Y0-CAS-109
801
C761c
Index
V1-155

CLC Cumulative Title Index, Vols 1-155

"The 2nd Sally" (Lem)
See "Second Sally"
"2nd Train for Frank O'Hara" (Carroll) **143**:41
"Indian Boy Love Song (#3)" (Alexie) **154**:4
"3rd Train (for The Summers)" (Carroll) **143**:41
Bach Cello Suite #4: Sarabande (Egoyan) **151**:175
"11th Train" (Carroll) **143**:41
"14th Voyage" (Lem) **149**:148
"The 18th Voyage" (Lem) **149**:150-51
"21st Voyage of Ijon Tichy" (Lem) **149**:134, 154
"22nd Voyage" (Lem) **149**:148
"28th Voyage" (Lem) **149**:155
"1934" (Hall) **151**:195
1973-nen no pinbōru (Murakami) **150**:72
"1975" (Castillo) **151**:3-4
"A" (Cummings) **15**:160, 162
"A" (Merrill) **8**:383-84, 386; **13**:377
"A" (Zukofsky) **1**:385; **2**:487; **4**:599; **11**:581; **18**:558-61
"A, a, a, Domine Deus" (Jones) **42**:245, 249
"A André Masson" (Cabral de Melo Neto) **76**:156
A Antonio Mairena, cantador (Cabral de Melo Neto) **76**:164
"'A' Bomb in Wardour Street" (Weller) **26**:444
A caso (Landolfi) **49**:213-14
A ciascuno il suo (Sciascia) **9**:474-75; **41**:388-90, 392-94
"A. D." (Burgess) **40**:126
"A extraordinária senhorita do país do Sonho" (Dourado) **23**:151
À haute flamme (Tzara) **47**:390, 395
"A la recherche d'un nouveau mode d'expression" (de Man) **55**:422
"Á la santé du serpent" (Char) **9**:166; **11**:118; **14**:128
"A la Víbora de la mar" (Fuentes) **113**:236
"A l'appel de la race de Saba" (Senghor) **130**:238, 241, 253, 259
A lume spento (Pound) **1**:276; **2**:343; **10**:407; **48**:288; **112**:329-31
"A. M." (Strand) **71**:280, 288
"A qué hora venderemos todo" (Zamora) **89**:368, 384
"'A Story' by John V. Marsh" (Wolfe) **25**:472
"A un pauvre écoeuré" (Reverdy) **53**:286
À une sérénité crispée (Char) **9**:162; **11**:115; **55**:288
Aa Went the Blaydon Races (Taylor) **27**:441, 443
"Aaron" (Theriault) **79**:408, 416
Aaron (Theriault) **79**:399-401, 405-06, 408, 413, 418, 419
"Abacus" (Seifert) **93**:317, 340
Abaddón, el exterminador (Sabato) **10**:446; **23**:381
Abaddon, the Exterminator (Sabato)
See *Abaddón, el exterminador*
Abahn Sabana David (Duras) **68**:94
"Abalone Soup" (Seth) **90**:338
"An Abandoned Place" (Jennings) **131**:240
"The Abandoned" (Abse) **29**:15, 17-18
"The Abandoned British Cemetery at Balasore, India" (Mahapatra) **33**:284
The Abandoned Men (Duhamel)
See *Les hommes abandonnés*
The Abandoned Woman (Condon) **8**:150
'Abath al aqdār (Mahfūz) **52**:292-93
Abath al-aqdar (Mahfouz) **153**:249, 258-59, 270, 272-74, 277, 309-10, 313-14, 336, 353-54, 372
"Abat-Jour" (Reverdy) **53**:281
ABBA ABBA (Burgess) **15**:103-04; **22**:78; **81**:303, 307, **94**:60
L'abbé C (Bataille) **29**:45
The Abbess of Crewe: A Modern Morality Tale (Spark) **5**:398-400; **8**:493-95; **40**:394-95; **94**:353
Abbey Road (Lennon and McCartney) **12**:364, 376-77, 380; **35**:278, 281-82, 289-90
"Abbeyforde" (Davie) **8**:164
Abbey's Road (Abbey) **36**:18-19; **59**:238, 241
"The Abbot" (Brown) **48**:57
"Abby, This Is Your Father" (Perelman) **49**:258
"ABC" (Bowering) **47**:31
"ABC" (Justice) **102**:250, 265-66
ABC de Castro Alves (Amado) **40**:34
The ABC Murders (Christie) **6**:108; **8**:142; **12**:113-14, 117, 119, 122-23; **48**:72-3; **110**:112, 122, 124
ABC of Economics (Pound) **7**:333
ABC of Reading (Pound) **4**:417
ABC: The Alpha Beth Book (Nichol) **18**:367, 369
ABCD (Slavitt) **5**:392
ABCDEFGHIJKLMNOPQRSTUVWXYZ (Disch) **36**:126-27
The ABC's of Astronomy: An Illustrated Dictionary (Gallant) **17**:127
The ABC's of Chemistry: An Illustrated Dictionary (Gallant) **17**:128
The ABC's of Cinema (Cendrars) **106**:194
"The Abduction" (Kunitz) **148**:110, 123, 125-26, 143
"The Abduction from the Seraglio" (Barthelme) **23**:48
"Abduction of the Endursky Enigma" (Iskander)
See "Umykanie, ili Zagadka Endurtsev"
"The Abduction; or, The Mystery of the Endurtsies" (Iskander)
See "Umykanie, ili Zagadka Endurtsev"
"Abdul and Ebenezer" (Kesey) **46**:224
Abe Lincoln Grows Up (Sandburg) **35**:357
Los abel (Matute) **11**:363-64
"Abel's Bride" (Levertov) **66**:238
"Abencaján el Bojarí, muerto en su laberinto" (Borges) **19**:47
Abend mit Goldrand: Eine Märchen Posse. 55 Bilder aus der Lä/endlichkeit fur Gönner der VerschreibKunst (Schmidt) **56**:397-400, 402, 404
Abeng (Cliff) **120**:90-94, 96, 99, 102, 108-09, 112-13, 115
"Abenjacán el-Bokhari, Dead in his Labyrynth" (Borges)
See "Abencaján el Bojarí, muerto en su laberinto"
"Abenjacán the Bojarí, Dead in His Labyrinth" (Borges)
See "Abencaján el Bojarí, muerto en su laberinto"
"Abenjacán the Buckharian, Dead in His Labyrinth" (Borges)
See "Abencaján el Bojarí, muerto en su laberinto"
"Das Abenteuer" (Boell) **72**:71, 77
Abenteuer eines Brotbeutels, und andere Geschichten (Boell) **15**:70; **27**:58
Das abenteuerliche Herz (Jünger) **125**:220, 222-23, 234, 249-51
Aber auch diese Sonne ist heimatlos (Sachs) **98**:321
"Abercrombie Station" (Vance) **35**:420
"Aberdarcy: The Chaucer Road" (Amis) **40**:41
"Aberdeen" (Smith) **64**:395-96
"Aberporth" (Fuller) **62**:186
Aberration of Starlight (Sorrentino) **22**:394-96; **40**:385, 391
"Abertackle" (Powys) **46**:325
Abgelegene Gehöfte (Eich) **15**:204
Abhijan (Ray) **16**:483
"Abide with Me" (Hoffman) **141**:282, 312-13
"The Abiding Vision" (West) **31**:454
"Abigail Adams: Peper-dulse Seaweed and Fever Talk, 1786" (Dubie) **36**:135
"Abiku" (Clark Bekedermo) **38**:117, 125, 128-29
"Abiku" (Soyinka) **36**:409
Abingdon Square (Fornés) **61**:138, 142-43
Abinger Harvest (Forster) **1**:104; **2**:135; **15**:226, 229; **45**:132, 144
Abismos de pasion (Bunuel) **80**:24, 28, 30, 47
"Ablazione de duodeno per ulcera" (Gadda) **11**:211
"Able, Baker, Charlie, Dog" (Vaughn) **62**:456-57, 459
Able Was I Ere I Saw Elba: Selected Poems (Hoffman) **13**:286-87
"Abnegation" (Rich) **36**:371
The Abolition (Schell) **35**:369-70
The Abolition of Man (Lewis) **6**:311; **27**:269; **124**:212, 225, 229, 247-48
The Abolitionist of Clark Gable Place (Webb) **7**:516
The Abominable Man (Wahlöö)
See *Den vedervaerdige mannen fraan saeffle*
"The Abomination" (Murray) **40**:335-36
"Abomunist Manifesto" (Kaufman) **49**:203-04
"Aborigine" (Williams) **42**:440
"Abortion" (Ai) **69**:16
"Abortion" (Selzer) **74**:270-72
"The Abortion" (Sexton) **123**:423
"The Abortion" (Walker) **27**:448; **103**:411
The Abortion: An Historical Romance, 1966 (Brautigan) **3**:86-9; **5**:71; **9**:124; **12**:60-3,

Pub
1/02

69-70; **34**:314-15, 317; **42**:50, 56-7, 60, 62
"abortion cycle #1" (Shange) **25**:402, 404
"Abortive Joy" (Tchicaya) **101**:347
"About a New Anthology Again..." (Avison) **97**:114
"About Atlanta" (Shange) **38**:394
About Centennial: Some Notes on the Novel (Michener) **5**:289
About Chinese Women (Kristeva)
See *Des chinoises*
"About Effie" (Findley) **102**:97, 105, 107-08, 111, 116
About Face (Fo)
See *Clacson, trombette e penacchi*
About Fiction: Reverent Reflections on the Nature of Fiction with Irreverent Observations on Writers, Readers, and Other Abuses (Morris) **7**:245, 247; **18**:351
About Harry Towns (Friedman) **5**:126-27; **56**:106-07, 109
"About Infinity and the Lenesdorf Pools" (Dubie) **36**:130
About Looking (Berger) **19**:40
"About Love and Money" (Cooper) **56**:71
"About Marriage" (Levertov) **66**:237
"About Money" (Ignatow) **40**:258
"About Religion" (Lorde) **71**:232
"About That Mile" (Smith) **64**:397
"About That Similarity" (Aksyonov) **101**:22
"About the House" (Auden) **1**:9; **3**:22, 24, 29; **6**:19; **9**:57
"About the Writer's Work" (Ehrenburg) **62**:178
"About These Germans" (Blunden) **56**:30
About Three Bricks Shy of a Load: A Highly Irregular Lowdown on the Year the Pittsburgh Steelers Were Super But Missed the Bowl (Blount) **38**:44-5
About Tilly Beamis (Elliott) **38**:182
"About Time" (Ostriker) **132**:329
"Above Calgary" (Bowering) **47**:20
"Above Dalton" (Mott) **15**:380
"Above Everything" (Ignatow) **40**:259
Above Suspicion (MacInnes) **27**:278-79; **39**:349-51
Above the Barriers (Pasternak)
See *Poverkh barierov*
"Above the City" (Laughlin) **49**:220
"Above the Gods" (Murdoch) **51**:291-92
Abra (Barfoot) **18**:35
"Abracadabra" (Livesay) **79**:332
"Abracadastra" (Connell) **45**:113
"Abraham and Orpheus" (Schwartz) **10**:464
"Abraham Darby's Bridge" (Fisher) **25**:161
Abraham in the Fire (Shamlu) **10**:470
"Abraham Lincoln and the Art of the World" (Moore) **47**:268
"Abraham Lincoln in Cleveland" (Crase) **58**:163, 165
"Abraham Lincoln of Rock Spring Farm" (Tolson) **105**:233
Abraham Lincoln: The Prairie Years (Sandburg) **10**:451; **35**:343-44, 350, 357
Abraham Lincoln: The War Years (Sandburg) **10**:451; **35**:348-51
"Abraham's Knife" (Garrett) **51**:144
Abraham's Knife and Other Poems (Garrett) **3**:192; **51**:144-45
Abram in the Salt (Sachs) **98**:322
Abraxas (Audiberti) **38**:22, 34
Abrégé de la nuit (Tzara) **47**:385
Abroad (Weller)
See *Split*
Abroad: British Literary Traveling between the Wars (Fussell) **74**:124, 128, 137, 146-47
"Abrupt Daylight Sadness" (Coles) **46**:113
Absalom, Absalom! (Faulkner) **3**:149, 153, 155-57; **6**:176-78, 180-81; **8**:207, 210-11; **9**:200-01; **11**:197, 202, 206-07; **14**:168-72, 176, 178-79; **18**:143-44, 147-50; **28**:138, 140, 143, 145-6; **52**:106-47
Absalom in the Tree (Mathias) **45**:237
"Abschied" (Boell) **72**:70, 73
"Abschied des Träumersvom Neunten Land" (Handke) **134**:162
Abschied von den Eltern: Erzählung (Weiss) **15**:563; **51**:389
"An Absence" (Ginzburg)
See "Un assenza"
"Absence" (McAuley) **45**:254
"Absence" (Thomas) **48**:381
Absence (Handke)
See *Die Abwesenheit*
An Absence (Johnson) **40**:263
"An Absence of Slaves" (Jacobsen) **102**:239
Absence of Unicorns, Presence of Lions (Mott) **15**:380
The Absence of War (Hare) **136**:257-59, 267-68, 270-75, 290, 306
"Absences" (Justice) **19**:234; **102**:252, 264
"Absences" (Larkin) **18**:295; **64**:260, 262, 266
"Absences" (MacEwen) **55**:168
Absences (Tate) **2**:431-32; **25**:429
Absent and Present (Kallman) **2**:221
Absent Friends (Ayckbourn) **5**:35-6; **8**:34; **18**:28; **33**:47-9; **74**:8, 19, 22
Absent in the Spring (Christie) **12**:114; **48**:78
"The absent One" (Senghor)
See "L'Absente"
"L'Absente" (Senghor) **54**:408; **130**:259
"Absentia animi" (Ekeloef) **27**:117
"An Absolute" (Jennings) **131**:233
Absolute Beginners (Griffiths) **52**:182-83
Absolute Beginners (MacInnes) **4**:314; **23**:282-87
"The Absolute Dance" (MacEwen) **13**:357
"The Absolute Ghost" (Redgrove) **41**:351
An Absolute Hero (Humphreys) **47**:190-91
"Absolute Zero" (Parra) **102**:351-53
Absolutely Free (Zappa) **17**:584, 588-89, 591
"Absolutely Inflexible" (Silverberg) **140**:363-64
Absolutely Live (Morrison) **17**:289-91, 295
Absolutely Nothing to Get Alarmed About (Wright) **49**:430-31
"An Absolutely Ordinary Rainbow" (Murray) **40**:340
"Absolution" (Sassoon) **36**:389; **130**:177, 180, 192, 212
"Absolution" (Thomas) **6**:534; **48**:374, 380
"The Absorbed" (Avison) **97**:77-8
Der Abstecher (Walser) **27**:462
"Abstinence Makes the Heart Grow Fonder" (Ammons) **57**:53
"The Abstract Calorie" (Ciardi) **40**:162
Absurd Person Singular (Ayckbourn) **5**:35-7; **8**:34; **18**:28; **33**:42, 47-9; **74**:3, 7-8, 18, 31, 34
"Absurd Prayer" (Cohen) **38**:131
"The Absurdist Moment in Contemporary Literary Theory" (White) **148**:222
The Absurdity of the Fates (Mahfouz)
See *Abath al-aqdar*
"Abu" (Randall) **135**:390
"El abuelo" (Guillén) **79**:244, 248-49
"Abundance" (Ciardi) **40**:155
"Abundance" (Kunene) **85**:165
"Abundance" (Moore) **47**:265
"The Abundant Dreamer" (Brodkey) **56**:62, 64, 67
"The Abused: Hansel and Gretel" (Smith) **42**:351
Die Abwesenheit (Handke) **134**:142-43, 155, 168-70, 176
Abwesenheit (Handke)
See *Die Abwesenheit*
"The Abyss" (Roethke) **3**:433; **8**:456-57; **101**:290, 309
The Abyss (Yourcenar)
See *L'oeuvre au noir*
Abyss: Two Novellas (Wilhelm) **7**:537
"Abyssinia" (Sillitoe) **6**:500
"Abzählreime" (Celan) **82**:52
"Acaba" (Aleixandre) **9**:14
Academia Nuts (Larson) **31**:239
Academic Squaw: Reports to the World from the Ivory Tower (Rose) **85**:312, 314
Academic Year (Enright) **31**:148, 151-52
L'Acadie pour quasiment rien (Maillet) **54**:304, 310; **118**:364
Acan (p'Bitek) **96**:300
"Acana" (Guillén) **48**:162; **79**:240
Acastos: Two Platonic Dialogues (Murdoch) **51**:291-92
"Accattone" (Pasolini) **20**:258-59; **37**:347
Accattone (Pasolini) **106**:206, 208-09, 219, 221-22, 225-26, 248, 251, 253, 263, 273
"The Accent of a Coming Foot" (Williams) **45**:454
"Accents of Death" (Farrell) **66**:112
Acceptable Losses (Shaw) **34**:369
"Acceptance" (Hughes) **108**:297
"Acceptance of Spring" (Tzara)
See "Acceptation du printemps"
The Acceptance World (Powell) **3**:400, 402; **9**:436; **10**:413
"Acceptation du printemps" (Tzara) **47**:390, 395
"Access to the Children" (Trevor) **71**:324
"The Accident" (Lem) **40**:295, 297
"Accident" (Munro) **95**:305, 308-09
"An Accident" (Narayan) **28**:293
"The Accident" (Strand) **18**:516, 518; **41**:437; **71**:283
Accident (Mosley) **43**:312-16, 319, 321
Accident (Pinter) **11**:443; **27**:391
The Accident (Wiesel)
See *Le jour*
Accident: A Day's News (Wolf) **58**:436-39; **150**:234-36, 248, 251, 255, 297, 301, 318, 329-30, 352
"Accident Zone" (Campbell) **42**:89
an Accidental Autobiography (Harrison) **144**:116-17, 119-21
"Accidental Bird Murder" (Hillis) **66**:193
Accidental Death of an Anarchist (Fo)
See *Morte accidentale di un anarchico*
An Accidental Man (Murdoch) **1**:237; **2**:297-98; **3**:347; **15**:388-89
The Accidental Tourist (Tyler) **44**:311-15, 317-21; **59**:201-08, 210; **103**:226-27, 244, 247-48, 250, 255-56, 260, 266, 271, 272, 275
"Accidentally on Purpose" (Frost) **9**:221; **13**:230
"Accidents Will Happen" (Costello) **21**:71
"An Accompanist" (Desai) **97**:150
"The Accompanist" (Pritchett) **15**:442
The Accomplice (Duerrenmatt)
See *Der Mitmacher*
Les accomplices (Simenon) **2**:398
"Accomplished Desires" (Oates) **19**:351; **134**:246-47
"Accomplishments" (Macdonald) **13**:356
"According to the Old Bards" (Padilla) **38**:349
"Account" (Milosz) **82**:298
"Account of the Journey by the Capibaribe River from Its Source to the City of Recife" (Cabral de Melo Neto) **76**:167
"Account Rendered" (Brittain) **23**:91
Account Unsettled (Simenon) **2**:399
"The Accountant's House" (Seth) **43**:388
"Accumulation" (Updike) **43**:436
"The Accursed Huntsman" (Garrett) **51**:140
"The Accusation" (Mahapatra) **33**:284
"The Accuser" (Milosz) **22**:306; **31**:262
"Ace in the Hole" (Simon) **17**:467
"Ace in the Hole" (Updike) **23**:473
Ace in the Hole (Wilder) **20**:456-57, 463
Ace of Clubs (Coward) **1**:65; **29**:139
"An Ace of Hearts" (Nemerov) **36**:306, 308
Ace of Pentacles (Wieners) **7**:535-36
"El acercamiento a Almotásim" (Borges) **1**:38; **3**:77; **8**:96; **48**:35, 45; **83**:164
"The Ache of Marriage" (Levertov) **66**:237, 250
"The Achieve of, the Mastery of the Thing" (Colwin) **23**:130; **84**:149

Achievement in American Poetry, 1900-1950 (Bogan) **39**:388; **46**:81; **93**:64, 100
"The Achievement of Desire" (Rodriguez) **155**:279, 308, 312
"The Achill Woman " (Boland) **113**:73, 90, 99, 111, 116-17, 126
"Achilles" (Harris) **25**:212
"Achilles' Last Stand" (Page and Plant) **12**:480, 483
Achimoona (Campbell) **85**:18
"Achronos" (Blunden) **56**:39
Achterloo (Duerrenmatt) **102**:69
"The Achziv Poems" (Amichai) **9**:24; **22**:30; **57**:37
The Achziv Poems (Amichai) **116**:97
"Acid" (Kelman) **58**:295
"Acid" (Oliver) **98**:278
"The Acid House" (Welsh) **144**:319, 336
The Acid House (Welsh) **144**:316-21, 324, 326-27, 336-37, 342-43, 345, 348
O acidente (Migueis) **10**:341
Acis in Oxford and Other Poems (Finch) **18**:154
"Acknowledgements and Dedication, Sort Of" (Berrigan) **4**:58
Ackroyd (Feiffer) **8**:217; **64**:151-52, 157-58, 162
"The ACLU: Bait and Switch" (Dworkin) **123**:101
"The Acolyte" (Levertov) **66**:237
The Acolyte (Astley) **41**:47-9
El acomador Felisberto Hernández y la literatura fantástics (Ferré) **139**:153
"Acon" (H. D.) **73**:115, 139
"Acorn, Yom Kippur" (Nemerov) **36**:306
El acoso (Carpentier) **11**:97; **38**:92; **110**:48-9
"Acquaintance with Time in Early Autumn" (Warren) **39**:258
"Acquainted with the Night" (Frost) **1**:110; **3**:170; **9**:219; **10**:194-95, 198; **15**:250; **26**:125
Acquainted with the Night (Boell)
See *Und Sagte kein einziges Wort*
Acque e terre (Quasimodo) **10**:427
Acquired Tastes: A Beginner's Guide to Serious Pleasures (Mayle)
See *Expensive Habits*
An Acre of Grass (Stewart) **7**:465
"An Acre of Land" (Thomas) **6**:530; **13**:542
Acres and Pains (Perelman) **9**:415; **49**:266
"The Acrobat" (Hirsch) **31**:215
Acrobats (Horovitz) **56**:150-51
The Acrobats (Richler) **5**:371-74; **13**:482-83, 485
The Acrophile (Kaniuk) **19**:238-39
Across (Handke)
See *Der Chinese des Schmerzes*
"Across a Crowded Room" (Pym) **111**:245
Across the Bitter Sea (Dillon) **17**:98-100
Across the Black Waters (Anand) **23**:14, 19; **93**:24, 31, 43
Across the Board on Tomorrow Morning (Saroyan) **10**:453
"Across the Bridge" (Boell)
See "An der Brücke"
"Across the Line" (Jünger)
See *Uber die Linie*
"Across the Lines" (Price) **63**:327
Across the Pacific (Huston) **20**:164
Across the River and into the Trees (Hemingway) **3**:231, 234, 242-43; **6**:225, 227, 231; **8**:283, 291; **13**:275, 278; **19**:218; **39**:399-400, 403, 428, 430-32, 434-35; **41**:197, 202, 205, 207; **50**:427; **61**:226; **80**:112, 117-18, 145-46
Across the Sea of Suns (Benford) **52**:69-71, 77
Across the Sea Wall (Koch) **42**:259-65
"Across the Street and into the Grill" (White) **10**:530
"Across the Wide Missouri" (Wideman) **34**:298
"Across the World the Beholder Come" (Gustafson) **36**:220
"The Act and Place of Poetry" (Bonnefoy)
See "L'acte et le lieu de la poésie"
The Act of Creation (Koestler) **33**:236-37
Act of Darkness (King) **53**:209-10, 212-13; **145**:353, 357, 361
"Act of Faith" (Shaw) **7**:411
Act of Faith and Other Stories (Shaw) **23**:396
"An Act of God" (Nemerov) **36**:309
The Act of Life (Cousteau) **30**:105-07
"The Act of Love" (Creeley) **2**:108
"Act of Love" (Scannell) **49**:327, 331
"The Act of Love: Poetry and Personality" (Carruth) **84**:115, 117
"An Act of Prostitution" (McPherson) **77**:361, 365
An Act of Terror (Brink) **106**:117-18, 133, 137
"Act of Union" (Heaney) **25**:245; **74**:157, 162
Act One (Stow) **23**:436
Act One: An Autobiography (Hart) **66**:180-82, 188, 191
Act without Words I (Beckett)
See *Actes sans paroles I*
Act without Words II (Beckett) **6**:46; **18**:41
Acta sanctorum (Lengyel) **7**:202
Acte (Durrell) **1**:86; **4**:145; **13**:184
"L'acte et le lieu de la poésie" (Bonnefoy) **58**:45, 50, 59
Actes sans paroles I (Beckett) **1**:20; **3**:47; **6**:46; **11**:42; **18**:41; **83**:117
"Actfive" (MacLeish) **8**:362
Actfive, and Other Poems (MacLeish) **8**:362; **68**:290
The Acting Person (John Paul II)
See *Osoba i czyn*
"Action" (Bukowski) **82**:27
"Action" (Levertov) **66**:250
"The Action" (Murray) **40**:336
The Action (King) **53**:213
Action (Shepard) **6**:496-97; **17**:448; **41**:410
"Action and Epilogue" (Ciardi) **40**:156
L'action de la justice est éteinte (Char) **14**:126
Active Antology (Pound) **112**:337
The Activists Papers (Bond) **23**:71
"Actor" (John Paul II) **128**:187
"The Actor" (Williams) **42**:440
"The Actor to the Audience" (Turner) **48**:399
"Actors and Sinners" (Cabrera Infante) **120**:80, 82
The Actor's Nightmare (Durang) **27**:91-3
An Actor's Revenge (Ichikawa)
See *Yukinojo henge*
"An Actor's War" (Williams) **42**:445
"Acts of God" (Boyle) **90**:63
The Acts of King Arthur and His Noble Knights: From the Winchester Manuscripts of Thomas Malory and Other Sources (Steinbeck) **13**:535; **21**:387; **124**:393
"Acts of Love" (McCarthy) **39**:487
Acts of Love (Kazan) **63**:220-21
Acts of Theft (Cohen) **31**:93-4
"Actue Crisis Identity" (Royko) **109**:405
"Acuérdate" (Rulfo) **80**:200, 216
"Acute Triangle" (Raphael) **14**:438
"Ad Castitatem" (Bogan) **93**:66
Ad horef, 1974 (Yehoshua) **31**:470
"Ad Libitum" (Elytis) **100**:179, 181
Ad m'avet (Oz) **8**:436; **54**:352
Ada; or, Ardor: A Family Chronicle (Nabokov) **1**:244-46; **2**:300-01, 304-05; **3**:352-53, 345-55; **4**:2497; **6**:352, 354-55, 357-58; **8**:407-16, 418; **11**:391-93, 395; **15**:393-94, 396; **44**:465-69, 473; **64**:348, 350-51
"Adagio" (Seth) **90**:350
L'adalgisa, disegni milanesi (Gadda) **11**:211
"Adam" (Tomlinson) **45**:393-94
"Adam and Eve" (Shapiro) **8**:486; **53**:330, 334
"Adam and the Sacred Nine" (Hughes) **37**:174, 177-78; **119**:272
Adam by Adam: The Autobiography of Clayton Powell, Jr. (Powell) **89**:210-11
Adam, Eve and the City (Gray) **153**:138-39, 142-46, 149
Adam, Eve, and the Serpent (Pagels) **104**:212-17, 229, 234
Adam in Moonshine (Priestley) **34**:361, 364
"Adam Kadmon" (Nye) **42**:308-09
"Adam, One Afternoon" (Calvino)
See "Un pomeriggio Adamo"
Adam, One Afternoon, and Other Stories (Calvino)
See *L'entrada en guerra*
"Adam Raised a Cain" (Springsteen) **17**:483, 490
Adam Resurrected (Kaniuk) **19**:239, 241
"Adam Snow" (Ashbery) **77**:68-69
Adam, Where Art Thou? (Boell)
See *Wo warst du, Adam?*
"Adam Yankev" (Simpson) **7**:429; **149**:228
"The Adamant" (Roethke) **8**:460
Adame miroir (Genet) **44**:390
"Adam's Bride" (Jolley) **46**:213
Adam's Dream (Belitt) **22**:54, 52
"Adam's Legacy" (MacNeice) **53**:233
Adam's Rest (Millin) **49**:246
"Adam's Rib: Fictions and Realities" (Gordimer) **123**:157
"Adam's Song to Heaven" (Bowers) **9**:122
Adam's Task: Calling Animals by Name (Hearne) **56**:128-32, 134
The Adaptable Man (Frame) **22**:144, 146; **96**:168-69, 190, 196-97, 211-12, 216-17
Addams and Evil (Addams) **30**:12
"Added Weight" (Bissett) **18**:58
"Addendum to 'The Block'" (Van Duyn) **116**:422, 427
"The Adder" (Chappell) **78**:116-17
Addictions (Enright) **4**:155; **8**:203
Addictions (Hyde) **21**:178-79
The Adding Machine (Rice) **7**:359-64; **49**:292-94, 299, 301-02, 304-05
The Adding Machine: Collected Essays (Burroughs) **42**:76-7
"Addio" (Ciardi) **40**:161
"Addio" (Gilliatt) **53**:146
Additional Dialogue (Trumbo) **19**:445
"Address for a Prize-Day" (Auden) **11**:18
"Address to Existence" (Wheelock) **14**:571
"An Address to the Literary Philosophical Society" (Wain) **46**:411
"Address to the Lord" (Berryman) **62**:45
"The Address to the Parents" (Bell) **31**:47
"Adelaide's Dream" (Middleton) **13**:389
"Adélia" (Condé) **92**:106
"Aden" (Hall) **51**:170
The Adept (McClure) **6**:316, 319
Adept's Gambit (Leiber) **25**:301
"Adiere" (Arghezi) **80**:9
"L'adieu" (Butor) **15**:117
"Adieu" (Endō) **99**:307
"Adieu á Charlot" (Ferlinghetti) **27**:137, 139
"Adieu, Mlle. Veronique" (Brodsky) **6**:96
"Adieu, New-York!" (Morand) **41**:301
"Adieu to Norman, Bon Jour to Joan and Jean-Paul" (O'Hara) **78**:335
"Un adieu, un salut" (Char) **9**:167
Adieux: A Farewell to Sartre (Beauvoir)
See *La céremonie des adieux: Suivi de entretiens avec Jean-Paul Sartre*
"Adios carnero" (Ulibarrí) **83**:416
Adios, Mr. Moxley (Jacobsen) **48**:196, 198-99
Los adioses (Onetti) **10**:376
"Adivinanzas" (Guillén) **48**:166
The Adjuster (Egoyan) **151**:126-30, 132, 134, 136, 139-41, 145, 147, 150-53, 156, 161, 167, 173
"Admass" (Priestley) **2**:347
An Admirable Woman (Cohen) **31**:94-5
"The Admiral and the Nuns" (Tuohy) **37**:427, 433
The Admiral and the Nuns with Other Stories (Tuohy) **37**:426-27, 430
Admiral Hornblower in the West Indies (Forester) **35**:171

Admiral of the Ocean Sea: A Life of Christopher Columbus (Morison) **70**:331, 335, 342, 344, 346, 350, 353
The Admiral on the Wheel (Thurber) **25**:440
"Admirals" (Chabon) **149**:8
Admiralteiskaia igla (Nabokov) **6**:358
"The Admiralty Spire" (Nabokov)
See *Admiralteiskaia igla*
"The Admirer" (Singer) **6**:511; **9**:487
"Admiring the Scenery" (O'Faolain) **14**:406
Admission to the Feast (Beckman)
See *Tillträde till festen*
"Adolescence" (Dove) **81**:134
"Adolescence of Day" (Elytis) **49**:114
"Adolescence—III" (Dove) **81**:137
Un adolescent d'autrefois (Mauriac) **9**:369; **56**:216
"The Adolescent Novel" (Kristeva) **140**:201-2
The Adolescent Savenko (Limonov) **67**:180
"Adolfo Miller" (Ulibarrí) **83**:415
"Adolpho's Disappeared and We Haven't a Clue Where to Find Him" (Rooke) **25**:392
"Adonis" (H. D.) **73**:119
"La adoración de los magos" (Cernuda) **54**:47
"Adoration" (Gilchrist) **48**:119, 121; **143**:305-06, 324
"Adoration" (Moure) **88**:227
"Adore Her" (Robison) **98**:307
"Adowe: We Return Thanks" (Kenny) **87**:240
The Adrian Mole Diaries (Townsend)
See *The Growing Pains of Adrian Mole*
The Adrian Mole Diaries (Townsend)
See *The Secret Diary of Adrian Mole, Aged 13 3/4*
"The Adriatic" (Prokosch) **48**:309
Adrienne Mesurat (Green) **77**:266-69, 274, 289-90, 294
Adrift in Soho (Wilson) **3**:537; **14**:588
"Adrift Just Off the Islets of Langerhans: Latitude 38 54'N, Longitude 00'13""" (Ellison) **13**:207; **42**:128-29; **139**:130
Adrift on the Nile (Mahfouz)
See *Tharthara fawq al-Nil*
"Adult Art" (Gurganus) **70**:191, 194, 196
"Adult Bookstore" (Shapiro) **8**:486; **15**:477-78
"Adult Grief" (Glück) **44**:217, 222
"The Adult Holiday" (Spencer) **22**:406
The Adult Life of Toulouse Lautrec (Acker) **45**:14-15; **111**:11, 21, 23, 25, 32-33, 37, 42
"The Adulterous Woman" (Camus)
See "La femme adultère"
"Adultery" (Banks) **72**:5, 9
"Adultery" (Dickey) **15**:174
"Adultery" (Dubus) **36**:143-46; **97**:199-202, 218-21, 226-27, 229
"Adultery" (Gunn) **32**:214
Adultery, and Other Choices (Dubus) **13**:184; **36**:143-44, 146-48; **97**:197-99, 207-09, 219, 231, 235
Adultery and Other Diversions (Parks) **147**:215, 219
"Adulthood" (Giovanni) **19**:190; **64**:185
"Adulthood (Fo Claudia)" (Giovanni) **117**:195
Adulthood Rites (Butler) **121**:88, 91-3, 96-99, 103, 105, 108, 118, 120, 135, 139
"Adults Only" (Stafford) **29**:382
"Advancing Luna—and Ida B. Wells" (Walker) **27**:448; **103**:407, 409, 411-12
Advancing Paul Newman (Bergstein) **4**:55
"Advent" (Grass) **32**:198-99
"Advent" (H. D.) **73**:136, 138
"Advent" (Merton) **83**:392
"Advent" (Rexroth) **112**:405
"Advent, 1966" (Levertov) **5**:248; **28**:239
"Advent Calendar" (Schnackenberg) **40**:382
"The Adventure" (Lagerkvist)
See "Äventyret"
"Adventure in a Room" (Green) **97**:292
"Adventure in an Antique Shop" (Akhmadulina)
See "Prikliuchenie v antikvarnom magazine"
Adventure in Baltimore (Isherwood) **44**:397
Adventure in Grey (Buero Vallejo)
See *Aventura en lo gris*
"The Adventure of a Bather" (Calvino) **33**:101-02
"The Adventure of a Clerk" (Calvino) **39**:314
"The Adventure of a Poet" (Calvino)
See "L'avventura di un poeta"
"The Adventure of a Reader" (Calvino) **33**:102
"The Adventure of Ricoletti of the Clubfoot" (Derleth) **31**:137
"The Adventure of the Bearded Lady" (Queen) **3**:422
"The Adventure of the Cheap Flat" (Christie) **110**:111
"The Adventure of the Glass-Domed Clock" (Queen) **11**:461
"The Adventure of the Late Mr. Faversham" (Derleth) **31**:137
"The Adventure of the Letter I" (Simpson) **149**:342
"The Adventure of the Norcross Riddle" (Derleth) **31**:137
The Adventure of the Unique Dickensians (Derleth) **31**:138
The Adventurer (Zweig) **34**:378; **42**:466-67
The Adventurers (Robbins) **5**:380
"Adventures" (Urdang) **47**:400
Adventures in Everyday Life (Oe)
See *Nichijōseikatsu no boken*
Adventures in the Alaskan Skin Trade (Hawkes) **49**:156-60
"Adventures in the Bohemian Jungle" (Kavanagh) **22**:240, 243
Adventures of a Columnist (Berton) **104**:47
"Adventures of a Haversack" (Boell) **72**:100
The Adventures of a Photographer in La Plata (Bioy Casares)
See *La aventura de un fotògraf en La Plata*
Adventures of a Young Man (Dos Passos) **4**:137; **11**:156; **15**:183, 187; **34**:420; **82**:72
The Adventures of Augie March (Bellow) **1**:27-30, 33; **2**:49-53; **3**:48-51, 60-2; **6**:53-8, 61; **8**:75-6; **10**:37, 44; **13**:69-73; **15**:47-50, 53, 52-6; **25**:85; **33**:65-6, 69, 71; **34**:545; **63**:28, 32-5, 37, 41; **79**:61-2, 76, 83-4
The Adventures of Baron Munchausen (Gilliam) **141**:244-49, 255, 260
The Adventures of Deke (Nwapa) **133**:229
The Adventures of Ellery Queen (Queen) **3**:422
The Adventures of Fathead, Smallhead, and Squarehead (Sanchez) **116**:301, 309
The Adventures of Gerard (Skolimowski) **20**:350, 354
"The Adventures of God in His Search for the Black Girl" (Brophy) **6**:99; **105**:6, 8, 12, 31
The Adventures of God in His Search for the Black Girl (Brophy) **6**:98-100
The Adventures of Gurudeva (Naipaul) **39**:356
"The Adventures of My Seven Uncles" (Cendrars)
See "Le Panama ou les aventures de mes sept oncles"
The Adventures of Robina, by Herself (Tennant) **52**:404-06
The Adventures of Solar Pons (Derleth) **31**:139
The Adventures of Strong Vanya (Preussler) **17**:375
Adventures of the Letter I (Simpson) **4**:500; **7**:428-29; **9**:486; **32**:379; **149**:303, 305, 309, 313, 315, 327-28, 331, 350
The Adventures of the Stainless Steel Rat (Harrison) **42**:204
The Adventures of Una Persson and Catherine Cornelius in the Twentieth Century (Moorcock) **27**:349; **58**:354-55
The Adventures of Wesley Jackson (Saroyan) **8**:467
The Adventures of William Saroyan (Saroyan) **8**:467
"The Adventuress" (O'Connor) **23**:331
The Adversary (Ray)
See *Pratidwandi*
Advertisements for Myself (Mailer) **1**:189-90, 192; **2**:258, 264-65; **3**:311-13, 315; **4**:323; **8**:366, 368-72; **11**:339-40, 343; **28**:255-57; **39**:416, 423, 425; **74**:203-04, 207, 212, 225; **111**:95, 104, 107, 118-20, 135, 137
"Advertising=Poetry" (Cendrars) **106**:179
"Advice" (Milosz) **56**:234
"Advice" (Singer) **69**:305
"Advice on Reading the Confessional Poet" (Kuzma) **7**:196
"Advice to a Discarded Lover" (Adcock) **41**:13
Advice to a God (Van Duyn) **63**:436
"Advice to a Lady" (Padilla) **38**:352
"Advice to a Prophet" (Wilbur) **3**:531; **6**:568; **53**:404; **110**:351, 359-60, 378
Advice to a Prophet and Other Poems (Wilbur) **3**:532; **6**:568; **53**:396, 398-99, 405, 410; **110**:352, 384
"'Advice' to a Young Poet" (Kunene) **85**:176
"Advice to King Lear" (Cassity) **42**:99
"Advice to My Friends" (Kroetsch) **57**:292-94
Advice to My Friends (Kroetsch) **57**:292-93
"Advice to the Old (Including Myself)" (Boyle) **58**:75-6
Advise and Consent (Drury) **37**:98-100, 102-08, 111
Aeducacão pela pedra (Cabral de Melo Neto) **76**:153-54, 156, 158-59, 163
"The Aegean" (Squires) **51**:381
"Aegean Route" (Elytis) **100**:179
"Aegeis" (Elytis) **49**:110
"Aegeodrome" (Elytis) **100**:187
Aegypt (Crowley) **57**:162-64
"Aeneas at Washington" (Tate) **2**:429; **11**:525
Aeneid (Day Lewis) **6**:127
The Aerial Letter (Brossard)
See *La lettre aérienne*
"Aerial Ways" (Pasternak) **7**:293; **18**:386
"Aerialist" (Plath) **51**:342
The Aerodrome: A Love Story (Warner) **45**:432-35, 437-41
"The Aeroplanes at Brescia" (Davenport) **6**:123; **14**:140; **38**:140
"El aeroplano" (Guillén) **48**:159
"Aesculapian Notes" (Redgrove) **41**:355
"Aesthetic" (Tomlinson) **13**:546; **45**:402
"Aesthetics" (MacCaig) **36**:285
Aesthetics (Olson) **28**:344
"Aesthetics after War" (Eberhart) **56**:91
The Aesthetics of Chaosmos (Eco) **60**:125
"Aesthetics of the Shah" (Olds) **85**:291
The Aesthetics of Thomas Aquinas (Eco) **142**:66
"Aet Beran Byrg" (Grigson) **7**:136
"Aether" (Ginsberg) **36**:183
"Los afanes" (Bioy Casares) **88**:94
"Afar a Bird" (Beckett) **29**:57
"Affabulazione" (Pasolini) **37**:347
"The Affair" (Bell) **8**:65-6
"An Affair" (Ezekiel) **61**:104
The Affair (Snow) **1**:316; **4**:502; **6**:516; **13**:512; **19**:427
"An Affair, Edited" (Gaitskill) **69**:203
"An Affair in the Country" (Simpson) **149**:360
"An Affair of Honor" (Nabokov) **3**:354
"The Affair of the Bungalow" (Christie) **110**:130, 144-46
"An Affair of the Heart" (Hope) **52**:208
"An Affair of the Heart" (Sargeson) **31**:364
An Affair with the Moon (White) **49**:399
Une affaire de viol (Himes) **2**:195; **18**:249; **108**:229
L'affaire Saint Fiacre (Simenon) **3**:451-52
Affairs in a Tent (Ayckbourn) **74**:20
L'affamée (Leduc) **22**:264
"Affection" (Barthelme) **46**:43; **59**:249-51
"Affinities" (Hersey) **81**:330
Affinities (Watkins) **43**:444, 447, 452-53
"Affinities II" (Blackburn) **9**:100
"Affinity" (Thomas) **48**:380

"Affirmation" (Allen) **84**:5
"Affirmation" (Wheelock) **14**:571
"Affirmations" (Pound) **7**:326
"Affirmative Action Berkeley, 1977" (Rose) **85**:316
Affliction (Banks) **72**:11-19, 22
Affliction (Weldon) **122**:275
"Afghanistan and South Vietnam" (Chomsky) **132**:33
An Afghanistan Picture Show: Or, How I Saved the World (Vollmann) **89**:285-87, 290-92, 297098, 301, 307
"Afin qu'il n'y soit rien changè" (Char) **9**:163
"Afloat" (Beattie) **40**:64, 66; **63**:2, 17, 19
Afrah al-qubba (Mahfouz) **153**:359-60
"Africa" (Giovanni) **117**:196-97
"Africa Emergent" (Gordimer) **33**:183; **123**:116
"Africa I" (Giovanni) **117**:196
"The African Ambassador" (Kallman) **2**:221
African Calliope (Hoagland) **28**:184-85
The African Child (Laye)
See *L'enfant noir*
"African China" (Tolson) **105**:240
An African Elegy (Okri) **87**:323
African Firebrand: Jomo Kenyatta (Archer) **12**:17
African Horse (Pownall) **10**:419
The African Image (Mphahlele) **25**:332-33, 335, 341; **133**:126, 128-29, 133, 136
African Laughter (Lessing) **94**:266-68
"African Literature" (Achebe) **152**:68
"African Literature: What Traditions?" (Mphahlele) **133**:143
"The African Magician" (Gordimer) **33**:180; **123**:114
The African Queen (Forester) **35**:159-61, 165-66, 169-70, 172, 174
The African Queen (Huston) **20**:161, 165-66
"African Question Mark" (Hughes) **15**:295
African Religions in Western Scholarship (p'Bitek) **96**:291, 294
African Songs of Love, War, Grief and Abuse (Damas)
See *Poèmes nègres sur des airs africains*
African Stories (Lessing) **2**:239; **3**:288; **22**:279; **94**:280
"African Suite" (Randall) **135**:398
"African Tea Ceremony" (Hope) **52**:209
"The African Trilogy" (Diamond) **30**:110-11
African Trio (Simenon) **18**:487
African Writing Today (Mphahlele) **133**:127-28
African-American (Shange) **74**:298
African-American Baseline Essays (Hillard) **70**:406
Africanus Instructus (Foreman) **50**:163, 165, 171
Africa's Cultural Revolution (p'Bitek) **96**:299, 310
Afrika My Music (Mphahlele) **133**:132, 150
Afrikanische Spiele (Jünger) **125**:222
L'Afrique fantôme de Dakar a Djibouti, 1931-1933 (Leiris) **61**:341, 352
"L'Afrique, un continent difficile" (Condé) **92**:112-13
"Afro-American" (Dumas) **62**:151
Afro-American Literature in the Twentieth Century: The Achievement of Intimacy (Cooke) **65**:365
Afro-American Literature: The Reconstruction of Instruction (Stepto) **65**:364, 379, 381, 386
The Afrocentric Idea (Asante) **70**:389-90
Afrocentricity: The Theory of Social Change (Asante) **70**:390
"After" (Angelou) **77**:28
"After" (Lane) **25**:288
"After 37 Years My Mother apologizes for My Childhood" (Olds) **85**:295, 304
"After a Day of Work" (Bly) **128**:14
"After a Death" (Stevenson) **33**:379
"After a Death" (Tomlinson) **13**:548
"After a Departure" (Abse) **7**:1; **29**:15
"After a Fifteenth-Century Miniature Showing King Mark Stabbing Tristram in the Presence of Ysolt" (Dacey) **51**:79
"After a Flight" (Montale) **7**:231; **9**:388
"After a Flight" (Montefiore)
See "Dopa una fuga"
"After a Journey" (Brodsky) **100**:61
"After a Nightmare" (Davison) **28**:99-100
"After a Phrase Abandoned by Wallace Stevens" (Justice) **102**:270, 277, 279-80, 283
"After All" (Bowie) **17**:57, 59
"After an Attack" (Transtroemer) **52**:410; **65**:219, 228
"After Apple-Picking" (Frost) **1**:110; **3**:170; **15**:245, 248; **26**:112, 115-16, 123, 128
"After Auschwitz" (Sexton) **6**:494; **123**:446
After Babel (Steiner) **24**:434, 437
"After Bakhtin" (Lodge) **141**:351, 355
After Bakhtin (Lodge) **141**:350-51, 355, 373
After Candlemas (Arthur) **12**:27, 29
"After Cavafy" (Mahon) **27**:286-88
"After Christmas" (Mathias) **45**:236
"After Consulting My Yellow Pages" (Wagoner) **3**:508
"After Dark" (Rich) **3**:428; **7**:365, 368; **125**:336
After Dark (Wellman) **49**:389-90, 394, 396
After Dark, My Sweet (Thompson) **69**:378, 387, 389
"After Death" (Aleixandre) **36**:29
"After Douglas" (Merwin) **88**:211
"After Drinking All Night with a Friend" (Bly) **10**:57
"After Eden" (Simmons) **43**:412, 414
After Every Green Thing (Abse) **29**:12-14, 16-17
"After Exile" (Brutus) **43**:88
After Experience: Poems and Translations (Snodgrass) **2**:405-06; **6**:513-14; **18**:491, 494; **68**:383, 388, 391, 393, 397
"After Feydeau" (Schuyler)
See "What to Do? A Problem Play"
"After Ford" (Burgess) **94**:76
"After Free Verse" (Perloff) **137**:302
"After Frost" (Creeley) **78**:160
"After Grief" (Plumly) **33**:313
After Hannibal (Unsworth) **127**:422-24
"After He Left" (Ding Ling)
See "Ta zou hou"
After Hours (Campion) **95**:6
After Hours (Scorsese) **89**:240-42, 260, 265-68
"After I Have Voted" (Jensen) **37**:187
"After Ikkyu" (Harrison) **143**:354
After Ikkyu (Harrison) **143**:354
"After Illness" (Ostriker) **132**:323, 326
"After Illness in Childhood" (Urdang) **47**:400
"After I'm Gone" (McGrath) **28**:280
"After Images: Autobiographical Sketches" (Snodgrass) **68**:394
After Julius (Howard) **29**:244-46
"After Keats" (Levine)
See "Having Been Asked 'What Is a Man?' I Answer"
"after Kent State" (Clifton) **66**:65, 67
After Lazarus: A Filmscript (Coover) **46**:121-22
After Leaving Mr. Mackenzie (Rhys) **2**:372-73; **4**:445; **6**:453-55; **14**:446, 450-51; **51**:357-59, 368, 370; **124**:330-31, 338, 340-41, 344, 348-49, 353, 365, 369-70
After Long Absence (Hospital) **145**:311, 315-16
After Lorca (Spicer) **8**:497; **18**:507, 512; **72**:348, 352-57, 359-65
After Lydia (Rattigan) **7**:355
"After Magritte" (Stoppard) **3**:470; **4**:524, 527; **8**:502-03; **29**:399-401; **91**:189
"After Making Love We Hear Footsteps" (Kinnell) **129**:270
After Many a Summer Dies the Swan (Huxley) **1**:150-52; **4**:238-40, 243; **8**:304; **35**:243-44; **79**:306, 328
After Martial (Porter) **5**:347
"After Mecca" (Brooks) **49**:28
"After Melville" (Rukeyser) **10**:442; **27**:411
After Moondog (Shapiro) **76**:114-18
After My Fashion (Powys) **46**:323-24
"After Nerval" (Mahon) **27**:287, 289-90
"After Paradise" (Milosz) **56**:246; **82**:290
"After Pasternak" (Creeley) **78**:160
"After Rain" (Page) **7**:291; **18**:379
"After Rain" (Trevor) **116**:394
After Rain (Trevor) **116**:394-96
"After Reading, I Go Outside to the Dwarf Orchard" (Wright)
See "After Reading Tu Fu, I Go Outside to the Dwarf Orchard"
"After Reading Mickey in the Night Kitchen for the Third Time before Bed" (Dove) **81**:150
"After Reading Tu Fu, I Go Outside to the Dwarf Orchard" (Wright) **146**:349-50, 365
"After Rilke" (Schwartz)
See "Late Autumn in Venice"
"After Saturday Night Comes Sunday" (Sanchez) **116**:306, 313
"After School" (Merwin) **88**:206
"After Soweto" (Brink) **36**:68
"After Spring Snow, What They Saw" (Dubie) **36**:137
After Strange Gods: A Primer of Modern Heresy (Eliot) **6**:165-66; **24**:162-63, 182-83; **34**:394, 403; **41**:156-59
After Such Knowledge (Blish) **14**:87
After Such Pleasures (Parker) **15**:414; **68**:325
"After Terror" (Oates) **33**:294
After the Act (Graham) **23**:193-94
"After the Alphabets" (Merwin) **88**:197, 206
"After the Anonymous Swedish" (Harrison) **143**:350
"After the April Festivals" (Disch) **36**:127
After the Armies Have Passed (Kessler) **4**:270
"After the Ball" (Colter) **58**:146-47
"After the Ball" (McCartney) **35**:286
After the Ball (Coward) **29**:140
After the Banquet (Mishima) **4**:357-58; **9**:382; **27**:336
"After the Big Parade" (Ginsberg) **109**:318
After the Bombing and Other Short Poems (Blunden) **56**:29, 34-5, 39, 41, 45, 47
"After the Crash" (MacNeice) **10**:323, 325
"After the Cries of the Birds" (Ferlinghetti) **27**:139; **111**:65
"After the Dance" (Gaye) **26**:132
"After the Death of Mdabuli, Son of Mhawu" (Kunene) **85**:176
"After the Defeat" (Ritsos) **6**:464
"After the Denim" (Carver) **22**:102
"After the Dinner Party" (Warren) **39**:265; **59**:298
After the Fairy Tale (Aitmatov)
See *Belyj parokhod*
"After the Faith Healings" (Appleman) **51**:17
After the Fall (Kazan) **63**:226, 235
After the Fall (Miller) **1**:216-18; **2**:279-80; **6**:326-33, 336; **10**:342-43; **15**:373-74, 376; **26**:322, 324, 327; **47**:254-56, 258; **78**:318-19, 325
After the First Death (Cormier) **30**:81-3, 85-6, 88-91
"After the First House" (Alexander) **121**:8
After the Funeral (Christie) **12**:124; **48**:72, 76
"After the Game" (Dubus) **97**:213, 216, 229
"After the Gold Rush" (Young) **17**:583
After the Gold Rush (Young) **17**:569-70, 572-73, 577-79
"After the 'I Ching'" (Spacks) **14**:511
"After the Killing" (Randall) **135**:398
After the Killing (Randall) **135**:385, 391-93, 398
"After the Last Dynasty" (Kunitz) **6**:287; **148**:89
After the Last Sky (Said) **123**:346-47, 352-53, 358, 383, 385
"After the Lecture" (Thomas) **48**:375
After the New Criticism (Lentricchia) **34**:574

"After the Persian" (Bogan) **4**:69; **39**:387, 393; **46**:90; **93**:65
After the Prize (Weldon) **36**:444-45
"After the Quarrel" (Rukeyser) **27**:411
"After the Rain" (Mahapatra) **33**:284
"After the Rats" (Purdy) **6**:428
After the Rehearsal (Bergman) **72**:59, 61
"After the Reunion" (Ostriker) **132**:323
"After the Riots" (Enright) **31**:150
"After the Sex Bomb" (Ewart) **13**:208
"After the Sirens" (Hood) **28**:187
"After the Storm" (Hemingway) **8**:285, 287; **30**:192
"After the Storm" (Santos) **22**:364
"After the Storm" (Simon) **26**:409
"After the Street Fighting" (Ciardi) **40**:155
After the Stroke (Sarton) **91**:244, 246
"After the Sun Has Risen" (Farrell) **66**:129
After the Sundown (Jordan) **37**:195
"After the Surgery" (Bottoms) **53**:30
"After the Surprising Conversions" (Lowell) **4**:295; **15**:344
After the Tale (Aitmatov)
See *Belyj parokhod*
"After the War" (Smith) **64**:388
"After Thomas Hardy" (McFadden) **48**:244
"After Three Photographs of Brassai" (Dubie) **36**:134
"After Thunder" (Johnston) **51**:240, 250-52
"After Two Years of Analysis: Reactions" (Dickey) **28**:119
"After Whistler" (Plumly) **33**:316
"After Winter" (Brown) **59**:266
"After Working" (Bly) **128**:15
"After Wyatt" (O'Hara) **5**:325
"After You, My Dear Alphonse" (Jackson) **60**:229
"After You've Gone" (Adams) **65**:348
After You've Gone (Adams) **65**:348-49
"After-Image" (Caldwell) **1**:51
"Afterimages" (Lorde) **71**:235
"Afterimages" (MacEwen) **55**:163-64, 169
Afterlife (Monette) **82**:324, 326-28, 331
The Afterlife (Updike) **139**:368-69
"Afterlives" (Mahon) **27**:290
"The Afterlives of Count Zeppelin" (Cassity) **42**:99
"Aftermath" (Alexander) **121**:9
"Aftermath" (Plath) **14**:426
"Aftermath" (Sassoon) **130**:187-88
Aftermath (Jagger and Richard) **17**:237, 239
"Afternoon" (Ellison) **11**:183; **114**:131
"Afternoon and Evening at Ohrid" (Wright) **5**:519
"An Afternoon at the Beach" (Bowers) **9**:121
"Afternoon Dancing" (Trevor) **7**:478; **116**:377
"Afternoon Happiness" (Kizer) **80**:182
Afternoon Men (Powell) **1**:277; **3**:400; **7**:339; **10**:409-11; **31**:319, 322
"Afternoon Nap" (Cortázar) **5**:109
"The Afternoon of a Faun" (Ferber) **93**:145, 180
Afternoon of a Faun (Hearon) **63**:163
Afternoon of a Pawnbroker (Fearing) **51**:110-11
The Afternoon of a Writer (Handke)
See *Nachmittag eines Schriftsellers*
"Afternoon of an American Boy" (White) **34**:430
An Afternoon of Pocket Billiards (Taylor) **44**:301
Afternoon of the Unreal (Salinas) **90**:326, 330
Afternoon Off (Bennett) **77**:86-9
"Afternoon on Elba" (O'Faolain) **47**:325
"The Afternoon Sun" (Durrell) **13**:188
"Afternoon Sun" (Willingham) **51**:403
"Afternoon Walk" (Miles) **34**:245
Afternoons (Hecht)
See *1001 Afternoons in Chicago*
Afternoons in Mid-America (Caldwell) **8**:123; **14**:95
"Afterthought" (Lowell) **37**:240; **124**:257, 260
"Afterthought" (Musgrave) **13**:401
"After-Thoughts" (MacEwen) **55**:163-64, 167, 169
"Afterthoughts of Donna Elvira" (Kizer) **80**:173
"Afterthoughts on the Rosenbergs" (Fiedler) **4**:163
Aftertones (Ian) **21**:186
"Afterward" (Appleman) **51**:15
"An Afterward" (Heaney) **14**:246; **74**:160, 164, 167; **91**:115
"Afterward" (Rich) **125**:330
"Afterward" (Warren) **39**:257, 262
"Afterwards" (Davison) **28**:101
"Afterwards" (Muske) **90**:312
Afterwards (Benet)
See *Despuúes*
"An Afterword: For Gwen Brooks" (Madhubuti) **73**:215
"Afterword on Rupert Brooke" (Prince) **22**:339-40
"An Afterword to 'Lolita'" (Nabokov) **64**:348
"An Afterword to My Father" (Bell) **8**:65; **31**:47
"Afterwords" (Gass) **15**:255
Afterworlds (MacEwen) **55**:163-69
Aftonland (Lagerkvist) **10**:313; **13**:330, 332-33
"Afw al-malik Userkaf" (Mahfouz) **153**:351
Agaguk (Theriault) **79**:399, 401, 403, 406-408, 410, 412, 415, 417-18, 420
"Again" (Raine) **103**:190
"Again, Again, Again" (Robison) **98**:306, 308
"Again and Again and Again" (Sexton) **123**:408
"Again at Waldheim" (Rexroth) **49**:277
Again Calls the Owl (Craven) **17**:80
"Again El cante flamenco" (Cabral de Melo Neto)
See "Ainda El cante flamenco"
"Again, Like Before" (Castillo) **151**:47
Again to the North (Mackenzie) **18**:313
Against a Darkening Sky (Lewis) **41**:253, 256-57, 263
Against a League of Liars (Acorn) **15**:10
"Against Botticelli" (Hass) **18**:213
"Against Confidences" (Davie) **31**:109
"Against Coupling" (Adcock) **41**:15, 18
"Against Destiny" (Tchicaya) **101**:347
"Against Dryness: A Polemical Sketch" (Murdoch) **2**:297; **3**:346; **6**:347-48
"Against Dullness" (Szirtes) **46**:393
"Against Elegies" (Hacker) **91**:110-11
Against Emptiness (Zweig) **34**:378; **42**:465-67
Against Entropy (Frayn) **3**:164; **7**:106
"Against Extremity" (Tomlinson) **13**:548; **45**:402
Against Forgetting: Twentieth-Century Poetry of Witness (Forché) **86**:142, 144
"Against Illuminations" (MacLeish) **68**:286
Against Infinity (Benford) **52**:68-9, 71-2, 77
"Against Interpretation" (Sontag) **105**:207-08
Against Interpretation and Other Essays (Sontag) **1**:322; **10**:484; **31**:405-06, 416-18; **105**:209, 215-18, 225
"Against Meaning" (Codrescu) **121**:160
"Against Memory" (Bunting) **47**:44
"Against Romanticism" (Amis) **40**:39, 44
"Against San Francisco" (Cassity) **42**:95
"Against Silence" (Hacker) **72**:191
"Against Stupidity" (Asimov) **19**:26
"Against the Age" (Simpson) **7**:426
Against the Circle (Ghiselin) **23**:169
"Against the Fall of Night" (Clarke) **136**:209
Against the Fall of Night (Clarke) **1**:59; **13**:153; **35**:121-22, 127; **136**:211, 213, 225, 238
Against the Grain: Selected Essays, 1975-1985 (Eagleton) **63**:106-07
"Against the Male Flood: Censorship, Pornography and Equality" (Dworkin) **123**:76, 102-03, 107
Against the Silences (Blackburn) **43**:66-8
"Against the Silences to Come" (Loewinsohn) **52**:283-84
"Against the Small Evil Voices" (Hulme) **130**:66
"Against the Wind" (Seger) **35**:384, 387
Against the Wind (Seger) **35**:384-87
"Against Your Beliefs" (Snodgrass) **68**:389
"Agamemnon" (Ritsos) **13**:488
Agamemnon (Berkoff) **56**:12
Agamemnon (Harrison) **129**:180, 211
Agantuk (Ray) **76**:360, 366
Agatha (Colegate) **36**:110-11, 113
Agatha (Duras) **68**:85, 92; **100**:143
Agatha Christie: A Biography (Morgan) **39**:436, 438-39, 441-43
"Agbor Dancer" (Clark Bekedermo) **38**:117, 121, 128
"Age" (Breton) **9**:126
"An Age" (Jensen) **37**:190
"Age" (Larkin) **64**:262
"Age" (Thomas) **48**:376
An Age (Aldiss) **14**:13
Age (Calisher) **134**:21, 23-4, 35-6, 40
"L'âge de discrétion" (Beauvoir) **124**:185-86
L'âge de discrétion (Beauvoir) **14**:70; **31**:45; **44**:345; **124**:127
L'âge de raison (Sartre) **1**:304-05; **44**:493; **50**:383
L'age d'homme (Leiris) **61**:341-54, 357-58, 360
L'age d'or (Bunuel) **16**:145-6; **80**:19-20, 27-34, 36-8, 40-1, 44-5, 47, 50, 56-7
"The Age of a Wart" (White) **69**:413-14
The Age of Amazement (Appelfeld)
See *Tor Hapela'ot*
The Age of Anxiety: A Baroque Eclogue (Auden) **1**:9-10; **2**:23-4; **3**:26-7; **4**:33; **11**:19; **14**:31; **43**:15, 20, 26-7; **123**:52-6
Age of Aquarius: You and Astrology (Branley) **21**:23-4
Age of Assassins: The Story of Prisoner No. 1234 (Soupault)
See *Le temps des assassins*
The Age of Defeat (Wilson) **14**:586
"The Age of Desire" (Barker) **52**:52-3, 55
The Age of Discretion (Beauvoir)
See *L'âge de discrétion*
"The Age of Dogma" (Blaga)
See "Eonul dogmatic"
Age of Eternal Peace (Haavikko)
See *Ikuisen rauhau aika*
The Age of Grief (Smiley) **53**:347-50; **76**:230, 233, 235; **144**:253
The Age of Happy Problems (Gold) **7**:122; **42**:189; **152**:122-23, 126, 144
"The Age of Herbert and Vaughan" (Blunden) **56**:39
"The Age of Innocence" (Hope) **51**:221
The Age of Innocence (Scorsese) **89**:268-70
"The Age of Iron" (Haavikko) **34**:175, 177-79
Age of Iron (Coetzee) **66**:101-04, 106-07; **117**:59-61, 75, 79-82, 85, 87-90, 92, 102
The Age of Jackson (Schlesinger) **84**:347-48, 352, 370-71, 375, 377, 379, 382, 384
"The Age of Kaie" (Harris) **25**:217
"The Age of Lead" (Atwood) **84**:96, 98
The Age of Longing (Koestler) **3**:271; **33**:234, 241-42
The Age of Miracles (Gilchrist) **143**:299-301, 308, 313-15, 325, 327, 329-30
The Age of Rainmakers (Harris) **25**:217
"The Age of Reason" (Graham) **118**:229, 259
The Age of Reason (Hope) **51**:226
The Age of Reason (Koestler) **3**:271
The Age of Reason (Sartre)
See *L'âge de raison*
The Age of Roosevelt (Schlesinger) **84**:375, 378
The Age of Scandal (White) **30**:449
The Age of Suspicion: Essays on the Novel (Sarraute)
See *L'ere du soupçon: Essais sur le roman*
Age of Thunder (Prokosch) **4**:420; **48**:312, 314
The Age of Wonders (Appelfeld)
See *Tor Hapela'ot*
"Age, Race, Class and Sex: Women Redefining Difference" (Lorde) **71**:244-45
"Age to Youth" (Wright) **53**:424
"The Aged" (Kuzma) **7**:196

"Aged Man Surveys the Past Time" (Warren) **13**:573
"The Ageing Lovers" (Dickey) **3**:127
The Agency (Fearing) **51**:110
"The Agency of the Letter in the Unconscious; or, Reason Since Freud" (Lacan)
See "L'instance de la lettre"
"The Agent" (Jones) **42**:242-43
"The Agent" (Wilbur) **6**:568; **53**:398
Agent (Hinde) **6**:242
Agent in Place (MacInnes) **27**:282
Agents and Patients (Powell) **10**:411-12
Agents and Witnesses (Newby) **2**:311; **13**:408, 410
Un agenzia matrimoniale (Fellini) **16**:276
L'aggrandissement (Mauriac) **9**:363
"Aggressivitly in Psychoanalysis" (Lacan) **75**:280, 294
"Aghwee the Sky Monster" (Oe)
See "Sora no kaibutsu Aguwee"
"Aging Female Reads Little Magazines" (Atwood) **84**:69
"Aging Into Death: Petrify then Dissolve" (Rose) **85**:314
"Agnes" (Gordon) **128**:118
"The Agnes Cleves Papers" (Avison) **97**:69-71, 76-7, 80-1, 84, 91, 105, 110, 127
Agoak, l'héritage d'Agaguk (Theriault) **79**:407
Agoak: The Legacy of Agaguk (Theriault)
See *Agoak, l'héritage d'Agaguk*
Agon: Towards a Theory of Revisionism (Bloom) **24**:81; **103**:20-1, 23-5, 30, 33-4, 37, 47-8, 54
"Agonia" (Ungaretti) **11**:556
"Agonie" (Tchicaya) **101**:350
"Agonist of the Acceleration Lane" (Fulton) **52**:158-59
"Agony" (Ungaretti)
See "Agonia"
The Agony and the Ecstasy (Stone) **7**:469, 471
"An Agony. As Now" (Baraka) **10**:20
The Agony of Flies (Canetti)
See *Die Fliegenpein*
The Agony of the American Left (Lasch) **102**:293
"Agoraphobia" (Prager) **56**:276
"Agosta the Winged Man and Rasha the Black Dove" (Dove) **81**:137
Agostino (Moravia) **7**:240, 244; **18**:343
"Agosto" (Aleixandre) **9**:12
Agrestes (Cabral de Melo Neto) **76**:160-61, 163-64, 166, 168
Agricola and the Fox (Haavikko)
See *Agricola ja kettu*
Agricola ja kettu (Haavikko) **18**:208; **34**:173
"Agricultural Caress" (Betjeman) **43**:43
Agrippa's Daughters (Fast) **131**:100
Agrippina (Neihardt) **32**:331
Agua (Arguedas) **10**:8; **18**:5-6
"Agua sexual" (Neruda) **1**:247
Água viva (Lispector) **43**:265-66
"As águas do Recife" (Cabral de Melo Neto) **76**:169
"El águila" (Cernuda) **54**:47-8
Aguirre, the Wrath of God (Herzog) **16**:322-25, 331, 333-35
"Agulhas" (Cabral de Melo Neto) **76**:168-69
The Agunah (Grade) **10**:246
"Agunot: A Tale" (Agnon) **14**:2
Ah! Ah! (Ducharme) **74**:61, 65-8
Ah, but Your Land Is Beautiful (Paton) **25**:362-63; **55**:311; **106**:294-95, 298, 300
"Ah Life, This Lowgrade Infection" (Honig) **33**:213
"Ah, mon bon château.?.?." (Yourcenar) **38**:462
"Ah, Nonny, Nonny" (Kherdian) **9**:318
Ah Pook Is Here and Other Texts (Burroughs) **15**:112
"Ah, Woe Is Me" (Gordimer) **70**:178
"Ahasuerus" (Nemerov) **36**:301
Ahasverus död (Lagerkvist) **7**:199; **10**:311-12; **13**:332; **54**:280-83, 285
"Ahavnu Kan" (Amichai) **116**:109
"Ahead" (Aldiss)
See "The Failed Men"
"Ahmet Ertegun" (Trow) **52**:421-22
"El ahogado más hermoso del mundo" (García Márquez) **2**:149; **27**:148, 154; **47**:148, 151
Ai no barei (Oshima) **20**:256-57
Ai no megane wa irogarasu (Abe) **81**:286
Ai-ch'ing ti san-pu ch u (Pa Chin) **18**:372-73
"Aïda in the Mirror" (Shamlu) **10**:470
"Aide-Memoire" (Forché)
See "El Salvador: An Aide Memoire"
AIDS and Its Metaphors (Sontag) **105**:206, 215, 219, 227
"Aigeltinger" (Williams) **42**:450
L'aigle à deux têtes (Cocteau) **8**:148-49; **16**:223, 225; **43**:105, 112
Aiiieeeee! (Chin)
See *The Big Aiiieeeee!: An Anthology of Chinese American and Japanese American Literature*
Aika (Endō) **54**:160
Aikin Mata (Harrison) **129**:189, 193
"Aile" (Reverdy) **53**:289
"Aim" (Randall) **135**:398
Aimé Césaire: Profil d'une oeuvre (Condé) **92**:100
Aimé Césaire: The Collected Poetry (Césaire) **32**:112-13; **112**:8
The Aimer Gate (Garner) **17**:150-51
Aimez-vous Brahms? (Sagan) **17**:421-22, 425
"The Aims of Education" (Eliot) **41**:155
The Aims of Interpretation (Hirsch) **79**:255, 257-58, 260-62
"Ainda El cante flamenco" (Cabral de Melo Neto) **76**:162
L'aîné des Fercheaux (Simenon) **47**:379
Ain't I a Woman: Black Women and Feminism (Hooks) **94**:132-40, 144, 154, 159-60
"Ain't It Strange" (Smith) **12**:539
"Ain't Nature Wonderful!" (Ferber) **93**:142, 145
"Ain't No Crime" (Joel) **26**:213
"Ain't No Love in These Streets" (Milner) **56**:225
"Ain't No Man Righteous, No Not One" (Dylan) **77**:186
Ain't Supposed to Die a Natural Death (Van Peebles) **2**:447-48
"Ain't That Peculiar" (Robinson) **21**:347
"Air" (Reverdy) **53**:289
"Air" (Walcott) **25**:451
"The Air" (Zappa) **17**:586
Air and Angels (Hill) **113**:318
"The Air and the Wind" (Galeano) **72**:139
"Air and Variations" (Daryush) **19**:122
Air Apparent (Gardner) **30**:153
L'air de l'eau (Breton) **54**:30; **9**:127-28, 132; **15**:91
"Air Hostess" (Amichai) **57**:38
Air Indien (Morand) **41**:304
"The Air of June Sings" (Dorn) **10**:159
"Air Raid" (Achebe) **7**:6; **11**:3; **26**:21
Air Raid (MacLeish) **68**:286
Air Surgeon (Slaughter) **29**:373
An Air That Kills (King) **53**:204
The Air We Breathe (Josipovici) **43**:222-23
Air with Armed Men (Simpson) **149**:341
Airborn (Paz)
See *Hijos del aire*
Airborn/Hijos del aire (Tomlinson) **45**:398, 400
The Air-Conditioned Nightmare (Miller) **4**:351
The Air-Line to Seattle (Lynn) **50**:426
"Airman's Virtue" (Meredith) **4**:348
"The Airport" (Lowell) **9**:335
Airport (Hailey) **5**:156-57
Airs above the Ground (Stewart) **7**:467; **35**:391
"The Airship Boys in Africa" (Cassity) **42**:99
Airships (Hannah) **23**:209, 211-12; **38**:232-35; **90**:126, 128-31, 138-39, 141, 143-48, 159-61, 163
Airshipwreck (Deighton) **46**:128
"Airwaves" (Mason) **154**:302-05
Airways (Pasternak) **63**:290
Airways, Inc. (Dos Passos) **4**:134; **15**:184; **25**:144
Airy Hall (D'Aguiar) **145**:114, 117, 121, 127
"Airy Hall at Night" (D'Aguiar) **145**:115
"Airy Hall Barrier" (D'Aguiar) **145**:115
"Airy Hall's Feathered Glories" (D'Aguiar) **145**:115
"The Airy Tomb" (Thomas) **6**:534; **48**:378
"Aisling" (Heaney) **74**:162
"Aix-en-Provence" (Rexroth) **49**:283
"Aja" (Becker and Fagen) **26**:84
Aja (Becker and Fagen) **26**:83-4
Ajaiyi and His Inherited Poverty (Tutuola) **29**:435, 442-43
"Ajanta" (Rukeyser) **6**:478; **27**:407-08, 410-11, 414
"Ajax" (Ritsos) **13**:488
"El ajolote" (Arreola) **147**:31
"Um ajuste de contas" (Dourado) **60**:85
"Akai mayu" (Abe) **8**:1; **81**:292
Akallabêth (Tolkien) **3**:481
"Akanishi Kakita" (Shiga) **33**:366
Aké: The Years of Childhood (Soyinka) **36**:413-14
Akhenaten: Dweller in Truth (Mahfouz) **153**:365-70, 374
Akhshav bara'ash (Amichai) **116**:123
Akhshav Uveyamim (Amichai) **116**:125
"Akiba" (Rukeyser) **15**:457
Akillesovo serdtse (Voznesensky) **57**:414-15, 418
"Akkayya" (Rao) **56**:312
"An Akoulina of the Irish Midlands" (Lavin) **4**:282; **18**:304
Akt przerywany (Rozewicz) **9**:464-65; **139**:229, 276-78, 280-83, 293
Aku-Aku: The Secret of Easter Island (Heyerdahl) **26**:191, 193
"Akueke" (Achebe) **75**:15-16
"Akuma" (Tanizaki) **8**:509
Al 'A'ish fi-al-haqiqah (Mahfouz) **153**:361, 374
"Al amor" (Aleixandre) **9**:15
"Al azar" (Otero) **11**:427
Al cielo se sube a pie (Ulibarrí) **83**:407, 412, 416
"Al Denny" (Keillor) **115**:286
Al di la delle navole (Antonioni) **144**:54, 56-58, 62-63, 65-67, 70-9, 81
Al paso (Paz) **119**:414
Al pie de la letra (Castellanos) **66**:45, 47, 52
Al que quiere! (Williams) **13**:603; **42**:450, 459
"Alabama" (Young) **17**:570, 572-73, 582
"Alabama Poem" (Giovanni) **19**:192; **117**:195
"Alabama Song" (Morrison) **17**:286-87
Aladdin Sane (Bowie) **17**:59-62, 64, 66-7
Aladdin's Problem (Jünger) **125**:251-52, 257, 261
"Alain Alain" (Simpson) **149**:345
Al'A'ish fi'al-haqiqah (Mahfouz) **153**:361, 374
"The Alamo Plaza" (Rooke) **25**:390
Alan and the Animal Kingdom (Holland) **21**:150, 154
Alan Mendelsohn, the Boy from Mars (Pinkwater) **35**:317-20
Alanna Autumnal (Barker) **48**:9-10, 22
"Alan's Psychedelic Breakfast" (Pink Floyd) **35**:305, 311
"Alarma para el año 2000" (Arreola) **147**:34
"The Alarming Revenge of a Domestic Pet" (Buzzati) **36**:92
Alarms and Diversions (Thurber) **11**:532
"Alas, Poor Richard" (Baldwin) **17**:38; **127**:142
Alaska (Michener) **60**:258-62; **109**:376-77, 381, 386
"Alaska Passage" (Birney) **11**:51
"Alaskan Meander" (Richards) **14**:453
"Alatus" (Wilbur) **53**:405; **110**:360
"Alba" (Spicer) **72**:364
"Alba after Six Years" (Middleton) **13**:387
El alba del alhelí (Alberti) **7**:8
"Alba innominata" (Pound) **10**:407

"Al-Bahw" (Mahfouz) **153**:373
"The Albanian Virgin" (Munro) **95**:319, 322, 324
"The Albatross" (Hill) **113**:281-82, 312
"The Albatross" (Lem) **149**:162
The Albatross and Other Stories (Hill) **4**:228; **113**:281, 291, 293, 297, 303, 310, 312, 325
Albatross Two (Thiele)
See *Fight against Albatross Two*
"Albergo Empedocle" (Forster) **13**:220
Albergo Empedocle, and Other Writings (Forster) **4**:166
Albert Angelo (Johnson) **6**:263; **9**:300, 302
"Albert des capitales" (Duras) **40**:118; **68**:75-6, 78, 80, 83, 90, 94
"Albert Giacometti (On a Postage Stamp or Medallion)" (Leiris) **61**:361
"Albert of the Capital/Ter of the Militia" (Duras)
See "Albert des capitales"
"Albert of the Capitals" (Duras)
See "Albert des capitales"
Alberta (Kroetsch) **132**:271
"Alberta Bound" (Lightfoot) **26**:278-79
Albertine in Five Times (Tremblay) **102**:378-79
"Albert's Bridge" (Stoppard) **4**:524; **15**:519; **29**:394, 397
"Albino" (Komunyakaa) **94**:246
"Albino Pheasants" (Lane) **25**:286-87
Albino Pheasants (Lane) **25**:285, 288
"The Album" (Day Lewis) **10**:131
"Album" (Miles) **34**:245
Album de familia (Castellanos) **66**:58
Albúm familiar (Alegria) **75**:44, 51-3
Album of Destiny (Stuart) **8**:507; **11**:509
"Album of Dreams" (Milosz) **31**:269; **56**:236, 240-41
The Album of the Soundtrack of the Trailer of the Film "Monty Python and the Holy Grail" (Monty Python) **21**:226
"Albuquerque" (Tomlinson) **45**:397
"Albuquerque" (Young) **17**:574
"Albuquerque Back Again, 12/6/74" (Ortiz) **45**:305
Alburquerque (Anaya) **148**:22, 26-36, 39
"Alcatraz" (Olds) **85**:296
"Alceste" (Hecht) **8**:266
"Alceste in the Wilderness" (Hecht) **8**:267, 269; **13**:269
The Alcestiad (Wilder) **1**:364; **6**:577; **10**:536; **82**:377
"Alcestis and the Poet" (Porter) **33**:321
"Alcestis on the Poetry Circuit" (Jong) **83**:290
"The Alchemist" (Bogan) **4**:68; **46**:83-4, 89; **93**:64, 66, 69, 81, 93
"The Alchemist" (Pound) **10**:406
"The Alchemist Lost to Human Gifts" (Lerman) **9**:329
"Alcide 'Slow Drag' Pavageau" (Matthews) **40**:321
"Alcohol" (Carver) **36**:100
"Alcohol" (Davies) **21**:92
"Alcohol" (Duras) **68**:100
"The Alcoholic Love Poems" (Alexie) **96**:8; **154**:27
The Alcoholics (Thompson) **69**:384, 386-87
Alcoholism (Silverstein and Silverstein) **17**:454
"Aldarion and Erendis" (Tolkien) **38**:432
"Alder Catkin" (Yevtushenko) **26**:468
"The Alderman's Day in the City" (Johnston) **51**:244
"Aldershot Crematorium" (Betjeman) **10**:52; **43**:47
"The Ale House Poems" (Blackburn) **43**:62
"Alec" (O'Connor) **23**:329
Aleck Maury, Sportsman (Gordon) **6**:204; **13**:242; **29**:186, 188-90; **83**:228-29, 233, 240, 242, 247, 253-54, 257, 260
Alehouse Sonnets (Dubie) **36**:129, 135, 139
"Aleluja" (Pasolini) **106**:233
"El aleph" (Borges) **2**:72, 76; **4**:73; **13**:108-09; **44**:353; **48**:33, 35, 39-40, 42, 45; **83**:166, 183, 185-86, 189
"The Aleph" (Borges)
See "El aleph"
El aleph (Borges) **2**:72, 74, 76-7; **4**:74; **9**:118, 120; **13**:105; **44**:356, 363, 368; **48**:33-5; **83**:156, 158, 160-61, 164, 171, 185, 189
The Aleph, and Other Stories, 1933-1969 (Borges)
See *El aleph*
"Alerted" (Heaney) **74**:169
"Alethia" (Johnson) **51**:236
"Alewives Pool" (Kinnell) **5**:216
"Alexander" (Bates) **46**:49-50, 67
Alexander Pope (Sitwell) **2**:404
Alexandra (Martin) **89**:107-09, 116, 125-26, 129
Alexandre Chenevert (Roy) **10**:441; **14**:465-66, 469
"Alexandria" (Shapiro) **15**:476
"Alexandria, 641 A.D." (Borges) **83**:169
Alexandria: A History and a Guide (Forster) **13**:221; **45**:134
"Alexandria and Henrietta" (Barthelme) **46**:42
The Alexandria Quartet (Durrell) **1**:83-7; **4**:144-47; **6**:151-53; **8**:190-93; **13**:185-88; **27**:95-8, 100
Alexis; ou, Le traité du vain combat (Yourcenar) **38**:460-61, 464; **50**:362-65; **87**:383-84, 394-97, 399-400
"al-Fajr al-kadhib" (Mahfouz) **153**:352, 361
"The Alfano Ending" (Cassity) **42**:99
"Alfansa" (Forché) **25**:170
De Alfonce Tennis (Donleavy) **45**:126-27
Alfred and Guinevere (Schuyler) **23**:387-88
"Alfred Chester's Wig" (Ozick) **155**:185
"Alfred Corning Clark" (Lowell) **124**:255
Alfred Dies (Horovitz) **56**:155-56
"Alfred Jarry in Boston" (Donnell) **34**:159
Alfred the Great (Gustafson) **36**:216
Alfred the Great (Horovitz) **56**:152, 155-56
"Algebra" (Theroux) **28**:425
"Algebra and Fire" (Barth) **51**:24
"Algera" (Pastan) **27**:369
The Algiers Motel Incident (Hersey) **81**:332, 334, 337
"Algo secretamente amado" (Moraga) **126**:308
"Alguien desordena estas rosas" (García Márquez) **3**:181-82
"Alguien que anda por ahí" (Cortázar) **33**:125, **34**:333
Alguma poesia (Andrade) **18**:4
"Algunos aspectos del cuento" (Cortázar) **92**:159
Al-Hubb fawq hadbat al-haram (Mahfouz) **153**:235
"Ali" (Merwin) **45**:274-75
Alí dagli occhi azzurri (Pasolini) **37**:346-47
Alianza y condena (Rodriguez) **10**:439-40
"L'alias du 'Non' et du néant" (Ferron) **94**:121, 129
"The Alias of the 'NO' and Nothingness" (Ferron)
See "L'alias du 'Non' et du néant"
Alibi (Kroetsch) **57**:284-87; **132**:248-50, 252-55, 270-73, 280, 293
"Alibis" (Longley) **29**:293, 296
"Alibis and Lullabies" (Peacock) **60**:292
"Alicante Lullaby" (Plath) **111**:201
"Alice" (Barthelme) **115**:71
"Alice" (Creeley) **11**:139
Alice (Fast) **131**:100
Alice (Potter) **123**:233
Alice Doesn't Live Here Any More (Scorsese) **20**:362-27, 329, 334, 338-39; **89**:221-22, 232, 240-41, 243, 245, 256, 260, 263, 266-67
"Alice, Falling" (Millhauser) **109**:157-58, 160-61
Alice Fell (Tennant) **52**:398-99, 406
Alice in Bed (Sontag) **105**:214, 223-25
"Alice Is Gone" (Auden) **43**:17
Alice K's Guide to Life (Knapp) **99**:52
"Alice Long's Dachsunds" (Spark) **8**:493; **40**:402
"Alice's Last Adventure" (Ligotti) **44**:54
"Alicia" (Cisneros) **118**:180
"Alicia and I Talking on Edna's Steps" (Cisneros) **118**:174, 180
"Alicia and the Underground Press" (Didion) **129**:77-78
"Alicia Who Sees Mice" (Cisneros) **69**:146; **118**:174, 177
The Alien (Mitchell) **25**:322
"The Alien Corn" (Maugham) **67**:219
"An Alien Craft" (Akhmadulina)
See "Chuzhoe remeslo"
An Alien Heat (Moorcock) **5**:294; **27**:348-49; **58**:347-48
The Alien Intelligence (Williamson) **29**:454
"Alien Territory" (Atwood) **84**:105
"Alienation and Affection" (Sadoff) **9**:467
" Alienation: Two Bees" (Ferlinghetti) **111**:60
"The Alienations of Mr. Cogito" (Herbert) **9**:275
The Alienist (Carr) **86**:41-9
"The Aliens" (Auden) **9**:59
"Aliens" (Leavitt) **34**:78-9
"The Aliens" (McCullers) **12**:433
"Alighieri's Dream" (Baraka)
See "A Chase"
"Los alimentos terrestres" (Arreola) **147**:17-18
"Alinsky No in Their League" (Royko) **109**:408
Alinsky's Diamond (McHale) **5**:281-83
"Alison" (Costello) **21**:66-7
"Alive" (Appleman) **51**:14
Alive (Read) **4**:445; **10**:435; **25**:377
"Alive and Dead" (Fuller) **62**:185
"Alive and Well on a Friendless Voyage" (Ellison) **42**:130
"Alive for an Instant" (Koch) **44**:251
Alive: Poems, 1971-1972 (Wright) **11**:578; **53**:429-30, 432
"Alive Together" (Mueller) **13**:400
al-Jarima (Mahfouz) **153**:359
Al-Karnak (Mahfouz) **153**:270, 305, 359-60
"Al-Khala'" (Mahfouz) **153**:234
"Alkmene" (Dinesen) **29**:159, 163; **95**:35, 47, 59
All (Campbell) **32**:80
"All about and to a Female Artist" (Delaney) **29**:146
"All About—And Back Again" (Knight) **40**:283-86
All against All (Adamov)
See *Tous contre tous*
"All along the Watchtower" (Dylan) **12**:185
"All Around the Mulberry Tree" (Hunter) **35**:226
"All at One Point" (Calvino) **8**:127
"All Attempts Will End in Failure" (Berriault) **54**:4
"All Avoidable Talk" (Narayan) **47**:305
All Bleeding (Barker) **37**:37
All Bloods (Arguedas)
See *Todas las sangres*
All Creatures Great and Small (Herriot) **12**:282
"All Day and All of the Night" (Davies) **21**:88
"all day i have seen you" (Young Bear) **94**:366, 369
"All Day Long" (Senghor) **130**:278
All Day on the Sands (Bennett) **77**:86, 88, 93
"All Day Sucker" (Wonder) **12**:660
All Dressed Up and Nowhere to Go; or, The Poor Man's Guide to the Affluent Society (Bradbury) **32**:55; **61**:41
All Fires the Fire, and Other Stories (Cortázar)
See *Todos los fuegos el fuego*
"All Fools' Eve" (Avison) **97**:70
"All Generations Before Me" (Amichai) **116**:127
All God's Children Need Traveling Shoes (Angelou) **64**:35-8; **77**:7, 13-15, 20, 22, 27-8, 31
All Good Men (Fleming) **37**:119-21

All Good Men (Griffiths) **52**:173, 181-84
"All Grass Is Flesh" (L'Heureux) **52**:272
"All Hallows" (Glück) **7**:119
"All He Needs Is Feet" (Himes) **7**:160; **108**:227, 235
All Heaven in a Rage (Duffy) **37**:116
All Her Children (Wakefield) **7**:503
All I Could Never Be (Yezierska) **46**:444-45, 447
"All I Gotta Do" (Giovanni) **19**:192; **64**:187-88
"All I Need Is a Girl" (Sondheim) **30**:377
"All I Really Want to Do" (Dylan) **77**:176
"All in Green Went My Love Riding" (Cummings) **68**:46
All in the Family (Lear) **12**:326-32, 336, 338
All in the Family (O'Connor) **14**:392-93
"All in the Streets" (Baraka) **5**:48
All Is But a Beginning (Neihardt) **32**:336
"All is Emptiness and I Must Spin" (Kinsella) **138**:102
"All Is Mine" (Guillén)
See "Tengo"
All Is Mine (Guillén)
See *Tengo*
"All Kinds of Caresses" (Ashbery) **77**:46
"All Legendary Obstacles" (Montague) **46**:264-66, 275-76
All Love (Seifert)
See *Samá láska*
"All Lovers Love the Spring" (Gordon) **83**:231
All Men Are Enemies (Aldington) **49**:14, 18
All Men Are Mortal (Beauvoir)
See *Tous les hommes sont mortels*
All Mod Cons (Weller) **26**:444-45
All My Children (Nixon) **21**:242-48, 250-53
All My Friends Are Going to Be Strangers (McMurtry) **2**:272; **3**:333; **7**:214-15; **11**:371; **27**:329-31; **44**:255; **127**:317, 320, 329, 231-32, 344
"All My Friends Died" (Carroll) **35**:79
All My Little Ones (Ewart) **46**:150
"All My Pretty Ones" (Sexton) **53**:318, 320, 322
All My Pretty Ones (Sexton) **4**:482-83; **8**:482-83; **15**:471-72; **53**:312, 316-18, 320-21, 324; **123**:408, 414, 416, 424, 435, 437, 440
All My Relations: An Anthology of Contemporary Native Fiction (King) **89**:92
All My Road Before Me (Lewis) **124**:226
"All My Sins" (Fuentes)
See "Todos mis pecados"
All My Sins Remembered (Haldeman) **61**:177, 182-83
All My Sons (Kazan) **63**:234
All My Sons (Miller) **1**:216, 218-19; **6**:327, 329-32; **10**:342, 344; **15**:371-74; **26**:321-22; **47**:251, 254-56; **78**:293, 301-02, 306, 312, 318, 324
"All Night, All Night" (Schwartz) **45**:355-56
All Night Long (Caldwell) **60**:50
"All of Which Isn't Singing Is Mere Talking" (Cummings) **15**:164
All One Horse (Breytenbach) **126**:90
All or Nothing (Powys) **46**:323, 325; **125**:293
All Our Yesterdays (Ginzburg)
See *Tutti i nostri ieri*
All Over (Albee) **2**:1-4; **5**:13-14; **9**:6, 9; **11**:12; **13**:4-5; **25**:36, 38, 40; **53**:21; **113**:15, 17, 22-3. 28
All Over Town (Schisgal) **6**:490-91
All Quiet on the Western Front (Remarque)
See *Im Westen nichts Neues*
"All Revelation" (Frost) **13**:225, 230; **26**:118
All Roads at Once (Corn) **33**:113-14
All Said and Done (Beauvoir)
See *Tout compte fait*
All Screwed Up (Wertmueller)
See *Everything's in Place, Nothing's in Order*
"All Set About with Fever Trees" (Durban) **39**:44-6
All Set About with Fever Trees (Durban) **39**:44-6
"All Shook Up" (Boyle) **36**:63
All Shot Up (Himes) **18**:246; **58**:264, 267
"All Sorts of Impossible Things" (McGahern) **48**:264
All Soul's Day (Konwicki)
See *Zaduszki*
"All Souls Night" (Day Lewis) **6**:129
All Souls' Rising (Bell) **102**:20-23
All Stories are True (Wideman) **122**:343, 345, 347
"All Strange Away" (Beckett) **29**:59
"All Summer Long" (Anderson) **23**:29-30, 33
"All Systems Break Down" (Bottoms) **53**:29
"All Systems Tower and Collapse" (Bottoms) **53**:29
All That Fall (Beckett) **6**:42, 44-5, 47; **10**:30; **11**:34; **14**:79; **18**:42; **29**:63; **57**:79; **59**:255
All That Glitters (Lear) **12**:337-38
"All That Is" (Wilbur) **53**:412; **110**:357
"All That Is Lovely in Men" (Creeley) **78**:136
"All That Is Perfect in Woman" (Williams) **42**:456
All That Jazz (Fosse) **20**:126-27
"All That Lies Buried" (Dobyns) **37**:80
All That Remains (Cornwell) **155**:61
All That Rises Must Converge (O'Connor)
See *Everything That Rises Must Converge*
"All That Time" (Swenson) **106**:337
"All the Animal inside Us" (Bottoms) **53**:31
All the Assholes in the World and Mine (Bukowski) **41**:69
All the Beauty of the World (Seifert) **93**:326
All the Best People (Wilson) **32**:447
"All the Birds Come Home to Roost" (Ellison) **42**:130
"All the Blood within Me" (Amis) **40**:43, 45
All the Brave Promises (Settle) **19**:410; **61**:371
All: The Collected Short Poems, 1923-1958 (Zukofsky) **1**:385; **4**:599
All the Conspirators (Isherwood) **1**:155-56; **9**:292-93; **11**:295, 298-300; **14**:280-81, 285; **44**:396-97, 400-01
"All the Critics Love U in New York" (Prince) **35**:326-27
"All the Days of Our Lives" (Smith) **25**:410; **73**:357
"All the Dead Dears" (Plath) **11**:445; **51**:344
"All the Earth, All the Air" (Roethke) **101**:328, 332
"All the Fine Young Horses" (MacEwen) **13**:357
"All the Fruits Had Fallen" (Schwartz) **45**:361
"All the Kinds of Yes" (Tiptree) **48**:388; **50**:357
All the King's Men (Warren) **1**:352-56; **4**:577, 580-83; **6**:555-56; **8**:536, 539-40, 543; **10**:518; **13**:574, 579; **39**:264, 266; **53**:359-67, 369, 372-85; **59**:296, 298-300, 303
"All the Lies That Are My Life" (Ellison) **42**:129-30
All the Little Live Things (Stegner) **9**:508-09; **49**:353; **81**:340, 348, 352
"All the Lonely People" (McPherson) **77**:359-60
"All the Lovely Ladies" (Lightfoot) **26**:281
All the News That's Fit to Sing (Ochs) **17**:329, 331-32
All the Nice People (Leonard)
See *Mick and Mick*
All the President's Men (Goldman) **48**:128
All the Pretty Horses (McCarthy) **101**:164-65, 168-69, 171, 173, 176, 180, 182-92, 194-97, 199-200, 202-05
"All the Pussy We Want" (Bukowski) **41**:68
All the Rest Have Died (Gunn) **5**:152
"All the Sounds of the Rainbow" (Spinrad) **46**:384
All the Strange Hours: The Excavation of a Life (Eiseley) **7**:92-3
"All the Strength We Got" (Cliff) **21**:65
All the Summer Voices (Corcoran) **17**:72
"All the Time in the World" (Dubus) **97**:236-37
All the Time in the World (Williams) **42**:440-41
"All the Universe in a Mason Jar" (Haldeman) **61**:174, 176
"All the Way" (Gaye) **26**:132
"All the Way in Flagstaff, Arizona" (Bausch) **51**:55-7
All the Way to Bantry Bay (Kiely) **23**:265
"All the Young Punks" (Clash) **30**:43-4
All These Women (Bergman)
See *For att ente tala om alla dessa kvinnor*
"All Things Are Water" (Mathews) **6**:315
All Things Bright and Beautiful (Herriot) **12**:283
All Things Bright and Beautiful (Waterhouse) **47**:417
All Things Considered (Baker) **31**:27
All Things Nice (Billington) **43**:53-4
All Things Wise and Wonderful (Herriot) **12**:283
"All This Review" (Dodson) **79**:193
All Times, All Peoples: A World History of Slavery (Meltzer) **26**:307
All Together, All United, But Excuse Me, Isn't This Guy the Boss? (Fo)
See *Tutti uniti! tutti insieme! ma scusa quello non e'il padrone?*
All Together Now (Bridgers) **26**:91-3
"All Tomorrow's Parties" (Reed) **21**:303, 314
"All Too Clearly" (Ferlinghetti) **27**:139
All United! All Together! Hey Wait a Minute, Isn't That the Boss? (Fo)
See *Tutti uniti! tutti insieme! ma scusa quello non e'il padrone?*
All Us Come Cross the Water (Clifton) **66**:67, 86-7
"All Wars Are Holy" (Codrescu) **46**:102
All We Need of Hell (Crews) **49**:76-9
All What Jazz: A Record Diary, 1961-68 (Larkin) **33**:262, 268; **39**:334, 340, 343-44
"All Winter" (Hogan) **73**:159
All Women Are Fatal (Mauriac)
See *Toutes les femmes sont fatales*
"All Worlds Have Halfsight, Seeing Either With" (Cummings) **15**:164
"All You Can Hold for Five Bucks" (Mitchell) **98**:169, 184
"All You Need Is Love" (Lennon and McCartney) **35**:287
"All You Wanna Do Is Dance" (Joel) **26**:215, 220
"All You Who Sleep Tonight" (Seth) **90**:351
All You Who Sleep Tonight (Seth) **90**:350-1, 353, 361
"All You Zombies" (Heinlein) **14**:253; **26**:165, 174, 178
"Alla noia" (Ungaretti) **11**:555; **15**:536-37
"Alla Tha's All Right, but" (Jordan) **114**:145
"Allal" (Bowles) **19**:59, 61; **53**:37
All-American (Tunis) **12**:593-94, 598
All-Bright Court (Porter) **70**:96-101
"Alle" (Bachmann) **69**:35, 37
"Alle Tage" (Bachmann) **69**:38
"Allegiance" (Taylor) **37**:407-08, 412; **44**:305-06
Allegiances (Stafford) **4**:520-21; **7**:460
"The Allegorical Method" (Warner) **45**:434, 439
Allegories of Reading (de Man) **55**:384, 386, 391, 400, 406, 409-10, 415
"Allegorizing Hitchcok" (Jameson) **142**:247
"Allegory for Seafaring Black Mother" (Dodson) **79**:196
The Allegory of Love: A Study in Medieval Tradition (Lewis) **6**:308; **14**:321-22; **27**:259; **124**:193, 218, 221-22, 224, 228, 232
"An Allegory of Man's Fate" (Hood) **28**:193
"Allegory of the Adolescent and the Adult" (Barker) **48**:21
"Allegre" (Walcott) **25**:448; **76**:279
L'allegria (Ungaretti) **7**:481-82, 484; **11**:556-60; **15**:536-39
"Allegro" (Transtroemer) **52**:410; **65**:224, 235
Allegro Postillions (Keates) **34**:201-03
Allen Verbatim (Ginsberg) **6**:201

"Allentown" (Joel) **26**:222-23
"Aller et retour" (Barnes) **29**:27, 30
"Aller et retour" (Sartre) **24**:416-17
Allergies (Silverstein and Silverstein) **17**:456
Allergy (Taylor) **27**:440, 443
Alley Jaggers (West) **7**:522-25; **96**:375, 380
The Alleys of Eden (Butler) **81**:123, 127
"Allhallows Eve" (Gustafson) **36**:219
"Allie" (Graves) **45**:166
"Allies: According to Herodotus" (Williams) **148**:348
The Alligation (Ferlinghetti) **2**:134; **111**:63
"The Alligator Bride" (Hall) **37**:142, 147; **151**:196
The Alligator Bride: Poems Selected and New (Hall) **1**:137; **37**:141-42; **59**:156
The Alligator Groom (Hall) **1**:137
"Alligator Playground" (Sillitoe) **148**:199
Alligator Playground (Sillitoe) **148**:199
The Alligator Report (Kinsella) **43**:257-58
"Alligators and Paris and North America" (Dickey) **28**:119
al-Liss w'l kilab (Mahfouz) **153**:239, 243, 250, 262, 264, 270-72, 301, 305, 324, 343-45, 347-49, 357-59
All-Night Visitors (Major) **19**:291-92, 294-95; **48**:212, 215, 217
"All-Nite Donuts" (Goldbarth) **38**:205
"Allons Mes Enfants" (Hannah) **90**:158
"Allons voir sil la rose" (Arreola) **147**:31
Allophanes (Bowering) **15**:84; **47**:22-3, 28-9, 32
"Allotments" (Harrison) **43**:175
The All-True Travels and Adventures of Lidie Newton (Smiley) **144**:284-85, 293-96, 301
"Alma" (Chappell) **78**:116
"Almanac" (Swenson) **14**:520; **61**:390
Almanac of the Dead: A Novel (Silko) **74**:331, 350-52; **114**:330-31, 334-37, 340-43
al-Maraya (Mahfouz) **153**:277, 289, 308, 342, 350, 359
"Almeyer's Mother" (Findley) **102**:111
"The Almond of the World" (Elytis) **100**:179
"The Almond Trees" (Walcott) **25**:451
Almost a Fairy Tale (Buero Vallejo) **15**:100-02
Almost a Life (Friedman) **7**:109
"Almost an Elegy" (Brodsky)
See "Pochti elegiia"
Almost April (Sherburne) **30**:360
Almost at the End (Yevtushenko) **51**:431-33
"Almost Aubade" (Hacker) **72**:184
Almost By Chance A Woman: Elizabeth (Fo)
See *Elisabetta: Quasi per Caso una Donna*
Almost Cinderella (Potter) **86**:346
"Almost Grown" (Berry) **17**:54
"Almost in Iowa" (Irving) **112**:172, 175
"Almost Noon" (Galvin) **38**:198
Almost Paradise (Isaacs) **32**:255-56
Alms for Oblivion (Dahlberg) **7**:68-70; **14**:136
Alms for Oblivion (Raven) **14**:440-43
"Almswomen" (Blunden) **56**:27-8, 32, 37, 48, 52
"El almuerzo" (Cortázar) **34**:332
Alnilam (Dickey) **47**:98-101; **109**:236, 240, 241, 257
Aloes (Fugard)
See *A Lesson from Aloes*
"Alone" (Angelou) **77**:29
"Alone" (Singer) **23**:418
Alone Against Tomorrow: Stories of Alienation in Speculative Fiction (Ellison) **139**:129, 136-9
L'alone grigio (Ortese) **89**:192
"Alone in Africa" (Rush) **44**:92, 94-5
"Alone in the Lumber Business" (Ashbery) **77**:62-3
Alone of All Her Sex (Warner) **59**:217
Alone on the Pacific (Ichikawa) **20**:179, 182
Alone with America (Howard) **7**:166
Aloneness (Brooks) **49**:35, 37
"Along Lake Michigan" (Leithauser) **27**:240-42
"Along the Edges" (McGahern) **48**:264
"Along the Road" (Van Duyn) **116**:405
Along the Road: Notes and Essays of a Tourist (Huxley) **3**:256; **11**:287; **18**:269
"Along the Scenic Route" (Ellison) **13**:203; **42**:127
"Along These Lines" (Williams) **42**:443
Along with Youth: Hemingway, the Early Years (Griffin) **39**:398-403
"L'alouette" (Char) **9**:161
L'alouette (Anouilh) **1**:7; **3**:11; **13**:17-18, 21-2; **40**:53, 56-7, 61; **50**:278-80
"O alpendre no canavial" (Cabral de Melo Neto) **76**:169
"Alpha" (Tolson) **105**:241, 247-48, 253, 263-64, 283-84
Alpha Alpha (Barker) **37**:32, 37
Alpha Beta (Whitehead) **5**:488-89
"The Alphabet Begins with AAA" (Derleth) **31**:133
An Alphabet for Gourmets (Fisher) **76**:341-42; **87**:119-20
Alphabet for the Lost Years (Schaeffer) **11**:491
The Alphabet of Grace (Buechner) **2**:82
"Alphabetical Africa" (Abish) **22**:16, 18, 22
Alphabetical Order (Frayn) **7**:107-08
"Alphabets" (Heaney) **74**:161-62, 175-77, 190, 193
Alphabets (Perec) **116**:251
Alphaville (Godard) **20**:133-34, 137, 149
Alpine (Oppen) **34**:359
"The Alpine Christ" (Jeffers) **54**:250-51
"An Alpine Idyll" (Hemingway) **3**:240-41; **13**:273; **30**:181, 184
Alpýdubókin (Laxness) **25**:295, 298, 300
al-qahira al-jadida (Mahfouz) **153**:249, 260, 267, 270-72, 274, 277, 318, 336, 350-52, 355
"al-Qay'" (Mahfouz) **153**:350-51
"Already One" (Young) **17**:580
Als das Wünschen noch geholfen hat (Handke) **134**:133
"Als der Krieg ausbrach" (Boell) **27**:62-3, 67; **72**:79
Als der Krieg zu Ende war (Boell) **27**:67; **72**:78, 80
Als der Krieg zu Ende war (Frisch) **9**:217; **14**:182-83; **18**:160-62; **44**:196, 199
Als Kind habe ich Stalin gesehen (Hein) **154**:56, 73-8, 80-2, 122, 159, 161, 178-80
al-Shaytan y'iz (Mahfouz) **153**:351
al-Sukkariayah (Mahfouz)
See *al-Sukkariyya*
al-Sukkariyya (Mahfouz) **153**:249, 252, 254, 256-58, 267, 272, 276, 282-83, 285, 287, 293-94, 296, 298, 301, 304, 337, 372
al-Summan w'l-kharif (Mahfouz) **153**:250, 276, 358-59
"Alta niña de caña y amapola" (Guillén) **79**:241
Altanima (Audiberti) **38**:23
"Altar Boy" (Fante) **60**:133
The Altar Steps (Mackenzie) **18**:314
al-Tariq (Mahfouz) **153**:250, 253, 271, 358
"Altarpiece" (Hoffman) **141**:274, 280, 285, 309
"Die Alte Frau, die alte Marshallin" (Dickey) **28**:119
Alte Meister (Bernhard) **61**:22
"Altele" (Singer) **6**:509
The Alteration (Amis) **8**:11-12; **13**:13-14; **40**:42; **129**:18
Altered States (Brookner) **136**:119-22
Altered States (Chayefsky) **23**:119-20
"Ein älterer Herr, federleicht" (Hein) **154**:164-65, 167, 181
An Alternate Life (Duncan) **55**:295
Alternating Current (Paz)
See *Corriente alterna*
"The Alternative" (Baraka) **33**:55
"Alternative Commencement Address at Dartmouth College" (Jordan) **114**:153
The Alternative Society: Essays from the Other World (Rexroth) **2**:371; **49**:277
"Altitudes" (Wilbur) **53**:410; **110**:348, 353
"Alto do Trapuá" (Cabral de Melo Neto) **76**:167
"L'alto veliero" (Quasimodo) **10**:428
Altogether: The Collected Stories of W. Somerset Maugham (Maugham)
See *East and West: The Collected Short Stories of W. Somerset Maugham*
"Altriuzine" (Lem) **149**:126, 275, 278
Alturas de Macchu Picchu (Neruda) **1**:247; **5**:301, 303-04; **7**:260; **28**:307-08, 314; **62**:325, 328
"The Alumnae Bulletin" (Prager) **56**:276-78
"Aluroid" (Birney) **6**:78
"The Alvordton Spa and Sweat Shop" (Kauffman) **42**:251
"Always" (Strand) **71**:280
Always Coming Home (Le Guin) **45**:219-21; **136**:316, 328-29, 331, 333-36, 338-44, 369, 374-75, 385, 392-93
"Always for the First Time" (Breton) **54**:30
Always on Sale (Aksyonov)
See *Vsegda v prodaže*
"Always the Effort to Gather It All" (Coles) **46**:108-09
Always the Young Strangers (Sandburg) **10**:451; **35**:353-54, 357, 360
Always Young and Fair (Richter) **30**:319-21, 325
"Alyx" (Delany) **141**:154-55
"Am I an Irishwoman?" (Brophy) **105**:12
"Am I Blue" (Henley) **23**:217
"Am I Blue?" (Walker) **58**:408
"Am I My Neighbor's Keeper?" (Eberhart) **3**:133; **11**:177; **19**:140-42
"Am I Not Your Rosalind?" (Thurber) **125**:413
"Am I Spoiling You" (Bambara)
See "The Apprentice"
"Am Ortler" (Bernhard) **32**:20
Am Sarazenenturm (Jünger) **125**:223
"Am Strande von Tanger" (Salter) **52**:367, 369; **59**:195-96, 198
Am ungenauen Ort (Wellershoff) **46**:435
Am Ziel (Bernhard) **61**:26
Amadeus (Shaffer) **18**:477-78; **37**:382-89
Amado mio (Pasolini) **106**:254-55
"Amahl and the Night Visitors: A Guide to the Tenor of Love" (Moore) **39**:85; **45**:279-80
"Amalfi" (Aldington) **49**:17
"Amalfi Days" (Parini) **133**:288
Amalgamemnon (Brooke-Rose) **40**:110-11
"Amalia" (Ferré) **139**:152, 163
Amam al'Arsh (Mahfouz) **153**:288, 361, 368-70, 373
"Amana Grass" (Silkin) **6**:498
Amana Grass (Silkin) **2**:396; **6**:498; **43**:404
"Amanda" (Waldman) **7**:509
"Amanda Dreams She Has Died and Gone to the Elysian Fields" (Kumin) **13**:327
Amanda/Miranda (Peck) **21**:300-01
Amanda's Choice (Holland) **21**:147-48
"L'amande croyable au lendemain neuf" (Char) **9**:162
"Amandine" (Tournier) **95**:383-86
Amandine ou les deux jardins (Tournier) **95**:367-68, 383
L'amant (Duras) **34**:162-63; **40**:185-87; **68**:73-4, 76-7, 79-85, 87, 90-5, 98-9; **100**:119-22, 126, 128-32, 134, 136, 138-39, 141-49
L'Amant de la Chine du Nord (Duras) **100**:121, 123, 131-33, 136, 138-42, 144-45, 149
La amante (Alberti) **7**:8-9
L'amante anglaise (Duras) **6**:149; **11**:166; **40**:175-76, 181-83; **68**:89
Amantes (Brossard) **115**:105, 107, 110-11, 114-18, 121-23, 132-36, 140
"Los amantes viejos" (Aleixandre) **9**:17
Les amants puérils (Crommelynck) **75**:150, 153, 155-56, 162-63, 166, 168
"Amanuensis" (Godwin) **31**:197
"Amao guniang" (Ding Ling) **68**:56
Amarcord (Fellini) **16**:288-90, 294-97, 299-300; **85**:51, 59-60, 63-4, 66, 69-71, 74-8, 81-2

"Amargura para tres sonámbulos" (García Márquez) **3**:181; **47**:148
"El amarte" (Arreola) **147**:31
"The Amateur" (Gustafson) **36**:220
The Amateur (Littell) **42**:276-77
Amateurs (Barthelme) **8**:52-3; **13**:61; **46**:35-6; **59**:247; **115**:71
"An Amateur's Guide to the Night" (Robison) **42**:342-43
An Amateur's Guide to the Night (Robison) **42**:342-43; **98**:306, 318
Amator (Kieslowski) **120**:202, 207, 209, 224, 243-44, 247, 252-53, 256-57, 260
"Amazed and Confused" (Diamond) **30**:113
"Amazement" (Milosz) **22**:308
"Amazing" (Fuller) **62**:199, 204
The Amazing Adventures of Kavalier & Clay (Chabon) **149**:25-35
"Amazing Grace" (Mueller) **13**:399
"Amazing Grace in the Back Country" (Warren) **18**:536-37
"Amazing Journey" (Townshend) **17**:526, 538
"Amazing Perfume Offer" (Redgrove) **41**:354
The Amazing Spider Man (Lee) **17**:259-60
"Amazonka" (Bagryana) **10**:12
"The Amazons" (Barker) **48**:9, 12, 20
"Amazons" (Selzer) **74**:273
Amazons: An Intimate Memoir by the First Woman Ever to Play in the National Hockey League (DeLillo) **27**:79-80
"The Ambassador" (Reid) **33**:350
The Ambassador (Brink) **106**:105-06, 124, 136
"The Amber Witch" (Nye) **42**:304
"Ambergris" (Graham) **48**:146
"Amberjack" (Tiptree) **48**:396
"Amberose Triste" (Broumas) **73**:17
The Amberstone Exit (Feinstein) **36**:168
"Ambience" (Graves) **45**:166
Ambit (Aleixandre)
See *Ambito*
"The Ambition Bird" (Sexton) **4**:483; **53**:313
Ambito (Aleixandre) **9**:10, 12, 15; **36**:23, 25, 28-9
Le ambizioni sbagliate (Moravia) **7**:240; **46**:281
"Amblyopia" (Bernstein) **142**:23
"Ambroise, la baleine et Gabrielle" (Theriault) **79**:408
"Ambrose His Mark" (Barth) **9**:66, 69; **89**:3, 7-8, 14, 16, 19, 22, 40-1, 43, 49, 54, 58-9
"Ambrose Syme" (McGrath) **55**:74, 76
"Ambroso" (Isherwood) **14**:284
"Ambulance Blues" (Young) **17**:573, 581-82
"Ambulances" (Larkin) **8**:332; **13**:337; **18**:298-99; **33**:260; **39**:342; **64**:266
"Ambush" (O'Brien) **103**:143
Ambush (Read) **4**:439
Ambush at Tether's End (Walker) **61**:424
Amédée; or, How to Get Rid of It (Ionesco)
See *Amédée; ou, Comment s'en débarrasser*
Amédée; ou, Comment s'en débarrasser (Ionesco) **4**:251; **6**:247-50, 253-54; **9**:287; **41**:227, 230; **86**:332-34
L'amélanchier (Ferron) **94**:104, 106-7, 109, 111, 113-15, 124, 126-27
"Amelia" (Mitchell) **12**:442
"Amelia Earheart" (Smith) **12**:535
"Amen" (Hogan) **73**:154
Amen (Amichai)
See *Me-horei Kol Zeh Mistater Osher Gadol*
"Amen and Out" (Aldiss) **14**:15
The Amen Corner (Baldwin) **5**:40; **17**:31, 34, 37; **50**:283, 294; **67**:8; **127**:91, 98, 102, 105, 108-09, 145
"Amena Karanova" (Ulibarrí) **83**:417
L'Amer (Brossard) **115**:105, 107, 114-15, 119, 123-24, 127-29, 133, 136, 155-56
Amer Eldorado (Federman) **47**:122, 127
"America" (Angelou) **77**:29
"America" (Diamond) **30**:113-14
"America" (Ginsberg) **6**:199; **13**:239-41; **36**:180, 187, 192; **69**:211, 215; **109**:337, 355
"America" (Prince) **35**:332
"America" (Simon) **17**:462-63
"America" (Sondheim) **30**:387
America (Baudrillard)
See *Amérique*
America a Prophecy: A New Reading of American Poetry from Pre-Columbian Times to the Present (Rothenberg) **57**:382
"America! America!" (Plath) **11**:451
"America! America!" (Schwartz) **10**:462, 466; **45**:353-55; **87**:334-36, 342, 43
America, America (Kazan) **6**:273; **16**:367-68, 370-71; **63**:213-15, 221-22, 233, 235
America at Last (White) **30**:449
"America Began in Houses" (Crase) **58**:159, 164
"America Competes" (Gurganus) **70**:190-91, 195-96
America Day by Day (Beauvoir) **44**:343; **124**:134
"America Drinks" (Zappa) **17**:588
"America Drinks and Goes Home" (Zappa) **17**:585, 588
América, fábula de fábulas, y otros ensayos (Asturias) **13**:39
America Hurrah (van Itallie) **3**:492-93
America in 1492 (Josephy) **70**:352
America Invulnerable (Carr) **86**:47
America Is Hard to Find (Berrigan) **4**:56
America, My Wilderness (Prokosch) **4**:422; **48**:317
"America, Seen through Photographs, Darkly" (Sontag) **10**:486
"America the Beautiful" (Leiber) **25**:304
America, Their America (Clark Bekedermo) **38**:117, 127-28
"America: Toward Yavneh" (Ozick) **28**:348
America Was Promises (MacLeish) **8**:362; **14**:338; **68**:286, 289-90, 293
The American (Fast) **23**:157; **131**:66, 69-70, 73, 97
"An American Adventure" (Oates) **3**:360
American Appetites (Oates) **108**:374, 381, 386, 388
"American Art and Non-American Art" (O'Hara) **78**:375
"The American Background" (Williams) **67**:420-21
"The American Bakery" (Apple) **33**:21
"American Beauty" (Canin) **55**:36, 38-9
American Beauty (Ferber) **93**:156-59, 164, 171-72, 189-90
The American Bicentennial Series (Jakes) **29**:248-49
"American Blood" (DeLillo) **54**:87
American Buffalo (Mamet) **9**:360-61; **15**:356, 357-58; **34**:218, 220-22, 224; **46**:246, 248-50, 252, 254-55
"American Buttons" (Voznesensky) **57**:421, 428
"The American Cancer Society or There Is More Than One Way to Skin a Coon" (Lorde) **71**:249-50
"American Change" (Ginsberg) **3**:195; **4**:181; **109**:364
American Characteristics, and Other Essays (Wilder) **15**:575-76; **82**:378, 386
An American Childhood (Dillard) **60**:77-81; **115**:179, 181, 189, 197, 200-01
"American Citizen" (Boyle) **58**:69
"American Classic" (Simpson) **149**:307, 322, 325
The American Communist Party: A Critical History (Howe) **85**:119-20
"The American Couple" (Butler) **81**:122-23, 127-29
American Dad (Janowitz) **43**:209-10; **145**:330-32, 340-42
American Days (Poliakoff) **38**:382-84
The American Drama Since 1918 (Krutch) **24**:285
The American Dream (Albee) **1**:4-5; **2**:2-4; **3**:6; **5**:10-11; **9**:2, 4-5, 9-10; **13**:7; **25**:35, 40; **53**:22, 24, 27; **86**:120, 125; **113**:3-5, 9, 15, 18, 26, 31, 34-5, 40, 47-8, 54
An American Dream (Mailer) **1**:190-93; **2**:258-59, 261, 263; **3**:312-13, 317-18; **4**:321, 323; **5**:268; **8**:364-66, 369, 372-73; **11**:340-43; **14**:350-52; **28**:256-57, 261; **39**:421; **74**:203-07, 209, 224, 226, 233-34, 236, 245; **111**:95, 98-9, 108, 117-18, 120-21, 141, 148-49
"American Dreams" (Carey) **40**:127-29, 133; **96**:24, 27-8, 30, 37, 66-7
"American Dreams" (Simpson) **149**:330
American Dreams (Sapphire) **99**:80-2, 84, 87-8
American Dreams, American Nightmares (Madden) **5**:265
American Dreams: Lost and Found (Terkel) **38**:425-26, 428
American Earth (Caldwell) **14**:93, 96; **50**:299-300; **60**:44, 46, 48
The American Earthquake (Wilson) **2**:478
American Energies (Birkerts) **116**:152-53, 157
The American Evasion of Philosophy: A Genealogy of Pragmatism (West) **134**:328, 330, 332-34, 336-39, 359, 369, 374, 376
"American Express" (Salter) **52**:368; **59**:194, 196-97
American Expression (Lezama Lima)
See *La expresión americana*
American Fictions, 1940-1980: A Comprehensive History and Critical Evaluation (Karl) **34**:551-54
"The American Flag" (Miles) **14**:370
American Folksong (Guthrie) **35**:184, 192
"American/French Poems" (Laughlin) **49**:224
American Gigolo (Schrader) **26**:394-96, 398-99
American Girl (Tunis) **12**:592-93
American Gothic (Bloch) **33**:84
American Graffiti (Lucas) **16**:408-11, 416-17
The American Gun Mystery (Queen) **11**:460
The American Health System (Ehrenreich) **110**:152-53, 177
American Heritage Picture History of the Civil War (Catton) **35**:90
"The American Hotel" (Brautigan) **12**:57
American Hunger (Wright) **9**:585-86; **74**:378-83, 388-89
An American in Washington (Baker) **31**:25 6
American Indian Fiction (Larson) **31**:239-40
American Indian Policy in the Twentieth Century (Deloria) **122**:115-16
"American Indian Songs" (Rexroth) **112**:377
American Indians, American Justice (Deloria) **122**:112-13
American Indians in the Pacific: The Theory behind the Kon-Tiki Expedition (Heyerdahl) **26**:190-91
The American Jitters (Wilson) **24**:486
"American Journal" (Hayden) **37**:159
American Journal (Hayden) **14**:240-41; **37**:153-58, 160
The American Kaleidoscope: Race, Ethnicity, and the Civil Culture (Fuchs) **70**:376, 382, 385, 410
American Landscape (Rice) **7**:360-61; **49**:298, 300, 302-03, 305
"American Landscapes" (Montague) **46**:265
"American Letter" (MacLeish) **68**:273, 287-88, 292
The American Liberals and the Russian Revolution (Lasch) **102**:292, 318
"American Light: A Hopper Perspective" (Sissman) **18**:488
"The American Loneliness" (Wilder) **82**:357
American Madness (Capra) **16**:163-64
"American Mantras and Songs" (Ferlinghetti) **6**:184; **27**:139
"An American Marriage" (Klein) **30**:236
An American Marriage (Masters) **48**:220
An American Memory (Larsen) **55**:69-72
An American Millionaire (Schisgal) **6**:490
American Mischief (Lelchuk) **5**:240-43, 245
"American Muse" (Walcott) **67**:348

The American Newness: Culture and Politics in the Age of Emerson (Howe) **85**:142-45, 150
"An American Nightingale" (Yevtushenko) **26**:463-64
American Outpost: A Book of Reminiscences (Sinclair) **63**:346, 349
American Pastoral (Roth) **119**:120-25, 127-35, 138, 140-43, 145-46
"American Plastic: The Matter of Fiction" (Vidal) **8**:527-28; **10**:504
"American Poetry" (Simpson) **7**:427; **149**:319, 321, 354
"American Poetry and American Life" (Pinsky) **94**:301-2; **121**:433, 438
American Poetry in the Twentieth Century (Rexroth) **49**:279; **112**:386
American Poetry Since 1970: Up Late (Codrescu) **121**:164-70
"American Poets" (Bell) **8**:66
American Pop (Bakshi) **26**:74-6
"American Portrait, Old Style" (Warren) **13**:582; **18**:534; **39**:260, 264
American Power and the New Mandarins (Chomsky) **132**:32, 38, 40
An American Prayer (Morrison) **17**:292-96
"American Primitive" (Smith) **6**:513
American Primitive (Oliver) **34**:246-49; **98**:258-50, 269, 272-73, 275-77, 279, 290, 295-96, 298, 300-02
An American Procession (Kazin) **34**:555-64; **119**:311, 315-16, 321, 332-33
American Psycho (Ellis) **71**:143-74; **117**:132-35, 138, 140-41, 143, 145-51, 153-61
"American Radio Company" (Keillor) **115**:296
"American Rhapsodies" (Fearing) **51**:106
"American Rhapsody" (Fearing) **51**:106; **51**:108
An American Romance (Casey) **59**:119-20, 122
"American Scenes (1904-1905)" (Justice) **102**:274, 285
American Scenes and Other Poems (Tomlinson) **2**:436-37; **4**:543-44, 546, 548; **13**:545, 547-48; **45**:401
American Scrapbook (Charyn) **5**:104
"American Sexual Reference: Black Male" (Baraka) **115**:47, 49
The American Shore (Delany) **141**:145, 148-49
"American Sketches" (Justice) **102**:260-61, 270
The American Soldier (Fassbinder)
See *Der Amerikanische Soldat*
American Stars 'n Bars (Young) **17**:576, 579
"An American Student in Paris" (Farrell) **66**:131
"American Suite" (Urdang) **47**:400
"The American Sun" (Kaufman) **49**:205
An American Takes a Walk (Whittemore) **4**:588
"American Tune" (Simon) **17**:466
"American Twilights, 1957" (Wright) **3**:543; **5**:519
The American University: How It Runs, Where It Is Going (Barzun) **51**:40-1; **145**:82-3, 88, 94
"An American View of Pasternak" (Simpson) **149**:356
American Voices (Mason) **154**:203
The American Way (Hart and Kaufman) **38**:261-62, 266; **66**:175, 189
The American Way in Sport (Tunis) **12**:597
An American Werewolf in London (Landis) **26**:276-77
"Americana" (Rakosi) **47**:344, 347
Americana (DeLillo) **10**:134-35; **13**:175-76, 178; **27**:76-9, 81; **39**:117, 125; **76**:182; **143**:170, 172, 174-75, 207-08
The Americanization of Emily (Chayefsky) **23**:117
"Americans" (Riding) **7**:374
The Americans (Jakes) **29**:249
"America's Color Blind: The Modeling of Minorities" (Reed) **60**:310
America's Coming of Age (Brooks) **29**:78, 81-3, 87
Amérika (Alegria) **57**:11
Der Amerikanische Soldat (Fassbinder) **20**:107, 116
Amérique (Baudrillard) **60**:24-5
Amers (Perse) **4**:399-401; **11**:433, 435-36; **46**:306, 308
Les ames fortes (Giono) **4**:184
The Amethyst Ring (O'Dell) **30**:277-78
Le amiche (Antonioni) **20**:19, 21-2, 24-5, 29; **144**:17, 36-37, 67-68, 74, 79
"Amid Mounting Evidence" (Ashbery) **77**:66
"Amigo Acres" (Jensen) **37**:186
"Amigos de corazon" (Middleton) **13**:387
Aminadab (Blanchot) **135**:76, 113-15, 117-19, 136-37
The Amis Collection (Amis) **129**:17
L'Amité (Blanchot) **135**:113
"Amithaine" (Smith) **43**:420
"Amitié du prince" (Perse) **11**:434; **46**:301, 307
"Amities" (Scannell) **49**:330
Amnesia (Cooper) **86**:50-60
"Amnesiac" (Plath) **51**:340; **111**:160, 163
"Amo, amas, amat, amamus, amatis, Enough" (Perelman) **49**:265
Amok Time (Sturgeon) **39**:364
"Among All These" (Blunden) **56**:48
"Among Artisans' Houses" (Davie) **31**:124
"Among Bells" (Merwin) **88**:208-09, 211
"Among Children" (Levine) **118**:304
Among Friends (Fisher) **76**:339-40; **87**:123, 125, 130
Among Friends (Wright) **44**:334
"Among Murderers and Madmen" (Bachmann)
See "Unter Mördern und Irren"
"Among Ourselves" (Lorde) **71**:244
"Among School Children" (Van Duyn) **116**:401
Among the Beasts/Parmi les monstres (Federman) **47**:128
Among the Believers: An Islamic Journey (Naipaul) **37**:319, 321-24, 328; **105**:155, 176
"Among the Bumble Bees" (Plath) **11**:451
Among the Dangs (Elliott) **2**:131
"Among the Gods" (Kunitz) **6**: **287**: **148**:77, 88
"Among the Impressionists" (Wiggins) **57**:433
"Among the Massagetae" (Hesse) **25**:259
"Among the Mourners" (Gilchrist) **143**:300-01
"Among the Narcissi" (Plath) **51**:349; **111**:203-04, 214
"Among the Ordained" (Zamora) **89**:369
"Among the Paths to Eden" (Capote) **3**:99; **13**:134-36
"Among the Roses" (Lessing) **94**:272, 275
"Among the Ruins" (Friel) **115**:216, 218-20
Amongst Thistles and Thorns (Clarke) **8**:143; **53**:85-7, 92
"Amongst Those Left Are You" (Johnson) **6**:265; **9**:301
"El amor iracundo" (Aleixandre) **9**:15
"Amor loci" (Auden) **14**:30
Amor mundo y todos los cuentos (Arguedas) **10**:9
"El amor no es relieve" (Aleixandre) **36**:31
"El amor padecido" (Aleixandre) **9**:15
De amor y de sombra (Allende) **57**:17, 19, 23, 25-9, 33; **97**:4, 19, 25, 27, 40, 42, 57, 59, 62
Amor y Ecuador (Ulibarrí) **83**:412, 416
"The Amoralists" (Colter) **58**:147
The Amoralists and Other Tales (Colter) **58**:146-47
"Amorality Tale" (Bova) **45**:75
"Amore" (Moure) **88**:227
Un amore (Buzzati) **36**:87-90, 94-6
L'amore coniugale, e altri racconti (Moravia) **2**:293; **7**:244
Gli amori difficili (Calvino) **11**:90; **33**:100-02; **39**:306, 310, 314-17; **73**:42
"Amorosa anticipación" (Borges) **6**:88
L'amorosa menzogna (Antonioni) **20**:28; **144**:77
"An Amorous Debate" (Gunn) **18**:202
"L'amour" (Char) **9**:165
L'amour (Duras) **3**:129; **40**:178, 180, 185; **68**:91
Amour au goût de mer (Theriault) **79**:401, 415-16, 419
L'amour au temps des solitudes (Gallo) **95**:99
L'amour fou (Breton) **9**:127-28, 130; **54**:21, 26-7, 31
L'ampélour (Audiberti) **38**:23
The Ampersand Papers (Stewart) **32**:420
Amphitryon Thirty-Eight (Behrman) **40**:88
"Amplitude" (Gallagher) **63**:123, 125
Amplitude: New and Selected Poems (Gallagher) **63**:122-26
Amputations (Macdonald) **13**:355-56; **19**:291
"The Amputee" (Dacey) **51**:79
Amras (Bernhard) **32**:17-18; **61**:9, 21
Amrita (Jhabvala) **29**:252-53, 255, 260; **94**:167, 169-70, 176, 180, 200; **138**:64
"Am-traking to the Adirondacks" (Kenny) **87**:247
Amulet (Rakosi) **47**:343, 346
"Amusement Park" (Mahfouz)
See "Luna bark"
"Amusing Our Daughters" (Kizer) **80**:174, 178, 180, 183-84
"Amy Son" (Bennett) **28**:29
"An den Wassern Babels" (Celan) **82**:55
"An der Angel" (Boell) **72**:70-1
"An der Brücke" (Boell) **72**:69
"L'an trentiesme de mon eage" (MacLeish) **68**:273, 285, 291
L'an V de la révolution algérienne (Fanon) **74**:71-2, 74, 80
"Ana" (Rodriguez) **155**:312
"Ana María" (Donoso) **32**:156, 158
"Ana María" (Guillén) **79**:229, 241
The Anabaptists (Duerrenmatt) **102**:55, 58, 60
The Anabaptists (Dürrenmatt)
See *Die Wiedertäufer*
Anabase (Perse) **4**:399-400; **11**:433-34; **46**:298-302, 305-09
"Anabasis" (Merwin) **45**:270
Anabasis (Perse)
See *Anabase*
Anabasis, a Journey to the Interior (Gilchrist) **143**:310, 312-13
"Anabasis I" (Merwin) **45**:270
"Anabasis II" (Merwin) **45**:270
"Anacleto morones" (Rulfo) **80**:200
"Anacreontic" (Winters) **32**:470
"Anadyomene" (Walcott) **67**:352
"The Anagogic Man" (Macpherson) **14**:346
"An Anagram of Ideas on Art, Form, and Film" (Deren) **102**:38, 47
Anagrams (Moore) **45**:280-84; **68**:296, 298-99
Anagrams (Slavitt) **5**:391-92; **14**:490
"Anahorish" (Heaney) **7**:148; **14**:243; **25**:245, 249; **74**:157
Anaïs Nin Reader (Nin) **4**:378-79
Analecta del reloj (Lezama Lima) **4**:288; **101**:110
Anales de los Xahil (Asturias) **13**:37
"Analogies" (Parks) **147**:215
"L'analyse structurale en linguistique et en anthropologie" (Lévi-Strauss) **38**:300
"Analysis" (Livesay) **79**:348
"Analysis of Baseball" (Swenson) **106**:331, 339
"The Analytical Language of John Wilkins" (Borges) **83**:193
Ananke (Lem) **40**:291, 295
"Anaphora" (Bishop) **32**:29, 34
"L'anapo" (Quasimodo) **10**:428
Anarchism (Forman) **21**:120
"Anarchism and the Religious Impulse" (Rexroth) **112**:402
Anarchism Is Not Enough (Riding) **3**:431
The Anarchist's Convention (Sayles) **14**:483-84
"Anarchy" (MacEwen) **55**:163, 168
"Anarchy and Authority in American Literature" (Howe) **85**:152
"The Anasazi Woman" (Lewis) **41**:260-61
Anastomòsi (Gadda) **11**:211
"Anathema" (Voznesensky) **15**:554

The Anathemata: Fragments of an Attempted Writing (Jones) **2**:216-19; **4**:259-62; **7**:187-91; **13**:307-12; **42**:237-44, 246-48
"Anatole France" (Howard) **47**:170
The Anatolian (Kazan) **63**:221-22, 233
Anatolian Tales (Kemal) **29**:265
"Anatomie gagu" (Havel) **123**:171
"Anatomy" (Sorrentino) **40**:384
Anatomy and Solidary: Interviews with Jürgen Habermas (Habermas) **104**:76-7, 87
"Anatomy Lab" (Ciardi) **40**:154
"The Anatomy Lesson" (Connell) **45**:106
The Anatomy Lesson (Roth) **31**:340-47; **47**:357-59, 362; **86**:256; **119**:129-30, 135
The Anatomy Lesson and Other Stories (Connell) **45**:106-07, 109
"The Anatomy of Bliss" (L'Heureux) **52**:279
Anatomy of Criticism (Frye) **24**:208-09, 211, 213, 215, 217, 219, 222-23, 229, 231; **70**:271, 273-77
"The Anatomy of Mind" (Gass) **39**:480; **132**:156
The Anatomy of Nonsense (Winters) **8**:552; **32**:458
An Anatomy of Reticence (Havel) **58**:244; **123**:174
The Anaya Reader (Anaya) **148**:32, 35-36
"Anbarlulu" (Mahfūz) **52**:292
"Ancestors" (Randall) **135**:390, 398
"The Ancestors" (Wright) **53**:419
The Ancestors and the Sacred Mountain (Kunene) **85**:171, 175, 177
Ancestral Vices (Sharpe) **36**:402
The Anchor Tree (Humphreys) **47**:182-83
Anchors Aweigh: The Story of David Glasgow Farragut (Latham) **12**:324
Ancia (Otero) **11**:425
Les anciennes odeurs (Tremblay) **29**:427; **102**:372, 374, 377-78
"Ancient Amphitheater" (Ritsos) **31**:325
"An Ancient Ballet" (Kinsella) **138**:89, 100
"The Ancient Briton Lay Ynder His Rock" (Hughes) **119**:279, 289
The Ancient Child (Momaday) **85**:270-71, 273-74
Ancient Evenings (Mailer) **28**:257-63; **39**:416, 421, 423; **74**:205, 207, 224, 231, 233, 237; **111**:116-18, 120, 135, 141
"An Ancient Goddess: Two Pictures" (Blunden) **56**:47
"The Ancient Heroes and the Bomber Pilot" (Hughes) **9**:285
"Ancient History" (Bausch) **51**:55
"Ancient History" (Sassoon) **130**:215
Ancient History: A Paraphase (McElroy) **5**:279; **47**:238-39, 241-42, 244-45
Ancient Light (Lightman) **81**:78
"Ancient Lights" (Clarke) **6**:113; **9**:168
Ancient Lights: Poems and Satires, First Series (Clarke) **6**:113; **9**:167, 169
The Ancient Ones (Lewis) **41**:260-61
"The Ancient Ones: Betátakin" (Lewis) **41**:260-61
"The Ancient Rain" (Kaufman) **49**:205-07
The Ancient Rain: Poems, 1956-1978 (Kaufman) **49**:204-06
"Ancient Rites and Mysteries" (Williams) **39**:101
"Ancient Signs" (Hirsch) **50**:197
"Ancient Slang" (MacEwen) **55**:163, 167
"Ancient Sorceries" (Blackwood) **71**:86
"The Ancient Woman" (Mueller) **51**:279
"The Ancre at Hamel: Afterwards" (Blunden) **56**:43
"And" (Creeley) **11**:138
"And" (Gass) **39**:481-82
"And" (Goldbarth) **38**:207
& (Cummings) **8**:156; **15**:155, 160; **68**:35
And (Cummings)
See &
"And a Few Negroes Too" (Madhubuti)
See "A Message All Blackpeople Can Dig (& A Few Negroes Too)"
And a Nightingale Sang (Taylor) **27**:442, 444
And a Threefold Cord (La Guma) **19**:272-73, 276
And Again? (O'Faolain) **14**:407; **70**:319-21
And All Between (Snyder) **17**:473-75
"And All Flows Past" (Zamora) **89**:392
And All the Stars a Stage (Blish) **14**:83
"And Another One" (Ortiz) **45**:306
"And Another Thing" (Giovanni) **4**:189
And Both Were Young (L'Engle) **12**:345
"And Call Me Conrad" (Zelazny) **21**:467
And Chaos Died (Russ) **15**:461
And Dangerous to Know (Daly) **52**:91
And Death White as Words (Breytenbach) **23**:84; **126**:61
"And Forty-second Street" (MacLeish) **68**:273
"And Give Us Our Trespasses" (Livesay) **79**:337, 350
And Grieve, Lesbia: Poems (Kenny) **87**:245
"And I Am Driftwood" (Brutus) **43**:97
"And I Awoke and Found Me Here on the Cold Hill's Side" (Tiptree) **48**:385; **50**:357
"And I Dreamt I Was a Tree" (Alegria) **75**:49
"And I Have Come upon This Place by Lost Ways" (Tiptree) **48**:389
"And I Moved" (Townshend) **17**:541
"And I Will Be Heard" (Beecher) **6**:48
"And in My Heart" (Cassill) **4**:95; **23**:106
And in the Human Heart (Aiken) **1**:4; **52**:20, 26
...And Ladies of the Club (Santmyer) **33**:358-62
"And Leave the Driving to Us" (Kenny) **87**:249
And Live Apart (Peacock) **60**:291, 295, 297
"And Men Decay" (Santos) **22**:364
"...And Mr. Ferritt" (Wright) **53**:428
"... And My Fear is Great" (Sturgeon) **39**:361
"And Narrating Them..." (Ritsos) **6**:464
And Never Said a Word (Boell)
See *Und Sagte kein einziges Wort*
And No Birds Sang (Mowat) **26**:345-47
And No One Knows Where to Go (Sachs)
See *Und Niemand weiss weiter*
"And Not in Utter Nakedness" (Yurick) **6**:583
"And Now" (Rich) **125**:335
And Now for Something Completely Different (Monty Python) **21**:223, 225
"And Now, Goodbye" (Seifert) **44**:422
And Now Here's Johnny (Ephron) **17**:110
...And Now Miguel (Krumgold) **12**:316-17, 319-21
"...And Now You Don't" (Asimov) **26**:60
"And of Clay Are We Created" (Allende) **97**:4, 63
"And of My Cuba, What?" (Cabrera Infante) **120**:82
And on the Eighth Day (Queen) **11**:461
"And Once More like the Lights of the Open-Hearth Furnace" (Akhmadulina) **53**:9
And One Day Lasts Longer than an Age (Aitmatov)
See *I dol'she veka dlitsia den'*
"And One for My Dame" (Sexton) **53**:316, 322
And Quiet Flows the Don (Sholokhov) **7**:418
"And Sarah Laughed" (Greenberg) **30**:162
"And Say of What You Saw in the Dark" (Lane) **25**:286
...And Searching Mind (Williamson) **29**:455-56
"And So Goodbye to Cities" (Merton) **83**:395
"And So I Go" (Grace) **56**:120
"And So I Grew up to Be Nineteen and to Murder" (Oates) **3**:359
"And So Today" (Sandburg) **35**:342
"And Socializing" (Ashbery) **125**:37
"And Some More" (Cisneros) **118**:187
"And Some of His Enemies" (Fenton)
See "The Fruit-Grower in War-Time"
"And Son" (Bell) **8**:67
"And Still I Rise" (Angelou) **35**:30; **77**:30
And Still I Rise (Angelou) **12**:14; **35**:29-30, 32; **64**:32; **77**:15, 22, 30
And Summer Nights (Wilson)
See *Summer Days*
"And That Night" (Ignatow) **7**:182
And That's the Truth (Tomlin) **17**:517
And the Air Didn't Answer (Kerr) **55**:377-80; **59**:400
And the Band Played On: Politics, People, and the AIDS Epidemic (Shilts) **85**:322, 324-29, 331, 339, 341-44
"And the Child Lied" (Nakos) **29**:322
"And the Children of Birmingham" (Merton) **83**:393
"And the Crooked Shall Become Straight" (Agnon)
See "Vehaya he'akov lemishor"
And the Day Lasts Longer Than a Century (Aitmatov)
See *I dol'she veka dlitsia den'*
"And the Moon Be Still as Bright" (Bradbury) **42**:38
"And the Rain Came Down!" (Ngũgĩ wa Thiong'o) **36**:317
And the Ship Sails On (Fellini)
See *E la nave va*
"And the Singer Sings His Songs" (Diamond) **30**:111
"And the Stars Were Shining" (Ashbery) **125**:30, 38-40
And the Stars Were Shining (Ashbery) **125**:32-4, 38-40
"And the Trains Go On" (Levine) **14**:315-16, 318-19; **118**:267, 301
"And the Wave Sings because It Is Moving" (Larkin) **64**:282
And the Wife Ran Away (Weldon) **11**:565; **36**:445, 448; **122**:247, 249, 254-55, 259, 268, 276
"And Then" (Barthelme) **115**:69-70
And Then I Told the President (Buchwald) **33**:90-1
And Then I Wrote (Nelson) **17**:305
And Then There Were None (Christie) **1**:58; **6**:108; **8**:142; **12**:113-14, 120, 122-23, 125; **48**:73; **110**:112, 116, 122-23, 138
And Then There Were None (Clair) **20**:71
"And Then There Were Three" (Shaw) **7**:412; **34**:370
"And Then Turn Out the Light" (Weldon) **122**:261
And Then We Heard Thunder (Killens) **10**:300
And Then We Moved to Rossenarra or The Art of Emigrating (Condon) **100**:102, 110
"And There Is Always One More Story" (Ortiz) **45**:304, 306
And They Put Handcuffs on the Flowers (Arrabal)
See *Et ils passèrent des menottes aux fleurs*
And Things That Go Bump in the Night (McNally) **7**:216-18; **41**:292; **91**:157
And This Damned Helplessness (Hein)
See *Und diese verdammte Ohnmacht*
"And Ut Pictura Poesis Is Her Name" (Ashbery) **15**:30; **77**:61
"And Wanton Optics Roll the Melting Eye" (Huxley) **5**:192
"And What About the Children" (Lorde) **71**:259
And Where Were You, Adam? (Boell)
See *Wo warst du, Adam?*
"And Why Should Not Old Men Be Mad?" (O'Faolain) **47**:331
And Yet (Neruda) **28**:315
"And Yet They Are Knocking at Your Door" (Buzzati) **36**:94
"And You Know" (Ashbery) **77**:58
And You, Thoreau! (Derleth) **31**:136
And You, Too (Endō)
See *Nanji mo mata*
"And You Were a Baby Girl" (Peacock) **60**:293
An Andalusian Dog (Bunuel)
See *Un chien andalou*

"Andar" (Otero) **11**:427
Der andere Prozeß: Kafkas Briefe an Felice (Canetti) **25**:111, 113; **75**:139; **86**:301, 303
"Eine andere Rede über Österreich" (Handke) **134**:162
"The Anderson Boy" (Hansen) **38**:240
The Anderson Tapes (Sanders) **41**:376-78, 381-82
Andersonville (Kantor) **7**:194-96
¡Ay vida!, no me mereces (Poniatowska) **140**:330
Andorra (Frisch) **3**:167; **9**:217-18; **14**:182-83; **18**:163; **32**:188, 191, 195; **44**:181-83, 193, 196-98, 200, 207
André Breton (Gracq) **48**:133-35
"Andrea" (O'Hara) **42**:319
"Andrée Rexroth" (Rexroth) **49**:281-82; **112**:391
Andrei Rublev (Tarkovsky) **75**:370-72, 374-76, 379, 382-86, 388-89, 396, 401-03, 407, 410, 412
"Andrew" (Bowles) **68**:9
"Andrew Marvell" (Eliot) **24**:171, 178
Andrew the Lion Farmer (Hall) **151**:182
"Andrina" (Brown) **48**:60-1; **100**:84, 86
Andrina and Other Stories (Brown) **48**:59, 61; **100**:84
Androgyne, mon amour (Williams) **39**:452; **45**:443-45
"The Android and the Human" (Dick) **72**:107
Android at Arms (Norton) **12**:463
"Andromache" (Dubus) **36**:144-45; **97**:208
"Andromeda Chained to Her Rock the Great Nebula in her Heart" (Rexroth) **112**:375
The Andromeda Strain (Crichton) **2**:108; **6**:119; **54**:63-5, 67, 69-70, 72, 74, 76; **90**:69-71, 82, 89
"Andrum juli" (Transtroemer) **52**:409
Andy (Nichol) **18**:370
"Andy Warhol" (Bowie) **17**:58
"Aneas and Dido" (Brodsky) **50**:121-23
"The Anecdotes" (Durrell) **27**:97
Anecdotes of Destiny (Dinesen) **10**:149; **29**:156; **95**:37, 53
"Der Anfang von etwas" (Lenz) **27**:245
Ange (Woolrich) **77**:392
"L'ange heurtebise" (Cocteau) **8**:146-47
"Das angebrochene Jahr" (Celan) **82**:51
"Angel" (Brodkey) **56**:57-9, 61-2, 68
"The Angel" (Hughes) **119**:278
"The Angel" (McFadden) **48**:246
"The Angel" (McGrath) **55**:73-75
"The Angel" (Springsteen) **17**:487
Angel (Jordan) **110**:268-76, 278
Angel (Taylor) **2**:432; **29**:408
"Angel and Man" (Watkins) **43**:452
Angel Arms (Fearing) **51**:103-05, 107-11, 117, 122
An Angel at My Table (Campion) **95**:5-8, 12, 14, 18, 25-26
An Angel at My Table (Frame) **66**:143-45, 150; **96**:174, 193-94, 196, 201-03, 208, 217-18, 220
"Angel Butcher" (Levine) **4**:288; **5**:252; **14**:318; **118**:298-99
Angel City (Shepard) **17**:445, 447-49; **41**:409, 412
"Angel Come Home" (Wilson) **12**:654
An Angel Comes to Babylon (Duerrenmatt) See *Ein Engel kommt nach Babylon*
An Angel Comes to Babylon (Dürrenmatt) See *Ein Engel kommt nach Babylon*
El ángel exterminador (Bunuel) **16**:133-34, 139, 141, 148; **80**:34-8
Angel Eyes (Estleman) **48**:103-04, 107
"Angel Face" (Woolrich) **77**:400
Angel Fire (Oates) **3**:361
"Angel Fix" (Tiptree) **48**:389, 393
"The Angel Heurtebise" (Cocteau) See "L'ange heurtebise"
Angel in Heavy Shoes (Weber) **12**:634
"The Angel in the Alcove" (Williams) **45**:452
Angel in the Forest: A Fairy Tale of Two Utopias (Young) **82**:397-98, 400, 404-06, 408-414
Angel in the Parlor: Five Stories and Eight Essays (Willard) **37**:463-64
Angel Landing (Hoffman) **51**:202-03
"Angel Levine" (Malamud) **1**:201; **11**:346-48; **27**:299, 306; **44**:412-13, 417, 420; **85**:191
"Angel of Fire and Genitals" (Sexton) **123**:442
The Angel of History (Forché) **86**:137-45
Angel of Light (Oates) **33**:286-88; **52**:331, 339; **108**:352
"The Angel of the Bridge" (Cheever) **15**:130; **64**:57, 61-3, 65
"The Angel of the Church" (Phillips) **28**:362
"The Angel of the Tar Sands" (Wiebe) **138**:329
Angel on Skis (Cavanna) **12**:100
Angel Pavement (Priestley) **34**:361, 363-65
"The Angel Poem" (Stern) **40**:410-11
"An Angel Sat on a Tomb-Stone Top ..." (Levi) **41**:243
Angel Street: A Victorian Thriller (Hamilton) See *Gaslight: A Victorian Thriller*
The Angel That Troubled the Waters, and Other Plays (Wilder) **5**:496; **10**:531, 533; **15**:569; **82**:362, 384
"Angela" (Lennon) **35**:264
"Angela" (Mukherjee) **53**:266, 270
Angela Davis (Davis) **77**:111, 113-14, 116, 128
Angela's Ashes (McCourt) **109**:146-55
"Los Angeles Notebook" (Didion) **129**:97, 101
The Angelic Avengers (Dinesen) **10**:152; **29**:154-56; **95**:37, 48, 68
"The Angelic Imagination: Poe as God" (Tate) **2**:429; **6**:527; **14**:528
"Angelica" (Blackwood) **100**:15
Angelici dolori (Ortese) **89**:195, 197-98
Angélique ou L'Enchantement (Robbe-Grillet) **128**:368, 376, 379-80, 382
"Angelita's Utility" (Zamora) **89**:394
"L'angelo nero" (Montale) **7**:225
"The Angels" (Kundera) **19**:269
"Angels" (Sexton) **123**:420
"The Angels" (Updike) **3**:485
Angels (Johnson) **52**:234-35, 237-41
Angels and Insects (Byatt) **136**:151, 153-55, 163, 180, 194
"Angels and Ministers of Grace" (O'Faolain) **14**:406
Angels and Other Strangers: Family Christmas Stories (Paterson) **30**:282-83
Angels Are So Few (Potter) **58**:391; **123**:231, 234-35
"Angels at the Ritz" (Trevor) **71**:323; **116**:374, 377
Angels at the Ritz, and Other Stories (Trevor) **7**:477-78; **9**:529; **25**:446; **71**:324; **116**:333, 374, 377
Angels Can't Do Better (De Vries) **28**:114-15
Angels Fall (Wilson) **36**:461-64
Angels Falling (Elliott) **47**:105-07
"The Angel's Gift" (Bova) **45**:75
Angels in America: A Gay Fantasia on National Themes (Kushner) **81**:197-99, 201-04, 206-13
Angels of Darkness (Woolrich) **77**:400
"The Angels of Detroit" (Levine) **2**:244; **4**:286; **118**:287
"Angels of the Love Affair" (Sexton) **53**:321
Angels on Toast (Powell) **66**:356, 358-59, 363, 370, 375-76
"The Angels Wanna Wear My Red Shoes" (Costello) **21**:67
The Angels Weep (Smith) **33**:378
"Angelus Domini" (Moure) **88**:227
"Anger" (Creeley) **78**:137
"Anger" (Dobyns) **37**:77-8
"Anger" (Jennings) **131**:233
Anger (Sarton) **49**:315-16; **91**:251
"Anger Lay by Me" (Daryush) **19**:120
Les anges du péché (Bresson) **16**:102-03
Les anges noirs (Mauriac) **56**:211-13
Angest (Lagerkvist) **13**:334; **54**:274
"Angie" (Jagger and Richard) **17**:228-29, 232, 240
L'anglais décrit dans le château fermé (Mandiargues) **41**:278-79
Angle of Ascent (Hayden) **9**:270; **14**:240; **37**:153, 157, 160
"Angle of Geese" (Momaday) **85**:230-31, 248-49, 262-63, 266-67, 280
Angle of Geese, and Other Poems (Momaday) **85**:247, 262, 281
Angle of Repose (Stegner) **9**:510; **49**:354-56, 360; **81**:344, 347-52
The Angled Road (Levine) **54**:291-92, 297
"An Angler at Heart" (Frazier) **46**:165
Angles and Circles (Grigson) **7**:136
"Anglo-Mongrels and the Rose" (Loy) **28**:249
Anglo-Saxon Attitudes (Wilson) **2**:471-74; **3**:535; **5**:514; **25**:463-64
"Anglosaxon Street" (Birney) **6**:72, 78
L'angoisse du Roi Salomon (Gary) **25**:191
Angry Abolitionist: William Lloyd Garrison (Archer) **12**:17
Angry Candy (Ellison) **139**:125-7
The Angry Exile (Krotkov) **19**:264
The Angry Hills (Uris) **32**:431, 433
The Angry Ones (Williams) **5**:497
"Angry Young Man" (Joel) **26**:215-16, 219
"The Angry Young Men" (Barthelme) **5**:55; **115**:85
"The Angry-Year" (Godwin) **31**:197-98
Angst (Cixous) **92**:53, 56
Die Angst des Tormanns beim Elfmeter (Handke) **5**:164-67; **10**:255-56, 258; **15**:268; **38**:216, 218-20, 223; **134**:118, 10, 130-31, 139, 162
Angst essen Seele auf (Fassbinder) **20**:106-07
Anguish (Lagerkvist) See *Angest*
"The Anguish of an Alien" (Endō) **99**:307
"Ani" (Thomas) **132**:382
Ani maamin: A Song Lost and Found Again (Wiesel) **5**:493
Ania Malina (Osborne) **50**:70-2
Aniara (Martinson) **14**:356
Anicet (Aragon) **22**:42
Anihtá hártia (Elytis) **49**:117, 119; **100**:187
"Anima" (Eberhart) **56**:87
"Animal" (Jensen) **37**:188
"Animal Behavior" (Colwin) **5**:108; **84**:146, 149
Animal Clocks and Compasses (Hyde) **21**:173
Animal Crackers (Kaufman) **38**:265
"Animal Crossing" (Squires) **51**:383
"Animal de luz" (Neruda) **28**:309
Animal Dreams (Kingsolver) **81**:191, 194; **130**:75-84, 89, 91, 93-6, 106-07, 110, 112-15, 120
The Animal Game (Tuohy) **37**:425-26, 428, 431
"Animal Hospital" (Moss) **7**:247
The Animal Inside (Jacobsen) **48**:190-91, 195, 197; **102**:236
"Animal Lover" (Donaldson) **46**:142-43
Animal Magnetism (Prose) **45**:324-25
"Animal of Light" (Neruda) See "Animal de luz"
Animal Spirits: Stories to Live By (McFadden) **48**:256-57
"The Animal That Drank Up Sound" (Stafford) **7**:461
The Animal, the Vegetable, and John D. Jones (Byars) **35**:74
"The Animal Trainer" (Berryman) **62**:71
"Animal, Vegetable, and Mineral" (Bogan) **46**:90
Animal, Vegetable, Mineral (Deutsch) **18**:118
The Animal-Lover's Book of Beastly Murder (Highsmith) **14**:260; **42**:214; **102**:197
"Animals" (Byrne) **26**:97-8
"Animals" (Levine) **118**:271
Animals (Pink Floyd) **35**:309-13, 315
"Animals All Around" (Soto) **80**:284

"Animals Are Passing from Our Lives" (Levine) **4**:287; **9**:332; **14**:317; **33**:273; **118**:271-73, 283
The Animals' Arrival (Jennings) **14**:292; **131**:232, 240
"The Animals at the Adelaide Zoo" (Ewart) **46**:152
"The Animals' Christmas" (Dacey) **51**:79
The Animals in That Country (Atwood) **2**:19; **8**:30, 32; **13**:44; **25**:63, 67
"Animula" (Eliot) **13**:201; **15**:217
"Animula" (Merwin) **1**:213; **88**:193
"Animula" (Rozewicz)
See "Duszyczka"
Anishinabe Adisokan (Vizenor)
See *Summer in the Spring: Ojibwe Lyric Poems and Tribal Songs*
Anishinabe Nagamon (Vizenor) **103**:296
"Ankor Wat" (Ginsberg) **6**:198
"Anmerkungen zu Cromwell" (Hein) **154**:136
Ann Lee's (Bowen) **118**:62, 75-76
Ann Lee's and Other Stories (Bowen) **22**:67
"Anna" (Dinesen) **10**:149-50
"Anna" (Dubus) **97**:223, 228
Anna (Almedingen) **12**:7
"Anna Fierling" (Shange)
See "How I Moved Anna Fierling to the Southwest Territories, or My Personal Victory over the Armies of Western Civilization"
Anna Hastings: The Story of a Washington Newspaperwoman (Drury) **37**:109
Anna Karenina and Other Essays (Leavis) **24**:305, 308
"Anna Liffey" (Boland) **113**:87, 89, 91, 94-5, 100-01, 111, 120, 127-28
"Anna Lisa's Nose" (Berriault) **54**:3; **109**:96
The Anna Papers (Gilchrist) **143**:297, 299, 310-11, 313, 315-16, 321-22, 328-29
"Anna, Part I" (Gilchrist) **48**:120, 122; **143**:279-80, 315
Anna Sophie Hedvig (Abell) **15**:1, 4
"Anna, soror" (Yourcenar) **87**:433
Anna, soror (Yourcenar) **87**:405, 412
"Anna Swanton" (Durcan) **43**:115
Annäherungen (Jünger) **125**:236
Annäherungen, Drogen und Rausch (Jünger) **125**:225
The Annals of Brekkukot (Laxness)
See *Brekkukotsannáll*
Annals of Innocence and Experience (Read) **4**:437
Annals of the Five Senses (MacDiarmid) **63**:251
"Annamalai" (Narayan) **121**:369-70, 420
"Anna's Song" (Gaye) **26**:133
"Anne" (Beauvoir) **31**:42
"Anne at the Symphony" (Shields) **113**:441
"Anne Boleyn's Song" (Sitwell) **67**:323
"Anne Frank Huis" (Motion) **47**:287, 294
"Anne Rey" (Kaplan) **50**:55-6
Anne Sexton: A Self-Portrait in Letters (Sexton) **10**:468-69; **15**:473; **53**:312-13; **123**:409
"Anne, Sylvia, Virginia, Adrienne" (Broumas) **10**:76
Les anneaux de Bicêtre (Simenon) **1**:309; **47**:379
L'annee derniére a Marienbad (Resnais) **16**:498, 500-11
L'année dernière à Marienbad (Robbe-Grillet) **1**:286-87; **2**:374, 376; **4**:449; **6**:465-66; **8**:453-54; **14**:455-56, 462; **43**:360, 366; **128**:326-28, 330, 332, 344, 354, 356, 362, 366
Annerton Pit (Dickinson) **12**:176-77
Annette (Caldwell) **14**:95
Anni mirabiles, 1921-1925 (Blackmur) **24**:65
"The Anniad" (Brooks) **49**:27
Annie Allen (Brooks) **1**:46; **5**:74-6; **15**:93; **49**:22, 26-7, 31-2, 35
"Annie Christian" (Prince) **35**:325-26, 328
Annie Hall (Allen) **16**:7-8, 10-11, 13-15, 17-18; **52**:38-40, 45-6, 48-50
"Annie John" (Johns) **137**:139
Annie John (Kincaid) **43**:249-51; **68**:205-12, 216-18, 220-28; **137**:137-38, 140-41, 144-52, 156, 161-64, 166-67, 169-70, 173-75, 179-84, 188, 195, 199
"Annie She" (Lane) **25**:289
"Annie Upside Down" (Fuller) **62**:196-97, 204
The Annihilation of Mylos (Ritsos) **6**:463
Annika and the Wolves (Zoline) **62**:462
"Anniversaries" (Dunn) **40**:172
"Anniversaries" (Justice) **102**:270
"Anniversaries" (Kinsella) **138**:102-03
"Anniversaries" (Motion) **47**:286, 289, 292-93
Anniversaries (Coles) **46**:108-09
Anniversaries: From the Life of Gesine Cresspahl (Johnson)
See *Jahrestage: Aus dem Leben von Gesine Cresspahl IV*
Anniversaries: From the Life of Gesine Cresspahl (Johnson)
See *Jahrestage: Aus dem Leben von Gesine Cresspahl III*
"An Anniversary" (Berry) **27**:34
"Anniversary" (Ciardi) **40**:156
"Anniversary" (Elytis) **49**:114; **100**:189
"Anniversary" (Jong) **83**:289
The Anniversary (Ray)
See *Pratidwandi*
"Anniversary Project" (Haldeman) **61**:176
"The Anniversary Song" (Kherdian) **9**:318
"Anniversary Words" (Randall) **135**:398
"Anno Domini" (Barker) **48**:24
"Anno Domini" (Brodsky) **13**:115; **50**:123, 131
"Anno Domini" (Raine) **103**:180, 189
Anno Domini (Barker) **48**:21-2
Anno Domini (Raine) **32**:349
Anno Domini MCMXXI (Akhmatova) **25**:24, 27; **64**:5, 10; **126**:5, 24-5, 33
"Annointed with Oils" (Nowlan) **15**:399
"An Annotated Exequy" (Sissman) **9**:490
"Annotations of Auschwitz" (Porter) **33**:322
"Annotations of Giant's Town" (Fuller) **62**:194
"Announcement" (Arreola)
See "Anuncio"
"Annual" (Swenson) **106**:347
"The Annual Heron" (Price) **43**:351
"Annunciation" (Livesay) **79**:334, 336
"Annunciation" (Morgan) **2**:294
"The Annunciation" (Mueller) **51**:281
"Annunciation" (Sarton) **14**:482
The Annunciation (Gilchrist) **34**:164-65; **48**:116-18, 120; **143**:273-80, 282-83, 286, 288, 290, 294, 297, 310-11, 313, 316, 321-22, 329
"Annunciation with a Bullet in It" (Graham) **118**:223, 257
"Annunciations" (Hill) **8**:295; **45**:178-79, 184, 187
"Annus Mirabilis" (Larkin) **8**:333; **9**:323-24; **64**:282
"Annus Mirabilis, 1961" (Montague) **46**:271
"Anodyne" (Mac Laverty) **31**:253-54
"Anoint the Ariston" (Elytis) **100**:187
"Anon" (Boland) **40**:98
"Anonymiad" (Barth) **3**:41; **5**:51-2; **9**:68, 70-1; **51**:23; **89**:6-11, 15-19, 21-4, 29-30, 32, 34, 36, 45-6, 48, 51, 55-6, 58-9, 63-4
"Anonymity" (Forster) **3**:160
"An Anonymous Affair" (Williams) **42**:440
The Anonymous Lover (Logan) **5**:254-55
"Anonymous Signature" (MacLeish) **68**:273
"Anonymous Sins" (Oates) **6**:367
Anonymous Sins and Other Poems (Oates) **1**:251; **3**:359; **6**:367
"The Anonymous Telephone Caller" (MacEwen) **55**:168
"Anorexic" (Boland) **40**:99-100; **67**:44, 46; **113**:58, 60-61, 109, 123
Another America/Otra America. (Kingsolver) **130**:84-85, 96, 101
"Another and Another and..." (Weiss) **14**:557
"Another Animal" (Swenson) **106**:347
Another Animal (Swenson) **4**:533-34; **61**:390, 398-99; **106**:317, 324, 331, 336, 340, 345-46
Another Antigone (Gurney) **50**:180, 184; **54**:219-20, 223
"Another April" (Stuart) **11**:514
"Another Brick in the Wall" (Pink Floyd) **35**:313
"Another Christmas" (Avison) **97**:72, 111
"Another Christmas" (Trevor) **14**:536; **71**:326, 337; **116**:338, 345-47, 360
"Another Country" (Hemingway)
See "Let It Go"
Another Country (Baldwin) **1**:14-16; **2**:31; **3**:32; **4**:40-2; **5**:41-2; **13**:48-50, 52; **15**:42; **17**:23-4, 28-32, 34, 36-7, 44-5; **42**:14, 18; **50**:283-84, 289, 293, 296; **67**:14; **90**:5, 31-2; **127**:119-23, 125, 130, 141, 144-45, 147, 151-52
"Another Day" (Larson) **99**:176
"Another Day Another Dollar" (Selby) **8**:475-76
"Another Day, Another Night" (McAuley) **45**:255
"Another Dog's Death" (Updike) **43**:436
"Another Dollar" (Williams) **148**:343
"Another Elegy" (Hall) **151**:200-02
"Another Fragment" (Laughlin) **49**:220
"Another Hanging" (Stuart) **11**:512
Another Heaven and Earth (Haavikko)
See *Toinen taivas ja maa*
"Another Hundred People" (Sondheim) **30**:391, 395; **147**:251-54
"Another Journey" (Livesay) **79**:337
"Another Journey from Béthune to Cuinchy" (Blunden) **56**:43
Another Kind (West) **50**:360
"Another Life" (Bidart) **33**:74
"Another Life" (Levine) **9**:332; **14**:316, 318
Another Life (Walcott) **4**:574-76; **9**:556; **14**:549, 551; **25**:452; **42**:418-23; **67**:342-44, 348-51, 354-55, 357-58; **76**:270, 272, 274-76, 278, 280, 282-85
Another Life. The House on the Embankment: Three Novellas (Trifonov)
See *Drugaia zhizn'*
"Another Little Boy" (Aldiss) **5**:15
Another Marvelous Thing (Colwin) **84**:141-43, 150, 153
"Another Merry Widow" (Klappert) **57**:66
Another Monty Python Record (Monty Python) **21**:224, 226
"Another National Anthem" (Sondheim) **147**:244-45
"Another Pair of Hands" (Spark) **40**:403
Another Part of the Forest (Hellman) **2**:187; **14**:258; **18**:221-22; **34**:349; **52**:191
Another Part of the Wood (Bainbridge) **18**:32-5; **22**:44; **62**:23-4, 30; **130**:20
Another Passenger (Simon) **26**:410-12
"Another Place" (Merwin) **88**:212-13
"Another Place" (Simic) **130**:297
Another Place (Priestley) **2**:347
"Another Poem for Me—After Recovering from an O.D." (Knight) **40**:286
"Another River: The Ebro" (Cabral de Melo Neto)
See "Otro rio: O Ebro"
Another Roadside Attraction (Robbins) **9**:453; **32**:366, 368-74; **64**:371-73, 376-78, 382
"Another September" (Kinsella) **138**:97-99, 105, 118, 133, 159, 161, 165
Another September (Kinsella) **138**:98, 108-9, 118, 136, 139, 141-42, 146
Another Side of Bob Dylan (Dylan) **12**:185, 198; **77**:167
"Another Snowstorm" (Zaturenska) **11**:580
Another Song (Cage) **41**:86
"Another Sorrowing Woman" (Belitt) **22**:52
"Another Space" (Page) **7**:292; **18**:379
"Another Star" (Wonder) **12**:662
"Another State" (Loewinsohn) **52**:285

"Another Suitcase in Another Hall" (Rice and Webber) **21**:432
"Another Sunday Morning" (Mahon) **27**:293
"Another Tempest" (Van Duyn) **116**:427
"Another Time" (Auden) **3**:22; **6**:23; **11**:14; **14**:26; **123**:47
"Another Time" (O'Brien) **65**:167, 169, 172
Another Time in Fragments (Eigner) **9**:180
"Another Try at It" (Bowering) **47**:19
"Another Unhappy Love Song" (Cryer) **21**:81
"Another Voice" (Wilbur) **3**:531
Another War, Another Peace (Glasser) **37**:134
Another World (Barker) **146**:38-40, 42
Another World (Hanley) **5**:167-68
Another World (Nixon) **21**:242
Another You (Beattie) **146**:78-9, 83-4
"Anothering" (Plumly) **33**:313
"Anoukis et plus tard Jeanne" (Char) **11**:116
Anpao: An American Indian Odyssey (Highwater) **12**:286-87
Anrufung des Grossen Bären (Bachmann) **69**:41
"Anschluss" (Boyle) **58**:70
"Ansell" (Forster) **2**:136
"Anseo" (Muldoon) **72**:266
Ansichten eines Clowns (Boell) **2**:68; **3**:74-5; **6**:83; **9**:102, 106-09; **11**:52-3, 55-6, 58; **27**:61, 67; **39**:292-96; **72**:68, 73
"Ansiedad para el día" (Aleixandre) **9**:15
Ansikte mot ansikte (Bergman) **16**:77-8, 81; **72**:53-7, 59, 61
Ansiktet (Bergman) **16**:47-9, 52, 62, 64-7, 81-2; **72**:31, 33, 40-1, 50
Ansprachen (Wolf) **150**:233
"Answer" (Achebe) **11**:4; **26**:22
"An Answer" (Bowers) **9**:122
"Answer" (Capote) **13**:137
"The Answer" (Jeffers) **54**:249-50
"The Answer" (Montague) **46**:268
The Answer (Lee) **105**:85
The Answer (Wylie) **43**:468
Answer as a Man (Caldwell) **28**:68-9; **39**:302-03
An Answer from Limbo (Moore) **1**:225; **5**:295-96; **7**:235; **19**:331; **32**:313; 90;238-41, 243-44, 247-48, 250-54, 261, 272, 277, 280-2,288
"Answer in the Affirmative" (Fisher) **87**:124
"An Answer to Some Questions on How I Write" (Giovanni) **64**:196; **117**:189, 204
Answer Yes or No (Mortimer) **28**:281
"Answering a Question in the Mountains" (Ashbery) **25**:58
"Answering the Deer: Genocide and Continuance in the Poetry of American Indian Women" (Allen) **84**:15, 36, 39, 41
"Answers" (Jennings) **131**:234
"Answers in Progress" (Baraka) **5**:48; **33**:55
The Ant Colony (King) **145**:356-58
"Ant Trap" (Kennedy) **42**:255
"Antaeus" (Heaney) **74**:158, 162
The Antagonists (Gann) **23**:167
Antarctic Fugue (Cendrars)
See *Le plan de l'aiguille*
Antarctic Traveller (Pollitt) **28**:367-68; **122**:201-02, 204-05, 208, 222
"Antebellum Boston" (Lowell) **124**:287
"Antecedents" (Tomlinson) **45**:396
Antechamber and Other Poems (McClure) **10**:334
"Antediluvian Customs" (Simic) **130**:306
"Antelación de amor" (Borges) **19**:45
"Antelope Standing, Some Lying" (Smith) **22**:387
"Antennae" (Gascoyne) **45**:148
Anteroom to Paradise (Zinoviev) **19**:488
"Antheap" (Breytenbach) **23**:86-7
Antheil and the Treatise on Harmony (Pound) **48**:292
"Anthem" (Auden) **2**:28
Anthem (Rand) **30**:297, 300-01, 304-05; **79**:369, 372-73, 378, 392-94
"Anthem of the Decades" (Kunene) **85**:162, 164-65
Anthem of the Decades: A Zulu Epic (Kunene) **85**:163-64, 171-72, 175, 178
"Anthem Sprinters" (Bradbury) **42**:35
"Anthem to Peacefulness" (Kunene) **85**:175, 177
Anthills of the Savannah (Achebe) **51**:7-10; **75**:2, 4-8, 12-13, 17-27; **127**:27-9, 40, 43-4, 46, 48; **152**:40, 93
Anthologie de la nouvelle poésie nègre et malgache de langue Française (Senghor) **54**:400, 404; **130**:278
Anthologie de la poésie nègre et malagache (Senghor) **130**:272
Anthologie Nègre (Cendrars) **106**:149, 185
Anthology of the New Black and Malagasy Poetry (Senghor)
See *Anthologie de la nouvelle poésie nègre et malgache de langue Française*
Anthony Rose (Feiffer) **64**:163
"Anthony's Song" (Joel)
See "Movin' Out"
"Anthracite Country" (Parini) **54**:360; **133**:252
Anthropologie structurale (Lévi-Strauss) **38**:294-98
An Anthropologist at Work (Mead) **37**:280
"An Anthropologist's Confession" (Porter) **33**:323
"The Anthropology Convention" (Rose) **85**:314
"Anthropology: What Is Lost in Rotation" (Wilson) **49**:416
"Anthropomorphosis" (Szirtes) **46**:391
The Anthropos-Specter-Beast (Konwicki)
See *Zwierzoczlekoupiór*
"Antibes: Variations on a Theme" (Jones) **10**:286, 289
Antic Hay (Huxley) **1**:151-52; **4**:238-40, 243-44; **5**:192-94; **8**:304; **11**:281-82, 284, 288; **18**:265, 267-69; **35**:232, 235, 244; **79**:304, 306, 312, 328
"Anticipation" (Schuyler) **23**:391
"Anticipation" (Simon) **26**:407, 410
The Anti-Death League (Amis) **2**:6, 8-9; **3**:8-9; **5**:23; **8**:12; **13**:12-13, 15; **40**:42; **129**:6-7
"Anti-Father" (Dove) **81**:138
"The Antifeminist Woman" (Rich) **18**:447
Anti-Galaxie Nebulae (Ludlam) **50**:344
Antigone (Anouilh) **3**:11; **8**:22; **13**:16-7, 19, 20-1; **40**:51-3, 56-8, 60; **50**:278-80
Antigone (Cocteau) **8**:144, 147; **43**:109, 111
"Antigone, This Is It" (Reed) **60**:313
"Antigua" (Soto) **80**:276
Antigua, Penny, Puce (Graves) **44**:476
The Antigua Stamp (Graves) **45**:171
"The Antihero" (Castillo) **151**:5-7, 34-35
Anti-Man (Koontz) **78**:200
Antimémoirs (Malraux) **57**:306, 308, 311, 318-19, 322-24
Anti-Memoirs (Malraux) **1**:203; **13**:366-69
Antimiry (Voznesensky) **1**:349; **15**:553-55; **57**:413-16, 420, 425-26
"L'antimonio" (Sciascia) **8**:473; **41**:392
"The Antinomies of Postmodernity" (Jameson) **142**:250, 252, 262
"Antinoüs: The Diaries" (Rich) **11**:475-76; **36**:366
Antiode (Cabral de Melo Neto) **76**:152
"The Antiphon" (Levertov) **66**:245
The Antiphon (Barnes) **3**:36; **4**:43-4; **8**:48; **29**:26-32; **127**:160-63, 176, 185-86, 189, 194, 201, 205-06, 210-11
L'antiphonaire (Aquin) **15**:17
Anti-Platon (Bonnefoy) **58**:57, 59
"Antipodes" (Soupault) **68**:405
"Anti-Poem" (Ewart) **46**:148
Antipoems: New and Selected (Parra) **102**:348
Antipolitics (Konrád) **73**:184-87
"Anti-Professionalism" (Fish) **142**:177, 180
"The Antiquary" (Reaney) **13**:473
"Antique Father" (Kizer) **39**:171
"Antique Harvesters" (Ransom) **4**:431; **11**:471
"Antiquity" (Dickey) **28**:118
Anti-Semite and Jew (Sartre) **52**:380
"The Anti-Soviet Soviet Union" (Voinovich) **49**:382-83
Antitheses (Berryman) **25**:95
Antiworlds (Voznesensky)
See *Antimiry*
The Ant-Nest Swells Up (Breytenbach) **126**:82-3
Antoine et Colette (Truffaut) **20**:399-400; **101**:398, 410-11
"Antoine et l'orpheline" (Truffaut) **101**:398-400
Antología clásica de la literatura Argentina (Borges) **44**:363
Antología de la literatura fantástica (Bioy Casares) **8**:94; **83**:176; **88**:92, 95
Antologia personal (Borges) **48**:46; **83**:159
Anton Pan (Blaga) **75**:65
Antonietta (Hersey) **81**:330-32, 334
Antonio Azorín (Azorín) **11**:27
"Antony in Behalf of the Play" (Burke) **24**:128
"Antonyin's" (Hill) **113**:330-31
"Antrim to the Boyne" (Boland) **113**:110
Antrobus Complete (Durrell) **41**:139
"The Ants" (Empson) **19**:155
"Antwerp, 1984" (Durcan) **70**:153
"Anuncio" (Arreola) **147**:4, 14, 34
"The Anvil of Jove" (Benford) **52**:63
"Anxiety" (Paley) **37**:334-35; **140**:209, 221, 263
Anxiety (Rozewicz)
See *Niepokój*
"Anxiety About Dying" (Ostriker) **132**:303
"Anxiety and Ashes" (Jensen) **37**:188
Anxiety and Ashes (Jensen) **37**:187
The Anxiety of Influence (Bloom) **24**:72, 74-6, 79; **103**:2, 4-6, 9, 11-13, 20, 22-6, 28, 33, 41, 44-6, 49-51, 53-4
Any Cold Jordan (Bottoms) **53**:33
"Any Day Now" (Derleth) **31**:131-33
Any Day of Your Life (Kherdian) **9**:317-18
Any God Will Do (Condon) **45**:94, 97; **100**:113
"Any History" (Kunitz) **148**:87
"Any Major Dude Will Tell You" (Becker and Fagen) **26**:79
Any Man's Death (Estleman) **48**:106-07
Any Minute I Can Split (Rossner) **6**:468; **9**:456-57
Any Old Iron (Burgess) **62**:133-39
Any Shape or Form (Daly) **52**:89
"Any Size We Please" (Frost) **9**:223
"Any Time" (Dunn) **36**:153
"Any Time" (Stafford) **29**:384
"Any Time at All" (Lennon and McCartney) **12**:375; **35**:274
"Any Vacation" (Stafford) **29**:384
Any Woman's Blues (Jong) **83**:316-17, 321
"Any World" (Becker and Fagen) **26**:80, 84
Anya (Schaeffer) **6**:488; **11**:492
Anya Kōro (Shiga) **33**:365, 369-71, 373
"Anybody Else like Me?" (Miller) **30**:264
Anybody's Woman (Arzner) **98**:70-1
Anyone Can Whistle (Sondheim) **30**:378-80, 385, 387, 392, 395-97, 400
"anyone lived in a pretty how town" (Cummings) **3**:119; **15**:162; **68**:48, 51
"Anyone with Yama-bushi Tendencies" (Snyder) **120**:347
"Anything" (Dorris) **109**:307
Anything for Billy (McMurtry) **127**:328, 331-33, 339-40, 342, 350
"Anything Long and Thin" (Zweig) **34**:379
Anything on Its Side (Eigner) **9**:181
"Anything Rather than the Angel" (Herbert) **9**:275
"Anything to Declare?" (Forster) **45**:134
"Anyway, Anyhow, Anywhere" (Townshend) **17**:525, 528, 530, 532
Anywhere but Here (Simpson) **44**:97-102; **146**:277-94, 296
"Apa mare" (Arghezi) **80**:13
"Apacalipsis de Solentiname" (Cortázar) **33**:124
"Apache Love" (Ortiz) **45**:311
Aparajito (Ray) **16**:474-78, 482-83, 485-86, 491; **76**:356, 360, 366

El apartamiento (Marqués) **96**:253, 260
Apartheid and the Archbishop: The Life and Times of Geoffrey Clayton, Archbishop of Cape Town (Paton) **25**:363
Apartment in Athens (Wescott) **13**:592
"The Apartment Next to the War" (Disch) **36**:127
"The Apathetic Bookie Joint" (Fuchs) **22**:157, 161
The Apathetic Bookie Joint (Fuchs) **22**:156, 160-61
Ape and Essence (Huxley) **1**:150-52; **4**:239, 243; **5**:193; **8**:303; **35**:234-35, 241; **79**:300
The Ape Inside Me (Platt) **26**:354, 356
"The Ape Judges" (Arghezi)
See "Maimuţoii judecători"
"The Ape Lady in Retirement" (Boyle) **90**:45
"Apellesova cherta" (Pasternak)
See "Il tratto di Apelle"
"El apellido" (Guillén) **48**:163; **79**:233, 237
Apel'siny iz Marokko (Aksyonov)
See *Oranges from Morocco*
"Apeman" (Davies) **21**:91
"Apeneck Sweeney" (Eliot) **13**:202
"Aperto, Chiuso" (Updike) **139**:368
"The Apes of God Revisited" (Sorrentino) **7**:451
"The Apex Animal" (Avison) **97**:88-9, 110, 122, 124
"Aphorisms" (Randall) **135**:398
"Aphrodissia, the Widow" (Yourcenar)
See "La veuve Aphrodissia"
"Aplauso humano" (Cernuda) **54**:59
Apo-33 Bulletin A Metabolic Regulator (Burroughs) **109**:184
"Apocalipsis" (Cardenal) **31**:75
"Apocalypse" (Cardenal)
See "Apocalipsis"
"Apocalypse" (MacEwen) **55**:163-64, 167-69
"Apocalypse at Solentiname" (Cortázar)
See "Apacalipsis de Solentiname"
"Apocalypse at the Plaza" (Klein) **30**:235-36
"The Apocalypse Commentary of Bob Paisner" (Moody) **147**:170, 189
"Apocalypse, For Spencer" (Moure) **88**:217
"The apocalypse is disappointing" (Blanchot) **135**:134
Apocalypse Now (Coppola) **16**:245-49; **126**:204, 214-15, 217-19, 223-27, 254-60, 267
"The Apocalypse of John" (Samarakis) **5**:382
Apocalypse Postponed (Eco) **142**:100, 103
"Apocalypse: Umbrian Master, about 1490" (Enzensberger) **43**:153
"Apocalyptics" (Avison) **97**:76, 90-1, 127
"Apocryphal Doubts of Marianne Moore" (Cabral de Melo Neto)
See "Dúvidas apócrifas de Marianne Moore"
L'apocryphe (Pinget) **37**:362-63
"Apollo and Daphne" (Rodgers) **7**:378
"Apollo and Marsyas" (Herbert) **9**:272; **43**:184, 188, 190, 194
Apollo and the Whores (Fuentes) **113**:263
"An Apollonian Elegy" (Duncan) **7**:88
Apollonius of Tyana (Olson) **11**:420
"Apollo's Harsher Songs" (Vendler) **138**:250
"Apologia" (Hirsch) **31**:215
"Apologia" (McGinley) **14**:367
"Apologia Pro Vita Sua" (Wright) **119**:180-81, 184, 186-89; **146**:355, 358-60, 368-69
"Apologies" (Piercy) **27**:376
"Apologies to All the People in Lebanon" (Jordan) **114**:147, 150
Apologies to the Iroquois (Wilson) **2**:475; **24**:487
"The Apologist's Evening Prayer" (Lewis) **124**:227
"Apologne" (Gustafson) **36**:218
"The Apology" (Barthelme) **46**:37-8
"Apology" (Mueller) **51**:280
"The Apology" (Voigt) **54**:431
"Apology for Apostasy?" (Knight) **40**:282
"Apology for Bad Dreams" (Jeffers) **2**:212; **11**:307, 312
Apology for Heroism (Anand) **93**:38-9, 43-4
"An Apology for Not Invoking the Muse" (Ciardi) **44**:383; **129**:46
"An Apology for the Revival of Christian Architecture in England" (Hill) **45**:178, 181-82, 190
"Apology of Genius" (Loy) **28**:246, 248, 251
Aposcalittici e Integrati (Eco) **142**:100
"Apostasy" (Robison) **42**:338
"The Apostate" (Kizer) **80**:172
"Apostle Birds" (Wright) **53**:423
"Apostle of Hope" (Kinsella) **138**:135, 137
Apostles of Light (Douglas) **73**:68-70, 72-5, 83, 85, 95
"Apostrophe to a Nephew" (McGinley) **14**:365
"An Apostrophe to One of the Landed Gentry" (Betjeman) **43**:32
The Apothecary's Shop (Enright) **31**:145-46
"Apotheosis" (Ekelöf) **27**:117
"Apotheosis" (Kingsolver) **130**:85
"Apotheosis of an Unhappy Hypocrite" (Waugh) **107**:371
"The Apotheosis of Myra" (Tevis) **42**:372, 377
"The Apotheosis of Tins" (Mahon) **27**:288-90
Appalachia (Wright) **119**:189; **146**:369, 372-73, 375-76, 378-81
Appalachian Wilderness (Abbey) **59**:244
"The Apparition" (Roethke) **101**:331
The Apparition (Eberhart) **56**:88
"Apparition d'aerea" (Char) **14**:127
"Apparitions" (Merwin) **45**:274-75
"An Appearance" (Plath) **111**:203, 214
"The Appearance of Metaphor and the Meaning of Culture" (Blaga)
See "Geneza metaforei şi sensul culturii"
"Appearances" (Mahapatra) **33**:279
"Appearances" (Swenson) **106**:345
Appearances Are Deceiving (Bernhard)
See *Der Schein trügt*
Appeuring Nightly (Tomlin) **17**:518, 520, 523
"L'appendice aux confitures de coing" (Ferron) **94**:125-26
"Appendix to 'Quince Jam'" (Ferron)
See "L'appendice aux confitures de coing"
"Appendix to the notebooks of Malte Laurids Brigge written by 'life itself'" (Rozewicz) **139**:273
"L'Appennino" (Pasolini) **106**:265
"Applause" (Muske) **90**:317
Applause (Mamoulian) **16**:418-20, 422-24
"The Apple" (Kinnell) **29**:284-85, 289
"Apple" (Peck) **3**:377
"The Apple" (Roddenberry) **17**:412-13
The Apple (Gelber) **6**:196; **79**:208-09, 211-15, 217, 221-24
"Apple and Mole" (Davidson) **19**:126
Apple Bough (Streatfeild) **21**:403
The Apple Broadcast and Other New Poems (Redgrove) **41**:358
An Apple from One's Lap (Seifert)
See *Jablko z klína*
An Apple From the Lap (Seifert)
See *Jablko z klína*
An Apple from Your Lap (Seifert)
See *Jablko z klína*
The Apple in the Dark (Lispector)
See *A maçã no escuro*
Apple of the Eye (Middleton) **38**:330
The Apple of the Eye (Wescott) **13**:590-92
"The Apple Tree" (Dunn) **40**:169
The Apple Tree: A Short Novel and Some Stories (du Maurier) **59**:286
"The Apple Trees" (Glück) **7**:119-20; **22**:174
"The Apple Trees at Olema" (Hass) **99**:143
Appleby and Honeybath (Stewart) **32**:422-23
"Apple-Doors" (Dacey) **51**:80
"Apple-Picking Time" (Bernstein) **142**:30
"Apples" (Bowering) **47**:22
"Apples" (Hall) **151**:196
"Apples" (Hartley) **22**:216
"Apples" (Merwin) **18**:336; **88**:203
"Apples and Pears" (Davenport) **38**:146-48
Apples and Pears, and Other Stories (Davenport) **38**:146-48
"Apples and Water" (Graves) **45**:166-67
"The Applicant" (Plath) **9**:428; **14**:423; **17**:348; **51**:346; **62**:396, 415; **111**:159, 172-74, 181-86, 203
"The Applicant" (Swados) **12**:557-58
"Applicaton of Terminology" (Burke) **24**:118
"The Appointment" (Kumin) **28**:220
Appointment in Samarra (O'Hara) **1**:260-62; **2**:324-25; **3**:371; **6**:384; **42**:311-18, 320-21, 323-24
Appointment with Death (Christie) **12**:125; **48**:74; **110**:114
"An Appointment with the General" (Greene) **125**:200
"Apprehension" (Van Doren) **10**:496
"Apprehensions" (Duncan) **15**:190; **41**:128-29
"Apprehensions" (Hecht) **13**:269; **19**:207
"Apprehensions" (Plath) **3**:390
"The Apprentice" (Bambara) **88**:22-23, 28, 43, 52-54
"The Apprentice" (Brown) **73**:24
"The Apprentice" (Dybek) **114**:62, 64-5, 71, 74
"The Apprentice Psychiatrist" (Green) **77**:263-64
The Apprentices (Garfield) **12**:233, 238-39
The Apprentices (Strugatskii and Strugatskii) **27**:433
"Apprentices of Freedom" (Gordimer) **123**:119
The Apprenticeship of Duddy Kravitz (Richler) **5**:373-75, 377-78; **9**:451-52; **13**:481, 486; **18**:453, 455-56; **46**:347-48, 350-51; **70**:220, 223, 232
"The Approach to al Mu'tasim" (Borges)
See "El acercamiento a Almotásim"
"The Approach to Almotasim" (Borges)
See "El acercamiento a Almotásim"
An Approach to Literature (Brooks) **110**:20, 29-30, 33
"The Approach to Montego Bay" (Lezama Lima)
See "Para llegar a Montego Bay"
"Approach to Thebes" (Kunitz) **148**:69, 78-79, 82-87, 89, 102-03
"The Approaches" (Merwin) **13**:386
"Approaches to How They Behave" (Graham) **29**:198
"Approaches to T.S. Eliot" (Leavis) **24**:310
Approaching Oblivion: Road Signs on the Treadmill Toward Tomorrow (Ellison) **13**:203; **139**:129
"The Approaching Obsolescence of Housework: A Working Class Perspective" (Davis) **77**:123
"Approaching Prayer" (Dickey) **109**:237, 273
Approaching Simone (Terry) **19**:440
"L'Approche de Clarice Lispector" (Cixous) **92**:74, 80-2
"The Approximate Size of My Favorite Tumor" (Alexie) **96**:12
"Approximations" (Hayden) **9**:270; **37**:159
Approximations, Drugs, and Intoxication (Jünger)
See *Annäherungen, Drogen und Rausch*
"Appunti per un poema popolari" (Pasolini) **37**:346
Après coup, précédé par Le Ressassement éternel (Blanchot) **135**:113, 137
L'après-midi de Monsieur Andesmas (Duras) **40**:180; **100**:146
"April" (Blaga) **75**:71
April (Gascoyne) **45**:158
"April 5, 1974" (Wilbur) **9**:570
"April 7, 1969" (Brautigan) **12**:72
"April 25th, as Usual" (Ferber) **93**:139
"April Fool's Day" (Shapcott) **38**:400
"April Fugue" (Shapcott) **38**:402
April Galleons (Ashbery) **77**:62-6, 68-70; **125**:35

"The April Hill" (Lewis) **41**:254-55
"April Inventory" (Snodgrass) **2**:404; **18**:491; **68**:390, 396
April, June, and November (Raphael) **2**:367; **14**:436
"April Kinney" (Derleth) **31**:138
April Morning (Fast) **131**:54, 60, 81, 85, 90
"April Rise" (Lee) **90**:191
April Snow (Linney) **51**:263-64
"An April Sunday" (Larkin) **64**:258
"The April Witch" (Bradbury) **42**:32
"April Woods: Morning" (Berry) **4**:59
"Aprille" (Keillor) **115**:267, 287-93
Apt Pupil (King) **26**:240-42; **61**:327, 331; **113**:338, 352
"Apuntes para una declaración de fe" (Castellanos) **66**:44, 49-51
Apur sansar (Ray) **16**:475-78, 480, 482, 485-86, 490-491; **76**:356, 358, 360, 366
"Aqua del recuerdo" (Guillén) **79**:240
"Aquafuerte" (Guillén) **79**:240
Aquarium (Soupault) **68**:404
"Aquarius" (Thomas) **13**:539; **37**:417; **107**:332
"The Aquatic Uncle" (Calvino)
See "Lo zio acquativo"
Aquí pasan cosas raras (Valenzuela) **31**:438; **104**:355, 370, 388
The Aquitaine Progression (Ludlum) **43**:276-77
Arabes et Israeliens (Friedlander) **90**:109
Arabeskot (Shammas) **55**:85-91
Arabesques (Shammas)
See *Arabeskot*
Arabian Days (O'Brien) **13**:415
The Arabian Nights (Pasolini)
See *Il fiore della Mille e una notte*
Arabian Nights and Days (Mahfouz) **153**:338-39
The Arabian Nights Murder (Carr) **3**:101
Arabs and Israelis: A Dialogue (Friedlander)
See *Arabes et Israeliens*
"The Arabs of Palestine" (Gellhorn) **60**:196
"Arachne" (Empson) **3**:147; **19**:155; **33**:141
"Arachne, Astonished" (Jacobsen) **48**:194
Aracoeli (Morante) **47**:280-84
Les Araignées (Lang) **103**:88
"Araki Thomas" (Endō) **99**:289-90, 293, 295
"La araña" (Cortázar) **92**:172
Aranyer din ratri (Ray) **16**:483, 485-89, 493; **76**:360, 362, 367
Ararat (Glück) **81**:166, 168, 171
Ararat (Thomas) **31**:431-35; **132**:340-42, 353-56, 377-78, 380
"Arawak Horizon" (Harris) **25**:217
Die Arbeit des Lebens: Autobiographische Texte (Wellershoff) **46**:438
Der Arbeiter (Jünger) **125**:221-22, 226, 231, 248, 259
La arboleda perdida (Alberti) **7**:9
Los árboles mueren de pie (Casona) **49**:42-3, 45, 49
"Arbor" (Willard) **37**:464
El árboyl y sus sombras (Ferré) **139**:153
"L'arbre" (Theriault) **79**:407
"Arbre de décision" (Bowering) **47**:29
L'arbre de guernica (Arrabal) **9**:33, 37, 41; **18**:19, 23; **58**:4, 7, 9, 12, 16, 24-5
L'arbre des voyageurs (Tzara) **47**:390, 393
"L'arbre, la lampe" (Bonnefoy) **15**:74
"The Arc Inside and Out" (Ammons) **5**:29; **25**:44; **108**:16-7, 54
Arc Musical (Tchicaya) **101**:348, 353
Arcadia (Reid) **33**:348-51
Arcadia (Stoppard) **91**:182-93
Arcadio (Goyen) **40**:215-16, 218
Arcady and Other Places (Buckley) **57**:126, 130-33
"Arcady Unheeding" (Sassoon) **130**:176, 191
Arcane 17 (Breton) **9**:127; **15**:87; **54**:21, 26, 28
L'arc-en-ciel, Journal 1981-1984 (Green) **77**:282, 284
"The Arch of Triumph" (Canetti) **75**:132
Arch of Triumph (Remarque) **21**:329-32
"The Archaelogy of Knowledge" (Foucault) **31**:177
"The Archaeologist" (Mahon) **27**:288
"The Archaeologist" (Simmons) **43**:414
Archaeologist of Morning (Olson) **5**:328; **9**:412; **29**:329
The Archaeology of Knowledge (Foucault)
See *L'archéologie du savoir*
"Archaeology of Snow" (Purdy) **6**:428; **14**:430; **50**:236, 244
"The Archaic Avant-Garde" (Eagleton) **132**:124
"The Archangel of the Suburb" (Ferron) **94**:103
"Archangel Returning Home" (Blaga) **75**:77
Archangels Don't Play Pinball (Fo) **109**:118-19, 121
L'archéologie du savoir (Foucault) **31**:177-79, 185; **34**:339, 341; **69**:170, 186
"Archeology" (Pollitt) **28**:367; **122**:201
"The Archer" (Smith) **15**:513
Archer in Hollywood (Macdonald) **41**:267
"Archetypal Criticism: Theory of Myths" (Frye) **24**:208
"Archetype and Signature: A Study of the Relationship between Biography and Poetry" (Fiedler) **4**:163; **13**:211; **24**:203
"The Archetypes" (Frye) **24**:216
"Archetypes" (Williams) **148**:366
Archibald of the Cross (Bunuel)
See *Ensayo de un crimen*
Archibaldo de la Cruz (Bunuel)
See *Ensayo de un crimen*
"Archipelago" (Glück) **7**:120
"Archistichs" (Voznesensky) **57**:425
The Architect (Haavikko)
See *Arkkitehti*
The Architect and the Emperor of Assyria (Arrabal)
See *L'Architecte et l'Empereur d'Assyria*
L'Architecte et l'Empereur d'Assyria (Arrabal) **2**:15-16; **9**:33, 38, 41; **18**:20-1; **58**:7, 9-11, 14-15, 17-19, 22
"Architecture" (Barthelme) **117**:5
"Architecture and the Critique of Ideology" (Jameson) **142**:230
"The Architecture of California" (Vaughn) **62**:457-58
The Architecture of Vision (Antonioni) **144**:59-60
Archives de ma tour d'ivoire (Cendrars) **106**:170
Archives du nord (Yourcenar) **19**:484; **87**:389, 396, 412, 417, 433
"Archways" (Oates) **6**:370
"Arco invisible de Viñales" (Lezama Lima) **101**:121
El arco y la lira: El poema. la revelación poetica, poesia,e historia (Paz) **3**:375; **4**:396-97; **6**:396-98; **10**:390; **51**:324, 326-27, 331, 336; **65**:176-77; **119**:423
"L'arcs" (Butor) **15**:114
Arctic Grail (Berton) **104**:50-1, 53-6
"The Arctic Landscape High above the Equator" (Bissoondath) **120**:13, 19
"Arctic Rhododendrons" (Purdy) **50**:245
Arctic Summer, and Other Fiction (Forster) **22**:136-37; **45**:131-33
"Arctic Syndrome: Dream Fox" (Atwood) **8**:32
"Arcturus" (Connell) **45**:106-07, 109
Ardabiola (Yevtushenko) **51**:427, 430-31; **126**:398
Ardele; or, The Daisy (Anouilh)
See *Ardèle; ou, La marguerite*
Ardèle; ou, La marguerite (Anouilh) **13**:21; **50**:280
The Ardent Slingsman (Neruda)
See *El hondero entusiasta, 1923-1924*
Les ardoises du toit (Reverdy) **53**:288
"Ardor/Awe/Atrocity" (Abish) **22**:17, 19, 22
"Are Canadians Politically Naive?" (Škvorecký) **69**:335-36
"Are Flowers Whores?" (Smart) **54**:421
"Are These Actual Miles?" (Carver) **53**:65
"Are You a Doctor?" (Carver) **22**:99; **126**:161, 179
Are You in the House Alone? (Peck) **21**:298-99
"Are You Listening?" (Ellison) **42**:127
"Are You Ready" (Dylan) **77**:190
"Are You Ready for the Country" (Young) **17**:571
Are You Ready for the Country (Jennings) **21**:203-04
"Are You Ready to Rock?" (Sapphire) **99**:81
"Are You Still There" (Harjo) **83**:278-79
"Are You the Right Size?" (Powell) **89**:207
Are You There God? It's Me, Margaret (Blume) **12**:44-7; **30**:20-3
"Are You Ticklish" (Simon) **26**:409
"Are You with Me?" (Swados) **12**:557
Are Your Teeth White? Then Laugh! (p'Bitek)
See *Lak tar miyo kinyero wi lobo*
"An Area in the Cerebral Hemisphere" (Major) **19**:298
An Area of Darkness (Naipaul) **4**:371, 373-74; **7**:253-54; **13**:406-07; **18**:363; **37**:319, 321; **105**:133-34, 151, 155, 159, 161, 171, 180
"Arena" (Rodriguez) **10**:440
Aren't You Rather Young to be Writing Your Memoirs? (Johnson) **6**:263; **9**:303
Aretheus (Krleža) **114**:177
Arfive (Guthrie) **23**:199
L'argent de la poche (Truffaut) **20**:404; **101**:384-87, 400, 403-04, 407
"The Argentine Ant" (Calvino)
See *La formica Argentina*
"The Argentine Writer and Tradition" (Borges)
See "El escritor argentino y la tradición"
"Argon" (Levi) **37**:223, 227
"Argonaut" (Seferis) **11**:495
The Argot Merchant Disaster: Poems New and Selected (Starbuck) **53**:354-56
"Argument" (Auden) **11**:18
"Argument" (Char) **11**:111
"Argument" (Hughes) **119**:269
"Argument" (Powys) **125**:274
"The Argument for the Benevolent God" (Ewart) **46**:150
Argument of Kings (Scannell) **49**:333-34
An Argument with My Mexican Father (Rodriguez)
See *Days of Obligation: An Argument with My Mexican Father*
"Argyle Street" (Mathias) **45**:235
"Argyria" (Aldington) **49**:6
"Aria" (Barthelme) **23**:47
"Ariadne" (Simic) **49**:337
Ariadne: Le chemin de Créte (Marcel) **15**:361
"Ariel" (Plath) **5**:339-345; **9**:433; **14**:424, 428; **17**:351, 353, 360-61, 363, 365-66; **50**:446; **51**:342-43, 352; **111**:161, 175-76, 178, 199
Ariel (Plath) **1**:269-70; **2**:335-38; **3**:388-91; **5**:339-40, 342-43, 345-46; **9**:424-25, 432-33; **11**:445-49; **14**:422-26; **17**:345-50, 352-53, 355-56, 361-64, 366-69; **50**:441, 444; **62**:386, 425; **111**:158, 160, 164, 167-69, 176-82, 185-86, 210, 216
Ariel Poems (Eliot) **1**:89; **2**:128; **15**:213-14
Arigato (Condon) **6**:115; **8**:150; **10**:111
Arilla Sun Down (Hamilton) **26**:151-52, 154-55
"Arion" (Herbert) **43**:183
An Aristocracy of Everyone: The Politics of Education and the Future of America (Barber) **141**:10-11
The Aristocrat (Richter) **30**:325
Aristocrats (Friel) **42**:174; **59**:145-49; **115**:224-25, 227-29, 234, 236, 241-42, 247
Aristofaniana s ljugaškami (Aksyonov) **37**:12
Aristophaniana with Frogs (Aksyonov)
See *Aristofaniana s ljugaškami*
The Aristos: A Self-Portrait in Ideas (Fowles) **2**:138; **4**:170-71; **6**:185; **9**:210-11, 213, 216; **10**:184, 189; **15**:233; **33**:160, 164, 166-67, 171, 173; **87**:141-42, 159, 175-77, 182, 186
"Aristotle and the Hired Thugs" (Gold) **152**:129
"Arizona Highways" (Welch) **52**:429-30

The Ark (Benary-Isbert) **12**:30-2, 35
"Ark of Bones" (Dumas) **6**:145; **62**:150, 153, 155, 161-64
Ark of Bones (Dumas) **6**:145; **62**:150-52, 158-60
"The ark of consequence" (Piercy) **128**:274
The Ark Sakura (Abe)
See *Hakobune sakura maru*
"The Arkansas Testament" (Walcott) **67**:359, 361; **76**:275
The Arkansas Testament (Walcott) **67**:342, 358-63; **76**:288
"Arkansas Traveler" (Wright) **146**:313, 317, 322
Arkhipelag GuLag, 1918-1956: Op' bit khudozhestvennopo issledovaniia (Solzhenitsyn) **4**:512-516; **7**:436-41, 443, 445-47; **10**:478-79; **34**:484-85, 489, 491, 493; **78**:386-87, 389, 401, 403-06, 410-11, 423-24, 426-27; **134**:289-90, 299, 304-05, 317
Arkkitehti (Haavikko) **34**:170
"An Arles, an Arles for My Hiring" (Bunting) **39**:300
Arlette (Freeling) **38**:187
The Arm and the Darkness (Caldwell) **28**:57-8; **39**:303
The Arm and the Flame (Seifert)
See *Ruka a plamen*
"Arm in Arm" (Simpson) **149**:345, 350
The Arm of Flesh (Salter) **52**:358-59, 363
The Arm of the Starfish (L'Engle) **12**:347, 351
Arm Yourself or Harm Yourself: A One-Act Play: A Message of Self-Defense to Black Men (Baraka) **115**:36
An Armada of Thirty Whales (Hoffman) **6**:243; **13**:286-87; **23**:237-38
"The Armadillo" (Bishop) **9**:93; **13**:88-9; **32**:37, 43
Armadillo in the Grass (Hearon) **63**:160, 166
"Armageddon" (Ransom) **4**:435
"Armageddon" (Scott) **22**:372
Armageddon (Uris) **7**:491; **32**:431-32, 434
"Armageddon, Armageddon" (Muldoon) **32**:318-19; **72**:265-66
Armageddon?: Essays 1983-1987 (Vidal) **72**:398, 400; **142**:308
"Armageddon News" (Bissett) **18**:58
"Armaja Das" (Haldeman) **61**:174, 176 78
"Armantrout" (Howe) **152**:159, 162
"Las armas secretas" (Cortázar) **10**:113; **13**:164; **33**:126; **34**:329
Armas y corações (Dourado) **23**:151
Armed Forces (Costello) **21**:71-2
Armed Love (Lerman) **9**:328-31
"Les armes miraculeuses" (Césaire) **32**:113; **112**:10, 12, 29
An Armful of Warm Girl (Spackman) **46**:376-78, 380-81
"Armidale" (Simpson) **149**:307
The Armies of the Moon (MacEwen) **13**:358; **55**:163, 166
The Armies of the Night: History as a Novel, the Novel as History (Mailer) **1**:191, 193; **2**:259-60, 263-65; **3**:312-15, 317, 319; **4**:321-23; **8**:367-73; **11**:340-41, 343-44; **14**:349-50, 352-53; **28**:256-57, 262; **39**:425; **74**:204-06, 213-17, 225, 231; **111**:103, 106-08, 110, 113-15, 120, 125-26, 131, 133, 148, 151
"Armistice" (Bowering) **32**:47
"Armistice Day" (Simon) **17**:461
L'armoireà glace un beau soir (Aragon) **22**:41
Les armoires vides (Ernaux) **88**:98-101, 105-06, 108, 114-15, 120
Armored Cav (Clancy) **112**:77
"Armor's Undermining Modesty" (Moore) **8**:401; **10**:350
The Armourer's House (Sutcliff) **26**:428, 433, 435, 439
"Arms" (Beer) **58**:32, 36
"Arms and the Man" (Sassoon) **130**:182
The Arms of Venus (Seifert) **34**:256; **93**:306, 315, 318, 335, 341
Armstrong's Last Goodnight (Arden) **6**:7-8, 11; **13**:24-5, 29; **15**:18, 25
"Army of Occupation" (Boyle) **58**:81-2
Arna Bontemps-Langston Hughes Letters, 1925-67 (Bontemps) **18**:65-6
"The Arno at Rovezzano" (Montale) **9**:387
Arnold and Degener, One Chase Manhattan Plaza (Auchincloss) **18**:24
"Arnold and Pater" (Eliot) **24**:166
Arnold Bennett (Drabble) **5**:117
Arnold Bennett (Wain) **2**:458
"Arnold, Burke and the Celts" (Deane) **122**:77
"The Arnold Crombeck Story" (McGrath) **55**:76
"Arnold Stone" (O'Hara) **42**:319
Arnoumai (Samarakis) **5**:381; **5**:381
Aromates chasseurs (Char) **55**:285, 288
Aromatic Hunters (Char)
See *Aromates chasseurs*
"Aromos" (Parra) **102**:340
"Around Pastor Bonhoeffer" (Kunitz) **6**:287; **148**:89, 127-28, 146
"Around the Bend in Eighty Days" (Perelman) **5**:338
"Around the Corner from Francis Bacon" (Durcan) **43**:118
Around the Day in Eighty Worlds (Cortázar)
See *La vuelta al día en ochenta mundos*
Around the Dead Sea (Endō) **99**:308
"Around the Dear Ruin" (Berriault) **54**:3
"Around the Dial" (Davies) **21**:107
"Around the Light House" (Durcan) **70**:151-52
Around the Mountain: Scenes from Montreal Life (Hood) **15**:284; **28**:188
"Around the World" (Graver) **70**:49, 52-3
Around the World in 80 Days (Welles) **80**:380, 386
Around the World in a Day (Prince) **35**:331-32
Around the World in Eighty Days (Perelman) **23**:335; **44**:500-02; **49**:269-70
El arpa y la sombra (Carpentier) **70**:347, 351; **110**:69, 74, 78
Arrabal celebrando la ceremonia de la confusión (Arrabal) **18**:18; **58**:6
Arrabal Celebrating the Ceremony of Confusion (Arrabal)
See *Arrabal celebrando la ceremonia de la confusión*
The Arrangement (Kazan) **6**:273; **16**:368, 370-71; **63**:215, 221, 223, 229, 233-34
"Arrangement in Black and White" (Parker) **15**:415; **68**:326, 330, 334, 336
"An Arrangement of Shadows" (Bissoondath) **120**:2, 4-5, 24
"Arras" (Page) **7**:292; **18**:380
"The Arrest of Oscar Wilde at the Cadogan Hotel" (Betjeman) **43**:32, 42
L'arrestation (Anouilh) **8**:24
"Arrests" (Samarakis) **5**:382
L'Arrêt de mort (Blanchot) **135**:87-88, 109-10, 132, 136-37, 141, 145, 148
L'arrière-pays (Bonnefoy) **9**:112; **58**:51-4, 60
"Arrival" (Celan) **19**:95
"Arrival" (Guillén) **48**:164, 166; **79**:230
"The Arrival" (Merwin) **88**:202
Arrival and Departure (Koestler) **15**:310-11; **33**:229-30, 233, 238, 240-41, 243-44
"Arrival at Santos" (Bishop) **13**:88, 93; **32**:37
"Arrival of My Cousin" (Jacobsen) **48**:191
"The Arrival of the Bee Box" (Plath) **9**:429, 431; **14**:425; **51**:342
Arrival of the Gods (Buero Vallejo)
See *Llegada de los dioes*
"Arrivals, Departures" (Larkin) **33**:256; **64**:262, 266
"Arrivals Wolfville" (Birney) **6**:74, 77
The Arrivants: A New World Trilogy (Brathwaite) **11**:67
"Arriving" (Piercy) **27**:376
"Arriving at the Point of Departure" (Plumly) **33**:311
"Arriving in the Country Again" (Wright) **3**:540
"Arriving Late for a Movie" (Dacey) **51**:82
The Arrivistes: Poems, 1940-1949 (Simpson) **4**:498; **32**:378; **149**:298, 326, 344, 349-50
"Arrogant" (Matthews) **40**:325
Arrogant Beggar (Yezierska) **46**:444
"Arrow" (Dove) **81**:152
Arrow in the Blue (Koestler) **15**:311-12; **33**:234-35, 243
An Arrow in the Wall: Selected Poetry and Prose (Voznesensky) **57**:426-28
Arrow of God (Achebe) **1**:1; **3**:1-3; **5**:1, 3; **7**:3-4, 6-7; **11**:1-5; **26**:13-20, 25, 27; **51**:2-3, 5, 7; **75**:3-4, 6, 8-10; **127**:18, 25 6, 28 9, 31, 34, 40, 51-2, 54, 57, 61-4, 70-2, 74-6; **152**:17, 45, 52-3, 56-7
Arrow Pointing Nowhere (Daly) **52**:89
Arrowroot (Tanizaki)
See *Yoshinokuzu*
Arrowsmith (Ford) **16**:303
Ars amandi (Arrabal) **9**:35; **18**:22
Ars longa, vita brevis (Arden) **15**:21
"Ars poetica" (Davie) **31**:118
"Ars poetica" (Dove) **81**:140, 150-51
"Ars poetica" (Dunn) **6**:148
"Ars poetica" (Kennedy) **42**:256
"Ars poetica" (Longley) **29**:296
"Ars Poetica" (MacLeish) **8**:360-61, 363; **14**:337-38; **68**:273, 284, 287, 290-91, 293-94
"Ars poetica?" (Milosz) **22**:308, 310; **56**:238, 242; **82**:303
"Ars poetica" (Richards) **14**:455
"Ars poetica" (Tomlinson) **4**:548
Ars Poetica: In the American Grain (Williams)
See *In the American Grain*
"Ars Poetica: Or; Who Lives in the Ivory Tower?" (McGrath) **59**:178, 181
"Ars poetica. Scrisori unei fetițe" (Arghezi) **80**:11
"Arse poetica" (Jong) **6**:267
Arse poetica: A Monologue by an Arsehole (Breytenbach) **23**:87
"Arsehole" (Raine) **103**:186, 190-91, 199, 209
Arsenal (Char) **11**:114; **55**:287
"Arsenal by Night" (Neruda)
See "Maestranzas de noche"
Arsenic and Old Lace (Kesselring) **45**:207-10
"Arsenio" (Montale) **7**:222; **9**.387, **18**.342
"Art" (Carver) **126**:119
"Art" (Levertov) **15**:337
"Art" (Major) **19**:297
Art and Ardor (Ozick) **28**:351-55; **62**:347; **155**:124, 128, 13, 178-80, 187, 190, 216, 226
"Art and Democracy" (Jones) **7**:190
"Art and Eros" (Murdoch) **51**:291-92
"Art and Evil" (Lowell) **124**:268
"Art and Extinction" (Harrison) **43**:180; **129**:166
"Art and Fortune" (Trilling) **9**:531; **11**:542; **24**:450-53, 461
"Art and Life" (Johnston) **51**:244
"Art and Mr. Mahoney" (McCullers) **12**:433
"Art and Neurosis" (Trilling) **24**:452, 456
Art and Outrage (Miller) **84**:250
"Art and Politics: The Editorship of Blast'" (Williams) **22**:464
"Art and Responsibility" (Bakhtin) **83**:36
Art and Revolution (Berger) **2**:54; **19**:37
"Art and Sacrament" (Jones) **7**:188-90; **42**:244
"Art and the Obvious" (Huxley) **79**:310
"Art and the Ravens" (Watkins) **43**:442
"Art and the Underground" (Sukenick) **48**:368, 370
Art and Value (Blaga)
See *Artă si valoare*
Art as Second Nature: Occasional Pieces, 1950-74 (Hamburger) **14**:234
Art Buchwald's Paris (Buchwald) **33**:87
Art Chronicles, 1954-1966 (O'Hara) **5**:325; **13**:423; **78**:359

Art Colony (Boyle) **121**:29
L'Art du roman (Kundera)
See *Unemí románu: Cesta Vladislava Vančuryza velkou epikou*
"Art for Art's Sake" (Forster) **4**:166; **77**:216
"Art History" (Gurganus) **70**:190-91, 194, 196
Art in Anchorage (Gray) **49**:147
"Art Lecture" (Ezekiel) **61**:97, 101, 103
An Art Lover's Collection (Perec)
See *Un cabinet d'amateur*
"Art Notes" (Pound) **112**:351
The Art of Asking (Handke)
See *Das Spiel vom Fragen oder Die Reise zum Sonoren Land*
"The Art of Bergotte" (Bowen) **15**:78
"The Art of Biography" (Lively) **32**:276
The Art of Birds (Neruda)
See *Arte de pájaros*
"The art of blessing the day" (Piercy) **128**:271
"The Art of Courtly Love" (Garrett) **51**:140
The Art of Darkness (McFadden) **48**:257-58
The Art of Dining (Howe) **48**:173-75
The Art of Easter Island (Heyerdahl) **26**:193
The Art of Eating: Five Gastronomical Works (Fisher) **76**:337, 339, 341-42; **87**:120, 122, 125
The Art of Fiction (Lodge) **141**:353, 373
"The Art of Fiction: An Interview" (Ellison) **114**:91, 102
The Art of Fiction: Notes on Craft for Young Writers (Gardner) **34**:547-50
The Art of Growing Old (Powys) **125**:293
"The Art of Happiness" (Powys) **125**:300
The Art of Happiness (Powys) **125**:302
The Art of Hunger (Auster) **131**:19, 21-2
"The Art of Ingratiating" (Yevtushenko) **126**:388
"The Art of Literature and Commonsense" (Nabokov) **23**:315
"The Art of Living" (Gardner) **28**:161
The Art of Living, and Other Stories (Gardner) **28**:161-63
"The Art of Love" (Fuller) **62**:186-87, 193
"The Art of Love" (Koch) **44**:244-45, 249-50
The Art of Love (Koch) **8**:323; **44**:246, 249, 251
"The Art of Needles and Sins" (Okudzhava) **59**:378-79
"Art of Poetry" (Ammons) **5**:29
"Art of Poetry" (Bonnefoy)
See "Art poétique"
"The Art of Poetry" (Koch) **8**:323; **44**:249, 251
"The Art of Response" (Lorde) **71**:260
The Art of Salad Gardening (Proulx) **81**:275
The Art of Seeing (Huxley) **3**:253
The Art of Shakespeare's Sonnets (Vendler) **138**:277-78, 282, 287, 296, 298, 300-02
"The Art of the Film" (Carpenter) **41**:103
The Art of the Impossible (Havel) **123**:218
The Art of the Novel: Vladislav Vancura's Search for the Great Epic (Kundera)
See *Unemí románu: Cesta Vladislava Vančuryza velkou epikou*
"The Art of the Octopus" (Levertov) **28**:243
"Art of the Possible" (Lowell) **37**:238
The Art of the Self (Kosinski) **53**:221, 225
Art of the Sonnet (Orlovitz) **22**:334, 336
"The Art of the Word and the Culture of Folk Humor (Rabelais and Gogol)" (Bakhtin) **83**:24
The Art of War (Walker)
See *The Power Plays*
The Art of Worldly Wisdom (Rexroth) **6**:450; **22**:344, 347; **49**:274, 279, 284; **112**:365, 374-76, 384
Art on My Mind (Hooks) **94**:159
"Art poétique" (Bonnefoy) **58**:42, 51
"Art Review" (Fearing) **51**:111, 116
Eine Art Schadensabwicklung (Habermas) **104**:87
"Art School" (Weller) **26**:443
"Art Student" (Spender) **5**:401
"Art Work" (Byatt) **136**:164
Artă si valoare (Blaga) **75**:80
Arte de pájaros (Neruda) **28**:312-14; **62**:331
"El arte narrativo y la magia" (Borges) **13**:108; **48**:47; **83**:163
Artefactos (Parra) **102**:334, 355-56
"Artemis" (Broumas) **73**:2, 4, 6, 9
"Artemis" (Williams) **56**:427
Artemis Hates Romance (Thesen) **56**:414-15, 417, 421
"Arthur" (Hellman) **52**:192
Arthur (Davies) **21**:91, 93, 100
"Arthur at Ampelos" (Forster) **45**:133
"Arthur Bond" (Goyen) **40**:216, 218
Arthur C. Clarke & Lord Dunsany: A Correspondence (Clarke) **136**:239
Arthur Dimmesdale (Larson) **31**:241
Arthur Miller's Collected Plays (Miller) **4**:2369, 2373; **6**:334; **15**:371; **26**:319, 321-22; **78**:309, 311, 314, 316, 319, 324
Arthur Rex: A Legendary Novel (Berger) **11**:46-8; **18**:57-8; **38**:39
"Arthur Rimbaud" (Char) **11**:115
"Arthur Snatchfold" (Forster) **22**:135
Articles of Faith (Harwood) **32**:224-25
Articulate Energy: An Inquiry into the Syntax of English Poetry (Davie) **8**:162, 167
"Articulation of Sound Forms in Time" (Howe) **152**:154, 203, 205-6, 242
Articulation of Sound Forms in Time (Howe) **72**:202-05, 207, 209; **152**:152, 157-58, 164-66, 168, 170, 172, 174, 192, 195, 216-17
"Artifact" (Rukeyser) **10**:442
Artifact (Benford) **52**:73-4
Artifacts (Parra)
See *Artefactos*
"Artifax in Extremis" (Davie) **31**:123-24
"Artifice of Absorption" (Bernstein) **142**:18, 20, 43, 56
"Artificer" (Kennedy) **42**:255
"Artificer" (Milosz) **56**:247
"Artificial Illuminations" (Urdang) **47**:399-400
The Artificial Jungle (Ludlam) **46**:244; **50**:342-44
The Artificial Kid (Sterling) **72**:372
"The Artificial Nigger" (O'Connor) **3**:365-66; **6**:381; **13**:419; **15**:410; **21**:256-57, 263-64; **104**:117, 123, 135, 190, 192
An Artificial Nigger (O'Connor)
See *A Good Man Is Hard to Find and Other Stories*
"Artificial Roses" (García Márquez) **47**:151
An Artificial Wilderness: Essays on Twentieth Century Literature (Birkerts) **116**:147-52
De Artificiali Perspectiva or Anamorphosis (The Brothers Quay) **95**:347
"The Artist" (Avison) **97**:76, 80, 84
"The Artist" (Heaney) **37**:165; **74**:169
"An Artist" (Jeffers) **54**:236
"The Artist" (Koch) **5**:219; **8**:322; **44**:243, 247-48
"The Artist" (Kunitz) **148**:69, 78-80, 83, 89
"The Artist as a Critic and a Witness" (Wiebe) **138**:388, 392, 394
"The Artist as Housewife/The Housewife as Artist" (Jong) **83**:298
"Artist at Home" (Faulkner) **3**:155-56; **18**:145-47
"The Artist at Work" (Camus)
See "Jonas ou l'artiste au travail"
Artist Descending a Staircase (Stoppard) **15**:519; **29**:397, 401, 404
An Artist in the Family (Millin) **49**:243-46
"An Artist in the North" (Transtroemer) **65**:236
An Artist of the Floating World (Ishiguro) **56**:158-61; **59**:159, 161, 163-65, 167; **110**:220, 222-26, 228, 231-34, 243-44, 246, 257-59, 261-62
"An Artist Waiting in a Country House" (Dunn) **40**:168
"Artists" (Smith) **25**:409-10; **73**:358
"The Artists' and Models' Ball" (Brooks) **49**:32; **125**:87
Artists in Crime (Marsh) **53**:249
"Artists' Letters" (Kinsella) **138**:110
"Artist's Model One" (Lowell) **11**:330
"Artists Only" (Byrne) **26**:96
"Artists, Providers, Places to Go" (Fisher) **25**:159
"Art-Luck-Risk" (Elytis) **100**:190
"Arts et métiers" (Butor) **15**:114
"The Arts in 1975" (Ciardi) **129**:54
An Arts of the Difficult World (Roberts) **76**:209, 212-13, 215, 219
Artsot hatan (Oz) **8**:436; **27**:358-61; **54**:352
Arturo's Island (Morante)
See *L'isola di Arturo*
"An Arundel Tomb" (Larkin) **8**:332; **18**:300; **33**:258, 261, 263; **39**:335, 344-45; **64**:263, 277, 279
Arztliche seelsorge (Frankl) **93**:209-10, 214, 216, 218-19, 223
"As" (Wonder) **12**:662
"As a Comment on Romans 1:10" (Avison) **97**:121
"As a Man Walks" (Simpson) **149**:319, 341
"As Birds Are Fitted to the Boughs" (Simpson) **149**:326
"As Birds Bring Forth the Sun" (MacLeod) **56**:198-99
As Birds Bring Forth the Sun and Other Stories (MacLeod) **56**:197-200
"As Breathing and Consciousness Return" (Solzhenitsyn)
See "Dykhanie"
"As Children Together" (Forché) **25**:172
"As Evening Lays Dying" (Salinas) **90**:332
As Ever: The Collected Correspondence of Allen Ginsberg and Neal Cassady (Ginsberg) **36**:185
"As Expected" (Gunn) **32**:214
"As facas Pernambucanas" (Cabral de Melo Neto) **76**:165
"As Fast As You Can" (Feldman) **7**:103
"As Flowers Are" (Kunitz) **148**:70, 137
As for Me and My House (Ross) **13**:490, 492-94
"As Freedom Is a Breakfast-Food" (Cummings) **15**:162
"As He Came Near Death" (Fisher) **25**:159
"As I Came from the Holy Land" (Ashbery) **6**:12; **25**:58
"As I Came, I Saw a Wood" (Hughes) **119**:270
"As I Grow Older" (Hughes) **108**:283
As I Lay Dying (Faulkner) **1**:98, 102; **3**:153; **6**:179-80; **8**:207; **9**:198-200; **11**:202, 204-06; **14**:173, 175, 178; **28**:140-43; **52**:107, 113, 138; **68**:109
"As I Step over the Puddle at the End of Winter, I Think of an Ancient Chinese" (Wright) **3**:541, 543; **28**:466
"As I Walked Out One Evening" (Betjeman) **43**:40
As I Walked Out One Midsummer Morning (Lee) **90**:188-91, 202-4, 206-7, 209-10
"As I Was Going Up the Stairs" (Chester) **49**:55-6
"As I Was Saying" (Parra) **102**:353-54
"As I Went Out One Morning" (Dylan) **12**:185
As If by Magic (Wilson) **3**:535-36; **5**:514-15; **25**:458-59, 461, 463-64
As If: Poems New and Selected (Ciardi) **40**:154, 156, 162; **44**:375, 379, 381; **129**:42
As imaginações pecaminosas (Dourado) **60**:85
"As in a Dream I Would Yet Remain" (Lerman) **9**:329
"As in a Gallery" (Ostriker) **132**:327
As Is (Breytenbach) **126**:89
As Is (Hoffman) **40**:254-56
"As It Should Be" (Mahon) **27**:288
"As It Was in the Beginning" (Richter) **30**:319
"As John to Patmos" (Walcott) **76**:278
"As Mortes e o Triunfo de Rosalinda" (Amado) **106**:74, 77

"As of July 6, I Am Responsible for No Other Debts than My Own" (Jones) **81**:65
"As Old as the Century" (Pritchett) **41**:332
"As on a Darkling Plain" (Taylor) **44**:302
"As One Put Drunk into the Packet Boat" (Ashbery) **13**:31; **15**:28; **125**:34
As Sad as She Is (Onetti)
See *Tan triste como ella*
"Às seis e meia no largo do carmo" (Dourado) **23**:151
As sete portas du Bahia (Amado) **106**:62
"As Sparks Fly Upward" (Hollander) **2**:197
As Ten, as Twenty (Page) **7**:291
As Testimony (Duncan) **55**:293
"As the 'Billy World Turns" (Jennings) **21**:204-05
"As the Crickets' soft autumn hum" (Snyder) **120**:325
"As the Dead Prey upon Us" (Olson) **29**:334
"As the Manatees Go to Drink at the Source" (Senghor) **54**:408
"As the Mist Leaves No Scar" (Cohen) **38**:132
"As the Night Goes" (Jiles) **58**:272
As the Third Millennium Draws Near (John Paul II) **128**:197-99
"As the Window Darkens" (Jensen) **37**:189
As the World Turns (Nixon) **21**:242, 246
As They Reveled (Wylie) **43**:462
As They Were (Fisher) **76**:340; **87**:122, 128
As Thousands Cheer (Hart) **66**:176, 178, 185, 190
As We Are Now (Sarton) **4**:471-72; **14**:480-81; **49**:322; **91**:240, 246-50
"As We Know" (Ashbery) **15**:33-4
As We Know (Ashbery) **15**:33-6; **25**:52-3, 58-9; **41**:38, 41
"As We Like It" (Auden) **14**:26
"As You Came from the Holy Land" (Ashbery) **6**:12; **15**:26; **77**:51-2
"As You Leave Me" (Knight) **40**:279, 286
Asakusa Kurenaidan (Kawabata) **9**:311; **107**:105, 107
"Ascending Image" (Donnell) **34**:156
"Ascension" (Levine) **33**:275
"Ascension" (Thomas) **107**:338, 340, 342, 346
Ascension (Konwicki)
See *Wniebowstapienie*
"The Ascent" (Kennedy) **42**:255
"Ascent" (Merwin) **88**:194
"The Ascent" (Randall) **135**:390, 397
"Ascent into Hell" (Hope) **51**:214, 224
Ascent into Hell (Greeley) **28**:177-78
The Ascent of F6 (Auden) **1**:9; **3**:26; **11**:18; **14**:30-1; **43**:21
The Ascent of F6 (Isherwood) **44**:396, 399
The Ascent of Mount Fuji (Aitmatov)
See *Voskhozhdenie na Fudzhiamu*
Ascent to Dmai (Harris) **25**:209-10, 216
Ascent to Orbit (Clarke) **35**:128; **136**:225
The Ascent to the Truth (Merton) **83**:403
El asesinato del perdedor (Cela) **122**:71
"El asesino" (Arreola) **147**:16
"El asesino desinteresado Bill Harrigan" (Borges) **83**:165
Ash (Walker) **14**:552
"The Ash and the Oak" (Simpson) **149**:345
Ash on a Young Man's Sleeve (Abse) **29**:11, 18, 20
Ash on an Old Man's Sleeve (King) **145**:365-67
"Ash Wednesday" (Jennings) **131**:234
"Ash Wednesday" (Seifert) **93**:332
Ashani sanket (Ray) **16**:488-89, 493-94; **76**:357, 360, 362, 367
"A-Sharr al-m'bud" (Mahfouz) **153**:17
Ashenden; or, The British Agent (Maugham) **67**:210
"Ashes" (Levine) **118**:299
"Ashes" (Peterkin) **31**:308
Ashes (Rudkin) **14**:470-71
Ashes and Diamonds (Wajda) **16**:577-79, 581-82, 584
"Ashes and Wrath" (L'Heureux) **52**:272
"The Ashes of a Poet" (Solzhenitsyn) **7**:432
The Ashes of Gramsci (Pasolini)
See *Le ceneri di Gramscí*
Ashes of Izalco (Alegria)
See *Cenizas de Izalco*
Ashes: Poems New and Old (Levine) **14**:320-21; **33**:270-72; **118**:284, 293, 295, 299-300
"Ashikari" (Tanizaki) **8**:510; **28**:414, 416, 418
Ashini (Theriault) **79**:399, 401, 406, 411-412, 416-418
"The Ashplant" (Heaney) **91**:125
"Ashtamudi Lake" (Alexander) **121**:21
"The Ashtray" (Carver) **36**:107
"Ashurnatsirpal III" (Sandburg) **15**:466
Ash-Wednesday (Eliot) **1**:90-2; **2**:128-29; **3**:137-39, 141; **6**:163, 165-66; **9**:183-84, 186-89; **10**:167-68, 170; **13**:194, 200-02; **15**:208, 213-17; **34**:524-25, 529-31; **41**:148, 151, 154-56, 162; **55**:350, 362, 371; **57**:179, 181, 186, 213
Ashworth Hall (Perry) **126**:340-41
Así en la paz como en la guerra (Cabrera Infante) **5**:96
Asian Figures (Merwin) **5**:287; **45**:273
The Asian Journal of Thomas Merton (Merton) **3**:337
"The Asian Shore: A Tale of Possession" (Disch) **7**:86
"The Asians Dying" (Merwin) **13**:385; **88**:206
The Asiatics (Prokosch) **4**:421; **48**:302-04, 307, 309, 312-15
"An Aside" (Blunden) **56**:48
Asimov on Science Fiction (Asimov) **26**:57
Asimov's Guide to Shakespeare (Asimov) **76**:312
Asimov's Guide to the Bible, Volume I: The Old Testament (Asimov) **76**:312
Asimov's Guide to the Bible, Volume II: The New Testament (Asimov) **76**:312
Asimov's Mysteries (Asimov) **26**:37
Asimov's New Guide to Science (Asimov) **76**:313
Asinamali! (Ngema) **57**:339-44
Ask Again (Johnston) **51**:248-49, 254
"Ask Him" (Carver) **53**:61
Ask Me No Questions (Schlee) **35**:374
Ask Me Now (Young) **19**:480
Ask Me Tomorrow, or The Pleasant Comedy of Young Fortunatus (Cozzens) **92**:203
Ask Me Tomorrrow (Cozzens) **11**:126, 128, 131; **92**:178, 180-82, 184-86, 194, 203-06, 208
Ask the Dust (Fante) **60**:129-30, 132-34
"Ask the Roses" (Levine) **14**:318; **118**:279, 300
Ask Your Mama: 12 Moods for Jazz (Hughes) **10**:279; **15**:294; **35**:216, 218, 220; **108**:283-84, 335
Asking Around (Hare) **136**:258-59, 271
Aslan Norval (Traven) **11**:537
"Asleep?" (Silkin) **6**:498
Asleep in the Sun (Bioy Casares)
See *Dormir al sol*
"Asleep: With Still Hands" (Ellison) **42**:127
Asmodée (Mauriac) **56**:212, 214-15
"Asmodeus" (Hill) **8**:294
"An Aspect of Love, Alive in the Fire and Ice" (Brooks) **49**:28
"Aspects" (MacCaig) **36**:288
"Aspects of a Play" (Bentley) **24**:47
Aspects of Eve (Pastan) **27**:369
Aspects of Feeling (Vansittart) **42**:398-401
"Aspects of God" (Broumas) **10**:76
"Aspects of Lilacs" (Moss) **45**:287
Aspects of the Dying Process (Wilding) **73**:398
Aspects of the Novel (Forster) **3**:160; **4**:165; **9**:208-09; **13**:219; **15**:224, 227; **45**:136, 138, 140, 143-44; **77**:205, 214-15, 222
Aspects of the Present (Mead) **37**:282
Aspects of the Presidency: Truman and Ford in Office (Hersey) **81**:332, 335
Aspects of the Theory of Syntax (Chomsky) **132**:6-7, 14
"Aspen Tree" (Celan) **82**:37-8, 47
"Aspen's Song" (Winters) **32**:469
"The Aspern Papers" (Ozick) **155**:197
Os ásperos tempos (Amado) **106**:59
Asphalt Georgics (Carruth) **84**:135
The Asphalt Jungle (Huston) **20**:160, 162, 165
"The Asphalt Orangery" (Aksyonov) **101**:22
"Asphodel" (Welty) **14**:562
"Asphodel, That Greeny Flower" (Williams) **9**:572-73, 575; **22**:465, 467-68; **42**:463-64
An Aspidistra in Babylon: Four Novellas (Bates) **46**:65
"Asra" (Muldoon) **72**:281
"Ass" (Salinas) **90**:326
"Assassin" (Mahapatra) **33**:277, 283
"Assassin" (Tomlinson) **4**:544; **13**:548-49; **45**:393, 404
The Assassin (O'Flaherty) **5**:321
The Assassin (Shaw) **23**:396
"Assassination Raga" (Ferlinghetti) **6**:184; **27**:137, 139
"The Assassins" (Epstein) **7**:97
"The Assassins" (Prokosch) **48**:304, 306
"Assassins" (Szirtes) **46**:393
The Assassins (Camus)
See *Les justes*
The Assassins (Kazan) **6**:273; **63**:216-18
Assassins (Mosley) **43**:313-14; **70**:204
The Assassins (Prokosch) **48**:302-04, 306-10
Assassins (Sondheim) **147**:238-40, 243-45, 247, 249-50, 254, 260
The Assassins: A Book of Hours (Oates) **6**:374; **9**:402-05; **19**:350, 353-54; **33**:289; **52**:338; **108**:386, 391
The Assault (Mulisch) **42**:289-92
Assault with Intent (Kienzle) **25**:276
"Assaut de la pitié" (Malraux) **13**:367
"Assay of the Infinite Man" (Neruda)
See *Tentativa del hombre infinito*
Assays (Rexroth) **22**:346
"The Assembly" (Borges)
See *El congreso*
"The Assembly" (Gallant) **38**:195
"Un assenza" (Ginzburg) **54**:198; **70**:283
Assez (Beckett) **6**:36, 38, 42; **18**:51-2
"Assia" (Trevor) **116**:388
The Assignation (Oates) **108**:374-76
"Assignment" (Carruth) **84**:136
The Assignment (Duerrenmatt) **102**:83, 85-90
Assignment in Brittany (MacInnes) **27**:279; **39**:349-51
Assignment: Sports (Lipsyte) **21**:208
"Assimilation" (Alexie) **154**:45, 48
"Assisi" (Celan) **19**:88
"The Assistance" (Blackburn) **43**:61
The Assistant (Malamud) **1**:195-98, 200-01; **2**:265-69; **3**:320-21, 323-24; **5**:269-70; **8**:374, 376; **9**:341-42, 346-50; **11**:345-46, 348-54; **18**:319, 321; **27**:295-98, 301; **44**:411-18, 420; **78**:247-86; **85**:200
Assorted Prose (Updike) **13**:557; **23**:463, 473; **34**:285-86; **139**:362
The Assumption of the Rogues and Rascals (Smart) **54**:413-14, 419-22, 425-26
Assumptions (Hacker) **72**:182-84, 189-90
"Assunta" (Chatwin) **57**:153
"Assunta 2" (Chatwin) **57**:153
Assured Survival (Bova) **45**:74, 76
The Assyrian, and Other Stories (Saroyan) **29**:361
"Asteroids" (Tallent) **45**:387
Ästhetik (Lukacs) **24**:332, 335
Die Ästhetik des Widerstands, Vol. 1 (Weiss) **51**:387-91, 395
Die Ästhetik des Widerstands, Vol. 2 (Weiss) **51**:388-91
Die Ästhetik des Widerstands, Vol. 3 (Weiss) **51**:388-91
El astillero (Onetti) **10**:374-76
The Astonished Man (Cendrars)
See *L'homme foudroyé*
The Astonishing World (Harrison) **144**:112-13, 115

The Astral Mirror (Bova) **45**:75
Astral Weeks (Morrison) **21**:231-32, 236-37, 240
"An Astrologer's Day" (Narayan) **28**:293; **121**:418
An Astrologer's Day and Other Stories (Narayan) **28**:293, 301, 303
Astrology: Sense or Nonsense? (Gallant) **17**:130
Astrology: Wisdom of the Stars (Kettelkamp) **12**:306
"Astrometaphysical" (Frost) **26**:118
Astronauci (Lem) **40**:289-90; **149**:148, 152, 165, 255, 259, 263, 282
"Astronauts" (Hayden) **37**:157
The Astronauts (Lem)
See *Astronauci*
"The Astronomer" (Schevill) **7**:400
The Astronomer and Other Stories (Betts) **3**:73; **28**:34
"The Astronomer Poems" (Wakoski) **9**:554
The Astronomers (Bowers) **9**:121
"The Astronomers at Mont Blanc" (Bowers) **9**:121
"Astronomersq1s Wife" (Boyle) **121**:60-1
"Astronomical Riddles" (Leithauser) **27**:242
Astronomy (Branley) **21**:21-2
"Astronomy Domine" (Pink Floyd) **35**:307
Astyanax (Mandiargues) **41**:275
Asu o Tsukuru Hitobito (Kurosawa) **119**:346
"Asunto de prinicpio" (Zamora) **89**:386
The Asutra (Vance) **35**:421
"Asylum" (Bernstein) **142**:55
"The Asylum" (Carruth) **4**:94; **84**:119, 128
Asylum Piece (Kavan) **82**:116-17, 119-20
"At a Bach Concert" (Rich) **7**:371; **73**:323; **125**:310
"At a Cathedral Service" (Blunden) **56**:39
"At a Difficult Time" (Ghose) **42**:179
"At a Funeral" (Brutus) **43**:91
"At a March against the Vietnam War" (Bly) **128**:6
"At a Party" (Bogan) **46**:83-4, 90; **93**:64
"At a Poetry Conference, Expo '67" (Wright) **53**:428
"At a Potato Digging" (Heaney) **5**:171; **14**:243; **25**:251; **74**:158
"At a Public Dinner" (Wright) **53**:429
"At a Ritual Worship on a Saturday Afternoon" (Mahapatra) **33**:282
"At a Slight Angle to the Universe" (Raine) **103**:205
"At a Yorkshire Bus Stop" (Dunn) **40**:165-66
"At Akitio" (Baxter) **14**:62
"At Assissi" (McAuley) **45**:254
"At Auden's Grave" (Shapiro) **53**:334
At Bertram's Hotel (Christie) **6**:108; **12**:116-17; **110**:116, 134-35, 137
"At Bickford's" (Stern) **40**:410
"At Bluebeard's Castle" (Howard) **10**:277
"At Breakfast" (Swenson) **106**:318-19
"At Briggflatts Meeting House" (Bunting) **47**:53
"At Brown Crane Pavilion" (Kennedy) **42**:256
"At Carnoy" (Sassoon) **36**:385, 392
"At Cove on the Crooked River" (Stafford) **29**:380
"at creation" (Clifton) **66**:83
"At Dawn" (Rulfo)
See "En la madrugada"
"At Dawn, Sitting in My Father's House" (Cook-Lynn) **93**:116
"At Daybreak" (Rulfo)
See "En la madrugada"
"At Delft" (Tomlinson) **45**:399
"At East River" (Swenson) **61**:399; **106**:325
"At Evergreen Cemetary" (Purdy) **6**:428
"At Every Gas Station There Are Mechanics" (Dunn) **36**:151
At Fever Pitch (Caute) **29**:108-09
"At First Sight" (Adams) **46**:17
"At First Sight" (Campbell) **42**:84
"At Ford's Theater" (Voznesensky) **59**:378
At Freddie's (Fitzgerald) **51**:123-25; **61**:117-18; **143**:238, 240, 254-55, 262, 264-65, 268
At Full Flame (Tzara)
See *À haute flamme*
"At Fumicaro" (Ozick) **155**:139
"at gettysburg" (Clifton) **66**:82-3
"At Grass" (Larkin) **5**:227; **8**:339; **39**:336, 339, 342, 345; **64**:260, 262, 266, 269-70, 279
"At Hand" (Zamora) **89**:387
At Heaven's Gate (Warren) **4**:578, 580, 582-83; **10**:519; **13**:574; **39**:266; **53**:359, 361, 376
"At Holwell Farm" (Tomlinson) **13**:549
"At Home" (Merwin) **88**:195
"At Home" (Reading) **47**:352
At Home (Weller)
See *Split*
At Home: Essays (Vidal)
See *Armageddon?: Essays 1983-1987*
"At Home with Ron Padgett" (Schuyler) **23**:388
"At Hotel Berlin" (Voznesensky) **57**:426
"At Jeanneret's Beach" (McAuley) **45**:254
"at jonestown" (Clifton) **66**:82
"At Karl Weilink's Exhibition" (Brodsky)
See "Na vystavke Karla Veilinka"
"At Kinosaki" (Shiga)
See "Kinosaki nite"
At Lady Molly's (Powell) **3**:400
At Land (Deren) **16**:251-53; **102**:28, 31, 37-40, 42, 44, 47-8
"At Last" (Kincaid) **43**:248; **68**:208; **137**:138
"At Last" (Montague) **46**:272, 277
"At Last" (Walcott) **9**:557; **76**:280, 285
"At Least I Have Made a Woman of Her" (Oates) **108**:348
"At Lemmons" (Day Lewis) **10**:131
"At Luca Signorelli's Resurrection of the Body" (Graham) **48**:148
"At Lunch with the Rock Critic Establishment" (Trow) **52**:419
"At Majority" (Rich) **7**:364
"At Martha's Deli" (Muldoon) **32**:319
"At Midsummer" (Dubie) **36**:142
"At Millstreet" (Buckley) **57**:134
"At Mitylene" (Aldington) **49**:6
"At Mrs. Preston's" (White) **49**:408
"At Muzat" (Sarton) **14**:482
At My Father's Wedding (Lee) **70**:422
At My Heart's Core (Davies) **42**:104
"at nagasaki" (Clifton) **66**:82
"At Night" (Dubus) **97**:235
At Night All Cats Are Grey (Boyle) **19**:67
"At Nightfall" (Silkin) **43**:404
"At No Distance" (Fisher) **25**:158
"At North Farm" (Ashbery) **41**:33, 35, 37; **77**:69; **125**:32
"At Once" (Fisher) **25**:159
At One's Goal (Bernhard)
See *Am Ziel*
"At Osborne House" (Hooker) **43**:202
At Paradise Gate (Smiley) **53**:345-46
"At Paso Rojo" (Bowles) **53**:36, 49
"At Pentre Ifan" (Walker) **13**:566
"At Père Lachaise" (Van Duyn) **63**:443
At Play in the Fields of the Lord (Matthiessen) **5**:274; **7**:210, 212; **11**:360; **32**:287-88, 290; **64**:302-04, 307, 309, 311, 321, 327-28
"At Pleasure Bay" (Pinsky) **94**:307; **121**:428, 434, 437-38, 447, 452, 454
"At Porthcothan" (Middleton) **13**:387
"At Risk" (Momaday) **85**:282
"At Roblin Lake" (Purdy) **6**:428
"At Rugmer" (Blunden) **56**:30, 44
"At Sallygap" (Lavin) **18**:302-03
"At Sea" (Hemingway) **6**:232; **8**:285
"At Sechelt" (Livesay) **79**:336
"At Seventeen" (Ian) **21**:185
At Seventy, Journal of a Solitude (Sarton) **91**:246-47, 250-51
"At Stoke" (Tomlinson) **6**:536; **13**:548; **45**:396
At Swim-Two-Birds (O'Brien) **1**:252; **4**:383; **5**:314-15, 317; **7**:268-70; **10**:362-64; **47**:311-17, 319-23
At Swords' Points (Norton) **12**:456
At Terror Street and Agony Way (Bukowski) **108**:113
At Terror Street and Agony Way (Bukowski) **5**:81; **41**:67; **108**:112
"At That Time; or, The History of a Joke" (Paley) **37**:333; **140**:236
"At the All-Night Cafe" (Soto) **80**:301
"At the Athenian Market" (Purdy) **50**:238
"At the Bar, 1948" (Sissman) **18**:490
"At the Beach" (Adams) **46**:17
"At the Beach" (Friedman) **56**:105
"At the Birth of an Age" (Jeffers) **54**:238; **11**:306, 310
"At the Bodega" (Ferlinghetti) **111**:65
"At the Bomb Testing Site" (Stafford) **29**:382
"At the Bottom of the River" (Kincaid) **68**:210-11; **137**:138-39
At the Bottom of the River (Kincaid) **43**:247-51; **68**:207-11, 217-18, 220, 225; **137**:137, 139-44, 148-50, 156, 161-64, 167, 169, 172-74, 182, 188
At the Building Site (Konwicki)
See *Przy budowie*
"At the Burning Ground" (Mahapatra) **33**:280
"At the Cabaret Now" (Graham) **118**:238
"At the Cafe" (Moss) **45**:287
"At the Call of the Race of Saba" (Senghor)
See "A l'appel de la race de Saba"
"At the Cemetery" (Harper) **7**:139
"At the Center" (Gunn) **3**:216
"At the Cinema" (Young) **82**:396
"At the Country Club" (Hope) **52**:208-09
"At the Court of Yearning" (Blaga) **75**:74
At the Court of Yearning (Blaga)
See *La curţile dorului*
"At the Crossroads" (Connell) **45**:109
"At the Crossroads" (Kinsella) **138**:94, 101
At the Crossroads (Connell) **45**:109-12
"At the Dam" (Didion) **129**:76, 78
"At the Dressing Table" (Szirtes) **46**:391
"At the Drug Store" (Taylor) **18**:527; **37**:409
"At the Edge" (Tomlinson) **45**:400
At the Edge of the Body (Jong) **18**:278
"At the Edge of the Jungle" (Lane) **25**:285, 287
"At the End of a Caboose" (Jensen)
See "To a Stranger"
At the End of the Open Road (Simpson) **4**:498-500; **7**:427-29; **32**:376-77, 379; **149**:294-95, 298, 305, 307, 309-13, 315, 321, 325, 327-31, 337, 340, 349-50
"At the End of the Open Road, 1963" (Simpson) **32**:378
"At the Executed Murderer's Grave" (Wright) **3**:543; **5**:519; **10**:545; **28**:470
"At the Exhumed Body of Santa Chiara, Assisi" (Graham) **118**:240, 244-45
"At the Fair" (Smith) **64**:391-92
"At the Fall of an Age" (Jeffers) **54**:237, 246; **11**:305, 310
"At the Fillmore" (Levine) **118**:300
"At the Fishhouses" (Bishop) **9**:95; **13**:92-3; **15**:59; **32**:37-9, 41
"At the Foot of the Hill, Birdie's School" (Hodgins) **23**:230
"At the Frick" (Hecht) **8**:266
At the Front Door of the Atlantic (Kerrigan) **4**:269; **6**:275-76
"At the Funeral of Great-Aunt Mary" (Bly) **38**:56; **128**:5
"At the Gate of the Valley" (Herbert) **9**:271, 273; **43**:188
At the Gates of Pompeii (Faludy) **42**:139-40
"At the German Writers Conference in Munich" (Dove) **81**:137
"At the Glass Factory in Cavan Town" (Boland) **113**:92
"At the Grave of Henry James" (Auden) **43**:27; **123**:35
"At the Grave of Marianne Moore" (Hirsch) **31**:215
"At the Grave of My Brother" (Stafford) **29**:379

"At the Grave of the Unknown African" (D'Aguiar) **145**:119
"At the Grave of Virgil Campbell" (Chappell) **40**:145
"At the Grave of Wallace Stevens" (Corn) **33**:117
"At the Head Table" (Kinsella) **138**:135, 152, 154-55, 159
"At the Hungarian Border" (Faludy) **42**:141
"At the Ibaru Family Tomb" (Snyder) **120**:325
"At the Ice Cream Parlor" (Parini) **54**:363-64
"At the Indian Killer's Grave" (Lowell) **4**:302; **8**:350-51; **124**:284-85
At the Jerusalem (Bailey) **45**:39-40, 42, 44, 46, 48-9
"At the Jewish Museum" (Pastan) **27**:368
"At the Landing" (Welty) **22**:460
"At the Long Island Jewish Geriatric Home" (Graham) **118**:231
"At the Masseurs's" (Moss) **7**:249-50
At the Moon's Inn (Lytle) **22**:299
"At the Movies: Virginia, 1956" (Voigt) **54**:433-34
"At the National Gallery" (Forster) **45**:133
"At the Night Court" (Simic) **49**:343
"At the Point of No Return" (Wagoner) **15**:560
"At the Portal" (Narayan) **47**:304
"At the Post Office" (Simmons) **43**:412
At the Rendezvous of Victory (James) **33**:223
"At the River" (Grace) **56**:111, 118
"At the Sale" (Smith) **64**:395
"At the San Francisco Airport" (Winters) **4**:591; **32**:468
"At the Screen Door" (Komunyakaa) **86**:193; **94**:242
"At the Seashore" (Blaga) **75**:76
At the Shores (Rogers) **57**:367-68
"At the Sight of Last Night's Fire" (Davison) **28**:100
"At the Sink" (Szirtes) **46**:391
At the Speed of Sound (McCartney) **35**:283-86
"At the Springs of Orlu" (Le Guin) **45**:219
"At the Summary of a Passion" (Tchicaya)
See "Au Sommaire d'une Passion"
"At the Swings" (Taylor) **44**:301
"At the Time of Peony Blossoming" (Bly) **128**:18
"At the Tolstoy Museum" (Barthelme) **3**:43; **6**:30; **46**:36, 40; **115**:56, 67-69, 80
"At the Tomb of the Czech Kings" (Seifert) **93**:335
"At the Tomb of Walt Whitman" (Kunitz) **148**:120
"At the Typewriter" (Thesen) **56**:417
"At the Villa Madeira" (Ewart) **46**:150
At the Water Divide (Blaga)
See *La cumpana apelor*
At the Watershed (Blaga)
See *La cumpana apelor*
"At the Well" (Piercy) **27**:376
"At the Western Ocean's Edge" (Kinsella) **138**:134, 157-58
At the White Monument and Other Poems (Redgrove) **41**:347, 349
"At The Zoo" (Simon) **17**:459, 463
"At Thirteen" (Stevenson) **7**:462
"At This Moment of Time" (Schwartz) **45**:355
"At Thurgarton Church" (Barker) **48**:22
"At Times in Flight" (Roth) **104**:249, 251
"At Usk" (Norris) **14**:388
"At Walden Pond" (Skelton) **13**:506
"At War With My Skin" (Updike) **139**:326
At War with the U.S. (Bowering) **15**:84; **47**:28-9
At Weddings and Wakes (McDonald) **90**:236-34
At West Point: The Men and Times of the United States Military Academy (Fleming) **37**:122-23
"At What Time Will We Sell Everything?" (Zamora)
See "A qué hora venderemos todo"
"At Will Rogers Beach" (Steele) **45**:366
"At Woodward's Garden: Resourcefulness Is More Than Understanding" (Frost) **4**:174
Atame! (Almodovar) **114**:26, 32, 37, 55
Atarashii hito yo mezameyo (Oe) **36**:350
Der Atem (Bernhard) **32**:25; **61**:11
Atemwende (Celan) **10**:101; **19**:90; **53**:72, 74, 76-7, 79-80, 82; **82**:32
El atentado (Ibarguengoitia) **37**:182-83
Athabasca (MacLean) **50**:348
Athena (Banville) **118**:27, 32-36, 38, 44
"Athene's Song" (Boland) **67**:46; **113**:96, 109
"Athens Apartment" (Purdy) **6**:429
"Athens, Florence" (Thomas) **13**:544
Atheological Summa (Bataille)
See *Somme athéologique*
"The Athlone Years" (Durcan) **43**:117
"At-Homeness in the Self" (Gregor) **9**:255
"The Atlantic" (Tomlinson) **45**:399
The Atlantic Abomination (Brunner) **8**:105
Atlantic City (Guare) **29**:205-06, 208; **67**:79, 81, 86
"Atlantic Coast Reggae" (Jordan) **114**:161-62
"Atlantic Crossing" (Gustafson) **36**:216
Atlantic High (Buckley) **37**:61
Atlantis (Dudek) **11**:159-60; **19**:138
Atlantis (Powys) **7**:348-49; **46**:322-23; **125**:281, 292, 295
"Atlantis and the Department Store" (Avison) **97**:76, 89
"Atlantis: Model 1924" (Delany) **141**:149, 159-60
Atlantis: Three Tales (Delany) **141**:149, 160
Atlas (Borges) **44**:360; **48**:48
"An Atlas of the Difficult World" (Rich) **125**:324
An Atlas of the Difficult World: Poems, 1988-1991 (Rich) **73**:333-34, 336-37; **76**:208-20
Atlas Shrugged (Rand) **3**:423; **30**:293-303; **44**:448, 450-54; **79**:358-62, 365, 367, 369-75, 389, 391-96
"Atmosfear" (o huigin) **75**:219-20
"Atmosphere Anthrax" (Rakosi) **47**:344
"Atmosphere in Weird Fiction" (Smith) **43**:421
Atom (Asimov) **76**:317
"Atom Heart Mother" (Pink Floyd) **35**:307
Atom Heart Mother (Pink Floyd) **35**:305-07, 311
The Atom Station (Laxness)
See *Alpýdubókin*
"Atomic Power" (Campbell) **32**:74
Atoms Today and Tomorrow (Hyde) **21**:172, 175
Atómstödin (Laxness)
See *Alpýdubókin*
"Atonal Blues" (Hope) **52**:209
The Atrocity Exhibition (Ballard) **3**:34; **6**:27; **14**:40-1; **36**:35-6, 46; **137**:5-8, 11-12, 16, 22-23, 25, 31, 33, 35, 39-40, 43, 69
"Atrophied Preface" (Burroughs) **15**:112
"Atsvut vesimha" (Amichai) **116**:122
Attachments (Rossner) **9**:457-58; **29**:356
"Attack" (Sassoon) **130**:216-17, 219
The Attack on Literature and Other Essays (Wellek) **28**:453-54
"An Attempt at an Explanation" (Sargeson) **31**:365
"An Attempt at Jealousy" (Raine) **103**:188, 190
"An Attempt at Self-Criticism" (Castellanos) **66**:56
"An Attempt to Hold Back History" (Amichai) **116**:97
An Attempted Escape (Strugatskii and Strugatskii)
See *Popytka k begstvu*
"Attempted Reconstruction" (Rozewicz)
See "Próba rekonstrukcji"
The Attempted Rescue: An Autobiography (Aickman) **57**:2
Attempted Suicide (Antonioni)
See *Tentato suicidio*
L'Attente l'oubli (Blanchot) **135**:99, 121, 132
Attention (Moravia)
See *L'attenzione*
L'attenzione (Moravia) **2**:292, 294; **7**:240-42, 244; **11**:383; **46**:284-85
Atti impuri (Pasolini) **106**:254-55
Attic (Dunn) **71**:132-35
"Attic Red-Figure Calyx, Revelling in Progress, circa 510 B.C." (Howard) **47**:170-71
"Attica State" (Lennon) **35**:264
"Attis; or, Something Missing" (Bunting) **10**:83-4; **47**:45, 52, 54
"Attitude" (Broumas) **73**:15-16
"Attitude" (Davies) **21**:105
"Attitude" (Keillor) **40**:274
"Attitude Dancing" (Simon) **26**:409-10
"Les attitudes spectrales" (Breton) **9**:127
"Attitudes toward Henry James" (Rahv) **24**:359
Attitudes toward History (Burke) **24**:125-27, 133
"Attracta" (Trevor) **14**:536; **71**:327; **116**:338-39, 342, 360, 376, 383
"Attractive Modern Homes" (Bowen) **22**:67; **118**:75
Atuan (Le Guin)
See *The Tombs of Atuan*
"Au" (Lennon) **35**:265
Au bout du rouleau (Simenon) **47**:379
Au château d'Argol (Gracq) **11**:244-45; **48**:133-37, 140-42
Au commencement était l'amour: Psychanalyse et foi (Kristeva) **77**:314
Au hasard, Balthazar (Bresson) **16**:110-12, 114
Au Moment Voulu (Blanchot) **135**:87
"Au Pair" (Weldon) **122**:269
"Au Sommaire d'une Passion" (Tchicaya) **101**:351
"Au tombeau de Charles Fourier" (Davenport) **38**:140
"Au vieux jardin" (Aldington) **49**:16
"Aubade" (Empson) **8**:202; **19**:159; **34**:336
"Aubade" (Hoffman) **6**:243
"Aubade" (Larkin) **33**:262; **39**:335, 337, 339, 341-44, 348; **64**:259-60, 263, 266-67, 272, 280, 285
"Aubade" (MacNeice) **53**:234, 239
"Aubade: Harlem" (Merton) **83**:392
"Aubade: Lake Erie" (Merton) **83**:392
"Aubades" (Shapcott) **38**:400
"Aubade—The Annunciation" (Merton) **83**:391
L'aube (Wiesel) **3**:530; **5**:491
Aube à la saison (Brossard) **115**:102
"L'aube fille des larmes" (Bonnefoy) **58**:45
"Auckland" (Baxter) **14**:62
"Audacity" (Scott) **22**:373
"Audacity of the Lower Gods" (Komunyakaa) **94**:247
"Audenesque for an Initiation" (Ewart) **13**:208; **46**:153
"Auden's Funeral" (Spender) **41**:427-28
"The Audible Reading of Poetry" (Winters) **4**:592
Audience (Havel) **58**:237-38, 240, 243; **123**:187
The Audience (Havel) **25**:224-25, 227, 230; **65**:413, 439-40; **123**:187, 191, 196, 199, 205
"Audience Dispersed" (Avison) **97**:128
"Audiencia privada" (Roa Bastos) **45**:346
"Audit at Key West" (Ciardi) **129**:52
Audrey Hepburn's Neck (Brown) **99**:37-41
Audubon, A Vision (Warren) **6**:557-58; **8**:539; **10**:520-21; **13**:574, 576-77, 581-82; **18**:533, 536; **39**:259, 264, 266-68; **59**:296, 298
Audun and the Polar Bear (Haavikko)
See *Audun ja jääkarhu*
Audun ja jääkarhu (Haavikko) **34**:170, 173
Aurélien (Aragon) **22**:37
"Auerbach's Literary History" (White) **148**:299
"Auf dass die Verfolgten nicht die Verfolger werden" (Sachs) **98**:328, 350
Auf dem Turm (Hofmann) **54**:225-26, 228
Auf dem Weg nach Taboo (Wolf) **150**:

"Auf den Brücken Friert es zuerst" (Hein) **154**:161, 165, 167
Auf den Marmorklippen (Jünger) **125**:219, 221-23, 233, 259-60
Auf der Mantuleasa-Strasse (Eliade) **19**:147
"Aufenthalt in X" (Boell) **72**:69, 79
Aufsätze zur Literatur (Grass) **22**:195
Der Auftrag oder Vom Beobachten des Beobachters der Beobachter: Novelle in vierundzwanzig Sätzen (Duerrenmatt) **102**:80
Aufzeichnungen, 1942-48 (Canetti) **14**:121-24; **25**:107-10, 114; **75**:127, 130-32, 134-35
"Die Augenbinde" (Lenz) **27**:257
Das Augenspiel: Lebensgeschichte 1931-1937 (Canetti) **75**:140, 143-44, 146; **86**:297-99, 301-02
L'augmentation (Perec) **56**:257
"Auguiano Religious Articles Rosaries Statues" (Cisneros) **69**:153; **118**:205
"Auguries" (Livesay) **79**:338
"Augury" (Heaney) **7**:148
"Augury for an Infant" (Randall) **135**:396
"August" (Carruth) **84**:136
"August" (Oliver) **34**:249; **98**:290, 298
"August" (Pasternak) **63**:313
"August" (Rich) **3**:429
"August" (Walker) **13**:566
August (Rossner) **29**:355-57
"August 19, Pad 19" (Swenson) **61**:392
"August 22, 1939" (Rexroth) **22**:345; **49**:284; **112**:396
"August, 1914" (Masefield) **11**:357-58; **47**:227, 233
August 1914 (Solzhenitsyn)
See *Avgust chetyrnadtsatogo*
"August, 1940" (Fuller) **28**:158
"August, 1968" (Auden) **3**:29
"August 1974: A Tapestry" (Muske) **90**:317
"August Afternoon" (Caldwell) **14**:96
August August August (Kohout) **13**:324
"August Eschenburg" (Millhauser) **54**:324-25, 327
"August for the People" (Auden) **43**:16
August Is a Wicked Month (O'Brien) **5**:313; **116**:178-79, 183, 185, 192-93, 227
"August Journal" (Hacker) **91**:110-11
"August Moon" (Warren) **39**:273
"August Night" (Swenson) **106**:347
"August Saturday" (Trevor) **71**:348
August Snow (Price) **63**:325
"Augusta née Hoffman" (Suknaski) **19**:434
"Augustine's Concubine" (Updike) **15**:546
Augustus (MacLennan) **92**:306
Aujourd'hui Michelet (Barthes) **24**:32
Aún es de día (Delibes) **18**:111
"Aunt Creasy, on Work" (Williams) **13**:600
Aunt Dan and Lemon (Shawn) **41**:399-403
"Aunt Helen" (Eliot) **41**:150
"Aunt Jennifer's Tigers" (Rich) **11**:477; **18**:445; **125**:310
Aunt Julia and the Scriptwriter (Vargas Llosa)
See *La tiá Julia y el escribidor*
"Aunt Justina" (Cheever) **3**:108
"Aunt Maggie, the Strong One" (Friel) **5**:128
"Aunt Maria and the Gourds" (Davidson) **13**:170
"Aunt Mary" (Oliver) **98**:266
"Aunt Rectita's Good Friday" (Kennedy) **42**:257
Aunts Aren't Gentlemen (Wodehouse) **5**:517
The Aunt's Story (White) **3**:522-23; **4**:583-85; **5**:486-87; **7**:531; **18**:544-45, 547; **65**:275-80, 282; **69**:392-97, 399-401, 405-08, 410-11
Aura (Fuentes) **8**:222-23; **41**:167, 169, 171-72; **60**:158, 162; **113**:242, 253
"Auras on the Interstate" (Vizenor) **103**:301
"Aurelia Paris" (Duras) **68**:90
Aurélia Steiner (Duras)
See *Aurélia Steiner, dite Aurélia Vancouver*
Aurélia Steiner (Duras)
See *Aurélia Steiner, dite Aurélia Melbourne*
Aurélia Steiner, dite Aurélia Melbourne (Duras) **68**:91-2, 96
Aurélia Steiner, dite Aurélia Vancouver (Duras) **68**:91-2, 96-7
"The Aurelian" (Nabokov) **1**:242
The Aurochs (Granin)
See *Zubr*
"Aurora" (Morand) **41**:295, 297, 308
Aurora (Fornés) **61**:129, 132
Aurora (Leiris) **61**:341
"Aurora Borealis" (Dove) **50**:153, 157; **81**:139
"Aurora Borealis" (Faludy) **42**:140
Aurora Dawn (Wouk) **38**:444-47
L'aurte par lui-même (Baudrillard) **60**:24-5
Aus dem Leben der Marionetten (Bergman) **72**:59, 61
Aus dem Leben eines Fauns: Kurzroman (Schmidt) **56**:390-91, 403-05
Aus dem Tagebuch einer Schnecke (Grass) **2**:174; **4**:205-07; **6**:208-09; **11**:250; **15**:262-63; **32**:202; **49**:137, 140
"Aus dem Zweiten Reich" (Bunting) **10**:83-4; **47**:45, 54
Aus der Fremde: Spredchoper in 7 szenen (Jandl) **34**:196-97, 199-200
"Aus meinem Tagebuch" (Hildesheimer) **49**:174
Auschwitz (Barnes)
See *Laughter!*
Ausgefragt (Grass) **32**:198-200
Ausgewählte Gedichte (Eich) **15**:204
Ausgewählte Gedichte (Sachs) **98**:322
"Ausländerhaß" (Hein) **154**:79
"The Auspice of Jewels" (Riding) **7**:375
"Auspicious Occasion" (Mistry) **71**:270-71, 273
Une aussi longue absence (Duras) **68**:94
"Austerities" (Simic) **49**:336; **68**:373
Austerities (Simic) **49**:335-37, 341, 343; **130**:306, 311-12, 318
"Australia" (Hope) **51**:216, 221, 226
"An Australian Garden" (Porter) **33**:320
Aut tunc aut Nunguam (Durrell) **13**:185
"La autentiticidad de la mujer en el arte" (Ferré) **139**:173-75
"Author and Director: A Delicate Situation" (Williams) **45**:446
"An Author and His Work" (Mauriac) **56**:219
"The Author and the Hero in Aesthetic Activity" (Bakhtin) **83**:12
"The Author Apologizes to His Readers" (Barth) **14**:50
Author from a Savage People (Pesetsky) **28**:359
"The Author in Truth" (Cixous) **92**:81-2
"The Author of Christine" (Howard) **7**:165
"The Author of the Acacia Seeds and Other Extracts from the 'Journal of the Association of Therolinguistics'" (Le Guin) **45**:213, 216
"An Author Speaks About His Novel" (Wiebe) **138**:309
"The Author to His Body on Their Fifteenth Birthday, 29 ii 80" (Nemerov) **36**:306
"Authors and Writers" (Barthes)
See "Écrivains et écrivants"
The Author's Dimension, Vol. I (Wolf) **150**:
"The Author's Last Words to His Students" (Blunden) **56**:40, 42
"An Autistic Poem" (Rozewicz)
See "Poemat autystyczny"
Auto da fé (Montale) **7**:223, 228; **9**:387
Auto do frade (Cabral de Melo Neto) **76**:155-56, 160-62, 168
"Auto Wreck" (Shapiro) **15**:476-77; **53**:330, 334
"Autobiografia in tempo di guerra" (Vittorini) **9**:549
"The Autobiographer as Torero" (Leiris) **61**:344
"Autobiographia literaria" (O'Hara) **13**:424, 427; **78**:345-46, 365
"An Autobiographical Essay: Family and Childhood" (Borges) **48**:33, 35; **83**:180
Autobiographical Fragment (Yglesias) **22**:492
An Autobiographical Novel (Rexroth) **11**:473; **22**:343-44; **49**:276, 280, 289; **112**:377, 380, 386-87, 389, 400, 402, 404
Autobiographical Writings (Hesse) **2**:190-91; **17**:216
Autobiographies (O'Casey) **15**:405
"Autobiography" (Ferlinghetti) **6**:184; **10**:176-77
"Autobiography" (Gunn) **18**:199, 204; **81**:177
"Autobiography" (Harjo) **83**:272, 274
"Autobiography" (MacLeish) **8**:362
"Autobiography" (MacNeice) **53**:232
"Autobiography" (Seifert) **93**:324
"Autobiography" (Steele) **45**:362
An Autobiography (Brooks) **29**:85
An Autobiography (Christie) **12**:125; **39**:439, 443; **48**:78; **110**:125-26, 128
Autobiography (Coward) **51**:76
An Autobiography (Davis)
See *Angela Davis*
Autobiography (Frame) **96**:219-20
Autobiography (Powys) **7**:349; **9**:439-40; **15**:433; **46**:322; **125**:276-77, 280-81, 290-91, 295-97, 300-02, 304
Autobiography (Trilling) **11**:540
Autobiography (Zukofsky) **11**:581-82; **18**:557
Autobiography: A Novel (Rechy) **107**:259
"Autobiography: A Self-Recorded Fiction" (Barth) **3**:41; **9**:66, 69; **51**:23; **89**:4-5, 8, 11-12, 15-16, 19, 27-30, 32-3, 43, 50-2, 57, 59, 61
"The Autobiography of a Dog" (Stuart) **34**:376
The Autobiography of a Gorgon (Hall) **51**:171
Autobiography of a Princess (Jhabvala) **29**:259-60; **94**:187, 194
Autobiography of a Princess (Jhabvala) **138**:64-7
The Autobiography of LeRoi Jones (Baraka) **115**:10, 39
The Autobiography of LeRoi Jones/Amiri Baraka (Baraka) **33**:60-2
The Autobiography of Malcolm X (Haley) **8**:259; **12**:243-46; **76**:345, 347-49, 352
The Autobiography of Malcolm X (Malcolm X) **82**:171, 173-76, 188-193, 195-201, 203-08, 210-14, 217-23, 226; **117**:295, 299, 301, 308, 317-18, 326-31, 340-41, 345-46, 350, 353-57, 359-61
The Autobiography of Miss Jane Pittman (Gaines) **3**:179; **11**:218; **18**:165, 167; **86**:171, 173, 175-78
The Autobiography of My Mother (Brown) **32**:64-6, 68-9
The Autobiography of My Mother (Kincaid) **137**:174-77, 179, 199-201, 209
"An Autobiography of Religious Development" (King) **83**:338
The Autobiography of W. E. B. Du Bois (Du Bois) **96**:138-39, 146-51
The Autobiography of William Carlos Williams (Williams) **22**:465, 468-69; **42**:452, 454, 460-61
Autobiology (Bowering) **15**:83; **47**:23
"Autocar" (Roberts) **14**:463
"Autocrítica" (Cabral de Melo Neto) **76**:158
Auto-da-Fé (Canetti)
See *Die Blendung*
"Automatic" (Prince) **35**:328
Automatic Pilot (Ritter) **52**:353-55, 357
"Automation Song" (Ochs) **17**:333
The Automobile Graveyard (Arrabal)
See *Le cimetière des voitures*
"The Automobile That Wouldn't Run" (Caldwell) **14**:96
O automobilista Infundioso (Cabral de Melo Neto) **76**:168
Los autonautas de la cosmopista (Cortázar) **34**:329, 331
The Autonauts of the Cosmohighway (Cortázar)
See *Los autonautas de la cosmopista*
"Autonomy" (Ammons) **57**:53

"La autopista del sur" (Cortázar) **5**:110; **13**:158
"The Autopsy" (Elytis) **49**:107, 113; **100**:156, 175, 192
"Autopsy Report 86-13504:" (Sapphire) **99**:81
"The Autopsy Room" (Carver) **55**:276
"Autorengespräch" (Hofmann) **54**:225
Un autoritratto (Buzzati) **36**:97
"Autorretrato" (Castellanos) **66**:53, 61
Auto-Stop (Havel) **123**:180
Autour de Mortin (Pinget) **13**:442
L'autre (Chedid) **47**:85
L'autre (Green) **3**:205
L'autre (Green) **77**:277-78
L'autre (Loewinsohn) **52**:284-85
"Autre Fois" (Soupault) **68**:406
L'autre sommeil (Green) **11**:260; **77**:269, 276, 277
"Autres" (Guillevic) **33**:194
Autres: Poèmes, 1969-1979 (Guillevic) **33**:194
"Autrui" (Arreola) **147**:17, 27-30
"Autumn" (Fugard) **48**:109
"Autumn" (Ignatow) **7**:182; **14**:275
"Autumn" (Landolfi) **11**:321
"Autumn" (Larkin) **64**:258
"Autumn" (Livesay) **79**:333, 340
"Autumn" (Morrison) **10**:354
"Autumn" (Neruda)
See "Otoño"
"Autumn" (Pasternak) **63**:313
"Autumn" (Sassoon) **130**:184-85, 221
"Autumn" (Shapcott) **38**:402
"Autumn" (Voznesensky) **57**:413, 415
Autumn (Mojtabai) **29**:318-20
"Autumn 1980" (Hacker) **72**:183-84
"Autumn Afternoon" (Farrell) **66**:129, 131
An Autumn Afternoon (Ozu) **16**:447-51, 454, 456
"Autumn Again" (Levine) **14**:316
"Autumn Begins in Martins Ferry, Ohio" (Wright) **3**:540; **28**:465
"The Autumn Bleat of the Weathervane Trombone" (Chappell) **40**:144; **78**:91
"Autumn Chapter in a Novel" (Gunn) **81**:185
"Autumn Chill" (Blaga) **75**:76
Autumn Day (Pa Chin)
See *Ch'iu*
"The Autumn Dog" (Theroux) **11**:528
"Autumn Equinox" (Rich) **6**:459; **125**:337, 339
"Autumn Evening" (Merwin) **88**:203
The Autumn Garden (Hellman) **2**:187; **8**:281; **14**:255-60; **18**:221, 223-24; **34**:349, 351
"Autumn in California" (Rexroth) **49**:277, 284; **112**:397
"Autumn in Florida" (Tremain) **42**:385-86
An Autumn in Italy (O'Faolain) **70**:315
"Autumn in Sigulda" (Voznesensky) **57**:420
"Autumn in the Skerries" (Transtroemer)
See "Höstlig skärgård"
Autumn Journal (MacNeice) **1**:186; **4**:315-18; **10**:327; **53**:232-33, 235-37, 239-40, 243-44
Autumn Landscape (Cummings) **15**:157
"Autumn Leaves" (Ginsberg) **109**:329
"Autumn Madrigal" (Shapcott) **38**:401
"Autumn Meadow" (Kiš) **57**:246
"Autumn of a Dormouse" (Gilliatt) **53**:147
The Autumn of the Patriarch (García Márquez) **8**:232-33; **10**:215-17; **15**:254; **27**:147-48, 150-51, 153, 155-57; **47**:146-47, 151; **55**:139, 144-47
"Autumn on Nan-Yueh" (Empson) **8**:202; **19**:152, 159
"An Autumn Park" (Gascoyne) **45**:158
An Autumn Penitent (Callaghan) **41**:89
The Autumn People (Arthur) **12**:27, 29
Autumn Quail (Mahfouz)
See *al-Summan w'l-kharif*
Autumn Quail (Mahfūz) **55**:181; **52**:304
"Autumn Scene" (Snodgrass) **68**:397
"Autumn Sequel" (MacNeice) **1**:186; **4**:317
Autumn Sequel: A Rhetorical Poem (MacNeice) **1**:186; **4**:317; **10**:325; **53**:232-33, 240
"Autumn Shade" (Bowers) **9**:121-22
Autumn Sonata (Bergman)
See *Höstsonaten*
"Autumn Song" (Morrison) **21**:234
"Autumn Song" (Watkins) **43**:450
"Autumn Sunshine" (Trevor) **71**:325; **116**:338, 342-43, 345, 385
Autumn Testament (Baxter) **14**:66
Autumn to Autumn (Alvarez) **13**:9
"Autumnal" (Scott) **22**:372
"Autumnal Equinox on Mediterranean Beach" (Warren) **13**:573
"Autumnal Sunset" (Blaga) **75**:76
"Aux arbres" (Bonnefoy) **58**:43
"Aux premiers âges" (Damas) **84**:179
"Aux Tirailleurs sénégalais morts pour la France" (Senghor) **130**:259
Available Light (Booth) **23**:76
Available Light (Currie) **44**:39-43
Available Light (Piercy) **62**:377-79; **128**:248, 273-74
Avalanche (Boyle) **19**:62; **58**:64, 73, 75-6; **121**:36, 44, 53-4
Avalanche Express (Polonsky) **92**:415
L'avalée des avalés (Ducharme) **74**:56-7, 60-1
"Avalon" (Davidson) **13**:168
Avanti (Wilder) **20**:464-65
Avarice House (Green)
See *Mont-Cinère*
The Avatar (Anderson) **15**:15
"Avatars" (MacEwen) **55**:163-64, 167, 169
"Avatars of the Tortoise" (Borges) **10**:64; **83**:156, 160, 162
"Ave Luna, Morituri Te Salutant" (Faludy) **42**:137, 140, 142
"Ave Maria" (O'Hara) **78**:333, 354
"Ave Maria" (Tanizaki) **28**:419
Ave Maria (Linney) **51**:263
"Ave Regina Coelorum" (Hill) **45**:180
L'avea (Adamov) **25**:16
"Avelino Arredondo" (Borges) **48**:41
L'avenir dure longtemps (Althusser) **106**:12, 16-17, 28, 31-2, 37-40, 42
L'Avenir est dans les oeufs (Ionesco) **4**:251; **6**:248
La aventura de un fotògraf en La Plata (Bioy Casares) **88**:91
Aventura en lo gris (Buero Vallejo) **15**:101-03; **46**:98; **139**:10, 18-19
Las aventuras de Robinson Crusoe (Bunuel) **16**:128-29, 148; **80**:23, 25, 28-9, 36
Aventuras sigilosas (Lezama Lima) **101**:121
Les aventures d'Ori d'Or (Theriault) **79**:412
"Äventyret" (Lagerkvist) **54**:286
"The Avenue" (Muldoon) **32**:320
"The Avenue Bearing the Initial of Christ into the New World" (Kinnell) **5**:215-17; **13**:320, 322; **29**:280-82, 284, 289-90; **129**:260, 266
The Avenue Bearing the Initial of Christ into the New World: Poems, 1946-1964 (Kinnell) **5**:217-18; **13**:320-22; **29**:286; **129**:248
"Avenue C" (Kinnell) **129**:267
"The Avenue of Poplars" (Williams) **42**:463
An Avenue of Stone (Johnson) **1**:161; **27**:215-16
"Avenue of the Americas" (Simic) **49**:343
"The Average Egyptian Faces Death" (Updike) **23**:475
"Average Person" (McCartney) **35**:292
"Averroes's Search" (Borges)
See "La busca de Averroes"
"Aversion/Perversion/Diversion" (Delany) **141**:149, 159
"Avey" (Toomer) **1**:341; **22**:425
Avgust chetyrnadtsatogo (Solzhenitsyn) **1**:321; **2**:408-13; **4**:508-12, 514-15; **7**:432-34, 436, 438, 442-45; **9**:503; **10**:479; **18**:498; **33**:483, 489-91; **34**:489; **59**:372-77; **78**:282, 398-99, 401, 413-21, 423; **134**:297
"Aviation" (Fulton) **52**:160
The Aviator (Gann) **23**:167-68
"Avie Loves Ric Forever" (Mazer) **26**:295
"Avila" (West) **96**:383
L'Aviva (Brossard) **115**:120
"Avocado Lake" (Soto) **80**:288
Avram Iancu (Blaga) **75**:64-5, 67
Avril brisé (Kadare)
See *Prilli i thyer*
Avsked till Hamlet (Johnson) **14**:294
L'avventura (Antonioni) **20**:19-21, 26, 31; **144**:4, 7, 9-12, 14-8, 26-7, 33-4, 37, 39, 42-3, 45-6, 48, 52-7, 59-60, 62-3, 66-75, 79-81, 84, 91-5, 97
"L'avventura di un poeta" (Calvino) **39**:314
"Aw baby you so pretty" (Shange) **126**:362
"Awaite Pawana" (Le Clézio) **155**:105-09
The Awaited Sign (Buero Vallejo)
See *La señal que se espera*
"Awaiting His Execution" (Ritsos) **6**:464
Awaiting Oblivion (Blanchot)
See *L'Attente l'oubli*
"Awake" (Harrison) **6**:223
Awake! and Other Wartime Poems (Rodgers) **7**:377-78
Awake and Sing! (Odets) **2**:318-19; **28**:323-30, 332-40; **98**:190, 193-95, 198-210, 212, 215-18, 220-25, 227-31, 234-40, 242, 245, 250, 252
Awake for Mourning (Kops) **4**:274
Awake in Spain (O'Hara) **78**:368-69
Awake in th Red Desert (Bissett) **18**:60
Awaken, Bells Falling: Poems, 1959-1967 (Turco) **11**:549-50; **63**:429-30
"Awakened before I Meant" (Corn) **33**:116
"Awakening" (Bly) **128**:5, 11
"Awakening" (Borges)
See "El despertar"
"The Awakening" (Clarke) **136**:209
"Awakening" (Kunene) **85**:175
"The Awakening" (Miller) **14**:373
The Awakening Land (Richter) **30**:324, 328
The Awakening of George Darroch (Jenkins) **52**:230
"The Awakening of the Mummy" (Mahfūz)
See "Yaqzat al mūmyā'"
"Awakening to Song Over Rooftops" (Transtroemer) **65**:222-23
Awakenings (Sacks) **67**:285, 287-91, 295-96, 298-99, 304
"Awatobi" (Lewis) **41**:260-62
"Away!" (Frost) **13**:227
"Away" (Miles) **34**:245; **39**:354
Away (Creeley) **36**:118
Away (Urquhart) **90**:394-9, 402
"Away from It All" (Heaney) **37**:169; **91**:118-19
"Away from the Numbers" (Weller) **26**:443-44
Away from the Vicarage (Streatfeild) **21**:408
"Away from Water" (Broumas) **73**:9
"Away in Airdrie" (Kelman) **58**:295
"Away, Melancholy" (Smith) **25**:422-23
"The Away-Bound Train" (Murray) **40**:340
"Awe and Devastation of Solomos" (Elytis) **100**:189
"A-W-F Unlimited" (Herbert) **44**:394
"Awful Music" (Merton) **83**:384
The Awful Rowing Toward God (Sexton) **6**:492-94; **8**:484; **53**:312, 319, 322; **123**:404, 406, 409, 416, 423, 425-27, 429, 431, 443-44, 446-47
An Awfully Big Adventure (Bainbridge) **62**:38-40; **130**:14-16, 20, 22-23, 26, 34
An Awkward Lie (Stewart) **14**:512
Awlad haratina (Mahfouz) **153**:235, 239-40, 250, 257, 260, 270, 272-73, 285, 304-5, 308, 323, 326, 335, 337-41, 365
Awlad haretna (Mahfouz) **153**:357, 359-60, 367, 372
Awlād hāretnā (Mahfūz) **52**:294-95, 300-01; **55**:171-76, 178, 183, 185
"Ax" (Simic) **49**:339; **68**:364
The Axe (Vaculik) **7**:494-95
"Axe Handles" (Snyder) **120**:324-25, 355
Axe Handles (Snyder) **32**:395, 397, 400;

120:322-25, 336-37, 342
Axe Time, Sword Time (Corcoran) **17**:76-7
"Axel" (Nye) **42**:304
Axel's Castle: A Study in the Imaginative Literature of 1870-1930 (Wilson) **1**:372-73; **2**:475; **3**:538; **8**:550; **24**:464-70, 472-74, 478-81, 483-86
The Axe's Edge (Gunnars) **69**:264
"The Ax-Helve" (Frost) **10**:197; **26**:112
The Axion Esti (Elytis) **49**:114; **100**:155-56, 158-63, 165, 167, 170, 175, 181, 183-84, 187-88, 190, 192
"Axis" (Paz) **51**:334-35
"Axolotl" (Cortázar) **33**:123, 131-32; **34**:331-32
"Ay negra, si tu supiera" (Guillén) **48**:161; **79**:245-46
"Aye, and Gomorrah" (Delany) **38**:154; **141**:126
"Aye, Black Lover, If You Only Knew" (Guillén)
See "Ay negra, si tu supiera"
"Ayer me dijeron negro" (Guillén) **48**:161
The Aylwin's (Stewart) **7**:466
Ázma iroikó ke pénthimo yia ton haméno anthipolohaghó tis Alvanías (Elytis) **49**:106-07, 114-15
Azrael (Warner) **19**:460
"Aztec" (McIntyre) **18**:327
"Aztec Angel" (Salinas) **90**:324, 327
"The Azure Steppe" (Sholokhov) **7**:417
"B" (Merrill) **8**:383-84
B (Figes) **31**:163
"B/ Betty Boop/ Boop-boop-a-doop/ Babel/ Bable" (Sorrentino) **7**:449
"B. C." (Moss) **7**:250
"B Negative" (Kennedy) **42**:254
"B. Traven is Alive and Well in Cuernavaca" (Anaya) **148**:14
"B. W., 1916-1979" (Cage) **41**:86
Baal Babylone (Arrabal) **9**:33; **18**:18; **58**:4, 6-7, 9-11
Der Baal tshuve (Singer)
See *Der Bal-tshuve*
Baalbec, a Stain (Benet)
See *Baalbec, una mancha*
Baalbec, una mancha (Benet) **28**:23
Baba Goya (Tesich) **40**:418-19, 421-22
"Baba O'Reilly" (Townshend) **17**:532, 535
"Las babas del diablo" (Cortázar) **2**:103; **3**:115; **13**:158; **15**:146, 148; **33**:125, 132-34, 136; **92**:149
Babble (Baumbach) **23**:55
Babbling April (Greene) **70**:292
Babe (Wiggins) **57**:430, 439
"Babe I'm Gonna Leave You" (Page and Plant) **12**:482
"Babel" (Simon) **39**:209
Babel (Smith) **12**:541-42
Babel to Byzantium (Dickey) **7**:79; **47**:97; **109**:245
Babel-17 (Delany) **14**:146; **38**:149-50, 153-54, 160-62; **141**:108-10, 112-13, 126, 129, 147-48, 152-53, 155, 158
"Babelogue" (Smith) **12**:543
"Babel's Children" (Barker) **52**:55
Babes and Sucklings (Wylie) **43**:460, 469
The Babe's Bed (Wescott) **13**:592
"Babette's Feast" (Dinesen) **10**:150
"Babi Yar" (Yevtushenko) **3**:547; **13**:620; **26**:461, 464; **51**:428, 431; **126**:386-88, 390, 393, 396, 398-400, 404, 406-10, 413-15
"Babies" (Fulton) **52**:161
"The Babies" (Strand) **18**:519; **41**:431; **71**:283
"Babočka" (Brodsky) **13**:117; **36**:76, 78; **50**:124-25, 131
"Baboons in the Perennial Bed" (Piercy) **62**:378
"Baby" (Barthelme) **59**:250
"Baby" (Campbell) **42**:88-9
"Baby" (Sontag) **13**:517
"Baby Blue" (O'Brien) **13**:416; **116**:208, 210
Baby Breakdown (Waldman) **7**:507
Baby, Come on Inside (Wagoner) **3**:508
"Baby Department" (Redgrove) **41**:354
"Baby Doll" (Berry) **17**:54
Baby Doll (Kazan) **16**:366, 368, 373-74; **63**:233, 235
Baby Doll (Williams) **39**:446
"Baby Driver" (Simon) **17**:460-61, 465
"Baby Face" (Reed) **21**:309
"Baby H. P." (Arreola) **147**:4, 13, 16, 34
"Baby I" (Armatrading) **17**:10
"Baby I'm a Star" (Prince) **35**:329
The Baby in the Icebox and Other Short Fiction (Cain) **28**:54
Baby Is Three (Sturgeon) **22**:410; **39**:361, 364-66
Baby, It's Cold Inside (Perelman) **3**:382; **5**:337; **23**:337; **49**:269, 272
Baby Love (Edgar) **42**:116, 124
Baby Love (Maynard) **23**:289-91
"Baby Pictures" (Giles) **39**:64-5
"Baby Pictures of Famous Dictators" (Simic) **68**:378; **130**:318
"Baby Sister" (Himes) **4**:229; **18**:249
Baby Snakes (Zappa) **17**:594
Baby, the Rain Must Fall (Foote) **51**:131
"Baby V" (Levine)
See "Baby Villon"
"Baby Villon" (Levine) **4**:287; **5**:252; **9**:332; **33**:273; **118**:288-89
Baby with the Bathwater (Durang) **38**:170-74
"Baby You're a Rich Man" (Lennon and McCartney) **12**:360
Babycakes (Maupin) **95**:192, 194-97, 199, 201, 203, 208
"Babylon" (Herbert) **43**:191
"Babylon" (Simic) **68**:377
"Babylon" (Tolson) **105**:288
Babylon by Bus (Marley) **17**:272
"The Babylon Lottery" (Borges)
See "La lotería en Babilonia"
"Babylon Revisited" (Baraka) **5**:48
"Babylon Sisters" (Becker and Fagen) **26**:85
"The Babylonian Event" (Škvorecký) **152**:329
"Babylonish Dialects" (Raine) **103**:197
"Baby's First Step" (Updike) **139**:369
"A Baby's Mouth" (Peterkin) **31**:306-08
"The Babysitter" (Coover) **7**:58
"The Babysitters" (Klappert) **57**:256-59, 265
"The Babysitters" (Plath) **5**:345; **51**:344
"Baby-Sitting" (Clarke) **61**:73-4
"Baccalaureate" (MacLeish) **8**:362
The Bacchae (Harrison) **129**:189
The Bacchae of Euripides: A Communion Rite (Soyinka) **36**:412; **44**:298
"Bacchus" (Empson) **3**:147; **8**:202; **19**:156; **33**:142
Bacchus (Cocteau) **15**:134; **43**:104-06, 112
"Bachanale" (Hayden) **37**:156
"The Bachelor" (O'Brien) **36**:336; **116**:186
Bachelor Girls (Wasserstein) **90**:429-30, 432, 435, 437
The Bachelor of Arts (Narayan) **7**:255; **28**:291, 299; **121**:352, 355-56, 383, 385
Bachelorhood: Tales of the Metropolis (Lopate) **29**:300-02
"Bachelors" (Williams) **42**:443
The Bachelors (Montherlant) **19**:324-25
The Bachelors (Spark) **2**:417; **3**:466; **13**:520-522; **18**:501; **40**:398, 400; **94**:326, 328-29, 332
Bachelors Anonymous (Wodehouse) **5**:516-17
"The Bachelor's Dilemma" (Gold) **42**:189
Back (Green) **2**:178; **13**:252, 255; **97**:243, 245-47, 249, 254-55, 257, 270, 279, 282-83, 288-90, 293
"Back Again, Home" (Madhubuti) **6**:313; **73**:194, 199, 207
Back Bog Beast Bait (Shepard) **4**:489-90; **17**:443
"The Back Country" (Snyder) **120**:324
The Back Country (Snyder) **1**:318; **2**:406; **5**:393-95; **9**:500; **32**:387-88, 391-92, 396, 399; **120**:317, 356
"Back Door Man" (Morrison) **17**:287, 292
"Back Down to Earth" (Simon) **26**:411
"The Back Drawing-Room" (Bowen) **118**:75
"Back from Australia" (Betjeman) **43**:46
"Back from Java" (Aldiss) **40**:19
"Back from teh Market" (Boland) **113**:96
"Back Gate" (Cabral de Melo Neto)
See "Postigo"
"Back Home" (Berry) **17**:51
"Back Home in Pompeii" (Ciardi) **40**:158; **44**:382
"Back in '72" (Seger) **35**:379
Back in '72 (Seger) **35**:379-80
"Back in the U.S.S.R." (Lennon and McCartney) **12**:379
Back in the World (Wolff) **64**:450-54, 456-57
"The Back Lane" (Kinsella) **138**:135, 156
The Back of the North Wind (Freeling) **38**:187-88
"Back Seat of My Car" (McCartney) **12**:372; **35**:279
"Back Street Girl" (Jagger and Richard) **17**:230, 234-35, 238
Back Talk (Weidman) **7**:517
"Back Then" (Komunyakaa) **94**:246-47
"Back to Africa" (Bennett) **28**:26-7, 29
Back to Barter (Proulx) **81**:275
Back to China (Fiedler) **4**:160
"Back to Kentucky" (Ferron) **94**:103
"Back to Life" (Gunn) **32**:208
"Back to Tahiti" (Honig) **33**:213
"Back to the Basics of Love" (Jennings)
See "Luckenbach, Texas"
"Back to the Beast" (Wellman) **49**:391
Back to the Egg (McCartney) **35**:286-88
"Back to the Land" (Davis) **49**:91
Back to the Night (Armatrading) **17**:7
"Back to Val d'Or" (Ferron) **94**:103
"Backatcha" (Robinson) **21**:346
"Backcasting" (Ammons) **57**:53
"Background, Casually" (Ezekiel) **61**:107
Background in Tennessee (Scott) **43**:382-85
Background to Danger (Ambler) **4**:18; **6**:2, 3; **9**:19
Background with Chorus (Swinnerton) **31**:426
"Background with Revolutionaries" (MacLeish) **68**:281
"Backlands" (Dorfman) **77**:141-45
"The Backlash Blues" (Hughes) **15**:292
Backlash: The Undeclared War Against Women (Faludi) **140**:80-4, 86-91, 95-11, 113, 115-16, 118, 122, 124, 127, 129-31
"Backseat" (Wideman) **122**:343, 347
"Backside to the Wind" (Durcan) **43**:114
"Backstreets" (Springsteen) **17**:480, 484, 489
"Backsweep/Black" (Blackburn) **43**:65
"Backtalk" (Chin) **135**:155, 176
Backtrack (Hansen) **38**:239
"The Backward Look" (Heaney) **7**:148
"The Backward Look" (Nemerov) **9**:395
The Backward Look (O'Connor) **14**:397
A Backward Place (Jhabvala) **4**:258; **29**:253, 255-57, 259-60; **94**:166, 169-70, 176-70, 181, 203; **138**:64
The Backward Shadow (Banks) **23**:41
"Backwards Traveller" (McCartney) **35**:288
"Backwaters" (Dunn) **40**:167
"Backyard Dramas with Mamas" (Loewinsohn) **52**:285
"Bad" (Matthews) **40**:324-25
Bad Apple (Bograd) **35**:63-4
Bad Attitudes (Carr) **86**:47
Bad Behavior (Gaitskill) **69**:198-206
Bad Blood (Tchicaya)
See *Le Mauvais Sang*
"Bad Boats" (Jensen) **37**:190
Bad Boats (Jensen) **37**:186-92
Bad Boy (Thompson) **69**:383-84, 388
Bad Boys (Cisneros) **69**:151; **118**:174
"Bad Characters" (Stafford) **19**:431; **68**:423, 437
Bad Characters (Stafford) **68**:431, 435
"Bad Company" (Gallagher) **63**:121

Bad Connections (Johnson) **58**:283-855
A Bad Day for Sales (Leiber) **25**:301
Bad Debts (Wolff) **41**:454-55, 457, 460
"Bad Dogs" (Sayles) **14**:483
"Bad Dreams" (Taylor) **18**:523; **37**:409, 411
"A Bad Example" (Maugham) **67**:220
"The Bad Girl" (Vollmann) **89**:296
Bad Habits (McNally) **4**:347; **7**:218-19; **41**:292
"A Bad Heart" (Rendell) **28**:384
The Bad Infinity (Wellman) **65**:242
Bad Luck under the Roof (Kohout) **13**:325
A Bad Man (Elkin) **4**:153-54; **6**:169; **9**:190; **27**:122-23; **51**:85, 88, 100; **91**:213
"A Bad Memory Block" (Moravia) **46**:286
"The Bad Music" (Jarrell) **13**:299
"Bad News" (Atwood) **84**:104
"A Bad Night: A Lexical Exercise" (Auden) **6**:19; **43**:27
"The Bad Old Days" (Rexroth) **112**:400
BAD: or, the Dumbing of America (Fussell) **74**:140-41, 143, 145-47
Bad Penny (Wellman) **65**:239, 241-42
The Bad Place (Koontz) **78**:218
The Bad Sister (Tennant) **13**:537; **52**:397
The Bad Sleep Well (Kurosawa) **16**:399, 401-03; **119**:338, 343, 351, 379
"Bad Vision at the Skagit" (Hugo) **32**:242
Badenheim 1939 (Appelfeld) **23**:35-7; **47**:2-4, 6-7
"The Badgers" (Heaney) **14**:246; **25**:247
"The Badgers" (Heaney) **74**:159
The Badgers (Leonov)
See *Barsuki*
"Badlands" (Springsteen) **17**:483-86
Badlands (Kroetsch) **23**:271; **57**:282-84, 288-91; **132**:224, 246-50, 252, 280
"Badlat al-asir" (Mahfouz) **153**:349, 352
Badly Sings the Nightingale (Seifert) **34**:259
Badon Parchments (Masefield) **11**:357
The Bag (Yurick) **6**:583
Baga (Pinget) **13**:442; **37**:360
"La bagarede" (Kinnell) **5**:216
"Bagatelles" (Spender) **5**:401
"Bagatelles" (Tomlinson) **45**:393
Bagatelles pour un massacre (Céline) **47**:79; **124**:60-61, 88, 96, 104, 108, 111, 116
Bagdad Saloon (Walker) **61**:424-28
"The Bagel" (Ignatow) **7**:178
"Bagel Shop Jazz" (Kaufman) **49**:203
"The Bagful of Dreams" (Vance) **35**:428
"Baggot Street Deserta" (Kinsella) **138**:89-90, 105, 118, 139, 141, 149, 161
"Baggs" (Blackburn) **43**:65, 69
The Bagman (Arden) **15**:21
"Bagpipe Music" (MacNeice) **53**:235
"Bagpipe Music" (Simmons) **43**:409
"The Bagpiping People" (Dunn) **40**:171
"Bahia, Brazil" (Carver) **53**:61
Bahia de todos os santos (Amado) **106**:57, 62
La Baie des anges (Gallo) **95**:98
Uma bailadora Sevilhana (Cabral de Melo Neto) **76**:161
"A bailarina" (Cabral de Melo Neto) **76**:151
"La bailarina" (Ferré) **139**:166
"The Bailbondsman" (Elkin) **6**:169; **14**:157-58; **27**:122; **51**:101
The Bailbondsman (Elkin) **91**:216
Bailegangaire (Murphy) **51**:307-08
"Le baiser" (Char) **9**:163
Le baiser au lépreux (Mauriac) **4**:341; **9**:367-68; **56**:204-06, 214, 217, 219
Baisers volés (Truffaut) **20**:385, 391-92, 397, 399; **101**:382, 386, 388, 390, 396, 398, 400, 410-11, 413
"Bait" (Heaney) **14**:243
"Baja" (Stern) **40**:414
Bajki Robotów (Lem) **149**:283
"Baked Potatoes" (Urdang) **47**:399
"Baker Street at Sunset" (Steele) **45**:362
The Baker, the Baker's Wife, and the Little Baker's Boy (Anouilh)
See *Le boulanger, la boulangère, et le petit mitron*
"The Bakery Poems" (Blackburn) **43**:62-3
Bakunin: Eine Invention (Bienek) **11**:48
Le bal des voleurs (Anouilh) **3**:11; **8**:24; **13**:16; **40**:54, 57; **50**:279
"La balada azul" (Guillén) **79**:251
Balada de Atta Troll (Casona) **49**:40
"Balada de los dos abuelos" (Guillén) **48**:162, 168; **79**:230, 232, 237, 248-49
"Balada del güje" (Guillén) **79**:231, 237, 248
Balade Petrice Kerempuha (Krleža) **114**:167, 176, 185-86
"Balakirevs dröm" (Transtroemer) **52**:409
"Balalaika" (Dubie) **36**:130
"The Balance" (Johnson) **7**:415
"The Balance" (Waugh) **107**:392-93
"Balance His, Swing Yours" (Stegner) **81**:346
Balance of Terror (Shaffer) **14**:484
"Balances" (Giovanni) **19**:191
Balancing Acts (Schwartz) **31**:389-90
Balancing Acts: Contemporary Stories by Russian Women (Goscilo) **59**:370-71, 379
"Balboa, The Entertainer" (Baraka) **115**:40
Le balcon (Genet) **1**:115; **2**:157-58; **5**:136-37; **10**:224-25, 227; **14**:198, 203, 205; **44**:385-90; **46**:172-73
Un balcon en forêt (Gracq) **11**:245; **48**:136, 139-41
"Balcony" (Bromell) **5**:74
The Balcony (Genet)
See *Le balcon*
The Bald Prima Donna (Ionesco)
See *La cantatrice chauve*
"The Bald Primaqueera" (O'Casey) **88**:260, 262
The Bald Soprano (Ionesco)
See *La cantatrice chauve*
Baldur's Gate (Clark) **19**:105-06
"La baleine" (Theriault) **79**:408
"The Balek Scales" (Boell)
See "Die Waage der Baleks"
"De balística" (Arreola) **147**:4, 16, 18
Balkan Trilogy (Manning) **5**:271; **19**:301, 304
"Ball der Wohltäter" (Lenz) **27**:245
A Ball of Malt and Madame Butterfly: A Dozen Stories (Kiely) **23**:260; **43**:239
"Ballad" (Ammons) **8**:14; **9**:29; **108**:12
"Ballad" (Arreola) **147**:5
"Ballad" (Cohen) **38**:131
The Ballad and the Source (Lehmann) **5**:235, 238
La ballad du grand macabre (Ghelderode) **11**:226
A Ballad for Hogskin Hill (Forman) **21**:122
"Ballad from Childhood" (Lorde) **71**:251
"Ballad of a Marriage" (Simmons) **43**:406, 413-14
Ballad of a Stonepicker (Ryga) **14**:472-73
"Ballad of a Sweet Dream of Peace" (Warren) **13**:575
"Ballad of a Thin Man" (Dylan) **77**:174-76, 179-81
"The Ballad of Barnaby" (Auden) **6**:18, 21
"A Ballad of Beauty and Time" (Boland) **113**:124
The Ballad of Benny Perhaps (Brinsmead) **21**:33
"The Ballad of Billie Potts" (Warren) **4**:578-80; **8**:539; **13**:573-76; **39**:264; **59**:298-99
"The Ballad of Billy the Kid" (Joel) **26**:213, 218
"The Ballad of Birmingham" (Randall) **1**:283; **135**:373, 386-87, 393-94, 396
"The Ballad of Blossom" (Van Duyn) **116**:410
The Ballad of Cable Hogue (Peckinpah) **20**:275-79, 282-84
"The Ballad of Chocolate Mabbie" (Brooks) **49**:22; **125**:79-83
"A Ballad of Despair" (Skelton) **13**:507
The Ballad of Dingus Magee (Markson) **67**:191-92, 194, 197
"Ballad of Donald White" (Dylan) **77**:166
"The Ballad of Edie Barrow" (Brooks) **125**:79, 101
"The Ballad of Erse O. Reilly" (Ewart) **46**:151
"The Ballad of Gerry Kelly: Newsagent" (Simmons) **43**:411-12
"Ballad of Henry, Bridegroom" (Jacobsen) **48**:190
"Ballad of Hollis Brown" (Dylan) **12**:180; **77**:166
"A Ballad of Home" (Boland) **113**:108
"Ballad of Jarvis Street" (Johnston) **51**:243
"The Ballad of Jesse Neighbors" (Humphrey) **45**:203-04
"The Ballad of Jimmy Governor" (Murray) **40**:336, 340
"Ballad of John Cable and Three Gentlemen" (Merwin) **88**:205
"A Ballad of Johnnie Question" (Skelton) **13**:507
"Ballad of Ladies Lost and Found" (Hacker) **72**:182-85, 190
"The Ballad of Late Annie" (Brooks) **125**:74, 76-7
"Ballad of Longwood Glen" (Nabokov) **8**:407
"The Ballad of Lord Timbal" (Fuller) **62**:184, 185
"Ballad of Mary's Son" (Hughes) **108**:299
"Ballad of Me" (Livesay) **79**:338, 341, 350
"Ballad of Mister Dutcher and the Last Lynching in Gupton" (Warren) **6**:556; **8**:537
"Ballad of Mr. Chubb" (Birney) **6**:75
"The Ballad of Nat Turner" (Hayden) **5**:168; **9**:270; **37**:155
"A Ballad of Nuggets" (Yevtushenko) **26**:464
"Ballad of Oedipus Sex" (Abse) **29**:16
"A Ballad of Oyo" (Mphahlele) **25**:339
"Ballad of Pearl May Lee" (Brooks) **49**:22; **125**:80, 84
The Ballad of Peckham Rye (Spark) **2**:414, 416; **3**:466; **8**:493; **13**:521, 523; **18**:501; **40**:393; **94**:326-28, 331-33
A Ballad of Remembrance (Hayden) **5**:168; **14**:241; **37**:156-57, 159-60
"The Ballad of Rudolph Reed" (Brooks) **125**:94, 96
"Ballad of Simón Caraballo" (Guillén) **48**:164, 166
The Ballad of Soapy Smith (Weller) **53**:391-92
"The Ballad of Sue Ellen Westerfield" (Hayden) **14**:240
"Ballad of Sweeney Todd" (Sondheim) **30**:394, 397-98; **147**:231
"The Ballad of the Big Stamp" (Yevtushenko) **126**:395, 397
"The Ballad of the Black Cloud" (Grass) **32**:200
"Ballad of the Carpenter" (Ochs) **17**:331
"The Ballad of the Children of the Czar" (Schwartz) **10**:465; **87**:336
"Ballad of the Crucified Rose" (MacDiarmid) **63**:252
"Ballad of the Despairing Husband" (Creeley) **36**:122
"The Ballad of the Flint" (Christie) **110**:127
"Ballad of the Full Stop" (Voznesensky) **57**:413
Ballad of the Ghost Train (Arrabal) **58**:23, 27
"Ballad of the Girl Whose Name Is Mud" (Hughes) **108**:330
"A Ballad of the Good Lord Baden-Powell" (Ewart) **46**:151
"Ballad of the Güije" (Guillén)
See "Balada del güje"
"The Ballad of the Hell Hound" (Faludy) **42**:141
"Ballad of the Hoppy Toad" (Walker) **1**:351
"Ballad of the Icondic" (Ciardi) **44**:383
"A Ballad of the Investiture, 1969" (Betjeman) **10**:53
"Ballad of the Landlord" (Hughes) **35**:222

"The Ballad of the Lonely Masturbator" (Sexton) **123**:408, 442
"Ballad of the Lord and Columbus" (McGinley) **14**:366
"Ballad of the Mari Lwyd" (Watkins) **43**:441, 445-46, 450-51, 454-56
Ballad of the Mari Lwyd and Other Poems (Watkins) **43**:440-43, 448-49, 453-54, 457
"Ballad of the Outer Dark" (Watkins) **43**:454-56
Ballad of the Outer Dark and Other Poems (Watkins) **43**:457
Ballad of the Phantom Train (Arrabal)
See *Ballad of the Ghost Train*
"Ballad of the Rattlesnake" (Tolson) **36**:427; **105**:231, 260
"Ballad of the River Spirit" (Guillén)
See "Balada del güje"
The Ballad of the Sad Café (Albee) **2**:2; **5**:13; **9**:5; **13**:5; **25**:38; **86**:120
The Ballad of the Sad Café (McCullers) **100**:245-46, 249-50, 252, 254-56, 259-64
The Ballad of the Sad Cafe: The Novels and Stories of Carson McCullers (McCullers) **1**:207-09; **4**:345-46; **10**:338-39; **12**:412-13, 415-16, 418, 421, 424, 426-29, 431-32; **48**:235, 241; **100**:260
"Ballad of the Throwaway People" (D'Aguiar) **145**:117
"Ballad of the Two Grandfathers" (Guillén)
See "Balada de los dos abuelos"
"The Ballad of the Wall" (Ratushinskaya) **54**:385
"Ballad of the World Extinct" (Celan)
See "Ballade von der erloschenen Welt"
The Ballad of Typhoid Mary (Federspiel) **42**:143-44, 146
"The Ballad of U.S. Steel" (Ochs) **17**:333
"The Ballad of William Worthy" (Ochs) **17**:324-30
"Ballad of Your Puzzlement" (Warren) **18**:539
"The Ballad of Yucca Flats" (Barker) **48**:18
"The Ballad Trap" (Murray) **40**:335
Ballada raboty (Voznesensky) **15**:555-56
"Ballade for Braque" (Deutsch) **18**:120
"A Ballade for Mr. Rhodes" (Cassity) **42**:95
"Ballade for the Duke of Orleans" (Wilbur) **53**:405
"Ballade of Lost Objects" (McGinley) **14**:367
"Ballade of the Sayings" (Merwin) **88**:205
"Ballade un peu banale" (Smith) **15**:515
"Ballade vom Auszug der drei" (Celan) **82**:54
"Ballade von der erloschenen Welt" (Celan) **82**:52-3
Ballads and Poems (Masefield) **47**:227
The Ballads of Petrica Kerempuh (Krleža)
See *Balade Petrice Kerempuha*
The Ballads of Villon (Faludy) **42**:139
"The Ballast Hole" (Blunden) **56**:52
Ballet Fever (Cavanna)
See *Take a Call, Topsy*
"The Ballet of Central Park" (Boyle) **121**:39
The Ballet or the Bullet (Malcolm X) **82**:228; **117**:354
Ballet Shoes (Streatfeild) **21**:396-97, 403, 405-07, 412-13, 416
Ballets sans musique, sans personne, sans rien (Céline) **47**:72
"The Balloon" (Barthelme) **13**:55; **46**:35
Balloon (Colum) **28**:88-9
"Balloon over the Rhondda" (Mathias) **45**:235
The Balloonist (Harris) **9**:261
"Balloons" (Plath) **9**:426, 428; **17**:360; **51**:342; **111**:167, 175
"The Ballroom at Sandover" (Merrill) **34**:229
"Ballroom Dancing" (McCartney) **35**:290-91, 293
"The Ballroom of Romance" (Trevor) **71**:339; **116**:332, 357, 363, 372, 376, 385
The Ballroom of Romance, and Other Stories (Trevor) **7**:476-77; **71**:322, 324; **116**:331-32, 374
"Balls-Up" (Epstein) **39**:465
"Ballydavid Pier" (Kinsella) **138**:118
Balm in Gilead (Wilson) **36**:465-66
Baltasar and Blimunda (Saramago)
See *Memorial do convento*
Baltasar and Blimunda (Saramago) **119**:149-52, 154, 164, 166, 168
"Baltasar Gérard (1555-1582)" (Arreola) **147**:5
Balthazar (Durrell) **1**:87; **4**:144, 146; **8**:191-92; **13**:185-86; **41**:136
"Balthazar's Marvelous Afternoon" (García Márquez)
See "La prodigiosa tarde de Baltazar"
The Balthus Poems (Dobyns) **37**:79-81
"The Baltic Night" (Morand) **41**:297
"Baltics" (Transtroemer) **65**:224, 237
Baltics (Transtroemer)
See *Österjöar*
The Baltimore Waltz (Vogel) **76**:262-69
Der Bal-tshuve (Singer) **38**:410-12; **69**:306-07, 315
Balún-Canán (Castellanos) **66**:43, 48-9, 60-1
"Balzac" (Carver) **36**:100
Balzac's Horse (Hofmann) **54**:229
La Bamba (Valdez) **84**:403-04, 407-08, 415
"Bambi" (Prince) **35**:323
I bambini ci guardano (De Sica) **20**:89, 91-2
"Bambini della creazione" (Ortese) **89**:194
"Bananafish" (Salinger)
See "A Perfect Day for Bananafish"
Bananas (Allen) **16**:2-5, 15-17; **52**:45
"Bananas-Slide" (Asturias) **8**:25
"Band Concert" (Sandburg) **10**:450
"Band Music" (Fuller) **62**:184
Band of Angels (Warren) **4**:581; **8**:540; **53**:366; **59**:298
Band of Brothers: E company, 506th Regiment, 101st Airborne, from Normandy to Hitler's Eagle's Nest (Ambrose) **145**:55
"The Band of Hope" (Kelman) **58**:302
Band of Outsiders (Godard)
See *Bande à part*
"Band on the Run" (McCartney) **35**:282-84
Band on the Run (McCartney) **12**:377, 380; **35**:282-86, 291
The Band Rotunda (Baxter) **14**:65
Bande à part (Godard) **20**:131, 138
Bandicoot (Condon) **10**:111
Bandido! (Valdez) **84**:414, 416-17
Bandits (Leonard) **71**:214-17, 219-21, 223, 225; **120**:266-68, 272-74, 286-88, 296
Bandits (Taylor) **27**:441, 444
"Bandit's Wives" (Jiles) **58**:276-77
"Bandung Conference" (Malcolm X) **117**:354
"Banff: An Exercise in Political Astronomy" (Avison) **97**:76
"Bang" (Muldoon) **32**:319
Bang the Drum Slowly (Harris) **19**:200, 203
"Bang-Bang You're Dead" (Spark) **8**:493; **40**:402
"Banging on My Drum" (Reed) **21**:312-13
Banished Children of Eve: A Novel of Civil War in New York (Quinn) **91**:72-85
"The Banished Gods" (Mahon) **27**:287-88
"The Banished One" (Agnon)
See "Ha nidah"
"Banishment" (Sassoon) **130**:184, 215
"Bank Holiday" (McGahern) **48**:273
Bank Shot (Westlake) **7**:528; **33**:438-40
Banker (Francis) **42**:151-52, 155; **102**:131, 160
Banket u Blitvi (Krleža) **8**:329; **114**:168, 176-77, 186
"Banking Potatoes" (Komunyakaa) **94**:241
"Bankrobber" (Clash) **30**:47-8
"Banks of a Stream Where Creatures Bathe" (Merrill) **13**:381
Le Banlieue de Paris (Cendrars) **106**:167, 173
"Banneker" (Dove) **81**:133, 137
Banners (Deutsch) **18**:118
The Banners (Krleža)
See *Zastave*
The Banquet (Slaughter) **56**:411
Banquet in Blithuania (Krleža)
See *Banket u Blitvi*
"The Banquet of Crow" (Parker) **68**:335
"Bans o' Killing" (Bennett) **28**:29-30
"Banyan" (Swenson) **61**:403
"The Banyan Tree, Old Year's Night" (Walcott) **76**:286
"A Baobab Tree in Recife" (Cabral de Melo Neto)
See "Um boabá no Recife"
"The Baptism" (Bishop) **32**:40
The Baptism (Baraka) **33**:59
Baptism of Desire (Erdrich) **120**:144
Baptismal (Tesich) **40**:421
"Baptizing" (Munro) **95**:294, 304
"Bar Giamaica" (Wright) **146**:364
"Bar Giamaica, 1959-60" (Wright) **146**:310, 338, 361
"Bar Italia" (Williams) **42**:443
"Bar Mitzvah" (Goldemberg) **52**:165
Barabbas (Lagerkvist) **54**:271, 275, 278-83, 285; **7**:198-99, 201; **10**:311-12; **13**:330
"Baraka pet be" (Krleža) **114**:167
"Barbados" (Marshall) **27**:311-12; **72**:227, 248
"Barbara" (Prévert) **15**:438
"Barbara Ann" (Wilson) **12**:647
Un barbare en Asie (Michaux) **8**:392
The Barbarian and the Geisha (Huston) **20**:163
A Barbarian in Asia (Michaux)
See *Un barbare en Asie*
Barbarian in the Garden (Herbert)
See *Barbarzyńca w ogrodzie*
"Barbarian Pastorals" (Dunn) **40**:168
"The Barbarians" (Highsmith) **102**:203
Barbarians (Dunn) **40**:167-68, 171
The Barbarous Coast (Macdonald) **14**:333; **41**:267, 272
Barbarous Knowledge (Hoffman) **6**:242; **23**:240
The Barbary Light (Newby) **2**:310
Barbary Shore (Mailer) **1**:187-92; **2**:258, 263; **3**:311, 315; **4**:319, 323; **8**:364, 368-69, 373; **11**:342-43; **28**:256-57; **74**:203-04, 206-07, 221-22, 224; **111**:94, 101, 108, 113, 136
Barbarzyńca w ogrodzie (Herbert) **9**:275; **43**:184, 189-90, 192-94
La barbe de François Hertel (Ferron) **94**:114
Barbe-Bleue (Tournier) **95**:379, 381
"The Barbecue" (Dixon) **52**:98
Barbedor (Tournier) **95**:369
"Barbed-Wire Entanglements" (Perloff) **137**:302
"The Barber" (O'Connor) **3**:366
"The Barber" (Raine) **103**:186
"The Barber of Bariga" (Mphahlele) **25**:339
"The Barber Whose Uncle Had His Head Bitten Off by a Circus Tiger" (Saroyan) **29**:363
The Barber's Trade Union and Other Stories (Anand) **93**:57
"Barbie" (Soto) **80**:298
"Barbie-Q" (Cisneros) **69**:153, 155
A barca dos homens (Dourado) **23**:150; **60**:85-9, 91-2
La barca sin pescador (Casona) **49**:44, 46-8
Barcarole (Neruda) **28**:313-15
"Barcelona" (Sondheim) **147**:251
The Barclay Family Theatre (Hodgins) **23**:235
"Bardon Bus" (Munro) **95**:305-06, 315, 318, 325
"The Bare Arms in Packing Cases" (Mahapatra) **33**:277
"Barefoot" (Sexton) **123**:440
"Barefoot and Pregnant" (Armatrading) **17**:10
"Barefoot and Pregnant in Des Moines" (Kinsella) **43**:253, 255-56
Barefoot in the Head: A European Fantasia (Aldiss) **14**:12-14
Barefoot in the Park (Simon) **6**:502-03; **11**:495; **31**:393, 396, 403; **39**:218; **70**:238, 240-41
Barely and Widely, 1956-1958 (Zukofsky) **4**:599
Barfly (Bukowski) **82**:23-6; **108**:88, 91, 94
"The Barfly Ought to Sing" (Sexton) **123**:412
"Bargain" (Guthrie) **23**:199

"The Bargain Sale" (Johnston) **51**:243
A Bargain with God (Savage) **40**:370
The Bark Tree (Queneau)
See *Le chiendent*
"The Barking" (Bachmann) **69**:47
"Barking Man" (Bell) **102**:7
Barking Man and Other Stories (Bell) **102**:5-7
"The Barn" (Blunden) **56**:37
Barn Blind (Smiley) **53**:344-45; **144**:258, 270, 296
"Barn Burning" (Faulkner) **6**:179; **11**:199
"Barn Burning" (Murakami) **150**:38, 52
"The Barn Cuts Off the View" (Ferber) **93**:180
Barn Fever and Other Poems (Davison) **28**:104
Bárnabo delle montagne (Buzzati) **36**:83, 91-2, 95
Barnabo of the Mountains (Buzzati)
See *Bárnabo delle montagne*
"The Barney Game" (Friel) **42**:166
"Barnum Museum" (Millhauser) **109**:158, 161
The Barnum Museum (Millhauser) **109**:157-60, 165, 167, 169-70, 174
Barometer Rising (MacLennan) **2**:257; **14**:339, 342, 344; **92**:298, 300-02, 304-14, 316-17, 321-22, 326, 340-42, 346
The Baron in the Trees (Calvino)
See *Il barone rampante*
Baron Munchausen (Gilliam)
See *The Adventures of Baron Munchausen*
Il barone rampante (Calvino) **5**:97; **8**:129-30; **11**:89, 91; **22**:87, 89-90; **33**:97; **39**:306-08, 314, 316-17; **73**:35, 54, 58
"Baroque Comment" (Bogan) **39**:388; **46**:81, 86; **93**:65, 79-81
Baroque 'n' Roll (Brophy) **105**:19-20, 29
"A Baroque Wall-Fountain in the Villa Sciarra" (Wilbur) **3**:530; **53**:398; **110**:356, 362, 374, 383, 387
"Barra de Navidad: Envoi" (Muske) **90**:318
"Barrack Room Fiddle Tune" (Ross) **13**:496
The Barracks (McGahern) **5**:280; **9**:370-71, 374; **48**:261-63, 267, 269, 271-72
"Barracks Apt. Fourteen" (Weiss) **3**:516
The Barracks Thief (Wolff) **39**:283-86
The Barracks Thief, and Selected Stories (Wolff) **64**:451, 454, 456-57
Barrage against the Pacific (Duras)
See *Un barrage contre le Pacifique*
Un barrage contre le Pacifique (Duras) **6**:149; **40**:176, 178-79, 185, 187; **68**:77, 82-3, 85, 91-2, 95-6, 98, 100; **100**:118, 129, 138, 140-41, 144-46
Barren Terrain (Neruda) **28**:315
"Barren Woman" (Plath) **51**:340
"Barricade Smith: His Speeches" (Klein) **19**:259
"The Barrie Cooke Show, May 1988" (Durcan) **70**:152
Barrier (Skolimowski) **20**:348-49, 351-54
Barrier Island (MacDonald) **44**:407
Barriers (Chomsky) **132**:38-9, 67
Barroco (Sarduy) **97**:374, 376-78, 405, 412, 414
"Bar-Room Matins" (MacNeice) **4**:318
Barry Lyndon (Kubrick) **16**:390-92
"Barrytown" (Becker and Fagen) **26**:79
"Bars" (Guillén) **79**:229
"Barstool Blues" (Young) **17**:579
Barsuki (Leonov) **92**:236-38, 242-43, 247-48, 253, 257, 259, 266, 270, 275-78
"Bart and Helene at Annie and Fred's" (Gold) **42**:197
The Bartered Bride (Harrison) **129**:169, 203
Bartleby (Albee) **113**:4
"Bartok and the Geraniums" (Livesay) **79**:345-46
Barton Fink (The Coen Brothers) **108**:147, 149, 151-64, 166-67, 169-71
"Barua a Soldani" (Dinesen) **95**:46
"Baruch" (Simpson) **9**:485; **149**:337, 347
Les bas fonds (Renoir) **20**:288, 303
Base Case (Rathbone) **41**:342-43
"Base Details" (Sassoon) **36**:391, 397; **130**:182-84, 192, 202, 214-15, 220
"Baseball" (Bowering) **47**:21
Baseball: A Poem in the Magic Number Nine (Bowering) **15**:83
"Baseball and the Meaning of Life" (Hall) **37**:149; **151**:200-02, 208
"Baseball and Writing" (Moore) **47**:261, 263
Baseball in April and Other Stories (Soto) **38**:189
Baseball in April, and Other Stories (Soto) **80**:298, 300
"The Baseball Spur" (Kinsella) **43**:253, 256-57
"Basement" (Bambara) **88**:48
"The Basement" (Lagerkvist) **54**:288
The Basement (Pinter) **11**:443; **15**:423; **27**:387, 394-95
The Basement: Meditations on a Human Sacrifice (Millett) **67**:254-57
"The Basement Room" (Greene) **3**:215; **70**:293-94
The Basement Tapes (Dylan) **77**:182
The Basement Window (Buero Vallejo)
See *El tragaluz*
"Básežn nejpokornější" (Seifert) **93**:338
"A Bash in the Tunnel" (O'Brien) **7**:270; **10**:362
Basi and Co. (Saro-Wiwa) **114**:258, 261, 267, 274-75
"Basic Dialogue" (Wright) **146**:372
Basic English (Richards) **24**:395
Basic Handbook for the Actor (Fo)
See *Manuale minimo dell'Attore*
Basic Movements (Gregor) **9**:254
Basic Training (Wiseman) **20**:473-74
The Basic Training of Pavlo Hummel (Rabe) **4**:425-28; **8**:449-51; **33**:341-44
"The Basilica at Vezelay" (Matthews) **40**:324
"Basilisk" (Ellison) **13**:206
Basin and Range (McPhee) **36**:298-99
"A Basin of Eggs" (Swenson) **4**:532
"Basis from Her Garden" (Barthelme) **115**:81
Basket Case (Peck) **17**:342
The Basketball Diaries (Carroll) **35**:78-80; **143**:28-31, 33-44, 46, 48-9
"Baskets" (Glück) **44**:217, 222
"Baskets" (Jensen) **37**:188
"The Basket-Weaver's Companion" (Char)
See "La compagne du vannier"
"The Basque and Bijou" (Nin) **60**:276; **127**:384, 388
Bas-relief and Other Poems (Rozewicz)
See *Płaskorzeźba*
The Bass Saxophone (Škvorecký)
See *Legenda emöke*
The Bassarids, Opera Seria with Intermezzo in One Act (Auden) **4**:34
"The Bastard" (Caldwell) **14**:93
The Bastard (Caldwell) **50**:299-300
The Bastard (Jakes) **29**:248-49
"The Bastard Bannerman" (Spillane) **13**:528
The Bastard King (Hibbert) **7**:156
Bastard Out of Carolina (Allison) **78**:3-6, 8-9, 11, 13; **153**:2-5, 7-10, 12-13, 15, 17-26, 28-35, 37-44, 46, 48, 51-3, 57
"Bastille Day on 25th Street" (Dybek) **114**:61, 66
"El bastón" (Marqués) **96**:233, 244
"De Bat He Fly in Me Face" (Simon) **26**:411
"A Bat in the Monastery" (L'Heureux) **52**:272, 274
"A Bat on the Road" (Heaney) **74**:167
La bataille de Pharsale (Simon) **4**:496-97; **9**:483; **15**:493-94, 496-97; **39**:203, 205-11, 214-15
Batailles dans la montagne (Giono) **4**:184-85; **11**:234
La bâtarde (Leduc) **22**:260-61
"Bateman Comes Home" (Thurber) **125**:397
"The Bath" (Carver) **36**:101, 104; **126**:125-26, 130-33, 135, 137-38, 141-42, 152-55, 163-64, 167-69, 182-83
"The Bath" (Snyder) **5**:395; **120**:327-29, 333, 350
"Bath after Sailing" (Updike) **23**:476
"The Bath House" (Gunn) **18**:200
"Bathers" (Prokosch) **48**:309
"Bathing at Glymenopoulo" (Motion) **47**:292-94
"Bathing Beauty" (Garrett) **3**:192
"Bathing in Diabolic Acid" (McFadden) **48**:246-48
"Bath-Sheba" (Shapiro) **53**:330
"De Bathsuit and de Cow" (Bennett) **28**:27
Batman: The Ultimate Evil (Vachss) **106**:366-67
Batman's Beachhead (Buzo) **61**:53-4
Bâtons, chiffres, et lettres (Queneau) **5**:360-61
The Bat-Poet (Jarrell) **2**:210; **13**:303
"Bats" (Jarrell) **9**:295
Bats Out of Hell (Hannah) **90**:158-60, 162-63
"Bats Out of Hell Division" (Hannah) **90**:161, 163-64
"Battaglia notturna alla biennale di Venezia" (Buzzati) **36**:86
"Battered" (Souster) **5**:395
"The Battered Wife" (Davie) **31**:124
"The Battery" (Kinsella) **43**:255
"Battery Park: High Noon" (Belitt) **22**:48-9
"The Battle" (Simpson) **7**:426; **149**:324, 350, 355
Battle as an Inner Experience (Jünger)
See *Der Kampf als inneres Erlebnis*
"The Battle Continues" (MacDiarmid) **19**:289
Battle Cry (Uris) **7**:490; **32**:430-31, 433
The Battle for Christabel (Forster) **149**:80-1
"The Battle for the Hill" (Amichai) **22**:30; **57**:38; **116**:106-07
"The Battle in the Hills" (Brown) **48**:61
The Battle Lost and Won (Manning) **19**:302-04
Battle of Angels (Williams) **5**:502; **11**:572, 575; **45**:452; **71**:263-65, 367; **111**:424
"The Battle of Aughrim" (Murphy) **41**:312-13, 317-19
The Battle of Aughrim (Murphy) **41**:312, 314-16
"The Battle of Britain Dinner, New York, 1963" (Coward) **29**:135
The Battle of Bubble and Squeak (Pearce) **21**:291, 293
"The Battle of Evermore" (Page and Plant) **12**:475, 477, 481-82
The Battle of Little Bighorn (Sandoz) **28**:404
A Battle of Nerves (Simenon) **47**:370, 374, 376, 383
"The Battle of Osfrontalis" (Hughes) **119**:262
The Battle of Pharsalus (Simon)
See *La bataille de Pharsale*
The Battle of San Pietro (Huston) **20**:158, 165
The Battle of Shrivings (Shaffer) **5**:387-88; **14**:486; **18**:475-77
"The Battle of the Sequins" (Boyle) **121**:59
"The Battle of the Trees" (Graves) **6**:210
The Battle of the Villa Fiorita (Godden) **53**:159-60
"A Battle of Wills Disguised" (Piercy) **27**:376
"Battle Piece" (Belitt) **22**:50
Battle Surgeon (Slaughter) **29**:373
The Battlefield (Mayne) **12**:390-91, 393, 407
Battlefield Earth: A Saga of the Year 3000 (Hubbard) **43**:204-08
Battlefield President: Dwight D. Eisenhower (Archer) **12**:15
"Battlefields" (Scannell) **49**:330
"Battlefields" (Sillitoe) **148**:199
"The Battler" (Hemingway) **13**:273; **30**:184, 189-90, 196; **39**:402
Battling Butler (Keaton) **20**:190, 196
Bau einer Laube (Wellershoff) **46**:435
"Baudelaire" (Eliot) **57**:182
Baudelaire (Sartre) **24**:404-06, 410; **50**:373, 383
"Baudelaire as Art Critic" (Paz) **51**:332
Baumgartner's Bombay (Desai) **97**:165-66, 168, 170, 172, 181-82, 185, 190, 192
Die Baumwollpflücker (Traven)
See *Der Wobbly*
"Bavaria" (Schnackenberg) **40**:378
"The Bay" (Baxter) **14**:62

The Bay at Nice (Hare) **58**:230-31; **136**:261, 267
"Bay Days" (Moss) **45**:292
The Bay Is Not Naples (Ortese)
See *Il mare non bagna Napoli*
Bay of Arrows (Parini) **133**:258-61
Bay of Noon (Hazzard) **18**:214-18
The Bay Psalm Book Murder (Harriss) **34**:192-93
Bayn al-Qasrayn (Mahfouz) **153**:236, 238-39, 241, 244, 246, 249, 251-52, 254-57, 265, 281-82, 285, 287, 293, 301-2, 304, 337, 372
Bayn al-Qasrayn (Mahfūz) **52**:293, 295, 300; **55**:171
Bayou Backwaters (Eckert) **17**:106
Bayt sayyi' al-su'a (Mahfouz) **153**:359
Bazaar and Rummage (Townsend) **61**:409-10
"Bazaar, Five P.M." (Mahapatra) **33**:284
"Be" (Diamond) **30**:111
Be a Farmer's Boy (Taylor) **27**:442
Be Angry at the Sun and Other Poems (Jeffers) **54**:246; **11**:309, 311
"Be Cool, Be Calm, and Keep Yourself Together" (Wonder) **12**:655
"Be Grave, Woman" (Riding) **7**:374
"Be Here in the Morning" (Wilson) **12**:641
"Be My Girl-Sally" (Police, The) **26**:363
Be My Guest! (Ewart) **13**:209
"Be Not Afraid!": André Frossard in Conversation with Pope John Paul II (John Paul II) **128**:166-67, 177, 183
"Be Not Amazed" (Senghor) **130**:281
"Be Still" (Wilson) **12**:641
"Be with Me" (Simon) **26**:410
Be Yourself (Connelly) **7**:56
The Beach (Sarduy)
See *La playa*
The Beach Boys Love You (Wilson) **12**:651-52
The Beach Boys Party Album (Wilson) **12**:643, 651
The Beach Boys Today! (Wilson) **12**:643, 650
"Beach Burial" (Slessor) **14**:493, 498
"Beach Glass" (Clampitt) **32**:115, 118
"The Beach Head" (Gunn) **18**:203; **32**:207
"The Beach Murders" (Ballard) **36**:38
"The Beach Party" (Grau) **9**:240; **146**:129
Beach Plovers (Kawabata)
See *Hamachidori*
"Beach Squatter" (Davis) **49**:91, 94-5
Beach Towels (Sachs) **35**:335
"The Beach Umbrella" (Colter) **58**:138, 140
The Beach Umbrella (Colter) **58**:138-40, 143, 146
The Beach Waifs (Amado)
See *Capitães da areia*
"Beach with White Cloud" (Gustafson) **36**:217
"The Beach Women" (Pinsky) **121**:435
"Beachcombers" (Williams) **42**:442
"Beachmaster" (Norris) **14**:388
The Beachmasters (Astley) **41**:49-50
"Beachworld" (King) **37**:207
"The Beacon" (Wilbur) **6**:570; **53**:405, 410; **110**:348, 353
"The Beaded Pear" (Simpson) **32**:377-78; **149**:305-7, 335
"Beagling" (Smith) **42**:356
An Béal Bocht (O'Brien) **4**:385; **5**:314-17; **7**:269; **47**:316-17
Beale Street Sundown (Lee) **52**:270
Beale Street: Where the Blues Began (Lee) **52**:265-69
"Beam Us Home" (Tiptree) **48**:385-86
"Beams" (Lorde) **71**:255, 260
"The Bean Eaters" (Brooks) **125**:53
The Bean Eaters (Brooks) **1**:46; **5**:75; **15**:93-4; **49**:22, 27, 30-2, 35-6; **125**:45, 53, 68, 74, 85, 87-8, 93-4, 97, 110-11
"Bean Spasms" (Berrigan) **37**:46
Bean Spasms (Berrigan) **37**:42-3
The Bean Trees (Kingsolver) **55**:64-8; **81**:191, 193-95; **130**:70, 72-3, 75-6, 78, 80, 84-5, 87-96, 101-03, 107, 110, 112, 114
"Beans" (Grace) **56**:116-18, 121
Beans: All about Them (Silverstein and Silverstein) **17**:455
The Beans of Egypt, Maine (Chute) **39**:37-43
"Beans with Garlic" (Bukowski) **5**:81; **108**:112
Beany and the Beckoning Road (Weber) **12**:632
Beany Has a Secret Life (Weber) **12**:633, 635
Beany Malone (Weber) **12**:632
"The Bear" (Faulkner) **1**:101; **6**:174, 176; **8**:211; **11**:201; **18**:149; **28**:143
"The Bear" (Frost) **10**:193-94, 196-97
"Bear" (Gunnars) **69**:257
"The Bear" (Kinnell) **2**:230; **3**:268-69; **5**:216; **13**:318-20, 322; **29**:284, 288; **129**:239, 251, 256, 259, 268
"The Bear" (Momaday) **85**:224-25, 231, 248, 262-64
"Bear" (Nowlan) **15**:398
Bear (Engel) **36**:159-62
"A Bear and a Love" (Ulibarrí)
See "Un oso y un amor"
"The Bear and the Kiss" (Dinesen) **10**:148-50; **95**:61
"A Bear Hunt" (Faulkner) **6**:179
Bear Island (MacLean) **3**:309; **13**:359, 361-63
"Bear News" (Frazier) **46**:165
"The Bear on the Delhi Road" (Birney) **6**:75, 78
"Bear Paw" (Hugo) **32**:240-41
"Bear Spirit in a Strange Land" (Wiebe) **138**:334, 379
Die Bearbeitung der mütze (Jandl) **34**:196, 198, 200
The Beard (McClure) **6**:317, 320; **10**:331-32
"A Beard for a Blue Pantry" (Hall) **151**:224
Bearded Ladies (Grenville) **61**:151-52, 154-56, 159, 161-62
"Bearded Lady" (Zamora) **89**:384-85, 387
"The Bearded Lady Tells Her Story Late at Night While Drunk in the Bar" (Moure) **88**:219
"Bearded Oaks" (Warren) **8**:539; **39**:264; **59**:301-02
"The Bearded Woman, by Ribera" (Muldoon) **32**:318
The Beardless Warriors (Matheson) **37**:244-45
Beard's Roman Women (Burgess) **8**:113; **15**:103; **81**:303
Beardsley and His World (Brophy) **105**:16
Bearheart--the Heirship Chronicles (Vizenor) **103**:311, 340
Bearing an Hourglass (Anthony) **35**:40-1
The Bear's Famous Invasion of Sicily (Buzzati) **36**:82-4
"The Beast" (Plath) **11**:448; **111**:159, 164
"The Beast" (Roethke) **46**:363; **101**:311
The Beast (Wilson) **33**:460-61, 463, 465
The Beast in Me, and Other Animals: A New Collection of Pieces and Drawings about Human Beings and Less Alarming Creatures (Thurber) **5**:439; **125**:416
Beast in View (Rukeyser) **27**:407-08, 410
The Beast Master (Norton) **12**:456-57, 461, 468
The Beast Must Die (Day Lewis) **6**:129
"Beast of Burden" (Jagger and Richard) **17**:239-40
A Beast Story (Kennedy) **66**:205-08
"The Beast That Etcetera" (Ellison)
See "The Beast That Shouted Love at the Heart of the World"
"The Beast That Shouted Love at the Heart of the World" (Ellison) **13**:206
The Beast That Shouted Love at the Heart of the World (Ellison) **42**:127
A Beast with Two Backs (Potter) **123**:233
The Beastly Beatitudes of Balthazar B (Donleavy) **1**:76; **4**:123-25; **6**:139, 141-42; **10**:153-54; **45**:125
"Beastly Manhattan" (Baker) **31**:31
Beastly Tales from Here and There (Seth) **90**:353
"Beasts" (Wilbur) **14**:578-79; **53**:411; **110**:355, 376
Beasts (Crowley) **57**:156-57, 162
Beasts of the Southern Wild and Other Stories (Betts) **3**:73; **6**:69
"The Beat" (Costello) **21**:68
The Beat Boys (Holmes)
See *Go*
Beat of the City (Brinsmead) **21**:26-8
Beat the Devil (Capote) **34**:322
Beat the Devil (Huston) **20**:163, 165
Beat the Last Drum: The Siege of Yorktown, 1781 (Fleming) **37**:120
Beat to Quarters (Forester) **35**:161-63, 166, 169-70
"The Beaters" (Gunn) **32**:207
"The Beating of a Drum" (Eliot) **15**:208
"Beating That Boy" (Ellison) **54**:141
Beating the Bushes: Selected Essays, 1941-1970 (Ransom) **4**:437
"Beatitude" (Moure) **88**:227
The Beatles (Lennon and McCartney) **12**:364
The Beatles VI (Lennon and McCartney) **35**:274
"Beatrice and Dante" (Graves) **45**:169
"Beatrice Passes" (Christie) **110**:126
"Beatrice Trueblood's Story" (Stafford) **19**:430; **68**:434
"The Beau Monde of Mrs. Bridge" (Connell) **45**:107, 109
Le beau serge (Chabrol) **16**:168, 170, 173-74, 178, 180-81, 183
Un beau ténébreux (Gracq) **11**:245; **48**:136-41
The Beaubourg Effect (Baudrillard) **60**:36
Beauford DeLancy Retrospective Exhibition: Harlem Studio Museum (Baldwin) **127**:109
"Beaufort Tides" (Beecher) **6**:49
La beauté du diable (Clair) **20**:64, 71
The Beauties and the Furies (Stead) **5**:403; **32**:411, 413-15; **80**:307, 317-18, 347, 349
Beautiful (Billington) **43**:55
"The Beautiful Amanita Muscaria" (Wakoski) **7**:505
"The Beautiful American Word, Sure" (Schwartz) **87**:347
"Beautiful and Cruel" (Cisneros) **69**:150; **118**:177, 217
"The Beautiful and the Sublime" (Sterling) **72**:372
"Beautiful Black Men (with compliments and apologies to all not mentioned by name)" (Giovanni) **19**:191; **64**:185, 187
"Beautiful Boy" (Lennon) **35**:272-74
"The Beautiful Changes" (Wilbur) **9**:569; **53**:399, 408
The Beautiful Changes and Other Poems (Wilbur) **3**:531; **6**:568; **9**:569; **14**:576; **53**:396-97, 401, 403-04, 406-07, 409-10; **110**:352, 380
Beautiful City (Walker)
See *The East End Plays*
"The Beautiful Comrade Furazhkin" (Aksyonov) **101**:10-11
A Beautiful Day (Wellershoff)
See *Ein schöner Tag*
The Beautiful Empire (Ghose) **42**:180-81
Beautiful Feathers (Ekwensi) **4**:151-52
The Beautiful Friend and Other Stories (Stolz) **12**:551-52
Beautiful Girl (Adams) **13**:2-3; **46**:16-17, 22
The Beautiful Inventions (Fuller) **62**:198-99, 201-02, 204
"Beautiful Loser" (Seger) **35**:380-81, 383
Beautiful Loser (Seger) **35**:380-81, 383
Beautiful Losers (Cohen) **3**:109; **38**:135, 137
"Beautiful Noise" (Diamond) **30**:112
Beautiful Noise (Diamond) **30**:112-13
The Beautiful People (Saroyan) **10**:454; **56**:376
"The Beautiful Poem" (Brautigan) **3**:87
The Beautiful Room is Empty (White) **110**:321. 323-32, 337, 339, 342-43

"The Beautiful Sewers of Paris, Alberta" (Wiebe) **138**:380
"Beautiful Speech" (Boland) **113**:100
"Beautiful Streamers" (Rabe) **8**:451
"Beautiful Thing" (Williams) **22**:466
The Beautiful Visit (Howard) **29**:242
Beautiful Women: Ugly Scenes (Bryan) **29**:105-06
The Beautiful Words (Jones) **52**:250-51, 254
"Beauty" (Christie) **110**:125
"The Beauty" (Ekelöf) **27**:119
"Beauty" (Huxley) **11**:283-84
Beauty and Sadness (Kawabata) **107**:102-03, 108
"Beauty and the Beast" (Broumas) **73**:5
"Beauty and the Beast" (Dove) **81**:137
Beauty and the Beast (Cocteau)
See *La belle et la bête*
Beauty and the Beast (Hunter) **31**:226-27
Beauty and the Beast (Page) **40**:355
"The Beauty of the Head" (Swenson) **61**:402; **106**:329, 344
The Beauty Part (Perelman) **44**:503, 505
"A Beauty that Rages" (Honig) **33**:211
The Beautyful Ones Are Not Yet Born (Armah) **5**:31; **33**:23-5, 27-9, 31-2; **136**:14-17, 19, 21, 23, 25, 38, 44, 50, 52-54, 56-57, 61, 68, 71-73
Les Beaux Draps (Céline) **47**:79; **124**:60, 88, 96, 104
Les beaux quartiers (Aragon) **22**:35, 37
The Beaver Men (Sandoz) **28**:407
"Beaver Tears" (Tiptree) **48**:389
"Beaverbank" (Hugo) **32**:243
"The Beavers of Renfrew" (Purdy) **50**:240-41, 246
"Bebop Boys" (Hughes) **35**:222
"Becalmed on Strange Waters" (Ashbery) **77**:67
"Because" (Pastan) **27**:369
"Because I Never Learned" (Lane) **25**:287
Because I Was Flesh (Dahlberg) **7**:63, 67, 69; **14**:135-38
Because I Was Invited (Wright) **11**:578
Because It Is Bitter and Because It Is My Heart (Oates) **108**:374-75, 378, 386, 388, 390
"Because My Father Always Said He Was the Only Indian Who Saw Jimi Hendrix Play 'The Star-Spangled Banner' at Woodstock" (Alexie) **96**:5, 13
Because of Love (Skelton) **13**:508
Because of Madeline (Stolz) **12**:550, 552-53
"Because of Me, Because of You" (Jarrell) **2**:209
Because of the Cats (Freeling) **38**:184
"Because One Is Always Forgotten" (Forché) **25**:172; **83**:214
"Because the Night" (Smith) **12**:543
"Because You Asked about the Line between Prose and Poetry" (Nemerov) **36**:306
Bech: A Book (Updike) **1**:345; **2**:440-41; **5**:456, 459-460; **9**:541; **13**:559; **43**:430-31; **139**:317, 328, 333, 335-36, 380-81
Bech at Bay (Updike) **139**:380-81
"Bech in Czech" (Updike) **139**:381
Bech Is Back (Updike) **43**:430-32; **139**:314, 317, 333, 380
"Bech Noir" (Updike) **139**:380-81
"Bech Presides" (Updike) **139**:381
"Bech Third Worlds It" (Updike) **43**:430
"Bech Wed" (Updike) **43**:430, 432
"Bechbretha" (Muldoon) **72**:273
The Becker Wives and Other Stories (Lavin) **18**:303; **99**:312
Becket; or, The Honor of God (Anouilh)
See *Becket; ou, L'honneur de Dieu*
Becket; ou, L'honneur de Dieu (Anouilh) **1**:7; **3**:12; **13**:17-18, 21-2; **40**:56-8, 61; **50**:278-80
"Beckoned" (Pearce) **21**:292
Beckonings (Brooks) **15**:93-4; **49**:23, 29, 35-8; **125**:45, 60-1, 88, 110
"Becky" (Toomer) **1**:341; **13**:552
Becky Sharp (Mamoulian) **16**:421-22, 424, 427
Becky Swan's Book (Musgrave) **54**:333
Becoming a Man: Half a Life Story (Monette) **82**:328-30
"Becoming the Characters in Your Novel" (Godwin) **125**:159
"The Bed" (Berry) **27**:35
"The Bed" (Gunn) **81**:178
"Bed among the Lentils" (Bennett) **77**:101
Bed and Board (Truffaut)
See *Domicile conjugal*
"Bed and Breakfast" (Gass) **132**:195
"Bed & Breakfast" (Raine) **103**:179
A Bed by the Sea (Gregor) **9**:254
"A Bed for the Night" (Yezierska) **46**:443
A Bed of Feathers (Davies) **23**:144
A Bed of Flowers (Waugh) **7**:514
The Bed Sitting Room (Lester) **20**:226, 228-29
Bed/Time/Story (Robinson) **10**:439
"Bedfordshire" (Davie) **31**:112, 116
"The Bedfordshire Clanger" (Bates) **46**:62
"The Bedroom Eyes of Mrs. Vansittart" (Trevor) **25**:445; **71**:326, 347
Bedroom Farce (Ayckbourn) **18**:28-30; **33**:41, 49; **74**:3, 7, 19, 29, 31, 34
"Bedroom of Music" (Williams) **42**:442
"Beds and Boards" (Chester) **49**:56
Beds in the East (Burgess) **4**:82; **22**:74; **81**:301
"The Bed's Too Big Without You" (Police, The) **26**:364
Bedside Manners (Valenzuela) **104**:390-92
"Bed-Time" (Johnston) **51**:243
"Bedtime" (Levertov) **66**:237
Bedtime Stories (Van Duyn) **3**:491-92; **63**:442-43; **116**:408, 417-18, 426
"Bedtime Story" (Abse) **29**:20
"A Bedtime Story" (Hughes) **119**:263
"Bedtime Story" (Simic) **22**:383
"A Bedtime Story for My Son" (Redgrove) **6**:445
"A Bedtime Story for My Wife" (Leyner) **92**:281
"The Bee Hive" (Rosenblatt) **15**:446
"The Bee Meeting" (Plath) **11**:450; **14**:429; **17**:360; **111**:176, 179
"The Bee of Words" (Dudek) **19**:136
Bee Tree and Other Stuff (Peck) **17**:339-40
"Beech Buds" (Clarke) **61**:73
"The Beech Tree" (Hoffman) **23**:238
The Beekeepers (Redgrove) **41**:356-57
"The Beekeeper's Daughter" (Plath) **9**:431; **111**:178
Been Down So Long It Looks Like Up to Me (Farina) **9**:195
"Been on a Train" (Nyro) **17**:313, 316, 318
"Beer at the Corner Bar" (Bukowski) **41**:73
"The Beer was Spilled on the Barroom Floor" (Keillor) **115**:277
"Bees Stopped" (Ammons) **25**:44
The Beet Queen (Erdrich) **54**:166-72; **120**:133-34, 138-39, 162-66, 168-70, 172, 174, 181, 184, 186-88, 192
"Beethoven" (Herbert) **9**:275; **43**:187
"Beethoven Attends the C Minor Seminar" (Tomlinson) **6**:536
"Beethoven Opus 111" (Clampitt) **32**:116
"Beethoven Triumphant" (Berryman) **3**:68, 70; **6**:64; **8**:91, 93; **25**:96
"Beethoven's Death Mask" (Spender) **41**:418, 428
The Beetle Leg (Hawkes) **2**:183; **3**:221, 223; **4**:215, 218; **7**:140, 142, 144, 146; **14**:237; **15**:270-71; **27**:191, 199; **49**:161
Beetlecreek (Demby) **53**:99-101, 103-06, 109-15
Der Befehl (Hochwälder) **36**:235-38
"Before a Cashier's Window in a Department Store" (Wright) **10**:544
"Before an Old Painting of the Crucifixion" (Momaday) **85**:225, 248, 266-67
"Before Dark" (Berry) **4**:59
Before Dawn (Rattigan) **7**:355
"Before Death" (Ali) **69**:31
"Before Disaster" (Winters) **4**:593; **32**:468, 470
"Before Hanging" (Simmons) **43**:408
"Before His Time" (Oz) **27**:360-62
"before leaving me, the poem: eagle butte and black river falls" (Young Bear) **94**:363
"Before March" (MacLeish) **68**:286
Before My Time (Howard) **5**:188-89; **14**:267; **46**:187; **151**:275
"Before Pentecost" (Buckley) **57**:130
Before Retirement (Bernhard)
See *Vor dem Ruhestand*
"Before Sex" (Gerstler) **70**:159
Before She Met Me (Barnes) **42**:26-8; **141**:31, 33-4, 44-5, 49, 61-4
"Before Sleep" (Kinsella) **138**:149-50
Before Sleep (Booth) **23**:77
"Before Snow Comes" (Sillitoe) **148**:158, 164, 166
"Before Spring" (Boland) **67**:45; **113**:108
"Before the Anaesthetic" (Betjeman) **34**:309; **43**:36
"Before the Battle" (Sassoon) **130**:180-81
"Before the Big Storm" (Stafford) **29**:380
Before the Blackout (Soyinka) **44**:286
Before the Brave (Patchen) **18**:392
"Before the Celtic Yoke" (Durcan) **43**:113
"Before the Deluge" (Browne) **21**:36-7, 40
Before the Flood (Dylan) **77**:175
"Before the Judgement" (Duncan) **41**:128, 130
"Before the Party" (Maugham) **67**:206
Before the Revolution (Bertolucci) **16**:83-8, 92-5, 99-100
"Before the Storm" (Campbell) **42**:92
"Before the Story" (Cohen) **38**:132
Before the Throne (Mahfouz)
See *Amam al'Arsh*
Before You Say "Hello" (Calvino) **39**:306
Die Befristeten (Canetti) **14**:121-22; **75**:124, 127, 129-30, 134, 146-47; **86**:303
"Beg, Sl Tog, Inc, Cont, Rep" (Hempel) **39**:67, 69-70
"Begat" (Sexton) **123**:442
The Beggar (Mahfouz) **153**:271, 301
The Beggar (Mahfūz) **55**:181; **52**:300
A Beggar in Jerusalem (Wiesel) **3**:527, 529; **37**:455
"Beggar in the Snow" (Baxter) **78**:28
"The Beggar Is King" (Harris) **25**:212
The Beggar Maid: Stories of Flo and Rose (Munro)
See *Who Do You Think You Are?*
Beggar on Horseback (Connelly) **7**:56
Beggar on Horseback (Kaufman) **38**:257, 264-66
The Beggar Queen (Alexander) **35**:28
"Beggarland" (Sillitoe) **148**:199
"Beggars Banquet" (Jagger and Richard) **17**:222-23, 226, 229, 233, 237, 240-41
The Beggar's Opera (Havel) **123**:184, 205
"Beggars Would Ride" (Bainbridge) **62**:36-7; **130**:28
"Begging the Dialect" (Skelton) **13**:507
Begin Here: The Forgotten Conditions of Teaching and Learning (Barzun) **145**:75-6, 80-1
Begin with Walking (Shapcott) **38**:401
The Beginners (Jacobson) **4**:253, 255; **14**:290
"Beginner's Guide" (Nemerov) **36**:301
Beginner's Love (Klein) **30**:243
"The Beginning" (Grau) **146**:151, 159, 161, 164
"The Beginning" (Van Duyn) **116**:422
"Beginning" (Wright) **3**:540; **28**:465
A Beginning and an End (Mahfūz)
See *Bidāya wa-nihāya*
"Beginning, and End" (Nichol) **18**:366
The Beginning and the End (Mahfouz)
See *Bidaya wa-nihaya*
"The Beginning Is Also the End" (Burroughs) **109**:196
"The Beginning Is Zero" (Giovanni) **64**:183

The Beginning of an Unknown Century (Paustovsky) **40**:368
"The Beginning of April" (Williams) **33**:443; **148**:312, 321
"The Beginning of Homewood" (Wideman) **122**:289-90, 305, 307
"The Beginning of September" (Hass) **99**:151
"The Beginning of Something" (Dixon) **52**:100
The Beginning of Spring (Fitzgerald) **61**:119-23; **143**:240-41, 244, 248-51, 253-54, 257, 261-62
"The Beginning of the End" (Achebe) **26**:22
The Beginning of the Journey: The Marriage of Diana and Lionel Trilling (Trilling) **129**:341, 348-52, 355, 357-63, 367
The Beginning of the Long Dash (Thesen) **56**:420, 422
The Beginning Place (Le Guin) **22**:274-75; **45**:215-16, 221; **136**:369-71, 374-75, 390
"Beginning to Say No" (Gallagher) **63**:123
"Beginning to See the Light" (Reed) **21**:318-19
Beginning with My Streets: Essays and Recollections (Milosz) **82**:308, 311
Beginning with O (Broumas) **10**:76-7; **73**:2, 4-13, 16
"Beginnings" (Adcock) **41**:16
"Beginnings" (Coover) **7**:58; **32**:127
"Beginnings" (Frame) **96**:189, 191
"Beginnings" (Haines) **58**:217
"Beginnings" (Hayden) **37**:153
Beginnings: Intention and Method (Said) **123**:357
"The Beginnings of a Fortune" (Lispector) **43**:267, 269
"The Beginnings of a Sin" (Mac Laverty) **31**:255
"Beginnings of Conservative Thought" (Barrett) **27**:23
Begleitumstände: Frankfurter Vorlesungen (Johnson) **40**:265, 270
"Begotten of the Spleen" (Simic) **22**:383; **68**:379; **130**:317
Begstvo Mistera Mak-Kinli (Leonov) **92**:252, 278-79
Begstvo Sandukova (Leonov)
See *Volk*
"Beguiled" (Abe) **81**:297
"Behaving like a Jew" (Stern) **40**:406
"Behaviorism" (Faludy) **42**:138
"The Behaviour of Dogs" (Raine) **103**:180
"The Behaviour of the Hawkweeds" (Barrett) **150**:5, 17
"Behemoth" (Huxley) **11**:283
"Behind a Shut Door" (MacCaig) **36**:285
Behind All This There's Great Happiness Hiding (Amichai) **22**:30; **116**:137
"Behind the Blue Curtain" (Millhauser) **109**:157, 160
"Behind the Curtained World (1942)" (O'Casey) **88**:267
Behind the Door (Bassani) **9**:76
Behind the Green Curtains (O'Casey) **5**:318; **9**:407; **88**:272-74
Behind the Lines: Gender and the Two World Wars (Higgonet, et al, eds.) **65**:327
Behind the Log (Pratt) **19**:376, 380, 383-84
Behind the Makeup (Arzner) **98**:69
"Behind the Mirror" (Gunn) **18**:201
"Behind the North Wind" (Davie) **10**:123
Behind the Scenes at the Museum (Atkinson) **99**:97-103
Behind the Trail of Broken Treaties: An Indian Declaration of Independence (Deloria) **21**:112-14
"Behold Goliath" (Chester) **49**:55-7
Behold Goliath (Chester) **49**:54-6
"Behold the Husband in His Perfect Agony" (Hannah) **38**:234; **90**:148, 150
"Behold the Lilies of the Field" (Hecht) **8**:268; **13**:269
Behold the Man (Moorcock) **27**:347-48; **58**:349, 352, 357
"Behührung" (Wolf) **58**:426; **150**:221
"The Beige Dolorosa" (Harrison) **143**:346-48, 353, 359
"Being a Lutheran Boy-God in Minnesota" (Bly) **38**:58
"Being a Man" (Theroux) **46**:401
"Being a Woman" (Urdang) **47**:400
"Being Adults" (Thesen) **56**:420, 423
"Being Alive" (Sondheim) **30**:392, 395, 400, 403; **147**:233, 251-52, 254
Being Alive: Poems, 1958-78 (Purdy) **14**:435; **50**:246
Being and Having (Marcel) **15**:359, 364
Being and Nothingness: An Essay on Phenomenological Ontology (Sartre)
See *L'être et le néant: Essai d'ontologie phénoménologique*
Being and Time (Heidegger)
See *Sein und Zeit*
"Being Blind" (Adcock) **41**:14
"Being Country Bred" (Oliver) **98**:291
"Being, Dwelling, Thinking" (Kroetsch) **132**:266
"Being for the Benefit of Mr. Kite" (Lennon and McCartney) **12**:358
Being Geniuses Together (Boyle) **58**:75, 77; **121**:35-7, 46, 66-8
Being Here: Poetry, 1977-80 (Warren) **18**:539; **39**:255-59, 264-66, 270-73
"Being Kind to Titina" (White) **69**:398
"Being Left" (Piercy) **62**:367-68
"Being Lost, As Usual" (Thesen) **56**:418
"Being of Hope and Rain" (Aleixandre) **36**:29
"Being of Three Minds" (Nemerov) **6**:362
Being Red (Fast) **131**:63, 66-7, 69-78, 82-7, 91-7, 99, 102
"Being Stolen From" (Trevor) **25**:446; **71**:326, 347
Being There (Kosinski) **1**:172; **2**:231-33; **3**:272-73; **6**:282-84; **10**:307; **15**:313-14; **53**:219-20, 222, 226, 228; **70**:297-98, 301, 306
Being Two Isn't Easy (Ichikawa) **20**:181, 186
Being with Children (Lopate) **29**:298-300
Being with You (Robinson) **21**:350-51
The Bejeweled Boy (Asturias) **13**:40
"Bela" (Stern) **100**:333
Bela Lugosi's White Christmas (West) **7**:524; **96**:380
"Belagerung" (Eich) **15**:202
Belaia staia (Akhmatova)
See *Belaya staya*
Belaia staja (Akhmatova)
See *Belaya staya*
Belaya staya (Akhmatova) **25**:24-7; **64**:3-4, 8-9; **126**:5, 24, 33
"Belderg" (Heaney) **14**:244; **25**:245
"Belfast" (Heaney) **25**:249
"Belfast" (MacNeice) **4**:316; **53**:238
"Belfast vs. Dublin" (Boland) **113**:114
Belfry (Ritsos) **13**:487
"Belief" (Levine) **118**:270-71, 285
"Believable Linden, Pumpkin, Cherry, Etc." (Bell) **31**:46
Believe Them (Robison) **98**:306-09, 318
"Believers" (Updike) **15**:546
Believing (Birch) **65**:444-48
"Believing in Literature" (Allison) **153**:5, 11, 52
Belinda (Rice) **128**:293
"Belize" (Gilchrist) **48**:119; **143**:316
The Bell (Murdoch) **1**:234-36; **2**:295-96, 298; **3**:345, 347-48; **6**:343, 345, 348; **15**:385; **22**:327; **51**:291-92
The Bell (O'Connor) **14**:398
"Bell Birds" (Wright) **53**:423
"Bell Boy" (Townshend) **17**:532
"Bell Buoy" (Merwin) **5**:288
"Bell Call" (Ashton-Warner) **19**:22
The Bell Family (Streatfeild) **21**:401, 405, 411
A Bell for Adano (Hersey) **1**:144; **7**:153; **40**:226-27, 238-39, 241; **81**:332-37; **97**:297-98, 301-02, 304-06, 324
The Bell Jar (Plath) **1**:270; **2**:336-37; **3**:390-91; **5**:342-44; **9**:423-24, 432; **11**:450-51; **17**:345, 350-54, 356-58, 361, 364-65, 368; **50**:439-42, 446, 448; **51**:343, 350-51; **62**:385-401, 404-429; **111**:157-59, 161, 163-64, 166, 168, 178, 184, 187-95, 197-99, 213, 215
"Bella dama sin piedad" (Castellanos) **66**:53
"La bella durmiente" (Ferré) **139**:150, 156, 158, 165-66, 188-90, 192
"Bella Fleace" (Waugh)
See "Bella Fleace Gave a Party"
"Bella Fleace Gave a Party" (Waugh) **27**:477
"The Bella Lingua" (Cheever) **11**:121
The Bellarosa Connection (Bellow) **63**:40-3
"Belle" (Simenon) **2**:399
La belle bête (Blais) **2**:63; **4**:67; **6**:81; **13**:96-7
La belle captive (Robbe-Grillet) **8**:454; **43**:367; **128**:361, 363, 378
Belle de jour (Bunuel) **16**:141; **80**:50-2, 56-7
"La belle époque" (Milosz) **82**:297, 310
La belle et la bête (Cocteau) **8**:145, 148; **15**:134; **16**:222, 225-26, 228-29
"Belle Isle" (Randall) **135**:373, 388
"Belle Isle, 1949" (Levine) **9**:333
"Belle Starr" (Guthrie) **35**:193
Bellefleur (Oates) **19**:354-56; **33**:289, 291-92, 295-96; **52**:331, 339; **108**:348, 371, 374-75, 378, 385, 391
"Bellerophoniad" (Barth) **5**:51-2; **14**:53, 55
Les belles images (Beauvoir) **14**:68; **71**:48, 51-3; **124**:127, 131-32, 137, 183-84
The Belles Lettres Papers (Simmons) **57**:408-10
Belles on Their Toes (Gilbreth and Carey) **17**:153-54, 156
Les belles-de-nuit (Clair) **20**:63, 71
Les belles-soeurs (Tremblay) **29**:419-20, 423, 426; **102**:360-63, 369, 371-72, 374-76, 381, 383-87
Bellisima (Visconti) **16**:564, 575
"Bellow Ellijay" (Dickey) **7**:80
The Bells (Reed) **21**:316-17
"Bells for John Whiteside's Daughter" (Ransom) **5**:365
"Bells in Winter" (Milosz) **31**:262-63
Bells in Winter (Milosz) **22**:308-10; **31**:262, 267, 269; **56**:239, 242; **82**:297-98
The Bells of Agony (Dourado) **60**:94
The Bells of Basel (Aragon)
See *Les cloches de bâle*
The Bells of Bicêtre (Simenon)
See *Les anneaux de Bicêtre*
"The Bells of Britany" (Christie) **110**:127
"Bells of the Evening" (Lightfoot) **26**:281
"Bells of Winter" (Milosz)
See "Bells in Winter"
"Bells on the Breeze" (Blunden) **56**:49
"The Belly" (Selzer) **74**:279
The Belly (Tchicaya)
See *Le Ventre*
"Belly Dancer at the Hotel Jerome" (Dunn) **36**:153-55
"Belly Song" (Knight) **40**:287
Belly Song and Other Poems (Knight) **40**:283, 285
"The Belonging Kind" (Gibson) **63**:130
Beloved (Morrison) **55**:195-213; **81**:231-32, 234-35, 237-40, 242, 244, 247, 252-53, 255-56, 258-63, 265-66, 268-69, 272; **87**:262-309
The Beloved Bandit (Hart) **66**:176, 180
"Below" (Berry) **46**:72
"Below" (Celan) **82**:46
"Below Freezing on Pinelog Mountain" (Bottoms) **53**:30
Below Grass Roots (Waters) **88**:328, 334, 337, 339, 345, 349, 360, 362
"Below the Ridge" (Hemingway) **80**:105
Below the Root (Snyder) **17**:473
Below the Salt (Costain) **30**:98
"Belsen, Day of Liberation" (Hayden) **37**:159
The Belting Inheritance (Symons) **14**:523
Le belvédère (Mandiargues) **41**:275, 278

Belyi dozhd (Aitmatov) **71**:7, 14-15
Belyj parokhod (Aitmatov) **71**:4, 7, 10-11, 13-15, 18-19, 21, 23
Ben Hur (Vidal) **142**:305, 325
"Ben Jonson" (Eliot) **24**:176
Ben Preserve Us (Bermant) **40**:90
"The Bench" (Dixon) **52**:99, 101
Bench of Desolation (Chabrol) **16**:178
"Benchmark" (Raphael) **14**:438
"Bend Down Low" (Marley) **17**:269
A Bend in the River (Naipaul) **13**:407; **18**:359-61, 363-64; **37**:321-22, 324, 328-29; **105**:158, 161-62, 170, 176, 181
Bend Sinister (Nabokov) **1**:240; **2**:300; **3**:353, 355; **6**:352, 355, 357; **8**:412, 415, 418; **15**:391, 396; **23**:312
The Bender (Scott) **9**:476-77
Bending the Bow (Duncan) **2**:122; **4**:141; **7**:89; **15**:190; **41**:129-30; **55**:293, 295
Bendingo Shafter (L'Amour) **25**:281
"Beneath My Hands" (Cohen) **38**:132
Beneath the Fortinaria (Bukowski) **108**:110
Beneath the Shadow of the Mountain (Ritsos) **13**:488
Beneath the Stone (Tabori) **19**:435
Beneath the Wheel (Hesse)
See *Unterm Rad*
"Benediction" (Kaufman) **49**:203
"Benedictory" (Riding) **7**:374
The Benefactor (Sontag) **1**:322; **13**:515; **31**:417-18; **105**:197, 207, 215, 225
Benefactors (Frayn) **47**:136-40
"Beneficiaries" (Gallagher) **63**:121
"The Benefit Concert" (Davies) **23**:142
Benefits (Fairbairns) **32**:162-63
"Benerci kendini nicin öldürdü" (Hikmet) **40**:244-45
Benighted (Priestley) **34**:361, 363
Benito Cereno (Lowell) **4**:299; **8**:352, 354-55; **11**:324-25
Benjamin's Crossing (Parini) **133**:286-88
Benjy (O'Connor) **14**:393
"Bennie" (Cook-Lynn) **93**:126
"Ben's Last Fight" (Merton) **83**:397
"Benson's Visitor" (Kelman) **58**:298
Bent (Miles) **39**:354
Bent (Sherman) **19**:415-16
"Bent Water in the Tasmanian Highlands" (Murray) **40**:341, 343
"Benzedrine" (Bowering) **47**:19
"Beowulf: The Monsters and the Critics" (Tolkien) **38**:439, 442
"Berck-Plage" (Plath) **9**:425, 428; **11**:450; **17**:348-49; **51**:341; **111**:168, 177
"The Bereaved" (Abse) **29**:18
"Bereaved Apartments" (Kingsolver) **130**:73
"Bereavement" (Beer) **58**:37
"Berechnungen I" (Schmidt) **56**:391-92, 404
"Bereft" (Frost) **13**:223; **26**:121, 124-25
"Bereft" (Reading) **47**:351
Bereitschaftsdienst Bericht uber die Epidemie (Nossack) **6**:365
"Berenda Slough" (Levine) **118**:289
Bérénice d'Egypte (Chedid) **47**:82, 87
Berenike (Rexroth) **11**:473
Berg (Quin) **6**:441
Berichte zur Gesinnungslage der Nation (Boell) **72**:85
"The Berkeley Concert" (Bruce) **21**:48
"Berkeley Eclogue" (Hass) **99**:142
"Berkeley House" (Adams) **46**:17
"Berkshire" (Davie) **31**:120
"The Berkshire Kennet" (Aldington) **49**:10
Berl Make Tea (Bermant) **40**:89-90
"Berlin" (Ferlinghetti) **27**:139
Berlin (Haviaras) **33**:202
Berlin (Reed) **21**:304, 306-07, 312
The Berlin Antigone (Hochhuth) **18**:253
"Berlin, Border of the Divided World" (Johnson) **15**:304
Berlin Days (Poliakoff) **38**:380, 385
The Berlin Ending (Hunt) **3**:251
Berlin Game (Deighton) **46**:129-32
"Berlin Is Hard on Colored Girls" (Lorde) **71**:262
Berlin Solstice (Fraser) **64**:178
The Berlin Stories (Isherwood) **14**:282 85; **44**:396-97, 400
The Berlin Wall Café (Durcan) **43**:117-18; **70**:150
The Berlin Warning (Guild) **33**:189
"Berliner Stadtansichten" (Hein) **154**:133, 165, 167
Berlioz and the Romantic Century (Barzun) **145**:92, 101
Bernabé (Valdez) **84**:404-07, 413
"Bernadette" (Gallant) **18**:172
Bernard Clare (Farrell) **66**:124-26
Bernard Shaw (Bentley) **24**:46
Bernice Bobs Her Hair (Silver) **20**:344
Beröringen (Bergman) **16**:71; **72**:47, 50, 53-5, 57, 59
Berries Goodman (Neville) **12**:449-52
Berro Dágua (Amado)
See "A Morte e a morte de Quincas Berro Dágua"
"A Berry Feast" (Snyder) **32**:387; **120**:336
"Berry Picking" (Layton) **15**:322
"The Berry Stain" (L'Heureux) **52**:275
Berryman's Sonnets (Berryman) **1**:33; **2**:56; **3**:65; **4**:63; **6**:62-5; **8**:89-91; **10**:49-50; **13**:78-9; **25**:93-5; **62**:43, 47, 50-2, 54, 56, 71, 75-6
Bert Breen's Barn (Edmonds) **35**:154, 156
Bertha and Other Plays (Koch) **5**:219; **44**:241
Berthe (Tremblay) **102**:364-66
Bertie and May (Norton) **12**:460
Bertie Makes a Break (Felsen) **17**:121
Bertie Takes Care (Felsen) **17**:120
Der Beruf des Dichters (Canetti) **25**:109
Die Berühmten (Bernhard) **61**:12, 20
"Beryl" (Metcalf) **37**:299
Beryll Gazes into the Night, or the Lost and Refound Alphabet (Sachs)
See *Beryll sieht in der Nacht*
Beryll Sees in the Night (Sachs)
See *Beryll sieht in der Nacht*
Beryll sieht in der Nacht (Sachs) **98**:322, 351
"Beseda" (Aksyonov) **101**:35
Det besegrade livet (Lagerkvist) **54**:274-75
Beside a Norman Tower (de la Roche) **14**:150
Beside the Ocean of Time (Brown) **100**:79-82, 84, 87
"Beside the Sea" (Johnston) **51**:243
"Beside the Seashore" (Betjeman) **43**:34, 40-2
"Beside the Seaside" (Smith) **25**:420-21
"Besides a Dinosaur, Whatta Ya Wanna Be When You Grow Up?" (Bradbury) **42**:42
"Besieged" (O Hehir) **41**:324
El beso de la mujer araña (Puig) **28**:371-72, 374; **65**:262, 269-72; **133**:300-01, 309-10, 313, 316-24, 331-33, 335-37, 344-50, 363-67, 371-74, 376, 378
"Bess" (Phillips) **139**:205-6
Eine bessere Welt (Lind) **4**:293; **82**:137-40, 142, 145
"Bessie Smith at Roy Thomson Hall" (Ondaatje) **51**:315
"Best" (Tate) **2**:432
The Best American Poetry 1989 (Hall) **151**:193
The Best and the Last of Edwin O'Connor (O'Connor) **14**:392
The Best Christmas (Kingman) **17**:243
"The Best Dog" (Govier) **51**:166-67
The Best Hour of the Night (Simpson) **32**:378-82, 384; **149**:309, 313-14, 316-17, 322, 325-27, 333-36, 340, 349, 351
The Best Man (Vidal) **4**:552, 559; **8**:528; **22**:438; **142**:305, 313, 326, 329, 332
The Best Man to Die (Rendell) **28**:383, 385
The Best Nightmare on Earth: A Life in Haiti (Gold) **152**:141-42, 144
The Best Of (Cliff) **21**:63
"Best of All Possible Worlds" (Kristofferson) **26**:266
The Best of Antrobus (Durrell) **41**:139
The Best of Arthur C. Clarke (Clarke) **18**:106; **136**:210
The Best of Carly Simon (Simon) **26**:410
The Best of Friends (Humphreys) **47**:182, 184, 190
The Best of Fritz Leiber (Leiber) **23**:303-04
The Best of H. E. Bates (Bates) **46**:59
The Best of Harry Harrison (Harrison) **42**:203
The Best of Henry Miller (Miller) **84**:241
The Best of Jack Vance (Vance) **35**:419
The Best of John W. Campbell (Campbell) **32**:77-8, 80
The Best of Myles: A Selection from "Cruiskeen Lawn" (O'Brien) **47**:312
The Best of Rhys Davies (Davies) **23**:148
The Best of Robert Silverberg (Silverberg) **140**:377-79
The Best of S. J. Perelman (Perelman) **49**:265
The Best of Simple (Hughes) **10**:278
The Best of Willie Nelson (Nelson) **17**:305
Best Science Fiction Stories (Aldiss) **5**:15
"The Best Shod" (Valenzuela) **104**:364, 388
The Best Short Stories of J.G. Ballard (Ballard) **14**:39; **36**:41
"Best Society" (Larkin) **64**:258, 263
The Best Times: An Informal Memoir (Dos Passos) **82**:108
Bestialitéérotique (Arrabal) **58**:18
Le bestiaries (Montherlant) **8**:393
"Bestiario" (Cortázar) **10**:113; **13**:164
"Bestiario" (Neruda) **28**:312
Bestiario (Arreola) **147**:3-4, 27, 40
Bestiario (Cortázar) **2**:104; **10**:118; **33**:125, 128; **34**:329, 332
"Bestiary" (Olds) **39**:187
Bestiary (Arreola)
See *Bestiario*
Bestiary (Cortázar)
See *Bestiario*
A Bestiary (Wilbur) **14**:577
"A Bestiary for My Daughters Mary and Katharine" (Rexroth) **112**:400
"Bestiary for the Fingers of My Right Hand" (Simic) **130**:311
"A Bestiary of the Garden for Children Who Should Have Known Better" (Gotlieb) **18**:191
Bestie del '900 (Palazzeschi) **11**:432
The Best-Loved Short Stories of Jesse Stuart (Stuart) **34**:376
Der Besuch der alten Dame (Duerrenmatt) **102**:69, 76-7
Der Besuch der alten Dame (Dürrenmatt) **1**:81; **4**:138; **8**:194, 197; **11**:168, 170; **15**:195-96, 200-01; **43**:120-21, 123-26, 128
"The Bet" (Abe) **81**:298
"Bet hakravot hatsva'i habriti behar hatsofim" (Amichai) **116**:110
"Beta" (Tolson) **105**:242, 254, 265, 272
La Bête humaine (Lang) **103**:85
La bête humaine (Renoir) **20**:287
La bête noire (Audiberti)
See *La fête noire*
"Les bêtes" (Gascar) **11**:220-22
"Bêtes" (Reverdy) **53**:289-90
Les bêtes (Gascar) **11**:220-22
"Beth Brant, 1981: Letter & Post Card" (Kenny) **87**:255
"Bethe" (Hellman) **52**:192
Beton (Bernhard) **32**:26-7; **61**:14-17, 19-20, 22-3, 29
The Betrayal (Hartley) **2**:182
Betrayal (Pinter) **15**:425-26; **27**:388-92, 395-96; **58**:373, 376, 384-85; **73**:276
Betrayed by F. Scott Fitzgerald (Carlson) **54**:35-6
Betrayed by Rita Hayworth (Puig)
See *La traición de Rita Hayworth*
"The Betrayer of Israel" (Singer) **38**:407; **69**:320

"The Betrothal" (Simic) **130**:314
"Betrothed" (Agnon) **14**:1
"Betrothed" (Bogan) **93**:65, 78, 82
Betsey Brown (Shange) **38**:395-96; **126**:358-60, 364, 380
The Betsy (Robbins) **5**:378-79
A Better Class of Person (Osborne) **45**:317-19
"Better Homes & Gardens" (Loewinsohn) **52**:284
Better Living (Walker)
See *The East End Plays*
"A Better Mousetrap" (Brunner) **8**:107
"The Better Part of Wisdom" (Bradbury) **42**:35
"Better Than Counting Sheep" (Warren) **39**:274
Better Than Sex (Thompson) **104**:345-47
"Better Things" (Davies) **21**:107
"Betty" (Moure) **88**:224
"Betty Lou's Gettin' Out Tonight" (Seger) **35**:384-85
"Betty's Ball Blues" (Reed) **13**:478
Le betullenane (Yevtushenko) **13**:620
"Between" (Johnston) **51**:253
Between (Brooke-Rose) **40**:105, 111
"Between Earth and Sky" (Grace) **56**:116, 119-20
Between Existenialism and Marxism (Sartre) **18**:472-73
Between Facts and Norms: Contributions to a Discourse Theory of Law and Democracy (Habermas)
See *Faktizität und Geltung: Beiträge zur Diskurstheorie des Techts und des demokratischen Rechtsstaats*
Between Famine and Agape (Pinget)
See *Entre fantoine et agapa*
"Between Friends" (Musgrave) **54**:334
Between Here and Now (Thomas) **48**:381
Between Life and Death (Sarraute)
See *Entre la vie et la mort*
"Between March and April Is the Cruelest Month" (Padilla) **38**:349, 352
"Between Men" (Lessing) **22**:278
Between Men (Govier) **51**:167-68
Between Mouthfuls (Ayckbourn) **33**:40
"Between Myself and Death" (Rexroth) **49**:284
"Between Our Selves" (Lorde) **71**:235, 259
Between Our Selves (Lorde) **71**:257
Between Past and Future (Arendt) **98**:6-9, 11, 26
Between Planets (Heinlein) **3**:225; **26**:171, 176; **55**:302
"Between Points" (Soto) **80**:291
Between Right and Right (Yehoshua) **31**:474
Between Sartre and Camus (Vargas Llosa) **42**:408
Between Silences (Jin) **109**:52-3
Between Stone and Flower (Paz) **119**:407
"Between Tears and Laughter" (Anand) **93**:57
Between Tears and Laughter (Anand) **93**:57
"Between the Bridges" (Hugo) **32**:247
Between the Buttons (Jagger and Richard) **17**:224, 232, 235, 237, 239
"Between the Lines" (Pinter) **1**:267
"Between the Lines" (Smith) **25**:410; **73**:359
Between the Lines (Ian) **21**:184-85
Between the Lines (Silver) **20**:343-45
Between the Lines (Wakefield) **7**:502
"Between the Living and the Dead" (Ignatow) **40**:259
Between the Numen and the Moha (Blackmur) **24**:59, 65-6
"Between the Pool and the Gardenias" (Danticat) **94**:98-9
"Between the Porch and the Altar" (Lowell) **4**:295; **8**:358
"Between the Porch and the Altar" (Stafford) **4**:518
"Between the Sheets" (Bowering) **47**:28-9
Between Time and Timbuktu; or, Prometheus-Five, a Space Fantasy (Vonnegut) **12**:625-26
Between Two Lives (Turner) **48**:398-99
"Between Two Nights" (Arghezi)
See "Între două nopţi"
"Between Two Nowheres" (MacCaig) **36**:285
"Between Two Prisoners" (Dickey) **109**:238
Between Two Rivers (Potter) **123**:229
Between Two Rivers: Selected Poems 1956-1984 (Kenny) **87**:244, 248-49
"Between Two Seas" (Broumas) **73**:16
"Between Two Shores" (Mac Laverty) **31**:252, 254
"Between Two Texts" (Porter) **33**:324
Between Two Tides (FitzGerald) **19**:176, 180
Between Two Worlds (Rice) **7**:360; **49**:300, 303-05
"Between What I See and What I Say" (Paz) **51**:335; **65**:190
"Between Zero and One" (Gallant) **38**:194
Beulah Land (Davis) **49**:85-6, 89-90, 97
The Beulah Quintet (Settle) **61**:369-74, 376, 378-79, 387
"Beverly Hills, Chicago" (Brooks) **49**:27
"A Bevy of Aunts" (Lavin) **99**:321-22
"Beware" (Fearing) **51**:110
"Beware" (Knight) **40**:279
"Beware My Love" (McCartney) **35**:284
Beware of the Trains (Crispin) **22**:110
"Beware, Soul Brother" (Achebe) **26**:22, 24
Beware, Soul Brother and Other Poems (Achebe) **7**:6; **11**:3-4
Beware the Months of Fire (Lane) **25**:284-85, 288
"Beware...The Vibes of Marx" (Raine) **103**:180
"Bewitched" (Edmonds) **35**:146
The Bewitched (Barnes) **5**:49-50; **56**:5-9
"The Bewlay Brothers" (Bowie) **17**:58
"Beyond" (Faulkner) **3**:152
Beyond (Richards) **24**:401
Beyond a Boundary (James) **33**:219, 222-25
Beyond a Reasonable Doubt (Lang) **20**:208, 216; **103**:89
Beyond All This Fiddle (Alvarez) **5**:17
Beyond Another Door (Levitin) **17**:265-66
Beyond Apollo (Malzberg) **7**:208
Beyond Criticism (Shapiro) **4**:485, 487
Beyond Culture (Trilling) **9**:530; **11**:546; **24**:458-59, 462-63
Beyond Dark Hills (Stuart) **14**:514; **34**:373, 375
Beyond Earth: The Search for Extraterrestrial Life (Gallant) **17**:131-32
Beyond Eurocentrism and Multiculturism (West) **134**:362
Beyond Feminist Aesthetics: Feminist Literature and Social Change (Felski) **65**:340
Beyond Formalism: Literary Essays, 1958-1970 (Hartman) **27**:179-80, 182-84, 187
"Beyond Harm" (Olds) **85**:306
"Beyond Howth Head" (Mahon) **27**:286-87, 290-91
"Beyond Lies the Wub" (Dick) **72**:113
Beyond Mozambique (Walker) **61**:426-27, 432
"Beyond Nationalism: A Prologue" (Kroetsch) **132**:219, 220, 270
"Beyond Power" (Rosenthal) **28**:394
Beyond Power: A Sequence (Rosenthal) **28**:391-92, 394-95
Beyond Power: On Women, Men, and Morals (French) **60**:138-40, 142-47
"Beyond Reason" (Kunitz) **148**:68, 87, 98, 103
"Beyond Sargasso" (Heaney) **14**:243
"Beyond Survival" (Levi) **50**:337
"Beyond the Alps" (Lowell) **8**:349; **15**:345-48; **124**:263, 273
Beyond the Bedroom Wall: A Family Album (Woiwode) **6**:578-79; **10**:540-41
Beyond the Blue Event Horizon (Pohl) **18**:413
"Beyond the Cave: Demystifying the Ideology of Modernism" (Jameson) **142**:226
Beyond the Clouds (Antonioni)
See *Al di la delle navole*
Beyond the Curve (Abe) **81**:296, 298
Beyond the Dead Reef (Tiptree) **48**:394-95
Beyond the Dragon's Mouth (Naipaul) **39**:355-58
"Beyond the End" (Barnes)
See "Spillway"
"Beyond the Eyelids" (Redgrove) **41**:352
Beyond the Fringe (Bennett) **45**:54-6; **77**:83, 85-6, 92-5, 98-9, 102, 104
"Beyond the Gentility Principle" (Alvarez) **5**:17
"Beyond the Glass Mountain" (Stegner) **49**:350
Beyond the Hundredth Meridian: John Wesley Powell and the Second Opening of the West (Stegner) **81**:347, 349, 351-52
"Beyond the Hunting Woods" (Justice) **102**:262
Beyond the Law (Mailer) **74**:217
Beyond the Limit (Ratushinskaya) **54**:381-82
"Beyond the Liss" (Montague) **46**:266, 268
"Beyond the Mexique Bay" (Huxley) **3**:255; **18**:269; **79**:310
Beyond the Mountains (Rexroth) **112**:373
Beyond the Mountains (Rexroth) **11**:472; **22**:345, 347; **49**:279-80; **112**:372, 376, 387
"Beyond the Novel" (Cioran) **64**:82, 84, 97
"Beyond the Pale" (Trevor) **25**:445-46; **71**:323, 326, 327, 337, 339, 342, 347; **116**:360, 367, 371-72, 376, 383, 385
Beyond the Pale, and Other Stories (Trevor) **25**:445-47; **71**:325, 346; **116**:348
Beyond the Palisade (Baxter) **14**:59-60
"Beyond the Peacock: The Reconstruction of Flannery O'Connor" (Walker) **58**:405
"Beyond the Pleasure Principle" (Nemerov) **2**:307
"Beyond the Red River" (McGrath) **59**:180
Beyond the Revolution: My Life and Times Since "Famous Long Ago" (Mungo) **72**:292
"Beyond the Snow Belt" (Oliver) **98**:266
Beyond the Vicarage (Streatfeild) **21**:411-12
Beyond the Wall (Abbey) **36**:20; **59**:238, 242
"Beyond the Zero" (Pynchon) **11**:452
Beyond Therapy (Durang) **27**:90, 92-3; **38**:171, 174
Beyond This Horizon (Heinlein) **3**:224-26; **14**:247, 249; **55**:304
Beyond This Place (Cronin) **32**:137-38
"Bez" (Rozewicz) **139**:294, 297
Bez konca (Kieslowski)
See *No End*
"The B-Flat Sonata" (Johnston) **51**:254
B.F.'s Daughter (Marquand) **10**:329
Biafra, Goodbye (Gold) **152**:132
The Biafra Story (Forsyth) **36**:174
Białe małżeństwo (Rozewicz) **23**:361-62; **139**:231-32, 239, 241, 263-68, 293
"Bialik's Hint" (Ozick) **62**:344, 349, 351; **155**:126, 129
"Bianca's Hands" (Sturgeon) **39**:361, 366
The Bible (Huston) **20**:170
The Bible of the Beasts of the Little Field (Schaeffer) **22**:369-70
Bibles du sexe (Ouologuem)
See *Les Milles et une bibles du sexes*
"Bibliographical Note" (Yourcenar) **87**:411
"A Bibliography of the King's Book, or, Eikon Basilike" (Howe) **152**:177, 195, 212
A Bibliography of the King's Book or, Eikon Basilike (Howe) **72**:208; **152**:196, 207, 218
"La biblioteca de Babel" (Borges) **1**:39; **2**:72, 77; **8**:96, 98, 101-02; **9**:116, 118; **13**:108-09; **19**:46; **44**:358, 362, 368; **48**:45-6; **83**:156-57, 164, 177-78, 183
Biblioteka XXI wieku (Lem) **149**:263
"De Bibliotheca" (Eco) **142**:74-6, 79
"Bicentennial Man" (Asimov) **26**:50, 56, 58
The Bicentennial Man, and Other Stories (Asimov) **26**:39, 50, 53-6; **92**:7, 9
Les biches (Chabrol) **16**:170-74, 180-81, 183
Les biches (Cocteau) **15**:134
Biciclettone (Pasolini) **106**:222, 224
"Bicoastal Journal" (Wright) **146**:339

"Bicultural" (Johnston) **51**:240, 242, 252
Bicycle Days (Schwartz) **59**:83-8
The Bicycle Thief (De Sica)
See *Ladri di biciclette*
"Bicycles" (Ritter) **52**:355
"Bicycles, Muscles, Cigarettes" (Carver) **53**:64
La bicyclette du condamné (Arrabal) **9**:35, 38; **58**:4, 6, 8, 17, 26-7
"The Bicyclist" (Schnackenberg) **40**:379
"A Bid" (Corn) **33**:117
Bid Me to Live (A Madrigal) (H. D.) **8**:258; **14**:223, 229; **31**:203, 207, 211; **34**:444; **73**:122-25, 127-33, 135
Bid Time Return (Matheson) **37**:247
Bidaya wa-nihaya (Mahfouz) **153**:238, 242, 244, 249, 262, 271, 274, 304-5, 337, 355-56
Bidāya wa-nihāya (Mahfūz) **52**:292-93, 300, 304; **55**:173-74, 181-82
"A Bidding Grace" (Hope) **51**:215
Il bidone (Fellini) **16**:274, 276, 298; **85**:59
Biedermann und die Brandstifter: Ein Lehrstück ohne Lehre (Frisch) **3**:166-68; **9**:217; **14**:182; **18**:161, 163; **32**:188, 191, 195; **44**:181-83, 196-97, 199-200
"Biedny August von Goethe" (Rozewicz) **139**:295
"Bien Pretty" (Cisneros) **69**:154-55; **118**:189, 201-02, 205-06
"Biens équaux" (Char) **9**:163
"Bientôt" (Damas) **84**:167, 169, 174, 177-78, 182
"Bienvenue" (Char) **14**:126
"Bière de pécheur" (Landolfi) **49**:214, 217
"Biesiada u hrabiny Kotlubaj" (Gombrowicz) **49**:127
The Bievres Desert (Duhamel) **8**:189
Biffures (Leiris) **61**:341-43, 347, 351-53, 355-57, 359
The Big Aiiieeeee!: An Anthology of Chinese American and Japanese American Literature (Chin) **135**:167-69, 175, 194-95
Big and Little (Strauss)
See *Gross und Klein*
"The Big Animal of Rock" (Hughes) **119**:277
Big as Life (Doctorow) **113**:152, 176
Big Bad Love (Brown) **73**:22-3
Big Bang (Sarduy)
See *Cocuyo*
The Big Barn (Edmonds) **35**:145, 148-49, 151, 156
"Big Barn Bed" (McCartney) **35**:281
Big Bear (Wiebe)
See *The Temptations of Big Bear*
"Big Bertha Stories" (Mason) **154**:295-96, 299
"Big Bessie Throws Her Son into the Street" (Brooks) **49**:27-8; **125**:45
"Big Black Good Man" (Wright) **21**:438, 443
"Big Blonde" (Parker) **15**:414-15; **68**:326, 329, 332, 334-35
The Big Bounce (Leonard) **71**:224; **120**:286-87, 296
"Big Boy Leaves Home" (Wright) **1**:380; **14**:596; **21**:444, 453
The Big Brass Ring (Welles) **80**:413
"Big Brother" (Wonder) **12**:657, 663
"Big Brother, Little Sister" (Ihimaera) **46**:200
"Big Business" (Guillevic) **33**:191
"The Big Cats" (Reading) **47**:352
"The Big Circus" (Bagryana) **10**:14
The Big City (Ray)
See *Mahanagar*
The Big Clock (Fearing) **51**:112-13, 115-16, 119-22
"The Big Country" (Byrne) **25**:96-8
Big David, Little David (Hinton) **111**:90
The Big Day (Unsworth) **127**:407-08
"A Big Day at Big House" (Iskander)
See "Bol'shoiden' Bol'shogo Doma"
The Big Dipper (Billington) **43**:53-4
"Big Elegy" (Brodsky)
See "The Great Elegy for John Donne"
"The Big Flash" (Spinrad) **46**:383
"Big Fleas and Little Fleas" (White) **49**:407
Big Fleas and Little Fleas (White) **49**:407
The Big Four (Christie) **6**:108; **48**:74; **110**:111
"The Big Front Yard" (Simak) **55**:320
The Big Funk: A Casual Play or Talk around the Polis (Shanley) **75**:331-32
"Big Game" (Boyle) **90**:62-3
"The Big Garage" (Boyle) **36**:57
The Big Glass (Josipovici) **153**:209-11
The Big Gold Dream (Himes) **58**:267
The Big Green Book (Graves) **39**:325
The Big H (Harrison) **129**:169, 227
"The Big Heart" (Sexton) **6**:492; **123**:428, 444
The Big Heart (Anand) **23**:12, 14-16; **93**:24, 30-2, 41-3, 50
The Big Heat (Lang) **20**:205, 207, 208; **103**:99
"The Big House" (Bowen) **118**:73, 104-05
"The Big House" (Muldoon) **32**:319; **72**:264-65
The Big House (Behan) **79**:25, 27
The Big House (Bowen) **118**:77
"The Big Hunger" (Miller) **30**:262-63, 265
"The Big It" (Guthrie) **23**:199
The Big It (Guthrie) **23**:198
A Big Jewish Book: Poems and Other Visions of the Jews from Tribal Times to Present (Rothenberg) **57**:382
"Big Joe and the Nth Generation" (Miller) **30**:262, 264-65
"Big Jules" (Callaghan) **41**:98
The Big Kill (Spillane) **3**:468; **13**:526
The Big Knife (Odets) **2**:318, 320; **28**:330-34, 339-40; **98**:201, 216-17, 224, 228, 235-36, 242, 244-48, 251-52
The Big Knives (Lancaster) **36**:245
"The Big Knockover" (Hammett) **47**:161
The Big Knockover: Selected Stories and Short Novels (Hammett) **5**:161-62
The Big Laugh (O'Hara) **42**:319, 322
"Big Leaguer" (Fante) **60**:133
"The Big Leagues" (Bowering) **47**:24
"Big Liz" (Muldoon) **32**:318
"Big Machine" (Hillis) **66**:195-200
Big Mama's Funeral (García Márquez)
See *Los funerales de la Mamá Grande*
The Big Man (McIlvanney) **42**:285
"Big Meadows in March" (Brosman) **9**:135
"Big Meeting" (Hughes) **108**:298
"Big Momma" (Madhubuti) **73**:213
The Big Money (Dos Passos) **1**:77; **4**:131-33, 135, 137; **11**:157; **15**:182-83; **34**:419, 422, 424; **82**:65-8, 71-5, 79, 82, 89, 91-2, 95, 97-103, 105, 107-10, 112
"Big My Secret, But It's Bandaged" (Swenson) **106**:341
The Big Names (Bernhard)
See *Die Berühmten*
The Big Nickel (Willingham) **5**:512; **51**:410-11
Big Night (Powell) **66**:366
"Big Numbers" (Szymborska) **99**:192
"The Big Outside World" (Beattie) **63**:14; **146**:52
Big Planet (Vance) **35**:423, 425-26
"The Big Plum" (Colwin) **5**:107; **84**:150
"The Big Pot Game" (Bukowski) **41**:68
Big River (Buzo) **61**:64-6
The Big Rock Candy Mountain (Stegner) **49**:348, 357, 360; **81**:339-40, 343, 347-50, 352
"The Big Rock-Candy Mountain" (Sissman) **9**:491
"Big Sam Was My Friend" (Ellison) **42**:126
The Big Sea: An Autobiography (Hughes) **10**:279; **15**:293; **44**:511; **108**:284, 290, 292, 295-96, 311-12, 314, 317, 323
The Big Sell (Berton) **104**:47
The Big Sell (Berton) **104**:45, 47
The Big Shave (Scorsese) **20**:326
"The Big Shot" (Faulkner) **18**:148
"Big Shot" (Joel) **26**:216-17, 220-21
"Big Sister's Clothes" (Costello) **21**:76
"Big Sky" (Davies) **21**:90
The Big Sky (Guthrie) **23**:195-96, 198-201
"The Big Space Fuck" (Vonnegut) **22**:451
A Big Storm Knocked It Over (Colwin) **84**:153
Big Sur (Kerouac) **14**:305; **29**:271-72; **61**:296, 308-09
Big Sur and the Oranges of Hieronymous Bosch (Miller) **14**:374; **84**:243, 258
The Big Time (Leiber) **25**:302-03, 305, 309, 311
The Big Time (Scannell) **49**:327
Big Time: Scenes from a Service Economy (Reddin) **67**:269-70
Big Toys (Buzo) **61**:62
"The Big Trip Up Yonder" (Vonnegut) **12**:617
"Big Two-Hearted River" (Hemingway) **3**:238, 240; **6**:234; **8**:289; **10**:268; **13**:270-71, 273, 278-79; **30**:180-81, 183-84, 190-95, 197-98, 200-02; **39**:401-02; **41**:197; **50**:412, 415, 421-22, 424, 427; **61**:194, 197, 203, 207, 214, 228; **80**:151
"Big Valley Vineyard" (Saroyan) **1**:301
The Big Wave (Buck) **127**:235-37
"Big Wheels: A Tale of the Laundry Game" (King) **37**:207
"Big Wind" (Roethke) **101**:287, 294-95
The Big Woods (Faulkner) **18**:149
Big World (Andrade)
See *Mundo grande*
"Big Yellow Taxi" (Mitchell) **12**:442
A Bigamist's Daughter (McDonald) **90**:214-22, 224-28, 230-33
"Bigfoot" (Muldoon) **72**:270
Bigfoot Dreams (Prose) **45**:326-28
"Big-Foot Sal" (Edmonds) **35**:157
"Bigfoot Stole My Wife" (Carlson) **54**:39
The Bigger Light (Clarke) **8**:143; **53**:90, 93-5
"The Bight" (Bishop) **9**:95; **13**:93; **32**:34, 37
Bijou (Madden) **5**:265-66; **15**:350
"Bike" (Pink Floyd) **35**:307
"The Bike" (Sillitoe) **57**:392
"The Bike" (Soto) **80**:301
"The Bilal's Fourth Wife" (Ousmane) **66**:347, 350
"Bildnis eines Dichters" (Hildesheimer) **49**:173-74
Bilete de papagal (Arghezi) **80**:3
"Biletul" (Arghezi) **80**:11
Bilgewater (Gardam) **43**:167-68
"Bi-Lingual" (Codrescu) **121**:157
"Bilingual Sestina" (Alvarez) **93**:17
"Bilking the Statues" (Ashbery) **77**:67
"Bill" (Masefield) **11**:358
"Bill" (Powers) **57**:349, 357-58
"Bill Boston" (Dickinson) **49**:104
"Bill Brand" (Griffiths) **52**:174, 182-84
"Bill of Fare" (Enzensberger) **43**:144
A Bill of Rites, a Bill of Wrongs, a Bill of Goods (Morris) **7**:247; **37**:313
Bill, the Galactic Hero (Harrison) **42**:199-200, 205-06
Billard um halbzehn (Boell) **2**:67; **3**:74; **6**:83; **9**:102-04, 106, 108-10; **11**:52, 55-56, 58; **27**:60; **39**:292-95; **72**:68, 72-3, 85
"Billboards" (Ondaatje) **51**:316
"Billboards Build Freedom of Choice" (Birney) **6**:75
"Billennium" (Ballard) **14**:41; **36**:36, 41
Billiards at Half-past Nine (Boell)
See *Billard um halbzehn*
"Billings and Cooings from 'The Berkeley Barb'" (Van Duyn) **63**:437, 439; **116**:408
The Billion Dollar Brain (Deighton) **4**:119; **7**:75; **46**:125
Billion Dollar Brain (Russell) **16**:541, 548
The Billion Dollar Sure Thing (Erdman) **25**:153-54
A Billion for Boris (Rodgers) **12**:494
Billion Year Spree: The History of Science Fiction (Aldiss) **14**:14; **40**:16
A Billionaire (Ichikawa) **20**:181-82
"Billons" (Glissant) **68**:181
Billy (French) **86**:61-7
Billy Bathgate (Doctorow) **65**:134-39, 141-45;

113:158, 161, 166, 168-70, 176-78
"Billy Boy" (Keillor) **115**:277
Billy Buck (Poole) **17**:372
"Billy Dee" (Kristofferson) **26**:267
"Billy Ducks among the Pharoahs" (DeMarinis) **54**:100
"Billy Hunt" (Weller) **26**:444
Billy Liar (Waterhouse) **47**:415-16, 418, 420-21
Billy Liar on the Moon (Waterhouse) **47**:420-21
Billy Phelan's Greatest Game (Kennedy) **28**:204-06; **34**:206-09; **53**:190, 192-94
Billy the Kid (Spicer) **8**:498; **18**:508-09
"Billy the Mountain" (Zappa) **17**:588
Biloxi Blues (Simon) **39**:216-19; **70**:236, 240, 243
Bilvav yamim (Agnon) **4**:12; **8**:8
"Bimini" (Hemingway) **6**:232; **8**:285
Bin; oder, Die Reise nach Peking (Frisch) **3**:167; **44**:193-95, 200
"Bin'arenu uvizkenenu" (Agnon) **14**:3
Binary (Crichton) **54**:68
The Binding Chair (Harrison) **151**:257
"Binding the Dragon" (Sarton) **91**:254
Bing (Beckett) **2**:48; **6**:38; **9**:83; **11**:40-1; **14**:78; **18**:50; **29**:57, 59
Bingo (Brown) **79**:167
The Bingo Palace (Erdrich) **120**:168-69, 181, 184, 187-90, 194-95
Bingo: Scenes of Money and Death (Bond) **4**:70; **6**:84-6; **13**:102; **23**:64
Binstead's Safari (Ingalls) **42**:232-33
"A Bintel Brief for Jacob Glatstein" (Ozick) **155**:216
Bio (Berry) **17**:53
Bio of a Space Tyrant (Anthony) **35**:39-40
Biochemistry and Human Metabolism (Asimov) **76**:315
"Biografía de Tadeo Isidoro Cruz (1829-1874)" (Borges) **13**:104-5
Biografie: Ein Spiel (Frisch) **3**:167; **14**:181-82; **18**:161-62; **32**:191; **44**:189, 193-96, 198-200, 203-04
Biograph (Dylan) **77**:186, 188, 190
The Biographer's Moustache (Amis) **129**:16-20
Biographia literaria (Brooks) **24**:104
"Biographical Note" (Simic) **130**:306
"A Biography" (Bell) **8**:66
"Biography" (Blaga) **75**:63, 70, 77
"Biography" (Ciardi) **40**:157
"Biography" (Gustafson) **36**:214
"Biography" (Herbert) **43**:183
"Biography" (Masefield) **47**:229-30
"Biography" (Ondaatje) **51**:310
"Biography" (Tomlinson) **45**:393
Biography (Behrman) **40**:74-6, 80, 82
Biography: A Game (Frisch)
See *Biografie: Ein Spiel*
Biography: A Play (Frisch)
See *Biografie: Ein Spiel*
"Biography in the First Person" (Dunn) **36**:152
Biography of a Buick (Morris)
See *Motor City*
"Biography of a Story" (Jackson) **87**:234
Biography of London (Ackroyd) **140**:69, 75, 77
"Biography of Tadeo Isidoro Cruz" (Borges)
See "Biografía de Tadeo Isidoro Cruz (1829-1874)"
Biography of T.H. White (Warner) **19**:460
"Biological Superiority: The World's Most Dangerous and Most Deadly Idea" (Dworkin) **123**:74
Bionics: Man Copies Nature's Machines (Silverstein and Silverstein) **17**:452
"Bio-poetics Sketch" (Harjo) **83**:270
"Biotherm (for Bill Berkson)" (O'Hara) **2**:323; **13**:431; **78**:359-64
"Bip Bop" (McCartney) **35**:280
"Birch Bark" (Ondaatje) **51**:318
"The Birch Tree of Iron" (Padilla) **38**:351
Birch Tree Thoughts (Fitzgerald) **143**:258
"Birches" (Frost) **3**:170; **4**:174; **9**:219, 229; **15**:242, 244-45, 248; **26**:111-12, 116, 122, 125
"Birches" (Leithauser) **27**:240-42
"The Birchwood" (Daryush) **19**:121
Birchwood (Banville) **46**:26-27, 32; **118**:2-6, 8-12, 24-25, 27
The Birch-Wood (Wajda) **16**:582-83
"Bird" (Harjo) **83**:280
"Bird" (Hesse) **25**:259
"The Bird" (Lane) **25**:284
"Bird?" (Lowell) **11**:329; **124**:265
"The Bird" (Simic) **9**:481; **22**:383
"The Bird" (Simpson) **149**:321, 344, 346, 349
"The Bird" (Smith) **15**:514
Bird (Hinde) **6**:241
Bird Alone (O'Faolain) **14**:402; **70**:316-17, 320-21
"Bird and the Muse" (Zaturenska) **6**:586
Bird at My Window (Guy) **26**:140-41
"The Bird Frau" (Dove) **81**:137
Bird in the Bush (Rexroth) **22**:346; **112**:371, 390
A Bird in the House (Laurence) **3**:278; **50**:314-15, 319-20, 322; **62**:267-68, 270-72, 278, 280, 282, 293, 296, 305-06
"Bird in the Lighted Hall" (Brown) **48**:60
"Bird Lament" (Swados) **12**:557
"Bird Life" (Willingham) **51**:403
The Bird of Dawning (Masefield) **11**:357
"The Bird of Jesus" (Colum) **28**:90
"The Bird of Night" (Jarrell) **13**:303
The Bird of Night (Hill) **4**:227-28; **113**:278-80, 282, 287, 292-93, 297, 301, 303-05, 322, 330
A Bird of Paper: Poems of Vicente Aleixandre (Aleixandre) **36**:32
"The Bird of Paradise" (Laing) **95**:127, 136
"Bird Song" (Kogawa) **78**:167
"The Bird Watcher" (Kotzwinkle) **35**:254
"Bird Watching" (Ciardi) **44**:382
"The Bird with the Dark Plumes" (Jeffers) **54**:237
"Birdbrain!" (Ginsberg) **36**:196
"Birdie" (Merwin) **88**:195
"Birdland" (Smith) **12**:537
"Birdland's Golden Age" (Stuart) **11**:510-11
"The Birdnesters" (Szirtes) **46**:392, 395
"The Birds" (Blackburn) **43**:64
"The Birds" (du Maurier) **59**:285, 287
"The Birds" (Jacobsen) **48**:190
"Birds" (Kenny) **87**:242
"The Birds" (Turner) **48**:398-99
The Birds (Hitchcock) **16**:343-44, 348, 350, 353, 359
Birds (Perse)
See *Oiseaux*
The Birds (Vesaas) **48**:407-10
Birds (Wright) **53**:423-24, 428, 431
"Birds/Amsterdam" (Blackburn) **9**:100
"The Birds and the Bees" (Vidal) **142**:329, 333
The Bird's Bright Ring (Alexander) **121**:3
"The Birds Complain" (Szirtes) **46**:395
"The Birds Do Thus" (Frost) **10**:199; **15**:246
The Birds Fall Down (West) **7**:525-26; **9**:560; **50**:394, 405, 408
"Birds in Winter" (Ignatow) **14**:275
"A Bird's Life" (Swenson) **14**:518
The Bird's Nest (Jackson) **60**:211-12, 216-17, 219-20, 229, 231
"A Bird's Nest Made of White Reed Fiber" (Bly) **15**:63
"Birds of a Feather" (Humphrey) **45**:205
"Birds of a Feather" (Lamming) **66**:220
Birds of America (McCarthy) **3**:328-29; **5**:276; **14**:363; **59**:291
The Birds of Paradise (Scott) **9**:476-77; **60**:328, 340
Birds of Passage (Kureishi) **135**:265
Birds of Passage (Rubens) **31**:351
The Birds of Pompeii (Ciardi) **44**:382; **129**:51
"Birds of Prey" (White) **49**:408
Birds of Prey (White) **49**:408
The Birds of the Air (Ellis) **40**:190-91, 193
"The Birds of Vietnam" (Carruth) **7**:41; **84**:134
"The Birds Poised to Fly" (Highsmith) **102**:203
The Birds Too Are Gone (Kemal)
See *Kuşlar da gitti*
"Birds Who Nest in the Garage" (Bell) **31**:50
"Birds with No Feet" (Barrett) **150**:5, 17
"Birds without Descent" (Aleixandre)
See "Pajaros sin descenso"
"Birdwatching" (Livesay) **79**:338
"Bird-Witted" (Moore) **8**:398
Birdy (Wharton) **18**:542-44; **37**:436-37, 439-43
"Birmingham" (MacNeice) **1**:186; **4**:316; **53**:231, 238
"Birmingham Sunday" (Hughes) **15**:295
"Birth" (Anand) **23**:18
"Birth" (Clarke) **61**:73
"Birth" (Hooker) **43**:197
"Birth" (MacBeth) **5**:265
"Birth" (Nin) **60**:267; **127**:365
"Birth Day" (Avison) **97**:92
"The Birth in a Narrow Room" (Brooks) **49**:26, 31; **125**:74, 76
"Birth of a Coachman" (Durcan) **43**:114
The Birth of a Grandfather (Sarton) **14**:482; **49**:312-13
Birth of a Hero (Gold) **42**:188, 191-92; **152**:124, 144
The Birth of a New Republic (Williamson) **29**:454
"Birth of a Notion" (Asimov) **26**:50
"Birth of a Salesman" (Tiptree) **48**:385; **50**:356
The Birth of a Story (Paustovsky) **40**:368
"The Birth of Black Boy" (Wright) **74**:389
The Birth of David (Robbe-Grillet) **14**:462
"Birth of Love" (Warren) **6**:556, 558; **8**:542-43; **39**:266
"Birth of Rainbow" (Hughes) **119**:271
The Birth of the Christ (Endō) **99**:285, 287
The Birth of the Clinic: An Archaeology of Medical Perception (Foucault)
See *Naissance de la clinique: Une archélologie du regard médical*
The Birth of the Modern: World Society 1815-1830 (Johnson) **147**:114-18, 120, 125-28, 130-31, 158
"The Birth of the Poet" (Acker) **111**:46
"Birth of the Virgin" (Swenson) **106**:349
"The Birth of Tragedy" (Oates) **6**:371
"The Birth of Venus" (Williams) **42**:456
Birth Rate: Biography of a Play (Rozewicz)
See *Przyrost naturalny: Biografia sztuki teatralnej*
"Birthday" (Ciardi) **40**:153; **129**:47
"Birthday" (Fuller)
See "Lines for a 21st Birthday"
"Birthday" (Louie) **70**:79
The Birthday Boys (Bainbridge) **130**:18, 20, 23-27, 30, 32-36, 39
"A Birthday Card" (Beer) **58**:36
"The Birthday Gift" (Deane) **122**:74
The Birthday Gift (Shapcott) **38**:404
Birthday Letters (Hughes) **119**:248, 250-52, 257
The Birthday Murderer (Bennett) **35**:44
"Birthday on the Acropolis" (Sarton) **49**:320
"The Birthday Party" (Berriault) **54**:3
"The Birthday Party" (Jackson) **60**:228
The Birthday Party (Pinter) **3**:386; **6**:407-08, 411, 413-14, 416-18, 420; **9**:420; **11**:437-38, 440-41, 444; **15**:422, 426; **27**:384-85, 387-89, 392-94, 396; **58**:371-72, 375-76, 384-85; **73**:249, 251-52, 256, 266, 276, 281
"Birthday Poem" (Simmons) **43**:411
"Birthday Poem" (Whalen) **29**:447
"Birthday Poem" (Young) **19**:477
"Birthday Poem (For Clifford Sealy)" (Lamming) **66**:220
"A Birthday Present" (Plath) **9**:426-27; **11**:447; **14**:423, 425; **17**:347-48, 366-67; **51**:345; **111**:168-69, 178
"Birthday Sestina" (Voigt) **54**:429
"Birthday Star Atlas" (Simic) **49**:341; **130**:311

"Birthday Thirty-Five: Diary Entry" (Chappell) **40**:143-44; **78**:92
The Birthgrave (Lee) **46**:233
"The Birthmark" (Ellison) **11**:182; **114**:93
"The Birthplace" (Heaney) **37**:168; **74**:168
Birthplace (Haavikko)
See *Synnyinmaa*
Birthplace: Moving into Nearness (Wilson) **49**:416-18
"Birthplace Revisited" (Corso) **11**:123
Birthright (Stribling) **23**:439, 445, 447-48
Births (Saroyan) **29**:363
"Birthstone" (Musgrave) **54**:341
Birthstone (Thomas) **22**:418
"Birthstones" (Van Duyn) **63**:443
"Bishop" (Barthelme) **23**:47
"Bishop Berkeley of Cloyne" (Young) **82**:396-397
"Bishop Erik Grave's Grave" (Gustafson) **36**:218
"Bishop of Cork Murders His Wife" (Durcan) **43**:114-15
The Bishop's Bonfire: A Sad Play within the Tune of a Polka (O'Casey) **5**:318, 320; **9**:407; **11**:409; **88**:257-58, 262-63, 270, 272-73
Bishop's Progress (Mano) **2**:270; **10**:327-28
"Bishopston Stream" (Watkins) **43**:444
Bison (Granin)
See *Zubr*
"Bison Crossing Near Mt. Rushmore" (Swenson) **61**:397
The Bit between My Teeth: A Literary Chronicle of 1950-1965 (Wilson) **8**:550; **24**:479, 481
A Bit of Singing and Dancing (Hill) **4**:227-28; **113**:281, 293, 297, 310, 312, 325, 330
"Bitch" (Dahl) **6**:121; **79**:183
"Bitch" (Jagger and Richard) **17**:224, 226, 229, 236
"Bitch" (Kizer) **80**:185
Bitches and Sad Ladies: An Anthology of Fiction by and about Women (Rotter) **65**:347, 350
"The Bite" (Stern) **40**:414
"Bite the Bullet" (Young) **17**:576
Bite the Dust (Rozewicz)
See *Do piachu*
"Bite-Me-Not; or, Fleur de Fur" (Lee) **46**:234
"Bites from the Bearded Crocodile" (Cabrera Infante) **120**:79-80
"The Biting Insects" (Kinnell) **129**:265
"Bitka kod Bistrice Lesne" (Krleža) **114**:167
"Bits and Pieces of Our Land" (Bell) **31**:49
Bitter Angel (Gerstler) **70**:155-59
The Bitter Box (Clark) **19**:104-05
"A Bitter Farce" (Schwartz) **10**:462; **87**:334
"Bitter Fruit of the Tree" (Brown) **59**:265
The Bitter Glass (Dillon) **17**:94
The Bitter Heritage: Vietnam and American Democracy, 1941-1966 (Schlesinger) **84**:361, 373
Bitter Lemons (Durrell) **8**:193; **13**:188
Bitter Medicine (Paretsky) **135**:324, 345, 354, 360-62, 364-65
"The Bitter Moon" (Winters) **32**:468
"The Bitter River" (Hughes) **108**:283
"Bitter Sorrow for Three Sleepwalkers" (García Márquez)
See "Amargura para tres sonámbulos"
Bitter Sweet (Coward) **1**:64; **29**:132, 137
The Bitter Tears of Petra von Kant (Fassbinder) **20**:106-09
"Bitter Thought in Exile" (Kunene) **85**:175
"Bitterness" (Ostriker) **132**:318
"Bitterness for Three Sleepwalkers" (García Márquez)
See "Amargura para tres sonámbulos"
Bivouac (Lopez y Fuentes)
See *Campamento*
Bizarre Behavior (Innaurato) **60**:200-01
Bizou (Klein) **30**:244
Den blaa Pekingeser (Abell) **15**:2, 7
"Blacamán el bueno vendedor de milagros" (García Márquez)
See "Blacamán the Good, Vendor of Miracles"
"Blacamán the Good, Vendor of Miracles" (García Márquez) **27**:147; **47**:151
The Black Aesthetic (Gayle) **65**:364
Black African Poems (Cendrars) **106**:190
The Black Album (Kureishi) **135**:267-69, 272-74, 276, 279-80, 283, 285-89, 293, 303
Black Alibi (Woolrich) **77**:389, 400, 404
Black Amber (Whitney) **42**:433
Black and Blue (Jagger and Richard) **17**:236, 238, 242
Black and Blue Magic (Snyder) **17**:470
"Black and Tan" (Bell) **102**:5-6
"The Black and White" (Pinter) **27**:387
Black and White (Brophy) **105**:16
Black and White (Naipaul) **32**:326-28; **39**:355-57
Black and White (Sorrentino) **7**:449
Black and White Keys (Hood) **28**:195-96
Black and White Minstrels (Taylor) **27**:443
"The Black Angel" (Montale)
See "L'angelo nero"
Black Angel (Cristofer) **28**:97
The Black Angel (Woolrich) **77**:389, 390-92, 394-95, 397-98, 400-01, 403-05
"Black Angels" (Friedman) **56**:97
Black Angels: Stories (Friedman) **3**:165
Black April (Peterkin) **31**:302-06, 309-12
"Black Art" (Baraka) **5**:48; **115**:39
"The Black Art" (Sexton) **10**:468; **53**:316, 319-20, 324
Black as He's Painted (Marsh) **53**:247, 249, 254
"Black as Ink" (Lee) **46**:234
Black Athena: The Afroasiatic Roots of Classical Civilization, Volume 1—The Fabrication of Ancient Greece, 1785-1985 (Bernal) **70**:363, 371, 387
Black Bagatelles (Hall) **51**:174-75
"The Black Ball" (Ellison) **114**:127
"Black Bart" (Dickinson) **49**:102-03
The Black BC's (Clifton) **66**:67, 86-7
The Black Beast (Audiberti)
See *La fête noire*
Black Beech and Honeydew: An Autobiography (Marsh) **53**:248, 257
Black Betty (Mosley) **97**:347-48, 350-54, 358, 361
"The Black Bird" (Ngũgĩ wa Thiong'o) **36**:317
Black Body Blues (Edwards) **43**:138-39
"The Black Book" (Smith) **43**:422
The Black Book (Durrell) **1**:84-5; **4**:147; **6**:154; **8**:192; **13**:184-85; **41**:136, 138
The Black Book (Morrison) **87**:264, 277-78
"The Black Box" (Ewart) **46**:154
Black Box (Oz) **54**:352-57
The Black Boxer (Bates) **46**:51
"Black Boy" (Boyle) **58**:66
Black Boy: A Record of Childhood and Youth (Wright) **1**:379-80; **3**:545; **4**:594, 597; **9**:583-86; **14**:596-98; **21**:434-35, 442-44, 448-49, 457; **74**:355-96
"The Black Boy Looks at the White Boy" (Baldwin) **13**:52; **42**:18; **50**:293; **127**:143
"Black Cargo Ships of War" (Ferron) **94**:103
The Black Cat Tavern (Mahfūz)
See *Khammārat al-qitt al-aswad*
The Black Cauldron (Alexander) **35**:23, 25
"The Black Christ" (Madhubuti) **73**:208-09
Black Cloud, White Cloud: Two Novellas and Two Stories (Douglas) **73**:65-7, 69, 73-5, 80-3, 87, 93, 95
Black Coach (Jordan) **37**:193
Black Coffee (Christie) **39**:437
Black Comedy (Shaffer) **5**:386-89; **14**:486; **18**:475
"The Black Cottage" (Frost) **10**:198
"Black Cow" (Becker and Fagen) **26**:84
"Black Critics and the Pitfalls of Canon Formation" (West) **134**:374, 383
"Black Crow" (Mitchell) **12**:443
The Black Curtain (Woolrich) **77**:389-90, 394, 397-98, 400, 404
"BLACK DADA NIHILISMUS" (Baraka) **5**:45, 48; **10**:19; **115**:39
"Black Dog" (Page and Plant) **12**:475, 480, 482
Black Dog, Red Dog (Dobyns) **37**:80-2
"Black Dominion" (Senghor)
See "Domaine noir"
Black Dougal (Walker) **14**:552
The Black Dudley Murder (Allingham)
See *The Crime at Black Dudley*
Black Eagle Child: The Facepaint Narratives (Young Bear) **94**:373-78
Black Easter (Blish) **14**:83, 87
"Black Edge" (Lee) **90**:177
Black Elk Speaks (Neihardt) **32**:335-36
Black Faces, White Faces (Gardam) **43**:166-67, 170
The Black Feast (Audiberti)
See *La fête noire*
Black Feeling, Black Talk (Giovanni) **117**:178, 190, 194
Black Feeling, Black Talk, Black Judgement (Giovanni) **19**:190-91; **64**:182, 185-86, 188, 190-91, 195; **117**:181-82, 185, 191
"The Black Ferris" (Bradbury) **42**:36
"The Black Filly" (Lane) **25**:285
Black Fire (Jones and Neal) **65**:371
"Black Flakes" (Celan)
See "Schwarze Flocken"
The Black Flame (Du Bois) **64**:117, 119; **96**:133
"Black for Dinner" (Colter) **58**:143
"Black Friday" (Becker and Fagen) **26**:80
Black Gangster (Goines) **80**:92, 95-7
The Black Gate (Arghezi)
See *Poarta neagră*
Black Genesis: Fortress of Evil (Hubbard) **43**:207
The Black Girl (Ousmane)
See *La Noire de...*
Black Girl Lost (Goines) **80**:93
"Black Goblet" (Pasternak) **7**:298
"Black Hair" (Soto) **80**:282-83, 288-89
"The Black Hand of the Raj" (McGrath) **55**:73
Black Hearts in Battersea (Aiken) **35**:17, 20
"The Black Helmet" (Glassco) **9**:237
The Black Hermit (Ngũgĩ wa Thiong'o) **7**:266; **36**:320
"The Black Hills" (Everson) **5**:123
"Black Hills Survival Gathering, 1980" (Hogan) **73**:148, 150
"Black Hole" (Swan) **69**:362-63
The Black Hole (Mowat) **26**:336
Black Holes and Baby Universes and Other Essays (Hawking) **105**:69, 71
"Black Holes Aren't Black" (Hawking) **105**:67
Black Holes, Black Stockings (Broumas) **73**:11-15
Black Holes, White Dwarfs, and Superstars (Branley) **21**:22
The Black Horses (Vesaas)
See *Dei svarte hestane*
Black Hosts (Senghor)
See *Hosties noires*
"The Black House" (Highsmith) **42**:215
The Black House (Highsmith) **42**:214; **102**:199
The Black House (Theroux) **5**:427-28; **8**:512; **11**:531; **28**:425-26; **46**:405
Black in America (Jackson) **12**:291
The Black Interpreters (Gordimer) **33**:183; **70**:163, 172
"Black Is My Favorite Color" (Malamud) **2**:266; **44**:416, 419
Black Is the Color of the Cosmos: Essays on Afro-American Literature and Culture, 1942-1981 (Davis) **65**:397
Black Island Memorial (Neruda)
See *Memorial de Isla Negra*
Black Jack (Garfield) **12**:217-18, 224-26, 230,

232, 234-35, 237, 240
"Black Jackets" (Gunn) **32**:208
The Black Jacobins: Toussaint L'Ouverture and the San Domingo Revolution (James) **33**:218-19, 221-22, 225
"The Black Jewel" (Merwin) **45**:275; **88**:205
The Black Joke (Mowat) **26**:339, 341-43
Black Judgement (Giovanni) **19**:191; **117**:178, 190, 195, 198
"Black Kettle Raises the Stars and Stripes" (Simpson) **7**:429
Black Lamb and Grey Falcon (West) **7**:525-26; **9**:561-63; **31**:455-56, 458, 460; **50**:394, 396, 398-402, 404-09
"Black Liberation/Socialist Revolution" (Baraka) **14**:49
Black Light (Kinnell) **3**:270; **5**:215
"The Black Lights" (Jones) **81**:62, 65, 67
Black Like Me (Griffin) **68**:202-03
Black Literature and Literary Theory (Gates) **65**:365, 378, 380, 398
Black Looks: Race and Representation (Hooks) **94**:150, 152-53, 156, 159-60
"Black Love" (Madhubuti) **73**:211
"The Black Madonna" (Lessing) **22**:279
"The Black Madonna" (Spark) **13**:522; **40**:401, 404
"Black magic" (Randall) **135**:396
"Black Magic" (Sanchez) **116**:277-78, 294
Black Magic (Morand)
See *Magie noire*
"The Black Magic of Barney Haller" (Thurber) **5**:429, 438
Black Magic: Sabotage, Target Study, Black Art; Collected Poetry, 1961-1967 (Baraka) **5**:46-8; **14**:45; **115**:10, 38-9
Black Magnificence (Walker) **19**:454
"Black Man" (Wonder) **12**:659-60, 662-63
"A Black Man Sings in New York City" (Guillén) **79**:230
"A Black Man Talks of Reaping" (Bontemps) **18**:65
"Black Man with a Horn" (Klein) **34**:71
"The Black Man's Lament" (Damas)
See "La complainte du nère"
"Black Maps" (Strand) **71**:285
Black Marina (Tennant) **52**:402-04
Black Marsden (Harris) **25**:210, 216
A Black Mass (Baraka) **5**:47-8; **115**:34, 36, 40-4
Black Mass (Bond) **23**:66
"The Black Mesa" (Merrill) **13**:381
"Black Messiah" (Davies) **21**:103-04
Black Mischief (Waugh) **1**:359; **3**:512; **13**:584-87; **27**:470, 477; **107**:357, 362, 370-71, 383, 393, 396
Black Misery (Hughes) **35**:219; **108**:336
"Black Money" (Gallagher) **18**:169
Black Money (Macdonald) **2**:255; **14**:334-35; **41**:266, 270
The Black Moon (Graham) **23**:194
"Black Mother Praying in the Summer of 1943" (Dodson) **79**:191
"Black Mother Woman" (Lorde) **71**:232, 245
Black Mountain Breakdown (Smith) **25**:407-08, 410-11; **73**:340-41, 343, 348, 358
"Black Mountain Side" (Page and Plant) **12**:479, 482
Black Music (Baraka) **14**:45; **33**:62; **115**:28, 39
Black Narcissus (Godden) **53**:150-53, 155-56, 160, 163-64
"Black Night" (Seger) **35**:380
Black Night Window (Newlove) **14**:377
Black Novel (with Argentines) (Valenzuela)
See *Novela negra con arentinos*
"A Black November Turkey" (Wilbur) **3**:530
"Black Nude" (Tomlinson) **13**:546
The Black Obelisk (Remarque) **21**:332
Black on Black: Baby Sister and Selected Writings (Himes) **4**:229; **7**:159; **18**:249; **108**:227
Black Opal (Prichard) **46**:330-32, 335-36, 338-41
Black Orpheus and Other Love Poems (Komunyakaa) **94**:223
The Black Path of Fear (Woolrich) **77**:404
The Black Pearl (O'Dell) **30**:270, 273
"The Black Pen" (Donnell) **34**:159
"The Black Pentecostal Fire" (Brown) **5**:78
"Black People!" (Baraka) **5**:48
Black Picture Show (Gunn) **5**:152-53
"The Black Pig" (Montague) **46**:277
"Black Poems, Poseurs and Power" (Giovanni) **19**:192; **64**:183; **117**:183
"Black Poet, White Critic" (Randall) **135**:389
"Black Poetics/for the many to come" (Madhubuti) **73**:198
Black Poetry: A Supplement to Anthologies Which Exclude Black Poets (Randall) **135**:374, 376-77, 382, 385, 393, 396
The Black Poets (Randall) **135**:382, 385, 395
"Black Pony Eating Grass" (Bly) **15**:68
Black Power (Wright) **4**:596; **14**:597
Black Pride (Madhubuti) **2**:238; **73**:191, 205, 207-10, 214-15
"The Black Prince" (Grau) **146**:126, 130, 148
The Black Prince (Murdoch) **3**:347-49; **4**:368, 370; **6**:343, 345, 348-49; **11**:384; **31**:287-88, 290; **51**:287-89, 291
The Black Prince, and Other Stories (Grau) **4**:207, 210; **146**:122, 125-26, 128-29, 132-35, 137, 142, 146, 149, 159-62
"The Black Rabbit" (White) **30**:452
Black Rain (Ibuse)
See *Kuroi ame*
Black Reconstruction: An Essay toward a History of the Part Which Black Folk Played in the Attempt to Reconstruct Democracy in America, 1860-1880 (Du Bois) **13**:180-81; **64**:105-07, 116; **96**:146, 149, 160
"The Black Rhino" (Hughes) **119**:291
The Black Rider (Burroughs) **109**:182
"Black River" (Kenny) **87**:248
Black Robe (Moore) **90**:263-69, 272-76, 283-89, 296, 298
"Black Rook in Rainy Weather" (Plath) **11**:447; **51**:344; **111**:202
The Black Rose (Costain) **30**:93, 95-8
Black Sea (Paustovsky) **40**:368
"The Black Sheep" (Boell)
See "Die schwarzen schafe"
Black Sheep (Rice) **7**:360; **49**:305
Black Ship to Hell (Brophy) **29**:92; **105**:3, 7, 9, 12, 30, 34
The Black Shrike (MacLean) **50**:348-49
"Black Shroud" (Ginsberg) **109**:364
"Black Shylock" (Auchincloss) **45**:30
"Black Silk" (Gallagher) **63**:116, 119
"Black Sketches" (Madhubuti) **73**:206
Black Skins and White Masks (Fanon)
See *Peau noire, masques blancs*
Black Skins, White Masks (Fanon)
See *Peau noire, masques blancs*
"Black Snakes" (Oliver) **98**:261, 265
Black Snow (Aquin)
See *Neige noir*
"Black Song" (Guillén)
See "Canto negro"
The Black Soul (O'Flaherty) **5**:321
The Black Spaniel Mystery (Cavanna) **12**:97
"The Black Spear" (Hayden) **5**:168-69
The Black Spectacles (Carr)
See *The Problem of the Green Capsule*
"black spots are white..." (Rozewicz)
See "czarne plamy s biale..."
Black Spring (Miller) **4**:351; **14**:375; **43**:298-99; **84**:234-36, 239, 241, 243, 262
"The Black Stag" (Char) **9**:166
The Black Stallion (Farley) **17**:115
The Black Stallion and Satan (Farley) **17**:116
The Black Stallion and the Girl (Farley) **17**:118
The Black Stallion Mystery (Farley) **17**:117
The Black Stallion Returns (Farley) **17**:115
The Black Stallion Revolts (Farley) **17**:117
The Black Stallion's Filly (Farley) **17**:116-17
The Black Stallion's Ghost (Farley) **17**:118
The Black Stallion's Sulky Colt (Farley) **17**:117
The Black Star Passes (Campbell) **32**:73, 76, 80
"The Black Stone" (Brooks) **125**:108
Black Sun (Abbey) **36**:17-19; **59**:242
Black Sun: Depression and Melancholia (Kristeva)
See *Soleil noir: Dépression et melancholie*
Black Sun: The Brief Transit and Violent Eclipse of Harry Crosby (Wolff) **41**:457-58
"The Black Swan" (Merrill) **13**:379; **91**:238
Black Swan (Hope) **52**:216
The Black Swan (Walser)
See *Der schwarze Schwan*
"Black Swans" (McAuley) **45**:254
Black Thunder (Bontemps) **1**:37; **18**:63-5
Black Tickets (Phillips) **15**:419-21; **33**:305-08; **139**:201-04, 206-07, 209, 215-16, 218, 220
"Black Tie" (Barthelme) **117**:6
The Black Tower (James) **18**:273; **46**:205-09; **122**:121, 128, 134, 145-46, 165, 183
"The Black Tsar" (Morand)
See "Le tsar noir"
"Black Tuesday" (Swenson) **106**:321
"The Black Underclass and Black Philosophers" (West) **134**:381
"The Black Unicorn" (Lorde) **18**:309
The Black Unicorn (Lorde) **18**:309; **71**:231-36, 240-41, 243, 246, 252, 254, 257-58, 260, 262
Black Venus (Carter) **41**:121-22
The Black Venus (Davies) **23**:143, 145
"The Black Virginity" (Loy) **28**:246, 253
Black Voices from Prison (Knight) **40**:281, 283, 285
Black Water (Oates) **108**:374, 395-96
"The Black Wedding" (Singer) **9**:487; **15**:504; **69**:306; **111**:305
"A Black Wedding Song" (Brooks) **15**:94; **49**:36
The Black Wine (Bennett) **5**:58-9
Black Wolf (Edmonds) **35**:146
"Black Woman" (Senghor) **130**:240
The Black Woman: An Anthology (Bambara) **88**:5
"Black Women and Feminism" (Hooks) **94**:144
"The Black Writer and the Southern Experience" (Walker) **103**:413
"A Black Writer's Burden" (Achebe) **26**:18
"Black Xmas" (Monette) **82**:333
Black Zodiac (Wright) **119**:180-89; **146**:355, 358, 360, 367-69, 371, 375-76, 378-81
"Blackberries" (Komunyakaa) **94**:241
"Blackberries" (Oliver) **98**:256
Blackberries (McClure) **10**:333
"Blackberry Eating" (Kinnell) **129**:235
"Blackberry Winter" (Warren) **1**:353; **4**:579
Blackberry Winter: My Earlier Years (Mead) **37**:279-80
"Blackberrying" (Plath) **3**:389; **9**:425; **51**:353; **111**:214
"Blackberry-Picking" (Heaney) **91**:119
"Blackbird" (Lennon and McCartney) **35**:279
"Blackbird" (Murakami) **150**:43
"Blackbird Bye Bye" (Bernard) **59**:45-6
Blackbird Bye Bye (Bernard) **59**:43-45
"Blackbird in a Bramble Bough" (Kiely) **43**:239, 244
"Blackbird in a Sunset Bush" (MacCaig) **36**:285
"Blackbird Pie" (Carver) **53**:62, 65; **55**:273, 275, 284
"A Blackbird Singing" (Thomas) **48**:379
The Blackboard Jungle (Hunter) **31**:217-18, 220-22, 225-26
"The Blackened Pot" (Ritsos) **31**:326, 328
The Blackened Pot (Ritsos) **13**:488
"Blackerchief Dick" (Allingham) **19**:11
Blackeyes (Potter) **58**:393-94, 397-98, 400; **86**:346, 352; **123**:243, 269, 275
"Blackgirl Learning" (Madhubuti) **73**:213

The Blackheath Poisonings: A Victorian Murder Mystery (Symons) **14**:523-24; **32**:428
"Blackie, the Electric Rembrandt" (Gunn) **3**:215
The Blacking Factory (Sheed) **2**:392-94; **10**:473; **53**:339
Black-Label (Damas) **84**:156-57, 159-164, 167, 176-78, 180, 182, 186
"Blackleaf Swamp" (Oliver) **19**:362; **98**:266
Blackmail (Hitchcock) **16**:352
The Blackmailer (Colegate) **36**:113-14
"Blackman/An Unfinished History" (Madhubuti) **73**:196, 212, 214
"Blackness" (Kincaid) **68**:208, 210-11; **137**:138, 142-43
"The Blackness of Blackness: A Critique on the Sign and the Signifying Monkey" (Gates) **65**:382, 393, 397, 399
Blackrobe: Isaac Jogues, b. March 11, 1607, d. October 18, 1646 (Kenny) **87**:241-43, 245, 252-53, 258
The Blacks: A Clown Show (Genet) See *Les nègres: Clownerie*
"Black-Shouldered Kite" (Wright) **53**:423
"Blacksnake" (Jiles) **58**:273, 281
"The Blackstone Rangers" (Brooks) **49**:30
"Blackstudies" (Lorde) **71**:232, 250
"The Blackthorn Bush in Spring" (Blunden) **56**:34
"Blackwater Mountain" (Wright) **6**:580
"Blackwater Wood" (Oliver) **98**:257, 267
Blade of Light (Carpenter) **41**:102-03
Blade on a Feather (Potter) **86**:346-47
"Blaen Crwt" (Clarke) **61**:73, 79-80
"Blaise Pascal Lip-syncs the Void" (Wright) **146**:350, 365
Blake (Ackroyd) **140**:55, 58, 62
Blake and Tradition (Raine) **7**:352
Blake's Apocalypse (Bloom) **103**:11, 13, 19
"Blake's Bible" (Frye) **70**:274
"Blake's Sunflower" (Smart) **54**:421
"Blame It on the Stones" (Kristofferson) **26**:266
Blaming (Taylor) **29**:409-12
Blanche ou l'oubli (Aragon) **3**:14
"Blanchi" (Damas) **84**:171, 176-77
Blanco (Paz) **3**:376; **6**:398; **10**:389, 391; **51**:327, 333-34; **65**:182-84, 196, 198-200
Les blancs (Hansberry) **17**:189-90, 192-93; **62**:242
"Blancura" (Aleixandre) **9**:14
Bland Beginning (Symons) **14**:523
"Blank ..." (Ellison) **42**:131; **139**:133
"A Blank" (Gunn) **81**:180-81
"The Blank Page" (Dinesen) **10**:145, 152; **95**:55
"Blank Thought" (Paz) See "El pensamiento en blanco"
The Blanket Word (Arundel) **17**:18
"Blankets" (La Guma) **19**:272
"Blanks" (Wittlin) **25**:469
"The Blasphemer" (Singer) **6**:509
The Blasphemer's Banquet (Harrison) **129**:173, 175-78, 183, 185, 210, 212
"Blast Off" (Grenville) **61**:154
"Blasting from Heaven" (Levine) **118**:299
Blasts and Benedictions (O'Casey) **15**:406; **88**:260, 267
Blätter aus dem Brotsack (Frisch) **44**:190-91, 193, 195
Blätter und Steine (Jünger) **125**:222, 251
Blaubart (Frisch) **32**:193-95; **44**:206-07
Blaze of Noon (Gann) **23**:162-63
The Blaze of Noon (Heppenstall) **10**:271-72
Blazing Saddles (Brooks) **12**:76-82
The Bleaching Ground (Vesaas) See *Bleikeplassen*
The Bleaching Place (Vesaas) See *Bleikeplassen*
The Bleaching Yard (Vesaas) See *Bleikeplassen*
"Bleating" (Zamora) **89**:394
Die Blechtrommel (Grass) **1**:125-26; **2**:171-73; **4**:201-04, 206; **6**:207-08; **11**:247-48, 251-52; **15**:259-60; **22**:189, 191; **32**:197-98, 200, 203-04; **49**:140, 142-43; **88**:134-82
"Bleecker Street, Summer" (Walcott) **42**:423; **67**:353
"Bleeding" (Swenson) **14**:519-21; **61**:393, 401; **106**:328, 349
"The Bleeding Heart" (Stafford) **68**:449
The Bleeding Heart (French) **18**:158-60; **60**:147
"Bleed-Through" (Harjo) **83**:268
Bleikeplassen (Vesaas) **48**:404, 406-07, 413
"Bleistein-Chicago Semite Viennese" (Eliot) **13**:202
Die Blendung (Canetti) **3**:98; **14**:119-21; **25**:107-14; **75**:120-21, 123-31, 134-37, 140, 142-44; **86**:293-95, 297-98, 301-03
"Bless Me, Father" (Dubus) **36**:147; **97**:211
Bless Me, Ultima (Anaya) **23**:22-5; **148**:3, 5-13, 15-16, 19-20, 25, 27-28, 29-30, 32-36, 39-40, 44, 48-51, 53-58, 60-63
Bless the Beasts and the Children (Swarthout) **35**:402-03
"Bless You" (Lennon) **35**:268
Blessed above Women (Johnson) **27**:213
"Blessed Are Those Who Mourn" (Maitland) **49**:235
Blessed Art Thou (Ingalls) **42**:232-35
"Blessed Assurance" (Hughes) **108**:329
Blessed Assurance: A Moral Tale (Gurganus) **70**:190-92, 194, 196
"Blessed Is the Man" (Moore) **47**:264
"Blessed Is the Name of the Lord Forever" (Dylan) **77**:186
"The Blessed Mary Fogarty" (Simmons) **43**:411
"The Blessed Virgin Mary Compared to a Window" (Merton) **83**:378, 389
"Blessing" (Hogan) **73**:149
"The Blessing" (Kizer) **39**:169
"A Blessing" (Wright) **3**:540, 543; **5**:521; **10**:543
The Blessing (Mitford) **44**:484, 489-92
The Blessing Way (Hillerman) **62**:256, 259-60
"Blessings" (Dubus) **97**:213, 236-37
Le bleu du ciel (Bataille) **29**:39
"Bleue maison" (Blunden) **56**:41
Des bleus à l'âame (Sagan) **6**:481-82; **17**:427
"Blickwechsel" (Wolf) **29**:464; **150**:237
"Blight" (Dybek) **114**:70-1, 76, 81-2
"Blighters" (Sassoon) **36**:385-86, 391, 397; **130**:175, 182 85, 192, 215
The Blind Beauty (Pasternak) **10**:382
"Blind Bird" (Breytenbach) **126**:78
The Blind Bow-Boy (Van Vechten) **33**:386-89, 392, 394-95, 397-98
Blind Chance (Kieslowski) See *Przypadek*
Blind Date (Foote) **51**:135
Blind Date (Kosinski) **10**:307-09; **15**:315-17; **53**:216-17, 219, 221, 223, 226-27; **70**:298, 303, 306
"Blind Dog" (Narayan) **28**:302; **121**:418
"Blind Euchre" (DeMarinis) **54**:100
Blind Eye (Edmonds) **35**:147
Blind Fireworks (MacNeice) **4**:317; **10**:324; **53**:233-34
"Blind Girls" (Phillips) **139**:201
"The Blind Leading the Blind" (Lowell) **8**:350
"The Blind Leading the Blind" (Mueller) **51**:279
The Blind Lion (Allen) **84**:9, 37
"Blind Love" (Pritchett) **13**:467-68; **41**:330, 333
"The Blind Man" (Wright) **53**:417-19, 428
The Blind Man (Duerrenmatt) See *Der Blinde*
The Blind Man (Dürrenmatt) See *Der Blinde*
"A Blind Man at the Museum" (Nemerov) **36**:309
Blind Man with a Pistol (Himes) **2**:194-95; **18**:246; **58**:258, 266-68, 270; **108**:234, 237-40, 242, 247, 249-52, 265, 268-72, 277, 278-79
"Blind Man's Buff" (Fuller) **62**:196, 201
Blind Man's Holiday (Everson) **27**:133-34
"A Blind Man's Tale" (Tanizaki) See "Mōmoku monogatari"
The Blind Mice (Friel) **42**:163
"A Blind Negro Singer" (Smith) **64**:398
Blind Photographer (Rosenblatt) **15**:447
"Blind School" (Buckley) **57**:136
"The Blind Seer of Ambon" (Merwin) **88**:209
"Blind Singer in a Train" (Mahapatra) **33**:282
Blind Understanding (Middleton) **38**:333-34
Der Blinde (Duerrenmatt) **102**:53
Der Blinde (Dürrenmatt) **8**:194; **11**:168-69; **15**:194-95, 199
"Der blinde junge" (Loy) **28**:246, 248, 251
"Blinded by the Light" (Springsteen) **17**:477, 487
Blinded by the Light (Brancato) **35**:66-9
Blindenschrift (Enzensberger) **43**:146, 151
Der Blindensturz (Hofmann) **54**:226, 227-28, 230
"Blinder" (Gordimer) **33**:185
The Blindfold (Hustvedt) **76**:56-63
Blindfolded (Saura) See *Los ojos vendados*
The Blinding (Canetti) See *Die Blendung*
"The Blindman Contradictions: an Interview with Rudy Wiebe" (Wiebe) **138**:380
"Blindness" (Borges) **48**:47
"Blindness" (Campbell) **32**:74, 78, 80
Blindness (Green) **13**:251, 254; **97**:242, 247, 251-57, 259-60, 262-64, 266, 287, 292
Blindness and Insight (de Man) **55**:384, 386, 396, 400-01, 409, 413-14
"Bliss" (Johnston) **51**:241, 243
Bliss (Carey) **40**:129-30, 132-33; **55**:114, 117; **96**:21-6, 28-31, 35-6, 39-43, 50, 52-5, 57, 59, 63, 65, 70, 72, 80-1
Blithe Spirit: An Improbable Farce (Coward) **29**:135, 137-39; **51**:70, 73, 77
Blitzkrieg (Deighton) **22**:117
Bliznets v tuchakh (Pasternak) **10**:387; **18**:381; **63**:289
"The Blizzard" (Dacey) **51**:81
The Blizzard (Leonov) See *Metel*
"Blk/Rhetoric" (Sanchez) **116**:272, 295, 327
"blk / wooooomen / chant" (Sanchez) **116**:295
"Block" (Carruth) **84**:136
"The Block" (Kelman) **58**:295
"The Block" (Van Duyn) **63**:445; **116**:413
Block-notes de un regista (Fellini) **16**:299; **85**:63-4, 73
Blomskryf: Uit die gedigte van Breyten Breyten-bach en Jan Blom (Breytenbach) **23**:83; **126**:79
The Blond Baboon (van de Wetering) **47**:407
"Blonde in the Bleachers" (Mitchell) **12**:437
Blonde on Blonde (Dylan) **4**:149; **6**:157; **12**:182, 184, 191, 199; **77**:168-69, 173, 177, 190
Blonde Venus (Sternberg) **20**:372
"Blood" (Hoffman) **141**:294
"Blood" (Murray) **40**:335-36, 340
"Blood" (Singer) **3**:458; **15**:504; **111**:296, 319
Blood & Family (Kinsella) **138**:127-28, 130-31, 136-37, 146, 148, 150, 152, 154
Blood and Grits (Crews) **23**:136; **49**:72-4, 76-7
Blood and Guile (Hoffman) **141**:316-17, 319-23, 325
Blood and Guts in High School Plus Two (Acker) **45**:15-19; **111**:5-6, 9-10, 18, 20, 24-5, 31, 34, 37-40, 42, 44-5
"Blood and Its Relationship to Water" (Carlson) **54**:39
Blood and Sand (Mamoulian) **16**:424, 426-28
"Blood and Water" (McGrath) **55**:73-4, 76
Blood and Water and Other Tales (McGrath) **55**:73-7
"Blood Bank" (Miller) **30**:263-64
The Blood Bay Colt (Farley) **17**:116
Blood, Bread, and Poetry: Selected Prose, 1979-1985 (Rich) **73**:319-22; **76**:215, 219

"Blood, Bread, and Poetry: The Location of the Poet" (Rich) **73**:323-24
Blood Brothers (Price) **12**:490-91
Blood Brothers (Shaffer) **60**:318, 320, 322
The Blood Countess (Codrescu) **121**:179, 181-82
"Blood Disease" (McGrath) **55**:73, 75
Blood Feud (Sutcliff) **26**:437
Blood Feud (Wertmueller) **16**:599-600
Blood for a Stranger (Jarrell) **2**:207-10; **6**:260; **13**:298-300
Blood for Blood (Gloag) **40**:212
The Blood Knot (Fugard) **5**:130; **9**:230, 232-34; **14**:190; **25**:175; **40**:196-97, 200-01, 203-04; **80**:61-6, 68-72, 74, 79-80, 83, 86
Blood Meridian, or, The Evening Redness in the West (McCarthy) **57**:337-38; **101**:142-46, 152-53, 157, 164-65, 168-70, 176-82, 186, 195-96, 198-99, 201-05
The Blood of a Poet (Cocteau)
See *Le sang d'un poète*
The Blood of Others (Beauvoir)
See *Le sang des autres*
Blood of Requited Love (Puig)
See *Sangre de amor correspondido*
"The Blood of Strangers" (Garrett) **3**:191
The Blood of the Bambergs (Osborne) **45**:313-14, 316
"Blood of the Conquistadores" (Alvarez) **93**:7
The Blood of the Lamb (De Vries) **1**:73; **2**:114; **7**:77; **28**:106, 109; **46**:134-35, 137
"Blood of Tyrants" (Bova) **45**:73
Blood on the Forge (Attaway) **92**:26-46
Blood on the Tracks (Dylan) **6**:157; **12**:191; **77**:172, 178
The Blood Oranges (Hawkes) **1**:139; **2**:185; **3**:223; **4**:214-19; **7**:140-46; **9**:268-69; **27**:190-92, 194-96, 199; **49**:161-64
The Blood Red Game (Moorcock)
See *The Sundered Worlds*
Blood Red, Sister Rose (Keneally) **5**:210-12; **10**:298; **19**:245-46; **43**:236; **117**:215, 217, 227-30, 234, 248
Blood Relations (Dillon) **17**:100
Blood Relations (Pollock) **50**:224-26
"Blood Relatives" (Apple) **33**:20-2
Blood Relatives (Chabrol) **16**:184
"Blood River Day" (Brutus) **43**:92, 96
"Blood, Sea" (Calvino)
See "Il sangue, il mare"
Blood Shot (Paretsky) **135**:324-26, 328-33, 335-37, 345, 363
Blood Simple (The Coen Brothers) **108**:120-30, 133, 135-40, 142, 145-47, 149, 151-52, 157-62, 165-70
"Blood Sisters" (Haldeman) **61**:181
Blood Sisters (De Palma)
See *Sisters*
Blood Sisters: An Examination of Conscience (Miner) **40**:326-28
"Blood Son" (Matheson) **37**:246
"Blood Soup" (Dybek) **114**:64-5, 71, 73-6
Blood Sport (Francis) **22**:151-52; **42**:148-50, 154-58; **102**:127, 131, 147
Blood Sport (Jones) **7**:192-93
"Blood, Taint, Flaw, Degeneration" (Coetzee) **66**:99, 101
"Blood Test" (Swenson) **61**:405
Blood Tie (Settle) **19**:410; **61**:373, 378, 385, 387-88
Blood Ties (Richards) **59**:187
"Bloodbirth" (Lorde) **71**:232
"Blood-Burning Moon" (Toomer) **13**:552; **22**:426
"Bloodchild" (Butler) **121**:103-04, 110-13, 123-24, 126-31, 141, 143-44
Bloodchild and Other Stories (Butler) **121**:141-43, 146
"Bloodfall" (Boyle) **90**:56
Bloodfire: A Poem (Chappell) **40**:142, 144-45, 147; **78**:91-2, 96, 111
"Bloodfire in the Garden" (Chappell) **78**:92, 96
The Bloodletters (Greenberg) **57**:226-28
Bloodline (Gaines) **3**:179; **18**:167; **86**:173, 177
Bloodlines (D'Aguiar) **145**:129-30
Bloodlines (Wright) **6**:581; **13**:612, 614; **28**:456-57, 460; **146**:304-05, 309, 312, 321-22, 326-27, 330, 333, 336, 360, 367-68, 373-74, 379
"Bloodshed" (Ozick) **7**:288; **62**:341-42, 353-54; **155**:178, 181, 183-84, 190-91, 193, 196, 209, 222
Bloodshed and Three Novellas (Ozick) **7**:288-89, 290; **28**:349-51, 355; **62**:350; **155**:170, 178, 180, 185, 191, 216
"Bloodsmiles" (Madhubuti) **73**:206
A Bloodsmoor Romance (Oates) **33**:290-91, 293, 295-96; **52**:329, 331, 339; **108**:348, 375, 385, 391
"The Bloodstained Bridal Gown; or, Xavier Kilgarvan's Last Case" (Oates) **108**:349-51, 353
"The Bloodstained Pavement" (Christie) **48**:72; **110**:130, 141, 145
Bloodstone (Ivask)
See *Verikivi*
"Bloodstream" (Brunner) **8**:110
"The Bloody Chamber" (Carter) **41**:118
The Bloody Chamber, and Other Stories (Carter) **41**:116-18, 121-22; **76**:326, 330
The Bloody Country (Collier and Collier) **30**:71-2
Bloody Marvellous (Rathbone) **41**:338
Bloody Murder (Symons) **32**:425
"The Bloody Past, The Wandering Future" (Hospital) **145**:303, 311, 313
The Bloody Sun (Bradley) **30**:29
The Bloom of Candles: Verse from a Poet's Year (Lee) **90**:182
The Bloomingdale Papers (Carruth) **7**:41; **10**:100; **18**:87; **84**:119
"The Blooms of Dublin" (Burgess) **40**:119-20
Bloomsbury (Luke) **38**:317-18
Bloomsbury: A House of Lions (Edel) **29**:173-75
"The Bloomsbury Group Live at the Apollo" (Frazier) **46**:163-64
"Blor" (Mitford) **44**:489
Blosch (Sterchi) **65**:100-04
"Blossom" (Plumly) **33**:315
Blossom (Vachss) **106**:361-62
"Blossoms" (Oliver) **34**:247, 249; **98**:257, 296
"Blots" (Hollander) **5**:186
Blott on the Landscape (Sharpe) **36**:400
"The Blouse" (Hersey) **81**:329
"The Blow" (Neruda)
See "El golpe"
"Blow and Counterblow" (Montale)
See "Botta e riposta"
Blow Job (Warhol) **20**:415, 421
Blow Out (De Palma) **20**:83
"Blow, West Wind" (Warren) **10**:525
Blow Wind, Come Wrack (Child) **19**:103
Blow, Wind of Fruitfulness (Baxter) **14**:60-1
Blow Your House Down (Barker) **32**:14; **94**:2, 5, 7, 9, 11, 13, 15; **146**:7, 29-33, 41
Blowfish Live in the Sea (Fox) **121**:198-99, 231
"Blowin' in the Wind" (Dylan) **4**:149; **12**:183; **77**:161, 166-67
"Blowing Eggs" (Muldoon) **32**:317; **72**:265
The Blowing of the Seed (Everson) **5**:122
Blow-Job (Wilson) **33**:460, 463-64
Blown Away (Sukenick) **48**:370
Blown Figures (Thomas) **7**:472-73; **13**:538, 540; **37**:417, 423-24; **107**:316, 318-19, 333-36, 340-41, 344-45, 348, 351
"Blow-Up" (Cortázar)
See "Las babas del diablo"
Blow-Up (Antonioni) **20**:30-3, 35-7; **144**:5-6, 21-22, 24-28, 30-36, 39, 41-43, 49, 55, 58-60, 62-3, 66-8, 72, 80-1, 85, 87-9, 91, 97
Blow-Up, and Other Stories (Cortázar)
See *End of the Game, and Other Stories*
"Blowups Happen" (Heinlein) **55**:302
Blubber (Blume) **12**:47
"Blue" (Hillis) **66**:195-99
"Blue" (Swenson) **106**:344
Blue (Mitchell) **12**:436-37, 443
Blue above the Trees (Clark) **12**:129-30
Blue Adept (Anthony) **35**:36-8
"Blue Africa" (Levertov) **66**:240
"The Blue Angel" (Ginsberg) **36**:182; **109**:358
The Blue Angel (Sternberg) **20**:369-73
"Blue Arab" (Wright) **53**:427
Blue at the Mizzen (O'Brian) **152**:295-96, 300
"The Blue Background" (Aldiss) **40**:21
Blue Belle (Vachss) **106**:355-61
"Blue Blood" (Ferber) **93**:153
The Blue Boat (Mayne) **12**:388-89, 395
"Blue Boom Ceremonial" (Vizenor) **103**:293
Blue Boy on Skates (Rosenthal) **28**:391, 394
"Blue Bug" (Moore) **13**:396
"The Blue Car" (Valenzuela) **104**:382
"Blue Chair in a Sunny Day" (MacCaig) **36**:281
Blue Chicory (Niedecker) **10**:361; **42**:296
A Blue Child for that Shadow (Marqués)
See *Un niño azul para esa sombra*
Blue City (Macdonald) **3**:307; **14**:333; **34**:416; **41**:271
Blue Collar (Schrader) **26**:389-93, 395, 399
Blue Day (Lustig) **56**:188-89
"Blue Dive" (Chappell) **40**:142; **78**:95
"Blue Dodge" (Leyner) **92**:281
"The Blue Dress" (Olds) **85**:294
"The Blue Dress" (Trevor) **116**:385
The Blue Estuaries: Poems, 1923-1968 (Bogan) **4**:68; **39**:387-88, 390-93, 396; **46**:86-90; **93**:71, 102
Blue Eyes (Charyn) **5**:105; **8**:135-36
Blue Eyes, Black Hair (Duras)
See *Les yeux bleux, cheveux noir*
"The Blue Feather" (Bates) **46**:63
Blue Fin (Thiele) **17**:494
Blue Fire (Whitney) **42**:433
"Blue Flames" (Lustig) **56**:182
The Blue Flower (Fitzgerald) **143**:243-50, 252-53, 259-66, 268-70
"Blue Fox" (Yevtushenko) **126**:396
The Blue Garden (Howes) **15**:289
Blue Gardenia (Lang) **20**:216; **103**:87, 96, 99, 101
"The Blue Geranium" (Christie) **110**:140, 143-44
"The Blue Ghazals" (Rich) **7**:366; **11**:476; **18**:446; **36**:366
"Blue Girls" (Ransom) **4**:431
"Blue Glass" (Adcock) **41**:17-18
The Blue Hammer (Macdonald) **14**:328; **34**:417; **41**:270
The Blue Hawk (Dickinson) **12**:174-76
"Blue Heron" (Oliver) **98**:303
Blue Highways: A Journey into America (Heat-Moon) **29**:222-26
"The Blue Hour" (Graver) **70**:52, 54
"The Blue House" (Gilchrist) **143**:300, 315
"The Blue House" (Transtroemer) **65**:228
"Blue Island" (Powers) **1**:282
"Blue Island Intersection" (Sandburg) **10**:450
Blue Jacket: War Chief of the Shawnees (Eckert) **17**:106
The Blue Jay's Dance: A Birth Year (Erdrich) **120**:180-81
The Blue Knight (Wambaugh) **3**:508-09; **18**:532
"The Blue Lake" (Gustafson) **36**:212
The Blue Light (Riefenstahl) **16**:520-22, 525-26
The Blue Machines of Night (Hillis) **66**:193-94
The Blue Macushla (Murphy) **51**:305
The Blue Man (Platt) **26**:348
"The Blue Meridian" (Toomer) **22**:424, 427-28
Blue Meridian: The Search for the Great White Shark (Matthiessen) **5**:273; **7**:210; **32**:292; **64**:305-06, 309
"Blue Moles" (Plath) **11**:446-47; **111**:203
Blue Monday (Wakoski) **9**:554
"Blue Moon" (Phillips) **139**:205-6
"Blue Motel Room" (Mitchell) **12**:442
The Blue Mountains of China (Wiebe) **11**:567-69; **14**:572-74; **138**:309, 311, 314, 316, 326,

330, 336, 351-57, 372, 387-89, 393-95
Blue Movie (Southern) **7**:454
Blue Movie (Warhol) **20**:419
"The Blue Nap" (Matthews) **40**:322
Blue of Noon (Bataille) **29**:48
Blue Pastoral (Sorrentino) **40**:387-89
The Blue Pekinese (Abell)
See *Den blaa Pekingeser*
"Blue Poles" (Crase) **58**:164-65
"Blue Red and Grey" (Townshend) **17**:536
Blue Remembered Hills (Potter) **58**:392; **86**:345-46, 348-49, 351; **123**:232, 237, 265, 271, 275-77
"Blue Ridge" (Voigt) **54**:430, 432
"The Blue Rim of Memory" (Levertov) **15**:339
The Blue Room (Hare) **136**:305
The Blue Room (Simenon) **1**:309; **18**:486; **47**:375
The Blue Rose (Straub) **107**:304
The Blue Rose Trilogy (Straub) **107**:302
"Blue Serge" (Ferber) **93**:140
"Blue Skies Motel" (Creeley) **78**:142
Blue Skies, No Candy (Greene) **8**:252
"Blue Skies, White Breasts, Green Trees" (Stern) **40**:407
The Blue Sky (Donnell) **34**:156-58
"Blue Sonata" (Ashbery) **77**:45
"Blue Spanish Eyes" (Thomas) **107**:339-40, 346
"The Blue Stones" (Carver) **36**:100
"Blue Suburban" (Nemerov) **6**:361
"Blue Suede Shoes" (Ai) **69**:9-10, 17
"The Blue Swallows" (Nemerov) **36**:302
The Blue Swallows (Nemerov) **2**:306-08; **9**:394; **36**:302
"The Blue Swan: An Essay on Music in Poetry" (Wakoski) **40**:454-55
Blue Thunder (Green) **25**:199-200
"The Blue Tick Pig" (Stuart) **14**:514
"Blue Toboggans" (Morgan) **31**:275
Blue Velvet (Lynch) **66**:261, 263-69, 271
Blue Voyage (Aiken) **10**:3; **52**:25
"The Blue Water Man" (Valenzuela)
See "El fontanero azul"
"Blue Window" (Pollitt) **28**:367-68; **122**:202-03
Blue Window (Lucas) **64**:288-89, 292, 295-96
Blue Wine (Hollander) **14**:265-66
A Blue Wing Tilts at the Edge of the Sea (Hall) **13**:259
"The Blue Yonder: A Tale of Cleanliness" (Vollmann) **89**:277-78, 302
"Bluebeard" (Barthelme) **59**:251; **115**:81
Bluebeard (Frisch)
See *Blaubart*
Bluebeard (Ludlam) **46**:239-42, 244; **50**:343-45
Bluebeard (Vonnegut) **111**:361
Bluebeard and After (Heppenstall) **10**:272
"Bluebeard's Egg" (Atwood) **84**:67-8
Bluebeard's Egg (Atwood) **84**:67, 96, 105
"Bluebell Meadow" (Kiely) **23**:266; **43**:245
"Bluebird" (McCartney) **35**:282
"Bluebirdbluebirdthrumywindow" (Sanchez) **116**:302
"The Blue-Eyed Buddhist" (Gilchrist) **48**:121; **143**:316
"Blue-Eyed Giant" (Hikmet) **40**:244
Bluegate Fields (Perry) **126**:328
"Bluegill" (Phillips) **139**:205-6
"The Blueprint" (Blunden) **56**:34
"Blueprint for a Monument of War" (Klein) **19**:259
"Blueprint for Negro Writing" (Wright) **14**:597; **21**:451, 456
"Blues" (Damas)
See "Limbé"
"Blues" (Hughes) **35**:214
"Blues" (Sanchez) **116**:303-04, 328
Blues (Hersey) **81**:335, 337
"Blues Ain't No Mockin Bird" (Bambara) **88**:21, 27
Blues and Roots/Rue and Bluets (Williams) **13**:600
A Blues Book for Blue Black Magical Women (Sanchez) **116**:272, 274, 280-81, 299, 301-02, 309-11, 313, 316, 321
The Blues Brothers (Landis) **26**:274-76
"Blues des projets" (Butor) **3**:93
"Blues for a Melodeon" (McGinley) **14**:364
"Blues for Benny Kid Paret" (Smith) **22**:386
"Blues/for J. C. " (Broumas) **73**:2
"Blues for John Coltrane" (Matthews) **40**:318
"Blues for Men" (Hughes) **15**:291
Blues for Mister Charlie (Baldwin) **2**:32; **4**:40; **5**:40; **17**:27, 31, 33-4, 37, 40; **50**:282-83, 290; **127**:105, 107, 129, 145, 148
"Blues for Warren" (McGrath) **59**:175
Blues, Ideology, and Afro-American Literature: A Vernacular Theory (Baker) **65**:365, 382, 385
"Blues I'm Playing" (Hughes) **108**:313, 315
"Blues Montage" (Hughes) **108**:335
Blues People: Negro Music in White America (Baraka) **10**:19; **14**:46; **33**:54, 58, 60, 62; **115**:5-7, 9-10, 28, 32, 39
"The Blues Roots of Contemporary African-American Poetry" (Williams) **89**:348, 355
"Blues Song for the Phoenix Bus Depot Derelict" (Ortiz) **45**:303
"Blues Songs" (Dumas) **62**:155
The Bluest Eye (Morrison) **4**:366; **10**:354-55; **22**:314-15, 318-19; **55**:196, 200, 205, 207-09; **81**:217-20, 225-29, 233-39, 254, 256, 260, 262, 267-68; **87**:263, 291-92, 294, 304
"Bluetit and Wren" (Clarke) **61**:82
"Blume" (Celan) **10**:103; **19**:92
"Blumenthal on the Air" (Chabon) **149**:3-4, 6
The Blunderer (Highsmith) **2**:193; **4**:225; **42**:211; **102**:170, 172, 185, 188, 211
"A Blunt Instrument" (Brown) **63**:56
The Blush (Taylor) **2**:432
Bo ni natta otako (Abe) **8**:1; **81**:291
"The Boa" (Duras)
See "Le Boa"
"Le Boa" (Duras) **40**:176, 184
"Um boabá no Recife" (Cabral de Melo Neto) **76**:167
"Board of Selection" (Enright) **31**:150
"The Boarder" (Simpson) **7**:426; **149**:325
"The Boarding House" (Trevor) **71**:322
The Boarding House (Trevor) **7**:475; **25**:443; **71**:345; **116**:331, 334-35, 348, 374, 377
Boarding House Rules (Farrell) **66**:131
The Boardinghouse Keeper (Audiberti)
See *La logeuse*
"The Boat" (Bowering) **15**:82
"The Boat" (MacLeod) **56**:192-96, 198, 200
The Boat (Buchheim) **6**:100-02
The Boat (Hartley) **22**:213
The Boat (Keaton) **20**:193
"Boat Animals" (Aldiss) **40**:19
The Boat in the Evening (Vesaas) **48**:411-13
A Boat Load of Home Folk (Astley) **41**:46, 48
"Boat Ride" (Gallagher) **63**:116, 118, 120
The Boat Who Wouldn't Float (Mowat) **26**:337, 347
Boating for Beginners (Winterson) **64**:427-29, 432-34
The Boatman (Macpherson) **14**:345-47
"Boats" (Dunn) **36**:153
"Boats" (Montague) **46**:269
Boaz and Ruth (Young) **5**:524
"Bob" (Williams) **148**:344, 354
"Bob, a Dog" (Smith) **73**:353, 356-58
"Bob and Bing Visit Saskatchewan" (Hillis) **66**:194
Bob Dylan (Dylan) **77**:166
Bob Dylan at Budokan (Dylan) **77**:173, 175
Bob the Gambler (Barthelme) **117**:27
"Bob Wills Is Still the King" (Jennings) **21**:202
"Bobby" (Jhabvala) **138**:78
"Bobby Brown" (Zappa) **17**:592
"bobby hutton" (Sanchez) **116**:294
"Bobby's Room" (Dunn) **40**:171
The Bobby-Soxer (Calisher) **134**:10, 14, 18, 35-7, 41
"Bobo's Metamorphosis" (Milosz) **56**:236
"La bocca della verità" (Davison) **28**:103
"Boccaccio: The Plague Years" (Dove) **81**:137
Bochkotara (Aksyonov)
See *The Tare of Barrels*
The Bodach (Hunter) **21**:157-58
Bodalsia telenok s dubom (Solzhenitsyn) **18**:497-500; **34**:481, 484, 487; **78**:394, 407; **134**:297, 305
Bödeln (Lagerkvist) **13**:333; **54**:267-68, 274-76, 286, 288, 290
Bodicea's Chariot: The Warrior Queens (Fraser) **107**:153, 155-59, 161
"Bodies" (Oates) **6**:370-71; **19**:348
Bodies and Souls (Rechy) **107**:256, 259
"Bodies like Flowers" (Cernuda) **54**:58
"Bodies of Water" (Cliff) **120**:89-90
Bodies of Water (Cliff) **120**:88-90, 94
"Bodies of Work" (Acker) **111**:46
Bodies of Work (Acker) **111**:46
Bodily Harm (Atwood) **25**:66, 68-70; **84**:80-1, 85, 97; **135**:7, 9-10, 13, 18-19, 58
"Bodily Secrets" (Trevor) **71**:333
"Body" (Broumas) **73**:9
"Body" (Jiles) **58**:280
The Body (Benedikt) **4**:54
The Body (King) **26**:240-42; **61**:331, 333; **113**:390-91
The Body (Sansom) **2**:383
"Body and Soul" (Broumas) **73**:8-9
Body and Soul (Polonsky) **92**:377-81, 383, 386, 393, 402, 404-05, 414-15
"The Body and the Earth" (Berry) **46**:75
The Body as Language: Outline of a "New Left" Theology (Eagleton) **63**:101
The Body Farm (Cornwell) **155**:63-4, 68-9
"Body Icons" (Phillips) **28**:363
"The Body in Grant's Tomb" (Woolrich) **77**:390
"The Body in Question" (D'Aguiar) **145**:117
The Body in the Library (Christie) **12**:120; **48**:77
The Body Is the Hero (Glasser) **37**:133
The Body Lovers (Spillane) **13**:528
"A Body Not Yet Born" (Bly) **15**:68; **128**:6
Body of Evidence (Cornwell) **155**:61
"The Body of Romulus" (Dobyns) **37**:78
"Body of Summer" (Elytis) **15**:218; **49**:106
Body of Summer (Elytis) **15**:218, 221
Body of This Death (Bogan) **39**:384, 390; **46**:77-80, 83, 85, 89; **93**:85, 90-1, 96, 105
Body of Waking (Rukeyser) **27**:408, 411
"The Body Opulent" (Fulton) **52**:161
"The Body Politic" (Barker) **52**:53-5
Body Rags (Kinnell) **1**:168; **2**:230; **3**:268-70; **5**:216, 218; **13**:320; **29**:283-84, 288, 290; **129**:256, 260, 267-68, 270
"The Body Shop" (Graver) **70**:53-4
"The Body Upstairs" (Woolrich) **77**:403
The Bodysnatcher (Onetti)
See "Just a Little One"
"Boeing Crossing" (Clark Bekedermo) **38**:129
"The Boeotian Count" (Murray) **40**:336
Boesman and Lena (Fugard) **5**:130; **9**:230, 232-34; **14**:189-91; **25**:175; **40**:197, 200, 203; **80**:62, 68-70, 74, 83-4, 86-7
Boetian Earth (Nakos) **29**:322-23
"Le boeuf sur le toit" (O'Hara) **13**:424
"The Bofors A A Gun" (Ewart) **46**:154
"The Bog Man" (Atwood) **84**:98
"Bog Oak" (Heaney) **5**:171; **14**:243; **25**:245
"The Bog People" (Heaney) **25**:250
"Bog Queen" (Heaney) **5**:172; **14**:244; **25**:243, 251
"Bogan, Louise, a Poetess" (Schwartz) **45**:361
The Bogey Man (Plimpton) **36**:354, 356
"Bogey Music" (Garner) **35**:288
"The Bogeyman" (Buzzati) **36**:94
"Bogland" (Heaney) **7**:148; **14**:243, 245; **25**:243, 245-46
"Bogland" (Heaney) **74**:154

Bogmail (McGinley) **41**:281-83
"Bogotá" (Didion) **129**:81
Bogue's Fortune (Symons) **14**:523
"Bogyman" (Adcock) **41**:14
Bohemia (Azorín) **11**:24
Bohemia (Gold) **152**:143-46
Bohin Manor (Konwicki) **117**:267, 275, 280, 291
O boi (Andrade) **18**:3
"The Boiling Water" (Koch) **44**:246
"Le bois de l'epte" (Char) **9**:159
Boises (Glissant) **68**:180
"A Boisterous Poem about Poetry" (Wain) **11**:563
The Bold and Magnificent Dream (Catton) **35**:95
The Bold Cavaliers (Brown) **47**:37
Bold John Henebry (Dillon) **17**:96
"Bolezn'" (Akhmadulina) **53**:12
"A Boll of Roses" (Dumas) **6**:145; **62**:150, 152, 155, 162-63
The Bollo Caper (Buchwald) **33**:94
"Bol'shoiden' Bol'shogo Doma" (Iskander) **47**:198
Bolt (Francis) **102**:126-28
Bomarzo (Mujica Lainez) **31**:279-84
"Bomb" (Corso) **1**:63
"The Bomb Shop" (O'Faolain) **70**:313-14
"Bombay Arrival" (Lee) **90**:182
Bombay Talkie (Jhabvala) **94**:192
"The Bomber" (Lowell) **124**:281-82, 285-86
Bomber: Events Relating to the Last Flight of an R.A.F. Bomber over Germany on the Night of June 31, 1943 (Deighton) **4**:119; **22**:115; **46**:127-28
"Bombers" (Day Lewis) **10**:133
"Bombinations of a Chimera" (MacDiarmid) **63**:244
"Bombing Casualties in Spain" (Read) **4**:439
"The Bombs" (Redgrove) **41**:357
Bombs Away: The Story of a Bomber Team (Steinbeck) **34**:405
"Bon Voyage" (Coward) **51**:74
"Bona and Paul" (Toomer) **4**:549; **13**:551, 556
"Bona Dea" (Scannell) **49**:334
Bona, l'amour et la peinture (Mandiargues) **41**:278
The Bonadventure: A Random Journal of an Atlantic Holiday (Blunden) **56**:33, 51
"Bonaventure" (Gallant) **38**:194
Bonchi (Ichikawa) **20**:182, 185
"The Bond" (Waddington) **28**:439
"Bond and Free" (Frost) **26**:113
A Bond Honoured (Osborne) **5**:332; **11**:421; **45**:313-14, 316
"Bondi" (Hospital) **145**:295, 303, 313
"Bone" (Selzer) **74**:283
Bone (Ng) **81**:81-8
"Bone Courts: The Natural Rights of Tribal Bones" (Vizenor)
See "Bone Courts: The Rights and Narrative Representations of Tribal Bones"
"Bone Courts: The Rights and Narrative Representations of Tribal Bones" (Vizenor) **103**:312
"Bone Dance: New and Selected Poems, 1965-1993" (Rose) **85**:317
"Bone Dreams" (Heaney) **14**:244
The Bone People (Hulme) **39**:158-67; **130**:41-9, 51-5, 57-63, 65-7
"Bone Poem" (Oliver) **98**:265, 274
"Bone Thoughts" (Starbuck) **53**:352
Bone Thoughts (Starbuck) **53**:352-53
The Bonebard Ballads (Harrison) **129**:171
Bonecrack (Francis) **2**:142-43; **22**:152; **42**:148-50, 155, 158; **102**:132
"The Bonefish in the Other Room" (McGuane) **127**:290
The Bonegrinder (Potter) **123**:233, 237
"Bones" (Aldington) **49**:12
"The Bones" (Merwin) **5**:288
"Bones of Contention" (O'Connor) **14**:398
Bones of Contention (O'Connor) **14**:398, 400; **23**:327
"The Bones of My Father" (Knight) **40**:283, 286
Bones of the Cuttlefish (Montale)
See *Ossi di seppia*
"The Bones Speak" (Wright) **53**:418
"Bonfire" (Gallagher) **63**:124
"Bonfire" (p'Bitek) **96**:272
"Bonfire" (Walker) **13**:565
A Bonfire (Johnson) **27**:222-23
The Bonfire of the Vanities (Wolfe) **35**:467; **51**:413-18, 420-23; **147**:303-04, 307, 310-13, 315, 317-18, 321-23, 325-26, 328, 338-45, 357, 366-68, 370-71, 373, 375
"Bongo Song" (Guillén)
See "La canción del bongo"
Le bonheur (Varda) **16**:555-59
"Le bonheur de Bolinka" (Gascar)
See "Les femmes"
Bonheur d'occasion (Roy) **10**:441; **14**:465-66, 468-69
Bonjour, là, bonjour (Tremblay) **29**:419, 421, 423; **102**:362, 372, 374-75
Bonjour tristesse (Sagan) **6**:481-82; **9**:468; **17**:416-17; **36**:380, 382-83
"Bonn Diary" (Boell)
See "Hauptstädtisches Journal"
"Bonnard: A Novel" (Howard) **7**:165; **10**:277
La bonne moitié (Gary) **25**:189
Les bonnes (Genet) **2**:157-58, 160; **5**:136; **10**:225; **14**:197; **44**:385-90; **46**:172-73, 182
Les bonnes femmes (Chabrol) **16**:170, 173-74, 177, 181
"The Bonnie Broukit Bairn" (MacDiarmid) **11**:336; **19**:289; **63**:252
"Bonny Chung" (Jenkins) **52**:226
Les bons débarreas (Ducharme) **74**:67
"Bonsai Poems" (Kaufman) **49**:207
"Bonus" (Ammons) **25**:42
A Bonus (Smart) **54**:421, 426
"Bonus for a Salesman" (Deighton) **46**:127
The Boo (Conroy) **74**:47, 49-51
"The Booby and the Noddy" (Appleman) **51**:17
"Boogey on Reggae Woman" (Wonder) **12**:661
"Boogie 1 a.m." (Hughes) **108**:299-304
"Boogie with Stu" (Page and Plant) **12**:477
Boogie Woogie Landscapes (Shange) **74**:294, 307-10; **126**:365, 370
A Book (Barnes) **29**:26-7; **127**:161, 169, 189
A Book (Brossard)
See *Un Livre*
The Book and the Brotherhood (Murdoch) **51**:293-94, 296-97
"The Book as a Container of Consciousness" (Gass) **132**:187
The Book as World (French) **18**:157
The Book Class (Auchincloss) **45**:33-4
"Book Codes: II" (Forché) **86**:144-45
"Book Codes: III" (Forché) **86**:142
"Book Ends" (Harrison) **43**:175; **129**:166, 211
"Book Ends I" (Harrison) **129**:200
"A Book from Venice" (Watkins) **43**:442
"The Book I Read" (Byrne) **26**:95
"A Book in the Ruins" (Milosz) **56**:245
The Book Lovers (Garfield) **12**:234
The Book of Absent People (Modarressi) **44**:82-5
"Book of Ancestors" (Atwood) **13**:44
"Book of Ayres" (Loewinsohn) **52**:285
"The Book of Balaam's Ass" (Jones) **7**:187, 191; **42**:242-43
A Book of Beasts (Ondaatje) **51**:316
The Book of Beasts (White) **30**:449
"The Book of Black Arts" (Brown) **48**:55
A Book of Canadian Poetry (Smith) **15**:514
A Book of Change (Morgan) **23**:296-97
The Book of Changes (Dillard) **5**:116
"A Book of Charms" (Livesay) **79**:339, 351
A Book of Common Prayer (Didion) **8**:174-77; **14**:151, 154-55; **32**:143, 145, 148; **129**:59-61, 65, 67, 80, 82, 84-85, 95, 102-03
The Book of Daniel (Doctorow) **6**:131-36; **11**:140, 142-43; **37**:84, 87, 90-4; **44**:167-68, 170, 172-76, 179; **65**:135; **113**:132-34, 137-39, 141, 143-45, 150-52, 156, 158-59, 165-66, 168-70, 172, 176-78, 180
The Book of Deeds (Agnon)
See *Sefer ha-Maasim*
Book of Dreams (Kerouac) **29**:270; **61**:296
The Book of Dreams (Vance) **35**:427
The Book of Ebenezer Le Page (Edwards) **25**:149-52
The Book of Embraces (Galeano) **72**:138-41, 143-44
"The Book of Ephraim" (Merrill) **8**:381-84, 386-88; **13**:376-77, 381-82; **18**:328-31; **34**:226-31, 234-36, 238, 240; **91**:235-237
The Book of Evidence (Banville) **118**:12, 14-15, 22-35, 38, 42, 44, 47-54
Book of Fables (Agnon)
See *Sefer ha-Maasim*
The Book of Fantasy (Bioy Casares)
See *Antología de la literatura fantástica*
The Book of Flights (Le Clézio) **31**:246-47, 249
The Book of Folly (Sexton) **2**:392; **4**:482-83; **6**:491-92, 494; **15**:471; **53**:312, 321-22; **123**:442
The Book of Forms: A Handbook of Poetics (Turco) **63**:430-31
Book of Friends: A Tribute to Friends of Long Ago (Miller) **43**:297-98
The Book of Fritz Leiber (Leiber) **25**:307
The Book of Fub (Frayn) **31**:189; **47**:135
"The Book of Galahad" (Spicer) **18**:513
"The Book of Gawain" (Spicer) **18**:513
The Book of Giuliano Sansevero (Giovene)
See *The Book of Sansevero*
The Book of God: A Response to the Bible (Josipovici) **153**:203-09, 213, 221
The Book of Gods and Devils (Simic) **68**:375-77; **130**:313, 316, 318, 336-37, 340
The Book of Guys (Keillor) **115**:285-86, 293-95
"The Book of Gwenivere" (Spicer) **18**:513
The Book of Imaginary Beings (Borges) **2**:70-2; **8**:96, 99; **83**:176
The Book of J (Bloom and Rosenberg) **65**:290-311
The Book of Jamaica (Banks) **37**:25; **72**:4, 14
The Book of Jessica: A Theatrical Transformation (Campbell) **85**:19, 25-8
A Book of Jesus (Goyen) **8**:251; **14**:213; **40**:218
"The Book of Juniper" (Paulin) **37**:355
"The Book of Kings and Fools" (Kiš) **57**:252-54
"The Book of Knowledge" (Nemerov) **36**:301
"The Book of Lancelot" (Spicer) **18**:513
The Book of Laughter and Forgetting (Kundera)
See *Le livre du rire et de l'oubli*
"The Book of Life" (Ostriker) **132**:322-23, 325-26
The Book of Lights (Potok) **26**:374-76; **112**:261-62, 266-67, 293
The Book of Lost Tales, Part I (Tolkien) **38**:441-43
The Book of Lost Tales, Part II (Tolkien) **38**:442
A Book of Lyrics (Krleža)
See *Knjiga lirike*
Book of Magazine Verse (Spicer) **8**:499; **18**:507; **72**:345-46, 351, 358
Book of Mercy (Cohen) **38**:137-38
"The Book of Merlin" (Spicer) **18**:513
The Book of Merlyn (White) **30**:449-51
Book of Moments (Burke) **2**:87
The Book of Mrs. Noah (Roberts) **48**:343-44
A Book of Music (Spicer) **8**:498
The Book of Newfoundland Verse (Pratt) **19**:376, 378, 381-82
The Book of Nightmares (Kinnell) **1**:168; **2**:229-30; **3**:268-70; **5**:218; **13**:318, 320-22; **29**:282, 284-85, 288-90; **129**:238-41, 243-44, 249-53, 255-57, 259, 264, 268-69, 271
The Book of Nods (Carroll) **143**:33-4, 37

A Book of Nonsense (Peake) **54**:373; **7**:301
The Book of Phoebe (Smith) **39**:97-9
"The Book of Pins" (Findley) **102**:108
Book of Questions (Neruda)
See *Libro de las preguntas*
The Book of Repulsive Women (Barnes) **29**:28; **127**:161, 207
The Book of Saints (Ricci)
See *Lives of the Saints*
"The Book of Sand" (Borges) **48**:38, 41
The Book of Sand (Borges) **9**:117; **13**:110; **19**:52; **44**:356, 365; **48**:37-41; **83**:189-90
The Book of Sansevero (Giovene) **7**:117
The Book of Sinera (Espriu) **9**:193
The Book of Skulls (Silverberg) **140**:365, 379
A Book of Spells (Maitland) **49**:236
The Book of Splendors (Foreman) **50**:169
The Book of the Body (Bidart) **33**:76-81
The Book of the Crime (Daly) **52**:92
"The Book of the Dead" (Rukeyser) **15**:457-59; **27**:404, 410
The Book of the Dead (Daly) **52**:89
"The Book of the Death of Arthur" (Spicer) **18**:513
Book of the Hopi (Waters) **88**:343, 347, 355-56, 363-65
The Book of the Lion (Daly) **52**:90
"The Book of the Market" (Raine) **103**:179
A Book of the Milky Way Galaxy for You (Branley) **21**:18
The Book of the New Sun (Wolfe) **25**:474-79
The Book of the Night (Lerman) **56**:179-80
A Book of the Planet Earth for You (Branley) **21**:21-2
The Book of Three (Alexander) **35**:23-6
A Book of Toys (Arghezi)
See *Cartea cujucării*
Book of Vagaries (Neruda)
See *Extravagario*
A Book of Venus for You (Branley) **21**:18
A Book of Voyages (O'Brian) **152**:280
The Book of Yaak (Bass) **143**:15-19, 21-2
Book: Part One (Breytenbach) **126**:87-8
Book That Doesn't Bite (Valenzuela)
See *Libro que no muerde*
"Book Titles" (Lopate) **29**:302
"The Bookcase" (Transtroemer) **52**:410
Bookends (Simon) **17**:459-60, 464, 466
"Booker T. and W. E. B." (Randall) **135**:386-87, 396
Booker T. Washington: The Making of a Black Leader, 1856-1901 (Harlan) **34**:184, 186, 189-91
Booker T. Washington: The Wizard of Tuskegee, 1901-1915 (Harlan) **34**:183-91
"Bookkeeping" (Brodkey) **56**:60, 64
"Books" (McFadden) **48**:244
"Books" (Phillips) **28**:363
"Books Are Bombs" (Breytenbach) **23**:84
Books Do Furnish a Room (Powell) **3**:402; **7**:339, 343; **9**:435, 437; **10**:416
The Books in Fred Hampton's Apartment (Stern) **4**:522
"The Books of Childhood" (Silverberg) **140**:396
"Books Which Have Influenced Me" (Rao) **56**:296
The Bookshop (Fitzgerald) **19**:172-73; **61**:115, 117, 120; **143**:237-38, 246, 249, 251, 253, 257, 260, 262, 264-66
"A Bookshop Idyll" (Amis) **40**:40, 44
"Bookworm" (Morrissy) **99**:78
"Boom!" (Nemerov) **6**:361
The Boom in Spanish American Literature: A Personal History (Donoso)
See *Historia personal del 'boom'*
"Boom Town" (Stafford) **29**:381
Boomerang (Hannah) **90**:139-45, 147, 159, 160
Boomerang! (Kazan) **63**:225
The Boomerang Clue (Christie)
See *Why Didn't They Ask Evans?*
"Boomtown Blues" (Seger) **35**:386-87
"Boon" (Muldoon) **32**:319
"A Boor" (Bukowski) **82**:14
"Boots" (Hood) **28**:193
Boots (Yevtushenko) **26**:466
"The Boot's Tale" (McGrath) **55**:74
"Booze, Cars, and College Girls" (Gray) **49**:148-49, 152
"Bop Bop against That Curtain" (Bukowski) **108**:87
Bopha! (Mtwa) **47**:297-99
Boquitas pintadas, follétín (Puig) **3**:407; **5**:354-56; **10**:420; **28**:369-71; **65**:266, 271-73; **133**:298-301, 306-08, 310, 315, 317, 320, 324, 335, 339-43, 347, 373, 376, 378
"Bora Ring" (Wright) **53**:418, 427, 431
"Bordeaux in My Pirough" (Berry) **17**:52
The Bordelais Natives (Audiberti)
See *Les naturels du Bordelais*
The Border (Feinstein) **36**:172-73
Border Hawk (Alexander) **35**:22
"Border Lord" (Kristofferson) **26**:267
Border Lord (Kristofferson) **26**:267
Borderline (Hospital) **42**:221-23; **145**:297-98, 300-01, 307-10, 320
Borderline (Kureishi) **135**:278, 280
Borderliners (Hoeg) **95**:111-15, 117-19
"Borders" (King) **89**:98-9, 102
Borders (Nichol) **18**:369
"Borealis" (Morand) **41**:308
"Borges" (Borges)
See "Borges y yo"
Borges: A Reader (Borges) **48**:44-7; **83**:162
"Borges and American Violence" (Dorfman) **77**:155
"Borges and I" (Borges)
See "Borges y yo"
"Borges and I" (Borges)
See "Borges y yo"
"Borges and Myself" (Borges)
See "Borges y yo"
Borges en/y/sobre cine (Borges) **83**:166
Borges In/And/On Film (Borges)
See *Borges en/y/sobre cine*
"Borges ou le voyant" (Yourcenar) **87**:424
"Borges y yo" (Borges) **13**:113; **48**:34-5, 45; **83**:157, 191
Ilborghese stregato (Buzzati) **36**:84
Borghesia (Ginzburg) **11**:230; **54**:198-99, 208
A Boring Afternoon (Hrabal) **67**:125
"Born 1925" (Brittain) **23**:91
"Born Bad" (Cisneros) **69**:147
Born Bad (Vachss) **106**:364
The Born Dancer (Olson) **11**:420
Born Free (Adamson) **17**:1-5
"A Born Genius" (O'Faolain) **1**:259; **14**:402
Born in Captivity (Wain) **2**:457; **15**:561-62; **46**:407-09, 419
"Born in the Fifties" (Police, The) **26**:363-64
Born in the Gardens (Nichols) **36**:328-29
"Born in Time" (Dylan) **77**:185
Born Indian (Kinsella) **27**:238-39; **43**:260
Born of a Woman: New and Selected Poems (Knight) **40**:282-87
Born on the Fourth of July (Stone) **73**:377-79, 381-82, 385
"Born to Run" (Springsteen) **17**:479, 489
Born to Run (Springsteen) **17**:478-86, 488-90
"Born to Win" (Cliff) **21**:60
Born to Win (Guthrie) **35**:185-88, 192, 194
"Born with the Dead" (Silverberg) **140**:343, 372, 379
"Born Yesterday" (Larkin) **13**:339; **64**:282
Born Yesterday (Kanin) **22**:229
Borom Sarret (Ousmane) **66**:334
Borrowed Time: An AIDS Memoir (Monette) **82**:316-22, 324-31
"Borrowed Tune" (Young) **17**:573
"Borrowing of Trees" (Buckley) **57**:131
Borstal Boy (Behan) **1**:26; **8**:64; **11**:44; **15**:44; **79**:24-7, 29, 34-5, 39-40, 47, 49-51, 55-8
Bosnian Chronicle (Andrić) **8**:19
Bosoms and Neglect (Guare) **14**:221-22; **29**:206, 209; **67**:79, 84-5, 88
The Boss Dog (Fisher) **76**:333, 335-36, 339, 341
Boss: Richard J. Daley of Chicago (Royko) **109**:399, 401-02, 404
Boston: A Documentary Novel of the Sacco-Vanzetti Case (Sinclair) **11**:498; **63**:346-47, 349, 351-53, 359-60, 362, 371-76
Boston Adventure (Stafford) **7**:455, 458; **19**:430; **68**:420-21, 423-24, 430, 434, 444, 446-49
The Boston Book (Forbes) **12**:208
"Boston Common" (Berryman) **3**:70
"The Boston Evening Transcript" (Eliot) **41**:160
"The Bostonians" (Stafford) **4**:517
The Bostonians (Jhabvala) **94**:185, 187; **138**:64
Boswell: A Modern Comedy (Elkin) **4**:154; **6**:170; **9**:190-91; **27**:120-21; **51**:85-90, 99; **91**:213-15
"The Botanic Gardens" (Freeman) **55**:55, 57
"Botanical Nomenclature" (Clampitt) **32**:118
"Botany" (Longley) **29**:295
"Botany Bay; or, The Rights of Women" (Hope) **51**:226
"Botella al mar" (Cortázar) **34**:333
"Both Sides Now" (Diamond) **30**:111
"Both Sides Now" (Mitchell) **12**:436, 438, 441
"Die Botschaft" (Boell) **72**:69, 73, 78
"Botta e riposta" (Montale) **7**:224; **9**:387
"Bottle Caps" (Dybek) **114**:68
The Bottle Factory Outing (Bainbridge) **5**:40; **8**:36-7; **10**:16-17; **18**:33-4; **22**:45; **62**:24-5, 29, 33, 36; **130**:7-8, 10, 20, 22-23, 34
"The Bottle Garden" (Boland) **67**:39-40; **113**:84
"Bottle Pickers" (Lane) **25**:285
"Bottleneck Blues" (Hillis) **66**:194
"The Bottles Become New, Too" (Wilbur) **53**:405
"Bottles of Beaujolais" (Louie) **70**:79, 81
Bottom Dogs (Dahlberg) **7**:61, 63, 65-6, 71; **14**:135, 137-38
"The Bottom Line" (Elkin) **14**:158
The Bottom of the Bottle (Simenon) **1**:309
"The Bottom of the Harbor" (Mitchell) **98**:182
The Bottom of the Harbor (Mitchell) **98**:159-61, 166-69, 171-73, 175, 177, 180-83, 187
Bottom: On Shakespeare (Zukofsky) **2**:488; **4**:599
Le boucher (Chabrol) **16**:177, 182-83
Les bouches inutiles (Beauvoir) **8**:59; **31**:40-1; **44**:343; **124**:164
"Bouclez-la" (Damas) **84**:178
Bouddha vivant (Morand) **41**:299-300, 304, 306-07
Boudu souvé des eaux (Renoir) **20**:291-94, 296, 301, 310
"Bought" (O'Faolain) **47**:328
Bought and Sold (Moravia)
See *Il paradiso*
Le boulanger, la boulangère, et le petit mitron (Anouilh) **13**:21; **40**:58-9
"Boulevard" (Browne) **21**:42
Le boulevards de ceinture (Modiano) **18**:337-38
Bound for Glory (Guthrie) **35**:182-84, 186-88, 190, 192, 194
Bound for the Rio Grande: The Mexican Struggle, 1845-1850 (Meltzer) **26**:302-03
Bound to Violence (Ouologuem)
See *Le #Devoir de violence*
"Boundaries" (Fuller) **62**:192
"Boundaries of Utopia" (Huxley) **79**:327
"The Boundary" (Berry) **46**:74
"The Boundary Commission" (Muldoon) **72**:268
"The Bounded Text" (Kristeva) **140**:183
The Bounty Hunters (Leonard) **120**:295
"Bouquet in Dog Time" (Carruth) **84**:131
"A Bouquet of Ten Roses" (Bly) **38**:54; **128**:17
Bourgeois Anonymous (Philipson) **53**:274
Le bourgeois avant-garde (Ludlam) **46**:243; **50**:342, 344
"A bourgeois death" (Rozewicz) **139**:273
Le Bourgeois Gentilhomme (The Brothers

Quay) **95**:349-50
Le bourgeois gentleman (Maillet) **54**:309, 313; **118**:329
"Bourgeois Poem" (Dacey) **51**:83
The Bourgeois Poet (Shapiro) **4**:485-86; **8**:485-86; **15**:478-79; **53**:329-34
Bourlinguer (Cendrars) **106**:167, 173, 181-84, 186-87, 190
"Bourn" (Ammons) **108**:21
The Bourne Identity (Ludlum) **22**:291; **43**:277-78
The Bourne Supremacy (Ludlum) **43**:277-78
A bout de souffle (Godard) **20**:128-29, 135, 143, 148
La boutique obscure (Perec) **116**:234, 246
Les bouts de bois de Dieu (Ousmane) **66**:333, 337-38, 343, 346, 349
The Bow and the Lyre: The Poem, the Poetic Revelation, and History (Paz)
See *El arco y la lira: El poema. la revelación poetica, poesia,e historia*
"Bow Down" (Barnes) **11**:30
Bow Harp (Tchicaya)
See *Arc Musical*
"Bow Lane" (Kinsella) **138**:140
Bowen's Court (Bowen) **11**:61-63; **118**:77-78, 103-04
"A Bower of Roses" (Simpson) **149**:306
"Bowery" (Ignatow) **40**:258
"Bowery Phoenix" (Miller) **14**:373-74
"The Bowl of Blood" (Jeffers) **11**:306; **54**:252
"A Bowler Hat" (Sondheim) **147**:258, 263
"Bowls" (Moore) **10**:348; **13**:396; **47**:260
"The Bowmen" (Haavikko) **34**:168, 175
"The Bowmen of Shu" (Davenport) **38**:146-47
"Box" (Creeley) **36**:122; **78**:141
"The Box" (Endō) **99**:296-98, 307
Box (Albee) **2**:2-4; **5**:13-14; **9**:6-9; **13**:5; **25**:38; **53**:22, 26; **113**:8-9, 22-3
"A Box for Tom" (Tate) **25**:428
The Box Garden (Shields) **113**:405-06, 408, 410, 412-13, 424, 437-38, 442-43, 445
The Box in Which Something Rattles (Aksyonov) **101**:22
The Box Man (Abe)
See *Hako otoko*
The Box of Delights; or, When the Wolves Were Running (Masefield) **11**:356
"A Box of Ginger" (Calisher) **134**:5
"Box Seat" (Toomer) **4**:550; **13**:551, 554; **22**:425
"Box Step" (Barthelme) **117**:14-15, 17-18
Boxcar Bertha (Scorsese) **20**:337; **89**:219, 221, 236, 239, 267
"The Boxer" (Simon) **17**:460-61, 463, 465
Der Boxer (Becker) **19**:35
"Los Boxers" (Cisneros) **118**:202
"A Boxer's Fate" (Yevtushenko) **26**:463
"Boxes" (Carver) **53**:62, 65, 67; **55**:274, 277
"A Boy" (Ashbery) **77**:58
"Boy" (Ciardi) **40**:160; **44**:380-81
"The Boy" (O'Connor) **14**:392
"Boy" (Sargeson) **31**:362
"The Boy" (Tanizaki) **14**:527
"Boy" (Voznesensky) **15**:555
Boy (Fry) **2**:144
Boy (Hanley) **5**:167
Boy (Oshima) **20**:245-46, 248, 253
"Boy and Dog" (Brown) **73**:20
"A Boy and His Dog" (Ellison) **139**:120-4, 145
A Boy and His Dog (Ellison) **13**:203; **42**:127; **139**:109, 128-29
Boy and Tarzan Appear in a Clearing! (Baraka) **115**:29-30
"The Boy and the Coyote" (Ortiz) **45**:305
The Boy and the Monkey (Garfield) **12**:235
"The Boy and the Sea" (Lamming) **66**:220
"A Boy Asks a Question of a Lady" (Barnes) **29**:27
Boy at the Window (Dodson) **79**:188-91, 199
"Boy by a River" (Walker) **13**:566
"Boy 'Carrying-In' Bottles in Glass Works" (Ryan) **65**:214-15
"The Boy Cried Wolf" (Woolrich) **77**:400
"The Boy Died in My Alley" (Brooks) **15**:94; **49**:23, 36, 38
"A Boy, Dreaming" (Hillis) **66**:193
The Boy Friend (Russell) **16**:543, 546, 548
"The Boy from Kingsburg" (Saroyan) **29**:363
Boy Gets Car (Felsen) **17**:123
"A Boy Grows Older" (Callaghan) **41**:98
"A Boy in Church" (Graves) **45**:166
Boy in Darkness (Peake) **54**:366, 373, 376-77
"Boy in Rome" (Cheever) **7**:49; **15**:131
The Boy in the Basement (Inge) **19**:230
"The Boy in the Green Hat" (Klein) **30**:235-36
"The Boy Knows the Truth" (Singer) **15**:507
"The Boy Made of Meat" (Snodgrass) **68**:388
The Boy on the Straightback Chair (Tavel) **6**:529
"The Boy on the Waggon" (Blunden) **56**:39
The Boy Scout Handbook, and Other Observations (Fussell) **74**:124-26, 129, 137
"The Boy Stood on the Burning Deck" (Forester) **35**:173
Boy: Tales of Childhood (Dahl) **79**:182
The Boy under the Bed (Dacey) **51**:80-1
"Boy Up a Tree" (Hoffman) **141**:285, 311-12
"Boy Walking Back to Find His Father's Cattle" (Klappert) **57**:259-60, 266
The Boy Who Could Make Himself Disappear (Platt) **26**:349-50, 356
"The Boy Who Fell Forty Feet" (Graver) **70**:49, 51
The Boy Who Followed Ripley (Highsmith) **42**:213-14; **102**:170, 173, 179, 182, 193, 195, 209, 220
"The Boy Who Talked with Animals" (Dahl) **79**:181
The Boy Who Waterskied to Forever (Tiptree) **48**:395
The Boy with a Cart (Fry) **10**:200
The Boy with a Trumpet (Davies) **23**:145-46
"Boy with Book of Knowledge" (Nemerov) **9**:395
"Boy with His Hair Cut Short" (Rukeyser) **27**:404, 406, 410
"Boy with Pigeons" (Dobyns) **37**:81
The Boyds of Black River (Edmonds) **35**:156
"The Boyfriend" (Oates) **108**:382
"Boyhood" (Farrell) **66**:129
Boyhood (Coetzee) **117**:102
"Boyhood in Tobacco Country" (Warren) **39**:264
"The Boyish Lover" (Colwin) **84**:146, 149
"Boys" (Moody) **147**:190-92
"Boys and Girls" (Cisneros) **118**:177
"Boys and Girls" (Farrell) **66**:129
"Boys and Girls" (Munro) **95**:298
Boys and Girls Come out to Play (Dennis) **8**:173
Boys and Girls Together (Goldman) **48**:124-25, 127-28
"Boys at a Picnic" (Oates) **6**:370
"Boys. Black." (Brooks) **49**:29, 36
"A Boy's Calendar" (Brown) **100**:82-3
"Boys in Dresses" (Komunyakaa) **94**:234, 241
"The Boys in the Back Room" (O'Hara) **3**:371
The Boys in the Back Room: Notes on California Novelists (Wilson) **24**:473
The Boys in the Island (Koch) **42**:259-62
Boys in the Trees (Simon) **26**:411-12
The Boys of Summer (Kahn) **30**:230-33
The Boys of Winter (Sheed) **53**:340-43
"The Boys on Their Bikes" (Brodkey) **56**:60-1
A Boy's Own Story (White) **27**:481-82; **110**:315-16, 318, 321, 323, 325, 327-29, 331, 336-37, 339, 341, 343
"Boys! Raise Giant Mushrooms in Your Cellar!" (Bradbury) **15**:86; **42**:33
"Boy's Room" (Oppen) **7**:281
"The Boys, The Broom Handle, the Retarded Girl" (Ostriker) **132**:326
The Boys Who Stole the Funeral (Murray) **40**:339
A Boy's Will (Frost) **4**:176; **10**:195-96; **13**:224; **15**:239, 246; **26**:116-19, 124, 128
Božena Němcová's Fan (Seifert)
See *Vejíř Boženy Němcové*
BP (Nichol) **18**:369
"Bracken Hills in Autumn" (MacDiarmid) **19**:289
"Bradford Tomb" (Harrison) **129**:210
"Bradshaw On: The Family" (Bradshaw) **70**:419, 422
"Bragg and Minna" (Findley) **102**:110
Braided Lives (Piercy) **27**:377-81; **62**:376; **128**:221, 236-42, 246
Brain 2000 (Gann) **23**:167
"Brain Damage" (Barthelme) **6**:30; **46**:36, 40
"Brain Damage" (Pink Floyd) **35**:306, 309
"Brain Dust" (Cohen) **19**:113
Brain Fever (Sayers) **122**:233, 240-41, 243-44
"Brain Stealers of Mars" (Campbell) **32**:75
Brainchild (Saul) **46**:368-69
The Brain's the Target (Acorn) **15**:8, 10
"Brainstorm" (Nemerov) **36**:305
"Brainsy" (O'Faolain) **32**:342
Brainwashing and Other Forms of Mind Control (Hyde) **21**:178
"Braly Street" (Soto) **80**:287-88, 293-94
"A Bramble Bush" (Simpson) **149**:353
"Bran" (Muldoon) **32**:320
"The Branch Line" (Beer) **58**:31
"The Branch Line" (Blunden) **56**:44
A Branch of the Blue Nile (Walcott) **67**:347; **76**:275
"A Branch of the Service" (Greene) **125**:200
The Branch Will Not Break (Wright) **3**:540-44; **5**:518-21; **10**:543-46; **28**:463-66, 468-71
"Branches" (Avison) **97**:78, 93
Branches of the Trees (Ray)
See *Shakha Proshakha*
The Brand (Olson) **28**:343
"Brand New Cadillac" (Clash) **30**:47
Brand New Morning (Seger) **35**:379
Brandbilen som foerwann (Wahlöö) **7**:502
"A Brand-New Approach" (Bioy Casares) **88**:78
Brand's Heide: Zwei Erzählungen (Schmidt) **56**:390, 405
Brandstetter and Others (Hansen) **38**:240
"Brasilia" (Plath) **9**:427; **51**:340, 345
"The Brass Atlas" (Jiles) **58**:275-76
The Brass Butterfly (Golding) **17**:160, 169, 174
The Brass Check: A Study of American Journalism (Sinclair) **11**:497; **15**:499, 502; **63**:346-47
The Brass Cupcake (MacDonald) **44**:407
"Brass Knuckles" (Dybek) **114**:61-2
Brass Knuckles (Dybek) **114**:61-3, 65, 72, 77, 81
"The Brass Ring" (Carver) **55**:279
"Brass Spittoons" (Hughes) **1**:149
Brassneck (Brenton) **31**:62, 67
Brassneck (Hare) **29**:214
"Bratsk Hydroelectric Station" (Yevtushenko) **126**:388, 394, 398
Bratsk Hydroelectric Station (Yevtushenko)
See *The Bratsk Station*
The Bratsk Station (Yevtushenko) **13**:619; **26**:462, 465-66
"Bravado" (Frost) **26**:118
The Brave African Huntress (Tutuola) **5**:443; **14**:539; **29**:438
Brave Are My People: Indian Heroes Not Forgotten (Waters) **88**:370-71
The Brave Coward (Buchwald) **33**:87-8
The Brave Cowboy (Abbey) **36**:11, 13-15, 18; **59**:239, 241-42
The Brave Free Men (Vance) **35**:421
Brave New World (Huxley) **1**:151-52; **3**:255-56; **4**:237-40, 243-44; **5**:192-94; **8**:304-06; **18**:265-66, 268; **35**:232-41, 243-45; **79**:283-329
Brave New World Revisited (Huxley) **4**:239-

241; **5**:194; **18**:266; **35**:235-37, 242-43; **79**:324
"Brave People" (Kunene) **85**:175
"Brave Strangers" (Seger) **35**:384
"Brave Words for a Startling Occasion" (Ellison) **114**:117
"Braveries" (Pinsky) **19**:372
A Bravery of Earth (Eberhart) **3**:134; **11**:178; **19**:143; **56**:74, 81, 86
Braving the Elements (Merrill) **2**:275; **3**:334-35; **6**:323; **8**:388; **13**:376, 381; **18**:331; **91**:228, 231
Bravo (Ferber) **93**:180-81
Bravoure (Carrere) **89**:69, 71-73
"Bravura Passage" (Reid) **33**:350
"The Brawler in Who's Who" (Pratt) **19**:380
The Brazen Head (Powys) **7**:349; **46**:322-23; **125**:281
Brazen Prison (Middleton) **38**:330
"Brazil" (Marshall) **27**:311-12; **72**:230
Brazil (Gilliam) **141**:240-47, 249, 251, 256, 259-60
Brazil (Updike) **139**:364-65, 375
"Brazil, January 1, 1502" (Bishop) **13**:89, 93-4; **32**:37
"Brazil-Copacabana" (Guillén) **79**:230
Brazzaville Beach (Boyd) **70**:132-45
"The Breach" (Murray) **40**:337
A Breach of Promise (Perry) **126**:344
"Bread" (Brand) **7**:30
"Bread" (Williams) **148**:314
Bread (Hunter) **31**:223
Bread and a Stone (Bessie) **23**:59-60, 62
Bread and a Sword (Scott) **43**:381-82, 384
Bread and Butter (Taylor) **27**:440, 443, 446
"Bread and Butter Smith" (Bainbridge) **62**:35
Bread and Jam for Frances (Hoban) **25**:266
Bread and Wine (Silone) **4**:492, 494
"Bread from Stones" (Garrett) **51**:152
Bread Givers (Yezierska) **46**:443-44, 446, 448
"The Bread God" (Montague) **46**:265, 270, 273
Bread in the Wilderness (Merton) **83**:387, 401
"The Bread of the World; Praises III" (McGrath) **59**:181, 183
The Bread of Those Early Years (Boell)
See *Das Brot der frühen Jahre*
The Bread of Time (Levine) **118**:306-08, 310
The Bread of Time to Come (Malouf)
See *Fly Away Peter*
The Bread of Truth (Thomas) **48**:374, 380
Bread Rather Than Blossoms (Enright) **31**:148-49
Bread upon the Waters (Shaw) **23**:399-401; **34**:369
Bread, Wine, and Salt (Nowlan) **15**:398
Bread—and Roses: The Struggle of American Labor, 1865-1915 (Meltzer) **26**:298-99
The Breadfruit Lotteries (Elman) **19**:151
The Breadwinner (Maugham) **1**:204; **67**:225-26
"The Break" (Sexton) **123**:409
Break a Leg, Betsy Maybe (Kingman) **17**:246-47
Break In (Francis) **42**:160-61; **102**:128, 148
Break in Harvest and Other Poems (Mathias) **45**:235-36
"Break of Day" (Avison) **97**:75
"The Break of Day" (Graham) **118**:223, 257, 262
"Break of Day" (Sassoon) **130**:184, 193
"Break On Through" (Jones) **81**:62, 65, 67
"Break on Through" (Morrison) **17**:295
Break the News (Clair) **20**:70
"Breakdancing" (Graham) **48**:151
The Breakdown (Duerrenmatt)
See *Die Panne*
"The Breakdown of the Bicultural Mind" (Moraga) **126**:296
"Breakfast" (Bowen) **22**:65-66; **118**:75
"Breakfast" (Williams) **31**:464
Breakfast (Delany) **141**:142
Breakfast at Tiffany's (Capote) **1**:55; **3**:99-100; **13**:134, 136-37; **19**:81-2, 85-7; **34**:320, 324-25; **38**:78, 82, 84, 87; **58**:120
A Breakfast for Barbarians (MacEwen) **13**:358
Breakfast in the Ruins (Moorcock) **5**:294
Breakfast of Champions; or, Goodbye, Blue Monday! (Vonnegut) **3**:501-04; **4**:568, 570; **5**:465-66, 468-70; **8**:530, 532-35; **12**:608-09, 613-14, 616-17, 619-20, 624-29; **40**:445-48; **60**:417, 432, 434; **111**:359-61, 363, 366, 371
Breakfast on Pluto (McCabe) **133**:120-23
Breakfast with the Nikolides (Godden) **53**:152-53, 157, 161
Breakheart Pass (MacLean) **13**:359, 361, 363; **50**:348
"The Break-In" (Adams) **46**:16-17
Breaking and Entering (Kennedy) **42**:255
Breaking Away (Tesich) **40**:421-23; **69**:368, 370-71, 373
Breaking Bread: Insurgent Black Intellectual Life (Hooks) **94**:150, 155-56
"Breaking Camp" (Piercy) **18**:406; **27**:374
Breaking Camp (Piercy) **3**:384; **6**:401-02; **18**:405; **27**:374; **62**:376; **128**:218, 228, 242-43, 246
"Breaking Glass" (Bowie) **17**:65
"Breaking Ground" (Gunn) **18**:199
Breaking Ice (McMillan) **112**:224-25, 228, 236
"The Breaking Mold" (Davidson) **19**:128
The Breaking of Bumbo (Sinclair) **2**:401
The Breaking of Style (Vendler) **138**:274-76, 294
"The Breaking of the Day" (Davison) **28**:99
The Breaking of the Day (Davison) **28**:99-100
The Breaking of the Vessels (Bloom) **24**:82; **103**:23-4, 31, 35, 37
"Breaking Open" (Rukeyser) **27**:413
Breaking Open (Rukeyser) **6**:478-80; **10**:442; **15**:458; **27**:410-12
"Breaking Out" (Ammons) **108**:56
"Breaking Out the Shovel" (Alexie) **96**:13
The Breaking Point (du Maurier) **59**:286
"Breaking the Ice with Poorer People" (Lebowitz) **36**:248
"Breaking the News" (Boell)
See "Die Botschaft"
"Breaking the News to Doll" (Kauffman) **42**:252
Breaking the Silence (Poliakoff) **38**:385
Breaking Up (Klein) **30**:241-42
"The Breaking Up of the Winships" (Thurber) **5**:431; **125**:402, 413
"Breaking Us" (Silkin) **43**:403
"Breaking Wood" (Deane) **122**:74, 83
Break-Neck (Céline)
See *Casse-pipe*
"The Breakthrough" (Aickman) **57**:3
Breakthrough Fictioneers (Kostelanetz) **28**:213, 219
The Breakthrough of Petushikhino (Leonov)
See *Petushikhinsky Prolom*
Breakthroughs in Science (Asimov) **26**:36-7
Breaktime (Chambers) **35**:98-9
"The Break-Up" (Klein) **19**:259
"The Breast" (Sexton) **123**:407, 441-42
The Breast (Roth) **2**:379-80; **3**:436-38; **4**:453, 455-57, 459; **6**:475-76; **9**:461-62; **15**:449, 452; **22**:353, 356; **47**:363; **66**:417; **86**:254
"Breast Milky" (Pink Floyd) **35**:311
"Breasts" (Gallagher) **18**:170
"Breasts" (Simic) **9**:479, 481; **68**:365; **130**:302, 307
"Breath" (Jacobsen) **48**:192
"Breath" (Levine) **5**:251; **118**:276
Breath (Beckett) **4**:51; **6**:36, 38-9, 43, 45; **9**:83; **10**:36; **29**:65
The Breath (Bernhard)
See *Der Atem*
Breath, Eyes, Memory (Danticat)
See *Le Cri de L'Oiseau Rouge*
"Breath from the Sky" (McCullers) **12**:432
A Breath of Air (Godden) **53**:156
The Breath of Clowns and Kings (Weiss) **8**:547
A Breath of Fresh Air (Cavanna) **12**:101
"A Breath of Lucifer" (Narayan) **28**:295; **121**:340
"Breathe" (Pink Floyd) **35**:307
Breathe upon These Slain (Scott) **43**:380-81, 384
Breathin' My Name with a Sigh (Wah) **44**:324, 326, 328
"Breathing" (Howes) **15**:289
"Breathing" (Solzhenitsyn)
See "Dykhanie"
"Breathing Is Key: Sarah, 1985" (McNally) **82**:262
"Breathing Jesus" (Hempel) **39**:70
Breathing Lessons (Tyler) **59**:199-210; **103**:249-50, 252-53, 255-56, 260, 265-67, 275
The Breathing Method (King) **26**:240, 242; **113**:343
"Breathing Room: July" (Transtroemer) **65**:223
"Breathing Room: Something About My Brother" (Gurganus) **70**:191, 195
"The Breathing, the Endless News" (Dove) **81**:151
Breathing the Water (Levertov) **66**:250-53
Breathing Tokens (Sandburg) **15**:470; **35**:358
"Breathing Trouble" (Busch) **10**:91-2
Breathing Trouble and Other Stories (Busch) **7**:38; **10**:91-2
Breathless (Godard)
See *A bout de souffle*
Breath-Turning (Celan)
See *Atemwende*
Brébeuf and His Brethren (Pratt) **19**:376-81, 383-84
"Brechfa Chapel" (Mathias) **45**:237
Brecht and Method (Jameson) **142**:265-66
"Breckenridge" (Silverberg)
See "Breckenridge and the Continuum"
"Breckenridge and the Continuum" (Silverberg) **140**:343
The Breed to Come (Norton) **12**:464-65
"The Breeder" (Highsmith) **102**:186, 197
"Breeders" (Thomas) **107**:340, 342-43
"Breeze" (Arghezi)
See "Adiere"
Breezeblock Park (Russell) **60**:317, 319-20
Brekkukotsannáll (Laxness) **25**:292, 300
Bremen Speech (Celan)
See *Speech on the Occasion of Receiving the Literature Prize of the Free Hanseatic City of Bremen*
Brendan Behan's Island (Behan) **79**:25-7, 37
Brendan Behan's New York (Behan) **79**:25, 52
"Brennbar's Rant" (Irving) **112**:173
"Brennende liebe, 1904" (Glück) **7**:120; **22**:174
"Brent's Deus ex machina" (Deighton) **46**:127
"The Brethren" (Deane) **122**:74
"Breughel's Two Monkeys" (Szymborska) **99**:195, 199
Breve for Afrika, 1914-34 (Dinesen) **95**:62
Una breve vacanza (De Sica) **20**:96-7
"Brewed and Filled by ..." (Bukowski) **41**:68
Brewster McCloud (Altman) **16**:21, 25, 28-9, 35, 38, 40-1, 43; **116**:3-5, 7, 11, 14, 21, 46, 59, 66
"Breyten Prays for Himself" (Breytenbach) **126**:81
"The Briar Patch" (Warren) **53**:359; **59**:298
Briarpatch (Thomas) **39**:246-47, 249
"The Bribe" (Borges) **48**:39
The Brickfield (Hartley) **2**:182
Bricklayer (Kieslowski) **120**:243
"The Bricklayers' Lunch Hour" (Ginsberg) **109**:353
Bricks to Babel (Koestler) **33**:243-44
The Bridal Canopy (Agnon)
See *Hakhnasat kalah*
"The Bridal Night" (O'Connor) **14**:399; **23**:332
"Bridal Photo, 1906" (Ciardi) **40**:156
"Bridal Piece" (Glück) **7**:119
"Bridal Suite" (Raphael) **14**:438
"Bride" (Broumas) **73**:9

"Bride and Groom Lie Hidden for Three Days" (Hughes) **37**:178; **119**:270
"A Bride in the 30's" (Auden) **123**:22
The Bride of Glomdale (Dreyer) **16**:259-62
"The Bride of Innisfallen" (Welty) **105**:324
The Bride of Innisfallen (Welty) **2**:461; **5**:479; **22**:461-62; **105**:307, 327, 335
The Bride of Texas (Škvorecký)
See *Nevesta z Texasu*
The Bride Price (Emecheta) **14**:159; **48**:97, 99, 101; **128**:54. 56-7, 61-4, 66-8, 74-6, 82-3
The Bride Price (Nwapa) **133**:175
The Bride Wore Black (Truffaut)
See *La mariée etait en noir*
The Bride Wore Black (Woolrich) **77**:389-90, 400, 403
The Bride Wore Red (Arzner) **98**:87, 91-2, 94
"The Bridegroom" (Gordimer) **33**:179-80
"The Bridegroom" (Smith) **15**:514, 516
A Bridegroom for Marcela (Klima) **56**:167-68
"The Bridegroom's Body" (Boyle) **19**:64-5; **58**:64, 67; **121**:31
"The Brides" (Hope) **3**:250; **51**:211, 214
The Bride's House (Powell) **66**:366
Brides of Reason (Davie) **5**:115; **8**:162; **10**:123, 125
Brideshead Revisited: The Sacred and Profane Memories of Captain Charles Ryder (Waugh) **1**:357-58, 360; **3**:510-14; **8**:543-44; **13**:585; **19**:461, 465; **27**:469-74, 476-77; **107**:357-58, 360-62, 368-70, 376, 385-86, 388-90, 400-01
"Bridestones" (Hughes) **119**:277
"Bridge" (Ammons) **8**:16-18; **9**:30; **108**:28
"The Bridge" (Blaise) **29**:75
"The Bridge" (Ferron) **94**:103, 124
"Bridge" (Okigbo) **84**:301, 305-06, 308
"The Bridge" (Walcott) **14**:550
"The Bridge" (Young) **17**:571
The Bridge (Mano) **10**:328
The Bridge (Talese) **37**:391, 403
The Bridge at Andau (Michener) **109**:375, 378-79, 382
"The Bridge at Arta" (Stewart) **32**:421
The Bridge at Arta and Other Stories (Stewart) **32**:420-21
The Bridge Builders (Sutcliff) **26**:430
The Bridge Builder's Story (Fast) **131**:81, 102
A Bridge for Passing (Buck) **127**:235-37
"Bridge Freezes before Roadway" (Hein)
See "Auf den Brücken Friert es zuerst"
The Bridge in the Jungle (Traven) **8**:519-20; **11**:536
The Bridge of Beyond (Schwarz-Bart)
See *Pluie et vent sur Télumée Miracle*
Bridge of Birds (Hughart) **39**:155-57
"The Bridge of Dreams" (Tanizaki)
See "Yume no ukihashi"
The Bridge of Lost Desire (Delany) **141**:99, 149
"Bridge of Music, River of Sand" (Goyen) **8**:250; **14**:212; **40**:216-17
The Bridge of San Luis Rey (Wilder) **1**:364-66; **6**:573-74, 576-78; **10**:536; **15**:572, 574; **35**:442; **82**:338-40, 344-45, 348, 350, 352-53, 355, 365, 367-68, 371-72, 376-77, 379, 382
The Bridge of Water (Berry) **46**:73
The Bridge of Years (Sarton) **49**:309-10; **91**:245
"Bridge over Troubled Waters" (Simon) **17**:464
Bridge over Troubled Waters (Simon) **17**:459-60, 464
"The Bridge, Palm Sunday, 1973" (Corn) **33**:114
"The Bridge Players" (Simmons) **43**:408
"Bridge through My Window" (Lorde) **71**:235, 252
Bridge to Terabithia (Paterson) **12**:485; **30**:282-87
A Bridge Too Far (Ryan) **7**:385
Bridgeport Bus (Howard) **5**:188, 190; **14**:267; **46**:186; **151**:261, 269-70, 272, 275, 283
"Bridges" (Kingsolver) **130**:85
"Bridges" (Tallent) **45**:388
Bridges (Haavikko)
See "Sillat"
The Bridges (Vesaas) **48**:409-10
The Bridges of Toko-Ri (Michener) **29**:311; **109**:376, 378-79, 382
Bridges-Go-Round (Clarke) **16**:215
Bridget Jones: The Edge of Reason (Fielding) **146**:108-11, 113-19
Bridget Jones's Diary (Fielding) **146**:89-96, 99-107, 109-19
"Bridging" (Apple) **30**:20-1
"The Bridle" (Carver) **36**:101, 104; **126**:107, 124, 158, 175, 177
Bridle the Wind (Aiken) **35**:21
Brief (Handke) **134**:164
Brief an einen jungen Katholiken (Boell) **9**:106; **11**:54
"Ein Brief an Sara" (Hein) **154**:77-8
Brief Diversions (Priestley) **34**:361
"Brief Encounter" (Coward) **29**:142
"A Brief Essay on the Subject of Celebrity: With Numerous Digressions and Particular Attention to the Actress Rita Hayworth" (Connell) **45**:115
"Brief for a Future Defense" (Belitt) **22**:49
"A Brief History of A Brief History" (Hawking) **105**:72
A Brief History of Time: From the Big Bang to Black Holes (Hawking) **63**:143-44, 151-52, 154-55; **105**:56-8, 61-3, 65-6, 69-72
A Brief Life (Onetti)
See *La vida breve*
Brief Lives (Brookner) **136**:91-94, 111, 116
Brief Moment (Behrman) **40**:74-6, 78
"Brief Reflection on Two Hot Shots" (Baraka) **115**:41
"Brief uit die vreemde aan slagter" (Breytenbach) **126**:79, 81-3
A Brief Vacation (De Sica)
See *Una breve vacanza*
"The Briefcase" (Muldoon) **72**:281
"The Briefcase" (Singer) **6**:509; **9**:486
The Briefcase (Abe) **81**:284, 286
Briefing for a Descent into Hell (Lessing) **2**:239-42; **3**:284-85, 289-91; **6**:295-97, 299, 303-04; **10**:313-15; **15**:334; **94**:253, 258, 261, 264, 270, 282, 284, 286, 288, 293, 295-96
Briefings: Poems Small and Easy (Ammons) **2**:12-14; **5**:26-7; **9**:26-7, 29; **25**:45; **57**:55, 58-9
"Brigade de cuisine" (McPhee) **36**:298
"Brigade-Leader Kiazym" (Iskander)
See "Brigadir Kiazym"
"Brigadier" (Smith) **15**:514
"The Brigadier and the Golf Widow" (Cheever) **64**:57
The Brigadier and the Golf Widow (Cheever) **3**:106-07; **64**:60, 62
"Brigadir Kiazym" (Iskander) **47**:198
Briggflatts (Bunting) **10**:83-4, 86; **39**:297-300; **47**:46, 48-56
"Bright" (Cummings) **15**:157
"Bright and Morning Star" (Wright) **1**:380; **14**:597; **21**:444, 453-55; **74**:390
Bright Angel (Ford) **99**:106
Bright Book of Life (Kazin) **34**:561; **38**:277-78, 281-82
Bright Center of Heaven (Maxwell) **19**:304-05
"The Bright Day" (Grau) **146**:127-28
"A Bright Day" (Montague) **46**:275-76
The Bright Day (Hocking) **13**:285
Bright Day (Priestley) **5**:351
"Bright Day in Boston" (Lowell) **11**:330; **37**:233
"The Bright Field" (Walcott) **14**:549
Bright Flows the River (Caldwell) **28**:68
Bright Journey (Derleth) **31**:133-34, 138
Bright Land (Ferber) **93**:178
"Bright Leaf" (Voigt) **54**:433
Bright Lights, Big City (McInerney) **34**:81-4; **112**:179-88, 196-97, 199-200, 202-04, 206, 208, 211, 215-17
"Bright New Day" (Mphahlele) **25**:340
Bright New Universe (Williamson) **29**:457-60
Bright Orange for the Shroud (MacDonald) **27**:275; **44**:408
"Bright Phoenix" (Bradbury) **98**:121
A Bright Room Called Day (Kushner) **81**:197, 206, 208, 210, 212
Bright Shadow (Priestley) **34**:362
Bright Shadow (Thomas) **35**:406-07
"The Bright Side" (Ammons) **57**:50
Bright Skin (Peterkin) **31**:304-06, 309-11
A Bright Star Falls (Weber) **12**:633
"The Bright Void of the Wind" (Le Guin) **45**:219
"Bright-Cut Irish Silver" (Boland) **113**:69
Brighten the Corner Where You Are (Chappell) **78**:101
The Brightfount Diaries (Aldiss) **14**:14
"Brightness as a Poignant Light" (Ignatow) **14**:275
Brightness Falls (McInerney) **112**:197-203, 212-13, 215, 218
Brightness Falls from the Air (Tiptree) **48**:392-94; **50**:355, 357
Brighton Beach Memoirs (Simon) **31**:400-02; **39**:216-17, 219; **70**:236, 238, 240-43
The Brighton Beach Trilogy (Simon)
See *Brighton Beach Memoirs*
The Brighton Belle and Other Stories (King) **53**:208
Brighton Rock (Greene) **1**:131-33, 135; **3**:207, 209-10, 212-14; **6**:213, 215, 217-19; **14**:216-19; **18**:197; **27**:173, 175-76; **37**:140; **70**:287, 290-91, 293; **72**:149-51, 155, 157-59, 161-63, 165, 178; **125**:180, 186, 193-94, 197-204, 208-09
Brighton Rock (Škvorecký) **15**:512
La brigitta (Audiberti) **38**:31
"Brigitte Bardot and the Lolita Syndrome" (Beauvoir) **124**:136
Brigitte Bardot and the Lolita Syndrome (Beauvoir) **124**:142
Brill Among the Ruins (Bourjaily) **62**:99-101, 104
"The Brilliant Leaves" (Gordon) **6**:203; **29**:189; **83**:231, 238
"Brimmer" (Cheever) **15**:131
Brimstone and Treacle (Potter) **58**:392, 400; **86**:346, 348, 350; **123**:227, 235, 240, 243, 250-55, 277
"Brimstone Yellow" (Szirtes) **46**:393
"Brindis" (Guillén) **48**:162
"Bring Down the Beams" (Bukowski) **41**:64
Bring Forth the Body (Raven) **14**:442
Bring Larks and Heroes (Keneally) **5**:210-11; **8**:318; **10**:298; **19**:243, 245, 247; **117**:209-11, 214-17, 221, 225, 227, 229-30, 232-34, 243-45, 248
Bring Me a Unicorn: Diaries and Letters of Anne Morrow Lindbergh, 1922-1928 (Lindbergh) **82**:150
"Bring Me My Bride" (Sondheim) **30**:378
Bring Me Sunshine (Taylor) **27**:443-45
Bring Me the Head of Alfredo Garcia (Peckinpah) **20**:279-82
"Bring Me the Sunflower" (Montale) **9**:388
Bring On the Bad Guys (Lee) **17**:261
"Bring on the Lucie" (Lennon) **35**:267
"Bring the Day" (Roethke) **101**:273, 279, 298, 335, 340
The Bringer of Water (Berry) **8**:85
Bringing It All Back Home (Dylan) **6**:155-57; **12**:181-82, 184, 199; **77**:168, 170, 188
"Bringing to Light" (Gunn) **18**:201, 204
"Bringing Up" (Harrison) **129**:197
"Brink of Darkness" (Winters) **8**:552
The Brink of Darkness (Winters) **8**:552; **32**:467
Brink of Life (Bergman)
See *Nära livet*
Brisées: Broken Branches (Leiris) **61**:361-62

"Bristol and Clifton" (Betjeman) **6**:68; **43**:32
The British Dramatists (Greene) **72**:153
"British Guiana" (Marshall) **27**:311-12; **72**:229
"British Migraine Association Poetry Competition" (Musgrave) **54**:335
"The British Military Cemetery on Tsofim Mountain" (Amichai)
See "Bet hakravot hatsva'i habriti behar hatsofim"
The British Museum Is Falling Down (Lodge) **36**:269-70; **141**:331-34, 344, 352, 367, 369, 372
British Sounds (Godard) **20**:150
British Subjects (D'Aguiar) **145**:116-18, 121, 128
The Broad Back of the Angel (Rooke) **25**:391-92
"The Broad Bean Sermon" (Murray) **40**:336, 341
"Broadcast" (Larkin) **33**:256; **39**:345; **64**:263
"Broadway Baby" (Sondheim) **30**:401
Broadway Bound (Simon) **70**:236-37, 240-43
Broadway, Broadway (McNally) **41**:292
"Broadway to Buenos Aires" (Ferber) **93**:141-42
"Broagh" (Heaney) **7**:148; **14**:242-43; **74**:157
Broca's Brain (Sagan) **30**:336-38, 343
"Brock" (Muldoon) **72**:273
"Broderie anglaise" (Gilliatt) **53**:146
Brodie (Borges)
See *El informe de Brodie*
Brodie's Report (Borges)
See *El informe de Brodie*
Brogg's Brain (Platt) **26**:356
The Broken Ark (Ondaatje)
See *A Book of Beasts*
"Broken Arrow" (Young) **17**:569, 572, 577-78
"Broken Blossoms" (Chappell) **40**:142
Broken Canes (Vansittart) **42**:390, 399
"Broken Chain" (Soto) **80**:300
The Broken Chariot (Sillitoe) **148**:199-200
"Broken Column" (Hollander) **5**:186
The Broken Connection: On Death and the Continuity of Life (Lifton) **67**:142, 152-55
"Broken Connections" (Oates) **9**:403
The Broken Cord: A Family's Ongoing Struggle with Fetal Alcohol Syndrome (Dorris) **109**:296-99, 304-05, 307-08, 310-11, 313
"Broken English" (Wright) **146**:347
"Broken Field Running" (Bambara) **19**:34; **88**:22, 28, 37, 53-55
"Broken Flag" (Smith) **12**:544
"Broken Freedom Song" (Kristofferson) **26**:268
The Broken Ground (Berry) **27**:34; **46**:69
"Broken Hearts Are for Assholes" (Zappa) **17**:592
"The Broken Home" (Merrill) **6**:323; **13**:380-81; **91**:229
"Broken Homes" (Trevor) **14**:536; **71**:326
"Broken Jar" (Paz)
See "El cántaro roto"
A Broken Journey (Callaghan) **14**:100; **41**:91
The Broken Jug (Banville) **118**:36
Broken Laws (Hoffman) **6**:243; **13**:286-87
"Broken Merchandise" (Bukowski) **41**:73
"The Broken Ones" (MacBeth) **5**:265
Broken Patterns (Jordan) **37**:194
The Broken Penny (Symons) **14**:523
"The Broken Pitcher" (Paz)
See "El cántaro roto"
The Broken Place (Shaara) **15**:474
The Broken Places (MacBeth) **5**:264
"Broken Promise" (MacLeish) **68**:286
"Broken Promises" (Jhabvala) **138**:78
"Broken Routine" (Archer) **28**:14
"The Broken Sandal" (Levertov) **5**:249
"The Broken Sea" (Watkins) **43**:441
Broken Soil (Colum)
See *The Fiddler's House*
The Broken Sword (Anderson) **15**:12
Broken Vessels (Dubus) **97**:231-33, 236
The Broken Wheel: Chung Kuo II (Wingrove) **68**:453, 456-57
"A Broken World" (O'Faolain) **1**:259; **32**:343
"Bromios" (Aldington) **49**:4
The Bronc People (Eastlake) **8**:198, 200
Brontë Wilde (Howe) **47**:174
The Bronx is Next (Sanchez) **116**:282, 301
El Bronx Remembered: A Novella and Stories (Mohr) **12**:446-47
"Bron-yr-aur" (Page and Plant) **12**:477, 479, 482
"Bronze" (Walcott) **76**:279
The Bronze Horseman (Thomas) **132**:340
"A Bronzeville Mother Loiters in Mississippi. Meanwhile a Mississippi Mother Burns Bacon" (Brooks) **15**:92; **49**:27, 32-3, 36; **125**:93, 96
"Bronzeville Woman in a Red Hat" (Brooks) **15**:93; **125**:90, 94
"The Brooch" (Hill) **113**:330-31
The Brood (Cronenberg) **143**:57, 65, 70-71, 76, 81, 94-98, 100, 108, 110, 113-114, 116, 138, 151-52
"Brooding" (Ignatow) **40**:258
"The Brook" (Blunden) **56**:44
"The Brook" (Davis) **49**:92
"Brooklyn" (Marshall) **27**:311-12
The Brooklyn Bridge (Miller) **84**:293
"Brooklyn from Clinton Hill" (Moore) **47**:270
"Brooklyn, Iowa, and West" (Miles) **14**:369
"Brooklyn Is My Neighborhood" (McCullers) **100**:260
"Brooklyn Pigeon" (Kenny) **87**:247
Brooklyn-Manhattan Transit: A Bouquet for Flatbush (Blackburn) **43**:63, 66
The Broom of the System (Wallace) **50**:92-6; **114**:347-51, 358-59, 361-62, 364, 367-68, 372
"Brooms" (Simic) **9**:479; **49**:337, 339; **68**:370, 379; **130**:330
Brosok na yug (Paustovsky) **40**:366, 368
Das Brot der frühen Jahre (Boell) **2**:68; **9**:109-11; **11**:54, 57; **27**:57-8; **39**:294
"Brothel-Going" (Faludy) **42**:140
"The Brother" (Coover) **7**:58; **15**:145
"Brother" (Davies) **21**:102
"Brother" (O'Brien) **65**:167-69; **116**:204
"The Brother" (Walcott) **76**:285
"Brother Alvin" (Lorde) **71**:247
"Brother and Sisters" (Wright) **53**:425, 427
"Brother André, Père Lamarche and My Grandmother Eugenie Blagdon" (Hood) **28**:189
Brother Cain (Raven) **14**:439
Brother, Can You Spare a Dime? The Great Depression, 1929-1933 (Meltzer) **26**:299, 305
Brother Dusty-Feet (Sutcliff) **26**:428, 433, 435
"Brother Fire" (MacNeice) **4**:315, 318
"Brother Jordan's Fox" (L'Heureux) **52**:275
"Brother Love's Traveling Salvation Show" (Diamond) **30**:111
Brother, My Brother (Santos) **22**:362, 365
"Brother of the Mount of Olives" (Monette) **82**:333-34
"The Brother Poems" (Urdang) **47**:399
Brother to Dragons (Warren) **1**:352; **4**:578-80; **10**:517-18; **13**:574-77, 581; **18**:535-38; **39**:260, 266; **59**:298
"Brother to Methusalem" (Still) **49**:366
Brotherhood (Ward) **19**:458
"Brotherhood in Pain" (Warren) **13**:578
"The Brotherhood Movement" (Bioy Casares) **88**:78
"The Brotherhood of Men" (Eberhart) **56**:80, 88
The Brotherhood of the Grape (Fante) **60**:132, 136
The Brotherhood of the Red Poppy (Troyat) **23**:460
Brotherly Love (Hoffman) **23**:241-43
"Brothers" (Cohen) **19**:113
"The Brothers" (King) **8**:322
"Brothers" (Merwin) **8**:390
"Brothers" (Sassoon) **130**:221
"The Brothers" (Smith) **64**:391
The Brothers (Barthelme) **117**:12-14, 19, 22-6
Brothers (Goldman) **48**:131
Brothers (Rubens) **31**:352
Brothers and Keepers (Wideman) **36**:456-57; **67**:370, 374-75, 379-82, 388; **122**:307, 323, 336, 342-44, 346-47, 350, 354, 356, 359-60, 363, 367, 369-70, 372
Brothers and Sisters (Compton-Burnett) **15**:135, 138; **34**:495-96, 499-500
The Brothers and Sisters of the Toda Family (Ozu) **16**:451
Brothers, I Loved You All: Poems, 1969-1977 (Carruth) **18**:87-9; **84**:119-20, 122-23, 130-31, 135
"Brothers in the Craft" (Kinsella) **138**:135, 156
Brothers Keepers (Westlake) **7**:529
Brothers of Earth (Cherryh) **35**:103-04
"Brothers of No Kin" (Richter) **30**:309
Brothers of No Kin and Other Stories (Richter) **30**:309, 323
The Brothers Rico (Simenon) **1**:309; **2**:399
"Brought Up to Be Timid" (Buckley) **57**:133
"Broward Dowdy" (Blaise) **29**:70-1
"Brown America in Jail: Kilby" (Hughes) **108**:318
"The Brown Book of the Hitler Terror" (Read) **4**:439
"The Brown Chest" (Updike) **139**:368
"Brown Dog" (Harrison) **66**:167-70; **143**:352-53
Brown Dog of the Yaak (Bass) **143**:22
"Brown Earth" (Nyro) **17**:313
Brown Girl, Brownstones (Marshall) **27**:308-09, 311-12, 314-16; **72**:212, 222-23, 226-27, 231-32, 243, 248-50, 252, 254-55
"The Brown Menace or Poem to the Survival of Roaches" (Lorde) **71**:248
Brown on Resolution (Forester) **35**:158, 165, 170, 174
"Brown Sugar" (Jagger and Richard) **17**:224, 226, 229-30, 235-38, 242
"Brown Tish" (Bowering) **47**:31
"Browning in Venice" (Watkins) **43**:452
The Browning Version (Rattigan) **7**:355-56
Brownout (Mo)
See *Brownout on Breadfruit Boulevard*
Brownout on Breadfruit Boulevard (Mo) **134**:210-15
"The Browns" (Barthelme) **117**:15, 17-18
"Brown's Descent" (Frost) **15**:248
"Brownshoes" (Sturgeon) **22**:411
"Brownstone" (Adler) **8**:6
Brownstone Eclogues and Other Poems (Aiken) **52**:21, 26
The Brownsville Raid (Fuller) **25**:180-81
A Browser's Dictionary and Native's Guide to the Unknown American Language (Ciardi) **44**:378-79, 383
Le bruissement de la langue (Barthes) **83**:88
"Un bruit de soie" (Hébert) **29**:228
"Brujerías o tonterías" (Ulibarrí) **83**:415
"El brujo postergado" (Borges) **13**:106
Brumby Innes (Prichard) **46**:337
"Bruno" (Warner) **7**:513
Bruno's Dream (Murdoch) **1**:236; **3**:345, 349; **6**:344, 349; **31**:293; **51**:288
"Bruns" (Rush) **44**:91-3, 95
"Brunswick Avenue" (Govier) **51**:166
Brunswick Gardens (Perry) **126**:344
"Brush Fire" (Rooke) **25**:390-91
Brush Fire (Tchicaya)
See *Feu de Brousse*
Brustein's Window (Hansberry)
See *The Sign in Sydney Brustein's Window*
The Brute (Bunuel)
See *El bruto*
El bruto (Bunuel) **16**:147; **80**:23
Brutus's Orchard (Fuller) **28**:148, 153, 157, 159

"Bubba" (Sanchez) **116**:302, 306, 313
The Bubble (Anand) **93**:52-53, 55-57
"Bubbs Creek Haircut" (Snyder) **32**:387; **120**:319, 321-22
"Bubnovy valet" (Leonov) **92**:262
"The Bubus" (Cendrars) **106**:159
Bucarest (Morand) **41**:304
Buchanan Dying (Updike) **5**:455-57; **15**:543; **23**:476-77; **43**:431
"Buchanan's Fancy" (Simmons) **43**:410
Bucharest (Morand)
See *Bucarest*
The Buchwald Stops Here (Buchwald) **33**:94
"The Buck" (Oates) **108**:383
Buck and the Preacher (Poitier) **26**:357-58, 360
"Buck Duke and Mama" (Taylor) **5**:426
"Buck in the Bottoms" (Derleth) **31**:132
"Buck Moon--From the Field Guide to Insects" (Oliver) **98**:290
Buck Private (Valdez)
See *Soldado razo*
Buckdancer's Choice (Dickey) **2**:115; **4**:122; **7**:79-80; **47**:93, 95; **109**:243-44
The Bucket of Blood (O'Hara) **42**:319
The Bucket Shop (Waterhouse) **47**:419
"Buckeye" (Rose) **85**:312
"Buckley at Mons" (Hemingway) **39**:398
Buckthorn (Akhmatova)
See *Podorozhnik*
Bucolic Comedies (Sitwell) **67**:312
"Bucolics" (Auden) **3**:23; **14**:29
"Bud" (Fuller) **62**:206
"Bud and Tom" (Kinsella) **43**:256
"The Buddha" (Soto) **80**:298
The Buddha of Suburbia (Kureishi) **64**:249-53; **135**:261-63, 265, 267-68, 272-73, 280, 284-89, 293, 297-98, 300, 303
"The Buddha's Last Instruction" (Oliver) **98**:280-81
"Buddhism" (Borges) **48**:47, 49
"Buddhism and the Coming Revolution" (Snyder) **120**:345
"The Buddhist" (Ferron) **94**:103, 125
The Buddhist Car and Other Characters (Schevill) **7**:401
Buddies (Kenny) **87**:249
Budding Prospects: A Pastoral (Boyle) **36**:60-3; **55**:106, 111; **90**:43-4, 47, 49
Buddy and the Old Pro (Tunis) **12**:597
"Buddy the Leper" (Keillor) **115**:295
"Budgie" (MacNeice) **4**:318
"Budilnikut" (Bagryana) **10**:13
Las buenas consciencias (Fuentes) **22**:164; **113**:230, 253
The Buenos Aires Affair (Puig) **5**:354-56; **10**:420; **28**:369-71; **65**:265-66, 269, 271-72; **133**:298-300, 302-03, 310, 317, 321, 332, 347-48, 350, 373
"Buenos Dias" (Broumas) **73**:9
La bufera e altro (Montale) **7**:222-26, 228-30, 232; **9**:387; **18**:340
Buff (Fuller) **28**:151, 153
"Buffalo" (Peacock) **60**:298
"Buffalo. 12.7.41" (Howe) **72**:202
Buffalo Bill (Breytenbach) **126**:89, 101
Buffalo Bill and the Indians; or, Sitting Bull's History Lesson (Altman) **16**:36, 41, 43; **116**:18-20, 26-8, 30-1, 35, 59, 72
"Buffalo Bill's Defunct" (Cummings) **8**:154; **12**:151
"Buffalo Climbs out of Cellar" (Willard) **7**:539
Buffalo Gals (Le Guin) **136**:329, 388
"Buffalo Gals, Won't You Come Out Tonight" (Le Guin) **136**:388
Buffalo Girls (McMurtry) **127**:334-35
The Buffalo Hunter (Straub) **107**:306-07
The Buffalo Hunters (Sandoz) **28**:403-04, 407
The Buffalo Shoot (Kuzma) **7**:197
Buffalo Springfield (Young) **17**:568
"Buffalo Story" (Silko) **74**:334-35, 338
"Buffs" (Pownall) **10**:419
Bug Jack Barron (Spinrad) **46**:383, 386
"The Bugbear of Relativism" (Barzun) **145**:73
"Bugle Song" (Stegner) **81**:345-46
The Bugles Blowing (Freeling)
See *What Are the Bugles Blowing For?*
"Bugs in the Bug" (Royko) **109**:406
"Buick" (Shapiro) **53**:330, 334
"Build Soil: A Political Pastoral" (Frost) **3**:170; **10**:193; **44**:460, 462
"The Builder and the Dream" (Stuart) **11**:510
"The Building" (Larkin) **5**:225-26, 230; **8**:332, 337; **9**:323; **13**:335; **18**:297-98; **33**:260, 262-63; **39**:341; **64**:266, 280, 282
"Building a Person" (Dunn) **36**:154
"Building a Teaching Community" (Hooks) **94**:156-57
"Building Bricks Without Straws" (Rhys) **124**:344
"Building Houses" (Smith) **42**:351
"The Building of the Prison" (Saro-Wiwa) **114**:254
"The Building Site" (Duras) **40**:184-85
"Building Speculation" (Calvino)
See "La speculazione edilizia"
The Build-Up (Williams) **5**:510
"Bujah and the Strong Force" (Amis) **62**:6-8, 10
"bukharin's Widow" (Yevtushenko) **126**:386-87
The Bukowski/Purdy Letters: A Decade of Dialogue, 1964-1974 (Bukowski) **108**:81, 114-15
"The Bulahdelah-Taree Holiday Song Cycle" (Murray) **40**:338-40
"The Bulgarian Poetess" (Updike) **15**:543; **139**:335
"The Bulge" (Johnston) **51**:245
"The Bull" (Wright) **53**:418-19
The Bull and the Spear (Moorcock) **5**:294
"The Bull Calf" (Frame) **96**:218
Bull Fire (Harris) **9**:261
The Bull from the Sea (Renault) **3**:425; **17**:394-97, 400-01
Bull Island (Smith) **22**:384-85
"The Bull Moose" (Nowlan) **15**:399
"The Bull Moses" (Hughes) **37**:176
"Bull of Bandylaw" (Plath) **17**:348, 366
"The Bull of Bendylaw" (Plath)
See "Bull of Bandylaw"
"The Bullaun" (Adcock) **41**:17-18
"The Bulldozer" (Francis) **15**:239
Bullet Park (Cheever) **3**:107, 109; **7**:50; **8**:138-39; **11**:120, 123; **25**:116-18; **64**:49-50, 57-9
"Bulletin" (Fearing) **51**:106
"Le bulletin des baux" (Char) **9**:164, 166
"Bulletin from the Writer's Colony" (Jacobsen) **48**:192
Bulletproof Buddhists (Chin) **135**:202
"The Bullets of Camden, North Carolina" (Smith) **22**:385
The Bullfighters (Montherlant) **19**:322
Bullies (Trow) **52**:419-20, 424
Bullivant and the Lambs (Compton-Burnett)
See *Manservant and Maidservant*
"Bullocky" (Wright) **53**:416, 423, 427, 430
"Bull-Ring: Plaza Mexico" (Belitt) **22**:49
The Bull's Hide (Espriu) **9**:193
"The Bully" (Reaney) **13**:473
"Bum Prayer" (Carrier) **78**:83
Bumazhnyī peīzazh (Aksyonov) **37**:13
Bumblebee Dithyramb (Rosenblatt) **15**:447
The Bumblebee Flies Anyway (Cormier) **30**:90-1
"Bumblebees" (Mason) **82**:244, 256; **154**:240
"Bums in the Attic" (Cisneros) **118**:172, 177
The Bundle (Bond) **23**:65, 67, 70
A Bundle of Myrrh (Neihardt) **32**:330
A Bundle of Nerves (Aiken) **35**:17
"The Bungalows" (Plomer) **4**:407
The Bungalows (Ashbery) **3**:16
"Bunkhouse North" (Lane) **25**:284
Le buono figlie (Buzzati) **36**:84
Burannyi polustanok (Aitmatov)
See *I dol'she veka dlitsia den'*
"Burbank with a Baedeker: Bleistein with a Cigar" (Eliot) **13**:193; **34**:394, 403; **41**:151; **55**:346-48, 355, 364-66, 370-71
"Burchfield's World" (Phillips) **28**:364
"Burden" (Eberhart) **11**:178
"A Burden for Critics" (Blackmur) **24**:61
"The Burden of Black Women" (Du Bois) **64**:114, 116
"Burden of Freedom" (Kristofferson) **26**:267
"The Burden of History" (White) **148**:217, 286, 293
The Burden of Our Time (Arendt)
See *The Origins of Totalitarianism*
"The Burdened Man" (Paley) **4**:392
Burger's Daughter (Gordimer) **18**:187-88; **51**:157-59, 161; **70**:163-64, 166-67, 170-76, 181, 186-88; **123**:119, 121, 127-28, 131, 134, 137, 141-42, 145, 157-58
The Burglar (Brophy) **105**:8-10, 30
"The Burglar of Babylon" (Bishop) **13**:89; **32**:38, 42
"Burglary" (Matthews) **40**:324
"A Burglary" (Ryan) **65**:209-12, 214-16
"Burial" (Lowell) **11**:331
"Burial" (Walker) **58**:405
"Burial at Sea" (Singer) **69**:311
"Burial by Salt" (Piercy) **62**:379; **128**:274
"The Burial of Saint Brendan" (Colum) **28**:90
"The Burial of the Dead" (Eliot) **2**:130; **6**:165; **9**:188; **10**:168; **15**:212; **113**:216
The Burial of the Sardine (Arrabal)
See *L'enterrement de la sardine*
"Burial Party" (Masefield) **11**:358
"Buried Although" (Johnson) **6**:265; **9**:301
Buried Child (Shepard) **17**:449; **34**:265, 267, 269; **41**:408-09, 411, 415-16; **44**:264-66, 268-69
Buried City (Moss) **7**:249-50; **14**:375-76; **45**:286
The Buried Day (Day Lewis) **6**:126; **10**:126
Buried for Pleasure (Crispin) **22**:109
"Buried in a Blue Suit" (Vizenor) **103**:297
"The Buried Lake" (Tate) **2**:429; **4**:451; **11**:525, 527; **14**:529
The Buried Mirror (Fuentes) **113**:255-56, 262
"The Buried Port" (Ungaretti) **7**:484; **11**:559
"Buriga" (Leonov)
See "Buryga"
"Burl" (Mosher) **62**:312
Burma Rifles: A Story of Merrill's Marauders (Bonham) **12**:54
The Burmese Harp (Ichikawa) **20**:176, 181
"The Burn" (Kinnell) **129**:268
The Burn (Aksyonov)
See *Ozhog*
"Burn and burn and burn" (Bukowski) **108**:113
"Burn Center" (Olds) **39**:189
Burn Marks (Paretsky) **135**:342-44, 346, 349, 354, 360, 363-64, 368-69
The Burn Ward (Glasser) **37**:130
"Burned" (Levine) **118**:304-05, 312
"Burnin' and Lootin'" (Marley) **17**:269, 271-72
"The Burning" (Momaday) **85**:269
"The Burning" (Welty) **22**:457
Burning (Johnson) **5**:198
"The Burning Babe" (Duncan) **41**:130
The Burning Book (Gee) **57**:219-22
The Burning Boys (Fuller) **62**:207-08
"Burning Brambles" (Mathias) **45**:238
Burning Brambles: Selected Poems, 1944-1979 (Mathias) **45**:236-37
Burning Bright: A Play in Story Form (Steinbeck) **1**:325; **13**:534; **21**:382; **34**:409; **45**:372, 374, 378
"The Burning Bush" (Turco) **63**:429-30
The Burning Cactus (Spender) **91**:261
"The Burning Child" (Clampitt) **32**:115
"Burning Chrome" (Gibson) **39**:139; **63**:129, 132, 134, 139
Burning Chrome (Gibson) **63**:139
The Burning Court (Carr) **3**:101
"The Burning Eyes" (Gordon) **29**:187; **83**:231

The Burning Flames, and Other Stories (Rulfo)
See *El llano en llamas, y otros cuentos*
The Burning Glass (Behrman) **40**:85-6
Burning Grass (Ekwensi) **4**:151-52
"Burning Hills" (Ondaatje) **51**:311-12, 315, 317
The Burning Hills (L'Amour) **25**:278; **55**:306, 308
"The Burning House" (Beattie) **40**:66; **63**:9, 12, 19; **146**:51, 84, 86
The Burning House (Beattie) **40**:63-6; **63**:2-3, 5, 9, 11-13, 15, 17; **146**:47, 54, 67, 69, 71, 76, 78
Burning in Water Drowning in Flame: Selected Poems 1955-1973 (Bukowski) **108**:110
The Burning Library (White) **110**:332, 334-35, 337-38,340
"Burning Love Letters" (Moss) **7**:247; **50**:353
The Burning Man (Millin) **49**:250
The Burning Mystery of Anna in 1951 (Koch) **44**:246, 248
"The Burning of Paper Instead of Children" (Rich) **6**:458; **36**:373; **125**:317-20
"The Burning of the Waters" (Still) **49**:368
"Burning Oneself In" (Rich) **3**:428; **11**:477
"Burning Oneself Out" (Rich) **3**:428; **7**:367; **11**:477
The Burning Perch (MacNeice) **4**:315-17; **10**:325; **53**:240, 242
The Burning Plain, and Other Stories (Rulfo)
See *El llano en llamas, y otros cuentos*
Burning Questions (Shulman) **10**:475-76
"Burning Sky" (Weller) **26**:446
"Burning the Cat" (Merwin) **5**:285
"Burning the Effects" (Buckley) **57**:126, 131
"Burning the Frankenstein Monster: Elegiac Letter to Richard Dillard" (Chappell) **78**:91
Burning the Ivy (Walker) **13**:566-67
"Burning the Letters" (Jarrell) **2**:210
"Burning the Letters" (Plath) **51**:340
"Burning the News" (Turco) **11**:549-50; **63**:429-30
"Burning the Small Dead" (Snyder) **32**:391
"Burning the Tomato Worms" (Forché) **25**:168, 170; **83**:207
Burning Water (Bowering) **47**:26, 29, 31, 34
"The Burning Wheel" (Huxley) **11**:282
The Burning Wheel (Huxley) **4**:243; **11**:282-84
The Burning Wind (Krleža)
See *Plameni vjetar*
The Burning Women of Far Cry (DeMarinis) **54**:99-100
Burnish Me Bright (Cunningham) **12**:165
"Burnished" (Stevenson) **33**:382
"Burns Unit" (Blackwood) **100**:2
"Burnt" (Levine) **118**:297
"Burnt Bird" (Breytenbach) **126**:78
"The Burnt Bridge" (MacNeice) **53**:242
"Burnt Norton" (Eliot) **1**:92; **2**:125; **3**:139; **6**:165; **9**:184; **10**:171; **13**:194; **15**:210-11, 215-16; **24**:174; **34**:399, 401, 527, 529-32; **41**:146, 152, 154-55, 160-61; **55**:367-68, 374; **57**:186; **113**:192
The Burnt Ones (White) **5**:486-87; **7**:532-33; **69**:397-98
Burnt Weenie Sandwich (Zappa) **17**:586-87
A Burnt-Out Case (Greene) **1**:130, 134-35; **3**:209, 213; **6**:213-16, 220; **14**:219; **27**:173, 175-76; **37**:137; **70**:289, 293; **72**:177; **125**:187-89, 197, 205-06, 208
Burr (Vidal) **4**:553-54, 556-57; **6**:548-50; **8**:525-26, 528; **10**:504; **33**:406-07, 409-11; **72**:377, 379-80, 382, 384-85, 387, 389, 391-92, 394-95, 398, 400-02, 404; **142**:296, 303, 320, 322, 334
Burr Oaks (Eberhart) **11**:178; **56**:79
"Burr Oaks: The Barn" (Eberhart) **56**:86
Bursting into Song (Purdy) **50**:248
"Bursting Rapture" (Frost) **9**:223
Bury Me at the Market Place (Mphahlele) **133**:148, 157
Bury My Heart at Wounded Knee: An Indian History of the American West (Brown) **18**:70-2; **47**:38-9
Bury the Dead (Shaw) **7**:411-12; **23**:394-95, 397; **34**:369
"Buryga" (Leonov) **92**:237, 242, 255, 261, 266, 275
"Burying an Enemy" (Wittlin) **25**:468
"Burying the Babies" (Macdonald) **19**:290
"The Bus" (Singer) **23**:421-22; **38**:410
The Bus Conductor Hines (Kelman) **58**:295-96, 299, 302; **86**:185
Bus Riley's Back in Town (Inge) **8**:310
Bus Stop (Inge) **1**:153; **8**:308; **19**:226, 228-29
"Bus Stop in Nevada" (Montague) **46**:265
"Bus Stop: Or, Fear and Loneliness on Potrero Hill" (Justice) **102**:283
"La busca de Averroes" (Borges) **6**:90; **19**:46-7, 52; **83**:164, 183
"Búscate plata" (Guillén) **48**:161, 168; **79**:245
"Bush" (Jacobsen) **48**:198
"Bush Christmas Eve" (Jacobsen) **48**:191; **102**:236
The Bush Garden (Frye) **70**:275
"A Bush League Hero" (Ferber) **93**:140
Bushūkō hiwa (Tanizaki) **28**:418-21
The Bushwhacked Piano (McGuane) **3**:329-31; **7**:213; **18**:323, 325; **45**:258, 262; **127**:245, 250, 257-58, 260, 262, 269, 274-75, 279-80, 298
Business (Ayckbourn)
See *A Small Family Business*
"Business as Usual" (Reid) **33**:351
"Business Girls" (Betjeman) **43**:41
"Business Is Business" (Boell)
See "Geschäft ist Geschäft"
"Business Is Business" (Friedman) **56**:107
"The Business Man of Alicante" (Levine) **4**:287
"The Business of Fancydancing" (Alexie) **96**:2
The Business of Fancydancing (Alexie) **96**:2-5, 7-8, 13, 16-17; **154**:3, 6-7, 13, 16, 17, 25-7, 29, 31, 35-6, 42, 44
The Business of Good Government (Arden) **6**:10; **13**:29; **15**:20
Business of Killing (Leiber) **25**:302
"Business Personals" (Ashbery) **15**:30; **77**:45
"Business Talk" (Apple) **33**:22
"Business Trip" (Hoffman) **141**:
"A Business Trip Home" (Mass) **59**:370
The Businessman (Disch) **36**:127-28
"Busride" (Cortázar)
See "Omnibus"
"Buster's Hand" (Masters) **48**:224
Bustin' Loose (Pryor) **26**:380
"Busy about the Tree of Life" (Zoline) **62**:462, 464
Busy about the Tree of Life (Zoline) **62**:461-64
"Busy Body under a Cherry Tree" (Enright) **31**:149
"Busy Doin' Nothin'" (Wilson) **12**:641, 650
"A Busy Man" (Nabokov) **15**:394
"The Busy Man Speaks" (Bly) **10**:57; **38**:58; **128**:8, 12
"But" (MacEwen) **55**:164-66
"But Alas Edgar" (Lamming) **66**:224
"But at Last" (Blunden) **56**:39
"But at the Stroke of Midnight" (Warner) **7**:513
But Beautiful (Dyer) **149**: :42-3, 45, 48, 54-5
"But Before" (Yevtushenko) **26**:467
But Do Blondes Prefer Gentlemen? (Burgess)
See *Homage to QWERT YUIOP, and Other Writings*
But for Bunter (Hughes) **48**:187-88
But for Whom Charlie (Behrman) **40**:88
"But He Was Cool; or, He Even Stopped for Green Lights" (Madhubuti) **6**:313; **73**:199, 210
"But in a Thousand Other Worlds" (Grayson) **38**:210
"But It Still Goes On" (Graves) **45**:171
But Not to Keep (Kahn) **30**:233-34
"But That Is Another Story" (Justice) **102**:261
But We Are Exiles (Kroetsch) **5**:220-21; **23**:269; **57**:282, 288; **132**:213, 243-44, 247, 250
"But We Hungry" (Marley)
See "Them Belly Full"
"But What Is the Reader to Make of This?" (Ashbery) **41**:36
But Who Wakes the Bugler (De Vries) **28**:112-13
Butch and Sundance: The Early Days (Lester) **20**:231-32
Butch Cassidy and the Sundance Kid (Goldman) **48**:126-28
Butch Cassidy and the Sundance Kid (Hill) **26**:196-97, 199-201, 203-05, 207-08, 211
"The Butcher" (Raine) **103**:186
"The Butcher" (Williams) **42**:440
The Butcher Boy (McCabe) **133**:105-07, 109-14, 116, 118-22
"Butcher Shop" (Simic) **49**:342; **68**:364; **130**:316
"Butcher's Dozen" (Kinsella) **138**:105, 116, 124, 159, 163, 167-68
Butcher's Dozen: A Lesson for the Octave of Widgery (Kinsella) **4**:271; **19**:251-52, 257; **138**:134
Butcher's Moon (Westlake) **33**:437
"The Butcher's Wife" (Erdrich) **54**:165
"Buteo Regalis" (Momaday) **85**:225, 231, 262, 264, 268
Butley (Gray) **9**:240-42; **36**:201-05, 207, 210
Der Butt (Grass) **11**:250-54; **32**:202, 204; **49**:140, 142-43
"A Buttefly on F Street" (Jones) **76**:65
The Butter and Egg Man (Kaufman) **38**:265-66
The Buttercup Chain (Elliott) **47**:103, 107
"Buttercups" (Lowell) **8**:358
Buttered Side Down (Ferber) **93**:140, 147
Butterfield Eight (O'Hara) **6**:384-86; **42**:311-12, 320-21, 324
"Butterflies" (Dickey) **15**:177
"Butterflies" (Grace) **56**:123
"Butterflies" (Kinsella) **27**:237
"The Butterfly" (Avison) **97**:68, 70-72, 75
"The Butterfly" (Brodsky)
See "Babočka"
"The Butterfly" (Giovanni) **64**:187
The Butterfly (Cain) **3**:96-7; **11**:84; **28**:47-8, 51, 53
"The Butterfly and the Traffic Light" (Ozick) **155**:178
"Butterfly Bones; or Sonnet Against Sonnets" (Avison) **97**:76, 85, 99, 104, 123, 129, 134-37
"The Butterfly Boy" (Vollmann) **89**:304, 313
"The Butterfly Collector of Corofin" (Durcan) **43**:114
"The Butterfly Farm" (McGuckian) **48**:277
The Butterfly Hunter (van de Wetering) **47**:409
Butterfly on Rock (Jones) **10**:286, 289
The Butterfly Plague (Findley) **27**:141; **102**:99-100, 104-05, 114
Butterfly Stories: A Novel (Vollmann) **89**:286, 304-05, 307-08, 311, 313, 315-16
The Button (McClure) **6**:317
"The Button Maker's Tale" (Szirtes) **46**:395
"Les buveurs d'horizons" (Reverdy) **53**:281
Buy Jupiter, and Other Stories (Asimov) **26**:50
Buy Me Blue Ribbons (Elliott) **38**:176
A Buyer's Market (Powell) **1**:277; **3**:400; **9**:438; **10**:412, 414-15; **31**:320-21
"Buying and Selling" (Levine) **118**:281
Buying Time (Haldeman) **61**:185-86
"Buzzard" (Clarke) **61**:82
"By a Frozen River" (Levine) **54**:297-98, 300-01
"By Al Liebowitz's Pool" (Nemerov) **36**:306-08
By Any Means Necessary (Lee) **105**:112
By Any Means Necessary (Malcolm X) **117**:319
"By any Other Name" (Donaldson) **138**:41
By Avon River (H. D.) **8**:258; **31**:202, 204, 208; **73**:115-17, 139
"By Candlelight" (Plath) **5**:345; **51**:353

By Cheating the Heart (Tchicaya)
See *A Triche-coeur*
"By Comparison" (MacCaig) **36**:279
"By Daylight and in Dream" (Wheelock) **14**:570
By Daylight and in Dream: New and Selected Poems (Wheelock) **14**:570
"By Destiny Denied" (Allen) **52**:42
"By Ferry to the Island" (Smith) **64**:388, 393, 398
"By Frazier Creek Falls" (Snyder) **120**:351
By Grand Central Station I Sat Down and Wept (Smart) **54**:411-15, 417-23, 425-26
By Heart: 101 Poems to Remember (Hughes) **119**:297-98
"By Himself" (Cocteau) **8**:146
"By His Bootstraps" (Heinlein) **26**:163; **55**:302
"By Lamplight" (Kunitz) **148**:75
By Land, By Sea (Hoffman) **141**:270-73, 275, 280, 283, 308-09
By Love Possessed (Cozzens) **1**:65-6; **4**:111, 113-16; **11**:126-27, 131-32; **92**:177-82, 184-86, 189-90, 193-94, 211
"By Means of a Reciprocal Correspondence" (Voinovich) **10**:506; **49**:373, 376; **147**:279
"By Means of Mutual Correspondence" (Voinovich)
See "By Means of a Reciprocal Correspondence"
"By Morning" (Swenson) **106**:319
By Night Unstarred: An Autobiographical Novel (Kavanagh) **22**:244
"By No Means Native" (Rich) **36**:365
"By Special Request" (Waugh) **27**:476
"By the Belgian Frontier" (Blunden) **56**:45
"By the Burn" (Kelman) **86**:185
"By the Falls" (Harrison) **42**:203
"By the Flooded Canal" (Ashbery) **77**:67
By the Highway Home (Stolz) **12**:554
"By the Lake" (Sitwell) **67**:335
"By the Light of an Apple" (Cixous) **92**:81
"By the North Gate" (Oates) **6**:370; **134**:248
By the North Gate (Oates) **6**:369-70; **108**:341, 368; **134**:247
By the Pricking of My Thumbs (Christie) **12**:117; **48**:71-2, 75
"By the Riverside" (Kizer) **80**:173, 185
"By the Road to the Air Base" (Winters) **32**:468
"By the Sea" (Adams) **46**:17
"By the Sea" (Gellhorn) **60**:189, 192
"By the Sea" (Smith) **64**:390, 393
"By the Sea" (Sondheim) **30**:394
By the Seashore (Akhmatova) **64**:11
By the Shores of Gitchee Gumee (Janowitz) **145**:346
"By the Snake River" (Stafford) **29**:382
"By the Waters of Babylon" (Celan)
See "An den Wassern Babels"
By the Waters of Manhattan (Reznikoff) **9**:450
By the Waters of Whitechapel (Kops) **4**:274
"By Way of Acknowledgment" (Castillo) **151**:47
"By Way of Private Correspondence" (Voinovich)
See "By Means of a Reciprocal Correspondence"
"By What Means" (Klappert) **57**:257
"Bye, Bye Love" (Simon) **17**:460, 465
Bye-Bye, Black Bird (Desai) **37**:66-7, 70-1; **97**:149, 160
"Bye-Child" (Heaney) **5**:170; **7**:148
"Bygones" (Wright) **146**:306
"Byl letnii polden" (Trifonov) **45**:408
The By-Pass Control (Spillane) **13**:528
"Bypassing Rue Descartes" (Milosz) **56**:244; **82**:301
"Byre" (MacCaig) **36**:282
"The Byrnies" (Gunn) **18**:203; **32**:208
"The Bystander" (Berriault) **54**:4-5; **109**:96
"Bystanders" (Matthews) **40**:323
Býti básníkem (Seifert) **44**:423, 426; **93**:308, 322, 331-32, 335-37
"Byzantium" (Kunitz) **148**:77
"Byzantium" (Thesen) **56**:422
Byzantium Endures (Moorcock) **27**:351-52; **58**:349, 352-59
"C" (Merrill) **8**:385-86
C (Reading) **47**:352-54
"C Major" (Transtroemer) **52**:410
"C Minor" (Wilbur) **53**:399
"C. Musonius Rufus" (Davenport) **38**:140
A Cab at the Door (Pritchett) **5**:352-53; **13**:465-66
Cab Calloway Stands In for the Moon (Reed) **60**:306-07
"Cabal" (Swenson) **106**:331
The Cabala (Wilder) **1**:366; **6**:576; **15**:571-74; **82**:339-40, 342, 344-45, 356, 362, 369-72, 376, 379, 382
"The Cabalist of East Broadway" (Singer) **6**:510; **38**:407
Caballo de copas (Alegria) **57**:10, 13-14
Cabaret (Fosse) **20**:122-23
"Cabbage" (Simic) **130**:318, 322
Cabbage Gardens (Howe) **152**:157, 220, 232, 235
Cabbagetown (Garner) **13**:236
"The Cabdriver's Smile" (Levertov) **15**:339
El cabellero inactual (Azorín) **11**:27
La cabeza de la hidra (Fuentes) **13**:231-32; **41**:167-68, 171; **60**:153, 170
"The Cabin" (Carver) **53**:67
"A Cabin in the Clearing" (Frost) **9**:224
The Cabin: Reminiscence and Diversions (Mamet) **91**:144, 146-47, 150
Cabin the in the Sky (Corcoran) **17**:76
Un cabinet d'amateur (Perec) **116**:238, 247, 250
"The Cabinet Maker" (Sayles) **14**:483
"The Cabinet of Edgar Allan Poe" (Carter) **41**:122
The Cabinet of Jan Svankmajer (The Brothers Quay) **95**:335, 341, 344-45, 348, 351, 353
"A Cabinet of Seeds Displayed" (Nemerov) **9**:394-95
Cab-Intersec (Walker) **14**:552
Cabiria (Fellini)
See *Le notti di Cabiria*
Cables to Rage (Lorde) **71**:260
"Cables to Rage, or I've Been Talking on This Street Corner a Hell of a Long Time" (Lorde) **71**:232
"Cables to the Ace" (Merton) **83**:384
Cables to the Ace; or, Familiar Liturgies of Misunderstanding (Merton) **1**:211; **3**:336; **83**:388-89, 397, 404
"Caboose Thoughts" (Sandburg) **35**:352
Cabot Wright Begins (Purdy) **2**:348-49; **4**:422-23; **10**:421, 423-24; **52**:343, 345, 347
"Cabras" (Blackburn) **43**:68
Cacao (Amado)
See *Cacáu*
Cacáu (Amado) **40**:24-7; **106**:71
"The Cachalot" (Pratt) **19**:377-79, 382-83
"Los cachorros" (Vargas Llosa) **31**:443-44
Los cachorros (Vargas Llosa) **10**:498; **31**:443-45; **85**:352
"El cacique Cruzto" (Ulibarrí) **83**:417
Cactus Country (Abbey) **36**:16-17
Cadastre (Césaire) **112**:15, 18
"Cadence" (Bowering) **15**:82
"Cadence" (Dubus) **36**:144; **97**:229
Cadenţe (Arghezi) **80**:6, 8
"Cadenza" (Hughes) **9**:280
"Cadieu" (Ferron) **94**:103, 120
The Cadillac Cowboys (Swarthout) **35**:400-01
"Cadillac Flambé" (Ellison) **86**:318; **114**:100
Cadillac Jack (McMurtry) **27**:332-34; **44**:254, 258
Le cadran lunaire (Mandiargues) **41**:275, 278-79
Cae la noche tropical (Puig) **65**:269, 272; **133**:342, 347-48
"Caer Arianrhod" (Fuller) **62**:192
"Caesar's Platter" (White) **49**:408
Caesar's Wife (Maugham) **1**:204; **11**:368; **15**:366; **67**:223
"Caeser's Quarry" (Powys) **125**:278
"Café" (Bowering) **32**:46
"Café" (Milosz) **31**:260
"Café: 3 A.M." (Hughes) **108**:329-30
Café de artistas (Cela) **122**:51
"The Café Filtre" (Blackburn) **43**:63
Café Myriam (Klima) **56**:166-68
"Cafe on the Left Bank" (McCartney) **35**:285
"Cafe Society" (Vanderhaeghe) **41**:450, 452
"Café Tableau" (Swenson) **106**:338
"The Cafeteria" (Singer) **38**:409; **69**:320
"Cafeteria in Boston" (Gunn) **81**:176, 178, 187
"The Cage" (Bissoondath) **120**:7, 27
"The Cage" (Montague) **46**:266-67, 277
The Cage (Cheever) **48**:64-5
"Cage, 1974" (Rozewicz) **23**:362
La cage aux folles (Fierstein) **33**:156-57
La cage de verre (Simenon) **2**:398
A Cage for Lovers (Powell) **66**:362-63
"The Cage of Sand" (Ballard) **14**:40
A Cage of Spines (Swenson) **61**:390, 399; **106**:314-16, 319, 325,340, 347
Cage without Grievance (Graham) **29**:193-94, 198
"Caged Bird" (Angelou) **77**:31
"Cages" (Vanderhaeghe) **41**:448-50
Cahena: A Dream of the Past (Wellman) **49**:397-98
Cahier d'un retour au pays natal (Césaire) **19**:95, 97-8; **32**:110, 113; **112**:6, 8-12, 21-4, 26-9, 31-3, 35-9
Cahiers pour une morale (Sartre) **50**:379, 382
Cahoot's Macbeth (Stoppard) **29**:395-97; **91**:190
"Cailleach" (Jones) **42**:242
Caimán (Buero Vallejo) **46**:98-100; **139**:10, 12, 25-7, 57
Cain His Brother (Perry) **126**:337-39
"Cain Rose Up" (King) **61**:331
Cain, Where Is Your Brother? (Mauriac) **56**:219
Cain x Three (Cain) **28**:52
The Caine Mutiny Court Martial (Altman) **116**:59
The Caine Mutiny Court-Martial (Wouk) **1**:375-77; **9**:579-80; **38**:444-48, 452
"Caino" (Ungaretti) **11**:555
The Cairo Trilogy (Mahfūz)
See *al-Thulatthiyya*
Caitaani mutharaba-ini (Ngũgĩ wa Thiong'o) **36**:319-20, 322-24
Cajetan et la taupe (Theriault) **79**:412
Cakes and Ale; or, The Skeleton in the Cupboard (Maugham) **1**:204; **11**:370; **15**:367; **67**:206, 210-15, 218-19, 229-30; **93**:257, 263
"Cakewalk" (Smith) **25**:409
Cakewalk (Smith) **25**:409-10; **73**:340, 355, 357-59
Cal (Mac Laverty) **31**:255-57
Cal y canto (Alberti) **7**:9
"El calamar opta por su tinta" (Bioy Casares) **88**:94
"Calamiterror" (Barker) **8**:46; **48**:10, 12, 17, 23-4
Calamity Town (Queen) **11**:458
"Calamus" (Sandburg) **4**:463
A Calander and an Hourglass (Konwicki)
See *Kalendarz i klepsydra*
"The Calculation of Probability" (Landolfi) **49**:212
"Calculations I" (Schmidt)
See "Berechnungen I"
The Calculta Chromosone (Ghosh) **153**:108-11, 113-15, 129
Calderón and the Seizures of Honor (Honig) **33**:213-14
Caldicott Place (Streatfeild) **21**:409-10
"Cale frîntă" (Arghezi) **80**:8
Cale sèche (Reverdy) **53**:282-83
Calendar (Egoyan) **151**:129-30, 134, 136, 139,

141-42, 146-47, 150, 152-53, 161, 166-67
Calendar of an Invisible April (Elytis) **49**:118-19
"A Calendar of Love" (Brown) **48**:52, 57
A Calendar of Love and Other Stories (Brown) **48**:51-2, 54, 57; **100**:84
A Calendar of Sin: American Melodramas (Scott) **43**:377-79, 385
"Calendrier lagunaire" (Césaire) **112**:31
"Caliban Remembers" (Weiss) **8**:545; **14**:553, 556-57
"Caliban über Setebos" (Schmidt) **56**:391
"Caliban's Daughter" (Cliff) **120**:92-93
Caliban's Fillibuster (West) **7**:523-24; **96**:375, 377, 384, 386
"Calico Shoes" (Farrell) **66**:129
Calico Shoes and Other Stories (Farrell) **66**:129-30
"California" (Mitchell) **12**:443
"California" (Zamora) **89**:370, 372-73, 376, 392-93
"California Dreaming" (Wright) **146**:313, 315, 317, 336, 359-60
The California Feeling: A Personal View (Beagle) **104**:5-7
"California Girls" (Wilson) **12**:644, 647, 649
California Split (Altman) **16**:30-1, 33-5; **116**:14, 16, 21-2, 48, 67
California Suite (Simon) **11**:496; **31**:403-04
"California, This is Minnesota Speaking" (Dunn) **36**:153
California Time (Raphael) **14**:437
"California Variations" (Carroll) **143**:33
Californians (Jeffers) **11**:305; **54**:233, 235-36, 244, 250
"Caligula" (Lowell) **4**:299; **8**:350-51, 355
Caligula (Camus) **1**:52; **2**:100; **9**:139, 141-42, 145-46, 152; **11**:93, 95; **14**:108, 114-15; **32**:84-6, 88-90, 92-3, 96, 98, 100-01; **63**:76-7; **69**:109; **124**:11, 21-2, 24, 31, 33
Caligula? (Vidal) **142**:304
Caligula, and Three Other Plays (Camus) **32**:84
"Ca'line's prayer" (Clifton) **66**:73
"Call" (Bagryana)
See "Zov"
"Call" (Lorde) **71**:255, 260-61
"The Call" (O'Brien) **36**:340
"The Call" (Williams) **148**:352
"The Call Across the Valley of Not-Knowing" (Kinnell) **129**:245, 251-53, 255, 264
The Call: An American Missionary in China (Hersey) **40**:240-42; **81**:335; **97**:324
"Call Any Vegetable" (Zappa) **17**:588
"Call at Corazón" (Bowles) **53**:37, 39, 49
Call at Corazón and Other Stories (Bowles) **53**:49
"Call First" (Campbell) **42**:87, 89
Call for a Miracle (Kiely) **23**:262; **43**:245
"A Call for Militant Resistance" (Hooks) **94**:145
A Call for Nixonicide and Glory to the Chilean Revolution (Neruda)
See *Incitación al Nixonicidio y alabanza de la revolución Chilena*
Call for the Dead (le Carré) **3**:281; **5**:233-34; **15**:325
A Call in the Midst of a Crowd (Corn) **33**:114-16, 118
"Call It a Good Marriage" (Graves) **45**:169
"Call It a Loan" (Browne) **21**:42
Call It Experience: The Years of Learning How to Write (Caldwell) **50**:299-300
"Call It Fear" (Harjo) **83**:266
Call It Sleep (Roth) **2**:377-78; **6**:470-74; **11**:487-90; **104**:238-58, 262-65, 268-70, 273-75, 277-79, 281-91, 294-300, 304, 306, 311-13, 315, 317-30
Call Me a Liar (Mortimer) **28**:283, 285
Call Me Charley (Jackson) **12**:289-91
"Call Me Comrade" (Clark) **5**:107
Call Me Ishmael: A Study of Melville (Olson) **5**:326-27; **29**:326-27, 332
Call Me Ishtar (Lerman) **56**:175-76, 178
"Call Me Lightning" (Townshend) **17**:530
Call Me Ruth (Sachs) **35**:334
"Call Me Sailor" (Sillitoe) **148**:199
Call My People Home (Livesay) **79**:345-46
"The Call of Nature" (Harrison) **43**:180
The Call of Service: A Witness to Idealism (Coles) **108**:207, 209
The Call of Stories (Coles) **108**:193, 201
"The Call of the Sea" (Neruda)
See "Llama el océano"
"The Call of the Wild" (Scott) **22**:372
"The Call of the Wild" (Snyder) **120**:341
"A Call on Mrs. Forrester" (Thurber) **11**:533
A Call to Order (Cocteau) **43**:99-100
"The Call Up" (Clash) **30**:47-9
"Callaghan Revisited" (Avison) **97**:108
"The Callalloo Interview" (Delany) **141**:116
Callander Square (Perry) **126**:325-26
"Calle Sierpes" (Cabral de Melo Neto) **76**:167
"Calle Vision" (Rich) **125**:335
"Called" (O Hehir) **41**:324
"Called Back" (Wright) **146**:308
"Called Home" (Beer) **58**:38
The Callender Papers (Voigt) **30**:419-20
"The Caller" (Scannell) **49**:327
Caller Anonymous (Hamilton) **51**:193
The Call-Girls (Koestler) **3**:271
"Calling Card" (Campbell)
See "First Foot"
Calling for Help (Handke)
See *Hilferufe*
Calling Myself Home (Hogan) **73**:149, 155-57
"The Calling of Names" (Angelou) **64**:32
Calling Out to Yeti (Szymborska) **99**:194, 199, 203, 207, 211
"Calling Sister Midnight" (Bowie) **17**:66
"Calling to the Badger" (Bly) **10**:59
"Callings" (Galeano) **72**:139
"The Calm" (Carver) **53**:64; **126**:108-09, 112, 125
"The Calm" (Gallagher) **63**:118
"Calm" (Hass) **99**:143
The Calm (Kieslowski)
See *Spokoj*
Calm Before the Storm (Kieslowski)
See *Spokoj*
"A Calm Rain" (Blunden) **56**:39
"Le Calmant" (Beckett) **4**:51; **10**:34, 36; **18**:49; **29**:63
"The Calmative" (Beckett)
See "Le Calmant"
"Calming Kali" (Clifton) **66**:80
"Calvin in the Casino" (Cassity) **42**:97
"Calypso" (Broumas) **73**:2
Calypso (Hunter) **31**:224
"The Camaldolese Come to Big Sur" (Beecher) **6**:49
"Camarillo Brillo" (Zappa) **17**:589
"Camberley" (Betjeman) **43**:40
"The Camberwell Beauty" (Pritchett) **5**:354; **13**:465, 467-68; **41**:332
The Camberwell Beauty, and Other Stories (Pritchett) **5**:352-54; **13**:465
Cambio de armas (Valenzuela) **31**:438-39; **104**:363, 370-72, 376-77, 385, 392
Cambio de piel (Fuentes) **3**:175-76; **8**:223; **22**:165-67; **41**:167, 169, 171; **60**:152-55, 164, 171; **113**:230-31, 233-34
Cambridge (Phillips) **96**:329-33, 342-52, 354-55, 357
" Cambridge Elegy" (Olds) **85**:295
"Camden Town" (Dickey) **47**:92
"Came Away with Betjeman..." (Ewart) **46**:154
"Came the Terrible Dark Lords" (Johnson) **7**:415
"Camelot" (Watkins) **43**:443
The Camel's Eye (Aitmatov)
See *Verbliuzhii glaz*
"Cameo Appearance" (Simic) **130**:346
The Camera Always Lies (Hood) **15**:283; **28**:188, 190, 195
Camera Buff (Kieslowski)
See *Amator*
Camera Lucida: Reflections on Photography (Barthes)
See *La chambre claire: Note sur la photographie*
The Cameraman (Keaton) **20**:196
"Camilla" (Robison) **42**:339
Camilla Dickinson (L'Engle) **12**:345
Camille: A Tear-Jerker (Ludlam) **46**:240-42; **50**:342-44, 346
"Caminado" (Guillén) **48**:162
El camino (Delibes) **18**:109-10, 112-13, 117
"Camino de amor" (Laughlin) **49**:224
"El Camino de Santiago" (Carpentier) **110**:48, 54, 57
Camino Real (Williams) **2**:465; **5**:498-500; **7**:543; **11**:571-73; **15**:581; **45**:446-47; **71**:269, 384, 386, 405; **111**:379-83, 388
"El camino verde" (Blackburn) **43**:64
Le camion: Suivi de entretien avec Michelle Porte (Duras) **20**:101-03; **40**:178, 183; **68**:90, 96
La camisa de fuerza (Parra) **102**:334, 343
"Camouflage" (Longley) **29**:292
Camouflage (Muske) **90**:310, 312
"Camouflaging the Chimera" (Komunyakaa) **94**:228-30, 240
"The Camp" (Davis) **49**:92
"Camp 1940" (Senghor) **130**:259
"Camp Cataract" (Bowles) **68**:6-7, 9, 11-14, 16, 19-21
Camp Concentration (Disch) **36**:123-24
"A Camp in the Prussian Forrest" (Jarrell) **6**:261
"The Camp in the Wood (Somme Battle, 1916)" (Blunden) **56**:44
"Camp Rose" (Freeman) **55**:56-7
The Campaign (Fuentes) **113**:252-54
"Campaigner" (Young) **17**:577
"Campaigning" (Steinem) **63**:384
Campamento (Lopez y Fuentes) **32**:279-81
The Campfire Reflection (Trifonov) **45**:420-21
"Camping at Split Rock" (Wright) **53**:425
"Camping in Madera Canyon" (Swenson) **106**:351
"Camping in the Valley" (Tate) **25**:427
"Camping Out" (Empson) **8**:201; **19**:155, 157
"Campo dei Fiori" (Milosz) **56**:247-48; **82**:278, 299
Campos de Níjar (Goytisolo) **23**:185; **133**:45-46
Campus Ethnoviolence and the Policy of Options (Ehrlich) **70**:378
"The Campus on the Hill" (Snodgrass) **2**:404; **18**:491; **68**:388
"Can a Woman Be a Shit?" (Ewart) **46**:154
Can Ethics Be Christian? (Gustafson) **100**:201, 229
"Can Graham Greene Write English?" (Fussell) **74**:125
"Can I Get A Witness" (Jordan) **114**:151
"Can I See Arcturus from Where I Stand?" (Warren) **8**:539; **13**:573, 577-78
"Can one live too long writing verse?" (Rozewicz)
See "więc jednak żyje się pisząc wiersze sa długo"
Can You Do It Until You Need Glasses? The Different Drug Book (Felsen) **17**:124-25
Can You Find Me (Fry) **14**:188-89
Can You Hear Me at the Back? (Clark) **29**:128-29
"'Can You Remember?'" (Blunden) **56**:30
Can You See Me Yet? (Findley) **102**:96-7, 103, 105
Can You Sue Your Parents for Malpractice? (Danziger) **21**:84-5
"Caña" (Guillén) **48**:163; **79**:240
"Canada: Case History, 1945" (Birney) **6**:76; **11**:49
"The Canada Council Poet" (Bowering) **47**:31
Canada Made Me (Levine) **54**:292, 294, 298-300

"The Canada of Myth and Reality" (Davies) **25**:132
Canada udner Siege (Berton) **104**:58
"The Canadian Authors Meet" (Scott) **22**:372, 376
"Canadian Experience" (Clarke) **53**:97
"The Canadian Prairies View of Literature" (Donnell) **34**:155, 157-59
"The Canadian Social Register" (Scott) **22**:372
Canadian Sunset (McFadden) **48**:258-59
"Canadian Writing: No Name Is My Name" (Kroetsch) **132**:208-9
"Canal Bank Walk" (Kavanagh) **22**:243
"The Canal Garden" (Seifert) **93**:337
Canal Zone (Wiseman) **20**:477
"Canaletto in the National Gallery of Ireland" (Boland) **113**:108
"Canals" (Sillitoe) **57**:388
"A Canary for One" (Hemingway) **6**:231
Canary in a Cat House (Vonnegut) **3**:500; **111**:351
"Canary in Bloom" (Dove) **50**:153, 155, 157
"O canavial e o mar" (Cabral de Melo Neto) **76**:168
Can-Can (Linney) **51**:263
Canção de berço (Andrade) **18**:4
Cancer (Silverstein and Silverstein) **17**:453-54
Cancer (Weller) **10**:525-26; **53**:386-93
"Cancer: A Dream" (Sissman) **18**:488, 490
"Cancer and Society" (Wolf) **150**:333
"The Cancer Cells" (Eberhart) **19**:144
The Cancer Journals (Lorde) **71**:237, 243, 248, 252-53
Cancer Lab (Berger) **12**:40
The Cancer Ward (Solzhenitsyn)
See *Rakovyi korpus*
"Cancerqueen" (Landolfi)
See "Cancroregina"
Cancerqueen and Other Stories (Landolfi) **11**:321; **49**:210-13
"Canción" (Parra) **102**:339
"Una canción de amor" (Neruda) **28**:309-10
"Canción de cuña" (Poniatowska) **140**:295
Canción de gesta (Neruda) **28**:312, 314
"La canción del bongo" (Guillén) **48**:162; **79**:233, 250
"La canción del oeste" (Cernuda) **54**:57
"La canciónde Peronelle" (Arreola) **147**:31
Canciones rusas (Parra) **102**:340, 356
Les cancrelats (Tchicaya) **101**:354-55, 357-58, 362-65
"Cancroregina" (Landolfi) **49**:209-10, 212
"The Candidate" (Tuohy) **37**:432
Candidate (Fuller) **25**:180
Candide (Hellman) **52**:201
Candide (Sondheim) **147**:256-57
Candido; or, A Dream Dreamed in Sicily (Sciascia) **41**:385, 387, 394
Candle (Akhmadulina) **53**:15
A Candle at Dusk (Almedingen) **12**:4
"The Candle Flame" (Lewis) **41**:255, 263
"A Candle for Pasch" (Gustafson) **36**:218
A Candle for St. Jude (Godden) **53**:155-56, 161
"A Candle in a Gale Wind" (Childress) **96**:114-15, 118
A Candle in Her Room (Arthur) **12**:24-6, 29
Candle in the Wind (Solzhenitsyn)
See *Svecha na vetru*
The Candle in the Wind (White) **30**:444-46
Candle of the Wicked (Wellman) **49**:388
"Candle Poems" (MacNeice) **53**:233
"Candles" (Plath) **5**:345; **11**:449; **111**:181
Candles in Babylon (Levertov) **28**:243; **66**:237-39, 250
"The Candles of Your Eyes" (Purdy) **52**:350
The Candles of Your Eyes (Purdy) **52**:349-50
Candy (Southern) **7**:453-54
The Candy Factory (Fraser) **64**:167-69, 171-75
"Candy Says" (Reed) **21**:314, 317, 322-23
"Candy Seller" (Bennett) **28**:26
"Candy Store Rock" (Page and Plant) **12**:480
"Candy-Man Beechum" (Caldwell) **1**:51; **60**:50, 67
"Candy's Room" (Springsteen) **17**:483, 485
Cane (Toomer) **1**:341; **4**:548-50; **13**:550-52, 556; **22**:423, 425-26, 429
"The Cane in the Corridor" (Thurber) **5**:432
"Canecutter's Song" (Dabydeen) **34**:148
"Canis Major" (Frost) **26**:118
"Canje" (Harris) **25**:212
"The Cannas" (Fugard) **48**:109
Cannery Row (Steinbeck) **1**:325; **9**:514, 517-18, 520; **21**:382, 391; **34**:405, 410, 412-14; **45**:370, 373; **59**:350-51; **75**:350; **124**:393, 424, 426, 428
"Cannery Row Revisited " (Naipaul) **105**:155
The Cannibal (Hawkes) **1**:138; **2**:183; **3**:221, 223; **4**:212-14; **7**:141-42, 145-46; **14**:238; **15**:270-71, 273; **27**:190-91, 195-96, 199; **49**:155-56, 161, 164
The Cannibal Galaxy (Ozick) **28**:354-56; **62**:341, 343, 346-47, 351-55, 357-58; **155**:138-39, 167, 169-70, 179-81, 183-85, 190, 196, 202, 216
A Cannibal in Manhattan (Janowitz) **145**:327-28, 332-33, 341, 344-45
The Cannibals (Tabori) **19**:437-38
Cannibals and Christians (Mailer) **1**:189-90, 192; **2**:258, 264; **3**:313, 320; **28**:256; **74**:212; **111**:95, 100
"Cannibals and Missionaries" (Fuller) **62**:186
Cannibals and Missionaries (Fuller) **62**:186-87, 194, 197, 201, 203
Cannibals and Missionaries (McCarthy) **14**:359-64; **39**:488; **59**:289
"Canning" (Piercy) **128**:231
"Can(n)on to the Right of Us, Can(n)on to the Left of Us: A Plea for Difference" (Perloff) **137**:289
"Canoeing at Night" (Leithauser) **27**:242
"The Canoes" (Dunn) **40**:170-71
"The Canonization" (Brutus) **43**:91
"Canons of Christianity" (Ochs) **17**:331
Canopus in Argos: Archives (Lessing) **15**:333-34; **22**:285-86; **40**:303-04, 306-07, 309, 315-16; **94**:252, 258, 261, 282, 286-87
"Canopus, Vega, Rigel, Aldeban" (Dickey) **3**:127
Can't Buy a Thrill (Becker and Fagen) **26**:79, 81
"Can't Depend on Love" (Lightfoot) **26**:279
Can't Pay? Won't Pay! (Fo) **32**:174; **109**:143
Can't Quit You, Baby (Douglas) **73**:90-2, 98-9
"Can't Stand Losing You" (Police, The) **26**:363-64
Cantares Mexicanos I (Cardenal) **31**:73
Cantares Mexicanos II (Cardenal) **31**:73
"El cántaro roto" (Paz) **65**:190-91
La cantatrice chauve (Ionesco) **1**:154; **4**:250-52; **6**:248, 252-54; **9**:286; **11**:290; **15**:298; **41**:224-25, 229-30, 232; **86**:331-33, 339
The Canterbury Tales (Pasolini)
See *I racconti di Canterbury*
Canti Barocchi (Piccolo) **13**:441
"Canticle" (Berry) **46**:70
"Canticle" (McAuley) **45**:250
"Canticle" (Nowlan) **15**:399
Canticle (Guillén)
See *Cántico*
"Canticle for Good Friday" (Hill) **45**:189
A Canticle for Leibowitz (Miller) **4**:352-53; **30**:253-58, 260-63, 265-66
"Canticle of St. John" (Smith) **15**:515
Cántico (Guillén) **11**:262-63
La cantidad hechizada (Lezama Lima) **101**:121
La cantidad hechizada (Lezama Lima) **4**:288
"The Cantina" (Soto) **80**:276
"Cantina Music" (Walcott) **25**:456
"Canto I" (Pound) **48**:282; **112**:334, 336, 345, 350, 354, 356-57
"Canto II" (Pound) **112**:323-25, 336
"Canto IV" (Pound) **10**:400; **112**:310-12
"Canto VII" (Pound) **48**:283; **112**:310, 312
"Canto VIII" (Pound) **10**:402; **112**:318, 337
"Canto IX" (Pound) **10**:402
"Canto XI" (Pound) **112**:337
"Canto XIII" (Pound) **48**:293; **112**:336-37
"Canto XXV" (Pound) **7**:327
"Canto XXXVI" (Pound) **48**:282
"Canto XXXIX" (Pound) **7**:328
"Canto XLII" (Pound) **112**:302
"Canto XLIV" (Pound) **112**:302
"Canto XLV" (Pound) **7**:330; **112**:357
"Canto XLVII" (Pound) **7**:328; **13**:462
"Canto XLIX" (Pound) **112**:343
"Canto LII" (Pound) **7**:327; **112**:332, 335
"Canto LXI" (Pound) **112**:332
"Canto LXII" (Pound) **112**:332
"Canto LXXI" (Pound) **112**:332, 335
"Canto LXXII" (Pound) **112**:335
"Canto LXXIV" (Pound) **1**:277; **7**:328; **48**:287; **112**:301-08, 322, 326, 337, 339, 350, 355
"Canto LXXVI" (Pound) **112**:304, 355, 357
"Canto LXXX" (Pound) **7**:326; **112**:355-57
"Canto LXXXI" (Pound) **7**:326, 328, 335; **48**:290
"Canto LXXXIV" (Pound) **48**:285; **112**:339
"Canto LXXXVII" (Pound) **112**:357
"Canto LXXXIX" (Pound) **48**:294
"Canto XCIX" (Pound) **48**:286
"Canto CXVI" (Pound) **7**:329
"Canto CXVII" (Pound) **112**:335
"Canto a las madres de los milicianos muertos" (Neruda) **62**:323
"Canto a Stalingrado" (Neruda) **62**:336
"Canto amor" (Berryman) **3**:70
"A canto da Andaluzia" (Cabral de Melo Neto) **76**:163
Canto for a Gypsy (Smith) **25**:412-13
Canto general de Chile (Neruda) **2**:309; **5**:301-04; **7**:258-59, 261-62; **9**:396-97; **28**:309-14; **62**:327, 329, 332-33
"Canto nacional" (Cardenal) **31**:77
"Canto negro" (Guillén) **48**:168; **79**:233
Cantos (Pound) **1**:274-76; **2**:339-45; **3**:394-99; **4**:407-18; **5**:348-49; **7**:323, 325-36, 338; **10**:400-03, 406-08; **13**:454, 456-57, 459, 461-62; **18**:422-23, 425-27; **34**:507, 509-1; **112**:30106, 308, 320-24, 327-29, 331-40, 343, 357
"Cantos LII-LXXXI" (Pound) **18**:423
Cantos ceremoniales (Neruda) **28**:314
Cantos para soldados y sones para turistas (Guillén) **48**:158-60, 162, 164; **79**:229, 251
"Canute" (Davies) **23**:148
"The Canyon Wren" (Snyder) **120**:326
"Canzon: Of Incense" (Pound) **10**:407
"Canzon: The Yearly Slain" (Pound) **10**:407
"Canzone" (Ashbery) **13**:35
"Canzone" (Ungaretti) **7**:481-82, 485; **11**:556
"La canzone clandestina della Grande Opera" (Morante) **47**:281
"Canzones" (Okigbo)
See "Four Canzones (1957-1961)"
Canzoni (Pound) **2**:343
O cão sem plumas (Cabral de Melo Neto) **76**:152-53, 156-57, 168
Cap of Darkness (Wakoski) **40**:452, 455-57
Capable of Honor (Drury) **37**:102-03, 105
The Cape (Eliade)
See *Die Pelerine*
"Cape Alava" (Hugo) **32**:237
"Cape Breton" (Bishop) **9**:95; **32**:31, 34, 42-3
"Cape Cod" (Brodsky)
See "A Cape Cod Lullaby"
"Cape Cod Autumn" (Starbuck) **53**:352
"A Cape Cod Lullaby" (Brodsky) **13**:117; **36**:75-78, 80; **50**:124-25, 128, 132; **100**:43, 48, 50, 54
"A Cape Cod Lullaby" (Brodsky)
See "A Cape Cod Lullaby"
"Cape Dread" (Merwin) **5**:288; **13**:383
Cape Drives (Hope) **52**:208

Cape Fear (MacDonald)
See *The Executioners*
Cape Fear (Scorsese) **89**:258, 261-63, 265-67, 269
"The Cape of Good Hope" (Morgan) **31**:277
Cape of Storms (Brink) **106**:126-33
"The Capibaribe Valley" (Cabral de Melo Neto)
See "Valo do Capibaribe"
Capitães da areia (Amado) **40**:26-7; **106**:60
"The Capital" (Auden) **43**:22
Capital (Duffy) **37**:117
Capital City (Sandoz) **28**:402, 406-07
"Capital, Just Capital" (Starbuck) **53**:354
"The Capital of the World" (Hemingway) **6**:229
"Capital Punishment" (Vizenor) **103**:311
"Capitalism, Modernism and Postmodernism" (Eagleton) **63**:107
Capitalism: The Unknown Ideal (Rand) **30**:304
"The Capitalist's Love Letter" (Dunn) **36**:154
Capitol (Card) **50**:143
"Capitol Air" (Ginsberg) **36**:196
"Capitol Radio" (Clash) **30**:43
Capitol: The Worthing Chronicle (Card) **47**:66-8
"Caplja" (Aksyonov)
See "The Heron"
Caplja (Aksyonov) **37**:12
Le caporal epinglé (Renoir) **20**:292-93, 297-98, 307
Cappella (Horovitz) **56**:151
Caprice (Bowering) **47**:33-4
"Caprichos" (Transtroemer) **52**:410
The Capricorn Bracelet (Sutcliff) **26**:437
Capricorn Games (Silverberg) **140**:343-44
"Caprilarología" (Asturias) **8**:25
"The Captain" (Dubus) **36**:147
"The Captain" (Hersey) **81**:330
"The Captain" (Michaels) **6**:325
The Captain (de Hartog) **19**:131
"Captain Ahab, A Novel by the White Whale" (West) **96**:375
The Captain and the Enemy (Greene) **70**:292, 294; **72**:177; **125**:184, 186
Captain Blackman (Williams) **5**:496-97
"Captain Blood" (Barthelme) **46**:43
"Captain Candelario's Heroic Last Stand" (Ferré)
See "La extraña muerte del capitancito Candelario"
"Captain Carpenter" (Ransom) **2**:363; **4**:431; **5**:365
Captain Cook (MacLean) **50**:350
"Captain Dobbin" (Slessor) **14**:496-97
The Captain from Connecticut (Forester) **35**:164-65
"Captain Haddock" (Szirtes) **46**:393
"Captain Hendrik's Story" (Ingalls) **42**:234
"Captain Holm" (Swenson) **61**:402; **106**:329
Captain Horatio Hornblower (Forester) **35**:161, 163, 170
"Captain Jack" (Joel) **26**:213, 218-19, 222, 215
Captain Maximus (Hannah) **38**:233-35; **90**:137-39, 144, 147, 159, 160
"Captain Nicholas Strong" (Ciardi) **40**:155-56
The Captain of Köpenick: A German Fairytale in Four Acts (Zuckmayer) **18**:553-56
Captain of the Discovery: The Story of Captain George Vancouver (Haig-Brown) **21**:139-41
Captain Pantoja and the Special Service (Vargas Llosa)
See *Pantaleón y las visitadoras*
Captain Quiros (McAuley) **45**:248-52, 254
"Captain Scuttle" (Scannell) **49**:331
Captain Shigemoto's Mother (Tanizaki)
See *Shōshō Shigemoto no haha*
Captain Slaughterboard Drops Anchor (Peake) **54**:369, 372-74
Captain S.O.S. (Simenon) **47**:374
The Captain with the Whiskers (Kiely) **23**:263; **43**:245
Captains and the Kings (Caldwell) **2**:95; **28**:65-6; **39**:302-03
The Captains and the Kings (Johnston) **7**:185-86; **150**:28, 30
"The Captain's Gift" (Stafford) **4**:518; **19**:431
"The Captain's Son" (Taylor) **18**:527; **50**:251; **71**:304, 308, 315, 317
The Captain's Verses (Neruda)
See *Versos del capitán*
The Captain's Watch (Garfield) **12**:235
"Captation" (Damas) **84**:159
Un captif amoureux (Genet) **46**:183
"The Captive" (Borges) **1**:39
"The Captive" (Gordon) **29**:187, 189; **83**:231
"The Captive" (Singer) **9**:486
The Captive (O'Dell) **30**:275-78
The Captive Mind (Milosz)
See *Zniewolony umysl*
The Captive of Kensington Palace (Hibbert) **7**:155
"The Captive Speaking" (Carroll) **38**:102-03
Captive Universe (Harrison) **42**:200, 205-06
"Captives of Our 'Classics'" (Goytisolo) **133**:60
"Captives of the Flame" (Delany) **14**:144
"Captivity" (Alexie) **96**:12
"The Captivity and REstoration of Mrs. Mary Rowlandson" (Howe) **152**:157, 159, 162, 213, 239, 241-42
"Captivity Captive" (Hall) **51**:179-81
The Captivity of Pixie Shedman (Linney) **51**:261
"Captivity of the Fly" (MacLeish) **8**:362
The Capture of Detroit (Berton) **104**:60
"The Captured Woman" (Barthelme) **46**:36; **115**:65
"The Capuchin from Toutes Aides" (Roy) **14**:467
"The Car" (Crews) **49**:73
Car (Crews) **6**:118; **23**:133, 138; **49**:67, 71-3, 76-7, 79
The Car Cemetery (Arrabal)
See *Le cimetière des voitures*
"Car Crazy Cutie" (Wilson) **12**:643
"The Car Factory Worker" (John Paul II) **128**:187
"Car Jamming" (Clash) **30**:50-2
"Car Journeys" (Abse) **29**:18
"Car Talk" (Bernard) **59**:46
"The Car We Had to Push" (Thurber) **125**:391
La cara de la desgracia (Onetti) **10**:377
Cara Massimina (Parks) **147**:207-08, 219
Les carabiniers (Godard) **20**:144, 149
"Les carabosses" (Hacker) **72**:188
Caracole (White) **110**:316-21, 323, 328, 337
"Caravan" (Longley) **29**:296
"Caravan of Silence" (Eberhart) **56**:76-7
The Caravan Passes (Tabori) **19**:436
Caravan to Vaccares (MacLean) **13**:359
"La caravane des férédjes" (Kadare) **52**:261
Caravans (Michener) **1**:214; **29**:311; **109**:376, 378-79, 382
"Carbon" (Levi) **37**:223, 227
"The Carcass" (Wagoner) **3**:508
"The Card Cheat" (Clash) **30**:46-7
The Card File (Rozewicz) **9**:464-65; **23**:359; **139**:227-29, 232, 241, 244-46, 248-50, 265-67, 292-93
"The Card Players" (Larkin) **5**:228; **8**:337; **13**:337, 341; **33**:261; **64**:275
"The Cardinal" (O'Connor) **14**:392-94
"A Cardinal" (Snodgrass) **2**:404; **18**:491; **68**:388
The Cardinal of the Kremlin (Clancy) **112**:52, 55-6, 62-3, 66, 69, 74-5, 77, 84, 88
The Cardinal Sins (Greeley) **28**:175-76
"The Cardinal's First Tale" (Dinesen) **10**:145, 152; **29**:153; **95**:49, 51-2, 55, 64
"The Cardinal's Third Tale" (Dinesen) **10**:152
"Cards" (Beattie) **63**:18
The Cards Face Down (Buero Vallejo)
See *Las cartas boca abajo*
Cards of Identity (Dennis) **8**:172-73
The Cards of the Gambler (Kiely) **23**:260, 262; **43**:245
Cards on the Table (Christie) **12**:113, 117, 122; **110**:111, 130
"Care" (Robison) **42**:339
"Care by Women" (Pesetsky) **28**:358
c/o Arnold's Corners (Newton) **35**:300-01
The Care of the Self: The History of Sexuality, Vol. 3 (Foucault)
See *Histoire de la sexualité, Vol. 3: Le souci de soi*
"A Career" (Narayan) **47**:305
Career in C Major (Cain) **28**:45-6, 52-3
"Career Opportunities" (Clash) **30**:44-5, 49
"Careers" (Yevtushenko) **126**:413
"Carefree" (Byrne) **26**:94
"Careful" (Carver) **36**:100, 102; **126**:123-24, 127, 169-73, 179, 183
Careful, He Might Hear You (Elliott) **38**:176-77, 181
"A Careful Passion" (Walcott) **25**:449; **76**:280
"Careful What You Let in the Door" (Kingsolver) **130**:113
"Careful with That Ax, Eugene" (Pink Floyd) **35**:305
Careless Love (Adams) **13**:2
"Careless Talk" (Bowen) **22**:65
"Carentan O Carentan" (Simpson) **7**:426; **32**:383; **149**:298, 321, 324, 327, 344, 350, 355
The Caretaker (Pinter) **1**:266-67; **3**:385-86; **6**:404-05, 407-08, 411, 413, 415, 417, 420; **9**:419-20; **11**:438-39, 441-43; **15**:422, 426; **27**:385, 387-88, 394, 396; **58**:373-74, 376, 380, 384; **73**:249, 256-58, 266, 281
The Carfitt Crisis and Two Other Stories (Priestley) **9**:441
Cargo of Eagles (Allingham) **19**:13
"Cargo Rap" (Phillips) **96**:322-23, 326, 343
"Cargoes" (Masefield) **47**:229, 233
"The Caribbean" (Guillén) **48**:159
Caribbean (Michener) **60**:262-63; **109**:377, 382, 386
"Caribbean: Culture or Mimicry" (Walcott) **76**:276-77, 281, 285, 287
Caribbean Discourse: Selected Essays (Glissant)
See *Le discours antillais*
A Caribbean Mystery (Christie) **6**:109; **48**:72
"The Caribbean Provedor" (Connell) **45**:114
"The Cariboo Horses" (Purdy) **50**:238
The Cariboo Horses (Purdy) **6**:428; **50**:237, 246
"Cariboo Winter" (Lane) **25**:284
La caricamás profunda (Cortázar) **10**:114
"Carillariology" (Asturias)
See "Caprilarología"
"Carillon" (Transtroemer) **65**:236
Carine ou la jeune fille folle de son âme (Crommelynck) **75**:153, 155-56, 169
"Caring" (Scott) **22**:372
"Caring for Animals" (Silkin) **43**:399, 401
"Caring for Surfaces" (Van Duyn) **116**:428
"Carioca Song" (Guillén) **79**:230
Caritas (Broumas) **73**:5, 7, 13-14, 16
Caritas (Wesker) **42**:429-30
"Caritas #2" (Broumas) **73**:7
"Caritas #3" (Broumas) **73**:7
Carl and the Passions—So Tough (Wilson) **12**:646, 650
Carl Rakosi: Collected Prose (Rakosi) **47**:348
"A Carlos Pena Filho" (Cabral de Melo Neto) **76**:163
Carlota (O'Dell) **30**:274
"Carlow Village Schoolhouse" (Murphy) **41**:321
Carly Simon (Simon) **26**:406-07, 410
"Carlyle and German Romanticism, 1929" (Wellek) **28**:446
"Carmel Point" (Jeffers) **54**:243
"Carmella, Adelina, and Florry" (Mazer) **26**:295
Carn (McCabe) **133**:111-13, 115-19, 122
Carnac (Guillevic) **33**:191-92, 194
Carnage (Audiberti) **38**:31, 33
The Carnal and the Crane (Hine) **15**:280, 282
The Carnal Island (Fuller) **28**:153-54

"Carnal Knowledge" (White) **49**:409
Carnal Knowledge (Feiffer) **8**:216; **64**:149-50, 159, 161, 163-64
The Carnal Myth (Dahlberg) **1**:72; **7**:64-8
"Carnal World" (Ritsos) **31**:332
"The Carnation" (Mansfield) **9**:303
"The Carnation" (Ponge) **18**:415
"Carnation" (Weller) **26**:447
The Carnation Gang (Poliakoff) **38**:374-75, 377, 379-80, 385
"Carnations" (Roethke) **101**:296
Carnaval afuera, carnaval adentro (Marqués) **96**:241-42
"Carnaval de maiz" (Ferlinghetti) **6**:183
"Carnegie, Oklahoma, 1919" (Momaday) **85**:281
Carnets (Camus) **1**:53; **4**:92; **9**:149; **32**:97; **63**:62-3; **69**:138; **124**:16
"Carnets de notes 1942-1948" (Yourcenar) **87**:412
Carnets II (Camus) **63**:74
"Carnival" (Dinesen) **10**:149-51; **95**:61-9
"Carnival" (Kroetsch)
See "Carnival and Violence: A Meditation"
Carnival (Everson) **27**:135
Carnival (Mackenzie) **18**:312, 314-15
The Carnival (Prokosch) **48**:306-07, 309-10
Carnival! (Rathbone) **41**:339
"Carnival and Violence: A Meditation" (Kroetsch) **132**:209-10, 221-22, 279
Carnival Country (Amado)
See *O país do carnaval*
"The Carnival Dog, the Buyer of Diamonds" (Canin) **55**:36
Carnival for the Gods (Swan) **69**:355-60, 363
The Carnival in My Mind (Wersba) **30**:434-35
Carnival Land (Amado)
See *O país do carnaval*
"The Carnival Man" (Lane) **25**:283
Carnival of Longing (Gunnars) **69**:265-68
"Carnival of Turtles" (Brosman) **9**:135
Carnival Outside, Carnival Inside (Marqués)
See *Carnaval afuera, carnaval adentro*
A Carnival Story (Amado)
See "História do Carnaval"
Carnivals: Entertainments and Posthumous Tales (Dinesen) **10**:148-50, 152-53; **95**:68, 71
Caro Michele (Ginzburg) **5**:141; **54**:196-200, 202-03, 205, 207-12
"Carol" (Blaga) **75**:77
"Carol" (Brown) **5**:77
Carol (Highsmith) **102**:210-11, 218
"Carol with Variations, 1936" (McGinley) **14**:366
Caroline (Maugham) **67**:223
Caroline England (Streatfeild) **21**:396-97
"Caroline Naked: A Husband to His Wife" (Dacey) **51**:80
"Caroline, No" (Wilson) **12**:646, 649-50
"Caroline's Wedding" (Danticat) **94**:93, 95-6, 98-9; **139**:86-7
Le carosse d'or (Renoir) **20**:288-89, 297, 302, 305
"Carousel" (Moody) **147**:191
La carpa de los raquachis (Valdez) **84**:398, 413-14
The Carpathians (Frame) **66**:146-49; **96**:186, 208-09, 212-13, 215-17
"Carpe Noctem, If You Can" (Thurber) **5**:433
"The Carpenter" (Lane) **25**:288
The Carpenter at the Asylum (Monette) **82**:314
Carpenter of the Sun (Willard) **7**:539-40; **37**:462
The Carpenter Years (Cohen) **7**:52; **31**:91-3
The Carpentered Hen and Other Tame Creatures (Updike) **23**:472-76
"Carpenters" (Cassity) **42**:97
"Carpenters" (Salinger)
See "Raise High the Roofbeam, Carpenters"
The Carpenters (Tesich) **40**:416-17, 422-23
Carpenter's Gothic (Gaddis) **43**:156-60, 162-63; **86**:148-49, 153, 155, 157-58, 164-67
"A Carpet Not Bought" (Merrill) **2**:273
The Carpetbaggers (Robbins) **5**:380
"Los Carpincheros" (Roa Bastos) **45**:345
"The Carpincho Hunters" (Roa Bastos)
See "Los Carpincheros"
La carreta (Marqués) **96**:224-25, 228, 233, 240-44, 250, 253-54, 256
"Carrickfergus" (MacNeice) **53**:231, 242
Carrie (King) **12**:309; **26**:234-37, 239, 242; **37**:199, 202, 204-07; **61**:321, 323, 326, 331, 335; **113**:335-36, 341, 343, 347, 355-56, 360-61, 368-69, 383-84, 386-89, 391
Carrie (De Palma) **20**:77-83
"Carried Away" (Munro) **95**:319, 321-22, 324
"Carrier" (Meredith) **55**:192
"The Carrier Bag Theory of Fiction" (Le Guin) **136**:328
The Carrier of Ladders (Merwin) **1**:213; **2**:277; **5**:288; **13**:384-86; **18**:332; **45**:273-74, 276-77; **88**:192-94, 197, 200, 205
The Carrier Pigeon (Seifert)
See *Poštovní holub*
"Carriers of the Dream Wheel" (Momaday) **85**:268
"Carrigskeewaun" (Longley) **29**:293
"The Carrion Spring" (MacLeish) **8**:360
"Carrion Spring" (Stegner) **81**:340, 352
"Carrots, Noses, Snow, Rose, Roses" (Gass) **15**:258; **132**:141, 165
Carry On, Mr. Bowditch (Latham) **12**:322, 325
"Cars Go By Outside, One after Another" (O Hehir) **41**:324
The Cars that Ate Paris (Weir) **20**:424-25
The Cart (Ferron)
See *La Charrette*
Cart and Cwidder (Jones) **26**:225-29
"A Cart with Apples" (Middleton) **13**:388
"Carta a un senorita en París" (Cortázar) **5**:109; **10**:114, 118; **33**:129; **34**:331-32
"Carta a un srta. en París" (Cortázar)
See "Carta a un senorita en París"
"Carta abierta" (Alberti) **7**:9
"Carta de creencia" (Paz) **65**:198
"Cartagena de Indias" (Birney) **6**:75, 78
"Cartas a una desconocida" (Parra) **102**:340-41
Las cartas boca abajo (Buero Vallejo) **15**:98-9, 101-02
"Carte postale" (Reading) **47**:352
La carte postale: De Socrate à Freud et au-delà (Derrida) **87**:93, 96, 104, 106-08
Cartea cujucării (Arghezi) **80**:6, 13
"Carter Fell" (Bowering) **47**:29
"Les cartes postales" (Carrier) **78**:59
Cartesian Linguistics (Chomsky) **132**:38
"Cartesian Sonata" (Gass) **132**:194
Cartesian Sonata and Other Novellas (Gass) **132**:194-95
Cărticica de seară (Arghezi) **80**:6, 8, 11
"The Cartographer of Meadows" (Ciardi) **44**:382
"Cartographies of Silence" (Rich) **11**:477
"Cartography" (Bogan) **46**:83; **93**:64
"Cartography Is an Inexact Science" (Cassity) **42**:97
"Cartoon" (Coover) **46**:121-22
Cartridge Music (Cage) **41**:78
"The Cartridges" (Levine) **4**:287
Carving a Statue (Greene) **70**:294
"The Caryatids" (Dinesen) **10**:152; **29**:155, 163; **95**:69
"Caryl Chessman Interviews the P.T.A...." (Kaufman) **49**:205
Un cas intéressant (Camus) **32**:100
"Casa al mare" (Ginzburg) **11**:229; **54**:198
"La casa de Asterión" (Borges) **4**:73; **48**:38
Casa de campo (Donoso) **32**:161; **99**:217, 219-20, 222, 231, 241, 267-68, 270-71
La casa de los espiritus (Allende) **39**:28-36; **57**:16-23, 25-33; **97**:4-6, 8-10, 17-20, 23-5, 27, 33, 36-7, 42, 44-8, 50-52, 55-7, 59, 62-3
"La casa dei doganieri" (Montale) **9**:387
"La casa del bosco" (Ortese) **89**:198
La casa en la tierra (Poniatowska) **140**:330
La casa sin reloj (Marqués) **96**:227-28, 242, 250, 252
"Casa sul mare" (Montale) **7**:228
"Casa tomada" (Cortázar) **10**:118; **33**:128, 332; **34**:332
"La casa vacía" (Castellanos) **66**:50
La casa verde (Vargas Llosa) **3**:493-94; **6**:544, 546-47; **9**:544, 546; **10**:498, 501; **15**:550-52; **31**:444-45, 447 449; **42**:408; **85**:352, 354, 356, 365, 370-71, 373-75, 381, 389, 392
"Casabianca" (Bishop) **32**:29, 37, 39
"Casablanca, Summer, 1940" (Faludy) **42**:142
Casanova (Fellini)
See *Casanova di Federico Fellini*
"Casanova and the Extra" (Hofmann) **54**:229
Casanova di Federico Fellini (Fellini) **16**:297-98, 300; **85**:51, 53, 60, 69-70, 74, 78, 81
Casanova's Chinese Restaurant (Powell) **3**:400; **7**:340, 345; **9**:435; **10**:408, 418
"Casarola" (Tomlinson) **13**:548; **45**:393
"The Casbah" (Faludy) **42**:140
"Cascadilla Falls" (Ammons) **5**:28; **25**:42; **57**:51, 59
"Cascando" (Beckett) **6**:43, 45, 47; **29**:62; **57**:99
"Cascob" (Mathias) **45**:235
La case du commandeur (Glissant) **68**:174-80, 184
"A Case for Political Inspectors" (Škvorecký) **152**:339
"The Case for the American Woman" (Trilling) **129**:345
"Case Histories" (Janowitz) **145**:325
"Case in Point" (Jordan) **114**:146
"The Case of Claus von Bulow" (Amis) **62**:2, 5
"A Case of Coincidence" (Rendell) **48**:320
"The Case of Comedy" (Thurber) **125**:398
"A Case of Conscience" (O'Connor) **23**:331
A Case of Conscience (Blish) **14**:83, 86
"The Case of Dimity Ann" (Thurber) **125**:413
The Case of Lena Smith (Sternberg) **20**:369, 371
The Case of Lucy Bending (Sanders) **41**:381
"The Case of Motorman Seventeen" (Davidson) **13**:170
"A Case of Murder" (Scannell) **49**:327
A Case of Need (Crichton) **54**:63
A Case of Rape (Himes)
See *Une affaire de viol*
A Case of Samples: Poems, 1946-1956 (Amis) **2**:5; **40**:40
"The Case of The" (Van Duyn) **116**:410
The Case of the Gilded Fly (Crispin) **22**:108, 110
The Case of the Late Pig (Allingham) **19**:15
The Case of the Midwife Toad (Koestler) **8**:325
The Case of The Murdered Mackenzie (Fast) **131**:101
The Case of the One-Penny Orange (Fast) **23**:160; **131**:101-02
"The Case of the Pietro Andromache" (Paretsky) **135**:364
The Case of the Poisoned Eclairs (Fast) **23**:161; **131**:102
The Case of the Russian Diplomat (Fast) **23**:160; **131**:101-2
The Case of The Sliding Pool (Fast) **131**:102
The Case of the Workers' Plane (Edgar) **42**:116
"Case Study" (Ezekiel) **61**:92, 100
The Case Worker (Konrád)
See *A látogáto*
A Casebook of Murder (Wilson) **14**:589
The Casement (Swinnerton) **31**:423
"Casey's Last Ride" (Kristofferson) **26**:266, 270
"Cash on Delivery" (Crispin) **22**:111
"The Cashier" (Voznesensky) **57**:414
The Cashier (Roy)
See *Alexandre Chenevert*
Casi un cuento de hadas (Buero Vallejo) **139**:16
Casing the Promised Land (Carr) **86**:47

Casino Royale (Fleming) **3**:159; **30**:130-33, 136, 138-39, 145, 147, 149
"La casita de sololoi" (Poniatowska) **140**:332-33
Un caso clinico (Buzzati) **36**:85, 93
El caso sabato (Sabato) **23**:378
"Cass and Me" (Muldoon) **32**:318; **72**:272
"Cassandra" (Barnard) **48**:26
"Cassandra" (Bogan) **39**:387, 392; **46**:83; **93**:64, 85, 87-88, 90, 92
Cassandra: A Novel and Four Essays (Wolf)
See *Voraussetzungen einer Erzählung: Kassandra*
"Cassation" (Barnes) **3**:37; **29**:27, 30-1
Cassava Song and Rice Song (Nwapa) **133**:229
Casse-pipe (Céline) **47**:79; **124**:60, 89
Cast a Cold Eye (McCarthy) **3**:326; **39**:491; **59**:289
"Cast and Cast Again" (Humphrey) **45**:205
"Cast rěci" (Brodsky) **13**:116; **36**:74-81; **50**:121, 124, 131, 137; **100**:52
Cast rěci (Brodsky) **13**:116-17; **36**:74-5, 77-81; **50**:121, 124, 131, 137; **100**:48-50, 52-5, 58, 61
Cast the First Stone (Himes) **2**:195; **4**:229; **18**:247-48; **58**:255-56, 263-64; **108**:228-29, 231, 259
"Castaway" (Clarke) **3**:125, 135-36, 149; **136**:210
"The Castaway" (Walcott) **25**:450; **67**:345, 357; **76**:280-81
Castaway (Cozzens) **1**:66-7; **4**:111; **11**:125, 128, 131; **92**:183-85, 189, 199-200
The Castaway, and Other Poems (Walcott) **25**:449-50, 452; **42**:421-22; **67**:346, 357, 360; **76**:274
Caste Marks: Style and Status in the U.S.A. (Fussell)
See *Class: A Guide through the American Class System*
"Castiliane" (Walcott) **25**:450
Castilla (Azorín) **11**:25
The Casting of Bells (Seifert)
See *Odlévání zvonů*
The Casting of the Bells (Seifert)
See *Odlévání zvonů*
Casting the Bells (Seifert)
See *Odlévání zvonů*
"The Castle" (Ali) **69**:31
"The Castle" (Prokosch) **48**:307
The Castle (Gold) **4**:192
The Castle (Klima) **56**:163, 166, 168, 170
Castle Conquer (Colum) **28**:87-8, 92
Castle in Sweden (Sagan)
See *Château en Suède*
Castle in the Air (Westlake) **33**:438-39
The Castle in the Sea (O'Dell) **30**:278
The Castle of Crossed Destinies (Calvino)
See *Il castello dei destini incrociati*
"The Castle of Glubbdubdrib" (Slessor) **14**:494
The Castle of Llyr (Alexander) **35**:23-5
"The Castle of Purity" (Paz) **19**:365
Castle of the Spider's Web (Kurosawa)
See *Throne of Blood*
Castle on the Border (Benary-Isbert) **12**:32
Castle Roogna (Anthony) **35**:37
Castle to Castle (Céline)
See *D'un château l'autre*
Castle Tzingal (Chappell) **40**:146-47, 149; **78**:97, 102, 106-08
"Castles and Distances" (Wilbur) **6**:570
"Castration or Decapitation?" (Cixous) **92**:57-8, 69, 72-3
"The Castrato Singer" (Squires) **51**:380
"Castroenteritis" (Cabrera Infante) **120**:75
A Casual Affair: A Modern Fairytale (Fraser) **64**:169-71
A Casual Brutality (Bissoondath) **120**:8-12, 15, 18; 21, 25, 27
Casual Condemnations (Wesker) **3**:519
"A Casual Encounter" (Plomer) **8**:446
"A Casual Incident" (Farrell) **66**:130
"The Casualties" (Clark Bekedermo) **38**:129
Casualties and Peace (O'Brien) **116**:179, 181, 183, 185, 192, 227
Casualties: Poems (Clark Bekedermo) **38**:125, 129
"Casualty" (Heaney) **25**:247; **74**:163-64
"Casualty" (Longley) **29**:292-93, 297
The Casuarina Tree (Maugham) **11**:370
"The Cat" (Turco) **11**:551
A Cat, a Man, and Two Women (Tanizaki)
See *The Cat, Shōzō, and Two Women*
Cat among the Pigeons (Christie) **12**:116; **48**:73-5
Cat and Mouse (Grass)
See *Katz und Maus*
The Cat and Shakespeare: A Tale of India (Rao) **25**:366-68, 370-73; **56**:289-90, 294, 298, 301, 306-07, 312
The Cat and the Blackbird (Duncan) **55**:293
"The Cat and the Casino" (Sagan) **36**:382
The Cat and the King (Auchincloss) **45**:31
"The Cat and the Saxophone" (Hughes) **35**:220
The Cat Ate My Gymsuit (Danziger) **21**:83-4
Cat Chaser (Leonard) **28**:236; **71**:213, 216-17, 221-23; **120**:265, 273, 276, 301
"Cat in an Empty Apartment" (Szymborska) **99**:197, 208, 211
"The Cat in the Attic" (Martin) **89**:111-12, 116
"Cat in the Garden" (Hall) **51**:170
"The Cat in the Hat for President" (Coover) **32**:122; **87**:25, 58
Cat in the Mirror (Stolz) **12**:555
"Cat in the Rain" (Hemingway) **6**:233; **19**:211, 218; **30**:189, 191; **39**:433; **50**:426
The Cat Inside (Burroughs) **109**:182
"The Cat Jumps" (Bowen) **11**:65; **22**:65, 67
The Cat Jumps and Other Stories (Bowen) **11**:66
Cat Man (Hoagland) **28**:179-80
Cat of Many Tails (Queen) **11**:462-63
Cat on a Hot Tin Roof (Kazan) **63**:222, 234
Cat on a Hot Tin Roof (Williams) **1**:368; **2**:465; **5**:499-501, 503-04; **7**:542-43, 545; **8**:547; **11**:572, 574, 576; **19**:472; **30**:466; **39**:446; **45**:444-46, 452-53, 455; **71**:268, 371, 380; **111**:377-78, 380, 384, 386, 388, 394, 408, 419, 422-24
Cat People (Schrader) **26**:398-99
"Cat Poem" (Zamora)
See "Gata Poem"
The Cat, Shōzō, and Two Women (Tanizaki) **28**:414
"The Cat Song" (Nyro) **17**:318-19
"Cat Spring" (Frame) **96**:201
The Cat Who Walks Through Walls (Heinlein) **55**:301, 303
The Cat Who Wished to Be a Man (Alexander) **35**:25-6, 28
"Cat Within" (Narayan) **28**:301
"The Cat Woman" (Dybek) **114**:62, 73, 75
"Cat Wood" (Amado) **40**:31
"Cataclysm" (Powys) **46**:325
The Catacombs (Demby) **53**:100-15
"The Catalan Night" (Morand)
See "La nuit Catalane"
The Catalans (O'Brian)
See *The Frozen Flame*
Catalina (Maugham) **1**:204; **15**:368
"Catalina Parra" (Parra) **102**:340
"The Catalogue of Charms" (Wakoski) **4**:572
"The Catalogues of Memory" (MacEwen) **13**:357
"The Catalonian Night" (Morand)
See "La nuit Catalane"
"Catalyst" (Ammons) **108**:6
"Cataract" (Baxter) **78**:17
"Catastrophe" (Buzzati)
See "Qualcosa era successo"
Catastrophe (Beckett) **29**:65-6; **59**:255, 258
Catastrophe Practice (Mosley) **43**:317-20, 322; **70**:199, 202-03, 205
Catastrophe: The Strange Stories of Dino Buzzati (Buzzati) **36**:88, 92, 94
"The Catbird Seat" (Thurber) **5**:432, 442; **11**:533; **125**:388, 394, 402, 410-11, 413, 415
"the catch" (Bukowski) **108**:114
"The Catch" (Gordimer) **18**:186; **33**:176
"Catch" (Kunitz) **148**:91, 128
"The Catch" (Rozewicz)
See "Złowiony"
"catch" (Sanchez) **116**:295
The Catch (Bowering) **47**:23
The Catch (Oe)
See *Shiiku*
The Catch (Oshima) **20**:247, 251
The Catch (Weiss) **14**:553, 556
Catch a Falling Spy (Deighton)
See *Twinkle, Twinkle, Little Spy*
"Catch a Fire" (Marley) **17**:270, 272
Catch as Catch Can (Anouilh)
See *La foire d'empoigne*
Catch as Catch Can (Poole) **17**:371-72
"Catch Me Now I'm Falling" (Davies) **21**:105
"Catch That Rabbit" (Asimov) **92**:4
"Catch That Zeppelin" (Leiber) **25**:307
Catch-22 (Heller) **1**:139-40; **3**:228-30; **5**:173-82; **8**:275-80; **11**:265-68; **36**:224-31; **63**:172-209
The Catcher in the Rye (Salinger) **1**:295-99; **3**:444-45; **8**:464-65; **12**:496-97, 502, 505, 514, 516-18; **56**:319-65; **138**:172-76, 180, 182-86, 192-98, 200, 202-04, 206, 213-17, 224-37
"Catcher in the Rye-and-Water" (Ritter) **52**:355
"Catching Geese" (McGuckian) **48**:278
Catchpenny Street (Cavanna) **12**:98
"Catechism for Cape Malays" (Cassity) **42**:96
"Categories" (Ekelöf)
See "Kategorier"
"Categories" (Giovanni) **64**:186-87; **117**:199, 202
"Category Z" (Abbott) **48**:6
The Cater Street Hangman (Perry) **126**:322, 324, 326-27, 330, 335
"Catering" (Gilliatt) **10**:230; **13**:237; **53**:147
A Caterpillar Anthology (Eshleman) **7**:98
"A Caterpillar on the Desk" (Bly) **15**:63
"The Catfish" (Bottoms) **53**:29
The Catfish Man (Charyn) **18**:100
"Cathay" (Millhauser) **54**:325-27, 329-30
Cathay (Pound) **10**:400; **34**:507; **48**:282, 284, 289, 293; **112**:340-46, 348-49
"Cathedral" (Carver) **36**:103-04, **53**:65, **55**:274, 276, 278, 281-82; **126**:105, 107, 109, 111-12, 114-19, 127-28, 141-42, 146-48, 150, 176-77, 183-85
Cathedral (Carver) **36**:100-05; **53**:60, 62-3; **126**:104-06, 110, 114, 120, 125, 127-31, 133, 135, 137, 141-42, 145-46, 149-50, 152, 155, 157-59, 161, 165, 173, 176-79, 181, 183-85
"The Cathedral Chair" (Silkin) **43**:402
Cathedral Wednesday (Mayne) **12**:388, 390, 403
Cathedrals in Space (Blish) **14**:86
Catherine Carmier (Gaines) **18**:165-66; **86**:173, 178
Catherine Carter (Johnson) **27**:216, 223
"Catherine of Alexandria" (Dove) **81**:135, 137
"Catherine of Siena" (Dove) **81**:135, 137
Catherine the Great (Troyat) **23**:462
The Catherine Wheel (Byrne) **26**:99
The Catherine Wheel (Stafford) **7**:455-58; **19**:430; **68**:421, 424, 434, 448-49
Cathleen Listens In (O'Casey)
See *Kathleen Listens In*
"Cathleen Sweeping" (Johnston) **51**:239, 250, 252
Catholic Boy (Carroll) **35**:79-80; **143**:29, 34
The Catholic Experience (Greeley) **28**:169
"Catholic Girls" (Zappa) **17**:593
"The Catholic Novelist in the Protestant South" (O'Connor) **13**:419

Catholic Social Ethics (John Paul II) **128**:209-12
Catholics (Moore) **3**:341; **5**:294, 297; **7**:236-37, 239; **8**:394; **19**:331-33; **32**:310-12; **90**:250, 255-56, 262, 264, 267, 269-70, 272-73, 289
La catira (Cela) **4**:96; **122**:19, 51, 66
"Catman" (Ellison) **13**:207
The Cat-Nappers (Wodehouse) **5**:517
"Cato" (Bioy Casares) **88**:94
Cato Street (Shaw) **5**:390
Cat-O-Nine-Deaths (Valenzuela)
See *El gato eficaz*
"Catrin" (Clarke) **61**:73
Cats and Bats and Things with Wings (Aiken) **52**:27
"Cats and Students, Bubbles and Abysses" (Bass) **79**:5-6, 11
"Cat's Cradle" (Leiber) **25**:307
Cat's Cradle (Vonnegut) **1**:348; **2**:453-55; **3**:495, 497-503, 505-06; **4**:561-63, 566-67, 569; **5**:466-69; **8**:530-35; **12**:601-04, 607, 609-11, 613-14, 617-19, 622-23, 625; **22**:445; **40**:44; **60**:416-17, 421, 432, 440; **111**:351, 355, 358-59, 363, 366, 368
Cat's Eye (Atwood) **84**:69-72, 78-9, 86, 88-9, 98-9, 104-08
Cat's Eye (King) **37**:206
"Cat's in the Well" (Dylan) **77**:182, 184-85
"The Cats of St. Nicholas" (Seferis) **11**:493
The Cat's Pajamas (De Vries) **28**:106
The Cat's Pajamas and Witch's Milk: Two Novels (De Vries) **1**:73; **2**:113; **28**:106-07
"Cats Pyre" (Dybek) **114**:61
Catseye (Norton) **12**:469
"Cat-Tails" (Lightfoot) **26**:278
"Cattle Dream" (Raine) **45**:341
"Cattle Egret" (p'Bitek) **96**:286
The Cattle Killing (Wideman) **122**:362-65, 367-70
The Cattlemen (Sandoz) **28**:404, 407
Catullus (Zukofsky) **4**:580; **11**:580-81; **18**:560
"Catullus on Friendship" (Davie) **31**:123
Caucasia (Senna) **119**:96-102
"Caught" (Rozewicz)
See "Złowiony"
Caught (Green) **2**:178; **13**:252-53, 255; **97**:243, 245-48, 254, 257, 268-70, 275-76, 280, 282-83, 288-91, 293
Caught on a Train (Poliakoff) **38**:385-86
"The Cauliflower" (Haines) **58**:216
"A Cauliflower in Her Hair" (Jackson) **60**:214
The Cause (Bernhard)
See *Die Ursache*
Cause Celeb (Fielding) **146**:88-9, 91, 112
Cause for Alarm (Ambler) **6**:2; **9**:19
Cause for Wonder (Morris) **1**:233; **37**:312-13
Cause of Death (Cornwell) **155**:67, 70
"Causerie" (Tate) **2**:428; **4**:535; **11**:523; **14**:528
"The Cautionary" (Williams) **148**:346-48, 352
The Cautious Heart (Sansom) **2**:383
Cavalcade (Coward) **1**:64; **29**:132, 135, 138; **51**:69
Cavalcanti (Pound) **13**:462
The Cavalier Case (Fraser) **107**:59
Il cavaliere inesistente (Calvino) **5**:97; **8**:128-30; **11**:91; **22**:87, 89-90; **33**:97; **39**:307, 314, 317; **73**:37, 58
Le cavaliseul (Audiberti) **38**:32
"Cavar un foso" (Bioy Casares) **88**:94
"The Cave" (Laughlin) **49**:221-23
"The Cave" (Turner) **48**:399
"The Cave" (Williams) **33**:445; **148**:344
The Cave and the Spring: Essays on Poetry (Hope) **51**:218-19, 222
Cave Birds: An Alchemical Cave Drama (Hughes) **9**:281; **14**:272; **37**:172-73, 175-76, 178; **119**:270, 277, 281, 288, 295
"Cave Call" (Clark Bekedermo) **38**:128
The Cave Dwellers (Saroyan) **10**:454
"The Cave of Making" (Auden) **123**:12, 39
"The Cave of Night" (Montague) **46**:271, 273-74, 276
Cave with Echoes (Elliott) **47**:103
"Caveat Emptor" (Stafford) **19**:431
Cavedweller (Allison) **153**:5, 17-18, 28-31, 33, 45-6
The Cavern (Anouilh) **50**:280
"La caverna" (Arreola) **147**:14
The Caves of Steel (Asimov) **9**:50; **19**:26, 28; **26**:39-43, 46-8, 53, 56, 58, 63; **76**:314; **92**:13
"Caviar and Bread Again" (Williams) **9**:571
Caviar and Cabbage (Tolson) **36**:432; **105**:281
"Caviare at the Funeral" (Simpson) **32**:378; **149**:325
Caviare at the Funeral (Simpson) **32**:376-79, 381; **149**:297, 304-07, 316, 325, 327, 331, 336, 351
"Cawdor" (Jeffers) **54**:233, 237-38, 248
Cawdor, and Other Poems (Jeffers) **11**:305; **54**:233, 236
"The Caxangá Driver" (Cabral de Melo Neto)
See "O motorneiro de Caxangá"
"Cayuga Lake in Winter" (Matthews) **40**:319
La caza (Saura) **20**:314-15, 317
"C.B. and Q." (Dorn) **10**:160-61
"C-dur" (Transtroemer) **65**:235
Ce formidable bordel! (Ionesco) **11**:292-94; **86**:341
Ce que je crois: Négritude, Francité et la civilisation de l'universel (Senghor) **130**:276
Ce qui était perdu (Mauriac) **56**:207, 212
Ce qu'il faut d'amour àL'homme (Green) **77**:284
Ce qu'ils disent ou rien (Ernaux) **88**:100
"Ce soir" (Char) **14**:127
Ce-ai cu mine, vîntule? (Arghezi) **80**:6, 11, 13
"Ceasing Upon the Midnight" (Seth) **90**:338
"Cecie" (Thomas) **13**:542
Cecil (Mujica Lainez) **31**:283
Cecile among Us (Duhamel) **8**:189
Cécile; ou, L'école des pères (Anouilh) **1**:7; **13**:17
"Cecilia" (Simon) **17**:460
Cecily (Holland) **21**:147-48
Cedartown, Georgia (Jennings) **21**:201
"Ceil" (Brodkey) **56**:57-60
"Cel ce gîndeste singur" (Arghezi) **80**:8
Cela s'appelle l'aurore (Bunuel) **16**:143, 147; **80**:25, 30, 40
The Celebrants (Feinstein) **36**:169
"Celebration" (Cohen) **38**:132
"The Celebration" (Dickey) **47**:95
"Celebration" (McGrath) **59**:183
Celebration (Settle) **61**:377-79, 385, 387-88
Celebration (Swados) **5**:420-23
Celebration (Waterhouse) **47**:416
"Celebration for June 24" (McGrath) **59**:181
"A Celebration for Northrop Frye" (Johnston) **51**:249
Célébration hasidique: Portraits et legendes (Wiesel) **11**:570; **37**:456-57, 459
"The Celebration of the Lizard" (Morrison) **17**:290-92
"Celebrations" (Sarton) **49**:310
Celebrations (Plomer) **4**:406
Celebrations after the Death of John Brennan (Kennedy) **8**:320
Celebrations and Attacks: Thirty Years of Literary and Cultural Commentary (Howe) **85**:137
Celebrations and Elegies (Jennings) **131**:242
Celebrities (Bernhard)
See *Die Berühmten*
The Celebrity (Hobson) **25**:271-72
La céleste bicyclette (Carrier) **78**:65
The Celestial Bicycle (Carrier)
See *La céleste bicyclette*
"Celestial Globe" (Nemerov) **36**:303
Celestial Navigation (Jiles) **58**:271-72, 275, 277-80
Celestial Navigation (Tyler) **7**:479-80; **18**:530; **28**:434; **44**:321; **59**:202, 204, 206; **103**:235, 237-39, 241, 243-45, 259, 261, 273
"The Celestial Omnibus" (Forster) **45**:136
The Celestial Omnibus (Forster) **15**:223
"The Celestial Plot" (Bioy Casares) **88**:59
The Celestial Plot (Bioy Casares)
See *La trama celeste*
Celestino antes del alba (Arenas) **41**:25-7
"Celia" (Baker) **8**:40
"Celia" (Brown) **48**:52
"Celia Is Back" (Hempel) **39**:68-70
"Celibacy" (Clarke) **9**:168
Les célibataires (Montherlant) **8**:393
The Cell (Bienek) **7**:28-9
"Cell Song" (Knight) **40**:281
"The Cellar" (Roth) **2**:378
"The Cellar" (Soto) **32**:403
The Cellar (Bernhard)
See *Der Keller*
"The Cellars" (Campbell) **42**:84, 92
"Celles" (Hacker) **72**:192
Cellophane (Wellman) **65**:242
The Cells of Love (Buckler)
See *The Cruelest Month*
"Celluloid Heroes" (Davies) **21**:94, 97
Celluloid Heroes (Williamson) **56**:439
Celtic Revivals (Deane) **122**:75, 77, 80-1
Celui qui ne m'accompagnait pas (Blanchot) **135**:78-80
"Cement" (Bova) **45**:75
The Cement Garden (McEwan) **13**:370-72; **66**:275-80, 282-83, 290, 294
El cementario de automóviles (Arrabal)
See *Le cimetière des voitures*
El cementerio de automóviles (Arrabal)
See *Le cimetière des voitures*
"Cemetary in Alagoas" (Cabral de Melo Neto)
See "Cemitério Alagoano"
"Cemetary in Paraiba" (Cabral de Melo Neto)
See "Cemitério Parabiano"
"Cemetary in Pernambucano" (Cabral de Melo Neto)
See "Cemitério Pernambucano (Floresta do navio)"
"Cemetery Angels" (Kinnell) **129**:248
"The Cemetery at Academy, California" (Levine) **118**:275, 278
The Cemetery of Annunciations (Arghezi)
See *Cimitirul Buna-Vestire*
"Cemetery of Whales" (Yevtushenko)
See "The Whales' Graveyard"
"Cemitério Alagoano" (Cabral de Melo Neto) **76**:168
"Cemitério Parabiano" (Cabral de Melo Neto) **76**:154, 168
"Cemitério Pernambucano (Floresta do navio)" (Cabral de Melo Neto) **76**:168
"Cenas da vida de Joaquim Cardozo" (Cabral de Melo Neto) **76**:165
"Le ceneri di Gramscí" (Pasolini) **37**:348; **106**:244-45, 253
Le ceneri di Gramscí (Pasolini) **37**:348; **106**:220, 232, 241, 243-44, 250, 262-63, 267
Cenizas de Izalco (Alegria) **75**:45, 47, 49-51
"The Censor" (Tanizaki) **28**:415
"The Censors" (Valenzuela) **104**:382
"Censorship" (Ciardi) **40**:162; **129**:45
"Censorship" (Simmons) **43**:408
"Censorship and Literature" (Brink) **36**:68; **106**:119
"Censorship From Left and Right" (Hooks) **94**:158
"Censorship is the Best Reader" (Yevtushenko) **126**:389, 398
"Census Taker" (Oates) **6**:370
Cent ans dans les bois (Maillet) **54**:310-12; **118**:336, 362
Cent jours (Audiberti) **38**:32
"The Centaur" (Swenson) **106**:316, 344, 346
The Centaur (Updike) **1**:344-45; **2**:440, 442; **3**:485-86, 488; **5**:450-53, 458-60; **7**:487-88; **9**:537-38, 541; **13**:557-59, 561; **23**:463, 465,

467-69, 476; **43**:433; **70**:249, 253; **139**:314, 324, 327, 335, 337-38, 368
Centaur Aisle (Anthony) **35**:37
"The Centaur Overhead" (Bowers) **9**:122
"Centaur Song" (H. D.) **73**:119
"The Centaurs" (Longley) **29**:295
"The Centaurs" (Muldoon) **32**:318-19
"A Centenary Ode: Inscribed to Little Crow, Leader of the Sioux Rebellion in Minnesota, 1862" (Wright) **10**:544
Centennial (Michener) **5**:289-91; **11**:375; **29**:311, 315; **109**:375, 377-79, 381, 383
Centennial Food Guide (Berton) **104**:47
The Centennial History of the Civil War (Catton) **35**:92-4
"Center" (Ammons) **5**:27; **25**:44
"Center" (Miles) **34**:245
"The Center of Attention" (Hoffman) **6**:243
The Center of Attention (Hoffman) **6**:242-44; **13**:286
"The Centerpiece" (Matthiessen) **64**:321, 323-24
Centesimus Annus (John Paul II) **128**:178-80
"Cento Virgilianus" (Strand) **71**:287-88
The Centogenarian (Eliade)
See *Der Hundertjärige*
El central (Arenas) **41**:28-9
"Central Heating System" (Spender) **5**:401
Central Line (Binchy) **153**:67
The Central Motion (Dickey) **47**:95-6, 98; **109**:245
"Central Park South" (Souster) **5**:396
"The Centre" (Silkin) **43**:400
Le Centre blanc (Brossard) **115**:103-04, 110-11, 121
"Centre Court" (McPhee) **36**:296
"The Centre of the Universe" (Durcan) **70**:151
"Century Oaks" (Williams) **42**:442
A Century of Hero-Worship (Bentley) **24**:43-5, 50
A Century of Sonnets (Michener) **109**:380
"Century Poem" (Morgan) **23**:299
The Century's Daughter (Barker) **94**:2, 9, 16; **146**:5, 29, 33-4, 36, 41
"The Century's Decline" (Szymborska) **99**:194, 200, 211
Century's Ebb (Dos Passos) **4**:138; **8**:181-82; **25**:146
Cenzura transcendenta (Blaga) **75**:80
"Ceol-Bag for James McAuley" (Buckley) **57**:134
"Cephalus" (Strand) **41**:439-40
Cerberus (Dudek) **19**:136
Cere perse (Bufalino) **74**:39
"Cereals for Roughage" (Bowering) **47**:23
"Cerebral Cortex" (Klappert) **57**:260
Cerebro y corazón (Guillén) **48**:157, 159, 165; **79**:240
Ceremonia de la confusión (Arrabal) **58**:7
Cérémonial de la violence (Chedid) **47**:82, 87
"The Ceremonial Motion of Indian Time: Long Ago, So Far" (Allen) **84**:14, 36
"Ceremonias de rechazo" (Valenzuela) **104**:372, 375-76
La céremonie des adieux: Suivi de entretiens avec Jean-Paul Sartre (Beauvoir) **31**:43-5; **44**:342, 345, 349-51; **71**:83; **124**:167
Cérémonie pour un noir assassiné (Arrabal) **58**:11, 17
"Ceremonies" (Oates) **6**:370
The Ceremonies (Klein) **34**:70-2
"Ceremony" (Mahapatra) **33**:277, 282
"Ceremony" (Wilbur) **110**:388
The Ceremony (Oshima) **20**:249-51, 254
Ceremony (Parker) **27**:367
Ceremony (Silko) **23**:406-08, 412; **74**:318, 320, 323, 329, 342-43, 347-48, 351; **114**:283-84, 286-89, 291, 293, 295, 297, 301-07, 309, 320, 322, 324, 326-27, 330, 335-36
Ceremony, and Other Poems (Wilbur) **6**:568; **14**:576-77; **53**:396-99, 404-07, 410; **110**:380
"Ceremony and Vision" (Berryman) **62**:71
Ceremony for a Murdered Black (Arrabal)
See *Cérémonie pour un noir assassiné*
"Ceremony for Any Beginning" (Pinsky) **38**:359
"Ceremony for Cedar, in an Old House" (Shapcott) **38**:399-400, 403
Ceremony in Lone Tree (Morris) **1**:231-33; **3**:342-43; **18**:349-52, 354; **37**:310-13
The Ceremony of Farewells (Beauvoir)
See *La céremonie des adieux: Suivi de entretiens avec Jean-Paul Sartre*
Ceremony of Innocence (Forman) **21**:118, 123
The Ceremony of Innocence (Ribman) **7**:358
Ceremony of the Innocent (Caldwell) **28**:67
Les cerfs-volants (Gary) **25**:190-91
"A Certain Death" (Nwapa) **133**:187
A Certain Distance (Francis) **15**:238
"Certain Distant Suns" (Greenberg) **30**:166
Certain Honorable Men (Serling) **30**:357
A Certain Justice (James) **122**:179-83, 185-87
"Certain Lesson" (Jennings) **131**:233
A Certain Lucas (Cortázar)
See *Un tal Lucas*
"Certain Mercies" (Graves) **2**:176; **44**:478
Certain Noble Plays of Japan (Pound) **48**:289
Un certain plume (Michaux) **8**:392; **19**:311
A Certain Plume (Michaux)
See *Un certain plume*
"A Certain Refrain" (Mahapatra) **33**:281, 284
"A Certain Silence" (Middleton) **13**:389
A Certain Smile (Sagan) **17**:417-21
"Certain Words, A Garden" (Moure) **88**:228
A Certain World: A Commonplace Book (Auden) **2**:26; **3**:22; **6**:16
Certaines choses naturelles (Laughlin) **49**:220
"Certainties" (Ciardi) **40**:155
"Certified Life" (Fearing) **51**:111
"Certs" (Lane) **25**:289
Cervantes; o, La crítica de la lectura (Fuentes) **10**:208; **60**:164
"Cervantes, or The Criticism of Reading" (Fuentes)
See *Cervantes; o, La crítica de la lectura*
Ces enfants de ma vie (Roy) **14**:469-70
Ces fruits si doux de l'arbre à pain (Tchicaya) **101**:355
César and Augusta (Harwood) **32**:225-26
Césarée (Duras) **68**:92, 96
C'est beau (Sarraute) **8**:470-71; **80**:241
Cet obscure objet du désir (Bunuel) **16**:151-52; **80**:52-3, 56
"C'était toi" (Joel) **26**:220-21
"Cette émotion appelée poésie" (Reverdy) **53**:284
Cette voix (Pinget) **13**:444
Cetyre temperamenta (Aksyonov) **37**:12
Ceux de la soif (Simenon) **3**:450
"Cezanne at Aix" (Tomlinson) **45**:392-93
"Chablis" (Barthelme) **59**:250-51
"Chac Mool" (Fuentes) **22**:170-71; **41**:166
Chacun pour soi (Crommelynck) **75**:152
Chad Hanna (Edmonds) **35**:150-53, 156-57
"Chaddeleys and Flemings" (Munro) **95**:302
"Chagall's 'Les Plumes en Fleur'" (Van Duyn) **116**:427
Chagrins précoces (Kiš)
See *Rani jadi*
"Chain" (Lorde) **71**:233
"The Chain of Aforgomon" (Smith) **43**:423, 425
The Chain of Chance (Lem) **15**:329-30; **40**:292, 296; **149**:118, 156, 161, 261, 284
"A Chain of Love" (Price) **3**:406
A Chain of Voices (Brink) **36**:65-9, 73; **106**:123-24, 126-27
Chain Reaction (Guild) **33**:188-89
Chaining the Lady (Anthony) **35**:37-8
"The Chair" (Davenport) **38**:146-48
"A Chair" (Popa) **19**:373
The Chair (Lieber) **6**:311
La chair et le sang (Mauriac) **56**:203-04, 206
"Chair Gallows" (Komunyakaa) **94**:246
"The Chair of Tears" (Vizenor) **103**:293, 297
The Chairs (Clarke) **16**:217
The Chairs (Ionesco)
See *Les chaises*
Les chaises (Ionesco) **4**:251-52; **6**:248, 251-53, 255-57; **9**:286; **11**:290; **41**:222-26, 229-30; **86**:331, 333-34, 340
"Chaka" (Prince) **22**:339
"Chaka" (Senghor) **54**:391-94, 400; **130**:234, 238, 246, 260
"Chalk" (Abse) **29**:16
"The Chalk Circle" (Rozewicz)
See "Kredowe koło"
The Chalk Garden (Bagnold) **25**:75-8
The Chalk Giants (Roberts) **14**:463-64
"Chalk Pebble" (Clarke) **61**:80
"The Challenge" (Borges) **13**:104; **48**:33
"The Challenge" (Vargas Llosa) **31**:443
"The Challenge of Fear" (Paton) **25**:364
"The Challenge of Our Time" (Forster) **9**:204
"A Challenge to Churches and Synagogues" (King) **83**:348
Challenge to the Learned Doctors (Arguedas) **18**:8
La chamade (Sagan) **17**:424-25
The Chamber (Grisham) **84**:199-201
Chamber Music (Grumbach) **13**:257-58; **64**:198-200
Chamber Music (Kopit) **18**:287-88; **33**:248-50
"Chamber of Commerce Tour" (Lieberman) **36**:264
"The Chamber of Poetry" (Brown) **48**:59
Chamber of Secrets (Rowling)
See *Harry Potter and the Chamber of Secrets*
"La chambre" (Bonnefoy) **15**:74
"La chambre" (Carrier) **78**:59
"La chambre" (Sartre) **52**:381
La chambre claire: Note sur la photographie (Barthes) **83**:89-90
"La chambre nuptiale" (Carrier) **78**:68
La chambre rouge (Mallet-Joris) **11**:355
La chambre verte (Truffaut) **20**:405-07; **101**:396-97, 407, 410
Les chambres de bois (Hébert) **4**:219; **29**:231-32, 236-38, 240-41
"Chameleon Condition" (Hospital) **145**:296, 303
"The Champ" (Boyle) **36**:57-8
Un champ d'îles (Glissant) **68**:179, 181
"Champagne Barn" (Levine) **54**:297, 301
"Champagne on the Terraces" (Townshend) **42**:379-80
"The Champion of the World" (Dahl) **79**:176, 178, 183
"The Champion Single Sculls" (Simpson) **149**:316
Champion's Choice (Tunis) **12**:593
Champions du monde (Morand) **41**:303-04, 306
"Champs Elysees of Broadway" (Hacker) **91**:110
Les champs magnétiques (Breton and Soupault) **2**:81; **9**:132; **54**:25, 28, 31-2; **68**:404, 408, 410-13
La chanca (Goytisolo) **23**:185, 189
"The Chance" (Carey) **55**:114; **96**:28, 39, 53, 55, 68
"Chance" (H. D.) **73**:119
"Chance and Order" (Lem) **149**:121-22, 161
A Chance Child (Paton Walsh) **35**:432-33
"Chance Encounters" (Yevtushenko) **26**:468
Chance, Luck, and Destiny (Dickinson) **12**:174-75
"A Chance Meeting" (Colter) **58**:146
Chance Meetings (Saroyan) **10**:456-57
"The Chance to Love Everything" (Oliver) **98**:258-59
The Chancellor Manuscript (Ludlum) **22**:289; **43**:275
A Chancer (Kelman) **58**:296-97, 299, 301; **86**:185
"The Chances of Rhyme" (Tomlinson) **45**:393
"Chances R" (Ginsberg) **109**:364
"Chanclas" (Cisneros) **118**:177

"Chandeliers and Shadows" (Pinter) **27**:387
"Chanel" (Durrell) **27**:96
The Chaneysville Incident (Bradley) **23**:80-2; **118**:117-18, 120-22, 125, 127-31, 138-39, 142, 145-46, 148-49, 151-52, 154-55, 160-63, 165-66
"The Change" (Berry) **4**:59
"Change" (Kunitz) **148**:87, 124
The Change (Greer)
See *The Change: Women, Aging and the Menopause*
A Change for the Better (Hill) **113**:288-90, 293, 297-99, 305, 309-11, 320-21, 325
"Change Is Not Always Progress" (Madhubuti) **73**:213
"The Change: Kyoto-Tokyo Express" (Ginsberg) **36**:184
"A Change of Air" (Auden) **9**:59
A Change of Climate (Mantel) **144**:220-23, 225, 230, 232-34, 239
A Change of Heart (Butor)
See *La modification*
A Change of Heart (Humphreys) **47**:187
"A Change of Life Style" (Aksyonov) **101**:9
A Change of Light, and Other Stories (Cortázar) **33**:123-24; **34**:329
A Change of Season (Ehrenburg)
See *The Thaw*
A Change of Skin (Fuentes)
See *Cambio de piel*
"A Change of Weather" (MacDiarmid) **63**:243
A Change of World (Rich) **3**:427; **7**:367, 370; **18**:445-46; **36**:365-66, 370, 372, 374, 378; **73**:314, 323, 325; **125**:310, 321, 330, 336
Change!: Seventy-One Glimpses of the Future (Asimov) **26**:57
The Change War (Leiber) **25**:308
The Change: Women, Aging and the Menopause (Greer) **131**:194, 196-99, 214, 218, 226
Change Your Bedding! (O'Hara) **78**:365-66
"A Changeable Report" (Josipovici) **153**:20
"Changed from Martial's Epigrams" (Porter) **33**:318
"Changeling" (Gunnars) **69**:260-61
The Changeling (Jenkins) **52**:223, 225-28
The Changeling (Snyder) **17**:471, 473-74
The Changeling (Williams) **31**:463-64
Changeling (Zelazny) **21**:478-79
"The Changeover" (Fisher) **87**:126
"Changes" (Bowie) **17**:58, 61
"Changes" (Heaney) **37**:165, 169
"Changes" (Kunene) **85**:175
"Changes" (Ochs) **17**:330-31, 333
"Changes of Name" (Parra)
See "Name Changes"
"Changes; or, Reveries at a Window Overlooking a Country Road with Two Women Talking Blues in the Kitchen" (Komunyakaa) **94**:247-49
Change-Up: New Poems (Souster) **14**:504
"Changing" (Cryer) **21**:81
"Changing a Way of Life" (Aksyonov) **101**:15
Changing Appearance (Olson) **28**:342-43
Changing Centuries: Selected Poems (Alegria) **57**:14
The Changing Forest: Life in the Forest of Dean Today (Potter) **86**:346; **123**:229-30
Changing Heaven (Urquhart) **90**:387, 389, 391-3, 395-6, 398, 402
The Changing Land (Zelazny) **21**:479
The Changing Light at Sandover (Merrill) **34**:226-32, 234-42; **91**:2228 232, 234-36, 238
Changing Mind (Aiken) **52**:28
"Changing Names" (Szirtes) **46**:395
The Changing of the Guard (Ehle) **27**:105
Changing Places (Lodge) **36**:271, 273, 277; **141**:336-39, 341, 343-49, 352-54, 356, 358-59, 367, 369-71
The Changing Room (Storey) **2**:425-26; **4**:528; **5**:414-16
"Changing Season" (Blaga) **75**:78
"Changing the Children" (Kumin) **28**:224
"Changing the Subject" (Enright) **31**:149
Changing Woman (Sainte-Marie) **17**:431
"Channels of Grace: A View of the Earlier Novels of Emyr Humphreys" (Mathias) **45**:238
Chanson de geste (Neruda)
See *Canción de gesta*
"Chanson de l'oiseleur" (Prévert) **15**:437
"Chanson Juive" (Celan) **82**:55-6
"Chanson of a Lady in the Shade" (Celan) **82**:37
"Chanson pathetique" (Barnard) **48**:27
"Chanson philosophique" (Steele) **45**:365
"Chanson un peu naïve" (Bogan) **4**:68; **46**:77-8, 81
Chansons (Soupault) **68**:408
"Le chant d l'homme" (Roumain) **19**:344
"Chant de l'initié" (Senghor) **54**:410
Le chant du monde (Giono) **4**:184, 186
Le chant du styréne (Resnais) **16**:496, 502-03, 506
Une chant et l'autre pas (Varda) **16**:559-60
"A Chant for Young/Brothas and Sistuhs" (Sanchez) **116**:295
The Chant of Jimmie Blacksmith (Keneally) **5**:210-11; **8**:319; **10**:298; **14**:301; **19**:242-46; **43**:233, 236; **117**:215, 217, 224, 229-31, 240, 243, 247-48
Chant of Saints: A Gathering of Afro-American Literature (Harper) **65**:364
"Chant of Seasons" (Turco) **63**:429
"Chant to Be Used in Processions around a Site with Furnaces" (Merton) **83**:384
"Chantal" (Beauvoir) **31**:42
Chanting at the Crystal Sea (Howe) **152**:220
Chants de la balandrane (Char) **14**:130; **55**:288
Chants d'ombre (Senghor) **54**:390-91, 407, 410; **130**:234, 238, 240-41, 243, 247-48, 256, 258-61, 263, 265-66, 268, 270, 278, 280
Chants pour Naëtt (Senghor) **54**:390, 396, 407-09; **130**:234-35, 237-38, 259-60
"Chants pour Signare" (Senghor) **130**:259-60
Chants pour signare (Senghor)
See *Chants pour Naëtt*
"Chaos" (Graham) **118**:231
Chaos (Lagerkvist)
See *Kaos*
Chaos and Night (Montherlant)
See *Le chaos et la nuit*
Le chaos et la nuit (Montherlant) **8**:393; **19**:326
Chaos: Making a New Science (Gleick) **147**:48-53, 56-8, 60, 63, 66, 68, 71, 75-8
Le chapeau de Paille (Clair) **20**:61
La chapelle ardente (Marcel) **15**:363
The Chapman of Rhymes (Priestley) **34**:362
The Chapman Report (Wallace) **7**:509; **13**:567-68
"Chapter 7" (Swenson) **61**:405
"Chapter 30" (Klappert) **57**:259-60
"Chapter Eleven" (Williams) **148**:353
"A Chapter on the Future" (Gubar) **145**:284
Chapter Two (Simon) **11**:496; **31**:398-99, 401, 403-04; **39**:217; **70**:238
Chapterhouse, Dune (Herbert) **44**:393-94
Chapters: My Growth as a Writer (Duncan) **26**:108
Chaque homme dans sa nuit (Green) **77**:270-71, 276-78, 290
"A Character Must Have a Name" (Barnard) **48**:27
"The Character of Our Addiction" (Young Bear) **94**:364
The Character of the Poet (Simpson) **149**:343, 354, 358
"The Character of Washington" (Goodman) **4**:197
"Characteristics of G. F." (Faludy) **42**:138
"Characters" (Oates) **134**:248
"Charades" (Fuller) **62**:196-97, 201
Charades (Hospital) **145**:292, 296-97, 305, 308-09, 311
Charades and Celebrations (Urdang) **47**:397-98
The Charcoal Burners (Musgrave) **54**:335-37, 340
"The Charge of History" (Hearne) **56**:126
"Chariot" (Kunitz) **148**:111
Chariot of Wrath (Leonov)
See *Vziatie Velikoshumska*
The Charioteer (Renault) **11**:472; **17**:393
Chariots of the Gods? (von Daniken) **30**:421-27
"Charity" (Dybek) **114**:64-5
"Charity" (Nissenson) **4**:381
"Charity" (Parks) **147**:215
Charivari (Hawkes) **4**:212; **7**:140, 145; **9**:263-64; **14**:239-40; **15**:272; **27**:191; **49**:161
"Charles Baudelaire" (Dubie) **36**:130
Charles Darwin: A Scientific Biography (Gallant) **17**:129
Charles Darwin and the Origin of the Species (Gallant) **17**:129
Charles Darwin: The Making of a Scientist (Gallant) **17**:129
Charles Lonceville's Fate (Paustovsky) **40**:367
"Charles Olson" (Bowering) **15**:83
Charles Olson Reading at Berkeley (Olson) **6**:387
"Charles River" (Lowell) **4**:304
Charles Ryder's Schooldays (Waugh)
See *Charles Ryder's Schooldays and Other Stories*
Charles Ryder's Schooldays and Other Stories (Waugh) **27**:476-77
"Charles Simic" (Simic) **49**:342
"Charles White" (Giovanni) **117**:202
"El charlestón" (Donoso) **4**:127; **8**:180; **32**:158
"Charleston" (Donoso)
See "El charlestón"
"Charleston" (Morand) **41**:301
Charley Starts from Scratch (Jackson) **12**:290
"Charlie" (Nowlan) **15**:398
Charlie and the Chocolate Factory (Dahl) **79**:177, 179
Charlie and the Great Glass Elevator: The Further Adventures of Charlie Bucket and Willy Wonka, Chocolate-Maker Extraordinary (Dahl) **79**:177
"A Charlie Brown Thanksgiving" (Schulz) **12**:531
Charlie Brown's Second Super Book of Questions and Answers: About the Earth and Space...from Plants to Planets! (Schulz) **12**:533
"Charlie Don't Surf" (Clash) **30**:49
"Charlie Freak" (Becker and Fagen) **26**:79, 82
Charlie in the House of Rue (Coover) **32**:122-25; **46**:116, 121-22
Charlie the Tramp (Hoban) **7**:162; **25**:266
"Charlie's Girl" (Reed) **21**:311
"Charlie's Greek" (O'Faolain) **32**:341, 344
"Charlotte Corday" (Tomlinson) **13**:550; **45**:401
"Charlotte Esmond" (Bates) **46**:51
Charlotte's Row (Bates) **46**:53
Charlotte's Web (White) **34**:425-28, 430, 432; **39**:369-70, 372-73, 375-77, 380
"Charlottetown Harbour" (Acorn) **15**:9
"The Charm" (Creeley) **36**:118; **78**:162
"A Charm against the Toothache" (Weiss) **8**:546; **14**:557
The Charm: Early and Uncollected Poems (Creeley) **2**:106-07; **8**:153
Le charme discret de la bourgeoisie (Bunuel) **16**:137, 141-43, 149, 152; **80**:49, 54, 56
Charmed Life (Jones) **26**:227-28, 230
A Charmed Life (McCarthy) **3**:326-27; **14**:357, 360, 363; **59**:289, 291, 293
"Charming" (Matthews) **40**:325
Charms for the Easy Life (Gibbons) **88**:132-33; **145**:153-55, 157, 164-65, 167-68, 184
"Charnel Ground" (Ginsberg) **109**:329
"Charnel House, Rothwell Church" (Scannell) **49**:329-30
The Charnel Rose, Senlin: A Biography, and Other Poems (Aiken) **52**:20, 28

"Charon" (MacNeice) **4**:316; **10**:325; **53**:243
"Charon's Cosmology" (Simic) **130**:302
Charon's Cosmology (Simic) **22**:380; **49**:340; **130**:295, 298, 311, 317-18
La Charrette (Ferron) **94**:113, 117, 120, 124-26
"The Chart" (Merwin) **8**:390
Charulata (Ray) **16**:480-87, 490, 492, 494-95; **76**:360, 362, 365-67
"Charwoman" (Belitt) **22**:48, 52
The Chas Addams Mother Goose (Addams) **30**:15-16
Chas Addams's Monster Rally (Addams) **30**:13
"A Chase" (Baraka) **33**:55
"The Chase" (Calvino) **5**:99; **73**:31-2
The Chase (Foote) **51**:130-31
Chase the Game (Jordan) **37**:195
"Chasing the Paper-Shaman" (Rose) **85**:313
"Chasms" (Squires) **51**:380, 382
"Chassidische Schriften" (Sachs) **98**:364-65
Chast' rechi (Brodsky)
See *Cast rěci*
Chat Show (White) **49**:410-11
"La châtaigne et le fruit à pain" (Condé) **92**:104
The Chateau (Maxwell) **19**:307
"Chateau d'If" (Vance) **35**:427
Château en Suède (Sagan) **6**:481-82; **17**:422-23, 426; **6**:481-82
"Chateau Hardware" (Ashbery) **2**:18
Chatsky; or, The Importance of Being Stupid (Burgess) **81**:302
"Chattanooga" (Reed) **5**:368; **6**:448
"Chattanooga-Choo-Choo" (Donoso) **8**:179-80; **32**:159; **99**:241
Chatter on the Nile (Mahfouz)
See *Tharthara fawq al-Nil*
Chatter on the Nile (Mahfūz)
See *Tharthara fawq al-Nīl*
Chatterton (Ackroyd) **52**:9-10, 12-16; **140**:5-10, 14, 20, 23-5, 27, 30, 32-3, 37, 39-42, 44-6, 48, 50, 57, 65-66
Chatting on the Nile (Mahfūz)
See *Tharthara fawq al-Nīl*
"Chatting with the Tide at Jaqueira" (Cabral de Melo Neto)
See "Prosas da maré na Jaqueira"
"Chaucerian" (Sargeson) **31**:370
Chaud et froid ou l'idée de Monsieur Dom (Crommelynck) **75**:154, 156, 159, 162-64, 166, 169
Che Guevara Speaks: Selected Speeches and Writings (Guevara) **87**:199-201
"Che Guevara's Cigars" (Berrigan) **37**:44
"Che vuoi pastore d'aria" (Quasimodo) **10**:428
"Cheap Thrills" (Zappa) **17**:585
Cheaper by the Dozen (Gilbreth and Carey) **17**:152-54, 156
"Cheapskate" (Clash) **30**:44
The Cheat (Jordan) **37**:195-96
Check (Barker) **37**:31, 34
"Checkbook Maternity: When is a Mother Not a Mother?" (Pollitt) **122**:224
Checkmate (Behan) **79**:27
Checkmates (Milner) **56**:227-28
"Checkpoint Charlie" (Durcan) **43**:118
"Cheepnis" (Zappa) **17**:591
The Cheer (Meredith) **22**:303; **55**:193
The Cheer Leader (McCorkle) **51**:273-76
"Cheerful-By Request" (Ferber) **93**:138
Cheerful--By Request (Ferber) **93**:138, 141-42
"Cheers!" (Guillén)
See "Brindis"
"Cheers" (Phillips) **15**:419
"The Cheery Soul" (Bowen) **118**:74
"A Cheery Soul" (White) **5**:486; **7**:532; **69**:398
"Cheesecake" (Muldoon) **32**:318-19
"Chefs and Spoons" (Grass) **15**:260
"Chef's House" (Carver) **36**:100, 104; **53**:67; **126**:105, 113-14, 121-23, 162, 180
"Chekhov" (Moss) **7**:250
"Chekhov on Sakhalin" (Heaney) **74**:175
"Chekhov on the West Heath" (Levertov) **15**:338
Chekhov's Grandmother (McClure) **6**:317
The Chelsea Girls (Warhol) **20**:416-18, 422
"Chelsea in Winter" (Ewart) **46**:148, 150
"Chelsea Morning" (Mitchell) **12**:435
The Chemicals We Eat and Drink (Silverstein and Silverstein) **17**:454, 456
"Chemin de fer" (Bishop) **32**:34, 36, 39
Le chemin des écoliers (Aymé) **11**:22
"Le Chemin du retour" (Robbe-Grillet) **128**:377
"Les chemins" (Bonnefoy) **15**:74
Les chemins de la liberté (Sartre) **1**:303-06; **7**:390, 398; **24**:411-12; **44**:494, 497; **50**:377, 380, 383; **52**:382, 388
Les chemins de la mer (Mauriac) **9**:368; **56**:212
"Chemistry" (Swift) **41**:443
"chemotherapy" (Clifton) **66**:84
Les chênes qu'on abat... (Malraux) **57**:307
The Chequer Board (Shute) **30**:374
Cher Antoine; ou, L'amour raté (Anouilh) **13**:20-2; **40**:59-61
Cherche tes mots, cherche tes pas (Carrier) **78**:65
Le Chercheur d'or (Le Clézio) **155**:83, 86, 99, 105, 108-09, 115
"Cherish" (Moure) **88**:227-28
"Cherish the Ladies" (Muldoon) **32**:322
Chernowitz! (Arrick) **30**:18-19
"Cherokee Bend" (Lightfoot) **26**:283
The Cherokee Trail (L'Amour) **25**:282
"Cherry Cherry" (Diamond) **30**:111
"Cherry Saplings" (Snodgrass) **68**:399
"The Cherry Stone" (Olesha) **8**:430, 432
The Cherry Stone (Olesha)
See *Vishnevaya kostochka*
"The Cherry Tree" (Gunn) **18**:199, 201
"Cherrylog Road" (Dickey) **7**:80, 84
Chers Zoiseaux (Anouilh) **40**:60
Chesapeake (Michener) **11**:374-76; **29**:311, 315; **60**:260; **109**:375, 377, 379, 381, 388
"Cheshire" (Betjeman) **43**:51
"Chesnut Tree--Three Storeys Up" (Avison) **97**:111
"The Chess Match" (Hood) **28**:192
The Chess Players (Ray)
See *Shatranj Ke Khilari*
The Chessmaster and His Moves (Rao) **56**:306-11
"The Chevalier of the Place Blanche" (Rhys) **14**:446
Les chevaliers de la table ronde (Cocteau) **16**:220; **43**:106, 111
"Les chevaux" (Gascar) **11**:220
La chevelure de Bérénice (Simon) **39**:215
"Chévere" (Guillén) **48**:161-63
Une chèvre sur un nuage (Arrabal) **18**:21
Cheyenne Autumn (Ford) **16**:309, 311-12, 319-20
Cheyenne Autumn (Sandoz) **28**:403-04, 407
Chez Charlotte and Emily (Baumbach) **23**:55
"Chez Jane" (O'Hara) **13**:426-27
Chez nous (Nichols) **5**:305-06, 309; **36**:329
"Chi" (Tolson) **105**:253, 276-77
"Chi in Igbo Cosmology" (Achebe) **152**:89
Ho Chi Minh: Legend of Hanoi (Archer) **12**:19
Chia (Pa Chin) **18**:371, 373
Chiaroscuro (Horovitz) **56**:148-49, 152
La chiave a stella (Levi) **50**:332-36, 339
"Chicago" (Sandburg) **4**:463; **10**:448-49; **15**:466, 469; **35**:347, 358
Chicago (Shepard) **4**:490; **6**:497; **17**:434-35, 439-40, 444
Chicago: City on the Make (Algren) **10**:6
"The Chicago Defender Sends a Man to Little Rock" (Brooks) **15**:94-5; **49**:36
"The Chicago Picasso" (Brooks) **49**:28; **125**:107
"The Chicago Picasso, 1986" (Brooks) **125**:107
Chicago Poems (Sandburg) **4**:463; **10**:447, 449-51; **15**:466-67; **35**:338-43, 347, 352, 358
The Chicago Race Riots, July, 1919 (Sandburg) **35**:355
A Chicano in China (Anaya) **148**:35
The Chicano Soldier (Valdez)
See *Soldado razo*
Chicanos (Coles) **108**:194
Chickamauga (Wright) **119**:180, 182, 189; **146**:344-50, 352-54, 356-58, 362, 365-67, 369-70, 35-76, 379-80
"The Chicken" (Lispector) **43**:269-70
"Chicken" (Sillitoe) **57**:388
"Chicken Fate" (Landolfi) **49**:217
Chicken Inspector No. 23 (Perelman) **23**:337
"The Chicken Killing" (Kogawa) **129**:319
The Chicken Run (Chambers) **35**:97
Chicken Soup with Barley (Wesker) **3**:518-19; **5**:482, 484; **42**:427, 430
"The Chicken without a Head" (Simic) **68**:379
Chickencoop (Chin)
See *The Chickencoop Chinaman*
The Chickencoop Chinaman (Chin) **135**:152, 154-55, 161, 165, 167, 170, 185-86, 190-91, 193-94, 197, 200
"Chickens" (Ferber) **93**:136, 141
"The Chicken's Egg" (Cabral de Melo Neto)
See "O ovo da galinha"
"Chickens the Weasel Killed" (Stafford) **29**:380-81
"El Chicle" (Castillo) **151**:104
"Chico King Popular Singer" (Rogin) **18**:457
Los chicos (Matute) **11**:363
Chido Guan, el Tacos de Oro (Esquivel) **141**:189
Chief (Bonham) **12**:52-3, 55
Chief Joseph of the Nez Perce (Warren) **39**:262-64
"Chief Justice Burger, Teen Idol" (Grayson) **38**:210
Un chien andalou (Bunuel) **16**:133-34, 138, 140-41, 149-50, 152; **80**:19-21, 25-6, 28, 31, 35, 37-8, 51, 55-6
Le chien couchant (Sagan) **36**:383
Le chien de coeur (Char) **9**:163
Le chiendent (Queneau) **2**:359; **5**:359-62; **10**:430; **42**:332-33
La chienne (Renoir) **20**:292-93, 301, 305-08, 310
"Chijin no ai" (Tanizaki) **8**:509; **28**:414, 418
"The Chiker" (Sillitoe) **148**:164
"Chike's School Days" (Achebe) **75**:13-14
"The Child" (Dudek) **11**:159
"The Child" (Eberhart) **56**:77
"The Child" (Ferron) **94**:103, 119
"Child" (Plath) **3**:391; **9**:434; **51**:345; **111**:167, 199, 206
"The Child" (Silkin) **43**:400
"The Child" (Wright) **53**:417
Child (Handke) **134**:158
"The Child and the Madman" (Wiesel) **5**:490
"The Child and the Shadow" (Le Guin) **71**:195-97, 199, 200
"Child and Wattle Tree" (Wright) **53**:417
"Child Asleep" (Clark Bekedermo) **38**:125
"The Child Asleep" (Rukeyser) **27**:404
"Child Beater" (Ai) **69**:4, 16
The Child Buyer (Hersey) **1**:144; **2**:188; **40**:232-34, 239-40; **81**:335; **97**:302
Child by Fever (Foote) **75**:230-31, 239, 243
"A Child Ill" (Betjeman) **43**:34, 41-2
The Child in Chains (Mauriac)
See *L'enfant chargé de chaînes*
The Child in Time (McEwan) **66**:286-94
"A Child Is Lost" (Fast) **131**:96
"The Child Is the Meaning of This Life" (Schwartz) **4**:478; **10**:462, 466; **45**:353-54; **87**:337
"The Child Looks Out" (Livesay) **79**:332
"A Child: Marginalia on an Epigraph" (Avison) **97**:78, 113
"Child Naming Flowers" (Hass) **18**:213
"The Child of Civilization" (Brodsky) **50**:134
"Child of Europe" (Milosz) **56**:237, 247-48
Child of Fire (O'Dell) **30**:270-71, 275
Child of Fortune (Spinrad) **46**:388-89
Child of God (McCarthy) **4**:341-43; **57**:330-33;

101:134-35, 144, 146-47, 149-54, 159-61, 163-64, 167, 176-77, 179, 183, 185, 195, 197-98, 201-04
"Child of Our Time" (Boland) **40**:99; **67**:43; **113**:96
Child of Our Time (del Castillo) **38**:163-64, 166-67
A Child of Queen Victoria (Plomer) **4**:406
Child of Rage (Thompson) **69**:384
A Child of the Century (Hecht) **8**:269, 272
Child of the Owl (Yep) **35**:469-71
"Child on Top of a Greenhouse" (Roethke) **3**:432; **101**:262, 295
Child o'War (Garfield) **12**:226-27, 230, 238
"Child Psychology" (Williams) **148**:343, 345-46, 348, 352
"The Child Screams and Looks Back at You" (Banks) **72**:4
"The Child/The Ring/The Road" (Willard) **37**:464
"Child Trapped in a Barber Shop" (Levine) **33**:273
"The Child Who Favored Daughter" (Walker) **19**:453; **58**:404, 406; **103**:359-64, 368, 407, 410-12
"Childbirth" (Hughes) **119**:266
Childe Byron (Linney) **51**:261-62
"Childe Horvald to the Dark Tower Came" (Ciardi) **40**:154, 157
"Childe Roland" (Howard) **7**:168
The Childhod of Ivan (Tarkovsky)
See *Ivanovo Detstvo*
"Childhood" (Aldington) **49**:6, 9, 16
"Childhood" (Farah) **137**:93
"Childhood" (Justice) **19**:235; **102**:251, 275, 277
"Childhood" (Walker) **6**:554
"Childhood" (Wright) **146**:337
Childhood (Sarraute)
See *Enfance*
Childhood (Wilder) **1**:366; **82**:363
"Childhood and Interruption" (Smith) **25**:421
Childhood and Other Neighborhoods (Dybek) **114**:62, 64, 67, 70-3, 75, 77-8
A Childhood in Agram (Krleža)
See *Djetinjstvo u Agramu, 1902-1903*
Childhood Is Not Forever (Farrell) **66**:129, 132
The Childhood of an Equestrian (Edson) **13**:190
"The Childhood of Hölderlin" (Watkins) **43**:452
"The Childhood of Luvers" (Pasternak) **7**:293; **10**:383; **18**:385-87; **63**:290
"The Childhood of Luvers" (Pasternak)
See "Detstvo Luvers"
Childhood of the Magician (Willard) **7**:539-40
"The Childhood of William Blake" (Padilla) **38**:349, 351-53
"The Childhood of Zhenya Luvers" (Pasternak)
See "Detstvo Luvers"
A Childhood: The Biography of a Place (Crews) **23**:134-37; **49**:68-71, 73-4, 76-7, 79
"Childhood's Body" (Wright) **146**:346
Childhood's End (Clarke) **1**:59; **4**:104-05; **13**:152-55; **18**:103-06; **35**:120, 122-27; **136**:198, 205-13, 217, 223-26, 232-34, 236, 238
"A Childish Prank" (Hughes) **4**:236
"Childless Woman" (Plath) **3**:391; **5**:345; **9**:427; **14**:424; **62**:404; **111**:168, 210
"Childlessness" (Merrill) **13**:379-81
The Childlike Life of the Black Tarantula (Acker) **45**:14-15; **111**:15-18, 21, 25, 32, 36
"The Child-Martyr" (Oates) **9**:403
"The Children" (Bell) **8**:67
"The Children" (Cheever) **15**:127
"Children" (Kizer) **39**:169
"The Children" (Lustig) **56**:182
"The Children" (Sexton) **6**:492; **123**:404
"Children" (Tanizaki)
See "Shōnen"
The Children (Fast) **131**:82, 86, 93
Children (Gurney) **32**:217-19; **50**:176-77
The Children (de Hartog) **19**:132
"Children and Art" (Sondheim) **30**:403; **39**:175
Children and Others (Cozzens) **92**:189
"Children Are Bored on Sunday" (Stafford) **7**:457; **19**:431; **68**:422
Children Are Bored on Sunday (Stafford) **68**:421
Children Are Civilians, Too (Boell) **27**:66-7; **72**:73
Children at the Gate (Banks) **23**:40
The Children at the Gate (Wallant) **5**:477; **10**:512-16
"Children Children" (McCartney) **35**:286
"Children, Dogs, and Desperate Men" (Colwin) **84**:150
Children from Their Games (Shaw) **23**:398
"Children in Exile" (Fenton) **32**:170
Children in Exile: Poems, 1965-1984 (Fenton) **32**:169
Children Is All (Purdy) **2**:348-49; **4**:422; **10**:421; **28**:378-79; **52**:350
Children of a Lesser God (Medoff) **23**:292-95
"Children of Choice" (Pollitt) **122**:223
Children of Crisis (Coles) **108**:186-88, 193-94, 203-05, 210, 214
"Children of Darkness" (Wilbur) **14**:579; **53**:398
Children of Dune (Herbert) **12**:277-78; **23**:221-24, 227; **35**:199, 201-02, 205, 207-09; **44**:393-94; **85**:88-9, 93-6, 100
The Children of Dynmouth (Trevor) **9**:528-29; **14**:535; **25**:444; **71**:326, 340, 346; **116**:334, 375, 377, 381-83
The Children of Gabalawi (Mahfūz)
See *Awlād hāretnā*
The Children of Gebelawi (Mahfouz)
See *Awlad haratina*
Children of God (Fisher) **7**:103
The Children of Ham (Brown) **30**:38-41
"Children of Light" (Lowell) **4**:297; **8**:350; **11**:326, 329; **37**:237
Children of Light (Stone) **42**:359-64
"The Children of Lir" (Durcan) **70**:150
"Children of Loneliness" (Yezierska) **46**:442, 449
Children of Loneliness (Yezierska) **46**:442-43
The Children of Men (James) **122**:169-73
Children of Men (Vesaas)
See *Menneskebonn*
Children of My Heart (Roy)
See *Ces enfants de ma vie*
"Children of Old Somebody" (Goyen) **14**:214; **40**:217-18
"Children of Our Age" (Szymborska) **99**:204
Children of Our Neighborhood (Mahfouz)
See *Awlad haretna*
Children of Our Neighborhood (Mahfūz)
See *Awlād hāretnā*
Children of Power (Shreve) **23**:403-04
Children of Primrose Lane (Streatfeild) **21**:412, 414
Children of Segu (Condé)
See *Ségou: La terre en miettes*
"Children of Strikers" (Chappell) **40**:142
Children of the Albatross (Nin) **1**:249; **4**:376, 379
Children of the Alley (Mahfouz)
See *Awlad haratina*
Children of the Arbat (Rybakov) **53**:295-302; **59**:368, 381-82, 387-89, 391, 393
Children of the Black Sabbath (Hébert)
See *Les infants du sabat*
"Children of the Corn" (King) **61**:331, 333-34; **113**:336-38, 380
The Children of the Dream (Bettelheim) **79**:109
Children of the Game (Cocteau)
See *Les enfants terribles*
"Children of the Headmaster" (Trevor) **71**:342; **116**:375
Children of the Holocaust (Lustig) **56**:186
The Children of the House (Pearce) **21**:282-84, 287, 291
"Children of the Kingdom" (Klein) **34**:71
The Children of the Man in the Moon (Carrier)
See *Les enfants du bonhomme dans la lune*
Children of the Mire: Modern Poetry from Romanticism to the Avant-Garde (Paz)
See *Los hijos del limo: Del romanticismo a la vanguardia*
"Children of the Mississippi" (Brown) **1**:47; **23**:96; **59**:266
"Children of the Moon" (Du Bois) **64**:110-11
Children of the Revolution: A Yankee Teacher in the Cuban Schools (Kozol) **17**:254-55
Children of the Rose (Feinstein) **36**:169
"Children of the Sea" (Danticat) **94**:93, 95-100
Children of Violence (Lessing) **1**:173-75; **2**:239-41; **3**:282-83, 286, 289, 290-91; **6**:290, 292, 295-96, 298, 300, 304; **22**:280-81, 283-86
"Children of Wealth in Your Warm Nursery" (Daryush) **19**:121-22
The Children on the Top Floor (Streatfeild) **21**:404, 407-08
"Children on Their Birthdays" (Capote) **1**:55; **3**:99; **13**:134, 139-40; **19**:79, 86; **58**:98
"Children Passing" (Blunden) **56**:47
"The Children: Proemio" (Berryman) **8**:93
"Children Walking Home from School through Good Neighborhood" (Justice) **102**:284
A Children's Biography of Langston Hughes (Walker) **103**:357
"The Children's Campaign" (Lagerkvist)
See "Det lilla fälttåget"
"Children's Court" (Hochman) **8**:297
"The Children's Crusade" (Levine) **14**:318
The Children's Crusade (Blaga) **75**:64-6
Children's Day (Waterhouse) **47**:419
"The Children's Game" (Stafford) **68**:422
The Children's Hell (Nakos)
See *The Children's Inferno*
The Children's Hour (Hellman) **2**:187; **8**:281; **14**:256, 258-60; **18**:220-21, 225; **34**:347-49; **44**:528-29, 532; **52**:191, 202, 205
The Children's Inferno (Nakos) **29**:321, 323
"The Children's Orchard" (Rukeyser) **15**:458
"Children's Rhymes" (Hughes) **10**:281
"Children's Story" (Handke)
See "Child's Story"
The Children's Story (Clavell) **25**:127-28; **87**:2-4, 19
"A Child's Calendar" (Brown) **48**:53-4, 57
A Child's Garden of Curses (Perelman) **49**:272
"The Child's Grave" (Blunden) **56**:39
"Child's Guide to Parents" (Nash) **23**:322
A Child's History (Newman) **8**:419
"A Child's Nightmare" (Wright) **53**:424
"Child's Park" (Hughes) **119**:257
"Child's Park Stones" (Plath) **111**:200
"Child's Play" (Malouf) **28**:268-69
Child's Play (Slavitt) **5**:392
Child's Play (Walser)
See *Ein Kinderspiel*
"A Child's Prayer" (Sassoon) **36**:385
"Child's Story" (Handke) **38**:225, 228-29
"Childsong" (Diamond) **30**:110
Childwold (Oates) **9**:404-05; **19**:349-50, 353; **33**:289; **52**:338; **108**:386, 391
"Childybawn" (O'Faolain) **32**:341, 344; **70**:318
"Chile" (Lane) **25**:286
The Chilean Spring (Alegria)
See *El Paso de los Gansos*
"Chiliastic Sapphics" (Hacker) **91**:109
Chi-liu (Pa Chin) **18**:371-72, 374
The Chill (Macdonald) **1**:185; **2**:256; **14**:332, 334-35; **41**:268
Chills and Fever (Ransom) **4**:436; **5**:365
Chills and Other Poems (Akhmadulina) **53**:15
Chilly Scenes of Winter (Beattie) **8**:54-7; **13**:64-5; **40**:66; **63**:3-4, 7-9, 13, 22; **146**:57-8, 51, 54, 56-7, 67, 69, 71, 74, 78, 83
"Chimera" (Howes) **15**:290
Chimera (Barth) **2**:37-9; **3**:42; **5**:51; **7**:22-5; **9**:74; **10**:24; **14**:52-4, 56; **27**:28; **51**:20-3, 26, 29; **89**:10-11, 24-5, 31-2, 39, 45, 47, 63

Chimes at Midnight (Welles) **20**:439-40, 443, 445, 448, 450-51; **80**:367-69, 373, 377, 391, 393, 409-12, 414
Chimes at Midnight (White) **49**:408
"Chimes for Yahya" (Merrill) **8**:381
"The Chimney" (Campbell) **42**:88-9
"Chimney Bluff" (Crase) **58**:163, 166
"Chimneys" (Cummings) **15**:159
"China" (Donoso) **8**:178; **11**:146; **32**:156
"China" (Johnson) **51**:234, 236
China Court: The Hours of a Country House (Godden) **53**:158-59, 161
China Diary (Spender) **91**:263
China Gold (Buck) **11**:77
China in the Twentieth Century (Archer) **12**:21
"China Mail" (Wright) **146**:377
China Men (Kingston) **19**:249-51; **58**:308-17, 327; **121**:255, 267, 295, 300, 308-14
"China Poems" (Lane) **25**:289
China Poems (Brutus) **43**:89
"China Trace" (Wright) **146**:362
China Trace (Wright) **13**:614-15; **28**:457-58; **146**:304-06, 309, 321, 326-27, 329-30, 333, 335-37, 343, 351, 359, 361, 373-74, 379-80
The Chinaberry Tree: A Novel of American Life (Fauset) **54**:169-71, 175, 177, 179-80, 182, 187, 189-90
"The Chinaman" (Wideman) **122**:289
The Chinaman Pacific and Frisco R.R. Co. (Chin) **135**:156-58, 165, 169
Chinatown (Polanski) **16**:470-73
Chinatown (Towne) **87**:353-54, 359, 361-66, 369-70, 373-78
Der Chinese (Handke)
See *Der Chinese des Schmerzes*
The Chinese Agent (Moorcock)
See *Somewhere in the Night*
The Chinese Americans (Meltzer) **26**:307-08
"Chinese and Japanese-American Literature" (Chin) **135**:155
The Chinese and the Americans (Archer) **12**:22
"The Chinese Banyan" (Meredith) **22**:302
Der Chinese des Schmerzes (Handke) **134**:118, 134, 144, 158, 162-64, 167
Chinese Dynasty Cantos (Pound) **112**:351, 358
"Chinese Finches" (Pollitt) **122**:202, 205
"Chinese Food" (Jong) **4**:264
"The Chinese Geomancer" (Chatwin) **57**:153
The Chinese Girl (Godard)
See *La Chinoise*
"The Chinese Insomniacs" (Jacobsen) **48**:194
The Chinese Insomniacs (Jacobsen) **48**:192-93, 195
"Chinese Journal" (Wright) **119**:187
"A Chinese Lady Dies" (Chin) **135**:156
"The Chinese Lobster" (Byatt) **136**:156, 164
"The Chinese Novel" (Buck) **7**:32
The Chinese Orange Mystery (Queen) **3**:422
"Chinese Poem" (Smith) **64**:400
The Chinese Prime Minister (Bagnold) **25**:76-8
"The Chinese Restaurant in Portrush" (Mahon) **27**:292
Chinese Roulette (Fassbinder) **20**:117
"The Chinese Statue" (Archer) **28**:14
"Chinese Tallow" (Plumly) **33**:315
The Chinese Wall (Frisch)
See *Die chinesische Mauer: Eine Farce*
Die chinesische Mauer: Eine Farce (Frisch) **3**:166-67; **9**:217; **14**:181-83; **18**:160; **44**:181, 195-97, 203
Der chinesische Mauer: Eine Farce (Frisch)
See *Die chinesische Mauer: Eine Farce*
"The Chink" (Stegner) **81**:346
Chinmoku (Endō) **7**:95-6; **14**:160, 162; **19**:160-61; **54**:152-55, 157, 159-60, 162; **99**:282-95, 298-300, 302, 305, 307-09
La Chinoise (Godard) **20**:138, 143
"Chinoiserie" (Fuller) **4**:178; **28**:151
"Chinoiserie" (Wright) **6**:581
"Chinook" (Muldoon) **72**:275
"A Chip of Glass Ruby" (Gordimer) **123**:114
The Chip-Chip Gatherers (Naipaul) **32**:324-25, 327; **39**:355-56, 358
"Chipping Away at Death" (Dunn) **36**:151
"Chips" (Durcan) **70**:149, 153
Chips with Everything (Wesker) **3**:517-18; **5**:482-83; **42**:425-28, 430
"Chirico" (Fisher) **25**:158
Chirundu (Mphahlele) **25**:340, 345-46; **133**:130-32, 155, 157
Chiryō-tō (Oe) **86**:244
"The Chiseller" (Callaghan) **41**:98
The Chisholms (Hunter) **11**:280; **31**:224
Chit-Chat on the Nile (Mahfūz)
See *Tharthara fawq al-Nīl*
Ch'iu (Pa Chin) **18**:371-72
Ch'i-yüan (Pa Chin) **18**:373, 375
Chloe in the Afternoon (Rohmer) **16**:532, 534-35
Chloris and the Creeps (Platt) **26**:351-53
Chloris and the Freaks (Platt) **26**:351-53
Chloris and the Weirdos (Platt) **26**:352-53
"Choc Bay" (Walcott) **76**:278-79
Chocky (Wyndham) **19**:475
"Chocolate Footballs" (Giles) **39**:64
"Chocolate Mabbie" (Brooks) **125**:81
"Chocolate Pudding" (Mazer) **26**:291
A Chocolate Soldier (Colter) **58**:146
The Chocolate War (Cormier) **12**:134-38; **30**:181-91
"Chocolates" (Simpson) **32**:377-78; **149**:321, 359
"Choice" (Ammons) **25**:44
"A Choice" (Christie) **110**:126
The Choice (Schell) **35**:366-67
A Choice Collection of Hymns and Spiritual Songs; Intended for the Edification of Sincere Christians, of all Denominations (Occom)
See *Hand to Mouth*
"A Choice of Butchers" (Trevor) **71**:348
A Choice of Dreams (Kogawa) **129**:300
A Choice of Enemies (Richler) **5**:371-74; **13**:484-85; **46**:349
A Choice of Gods (Simak) **55**:320
"A Choice of Profession" (Malamud) **44**:420
A Choice of Shelley's Verse (Spender) **91**:263
"Choices" (Cunningham) **31**:102, 104
"The Choir and Music of Solitude and Silence" (Schwartz) **45**:355
The Choirboys (Wambaugh) **18**:532-33
"Le choix" (Theriault) **79**:407
"Cholera" (Dove) **81**:137
"Chomei at Toyama" (Bunting) **10**:83-4; **39**:299; **47**:44-5, 52, 55
"The Chomsky File" (Stewart) **32**:421
Chomsky Reader (Chomsky) **132**:31, 33-4, 36, 54-5, 68-9
"Choose Something like a Star" (Frost) **9**:222
"Choosing a Homesite" (Booth) **23**:74-5
Choosing Equality: The Case for Democratic Schooling (Bastian) **70**:366
"Chopin in Winter" (Dybek) **114**:69-70, 72, 74-5, 81-2
"Chor der Stern" (Sachs) **98**:327, 349, 355
"Chor der Ungeborenen" (Sachs) **14**:475; **98**:327, 349
"Chor der Waisen" (Sachs) **98**:327, 349
"The Choral Union" (Sassoon) **130**:178, 183
"Chorale" (Hope) **51**:212, 216
"Chorale" (McAuley) **45**:246, 248
"A Chorale of Cherokee Night Music as Heard through an Open Window Long Ago" (Williams) **13**:600
"Chord" (Merwin) **88**:206
"Chords of Fame" (Ochs) **17**:333-35
"Chöre nach Mitternacht" (Sachs) **98**:325, 327, 355
"Choricos" (Aldington) **49**:2-4, 6, 9, 12, 16
Chorister's Cake (Mayne) **12**:387-88, 390, 403
"Choros Sequence from Morpheus" (H. D.) **73**:114
"Choros Translations" (H. D.) **73**:121
"Chorus" (Ciardi) **40**:157
"Chorus" (Lorde) **71**:248
"Chorus for One Voice" (Simic) **130**:316
"Chorus for the Untenured Personnel" (Bowers) **9**:122
A Chorus Line (Kirkwood) **9**:319-20
"Chorus of Clouds" (Sachs) **98**:327
A Chorus of Disapproved (Ayckbourn) **74**:7, 15, 21, 23, 31, 34-5
"Chorus of Furies—Overheard—guarda, mi disse, le feroce Erine" (Bunting) **47**:44
"Chorus of Invisible Things" (Sachs) **98**:327
"Chorus of Orphans" (Sachs)
See "Chor der Waisen"
"Chorus of Shades" (Sachs) **98**:327
"Chorus of Stars" (Sachs)
See "Chor der Stern"
"Chorus of Stones" (Sachs) **98**:327
"Chorus of the Saved" (Sachs) **98**:327
"Chorus of the Unborn" (Sachs)
See "Chor der Ungeborenen"
"Chorus of Things Left Behind" (Sachs) **98**:327
"Chorus of Trees" (Sachs) **98**:327
"Chorus of Wanderers" (Sachs) **98**:327
"Choruses After Midnight" (Sachs)
See "Chöre nach Mitternacht"
"Choruses Describing the States of Mind of Dido" (Ungaretti)
See "Cori descrittivi d'anima di Didone"
"The Chosen" (Voigt) **54**:433
The Chosen (Potok) **2**:338-39; **7**:321; **26**:367-72, 374, 376; **112**:256-61, 263-64, 266-67, 269-75, 277-80, 282-83, 289-91, 293, 295
Chosen Country (Dos Passos) **15**:186; **25**:140-41, 146; **34**:422; **82**:76
Chosen Defects (Neruda)
See *Defectos escogidos: 2000*
A Chosen Light (Montague) **13**:391; **46**:264-68, 271-72, 275, 278
"The Chosen One" (Davies) **23**:147-48
The Chosen One and Other Stories (Davies) **23**:146
The Chosen Place, the Timeless People (Marshall) **27**:309-13, 315; **72**:212-13, 216, 219, 231, 233, 235, 247-48, 250-51, 254
Chosen Poems: Old and New (Lorde) **71**:235, 246, 260
Les Choses: A Story of the Sixties (Perec)
See *Les choses: Une histoire des années soixante*
Choses et autres (Prévert) **15**:440
Les choses: Une histoire des années soixante (Perec) **56**:253-54, 260, 268; **116**:231-322, 236, 242, 245, 252-53, 261
"Chosun" (Fenton) **32**:166, 169
"Choteau" (Bass) **79**:3-6, 17
Chou En-Lai (Archer) **12**:20
"Choughs" (Clarke) **61**:79, 82
Chris Axelson, Blacksmith (Ringwood) **48**:330, 334-36
"Chris's Last Party" (Highsmith) **42**:216
Christ and the Moral Life (Gustafson) **100**:220, 229
"Christ Climbed Down" (Ferlinghetti) **111**:64
"Christ in Alabama" (Hughes) **1**:147; **10**:279; **35**:218; **108**:298, 328
Christ Sein (main title) (Kung) **130**:127, 129, 131, 133-34, 136, 155, 167
Christabel (Potter) **58**:399-400; **86**:346, 352-53
Christian Behavior (Lewis) **27**:260-61
The Christian Challenge (Kung) **130**:155
"The Christian in the Diaspora" (Merton) **83**:383
"Christian Island" (Lightfoot) **26**:278-79
"Christianity and I" (Endō) **54**:158
"Christianity and Revolution" (Arendt) **98**:51
Christianity and the World Religions: Paths of Dialogue with Islam, Hinduism, and Buddhim (Kung) **130**:133, 146
Christianity: Essence, History, and Future (Kung) **130**:166-70

"Christians" (Scott) **43**:370
"The Christian's Year in Miniature" (Avison) **97**:86
Christie in Love (Brenton) **31**:56-7, 59, 62, 65-6, 69
Christie Malry's Own Double-Entry (Johnson) **6**:263; **9**:301-02
Christifideles Laici (John Paul II) **128**:178, 180
A Christina Stead Reader (Stead) **32**:411
"Christine" (Green) **77**:266
Christine (King) **26**:244; **37**:206; **61**:325, 328, 336; **113**:336, 344, 347, 388, 391
Christine, and Other Stories (Green)
See *Le voyageur sur la terre*
"Christmas" (Betjeman) **6**:69; **43**:45, 51
"Christmas" (McGahern) **48**:263
Christmas (Dürrenmatt)
See *Weihnacht*
Christmas and the Beads of Sweat (Nyro) **17**:313-14, 317, 319-20
"Christmas at Beaconsfield" (Deane) **122**:74
Christmas at Fontaigne's (Kotzwinkle) **35**:256-58
"Christmas at Rillingham's" (Wain) **46**:411
"Christmas at the End of a Decade" (Squires) **51**:378, 381
"A Christmas Ballad" (Brodsky) **4**:77
"Christmas Ballad" (Wright) **53**:426
"Christmas Beaches" (Voznesensky) **57**:421
A Christmas Birthday Story (Laurence) **50**:314
"A Christmas Card" (Merton) **83**:392
"A Christmas Card after the Assassinations" (Van Duyn) **7**:498
"A Christmas Carol" (Ciardi) **40**:157
"Christmas Cold" (Buckley) **57**:133
"A Christmas Conspiracy Tale" (Klima) **56**:171
"Christmas Eve" (Ammons) **108**:51, 53, 58
"Christmas Eve" (Ciardi) **40**:157
"Christmas Eve" (Morgan) **31**:275
Christmas Eve (Brennan) **5**:72-3
"Christmas Eve at Johnson's Drugs N Goods" (Bambara) **88**:22, 28
"Christmas Eve in the Time of War" (Lowell) **124**:281, 283
"Christmas Eve Service at Midnight at St. Michael's" (Bly) **15**:63; **38**:57
"Christmas Eve under Hooker's Statue" (Lowell) **124**:283
"Christmas Every Day" (Boell)
See "Nicht nur zur Weihnachtzeit"
"Christmas from Summertime Seen" (Avison) **97**:117-18
"Christmas Gift" (Himes) **7**:160; **108**:235
"A Christmas Gift for the President of the United States, Chicano Poets and a Marxist or Two" (Castillo) **151**:11, 20, 102
"A Christmas Greeting" (Wright) **5**:520
A Christmas Holiday (Maugham) **1**:204
"A Christmas Hymn" (Wilbur) **53**:405, 411; **110**:356, 385
"Christmas in Biafra" (Achebe) **7**:6; **11**:3-4; **26**:21; **127**:10
Christmas in Biafra and Other Poems (Achebe) **7**:6; **26**:20-21, 24; **127**:10, 29, 31
"Christmas in My Soul" (Nyro) **17**:316, 318
"Christmas Is Coming" (Hecht) **8**:267; **13**:269
"A Christmas Letter from Ted and Jean Just to Catch Up and Let You All Know How We All Are ... Doing" (Gray) **49**:147
"Christmas Lunch" (Bissoondath) **120**:3, 18
"A Christmas Memory" (Capote) **13**:134-36; **19**:82, 87; **34**:321-22; **38**:84, 87
"A Christmas Memory" (Giovanni) **117**:192
"Christmas Morning" (O'Connor) **14**:399
"Christmas Poem" (O'Hara) **6**:385
"Christmas Poem, 1965" (Ondaatje) **14**:407
"Christmas Present for a Poet" (Van Duyn) **116**:425
Christmas Pudding (Mitford) **44**:492
"A Christmas Recalled" (Porter) **33**:317
"The Christmas Robin" (Graves) **45**:169
"Christmas Roses" (O'Brien) **36**:341
"Christmas Sermon" (Levi) **41**:245, 248
"Christmas Shopping" (MacNeice) **53**:231
The Christmas Sky (Branley) **21**:17
"Christmas Snow" (Hall) **151**:187
"Christmas Star" (Pasternak) **63**:312-13, 315, 317
"A Christmas Storm" (Nemerov) **36**:306-08
"A Christmas Story" (Naipaul) **105**:150
"Christmas Story of the Golden Cockroach" (Castillo) **151**:48
"A Christmas Suite in Five Movements" (Jennings) **131**:234
"A Christmas Thought" (Hannah) **90**:158
"A Christmas Tragedy" (Christie) **110**:141-42, 144-45
"Christmas Tree" (Weldon) **36**:444; **122**:254
The Christmas Tree (Johnston) **150**:22-3, 31
"Christmas Trees" (Frost) **15**:246, 248
"The Christmas Virgin" (Derleth) **31**:138
"Christmas with Two Children's Stories" (Hesse) **25**:260-61
Christopher and His Kind, 1929-1939 (Isherwood) **14**:286; **44**:397-401
Christopher Blake (Hart) **66**:178, 182-83, 189-90
Christopher Columbus (Granzotto) **70**:351
Christopher Columbus, Mariner (Morison) **70**:351
Christopher Columbus: Master of the Atlantic (Thomas) **70**:338
Christopher Strong (Arzner) **98**:62-6, 70-1, 74, 81, 85-7
Christopher Unborn (Fuentes)
See *Cristóbal nonato*
"Christo's" (Muldoon) **72**:273-74, 277
Chroma (Barthelme) **117**:5-6
"A Chromatic Passing-Note" (Amis) **40**:41
"Chromium" (Levi) **37**:223
Chromos (Alfau) **66**:8-13
"Chronic" (Avison) **97**:76, 128
"Chronic" (Ezekiel) **61**:108
"A Chronic Condition" (Wilbur) **3**:534; **110**:351
The Chronicle and the Chant of the Ages (Blaga) **75**:61
Chronicle in Stone (Kadare) **52**:261-63
Chronicle of a Death Foretold (García Márquez)
See *Crónica de una muerte anunciada*
"Chronicle of a Decade" (Elytis) **100**:190-91
"Chronicle of a Demise" (Williams) **15**:579
"Chronicle of Anse Saint-Roch" (Ferron) **94**:124-25
Chronicle of Dawn (Sender)
See *Crónica del alba*
Chronicle of Early Youth (Sender)
See *Crónica del alba*
A Chronicle of Love Affairs (Konwicki)
See *Kronika wypadków milosnych*
A Chronicle of Love Events (Konwicki)
See *Kronika wypadków milosnych*
Chronicle of Our Time (Ehrenburg) **62**:179
"A Chronicle of the Coming of the New Ice Age" (Haavikko) **34**:178
Chronicle of Youth (Brittain) **23**:93
"Chronicler's Notice" (Arghezi)
See "Tableta de cronicar"
Chronicles of Bustos Domecq (Bioy Casares)
See *Crónicas de Bustos Domecq*
Chronicles of Dissent (Chomsky) **132**:68, 72
Chronicles of Hell (Ghelderode)
See *Fastes d'enfer*
"The Chronicles of Narnia" (Lewis) **124**:192-94, 213, 225, 229, 232, 236-37, 247
Chronicles of Our Peaceful Kitchen (Tanizaki) **28**:414
Chronicles of Prydain (Alexander) **35**:26, 28
The Chronicles of Robin Hood (Sutcliff) **26**:428, 433, 435
Chronicles of Solar Pons (Derleth) **31**:138
The Chronicles of Thomas Covenant, the Unbeliever (Donaldson) **46**:140, 142, 144; **138**:8, 12-13, 15-18, 20, 23-8, 31, 34-5
Chronique (Perse) **4**:400; **46**:308
Chronique de la ville de pierre (Kadare) **52**:261
Chronique des Pasquier (Duhamel) **8**:186
Chroniques (Giono) **4**:184
Chroniques du plateau Mont-Royal (Tremblay) **29**:424, 427
Chroniques du XXme siècle (Morand) **41**:305
Chroniques romanesques (Giono) **4**:187
"Chronologues" (Goldbarth) **38**:205-06
The Chrysalids (Wyndham) **19**:475-76
"Chrysallis" (Montale) **9**:386
"Chrysanthemum Show" (Day Lewis) **10**:131
"Chrysanthemum Tea" (Sondheim) **30**:397; **147**:258
"The Chrysanthemums" (Steinbeck) **9**:516, 519; **21**:391-92; **34**:415; **45**:382
Chrysothemis (Ritsos) **13**:488
"The Chuck Show of Television" (Keillor) **115**:286, 295
"Chudala" (Narayan) **121**:334
"Chun" (Le Guin) **45**:213
Ch'un (Pa Chin) **18**:371
Chung Kuo (Antonioni) **20**:38; **144**:80
Chung Kuo: The Middle Kingdom, Book One (Wingrove) **68**:451-57
Chunga's Revenge (Zappa) **17**:587
"The Chuppah" (Piercy) **62**:371; **128**:230-31, 273
The Church as Moral Decision Maker (Gustafson) **100**:195
"Church Going" (Larkin) **3**:277; **5**:223, 230; **8**:332, 335, 337-38, 339; **13**:335-36, 340; **18**:294, 297; **33**:256, 259-60, 263; **39**:340-42, 345; **64**:261, 265, 269-70, 277, 282-83
"The Church in High Street" (Campbell) **42**:83, 92
"Church of England: Thoughts Occasioned by Hearing the Bells of Magdalen Tower from the Botanic Garden, Oxford on St. Mary Magdalen's Day" (Betjeman) **43**:50
Church Poems (Betjeman) **34**:306, 309; **43**:49-50
Churchill Barriers (Brown) **100**:85
The Churchill Play (Brenton) **31**:58, 62-7
The Church--Maintained in Truth: A Theological Meditation (Kung) **130**:153
"The Churchyard at Creggan" (Deane) **122**:83
"Churn Milk Joan" (Hughes) **14**:273
"Churning Day" (Heaney) **25**:244; **91**:119
"The Chute" (Olds) **85**:298
La chute (Camus) **1**:52-4; **2**:97-8; **4**:91-2; **9**:144-46, 150; **11**:95; **14**:107, 110, 113-14; **32**:86-7, 91; **63**:63, 68, 71, 75, 77, 83-90; **69**:135; **124**:7, 10, 13, 21, 31-5
La chute dans le temps (Cioran) **64**:82-5, 87-8, 92
"Chuy" (Soto) **80**:278, 291-92, 296
"Chuzhoe remeslo" (Akhmadulina) **53**:11
"Ciant da li ciampanis" (Pasolini) **106**:233
"Ciants di muart" (Pasolini) **106**:233
A ciascuno il suo (Sciascia) **9**:474; **41**:389-90
"Cicada" (Ihimaera) **46**:200
"Cicada" (Wright) **146**:354, 358, 366, 372
Cicada (Haines) **58**:217-19, 221
"Cicada Blue" (Wright) **146**:
"Cicada Queen" (Sterling) **72**:368
"Cicadas" (Mueller) **51**:281
Le Cid maghané (Ducharme) **74**:63-7
A cidade sitiada (Lispector) **43**:261, 265
"Cider Hill" (Williams) **45**:445
The Cider House Rules (Irving) **38**:251-55; **112**:154-58, 165
Cider with Rosie (Lee) **90**:182-85, 187-88, 190-92, 195-96, 198-99, 201, 204, 207, 209
Le Ciel de Québec (Ferron) **94**:108, 112-17, 122, 124-25, 127
La Ciel et la merde (Arrabal) **58**:18
Cien años de soledad (García Márquez) **2**:148-50; **3**:179-83; **8**:230, 232-33; **10**:214-17; **15**:254; **27**:147-55; **47**:143-44, 146-51, 153-

54; **55**:134, 136, 138-39, 144-47; **68**:139-168
Cien sonetos de amor (Neruda) **28**:313-14; **62**:334
La cifra (Borges) **44**:356
Cigarettes (Mathews) **52**:311-12, 316-18
"Cigarettes and Whisky and Wild, Wild Women" (Sexton) **123**:405
"Cigars Clamped Between Their Teeth" (Simic) **130**:326
Cimarron (Ferber) **18**:151; **93**:153-56, 159, 164, 171, 174, 176, 179, 181, 185-87, 189-90
Le cimetière des voitures (Arrabal) **9**:34, 38; **18**:19; **58**:3-4, 7-8, 11, 16-17, 21, 24-6
Cimitirul Buna-Vestire (Arghezi) **80**:6
"Cina" (Arghezi) **80**:7
"Cînatre omului" (Arghezi) **80**:4
Cinco horas con Mario (Delibes) **8**:169; **18**:113
5 narraciones y 2 fábulas (Benet) **28**:25
Cinder (DeMarinis) **54**:97-8
"Cinderella" (Jarrell) **13**:302
Cinderella (Potter) **123**:231
"Cinderella and the Mob" (Woolrich) **77**:390
"The Cinderella Waltz" (Beattie) **40**:66; **63**:19; **146**:81, 85
"The Cinema" (Salter) **52**:369
"Cinema and Ballad of the Great Depression" (Justice) **102**:285
"Cinema as an Art Form" (Deren) **102**:43
"Cinema of a Man" (MacLeish) **68**:273
"Cinematography: The Creative Use of Reality" (Deren) **102**:43-4
Cingiz Ajtmatov: Povesti i rasskazy (Aitmatov) See *Povestri i rasskazy*
A cinkos (Konrád) **73**:175-84
"The Cinnamon Peeler" (Ondaatje) **51**:318
Cinnamon Skin (MacDonald) **27**:275-76
Cinque romanzi brevi (Ginzburg) **11**:229
"Cinquevalli" (Morgan) **31**:276
Cîntare omului (Arghezi) **80**:6, 8
Cîntece noi (Arghezi) **80**:6
La ciociara (Moravia) **7**:240-41; **11**:382; **18**:344, 349
La ciociara (De Sica) **20**:89-90, 94
CIOPW (Cummings) **12**:146; **68**:35
"Cipango's Hinder Door" (Dahlberg) **7**:63
Cipango's Hinder Door (Dahlberg) **7**:63
The Cipher (Borges) See *La cifra*
Cipher (Mosley) **43**:317
Los cipreses creen en Dios (Gironella) **11**:234, 237
Circa 1492: Art in the Age of Exploration (Levenson) **70**:355
"Circe" (Auden) **6**:18
"Circe" (Broumas) **10**:77; **73**:8
"Circe" (H. D.) **73**:105
"Circe" (Hope) **51**:212, 220
"Circe" (Miller) **14**:373
"Circle" (Moss) **14**:376
"The Circle" (Nabokov) **3**:354
The Circle (Feinstein) **36**:167-68
The Circle (Maugham) **1**:204; **11**:368-70; **67**:223-25, 227; **93**:244
"The Circle Game" (Atwood) **4**:27
"The Circle Game" (Mitchell) **12**:436
The Circle Game (Atwood) **4**:24, 26-27; **8**:30; **13**:42; **15**:37; **25**:63-4, 66-7; **84**:68; **135**:13, 30
The Circle Game (Lieber) **6**:311
The Circle Home (Hoagland) **28**:180
Circle in the Dirt (Moraga) **126**:301
"The Circle Is Small" (Lightfoot) **26**:282
"Circle of Chalk" (Rozewicz) See "Kredowe koło"
"A Circle of Fire" (O'Connor) **1**:257; **15**:412; **21**:256-57
"A Circle of Friends" (Voinovich) **49**:376-77; **147**:272, 285
Circle of Friends (Binchy) **153**:64-8, 71, 73-6, 78
"Circle of Prayer" (Munro) **50**:211, 215-16, 218, 220
A Circle of Quiet (L'Engle) **12**:349-50
The Circle of Reason (Ghosh) **44**:44-8; **153**:83, 85, 97-100, 102, 107, 110, 114, 129
"Circle of Steel" (Lightfoot) **26**:280, 283
"Circle One" (Dodson) **79**:193
"A Circle Tour of the Rockies" (Dudek) **11**:161
"Circle Two" (Dodson) **79**:193
"Circles" (Van Doren) **6**:541
Circles on the Water (Piercy) **27**:380-81; **62**:373; **128**:227-28, 246, 272-73
"The Circling Hand" (Kincaid) **43**:249
El circo (Goytisolo) **23**:186; **133**:90, 93
"Circolo della caccia" (Davison) **28**:103
"Circonstances de la poésie" (Reverdy) **53**:283
"The Circuit" (Avison) **97**:115
Circuit by the Moon and Color (Tzara) See *Circuit par la lune et par la couleur*
Circuit par la lune et par la couleur (Tzara) **47**:390
"Circular from America" (Barker) **48**:18
"The Circular Ruins" (Borges) See "Las ruinas circulares"
Circular Stairs, Distress in the Mirrors (Klappert) **57**:259-60, 264
"The Circular Valley" (Bowles) **19**:61; **53**:37, 42
"Circulation of the Song" (Duncan) **41**:127, 130; **55**:298-99
Circulatory Systems: The Rivers Within (Silverstein and Silverstein) **17**:451
"The Circus" (Gustafson) **36**:220
"The Circus" (Koch) **8**:323; **44**:249, 251
"Circus" (MacNeice) **53**:231
"The Circus" (Porter) **7**:317; **15**:429
The Circus (Chaplin) **16**:187-89, 199-201, 204
Circus (MacLean) **13**:363; **63**:265
"The Circus Animals' Desertion" (Van Duyn) **116**:401, 417, 426
"The Circus at Luxor" (Naipaul) **105**:157
The Circus in the Attic, and Other Stories (Warren) **1**:353
"Circus in Three Rings" (Plath) **17**:362; **111**:178
The Circus Is Coming (Streatfeild) **21**:398, 402, 404-06, 414, 416
A Circus of Needs (Dunn) **36**:153-55
Circus Shoes (Streatfeild) See *The Circus Is Coming*
"The Circuses" (Jennings) **131**:233
"Cirque d'hiver" (Bishop) **9**:92, 94-6
"Ciruelo silvestre" (Rodriguez) **10**:440
Cistercian Contemplatives (Merton) **34**:465
Cistercian Life (Merton) **34**:465
"Cistercians in Germany" (Lowell) **4**:302; **124**:281, 283-86
The Cistern (Seferis) **5**:384
"The Citadel" (L'Heureux) **52**:274
"Citadel" (Jagger and Richard) **17**:221
The Citadel (Cronin) **32**:133-36, 138, 140
The Citadel of the Autarch (Wolfe) **25**:477-79
La cité dans l'oeuf (Tremblay) **29**:425-26; **102**:372
La cité fertile (Chedid) **47**:85-6
"Citez-m'en" (Damas) **84**:160
"Cities" (Byrne) **26**:97
"The Cities" (H. D.) **73**:105
The Cities (Blackburn) **9**:100; **43**:61-3, 65
Cities Burning (Randall) **1**:283; **135**:374, 377, 389-90, 392, 394-95
Cities in Bezique (Kennedy) **66**:205, 208-09
Cities in Flight (Blish) **14**:82
Cities of the Interior (Nin) **1**:248; **4**:376-77; **14**:382-84, 386; **60**:275-76, 278, 280; **127**:377, 379
"The Cities of the Plain" (Van Duyn) **63**:439; **116**:404, 430
Cities of the Red Night: A Boys' Book (Burroughs) **22**:84-6; **42**:73, 80
"Cities, Plains and People" (Durrell) **27**:97
"Citified" (Ammons) **57**:53
Citizen Kane (Welles) **20**:431-36, 438-54; **80**:371-72, 374, 378, 382, 386, 391, 393, 396, 402-04, 406-09, 411, 413-17, 419-23
"A Citizen of Mondath" (Le Guin) **136**:330
Citizen of the Galaxy (Heinlein) **3**:225; **14**:247; **26**:161, 165-66, 173, 177; **55**:301
"CITIZEN RESPONSIBILITY (Hey! I'm Running for Office!)" (Giovanni) **117**:204
"Citizen Ship" (Smith) **12**:544
Citizen Soldiers: The U.S. Army from the Normandy Beaches to the Bulge to the Surrender of Germany (Ambrose) **145**:55-7
Citizens (Levin) **7**:204
Citizens: A Chronicle of the French Revolution (Schama) **150**:103-30, 133-35, 137, 140-41, 143-50, 161-62, 168, 172, 178-80, 183-86, 188
Citizens of Ohio (Edmonds) **35**:146
"Citre et Trans" (Delany) **141**:160
La città delle donne (Fellini) **85**:53, 60, 66, 70, 74, 76, 79-81
La città e la casa (Ginzburg) **54**:201-02, 205, 209-13; **70**:280
Le città invisibili (Calvino) **5**:99-101; **8**:126-27, 129, 131-32; **11**:92; **22**:89, 93; **33**:98-101; **39**:306-07, 309-10, 314-17; **73**:41, 48, 51-2, 57-8
"City" (Fisher) **25**:157-59, 161
"The City" (Wright) **53**:426
City (Simak) **55**:319-21
"City Afternoon" (Ashbery) **15**:32
The City and the Dogs (Vargas Llosa) See *La ciudad y los perros*
The City and the House (Ginzburg) See *La città e la casa*
The City and the Island (Davison) **28**:100
The City and the Pillar (Vidal) **2**:449; **4**:557-58; **6**:550; **22**:432-33; **33**:406; **72**:378, 387; **142**:294, 304-05, 307, 309, 313, 315, 319-22, 326, 331-32, 334, 338
The City and the Stars (Clarke) **4**:105; **35**:121-22, 127; **136**:209, 225
"City Boy" (Michaels) **25**:315-16
The City Boy (Wouk) **38**:445-47
The City Builder (Konrád) See *A városalapító*
"City Drops" (Carroll) **143**:40, 44
A City for Lincoln (Tunis) **12**:595, 598
"A City Garden in April" (Swenson) **61**:400; **106**:326
The City in Tears (Seifert) See *Město v slzách*
The City in the Mist (Trow) **52**:422-24
"The City Is in Total Darkness" (Shaw) **7**:412
"City Life" (Barthelme) **13**:55; **46**:40; **115**:63, 70
City Life (Barthelme) **1**:18; **3**:43; **6**:28-30; **8**:50, 52-3; **13**:55; **46**:35-6; 40; **59**:247, 249; **115**:56, 60, 63, 68
"City Lights" (Reed) **21**:317
City Lights (Chaplin) **16**:188-89, 195, 198-201, 203-04
"The City Limits" (Ammons) **5**:27; **9**:27; **25**:43; **108**:11
"The City Lost in the Snow" (Calvino) **33**:100
"City of a Thousand Suns" (Delany) **14**:144
"The City of Acknowledgement" (Shapcott) **38**:400-01
City of Angels (Gelbart) **61**:147-50
City of Darkness (Bova) **45**:68-9
City of Darkness, City of Light (Piercy) **128**:268-70
"City of Fire" (Harjo) **83**:283
City of Glass (Auster) **47**:12-16; **131**:3-5, 7, 9-15, 18, 21-4, 26-7, 33-8
City of Night (Rechy) **7**:356-57; **14**:443-45; **107**:223-39, 243, 254, 256-58, 260
The City of Satisfactions (Hoffman) **6**:243; **13**:287
"The City of Silence" (Matthews) **40**:320
City of Spades (MacInnes) **4**:314; **23**:281-87

City of Splintered Gods (Faludy)
See *Karoton*
City of the Chasch (Vance) **35**:422, 424
"A City of the Dead, a City of the Living" (Gordimer) **33**:185; **123**:118, 131
"The City of the End of Things" (Thesen) **56**:417
"A City of the Living" (Gordimer) **33**:185
"The City of the Living" (Stegner) **49**:351; **81**:346
The City of the Living, and Other Stories (Stegner) **49**:351; **81**:346
The City of the Olesha Fruit (Dubie) **36**:133-34, 140, 142
City of the Seven Serpents (O'Dell) **30**:276
"The City of the Singing Flame" (Smith) **43**:420-22, 424-25
The City of Trembling Leaves (Clark) **28**:77, 80-3
City of Women (Fellini)
See *La città delle donne*
The City of Yes and the City of No (Yevtushenko) **126**:400
A City on a Hill (Higgins) **7**:157-58
"City on Fire" (Sondheim) **30**:394, 398; **147**:236
"City on the Edge of Forever" (Ellison) **139**:129, 133
City on the Edge of Forever (Ellison) **139**:143
City Primeval: High Noon in Detroit (Leonard) **28**:234, 236; **71**:207, 219, 222, 224; **120**:270-71, 275-76, 286-87, 289, 291
"City Seasons" (Denby) **48**:84
"City Song" (Gustafson) **36**:216
City Streets (Mamoulian) **16**:420-21, 423-24
City Sugar (Poliakoff) **38**:375, 378, 380-83, 385-86
A City Winter (O'Hara) **13**:427
"City without a Name" (Milosz) **11**:377; **56**:249
"City without Smoke" (Denby) **48**:81, 84
"City without Walls" (Auden) **11**:17; **14**:27
City without Walls and Other Poems (Auden) **2**:25-6; **3**:22, 24, 29; **4**:33; **6**:17-19; **14**:27; **43**:18
"CITYCity-city" (Kerouac) **29**:271
"A City's Death by Fire" (Walcott) **25**:450; **76**:273, 280
"The City's Life" (Waddington) **28**:437
"Ciudad ajena" (Valenzuela) **104**:355, 386
Ciudad Real (Castellanos) **66**:60
La ciudad y los perros (Vargas Llosa) **3**:493; **6**:545-46; **10**:498-500; **31**:445, 447, 449; **42**:409; **85**:352, 358, 364, 366, 370-71, 375, 389
"Ciudades" (Otero) **11**:427
Ciugrena (Arrabal) **18**:19; **58**:7-8
"Civil Disobedience" (Arendt) **98**:12
"Civil Peace" (Achebe) **26**:23; **75**:15
"Civil Rights Poem" (Baraka) **5**:48
Civil to Stangers (Pym) **111**:284, 287
"Civil War" (O'Flaherty) **34**:356
The Civil War: A Narrative (Foote) **75**:232, 240, 243-248, 251, 257-60, 262-63
Civil Wars (Brown) **32**:68-70
Civil Wars (Jordan) **23**:256-57; **114**:152-53
"Civilian and Soldier" (Soyinka) **36**:409
La civilisation du bossale (Condé) **92**:100
"The Civilisation of Iron" (Kunene) **85**:166
"Civilities of Lamplight" (Tomlinson) **45**:392
"Civility a Bogey" (Avison) **97**:72, 109
"Civilization" (Summers) **10**:494
"Civilization and Its Discontents" (Ashbery) **9**:43; **41**:40
"Civilization and Its Discontents" (Matthews) **40**:324
"Civilization and Its Discontents" (Roth) **66**:386
The Civilization of Ancient Egypt (Johnson) **147**:160
Clacson, trombette e penacchi (Fo) **32**:176; **109**:109-11, 119-20, 136-37, 139, 143, 146
Clad in Light (Seifert)
See *Světlem oděná*
Clad in Light (Seifert) **34**:257
Claiming an Identity They Taught Me to Despise (Cliff) **120**:90, 126
"Claiming Kin" (Voigt) **54**:429-30
The Claiming of Sleeping Beauty (Rice) **128**:293-94
Clair de femme (Gary) **25**:191
"Clair de terre" (Breton) **9**:126
Claire de Lune (Linney) **51**:263
Claire de terre (Breton) **54**:17, 29-30, 32-3
Claire's Knee (Rohmer)
See *Le genou de Claire*
"Clairvoyance" (Gerstler) **70**:157
"The Clairvoyant" (Gass) **8**:242; **15**:255
"The Clam Digger" (Bowering) **47**:29-30
The Clam Shell (Settle) **61**:374, 385
The Clam Theater (Edson) **13**:190
Clamor (Guillén) **11**:262
"Clampdown" (Clash) **30**:46
Le clan des Ostendais (Simenon) **18**:482
The Clan of the Cave Bear (Auel) **31**:22-3; **107**:3-5, 7-9, 11-6, 18, 21-4
"Clancy" (Young) **17**:568-69
"Clancy in the Tower of Babel" (Cheever) **64**:65
The Clang Birds (L'Heureux) **52**:276-77, 279
Clans of the Alphane Moon (Dick) **30**:123, 125; **72**:109, 121
"Clap Hands, Here Comes Charlie" (Bainbridge) **62**:37
"Clapp's Pond" (Oliver) **34**:247; **98**:256
"Clara" (O'Brien) **13**:416
Clara (Valenzuela) **104**:376-77, 382
Clara's Ole Man (Bullins) **5**:82-3
"Clare Savage as Crossroads Character" (Cliff) **120**:92-93
Claremont Essays (Trilling) **129**:330-31, 337, 342, 356, 363
"Clarendon Whatmough" (Adcock) **41**:14
"Clarice Lispector: The Approach" (Cixous)
See "L'Approche de Clarice Lispector"
"Clarifications for Robert Jacoby" (Matthias) **9**:362
The Clarinet and Saxophone Book (Berger) **12**:40
"Clarisa" (Allende) **97**:11
"Clarissa" (Morand) **41**:295, 297, 308
Clark Gifford's Body (Fearing) **51**:109-10, 121
Clarkton (Fast) **131**:83, 97
Claro enigma (Andrade) **18**:5
"Clartés terrestres" (Reverdy) **53**:290
The Clash (Clash) **30**:43-6
Clash by Night (Lang) **20**:207
Clash by Night (Odets) **2**:320; **28**:329-30, 332-33; **98**:197-99, 229, 237, 241, 244
"Clash City Rockers" (Clash) **30**:43-4
"Class" (Alexie) **154**:45, 47-8
"Class" (Bukowski) **41**:74; **108**:85-6
"The Class" (Ostriker) **132**:321
"Class" (Tomlinson) **6**:535
Class: A Guide through the American Class System (Fussell) **74**:127-28, 137, 142, 146-47
"Class and Allegory in Contemporary Mass Culture: Dog Day Afternoon as a Political" (Jameson) **142**:247, 258
The Class of '49 (Carpenter) **41**:107-08
"Class of 1949" (Levine) **54**:298-99
Class Pictures (Sachs) **35**:334
"The Class Reunion" (Amichai) **116**:107
"Class with No Class" (Levine) **118**:307
"Classic" (Ammons) **2**:14
"Classic Ballroom Dances" (Simic) **49**:338; **130**:305, 317
Classic Ballroom Dances (Simic) **22**:381, 383; **49**:341; **68**:369; **130**:298, 305, 311, 318-19
Classic, Romantic, and Modern (Barzun)
See *Romanticism and the Modern Ego*
"The Classic Touch" (Powys) **125**:291
"A Classic Waits for Me" (White) **10**:528
"Classical Portrait" (Gustafson) **36**:220
Classics and Commercials: A Literary Chronicle of the Forties (Wilson) **3**:538; **8**:550; **24**:479, 481, 487
"The Classics and the Man of Letters" (Eliot) **41**:155
Classics Revisited (Rexroth) **22**:346; **49**:286; **112**:387
"Classified" (Ferber) **93**:153
"A Class-Room" (Jennings) **131**:234
"Classroom Windmills" (Vizenor) **103**:288
"Claude Emerson, Reporter" (O'Hara) **42**:319
"Claude Gauvreau" (Ferron) **94**:126
"Claude Glass" (Ondaatje) **51**:313
"The Claude Glass" (Szirtes) **46**:393-94
"Claudius' Diary" (Shiga)
See "Kurōdiasu no nikki"
"Claudius' Journal" (Shiga)
See "Kurōdiasu no nikki"
Claudius the God and His Wife Messalina (Graves) **1**:128; **6**:211; **39**:322-23, 325; **45**:173
"Claud's Dog" (Dahl) **79**:178
"Claudy" (Simmons) **43**:411
"Claus Von Stauffenberg" (Gunn) **18**:201; **32**:208
"Cláusula III" (Arreola) **147**:10
Claw (Barker) **37**:32, 34-5, 37
The Claw of the Conciliator (Wolfe) **25**:474-78
The Clay and the Wheel (Vesaas)
See *Leiret og hjulet*
"Clay Bertrand Is Alive and in Camelot" (Cassity) **42**:95
Clay's Ark (Butler) **38**:66; **121**:89, 95, 97-8, 100, 103, 106-7, 111-13, 115, 117, 119, 122, 131
Clea (Durrell) **1**:87; **4**:144; **8**:190-92; **13**:185-86, 188
Clea and Zeus Divorce (Prager) **56**:278-81
"A Clean Quiet House" (Fuchs) **22**:157
"A Clean, Well-Lighted Place" (Hemingway) **6**:231; **8**:285; **10**:268, 270; **13**:272, 279; **30**:192; **34**:478; **41**:198; **61**:203
Cleaned Out (Ernaux)
See *Les armoires vides*
"Cleaning the Well" (Chappell) **78**:96
"Cleanup Time" (Lennon) **35**:272-74
Clear and Present Danger (Clancy) **112**:53-6, 65, 77, 84, 90
"Clear Autumn" (Rexroth) **49**:283
A Clear Introduction to Later History (Haavikko)
See *Selvä johdatus myöhempään historiaan*
Clear Light of Day (Desai) **19**:134-35; **37**:70-2; **97**:139-40, 14549, 166, 168, 178-80
"Clear Morning" (Glück) **81**:167, 170, 173
"Clear Night" (Paz)
See "Noche en claro"
"Clear Night" (Wright) **146**:335, 374
Clear Pictures: First Loves, First Guides (Price) **63**:337-38
Clear Springs (Mason) **154**:300-01
"Clearances" (Heaney) **74**:160-62, 174-75, 191, 194
"The Clearest Day" (Cook-Lynn) **93**:124
"Clearfield" (Freeman) **55**:57-8
"The Clearing" (Baraka) **14**:42
"The Clearing" (Kinsella) **138**:87, 94
"The Clearing" (Slavitt) **14**:491
"The Clearing" (Thomas) **31**:430
Clearing (Berry) **27**:35-6
Clearing in the Sky and Other Stories (Stuart) **34**:373, 376
"Clearing the Air" (Willard) **37**:463
"Clearness" (Wilbur) **6**:570; **9**:569
"Les clefs de la mort" (Green) **77**:264-66
"The Cleggan Disaster" (Murphy) **41**:311-12, 314, 316
Clem Anderson (Cassill) **4**:95; **23**:102-04
"Clem Maverick" (Vliet) **22**:441
Clemmons (Masters) **48**:222-24
"Clenched Fist" (Ihimaera) **46**:200
The Clenched Fist (Lagerkvist)
See *Den knutna näven*
Cléo de 5 à 7 (Varda) **16**:554, 557-59

Cleo from Five to Seven (Varda)
See *Cléo de 5 à 7*
"Cleopatra" (Akhmatova) **64**:16
"Clepsydra" (Ashbery) **2**:19; **41**:40-1; **77**:60-1; **125**:40
"The Cleric" (Heaney) **74**:169
The Clerk's Journal: Being the Diary of a Queer Man (Aiken) **52**:21-2
"The Cleveland Wrecking Yard" (Brautigan) **12**:59, 63-4
"The Clever One" (Gellhorn) **60**:187
Clever Soldiers (Poliakoff) **38**:375-77, 380, 385
"A Clever-Kids Story" (Beattie) **146**:65
The Clewiston Test (Wilhelm) **7**:538
"A Client" (Rao) **56**:291, 293
The Client (Grisham) **84**:195-99
"The Cliff" (Baxter) **78**:17
"Cliff and Wave" (Graves) **45**:169
The Cliff of Time (Abe) **81**:291
"Cliffdwellers" (Gilliatt) **53**:146
Cliffs of Fall and Other Stories (Hazzard) **18**:213, 215-18
"The Cliff-Temple" (H. D.) **73**:104, 139
The Climate of Eden (Hart) **66**:178-79, 182, 189-90
"The Climate of Insomnia" (Shaw) **7**:412
"The Climber" (Mason) **154**:231, 322
"Climbers" (Wild) **14**:581
"Climbing Alone" (Wagoner) **15**:560
The Climbing Frame (Hocking) **13**:285
Climbing into the Roots (Saner) **9**:468-69
"Climbing Katahdin" (Hoffman) **6**:243
"Climbing Milestone Mountain" (Rexroth) **112**:383
"Climbing the Chagrin River" (Oliver) **34**:249
"Climbing the Streets of Worcester, Mass." (Harjo) **83**:281-82
"Climbing the Tower" (Crews) **49**:68, 75
"Climbing This Hill Again" (Stern) **40**:406
"Clinamen; or, Poetic Misprision" (Bloom) **24**:77
Clinging to the Wreckage: A Part of Life (Mortimer) **28**:288-89; **43**:308
A Clinical Case (Buzzati)
See *Un caso clinico*
"Clio" (Barthelme) **117**:5
Clio and the Doctors: Psycho-History, Quanto-History, and History (Barzun) **51**:43, 45-6; **145**:72
Clive Barker's Books of Blood, Vols. I-III (Barker) **52**:51-4, 56-7
Clive Barker's Books of Blood, Vols. IV-VI (Barker) **52**:52-3, 56-7
"C.L.M." (Masefield) **47**:233
Cloak and Dagger (Lang) **20**:207, 216
"Cloak of Aesir" (Campbell) **32**:75-6, 78, 80
Cloak of Darkness (MacInnes) **27**:284-85
A Cloak of Light (Morris) **37**:316-17
"Clochard" (Szymborska) **99**:200
"Un clochard m'a demandé dix sous'" (Damas) **84**:177
"Un clochard m'a demandé dix sous" (Damas) **84**:177
Les cloches de bâle (Aragon) **3**:13; **22**:34, 37
Les cloches sur le coeur (Char) **11**:113
"The Clock" (Abse) **29**:13
"The Clock" (Beer) **58**:38
"The Clock above the Kitchen Door Says One" (Ostriker) **132**:302
Clock Analect (Lezama Lima)
See *Analecta del reloj*
"Clock and Heart" (Wright) **53**:426
"A Clock in the Square" (Rich) **36**:365
"Clock Invention" (Goldbarth) **38**:200
The Clock Winder (Tyler) **11**:552; **28**:431; **103**:237-38, 243-44, 259, 263-65, 267-69, 273
"A Clock with No Hands" (Nemerov) **36**:303
Clock without Hands (McCullers) **1**:209-10; **4**:346; **10**:335, 338; **12**:418-21, 424-25, 427, 430; **48**:232, 234; **100**:251-52, 255-56
Clockers (Lee) **105**:120-21, 127, 129
The Clocks (Christie) **12**:122; **48**:74-5
The Clocks (Hildesheimer)
See *Die Uhren*
"The Clocks of the Dead" (Simic) **130**:334
A Clockwork Orange (Burgess) **2**:85-7; **4**:80-1, 84-5; **5**:87-8, 90-1; **8**:112; **10**:86-8, 90; **13**:124-128; **15**:104, 106-07; **22**:69-70, 74, 76-8; **40**:114-17, 125; **62**:127-32, 138; **81**:300-02, 305-06, 310; **94**:23-88
A Clockwork Orange (Kubrick) **16**:383-84, 386, 388-91
A Clockwork Orange 2004 (Burgess) **94**:81
A Clockwork Orange: A Play with Music (Burgess) **94**:80, 82-85
The Clockwork Testament; or, Enderby's End (Burgess) **4**:84; **5**:88-91; **8**:112-13; **40**:115, 122-23; **62**:125, 130, 132; **94**:57, 65, 69-70, 84
"The Cloister of the Lilies" (Wiebe) **14**:575
"Cloistered" (Heaney) **74**:193
"Clone" (Cortázar) **33**:126-30
The Cloning (Wild) **14**:581
The Cloning of Joanna May (Weldon) **122**:259, 262, 264-66
Clonk Clonk (Golding) **2**:169; **17**:177; **81**:325
Clope au dossier (Pinget) **13**:442; **37**:363
Close Encounters of the Third Kind (Spielberg) **20**:360-62, 364-67
Close Harmony (Rice) **7**:360
"Close Listening" (Birkerts) **116**:164, 167
Close Listening (Bernstein) **142**:51
Close of Play (Gray) **14**:215; **36**:205, 207
Close of Play (Raven) **14**:440, 443
Close Quarters (Golding) **81**:317-18, 320, 324-26
Close Quarters (Heinemann) **50**:187, 191
Close Relations (Isaacs) **32**:254-55
Close Sesame (Farah) **53**:134-35, 138-39; **137**:96-97, 105-09, 112, 114-15, 117, 119-26, 128-29
Close the Sky, Ten by Ten (Mahapatra) **33**:281, 284
"Close to the Borderline" (Joel) **26**:220
Close to the Sun Again (Callaghan) **41**:88-90, 94-5
Closed All Night (Morand)
See *Fermé la nuit*
The Closed Chaplet (Riding) **3**:432
"The Closed Door" (Donoso)
See "La puerta cerrada"
A Closed Eye (Brookner) **136**:94-96, 111, 114-16, 126-28, 131
The Closed Garden (Green) **77**:262, 264, 270
The Closed Garden (Green) **77**:262, 264, 270
The Closed Harbour (Hanley) **3**:220
Closely Observed Trains (Hrabal)
See *Ostře sledované vlaky*
Closely Watched Trains (Hrabal)
See *Ostře sledované vlaky*
The Closest of Strangers: Liberalism and the Politics of Race in New York (Sleeper) **70**:374
"Closets" (Shange) **25**:399
"Close-Up" (Ammons) **108**:21
Close-Up (Deighton) **46**:126-27
"Closing" (Blaga) **75**:78
"The Closing Down of Summmer" (MacLeod) **56**:196-200
"Closing in New Haven" (Klappert) **57**:259
The Closing of the American Mind: How Higher Education Has Failed Democracy and Impoverished Souls of Today's Students (Bloom) **70**:364, 400
"Closing the Time-Lid" (Card) **47**:67
"Cloteel" (Brown) **59**:265
"Clothe the Naked" (Parker) **15**:415; **68**:327, 334-35, 340
Clothed in Light (Seifert)
See *Světlem oděná*
"Clothes" (Szymborska) **99**:196
Clothes for a Summer Hotel: A Ghost Play (Williams) **19**:473; **45**:447, 449, 455
"Clothes Make the Man" (Matheson) **37**:246
"The Clothes Pit" (Dunn) **40**:166
"Clotheslines" (Jones) **10**:285
"Clothespin" (Dybek) **114**:61
"La clôture" (Perec) **56**:254
La clôture et autres poémes (Perec) **56**:254-55
"The Cloud" (Elytis) **49**:110
"The Cloud" (Fowles) **6**:187-89; **15**:232; **87**:157, 163
"The Cloud" (Walcott) **14**:549
The Cloud Catchers (Holden) **18**:258
Cloud Chamber (Dorris) **109**:296-300, 311-13
The Cloud Forest; A Chronicle of the South American Wilderness (Matthiessen) **11**:360; **32**:286, 290
Cloud Handkerchief (Tzara)
See *Mouchoir de nuages*
Cloud Nine (Churchill) **31**:84-9; **55**:122
A Cloud on Sand (De Ferrari) **65**:42-6
"The Cloud Parade" (Jensen) **37**:187, 190
Cloud, Stone, Sun, and Vine (Sarton) **91**:241
"The Cloud-Gatherer" (Elytis) **49**:110
"Clouds" (Ashbery) **77**:54
"Clouds" (Jacobsen) **48**:198
"Clouds" (Levine) **118**:283
"The Clouds" (Williams) **9**:572; **42**:450
The Clouds (Cernuda)
See *Las nubes*
Clouds (Frayn) **31**:191
Clouds (Mitchell) **12**:435-36
"The Clouds Go Soft" (O'Hara) **13**:430
The Clouds over Metapontion (Johnson)
See *Molnen över Metapontion*
"Cloudy" (Simon) **17**:459
The Cloven Viscount (Calvino)
See *Il visconte dimezzato*
The Cloven Viscount (Calvino)
See *Il visconte dimezzato*
"The Clown" (Jennings) **131**:232
"Clown" (Michaux) **8**:391
"The Clown" (Tanizaki) **28**:414
The Clown (Boell)
See *Ansichten eines Clowns*
The Clown (Corcoran) **17**:74-5
I clowns (Fellini) **16**:284-86, 299; **85**:55, 59, 64-6, 69, 74, 76, 78-81
The Clowns (Fellini)
See *I clowns*
Clown's Houses (Sitwell) **67**:312
Les clowns lyriques (Gary) **25**:190
The Clowns of God (West) **33**:432-33
The Club (Williamson) **56**:435, 437, 442-43
"Club Dread" (Ritter) **52**:355
"Clubland" (Costello) **21**:75
"Clues" (Rukeyser) **15**:459
Clues of the Caribbees (Stribling) **23**:445
Clunie (Peck) **17**:343
Cluster (Anthony) **35**:37
"Clusters Traveling Out" (Graham) **29**:196
Clutch of Constables (Marsh) **53**:247, 250-51, 253
A Clyack-Sheaf (MacDiarmid) **4**:313
"Clywedog" (Clarke) **61**:80
"C-Minor" (Transtroemer)
See "C-dur"
"Coach" (Robison) **42**:342; **98**:306
"Coal" (Lorde) **71**:232
Coal (Lorde) **18**:309; **71**:235, 248, 251-52, 262
"Coal and Fire" (MacNeice) **10**:324; **53**:233
"Coal Train" (Parini) **54**:362
"The Coalman" (Williams) **42**:440
"Coals" (Hoffman) **141**:282, 311-13
The Coast of Chicago (Dybek) **114**:68, 70, 72-3, 77, 79-81
The Coast of Illyria (Parker) **68**:340-41
"Coast of Texas" (Sorrentino) **40**:386
"Coast of Trees" (Ammons) **108**:56
A Coast of Trees (Ammons) **25**:45; **57**:51, 59; **108**:24, 55
Coastal Disturbances (Howe) **48**:176-79
"The Coast-Range Christ" (Jeffers) **11**:309
"The Coasts of Cerigo" (Hope) **3**:250; **51**:223

The Coat (Fugard) **80**:66
"The Coat of Arms" (Bell) **31**:46
A Coat of Varnish (Snow) **19**:427-30
"The Coat Without a Seam" (Kunitz) **148**:70
The Coat Without a Seam (Kunitz) **148**:67
"The Coats" (Gallagher) **63**:124
"Cobbler" (Carroll) **38**:103
"The Cobbler and the Machine" (Anand) **23**:18
Cobra (Sarduy) **6**:485-87; **97**:367-69, 372-78, 380-81, 393-95, 397, 399-403, 406, 409-17
"Cobra amor" (Aleixandre) **9**:14
The Cobweb (Gibson) **23**:173
"Cocaine" (Browne) **21**:40
Cocaine Nights (Ballard) **137**:68-69, 74-75
Cochise (Wild) **14**:580-81
"La cocina de la escritura" (Ferré) **139**:149, 157, 159-60, 174, 178-81, 188
"Cock Crow" (Gordon) **83**:250, 259
Cock Pit (Cozzens) **11**:131; **92**:196-98
Cock Robin (Rice) **49**:301
Cock Robin; or, A Fight for Male Survival (Billington) **43**:54
Cock-a-Doodle Dandy (O'Casey) **5**:318, 320; **9**:409, 411; **11**:408-09; **15**:404-05; **88**:257-58, 260, 262, 269-71
"Cockadoodledoo" (Singer) **9**:487
"The Cockatoos" (White) **7**:533
The Cockatoos (White) **4**:587; **5**:485-87; **7**:533; **65**:275
"Cockfight" (Beagle) **104**:5
"Cockles and Mussels" (Hill) **113**:291
Cockpit (Kosinski) **6**:285; **10**:305-07, 309; **15**:313-14, 316-17; **53**:216-17, 220-23, 226-27; **70**:298, 304, 306
"Cocks" (Hirsch) **31**:214, 216
Cocksfoot, Crested Dog's Tail, Sweet Vernal Grass (Norris) **14**:388
Cocksure (Richler) **5**:375-76, 378; **13**:481, 484, 486; **18**:451-52, 455; **46**:347-50; **70**:232
The Cocktail Hour (Gurney) **54**:221-23
"Cocktail Party" (Arreola) **147**:16
"Cocktail Party" (Warren) **39**:256, 273
The Cocktail Party (Eliot) **2**:126, 129; **3**:140; **6**:164, 167; **9**:186; **13**:194-95; **15**:208-09; **24**:172; **34**:394; **41**:143-46; **55**:346, 352-53, 360, 367
"Cocktails at Doney's" (Trevor) **71**:340
"Cocktails at the Mausoleum" (Musgrave) **54**:341
"The Cocky Walkers" (Peake) **54**:372
The Cocoanuts (Kaufman) **38**:265
"Cocu et content" (Damas) **84**:179
Le cocu magnifique (Crommelynck) **75**:150-53, 156, 159, 161-63, 168-69
Cocuyo (Sarduy) **97**:417
"Coda" (Allen) **84**:37
"Coda" (Bernard) **59**:46
"Coda" (Carroll) **143**:45
"Coda" (Robbe-Grillet) **8**:454; **14**:462
"coda for innocent persons" (Moure) **88**:229
"Coda: The Faustian Pact" (Birkerts) **116**:167
"The Code" (Frost) **26**:111-12
"Code Book Lost" (Warren) **13**:582; **39**:270
Code Name Valkyrie (Forman) **21**:119-20
"Codes" (Howard) **47**:169
"Codex" (Transtroemer) **65**:237
"Codger" (Coles) **46**:108
Il codice di Perela (Palazzeschi) **11**:432
"Codicil" (Walcott) **42**:418; **67**:357, 360
"Cod'ine" (Sainte-Marie) **17**:430
"Coed Anghred" (Mathias) **45**:235
Coeur à cuir (Audiberti) **38**:30
Le coeur des autres (Marcel) **15**:363
"Le coeur écartelé" (Reverdy) **53**:281
"Le coeur, l'eau non troublée" (Bonnefoy) **15**:74
"Coffee" (Brautigan) **12**:65
"Coffee" (Moure) **88**:219
"Coffee with Oliver" (Trevor) **71**:342, 349
The Coffer Dams (Markandaya) **38**:324
A Coffin for Dimitrios (Ambler)
See *The Mask of Dimitrios*
"Cofiant" (Clarke) **61**:84
Cogan's Trade (Higgins) **4**:224-25; **7**:158
La cognizione del dolore (Gadda) **11**:209, 211, 213-15
"Cohen on the Telephone" (Hollander) **8**:299
"Cohere Britania" (Codrescu) **121**:161
"Cohorts" (Gold) **42**:198
Coils (Eshleman) **7**:98-9
"A Coin for the Ferryman" (MacEwen) **55**:169
A Coin in Nine Hands (Yourcenar)
See *Denier du rêve*
Coincidence (Kieslowski)
See *Przypadek*
Coins and Coffins (Wakoski) **7**:507; **40**:454, 457
"Coisas de cabeceira, Recife" (Cabral de Melo Neto) **76**:168
"Coisas de cabeceira, Sevilha" (Cabral de Melo Neto) **76**:168
"The Cokboy" (Rothenberg) **57**:374
"The Coke Factory" (Jones) **131**:269
Cola de lagartija (Valenzuela) **31**:438-39; **104**:364-65, 380, 382, 388, 390, 392
"Cold" (Byatt) **136**:194
"A Cold and Married War" (Piercy) **27**:374
Cold Chills (Bloch) **33**:84
"A Cold Coming" (Harrison) **129**:202, 211, 215
A Cold Coming: Gulf War Poems (Harrison) **129**:210, 213
The Cold Country and Other Plays for Radio (Hill) **113**:283-84, 295
"Cold Didn't Keep the Stuff" (Ammons) **57**:57
Cold Feet (McGuane) **127**:263-63, 270
Cold Fire (Breytenbach) **126**:81
Cold Fire (Koontz) **78**:218
Cold Gradations (Middleton) **38**:331, 333
The Cold Green Element (Layton) **15**:318
"Cold Ground Was My Bed Last Night" (Garrett) **51**:147
Cold Ground Was My Bed Last Night (Garrett) **51**:146-47
Cold Hand in Mine: Strange Stories (Aickman) **57**:3
Cold Heaven (Moore) **32**:311-14; **90**:259-60, 263, 265, 268, 273-75, 289-90, 292-3
"Cold Journey" (Haines) **58**:220
Cold Lazarus (Potter) **86**:343-46, 348; **123**:277-80
Cold Morning Sky (Zaturenska) **11**:579
Cold Mountain (Frazier) **109**:48-51
Cold Nights (Pa Chin) **18**:373, 375
Cold on the Shoulder (Lightfoot) **26**:280-81
"Cold Poem" (Oliver) **98**:266, 273
"Cold Print" (Campbell) **42**:83-5, 92
Cold Print (Campbell) **42**:91-2
"Cold Rains" (Salinas) **90**:322-23
A Cold Red Sunrise (Kaminsky) **59**:170-72
"Cold Rheum" (Ammons) **108**:61
"Cold Spell" (Scannell) **49**:329-30
"A Cold Spring" (Bishop) **4**:65; **13**:91; **32**:38, 41
"The Cold Spring" (Levertov) **28**:239
Cold Spring Harbor (Joel) **26**:217
"Cold Turkey" (Lennon) **35**:265, 270-71
The Cold War and the Income Tax (Wilson) **24**:487
"The Cold Wind and the Warm" (Bradbury) **42**:34
The Cold Wind and the Warm (Behrman) **40**:84
"Cold Wind in August" (Morrison) **21**:237
"Cold-Blooded" (Atwood) **84**:105
"The Cold-Blooded Romantics" (Huxley) **8**:305
"The Colder the Air" (Bishop) **32**:43
"Coldness" (Montague) **46**:272
"The Coldness" (Silkin) **43**:399-400
"Coldwater Morning" (Diamond) **30**:111
"Coleman A. Young: Detroit Renaissance" (Randall) **135**:391
"Coleraine, 1977" (Simmons) **43**:413-14
"Coleridge Crossing the Plain of Jars, 1833" (Dubie) **36**:135, 139
Coleridge on the Imagination (Richards) **24**:387, 389, 393-94, 400-01
Colibrí (Sarduy) **97**:404-07, 409-10
Collaborators (Kauffman) **42**:252-53
"Collage" (Brooks) **4**:78
Collages (Nin) **4**:378; **14**:381, 383; **60**:281
Colleagues (Aksyonov) **101**:6, 9, 13-15, 17, 29
Collect Your Hand Baggage (Mortimer) **28**:283-86
Collected and New Poems, 1924-1963 (Van Doren) **6**:541-42
The Collected Books of Jack Spicer (Spicer) **8**:497; **18**:506; **72**:345, 348, 352
Collected Earlier Poems (Williams) **42**:450, 452
Collected Earlier Poems 1940 to 1960 (Levertov) **28**:241-42; **66**:251
Collected Early Poems of Ezra Pound (Pound) **10**:407
Collected Essays (Greene) **6**:217; **125**:179, 198
Collected Essays (Huxley) **35**:242
Collected Essays (Schwartz) **87**:335
The Collected Essays and Occasional Writings of Katherine Anne Porter (Porter) **1**:274; **101**:223-24, 237
The Collected Essays of J.V. Cunningham (Cunningham) **31**:103, 105
The Collected Essays of Leslie Fiedler (Fiedler) **4**:161-63
The Collected Essays of Ralph Ellison (Ellison) **114**:122-23, 131
The Collected Essays of Robert Creeley (Creeley) **78**:160
The Collected Ewart, 1933-1980 (Ewart) **46**:147, 149-52
The Collected Greed, Parts 1-13 (Wakoski) **40**:457
Collected Impressions (Bowen) **3**:84
Collected Later Poems (Clarke) **6**:110-11; **9**:167
Collected Later Poems (Williams) **42**:450, 455-56
The Collected Letters of a Nobody (Waterhouse) **47**:424
The Collected Longer Poems of Kenneth Rexroth (Rexroth) **2**:371; **6**:451; **22**:347-48; **112**:364, 369, 386, 395
"Collected Novels" (Hollander) **14**:264
Collected Papers (Eco) **142**:
Collected Plays (Maugham) **67**:225
Collected Plays (Soyinka) **44**:286
The Collected Plays and Writings on Theater (John Paul II) **128**:165, 168
The Collected Plays of Gwen Pharis Ringwood (Ringwood) **48**:338-39
Collected Poems (Aiken) **3**:5; **52**:19, 21
Collected Poems (Aldington) **49**:6-9, 14-15
The Collected Poems (Ammons) **108**:24, 28, 55
Collected Poems (Auden) **6**:24; **9**:56-8; **11**:21; **14**:33-4; **43**:15-17, 19, 26; **123**:48, 50
Collected Poems (Barker) **48**:23-4
Collected Poems (Barnard) **48**:25-8
Collected Poems (Beecher) **6**:49
Collected Poems (Beer) **58**:38
Collected Poems (Betjeman) **6**:65-6, 68; **34**:305; **43**:34-5, 41, 43-4, 46
The Collected Poems (Bishop) **4**:66; **9**:93
Collected Poems (Boyle) **19**:64; **58**:69
Collected Poems (Brown) **63**:57
Collected Poems (Bunting) **39**:298; **47**:50-1, 53, 55
Collected Poems (Clarke) **6**:110-12; **9**:167
Collected Poems (Cummings) **3**:116; **12**:144; **15**:162; **68**:29, 35, 39, 49
Collected Poems (Daryush) **19**:120-22
Collected Poems (Denby) **48**:82-4
Collected Poems (Dugan) **2**:121; **6**:144
Collected Poems (Eberhart) **3**:135; **19**:143
Collected Poems (Eich)
See *Ausgewählte Gedichte*
Collected Poems (Empson) **8**:202; **34**:335-36
Collected Poems (Enright) **31**:153-55
Collected Poems (Faludy) **42**:141
Collected Poems (Frost) **10**:198; **44**:457
Collected Poems (Gascoyne) **45**:149-52, 154

Collected Poems (Goodman) **4**:197; **7**:128
Collected Poems (Grass)
See *Gesammelte Gedichte*
Collected Poems (Haavikko) **34**:174
Collected Poems (Hayden)
See *Robert Hayden: Collected Poems*
Collected Poems (Hill) **45**:189-90
Collected Poems (Jarrell) **6**:261; **9**:295
Collected Poems (Jennings) **5**:197; **14**:292; **131**:233-41
Collected Poems (Kavanagh) **22**:235, 240
Collected Poems (Koch) **44**:248
Collected Poems (Larkin) **64**:256-87
Collected Poems (Layton) **15**:321
Collected Poems (MacDiarmid) **2**:253; **4**:309, 313; **11**:334; **63**:244, 246, 256
Collected Poems (Milosz)
See *Czeslaw Milosz: The Collected Poems, 1931-1987*
Collected Poems (Moore) **8**:398; **19**:339, 342; **47**:264-65
Collected Poems (Neihardt) **32**:330-31
Collected Poems (Oppen) **7**:285-86; **13**:434; **34**:358-59
Collected Poems (Pasternak) **63**:289-90
The Collected Poems (Patchen) **18**:394
The Collected Poems (Plath) **51**:339-45, 350-53
Collected Poems (Plomer) **8**:446-47
Collected Poems (Popa) **19**:375
Collected Poems (Porter) **33**:320-26
Collected Poems (Pound) **7**:335
Collected Poems (Prince) **22**:339
Collected Poems (Read) **4**:440
Collected Poems (Riding) **7**:373, 375
Collected Poems (Rodgers) **7**:377-78
Collected Poems (Sandburg) **15**:468
Collected Poems (Sarton) **91**:243
Collected Poems (Sillitoe) **148**:195
Collected Poems (Simpson) **149**:349, 352, 355, 358-59, 361
Collected Poems (Sitwell) **67**:317, 355
Collected Poems (Smith) **15**:513-15
Collected Poems (Spender) **91**:264
Collected Poems (Tomlinson) **45**:404-05
Collected Poems (Transtroemer) **65**:226
Collected Poems (Van Doren) **6**:542
Collected Poems (Winters) **32**:467-69
Collected Poems (Wright) **3**:541-42; **5**:520; **10**:542, 544; **28**:463, 465, 471-72
Collected Poems (Young) **5**:526
Collected Poems (Zaturenska) **6**:585; **11**:579-80
Collected Poems, 1938 (Graves) **45**:163, 165
Collected Poems, 1954 (Day Lewis) **6**:128
Collected Poems, 1955 (Graves) **1**:127, 127; **2**:174; **6**:212
Collected Poems, 1959 (Graves) **39**:328; **45**:163
Collected Poems, 1965 (Graves) **45**:166
Collected Poems, 1968 (Fisher) **25**:157-59
Collected Poems, 1919-62 (Deutsch) **18**:119-20
Collected Poems, 1930-83 (Miles) **34**:243-45; **39**:352-54
Collected Poems, 1908-1956 (Sassoon) **36**:388, 391
Collected Poems, 1909-1935 (Eliot) **15**:206, 211-12; **41**:155
Collected Poems, 1917-1952 (MacLeish) **68**:288-89, 293
Collected Poems, 1919-1976 (Tate) **11**:526-27; **14**:530
Collected Poems, 1923-1953 (Bogan) **39**:390; **46**:82-3, 85, 87; **93**:87
Collected Poems, 1924-1962 (Grigson) **7**:135; **39**:330
Collected Poems, 1928-1953 (Spender) **5**:401; **41**:418, 420, 427-29; **91**:264
Collected Poems, 1930-1955 (Barker) **48**:17
Collected Poems, 1930-1960 (Eberhart) **56**:84, 87-8
Collected Poems, 1930-1965 (Barker) **8**:46
Collected Poems, 1930-1965 (Hope) **3**:250; **51**:218
Collected Poems, 1930-1973 (Sarton) **4**:472; **14**:480; **49**:314
Collected Poems, 1930-1976 (Eberhart) **11**:178
Collected Poems (1930-1993) (Sarton) **91**:253
Collected Poems, 1931-1974 (Durrell) **27**:96-7
Collected Poems, 1935-1980 (Raine) **45**:340-41
Collected Poems, 1936-1960 (Fuller) **4**:177; **28**:149-51, 158-59
Collected Poems, 1936-1970 (McAuley) **45**:250, 252-53
Collected Poems, 1937-1971 (Berryman) **62**:71, 75
Collected Poems, 1940-1978 (Shapiro) **15**:477-79
Collected Poems, 1942-1970 (Wright) **53**:426, 428-29, 432
Collected Poems, 1942-1977 (Graham) **29**:197-99
Collected Poems, 1944-1979 (Amis) **40**:39-40, 44
Collected Poems, 1947-1980 (Ginsberg) **36**:193-99; **109**:331, 338, 352, 356, 358, 364
Collected Poems, 1948-1976 (Abse) **29**:17-19
Collected Poems, 1948-1984 (Walcott) **42**:418-21, 423; **67**:349, 352, 354, 357-58; **76**:296
Collected Poems, 1950-1970 (Davie) **5**:114-16; **8**:166; **10**:123, 125; **31**:117
Collected Poems, 1951-1971 (Ammons) **2**:13-14; **3**:10-11; **5**:28-9, 31; **8**:14, 17, 19; **9**:27; **25**:42-4, 48; **57**:49, 58; **108**:5-6, 8-9, 24, 27
Collected Poems, 1951-1975 (Causley) **7**:41-2
The Collected Poems, 1952-1990 (Yevtushenko) **126**:388, 390-91, 393, 395-96
Collected Poems, 1955-1975 (Levi) **41**:246-48
The Collected Poems, 1956-1974 (Dorn) **10**:156-57; **18**:129
Collected Poems 1956-1994 (Kinsella) **138**:159-61, 162-65, 167
Collected Poems, 1957-1982 (Berry) **46**:72-3
Collected Poems, 1958-1970 (MacBeth) **2**:251-52; **5**:263
Collected Poems, 1963-1980 (Grigson) **39**:330
Collected Poems, 1970-1983 (Davie) **31**:123-24
Collected Poems and Epigrams (Cunningham) **3**:122; **31**:102
Collected Poems and Selected Translations (Sisson) **8**:491
The Collected Poems of Al Purdy (Purdy) **50**:235, 243-48
The Collected Poems of A.M. Klein (Klein) **19**:260
The Collected Poems of Carl Rakosi (Rakosi) **47**:347-48
The Collected Poems of E. J. Pratt (Pratt) **19**:376
The Collected Poems of Earle Birney (Birney) **11**:49, 51
The Collected Poems of Frank O'Hara (O'Hara) **2**:322-23; **5**:323, 325; **13**:430; **78**:339
The Collected Poems of George Garrett (Garrett) **51**:151
Collected Poems of H. D. (H. D.) **8**:257; **14**:223; **31**:201, 208; **73**:109, 115, 117, 119
The Collected Poems of Howard Nemerov (Nemerov) **36**:300-04
The Collected Poems of Kathleen Raine (Raine) **45**:332-34, 336-37, 340-41
Collected Poems of Kenneth Fearing (Fearing) **51**:108-09, 111
The Collected Poems of Langston Hughes (Hughes) **108**:334-35
The Collected Poems of Louis MacNeice (MacNeice) **1**:186; **4**:316; **53**:238, 243-44
Collected Poems of Lucio Piccolo (Piccolo) **13**:440-41
The Collected Poems of Muriel Rukeyser (Rukeyser) **15**:456-58, 460
The Collected Poems of Octavio Paz, 1957-1987 (Paz) **51**:332, 334, 336; **65**:195 201; **119**:408, 410
Collected Poems of Padraic Colum (Colum) **28**:90
The Collected Poems of Paul Blackburn (Blackburn) **43**.68-9
The Collected Poems of Robert Creeley, 1945-1975 (Creeley) **36**:116-17, 119-21; **78**:135
The Collected Poems of Sterling A. Brown (Brown) **23**:100-01; **59**:265-69
The Collected Poems of Stevie Smith (Smith) **8**:491; **25**:417-18, 422
The Collected Poems of Theodore Roethke (Roethke) **1**:291; **3**:433; **8**:457, 460; **101**:271, 273
The Collected Poems of Thomas Merton (Merton) **11**:374; **83**:384-85, 397
Collected Poems: The Two Seasons (Livesay) **4**:294; **79**:340-41
Collected Poetry (Dudek) **11**:160; **19**:138
The Collected Poetry of Aldous Huxley (Huxley) **5**:192
The Collected Poetry of W. H. Auden, 1945 (Auden) **2**:23; **11**:20; **123**:53
The Collected Prose (Bishop) **32**:40, 43-4
Collected Prose (Celan) **53**:82-3
Collected Prose (Hayden) **37**:159
Collected Prose (Lowell) **124**:265-68, 275, 281, 286
The Collected Prose of Robert Creeley (Creeley) **36**:122
Collected Short Stories (Amis) **40**:43-5
The Collected Short Stories (Dahl) **79**:183
Collected Short Stories (Forster) **45**:132
Collected Short Stories (Huxley) **35**:242
The Collected Short Stories of Julia Peterkin (Peterkin) **31**:306-07
The Collected Short Stories, Volume 2 (Coward) **51**:74
Collected Shorter Poems (Auden) **6**:21; **123**:16, 19
Collected Shorter Poems, 1930-1944 (Auden) **43**:26
Collected Shorter Poems, 1946-1991 (Carruth) **84**:134, 136
The Collected Shorter Poems of Kenneth Rexroth (Rexroth) **2**:369; **22**:347; **49**:277, 280; **112**:364 65, 369, 376, 386, 395, 398
The Collected Stories (Boyle) **90**:61
Collected Stories (García Márquez) **47**:145-48, 150-51
Collected Stories (Greene) **3**:211-13
Collected Stories (Malamud)
See *The Stories of Bernard Malamud*
Collected Stories (Paley)
See *Grace Paley: The Collected Stories*
Collected Stories (Pritchett) **41**:331-33, 335
Collected Stories (Sargeson) **31**:364-65
Collected Stories (Sillitoe) **148**:198
The Collected Stories (Trevor) **116**:362-63, 371, 394
Collected Stories (Williams) **45**:452-56
Collected Stories: 1939-1976 (Bowles) **19**:60-1; **53**:36, 45
The Collected Stories of Caroline Gordon (Gordon) **29**:187-90
The Collected Stories of Chester Himes (Himes) **108**:227-28, 234-35, 241
The Collected Stories of Elizabeth Bowen (Bowen) **22**:64-5, 67-8
The Collected Stories of Eudora Welty (Welty) **22**:458; **105**:297-300
The Collected Stories of Frank Tuohy (Tuohy) **37**:432-33
The Collected Stories of Hortense Calisher (Calisher) **8**:124-25; **134**:7-8, 33, 41
The Collected Stories of Isaac Bashevis Singer (Singer) **38**:407-10; **69**:306
The Collected Stories of Jean Stafford (Stafford) **4**:517; **19**:430-31; **68**:422, 424, 430, 433-35, 449

Collected Stories of John O'Hara (O'Hara) **42**:325-27
The Collected Stories of Katherine Anne Porter (Porter) **3**:393
The Collected Stories of Noël Coward (Coward) **29**:141; **51**:74
The Collected Stories of Peter Taylor (Taylor) **4**:542; **18**:523-24, 526; **37**:411-13; **44**:305; **71**:299, 308
The Collected Stories Of Seán O'Faoláin (O'Faolain) **70**:320-21
The Collected Stories of Seán O'Faoláin, Volume 2 (O'Faolain) **32**:340
The Collected Stories of Seán O'Faoláin, Volume 3 (O'Faolain) **32**:341-44
Collected Stories of Wallace Stegner (Stegner) **81**:339, 346-47
Collected Stories of William Faulkner (Faulkner) **6**:179-80; **18**:148-49
The Collected Stories of William Goyen (Goyen) **8**:250; **14**:211, 213-14; **40**:215
The Collected Stories of William Humphrey (Humphrey) **45**:203-04
The Collected Stories of Wolfgang Hildesheimer (Hildesheimer) **49**:179-80
Collected Stories to Collected Short Stories (Huxley)
See *Collected Short Stories*
The Collected Tales of E. M. Forster (Forster) **22**:129
Collected Verse (Smith) **15**:515
Collected Verse Translations (Gascoyne) **45**:153
Collected Works (Pa Chin) **18**:373
Collected Works (Tanizaki) **28**:421
The Collected Works of Billy the Kid (Nichol) **18**:366
The Collected Works of Billy the Kid: Left Handed Poems (Ondaatje) **14**:408-10; **29**:339-42; **51**:310-13, 317-19; **76**:204
The Collected Works of Jane Bowles (Bowles) **68**:4-5, 7
The Collected Works of John Masefield (Masefield) **47**:230
Collecting Himself (Thurber) **125**:404-05
"Collecting Pictures" (Coles) **46**:113
The Collection (Pinter) **3**:385-86; **6**:413; **11**:441; **15**:423; **27**:385-86, 394-95; **58**:373, 376; **73**:251, 257
A Collection of Great Dance Songs (Pink Floyd) **35**:313
A Collection of Sand (Calvino)
See *Collezione di sabbia*
La collectionneuse (Rohmer) **16**:529-31, 533-34
"Collective Dawns" (Ashbery) **13**:36; **77**:45
"The Collector" (Redgrove) **41**:351
The Collector (Fowles) **1**:109; **2**:138-39; **3**:163; **4**:171; **6**:184, 186-89; **9**:213-15; **10**:184, 187-88; **15**:234; **33**:159-67, 169-75; **87**:147-48, 154, 159-62, 175, 178, 181, 184, 187
The Collector and Other Poems (Redgrove) **41**:347-48, 351
"The Collector of Treasures" (Head) **67**:93-5, 98, 107
The Collector of Treasures (Head) **25**:237; **67**:96-8, 111
"Collectors" (Carver) **22**:96, 99; **55**:281; **126**:123, 142-43
"The Collectors" (Mistry) **71**:270, 272
"Collector's Item" (Brodsky) **100**:70
College (Keaton) **20**:189, 191, 193, 196
"The College Ghost" (Fuller) **62**:200, 204
"College of Cashier Education" (Bogosian) **141**:86
"College of Religious Misunderstandings" (Montague) **46**:274
Collezione di sabbia (Calvino) **39**:315
Collin (Heym) **41**:218-19
Colline (Giono) **4**:186; **11**:232
"Collision" (Shields) **113**:404, 408, 413, 432
Collision (Tiptree) **48**:394-95
Collision Orbit (Williamson) **29**:455
Collisions (Caute) **29**:118-19, 122
"Colloquy" (Jackson) **60**:211, 217
Colloquy for the States (MacLeish) **14**:338
"Colloquy in Black Rock" (Lowell) **4**:303; **8**:348; **15**:346; **124**:268
Colmain (Gray) **36**:200
La colmena (Cela) **4**:96-7, 98; **13**:145-47; **59**:126-27, 129, 134-44; **122**:2-3, 4, 9, 19, 28-30, 32-37, 39, 41, 45, 53, 61, 65, 68, 70
Colombe (Anouilh) **1**:7; **3**:11; **8**:24; **13**:17; **40**:54, 59-60
Il colombre (Buzzati) **36**:97
"A Colonel" (Blunden) **56**:43
"The Colonel" (Forché) **25**:171-72; **83**:197, 201, 212, 214, 216, 221, 223; **86**:140
"Colonel Fantock" (Sitwell) **67**:335
The Colonel Has No One to Write Him (García Márquez)
See *El colonel no tiene quien le escribe*
Colonel Mint (Mano) **10**:328
Colonel Mint (West) **7**:524-25; **14**:568; **96**:374
El colonel no tiene quien le escribe (García Márquez) **2**:148, 150; **3**:183; **10**:216; **27**:147, 155; **47**:145-46, 149, 153; **55**:140; **68**:140, 145, 151, 153
"Colonel Shaw and the Massachusetts' Fifty-Fourth" (Lowell) **8**:350; **124**:295
Colonel Sun: A James Bond Adventure (Amis) **2**:8, 10; **3**:9; **129**:18
"The Colonel's Daughter" (Tremain) **42**:386
The Colonel's Daughter (Aldington) **49**:11
The Colonel's Daughter and Other Stories (Tremain) **42**:385-86
"The Colonel's Hash Resettled" (Munro) **95**:295
"The Colonel's Wife" (Dubus) **97**:234, 236, 238
The Colonial Harem (Alloula) **65**:329
"Colonialist Criticism" (Achebe) **75**:2; **127**:80
"Colonisation in Reverse" (Bennett) **28**:28
"Colonoscope Nite" (Leyner) **92**:283
"Colony" (Dick) **72**:108
"The Colony" (Singer) **3**:454
Colony (Bova) **45**:70, 72
"El coloquio de las perras" (Ferré) **139**:151
El coloquio de las perras (Ferré) **139**:150
The Color Curtain (Wright) **4**:596; **21**:449
"Color Me Real" (Cooper) **56**:70
Color of Darkness (Purdy) **2**:348-49; **10**:421; **28**:376-79; **52**:350
The Color of Light (Goldman) **48**:129-30
The Color of Money (Scorsese) **89**:242-43, 249, 260
The Color of Money (Tevis) **42**:377
"The Color of Time" (Williams) **33**:449
The Color Purple (Walker) **27**:449-51, 454; **46**:424-25, 427-32; **58**:405-15; **103**:366-68, 372, 374-76, 380, 383, 385, 387-89, 391-93, 395-98, 405, 411, 417, 419, 422, 428
Color Struck! (Hurston) **30**:223
"Colorado" (Beattie) **13**:64; **146**:64, 81
"Colorado" (Cernuda) **54**:55
"Colorado" (Van Duyn) **116**:400
The Colorado (Waters) **88**:331-36, 341, 351, 360, 362-64, 366
The Colored Museum (Wolfe) **49**:419-24
"Colored Spade" (Ragni and Rado) **17**:385
The Colorist (Daitch) **103**:62-4, 66-78
"The Colors" (Disch) **7**:87
"The Colors of Night" (Momaday) **85**:268
"The Colors of Our Age: Pink and Black" (Smith) **42**:353
"Colors of the Sun" (Browne) **21**:37
"Colors without Objects" (Swenson) **61**:392; **106**:331
"Colossus" (Plath) **111**:178
The Colossus, and Other Poems (Plath) **1**:270; **2**:335-37; **3**:391; **5**:339, 343, 345; **9**:425, 432-33; **11**:445-47; **14**:422-25; **17**:344-45, 347-50, 352, 366-68; **50**:442, 449; **51**:340, 343-44, 347; **62**:386, 389; **111**:159, 164-65, 167, 177-78, 185
The Colossus of Maroussi (Miller) **1**:223-24; **9**:381; **14**:374
"Colour" (D'Aguiar) **145**:117
"Colour Bar" (Bennett) **28**:29
The Colour of Blood (Moore) **90**:268-70, 272, 274-75, 289-90
The Colour of Memory (Dyer) **149**:42, 44-5, 52
The Colour of the Times (Souster) **14**:502
Colour Scheme (Marsh) **53**:249-51, 253, 255-56, 258-59
Colour the Flesh the Colour of Dust (Cook) **58**:150-51, 153-58
"The Colour-Machine" (Gunn) **32**:208
Colours in the Dark (Reaney) **13**:472, 475
The Colours of the Day (Gary) **25**:184
The Colours of War (Cohen) **19**:112-13, 115
La Colpa é sempre del diavolo (Fo) **109**:115
"The Colt" (Stegner) **81**:346
"A Coltrane Poem" (Sanchez) **116**:296
"Columba" (Cliff) **120**:89-90
Columba (Slaughter) **56**:408, 411
Columbella (Whitney) **42**:433-34
Columbia and Beyond: The Story of the Space Shuttle (Branley) **21**:23
The Columbia History of American Poetry (Parini) **133**:266-71, 273, 275, 277-82
The Columbia: Power House of North America (Latham) **12**:324
Columbus (Fernandez-Armesto) **70**:338, 346, 354
Columbus and the Age of Discovery (Dor-Ner) **70**:343
"Columbus and the Fat Lady" (Cohen) **19**:113
The Columbus Encyclopedia (Bedini) **70**:341
Columbus: For Gold, God, and Glory (Dyson) **70**:343
Columbus: His Enterprise (Koningsberger) **70**:339
"Columbus in Chains" (Kincaid) **43**:249
The Columbus Myth: Did Men of Bristol Reach America Before Columbus? (Wilson) **70**:338
The Columbus Papers (Obregon) **70**:331
Columbus: The Great Adventure—His Life, His Times, and His Voyages (Taviani) **70**:331, 340, 351, 353
"Columns and Caryatids" (Kizer) **80**:177
"Coma" (Williams) **148**:360
Coma (Cook) **14**:131
Coma (Crichton) **54**:71; **90**:69
The Comb (The Brothers Quay)
See *The Comb from the Museum of Sleep*
The Comb from the Museum of Sleep (The Brothers Quay) **95**:347-49, 351, 353-55
"The Combat" (Thomas) **48**:379
"Combat" (Williams) **33**:447; **148**:319, 324, 344
"Combat Cultural" (Moore) **47**:263
"Combat Pay for Jodie" (Komunyakaa) **94**:226, 233
Combat Rock (Clash) **30**:50-2
"The Combine" (Weller) **26**:443
"Combustion" (Blaga) **75**:62
"Come Again Tomorrow" (Gordimer) **70**:166
Come Alive at 505 (Brancato) **35**:68-9
"Come All Ye Asian American Writers of the Real and the Fake" (Chin) **135**:175, 177
"Come Along, Marjorie" (Spark) **8**:493
Come Along with Me (Jackson) **60**:213-214, 217, 233, 235
"Come and Buy My Toys" (Bowie) **17**:65
Come and Get It (Ferber) **93**:163-64, 171
"Come as You Are" (Bernard) **59**:45
Come As You Are (Mortimer) **28**:286
"Come Away, Death" (Pratt) **19**:385
"Come Back" (Merwin) **45**:278
Come Back, Dr. Caligari (Barthelme) **2**:39, 41; **3**:43; **6**:31; **8**:49-50, 53; **23**:44, 47; **46**:35, 39-40; **59**:247, 249; **115**:56-7, 65
Come Back, Little Sheba (Inge) **1**:153; **8**:308; **19**:226-30
Come Back to Erin (O'Faolain) **7**:275; **14**:402,

404; **70**:312, 317, 321
Come Back to the Fiva and Dime, Jimmy Dean, Jimmy Dean (Altman) **116**:39, 47, 59, 67, 73
"Come Back to the Raft Ag'in Huck Honey!" (Fiedler) **4**:163; **13**:211; **24**:195, 203
Come Back Wherever You Are (Weber) **12**:634
"Come before His Countenance with a Joyful Leaping" (Wagoner) **5**:474
Come Blow Your Horn (Simon) **6**:502; **31**:396-97, 400, 403; **70**:238, 240
"Come Break with Time" (Bogan) **46**:77, 89-90; **93**:65, 96
Come Dance with Kitty Stobling (Kavanagh) **22**:235
Come Gentle Spring (Stuart) **34**:376
Come Home Early, Child (Dodson) **79**:198
"Come In" (Frost) **10**:194; **26**:118, 123
"Come Inside" (Waugh) **107**:369
"Come into Animal Presence" (Levertov) **15**:337
"Come into My Cellar" (Bradbury) **15**:86; **42**:33-4
"Come into My Parlour" (Muldoon) **72**:267
"Come, Lady Death" (Beagle) **104**:5, 25
"Come Live with Me Angel" (Gaye) **26**:132
Come Nineveh, Come Tyre (Drury) **37**:106-07
"Come on a Coming" (Dixon) **52**:100
"Come On Back" (Gardner) **28**:161-62
"Come On, My Lucky Lads" (Blunden) **56**:38, 43
"Come On, Ye Sons of Art" (Paley) **37**:337; **140**:255
"Come Out the Wilderness" (Baldwin) **17**:33
Come Out to Play (Comfort) **7**:54
"Come Round Here" (Robinson)
See "If You Wanna Make Love"
Come si fa una tesi di laurea (Eco) **142**:100
"'Come Sleep . . .'" (Bogan) **39**:391, 393; **93**:67
Come Softly to My Wake: The Poems of Christy Brown (Brown) **63**:51
Come, Tell Me How You Live (Christie) **6**:110; **48**:78
Come, the Restorer (Goyen) **5**:149; **8**:250-51; **14**:212, 214; **40**:218
Come the Sweet By and By (Lerman) **9**:329-31
"Come Then to Prayers" (Larkin) **64**:282
"Come Thunder" (Okigbo) **25**:354, 356; **84**:316
"Come to My Merry Grave" (Yevtushenko) **51**:432
Come to the Edge (Cunningham) **12**:166
"Come Together" (Lennon and McCartney) **12**:364, 380
Come Unto These Yellow Sands (Carter) **76**:329
"Come Upstairs" (Simon) **26**:413
Come Upstairs (Simon) **26**:413
Come Wind, Come Weather (du Maurier) **59**:286
Come Winter (Hunter) **11**:279
"Come with Me" (Bly) **5**:64
"Comeback" (Scannell) **49**:329-31
Comeback (Francis) **102**:142-43, 158
The Comedians (Greene) **1**:134; **3**:207, 210, 212-14; **9**:246-51; **18**:194; **27**:173, 175-76; **37**:136; **70**:289-90, 293; **72**:156-57, 163, 165; **125**:175, 178-80, 183, 187
Comedians (Griffiths) **13**:256-57; **52**:174-79, 185
Comedy: American Style (Fauset) **19**:170-71; **54**:177, 187-90
"Comedy Cop" (Farrell) **66**:131
"Comedy Events You Can Do" (Martin) **30**:248
Comedy Is Not Pretty (Martin) **30**:249
The Comedy of Neil Simon (Simon) **31**:396
"The Comedy of the White Dog" (Gray) **41**:181, 183
Comedy of Vanity (Canetti)
See *Die Komödie der Eitelkeit*
Comedy of Vanity & Life-Terms (Canetti) **75**:145
"Comedy Tonight" (Sondheim) **30**:378
"Comemos sombra" (Aleixandre) **9**:12
"The Come-On" (Dunn) **40**:168
"Comes a Time" (Young) **17**:583
Comes a Time (Young) **17**:579-80
Comes the Blind Fury (Saul) **46**:366, 369
"Comes Winter: The Sea Hunting" (Dubie) **36**:135, 141-42
"The Comet" (Aleixandre) **36**:28
"Comet Watch on Indian Key" (Swenson) **61**:403
The Cometeers (Williamson) **29**:455, 458-59
Comets, Meteoroids, and Asteroids (Branley) **21**:20
"Comfort" (Kaplan) **50**:55-7
Comfort (Kaplan) **50**:55-7
"Comfort at Fifty" (Levi) **41**:248
Comfort Me with Apples (De Vries) **1**:73; **28**:106, 108, 112
The Comfort of Strangers (McEwan) **66**:282-85, 288, 292-94
Comfort Woman (Keller) **109**:63-6
The Comfortable Pew (Berton) **104**:44, 47, 57
The Comforters (Spark) **2**:414-18; **3**:465-66; **5**:400; **8**:496; **13**:520, 522-23; **18**:501; **40**:393, 395, 398-400; **94**:326, 328,k 330-334, 336, 350, 353-54
"The Comforts of Home" (O'Connor) **6**:377, 382; **15**:410; **21**:263-64, 269, 276; **104**:107-08, 110, 115, 123-24, 135-36, 155, 179-80, 184, 194-96
The Comic (Glanville) **6**:202
"Comic at the Palladium" (Bruce) **21**:48, 53-4
Comic Mystery Play (Fo)
See *Mistero Buffo*
"Comin' Down Again" (Jagger and Richard) **17**:228-29
"Comin' Home" (Seger) **35**:386-87
"The Coming" (Ciardi) **40**:157
"Coming" (Larkin) **5**:227; **8**:333; **33**:256, 259-60; **64**:262, 266, 274
"Coming Apart" (Walker) **27**:448, 450; **103**:366, 407-08, 411-12, 423
"Coming Attraction" (Leiber) **25**:301-04
"Coming Attractions" (Wolff) **64**:450, 452-54
Coming Attractions (Tally) **42**:366-67
"Coming Back in Spring" (Merwin) **45**:274
"Coming Close" (Levine) **118**:321
"Coming Close to Donna" (Hannah) **90**:145, 146
"Coming Down from the Acropolis" (Snodgrass) **68**:399
Coming Down from Wa (Thomas) **107**:350-52
"Coming Down through Somerset" (Hughes) **37**:175; **119**:272, 289
"Coming Events" (Montague) **46**:269
The Coming Forth by Day of Osiris Jones (Aiken) **52**:20, 26-7
The Coming Fury (Catton) **35**:89-94
"Coming Home" (Gallagher) **18**:168
"Coming Home" (Hecht) **13**:269
Coming Home (Le Guin)
See *Always Coming Home*
Coming Home (Jones) **52**:255
"Coming Home, Detroit, 1968" (Levine) **118**:284, 290, 297
"Coming Home from the Post Office" (Levine) **118**:304
"Coming Home on the 5:22" (Ciardi) **44**:381
"Coming in for Supper" (Bly) **10**:62
"Coming in from the Cold" (Marley) **17**:273
"Coming in from the Cold" (Walker) **58**:409
Coming into Eighty (Sarton) **91**:245
"Coming into His Kingdom" (McGahern) **48**:267
Coming into the Country (McPhee) **36**:296-99
"Coming into Town, Cold" (Musgrave) **54**:341
"Coming of Age" (Musgrave) **54**:338
The Coming of Age (Beauvoir)
See *La vieillesse*
"Coming of Age in Michigan" (Levine) **118**:305
Coming of Age in Samoa (Mead) **37**:268-71, 275, 277, 281, 283-85
Coming of Age in SoHo (Innaurato) **60**:201-04, 206-07
Coming of Age: New and Selected Poems (Deutsch) **18**:119
"The Coming of Kali" (Clifton) **66**:80
"The Coming of Light" (Strand) **18**:521; **41**:432
"The Coming of Spring" (Behan) **79**:39
The Coming of Stork (Williamson) **56**:431-33, 435
"The Coming of the Cat" (Beer) **58**:32
"The Coming of the Eagles" (Dumas) **62**:155
The Coming of the Lord (Millin) **49**:244-46, 252
The Coming of the New Deal (Schlesinger) **84**:352-55, 382
"The Coming of War" (MacNeice) **53**:237
The Coming of Winter (Richards) **59**:187, 189, 192
"Coming Over Coldwater" (Muske) **90**:313
"Coming Round" (Ammons) **57**:57
"Coming Round" (Hope) **52**:209
Coming through Slaughter (Ondaatje) **14**:410; **29**:339-40, 342-43; **51**:314, 317-20; **76**:204
"Coming to Canada" (Shields) **113**:442
Coming to Canada (Shields) **113**:441-42
"Coming to Get You" (Simon) **26**:413
"Coming to Summer" (Ammons) **108**:19
"Coming to Terms" (Mohr) **12**:447
Coming to Terms (Miles) **34**:244
"Coming to This" (Strand) **71**:285
"Coming to Writing" (Cixous) **92**:80-3, 95
"Coming to Writing" and Other Essays (Cixous) **92**:80-1, 83, 95
"The Coming Triumph of the Free World" (DeMarinis) **54**:101
"Coming Up" (McCartney) **35**:287-88
"Comings and Goings" (Tallent) **45**:387
Comings and Goings (Terry) **19**:440
Comings Back: A Sequence of Poems (Goldbarth) **38**:200-01, 203
Command, and I Will Obey You (Moravia)
See *Una cosa è una cosa*
"Command Performance" (Miller) **30**:263-64
Command the Morning (Buck) **11**:77; **127**:233-35
The Commandant (Anderson) **37**:19
"Commander Lowell 1887-1950" (Lowell) **3**:300; **124**:285
"Commands of Love" (Peacock) **60**:298
La commare secca (Bertolucci) **16**:84-5
La commare secca (Bertolucci) **16**:84-85
Comme l'eau qui coule (Yourcenar) **50**:363-64; **87**:396-97, 399, 404
Comme nous avons été (Adamov) **25**:12
"Commemoration" (Elytis) **49**:114
"The Commencement" (Dickey) **3**:127
"A Commencement Address" (Brodsky) **50**:132, 136
"Commencement, Pingree School" (Updike) **43**:430
"A Comment" (Ezekiel) **61**:107
Comment ca va (Godard) **20**:153
Comment c'est (Beckett) **1**:22; **3**:44; **6**:36, 41; **9**:78, 83-4, 88; **10**:27, 29, 31-4; **11**:32, 34, 37, 39-40; **14**:70, 74, 77, 79-80; **18**:42, 52; **29**:56-7, 59, 65-6
"Comment parler" (Kristeva) **140**:197
"Commentary" (Auden) **43**:18
Commentary on a Falling Star (Johnson) **14**:294
"Commercial" (Updike) **15**:546
"Commercialization" (Cliff) **21**:60-1
Les commettants de Caridad (Theriault) **79**:401, 408, 417
"A Commination" (Hope) **51**:215, 221
"La commission des fêtes" (Kadare) **52**:261
"Commitment" (Ezekiel) **61**:92, 100
The Commitments (Doyle) **81**:158-61
"Committee of the Whole" (Herbert) **44**:394
The Commodore (Forester)
See *Commodore Hornblower*
The Commodore (O'Brian) **152**:270, 272-74, 276-77, 281-82, 288
Commodore Hornblower (Forester) **35**:165-67, 170

The Common Asphodel: Collected Essays on Poetry, 1922-1949 (Graves) **45**:174
The Common Chord (O'Connor) **14**:399
The Common Chorus (Harrison) **129**:172, 194, 223, 226
"The Common Fate of Objects" (Lerman) **9**:331
The Common Glory (Green) **25**:197
A Common Grace (MacCaig) **36**:280, 288
The Common Heart (Horgan) **53**:175-76
"The Common Life" (Auden) **123**:12
"The Common Man" (Smith) **15**:517
"Common Mannerism" (Davie) **10**:124
Common One (Morrison) **21**:239-40
The Common Pasture (Masters) **48**:219
The Common Pursuit (Gray) **36**:209-10
The Common Pursuit (Leavis) **24**:295, 297-98, 308
A Common Room, Essays 1954-1987 (Price) **63**:323, 326-28, 333-35
"Common Words in Uncommon Orders" (Williams) **13**:601
Commonplace Book (Forster) **45**:134, 143-44
"The Commonwealth Air Training Plan" (Johnston) **51**:253
Communalism: From Its Origins to the Twentieth Century (Rexroth) **11**:473
La Communauté inavouable (Blanchot) **135**:89, 134
"Commune présence" (Char) **14**:126
The Communicants (Bergman)
See *Nattvardsgästerna*
The Communication Cord (Friel) **42**:173; **115**:221-23, 230-31, 239, 241-42, 245
"Communication in White" (Madhubuti) **73**:209
"Communications Breakdown" (Page and Plant) **12**:473, 475, 477-78
"Communion" (Ignatow) **7**:177, 179
"The Communion" (Levertov) **15**:337
"Communion" (Tchicaya) **101**:353
La communion solonelle (Arrabal) **9**:39; **18**:21; **58**:10, 16-18, 22
"Communionism" (Snyder) **32**:392
"Communism and Christianism" (Cowley) **39**:461
Communism and the French Intellectuals, 1914-1960 (Caute) **29**:109-10
"Communist" (Ford) **46**:161
"Communist Cardinal Visits Dublin" (Durcan) **43**:115
"Communist Mentalities" (Scott) **43**:385
"The Communist Party to Youth" (Pasolini) **106**:225
"Communist Women" (Davis) **77**:120-21
Les communistes (Aragon) **3**:13; **22**:37
"Les Communistes et la paix" (Sartre) **50**:374
The Communists and the Peace (Sartre)
See "Les Communistes et la paix"
"Community" (Clarke) **61**:73
"Community" (Piercy) **27**:375
"Community" (Silkin) **43**:397
"Commuters" (Hirsch) **50**:198
Como agua para chocolate (Esquivel) **141**:166-237
"Como el viento" (Cernuda) **54**:59
Como en la guerra (Valenzuela) **31**:436-39; **104**:354, 356-58, 360, 370, 374, 377-79, 388
"Como lavoro" (Gadda) **11**:211
"Como les iba diciendo" (Parra) **102**:342
"De como o Mulato Porciúncula Descarregou seu Defunto" (Amado) **106**:74-76
Como quien espera el alba (Cernuda) **54**:45, 53, 61
"Comp Lit 101: Walt Grows Up" (Shields) **97**:430
"The Compact: At Volterra" (Tomlinson) **45**:392
"La compagne du vannier" (Char) **9**:164
"Compagnie de l'écolière" (Char) **14**:127
"Le compagnon de la dernière heure" (Chedid) **47**:87
Les compagnons dans le jardin (Char) **9**:159
"The Companion" (Campbell) **42**:86, 89
"The Companion" (Christie) **110**:141-42, 145
"The Companions" (Nemerov) **2**:307
"Companions" (Rao) **56**:291
Companions of the Day and Night (Harris) **25**:210, 216
Companions of the Left Hand (Tabori) **19**:435
"Company" (Dove) **81**:139, 146
"Company" (Longley) **29**:296
"The Company" (Raine) **45**:333, 338
Company (Beckett) **29**:57-62, 67; **59**:255, 260
The Company (Creeley) **78**:160
Company (Sondheim) **30**:380-92, 395-97, 399-402; **39**:175; **147**:233, 240, 251-54, 261, 263
"The Company I Keep" (Ezekiel) **61**:95
The Company I've Kept (MacDiarmid) **63**:255
Company Limited (Ray)
See *Simabaddha*
The Company of Children (Spacks) **14**:510
The Company of Eagles (Gann) **23**:166-67
"A Company of Laughing Faces" (Gordimer) **33**:180-81; **123**:113, 115, 144, 147-48
"The Company of Lovers" (Wright) **11**:578; **53**:423, 427, 430-31
The Company of Men (Gary) **25**:183-85
A Company of Poets (Simpson) **149**:310, 314, 316, 319-20, 358
"The Company of Wolves" (Carter) **41**:117, 119
The Company of Wolves (Carter) **76**:324
The Company of Wolves (Jordan) **110**:275-76, 278, 280-82
The Company of Women (Gordon) **22**:184-86; **128**:90, 92-4, 96-102, 111-14, 116, 118-24, 126-28, 140, 144, 147, 149, 151
The Company She Keeps (McCarthy) **1**:206; **3**:326-28; **14**:360, 363; **24**:342; **59**:289-91, 293
"Comparatives" (Momaday) **85**:248, 263
"Comparing X-Rays" (Spacks) **14**:510
"Comparison" (Nowlan) **15**:399
"A Comparison" (Plath) **11**:451
"A Comparison of the Conceptions of God in the Thinking of Paul Tillich and Henry Nelson Wieman" (King) **83**:339
Compartiment tueurs (Japrisot) **90**:167-69
"The Compartment" (Carver) **36**:104; **126**:107, 122, 127, 163-65, 167, 169, 171, 173, 179, 185
The Compass Flower (Merwin) **8**:389-90; **13**:383; **18**:334-37; **45**:274, 277-78; **88**:194, 197, 200, 202-03, 205
The Compass Rose (Le Guin) **45**:216-17
"A Compassionate Leave" (Yates) **23**:483
"Complaint" (Wright) **28**:470
"The Complaint of the Morpethshire Farmer" (Bunting) **39**:300; **47**:45
"La complainte de nègre" (Damas) **84**:176
"La complainte du nère" (Damas) **84**:176
"The Complaisant Husband" (Simmons) **43**:408
The Complaisant Lover (Greene) **3**:211; **6**:213-15; **70**:292, 294
A Completa verdade sobre as discutides aventuras do comandante Vasco Moscoso d'Aragão (Amado) **106**:57
The Complete Bolivian Diaries of Che Guevara, and Other Captured Documents (Guevara)
See *El diario de Che en Bolivia: noviembre 7, 1966, a octubre 7, 1967*
"Complete Control" (Clash) **30**:43-5, 47
The Complete Knowledge of Sally Fry (Murphy) **34**:91-2
The Complete Memoirs of George Sherston (Sassoon) **130**:193-94
Complete Plays (Behan) **79**:58
The Complete Poems (Bishop) **4**:66; **13**:95; **15**:59-61; **32**:33, 35, 38, 41
Complete Poems (Cendrars) **106**:188
Complete Poems (Cummings) **3**:119
The Complete Poems (Denby) **48**:84-5
Complete Poems (Jarrell) **6**:259; **9**:296
Complete Poems (Sandburg) **15**:466; **35**:351-52, 359
The Complete Poems (Sexton) **53**:312-14, 316, 320-23; **123**:419, 447
The Complete Poems (Yevtushenko) **126**:387
Complete Poems, 1910-1962 (Cummings) **68**:52
Complete Poems, 1920-1976 (MacDiarmid) **19**:289
Complete Poems, 1923-1962 (Cummings) **68**:42
The Complete Poems and Plays, 1909-1950 (Eliot) **34**:392
The Complete Poems of Anna Akhmatova (Akhmatova) **64**:17-20
The Complete Poems of Marianne Moore (Moore) **8**:399; **19**:340, 342-43; **47**:260-61, 270
The Complete Poems of Richard Aldington (Aldington) **49**:16
Complete Poems of Robert Frost (Frost) **13**:225; **26**:114, 117
The Complete Prose of Marianne Moore (Moore) **47**:267-69, 271
The Complete Robot (Asimov) **26**:58
The Complete Short Stories of L.P. Hartley (Hartley) **22**:215-16
A Complete State of Death (Gardner) **30**:152-53
The Complete Stories (O'Connor) **2**:318; **3**:366
The Complete Stories of Alice Walker (Walker) **103**:422
The Complete Stories of Erskine Caldwell (Caldwell) **14**:96
"The Complete Works" (Berrigan) **37**:43
Complete Works (Aleixandre)
See *Obras completas*
Complete Works (Auden) **123**:41
Complete Works (Borges)
See *Obras completas*
"Completed" (Williams) **5**:502; **45**:453
Completed Field Notes: The Long Poems of Robert Kroetsch (Kroetsch) **132**:284, 286
"Complex Autumnal" (Kizer) **80**:172
"Complexion" (Rodriguez) **155**:266-67, 272-73, 279, 304, 312
"Compleynte, Etc." (Rosenthal) **28**:395
"A Complicated Nature" (Trevor) **71**:326
Complicity (Cooke) **55**:46-8
Complimentaries: Uncollected Essays (Richards) **14**:454; **24**:401
"Compline" (Berryman) **3**:71
"The Composer's Winter Dream" (Dubie) **36**:135
"Composition" (Simic) **130**:294, 296, 304
"Composition in Black and White" (Pollitt) **28**:367
"Composition in Retrospect" (Cage) **41**:86
The Composition Reader (Tanizaki) **28**:414
"The Compost Heap" (Watkins) **43**:450
Comprador (Cudlip) **34**:38-9
"Compression" (Thomas) **107**:340-41, 346
Compromising Positions (Isaacs) **32**:253-54
Compulsion (Levin) **7**:203-04, 205
"Compulsive Qualifications" (Howard) **10**:275-76
"Compulsory Heterosexuality and Lesbian Existence" (Rich) **73**:320, 323
The Computer That Went on Strike (Asimov) **19**:25
"The Computer's First Christmas Card" (Morgan) **31**:275-76
"Comrade" (Soupault) **68**:406
Comrade Jacob (Caute) **29**:108, 121
Comrade Kirillov (Rao) **56**:298, 314-16
"Comrade Past and Mister Present" (Codrescu) **46**:105
Comrade Past and Mister Present (Codrescu) **46**:105; **121**:155, 157, 159-62, 175-8
"Comrade Smart-hat" (Aksyonov) **101**:18
Comstock Lode (L'Amour) **25**:281-82
"Con la señora du gast" (Azorín) **11**:24
Con las horas contadas (Cernuda) **54**:58, 60
"Con los ojos cerrados" (Arenas) **41**:28

"Con Quevedo en primavera" (Neruda) **28**:310; **62**:334
"Con Sequences" (Livesay) **79**:340
Concealed Enemies (Whitemore) **37**:445-47
"The Concealed Side" (Gordimer) **123**:161
Conceived in Liberty (Fast) **23**:154, 157; **131**:65, 90, 93, 97
"The Concentration City" (Ballard) **36**:36, 41
"Concentration Moon" (Zappa) **17**:589, 593
Concentric Circles (Bowering) **47**:25
"The Concept in Fiction" (Gass) **2**:155
"The Concept of Baroque in Literary Scholarship" (Wellek) **28**:445
"The Concept of Character in Fiction" (Gass) **15**:258; **132**:165
The Concept of Nation and the African View of Socialism (Senghor)
See *Nation et voie africaine du socialisme*
"The Concept of Time in Historiography" (Heidegger) **24**:279
"Conception" (Sarton) **49**:309
Concepts of Criticism (Wellek) **28**:445-46, 449, 454
"Conceptual Lesbianism" (Allison) **153**:4, 11
"Concerning My Neighbors the Hittites" (Simic) **68**:378
"Concerning Nature" (Ashbery) **77**:63
"Concerning the Bodyguard" (Barthelme) **13**:59; **59**:250-51
"Concerning the case of Bobby T." (Oates) **134**:246
"Concerning the Greek Tyrant" (Carey) **96**:35
"Concerning the Right to Life" (Graham) **118**:223, 262
"Concert" (Wideman) **67**:385
"Concert at Long Melford Church" (Beer) **58**:31, 36
The Concert at Saint Ovide (Buero Vallejo)
See *El concierto de San Ovidio*
Concert dans oeuf (Arrabal) **9**:33; **58**:9, 11
"The Concert of Hyacinths" (Elytis) **49**:111
Concert on the Island (Seifert)
See *Koncert na ostrově*
"The Concert: Oratorio for a Season of Wrath" (L'Heureux) **52**:273
"Concert Party" (Sassoon) **130**:186-87
"Concert Party: Busseboom" (Blunden) **56**:52
Concerto in B Goode (Berry) **17**:51
"The Concession" (Thomas) **48**:375
"The Concessions" (Ondaatje) **51**:315
"Conch-Shell" (Wright) **53**:418
"Una conciencia musical" (Ferré) **139**:188
Concierto barroco (Carpentier) **11**:102, 107; **110**:57-8, 69-70, 72-4
El concierto de San Ovidio (Buero Vallejo) **15**:98, 101-02; **46**:95-8; **139**:10, 15, 33, 43-5, 57-60
Concluding (Green) **2**:178; **13**:252-53, 255; **97**:243-51, 254-57, 267, 270, 272, 279-82, 288-90, 293
"Conclusion" (Leffland) **19**:280
"The Conclusion" (Yehoshua) **31**:472
Conclusive Evidence: A Memoir (Nabokov)
See *Speak, Memory: An Autobiography Revisited*
"Concord" (Lowell) **4**:300
"Concord" (Paz) **65**:182
Concrete (Bernhard)
See *Beton*
Concrete Island (Ballard) **6**:28; **14**:39, 41; **137**:5, 8, 14, 38, 41
The Concrete Island (Bowering) **15**:83; **47**:22
"Concrete Jungle" (Marley) **17**:271-72
"Concrete Relations with Others" (Sartre) **13**:498, 501
"The Concrete Universal" (Ransom) **2**:364; **5**:367
Concurring Beasts (Dobyns) **37**:74-8
"Concussion" (Campbell) **42**:84, 92
"Concussion" (MacLennan) **92**:340
"Le condamnéà mort" (Genet) **44**:389-90; **46**:173
Un condamné a mort s'est echappé (Bresson) **16**:105, 107-08, 111
Conde Julián (Goytisolo)
See *La reivindicación del Conde Don Julián*
"The Condemned" (Allen) **52**:42
"Condemned Door" (Cortázar) **5**:109
The Condemned Man's Bicycle (Arrabal)
See *La bicyclette du condamné*
The Condemned of Altona (Sartre)
See *Les séquestrés d'Altona*
The Condemned of Altona (De Sica)
See *Les séquestrés d'Altona*
"Condemned Site" (Van Duyn) **116**:411
"The Condemned Well" (Brown) **5**:78; **48**:57
Condenados a vivir (Gironella) **11**:237
"The Condensed Shorter Testament" (Mahon) **27**:291
"The Condiment" (Corman) **9**:169
"La condition botanique" (Hecht) **8**:266
La condition humaine (Malraux) **1**:203; **4**:324-25, 327-31, 333-36; **9**:353-55, 358; **13**:365-69; **15**:351-53; **57**:300-02, 304-05, 307, 309-17, 321, 324
The Condition of Muzak (Moorcock) **27**:349-50; **58**:348-49, 357
"The Condition of the Working Classes, 1970" (Bly) **10**:59
"The Condition We Call Exile" (Brodsky) **100**:69
"Conditional" (Richards) **14**:455
Conditionally Human (Miller) **30**:260, 262-64
"The Conditioned Reflex" (Lem) **40**:291
"Conditions for Leaving" (Jordan) **5**:203
"Conditions of a Narrative: Cassandra" (Wolf)
See *Voraussetzungen einer Erzählung: Kassandra*
"The Condolence" (Pound) **112**:309
"Condolence Visit" (Mistry) **71**:272
"Condolences to Every One of Us" (Gurganus) **70**:190, 192, 195
"The Condominium" (Elkin) **4**:154; **6**:169; **27**:122; **51**:99-100
Condominium (MacDonald) **44**:407-09
"The Condor" (Jeffers) **54**:234
"El cóndor" (Ulibarrí) **83**:417
"El Condor" (Ulibarrí)
See "El conejo pionero"
El cóndor, and Other Stories (Ulibarrí) **83**:418
The Condor and the Cows (Isherwood) **14**:279; **44**:397-98
"El condor pasa" (Simon) **17**:461
A Condor Passes (Grau) **4**:208-09; **146**:121, 128-29, 133, 136-38, 140-42, 149-52, 160-61, 163, 165
The Condor Passes (Grau)
See *A Condor Passes*
Conduct Unbecoming: Lesbians and Gays in the U.S. Military, Vietnam to the Persian Gulf (Shilts) **85**:329-32, 334-38, 342-43
Conducting Bodies (Simon)
See *Les corps conducteurs*
"The Conductor or Nothing" (Levine) **118**:279
The Cone-Gatherers (Jenkins) **52**:220, 225-27, 229
"El conejo pionero" (Ulibarrí) **83**:416
"The Coney" (Muldoon) **72**:273, 277
"Coney Island" (Beattie) **63**:14, 18; **146**:63
"Coney Island Baby" (Reed) **21**:311-12, 314, 316
Coney Island Baby (Reed) **21**:310-13, 315
A Coney Island of the Mind (Ferlinghetti) **6**:183; **10**:174-77; **27**:137-39; **111**:50-1, 53-8, 60, 64, 72
Confabulario (Arreola) **147**:4-7, 9-10, 15-16, 18, 27-31, 35
Confabulario Total, 1941-61 (Arreola) **147**:3-4, 6
Confabulations: Poems for Malcolm Lowry (Thesen) **56**:415-16, 419-22
The Confederacy (Green) **25**:198
A Confederacy of Dunces (Toole) **19**:441-43; **64**:404-24
A Confederate General from Big Sur (Brautigan) **3**:87-9; **5**:71; **12**:57, 59, 62, 66-8, 70; **34**:315-16; **42**:50, 57, 60, 62-3, 65
Confederates (Keneally) **14**:302-03; **19**:247-49; **27**:232; **43**:230, 234; **117**:225, 227, 229, 231, 241
"The Conference" (Singer) **69**:306
La conférence inachevée (Ferron) **94**:128-29
Conference of Victims (Berriault) **54**:2; **109**:90
Las confesiones de un pequeño filósofo (Azorín) **11**:27
"Confession" (Arghezi)
See "Duhovnicească"
"The Confession" (Justice) **102**:251, 265
"The Confession" (Nyro) **17**:312, 319
The Confession (Adamov) **25**:20
The Confession of a Child of the Century by Samuel Heather (Rogers) **57**:364-67
Confession of a Lover (Anand) **93**:32-34, 36, 56
The Confession of Joe Cullen (Fast) **131**:86
"The Confession of the Flesh" (Foucault) **69**:184
"Confession Overheard in a Subway" (Fearing) **51**:110
The Confession Stone (Dodson) **79**:199
"The Confessional" (Bidart) **33**:78-81
"The Confessional" (O'Faolain) **32**:341
The Confessional (Simenon) **8**:487
Confessional (Williams) **2**:465-66; **5**:502; **45**:448
"Confessional Poem" (Scannell) **49**:328, 330
The Confessional Poets (Phillips) **28**:362
Confessions (Rodriguez) **155**:
Les confessions de Dan Yack (Cendrars) **18**:95, 97; **106**:169, 183, 185-86, 190
Confessions from Left Field: A Baseball Pilgrimage (Mungo) **72**:291-92
Confessions of a Bad Girl (Pesetsky) **65**:349-50
"Confessions of a Former Anti-Semite" (Baraka) **115**:10
Confessions of a Knife (Selzer) **74**:279, 281
Confessions of a Mask (Mishima)
See *Kamen no kokuhaku*
Confessions of a Native-Alien (Ghose) **42**:177
"Confessions of a Pornographer's Shroud" (Barker) **52**:54
Confessions of a Spent Youth (Bourjaily) **62**:90-3, 95-6, 98, 104, 107
Confessions of a Teenage Baboon (Zindel) **26**:474-75, 480
Confessions of a Toe-Hanger (Harris) **12**:262
Confessions of an Irish Rebel (Behan) **79**:28, 34
The Confessions of Edward Dahlberg (Dahlberg) **7**:68-9
The Confessions of Josef Baisz (Jacobson) **14**:290-91
The Confessions of Nat Turner (Styron) **1**:331; **3**:473-74; **5**:418-20; **11**:515-16, 518-19, 521; **15**:526; **60**:392-93, 398, 400
"The Confessions of St. Jim-Ralph: Our Patron of Falling Short, Who Became a Prayer" (Johnson) **52**:234
Confessions of Summer (Lopate) **29**:300
Confessions of Two Brothers (Powys) **125**:265-66
"A Confessor's Words" (Arghezi)
See "Cuvinte duhovniceşti"
The Confidence Course (Potter) **58**:400; **123**:231
The Confidence Man (Garfield) **12**:241
The Confident Years (Brooks) **29**:84, 89
The Confidential Agent (Greene) **1**:131; **3**:212; **9**:250; **18**:194; **27**:175; **37**:140; **72**:148, 151, 155, 169, 171-72, 176, 179
The Confidential Clerk (Eliot) **1**:90; **13**:194-95; **15**:209; **34**:389; **41**:143, 145
"Confidential Report" (Laughlin) **49**:220

Confidential Report (Welles)
See *Mr. Arkadin*
Confieso que he vivido: memorias (Neruda) **9**:389-99; **28**:310; **62**:327, 329, 332
"Configurations" (Ammons) **108**:11, 23
Configurations (Paz) **4**:398; **6**:397-98
Confirmation: An Anthology of African-American Women (Baraka) **115**:10
Les confitures de coings (Ferron)
See *La nuit*
Conflagration (Ichikawa)
See *Enjo*
"The Conflict" (Day Lewis) **10**:128
"Conflict" (Scott) **22**:372, 374
Conflicts of Spring (Gustafson) **36**:222
The Conformist (Bertolucci)
See *Il conformista*
The Conformist (Duerrenmatt) **102**:58, 60
The Conformist (Moravia)
See *Il conformista*
Il conformista (Bertolucci) **16**:85-8, 90, 92-5, 97-8, 100
Il conformista (Moravia) **7**:243; **11**:383; **27**:356; **46**:282-83
"Conformity" (Parks) **147**:215
"Confrontation" (Sillitoe) **57**:391, 396; **148**:159
The Confrontation (Caute) **29**:114
Confrontation (Lengyel) **7**:202
Confrontations: Studies in the Intellectual and Literary Relations between Germany, England, and the United States during the Nineteenth Century (Wellek) **28**:446-47
"Confused" (Singer) **69**:306, 308-09
"Confusion" (Cozzens) **11**:124, 128, 131; **92**:196-97, 201
"Confusion and Poetry" (Tate) **24**:445
"Confusion in Language" (Shapiro) **53**:327
"The Confusion of Belief" (Shapiro) **53**:327
"Confusion of the Senses" (Rexroth) **112**:404
La confusione degle stili (Pasolini) **37**:344
"La confusione degli stili" (Pasolini) **106**:245
Confusions (Ayckbourn) **18**:28; **33**:40-1
"Congenital" (Wright) **6**:579, 581
"Congo" (Senghor) **54**:410; **130**:234
Congo (Crichton) **54**:72-3; **90**:93
"Congratulations" (Simon) **17**:461
Congratulations! You're Not Pregnant: An Illustrated Guide to Birth Control (Mayle)
See *We're Not Pregnant: An Illustrated Guide to Birth Control*
"Congregation of the Story-Tellers at a Funeral of Soweto Children" (Kunene) **85**:175
El congreso (Borges) **2**:72; **9**:117; **13**:110; **48**:37-41
"The Congress" (Borges) **83**:189-90
The Congress (Borges)
See *El congreso*
The Congressman Who Loved Flaubert and Other Washington Stories (Just) **4**:265-67
"Coniagui Women" (Lorde) **18**:309; **71**:232, 247, 254
Conjectures of a Guilty Bystander (Merton) **83**:402-03
Conjugal Love (Moravia)
See *L'amore coniugale, e altri racconti*
"A Conjugation" (Ezekiel) **61**:93
"The Conjugial Angel" (Byatt) **136**:151, 154-55
Conjunciones y disyunciones (Paz) **4**:396-397; **10**:390; **51**:331; **65**:181-82, 184
Conjunctions and Disjunctions (Paz)
See *Conjunciones y disyunciones*
Los conjurados (Borges) **44**:353
"Conjuration" (Wilbur) **53**:405
Conjure: Selected Poems, 1963-1970 (Reed) **2**:369; **3**:424; **5**:368-370; **6**:448; **13**:478
Conjure Wife (Leiber) **25**:301, 305-06, 310
Conjuros (Rodriguez) **10**:439
"A Connacht Doctor Dreams of an African Woman" (Durcan) **43**:115
Connaissance par les gouffres (Michaux) **8**:393; **19**:312-13
Connecting Times: The Sixties in Afro-American Fiction (Harris) **65**:379
"Connection" (Gaitskill) **69**:199
"Connection" (Jagger and Richard) **17**:232
"Connection" (Munro) **95**:306
"Connection" (Transtroemer) **65**:223
The Connection (Clarke) **16**:215-18
The Connection (Gelber) **1**:114; **6**:196-97; **79**:202-08, 210, 212-25
"Connections" (Simmons) **43**:406
"The Conning Tower" (Parker) **15**:417
"A Connoisseur" (Blunden) **56**:47
The Connoisseur (Connell) **4**:110; **6**:115-17; **45**:112
"The Connoisseur of Jews" (Rothenberg) **57**:374
"The Connoisseuse of Slugs" (Olds) **85**:289
"The Connor Girls" (O'Brien) **36**:339, 341; **116**:186
"Conon in Exile" (Durrell) **27**:97
Les conquérants (Malraux) **4**:324-25, 327, 329-31, 335; **9**:353-54, 356; **13**:364-66, 368; **15**:352; **57**:300-05, 311
The Conquering Hero (Gelbart) **21**:124-25
"The Conquering Hero Is Tired" (Simic) **130**:346
"The Conqueror Worm" (Donaldson) **46**:143
"The Conquerors" (Breytenbach) **126**:85
The Conquerors (Costain) **30**:95, 97, 99
The Conquerors (Eckert) **17**:107
The Conquerors (Malraux)
See *Les conquérants*
"The Conquest" (Murray) **40**:336
"The Conquest" (Samarakis) **5**:382
"Conquest of Dawn" (Kunene) **85**:166
Conquest of Eden 1493-1515: The Other Voyages of Columbus (Paiewonsky) **70**:331, 355
The Conquest of Mt. Everest (Kopit) **33**:249-50
The Conquest of Paradise: Christopher Columbus and the Columbian Legacy (Sale) **68**:354-58, 360
The Conquest of Paradise: Christopher Columbus and the Columbian Legacy (Sale) **70**:331, 345, 349, 351, 353
The Conquest of Politics: Liberal Philosophy in Democratic Times (Barber) **141**:4
Conquest of the Universe (Ludlam) **46**:239; **50**:342, 344
"Conquistador" (Hope) **3**:250; **51**:216, 221
Conquistador (MacLeish) **8**:361-63; **14**:336-37; **68**:275-79, 284-90, 292
"Conrad in Twilight" (Ransom) **11**:466
"Conrad Martins in 1850" (Shapcott) **38**:404
"Conrad's Darkness" (Naipaul) **37**:321; **105**:155
"Conrad's Journey" (Berryman) **10**:46; **13**:76
La consagración de la primavera (Carpentier) **110**:74-5, 77
"Conscience" (Williams) **56**:429
The Conscience (Fuentes) **60**:156-57, 160
The Conscience of the Rich (Snow) **1**:317; **6**:516; **13**:508-10; **19**:426
The Conscience of Words (Canetti)
See *Das Gewissen der Worte*
"Les consciences atténuantes" (Tzara) **47**:394
"Consciousness" (Milosz)
See "Świadomość"
"The Conscript" (MacNeice) **4**:318
"Conscripts" (Sassoon) **130**:178, 185
"A Consecration" (Masefield) **11**:358; **47**:230
"The Consent" (Nemerov) **9**:394-95
Consenting Adult (Hobson) **7**:163-64
Consenting Adults; or, The Duchess Will Be Furious (De Vries) **28**:105-08, 111
"Consequences" (Fish) **142**:175, 185, 210
"Consequences" (Meredith) **13**:375
Consequently I Rejoice (Jennings) **14**:293; **131**:241
"The Conservation of Races" (Du Bois) **96**:154, 160
The Conservationist (Gordimer) **5**:145-48; **7**:131-32; **10**:239-40; **33**:183; **51**:156, 158, 161; **70**:163-65, 167, 170, 172, 182-83; **123**:119, 128, 131, 145-46, 148
Conservatism: From John Adams to Churchill (Viereck) **4**:560
Conservatism Revisited (Viereck) **4**:560
"Conservatory" (Barthelme) **115**:81
"Conserving the Magnitude of Uselessness" (Ammons) **108**:28
"Consider" (Auden) **43**:21
"Consider the Lilies" (Ferber) **93**:153
Consider the Lilies (Hill) **113**:285-86
Consider the Lilies (Smith) **64**:389, 393
Consider the Lillies (Waugh) **7**:514
Consider the Oyster (Fisher) **76**:337-38, 340-41; **87**:118, 120
"Consider This and In Our Time" (Auden) **14**:32; **43**:15
"A Considerable Speck" (Frost) **10**:196-97
A Considerable Town (Fisher) **76**:341; **87**:120-21
"Considering the Snail" (Gunn) **32**:209
Il consiglio d'Egitto (Sciascia) **8**:474; **9**:474; **41**:389, 393
"The Consolation of Nature" (Martin) **89**:118
The Consolation of Nature, and Other Stories (Martin) **89**:110-13, 116, 118, 121, 125, 128-29, 137
"Consolations of Age" (Aldiss) **40**:21
"The Consolations of Horror" (Ligotti) **44**:53
"Consolations of Philosophy" (L'Heureux) **52**:279
"Consolations of Philosophy" (Mahon) **27**:288, 290-91
"A Consolatory Tale" (Dinesen) **29**:159, 161-62; **95**:35, 51
"Consorting with Angels" (Sexton) **53**:321; **123**:442
"The Conspiracy" (Spinrad) **46**:384
"The Conspiracy" (Tomlinson) **45**:398
The Conspiracy (Hersey) **2**:188; **7**:154; **40**:240
The Conspiracy of Equals (Ehrenburg) **62**:176
Conspiracy of Knaves (Brown) **47**:40-2
"The Conspiracy of Us" (Bernstein) **142**:9
Conspirator (Benson) **17**:49
"The Conspirators" (Burke) **2**:87
"The Conspirators" (Prokosch) **48**:309
The Conspirators (Borges)
See *Los conjurados*
The Conspirators (Havel) **25**:224-27, 229; **123**:172, 205
The Conspirators (Prokosch) **4**:420; **48**:311-12
Conspirators and Poets (Enright) **31**:147-48
"A Constable Calls" (Heaney) **7**:149; **74**:167
Constance Markievicz (O'Faolain) **70**:316-17
Constance; or, Solitary Practices (Durrell) **27**:97-100; **41**:134-38
"Constancia" (Fuentes) **113**:242-43
"The Constant Symbol" (Frost) **1**:111; **26**:119
The Constant Wife (Arzner) **98**:69
The Constant Wife (Maugham) **67**:223-27
Constantly Singing (Simmons) **43**:412-14
Constellations (Breton) **54**:29-30; **9**:132-34; **15**:91
The Constellations: How They Came to Be (Gallant) **17**:133
"The Constipated Frenchman" (Singh) **11**:505
"Constipation" (Breytenbach) **126**:62
"Constituents of a Theory of the Media" (Enzensberger) **43**:149
"The Constraints of Postmodernism" (Jameson) **142**:253
"Construction" (Barthelme) **115**:81
Constructions (Frayn) **7**:107
The Consul's Daughter (Schlee) **35**:372
The Consul's File (Theroux) **11**:528-29; **15**:533; **28**:428
"Consultation" (Dorfman) **77**:142
"The Consumer Bulletin Annual" (Barthelme) **5**:54

Consumer Society (Baudrillard)
See *La société de consommation*
"A Consumer's Report" (Porter) **33**:319
"The Consuming Fire" (Callaghan) **41**:98
"The Consumptive, Belsen, 1945" (Peake) **54**:375
"Contact" (Dunn) **36**:154
"Contam de Clarice Lispector" (Cabral de Melo Neto) **76**:163
The Contaminated Man (Keyes)
See *The Touch*
"The Contemplative Soul" (Huxley) **11**:283
The Contemporaneity Game (Oe)
See *Dōjidai gēmu*
"Contemporaneous Poem" (Rozewicz)
See "Poemat równoczesny"
Contemporaries (Kazin) **38**:274-75, 279
"A Contemporary" (Merwin) **88**:204
"A Contemporary Film of Lancasters in Action" (Ewart) **46**:153
"Contemporary Poem" (Rozewicz)
See "Poemat równoczesny"
Contemporary Realism (Lukacs) **24**:319
Contemporary Scottish Studies (MacDiarmid) **19**:287
"Contemporary Standards in the canadian Novel" (Kroetsch) **132**:222
"Contemporary Trends in French Literature" (de Man) **55**:421
Contempt (Godard)
See *Le mépris*
"Contend in Vain" (Asimov) **19**:26
"The Contender" (Davies) **21**:91
"The Contender" (Hughes) **9**:284; **37**:177
"The Contender" (Santos) **22**:365
The Contender (Lipsyte) **21**:207-09
The Contenders (Wain) **2**:457; **46**:408-09
"Content" (Ignatow) **14**:275
"Content" (Townshend) **17**:528
The Content of the Form: Narrative Discourse and Historical Representation (White) **148**:234-35, 237-38, 240-41, 244-48, 250-51, 253, 256, 267-68, 270, 282, 286-88, 291-92, 296, 299
Content's Dream: Essays 1975-1984 (Bernstein) **142**:8-9, 18, 22-3, 26, 31, 48, 56
Contes anglais et autres (Ferron) **94**:108, 123-24
Les Contes du chat perché (Aymé) **11**:22
Contes du pays incertain (Ferron) **94**:103-4, 106, 110, 123-24
Contes inédits (Ferron) **94**:123-24
Contes pour buveurs attardés (Tremblay) **29**:426
Contes pour milles oreilles (Carrier) **78**:59, 63, 67
Contes pour un homme seul (Theriault) **79**:400, 410-12
Contes: Tales from the Uncertain Country (Ferron)
See *Contes du pays incertain*
"The Contest" (Paley) **37**:337; **140**:219, 277
"Contest of the Bards" (Ginsberg) **36**:191, 196
Il contesto (Sciascia) **8**:474; **9**:475; **41**:388-91, 393-94
"Context" (Allison) **153**:19
"context" (Plath) **111**:217, 220
"Contexts" (Monette) **82**:315
Contexts of Poetry: Interviews 1960-1970 (Creeley) **78**:120
"The Continent as the Letter M" (Crase) **58**:160, 162
"Continent of Strangers" (Blaise) **29**:75
"The Continental College of Beauty" (Strand) **71**:287
"Continental Drift" (Bissoondath) **120**:3, 5
Continental Drift (Banks) **37**:28-30; **72**:2-5, 7, 9, 11-12, 14, 16-18, 22
The Continental Op (Hammett) **5**:160-62
"Continent's End" (Jeffers) **54**:236, 244
"Contingencies" (Dobyns) **37**:75
"Continuación" (Alonso) **14**:26
"Continue by Waking" (Dobyns) **37**:75
"La continuidad histórica" (Azorín) **11**:24
"Continuing" (Ammons) **25**:45
A Continuing Journey (MacLeish) **14**:338
"Continuing to Live" (Larkin) **39**:340
Continuities in Cultural Evolution (Mead) **37**:274
"Continuity" (Levine) **54**:299
"The Continuity of Norman Mailer" (Oe) **86**:214
Continuous: Fifty Sonnets from "The School of Eloquence" (Harrison) **43**:177-80; **129**:165
"The Continuous Life" (Strand) **71**:288
The Continuous Life (Strand) **71**:278, 286-90
"Continuous Performance" (Fearing) **51**:119
"Continuous Performances" (Rozewicz) **139**:289
"Continuum" (Kumin) **28**:224
"Continuum" (Rich) **125**:337
"Contra mortem" (Carruth) **4**:94
Contra Mortem (Carruth) **84**:119
"Contra naturam" (Howard) **10**:274
"Contra prudentium" (Ekelöf) **27**:110
Contraataque (Sender) **8**:478
"A Contract" (Baraka) **5**:45
The Contract (Carlisle) **33**:103
Contract with the World (Rule) **27**:421-22
The Contractor (Storey) **2**:424-25; **4**:529-30; **5**:414-17; **8**:505
"Contracts and Apple Pie: the Strange Case of Baby M" (Pollitt) **122**:224
The Contradictions (Ghose) **42**:177-78
Contraries (Oates) **33**:287-89; **108**:388
The Contrary Experience: Autobiographies (Read) **4**:440-41
Contrasto for a Solo Voice (Fo) **32**:176
"Contrasts" (Cendrars) **106**:180
"Contrasts" (Smith) **64**:396
Contre la mélancolie: Célébration hassidique II (Wiesel) **37**:451, 455-56
"Contre notre amour qui ne voulait rien d'autre" (Damas) **84**:186
Le contrebandière (Maillet) **54**:311
Contre-Jour: A Triptych after Pierre Bonnard (Josipovici) **43**:227-28; **153**:209-10
"Contribution to the Second Bitterfeld Conference" (Wolf) **150**:296
"Contrition" (Bausch) **51**:55-7
"Contrition" (Dubus) **97**:211
Control (Goldman) **48**:129
Controlling Interests (Bernstein) **142**:27, 34, 43
"Controversy" (Prince) **35**:324
Controversy (Prince) **35**:324-28, 331-32
"Contusion" (Plath) **9**:426-27; **14**:424; **51**:341; **62**:406; **111**:163, 199
"Contusion" (Wonder) **12**:660, 662
"Convalescence" (Dybek) **114**:67
"Convalescing" (Oates) **19**:348
"Convenience" (Murphy) **41**:320
La convention belzébir (Aymé) **11**:22
"The Conventional Wisdom" (Elkin) **14**:157-58
Convergences (Paz) **119**:410
"Converging City" (Okri) **87**:314
"Conversa de Sevilhana" (Cabral de Melo Neto) **76**:161
Conversación en la catedral (Vargas Llosa) **6**:544-48; **9**:542-44; **10**:496-98, 501; **15**:549-52; **31**:444-45; **42**:404, 409; **85**:350, 352-56, 358-60, 362, 364, 395
"Conversación galante" (Parra) **102**:341
"Conversation" (Ai) **69**:9
"Conversation" (Giovanni) **4**:189
The Conversation (Coppola) **16**:237-39, 242, 244-45, 249; **126**:196, 262
"A Conversation about Balzac's Horse" (Hofmann) **54**:229
"Conversation at Tea" (Kinnell) **13**:321
"Conversation et sous-conversation" (Sarraute) **2**:385
"Conversation Galante" (Eliot) **1**:92
"Conversation in a Bedroom" (Davidson) **19**:128
"A Conversation in Rome" (Voznesensky) **57**:427
Conversation in the Cathedral (Vargas Llosa)
See *Conversación en la catedral*
"Conversation in the Mountains" (Celan)
See "Gespräch im Gebirge"
"Conversation in the Park" (Hacker) **72**:188
The Conversation of the Three Walking Men (Weiss) **15**:563
"Conversation on a Country Path about Thinking" (Heidegger) **24**:266-69
"Conversation on V" (Dodson) **79**:194
"Conversation Piece" (Ewart) **46**:151
Conversation Piece (Keane) **31**:232-33
Conversation Piece (Visconti) **16**:573, 575-76
La conversation souveraine (Char) **11**:113
"Conversation with a Fireman from Brooklyn" (Gallagher) **63**:118
"Conversation with a Friend" (Rozewicz)
See "rozmowa z Przyjacielem"
"A Conversation with Anthony Davis" (Delany) **141**:116, 118
Conversation with Calliope (Hope) **51**:217
"Conversation With Death" (Seifert) **93**:342
"Conversation with Langston Hughes" (Guillén) **48**:167
"A Conversation with My Father" (Paley) **4**:392; **6**:392-93; **37**:332; **140**:211-14, 216, 224-25, 231, 243, 245, 248, 263-64, 268, 277, 282
"Conversation with My Uncle" (Sargeson) **31**:363, 373
Conversation with My Uncle (Sargeson) **31**:364, 369
"A Conversation with Myself" (Knight) **40**:282
"Conversation with the Prince" (Rozewicz) **139**:289, 291
Conversation with the Prince and Other Poems (Rozewicz) **139**:291
Conversations (Rothenberg) **6**:477
Conversations in Another Room (Josipovici) **43**:226
Conversations in Bloomsbury (Anand) **93**:35, 44
"Conversations in Moscow" (Paley) **140**:285-86, 291
Conversations in Sicily (Vittorini)
See *Conversazione in Sicilia*
"Conversations of the Tide at Jaqueira" (Cabral de Melo Neto)
See "Prosas da maré na Jaqueira"
Conversations on a Homecoming (Murphy)
See *The White House*
Conversations with Algren (Algren) **33**:12
"Conversations with an Absent Lover on a Beachless Afternoon" (Castillo) **151**:48
Conversations with Children (Laing) **95**:157
"Conversations with Goethe" (Barthelme) **46**:39, 42
"Conversations with Helmholtz" (Allen) **52**:35
Conversations with Isaac Bashevis Singer (Singer) **69**:308
"Conversations with Jan" (Wakoski) **4**:572
Conversations with Professor Y (Céline)
See *Entretiens avec le Professeur Y*
"Conversations with Unicorns" (Carey) **40**:128; **96**:25
Conversazione in Sicilia (Vittorini) **6**:551; **9**:546-52; **14**:543-47
"Converse at Night in Copenhagen" (Dinesen) **10**:152; **95**:50
"Conversió i mort d'en quim federal" (Espriu) **9**:192
"The Conversion" (Banks) **37**:24
"Conversion" (Toomer) **22**:426
"The Conversion of William Kirkwood" (McGahern) **48**:272-73
The Conversions (Mathews) **6**:314-16; **52**:307-10, 315-18
"The Convert" (Ciardi) **40**:157

"The Convert" (Shapiro) **4**:486
The Converts: A Novel of Early Christianity (Warner) **45**:440-41
The Convict Bird (Vollmann) **89**:304
Convict Thirteen (Keaton) **20**:192
"Conviction" (Smith) **44**:444
"Los convidados de agosto" (Castellanos) **66**:48
Los convidados de agosto (Castellanos) **66**:48
"Convocation Address: Queen's University, 29/5/71" (Johnston) **51**:245, 253
Convoy (Altman) **16**:43
Convoy (Peckinpah) **20**:282
"Conway Burying Ground" (MacLeish) **8**:363
"The Cooboo" (Prichard) **46**:333, 345
"The Cook" (Young Bear) **94**:361, 366
"Cook County" (MacLeish) **68**:285, 288
"Cook of the House" (McCartney) **35**:285
"Cookie" (Taylor) **18**:522; **37**:409
"A Cooking Egg" (Eliot) **15**:210-11
"The Cooking Lesson" (Castellanos) See "Lección de cocina"
The Cooking of Provincial France (Fisher) **76**:342
Cooking Together: Recipes and Recollections (Hellman) **34**:347
"The Cook's Lesson" (Fuller) **62**:185, 194-95
Cool Cat (Bonham) **12**:52-3
Cool Country (Barnard) **48**:26-7
The Cool Crazy Committed World of the '60s (Berton) **104**:47
"Cool Dark Ode" (Justice) **102**:258
Cool Memories 1980-1985 (Baudrillard) **60**:24
Cool Repentance (Fraser) **32**:186
"Cool Tombs" (Sandburg) **10**:448-49; **35**:352
"The Cool Web" (Graves) **1**:128; **45**:169-70, 173
The Cool World (Clarke) **16**:217-19
Cool Zebras of Light (Peters) **7**:303
Coolie (Anand) **23**:13, 15; **93**:24, 29, 31-32, 42, 50
"Coon Song" (Ammons) **25**:43; **108**:5, 8, 30
Coonardoo: The Well in the Shadow (Prichard) **46**:328-29, 331-32, 334-38, 341, 343-45
"Cooney on World Affairs" (Carpenter) **41**:108
Coonskin (Bakshi) **26**:70-5
Co-Op (Sinclair) **15**:498
"Cooped Up" (Baker) **31**:28
Cooper (Masters) **48**:224-25
"Cootchie" (Bishop) **32**:38, 42
Cop Hater (Hunter) **31**:224
Cop Killer (Wahlöö) See *Polismördaren*
Cop Out (Queen) **11**:464
"Cop Tales" (Paley) **140**:245
Copacetic (Komunyakaa) **94**:217-20, 224, 246-47
"Copacetic Mingus" (Komunyakaa) **94**:247
"Copenhagen Season" (Dinesen) **10**:152; **95**:52
"Copla" (Alonso) See *Oscura noticia*
Cop-Out (Guare) **29**:203-05
"Cop-Out Session" (Knight) **40**:287
"The Copper Beech" (Hine) **15**:282
The Copper Beech (Binchy) **153**:66, 68, 78
"The Copperhead" (Bottoms) **53**:33
"Coppersmith" (Murphy) **41**:317
Coppia aperta (Fo) **109**:109
Coprolites (Goldbarth) **5**:143
Cops (Keaton) **20**:192, 195
Cops and Robbers (Westlake) **7**:528
"Cops of the World" (Ochs) **17**:330
Copse (Jünger) **125**:252
"Coq au vin" (Ciardi) **40**:159
Le coq de bruyère (Tournier) **23**:452-53; **36**:440; **95**:361-62, 367-68, 377-78, 382-83
"le coq pondeur" (Theriault) **79**:408
Coquette (Swinnerton) **31**:422-23
Cora Fry (Brown) **32**:66-7
"Coral Atoll" (Randall) **135**:397
"Coral Sea, 1945" (Muske) **90**:309-10
Coralie Lansdowne Says No (Buzo) **61**:52-6, 58-9, 61-6, 68-9
"Coralles 1948" (Honig) **33**:211
El corazón amarillo (Neruda) **28**:310; **62**:333-34, 336
"Le Corbillard" (Tchicaya) **101**:351
La corde et les souris (Malraux) **57**:306
La corde raide (Simon) **39**:206, 209, 211
Cordélia (Mallet-Joris) **11**:355
"Cordelia's Song" (Zaturenska) **11**:580
Les cordes-de-bois (Maillet) **54**:303-04, 306-08, 311; **118**:327, 329, 336-37, 339, 341, 343, 345
A Cordiall Water: A Garland of Odd & Old Recipes to Assuage the Ills of Man or Beast (Fisher) **76**:338, 342; **87**:123, 125-26
"Cori descrittivi d'anima di Didone" (Ungaretti) **7**:481, 485; **15**:537
The Coriander (Dillon) **17**:95
"Coriolan" (Eliot) **41**:161
Coriolanus (Berkoff) **56**:20-3
"Coriolanus and His Mother" (Schwartz) **10**:464-65
"Coriolanus Leaves Home" (Beer) **58**:38
"Corkscrew" (Hammett) **47**:161
"Corky's Car Keys" (Ashbery) **25**:54
Corn (Ludlam) **46**:240-41
"Corn Close" (Creeley) **78**:150-51
"Corn Flakes" (Phillips) **28**:364
The Corn Is Green (Williams) **15**:576-77
Cornelius (Priestley) **2**:346
"The Corner" (Capote) **13**:137
"The Corner of the Eye" (Warren) **39**:259
The Corner That Held Them (Warner) **7**:511; **19**:460
The Cornerman (Gardner) **30**:154
Corners in the Glass (Gustafson) **36**:217-19, 222
"Cornet at Night" (Ross) **13**:493-94
The Cornet Player Who Betrayed Ireland (O'Connor) **23**:330-31
"Cornet Solo" (Day Lewis) **10**:131
"Cornfields" (Watkins) **43**:450
Cornhuskers (Sandburg) **10**:448-49, 451; **15**:466; **35**:339-41, 343, 352
Cornish Trilogy (Davies) **91**:201, 204
"Cornwall" (Corn) **33**:117
"Cornwall" (Davie) **8**:165
"Corona" (Celan) **19**:89; **53**:71
"Corona" (Delany) **38**:154
Corona de amor y muerte (Casona) **49**:49
Coronación (Donoso) **4**:126-27; **8**:178-79; **11**:145-46; **32**:151-54, 158; **99**:216, 218-19, 221-23, 232, 239, 263
"Coronary Thrombosis" (Oates) **15**:402
The Coronation (Arrabal) See *Le couronnement*
Coronation (Donoso) See *Coronación*
The Coronation Murder Mystery (O'Hara) **78**:364
Coroner's Pidgin (Allingham) **19**:17
Coronis (Booth) **13**:103
"The Corporal" (Gunn) **18**:199
"Corporate Entity" (MacLeish) **68**:270, 290
"The Corporation Gardener's Prologue" (Raine) **103**:180
Les corps conducteurs (Simon) **4**:497; **9**:482; **15**:493-95; **39**:205-06, 208-11
"Corps d'Energie/Rituels d'Ecriture" (Brossard) **115**:126
Les corps etrangers (Cayrol) **11**:107
Corps perdu (Césaire) **112**:13, 15, 29
The Corpse on the Dike (van de Wetering) **47**:405-06, 412
"The Corpses at Zinderneuf" (Cassity) **42**:96
Correction (Bernhard) See *Korrektur*
"Corrections: Executive Suite" (Moure) **88**:232
"Corrections to the Saints: Transubstantial" (Moure) **88**:232
Corregidora (Jones) **6**:265-66; **9**:307; **131**:249-51, 253-6, 259-62, 264-7, 270, 273-4, 278-87, 289, 291, 293-4, 296-329, 338-9, 341
"Correspondence" (McCullers) **12**:433
"A Correspondence Course" (Gordimer) **123**:118
The Correspondence of Thomas Percy and Richard Farmer (Brooks) **110**:31
"The Correspondence School Instructor Says Goodbye to His Poetry Students" (Kinnell) **29**:290
"Correspondences" (Rukeyser) **27**:411
Correspondences: A Family History in Letters (Stevenson) **7**:462-64
"Correspondencias" (Ferré) **139**:181-82
The Corrida at San Felíu (Scott) **9**:476; **60**:329, 340
"The Corridor" (Gunn) **18**:201
Corridor and Stairs (Ritsos) **31**:327
Corridors of Power (Snow) **1**:317; **4**:500, 502; **9**:496-97; **19**:427
Corridos (Valdez) **84**:403-04, 406, 410, 414-15
Corriente alterna (Paz) **3**:375, 377; **4**:396-97; **6**:396-98; **10**:390; **51**:331; **65**:182
Corrigan (Blackwood) **100**:7, 9-10, 15, 28
Corrosive Sublimate (Sorrentino) **3**:461; **7**:448, 451
"Corruption" (Lively) **32**:277
Corruption (Mosley) **43**:311, 319, 321
"The Corset" (Connell) **45**:110
"Corson's Inlet" (Ammons) **5**:26-7, 29; **8**:16-19; **9**:26, 30; **25**:43, 47-8; **108**:10, 14-17, 28, 45
Corson's Inlet (Ammons) **2**:12; **5**:25-6, 28; **8**:15; **108**:5, 24, 46, 60
Le cortège des vainqueurs (Gallo) **95**:96-8
"Cortés and Montezuma" (Barthelme) **13**:59; **46**:35
"Cortez the Killer" (Young) **17**:575, 579, 583
"Corymba" (Davidson) **13**:168; **19**:129
"Coś takiego" (Rozewicz) **139**:296, 299
Una cosa è una cosa (Moravia) **18**:346
The Cosmic Carnival of Stanislaw Lem (Lem) **40**:296
The Cosmic Connection (Sagan) **30**:331-33, 343; **112**:413, 416
The Cosmic Engineers (Simak) **55**:319
The Cosmic Express (Williamson) **29**:454
Cosmic Profit: How to Make Money without Doing Time (Mungo) **72**:291
The Cosmic Rape (Sturgeon) **22**:413; **39**:361
"Cosmic Sleepwalker" (Ekelöf) **27**:117
Le cosmicomiche (Calvino) **5**:99, 101; **8**:127, 129-31; **11**:89, 91-2; **22**:89, 93; **33**:98-9; **39**:306-07, 309, 313-15, 317; **73**:40-4, 47-8, 54, 57-8
Cosmicomics (Calvino) See *Le cosmicomiche*
"Cosmogony" (Borges) **44**:354
The Cosmological Eye (Miller) **43**:298; **84**:252
"The Cosmology of Finding Your Place" (Dorn) **10**:159
Cosmopolatain Greetings (Ginsberg) **109**:316, 318, 329
The Cosmopolitan Girl (Drexler) **6**:142-43
"Cosmopolitan Lady" (Coward) **29**:139
"Cosmos" (Beattie) **146**:85
Cosmos (Gombrowicz) See *Kosmos*
Cosmos (Sagan) **30**:338-39, 340, 342-44; **112**:409-15, 418-19, 423-30, 433, 437, 442
"The Cost" (Hecht) **13**:270
"The Cost of Seriousness" (Porter) **33**:320
The Cost of Seriousness (Porter) **13**:452-53; **33**:320-21, 323, 325
"The Costa San Giorgio" (Loy) **28**:249
"La Côte Basque, 1965" (Capote) **8**:133; **34**:321, 323
"Côte d'Azur" (Simpson) **149**:295
Cotnoir (Ferron) **94**:106-07, 118, 120, 124, 126-27
Coto vedado (Goytisolo) **133**:86, 95-97, 99-100
"Cottage for Sale" (Murphy) **41**:319
"The Cottage Hospital" (Betjeman) **43**:36

"Cottage Street, 1953" (Wilbur) **14**:579; **110**:361-62, 369, 385-86
Cotter's England (Stead)
See *Dark Places of the Heart*
"Cotton Avenue" (Mitchell) **12**:443
"Cotton Candy" (Giovanni) **64**:195
Cotton Candy on a Rainy Day (Giovanni) **64**:188, 191, 194-95; **117**:184, 186, 192-93, 197-98, 205
The Cotton Club (Coppola) **126**:242, 267
The Cotton Club (Puzo) **107**:213
The Cotton Club: New Poems (Major) **19**:293
Cotton Comes to Harlem (Himes) **4**:229; **7**:159; **18**:246; **58**:258, 267; **108**:233, 239, 256, 269, 276-77
"Cotton Gonna Kill Me Yet" (Himes) **7**:159
"Cotton Jenny" (Lightfoot) **26**:283
The Cotton Pickers (Traven) **11**:536
"Cottonfields" (Wilson) **12**:645
"Cottonwood: Part I" (Silko) **114**:314
"Cottonwood: Part II Buffalo Man" (Silko) **74**:345; **114**:314
Couch (Warhol) **20**:415
"Cougar Meat" (Gallagher) **63**:125
"Could Have" (Szymborska) **99**:200
Could Have (Szymborska) **99**:199
"Could I Leave You?" (Sondheim) **30**:382
"Could You Be Loved" (Marley) **17**:273
The Council of Egypt (Sciascia)
See *Il consiglio d'Egitto*
"Counsel" (Bukowski) **41**:66
Counsellor-at-Law (Rice) **7**:359-63; **49**:298-300, 302
"Counsels" (Milosz) **5**:293
Count Belisarius (Graves) **39**:322; **45**:172
Count Bruga (Hecht) **8**:269
"Count Fersen to the Queen" (Christie) **110**:126
Count Julian (Goytisolo)
See *La reivindicación del Conde Don Julián*
"Count Lothar's Heart" (Boyle) **58**:66
Count Öderland (Frisch)
See *Graf Öderland*
"Count the Clock That Tells the Time" (Ellison) **42**:130
Count Zero (Gibson) **39**:143; **63**:129-32, 134-39
Countdown (Altman) **16**:19, 41; **116**:11, 35, 47
Countdown (Slaughter) **29**:377
Countdown to Ecstasy (Becker and Fagen) **26**:79-80
"Countee Cullen" (Dodson) **79**:193
"Counter-Attack" (Sassoon) **130**:181, 188, 193, 213-14, 219
Counter-Attack and Other Poems (Sassoon) **36**:385-86, 390-93; **130**:181, 184, 191, 193, 202, 208, 212-14, 218-19, 222-24
Counterblast (McLuhan) **83**:366
CounterBlasts No. 9: Mr. Bevan's Dream (Townsend) **61**:421
Counter-Clock World (Dick) **30**:115, 117, 124; **72**:121-22
Counterfeit Nazi: The Ambiguity of Good (Friedlander)
See *Kurt Gerstein ou l'ambiguité du bien*
A Counterfeit of Silence (Stow) **23**:436
"Counter-Hegemonic Art: Do the Right Thing" (Hooks) **94**:145
"Countering" (Ammons) **9**:27
The Counterlife (Roth) **47**:360-67; **86**:248, 250, 253, 255-57, 259-63; **119**:129-30
"Counterparts" (Dobyns) **37**:75
Counterparts (Fuller) **28**:153, 159
"Counterpoint" (Haldeman) **61**:174, 176
Counterpoint (Holland) **21**:154
"A Counter-Revolutionary Proposition" (Castillo) **151**:3-4
Counter-Statement (Burke) **24**:118-20, 127-28, 132
Countess from Hong Kong (Chaplin) **16**:203
"The Countess of Pembroke's Dream" (Hope) **51**:222
Counties of Contention (Kiely) **43**:245
"Counting" (Deane) **122**:81
"Counting" (Larkin) **64**:262
Counting (Phillips) **139**:201-2
"Counting Birds" (Harrison) **143**:352
"Counting Coup" (Plumly) **33**:312
"The Counting Game" (Graver) **70**:52, 54
"The Counting Houses" (Merwin) **18**:334
"Counting Months" (Leavitt) **34**:78-9
Counting My Steps: An Autobiography (Lind) **2**:245; **4**:293; **27**:271, 273; **82**:140-43
"Counting the Mad" (Justice) **102**:278-79
Counting the Ways: A Vaudeville (Albee) **11**:13; **53**:21-2; **86**:121; **113**:24, 31
"Counting the Wind" (Bissoondath) **120**:3, 5, 7
Country (Griffiths) **52**:179-80
The Country (Plante) **23**:345-47; **38**:365-67, 370-71
The Country Ahead of Us, the Country Behind (Guterson) **91**:104
"Country & Western I" (Hacker) **72**:192
"Country & Western II" (Hacker) **72**:192
"Country Bedroom" (MacCaig) **36**:281
The Country between Us (Forché) **25**:170-72; **83**:198, 207, 210-14, 219, 221; **86**:138-39, 141-42, 144
"Country Burial" (Lewis) **41**:254, 263
"Country Church" (Thomas) **13**:543
"Country Churchyard" (Warner) **19**:460
"The Country Clergy" (Thomas) **13**:544; **48**:379
"The Country Club" (Muldoon) **32**:319; **72**:265
Country Cooking and Other Stories (Mathews) **52**:307-08
"Country Cooking from Central France: Roast Boned Rolled Stuffed Shoulder of Lamb" (Mathews) **52**:307, 313
The Country Cousin (Auchincloss) **18**:24-5
"Country Dance" (MacCaig) **36**:285
"A Country Festival" (Mahapatra) **33**:283
"The Country Fiddler" (Montague) **46**:266
"Country Full of Swedes" (Caldwell) **1**:51; **60**:49-50
"Country Girl" (Brown) **48**:57
"Country Girl" (Young) **17**:569-70
The Country Girl (Odets) **2**:319-20; **28**:334, 339-40; **98**:195-96, 198-99, 209, 211-12, 215-17, 228, 230-32, 236-37, 251-52
Country Girls (O'Brien) **3**:365; **5**:313; **36**:337; **116**:182, 187, 190-93, 205-06, 214
The Country Girls Trilogy (O'Brien) **65**:170, 172; **116**:189, 195-96, 226-27
"A Country God" (Blunden) **56**:37-8, 41
Country Growth (Derleth) **31**:132-33
"The Country Houses" (Prokosch) **48**:310
"The Country Husband" (Cheever) **64**:53-4
"Country Junction" (Garrigue) **8**:240
"A Country Life" (Jarrell) **2**:209
Country Life (Ackroyd) **140**:9, 21
"A Country Love Story" (Stafford) **4**:518; **68**:449
"Country Matters" (Montague) **46**:267, 275
"The Country Mouse" (Bishop) **32**:40-1, 43
"Country Mouse, City Mouse" (Price) **63**:336
"Country Music" (Cohen) **19**:115-16
Country Music: Selected Early Poems (Wright) **28**:460; **119**:180, 189; **146**:321, 325, 328, 341, 369, 373-75, 378-79, 381
"Country Night" (Ondaatje) **51**:317
"The Country North of Belleville" (Purdy) **14**:433; **50**:237
The Country of a Thousand Years of Peace and Other Poems (Merrill) **2**:272; **13**:379; **91**:228
The Country of Her Dreams (Elliott) **47**:113-14
The Country of Marriage (Berry) **6**:61; **27**:33-4, 36
The Country of Purple Clouds (Strugatskii and Strugatskii) **27**:432
A Country of Strangers (Richter) **30**:322-23
The Country of the Heart (Wersba) **30**:431-32
Country of the Minotaur (Ghiselin) **23**:169-72
Country of the Open Heart (McFadden) **48**:257-58
"Country Pie" (Dylan) **12**:186
"A Country Place" (Bitov) **57**:119
Country Place (Petry) **1**:266; **7**:305; **18**:403-04
Country Places (Andrade) **18**:4
"Country Pleasures" (Grenville) **61**:152
Country Pleasures (Brammer) **31**:53-4
Country Poems (Derleth) **31**:138
"The Country Ride" (Slessor) **14**:493
"Country Road H" (Baxter) **78**:25
The Country Scene (Masefield) **11**:357
Country Sentiment (Graves) **6**:210; **45**:163, 166
"Country Station" (Adcock) **41**:14
"A Country Tale" (Dinesen) **10**:152
"Country Town" (Buckley) **57**:129
"Country Town" (Wright) **11**:578; **53**:427
"Country Towns" (Slessor) **14**:496
"A Country Walk" (Kinsella) **4**:271; **19**:251, 255; **138**:109, 116, 118, 121, 136, 148, 156
Country without Maps (Garrigue) **2**:153-54; **8**:239
Country You Can't Walk In (Kelly) **55**:159
"Countrymen" (Kennedy) **8**:320
"County" (Betjeman) **43**:47
"The County Engineer" (Durcan) **43**:114-15
"County Fair" (Ryan) **65**:211, 215
"County Ward" (Soto) **80**:286
"The Coup" (Archer) **28**:14
"The Coup" (Chatwin) **59**:279
The Coup (Updike) **13**:559-63; **15**:544, 548; **23**:470; **34**:289; **43**:431; **70**:249; **139**:315-16, 324, 328, 334, 336-37, 364
Le coup de grâce (Yourcenar) **19**:482; **38**:454, 456, 464; **50**:363, 365; **87**:387, 390-91, 394, 396-98, 413-17, 419, 421
Coup de Grâce (Yourcenar)
See *Le coup de grâce*
Le coupable (Bataille) **29**:38-9
"Couperin-Le-Grand in Turkey" (Gustafson) **36**:213
"A Coupla Scalped Indians" (Ellison) **114**:93, 94, 126, 138
"The Couple" (Strand) **71**:286, 288
"A Couple" (Swenson) **106**:337
"The Couple" (Voigt) **54**:431
A Couple of Blaguards (McCourt) **119**:83
A Couple of Comedians (Carpenter) **41**:105-08
"A Couple of Fools" (Bates) **46**:67
"A Couple of Hamburgers" (Thurber) **125**:415
Couples (Updike) **1**:343-45; **2**:440, 442-44; **3**:488; **5**:449-52, 456, 458-59; **7**:485, 489-90; **9**:537-38; **13**:557-59, 561-62; **15**:541, 545; **23**:456-67, 471, 477; **34**:284, 286, 293; **70**:249, 252; **139**:314, 327, 329, 331-32, 334-35, 337-38, 347-48, 352, 357, 368
Couplings and Groupings (Terry) **19**:441
"Coups de couteaux" (Mauriac) **56**:206
"Courage" (Akhmatova) **25**:25; **64**:15
Courage (Akhmatova) **25**:29-30
"Courage Means Running" (Empson) **34**:540
"The Courage of Her Afflictions" (Harrison) **144**:107
"The Courage of Shutting Up" (Plath) **51**:340, 344
The Courage of Turtles (Hoagland) **28**:180-81, 186
"The Courage to See" (Solzhenitsyn) **78**:405
"La courageuse" (Theriault) **79**:408
"The Couriers" (Plath) **111**:204
Le couronnement (Arrabal) **9**:34, 38; **18**:20; **58**:11
"A Course in Filmmaking" (Mailer) **1**:193
Court and Spark (Mitchell) **12**:438, 440, 442
The Court and the Castle (West) **7**:526; **9**:562; **31**:458
"Court Day" (Still) **49**:362
"The Court Historian (A Satirical Composition)" (MacNeice) **53**:233
"Court Martial" (Warren) **39**:268
Court of Appeal (Richards) **14**:453
Court of Chaos (Zelazny) **21**:471-73
"The Court of Divine Justice" (Klappert) **57**:266
"Court of Inquiry" (Amis) **40**:43, 45

"Courtesies of the Interregnum" (Gunn) **81**:187
"Courting Disaster" (Roth) **4**:459
The Courting of Marie Jenvrin (Ringwood) **48**:329-30, 335, 337-39
"Courtly Vision" (Mukherjee) **53**:267, 269
The Courts of Love (Gilchrist) **143**:313-15
"Courts-circuits" (Simon) **15**:497
"Courtship" (Dove) **50**:156-57
"Courtship" (O'Brien) **116**:186
"Courtship" (Strand) **18**:519; **41**:438; **71**:285
"Courtship, Diligence" (Dove) **50**:156
The Courtyard (L'vov) **59**:368
"The Courtyards" (Szirtes) **46**:395-96
Courtyards in Delft (Mahon) **27**:292
Cousin Angélica (Saura)
See *La prima Angélica*
"Cousin Harriet" (Eliot) **13**:202
"Cousin Larry" (Parker) **68**:334, 336
Cousin Rosamund (West) **50**:397
"Cousins" (Bellow) **33**:67-8; **63**:42
"Cousins" (Ihimaera) **46**:200
Les cousins (Chabrol) **16**:167-68, 173-74, 180, 183
"Couvade" (Harris) **25**:217
The Covenant (Michener) **29**:311-14; **109**:375, 379, 381, 386
"Covenant Woman" (Dylan) **77**:185-87, 190
"Coventry" (Heinlein) **55**:302
Cover Charge (Woolrich) **77**:387
"Cover Her Face" (Kinsella) **138**:159, 165-66
Cover Her Face (James) **18**:272; **46**:205, 207, 210; **122**:120, 126, 134, 137
"Cover Note" (Merwin) **88**:209
"Covered Bridge" (Warren) **39**:265
"Covered Bridges" (Kingsolver) **130**:80
The Covered Wagon (Ford) **16**:302
Covering Islam (Said) **123**:347, 358
"The Covering of Light" (Strand) **18**:518
"The Covert" (Blunden) **56**:48
"The Cow" (Ciardi) **40**:157
"The Cow" (Prichard) **46**:332-33, 343, 345
Cow (Sterchi)
See *Blosch*
"The Cow in Apple-Time" (Frost) **26**:112
"Cow in Calf" (Heaney) **14**:243
A Cow in the House and Other Stories (Kiely) **23**:265
The Cow Jumped over the Moon (Birney) **6**:79
"The Cow of the Barricades" (Rao) **56**:291, 312, 314
The Cow of the Barricades and Other Stories (Rao) **56**:287, 291, 294, 296, 306
"The Cow That Swam Lake Ontario" (McFadden) **48**:257
"Coward" (Avison) **97**:80
Coward Plays (Coward) **29**:137
The Cowards (Škvorecký)
See *Zbabělci*
"Cowards from the Colleges" (Hughes) **108**:319
"Cowboy" (Steele) **45**:362
Cowboy Mouth (Shepard) **6**:495; **17**:441, 443-45
Cowboy Mouth (Smith) **12**:534
"Cowboys" (Williams) **56**:427
Cowboys #2 (Shepard) **17**:440-41; **41**:409, 412
"Cowboys and Indians" (Stafford) **4**:517
"Cowgirl in the Sand" (Young) **17**:569
"Cowpats" (Sargeson) **31**:362, 370
"Cows" (Plumly) **33**:313
"Cows: A Vision" (Gallagher) **18**:169
"The Cows at Night" (Carruth) **7**:40; **84**:132
"Cows in Trouble" (Martin) **30**:248
"The Cowshed Blues" (Carruth) **84**:129
"The Cowslip Field" (Bates) **46**:67
"Cowtown" (Simon) **26**:410
"Coyote" (Mitchell) **12**:441-42
"Coyote and the Stro'ro'ka Dancers" (Silko) **74**:348
A Coyote Columbus Story (King) **89**:92, 94, 97-8, 101
"Coyote Holds a Full House in His Hand" (Silko) **23**:411; **74**:349
"Coyote-Mind" (Snyder) **120**:343
"Coyotes" (Mason) **82**:244; **154**:240
Coyote's Daylight Trip (Allen) **84**:3, 11, 38
"Crab" (Adcock) **41**:18
"A Crab" (Gunn) **18**:200
"Crab" (Smith) **42**:347-48
Crab Apple Jelly (O'Connor) **14**:395, 398-400
"Crab Boil" (Dove) **81**:147
"Crab Crack" (Updike) **43**:436
"The Crab Feast" (Malouf) **28**:268
"Crab Orchard Sanctuary: Late October" (Kinsella) **138**:121
"Crabs" (Carey) **96**:27-8, 30, 36, 67
"Crabs" (Piercy) **27**:375
"The Crabs Are Crazy" (Ochs) **17**:335
Crache-à-pic (Maillet) **54**:317-18; **118**:336, 348-49
The Crack in Everything (Ostriker) **132**:320-22, 324-26, 328
The Crack in Space (Dick) **72**:121
Crack Steppin' (Milner) **56**:225
"Cracked Actor" (Bowie) **17**:60
"The Cracked Looking-Glass" (Porter) **101**:211
Crackers: This Whole Many-Angled Thing of Jimmy, More Carters, Ominous Little Animals, Sad Singing Women, My Daddy and Me (Blount) **38**:45-8
A Cracking of Thorns (Hollander) **8**:298
"Cracklin' Rose" (Diamond) **30**:110-11, 113-14
"The Cracks" (Creeley) **78**:143
Cracks (Purdy) **4**:422; **10**:421; **28**:378-79
"Cracks and Keyholes" (Bissoondath) **120**:13, 15, 19
The Crackwalker (Thompson) **39**:253
"Cradle Catholic" (Jennings) **131**:241
"Cradle of Glasnost" (Yevtushenko) **126**:398
"Cradle Song" (Chester) **49**:55
Cradle Song (Andrade)
See *Canção de berço*
"The Cradle Trap" (Simpson) **149**:295, 328, 330
Craft Slices (Bowering) **47**:30-1
The Crafte So Longe to Lerne (Purdy) **3**:408; **6**:428
Craig's Wife (Arzner) **98**:63, 71, 74, 81-3, 86
Crampton Hodnet (Pym) **37**:378-79; **111**:263, 268, 270, 275, 277-78, 283-85
"The Crane" (Watkins) **43**:444
"A Cranefly in September" (Hughes) **37**:180
The Cranes Fly Early (Aitmatov)
See *Rannie zhuravli*
"The Crank" (Baxter) **45**:52; **78**:17
"The Crank That Made the Revolution" (Gray) **41**:183
"Craps" (Oates) **108**:384
Crash (Ballard) **3**:34-5; **6**:27-8; **14**:41; **137**:3, 5, 7-9, 12, 14-16, 18, 21-25, 30-31, 33, 39, 43, 61-62, 69, 74-78
Crash (Cronenberg) **143**:134-35, 137-40, 142, 144-46, 148-49, 152-55, 158
Crash Club (Felsen) **17**:122-23
The Crash of '79 (Erdman) **25**:154-55
Les crasseux (Maillet) **54**:305-07, 310-11, 313-17; **118**:329-32, 334-36, 344, 346
"Crate" (Sturgeon) **22**:411
"Crátion du Monde" (Crase) **58**:164
Craven House (Hamilton) **51**:183, 190, 194
"A Craving for Innocence" (Gary) **25**:186
A Craving for Swan (Codrescu) **46**:105; **121**:157
"Crawfish Love" (Castillo) **151**:65
Crawl (Williams) **33**:444
"Crawling" (Snyder) **120**:358
Crawling Arnold (Feiffer) **64**:159-60
"Crawling Out at Parties" (Bottoms) **53**:29, 31
"Crazy" (Olson) **28**:343
"Crazy as a Soup Sandwich" (Ellison) **139**:144
"Crazy Carlson's Meadow" (Bly) **38**:55, 57
Crazy Cock (Miller) **84**:261
"Crazy, Crazy, Now Showing Everywhere" (Gilchrist) **34**:165; **143**:316
"Crazy Diamonds" (Delany) **141**:146
"Crazy Gypsy" (Salinas) **90**:322, 324, 327
Crazy Gypsy (Salinas) **90**:323-24, 326, 330, 332
"Crazy Horse Dreams" (Alexie) **154**:6
"Crazy Horse names his daughter" (Clifton) **66**:82
"Crazy Horse Speaks" (Alexie) **154**:27
Crazy Horse: The Strange Man of Oglalas (Sandoz) **28**:402-03, 407
"The Crazy Hunter" (Boyle) **19**:64-5; **58**:67
Crazy in Berlin (Berger) **3**:63; **5**:60; **8**:83; **18**:53-4, 57; **38**:36-8
"Crazy in the Stir" (Himes) **58**:265, 267; **108**:227
Crazy John and the Bishop (Eagleton) **132**:137
The Crazy Kill (Himes) **18**:245; **58**:257, 261, 265, 267
Crazy Like a Fox (Perelman) **23**:334, 339; **49**:264
"The Crazy Old Man" (Nissenson) **4**:381
"Crazy Pigeon" (Knight) **40**:279
The Crazy Ray (Clair)
See *Paris qui dort*
Crazy Salad (Ephron) **17**:111-13; **31**:159
"Crazy Times" (Waddington) **28**:440
Cream in My Coffee (Potter) **86**:346
Creamy and Delicious: Eat My Words (Katz) **47**:216, 218, 222
"La créance" (Ferron) **94**:126
"Creating a Personal Mythology" (Wakoski) **40**:454
"Creation" (Harris) **25**:212
"Creation" (Tanizaki) **28**:415
"The Creation" (Van Duyn) **63**:441; **116**:402, 408, 429
Creation (Vidal) **22**:436-40; **33**:407; **72**:385, 387, 301, 303, 322, 329, 333
"The Creation, according to Coyote" (Ortiz) **45**:306
La création culturelle dans la société moderne (Goldmann) **24**:242, 250
La Création de Monde (Cendrars) **106**:190
"Creation of Anguish" (Nemerov) **2**:306-07
"The Creation of the Animals" (Tillinghast) **29**:415
The Creation of the World and Other Business (Miller) **2**:280; **15**:373
The Creative Element: A Study of Vision, Despair and Orthodoxy Among Some Modern Writers (Spender) **91**:261
Creative Fidelity (Marcel) **15**:359
"The Creative Impulse" (Maugham) **67**:219
"The Creative Instinct" (Maugham) **67**:205
"Creative Jive" (Codrescu) **46**:104
Creative Mythology (Campbell)
See *The Masks of God: Creative Mythology*
The Creative Writer (Birney) **11**:50
"The Creator and the Commissars" (Heym) **41**:217
Creature Comforts (Addams) **30**:16
"The Creature from the Black Lagoon" (Jensen) **37**:192
"Creatures" (Jacobsen) **48**:198
Creatures (Colum) **28**:91
Les creátures (Varda) **16**:558
"The Creature's Claim" (Johnston) **51**:243, 245, 247, 252
Creatures in an Alphabet (Barnes) **29**:32; **127**:163
Creatures of Light and Darkness (Zelazny) **21**:464
"Credences of Summer" (Ashbery) **77**:65-66
Credentials of a Sympathiser (Barker) **37**:37
"Credit Due" (Ferron)
See "La créance"
"Credo" (Cohen) **38**:131
"Credo" (McAuley) **45**:253
"Credo" (Rodriguez) **155**:279, 304, 312
Credo: The Apostles' Creed Explained for Today (Kung) **130**:161, 165-66
Credos and Curios (Thurber) **125**:387-88

A Creed for the Third Millennium (McCullough) **107**:139-40, 154
Creek Mary's Blood (Brown) **18**:70-2; **47**:40
Creepshow (King) **26**:239-40, 243-44; **37**:206
"Creon's Mouse" (Davie) **10**.121-22
"Crepe Myrtle" (Aiken) **52**:24
Crépusale (Gallo) **95**:98
Crepúsculario (Neruda) **28**:312-13; **62**:322-23
Le crépuscule des dieux de la steppe (Kadare) **52**:259
"Crepuscule with Nellie" (Simic) **130**:336
Crépuscules (Soupault) **68**:408
"Crescent Moon like a Canoe" (Piercy) **27**:376, 381; **128**:243
Cress Delahanty (West) **7**:521; **17**:545-48, 551
Cressida (Baxter) **14**:62
The Crest on the Silver: An Autobiography (Grigson) **39**:331
"The Cretan Woman" (Jeffers) **54**:242
The Cretan Woman (Jeffers) **11**:306
"Crevasse" (Faulkner) **8**:213
"Crevasses" (Césaire) **112**:20, 22-3, 25
"Crèvecoeur" (Niedecker) **42**:299
"Crèvecoeur" (Reverdy) **53**:283
Le crève-coeur (Aragon) **22**:37
"Crew" (Willard) **37**:463
"Crew-Cuts" (Hall) **37**:142
Le Cri de L'Oiseau Rouge (Danticat) **94**:90-2, 94-6, 98; **139**:85-9, 91-2, 97-9
Cria! (Saura) **20**:316-20
Cria cuervos (Saura)
See *Cria!*
Cría ojos (Dorfman) **77**:141-44
The Cricket beneath the Waterfall and Other Stories (Krleža) **8**:330; **114**:185
Cricket Country (Blunden) **56**:34, 48
"Cricket Master" (Betjeman) **43**:43
"Crickets" (Butler) **81**:129
"Criers and Kibitzers, Kibitzers and Criers" (Elkin) **51**:98
Criers and Kibitzers, Kibitzers and Criers (Elkin) **4**:152, 154; **51**:88, 98-9; **91**:213-14
Cries and Whispers (Bergman)
See *Viskningar och rop*
Cries for Help (Handke)
See *Hilferufe*
The Crime (Mahfouz)
See *al-Jarima*
Crime and Justice in Our Time (Hyde) **21**:180
"Crime & Punishment" (Dybek) **114**:61
"Crime and the Law" (MacInnes) **23**:286
The Crime at Black Dudley (Allingham) **19**:13
The Crime at Lock 14 (Simenon) **47**:369
"Crime at the Tennis Club" (Moravia)
See "Delitto al circolo di tennis"
Le crime de M. Lange (Renoir) **20**:291, 294, 296-98, 306, 309-10
"Le crime de Suzana" (Kadare) **52**:261
A Crime in Holland (Simenon) **47**:370
Crime na Calle Relator (Cabral de Melo Neto) **76**:161
The Crime of Monsieur Lange (Renoir)
See *Le crime de M. Lange*
"The Crime of S. Karma" (Abe)
See "S. Karuma-shi no hanzai"
The Crime of S. Karma (Abe)
See *S. Karuma-shi no hanzai*
The Crime of the Century (Amis) **129**:18
"The Crime of the Mathematics Professor" (Lispector) **43**:269
Crime on Relator Street (Cabral de Melo Neto)
See *Crime na Calle Relator*
Crime Partners (Goines) **80**:94, 96
Crime Passionel (Sartre)
See *Les mains sales*
"Crimes of Conscience" (Gordimer) **33**:184
Crimes of Passion (Orton) **43**:330
Crimes of the Future (Cronenberg) **143**:87, 94, 108, 152
Crimes of the Heart (Henley) **23**:214-17
Crimes Times Three: Cover Her Face. A Mind to Murder. Shroud for a Nightingale (James) **18**:273
"The Criminal" (Tanizaki) **28**:417
The Criminal (Thompson) **69**:386
"A Criminal Act" (Harrison) **42**:203
"Criminal Ballad" (Hughes) **9**:284; **119**:259
"The Criminal Child" (Genet) **14**:197
Criminal Conversation (Freeling) **38**:184-85
The Criminal Life of Archilbaldo de la Cruz (Bunuel)
See *Ensayo de un crimen*
Criminals in Love (Walker)
See *The East End Plays*
The Crimson Gang of Asakusa (Lacey)
See *Asakusa Kurenaidan*
Crimson Ramblers (West) **7**:521; **17**:550
"Crinkle, Near Birr" (Durcan) **70**:147
"The Crinoid" (Watkins) **43**:450
"A Crippen Case in Japan" (Tanizaki) **14**:527
"The Cripple" (Hein) **154**:
"Cripple Creek Ferry" (Young) **17**:569-71, 582
"Crippled Inside" (Lennon) **35**:263-64
"Crise de coeur" (Hollander) **5**:186
Crises of the Republic (Arendt) **98**:11
"The Crisis" (Barthelme) **13**:59; **46**:41
"Crisis" (Berryman) **62**:58
"Crisis" (Marley) **17**:271
Crisis (Bergman)
See *Kris*
Crisis in the Church: A Study of Religion in America (Greeley) **28**:174
"The Crisis of Black Leadership" (West) **134**:359
"The Crisis of Man" (Camus) **69**:104
The Crisis of the Old Order: 1919-1933 (Schlesinger) **84**:351, 380, 382
Crisis: Pages from a Diary (Hesse)
See *Krisis: Ein Stuck Tagebuch*
"Crisscross" (Sommer) **25**:425
Cristo versus Arizona (Cela) **122**:68, 70
Cristóbal nonato (Fuentes) **60**:161, 168-69, 171-73; **113**:251-53
"Cristo's" (Muldoon)
See "Christo's"
Cristoval Colon (Krleža)
See *Kristofor Kolombo*
"Criteria for Negro Art" (Du Bois) **64**:120, 123; **96**:146
"The Critic" (O'Hara) **13**:427; **78**:356
The Critic (Brooks) **12**:76
"The Critic as Clown" (Eagleton) **63**:107
"La critica" (Ginzburg) **54**:207
"Critical Can-Opener" (Brautigan) **3**:89
Critical Condition: Feminism at the Turn of the Century (Gubar) **145**:280, 283-84, 288
Critical Essays (Barthes)
See *Essais critiques*
Critical Essays (Enzensberger) **43**:153-54
"Critical Languages" (Acker) **111**:47
"The Critical Method of R. P. Blackmur" (Schwartz) **10**:462
The Critical Path (Frye) **24**:231; **70**:277
"Critical Self-Consciousness" (Fish) **142**:170
"Critical Theory and Christian Faith" (West) **134**:379
Critical Understanding: The Powers and Limits of Pluralism (Booth) **24**:97-9
Critical Writings, 1953-1978 (de Man) **55**:413-14
"Criticism and Crisis" (de Man) **55**:397
Criticism and Idealogy (Eagleton) **132**:89-90, 93, 122, 131
Criticism and Ideology: A Study in Marxist Literary Theory (Eagleton) **63**:94, 96-7, 101-04, 112-13
Criticism and Social Change (Lentricchia) **34**:571-75
Criticism and Truth (Barthes)
See *Critique et vérité*
"Criticism as Pure Speculation" (Ransom) **4**:434
"Criticism, History, and Critical Relativism" (Brooks) **110**:9, 35
"Criticism in a Mass Society" (Auden) **123**:6-8, 20
"Criticism in the Jungle" (Gates) **65**:366, 378, 398
Criticism in the Wilderness: The Study of Literature Today (Hartman) **27**:185-88
"Criticism, Inc." (Ransom) **24**:368
"Il critico d'arte" (Buzzati) **36**:86
"Critics" (Busch) **47**:62
"Critics and Connoisseurs" (Moore) **47**:262
Critics and Criticism (Crane) **27**:71
"Critics and Thinkers" (Birkerts) **116**:148
"Critics Can Bleed" (Fisher) **25**:160
"A Critic's Job of Work" (Blackmur) **24**:56-7, 62
Critique de la raison dialectique, Volume I: Théorie des ensembles pratiques (Sartre) **4**:474; **7**:390-91, 393-94, 397; **9**:470; **24**:410, 412, 421; **44**:494-95, 498; **50**:382-84; **52**:373, 380, 384-85, 388-89
"Critique de la vie quotidienne" (Barthelme) **3**:43-4; **13**:55-6; **23**:49; **115**:60
Critique et vérité (Barthes) **24**:37; **83**:77-8, 80, 89
Critique of Dialectical Reason: Theory of Practical Ensembles (Sartre)
See *Critique de la raison dialectique, Volume I: Théorie des ensembles pratiques*
"A Critique of Political Ecology" (Enzensberger) **43**:149-50, 154
Critique of the Pyramid (Paz) **119**:411
The Croatian God Mars (Krleža)
See *Hrvatski bog Mars*
"Croatoan" (Ellison) **13**:207; **139**:131-2
"The Crocodile and the Monkey" (Seth) **90**:353
"Crocodile Tears" (Byatt) **136**:194
"The Crocodiles of Yamoussoukro" (Naipaul) **37**:325, 327-29
The Crofter and the Laird (McPhee) **36**:294
Croissez et multipliez (Marcel) **15**:360
Il crollo della baliverna (Buzzati) **36**:91
Crome Yellow (Huxley) **1**:150-51; **4**:238-44; **5**:194; **8**:304; **11**:281-82, 284, 288; **18**:265, 267-69; **35**:235, 240, 243; **79**:287, 306, 309, 326-28
Cromedeyre-le-viel (Romains) **7**:381
Cromwell (Hein) **154**:53, 71, 135, 188
Cromwell (Storey) **4**:529; **5**:416
Cromwell: Our Chief of Men (Fraser) **32**:180-83, 185; **107**:35-38
Cromwell: The Lord Protector (Fraser)
See *Cromwell: Our Chief of Men*
Cronaca di un amore (Antonioni) **20**:19, 21-2, 24, 28; **144**:10, 16, 36, 55, 65, 67, 69, 74, 78-9
Crónica de una muerte anunciada (García Márquez) **27**:148-53, 156-58; **47**:146-48, 151, 153-54; **55**:134; **68**:158, 161
Crónica del alba (Sender) **8**:478, 481
Crónicas de Bustos Domecq (Bioy Casares) **88**:64, 78
Crónicas reales (Mujica Lainez) **31**:281
"Cronkhite Beach" (Tomlinson) **45**:400
Cronopios and Famas (Cortázar)
See *Historia de cronopios y de famas*
Crooked House (Christie) **12**:117, 120; **48**:74-5; **110**:137
The Crooked Lines of God: Poems, 1949-54 (Everson) 1:96; **14**:166
"The Crooked Made Straight" (Agnon)
See "Vehaya he'akov lemishor"
"A Crooked Prayer" (Okri) **87**:314
Crooklyn (Lee) **105**:115-20, 127-28, 130
"Crop Campers" (Davis) **49**:93
Cropper's Cabin (Thompson) **69**:384
"Cross" (Hughes) **10**:280; **108**:314, 334-35
"The Cross" (Tate) **2**:430; **4**:536; **6**:525
Cross Channel (Barnes) **141**:58, 60-2, 69-70
Cross Country (MacLennan) **92**:304, 306, 330, 341, 346, 349
"Cross Cut" (Davison) **28**:103

"Cross Examination" (Sukenick) **48**:369
"Cross My Heart" (Ochs) **17**:334
Cross of Iron (Peckinpah) **20**:282-83
Cross Purpose (Camus)
See *Le malentendu*
"Cross Ties" (Kennedy) **42**:256-57
Cross Ties: Selected Poems (Kennedy) **42**:255-58
Cross Town (Kesselring) **45**:207
Crossbloods: Bone Courts, Bingo, and Other Reports (Vizenor) **103**:311-12
"Crossbones" (Michaels) **25**:314
"Cross-Country Snow" (Hemingway) **1**:143; **10**:269; **30**:181, 191, 197-98
"The Crossed Apple" (Bogan) **39**:393; **46**:78, 83, 86; **93**:64, 96
Cross-Examined (Grass)
See *Ausgefragt*
"The Crossing" (Dumas) **6**:145
The Crossing (McCarthy) **101**:183-85, 187-89, 191-97, 199-205
"Crossing a River" (Wagoner) **15**:560
"Crossing into Eden" (Stegner) **81**:347
Crossing Over (Bass) **143**:11-12
Crossing Over (Elman) **19**:151
"Crossing the Border" (Hillis) **66**:194
Crossing the Border (Oates) **11**:403-04
"Crossing the Great Void" (Abish) **22**:19
"Crossing the Line" (Muldoon) **72**:273
Crossing the Mangrove (Condé)
See *Traversée de la mangrove*
"Crossing the Mississippi" (Hemingway) **30**:197
Crossing the River (Phillips) **96**:350-55, 357
Crossing the River Twice (Haviaras) **33**:202
"Crossing the Rubicon" (Thomas) **37**:419-21; **107**:327-28, 330-31, 349-50
"Crossing the Swamps" (Oliver) **34**:247; **98**:274, 297
Crossing the Threshold of Hope (John Paul II) **128**:181-83, 188-91, 193, 195-200
"Crossing the Water" (Plath) **51**:349; **111**:210, 214-15
Crossing the Water: Transitional Poems (Plath) **1**:270-71; **2**:337-38; **3**:389, 391; **5**:339, 343, 345; **9**:433; **11**:447-49; **14**:424-26; **17**:352-54, 362-64; **62**:389; **111**:158, 166-67, 180-81, 185
Crossing to Safety (Stegner) **49**:360-61; **81**:345, 349-50
"Crossing Water" (Harjo) **83**:282
"Crossings" (Dorfman) **77**:142, 144
"Crossings" (Heaney) **74**:188-89
Crossings (Rovit) **7**:383-84
"Crossover" (Butler) **121**:142
The Crossroad Murders (Simenon) **47**:369, 379
"Crossroads" (Dobyns) **37**:77
"Crossroads" (Gunn) **32**:212
"Crossroads" (Hemingway) **39**:399, 401-02
"Crossroads Inn" (Ryan) **65**:213, 215
"The Crossroads of the World, Etc." (Merwin) **5**:288
The Crossroads of Time (Norton) **12**:467, 470-71
"Cross-Stitch" (Graham) **48**:145
Crosstime Agent (Norton) **12**:469
"Crosswords" (Le Guin) **136**:346
"Crotch Lake" (Sanders) **53**:304
"Crow" (Carroll) **35**:80
"Crow" (Ezekiel) **61**:109
"Crow" (Hogan) **73**:154
Crow (Booth) **13**:103
Crow (Kroetsch)
See *What the Crow Said in his Crow Journal*
"Crow and Mama" (Hughes) **119**:259
The Crow and the Heart (Carruth) **4**:93; **84**:128, 135
"Crow babies" (Piercy) **128**:274
"Crow Blacker Than Ever" (Hughes) **119**:261
"The Crow Catcher" (Arreola) **147**:4-5
"the crow children walking circles in the snow" (Young Bear) **94**:363
Crow: From the Life and Songs of the Crow (Hughes) **2**:199-205; **4**:235-37; **9**:280-81, 283; **14**:272-73; **37**:171-72, 174-81; **119**:252, 258-68, 273, 277, 281, 284-85, 287-88, 291, 295
"Crow Goes Hunting" (Hughes) **119**:259
"Crow Jane in High Society" (Baraka) **115**:39
The Crow Journal (Kroetsch)
See *What the Crow Said in his Crow Journal*
Crow Journals (Kroetsch)
See *What the Crow Said in his Crow Journal*
"Crow Tries the Media" (Hughes) **119**:264
Crowbar (Wellman) **65**:240-41
"The Crowd Punk Season Drew" (Hannah) **90**:127, 130
Crowds and Power (Canetti)
See *Masse und Macht*
"Crowds and Power in the Early Victorian Novel" (Lodge) **141**:351
"Crowing-Hen Blues" (Hughes) **15**:292
The Crown and the Cross (Slaughter) **29**:376
"Crown Fire" (Caldwell) **60**:48
The Crown of Columbus (Dorris) **109**:296-98, 307-09
The Crown of Columbus (Dorris and Erdrich) **70**:332, 348, 355
The Crown of Columbus (Erdrich) **120**:181, 183, 187
A Crown of Feathers, and Other Stories (Singer) **3**:457-59; **6**:509-11; **9**:486-87; **11**:499; **15**:507; **23**:422
"The Crown of Frogs" (Ryan) **65**:209-10, 215-16
"Crown of Thorns" (Celan)
See "Dornenkranz"
"Crown Point Pensioners" (Hughes) **37**:172; **119**:289
The Crown Princess and Other Stories (Brophy) **29**:90-1; **105**:8, 15, 30
Crowned Heads (Tryon) **11**:548-49
"Crowned Out" (Celan) **82**:37
Crownfire (Caldwell) **50**:301
"The Crowning" (Broumas) **73**:16
"Crows" (Carroll) **38**:103
"The Crows" (Ezekiel) **61**:104
"Crows" (Mahapatra) **33**:283
"Crows" (Simic) **49**:336-37
Crows (Dickinson) **49**:101-03
"Crow's Account of St. George" (Hughes) **4**:236; **9**:284; **119**:262, 281
"Crow's Account of the Battle" (Hughes) **4**:236
"Crow's Account of the Battle" (Hughes) **119**:259
"Crows at Paestum" (Garrett) **11**:219; **51**:147
"Crow's First Lesson" (Hughes) **2**:200-01; **119**:259, 262
"Crow's Last Stand" (Hughes) **119**:262
"Crow's Theology" (Hughes) **2**:204; **4**:236
"Crow's Undersong" (Hughes) **119**:259
"Crowson" (Nye) **42**:304
"Croydon" (Betjeman) **43**:52
The Crozart Story (Fearing) **51**:119
Le cru et le cuit (Lévi-Strauss) **38**:297-301, 304, 306, 309
Crucial Conversations (Sarton) **14**:480-81; **91**:245
The Crucible (Miller) **1**:216-17, 219; **2**:278, 280; **6**:326, 328-32; **10**:342, 346; **15**:372-73; **26**:312-15, 319, 324-25, 327; **47**:251, 254, 256; **78**:287-329
Crucible of Power (Williamson) **29**:455
"The Crucifix" (Read) **4**:439
Crucifix in a Deathhand: New Poems, 1963-1965 (Bukowski) **5**:80-1; **41**:67; **82**:15; **108**:81, 110
"The Crucifixion" (Akhmatova) **64**:12
"Crucifixion" (Ochs) **17**:333, 335
"Crucifixions" (Walker) **9**:558
"Crucifixus etiam" (Miller) **30**:262-65
Cruel and Unusual (Cornwell) **155**:62
"The Cruel Falcon" (Jeffers) **54**:244
"Cruel Shoes" (Martin) **30**:246
Cruel Shoes (Martin) **30**:248
"The Cruel Suitor" (Oates) **108**:350-51
The Cruelest Month (Buckler) **13**:121-22
Cruelty (Ai) **4**:16; **14**:7-8; **69**:3-6, 8, 11-13, 16-17
"The Cruise" (Rukeyser) **27**:404
"Cruise (Letters from a Young Lady of Leisure)" (Waugh) **27**:477
The Cruise of "The Breadwinner" (Bates) **46**:61, 63-5
The Cruise of the Cashalot (Edmonds) **35**:147
The Cruise of the Santa Maria (Dillon) **17**:97
"The Cruising Auk" (Johnston) **51**:239, 249-51
The Cruising Auk (Johnston) **51**:238-45, 247-52
"Cruising for Burgers" (Zappa) **17**:585
Cruising Speed (Buckley) **7**:34; **37**:61
Cruising with Reuben and the Jets (Zappa) **17**:585, 589
Crump's Terms (Ghose) **42**:181
"The Crunge" (Page and Plant) **12**:477, 482
"Crusade" (Oz) **5**:335; **8**:436-37
The Crusaders (Heym) **41**:212-13, 216
"A Crusader's Christmas" (Brown) **100**:83
"The Crushed Nettle" (Duras) **68**:90
"Crushing a Butterfly" (McCarthy) **24**:346
"Crusoe in England" (Bishop) **9**:96-7; **13**:89-91, 94-5; **15**:61; **32**:31, 33, 37, 39
Crusoe's Daughter (Gardam) **43**:172-73
"Crusoe's Island" (Walcott) **25**:451-52; **76**:274, 280
"Crusoe's Journal" (Walcott) **76**:281
Crust (Popa) **19**:373
"La cruz" (Parra) **102**:343
"Cruz Alta" (Soupault) **68**:407
"Cruzto, Indian Chief" (Ulibarrí)
See "El cacique Cruzto"
"Cry" (Bagryana)
See "Vik"
"A Cry" (Oe) **86**:241
"The Cry" (Smith) **64**:392
"Cry Ararat!" (Page) **7**:291; **18**:377
"Cry Baby Cry" (Lennon and McCartney) **35**:274
Cry Evil (Rooke) **25**:392-93
"Cry for Me" (Kelley) **22**:247
The Cry for the Dead (Wright) **53**:432
Cry for the Strangers (Saul) **46**:366
"The Cry Going Out over Pastures" (Bly) **10**:62
"Cry Hope, Cry Fury!" (Ballard) **137**:64, 66
A Cry of Absence (Jones) **4**:263
A Cry of Angels (Montgomery) **7**:233
"Cry of Birth" (Clark Bekedermo) **38**:126-27
A Cry of Players (Gibson) **23**:179-80
The Cry of the Crow (George) **35**:178-79
The Cry of the Halidon (Ludlum) **43**:274-75
The Cry of the Owl (Highsmith) **2**:192-93; **102**:170, 172
A Cry of Whiteness (Fleming) **37**:122
Cry Softly! The Story of Child Abuse (Hyde) **21**:180
Cry, the Beloved Country: A Story of Comfort in Desolation (Paton) **4**:395; **10**:387; **25**:357-62; **55**:310-14; **106**:278-79, 281-83, 288, 293-94, 297-300, 304-06, 311
Cry, the Peacock (Desai) **37**:64-70; **97**:142, 149, 151-52, 154, 160-62
Cry to Heaven (Rice) **41**:364-65; **128**:278, 312
"Cry to Me" (Marley) **17**:269
Cry Wolf (Smith) **33**:375-76
Cryer and Ford: You Know My Music (Cryer) **21**:80
The Crying Game (Braine) **1**:43
The Crying Game (Jordan) **110**:282-89, 291-93, 295-309
Crying in the Wilderness: The Struggle for Justice in South Africa (Tutu) **80**:356-57
The Crying of Lot 49 (Pynchon) **2**:354-55, 357; **3**:409-12, 414-15, 417-20; **6**:434-36, 438-

39; **9**:444-45; **11**:452, 455-57; **18**:429-34, 436-37; **33**:327-31, 333-35, 338; **62**:432-33, 436, 439, 443, 445-46, 448-49, 451, 453; **72**:294-342; **123**:294-95, 297, 300, 306-07, 311, 317-18, 320-25, 327-31
The Cryptogram (Mamet) **91**:144-54
Cryptozoic (Aldiss)
See *An Age*
"The Crystal" (Aiken) **52**:24, 26-7
Crystal and Fox (Friel) **5**:128-29; **42**:168; **115**:229, 241
"Crystal Cage" (Kunitz) **148**:90
The Crystal Cave (Stewart) **7**:462; **35**:391, 393-96; **117**:368-69, 376, 385-86, 390-92, 394
Crystal Express (Sterling) **72**:372
"The Crystal Fantasy" (Kawabata)
See "Suishō Gensō"
"The Crystal Garden" (Ballard) **137**:66
The Crystal Garden (Feinstein)
See *The Glass Alembic*
The Crystal Gryphon (Norton) **12**:463, 465
"The Crystal Interior of a Filthy Man" (Rozewicz) **23**:362
"Crystal Lake" (Harjo) **83**:276
The Crystal Lithium (Schuyler) **5**:383
"Crystal Night" (Levertov) **66**:239
"A Crystal Principle" (Young) **82**:396, 412
"The Crystal Ship" (Vinge) **30**:410
"The Crystal Skull" (Raine) **45**:337
Crystal Vision (Sorrentino) **40**:384-87, 389
The Crystal World (Aldington) **49**:15, 18
The Crystal World (Ballard) **6**:27-8; **14**:41; **36**:35-7, 45; **137**:8, 11-13, 17-18, 23, 35, 37, 39, 43, 56, 58-59, 61, 70
C'tà ton tour Laura Cadieux (Tremblay) **102**:375
"Ctesiphon" (Christie) **110**:127
Cuaderno de bitácora de 'Rayuela' (Cortázar) **92**:169, 171-73
Cuaderno San Martín (Borges) **19**:45; **44**:367
"Cualquier tiempo pasado fue peor" (Guillén) **48**:159
"Cuando las mujeres quieren a los hombres" (Ferré) **139**:151, 153-54, 156, 190
La cuarentena (Goytisolo) **133**:84, 86-87
"Cuarta versión" (Valenzuela) **31**:438, 440; **104**:372, 377-78
"Un cuarteto y su desenlace" (Ferré) **139**:175
Cuatro para Delfina (Donoso) **99**:242
"Cuba" (Hemingway) **6**:232; **8**:285
"Cuba" (Muldoon) **32**:321; **72**:266
Cuba (Lester) **20**:232
"Cuba, 1962" (Ai) **69**:3-4, 8, 11, 13
Cuba and His Teddy Bear (Povod) **44**:86-90
"Cuba Confrontation" (Clark Bekedermo) **38**:129
"Cuba libre" (Baraka) **14**:48
Cuba Libre (Leonard) **120**:301
"Cuba: Púeblo y poesía" (Guillén) **79**:238
"Cuba Revisited" (Gellhorn) **60**:191
Cuba, Yes? (Caute) **29**:119
The Cuban Thing (Gelber) **1**:114
The Cube Root of Uncertainty (Silverberg) **7**:425
"The Cubs" (Vargas Llosa)
See "Los cachorros"
The Cubs, and Other Stories (Vargas Llosa)
See *Los cachorros*
Cuchama and Sacred Mountains (Waters) **88**:365
"El cuchillo y la piedra" (Marqués) **96**:227, 244
"Cuckold's Song" (Cohen) **38**:131
"Cuckoo Corn" (Muldoon) **72**:265
The Cuckoo Tree (Aiken) **35**:17
"The Cuckoo-Spit" (Lavin) **4**:281; **99**:321-22
Cuckooz Countrey (Slessor) **14**:492, 495
"Cud dnia poweszedniego" (Rozewicz) **139**:262
Cue for Passion (Rice) **7**:363; **49**:301-02
"Cuento de dos jardines" (Paz) **65**:183, 198; **119**:419-20
Cuentos (Donoso) **4**:127; **8**:180; **99**:223
Cuentos (Moraga) **126**:270-72, 274
Cuentos breves y extraordinarios (Bioy Casares) **88**:64
Los cuentos de Juan Bobo (Ferré) **139**:153
Los cuentos de Lilus Kikus (Poniatowska) **140**:330
Cuentos puertorriqueños de hoy (Marqués) **96**:229
Cuentos: Stories by Latinas (Moraga) **126**:289
Cugel's Saga (Vance) **35**:428
"The Cuirassiers of the Frontier" (Graves) **45**:162
Cuisine Novella (Laurent) **50**:59-61
Cujo (King) **26**:238-42; **37**:203, 208; **61**:319, 321, 331; **113**:335, 342-45, 347, 355-56, 358-59, 369, 388, 390
"Cul De Sac Valley" (Walcott) **67**:360
"Culag Pier" (MacCaig) **36**:282
Cul-de-sac (Polanski) **16**:463-68, 471-72
Cul-de-sac (Theriault) **79**:400, 403, 412
"Cullen" (Page) **18**:377
"Culloden and After" (Smith) **64**:394
"The Cult of Experience in American Writing" (Rahv) **24**:352, 355-56
"The Cult of Power" (Warner) **45**:435
The Cult of Power (Warner) **45**:433-34, 441
"The Cultivated Man" (Phillips) **28**:362-63
"The Cultivation of Christmas Trees" (Eliot) **41**:152
"El culto de los libros" (Borges) **83**:169
"Cultural Center" (Montague) **46**:266
"Cultural Conservatism and Democratic Education" (Barber) **141**:5, 7
Cultural Creation (Goldmann)
See *La création culturelle dans la société moderne*
"Cultural Directives" (Szirtes) **46**:395
"A Cultural Exchange" (Godwin) **31**:198
"Cultural Exchange" (Hughes) **35**:218
"Cultural Exchanges" (Hacker) **72**:192
"Cultural Freedom" (Enright) **31**:150, 155
"Cultural History as a Synthesis" (Barzun) **145**:101
"Cultural Literacy" (Hirsch) **79**:267
Cultural Literacy (Hirsch) **79**:265, 270-71, 273-77, 279-80
"'Cultural Literacy' Does Not Mean 'Core Curriculum'" (Hirsch) **79**:267
"Cultural Man" (Mead) **37**:280
"Cultural Mis-readings by American Reviewers" (Kingston) **121**:282, 297, 301, 304, 320
"Cultural Notes" (Fearing) **51**:117
The Cultural Turn (Jameson) **142**:264-65
"Culture and Anarchy" (Rich) **36**:376; **125**:322
Culture and Commitment: A Study of the Generation Gap (Mead) **37**:275-77
"Culture and Destiny" (Powys) **125**:270
Culture and Environment (Leavis) **24**:301
"Culture and Futurology" (Lem) **149**:123, 278
"Culture and Human Relations" (Powys) **125**:270
Culture and Imperialism (Said) **123**:358, 374, 376-77, 379-81, 383, 385, 390, 392, 396-97
"Culture and Love" (Powys) **125**:270
"Culture and Nature" (Powys) **125**:269
"Culture and the Art of Reading" (Powys) **125**:270
"Culture High and Dry" (Barzun) **145**:72
"Culture Now: Some Animadversions, Some Laughs" (Bellow) **8**:74
The Culture of Narcissism (Lasch) **102**:289-90, 293-94, 301, 319
The Culture of Terrorism (Chomsky) **132**:32, 36, 40, 67
"Culture or Mimicry" (Walcott)
See "Caribbean: Culture or Mimicry"
"Culture, Self, and Style" (Gass) **39**:482; **132**:167
"Culture: The Antinomy of the Scientific Method" (Percy) **6**:401
The Culture We Deserve (Barzun) **145**:69-72, 74, 76
The Cultures of Globalizatione (Jameson) **142**:267
"Cumberland Station" (Smith) **22**:385-86
Cumberland Station (Smith) **22**:384-87, 389; **42**:346, 348, 350, 352-53
"Cummings" (Davenport) **38**:141
La cumpana apelor (Blaga) **75**:77-8
Cumpleaños (Fuentes) **41**:167; **60**:158; **113**:253
The Cunning Man (Davies) **91**:198, 200-3, 207, 209, 210
"Cunt and Kant and a Happy Home" (Bukowski) **41**:68
"El cuòr su l'agua" (Pasolini) **106**:260
Cup of Gold: A Life of Henry Morgan, Buccaneer, with Occasional References to History (Steinbeck) **1**:325-26; **5**:407; **9**:512; **21**:380, 390; **34**:409, 411; **45**:374; **59**:322, 333; **75**:349-50
The Cupboard (Tremain) **42**:384-85
"Cupid and Psyche" (Elytis) **100**:189
"The Cupola" (Bogan) **93**:90-2, 96, 102-03, 105
"Cups with Broken Handles" (Ashbery) **41**:37
"Cura pastoralis" (Hood) **28**:189, 193
"The Curable Romantic" (Fuller) **62**:206
"The Curb in the Sky" (Thurber) **125**:410-11
"The Cure" (King) **8**:321
"Cure" (Moure) **88**:224
"The Cure" (Simic) **22**:380
The Cure (Foreman) **50**:160-62, 164-65, 168-69
The Cure at Troy: A Version of Sophocles' Philoctetes (Heaney) **74**:195-96; **91**:124
A Cure for Cancer (Moorcock) **27**:349-50; **58**:347-49
A Cure for Dreams (Gibbons) **88**:127-28, 131-32; **145**:147, 149-50, 152-54, 159-67, 169-70, 172-73, 175, 184
"The Cure for Warts" (Muldoon) **32**:315
Curfew (Donoso)
See *La Desesperanza*
Curious (Bowering) **15**:83; **47**:22, 28
"The Curious Child" (Matheson) **37**:246
"Curlew" (Clarke) **61**:82
"The Curlew" (Watkins) **43**:454
"Curls and a Quiet Country Face" (Bowles) **68**:9
"The Current" (Merwin) **88**:202
"Current Account" (Tremain) **42**:386
"Current Status 1/22/87" (Monette) **82**:321, 332
The Currents of Space (Asimov) **19**:25; **26**:48, 64
A Curriculum of Inclusion: Report of the Commissioner's Task Force on Minorities (New York Dept. of Ed.) **70**:371, 374, 378
"Curriculum vitae" (Hirsch) **50**:196
Curries and Other Indian Dishes (Anand) **93**:23-4
"A Curse" (Morrissy) **99**:78
"The Curse" (Prichard) **46**:332, 343, 345
"A Curse against Elegies" (Sexton) **123**:446
"The Curse of Eve" (Atwood) **84**:89
The Curse of Lono (Thompson) **40**:430-31
"Curse of the Earth Magician" (Piercy) **14**:406; **27**:375
Curse of the Starving Class (Shepard) **17**:446-47; **34**:267, 269, 271; **41**:409-11, 413-14, 416; **44**:264-66, 268-69
The Curse of the Viking Grave (Mowat) **26**:336-37, 342-43
"The Cursed Play" (Tanizaki) **28**:417
"The Curtain" (Wright) **53**:426
Curtain (Christie) **6**:108, 110; **8**:140-42; **12**:120-22; **48**:71, 77-8; **110**:120-21, 123
"A Curtain of Green" (Welty) **105**:368
A Curtain of Green and Other Stories (Welty) **1**:362; **14**:561-62; **22**:458-59; **33**:414; **105**:298
Curtain Up (Streatfeild) **21**:407, 416
La curţile dorului (Blaga) **75**:67, 78
Curtmantle (Fry) **2**:143-44; **10**:200-01; **14**:186
"Curva minore" (Quasimodo) **10**:427

"Curve of Binding Energy" (McPhee) **36**:295, 297
"Cushendun" (MacNeice) **53**:237
"Cuss-Cuss" (Bennett) **28**:29
"The Custard Heart" (Parker) **68**:327, 334-35, 340
"Custard Pie" (Page and Plant) **12**:477
Custer Died for Your Sins: An Indian Manifesto (Deloria) **21**:108-11; **122**:108-10, 113, 117
"The Custodian" (Hill) **113**:281, 294, 297, 310
The Custom House (King) **53**:205-07; **145**:351
"The Custom of the World" (Simpson) **149**:321
"Customers" (Lively) **32**:277
The Customs Collector in Baggy Pants (Ferlinghetti) **111**:63
"Customs of the Country" (Bell) **102**:6
"The Customs-Collector's Report" (Kunitz) **148**:89
"The Customs-Officer's House" (Montale) See "La casa dei doganieri"
"Cut" (Dixon) **52**:95, 97
"Cut" (Plath) **9**:426-27; **17**:348, 351, 359; **51**:340, 342-43; **111**:160-63, 182, 185, 203
"Cut Flower" (Peacock) **60**:293
"Cut Glass" (Barthelme) **117**:5
"Cut Grass" (Larkin) **5**:229-30; **8**:333, 339; **39**:333, 345; **64**:282
"Cut of Mind" (Broumas) **73**:9
The Cut Pages (Fisher) **25**:160, 162
"Cut the Grass" (Ammons) **9**:27; **25**:44
"Cut Worm" (Fisher) **25**:160
"Cute Chick!" (Kelman) **58**:301-02
The Cut-Rate Kingdom (Keneally) **43**:233-34; **117**:225
Cuts (Bradbury) **61**:40-2, 44-7
"The Cutter-Off of Water" (Duras) **68**:100-02
Cutter's World (Ellison) **139**:129
"Cuttin Down to Size" (Dumas) **6**:145
"The Cutting Edge" (Levine) **4**:286
The Cutting Edge (Gilliatt) **13**:238-39
"Cutting Greens" (Clifton) **66**:88
Cutting Lisa (Everett) **57**:217
Cutting Timber (Bernhard) See *Holzfällen: Eine Erregung*
"Cuttings" (Hoffman) **141**:270, 273
"Cuttings" (Roethke) **11**:485; **19**:397; **11**:485
"Cuttings (Later)" (Roethke) **101**:293, 334
Cuttlefish Bones (Montale) See *Ossi di seppia*
"Cuvinte duhovniceşti" (Arghezi) **80**:3
Cuvinte potrivite (Arghezi) **80**:6-11
"Cy" (Dixon) **52**:98, 100
Cybele (Oates) **33**:289
Cyberiad: Fables for the Cybernetic Age (Lem) **8**:344; **15**:327-28; **40**:296; **149**:123-27, 154, 156-57, 159, 165, 243, 255, 272, 274-75, 278
"Cybernetics and Ghosts" (Calvino) **73**:45, 48
"The Cycads" (Wright) **53**:418
"Cyclamen" (Thomas) **48**:380
"Cycle" (Kunene) **85**:165
"The Cycle" (Roethke) **19**:397; **46**:362
"Cycle Number Twenty-Two" (Nichol) **18**:369
Cycle of the Werewolf (King) **37**:205; **61**:331; **113**:361, 365, 388
A Cycle of the West (Neihardt) **32**:334-35, 337-38
Cycle Smash (Chambers) **35**:98
"The Cycles of American History" (Schlesinger) **84**:379
The Cycles of American History (Schlesinger) **84**:379-81, 383, 385-86
"The Cycles of American Politics" (Schlesinger) **84**:385
"The Cyclical Night" (Borges) See "La noche cíclica"
"Cycling in the Lake District" (Murray) **40**:336
"A Cyclist" (Goodman) **4**:197
"The Cyclone" (Hesse) **6**:237
The Cyclone (Asturias) **3**:18; **8**:27-8
"Cynddylan on a Tractor" (Thomas) **48**:375
"Cynic Song" (Eberhart) **56**:75
"Cynthia" (Simpson) **7**:429
"Cynthis in California" (Laughlin) **49**:221
Cypress and Acacia (Watkins) **43**:442-43, 451-52, 456
"Cypress & Cedar" (Harrison) **129**:219
The Cypresses Believe in God (Gironella) See *Los cipreses creen en Dios*
Cyrano (Burgess) **81**:301
"Cyril" (Willingham) **51**:403
Cyrion (Lee) **46**:232
Cyrion in Stone (Lee) **46**:232
"Cyrion in Wax" (Lee) **46**:231
"czarne plamy s biale..." (Rozewicz) **139**:297
"The Czar's Last Christmas Letter: A Barn in the Urals" (Dubie) **36**:132
Czas Nietracony (Lem) **149**:165, 255, 263, 282
Czerwona rękawiczka (Rozewicz) **23**:358
Czeslaw Milosz: The Collected Poems, 1931-1987 (Milosz) **56**:246, 249, 251; **82**:290, 296-99, 303, 309-11
Czlowiek z Marsa (Lem) **149**:260-61, 282
"Czy pan instnenije, Mr. Johns?" (Lem) **149**:149
"Czytanie ksiązQDOTek" (Rozewicz) **139**:295
"D" (Cummings) **15**:160
"D" (Merrill) **8**:383-85
"D. D. Byrde Callyng Jennie Wren" (Snodgrass) **68**:399
D. H. Lawrence (West) **50**:360
D. H. Lawrence: An Unprofessional Study (Nin) **4**:379
D. H. Lawrence, Novelist, Poet, Prophet (Spender) **91**:263
Da (Leonard) **19**:281, 283
"Da Da Da Da Da" (McGrath) See "After I'm Gone"
Da Silva da Silva's Cultivated Wilderness (Harris) **25**:211, 216
Da Vinci's Bicycle (Davenport) **14**:142; **38**:139, 148
"D'Accord, Baby" (Kureishi) **135**:284
"The Dacey Players...." (Dacey) **51**:83
Dad (Wharton) **37**:435-38, 441-43
"Dada" (Boyle) **36**:57
"Daddy" (Clifton) **66**:74
"Daddy" (Plath) **2**:336; **3**:390; **5**:341, 343; **9**:424-26, 430; **11**:445-50; **14**:423-26, 428; **17**:346-48, 350, 353, 356, 359, 363, 369; **50**:440; **51**:342-45, 353; **62**:404-05, 415; **111**:159, 166, 173-76, 178-79, 181-82, 208-09, 211, 216-19, 221
"Daddy" (Tevis) **42**:372, 377
Daddy (Greer) See *Daddy, We Hardly Knew You*
Daddy Boy (Cameron) **59**:47-51
Daddy Cool (Goines) **80**:93, 98
Daddy, Daddy (Durcan) **70**:146-54
"Daddy Don't Live in That New York City No More" (Becker and Fagen) **26**:79-80
"Daddy, Don't Strike the Match" (Nwapa) **133**:187
"Daddy Garbage" (Wideman) **36**:455; **122**:289
Daddy, We Hardly Knew You (Greer) **131**:190, 192, 212
"Daddy with Chesterfields in a Rolled Up Sleeve" (Castillo) **151**:11
"Daddy Wolf" (Purdy) **28**:378-79
Daddyji (Mehta) **37**:292, 294-95
Daddy's Girl (Savage) **40**:372-73
"Daddy's Song" (Kristofferson) **26**:270
"Daddy's Tune" (Browne) **21**:39
Dador (Lezama Lima) **101**:121
"Daedalus" (Barker) **48**:9
"Daedalus" (Squires) **51**:380
Daedalus (Squires) **51**:378
"Daedalus Broods on the Equestrian Olympic Trials" (Hearne) **56**:127
"The Daemon" (Bogan) **46**:81; **93**:65
"The Daemon Lover" (Jackson) **60**:212, 235
The Daffodil Fields (Masefield) **11**:357; **47**:226-28, 230
"The Daffodil Murderer" (Sassoon) **130**:189-91, 193
The Daffodil Murderer (Sassoon) **36**:389; **130**:181, 192, 212
"Daffodildo" (Swenson) **106**:341
"Daffodils" (Brown) **100**:87
"Daffy Duck in Hollywood" (Ashbery) **15**:30; **77**:46, 48, 61
Dage paa en sky (Abell) **15**:1, 6
Dagger of the Mind (Fearing) **51**:109, 112, 116
Daggers and Javelins: Essays, 1974-1979 (Baraka) **33**:61-2; **115**:14, 30
Dago Red (Fante) **60**:130-31, 133
Dagon (Chappell) **40**:138-40; **78**:97-100, 110, 112, 114, 116
"Daguerreotypes" (Dinesen) **95**:61
Daguerreotypes (Varda) **16**:559
Daguerreotypes, and Other Essays (Dinesen) **95**:58, 61
The Dahomean (Yerby) **22**:490
"Dahomey" (Lorde) **71**:232
The Daily Round (Lopate) **29**:299
The Dain Curse (Hammett) **3**:218-19; **10**:252; **19**:193, 195-96; **47**:156, 159-61
The Dainty Monsters (Ondaatje) **14**:407-08; **29**:341; **51**:310, 316
"Daisy" (Johnston) **51**:243
"Daisy" (Maugham) **67**:220
"Daisy's Valentine" (Gaitskill) **69**:199
Daiyon kampyoki (Abe) **22**:12; **53**:5-6; **81**:285, 290
"Dakar Hieroglyphs" (Armah) **1**:52; **136**:73
Dal fondo delle comagne (Luzi) **13**:352
"Dal laboratorio" (Pasolini) **106**:247
The Dalkey Archive (O'Brien) **1**:252; **4**:383, 385; **7**:270; **10**:362-63; **47**:313-14, 316, 318-20
Dal'she...Dal'she...Dal'she! (Shatrov) **59**:358, 361-62
Dalva (Harrison) **66**:159-60, 163-66, 168-69, 171; **143**:341-45, 351, 353, 355, 359-60
"Dam Neck, Virginia" (Eberhart) **19**:144; **56**:79
La dama del alba (Casona) **49**:42-6, 49-52
Damage (Hare) **136**:256
Damage (Hart) **70**:59-64
Damaged Goods: The Great Play "Les avariés" by Brieux, Novelized with the Approval of the Author (Sinclair) **63**:348
The Damages (Howard) **7**:165, 168; **10**:276; **47**:167-68
"Damals in Odessa" (Boell) **72**:69, 79
The Damask Drum (Mishima) **27**:343-45
"Damastes z przydomkiem Prokustes mówi" (Herbert) **43**:186
"Damballah" (Wideman) **122**:304, 307, 309, 314, 320-21, 323, 344
Damballah (Wideman) **34**:298, 300; **36**:454-55; **67**:374, 380; **122**:289-90, 292, 303, 305, 307, 315-17, 319, 322, 327-32, 335-36, 340, 343, 345-48, 355, 363, 367
Dam-Burst of Dreams (Nolan) **58**:361-62, 366
La dame dans l'auto avec des lunettes et un fusil (Japrisot) **90**:168, 170
"Dame of the British Empire, BBC" (Gilliatt) **53**:145
La dame qui avait des chaînes aux chevilles (Carrier) **78**:73
Les dames du Bois de Boulogne (Bresson) **16**:103, 107-09, 111
"Dämmerung" (Celan) **82**:52
"The Damnation" (Kizer) **80**:173
"Damnation Alley" (Zelazny) **21**:479
Damnation Alley (Zelazny) **21**:464-65, 479
The Damnation Game (Barker) **52**:52, 55-7
"Damnation of Vancouver" (Birney) **6**:74-5
"Damned" (Berryman) **10**:51; **62**:74
The Damned (Fanon) See *Les damnés de la terre*
The Damned (Visconti) **16**:568-70, 574-75
Damnée Manon, sacrée Sandra (Tremblay) **29**:419, 422-25, 427; **102**:375
Les damnés de la terre (Fanon) **74**:71-2, 74-86

"Damoetas" (Hollander) **5**:186
"Der Dampfkessel-Effekt" (Grass) **32**:199
Dan Leno and the Limehouse Golem (Ackroyd) **140**:50
Dan Yack (Cendrars)
See *Les confessions de Dan Yack*
"Danae" (Le Guin) **45**:212
"Danae" (Howes) **15**:289
"The Dance" (Duncan) **15**:192
"Dance" (Kenny) **87**:240
"The Dance" (Larkin) **64**:258, 260, 263-64, 280-81
"The Dance" (Strand) **71**:285
"The Dance" (Thomas) **107**:333
The Dance and the Railroad (Hwang) **55**:151-52
"The Dance Called David" (Weiss) **14**:556
"Dance, Dance" (Shapcott) **38**:399, 401
"Dance, Dance, Dance" (Wilson) **12**:644, 647, 651
Dance, Dance, Dance (Murakami)
See *Dansu, Dansu, Dansu*
Dance, Girl, Dance (Arzner) **98**:63-4, 73-8, 81, 84, 86-7, 90-1
"Dance Hall" (Miller) **14**:373
Dance Hall of the Dead (Hillerman) **62**:251-54, 256-57, 259
Dance in the Desert (L'Engle) **12**:348-49
A Dance in the Sun (Jacobson) **4**:255-56
The Dance Is One (Scott) **22**:376
Dance Lessons for Adult and Advanced Pupils (Hrabal)
See *Taneční hodiny pro starší a pokročilé*
Dance Me Outside (Kinsella) **27**:235-37; **43**:258, 260
"Dance: Nicaragua" (Jordan) **114**:146
Dance Night (Powell) **66**:366
The Dance of Death (Auden) **11**:18; **14**:30-1; **43**:15-16, 18, 29
"The Dance of Death and Human Inequality" (Milosz) **56**:232
The Dance of Genghis Cohn (Gary) **25**:186
A Dance of the Forests (Soyinka) **3**:462; **5**:396; **14**:506-07; **36**:410; **44**:279-83, 285, 287
"Dance of the Girls' Chemises" (Seifert) **93**:333
"Dance of the Happy Shades" (Munro) **95**:284, 287
Dance of the Happy Shades and Other Stories (Munro) **6**:341-42; **10**:357; **19**:343-44; **50**:210; **95**:284, 295-97, 300, 302, 312-13
The Dance of the Intellect: Studies in the Pound Tradition (Perloff) **137**:271-73, 276, 282, 288, 290, 293-94
"The Dance of the Solids" (Updike) **23**:475
Dance of the Years (Allingham) **19**:12
"Dance of Words" (Graves) **11**:256
Dance on My Grave (Chambers) **35**:100-01
Dance on the Earth (Laurence) **50**:314, 320; **62**:304-08
"Dance Piece" (Belitt) **22**:49
"Dance Script with Electric Ballerina" (Fulton) **52**:159
Dance Script with Electric Ballerina (Fulton) **52**:157-61
Dance the Eagle to Sleep (Piercy) **3**:383-84; **62**:362-65, 381; **128**:218-20, 240-41, 244
"Dance the Night Away" (Carroll) **35**:81
Dance: The Ritual of Experience (Highwater) **12**:287-88
A Dance to Still Music (Corcoran) **17**:73-4
A Dance to the Music of Time (Powell) **1**:277-78; **3**:400-04; **7**:338-46; **9**:435-39; **10**:408-18; **31**:314, 316-23
A Dance, with Some Many Words (Olson) **11**:420
"The Dancer" (Cabral de Melo Neto)
See "A bailarina"
"The Dancer" (Govier) **51**:166
"Dancer" (Hoffman) **141**:279, 310
"The Dancer" (Swados) **5**:420
The Dancer (Kawabata)
See *Maihime*
The Dancer from Atlantis (Anderson) **15**:15
Dancer from the Dance (Holleran) **38**:245-47
Dancer with One Leg (Dobyns) **37**:79
Dancers at Night (Richards) **59**:187, 189
"Dancers at the End of Time" (Moorcock) **5**:294
"Dancers at the Moy" (Muldoon) **72**:264
Dancers, Buildings, and People in the Streets (Denby) **48**:82
"Dancers Exercising" (Clampitt) **32**:116
Dancers in Mourning (Allingham) **19**:15
Dancers in the Scalp House (Eastlake) **8**:200
Dancers on the Shore (Kelley) **22**:246, 250
Dances of Death (Tindall) **7**:474
"Dancey" (Brown) **100**:82-3
Dancin' (Fosse) **20**:126
"Dancin' with Mr. D" (Jagger and Richard) **17**:228, 238
"Dancing" (Bissoondath) **120**:3-4, 7
"The Dancing" (Stern) **40**:413-14
Dancing (Young) **19**:477, 480
Dancing After Hours (Dubus) **97**:234-38
Dancing at Lughnasa (Friel) **115**:233, 236-39, 241, 245, 250
Dancing at the Edge of the World (Le Guin) **136**:326-29, 334, 336-40, 342, 362, 364-68, 387
Dancing Aztecs (Westlake) **33**:437-38
Dancing Back Strong the Nation (Kenny) **87**:238-41
"Dancing Barefoot" (Smith) **12**:544
"Dancing Bear" (Vanderhaeghe) **41**:449
The Dancing Bear (Dickinson) **12**:170-71, 174-75
The Dancing Bears (Merwin) **1**:212; **2**:276; **5**:284; **8**:389; **13**:384; **45**:268; **88**:205
The Dancing Chicken (Musgrave) **54**:341-42
"Dancing Days" (Page and Plant) **12**:476, 482
"The Dancing Dwarf" (Murakami) **150**:56, 61
"The Dancing Girls" (Ferber) **93**:139
Dancing Girls, and Other Stories (Atwood) **13**:44-46; **25**:61-2, 70; **84**:70, 96
Dancing in Cambodia, At Large in Burma (Ghosh) **153**:116-17
"The Dancing Mistress" (Bowen) **118**:75, 98
"Dancing on Park Avenue" (Dunn) **36**:151-52
Dancing on the Grave of a Son of a Bitch (Wakoski) **4**:574; **9**:554; **40**:455
"The Dancing Party" (Gordon) **128**:110
"Dancing Sam" (Browne) **21**:41
Dancing Shoes (Streatfeild)
See *Wintle's Wonders*
"Dancing To Ganam" (Le Guin) **136**:385
"Dancing with Poets" (Voigt) **54**:432
Dandelion on the Acropolis (Stuart) **34**:375
Dandelion Wine (Bradbury) **1**:42; **10**:68-70; **15**:84; **42**:36, 42, 44; **98**:111, 144
"Dandelions" (Silkin) **43**:398
"Dandy; or, Astride the Funky Finger of Lust" (Bullins) **7**:37
"The Dane's Place" (Donoso)
See "Dinamarquero"
The Danger (Francis) **42**:152-53; **102**:162
"The Danger at Funny Junction" (Bell) **8**:65
Danger: Memory! (Miller) **47**:255-58
Danger Signal (Samarakis)
See *Sima kindynou*
The Danger Tree (Manning) **19**:302, 304
Dangerous Corner (Priestley) **2**:346; **5**:351; **34**:361, 363-64
Dangerous Crossings (Donnell) **34**:156, 158
"Dangerous Dads" (Leyner) **92**:293-94
A Dangerous Encounter (Jünger) **125**:258, 261
Dangerous French Mistress, and Other Stories (Colwin)
See *Passion and Affect*
"The Dangerous Gift" (Graves) **1**:129
"A Dangerous Man" (Faulkner) **18**:149
A Dangerous Mourning (Perry) **126**:340
"Dangerous Play" (Motion) **47**:293-94
Dangerous Play: Poems, 1974-1984 (Motion) **47**:290-93
"A Dangerous Remedy" (Davies) **23**:142
Dangerous Spring (Benary-Isbert) **12**:33, 35
The Dangerous Summer (Hemingway) **6**:226; **41**:201-04
Dangerous Visions (Ellison) **13**:203
"Dangerous Woman" (Rooke) **25**:391
"The Dangling Conversations" (Simon) **17**:458-59, 464-66
Dangling in the Tournefortia (Bukowski) **41**:69-70; **82**:5, 13
Dangling Man (Bellow) **1**:28-32; **2**:49, 51, 53; **3**:48-52, 55; **6**:56-7, 60; **8**:69-71, 74, 78; **10**:39, 43; **13**:71-2; **15**:47-50, 52-56; **25**:80, 85; **33**:65-6; **63**:31-2; **79**:76, 80, 82
The Dangling Witness (Bennett) **35**:44-5
Daniel Come to Judgement (Hocking) **13**:285
Daniel Martin (Fowles) **9**:213-16; **10**:188-90; **15**:232-33; **33**:164, 166, 171-75; **87**:141, 148, 158, 161-62, 164, 167-70, 172, 178-84
Danny and the Deep Blue Sea: An Apache Dance (Shanley) **75**:320, 328
Danny Boy (Jordan)
See *Angel*
Danny Hill (King) **53**:213
"Danny in Transit" (Leavitt) **34**:77
Danny O'Neill (Farrell) **11**:195
"Danny's Girls" (Mukherjee) **115**:363
"Dans la marche" (Char) **9**:164
Dans la pluie giboyeuse (Char) **14**:126
Dans le labyrinthe (Robbe-Grillet) **1**:286, 289-90; **2**:374; **4**:447-48, 450; **6**:465-68; **8**:451-52; **10**:437; **14**:456-57, 461; **43**:360, 362; **128**:326-27, 331-33, 344-46, 354, 356-57, 359, 362, 368, 382
Dans le leurre du seuil (Bonnefoy) **9**:114; **15**:73; **58**:50-1, 54, 56-7, 60-1
"Dans le restaurant" (Eliot) **57**:206
"Dans les années profondes" (Jouve) **47**:204
Dans les années sordides (Mandiargues) **41**:275
"Danse Macabre" (Faludy) **42**:139, 142
"Danse Macabre" (Raine) **32**:349
Danse Macabre (King) **113**:336, 338, 355, 366, 390, 392
Dansu, Dansu, Dansu (Murakami) **150**:51-5, 63, 65, 67, 86-7, 92
"Dante" (Akhmatova) **64**:16
Dante (Baraka)
See *The Eighth Ditch*
Dante (Eliot) **24**:182-83
"Dante and the Lobster" (Beckett) **10**:29
"Dante... Bruno. Vico.. Joyce" (Beckett) **11**:34; **29**:67; **59**:260
"Dante Etudes" (Duncan) **41**:128-30; **55**:298
The Danzig Trilogy (Grass) **15**:259; **22**:193; **88**:175
Danziger Trilogie (Grass)
See *The Danzig Trilogy*
Daphne du Maurier: The Secret Life of the Renouwned Storyteller (Forster) **149**:83, 85, 87, 89, 94-5
"Daphne with Her Thighs in Bark" (Boland) **40**:100; **113**:70-1, 124
Dar (Nabokov) **1**:242; **2**:299-300, 305; **3**:355; **6**:355; **8**:415, 417-18; **11**:392; **23**:309; **44**:467, 469; **46**:291; **64**:366
Darconville's Cat (Theroux) **25**:432-34
D'arcs de cycle la dérive (Brossard) **115**:121
Darcy's Utopia (Weldon) **122**:266
"Darfsteller" (Miller) **30**:260, 262, 265
Daria (Blaga) **75**:65-6
"Darien" (Graves) **2**:175
"The Daring Young Man on the Flying Trapeze" (Saroyan) **1**:301; **8**:468; **29**:361; **34**:457; **56**:374-75
"The Dark" (Jones) **76**:65
"The Dark" (Oates) **6**:367
The Dark (McGahern) **5**:280; **9**:371-72; **48**:260-63, 269-72
Dark Adaptation (Transtroemer)
See *Mörkerseende*
"Dark Ages" (Reid) **33**:350
The Dark Ages (Asimov) **76**:312
The Dark and Feeling: Black American

Writers and Their Work (Major) **19**:293, 295
"The Dark and the Fair" (Kunitz) **148**:70, 73, 88
The Dark and the Light (Vittorini) **6**:551; **14**:544
The Dark Arena (Puzo) **1**:282; **2**:352; **6**:429; **36**:358, 362; **107**:174-76, 199, 212, 215
"Dark Arm, Hanging over the Edge of Infinity" (Williams) **45**:443-44
"Dark around Light" (Bowering) **47**:19
The Dark at the Top of the Stairs (Inge) **1**:153; **8**:307-08; **19**:226-30
The Dark at the Top of the Stairs (Kazan) **63**:234
"Dark Benediction" (Miller) **30**:263-64
"The Dark Brain of Piranesi" (Yourcenar) **38**:461
The Dark Brain of Piranesi, and Other Essays (Yourcenar)
See *Sous bénéfice d'inventaire*
Dark Bridwell (Fisher) **7**:105
Dark Brown (McClure) **6**:320
The Dark Canoe (O'Dell) **30**:268-70
The Dark Child (Laye)
See *L'enfant noir*
"Dark City" (Bernstein) **142**:29-30
Dark City (Bernstein) **142**:21-31
Dark Companions (Campbell) **42**:90-1
Dark Conceit: The Making of Allegory (Honig) **33**:209-10
"Dark Continent" (Reading) **47**:352
"A Dark Country" (Mahon) **27**:288
The Dark Crusader (MacLean) **50**:349-50
The Dark Dancer (Prokosch) **48**:315
The Dark Daughters (Davies) **23**:142-43
Dark Entries (Aickman) **57**:2
The Dark Eye in Africa (van der Post) **5**:463
"Dark Eye in September" (Celan) **82**:36
"Dark Farmhouses" (Simic) **130**:312
Dark Fields of the Republic (Rich) **125**:335-37
The Dark Frontier (Ambler) **4**:19
"Dark Gift" (Wright) **53**:428
"Dark Glasses" (Longley) **29**:293
Dark Glasses (Hood) **28**:191-92
The Dark Glasses (King) **53**:204-05
Dark Green, Bright Red (Vidal) **33**:406
Dark Habits (Almodovar)
See *Entre Tinieblas*
The Dark Half (King) **61**:337; **113**:388, 390-92
Dark Harvest (Ringwood) **48**:329-30, 334-39
Dark Horse (Knebel) **14**:309
"Dark Horse of Darran" (Prichard) **46**:333
"Dark House" (Plath) **11**:446, 448; **111**:164, 167, 179
"Dark Houses" (Davison) **28**:102
The Dark Is Light Enough (Fry) **2**:143-44; **10**:200-02; **14**:186-87
The Dark Is Not So Dark (Everson) **27**:134
Dark Is the Sun (Farmer) **19**:168
The Dark Journey (Green)
See *L'eviathan*
The Dark Kingdom (Patchen) **1**:265
The Dark Labyrinth (Durrell) **1**:85
The Dark Lady (Auchincloss) **9**:55
"Dark Lagoon" (Reaney) **13**:473
"The Dark Men" (Dubus) **97**:204-05
The Dark Mountains (Hoffman) **141**:264, 266, 272, 276, 281, 296-97, 301
The Dark Night of Resistance (Berrigan) **4**:57
A Dark Night's Passing (Shiga)
See *Anya Kōro*
"Dark O' the Moon" (Brown) **59**:262
"Dark Odyssey of Soosie" (Mowat) **26**:344-45
Dark of the Woods (Koontz) **78**:199
"Dark Pines under Water" (MacEwen) **13**:358
Dark Piper (Norton) **12**:458, 461, 464, 467
"The Dark Place Inside" (Potok) **112**:280
Dark Places of the Heart (Stead) **2**:421-22; **5**:403; **32**:408-09, 412, 414; **80**:305, 307, 311-12, 316, 331, 339, 341, 345
Dark Pony (Mamet) **15**:358; **46**:250-51
Dark Princess (Du Bois) **64**:113-14, 117-18
"Dark Prophecy: I Sing of Shine" (Knight) **40**:284
Dark Quartet (Banks) **23**:42
"Dark Rings" (Levine) **4**:286
The Dark River (Millin) **49**:238-39, 243, 246
"Dark Room" (H. D.) **31**:213
"The Dark Room" (Williams) **45**:454
The Dark Room (Narayan) **28**:299; **121**:357, 360
The Dark Root of a Scream (Valdez) **84**:397-98, 406, 413
"Dark Sheila" (Christie) **110**:126, 128
The Dark Side of Genius: The Life of Alfred Hitchcock (Spoto) **39**:445, 451-52
"The Dark Side of the Earth" (Zweig) **42**:467
The Dark Side of the Earth (Zweig) **34**:378; **42**:466-67
The Dark Side of the Moon (Pink Floyd) **35**:306-13, 315
"The Dark Smoke" (Dorris) **109**:309-10
"Dark Song" (Ammons) **108**:8
"The Dark Song" (Shamlu) **10**:471
The Dark Store (Perec)
See *La boutique obscure*
"Dark Summer" (Bogan) **93**:95
Dark Summer (Bogan) **39**:390; **46**:77-80, 89-90; **93**:90, 92-4, 96, 103
"The Dark Sun" (Hirsch) **31**:215
"Dark Symphony" (Tolson) **36**:424-25, 427; **105**:239, 260, 282, 288
The Dark Symphony (Koontz) **78**:197
Dark Symphony (Tolson) **105**:282
Dark Testament (Abrahams) **4**:1
"Dark They Were, and Golden-Eyed" (Bradbury) **42**:32
The Dark Tower (MacNeice) **53**:239-40
The Dark Tower: The Gunslinger (King) **61**:337; **113**:381-82, 388-89, 393
The Dark Tunnel (Macdonald) **14**:332-33; **34**:416; **41**:265
"A Dark Walk" (Taylor) **18**:526-27
"Dark Waters of the Beginning" (Okigbo) **84**:312
"Dark Ways We Lead Each Other" (Livesay) **79**:344
Dark Wedding (Sender)
See *Epitalamio del prieto Trinidad*
"Dark Well" (Thomas) **48**:380
"Dark Wild Honey" (Swenson) **106**:339
The Dark Wind (Hillerman) **62**:255-56, 258
A Dark-Adapted Eye (Rendell) **48**:326-27
A Dark-Adapted Eye (Vine) **50**:263-64
"The Darkened Room" (Hoffman) **141**:283, 285, 287-88
"Darkening Hotel Room" (Corn) **33**:115
"The Darkening Moon" (Stafford) **68**:434
"Darker" (Strand) **41**:438
"Darker Ends" (Nye) **42**:305
Darker Ends (Nye) **13**:412; **42**:304-05
Darker: Poems (Strand) **6**:521-22; **18**:515, 517-19; **41**:436; **71**:278, 284-86
The Darker Proof (White) **110**:324-26
Darker Than Amber (MacDonald) **27**:275; **44**:408
Darker than You Think (Williamson) **29**:455-56, 459-60
Darkfall (Koontz) **78**:197, 202-03, 206-07, 209-17
"Darkmotherscream" (Voznesensky) **57**:421
"The Darkness" (Purdy) **50**:240-41
"Darkness" (Wain) **46**:415
Darkness (Brink)
See *Kennis van die Aand*
Darkness (Mukherjee) **53**:265-68, 270-71; **115**:365, 386
Darkness and Day (Compton-Burnett) **34**:500
"Darkness and Light" (Spender) **10**:492
The Darkness and the Dawn (Costain) **30**:99
Darkness at Noon (Kingsley) **44**:235-36, 238
Darkness at Noon (Koestler) **1**:170; **3**:270-71; **6**:281; **8**:324-25; **15**:310, 312; **33**:227-30, 233-35, 239-44
Darkness at Noon (Solzhenitsyn) **78**:380
Darkness Casts No Shadow (Lustig) **56**:184-85
A Darkness in My Soul (Koontz) **78**:199, 203
Darkness in Saint Louis Bearheart (Vizenor) **103**:284-85, 288, 294-96, 298, 304, 310, 314-19, 323-25, 327-28, 330, 332-33, 348-52
"The Darkness of Practical Reason" (Murdoch) **6**:349
The Darkness of the Body (Plante) **7**:307; **23**:344
Darkness on the Edge of Town (Springsteen) **17**:482, 484-86, 490
"A Darkness on the Mountain" (Hoffman) **141**:309
"The Darkness Out There" (Lively) **32**:277
The Darkness Surrounds Us (Sorrentino) **7**:449; **22**:391
"Darkness 'til Dawn" (Simon) **26**:410
"Darkness under the Trees" (Salinas) **90**:332
Darkness under the Trees/Walking behind the Spanish (Salinas) **90**:331
Darkness Visible (Golding) **17**:178-81; **27**:161-64, 166-67, 169; **81**:317-20, 323, 325
Darkover (Bradley) **30**:26-7, 29, 32
Darkover Landfall (Bradley) **30**:26, 28, 30
"Darkroom" (McCartney) **35**:288
"The Darkwater Hall Mystery" (Amis) **40**:43-5
Darkwater: Voices from within the Veil (Du Bois) **64**:104, 116; **96**:138
"Darlin'" (Wilson) **12**:643, 645, 651
"Darling" (Dixon) **52**:100
Darling (Raphael) **14**:436-37
"Darling Boy" (Lennon)
See "Beautiful Boy"
The Darling Buds of May (Bates) **46**:58-60
"Darling, It's Frightening! When a Poet Loves ..." (Pasternak) **10**:383
"Darling Nikki" (Prince) **35**:331-32
Darrell (Montgomery) **7**:232
"Darryl and the Moose" (McFadden) **48**:243
The D'Arthez Case (Nossack)
See *Der Fall d'Arthez*
"Dartmoor" (Christie) **110**:127
"Darwin" (Niedecker) **42**:296, 300
"Darwin in 1881" (Schnackenberg) **40**:378-80
Darwin, Marx, Wagner: Critique of a Heritage (Barzun) **51**:35, 50; **145**:71-2, 101
"Darwin's Ark" (Appleman) **51**:17
Darwin's Ark (Appleman) **51**:16-17
"Darwin's Bestiary" (Appleman) **51**:17
"Darwin's Rubber Plant" (Faludy) **42**:137, 140
"Dash It" (Dillard) **115**:210
Dashiell Hammett: A Life (Johnson) **48**:203-04
Dasma (Kadare) **52**:258-59
A Date for Diane (Cavanna) **12**:97-9
"Date with a Bird" (Tolstaya) **59**:371
Dateless Diary (Narayan) **121**:353
"Dates: Penkhull New Road" (Tomlinson) **6**:536
"Dating Your Mom" (Frazier) **46**:163-65
Dating Your Mom (Frazier) **46**:163-65
"Dative Haruspices" (Rexroth) **112**:397
Dauber (Masefield) **11**:357-58; **47**:225-31, 233
"Daughter" (Caldwell) **60**:60
"Daughter" (Fuller) **62**:206
"Daughter" (Voigt) **54**:430
Daughter Buffalo (Frame) **2**:142; **3**:164; **6**:190; **22**:145-46; **66**:145; **96**:179, 181-82, 184-86, 191-92, 194, 197, 199, 217
"The Daughter Finds Her Father Dead" (Durcan) **43**:118
"Daughter in the House" (Kennedy) **42**:257
"Daughter, Last Glimpses Of" (Updike) **15**:547
"Daughter of Invention" (Alvarez) **93**:9
Daughter of Jerusalem (Maitland) **49**:230-31, 234
Daughter of Regals and Other Tales (Donaldson) **46**:142-43; **138**:41
Daughter of Silence (West) **33**:427-28
Daughter of the Legend (Stuart) **11**:514; **34**:377

"A Daughter of the Sun Is She" (Kunitz) **148**:87
Daughters (Marshall) **72**:254-60
A Daughter's a Daughter (Christie) **1**:58; **39**:442
Daughters and Sons (Compton-Burnett) **15**:137-38, 141; **34**:500
A Daughter's Geography (Shange) **38**:394; **126**:364
Daughters, I Love You (Hogan) **73**:148, 150, 152, 156
"The Daughters of Blossom Street" (Plath) **3**:390; **11**:450
Daughters of Earth (Enright) **31**:150
Daughters of Eve (Duncan) **26**:106-07
"The Daughters of Mama Sea" (Shamlu) **10**:471
Daughters of Men (Orton) **13**:437
"Daughters of Passion" (O'Faolain) **47**:328
Daughters of Passion (O'Faolain) **47**:327-28, 331
"Daughters of the Vieux Carré" (Rooke) **25**:390
"Daumier" (Barthelme) **46**:36, 41; **115**:65, 70, 89
"De Daumier-Smith's Blue Period" (Salinger) **138**:183, 202
"Dauntless Little John" (Calvino) **22**:90
"D'autres chants" (Senghor) **54**:409
"Dave Loves Macker 14.2.83" (Durcan) **43**:117
Dave Sulkin Cares (Knebel) **14**:309
Davey Logan, Intern (Felsen) **17**:121
"David" (Birney) **6**:72, 74-6, 79; **11**:51
"David" (Pasolini) **106**:228
"David" (Pastan) **27**:369
David (John Paul II) **128**:163, 168
David and Broccoli (Mortimer) **28**:283-85
David and Other Poems (Birney) **6**:72
David Bowie (Bowie) **17**:67
David Knudsen (Elliott) **2**:130-31
David Live (Bowie) **17**:63-4, 68
"David Lynch Keeps His Head" (Wallace) **114**:388
"David Riesman Reconsidered" (Mailer) **111**:104
The David Show (Gurney) **50**:175, 184
David Starr, Space Ranger (Asimov) **26**:35, 41
David Sterne (Blais) **4**:67; **6**:82
"David Watts" (Davies) **21**:91
Davita's Harp (Potok) **112**:266-67, 269, 293
Davor (Grass) **2**:173; **4**:204; **11**:248; **49**:139
"Dawn" (Dudek) **19**:136
"Dawn" (Lowell) **4**:304
"Dawn" (Mahapatra) **33**:277-78, 282
"Dawn" (Powers) **1**:280
"Dawn" (Williams) **148**:340
Dawn (Buero Vallejo)
See *Madrugada*
Dawn (Butler) **121**:88-100, 103, 105, 108-09, 111, 117-18, 120, 136-37, 139, 143
Dawn (Wiesel)
See *L'aube*
"Dawn at Puri" (Mahapatra) **33**:283
Dawn Ginsbergh's Revenge (Perelman) **5**:337; **23**:334-35, 337; **44**:501-02; **49**:257-59, 261, 264, 270
"The Dawn in Erewhon" (Davenport) **6**:125; **14**:139; **38**:140, 147-48
"The Dawn of Phallocentrism" (Cixous) **92**:85, 87
Dawn of Remembered Spring (Stuart) **34**:376
Dawn O'Hara (Ferber) **93**:135, 140, 146, 172
Dawn to the West: Japanese Literature of the Modern Era (Keene) **34**:566-70
"Dawn Travellers" (Miller) **14**:373
"Dawn Walk" (Hirsch) **50**:197
Dawn Wind (Sutcliff) **26**:429-31, 433-36, 439
"Dawnings" (Livesay) **79**:348
"Dawns" (Milosz) **82**:297-98
"The Daws" (Thurber) **5**:435
"The Day" (Fuller) **28**:149
"The Day" (Lowell) **9**:336
"Day" (Tomlinson) **45**:398, 400-01
"A Day" (Trevor) **116**:395
"The Day After" (Soto) **80**:290
"Day after Chasing Porcupines" (Welch) **52**:428
Day after Day (Quasimodo)
See *Giorno dopo giorno*
The Day after Judgment (Blish) **14**:83, 87
"The Day after My Friends became Godly and Great" (Mahapatra) **33**:284
The Day after Sunday (Summers) **10**:493-94
"The Day After Superman Died" (Kesey) **46**:224-26, 228
"Day and Night" (Césaire) **32**:111
Day and Night (Livesay) **15**:339, 341; **79**:332, 342, 345-46
The Day and the Way We Met (Stolz) **12**:549-50
"a day at the oak tree meet" (Bukowski) **108**:75
"The Day Bed" (Eberhart) **11**:178
"The Day Before" (Endō)
See "Sono zenjitsu"
"The Day Before" (Spencer) **22**:402
"The Day before the Revolution" (Le Guin) **13**:348; **136**:311-12, 343
The Day before Tomorrow (Hikmet) **40**:248
A Day Book (Creeley) **2**:108; **4**:118; **8**:153; **11**:138; **15**:151; **78**:128-30, 133
"Day by Day" (Lowell) **124**:298
Day by Day (Lowell) **8**:357; **9**:336, 339; **11**:330-31; **15**:344; **37**:232, 236, 238-39; **124**:254-55, 263, 290-91, 297-98, 301-03
Day by Night (Lee) **46**:231
"Day Dream" (Thesen) **56**:421
"Day Falcon" (Gotlieb) **18**:191
"A Day for Anne Frank" (Williams) **33**:441-43; **148**:343
Day for Night (Truffaut)
See *La nuit américaine*
"The Day He Died" (Hughes) **37**:176; **119**:271
"The Day He Himself Shall Wipe My Tears Away" (Oe)
See "Mizu kara waga namida o nuguitamo hi"
"The Day I Don't Remember" (Rule) **27**:423
The Day I Met a Lion (Kantor) **7**:195
"The Day I Was Conceived" (Rose) **85**:313
"A Day in Africa" (Du Bois) **64**:114, 117
"A Day in Late October" (Van Duyn) **7**:498; **63**:439; **116**:402-03
"A Day in Salamanca" (Squires) **51**:379, 381-82
The Day in Shadow (Sahgal) **41**:371
"A Day in the Country" (Millhauser) **54**:324-27
"A Day in the Dark" (Bowen) **22**:65-6
A Day in the Death of Joe Egg (Nichols) **5**:305-08; **36**:326-27, 329-34; **65**:161-62, 164
"A Day in the Jungle" (Jackson) **60**:213
"A Day in the Life" (Lennon and McCartney) **12**:357-58, 368, 374; **35**:264
"A Day in the Life of a Doe" (Allen) **52**:35
"A Day in the Open" (Bowles) **68**:6-7
The Day Is Dark (Blais)
See *Le jour est noir*
"The Day Itself" (Merwin) **88**:210, 212
"The Day Lady Died" (O'Hara) **5**:325; **78**:337-38, 344, 349, 376
The Day Lasts More than a Century (Aitmatov)
See *I dol'she veka dlitsia den'*
The Day Lasts More than a Hundred Years (Aitmatov)
See *I dol'she veka dlitsia den'*
"A Day Like Rousseau's Dream" (Swenson) **61**:405
"A Day Marked With A Small White Stone" (Simic) **130**:294-95
A Day Marked X (Heym)
See *Five Days in June*
A Day No Pigs Would Die (Peck) **17**:336-39, 341
Day of Absence (Ward) **19**:456-58
The Day of Creation (Ballard) **137**:3-4, 10-11, 13-14, 16-17, 50, 61
"Day of Foreboding" (Kunitz) **148**:107-08
"The Day of Forever" (Ballard) **3**:33
Day of Freedom—Our Armed Forces (Riefenstahl) **16**:522, 525
"A Day of Old Age" (Le Clézio) **31**:243
A Day of Pleasure: Stories of a Boy Growing Up in Warsaw (Singer) **111**:311
"A Day of Rain" (Mahapatra) **33**:281, 284
"Day of Success" (Plath) **11**:450
The Day of the Burning (Malzberg) **7**:209
"Day of the Butterfly" (Munro) **95**:291
The Day of the Dog (Frayn) **31**:188; **47**:135
"The Day of the Dying Rabbit" (Updike) **2**:445
The Day of the Jackal (Forsyth) **2**:136-37; **5**:125; **36**:174-75, 177
The Day of the Owl (Sciascia)
See *Il giorno della civetta*
"Day of the Rat" (Sondheim) **30**:390
The Day of the Scorpion (Scott)
See *The Raj Quartet*
"The Day of the Small Winds" (Souster) **14**:505
"The Day of the Starter" (Durcan) **43**:114
The Day of the Triffids (Wyndham) **19**:474-76
"The Day of Treachery" (Kunene) **85**:162
"Day of Wrath" (Davison) **28**:103
"Day of Wrath" (Jhabvala) **94**:173
Day of Wrath (Child) **19**:100
Day of Wrath (Dreyer) **16**:256-61, 263-66, 269
"The Day Off" (Sondheim) **39**:174
"A Day on the Big Branch" (Nemerov) **36**:303, 305
The Day Room (DeLillo) **54**:85
"The Day Slats Fell for a Girl" (Royko) **109**:407
"The Day Stalin Died" (Lessing) **22**:277
"The Day That Beaumont Became Aquainted with His Pain" (Le Clézio) **31**:243-44
"The Day the American Empire Ran Out of Gas" (Vidal) **142**:331
"The Day the Buffalo Danced" (Martin) **30**:248
The Day the Call Came (Hinde) **6**:239, 241
"The Day the Dancers Came" (Santos) **22**:365-66
The Day the Leader Was Killed (Mahfouz)
See *Yawm qutila'l-z'im*
"The Day the Pig Fell into the Well" (Cheever) **7**:49
The Day the Whales Shall be Annihilated (Oe)
See *Kujira no shimetsu suru hi*
The Day the Whores Came Out to Play Tennis (Kopit) **18**:286-87, 289; **33**:248, 250
"The Day They Burned the Books" (Rhys) **14**:447; **51**:370, 375
The Day They Came to Arrest the Book (Hentoff) **26**:187-88
"The Day We Got Drunk on Cake" (Trevor) **116**:384
The Day We Got Drunk on Cake, and Other Stories (Trevor) **7**:475; **71**:324; **116**:332
"Day without Night" (Glück) **44**:215, 222-23
"Daybreak" (Aldington) **49**:7
"Daybreak" (Kinnell) **129**:241
"Daybreak" (Leithauser) **27**:242
"Daybreak" (Pasternak) **63**:312-13
"Daybreak" (Soto) **80**:286-87
Daybreak (Slaughter) **29**:376
"Daybreak at Pisa" (Findley) **102**:108
"Daybreak at the Maternity Ward" (Everson) **27**:133
"Daybreak in Alabama" (Hughes) **108**:332-33
The Daybreakers (L'Amour) **25**:280
Daydream Mechanics (Brossard)
See *Mécanique jongleuse*
"Daydreams" (O'Connor) **23**:325
Daylight (Milosz) **82**:298
"Daylight Katy" (Lightfoot) **26**:282
"Daylilies on the Hill" (Hall) **151**:208
"Daynights" (MacEwen) **55**:164
"Days" (Davies) **21**:107
"Days" (Larkin) **8**:332; **39**:344; **64**:268-69, 271, 285
Days (Figes) **31**:163-64
Days (Robison) **42**:338-43; **98**:318
"Day's Affirmation" (Read) **4**:439
"Days and Nights" (Koch) **44**:248-49
Days and Nights (Koch) **44**:248
Days and Nights in Calcutta (Blaise) **29**:71

Days and Nights in the Forest (Ray)
See *Aranyer din ratri*
Days and Nights of Love and War (Galeano) **72**:129-31, 143-44
Days and Occasions (Paz)
See *Días hábiles*
The Days Before (Porter) **13**:447; **101**:223
Days between Stations (Erickson) **64**:137-40, 142, 144
"Day's End" (Bates) **46**:49
Day's End and Other Stories (Bates) **46**:49, 53
The Days In Yellow Leaf (Hoffman) **141**:264-65, 272, 274, 276, 293, 296-97, 307
"Days of 1935" (Merrill) **2**:275; **6**:323
"Days of 1992" (Hacker) **91**:110
Days of 1945-1951: A Poet's Journal (Seferis) **5**:385; **11**:493-94
The Days of Awe (Agnon) **8**:9
Days of Grass (Lee) **46**:232
"Days of Heaven" (Bass) **143**:10, 13, 21
Days of Man (Bitov)
See *Dni cheloveka*
"The Days of Nietzsche" (Stern) **40**:406, 408
Days of Obligation: An Argument with My Mexican Father (Rodriguez) **155**:252, 254-55, 257, 260-63, 265, 268, 272, 274-76, 281, 287-93, 295-97, 299-300, 303, 305, 315, 319, 335
"Days of the Dancing" (McKuen) **3**:332
Days of the Year (Johnson)
See *Jahrestage: Aus dem Leben von Gesine Cresspahl*
Days of Thunder (Towne) **87**:374
Days of Wine and Neuroses (Mull) **17**:299
Days of Wrath (Malraux)
See *Le temps du mépris*
Days on a Cloud (Abell)
See *Dage paa en sky*
The Days Run Away Like Wild Horses over the Hills (Bukowski) **82**:4, 15; **108**:81
"Days through Starch and Bluing" (Fulton) **52**:161
Days to Come (Hellman) **2**:187; **14**:258-59; **18**:221, 226; **34**:348; **52**:191
"A Day's Wait" (Hemingway) **6**:231
"A Day's Work" (Capote) **19**:85
The Daysman (Middleton) **38**:334-35
"Daystar" (Deane) **122**:83
"Daystar" (Dove) **50**:154; **81**:139
"Daytona" (Cernuda) **54**:55
"Dazed and Confused" (Page and Plant) **12**:478
"Dazzle" (Capote) **19**:85
"D-Day and After: Temembering a Scrapbook I Cannot Find" (Kroetsch) **132**:281
D-Day, June 6, 1944: The Climactic Battle of World War II (Ambrose) **145**:37, 39-42, 53, 55
Un de baumugnes (Giono) **4**:186; **11**:233
"The de Cats Family" (Dinesen) **10**:149-50; **95**:67
"La dea cieca e veggente" (Landolfi) **49**:214
"The Deacon" (Updike) **7**:488
"Deacon Blues" (Becker and Fagen) **26**:84
"The Deacon's Tale" (Rooke) **25**:392-93
"The Dead" (Dudek) **11**:158
"The Dead" (Oates) **108**:354, 368, 370-71
"The Dead" (Senghor) **130**:280
Dead and Buried (Rozewicz)
See *Do piachu*
The Dead and the Living (Olds) **32**:346-47; **39**:186-93; **85**:287-88, 291-92, 300, 305
"Dead as They Come" (McEwan) **66**:275, 279, 280-81
"The Dead Astronaut" (Ballard) **137**:39
Dead Babies (Amis) **9**:26; **38**:11-13; **62**:5, 7, 12, 17; **101**:59-63, 86-89
"Dead Baby" (Dobyns) **37**:82
The Dead Beat (Bloch) **33**:83
"A Dead Boche" (Graves) **45**:166
Dead Cert (Francis) **2**:142-43; **22**:154; **42**:148-49, 153; **102**:131-32, 140-41, 144-47, 153, 159-60
Dead Certainties (Unwarranted Speculations) (Schama) **150**:131-39, 141-42, 160, 162, 164, 172-73, 178
"Dead Color" (Wright) **146**:302, 309
"The Dead Cow in the Canyon" (Ferron) **94**:128
"Dead doe lying in the rain" (Snyder) **120**:325
"Dead Dog" (Scannell) **49**:326
"Dead Elms by a River" (Leithauser) **27**:241-42
Dead End (Kingsley) **44**:231-34, 237-38
"Dead End Street" (Davies) **21**:97
"Dead Every Enormous Piece" (Cummings) **15**:162
The Dead Father (Barthelme) **6**:31; **8**:49-52, 54; **13**:58; **46**:35, 45; **59**:247, 249; **115**:63-5, 67, 78-9, 81, 87, 92-6, 98-9
Dead Fingers Talk (Burroughs) **75**:93
"Dead Flowers" (Jagger and Richard) **17**:230
"Dead Gallop" (Neruda)
See "Galope muerto"
The Dead Girls (Ibarguengoitia)
See *Las muertas*
"Dead Horses and Live Issues" (Simpson) **149**:319
The Dead House (Ritsos) **31**:325-26; **13**:488-89
"The Dead in Korea" (Dybek) **114**:74
"The Dead in Melanesia" (Jarrell) **9**:298
The Dead Kingdom (Montague) **46**:277, 279
"The Dead Lad" (Pasolini) **106**:260
"Dead Lakes" (Waddington) **28**:438
Dead Languages (Shields) **97**:421-34
"A Dead Leaf" (Moss) **45**:292
"Dead Leaf in May" (Aiken) **52**:28
Dead Leaves (García Márquez)
See *La hojarasca*
The Dead Lecturer (Baraka) **3**:35; **5**:44-6; **10**:20; **115**:31, 38-9
"Dead Letters" (Blunden) **56**:40
Dead Letters (King) **145**:368
Dead Letters Sent, and Other Poems (Kenny) **87**:245
"Dead Mabelle" (Bowen) **118**:75
"The Dead Man" (Borges)
See "El muerto"
"Dead Man" (McPherson)
See "The Story of a Dead Man"
Dead Man Blues (Woolrich) **77**:400
A Dead Man in Deptford (Burgess) **81**:303, 312-13
Dead Man Leading (Pritchett) **41**:335
Dead Man's Folly (Christie) **12**:124
"Dead Man's Path" (Achebe) **26**:21-3
"The Dead Man's Room" (Logan) **5**:255
Dead Man's Walk (McMurtry) **127**:351-52
Dead Men Don't Wear Plaid (Martin) **30**:251-52
"Dead Men's Fingers" (Longley) **29**:294
"Dead Musicians" (Sassoon) **130**:185, 222
The Dead of the House (Greenberg) **3**:202
"Dead on Her Feet" (Woolrich) **77**:403
"The Dead Poet" (Purdy) **50**:248
"The Dead Poets of Vancouver" (Bowering) **47**:33
The Dead Priestess Speaks (H. D.) **31**:208
"Dead Reckoning" (Shacochis) **39**:199-200
Dead Reckoning (Fearing) **51**:106-07, 110
Dead Ringers (Cronenberg) **143**:57-61, 63-65, 70-73, 83, 88, 94-98, 100-09, 116, 118, 126, 138-39, 143, 147, 152
"Dead Roses" (White) **69**:398
"Dead Roses" (Woolrich) **77**:389, 398
The Dead School (McCabe) **133**:107-11; 113, 119-21
The Dead Sea Scrolls (Wilson) **2**:477
The Dead Seagull (Barker) **8**:43; **48**:21
"The Dead Seal near McClure's Beach" (Bly) **15**:63; **128**:16, 32
"The Dead Shall Be Raised Incorruptible" (Kinnell) **129**:244, 258
Dead Snowmen (Foreman) **50**:169
"Dead Soldiers" (Chappell) **40**:145; **78**:91, 95
"Dead Soldiers" (Fenton) **32**:166, 169
Dead Star Station (Williamson) **29**:454
"Dead Still" (Voznesensky) **57**:414
"The Dead Time" (Ballard) **36**:47; **137**:14, 16, 37-38
Dead Voices: Natural Agonies in the New World (Vizenor) **103**:312, 320, 334-37, 340
Dead Water (Marsh) **53**:250-51
"The Dead Wingman" (Jarrell) **9**:299; **13**:300
The Dead Without Burial (Sartre)
See *Morts sans sépulture*
Dead Yesterdays (Ginzburg)
See *Tutti i nostri ieri*
The Dead Zone (Cronenberg) **143**:57, 70, 77-83, 94-95, 97-98, 100-01, 107, 116, 118-19, 152
The Dead Zone (King) **26**:234, 237-39, 242; **37**:201-02, 204; **61**:319, 329; **113**:336, 342, 344-45, 347, 360, 363, 388, 390
Dead-End Werther (Fiedler) **24**:188
Deadeye Dick (Vonnegut) **40**:441-46
The Deadline (Duerrenmatt)
See *Die Frist*
Deadline at Dawn (Odets) **98**:197, 245-46
Deadline at Dawn (Woolrich) **77**:389-91, 393-94, 396, 398-99, 404-05
The Deadlined (Canetti)
See *Die Befristeten*
Deadlock (Paretsky) **135**:308-09, 324, 334-35, 349, 363-64
The Deadly Companions (Peckinpah) **20**:272, 283
The Deadly Gift (Bennett) **35**:42-3
Deadly Hall (Carr) **3**:101
"Deadly Leap" (Alegria) **75**:49
Deadly Nightshade (Daly) **52**:87
A Deadly Shade of Gold (MacDonald) **44**:408
"Deaf Cities" (Ostriker) **132**:326
Deafman Glance (Wilson) **7**:549
"Deaf-Mutes at the Ballgame" (Jacobsen) **48**:190, 195; **102**:237
Dealing in Futures (Haldeman) **61**:181-82
Dealing; or, The Berkeley-to-Boston Forty-Brick Lost-Bag Blues (Crichton) **54**:66
"Dealing with the Mystics" (Cioran) **64**:79, 82
"Dean of Men" (Taylor) **18**:523; **50**:251
The Dean's December (Bellow) **25**:81-6; **33**:67, 70-1; **34**:546; **63**:32-4
"Dear Alexandros" (Updike) **23**:473
"Dear Amnesty" (Hospital) **145**:304-05
Dear and Glorious Physician (Caldwell) **28**:61-2; **39**:302-03
Dear Antoine; or, The Love That Failed (Anouilh)
See *Cher Antoine; ou, L'amour raté*
Dear Bill, Remember Me? and Other Stories (Mazer) **26**:291, 295
Dear Carolyn: Letters to Carolyn Cassady (Kerouac) **29**:278
"Dear David" (Breytenbach) **126**:76
The Dear Deceit (Brooke-Rose) **40**:103-04
Dear Departed (Yourcenar)
See *Souvenirs pieux*
Dear Diego, with hugs from Quiela (Poniatowska)
See *Querido Diego, te abraza Quiela*
Dear Digby (Muske) **90**:315-17
"Dear Dorothy" (Creeley) **78**:141
"Dear Dr. Husak" (Havel) **123**:167
"Dear Elizabeth" (Swenson) **106**:321
"Dear Freud" (Major) **19**:297
"Dear Friend" (McCartney) **12**:372; **35**:280
Dear Future (D'Aguiar) **145**:120-21, 123-25, 127-28
"Dear Helen" (Simic) **49**:341, 343
"Dear Illusion" (Amis) **40**:43-5
"Dear Isaac Newton" (Simic) **130**:306
"Dear John" (Kaufman) **49**:203
Dear John, Dear Coltrane (Harper) **22**:207
"Dear John Wayne" (Alexie) **154**:48
"Dear Jool, I Miss You in Saint-Saturnin" (Hacker) **72**:192

"Dear Judas" (Jeffers) **54**:237; **11**:310
Dear Judas and Other Poems (Jeffers) **54**:237; **11**:305, 310-11
"The Dear Ladies of Cincinnati" (Stevenson) **7**:463
"Dear Landlord" (Dylan) **12**:185
"Dear Mama" (Sanchez) **116**:307, 311
"Dear Masoch" (Codrescu) **46**:106; **121**:157
"Dear Men and Women" (Wheelock) **14**:571
"Dear Mother" (Cliff) **21**:63
Dear Mr. Capote (Lish) **45**:225-31
"Dear Mr. President" (Whalen) **6**:566
"The Dear Old Village" (Betjeman) **6**:68; **43**:37
"Dear Paul: Four Versions" (Niedecker) **42**:299
"Dear People" (Kaufman) **49**:207
"Dear Phil Donahue" (Smith) **25**:409; **73**:357
"Dear Pop" (Carroll) **38**:102-03
"Dear Pope" (Schwartz) **45**:361
Dear Rat (Cunningham) **12**:164
Dear Shadows: Portraits from Memory (Wain) **46**:420
"Dear Soul" (Rozewicz)
See "Duszyczka"
"Dear Strager Extant in Memory by the Blue Juaniata" (Kinnell) **129**:244
Dear Summer Sister (Oshima) **20**:251
"Dear Yoko" (Lennon) **35**:272, 274
Dearly Beloved (Lindbergh) **82**:166-67
"A Death" (Creeley) **11**:136
"Death" (Mailer) **111**:96
Death (Allen) **52**:37, 43
"Death II" (Mphahlele) **25**:336
"A Death Alive" (Jennings) **131**:233
"Death Alone" (Neruda)
See "Sola la muerte"
Death along the Wabash (Saroyan) **10**:453-54
"The Death and Birth of Doctrines" (Mahfouz)
See "Ihtidar M'taqadat wa Tawallud M'taqadat"
"Death and Co." (Plath) **2**:336; **11**:445; **14**:424; **17**:347-48; **51**:342, 345-46; **111**:203
Death and Friends (Anderson) **9**:31
Death and Letters (Daly) **52**:91-2
Death and Life of a Severino (Cabral de Melo Neto)
See *Morte e vida severina e outraos poemas em voz alta*
The Death and Life of Harry Goth (Mano) **2**:270; **10**:328
Death and Resurrection of Konstandinos Paleologhos (Elytis) **49**:108; **100**:175
Death and Taxes (Parker) **68**:325
Death and the Children (Horgan) **9**:278
"Death and the Compass" (Borges)
See "La muerte y la brújula"
Death and the Dancing Footman (Marsh) **53**:249-51
"Death and the Good Life" (Hugo) **32**:241-42
Death and the King's Horseman (Soyinka) **36**:411; **44**:287-90
"Death and the Maiden" (Lowell) **4**:304; **124**:255
"Death and the Maiden" (Nemerov) **9**:394; **36**:305
Death and the Maiden (Dorfman) **77**:154-55
"Death and the Professor" (Kinsella) **138**:98
"Death at a Great Distance" (Oliver) **98**:292
Death at an Early Age (Kozol) **17**:249-51, 254
Death at Crane's Court (Dillon) **17**:95
"Death at Dawn" (Soyinka) **36**:410; **44**:280
Death at Sea (Prokosch) **48**:308-10
Death at the Bar (Marsh) **53**:250
Death at the President's Lodging (Stewart)
See *Seven Suspects*
"The Death Baby" (Sexton) **53**:322-23
"Death Ballad" (Berryman) **62**:74
"Death Be Not Proud" (Simmons) **43**:411
Death before Bedtime (Vidal) **22**:434
"Death behind Bars" (Crispin) **22**:111
"The Death Bell" (Watkins) **43**:446, 451
The Death Bell: Poems and Ballads (Watkins) **43**:442, 447, 449
"Death by Drowning" (Christie) **110**:141, 143
"Death by Drowning" (Eberhart) **11**:177
Death by Hanging (Oshima)
See *Koshikei*
"Death by Landscape" (Atwood) **84**:95, 98
"Death by Rarity" (Young) **82**:397
"Death by Water" (Eliot) **15**:214
"Death by Water" (Smith) **12**:535
"Death Chant for Mr. Johnson's America" (Souster) **14**:504
Death Claims (Hansen) **38**:236-37
Death Comes as the End (Christie) **6**:109; **8**:142; **12**:114-15; **48**:74-5
"Death Comes to a Hero" (Gilchrist) **143**:301
"Death Constant beyond Love" (García Márquez)
See "Muerte constante más allá der amor"
"The Death Dance" (Madhubuti) **73**:208
The Death Dealers (Spillane) **13**:528
"Death, etc." (Hogan) **73**:157
Death Flight (Hunter) **31**:228
"Death Fugue" (Celan)
See "Todesfuge"
"The Death Ghazals" (Ostriker) **132**:328
"Death Goes to a Party" (Martin) **89**:110, 112-13, 118
"Death, Great Smoothener" (Swenson) **106**:350
Death in a Tenured Position (Heilbrun) **25**:256-57
Death in a White Tie (Marsh) **53**:249-50
Death in April (Greeley) **28**:175
Death in Don Mills (Garner) **13**:237
"Death in Dreams: The Interpretation of Nightmares" (Leet) **11**:323
Death in Ecstasy (Marsh) **7**:209; **53**:250, 254
"Death in Ilium: in Yeats's Centenary Year" (Kinsella) **138**:86, 118
"Death in January" (Buckley) **57**:131
"Death in Jerusalem" (Trevor) **116**:363
"Death in Leamington" (Betjeman) **43**:32, 40, 52
Death in Life: Survivors of Hiroshima (Lifton) **67**:137-40, 142, 153-54
"Death in Mexico" (Levertov) **66**:253
"Death in Miami Beach" (Gold) **42**:195
Death in Midsummer, and Other Stories (Mishima) **6**:338-39
"Death in Spring" (Bates) **46**:51
Death in the Afternoon (Hemingway) **1**:141; **3**:235, 241; **6**:226, 228, 230; **8**:283, 290; **13**:271; **19**:218; **30**:179, 189-90; **34**:477-79; **39**:400, 403, 430, 433; **41**:199, 201, 203; **50**:422, 429; **61**:225; **80**:137, 150
Death in the Air (Christie) **12**:122; **39**:439; **48**:72
"A Death in the Aquarium" (Hugo) **32**:252
Death in the Clouds (Christie)
See *Death in the Air*
A Death in the Faculty (Heilbrun)
See *Death in a Tenured Position*
Death in the Fifth Position (Vidal) **22**:434
"Death in the Lounge Bar" (Scannell) **49**:328
"A Death in the North" (MacBeth) **5**:265
Death in This Garden (Bunuel)
See *La mort en ce jardin*
Death in Venice (Visconti) **16**:569-73, 575
"Death in Vietnam" (Salinas)
See "Death of Vietnam"
"Death Invited" (Swenson) **106**:350
"Death Is a Happy ending: A Dialogue in Thirteen Parts (with Diane Bessai)" (Kroetsch) **132**:203
Death Is a Lonely Business (Bradbury) **42**:45-6; **98**:144
"Death Is the Star" (Clash) **30**:51-2
Death Kit (Sontag) **1**:322; **2**:413-14; **13**:515; **31**:418; **105**:197, 207, 225
Death Likes It Hot (Vidal) **22**:434
Death List (Bullins) **1**:47
Death List (Goines) **80**:91, 94
"Death Mother" (Morgan) **23**:301
Death Mother and Other Poems (Morgan) **23**:299-301
The Death Notebooks (Sexton) **4**:483-84; **6**:492, 494; **8**:483; **15**:472; **53**:322; **123**:406, 409, 439-41, 443-44
"Death of a Bird" (Silkin) **43**:399-400
"Death of a Bomber" (Ciardi) **40**:152
Death of a Career Girl (Lang) **20**:212
"Death of a Chieftain" (Montague) **46**:264
Death of a Chieftain and Other Stories (Montague) **46**:264, 278
"Death of a Chleuch Dancer" (Faludy) **42**:138, 140
"Death of a Critic" (Lowell) **11**:331; **37**:238
"Death of a doe on Chequesset Neck" (Piercy) **128**:274
"Death of a Favorite" (Powers) **57**:356
Death of a Fool (Marsh) **53**:249-51
"Death of a Friend" (Cohen) **19**:113
"Death of a Ghost" (Allingham) **19**:11, 14
"The Death of a Good Man" (Phillips) **28**:362
Death of a Harbour Master (Simenon) **18**:481; **47**:372
Death of a Hawker (van de Wetering) **47**:406-07, 411-12
Death of a Hero (Aldington) **49**:9, 11
Death of a Hero (Anand) **23**:18
Death of a Huntsman (Bates) **46**:61
"The Death of a Kinsman" (Taylor) **37**:408, 411; **44**:305; **50**:260; **71**:295
Death of a Lady's Man (Cohen) **38**:136-37
"Death of a Lesser Man" (Berriault) **54**:3, 5
"Death of a Man" (L'Heureux) **52**:272
Death of a Man (Boyle) **58**:64; **121**:30, 45-7, 50, 52
"The Death of a Mormon Elder" (Freeman) **55**:57-8
"Death of a Naturalist" (Heaney) **25**:241
Death of a Naturalist (Heaney) **5**:171-72; **7**:147, 149-50; **14**:242-43, 245; **25**:241-42, 244, 246, 248, 250; **37**:165; **74**:156-57, 163, 167, 170, 188, 192, 194; **91**:121, 123, 125, 127
"Death of a Peasant" (Thomas) **6**:534; **13**:543
Death of a Peer (Marsh) **7**:210; **53**:251-52, 254, 258
"Death of a Pig" (White) **34**:430
"Death of a Poet in Battle-Dress" (Simmons) **43**:407
Death of a Politician (Condon) **45**:98-9; **100**:100, 110, 113
"Death of a Public Servant" (Kizer) **80**:172, 185
"Death of a Queen" (Kinsella) **138**:97-98, 133
Death of a Salesman (Kazan) **63**:222, 231, 234
Death of a Salesman (Miller) **1**:216-19; **2**:278-80; **6**:326-37; **10**:342-44; **15**:370-74, 376; **26**:310-24, 327; **47**:250-51, 253-55; **78**:288-90, 293, 295, 297-99, 301-02, 305-06, 309, 311-13, 318, 324-25, 328
"Death of a Son" (Silkin) **6**:498; **43**:398, 400-01, 404
"Death of a Spaceman" (Miller) **30**:263-65
"The Death of a Toad" (Wilbur) **6**:569
"The Death of a Traveling Salesman" (Welty) **2**:462; **14**:561; **33**:414, 424; **105**:306-07, 325
"Death of a Vermont Farm Woman" (Howes) **15**:290
Death of a Young, Young Man (Russell) **60**:320
The Death of Ahasuerus (Lagerkvist)
See *Ahasverus död*
"Death of an Actor" (Williams) **42**:445
Death of an Expert Witness (James) **18**:273; **46**:205-06; **122**:128, 130, 135-36, 186
"Death of an Explorer" (Gascoyne) **45**:158
"Death of an Old Lady" (MacNeice) **53**:238
The Death of Artemio Cruz (Fuentes)
See *La muerte de Artemio Cruz*
"The Death of Assia G." (Amichai)
See "Mota Shel Assia G."
"The Death of Aunt Alice" (Abse) **29**:18
The Death of Bessie Smith (Albee) **2**:4; **5**:10;

9:2-3, 5; **25**:33; **113**:3-6, 43
"The Death of Celan" (Amichai)
See "Moto Shel Celan"
"Death of Childhood Beliefs" (Blunden) **56**:49
"The Death of Cock Robin" (Snodgrass) **68**:398
The Death of Cock Robin (Snodgrass) **68**:388, 393-94
The Death of Communal Liberty (Barber) **141**:2
"The Death of Crazy Horse" (Clifton) **66**:82
The Death of Dickey Draper and Nine Other Stories (Weidman) **7**:517
"The Death of Don Quixote" (Glassco) **9**:237
A Death of Dreams (Hoffman) **141**:276, 280, 296-97, 302-03, 319
"The Death of Edward Lear" (Barthelme) **13**:59, 63; **46**:35
"The Death of Egorushka" (Leonov)
See "Ghibel' Egorushki"
"The Death of Elsa Baskoleit" (Boell)
See "Der Tod der Elsa Baskoleit"
"The Death of Emmit Till" (Dylan) **77**:166
"The Death of Francisco Pizarro" (Ai) **69**:8
"The Death of Fred Clifton" (Clifton) **66**:82
The Death of Jim Loney (Welch) **52**:426, 430-36, 438
"The Death of Justina" (Cheever) **15**:127, 130; **25**:120
"The Death of Keats" (Watkins) **43**:452
"Death of King George V" (Betjeman) **2**:60; **34**:306
"The Death of Kropotkin" (Read) **4**:442
"The Death of Leon Trotsky" (Goodman) **4**:197
"Death of Little Boys" (Tate) **2**:429
The Death of Malcolm X (Sanchez) **116**:301
"The Death of Marilyn Monroe" (Olds) **39**:190
"The Death of Marilyn Monroe" (Trilling) **129**:336
"The Death of Mary Queen of Scots" (Monty Python) **21**:227
"The Death of Me" (Malamud) **9**:348; **44**:419
The Death of Methusaleh, and Other Stories (Singer) **69**:309-11, 313-14, 316
"The Death of Methuselah" (Singer) **69**:310, 312-14
The Death of Mr. Baltisberger (Hrabal) **13**:290-91; **67**:121, 126
"The Death of Myth-Making" (Plath) **9**:432
"Death of Narcissus" (Lezama Lima)
See "Muerte de Narcisco"
"The Death of Pan" (Blaga) **75**:76
"The Death of Picasso" (Davenport) **38**:144-45
"The Death of Randall Jarrell" (Shapiro) **53**:328
"The Death of Reason" (Boland) **113**:110, 126
"The Death of Robert Browning" (Urquhart) **90**:384-5
The Death of Robin Hood (Vansittart) **42**:397-98
"The Death of Saint Narcissus" (Eliot) **57**:204
The Death of Seneca (Hine) **15**:282
"The Death of St. Catherine of Siena" (Buckley) **57**:129
"The Death of the Author" (Barthes)
See "La mort de l'auteur"
"The Death of the Author" (Gass) **39**:481-82
"The Death of the Ayatollah Khomenei" (Durcan) **70**:147
"The Death of the Ball Turret Gunner" (Jarrell) **2**:211; **9**:298; **13**:300, 302-03; **49**:201
"Death of the Band" (Katz) **47**:220, 222
"The Death of the Bird" (Hope) **51**:216, 221
"Death of the Creative Process" (Olsen) **4**:386
"The Death of the Fathers" (Sexton) **4**:483; **6**:495; **15**:472; **53**:314, 321-23; **123**:420
Death of the Fox (Garrett) **3**:189-90, 193; **11**:220; **51**:148-49, 151, 153
The Death of the Heart (Bowen) **1**:39-41; **3**:82-3; **6**:94-5; **11**:59-62, 64; **15**:78-79; **118**:63, 83, 92, 97, 105, 107-08, 110-11
Death of the Hind Legs and Other Stories (Wain) **46**:415
"The Death of the Hired Man" (Frost) **3**:170; **9**:218; **13**:230; **15**:246-47; **26**:112-13, 123, 127-28
Death of the Inquisitor (Sciascia)
See *La morte dell'inquisitore*
"Death of the Kapowsin Tavern" (Hugo) **32**:246-47
Death of the Kapowsin Tavern (Hugo) **32**:234-35, 237-38, 244, 247, 249
"The Death of the King of France" (Landolfi) **49**:209-10
"Death of the Miners or the Widows of the Earth" (Kunene) **85**:176
"Death of the Nazarene" (Shamlu) **10**:471
The Death of the Novel and Other Stories (Sukenick) **3**:475; **4**:531
"The Death of the Old Man" (Yehoshua) **31**:472
The Death of the Old Man (Yehoshua) **13**:617; **31**:468, 472
"The Death of the Old Men" (Fiedler) **24**:194
"The Death of the Pythia" (Duerrenmatt)
See "Das Sterben der Pythia"
"The Death of the Right Fielder" (Dybek) **114**:68, 83
"The Death of the Small Commune" (Piercy) **18**:406; **27**:375
The Death of Tragedy (Steiner) **24**:425-27
"The Death of Uncle Silas" (Bates) **46**:52
"Death of Vietnam" (Salinas) **90**:324, 327
The Death of Virgil (Škvorecký) **15**:511
The Death of William Posters (Sillitoe) **3**:448; **6**:500; **19**:421; **148**:156-57, 163, 166, 171, 185, 189-93, 201, 208
"Death of Women" (Coles) **46**:108
"Death on All Fronts" (Ginsberg) **36**:185
"A Death on the East Side" (Gold) **42**:193; **152**:126
Death on the Installment Plan (Céline)
See *Mort à crédit*
Death on the Nile (Christie) **12**:113-14, 117; 122-23; **39**:438; **48**:72, 74, 76-7; **110**:121-22
"Death or Glory" (Clash) **30**:46-7
"Death or the Waiting Room" (Aleixandre) **36**:29
"A Death Road for the Condor" (Macdonald) **41**:270
Death Sentence (Blanchot)
See *L'Arrêt de mort*
Death Shall Not Enter the Palace (Marqués)
See *La muerte no entrará en palacio*
The Death Ship (Traven)
See *Das Totenschiff*
"Death Sits in the Dentist's Chair" (Woolrich) **77**:401
Death, Sleep, and the Traveler (Hawkes) **4**:215-19; **7**:140-46; **9**:269; **27**:190-91, 194-96, 199; **49**:162-64
Death Suite (Rooke) **25**:393-95
Death Takes a Stroll (Ghelderode)
See *La ballad du grand macabre*
Death to the Death of Poetry (Hall) **151**:204, 206, 208
Death to the French (Forester)
See *Rifleman Dodd*
"A Death to Us" (Silkin) **43**:400-01
"Death to Van Gogh's Ear!" (Ginsberg) **6**:199; **13**:239-40
"Death Valley" (Oates) **108**:384
"Death Valley Scotty" (Guthrie) **35**:193
Death Wears a Red Hat (Kienzle) **25**:275
"The Deathbird" (Ellison) **13**:207; **42**:128-29; **139**:136, 138, 140
Deathbird Stories: A Pantheon of Modern Gods (Ellison) **13**:203, 206, 208; **42**:128; **139**:129
"Deathe" (Wright) **146**:305, 335
"The Death-in-Life of Benjamin Reid" (Styron) **60**:393
"The Deathmaker at San Quentin" (Bowering) **47**:33
Deathman, Do Not Follow Me (Bennett) **35**:42, 45
"Deaths" (Swenson) **106**:350
"The Deaths about You When You Stir in Sleep" (Ciardi) **40**:157-58
"The Deaths and the Victory of Rosalinda" (Amado)
See "As Mortes e o Triunfo de Rosalinda"
"Deaths at Sea" (Dubus) **97**:214, 216, 218
Death's Deputy (Hubbard) **43**:203-04
"Death's Door" (Gunn) **81**:180, 187
"Death's Echo" (Auden) **6**:21
"Death's Head" (Gotlieb) **18**:193
"Death's Head Revisited" (Serling) **30**:358
Death's Master (Lee) **46**:231-34
"The Deaths of Uncles" (Kumin) **13**:327
Deathwatch (Genet)
See *Haute surveillance*
The Deathworld Trilogy (Harrison) **42**:205
Debate (Chomsky) **132**:20-1
"Debates" (Corn) **33**:116
"Debbie Go Home" (Paton) **25**:360
"Debout" (Tchicaya) **101**:350
Debridement (Harper) **7**:139; **22**:207-08
"Debriefing" (Sontag) **13**:516-17
The Debriefing (Littell) **42**:276
"Debris" (Ammons) **57**:49
"Dèbris" (Césaire) **19**:98
"Debris" (Fearing) **51**:106
"Debris of Shock/Shock of Debris" (Bernstein) **142**:28
Debt of Honor (Clancy) **112**:76-80, 82, 84, 90
"A Debt of Honour" (Pritchett) **41**:333
The Debt to Pleasure (Lanchester) **99**:54-61
"Debtors' Lane" (Okigbo) **25**:350; **84**:328, 330-31
"Debts" (Paley) **37**:337; **140**:222-24, 268, 277, 282
"Debut" (Hunter) **35**:226
The Debut (Brookner) **136**:90, 103, 113
The Debut (Brookner)
See *A Start in Life*
Debutante Hill (Duncan) **26**:100
Decade (Young) **17**:577-80, 582
"Decades" (Howard) **7**:170; **10**:275-76
Decalogue (Kieslowski)
See *Dekalog*
Decalogue Eight: Thou Shalt Not Bear False Witness (Kieslowski)
See *Dekalog osiem*
Decalogue Five: Thou Shalt Not Kill (Kieslowski)
See *Dekalog piec*
Decalogue Four: Honor Thy Father and Thy Mother (Kieslowski)
See *Dekalog cztery*
Decalogue Nine: Thou Shalt Not Covet THy Neighbor's Wife (Kieslowski)
See *Dekalog dziewiec*
Decalogue One: Thou Shalt Worship One God (Kieslowski)
See *Dekalog jeden*
Decalogue Seven: Thou Shalt Not Steal (Kieslowski) **120**:211-12, 215, 258-59
Decalogue Six: Thou Shalt Not Commit Adultery (Kieslowski)
See *Dekalog szesc*
Decalogue Ten: Thou Shalt Not Covet Thy Neighbor's Goods (Kieslowski) **120**:213-14, 221, 254, 258-59
Decalogue Three: Honor the Sabbath Day (Kieslowski)
See *Dekalog trzy*
Decalogue Two: Thou Shalt Not Take the Name of the Lord Thy God in Vain (Kieslowski) **120**:210, 214, 257-58, 260
The Decameron (Pasolini)
See *Il Decamerone*
Il Decamerone (Pasolini) **20**:266-68; **106**:224, 226
The Decay of the Angel (Mishima) **4**:356-58; **6**:337; **27**:341-42
"December" (Akhmadulina) **53**:11
"December" (Oliver) **98**:303
"December" (Simic) **49**:341
"December 6th" (Forester) **35**:173
"December 9th" (Sexton) **123**:409

"December 29, 1890: Wounded Knee Creek" (Momaday) **85**:281
"December 1920" (Seifert) **93**:339
"December at Yase" (Snyder) **120**:356
"December Evening 1972" (Transtroemer) **65**:221, 230
"December in Florence" (Brodsky) **13**:117; **50**:125; **100**:52
"December Journal" (Wright) **146**:352, 365
"December of My Springs" (Giovanni) **64**:191
"December Thirty-one St. Silvester" (Warner) **19**:461
A Decent Birth, a Happy Funeral (Saroyan) **8**:467
"Deception" (Corn) **33**:116
The Deception (Canetti)
See *Die Blendung*
Deception (Roth) **86**:248-49, 252-53; **119**:129
"Deception Bay" (Malouf) **28**:268
"Deceptions" (Larkin) **8**:332, 340; **18**:294; **33**:261; **39**:336; **64**:262, 266, 268, 270
Deceptive Distinctions (Epstein) **65**:325
The Deceptive Grin (Ewart) **13**:209
Decider (Francis) **102**:150-52
"Deciduous Branch" (Kunitz) **14**:312-13
"Decipherings" (Levertov) **66**:240
The Decision (Drury) **37**:111-12
Decision at Delphi (MacInnes) **27**:281; **39**:350
Decision at Doona (McCaffrey) **17**:280
"Decision on King Street" (Souster) **5**:396
"Decisions to Disappear" (Dunn) **36**:151
"The Decisive Moment" (Auster) **131**:19
"Declaration" (Lessing) **3**:292; **6**:295
"A Declaration for 1955" (Boyle) **58**:74; **121**:60
"Declaration, July 4" (Corn) **33**:116
Declarations of War (Deighton) **4**:119; **46**:127
Declensions of a Refrain (Gregor) **9**:254
"Decline and Fall" (Swan) **69**:361-62
Decline and Fall (Waugh) **1**:357-59; **3**:510-13; **8**:543-44; **13**:584-85; **19**:461; **44**:520; **107**:357, 362-64, 370-71, 378, 383, 385, 393, 397, 399, 401, 406
"The Decline and Fall of Frankie Buller" (Sillitoe) **6**:501; **57**:387; **148**:199
The Decline and Fall of the American Empire (Vidal) **142**:290
"The Decline and Fall of the King's English" (Thurber) **125**:403
"The Decline and the Validity of the Idea of Progress" (Tillich) **131**:345
"The Decline of the Argo" (Ritsos) **6**:464
Decline of the New (Howe) **85**:121-22
The Decline of the West (Caute) **29**:111-14, 121-22
"The Decolonization of American Literature" (Shapiro) **53**:328
Deconstruction and Criticism (Bloom) **103**:20, 25, 28
"The Deconstruction of Emily Dickinson" (Kinnell) **129**:271
"Decoration" (Bogan) **46**:85-6
Découvertes (Ionesco) **41**:229
"Decoy" (Ashbery) **25**:58; **77**:48, 57
"Decreator" (Redgrove) **6**:445; **41**:351, 353
Dedans (Cixous) **92**:90
Dedica (Pasolini) **106**:233
"Dedicated" (Leavitt) **34**:78-9
"Dedicated Follower of Fashion" (Davies) **21**:97, 103
A Dedicated Man (Taylor) **2**:432
"Dedication" (Boland) **40**:100
"Dedication" (Graham) **118**:225
"A Dedication" (Merrill) **34**:239
"Dedication" (Milosz) **31**:259; **56**:233; **82**:289, 296
Dedication (Ekeloef) **27**:109-11
"Dedication for a Plot of Ground" (Williams) **42**:452
"Dedication: The Other Woman and the Novelist" (Boland) **113**:115
"Dedication to a Poet" (Kunene) **85**:166
"Dedication to Hunger" (Glück) **22**:175; **44**:216; **81**:173
"Dedications" (Rich) **73**:336-37; **76**:218; **125**:311
Dedications and Other Darkhorses (Komunyakaa) **94**:218, 230, 239, 246
"Dedicatory Epistle" (Fuller) **28**:158
"Dedicatory Stanzas" (Day Lewis) **10**:134
"Deductible Yacht" (Auchincloss) **9**:52
Deenie (Blume) **12**:47; **30**:20, 23
The Deep (Benchley) **8**:82
The Deep (Crowley) **57**:156, 162, 164
The Deep (Spillane) **13**:527-28
"Deep Analysis" (Larkin) **64**:282
The Deep Blue Goodbye (MacDonald) **3**:307; **44**:407-08
The Deep Blue Sea (Rattigan) **7**:355
"A Deep Breath at Dawn" (Hecht) **8**:268
"The Deep End" (Mac Laverty) **31**:253
Deep End (Skolimowski) **20**:349, 352-54
"Deep Forbidden Lake" (Young) **17**:577
The Deep Has Many Voices (Ringwood) **48**:330-31, 334-37, 339
"Deep Measure" (Wright) **146**:368
"The Deep Museum" (Sexton) **123**:418
Deep River (Endō) **99**:284, 288, 297, 299-310
"The Deep River: A Story oF Ancient Tribal Migration" (Head) **67**:98
Deep Rivers (Arguedas)
See *Los ríos profundos*
The Deep Sleep (Morris) **1**:233; **3**:343; **18**:352; **37**:311
"The Deep Supermarket" (Durcan) **70**:147
The Deep Tangled Wildwood (Connelly) **7**:56
The Deep Tangled Wildwood (Kaufman) **38**:257
Deep Torrent, Dark River (Yourcenar)
See *Fleuve profond, sombre rivière*
Deep Water (Highsmith) **2**:193; **42**:211, 215; **102**:170, 172-73, 201-02, 204
"Deep Woods" (Nemerov) **36**:305
"The Deeper Friendship" (Blunden) **56**:38
"The Deeper Lesson" (Carroll) **10**:98
Deeper than the Darkness (Benford)
See *The Stars in Shroud*
"The Deeps" (Roberts) **14**:464
"Deep-Sea Fish" (Turner) **48**:399
"Deer among Cattle" (Dickey) **7**:81
The Deer at Our House (Caldwell) **50**:302
"Deer Dance/For Your Return" (Silko) **74**:330, 347; **114**:316
"Deer Dancer" (Harjo) **83**:272, 274, 280-81
"Deer Dancers at Santo Domingo" (Lewis) **41**:260-61
"Deer Ghost" (Harjo) **83**:273, 282
The Deer Hunter (Cimino) **16**:209-14
"The Deer of Providencia" (Dillard) **60**:74-5; **115**:197
"Deer on the High Hills" (Smith) **64**:388, 394, 396, 398
"Deer on the High Hills—A Meditation" (Smith)
See "Deer on the High Hills"
The Deer Park (Mailer) **1**:187-90, 192-93; **2**:258-59, 263; **3**:311, 313, 318; **4**:319, 321-23; **5**:268; **8**:364, 366, 370, 373; **11**:339-40, 342-43, 345; **14**:348, 352; **28**:257; **74**:203, 206, 222-24, 233; **111**:94-5, 98, 100, 103, 108, 120, 130, 133, 135, 148
"Deer Park at Sarnath" (Alexander) **121**:21
The Deer Pasture (Bass) **79**:2, 10, 15-18; **143**:4-5, 9, 18, 21
"Deer Season" (Beattie) **146**:64
"Deer Song" (Silko) **74**:330; **114**:316
"Deer Trails in Tzityonyana" (Rooke) **25**:394
"Deerslayer's Campfire Talk" (Stafford) **4**:520
"De-Evolution" (Livesay) **79**:338, 350
"Defeat" (Aldington) **49**:7
"Defeat" (Boyle) **58**:66; **121**:33
"The Defeat of Youth" (Huxley) **11**:282, 284
The Defeat of Youth, and Other Poems (Huxley) **11**:282, 284
"The Defeated" (Gordimer) **18**:185; **33**:177
"The Defeated" (Kavanagh) **22**:243
"Defection of a Favorite" (Powers) **57**:356
The Defection of A. J. Lewinter (Littell) **42**:274-76
"Defective Story" (Raine) **103**:180
Defectos escogidos: 2000 (Neruda) **28**:310; **62**:333-34, 336
"Defence" (Bernstein)
See "A Defence sic of Poetry"
"Defence" (Silkin) **43**:397, 400
"A Defence sic of Poetry" (Bernstein) **142**:56-7
The Defendant (Mahfūz) **52**:298
"Defender of the Faith" (Roth) **2**:380; **22**:357; **31**:335
"Defender of the Little Falaya" (Gilchrist) **34**:164
Defending Ancient Springs (Raine) **7**:351
"Defending Walt Whitman" (Alexie) **154**:21
Defenestration of Prague (Howe) **72**:195, 197-98, 208; **152**:150-52, 164-69, 176, 196-97, 214, 235-36
"Defensa de Violeta Parra" (Parra) **102**:340
The Defense (Nabokov)
See *Zashchita Luzhina*
The Defense (Nabokov)
See *Zashchita Luzhina*
The Defense of Granada (Brandys) **62**:112
The Defense of the Sugar Islands: A Recruiting Post (Cassity) **42**:96-7
"The Defenseman" (Banks) **72**:4
"Defensio in extremis" (Berryman) **25**:96
The Defiant Agents (Norton) **12**:467
"Define This Word" (Fisher) **76**:338
"Defining the Poet" (Turco) **11**:551
Definitely Maybe (Strugatskii and Strugatskii) **27**:435-37
"Definition" (Dodson) **79**:194
"definition for blk / children" (Sanchez) **116**:295
"Definition in the Face of Unnamed Fury" (Dove) **81**:139
Definition of Blue (Ashbery) **13**:33
"Definitions" (Wright) **6**:580
"Definitions of Poetry" (Sandburg) **35**:352
"Definitive Dialogue" (Ali) **69**:32
The Deflowered One (Nakos)
See *Le livre de mon pierrot*
"Defrauded Woman" (Scannell) **49**:331
Defy the Wilderness (Banks) **23**:42
"Degas's Laundresses" (Boland) **40**:101; **113**:109, 123
Le degré zéro de l'écriture (Barthes) **24**:22, 25-7, 30-1, 33, 37, 39-41; **83**:67-9, 83, 85, 90, 100
Degree of Trust (Voinovich)
See *Stepen' doveriia*
"Degrees" (Thomas) **37**:423; **107**:320-21, 333
Degrees (Butor)
See *Degrés*
Degrees of Freedom (Byatt) **65**:131
"Degrees of Gray in Philipsburg" (Hugo) **32**:240, 248, 250
Degrés (Butor) **3**:92-3; **8**:116-18, 120-21; **11**:79-80; **15**:115, 117-19
"Dehorning" (Hughes) **37**:175; **119**:271
Dei svarte hestane (Vesaas) **48**:404-05, 407
Dei ukjende mennene (Vesaas) **48**:405
"Dein Leib im Rauch durch die Luft" (Sachs) **98**:327
"Dein Schimmer" (Celan) **82**:51-3
"Deities" (Montague) **46**:277
"Deity Considered as Mother Death" (Hulme) **130**:66
"Deja vu" (Urdang) **47**:400
Déjà vu (Young) **17**:569-70
"Déjeuner sur l'herbe" (Thomas) **37**:421; **107**:328
Le déjeuner sur l'herbe (Renoir) **20**:290-93, 297, 303-04
"Dekabr' vo Florentsii" (Brodsky)
See "December in Florence"
Dekachtō lianotragouda tēs pikrēs patridas (Ritsos) **6**:463; **13**:487

Dekalog (Kieslowski) **120**:209-13, 216-21, 224-27, 234-35, 245, 249-51, 253, 256-61
Dekalog cztery (Kieslowski) **120**:212, 220, 233, 257-58, 260
Dekalog dziewiec (Kieslowski) **120**:210, 215, 233, 258-60
Dekalog jeden (Kieslowski) **120**:210-14, 235, 257-60
Dekalog osiem (Kieslowski) **120**:211-12, 215, 235, 258, 260
Dekalog piec (Kieslowski) **120**:211, 213, 232, 257-60
Dekalog szesc (Kieslowski) **120**:210, 232, 258-60
Dekalog trzy (Kieslowski) **120**:214, 257, 260
Del Corso's Gallery (Caputo) **32**:106
Del pozo y del Numa: Un ensayo y una leyenda (Benet) **28**:23-4
Delano: The Story of the California Grape Strike (Dunne) **28**:120-21, 125
"Delay" (Jennings) **131**:237, 240
The Delay (Hildesheimer)
See *Die Verspätung*
The Delectable Mountains (Malone) **43**:281
"The Delegate" (Porter) **13**:452-53; **33**:322-23
"The Delhi Division" (Moorcock) **58**:347
"Delia" (Gordon) **128**:118
"Delia's Father" (Colwin) **84**:146, 150
A Deliberate Policy (Schell) **35**:369
A Delicate Balance (Albee) **1**:4-5; **2**:1, 3-4; **3**:6-7; **5**:11, 13; **9**:4-6, 9; **11**:13; **13**:3, 5, 7; **25**:35-8, 40; **53**:20-1, 24; **86**:119-20, 124-25; **113**:9-10, 12-15, 17, 21-2, 28, 40
"The Delicate Bird Who Is Flying Up Our Asses" (Bell) **8**:65-6
"Delicate Criss-Crossing Beetle Trails Left in the Sand" (Snyder) **32**:395
"The Delicate Prey" (Bowles) **53**:36, 43, 46
A Delicate Prey and Other Stories (Bowles) **1**:41-2; **2**:79; **19**:56; **53**:37-40
"Delight" (Warren) **13**:577
"The Delight Song of Tsoai-talee" (Momaday) **85**:247, 265
"Delights of France or Horrors of the Road" (Weldon) **122**:261
"Delights of Winter at the Shore" (Whalen) **29**:445
Delinquent Chacha (Mehta) **37**:290
The Delinquents (Altman) **16**:41; **116**:12-13, 46
"Delirious" (Prince) **35**:327
Delirium's Mistress (Lee) **46**:234
"Delito por bailer el chachachá" (Cabrera Infante) **120**:83
Delito por bailer el chachachá (Cabrera Infante) **120**:83-84
"Delitto al circolo di tennis" (Moravia) **7**:240
"Deliverance" (Graves) **45**:166, 168
Deliverance (Dickey) **1**:73-4; **2**:116; **4**:121-23; **7**:81, 84-6; **10**:139-40, 142-43; **15**:176-77; **47**:91, 93, 98-100; **109**:243, 245, 257-63, 276-77, 279-80, 282-83, 285-86
"Delivering" (Dubus) **36**:145-46; **97**:202, 208, 223
"The Delivery" (Smith) **22**:385
"The Delivery" (Van Duyn) **116**:421, 427
"Della's Modesty" (Gerstler) **70**:156, 159
"Delphi: Commentary" (Kroetsch) **57**:292-93
"Delphine" (Morand) **41**:295, 297, 308
"Delta" (Tolson) **105**:274
The Delta Decision (Smith) **33**:377
The Delta Factor (Spillane) **13**:528
Delta of Venus (Nin) **8**:425; **11**:398; **14**:387; **60**:269, 274-77; **127**:383-90, 397
Delta of Venus (Nin) **127**:383-84, 386, 388-90
Delta Wedding (Welty) **1**:361; **2**:462-63; **5**:478; **14**:561; **22**:457, 461; **33**:421-24; **105**:303, 316, 325, 336-38, 340, 360, 382, 389
"The Deltoid Pumpkin Seed" (McPhee) **36**:295, 297
Le déluge (Le Clézio) **31**:243, 245-46, 249
"The Deluge at Norderney" (Dinesen) **10**:146; **29**:162; **95**:35-6, 48, 50-2, 64, 67
The Delusion (Canetti)
See *Die Blendung*
"Delusion for a Dragon Slayer" (Ellison) **42**:126, 128-29
Delusions, Etc. of John Berryman (Berryman) **2**:57-9; **3**:66-71; **4**:62-3; **6**:63-4; **8**:91-2; **10**:51; **13**:82-3; **25**:91-2, 95-7; **62**:45-6, 74-5
Delusion's Master (Lee) **46**:231, 234
Dem (Kelley) **22**:247-49
Dem unbekannten Sieger (Nossack) **6**:364-66
"The Demagogue" (Williams) **148**:361
Demain matin, Montréal m'attend (Tremblay) **29**:419, 425; **102**:372, 374, 376
"Demands of the Muse" (Watkins) **43**:452-53
"Demands of the Poet" (Watkins) **43**:452-53
The deMaury Papers (Holland) **21**:151
Demelza (Graham) **23**:191
"Le déménagement" (Roy) **10**:440
Le déménagement (Simenon) **47**:379
Dementia Thirteen (Coppola) **16**:231, 244, 249
"Demeter" (Broumas) **73**:2
"Demeter" (H. D.) **73**:105, 128
Demian (Hesse) **1**:145-47; **2**:189-90; **3**:245, 248; **6**:236-37; **11**:270, 272; **17**:195, 198, 201-02, 204-06, 211-12, 217-18; **25**:261; **69**:272, 287, 289, 294, 296
"The Demiurge" (Cioran) **64**:80, 89, 94
"Demiurges" (Sherwood) **81**:102
"The Demiurge's Laugh" (Frost) **26**:117
"Demo against the Vietnam War, 1968" (Abse) **7**:2; **29**:18-19
Democracy (Didion) **32**:146-50; **129**:83-5, 87-8, 90-2, 103
Democracy and Esther (Linney) **51**:259, 265
Democracy and Poetry (Warren) **10**:520; **13**:582
"Democracy in America" (Oates) **6**:371
"Democratic Party Poem" (Williams) **13**:604
"A Democratic School" (Cozzens) **92**:201
"Demolition with Tobacco Speck" (Raine) **103**:186
"A Demon" (O'Brien) **65**:170, 172; **116**:203
"Demon" (Sexton) **123**:404
The Demon (Selby) **8**:477
Demon Box (Kesey) **46**:224-29
"Demon Dance" (Sondheim) **147**:258
A Demon in My View (Rendell) **28**:384; **48**:320-21
A Demon in My View (Vine) **50**:264
"The Demon Love" (Rich) **73**:328
"The Demon Lover" (Bowen) **15**:77-8; **22**:65; **118**:74, 100-03
"The Demon Lover" (Rich) **6**:458; **7**:366; **125**:317, 336-37
The Demon Lover and Other Stories (Bowen) **11**:63; **15**:77; **22**:63-4, 68; **118**:65, 100, 103
The Demon of Scattery (Anderson) **15**:15
Demon Princes (Vance) **35**:421, 423, 426-27
Demon Seed (Koontz) **78**:199, 203
"Demon With a Glass Hand" (Ellison) **139**:129, 133
The Demon-Haunted World (Sagan) **112**:437-38, 440, 443
Demonology (Moody) **147**:190-91
"Demons" (Oates) **6**:367
Demons by Daylight (Campbell) **42**:83-4, 87-90
"The Demonstration" (Ostriker) **132**:302
The Demonstration (Caute) **29**:113-15, 122
"The Demonstrators" (Welty) **105**:299, 311-13
The Den of Beasts (Kurosawa) **119**:399
"Dendrocacalia" (Abe) **81**:297
"Denial" (Gustafson) **36**:211
Denier du rêve (Yourcenar) **38**:457-60, 464-65; **50**:363-64; **87**:383, 390, 404
"Denis le boiteux" (Theriault) **79**:408
"Dennis Martinez and the Uses of Theory" (Fish) **142**:169, 182-83
"Denouement" (Fearing) **51**:105, 117
"The Deodand" (Hecht) **19**:207-10
Le départ (Skolimowski) **20**:347-49, 352-53
"The Departed" (Davie) **31**:117
"Departing Song" (Young) **82**:411
The Department (Williamson) **56**:434-35, 441
"Department of Public Monuments" (Simic) **49**:343
"Departmental" (Frost) **10**:196; **34**:475
"Departure" (Fast) **23**:156
"The Departure" (Olds) **39**:189-90; **85**:289
"Departure" (Plath) **111**:201
"Departure" (Scott) **22**:376
"Departure" (Tomlinson) **45**:394
Departure and Other Stories (Fast) **23**:156
"Departure from the Bush" (Atwood) **8**:32
"Departure in Middle Age" (Mathias) **45**:238
"Departure in the Dark" (Day Lewis) **6**:127; **10**:131
Departure of a Hunger Artist (Rozewicz)
See *Odejście Głodomora*
"Departure Platforms" (Kinsella) **138**:135
"Departures" (Barthelme) **115**:65, 68-9
"Departures" (L'Heureux) **52**:279
Departures (Justice) **6**:271-72; **19**:233; **102**:249-50, 261, 264, 270, 277, 280-81, 283
Dependencies (Mueller) **51**:279-81
Depends: A Poet's Notebook (Montale)
See *Quaderno de quattro anni*
Le dépeupleur (Beckett) **2**:47-8; **3**:45; **4**:50, 52; **6**:36, 38, 40, 42; **9**:83; **11**:39-40; **18**:49-51; **29**:57, 59-60, 62, 67
"Deposition: Testimony Concerning a Sickness" (Burroughs) **15**:111
"Depot Bay" (Levine) **33**:275
The Depraved Sleepers (Ruyslinck)
See *De ontaarde slapers*
"Depravity: Two Sermons" (Davie) **31**:116
"The Depreciated Legacy of Cervantes" (Kundera) **68**:242; **115**:321
"Depressed by a Book of Bad Poetry, I Walk Toward an Unused Pasture and Invite the Insects to Join Me" (Wright) **3**:540
"Depression" (Bly) **5**:63; **10**:56; **128**:4
The Deptford Trilogy (Davies) **42**:101-03, 106-07, 109; **75**:180, 184, 190, 192, 199, 214; **91**:201-04
Depth of Field (Heyen) **13**:281; **18**:230
"The Depths" (Levertov) **5**:246
"Depths" (Silkin) **43**:396, 400, 404
"Depths" (Williams) **148**:367
The Deputy (Hochhuth)
See *Der Stellvertreter*
"Derbyshire" (Davie) **31**:120
"Derelict" (Day Lewis) **6**:128; **10**:131
"Dereliction" (Achebe) **11**:4
"The Derelicts of Ganymede" (Campbell) **32**:73
"DeRerum Natura" (Codrescu) **121**:158
Dereva detstva (Iskander) **47**:199
"Dereviannaia koroleva" (Leonov) **92**:237, 242, 256, 262-63
Derivations (Duncan) **2**:123; **15**:187-8; **55**:294
"Derm Fool" (Sturgeon) **22**:410
Le dernier havre (Theriault) **79**:415
Le dernier homme (Blanchot) **135**:80-81
Le dernier milliardaire (Clair) **20**:61-2, 70
"Le Dernier Mot" (Blanchot) **135**:99, 113, 117
La dernier reveillon (Renoir) **20**:300
Le dernier tableau ou le portrait de Dieu (Cixous)
See "The Last Painting or the Portrait of God"
"Dernières cartouches" (Soupault) **68**:407
Les dernières nuits de Paris (Soupault) **68**:416
Les dernières paroles d'un impie (Pasolini) **106**:254-55
Les derniers jours (Queneau) **5**:360; **42**:335-36
Les Derniers Jours de Corinthe (Robbe-Grillet) **128**:376-82
Les derniers rois mages (Condé) **92**:125-26, 131-34
"Derry" (Deane) **122**:82
Dersu Uzala (Kurosawa) **119**:340, 380, 383, 397, 399-400
Des chinoises (Kristeva) **65**:328; **77**:303-05, 312; **140**:151
Des Clefs et des serrures (Tournier) **95**:361, 365, 381

Des journées entières dans les arbres (Duras) **6**:149; **40**:175, 184; **68**:92; **100**:145
Des mois (Landolfi) **49**:215
Des Teufels General (Zuckmayer) **18**:553-54, 556-57
Des tonnes de semence (Audiberti) **38**:21
Des traces de pas (Simenon) **8**:488
A Descant for Gossips (Astley) **41**:43-4, 48-9
Descant on Rawley's Madrigal (Bunting) **39**:298
"Descartes and the Stove" (Tomlinson) **45**:392
Descending Figure (Glück) **22**:175-77; **44**:214, 216, 221-22, 224; **81**:173
"Descent" (Ritsos) **31**:330
"Descent" (Weiss) **14**:556
"The Descent" (Williams) **42**:452
The Descent (Berriault) **54**:1; **109**:90
"The Descent Beckons" (Williams) **13**:604
"Descent in a Parachute" (Belitt) **22**:49
"Descent of Man" (Boyle) **36**:57-8
Descent of Man, and Other Stories (Boyle) **36**:56-9, 61, 63; **90**:45, 49-50
The Descent of Winter (Williams) **2**:468-69; **42**:462
Descent to the Dead: Poems Written in Ireland and Great Britain (Jeffers) **54**:237, 244, 246
"Descoberta da literatura" (Cabral de Melo Neto) **76**:164
A Descoberta de América pelos Turcos (Amado) **106**:91
"Description" (Simic) **130**:295
"Description of a Masque" (Ashbery) **41**:34, 37-40
"Description of a Pain in the Solar Plexus" (Akhmadulina) **53**:12
"Description of a View" (Empson) **19**:157
Description of San Marco (Butor) **8**:118; **15**:117-18
"A Description of Some Confederate Soldiers" (Jarrell) **2**:209
"Descriptive Passages" (Matthews) **40**:324
"La Desdichada" (Fuentes) **113**:242-43
"Desecration" (Jhabvala) **8**:313
"The Desert" (Faludy) **42**:140
"Desert" (Hogan) **73**:151
Désert (Le Clézio) **31**:251; **155**:84, 86, 93-5, 99-104, 110-15, 119
"The Desert as Garden of Paradise" (Rich) **73**:331
"Desert Breakdown, 1968" (Wolff) **64**:450-51, 454
Le désert de l'amour (Mauriac) **4**:338-41; **9**:368; **56**:204-07, 214, 216
Desert Drum (Schlee) **35**:372
"Desert Elm" (Bowering) **47**:23
A Desert Incident (Buck) **11**:77; **18**:80; **127**:233
"Desert Island Discs" (Townshend) **17**:533
Desert Love (Montherlant)
See *La rose de sable*
Le désert mauve (Brossard) **115**:119-20, 122-23, 135-36, 155
"The Desert Music" (Williams) **9**:575; **22**:465-66; **42**:455, 463
The Desert Music, and Other Poems (Williams) **22**:465; **42**:451, 454, 463
The Desert of Love (Mauriac)
See *Le désert de l'amour*
The Desert of Stolen Dreams (Silverberg) **140**:300
The Desert of the Heart (Rule) **27**:416-17, 421
"Desert Places" (Frost) **1**:110; **9**:227-28; **13**:225; **15**:244; **26**:121
"Desert Places" (Haines) **58**:214
The Desert Rose (McMurtry) **44**:259
Desert Solitaire: A Season in the Wilderness (Abbey) **36**:12-13, 16, 18-19, 21; **59**:238-45
The Desert Year (Krutch) **24**:290
"Deserters" (Rozewicz)
See "Dezerterzy"
"Desertion" (Simak) **55**:320
"Desertions" (Honig) **33**:212
"Desertmartin" (Paulin) **37**:355
Il deserto dei tartari (Buzzati) **36**:83-9, 91-5
Il deserto rosso (Antonioni) **20**:29-31, 34-5; **144**:2, 5, 7-8, 11-15, 19, 26 27, 34, 36, 40, 45, 48, 52-54, 54, 59, 63, 66, 72-3, 76, 80-81, 84, 91, 93, 95-96
Les désespéranto (Tzara) **47**:385, 387, 390, 394
La Desesperanza (Donoso) **99**:217, 219, 222-23, 232, 242, 256-69
"Désespoir d'un volontaire libre" (Senghor) **54**:410; **130**:259
"Deshoras" (Cortázar) **33**:134; **34**:333
"Design" (Frost) **1**:110; **3**:174; **9**:221, 228; **13**:228; **15**:250; **26**:124-25
Design for Living (Coward) **1**:64; **29**:132-33, 135-36, 138; **51**:69-73, 75, 77
"Design in Living Colors" (Rich) **36**:365
The Designated Heir (Kumin) **5**:222
"Desire" (Beattie) **40**:66; **63**:2, 9
"Desire" (Hughes) **108**:332
"Desire" (Peacock) **60**:293-94, 297
"Desire" (Raine) **45**:337
"Desire" (Wilson) **49**:416
Desire (Dylan) **12**:192; **77**:178
"Desire and the Black Masseur" (Williams) **15**:579-80; **45**:453-54, 456; **71**:363; **111**:419, 419
Desire in Language: A Semiotic Approach to Literature and Art (Kristeva) **77**:309-10, 312, 320; **140**:146-48, 150-51, 154, 168, 174, 180, 184, 197
"Desire in November" (Calvino) **33**:102
"Desire Is a World by Night" (Berryman) **62**:56
"Desire on Domino Island" (Smith) **73**:357
Desires (L'Heureux) **52**:279
Desmonde (Cronin) **32**:141
Desolación de la quimera (Cernuda) **54**:58, 60
"A Desolation" (Ginsberg) **36**:182
Desolation Angels (Kerouac) **3**:264; **29**:270, 272
Desolation Island (O'Brian) **152**:278, 282, 285, 287, 297, 300
"Desolation Row" (Dylan) **3**:130; **4**:149; **6**:156; **12**:181; **77**:161-62, 164, 187
Le désordre de la mémoire: Entretiens avec Francine Mallet (Mandiargues) **41**:278
"Despair" (Berryman) **25**:95-6
Despair (Crumb) **17**:84
Despair (Donoso)
See *La Desesperanza*
Despair (Fassbinder) **20**:117
Despair (Nabokov)
See *Otchaianie*
Despair (Nabokov)
See *Otchaianie*
Despair and Orthodoxy Among Some Modern Writers (Spender) **91**:261
"Despair in Being Tedious" (Duncan) **41**:128, 130
"Despair of a free volunteer" (Senghor)
See "Désespoir d'un volontaire libre"
The Despairing (Tzara)
See *Les désespéranto*
"La Despedida" (Moraga) **126**:297
"Desperadoes: Missouri 1861-1882 (or The James Gang and Their Relations)" (Jiles) **58**:276-77
Desperate Characters (Fox) **2**:139-40; **8**:217-18; **121**:188, 191-97, 218
"Desperate Measures" (Gallagher) **63**:121-22
"Desperate Measures" (Starbuck) **53**:353
Desperate Measures (Starbuck) **53**:353-54
The Desperate People (Mowat) **26**:334
"A Desperate Vitality" (Pasolini)
See "Una Disperata Vitalita"
Desperation (Donoso)
See *La Desesperanza*
"El despertar" (Borges) **3**:80
Despierta, mi bien, despierta (Alegria) **75**:46
"Despisals" (Rukeyser) **15**:458; **27**:412-13
"Despondency and Madness: On Lowell's 'Skunk Hour'" (Berryman) **13**:76
"Despues de la muerte" (Aleixandre) **9**:16
Despuúes (Benet) **28**:23-4
Dessa Rose (Williams) **89**:324-28, 330-36, 338, 340-45, 348, 350, 358
"Destierro" (Castellanos) **66**:50
Le destin (Tchicaya) **101**:365
"Le destin de la Flandre" (de Man) **55**:423
Le destin glorieux du Maréchal Nnikon Nniku, prince qu'on sort (Tchicaya) **101**:365
Destination Biafra (Emecheta) **48**:97-8; **128**:67-9
Destination Moon (Heinlein) **55**:304
Destination Unknown (Christie) **110**:113
Destination: Void (Herbert) **23**:219-20, 224, 226; **35**:197-98, 209; **44**:393-94
"Destinies" (Schaeffer) **22**:368-69
Destinies (Mauriac)
See *Destins*
The Destinies of Darcy Dancer, Gentleman (Donleavy) **10**:154-55; **45**:123, 125
"Destino" (Castellanos) **66**:50
"Destino de la carne" (Aleixandre) **9**:16; **36**:27
"Destino trágico" (Aleixandre) **9**:16
Destins (Mauriac) **4**:341; **56**:206, 212
"Destiny" (Parks) **147**:216-21
Destiny (Edgar) **42**:112-13, 115-17, 121-24
Destiny (Lang) **20**:200, 203
Destiny (Parks) **147**:215
Destiny Express (Rodman) **65**:89-94
Destiny Times Three (Leiber) **25**:301-03
Deštník z Piccadilly (Seifert) **93**:308-09, 320-25, 330-31, 337, 344
Destroy, She Said (Duras)
See *Détruire, dit-elle*
La destrucción o el amor (Aleixandre) **9**:11, 15; **36**:23-30
Destruction (Pa Chin) **18**:373
"The Destruction of Kreshev" (Singer) **6**:508; **9**:488; **38**:408; **69**:310 11; **111**:305-06
"The Destruction of Long Branch" (Pinsky) **121**:433-34, 436-38
"The Destruction of Pompeii" (Aksyonov) **101**:41
The Destruction of Reason (Lukacs) **24**:319-20
"The Destruction of the Goetheanum" (Salter) **52**:367, 369
Destruction or Love (Aleixandre)
See *La destrucción o el amor*
The Destructive Element: A Study of Modern Writers and Beliefs (Spender) **10**:490; **91**:261, 264
"Destructive Forces in Life" (Thurber) **125**:391
Details (Enzensberger)
See *Einzelheiten*
Details of a Sunset, and Other Stories (Nabokov) **8**:417; **15**:393
Detained: A Writer's Prison Diary (Ngũgĩ wa Thiong'o) **36**:318-19
The Detainee (Soyinka) **44**:285
"The Detective" (Ai) **69**:17
"The Detective" (Plath) **3**:390; **11**:449; **51**:340; **111**:169, 203
Detective Story (Kingsley) **44**:234-35, 238
Deterring Democracy (Chomsky) **132**:50, 55, 60, 67, 74
The Detling Secret (Symons) **32**:428
La detonación (Buero Vallejo) **139**:7-8, 10-12, 19, 23-7, 40, 42, 45-6
Detour (Brodsky) **19**:69-70
The Detour (Walser)
See *Der Abstecher*
"Detroit Abe" (Friedman) **56**:107
"Detroit Conference of Unity and Art" (Giovanni) **64**:194
"Detroit Skyline, 1949" (Mason) **43**:288; **82**:254-55; **154**:231, 234, 236, 285, 321-22
Détruire, dit-elle (Duras) **6**:150; **20**:98-101; **40**:179; **68**:87, 98; **100**:146
"Detstvo Luvers" (Pasternak) **7**:293; **10**:383; **18**:385-87; **63**:290

The Deuce (Butler) **81**:123, 126
Deus Irae (Dick) **10**:138; **72**:108
Deus irae (Zelazny) **21**:470
"Deutsch Durch Freud" (Jarrell) **9**:296
"Deutsches Requiem" (Borges) **1**:39; **19**:45, 47; **83**:157
Deutschland, Deutschland unter anderm (Enzensberger) **43**:154
Deutschstunde (Lenz) **27**:246-52
Deux Anglaises et le continent (Truffaut) **20**:392, 394-96; **101**:380, 382-84, 396-97
Les deux bourreaux (Arrabal) **9**:33-37; **18**:17-18; **58**:3-7, 10, 12, 16, 21, 24-6
"Les deux critiques" (Barthes) **24**:26
Deux hommes (Duhamel) **8**:186
"Les deux lys" (Ferron) **94**:129
"Les deux mains" (Hébert) **29**:227
Deux ou trois choses que je sais d'elle (Godard) **20**:140, 144, 146-48
Deux sous de violettes (Anouilh) **50**:279
Les deux timides (Clair) **20**:61, 66, 69
Deuxième bélvèdere (Mandiargues) **41**:278
Le deuxième sexe (Beauvoir) **1**:19; **2**:43-4; **4**:45-9; **8**:58, 60-1; **31**:33-9, 41-3; **44**:341-51; **50**:387-92; **71**:37-43, 45-50, 53-4, 56-61, 63-5, 67, 72-8, 83-7; **124**:133-36, 138-43, 149-51, 153, 157-59, 161-64, 166-69, 171-76, 179, 181
Le deux-millième étage (Carrier) **13**:143-44; **78**:50-1, 57-8, 60, 62, 67-70
Dévadé (Ducharme) **74**:68
DeValera (O'Faolain) **70**:317
"Development of Language" (John Paul II) **128**:187
Devi (Ray) **16**:479-80, 483, 486, 491, 493; **76**:357
Devices and Desires (James) **122**:163-64, 166, 168-69, 174, 183
"The Devil" (Tanizaki)
See "Akuma"
"The Devil and Irv Cherniske" (Boyle) **90**:45
The Devil and the Good Lord (Sartre)
See *Le diable et le bon Dieu*
The Devil at the Long Bridge (Bacchelli)
See *Diavolo al pontelungo*
The Devil Came from Dublin (Carroll) **10**:97-100
"Devil Car" (Zelazny) **21**:465
The Devil Doll (Browning) **16**:121
The Devil Finds Work (Baldwin) **8**:40-2; **17**:40-1; **42**:16, 18-19, 22; **90**:31; **127**:90, 108, 141
Devil in a Blue Dress (Mosley) **97**:327-35, 337-44, 347-48, 351-54, 358-60
The Devil in a Forest (Wolfe) **25**:473
A Devil in Paradise (Miller) **2**:281
The Devil in the Desert (Horgan) **53**:176-77
The Devil Is a Woman (Sternberg) **20**:371-73, 378
The Devil Is Loose! (Maillet)
See *Crache-à-pic*
Devil of a State (Burgess) **2**:85; **4**:81; **22**:77; **40**:113-15; **81**:301; **94**:23-24, 40
Devil on the Cross (Ngugi)
See *Caitaani mutharaba-ini*
The Devil on the Road (Westall) **17**:558-60
The Devil Rides Outside (Griffin) **68**:194-201
The Devil Soldier (Carr) **86**:42, 47
The Devil to Pay (Queen) **11**:458
The Devil to Pay in the Backlands (Rosa)
See *Grande Sertão: Veredas*
The Devil Tree (Kosinski) **2**:232-33; **3**:272-74; **6**:283-84; **10**:307; **15**:313-14, 316; **53**:219-20, 225-26, 228; **70**:298, 306
Devil with Boobs (Fo) **109**:143
Devilhorn (Bonham) **12**:55
Devil-in-the-Fog (Garfield) **12**:216-17, 224-25, 227-28, 230, 234-36, 240
The Devils (Russell) **16**:543-44, 546-50
"The Devil's Advice to Poets" (Kennedy) **42**:256
The Devil's Advocate (Caldwell) **28**:60; **39**:303
The Devil's Advocate (West) **6**:564; **33**:427-29, 431-33
The Devil's Alternative (Forsyth) **36**:175-76
The Devils and Canon Barham (Wilson) **3**:540
The Devil's Children (Dickinson) **12**:169-70, 172
The Devil's Eye (Bergman)
See *Djävulens öga*
The Devil's General (Zuckmayer)
See *Des Teufels General*
"Devil's Half-Acre; or, The Mystery of the 'Cruel Suitor'" (Oates) **108**:349
The Devil's Mode (Burgess) **62**:139
The Devils of Loudun (Huxley) **3**:253; **4**:240, 243; **5**:195; **35**:239
The Devil's Picture Book (Hine) **15**:281, 283
"The Devil's Spittle" (Cortázar)
See "Las babas del diablo"
The Devil's Stocking (Algren) **33**:17
"Devils Talk in Broad Daylight" (Tanizaki) **28**:414
The Devil's Wanton (Bergman)
See *Fängelse*
Le #Devoir de violence (Ouologuem) **146**:169-71, 173-80, 182-94, 196-97, 199-200, 206-19, 221, 223-29, 231-37, 239-55, 257-58, 261, 270
"Devonshire" (Davie) **8**:165-66
"Devonshire Street, W. 1" (Betjeman) **43**:34, 50
"The Devoted" (Howard) **7**:165
Devoted Ladies (Keane) **31**:232-33
"Devoted Son" (Desai) **97**:150
Devotion (Strauss)
See *Die Widmung*
"Devotion: That It Flow; That There Be Concentration" (Gallagher) **63**:118-20, 126
"Devyatsat pyaty god" (Pasternak) **18**:382; **63**:288-89, 293, 308
"Dezerterzy" (Rozewicz) **139**:297
D.H. Lawrence, Novelist (Leavis) **24**:297, 300, 305, 308-10
Dhalgren (Delany) **8**:168-69; **14**:144; **38**:151-54, 159, 161-62; **141**:101, 106, 115, 126, 128-30, 141-44, 148, 152-53, 155, 158-60
The Dharma Bums (Kerouac) **1**:166; **2**:226-27, 229; **3**:263-65; **14**:303-07; **61**:286, 293, 296, 306-09
"Dharma Queries" (Snyder) **120**:328
Dhiádhromos ke skála (Ritsos) **6**:463
"D.H.S.S." (Lessing) **94**:265
Di Familie Moskat (Singer) **1**:312-13; **3**:455-56; **6**:507; **11**:501; **15**:503-06; **23**:414, 417-20; **111**:293-94, 305, 340
Un dia en la vida (Argueta) **31**:19-21
"Diabetes" (Dickey) **47**:96
Le diable et le bon Dieu (Sartre) **4**:476; **7**:392; **9**:471; **13**:498-99, 502; **18**:470; **50**:381, 385
Le diable, probablement (Bresson) **16**:119
Diadème (Jouve) **47**:206
Diadia Sandro i konets kozlotura (Iskander) **47**:197, 200
"Diagrams" (Goldbarth) **38**:205
Dial M for Murder (Hitchcock) **16**:341, 346
"The Dialect of the Tribe" (Mathews) **52**:308, 313-14
"Dialectics" (Vollmann) **89**:284
"The Dialectics of Love" (McGrath) **28**:275, 279; **59**:177
"Dialectics of Rationalization" (Habermas) **104**:87
"Dialing for Dollars" (Mull) **17**:300
The Dialogic Imagination (Bakhtin)
See *Voprosy literatury i estetiki*
"Diálogo" (Cabral de Melo Neto) **76**:158
"Diàlogo" (Fuentes) **113**:244
Dialogo dei massimi sistemi (Landolfi) **49**:215
"Diálogo del espejo" (García Márquez) **3**:181; **15**:252
Diálogo secreto (Buero Vallejo) **139**:26-8, 31-2, 39-43, 57-60
"El diálogo y el ruido" (Paz) **65**:190
Diálogos con los hombres más honrados (Castellanos) **66**:53
Diálogos del conocimiento (Aleixandre) **9**:17; **36**:27, 30-2
"Dialogue" (Dickey) **28**:118
"Dialogue" (Garrigue) **8**:240
"Dialogue" (Scott) **22**:374
A Dialogue (Baldwin) **127**:104
"Dialogue III" (Barker) **8**:47
"Dialogue and Noise" (Paz)
See "El diálogo y el ruido"
"Dialogue at an Exhibition" (Wiebe) **138**:379
"Dialogue at Three in the Morning" (Parker) **15**:417
Dialogue de Rome (Duras) **68**:92
"Dialogue in a Mirror" (García Márquez)
See "Diálogo del espejo"
"Dialogue in the Stoneworks" (Ciardi) **40**:156
A Dialogue: James Baldwin and Nikki Giovanni (Giovanni) **117**:183-84, 192
"Dialogue of the Greater Systems" (Landolfi) **49**:215, 217
"A Dialogue of Watching" (Rexroth) **112**:400
"Dialogue on the Art of Composition" (Kundera) **68**:247-49; **115**:321
"Dialogue on the Art of the Novel" (Kundera) **115**:321
"Dialogue on the Greater Harmonies" (Landolfi) **49**:210
Dialogue with Death (Koestler) **15**:309; **33**:229
Dialogues (Lem)
See *Dialoqi*
"Dialogues des règnes" (Butor) **3**:93
Dialogues, Etc. (Barker) **8**:47; **48**:24
"Dialogues of Gog and Magog" (Barker) **48**:24
Dialogues of Knowledge (Aleixandre)
See *Diálogos del conocimiento*
Dialogues with the Devil (Caldwell) **28**:65; **39**:303
Dialoqi (Lem) **149**:111, 149, 156, 255, 289
"El diamante" (Arreola) **147**:16
Diamantes y pedernales (Arguedas) **10**:8
"The Diameter of the Bomb" (Amichai) **57**:46
"Diamond Body" (MacDiarmid) **4**:310
"The Diamond Cutters" (Rich) **7**:373
The Diamond Cutters, and Other Poems (Rich) **7**:368, 370; **18**:446, 449; **36**:366, 372, 374, 378; **73**:325, 328, 330; **76**:211; **125**:310
Diamond Dogs (Bowie) **17**:61-3, 65-8
"A Diamond Guitar" (Capote) **13**:134; **19**:82
Diamond Head (Waters) **88**:362
The Diamond Hunters (Smith) **33**:374
"The Diamond Merchant" (Wakoski) **9**:554-55
The Diamond Smugglers (Fleming) **30**:131
Diamonds and Flints (Arguedas)
See *Diamantes y pedernales*
Diamonds Are Forever (Fleming) **30**:131-32, 136, 142, 147-49
Diamonds Bid (Rathbone) **41**:337
Diamonds of the Night (Lustig) **56**:185-86
"Diana and Actaeon" (Porter) **33**:319, 324
Diana: The Goddess Who Hunts Alone (Fuentes) **113**:269
"The Dianas" (Stead) **32**:408; **80**:305
Diane (Isherwood) **44**:397
La diane Française (Aragon) **22**:37
"Diaper" (Birney) **6**:75
Diaries (Guevara)
See *El diario de Che en Bolivia: noviembre 7, 1966, a octubre 7, 1967*
Diaries (Lem) **149**:112
Diaries (Sassoon) **130**:224, 226-27
The Diaries of Evelyn Waugh (Waugh) **27**:475; **44**:520, 524-25
The Diaries of Jane Somers (Lessing) **40**:316; **94**:258-60, 272
"Diario" (Otero) **11**:427
"El diario como forma femenina" (Ferré) **139**:174
El diario de Che en Bolivia: noviembre 7, 1966, a octubre 7, 1967 (Guevara) **87**:206, 210

Diario de la guerra del cerdo (Bioy Casares) **4**:63-4; **13**:84-5; **88**:60, 90, 92
Diario de un cazador (Delibes) **18**:113
Diario de un enfermo (Azorín) **11**:27
Diario del '71 e del '72 (Montale) **7**:231; **9**:387; **18**:340
Diario in pubblico (Vittorini) **9**:551; **14**:543
"Diario para un cuento" (Cortázar) **33**:135; **34**:333
El diario que a diario (Guillén) **48**:160
Diario: Una sua bella biografia (Ungaretti) **7**:482
"The Diarrhea Gardens of El Camino Real" (Martin) **30**:248
"Diarrhea of a Writer" (Grayson) **38**:211
"Diary" (Stern) **100**:345
Diary (Gombrowicz)
See *Dziennik*
Diary (Nin) **1**:247-48; **4**:377-78; **8**:424; **11**:396-99; **14**:384-85; **127**:360. 364-65, 371-72, 375-76, 384-86, 397, 399-01, 403
Diary 1928-1957 (Green) **77**:270
"The Diary as Feminine Form" (Ferré)
See "El diario como forma femenina"
"Diary: Audience, 1966" (Cage) **41**:78
Diary: How to Improve the World (Cage) **41**:77-8, 80, 82, 85
Diary of '71 and '72 (Montale)
See *Diario del '71 e del '72*
Diary of a Chambermaid (Bunuel)
See *Le journal d'une femme de chambre*
The Diary of a Chambermaid (Renoir) **20**:303-04
Diary of a Country Priest (Bresson)
See *Journal d'un curé de campagne*
The Diary of a Good Neighbour (Lessing) **40**:308-10, 315; **94**:258, 261
Diary of a Hunter (Delibes)
See *Diario de un cazador*
Diary of a Mad Housewife (Kaufman) **3**:263; **8**:317
Diary of a Mad Old Man (Tanizaki)
See *Futen rojin nikki*
"Diary of a Myth-Boy" (Thomas) **132**:382
"Diary of a Naturalist" (Milosz) **31**:261 62; **82**:295
"Diary of a New York Apartment Hunter" (Lebowitz) **36**:249
The Diary of a Rapist (Connell) **4**:109; **45**:110-11
The Diary of a Seducer (Rothenberg) **6**:477
Diary of a Shinjuku Thief (Oshima) **20**:246, 248-49, 251, 254
Diary of a Yunbogi Boy (Oshima) **20**:250
Diary of a Yuppie (Auchincloss) **45**:36-7
"The Diary of Abraham Segal, Poet" (Klein) **19**:258
The Diary of Alexander Patience (Orlovitz) **22**:332
"The Diary of an African Nun" (Walker) **19**:450; **103**:406-07, 410-11
"Diary of an Invisible April" (Elytis) **100**:175, 182-83, 185-86
Diary of an Old Man (Bermant) **40**:90-2
The Diary of Anaïs Nin, 1931-1934, Vol. 1 (Nin) **8**:423; **11**:397, 399; **14**:384
The Diary of Anaïs Nin, 1934-1939, Vol. 2 (Nin) **4**:380; **11**:397; **14**:384
The Diary of Anaïs Nin, 1939-1944, Vol. 3 (Nin) **8**:425; **11**:397; **14**:384; **127**:364-65, 383, 385
The Diary of Anaïs Nin, 1944-1947, Vol. 4 (Nin) **4**:377; **11**:397-98; **14**:384-85
The Diary of Anaïs Nin, 1947-1955, Vol. 5 (Nin) **4**:379-80; **11**:398; **14**:385
The Diary of Anaïs Nin, 1955-1966, Vol. 6 (Nin) **8**:423; **11**:398; **14**:385
The Diary of Anaïs Nin: Vols. I-VII (Nin) **60**:275, 277-78; **127**:391
The Diary of Che Guerara; Bolivia: November 7, 1966—October 7, 1967 (Guevara)
See *El diario de Che en Bolivia: noviembre 7, 1966, a octubre 7, 1967*
The Diary of Dr. Eric Zero (Orlovitz) **22**:332
"The Diary of K. W." (Berriault) **54**:3-5; **109**:96-7
"The Diary of Miss Sophie" (Ding Ling)
See "Shafei nüshi de riji"
The Diary of Samuel Marchbanks (Davies) **13**:173; **25**:129; **42**:103, 105; **75**:182-83
"The Diary of the Rose" (Le Guin) **45**:213, 216-17
Diary of the War of the Pig (Bioy Casares)
See *Diario de la guerra del cerdo*
A Diary without Dates (Bagnold) **25**:72-3
Los días enmascarados (Fuentes) **8**:223; **41**:166, 171
Días hábiles (Paz) **65**:181
"Los días y los temas" (Otero) **11**:427
Días y noches de amor y de guerra (Galeano)
See *Days and Nights of Love and War*
"Diaspora" (Lorde) **71**:258, 260
Diavolo al pontelungo (Bacchelli) **19**:30
The (Diblos) Notebook (Merrill) **2**:275; **91**:234
Diccionario secreto (Cela)
See *Dicciones secreto*
Dicciones secreto (Cela) **122**:21-2, 66
The Dice of War (Giovene) **7**:117
Diceria dell'untore (Bufalino) **74**:38-9
Dicey's Song (Voigt) **30**:418-20
"Dichtung und Wahrheit" (Hecht) **8**:269
The Dick (Friedman) **3**:165; **5**:127; **56**:99-102, 107
Dick Deterred (Edgar) **42**:111-12, 116, 121
"Dick Donnelly" (Buckley) **57**:135
The Dick Francis Treasury of Great Horseracing Stories (Francis) **102**:141
The Dick Gibson Show (Elkin) **4**:154; **6**:169; **9**:190-91; **14**:158; **27**:122-23, 125; **51**:85, 89, 91, 96-7; **91**:213
Dickens (Ackroyd)
See *Dickens: Life and Times*
"Dickens Digested" (Davies) **42**:103
Dickens: Life and Times (Ackroyd) **140**:10, 13-14, 28, 30, 32, 50
"The Dickies" (Gardam) **43**:169
The Dictators (Archer) **12**:16
The Dictatorship of the Conscience (Shatrov)
See *Diktatura sovesti*
The Dictionary of Cultural Literacy: What Every American Needs To Know (Hirsch) **70**:363, 396
Dictionary of the Khazars: A Lexicon Novel in 100,000 Words (Pavic)
See *Hazarski recnik*
"Dictum: For a Masque of Deluge" (Merwin) **8**:388; **88**:207
"Did I Say" (Stern) **100**:344
"Did Jesus Ever Laugh?" (Wiebe) **138**:326
"Did She Mention My Name?" (Lightfoot) **26**:278
Did She Mention My Name? (Lightfoot) **26**:278
"Did You Ever Slip on Red Blood?" (Oates) **134**:246
"Did You Say the War Is Over?" (McKuen) **3**:333
"Didactic Piece" (Bogan) **93**:65, 67, 69, 90-91
"Didn't He Ramble" (Simmons) **43**:410
"Dido's Lament" (Castellanos)
See "Lamentación de Dido"
"Didymus" (MacNeice) **4**:316
"An die Sonne" (Bachmann) **69**:42
Died in the Wool (Marsh) **53**:250-51, 255-56, 259-60
"Died of Wounds" (Sassoon) **130**:182
Died on a Rainy Sunday (Aiken) **35**:16-17
Dien cai dau (Komunyakaa) **86**:191; **94**:225-26, 228-29, 231-34, 236, 240
"Dienstag, den 27. September" (Wolf) **29**:464; **150**:237, 296, 321-22
"Dies irae" (Lowell) **1**:182
"Dies irae" (Morgan) **31**:276
"Diese Kette von Rätseln" (Sachs) **98**:341
Le Dieu bleu (Cocteau) **15**:134
Le Dieu caché (Goldmann) **24**:234, 236, 238-39, 241, 243, 245, 247, 251, 254
Dieu nous l'a donné (Condé) **52**:79-81; **92**:99-100
Dieu tenté par les mathematiques (Arrabal) **9**:35
"Difference" (Aldiss) **14**:15
"Difference" (Derrida) **24**:145
The Difference Engine (Sterling) **72**:372-73
A Difference of Design (Spackman) **46**:378-80
The Difference Within: Feminism and Critical Theory (Meese and Parker) **65**:338
"The Differences" (Gunn) **81**:178
A Different Drummer (Kelley) **22**:248, 250
A Different Face (Manning) **19**:300
"Different Finger" (Costello) **21**:76
Different Fleshes (Goldbarth) **38**:202-04
"A Different Image" (Randall) **135**:389
A Different Kind of Christmas (Haley) **76**:347
"Different Kinds of Plays" (Bentley) **24**:47
A Different Person (Merrill) **91**:227-28 230, 236
Different Seasons (King) **26**:240-43; **37**:207; **61**:327-28; **113**:338, 343, 351-52
A Different World (Ghose) **42**:181-82
"Differently" (Munro) **95**:310-11, 314-15
"Difficult" (Jennings) **131**:239-40
The Difficult Hour (Lagerkvist) **54**:277
Difficult Loves (Calvino)
See *Gli amori difficili*
The Difficult Ones (Frisch)
See *Die Schwierigen; oder, J'adore ce qui me brûle*
Difficult Women: A Portrait of Three (Plante) **38**:368-72
Difficulties with Girls (Amis) **129**:3, 19
Dig a Grave and Let Us Bury Our Mother (Smart) **54**:425-26
"Dig, He Said, Dig" (Musgrave) **54**:335
Dig the New Breed (Weller) **26**:447
The Digestive System: How Living Creatures Use Food (Silverstein and Silverstein) **17**:451
The Digger's Game (Higgins) **4**:222-24; **7**:158; **10**:274
"Digging" (Hall) **37**:142
"Digging" (Heaney) **25**:244, 248, 250-51; **74**:150-51, 155, 163, 165, 180
"Digging for China" (Wilbur) **53**:410; **110**:348, 353
"Digging In" (Piercy) **62**:367; **128**:230
Digging Out (Roiphe) **3**:435
"The Digging Skeleton (after Baudelaire)" (Heaney) **74**:158
"Digging Up the Mountains" (Bissoondath) **120**:4, 8, 18
Digging Up the Mountains (Bissoondath) **120**:2-3, 5-11, 15, 18, 26
"Digital Dexterity of the Dental Demonstrator Holds Audience in Awe" (Barnes) **127**:164
Dijalekticki antibarbarus (Krleža) **114**:174
Diktatura sovesti (Shatrov) **59**:358, 360-61, 364
"The Dileas" (MacLean) **63**:270
"The Dilemma (My poems are not sufficiently obscure? To please the critics—Ray Durem)" (Randall) **135**:390, 398
The Dilemma of Love (Giovene) **7**:117
"The Dilemma of the Black Intellectual" (West) **134**:375, 383
The Dilemma of the Contemporary Novelist (Wilson) **34**:580-81
"Díles que no me maten!" (Rulfo) **80**:201, 222
"Dili" (Pasolini) **106**:228
"Diligence Is to Magic As Progress Is to Flight" (Moore) **19**:341
Dilli ki Sham (Ali) **69**:25
"Dillingham, Alaska, the Willow Tree Bar" (Snyder) **120**:325-26
"Dilton Marsh Halt" (Betjeman) **43**:46
Le dimanche de la vie (Queneau) **2**:359; **5**:358-

59, 362; **10**:432; **42**:332, 334
Dimanche m'attend (Audiberti) **38**:32
Die Dimension des Autors: Essays und Aufsätzes, Reden und Gespräche (Wolf) **58**:430-31; **150**:296-97, 300, 302, 314-17, 337, 339, 342
"The Dimensions of a Tiger" (MacEwen) **13**:357
Dime-Store Alchemy: The Art of Joseph Cornell (Simic) **130**:326-28, 332, 338
Dimetos (Fugard) **9**:232-33; **80**:62, 68-9
"Dimitri" (Theriault) **79**:408
Dinah and the Green Fat Kingdom (Holland) **21**:153
"Dinamarquero" (Donoso) **32**:158
Le dîner en ville (Mauriac) **9**:363-64
Dingley Falls (Malone) **43**:281-82, 284
"Dining from a Treed Condition: An Historical Survey" (Harper) **22**:209
The Dining Room (Gurney) **32**:218-20; **50**:177-79, 183-84; **54**:216-22
Dinky Hocker Shoots Smack! (Kerr) **12**:296-98, 301; **35**:250
"Dinner" (Arghezi)
See "Cina"
"The Dinner" (Lispector) **43**:269
"Dinner Along the Amazon" (Findley) **102**:107-08
Dinner Along the Amazon (Findley) **102**:107, 109-11
"Dinner at Eight" (Mphahlele)
See "We'll Have Dinner at Eight"
Dinner at Eight (Ferber) **93**:159-61, 165
Dinner at Eight (Kaufman) **38**:259
Dinner at the Homesick Restaurant (Tyler) **28**:432-35; **44**:313, 315, 321; **59**:202-08, 210; **103**:217-18, 220-21, 223-30, 233-35, 238-44, 247-48, 260-61, 263-64, 268-71, 275
"Dinner at the Sea-View Inn" (Simpson) **149**:351
"Dinner for One" (Tremain) **42**:386
"Dinner in Audoghast" (Sterling) **72**:372
"Dinner in Donnybrook" (Binchy) **153**:65
The Dinner Party (Fast) **131**:56-7, 59-61, 86, 102
The Dinner Party (Mauriac)
See *Le dîner en ville*
Dinny and the Witches (Gibson) **23**:177, 180
Dinosaur Planet (McCaffrey) **17**:283
Dinosaur Tales (Bradbury) **42**:42
Dintr-un foişor (Arghezi) **80**:13
The Dionne Years: A Thirties Melodrama (Berton) **104**:46-7, 57
Dionysus in '69 (De Palma) **20**:78
"El dios de los toros" (Bioy Casares) **88**:67-8
De dioses, hombrecitos, y policías (Costantini) **49**:61-2
Dioses y hombres de huarochiri (Arguedas) **10**:9
Diplomacy (Kissinger) **137**:232, 235, 238, 240-41, 250, 256, 258
"Diplomacy: The Father" (Snodgrass) **68**:381-82
"Diplomatic Relations" (Theroux) **11**:528
Diplopic (Reading) **47**:352-53
"Diptych: Jesus and the Stone" (Baxter) **78**:28
"Diptych with Votive Tablet" (Paz)
See "Preparatory Exercise (Dyptych with Votive Tablet)"
The Dirdir (Vance) **35**:422, 424
Dire Coasts (Holmes) **56**:145
"Direadh" (MacDiarmid) **4**:309; **11**:333
Le directeur de l'opéra (Anouilh) **40**:57, 59
"Direction" (Macdonald) **13**:356
The Direction of the March (Adamov)
See *Le sens de la marche*
"The Direction of the Treatment and the Principles of its Power" (Lacan) **75**:295
"Directions" (Deane) **122**:74, 83
"Directions to a Rebel" (Rodgers) **7**:378
Directionscore: Selected and New Poems (Madhubuti) **73**:205, 215
"Directive" (Frost) **1**:110; **4**:176; **9**:221, 228; **15**:245, 250; **26**:119-20, 124, 126
"Directive" (Haines) **58**:214
"Directive" (Redgrove) **41**:352
"Director of Alienation" (Ferlinghetti) **27**:137; **111**:59
A Director's Notebook (Fellini)
See *Block-notes de un regista*
Direption (Booth) **13**:103
"Dirge" (Dylan) **4**:150
"Dirge" (Eliot) **55**:366
"Dirge" (Fearing) **51**:117
"Dirge for a Penny Whistle" (Gustafson) **36**:216
"Dirge for the New Sunrise (August 6, 1945)" (Sitwell) **67**:333, 336
"Dirge Notes" (Huddle) **49**:183
"Dirge of the Palm Race" (Kunene) **85**:166
"Dirge over a Pot of Pâté de Foie Grass" (McGinley) **14**:366
Dirk Gently's Holistic Detective Agency (Adams) **60**:3-6
"Dirt" (Salter) **52**:369; **59**:197
"The Dirty Hand" (Strand) **71**:284
Dirty Hands (Sartre)
See *Les mains sales*
Dirty Hearts (Sanchez) **116**:301
Dirty Linen (Stoppard) **8**:503-04; **29**:397, 400
"Dirty Mind" (Prince) **35**:323, 328
Dirty Mind (Prince) **35**:323-25, 327-28, 330
Dirty Story (Ambler) **4**:19; **9**:19
Dirty Tricks; or, Nick Noxin's Natural Nobility (Seelye) **7**:407
"The Dirty Word" (Shapiro) **53**:332
Dirty Work (Brown) **73**:20-3, 27
A Disaffection (Kelman) **58**:302-05; **86**:181, 185, 188-89
The Disappearance (Guy) **26**:144-45
The Disappearance (Perec)
See *La disparition*
The Disappearance (Trifonov) **59**:382
The Disappearance (Wylie) **43**:466-67, 470, 472
"The Disappearance of an Absolute Destroys" (Rozewicz)
See "Wygasnięcic Absolutu niszczy"
"The Disappearance of the Fireflies" (Pasolini) **106**:251
The Disappearance of the Outside (Codrescu) **121**:155, 159-60
"Disappearances" (Hogan) **73**:152
Disappearances (Mosher) **62**:310-15
"The Disappeared" (Baxter) **78**:25-27, 30
Disappearing Acts (McMillan) **61**:364-67; **112**:222, 225-28, 230, 234, 236, 239-41, 243, 246-48, 250, 252
"The Disappearing Island" (Heaney) **74**:190
"Disappointment" (Newlove) **14**:378
"A Disaster" (Hughes) **2**:205; **119**:262, 264
Disaster (O'Brien) **17**:324
"Disasters" (Fuller) **4**:178
"Disasters of the Sun" (Livesay) **79**:351-52
The Discarded Image: An Introduction to Medieval and Renaissance Literature (Lewis) **3**:296; **6**:308; **124**:193
"The Disciple of Bacon" (Epstein) **27**:128
"A Discipline" (Berry) **27**:34
"Discipline" (Brown) **73**:23
"The Discipline" (Clarke) **53**:91
"Discipline and Honor" (Berry) **46**:75
"Discipline and Hope" (Berry) **27**:38-9
Discipline and Punish: The Birth of the Prison (Foucault)
See *Surveiller et punir: Naissance de la prison*
"El discípulo" (Arreola) **147**:15
Disclosure (Crichton) **90**:88-95, 97
"Disco Apocalypse" (Browne) **21**:42
"Disco Mystic" (Reed) **21**:317
Le discours antillais (Glissant) **68**:175, 178-80, 184-87, 189-90
Discours dc la méthode (Ionesco) **6**:252
"Discours de Rome" (Lacan)
See "Fonction et champ de la parole et du langage en psychanalyse"
Discours sur le colonialisme (Césaire) **112**:6-7, 20, 39
"Discourse" (Thesen) **56**:415
"A Discourse concerning Temptation" (Hecht) **8**:267
"Discourse Ethics, Law and Sittlichkeit" (Habermas) **104**:87
"Discourse in Life and Discourse in Art" (Bakhtin) **83**:14, 28
"Discourse in the Novel" (Bakhtin) **83**:11, 14, 25, 44-6, 58-9
"The Discourse of the Good Thief" (Parra) **102**:353-54
The Discourse of the Great Sleep (Cocteau) **8**:146
"Discourse on Beauty" (Elytis) **49**:110
Discourse on Colonialism (Césaire)
See *Discours sur le colonialisme*
"The Discourse on Language" (Foucault) **31**:177
The Discourse on Language (Foucault)
See *L'orare du discours*
"Discourse on Poetry" (Quasimodo) **10**:427
Discourse on Thinking (Heidegger) **24**:266
Discourse on Vietnam (Weiss)
See *Viet Nam Diskurs*
"Discoveries, Trade Names, Genitals, and Ancient Instruments" (Rakosi) **47**:348
"Discovering Literature" (Cabral de Melo Neto)
See "Descoberta da literatura"
"Discovering Obscenities on Her Wall" (Smith) **42**:346
"The Discovery" (Barthelme) **115**:71
"The Discovery" (MacEwen) **13**:358
"Discovery of Chile" (Neruda) **1**:247
"The Discovery of Mexico" (Fuentes) **113**:256
A Discovery of Strangers (Wiebe) **138**:372-74, 379, 381, 386
"A Discreet Miracle" (Allende) **97**:9, 11
Discrepancies and Apparitions (Wakoski) **7**:507; **40**:454
Discrete Series (Oppen) **7**:283, 285; **34**:389-59
"Discretions of Alcibiades" (Pinsky) **121**:435
Discriminations (Wellek) **28**:451-52
"The Discriminator" (Scannell) **49**:330
"The Discursive Mode" (Hope) **51**:215, 217-18, 222
Discusión (Borges) **83**:162-63, 165-66
"A Discussion of Feminine Types" (Thurber) **125**:402
Discussions (Borges)
See *Discusión*
"Disdain" (Aldington) **49**:4, 7
"Disease" (Tate) **25**:428
Disease and the Novel (Meyers) **39**:433
Disease Detectives (Berger) **12**:42
"The Diseases of Costume" (Barthes) **83**:70
"The Disembodied Lady" (Sacks) **67**:301
The Disenchanted (Schulberg) **7**:402-03; **48**:347-50, 352-53
Disent les imbéciles (Sarraute) **8**:472-73; **10**:460; **31**:386; **80**:257-58
"Disfiguration" (Ghose) **42**:179
"The Disgrace of Jim Scarfedale" (Sillitoe) **57**:388, 392, 394
"Disguise" (Singer) **69**:313
"Disguised Zenith" (Ashbery) **77**:68
"Disguises" (Townshend) **17**:529
"Dishonest Modesty" (Simon) **26**:410
Dishonored (Sternberg) **20**:369-70, 372, 378-79
"The Disincarnation" (Sisson) **8**:491
"Disinheritance" (Jhabvala) **138**:65, 67, 69
"The Disinherited" (Bowen) **22**:62-3, 66-7
The Disinherited (Cohen) **19**:112-14, 116
The Disinherited (del Castillo) **38**:165-67
"Disintegration" (Kostelanetz) **28**:218

"The Disinterested Killer Bill Harrigan" (Borges)
See "El asesino desinteresado Bill Harrigan"
"Disjecta Membra" (Wright) **119**:180-82, 184-88
Disjecta: Miscellaneous Writings and a Dramatic Fragment (Beckett) **29**:67
Disjointed Fictions (Grayson) **38**:208-09, 211-12
Dislocations (Hospital) **145**:295, 297, 311-12, 315, 320
"Disloyal to Civilzation: Feminism, Racism, Gynephobia" (Rich) **73**:323
"Dismantling the Silence" (Simic) **9**:480
Dismantling the Silence (Simic) **6**:502; **9**:478-79, 481; **22**:379-80, 382; **68**:368, 379; **130**:293, 298, 305, 316-17, 332
"Disnae Matter" (Welsh) **144**:319
"Disneyad" (Apple) **33**:19
"Disobedience" (Moravia) **46**:282
Disobedience (Moravia)
See *La disubbidienza*
"Disobedience and Women's Studies" (Rich) **73**:322
"Disparities" (Okri) **87**:315
La disparition (Perec) **56**:254-56, 258, 260-63, 265, 268-72; **116**:233-34, 240, 243, 245-46, 248, 250-52, 254, 262-67, 269-70
La disparition d'Odile (Simenon) **2**:399
Dispatches (Swados) **12**:560-62
"Una Disperata Vitalita" (Pasolini) **106**:220, 239, 241, 249, 253, 264
"The Dispersal" (Avison) **97**:128
"Dispersed Titles" (Avison) **97**:76, 83, 88, 94, 96, 98, 109, 111, 122-23, 125, 127-29, 131-32
"Displaced Person" (Murphy) **41**:319
"The Displaced Person" (O'Connor) **1**:255, 257; **3**:366; **13**:419; **15**:410, 412; **21**:256, 261-62, 266-67, 269-71, 278; **104**:105, 124, 137, 179
"Displacement" (Allen) **84**:5
"Displacement" (Louie) **70**:78
"Disposal" (Snodgrass) **68**:382
"The Dispossessed" (Berryman) **10**:50; **13**:78
"The Dispossessed" (Kinsella) **138**:120
The Dispossessed (Berryman) **2**:56; **3**:70; **8**:91; **10**:48; **13**:75, 77-8; **25**:89; **62**:71, 75-6
The Dispossessed: An Ambiguous Utopia (Le Guin) **8**:341-43; **13**:348, 350-51; **22**:268-69; **45**:213-15, 217, 220-23; **136**:312, 330, 335, 338, 340-41, 343, 348-54, 383-85, 392-93
Disputed Questions (Merton) **83**:403
"Le disque de Caruso" (Theriault) **79**:407
"The Disquieted Muses" (Plath)
See "The Disquieting Muses"
"The Disquieting Muses" (Plath) **2**:336; **17**:360; **51**:344
Disquietude (Rozewicz)
See *Niepokój*
"Dissect This Silence" (Kunitz) **148**:87
"The Dissecting Table" (Szirtes) **46**:392
La dissémination (Derrida) **24**:141, 155; **87**:72, 88-9, 91-2, 103
Dissemination (Derrida)
See *La dissémination*
Dissentient Voice: The Ward-Phillips Lectures for 1980 with Some Related Pieces (Davie) **31**:120-22
"Dissertation by Wax Light" (Eberhart) **56**:80
"Disseverings, Divorces" (Nemerov) **36**:309
"The Dissolving Fabric" (Blackburn) **43**:69
The Dissolving Fabric (Blackburn) **43**:63
"Distance" (Boland) **113**:94
"Distance" (Carver) **53**:64; **126**:133
"A Distance" (Merwin) **88**:212
"Distance" (Paley) **140**:219, 232, 238, 255, 277, 281
The Distance (Seger) **35**:386-87
"Distance and a Certain Light" (Swenson) **61**:397, 400; **106**:326
The Distance and the Dark (White) **49**:404-05
The Distance Anywhere (Hanson) **13**:264
The Distance Between Us (Sayers) **122**:231-36, 238-39, 242
"A Distance of Half a Kilometer" (Voinovich) **10**:505; **147**:270
"Distances" (Alexie) **96**:4
"The Distances" (Carroll) **35**:78; **143**:27
"The Distances" (Cortázar)
See "Lejana"
"Distances" (Goldbarth) **38**:205
"Distances" (Hugo) **32**:252
"Distances" (Okigbo) **84**:302, 307, 312, 314-22, 324-27, 329, 332-33, 336, 341-42
Distances (Josipovici) **153**:208, 218
Distances (Okigbo) **25**:349, 352, 356
The Distances (Olson) **2**:326; **11**:415
"Distancia del amigo" (Castellanos) **66**:50
"The Distant" (Ritsos) **31**:331
The Distant, 1975 (Ritsos) **31**:328-30
"Distant Chirping Birds" (Matthews) **40**:324
"A Distant Episode" (Bowles) **19**:57, 60
"Distant Fingers" (Smith) **12**:539
The Distant Lands (Green)
See *Les pays lointains*
A Distant Likeness (Bailey) **45**:41-2, 44, 46
"Distant Lover" (Gaye) **26**:133
The Distant Lover (Hein)
See *Der fremde Freund*
"Distant Music" (Beattie) **13**:65; **146**:52, 62-3
The Distant Music (Davis) **49**:91-2, 97
"The Distant Past" (Trevor) **7**:478; **116**:338-39, 359
Distant Relations (Fuentes)
See *Una familia lejana*
The Distant Shore (de Hartog) **19**:130
Distant Stars (Delany) **38**:154
Distant Thunder (Ray)
See *Ashani sanket*
A Distant Trumpet (Horgan) **53**:177-79, 181
Distant Years (Paustovsky) **40**:368
"Dístico español" (Cernuda) **54**:46
"Distinctions" (Tomlinson) **45**:399
Distinctions (Wesker) **42**:429-30
"The Distinguished Elephant" (Keates) **34**:202-03
Distortions (Beattie) **8**:54-7; **13**:65; **40**:63, 66; **63**:3, 9-12, 15, 17-19; **146**:47, 53-4, 69, 78, 83-4, 86
Distractions (Middleton) **7**:220-21
"The Distractions; the Music" (Loewinsohn) **52**:285
"Distractions of a Fiction Writer" (Bellow) **8**:74; **25**:87
"Los distraídos" (Castellanos) **66**:52
"Distress Sale" (Carver) **36**:107; **55**:273
"A District in the City" (Hugo) **32**:236
District of Columbia (Dos Passos) **4**:133, 137; **25**:145-46; **34**:420, 422; **82**:76, 85
Disturbances (Bernhard)
See *Verstörung*
Disturbances in the Field (Schwartz) **31**:390-92
Disturbing the Peace (Yates) **7**:555-56; **8**:555-56
Disturbing the Peace: A Conversation with Karel Hvízdala (Havel) **65**:433-38, 441-43; **123**:172, 175-77, 185, 196, 214
La disubbidienza (Moravia) **7**:244; **18**:343; **27**:354
The Disuniting of America: Reflections on a Multicultural Society (Schlesinger) **70**:405; **84**:387, 389, 391
"Disunity as Unity" (Kroetsch) **132**:285
"A Disused Shed in Co. Wexford" (Mahon) **27**:287-89, 291-93
"Dit du péégrin" (Guillevic) **33**:193-94
Dita Sax (Lustig) **56**:182
"The Ditch" (Ryan) **65**:216
The Ditch: A Spiritual Trial (Voznesensky) **57**:425
"Dithyramb" (Ekeloef) **27**:110
"The Diver" (Hayden) **5**:169; **37**:155, 158
"The Diver" (Pritchett) **13**:468; **41**:331
"Divergence" (Char) **11**:116
"The Diver's Vision" (Merwin) **88**:198
"The Diverse Causes" (Ondaatje) **14**:407
Diversifications (Ammons) **8**:14, 17; **9**:29-30; **25**:44; **108**:12, 24, 55
"Diversions" (Fisher) **25**:161
The Diversions of Purley and Other Poems (Ackroyd) **52**:9; **140**:9
Diversity and Depth in Fiction: Selected Critical Writings of Angus Wilson (Wilson) **34**:579-83
Dives in Misericordia (John Paul II) **128**:177, 193
"The Divestment of Beauty" (Riding) **7**:375
"Divided Heaven" (Wolf) **150**:319
The Divided Heaven (Wolf)
See *Der geteilte Himmel*
"The Divided Life Re-Lived" (Fuller) **28**:153
A Divided People (Lynn) **50**:426
The Divided Self: A Study of Sanity and Madness (Laing) **95**:124, 129-35, 137-41, 144, 153-54, 156, 166, 168-74, 177, 179, 181-82, 184-86, 188
Divided Soul: The Life of Gogol (Troyat) **23**:461
"Divided Twins" (Yevtushenko) **126**:399
"Dividends" (O'Faolain) **14**:405; **70**:319
The Dividing Night (Scannell) **49**:325-26
The Dividing Stream (King) **53**:203-04
Divina commedia (MacDiarmid) **4**:310; **11**:334
"Divination by a Cat" (Hecht) **8**:266
"The Divine Claudius" (Herbert) **43**:191
Divine Comedies: Poems (Merrill) **8**:380-81, 384, 386, 388; **13**:376-78, 381-82; **18**:328; **34**:226-27, 231; **91**:228, 232
"The Divine Comedy" (Borges) **48**:47, 49
"Divine Comedy" (Dodson) **79**:193
The Divine Comedy (Ciardi) **129**:54
Divine Comedy (Dodson) **79**:188, 193, 197
Divine Disobedience: Profiles in Catholic Radicalism (Gray) **22**:199-200; **153**:138
The Divine Enchantment (Neihardt) **32**:332-33
Divine Horsemen: The Living Gods of Haiti (Deren) **16**:254; **102**:26-7, 31, 36-8, 44-9
The Divine Invasion (Dick) **72**:113, 119-20
The Divine Mimesis (Pasolini) **106**:265
The Divine Pilgrim (Aiken) **52**:22, 26
"The Diviner" (Heaney) **25**:244; **74**:153, 167
The Diviners (Laurence) **6**:289-90; **13**:342; **50**:312-15, 319-22; **62**:266-84, 287-88, 290, 293-308
Diving for Sunken Treasure (Cousteau) **30**:105
"Diving into the Wreck" (Rich) **3**:428; **6**:459; **7**:371, 373; **11**:475-77; **36**:374; **76**:210-11; **125**:319, 332
Diving into the Wreck: Poems, 1971-1972 (Rich) **3**:427-29; **6**:459; **7**:367-69, 371-73; **11**:476, 478; **18**:447; **36**:368, 372-73, 375, 377; **73**:314, 325-27, 331; **76**:217; **125**:317, 319, 322, 336
A Diving Rock on the Hudson (Roth) **104**:324-26, 329-30
"Divinità in incognito" (Montale) **9**:386
"Divinities" (Merwin) **88**:191
"Division" (Bogan) **46**:90; **93**:81, 90-2, 98
"Division" (Merwin) **3**:339
"The Division of Parts" (Sexton) **123**:435
A Division of the Spoils (Scott)
See *The Raj Quartet*
Division Street (Tesich) **40**:421-23; **69**:368, 370-71, 373
Division Street: America (Terkel) **38**:418-23, 425
"Divisions" (Silkin) **43**:404
Divisions on a Ground (Frye) **70**:275
Divisions on a Ground (Nye) **42**:305
"Divorce" (Gilchrist) **143**:300
"Divorce" (Jong) **83**:289
"The Divorce" (Smith) **22**:384
Divorce American Style (Lear) **12**:326

"Divorce as a Moral Act" (Gold) **42**:189
"Divorce of Lovers" (Sarton) **91**:254
"The Divorce Papers" (Sexton) **15**:473
"Divorced Child" (Coles) **46**:113
Dīwān (Ekeloef)
See *Dīwān över fursten av Emigón*
Dīwān över fursten av Emigón (Ekeloef) **27**:116-17
Dix heures et demie du soir en été (Duras) **6**:149; **11**:166; **40**:179-81; **68**:74, 85
Dixiana Moon (Fox) **22**:141-42
Dix-neuf poèmes élastiques (Cendrars) **18**:94; **106**:163, 177, 181, 185-86, 190-91, 197-98
"D.J." (Bowie) **17**:66
"Django" (Ellison) **42**:129
Djävulens öga (Bergman) **72**:40
Djetinjstvo u Agramu, 1902-1903 (Krleža) **8**:330; **114**:166, 171
Djinn (Robbe-Grillet) **43**:362-64; **128**:360-61, 363, 370, 377
"The Djinn in the Nightingale's Eye" (Byatt) **136**:163
The Djinn in the Nightingale's Eye (Byatt) **136**:162-63
"The Djinn Who Watches Over the Accursed" (Donaldson) **138**:41
Dlia pol'zy dela (Solzhenitsyn) **4**:507; **7**:432; **134**:284
"D.M.S.R." (Prince) **35**:327-28
"The DNA Molecule Is the Nude Descending a Staircase" (Swenson) **14**:521
Dni cheloveka (Bitov) **57**:115
"Do" (Tolson) **105**:262-63, 283
Do Androids Dream of Electric Sheep? (Dick) **30**:123, 125-28; **72**:104, 108, 110, 113, 117-24
Do Black Patent Leather Shoes Really Reflect Up? (Powers) **66**:380-83
"De Do Do Do, De Da Da Da" (Police, The) **26**:365-66
"Do I Hear a Waltz?" (Sondheim) **30**:379
Do I Hear a Waltz? (Sondheim) **30**:379, 385, 387, 389, 392, 395
"Do It Again" (Becker and Fagen) **26**:79-81
"Do It Again" (Wilson) **12**:650
"Do It All Night" (Prince) **35**:323
Do, Lord, Remember Me (Garrett) **3**:190; **11**:219; **51**:147
Do Me a Favour (Hill) **113**:288-90, 309-10, 320
"Do Me Baby" (Prince) **35**:324-26
"do not be afraid of no" (Brooks) **125**:74, 76
"Do Not Touch" (Pasternak) **63**:280
Do piachu (Rozewicz) **139**:227, 231, 239, 286, 293
"Do polityka" (Milosz) **56**:238
"Do Re Mi" (Guthrie) **35**:193
Do Re Mi (Kanin) **22**:230
"Do Right to Me Baby (Do unto Others)" (Dylan) **77**:186
"Do the Dead Sing?" (King)
See "The Reach"
"Do the Dog" (Mull) **17**:299
Do the Right Thing (Lee) **105**:84-89, 93, 95, 98, 101-03, 106, 108-09, 111, 113, 123-24, 126, 128, 129
Do These Bones Live (Dahlberg) **7**:67, 69-70; **14**:134, 137
Do What You Will (Huxley) **4**:238; **35**:241; **79**:310
Do with Me What You Will (Oates) **3**:362-64; **6**:368-69, 373; **9**:405; **14**:401; **19**:351-52; **52**:338; **108**:344, 391
"Do You Believe in Cabeza de Vaca?" (Swan) **69**:363-65
Do You Believe in Cabeza de Vaca? (Swan) **69**:363
Do You Hear Them? (Sarraute)
See *Vous les entendez?*
"Do You Love Me?" (Carey) **96**:21, 38-9
Do You Love Me? An Entertainment in Conversation and Verse (Laing) **95**:155
"Do You Really Think It's Fair?" (Mazer) **26**:295
"Do You Think..." (Creeley) **2**:108; **4**:117
La doble historia del Doctor Valmy (Buero Vallejo) **15**:101; **46**:95-6; **139**:3, 6, 12, 15, 19, 33, 83
Doc (Pollock) **50**:223-27
"Doc For Doc" (McPherson)
See "A Solo Song: For Doc"
"Doc Mahoney and the Laughter of War" (Klappert) **57**:268
"Doc Rivers" (Williams)
See "Old Doc Rivers"
"Las doce figuras del mundo" (Bioy Casares) **88**:68
Docherty (McIlvanney) **42**:283-86
The Docile Puerto Rican (Marqués) **96**:233
The Dock Brief (Mortimer) **28**:282-84, 286
Dock Ellis in the Country of Baseball (Hall) **37**:143, 149
"Docker" (Heaney) **74**:167
Le docker noir (Ousmane) **66**:334
"Dockery and Son" (Larkin) **5**:227; **8**:332, 339; **18**:294, 298-99; **33**:256-57; **39**:335, 341; **64**:260, 264, 266, 268
Docking at Palermo (Hugo) **32**:236
"The Dock-Witch" (Ozick) **7**:287-88; **62**:350-51; **155**:177-78, 183-84
"The Dock-Witch" (Ozick) **155**:
"Dockyards at Night" (Neruda)
See "Maestranzas de noche"
"Doc's Story" (Wideman) **67**:379-81, 384; **122**:343
Docteur Popaul (Chabrol) **16**:182
"The Doctor" (Dubus) **97**:195, 204-05
"Doctor" (Ignatow) **7**:182
Doctor Anaconda's Solar Fun Club (Rosenblatt) **15**:448
"The Doctor and the Doctor's Wife" (Hemingway) **10**:269; **30**:186-87, 190, 192, 196, 199, 201-02
The Doctor and the Soul: An Introduction to Logotherapy (Frankl)
See *Arztliche seelsorge*
"Doctor Blanke's First Command" (Forester) **35**:173
Doctor Brodie's Report (Borges)
See *El informe de Brodie*
Doctor Cobb's Game (Cassill) **4**:95; **23**:108
Doctor Copernicus (Banville) **46**:28; **118**:10, 12, 15-16, 23, 26-27, 31, 35, 38, 47-48, 53-54
"Doctor Crombie" (Greene) **3**:213
Doctor DeMarr (Theroux) **46**:399-401
Doctor Detroit (Friedman) **56**:108
"Doctor Diagoras" (Lem) **149**:148
Doctor Fischer of Geneva; or, The Bomb Party (Greene) **18**:195-98; **27**:177; **70**:294
Doctor Frigo (Ambler) **6**:3-4
"Doctor Havel after Ten Years" (Kundera) **32**:260
"Doctor Havel Ten Years Later" (Kundera)
See "Doctor Havel after Ten Years"
The Doctor Is Sick (Burgess) **22**:69, 74; **40**:115; **94**:52
Doctor Mirabilis (Blish) **14**:83, 87
"Doctor My Eyes" (Browne) **21**:35
"The Doctor of Starlight" (Levine) **33**:275
"The Doctor of the Heart" (Sexton) **4**:483
Doctor Rat (Kotzwinkle) **14**:309-10; **35**:255-56, 258
Doctor Sax: Faust Part Three (Kerouac) **1**:167; **2**:228; **3**:264; **14**:307; **29**:270; **61**:299, 308-10, 314
Doctor Slaughter (Theroux)
See *Half Moon Street*
Doctor Sleep (Bell) **102**:8-10
The Doctor Stories (Williams) **42**:457-58
"The Doctor Will See You Now" (Fearing) **51**:108
"Doctor Wu" (Becker and Fagen) **26**:80
Doctor Zhivago (Pasternak)
See *Dr. Zhivago*
"The Doctors" (Barnes) **3**:37; **11**:30
Doctors and Women (Cheever) **48**:67-8
Doctors at Risk (Slaughter) **29**:378
"The Doctor's House" (Collins) **44**:37
"A Doctor's Illness" (Mahfouz)
See "Marad tabib"
"A Doctor's Journal Entry for August 6, 1945" (Seth) **90**:351
Doctors of Philosophy (Spark) **3**:467
"The Doctor's Son" (O'Hara) **42**:312
"The Doctor's Son" (Stewart) **32**:422
The Doctor's Son, and Other Stories (O'Hara) **42**:320
Doctors Wear Scarlet (Raven) **14**:440
"The Doctor's Wife" (Ozick) **155**:233
The Doctor's Wife (Moore) **8**:394-96; **32**:310-11, 313; **90**:251, 257, 259, 268, 277-8, 281-2, 304
The Doctor's Wife Comes to Stay (Swinnerton) **31**:426
"Doctrinal Point" (Empson) **19**:157
"The Doctrine of the Leather-Stocking Jesus" (Willard) **37**:464
"Docu-fiction" (Birkerts) **116**:148
Documentaires (Cendrars)
See *Kodak*
"Documentary" (Alegria) **75**:49
"A Documentary from America" (Stafford) **29**:382
"Documentation" (Wolf) **150**:221
Documents Relating to the Sentimental Agents in the Volyen Empire (Lessing) **40**:305-07, 309, 312-15
Dodes'ka-den (Kurosawa) **16**:404; **119**:338, 378-79, 382
"Dodging Apples" (Price) **43**:346
"Doe Season" (Kaplan) **50**:55-7
"Does a High Wind Make Me Reel?" (Voznesensky) **57**:427
"Does Daniel Believe in Order?" (Klappert) **57**:268
Does God Exist? (Kung) **130**:131, 136, 167
"Does It Matter?" (Sassoon) **36**:391; **130**:182, 184, 216, 220
Does This School Have Capital Punishment? (Hentoff) **26**:185-86
"The Dog" (Dürrenmatt)
See "Der Hund"
"Dog" (Ferlinghetti) **111**:64
"The Dog" (Newlove) **14**:378
"The Dog" (Williams) **33**:448; **148**:328, 359
"A Dog after Love" (Amichai) **22**:33
"A Dog at Dinner" (Breytenbach) **126**:94
The Dog beneath the Skin (Isherwood) **44**:396, 399
The Dog beneath the Skin; or, Where Is Francis? (Auden) **1**:9; **6**:23; **11**:18; **14**:32; **43**:16, 21
"Dog Breath" (Zappa) **17**:585, 588
"The Dog Carla" (Szirtes) **46**:393
"Dog Creek Mainline" (Wright) **6**:580-81; **146**:326, 374
"Dog Day Vespers" (Wright) **146**:302-03
Dog Days (Gray) **36**:202
"Dog Dream" (Smith) **12**:535
"The Dog Explosion" (Hood) **28**:189
"Dog Heaven" (Vaughn) **62**:456, 458
"Dog Life" (Strand) **41**:439 41
"A Dog Lover's Confession" (Van Duyn) **116**:420
"Dog Prospectus" (Redgrove) **41**:354
A Dog So Small (Pearce) **21**:282, 284-87
Dog Soldiers (Stone) **5**:409-11; **23**:426, 428-31; **42**:358-63
"Dog Star" (Musgrave) **54**:341
"Dog Wearing Baby Clothes" (Simic) **130**:327
The Dog Who Wouldn't Be (Mowat) **26**:333, 335-36, 338-39, 343-44
"The Dog with the Wooden Leg" (Woolrich) **77**:389-90

Dog Years (Grass)
See *Hundejahre*
"Dog Yoga" (Wright) **146**:308
"The Dog-Days" (Cunningham) **31**:97-9, 101
"Dogface Poetics" (Simpson) **149**:331, 359
"Dogfight" (Gibson) **63**:134
"Dogfish" (Oliver) **98**:259
Dogg's Hamlet (Stoppard) **15**:520; **29**:395-98
Dogg's Hamlet, Cahoot's Macbeth (Stoppard) **29**:396-97
"Dogg's Our Pet" (Stoppard) **29**:395
"The Dogg's Troupe 'Hamlet'" (Stoppard) **29**:397
"Dogs" (Pink Floyd) **35**:311
"Dogs" (Townshend) **17**:529-30
"Dogs and Books" (Kiš)
See "Psi i knjige"
"The Dogs are Eating Your Mother" (Hughes) **119**:296
"Dogs Are Shakespearean, Children Are Strangers" (Schwartz) **87**:347
The Dogs Bark: Public People and Private Places (Capote) **3**:100; **8**:132-33; **34**:320; **38**:85
"Dog's Death" (Updike) **3**:485
Dogs Enjoy the Morning (Kiely) **23**:259-60, 263-64; **43**:245
"Dogs in My Nose" (Martin) **30**:248
"The Dogs in the Great Glen" (Kiely) **23**:267-68; **43**:244
A Dog's Life (Mayle) **89**:154
The Dogs of Paradise (Posse) **70**:351
The Dogs of Pavlov (Abse) **7**:2
The Dogs of War (Forsyth) **5**:125; **36**:175, 177
A Dog's Ransom (Highsmith) **2**:194; **42**:213; **102**:185, 209
Dogsbody (Jones) **26**:226-27, 230
Dogtown (Bonham) **12**:51-2
The Dogtown Tourist Agency (Vance) **35**:422
"The Dogwood Tree" (Updike) **23**:463; **139**:327
"Doing It Differently" (Piercy) **27**:375; **128**:272
"Doing Lennon" (Benford) **52**:75-6
"Doing Right" (Clarke) **53**:97
"Doing the Twist on Nails" (Yevtushenko) **3**:547
Doing What Comes Naturally: Change, Rhetoric, and the Practice of Theory in Literary and Legal (Fish) **142**:162, 164, 169-70, 176-81, 184-86, 191-92, 197-98
"Dois castelhanos em Sevilha" (Cabral de Melo Neto) **76**:163
Dois palamentos (Cabral de Melo Neto) **76**:158, 169
Dōjidai gēmu (Oe) **36**:350; **86**:226, 228, 230, 232, 234, 239-41, 244
"Dōjōji" (Mishima) **27**:341
"Dōke to saisei e no sōzōryku" (Oe) **86**:215, 223
Doktor Murkes gesammeltes Schweigen, und andere Satiren (Boell) **15**:70; **27**:59, 61, 64; **39**:296; **72**:72, 73, 80, 101
La dolce vita (Fellini) **16**:272-74, 276-82, 284, 287, 290-91, 293-94, 298, 300; **85**:51, 58-60, 64, 67, 69, 71, 73-6, 78-82
Dolgoe proshchanie (Trifonov) **45**:408, 417, 423
Dolina Issy (Konwicki) **117**:283
Dolina Issy (Milosz) **11**:378; **22**:305-07, 312-13; **31**:260-61, 264, 270; **82**:280-81, 285, 289
"The Doll" (O'Brien) **36**:336, 339; **116**:201-03
"The Doll" (Summers) **10**:493
"The Doll House" (McGinley) **14**:364
"The Doll Queen" (Fuentes)
See "La muñeca reina"
"The Doll That Does Everything" (Matheson) **37**:246
The Doll Who Ate His Mother (Campbell) **42**:86-7, 90, 92-3
The $ Value of Man (Wilson) **7**:551
"The Dollar Value of Poetry" (Bernstein) **142**:43
The Dollmaker (Arnow) **2**:14; **7**:15-6; **18**:11-6
The Dolls (Haavikko)
See *Nuket*
"Dolls, Dolls, Dolls, Dolls" (Shields) **113**:430
A Doll's House (Rozewicz) **139**:279
"The Dolls Museum in Dublin" (Boland) **113**:92-3
Dolly (Brookner) **136**:105-07, 117
"Dolor" (Roethke) **19**:397, 401; **46**:356; **101**:263, 291
Il dolore (Ungaretti) **7**:481-82, 485; **11**:556
Dolores (Compton-Burnett) **3**:112; **10**:110; **15**:135, 138; **34**:495, 499
Dolores Claiborne (King) **113**:384-85, 388, 392-93
"Dolphin" (Lowell) **124**:299
The Dolphin (Lowell) **3**:302-06; **4**:301, 304; **5**:257-59; **8**:355-58; **9**:336; **11**:328, 330-31; **37**:236-38; **124**:256, 286, 290-91, 300
"A Dolphin in the Forest, a Wild Board on the Waves" (Newman) **8**:419
Dolphins (Cousteau) **30**:106
The Dolphins (Spender) **91**:262, 264, 269
"The Dolt" (Barthelme) **115**:56, 69, 94
Dom na naberezhnoi (Trifonov) **45**:408-11, 413-14, 416-19, 421-23; **59**:383
"Dom tvorchestva" (Akhmadulina) **53**:12
"Domain of the Marvelous Prey" (Simic) **130**:296
"Domaine noir" (Senghor) **54**:401
"Domaine Public" (Hill) **45**:178
"Dome of Sunday" (Shapiro) **15**:476-77
"The Dome Poem" (Smith) **22**:385
"La Domenica Uliva" (Pasolini) **106**:233
"Domesday Book" (Lowell) **11**:331; **37**:238
"Domestic" (Johnston) **51**:244-45
"Domestic and Personal" (Simmons) **43**:414
A Domestic Animal (King) **53**:208; **145**:351, 365
Domestic Arrangements (Klein) **30**:242
"A Domestic Dilemma" (McCullers) **12**:413, 425, 433; **100**:246
"Domestic Flight" (D'Aguiar) **145**:119
Domestic Fuel (Moure) **88**:219-23, 227, 229-30
"Domestic Interior" (Boland) **113**:71-2, 92, 94, 98, 109, 124
"Domestic Life in America" (Updike) **15**:545-46
Domestic Particulars (Busch) **10**:91-3
Domestic Relations: Short Stories (O'Connor) **23**:325
Domicile conjugal (Truffaut) **20**:389, 392, 399-401; **101**:382, 386, 396, 398, 411, 413
"Dominant Margins" (Ammons) **57**:53, 57
Domingo 7 (Poniatowska)
See *Domingo siete*
Domingo siete (Poniatowska) **140**:304, 330
"Dominican Shoe Tinkers" (Lieberman) **36**:262
"The Dominicans" (Brodsky) **36**:77
"Dominion Square" (Souster) **5**:396
"Domino" (Morrison) **21**:232-33
Domino (Whitney) **42**:436
Le dompteur d'ours (Theriault) **79**:399-400, 402, 408, 412
"Don" (Dixon) **52**:100
Don Bueno (Ghose) **42**:184
Don de la ebriedad (Rodriguez) **10**:439
Don Fernando (Maugham) **67**:216, 219, 222
"Don Giovanni" (Keillor) **115**:294
"Don Gustano" (Padilla) **38**:349
Don Juan (Camus) **32**:91
Don Juan; oder, Die Liebe zur Geometrie (Frisch) **3**:167; **9**:217; **14**:182; **18**:161; **32**:195; **44**:182-83, 197-98
Don Juan; or, The Love of Geometry (Frisch)
See *Don Juan; oder, Die Liebe zur Geometrie*
"Don Juan y el diablo" (Casona) **49**:47
"Don Juan's Reckless Daughter" (Mitchell) **12**:443
Don Juan's Reckless Daughter (Mitchell) **12**:443-44
Don Julián (Goytisolo)
See *La reivindicación del Conde Don Julián*
"A Don Looks at His Fellows" (Betjeman) **43**:32
Don l'Orignal (Maillet) **54**:303-08; **118**:327, 329-30, 344
"Don Marquis" (White) **10**:528
"Don Nicomedes" (Ulibarrí) **83**:415
Don Q (Lopez Portillo) **46**:235-37
Don Quixote (Acker) **45**:18-20; **111**:3-4, 6-8, 11-12, 18-19, 21 2, 25-6, 28, 31-3, 34-5, 37-9
Don Quixote (Lightfoot) **26**:278-79
Don Quixote (Welles) **80**:367, 371, 413
The Don Tales (Sholokhov)
See *Donskie rasskazy*
"Don: The True Story of a Young Person" (Keillor) **40**:274
"Don Tómas Vernes" (Ulibarrí) **83**:415
Dona Flor and Her Two Husbands (Amado)
See *Dona Flor e seus dois maridos*
Dona Flor e seus dois maridos (Amado) **13**:11; **40**:32-5; **106**:54-5, 57, 61, 65, 73, 78-9, 81, 84, 86
Doña inés (Azorín) **11**:25
Donadieu (Hochwälder) **36**:235-38
Donald Duk (Chin) **135**:165-67, 169, 171-72, 174, 177, 202
A Donald Justice Reader (Justice) **102**:277, 283
"Donat" (Ortese)
See "Le sei della sera"
"La doncella y la muerte" (Parra) **102**:342
Donde esta la casa de Dios (Shange)
See *Sanctuary*
Donde habite el olvido (Cernuda) **54**:41, 55, 60
De donde son los cantantes (Sarduy) **6**:486; **97**:366-67, 369, 372, 376, 384, 386-92, 395-98, 409-10, 415, 417
Donde viven las águilas (Valenzuela) **104**:376-77
"Done Too Soon" (Diamond) **30**:111
Donna mi prega (Pound) **4**:418
"Donne ch'avete intelletto d'amore" (Ciardi) **44**:383
Le donne di Messina (Vittorini) **6**:551-52; **9**:548; **14**:547
"Donnerbach mühle" (Char) **9**:165
The Do-Nothing Bar (Cocteau) **8**:148
Donovan's Reef (Ford) **16**:312-13, 319
Don's Party (Williamson) **56**:431-32, 435, 439, 443
Donskie rasskazy (Sholokhov) **7**:416, 420; **15**:483-85
"Don't" (Williams) **33**:441
Don't Ask (Levine) **33**:273; **118**:279, 288, 292, 294-95, 307
"Don't Ask Me Why" (Joel) **26**:221
"Don't Be Denied" (Young) **17**:571-72, 582
Don't Bite the Sun (Lee) **46**:230
"Don't Bring Me Oscars" (Perelman) **5**:338
Don't Call Me Katie Rose (Weber) **12**:633
"Don't Cry, Darling, It's Blood All Right" (Nash) **23**:322
"Don't Cry for Me, Argentina" (Rice and Webber) **21**:431
"Don't Cry, Old Man" (Ian) **21**:186
Don't Cry, Scream (Madhubuti) **2**:238; **73**:193, 195, 198, 205, 207, 209-15
Don't Die Before Dying (Yevtushenko) **126**:406
Don't Die Before You're Dead (Yevtushenko) **126**:400, 402, 404-08, 411-12
Don't Drink the Water (Allen) **52**:48
Don't Forget to Write (Buchwald) **33**:89
Don't Gag On It ... Goof On It (Crumb) **17**:84
Don't Get God Started (Milner) **56**:226-27
Don't Go Away Mad (Saroyan) **8**:467
Don't Go Gentle (Inge) **8**:308
Don't Grow Old (Ginsberg) **109**:338
"Don't Have a Baby Till You Read This" (Giovanni) **19**:192; **64**:183; **117**:191
"Don't Interrupt the Sorrow" (Mitchell) **12**:439

"Don't Leave Me Now" (Pink Floyd) **35**:311
Don't Let Him Die: An Anthology of Memorial Poems for Christopher Okigbo (1932-1967) (Achebe) **127**:29
"Don't Let It Bring You Down" (McCartney) **35**:285-86
"Don't Let It Bring You Down" (Young) **17**:569-70
"Don't Let Me Down" (Lennon and McCartney) **35**:274
Don't Look and It Won't Hurt (Peck) **21**:295
Don't Look Back (Dylan) **77**:161
Don't Look Now (du Maurier)
See *Not after Midnight*
"Don't Make Me Hate You!" (Ewart) **46**:154
Don't Never Forget: Collected Views and Reviews (Brophy) **29**:94; **105**:5, 8
Don't Play Dead before You Have To (Wojciechowska) **26**:455
Don't Play Us Cheap (Van Peebles) **2**:448
Don't Sit under the Apple Tree (Brancato) **35**:65, 67
Don't Slam the Door When You Go (Corcoran) **17**:72
"Don't Stand So Close to Me" (Police, The) **26**:365
Don't Stop the Carnival (Wouk) **38**:449
"The Don't Swear Man" (Mitchell) **98**:186
"Don't Take Me Alive" (Becker and Fagen) **26**:82-3
Don't Take Teddy (Friis-Baastad) **12**:213-14
"Don't Talk" (Wilson) **12**:646
Don't Tell Alfred (Mitford) **44**:490-92
"Don't Tell Me You Don't Know" (Allison) **78**:3
"Don't Think Twice, It's All Right" (Dylan) **77**:173
"Don't Think...Feel" (Diamond) **30**:112
Don't Tread on Me: The Selected Letters of S. J. Perelman (Perelman) **49**:269-70
"Don't Wanna Be" (Sanchez) **116**:301
"Don't Worry about the Government" (Byrne) **26**:94-5, 98
"Don't Worry Baby" (Wilson) **12**:644, 649
"Don't Worry Kyoko" (Lennon) **35**:265
"Don't Write about the Storm" (Akhmadulina)
See "Ne pisat' o groze"
"Don't You Ever Wash That Thing" (Zappa) **17**:591
"Don't You Hear the Dogs Barking?" (Rulfo)
See "No oyes ladrar los perros"
"Don't you talk about My Momma" (Jordan) **114**:152
Don't You Turn Back (Hughes) **35**:219
Don't You Want to Be Free? (Hughes) **108**:295
"Don't You Worry 'bout a Thing" (Wonder) **12**:657
"Doo Doo Doo Doo Doo" (Jagger and Richard) **17**:229
"Doodle Bugs" (Harrison) **43**:176
Doom (Gerhardie) **5**:140
"Doom Is Dark and Deeper than Any Sea Dingle" (Auden) **3**:24; **6**:20
"The Doom of Antarion" (Smith) **43**:419
Doomed (Kurosawa)
See *Ikiru*
"The Doomed in Their Sinking" (Gass) **15**:258
Doomsday (Harrison) **129**:192
The Doomsday Gang (Platt) **26**:352-53
The Doomsters (Macdonald) **14**:334; **41**:272
Doonesbury (Trudeau) **12**:588-91
The Doonesbury Chronicles (Trudeau) **12**:590
"The Door" (Barthelme) **13**:63
"The Door" (Bitov) **57**:114-15
"The Door" (Creeley) **8**:153; **15**:149; **78**:124, 130, 132
"Door" (Hoffman) **6**:244
"A Door" (Merwin) **5**:286
"The Door" (Strand) **18**:516; **41**:431; **71**:283
"The Door" (Turco) **11**:551
"The Door: A Prologue of Sorts" (Coover) **7**:58; **15**:145; **32**:121
The Door Between (Queen) **11**:461-63
The Door into Summer (Heinlein) **1**:139; **26**:165; **55**:304
Door into the Dark (Heaney) **5**:170-72; **7**:146-48, 150; **14**:242-43, 245; **25**:243-46; **37**:165; **74**:153-54, 156-57, 162, 170-71, 179, 193; **91**:117, 121, 123, 128
The Door of Life (Bagnold) **25**:73-4
"The Door Prohibited" (Dacey) **51**:81
"Doors" (Hoffman) **141**:294
Doors (Hoffman) **141**:293-95
The Doors (Morrison) **17**:287, 291, 295-96
The Doors (Stone) **73**:380-83
"The Doors of His Face, the Lamps of His Mouth" (Zelazny) **21**:468
The Doors of His Face, the Lamps of His Mouth and Other Stories (Zelazny) **21**:465, 468, 474-75
The Doors of Perception (Huxley) **4**:239, 241; **5**:194; **8**:303; **18**:270; **35**:241, 243
The Doors of Stone (Prince) **22**:338
"The Doorway" (Glück) **81**:164, 167
"Doorways" (McGahern) **48**:263-64, 271
Doorways in the Sand (Zelazny) **21**:469-70
"Dopa una fuga" (Montale) **7**:228
Dopefiend: The Story of a Black Junkie (Goines) **80**:92, 95
"Der Doppelgänger" (Dürrenmatt) **15**:195
"El Dorado Update" (D'Aguiar) **145**:115, 127
"Dordogne" (Ekelöf) **27**:118-19
Doris and Doreen (Bennett) **77**:86, 88
"Doris Lessing" (Didion) **129**:81
"Dorking Thigh" (Plomer) **4**:407
Dormir al sol (Bioy Casares) **13**:84; **88**:64-5
"Dornenkranz" (Celan) **82**:56-7
Doroga na okean (Leonov) **92**:240, 246-47, 249-55, 259, 261, 276-77
"Dorot ba'arets" (Amichai) **116**:117
Dorothea Lange: A Photographer's Life (Meltzer) **26**:305-06
Dorothy and Me (Ayckbourn) **33**:44
Dorp Dead (Cunningham) **12**:163-65
"Dorset" (Davie) **8**:167-68
"Dos, caddy d'aisselles" (Perec) **56**:258
Las dos caras del patroncito (Valdez) **84**:395
"Dos cartas" (Donoso) **32**:156, 158
Dos crímenes (Ibarguengoitia) **37**:183-85
"Las dos Elenas" (Fuentes) **8**:222; **22**:167-68; **113**:236
Dos españoles del siglo de oro (Alonso) **14**:20
"Dos niños" (Guillén) **79**:250
Dos Passos: A Life (Carr) **34**:419-23
"Dos poemas" (Castellanos) **66**:50
"Las dos Venecias" (Ferré) **139**:153, 162, 181-82
Las dos Venecias (Ferré) **139**:181-83
Los dos verdugos (Arrabal)
See *Les deux bourreaux*
"Dos vidas" (Aleixandre) **9**:17
The Dosadi Experiment (Herbert) **12**:279; **23**:219, 221; **35**:209; **44**:393-94
"Dossy" (Frame) **96**:185
Dostoevsky (Bakhtin)
See *Problemy tvorčestva Dostoevskogo*
"Dostoievski and the Collapse of Liberalism" (Warner) **45**:433-34
Doting (Green) **2**:178; **13**:252, 254; **97**:245, 248, 250, 254, 257, 276, 278-79, 283, 286, 290-91, 293
"The Dotted Line of Progress" (Aksyonov) **101**:20
"The Double" (Dürrenmatt)
See "Der Doppelgänger"
The Double Agent (Blackmur) **24**:53, 56-7
The Double Axe and Other Poems (Jeffers) **2**:212; **3**:260; **11**:305, 311; **15**:301; **54**:240-41, 246
"Double Bird" (Ignatow) **14**:276-77
The Double Case History of Doctor Valmy (Buero Vallejo)
See *La doble historia del Doctor Valmy*
"Double Charley" (Stern) **39**:244
"The Double Corner" (Stegner) **49**:350
Double Dare (Potter) **58**:391; **123**:234-35, 237, 263
The Double Dealer (Faulkner) **9**:201
"Double Derivation, Association, and Cliché: From the Great Tournament Roll of Westminster" (Matthias) **9**:362
"Double Dialogue: Homage to Robert Frost" (Rukeyser) **15**:457
Double, Double (Queen) **11**:463
The Double Dream of Spring (Ashbery) **2**:17-19; **4**:21-4; **9**:41, 44; **13**:30-1, 33; **15**:26-7, 31-3; **25**:58; **41**:40; **77**:47, 50, 52, 54; **125**:11
"The Double Dying of an Ordinary Criminal" (Breytenbach) **126**:70-1
"Double Exposure" (Swenson) **106**:332
Double Exposure (Plath) **50**:450
Double Fantasy (Lennon) **35**:270, 272-76
"Double Feature" (Hayden) **37**:156
"Double Feature" (Roethke) **19**:397
The Double Flame (Paz) **119**:408, 417-19, 424
Double Honeymoon (Connell) **45**:112
The Double Hook (Kroetsch) **132**:258
"The Double Horror" (Ezekiel) **61**:104
"The Double Image" (Sexton) **15**:472; **53**:312, 316, 318, 320; **123**:412, 416, 435-36, 441, 451
The Double Image (Levertov) **28**:241-42; **66**:251
The Double Image (MacInnes) **27**:281-82; **39**:351
Double Indemnity (Cain) **3**:96; **28**:45-7, 49-53
Double Indemnity (Wilder) **20**:456, 460
"Double Jeopardy: Making Sense of AIDS" (Amis) **62**:2, 4, 6
"The Double Life of Robertson Davies" (Davies) **75**:183
The Double Life of Veronique (Kieslowski)
See *Podwojne zycie Weroniki*
"The Double Looking Glass" (Hope) **51**:224
The Double Man (Auden) **123**:9, 25
"Double Monologue" (Rich) **36**:374
"Double Nigger" (Dumas) **6**:145; **62**:153-54
Double or Nothing (Federman) **6**:181; **47**:119-24, 127-29, 131-32
Double Persephone (Atwood) **25**:64-5; **84**:89; **135**:68
The Double Room (Klima) **56**:168-69
"The Double Session" (Derrida) **87**:89
A Double Shadow (Turner) **48**:400
The Double Shadow and Other Fantasies (Smith) **43**:417
"The Double Shame" (Spender) **41**:428; **91**:269
Double Solitaire (Anderson) **23**:33
"Double Sonnet for Minimalists" (Van Duyn) **116**:415
Double Star (Heinlein) **1**:139; **14**:254; **26**:163, 165; **55**:300, 303
"The Double Thumb" (Bates) **46**:62
Un double tour (Chabrol) **16**:169-70, 174, 178, 181
The Double Tree: Selected Poems, 1942-1976 (Wright) **11**:578; **53**:430
La Double Vie de Véronique (Kieslowski)
See *Podwojne zycie Weroniki*
Double Vision: American Thoughts Abroad (Knowles) **26**:258-59
The Double Witness (Belitt) **22**:54-6
Double Yoke (Emecheta) **48**:98-100; **128**:67-72, 79
"Doubled Mirrors" (Rexroth) **112**:399
The Doubleman (Koch) **42**:266-68
"Doubles" (Hood) **28**:195
"Doubling" (Daitch) **103**:77
Doubling the Point (Coetzee) **117**:68-9, 73
"Doubt" (Aldington) **49**:7
"Doubt" (Dobyns) **37**:76
"Doubt" (Gerstler) **70**:156-57
Doubtfire (Nye) **13**:412; **42**:302-04
"The Doubtful Passage" (Cardenal)
See "El estrecho dudoso"

"The Doubtful Passage" (Cardenal)
See "El estrecho dudoso"
"The Doughty Oaks" (Piercy) **27**:376
"The Doukhubor" (Newlove) **14**:378
"La douleur" (Duras) **68**:76, 80-2, 90; **100**:120-21, 126, 135, 149
La douleur (Duras) **68**:73-82, 84-5, 90-5, 99
The Dove (Barnes) **127**:185-86, 189, 191-94
The Dove (Beagle) **104**:5
"The Dove Breeder" (Hughes) **119**:258
"A Dove in Santiago" (Yevtushenko) **26**:469; **126**:395
Dove Inside (Neruda)
See *Paloma por dentro*
Dov'è la mia patria (Pasolini) **106**:232
The Dove of Popular Flight—Elegies (Guillén)
See *La paloma de vuelo popular: Elegiás*
A Dove of the East and Other Stories (Helprin) **7**:152; **10**:260, 262; **22**:222
"Dove sta memoria" (Tomlinson) **45**:402
"Dover" (Auden) **43**:16; **123**:42
"Dover Beach" (Jarrell) **13**:298
"Dover Beach" (Van Duyn) **116**:417
Dover Beach (Betjeman) **10**:52
"Dover Beach—A Note to That Poem" (MacLeish) **8**:363; **68**:288
The Doves of Venus (Manning) **19**:300
"Dowager" (Montague) **46**:274
"The Dower Chest" (Richter) **30**:329
"Down" (Graves) **1**:128; **45**:167
Down a Dark Hall (Duncan) **26**:103-05
Down All the Days (Brown) **63**:48-56
"Down along the Cove" (Dylan) **12**:185
Down among the Women (Weldon) **6**:562; **11**:565; **19**:466-67; **36**:447; **122**:247-51, 254-55, 268
Down and In (Sukenick) **48**:370-72
"Down and Out" (Hughes) **35**:221
"Down at the Cross" (Baldwin) **13**:52; **42**:14; **127**:107
"Down at the Dinghy" (Salinger) **12**:499; **56**:329
"Down at the Docks" (Koch) **5**:219
"Down at the Dump" (White)
See "Down in the Dump"
Down by the River (Adler) **35**:11-12
Down by the River (O'Brien) **116**:225-28
"Down by the Riverside" (Wright) **21**:442, 444, 453-54
"Down by the Seaside" (Page and Plant) **12**:477, 479
"Down by the Station, Early in the Morning" (Ashbery) **41**:37, 40
"Down Cemetery Road" (Porter) **33**:324
"Down East" (Laurence) **62**:280
"Down from Another Planet They Have Settled to Mend" (Miles) **14**:369
Down From the Hill (Sillitoe) **57**:398-99; **148**:
"Down From Troy" (Selzer) **74**:263, 279
"Down Here on Greene Street" (Mazer) **26**:296
"Down in a Tube Station at Midnight" (Weller) **26**:444-46
"Down in the Dump" (White) **69**:398
"Down in the Wood" (Christie) **110**:126, 128
Down in the Zero (Vachss) **106**:364-65
"Down on the Funny Farm" (Raine) **32**:350, 353
"Down Our Way" (Wain) **46**:415
"Down, Satan!" (Barker) **52**:53
Down Second Avenue (Mphahlele) **25**:333, 336-37, 341, 343; **133**:125, 132, 136-37, 149, 154, 157-59, 162
"Down the Clinical Disco" (Weldon) **122**:268
"Down the Line with the Annual" (Barthelme) **6**:29
Down the Long Table (Birney) **6**:70-2; **11**:49-50
Down the River (Abbey) **36**:19-20; **59**:238, 242
"Down the River with Henry Thoreau" (Abbey) **36**:21
Down the Seine and up the Potomac with Art Buchwald (Buchwald) **33**:94-5
"Down Then by Derry" (Kiely) **43**:244-45
"Down There" (Campbell) **42**:87, 89
Down There on a Visit (Isherwood) **1**:155; **9**:294; **11**:296-98, 300; **14**:278, 280, 282-84, 286; **44**:397-98, 402
Down These Mean Streets (Thomas) **17**:497-502
"Down to the Wire" (Young) **17**:577
"Down to You" (Mitchell) **12**:438
"Down to Zero" (Armatrading) **17**:10
"Down, Wanton, Down!" (Graves) **45**:161, 169
Down Where the Moon Is Small (Llewellyn) **7**:207
"Down with the Restoration!" (Perelman) **49**:258
"Down-and-Out" (Queneau) **42**:337
Downbelow Station (Cherryh) **35**:106-07, 109, 113
Downerstag (Hochwälder) **36**:236-38
"The Downfall of Fascism in Black Ankle County" (Mitchell) **98**:187
"Downhill" (Beattie) **63**:17, 19, **146**:77
Downriver; or, The Vessels of Wrath (Sinclair) **76**:221-28
"Downstairs" (Ostriker) **132**:327
"Downstairs at Fitzgerald's" (Trevor) **25**:446
"Downstream" (Kinsella) **4**:271; **19**:255; **138**:84, 99, 105, 116-17, 129, 132, 136, 159
Downstream (Kinsella) **138**:134, 136, 141-42, 146-49, 158, 163, 165
"Downtown, America" (Montague) **46**:265, 270
Downtown Diaries (Carroll)
See *Forced Entries: The Downtown Diaries, 1971-1973*
"downtown vaudeville" (Brooks) **125**:74
"Downward" (Swenson) **61**:391
"Downward" (Williams) **33**:441; **148**:328
Downward (Silverberg)
See *Downward to the Earth*
"The Downward Path to Wisdom" (Porter) **7**:311; **27**:399; **101**:210-12
Downward to the Earth (Silverberg) **140**:343, 345-46, 365, 368, 372, 378, 390-91
"The Dowser" (Redgrove) **41**:357
"Dowson and Company" (Mahon) **27**:290
"Doxology" (Ammons) **108**:19
"Dr. Beeber" (Singer) **3**:453
Dr. Bloodmoney, or How We Got Along After the Bomb (Dick) **30**:124-25, 127; **72**:107, 110, 114, 121
Dr. Brodie's Report (Borges)
See *El informe de Brodie*
"Dr. Cooper's Story" (Reading) **47**:350
Dr. Cotnoir (Ferron)
See *Cotnoir*
"Dr. Faust's Sea-Spiral Spirit" (Redgrove) **41**:353
Dr. Faust's Sea-Spiral Spirit and Other Poems (Redgrove) **41**:349, 351-52
Dr. Futurity (Dick) **72**:120
Dr. Golf (Fox) **22**:140
Dr. Gruber's Daughter (Elliott) **47**:115-17
"Dr. Hachiyas Tagebuch aus Hiroschima" (Canetti) **75**:129
Dr. Heart: A Novella and Other Stories (Clark) **5**:105-07
Dr. Hero (Horovitz) **56**:151-52
Dr. Jekyll and Mr. Holmes (Estleman) **48**:103
Dr. Jekyll and Mr. Hyde (Mamoulian) **16**:420-21, 423-25
Dr. Kane of the Arctic Seas (Berton) **104**:60
Dr. Kheal (Fornés) **39**:138; **61**:130-31, 137
Dr. Mabuse the Gambler (Lang) **20**:202; **103**:85
Dr. Murke's Collected Silences (Boell)
See *Doktor Murkes gesammeltes Schweigen, und andere Satiren*
Dr. No (Fleming) **30**:133-34, 139, 149-50
Dr. Ox's Experiment (Egoyan) **151**:155, 175
"Dr. Perelman, I Presume; or, Small Bore in Africa" (Perelman) **23**:336
Dr. Strangelove; or, How I Learned to Stop Worrying and Love the Bomb (Kubrick) **16**:378-89, 391
"Dr. Voke and Mr. Veech" (Ligotti) **44**:53-4
"Dr. Woolacott" (Forster) **3**:161; **15**:231; **45**:140, 143
Dr. Zhivago (Pasternak) **7**:293-301; **10**:383-85, 387; **18**:382-85, 388-89; **59**:382, 384, 388, 391; **63**:282-83, 286-87, 289, 292-96, 299, 301, 304, 306-13, 318
Drachenblut (Hein)
See *Der fremde Freund*
"Draco, Draco" (Lee) **46**:232
Dracula (Browning) **16**:121-22, 124-26
Dracula (Coppola) **126**:266-68
Dracula (Welles) **80**:379
Dracula, Go Home! (Platt) **26**:353-54, 356
"Draft Dodger Rag" (Ochs) **17**:331, 333, 339
A Draft of XVI Cantos (Pound) **4**:412; **112**:332
A Draft of XXX Cantos (Pound) **10**:400; **50**:437
"A Draft of Shadows" (Paz) **119**:409
A Draft of Shadows (Paz)
See *Pasado en claro*
Drafts and Fragments of Cantos CX to CXVII (Pound) **2**:343; **4**:413-14; **13**:463; **34**:505; **48**:282-85, 299
"Dragged Fighting from His Tomb" (Hannah) **90**:130, 148, 150
"Dragger Captain" (Mitchell) **98**:160-61, 182
"The Dragon" (Barthelme) **115**:65, 68-9
"The Dragon" (Govier) **51**:166
"Dragon" (Ondaatje) **51**:310, 316
"The Dragon" (Spark) **40**:402
"The Dragon and the Undying" (Sassoon) **130**:180
"The Dragon and the Unicorn" (Rexroth) **49**:276-77, 279-80, 282, 285; **112**:386, 394, 402-04
The Dragon and the Unicorn (Rexroth) **6**:450-51; **22**:346-47; **49**:277; **112**:373, 376-77, 387
The Dragon Can't Dance (Lovelace) **51**:267-68, 271
Dragon Country (Williams) **45**:450-51
Dragon, Dragon and Other Tales (Gardner) **8**:238
Dragon Harvest (Sinclair) **63**:358
"Dragon Head" (Jin) **109**:52, 54
The Dragon in the Sea (Herbert)
See *Twenty-First Century Sub*
Dragon Magic (Norton) **12**:462
The Dragon Masters (Vance) **35**:417-19, 423, 426
Dragon of the Lost Sea (Yep) **35**:473
Dragon on a Pedestal (Anthony) **35**:39-40
Dragon Seed (Buck) **11**:75-7
Dragon Summer (Arthur) **12**:24, 28
Dragon Tears (Koontz) **78**:219
Dragondrums (McCaffrey) **17**:283-84
Dragonflight (McCaffrey) **17**:280-81, 283
"Dragonfly" (Bogan) **46**:90-1; **93**:65
"The Dragonfly-Mother" (Levertov) **66**:240
Dragonquest: Being the Further Adventures of the Dragonriders of Pern (McCaffrey) **17**:281, 283
The Dragonriders of Pern (McCaffrey) **17**:281
"Dragons" (Barnes) **141**:
Dragons in the Waters (L'Engle) **12**:351
Dragon's Island (Williamson) **29**:450, 459-60
The Dragons of Eden: Speculations on the Evolution of Human Intelligence (Sagan) **30**:333-36, 343-44; **112**:413, 419, 431
"Dragon's Seed" (Bell) **102**:5, 7
The Dragon's Tail (Kurosawa) **119**:399
"The Dragon's Teeth" (Gordon)
See "One against Thebes"
The Dragon's Teeth (Queen) **11**:458
Dragon's Teeth (Sinclair) **11**:497; **15**:500; **63**:355-56, 359, 376
Dragon's Teeth: Literature in the English Revolution (Wilding) **73**:399
Dragonsinger (McCaffrey) **17**:282-84
Dragonsong (McCaffrey) **17**:282-83
Dragonwings (Yep) **35**:468, 470-71

Drake, The Man They Called a Pirate (Latham) **12**:323
"Drama o puerta cerrada" (Cernuda) **54**:56
"Dramas" (O'Brien) **65**:167, 171
Dramatic Verse 1973-1985 (Harrison) **129**:167
"Dramaturgie des Labyrinths" (Duerrenmatt) **102**:61-2
"Drame Bourgeoise" (Ashbery) **13**:36
Dramen (Canetti) **86**:303
Dramen (Hochwälder) **36**:235
Dramouss (Laye) **4**:284-85; **38**:285, 288-91
"The Draped Mirrors" (Borges) **8**:99
"The Drawer" (Klappert) **57**:258, 266
"Drawing Lessons" (Nemerov) **36**:304
"The Drawing Master" (Urquhart) **90**:384, 386
"Drawing Names" (Mason) **82**:234; **154**:233, 241, 254-55, 317-18
The Drawing of the Three (King) **113**:382
"Drawing Room" (Ezekiel) **61**:104
"Drawing the Triangle" (Simic) **49**:337
"Drawing Wildflowers" (Graham) **48**:145, 147
"Drawings by Children" (Mueller) **51**:282
Drawn and Quartered (Addams) **30**:11-12
Drawn and Quartered (Cioran)
See *Écartèlement*
"Dread" (Barker) **52**:51, 53
Dread Companion (Norton) **12**:459, 462-63, 467
"The Dread Redeemer Lazarus Morrell" (Borges)
See "El espantoso redentor Lazarus Morell"
"Dreaded Hell" (Onetti)
See "El infierno tan temido"
"The Dreadful Day of Judgement" (Rendell) **48**:320
The Dreadful Lemon Sky (MacDonald) **27**:275
"The Dream" (Bogan) **46**:81-4; **93**:64, 67-8, 81
"The Dream" (Bowers) **9**:122
"A Dream" (Ciardi) **40**:156
"The Dream" (Ekelöf) **27**:110, 114
"Dream" (Livesay) **79**:338, 341, 343
"The Dream" (Roethke) **46**:363; **101**:315, 328
"Dream" (Sarton) **91**:254
"The Dream" (Sassoon) **130**:185, 222
"Dream" (Thomas) **13**:541-42
"The Dream" (Williams) **148**:317
"Dream" (Wright) **53**:419
The Dream (Montherlant)
See *Le songe*
The Dream (Smith) **64**:401-02
"The Dream, 1863" (Hayden) **9**:270; **14**:240; **37**:157
"Dream after Nanook" (Swenson) **61**:398
Dream and the Leg (Michaux)
See *Les rêves et la jambe*
"The Dream and the Triumph" (Buckler) **13**:119
"Dream as a Metaphor of Survival" (Harrison) **143**:358
A Dream Awake (Dodson) **79**:190
"Dream: Bluejay or Archeopteryx" (Atwood) **8**:31
"Dream Boogie" (Hughes) **108**:299-300, 302-04
"Dream Boogie: Variation" (Hughes) **108**:299, 301, 303-04
"Dream Children" (Godwin) **8**:248-49
Dream Children (Godwin) **8**:248-49; **22**:180; **31**:195; **69**:232-33, 243, 247; **125**:168
Dream Craters (Rosenblatt) **15**:447-48
"A Dream Deferred" (Hughes) **35**:218, 221
The Dream Department (Perelman) **49**:258-59
"Dream Dogs" (Codrescu) **46**:102
"Dream Flight" (Smith) **42**:348
Dream Flights (Smith) **42**:346-51, 353
A Dream Fulfilled, and Other Stories (Onetti)
See *Un sueño realizado y otros cuentos*
Dream Girl (Rice) **7**:361, 363; **49**:299-300
"The Dream Habitues" (Jacobsen) **48**:194
"Dream III" (Jiles) **58**:279
A Dream in the Luxembourg (Aldington) **49**:11-15, 18
"A Dream in the Woods of Virginia" (Simpson) **7**:427
A Dream Journey (Hanley) **8**:265-66; **13**:261
"Dream Journeys" (Hesse) **3**:248
"The Dream Keeper" (Hughes) **35**:214
The Dream Keeper and Other Poems (Hughes) **35**:214; **108**:283
A Dream Like Mine (Kelly) **55**:156-61
The Dream Master (Zelazny) **21**:463, 470
"Dream Objects" (Updike) **3**:485
The Dream of a Beast (Jordan) **110**:274-75, 278
The Dream of a Common Language: Poems, 1974-1977 (Rich) **11**:478-79; **18**:448-51; **36**:368, 373-74, 376; **73**:315, 317, 326, 332; **76**:217; **125**:308-11, 315-16, 321, 336, 337, 339
"The Dream of a House" (Price) **43**:351
"Dream of a Large Lady" (Kizer) **39**:169
"Dream of a Mannikin; or, The Third Person" (Ligotti) **44**:53-5
A Dream of Africa (Laye)
See *Dramouss*
"A Dream of Beauty" (Smith) **43**:424
"A Dream of Birth" (Jennings) **131**:232
Dream of Dark Harbor (Kotzwinkle) **35**:255
Dream of Fair to Middling Women (Beckett) **29**:67
"A Dream of Fair Women" (Amis) **40**:39-40, 44
A Dream of Ghosts (Bonham) **12**:54
A Dream of Governors (Simpson) **4**:499; **7**:426-428; **32**:378; **149**:306, 309, 326, 345-46, 349
The Dream of Heroes (Bioy Casares)
See *El sueño de los héroes*
"A Dream of Jealousy" (Heaney) **14**:246; **74**:164
"Dream of Judgement" (Dunn) **40**:167
"The Dream of Lee" (Price) **43**:350-51
"A Dream of Mind" (Williams) **148**:345, 347, 349, 353, 359-61
A Dream of Mind (Williams) **148**:331, 343-45, 347-52, 356-57, 359, 361
Dream of Orchids (Whitney) **11**:437
"Dream of Pairing" (Shange) **74**:311
"Dream of Planets" (Kunene) **85**:175
"The Dream of Private Clitus" (Jones) **7**:191
"The Dream of South" (Williams) **39**:101
"A Dream of Springtime" (Ostriker) **132**:302
A Dream of Springtime (Ostriker) **132**:302, 318
The Dream of Success (Lynn) **50**:426
"Dream of the Butterflies" (Danticat) **94**:100
"Dream of the Future" (Jeffers) **54**:235
"The Dream of the Gods" (Hesse) **25**:260
"The Dream of the Islanders of Thomas Mann" (Dubie) **36**:136
The Dream of the Unified Field: Selected Poems 1974-1994 (Graham) **118**:258, 261, 263
"A Dream of Whitman Paraphrased, Recognized, and Made More Vivid by Renoir" (Schwartz) **45**:355
"Dream of Winter" (Brown) **48**:51
"A Dream of Winter" (Lehmann) **5**:240
Dream on Monkey Mountain (Walcott) **76**:276-77, 282, 286
The Dream on Monkey Mountain, and Other Plays (Walcott) **2**:459-60; **4**:574; **9**:556; **25**:451-52, 454-55; **67**:347, 350, 352
"A Dream Pang" (Frost) **26**:116-17
"Dream Record: June 1955" (Ginsberg) **109**:358
"The Dream Sleepers" (Grace) **56**:116
The Dream Sleepers and Other Stories (Grace) **56**:116-17, 119, 123
"Dream Song 2" (Berryman) **62**:60
"Dream Song 3" (Berryman) **62**:69
"Dream Song 4" (Berryman) **62**:54
"Dream Song 13" (Berryman) **62**:62
"Dream Song 15" (Berryman) **62**:73
"Dream Song 20" (Berryman) **62**:44
"Dream Song 23" (Berryman) **62**:63, 73
"Dream Song 25" (Berryman) **62**:61, 65
"Dream Song 26" (Berryman) **62**:61, 65
"Dream Song 27" (Berryman) **62**:45, 61
"Dream Song 29" (Berryman) **62**:48, 62
"Dream Song 36" (Berryman) **62**:65
"Dream Song 50" (Berryman) **62**:61-2
"Dream Song 53" (Berryman) **62**:70
"Dream Song 56" (Berryman) **62**:45
"Dream Song 66" (Berryman) **62**:48, 69
"Dream Song 69" (Berryman) **62**:61, 63
"Dream Song 71" (Berryman) **62**:63
"Dream Song 75" (Berryman) **62**:63
"Dream Song 76" (Berryman) **62**:61-2
"Dream Song 78" (Berryman) **62**:66, 68-9
"Dream Song 81" (Berryman) **62**:66
"Dream Song 82" (Berryman) **62**:66
"Dream Song 85" (Berryman) **62**:66
"Dream Song 86" (Berryman) **62**:65-6
"Dream Song 97" (Berryman) **62**:57
"Dream Song 100" (Berryman) **62**:58
"Dream Song 159" (Berryman) **62**:74
"Dream Song 162" (Berryman) **62**:70
"Dream Song 163" (Berryman) **62**:70
"Dream Song 171" (Berryman) **62**:64
"Dream Song 175" (Berryman) **62**:64
"Dream Song 180" (Berryman) **62**:70
"Dream Song 181" (Berryman) **62**:70
"Dream Song 185" (Berryman) **62**:74
"Dream Song 191" (Berryman) **62**:48
"Dream Song 219" (Berryman) **62**:59
"Dream Song 242" (Berryman) **62**:58
"Dream Song 256" (Berryman) **62**:65
"Dream Song 258" (Berryman) **62**:48
"Dream Song 303" (Berryman) **62**:44
"Dream Song 319" (Berryman) **62**:65
"Dream Song 373" (Berryman) **62**:63
"Dream Song 384" (Berryman) **62**:62, 65
The Dream Songs (Berryman) **1**:33-4; **2**:56-9; **3**:66-72; **4**:60-3; **6**:63-5; **8**:87-92; **10**:45-52; **13**:76, 78-9, 81-3; **25**:89-99; **62**:43-50, 54-7, 59-61, 63-74, 76-7
"The Dream Spinners" (Christie) **110**:125
Dream Street Rose (Lightfoot) **26**:282
The Dream Team (McGinniss) **32**:300-01
"Dream Variations" (Hughes) **108**:296, 300
"The Dream Vendor's August" (Okri) **87**:314-15
The Dream Watcher (Wersba) **30**:429-31, 433
The Dream Weaver (Buero Vallejo) **15**:100-02
"A Dream with No Stump Roots in It" (Huddle) **49**:181-2
Dream Work (Oliver) **98**:259-61, 267, 272, 276-77, 282, 286, 302
A Dreambook for Our Time (Konwicki)
See *Sennik współczesny*
Dreamchild (Potter) **58**:391-92; **86**:346, 353; **123**:249
"The Dreamer" (Fante) **60**:133
"The Dreamer" (Soyinka) **36**:411
The Dreamer (Green)
See *Le visionnaire*
"The Dreamer and the Watcher" (Glück) **44**:220
The Dreamer Examines His Pillow: A Heterosexual Homily (Shanley) **75**:321
A Dreamer for a People (Buero Vallejo)
See *Un soñador para un pueblo*
"Dreamer in a Dead Language" (Paley) **37**:336, 339; **140**:210, 231-32, 235, 257, 282
"The Dreamers" (Dinesen) **29**:157-58, 164; **95**:42-4, 47, 55, 64, 73
"Dreamers" (Sassoon) **130**:186, 216, 220
"Dreamers" (Smith) **73**:353, 356
"Dreamers of the Absolute, Part I: Pamphlets and Bombs" (Enzensberger) **43**:150
"Dreamers of the Absolute, Part II: The Beautiful Souls of Terror" (Enzensberger) **43**:150
Dreamhouse (Grenville) **61**:155-63
Dreaming (Gold) **152**:138-40
"The Dreaming Child" (Dinesen) **29**:159; **95**:35
"Dreaming Crew" (Swan) **69**:365
"Dreaming from the Waist" (Townshend) **17**:536
Dreaming in Bronze (Thomas) **31**:430; **132**:382

Dreaming in Cuban (Garcia) **76**:39-45
"Dreaming in Daylight" (Warren) **39**:274
The Dreaming Jewels (Sturgeon) **39**:361, 364
Dreaming My Dreams (Jennings) **21**:202, 204, 206
Dreaming of Babylon: A Private Eye Novel, 1942 (Brautigan) **9**:124-25; **12**:74; **42**:56-7, 60-1
"Dreaming of Her" (Ostriker) **132**:327
"Dreaming of Horses" (Jensen) **37**:190
"Dreaming of Immortality in a Thatched Hut" (Stevenson) **33**:379
"Dreaming of You" (Monette) **82**:323, 332
"Dreaming the Beasts" (Sexton) **123**:437
"Dreaming the Middle Ages" (Eco) **142**:93
"Dreaming Winter" (Welch) **52**:428
"Dreamland" (Lightfoot) **26**:282
"Dreamland" (Mitchell) **12**:443
Dreamland (Higgins) **10**:273-74
Dreamland Lake (Peck) **21**:296
"Dreams" (Creeley) **36**:121
"Dreams" (Findley) **102**:111
"Dreams" (Galeano) **72**:130
"Dreams" (Giovanni) **64**:185
"Dreams" (Oliver) **98**:265, 268, 271, 276
Dreams (Bergman)
See *Kvinnodröm*
Dreams (Eich)
See *Träume*
Dreams (Kettelkamp) **12**:305
Dreams (Kurosawa) **119**:340, 378, 380-81, 384-85, 394, 396, 398
"Dreams and Dollars" (Yezierska) **46**:443
Dreams from Bunker Hill (Fante) **60**:133-34
"Dreams Must Explain Themselves" (Le Guin) **13**:347; **71**:188, 199; **136**:318
Dreams of a Summer Night (Barker) **48**:18, 21-2
"Dreams of Adulthood" (Ashbery) **77**:65-6
Dreams of Dark and Light: The Great Fiction of Tanith Lee (Lee) **46**:234
Dreams of Glory (Fleming) **37**:128-29
Dreams of Leaving (Hare) **29**:215; **136**:261, 279-80, 282-83
Dreams of Roses and Fire (Johnson)
See *Drömmar om rosor och eld*
Dreams of Sleep (Humphreys) **34**:63-6; **57**:234-36, 238
"Dreams of the Animals" (Atwood) **84**:68
Dreams of the Kalahari (Slaughter) **56**:409-10
"Dreams of Water" (Justice) **102**:263
Dreamsnake (McIntyre) **18**:326
The Dreamstone (Cherryh) **35**:112-13
"Dreamtigers" (Borges)
See "El hacedor"
Dreamtigers (Borges)
See *El hacedor*
Die drei Grazien (Eliade) **19**:148
"Dreiser's Sister Carrie" (Farrell) **66**:139
"Das dreissigste Jahr" (Bachmann) **69**:37
Das dreissigste Jahr (Bachmann) **69**:35, 37, 44
"Drenched in Light" (Hurston) **7**:172; **30**:211
The Dresden Green (Freeling) **38**:184
"The Dress" (Creeley) **78**:126
"The Dress" (Strand) **71**:278, 285-86
Dress Her in Indigo (MacDonald) **44**:408
"Dress Me Up as a Robber" (McCartney) **35**:289-91
"Dressed All in Pink" (Randall) **135**:373, 394, 396
Dressed in Light (Seifert)
See *Světlem oděná*
"Dressed Like Summer Leaves" (Dubus) **97**:214, 216
Dressed to Kill (De Palma) **20**:81-2
"Dressed Up" (Hughes) **1**:148
The Dresser (Harwood) **32**:227-28
A Dressing of Diamond (Freeling) **38**:186-87
"Dressing Up for the Carnival" (Shields) **113**:408
Dressing Up: Transvestism and Drag, the History of an Obsession (Ackroyd) **52**:5, 14; **140**:20
The Dressmaker (Bainbridge) **4**:39; **5**:39-40; **8**:37; **10**:16; **18**:33; **22**:46; **62**:24, 29, 38; **130**:6-7, 20, 26
Dried Hand (Tchicaya)
See *La main sèche*
"The Dried Sturgeon" (Bly) **128**:44
The Drifters (Michener) **109**:375, 378-79
"The Drifter's Escape" (Dylan) **12**:185
Driftglass (Delany) **14**:147; **38**:154, 160-61
"The Drifting" (Bell) **8**:66
"Drifting" (Grace) **56**:116
Drifting Home (Berton) **104**:47
Drifting into War (Bissett) **18**:59
"Drifting Off" (Heaney) **74**:169
"Driftwood" (Wilbur) **6**:570; **110**:383
"A Driftwood Altar" (Ashbery) **125**:37
"A Drink in the Passage" (Paton) **25**:359-60
"A Drink of Water" (Heaney) **7**:151
"Drink to Me Only with Labyrinthine Eyes" (Ligotti) **44**:54
"Drink Ye All of It" (Wiebe) **14**:574
"The Drinker" (Lowell) **1**:181
Drinking: A Love Story (Knapp) **99**:47-53
Drinking Companion (Ayckbourn) **33**:40
"Drinking From a Helmet" (Dickey) **109**:237
The Drinking Gourd (Hansberry) **17**:191-93
Drinking in America (Bogosian) **45**:62-4; **141**:82-5, 89
Drinking Sapphire Wine (Lee) **46**:230
"Drinking Song" (Hecht) **8**:267; **13**:269
Drinks before Dinner (Doctorow) **15**:179-80; **37**:91; **113**:149, 176
"Drinks with X" (Moss) **45**:292
Das Dritte Buch über Achim (Johnson) **5**:200-01; **10**:283-84; **15**:304-06; **40**:268
"The Drive" (Bullins) **7**:37
"Drive Back" (Young) **17**:575
"The Drive Home" (Banks) **37**:23
"The Drive Home" (Merwin) **18**:334; **88**:205
"A Drive in the Country/Henri Toulouse-Lautrec" (Middleton) **13**:388
"Drive My Car" (Lennon and McCartney) **35**:268
"A Drive through Hell" (Bukowski) **82**:23
"A Drive through Spring" (Ciardi) **40**:157
"Driven to Tears" (Police, The) **26**:365
"Driver" (Barthelme) **117**:5, 7
"The Driver" (Voznesensky) **57**:427
The Driver's Seat (Spark) **2**:416-19; **3**:464-65; **5**:400; **8**:495; **13**:524; **40**:395, 397, 399-400
"Drivin'" (Davies) **21**:91
"Driving across the American Desert and Thinking of the Sahara" (Ciardi) **40**:161
"Driving across the Prairie" (Dorn) **10**:161
"Driving Back from the Funeral" (Collins) **44**:38
Driving Force (Francis) **102**:143-44, 149
"Driving Home" (Waddington) **28**:438
Driving Home (Waddington) **28**:437-38
"Driving Home in Breaking Season" (Smith) **22**:387
"Driving in from Muskoka Slow Rain Blues" (Donnell) **34**:159
Driving Miss Daisy (Uhry) **55**:264-67
"Driving My Parents Home at Christmas" (Bly) **15**:68; **38**:57; **128**:15
"Driving on the A 30" (Williams) **42**:443
"Driving Through" (Ammons) **108**:19
"Driving Through Minnesota During the Hanoi Bombings" (Bly) **128**:21
"Driving through Ohio" (Bly) **5**:61
"Driving Through Oregon" (Haines) **58**:222
"Driving through Sawmill Towns" (Murray) **40**:340-41
"Driving Through Tennessee" (Wright) **146**:304
Driving Today and Tomorrow (Hyde) **21**:171-72
"Driving Toward Boston I Run Across One of Robert Bly's Old Poems" (McGrath) **59**:179-81
"Driving toward the Lac Qui Parle River" (Bly) **5**:61; **128**:12-13, 15, 20
"Driving toward the Moon" (Kinsella) **43**:253, 255-56
"Driving West" (Beer) **58**:33, 38
Driving West (Beer) **58**:32-3, 36, 39
"Drogo" (Strand) **41**:440
Les drôlatiques, horrifiques, et épouvantables aventures de Panurge, ami de Pantagruel, d'aprés Rabelais (Maillet) **54**:313, 317
Drôle de baraque (Kennedy)
See *Funnyhouse of a Negro*
Drôles de journal (Rakosi) **47**:347
Drömmar om rosor och eld (Johnson) **14**:295
"Drømmerne" (Dinesen)
See "The Dreamers"
A Drop of Patience (Kelley) **22**:247-48, 251
"A Drop of Pure Liquid" (Willingham) **51**:403
"Droplets" (Williams) **148**:366
"Dropping Dance" (Grenville) **61**:162
The Drought (Ballard) **3**:34; **6**:28; **14**:41; **36**:33-6; **137**:14-15, 23, 37, 41, 56
"A Drover" (Colum) **28**:90
"Drover's Song" (Mathias) **45**:235
"The Drowned" (Bottoms) **53**:32
Drowned Ammet (Jones) **26**:227-29
The Drowned and the Saved (Levi)
See *I sommersi e i salvati*
"The Drowned Child" (Glück) **44**:214
"The Drowned Giant" (Ballard) **3**:33; **14**:41; **36**:36, 39-41; **137**:13
"The Drowned Man: Death between Two Rivers" (McGrath) **28**:275
The Drowned World (Ballard) **3**:32-4; **6**:27; **14**:41; **36**:35-6, 42, 45; **137**:8, 11-12, 14-15, 17-18, 23, 35, 37-38, 41, 43-47, 49-51, 56, 70-73, 76
"Drowning" (Boyle) **36**:57-8
"Drowning" (Olds) **32**:346
"Drowning 1954" (Keillor) **40**:275
"Drowning Another Peasant Inquisition" (Codrescu) **121**:160
The Drowning of Wasyl Nemitchuk; or, A Fine Colored Easter Egg (Ringwood) **48**:334-36, 339
The Drowning Pool (Macdonald) **2**:256; **14**:334; **41**:265, 271
"Drowning Puppies" (Simmons) **43**:408
The Drowning Season (Hoffman) **51**:201-02, 207
Drowning with Others (Dickey) **7**:80, 82-3; **109**:244-45
"The Drowning Young Man" (Rukeyser) **27**:404
"Drowsing Over the Arabian Nights" (Kinsella) **138**:94, 121
"Droysen's Historik: Historical Writing as a Bourgeois Science" (White) **148**:267
"Drüben auf den Inseln" (Lenz) **27**:245
"A Drug Called Tradition" (Alexie) **154**:6
"Drug Store" (Shapiro) **4**:486; **15**:476
Drugaia zhizn' (Trifonov) **45**:408-10, 416-20
"Drugged" (Hall) **51**:172
"Drugoe" (Akhmadulina) **53**:12
"Drugs" (Byrne) **26**:97
"Drugs and Ecstasy" (Jünger) **125**:232
"Drug-Stabbing Time" (Clash) **30**:43
"A Drugstore in Winter" (Ozick) **28**:353-54
The Druid's Rest (Williams) **15**:577
"The Drum" (Bogan) **93**:90
"Drum" (Voznesensky) **57**:424
"Drummer" (Vanderhaeghe) **41**:448-50
The Drummer (Fugard) **80**:80
The Drummer Boy (Garfield) **12**:218, 221, 223-27, 235, 237
"The Drummer of All the World" (Laurence) **62**:274
"Drums" (Kenny) **87**:240
"Drums" (Okigbo) **84**:315
Drums along the Mohawk (Edmonds) **35**:147-51, 153, 155-56
Drums along the Mohawk (Ford) **16**:304, 310

Drums and Colours: An Epic Drama (Walcott) **25**:453-54
Drums at Dusk (Bontemps) **1**:37; **18**:63, 65
Drums Beneath the Window (O'Casey)
See *Drums Under the Window*
"Drums in Scotland" (Hugo) **32**:242
The Drums of Father Ned (O'Casey) **5**:318; **11**:406-07, 409-10; **15**:405; **88**:241-42, 270, 273-75
Drums, Rattles, and Bells (Kettelkamp) **12**:304
Drums Under the Window (O'Casey) **88**:239
"Drumtochty Castle School" (Barker) **48**:19
"Drunk" (Plumly) **33**:312
"The Drunk Hunter" (Bottoms) **53**:29-30
The Drunk in the Furnace (Merwin) **1**:212-13; **2**:276; **5**:288; **8**:388-89; **13**:383; **18**:333, 335; **45**:268, 270, 276-77; **88**:186, 205-06
A Drunk Man Looks at the Thistle (MacDiarmid) **2**:254; **4**:309-13; **11**:333-38; **19**:288-90; **63**:239, 241-42, 244, 249; 251-52
"Drunk with Love" (Gilchrist) **48**:119, 121
Drunk with Love (Gilchrist) **48**:119-22; **143**:283, 294, 301, 311, 315-16, 324, 330
"Drunk with the Buddha" (Bukowski) **82**:27
"The Drunkard" (O'Connor) **14**:398
"The Drunkard's Sunday" (Keillor) **40**:274
Drunken Angel (Kurosawa) **16**:402-03; **119**:340, 342, 345-47, 349, 352, 379-80, 382
"The Drunken Fisherman" (Lowell) **1**:181; **4**:303
"The Drunken Poet" (Nowlan) **15**:399
The Drunken Sisters (Wilder) **10**:536
"Drunks" (Smith) **22**:386
The Drunks (Newlove)
See *Leo and Theodore*
"Drunks in the Bass Boat" (Bottoms) **53**:32
Drury Lane's Last Case (Queen) **11**:460
Dry Dreams (Carroll) **35**:80; **143**:34
"Dry Foot Bwoy" (Bennett) **28**:26, 30
The Dry Heart (Ginzburg)
See *E stato cosí*
Dry Lips Oughta Move to Kapuskasing (Highway) **92**:218-20, 224-25, 227-32
"The Dry Prophet" (Watkins) **43**:454, 457
"The Dry Salvages" (Eliot) **1**:92; **6**:164-65; **13**:194; **15**:215-16; **24**:174; **34**:525, 529-30; **41**:152; **55**:347, 362; **57**:206, 211
"Dry September" (Faulkner) **3**:156; **18**:147; **52**:142
Dry Summer in Provence (Brand) **7**:29
Dry Sun, Dry Wind (Wagoner) **3**:508; **5**:473
Dry Victories (Jordan) **11**:312
A Dry White Season (Brink) **18**:69-70; **36**:65, 67; **106**:98-9, 104, 119, 124, 130, 133, 137, 139, 142, 143, 145
"Dry Your Eyes" (Diamond) **30**:112
"Dryad" (Davidson) **13**:168; **19**:124, 129
"The Dryad War" (Paz) **65**:200
"Dryads" (Sassoon) **130**:176-77, 191
Drypoints of the Hasidim (Prince) **22**:338-39
"DTNB" (Weller) **26**:448
Du domaine (Guillevic) **33**:192-94
The Du Mauriers (du Maurier) **59**:286
Du mouvement et de l'immobilité de Douve (Bonnefoy) **9**:112, 114; **58**:41-54, 57-60
Du surréalisme en ses oeuvres vives et d'ephemerides surréalistes (Breton) **54**:16, 28
"Du wanxiang" (Ding Ling) **68**:67-9
The Dual Tradition (Kinsella) **138**:143-46
"Duality" (Abse) **29**:16
An Duanaire (Kinsella) **138**:96, 121-22, 124, 126, 130, 145
Duas aguas (Cabral de Melo Neto) **76**:153
"Dubieties" (Cassity) **6**:107
Dubin's Lives (Malamud) **18**:319-22; **27**:302; **44**:413, 415, 419-20
Dubious Honors (Fisher) **76**:341
"Dublin" (MacNeice) **53**:237
Dubliners (Swinnerton) **31**:421
"Dublinesque" (Larkin) **5**:227; **8**:333
Ducdame (Powys) **7**:348; **46**:314-15, 324; **125**:279, 294
"The Duchess" (Cheever) **11**:121
"The Duchess' Red Shoes" (Schwartz) **10**:462
La duchesse de Langeais (Tremblay) **29**:419-20, 425; **102**:362-65, 370, 376
La duchesse et le roturier (Tremblay) **29**:424, 427-28; **102**:370
"Duck Blind" (Hass) **99**:141
Duck Song (Mercer) **5**:284
The Duck Variations (Mamet) **15**:356-58; **46**:247, 249-50
"Duck-Chasing" (Kinnell) **5**:217
"The Ducking Stool" (Muldoon) **32**:319; **72**:265
"The Ducks" (Carver) **22**:96; **36**:106
"Ducks On the Wall" (Davies) **21**:99
"Duck's Yas Yas" (Crumb) **17**:83
"Duckweed" (Leithauser) **27**:240, 242
Dude (Ragni and Rado) **17**:386
Due East (Sayers) **50**:82-7; **122**:227-31, 233-34, 237-38, 240, 242
"Due Process" (Musgrave) **54**:334
"The Duel" (Belitt) **22**:48
"The Duel" (Borges)
See "El duelo"
Duel (Spielberg) **20**:357-58
"Duel in Pernambucan Fashion" (Cabral de Melo Neto)
See "Duelo à pernambucana"
The Dueling Machine (Bova) **45**:66
"El duelo" (Borges) **10**:67; **13**:105; **83**:189
Duelo (Benet) **28**:23
"Duelo à pernambucana" (Cabral de Melo Neto) **76**:165
Duelo en el paraíso (Goytisolo) **23**:186; **133**:89, 93, 97
"The Duet" (Auden) **14**:28
"Duet" (Oates) **6**:367
Duet for Cannibals (Sontag) **31**:409
"Duffy's Circus" (Muldoon) **32**:319; **72**:275
"The Dufluflu Bird" (Johnston) **51**:239
Dúfnaveislan rónika (Laxness) **25**:300
"The Dugong" (Wright) **53**:425
"The Dug-Out" (Sassoon) **130**:186, 217
"Duhovnicească" (Arghezi) **80**:2, 6
Duishen (Aitmatov)
See *Pervyi uchitel'*
Duke Decides (Tunis) **12**:594
"The Duke Imlach Story" (Faust) **8**:215
The Duke in Darkness (Hamilton) **51**:189
"The Duke in His Domain" (Capote) **8**:132; **13**:139
The Duke of Deception: Memories of My Father (Wolff) **41**:459-61
Dulcy (Connelly) **7**:55
Dulcy (Kaufman) **38**:257-58, 264-66
"Dull Tale" (Faulkner) **18**:148
"Dulse" (Munro) **95**:302, 306, 315, 318
The Duluoz Legend (Kerouac) **61**:309-10
Duluth (Vidal) **33**:408-09; **72**:384-87, 389; **142**:292, 296, 300, 307, 322, 326, 332, 334
"La dumaiu: kak ia byla glupa" (Akhmadulina) **53**:12
"The Dumb Dutchman" (Forester) **35**:173
"Dumb Show" (Aldiss) **14**:10
"Dumb Waiter" (Miller) **30**:261
The Dumb Waiter (Altman) **116**:59
The Dumb Waiter (Pinter) **6**:407-08, 411, 413, 416-18, 420; **11**:437-38, 441; **15**:422; **27**:385, 387-88, 393; **73**:276
Dumb Witness (Christie) **48**:73
"The Dumbfounding" (Avison) **97**:85, 87, 121
The Dumbfounding (Avison) **2**:29; **4**:36; **97**:73, 77, 79-86, 88, 92-3, 99-100, 104-05, 108, 110-17, 128
"The Dummy" (Sontag) **13**:518
"The Dummy in the Window" (Walker) **58**:409
"The Dump: A Dream Come True" (Sissman) **9**:491
"Dump Gull" (Howe) **47**:173-74
The Dumplings (Lear) **12**:334
D'un château l'autre (Céline) **3**:103-05; **4**:98, 100, 102-03; **7**:45; **9**:158; **47**:74-5, 77-9; **124**:72-3, 78, 89, 92-4, 112; **124**:60, 63-4, 89, 94, 103, 107-08
"The Dun Cow and the Hag" (Dubie) **36**:134
"The Dun Dakotas" (Roth) **104**:250-51
"Dunbarton" (Lowell) **124**:278-79
"Duncan" (Simon) **17**:461, 466
"Duncan Spoke of a Process" (Baraka) **5**:45
Dunciad Minimus (Hope)
See *Dunciad Minor: An Heroick Poem*
Dunciad Minor: An Heroick Poem (Hope) **51**:211, 215, 217, 226
Dune (Herbert) **12**:270-81; **23**:221-27; **35**:196, 198-208, 210; **44**:392-95; **85**:85-112
Dune (Lynch) **66**:264, 269, 271
"D'une jeunesse européenne" (Malraux) **57**:301-02
Dune Messiah (Herbert) **12**:271-73, 276-77; **23**:221-24, 226-27; **35**:196, 199, 201, 207-08; **44**:393-94; **85**:88-9, 93-6, 110-11
Dunelawn (McNally) **4**:347; **7**:218
"Dunes" (Ammons) **25**:43-4; **108**:23
Dunfords Travels Everywheres (Kelley) **22**:249, 251-52
Dunkirk (Pratt) **19**:385
The Dunne Family (Farrell) **8**:205; **11**:194-95
Dunnigan's Daughter (Behrman) **40**:83
Dunya'llah (Mahfouz) **153**:234, 359
"Dunyazadiad" (Barth) **5**:51; **14**:52; **51**:22; **89**:10
The Duplex: A Black Love Fable in Four Movements (Bullins) **5**:82-3; **7**:36
Duplicate Keys (Smiley) **53**:346-47; **144**:247-51, 255
The Duplications (Koch) **8**:324; **44**:246, 248, 250
A Durable Fire (Sarton) **4**:471
"Durango" (Cernuda) **54**:55
Durango Street (Bonham) **12**:49, 53
Durdane (Vance) **35**:427
"Durham" (Harrison) **43**:175; **129**:171
"During a Solar Eclipse" (Nemerov) **36**:306
"During a Transatlantic Call" (Lowell) **124**:256
"During Days of Horror, Despair, and World Change" (Parker) **68**:334
"During Fever" (Lowell) **37**:243; **124**:278
"Dusie" (Barnes) **3**:37
"Dusk" (Harrison) **33**:198
"Dusk" (Ritsos) **13**:488
"Dusk" (Salter) **59**:196
Dusk and Other Stories (Salter) **52**:368-69; **59**:194-98
"Dusk before Fireworks" (Parker) **68**:326, 335, 337, 339
"Dusk: Elegy for the Dark Sun" (Hirsch) **31**:215
Dusk of Dawn (Du Bois) **64**:127; **96**:138, 146, 148
A Dusk of Idols (Blish) **14**:86
"Dusk on the Bay" (Birney) **6**:74
"Dusk Shows Us What We Are and Hardly Mean" (Schwartz) **87**:347
Dusklands (Coetzee) **23**:121-22; **66**:90-2, 95, 99; **117**:32-5, 38-9, 44-5, 47, 65, 67, 79-81, 83, 85
"Dust" (Johnston) **51**:244-45
"Dust" (Williams) **42**:442
"Dust" (Wright) **11**:578
Dust Bowl Ballads (Guthrie) **35**:184
"The Dust Garden" (Ferré) **139**:151
Dust on the Paw (Jenkins) **52**:219-22, 225-27
"Dust on the Pearls" (Daly) **17**:91
Dust Tracks on a Road (Hurston) **30**:213-14, 226; **61**:256-57, 267, 269, 275
The Dust within the Rock (Waters) **88**:328-29, 335, 337-40, 345, 360-62
"Dusting" (Dove) **50**:153, 158; **81**:139
Dustland (Hamilton) **26**:155-56
Dusty Answer (Lehmann) **5**:235, 239
"Duszyczka" (Rozewicz) **139**:297, 299
Dutch Interior (O'Connor) **14**:397; **23**:328-29
Dutch Shea, Jr. (Dunne) **28**:125-29
The Dutch Shoe Mystery (Queen) **3**:421

Dutch Uncle (Gray) **9**:241; **36**:201-04, 207
Dutchman (Baraka) **1**:163; **2**:35; **3**:35-6; **5**:44-7; **14**:43-4, 46, 49; **33**:54, 57-60, 62; **115**:10, 32-3, 37-8, 44-50
"Duties of a Black Revolutionary Artist" (Walker) **103**:376
A Dutiful Daughter (Keneally) **5**:209-11; **8**:319; **14**:302; **19**:245; **117**:215, 226-27
"Duty" (Ritsos) **31**:325
Duveen (Behrman) **40**:83, 85, 88
"Dúvidas apócrifas de Marianne Moore" (Cabral de Melo Neto) **76**:160, 166
"Duwamish Head" (Hugo) **32**:237-38, 247
"Duwamish No. Two" (Hugo) **32**:242
"Dużo śpiè" (Milosz) **56**:244
Dva tovarishcha (Voinovich) **10**:506-07; **49**:373; **147**:271-72, 275
Dvärgen (Lagerkvist) **10**:311; **13**:334; **54**:270-71, 275, 278, 288
"Dvojnik" (Coles) **67**:179
"Dvonya" (Simpson) **149**:325
Dvořák in Love (Škvorecký)
See *Scherzo capriccioso*
"Dwa wyroki" (Rozewicz) **139**:306
The Dwarf (Lagerkvist)
See *Dvärgen*
"The Dwarf and the Doll" (Boell)
See "Der Zwerg und die Puppe"
"Dwarf Birches" (Yevtushenko) **126**:415
"Dwarf House" (Beattie) **146**:76
The Dwarfs (Pinter) **6**:411; **11**:438; **15**:423; **27**:385-86; **73**:249
Dwell in the Wilderness (Bessie) **23**:58-9, 61
"The Dweller in the Gulf" (Smith) **43**:420
"Dweller in the Martian Depths" (Smith) **43**:422
Dweller in Truth (Mahfouz)
See *Akhenaten: Dweller in Truth*
Dwellers in the Land: The Bioregional Vision (Sale) **68**:352-54
"The Dwelling" (Ammons) **57**:53, 55
"The Dwelling House" (Turco) **11**:550-51
The Dwelling Places of God (Vesaas)
See *Guds bustader*
"Dwellings" (Guillevic) **33**:192
"Dyâli" (Césaire) **112**:19
"D'yer Maker" (Page and Plant) **12**:476, 482
The Dyer's Hand and Other Essays (Auden) **2**:22, 24-5; **3**:24-5; **4**:34; **6**:16; **14**:27, 31; **123**:16, 23
"Dying" (Oates) **6**:370
"Dying" (Stern) **39**:237
"Dying: An Introduction" (Sissman) **9**:492
Dying: An Introduction (Sissman) **9**:489-90, 492; **18**:488
"A Dying Art" (Mahon) **27**:290
A Dying Colonialism (Fanon)
See *L'an V de la révolution algérienne*
The Dying Earth (Vance) **35**:417-23, 425-28
"Dying for Love" (Shields) **113**:408, 426, 429-30
"Dying for Survival" (Cousteau) **30**:106
"The Dying Garden" (Nemerov) **36**:306
The Dying Gaul and Other Writings (Jones) **13**:312; **42**:238-39
"The Dying Goddess" (Kizer) **15**:309; **39**:169; **80**:184
Dying, in Other Words (Gee) **57**:218-21
Dying Inside (Silverberg) **7**:425; **140**:358, 365, 371-72, 374-76, 379-80
"The Dying Man" (Roethke) **8**:455, 460; **101**:286
"The Dying Miner" (Guthrie) **35**:193
"The Dying Night" (Asimov) **26**:44-5
"A Dying Race" (Motion) **47**:286, 293
Dying Young (Leimbach) **65**:63-6
"Dykhanie" (Solzhenitsyn) **78**:403-04
Dylan Thomas: No Man More Magical (Sinclair) **14**:488
Dymer (Lewis) **27**:258, 265; **124**:227
Dymkov's View of the Universe (Leonov) **92**:278
"Dynamite" (Smiley) **53**:348-49
Dynamite Voices I: Black Poets of the 1960's (Madhubuti) **73**:196, 202-04, 207
"The Dynasts" (Blunden) **56**:38
Dynasty of Death (Caldwell) **28**:55-7, 59-60, 65, 67; **39**:302-03
"Dyslexia" (Pesetsky) **28**:358
"Dysraphism" (Bernstein) **142**:7
Dzhamilia (Aitmatov) **71**:3, 6, 10, 13, 16
Dziennik (Gombrowicz) **7**:124; **49**:122-23, 131
Dzienniki gwiazdowe (Lem) **149**:149
Dziura w niebe (Konwicki) **117**:285
Dziura w niebie (Konwicki) **8**:326; **117**:257, 284
"E" (Merrill) **8**:384-85
"E & O E" (Tolson) **105**:265, 271, 284
E la nave va (Fellini) **85**:51, 60, 71, 75, 78, 81-2
E. M. Forster: The New Collected Short Stories (Forster) **45**:140
"E muet mutant" (Brossard) **115**:141
"E se" (Buzzati) **36**:97
E stato cosí (Ginzburg) **11**:228-29; **54**:193, 198, 206; **70**:281, 283
"E Unibus Plurnam: Television and U. S. Fiction" (Wallace) **114**:388
"Each Bird Walking" (Gallagher) **63**:117
"Each Dawn" (Levine) **33**:275
"Each Day of Summer" (Swenson) **106**:339
Each Man in His Darkness (Green)
See *Chaque homme dans sa nuit*
Each Man's Son (MacLennan) **2**:257; **14**:340, 342; **92**:322, 326-27, 341-42, 347
"Each Night" (Ignatow) **40**:258
"Each Other" (Lessing) **22**:278
"The Eagle" (Castellanos) **66**:60
"The Eagle" (Tate) **14**:532
The Eagle and the Iron Cross (Swarthout) **35**:401, 403
The Eagle and the Raven (Michener) **109**:326
"Eagle Descending" (Warren) **39**:274
Eagle Eye (Calisher) **4**:87-8; **134**:19, 24, 28-31, 35
"Eagle Flies on Friday; Greyhound Runs at Dawn" (Hillis) **66**:197
Eagle Fur (Peck) **17**:343
The Eagle Has Two Heads (Cocteau)
See *L'aigle à deux têtes*
Eagle in the Sky (Smith) **33**:375
The Eagle Kite (Fox) **121**:240-41
The Eagle of the Ninth (Sutcliff) **26**:425-30, 432-35, 437, 439-40
The Eagle on the Coin (Cassill) **23**:102
Eagle or Sun? (Paz) **3**:375; **6**:398
"Eagle Poem" (Harjo) **83**:286
"Eagle Squadron" (Forester) **35**:173
"The Eagles" (Guillén) **48**:159
Eagles and Traces (Transtroemer)
See *Klanger och spår*
The Eagles Gather (Caldwell) **28**:56-7; **39**:302-03
"The Eagle's Mile" (Dickey) **109**:246-47, 251, 273
The Eagle's Mile (Dickey) **109**:236, 245-46, 264
Eagle's Nest (Kavan) **13**:316
"Eaglet Tricks" (Musgrave) **54**:341
Ealdwood (Cherryh) **35**:113
"The Ear" (Ayrton) **7**:18
An Ear in Bartram's Tree: Selected Poems, 1957-1967 (Williams) **13**:600
"Ear of Corn" (Lowell) **11**:331
The Ear of the Other (Derrida)
See *L'oreille de l'autre*
"Ear To the Ground" (Sillitoe) **57**:396
"Earl Casillis's Lady" (Warner) **19**:461
"Earl Grey" (Keillor) **115**:295
"Earliest Recollection" (Ammons) **57**:54
"Early Americana" (Richter) **30**:329
Early Americana and Other Stories (Richter) **30**:306-07, 311, 314-15, 319, 323
The Early Asimov; or, Eleven Years of Trying (Asimov) **3**:16; **26**:38
Early Autumn (Parker) **27**:367
The Early Ayn Rand (Rand) **79**:373
"Early Copper" (Sandburg) **35**:356
The Early Cranes (Aitmatov)
See *Rannie zhuravli*
Early Dark (Price) **43**:347; **63**:325
"Early Darkness" (Glück) **81**:167, 170
Early Elkin (Elkin) **51**:96
"Early Evening Algebra" (Simic) **49**:343; **68**:378
"Early Evening Quarrel" (Hughes) **15**:292
"Early Frost" (Bernstein) **142**:30
"Early Frost" (Norris) **14**:387
"Early Grave" (Major) **19**:298
"Early Harvest" (Santos) **22**:363
"Early in the Morning" (Lustig) **56**:185-86
"Early in the Summer of 1970" (Yehoshua) **13**:617; **31**:471, 473
Early in the Summer of 1970 (Yehoshua) **13**:617-18; **31**:471
The Early Life and Adventures of Sylvia Scarlett (Mackenzie) **18**:314
Early Man and the Ocean: A Search for the Beginnings of Navigation and Seaborne Civilizations (Heyerdahl) **26**:194
"Early Marriage" (Richter) **30**:307
"Early Mondrian" (O'Hara) **78**:344
Early Moon (Sandburg) **35**:357
Early Morning (Bond) **4**:69-70; **6**:86; **13**:98, 102; **23**:66
"Early Morning: Cape Cod" (Swenson) **106**:339
"Early Morning Feed" (Redgrove) **6**:445
"Early Morning in Early April" (Ammons) **57**:58-9
"Early Morning Rain" (Lightfoot) **26**:279
"Early Noon" (Bachmann)
See "Früher Mittag"
"Early Poems" (Tate) **14**:532
Early Poems, 1935-1955 (Paz) **4**:397; **6**:398; **10**:390; **51**:333; **65**:197
"Early Pompeian" (Walcott) **25**:456; **42**:423
"The Early Purges" (Heaney) **25**:244
Early Ripening: American Women Poets Now (Piercy) **128**:272
Early Selected y mas: Poems, 1949-1966 (Blackburn) **43**:62-4
The Early Spanish Main (Sauer) **70**:331, 351
Early Spring (Ozu) **16**:448, 450, 455
Early Summer (Ozu) **16**:449, 451
"Early Waking" (Zweig) **34**:379
"Early Walk" (Pastan) **27**:368
The Early Williamson (Williamson) **29**:456-57
The Early Years (Derleth) **31**:126
"Earnest Money" (Dorris) **109**:307, 310
The Earp Brothers of Tombstone: The Story of Mrs. Virgil Earp (Waters) **88**:359-60
"The Earring" (Woolrich) **77**:389
"The Ears of Johnny Bear" (Steinbeck) **13**:530
"Earth" (Creeley) **78**:154
"The Earth" (Pasternak) **63**:312
"Earth" (Redgrove) **6**:445
"The Earth" (Sexton) **6**:494; **123**:425
"Earth" (Voznesensky) **57**:419
"Earth" (Walcott) **9**:557
"Earth and I Give You Turquoise" (Momaday) **85**:231, 262
"Earth and the Overlords" (Clarke) **136**:212
The Earth Compels (MacNeice) **10**:326; **53**:231, 234-35
"Earth Dweller" (Stafford) **29**:383
"The Earth Eats Everything" (Smith) **64**:393
Earth Erect (Popa)
See *Uspravna zemlja*
"The Earth Falls Down" (Sexton) **123**:446
"The Earth from this Distance" (Dobyns) **37**:82
Earth House Hold: Technical Notes and Queries to Fellow Dharma Revolutionaries (Snyder) **5**:393; **32**:389, 391, 394, 396, 399; **120**:310-11, 323, 325, 340, 345, 353
Earth Is Room Enough: Science Fiction Tales of Our Own Planet (Asimov) **26**:40

The Earth Is the Lord's (Caldwell) **28**:57; **39**:302-03
"The Earth Lover" (Prichard) **46**:337
The Earth Lover and Other Verses (Prichard) **46**:337
"The Earth Men" (Bradbury) **42**:38
"Earth, Moon" (Boyle) **36**:58
"The Earth of July" (Mahapatra) **33**:279
The Earth: Planet Number Three (Branley) **21**:17-18
"Earth Psalm" (Levertov) **15**:337
Earth Stopped (White) **30**:449
"The Earth That Falls Away" (Avison) **97**:79, 84, 93
Earth upon Earth (Tzara)
See *Terre sur terre*
"Earth Walk" (Meredith) **13**:375
Earth Walk: New and Selected Poems (Meredith) **4**:347-49; **13**:375; **55**:193
Earth Worms (Innaurato) **21**:193-94
"Earth Your Dancing Place" (Swenson) **106**:346
The Earth-Bound, 1924-1944 (Lewis) **41**:254
"Earth-Bread" (Still) **49**:365
Earthdivers (Vizenor) **103**:285, 288-89, 292-93, 296-98, 310, 327
Earthfasts (Mayne) **12**:392-93, 396, 398, 401-02, 404-06
Earthlight (Clarke) **13**:155; **35**:121
Earthlight (MacEwen) **55**:163
Earthly Bread (Mewshaw) **9**:376-77
Earthly Possessions (Tyler) **11**:553-54; **18**:529-30; **28**:432; **44**:315; **59**:202; **103**:216-17, 222-25, 228, 235, 237, 240-44, 256, 259, 270, 273
Earthly Powers (Burgess) **22**:75-9; **40**:119, 122, 124; **62**:124-25, 127, 132-33, 136; **81**:303-04, 307, 310
Earthman, Come Home (Blish) **14**:85
"Earth-Numb" (Hughes) **37**:177-78; **119**:272
Earthquake (Puzo) **107**:211, 213
An Earthquake in My Family (Federspiel) **42**:145-46
Earth's Changing Climate (Gallant) **17**:132-33
Earth's Children (Auel) **31**:23
Earth's Other Shadows (Silverberg) **140**:352, 354-56
"Earthsea Revisioned" (Le Guin) **136**:381, 387-90
Earthsea Trilogy (Le Guin) **13**:347, 350; **22**:270
"Earthset and the Evening Star" (Asimov) **19**:28
Earthsleep: A Poem (Chappell) **40**:143-45; **78**:91-3, 96, 111
"Earth-Visitors" (Slessor) **14**:497
Earth-Visitors (Slessor) **14**:495-96
"The Earthwoman and the Waterwoman" (Levertov) **66**:238
Earthworks (Aldiss) **14**:12-13
Earthworks: Poems, 1960-1970 (Hochman) **3**:250; **8**:297
Earthworms (Innaurato) **60**:201
Earthy Delights, Unearthly Adornments: American Writers as Image Makers (Morris) **18**:353; **37**:316
"Earwigs" (Carver) **55**:276
Earwitness: Fifty Characters (Canetti)
See *Der Ohrenzeuge: Fünfzig Charaktere*
"East" (Hoffman) **6**:244; **13**:289
East and West (Buck) **7**:34
East and West: Selected Poems of George Faludy (Faludy) **42**:136-41
East and West: The Collected Short Stories of W. Somerset Maugham (Maugham) **1**:204; **67**:205, 209
"East Berlin Diary" (Hein) **154**:65
"East Coast Journey" (Baxter) **14**:63
"East Coker" (Eliot) **1**:92; **3**:139; **6**:165; **10**:168; **13**:201-02; **15**:215-16; **34**:527, 530; **55**:374
East: Elegy for the East End and Its Energetic Waste (Berkoff) **56**:12-14, 16
The East End Plays (Walker) **44**:329-33; **61**:431-33
"East European Cooking" (Simic) **49**:335-36
East India and Company (Morand) **41**:298-99
East into Upper East: Plain Tales from New York and New Delhi (Jhabvala) **138**:77-9
East Is East (Boyle) **90**:49-61
East of Eden (Kazan) **16**:364-69; **63**:226-27, 233
East of Eden (Steinbeck) **1**:325-27; **5**:407; **9**:512-15, 517-20; **21**:367, 371, 374-75, 378, 382-83, 385-86, 391; **34**:405-07, 409-10, 413-15; **45**:369-85; **59**:350-51, 353; **124**:386, 388-93, 402
The East of Eden Letters (Steinbeck) **59**:348
East of Farewell (Hunt) **3**:252
East of Suez (Maugham) **11**:369
"East of the Blue Ridge, Our Tombs Are in the Dove's Throat" (Wright) **146**:
East of the City (Dudek) **11**:159; **19**:136
"East of the Sun and West of the Moon" (Merwin) **8**:389; **88**:205
East Side General (Slaughter) **29**:375
"East Side Story" (Seger) **35**:380, 382
East Slope (Paz)
See *Ladera este*
"East Texas Red" (Guthrie) **35**:190-91, 193
East, West (Rushdie) **100**:287, 290, 293, 315
"The East West Interview" (Snyder) **120**:330
East Wind: West Wind (Buck) **11**:70-2, 76
"Eastbourne" (Montale) **9**:387-88
"Easter" (Avison) **97**:90
"Easter" (Broumas) **73**:8
"Easter" (Kinnell) **5**:217
"Easter" (Nemerov) **36**:306
"Easter" (O'Hara) **2**:323; **13**:426; **78**:355
Easter (Smith) **12**:543
"Easter 1918" (Christie) **110**:125, 127
"Easter 1989" (Wright) **146**:357, 366
"An Easter Carol" (Clarke) **53**:95
The Easter Egg (Reaney) **13**:472, 475
"The Easter Egg Party" (Bowen) **118**:110
"Easter Hymn" (Hope) **51**:211, 220-21
Easter in New York (Cendrars)
See *Les pâques*
"Easter in Pittsburgh" (Laughlin) **49**:220, 225
"Easter Island" (Kristofferson) **26**:269
Easter Island (Kristofferson) **26**:269
"The Easter Lilies" (Gardam) **43**:171
"Easter Morning" (Ammons) **25**:46; **57**:49, 51; **108**:56-7
"Easter Morning" (Clampitt) **32**:114
"Easter Morning Aubade" (Graham) **118**:262
Easter Parade (Yates) **8**:555-56
"Easter Rising" (MacDiarmid) **11**:336
"Easter Sunday" (Ginsberg) **36**:185
"Easter Sunday" (Souster) **14**:503
Eastern Slope (Paz)
See *Ladera este*
Eastern Standard (Greenberg) **57**:229-32
"The Eastmill Reception Centre" (Metcalf) **37**:306
"Eastward Across Texas" (Snyder) **120**:325
Eastward Ha! (Perelman) **9**:415-16; **15**:417-18
"Easy Boogie" (Hughes) **108**:299-304
"The Easy House" (Dickey) **28**:118
"Easy in the Islands" (Shacochis) **39**:198-200
Easy in the Islands (Shacochis) **39**:198-201
"Easy Knowledge" (Fuller) **62**:193
"Easy Morning" (Lightfoot) **26**:279
"An Easy One" (Weidman) **7**:516
"Easy Rider" (Brautigan) **12**:64, 67
"Easy Skanking" (Marley) **17**:270-71
"Easy to Be Hard" (Ragni and Rado) **17**:385
Easy to Kill (Christie) **110**:112
Easy Travel to Other Planets (Mooney) **25**:329-30
Easy Virtue (Coward) **29**:131, 137, 139; **51**:69, 77
"Eat" (Sapphire) **99**:80
Eat (Warhol) **20**:415-16
"The Eat and Run Midnight People" (Chin) **135**:156, 158
"Eat at Home" (McCartney) **35**:279
The Eaten Heart (Aldington) **49**:8, 10-13, 18
Eaters of the Dead: The Manuscript of Ibn Fadlan, Relating His Experience with the Northmen in A.D. 922 (Crichton) **54**:70; **90**:91
"Eating Alone in Restaurants" (Friedman) **56**:105
Eating at Arby's (Grayson) **38**:211-12
"Eating Fish" (Johnston) **51**:239, 246
"The Eating Match" (Bates) **46**:62
"Eating Out" (Michaels) **6**:324
"Eating Out the Angel of Death" (Simic) **9**:481
Eating Pavlova (Thomas) **132**:384-85
Eating People Is Wrong (Bradbury) **32**:49-51, 53; **61**:34, 39-40, 42, 45
"Eating Poetry" (Strand) **18**:516, 518; **41**:438; **71**:284, 286
"Eating Sparrows" (Gallagher) **63**:120
"Eating the Bread of Affliction" (Gubar) **145**:285
"Eating the Leftovers" (Sexton) **123**:436
"Eating the Other" (Hooks) **94**:150
"Eating the Pig" (Hall) **13**:259; **151**:192
"Eating the Placenta" (Dixon) **52**:100
"L'eau de Pâques" (Theriault) **79**:407
L'eau vive (Giono) **11**:232
"Eaux-meres" (Char) **55**:289
"Eavesdropper" (Plath) **51**:343; **111**:215
E.B. White: A Biography (Elledge) **34**:425-32
"Ebano real" (Guillén) **48**:162; **79**:234, 240
"Ebb at Evening" (Everson) **5**:123
Ebony and Crystal (Smith) **43**:417
"Ebony and Ivory" (McCartney) **35**:289-92
"Ebony Eyes" (Wonder) **12**:660, 662
The Ebony Tower (Fowles) **6**:186-89; **9**:213, 216; **10**:188; **15**:23-32; **33**:171, 173-74; **87**:147, 151-52, 158, 162-63, 177-78
"éboulis" (Césaire) **112**:30
Écartèlement (Cioran) **64**:94-6
"Ecce homo" (Berryman) **6**:64
"Ecce homo" (Corso) **11**:123
"Ecce homo" (Gascoyne) **45**:147-49, 157-58
"Ecce homo" (Raine) **45**:330
"Ecce Tempus" (Blaga) **75**:79
"Eccentric Motion" (Rukeyser) **27**:405
Eccentric Neighborhoods (Ferré) **139**:162, 194-95
The Eccentricities of a Nightingale (Williams) **8**:548-49
Ecclesiastes (Mahon) **27**:287-88
L'échange symbolique et la mort (Baudrillard) **60**:12-15, 18, 24, 33
Echec à la reine (Chedid) **47**:82-3
"Echec et mât" (Damas) **84**:179
"Echo" (Barth) **3**:41; **9**:67, 70; **51**:23-4; **89**:4-5, 9-10, 12, 16, 19-20, 22-3, 26-7, 34, 43-4, 48, 50, 54, 61, 63
"The Echo" (Bowles) **19**:60; **53**:46, 49
"The Echo and the Nemesis" (Stafford) **7**:459; **19**:430; **68**:422, 434, 449
The Echo at Coole (Clarke) **6**:112; **9**:167
The Echo Chamber (Josipovici) **43**:221-22
"Echo for the Promise of Georg Trakl's Life" (Wright) **5**:520
The Echo Gate (Longley) **29**:294-96
"Echo Of" (Creeley) **36**:121
"Echo Tree" (Dumas) **6**:145; **62**:153, 155, 162
"Echoes" (Creeley) **36**:121; **78**:140, 161
"Echoes" (Dinesen) **10**:152; **95**:47-8
"Echoes" (Pink Floyd) **35**:306, 311
Echoes (Binchy) **153**:67, 71, 78
Echoes (Creeley) **36**:121
Echoes and Traces (Transtroemer)
See *Klanger och spår*
"Echoes from the Great War" (Blunden) **56**:44
Echoes Inside the Labyrinth (McGrath) **59**:175
Echoes of an Autobiography (Mahfouz) **153**:341-42, 367
The Echoing Green: Three Elegies (Levi) **41**:249
The Echoing Grove (Lehmann) **5**:235, 238
"Echo's Bones" (Beckett) **9**:81
Echo's Bones and Other Precipitates (Beckett)

9:80-1; **14**:78
"Une eclaircie" (Reverdy) **53**:290
"Eclipse" (Fuller) **28**:149
"Eclipse" (Pink Floyd) **35**:306-07
The Eclipse (Antonioni)
See *L'eclisse*
Eclipse (Hogan) **73**:149-50, 154
The Eclipse (Oates) **108**:376
Eclipse (Trumbo) **19**:446-47
"Eclipse Calypso" (Thesen) **56**:420
"Eclipse Morning" (Swenson) **61**:405
Eclipse of Stars (Sachs)
See *Sternverdunkelung*
"Eclipses" (Breton) **54**:28
L'eclisse (Antonioni) **20**:23, 26-8, 30-2; **144**:7-8, 11-15, 17-19, 27, 34-37, 39-43, 46, 48-50, 52, 54-6, 59, 67, 72, 77, 80-81, 84, 91, 93-96
"Eclogue" (Ashbery) **77**:43
"Eclogue" (Hall) **59**:151, 153, 155-56
"Eclogue" (Ransom) **11**:470
"Eclogue between the Motherless" (MacNeice) **53**:231
"An Eclogue for Christmas" (MacNeice) **4**:315; **10**:324; **53**:231, 233
"Eclogue from Iceland" (MacNeice) **53**:231, 234
"Eclogue IV: Winter" (Brodsky) **100**:43-4, 49-50
Eclogues (Davenport) **38**:144-45, 148
Eclogues (MacNeice) **4**:317
Eclogues (Read) **4**:442
L'École des Cadavres (Céline) **3**:104; **47**:79; **124**:60, 88, 96, 104
"Ecologue" (Ginsberg) **3**:195; **36**:185; **109**:364
"Economía doméstica" (Castellanos) **66**:61
"Economics" (Auden) **6**:18
"The Economist's Song" (Kunitz) **6**:287
Ecopoemas (Parra) **102**:347, 355
Ecopoems (Parra)
See *Ecopoemas*
"Ecossaise, Berceuse, Polonaise" (Fuchs) **22**:159
Ecrire (Duras) **100**:134-35, 148
Ecrits (Lacan) **75**:280, 284, 288, 290, 298, 314-15
Écrits: A Selection (Lacan)
See *Ecrits*
L'Ecriture du désastre (Blanchot) **135**:89, 96, 99, 102, 110, 134, 145,
L'écriture et la différence (Derrida) **24**:153; **87**:72, 88, 104
"Écrivains et écrivants" (Barthes) **24**:34; **83**:98
"Ecstasy" (Hooks) **94**:157
"Ecstasy" (Olds) **39**:187, 189
The Ecstasy Business (Condon) **45**:94-5, 97
"Ecstasy of a Song" (Kunene) **85**:175
The Ecstasy of Communication (Baudrillard) **60**:36
The Ecstasy of Dr. Miriam Garner (Feinstein) **36**:170
The Ecstasy of Matter (Le Clézio)
See *L'extase matérielle*
The Ecstasy of Rita Joe (Ryga) **14**:472
Ecstasy: Three Tales of Chemical Romance (Welsh) **144**:320-25, 327-28, 334, 348
"Ecstatic" (Johnston) **51**:254
Ecuador (Michaux) **8**:392
Ecue-yamba-ó! (Carpentier) **11**:102-04; **38**:95-6, 98; **110**:69, 75-7
"Ed" (Simpson) **149**:323
"Ed è subito sera" (Quasimodo) **10**:427
Ed è subito sera (Quasimodo) **10**:428-29
"Eddie, Are You Kidding" (Zappa) **17**:588
"Eddie Mac" (McGahern) **48**:272
"Eddie the Eunuch" (Kristofferson) **26**:269
"Eddy" (Musgrave) **54**:334
The Eddy Duchin Story (Hart) **66**:182
"Eden" (Scott) **22**:372, 375
Eden (Lem) **40**:290; **149**:118, 144, 167-68, 172, 208, 220, 255, 260, 263, 282, 284, 289
Eden and After (Robbe-Grillet)
See *L'Eden et après*
Eden Cinema (Duras)
See *L'éden cinéma*
L'éden cinéma (Duras) **40**:176 78; **69**:92, 95-6
"Eden, Eden" (MacEwen) **13**:357
Eden End (Priestley) **2**:346; **5**:350-51; **34**:365
L'Eden et après (Robbe-Grillet) **1**:289; **4**:449; **43**:367; **128**:363
Eden: Graphics and Poetry (Tomlinson) **45**:394, 404-05
Edens Lost (Elliott) **38**:178-79, 181
Edgar Allan Poe: A Study in Genius (Krutch) **24**:286-87
Edgar Allen (Neufeld) **17**:307-08, 311
"The Edgar Era" (Keillor)
See "WLT"
"Edgar Jené and the Dream about the Dream" (Celan)
See "Edgar Jené und der Traum vom Traume"
"Edgar Jené und der Traum vom Traume" (Celan) **19**:89; **82**:53
"Edgar Poe's Tradition" (McLuhan) **83**:360
"Edge" (Gunnars) **69**:260
"The Edge" (Komunyakaa) **94**:230
"Edge" (Montague) **46**:275-76
"The Edge" (Narayan) **28**:301; **121**:420
"Edge" (Plath) **5**:344; **9**:427, 433-34; **14**:424, 426; **17**:360, 366; **62**:406; **111**:168, 206
The Edge (Francis) **102**:131, 133-36, 139, 147-48, 158
An Edge in My Voice (Ellison) **139**:129
An Edge in My Voice (Ellison) **42**:133
The Edge of Being (Spender) **2**:420; **5**:401
Edge of Being: Poems (Spender) **91**:261
The Edge of Darkness (Chase) **2**:101
The Edge of Day (Lee)
See *Cider with Rosie*
The Edge of Impossibility: Tragic Forms in Literature (Oates) **3**:361; **134**:239
"Edge of Love" (Aleixandre)
See "Filo del amor"
The Edge of Next Year (Stolz) **12**:554-55
The Edge of Sadness (O'Connor) **14**:389-90, 392-94
The Edge of the Alphabet (Frame) **6**:190; **22**:145-46, 148; **96**:167, 174-76, 178-79, 182, 190-91, 195-96, 203, 217
"The Edge of the Forest" (Murray) **40**:336-37
The Edge of the Paper (Tindall) **7**:473
The Edge of the Sea (Carson) **71**:94, 101-09
"The Edge of the World" (Cheever) **64**:66
"Edge of the World" (Oates) **134**:245
The Edible Woman (Atwood) **2**:19-20; **3**:19; **4**:26, 28; **8**:30-1, 34; **13**:42, 44, 46; **15**:37, 39; **25**:63-4, 68; **44**:146-47, 152-53; **84**:50-2, 71, 78-9, 86, 90, 99, 107; **135**:7, 9, 13, 18, 31, 38, 71
Edipo Re (Pasolini) **20**:260-61, 263-65, 267, 269; **106**:226, 256
Edisto (Powell) **34**:97-101
Edith Jackson (Guy) **26**:143-45
"Edith Piaf Among the Pygmies" (Paz) **119**:410
Edith's Diary (Highsmith) **14**:260; **42**:215; **102**:172-73, 190-91, 209
"Editorial" (Reading) **47**:352
"Editorial Impressions" (Sassoon) **130**:183, 221
Edmond (Mamet) **46**:252-55
Edmund Campion (Waugh) **107**:358, 361
Edmund Husserl's "Origin of Geometry": An Introduction (Derrida)
See *Traduction et introduction à l'origine de la géométrie d'Edmund Husserl*
"Edmund to Gloucester" (Snodgrass) **68**:397
"Edna's Ruthie" (Cisneros) **118**:177
Edsel (Shapiro) **4**:487; **53**:333
"Eduard Munch" (Mahon) **27**:286, 288
"A educão pela pedra" (Cabral de Melo Neto) **76**:160, 164, 168
The Educated Imagination (Frye) **24**:214, 226; **70**:278
Educating Rita (Russell) **60**:317-25
"Educating the Rider and the Horse" (Bly) **128**:41-42
"Education" (Davies) **21**:101
"Education" (Madhubuti) **73**:207
"An Education" (Ozick) **7**:288; **62**:353-54; **155**:182, 184
Education and the University (Leavis) **24**:308
"Education by Poetry" (Frost) **9**:221
Education by Stone (Cabral de Melo Neto)
See *Aeducacão pela pedra*
L'éducation des filles (Mauriac) **9**:369
Education Européenne (Gary) **25**:184-86
An Education in Blood (Elman) **19**:150
"Education of a Novelist" (Rich) **73**:330
"The Education of Mingo" (Johnson) **51**:234-36
The Education of Patrick Silver (Charyn) **8**:136
"The Education of Richard Rodriguez" (Rodriguez)
See *Hunger of Memory: The Education of Richard Rodriguez, An Autobiography*
The Education of Skinny Spew (Brenton) **31**:57
Education through Art (Read) **4**:443
"The Educational Experience" (Barthelme) **8**:53; **115**:80
Edukacja Cyfrania (Lem) **149**:114
"Edward" (Hughes) **4**:236
"Edward and God" (Kundera) **32**:260; **68**:241, 261
The Edward Dahlberg Reader (Dahlberg) **7**:63-4
The Edward Hoagland Reader (Hoagland) **28**:183-85
"Edward the Conqueror" (Dahl) **79**:176
Edward: The Final Days (Barker) **37**:34
"Edward Weston in Mexico City" (Dacey) **51**:80
Edwin (Mortimer) **43**:308
Edwin Arlington Robinson (Winters) **32**:460
Edwin Mullhouse: The Life and Death of an American Writer, 1943-1954, by Jeffrey Cartwright (Millhauser) **54**:319-28, 330-31; **21**:215-19; **109**:161-62, 165-70, 173-74
"The Eel" (Montale)
See "L'anguilla"
"The Eel Teller" (Shapcott) **38**:404
"The Eemis Stane" (MacDiarmid) **19**:285-86, 288; **63**:252
"Eena Wales" (Bennett) **28**:29
"The Effect" (Sassoon) **130**:182, 214, 220
The Effect of Gamma Rays on Man-in-the-Moon Marigolds (Zindel) **6**:586; **26**:472-73
"L'effet du réel" (Barthes) **83**:90
L'effet Glapion (Audiberti) **38**:23
Effi Briest (Fassbinder) **20**:108-09, 113-14, 116
The Efficient Cat (Valenzuela)
See *El gato eficaz*
Effluences from the Sacred Cave: More Selected Essays and Reviews (Carruth) **84**:125, 127, 129
"Effort at Speech" (Meredith) **4**:348; **13**:375
"Effort at Speech between Two People" (Rukeyser) **27**:404-05
"Efforts of Affection" (Bishop) **32**:44
"Efforts of Affection" (Moore) **1**:230; **19**:340; **47**:264
L'effroi la joie (Char) **14**:124
Efuru (Nwapa) **65**:329-33; **133**:165-66, 169-71, 180-83, 190-93, 195-96, 201, 211, 214, 216, 219, 222-23, 226-27, 229-31, 233, 235, 238, 241-47
"Egg" (Hoffman) **6**:244
"The Egg" (Snyder) **5**:395; **120**:313
"The Egg and the Hen" (Lispector)
See "O ovo e a galinha"
"The Egg and the Machine" (Frost) **10**:193
"The Egg Boiler" (Brooks) **49**:32; **125**:86-7
"An Egg for the Major" (Forester) **35**:173
"The Egg Race" (Updike) **15**:547-48
"Egg-Head" (Hughes) **14**:270

The Egghead Republic: A Short Novel from the Horse Latitudes (Schmidt)
See *Die Gelehrtenrepublik: Kurzroman aus den Rossbreiten*
"Eggplant" (Pollitt) **122**:204
"The Eggplant Epithalamion" (Jong) **6**:267
"Eggs" (Olds) **85**:289
Eggs (Howe) **47**:174
"The Eggs Speak Up" (Arendt) **98**:55
"Eggshell Expressway" (Hospital) **145**:295, 303, 305, 313
L'église (Céline) **3**:104-05; **7**:43; **9**:154; **124**:60, 72
The Ego and the Centaur (Garrigue) **2**:153
"Ego Confessions" (Ginsberg) **109**:333
"The Ego Is Always at the Wheel" (Schwartz) **87**:348
The Ego Is Always at the Wheel: Bagatelles (Schwartz) **45**:359-60; **87**:344, 348
"Ego Tripping" (Giovanni) **64**:195; **117**:184, 197, 200
"The Egoist" (Neruda)
See "El egoísta"
"The Egoist" (Nowlan) **15**:398
"El egoísta" (Neruda) **62**:335
"The Egoist's Prayer" (Ezekiel) **61**:108
"Egorushka's Destruction" (Leonov)
See "Ghibel' Egorushki"
"Egorushka's Undoing" (Leonov)
See "Ghibel' Egorushki"
Ego-Tripping and Other Poems for Young People (Giovanni) **117**:168, 184, 191
"The Egret" (Oliver) **98**:289
"Egrets" (Oliver) **34**:247; **98**:257
"Egypt" (H. D.) **73**:105
"Egypt from My Inside" (Golding) **3**:199; **27**:169
The Egypt Game (Snyder) **17**:470-72
"Egypt, Tobago" (Walcott) **42**:423
An Egyptian Bondage and Other Stories (Kessler) **4**:269
The Egyptian Cross Mystery (Queen) **11**:460
"Egyptian Gold" (Garrett) **3**:192; **11**:219; **51**:148
An Egyptian Journal (Golding) **81**:323-24
"An Egyptian Passage" (Weiss) **14**:556
The Egyptians (Asimov) **76**:312
Egyptology (Foreman) **50**:163, 168
Eh Joe (Beckett) **6**:39, 45; **9**:83-4; **18**:42-3
Die Ehe des Herrn Mississippi (Duerrenmatt) **102**:53, 56-7, 74, 76-8, 80
Die Ehe des Herrn Mississippi (Dürrenmatt) **4**:140; **8**:194; **11**:168-69; **15**:194-95, 198; **43**:125
Die Ehen in Philippsburg (Walser) **27**:456-60, 467
"Ehrengard" (Dinesen) **10**:145; **29**:156; **95**:52-4
Eiche und Angora (Walser) **27**:455, 461-62, 465
Eichmann in Jerusalem: A Report on the Banality of Evil (Arendt) **66**:26-7, 31; **98**:6, 11, 18, 27, 30-1, 34, 43, 48-9, 53, 55
"Eidolon" (H. D.) **31**:207
"Eidolon (Phantom) Parade" (Scannell) **49**:331
"The Eiffel Tower" (Buzzati) **36**:94
The Eiger Sanction (Trevanian) **29**:429-32
"VIII" (Kinnell) **3**:268; **13**:322
8 1/2 (Fellini)
See *Otto e Mezzo*
"Eight Arms to Hold You" (Kureishi) **135**:286
"Eight Aspects of Melissa" (Durrell) **27**:97
Eight Days (Seifert)
See *Osm dnů*
"Eight Days a Week" (Lennon and McCartney) **35**:275
Eight Days of Luke (Jones) **26**:225, 230
"Eight for Ornette's Music" (Rexroth) **22**:346
"Eight Fragments for Kurt Cobain" (Carroll) **143**:44, 46
"Eight Games of Strategy" (Morgan) **2**:295
Eight Hours Don't Make a Day (Fassbinder) **20**:106
Eight Hundred Rubles (Neihardt) **32**:331
Eight Men (Wright) **3**:545; **9**:584-85; **14**:596, 598; **21**:437; **74**:382, 390
8 Million Ways to Die (Stone) **73**:382
Eight Months on Ghazzah Street (Mantel) **144**:210-13, 220, 222, 224, 230, 232-33, 239
Eight Mortal Ladies Possessed (Williams) **5**:502-03; **7**:544
"Eight O'Clock One Morning" (Grau) **9**:240; **146**:128
"Eight People on a Golf Course and One Bird of Freedom Flying Over" (Ferlinghetti) **111**:66
"Eight Plus" (Creeley) **78**:161
Eight Plus One: Stories (Cormier) **30**:87
"Eight Poems on Portraits of the Foot" (Logan) **5**:253
"Eighteen Days without You" (Sexton) **6**:492
1876: A Novel (Vidal) **8**:525-26; **33**:407, 409-11; **72**:377, 382-85, 387, 389, 391-93, 395-96, 399-402, 404; **142**:322, 334
Eighteen Short Songs of the Bitter Motherland (Ritsos)
See *Dekachtō lianotragouda tēs pikrēs patridas*
18 Stories (Boell) **27**:63; **72**:67, 73
"Eighteen West Eleventh Street" (Merrill) **6**:323
"1889 and the Devil's Mode" (Burgess) **62**:139
Eighteenth-Century Women Poets: An Oxford Anthology (Lonsdale) **65**:316-17, 343
"1830" (Davenport) **6**:125
An Eighteen-Year-Old Looks Back on Life (Maynard) **23**:289
"Eighth Air Force" (Jarrell) **9**:299; **13**:300, 302-03; **49**:193
"The Eighth and the Thirteenth" (Ostriker) **132**:321, 326
The Eighth Day (Wilder) **1**:366; **6**:576-78; **10**:533, 535; **15**:575; **82**:354-56, 367-68, 375, 378
"The Eighth Ditch" (Baraka) **115**:17
The Eighth Ditch (Baraka) **33**:59; **115**:10, 17
"The Eighth Voyage" (Lem) **149**:148, 157, 274
"The Eighth Voyage of Sinbad" (Millhauser) **109**:157-59, 161
"Eighty" (Berryman) **13**:81
"Eighty Acres" (Wright) **53**:425
"The Eighty Yard Run" (Shaw) **34**:369-70
Eighty-Eight Poems (Hemingway) **19**:219
The Eighty-Minute Hour: A Space Opera (Aldiss) **5**:15-16; **14**:14
Eighty-Seventh Precinct Series (Hunter) **31**:225
Eighty-Sixed (Feinberg) **59**:59-62
"Eileann Chanaidh" (Raine) **45**:341
"Eileen" (Gordon) **128**:118
Eimi (Cummings) **1**:68; **12**:142-43, 145, 161; **15**:161; **68**:32, 35, 38-9, 48-50
"Der eine hauet Silber, der andere rotes Gold" (Hein) **154**:165
Einer fur alle, alle fur einen (Fo) **32**:172
Einführung in die Metaphysik (Heidegger) **24**:264
Das Einhorn (Walser) **27**:456, 459-61, 464, 467
Einladung an alle (Wellershoff) **46**:435-36
"Einladung zum Lever Bourgeois" (Hein) **154**:133-35, 164-65, 194
Einladung zum Lever Bourgeois (Hein) **154**:
"Der Einsame" (Celan) **10**:104
"Einst hab ich die Muse gefragt..." (Rozewicz) **139**:294
"Einstein" (MacLeish) **8**:359; **14**:337; **68**:271, 273-76, 286, 289-90
The Einstein Intersection (Delany) **8**:168-69; **14**:146; **38**:149-50, 152, 154, 160-61; **141**:97, 126, 142, 153-55, 158
Einstein on the Beach (Wilson) **9**:577
Einstein überquert die Elbe bei Hamburg (Lenz) **27**:251-52
"Einstein's Bathrobe" (Moss) **45**:289
Einstein's Dreams (Lightman) **81**:71-80
Einstein's Monsters (Amis) **62**:6-11, 15-16
"Einundzwanzig Punkte du zen Physikern" (Dürrenmatt) **15**:196
Einzelheiten (Enzensberger) **43**:154
Eirei no koe (Mishima) **27**:342
"Eisenheim the Illusionist" (Millhauser) **109**:157-58, 161, 171
Eisenhower and the German POWS (Ambrose) **145**:36
Eisenhower, My Eisenhower (Charyn) **5**:104
Eisenhower: Soldier, General of the Army, President-Elect 1890-1952 (Ambrose) **145**:3, 29
Eisenhower: The President (Ambrose) **145**:5, 7
"Eisenhower's Visit to Franco, 1959" (Wright) **3**:540
"The Ejection Seat" (Aksyonov) **101**:15
Eklips (Breytenbach) **126**:89, 101
"Ekloga 4-aya: Zimnyaya" (Brodsky)
See "Eclogue IV: Winter"
El (Bunuel) **16**:135, 147, 150-51; **80**:23-4, 27-31, 34, 47, 50
"El Greco" (Dubie) **36**:130, 137
"El Greco: Espolio" (Birney) **6**:77; **11**:50
El hermano (Linney) **51**:260
"Elaboration" (Carruth) **84**:129
"Elaine in a Bikini" (Johnston) **51**:240, 245-46
Elämä ja aurinko (Sillanpaa) **19**:417-19
"L'élan vital" (Montale) **9**:388
"Elbow Room" (McPherson) **77**:357-59, 362-63, 372-73, 375, 377-78, 382-85
Elbow Room (McPherson) **19**:310; **77**:355-57, 362, 364, 366, 374, 378, 382, 384
Elbowing the Seducer (Gertler) **34**:49-53
"The Elder Gods" (Campbell) **32**:75
"The Elder Lady" (Borges) **10**:67
The Elder Sister (Swinnerton) **31**:423
The Elder Statesman (Eliot) **1**:91; **6**:168; **13**:195; **15**:209-10; **41**:143, 145-46, 148, 152
"Elderly Politicians" (Hughes) **10**:279
Elders and Betters (Compton-Burnett) **15**:140; **34**:496
"The Eldest" (Ferber) **93**:138, 141
"The Eldest of Things" (Abbott) **48**:4, 7
Eldorado Red (Goines) **80**:96
Eleanor (Lerman) **56**:178-79
"Eleanor on the Cliff" (Wakoski) **40**:456
"Eleanor Rigby" (Lennon and McCartney) **35**:293
The Elected Member (Rubens) **19**:402; **31**:351-52
Elected Silence: The Autobiography of Thomas Merton (Merton) **3**:336
"Election Day" (Hansen) **38**:240
"Elective Affinities" (Jacobsen) **48**:192, 194
"Electra Currents" (Castillo) **151**:11
"Electra on Azalea Path" (Plath) **17**:360; **50**:448; **51**:344; **111**:178, 219, 221
"Electric Aunt Jemima" (Zappa) **17**:586
"An Electric Blanket" (Frame) **96**:215
Electric City and Other Stories (Grace) **56**:122-23
"Electric Guitar" (Byrne) **26**:98
The Electric Kool-Aid Acid Test (Wolfe) **2**:482; **9**:578; **35**:451-56, 459-66; **51**:419-20; **147**:301, 304, 310, 320, 328-30, 333-37, 357-59, 361-65
The Electric Life (Birkerts) **116**:152, 157
"An Electric Sign Goes Dark" (Sandburg) **35**:341
"Electrical Storm" (Hayden) **37**:151
The Electrification of the Soviet Union (Raine) **103**:196-97, 199
The Electromagnetic Spectrum: Key to the Universe (Branley) **21**:23
The Electronic Nigger (Bullins) **1**:47; **5**:82
"The Electronic Siege" (Campbell) **32**:73
El elefante (Arreola) **147**:40, 42, 44
"Elegi" (Transtroemer) **65**:235-36
"Elegía" (Castellanos) **66**:50-1
Elegía (Neruda) **28**:310; **62**:333, 336
"Elegia na powrót umarłych poetów"

(Rozewicz) **139**:283
"Elegía para cantar" (Neruda) **62**:336
"Elegiac Calculation" (Szymborska) **99**:200
Elegiac Feelings American (Corso) **1**:64
"Elegiac Stanzas for Alban Berg" (Gascoyne)
See "Strophes elegiaque: A la memoire d'Alban Berg"
"Elegías del amado fantasma" (Castellanos) **66**:50
"Elegie" (Smith) **12**:537
"Elégie des alizés" (Senghor) **130**:260-61, 275
"Elégie des circoncis" (Senghor) **54**:391; **130**:253, 260
"Elégie des eaux" (Senghor) **54**:391; **130**:234
"Elégie pour Georges Pompidou" (Senghor) **130**:261
"Elégie pour Jean-Marie" (Senghor) **130**:261
"Elégie pour Martin Luther King" (Senghor) **130**:261, 284-85
"Elegies" (Alexie) **154**:21
"Elegies" (Ekelöf) **27**:110
"Elegies" (Levertov) **5**:249
"Elegies" (Rukeyser) **27**:408
"Elégies" (Senghor) **130**:238, 260
Elegies (Dunn) **40**:170-72
Elegies (Rukeyser) **27**:407
"Elegies for Paradise Valley" (Hayden) **14**:241; **37**:154, 156, 158
"Elegies for the Ochre Deer on the Walls at Lascaux" (Dubie) **36**:139-40, 142
Elégies majeures (Senghor) **130**:260-61
"The Elegies of Jutting Rock" (Elytis) **100**:190
"Elegy" (Auden) **4**:33
"Elegy" (Berry) **46**:71-3
"Elegy" (Bidart) **33**:76
"Elegy" (Broumas) **73**:8
"Elegy" (Brown) **5**:77
"Elegy" (Cohen) **38**:131
"Elegy" (Ekeloef)
See *En Mölna-elegi*
"Elegy" (Forché) **86**:139, 142
"Elegy" (Heaney) **25**:245; **74**:159
"The Elegy" (Hope) **51**:217, 221
"Elegy" (Johnston) **51**:249
"Elegy" (Kunene) **85**:160, 162
"Elegy" (Morgan) **2**:295
"Elegy" (Roethke) **101**:269, 271
"Elegy" (Simic) **22**:381
"Elegy" (Stafford) **29**:385
"Elegy" (Transtroemer)
See "Elegi"
"Elegy" (Walcott) **42**:421; **76**:279-82
"Elegy" (Young) **19**:480
Elegy (Neruda)
See *Elegía*
Elegy (West) **9**:562
"Elegy 1969" (Strand) **71**:284
An Elegy and Other Poems (Blunden) **56**:47
"Elegy Anticipating Death" (Barker) **48**:9
"Elegy Asking That It Be the Last" (Dubie) **36**:130
"Elegy at the Year's End" (Baxter) **14**:62
"Elegy for a Cricket" (Cunningham) **31**:98
"Elegy for a Dead Soldier" (Shapiro) **15**:475, 478
"Elegy for a Freelance" (Carter) **5**:103
Elegy for a Lady (Miller) **47**:253
"Elegy for a Warbler" (Pack) **13**:439
"Elegy for a Youth Changed to a Swan" (Boland) **67**:43
"Elegy for Aldous Huxley" (Jennings) **131**:241
"Elegy for Alto" (Okigbo) **25**:353, 356; **84**:312, 316, 321, 331-32
"Elegy for Camagüey" (Guillén) **79**:230
"Elegy for Dead Animals" (Martin) **89**:111, 118
"Elegy for Father Stephen" (Merton) **83**:395
"An Elegy for Five Old Ladies" (Merton) **83**:395
"Elegy for Georges Pompidon" (Senghor)
See "Elégie pour Georges Pompidou"
"Elegy for Jake" (Simpson) **149**:323
"Elegy for Jane" (Roethke) **8**:455; **11**:483; **46**:363; **101**:269, 304, 327, 329-30, 333
"Elegy for Jean-Marie" (Senghor)
See "Elégie pour Jean-Marie"
"Elegy for John Donne" (Brodsky)
See "The Great Elegy for John Donne"
"Elegy for Margaret" (Spender) **41**:426, 428; **91**:261
"Elegy for Martin Luther King" (Senghor)
See "Elégie pour Martin Luther King"
"Elegy for Mitch Stuart" (Stuart) **34**:375
"Elegy for Msizi" (Kunene) **85**:165-66
"Elegy for My Father" (Moss) **7**:247; **45**:290, 292; **50**:353
"Elegy for My Father" (Strand) **6**:521-22; **18**:519; **71**:279
"Elegy for My Friend E. Galo" (Kunene) **85**:165
"Elegy for My Sister" (Moss) **45**:286, 289, 292; **50**:353
"Elegy for Sam" (Ciardi) **40**:154; **129**:48
"Elegy for Singing" (Neruda)
See "Elegía para cantar"
"Elegy for Slit-Drum" (Okigbo) **25**:354, 356; **84**:314, 316, 321
"Elegy for Sylvia Plath" (Schaeffer) **6**:489
"Elegy for the Gas Dowsers" (MacBeth) **9**:340
"Elegy for the Giant Tortoises" (Atwood) **15**:37
"Elegy for the Labouring Poor" (Hooker) **43**:196-97, 199-200
"Elegy for the Lost Parish" (Dunn) **40**:168
"Elegy for the Monastery Barn" (Merton) **83**:394
"Elegy for the Queen of Sheba" (Senghor) **130**:261
"An Elegy for the Unknown Man Nicknamed Donda" (Kunene) **85**:165
"Elegy for Thelonious" (Komunyakaa) **86**:191
"Elegy for Wesley Wells" (Hall) **37**:143; **151**:207
"Elegy for Y. Z." (Milosz) **82**:299, 304
"Elegy in a Botanic Garden" (Slessor) **14**:492
"Elegy in a Kensington Churchyard" (Spark) **40**:393
"Elegy in a Rainbow" (Brooks) **49**:36, 38
"Elegy in an Abandoned Boatyard" (Smith) **42**:349, 353-54
"Elegy Just in Case" (Ciardi) **40**:157; **44**:381, 383; **129**:45
"Elegy of a Plain Black Boy" (Brooks) **125**:107
"Elegy of Carthage" (Senghor) **130**:261
"Elegy of Fortinbras" (Herbert)
See "Tren Fortynbrasa"
"Elegy of Midnight" (Senghor) **54**:391
"Elegy of the Circumcised" (Senghor)
See "Elégie des circoncis"
"Elegy of the Trade Winds," (Senghor)
See "Elégie des alizés"
"Elegy of the Waters" (Senghor)
See "Elégie des eaux"
"Elegy of the Wind" (Okigbo) **25**:354; **84**:316
Elegy on Dead Fashion (Sitwell) **9**:493-96; **67**:313
"Elegy on Spain" (Barker) **48**:10-11, 15, 20, 23
"Elegy on the Closing of the French Brothels" (Durrell) **27**:97
"An Elegy on the Death of Kenneth Patchen" (Ferlinghetti) **6**:184; **111**:65
"Elegy on the Dust" (Gunn) **32**:214
"Elegy on the Lost Child" (Amichai) **22**:29
"The Elegy on the Lost Child" (Amichai) **57**:44
"An Elegy on the Return of Dead Poets" (Rozewicz)
See "Elegia na powrót umarłych poetów"
"An Elegy: R. R. 1916-1941" (Gascoyne) **45**:157
"Elegy to Emmett Till" (Guillén) **48**:164; **79**:230
Elegy to John Donne and Other Poems (Brodsky) **100**:58-9
"An Elegy to the Guevera" (Rosenblatt)
See "The Bee Hive"
"Elegy to the Pulley of Superior Oblique" (Dubie) **36**:133
"Elegy to the Sioux" (Dubie) **36**:133
"Elegy—The Streets" (Denby) **48**:82
"The Element" (Merwin) **8**:390
"Element" (Page) **18**:379
The Elemental Odes (Neruda)
See *Odas elementales*
Elementals (Byatt) **136**:194
"Elementary Attitudes" (Van Duyn) **63**:440; **116**:420
"Elementary Comments" (Chomsky) **132**:37
"Elementary Cosmogony" (Simic) **9**:478; **68**:373
Elementary Odes (Neruda)
See *Odas elementales*
"An Elementary School Classroom" (Spender) **91**:263
The Elements (Hooker) **43**:196-97
"Elements constitutifs d'une civilisation d'inspiration négro-af ricaine" (Senghor) **54**:409
Eléments de sémiologie (Barthes) **24**:26, 42; **83**:85, 94
"Elements of Immortality" (Rudnik) **7**:384
The Elements of Poetry (FitzGerald) **19**:178
The Elements of San Joaquin (Soto) **32**:401-02, 404-05; **80**:277-79, 281-83, 285, 292-95, 298
Elements of Semiology (Barthes)
See *Eléments de sémiologie*
The Elements of Style (White) **10**:528; **34**:425, 428; **39**:369-71, 373, 377, 379
"Elena" (Nin) **127**:386-87, 390
"Elenita, Cards, Palm Water" (Cisneros) **118**:177
"Elephant" (Carver) **53**:62, 64-7; **55**:278
"Elephant" (Neruda) **7**:260
The Elephant (Arreola)
See *El elefante*
Elephant, and Other Stories (Carver) **53**:62, 66-7
The Elephant and the Kangaroo (White) **30**:442, 449
Elephant Bangs Train (Kotzwinkle) **5**:220; **14**:309; **35**:253-54
"Elephant Hunt" (Cendrars) **106**:158
The Elephant Man (Lynch) **66**:257, 259-60, 269, 271
The Elephant Man (Pomerance) **13**:444-46
"The Elephant Shooter" (Paton) **25**:360
"The Elephant Vanishes" (Murakami) **150**:51, 56, 58, 61
The Elephant Vanishes (Murakami) **150**:38, 50-3, 55-8, 61, 65, 86, 88
"The Elephant-Man" (Hill) **113**:281
Elephants Can Remember (Christie) **48**:72; **110**:123
"Elephants in Heat" (Alexander) **121**:21
"Elethia" (Walker) **103**:410-12, 423
Eleuthéria (Beckett) **57**:99; **59**:254; **83**:115
"The Elevator" (Bowering) **47**:22
"Eleven" (Cisneros) **118**:215
"Eleven" (MacLeish) **68**:285
Eleven (Highsmith) **102**:172
"Eleven Addresses to the Lord" (Berryman) **3**:68, 70; **6**:64; **25**:92, 95; **62**:44, 66, 74-5
Eleven Declarations of War (Deighton)
See *Declarations of War*
Eleven Kinds of Loneliness (Yates) **7**:554; **23**:481-82
"Eleven O'Clock at Night" (Bly) **38**:54; **128**:23
"Eleven Poems of Exhaustion" (L'Heureux) **52**:273
Eleven Poems on the Same Theme (Warren) **4**:579; **13**:573-77
"Eleven Political Poems" (Buckley) **57**:126, 131
Eleven Stained-Glass Segments (Endō) **54**:160
"11Outlined Epitaphs" (Dylan) **6**:157; **77**:178
"Eleventh Avenue Racket" (Sandburg) **35**:352
"The Eleventh Commandment" (Simpson) **149**:349
"The Eleventh Floor" (Baxter) **45**:53; **78**:18

"11th R. S. R." (Blunden) **56**:41, 43
The Eleventh Summer (Gébler) **39**:60-2
"The Eleventh Voyage" (Lem) **149**:273
Elfenbeinturms (Handke) **134**:151
"El-Hajj Malik El-Shabazz" (Hayden) **37**:155
Eli: A Mystery Play on the Sufferings of Israel (Sachs) **14**:475; **98**:322, 332, 334-36, 344-45
Eli and the Thirteenth Confession (Nyro) **17**:312-13, 315, 317-21
"Eli the Fanatic" (Roth) **66**:418
Elia Kazan: A Life (Kazan) **63**:223-33
"Elias Schneebaum" (Kaplan) **50**:55, 57
Elidor (Garner) **17**:134-40, 142-44, 149, 151
Eliduc (Fowles) **87**:150, 153
Eligible Men (Elkin)
See *Searches and Seizures*
The Eligible Men (Elkin) **6**:169
"El eliglia" (Cernuda) **54**:48
"Elimination" (Campbell) **32**:78, 80
Elimination Dance (Ondaatje) **51**:317
"Eli's Comin'" (Nyro) **17**:318
"Elisa and Mary" (Musgrave) **54**:334
"Elisabetta, Carlotta, Catherine" (Kaplan) **50**:55, 57
Elisabetta: Quasi per Caso una Donna (Fo) **109**:101, 116, 119, 140
"Elite 6" (Wah) **44**:327
"Elite 9" (Wah) **44**:324
"The Elite Viewer" (Colwin) **84**:150
"Elixir" (Murphy) **41**:319
"Elizabeth" (Adams) **46**:21
"Elizabeth" (Hill) **113**:330-31
"Elizabeth" (Jackson) **60**:211, 235
"Elizabeth" (Muldoon) **72**:265-66
"Elizabeth" (Ondaatje) **14**:408
Elizabeth Alone (Trevor) **7**:477; **9**:529; **71**:326, 345-46; **116**:334-35, 338
Elizabeth Appleton (O'Hara) **42**:319, 322-24
Elizabeth Barrett Browning (Forster) **149**:71-2, 77, 79
Elizabeth Cree (Ackroyd)
See *The Trial of Elizabeth Cree*
"Elizabeth of England" (Christie) **110**:127
Elizabethan Essays (Eliot) **24**:181
"Elizabeth's War with the Christmas Bear, 1601" (Dubie) **36**:133
"The Elk Song" (Hogan) **73**:158
Elle est là (Sarraute) **31**:381
"Elle est pour moi" (Theriault) **79**:408
"Elle est trois," (Lee) **46**:234
"Elle me force sans jamais répit" (Senghor) **54**:396
Ellen (Almedingen) **12**:5-7
Ellen Foster (Gibbons) **50**:46-9; **88**:123-24, 126, 128-30, 132; **145**:136, 146-48, 150-51, 153-57, 164, 167, 175-76, 184-88, 192, 194-98, 200-01
Ellen Rogers (Farrell) **66**:128-29
"Ellen Terhune" (Wilson) **8**:551
"Ellen West" (Bidart) **33**:76
Elliot Loves (Feiffer) **64**:163-64
"Ellis Island" (Helprin) **22**:220-23
Ellis Island and Other Stories (Helprin) **22**:221-22; **32**:229-30, 232
Ellison Wonderland (Ellison) **139**:129
"Elm" (Plath) **1**:270; **9**:427; **50**:446; **51**:344; **111**:159, 203, 213-15
"Elm Buds" (Sandburg) **35**:356
The Elm Street Lot (Pearce) **21**:291
"Elms" (Glück) **44**:218, 222
"Elms" (Williams) **56**:425
Éloges (Perse) **11**:433; **46**:298, 300, 302-10
"Elogio de la madrastra" (Vargas Llosa) **85**:379, 385-86
Elogio de la sombra (Borges) **3**:82; **4**:75; **6**:89-90, 92-3; **8**:103; **9**:120
"Elohim merakhem 'al yaldei hagan" (Amichai) **22**:30; **57**:40-1, 46; **116**:111
"Else a Great Prince in Prisons Lies" (Levertov) **66**:250
"Elsewhen" (Heinlein) **26**:165
"Elsewhere" (Bishop) **13**:89
"Elsewhere" (Walcott) **67**:359, 361
Elsewhere, Perhaps (Oz)
See *Makom aher*
Elsewhereless (Egoyan) **151**:155, 175
"Elsewheres" (Justice) **102**:258
"Elvis Presley: He Did It His Way" (Amis) **62**:5
"Ely Place" (Kinsella) **138**:94, 149
"Elysian Fields" (Hacker) **91**:110
"Em" (Dixon) **52**:97
"The Emancipator" (Gilchrist) **48**:119-22
"The Emasculation of Ted Roper" (Lively) **32**:277
"The Embalmer's Art" (Musgrave) **54**:338
Embarkation (Salamanca) **4**:462; **15**:463-65
The Embarrassment of Riches: An Interpretation of Dutch Culture in the Golden Age (Schama) **150**:98-100, 102, 111-13, 132, 134-35, 137, 161-62, 168, 179-81, 188, 190-91, 197
Embers (Beckett) **6**:45, 47; **18**:42; **29**:61; **57**:89
The Embezzler (Auchincloss) **4**:29-30; **9**:53
The Embezzler (Cain) **3**:96; **28**:45-6, 54
"Emblem of a Virtuous Woman" (Castellanos)
See "Emblema de la virtuosa"
"Emblema de la virtuosa" (Castellanos) **66**:46
"Emblems" (Tate) **14**:529
Emblems of a Season of Fury (Merton) **83**:394
"Emblems of Exile" (McGrath) **59**:178, 180
"Emblems of Passion" (Causley) **7**:42
The Embodiment of Knowledge (Williams) **42**:453
"The Embrace" (Bell) **8**:66
"The Embrace" (Glück) **44**:214, 222-23
"Embrace Me You Child" (Simon) **26**:408
"Embracing Change" (Hooks) **94**:156
"Embryos" (Piercy) **27**:375
"Emden" (Narayan) **121**:418
Emeka: The Driver's Guard (Nwapa) **133**:201, 229-30
"The Emerald" (Merrill) **13**:381
Emerald (Whitney) **42**:436-37
Emerald City (Williamson) **56**:443-44
The Emerald City of Oz (Thurber) **25**:438
"The Emerald Essay" (Wakoski) **7**:504; **40**:453
"Emergancy Room" (Van Duyn) **116**:421
The Emergence of African Fiction (Larson) **31**:237-38
"Emergence of Ernest Hemingway" (Wilson) **24**:481
The Emergence of Metaphor and the Meaning of Culture (Blaga)
See *Geneza metaforei si sensul culturii*
Emergences—Résurgences (Michaux) **19**:314, 317
"Emergency" (Graham) **118**:263-64
"Emergency Commission" (Clark Bekedermo) **38**:125
Emergency Exit (Major) **19**:295; **48**:211-16
Emergency Exit (Silone) **4**:493
"Emergency Haying" (Carruth) **7**:41
Emergency Poems (Parra) **2**:331; **102**:334, 342, 353-56
Emergency Ward 9 (Potter) **123**:228, 231, 236
"Emerging" (Thomas) **48**:379, 381, 383
"Emerson and German Philosophy, 1943" (Wellek) **28**:446
"Emerson and the Essay" (Gass) **39**:477, 480, 482
"The Emigrant Irish" (Boland) **113**:82
"The Emigrants" (Brand) **7**:30
The Emigrants (Lamming) **2**:235; **4**:279; **66**:218, 221, 223, 227-30; **144**:126, 140, 143, 165
"The Emigre" (Ai) **69**:9-10
"Emigre" (Merwin) **88**:195
Emilia Galotti (Duerrenmatt) **102**:61
"Emily" (Benson) **17**:47
Emily (Benson) **17**:47
"Emily Dickinson" (Pastan) **27**:369
"Emily Dickinson" (Tate) **4**:537
"Emily Dickinson in Southern California" (Kennedy) **42**:257-58
"Emily Dickinson's Horses" (Donnell) **34**:159
Emily L. (Duras) **68**:91, 97-9, 101-02; **100**:136, 144
Emily Stone (Redmon) **22**:341-42
Emlyn: An Early Autobiography (Williams) **15**:578
"Emma Enters a Sentence of Elizabeth Bishop's" (Gass) **132**:195
"Emma, Flaubert and the Pleasure Principle" (Vargas Llosa) **85**:366
Emma in Love (Arundel) **17**:14, 16
Emma McChesney and Co. (Ferber) **93**:137, 140-42
Emma McChesney Stories (Ferber) **93**:185
Emma Tupper's Diary (Dickinson) **12**:169-70
"Emma Zunz" (Borges) **2**:70; **6**:88; **19**:49-50; **83**:186, 188
Emmanuel à Joseph à Dâvit (Maillet) **118**:327, 345
"Emmanuele! Emmanuele!" (Gordon) **13**:245; **29**:187-90
Emma's Island (Arundel) **17**:14, 18
Emmeline (Rossner) **29**:352-55
Emmène-moi au bout du monde! (Cendrars) **18**:97; **106**:176, 178, 187
"Emmy Moore's Journal" (Bowles) **68**:9
Emöke (Škvorecký)
See *Legenda emöke*
Emotional Rescue (Jagger and Richard) **17**:242
"Emotions of Normal People" (Bernstein) **142**:23, 27-8
"Empedoklean Reveries" (Duncan) **41**:130
"The Emperor" (Simic) **130**:346
The Emperor Alexander I (Almedingen) **12**:2
Emperor of America (Condon) **100**:95-102, 111
The Emperor of Ice-Cream (Moore) **1**:225; **3**:341; **5**:296; **7**:235-36, 239; **19**:331, 334-35; **90**:243-5, 247-8, 250-1, 253-5, 258, 263, 273, 277-8
"Emperor of the Air" (Canin) **55**:35-6, 38
Emperor of the Earth: Modes of Eccentric Vision (Milosz) **56**:250; **82**:281
Emperor Shaka the Great: A Zulu Epic (Kunene) **85**:164, 166, 168-72, 174-75, 179-80, 182-84, 187
"The Emperor with the Golden Hands" (Bunting) **47**:49
The Emperors (Forsyth) **36**:177
The Emperor's Clothes (Tabori) **19**:437
"Emperors of the Island" (Abse) **29**:16
The Emperor's Snuff Box (Carr) **3**:101
The Emperor's Virgin (Fraser) **64**:170
Emphyrio (Vance) **35**:427
Empire (Vidal) **72**:391-404; 322, 328, 330, 333
Empire (Warhol) **20**:416-17, 421
"Empire Builders" (MacLeish) **68**:290
L'empire céleste (Mallet-Joris) **11**:355
The Empire City (Goodman) **1**:123; **4**:197-98; **7**:128
L'empire de sens (Oshima) **20**:251-53, 255-56
L'empire des signes (Barthes) **24**:36; **83**:78
"L'empire et la trappe" (Audiberti) **38**:21
"Empire of Dreams" (Simic) **49**:337, 339
Empire of Passion (Oshima)
See *Ai no barei*
Empire of Signs (Barthes)
See *L'empire des signes*
"The Empire of the Necromancers" (Smith) **43**:424
Empire of the Senseless (Acker) **111**:9-11, 16-17, 20, 25, 32-4, 37-40
Empire of the Sun (Ballard) **36**:47-8; **137**:3-5, 8-9, 14, 20-1, 26, 28, 32-3, 35-42, 50, 74
Empire Star (Delany) **8**:169; **38**:150-54, 161; **141**:118
Empire, York Street (Moure) **88**:216, 219, 227, 229
"Empires" (Williams) **42**:442
The Empire's Old Clothes: What the Lone

Ranger, Babar, and Other Innocent Heroes Do to Our Minds (Dorfman)
See *Reader's nuestro que estás en la tierra: Ensayos sobre el imperialismo cultural*
"Empiricists of Crimson" (Dubie) **36**:139
Empirismo eretico (Pasolini) **106**:224-25, 235, 245-47
L'emploi du temps (Butor) **3**:92; **8**:114-19; **11**:78-82; **15**:114-17
"Employment and Truth" (White) **148**:293
"Employment for the Castes in Abeyance" (Murray) **40**:338
"Empress" (Livesay) **79**:337
"Empson Lieder" (Sissman) **9**:491
The Empty Canvas (Moravia)
See *La noia*
"An Empty Chair" (Blunden) **56**:40
The Empty Copper Sea (MacDonald) **27**:275
Empty Cupboards (Ernaux)
See *Les armoires vides*
"The Empty Day" (Laughlin) **49**:220
The Empty Fortress: Infantile Autism and the Birth of the Self (Bettelheim) **79**:111, 124
"Empty Glass" (Townshend) **17**:542
Empty Glass (Townshend) **17**:540-42
"The Empty Hills" (Winters) **32**:469
Empty Mirror (Ginsberg) **1**:119; **3**:194; **4**:182-83; **36**:181-85, 195; **109**:340, 353, 371
The Empty Mirror: Experiences in a Japanese Zen Monastery (van de Wetering) **47**:402-05
"An Empty Place" (Bly) **128**:15
"Empty Provinces" (Prokosch) **48**:309
"Empty Rooms" (Sorrentino) **7**:449
Empty Swings (Vizenor) **103**:296
"An Empty Threat" (Frost) **13**:225
"Empty Vessel" (MacDiarmid) **11**:337; **63**:252
"Empty Water" (Merwin) **88**:206
"Empty White Blotch on Map of Universe: A Possible View" (Warren) **18**:539
"Empty Words" (Cage) **41**:84
Empty Words: Writings, '73-'78 (Cage) **41**:82-4, 86
En attendant Godot (Beckett) **1**:20-4; **2**:44-7; **3**:44, 46-7; **4**:49-52; **6**:33, 35, 37-40, 42-7; **9**:78, 81, 83-5, 87; **10**:25, 29-30, 33; **11**:32-3, 37-8, 42-3; **14**:70, 73, 75, 78-9; **18**:41-4, 48-9; **57**:62-112; **59**:252-58, 260; **83**:108-09, 111-13, 115-17, 129-30, 132-35, 142-44, 147, 150-51
En castellano (Otero) **11**:425
"En el día de los difuntos" (Alonso) **14**:25
"En el gran ecbó" (Cabrera Infante) **120**:83
En esta tierra (Matute) **11**:364
En etrange pays dans mon pays lui-même (Aragon) **22**:42
"En face" (Reverdy) **53**:289
"En file indienne" (Damas) **84**:176
En la ardiente oscuridad (Buero Vallejo) **15**:100; **46**:93, 95; **139**:14-15, 18-20, 26, 33-4, 36-8, 43
En la cuerda floja (Arrabal) **58**:17, 27-8
"En la madrugada" (Rulfo) **80**:200
"En la popa hay un cuerpo reclinado" (Marqués) **96**:229, 241, 244
En la tierra de en medio (Castellanos) **66**:53
En lektion i kärlek (Bergman) **16**:60-1; **72**:40-1, 48, 52, 62
En los reinos de taifa (Goytisolo) **133**:66, 69, 86, 95-97, 99-101
"En medio de la multitud" (Cernuda) **54**:52
En México (Dudek) **11**:159-61; **19**:137-38
En mi jardín pastan los héroes (Padilla) **38**:350-51, 354
"En Mi-Careme" (Walcott) **25**:450
En Passion (Bergman) **16**:63-4, 68-9, 74-5; **72**:49-50, 53, 57, 59
En pèlerin et en étranger (Yourcenar) **87**:412, 419, 424
En pièces détachées (Tremblay) **29**:419-20, 422; **102**:361-62, 364-65, 371-72, 374-77
"En roulant ma boute, roulant" (McNickle) **89**:183
En un vasto dominio (Aleixandre) **9**:12, 17; **36**:24, 26
"En una ciudad llamada San Juan" (Marqués) **96**:227
"En verdad os digo" (Arreola) **147**:6, 13, 16, 18, 31
En vrac: Notes (Reverdy) **53**:286
"An Encampment at Morning" (Merwin) **13**:383
The Enchaféd Flood; or, The Romantic Iconography of the Sea (Auden) **14**:27
The Enchanted Echo (Purdy) **50**:235-36
"An Enchanted Garden" (Calvino)
See "Un giardino incantato"
"The Enchanted Nurse" (Goyen) **14**:211-12
The Enchanted Pig (Ludlam) **46**:241-42; **50**:342, 344
The Enchanted Pimp (Callaghan) **41**:90-2, 97-8
The Enchanted Quantity (Lezama Lima)
See *La cantidad hechizada*
The Enchanter (Nabokov)
See *Volshebnik*
Enchantment (Merkin) **44**:62-6
Enciklopedia mrtvih (Kiš) **57**:249, 251-54
"Encloser" (Howe) **152**:176, 180, 199, 213, 217-18, 233, 250
The Enclosure (Hill) **113**:287-88, 291, 295, 309, 320
"Encontro com um poeta" (Cabral de Melo Neto) **76**:163
"Encore" (Purdy) **28**:378-79
Encore (Lacan)
See *Séminaire XX*
Encore: A Journal of the 80th Year (Sarton) **91**:245-46, 252-53
"An Encounter" (Auden) **6**:18; **43**:18
"An Encounter" (Coover) **32**:127
"An Encounter" (Frost) **26**:117, 122
"The Encounter" (Howard) **7**:165
"Encounter" (Milosz) **82**:293
"Encounter" (Olds) **32**:346
"An Encounter" (Prichard) **46**:333
"Encounter" (Yevtushenko) **1**:382
Encounter in April (Sarton) **49**:307, 320; **91**:245
"Encounter in Buffalo" (Barnard) **48**:27
"Encounter on the 7:07" (Simpson) **149**:334
"Encounter With a Poet" (Cabral de Melo Neto)
See "Encontro com um poeta"
"Encounter with a Red Circle" (Cortázar) **33**:124
"Encounter with Silence" (Gascoyne) **45**:151
"Encounter with the Ancestors" (Kunene) **85**:175-77
Encounters (Berrigan) **4**:56
Encounters (Bowen) **22**:67; **118**:98
Encounters (Ringwood) **48**:331
"Encounters with Suicide" (Cioran) **64**:89, 94
Encounters with the Archdruid (McPhee) **36**:295
"Encuentros" (Castillo) **151**:11
The Encyclopaedist (Mortimer) **28**:284
An Encyclopaedia of Murder (Wilson) **14**:589
"The Encyclopedia of the Dead" (Kiš)
See "L'encyclopedie des morts"
The Encyclopedia of the Dead (Kiš)
See *Enciklopedia mrtvih*
Encyclopédie de la pléiade (Queneau) **5**:360
"L'encyclopedie des morts" (Kiš) **57**:249, 251, 253-54
Encyclopedie des morts (Kiš)
See *Enciklopedia mrtvih*
"The Encyclopedists" (Asimov) **19**:26; **26**:63
"The End" (Beckett)
See "La Fin"
"The End" (Lennon and McCartney) **35**:278
"The End" (Morrison) **17**:285-86, 289, 292, 295
"The End" (Neruda) **28**:312
"The End" (Smith) **12**:539
"The End" (Strand) **71**:288-89
The End and the Beginning (Szymborska) **99**:194, 199, 203, 208, 211
"The End" Appendix (Kostelanetz) **28**:218
End as a Man (Willingham) **51**:399-408, 410
"The End" Essentials (Kostelanetz) **28**:218
"The End of 1968" (Montale)
See "Fine del '68"
"End of a Beginning" (Kelman) **58**:301
"The End of a Career" (Stafford) **7**:459; **19**:430; **68**:434
The End of a Fine Epoch (Brodsky)
See *Konets prekrasnoy epokhi*
"The End of a Good Man" (O'Faolain) **32**:341
The End of a Little Man (Leonov)
See *Konets melkogo cheloveka*
End of a Mission (Boell)
See *Ende einer Dienstfahrt*
The End of a Petty Man (Leonov)
See *Konets melkogo cheloveka*
The End of a Primitive (Himes) **108**:230, 232
"End of a Season" (Scannell) **49**:329
"End of a Summer's Day" (Campbell) **42**:85-6
The End of a Trivial Man (Leonov)
See *Konets melkogo cheloveka*
"The End of a War" (Read) **4**:439
"End of a World" (Rodgers) **7**:378
The End of an Insignificant Man (Leonov)
See *Konets melkogo cheloveka*
The End of Beauty (Graham) **48**:150-55; **118**:222, 229-31, 236-37, 248-51, 253-54, 260-61, 263
"End of Drought" (Williams) **148**:326
"The End of Enoch" (Sillitoe) **148**:
The End of Eternity (Asimov) **9**:50; **19**:26-7; **26**:48, 64
End of Exile (Bova) **45**:68
"The End of Fiction" (Hildesheimer) **49**:173, 175
"The End of Grief" (Abbott) **48**:6
"The End of History?" (Fukuyama) **131**:106-10, 114, 116, 118, 120, 126, 136, 147, 149, 164, 168-69
The End of History (Fukuyama)
See *The End of History and the Last Man*
The End of History and the Last Man (Fukuyama) **131**:111-12, 114, 116, 126, 128, 138, 147, 154-57, 159, 161, 164, 169
The End of Intelligent Writing (Kostelanetz) **28**:213, 215-18
The End of Lieutenant Boruvka (Škvorecký) **69**:333, 345-47; **152**:315
"The End of Love" (Raine) **45**:338
"End of Magna" (Dixon) **52**:99
"The End of March" (Bishop) **9**:97-8; **13**:95; **32**:30, 37
The End of Me Old Cigar (Osborne) **5**:333-34; **45**:319
The End of Modernity (McAuley) **45**:250-51
The End of My Life (Bourjaily) **8**:103; **62**:80-5, 88-9, 92-5, 98-9, 103, 107
"End of Play" (Graves) **45**:165
"End of Play" (Taylor) **18**:526
"The End of Romance" (Brown) **73**:20
"The End of Science Fiction" (Mueller) **51**:281
The End of Solomon Grundy (Symons) **14**:523
"The End of Something" (Hemingway) **3**:242; **10**:269; **30**:186-87, 189-90, 192, 195-98
"End of Summer" (Glück) **81**:167-68
"The End of Summer" (Haines) **58**:213
"End of Summer" (Kunitz) **148**:117, 132
End of Summer (Behrman) **40**:78-80, 82, 87
The End of Summer (Hill) **113**:295
The End of Summer (Ozu) **16**:454, 456
The End of the Affair (Greene) **1**:131-32, 134; **3**:207, 209-11, 213-14; **6**:213-16, 220; **9**:251; **14**:217-19; **27**:173; **70**:289; **72**:155, 167, 169, 177-78; **125**:187-89, 191-92
"The End of the Avant-Garde" (Pasolini) **106**:258
"The End of the Axletree" (Gray) **41**:181, 183
"The End of the Beginning" (O'Casey) **11**:405

"The End of the Book and the Beginning of Writing" (Derrida) **24**:147
The End of the Dream (Wylie) **43**:472
"The End of the Duel" (Borges) **4**:75; **10**:67; **44**:353
End of the Game (Cortázar)
See *Final del juego*
End of the Game, and Other Stories (Cortázar) **92**:139
"The End of the Indian Poems" (Plumly) **33**:313
"End of the Line" (Weldon) **122**:278, 281
The End of the Musketeers (Yevtushenko) **126**:398
The End of the Night (Mauriac)
See *La fin de la nuit*
The End of the Nylon Age (Škvorecký) **152**:314
"The End of the Owls" (Enzensberger) **43**:144-45
"The End of the Party" (Greene) **3**:215
"The End of the Rainbow" (Jarrell) **9**:296
The End of the Ring (Llewellyn) **7**:207
The End of the Road (Barth) **1**:17-18; **2**:36; **3**:38-9, 42; **5**:51; **7**:23; **9**:68, 72; **14**:49, 51, 56; **27**:26, 29; **51**:20-1, 29; **89**:9, 17, 24
The End of the Row (Green) **25**:192
"The End of the Story" (Smith) **43**:420, 424-25
"The End of the Towpath" (Edmonds) **35**:155
"The End of the World" (Branley) **21**:20
"The End of the World" (Glück) **44**:222
"The End of the World" (Hildesheimer)
See "Das Ende einer Welt"
"The End of the World" (MacLeish) **14**:338; **68**:291, 294
"The End of the World" (McGrath) **28**:280
End of the World (Kopit) **33**:252-54
The End of the World (Valdez)
See *El fin del mundo*
"The End of the World, 1843" (Schnackenberg) **40**:380
The End of the World Filmed by the Angel of Notre Dame (Cendrars) **106**:191
The End of the World in Our Usual Bed in a Night Full of Rain (Wertmueller) **16**:597-99
The End of the World News (Burgess) **40**:120-21, 123; **62**:130-33; **81**:304
The End of White World Supremacy (Malcolm X) **117**:320, 341
"End of Winter" (Glück) **81**:167
"The End of Your Life" (Levine) **14**:320
End Papers (Breytenbach) **126**:74-8, 87, 90, 94
"An End to Audience?" (Atwood) **135**:18
An End to Innocence (Fiedler) **4**:163; **13**:211; **24**:188, 203
"End to Laughter" (Santos) **22**:364
An End to Perfect (Newton) **35**:303
End to Torment: A Memoir of Ezra Pound (H. D.) **31**:207-08, 212; **73**:135-37, 139, 141, 143-44
End Zone (DeLillo) **8**:171-72; **10**:134-35; **13**:175-79; **27**:76-80, 82, 84, 86; **39**:116-17, 125; **54**:79-83, 85; **76**:171, 180, 182; **143**:171, 187, 212
"The Endangered Roots of a Person" (Rose) **85**:314
Das Ende der Fiktionen: Reden aus fünfundzwanzig Jahren (Hildesheimer) **49**:179
Ende einer Dienstfahrt (Boell) **6**:83-4; **11**:58; **39**:294; **72**:89, 93
"Das Ende einer Welt" (Hildesheimer) **49**:174, 179
"Ende eines Sommers" (Eich) **15**:202
Endeavors of Infinite Man (Neruda)
See *Tentativa del hombre infinito*
Endecott and the Red Cross (Lowell) **8**:352; **11**:324-25
Enderby (Burgess) **2**:86; **4**:80-1; **5**:88, 90-1; **10**:87-8; **13**:127; **22**:71, 78; **40**:114, 116-18; **81**:302; **94**:40
Enderby Outside (Burgess) **5**:85, 88-9; **8**:112; **40**:114, 118, 123; **62**:130
Enderby's Dark Lady; or, No End to Enderby (Burgess) **40**:122-23; **62**:130, 132
Ender's Game (Card) **44**:163-65; **47**:67, 69; **50**:142-45, 147-51
"Endfray of the Ofay" (Leiber) **25**:307
Endgame (Beckett)
See *Fin de partie*
Endgame: A Journal of the Seventy-ninth Year (Sarton) **91**:251-52
"Ending" (Grau) **146**:132, 137-38, 153, 157
"Ending" (Swenson) **61**:395; **106**:335
Ending (Wolitzer) **17**:561-62
Ending Up (Amis) **5**:21-4; **8**:10-11; **13**:13-14; **44**:135, 139, 142, 144; **129**:10
"Endings" (Adcock) **41**:16
"Endings" (Boland) **67**:45-6
"Endings" (Lowell) **124**:298
"Endings" (Van Duyn) **116**:422
"Endings" (Walcott) **14**:549
"Endless" (Rukeyser) **27**:409
"Endless Life" (Ferlinghetti) **27**:139
Endless Life: Selected Poems (Ferlinghetti) **27**:136-37, 139
Endless Love (Spencer) **30**:405-08
Endless Night (Christie) **1**:58; **48**:71-2; **110**:132
Endless Race (Holden) **18**:257
The Endless Short Story (Sukenick) **48**:370
"Endless Wire" (Lightfoot) **26**:282
"The Endochronic Properties of Resublimated Thiotimoline" (Asimov) **9**:50
"Ends" (Beckett) **9**:84
Ends and Means (Huxley) **11**:286; **18**:269; **79**:286
Ends and Means (Middleton) **38**:331
Ends and Odds (Beckett) **9**:83-4; **14**:74; **18**:43; **29**:61
"Endure No Conflict: Crosses Are Keepsakes" (Graham) **29**:193
"The Enduring Chill" (O'Connor) **6**:382; **10**:365-66; **13**:419-20; **15**:412; **21**:257, 263, 267, 272; **104**:107, 110, 115, 124, 135-36, 152, 179, 183-84, 188, 194
"Endymion" (Kinsella) **138**:94, 101
"Eneboerne" (Dinesen) **95**:69-71
"Enemies" (Gordimer) **123**:116
"The Enemies" (Gordon) **29**:187; **83**:231
"Enemies" (O'Brien) **103**:140
"Enemies" (Sassoon) **130**:178, 186-87
The Enemies (Broner) **19**:70
Enemies: A Love Story (Singer)
See *Sonim, di Geschichte fun a Liebe*
Enemies of Society (Johnson) **147**:84-5, 106-08
Enemies of the System: A Tale of Homo Uniformis (Aldiss) **14**:14
Enemigo rumor (Lezama Lima) **101**:121
"The Enemy" (Rosenthal) **28**:394
"The Enemy" (Singer) **69**:305
The Enemy (Garfield) **12**:241
The Enemy (Green)
See *L'ennemi*
Enemy (Wiebe)
See *My Lovely Enemy*
The Enemy Camp (Weidman) **7**:516
"Enemy Detail" (Boyle) **121**:53, 55
The Enemy in the Blanket (Burgess) **22**:73; **81**:300
The Enemy Joy (Belitt) **22**:49-50, 52
"An Enemy of the People" (Callaghan) **41**:98
An Enemy of the People (Miller) **78**:308, 322
An Enemy of the People (Ray)
See *Ganashatru*
The Enemy Sea (Polonsky) **92**:374
The Enemy Stars (Anderson) **15**:11
"Enemy Territory" (Kelley) **22**:250, 252
The Enemy Within (Friel) **42**:173-74; **115**:246, 249
"Energies" (Boland) **113**:72
The Energies of Art (Barzun) **51**:39; **145**:94
"The Energized Man" (Dickey) **109**:249
Energy for the Twenty-First Century (Branley) **21**:21-2
"Energy is Eternal Delight" (Snyder) **120**:344, 351
The Energy of Slaves (Cohen) **3**:110; **38**:137
Energy to Burn (Simmons) **43**:408-09, 413
Enfance (Sarraute) **31**:384-86; **80**:243, 245, 255, 257
L'enfance d'un chef (Sartre) **7**:395-96; **9**:472
L'enfant chargé de chaînes (Mauriac) **9**:368; **56**:203, 206
L'enfant noir (Laye) **4**:282, 284-85; **38**:284-91
L'enfant sauvage (Truffaut) **20**:386, 389, 393, 397; **101**:375, 381-82, 384, 386, 395-97, 400, 407, 411, 413
"L'enfantillage" (Mandiargues) **41**:278
Les enfantômes (Ducharme) **74**:59-61, 68
Les enfants (Duras) **68**:96
Les enfants du bonhomme dans la lune (Carrier) **78**:62-7, 72, 77
Les enfants terribles (Cocteau) **1**:59; **8**:145, 147; **15**:132-33; **43**:102-05, 111
El enfermo (Azorín) **11**:27
Engaged in Writing (Spender) **41**:418
"Engagements" (Janowitz) **43**:212; **145**:326, 343
Ein Engel kommt nach Babylon (Duerrenmatt) **102**:55, 57, 74, 77, 79, 83
Ein Engel kommt nach Babylon (Dürrenmatt) **8**:194; **11**:168-69, 171-72; **15**:196
"L'engendrement de la formule" (Kristeva) **77**:301
O engenheiro (Cabral de Melo Neto) **76**:150, 152-54, 156-57, 159, 169
"Engführung" (Celan) **10**:102; **19**:90, 95; **53**:77; **82**:42, 45
"Enghcantment" (Christie) **110**:125
"The Engine at Heartspring's Center" (Zelazny) **21**:479
Engine Summer (Crowley) **57**:157-62
Engine Trouble (Narayan) **28**:296
The Engineer (Cabral de Melo Neto)
See *O engenheiro*
The Engineer of Human Souls: An Entertainment of the Old Themes of Life, Women, Fate, Dreams, the Working Class, Secret Agents, Love, and Death (Škvorecký)
See *Příběh inženýra lidských duší*
"Engineer-Private Paul Klee Misplaces an Aircraft between Milbertschofen and Cambrai, March 1916" (Barthelme) **3**:44; **13**:57; **59**:251; **115**:69
"England" (Davie) **5**:114; **8**:165, 167
"England" (Stevenson) **7**:462
England, England (Barnes) **141**:71-2, 76
"England: Eulogy and Lament" (Ginzburg) **54**:202
England Have My Bones (White) **30**:449
England Made Me (Greene) **3**:209; **27**:173, 175; **72**:148, 150-51, 161
England, Our England (Waterhouse) **47**:417
"England versus England" (Lessing) **22**:278
"Englands of the Mind" (Heaney) **25**:249-50
The English (Priestley) **5**:350
"English and the Afrikaans Writer" (Brink) **36**:69
"English and Welsh" (Tolkien) **38**:442
English as a Second Language (Mueller)
See *Second Language*
The English Assassin: A Romance of Entropy (Moorcock) **27**:349-50; **58**:347-48
The English Auden: Poems, Essays, and Dramatic Writings, 1927-1939 (Auden) **14**:31-4; **43**:14-17; **123**:6, 48
"English Civil War" (Clash) **30**:43, 46
The English Comic Characters (Priestley) **34**:361-62
"English Days" (Wright)
See "A Journal of English Days"
"The English Fiction of Samuel Beckett: An Essay in Stylistic Analysis" (Coetzee) **117**:48
"The English Garden" (Abish) **22**:17, 19

"An English Garden in Austria" (Jarrell) **9**:297
The English Gentleman (Raven) **14**:439, 442
"The English Girl" (Levine) **54**:294
"English Journal" (Wright)
See "A Journal of English Days"
English Journey (Priestley) **34**:361, 363-64, 366
English Journey: or, The Road to Milton Keynes (Bainbridge) **62**:25-8; **130**:3, 14
"The English Language of the South" (Brooks) **86**:279
"The English Lesson" (Mohr) **12**:447
"English Lessons" (Pasternak) **10**:383
"English Literature and the Small Coterie" (Kelman) **86**:186
English Literature in Our Time and the University (Leavis) **24**:306, 308
English Literature in the Sixteenth Century, Excluding Drama (Lewis) **6**:308; **27**:261-62; **124**:193, 195, 205, 228, 232
English Made Plain (Burgess)
See *Language Made Plain*
English Music (Ackroyd) **140**:18, 29-36, 38-9, 43-5, 47-8, 65
The English Novel (Priestley) **34**:362
"The English Novel of the Future" (Green) **97**:260
English Novelists (Bowen) **11**:62
"English Now" (Paulin) **37**:356-57
"The English Orphan's Monologue" (Reaney) **13**:473
English Pastoral Poetry (Empson)
See *Some Versions of Pastoral*
The English Patient (Ondaatje) **76**:196-207
English Poems (Blunden) **2**:65; **56**:36-7, 47
"The English Professor as Turkey" (Harrison) **129**:211
"The English Pupil" (Barrett) **150**:5
"English Rose" (Weller) **26**:444
"The English Spirit" (Sassoon) **130**:188
English Subtitles (Porter) **33**:320-21, 325
The English Teacher (Narayan) **7**:254-55; **28**:291-92, 294, 297, 299; **121**:351-52, 356-57, 359-61, 372, 382, 400-04, 406
"English Threnody and American Tragedy" (Spender) **5**:402
An Englishman Abroad (Bennett) **77**:90, 95, 97, 100
"An Englishman in Texas" (Middleton) **13**:388
"Englishman's Road" (Hooker) **43**:198, 200
Englishman's Road (Hooker) **43**:198-201
Englishmen (Hope) **52**:213-14
"An English-Speaking Quebecker Looks at Quebec" (MacLennan) **92**:306
"The Englishwoman" (Jhabvala) **29**:259
Enid Bagnold's Autobiography (Bagnold) **25**:77
"The Enigma" (Camus)
See "L'Enigme"
"The Enigma" (Fowles) **6**:189; **33**:174; **87**:151, 155, 157-58, 176-77
"Enigma" (Thomas) **48**:376
The Enigma of Arrival (Naipaul) **105**:159-61, 173, 178-79, 181-82
"The Enigma of Edward FitzGerald" (Borges) **83**:161
The Enigma of Stonehenge (Fowles) **87**:176-77
"The Enigma: Rilke" (Hirsch) **31**:216
"L'Enigme" (Camus) **14**:110; **124**:18, 25
Enjo (Ichikawa) **20**:177, 179, 186
Enjoy (Bennett) **45**:58
Enjoying Opera (Streatfeild) **21**:408
Enjoyment of Literature (Powys) **125**:272-73, 279
Enken i spejlet (Abell) **15**:1
Det enkla och det svåra (Martinson) **14**:355
Enlarging the Change: The Princeton Seminars in Literary Criticism, 1949-1951 (Fitzgerald) **39**:318, 471-73, 475
"Enlightenment" (Miles) **34**:245
L'ennemi (Green) **77**:271, 277
"Enoch's Two Letters" (Sillitoe) **148**:198
"Uma enorme rês deitada" (Cabral de Melo Neto) **76**:164
"Enormous Changes at the Last Minute" (Paley) **140**:212, 227, 232, 234
Enormous Changes at the Last Minute (Paley) **4**:391-94; **18**:391-93; **37**:332, 334-35, 337-38; **140**:207, 209, 227, 231-34, 238, 240, 247, 252, 255, 261-62, 265, 276-77, 281, 283
"The Enormous Gas Bill at the Dwarf Factory. A Horror Movie to Be Shot with Eyes." (Kaufman) **49**:205
"The Enormous Radio" (Cheever) **3**:107; **11**:120; **15**:127-29; **64**:65
The Enormous Radio, and Other Stories (Cheever) **7**:49; **15**:127
The Enormous Room (Cummings) **1**:68; **8**:158-60; **12**:139, 142-46, 156-57, 161; **15**:158; **68**:25, 35, 38, 43, 50
"The Enormous Space" (Ballard) **137**:38
"Enough" (Creeley) **15**:151
Enough (Beckett)
See *Assez*
Enough! (Westlake) **33**:438
"Enough for You" (Kristofferson) **26**:268
Enough of Green (Stevenson) **33**:380-81
Enough Rope (Parker) **68**:324
Enough Said: Poems, 1974-1979 (Whalen) **29**:447
Enquiry (Francis) **42**:148, 155
"An Enquiry into Two Inches of Ivory" (Raine) **103**:179, 182, 186
Ensayo de un crimen (Bunuel) **16**:129, 136, 139; **80**:22, 24, 26-9, 34, 36, 47
Ensayos (Marqués) **96**:242, 245
"Enshroud" (Roethke) **11**:486
Enslaved (Masefield) **11**:357
"Enslavement: Three American Cases" (Berryman) **8**:90
Enter a Free Man (Stoppard) **5**:413-14; **15**:518; **29**:394, 397-99
Enter a Murderer (Marsh) **53**:247, 249
Enter and Exit (Boell)
See "Als der Krieg ausbrach"
Enter Solly Gold (Kops) **4**:274
"Enter Your Garden" (Tillinghast) **29**:414
"Entering the garden" (Arreola)
See "Para entrar al jardín"
"Entering the Kingdom" (Oliver) **19**:363; **98**:266, 287, 290, 294
"Entering the Temple in Nîmes" (Wright) **28**:467
Entering the War (Calvino)
See *L'entrada en guerra*
"Enterprise" (Ezekiel) **61**:91
"Enterprise" (Montague) **46**:270
L'enterrement de la sardine (Arrabal) **9**:39; **18**:17-18
"The Entertainer" (Joel) **26**:214, 219
The Entertainer (Osborne) **1**:263; **2**:327-28; **5**:333; **11**:422, 424; **45**:313-16, 321
"Entertaining God" (Walker) **103**:410-12
Entertaining Mr. Sloane (Orton) **4**:387-88; **13**:435-36; **43**:326-29, 331-34
Entertaining Strangers (Gurney) **32**:218
An Entertainment (Williams)
See *This Is*
"The Entertainment of the Senses" (Auden) **6**:19
"The Entertainment of War" (Fisher) **25**:158
Entfernung von der Truppe (Boell) **2**:68; **3**:75; **11**:53-5, 58; **27**:61-2; **39**:294; **72**:68, 93
"The Enthusiast" (Leet) **11**:323
"Enthusiastic Fires" (Keates) **34**:202-03
The Enthusiastic Slinger (Neruda)
See *El hondero entusiasta, 1923-1924*
El entierro de la sardina (Arrabal)
See *L'Eterrement de la sardine*
"The Entire Fabric" (Kinsella) **138**:128
The Entire Son (Guillén)
See *El son entero*
"Entitled Story" (Lish) **45**:230
"Entitlement" (Bernstein) **142**:46
"The Entombment" (Hine) **15**:280
"Entomology" (Longley) **29**:295
Entr'acte (Clair) **20**:57, 61, 69
L'entrada en guerra (Calvino) **33**:98-9; **39**:314; **73**:42
"Entrance" (Elytis) **100**:187
Entrance of the Celebrant (Musgrave) **13**:400; **54**:341
"The Entrance of Winifred into Valhalla" (Cassity) **42**:97
The Entrance to Porlock (Buechner) **4**:79
"Entranceways" (Ammons) **57**:57
"Entrapped and Abondoned" (Sommer) **25**:425
"Entre chiens et loups" (Gascar) **11**:221, 223
Entre fantoine et agapa (Pinget) **37**:359, 364-66
Entre la vie et la mort (Sarraute) **2**:386; **4**:466-70; **8**:472; **31**:378-80, 382-83; **80**:238, 240, 245-47, 250
Entre l'écriture (Cixous) **92**:90, 96
"Entre oui et non" (Camus) **124**:14
Entre Tinieblas (Almodovar) **114**:4-5, 11-14, 17-8, 22-3, 25
"L'entrée" (Butor) **15**:117
El entremés del mancebo que casó con mujer brava (Casona) **49**:40
L'entretien infini (Blanchot) **135**:122
Entretiens avec le Professeur Y (Céline) **9**:152; **47**:77, 79-80; **124**:97; **124**:58, 60, 62, 65, 97
Entretiens sur la poésie (Bonnefoy) **58**:60
"Entrevista" (Ferré) **139**:188
"Entries" (Tate) **2**:432
"Entropy" (Mahon) **27**:287-88, 290-91
"Entropy" (Pynchon) **6**:430, 432, 434-35; **11**:452; **33**:329, 334, 338-40; **62**:433, 446, 450; **72**:302-04; **123**:303
"Entropy" (Silverberg)
See "In Entropy's Jaws"
"Entropy at Hartburn" (Silkin) **43**:400
"Entry" (Elytis) **100**:170
Entry into Jerusalem (Middleton) **38**:334
Die Entscheidung (Seghers) **7**:408
"Enueg I" (Beckett) **9**:80
"L'envers du monde" (Hébert) **29**:228
L'envers et l'endroit (Camus) **9**:145; **14**:107, 111, 114, 116; **32**:86, 88, 96; **69**:112, 117; **124**:9, 14, 16, 20, 31-2
"Envidia" (Azorín) **11**:24
"Envies and Identifications: Dante and the Modern Poet" (Heaney) **74**:181
"The Environmental Revolution" (Hughes) **37**:173
"Envoi" (Boland) **67**:40, 46; **113**:82, 85-86, 106-08
"Envoi" (Pound) **112**:309-14
"Envoi" (Wright) **119**:181
"Envoi: The Search for Beauty" (Montague) **46**:274
Envoy Extraordinary (Golding) **2**:169; **17**:177; **81**:325
"Envoy from D'Aubigné" (Merwin) **1**:213; **88**:194
The Envoy from Mirror City (Frame) **66**:146, 150; **96**:194, 202-03, 217-20
"The Envoy of Mr. Cogito" (Herbert) **9**:276; **43**:189
"Envoys Are Going to Lenin" (Yevtushenko) **26**:462
"Envy" (Yevtushenko) **26**:461
Envy (Olesha)
See *Zavist'*
"Envy: or, Yiddish in America" (Ozick) **7**:287-88; **28**:347-48; **62**:345, 353-54, 357; **155**:125, 128-29, 134, 160, 167, 170, 172-73, 175, 177-80, 183, 197, 214-16, 226, 229
Enzymes in Action (Berger) **12**:39
"Eonul dogmatic" (Blaga) **75**:80
"L'epaule" (Bonnefoy) **15**:74
Epaves (Green) **11**:261; **77**:267-68
Eperons: Les styles de Nietzsche (Derrida) **24**:151; **87**:92

"The Epic and the Novel" (Bakhtin) **83**:5, 14, 16, 18, 34, 60-1
Epic Fantasy in the Modern World (Donaldson) **138**:27-8
"The Epic Love of Elmii Banderii" (Laurence) **62**:280
The Epic of Gilgamesh (The Brothers Quay) See *Little Songs of the Chief Officer of Hunar Louse, or This Unnameable Little Broom*
"The Epic of Sheik Bedreddin" (Hikmet) See "Seyh Bedreddin destani"
The Epic of Sheik Bedreddin and Other Poems (Hikmet) **40**:247-48, 250
"Epic of the War of Liberation" (Hikmet) **40**:244
"Epic Theatre and Dramatic Theatre" (Sartre) **52**:373
Epics of the West (Neihardt) **32**:330-31
"The Epidemic" (Buzzati) **36**:92
Epidemic! (Slaughter) **29**:377
Epidemic! The Story of the Disease Detectives (Archer) **12**:23
"Epidermal Macabre" (Roethke) **46**:357
"Epifanía del cuento" (Ferré) **139**:182-83
"Epigram" (Lowell) **8**:350
"Epigram Eight" (Cunningham) **31**:102
"Epigram Forty-Three" (Cunningham) **31**:104
Epigramas (Cardenal) **31**:71
"Epigrams" (H. D.) **73**:108
Epigrams (Cardenal) See *Epigramas*
"Epigraph" (Atwood) **84**:106
"Epigraphs Written on Air" (Sachs) See "Grabschriften in die Luft geschrieben"
"Epilog" (Rose) **85**:312-13
"Epilog" (Transtroemer) **65**:222, 224, 233, 235
"Epilog to Stifters 'Nachsommer'" (Boell) See "Epilog zu Stifters 'Nachsommer'"
"Epilog zu Stifters 'Nachsommer'" (Boell) **6**:83; **72**:77
"Epilogue" (Akhmatova) **25**:28
"Epilogue" (Aldington) **49**:3-4, 7, 18
"Epilogue" (Ciardi) **44**:381
"Epilogue" (Gascoyne) **45**:148
"Epilogue" (Ignatow) **14**:277
"Epilogue" (Lowell) **8**:358; **11**:331; **37**:232, 239; **124**:255, 299
"Epilogue" (MacNeice) **53**:231
"Epilogue" (Silkin) **43**:401
"The Epilogue" (Tomlinson) **45**:397, 403
"Epilogue" (Transtroemer) See "Epilog"
"Epilogue from a New Home: For Tony Barkan" (Matthias) **9**:362
Epilogue III (Graves) **45**:165
"Epilogue: Nevertheless" (Ostriker) **132**:322
"Epilogue: Romanticism in 1960" (Barzun) **51**:39
"Epilogue: The Photographer" (Munro) **95**:304
"Epilogue: Women Like Us" (Danticat) **94**:99
"Epiphany" (Ellison) **139**:115
"Epiphany" (Moure) **88**:227, 229
"Epiphany" (Sondheim) **30**:398; **147**:231
"An Epiphany" (Stafford) **29**:382
"An Epiphany Tale" (Brown) **48**:59
"Episode" (Durrell) **27**:96
"Episode at Gastein" (Sansom) **2**:383; **6**:484
Episode in Palmetto (Caldwell) **60**:53
"Episode in the Life of an Ancestor" (Boyle) **19**:62; **121**:25-6, 40-1
"An Episode in the Life of Professor Brooke" (Wolff) **64**:446-47, 449-50
An Episode of Sparrows (Godden) **53**:157, 161
"Episode, Scene, Speech, and Word: The Madness of Lear" (Maclean) **78**:235
Episodes of the Revolutionary War (Guevara) See *Pasajes de la guerra revolucionaria*
"Epistemology" (Wilbur) **53**:404-05; **110**:350
"Epistle" (Cardenal) **31**:77
"An Epistle: Edward Sackville to Venetia Digby" (Hope) **51**:213, 215, 217-18, 220
"An Epistle from Holofernes" (Hope) **3**:250; **51**:215, 217-18, 220-21
"Epistle to a Godson" (Auden) **14**:27
Epistle to a Godson and Other Poems (Auden) **2**:27-8; **3**:22-4, 29; **6**:16-19; **43**:18, 27
"An Epistle to a Patron" (Prince) **22**:338, 340
"Epistle to Angus Macintyre" (Fuller) **62**:203
"Epistle To Be Left in the Earth" (MacLeish) **68**:294
"Epistle to His Verses" (Brodsky) See "Poslanie k stikham"
"Epistle to Sabin Drăgoi" (Arghezi) See "Epistolă lui Sabin Drăgoi"
Epistles to Several Persons (Fuller) **62**:188-91, 194-95, 197, 201-03
"Epistolă lui Sabin Drăgoi" (Arghezi) **80**:3
"Epitafio" (Arreola) **147**:4
Epitalamio del prieto Trinidad (Sender) **8**:478
"Epitaph" (Alegria) **75**:46
"Epitaph" (Arreola) See "Epitafio"
"Epitaph" (Blaga) **75**:78
"Epitaph" (H. D.) **73**:119
"Epitaph" (O'Brien) **65**:167-69, 171-2
"Epitaph" (Parra) **102**:345
"Epitaph" (Pound) **2**:343
"Epitaph" (Smith) **15**:514
"The Epitaph" (Thomas) **6**:530
Epitaph for a Dead Beat (Markson) **67**:191
"Epitaph for a Lady's Man" (Wagoner) **3**:508
"Epitaph for a Negro Woman" (Dodson) **79**:187, 191
Epitaph for a Spy (Ambler) **6**:4; **9**:18
Epitaph for a Tramp (Markson) **67**:191
"Epitaph for an Old Woman" (Paz) **51**:335
"Epitaph for Anton Schmidt" (Gunn) **18**:203
"Epitaph for Biafra" (Saro-Wiwa) **114**:253
"Epitaph for Fire and Flower" (Plath) **17**:368
"Epitaph for Flann O'Brien" (Mahon) **27**:287, 290
Epitaph for George Dillon (Osborne) **5**:331-33; **45**:313-15, 317
Epitaph for the Young: A Poem in XII Cantos (Walcott) **25**:452; **76**:273, 284
"Epitaph in a Country Churchyard" (Beer) **58**:36
"Epitaph on a Tyrant" (Auden) **43**:22
"Epitaph: 'The Man with the Golden Arm'" (Algren) **33**:15
Epitáphios (Ritsos) **13**:428; **31**:324, 328
"Epitaphs" (Matthews) **40**:324
Epitaphs and Occasions (Fuller) **28**:147-48, 152-53, 158
Epitaphs for Our Times: The Letters of Edward Dahlberg (Dahlberg) **7**:64
"Epithalamion" (Abse) **29**:14, 19
"Epithalamion" (Cummings) **12**:146; **15**:159
"Epithalamion" (Kizer) **80**:174
"Epithalamion" (Longley) **29**:296
"Epithalamion" (Raine) **32**:349
"Epithalamion" (Wright) **6**:580
"Epithalamion after a War" (Ciardi) **44**:380
"Epithalamium" (Reading) **47**:352
Epithalamium in Time of War (Gustafson) **36**:216
Epithets of War (Scannell) **49**:327-28, 331
Epitomé (Tchicaya) **101**:345-48, 350-53, 358-60
Epitome/Epigraphs for the Summary of a Passion (Tchicaya) See *Epitomé/Les Mots de Tête pour le Som- maire d'une Passion*
Epitomé/Les Mots de Tête pour le Sommaire d'une Passion (Tchicaya) **101**:351
"Epîtres à la Princesse" (Senghor) **54**:390-91, 396, 410; **130**:259
Epoch and Artist: Selected Writings (Jones) **4**:259, 262; **7**:187-88, 190; **13**:309, 312; **42**:238, 243, 245, 247
"Epode: The New Bus Terminal" (Goodman) **4**:198
Épreuves du vivant (Chedid) **47**:82
"Epsilon" (Tolson) **105**:241, 269, 274
Epsom Downs (Brenton) **31**:65, 67
"Epstein" (Roth) **15**:449-50
Equal Danger (Sciascia) See *Il contesto*
"Equal in Paris" (Baldwin) **42**:18
"Equal Opportunity" (Lorde) **71**:260
"Equal, That Is, to the Real Itself" (Olson) **29**:338
"The Equaliser" (Clash) **30**:48-9
The Equalizer (Williamson) **29**:452, 455
"Equals" (Seth) **90**:350
"Equanimity" (Murray) **40**:342-43
The Equations of Love (Wilson) **13**:607-08, 611
Equator (Aldiss) **14**:12
"Equilibrist" (Swenson) **106**:336-37, 347
"The Equilibrists" (Ransom) **2**:363; **4**:431, 435; **5**:365; **11**:467
Equinox (Figes) **31**:161-62
Equinox Flower (Ozu) **16**:451, 453
L'équinoxe de Septembre (Montherlant) **8**:394
"Equinoxiale" (Tchicaya) **101**:350
Equus (Shaffer) **5**:386-90; **14**:486-87; **18**:475-78; **37**:383-84; **60**:355-81
"Er kam als Bierfahrer" (Boell) **72**:77
"Era proibito" (Buzzati) **36**:86
Erään elämän Sotoa (Sillanpaa) **19**:419
"Eramos Tres" (Alegria) See "We Were Three"
Eras and Modes in English Poetry (Miles) **2**:278
"Eraser" (Simic) **130**:296
Eraserhead (Lynch) **66**:257, 259-61, 263-65, 268-71
The Erasers (Robbe-Grillet) See *Les gommes*
Erasmus of Rotterdam (Faludy) **42**:139-40
"Erasure" (Piercy) **128**:229
"Ercole the Butcher" (Turco) **11**:552
L'ere du soupçon: Essais sur le roman (Sarraute) **2**:384, 386; **4**:465; **8**:469; **31**:377, 385-86; **80**:229, 236, 239-40, 242, 244-45, 248, 250, 254
"Erect" (Tchicaya) **101**:346
Erections, Ejaculations, Exhibitions, and General Tales of Ordinary Madness (Bukowski) See *Life and Death in the Charity Ward*
"Das Ereignis" (Heidegger) **24**:276
Ere-Voice (Rakosi) **47**:344-45
"Erfurt 1970 and 1891" (Grass) **49**:137
Ergo (Lind) See *Eine bessere Welt*
"Eric, Gwen, and D. H. Lawrence's Esthetic of Unrectified Feeling" (Delany) **141**:160
Erica (Vittorini) **9**:549
Erie Water (Edmonds) **35**:146, 149, 151, 156-57
"Erige Cor Tuum ad Me in Coelum" (H. D.) **73**:118
Erik Dorn (Hecht) **8**:269, 272-73
Erin Brockovich (Soderbergh) **154**:346, 348-54, 356
Erkenntnis und Interesse (Habermas) **104**:69, 75
"Erlanger Rede über das absurde Theater" (Hildesheimer) **49**:167-68
Erlaüterungen zu Hölderlins Dichtung (Heidegger) **24**:260
"Erlinda and Mr. Coffin" (Vidal) **33**:407
The Erlking (Tournier) See *Le roi des Aulnes*
The Ermine (Anouilh) See *L'hermine*
Die Ermittlung: Oratorium in Elf Gesëngen (Weiss) **3**:515; **15**:564, 566; **51**:387-88, 391, 394, 396
Ernest Hemingway and His World (Burgess) **13**:125
Ernest Hemingway: Selected Letters, 1917-1961 (Hemingway) **30**:201; **41**:203
Ernest K. Gann's Flying Circus (Gann) **23**:167
"Eroded Hills" (Wright) **53**:419
"Eros" (Broumas) **73**:17

"Eros" (Oppen) **7**:281
"Eros absconditus" (Gascoyne) **45**:147
"Eros and Agape" (Auden) **4**:35
"Eros and Psyche" (Aldington) **49**:16
Eros at Breakfast, and Other Plays (Davies) **42**:104
"Eros at Temple Stream" (Levertov) **28**:239
"Eros at the World Kite Pageant" (Lieberman) **36**:262-63
Eros at the World Kite Pageant: Poems, 1979-82 (Lieberman) **36**:262-65
Eros e Priapo (Gadda) **11**:213
"Eros, Eroticism, and the Pedagogical Process" (Hooks) **94**:157
Eros in Dogma (Barker) **48**:16, 20
"Éros suspendu" (Char) **14**:128
"Eros to Howard Nemerov" (Van Duyn) **63**:437, 439
"Eros Turannos" (Walker) **103**:410
"Erosion" (Graham) **48**:148-49; **118**:239
Erosion (Graham) **48**:147-54; **118**:226, 228, 230-31, 236, 239-40, 242-44, 248-50, 252, 254, 261
"Erosion: Transkei" (Brutus) **43**:92
"An Erotic Beyond" (Paz) **119**:422
An Erotic Beyond: Sade (Paz) **119**:422
"The Erotic Poetry of Sir Isaac Newton" (Randall) **135**:399
"The E(rot)ic Potato" (McGrath) **55**:73-4
Erotic Tales (Moravia) **46**:285-87
"Erotica" (Creeley) **78**:141
Erotica (Nin) **127**:383-84, 386, 388-90
Erotica (Ritsos) **31**:332
"Erotica vs. Pornography" (Steinem) **63**:381
Eroticism (Bataille)
See *L'erotisme*
"An Erotics of Space" (Kroetsch)
See "The Fear of Women in Prairie Fiction: An Erotics of Space"
L'erotisme (Bataille) **29**:43, 45
The Erpingham Camp (Orton) **43**:326-27, 330, 332-34
"The Errancy" (Graham) **118**:262-64
"Errand" (Carver) **53**:65-7; **55**:278, 283
"Errata" (Queneau) **42**:333
"The Errigal Road" (Montague) **46**:274-75
"Error" (Singer) **9**:487
An Error of Judgement (Johnson) **27**:219-20, 224
"The Errors" (Goldbarth) **38**:201, 205-06
"Erschaffung der eva" (Jandl) **34**:198
Az értlemiség utja az oszatályhatalomhoz (Konrád) **73**:167-68, 171-72, 174, 176, 187
"Eruntics" (Lem) **40**:298
"Eruption" (Van Duyn) **116**:422
Erzählungen, 1950-1970 (Boell) **72**:76
"Es olvido" (Parra) **102**:340
"Es que somos muy pobres" (Rulfo) **80**:200-01, 216
Es steht geschrieben (Duerrenmatt) **102**:76
Es steht geschrieben (Dürrenmatt) **4**:140; **8**:194; **11**:168-71; **15**:194
"Es tan corto el amor, y es tan largo el olvido" (Neruda) **7**:257
"Es wird etwas geschehen" (Boell) **15**:69-70; **72**:72
L'Escadron blindé (Škvorecký) **69**:336, 340-43
"The Escapade" (Ignatow) **7**:173
Escapade (Scott) **43**:372-73, 383-85
Escapade (Warner) **45**:438-39
"Escape" (Asimov) **92**:4, 12
"Escape" (Blunden) **56**:43
"Escape" (Bova) **45**:73
"The Escape" (Campbell) **32**:74
"Escape" (Huxley) **11**:282
"Escape" (Johnston) **51**:243
"The Escape" (Levine) **118**:313
"The Escape" (Saro-Wiwa) **114**:253
Escape! (Bova) **45**:67
The Escape Artist (Wagoner) **3**:507; **5**:474
Escape Attempt (Strugatskii and Strugatskii)
See *Popytka k begstvu*
Escape from Five Shadows (Leonard) **120**:287
Escape from the Evil Prophecy (Kingman) **17**:246
"Escape from the Planet of the Humanoids" (Grayson) **38**:212
The Escape into You (Bell) **8**:66-67; **31**:46-9
Escape Plus (Bova) **45**:73
"Escape the Close Circle" (Major) **19**:298
"Escaping Again" (Dobyns) **37**:76-7
"Escapist—Never" (Frost) **9**:224
Escarmouches (Ferron) **94**:126, 128
"Escarpment" (Ondaatje) **51**:315
"A escola das facas" (Cabral de Melo Neto) **76**:160
A escola das facas (Cabral de Melo Neto) **76**:153, 155, 158, 160, 163, 165
"Escribir en España" (Goytisolo) **133**:45, 71
"Escrito en el agua" (Cernuda) **54**:47
Escrito sobre un cuerpo (Sarduy) **6**:486; **97**:367, 393, 405
El escritor (Azorín) **11**:27
"El escritor argentino y la tradición" (Borges) **48**:44; **83**:192-93
"Escritura" (Paz) **119**:422
"La escritura del Dios" (Borges) **8**:98-9; **9**:116; **44**:353-54; **83**:166
"Escuela de noche" (Cortázar) **33**:135
La esfera (Sender) **8**:478, 480-82
"Eskimo" (Munro) **50**:210, 216, 219
"Eskimo Love" (Apple) **33**:22
"The Eskimo Motor in the Detention Cell" (West) **96**:395
"Eskimo Pie" (Hollander) **2**:197
"Esmé" (Salinger)
See "For Esmé—with Love and Squalor"
Esmond in India (Jhabvala) **4**:258; **29**:255-58; **94**:169-70, 176-77, 180-81, 184, 189-91, 193, 200; **138**:64
El esoritor y sus fantasmas (Sabato) **10**:446; **23**:379
L'Espace littéraire (Blanchot) **135**:89, 95-96, 98-99, 108, 121-24, 127, 145
La espada encendida (Neruda) **7**:257
Espadas como labios (Aleixandre) **9**:11, 13; **36**:23, 25-6, 30
"Espagne" (Cocteau) **8**:145
The Espalier (Warner) **19**:460
España en el corazón: himno a las glorias del pueblo en la guerra (1936-1937) (Neruda) **7**:258-59; **28**:314; **62**:323
España: Poema en cuatro angustias y una esperanza (Guillén) **48**:158; **79**:229
España y los españoles (Goytisolo) **133**:39
"Un español habla de su tierra" (Cernuda) **54**:61
"El espantoso redentor Lazarus Morell" (Borges) **48**:36; **83**:166
Espèces d'espaces (Perec) **116**:234
An Especially Tricky People (Trudeau) **12**:590
Un especie de memoria (Alegria) **57**:14
"Los espejos" (Borges) **3**:81
"Espérance, o savanes" (Tchicaya) **101**:349
"Esperimento di magia" (Buzzati) **36**:86
"L'espion des pouilles" (Mandiargues) **41**:279
Les Espions (Lang) **103**:88
"The Esplanade" (Zweig) **34**:379; **42**:469
"L'espoir" (Malraux) **9**:356
L'espoir (Malraux) **1**:203; **4**:325-29, 333, 335-36; **9**:354, 356-58; **13**:366-69; **15**:352; **57**:303-04, 306, 308-10, 321, 323-24
"Espresso" (Transtroemer) **65**:224
Ésprit de corps: Sketches from Diplomatic Life (Durrell) **41**:139
"L'esprit de l'escalier" (Murray) **40**:337
Essai sur la situation de la poésie (Tzara) **47**:395
Essais (Camus) **63**:75
Essais critiques (Barthes) **24**:27, 41; **83**:67, 70, 73-4, 78, 88
"An Essay at War" (Duncan) **41**:128
Essay on Blindness (Saramago) **119**:173-77
"An Essay on Criticism" (Van Duyn) **63**:438
"Essay on Death" (Carruth) **84**:136
An Essay on French Verse (Barzun) **145**:78-9
"Essay on Memory" (FitzGerald) **19**:178-79, 181-82
An Essay on Morals (Wylie) **43**:465, 472
"Essay on Poetics" (Ammons) **2**:13; **8**:14-16, 18-19; **9**:28-9; **25**:44-5, 47; **57**:57, 59; **108**:11, 32-3, 35-6, 40, 43, 46
"Essay on Psychiatrists" (Pinsky) **9**:417; **38**:360, 362; **121**:432, 435, 446
Essay on Rime (Shapiro) **53**:326-30, 332; **4**:486
"Essay on Sanity" (Dunn) **36**:154-55
"Essay on Stone" (Carruth) **18**:89
"Essay on Style" (O'Hara) **78**:350, 356, 360
Essay on the Essay (Lukacs) **24**:326
Essay on Tragedy (Lukacs) **24**:326
Essays About Storytelling (Handke) **134**:171-73
Essays in Craft and Elucidation (Blackmur) **24**:56
Essays in Poetry: Mainly Australian (Buckley) **57**:132
Essays in Self-Criticism (Althusser) **106**:41
Essays in Understanding, 1930-1954 (Arendt) **98**:51, 54
Essays of E. B. White (White) **10**:531; **39**:370, 377
Essays of Four Decades (Tate) **14**:531
Essays on Contemporary Issues (Oe)
See *Ōe Kenzaburo dojidai ronshu*
Essays on Culture and Politics (Fiedler) **24**:203
Essays on Literature and Politics, 1932-1972 (Rahv) **24**:356-57, 360-61
Essays on Mexican Art (Paz) **119**:410, 414-15
Essays on Realism (Lukacs) **24**:339
"Esse" (Milosz) **82**:298
"Esse est percipi" (Bioy Casares) **88**:78
Essene (Wiseman) **20**:473-74, 477
"Die Essenholer" (Boell) **72**:69
"Essential Beauty" (Larkin) **8**:332, 340; **64**:269
The Essential Ellison: A 25-Year Retrospective (Ellison) **139**:129, 136-41
"The Essential Gesture" (Gordimer) **123**:136
The Essential Gesture (Gordimer) **70**:168-71, 186
The Essential Gore Vidal (Vidal) **142**:331-32
The Essential Haiku (Hass) **99**:150, 155, 157
The Essential Lenny Bruce (Bruce) **21**:51
Essential Reading (Reading) **47**:354
"The essential solitude" (Blanchot) **135**:107, 123
The Essential Whitman (Kinnell) **129**:268
"Essentialism and Experience" (Hooks) **94**:157
"Essentials of Spontaneous Prose" (Kerouac) **29**:273-74; **61**:309, 312
"Essex" (Davie) **8**:165; **31**:117
Essex Poems, 1963-1967 (Davie) **5**:113-14; **8**:162, 165-66; **31**:117
"Esta mano" (Castillo) **151**:20
"Esta muy caliente" (Bowering) **47**:28
Esta puente, mi espalda (Moraga) **126**:274, 288-89, 298, 311
The Establishment (Fast) **23**:161; **131**:86
The Establishment Is Alive and Well in Washington (Buchwald) **33**:92-3
"La estampa antiqua" (Aleixandre) **9**:17
The Estate (Singer) **3**:454-56; **6**:511; **9**:488; **15**:505
"Estatura del vino" (Neruda) **7**:258
Este Domingo (Donoso) **4**:126-28; **8**:178; **11**:145-46; **32**:152-54, 156, 158; **99**:216, 239
"Estelí" (Alegria) **75**:34
"Esther" (Toomer) **13**:552; **22**:426
Esther (Hochwälder) **36**:235, 238
"Esther's Tomcat" (Hughes) **9**:280
"Esthetics and Loss" (White) **110**:333, 341
"Estienne Redivivus" (Klappert) **57**:268
"Estoy cansado" (Cernuda) **54**:55
"Estoy-eh-muut and the Kunideeyahs" (Silko) **74**:347
"The Estrangement" (Blunden) **56**:41

"El estrecho dudoso" (Cardenal) **31**:74-6
"La estrella" (Neruda) **62**:335
"The Estuary" (Beer) **58**:31-2
"Estuary" (MacCaig) **36**:283
"Estuary" (Merwin) **18**:335
The Estuary (Beer) **58**:31-2, 36
"Estudos para uma bailadora andaluza" (Cabral de Melo Neto) **76**:161
"Et caetera" (Damas) **84**:177-78
"Et Cetera" (Damas)
See "Et caetera"
Et ils passèrent des menottes aux fleurs (Arrabal) **2**:15; **9**:36; **58**:12, 15-17, 23, 26-7
"Et in arcadia ego" (Rozewicz) **23**:358; **139**:253, 290
Et les chiens se taisaient: Tragédie (Césaire) **112**:21, 26-30
"Et maintenant" (Damas) **84**:180
E.T.: The Book of the Green Planet (Kotzwinkle) **35**:258-59
E.T., the Extra-Terrestrial in His Adventure on Earth (Kotzwinkle) **35**:256-58
Et Tu, Babe (Leyner) **92**:284-94
"Eta" (Tolson) **105**:272, 284
"Etape" (Reverdy) **53**:289
L'état de siège (Camus) **1**:54; **9**:146; **14**:114-15; **32**:84-8, 90-1, 94, 96-8, 100-01; **63**:63
Les états-généraux (Breton) **9**:126
"Etcetera" (Borges) **48**:36
L'été (Camus) **1**:53; **14**:111; **32**:86; **124**:7
L'ete meurtrier (Japrisot) **90**:168-70
"Eterna" (Lavin) **99**:320
"Eternal Contemporaries" (Durrell) **27**:97
Eternal Curse on the Reader of These Pages (Puig) **28**:373-74; **65**:268, 271; **133**:305, 318, 321, 371
The Eternal Day of Michel de Ghelderode (The Brothers Quay) **95**:330, 340-41, 353
"The Eternal Feminine" (Castellanos)
See *El eterno femenino*
Eternal Fire (Willingham) **5**:511-12; **51**:407-08, 410
"The Eternal Kansas City" (Morrison) **21**:237
Eternal Life (Kung) **130**:131
"The Eternal Moment" (Forster) **3**:162; **45**:132
"The Eternal Province" (Landolfi) **49**:216-17
"The Eternal Rectangle" (Willingham) **51**:403
The Eternal Return (Cocteau)
See *L'êternel retour*
The Eternal Smile and Other Stories (Lagerkvist) **54**:276; **7**:199, 201
"Eternal Snow" (Govier) **51**:165-67
"The Eternal Wager" (Elytis) **49**:109-10, 118
"Eternal Woman" (Ferlinghetti) **111**:65
Eternal Worry (Dabrowska)
See *Wieczne zmartwiene*
"Eternamente" (Aleixandre) **9**:17
L'êternel retour (Cocteau) **16**:229; **43**:107
Eternity to Season (Harris) **25**:204, 212-13
"Eternity's Woods" (Zweig) **42**:470
Eternity's Woods (Zweig) **34**:379-80; **42**:469
El eterno femenino (Castellanos) **66**:47, 59-61
L'Eterrement de la sardine (Arrabal) **58**:4-6
"Ether" (Ginsberg) **109**:325
"The Ether Breather" (Sturgeon) **22**:410; **39**:361, 366
"Ether, OR" (Le Guin) **136**:376
"The Ethic of Care for the Self as a Practicc of Freedom" (Foucault) **69**:192
"Ethical Criticism: Theory of Symbols" (Frye) **24**:230
"The Ethical Dimensions of Marxist Thought" (West) **134**:349
Ethics from a Theocentric Perspective (Gustafson) **100**:199-201, 205-07, 212-14, 216, 222-23, 229, 232, 235
The Ethics of Ambiguity (Beauvoir) **1**:19; **124**:134-35, 137-38, 149-50, 159-60
"The Ethics of Linguistics" (Kristeva) **77**:312-14
"The Ethics of Living Jim Crow" (Wright) **9**:584; **21**:453; **74**:380, 388, 390, 393
Éthiopiques (Senghor) **54**:390, 407-09; **130**:234-35, 238, 259-61, 280, 286
Ethnic Identity: The Transformation of White America (Alba) **70**:379, 410
Ethnic Options: Choosing Ethnic Identities in America (Waters) **70**:381
Ethnic Radio (Murray) **40**:338
"The Ethnographer Faced with Colonialism" (Leiris) **61**:361
Étier: Poèmes, 1965-1975 (Guillevic) **33**:193-94
"Les etiquettes jaunes" (O'Hara) **13**:427
Eto ja—Edichka (Coles) **67**:168-73, 175-82
"L'etoile" (Wilbur) **53**:407
Étoile errante (Le Clézio) **155**:84-6, 99, 110-15, 119-21
Les ètoiles du sud (Green) **77**:293-94
"Eton Rifles" (Weller) **26**:445-46
"L'Etrange Agonie" (Tchicaya) **101**:350
L'étranger (Camus) **1**:52-4; **2**:97-9; **4**:90; **9**:139-41, 144-50, 152; **11**:93-5; **14**:104-08, 110-14, 116-18; **32**:86, 88-90, 96, 100; **63**:60-2, 64-6, 68, 71-3, 75-83; **69**:103-41; **124**:9-10, 14-5, 18, 21-2, 26, 27-31, 33-5
Etrangers à nous-mêmes (Kristeva) **77**:323, 325-26, 330, 332, 336; **140**:164
L'être et le néant: Essai d'ontologie phénoménologique (Sartre) **1**:303-05; **4**:473-75, 477; **7**:389, 396; **9**:470; **13**:498; **18**:473; **24**:406, 409, 412-14; **44**:494-95, 497; **50**:375, 378-80, 382-83; **52**:373, 376-79, 381, 383-84, 388
L'etreinte de Vénus (Theriault) **79**:415
"An Étude for Emma" (Ferber) **93**:140
"Etude in F" (Jandl) **34**:197
"L'Eubage" (Cendrars) **106**:170
"Eucharist" (Buckley) **57**:129
"Euclid Avenue" (Simic) **130**:295-96, 317
"Euclidians" (Guillevic)
See "Euclidiennes"
"Euclidiennes" (Guillevic) **33**:192, 194
Eugene Onegin (Nabokov) **1**:244; **3**:351; **8**:412, 417
"Eugene Thornton" (Johnston) **51**:253
"Eulogy" (Pryor) **26**:378
Eulogy for a Small Time Thief (Piñero) **55**:316-18
"Eulogy for Alvin Frost" (Lorde) **71**:323-33, 247
"Eulogy on Vladimír Holan" (Seifert)
See "Pocta Vladimíru Holanovi"
"Eumenides" (Aldington) **49**:7
Eumeswil (Jünger) **125**:251, 261-62
Eunuch (Greer)
See *The Female Eunuch*
Eunuchs of the Forbidden City (Ludlam) **46**:239-40; **50**:342
"The Euphemisms" (Reading) **47**:351
"Euphoria" (Ekeloef) **27**:113-14, 119
"Eurasian Girl My Love" (Kerrigan) **6**:276
"Euripides and Professor Murray" (Harrison) **129**:167
The Euro-Killers (Rathbone) **41**:341, 343
"Europa" (Walcott) **42**:423
Europa (Gary) **25**:189
Europa (Parks) **147**:210-16, 218, 222
Europa and the Bull (Rodgers) **7**:377-78
Europa's Lover (Dunn) **40**:169-70
"Europe" (Ashbery) **2**:18; **4**:23; **9**:43; **25**:49-50, 58; **77**:42; **125**:10-11
"Europe" (Ehrenburg) **62**:170
"Europe" (Kunene) **85**:166, 177
"Europe" (Parks) **147**:216
Europe (Dudek) **11**:158-60; **19**:136, 138
"Europe and America" (Ignatow) **40**:258
Europe at Love (Morand)
See *L'Europe galante*
L'Europe galante (Morand) **41**:302-05
The Europe of Trusts (Howe) **72**:208; **152**:192-93, 196-97, 204, 207, 235, 237-38, 244
Europe; or, Up and Down with Baggish and Schreiber (Stern)
See *Europe; or, Up and Down with Schreiber and Baggish*
Europe; or, Up and Down with Schreiber and Baggish (Stern) **4**:523; **39**:236
Europe without Baedeker (Wilson) **8**:550; **24**:487
A European Education (Gary)
See *Education Européenne*
"The European Scene" (Phillips) **28**:363
"European Son" (Reed) **21**:304, 323
The European Tribe (Phillips) **96**:319-20, 322, 328, 330, 332, 335, 352, 354, 356
European Witness (Spender) **41**:422-23; **91**:261
The Europeans (Jhabvala) **94**:185, 187
"Eurotrash" (Welsh) **144**:316-17, 319, 336
"Euryclea's Tale" (Rich) **11**:475-76; **36**:366
"Eurydice" (H. D.) **73**:104
"Eurydice" (Sitwell) **67**:324
Eurydice (Anouilh) **8**:22; **13**:16-17; **40**:50, 52, 55-7; **50**:278-80
"Eurydice in Darkness" (Davison) **28**:100
"Eurydice in the Underworld" (Acker) **111**:46-7
Eurydice in the Underworld (Acker) **111**:46
"Eustace" (Malouf) **28**:269
Eustace and Hilda (Hartley) **22**:213, 217
Eustace Chisholm and the Works (Purdy) **2**:349; **10**:424; **28**:380; **52**:344, 347
"Euthanasia" (Jennings) **131**:241
"Eva" (Arreola) **147**:10
Eva (Levin) **7**:204-05
Eva aftjener sin barnepligt (Abell) **15**:1
"Eva está dentro de su gato" (García Márquez) **3**:181; **47**:150
Eva Gay: A Romantic Novel (Scott) **43**:379-80, 384-85
"Eva Inside Her Cat" (García Márquez)
See "Eva está dentro de su gato"
Eva Luna (Allende) **57**:33-4; **97**:2, 4, 9-11, 13, 17-18, 20, 23, 25, 27-8, 42, 51-2, 55-7, 59
"Eva María" (Ferré) **139**:166
Eva Trout; or, Changing Scenes (Bowen) **6**:94; **11**:59-61, 63-64; **118**:107
"Evaluation of an Unwritten Poem" (Szymborska)
See "Unwritten Poem Review"
An Evaluation of the Possibility of Constructing Christian Ethics on the Assumptions of Max Scheler's Philosophical System. (John Paul II)
See *Ocena mozliwooeci zbudowaniaetyki chrzeoecijańskiej przy zakozeniach systemu Maksa Schelera*
"An Evaluation under a Pine Tree, Lying on Pine Needles" (Eberhart) **11**:178
"Evangeline" (Faulkner) **18**:148-50
Evangéline deusse (Maillet) **54**:304, 309, 312, 314-16; **118**:329-30, 332, 334-35, 344, 358, 364
"Evangelist" (Davie) **5**:113
"The Evans Country" (Amis) **2**:6; **40**:40-1
Evaristo Carriego (Borges) **44**:363; **83**:165-66
Eva's Man (Jones) **9**:306-08; **131**:249-51, 253-67, 269-72, 275-77, 286-89, 291-94, 297-98, 307-10, 312-13, 315, 328-31, 335-36, 338-41
Evasion (West)
See *The American Evasion of Philosophy: A Genealogy of Pragmatism*
"Eve" (Livesay) **79**:337
The Eve of Manhood (Marqués)
See *La víspera del hombre*
Eve of Retirement (Bernhard)
See *Die Berühmten*
The Eve of St. Venus (Burgess) **2**:86; **22**:71; **40**:115-17
The Eve of the Green Grass (Dowell) **60**:99
"Eve the Fox" (Allen) **84**:24
Evelyn Brown (Fornés) **39**:138; **61**:137
Evelyn Waugh (Lodge) **141**:333

Evelyn Waugh: The Early Years, 1903-39 (Stannard) **44**:520-22
Even a Fist (Amichai)
See *Gam ha'egrof haya pa'am yad ptuba ve'etsba'ot*
Even Cowgirls Get the Blues (Robbins) **9**:454; **32**:366-74; **64**:371-73, 377-80, 382-83
Even Dwarfs Started Small (Herzog) **16**:322-23, 325, 327, 331-32
"Even Greenland" (Hannah) **38**:234-35; **90**:138
Even If I Could (Williams) **33**:442
"Even in Communal Pitches" (Kelman) **58**:301
"Even Now" (Seger) **35**:386-87
"The Even Sea" (Swenson) **106**:315
"Even Song" (Sissman) **9**:491
"Even The Devil Can't Save the World" (Moravia) **46**:286-87
Even the Fist Once Was an Open Hand and Fingers (Amichai)
See *Gam ha'egrof haya pa'am yad ptuba ve'etsba'ot*
"Even Then" (Steele) **45**:362
Even Tide (Woiwode) **10**:542
"Even Venus Turns Over" (Barker) **8**:47
"Evenin' Air Blues" (Hughes) **35**:221
"Evening" (Merton) **83**:392
"Evening" (Prokosch) **48**:309
Evening (Akhmatova)
See *Vecher*
"Evening, after the Auction" (Steele) **45**:362
"An Evening Alone at Bunyah" (Murray) **40**:334, 337
"The Evening and the Morning and the Night" (Butler) **121**:110-11, 113-16, 141
Evening at Grinde (Vesaas)
See *Grinde-kveld; eller, Den gode engelen*
"Evening at Wolf Trap" (Taylor) **44**:302
"Evening Chess" (Simic) **130**:336
Evening Class (Binchy) **153**:73-5, 78
Evening Dawns (Konwicki)
See *Zorze wieczorne*
Evening Edged in Gold: A FairytalefArse. 55 Scenes from the Countryside for Patrons of Errata (Schmidt)
See *Abend mit Goldrand: Eine Märchen Posse. 55 Bilder aus der Lä/endlichkeit fur Gönner der VerschreibKunst*
"The Evening Grass" (Boyle) **58**:69
"Evening Hawk" (Warren) **8**:540; **13**:578; **18**:536; **39**:266
Evening in Byzantium (Shaw) **7**:413
"Evening in Connecticut" (Tuohy) **37**:432
Evening in Spring (Derleth) **31**:127, 135
"Evening in the Country" (Ashbery) **2**:17; **4**:23; **15**:30; **41**:40
"Evening in the Sanitarium" (Bogan) **46**:83, 90; **93**:64, 78
"The Evening Journey of Yatir" (Yehoshua) **31**:467, 470
Evening Land (Lagerkvist)
See *Aftonland*
"The Evening of Ants" (Soto) **80**:287-88
"An Evening of Russian Poetry" (Nabokov) **8**:407
The Evening of the Holiday (Hazzard) **18**:214, 217-18
"The Evening of the Mind" (Justice) **19**:233
"The Evening of the Second Day" (Chappell) **40**:147
"Evening of the Visitation" (Merton) **83**:391
"Evening People" (Breytenbach) **126**:81
An Evening Performance: New and Selected Short Stories (Garrett) **51**:151-52
"The Evening Primrose" (Parker) **68**:325
Evening Primrose (Sondheim) **30**:389
"Evening Signs at Gallt-y-Celliog" (Fuller) **62**:192
"Evening Song" (Toomer) **22**:426
"Evening Star" (McFadden) **48**:246, 248
The Evening Star (McMurtry) **127**:342
Evening Star (Sherburne) **30**:361
"Evening Talk" (Simic) **68**:377
Evening Verses (Arghezi) **80**:10
"Evening Walk" (Soto) **80**:301
An Evening with Dead Essex (Kennedy) **66**:214
"An Evening with Jackie Kennedy, or, The Wild West of the East" (Mailer) **111**:106-07
"An Evening with John Joe Dempsey" (Trevor) **71**:322; **116**:333, 358-59, 363-64
An Evening with Richard Nixon and ... (Vidal) **2**:449-50
"The Evening's at Seven" (Thurber) **5**:430
An Evening's Frost (Frost) **1**:110
"The Event" (Dove) **50**:153, 155, 157-58; **81**:138
"Event" (Ezekiel) **61**:92, 97
"The Event" (Heidegger)
See "Das Ereignis"
"Event" (Plath) **3**:390; **51**:340, 346; **111**:203
"An Event" (Wilbur) **14**:577; **53**:408, 410, 412; **110**:351, 353, 357, 383
"The Event Horizon" (Antonioni) **144**:65
Eventail de fer (Montherlant) **19**:325
Events and Celebrations (Vliet) **22**:441
Events and Signals (Scott) **22**:371
Events and Wisdoms: Poems, 1957-1963 (Davie) **5**:114; **8**:164; **10**:123
"Events at Drimaghleen" (Trevor) **71**:341, 343, 348; **116**:379-80
"The Events at Poroth Farm" (Klein) **34**:71
Events following the Closure of a Motorcycle Factory (Edgar) **42**:116
"Eventual Proteus" (Atwood) **4**:27; **8**:32
"Eventually the Poem for Keewaydin" (Ondaatje) **51**:310
"Ever a Bridegroom: Reflections on the Failure of Texas Literature" (McMurtry) **127**:333
"Ever After" (Gallagher) **18**:170
Ever After (Swift) **88**:313-18, 320-23
Ever the Winds of Chance (Sandburg) **35**:360
The Everest Hotel (Wilson) **33**:461, 464
"Evergreen Cemetery" (Purdy) **50**:245
The Everlasting Mercy (Masefield) **11**:357-58; **47**:225-31, 233
The Everlasting Sky: New Voices from the People Named the Chippewa (Vizenor) **103**:296-97
The Everlastings (Dubie) **36**:134-35, 137-38, 141
"Evermore" (Barnes) **141**:69
"Every Breath You Take" (Police, The) **26**:366
Every Brilliant Eye (Estleman) **48**:106-07
"Every Bullet Has Its Billet" (Bates) **46**:56
Every Changing Shape (Jennings) **131**:238
"Every Day a Little Death" (Sondheim) **30**:389, 400; **147**:261
Every Day Except Christmas (Anderson) **20**:11, 16-17
Every Day is Mother's Day (Mantel) **144**:209-10, 212, 220, 222, 228, 239
Every Day Is Saturday (White) **10**:528-29
"Every Day of His Life" (Hodgins) **23**:230
"Every Evening When the Sun Goes Down" (Ashbery) **25**:59
Every Form of Refuge Has Its Price (Piñero) **55**:316-18
Every Good Boy Deserves Favour: A Piece for Actors and Orchestra (Stoppard) **15**:518; **29**:395-97, 402, 404; **34**:272; **91**:190
"Every Little Hurricane" (Alexie) **96**:4
"Every Little Thing" (Lennon and McCartney) **35**:274
"Every Little Thing She Does Is Magic" (Police, The) **26**:365-66
Every Man for Himself (Bainbridge) **130**:30-33, 35-36, 39
Every Man for Himself (Godard)
See *Sauve qui peut (La vie)*
Every Man for Himself and God against All (Herzog) **16**:324-26, 329-32, 334
"Every Man His Own Critic" (Crane) **27**:74
"Every Night" (McCartney) **35**:278-79
Every Night's a Bullfight (Gardner)
See *Every Night's a Festival*
Every Night's a Festival (Gardner) **30**:153
"Every Other Thursday" (Ferber) **93**:153, 180
"Every Person Is a Superpower" (Yevtushenko) **126**:398
"Every Traveler Has One Vermont Poem" (Lorde) **71**:258
"Every Woman Her Own Theology" (Ostriker) **132**:328
"Everybody Has a Dream" (Joel) **26**:215
"Everybody, I Love You" (Young) **17**:569-70
"Everybody Knew Bubba Riff" (Wideman) **122**:343-44, 347
Everybody Knows This Is Nowhere (Young) **17**:569-70, 572, 579
"Everybody Loves You Now" (Joel) **26**:217, 222
"Everybody Ought to Have a Maid" (Sondheim) **30**:378
"Everybody Says Don't" (Sondheim) **30**:379
"Everybody's a Star" (Davies) **21**:99
"Everybody's Gonna Be Happy" (Davies) **21**:89
Everybody's in Showbiz (Davies) **21**:94-5
"Everybody's Lib" (Brophy) **105**:13
"Everybody's Protest Novel" (Baldwin) **4**:40-2; **15**:42; **17**:33; **42**:14; **50**:291; **67**:5, 14; **127**:105, 142
"Everyday Use" (Walker) **103**:361, 407
"The Everydayness of the Soul" (Herbert) **9**:275
"Everyone Knows the World Is Ending" (Fulton) **52**:161
"Everyone Knows Whom the Saved Envy" (Galvin) **38**:198
Everyone Sang (Sassoon) **36**:391
"Everyone's Gone to the Movies" (Becker and Fagen) **26**:80
Everyone's Trash Problem (Hyde) **21**:179-80
"Everything" (Bachmann)
See "Alle"
"Everything" (Levine) **14**:321
"Everything and Nothing" (Borges) **1**:39; **2**:75; **83**:172
"Everything: Eloy, Arizona, 1956" (Ai) **69**:11
Everything for Sale (Wajda) **16**:579-80
Everything in the Garden (Albee) **3**:7; **5**:13; **13**:5; **25**:38
"Everything is Green" (Wallace) **114**:347, 349
"Everything Is Nice" (Bowles) **68**:6, 8, 11
Everything Must Go (Waterhouse)
See *The Bucket Shop*
"Everything Stuck to Him" (Carver)
See "Distance"
"Everything That Acts Is Actual" (Levertov) **15**:337
Everything That Moves (Schulberg) **48**:350-51
"Everything That Rises Must Converge" (O'Connor) **13**:419; **15**:410, 413; **21**:269, 276; **104**:112, 115, 126-29, 131, 133, 135, 137, 143, 145, 148, 151, 162-63, 168-69, 171-80, 182-84, 186, 190, 199, 200-02
Everything That Rises Must Converge (O'Connor) **3**:369; **6**:377; **21**:262, 264, 267, 276; **104**:102-03, 106-07, 113, 116, 125, 127, 135, 138, 161, 165, 178-79, 187-90
Everything to Live For (Horgan) **53**:182-83, 185
"Everything Went Still" (Van Doren) **10**:496
Everything You Always Wanted to Know about Sex (Allen) **16**:4-5; **52**:38-9, 45
"Everything You Did" (Becker and Fagen) **26**:83
Everything You've Heard Is True (Sherwood) **81**:102, 109
"Everything's All Right" (Rice and Webber) **21**:426
"Everything's Alright" (Wonder)
See "Uptight"
"Everything's Coming Up Roses" (Sondheim) **30**:377, 395
"Everything's Foreseeable" (Simic) **68**:379

Everything's in Place, Nothing's in Order (Wertmueller) **16**:591, 595, 598
"Everywhere" (Matthews) **40**:322, 324
Eves (Ehrenburg) **62**:175
Evgenia Ivanova (Leonov) **92**:253, 261, 265, 268-69, 278
L'eviathan (Green) **77**:262-65, 267, 269-71, 290
"Evidence" (Asimov) **26**:50, 54, 56; **92**:4, 8, 12
"The Evidence" (Jong) **6**:268
Evidence of Love (Grau) **9**:240; **146**:122, 124, 128, 130-31, 133, 136, 138, 141, 149-51, 155, 161, 163, 165
Evidence of Love (Jacobson) **4**:255; **14**:289
The Evidence of Things Not Seen (Baldwin) **42**:15-16, 18, 20-3; **50**:283, 293, 297
Evidence of Things Seen (Daly) **52**:88-9
The Evidence That Wasn't There (Adler) **35**:12-13
Det eviga leendet (Lagerkvist) **13**:333; **54**:266-68, 274, 286, 288-89
"Evil" (Wonder) **12**:656, 663
"Evil and the English Novel" (Wilson) **34**:582
"The Evil Angel" (Lagerkvist)
See "Den onda ängeln"
"Evil Days" (Pasternak) **63**:313
The Evil Demon of Images (Baudrillard) **60**:36
"The Evil Eye" (Ciardi) **40**:154
The Evil Hour (García Márquez)
See *La mala hora*
Evil Is Abroad (Audiberti)
See *Le mal court*
The Evil Runs (Audiberti)
See *Le mal court*
Evil Sagas (Lagerkvist)
See *Onda sagor*
Evil Tales (Lagerkvist)
See *Onda sagor*
Evil under the Sun (Christie) **6**:110; **12**:123; **48**:72-3, 75; **110**:114
"Evil Worshipped" (Mahfouz)
See "A-Sharr al-m'bud"
Evita (Rice and Webber) **21**:431-33
"The Evitable Conflict" (Asimov) **26**:54, 56, 64; **92**:4, 8-9, 12, 19
"Evocation" (Thesen) **56**:418
"Evolution" (Swenson) **106**:314, 337, 346, 348-49
"Evolution" (Townshend) **17**:528, 531
Evolution and Genetics: The Code of Life (Silverstein and Silverstein) **17**:453, 456
"Évolution de rêve, rêve et révolution: Réalité" (Prévert) **15**:440
"Evolution from the Fish" (Bly) **128**:7
"Evolution in Light and Water" (Hogan) **73**:150
"The Evolution of Birds of Paradise" (Tallent) **45**:387-88
"The Evolution of Federal Indian Policy Making" (Deloria) **122**:115-16
"Evolutionary Hymn" (Lewis) **124**:213
"Evolutionary Poem No. 1" (Knight) **40**:285
"Evolutionary Poem No. 2" (Knight) **40**:285
"Evolutions" (Arghezi) **80**:2
The Ewings (O'Hara) **2**:324-25; **42**:324
Ex cathedra (Connelly) **7**:56
Ex Corde Ecclesiae (John Paul II) **128**:181
Ex Cranium, Night (Rakosi) **47**:345-46
"Ex Nihilo" (Chappell) **78**:96
"Ex ponto" (Ekeloef) **27**:119
"The Exact Location of the Soul" (Selzer) **74**:264, 271
The Exact Name (Ezekiel) **61**:91, 93-4, 96, 100-01, 103
"The Exact Nature of Plot" (Schaeffer) **22**:369-70
"The Exacting Ghost" (Watkins) **43**:452
"The Exaggeration of Despair" (Alexie) **154**:21
The Exaggerations of Peter Prince (Katz) **47**:215-17
"Das Examen" (Lenz) **27**:252
"Examen de la obra de Herbert Quain" (Borges) **3**:77; **83**:164, 180
"The Examination" (Snodgrass) **6**:514; **68**:388, 397
The Examination (Pinter) **27**:388
"Examination at the Womb-Door" (Hughes) **2**:203; **9**:281; **119**:261
"An Examination of the Work of Herbert Quain" (Borges)
See "Examen de la obra de Herbert Quain"
"Examiner" (Scott) **22**:377
"Examples" (Hollander) **8**:299
"Exaugeral Address" (Baraka) **14**:43
"Ex-Basketball Player" (Updike) **23**:473
"La excavación" (Roa Bastos) **45**:345-47
"The Excavation" (Roa Bastos)
See "La excavación"
Excavations (Van Vechten) **33**:390
"Excellence and the Pleasure Principle" (Stegner) **49**:359
"The Excellent Irony" (Blunden) **56**:47
Excellent Women (Pym) **13**:469-71; **37**:370, 375-76; **111**:225-27, 229, 232, 234-39, 243, 245-48, 263-65, 269-70, 273, 278-79, 281-87
"Excelsior! We're Going to the Moon! Excelsior!" (Vonnegut) **12**:610
Except for Me and Thee (West) **7**:521; **17**:550-53
"Except That She Smokes, Drinks Booze and Talks Rough, Miss Mazie Is a Nun" (Mitchell) **98**:154, 164, 177, 180
"Excerpt from a Letter" (Seifert)
See "Úryvek z dopisu"
"Excerpt from Work in Progress..." (Avison) **97**:70-1
Excerpts from a Life (Buckler) **13**:120
"Excerpts from a Poem for Samuel Beckett" (Boyle) **58**:76
Excerpts from the Real World: A Prose Poem in Ten Parts (Kroetsch) **57**:296-98
Excerpts from Visions of Cody (Kerouac) **29**:274
"Exchange" (Cixous) **92**:78-9
"The Exchange" (Ostriker) **132**:303
The Exchange (Trifonov)
See *Obmen*
"An Exchange between the Fingers and the Toes" (Fuller) **62**:185
"An Exchange of Views" (Fussell) **74**:140
"Exchange Value" (Johnson) **51**:235-36
"Exchanges" (Dickey) **15**:178; **47**:92-3, 95, 98
"Exchanging Glances" (Wolf) **150**:298, 301, 320
"Excitement in Ergo" (Willingham) **51**:403
"Exclamación" (Paz) **10**:392; **51**:327
"El excluido" (Castellanos) **66**:52
The Exclusions of a Rhyme (Cunningham) **31**:97-9, 106
"Exclusive" (Olds) **32**:347
"The Excruciating Final Days of Dr. Jekyll, Englishman" (Ligotti) **44**:54
"Excursion" (Garrett) **51**:148
"Excursion in Reality" (Waugh) **27**:477
"The Excursionists" (Santos) **22**:364
Excursions in the Real World (Trevor) **116**:378, 386
"Excursions, Incursions" (Piercy) **27**:376
Excuses, Excuses (Edgar) **42**:116
"Execution" (Guillén) **79**:229
"The Execution" (Nowlan) **15**:399
"L'exécution de Maski" (Ferron) **94**:118, 121, 127
Execution Eve (Buckley) **7**:34
"The Execution of Clemmie Lake" (Nowlan) **15**:398
"The Execution of Cornelius Vane" (Read) **4**:437, 439
"The Execution of Imre Nagy" (Faludy) **42**:138
The Execution of Justice (Duerrenmatt) **102**:83-4
"The Execution of Maski" (Ferron)
See "L'exécution de Maski"
"The Execution of Stenka Razin" (Yevtushenko) **26**:462
The Executioner (Bennett) **35**:45
The Executioner (Lagerkvist) **54**:271
The Executioner Waits (Herbst) **34**:449, 451, 455
The Executioners (Arrabal)
See *Les deux bourreaux*
The Executioners (MacDonald) **44**:408
The Executioner's Block (Aitmatov)
See *Plakha*
The Executioner's Song (Mailer) **14**:351-54; **28**:260, 262; **39**:416, 419; **74**:202, 205-06, 210, 225, 228-31, 237; **111**:118, 120-21, 123-35, 148-49
"Executive" (Betjeman) **34**:306; **43**:47
Executive Orders (Clancy) **112**:80-6
Exécutoire (Guillevic) **33**:191, 194
"The Executor" (Spark) **40**:403
"Exekution eines Kalbes" (Hein) **154**:194
Exekution eines Kalbes (Hein) **154**:164-65, 175, 181
An Exemplary Life (Lenz)
See *Das Vorbild*
"An Exequy" (Porter) **13**:453; **33**:321-25
Exercices de style (Queneau) **2**:359; **5**:359, 361; **10**:429-30; **42**:331, 333-34
"The Exercise" (Mac Laverty) **31**:252, 254
"Exercise on a Sphere" (Hope) **51**:222
Exercises in Style (Perec) **56**:267
Exercises in Style (Queneau)
See *Exercices de style*
"Exeunt the Humanities" (Barzun) **145**:70-1
"Exhaustion" (Barth)
See "The Literature of Exhaustion"
"Exhaustion Now Is a More Frequent Guest" (Brodsky) **36**:81
"The Exhibition" (Stevenson) **33**:381
"Exhibitionist" (Boland) **113**:60, 62-3
"Exhortation" (Bogan) **46**:83; **93**:64
"The Exhortation" (Gustafson) **36**:214
"Ein Exil" (Hein) **154**:166
"Exil" (Perse) **46**:304
L'exil (Laye) **38**:292
L'exil (Montherlant) **19**:328
Exil (Perse) **4**:399-400; **11**:433-34; **46**:302-05, 307-09
L'Exil de James Joyce ou l'art du remplacement (Cixous) **92**:50, 70
L'éxil et le royaume (Camus) **1**:52; **9**:144-45, 150-51; **14**:107, 110, 114; **63**:71, 77; **124**:30, 42
"Exile" (Aldington) **49**:9
"Exile" (Feinstein) **36**:168
"Exile" (Gellhorn) **60**:183-84
"Exile" (Guillén) **79**:229
"Exile" (Hall) **151**:195
"Exile" (Hein)
See "Ein Exil"
"Exile" (Lane) **25**:286
"Exile" (Perse)
See "Exil"
The Exile (Buck) **7**:32; **11**:74-5; **127**:226
An Exile (Jones) **4**:262
Exile (Weiss) **3**:514
Exile and Other Poems (Aldington) **49**:5, 10, 17
Exile and Other Poems (Perse)
See *Exil*
Exile and the Kingdom (Camus)
See *L'éxil et le royaume*
Exile Ends in Glory: The Life of a Trappestine, Mother M. Berchmans (Merton) **34**:465
The Exile of James Joyce or the Art of Replacement (Cixous)
See *L'Exil de James Joyce ou l'art du remplacement*
Exile on Main Street (Jagger and Richard) **17**:224-25, 228-29, 232-33, 235-36
"Exile Prolonged by Real Reasons" (Murray) **40**:344
"Exiled by a Dead Script!" (Alexander) **121**:2, 6
Exiled from Earth (Bova) **45**:67

"The Exiles" (Auden) **11**:16
"The Exiles" (Bradbury) **98**:111
"Exiles" (Strand) **18**:518, 520; **41**:434
Exiles (Kroetsch)
See *But We Are Exiles*
Exiles and Emigrés: Studies in Modern Literature (Eagleton) **63**:93, 101-02
Exiles and Marriages (Hall) **59**:154; **151**:207, 213
"Exiles from Their Land, History Their Domicile" (Spender) **41**:427
"The Exiles Letter" (Pound) **2**:343; **112**:343, 345
Exiles of the Stars (Norton) **12**:460, 462, 469
"The Exile's Return" (Lowell) **9**:335; **11**:325
Exile's Return (Cowley) **39**:458, 461
The Existence and Discovery of Beauty (Kawabata) **107**:108, 110
"Existence and Presence" (Graham) **118**:262
"The Existence of Italy" (Jameson) **142**:248
The Existential Background of Human Dignity (Marcel) **15**:364
Existential Errands (Mailer) **2**:263-64; **111**:126
The Existential Vacuum: A Challenge to Psychiatry (Frankl) **93**:208
"L'existentialisme" (Behan) **79**:39-40
L'existentialisme et la sagesse des nations (Beauvoir) **44**:344
eXistenZ (Cronenberg) **143**:134-35, 142-45, 152-58
"The Exit" (Elytis) **100**:171, 187
Exit Lady Masham (Auchincloss) **45**:33
"Exit Line" (Ciardi) **44**:381
"Exit Molloy" (Mahon) **27**:290
Exit the King (Ionesco)
See *Le roi se meurt*
Exit to Eden (Rice) **128**:293-94
"Ex-Judge at the Bar" (Tolson) **105**:259
"Exodo" (Castellanos) **66**:50
"Exodus" (Cohen) **38**:131
"Exodus" (Kizer) **39**:170
Exodus (Marley) **17**:269-72
Exodus (Uris) **7**:490-91; **32**:433, 435-38
"Exorcised" (Blunden) **56**:45
"Exorcising Ghosts and Ancestors" (Shapcott) **38**:404
"The Exorcism" (Roethke) **19**:399; **101**:263, 265
"The Exorcism" (Smith) **64**:391
Exorcismos de esti(l)o (Cabrera Infante) **25**:102; **120**:49, 60
The Exorcist (Blatty) **2**:63-4
"Exotic Nile" (Barthelme) **117**:17
"The Exotic Nouns" (Reid) **33**:350
"Exotic Pleasures" (Carey) **40**:133; **96**:27, 39
Exotic Pleasures (Carey) **96**:36
Exotica (Egoyan) **151**:132-37, 139, 142-48, 150, 152-57, 159, 161, 165-67, 173
Expanded Universe: The New Worlds of Robert A. Heinlein (Heinlein) **55**:301, 303
"An Expanded Want Ad" (Leithauser) **27**:242
"The Expansion of the Universe" (Gilchrist) **48**:119; **143**:295, 303
"The Expatriate" (Forché) **25**:171
"The Expatriates" (Williams) **42**:442
The Expatriates (Jenkins) **52**:224-25, 228
"The Expatriates' Party" (Vanderhaeghe) **41**:449-50, 453
L'expatrié (Green) **77**:293
"Expectation of Life" (Watkins) **43**:444
"Expecting to Fly" (Young) **17**:569, 577
"The Expedition" (Barthelme) **46**:36
"An Expedition at the Pole" (Dillard)
See "An Expedition to the Pole"
"Expedition to Earth" (Clarke) **3**:150; **136**:211-12
Expedition to Earth (Clarke) **3**:124, 135, 149-50; **136**:212
"An Expedition to the Pole" (Dillard) **60**:74-5; **115**:198, 206
"The Expelled" (Beckett)
See "L'Expulsé"
"Expelled" (Cheever) **64**:66
The Expense of Greatness (Blackmur) **24**:54-5, 61, 66
"The Expense of Spint" (Oates) **6**:370; **108**:368, 370-71
"The Expense of Spirit in a Waste of Shame" (Mueller) **51**:280
Expensive Habits (Howard) **46**:188-91; **151**:262-63, 269, 275, 285
Expensive Habits (Mayle) **89**:147-48, 150
"The Expensive Moment" (Paley) **37**:333, 336, 338; **140**:229, 277, 282
Expensive People (Oates) **1**:251; **2**:314-16; **3**:359-60; **6**:368, 371; **11**:402; **15**:400; **19**:349-51; **52**:338; **108**:343, 385, 391
An Expensive Place to Die (Deighton) **46**:126
"Experience" (Simmons) **43**:412
Experience and Art (Krutch) **24**:283, 289
"Experience and Fiction" (Jackson) **60**:213
Experience and Religion: A Lay Essay in Theology (Mosley) **43**:321
"Experience and the Objects of Knowledge in the Philosophy of F. H. Bradley" (Eliot) **24**:172; **113**:205, 207, 209-10
"Experience by Battle" (Hersey) **97**:304-05
"Experience Evoked" (Eberhart) **56**:78
L'expérience intérieure (Bataille) **29**:38, 44, 48-9
"An Experience of India" (Jhabvala) **94**:181-82, 185
An Experience of India (Jhabvala) **4**:257-58; **29**:258
The Experience of Literature (Trilling) **9**:532
"The experience of Poetry in a Scientific Age" (Swenson) **106**:334
"Experience of the Theatre" (Ionesco) **86**:331
"Experiences with Images" (MacNeice) **10**:324
"Experiment" (Barnes) **141**:58
"Experiment" (Kogawa) **78**:167
"Experiment" (Szymborska) **99**:192
An Experiment in Criticism (Lewis) **3**:295; **27**:264
An Experiment in Love (Mantel) **144**:225-30, 232-34, 239
"The Experiment That Failed" (Logan) **5**:253
"Experimental" (Kavan) **82**:120
"Experimental Death Unit #1" (Baraka) **115**:35-6
Experimental Death Unit #1 (Baraka) **5**:46
Experimenting with an Amen (Thomas) **48**:383
Experiments in Optical Illusions (Branley) **21**:16
Experiments in Science (Branley) **21**:15
Experiments in Sky Watching (Branley) **21**:17
Experiments with a Microscope (Branley) **21**:16
Experiments with Atomics (Branley) **21**:16
Experiments with Electricity (Branley) **21**:15
Experts Are Puzzled (Riding) **3**:431
"Expiation" (Hoffman) **141**:316
"Expiation" (Jhabvala) **94**:209; **138**:77-8
"Explaining a Few Things" (Neruda)
See "Explico algunas cosas"
"Explaining a Few Things" (Simic) **130**:345
"The Explanation" (Barthelme) **59**:251; **115**:56
"Explanation" (Enright) **31**:154
"Explanation" (Livesay) **79**:341
"Explanation" (Pasternak) **63**:313
"Explanation of a Map" (Graham) **29**:198
"Explico algunas cosas" (Neruda) **62**:336
An Exploded View (Longley) **29**:292-94, 296
"Exploding" (Kroetsch)
See "The Exploding Porcupine: Violence of Form in English-Canadian Fiction"
"The Exploding Porcupine: Violence of Form in English-Canadian Fiction" (Kroetsch) **132**:205, 209, 222
The Exploration of Space (Clarke) **35**:117, 121; **136**:208,236
Exploration of the Moon (Branley) **21**:17
"Exploration over the Rim" (Dickey) **28**:117
The Explorer (Maugham) **15**:365; **93**:230
"The Explorers" (Hope) **51**:214
"Explorers" (Simic) **22**:380; **130**:305
"The Explorers" (Weidman) **7**:516
Explorers of the Atom (Gallant) **17**:130
Exploring by Astronaut: The Story of Project Mercury (Branley) **21**:17
Exploring Chemistry (Gallant) **17**:127
Exploring Mars (Gallant) **17**:126
Exploring the Brain (Silverstein and Silverstein) **17**:454, 456
Exploring the Earth and the Cosmos (Asimov) **26**:58-9
Exploring the Moon (Gallant) **17**:126
Exploring the Planets (Gallant) **17**:127-28
Exploring the Sun (Gallant) **17**:127
Exploring the Universe (Gallant) **17**:126
Exploring the Weather (Gallant) **17**:126
Exploring under the Earth (Gallant) **17**:127
"The Explosion" (Aleixandre)
See "La explosión"
"La explosión" (Aleixandre) **36**:28
"The Explosion" (Larkin) **5**:230; **8**:332-33, 339; **13**:335; **18**:300-01; **39**:336; **64**:266, 280, 285
Explosion in the Cathedral (Carpentier)
See *El siglo de las luces*
"The Explosion of Black Poetry" (Major) **19**:293
Exposition of the Orthodox Faith (John)
See "Isolt of Brittany"
"Exposure" (Heaney) **7**:151; **25**:246; **74**:159-60, 163-64, 167, 169, 180, 184
"Exposure" (Musgrave) **13**:400
Exposure (Harrison) **151**:238-43, 249, 251
Exposure (Rozewicz)
See *Ujawnienie*
"Exposures" (Benford) **52**:76
La expresión americana (Lezama Lima) **101**:121-22
"Expression" (Gunn) **32**:214
Expressions of Sea Level (Ammons) **2**:12; **5**:25-6; **25**:43, 48; **108**:2, 5, 7, 26, 46
"L'Expulsé" (Beckett) **3**:45; **10**:34-5
"The Expulsion" (Stern) **40**:412-13
"The Ex-Queen among the Astronomers" (Adcock) **41**:15, 17-18
The Exquisite Corpse (Chester) **49**:57-60
L'extase matérielle (Le Clézio) **31**:247, 249
"Extelopedia" (Lem) **40**:298-99
Extending the Territory (Jennings) **131**:233, 242
Extending upon the Kingdom (Booth) **13**:104
Exterminating Angel (Bunuel)
See *El ángel exterminador*
"The Extermination of the Jews" (Bell) **8**:65
The Exterminator (Burroughs) **2**:93; **5**:92-3; **22**:86; **42**:75, 79-80; **75**:93
Exterminator! (Burroughs)
See *The Exterminator*
"Extinct Birds" (Wright) **53**:428
"The Extinction Tales" (Boyle) **36**:57-8
"Extra Gang" (Davis) **49**:91, 94, 97
"Extra Innings" (Hall) **151**:201
Extra Innings: New Poems (Souster) **14**:504-05
"An Extra Joyful Chorus for Those Who Have Read This Far" (Bly) **10**:61
"Extractions and Contractions" (Blaise) **29**:70, 75
"Extracts from a Private Life" (Rakosi) **47**:343
"Extracts from Addresses to the Academy of Fine Ideas" (Pinsky) **38**:357
"Extracts from the Journal of Elisa Lynch" (Stanton) **9**:507
"La extraña muerte del capitancito Candelario" (Ferré) **139**:159, 179
La extranjera (Moraga) **126**:275-76
The Extraordinary Adventures of Julio Jurenito and His Disciples (Ehrenburg) **18**:130, 134, 136; **34**:435-39; **62**:174-75, 178-80
"The Extraordinary Patience of Things" (Zamora) **89**:393
Extraordinary Tales (Bioy Casares)
See *Cuentos breves y extraordinarios*
Extraordinary Women (Mackenzie) **18**:314

"The Extraterrestrial" (Ostriker) **132**:323
Extraterrestrial Civilizations (Asimov) **26**:50-1
"Extraterrestrial Relays" (Clarke) **35**:118
Extraterritorial (Steiner) **24**:432-33
"An Extravagance of Laughter" (Ellison) **114**:125
"The Extravagance of the Dead" (Oe)
See "Shisha no ogori"
Extravagario (Neruda) **1**:247; **2**:309; **5**:303-05; **7**:261; **28**:310-15
"Extremes and Moderations" (Ammons) **2**:13; **8**:16, 18; **9**:29-30; **57**:59; **108**:9, 11, 38, 44
The Extremists: Gadflies of American Society (Archer) **12**:17
The Extremities (Mastrosimone) **36**:289-92
Exultate! Jubilate! (Kotzwinkle) **5**:220
Exultations (Pound) **2**:343
"An Ex-Voto in an Old Roman Town" (Kerrigan) **6**:276
"The Eye" (Hillis) **66**:194, 197, 199
"The Eye" (Olds) **32**:347; **39**:187
"The Eye" (Powers) **1**:280, 282; **4**:419
"The Eye" (Tate) **11**:528; **14**:530
"The Eye" (Wilbur) **9**:568
The Eye (Nabokov)
See *Sogliadatai*
"The Eye Altering" (Le Guin) **45**:213
Eye among the Blind (Holdstock) **39**:152
"Eye and Tooth" (Lowell) **8**:351; **11**:327; **124**:264, 299, 302
The Eye in the Door (Barker) **94**:15, 17-19; **146**:2, 5-7, 9-11, 13, 30, 38, 41
The Eye in the Pyramid (Wilson) **9**:576
Eye in the Sky (Dick) **30**:116; **72**:104, 108, 120, 122
The Eye of a Needle (Scott) **22**:371
The Eye of Conscience: Photographers and Social Change (Meltzer) **26**:302
"The Eye of Innocence: Some Notes on the Role of the Child in Literature" (Fiedler) **24**:203
"Eye of the Beholder" (Brunner) **8**:109
The Eye of the Camel (Aitmatov)
See *Verbliuzhii glaz*
The Eye of the Heron (Le Guin) **45**:214-15, 217-18
"The Eye of the Hurricane" (Brown) **48**:52
Eye of the Monster (Norton) **12**:467
Eye of the Needle (Follett) **18**:155-56
The Eye of the Scarecrow (Harris) **25**:204, 215
The Eye of the Storm (White) **3**:521-25; **4**:584-87; **5**:484-88; **7**:532; **9**:567; **65**:274-77, 279, 282; **69**:401-02, 405, 411
The Eye of the Story (Welty) **14**:565-67; **33**:423
The Eye of the Tiger (Smith) **33**:375
"Eye to Eye" (Lorde) **71**:244
"The Eye-Beaters" (Dickey) **2**:117; **10**:142; **15**:174; **109**:267-68, 273, 292
The Eye-Beaters, Blood, Victory, Madness, Buckhead, and Mercy (Dickey) **2**:116-17; **4**:120-21; **10**:141; **47**:92, 95-6; **109**:245, 264, 267-69, 272
The Eyeglass of Love Is Colored Glass (Abe)
See *Ai no megane wa irogarasu*
Eyeless in Gaza (Huxley) **1**:151; **4**:237-40, 243-44; **5**:194; **8**:304-05; **11**:281-82, 286; **18**:265, 267; **35**:240-41, 243-44; **79**:327-28
"The Eyeless Saying Yes" (Santos) **22**:361
"The Eye-Mote" (Plath) **5**:345; **17**:348; **111**:160
"Eyes" (Amichai) **116**:98
"Eyes" (Blaise) **29**:70
Eyes and Memory (Aragon)
See *Les yeux et la memoire*
Eyes at the Back of Our Heads (Levertov)
See *With Eyes at the Back of Our Heads*
Eyes, Etc. (Clark) **19**:107
"Eyes Fastened with Pins" (Simic) **68**:379
Eyes in the Fishbowl (Snyder) **17**:470-71
Eyes of a Blue Dog (García Márquez) **47**:147
Eyes of Amber (Vinge) **30**:415
"Eyes of Amber" and Other Stories (Vinge) **30**:410
"The Eyes of Children at the Brink of the Sea's Grasp" (Jacobsen) **102**:240
The Eyes of Darkness (Koontz) **78**:200-01
"Eyes of Dust" (Ellison) **42**:126
The Eyes of Heisenberg (Herbert) **23**:226-27; **35**:196-98; **44**:393-94
"Eyes of Night Time" (Rukeyser) **27**:408
The Eyes of Reason (Heym) **41**:213-16
The Eyes of the Dragon (King) **113**:366, 381
"The Eyes of the Drowned Watch Keels Going Over" (Merwin) **5**:285
The Eyes of the Interred (Asturias) **3**:18; **8**:27-8
The Eyes of the Madonna (Arghezi)
See *Ochii Maicii Domnului*
The Eyes of the Overworld (Vance) **35**:417-20, 423, 427-28
"The Eyes of the World" (Beer) **58**:31, 36
"Eyes of Zapata" (Cisneros) **69**:153; **118**:206, 211
Eyes on the Harem (Fornés) **39**:138; **61**:128-29
"Eyes Only" (Pastan) **27**:371
"Eyes That Last I Saw in Tears" (Eliot) **15**:213
"Eyes That Open" (Bowering) **15**:82
"Eyes to See" (Cozzens) **92**:189
"Eyes to Wonder" (Bachmann) **69**:47
"Eyesight" (Ammons) **2**:14; **25**:42
Eyewitness (Hall) **51**:170
"Eyze min adam" (Amichai) **116**:122
"Ezra Pound" (MacDiarmid) **63**:256
Ezra Pound and His World (Ackroyd) **52**:5; **140**:20, 30
"Ezra Pound and the Great Style" (Carruth) **84**:124
Ezra Pound: Poet as Sculptor (Davie) **31**:109-13
Ezra Pound: The Solitary Volcano (Tytell) **50**:434-35, 437-38
"F" (Merrill) **8**:384
F for Fake (Welles) **20**:452-53; **80**:391, 396-97, 413, 416
"F. H. Underhill, 1889-1971" (Johnston) **51**:253
"F. Scott Fitzgerald" (Wilson) **24**:481
"Fa" (Tolson) **105**:262
Faabeleita vuodelta 1965 (Haavikko) **34**:170
"The Fabbri Tape" (Auchincloss) **45**:33
The Faber Book of Pop (Kureishi) **135**:269-72, 275, 279
"A Faber Melancholy" (Dunn) **40**:167
"A Fable" (Deane) **122**:74
"Fable" (Golding) **58**:194, 199; **81**:315-16, 319
"Fable" (Ponge) **18**:417
"A Fable" (Walker) **103**:366, 411
"A Fable" (Wilbur) **53**:412; **110**:357, 371
Fable (Cabral de Melo Neto)
See *Fabúe Anfion*
A Fable (Faulkner) **3**:153; **9**:203; **11**:202; **14**:171, 175; **28**:140
Fable (Pinget) **7**:305; **37**:361, 363
Fable (Taylor) **27**:439, 441
"Fable from the Cayoosh Country" (Barnard) **48**:25
The Fable of Amphion (Cabral de Melo Neto)
See *Fabúe Anfion*
"The Fable of Anfion" (Cabral de Melo Neto)
See "Fábula de Anfion"
"A Fable of Joan Miro" (Paz) **65**:200
"Fables about Error" (Meredith) **13**:375; **21**:302
"Fables for Our Time" (Thurber) **125**:395
Fables for Our Time and Famous Poems Illustrated (Thurber) **5**:430, 432-35, 442; **25**:437; **125**:386, 388, 395
Fables from the Year 1965 (Haavikko)
See *Faabeleita vuodelta 1965*
Fables of Aggression: Wyndham Lewis, the Modernist as Fascist (Jameson) **142**:219-20, 222-23, 241
Fables of Brunswick Avenue (Govier) **51**:165-67
Fables of Identity (Frye) **24**:216; **70**:275
The Fables of La Fontaine (Moore) **4**:359, 363
"The Fabric of African Culture" (Mphahlele) **133**:134
Fabrications (Ayrton) **7**:18, 20
La fabrique du pré (Ponge) **18**:417
"Fabrizio's: Criticism and Response" (Allen) **52**:41-2, 48
Fabryka (Kieslowski)
See *The Factory*
Fabúe Anfion (Cabral de Melo Neto) **76**:152, 157, 162, 168
"Fábula de Anfion" (Cabral de Melo Neto) **76**:152
Fábulas de la garza desagrada (Ferré) **139**:153, 173
"La Fabulosa: A Texas Operetta" (Cisneros) **118**:202, 217, 219
"The Fabulous Eddie Brewster" (Blaise) **29**:70
The Fabulous Invalid (Hart and Kaufman) **38**:266; **66**:175, 182, 188-89
The Fabulous Miss Marie (Bullins) **5**:82-3; **7**:36
The Fabulous Riverboat (Farmer) **19**:165-67
Uma faca só lâmina (Cabral de Melo Neto) **76**:153, 156, 158, 160, 165, 167
"La façade" (Butor) **15**:117
"Façade" (Reverdy) **53**:281
Façade (Sitwell) **9**:493; **67**:312, 324, 335, 337
"The Face" (Jarrell) **13**:302
"The Face" (Levine) **118**:277, 290, 301
"A Face" (Moore) **8**:397; **10**:350
"The Face" (Smith) **15**:517
The Face (Bergman)
See *Ansiktet*
Face (Pineda) **39**:94-6
The Face (Vance) **35**:426
Face à ce qui se dérobe (Michaux) **19**:316-17
"The Face and the Image" (Agnon)
See "Ha-panim la-panim"
The Face behind the Face (Yevtushenko) **26**:466-68
The Face beside the Fire (van der Post) **5**:463
A Face for a Clue (Simenon) **47**:370
"The Face in the Bar Room Mirror" (Fearing) **51**:119
"A Face in the Crowd" (Davies) **21**:99
A Face in the Crowd (Kazan) **16**:367-69; **63**:226-27, 229, 233, 235
A Face in the Crowd (Schulberg) **7**:403
"The Face in the Mirror" (Graves) **39**:321; **45**:169
"A Face in the Trash" (Benedikt) **14**:82
La face intérieure (Tzara) **47**:388
"Face Lift" (Plath) **17**:365-66; **111**:210
Face of a Fighter (Nelson) **17**:305
The Face of a Stranger (Perry) **126**:322
The Face of Another (Abe)
See *Tanin no kao*
The Face of England in a Series of Occasional Sketches (Blunden) **56**:38
The Face of Fear (Koontz) **78**:203
"The Face of Hate" (Lavin) **99**:321-22
"The Face of Helen" (Christie) **110**:112
The Face of Innocence (Sansom) **6**:483
The Face of Misfortune (Onetti)
See *La cara de la desgracia*
The Face of the Enemy (Scannell) **49**:325
"The Face of the Waters" (FitzGerald) **19**:175-77, 179, 182-83
The Face of Trespass (Rendell) **28**:384; **48**:321
The Face of War (Gellhorn) **60**:185-86,190, 193-95
A Face of War (Maysles and Maysles) **16**:440
The Face That Must Die (Campbell) **42**:87, 90-1, 93
Face the Music (Hart) **66**:176, 182
"Face to Face" (Rich) **11**:475-76; **125**:336
"Face to Face" (Wolff) **64**:446, 449
Face to face (Aitmatov)
See *Litsom k litsu*
Face to Face (Bergman)
See *Ansikte mot ansikte*
Face to Face (Davies) **21**:88-9
Face to Face (Mehta) **37**:287-88, 292, 294
Face to Face (Queen) **11**:464
Faceache (Barker) **37**:32
The Faceless Man (Vance) **35**:421

"Face-Lift" (Mueller) **51**:284
"Faces" (Ciardi) **129**:54
"Faces" (Koch) **44**:243
"Faces" (Randall) **135**:396
Faces (Cassavetes) **20**:45, 47
"The Faces at Pine Dunes" (Campbell) **42**:92
"Faces at the Window" (Hoffman) **141**:274, 280
"The Faces I Love" (Stern) **100**:338
Faces in My Time: The Memoirs of Anthony Powell (Powell) **31**:317-20, 322
Faces in the Water (Frame) **2**:141; **6**:190; **22**:146; **66**:143-46; **96**:166-67, 174-75, 178-79, 190-92, 195, 202, 209, 218, 220
"Faces of an Age" (Blaga) **75**:75
Faces of Anxiety (Rozewicz) **9**:463; **23**:358
The Faces of Blood Kindred: A Novella and Ten Stories (Goyen) **14**:210; **40**:218
"The Faces of the Medal" (Cortázar) **33**:123-25
Les fâcheux (Cocteau) **15**:134
Facial Justice (Hartley) **22**:212
The Facilitators; or, Mister Hole-in-the-Day (Redgrove) **41**:357-58
"Facing" (Swenson) **106**:348-49
"Facing It" (Le Guin) **136**:334
"Facing It" (Komunyakaa) **86**:191; **94**:226-27, 230, 233
Facing It (Brancato) **35**:70
Facing Nature (Updike) **43**:435-36
"Facing Oneself" (Lowell) **124**:286
"Facing Shadows" (Jin) **109**:53
Facing the Chair: Story of the Americanization of Two Foreignborn Workmen (Dos Passos) **25**:140; **82**:108
"Facing the Forests" (Yehoshua) **31**:474
Facing the Forests (Yehoshua) **31**:467, 469-70, 472-73
"Facing the Funerals" (Nemerov) **36**:309
Facing the Lions (Wicker) **7**:533-34
Facing the Music (Brown) **73**:20, 22
Facing the Tree (Ignatow) **7**:178-79, 181-82; **14**:275-76
Facing What Is Disappearing (Michaux)
See *Face à ce qui se dérobe*
Facism (Forman) **21**:120
Die Fackel im Ohr: Lebensgeschichte 1921-1931 (Canetti) **25**:113-14; **75**:141-42, 144; **86**:294, 297, 300-02
"Fackelzug" (Celan) **82**:54-5
Façons d'endormi, façons d'éveillé (Michaux) **8**:392
"The Fact in Fiction" (McCarthy) **14**:360
The Fact of a Doorframe: Poems Selected and New, 1950-1984 (Rich) **36**:366, 378-79; **73**:325-26, 330
"Facteur Cheval" (Breton) **54**:27
"Factoring" (Avison) **97**:70-2
"Factory" (Simic) **130**:318
"The Factory" (Springsteen) **17**:483-84
The Factory (Kieslowski) **120**:209, 243, 244-45
Factotum (Bukowski) **9**:137; **41**:68, 70-1; **82**:10-13, 17-19, 22-28; **108**:72, 97-8, 103-04, 106, 108
"The Facts" (Althusser) **106**:32, 37
"Facts" (L'Heureux) **52**:275
The Facts (Althusser) **106**:40-1
The Facts: A Novelist's Autobiography (Roth) **86**:249-50, 257; **119**:121-22, 129-30, 132
Facts about Sex: A Basic Guide (Gordon) **26**:136-37, 139
Facts about Sex for Today's Youth (Gordon) **26**:137, 139
Facts about Veneral Disease for Today's Youth (Gordon) **26**:137, 139
"The Facts and Issues" (Berryman) **13**:82; **25**:92; **62**:45
The Facts in the Case of E.A. Poe (Sinclair) **14**:489-90
"The Facts of Life" (Kumin) **28**:222
"Facts of Life" (Raine) **103**:182
Facts of Life (Howard) **14**:268; **46**:185, 187-90; **151**:262, 269-70, 272, 275-76, 278, 280-81
The Facts of Life: An Essay in Feelings, Facts, and Fantasy (Laing) **95**:154, 169
The Facts of Life and Other Fictions (Nye) **42**:308-09
The Faded Sun: Kesrith (Cherryh) **35**:105-06, 111
The Faded Sun: Kutath (Cherryh) **35**:106, 111
The Faded Sun: Shon'jir (Cherryh) **35**:105-06, 111
Fadensonnen (Celan) **10**:101; **19**:91; **53**:70, 73, 76, 79; **82**:34
Fadeout (Hansen) **38**:236-37, 239
Fading, My Parmacheene Belle (Scott) **50**:88-90
"A Fading Phantom" (Blunden) **56**:47
"Fafnir" (Hope) **3**:250
Faggots (Kramer) **42**:269-70
"Fah" (Abse) **29**:16
Fahrenheit 451 (Bradbury) **10**:68, 70; **42**:35-6, 40-2; **98**:103-05, 107-13, 115-18, 120-29, 133, 136-38, 141-48
Fahrenheit 451 (Truffaut) **20**:384, 387, 390-91; **101**:375, 377-79, 383, 386, 391, 395-97, 406-07, 412
Fahrt ins Staublose (Sachs) **98**:322-24, 328
"The Failed Men" (Aldiss) **14**:10-11
"Failing Perspective" (Young) **82**:412
"A Failure" (Day Lewis) **6**:127
"The Failure" (Kelman) **58**:298
"Failure" (Pollitt) **28**:367-68; **122**:204
"Failure" (Williams) **148**:340
Failure to Zigzag (Vandenburgh) **59**:100-04
"The Faint" (Updike) **15**:547
"Faint Music" (Hass) **99**:155
"Faint Praise" (Williams) **33**:442
"The Fair" (Arreola) **147**:26
"Fair" (Brunner) **8**:105
Fair and Tender Ladies (Smith) **73**:350-52, 354-59
Fair Blows the Wind (L'Amour) **25**:281
"Fair Exchange" (Santos) **22**:361
"Fair Exchange" (White) **49**:408
Fair Game (Johnson) **5**:198; **48**:201
"The Fair in St. Giles" (Raine) **103**:186
"The Fair in the Woods" (Gunn) **3**:216
The Fair Sister (Goyen) **5**:149; **14**:210-12, 214; **40**:218
Fair Slaughter (Barker) **37**:33-4, 41
Fair Stood the Wind for France (Bates) **46**:57-61
"Fair Warning" (Brunner) **8**:108
"Fair Weather" (Parker) **68**:324
"Fairbanks Under the Solstice" (Haines) **58**:222
"The Fairground" (Longley) **29**:293, 296
"Fairground Music" (Fuller) **62**:184
Fairground Music (Fuller) **62**:184-86, 200
"The Fairies" (Enright) **31**:148
"The Fairies" (Shamlu) **10**:470-71
Fairies and Fusiliers (Graves) **45**:166
A Fairly Conventional Woman (Shields) **113**:401, 403, 405-06, 410, 411, 414, 438, 446
A Fairly Good Time (Gallant) **7**:110-11; **38**:194
"Fairly High Assimilation Rag" (Ammons) **57**:49
A Fairly Honourable Defeat (Murdoch) **2**:297; **3**:347; **31**:289, 293
"Fairweather Father" (Simon) **26**:410
"Fairy Flood" (Hughes) **37**:180
"A Fairy Story" (Smith) **25**:419
"Fairy Tale" (Brunner) **8**:107
"Fairy Tale" (Butler) **81**:122, 127
"Fairy Tale" (Fuller) **62**:184-85
"A Fairy Tale" (Pasternak)
See "Skazka"
A Fairy Tale of New York (Donleavy) **4**:123, 125-26; **6**:140-41; **10**:153; **45**:128
Fairy Tales for Robots (Lem)
See *Bajki Robotów*
"A Fairytale about the Rain" (Akhmadulina) **53**:10-15
Faites vos jeux (Tzara) **47**:390
"The Faith" (Mahapatra) **33**:282-83
Faith and the Good Thing (Johnson) **7**:183; **51**:228-29, 233; **65**:152, 156-57
Faith and Treason: The Story of the Gunpowder Plot (Fraser) **107**:66-67
Faith Healer (Friel) **42**:169-70, 174-75; **59**:149; **115**:224-26, 228-29, 231, 234-35, 241-42, 244, 248
"The Faith Healer Come to Rabun County" (Bottoms) **53**:29
"Faith Healing" (Larkin) **8**:332; **18**:294; **33**:258; **39**:334
"Faith, Hope, and Charity" (McGahern) **48**:264, 271
"Faith in a Tree" (Paley) **140**:211-12, 227, 232, 255-57, 261, 264, 282
Faith in Fakes (Eco) **142**:63
Faith in Life (Guillén)
See *Cántico*
"Faith in the Afternoon" (Paley) **4**:392; **37**:332, 337-38; **140**:227, 231, 249, 257, 262-63, 265, 282
"Faith Is a Concrete Object" (Gustafson) **36**:215
The Faith of Graffiti (Mailer) **4**:322; **14**:351
"The Faith That Illuminates" (Eliot) **24**:177
"The Faithful" (Enright) **31**:155
"The Faithful" (Jacobsen) **102**:236
"The Faithful" (McPherson) **19**:310; **77**:359, 365-66
Faithful Are the Wounds (Sarton) **49**:312, 322; **91**:242
"The Faithful Mouse" (Seth) **90**:353
The Faithful Ruslan (Vladimov) **59**:384, 388
"Faithful to Thee, Terra, in Our Fashion" (Tiptree) **48**:385
"The Faithful Wife" (Beer) **58**:31-2
"The Faithless Wife" (O'Faolain) **14**:406
Les Faits (Althusser) **106**:12
The Fake Fish (Abe) **81**:284, 286, 289
"A Fake Novel about the Life of Rimbaud" (Spicer) **18**:510
"Fakin' It" (Simon) **17**:459, 461
Faktizität und Geltung: Beiträge zur Diskurstheorie des Techts und des demokratischen Rechtsstaats (Habermas) **104**:83-4, 86-7, 92, 94, 96-7
"The Falcon and the Dove" (Read) **4**:439
A Falcon Flies (Smith) **33**:376-78
Falconer (Cheever) **8**:136-40; **11**:120, 123; **15**:129; **25**:118-21; **64**:49-51, 57, 59, 65-8
"A Fall" (Moss) **45**:287
"The Fall" (Mueller) **51**:280
"The Fall" (Murphy) **41**:314
"Fall" (Neruda)
See "Otoño"
"The Fall" (Raine) **45**:337
"The Fall" (Smith) **64**:390
The Fall (Camus)
See *La chute*
The Fall (Duerrenmatt) **102**:54
"Fall 1961" (Lowell) **11**:327
Fall and Rise (Dixon) **52**:101-02
"The Fall and Rise of Mrs. Habgood" (Gellhorn) **60**:187
"Fall Comes in Back-Country Vermont" (Warren) **13**:573
Der Fall d'Arthez (Nossack) **6**:365
"A Fall Day" (Simic) **130**:318
Der Fall Franza (Bachmann) **69**:36, 47-8, 59-60
"A Fall from Grace" (Maitland) **49**:236
The Fall into Time (Cioran)
See *La chute dans le temps*
"Fall of a City" (Spender) **41**:419
"Fall of a House" (Honig) **33**:211
The Fall of America: Poems of These States 1965-1971 (Ginsberg) **3**:195; **4**:181-82; **6**:200-01; **36**:181, 184-85, 188, 191, 194, 196; **109**:357, 362
"The Fall of Edward Barnard" (Maugham) **15**:370

The Fall of Kelvin Walker: A Fable of the Sixties (Gray) **41**:183-84
"The Fall of Literary History" (Wellek) **28**:453
A Fall of Moondust (Clarke) **35**:124, 127
"The Fall of Night" (Merton) **83**:392
The Fall of Paris (Ehrenburg) **18**:131; **62**:169, 177-80
"The Fall of Rome" (Auden) **43**:20
The Fall of the City (MacLeish) **68**:286
The Fall of the Dream Machine (Koontz) **78**:201, 203
The Fall of the House of Usher (Berkoff) **56**:15
"The Fall of the Roman Empire . . ." (Murakami) **150**:56
The Fall of the Towers (Delany) **38**:150; **141**:152, 158
"Fall Pageant" (Ashbery) **77**:65
"The Fall River Axe Murders" (Carter) **41**:122
"Fall, Sierra Nevada" (Rexroth) **49**:280-81; **112**:390
"Fall Song" (Oliver) **34**:249; **98**:256
Die Falle (Duerrenmatt)
See *Der Nihilist*
"Fallen Angel" (Van Duyn) **116**:422
The Fallen Angel (Fast) **131**:98
"The Fallen Angels" (Sexton) **123**:446
Fallen Angels (Coward) **1**:64; **51**:69, 77
Fallen Asleep While Young (Sillanpaa) **19**:417-18
The Fallen Curtain (Rendell) **28**:384
"The Fallen, Fallen World" (Avison) **97**:89, 109
The Fallen House (Baxter) **14**:60-1
The Fallen Idol (Greene) **70**:289, 294; **72**:165
"Fallgesetze" (Lenz) **27**:252
"Falling" (Dickey) **2**:115, 117; **7**:82; **10**:141; **15**:177; **109**:246-48, 250-52, 254-56, 266, 283, 293
"Falling" (Rozewicz)
See "Spadanie czyli; o, Elementach wertykalnych i horyzontalnych w życiu czlowieka wspolczesnego"
Falling (Dickey) **47**:95
Falling (Schaeffer) **6**:488; **11**:492; **22**:367
"Falling Asleep over Scott" (Starbuck) **53**:354
"Falling Asleep over the 'Aeneid'" (Lowell) **4**:301; **8**:349, 356; **9**:336
The Falling Astronauts (Malzberg) **7**:208
Falling Bodies (Kaufman) **3**:263; **8**:317
"The Falling Dog" (Barthelme) **46**:35; **115**:60
"The Falling Girl" (Buzzati) **36**:94
"Falling in Love" (Dubus) **97**:235
"Falling in Love Again" (Gaye) **26**:134
"Falling in Love at Sixty-Five" (Van Duyn) **63**:445; **116**:411, 423
Falling in Place (Beattie) **18**:37-40; **40**:66, **63**:4-5, 7-9, 13; **146**:47, 51-2, 54, 58, 62-3, 68, 77-8
The Falling of the Grain (Everson) **14**:165
"Falling of the Rain" (Joel) **26**:217-18
"Falling; or, On the Vertical and Horizontal Elements in the Life of Contemporary Man" (Rozewicz)
See "Spadanie czyli; o, Elementach wertykalnych i horyzontalnych w życiu czlowieka wspolczesnego"
"Falling out of Love" (Brown) **73**:23
"Falling Rocks, Narrowing Road, Cul-de-sac, Stop" (O'Faolain) **70**:314
"The Falling Sky" (Levine) **14**:316
Falling Slowly (Brookner) **136**:132
Falling through Space: The Journals of Ellen Gilchrist (Gilchrist) **143**:311
The Fallow Land (Bates) **46**:50-1, 53, 56
"Falls" (Van Duyn) **116**:422, 426, 431
"The Falls of Love" (Moss) **50**:353
"Falsche Schönheit" (Grass) **32**:199
The False and True Green (Quasimodo)
See *Il falso e vero verde*
"The False Bride's Story" (Mueller) **51**:282
False Coin (Swados) **5**:420, 422
False Country of the Zoo (Garrigue) **8**:239
"False Dawn" (Mahfouz)
See "al-Fajr al-kadhib"
"False Documents" (Doctorow) **113**:156
False Entry (Calisher) **2**:96; **4**:88; **38**:68-9, 74; **134**:3-7, 11-2, 19, 32-6, 39
"False Leads" (Komunyakaa) **94**:239
"False Lights" (Godwin) **8**:249
"False Notes" (Reverdy)
See "Fausses notes"
"False Shuffles" (Urquhart) **90**:373-5, 381
False Shuffles (Urquhart) **90**:398
"A False Spring" (Boland) **113**:89
A False Spring (Jordan) **37**:194-95
The False Start (Mahapatra) **33**:280, 284
"False Youth, Autumn, Clothes of the Age" (Dickey) **15**:177; **47**:91-2, 95
"Falsification and Consensus" (Eco) **142**:63
Il falso e vero verde (Quasimodo) **10**:428
Falstaff (Nye) **13**:413; **42**:305-06, 308
Falstaff (Welles)
See *Chimes at Midnight*
FAM and YAM: An Imaginary Interview (Albee) **113**:32
"Fame" (Bowie) **17**:62
"Fame" (Miller) **47**:250
"Fame" (Walker) **27**:449; **103**:366, 407-08, 410, 412, 423
Fame & Folly (Ozick) **155**:201
Fame and Love in New York (Sanders) **53**:308-09
Fame and Obscurity (Talese) **37**:393, 403
Fame Became of Him: Hemingway as Public Writer (Raeburn) **34**:477-78
Famiglia (Ginzburg) **11**:230; **54**:198-200, 208; **70**:279
La famiglia Manzoni (Ginzburg) **54**:200-02, 209-13; **70**:280
"La familia" (Cernuda) **54**:61
La familia de Pascual Duarte (Cela) **4**:96-8; **13**:145-47; **59**:126-29, 132-34, 141-44; **122**:2, 4-13, 15-20, 44, 48, 51, 55, 61-3, 65, 68, 70
La familia del héroe (Cela) **4**:96; **122**:19
Una familia lejana (Fuentes) **41**:164-68, 171; **60**:155, 170; **113**:262
"Una familia para Clotilde" (Valenzuela) **104**:357
"Familiär" (Grass) **32**:198
"Familiar Poem" (Chappell) **78**:111
Familiaris Consortio (John Paul II) **128**:178, 180
"Familien de Cats" (Dinesen)
See "Eneboerne"
"Families" (Reed) **21**:317, 320-21
Families and Survivors (Adams) **6**:1-2; **13**:1-2; **46**:13-14
The Families of Schizophrenics (Laing)
See *Sanity, Madness and the Family*
"La Famille Adam" (Tournier) **95**:362
"The Family" (Boyle) **58**:74; **121**:37
"Family" (Miles) **14**:369; **34**:245
"Family" (Oates) **108**:384-85
"The Family" (Oliver) **19**:362
Family (Donovan) **35**:142-43
Family (Ginzburg)
See *Famiglia*
A Family (Harwood) **32**:226-27
Family (Hill) **113**:327
Family (Pa Chin)
See *Chia*
The Family (Plante) **23**:343-47; **38**:365-67, 370-71
Family: A Novel in the Form of a Memoir (Gold) **42**:195, 197; **152**:122, 132, 141
"A Family Affair" (L'Heureux) **52**:278
"Family Affair" (Murakami) **150**:57-8
A Family Affair (Mehta) **37**:296
A Family Affair (Stewart) **14**:512
"Family Affairs" (Angelou) **35**:32
Family Affairs (L'Heureux) **52**:277-78
"Family Album" (Fearing) **51**:117
"Family Album" (Harjo) **83**:286
"Family Album" (Porter) **13**:452
Family Album (Castellanos)
See *Album de familia*
Family Album: Three Novellas (Alegria)
See *Albúm familiar*
A Family and a Fortune (Compton-Burnett) **3**:111; **10**:110; **15**:137; **34**:495
Family and Friends (Brookner) **51**:59-60, 62-4; **136**:85, 89, 105, 111, 116
The Family Arsenal (Theroux) **8**:513-14; **11**:529, 531-32; **28**:425-26; **46**:399, 405
The Family at Caldicott Place (Streatfeild)
See *Caldicott Place*
"Family Attractions" (Freeman) **55**:55
Family Business (Ayckbourn)
See *A Small Family Business*
"A Family Chat" (Landolfi) **49**:212
"Family Circle" (Dorfman) **77**:141-43
Family Circle (Hocking) **13**:285
Family Circles (Ayckbourn) **33**:41-2
"Family Conference" (Montague) **46**:267, 277
"The Family Cycle" (Kiš) **57**:249
"Family Dancing" (Leavitt) **34**:78
Family Dancing (Leavitt) **34**:77-9
Family Devotions (Hwang) **55**:151-52
"A Family Discourse (Or, John Constable's Painting 'The Valley Farm')" (Blunden) **56**:37-8
A Family Failing (Arundel) **17**:16, 18-19
Family Feeling (Yglesias) **7**:558-59; **22**:493
"A Family for Clotilde" (Valenzuela)
See "Una familia para Clotilde"
A Family Gathering (Broughton) **19**:72-4
"Family Happiness" (Colwin) **84**:146-47, 150
Family Happiness (Colwin) **84**:139-41, 143, 146-47, 150, 153
The Family Idiot: Gustave Flaubert, 1821-1857 (Sartre)
See *L'idiot de la famille: Gustave Flaubert de 1821 à 1857*
"The Family in Modern Drama" (Miller) **10**:345; **15**:373
"The Family Jewels" (Blount) **38**:46
Family Letters of Robert and Elinor Frost (Frost) **44**:459
The Family Lie (Simenon) **18**:486
"Family Life" (Urdang) **47**:399
Family Life (Altman) **16**:24
Family Life (Banks) **37**:23; **72**:14
"A Family Likeness" (Lavin) **99**:322-23
A Family Likeness (Lavin) **99**:321-22
Family Linen (Smith) **73**:343-44, 350, 352, 357-58
A Family Madness (Keneally) **43**:234-37; **117**:224-26, 231, 234-36, 243
"A Family Man" (Pritchett) **15**:443
"Family Matters" (Grass)
See "Familiär"
The Family Moskat (Singer)
See *Di Familie Moskat*
"The Family Name" (Guillén)
See "El apellido"
"The Family Novel" (Jiles) **58**:272, 279, 281
A Family of Foxes (Dillon) **17**:95-6, 101
"The Family of Little Feet" (Cisneros) **118**:173, 186, 209, 216
"The Family of Love" (McAuley) **45**:249
The Family of Pascual Duarte (Cela)
See *La familia de Pascual Duarte*
Family Pictures (Brooks) **15**:92-3; **49**:23, 28 30, 35, 37; **125**:45, 88, 110
Family Planning (Parks) **147**:199
Family Plot (Hitchcock) **16**:353-54, 359
"Family Portrait" (Alexie) **96**:9; **154**:6
"The Family Reunion" (Eliot) **1**:90; **13**:194-95; **15**:207-09; **24**:172; **34**:397, 529, 531; **41**:143-46, 152; **55**:346, 356; **57**:193
"Family Reunion" (Erdrich) **120**:138
"Family Reunion" (Steele) **45**:362
A Family Reunion (Albee) **25**:36
Family Reunion (Nash) **23**:321
A Family Romance (Brookner) **136**:102, 107

Family Sayings (Ginzburg)
See *Lessico famigliare*
"Family Seat" (Murphy) **41**:320
"Family Secrets" (Shields) **113**:411, 432
Family Shoes (Streatfeild)
See *The Bell Family*
"Family Sins" (Trevor) **71**:341-2, 348-50
Family Sins, and Other Stories (Trevor) **71**:341; **116**:347-48, 378-79
"A Family Supper" (Ishiguro) **110**:224
"The Family Sweetheart" (Dourado)
See "Queridinha da familia"
The Family: The Story of Charles Manson's Dune Buggy Attack Battalion (Sanders) **53**:304-07, 310
"Family Ties" (Lispector) **43**:268-69
Family Ties (Lispector)
See *Laços de família*
Family Trade (Carroll) **38**:107-08
"The Family Tree" (Boland) **40**:96
A Family Trust (Just) **27**:228
Family Viewing (Egoyan) **151**:122-29, 134, 136, 139-40, 142, 147-49, 151-52, 154, 161, 166, 173-74
Family Voices (Pinter) **27**:393, 396; **58**:369-70, 372, 374-75, 381-84; **73**:277
"Family Walls" (Brennan) **5**:73
A Family's Affairs (Douglas) **73**:63-6, 73-5, 79-85, 92-3
The Famine (Creasey) **11**:134
Famine (Murphy) **51**:305
Famine (O'Flaherty) **34**:355-57
"The Famine Road" (Boland) **40**:96; **67**:46; **113**:122
The Famished Road (Okri) **87**:323-26, 328-31
Famous All Over Town (Santiago) **33**:352-54
Famous American Negroes (Hughes) **108**:286
"The Famous Final Scene" (Seger) **35**:383
"Famous Groupies" (McCartney) **35**:285-86
Famous Last Words (Findley) **27**:144-45; **102**:109-10, 114-18
Famous Long Ago: My Life and Hard Times with Liberation News Service (Mungo) **72**:285-89, 291
Famous Men of Modern Biology (Berger) **12**:37
Famous Negro Heroes of America (Hughes) **108**:286
Famous Negro Music Makers (Hughes) **108**:283
The Famous Ones (Bernhard)
See *Die Berühmten*
"Famous Poet" (Hughes) **9**:280
"The Famous Poll at Jody's Bar" (Gilchrist) **143**:283, 314, 319
The Famous Stanley Kidnapping Case (Snyder) **17**:475
Famous Young Rebels (Archer) **12**:20
The Fan Club (Wallace) **7**:510; **13**:568-69
The Fan Man (Kotzwinkle) **5**:219-20; **35**:257
The Fanatic (Levin) **7**:205
A Fanatic Heart: Selected Stories of Edna O'Brien (O'Brien) **36**:338-41; **116**:186-87, 195, 208-09
"Fancy" (Cunningham) **31**:97, 102
"Fancy" (Davies) **21**:88
"Fancy and Memory" (Blunden) **56**:44
The Fancy Dress Party (Moravia) **7**:244; **46**:282-83
"Fancy Flights" (Beattie) **8**:57; **63**:17
Fancy Goods (Morand)
See *Tendres stocks*
Fancy Goods. Open All Night (Morand) **41**:307-08
Fancy Meeting You Again (Kaufman) **38**:267
Fancy Strut (Smith) **25**:406-07, 410
"The Fancy Woman" (Taylor) **18**:523; **37**:407, 409
Fando and Lis (Arrabal)
See *Fando et Lis*
Fando et Lis (Arrabal) **58**:3, 7-9, 10, 18-19, 21
Fando y Lis (Arrabal)
See *Fando et Lis*
"Fan-Fare" (Waugh) **107**:399
Fanfare for Elizabeth (Sitwell) **67**:325-27
Fängelse (Bergman) **72**:39, 52
Fanny (Almedingen) **12**:5-7
Fanny and Alexander (Bergman)
See *Fanny och Alexander*
Fanny: Being the True History of the Adventures of Fanny Hackabout-Jones (Jong) **18**:278-79; **83**:307-08, 311, 315, 321
Fanny Herself (Ferber) **18**:150, 153; **93**:137-38, 147, 171
Fanny och Alexander (Bergman) **72**:57-61
Fanny Otcott (Wilder) **82**:384
Fanny Peculiar (Waterhouse) **47**:422
"Fans" (Hannah) **38**:234; **90**:138
A Fan's Notes (Exley) **6**:170-72; **11**:186-87
Fanshen (Hare) **29**:212-14; **136**:286
"Fantasia" (Livesay) **79**:342
"Fantasia on 'The Nut-Brown Maid'" (Ashbery) **13**:30, 35; **15**:29-30, 32, 34; **41**:37, 40; **77**:44-5, 68; **125**:18, 35
"Fantasia on the Seventies" (White) **110**:332, 341-42
The Fantasies of Harlan Ellison (Ellison) **139**:136-41
Los fantasmos de mi cerebo (Gironella) **11**:236
The Fantastic Four (Lee) **17**:257-58
Fantastic Lives (Ellison) **139**:129
Fantastic Mr. Fox (Dahl) **79**:177
"Fantastic Voyage" (Bowie) **17**:66
Fantastic Voyage (Asimov) **76**:315
"Fantastic World's End" (Moure) **88**:218
Fantastyka i futurologia (Lem) **40**:300; **149**:111, 114-16, 119, 156, 160, 188-92, 194-95, 198, 209, 245, 248, 256, 261
"Fantasy" (O'Hara) **78**:333
Fantasy and Fugue (Fuller) **4**:178; **28**:148
The Fantasy Poets: Philip Larkin (Larkin) **64**:257
Fantomas against the Multinational Vampires (Cortázar)
See *Fantomas contra los vampiros multinacionales*
Fantomas contra los vampiros multinacionales (Cortázar) **10**:117-18; **33**:123
Le fantôme de la liberté (Bunuel) **16**:144, 148, 152; **80**:57
Le fantôme de Marseille (Cocteau) **43**:107
"Les fantômes du temps des feuilles mortes" (Carrier) **78**:69
"Far and Scattered Are the Tribes that Industrialization Has Left Behind" (Jiles) **58**:281
"Far Away" (Durrell) **13**:188
Far Away from Anywhere Else (Le Guin)
See *Very Far Away from Anywhere Else*
"Far Cry" (Gaye) **26**:135
"The Far Cry" (Yevtushenko) **26**:462
Far Cry (MacCaig) **36**:284
A Far Cry (Rovit) **7**:383
"A Far Cry after a Close Call" (Howard) **7**:165; **10**:277; **47**:167
"A Far Cry from Africa" (Walcott) **25**:451-52; **42**:418, 421; **67**:347, 352, 354; **76**:273
"A Far Cry from Bowmore" (Jenkins) **52**:226
"The Far Field" (Roethke) **8**:460; **11**:484-85; **19**:396, 398, 400; **46**:364; **101**:289, 304-05, 307, 319-20, 326
The Far Field (Roethke) **1**:291; **3**:432-34; **8**:455, 457; **11**:485; **19**:396, 398; **46**:355, 357, 361, 364; **101**:267, 286-90, 296, 304, 310, 327, 330, 332-33
"Far Floridas" (Mott) **15**:381
Far from Cibola (Horgan) **53**:174
Far from Home (Sebestyen) **30**:346-47, 349-51
Far from Home (Tevis) **42**:372, 377
Far from Shore (Major) **26**:286-88
"Far from the City" (Santos) **22**:364
Far from the City of Class and Other Stories (Friedman) **3**:165; **56**:95-6
"Far from the Opposite Shore" (Steinem) **63**:379
Far from the Sea (Hunter) **31**:226
Far in the Day (Cunningham) **12**:166
Far Journey of Oudin (Harris) **25**:203, 205, 214
"Far Off" (Guillén) **79**:230
"Far Out" (Larkin) **64**:258
The Far Pavilions (Kaye) **28**:198-202
Far Rainbow (Strugatskii and Strugatskii) **27**:434, 437
Far Side of the Dollar (Macdonald) **2**:256; **3**:308; **14**:334-35; **41**:266, 270
The Far Side of the World (O'Brian) **152**:282, 299
The Far Side of Victory (Greenberg) **30**:167-68
Far to Go (Streatfeild) **21**:413, 416
Far Tortuga (Matthiessen) **5**:274-75; **7**:210-12; **11**:359-60; **32**:290, 297; **64**:307, 309, 311-14, 316, 320, 324-25, 327-28
Far Voyager: The Story of James Cook (Latham) **12**:325
"Far West" (Cendrars) **106**:175
"Far West" (Smith) **15**:516-17
"Faraway Image" (Cortázar)
See "Lejana"
The Faraway Island (Corcoran) **17**:76
"Far-Away Meadow" (Frost) **4**:175
"Farce Double" (Mathews)
See "Country Cooking from Central France: Roast Boned Rolled Stuffed Shoulder of Lamb"
"The Farcical History of Richard Greenow" (Huxley) **79**:326
"Fare Well" (Berryman) **62**:71,75
"The Farenheit Man" (Frame) **96**:189
"Farewell" (Amichai) **116**:138
"Farewell" (Dybek) **114**:72
"Farewell" (Powers) **8**:448; **57**:349
"Farewell at the Station" (Young) **82**:396
"Farewell Blues" (Amis) **40**:41
Farewell, Gul'sary! (Aitmatov)
See *Proschai, Gul'sary!*
Farewell Happy Fields (Raine) **7**:353
"Farewell, My Lovely!" (White) **10**:527; **34**:426
"The Farewell Party" (Desai) **97**:150, 152-53
The Farewell Party (Kundera)
See *La valse aux adieux*
"Farewell Rehearsed" (Tate) **14**:531
Farewell, Spring! (Seifert)
See *Jaro sbohem*
"A Farewell Thing While Breathing" (Bukowski) **41**:66
"Farewell to America" (Powys) **125**:297
"Farewell to Annabel" (Lightfoot) **26**:279
A Farewell to Arms (Hemingway) **1**:141, 143-44; **3**:231, 234-35, 239-40; **6**:225-27, 230, 234; **8**:283, 290-91; **10**:266-67, 271; **13**:271, 273-75, 277-79; **19**:218; **30**:179, 181, 195, 198-99; **34**:477-79; **61**:196, 201, 218; **80**:104, 113, 115, 117-18, 128, 134, 136-37, 142, 146-49
"Farewell to Earth" (Clarke) **35**:122
"Farewell to Europe" (Boyle) **121**:59
Farewell to Greatness! (Carroll) **10**:97-8
Farewell to Hamlet (Johnson)
See *Avsked till Hamlet*
"Farewell to New York" (Boyle) **121**:37, 59
"A Farewell to Omsk" (Perelman) **15**:417; **49**:265
"Farewell to September" (Herbert) **43**:183
"A Farewell to Speech" (Thurber) **125**:403
Farewell to the Sea: A Novel of Cuba (Arenas)
See *Otra vez el mar*
A Farewell to the Twentieth Century: A Compendium of the Absurd (Berton) **104**:62
Farewell Victoria (White) **30**:449
"Farewells" (Alegria) **75**:49
Farewells (Onetti)
See *Los adioses*
La farfalla di Dinard (Montale) **7**:223, 226
Fargo (The Coen Brothers) **108**:165-71
"The Faring" (Davidson) **13**:169

"The Farm" (Hall) **37**:142
"The Farm" (MacLeish) **68**:286-87, 292
The Farm (Storey) **4**:529; **5**:415
The Farm at Grinde (Vesaas) **48**:405, 411
"Farm behind Battle Zone" (Blunden) **56**:44
"Farm Country" (Oliver) **98**:266
"Farm Implements and Rutabagas in a Landscape" (Ashbery) **15**:32
"The Farm Novels of C. M. van den Heever" (Coetzee) **66**:99
"The Farm on the Great Plains" (Stafford) **29**:380
"Farm Wife" (Thomas) **48**:379
Farmer (Harrison) **14**:235; **33**:199-201; **66**:154-56, 158, 160-61, 163; **143**:345
Farmer Giles of Ham (Tolkien) **12**:574
"Farmer in the Dell" (Ferber) **93**:139
Farmer in the Sky (Heinlein) **3**:226; **26**:171, 175-76; **55**:302
Farmer of the Clouds and Poetry until Now (Andrade)
See *Fazendeira do ar y poesia até agora*
The Farmer Takes a Wife (Connelly) **7**:57
"The Farmers" (Bottoms) **53**:31
"Farmers" (Lane) **25**:288
"The Farmer's Children" (Bishop) **32**:40
The Farmers Hotel (O'Hara) **2**:325
"The Farmer's Wife" (Sexton) **53**:317; **123**:423, 441
Farming: A Handbook (Berry) **6**:61; **8**:85; **27**:32-3, 36; **46**:73
The Farming of Bones (Danticat) **139**:98-100, 102-3
Farmstead of Time (Celan)
See *Zeitgehöft*
Farmyard (Kroetz)
See *Stallerhof*
Farnham's Freehold (Heinlein) **14**:254; **26**:172; **55**:303
A Far-Off Place (van der Post) **5**:463-64
The Farolitos of Christmas (Anaya) **148**:35
Farragan's Retreat (McHale) **3**:332; **5**:281-82
Far-Ranging Beetleology (Neruda) **62**:327
Farrier's Lane (Perry) **126**:331
Fars reise (Vesaas) **48**:405
Farther Off from Heaven (Humphrey) **45**:199-200, 202-03, 205
"Farther On" (Browne) **21**:40
The Farthest Shore (Le Guin) **13**:347; **22**:266, 271; **71**:180-82, 186-88, 190-91, 194-96, 198, 200, 203-04
Farthest Star (Williamson) **29**:462
"Fascinating Fascism" (Sontag) **105**:197, 216-19
"Fascination" (Le Clézio) **155**:83
"Fascination" (Schuyler) **23**:391
"Fascinations" (Bowie) **17**:62
"Fascist Honeymoon" (Dybek) **114**:67
"Las fases de Severo" (Cortázar) **13**:164; **33**:124
The Fashion in Shrouds (Allingham) **19**:12, 16
"Fashion in the 70's" (Swenson) **106**:330
The Fashion System (Barthes)
See *Système de la mode*
Fashions for Women (Arzner) **98**:62-3, 69, 74
"The Fast" (Singer) **15**:504; **111**:295
"Fast Break" (Hirsch) **50**:195, 198
"The Fast Bus" (Strand) **71**:283
Fast, Fast Relief (Berton) **104**:47
"Fast Forward" (Cameron) **44**:33
"Fast Lanes" (Phillips) **139**:203
Fast Lanes (Phillips) **139**:201, 203-06, 216, 220
Fast Sam, Cool Clyde, and Stuff (Myers) **35**:295-96
"Fast Speaking Woman" (Waldman) **7**:508
Fast Speaking Woman (Waldman) **7**:508
Faster: The Acceleration of Just About Everything (Gleick) **147**:74-8
Fastes d'enfer (Ghelderode) **11**:226
"The Fastest Runner on Sixty-First Street" (Farrell) **66**:131
"Fastitocalon" (Borges) **8**:96
"Fat" (Carver) **53**:65; **126**:144
The Fat and the Lean (Polanski) **16**:468, 471
Fat City (Huston) **20**:172
"The Fat Girl" (Dubus) **36**:144-45; **97**:198, 204, 207, 216, 221
The Fat Girl (Sachs) **35**:335-36
"The Fat Lady" (Carruth) **84**:135
"Fat Lip" (Guillén)
See "Negro bembón"
"The Fat Man" (Dinesen) **10**:152
"The Fat Man" (Newlove) **14**:378
"The Fat Man in History" (Carey) **96**:25, 28, 36, 38, 67
The Fat Man in History (Carey) **40**:127-30, 134; **96**:22, 24, 36-8, 53-4, 63-4, 68, 70
Fat Man Poems (Wild) **14**:580
The Fat Man: Selected Poems, 1962-1972 (Newlove) **14**:378
Fat Men from Space (Pinkwater) **35**:320
"Fat Molly" (Durcan) **43**:114
"The Fat of the Land" (Yezierska) **46**:441, 449
Fat Woman (Rooke) **25**:392-94; **34**:251, 254
The Fat Woman Next Door Is Pregnant (Tremblay)
See *La grosse femme d'à côté est enciente*
The Fat Woman's Joke (Weldon)
See *And the Wife Ran Away*
Fata Morgana (Breton) **54**:30
Fata Morgana (Herzog) **16**:321-23, 327
Fata Morgana (Kotzwinkle) **14**:311; **35**:255-57
Fatal Half Measures (Yevtushenko) **126**:391, 395, 397-98
"Fatal Interview: Penthesilea and Achilles" (Warren) **13**:573
A Fatal Inversion (Rendell) **48**:326-27
Fatal Strategies (Baudrillard)
See *Les stratégies fatales*
Fatal Vision (McGinniss) **32**:304-06
The Fatal Woman (Glassco) **9**:237
"Fate" (Olds) **39**:191; **85**:288
Fate (Ai) **69**:18
Fate Is the Hunter (Gann) **23**:166
"The Fate of Flesh" (Aleixandre) **36**:27
The Fate of Mary Rose (Blackwood) **100**:2-4, 9, 13-14, 27, 31
"The Fate of Pleasure" (Trilling) **24**:462
The Fate of Reading and Other Essays (Hartman) **27**:180, 182-84
The Fate of the Earth (Schell) **35**:365-70
"The Fate of Women of Genius" (Gordon) **128**:120
The Fateful Triangle: The United States, Israel and the Palestinians (Chomsky) **132**:25-7, 35-6, 67, 74
Fate's Play (Mahfouz)
See *Abath al-aqdar*
Fates Worse than Death (Vonnegut) **111**:368-70, 373
"The Father" (Carver) **22**:99; **55**:275
"The Father" (Cassill) **4**:95; **23**:105
"Father" (Levine) **118**:284
"A Father" (Mukherjee) **53**:270
"Father" (Plath) **51**:348
"Father" (Soto) **80**:284
"Father" (Walker) **58**:409
The Father (Olds) **85**:305-08
"Father and Daughter" (Eberhart) **11**:177
"Father and Daughter" (Sanchez) **116**:278-79, 281, 301
A Father and His Fate (Compton-Burnett) **34**:500
"A Father and His Son" (Wiesel) **37**:450
"Father and I" (Lagerkvist) **54**:276
The Father and Other Stories (Cassill) **23**:106
"Father and Son" (Ai) **69**:7
"Father and Son" (Buckley) **57**:130
"Father and Son" (Eberhart) **11**:177
"Father and Son" (Hughes) **108**:315, 317, 327
"Father and Son" (Kunitz) **148**:77, 82, 85, 88, 96, 98-99, 104, 107, 132, 138, 141, 149
"Father and Son" (Santos) **22**:361
Father and Son (Compton-Burnett) **10**:109
Father and Son (Farrell) **66**:114, 116-17
"A Father at His Son's Baptism" (Gerstler) **70**:158
"Father Ch., Many Years Later" (Milosz) **56**:240; **82**:303, 306
"Father Christmas" (Davies) **21**:103
The Father Christmas Letters (Tolkien) **8**:515
Father Come Home (Mphahlele) **133**:135, 154, 159, 162
"Father Coming Home" (Alexie) **154**:4
Father Figure (Peck) **21**:299
"Father Guzman" (Stern) **100**:333
"Father in the Library" (Milosz) **56**:232
Father Is a Pillow Tied to a Broom (Soto) **80**:277
"Father Mat" (Kavanagh) **22**:240
Father Melancholy's Daughter (Godwin) **69**:252-55; **125**:152, 165, 168
"Father/Mother Haibun #9" (Wah) **44**:327
Father Ned (O'Casey)
See *The Drums of Father Ned*
"The Father of My Country" (Wakoski) **7**:506; **40**:454
"A Father out Walking on the Lawn" (Dove) **81**:138
"Father Philip" (Dabrowska) **15**:169
"Father Son, and Holy Ghost" (Lorde) **71**:245
Father Stafford (Hope) **83**:170
"Father, the Cavalier" (Davie) **31**:116
"The Father to His Children" (Simmons) **43**:414
"Father to Sons" (Day Lewis) **10**:130
Fatheralong: A Meditation on Fathers and Sons, Race and Society (Wideman) **122**:357-61, 363, 366-67
"Fatherhood" (Wilson) **49**:415-16
"Fathering" (Mukherjee) **53**:270-71
Fathering (Delbanco) **6**:129-30
"The Fathers" (Rothenberg) **57**:374
"The Fathers" (Sassoon) **130**:183, 185, 220
The Fathers (Tate) **2**:427; **4**:537; **6**:527; **9**:523, 525; **11**:522, 526-27; **14**:530-31, 533; **24**:442
Fathers: A Novel in the Form of a Memoir (Gold) **4**:192; **7**:120, 122; **42**:192, 194-95, 197-98; **152**:118, 121-22, 126-29, 137-38, 141
"Fathers and Bridges over Hell: Deep Rivers" (Dorfman) **77**:156
Fathers and Crows (Vollmann) **89**:283, 285-86, 288, 291-97, 300, 306, 309-13
"Fathers and Daughters" (Hoffman) **141**:280
"Fathers and Sons" (Hemingway) **10**:270; **30**:181, 194, 197, 199
"Father's Bedroom" (Lowell) **37**:243; **124**:267
"The Fathers' Daughters" (Spark) **40**:401
"Father's Day" (Shields) **97**:433
Father's Day (Goldman) **48**:125, 128
"A Father's Ear" (Yevtushenko) **26**:468
"Father's Help" (Narayan) **121**:354
A Father's Hours (Mahapatra) **33**:277, 281, 283
Father's Journey (Vesaas)
See *Fars reise*
Fathers Playing Catch with Sons: Essays on Sport (Hall) **37**:148-49
"A Father's Son" (Yevtushenko) **26**:467
"Fathers, Sons and Lovers" (Thomas) **132**:382
"A Father's Story" (Dubus) **36**:147-48; **97**:199-200, 218, 222, 224, 226, 228-29, 233
A Father's Words (Stern) **39**:245
"The Fatigue" (Jones) **4**:259; **7**:191
"Fatra min al-shabab" (Mahfouz) **153**:349-50
"Fatty" (Gunn) **81**:185
Fatu-Hiva (Heyerdahl) **26**:193
"Faulkner and the Fugitive-Agrarians" (Brooks) **86**:288
"The Fault" (Montague) **46**:270
"Fault Lines" (Kingsolver) **130**:101
Fault Lines (Alexander) **121**:12-13, 19-20
Fault Lines (Carroll) **38**:106-08
The Fault of Angels (Horgan) **53**:169-71, 176
"Fauna of Mirrors" (Borges) **8**:99
"Fausse porte ou portrait" (Reverdy) **53**:290

"Fausses notes" (Reverdy) **53**:291
Faust (Nye) **42**:306-08
"Faust: A Skit" (Justice) **102**:254
A Faust Book (Enright) **31**:153-55
"The Faustian Pact" (Birkerts) **116**:157, 163
"Faustian Sketches" (Fuller) **28**:150
"Faustina; or, Rock Roses" (Bishop) **32**:33, 38, 42
Faustrecht der Freiheit (Fassbinder) **20**:108
"Faustus Kelly" (O'Brien) **7**:270; **10**:362
"The Fauve" (Humphrey) **45**:193, 203
Faux pas (Blanchot) **135**:122, 130, 132
The Favor (Guild) **33**:187-88
The Favorite (Wright) **44**:334
Favorite Haunts (Addams) **30**:16
"The Favourite" (O'Brien) **5**:311-12
The Favourite Game (Cohen) **3**:109; **38**:132-34
Favourite Nights (Poliakoff) **38**:384, 386
"A Favourite Scene (Recalled on Looking at Birket Foster's Landscape)" (Blunden) **56**:37
Favours (Rubens) **19**:404-05
"Fawn" (Davison) **28**:104
"Fawn" (Kinsella) **27**:237
"The Fawn" (Oliver) **98**:266
Fawn (Peck) **17**:338-39
Fay's Circus (Prichard)
See *Haxby's Circus: The Lightest, Brightest Little Show on Earth*
Fazendeira do ar y poesia até agora (Andrade) **18**:5
FBI (Berger) **12**:41
"Fear" (Carver) **36**:107
"Fear" (Dobyns) **37**:76-7
"The Fear" (Frost) **1**:110; **15**:240; **26**:119
"Fear" (Merwin) **88**:200
"Fear" (Read) **4**:439
"The Fear" (Tanizaki)
See "Kyofu"
"The Fear" (Williams) **148**:346
Fear (Hubbard) **43**:203, 205, 207
The Fear (Keneally) **5**:210; **19**:245-46; **117**:210, 213-15
Fear and Desire (Kubrick) **16**:376, 380, 385-86, 388-89
"Fear and Fame" (Levine) **118**:296, 304
Fear and Hope of the Federal Republic of Germany (Kroetz) **41**:240
Fear and Loathing in Las Vegas (Gilliam) **141**:255-56, 260-61
Fear and Loathing in Las Vegas: A Savage Journey to the Heart of the American Dream (Thompson) **9**:526-27; **17**:504-05, 510, 514-15; **40**:426-31; **104**:334-35, 338, 340, 343, 345-51
The Fear and Loathing Letters, Vol. 1 (Thompson) **104**:348, 350
Fear and Loathing: on the Campaign Trail, '72 (Thompson) **9**:527-28; **17**:505, 507-09, 511-12; **40**:427-28; **104**:334-36, 338, 340, 345, 347
"Fear and Trembling" (Warren) **39**:257, 259, 262
"Fear and Trespass" (Bernstein) **142**:46
Fear Eats Up Souls (Fassbinder)
See *Angst essen Seele auf*
"Fear: Four Examples" (Lish) **45**:228-30
"Fear in the Streets" (Wideman) **122**:354
Fear Is the Key (MacLean) **13**:361; **50**:348-50
"Fear Not Your Enemies" (Ellison) **139**:115
"The Fear of Bo-talee" (Momaday) **85**:247
"The Fear of Burial" (Glück) **22**:175-177
"Fear of Death" (Ashbery) **15**:28; **25**:52
Fear of Dreaming (Carroll) **143**:37
Fear of Falling (Ehrenreich) **110**:164, 166-67, 169, 173, 176, 178-81
Fear of Fear (Fassbinder) **20**:114
Fear of Fifty (Jong) **83**:319
"The Fear of Flying" (Van Duyn) **63**:438-39; **116**:407
Fear of Flying (Jong) **4**:263-65; **6**:267, 269-70; **8**:313-15; **83**:290-91, 296-97, 300-04, 307-11, 316-20
Fear of Heaven (Mortimer) **43**:307
"Fear of Math" (Cameron) **44**:33, 35
Fear of Music (Byrne) **26**:97-8
"Fear of Women" (Kroetsch)
See "The Fear of Women in Prairie Fiction: An Erotics of Space"
"The Fear of Women in Prairie Fiction: An Erotics of Space" (Kroetsch) **132**:201-02, 204, 219,20, 256, 258-59, 279
"The Fearful" (Plath) **14**:424; **51**:341; **111**:168, 204
"Fearful Rock" (Wellman) **49**:388, 395
Fearful Symmetry: A Study of William Blake (Frye) **24**:207, 231; **70**:273, 275-76
"Fearless" (Pink Floyd) **35**:306
The Fearless Treasure (Streatfeild) **21**:401, 411
The Fearless Vampire Killers; or, Pardon Me, But Your Teeth Are In My Neck (Polanski) **16**:464, 466-67, 473
"Fears" (Collins) **44**:38
"Fears" (Yevtushenko) **126**:408, 413
"The Feast at Countess Fritter's" (Gombrowicz)
See "Biesiada u hrabiny Kotlubaj"
"The Feast at Paplay" (Brown) **48**:60
"Feast Day" (Voigt) **54**:433
A Feast for Boris (Bernhard)
See *Eine Fest für Boris*
The Feast of All Saints (Rice) **41**:363-64; **128**:278, 312
Feast of Friends (Morrison) **17**:288
The Feast of Lupercal (Moore) **1**:225; **3**:341; **5**:295-96; **19**:330, 334; **32**:314; **90**:238-40, 246, 251-4, 262, 288
A Feast of Snakes (Crews) **23**:132, 134, 139; **49**:68-72, 74, 76-9
The Feast of St. Dionysus (Silverberg) **140**:343-44, 378
Feast of Stephen (Davies) **75**:209
Feast of Victors (Solzhenitsyn) **10**:479
Feast or Famine? The Energy Future (Branley) **21**:24
A Feast Unknown (Farmer) **19**:164, 167
Feather Crowns (Mason) **82**:258-60; **154**:260-61, 272-73, 279, 284-85, 207-88, 300
"A Feather for Voltaire" (Graham) **118**:225, 248-49
Feather Woman of the Jungle (Tutuola) **14**:540, 542
"A Feather-Bed for Critics" (Blackmur) **24**:56-7
The Feathered Serpent (O'Dell) **30**:276-78
The Featherless Dog (Cabral de Melo Neto)
See *O cão sem plumas*
"Featherly" (Cummings) **68**:37
"Feathers" (Carver) **53**:65; **36**:103, 106; **55**:278; **126**:105-06, 110, 113, 120-22, 147-49, 151, 160-62, 181
"Feathers" (Kinsella) **27**:236
"Feathers" (Ortiz) **45**:310
"Feathers from the Hill" (Merwin) **45**:273
Feathers from the Hill (Merwin) **18**:336-37
The Feathers of Death (Raven) **14**:439, 443
"Februar" (Eich) **15**:204
"February" (Merwin) **88**:192
"February" (Simic) **49**:337
February Dragon (Thiele) **17**:493, 495
"February Ground" (Dahlberg) **7**:63
"February Seventeenth" (Hughes) **37**:174-76, 180; **119**:271
"February the 20th Street" (Williams) **42**:441
"February: The Boy Breughel" (Dubie) **36**:131, 136
"February's Full Moon" (Akhmadulina) **53**:15
"The Fecund Complain They Are Not Honored" (Piercy) **62**:378
Federico Fellini's intervista (Fellini) **85**:59-60, 66, 73-6, 78-82
Fedora (Wilder) **20**:466
"Feeders" (Barthelme) **117**:14
"Feeding Ducks" (MacCaig) **36**:283
"Feeding Out Wintery Cattle at Twilight" (Hughes) **119**:271
Feeding the Ghosts (D'Aguiar) **145**:126, 128
"Feeding Time" (Kumin) **28**:224
"Feel All My Love Inside" (Gaye) **26**:132
"Feel Like a Number" (Seger) **35**:383-84
"Feel Like Fucking" (Smith) **12**:541
"Feel Me" (Swenson) **4**:534; **14**:518; **61**:393; **106**:344-45
"The Feel of a Face" (Plumly) **33**:311
"The Feel of Hands" (Gunn) **6**:220
"The Feel of the Trigger" (Westlake) **33**:440
"Feeling and Precision" (Moore) **47**:270, 272
"Feeling for Life" (Cooper) **56**:71
"Feeling Fucked Up" (Knight) **40**:283, 286-87
"Feeling Groovy" (Simon) **17**:458-59, 464, 466
"Feeling into Words" (Heaney) **25**:249; **74**:156, 179
"Feeling Old" (Ortiz) **45**:310
"Feeling Sorry for Yourself" (Peacock) **60**:298
Feeling You're Behind (Nichols) **33**:332
Féerie pour une autre fois (Céline) **1**:56; **4**:102; **47**:76-7; **124**:62-3, 89, 92, 94
Féerie pour une autre fois I (Céline) **124**:97
Féerie pour une autre fois II: Normance (Céline) **4**:102; **47**:76-7
Feet in Chains (Roberts)
See *Traed mewn cyffion*
"Feet on the Ground" (Wakoski) **2**:459
Fefu and Her Friends (Fornés) **39**:138; **61**:126-29, 133-38, 141
Feiffer: Jules Feiffer's America from Eisenhower to Reagan (Feiffer) **64**:156
Feiffer on Civil Rights (Feiffer) **64**:153
Feiffer on Nixon: The Cartoon Presidency (Feiffer) **64**:153
Feiffer's Album (Feiffer) **64**:158
Feiffer's Marriage Manual (Feiffer) **64**:158
Felicia's Journey (Egoyan) **151**:155, 168-76
Felicia's Journey (Trevor) **116**:389-93
"La felicidad" (Poniatowska) **140**:322-23
"Felicity in Turin" (Durcan) **70**:152-53
"Felis Catus" (Berriault) **54**:3; **109**:96
"Felix" (Aleixandre) **36**:26
"The Fell of Dark" (Skelton) **13**:507
Fell Purpose (Derleth) **31**:138
"Fellatio" (Updike) **3**:485
Fellini: A Director's Notebook (Fellini)
See *Block-notes de un regista*
"Fellini on Fellini" (Fellini) **85**:82
Fellini Roma (Fellini)
See *Roma*
Fellini's Casanova (Fellini)
See *Casanova di Federico Fellini*
Fellini's Roma (Fellini)
See *Roma*
Fellini's Satyricon (Fellini)
See *Satyricon*
Fellow Feelings (Howard) **7**:169; **10**:275-76; **47**:168
The Fellowship of the Ring (Tolkien) **12**:563-65; **38**:431
The Fellow-Travellers (Caute) **29**:116-18
"Fem strofer till Thoreau" (Transtroemer) **52**:410; **65**:222-23
"female" (Clifton) **66**:87
"Female" (Smith) **12**:534
The Female Eunuch (Greer) **131**:177-9, 181, 183-5, 187-90, 192-4, 197, 199-218, 223-26
Female Friends (Weldon) **6**:562-63; **9**:559-60; **11**:565; **19**:466-69; **36**:446-47; **122**:247-49, 250-52, 254, 268
The Female Man (Russ) **15**:461-62
Female Parts (Fo) **32**:175
"Feminine Intuition" (Asimov) **19**:25; **26**:50, 56
"The Feminine Landscape in Leslie Marmon Silko's Ceremony" (Allen) **84**:31
The Feminine Mystique (Friedan) **74**:90-3, 96-9, 102-03, 105-08, 110-11
"The Feminine Note in Literature" (Forster) **45**:132

Feminine Wiles (Bowles) **68**:9
"Feminism: An Agenda" (Dworkin) **123**:74-5
Feminism/Postmodernism (Nicholson) **65**:342-43
Feminism Unmodified: Discourses on Life and Law (MacKinnon) **65**:324
"A Feminist Challenge" (Hooks) **94**:152
Feminist Revision and the Bible (Ostriker) **132**:318, 321, 328
"feminist scholarship: ethical questions" (Hooks) **94**:143
Feminist Theory: From Margin to Center (Hooks) **94**:140-42, 144
"Femme" (Allison) **153**:4, 11
Une femme (Ernaux) **88**:98-100, 106-12, 115-17
"La femme adultère" (Camus) **9**:144; **14**:114; **63**:71, 77; **124**:20
"La femme Anna" (Theriault) **79**:408
La femme Anna, et autres contes (Theriault) **79**:407-08
Une femme douce (Bresson) **16**:115
La femme du Gange (Duras) **20**:99-101; **40**:178; **68**:91
Une femme est une femme (Godard) **20**:130, 140, 148
"Femme Fatale" (Reed) **21**:303, 314, 319, 321
La femme gelée (Ernaux) **88**:100, 120
Le femme infidele (Chabrol) **16**:172-75, 179
Une femme mariée (Godard) **20**:131, 133, 136, 149
"Femme noire" (Senghor) **130**:237, 241, 253, 258, 261, 275
Une femme qu'a le coeur trop petit (Crommelynck) **75**:154, 161, 169
"La femme rompue" (Beauvoir) **124**:185
La femme rompue (Beauvoir) **2**:43; **8**:63; **14**:70; **31**:43; **44**:343, 350-51; **71**:48-53; **124**:127, 144, 183, 185-86
La Femme sur la Lune (Lang)
See *Die Frau im Mond*
"Les femmes" (Gascar) **11**:220-21
Les femmes (Gascar) **11**:221-22
Femmes (Simon) **39**:208, 215
"Femmes de France" (Senghor) **130**:259
Les femmes du boeuf (Audiberti) **38**:22-3, 28
Fen (Churchill) **31**:88-9; **55**:126
Fen Country (Crispin) **22**:111
Fences (Wilson) **50**:267-71; **63**:447-49, 451, 453-54, 456-58; **118**:372-77, 379, 382, 388-89, 399, 403, 405-07, 412
The Fencing Master and Other Stories (Rogin) **18**:457
"Fencing with a Pile of Dung" (Yevtushenko) **126**:391
Fenella Phizackerley (Forster) **149**:63
Fenêtres dormantes et porte sur la toit (Char) **55**:288
Feng (Wain) **11**:561; **15**:561
"Fenstad's Mother" (Baxter) **78**:26-30
Fer-de-lance (Stout) **3**:471
Ferdinand (Zukofsky) **2**:487
Ferdydurke (Gombrowicz) **4**:193, 195; **7**:122-26; **11**:241; **49**:121-23, 126-29, 133
Fergus (Moore) **1**:225-26; **3**:340; **5**:296-97; **7**:238; **19**:331-32, 334; **32**:311, 313-14; **90**:243, 247, 249-51, 254-5, 272-3, 277, 281
"Fergus Falling" (Kinnell) **29**:285; **129**:240-41, 256
Fergus Lamont (Jenkins) **52**:229
The Ferguson Affair (Macdonald) **14**:334
La feria (Arreola) **147**:6, 19-24, 34, 36, 38-40
The Ferlie (Hunter) **21**:157
Fermé la nuit (Morand) **41**:298, 303, 306
"Fern" (Hughes) **14**:271
"Fern" (Toomer) **1**:341; **22**:426
"Fern Beds in Hampshire County" (Wilbur) **53**:407; **110**:359
"Fern Dying" (Moss) **14**:376; **45**:292
Fernwood 2-Night (Lear) **12**:337-38; **17**:300-01
Ferraille (Reverdy) **53**:279, 281, 285
Ferrements (Césaire) **19**:95; **32**:112-13; **112**:29
"The Ferris Wheel" (Van Duyn) **116**:412, 415
"The Ferry; or, Another Trip to Venice" (Cortázar) **33**:123-25
"Ferry Port" (Merwin) **88**:194
Ferryman's Song (Ekelöf) **27**:110
Fertig (Yurick) **6**:584
"Fertilizing the Continent" (Oates) **33**:294
Fervor de Buenos Aires (Borges) **6**:88; **8**:95; **19**:44, 49; **44**:361, 367
Fervor of Buenos Aires (Borges)
See *Fervor de Buenos Aires*
Fest der Schoneit (Riefenstahl) **16**:521
Fest der Volker (Riefenstahl) **16**:521
Eine Fest für Boris (Bernhard) **32**:24; **61**:12
Festianus, Martyrer (Eich) **15**:203
"Festival" (Beer) **58**:36
"Festival" (Berry) **17**:52
Festival at Farbridge (Priestley) **34**:361
Festival of Beauty (Riefenstahl)
See *Fest der Schoneit*
"The Festival of the Dead" (King) **53**:212
Festival of the People (Riefenstahl)
See *Fest der Volker*
"A Festive Day" (Seifert)
See "Slavnostní den"
The Festivities of the Dome (Mahfouz)
See *Afrah al-qubba*
The Festivity (Haavikko)
See *Juhlat*
"The Festubert Shrine" (Blunden) **56**:41
"Festubert: The Old German Line" (Blunden) **56**:41
"Die Festung" (Lenz) **27**:245
"Fetal rights, Women's Wrongs" (Pollitt) **122**:215, 219, 223
"The Fetch" (Aickman) **57**:6-7
"Fête des arbres et du chasseur" (Char) **11**:116
La fête noire (Audiberti) **38**:22, 24, 26-30, 32
Les fetes galantes (Clair) **20**:66
"Le Fétischiste" (Tournier) **95**:361, 383
Fetish (Harris) **25**:212
"Fetishes" (Selzer) **74**:273
The Fetishist and Other Stories (Tournier) **36**:438
"Fetus" (Lowell) **37**:234
Feu de braise (Mandiargues) **41**:278
Feu de Brousse (Tchicaya) **101**:346-47
Feu froid (Breytenbach) **23**:83
Le feu sur la terre (Mauriac) **56**:215
"Feud" (Roethke) **19**:397
The Feud (Berger) **38**:38-42
Feuer und Blut (Jünger) **125**:222, 248, 254
"Feuer-Nacht" (Bogan) **46**:86; **93**:92-3, 95
Feuilles de route (Cendrars) **18**:95; **106**:185, 198
Feuilles de température (Morand) **41**:303
Feuillets d'Hypnos (Char) **9**:159-60; **14**:127; **55**:287-89
Feux (Yourcenar) **38**:455-57, 459, 461, 464; **50**:363-64; **87**:383, 385-87, 390, 399
"Fever" (Akhmadulina)
See "Oznob"
"Fever" (Boland) **113**:82, 84, 92
"Fever" (Carver) **36**:103-04; **126**:127-28, 174-75, 177, 180
"Fever" (Le Clézio) **31**:243
"Fever" (Hirsch) **50**:195, 197
"Fever" (Updike) **23**:474
"Fever" (Wideman) **67**:379-83, 385; **122**:316-17, 368
Fever (Le Clézio)
See *Le fièvre*
"Fever 103°" (Plath) **2**:336; **3**:390; **9**:425, 428, 433; **14**:428; **17**:355, 365-66; **51**:342, 345; **111**:160, 163, 176-78, 181, 199, 209, 219
"Fever and Chills" (Elliott) **2**:131
Fever and Other New Poems (Akhmadulina)
See *Chills and Other Poems*
"Fever Dream" (Bradbury) **15**:85-6; **42**:35
"Fever Flower" (Grau) **146**:128, 137
"The Fever Monument" (Brautigan) **12**:59
Fever Pitch (Waters) **88**:326, 359
"The Fever Toy" (Wright) **6**:580
"The Fever Tree" (Rendell) **48**:320
The Fever Tree and Other Stories (Rendell) **48**:320
Fever: Twelve Stories (Wideman) **67**:378, 380-82, 384-85, 388, 390; **122**:31, 341, 343, 345, 347-48, 365, 367
"Fever-Chills" (Masefield) **11**:358
"Feverish" (Adcock) **41**:15
"Das Feverschiff" (Lenz) **27**:249, 252-54
"A Few Day's War Which One is Not Certain Happened" (Konwicki)
See "Kilka dni wojny o ktorej nie wiadomo, czy byla"
"A Few Don'ts by an Imagiste" (Pound) **4**:410; **13**:457; **48**:289
"A Few Drinks with Alcock and Brown" (Wain) **46**:411
A Few Enquiries (Sackler) **14**:479
A Few Fair Days (Gardam) **43**:165-66
A Few Green Leaves (Pym) **19**:387-88; **37**:376-77; **111**:227-29, 234, 236, 238, 240, 242-48, 263-66, 270-71, 273, 281-82, 287-88
A Few Hours of Sunlight (Sagan) **17**:426
A Few Late Chrysanthemums (Betjeman) **34**:306, 309; **43**:33-4
"A Few Minutes" (Transtroemer) **65**:222
"A Few Notes about Aunt Gwen" (Fisher) **87**:131
"A Few Notes of Poetry" (Thesen) **56**:421
A Few Poems (Barnard) **48**:26
"A Few Recollections on Teaching and Writing" (Paley) **140**:291
"A Few Too Few Words" (Ellison) **139**:116
"A Few Words about Fascism" (Levi) **41**:246
"The Fez" (Becker and Fagen) **26**:83
Fiabe italiene (Calvino) **11**:91; **22**:89-90, 92; **33**:100; **39**:306-07, 309, 314; **73**:42, 53-4
"Fiammetta Breaks Her Peace" (Dove) **81**:137
"The Fiancés" (Kiš) **57**:246
Fiasco (Lem) **149**:114, 116, 118, 156-57, 166, 173, 175, 208, 215, 217-19, 252-53, 262-63, 276
"Fiat homo" (Miller) **30**:254, 259
"Fiat lux" (Miller) **30**:254
"Fiat voluntas tua" (Miller) **30**:254
"Fiber" (Bass) **143**:22
Fibrilles (Leiris) **61**:343-44, 347, 350-51, 356
Ficciones, 1935-1944 (Borges) **2**:72, 75-7; **3**:77; **4**:74; **6**:93-4; **8**:99, 101-02; **9**:118-19; **13**:105; **19**:49; **44**:356, 363, 368; **48**:37, 42, 44, 46; **83**:156, 158, 160-61, 184
"Fiction" (Nemerov) **9**:395
"Fiction" (Strand) **71**:280
Fiction (Reading) **47**:350, 354
"Fiction: A Lens on Life" (Stegner) **49**:359
Fiction and the Colonial Experience (Meyers) **39**:433
"Fiction and the Criticism of Fiction" (Rahv) **24**:354, 361
Fiction and the Figures of Life (Gass) **2**:155; **8**:240; **11**:225; **15**:255; **39**:477; **132**:142-44, 146-48
Fiction and Wisdom (McCarthy) **59**:290
"Fiction for Teenagers" (Hentoff) **26**:184
"Fiction Today; or, The Pursuit of Non-Knowledge" (Federman) **47**:126
"The Fiction Writer" (Jacobsen) **48**:195
"The Fiction Writer and his Country" (O'Connor) **21**:262
Fictions (Borges)
See *Ficciones, 1935-1944*
"The Fictions of Fatual Representation" (White) **148**:291
"Fictions of the Feminine" (Fulton) **52**:161
Fictive Certainties (Duncan) **55**:294-95
"The Fiddle" (Sillitoe) **57**:391, 396
"The Fiddle and the Drum" (Mitchell) **12**:435
The Fiddler (Millin) **49**:245-46
"Fiddler Crabs" (Brosman) **9**:135
"The Fiddler on Twenty-Third Street" (Callaghan) **41**:98
Fiddler's Green (Gann) **23**:163

The Fiddler's House (Colum) **28**:86-7
Fidelities (Watkins) **43**:449-50, 453
"Fidelity" (Jhabvala) **138**:77-8
"Fidelity" (Parks) **147**:215
"Field" (Abse) **29**:15
"Field" (Broumas) **73**:15, 17
"Field" (Soto) **80**:286, 294
"Field Burning Debates. Salmon Fate Discussed" (Le Guin) **136**:395
"A Field by the River" (Davis) **49**:93
Field Day Anthology of Irish Writing (Deane) **122**:85, 89-91, 96
"Field Events" (Bass) **143**:8-9
"Field Flowers" (Glück) **81**:167-68
The Field God (Green) **25**:193, 199-200
Field Guide (Hass) **18**:208-13; **99**:139-141, 148-150, 154-55, 157
"Field Guide to the Western Birds" (Stegner) **49**:351
Field Guide to the Western Birds (Stegner) **81**:345-46
"Field Hospital" (Jarrell) **9**:299
"The Field Hospital" (Muldoon) **32**:317
"Field Music" (Smith) **42**:356
Field Notes (Kroetsch) **23**:273-75; **57**:292-94; **132**:275
"Field of Battle" (Trevor) **116**:378, 387
"The Field of Blue Children" (Williams) **5**:502; **45**:447, 452-54
"A Field of Carnations" (Enzensberger) **43**:145
"A Field of Light" (Roethke) **11**:480, 485; **46**:362; **101**:274, 283, 324, 335-37, 339
"Field of Opportunity" (Young) **17**:580
"The Field of Roses" (Simmons) **43**:408
"A Field of Snow on a Slope of the Rosenberg" (Davenport) **38**:140
"The Field of Vision" (Le Guin) **8**:343
"Field of Vision" (Heaney) **74**:192
The Field of Vision (Morris) **1**:231, 233; **3**:342-43; **7**:246; **18**:350, 352, 354; **37**:310-12
"A Field of Wheat" (Ross) **13**:492-93
"Field Poem" (Soto) **32**:404; **80**:279, 287, 294
"The Field Trip" (Voigt) **54**:433
"Field Work" (Heaney) **74**:164
Field Work (Heaney) **14**:244-46; **25**:242-44, 246-51; **37**:162, 164-67; **74**:157, 159-60, 162-67, 171-73, 175, 177, 188, 190, 193, 197; **91**:115, 117-18, 122-23
Fielding Gray (Raven) **14**:441
"Fields" (Johnston) **51**:243
"The Fields" (Merwin) **45**:274, 276
The Fields (Richter) **30**:310-15, 318-19, 324-25
"Fields at Dusk" (Salter) **59**:194
Fields of Fire (Webb) **22**:453-55
Fields of Grace (Eberhart) **3**:135
Fields of Peace (Brand) **7**:30
"The Fiend" (Dickey) **15**:173
"Fiend's Weather" (Bogan) **46**:78; **93**:93
The Fierce Dispute (Santmyer) **33**:356-57
"Fierce Girl Playing Hopscotch" (Fulton) **52**:162
The Fiery Hunt (Olson) **11**:420
The Fiery Hunt, and Other Plays (Olson) **11**:420
"Fiesta" (Pasolini) **106**:230
Fiesta (Hemingway)
See *The Sun Also Rises*
Fiesta al noroeste (Matute) **11**:362-64
"Fiesta en grande" (Donoso) **11**:145; **32**:158
"Fiesta for an eye" (Breytenbach) **126**:63
"A Fiesta for the Form" (Gass) **132**:187
Fiestas (Goytisolo) **23**:186; **133**:89-91, 93
"Las fiestas en el campo" (Azorín) **11**:24
Le fièvre (Le Clézio) **31**:243-45; **155**:79-80
La fièvre monte à El Pao (Bunuel) **80**:36, 40, 42-4, 52
"Fifine Answers" (Pound) **48**:288
Fifteen Big Ones (Wilson) **12**:648, 650-52
Fifteen Dead (Kinsella) **138**:99, 102-03
Fifteen Essays (Ciardi) **129**:56
"15 Flower World Variations" (Rothenberg) **57**:381
"The Fifteen-Dollar Eagle" (Plath) **3**:390; **11**:451; **62**:395
"Fifteenth Farewell" (Bogan) **4**:68; **46**:78
"Fifth Avenue, Uptown" (Baldwin) **42**:16; **127**:113
Fifth Business (Davies) **2**:113; **7**:72-4; **13**:173-74; **25**:131, 133-35; **42**:101-03, 105-07, 109; **75**:178, 180-81, 184-85, 187, 190, 192, 199, 204-05, 211-12, 214-16, 224; **91**:198, 200-2, 204, 206
The Fifth Child (Lessing) **94**:287
Fifth Chinese Daughter (Wong) **17**:565-67
The Fifth Column (Hemingway) **13**:274, 278; **80**:101, 105, 121, 149
"Fifth Commandment" (Brunner) **8**:107
"Fifth Day" (FitzGerald) **19**:177, 179
"The Fifth Day" (Matthiessen) **64**:321, 323-24
Fifth Decad of Cantos (Pound) **48**:284
"The Fifth Gospel" (Morgan) **31**:275
"The Fifth Head of Cereberus" (Wolfe) **25**:472
The Fifth Head of Cereberus (Wolfe) **25**:472-74, 476
The Fifth of July (Wilson) **14**:590-92; **36**:459-61, 463-65
The Fifth Sally (Keyes) **80**:165
"The Fifth Season" (Kinsella) **138**:141
"The Fifth Sense" (Beer) **58**:38
The Fifth Son (Wiesel) **37**:458-59
Fifth Sunday (Dove) **81**:140-41, 146
"Fifth Sunday After Easter" (Kinsella) **138**:136
"Fifty Dollars" (Elkin) **51**:96
"Fifty Grand" (Hemingway) **3**:233; **30**:179; **80**:104
"Fifty Males Sitting Together" (Bly) **38**:57
Fifty Poems (Cummings) **8**:154; **12**:154-53; **15**:162; **68**:35, 48
Fifty Poems Fifty (Whittemore) **4**:588
Fifty Roads to Turn (Hamner) **12**:257
Fifty Stories (Boyle) **19**:66; **58**:74, 76; **121**:35
"Fifty Ways to Leave Your Lover" (Simon) **17**:465-66
Fifty Works of English Literature We Could Do Without (Brophy) **6**:99; **29**:95-6; **105**:5-6, 29-30
"A Fifty Year Old Man" (Endō) **99**:288, 297, 301
"Fifty-Fifty" (Sandburg) **35**:356
"Fifty-Fifty" (Zappa) **17**:590
"59x: A True Tale" (Nye) **42**:309
"The Fifty-Ninth Bear" (Plath) **3**:390
"The Fifty-Ninth Street Bridge Song" (Simon) **17**:461, 464, 466
Fifty-Second Street (Joel) **26**:216-17, 220-21
"Fifty-Seven Views of Fujiyama" (Davenport) **38**:145-47
53 Days (Perec)
See *53 Jours*
53 Jours (Perec) **116**:238, 254-55
52 Pick-Up (Klappert) **57**:64
Fifty-two Pickup (Leonard) **28**:233; **71**:223; **120**:271, 287, 301
"The Fifty-Yard Dash" (Saroyan) **8**:468
"The Fig Tree" (Porter) **27**:402
"The Fig Tree" (Pritchett) **15**:443
"Fight" (Bukowski) **82**:14
The Fight (Mailer) **11**:344; **14**:351; **28**:259
Fight against Albatross Two (Thiele) **17**:495
Fight Back: For the Sake of the People, for the Sake of the Land (Ortiz) **45**:308-10
Fight for Freedom (Hughes) **108**:284, 286
Fight Night on a Sweet Saturday (Settle) **19**:409-10; **61**:373-74, 376, 383
"Fight to a Finish" (Sassoon) **130**:183, 216, 220
"The Fighter" (Kristofferson) **26**:269
Fighter (Deighton) **22**:117
Fightin': New and Collected Stories (Ortiz) **45**:309-11
Fighting Angel (Buck) **7**:32; **11**:74-5; **127**:226
The Fighting Cock (Anouilh) **50**:278
"Fighting Depression, I Take My Family on a Picnic" (Baxter) **78**:25
"Fighting for the Rebound" (Mukherjee) **115**:364
The Fighting Indians of the West (Brown) **47**:37
Fighting International Fat (Reynolds) **38**:390-91
Fighting Terms: A Selection (Gunn) **3**:215; **18**:200; **32**:207, 210-11; **81**:177, 183, 185
"Fighting the Bureaucracy" (Appleman) **51**:15
"The Fights" (Acorn) **15**:8-9
Figleafing through History: The Dynamics of Dress (Harris) **12**:263
"La figlia che piange" (Eliot) **1**:90; **9**:187, 189; **13**:201; **15**:213; **41**:146, 150-51
Figural Realism: Studies in the Mimesis Effect (White) **148**:296-99, 302-03
"Figure" (Summers) **10**:494
"The Figure a Poem Makes" (Frost) **4**:177
"Figure in a Landscape" (Gascoyne) **45**:148
"The Figure in the Carpet" (Hollander) **5**:186
"The Figure in the Carpet" (Stevenson) **33**:382
Figure in the Door (Gregor) **9**:253
"The Figure in the Doorway" (Frost) **9**:228
A Figure of Speech (Mazer) **26**:289-90, 292, 296
"The Figure of the Woods" (Hall) **151**:187
"Figure over the Town" (Goyen) **40**:216-17
"The Figured Wheel" (Pinsky) **38**:355, 361; **94**:299, 306, 308; **94**:299, 306, 308; **121**:435-36, 438, 446
The Figured Wheel (Pinsky) **121**:445, 448, 450
"The Figurehead" (Shapiro) **53**:331
Figures Capable of Imagination (Bloom) **103**:4, 14, 24-5
Figures for an Apocalypse (Merton) **83**:400
Figures in Black: Words, Signs and the 'Racial' Self (Gates) **65**:379, 381-82, 393-94,398
Figures in Bright Air (Plante) **7**:308; **23**:344
Figures in Modern Literature (Priestley) **34**:361
Figures in the Foreground (Swinnerton) **31**:426
Figures of Enchantment (Ghose) **42**:185
The Figures of Human (Ignatow)
See *Figures of the Human*
"Figures of Space" (Young) **82**:412
Figures of Speech (Enright) **31**:146-47, 152
Figures of the Human (Ignatow) **7**:174-76; **14**:276; **40**:258
Figures of Thought: Speculations on the Meaning of Poetry and Other Essays (Nemerov) **36**:303-04
Figures of Time (Hayden) **37**:156, 160
Figuro in the Night (O'Casey) **5**:318; **88**:268
La fijeza (Lezama Lima) **101**:121
File on a Diplomat (Brink) **18**:67-8; **36**:67, 69; **106**:99, 124, 126-27, 136-37
The File on Stanley Patton Buchta (Faust) **8**:215
Files on Parade (O'Hara) **42**:312, 320
"Filet" (Montague) **46**:270
La fille de Christophe Colomb (Ducharme) **74**:57
La fille de l'eau (Renoir) **20**:291, 301
"La fille Eva" (Theriault) **79**:407
La fille laide (Theriault) **79**:400, 408, 411-12, 419
"La fille noire" (Theriault) **79**:408
"Filling Night with the Name: Funeral as Local Color" (Warren) **39**:256, 272
"Filling Station" (Bishop) **9**:92; **32**:33, 38-9
"Filling the Boxes of Joseph Cornell" (Wakoski) **4**:571
"Filling the Forms" (Hoffman) **6**:243; **13**:289
Fillmore East (Zappa) **17**:587, 593
"A Film" (Barthelme) **115**:65
Film (Beckett) **6**:36; **9**:82, 84; **18**:43, 47; **59**:253, 255
Un film comme les autres (Godard) **20**:150
"Film Digression" (Sukenick) **48**:370
Film Flam (McMurtry) **127**:327-28
Film Is Evil: Radio Is Good (Foreman) **50**:160, 164-71, 173
A Film Like Any Other (Godard)
See *Un film comme les autres*

"Film Preview in the Morning" (Shiga) **33**:366
The Films in My Life (Truffaut) **101**:407
"Filo del amor" (Aleixandre) **9**:15
Filozofia przypadku (Lem) **149**:111, 120, 142, 156, 164, 256, 261
Fils de personne (Montherlant) **19**:327
Filth (Welsh) **144**:341-48
Filthy Lucre: or, The Tragedy of Andrew Ledwhistle and Richard Soleway (Bainbridge) **62**:36; **130**:27
Filthy Rich (Walker)
See *The Power Plays*
"Filthy with Things" (Boyle) **90**:62-3
"La Fin" (Beckett) **4**:51; **10**:34, 36
Fin de fiesta (Goytisolo)
See *The Party's Over*
La fin de la nuit (Mauriac) **56**:207-09
Fin de mundo (Neruda) **7**:257; **28**:310, 312
Fin de partie (Beckett) **1**:20, 24; **2**:44-6; **3**:44, 46-7; **4**:51; **6**:39-43, 47; **9**:84-5, 87; **10**:26, 30-1; **11**:37, 42-3; **14**:79; **18**:45, 47; **29**:54, 61, 65, 67; **59**:252-55, 257-59; **83**:108-51
El fin del mundo (Valdez) **84**:400, 406
El fin del viaje (Neruda) **62**:336
"Fin du monde" (Hébert) **29**:237
"Final" (Neruda) **28**:310
The Final Addiction (Condon) **100**:102-05
The Final Adventures of the Robber Hotzenplotz (Preussler) **17**:377
Final Analysis (Gould) **4**:200-01; **10**:241
Final Blackout (Hubbard) **43**:203-04, 206
"The Final Choruses for the Promised Land" (Ungaretti) **7**:485
The Final Circle of Paradise (Strugatskii and Strugatskii) **27**:435
Final Concrete Testament (Nichol) **18**:369
Final Curtain (Marsh) **53**:247, 254
The Final Cut (Pink Floyd) **35**:314-16
Final del juego (Cortázar) **2**:103-04; **13**:157; **33**:123, 126, 130; **34**:329, 332
"Final Dwarf" (Roth) **104**:284, 311
The Final Folly of Captain Dancy (Evans) **70**:332
The Final Hour (Caldwell) **28**:63; **39**:303
"The Final Martyrs" (Endō) **99**:298
The Final Martyrs (Endō) **99**:284, 288, 298, 300-01, 306-07
"Final Meeting" (Kizer) **80**:183
"The Final Night" (Faludy) **42**:140
"Final Notations" (Rich) **76**:212, 214, 218
The Final Opus of Leon Solomon (Badanes) **59**:38-42
The Final Passage (Phillips) **96**:315-17, 323-24, 329-30, 332, 335, 338, 341, 343, 352, 354
Final Payments (Gordon) **13**:249-50; **22**:185, 187-88; **128**:90-94, 96, 98-105, 107, 111-12, 114, 116-23, 125-28, 131-32, 134, 139-40, 142, 144, 146-47, 149, 151
The Final Programme (Moorcock) **27**:349-50; **58**:347-48, 357
"The Final Proof of Fate and Circumstance" (Abbott) **48**:5, 7
"the final solution" (Sanchez) **116**:278, 294
Final Solutions (Seidel) **18**:474-75
"A Final Sonnet" (Berrigan) **37**:42
"Final Trophy" (Ellison) **42**:131
"Finale: Presto" (Davison) **28**:100
"Finale/Your Eycs" (Larson) **99**:180
"Finally" (Jacobsen) **48**:193
"Finally I See Your Skin" (Lerman) **9**:329
The Financial Expert (Narayan) **7**:255; **28**:291, 299; **47**:301, 304, 307; **121**:331, 351-52, 356-57, 359-62, 371
"Financial Statement" (Slavitt) **14**:491
"The Financial World" (Brophy) **29**:91
"Financially the Paper..." (Barthelme) **46**:42
Finbar's Hotel (Johnston) **150**:26
"A Find" (Gordimer) **123**:129
Find a Victim (Macdonald) **41**:265, 268, 272
Find My Killer (Wellman) **49**:387, 391
Find the Changeling (Benford) **52**:67
Find Your Way Home (Hopkins) **4**:233-34
"The Finder" (Spencer) **22**:405
Finders (Friel)
See *Winners*
"Finding" (Davenport) **38**:141
Finding a Form (Gass) **132**:185-87, 195
"Finding a Girl in America" (Dubus) **36**:145-47; **97**:199, 201, 220, 226
Finding a Girl in America (Dubus) **36**:146, 148; **97**:198, 205, 208-09, 220, 231, 235
"Finding a Poem" (Snodgrass) **68**:384
"Finding a Remedy" (Longley) **29**:295
"Finding a Voice" (Welty) **105**:320-22, 378, 382
"Finding an Old Ant Mansion" (Bly) **38**:54-5, 58-60; **128**:45
Finding Gold (Norris) **14**:387
Finding Losses (Bronk) **10**:75
"Finding Natasha" (Bell) **102**:6, 8
"The Finding of the Way" (MacLennan) **92**:344
Finding the Centre (Naipaul) **37**:325-29; **105**:172-73, 179
"Finding the Haystack in the Needle" (Jordan) **114**:153
Finding the Islands (Merwin) **45**:273, 278; **88**:194-95
Finding the Sun (Albee) **53**:23-4; **86**:120-21, 124
Finding Them Lost, and Other Poems (Moss) **45**:292; **50**:353
Findings (Berry) **8**:85; **46**:69-70
Findings (Howard) **7**:166, 168; **10**:276; **47**:168
A Fine and Private Place (Beagle) **7**:25-6; **104**:2-7, 10, 24-5
A Fine and Private Place (Callaghan) **14**:102; **41**:88-90, 94-6; **65**:245, 248-50, 253
A Fine and Private Place (Queen) **11**:465
"Fine As Fine Can Be" (Lightfoot) **26**:281
Fine Clothes to the Jew (Hughes) **1**:147; **10**:279; **44**:508, 511; **108**:293-94, 310, 319, 323
A Fine Day (Vesaas)
See *Ein vakker dag*
"Fine del '68" (Montale) **9**:387
A Fine Madness (Baker) **8**:38-9
"Fine Memory" (Seger) **35**:380
Fine Mess (Céline)
See *Les Beaux Draps*
"A Fine Old Firm" (Jackson) **60**:229
A Fine Red Rain (Kaminsky) **59**:171
A Fine Romance (Seton) **27**:425-29
A Fine, Soft Day (Forman) **21**:122
"A Fine Son" (Dahl)
See "Genesis and Catastrophe"
"Fine Western Land: Cloud-Light" (Buckley) **57**:136
"The Fine White Mist of Winter" (Oates) **134**:245
Finest Short Stories of Seán O'Faoláin (O'Faolain) **31**:340; **70**:318
"The Finger" (Creeley) **36**:121
Finger of Fire (Braine) **41**:60
"Finger Prints" (Seifert) **93**:325, 331
"Finger Wet, Finger Dry" (Bates) **46**:62
"Fingernail Sunrise" (Watkins) **43**:450
"Fingers and Toes" (Michaels) **25**:315
Fingers at Air: Experimental Poems, 1969 (Shapcott) **38**:399-401
Fingers in the Door (Tuohy) **37**:428-30, 432
Fingers of Hermes (Squires) **51**:377, 381
Finian's Rainbow (Coppola) **16**:232, 244
"Finis Not Tragedy" (Smith) **64**:399
The Finished Man (Garrett) **3**:190; **11**:220; **51**:141-42, 145-46
The Finishing School (Godwin) **69**:236-39, 243, 246, 252; **125**:141-45, 149, 167-69
"Finishing the Hat" (Sondheim) **30**:403;
The Finishing Touch (Brophy) **29**:92-4; **105**:7-8, 12, 30, 38-9, 41-2
Finishing Touches (Kerr) **22**:257-58
"Finistère" (Kinsella) **138**:102-03, 121, 162
"Finisterre" (Plath) **111**:214
Finisterre (Montale) **7**:221-22, 226
Finn and Hengest: The Fragment and the Episode (Tolkien) **38**:440, 442
Finnegan's Funeral Parlor and Ice Cream Shoppe (Kerr) **59**:400-02
"Finnish Rhapsody" (Ashbery) **77**:69-70
A Finnish Suite (Haavikko)
See *Suomalainen sarja*
Finnley Wren (Wylie) **43**:461-63, 469-71
"Fiona the First" (Kinsella) **27**:237
Il fiore della Mille e una notte (Pasolini) **20**:270; **106**:226, 241, 248, 250, 266, 270
"Fire" (Creeley) **78**:135
"The Fire" (Dickinson) **49**:102
"The Fire" (Duncan) **15**:190-91; **41**:124, 130
"Fire" (Hoffman) **6**:244
"Fire" (Hughes) **108**:297
"Fire" (Levine) **118**:296
"Fire" (Ryan) **65**:216
"Fire" (Williams) **148**:362
Fire (Pa Chin) **18**:374
Fire and Blood (Jünger)
See *Feuer und Blut*
"Fire and Cloud" (Wright) **14**:596-97; **21**:444, 453-54
Fire and Ice (Stegner) **49**:347
The Fire and the Anvil (Baxter) **14**:60, 62-3
The Fire and the Sun: Why Plato Banished the Artists (Murdoch) **51**:289, 291
"Fire and the Tide" (Stevenson) **33**:381
"The Fire Autumn" (Murray) **40**:334-36
"The Fire Balloons" (Bradbury) **10**:71
"The Fire Down Below" (Seger) **35**:382, 386
Fire Down Below (Golding) **81**:317-18, 320, 325-26
"The Fire Eaters" (Bates) **46**:63
The Fire Engine That Disappeared (Wahlöö)
See *Brandbilen som foerwann*
"Fire Escape" (Woolrich) **77**:390
Fire from Heaven (Renault) **3**:426; **17**:400
"The Fire i' the Flint" (Heaney) **74**:178
Fire in the Basement (Kohout) **13**:325
Fire in the Belly: On Being a Man (Keen) **70**:420, 422-23, 425-26, 458
"Fire in the Hole" (Becker and Fagen) **26**:84
Fire in the Morning (Spencer) **22**:398-400, 403
Fire in the Stone (Thiele) **17**:494-95
"Fire in the Vineyards" (Boyle) **58**:71
"Fire Island" (Swenson) **14**:519; **106**:349-50
"Fire Lake" (Seger) **35**:384-86
"The Fire Next Time" (Baldwin) **42**:15-17, 19; **50**:284; **127**:144
The Fire Next Time (Baldwin) **2**:32-3; **3**:31; **4**:41; **5**:41; **8**:41-2; **13**:52-3; **15**:42-3; **17**:25, 28, 34, 36, 38, 42; **42**:14-19, 22-3; **50**:282, 291-93, 295; **67**:8, 27; **127**:104-08, 112, 114, 116, 144, 148
"Fire Now Wakening on the River" (Chappell) **78**:96
"The Fire of Despair Has Been Our Saviour" (Bly) **38**:60
"Fire on Belmont Street" (Davidson) **19**:127
"Fire on Greenstone" (Ihimaera) **46**:195
Fire on Stone (Gustafson) **36**:215-18
Fire on the Mountain (Abbey) **36**:13, 15-16; **59**:241
Fire on the Mountain (Desai) **19**:133; **37**:70, 72; **97**:144, 149-50, 159, 161-63, 168-69, 171, 177, 180, 186
The Fire Screen (Merrill) **2**:274-75; **6**:323; **13**:380-82; **91**:228, 230
Fire Sequence (Winters) **32**:468
"The Fire Sermon" (Eliot) **9**:183; **10**:169; **15**:212; **41**:155-56; **113**:223
Fire Sermon (Morris) **3**:343; **7**:245-46; **37**:313
"Fire Station" (Bukowski) **82**:14, 17, 22
"Fire Storm" (Alexie) **96**:10; **154**:28
"Fire: The People" (Corn) **33**:116
"A Fire Truck" (Wilbur) **53**:410; **110**:353, 384
"The Firebombing" (Dickey) **1**:73; **2**:115; **7**:80-1, 84; **47**:93; **109**:238, 244, 266, 272, 281-82

Firebrand (Troyat) **23**:457
"The Firebug" (Sillitoe) **57**:388; **148**:198
The Firebugs: A Learning Play without a Lesson (Frisch)
See *Biedermann und die Brandstifter: Ein Lehrstuck ohne Lehre*
Firecracker (Henley)
See *The Miss Firecracker Contest*
Firecrackers (Van Vechten) **33**:388, 397-98
"Fire-Damp" (Sciascia)
See "L'antimonio"
The Fire-Dwellers (Laurence) **3**:281; **50**:312, 314-15, 319, 321; **62**:269-72, 279, 282, 284-86, 291-92, 306
The Fire-Eaters (MacEwen) **13**:358; **55**:164
Firefall (Van Duyn) **116**:417-18, 420-23, 426-27
"The Firefighter" (Kinsella) **43**:256-57
"Fireflies" (Hollander) **2**:197
"Fireflies" (Muske) **90**:309-10, 312
Fireflies (Naipaul) **32**:323-25, 327; **39**:355-56, 358
Fireflood, and Other Stories (McIntyre) **18**:327
Firefly Summer (Binchy) **153**:67, 70, 76, 78
Firekeeper (Medoff) **23**:294
"The Fireman" (Bradbury) **98**:108-09, 111, 114-15, 144
Fireman Flower and Other Stories (Sansom) **2**:383
"Fires" (Carver) **36**:103, 107; **55**:283; **126**:142-43, 157, 164, 168
"The Fires" (Shiga) **33**:367
Fires (Yourcenar)
See *Feux*
Fires: Essays, Poems, Stories, 1966-1982 (Carver) **39**:99, 106; **53**:66; **126**:131, 133, 135, 141-43, 145, 148, 151, 157
Fires in th tempul OR th jinx ship nd othr trips (Bissett) **18**:60
Fires in the Mirror: Crown Heights, Brooklyn and Other Identities (Smith) **86**:266, 268-72
Fires in the Sky: The Birth and Death of Stars (Gallant) **17**:132
Fires of Azeroth (Cherryh) **35**:106, 112
The Fires of Spring (Michener) **29**:309-11; **109**:377
"Fires on Llyrn" (Clarke) **61**:79-81
Fires on the Plain (Ichikawa)
See *Nobi*
The Fire's Reflection (Trifonov)
See *The Campfire Reflection*
"The Fires Within" (Clarke) **3**:125, 129, 135, 143, 149; **136**:210
Fireship (Vinge) **30**:409-10
Fireship and Mother and Child (Vinge) **30**:409
Firestarter (King) **26**:236-37, 241; **37**:199, 201, 203, 205; **61**:319, 331; **113**:335-36, 338, 343, 345, 347, 369-70, 388, 391
"Firesticks" (Kunitz) **148**:91
The Firewalkers (King) **145**:350
"Firewater" (Chappell) **40**:145
Fireweed (Paton Walsh) **35**:430, 433
Fireweeds (Weiss) **8**:546; **14**:553-54, 556-57
"Firewood" (Banks) **72**:5
"Firewood" (Chappell) **40**:144
"Firewood" (McPhee) **36**:296
"Fireworks" (Shapiro) **15**:475
Fireworks (Thompson) **69**:388
Fireworks: A History and Celebration (Plimpton) **36**:357
Fireworks: Nine Profane Pieces (Carter) **5**:101-03; **41**:121
The Firm (Grisham) **84**:190-97, 199
Firm Beliefs of William Faulkner (Brooks)
See *On the Prejudices, Predilections, and Firm Beliefs of William Faulkner*
Firozsha Baag (Mistry)
See *Tales from Firozsha Baag*
"First" (Avison) **97**:82
"The First" (Soto) **80**:277
"The First Adam" (Gardam) **43**:171
"First Advertisements for Myself" (Mailer) **111**:120
"First American Ode" (Barker) **48**:13
"A First American Views His Land" (Momaday) **85**:265, 268
First and Last Loves (Betjeman) **6**:67; **34**:311; **43**:38, 43
First and Last Words (Chappell) **78**:98
First and Vital Candle (Wiebe) **14**:574; **138**:309, 330, 351
First Blues: Rags, Ballads, and Harmonium Songs (Ginsberg) **36**:196
The First Book of Ballet (Streatfeild) **21**:401
The First Book of Jazz (Hughes) **108**:300
The First Book of Negroes (Hughes) **108**:291-92
First Book of Odes (Bunting) **39**:297
The First Born Son (Buckler) **13**:120
"First Boyfriend" (Olds) **85**:294
The First Chronicles of Thomas Covenant: The Unbeliever (Donaldson)
See *The Chronicles of Thomas Covenant, the Unbeliever*
The First Circle (Solzhenitsyn)
See *V kruge pervom*
The First Cities (Lorde) **18**:307; **71**:240, 257
First Comes Courage (Arzner) **98**:69, 73-4, 87, 93-5
"First Communion" (Fante) **60**:133
"First Communion" (Kinnell) **5**:217; **129**:255
"The First Communion" (Suknaski) **19**:432
First Communion (Arrabal)
See *La communion solonelle*
"First Confession" (Kennedy) **42**:255
"First Conjugation" (O'Faolain) **47**:325
"First Dark" (Spencer) **22**:405-06
"The First Day" (Jones) **76**:64-5, 67
"The First Day" (Nemerov) **36**:304
"First Day after the War" (Kunene) **85**:175
"First Day of School" (Squires) **51**:381, 383
"The First Day of Summer" (Saroyan) **29**:362
"First Day of the Future" (Kinnell) **129**:249
"First Day of Winter" (Pancake) **29**:348, 350
"The First Day Out from Troy" (Squires) **51**:381
The First Deadly Sin (Sanders) **41**:377-79
"First Death" (Justice) **102**:269, 285
"First Death in Nova Scotia" (Bishop) **9**:91; **32**:33-4, 37-8
The First Decade (Duncan) **15**:187-88; **55**:294
"The First Declension" (Gardam) **43**:167
"First Draft of Cantos I-III" (Pound) **10**:400
"First Dream" (Guillén)
See "Primero sueño"
"First Encounter" (Clarke) **35**:122
First Encounter (Dos Passos)
See *One Man's Initiation—1917*
First Encounters (Ulibarrí)
See *Primeros encuentros/First Encounters*
"First Essay on Interest" (Murray) **40**:343
"First Exercise" (Ryan) **65**:209
"First Fall" (Bernard) **59**:44
The First Fast Draw (L'Amour) **25**:280
"First Fight. Then Fiddle" (Brooks) **5**:76
"The First Flight" (Heaney) **91**:117
"First Flight" (Van Duyn) **7**:498; **63**:436; **116**:402, 406, 412
"First Foot" (Campbell) **42**:89
The First Four (Merwin) **88**:205
The First Freedom: The Tumultuous History of Free Speech in America (Hentoff) **26**:185-87
"First Frost" (Simic) **49**:341
"First Frost" (Voznesensky) **57**:414-15
"First Goodbye" (Glück) **44**:216
"First Heat" (Taylor) **71**:309-11, 313-15
"First Hippy Revolution" (Garnett) **3**:189
First Holy Communion (Arrabal)
See *La communion solonelle*
"First Hymn to Lenin" (MacDiarmid) **2**:255; **19**:289; **63**:245, 253-54
"A 'First Impression' (Tokyo)" (Blunden) **56**:39, 46
First Indian on the Moon (Alexie) **96**:5, 7-12, 17; **154**:7, 9-14, 26-7
"First Inning" (Hall) **151**:200
"The First Invasion of Ireland" (Montague) **46**:266
"The First Kingdom" (Heaney) **74**:169
First Lady (Endō) **99**:285
"First Lesson" (Willard) **37**:463
First Lesson (White) **30**:449
"First Lesson about Man" (Merton) **83**:396-97
"First Light" (Kinsella) **138**:97-98
First Light (Ackroyd) **140**:9, 28-9, 32-3, 39, 41-5, 49
First Light (Baxter) **78**:19-21, 25-26, 30-32
"The First Line" (Moss) **45**:287-88, 293
"First Love" (Olds) **85**:295
"First Love" (Welty) **1**:361; **105**:298, 385
First Love (Beckett)
See *Premier amour*
"First Love and Other Sorrows" (Brodkey) **56**:55-6, 63
First Love, and Other Stories (Beckett) **3**:47; **6**:38-9; **29**:56
First Love, Last Rites (McEwan) **13**:369-71; **66**:275-76, 280, 292, 294
First Lover, and Other Stories (Boyle) **58**:64
"The First Madam" (Schaeffer) **11**:491
The First Man in Rome: Marius (McCullough) **107**:153, 155-58, 163-66
"First Manhattans" (Gilchrist) **48**:120; **143**:316
First Manifesto (McGrath) **59**:177
First Marriage (Howe) **47**:175
"First Meditation" (Roethke) **101**:312
"First Meeting with Ivan Shark" (Dobyns) **37**:77
"The First Men on Mercury" (Morgan) **31**:275
"First Names and Empty Pockets" (Kinsella) **27**:237
"First Night" (Olds) **32**:346; **85**:286
"The First Night of Fall and Falling Rain" (Schwartz) **45**:355
First Papers (Hobson) **25**:272
First Person Singular (Maugham) **67**:209
First Poems (Merrill) **2**:272, 274-75; **3**:335; **13**:379; **91**:228, 230
First Poems (Turco) **11**:550; **63**:428, 430
First Poems, 1946-1954 (Kinnell) **13**:321
"First Prayer" (Atwood) **13**:44
"First prayer for the hottentotsgod" (Breytenbach) **126**:64
"First Principal" (Guthrie) **23**:199
"The First Report of the Shipwrecked Foreigner to the Kadanh of Derb" (Le Guin) **45**:213
The First Sally or The Trap of Gargantius (Lem) **149**:274
"The First Seven Years" (Malamud) **27**:306; **44**:412
"First Sex" (Olds) **85**:297
"The First Shot" (Achebe) **7**:6; **11**:3; **26**:24
"First Sight" (Larkin) **5**:227; **39**:336
"First Snow" (Mosher) **62**:313
"First Snow" (Nemerov) **36**:304
"First Snow" (Oliver) **34**:246
"First Snow" (Sarton) **49**:320
"The First Snow in Alsace" (Wilbur) **6**:570; **53**:397; **110**:381
"First Sonata for Karlen Paula" (Sandburg) **35**:356
The First Songs (Nyro) **17**:313
"First South and Cambridge" (Hugo) **32**:236
"The First Spade in the West" (Fiedler) **13**:214
"The First Sunday" (Blaga) **75**:62
The First Teacher (Aitmatov)
See *Pervyi uchitel'*
"The First Thing the Baby Did Wrong..." (Barthelme) **46**:42
"First Things, and Last" (Nemerov) **36**:308
"First Things First" (Elytis) **100**:191
First Things Last (Malouf) **28**:268
"The First Time" (Creeley) **78**:135
"First Trip through the Automatic Carwash" (Van Duyn) **63**:444-45; **116**:413

First Will and Testament (Patchen) **18**:392
"The First Year of My Life" (Spark) **40**:403
"Firstborn" (Wright) **6**:580
The Firstborn (Fry) **2**:144; **10**:200-01; **14**:186, 188
Firstborn (Glück) **7**:118-19; **22**:173-76; **44**:216
"Firsts" (Ciardi) **40**:162; **129**:47
"The Fish" (Banks) **72**:3, 5
"Fish" (Barthelme) **117**:18
"The Fish" (Bishop) **1**:34-5; **4**:66; **32**:29, 32, 37-8, 42-3
"The Fish" (Clark) **5**:105
"The Fish" (Dinesen) **29**:159
"The Fish" (Moore) **2**:291; **4**:362; **10**:353; **47**:260, 262, 266
"The Fish" (Oliver) **34**:249; **98**:257, 272, 290, 297
"The Fish Are All Sick" (Stevenson) **33**:383
"Fish Bones" (Oliver) **98**:283
The Fish Can Sing (Laxness)
See *Brekkukotsannáll*
"The Fish Counter at Bonneville" (Stafford) **29**:381
"Fish Crier" (Sandburg) **15**:468; **35**:355
"Fish Fry" (Bass) **143**:4
"The Fish of His Woman" (Dacey) **51**:80
"Fish Shop" (Townshend) **42**:379-81
Fish, Sweet Giraffe, the Lion Snake and Owl (Dacey) **51**:78
Fish Tales (Jones) **34**:67-9
"The Fish Tales: A Conversation with 'Contemporary Sophist'" (Fish) **142**:187
"The Fish that Walked" (Sexton) **123**:425
"Fish, Tomatoes, Mama, and Book" (Major) **19**:298
"The Fish Who Could Close His Eyes" (Clark) **28**:79
The Fisher King (Gilliam) **141**:249-50, 255-56, 259
"The Fisherman" (Banks) **37**:26
"Fisherman" (Dunn) **40**:170
"Fisherman" (Kinnell) **129**:237
"The Fisherman" (O'Brien) **103**:146, 148
"Fisherman" (Watkins) **43**:450
The Fisherman and His Wife (DeMarinis) **54**:98
"The Fisherman from Chihuahua" (Connell) **45**:114
"A Fisherman of the Inland Sea" (Le Guin) **136**:385
A Fisherman of the Inland Sea (Le Guin) **136**:383-85
Fisherman's Spring (Haig-Brown) **21**:137
Fisherman's Summer (Haig-Brown) **21**:138, 142
The Fisherman's Whore (Smith) **22**:384-85, 387, 389; **42**:352, 356
Fisherman's Winter (Haig-Brown) **21**:137-38
"The Fishermen at South Head" (Murray) **40**:343
"The Fishermen of the Seine" (Humphrey) **45**:205
Fishermen with Ploughs: A Poem Cycle (Brown) **5**:76-8; **48**:53-4, 57; **100**:84
"The Fisher's Wish" (Goldbarth) **5**:144
"The Fisherwoman's Daughter" (Le Guin) **136**:326-27, 333, 364, 366, 369, 374
"The Fish-Hawk" (Wheelock) **14**:571
"Fishing" (Nye) **42**:305
"Fishing" (Thomas) **13**:545
Fishing (Weller) **10**:525-26; **53**:389-90, 392
"Fishing Fever" (Davis) **49**:92
"Fishing for Albacore" (Smith) **6**:513
"The Fishing Lake" (Spencer) **22**:406
"Fishing Off Nova Scotia" (Olds) **32**:346
"The Fishing Pole of the Drowned Man" (Carver) **36**:107
"Fishing the Olearia Tree" (Hulme) **130**:66
"Fishing the White Water" (Lorde) **71**:257
"The Fishing-Boat Picture" (Sillitoe) **57**:388; **148**:165, 198
"Fishnet" (Lowell) **8**:355; **124**:256
Fiskadoro (Johnson) **52**:235-41
"Fission" (Graham) **118**:252
"Fission" (Sayles) **14**:483
"Fist" (Levine) **118**:283, 299, 303
"The Fist" (Walcott) **14**:549; **42**:422; **76**:285
The Fist Too Was Once the Palm of an Open Hand and Fingers (Amichai)
See *Gam ha'egrof haya pa'am yad ptuba ve'etsba'ot*
Die Fistelstimme (Hofmann) **54**:224
Le fiston (Pinget) **7**:305; **13**:442
"A Fit against the Country" (Wright) **28**:462
"Fits" (Munro) **50**:208, 210, 214-16, 218, 220
"Fitter's Night" (Miller) **47**:249-50
"The Fitting" (Barnard) **48**:25-6
"The Fitting of the Mask" (Kunitz) **148**:69, 88
Fitting Words (Arghezi)
See *Cuvinte potrivite*
"Five" (Cummings) **15**:161
"5" (Fearing)
See "American Rhapsody"
5 (Reading) **47**:352-54
"Five Accounts of a Monogamous Man" (Meredith) **13**:375; **22**:302; **55**:191
Five Acre Virgin, and Other Stories (Jolley) **46**:214
Five Ages (Levi) **41**:247-48
"Five Ages of a Poet" (Levi) **41**:248
Five Alone (Derleth) **31**:127-28
"Five A.M." (Fearing) **51**:119
"Five A.M. in the Pine Woods" (Oliver) **98**:283, 292
"Five American Sonnets" (Simmons) **43**:412, 414
"Five Bells" (Slessor) **14**:493-95, 498
Five Bells (Slessor) **14**:495-96
Five Biblical Portraits (Wiesel) **37**:455, 457
Five Boyhoods (Updike) **23**:463
"Five Chinese Songs" (Guillén) **79**:229
Five Corners (Shanley) **75**:322-23, 326-28, 330, 332
Five Days in June (Heym) **41**:216-18
Five Decades (Shaw) **34**:369
Five Decades, a Selection: Poems, 1925-1970 (Neruda) **5**:303; **7**:260
"Five Domestic Interiors" (Scannell) **49**:330
"The Five Faces of Pity" (Barker) **8**:46; **48**:14
Five Finger Exercise (Shaffer) **5**:386, 388-89; **14**:484-86; **18**:475-76
"Five Flights Up" (Bishop) **32**:37
Five for Sorrow, Ten for Joy (Godden) **53**:162
Five Gates to Hell (Clavell) **87**:18
"Five Generations" (Porter) **33**:318
"The Five Gold Bands" (Vance) **35**:419
"Five Green Waves" (Brown) **48**:52
"Five Highways" (Moure) **88**:221, 227
Five Hours with Mario (Delibes)
See *Cinco horas con Mario*
Five Hundred Scorpions (Hearon) **63**:166-68
"Five Letters from an Eastern Empire" (Gray) **41**:179, 183
Five Little Pigs (Christie)
See *Murder in Retrospect*
"The Five Master Terms" (Burke) **24**:127
Five Masters: A Study in the Mutation of the Novel (Krutch) **24**:281
"Five Meals" (Hacker) **72**:192
"Five Men" (Herbert) **43**:190
"Five Men against the Theme, 'My Name is Red Hot. Yo Name ain Doodley Squat'" (Brooks) **49**:36, 38
"Five O'Clock Shadow" (Betjeman) **6**:69
Five Patients (Crichton) **2**:108
"Five Pedantic Pieces" (Ashbery) **15**:34
Five Plays (Mortimer) **28**:286
Five Plays (Shepard) **4**:489; **17**:436
Five Plays of Langston Hughes (Hughes) **35**:217
Five Poems (Avison) **97**:67
"Five Poems about Poetry" (Oppen) **7**:281
"Five Poems from Japanese Paintings" (Pollitt) **28**:367-68; **122**:202
"Five Poems on Film Directors" (Morgan) **31**:276
"Five Points" (Munro) **95**:307, 310, 314
Five Seasons (Angell) **26**:30-2
"Five Senses" (Wright) **53**:424, 428-29
"The Five Senses: A Bestiary" (Dacey) **51**:79
Five Senses: Selected Poems (Wright) **53**:423-25, 431
"Five Short Moral Poems" (Levi) **41**:248
Five Signs of God's Decay (Mishima)
See *The Decay of the Angel*
The Five Stages of Grief: Poems (Pastan) **27**:369-70
"Five Stanzas to Thoreau" (Transtroemer)
See "Fem strofer till Thoreau"
Five Stories of Ferrara (Bassani) **9**:76
5 Tales and 2 Fables (Benet)
See *5 narraciones y 2 fábulas*
"Five Visions of Captain Cook" (Slessor) **14**:492, 494-95
"The Five Voyages of Arnor" (Brown) **48**:57
"Five Walks on the Edge" (Viereck) **4**:559
"Five Ways of Facing the Deep" (Booth) **23**:75
A Five Year Sentence (Rubens) **19**:404
"Five Years" (Bowie) **17**:59
Five Years (Goodman) **2**:171; **4**:196-97
Five Years (Levinson) **49**:226-27
The Five-Fold Mesh (Belitt) **22**:48, 52
"The Five-Forty-Eight" (Cheever) **15**:130; **64**:48, 65
Fives (Dacey) **51**:82
"The Five-Thousandth Baritone" (Newman) **8**:419
"Five-Twenty" (White) **5**:487; **7**:533
"Fixed" (Dunn) **40**:166
"Fixed Ideas" (Slessor) **14**:493
"Fixed Opinions" (Slessor)
See "Fixed Ideas"
The Fixer (Malamud) **1**:198-99; **2**:266, 268-69; **3**:321-23; **5**:269-70; **9**:348-49; **11**:348-51, 354; **18**:319-20; **27**:295-98, 301-02; **44**:411, 413, 415, 417, 419; **78**:271; **85**:200
"Fixing a Hole" (Lennon and McCartney) **12**:359
Fixity (Lezama Lima)
See *La fijeza*
Fizzles (Beckett)
See *Foirades*
A Flag for Sunrise (Stone) **23**:426-31; **42**:359-63
A Flag on the Island: A Fantasy for a Small Screen (Naipaul) **13**:404-05; **105**:157
"The Flag Rave" (Murray) **40**:338
Flagons and Apples (Jeffers) **54**:233-35, 244, 250; **11**:305
"Flags" (Moure) **88**:217
Flags in the Dust (Faulkner)
See *Sartoris*
"Flake" (Morgan) **31**:275
"Flakes" (Zappa) **17**:593
"The Flame" (Pound) **48**:288
Flame into Being (Burgess) **40**:124
The Flame of Life (Sillitoe) **6**:500; **148**:157, 189
The Flame of New Orleans (Clair) **20**:70
The Flames (Ali)
See *Sholay*
Flames Across the Border: The Canadian-American Tragedy, 1813-1814 (Berton) **104**:42-3, 46, 59
"Flames and Generosities" (Howe) **152**:183, 213
Flames Going Out (Platt) **26**:354-56
Flaming Bodies (Wilson) **33**:463-64
"Flaming Eternity" (p'Bitek) **96**:287
The Flaming Sword (Neruda) **28**:314
Flamingo Feather (van der Post) **5**:463
"Flamingos Fly" (Morrison) **21**:237
"Flamingos of the Soda Lakes" (Lieberman) **36**:261
The Flanders Road (Simon)
See *La route des Flandres*

A Flann O'Brien Reader (O'Brien) **47**:317
Flannery O'Connor's South (Coles) **108**:179, 180, 183
Flare Path (Rattigan) **7**:354
"Flash" (Arreola) **147**:13, 16, 18, 34
Flash and Filigree (Southern) **7**:452
"Flash Flood" (Snodgrass) **68**:397
"The Flash of Fireflies" (Gordimer) **123**:144-45
A Flash of Green (MacDonald) **44**:408
"A Flashing Cliff" (Rukeyser) **27**:406
"The Flashing Pigeons as They Wheel" (Goodman) **4**:197
The Flashman Papers (Fraser) **7**:106
"Flat in Ringsend" (Binchy) **153**:65
"A Flat One" (Snodgrass) **68**:388
Flats (Wurlitzer) **2**:482-84; **4**:597-98; **15**:588-89
"The Flats Road" (Munro) **95**:300, 303
"Flatted Fifth" (Hughes) **35**:222
"Flattery" (Lopate) **29**:302
"Flaubert in Egypt" (Warren) **6**:555; **8**:538
"The Flaubert Pavilion" (Simpson) **149**:353
Flaubert y "Madame Bovary" (Vargas Llosa)
See *La orgía perpetua: Flaubert y "Madame Bovary"*
"Flaubert's Early Prose" (Creeley) **78**:141
Flaubert's Parrot (Barnes) **42**:27-30; **141**:31-3, 39, 48, 53-4, 58-67, 71, 73-7
Flavio (Parks) **16**:460
The Flavor of Green Tea over Rice (Ozu) **16**:450
"The Flaw" (Lowell) **8**:354; **124**:298
The Flaw (Samarakis) **5**:381-82
"Flawless Play Restored: The Masque of Fungo" (Sorrentino) **14**:500
Flaws in the Glass (White) **65**:274, 276; **69**:406-07, 410
The Flea Circus (Brammer) **31**:53-4
A Flea in Her Ear (The Brothers Quay) **95**:347, 350
The Flea of Sodom (Dahlberg) **7**:67; **14**:137
Flèche d'Orient (Morand) **41**:304
"Flee on Your Donkey" (Sexton) **6**:493; **10**:468; **123**:444
"Fleecing" (Gilliatt) **10**:230
"Fleeting Friendships" (Castellanos) **66**:60-1
"Fleetwood Cafe" (Baxter) **78**:28
"Flemish Rain" (Szirtes) **46**:393, 395
The Flemish Shop (Simenon) **47**:371
"Flesh" (Thomas) **132**:382
"Flesh" (Wright) **53**:420, 424
Flesh (Brophy) **6**:100; **11**:68; **29**:92, 97-8; **105**:10, 29-30, 32-33
Flesh (Farmer) **19**:164
Flesh and Blood (Hamill) **10**:251
Flesh and Blood (Humphreys) **47**:181-82, 184, 187, 190
Flesh and Blood (Williams) **56**:425-29; **148**:311, 314, 317-18, 320, 325-27, 329, 332, 338, 340-41, 344, 356, 359, 361
"Flesh and the Mirror" (Carter) **5**:103
The Flesh in the Furnace (Koontz) **78**:199-200
"Fleshing-out the Season" (Komunyakaa) **94**:234
"La fleur qui disait amour" (Theriault) **79**:408
"Les fleurs" (Ligotti) **44**:54
Les fleurs bleues (Queneau) **10**:430-32
Fleuve profond, sombre rivière (Yourcenar) **50**:364; **87**:401
Le fleuvre de feu (Mauriac) **56**:204, 206
"Flexion" (Zamora) **89**:363
Die Fliegenpein (Canetti) **86**:301
Ein fliehendes Pferd (Walser) **27**:463-64
"Flies" (Grace) **56**:122
"The Flies" (Kureishi) **135**:276, 284, 291
"Flies" (Silverberg) **140**:378
The Flies (Sartre)
See *Les mouches*
"Flight" (Grau) **146**:151
"Flight" (Johnston) **51**:239, 244, 251
"Flight" (Kenny) **87**:255
"Flight" (McGuane) **45**:266
"The Flight" (Neruda) **62**:332
"The Flight" (Roethke) **11**:481
"Flight" (Steinbeck) **21**:369, 381, 389, 391-92; **124**:394, 396
"Flight" (Swan) **69**:360-61, 363-64
"Flight" (Williams) **148**:325
Flight 115 (O'Hara) **78**:364
"Flight from Byzantium" (Brodsky) **50**:132
Flight from Fiesta (Waters) **88**:358
Flight from Nevèrÿon (Delany) **141**:149, 154-57
The Flight from the Enchanter (Murdoch) **1**:233-34, 236; **2**:295; **3**:345, 347; **6**:345-48; **11**:386-87; **15**:381-84; **31**:293, 295
Flight into Camden (Storey) **2**:423; **4**:528
"Flight into Darkness" (Gustafson) **36**:211, 214, 216, 218
"The Flight Into Egypt" (Buckley) **57**:129
"The Flight into Egypt" (Merton) **83**:378
"Flight into Super-Time" (Smith) **43**:422
"The Flight of Apollo" (Kunitz) **148**:89, 96, 100-02, 133
Flight of Exiles (Bova) **45**:67
The Flight of Icarus (Queneau)
See *Le vol d'Icare*
The Flight of Mr. MacKinley (Leonov)
See *Begstvo Mistera Mak-Kinli*
"The Flight of Pigeons from the Palace" (Barthelme) **46**:36; **115**:80
"A Flight of Ravens" (Bradbury) **42**:33
The Flight of Sandukov (Leonov)
See *Volk*
"The Flight of the Earls" (Boland) **67**:46
The Flight of the Falcon (du Maurier) **59**:280-81, 284
Flight of the Falcon (Smith)
See *A Falcon Flies*
The Flight of the Wild Gander: Explorations in the Mythological Dimension (Campbell) **69**:76
"Flight Pattern" (Greenberg) **30**:166
Flight to Africa (Clarke) **6**:110-11; **9**:167
Flight to Canada (Reed) **13**:479-80; **32**:355-56, 358-59, 364; **60**:302, 313
Flight to the West (Rice) **7**:360-61; **49**:300, 302, 304
Flight Today and Tomorrow (Hyde) **21**:171, 175
"Flighting for Duck" (Empson) **19**:158
Flightpoint (Weiss)
See *Fluchtpunkt*
Flights (King) **8**:321
Flights (Shepard) **36**:405-07
Flights of Angels (Gilchrist) **143**:309
"Flights of Fancy" (Trevor) **14**:537
"Fling" (Hersey) **81**:329
Fling, and Other Stories (Hersey) **81**:329-30, 332
The Flint Anchor (Warner) **7**:511-12; **19**:460
"The Flitting" (McGuckian) **48**:276
Floaters (Ezekiel) **34**:46-8
"Floating" (Rexroth) **112**:398
Floating Bear (Baraka) **115**:3
"The Floating Bridge of Dreams" (Tanizaki)
See "Yume no ukihashi"
Floating Dragon (Straub) **28**:411; **107**:265, 267-68, 271, 274-78, 280-83, 285, 288-90, 302, 304-10
"The Floating Feathers Shield" (Momaday) **85**:280
The Floating Light Bulb (Allen) **52**:44-5
The Floating Opera (Barth) **2**:36; **3**:38, 42; **7**:23; **9**:68, 72; **10**:21-2; **14**:49-51, 56; **27**:26-7, 29; **51**:20-1; **89**:8-9, 17, 27, 47-8
"The Floating Poem, Unnumbered" (Rich) **73**:331; **125**:312-13
"The Floating Truth" (Paley) **37**:337
The Floating World (Kadohata) **59**:63-69; **122**:190-99
The Floating World (Michener) **109**:376, 379, 382
"The Flock" (Walcott) **42**:422
"A Flock of Trouble" (Davis) **49**:94
"The Flood" (Clark Bekedermo) **38**:129
"The Flood" (Richter) **30**:329
"The Flood" (Tomlinson) **45**:397-98, 400-01, 403
"The Flood" (Wright) **53**:417
The Flood (Le Clézio)
See *Le déluge*
Flood (Grass) **4**:202; **15**:260
Flood (Matthews) **40**:322, 324
The Flood (Tomlinson) **45**:396-98, 400-04
Flood (Vachss) **106**:354, 357-59, 361, 365
Flood (Warren) **59**:302
Flood: A Romance of Our Time (Warren) **1**:356; **4**:578; **8**:540
"Flood Burial" (Foote) **75**:230-31
"Flood Light" (Matthews) **40**:322
"Flood Plain" (Matthews) **40**:324
"Flood Tide" (Yehoshua) **31**:468-69
The Flood unto my Soul (Oe)
See *Kōzui wa waga tamashii ni oyobi*
"Flooded Meadows" (Gunn) **3**:216
"The Flooded Valley" (Mathias) **45**:235, 238
The Flooded Valley (Mathias) **45**:234-35
"Floods" (Raine) **103**:194
"Floods of Florence" (Ochs) **17**:332
"Floodtide" (Bova) **45**:73
Floodtide (Yerby) **1**:381
"Floor" (Williams) **33**:448; **148**:315
"Flophouse" (Fearing) **51**:106
"Una flor amarilla" (Cortázar) **34**:332
La 'Flor de Lis' (Poniatowska) **140**:309-10, 330
La flor de mi secreto (Almodovar) **114**:55, 58
Floralie, où es-tu? (Carrier) **13**:140-41, 143-44; **78**:38-40, 45-6, 49, 53-6, 59-61, 63, 67-71, 79, 82-3
Floralie, Where Are You? (Carrier)
See *Floralie, où es-tu?*
"Florence" (Denby) **48**:84
Florence (Childress) **86**:309, 311, 314; **96**:88, 103-04, 109, 112
"Florence Green is 81" (Barthelme) **3**:43; **5**:57; **46**:35; **115**:66
"Florence Nightingale" (Longley) **29**:297
The Florence Poems (Olson) **28**:344
"Florentines" (Hill) **18**:239
Flores del volcán/Flowers from the Volcano (Alegría) **75**:35-8, 40-2, 46, 49, 53
Flori de mucigai (Arghezi) **80**:6-7, 9-10
"Florida" (Bishop) **4**:65; **9**:94; **13**:92-3; **32**:38
Florida Frenzy (Crews) **49**:73-4, 77
"Florizel's Complaint" (Fuller) **62**:184
Flotsam (Remarque) **21**:328, 330
The Flounder (Grass)
See *Der Butt*
Flow Chart (Ashbery) **77**:70-6; **125**:7-12, 16-29, 38
Flow My Tears, the Policeman Said (Dick) **30**:123, 125; **72**:104, 106
"The Flower" (Creeley) **36**:118; **78**:144
"The Flower" (Warren) **13**:578
The Flower and the Leaf: A Contemporary Record of American Writing since 1941 (Cowley) **39**:457-62
The Flower and the Nettle: Diaries and Letters of Anne Morrow Lindbergh, 1936-1939 (Lindbergh) **82**:153, 155, 160
"Flower Bulbs" (Dudek) **11**:160
"Flower Dump" (Roethke) **3**:432; **11**:481; **101**:296
Flower, Fist, and Bestial Wail (Bukowski) **41**:63; **82**:15; **108**:81
"The Flower Garden" (Jackson) **60**:211, 229
Flower Herding on Mount Monadnock (Kinnell) **3**:269; **5**:216; **13**:321; **29**:283; **129**:267
"Flower Herding on the Mountain" (Kinnell) **5**:216; **29**:280
"Flower Lady" (Ochs) **17**:333
The Flower Master (McGuckian) **48**:275-77, 279
"Flower Music" (Livesay) **15**:340; **79**:338
"The Flower of Coleridge" (Borges) **83**:160
"The Flower of Kiltymore" (Friel) **115**:252-53

The Flower of My Secret (Almodovar)
See *La flor de mi secreto*
"The Flower Piece" (Bates) **46**:51
"Flower Poems" (Silkin) **2**:396; **43**:397, 404
"Flower Punk" (Zappa) **17**:591
Flower Wreath Hill: Later Poems (Rexroth) **112**:392, 395
"The Flower-Cart and the Butcher" (Klappert) **57**:264
"The Flower-Gatherers" (Blunden) **56**:37
"Flower-Gathering" (Frost) **26**:113
The Flowering and Subsequent Deflowering of New England (Angell) **26**:29
Flowering Cactus (Hamburger) **5**:158
Flowering Cherry (Bolt) **14**:87-9
"Flowering Death" (Ashbery) **15**:33-4
"The Flowering Dream: Notes on Writing" (McCullers) **4**:345; **10**:335; **12**:427; **100**:262
"Flowering Eucalypt in Autumn" (Murray) **40**:343
"Flowering Judas" (Porter) **3**:393; **7**:310, 315, 320; **10**:396, 399; **13**:448-49; **15**:432; **27**:401; **101**:209-10, 212, 224-28, 235-39, 242, 253
Flowering Judas, and Other Stories (Porter) **1**:272; **13**:447; **101**:209-10, 212, 215, 222, 249, 255
The Flowering of New England (Brooks) **29**:81-2, 88
Flowering of the Cumberland (Arnow) **7**:15-16; **18**:12
"The Flowering of the Rod" (H. D.) **8**:255, 257-58; **14**:223, 225, 227; **31**:201-03, 208; **34**:445
The Flowering Peach (Odets) **2**:320; **28**:334-35, 339-40; **98**:198-200, 210-13, 217, 228-31, 234-37, 241, 252-53
"Flowering Plum" (Glück) **22**:174
"Flowering Quince" (Ciardi) **40**:157
"Flowering Sudden" (L'Heureux) **52**:272
The Flowering Suns (Ferron)
See *Les grands soleils*
"Flowers" (Akhmadulina)
See "Tsvety"
"The Flowers" (Walker) **103**:406, 411-12
Flowers and Insects (Hughes) **119**:290
Flowers and Shadows (Okri) **87**:313-14, 322, 325
Flowers for Algernon (Keyes) **80**:162-68
"Flowers for Grandmother" (Yevtushenko) **126**:396
Flowers for Hitler (Cohen) **38**:132, 134-37
Flowers for the Judge (Allingham) **19**:15
"Flowers for the Void" (Snyder) **32**:388
"Flowers from the Volcano" (Alegria) **75**:34, 39, 41, 53
Flowers from the Volcano (Alegria)
See *Flores del volcán/Flowers from the Volcano*
"The Flowers Grow High" (Guillén) **79**:229-30
"Flowers in the Interval" (MacNeice) **4**:316
"The Flowers of Boredom" (DeMarinis) **54**:101
Flowers of Darkness (Cohen) **19**:116
"Flowers of Edo" (Sterling) **72**:372
Flowers of Mildew (Arghezi)
See *Flori de mucigai*
Flowers of Mold (Arghezi)
See *Flori de mucigai*
"The Flowers That Bloom in Spring" (Metcalf) **37**:300
"The Flower-Women" (Smith) **43**:422
"The Flowing" (Snyder) **120**:358
Flucht und Verwandlung (Sachs) **98**:322, 324
Der Flüchtling (Hochwälder) **36**:234-36
Fluchtpunkt (Weiss) **15**:563; **51**:389
Fludd (Mantel) **144**:213-14, 218, 220, 222-24, 227, 233-34, 239
Fluff (Olson) **11**:420
Ein Flugzeug über dem Haus (Walser) **27**:456-57
"The Flume" (Bogan) **46**:78-9; **93**:90, 94-5, 97
The Flute Book (Berger) **12**:39-40
"Flute Maker's Story" (Cook-Lynn) **93**:116
"The Flute Player of Brindaban" (Ezekiel) **61**:104
The Flute-Player (Thomas) **22**:417-18; **31**:435; **132**:334, 339, 341
The Flutes of Autumn (Levi) **41**:248
"Fly" (Merwin) **88**:206
"The Fly" (Shapiro) **15**:475, 478; **53**:334
"Fly" (Weller) **26**:444
The Fly (Clavell) **87**:18
The Fly (Cronenberg) **143**:57-58, 65, 70, 72, 76, 83, 86, 94-98, 100-01, 103-04, 107-08, 115-120, 123, 125-26, 139, 156-7
Fly (Lennon) **35**:267
Fly and the Fly-Bottle: Encounters with British Intellectuals (Mehta) **37**:289-90
Fly Away Home (Piercy) **62**:366-69, 373; **128**:222, 234, 246, 256
Fly Away Home (Tindall) **7**:473-74
Fly Away Peter (Malouf) **28**:268-70
Fly Free (Adler) **35**:14-15; **77**:
A Fly Hunt (Wajda) **16**:580
"The Fly in the Coffin" (Caldwell) **14**:96
A Fly on the Wall (Hillerman) **62**:251, 262-63
"Fly Paper" (Hammett) **47**:159
Flycatcher and Other Stories (Bowering) **47**:22
"Flying" (Mahon) **27**:288
Flying (Millett) **67**:241-53, 256, 258
"Flying a Red Kite" (Hood) **28**:187, 193
Flying a Red Kite (Hood) **15**:284; **28**:187, 190
The Flying Boy: Healing the Wounded Man (Lee) **70**:421, 423
"The Flying Bum" (Plomer) **4**:407
"The Flying Change" (Taylor) **44**:302-03
The Flying Change (Taylor) **44**:300, 302-03
Flying Colors (McGuane) **127**:262
Flying Colours (Forester) **35**:163, 166, 170
Flying Correspondent (Felsen) **17**:120
"Flying Crooked" (Graves) **45**:174
Flying Finish (Francis) **42**:148-50, 155, 158; **102**:131, 144, 154-55
"The Flying Goat" (Bates) **46**:55
The Flying Goat (Bates) **46**:55-6
Flying Hero Class (Keneally) **117**:239
"Flying Home" (Ellison) **86**:324; **114**:94, 95, 102, 108, 131
"Flying Home" (Kinnell) **29**:285; **129**:238, 240
Flying Home and Other Stories (Ellison) **114**:124, 126, 130, 137-38
"Flying House" (Swenson) **4**:533
Flying In to Love (Thomas) **132**:379-80
Flying Inland (Spivack) **6**:520-21
"Flying on the Ground" (Young) **17**:568
"Flying out of It" (Ferlinghetti) **10**:175
The Flying Swans (Colum) **28**:89, 92-3
"Flying Switch" (Davis) **49**:91, 94
"Flying to Belfast, 1977" (Raine) **32**:351; **103**:181, 184
Flying to Nowhere (Fuller) **62**:199-200, 202-05
"Flying Underground" (Giovanni) **117**:198
The Flying Wasp (O'Casey) **88**:260
"The Flynch Cows" (Nowlan) **15**:398
F.M. (Linney) **51**:262
"Foal" (Watkins) **43**:453
"Foam" (Enzensberger) **43**:145-46
FOB (Hwang) **55**:152
Foco novo (Pomerance) **13**:444
Focus (Miller) **47**:248-49
"Fodder" (Heaney) **5**:172
Fodor's Indian America (Highwater) **12**:285
Foe (Coetzee) **66**:90-6, 98-9, 106; **117**:34, 46-7, 49-50, 59-60, 67, 75-6, 80-1, 86-7, 102
"Foetal Song" (Oates) **6**:367
"Fog" (Kavan) **5**:206; **82**:120
"Fog" (Sandburg) **10**:449, **15**:468
"Fog" (Soto) **80**:287, 294
"Fog" (Warren) **10**:521
Fog (Pa Chin) **18**:372-73
The Fog Comes on Little Pig Feet (Wells) **12**:637-38
"Fog Envelops the Animals" (Dickey) **7**:83
"The Fog Horn" (Bradbury) **42**:35, 42; **98**:115
"The Fog Man" (Boyle) **90**:64
"Fog Report" (Lorde) **71**:234, 252
Fogarty (Neville) **12**:451-52
Foggage (McGinley) **41**:284-86
"The Foggy Lane" (Simpson) **7**:428-29; **149**:338
"Foggy Street" (Voznesensky) **57**:419
"Foghorn in Horror" (Rukeyser) **15**:459
The Foibles and Fables of an Abstract Man (Honig) **33**:216
"Le foin de Martial" (Theriault) **79**:408
Foirades (Beckett) **9**:83-4; **14**:74, 80; **29**:61
La foire d'empoigne (Anouilh) **1**:7; **13**:21-2; **40**:56-7
The Folded Leaf (Maxwell) **19**:305-06
"Folding a Shirt" (Levertov) **5**:246
The Folding Screens (Genet)
See *Les paravents*
"Folding Sheets" (Piercy) **128**:231
The Folding Star (Hollinghurst) **91**:132-42
"Folie à deux" (Adcock) **41**:15
La Folie du jour (Blanchot) **135**:87-88, 90-93, 136-37, 145, 148
La folie en tête (Leduc) **22**:262
Folie et déraison: Histoire de la folie à l'âge classique (Foucault) **31**:171, 173, 176, 178, 184-85; **34**:340-42, 345; **69**:158, 165, 169-70
The Folk of the Air (Beagle) **104**:23-5, 27, 32, 34
"Folk Tale" (Jiles) **58**:277
"Folk Tale" (Pastan) **27**:369
The Folks That Live on the Hill (Amis) **129**:13, 25
"Folksong" (Hogan) **73**:150, 153
Follies (Sondheim) **30**:381-91, 396-97, 399-402; **39**:175; **147**:228, 230-31, 234, 240, 252, 263-64
"Follow Me, Comrades" (Blaga) **75**:69
Follow Me Down (Foote) **75**:230-31, 237, 243, 251
Follow Me Home (Hoffman) **141**:282-83, 295, 308-10, 315
Follow My Mind (Cliff) **21**:63
"Follow the Eagle" (Kotzwinkle) **35**:254
Follow the Footprints (Mayne) **12**:388, 397
"Follow the Leader" (Reed) **21**:312-13
Follow the Yellow Brick Road (Potter) **58**:391-92; **123**:234
The Followed Man (Williams) **14**:583
"Follower" (Heaney) **74**:180, 194
Following a Lark (Brown) **100**:84, 87-8
"Following Pine" (Harrison) **129**:216, 219
"Following the Guide" (Rozewicz) **139**:226
"Der Folterknecht" (Dürrenmatt) **8**:195; **15**:193
Fombombo (Stribling) **23**:445
"Fon" (Dumas) **6**:145; **62**:155, 160, 162
"Fonction et champ de la parole et du langage en psychanalyse" (Lacan) **75**:284, 293, 295, 300
"Fond Farewell to the 'Chicago Quarterly'" (Whalen) **29**:446
"Fond Memory" (Boland) **67**:39; **113**:108
"Fondo con figuras" (Aleixandre) **36**:31
Fong and the Indians (Theroux) **8**:513
La Fontaine des innocents (Gallo) **95**:98-9
La fontaine narrative (Char) **14**:125
Fontamara (Silone) **4**:492, 494
"Fontan" (Brodsky) **13**:115
"El fontanero azul" (Valenzuela) **104**:388
"La fonte" (Alonso) **14**:25
"Food" (Jacobsen) **48**:194, 199
"Food for All His Dead" (Chin) **135**:152, 155
Food for Centaurs (Graves) **11**:254
"Food for Love" (Kizer) **39**:169-70
"Food for Thought" (Robinson) **21**:350-51
"The Food of Love" (Dickey) **28**:119
"Food Packages: 1947" (Rich) **125**:336
"The Food Thief" (Olds) **85**:293, 301
"The Fool" (MacDiarmid) **63**:251
The Fool (Bond) **13**:103

The Fool (Garfield) **12**:235, 238
The Fool and the Madman (Bernhard)
See *Der Ignorant und der Wahnsinnige*
Fool for Love (Altman) **116**:49, 59, 73
Fool for Love (Shepard) **34**:265-71; **41**:412, 414-16; **44**:264-65, 268-70
A Fool i' the Forest: A Phantasmagoria (Aldington) **49**:5-6, 8-11, 13, 15-17
"The Fool on the Hill" (Lennon and McCartney) **12**:362
"A Fool Too Fast" (Ciardi) **40**:161
The Fooleen: A Crucial Week in the Life of a Grocer's Assistant (Murphy) **51**:306-07
"Fooling Marie" (Bukowski) **41**:73
"Foolish" (Spacks) **14**:511
"Foolish Pride" (Cliff) **21**:63
"The Foolish Wing" (Ciardi) **40**:151
Fools (Simon) **31**:399-400, 403-04; **39**:219; **70**:235
Fools Are Passing Through (Dürrenmatt)
See *Die Ehe des Herrn Mississippi*
Fools Crow (Welch) **52**:435-38
Fools Die (Puzo) **36**:359-62; **107**:193, 213
"Fool's Education" (Price) **6**:423; **43**:345
"A Fool's Love" (Tanizaki)
See "Chijin no ai"
Fools of Fortune (Trevor) **71**:321, 323-25, 327, 329, 340, 342, 346, 349-350; **116**:348, 351-52, 365, 367-72, 376-77, 382-83
Fools of Time (Frye) **70**:277
The Fool's Progress (Abbey) **59**:238-39, 242
Fool's Sanctuary (Johnston) **150**:32
Fools Say (Sarraute)
See *Disent les imbéciles*
"A Foot in the Door" (Friedman) **56**:96
"Foot Notes" (Phillips) **28**:363
The Football Game of the First Year of Manen (Oe)
See *Man'en gan'nen no futtobōru*
"Footfalls" (Ashbery) **125**:40
Footfalls (Beckett) **9**:84; **11**:43; **14**:74, 78; **18**:46; **29**:63-4; **59**:253
"Foothold" (Bowen) **22**:64
Footmen's Quartet (Coward) **29**:138
"Footnote" (Rosenthal) **28**:394
"A Footnote on Monasticism: Dingle Peninsula" (Montague) **46**:265
"Footnote to a Laundry List" (Santos) **22**:365
"Footnote to a Pretentious Book" (Baraka) **5**:45
"Footnote to Howl" (Ginsberg) **69**:212, 214, 219, 221, 223, 225-26; **109**:347, 350, 359, 370
"Footnote to Wisdom" (Santos) **22**:361
Footprints (Levertov) **3**:292-93; **66**:251
"Footprints in the Jungle" (Maugham) **67**:206
The Footprints of the Prophet (Blaga)
See *Paşii profetului*
"Footsteps" (Dobyns) **37**:79
"Footsteps in the Dark" (Nowlan) **15**:398
"Footsteps in the Footprints" (Cortázar) **33**:123
Footsteps of the Hawk (Vachss) **106**:365-66
Footsteps on the Stairs (Adler) **35**:12
"The Foot-Washing" (Ammons) **108**:51
Footwriting (Breytenbach) **126**:84
"For A" (Bowering) **15**:82; **47**:19
"For a Birthday" (Plath) **11**:446
"For a Birthday" (Wright) **53**:428
"For a Bitter Season" (Garrett) **3**:192
For a Bitter Season: New and Selected Poems (Garrett) **11**:219, 219; **51**:147-48
"for a black prostitute" (Sanchez) **116**:307, 322
"For a Breath I Tarry" (Zelazny) **21**:466-67, 479
"For a Brother in Asia" (Celan) **82**:34
"For a Child Born Dead" (Jennings) **131**:238
"For a Child Pronounced Mentally Defective" (Silkin) **43**:398
"For a Coming Extinction" (Merwin) **13**:385; **88**:202, 206
For a Critique of the Political Economy of the Sign (Baudrillard)
See *Pour une critique de l'économie politique du signe*
"For a Dancer" (Browne) **21**:36-7, 39, 41
"For a Dead African" (Brutus) **43**:96
"For a Fatherless Son" (Plath) **3**:391; **51**:345
"For a few Hopi Ancestors" (Rose) **85**:312
"For a Five-Year-Old" (Adcock) **41**:13, 18
"For a Friend" (Ignatow) **7**:180
"For a Friend Who Was Killed in the War" (Kunene) **85**:166
"For a Lamb" (Eberhart) **56**:84
"For a Man Your Age" (Dixon) **52**:99
"For a Mexican Painter" (Rukeyser) **27**:408
For a Nameless Tomb (Onetti)
See *Para una tumba sin nombre*
For a New Novel (Robbe-Grillet)
See *Pour un nouveau roman*
"For a Place in the Sun" (Grau) **146**:124-25
"For a Poet I Know" (Giovanni) **19**:190
"For a Russian Poet" (Rich) **6**:458
"For a Singer" (Acorn) **15**:9
"For a Young Artist" (Hayden) **9**:270; **37**:160
"For Abe Klein: Poet" (Livesay) **79**:351
"For Adrian" (Walcott) **67**:361
"For All" (Snyder) **120**:324, 326, 355
For All That I Found There (Blackwood) **6**:79-80
For All the Seasons of Your Mind (Ian) **21**:182
For All the Wrong Reasons (Neufeld) **17**:310
"For an Unmarked Grave" (Mathias) **45**:238
"For Andrew" (Adcock) **41**:13, 18
"For Angus MacLeod" (Smith) **64**:389
"For Anna Akmatova" (Lowell) **1**:182
"For Anna Mae Pictou Aquash, Whose Spirit Is Present Here and in the Dappled Stars (For We Remember the Story and Tell It Again So that We May All Live)" (Harjo) **83**:274, 281-82
"For Anne" (Cohen) **38**:132
"For Any Member of the Security Police" (Jacobsen) **48**:190
For att ente tala om alla dessa kvinnor (Bergman) **16**:55-6, 70; **72**:40
"For Better for Worse" (Gellhorn) **14**:195; **60**:184
"for Black history month/February 1986" (Sanchez) **116**:318
"For Black People" (Madhubuti) **73**:214-15
"For Black Poets Who Think of Suicide" (Knight) **40**:285
"For Bonfires" (Morgan) **31**:275
"For Brigid" (Buckley) **57**:131
"For C" (Whalen) **29**:446
"For C. P. F." (Cabral de Melo Neto)
See "A Carlos Pena Filho"
"For Charlie Beaulieu in Yellowknife" (Musgrave) **54**:338
"For Chekhov" (Hass) **18**:212
for colored girls who have considered suicide/ when the rainbow is enuf: A Choreopoem (Shange) **8**:484-85; **25**:396-99, 401-05; **38**:393, 395; **74**:291, 293-99, 302, 307-11, 313; **126**:348-49, 354, 357, 359-60, 364-70, 373, 375-76, 381
For Continuity (Leavis) **24**:308
"For Danton" (Tomlinson) **13**:550
"For David Emmanuel" (Silkin) **6**:498
"For David Kalstone" (Van Duyn) **116**:411
"For David St. John Who's Written a Poem" (Dubie) **36**:130
"For Dear Life" (Gordimer) **18**:189
"For deLawd" (Clifton) **66**:73
"For Denise Levertov" (Kinnell) **29**:288
"for domestic workers in the african diaspora" (Sanchez) **116**:307
"For Dudley" (Wilbur) **53**:406, 413; **110**:384, 386
"For Each of You" (Lorde) **71**:254
"For Edward Thomas" (Jennings) **131**:241
"For Eleanor and Bill Monahan" (Williams) **22**:465
"For Eli Jacobsen" (Rexroth) **49**:285
"For Ellen" (Wilbur) **53**:412; **110**:357
"For Emily, Whenever I May Find Her" (Simon) **17**:461
"For Eric Dolphy" (Knight) **40**:284
"For Esmé—with Love and Squalor" (Salinger) **1**:298; **12**:497, 510; **138**:176, 183, 202, 209-13
"For Ever and Ever, Amen" (Smith) **15**:517
For Everyman (Browne) **21**:35, 37, 40
"For Everyone" (Neruda) **7**:261
"For Fear of Little Men" (Wellman) **49**:393
"For Fran" (Levine) **118**:290
"For Françoise Adnet" (Jones) **10**:287
"For Freckle-Faced Gerald" (Knight) **40**:286
"For Free" (Mitchell) **12**:442
"For/From Lew" (Snyder) **32**:400; **120**:324
"For Futures" (Miles) **39**:354
"For Gabriela Mistral" (Le Guin) **136**:395
"For George Lamming" (Birney) **6**:76
"For George Santayana" (Lowell) **8**:349
"For Good Measure" (Elytis) **100**:190
For Good Measure: The Story of Modern Measurement (Berger) **12**:37-8
"For Granny" (Clark Bekedermo) **38**:117, 121, 126-27
"For Gwendolyn Brooks, Teacher" (Randall) **135**:398
"For Harold Bloom" (Ammons) **25**:44; **108**:17
"For Helen" (Hecht) **19**:208
"For Her" (Strand) **18**:518; **41**:432
"For Her First Exhibition with Love" (Cage) **41**:86
For Her Own Good: One Hundred Fifty Years of Experts' Advice to Women (Ehrenreich) **110**:177-78
"For His Father" (Meredith) **4**:347
"For Instance" (Ciardi) **129**:46
For Instance (Ciardi) **40**:162; **129**:44, 47, 51, 55
"For James Dean" (O'Hara) **13**:423
"For Jan, In Bar Maria" (Kizer) **80**:175, 180, 182
"For Jean Rhys" (Castillo) **151**:11
"For Jenny and Roger" (Garrigue) **8**:240
"For Jeromé—With Love and Kisses" (Lish) **45**:228-30
"For Jessica, My Daughter" (Strand) **18**:518, 521; **41**:438
"For John, after His Visit: Suffolk, Fall" (Matthias) **9**:362
"For John Berryman" (Ignatow) **14**:275
"For John Berryman" (Lowell) **11**:330
"For John, Who Begs Me Not to Enquire Further" (Sexton) **53**:320; **123**:403, 405, 413-15, 433
"For Johnny Pole on the Forgotten Beach" (Sexton) **10**:469; **123**:409
"For Julia Li Qiu" (Van Duyn) **116**:422
"For K. J., Leaving and Coming Back" (Hacker) **72**:192
"For Keats" (Smith) **64**:399
For Kicks (Francis) **22**:150, 152-53; **42**:149 50, 153, 156, 158; **102**:154
"For Koras and Balafong" (Senghor) **130**:248
"For L. G.: Unseen for Twenty Years" (Rich) **6**:459
For Lancelot Andrewes: Essays on Style and Order (Eliot) **24**:182; **57**:213
"For Langston Hughes" (Knight) **40**:279
För levande och döda (Transtroemer) **65**:229, 233, 237
"For Lil' Bit" (Jordan) **114**:146
For Living and Dead (Transtroemer)
See *För levande och döda*
For Lizzie and Harriet (Lowell) **3**:302-04, 306; **4**:301; **5**:257, 259; **8**:358; **9**:336; **11**:328; **15**:344; **124**:290
"For Love" (Creeley) **36**:119-20; **78**:162
For Love Alone (Stead) **2**:422-23; **32**:406-09,

411-12, 414-15; **80**:307-08, 317-19, 324-27, 330-33, 336, 342, 346, 348
"For Love of Eleanor" (Rooke) **25**:391
"For Love of Gomez" (Rooke) **25**:391-92
For Love of Imabelle (Himes) **58**:257-58, 262, 266-70; **108**:232, 241, 264; **108**:232, 236-39, 241, 264, 267-70, 275
"For Love of Madeline" (Rooke) **25**:391
For Love: Poems, 1950-1960 (Creeley) **1**:67; **2**:106-07; **8**:151-53; **11**:137-38; **15**:150-51; **36**:119-20; **78**:124-26, 134-38, 143-44, 147
"For Lucy" (Mueller) **51**:280
"For Ma" (Dabydeen) **34**:150
"For Malcolm, a Year After" (Knight) **40**:279, 284
For Malcolm X (Randall) **135**:373-77, 380, 382, 385, 387-89, 394, 396
"For Margaret Danner/ In Establishing Boone House" (Randall) **135**:388
"For Marguerite, Real Love" (Codrescu) **46**:102
"For Marianne Moore" (Ignatow) **14**:275
"For marilyn m" (Bukowski) **108**:111
"For Mars and her children returning in March" (Piercy) **128**:274
For Marx (Althusser)
See *Pour Marx*
"For Mary Ann Youngren" (Bidart) **33**:80
For Mary, with Love (Savage) **40**:376-77
"For May Swenson" (Van Duyn) **116**:427
"For Men, Freedom of Speech; For Women, Silence Please" (Dworkin) **123**:76
"For Miriam" (Tomlinson) **45**:397-98, 400-01, 403
"For My American Family" (Jordan) **114**:151
"For My Brother Reported Missing in Action, 1943" (Merton) **83**:379, 393
"For my Daughter" (Ignatow)
See "For My Daughter in Reply to a Question"
"For My Daughter" (Wright) **53**:424, 431
"For My Daughter in Reply to a Question" (Ignatow) **7**:178
"For My Daughter, Now Seven Years Old" (Coles) **46**:107, 113
"For My Father" (Kherdian) **6**:281
"For My Father" (Whalen) **6**:565
For My Great Folly (Costain) **30**:92
"For My Husband" (Voigt) **54**:431
"For My Lady" (Sanchez) **116**:295
"For My Lover, Returning to His Wife" (Sexton) **123**:409, 439, 450
"For My Mother" (Creeley) **8**:153
"For My Mother" (Jennings) **131**:243
"For My Mother" (Smith) **64**:389, 393, 396
"For My Mother" (Steele) **45**:363
"For My Mother" (Voigt) **54**:431
"For My People" (Walker) **6**:554
"For My Sister Molly Who in the Fifties" (Walker) **19**:453
"For my Sister, now a Widow" (Jennings) **131**:243
"For My Son" (Rukeyser) **15**:458
"For My Son Noah, Ten Years Old" (Bly) **38**:58; **128**:44
"For My Son When He Can Read" (Zukofsky) **18**:560
"For My Sons" (Garrett) **51**:144
"For Myra out of the Album" (Ciardi) **129**:56
"For Neruda" (Galvin)
See "Lemon Ode"
"For New England" (Wright) **53**:427
For No Good Reason (Sarraute) **80**:244-45
"For Norman Mailer" (Lowell) **5**:256
"For Old Times' Sake" (Simon) **26**:412
"For Once in My Life" (Wonder) **12**:661
"For Once, Then, Something" (Frost) **10**:198; **15**:245
"For One Moment" (Ignatow) **40**:258
"For Our Brothers: Blue Jay, Gold Finch, Flicker, Squirrel" (Ortiz) **45**:307
"For Our Country" (Wolf) **150**:272
"For P. da C." (Cabral de Melo Neto)
See "A Pereira da Costa"
"For Paul" (Niedecker) **42**:299-300
"(For Peppe, Who Will Ultimately Judge Our Efforts)" (Giovanni) **117**:194
"For Peter Taylor" (Lowell) **3**:302
"For Pharish Pinckney, Bindle Stiff During the Depression" (Randall) **135**:397
"For Play and Entrance: the Contemporary Canadian Long Poem" (Kroetsch) **132**:201, 219-20, 282-83, 286
For Pollution Fighters Only (Hyde) **21**:175
"For Precision" (Wright) **53**:420
"For Real" (Robison) **98**:307-08
"For Realism" (Fisher) **25**:157
"For Richer for Poorer" (Gellhorn) **14**:195; **60**:184-85
"For Robert Frost" (Kinnell) **29**:281, 283, 287-88
"For Robert Frost" (Levi) **41**:242
"For Rupert—With No Promises" (Lish) **45**:229
"For Sale" (Lowell) **37**:243
"For Sarah" (Codrescu) **46**:102
"For Saundra" (Giovanni) **64**:182, 193-94; **117**:195
"For Saying that It Won't Matter" (Merwin) **88**:193
For Services Rendered (Maugham) **1**:204; **15**:366; **67**:225-26
"For Seurat, 1859-1891" (Plumly) **33**:311
"For Sidney Bechet" (Larkin) **33**:259
"For Some Time Now" (Rozewicz) **139**:226
"For Someone" (Weller)
See "I Need You"
For Special Services (Gardner) **30**:157-58
"For Strong Women" (Piercy) **27**:377
"For Such a Bird He Had No Convenient Cage" (Garrigue) **8**:239
"For Sydney Bechet" (Larkin) **64**:278
"For Sylvia or Amina (Ballad Air & Fire)" (Baraka) **115**:38
"For the Altarpiece of the Roseau Vally Church" (Walcott) **76**:285-86
"For the Anniversary of My Death" (Merwin) **88**:191, 206
For the Birds (Cage) **41**:83
"For the Chinese New Year and for Bill Berkson" (O'Hara) **2**:323
"For the Color of My Mother" (Moraga) **126**:277
"For the Concerned" (Bukowski) **82**:23
"For the Conjunction of Two Planets" (Rich) **36**:365
"For the Country" (Levine) **118**:282
"For the Daughters" (Ostriker) **132**:302
"For the Dead" (Rich) **3**:427
"For the Death of Lombardi" (Dickey) **15**:177-78; **47**:91-2, 98; **109**:245
For the Defense (Rice) **49**:302
"For the Fallen" (Levine) **9**:333; **14**:316, 318-19
"For the Father of Sandro Gulotta" (Lewis) **41**:261-62
For the Good of the Cause (Solzhenitsyn)
See *Dlia pol'zy dela*
"For the Good Times" (Kristofferson) **26**:266
"For the Inmost Lost" (Graham) **29**:194
For the Just Cause (Grossman) **41**:188, 193
"For the Lost Generation" (Kinnell) **29**:288
For the Love of a Cat (Codrescu) **121**:161
For the Municipality's Elderly (Reading) **47**:349-51
"For the New Year" (Creeley) **78**:135
"For the Poet Who Said Poets Are Struck by Lightning Only Two or Three Times" (Klappert) **57**:258
"For the Previous Owner" (McGuckian) **48**:278
"For the Rain in March: The Blackened Hearts of Herons" (Young Bear) **94**:361-63, 371
"For the Record" (Lorde) **71**:260
"For the Roses" (Mitchell) **12**:440
For the Roses (Mitchell) **12**:437, 440, 442
"For the Running of the New York Marathon" (Dickey) **15**:177; **47**:92
"For the sake of Amelia" (Simic) **130**:312
For the Sleepwalkers (Hirsch) **31**:214-16; **50**:195-97
"For the Stranger" (Forché) **83**:209
"For the Student Strikers" (Wilbur) **110**:382
"For the Tears in Your Eyes" (Prince) **35**:332
For the Time Being (Auden) **1**:9; **2**:23-4; **3**:27; **4**:33; **9**:55; **11**:19-20; **14**:31; **43**:15; **123**:52-3, 56-7
"For the Turnstiles" (Young) **17**:573, 581
For the Unfallen: Poems, 1952-1958 (Hill) **8**:293-94, 296; **45**:178-79, 181, 184, 186-87
"For the Union Dead" (Lowell) **1**:179-82, 184; **2**:246-49; **3**:300-02; **4**:297-98, 301-03; **5**:257-58; **8**:350-51, 353, 357; **9**:336-37; **11**:325-27; **15**:343-44, 347-48; **37**:234, 236-37, 240; **124**:258, 263, 291-92, 294, 304-05
For the Union Dead (Lowell) **1**:179-82, 184; **2**:247-49; **3**:300-02; **4**:297-98, 301-03; **5**:257-58; **8**:350-51, 353, 357; **11**:325, 327-28; **15**:343-44, 347-48; **37**:234; **124**:255, 264, 274, 298-99, 302-03
"For the Unknown Seamen of the 1939-45 War Buried in Iona Churchyard" (Smith) **64**:388, 393
"For the Word is Flesh" (Kunitz) **148**:77, 78, 96, 148
"For the Year" (Merwin) **88**:211
"For There Is No Help in Them" (Blunden) **56**:46
"For Theresa" (Giovanni) **19**:190
"For Thomas Moore" (Simmons) **43**:411
"For Tinkers Who Travel on Foot" (Avison) **97**:93
For to end yet again and Other Fizzles (Beckett)
See *Foirades*
For to End Yet Again, and Other Fizzles (Beckett) **29**:57, 59
For Tonight (Onetti)
See *Para esta noche*
"For Unborn Malcolms" (Sanchez) **116**:277, 294
For Us the Living (Lancaster) **36**:242-43
"For Vivian" (Randall) **135**:398
"For W. C. W." (Creeley) **15**:152; **78**:125, 137
"For WCW" (Bowering) **15**:82
For Whom the Bell Tolls (Hemingway) **1**:141, 143; **3**:236-37, 239-40; **6**:225, 229-31, 234; **8**:283-84, 286, 288, 292-93; **10**:266; **13**:271, 275, 277-79; **19**:220-21, 224; **30**:179, 183; **34**:479; **39**:430; **61**:194, 201, 215; **80**:101-59
"For William Carlos Williams" (Kinnell) **29**:288
"For You" (Prince) **35**:323
"For You" (Springsteen) **17**:484, 487
For You (Prince) **35**:323-24, 330
For You Departed (Paton)
See *Kontakion for You Departed*
For You: Poems (Carruth) **4**:94; **7**:40; **84**:119, 131
"For You, Who Didn't Know" (Willard) **37**:464
"For Your Information" (O'Hara) **13**:431
"For Your Life" (Page and Plant) **12**:480
"For Your Viewing Entertainment" (Friedman) **3**:166
"El forastero gentil/The Gallant Stranger" (Ulibarrí) **83**:415
"The Forbidden" (Barker) **52**:55
Forbidden Colors (Mishima) **2**:286, 288; **9**:382-83; **27**:337, 343
"Forbidden Dances" (Urquhart) **90**:384-5
Forbidden Disappointments (Carroll) **38**:102-03
The Forbidden Forest (Eliade)
See *Forêt interdite*
Forbidden Frontier (Harris) **12**:262-64, 267
Forbidden Fruit, and Other Stories (Iskander)
See *Trinadtsaty podvig Gerakla*
Forbidden Ground (Goytisolo)
See *Coto vedado*

"Forbidden Love" (Daryush) **19**:120
Forbidden Pleasures (Cernuda)
See *Los placeres prohibidos*
Forbidden Territory (Goytisolo)
See *Coto vedado*
The Forbidden Tower (Bradley) **30**:27-9
"Force" (Walcott) **9**:557
The Force and Other Poems (Redgrove) **6**:445; **41**:348-49, 351-52
La force de l'âge (Beauvoir) **1**:19; **31**:42; **44**:345, 349-50; **50**:390; **71**:56, 60, 76, 78, 80; **124**:134, 144, 146-48, 159, 166
La force des choses (Beauvoir) **4**:47; **8**:62; **14**:67; **31**:34; **44**:343, 345, 349-50; **50**:388, 390; **71**:56, 67, 72-4, 78, 81-2; **124**:144, 149, 155, 164
Force of Circumstance (Beauvoir)
See *La force des choses*
Force of Evil (Polonsky) **92**:375, 377-83, 387-88, 391, 393-406, 408-15
The Force of Habit (Bernhard)
See *Die Macht der Gewohnheit*
Force of Light (Celan)
See *Lichtzwang*
Force Ten from Navarone (MacLean) **50**:348-49; **63**:264-65
Forced Entries: The Downtown Diaries, 1971-1973 (Carroll) **143**:33-40, 43-5
"Forced Retirement" (Giovanni) **64**:191
The Forces of Plenty (Voigt) **54**:430-32, 434
"Forcing House" (Roethke) **3**:432; **101**:293-94
"Forcing the End" (Nissenson) **4**:381
"Fordie" (Brophy) **29**:91; **105**:8
"Fording and Dread" (Harrison) **143**:355, 357
"Foreboding" (Ashbery) **15**:28
"Forefathers" (Blunden) **56**:32, 51
A Foreign Affair (Hunt) **3**:252
A Foreign Affair (Wilder) **20**:455-56, 460, 465
Foreign Affairs (Lurie) **39**:177-85
Foreign Affairs, and Other Stories (O'Faolain) **7**:273-74, 276; **32**:343; **70**:314, 319
Foreign Bodies (Aldiss) **40**:19
Foreign Bodies (Harrison) **144**:111-12, 114
"The Foreign City" (Valenzuela)
See "Ciudad ajena"
Foreign Correspondent (Hitchcock) **16**:359
Foreign Devils (Enright) **31**:150
Foreign Devils (Faust) **8**:214-15
"The Foreign Lands" (Jacobsen) **48**:191
"The Foreign Legation" (Doctorow) **37**:91, 93-4; **113**:153
The Foreign Legion (Lispector) **43**:272
"Foreign Market" (Castillo) **151**:47
"Foreign Shores" (Salter) **52**:368; **59**:196
The Foreign Student (Choi) **119**:41-45
Foreign Studies (Endō)
See *Ryugaku*
"The Foreigner" (Nowlan) **15**:399
"Foreigner" (Page) **7**:291
"The Foreigner" (Urdang) **47**:399
The Foreigner (Plante) **38**:371-73
The Foreigner (Shue) **52**:390-93
"The Foreman" (Peterkin) **31**:306, 308
"The Foreman Kyazym" (Iskander) **47**:196
Forensic and the Navigators (Shepard) **17**:437-38, 440, 444
Forerunner Foray (Norton) **12**:465
"The Forest" (Bitov) **57**:114-15
"Forest" (Simic) **9**:480; **130**:302, 305
"Forest" (Swenson) **14**:521; **106**:334
"The Forest" (Wright) **53**:429
"The Forest beyond the Glass" (Turco) **11**:551
"The Forest Hit by Modern Use" (Murray) **40**:343
A Forest in Flower (Mishima)
See *Hanazakari no mori*
The Forest in Full Bloom (Mishima)
See *Hanazakari no mori*
Forest Moon (Paz)
See *Luna silvestre*
"Forest Mould" (Richter) **30**:323
"Forest of Europe" (Walcott) **67**:357
A Forest of Flowers (Saro-Wiwa) **114**:252
"The Forest of Men" (Elytis) **49**:110
"The Forest of the South" (Gordon) **83**:231, 234, 239
The Forest of the South (Gordon) **13**:247; **29**:189; **83**:230, 232, 242, 251
"The Forest Path" (Wright) **53**:419
Forestilling om det Tyvende Århundrede (Hoeg) **95**:116, 118-19
"The Forests" (Davis) **49**:92
The Forests of Lithuania (Davie) **5**:114; **8**:163, 167; **10**:123
Forêt interdite (Eliade) **19**:144-45
Foretaste of Glory (Stuart) **11**:512; **34**:377
"Foretelling the Future" (Atwood) **25**:69
"The Forethought" (Du Bois) **64**:132
Forever (Blume) **12**:44-6; **30**:21-5
Forever and a Day (Isherwood) **44**:397
"Forever and the Earth" (Bradbury) **42**:35
Forever England: North and South (Bainbridge) **130**:14, 38-39
Forever Fernwood (Lear) **12**:338
Forever Flowing (Grossman) **41**:186-89
Forever Free (Adamson) **17**:4
"Forever Hold Your Peace" (Cheever) **15**:127
Forever Morning (Davison) **15**:170
"Forever My Love" (Simon) **26**:409
"Forever O'Clock" (Warren) **8**:536
Forever Panting (De Vries) **3**:125-26; **28**:110
"Forever to a Hudson Bay Blanket" (Tiptree) **50**:357
The Forever War (Haldeman) **61**:170-71, 173-75, 177, 181-85
"Forever Young" (Dylan) **4**:150
"Forevermore" (Agnon) **4**:12
"Foreword" (Merwin) **88**:192
"Foreword" (Pinsky) **94**:302
"Foreword to the Reader of (Some) General Culture" (Ciardi) **44**:375
"A Foreword to Three Pieces" (Shange) **74**:308-09
Forewords and Afterwords (Auden) **3**:23-5; **6**:17; **14**:31
Forfeit (Francis) **22**:150; **42**:148-51, 153, 157-58; **102**:128, 132
"The Forge" (Heaney) **25**:241; **91**:121
"La forge" (Theriault) **79**:407
The Forge (Stribling) **23**:440, 442, 444, 449
"Forgers of Myth" (Sartre) **13**:502
Forget Foucault (Baudrillard)
See *Oublier Foucault*
"Forget What Did" (Larkin) **8**:333; **64**:282
"Forgetfulness" (Campbell) **32**:75, 78, 80
Forget-Me-Not Lane (Nichols) **5**:305-07; **36**:329-30, 333; **65**:161
"Forgetting" (O'Brien) **116**:193
"Forgetting" (Williams) **56**:429
Forgetting Elena (White) **27**:478-80, 482; **110**:316, 318, 320, 327-28, 336
"Forgetting This World" (Sadoff) **9**:466
"Forgetting to Mention Allende" (Kelman) **58**:298
"(Forgive Me) My Little Flower Princess" (Lennon) **35**:275-76
"Forgiven" (Brautigan) **3**:88; **12**:65
"Forgiveness in Families" (Munro) **10**:357; **95**:287
"The Forgotten Captain" (Transtroemer) **65**:237
The Forgotten Man (Hikmet)
See *Unutulan adam*
"Forgotten Sex" (Ashbery) **77**:62-3, 69
"Forgotten Song" (Ashbery) **77**:65, 67; **125**:36
The Forgotten Victory: The Battle for New Jersey, 1780 (Fleming) **37**:125
"Fork" (Simic) **22**:383; **49**:337, 339, 341-42; **68**:370-71, 374, 379; **130**:311, 330
The Fork River Space Project (Morris) **18**:351
Forked Tongue: the Politics of Bilingual Education (Porter) **70**:377-78, 384
"The Forks" (Powers) **1**:282; **57**:358
"Forks with Points Up" (Ignatow) **7**:180
"Forlesen" (Wolfe) **25**:475
Den förlorade jaguaren (Martinson) **14**:355
The Forlorn Demon: Didactic and Critical Essays (Tate) **24**:442-43
Form and Fable in American Fiction (Hoffman) **23**:240
"The Form and Function of the Novel" (Goldbarth) **38**:206
"Form, Ideology and 'The Secret Agent'" (Eagleton) **63**:107
The Form of Loss (Bowers) **9**:121
A Form of Women (Creeley) **2**:106; **15**:149
"Form, Reference, and Ideology in Musical Discourse" (White) **148**:297, 300
"Form Rejection Letter" (Dacey) **51**:79
"Form that is Neither In nor Out" (Bly) **128**:24
"Forma" (Borges)
See "La forma de la espada"
"La forma de la espada" (Borges) **10**:66; **19**:47
Formal Defect (Levi)
See *Vizio di forma*
A Formal Feeling (Oneal) **30**:280-81
The Formal Method in Literary Scholarship (Bakhtin)
See *Formal'nyj metod v literaturovedenii*
"Formalist and Contextualist Strategies in Historical Explanation" (White) **148**:299
Formal'nyj metod v literaturovedenii (Bakhtin) **83**:3, 6-7, 21-2, 26-7, 31-4, 45
"The Formation of a Separatist, I" (Howe) **152**:164
La formica Argentina (Calvino) **5**:98; **11**:89, 91; **39**:315
"Forms and Citizens" (Ransom) **5**:364
Forms in Relief (Rozewicz)
See *Płaskorzeźba*
Forms of Discovery (Winters) **4**:591-92; **32**:463-64, 466
Forms of Exile (Montague) **13**:390; **46**:265-66, 278
"Forms of the Earth at Abiquiu" (Momaday) **85**:269-70
"Forms of Time and Chronotope in the Novel" (Bakhtin) **83**:5, 15, 34, 60, 62
The Forms of Water (Barrett) **150**:3-5, 8
"The Forms of Wildness: Archaeology of an Idea" (White) **148**:286
"Formulation" (Raine) **45**:335
"Fornalutx" (Layton) **15**:322
"The Forsaken" (Livesay) **79**:340
Forsaking All Others (Breslin) **43**:74-6, 78
Fort Apache (Ford) **16**:311, 315
Fort Everglades (Slaughter) **29**:374
The Fort of Gold (Dillon) **17**:94-5
"Fort Sill: Set-angia" (Momaday) **85**:281
"Fortitude" (Vonnegut) **12**:611
Fortællinger om Natten (Hoeg) **95**:116
"The Fortress" (Glück) **7**:119
"The Fortress" (Sexton) **53**:319
Fortress Besieged (Ch'ien) **22**:105-07
"Fortuna lo que ha querido" (Fuentes) **113**:237
A Fortunate Madness (Shreve) **23**:402
A Fortunate Man (Berger) **19**:37
The Fortunate Pilgrim (Puzo) **2**:352; **36**:358-60, 362; **107**:174-76, 182, 199, 207, 212, 215
"The Fortunate Traveller" (Walcott) **25**:456-57; **42**:423; **76**:275, 297
The Fortunate Traveller (Walcott) **25**:455-57; **42**:418-19, 421-22; **67**:348, 355-56, 358, 360, 362
"Fortune Always has Her Way" (Fuentes)
See "Fortuna lo que ha querido"
The Fortune Cookie (Wilder) **20**:461
Fortune Heights (Dos Passos) **4**:134; **15**:185; **25**:144-45
Fortune Is a Woman (Graham) **23**:191
Fortune, My Foe (Davies) **42**:104
The Fortune of War (O'Brian) **152**:259, 276, 282, 297, 299
"The Fortune Teller" (Spark) **40**:402
"Fortunes" (Waddington) **28**:438

"Fortune's Always Hiding: A Corporate Drug Romance" (Welsh) **144**:320-21, 328, 334
Fortune's Daughter (Hoffman) **51**:204-08
Fortune's Favorites (McCullough) **107**:164-66
Fortunes of a Fool (Megged) **9**:375
Forty Beads on a Hangman's Rope (Hall) **51**:170-71, 175
Forty Lashes Less One (Leonard) **120**:286-87
"Forty Something" (Hass) **99**:154
Forty Stories (Barthelme) **59**:250-51; **115**:80-1
Forty Thousand in Gehenna (Cherryh) **35**:113-14
"Forty Whacks" (Howe) **47**:172-74
Forty Whacks (Howe) **47**:172-74
"Forty Years On" (Auden) **6**:18
Forty Years On (Bennett) **45**:55-6, 58; **77**:84, 96, 99
Forty Years On. Getting On. Habeas Corpus (Bennett) **45**:58; **77**:99
"Forty-Five a Month" (Narayan) **28**:293
Forty-Five Mercy Street (Sexton) **8**:483-84; **10**:467; **15**:473; **53**:313; **123**:404-05, 411, 435-36
.44 (Breslin) **43**:73-4
XLI Poems (Cummings) **8**:156; **12**:139, 156; **15**:160; **68**:35, 45
The 42nd Parallel (Dos Passos) **1**:77; **8**:181; **11**:152, 157; **34**:419, 424; **82**:61-2, 64-8, 71, 73, 83-5, 89, 91-2, 95, 97-8, 100-03, 107-11
"47 Beds" (Gray) **49**:152; **112**:111
"The Forty-Seventh Saturday" (Trevor) **116**:338, 385
"A Forty-Year-Old Man" (Endō) **54**:157
Forward from Liberalism (Spender) **10**:491; **91**:261, 263, 265-66
Forward in Time (Bova) **45**:69
Forward the Foundation (Asimov) **76**:313-14
"Forward to the Reader" (Parra) **102**:345
"Fossil, 1975" (Lewis) **41**:263
"Fossil Gathering" (Porter) **5**:346
"Fossil Inscription" (Ekelöf) **27**:110
"Fossils" (McGuckian) **48**:276
"Fosterage" (Heaney) **25**:246
"Fosterling" (Heaney) **74**:190, 194; **91**:125
"Fotografia do engenho Timbó" (Cabral de Melo Neto) **76**:169
"Foucault Decoded: Notes from Underground" (White) **148**:217, 249
"Foucault's Discourse: The Historiography of Anti-Humanism" (White) **148**:241, 249
Foucault's Pendulum (Eco)
See *Il pendolo di Foucault*
The Foul (Donaldson)
See *Lord Foul's Bane*
"Foul Shots: A Clinic" (Matthews) **40**:322
Foul's Bane (Donaldson)
See *Lord Foul's Bane*
"Found a Job" (Byrne) **26**:96-7
Found a Peanut (Margulies) **76**:194
"The Found Boat" (Munro) **95**:302
"Found in the Bowery" (Barnes) **127**:164
"Found in the Cabbage Patch" (Mueller) **51**:282
Found in the Street (Highsmith) **42**:216; **102**:197-201, 209
Found, Lost, Found: The English Way of Life (Priestley) **9**:442
"Found Paradise" (Keillor) **40**:274
"The Found Picture" (Graham) **29**:199
"Foundation" (Asimov) **26**:60-2
"Foundation" (Masters) **48**:223
"Foundation" (Redgrove) **6**:445
Foundation (Asimov) **76**:313-14, 316-17; **92**:18, 20-2
The Foundation (Buero Vallejo)
See *La fundación*
Foundation and Earth (Asimov) **76**:313; **92**:18
Foundation and Empire (Asimov) **3**:17; **19**:26; **26**:46; **76**:313-14; **92**:21-2
The Foundation Trilogy: Three Classics of Science Fiction (Asimov) **1**:8; **3**:17; **19**:26, 28; **26**:38-9, 45-6, 48, 50, 59-64; **76**:313, 316, 318
Foundation's Edge (Asimov) **26**:58-9, 63-5; **76**:313
The Foundations of Aesthetics (Richards) **24**:389, 397
"The Foundations of American Industry" (Hall) **37**:142
Founder Member (Gardner) **30**:152
The Founders (Green) **25**:198
Founder's Praise (Greenberg) **30**:165
The Founding of Montreal (Scott) **22**:371
"A Foundling" (Atwood) **25**:67
The Foundling and Other Tales of Prydain (Alexander) **35**:26
"The Foundry House" (Friel) **5**:128; **42**:163; **115**:216, 218
"Fountain" (Jennings) **131**:238-39
Fountain and Tomb (Mahfouz)
See *Hikayat haratina*
"The Fountain of Arethusa" (Davie) **31**:119, 124
"The Fountain of Cyanë" (Davie) **31**:119, 124
The Fountain of Youth (Welles) **20**:447
The Fountain Overflows (West) **7**:525, 528; **9**:562; **31**:456-58; **50**:394-95, 397, 399, 408
"Fountain Piece" (Swenson) **4**:533; **61**:399; **106**:325
"Fountainebleau" (Young) **17**:576
The Fountainhead (Rand) **30**:292-95, 297-98, 300-03; **44**:448, 450-52, 454; **79**:357-58, 361-65, 369, 371-75, 378-83, 389-95
"The Fountains of Aix" (Swenson) **106**:320-21, 349-50
The Fountains of Paradise (Clarke) **13**:155; **18**:107; **35**:124, 126-27; **136**:199, 202, 237
"Four" (Cummings) **15**:161
4 (Cage) **41**:79
"4 A.M." (Fearing) **51**:114
"4 A.M. Traffic" (Ghose) **42**:179
"The Four Apples" (Apple) **33**:21
"Four Archetypes" (Soyinka) **36**:415, 417; **44**:285
"Four Auguries" (Atwood) **15**:37
"The Four Beauties" (Bates) **46**:61
"Four California Deaths" (Bowering) **47**:29
"Four Canzones (1957-1961)" (Okigbo) **25**:350-51, 354; **84**:310, 324-25, 328-29, 331-32, 336
"Four Changes" (Snyder) **120**:339, 346-47
"Four Classic Texts" (Hall) **151**:181-82, 188, 190
"Four Cycles of Love Poems" (Barker) **8**:46
Four Days (Buell) **10**:82-3
"Four Dead Beats to a Bar" (Scannell) **49**:332
Four Dubliners: Wilde, Yeats, Joyce, and Beckett (Ellmann) **50**:306-07
"Four Exposures: Light Meter" (Eberhart) **11**:178
"Four Eyes" (Ondaatje) **14**:407; **51**:310, 312, 316
Four for Delfina (Donoso)
See *Cuatro para Delfina*
"Four for Sir John Davies" (Roethke) **46**:363; **101**:286, 289, 304
Four for Tomorrow (Zelazny) **21**:468
Four Friends (Tesich) **69**:371
The Four Fundamental Concepts of Psycho-anaylsis (Lacan) **75**:290, 293-94, 298
Four Hasidic Masters and Their Struggle against Melancholy (Wiesel)
See *Contre la mélancolie: Célébration hassidique II*
"Four Horsemen" (Clash) **30**:46-7
The 400 Blows (Truffaut)
See *Les quatre cents coups*
The 400 Eels of Sigmund Freud (Mojtabai) **9**:385-86; **15**:379
"Four Hundred Miles" (Ciardi) **129**:47
"Four in Blue" (Robinson) **21**:343
"Four Introductions" (Giovanni) **64**:196
Four Kings and a Queen (Sturgeon) **39**:365
"Four Lakes' Days" (Eberhart) **56**:75, 80, 87-8
The Four Loves (Lewis) **3**:296; **6**:308; **124**:228, 241-43, 246
"Four Men" (Harmon) **38**:243
The Four Musketeers (Lester) **20**:230
Four Nights of a Dreamer (Bresson) **16**:117-18
"Four Notions of Love and Marriage" (Momaday) **85**:247
The Four of Hearts (Queen) **11**:461-62
Four Past Midnight (King) **113**:366, 385
"Four Penny" (Cohen) **38**:131
"Four Personal Lectures" (Snodgrass) **10**:477-78
Four Plays (Inge) **19**:226-27
"Four Poems" (Bishop) **13**:88
"Four Poems for Robin" (Snyder) **120**:356
"Four Poems of Departure" (Pound) **112**:343
"Four Preludes on Playthings of the Wind" (Sandburg) **10**:448; **35**:352
The Four Quartets (Eliot) **1**:89-92; **2**:125, 129; **3**:137-39; **6**:160-64, 166, 168; **9**:184, 186, 188; **10**:168-70; **13**:191-94, 200-02; **15**:210, 213-17; **24**:181; **34**:387-88, 390, 392, 395, 39; **55**:346, 350, 353, 360, 362, 374; **57**:201, 208-09; **113**:207-225
"Four Quartz Crystal Clocks" (Moore) **2**:291
Four Reforms (Buckley) **37**:59
Four Rooms (Tarantino) **125**:357, 366, 373
Four Screenplays of Ingmar Bergman (Bergman) **72**:31, 33, 35
"The Four Seasons" (Shields) **113**:442
The Four Seasons (Wesker) **5**:483; **42**:427, 429
The Four Seasons of Success (Schulberg) **48**:349-50
"Four Sketches for Herbert Read" (Spender) **5**:401
"Four Skinny Trees" (Cisneros) **118**:176-77, 179
"Four Soldiers" (Nemerov) **36**:308
"Four Songs" (Livesay) **79**:337, 343, 351
"4 Songs of Life" (Young Bear) **94**:362, 364
"Four Spells" (Beer) **58**:38
Four Spot (Cabral de Melo Neto)
See *Quaderna*
Four Springs (Honig) **33**:213-14, 216
"Four Stations in His Circle" (Clarke) **53**:87
"Four Sticks" (Page and Plant) **12**:475, 477, 481
"Four Summers" (Oates) **134**:248
"The Four Suspects" (Christie) **110**:140, 142-43
"The Four Temperaments" (Aksyonov) **101**:41
"The Four Temperaments" (Transtroemer) **65**:223, 226
Four Twelves Are Forty-eight (Kesselring) **45**:208-09
"Four Walks in the Country near Saint Brieve" (Mahon) **27**:290
"Four Ways of Knowledge" (Bly) **38**:55; **128**:32
The Four Winds of Love (Mackenzie) **18**:313, 315-16
The Four Wise Men (Tournier) **36**:433-37, 440; **95**:361-64, 368-71, 381-82
"A Four Years' Harvest" (MacDiarmid) **63**:251
The Four Years' Notebook (Montale)
See *Quaderno de quattro anni*
Fourbis (Leiris) **61**:341-43, 347, 351, 356-57
The Four-Chambered Heart (Nin) **4**:376; **14**:386; **60**:279
The Four-Dimensional Nightmare (Ballard) **3**:33
Four-Fifty from Paddington (Christie) **12**:117
The Four-Gated City (Lessing) **1**:175; **2**:239-42; **3**:282-83, 285, 287, 289-90, 292; **6**:291-92, 295-97, 302-04; **10**:314-15; **15**:332, 334; **22**:281, 284; **40**:303-04, 312; **94**:253, 257, 282, 284, 286
"The Four-Night Fight" (Beattie) **146**:85
The Fourposter (de Hartog) **19**:130
Fourskin (Vizenor) **103**:288
The Foursome (Whitehead) **5**:488
"Fourteen" (Hacker) **72**:182

Fourteen (Sachs) **35**:335
"Fourteen Elegies: Eleven" (Deane) **122**:82
Fourteen Hundred Thousand (Shepard) **17**:435-36, 439; **41**:409
"Fourteen Minutes to Go" (Voinovich) **49**:375
"1492" (D'Aguiar) **145**:116
"Fourteen Rulers" (Haavikko) **34**:175
14 Stories (Dixon) **52**:95-9, 101
1492: The Decline of Medievalism and the Rise of the Modern Age (Litvinoff)
See *1492: The Year and the Era*
1492: The Life and Times of Juan Cabezón of Castille (Aridjis)
See *1492: Vida y tiempas de Juan Cabeóz de Castilla*
1492: The Year and the Era (Litvinoff) **70**:338, 344, 353
1492: Vida y tiempas de Juan Cabeóz de Castilla (Aridjis) **70**:339, 347, 359
The Fourteenth Cadillac (Jackson) **12**:290-91
The Fourteenth Chronicle (Dos Passos) **4**:136-38; **8**:181
"The Fourteenth Street Poem" (Simic) **68**:376
4-Telling (Piercy) **128**:244, 246
The Fourth (Puzo) **107**:204, 213
"Fourth Act" (Jeffers) **54**:242
The Fourth Angel (Rechy) **7**:356; **107**:225, 228, 239, 256
"The Fourth Day Out from Santa Cruz" (Bowles) **19**:60
The Fourth Deadly Sin (Sanders) **41**:382
The Fourth Dimension (Wolf) **150**:235-36
The Fourth Dimension: Selected Poems of Yannis Ritsos (Ritsos) **13**:488; **31**:326-28, 331
"The Fourth Month of the Landscape Artist" (Rich) **7**:369
"The Fourth of July" (Codrescu) **121**:159
"The Fourth of July" (Lowell) **124**:305
"Fourth of July" (Snodgrass) **68**:382, 389
"The Fourth of July" (Wilbur) **9**:571; **53**:405
"Fourth of July at Santa Ynez" (Haines) **58**:218
"Fourth of July in Maine" (Lowell) **1**:181; **9**:337; **15**:343; **124**:294
"Fourth Poem from Niceragua Libre: Report from the Frontier" (Jordan) **114**:162
The Fourth Protocol (Forsyth) **36**:177-78
"Fourth Psalm" (Merwin) **88**:194
"Fourth Psalm" (Sexton) **123**:422
Fourth Quarter and Other Poems (Wright) **53**:432; **11**:578
The Fourth Side of the Triangle (Queen) **11**:464
"The Fourth Sparrow" (Ozick) **62**:351; **155**:181
Fourth Street East (Weidman) **7**:517
"Fourth Version" (Valenzuela)
See "Cuarta versión"
"Fourth Voice: The Grandmother" (Davison) **28**:101
"The Fourth Wonder of the World" (Shields) **97**:431
"Four-Word Lines" (Swenson) **106**:337
Les fous de Bassan (Hébert) **29**:239
"The Fox" (Clarke) **61**:73
"The Fox" (Day Lewis) **10**:131
"The Fox" (Jeffers) **54**:234
"The Fox" (Levine) **33**:275; **118**:271, 285
"The Fox" (Muldoon) **72**:276
"Fox" (Robbins) **21**:340
"The Fox" (Tomlinson) **13**:549
Fox and His Friends (Fassbinder) **20**:108
The Fox and the Camellias (Silone) **4**:493
"Fox Hunters" (Pancake) **29**:346, 348-49
The Fox in the Attic (Hughes) **1**:149; **11**:278
"The Fox of Peapack" (White) **39**:377
The Fox of Peapack and Other Poems (White) **10**:529
Fox on a Barn Door (Walker) **13**:565
Fox Prints (McGinley) **41**:284, 286-87
"The Foxes" (Bates) **46**:62-3
"Foxes" (Findley) **102**:111
"The Foxes" (Oliver) **98**:292
"Foxes' Moon" (Tomlinson) **13**:548
The Foxes of Harrow (Yerby) **1**:381; **7**:556-57; **22**:487-88
Foxfire: Confessions of a Girl Gang (Oates) **108**:393
The Foxglove Saga (Waugh) **7**:513-14
"Foxhunt" (Hughes) **37**:172
"Foxtail Pine" (Snyder) **120**:317
Foxybaby (Jolley) **46**:218-19, 221
"fPot-au-Feu" (Van Duyn) **116**:429
"Eine Frage der Macht" (Hein) **154**:167
"The Fragile Age" (Grau) **146**:125-26
"Fragment" (Ashbery) **77**:44, 50-1; **125**:11
"A Fragment" (Carroll) **143**:27
"Fragment" (Ortiz) **45**:307
"Fragment" (Williams) **148**:362
"A Fragment" (Winters) **32**:468
"Fragment" (Zweig) **34**:379
Fragment (Ashbery) **2**:19; **3**:16; **4**:24; **13**:30, 33; **15**:32; **41**:40
"fragment 3" (Sanchez) **116**:307
"Fragment from Public Secret" (Kaufman) **49**:207
"Fragment: Little N.Y. Ode" (Carroll) **143**:29
"Fragment of a Letter" (Seifert) **93**:324
"Fragment of Autobiography" (Brophy) **105**:22
"Fragment Thirty-Six" (H. D.) **31**:201
"Fragment: To a Mirror" (Justice) **19**:235; **102**:249-50, 256
The Fragmented Life of Don Jacobo Lerner (Goldemberg) **52**:163-65, 167-69
Fragmentos a su imán (Lezama Lima) **101**:121
"Fragments" (Creeley) **11**:138
"Fragments" (Dobyns) **37**:78
"The Fragments" (Lagerkvist) **54**:287
Fragments (Armah) **5**:31; **33**:25, 27, 29, 31-2, 36-8; **136**:3-8, 14, 17-19, 21-26, 38, 44, 52-54, 56-59, 71-73
Fragments: A Concerto Grosso (Albee) **86**:124
Fragments d'un déluge (Giono) **4**:188
Fragments d'un discours amoureux (Barthes) **24**:35-6; **83**:80-5, 89, 102, 104
Fragments d'un paradis (Giono) **4**:188
"Fragments from a Parable(of the 1950's)" (Jordan) **114**:149
"Fragments from Italy" (Ciardi) **40**:158
"Fragments from the Deluge" (Okigbo) **25**:350, 352; **84**:301, 309, 312, 314, 322, 326, 328, 331, 334, 341-42
"Fragments of a Growing Awareness" (Breytenbach) **126**:94
"Fragments of a Hologram Rose" (Gibson) **63**:129
Fragments of a Journal (Ionesco) **6**:253; **11**:290; **86**:332
"Fragments of a Liquidation" (Howe) **72**:195
"Fragments towards a Religio Poetae" (Gascoyne) **45**:147, 149
Fragola e panna (Ginzburg) **54**:207
"The Frailty" (Sassoon) **130**:221
"The Frame" (Dixon) **52**:98, 100
"Frame" (Rich) **36**:370; **73**:330
"Frame Lock" (Bernstein) **142**:57
"Frame Structures" (Howe) **152**:220, 235
Frame Structures: Early Poems, 1974-1979 (Howe) **152**:220, 232, 236-37
"Frames of Reference" (Bernstein) **142**:9
"Frame-Tale" (Barth) **3**:41; **9**:66; **51**:23; **89**:4, 7, 10, 15, 18, 22-23, 30, 32, 34, 38-9, 41, 43, 47, 49, 54-5, 59, 61
The Fran Lebowitz High Stress Diet (Lebowitz) **36**:249
"France" (Sassoon) **130**:180, 192, 212
France-la-doulce (Morand) **41**:304, 306
The Frances Ann Lebowitz Collection (Lebowitz) **36**:250
The Franchise (Gent) **29**:182-83
The Franchiser (Elkin) **9**:190-92; **14**:159; **27**:122-23; **51**:85, 88-9, 95-6, 99-101; **91**:213, 223
"Francis" (Nowlan) **15**:399
"Francisco, I'll Bring You Red Carnations" (Levine) **14**:320; **33**:274; **118**:279, 285, 302, 317
The Francoeur Novels (Plante) **38**:371
François Truffaut: Correspondence 1945-1984 (Truffaut) **101**:404
"Frank and Billy" (Colwin) **84**:141
Frank and Maisie: A Memoir with Parents (Sheed) **53**:338-40, 342
Frank and Stein and Me (Platt) **26**:356
Frank der Fünfte (Dürrenmatt) **15**:195-96, 199
Frank O'Hara: Poet among Painters (Perloff) **137**:262-64, 273
Frank Pig (McCabe)
See *Frank Pig Says Hello*
Frank Pig Says Hello (McCabe) **133**:113, 116
"Frank Sinatra or Carleton Carpenter" (Lish) **45**:229-30
Frank V (Duerrenmatt) **102**:54-5
Frank V (Dürrenmatt)
See *Frank der Fünfte*
"Frank Worley, D.C.M., July, 1954" (Blunden) **56**:40
"Frankenstein: A Political Version of the Myth of Motherhood" (Ferré) **139**:175
Frankenstein Unbound (Aldiss) **5**:15; **14**:14
"Frankforter Poetic-Vorlesungen" (Bachmann) **69**:58
"The Frankfurt Hauptbahnhof" (Kroetsch) **57**:292-93
Frankie and Johnny in the Clair de Lune (McNally) **91**:159
The Franklin Scare (Charyn) **18**:98
"The Franklin Stove" (Dixon) **52**:97
"Franny" (Salinger) **1**:299; **12**:512-13; **138**:172-73, 178, 216
Franny and Zooey (Salinger) **1**:298; **8**:463; **12**:512, 518; **56**:342, 348
Frantz Fanon (Caute) **29**:113
"Franz, a Goose" (Sarton) **14**:482
"Franz Grillparzer und der Clochard von Javel" (Handke) **134**:161
The Franza Case (Bachmann)
See *Der Fall Franza*
Fraternité de la parole (Chedid) **47**:81
A Fratricide/Ein Brudermord (The Brothers Quay) **95**:330, 333, 339-40
"Frau Bauman, Frau Schmidt, and Frau Schwartze" (Roethke) **101**:269-70, 286, 295
Die Frau im Mond (Lang) **20**:204, 211; **103**:88-9, 95
Fraud (Brookner) **136**:96, 108, 116-17, 121, 126-31
"Fraulein" (Ferber) **93**:162
"Fraying Paradise" (Blaga) **75**:68
"The Freak" (Wojciechowska) **26**:457
The Freak Mamma (Fo) **32**:176
Freak Out (Zappa) **17**:588-91, 593
"The Freak Show" (Willard) **7**:540
Freaks (Browning) **16**:122, 124-26
Freaks (Fiedler) **13**:214
Freaky Deaky (Leonard) **71**:217-18, 221-23, 225-26; **120**:275, 287, 303
Freaky Friday (Rodgers) **12**:493-95
The Fred Chappell Reader (Chappell) **78**:116
"Freda People" (Lennon)
See "Bring on the Lucie"
Freddy's Book (Gardner) **18**:180-84; **28**:166-68; **34**:550
Freddy's Book (Neufeld) **17**:309-10
"Freddy's Store" (Carroll) **35**:81
"Frederick" (Smith) **12**:543
"Frederick Douglass" (Hayden) **5**:168; **37**:153, 155, 157
"Frederick Douglass and the Slavebreaker" (Randall) **135**:386-87
"Frederick Jameson's American Marxism" (West) **134**:375
Frederick the Great (Mitford) **44**:485
"Fredericksted Dusk" (Walcott) **76**:285
"Frederiksted Nights" (Walcott) **14**:551; **76**:285

Fredi and Shirl and the Kids (Elman) **19**:150-51
"The Free" (Merwin) **13**:385
"Free" (Prince) **35**:328
Free Agents (Apple) **33**:20-2
"The Free and the Caged" (Cooper) **56**:70
Free at Last (Bontemps) **18**:64
Free Enterprise (Cliff) **120**:90-91, 113-18
Free Fall (Golding) **1**:121-22; **2**:166-68; **3**:196, 198-200; **10**:232-33, 237; **17**:161, 163, 166, 172, 174, 177-78, 180; **27**:162-64, 167; **58**:184-85; **81**:317, 323
"Free Fantasia: Tiger Flowers" (Hayden) **37**:158
"Free Flight" (Jordan) **114**:156
"Free Life" (Diamond) **30**:111
The Free Man (Richter) **30**:308, 310-12, 319-21
The Free Men (Ehle) **27**:103
"Free Money" (Smith) **12**:535, 538
Free Schools (Kozol) **17**:251-52
Free to Be Muhammad Ali (Lipsyte) **21**:212-13
"A Free Translation" (Raine) **103**:186, 188
A Free Translation (Raine) **32**:353-54; **103**:184
"Free Translation Of Reverdy" (Cabral de Melo Neto)
See "Paráfrase de reverdy"
"Free Will and the Commendatore" (Borges) **48**:43
"Free Women" (Lessing) **6**:292-93
"Freedman" (Heaney) **37**:162
Freedom Comes to Mississippi: The Story of Reconstruction (Meltzer) **26**:299-300
The Freedom Drum (Childress) **86**:309
"The Freedom Kick" (Foote) **75**:230-31
"Freedom New Hampshire" (Kinnell) **29**:281, 289; **129**:236, 257, 266
"Freedom Now" (Paley) **140**:244
Freedom of Action (Michaux)
See *Liberté d'action*
The Freedom of the City (Friel) **5**:129-30; **42**:168-69, 173-74; **115**:231, 234-36, 242, 244, 246, 248, 250, 256-57
The Freedom of the Poet (Berryman) **8**:87, 90-1; **10**:45-6; **13**:76; **62**:59
Freedom Road (Fast) **23**:155; **131**:55, 59-61, 64, 66, 69-70, 73, 79, 81, 85-6, 91-5
Freedom Road (Forman)
See *Freedom's Blood*
Freedom under Parole (Paz)
See *Libertad bajo palabra*
Freedom's Blood (Forman) **21**:122-23
"Freedom's Last Stand" (Bochco and Kozoll) **35**:58
"Freedom's Plow" (Hughes) **10**:282; **108**:283
The Freeing of the Dust (Levertov) **8**:348; **66**:238, 243
The Free-Lance Pallbearers (Reed) **2**:368-69; **3**:424; **5**:368-70; **6**:448-50; **13**:476-77; **32**:363; **60**:300, 305, 307, 311
Freely Espousing (Schuyler) **23**:388, 391
The Freeway (Nichols) **5**:306-09; **36**:329
The Freewheelin' Bob Dylan (Dylan) **4**:149; **12**:184, 198; **77**:168
Freewheeling Frank (McClure) **10**:332
"The Freeze" (Kuzma) **7**:196
"The Freeze" (Martin) **89**:111, 118
"Freezing to death" (Muske) **90**:308
Freidizm: Kriticheskii ocherk (Bakhtin) **83**:3, 7, 13, 23, 25, 29-30
"Freies Hörspiel" (Jandl) **34**:200
"The Freighters" (Lewis) **41**:261
"Freitzke's Turn" (Vance) **35**:422
Frêle bruit (Leiris) **61**:349, 351
Der fremde Freund (Hein) **154**:54-56, 58-9, 61, 64-72, 84-91, 94-104, 123, 125-26, 129, 134-36, 138-39, 141-42, 144, 149-50, 155, 160, 167, 176-78, 180, 188, 191, 193-94
"French as a Language of Culture" (Senghor) **130**:248
French Cancan (Renoir) **20**:288-89
French Connections: Voices from the Women's Movement in France (Duchen) **65**:325
French Dressing (Russell) **16**:541
"French Garden" (Senghor)
See "Jardin de France"
French Girls Are Vicious and Other Stories (Farrell) **66**:130
"French Intellectuals, 1946" (Faludy) **42**:140
French Kiss (Brossard) **115**:103-08, 110-11, 117-18, 148, 150-51, 154
"French Kissing" (Johnston) **51**:240-41, 245
"French Lessons" (Rasputin) **59**:379
"French Letters: Theories of the New Novel" (Vidal) **8**:527
The French Lieutenant's Woman (Fowles) **1**:109; **2**:137-39; **3**:163; **4**:170, 172-73; **6**:184-89; **9**:213-16; **10**:184, 186-90; **15**:234; **33**:166, 169, 171-75; **87**:138, 142-44, 147, 149-50, 156, 158, 161-62, 173-74, 176, 178-83
The French Lieutenant's Woman (Pinter) **27**:391
"The French Master" (Abse) **29**:15-16
French Persian Cats Having a Ball (Morgan) **31**:272
"A French Poem" (Merton) **83**:384
French Postcards (Klein) **30**:241
The French Powder Mystery (Queen) **3**:422
French Reveille (Aragon)
See *La diane Française*
The French Revolution and Enlightenment in England (Deane) **122**:84
French without Tears (Rattigan) **7**:354-55
A Frenchman Must Die (Boyle) **58**:64; **121**:53-4
Frenchman's Creek (du Maurier) **6**:147; **11**:162; 59;280-84, 286-87
"Freneau, Whitman, and Williams" (Pinsky) **94**:301, 303
Frenzy (Bergman)
See *Hets*
Frenzy (Hitchcock) **16**:350-54
Frequencies (Thomas) **13**:544-45; **48**:380-82
Frequent Hearses (Crispin) **22**:109
Frère bois (Tzara) **47**:396
Frère François (Green) **77**:282-83
"Fresco: Departure for an Imperialist War" (McGrath) **59**:181
"Frescoes for Mr. Rockefeller's City" (MacLeish) **68**:288
Frescoes for Mr. Rockefeller's City (MacLeish) **8**:362; **14**:338; **68**:279, 281-82, 284-85, 288-89, 292
"Frescoes of the New World II" (Walcott) **76**:274
"Fresh" (Pearce) **21**:289
"Fresh Air" (Koch) **8**:322; **44**:241, 243, 245-47, 249-51
The Fresh Air (Shamlu) **10**:470
"Fresh Spring in Whose Deep Woods I Sought" (Daryush) **19**:123
Fresh Water, Sea Water (Levi) **41**:244
"The Fresh-Ploughed Hill" (Nowlan) **15**:398
"Freshwater West" (Mathias) **45**:235
Freud (Huston) **20**:168-69, 173
"Freud and Literature" (Trilling) **24**:454, 456
Freud and Man's Soul (Bettelheim) **79**:134
"Freud and the Analysis of Poetry" (Burke) **24**:127, 130
"Freud and the Crisis of Our Culture" (Trilling) **24**:457
The Freud Scenario (Sartre) **52**:385
Freudianism: A Marxist Critique (Bakhtin)
See *Freidizm: Kriticheskii ocherk*
Freudism (Bakhtin)
See *Freidizm: Kriticheskii ocherk*
"Freud's Tropology of Dreaming" (White) **148**:299
The Friar (Cabral de Melo Neto)
See *Auto do frade*
The Friar's Way (Cabral de Melo Neto)
See *Auto do frade*
"Friday" (Grass) **32**:200
Friday (Heinlein) **26**:178-79; **55**:303
The Friday Book; or, Book-Titles Should Be Straightforward and Subtitles Avoided: Essays and Other Nonfiction (Barth) **51**:24-6, 29; **89**:57
"Friday Morning: The Orderly's Tale" (Klima) **56**:170
"Friday Night" (Hogan) **73**:150
"Friday Night in the Royal Station Hotel" (Larkin) **8**:332, 337; **64**:266
Friday; or, The Other Island (Tournier)
See *Vendredi; ou, La vie sauvage*
Friday the Rabbi Slept Late (Kemelman) **2**:225
"Friday the Thirteenth" (Ginsberg) **36**:185
"Friday's Child" (Livesay) **79**:348
"Friday's Child" (Pastan) **27**:371
"Friday's Footprint" (Gordimer) **33**:180
Friday's Footprint (Gordimer) **18**:185; **33**:179-80; **70**:162
Friday's Hiding (Arden) **15**:21
Der Friede (Jünger) **125**:221, 257
"Fried-Egg Deal" (Bogosian) **141**:85
"A Friend and Protector" (Taylor) **18**:522; **37**:411-13; **44**:305, 310; **50**:260; **71**:295
A Friend from England (Brookner) **51**:63-6; **136**:88, 92, 113-15, 127
"A Friend of Kafka" (Singer) **23**:419
A Friend of Kafka, and Other Stories (Singer) **3**:453, 455; **6**:509; **9**:488; **23**:419
"Friend of My Youth" (Munro) **95**:310, 315
Friend of My Youth (Munro) **95**:306-09, 311, 313, 318, 320, 322, 324
"A Friend of Ours Who Knits" (Shields) **113**:441
"A Friend of the Earth" (Thurber) **5**:432
"Friend of the Family" (Boyle) **19**:63
"A Friend of the Family" (Dybek) **114**:67
"A Friend of the Family" (Simpson) **7**:429; **149**:309, 321
"The Friend of the Fourth Decade" (Merrill) **6**:323; **13**:380-81
Friend to Friend (Buck) **127**:231-32
Friendly Fire (Bryan) **29**:102-04
The Friendly Persuasion (West) **7**:519-21; **17**:543-48, 550-52
The Friendly Young Ladies (Renault) **17**:390-91
"Friends" (Beattie) **146**:65
"Friends" (Ian) **21**:183
"Friends" (O'Brien) **103**:140
"Friends" (Page and Plant) **12**:475
"Friends" (Paley) **37**:334, 336, 339; **140**:208-10, 212, 214-16, 220, 223, 228, 234-35, 271, 277
"Friends" (Wilson) **12**:641
Friends (Abe)
See *Tomodachi, enemoto takekai*
The Friends (Guy) **26**:141-45
The Friends (Wesker) **3**:519-20; **42**:426-30
Friends (Wilson) **12**:641-42, 644, 649-50, 652
Friends and Heroes (Manning) **19**:301
Friends and Lovers (MacInnes) **27**:280
"Friends and Occasions" (Johnston) **51**:248-49, 254
Friends and Relations (Bowen) **3**:84; **11**:62; **15**:78; **118**:81, 88-97
Friends in Low Places (Raven) **14**:441
The Friends of Eddie Coyle (Higgins) **4**:222-24; **7**:158; **10**:273-74; **18**:233-35
The Friends of God (Vansittart)
See *The Siege*
"Friends of Miss Reece" (Hill) **113**:291, 310, 312, 325
"The Friends of Plonk" (Amis) **40**:43
"The Friends of the Family" (Barthelme) **115**:86
The Friends of the Loony Lake Monster (Bonham) **12**:53
"Friendship" (Katz) **47**:220, 223
Friendship (Blanchot) **135**:133-34, 148
"Friendship and Poverty" (Rooke) **25**:392
"Friendship on Visit" (Riding) **7**:374
A Friendship: The Letters of Dan Rowan and John D. MacDonald (MacDonald) **44**:408-09
"The Frightened Man" (Bogan) **46**:77; **93**:65
"Frightening Civil Servants" (Priestley) **34**:362
"Frigidity in Men" (Thurber) **125**:402

Fringe (Bennett)
See *Beyond the Fringe*
A Fringe of Leaves (White) **9**:566-68; **65**:275-76, 278-79, 282; **69**:405
Die Frist (Duerrenmatt) **102**:61, 64
"Fritz" (Stern) **40**:413, 415
"Fritz Bugs Out" (Crumb) **17**:82
Fritz the Cat (Bakshi) **26**:66-70, 73-5
Fritz the Cat (Crumb) **17**:82
"The Frivolous Cake" (Peake) **54**:369
"Frog Autumn" (Plath) **11**:447; **111**:185, 200
"The Frog Hunters" (Colter) **58**:147
"Frog Pond" (Muske) **90**:318
"Frog Trouncin' Contest" (Stuart) **11**:512
"Frogfather" (Wellman) **49**:393
The Frogs (Sondheim) **30**:389, 402
"Frog's Woman" (Bowering) **32**:47
"The Frolic" (Ligotti) **44**:53
A Frolic of His Own (Gaddis) **86**:146-69
Der Fröliche Weinberg (Zuckmayer) **18**:553-55
"From a Berkeley Notebook" (Johnson) **52**:232
"From a Certain Protocol" (Tanizaki) **28**:415
From a Crooked Rib (Farah) **53**:132-33, 135-36; **137**:82-84, 86-89, 105, 107, 120, 130
"From a Daybook" (Swenson) **106**:333
"From a Diary" (Voznesensky) **57**:421
"From a Distance" (Bell) **8**:67
"From a Forthcoming Blue Book" (Forster) **45**:134
"From a French Prison" (Rhys) **124**:337, 354
"From a Grown-Up to a Child" (Christie) **110**:125
From a Land Where Other People Live (Lorde) **18**:307-08; **71**:231, 254
"From a Litany" (Strand) **6**:522; **18**:515-16; **71**:285
"From a Long Distance" (Ezekiel) **61**:104
"From a Lost Diary" (Strand) **71**:286
From a Night Porter's Point of View (Kieslowski) **120**:245-46
"From a Notebook" (Justice) **6**:271
"From a Notebook, October '68—May '69" (Levertov) **5**:249; **28**:240
"From a Provincial" (Avison) **97**:74-5, 80, 123
"From a Refugee's Notebook" (Ozick) **28**:350-51; **62**:351
From a Seaside Town (Levine) **54**:293-95, 297, 300
"From a Suburban Window" (Abse) **29**:16
"From a Survivor" (Rich) **3**:427, 429; **36**:366
"From a Traveller" (Seth) **43**:388
From a View to a Death (Powell) **3**:404; **10**:411-12; **31**:320
From a Watch Tower (Arghezi)
See *Dintr-un foişor*
"From a Window" (Olson) **28**:343
"From a Writer's Notebook" (Cisneros) **69**:145
"From Action to Image: Theories of the Lyric in the Eighteenth Century" (Maclean) **78**:235-36
"From Allegories to Novels" (Borges) **83**:161
From an Abandoned Work (Beckett) **6**:38, 42; **11**:39-40; **29**:56
"From an Airplane" (Cabral de Melo Neto)
See "De um avião"
"From an Almanac" (Baraka) **5**:45
"From an Exchange of Letters" (Voinovich) **49**:376-77; **147**:270, 284
"From an Old House in America" (Rich) **6**:459; **7**:372; **11**:475; **36**:366, 375; **73**:328; **76**:218
"From Athens County, Ohio" (Plumly) **33**:311
From Bauhaus to Our House (Wolfe) **35**:460, 464; **51**:416, 420; **147**:310, 321, 335, 342-43
From Beginning to End (Lengyel) **7**:202
From Behind the Veil (Stepto) **65**:379, 381
From Bondage (Roth) **104**:327-31
From Bourgeois Land (Smith) **64**:390, 395, 398-99
From Centre City (Kinsella) **138**:134-38, 146, 148, 153-54, 156
From Cliché to Archetype (McLuhan) **83**:366
From Cuba with a Song (Sarduy)
See *De donde son los cantantes*
"From Dawn 'til Dusk" (Aksyonov) **101**:9
From Dawn to Decadence: 500 Years of Western Cultural Life, 1500 to the Present (Barzun) **145**:91-4, 97, 100-01, 103-06, 110
From Death-Camp to Existentialism: A Psychiatrist's Path to a New Therapy (Frankl)
See *Ein psycholog erlebt das konzentrationslager*
From Desire to Desire (Yevtushenko) **13**:620
"From Don Giovanni" (Thomas) **31**:434
From Doon with Death (Rendell) **28**:385, 387; **48**:319
From Dusk Till Dawn (Tarantino) **125**:367
"From: Elephant" (Neruda) **28**:307
"From Elfland to Poughkeepsie" (Le Guin) **13**:347; **22**:274
"From Em, Me" (Johnson) **6**:264
From Every Chink of the Ark and Other New Poems (Redgrove) **41**:354-55
From Fear Set Free (Sahgal) **41**:370
"From Feathers to Iron" (Kunitz) **148**:97
From Feathers to Iron (Day Lewis) **6**:128; **10**:126-27, 131-32
From Flushing to Calvary (Dahlberg) **7**:66, 68; **14**:135-37
"from Four Seasons in the American Woods" (Bly) **128**:17
"From Gloucester Out" (Dorn) **10**:159
From Heaven Lake: Travels through Sinkiang and Tibet (Seth) **43**:386-87; **90**:335-36, 349, 356-7
From Here to Eternity (Jones) **1**:161-62; **3**:260-62; **10**:290-94; **39**:405-10, 412-15
"From His Dream" (Young Bear) **94**:362
"From Hospital" (Clark Bekedermo)
See "For Granny"
"From Huesca with Love and Kisses" (O'Faolain) **32**:341
"From Humaweepi: Warrior Priest" (Silko) **23**:408
From Lexington to Liberty (Lancaster) **36**:244-45
"From Lines of Swinburne" (Bernstein) **142**:46
"From Memory" (Forché) **25**:169
From Morn to Midnight (Rice) **7**:359
"From Morning Poems" (Le Guin) **136**:395
"From My Window" (Williams) **33**:448; **148**:308-09, 329
"From Okra to Greens: A Different Kinda Love Story" (Shange) **38**:394
"From One Identity to Another" (Kristeva) **77**:320; **140**:185
"From Orient Point" (Hacker) **72**:192
"From P Forward" (Pesetsky) **28**:357
"From Pierced Darkness" (Rich) **125**:335
From Plan to Planet (Madhubuti) **65**:403
"From Poe to Valéry" (Eliot) **113**:194-211
From Potter's Field (Cornwell) **155**:64-7, 70
"From Proust to Dada" (Gold) **42**:197
"From Raven's Road" (Allen) **84**:28
"From Realism to Reality" (Robbe-Grillet) **43**:360
From Rockaway (Eisenstadt) **50**:38-42
From Russia, with Love (Fleming) **3**:15; **30**:131, 132, 137, 142, 148-50
From Sand Creek: Rising in This Heart Which Is Our America (Ortiz) **45**:308
"From Shannon" (Brutus) **43**:90
"From Silver Lake" (Browne) **21**:34, 37
From Sleep Unbound (Chedid)
See *Le sommeil délivré*
From Snow and Rock, from Chaos: Poems, 1965-1972 (Carruth) **4**:94; **7**:40-1; **84**:119
"From Someone to Nobody" (Borges) **83**:162
"From Spiralling Ecstatically This" (Cummings) **68**:41
From Submarines to Satellites (Hyde) **21**:172
"From Superstition" (Pasternak) **10**:382; **63**:280
"From the African Diary" (Transtroemer)
See "Ur en afrikansk dagbok"
"From the Arsonist" (Muske) **95**:314
"From the Attic" (Davies) **75**:197
"From the Babur-Nama" (Seth) **43**:388
From the Berkeley Hills (Elliott) **2**:131
"From the Canton of Expectation" (Heaney) **74**:161, 174-75, 177
"From the Cave" (Lorde) **71**:262
"From the Childhood of Jesus" (Pinsky) **94**:306, 308, 312; **121**:436-37, 446, 452
"From 'The Chronicles of Knarn'" (Nichol) **18**:368
From the City of Lodz (Kieslowski)
See *Lodz--The Town*
"From the Crypts of Memory" (Smith) **43**:424
"From the Cupola" (Merrill) **2**:273; **13**:376, 381
"From the Dalva Notebooks, 1985-87" (Harrison) **143**:355
"From the Depth" (Blaga) **75**:61
"From the Diary of a New York Lady" (Parker) **68**:334
From the Diary of a Snail (Grass)
See *Aus dem Tagebuch einer Schnecke*
"From the Diary of a Young Lady" (Parker) **68**:330
"From the Dressing Room" (McGuckian) **48**:277
From the Fifteenth District (Gallant) **18**:172-73
From the First Nine (Merrill) **34**:235
"From the Flying-Boat" (Blunden) **56**:49
"From the Foundry of the Soul" (Eklöf) **27**:110
"From the Frontier of Writing" (Heaney) **74**:162, 172
"From the Hazel Bough" (Birney) **6**:75
From the Heart of the Country (Coetzee)
See *In the Heart of the Country*
"From the Hot Hills" (Lane) **25**:288
"From the House of Yemanjá" (Lorde) **71**:233, 250-51
"From the Image Flow—Summer of 1986" (Levertov) **66**:251
"From the Imperial" (Motion) **47**:289
From the Irish (Simmons) **43**:414-15
"From the Irish of Pangur Ban" (Boland) **67**:43
"From the Japanese" (Glück) **44**:216, 222
"From the Joke Shop" (Fuller) **28**:157
From the Joke Shop (Fuller) **28**:154-55, 159
"From the Journal of a Leper" (Updike) **15**:544, 546-47
"From the Journals of a Poet" (Bogan) **39**:394
"From the Land of the Dead" (Kinsella) **138**:159
From the Life of the Marionettes (Bergman)
See *Aus dem Leben der Marionetten*
"From the Masque Hyacinth" (H. D.) **73**:108
From the Memoirs of Ijon Richy (Lem) **149**:148
"From the New World" (Graham) **118**:231-33, 237-38, 252, 260
"From the Painting 'Back from the Market'" (Boland) **40**:100; **113**:89, 93, 109
"From the Phoenix to the Unnamable, Impossibly Beautiful Wild Bird" (Chester) **49**:55-6
"From the Pillar" (Huxley) **11**:284
"From the Prado Rotunda" (Ostriker) **132**:328
"From the Prehistory of Novelistic Discourse" (Bakhtin) **83**:5, 59, 61
"From the Prehistory of the Novel-Word" (Bakhtin)
See "From the Prehistory of Novelistic Discourse"
"From the Questions to Mary" (Redgrove) **41**:352
"From the Ravages of Life We Create" (Kunene) **85**:165
From the Realm of Morpheus (Millhauser) **54**:329-331; **109**:157, 170, 174
"From the Reflections of Mr. Glass" (Redgrove) **41**:352
"From the Republic of Conscience" (Heaney) **74**:174

"From the Rising of the Sun" (Milosz)
See "From Where the Sun Rises"
From the River's Edge (Cook-Lynn) **93**:124-30, 132
"From the Roof" (Levertov) **66**:236, 250
"From the Rooftops" (Haines) **58**:216
From "The School of Eloquence" and Other Poems (Harrison) **43**:175-77, 180-81
"From the Secret Notebook of Fellow-Traveler Sand" (Olesha) **8**:430
"From the Song of Ullikummi" (Olson) **11**:416
From the Terrace (O'Hara) **2**:324-25; **6**:385; **42**:313, 316-18, 322
"From the Testament of Tourmaline: Variations of Themes of 'The Tao Teh Ching'" (Stow) **23**:436
"From the Town Guide" (Fisher) **25**:161
"From the Very First Coming Down" (Auden) **14**:32; **43**:15
"From the Vestibule" (Zamora) **89**:369
From the Wilderness (MacLean) **50**:349
"From the Winter of 1947" (Transtroemer) **52**:417; **65**:230
From This Condensery: The Complete Writings of Lorine Niedecker (Niedecker) **42**:297-300
From Threshold to Threshold (Celan)
See *Von Schwelle zu Schwelle*
From Time to Time (Ciardi) **40**:153-54; **44**:378, 382
"From 'Twelfth Night'" (Burke)
See "Trial Translation"
From under the Rubble (Solzhenitsyn) **34**:486; **78**:403, 405-06, 427-28
"From Where the Sun Rises" (Milosz) **11**:377, 380-81; **22**:308, 310; **56**:237; **82**:293-95, 297, 304-06, 309
"From William Tyndale to John Frith" (Bowers) **9**:122
"From Work to Text" (Barthes) **83**:88
"From Yellow Lake: An Interview" (Van Duyn) **116**:415
"A Front" (Jarrell) **13**:300
"Front de la rose" (Char) **14**:125
"Front Lines" (Snyder) **120**:340, 346
The Front Page (Hecht) **8**:270
"A Front Page Story" (Farrell) **66**:112
The Front Room Boys (Buzo) **61**:53-61, 64, 67-9
"Front Seat" (Rendell) **48**:320
"Front Tooth Crowned with Gold" (Simic) **49**:337; **130**:306
Frontier Wolf (Sutcliff) **26**:437
"Frontier Woman" (Richter) **30**:307
"Frontiers" (Aldiss) **40**:19
"The Frontiers of Criticism" (Eliot) **24**:178
"Frontiers of Writing" (Heaney) **91**:129
"The Frontiersman" (Turner) **48**:398
"Frontispiece" (Swenson) **106**:315
"Frontispoem" (Rose) **85**:313
"Frontline Chronicle" (D'Aguiar) **145**:115
Frontline General: Douglas MacArthur (Archer) **12**:15
Frossia (Almedingen) **12**:7
"Frost" (Johnston) **51**:249
Frost (Bernhard) **32**:17-20, 27; **61**:9, 21
Frost: A Literary Life Reconsidered (Pritchard) **34**:468-74
Frost on the Sun (Jones) **10**:285, 288
"Frost Still in the Ground" (Bly) **15**:68
"Frosty Night" (Graves) **45**:167
"The Frozen Fields" (Bowles) **2**:79; **53**:46, 48-9
The Frozen Flame (O'Brian) **152**:278
"Frozen Jap" (McCartney) **35**:289
Frozen Music (King) **53**:212-13; **145**:350-51, 358
"The Frozen Wedding Party" (Kadare) **52**:263
A Frozen Woman (Ernaux)
See *La femme gelée*
"Früh die Meere" (Sachs) **98**:359
"Früher Mittag" (Bachmann) **69**:39, 54
Das Frühwerk (Celan) **82**:48
"Fruit" (Ezekiel) **61**:101
"The Fruit" (Urdang) **47**:399
Fruit (Brenton) **31**:56-7, 60
"The Fruit Man, the Meat Man, and the Manager" (Hood) **28**:193
The Fruit Man, the Meat Man, and the Manager (Hood) **28**:188-90
"Fruit on a Straight-Sided Tray" (Boland) **40**:101; **67**:45
Le fruit permis (Tzara) **47**:390
Fruitful and Responsible Love (John Paul II) **128**:161
"The Fruit-Grower in War-Time" (Fenton) **32**:164, 166
"Fruition at Forty" (Narayan) **28**:293
Fruits and Vegetables (Jong) **4**:263; **6**:267; **8**:313-15; **18**:277; **83**:291, 299
Les fruits d'or (Sarraute) **2**:384-86; **4**:464-70; **8**:469, 472; **31**:379, 383, 386; **80**:236, 238, 240, 252
Früjesång (Ekelöf) **27**:112, 114
Frunze (Arghezi) **80**:6, 8
"Frutta" (Viereck) **4**:559
"The Fuck Machine" (Bukowski) **41**:68, 75; **108**:85
Fucking Martin (Peck)
See *Martin and John*
"Fuda-no-Tsuji" (Endō) **54**:161; **99**:301
"Fuego fatuo" (Ulibarrí) **83**:412
"Fuel for the Fire" (Shields) **113**:408, 432
"Fuel Stoppage on Gladesville Road Bridge in the Year 1980" (Murray) **40**:343
Fuera del juego (Padilla) **38**:353
Fuerte es el silencio (Poniatowska) **140**:298, 304, 309, 319, 331
"La Fuerza Feminina" (Moraga) **126**:296
"Fuga a caballo" (Aleixandre) **9**:13
Le fugitif (Gascar) **11**:222-23
"Fugitive" (Fulton) **52**:160
The Fugitive (Ford) **16**:312-13
Fugitive (Montgomery) **7**:233-34
Fugitive Kind (Williams) **111**:424
The Fugitive Pigeon (Westlake) **7**:528
"Fugitives Return" (Warren) **13**:581
"Los fugitivos" (Carpentier) **110**:76
"Fugue" (O'Faolain) **32**:340, 343; **70**:314-15
"La Fugue du petit Poucet" (Tournier) **95**:367, 378, 383-87, 389
Fugue in a Nursery (Fierstein) **33**:152-53
A Fugue in Time (Godden)
See *Take Three Tenses*
"A Fugue on Memory" (Hospital) **145**:294, 302
"The Führer Bunker" (Snodgrass) **68**:388
The Führer Bunker: A Cycle of Poems in Progress (Snodgrass) **10**:478; **18**:492, 494-95; **68**:383-86, 391, 398
"Fuku" (Yevtushenko) **51**:431-33
"Fulani Cattle" (Clark Bekedermo) **38**:121, 126, 128
"The Fulfilled Destiny of Electra" (Glassco) **9**:237
Fulfillingness' First Finale (Wonder) **12**:657
"Fulfillment" (Hughes) **108**:332
"The Fulfillment" (Schwartz) **45**:361
"Fulfilment" (Blunden) **56**:48
Fulgor y muerte de Joaquín Murieta (Neruda) **5**:301, 305; **28**:312
"The Full Belly" (White) **5**:487; **7**:532
Full Disclosure (Safire) **10**:446-47
"Full Fathom Five" (Plath) **9**:425; **17**:360; **51**:344; **111**:178, 209
Full House (Keane) **31**:232
"Full Moon" (Davies) **21**:102
Full of Life (Fante) **60**:131-36
Full of Lust and Good Usage (Dunn) **36**:152-53, 155
"Full Sail" (Wilson) **12**:654
Full Term (Stewart) **14**:512
Fullerton Street (Wilson) **118**:398
Fully Empowered (Neruda) **7**:260-62; **9**:398; **28**:314
"The Fully-Licensed Whore" (Highsmith) **102**:186, 197
The Fume of Poppies (Kozol) **17**:248-49
"Fumiko no ashi" (Tanizaki) **8**:509
"Fumiko's Feet" (Tanizaki)
See "Fumiko no ashi"
"Fun" (Johnston) **51**:244
"Fun and Games" (Major) **19**:298
"Fun, Fun, Fun" (Wilson) **12**:646, 649-50, 653
Fun in a Chinese Laundry (Sternberg) **20**:375
The Fun of It: A Love Story (Neufeld) **17**:310-11
"The Function and Field of Speech and Language in Psychoanalysis" (Lacan)
See "Fonction et champ de la parole et du langage en psychanalyse"
"Function of Blizzard" (Warren) **39**:273
"The Function of Criticism" (Eliot) **113**:207
"The Function of Criticism" (Vendler) **138**:264-65, 270-71
Function of Criticism (Eagleton) **132**:87, 100
The Function of Criticism (Winters) **32**:462-63
The Function of Criticism: From 'The Spectator' to Post-Structuralism (Eagleton) **63**:98-9
"The Function of the Poet in Society" (Rexroth) **49**:287
"Functional Poetry: A Proposal" (Dudek) **11**:159; **19**:137
La fundación (Buero Vallejo) **46**:94, 98-100; **139**:10, 14-16, 18-20, 22-27, 38, 40-2, 57-60, 72
"Fundamental Disagreement with Two Contemporaries" (Rexroth) **49**:278; **112**:372
"The Fundamental Project of Technology" (Kinnell) **129**:258, 264
"The Funeral" (Matheson) **37**:246
"The Funeral" (Redgrove) **41**:359
"The Funeral" (Spender) **41**:427-28
Funeral at Rutland Place (Perry) **126**:326, 328-29
Funeral Games (Orton) **13**:435; **43**:326, 330, 332, 335
Funeral Games (Scannell) **49**:334
Funeral in Berlin (Deighton) **7**:74-5; **22**:114; **46**:125-26, 128-30
A Funeral in Teresienburg (Krleža) **8**:329
"Funeral Music" (Hill) **8**:295; **45**:178-80, 185-87, 189
"Funeral na Inglaterra" (Cabral de Melo Neto) **76**:161
"The Funeral of Ally Flett" (Brown) **5**:77
"The Funeral of Bobo" (Brodsky) **36**:79-80
The Funeral of Mama Grand (García Márquez)
See *Los funerales de la Mamá Grande*
A Funeral Polish Style (Rozewicz)
See *Pogrzeb po polsku*
"Funeral Prayer" (Carrier) **78**:83
"Funeral Rites" (Heaney) **7**:148, 151; **14**:242, 244; **25**:246; **74**:162; **91**:116
Funeral Rites (Genet)
See *Pompes funèbres*
Los funerales de la Mamá Grande (García Márquez) **2**:148; **3**:183; **27**:151; **47**:148, 150; **68**:141, 150-51, 153
Funerals Are Fatal (Christie)
See *After the Funeral*
"Funes" (Borges)
See "Funes el memorioso"
"Funes el memorioso" (Borges) **1**:39; **2**:71-2; **6**:90; **8**:97; **48**:42, 45-6; **83**:157, 168-69, 183
"Funes, His Memory" (Borges)
See "Funes el memorioso"
"Funes the Memorious" (Borges)
See "Funes el memorioso"
"Fun-Fair of Words" (Rodgers) **7**:378
"Die fünfte Grundrechenart" (Hein) **154**:73, 133-34
Die fünfte Grundrechenart (Hein) **154**:66, 188
"Funghi in città" (Calvino) **33**:100; **73**:33

"Funhouse" (Barth)
See "Lost in the Funhouse"
Funhouse (Barth)
See *Lost in the Funhouse: Fiction for Print, Tape, Live Voice*
Funhouse (Bogosian) **45**:61-2; **141**:82-3, 85
The Funhouse (Koontz) **78**:202
"Funky Dung" (Pink Floyd) **35**:311
"A Funky Space Reincarnation" (Gaye) **26**:134
"Funland" (Oates) **33**:296
Funland and Other Poems (Abse) **7**:1-2; **29**:18-19
"Funny Girl" (Wasserstein) **59**:223
The Funny Man (Chaplin) **16**:200
The Funny Old Man (Rozewicz)
See *Śmieszny staruszek*
"Funny Papers by Hiram Handspring" (Laughlin) **49**:224
"A Funny Thing" (Bates) **46**:55-6, 62
A Funny Thing Happened on the Way to the Forum (Gelbart) **21**:125-26; **61**:147-49
A Funny Thing Happened on the Way to the Forum (Lester) **20**:223, 226
A Funny Thing Happened on the Way to the Forum (Sondheim) **30**:378, 383, 385, 395, 401-02; **147**:228, 253, 255, 259, 261
Funnyhouse of a Negro (Kennedy) **66**:205, 209-10, 212-14
"The Fur Coat" (O'Faolain) **32**:343
The Fur Hat (Voinovich) **147**:287-90
Fureur et mystère (Char) **9**:163; **11**:115; **14**:127
El furgón de cola (Goytisolo) **23**:185, 187
"Las furias y las penas" (Neruda) **62**:329-31
Die Furie des Verschwindens (Enzensberger) **43**:151
"The Furies" (Sexton) **53**:320, 322-23; **123**:420
"The Furies" (Zelazny) **21**:468
The Furies (Jakes) **29**:248
The Furies (Ringwood) **48**:339
"The Furies and the Pains" (Neruda)
See "Las furias y las penas"
Furious (Moure) **88**:223-26, 231
"The Furious Seasons" (Carver) **55**:275
Furious Seasons, and Other Stories (Carver) **22**:97; **55**:275; **126**:131-33
"The Furlough" (Tolson) **105**:282
"The Furnace" (Kinsella) **138**:163
"Furnished Lives" (Silkin) **43**:398-400
"Furnished Room" (Corso) **11**:123
"Furor Scribendi" (Butler) **121**:142
Furors Die (Hoffman) **141**:274-76, 281-82, 296-97, 307-08
"Furry Sings the Blues" (Mitchell) **12**:441
Fürsorgliche Belagerung (Boell) **27**:67-9; **39**:293
The Further Adventures of Huckleberry Finn (Matthews) **45**:240-44
The Further Adventures of the Robber Hotzenplotz (Preussler) **17**:375-76
"further attempt at a poem" (Rozewicz)
See "jesze próba"
Further Fables for Our Time (Thurber) **5**:430-32, 434, 442
"The Further Off from England" (McGinley) **14**:365
A Further Range (Frost) **3**:174; **4**:174; **9**:220, 228; **10**:196; **26**:117, 119; **34**:475
"Further Recollections" (Lem) **40**:294
"Further Reminiscences" (Lem) **149**:159
"Further Reminiscences of Ijon Itchy: II" (Lem) **149**:150, 162
"Further Reminiscences of Ijon Tichy" (Lem) **149**:158
Further Sightings (Rothenberg) **6**:477
Further Tales of the City (Maupin) **95**:191-92, 194-95, 197, 199, 203
Further...Further...Further! (Shatrov)
See *Dal'she...Dal'she...Dal'she!*
"Fury" (Theroux) **46**:398
Fury (Lang) **20**:206, 216; **103**:85
The Fury (De Palma) **20**:79-80
"The Fury of Aerial Bombardment" (Eberhart) **11**:176, 178; **19**:140, 144; **56**:88-9, 91
"The Fury of Rain" (Harjo) **83**:274, 276, 283
"The Fury of the Cocks" (Sexton) **123**:439
"The Fuse" (Browne) **21**:39
Le fusil-harpon et autres nouvelles (Vassilikos) **4**:552
Futen rojin nikki (Tanizaki) **14**:526-27; **28**:414-15, 418
Futility (Gerhardie) **5**:139-40
"The Future" (Ignatow) **7**:178; **14**:275
"The Future" (Murray) **40**:341
"A Future for the Novel" (Robbe-Grillet) **43**:360
"Future Green" (Jacobsen) **48**:191
Future History (Heinlein) **26**:164
"The Future, If Any, of Comedy; or, Where Do We Not-Go from Here?" (Thurber) **125**:387
The Future in the Present: Selected Writings (James) **33**:221-22
Future Indefinite (Coward)
See *Autobiography*
The Future Is in Eggs (Ionesco)
See *L'Avenir est dans les oeufs*
The Future Is Ours, Comrade: Conversations with the Russians (Kosinski) **2**:232; **53**:220; **70**:298, 300, 305
The Future Lasts a Long Time (Althusser)
See *L'avenir dure longtemps*
The Future Lasts Forever (Althusser)
See *L'avenir dure longtemps*
"Future Legend" (Bowie) **17**:68
"The Future of Literacy" (Eco) **142**:100, 103
"The Future of Music" (Cage) **41**:84
"The Future of Poetry" (Ransom) **4**:436; **5**:365
The Future of Religions (Tillich) **131**:345
"The Future of Science: Prometheus, Apollo, Athena" (Bova) **45**:75
The Future of Social Studies (Michener) **109**:376
"The Future of the Novel as an Art Form" (MacLennan) **92**:306
Future Perfect (Abish)
See *In the Future Perfect*
Futures (Hochman) **8**:297
The Futurist Moment (Perloff) **137**:271, 273-75, 277, 288
The Futurological Congress (Lem) **15**:327-28; **40**:289, 296; **149**:118-19, 132-38, 151, 159, 165, 168-71, 208, 261, 263, 270-72, 274-75, 277, 289
Futz (Owens) **8**:434
"G" (Berger) **2**:54; **19**:38, 40
"G" (Merrill) **8**:385
"Gabon" (Kinsella) **43**:258
"Gabor" (Swift) **41**:443
"Gabriel and the Water Shortage" (Olds) **85**:297
"Gabriel García Márquez and the Invention of America" (Fuentes) **60**:162
Gabriel García Márquez: Historia de un deicidio (Vargas Llosa) **10**:500; **85**:355, 378
The Gabriel Hounds (Stewart) **35**:391
Gabriela, Clove and Cinnamon (Amado)
See *Gabriela, cravo e canela*
Gabriela, cravo e canela (Amado) **13**:11-12; **40**:28-9, 31-5; **106**:54-5, 57, 60-2, 65, 73, 77-8, 84-6, 89
Gabriel's Lament (Bailey) **45**:47-9
Gaby Brimmer (Poniatowska) **140**:304, 330-31
"The Gadget Lover" (McLuhan) **83**:367
"Gaeltacht" (Buckley) **57**:134, 136
Gagner (Guillevic) **33**:191-92, 194
Le gai savoir (Godard) **20**:140
"Gaiety" (Sitwell) **67**:312
Gai-jin (Clavell) **87**:7, 16-18
Gaily, Gaily (Hecht) **8**:273
"Gaily Teetering on the Bath's Edge" (Brutus) **43**:91
"Gain" (Montague) **46**:270, 274
"Gaines Mill" (Mott) **15**:380-81
Gaining Ground (Barfoot) **18**:36
Gaining Ground (Kroetsch) **132**:199
Gala (West) **14**:568-69; **96**:368, 373, 375
"Galactic Consumer Reports" (Brunner) **8**:108
Galactic Derelict (Norton) **12**:463, 467
Galactic Effectuator (Vance) **35**:422
Galactic Pot-Healer (Dick) **30**:125; **72**:121
"Galán" (MacLeish) **68**:290
"Galanta" (O'Hara) **78**:333
The Galantrys (Allingham)
See *Dance of the Years*
Galápagos (Vonnegut) **40**:446-50; **111**:361
Galas: A Modern Tragedy (Ludlam) **46**:242; **50**:342-44
"Galatea" (Thomas) **37**:419-20; **107**:328
Galatea (Cain) **28**:48-9, 51, 53-4
Galatea 2.2 (Powers) **93**:295, 297-302
Galaxies like Grains of Sand (Aldiss) **14**:11
"Gale in April" (Jeffers) **54**:236
"Galician Nights, or, a Novel in Progress" (Rothenberg) **57**:383
The Galileans (Slaughter) **29**:375
The Galilee Hitch-Hiker (Brautigan) **12**:57, 61
"Galileo Galilei" (Smith) **6**:513
"The Gallery" (Murray) **40**:338
"The Gallery" (Transtroemer) **52**:414
A Gallery of Harlem Portraits (Tolson) **36**:429-30; **105**:237-40, 249, 256, 258-63, 281, 283-84
"Gallery Walk: Art and Nature" (Moss) **45**:290
"Galley Slave" (Asimov) **76**:320; **92**:13-4
Gallipoli (Masefield) **11**:358
Gallipoli (Williamson) **56**:437
Die Gallistl'sche Krankheit (Walser) **27**:460-61, 464, 466
"A Gallon of Gas" (Davies) **21**:104
"Galloping Foxley" (Dahl) **79**:178, 180
"Gallows Pole" (Page and Plant) **12**:475
Gallows Songs (Snodgrass) **6**:514
Galoots (Sandburg) **35**:340
"Galop" (Davison) **28**:100
"Galope muerto" (Neruda) **62**:322
The Galton Case (Macdonald) **1**:185; **2**:255; **14**:333-34; **34**:416; **41**:268-69, 271-72
The Galvanized Yankees (Brown) **47**:37
"Galway" (MacNeice) **53**:237
Gam ha'egrof haya pa'am yad ptuba ve'etsba'ot (Amichai) **116**:121
The Gambler (Alvarez) **13**:9
"The Gambler: A Ballet with Words" (Kavanagh) **22**:240
"The Gambler, the Nun, and the Radio" (Hemingway) **30**:179, 185; **80**:110
"The Gamblers" (Stoppard) **15**:518
"The Game" (Abse) **29**:16-17
"A Game" (Adcock) **41**:14
"The Game" (Barthelme) **8**:50; **23**:45; **115**:76
"The Game" (Glück) **22**:173
"The Game" (Kiš) **57**:246
"The Game" (Williams) **148**:358, 362
The Game (Byatt) **19**:75; **136**:130, 140-43, 145, 157-58
The Game and the Ground (Vansittart) **42**:389-90, 400
"A Game at Salzburg" (Jarrell) **13**:298
Game Crossing (Kroetz) **41**:239
A Game for the Living (Highsmith) **2**:193
Game in Heaven with Tussy Marx (Read) **4**:444; **25**:375
A Game Men Play (Bourjaily) **62**:104-06
"The Game of Blood and Dust" (Zelazny) **21**:479
"The Game of Chess" (Borges) **19**:46; **83**:177
"A Game of Chess" (Eliot) **6**:164; **15**:212; **34**:401; **41**:155
"A Game of Clue" (Millhauser) **109**:158, 160
A Game of Dark (Mayne) **12**:395, 398-99, 401-03
A Game of Football (Oe)
See *Man'en gan'nen no futtobōru*
A Game of Hide and Seek (Sargeson) **31**:367, 374
A Game of Hide and Seek (Taylor) **29**:410

A Game of Patience (King) **8**:321
A Game of Simultaneity (Oe)
See *Dōjidai gēmu*
"The Game of Time and Pain" (Delany) **141**:156-57
A Game of Touch (Hood) **28**:187, 190
"A Game of Truth" (Klima)
See "Hra na pravdu"
"Games" (Fowles) **15**:232
"Games" (Randall) **135**:399
Games (Klima) **56**:168-70
Games (Popa)
See *Igre*
"Games Are the Enemies of Beauty, Truth, and Sleep, Amanda Said" (Barthelme) **13**:56
"Games at Sunlight" (Desai) **97**:153
"Games at Twilight" (Desai) **19**:134; **97**:149, 151, 171, 176
Games of Chance (Gunn) **32**:214
Games of Chance (Hinde) **6**:239
Games of Choice (Gee) **29**:177
Gamma Rays (Zindel)
See *The Effect of Gamma Rays on Man-in-the-Moon Marigolds*
"The Gamut" (Angelou) **77**:28
Ganashatru (Ray) **76**:356, 360, 362
"Gandhi" (Mahapatra) **33**:281
"Gandy Dancing" (Wiggins) **57**:433-34
The Gang That Couldn't Shoot Straight (Breslin) **4**:76; **43**:70-1, 74, 76, 78
"The Ganges" (Dubie) **36**:136-37
"Gangrene" (Levine) **5**:251; **14**:316-17
The Gangs of Kosmos (Bowering) **15**:82
"A Gangsterdom of the Spirit" (Doctorow) **113**:177
Le gant de crin (Reverdy) **53**:280, 283-86, 290-91
"The Gap" (Tomlinson) **13**:548
"The Gap" (Williams) **148**:346-47
"The Gap in the Hedge" (Thomas) **6**:534
The Gap into Ruin (Donaldson) **138**:41
Gapi (Maillet) **54**:306, 315-16; **118**:329, 331-32, 334, 336
Gapi et Sullivan (Maillet) **54**:314; **118**:329
Garage Sale (Ringwood) **48**:339
"Garageland" (Clash) **30**:45
Garbage (Ammons) **108**:46-9, 59, 60-1
The Garbage Man (Dos Passos)
See *The Moon Is a Gong*
"The Garbageman Is Drunk" (Acorn) **15**:10
García Lorca (Honig) **33**:208-09
Les garçons (Montherlant) **8**:393
"The Garden" (Bitov) **57**:114-15
"The Garden" (Borges)
See "El jardín de senderos que se bifurcan"
"The Garden" (Dunn) **40**:166
"The Garden" (Glück) **22**:175, 77
"The Garden" (Govier) **51**:166
"Garden" (H. D.) **14**:223; **31**:205, 207; **34**:445; **73**:118, 121
"Garden" (Johnson) **7**:415
"The Garden" (Oliver) **98**:265
"A Garden" (Peacock) **60**:295
"The Garden" (Simon) **26**:407
"The Garden" (Stevenson) **33**:383
"The Garden" (Strand) **18**:520; **41**:432
"The Garden" (Thomas) **48**:376
The Garden (Summers) **10**:493
Garden, Ashes (Kiš) **57**:239, 242-49
"The Garden at St. John's" (Swenson) **106**:317
"The Garden House" (L'Heureux) **52**:272
"Garden in the Wind" (Roy) **14**:469
Garden in the Wind (Roy) **14**:469
The Garden Next Door (Donoso)
See *El jardín de al lado*
The Garden of Adonis (Gordon) **6**:203-04; **13**:242; **29**:186; **83**:233-34, 243, 247, 252-54
Garden of Broken Glass (Neville) **12**:453-54
"The Garden of Delight" (Hass) **18**:211
The Garden of Delights (Carrier)
See *Le jardin des délices*
The Garden of Delights (Saura) **20**:314, 317, 320, 322
"The Garden of Earthly Delights" (Milosz) **56**:251
"Garden of Earthly Delights" (Oe) **86**:231
"The Garden of Earthly Delights" (Porter) **33**:321
"The Garden of Earthly Delights" (Simic) **6**:502
The Garden of Earthly Delights (Arrabal)
See *Le jardin des délices*
A Garden of Earthly Delights (Oates) **1**:252; **2**:314; **3**:359; **6**:368; **9**:406; **19**:353; **33**:291; **52**:336, 338; **108**:341-42, 391
The Garden of Eden (Hemingway) **6**:230; **8**:285; **41**:204-08; **50**:412-14, 417, 419, 422, 426-29, 431; **80**:146, 150-51, 153, 156
"The Garden of Eros" (Squires) **51**:383
The Garden of Forking Paths (Borges)
See *El jardín de senderos que se bifurcan*
"The Garden of Gethsemane" (Pasternak) **7**:294
"The Garden of Hecate" (Squires) **51**:383
"The Garden of Love" (Livesay) **79**:340-41
"The Garden of Maia" (Squires) **51**:383
"The Garden of Medusa" (Squires) **51**:382-83
"The Garden of Niobe" (Squires) **51**:382
"The Garden of Prometheus" (Squires) **51**:382
Garden of Rest (Pa Chin)
See *Ch'i-yüan*
"The Garden of Stubborn Cats" (Calvino) **33**:100
The Garden of the Finzi-Continis (Bassani) **9**:74-7
The Garden of the Finzi-Continis (De Sica) **20**:95
"The Garden of the Forking Paths" (Borges)
See "El jardín de senderos que se bifurcan"
"The Garden of the Gods" (Gunn) **18**:200; **32**:208
The Garden of the Savage Beasts (Duhamel) **8**:188-89
"The Garden of Time" (Ballard) **137**:17
Garden of Time (Dodson) **79**:186
The Garden of Weapons (Gardner) **30**:156
"The Garden: On prospect of a fine day in early autumn" (Warren) **13**:573
"The Garden Party" (Davie) **5**:114; **8**:164; **10**:125
The Garden Party (Havel)
See *Zahradni Slavnost*
"The Garden Sees" (Elytis) **100**:179
"The Garden Shukkei-en" (Forché) **86**:139-41, 143
Garden Spot, U.S.A. (Garrett) **51**:145-46
"Garden State" (Ginsberg) **36**:192
Garden State (Moody) **147**:167, 171-72, 174, 181, 183-84, 186-87, 190
"The Gardener" (Haines) **58**:214
"The Gardener" (Raine) **32**:351-52
"The Gardener" (Wheelock) **14**:571
"The Gardener to His God" (Van Duyn) **116**:403
The Gardener's Song (McCarthy) **101**:202
Gardenia (Guare) **29**:207-08; **67**:78-81
"The Gardens" (Oliver) **34**:247, 249; **98**:273, 299-300
Gardens of Stone (Coppola) **126**:260-61
"The Gardens of the Villa d'Este" (Hecht) **8**:266-67
Gardens of the World (Squires) **51**:381-83
"Gare du midi" (Auden) **43**:22
"Gargantua" (Calisher) **38**:76; **134**:10
Gargoyle Cartoons (McClure) **6**:320
Gargoyles (Bernhard)
See *Verstörung*
La Garibaldina (Vittorini) **9**:549
The Garish Day (Billington) **43**:58
Garito de hospicianos (Cela) **4**:96; **122**:19
"A Garland for Christopher Smart" (Van Duyn) **116**:403, 418
A Garland for the Appalachians (Williams) **13**:600
"A Garland for Thomas Eakins" (Tomlinson) **13**:546
"Garland for You" (Warren) **13**:575
A Garland of Love (Bioy Casares)
See *Guirnalda con amores*
The Garnett Family (Heilbrun) **25**:252
Il garofano rosso (Vittorini) **9**:548-49
"The Garret" (Hildesheimer) **49**:180
The Garrick Year (Drabble) **2**:118; **5**:117; **8**:184; **22**:120; **53**:117-18, 121; **129**:111, 114, 118
Garrochés en paradis (Maillet) **54**:304
Garten und Strassen (Jünger) **125**:219
"Gas" (Adcock) **41**:14
Gas House McGinty (Farrell) **4**:157; **66**:114, 116, 122, 127, 135
"The Gas Station" (Williams) **148**:308, 312
"Gases" (Bernard) **59**:44
Gaslight: A Victorian Thriller (Hamilton) **51**:187, 189-90, 192-94, 196-98
Gasoline (Corso) **1**:64; **11**:123
"Gaspard de la nuit" (Donoso) **8**:180; **32**:160; **199**:241
Gaspard, Melchior, et Balthazar (Tournier)
See *The Four Wise Men*
Gäst hos verkligheten (Lagerkvist) **13**:330; **54**:267-68, 271-72, 274, 276, 286, 288-89
The Gastronomical Me (Fisher) **76**:335-36, 338-41; **87**:120, 122-23, 125, 129
"Gata Poem" (Zamora) **89**:370, 373-76, 386, 389, 394
The Gate (Day Lewis) **10**:128-29, 131
"The Gate at the Center" (Olson) **11**:419
"Gate City Breakdown" (Wright) **146**:340, 343
"The Gate in His Head" (Ondaatje) **51**:311-12, 315
"The Gate of a Great Mansion" (Sillitoe) **57**:396
The Gate of Angels (Fitzgerald) **143**:234-35, 238, 241-42, 244, 248-50, 253-55, 257, 262, 266
Gate of Ivrel (Cherryh) **35**:102-04, 112
"The Gate of Morning" (Milosz) **11**:380
"The Gateman's Gift" (Narayan) **121**:346-48, 350, 354
"The Gates" (Rukeyser) **10**:443
The Gates (Johnston) **7**:185-86; **150**:30
The Gates (Rukeyser) **10**:442
"Gates of Eden" (Dylan) **6**:155
The Gates of Hell (Willingham) **51**:403, 410-11
The Gates of Ivory (Drabble) **129**:133, 138-57, 159-160, 162
The Gates of November (Potok) **112**:295-96
"The Gates of the Arsenal" (Milosz) **82**:297
The Gates of the Forest (Wiesel)
See *Les portes de la forêt*
"Gates of the West" (Clash) **30**:45
The Gates of Wrath: Rhymed Poems, 1948-1952 (Ginsberg) **6**:199-201; **36**:181; **69**:223, 225; **109**:352-53
"The Gateway" (Hope) **51**:224
"The Gateway" (Wright) **53**:419, 431
Gateway (Pohl) **18**:411-13
The Gateway (Wright) **53**:419-20, 423, 428, 431
Gather, Darkness! (Leiber) **25**:301-02, 305, 310
Gather Together in My Name (Angelou) **12**:11-12; **35**:30-1; **64**:24, 27, 29-30, 34, 36, 38-9; **77**:4-15, 22-4
A Gathered Church: The Literature of the English Dissenting Interest, 1700-1930 (Davie) **31**:113-14, 117, 120-21
"Gathering" (Voigt) **54**:429
The Gathering (Hamilton) **26**:156-57
Gathering Evidence: A Memoir (Bernhard) **61**:19-22, 30
"Gathering Mushrooms" (Muldoon) **32**:321-22; **72**:282
"The Gathering of Californians" (Brautigan) **3**:90; **12**:65
"A Gathering of Men" (Moyers) **70**:416, 418-20, 423, 429-30, 435, 457
A Gathering of Old Men (Gaines) **86**:176-77
"Gathering of Shields" (Momaday) **85**:280
"The Gathering of the Whakapapa" (Ihimaera) **46**:201

The Gathering Storm (Empson) **19**:152, 156-57; **33**:141-42; **34**:335
Gathering the Tribes (Forché) **25**:168-71; **83**:206, 210-12; **86**:139, 142
"Gatineau" (Avison) **97**:71-4
El gato eficaz (Valenzuela) **31**:439-40; **104**:354-61, 366-70, 377-79, 387
Gatsby (Coppola) **126**:204
"GATSBY'S THEORY OF AESTHETICS" (Baraka) **115**:38-9
La gauche divine (Baudrillard) **60**:33
"Gaucho" (Becker and Fagen) **26**:85
Gaucho (Becker and Fagen) **26**:84-5
"The Gauchos" (Borges) **8**:103
Gaudete (Hughes) **9**:282; **14**:272-73; **37**:171-72, 174-76, 178-79; **119**:260, 264-71, 277, 279, 281, 288, 295
Gaudier-Brzeska: A Memoir (Pound) **10**:401; **13**:458
The Gaudy (Stewart) **7**:466
The Gaudy Place (Chappell) **40**:140-41; **78**:97
"Gaugin" (Walcott) **67**:360
"Gauguin" (Raine) **103**:186, 188
Gauguin (Resnais) **16**:505
"The Gauzy Edge of Paradise" (Gilchrist) **34**:164-65; **143**:296, 315
The Gavin Ewart Show: Selected Poems, 1939-1985 (Ewart) **13**:209; **46**:148, 153-54
"Gay Chaps at the Bar" (Brooks) **49**:35-6; **125**:50, 52, 90
The Gay Desperado (Mamoulian) **16**:423-24
"The Gay Old Dog" (Ferber) **93**:138, 141, 146-47, 180
"Gay Paree" (Bennett) **28**:27, 29
"The Gay Philosopher" (White) **110**:332, 336, 341
The Gay Place (Brammer) **31**:53-5
"Gay Talese: Sex Affirmative" (Amis) **62**:5
The Gay Vineyards (Zuckmayer)
See *Der Fröliche Weinberg*
The Gayden Chronicles (Cook) **58**:154
The Gazabos: Forty-One Poems (Honig) **33**:210-11, 213, 215
Gaze (Blanchot)
See *The Gaze of Orpheus and Other Literary Essays*
The Gaze (Marqués)
See *La Mirada*
"The Gaze of Orpheus" (Blanchot) **135**:87, 121, 124
The Gaze of Orpheus and Other Literary Essays (Blanchot) **135**:87-88, 141
"The Gaze of The Gorgon" (Harrison) **129**:212
The Gaze of The Gorgon (Harrison) **129**:202
"Gazebo" (Carver) **55**:275; **126**:127
"Gde, vysokaya, tvoy tsyganyonok" (Akhmatova) **64**:9
"Le géant blanc lépreux du paysage" (Tzara) **47**:394-95
"Gebete für den toten Bräutigam" (Sachs) **98**:325, 327, 347, 353
Gedichte 1938-1944 (Celan) **82**:48-49, 52, 57
"Gee, Officer Krupke" (Sondheim) **30**:376, 387; **147**:259
The Geek (Nova) **31**:296-97, 299
Geek Love (Dunn) **71**:133-40
"Geese" (Dobyns) **37**:79
"The Geese" (Graham) **48**:145, 154; **118**:259
Eine gefährliche Begegnung (Jünger) **125**:250, 259-61
Das Geheimherz der Uhr: Aufzeichnungen 1973-1985 (Canetti) **75**:144-45; **86**:296-97, 300-01
Gehen (Bernhard) **61**:9
"Geisenhausen" (Eich) **15**:203
Geisterbahn (Kroetz) **41**:234
Gelassenheit (Heidegger) **24**:277
Der Gelbe hund (Jandl) **34**:198-200
"Das Geld" (Hein) **154**:100
Die Gelehrtenrepublik: Kurzroman aus den Rossbreiten (Schmidt) **56**:393, 396-97, 399-402, 404-405
"Gemcrack" (Phillips) **15**:420-21
Gemini (Innaurato) **21**:191-92, 196-97; **60**:199-206
Gemini (Tournier) **23**:453-56; **36**:437, 441; **95**:371-73, 381
Gemini: An Extended Autobiographical Statement on My First Twenty-Five Years of Being a Black Poet (Giovanni) **2**:164-65; **19**:191; **64**:183-85, 187-89, 191-92; **117**:167-68, 181-84, 186, 191, 194, 201
The Gemini Contenders (Ludlum) **22**:289
"Gemini--A Prolonged Autobiographical Statement on Why" (Giovanni) **64**:184; **117**:183
"Gemistus Pletho" (Forster) **45**:132
"Gemona-del-friuli, 1961-1976" (Davie) **31**:117
Gender and the Politics of History (Scott) **65**:327
Gene Green--The Untouchable (Aksyonov) **101**:22
Gene Wolfe's Book of Days (Wolfe) **25**:475-76
"The General" (Asimov) **26**:61, 63
"The General" (Head) **67**:111
"The General" (Sassoon) **36**:388, 391, 393; **130**:182-83, 214-15, 220
"General" (Strand) **18**:516
The General (Forester) **35**:160-63, 166, 170, 174
The General (Keaton) **20**:189, 191-92, 194-97
The General (Sillitoe) **1**:307; **3**:448
The General and the President (Schlesinger) **84**:373
General Confession (Davies) **7**:73
The General Danced at Dawn (Fraser) **7**:106
Le général de l'armée morte (Kadare)
See *Gjenerali i ushtrisë së vdekur*
The General Died at Dawn (Odets) **28**:337; **98**:207, 242-44
"General Electric" (Scott) **22**:373
General Ludd (Metcalf) **37**:303-07
"The General Nature of Ritual" (Burke) **24**:126
General Relativity: An Einstein Centenary Survey (Hawking) **105**:46-7
The General Returns from One Place to Another (O'Hara) **13**:431; **78**:364, 370-71
General Song (Neruda)
See *Canto general de Chile*
Generalerna (Wahlöö) **7**:501-02
Generally a Virgin (Hinde) **6**:241-42
The Generals (Wahlöö)
See *Generalerna*
"The General's Day" (Trevor) **71**:322, 324, 339; **116**:332
The General's Lady (Forbes) **12**:204
The General's Wife (Straub) **107**:304-05
"Generation" (Alexander) **121**:21
A Generation (Wajda) **16**:578, 581
"Generation III" (Lorde) **71**:262
"Generation Gap" (Ciardi) **40**:161
"Generation of '45" (Cabral de Melo Neto)
See "A geração de '45"
Generation of Swine (Thompson) **104**:335-36, 347
Generation of Vipers (Wylie) **43**:463-66, 471-72
Generation without Farewell (Boyle) **58**:68, 70; **121**:33-4, 46, 52
Generation X: Tales for an Accelerated Culture (Coupland) **85**:30-41; **133**:2-8, 10-16, 19-20
"Generations" (Kenny) **87**:252, 254
"Generations" (Sanchez) **116**:315
"Generations" (Stevenson) **7**:462
Generations (Pollock) **50**:224
Generations: A Memoir (Clifton) **19**:110-11; **66**:66-7, 74, 78, 80, 84-6
"The Generations of Men" (Lowell) **124**:258
The Generations of Men (Wright) **53**:421-22
Generations of Winter (Aksyonov) **101**:47-53, 55
"Générique" (Simon) **15**:496-97
The Generous Days (Spender) **2**:419-20; **5**:401; **91**:264
The Generous Heart (Fearing) **51**:116, 121
A Generous Man (Price) **3**:405-06; **43**:342-44, 346; **50**:231-32; **63**:341
"Generous Pieces" (Gilchrist) **143**:320, 331-32
"Genesis" (Elytis) **100**:156, 159, 161, 163-64, 166
"Genesis" (Hill) **8**:294; **45**:184, 186-87, 189
Genesis (Stegner) **81**:340, 345-46
"Genesis 2" (MacEwen) **55**:167
"Genesis 1-2: 4" (Bidart) **33**:80
"Genesis and Catastrophe" (Dahl) **79**:181
Genesis, Book II (Schwartz) **87**:344, 347
Genesis: Book One (Schwartz) **4**:479; **10**:464-65; **45**:358-59; **87**:334, 347
Genesis of the Clowns (Harris) **25**:211
"The Genesis of the Metaphor and the Sense of Culture" (Blaga)
See "Geneza metaforei şi sensul culturii"
"Genesis on an Endless Mosaic" (Dumas) **62**:155
"Genessee Falls" (Crase) **58**:162-63, 165
"Genetic Expedition" (Dove) **81**:141, 151
"Genetics" (Alexie) **96**:10; **154**:28
The Genetics Explosion (Silverstein and Silverstein) **17**:457
Genève (Bowering) **15**:83; **47**:21
"Genevieve" (Lorde) **71**:260
"Geneza metaforei şi sensul culturii" (Blaga) **75**:59, 63, 74
Geneza metaforei si sensul culturii (Blaga) **75**:80
Gengoedelsens veje (Dinesen) **95**:68
Génie (Jouve) **47**:206
Le génie de lieu (Butor) **8**:116; **15**:118
"Genie's Prayer under the Kitchen Sink" (Dove) **81**:152
Génitrix (Mauriac) **4**:339-40; **9**:367-68; **56**:204-06, 214, 217, 219
"The Genius" (Barthelme) **3**:43-4; **59**:250
"Genius" (Levine) **33**:272
"The Genius" (MacLeish) **8**:362
The Genius (Brenton) **31**:69
Genius and Lust (Mailer) **74**:225-27
The Genius and the Goddess (Huxley) **4**:243; **5**:195; **35**:242
"The Genius Freaks" (McIntyre) **18**:327
"The Genius of Smalltown America" (Williams) **39**:100
Genius The Life and Science of Richard Feynam (Gleick) **147**:62-8, 71-3, 75, 77-8
Geniuses (Reynolds) **38**:387-91
Geniusz sierocy (Dabrowska) **15**:169
The Genoa Ferry (Harwood) **32**:225-26
The Genocidal Mentality: Nazi Holocaust and Nuclear Threat (Lifton) **67**:162-65
Genocide in Nigeria (Saro-Wiwa) **114**:261
The Genocides (Disch) **36**:123
A Genoese Fancy (Hughes) **48**:184
Le genou de Claire (Rohmer) **16**:531-34, 536, 540
Genshuku natsunawatari (Oe) **36**:349; **86**:215, 224, 226-27
Gente del po (Antonioni) **20**:24; **144**:12, 40, 61, 77
"Gentians" (McGuckian) **48**:276
"The Gentle Art" (Gordimer) **18**:185; **123**:116
"Gentle as Flowers Make the Stones" (Metcalf) **37**:299, 301
The Gentle Barbarian: The Life and Work of Turgenev (Pritchett) **13**:467-69
A Gentle Creature (Bresson) **16**:113-14
The Gentle Insurrection (Betts) **28**:32-4
The Gentle Island (Friel) **5**:129; **42**:173-74
A Gentle Occupation (Bogarde) **19**:43
"The Gentle People" (Shaw) **23**:395
"Gentle Reader" (Jacobsen) **48**:195
"Gentle Reader" (Loewinsohn) **52**:284
"The Gentle Sex" (Ewart) **13**:210; **46**:149, 153
"The Gentle Snorer" (Van Duyn) **116**:399, 406, 429

The Gentle Tamers: Women of the Old Wild West (Brown) **47**:36
The Gentle Weight Lifter (Ignatow) **7**:173-75; **14**:276; **40**:258
Gentlehands (Kerr) **12**:300-01, 303; **35**:250-51
Gentleman and Ladies (Hill) **113**:288-90, 297-98, 303, 305, 308-10, 320
"The Gentleman Arms" (Wiggins) **57**:433-34, 436
The Gentleman Caller (Bullins) **1**:47
The Gentleman Caller (Williams) **71**:364, 373
"The Gentleman from Cracow" (Singer) **3**:453; **38**:410; **69**:306
"The Gentleman from Shallot" (Bishop) **9**:96; **32**:29, 44-5
The Gentleman Host (Chabon) **149**:16, 18
"The Gentleman of Shallot" (Bishop)
See "The Gentleman from Shallot"
"Gentleman without Company" (Neruda) **1**:247
Gentleman's Agreement (Hobson) **7**:163-64; **25**:269-71
Gentleman's Agreement (Kazan) **63**:223, 225, 229, 234
Gentlemen, I Address You Privately (Boyle) **19**:64; **58**:64-5; **121**:27, 29, 46, 50
Les génts (Le Clézio) **31**:248-49; **155**:87
"Genuine and Poignant" (Hearne) **56**:125
"Geographer" (Hacker) **91**:109
"Geography" (Olds) **32**:346
Geography III (Bishop) **9**:97; **13**:89-91, 94-5; **15**:60-1; **32**:29-31, 33, 35, 37-9, 41-2
Geography of a Horsedreamer (Shepard) **4**:491-92; **6**:495, 497; **17**:443-44
The Geography of Lograire (Merton) **3**:335-36; **11**:372; **83**:398, 404
"The Geography of the House" (Auden) **14**:29; **123**:12
The Geography of the Imagination (Davenport) **38**:140-46
Geography of the Near Past (Young) **19**:480
"Geometaphysics" (Avison) **97**:67-8, 70, 72, 111
"Geometry of Goods" (Kunitz) **148**:86
"The Geometry of Love" (Cheever) **64**:46-8
"Georg Heym—przygoda prawie metafizyczna" (Herbert) **9**:275; **43**:187
"Georg Heym—The Almost Metaphysical Adventure" (Herbert)
See "Georg Heym—przygoda prawie metafizyczna"
Georg Trakl (Heidegger) **24**:255
"George" (Randall) **135**:386, 393, 396
"George" (Stead)
See "The Girl from the Beach"
George: An Early Autobiography (Williams) **15**:578
"George and the Seraph" (Brooke-Rose) **40**:106
"George Bowering" (McFadden) **48**:244
"George Bush" (Keillor) **115**:295
"George Eliot and Radical Evil" (Howe) **85**:153
"George Meredith, 1861" (Day Lewis) **10**:131
George Mills (Elkin) **27**:124-26; **51**:93, 98, 101; **91**:213-14, 223-24
"George Oppen" (Bowering) **47**:28
George Seferis: A Poet's Journal (Seferis)
See *Days of 1945-1951: A Poet's Journal*
George, Vancouver: A Discovery Poem (Bowering) **15**:83; **47**:23, 28
George Washington Crossing the Delaware (Koch) **5**:218
"George Washington Meets the King of Spain" (Wakoski) **9**:555
The George Washington Poems (Wakoski) **2**:459; **4**:572; **7**:505; **9**:555; **40**:454
George Washington September, Sir! (Harwood) **32**:222
George Washington Slept Here (Hart and Kaufman) **38**:265; **66**:175, 182-86
Georges Bataille's Bathrobe (Foreman) **50**:171
Georgia (Soupault) **68**:404-07
Georgia Boy (Caldwell) **14**:96; **50**:300, 302; **60**:49, 55
"Georgia Dusk" (Toomer) **13**:551; **22**:423, 426
Georgia, Georgia (Angelou) **77**:15, 18, 21
"A Georgia Song" (Angelou) **77**:31
The Georgian House: A Tale in Four Parts (Swinnerton) **31**:424
The Georgian Literary Scene: A Panorama (Swinnerton) **31**:424-25, 428
The Georgian Scene: A Literary Panorama (Swinnerton)
See *The Georgian Literary Scene: A Panorama*
Georgics (Day Lewis) **6**:127; **10**:134
"Georgie and Fenwick" (Nowlan) **15**:398
"Georgie Grimes" (Brown) **59**:265
Georgina and the Dragon (Kingman) **17**:246
Les géorgiques (Simon) **39**:212
Georgy Girl (Forster) **149**:68, 77, 98-9
Georgy Girl (Nichols) **65**:162
"A geração de '45" (Cabral de Melo Neto) **76**:157
"Gerald" (Lane) **25**:284
Gerald: A Portrait (du Maurier) **59**:286
Geraldine Bradshaw (Willingham) **51**:401-05, 407-09, 411
"Geraldo No Last Name" (Cisneros) **118**:186
Gerald's Party (Coover) **46**:116-22; **87**:41-2, 58-61, 63-4
"The Geranium" (Grace) **56**:122-23
"The Geranium" (O'Connor) **3**:366; **6**:382; **21**:277; **104**:188
"Geraniums" (Hogan) **73**:158-59
"Gerard" (Spacks) **14**:511
Gerard Manley Hopkins Meets Walt Whitman in Heaven and Other Poems (Dacey) **51**:82
Gerard's Game (King) **113**:388-89, 392-93
"Gerbil Funeral" (Olds) **85**:295-96
"The Gerbil That Ate Los Angeles" (Kinsella) **43**:258
Gerbils: All about Them (Silverstein and Silverstein) **17**:455
"Gerda in the Eyrie" (Hacker) **72**:182
Die gerettete Zunge: Geschichte einer Jugend (Canetti) **25**:110-14; **75**:130, 133, 141, 144; **86**:294-95, 297, 301-02
"Geriatrics" (Enright) **8**:203
"German and English Romanticism: A Confrontation, 1963" (Wellek) **28**:447
"A German Idyll" (Bates) **46**:52
The German Lesson (Lenz)
See *Deutschstunde*
A German Love Story (Hochhuth)
See *Eine Liebe in Deutschland*
"The German Refugee" (Malamud) **8**:375; **44**:415
"A German Requiem" (Fenton) **32**:166-67, 170
"The Germanic Day" (Ewart) **46**:152-53
Germany, Germany among Other Things (Enzensberger)
See *Deutschland, Deutschland unter anderm*
Germfree Life: A New Field in Biological Research (Silverstein and Silverstein) **17**:451
"Germinal" (Hogan) **73**:159
"The Gernsback Continuum" (Gibson) **63**:129-30, 132
Geronimo Rex (Hannah) **23**:207-08, 211; **38**:232-34; **90**:126-28, 130, 134, 136, 139-40, 143-44, 152, 155-59
"A Geronimo Story" (Silko) **74**:349; **114**:317-18
"Gerontion" (Eliot) **3**:137; **6**:160-62, 167; **10**:167-68; **13**:192-93, 195-96, 199-201; **15**:213, 217; **24**:163; **34**:393-94, 529; **41**:151-52, 154-55; **55**:346, 348, 351-52, 355, 364-65, 371, 374; **57**:174-75, 190, 202, 208, 210; **113**:219
Gerpla (Laxness) **25**:293, 298, 300
"Gershwin's Second Prelude" (Baxter) **78**:16
Gertrud (Dreyer) **16**:262-65, 269
Gertrude (Hesse) **17**:195, 202, 216
Gertrude and I (Hesse)
See *Gertrude*
"Gertrude Stein and the Geography of the Sentence" (Gass) **15**:258
Gesammelte Erzählungen (Wolf) **29**:464; **150**:237
Gesammelte Gedichte (Grass) **2**:173; **32**:200
Gesammelte Werke (Celan) **53**:81; **82**:52
Gesang vom lusitanischen Popanz (Weiss) **15**:565; **51**:387, 391-92, 394
"Geschäft ist Geschäft" (Boell) **27**:58; **72**:70, 101
Die Geschichte des Bleistifts (Handke) **134**:153
"Geshem bisdeh hakrav" (Amichai) **116**:110
"Gespräch im Gebirge" (Celan) **53**:81, 83
"Gespräch mit Horst Bienek" (Canetti) **86**:295
"Gespräch mit Joachim Schickel" (Canetti) **86**:295
Gespräch über Balzac's Pferd: Vier Novellen (Hofmann) **54**:224
"Gestalt at Sixty" (Sarton) **14**:482
Gestalt Therapy (Goodman) **4**:197-98
"Gestes, ponctuation, et langage poétique" (Tzara) **47**:386
"Gesthemane" (Pasternak) **63**:313
Die gestohlene Melodie (Nossack) **6**:364
Gestos (Sarduy) **6**:486; **97**:365, 367, 372, 390, 417
Die gestundete Zeit (Bachmann) **69**:36-9, 41
"The Gesture" (McClure) **6**:319
"Gestures" (Hoffman) **6**:243
Gestures (Sarduy)
See *Gestos*
Gestures and Other Poems (Ritsos) **31**:326
"Get a Seeing-Eyed Dog" (Hemingway) **30**:182
Get Happy!! (Costello) **21**:74
Get Home Free (Holmes) **56**:137-38
"Get It" (McCartney) **35**:289-91
"Get Off My Cloud" (Jagger and Richard) **17**:226, 234-35
Get Off the Unicorn (McCaffrey) **17**:282-83
Get on the Bus (Lee) **105**:127-30
"Get on the Right Thing" (McCartney) **35**:281
"Get Ready" (Robinson) **21**:348
Get Ready for Battle (Jhabvala) **29**:253-55; **94**:166-70, 181
Get Shorty (Leonard) **71**:223-24; **120**:282-84, 291, 295-97, 299, 303
Get to Know Your Rabbit (De Palma) **20**:74
"Get Up" (Davies) **21**:103-04
"Get Up in The Morning" (Jiles) **58**:271
Get Your Man (Arzner) **98**:63, 87
The Getaway (Peckinpah) **20**:276-80, 282
The Getaway (Thompson) **69**:378-81, 383, 386, 389
Der geteilte Himmel (Wolf) **14**:593; **58**:432; **150**:227, 271, 278, 289, 291-92, 321-22, 343
"Die geteilte Zukunft" (Canetti) **86**:295
"Gethsemane" (Raine) **103**:179
"Gettin' By High and Strange" (Kristofferson) **26**:267
"Gettin' Hungry" (Wilson) **12**:643
"Getting an Education" (Swan) **69**:360
"Getting around Town" (Dobyns) **37**:77
"Getting Away from Already Being Pretty Much Away from It All" (Wallace) **114**:388
"Getting Away from It All" (Dobyns) **37**:76-7
Getting Away with It (SODERBERGH) **154**:344, 354
"Getting Better" (Lennon and McCartney) **12**:358
"Getting Closer" (McCartney) **35**:286-87
Getting Even (Allen) **52**:35-6, 40, 45, 47
Getting High in Government Circles (Buchwald) **33**:93
"Getting in the Wood" (Snyder) **32**:397; **120**:354
"Getting into Death" (Disch) **7**:86
Getting into Death and Other Stories (Disch) **7**:86-7; **36**:123

Getting It Right (Howard) **29**:246-47
"Getting Married Today" (Sondheim) **30**:386; **147**:240, 251-54
Getting Off (Carpenter) **41**:104
Getting On (Bennett) **45**:58; **77**:98
Getting Out (Norman) **28**:317-21
"Getting Out of History: Jameson's Redemption of Narrative" (White) **148**:249
"Getting Outside" (Kelman) **58**:298
"Getting Ready" (Hannah) **38**:233-35; **90**:137
"Getting the Words Out" (Updike) **139**:326
"Getting There" (Plath) **5**:345; **9**:433; **14**:428; **17**:366; **51**:345; **111**:204, 221
"Getting There" (Wagoner) **15**:560
"Getting Things Straight" (Welch) **52**:429
Getting Through (McGahern) **48**:263-64, 271
"Getting Through Sunday Somehow" (Bradbury) **42**:35
"Getting Through to the End" (Dobyns) **37**:76
"Getting Through Winter" (Dobyns) **37**:78-9
"Getting to Know All about You" (Oates) **108**:384
Getting to Know the General (Greene) **37**:137-38; **72**:177
"Getting to the End" (Macdonald) **13**:356
"Getting to Williamstown" (Hood) **28**:193
"Getting Up" (Dobyns) **37**:80
"Getting Used to It" (Dunn) **40**:171
"Gettysburg" (Coupland) **85**:36
Das Gewicht der Welt (Handke) **38**:223-27; **134**:118, 123, 146, 151, 156, 181-82
Das Gewissen der Worte (Canetti) **25**:114; **75**:129-30, 132, 142; **86**:293, 301
"Der Gewöhnliche Rilke" (Jandl) **34**:196
"The Geysers" (Gunn) **18**:199-201; **32**:209, 211; **81**:179
"Ghalib, Two Years after the Mutiny" (Seth) **90**:351
Ghare Bahire (Ray) **76**:360, 362
"Ghastly Good Taste" (Betjeman) **43**:43
"Ghazal at Full Moon" (Jordan) **114**:150
"Ghazals" (Harrison) **33**:198
"Ghazals" (Rich) **6**:458; **18**:446
"The Ghetto" (Ehrenburg) **62**:171
Ghetto (Sobol) **60**:382-90
"Ghetto Defendant" (Clash) **30**:50-2
"Ghetto Funeral" (Reznikoff) **9**:450
"Ghibel' Egorushki" (Leonov) **92**:237, 263
Ghláfkos thrassákis (Vassilikos) **8**:524
"The Ghost" (Peacock) **60**:297-98
"The Ghost" (Slessor) **14**:497
"Ghost and Flesh" (Goyen) **40**:216
Ghost and Flesh: Stories and Tales (Goyen) **14**:212; **40**:218
A Ghost at Noon (Moravia) **7**:244
The Ghost Belonged to Me (Peck) **21**:297, 299
"Ghost Dance" (Smith) **12**:543
Ghost Dance (Maso) **44**:57-61
The Ghost Downstairs (Garfield) **12**:226-27, 232, 234-35, 237
The Ghost Front (Bonham) **12**:50
"A Ghost Garden" (Tuohy) **37**:431
The Ghost Goes West (Clair) **20**:62
"The Ghost Hammer" (Pinsky) **94**:308, 312
"The Ghost Horses" (Dinesen) **10**:148-49
The Ghost in the Machine (Koestler) **1**:169; **33**:237-38, 240, 242
Ghost in the Machine (Police, The) **26**:365-66
A Ghost in the Music (Nichols) **38**:343
Ghost in the Wheels (Birney) **11**:51
"A Ghost May Come" (Ginsberg) **36**:182
Ghost of a Chance (Burroughs) **109**:182
"The Ghost of a Flea" (Lively) **32**:276
"The Ghost of a Ghost" (Leithauser) **27**:240, 242
Ghost of Ballyhooly (Cavanna) **12**:101
The Ghost of Hellsfire Street (Platt) **26**:354-55
The Ghost of Henry James (Plante) **23**:341-42, 344
"The Ghost of Magnetism" (Vollmann) **89**:296
The Ghost of Monsieur Scarron (Lewis) **41**:255-59, 262
The Ghost Road (Barker) **94**:17-20; **146**:3, 5-11, 13-16, 30, 38
"The Ghost Ship" (Strand) **71**:283
"A Ghost Story" (Butler) **81**:129
Ghost Story (Straub) **28**:410-11; **107**:265-66, 268, 271, 274, 276, 278, 280-82, 287, 288, 291, 302, 304-10
Ghost Tantras (McClure) **6**:319-20
"Ghost Town" (Longley) **29**:296
Ghost Trio (Beckett) **9**:84
"Ghost Village" (Fuller) **62**:186, 193, 203
"Ghost Voice" (Fuller) **28**:157
The Ghost Way (Hillerman) **62**:258-59
"The Ghost Who Vanished by Degrees" (Davies) **42**:103
The Ghost Writer (Roth) **15**:450-55; **22**:354-56, 360; **31**:337-41, 345, 347-49; **47**:357-59, 366; **86**:250, 253, 261-63; **119**:120, 129, 138
"Ghosts" (O'Brien) **36**:336, 341
"Ghosts" (O'Connor) **23**:331
"Ghosts" (Oliver) **34**:249; **98**:257, 272, 274, 287
"Ghosts" (Weller) **26**:447-48
Ghosts (Auster) **47**:13-16; **131**:5, 7, 9, 12-5, 18, 23-4, 26, 33, 36-8
Ghosts (Banville) **118**:22-32, 34-35, 44, 47-53
Ghosts (Hunter) **31**:224
The Ghosts (Perec)
See *Les revenentes*
The Ghosts Call You Poor (Suknaski) **19**:433-34
Ghosts I Have Been (Peck) **21**:299-300
"Ghosts in England" (Jeffers) **54**:246
Ghosts in the Mirror (Robbe-Grillet)
See *Le miroir qui revient*
"The Ghost's Leave-taking" (Plath) **2**:335; **51**:340; **111**:178
"Ghosts of Cape Horn" (Lightfoot) **26**:283
The Ghosts of Forever (Bradbury) **42**:41
The Ghosts of Glencoe (Hunter) **21**:156, 162, 167
The Ghosts of Stone Hollow (Snyder) **17**:475
"Ghosts of the Missionaries" (Starbuck) **53**:352
"Ghosts: Some Words before Breakfast" (Harrison) **43**:175; **129**:165
"The Ghoul" (Smith) **43**:422
"Giacometti's Race" (Phillips) **28**:364
"Giacomo Leopardi" (Wright)
See "To Giacomo Leopardi in the Sky"
An Giall (Behan) **1**:26; **8**:63-4; **11**:44-5; **15**:45-6; **79**:25-7, 29-31, 33-4, 40-2, 44, 47-9, 52, 54-5, 58
Giant (Ferber) **18**:151; **93**:181-83, 185, 187-88, 190
Giant in Gray: A Biography of Wade Hampton of South Carolina (Wellman) **49**:392
The Giant, O'Brien (Mantel) **144**:234-35, 237-38, 240
"The Giant on Giant-Killing" (Howard) **10**:275-76
"The Giant Puff Ball" (Blunden) **56**:26
"Giant Snail" (Bishop) **32**:42
"A Giant Step for Mankind" (Allen) **52**:41
"Giant Streak Snarls Race" (Willard) **7**:539
"Giant Toad" (Bishop) **32**:42
"Giant Tortoise" (Leithauser) **27**:240, 242
The Giants (Le Clézio)
See *Les géants*
Giant's Bread (Christie) **12**:112
Giants from Eternity (Wellman) **49**:387
Giants of Jazz (Terkel) **38**:418
"Un giardino incantato" (Calvino) **33**:99, 101
"The Gibber" (Roethke) **11**:481; **46**:362
"Gibson Street" (Nyro) **17**:316, 318
Gideon (Chayefsky) **23**:114, 117
Gideon's Fire (Creasey) **11**:134
Gideon's Power (Creasey) **11**:134
"The Gift" (Carver) **55**:273
"The Gift" (Ciardi) **10**:107; **40**:155
"The Gift" (Creeley) **36**:118
"The Gift" (Daly) **17**:91
"The Gift" (Ferré) **139**:154, 157, 179
"The Gift" (Glück) **22**:176
"The Gift" (L'Heureux) **52**:275
"Gift" (Merwin) **3**:339
"Gift" (Milosz) **5**:293; **56**:248
"The Gift" (Oliver) **98**:284
"The Gift" (Raine) **103**:189
"The Gift" (Steinbeck) **9**:515
"The Gift" (Swan) **69**:365
"Gift" (Urquhart) **90**:386
The Gift (Dickinson) **12**:171-72, 174
The Gift (H. D.) **31**:208, 212-13
The Gift (Hamill) **10**:251
The Gift (Humphreys) **47**:180, 186, 188-89
The Gift (Nabokov)
See *Dar*
The Gift (Weller) **26**:447
"Gift for a Believer" (Levine) **14**:318; **118**:279, 284, 295, 299, 302, 316
A Gift from Nessus (McIlvanney) **42**:281
A Gift from the Boys (Buchwald) **33**:88
Gift from the Sea (Lindbergh) **82**:154-55, 158-60, 163-67
"Gift from the Stars" (Clarke) **3**:128; **35**:122; **136**:197
"A Gift of a Rose" (D'Aguiar) **145**:116-17
The Gift of Asher Lev (Potok) **112**:290-93
"The Gift of Fire" (Mueller) **13**:399
The Gift of Good Land (Berry) **27**:37-9
"Gift of Grass" (Adams) **13**:2
"A Gift of Great Value" (Creeley) **78**:162
"The Gift of Laughter" (Fauset) **54**:181
"A Gift of Light" (Belitt) **22**:50
A Gift of Magic (Duncan) **26**:102
"A Gift of Mercy" (Findley) **102**:110
"The Gift of the Prodigal" (Taylor) **37**:411-13; **44**:305-06; **50**:251; **71**:304, 306
"The Gift of the Second Snow" (Smith) **22**:385
A Gift of Time (Kanin) **22**:230-31
"The Gift of Wilderness" (Stegner) **49**:359
A Gift of Wings (Bach) **14**:35
"The Gift Outright" (Frost) **1**:110; **44**:459, 462
The Gift to Be Simple: A Garland for Ann Lee (Peters) **7**:303-04
Gifts (Farah) **137**:97-98, 104, 110-11, 114, 116-18
"The Gifts of Iban" (Steinbeck) **21**:390
"Gifts of Rain" (Heaney) **5**:172; **14**:243; **37**:169; **74**:157
"Gifts without Recipients" (Kunene) **85**:162
"Gigamesh" (Lem) **15**:330
The Gigli Concert (Murphy) **51**:303-06
"Gigolo" (Ferber) **93**:145-46
"Gigolo" (Plath) **5**:342; **111**:206
"The Gigolo" (Sagan) **17**:428
"Gila Flambé" (Barthelme) **36**:52; **117**:7, 14, 18
"Gilbert's Mother" (Trevor) **116**:376, 395
"The Gilded Man" (Ai) **14**:8; **69**:4-6, 11-12, 17
"The Gilded Six-Bits" (Hurston) **7**:172; **30**:211, 215, 219, 223; **61**:263
Gilden-Fire (Donaldson) **46**:141, 143
Giles Goat-Boy; or, The Revised New Syllabus (Barth) **1**:17-18; **2**:36-9; **3**:39-40, 42; **7**:22-3; **9**:61-3, 65, 68-9, 71; **10**:22-4; **14**:49-51, 55-6; **51**:20-1, 23, 25-6, 28; **89**:7, 11, 14, 17, 27
"Gilgamesh and Friend" (Purdy) **6**:428; **50**:236
Gilles et Jeanne: Récit (Tournier) **36**:438; **95**:372, 374-75, 390-91, 395
"Gills" (Moure) **88**:220
"Gimme Shelter" (Jagger and Richard) **17**:226
Gimme Shelter (Maysles and Maysles) **16**:440-43
"Gimme Some Truth" (Lennon) **12**:367; **35**:263-64, 267
"Gimpel Tam" (Singer) **1**:310, 312; **3**:452-53, 455, 458-59; **6**:508; **11**:500; **23**:414, 418, 422; **38**:407; **69**:306, 309, 311, 320; **111**:292, 294, 296, 312-13, 344-46
Gimpel Tam und andere Dertseylungen

(Singer) **3**:453; **11**:502
"Gimpel the Fool" (Singer)
See "Gimpel Tam"
Gimpel the Fool, and Other Stories (Singer)
See *Gimpel Tam und andere Dertseylungen*
"Gin" (Blackburn) **9**:100
"Gin" (Levine) **118**:297
The Gin Game (Coburn) **10**:107-08
"Gin the Goodwife Stint" (Bunting) **47**:45, 49
Ginger and Fred (Fellini)
See *Ginger e Fred*
Ginger Coffey (Moore)
See *The Luck of Ginger Coffey*
Ginger e Fred (Fellini) **85**:53-7, 60, 66, 71-2, 76, 81-2
"Ginger from Next Door" (Aksyonov) **101**:18
The Ginger Horse (Daly) **17**:91
The Ginger Man (Donleavy) **1**:75-6; **4**:123-26; **6**:139-42; **10**:153-55; **45**:123-25, 128-29
Ginger, You're Barmy (Lodge) **36**:266-67; **141**:331, 333
"The Gingerbread House" (Coover) **7**:58; **15**:145
The Gingerbread Lady (Simon) **6**:505; **11**:495; **31**:395-96, 400, 403; **70**:244
The Gingerbread Woman (Johnston) **150**:33-5
"Ginger's Friday" (Harrison) **43**:175
The Gingham Dog (Wilson) **7**:547
Il gioco segreto (Morante) **47**:279
"Gioconda and Si-Ya-U" (Hikmet)
See "Jokund ile Si-Ya-U"
The Gioconda Smile (Huxley) **5**:195
La giornato d'uno scruttatore (Calvino) **5**:98, 99, 101; **8**:127, 129-30; **11**:89, 91; **39**:308, 314-16
Il giorno della civetta (Sciascia) **8**:474; **9**:475; **41**:388-89, 393
Giorno dopo giorno (Quasimodo) **10**:428-29
Giorno per giorno dal 1922 al 1966 (Bacchelli) **19**:32
"Giotto's Joy" (Kristeva) **77**:312
"Giovanni and His Wife" (Landolfi) **49**:210
"Giovanni Franchi" (Loy) **28**:251, 253
Giovanni Pisano, Sculptor (Ayrton) **7**:18
Giovanni's Room (Baldwin) **1**:13-14, 16; **2**:32; **3**:32; **4**:40-1; **5**:41-3; **13**:51-2; **15**:41-2; **17**:21, 29-30, 32, 36, 41, 44-5; **42**:21; **50**:283, 293-94, 296; **90**:5, 31-2; **127**:99, 109, 119, 132-38, 143, 147, 149-51, 153
"Gipsies Revisited" (Mahon) **27**:288, 290
"Giraffe" (Plumly) **33**:312
"Giraffe" (Swenson) **61**:405
"The Giraffe" (Young) **82**:412
Giraffe: Poems by Stanley Plumly (Plumly) **33**:311-13
"Girl" (Kincaid) **43**:247-48, 250; **137**:162-64, 169, 172, 174
"The Girl" (Olds) **85**:293
Girl 6 (Lee) **105**:122-23, 127-28
"The Girl across the Room" (Adams) **46**:17
"The Girl and the Train" (Cabral de Melo Neto) **76**:169
"Girl at the Piano" (Graham) **48**:145; **118**:224
"Girl at the Seaside" (Murphy) **41**:312
"Girl Bathing" (Clark Bekedermo) **38**:117, 127-28
"Girl Beatnik" (Yevtushenko) **26**:463-64
The Girl beneath the Lion (Mandiargues) **41**:273-74, 276
"Girl Blue" (Wonder) **12**:656
A Girl Can Dream (Cavanna) **12**:98-9
"Girl Don't Tell Me" (Wilson) **12**:647
"Girl Friend" (Colter) **58**:140
The Girl Friends (Antonioni)
See *Le amiche*
"The Girl from California" (O'Hara) **42**:326
"The Girl from Ipanema" (Murakami) **150**:62
The Girl from Mars (Williamson) **29**:456
"The Girl from the Beach" (Stead) **32**:409; **80**:306
The Girl Green as Elderflower (Stow) **23**:437-38; **48**:358-61
The Girl Hunters (Spillane) **13**:526, 528
The Girl I Left Behind (Endō) **99**:285-86, 299-300, 305-06
"A Girl in a Library" (Jarrell) **9**:297; **13**:298; **49**:197, 201
The Girl in a Swing (Adams) **18**:2
"A Girl in a Window" (Wright) **28**:462
The Girl in Blue (Wodehouse) **10**:537
Girl in Gingham (Metcalf) **37**:301-03, 305
The Girl in Melanie Klein (Harwood) **32**:223
"The Girl in the Field" (Monette) **82**:315
The Girl in the Grove (Duncan) **26**:103
Girl in the Mirror (Sherburne) **30**:362
The Girl in the Moon (Lang)
See *Die Frau im Mond*
The Girl in the Opposite Bed (Arundel) **17**:14, 17
The Girl in the Plain Brown Wrapper (MacDonald) **44**:408
"Girl in Time Lost" (Derleth) **31**:132
"Girl in White" (Dobyns) **37**:81
A Girl in Winter (Larkin) **5**:223-24, 229; **8**:337-38; **9**:324; **13**:335, 337-38; **33**:263, 265-66; **39**:334, 340, 347; **64**:260, 280
"The Girl Next Door" (Levine) **54**:298, 301
A Girl of Forty (Gold) **42**:198; **152**:121, 126, 134-35, 137-38, 141
"The Girl of My Dreams" (Malamud) **8**:375; **44**:419
"Girl of My Dreams" (Matheson) **37**:245
"Girl of my Dreams" (Okudzhava) **59**:378-79
"Girl of the North Country" (Dylan) **4**:149; **12**:186; **77**:172-73
"Girl on the Beach" (Williams) **42**:440
"A Girl Sewing" (Szirtes) **46**:393-94
"A Girl Skating" (Colwin) **23**:129; **84**:150
The Girl That He Marries (Lerman) **56**:176-78
"Girl Trouble" (Smith) **12**:535
Girl, Twenty (Amis) **1**:6; **2**:10-11; **3**:7-8; **5**:22; **8**:12; **40**:42; **129**:3, 19
Girl Waiting in the Shade (Davies) **23**:147
"A Girl Walking into a Shadow" (Wright) **3**:542
"The Girl Who Approached the Fire" (Kawabata) **107**:107
The Girl Who Knew Tomorrow (Sherburne) **30**:362
"The Girl Who Knew What They Meant" (Sturgeon) **22**:411
"The Girl Who Raised Pigeons" (Jones) **76**:65, 69
"The Girl Who Sang" (Aldiss) **40**:21
The Girl Who Wanted a Boy (Zindel) **26**:481
The Girl Who Was Plugged In (Tiptree) **48**:388-89, 395; **50**:357
"The Girl Who Went to Mexico" (Nowlan) **15**:399
Girl with a Monkey (Astley) **41**:43-4, 48-9
"Girl with Coffee Tray" (Fuller) **62**:197
"Girl with Curious Hair" (Wallace) **114**:348, 352
Girl with Curious Hair (Wallace) **114**:349-52, 359, 361, 368
The Girl with Green Eyes (O'Brien) **3**:364; **116**:182
"The Girl with Harlequin Glasses" (Colwin) **5**:108
"The Girl with the Flaxen Hair" (Grau) **146**:127
"The Girl with the Hungry Eyes" (Leiber) **25**:303
The Girl with the Incredible Feeling (Swados) **12**:558, 560
The Girl with the Scar (Lustig) **56**:188-89
"The Girl with the Silver Eyes" (Hammett) **47**:164
Girlfriend (Coupland)
See *Girlfriend in a Coma*
Girlfriend in a Coma (Coupland) **133**:19-20
"Girlfriend Is Better" (Byrne) **26**:99
"Girlhood of Jane Harrison" (Levertov) **66**:238
"The Girls" (Elytis) **100**:191
"Girls" (Gallagher) **63**:121
The Girls (Ferber) **93**:142, 144-45, 147-48, 164, 180
Girls Are Girls and Boys Are Boys: So What's the Difference? (Gordon) **26**:137
Girls at Play (Theroux) **8**:512; **28**:423-24
"The Girls at the Sphinx" (Farrell) **66**:131
"Girls at War" (Achebe) **26**:23; **75**:14, 16
Girls at War, and Other Stories (Achebe) **3**:2; **7**:6; **26**:20-2; **75**:14, 17
"Girls Bathing, Galway, 1965" (Heaney) **25**:245
"Girls Fighting Broadway" (Shapiro) **53**:330
Girls in Their Married Bliss (O'Brien) **5**:313; **116**:182-83, 193, 197, 199
"The Girls in Their Summer Dresses" (Shaw) **7**:412; **23**:395; **34**:368, 370
The Girls of Slender Means (Spark) **2**:415; **3**:463, 467; **13**:524-25; **18**:501-02; **40**:394, 396, 399-400; **94**:350, 353
"The Girls of Summer" (Sondheim) **30**:398
"Girls on the Beach" (Wilson) **12**:644
A Girl's Own Story (Campion) **95**:2, 6, 11
"Girl's Song" (Bogan) **46**:81; **93**:92, 98
"A Girl's Story" (Bambara) **88**:8, 22, 28, 42
Girls Turn Wives (Klein) **30**:239
"The Girls Want to Be with the Girls" (Byrne) **26**:96
"Girovago" (Ungaretti) **11**:555
Le gisant mis en lumiere (Char) **55**:288-89
"Git Dough" (Guillén)
See "Búscate plata"
"Giulia Lazzari" (Maugham) **67**:216
Giulietta degli spiriti (Fellini) **16**:278-80, 286-87, 293, 299; **85**:51, 54, 59, 62-3, 68, 74, 76, 79-82
La giullarata (Fo) **109**:114-15
Il giusto della vita (Luzi) **13**:352
Give Birth to Brightness: A Thematic Study in Neo-Black Literature (Williams) **89**:319, 323, 340
Give 'Em Enough Rope (Clash) **30**:43, 45-6, 51
"Give Ireland Back to the Irish" (McCartney) **35**:292
"Give It Time to Be Tender" (Kristofferson) **26**:268
"Give Me a Body You Mountains" (Blaga) **75**:69
Give Me One Good Reason (Klein) **30**:237-38
"Give Me Time and I'll Tell You" (Buckley) **57**:133
Give My Regards to Broad Street (McCartney) **35**:293
"Give Peace a Chance" (Lennon) **35**:261, 267, 270-71
Give Thankx (Cliff) **21**:65
Give the Boys a Great Big Hand (Hunter) **31**:220
Give the People What They Want (Davies) **21**:107
"Give to the Rich" (Jacobsen) **48**:190
"Give Us Our Peace" (Hughes) **108**:334
"Give Us This Day" (Kogawa) **78**:167
"Give Way, Ye Gates" (Roethke) **8**:455; **101**:262, 273, 277, 280-81, 335, 340
"Give Your Heart to the Hawks" (Jeffers) **54**:237-38, 245-46
Give Your Heart to the Hawks and Other Poems (Jeffers) **11**:307; **54**:237, 245
The Giveaway (Jellicoe) **27**:210
The Given and the Made (Vendler) **138**:274-76, 292, 294
"A Given Grace" (Tomlinson) **2**:437; **6**:536
"The Given Note" (Heaney) **25**:249
Giver (Lezama Lima)
See *Dador*
Giving Back Diamonds (Bowering) **32**:48
"Giving Birth" (Atwood) **13**:46-7
"Giving Blood" (Alexie) **154**:29
"Giving Blood" (Updike) **139**:337
Giving Good Weight (McPhee) **36**:298
"Giving It Up" (Williams) **33**:441, 344
Giving Offense: Essays on Censorship (Coetzee) **117**:93-4, 96, 101

Giving up the Ghost (Moraga) **126**:275, 277, 280, 288, 293-94, 302, 305-07, 311-13, 315, 318
"Givings" (Ammons) **108**:56
Gjenerali i ushtrisë së vdekur (Kadare) **52**:257, 261
"Gkragkâta" (Ritsos) **6**:463
The Glad Hand (Wilson) **33**:462-64
"Glad Heart at the Supermarket" (Van Duyn) **116**:411, 413
Gladiator (Wylie) **43**:460, 462
"Gladiators" (La Guma) **19**:272
The Gladiators (Koestler) **1**:170; **3**:270; **15**:309-10; **33**:227, 239-40, 243
"Gladness and Madness" (Hall) **37**:145
"Glamour" (Ferber) **93**:161
"Glamour Profession" (Becker and Fagen) **26**:84
A Glance Away (Wideman) **36**:450-53, 455; **122**:311, 352, 354, 363
"A Glance from the Bridge" (Wilbur) **53**:413; **110**:382
"Glanmore Revisited" (Heaney) **74**:188, 190, 193, 195, 197
"Glanmore Sonnets" (Heaney) **14**:246; **25**:247-48; **74**:175, 190, 195
The Glapion Effect (Audiberti)
See *L'effet Glapion*
Glas (Derrida) **24**:153-55; **87**:72, 93, 96-7, 103-10
Gläserne Bienen (Jünger) **125**:223
Glasgow is Like the Sea (MacDiarmid) **63**:248
"Glasgow Schoolboys, Running Backwards" (Dunn) **40**:168
Glasgow Sonnets (Morgan) **31**:273, 275-77
Glasnost in Action: Cultural Renaissance in Russia (Nove) **59**:396
Das Glasperlenspiel (Hesse) **1**:146-47; **2**:190-92; **3**:243-47; **6**:237-38; **11**:270-72; **17**:195, 197-98, 204-07, 216-18; **25**:259, 261, **69**:278-83, 287, 290-92
"Glass" (Kawabata) **107**:107
"Glass" (Williams) **148**:366
The Glass Alembic (Feinstein) **36**:169
"The Glass and the Bowl" (Erdrich) **120**:145
The Glass Bead Game (Hesse)
See *Das Glasperlenspiel*
The Glass Bees (Jünger) **125**:251-52, 261
The Glass Blowers (du Maurier) **6**:146
The Glass Cage (Wilson) **3**:537
The Glass Cell (Highsmith) **42**:212; **102**:170, 172-73, 202-04, 209
The Glass Cottage: A Nautical Romance (Redgrove) **41**:353
A Glass Face in the Rain (Stafford) **29**:387-88
The Glass Flame (Whitney) **42**:436
"The Glass Floor" (King) **37**:202
"Glass Grain" (Tomlinson) **4**:543
The Glass Highway (Estleman) **48**:104, 107
Glass Houses (Joel) **26**:220-22
The Glass Key (Hammett) **3**:218-20; **5**:162; **19**:193-95; **47**:156-57, 162-65
The Glass Key (Welles) **80**:380
"The Glass King" (Boland) **67**:46; **113**:86, 98
The Glass Lake (Binchy) **153**:69-71, 76, 78
The Glass Menagerie (Williams) **1**:367, 369; **2**:465-66; **5**:498-99, 501, 503-04; **7**:540-41, 543, 545; **8**:547, 549; **11**:571-76; **15**:580; **19**:470, 473-74; **30**:455-58, 461, 464-66, 469-70; **39**:446; **71**:354-406; **111**:379-80, 388-89, 391, 393, 395, 397, 404, 408, 414, 417-24
"The Glass Mountain" (Barthelme) **1**:18; **6**:29; **13**:57; **46**:35, 40, 45; **115**:65, 68-9, 77
A Glass of Blessings (Pym) **13**:469-70; **19**:387; **37**:373; **111**:227-28, 230-31, 239, 243-48, 258, 263-64, 266, 269, 271, 278, 283-85
"The Glass of Madeira" (Rakosi) **47**:348
"The Glass of Pure Water" (MacDiarmid) **4**:312
"A Glass of Tea" (White) **5**:486
"A Glass of Wine" (La Guma) **19**:274
The Glass on the Table of Claudius Civilis's Conspirers (Haavikko)
See *Lasi Claudius Civiliksen salaliittolaisten pöydällä*
The Glass Palace (Ghosh) **153**:124-31
Glass People (Godwin) **5**:142; **8**:248; **22**:182-83; **69**:247; **125**:123, 128, 167-69
The Glass Teat: Essays of Opinion on the Subject of Television (Ellison) **13**:205; **139**:115, 129
The Glass Trumpet (Waddington) **28**:437
The Glass Village (Queen) **11**:464
"The Glassblowers" (Peake) **54**:366, 369
The Glassblowers (du Maurier) **59**:286
"The Glassblower's Breath" (Ostriker) **132**:321
The Glass-Sided Ants' Nest (Dickinson) **12**:168, 171; **35**:130-31, 133, 137
The Glassy Sea (Engel) **36**:162-63
"A Glastonbury Cricket Match" (Ewart) **46**:152
A Glastonbury Romance (Powys) **7**:348-50; **9**:440-41; **15**:433, 436; **46**:316-18, 320-22, 324; **125**:271-72, 276, 278, 280-82, 289-90, 292, 294-304
"Glazunoviana" (Ashbery) **77**:58
"The Gleaner" (Bates) **46**:52-3, 61
"Gleaning" (Blunden) **56**:37
"Gleanings from Snow Country" (Kawabata) **107**:104, 107-08
Gleisdreieck (Grass) **15**:263; **32**:198, 200-01
Gleiwitzer Kindheit: Gedicte aus zwanzig Jahren (Bienek) **11**:48
Glembajevi (Krleža) **8**:329; **114**:167, 175
The Glembays (Krleža)
See *Glembajevi*
"Glen Albyn" (MacDiarmid) **63**:242
"Glencull Waterside" (Montague) **46**:274
Glenda (Cortázar)
See *Queremos tanto a Glenda*
"Glendower" (Nye) **42**:309
Glengarry Glen Ross (Mamet) **34**:218-24; **46**:254-55
"Glengormley" (Mahon) **27**:288, 291
"Glenna—A Child of the 60's" (Tomlin) **17**:522-23
"Glenthorne Poems" (Fisher) **25**:160
"Glenway Wescott's War Work" (Wilson) **24**:481
Glide Path (Clarke) **136**:197
"Glimmerings" (Schaeffer) **11**:491
"Glimpse" (Hughes) **119**:262-63
"Glimpse at a Jockey" (Miller) **47**:250
A Glimpse of Nothingness: Experiences in an American Zen Community (van de Wetering) **47**:404
The Glimpses of the Moon (Crispin) **22**:110
Glissements progressifs du plaisir (Robbe-Grillet) **8**:454; **43**:367; **128**:363, 377
"Glitter: A Memory" (Carpenter) **41**:107-08
The Glittering Clouds (Paustovsky) **40**:367
The Glittering Coffin (Potter) **86**:345, 349; **123**:222, 224-26, 229, 273
"Glittering Pie" (Miller) **43**:298
The Glittering Prizes (Raphael) **14**:437-38
Glitz (Leonard) **71**:208-10, 212-18, 221-24, 226-27; **120**:264-67, 270-71, 275, 277-79, 287, 304
Global Dumping Ground: The International Traffic in Hazardous Waste (Moyers) **74**:257
A Global Ethic: The Declaration of the Parliament of the World's Religions (Kung) **130**:162
"The Global Fidget" (Dunn) **6**:148-49
Global Responsibility (Kung) **130**:146-47, 149
"The Globe" (Olson) **28**:343
"Globule" (Ostriker) **132**:321
"La gloire des rois" (Perse) **46**:300-01
"The Gloomy Tune" (Paley) **4**:392; **37**:337; **140**:262, 277
"Gloria" (Elytis) **100**:156, 159, 161, 163-64, 166
Gloria (Cassavetes) **20**:55-6
Gloria mundi (Clark) **19**:107-08
Gloria Star (Tremblay) **102**:365-66
"Gloria Steinem and the Feminist Utopia" (Amis) **62**:2
Gloriana; or, The Unfulfill'd Queen (Moorcock) **27**:351; **58**:349
La glorie de Dina (del Castillo) **38**:169
The Glorious Destiny of Marshal Nnikon Nniku (Tchicaya)
See *Le destin glorieux du Maréchal Nnikon Nniku, prince qu'on sort*
The Glorious Ones (Prose) **45**:323-24, 326
A Glorious Third (Seton) **27**:427-29
"The Glory" (Ciardi) **44**:381
"Glory" (Komunyakaa) **94**:237, 241
"Glory" (Larson)
See "One Song Glory"
Glory (Nabokov) **1**:246; **2**:301-02, 304; **11**:393-94; **15**:396; **44**:469
The Glory and the Dream (Hilliard) **15**:280
Glory and the Lightning (Caldwell) **28**:67
The Glory Girl (Byars) **35**:75-6
"Glory in the Daytime" (Parker) **68**:326, 334, 337
The Glory of Hera (Gordon) **6**:206; **29**:190; **83**:258, 261
"The Glory of Kings" (Perse)
See "La gloire des rois"
The Glory of the Hummingbird (De Vries) **7**:76-7
"Glory of Women" (Sassoon) **130**:183, 186-87, 216, 221
Glory Road (Catton) **35**:85-6
Glory Road (Heinlein) **14**:251; **26**:165; **55**:303
"The Glory Trumpeter" (Walcott) **25**:449; **67**:353-54
"Gloss Gimel" (Klein) **19**:262
"Glossolalia" (Barth) **9**:68; **51**:23; **89**:5-7, 9, 15, 21, 44, 61-2
"Gloucestershire" (Davie) **8**:166
"The Glove" (Dinesen) **10**:152
"The Gloves" (Middleton) **13**:389
Gloves to the Hangman (Walker) **13**:566
"Glow Girl" (Townshend) **17**:534
"Glowing Enigmas" (Sachs)
See *Glühende Rätsel*
"A Glowing Future" (Rendell) **48**:320
"Glowing Riddles" (Sachs)
See *Glühende Rätsel*
"A Glowworm Illuminates the Night" (Ritsos) **31**:324
"Gloze" (Corn) **33**:117
"Glubokim golosom proroka" (Akhmadulina) **53**:11
Glühende Rätsel (Sachs) **14**:476-77; **98**:324, 328, 334-35
"La Glutton, in Suburb" (Shapcott) **38**:400
"Gluttony" (Dobyns) **37**:76
The Gnädiges Fräulein (Williams) **2**:465; **5**:502, 504; **15**:580; **19**:471-72; **30**:470; **45**:450-51
"Gnat-Psalm" (Hughes) **37**:179
"Gnome" (Pink Floyd) **35**:307
Gnomes and Occasions (Nemerov) **6**:362-63; **9**:395; **36**:302
"Gnomic Variations for Kenneth Burke" (Nemerov) **36**:309
The Gnomobile (Sinclair) **11**:497
The Gnostic Gospels (Pagels) **104**:205-08, 210-11, 214, 217, 220-21, 224, 229, 234
Go (Holmes) **56**:136, 138-42, 145
"Go and Look for Bread" (Guillén)
See "Búscate plata"
Go Back for Murder (Christie) **12**:125
"Go Cry on Somebody Else's Shoulder" (Zappa) **15**:588
"Go Down Matthew" (Barnes) **11**:31
Go Down, Moses and Other Stories (Faulkner) **1**:102; **3**:151-52; **6**:174; **8**:210-14; **14**:172, 175, 179; **18**:149; **28**:140, 143, 145; **68**:129
"Go Get Money" (Guillén)
See "Búscate plata"

Go in Beauty (Eastlake) **8**:198, 200
"Go like This" (Moore) **39**:82-4; **45**:279
"Go, Lovely Rose" (Eberhart) **56**:84
"Go Not to Lethe Celebrates Its Twenty-Seventh Anniversary: A Soap Opera Journal Special" (Grayson) **38**:209
Go Saddle the Sea (Aiken) **35**:18, 21
Go, Team, Go! (Tunis) **12**:597
Go Tell It on the Mountain (Baldwin) **1**:13-14, 16; **2**:31-2; **3**:31-2; **4**:40-1; **5**:40-1, 43; **8**:41; **13**:51-2; **15**:41; **17**:20, 29, 31-2, 36-7, 42-4; **42**:14, 17-18; **50**:283-84, 293-95; **67**:3-30; **90**:5, 10, 12, 31; **127**:99, 105-06, 109, 112, 119, 143
Go Tell the Lemming (Rubens) **19**:403
Go to the Widow-Maker (Jones) **1**:162; **3**:261; **10**:292; **39**:406-07, 409
"Go Wake Jessie Up. We Are Going to the Beach!" (Gray) **49**:147
Go West (Keaton) **20**:188
"Go West Young Man" (Laughlin) **49**:220
Go When You See the Green Man Walking (Brooke-Rose) **40**:106
The Goal Attained (Bernhard)
See *Am Ziel*
The Goalie's Anxiety at the Penalty Kick (Handke)
See *Die Angst des Tormanns beim Elfmeter*
The Goat (Keaton) **20**:194
Goat Dances: Poems and Prose (Loewinsohn) **52**:285
"A Goat for Azazel" (Porter) **101**:223
A Goat on a Cloud (Arrabal)
See *Une chèvre sur un nuage*
Goat Song (Yerby) **22**:488-89
Goatfoot, Milktongue, Twinbird (Hall) **37**:145-47
"A Goatherd at Luncheon" (Calvino) **39**:314
The Goatibex Constellation (Iskander)
See *Sozvezdie Kozlotura*
"Goats and Monkeys" (Walcott) **25**:449; **42**:423; **67**:350, 352-53; **76**:270
Goat's Head Soup (Jagger and Richard) **17**:228-29, 232-33, 236, 238
"The Go-Away Bird" (Spark) **8**:493; **13**:520; **40**:401, 404
The Go-Away Bird, and Other Stories (Spark) **13**:519
"Gobegger Foriu Tostay" (Cabrera Infante) **120**:73
"El gobernador Glu Glu" (Ulibarrí) **83**:416
The Go-Between (Hartley) **2**:181-82; **22**:211, 213-14, 217-19
The Go-Between (Pinter) **27**:391; **58**:376
The Goblet of Fire (Rowling)
See *Harry Potter and the Goblet of Fire*
Goblin Reservation (Simak) **55**:320
"Goblin Revel" (Sassoon) **130**:176
"Una goccia" (Buzzati) **36**:96-7
"The God" (H. D.) **73**:120
"God" (Lennon) **35**:261-62, 266
"God" (Prince) **35**:331
"God" (Swenson) **61**:400; **106**:316, 327, 345-46, 350
God (Allen) **52**:36-7, 43-4, 48
God: A Biography (Miles) **100**:275-83
A God against the Gods (Drury) **37**:108-09
"God and Gods" (Endō) **54**:158; **99**:285
A God and His Gifts (Compton-Burnett) **3**:111-12; **15**:140
God and Mammon (Mauriac) **56**:218
God and Man at Yale (Buckley) **37**:53, 55-7, 61
God and the American Writer (Kazin) **119**:316-18, 320, 325, 334
"God and the Article Writer" (Berriault) **109**:92-3, 95
"God and the Cobbler" (Narayan) **28**:301; **121**:355
The God beneath the Sea (Garfield) **12**:219, 222, 229-30, 235
God Bless (Feiffer) **8**:216; **64**:149-50
"God Bless America" (Fuller) **62**:186, 193
God Bless the Child (Hunter) **35**:223-27
God Bless You, Mr. Rosewater; or, Pearls before Swine (Vonnegut) **1**:347; **2**:453, 455; **3**:495, 497, 499-500, 505-06; **4**:561-64, 567; **5**:466, 469; **8**:531-32; **12**:601-02, 604-05, 607, 614, 618-19, 623; **40**:446-47; **60**:417, 424, 427, 431; **111**:351, 354, 359, 371
God Emperor of Dune (Herbert) **23**:221-23; **35**:199, 201-03, 206-09; **44**:393-94; **85**:93-6
"God Full of Mercy" (Amichai) **116**:100, 128
"God Has Manifested Himself unto Us As Canadian Tire" (Hood) **28**:194
"God Has Mercy on Kindergarten Children" (Amichai)
See "Elohim merakhem 'al yaldei hagan"
"God Has Pity on the Kindergarten Children" (Amichai)
See "Elohim merakhem 'al yaldei hagan"
"God Hunger" (Ryan) **65**:211
God Hunger (Ryan) **65**:208-16
God in the Dock (Lewis) **124**:194
"A God in the Garden" (Sturgeon) **22**:410; **39**:360, 366
"God Is" (Mathias) **45**:238
"God Is a Helicopter with a Big Searchlight" (Wild) **14**:580
"God Is Love" (Gaye) **26**:130
God Is Red (Deloria) **21**:111-12; **122**:111, 118
"God Knows" (Dylan) **77**:183-84
God Knows (Heller) **36**:228-31
God Made Alaska for the Indians (Reed) **32**:361-62
The God Makers (Herbert) **12**:272; **35**:209; **44**:394; **85**:88
"The God of Dostoyevsky" (Richards) **24**:395
"The God of Flowers" (Levertov) **66**:241
The God of Glass (Redgrove) **41**:355-56
The God of Small Things (Roy) **109**:68-78
The God of Tarot (Anthony) **35**:35
"The God of the Bulls" (Borges) **48**:42
God of the Labyrinth (Wilson) **14**:584
God on the Rocks (Gardam) **43**:168-69
"God Only Knows" (Wilson) **12**:643
God Perkins (Pownall) **10**:419-20
"God Pities the Kindergarten Children" (Amichai)
See "Elohim merakhem 'al yaldei hagan"
The God Project (Saul) **46**:367
"God Rest Ye Merry, Gentleman: Part II" (Walcott) **67**:359
"God Rest You Merry, Gentlemen" (Hemingway) **3**:242; **19**:219
God Save the Child (Parker) **27**:363, 365-67
"God Save You, Future Humanity" (Asturias) **8**:26
God Sends Sunday (Bontemps) **1**:37; **18**:62-3
The God That Failed (Koestler) **33**:238
The God That Failed (Wright) **74**:382
"God, The" (McFadden) **48**:249
"The God Who Eats Corn" (Murphy) **41**:312-13, 317-18
God without Thunder: An Unorthodox Defense of Orthodoxy (Ransom) **2**:362; **4**:433-34, 436-37; **5**:363-64
Godbody (Sturgeon) **39**:361
"Goddamn Pussycats" (Thurber) **25**:436
Godded and Codded (O'Faolain) **47**:325-26, 330; **108**:399, 425
"The Goddess" (Levertov) **66**:238, 245
The Goddess (Chayefsky) **23**:113
The Goddess (Ray)
See *Devi*
The Goddess and Other Women (Oates) **6**:373; **19**:353; **108**:372
Goddess of the Americas: Writings on the Virgin of Guadalupe (Castillo) **151**:46, 74, 76, 103
Le godelureaux (Chabrol) **16**:183
"Godfather" (Dorfman) **77**:141, 143
The Godfather (Coppola) **16**:233-42, 244, 248-49; **126**:189, 191-93, 196-214, 228-32, 234-35, 240, 245, 254, 260, 262-63, 265-66
The Godfather (Puzo) **2**:351-52; **6**:429-30; **36**:359-63; **107**:175-76, 178-203, 205-16, 218
The Godfather Papers and Other Confessions (Puzo) **2**:352; **36**:360; **107**:175, 189, 213
The Godfather, Part II (Coppola) **16**:240-45, 249; **126**:196-98, 200-02, 204, 208-14, 244-45, 249, 254, 260, 262-63, 265
The Godfather: Part II (Puzo) **107**:202, 213
The Godfather, Part III (Coppola) **126**:262, 264-66
The Godfather: Part III (Puzo) **107**:193, 208, 213
Godfires (Hoffman) **141**:268-71, 274-75, 279, 281, 296-97, 306-07
"Godmother" (Parker) **68**:340
The Godmother (Elliott) **47**:104
"Gods" (Sexton) **6**:494
Gods and Devils (Simic) **130**:331
Gods and Generals (Shaara) **119**:104-06
God's Bits of Wood (Ousmane)
See *Les bouts de bois de Dieu*
God's Country and Mine (Barzun) **145**:73, 94
God's Country and My People (Morris) **7**:247; **37**:312-13
Gods, Demons, and Others (Narayan) **28**:299, 302; **121**:334, 353, 358, 394-96
God's Ear (Lerman) **56**:180
God's Favorite (Simon) **6**:505-06; **11**:496
God's Fool: The Life and Times of Francis of Assisi (Green)
See *Frère François*
Gods from Outer Space (von Daniken) **30**:423-24
God's Grace (Malamud) **27**:298-302; **44**:413, 416, 419
God's Images (Dickey) **10**:142
"The Gods in Flight" (Aldiss) **40**:21
God's Little Acre (Caldwell) **14**:95, 97-9; **50**:298-303; **60**:44-8, 50, 54, 58-60, 64-5
God's Measurements (Lieberman) **36**:261-64
God's Mistress (Galvin) **38**:198-99
"The Gods of the Earth Beneath" (Blunden) **56**:48
Gods of the Plague (Fassbinder) **20**:113, 116
God's Pocket (Dexter) **34**:43-5
God's Radar (Arrick) **30**:19
"The God's Script" (Borges)
See "La escritura del Dios"
God's Snake (Spanidou) **44**:104-10
God's Sparrows (Child) **19**:100, 103
"God's Spies" (Howe) **152**:152
God's Stepchildren (Millin) **49**:240-41, 243, 245-46, 249, 251-55
The Gods, the Little Guys, and the Police (Costantini)
See *De dioses, hombrecitos, y policías*
"The Gods Themselves" (Asimov) **19**:26
The Gods Themselves (Asimov) **19**:26, 28; **26**:37-40, 47-50, 63; **76**:313
"God's Typhoon" (Hersey) **81**:329
God's Warrior (Slaughter) **29**:377
God's World (Mahfouz)
See *Dunya'llah*
God's World (Mahfūz) **55**:183, 188
The Godstone and the Blackymor (White) **30**:449
The Godwulf Manuscript (Parker) **27**:363-65
"Gog" (Hughes) **119**:281, 284
Gog (Sinclair) **2**:400-02; **14**:488
"Gog II and III" (Hughes) **37**:173
Gogo no eiko (Mishima) **2**:286; **4**:354, 357; **27**:337, 340-41, 343
"Gogol's Wife" (Landolfi) **49**:209-11
Gogol's Wife and Other Stories (Landolfi) **11**:321; **49**:209-10, 212
"Gogo's Late Wife Tranquilla" (Durcan) **43**:114
Goin a Buffalo (Bullins) **7**:36
"Goin' Down This Road" (Guthrie) **35**:184
"Goin' Home" (Smith) **12**:539

"Goin' to Town" (Storm)
See "Going to Town"
"Going" (Larkin) **64**:257, 259, 261, 274
Going (Elliott) **38**:180
"Going After Cacciato" (O'Brien) **103**:144, 146
Going After Cacciato (O'Brien) **19**:356-59; **40**:345-48; **103**:131-39, 141, 143-49, 152, 159-60, 163-64, 166, 168-69, 172-75
Going All the Way (Wakefield) **7**:502-03
"Going Away" (Nemerov) **36**:305
Going Away: A Report, a Memoir (Sigal) **7**:424-25
"Going Back" (Stanton) **9**:508
"Going Back to Cape de Santo Agostinho" (Cabral de Melo Neto)
See "De volta ao Cabro de Santo Agostinho"
"Going Back to Sleep" (Sadoff) **9**:466
Going Back to the River (Hacker) **72**:191-92
"Going Back West" (Cliff) **21**:62
Going Down (Markson) **67**:185-86, 191-94
Going Down Fast (Piercy) **3**:384; **27**:372; **62**:362-63, 365, 369; **128**:218, 240, 242-43
"Going Down on Love" (Lennon) **35**:268
Going Down Slow (Metcalf) **37**:298-300, 304
"Going Dutch" (Moss) **7**:249
"Going for the Bread" (Grace) **56**:122
Going for the Rain (Ortiz) **45**:300-02, 304-08
"Going for Water" (Frost) **26**:116
"Going, Going" (Larkin) **5**:226; **8**:333, 340; **18**:294, 298-99; **33**:261, 269; **39**:346; **64**:266, 274
"Going, Going, Gone" (Dylan) **77**:182
"Going Home" (Didion) **129**:97
"Going Home" (Kenny) **87**:248
"Going Home" (Trevor) **116**:375
Going Home (Lessing) **94**:266, 276
"Going Home: Ben's Church, Virginia" (Smith) **42**:350
"Going Home to Mayo, Winter, 1949" (Durcan) **43**:114-15
"Going Home to Russia" (Durcan) **70**:152
"Going Home with Uccello" (Beattie) **146**:86
"Going Mad" (Cliff) **21**:63
"Going North" (Salinas) **90**:325
Going on Sixteen (Cavanna) **12**:97, 99
"Going Out as a Ghost" (Hood) **28**:192
"Going Out to Sea" (Freeman) **55**:55, 58
"Going Places" (Harrison) **143**:351
"Going Places" (Michaels) **25**:314, 316-17
Going Places (Michaels) **6**:324; **25**:314-16
Going Solo (Dahl) **79**:182-83
Going through the Motions (Govier) **51**:164-66
Going thru Changes (Wesley) **7**:518
"Going to California" (Page and Plant) **12**:475
"Going to Church" (Jiles) **58**:275-76
"Going to Europe" (Govier) **51**:166
Going to Extremes (McGinniss) **32**:303-04
"Going to Headquarters" (Calvino) **33**:99
"Going to India" (Blaise) **29**:73
Going to Jerusalem (Charyn) **5**:103
"Going to Massachusetts" (Bowles) **68**:9-10, 18
"Going to Meet the Man" (Baldwin) **8**:40
Going to Meet the Man (Baldwin) **8**:40; **17**:33; **50**:296; **90**:2, 19, 33
"Going to Naples" (Welty) **105**:299
"Going to Russia" (Vanderhaeghe) **41**:449
"Going to School" (McNickle) **89**:180
Going to School: The African-American Experience (Lomotey) **70**:375-76
"Going to See the Leaves" (Collins) **44**:37
Going to See the Leaves (Collins) **44**:36-8
"Going to Sleep in the Country" (Moss) **45**:291
"Going to the Bakery" (Bishop) **9**:93; **32**:37
Going to the Sun (George) **35**:178
Going to the Territory (Ellison) **86**:319, 323, 326; **114**:123, 128
"Going to Town" (Stegner) **81**:346
Going to War with All My Relations: New and Selected Poems (Rose) **85**:317
"Going Under" (Dubus) **97**:200, 202, 209, 218
"Going West Alone" (Holmes) **56**:143
"Going with the Current" (Transtroemer) **65**:229
"The Going Away Clothes" (Pownall) **10**:419
"Gold" (Brown) **32**:64
"Gold" (Hall) **37**:142; **151**:196
"Gold" (Muldoon) **72**:272
Gold (Cendrars)
See *L'or*
Gold (Diamond) **30**:111
"Gold and Silver" (Tanizaki) **28**:417
Gold and Silver Waltz (Linney) **51**:263
Gold and Work (Pound) **112**:357
"The Gold Bride" (Stead) **80**:334
The Gold Bug Variations (Powers) **93**:282, 286-99, 301
The Gold Cell (Olds) **85**:291-93, 296, 298-300, 302, 305, 308
"Gold Coast" (McPherson) **77**:351-52, 358, 360, 373-74, 377
Gold Coast (Leonard) **120**:271, 277, 287
"Gold Coast Customs" (Sitwell) **9**:493; **67**:317, 322, 325, 335
"The Gold Diggers" (Creeley) **11**:136; **36**:122
The Gold Diggers (Creeley) **4**:118; **8**:151; **11**:136-37; **78**:126, 128, 130, 144, 147
The Gold Diggers (Monette) **82**:315-16, 328
Gold from Crete (Forester) **35**:173
The Gold in the Sea (Friel) **42**:164-65; **115**:216, 252
"The Gold Lily" (Glück) **81**:172
Gold Mine (Smith) **33**:374
"Gold Nuggets" (Brown) **73**:23
The Gold of the Gods (von Daniken) **30**:424
The Gold of the Tigers: Selected Later Poems (Borges)
See *El oro de los tigres*
"The Gold of Tomas Vargas" (Allende) **97**:12, 31-2
The Gold Rush (Chaplin) **16**:187, 189, 198-201, 206-07
Gold through the Trees (Childress) **86**:309, 311, 314; **96**:103, 109-10
"The Gold Watch" (Anand) **23**:21
"The Gold Watch" (McGahern) **48**:273
The Golden Age (Bunuel)
See *L'age d'or*
The Golden Age (Gurney) **32**:221
The Golden Age (Vidal) **142**:339
"Golden Apple" (Kundera)
See "The Golden Apple of Eternal Desire"
"The Golden Apple" (Kundera)
See "The Golden Apple of Eternal Desire"
The Golden Apple (Wilson) **9**:576
"The Golden Apple of Desire" (Kundera)
See "The Golden Apple of Eternal Desire"
"The Golden Apple of Eternal Desire" (Kundera) **4**:278; **32**:260
"The Golden Apples" (Welty) **1**:361; **2**:463; **5**:479-80; **14**:562, 565; **22**:458, 461; **33**:419-20
The Golden Apples (Welty) **105**:299, 303, 319, 321, 325, 327, 333, 336, 338, 340, 349, 383-86
The Golden Apples of the Sun (Bradbury) **10**:70; **42**:32
The Golden Barge (Moorcock) **58**:350-51
The Golden Bees of Tulami (Bonham) **12**:54
"The Golden Bird" (Brown) **100**:81
The Golden Bird: Two Orkney Stories (Brown) **48**:61
"The Golden Bough" (Heaney) **74**:194
"The Golden Bough" (Mahon) **27**:291
"The Golden Boy" (Hughes) **119**:265, 268
Golden Boy (Gibson) **23**:179
Golden Boy (Odets) **2**:318, 320; **28**:326-27, 330, 332-33, 336, 340-41; **98**:196, 198-202, 205, 208-10, 229, 235, 237, 241, 243-44, 251-52
The Golden Breath: Studies in Five Poets of the New India (Anand) **93**:24
"Golden Builders" (Buckley) **57**:132-33
Golden Builders and Other Poems (Buckley) **57**:132-33
The Golden Chains (Barker) **48**:19, 21, 24
The Golden Chalice (Gustafson) **36**:217
The Golden Child (Fitzgerald) **19**:172; **61**:115, 117; **143**:236-37, 262, 265
The Golden Coach (Leonov)
See *Zolotaya kareta*
The Golden Coach (Renoir)
See *Le carosse d'or*
The Golden Country (Endō) **54**:151; **99**:285, 297
The Golden Door (Scott) **43**:373-74
The Golden Dream: Seekers of El Dorado (Silverberg) **140**:396
The Golden Droplet (Tournier)
See *La Goutte d'or*
Golden Earring (Polonsky) **92**:378, 383, 416
The Golden Evening (Middleton) **38**:330
The Golden Fleece (Gurney) **50**:183
The Golden Fortress (Ray)
See *Sonar Kella*
The Golden Fruits (Sarraute)
See *Les fruits d'or*
The Golden Gate (MacLean) **13**:359, 363; **63**:266
The Golden Gate (Seth) **43**:388-94; **90**:336, 338-41, 343-50, 353-8, 361, 365, 367-71
"The Golden Gift of Grey" (MacLeod) **56**:194
Golden Girls (Page) **40**:352-55
The Golden Gizmo (Thompson) **69**:383, 386-87
"Golden Gloves" (Oates) **52**:332
The Golden Harvest (Amado) **106**:86, 89
The Golden Hawk (Yerby) **7**:556
The Golden Helix (Sturgeon) **39**:364
The Golden Honeycomb (Markandaya) **8**:377-78
"The Golden Horseshoe" (Hammett) **10**:252
"The Golden Idol" (Kristofferson) **26**:269
The Golden Isle (Slaughter) **29**:374
"The Golden Mean" (Ammons) **108**:22
Golden Miles (Prichard) **46**:334, 338, 342-43
The Golden Notebook (Lessing) **1**:173-75; **2**:239-41; **3**:282-90, 292; **6**:290, 292-300, 302-03; **10**:314-15; **15**:331, 334-35; **22**:280-81; **40**:314-15; **94**:252-53, 257, 260, 262, 265, 272, 277, 282-84, 286-91, 293
The Golden Ocean (O'Brian) **152**:276, 278, 280, 293
Golden Ophelia (Ruyslinck) **14**:471-72
The Golden Rendezvous (MacLean) **13**:361
"Golden Retriever" (Muske) **90**:308
The Golden Rose: Literature in the Making (Paustovsky) **40**:359, 368
Golden Sardine (Kaufman) **49**:203, 205
The Golden Shadow (Garfield) **12**:229-30, 235
The Golden Spur (Powell) **66**:362-64, 368, 372-73, 375-76
"Golden State" (Bidart) **33**:75
"Golden State" (Sayles) **14**:483
Golden State (Bidart) **33**:73-7, 79-81
Golden States (Cunningham) **34**:40-2
"The Golden Treasury of Knowledge" (McFadden) **48**:246
Golden Tripe (Crommelynck)
See *Tripes d'or*
The Golden Unicorn (Whitney) **42**:435
"Golden Wasp" (Transtroemer)
See "Guldstekel"
"The Golden West" (Fuchs) **22**:156
"Golden Years" (Bowie) **17**:63
Goldengrove (Paton Walsh) **35**:430-33
"Goldenrod" (Oliver) **98**:287
Goldfinger (Fleming) **30**:137, 146, 149
The Goldfish (Anouilh)
See *Les poissons rouges; ou, Mon père, ce héros*
Goldilocks (Hunter) **11**:280; **31**:226-27
Goldilocks (Kerr) **22**:255
"The Gold-Rimmed Eyeglasses" (Bassani) **9**:77
"The Golem" (Borges) **19**:46
The Golem (Singer) **69**:306
The Golem (Wiesel) **37**:457
Golem XIV (Lem) **149**:113-14, 156, 173, 261-62, 277

The Golf Omnibus (Wodehouse) **5**:516
"Golgotha" (Kennedy) **42**:255
"Golgotha Is a Mountain" (Bontemps) **18**:65
"Goliath and David" (Graves) **45**:166
Golk (Stern) **4**:523; **39**:235-36
"El golpe" (Neruda) **7**:261
Les gommes (Robbe-Grillet) **1**:287-90; **2**:373-74; **6**:465-66; **8**:453; **10**:437; **14**:455, 458-62; **43**:360, 364, 366; **128**:325-27, 329-30, 332-35, 339-41, 348, 355, 357-59, 361-62, 368, 376, 379, 382
"Gondwanaland" (Purdy) **50**:247
"Gone" (Sandburg) **15**:468; **35**:358
"Gone at Last" (Simon) **17**:466
"Gone Away" (Levertov) **66**:239
"Gone Away Blues" (McGrath) **28**:277
"Gone Clear" (Cliff) **21**:65
Gone Fishin' (Mosley) **97**:352
Gone in January (Abse) **29**:21
"Gone in October" (Holmes) **56**:143-44
Gone in October: Last Reflections on Jack Kerouac (Holmes) **56**:143-44
Gone Indian (Kroetsch) **5**:221; **23**:273; **57**:283, 288, 294-96; **132**:200, 202, 205-15, 244, 246-48, 256-57, 261, 275-76, 278-79
"Gone Three Days" (Hood) **28**:195
Gone to Ground (White) **30**:449
Gone to Soldiers (Piercy) **62**:372-77; **128**:233-35, 246-48, 270
"The Gong of Time" (Sandburg) **35**:356
"Gonna change My Way of Thinking" (Dylan) **77**:186
"Gonna Roll the Bones" (Leiber) **25**:304, 307
Gonna Take a Miracle (Nyro) **17**:316-17
"Good" (Matthews) **40**:324-25
Good (Taylor) **27**:443-47
Good and Bad at Games (Boyd)
See *School Ties: Good and Bad at Games, and Dutch Girls*
"Good and Bad Dreams" (Price) **6**:423; **43**:345
The Good and Faithful Servant (Orton) **43**:326, 329, 332-33
The Good Apprentice (Murdoch) **51**:287-90, 292, 296-97
Good As Gold (Heller) **11**:268-69; **36**:223-28, 230-31
"The Good Author" (Kizer) **80**:185
Good Behaviour (Keane) **31**:233-35
Good Bones (Atwood) **84**:104-05
"A Good Boy" (Sargeson)
See "Sketch from Life"
Good Boys and Dead Girls and Other Essays (Gordon) **128**:140
"Good Brothers" (Cohen) **38**:131
"Good Bye to All That" (Scott) **22**:373
"A Good Chance" (Cook-Lynn) **93**:124, 126
"Good Citizens" (Didion) **129**:62, 80-81
"Good Climate, Friendly Inhabitants" (Gordimer) **123**:114
The Good Companions (Priestley) **2**:346-47; **34**:361-66
The Good Conscience (Fuentes)
See *Las buenas consciencias*
"Good Copy" (Rand) **79**:374
"Good Country People" (O'Connor) **1**:257; **2**:317; **13**:421; **15**:408, 412; **21**:255-56, 262-64, 266, 272; **66**:310; **104**:106, 124, 135, 173
"A Good Daughter" (Moravia) **7**:244
"Good Day Sunshine" (Lennon and McCartney) **35**:293
A Good Day to Die (Harrison) **6**:225; **33**:200; **66**:153, 155, 158; **143**:342, 344, 351
The Good Doctor (Simon) **6**:504; **31**:399, 403; **70**:238
The Good Earth (Buck) **7**:32-3; **11**:70-4, 76-7; **18**:76-80; **127**:228-29, 231, 241
A Good Enough Parent: A Book on Child Rearing (Bettelheim) **79**:142
Good Ethan (Fox) **121**:200
The Good European (Blackmur) **2**:61
The Good Fellow (Kaufman) **38**:265
"The Good Fight" (Kinsella) **138**:116
The Good Fight (Kinsella) **138**:120
"Good for Me" (Seger) **35**:384
"Good Form" (O'Brien) **103**:139, 143, 174
"Good Frend" (H. D.) **31**:204; **73**:116, 139
"Good Friday" (Clampitt) **32**:114-15
"Good Friday" (Dybek) **114**:75
"Good Friday" (Smith) **15**:515
"Good Friday" (Watkins) **43**:447
"Good Friday 1971. Riding Westward" (Muldoon) **72**:264-65
Good Friday and Other Poems (Masefield) **11**:358; **47**:227, 229
"The Good Girl" (Bowen) **118**:58
A Good Girl Is Hard to Find (Baraka) **33**:59
The Good God of Manhattan (Bachmann)
See *Der gute Gott von Manhattan*
Good Hearts (Price) **63**:323-25, 327-33, 335-36, 339, 341
"The Good Herdsman" (Davison) **15**:170
"Good Hours" (Frost) **15**:248
The Good Husband (Godwin) **125**:163-64
Good Intentions (Nash) **23**:319
A Good Journey (Ortiz) **45**:301, 304-08, 311
"The Good Life" (Lowell) **4**:304
"The Good Life" (Strand) **71**:285
The Good Listener (Johnson) **7**:184-85; **27**:224
Good Luck in Cracked Italian (Hugo) **32**:235, 238, 242, 244-45
Good Luck, Miss Wyckoff (Inge) **8**:309
"The Good Man" (Van Duyn) **116**:403
A Good Man in Africa (Boyd) **28**:37-42; **53**:50-1, 53, 55-6; **70**:132, 134-35, 138, 140-42
"A Good Man Is Hard to Find" (O'Connor) **1**:255, 257; **2**:317; **3**:366, 368; **6**:381; **10**:368; **15**:408, 412; **21**:256, 263, 270, 272; **66**:313, 330; **104**:105, 117, 128, 138, 173, 175
A Good Man Is Hard to Find and Other Stories (O'Connor) **10**:367; **13**:417; **15**:408; **21**:256-57, 262, 266; **104**:108, 120, 137, 165, 179, 190
"Good Mirrors Are Not Cheap" (Lorde) **71**:232
"Good Morning" (Codrescu) **46**:103
"Good Morning" (Schuyler) **23**:391
"Good Morning" (Van Doren) **6**:542
Good Morning (Ozu)
See *Ohayo*
Good Morning America (Sandburg) **15**:466; **35**:345-46, 352
Good Morning Blues: The Autobiography of Count Basie (Murray) **73**:242
"Good Morning, Good Morning" (Lennon and McCartney) **12**:357-58; **35**:276
Good Morning: Last Poems (Van Doren) **6**:541-43; **10**:496
Good Morning, Midnight (Rhys) **2**:371-73; **6**:453-55, 457; **14**:446-47, 449-51; **19**:393-94; **51**:360-61, 366-70, 375; **124**:317, 322, 330, 333, 339, 341, 344, 346-47, 354, 356, 371-72
"Good Morning Revolution" (Hughes) **108**:294, 296
Good Morning, Revolution: Uncollected Social Protest Writings (Hughes) **5**:191; **108**:318-21
Good Morning to You (Mahfouz) **153**:289
The Good Mother (Miller) **44**:67-76
"Good Neighbors" (Richter) **30**:320
"The Good New Days" (Leiber) **25**:304
"Good News" (Kuzma) **7**:197
"Good News" (Voigt) **54**:433
Good News (Abbey) **59**:238, 242
Good News About the Earth (Clifton) **19**:109; **66**:64-5, 67, 79-81, 84-6
"Good News from the Vatican" (Silverberg) **140**:379
"Good News of Death" (Simpson) **149**:345
Good News of Death and Other Poems (Simpson) **4**:498; **7**:427; **32**:378; **149**:298, 309, 326, 344, 350
Good News: Poems (Kuzma) **7**:196-97
"Good Night" (Kinsella) **138**:102, 105
"A Good Night" (Montague) **46**:270, 274
"Good Night Mr. James" (Simak) **55**:320
Good Night Sweet Ladies (Blackwood) **100**:4
Good Night, Sweetheart (Tiptree) **48**:394-95
"Good Night, Willie Lee, I'll See You in the Morning" (Walker) **103**:382
Good Old James (Donovan) **35**:142
The Good Parts (Horovitz) **56**:155
"Good Samaritan" (O'Hara) **6**:385
"The Good Samaritan" (Sargeson) **31**:363
Good Samaritan, and Other Stories (O'Hara) **6**:384-85
A Good Scent from a Strange Mountain (Butler) **81**:121-30
A Good School (Yates) **23**:480, 482
"A Good Shellacking" (Lem) **149**:125
The Good Shepherd (Fleming) **37**:124-25
The Good Shepherd (Forester) **35**:171, 174
"The Good Shepherd: Atlanta, 1981" (Ai) **69**:9, 15
"Good Ships" (Ransom) **4**:431
"The Good Silence" (Bly) **128**:32
The Good Son (Nova) **31**:298-300
The Good Spirit of Laurel Ridge (Stuart) **11**:511; **14**:517
"A Good Story" (Alexie) **154**:6, 9
"A Good Story" (Moody) **147**:170
"Good Taste" (Asimov) **19**:28
"The Good Tenor Man" (Hood) **28**:193
The Good Terrorist (Lessing) **40**:310-17; **94**:258, 286
"The Good Thing" (Byrne) **25**:96
"Good Tidings for the Blooming Apple" (Blaga) **75**:77
"Good times" (Clifton) **19**:108-09; **66**:66-8, 75, 80-1, 84-5
Good Times/Bad Times (Kirkwood) **9**:319
"Good Timin'" (Wilson) **12**:653
"Good Vibes" (Porter) **13**:451
"Good Vibrations" (Wilson) **12**:642-45
"The Good Virgin, Then...by Crivelli" (Kerrigan) **6**:276
"The Good War": An Oral History of World War II (Terkel) **38**:426-29
"Good Wars" (DeMarinis) **54**:100
"Good, Wild, Sacred" (Snyder) **120**:323
Good Will (Smiley) **76**:236, 000; **144**:251, 296
Good Woman: Poems and a Memoir, 1969-1980 (Clifton) **66**:81, 84-6
"The Good Women" (Sillitoe) **57**:392; **148**:167, 169, 172
The Good Word and Other Words (Sheed) **53**:336-38
Good Work (Schumacher) **80**:269-70
Good-By My Shadow (Stolz) **12**:550, 553
"Good-Bye" (Betjeman) **6**:69
"Goodbye" (Kinnell) **129**:270
"Goodbye" (Levine) **118**:277, 284
"Goodbye" (Miles) **34**:245
"A Goodbye" (Van Duyn) **116**:408
Goodbye (Sansom) **6**:484
"Goodbye and Good Luck" (Paley) **37**:331, 337; **140**:216, 219, 233, 246-48, 252, 261, 263, 266-67, 277, 281
Goodbye California (MacLean) **13**:364; **50**:348
"Goodbye, Cape Town" (Breytenbach) **126**:61
Goodbye, Chicken Little (Byars) **35**:73
"Goodbye Christ" (Hughes) **1**:147; **44**:511-12; **108**:294, 297, 320
Goodbye, Columbus (Roth) **1**:292-93; **2**:378-80; **3**:435-38, 440; **4**:451-52, 454-57, 459; **6**:474-76; **9**:459, 462; **15**:449, 452-53, 455; **22**:350; **31**:334-35, 342, 346; **86**:250, 252, 254
Goodbye, Columbus, and Five Short Stories (Roth) **47**:364; **66**:386, 389, 421
"Goodbye Cruel World" (Pink Floyd) **35**:312
Goodbye Earth (Richards) **14**:452, 455
"A Goodbye for Evadne Winterbottom" (Bradbury) **32**:53

The Goodbye Girl (Simon) **70**:237-38, 240
"Goodbye, Goldeneye" (Swenson) **61**:403
"Goodbye, Goodbye, Be Always Kind and True" (Garrett) **3**:191
Goodbye Harold, Good Luck (Thomas) **107**:333,337
Goodbye, Howard (Linney) **51**:262
The Goodbye Look (Macdonald) **2**:256; **14**:335-36; **41**:267, 269
"Goodbye Marcus, Goodbye Rose" (Rhys) **14**:446; **19**:390-91; **51**:370; **124**:336
"Goodbye Margery" (Derleth) **31**:132-33
Goodbye, Mickey Mouse (Deighton) **46**:128-29
"Goodbye Morbid Bear" (Stern) **100**:329
"Goodbye, My Brother" (Cheever) **15**:127; **64**:53, 65
"Good-Bye, New York" (Morand)
See "Adieu, New-York!"
"Goodbye Our Old Red Flag" (Yevtushenko) **126**:409
"Goodbye Party for Miss Pushpa T. S." (Ezekiel) **61**:95, 110
The Goodbye People (Gardner) **44**:210
"Goodbye, Shirley Temple" (Mitchell) **98**:157
"Good-bye, Son" (Lewis) **41**:254
Good-bye, Son and Other Stories (Lewis) **41**:253
Goodbye Spring (Seifert)
See *Jaro sbohem*
"Goodbye, Sweetwater" (Dumas) **62**:159, 162
Goodbye, Sweetwater (Dumas) **62**:157, 159, 161, 163-64
Good-Bye to All That (Graves) **2**:177; **39**:322-28; **44**:477, 479-80; **45**:170-74
Goodbye to Berlin (Isherwood) **1**:156; **9**:291, 293; **11**:298-300; **14**:283, 286; **44**:396-97, 400, 402-04
"Goodbye to Goodbye" (Dixon) **52**:100
"Goodbye to London" (MacNeice) **53**:239
"Goodbye to the Flowerclock" (Haines) **58**:217
"Goodbye to the Garden" (Fuller) **62**:185
"Good-bye to the Mezzogiorno" (Auden) **6**:20; **123**:17
Goodbye to the Summer (Carroll) **10**:97-8
Goodbye, Wisconsin (Wescott) **13**:591-92
Goodbye without Leaving (Colwin) **84**:143-47, 150-52
The Goodbyes (Onetti)
See *Los adioses*
Goodfellas (Scorsese) **89**:254-59, 261-63, 265, 267
A Goodly Fellowship (Chase) **2**:101
A Goodly Heritage (Chase) **2**:100
"Goodman Jacksin and the Angel" (Barker) **8**:46; **48**:15, 24
Goodness (Parks) **147**:199-200, 204-05, 209
"Goodness and Mercy" (Munro) **95**:310, 314
"The Goodnight" (Simpson) **7**:428; **149**:342
"Goodnight" (Smith) **25**:420; **44**:440
"Goodnight Ladies" (Reed) **21**:304-05
"Goodnight, Mr. Shade" (Bissoondath) **120**:13
Goodnight, Nebraska (McNeal) **119**:85-88
"Goodnight, Old Daisy" (Wain) **46**:415
"Goodnight Saigon" (Joel) **26**:222-23
"Goodnight Sweetheart" (Purdy) **28**:378
"Goodnight Tonight" (McCartney) **35**:287-89
Goodnight Willie Lee, I'll See You in the Morning (Walker) **19**:452; **58**:405; **103**:357, 371
"Goodwill to Men" (Gellhorn) **60**:179-81
"Goodwood Comes Back" (Warren) **39**:260
"Goong Hai Fot Choy" (Chin) **135**:152-55
Goopy gyne bagha byne (Ray)
See *Goupi gyne bagha*
Goose and Tomtom (Rabe) **33**:342-43, 346
"The Goose Fish" (Nemerov) **36**:305
"Goose Moon" (Kinsella) **27**:236
The Goose on the Grave (Hawkes) **2**:183, 185; **3**:221, 223; **4**:212-13; **7**:141; **15**:270, 273; **27**:190; **49**:161, 164
"Goose Pond" (Kunitz) **148**:77, 94
Goosefoot (McGinley) **41**:282-84, 286
The Goose-Step: A Study of American Education (Sinclair) **15**:499; **63**:346-47
The Goosesteppers (Alegria)
See *El Paso de los Gansos*
Gor Saga (Duffy) **37**:116
"Gorboduc" (Ashbery) **77**:64, 68
"Gorbunov and Gorchakov" (Brodsky) **4**:78; **36**:81; **50**:122, 125; **100**:51
Der Gordische Knoten (Jünger) **125**:233
Gord's Gold (Lightfoot) **26**:281
Gore and Igor (Levin) **7**:206
Gore Vidal: Writer Against the Grain (Parini) **133**:266, 283-84, 286
"The Gorge" (Belitt) **22**:50
A Gorgeous Bird like Me (Truffaut) **20**:393; **101**:379-84, 396, 410
The Gorgon and Other Beastly Tales (Lee) **46**:232
"Gorgon Planet" (Silverberg) **140**:376
"The Gorilla Girl" (Motion) **47**:292
"Gorilla, My Love" (Bambara) **88**:3, 8, 12, 17, 20-1, 39, 42, 46
Gorilla, My Love (Bambara) **19**:32; **88**:3, 11-12, 18-20, 22, 27-28, 41-42, 49
Gorilla Queen (Tavel) **6**:529
"Gorillas" (Ondaatje) **51**:310
Le gorille roi (Simenon) **47**:374
Gorky (Tesich) **40**:419-21
Gorky Park (Potter) **86**:346; **123**:249, 273
Gorky Park (Smith) **25**:412-15
The Gorky Poems (Rothenberg) **6**:477; **57**:376
Gormenghast (Peake) **54**:366-68, 370-72, 374-75, 377-78
The Gormenghast Trilogy (Peake) **7**:302
"Gornyy rodnichok" (Voznesensky) **57**:417
Gosforth's Fête (Ayckbourn) **33**:41
The Goshawk (White) **30**:442-43, 449
"Goshawk, Antelope" (Smith) **22**:389
Goshawk, Antelope (Smith) **22**:387-90; **42**:345-49, 352-53, 357
"Gospel" (Dove) **50**:155; **81**:144
"Gospel" (John Paul II) **128**:187
"Gospel" (Jones) **76**:65-6
"Gospel" (Piñero) **55**:317
The Gospel according to Chegem (Iskander)
See *Sandro iz Chegema*
The Gospel According to Jesus Christ (Saramago)
See *O Evangelho segundo Jesus Cristo*
The Gospel according to Joe (Gurney) **32**:217
"The Gospel according to Mark" (Borges) **10**:66; **83**:193
The Gospel according to St. Matthew (Pasolini)
See *Il vangelo secondo Matteo*
The Gospel According to Steiner (Tarkovsky) **75**:399
"Gospel Birds and Other Stories of Lake Wobegon" (Keillor) **115**:296
The Gospel of Life (John Paul II) **128**:200-02
The Gospel Singer (Crews) **6**:117-18; **23**:131, 134, 138; **49**:68-73, 77
"Gospel Song (Allison) **153**:18-19
The Goss Women (Cassill) **4**:95; **23**:108-09
"The Gossamers" (Tomlinson) **4**:545
Gossip (Walker)
See *The Power Plays*
Gossip from the Forest (Keneally) **8**:318-19; **10**:298; **14**:303; **19**:246; **43**:230, 233, 236; **117**:215, 224-25, 231-35
"Got to Be Free" (Davies) **21**:92
"Got to Begin Again" (Joel) **26**:218
"Got to Have Will Power" (Guillén)
See "Hay que tené boluntá"
"The Gothic Dusk" (Prokosch) **48**:309
Gothic Romance (Carrere)
See *Bravoure*
Gothic Tales (Dinesen) **95**:49
"Gotta Broken Heart Again" (Prince) **35**:323-24
"Gotta Get to Boston" (Guthrie) **35**:183
"Gotta Serve Somebody" (Dylan) **77**:186, 190
"Gottschalk and the Grande Tarantelle" (Brooks) **125**:96
Goupi gyne bagha (Ray) **16**:492
"The Gourd Dancer" (Momaday) **85**:268
The Gourd Dancer (Momaday) **19**:318; **85**:256, 262-67, 269-70, 281
La Goutte d'or (Tournier) **95**:374-75, 377, 382
"The Governess" (Gray) **153**:138
Government (Traven) **8**:520
"The Government Bears" (Bass) **79**:6, 12; **143**:12
The Government of Egypt (Forster) **77**:238
The Government of the Tongue: Selected Prose, 1978-1987 (Heaney) **74**:183-84, 189-90; **91**:223-24
"Governmentality" (Foucault) **69**:179
"Governor" (Guillén) **79**:229
"The Governor's Ball" (Carlson) **54**:37
The Governor's Bridge Is Closed (Hood) **28**:192
The Goy (Harris) **19**:201-02, 204
"Goya's 'Two Old People Eating Soup'" (Van Duyn) **116**:410
Gozos de la vista (Alonso) **14**:17, 23
Graal Flibuste (Pinget) **7**:305; **13**:442
The Grabber (Ehrenburg)
See *Rvach*
"Grabschriften in die Luft geschrieben" (Sachs) **98**:325, 327, 354
"Grace" (Arghezi) **80**:10
"The Grace" (Creeley) **4**:118
"Grace" (Harjo) **83**:271-72
"Grace" (Wilbur) **53**:397, 409
"Grace" (Wright) **53**:429
Grace (Gee) **57**:223-25
La grâce (Marcel) **15**:360, 363
"Grace Abounding" (Ammons) **25**:46; **57**:52; **108**:57
Grace Abounding (Howard) **46**:185-87; **151**:275, 285
Grace after Meat (Ransom) **4**:436
"Grace and Faigel" (Levine) **54**:297
"Grace at World's End" (Buckley) **57**:131
Grace before Ploughing (Masefield) **11**:357
"Grace before Song" (Pound) **48**:288
The Grace Divorce (Swinnerton) **31**:427
"Grace Notes" (Smith) **64**:397
Grace Notes (Dove) **81**:140, 147, 149-51
Grace Paley: The Collected Stories (Paley) **140**:260-63, 265-66, 268, 276-77, 281
"The Graceless Years" (Lerman) **9**:328
"Grace's House" (Merton) **83**:392-93
Gracias Haus (Merton) **83**:393
"Gracie" (Fisher) **87**:131
"A Gracious Rain" (Tilghman) **65**:106, 108-09, 111-12
"Grackles, Goodbye" (Warren) **39**:272
Gradations of Grandeur (Gustafson) **36**:221
"Gradual of the Northern Summer" (Davidson) **2**:113
Gradual Wars (Deane) **122**:73, 81-2
The Graduate (Webb) **7**:514-16
The Graduate (Willingham) **5**:512
"Graduate School" (Lerman) **9**:328
The Graduate Wife (Raphael) **2**:367
"Graduation" (Dubus) **36**:144-45
"Graduation Nite" (Shange) **25**:402
Graf Öderland (Frisch) **3**:167; **9**:217; **14**:182-83; **44**:181, 194, 196-97, 199-200
"Graffiti" (Cortázar) **33**:130, 132
"Graffiti" (Nemerov) **36**:309
Graffiti (Damas) **84**:156, 159-60, 179
"Graffiti from the Gare Saint-Manqué" (Hacker) **72**:182-84, 190
"Grafton Street" (Behan) **79**:38
Graham Greene on Film: Collected Film Criticism, 1935-1940 (Greene)
See *The Pleasure-Dome: The Collected Film Criticism, 1935-40*
"Grail" (Ellison) **42**:131
"The Grail Mass" (Jones) **42**:242
Le grain de la voix: Entretiens 1962-1980 (Barthes) **83**:88-90

"Grain de sel" (Damas) **84**:179
"The Grain Kings" (Roberts) **14**:464
A Grain of Mustard Seed (Sarton) **49**:314, **91**:244
"A Grain of Rice" (Scott) **22**:376
The Grain of the Voice: Interviews, 1962-1980 (Barthes)
See *Le grain de la voix: Entretiens 1962-1980*
A Grain of Wheat (Ngũgĩ wa Thiong'o) **3**:358; **7**:263-66; **36**:310, 312-17, 321, 323
La graine (Gascar) **11**:222
Grains et issues (Tzara) **47**:389-91
"Graiul noptii" (Arghezi) **80**:2
Grammar and Money (Codrescu) **121**:160
"Grammar Lesson" (Kunitz) **148**:88
A Grammar of Metaphor (Brooke-Rose) **40**:103
A Grammar of Motives (Burke) **24**:124, 127-28, 134
"The Grammar of Silence: Narrative Pattern in Ethic Writing" (Kroetsch) **132**:221-22
The Grammar of the Real: Selected Prose, 1959-1974 (McAuley) **45**:253
The Grammelot of Zanni (Fo) **109**:102
Gran Casino (Bunuel) **16**:149; **80**:21
El gran serafín (Bioy Casares) **13**:84
El gran zoo (Guillén) **48**:156, 158-59; **79**:229
"Granate" (Guillén) **79**:240
Grand Canary (Cronin) **32**:131-32
Le grand cerémonial (Arrabal) **9**:33; **18**:20; **58**:9-10, 17-18
The Grand Ceremony (Arrabal)
See *Le grand cerémonial*
"Grand Coulee Dam" (Guthrie) **35**:193
"The Grand Dance" (MacEwen) **55**:165
The Grand Design (Dos Passos) **4**:133; **11**:156; **15**:187; **34**:420
Le grand écart (Cocteau) **15**:132; **43**:102-03
"Grand Entrance" (Dybek) **114**:67
"Grand Galop" (Ashbery) **13**:34; **15**:28; **41**:40; **77**:60
"Grand Illusion" (Dubie) **36**:135
The Grand Illusion (Renoir)
See *La grande illusion*
The Grand Macabre's Stroll (Ghelderode)
See *La ballad du grand macabre*
Grand Manoeuvres (Ellis) **7**:93-5
Grand National (Tunis) **12**:599
"Grand Prairie: So Far from Poland" (Moure) **88**:217
The Grand Tarot (Ludlam) **46**:239; **50**:346
Le grand théâtre (Giono) **11**:230
The Grand Tour (Rice) **49**:300-01
Le grand troupeau (Giono) **4**:184, 186
"The Grand View" (Abse) **7**:1; **29**:15
The Grand Wazoo (Zappa) **17**:590
La grande Claudine (Hébert) **4**:219; **13**:267
La grande et la petite manoeuvre (Adamov) **25**:12, 14, 17-19
La grande gaieté (Aragon) **3**:15; **22**:37, 41
La grande illusion (Renoir) **20**:287-90, 292-93, 295, 297, 300, 302-03, 307-08
"The Grande Malade" (Barnes) **3**:37; **29**:27
"La grande mélancolie d'une avenue" (Soupault) **68**:404
Il grande ritratto (Buzzati) **36**:86-91, 96-7
Grande Sertão: Veredas (Rosa) **23**:348-50, 353, 355-57
Les grandes épreuves de l'esprit (Michaux) **8**:392; **19**:312
Les grandes manoeuvres (Clair) **20**:64
"The Grandfather" (Guillén)
See "El abuelo"
"Grandfather" (Mahon) **27**:290
"The Grandfather" (Soto) **80**:298, 301
"Grandfather and Grandson" (Singer) **3**:457; **6**:511; **38**:408
"The Grandfather Poem" (Dobyns) **37**:77
"The Grandfathers" (Justice) **102**:277, 282-83
The Grandfathers (Richter) **30**:318-19, 321, 325
"A Grandfather's Last Letter" (Dubie) **36**:142
"Grandma" (Adcock) **41**:14
"Grandma's Man" (Welch) **14**:559
"Grandmother" (Alexie) **154**:26
"Grandmother" (Allen) **84**:6, 30
"Grandmother" (McIlvanney) **42**:282
"grandmother" (Young Bear) **94**:363, 371
"Grandmother Dying" (Merwin) **45**:277
"Grandmother in Heaven" (Levine) **118**:284
"Grandmother in the Garden" (Glück) **22**:173
"Grandmother Watching at Her Window" (Merwin) **88**:205
"The Grandmothers" (Rothenberg) **57**:373
The Grandmothers: A Family Portrait (Wescott) **13**:590-92
Grandmothers of the Light: A Medicine Woman's Sourcebook (Allen) **84**:45-6
The Grandmother's Tale (Narayan) **121**:417-19
"Grandparenting" (Updike) **139**:368
"Grandparents" (Lowell) **124**:278, 289
"Grandparents: Can They Love Too Much?" (Coles) **108**:194
"Grand-père n'avait peur de rien ni de personne" (Carrier) **78**:63
Les grands chemins (Giono) **4**:186, 188
"Les Grands Réducteurs" (Blanchot) **135**:113, 134
Les grands soleils (Ferron) **94**:110, 114, 120, 124-25
"The Grange" (Smith) **25**:419
"La grange d'Emilien" (Theriault) **79**:408
"Granite and Cypress" (Jeffers) **54**:233, 244
"Granite and Steel" (Moore) **47**:263
Granite Lady (Schaeffer) **6**:489; **11**:491
The Granite Pail: The Selected Poems of Lorine Niedecker (Niedecker) **42**:296-99
"Granma" (Sargeson) **31**:362
Granny (Poliakoff) **38**:379
Granny Reardun (Garner) **17**:149-50
"Granny Weatherall" (Porter)
See "The Jilting of Granny Weatherall"
"Granny's Old Junk" (Welsh) **144**:336
Grant Moves South (Catton) **35**:88-9
"Grantchester Meadows" (Pink Floyd) **35**:305
"Grantchester Meadows" (Plath) **17**:350
"The Granton Star Cause" (Welsh) **144**:316-17, 319, 336
"Grape Sherbet" (Dove) **81**:135, 138
"The Grapes" (Hecht) **19**:207-10
The Grapes and the Wind (Neruda)
See *Las uvas y el viento*
The Grapes of Paradise: Four Short Novels (Bates)
See *An Aspidistra in Babylon: Four Novellas*
The Grapes of Wrath (Ford) **16**:304, 313-14
The Grapes of Wrath (Steinbeck) **1**:324-26; **5**:405-08; **9**:512-20; **13**:529-34; **21**:367-69, 371-74, 376, 381-84, 386, 390-91; **34**:404-05, 407-15; **45**:369-71, 373-77, 382-83; **59**:315-33, 335-37, 339-54; **75**:341, 343, 350, 357; **124**:379, 385-88, 394, 396-97, 399-402, 407-11, 413-19, 423-25
"Grapette" (Barthelme) **117**:14, 16, 18
"The Graph" (Ciardi) **10**:106; **44**:381
"Grasp the Sparrow's Tail" (Wah) **44**:326
"The Grass" (Bowering) **47**:20
"Grass" (Corn) **33**:117, 120
"Grass" (Sandburg) **4**:463; **10**:448-49
The Grass (Simon)
See *L'herbe*
The Grass Crown (McCullough) **107**:155, 163-66
The Grass Dancer (Power) **91**:67-71
The Grass Dies (Dowell)
See *One of the Children Is Crying*
"Grass Fires" (Lowell) **37**:238; **124**:299, 300
The Grass Harp (Capote) **1**:55; **8**:133; **13**:134-35, 137, 139; **19**:80-1, 86-7; **34**:320-22; **38**:78-9, 84, 87; **58**:86
The Grass Is Singing (Lessing) **1**:173; **3**:283, 290-91; **6**:292, 294, 298, 303-04; **22**:280; **40**:310, 315; **94**:253, 255-56, 266-67, 277, 280-81, 284-86
A Grass Rope (Mayne) **12**:387-89, 392, 398, 400, 407
"The Grass Still Grows, the River Still Flows" (Dorris) **109**:310
"The Grass Was Gone for Miles around Where Lil's White Arse Had Bumped the Ground" (Cummings) **68**:29
"The Grass Widows" (Trevor) **116**:333, 338, 375
Grasse (Delbanco) **6**:130
"La grasse matinée" (Prévert) **15**:439
"Grasse: The Olive Trees" (Wilbur) **53**:413
"The Grassfire Stanzas" (Murray) **40**:343
"Grasshoppers" (Jolley) **46**:213
"Grateful to Life and Death" (Narayan) **121**:331, 335
Grateful to Life and Death (Narayan)
See *The English Teacher*
"Gratified Desires" (Davison) **28**:103
"Gratitude" (Glück) **7**:120
"Gratitude, Need, and Gladness" (Davie) **31**:124
"The Grauballe Man" (Heaney) **14**:242; **25**:242-43, 250-51; **74**:158
"The Grave" (Gardner) **18**:178
"A Grave" (Moore) **4**:362; **19**:340; **47**:267
"The Grave" (Porter) **7**:315-16, 320; **10**:397; **15**:430
"The Grave Dwellers" (Oates) **3**:359
"The Grave of Lost Stories" (Vollmann) **89**:283, 302
"Grave of Signor Casanova" (Seifert) **34**:261
"The Grave of the Famous Poet" (Atwood) **25**:62
"The Grave of the Right Hand" (Wright) **6**:580
The Grave of the Right Hand (Wright) **6**:579-81; **13**:612, 614; **146**:305-06, 321, 326, 349, 373, 379
"The Grave Rubbings" (Lieberman) **36**:262
"A Grave Unvisited" (Thomas) **48**:375
Grave Witness (Levi) **41**:250
Gravedigger (Hansen) **38**:239
"Grave-Dirt" (Musgrave) **13**:401
Grave-Dirt and Selected Strawberries (Musgrave) **54**:341; **13**:400-01
"Gravel" (Moss) **45**:286-87
"The Gravel Ponds" (Levi) **41**:242-43
The Gravel Ponds (Levi) **41**:242-43, 246
"Gravelly Run" (Ammons) **8**:16; **9**:30; **108**:20
"The Gravel-Pit Field" (Gascoyne) **45**:147, 153-54, 157-59
Graven Images (Thomas) **107**:342-45, 351
Graves and Resurrections (Scannell) **49**:332
"Graveyard Day" (Mason) **28**:271; **154**:235-37, 239, 242-44, 247-51, 253, 257-58, 260, 267, 272-74, 228, 285-87, 295-97, 299-301, 306, 232
"The Graveyard Heart" (Zelazny) **21**:468
"Graveyard in Norfolk" (Warner) **19**:460-61
"The Graveyard Shift" (King) **113**:336
"Gravity" (Alexie) **154**:3
"Gravity" (Beattie) **40**:64; **63**:19
"Gravity" (Montague) **46**:277
"Gravity" (Simic) **130**:318
Gravity's Rainbow (Pynchon) **2**:354-58; **3**:412-20; **6**:432-39; **9**:443-47; **11**:452, 454-55; **18**:430-41; **33**:330-40; **62**:432, 435-40, 443, 445-48, 451, 453; **72**:332, 335-36, 340; **123**:283-90, 293-95, 298, 300, 303-09, 311-14, 328-29, 331
"Gray Matter" (King) **26**:237
Gray Soldiers (Smith) **42**:354
Gray's Anatomy (Gray) **112**:127, 132-36
Gray's Anatomy (Soderbergh) **154**:344
The Graywolf Annual Five: Multi-Cultural Literacy (Simonson) **70**:363
"Grazing Locomotives" (MacLeish) **68**:290
Grease (Jacobs and Casey) **12**:292-95
"Greaseball" (McFadden) **48**:258
"Greasy Lake" (Boyle) **90**:61-3
Greasy Lake, & Other Stories (Boyle) **90**:44-6, 49, 57
The Great American Fourth of July Parade: A

Verse Play for Radio (MacLeish) **14**:338
The Great American Jackpot (Gold) **4**:192; **14**:208; **42**:192; **152**:137
The Great American Novel (Roth) **3**:436-40; **4**:457, 459; **6**:474-75; **9**:461; **15**:449, 452; **22**:352-53; **31**:334-35; **47**:363
The Great American Novel (Williams) **2**:468-69; **5**:509; **9**:572; **42**:454
"The Great American Novel: Winter, 1927" (Dubie) **36**:132
The Great Auk (Eckert) **17**:103-05
"The Great Automatic Grammatisator" (Dahl) **79**:175, 183
"The Great Bear Cult" (Gray) **41**:181, 183
"The Great Blackberry Pick" (Pearce) **21**:289
"The Great Blue Heron" (Kizer) **80**:171-72, 181-82
The Great Canadian Sonnet (McFadden) **48**:249
"The Great Carbuncle" (Plath) **111**:202
The Great Ceremony (Arrabal)
See *Le grand cerémonial*
The Great Chain of Life (Krutch) **24**:290
"The Great Chinese Dragon" (Ferlinghetti) **111**:64
Great Circle (Aiken) **5**:9; **10**:3; **52**:31
Great Climate (Wilding) **73**:404
The Great Cloak (Montague) **13**:392; **46**:272-73, 275, 277, 279
The Great Code: The Bible and Literature (Frye) **24**:231; **70**:271-73, 275-77
"The Great Dam Disaster, a Ballad" (Starbuck) **53**:354
"A Great Day" (Sargeson) **31**:365, 370
"A Great Day for a Bananafish" (Salinger)
See "A Perfect Day for Bananafish"
"Great Days" (Barthelme) **46**:41
Great Days (Barthelme) **13**:59-64; **23**:51; **46**:35, 37-8, 41; **59**:247; **115**:64
The Great Days (Dos Passos) **4**:132, 135; **15**:186; **25**:140-41, 145-46; **34**:422
"The Great Deception" (Morrison) **21**:234-35
The Great Depression, 1929 to 1939 (Berton) **104**:56-8
The Great Dethriffe (Bryan) **29**:101-02
The Great Dictator (Chaplin) **16**:192, 195-96, 201, 203-04
"The Great Difference" (Singh) **11**:505
The Great Disruption (Fukuyama) **131**:162-64, 167-70, 172
The Great Divorce (Lewis) **3**:299; **27**:261, 266; **124**:196-99, 212, 222-23, 236, 241, 246
The Great Divorce (Martin) **89**:135, 137-38
"The Great Duck" (Middleton) **13**:389
"The Great Ekbo" (Cabrera Infante)
See "En el gran ecbó"
"The Great Elegy for John Donne" (Brodsky) **50**:121, 123, 128
The Great Escape (Clavell) **87**:18
The Great Exhibition (Hare) **29**:213-14; **136**:259
"Great Expectations" (Jhabvala) **138**:77-8
"Great Expectations" (Ritter) **52**:356
Great Expectations (Acker) **45**:14-17, 19-20; **111**:3, 5-6, 8-9, 21, 25, 31-5, 41
The Great Fake Book (Bourjaily) **62**:106-08
The Great Fear: The Anti-Communist Purge under Truman and Eisenhower (Caute) **29**:119-20
"Great Fennville Swamp" (Crase) **58**:159, 162-63, 166
"The Great Feud" (Pratt) **19**:377-78, 382, 385
"The Great Fillmore Street Buffalo Drive" (Momaday) **85**:281
"The Great Fire" (Bradbury) **42**:32
The Great Fire of London (Ackroyd) **52**:2-4, 6-7, 15-16; **140**:6, 14, 21, 23, 25, 29, 33-4, 39, 66
The Great Fortune (Manning) **19**:300-01
Great Fun (Aragon)
See *La grande gaieté*
The Great Game (Vesaas)
See *Det store spelet*
"A Great Generation" (Kunene) **85**:166
"The Great Genius" (Berrigan) **37**:44
"The Great Gig in the Sky" (Pink Floyd) **35**:306
The Great Gilly Hopkins (Paterson) **12**:486-87; **30**:283, 285, 287
"The Great Godalmighty Bird" (Dowell) **60**:107, 109
"A Great God's Angel Standing" (Kiely) **23**:260; **43**:239
Great Goodness of Life (A Coon Show) (Baraka) **115**:35
"The Great, Grand, Soap-Water Kick" (Gardam) **43**:169
Great Granny Webster (Blackwood) **100**:2, 9, 14, 19
"The Great Horned Owl" (Piercy) **27**:379
"The Great Horned Owl" (Simic) **49**:336; **130**:306
"Great House" (Walcott)
See "Ruins of a Great House"
"The Great Hug" (Barthelme) **8**:52
The Great Hunger (Kavanagh) **22**:234-35, 237-38, 242
Great Ideas in Physics (Lightman) **81**:78
Great Ideas of Science (Asimov) **26**:37
The Great Indian Novel (Tharoor) **70**:103-12
"Great Infirmities" (Simic) **22**:382; **49**:338; **68**:369
Great Jones Street (DeLillo) **54**:80-2; **8**:172; **10**:134-35; **13**:175-76, 178-79; **27**:77-9; **39**:117, 119, 123, 125; **76**:180, 182, 185; **143**:187, 206-07
The Great Letter E (Schor) **65**:95-9
Great Lion of God (Caldwell) **2**:95; **39**:302-03
The Great Lost Kinks Album (Davies) **21**:94-5
"The Great Man" (Motion) **47**:288, 294
"The Great Mountains" (Steinbeck) **9**:515-16
"The Great Music Robbery" (Baraka) **115**:12
"Great Nights Returning" (Watkins) **43**:447, 454
The Great Occasion (Colegate) **36**:108-09, 113-14
The Great O'Neill (O'Faolain) **14**:402, 404; **70**:321
The Great Ordeals of the Mind (Michaux)
See *Les grandes épreuves de l'esprit*
"The Great Palace of Versailles" (Dove) **50**:154; **81**:139
The Great Passage (Blaga)
See *În marea trecere*
"Great Poets Die in Steaming Pots of Shit" (Bukowski) **41**:68, 75; **108**:85
"Great Praises" (Eberhart) **3**:133; **11**:178; **19**:144; **56**:84, 87
The Great Quillow (Thurber) **5**:430, 438, 442; **25**:437
The Great Railway Bazaar: By Train through Asia (Theroux) **8**:512-13; **15**:533-35; **28**:425; **46**:402
"The Great Reducers" (Blanchot)
See "Les Grands Réducteurs"
"The Great Rememberer" (Holmes) **56**:143-44
Great River: The Rio Grande in North American History (Horgan) **9**:279; **53**:178
"The Great Rubble Lady Speaks" (Grass) **32**:200
The Great Santini (Conroy) **30**:77-8, 80; **74**:44-52
The Great Shark Hunt: Strange Tales from a Strange Time (Thompson) **17**:513-15; **40**:426-27, 431; **104**:347
The Great Sinner (Isherwood) **44**:397
Great Sky River (Benford) **52**:76-7
"The Great Slow Kings" (Zelazny) **21**:465-66
"The Great Society" (Bly) **10**:55
Great Son (Ferber) **93**:176-77, 179, 187-88, 190
"The Great Suburban Showdown" (Joel) **26**:214, 217-18
"The Great Switch" (Barzun) **145**:72
"The Great Switcheroo" (Dahl) **6**:121
The Great Tradition (Leavis) **24**:294, 297-98, 300, 303, 308, 313
The Great Train Robbery (Crichton) **6**:119; **54**:68-71, 76; **90**:69, 71
"Great Tranquillity" (Amichai) **57**:38
Great Tranquillity: Questions and Answers (Amichai)
See *Shalvah gedolah: She'elot utshuvot*
The Great Transfer (Yanovsky) **18**:551-52
"Great Uncle Crow" (Bates) **46**:59-60, 67
"Great Unexpectations" (Atwood) **84**:92
The Great Victorian Collection (Moore) **5**:297-98; **7**:236-39; **8**:394; **19**:331-33; **32**:309, 311, 313-14; **90**:250, 255-6, 263, 265, 269, 272, 289
The Great Waldo Pepper (Hill) **26**:203-05, 207-08, 211
The Great Wall of China (Silverberg) **140**:396
"The Great War" (Scannell) **49**:326
The Great War and Modern Memory (Fussell) **74**:120-23, 125, 128, 133-34, 137, 139-40, 143-44
"The Great Wave" (Levertov) **28**:243
The Great Wave, and Other Stories (Lavin) **18**:302, 307
The Great White Hope (Sackler) **14**:478-80
The Great Winter (Kadare) **52**:262
The Great World (Malouf) **86**:207
The Great World and Timothy Colt (Auchincloss) **4**:28; **9**:54; **45**:26-7, 29, 37
Great World Circus (Kotzwinkle) **35**:257
The Greater Apollo (FitzGerald) **19**:176, 181
"The Greater Festival of Masks" (Ligotti) **44**:53-4
"The Greater Music" (Weiss) **14**:556
"The Greater Whiteness" (Swenson) **4**:533
The Greatest Battle (Glasser) **37**:133
The Greatest Crime (Wilson) **32**:449
Greatest Hits Volume Two (Dylan) **77**:172
"The Greatest Living Patagonian" (Shapiro) **8**:486
"The Greatest Man in the World" (Thurber) **11**:533; **125**:388, 398-99
"The Greatest People in the World" (Bates) **46**:57
"The Greatest Poet Writing in English Today" (Bogan) **93**:105
"El Greco" (Peake) **54**:369
"Greece" (Ekeloef) **27**:119
"Greed" (Williams) **56**:425
Greed (Wakoski) **7**:506
"Greed and Aggression" (Olds) **39**:193; **85**:292, 297
"Greed Park" (Wiggins) **57**:434
Greed, Part 9 (Wakoski) **4**:573; **7**:504
Greed, Parts 8, 9, 11 (Wakoski) **4**:573
Greed, Parts 5-7 (Wakoski) **4**:572
"The Greed to Be Fulfilled" (Wakoski) **40**:457
Greek (Berkoff) **56**:16-17, 19-20
The Greek (Nova) **7**:267
The Greek Coffin Mystery (Queen) **3**:421; **11**:460-61
Greek Fire (Graham) **23**:192
The Greek Islands (Durrell) **13**:188-89
Greek Man Seeks Greek Maiden (Duerrenmatt) **102**:59
The Greek Myths (Graves) **1**:128; **6**:211; **11**:255, 257
"Greek Portrait" (Milosz) **56**:237
"The Greek Pothole" (Howard) **47**:171
The Greek Treasure (Stone) **7**:471
The Greeks (Asimov) **76**:312
Green Age (Ostriker) **132**:318-19, 328
"Green: An Epistle" (Hecht) **13**:269
"Green Atom Number Five" (Donoso) **8**:179-80; **32**:160
The Green Brain (Herbert) **23**:221, 226; **44**:393-94
"Green Breeks" (Dunn) **40**:169
"Green Candles" (Kinsella) **43**:253
Green Cars Go East (Carroll) **10**:98
"Green Categories" (Thomas) **6**:534
Green Centuries (Gordon) **6**:203-06; **29**:185, 189; **83**:230, 233-34, 242-43, 251-54, 258-59, 261

"The Green Chapel" (Mathias) **45**:238
The Green Child (Read) **4**:438, 440-44
The Green Cow (O'Casey) **88**:260
"Green Days in Brunei" (Sterling) **72**:372
"Green Earrings" (Becker and Fagen) **26**:83
Green Eyes (Shepard) **34**:108-10
"Green Finch and Linnet Bird" (Sondheim) **147**:263
"Green Fingers" (Fuller) **62**:185
"Green Flows the River of Lethe-O" (Sitwell) **67**:317
The Green Fool (Kavanagh) **22**:234, 242
The Green Gene (Dickinson) **35**:131, 133-34
The Green Girl (Williamson) **29**:454
Green Grass, Blue Sky, White House (Morris) **7**:247
Green Grass, Running Water (King) **89**:91-7, 99-101
"The Green Grave and the Black Grave" (Lavin) **18**:302
Green, Green My Valley Now (Llewellyn) **7**:207
"Green Hell" (Boyle) **36**:56-7
The Green Hills of Africa (Hemingway) **1**:141; **3**:234, 239, 241; **6**:226, 228; **8**:283-84; **10**:267; **13**:281; **19**:219; **34**:477-78; **39**:430, 433; **41**:198, 203; **80**:101, 140, 143
"The Green Hills of Earth" (Heinlein) **55**:301-02
"Green Holly" (Bowen) **118**:74
The Green House (Vargas Llosa)
See *La casa verde*
"Green Lampshade" (Simic) **22**:383
"The Green Lanes" (Kiely) **23**:260
"Green Lantern's Solo" (Baraka) **5**:45
"Green Light" (Fearing) **51**:117, 119, 122
"Green Magic" (Vance) **35**:427
The Green Man (Amis) **2**:8-9; **3**:9; **5**:22; **8**:12; **13**:12-13; **40**:42-3; **129**:14, 18, 25
The Green Man (Young) **5**:524
The Green Mare (Aymé)
See *La jument verte*
"Green Memory" (Hughes) **35**:222
The Green Millennium (Leiber) **25**:301, 303
"A Green Mother" (Hughes) **119**:270
"Green Mountain, Black Mountain" (Stevenson) **33**:382-83
The Green Pastures (Connelly) **7**:55
Green Pitcher (Livesay) **15**:339, 341; **79**:332, 340
"A Green Place" (Smith) **6**:513
The Green Pope (Asturias) **3**:18; **8**:27-8
"Green Rain" (Livesay) **79**:353
The Green Ripper (MacDonald) **44**:408
The Green Room (Truffaut)
See *La chambre verte*
"The Green Shepherd" (Simpson) **7**:426; **149**:295
Green Shoots (Morand)
See *Tendres stocks*
"Green Song" (Sitwell) **2**:402; **67**:320, 324
Green Song (Sitwell) **67**:317
"Green Stain" (MacCaig) **36**:284
"Green Stakes for the Garden" (Thomas) **13**:540
"The Green Step" (Koch) **44**:248
Green Street (Arundel) **17**:12, 17
"Green Thumb" (Levine) **118**:289
"Green Thursday" (Peterkin) **31**:308
Green Thursday (Peterkin) **31**:301, 303, 306-08, 310-11
"The Green Torso" (Warner) **7**:512
"The Green Twig and the Black Trunk" (Rahv) **24**:359
The Green Wall (Wright) **3**:540-43; **5**:519; **10**:542, 545; **28**:461, 468, 470
Green Water, Green Sky (Gallant) **18**:171
"Green Water Tower" (Merwin) **45**:276
The Green Wave (Rukeyser) **6**:478; **27**:408, 410
"Green Ways" (Kunitz) **148**:70, 88, 125
Green with Beasts (Merwin) **1**:213; **2**:276; **5**:285; **8**:389; **13**:384; **45**:268-70, 276; **88**:205-06
"The Green Woods of Unrest" (Graves) **45**:169
Green World (Waddington) **28**:436, 438-39
"Green World One" (Waddington) **28**:438-39
The Green Years (Cronin) **32**:136, 139
"The Greenest Island" (Theroux) **28**:425
The Greengage Summer (Godden) **53**:158, 163
A Greenish Man (Wilson) **33**:464
The Greenlanders (Smiley) **53**:349-51; **76**:235, 237-38; **144**:246-47, 270-71
"Greenleaf" (O'Connor) **1**:257; **15**:412-13; **21**:267, 269, 271, 276; **104**:103, 109, 115, 124, 135-36, 154, 166, 173, 179-80, 182-84, 191-92, 195
"Green's Book" (Chabon) **149**:22-4
"Greenstone" (Ashton-Warner) **19**:22
"The Greenstone Patu" (Ihimaera) **46**:201
Greenvoe (Brown) **5**:77; **48**:53-4, 57-8, 60; **100**:80-1, 83, 86
"Greenwich Time" (Beattie) **63**:3, 8; **146**:67
"Greenwich Village: A Memory" (Dunn) **36**:154-55
"Greenwich Village Saturday Night" (Feldman) **7**:102
Greetings (De Palma) **20**:72-5, 78
Greetings from Ashbury Park, NJ (Springsteen) **17**:477-78, 480, 484, 486-87
"Greggery Peccary" (Zappa) **17**:592
"Grenada Revisited: An Interim Report" (Lorde) **71**:245
Grendel (Gardner) **2**:151-53; **3**:184, 187; **5**:131, 133-35; **7**:112-15; **8**:233-34, 236-238; **10**:218-22; **18**:173-183; **28**:162-63, 166-67
Grenelle (Holland) **21**:150
Ein grenzenloser Nachmittag (Walser) **27**:462
"Ein Grenzfall" (Lenz) **27**:252
The Grey Among the Green (Fuller) **62**:206
"The Grey and the Green" (Fuller) **62**:206
"The Grey Boy" (Raine) **103**:190
Grey Eminence (Huxley) **1**:150; **3**:253; **4**:240, 243; **5**:193; **8**:303
Grey Gardens (Maysles and Maysles) **16**:444
"Grey Heat" (Hamburger) **5**:159
"The Grey Heron" (Kinnell) **29**:285; **129**:241
"The Grey Horse" (Prichard) **46**:332-33, 345
Grey Is the Color of Hope (Ratushinskaya) **54**:382-83, 386-87
"Grey John" (Lane) **25**:285
"The Grey Land" (Stevenson) **33**:380
"The Grey Ones" (Priestley) **2**:347
Greybeard (Aldiss) **14**:12
"Greyday" (Angelou) **77**:29
"The Grey-Eyed King" (Akhmatova) **25**:25
"Greyhound for Breakfast" (Kelman) **58**:299-303
Greyhound for Breakfast, and Other Stories (Kelman) **58**:297-302; **86**:189
"Greyhound People" (Adams) **46**:16
"Greyhounding" (Kenny) **87**:247
Greystoke: The Legend of Tarzan, Lord of the Apes (Towne) **87**:369-70, 374
The Grid of Language (Celan)
See *Sprachgitter*
Il grido (Antonioni) **20**:20, 22, 25; **144**:5, 9, 36, 66, 74-5, 79, 81, 91
Un grido e paesaggi (Ungaretti) **7**:483; **11**:556
Grieche sucht Griechin (Duerrenmatt) **102**:62
Grieche sucht Griechin (Dürrenmatt) **1**:81; **4**:140; **8**:195-96; **43**:120-21, 128
"Grief" (Dobyns) **37**:76
"Grief" (Muldoon) **72**:267, 269
"Grief" (Williams) **148**:359-60
The Grief (Ungaretti)
See *Il dolore*
Grief and Stars (Ekelöf) **27**:110
A Grief Observed (Lewis) **124**:228, 232, 241-42
"The Grief of Men" (Bly) **38**:57-8
"Griefs of the Sea" (Watkins) **43**:441, 447
"Grieg on a Stolen Piano" (Mphahlele) **25**:339
Grierson's Raid (Brown) **47**:35, 37
"Grieve For the Dear Departed" (Moore) **90**:277-8
Griever: An American Monkey King in China (Vizenor) **103**:300, 309-12, 328-29, 332-33, 340
"Griff" (Clarke) **53**:89, 91
Griffin's Way (Yerby) **7**:557
"Griffon" (Dobyns) **37**:77
Griffon (Dobyns) **37**:76-8
The Grifters (Thompson) **69**:385
The Grim Reaper (Bertolucci)
See *La commare secca*
"Grimoire" (Dobyns) **37**:76-7
Grimus (Rushdie) **23**:364; **55**:216, 218
Grindegard: Morgonen (Vesaas)
See *The Farm at Grinde*
Grinde-kveld; eller, Den gode engelen (Vesaas) **48**:411
Grindekveld; eller, Den gode engelen (Vesaas) **48**:405, 411
El gringo viejo (Fuentes) **41**:172-75; **60**:155-60, 165, 170; **113**:239-42, 251, 265, 267-68
"The Grip of the Geraghty's" (O'Connor) **23**:330
"Gristmill" (Komunyakaa) **94**:241
"Gritty" (Ewart) **46**:152
"Grizzly Cowboys" (Bass) **79**:17
The Groaning Board (Addams) **30**:15
Die Große Wut de Philipp Hotz (Frisch) **14**:182-83
"Groom" (Dybek) **114**:67
"Groping" (Thomas) **48**:382
Groping for Words (Townsend) **61**:409-10
"Gros Islet" (Walcott) **67**:360; **76**:299
"Le Gros Sang" (Tchicaya) **101**:349
Gros-câlin (Gary) **25**:188
Gross Misconduct (Egoyan) **151**:135, 152
Gross und Klein (Strauss) **22**:408
La grosse femme d'à côté est enciente (Tremblay) **29**:419, 423-25, 427; **102**:370, 373-75, 377, 379
"La grosse fifi" (Rhys) **51**:355; **124**:337
"Grosse Landschaft bei Wien" (Bachmann) **69**:40
"Der Grosse Lübbe-See" (Eich) **15**:202
"Der Grosse Wildenberg" (Lenz) **27**:245
"Grosses Geburtstagsblaublau mit Reimzeug und Assonanz" (Celan) **82**:52
"Grotesques" (Strand) **71**:286-89
"La grotte" (Mandiargues) **41**:278
La grotte (Anouilh) **40**:58-9
"Ground" (Davison) **28**:103
The Ground We Stand On (Dos Passos) **15**:183; **25**:137, 145
Ground Work: Before the War (Duncan) **41**:127-31; **55**:290-91, 293, 295, 298
Ground Work II: In the Dark (Duncan) **55**:293-95
"The Groundhog" (Eberhart) **11**:177; **19**:140, 143; **56**:76-7, 79-80, 87, 90
Groundwork (Auster) **131**:42
The Group (McCarthy) **1**:205-06; **3**:326-29; **5**:276; **14**:357-58, 360, 363; **24**:349; **59**:289, 291-93
"Group Life: Letchworth" (Betjeman) **6**:68; **43**:36-7
"Group of Progressive Catholics" (Boell) **9**:108
Group Portrait with Lady (Boell)
See *Gruppenbild mit Dame*
Group Therapy (Hearon) **63**:164-67
"Groups and Series" (Denby) **48**:83
"Grove and Building" (Bowers) **9**:122
"Grove of Academe" (H. D.) **14**:224
The Grove of Eagles (Graham) **23**:193
"Groves of Academe" (Hacker) **91**:111
The Groves of Academe (McCarthy) **1**:206; **3**:326; **5**:275; **14**:357, 363; **39**:486
"Grow Old Along with Me: The Best Is Yet to Be" (Lively) **32**:277
"Grow Old with Me" (Lennon) **35**:275-76
"Growin' Up" (Springsteen) **17**:487
"Growing Boys" (Aickman) **57**:6-7
Growing into Love (Kennedy) **8**:319-20; **42**:255
Growing Pains (du Maurier) **11**:164; **59**:285-88

The Growing Pains of Adrian Mole (Townsend) **61**:410-16, 418-21
Growing Points (Jennings) **14**:292-93; **131**:241
"The Growing Stone" (Camus)
See "La pierre qui pousse"
The Growing Summer (Streatfeild)
See *The Magic Summer*
"Growing Up" (Boland) **113**:77
Growing Up (Baker) **31**:30-1
Growing Up Absurd (Goodman) **2**:171; **4**:195, 198; **7**:129-30, 131
"Growing Up Female" (Bettelheim) **79**:125
Growing Up in New Guinea (Mead) **37**:270-71
Growing Up in Public (Reed) **21**:319-21
Growing Up Stupid under the Union Jack (Clarke) **53**:89-91, 93, 95
"Growltiger's Last Stand" (Eliot) **55**:347
Grown Ups (Feiffer) **64**:155-56, 161-64
"Grownup" (Simon) **26**:409
Grown-ups and Other Problems: Help for Small People in a Big World (Mayle) **89**:143
"Growth" (Levine) **118**:304
"Growth" (Lowell) **124**:256
"The Gruagach" (Montague) **46**:267-68
"Grub First, Then Ethics" (Auden) **123**:40
"Grumootvodite" (Bagryana) **10**:13
Grupa Laokoona (Rozewicz) **139**:228-29, 232, 240, 251-55, 257 267, 293
"Gruppa 'Konkret'" (Coles) **67**:174
Gruppenbild mit Dame (Boell) **2**:66-7; **3**:73-6; **6**:84; **11**:55-6, 58; **27**:64; **39**:292-93, 295-96; **72**:78, 85, 89, 100
"Gruzinskiye beryozy" (Voznesensky) **57**:417
"Gruzinskiye dorogi" (Voznesensky) **15**:555
"Guadalajara Hospital" (Ai) **69**:6, 14
"Guadalcanal" (Randall) **135**:397
Guadeloupe (Condé) **92**:132
"Guadeloupe, W.I." (Guillén) **48**:157, 166
"The Guanajuato Mummies" (Belitt) **22**:54
"Guard Duty" (Transtroemer) **52**:410; **65**:223-24
Guard of Honor (Cozzens) **1**:67; **4**:112, 114-16; **11**:124, 127, 132-33; **92**:176, 178, 181-82, 184, 186-89, 194, 212
"El guardagujas" (Arreola) **147**:3-5, 14-15, 18, 28-29
"Guardian Angel" (Clarke) **136**:210-12, 217, 222, 225
"Guardian Angel" (Simic) **130**:306
"The Guardian Angel" (Soto) **80**:300
"Guardian Angel" (Willingham) **51**:403
The Guardian Angel (Havel) **25**:224
Guardian Angel (Paretsky) **135**:354, 361-65, 367
"The Guardian Angel of Point of View" (Graham) **118**:263
"The Guardian Angel of Self-Knowledge" (Graham) **118**:263
"Guardian Dragon" (Humphrey) **45**:205
The Guardian of the Word (Laye)
See *Le maître de la parole: Kouma lafôlô kouma*
"The Guardians" (Merwin) **18**:335; **88**:200
The Guardians (Stewart) **7**:464
"The Guards" (Rozewicz)
See "Straż prozdkowa"
The Guards (Rozewicz) **139**:293
Guatemala: Occupied Country (Galeano) **72**:129
"A Guatemalan Idyll" (Bowles) **68**:6-7, 12
"Guayaquil" (Borges) **4**:75; **10**:67
Gudgekin the Thistle Girl and Other Tales (Gardner) **8**:238
Guds bustader (Vesaas) **48**:411
"Le gué dans le torrent" (Theriault) **79**:407
"La Guera" (Moraga) **126**:302
"La güera" (Ulibarrí) **83**:415
"Guerillas" (Deane) **122**:82
Guerillas (Naipaul) **7**:252-54; **9**:391-93; **13**:407; **18**:359, 361, 363-65; **37**:324; **105**:139-42, 157, 161-71, 176, 181
Les guerillères (Wittig) **22**:473-77
Guernica (Arrabal)
See *L'arbre de guernica*
Guernica (Resnais) **16**:502, 505-06
"The Güero" (Donoso)
See "El güero"
"El güero" (Donoso) **4**:127; **8**:178; **32**:158
La guerra de guerrillas (Guevara) **87**:199, 201, 203, 207, 212
La guerra del fin del mundo (Vargas Llosa) **31**:448-49; **42**:403-07, 409, 411; **85**:350, 352-53, 355, 362-63, 379-80, 382-83, 389-95
Guerra del tiempo (Carpentier) **11**:100; **38**:92, 94-5; **110**:48, 53
La guerre est finie (Resnais) **16**:504-06, 509-13
La guerre, Yes Sir! (Carrier) **13**:140-44; **78**:37-41, 44-9, 51-2, 54-7, 60-1, 67-71, 73, 79-80, 82-4, 87-9
Guerrilla Warfare (Guevara)
See *La guerra de guerrillas*
"Guerrilla Warfare: A Method" (Guevara) **87**:212
Guerrillas (Hochhuth) **18**:254
"Guess" (Pearce) **21**:292
"Guess Whose Loving Hands" (Mazer) **26**:291
"Guessers" (Sandburg) **35**:358
"The Guest" (Camus)
See "L'hôte"
"Guest" (Enright) **31**:154
"The Guest" (Middleton) **13**:387
"The Guest" (Watkins) **43**:450, 453
A Guest and His Going (Newby) **2**:311; **13**:407-08
"A Guest at the Spa" (Hesse) **2**:191; **11**:270; **17**:216
A Guest for the Night (Agnon)
See *Ore'ah natah lalun*
A Guest of Honour (Gordimer) **3**:201; **5**:145, 147; **7**:132; **10**:239; **18**:187; **33**:182-83; **51**:161; **70**:163, 165, 170, 184; **123**:131, 137
Guest of Reality (Lagerkvist)
See *Gäst hos verkligheten*
Guests (Dorris) **109**:309
The Guests (Harwood) **32**:224
"Guests in the Promised Land" (Hunter) **35**:226
Guests in the Promised Land (Hunter) **35**:226-27
The Guests of August (Castellanos)
See *Los convidados de agosto*
"Guests of the Nation" (O'Connor) **23**:328, 330
Guests of the Nation (O'Connor) **14**:398, 400-01; **23**:327, 329, 332
Guests of War (Jenkins) **52**:223, 225, 227-28
"Guevara" (Salinas) **90**:322, 324, 329
Guevle de Pierre (Queneau) **5**:360-61
Guiana Quartet (Harris) **25**:203, 213
"Guide" (Ammons) **5**:27; **8**:16; **9**:30; **108**:21, 50
The Guide (Narayan) **7**:255; **28**:292, 295, 300; **47**:304; **121**:341, 351-54, 356-58, 366-67, 383, 385-86, 389-92, 397
"Guide Book" (Coles) **46**:108-09
"Guide for the Misfortune Hunter" (Lebowitz) **36**:250
A Guide for the Perplexed (Levi) **76**:71-6
A Guide for the Perplexed (Schumacher) **80**:265-66, 268, 273
"Guide through the Aegean" (Elytis) **100**:171
"A Guide to Berlin" (Nabokov) **15**:393
Guide to Kulchur (Pound) **4**:414; **7**:334; **13**:461; **112**:321, 328, 332
"A Guide to Poetry" (Ciardi) **10**:107; **40**:152, 157
"A Guide to Some of the Lesser Ballets" (Allen) **52**:35
"A Guide To Switzerland" (Thomas) **132**:382
Guide to the Ruins (Nemerov) **6**:361; **36**:304
"A Guided Tour through the Zoo" (Ignatow) **40**:258
The Guiding Light (Nixon) **21**:242
"The Guiding Miss Gowd" (Ferber) **93**:142
"Guido the Ice House Man" (Turco) **11**:552
Guignol's Band (Céline) **1**:56; **4**:101; **9**:152, 154; **47**:71-2, 74; **124**:52, 60-2, 66-8, 70, 78, 88-9, 93, 96, 110-11
Guignol's Band I (Céline) **124**:95
Guignol's Band II (Céline) **124**:95-6
"GuíL an rannaire" (Behan) **79**:38-9
"The Guild" (Olds) **39**:193
"Guillaume de Lorris" (Pound) **7**:337
Guillevic (Guillevic) **33**:191, 193
"Guillotine" (Woolrich) **77**:403
"Guilt" (Betjeman) **43**:51
"Guilt" (Lish) **45**:229
"Guilt" (Oates) **15**:402
"Guilt" (Ritter) **52**:355-56
"Guilt Gems" (Updike) **15**:546-47
The Guilt Merchants (Harwood) **32**:223
"Guiltiness" (Marley) **17**:269
The Guilty (Bataille)
See *Le coupable*
"The Guilty Man" (Kunitz) **148**:68
Guilty Pleasures (Barthelme) **5**:54-5; **6**:29; **46**:36; **59**:247; **115**:63, 68
A Guilty Thing Surprised (Rendell) **28**:385, 387
"The Guinea Pig Lady" (Banks) **37**:26
The Guinea Pigs (Vaculik)
See *Sekrya*
The "Guinguette" by the Seine (Simenon) **47**:371
Guirnalda con amores (Bioy Casares) **13**:84, 86; **88**:94
"The Guitar" (Bottoms) **53**:34
"Guitar" (Dodson) **79**:191
"Guitar" (Williams) **148**:360
"Guitar or Moon" (Aleixandre)
See "Guitarra o luna"
"Guitar Recitivos" (Ammons) **5**:29
"Guitarra o luna" (Aleixandre) **36**:30
The Gulag Archipelago, 1918-1956: An Experiment in Literary Investigation (Solzhenitsyn)
See *Arkhipelag GuLag, 1918-1956: Op' bit khudozhestvennopo issledovaniia*
Gulag Archipelago Three (Solzhenitsyn) **78**:385
"Guldstekel" (Transtroemer) **65**:233
"Gulf" (Heinlein) **3**:226; **26**:165; **55**:302-03
"The Gulf" (Walcott) **25**:451; **67**:354; **76**:274, 281
The Gulf, and Other Poems (Walcott) **2**:460; **14**:549, 551; **25**:450-52; **42**:421; **67**:346
"The Gulf Between" (Calisher) **38**:71; **134**:7
Los gulfos (Saura) **20**:313
"Gulfport" (Smith) **25**:410
Gull Number 737 (George) **35**:176
"Gull on a Post" (Hooker) **43**:197
The Gull Wall (Eshleman) **7**:100
Gullah (Childress)
See *Sea Island Song*
"Gulliver" (Plath) **9**:428
"Gulliver" (Slessor) **14**:494
"Gulliver" (Soyinka) **36**:415-17; **44**:285
Gulliver (Simon) **4**:495; **9**:483-84; **15**:490-92; **39**:203-06, 209, 211
"Gulls" (Guillevic) **33**:191
"The Gulls" (Livesay) **79**:341
"The Gulls at Longbird Island" (Bronk) **10**:75
"Gulls from a Fantail" (Ciardi) **40**:157
"The Gully" (Banks) **72**:5
"The Gum Forest" (Murray) **40**:338
"Gum-Trees Stripping" (Wright) **53**:431
"The Gun" (Dobyns) **37**:81
The Gun (Forester) **35**:159, 161-62, 168, 170
Gun before Butter (Freeling) **38**:183
A Gun for Sale (Greene) **1**:130; **3**:213; **27**:173; **70**:290; **72**:148; **125**:196, 208
"Gun in the Grass at Your Feet" (Shields) **97**:433
"Gun Law at Vermilion: Anna, 1988" (McNally) **82**:262
"The Gun Shop" (Updike) **15**:545; **139**:338
"Gun Song" (Sondheim) **147**:249

"Gun, White Castle" (Klappert) **57**:259
Gunga Din Highway (Chin) **135**:172-75, 202
The Gunman (O'Casey)
See *The Shadow of a Gunman*
"The Gunner's Dream" (Pink Floyd) **35**:315
"Gunners' Passage" (Shaw) **7**:411; **23**:396
"Gunpowder Morning in a Gray Room" (Crase) **58**:165
"Gunpowder Plot" (Scannell) **49**:324, 328, 331-32
Guns in the Afternoon (Peckinpah)
See *Ride the High Country*
The Guns of Avalon (Zelazny) **21**:466, 473
"Guns of Brixton" (Clash) **30**:46, 50
Guns of Burgoyne (Lancaster) **36**:241-44
The Guns of Darkness (Schlee) **35**:372
The Guns of Navarone (MacLean) **13**:360-62; **50**:347, 349; **63**:261-62, 264-70
"Guns of the Enemy" (Cozzens) **92**:201
Guns on the Roof (Clash) **30**:43-4, 46
Gunsight (Weiss) **3**:516; **8**:545; **14**:556-57
Gunsights (Leonard) **120**:275, 286-87
Gunslinger (Dorn) **10**:155-59; **18**:128
Gunslinger, Book II (Dorn) **10**:158
"Gura vetrei" (Arghezi) **80**:5-6
Gurney (Silkin) **43**:405
The Guru (Jhabvala) **29**:259; **94**:189
Gus and Al (Innaurato) **60**:205-08
"De Gustibus Ain't What Dey Used to Be" (Perelman) **44**:505
Der gute Gott von Manhattan (Bachmann) **69**:48-50
The Gutenberg Elegies: The Fate of Reading in an Electronic Age (Birkerts) **116**:154-58, 161-64, 167, 173
The Gutenberg Galaxy: The Making of Typographic Man (McLuhan) **37**:253-57, 259-63; **83**:359-60, 362-63, 373-74
"The Gutting of Couffignal" (Hammett) **47**:156, 159, 164
"The Guttural Muse" (Heaney) **25**:244
"The Gut-Wrenching Machine" (Bukowski) **41**:75; **108**:85
"The Guy with the Crutch" (Kelman) **58**:301
"Guzman, Go Home" (Sillitoe) **57**:388-89
Guzman, Go Home and Other Stories (Sillitoe) **57**:388, 392; **148**:163
"Gwen" (Kincaid) **43**:249
"Gwendolyn" (Bishop) **32**:40
Gwiazda zaranna (Dabrowska) **15**:166, 170
"Gwilan's Harp" (Le Guin) **45**:213, 216, **136**:376
Gycklarnas afton (Bergman) **16**:46, 49, 51, 53, 61, 66, 70, 73, 81; **72**:29-30, 40-1, 48, 62
"The Gymnast" (Voigt) **54**:431-32
"The Gymnosophist" (Ekeloef) **27**:119
Gyn/Ecology (Sarton) **91**:246
Gypsy (Sondheim) **30**:376-78, 385, 387, 389, 390, 395, 400
"The Gypsy Girl" (Davis) **49**:83, 93
Gypsy, Gypsy (Godden) **53**:151-52
Gypsy in Amber (Smith) **25**:412-13
The Gypsy's Curse (Crews) **6**:118-19; **49**:71-2, 76-7
"The Gyroscope" (Rukeyser) **27**:408
The Gyrth Chalice Mystery (Allingham) **19**:14
"H" (Merrill) **8**:384
H. G. Wells: Aspects of a Life (West) **50**:359-60
H siao-jen, h siao shih (Pa Chin) **18**:374
"The H Street Sledding Record" (Carlson) **54**:39
"Ha chi je na I Am Coming" (Forché) **25**:170
Ha! Ha! (Ducharme)
See *Ah! Ah!*
"Haarlem" (Corso) **11**:123
Ha-atalef (Megged) **9**:375
The HAB Theory (Eckert) **17**:108
La Habana para un infante difunto (Cabrera Infante) **25**:104; **45**:78-83; **120**:52-57, 59, 63, 69, 78, 80-82
Habeas Corpus (Bennett) **45**:57-8; **77**:87
The Habit of Being: Letters of Flannery O'Connor (O'Connor) **13**:421-22; **15**:413; **21**:278
The Habit of Empire (Horgan) **53**:178
"The Habit of Loving" (Lessing) **6**:298; **10**:316; **22**:277
"Les habitants du continent des chas sans aiguilles" (Arp) **5**:34
"Habitar o tempo" (Cabral de Melo Neto) **76**:168
"Habitat" (Auden) **123**:40
"Habitations of the Word" (Gass) **39**:480; **132**:174
Habitations of the Word (Gass) **39**:477-82
"Habits" (Giovanni) **64**:195
"The Habits" (MacNeice) **10**:324
El hablador (Vargas Llosa) **85**:376, 395-98
"Hablar y decir" (Paz) **65**:177
Háblenme de Funes (Costantini) **49**:61
"El hacedor" (Borges) **3**:81; **6**:93; **8**:101; **9**:120; **13**:107; **84**:158
El hacedor (Borges) **2**:71-2; **3**:77; **8**:101; **13**:106-07; **44**:356; **83**:158-59, 171, 191
"Hacienda" (Porter) **7**:311; **13**:449; **27**:402; **101**:214
Hacienda (Porter) **101**:215
The Hack (Sheed) **4**:487
"Hack Wednesday" (Atwood) **84**:95, 97
Hackenfeller's Ape (Brophy) **11**:67-8; **29**:91-3, 97-8; **105**:7-8, 11, 29-30
"Had I a Hundred Mouths" (Goyen) **40**:217-18
Had I a Hundred Mouths: New and Selected Stories, 1947-1983 (Goyen) **40**:218-19
"Had to Phone Ya" (Wilson) **12**:648
"Hades and Euclid" (Martinson) **14**:357
Hadith al-sabah w'l-masa' (Mahfouz) **153**:359
Hadrian VII (Luke) **38**:313-18
Hadrian's Memoirs (Yourcenar)
See *Mémoires d'Hadrien*
"Haecity" (Cunningham) **31**:98
"The Hag of Beare" (Montague) **46**:268-69
Hagakure nyūmon (Mishima) **9**:385; **27**:342
"Hagibor ha'amiti shel ha'agedah" (Amichai) **116**:112-13
"Haha naru mono" (Endō) **54**:158, 161
"Haha no kouru ki" (Tanizaki) **28**:420
Haï (Le Clézio) **31**:251; **155**:108
"Haibun" (Ashbery) **41**:34
"Haig" (Smith) **64**:388
"Haiku" (Sanchez) **116**:302, 328
"Hail Mary" (Fante) **60**:133
Hail to the Chief (Hunter) **11**:279
"Hailstones" (Heaney) **74**:162, 174, 191
La haine de la poésie (Bataille) **29**:39
"Haines" (Soupault) **68**:405
"Hair" (Bly) **10**:55
"Hair" (Olson) **28**:343
Hair (Ragni and Rado) **17**:378-88
Hair (Weller) **53**:393
"Hair Jewellery" (Atwood) **13**:45
The Hair of Harold Roux (Williams) **14**:582-83
"Hairball" (Atwood) **84**:96-7
"A Haircut" (Carver) **55**:273
Haircut (Warhol) **20**:416, 421
The Haircutting (Hrabal)
See *Postřižiny*
"The Hairless Mexican" (Maugham) **67**:219
"A Hairline Fracture" (Clampitt) **32**:115-16
"A Hairpin Turn above Reading, Jamaica" (Matthews) **40**:321
"Hairs" (Cisneros) **118**:175
The Hairs of My Grandfather's Head (Laughlin) **49**:220
"Hairy Belly" (Ammons) **57**:57
"Haitian Divorce" (Becker and Fagen) **26**:83
Haitian Earth (Walcott) **67**:342
"Haitian Gentleman" (Gold) **152**:121
The Haj (Uris) **32**:436-37
Hakai (Ichikawa) **20**:182
Hakhnasat kalah (Agnon) **4**:11-12; **8**:8; **14**:3
Hako otoko (Abe) **8**:1-2; **53**:2, 5-6; **81**:285, 287, 293
Hakobune sakura maru (Abe) **53**:2-7; **81**:294-95
Hakuchi (Kurosawa)
See *The Idiot*
Halbzeit (Walser) **27**:456-61, 465, 467
"Halcyon" (H. D.) **73**:121
"Halcyon" (Ihimaera) **46**:199
"Hale Hardy and the Amazing Animal Woman" (Beattie) **8**:55; **63**:3, 17
"Half a Century Gone, 5" (Lowell) **124**:255
Half a Kilometre Away (Voinovich)
See *Rasstoyanie v polkilometra*
"Half a Mile Away" (Joel) **26**:217
"Half an Hour Before He Died" (Kelman) **58**:298
"Half Life" (Carlson) **54**:37
"Half Life" (Monette) **82**:320, 322, 332
"Half Light" (Szirtes) **46**:391
"Half Measure" (Yevtushenko) **126**:391
Half Moon Street (Theroux) **46**:398-401, 404
"Half Pass Four" (Le Guin) **136**:376
Half Portions (Ferber) **93**:139, 142, 147
Half Remembered (Davison) **28**:101-02
Half Sun Half Sleep (Swenson) **4**:533; **14**:518; **61**:392; **106**:320-21, 348-49
Half Time (Walser)
See *Halbzeit*
"Half-Breed" (Asimov) **26**:39
Halfbreed (Campbell) **85**:2-5, 8-9, 11-2, 14, 17, 20-5
"Half-Breeds on Venus" (Asimov) **26**:39
"Half-Caste Girl" (Wright) **53**:427
"Half-Deity" (Moore) **10**:350
The Half-Finished Heaven (Transtroemer)
See *Den halvfärdiga himlen*
"A Half-Grown Porcupine" (Bly) **15**:63
"Halfjack" (Zelazny) **21**:479
Half-Lives (Jong) **4**:263-64; **6**:267-68; **8**:313-15; **18**:277; **83**:289, 291, 299-300
The Half-Made Heaven (Transtroemer)
See *Den halvfärdiga himlen*
"The Half-Moon Blackbird" (Durcan) **70**:151-52
The Half-Mother (Tennant)
See *Woman Beware Woman*
"A Half-Private Letter on Poetry" (Milosz) **56**:237
The Half-Ready Sky (Transtroemer)
See *Den halvfärdiga himlen*
"Half-Scissors" (Redgrove) **41**:352
The Half-Sisters (Seton) **27**:425-27
"Hälfte des Lebens" (Hildesheimer) **49**:179
"Halfway" (Ammons) **108**:24
Halfway Down the Coast (Blackburn) **43**:64-5
Halfway Home (Monette) **82**:327-28, 331
"Halfway House" (Silverberg) **7**:425
Halfway House (Queen) **11**:458, 461
Halfway House: A Miscellany of New Poems (Blunden) **56**:44, 48
Halfway to Silence (Sarton) **49**:314
"Halfway to the Moon" (Aksyonov) **101**:9-10, 15, 20, 30
"A Hall of Mirrors" (Rosenblatt) **15**:446
A Hall of Mirrors (Stone) **5**:409-10; **23**:424-26, 429-30; **42**:358-63
Halleck: Lincoln's Chief of Staff (Ambrose) **145**:38
"Les halles d'Ypres" (Blunden) **56**:41
Halleyova kometa (Seifert)
See *Halleyová kometa*
Halleyová kometa (Seifert) **34**:257; **93**:319, 336-37, 343
"Halley's Comet" (Kunitz) **148**:127, 149
Halley's Comet (Seifert)
See *Halleyová kometa*
"Halloran's Child" (Hill) **113**:282
Halloran's Little Boat (Keneally) **117**:213
"Hallow Eve with Spaces for Ghosts" (Piercy) **27**:374
"Hallowe'en" (Aiken) **10**:4; **52**:26
Hallowe'en (Christie) **48**:74; **110**:137
"Halloween Delight" (Smith) **42**:353

"The Halloween Party" (Chabon) **149**:3, 6, 8
"Halloween Poem" (Cohen) **38**:131
"Hallowind" (Chappell) **78**:96
Hallucinations (Arenas)
See *El mundo alucinante: Una novela de aventuras*
"Halmaherra" (Randall) **135**:397
"Haloes" (Abse) **29**:18
"The Halt" (Miles) **14**:369
"A Halt in the Desert" (Brodsky)
See "Ostanovka v pustyne"
Halt in the Wilderness (Brodsky) **13**:114
"The Halted Battalion" (Blunden) **56**:45
"Halves" (Williams) **148**:320, 328, 343
Den halvfärdiga himlen (Transtroemer) **52**:409-10, 412, 415; **65**:222-23, 225, 229, 233, 236
The Ham Funeral (White) **7**:532
Ham on Rye (Bukowski) **41**:70-3; **82**:6, 8-10, 28; **108**:88, 102
Hamachidori (Kawabata) **107**:121
"Hamari Gali" (Ali) **69**:25
"Hamatsa" (Bowering) **15**:82
"A Hambledon Sequence" (Hooker) **43**:199
"The Hambone and the Heart" (Sitwell) **67**:313, 325
Hamilton County (Kantor) **7**:196
Hamilton Stark (Banks) **37**:23-4, 26-7; **72**:4-5
"Hamlen Brook" (Wilbur) **110**:361
"Hamlet" (Honig) **33**:215-16
"Hamlet" (Pasternak) **63**:312-13
"Hamlet" (Soyinka) **36**:416-17; **44**:285
The Hamlet (Faulkner) **1**:101-02; **3**:149, 151-52, 156; **6**:174, 179; **8**:211; **11**:197, 203-04; **14**:178-79; **18**:148-49; **28**:138, 140, 145; **52**:114, 139
Hamlet (Olivier) **20**:234-37, 242-43
"Hamlet and His Problems" (Eliot) **24**:172, 176
"Hamlet and the Party Secretary" (Hein) **154**:53
Hamlet in Autumn (Smith) **64**:399
The Hamlet of A. MacLeish (MacLeish) **3**:310; **14**:336; **68**:271-73, 275, 284, 286, 289-90
The Hamlet of Stepney Green (Kops) **4**:274
Hamlet, Revenge! (Stewart) **14**:511
Hamlet's Mother and Other Women (Heilbrun) **65**:344
"Hamlets of the World" (Shaw) **23**:396
Hamlet's Twin (Aquin)
See *Neige noir*
"A Hammer" (Guillevic) **33**:191
The Hammer (Fast) **131**:78, 98
"The Hammer Man" (Bambara) **19**:33; **88**:16
The Hammerhead Light (Thiele) **17**:496
Hammertown Tales (Masters) **48**:223-24
"Hammond, England" (Blunden) **56**:37
"Hamnavoe Market" (Brown) **48**:57, 60
Hamnstad (Bergman) **16**:46-7, 50-1, 60; **72**:52, 62
"Hampshire" (Davie) **8**:165
"Hampstead: The Horse Chestnut Trees" (Gunn) **18**:199, 202
"Hamrick's Polar Bear" (Caldwell) **60**:50
"Hams al-junun" (Mahfouz) **153**:336, 352-53, 372
Hams al-junūn (Mahfūz) **55**:174, 176
"Ham's Departure" (Leonov)
See "Ukhod Khama"
"Ham's Gift" (Dowell) **60**:107-08
Hamsters (Silverstein and Silverstein) **17**:456
"Hamuel Gutterman" (Tolson) **105**:237
"Han no hanza" (Shiga) **33**:366
Han som fik leva om sitt liv (Lagerkvist) **54**:269-70, 272, 275, 278
Hanazakari no mori (Mishima) **2**:286; **27**:338
"The Hand" (Sexton) **123**:407
"The Hand" (Thomas) **48**:379
The Hand (Stone) **73**:363-64, 382
A Hand at the Shutter (King) **145**:367
A Hand Full of Feathers (Breytenbach) **126**:102
"Hand in Glove" (Bowen) **118**:74
Hand in Glove (Marsh) **53**:248
"Hand in Hand" (Costello) **21**:68
"Hand of a Wanker" (McGrath) **55**:73, 75
The Hand of Oberon (Zelazny) **21**:470-71, 473
"A Hand of Solo" (Kinsella) **138**:121, 142-43, 156, 166
"Hand of the Mind" (Spacks) **14**:511
Hand Out (Rathbone) **41**:337
"Hand Poem" (Phillips) **28**:363
"The Hand That Cradles the Rock" (Perelman) **49**:263
The Hand That Cradles the Rock (Brown) **79**:153
Hand to Mouth (Auster) **131**:42
Die hand vol vere (Breytenbach) **126**:102
A Handbook For Drowning (Shields) **97**:428-34
A Handbook for Visitors from Outer Space (Kramer) **34**:74-6
A Handbook of Practical Morality (Arghezi)
See *Manual de morală practică*
"Handcarved Coffins: A Nonfiction Account of an American Crime" (Capote) **19**:84-5
"The Handcuff Manual" (Vollmann) **89**:283, 296
A Handful of Dust (Waugh) **1**:357-60; **3**:509-13; **8**:544-45; **13**:585-88; **19**:462-64; **27**:470-71, 476-77; **44**:524; **107**:360-62, 364, 366, 370-71, 378, 380, 398, 400-01
A Handful of Rice (Markandaya) **38**:323
"The Handgun" (DeMarinis) **54**:101-02
"The Handing Down" (Berry) **46**:70
Handkerchief of Clouds (Tzara)
See *Mouchoir de nuages*
"The Handkerchief of Ghost Tree" (Thomas) **31**:430
Handling Sin (Malone) **43**:282-85
The Handmaid's Tale (Atwood) **44**:146-51, 153-62; **84**:67, 69, 71, 79, 86, 97-104, 107; **135**:3-71
The Hand-Reared Boy (Aldiss) **5**:14; **14**:14
"Hand-Rolled Cigarettes" (Kunitz) **6**:287
"Handrolled Cigarettes" (Yevtushenko) **126**:395
"Hands" (Birney) **6**:74
"Hands" (Brautigan) **3**:86
"The Hands" (Campbell) **93**:95
"Hands" (Hughes) **119**:272, 290
"Hands" (Landolfi) **11**:321; **49**:212
"Hands" (Purdy) **50**:246
Hands across the Sea (Coward) **51**:70
"The Hands around the Neck" (Moravia) **46**:286
The Hands of Day (Neruda)
See *Las manos del día*
The Hands of Venus (Seifert)
See *The Arms of Venus*
"Hands Off, Foreign Devil" (Enright) **31**:155
"Hands over Head" (Clark Bekedermo) **38**:125
Hands Up! (Skolimowski) **20**:352-53
The Handsome Heart (De Vries) **28**:113-14
"Handsome Is as Handsome Does" (Pritchett) **41**:333
A Handsome Man (Cheever) **48**:63-4
"The Handsomest Drowned Man in the World: A Tale for Children" (García Márquez)
See "El ahogado más hermoso del mundo"
"Handsworth Liberties" (Fisher) **25**:160-61
"Handwritten News" (Char) **55**:289
"Handy Dandy" (Dylan) **77**:182
"Hanefesh" (Amichai) **116**:122
Hang for Treason (Peck) **17**:340-41
"Hang of It" (Salinger) **12**:498
The Hang of the Gaol (Barker) **37**:37, 39
"Hang On to the Good Times" (Cryer) **21**:81
"Hang On to Yourself" (Bowie) **17**:59, 65
"Hangdog Hotel Room" (Lightfoot) **26**:282
"A Hanged Man" (Cliff) **120**:90
"The Hanged Man" (Cohen) **19**:113
"The Hanged Man's Prayer" (Carrier) **78**:83
"Hangin' Round" (Reed) **21**:305
"Hanging Fire" (Lorde) **71**:232, 247
"The Hanging Judge" (Boland) **40**:96; **113**:122
"The Hanging Man" (Davison) **28**:103
"The Hanging Man" (Plath) **9**:427-28
"Hanging on a Sunrise" (Gordimer) **123**:157
"Hanging Out in America" (Allen) **84**:5
"Hanging Out with the Magi" (Rooke) **25**:394
The Hanging Stones (Wellman) **49**:393, 396
"Hangman" (Ai) **69**:11
Hangmen Also Die (Lang) **20**:207, 216
The Hangover (Sargeson) **31**:365-67, 374
Hangover Square; or, The Man with Two Minds: A Story of Darkest Earl's Court in the Year 1939 (Hamilton) **51**:187-88, 190, 193-94, 196-98
Hangsaman (Jackson) **60**:216-20, 229-31, 234
"Hanka" (Singer) **6**:511; **11**:499
Hanky Panky (Poitier) **26**:362
Hannah Arendt--Karl Jaspers: Correspondence, 1926-1969 (Arendt) **98**:47
Hannah's House (Hearon) **63**:159-60, 162
"Hannes" (Hesse) **25**:262
Hanoi (McCarthy) **14**:358-59
"Hanoi Hannah" (Komunyakaa) **94**:226, 232, 245
"Han's Crime" (Shiga)
See "Han no hanza"
Hans Feet in Love (Sansom) **2**:383; **6**:482-84
Hans nådes tid (Johnson) **14**:296
"Hänsel to Gretel" (Monette) **82**:314
"Ha-panim la-panim" (Agnon) **8**:8
"Hapax" (Rexroth) **112**:395, 400, 402
"Ha'penny" (Paton) **25**:359; **55**:313
"Hapless Dancer" (Townshend) **17**:532
"Happening" (Ezekiel) **61**:109
"Happening" (Honig) **33**:216
"Happenings" (Phillips) **28**:364
Happenstance (Shields) **113**:401, 404-08, 410, 412, 424, 431, 437-39, 441, 445-46
"The Happier Life" (Dunn) **40**:166
The Happier Life (Dunn) **6**:148; **40**:165-67
"The Happiest I've Been" (Updike) **34**:291
"Happily Ever After" (Sondheim) **147**:252
"Happiness" (Ciardi) **44**:381
"Happiness" (Glück) **22**:177
"Happiness" (Lavin) **18**:305; **99**:312-15, 319, 322
"Happiness" (Oliver) **34**:246, 249; **98**:299-300
"Happiness" (Prichard) **46**:332, 345
"Happiness" (Sandburg) **35**:355
"Happiness" (Warner) **7**:512
Happiness (Lavin) **99**:322
"Happiness Does Not Come in Colors" (Cooper) **56**:70
"Happiness in Herat" (Paz) **65**:200
"Happiness Is..." (Jones) **52**:250
Happiness Is Too Much Trouble (Hochman) **8**:298
Happiness: Selected Short Stories (Prichard) **46**:345
"Happy" (Beattie) **40**:65-6
Happy All the Time (Colwin) **13**:156-57; **84**:139-40, 142, 146-47, 149-53
Happy As Larry (Hinde) **6**:238-39
"Happy August the Tenth" (Williams) **5**:502-03; **45**:452
"The Happy Autumn Fields" (Bowen) **22**:64-66, 68; **118**:103, 111, 113-15
"Happy Birthday" (Bambara) **88**:12, 15, 46
"Happy Birthday" (Bidart) **33**:76
"Happy Birthday" (Lispector) **43**:268-69
Happy Birthday, Wanda June (Vonnegut)
See *Penelope*
A Happy Childhood (Matthews) **40**:323-25
"Happy Clouds" (Aleixandre)
See "Nube feliz"
"Happy Day" (Byrne) **26**:95
Happy Days (Beckett) **3**:45; **4**:51; **6**:36, 39, 43, 46-7; **9**:83, 85; **10**:29-34; **11**:33, 37-8; **14**:70-1, 80; **18**:43, 47-8; **57**:78-9, 109; **59**:252, 255; **83**:138
Happy Days (Marshall) **17**:275-78
Happy Days (Nash) **23**:317
Happy Days Are Here Again (Taylor) **27**:439-40
"A Happy Death" (Jennings) **131**:236
A Happy Death (Camus)
See *La mort heureuse*
"Happy Diwali" (Hospital) **145**:312

"Happy Ending" (Beer) **58**:31
Happy Ending (Ward) **19**:456-57
Happy Endings Are All Alike (Scoppettone) **26**:402-03
"Happy Enough" (Johnston) **51**:245-46, 248, 253-54
Happy Enough: Poems, 1935-1972 (Johnston) **51**:245-48, 250, 252-54
Happy Families (Maloff) **5**:270-71
"A Happy Family" (Trevor) **116**:361, 371
The Happy Family (Swinnerton) **31**:423
"The Happy Farmer" (Thomas) **107**:338, 340, 342
"Happy Feet" (Martin) **30**:246
Happy for the Child (Jenkins) **52**:219-20, 222, 225
The Happy Foreigner (Bagnold) **25**:71-2
"A Happy Ghost" (Johnston) **51**:240
The Happy Girls (Vollmann) **89**:302, 304
The Happy Haven (Arden) **6**:4-6, 8-9; **13**:23, 29
"The Happy Highway" (Phillips) **28**:362
Happy Homecoming (Condé)
See *Hérémakhonon: On doit attendre le bonheur*
The Happy Island (Powell) **66**:354-55, 369
Happy Jack (Townshend) **17**:530, 534
The Happy Journey to Trenton and Camden (Wilder) **6**:577; **10**:531-32; **35**:441, 446; **82**:352, 363-64, 387
Happy Lies (Taylor) **27**:445
The Happy Man (Hall) **59**:152-54; **151**:181-82, 193, 197-98, 204, 213
The Happy Marriage, and Other Poems (MacLeish) **8**:359; **68**:270, 272, 277
"Happy New Year" (Auden) **43**:16
"The Happy Onion" (Oates) **6**:370
The Happy Return (Forester)
See *Beat to Quarters*
"The Happy Three" (Roethke) **46**:364; **101**:332-33
Happy to Be Here: Stories and Comic Pieces (Keillor) **40**:273-74
"Happy Together" (Weller) **26**:447
Happy Valley (White) **5**:486; **7**:530-32; **65**:275, 277, 279; **69**:392-96, 399, 407
"A Happy View" (Day Lewis) **10**:131
"The Happy Warrior" (Read) **4**:439
The Happy Warriors (Laxness)
See *Gerpla*
"The Happy Worrier" (Simmons) **43**:413
"Happy Xmas" (Lennon) **35**:270-71
"Hapworth 16, 1924" (Salinger) **8**:463; **12**:518; **138**:182, 201, 216
Harafish (Mahfouz)
See *Malhamat al-Harafish*
Harald (Haavikko) **34**:173
The Harangues (Walker) **19**:454-55
"The Harbor at Seattle" (Hass) **99**:141
"The Harbour" (Walcott) **76**:278, 280
"The Harbour in the Evening" (Paulin) **37**:353
"Hard and Soft" (Laughlin) **49**:220, 222-23
The Hard Blue Sky (Grau) **4**:207; **146**:122, 128, 133-34, 138-39, 142, 146-47, 151, 161-62
Hard Candy (Vachss) **106**:359-61, 365
Hard Candy: A Book of Stories (Williams) **45**:447
"The Hard Core of Beauty" (Williams) **42**:456
"The Hard Core of Love" (Livesay) **79**:347
"Hard Daddy" (Hughes) **108**:329
A Hard Day's Night (Lennon and McCartney) **12**:356, 359, 375; **35**:293
A Hard Day's Night (Lester) **20**:218-19, 228
"A Hard Death" (Sarton) **91**:244
Hard Facts: Excerpts (Baraka) **10**:21; **33**:58; **115**:27, 39
Hard Feelings (King) **8**:322
Hard Freight (Wright) **6**:579-81; **13**:612, 614; **146**:304-06, 312, 321, 326, 330-31, 333, 373-74, 379
The Hard Hours (Hecht) **8**:268; **13**:269; **19**:207-08
The Hard Life: An Exegesis of Squalor (O'Brien) **1**:252; **4**:383; **7**:270; **10**:364; **47**:313-14, 316, 320
Hard Lines (Nash) **23**:316-17
Hard Loving (Piercy) **3**:384; **18**:406; **27**:375; **62**:376; **128**:229, 244, 246
Hard Nose the Highway (Morrison) **21**:234, 236, 238
Hard Rain (Dorfman)
See *Moros en la costa*
Hard Rain (van de Wetering) **47**:412-13
Hard Rain Falling (Carpenter) **41**:100-03
"A Hard Rain's A-Gonna Fall" (Dylan) **4**:149; **12**:189; **77**:164, 184, 187
"Hard Riding" (McNickle) **89**:182-83
"Hard Road to Travel" (Cliff) **21**:60
"Hard Rock Returns to Prison" (Knight) **40**:286
"A Hard Row to Hoe" (Garrett) **51**:140
"Hard Sell" (Boyle) **90**:45, 48
"Hard Time" (Piercy) **62**:378
Hard Times: An Oral History of the Great Depression (Terkel) **38**:420-25, 428
Hard to Be a God (Strugatskii and Strugatskii) **27**:432-37
"Hard Traveling" (Guthrie) **35**:185, 190, 193
A Hard Winter (Queneau)
See *Un rude hiver*
Hard Words, and Other Poems (Le Guin) **45**:212-13, 216
Hard-Boiled Wonderland and the End of the World (Murakami)
See *Sekai no owari to hādoboirudo wandārando*
"Hardcastle Crags" (Plath) **11**:446; **17**:367; **111**:200, 202, 206
Hardcore (Schrader) **26**:392-96, 398-99
Hardcore (Thompson) **69**:382-83
Hardcover (Shammas) **55**:86
The Harder They Come (Cliff) **21**:61, 63-4
The Harder They Come (Thelwell) **22**:415-16
The Harder They Fall (Schulberg) **7**:402; **48**:350
"Hardest It Is" (Scott) **22**:372
"Hardham" (Blunden) **56**:49
"Hard-Luck Stories" (Munro) **95**:315-19
"Hardly Ever" (Boyd) **28**:38
"Hardship aboard American Sloop the Peggy, 1765" (Reading) **47**:351
Hardwater Country (Busch) **18**:84-5
"Hardweed Path Going" (Ammons) **108**:4
"Hardy and the Hag" (Fowles) **87**:178-80
"The Hardys" (Humphrey) **45**:203
"Hare" (Clarke) **61**:79
Hare and Hornbill (p'Bitek) **96**:278, 301
"The Hare and the Tortoise" (Seth) **90**:353
The Harlan Ellison Hornbook (Ellison) **139**:129, 134, 137
Harlan Ellison's Movie (Ellison) **139**:129
Harlan Ellison's Watching (Ellison) **139**:126, 129, 134
"Harlem" (Hughes) **108**:333
"Harlem" (Tolson) **105**:281
The Harlem Book of the Dead (Dodson) **79**:196
Harlem Gallery: Book I, The Curator (Tolson) **36**:426-28, 430-31; **105**:234-35, 240-42, 244-45, 247-50, 253-58, 262-66, 269-72, 274-77, 279-88, 290, 292, 294
"A Harlem Game" (Dumas) **6**:145; **62**:150, 154, 161
"The Harlem Ghetto" (Baldwin) **2**:32; **42**:16, 20-2; **127**:141
"The Harlem Group of Negro Writers" (Tolson) **105**:280
"Harlem Hopscotch" (Angelou) **77**:28-9
"Harlem Montana: Just Off the Reservation" (Welch) **52**:429
Harlem Quartet (Baldwin) **127**:100
"A Harlequin" (Tanizaki)
See "Hokan"
Harlequin (Fo) **109**:129-34
Harlequin (West) **6**:564-65
"The Harlequin Tea Set" (Christie) **110**:128
"Harlequinette" (Tournier) **95**:379
"Harlequin's Lane" (Christie) **110**:128
Harlequin's Stick—Charlie's Cane (Madden) **15**:350
"Harley Talking" (Hood) **28**:189
Harlot's Ghost (Mailer) **74**:231, 233-34, 236-37, 240, 242-43, 245-46; **111**:134-38
"Harm" (Williams) **148**:345-48
L'harmattan (Ousmane) **66**:334
"Harmony" (Kauffman) **42**:251-52
"Harmony of the World" (Baxter) **45**:50-2
Harmony of the World (Baxter) **45**:50-2; **78**:16-17, 19, 21-22, 25-7, 32
Harm's Way (Wellman) **65**:242
"The Harness" (Steinbeck) **45**:382
Harold Muggins Is a Martyr (Arden) **15**:21
Harold of Orange (Vizenor) **103**:298, 302, 321, 341
Harold Urey: The Man Who Explored from Earth to Moon (Silverstein and Silverstein) **17**:452
Harold's Leap (Smith) **25**:420
Haroun and the Sea of Stories (Rushdie) **100**:287, 301, 315
The Harp and the Shadow (Carpentier)
See *El arpa y la sombra*
"Harp, Anvil, Oar" (Graves) **39**:326
Harp of a Thousand Strings (Davis) **49**:83-5, 89-90, 96-7
"The Harp of Wales" (Williams) **45**:443
"Harper's Bazaar" (Findley) **102**:97
"Harpers Ferry" (Rich) **73**:330-32
The Harpoon Gun and Other Stories (Vassilikos)
See *Le fusil-harpon et autres nouvelles*
"Harriet" (Lorde) **71**:241
Harriet (Kazan) **63**:225, 234
Harriet Hume (West) **31**:454, 457, 459
Harriet Said (Bainbridge) **4**:39; **5**:39-40; **8**:37; **10**:16; **18**:34; **22**:44-5; **62**:24, 30; **130**:5-8, 20, 34
"The Harris Fetko Story" (Chabon) **149**:25
"Harrison Bergeron" (Vonnegut) **12**:617
Harrison, Texas (Foote) **51**:130
Harris's Requiem (Middleton) **38**:332
"The Harrow" (Davie) **31**:116
"Harrow Street at Linden" (Oates) **52**:331
"Harry" (Newlove) **14**:378
"Harry and Barney" (Farrell) **66**:127
"Harry and Violet" (Thomas) **37**:419, 422; **107**:327
Harry Dernier: A Play for Radio Production (Walcott) **25**:453
Harry, Noon and Night (Ribman) **7**:357
Harry Potter and the Chamber of Secrets (Rowling) **137**:306-08, 310, 313-14, 323, 326-27, 331, 333, 337
Harry Potter and the Goblet of Fire (Rowling) **137**:332-38, 340-41
Harry Potter and the Philosopher's Stone (Rowling) **137**:306, 308-10, 313-15, 318, 322, 326-29, 331, 333, 337, 339
Harry Potter and the Prisoner of Azkaban (Rowling) **137**:310-13, 315, 318, 323, 326, 328, 331-33, 336-37
Harry Potter and the Sorcerer's Stone (Rowling)
See *Harry Potter and the Philosopher's Stone*
"Harry's Death" (Carver) **36**:106
"Harsh Climate" (Simic) **22**:383
"The Harsh Judgment" (Kunitz) **148**:88, 101
The Harsh Voice (West) **31**:453-54, 457; **50**:405-06
"Hart Crane" (Creeley) **36**:120
"The Hartford Girl" (Selzer) **74**:261
Hart-Lam (Breytenbach) **126**:94
"The Hartleys" (Cheever) **15**:129
Hart's Hope (Card) **47**:68-9
Haruka/Love Poems (Jordan) **114**:153-55
"Harv Is Plowing Now" (Updike) **15**:543; **139**:338

Harvard Anthology of Contemporary American Poetry (Vendler) **138**:273
Harvard Book of Contemporary American Poetry (Vendler) **138**:254, 260
Harvard Diaries (Coles) **108**:194
"Harvard Yard in April: April in Harvard Yard" (Richards) **14**:453-54
"Harvest" (Blunden) **56**:38
"Harvest" (Fowles) **15**:232
"Harvest" (Matthews) **40**:321
"Harvest" (p'Bitek) **96**:299
"Harvest" (Sitwell) **67**:319
"Harvest" (Soto) **80**:286
"Harvest" (Voigt) **54**:428
"Harvest" (Young) **17**:582
Harvest (Young) **17**:570, 572, 574, 577-80, 583
"Harvest at Mynachlog" (Clarke) **61**:74, 79, 81-3
"The Harvest Bow" (Heaney) **14**:246; **25**:243-44, 246-47, 250; **37**:164; **74**:165, 177, 195
Harvest Comedy (Swinnerton) **31**:426
"Harvest for Bergson" (Graham) **118**:224
"Harvest Home" (Baxter) **78**:25
Harvest Home (Tryon) **3**:483-84; **11**:548
"Harvest Hymn" (Betjeman) **43**:45-6
"The Harvest Knot" (Heaney)
See "The Harvest Bow"
The Harvest of a Life (Sillanpaa)
See *Erään elämän Sotoa*
Harvest of Youth (Stuart) **8**:507; **34**:373, 375-76
Harvest on the Don (Sholokhov) **7**:418
"Harvest Song" (Toomer) **4**:549-50; **22**:424
"Has Pinochle Lost Its Whack?" (Royko) **109**:406
"The Hashish-Eater; or, The Apocalypse of Evil" (Smith) **43**:416, 418
"Hasidic Tales" (Allen) **52**:35, 45
"Haskell's Mill" (Davison) **28**:103
"Hassan in England" (Forster) **45**:133
Hasta no verte, Jesús mío (Poniatowska) **140**:294, 97, 299, 304, 309, 313-14, 319-21, 327, 330-31, 338
"The Hat Act" (Coover) **3**:113; **7**:58; **15**:145; **46**:116
"The Hat Factory" (Durcan) **43**:113
"Hate and War" (Clash) **30**:44
"Hate Blows a Bubble of Despair into" (Cummings) **68**:44
"Hateful" (Clash) **30**:46-7
Hatfield, the Rainmaker (Ringwood) **48**:329-30, 333, 335-38
Hath Not a Jew (Klein) **19**:260-61
"Hatred of Men with Black Hair" (Bly) **10**:55; **128**:6, 22
Hatter's Castle (Cronin) **32**:128-33, 140
The Hatter's Phantoms (Simenon) **8**:487
"A Haul" (Heaney) **74**:197
"The Haulier's Wife" (Durcan) **43**:118
"Haunted" (Sassoon) **130**:176
"The Haunted Armchair" (Redgrove) **41**:348, 351
"The Haunted Boy" (McCullers) **12**:433
The Haunted Earth (Koontz) **78**:200
"Haunted House" (Graves) **45**:166-67
Haunted Houses (Kettelkamp) **12**:305
The Haunted Land (Stow) **23**:432
"Haunted Landscape" (Ashbery) **15**:34; **25**:53
The Haunted Mesa (L'Amour) **55**:307-08
The Haunted Mountain (Hunter) **21**:159, 162
"Haunting" (Simon) **26**:411
The Haunting of Hill House (Jackson) **11**:302; **60**:211, 216-17, 220, 229, 234-35
The Haunting of Julia (Straub) **107**:288
"Hauptstädtisches Journal" (Boell) **72**:68, 72
"Ein Haus aus lauter Liebe" (Lenz) **27**:245
Haus ohne Hüter (Boell) **6**:83; **11**:52, 57-8; **72**:72
Der Hausierer (Handke) **5**:163; **134**:128, 130
Hausipungo (Arguedas) **18**:7
Hausmusik (Neruda) **2**:309
Haussuchung (Lenz) **27**:246
Haute surveillance (Genet) **2**:158; **10**:225; **14**:198, 201; **44**:385-87, 390; **46**:173
"Havana Dreams" (Hughes) **108**:324
The Havana Inquiry (Enzensberger)
See *Das Verhör von Habana*
"Havana Moon" (Berry) **17**:56
Havana Treatises (Lezama Lima)
See *Tratados en la habana*
"Have a Cigar" (Pink Floyd) **35**:307-08
"Have a Cuppa Tea" (Davies) **21**:92
"Have a Good Rest" (Nagy) **7**:251
"Have a Good Time" (Simon) **17**:465
"Have a Havana" (Cabrera Infante) **120**:75
"Have a Talk with God" (Wonder) **12**:660, 664
"Have a Wonderful Nice Walk" (Gilchrist) **143**:309
"H'ave Caesar; or, Boadicea's Revenge" (Nash) **23**:323
Have I Ever Lied to You? (Buchwald) **33**:92
"Have I Got a Chocolate Bar for You!" (Bradbury) **42**:35
"Have I Outgrown You?" (Miles) **14**:369
"Have Mercy Judge" (Berry) **17**:55
Have Space Suit—Will Travel (Heinlein) **3**:225; **14**:249-51; **26**:161-62, 165, 173, 177
Have the Men Had Enough? (Forster) **149**:75-6, 78, 81
"have you ever kissed a panther" (Bukowski) **108**:74
"Have You Forgotten" (Moss) **45**:289
"Have You Seen Me?" (Graver) **70**:49, 52-3
"Have You Seen Me?" (Van Duyn) **116**:430-31
Have You Seen Me? (Graver) **70**:48-54
"Have You Seen Your Mother, Baby" (Jagger and Richard) **17**:235
Haven in a Heartless World (Lasch) **102**:293, 301, 327
Haven's End (Marquand) **10**:330
"Haven't Got Time for the Pain" (Simon) **26**:408-09, 411
"Having Been Asked 'What Is a Man?' I Answer" (Levine) **33**:273-74; **118**:279
"Having Fallen into Place" (Fisher) **87**:122
"Having No Ear" (Davie) **31**:124-25
"Having Replaced Love with Food and Drink: A Poem for Those Who've Reached Forty" (Wakoski) **40**:455
"Having the Human Thing of Joy" (Abbott) **48**:5, 7
"The Haw Lantern" (Heaney) **74**:176-77
The Haw Lantern (Heaney) **74**:160-62, 172-75, 183, 186, 189-92, 194; **91**:122, 124
Hawaii (Michener) **5**:289-90; **11**:375; **29**:311; **60**:260-61; **109**:375-81, 383, 385-86, 388
"Hawaii Dantesca" (Wright) **146**:338
Hawaii: The Sugar-Coated Fortress (Gray) **22**:201; **153**:138
"The Hawk" (Ciardi) **40**:157
"Hawk" (Oliver) **98**:288
"Hawk" (Williams) **148**:357, 360
"The Hawk in the Rain" (Hughes) **14**:270
The Hawk in the Rain (Hughes) **2**:197-98, 201-02; **4**:235-37; **9**:281-82, 284-85; **14**:269-70; **37**:171, 175; **119**:248, 251, 258, 265, 288, 290
The Hawk Is Dying (Crews) **6**:118; **23**:133, 138; **49**:73, 76, 79
"The Hawk Is Flying" (Crews) **49**:73
"The Hawk Is Hungry" (McNickle) **89**:183
The Hawk Is Hungry, and Other Stories (McNickle) **89**:179
Hawk Moon (Shepard) **4**:490
"Hawk on the Wind" (Derleth) **31**:130-31, 133
"Hawk Roosting" (Hughes) **4**:235; **119**:261, 271
The Hawk that Dare Not Hunt by Day (O'Dell) **30**:273
"Hawkfall" (Brown) **48**:55, 60
Hawkfall and Other Stories (Brown) **48**:55; **100**:84
The Hawkline Monster: A Gothic Western (Brautigan) **5**:70-2; **12**:70; **34**:315, 317; **42**:50, 56-8, 60
Hawkmistress! (Bradley) **30**:29, 32
The Hawks and the Sparrows (Pasolini)
See *Uccellacci e uccellini*
"The Hawk's Cry in Autumn" (Brodsky) **100**:43-4, 67
"A Hawk's Cry in Winter" (Brodsky) **100**:47
Hawks, Doves, and the Eagle (Archer) **12**:17
"Hawk's Shadow" (Glück) **44**:216, 218
"Hawksbill Station" (Silverberg) **140**:377-78
Hawksbill Station (Silverberg) **140**:364
Hawksmoor (Ackroyd) **52**:6-15; **140**:3-8, 14, 18-19, 22-24, 29, 32-33, 36-37, 39-42, 44-48, 50-52, 57, 65, 69
"The Hawthorn Hedge" (Wright) **53**:416, 427
"The Hawthorn Tree" (Glück) **81**:168
"The Hawthorn Tree" (Sassoon) **130**:186, 221
"Hawthorn Trees in Spring: A Lament of Women" (Christie) **110**:127
"Hawthorne" (Lowell) **8**:351
"Hawthorne in Our Time" (Trilling) **11**:547
Haxby's Circus: The Lightest, Brightest Little Show on Earth (Prichard) **46**:329-32, 337, 341
"Hay Fever" (Hope) **51**:227
Hay Fever (Coward) **1**:64; **9**:172; **29**:131, 133, 135, 137, 139; **51**:69-70, 73-5, 77
"Hay for the Horses" (Snyder) **120**:354
Hay que sonreír (Valenzuela) **31**:438-40; **104**:356, 387
"Hay que tené boluntá" (Guillén) **79**:246
"Hayat l'l-ghayr" (Mahfouz) **153**:352
Haydn and the Valve Trumpet (Raine) **103**:202-04
Hayduke Lives (Abbey) **59**:238, 245
"The Hayfield" (Bowering) **47**:24
"Hayfork Point" (Murray) **40**:335
"Haying before Storm" (Rukeyser) **27**:408
The Hazard and the Gift (McAuley) **45**:253
Hazard, the Painter (Meredith) **13**:372-73; **22**:303; **55**:193
"Hazardous Occupations" (Sandburg) **10**:450
The Hazards of Holiness (Everson) **5**:121; **14**:166
"Hazard's Optimism" (Meredith) **13**:373; **55**:192
Hazarski recnik (Pavic) **60**:282-90
"Haze" (Sandburg) **35**:352
"Hazel" (Shields) **113**:408
"Hazel" (Wideman) **122**:289
"A Hazel Stick for Catherine Ann" (Heaney) **37**:165; **74**:167
Ha-Zeman (Amichai) **22**:31-2; **116**:95, 97-9
"A Hazy Shade of Winter" (Simon) **17**:463
"H.D." (Duncan) **41**:128
H.D. Book (Duncan) **55**:291
"He" (Ashbery) **15**:27
"He" (Ferlinghetti) **10**:175; **111**:65
"He" (Josipovici) **153**:209
"He" (Porter) **7**:317; **101**:209-10
"He and I" (Ginzburg) **54**:208
"He and It" (Stevenson) **33**:382-83
"He and the Cat" (Mphahlele) **25**:344
"He Beats His Women" (Bukowski) **108**:84
"He 'Digesteth Harde Yron'" (Moore) **10**:347; **47**:262, 267
"He Don't Plant Cotton" (Powers) **1**:282
"He Held Radical Light" (Ammons) **9**:27; **57**:59
"He Hoho" (Hulme) **130**:44
"He Is a Strange Biological Phenomenon" (Atwood) **25**:67
"He Is Last Seen" (Atwood) **25**:67
"He Kept on Burning" (Ai) **69**:7
"He Knew" (Himes) **58**:265
He Left Home (Rozewicz)
See *Wyszedł z domu*
"He Loves Me, He Loves Me Not" (Achebe) **26**:21
"He na tye Woman" (Allen) **84**:4
"He of the Assembly" (Bowles) **53**:41
"He Reappears" (Atwood) **25**:67
"He Resigns" (Berryman) **8**:93; **13**:83; **25**:95-6; **62**:46

"He Sees Through Stone" (Knight) **40**:279, 281, 286
He/She (Gold) **42**:193-94; **152**:121, 126, 138
He, She, and It (Piercy) **128**:248-49, 256, 259-62
"He Shuttles" (Sturgeon) **22**:410
"He Tauware Kawa, He Kawa Tauware" (Hulme) **130**:48
"He Tears Easily . . ." (Rozewicz) **9**:465
"He that None could Capture" (Swenson) **106**:337
"He Was Such a Nice Chap—Why Did He Do It?" (Brunner) **8**:110
He Who Hunted Birds in His Father's Village: The Dimensions of a Haida Myth (Snyder) **32**:393
He Who Lived His Life Over Again (Lagerkvist)
See *Han som fik leva om sitt liv*
He Who Lives in the Truth (Mahfouz)
See *Al 'A'ish fi-al-haqiqah*
He Who Must Die (Capra) **16**:157
He Who Searches (Valenzuela)
See *Como en la guerra*
"He Who Shapes" (Zelazny) **21**:467, 479
"he wrote in lovely blood" (Bukowski) **108**:75
"The Head" (Phillips) **28**:363-64
"Head" (Prince) **35**:323-25
Head above Water (Emecheta) **48**:101;
Head and Heart (Guillén)
See *Cerebro y corazón*
Head Comix (Crumb) **17**:82
The Head, Guts and Soundbone Dance (Cook) **58**:149-50, 154-58
"Head Hewn with an Axe" (Tomlinson) **13**:546
Head in the Clouds (Troyat) **23**:461
The Head in the Soup (Levi) **41**:246
"Head in the void" (Rozewicz) **139**:273
Head o' W-Hollow (Stuart) **14**:513; **34**:373, 376
"Head of a Girl, at the Met" (Updike) **43**:436
"The Head of Babylon" (Barnes) **29**:32
"The Head of Joaquín Murrieta" (Rodriguez) **155**:254
"The Head of the Bed" (Hollander) **5**:187; **8**:300, 302; **14**:264
"The Head on the Pole" (Neruda) **1**:247
Head over Heels (Silver) **20**:345-46
Head over Wheels (Kingman) **17**:247
Head to Toe (Orton) **43**:325, 328, 330
"The Head Transplant" (Durcan) **43**:113
"The Headache" (Gibbons) **145**:150
Headbirths; or, The Germans Are Dying Out (Grass) **32**:202-05; **49**:142
Headed for the Blues (Škvorecký) **152**:337, 339
Headhunter (Findley) **102**:117-18, 121
"Heading for Nandi" (Updike) **23**:476
"Heading Home" (Campbell) **93**:106
"Heading Home" (Endō) **99**:297, 307
Heading Home (Hare) **136**:279-80, 282-83
Heading West (Betts) **28**:35-6
The Headless Cupid (Snyder) **17**:471-72
"The Headless Hawk" (Capote) **13**:133-34, 136, 140; **38**:81; **58**:86
Headman (Platt) **26**:351-52, 355
"The Headmaster" (McPhee) **36**:296-97
"The Head-Rape" (Thomas) **13**:541
Heads (Brenton) **31**:57
"Heads Float about Me" (Peake) **54**:369
"Heads in the Women's Ward" (Larkin) **64**:264
"Heads of Houses" (Taylor) **37**:413
The Heads of the Town up to the Aether (Spicer) **8**:498; **18**:510; **72**:348, 350, 357
Heads You Win, Tails I Lose (Holland) **21**:148
"Headwaiter" (Himes) **108**:235, 241
"Headwaters" (Momaday) **85**:233, 266, 277
Healer (Dickinson) **35**:136, 138
The Healer (Slaughter) **29**:375
The Healers (Armah) **33**:29, 32-4; **136**:3, 7-8, 11-12, 18, 21, 26, 36-38, 40-42, 52, 56-57, 60-68, 70, 73
The Healing (Jones) **131**:339-42
"Healing Animal" (Harjo) **83**:275
The Healing Art (Wilson) **33**:452
The Healing Arts (Kettelkamp) **12**:308
"The Healing of Mis" (Clarke) **6**:112
"Healing Our Wounds: Liberatory Mental Health Care" (Hooks) **94**:159
Health (Altman) **116**:59
"The Health of the Sick" (Cortázar) **5**:110
A Health unto His Majesty (Hibbert) **7**:156
"The Healthiest Girl in Town" (Stafford) **7**:457; **68**:423, 431, 449
"Healthy Kate" (Markson) **67**:193
Hear and Forgive (Humphreys) **47**:178, 185, 187
"Hear Me" (Levine) **118**:285, 300
Hear, My Country, My Affliction (Arrabal)
See *Oye, patria, mi aflicción*
Hear That Lonesome Whistle Blow: Railroads of the West (Brown) **47**:38-9
"Hear the Dogs Barking" (Rulfo)
See "No oyes ladrar los perros"
"Hear the Voice of the Bard" (Ewart) **46**:153
Hear the Wind Blow! (Beecher) **6**:48
Hear the Wind Sing (Murakami)
See *Kaze no uta o kike*
"Hear Us O Lord and the Orpheus Occasion" (Kroetsch) **132**:220
"Heard by a Girl" (Bogan) **46**:83; **93**:64
"Hearing" (Merwin) **45**:274
Hearing (Page) **40**:350-51
"Hearing 'Here': Robert Creeley's Poetics of Duration" (Bernstein) **142**:9
"Hearing of the End of the War" (Tillinghast) **29**:416
Hearing Secret Harmonies (Powell) **7**:338-41, 343-45; **9**:435-38; **10**:416-17; **31**:320
"Hearing Steps" (Simic) **68**:364
"The Hearse" (Tchicaya)
See "Le Corbillard"
"The Heart" (Merwin) **88**:205
"Heart" (Seth) **90**:350
The Heart (Ichikawa) **20**:181-82
"Heart and Mind" (Sitwell) **67**:320
"Heart and Soul" (Giles) **39**:64
"Heart Believes with Blows" (Broumas) **73**:9
Heart Disease (Silverstein and Silverstein) **17**:455
A Heart for the Gods of Mexico (Aiken) **52**:25
The Heart Hears Songs of Home (Vesaas)
See *Hjarta høyrer sine heimlandstonar*
"Heart in My Eye" (Bernstein) **142**:29
The Heart Is a Lonely Hunter (McCullers) **1**:207-09; **4**:345-46; **10**:335-36, 338-40; **12**:408-09, 412-14, 422-28, 430, 432; **48**:230-31, 234-35, 237-38, 240; **100**:240-41, 245-49, 251, 254, 256, 258-60, 264, 268, 272
"The Heart Never Fits Its Wanting" (Abbott) **48**:3
The Heart Never Fits Its Wanting (Abbott) **48**:3
"Heart of a Champion" (Boyle) **36**:57; **90**:63
"Heart of a Dybbuk" (Shields) **97**:431, 433
"The Heart of a King" (Plomer) **4**:406
The Heart of a Woman (Angelou) **35**:30-2; **64**:24-5, 27, 33, 36, 39; **77**:4-7, 13-5, 18, 22, 26-7
The Heart of Another (Gellhorn) **60**:179-181, 191
"Heart of Autumn" (Warren) **13**:582; **18**:534; **39**:258, 266; **59**:297
Heart of Aztlan (Anaya) **23**:25-6; **148**:6-9, 11, 13-14, 19, 27, 30-35, 39, 44
Heart of Glass (Herzog) **16**:328, 331, 333
"Heart of Gold" (Lavin) **99**:321
"Heart of Gold" (Young) **17**:571
"The Heart of Hialmar" (Walker) **13**:566
"The Heart of the Artichoke" (Gold) **152**:124, 138, 144
"Heart of the Backlog" (Warren) **18**:537
Heart of the Comet (Benford) **52**:74-7
"Heart of the Country" (McCartney) **35**:279
Heart of the Country (Matthews) **45**:243-44
The Heart of the Country (Weldon) **59**:229-34; **122**:258-59
"The Heart of the Game" (McGuane) **127**:289
The Heart of the Matter (Greene) **1**:131-33, 135; **3**:206, 209-10, 213-14; **6**:213, 216-20; **9**:244, 250-51; **14**:216-18; **27**:173; **37**:136, 140; **70**:289-91, 293-95; **72**:148-49, 151-52, 155, 177-78; **125**:187-92, 194, 209
Heart of the Night (Mahfouz)
See *Qalb allayl*
Heart of the River (Slaughter) **56**:410
"The Heart of Thomas Hardy" (Betjeman) **43**:34, 44
"The Heart on the Water" (Pasolini) **106**:260
Heart Songs, and Other Stories (Proulx) **81**:275
"Heart to Hang Onto" (Townshend) **17**:537
"Heartache" (Townshend) **17**:528, 531
"Heartbeat" (Harjo) **83**:271
Heartbreak (Aragon)
See *Le crève-coeur*
The Heartbreak Kid (May) **16**:432-37
Heartbreak Tango (Puig)
See *Boquitas pintadas, folletín*
"Heartbreaker" (Jagger and Richard)
See "Doo Doo Doo Doo Doo"
"Heartbreaker" (Page and Plant) **12**:474
Heartbreaks along the Road (Carrier)
See *De l'amour dans la ferraille*
"Heartburn" (Calisher) **38**:67
"Heartburn" (Taylor) **44**:302
Heartburn (Ephron) **31**:157-59
"The Hearth" (Arghezi)
See "Gura vetrei"
The Heartkeeper (Sagan) **17**:425-26
"Heartland" (Hogan) **73**:150
"Heartland" (Phillips) **96**:321-22, 326
Heartland (Harris) **25**:204, 214
Heartland (Maloff) **5**:271
Heartlight (Diamond) **30**:114
"The Hearts" (Pinsky) **94**:306, 310; **121**:428, 434, 437-38
"The Heart's Advantage" (Shacochis) **39**:199
The Hearts and Lives of Men (Weldon) **122**:257-59
"The Heart's Garden/The Garden's Heart" (Rexroth) **49**:276, 279; **112**:386, 402
The Heart's Garden/The Garden's Heart (Rexroth) **2**:370; **6**:450; **22**:347-49; **49**:278; **112**:372-73, 387
The Heart's Journey (Sassoon) **36**:392; **130**:193
"Heart's Needle" (Snodgrass) **6**:514; **18**:494; **68**:383, 388, 390, 395-96
Heart's Needle (Snodgrass) **2**:404-06; **6**:513-14; **18**:490-92; **68**:382-83, 387-88, 390-92, 395-98
The Hearts of Men: American Dreams and the Flight from Commitment (Ehrenreich) **110**:156, 161, 165, 176-77
"Hearts of Oak and Bellies of Brass" (McGahern) **48**:263, 266-68
"Hearts Together" (Betjeman) **43**:48
Heartsease (Dickinson) **12**:168, 170, 172-74
Heart-Shape in the Dust (Hayden) **37**:155-56, 160
Heartstones (Rendell) **48**:327
Heartway Guide (Tzara)
See *Indicateur des chemins de coeur*
"Heat" (H. D.)
See "Garden"
"Heat" (Johnson) **52**:232, 234
"Heat" (Moure) **88**:230
Heat (Goldman) **48**:130
Heat (Hunter) **31**:226
"Heat 2" (Moure) **88**:230
"Heat 3" (Moure) **88**:230
Heat and Dust (Jhabvala) **8**:311-12; **29**:259-60, 262-63; **94**:171, 174, 179, 183-89, 193-94, 196-99, 201-6, 212; **138**:45, 50, 52, 55, 57-9, 62-70, 78
Heat and Other Stories (Oates) **108**:374, 379, 383, 385
Heat Death (Dobyns) **37**:78-9

"The Heat Death of the Universe" (Zoline) **62**:460-64
The Heat Death of the Universe, and Other Stories (Zoline)
See *Busy about the Tree of Life*
"Heat Haze" (Weldon) **122**:282
"Heat Lightning" (Jiles) **58**:279
"Heat Lightning" (Smith) **25**:411
The Heat of the Day (Bowen) **1**:39; **3**:82; **11**:62-64; **15**:79-80; **118**:63, 81, 85, 88, 97
The Heat of the Sun: Stories and Tales (O'Faolain) **14**:404; **32**:340; **70**:319
"The Heat Rises in Gusts" (Stern) **40**:414
"Heat Wave Breaks" (Warren) **13**:582
Heathcliff and the Great Hunger (Eagleton) **132**:123-26, 130-34, 138
"The Heathen" (Marley) **17**:269-70
Heathen Valley (Linney) **51**:257
The Heat's On (Himes) **18**:246; **58**:258, 267; **108**:233, 236, 238-39, 268
"Heatwave/St. Louis" (Jiles) **58**:272, 280
"Heaven" (Byrne) **26**:98
"Heaven" (Gaitskill) **69**:199-200, 203
"Heaven" (Levine) **14**:317; **118**:275
Heaven (Barker) **37**:39
Heaven and Crap (Arrabal) **58**:17
"Heaven and Earth" (Glück) **81**:167
Heaven and Hell (Huxley) **4**:239, 241; **18**:270; **35**:241
"Heaven as Anus" (Kumin) **13**:326; **28**:224
"Heaven Help the Devil" (Lightfoot) **26**:283
"Heaven, in a Way" (Hall) **51**:173
Heaven, in a Way (Hall) **51**:172-73
"Heaven Is Ten Zillion Light Years Away" (Wonder) **12**:657
"Heaven is Under Our Feet" (McGuane) **127**:281
Heaven Knows Where (Enright) **31**:151-52
The Heaven Makers (Herbert) **12**:278; **35**:196, 198-99; **44**:393-94
"The Heaven of Animals" (Dickey) **1**:73; **7**:83
"Heaven on a Summer Night" (Beattie) **63**:18
Heaven on Earth (Elliott) **47**:108-10
"The Heavenly Animal" (Phillips) **15**:421
Heavenly Breakfast (Delany) **141**:142, 150, 160
"Heavenly City, Earthly City" (Duncan) **7**:88
The Heavenly Ladder (Mackenzie) **18**:314
Heaven's My Destination (Wilder) **1**:364, 366; **5**:496; **6**:575-77; **15**:572-73, 575; **82**:342-43, 345, 349, 365, 373-74, 376, 378
Heaven's Secret (Lagerkvist)
See *Himlens hemlighet*
Heavensgate (Okigbo) **25**:347, 349, 351, 354-55; **84**:299-302, 304, 306-07, 309, 313, 317-18, 321-22, 327, 330, 336-37
"The Heaviness of Clay" (Seifert) **93**:337
"The Heaviness of His Wisdom" (Berry) **46**:70
"The Heavy" (Ferlinghetti) **111**:65
"The Heavy Bear That Goes with Me" (Schwartz) **10**:462, 465; **45**:356
"Heavy Breathing" (Hughes) **108**:331
Heavy Breathing (Whalen) **29**:447
"Heavy Connection" (Morrison) **21**:237
Heavy Laden (Wylie) **43**:459-60, 462, 469
"Heavy Music" (Seger) **35**:378-81, 383, 386
Heavy Sand (Rybakov)
See *Heavy Sands*
Heavy Sands (Rybakov) **23**:370-74; **53**:295
"The Heavy Sugar" (Woolrich) **77**:402
Heavy Traffic (Bakshi) **26**:68-70, 73-5
"Heavy Women" (Plath) **5**:340; **111**:167
"The Hebrides" (Longley) **29**:293, 296
Hécate (Jouve) **47**:203
Hechima kun (Endō) **54**:159
The Heckler (Hunter) **31**:220
"Hector and Freddie" (Wilding) **73**:395, 398
"The Hector Quesadilla Story" (Boyle) **36**:63
"Hedge Tutor" (Fuller) **62**:203
"The Hedgeapple" (Bell) **31**:51
"The Hedgehog Killed on the Road" (Blunden) **56**:41
"Hedges in Winter" (Muldoon) **32**:317
Hedy (Warhol) **20**:422
Hedylus (H. D.) **31**:207-08, 210; **73**:112-13, 122-23, 131-33
Heed the Thunder (Thompson) **69**:383
The Heel of Achilles: Essays, 1968-1973 (Koestler) **6**:281
"Heemskerck Shoals" (FitzGerald) **19**:175, 179
The Heidi Chronicles (Wasserstein) **59**:218-27
The Heidi Chronicles, and Other Plays (Wasserstein) **90**:424-25, 427, 430-37, 439
"Heigh-Ho on a Winter Afternoon" (Davie) **5**:114
The Height of the Scream (Campbell) **42**:86, 88-90
"Heights of Folly" (Simic) **68**:377; **130**:318
The Heights of Macchu Picchu (Neruda)
See *Alturas de Macchu Picchu*
"The Heights of Trapua" (Cabral de Melo Neto)
See "Alto do Trapuá"
Das Heilige Experiment (Hochwälder) **36**:232-40
Heimatmuseum (Lenz) **27**:254-56
Heimkehr (Handke) **134**:164
Heimsljós (Laxness) **25**:293, 296, 299
"Heine Dying in Paris, I: Death and Morphine" (Lowell) **124**:256
Heine's Germany (Faludy) **42**:139
"The Heiress" (Akhmatova) **64**:13
"The Heiress of All the Ages" (Rahv) **24**:354
"Heirloom" (Spinrad) **46**:384
The Heirs of Columbus (Vizenor) **70**:348; **103**:312, 319-20, 334, 340
Heirs of Darkness (Snyder) **17**:475
"The Heirs of Stalin" (Yevtushenko)
See "Stalin's Heirs"
The Heirs of Stalin (Yevtushenko) **126**:393, 396, 398, 406
"Heirs of the Living Body" (Munro) **95**:300
"Hejira" (Mitchell) **12**:442
Hejira (Mitchell) **12**:440, 443
"The Helanders and the Moonies: A Family Story" (Harrison) **144**:107
"Hélas" (Creeley) **78**:134
Hélas (Simenon) **47**:374
"Heldensagen" (Hope) **51**:211
Held's Angels (Gilbreth and Carey) **17**:154
"Helen" (Elytis) **49**:110; **100**:172
"Helen" (Gustafson) **36**:222
"Helen" (H. D.) **73**:118
"Helen" (Hellman) **52**:201-02
"Helen" (Jeffers) **11**:305
"Helen" (Lowell) **1**:182
"Helen" (Wilbur) **14**:577; **110**:348
"Helen" (Williams) **148**:345-46, 348-49, 351
Helen (Fast) **131**:100
Helen (Ritsos) **13**:488
"Helen Grown Old" (Lewis) **41**:255
"Helen, I Love You" (Farrell) **66**:131
Helen in Egypt (H. D.) **3**:217; **8**:258; **14**:223, 230; **31**:204, 206-08, 211-12; **34**:442; **73**:121, 123-27, 139-41, 143
Helen of Troy, N.Y. (Connelly) **7**:56
"Helen, Thy Beauty Is to Me—" (Fante) **60**:133
"Helen Wheels" (McCartney) **35**:282
Helena (Waugh) **27**:470, 472; **44**:522-23; **107**:360, 367, 369-70
"Helen's Exile" (Camus) **2**:99
"Helicinas, Mollusles, and Wentletraps" (Dubie) **36**:135
"A Helicopter View of Terrestrial Stars" (Murray) **40**:336
Det heliga landet (Lagerkvist) **10**:312; **13**:332-33
"Heliodora" (H. D.) **31**:201; **73**:107, 120
Heliodora, and Other Poems (H. D.) **31**:208; **73**:107-10, 113, 120
"Heliogabalus" (Squires) **51**:379
Heliopolis (Jünger) **125**:223, 250-51, 259-61
"Hell" (Graves) **45**:165
"Hell" (Justice) **102**:281
"The Hell Cantos" (Pound) **112**:350-51, 356-57
Hell Has No Limits (Donoso)
See *El lugar sin límites*
Hell House (Matheson) **37**:247
A Hell of a Mess (Ionesco)
See *Ce formidable bordel!*
A Hell of a Woman (Thompson) **69**:379, 381, 383, 387, 389
Hell on Ice (Welles) **80**:379-80
"The Hell Poem" (Berryman) **62**:58
"Hellas Is Florida" (Benford) **52**:62
The Hellenic Secret (Strugatskii and Strugatskii) **27**:432
Heller in Pink Tights (L'Amour) **55**:306
"Hell-Fire" (Asimov) **26**:40
Hellfire (Saul) **46**:369
The Hellfire Club (Straub) **107**:301-04
Helliconia Spring (Aldiss) **40**:18-22
Helliconia Summer (Aldiss) **40**:19-22
Helliconia Winter (Aldiss) **40**:21-2
"Hello" (Corso) **11**:123
Hello (Creeley) **11**:139; **78**:140, 147
Hello: A Journal, February 29-May 3, 1976 (Creeley)
See *Hello*
"Hello Again" (Diamond) **30**:113
Hello America (Ballard) **36**:42; **137**:14, 43-47, 49-51, 58-59, 61, 69
Hello and Goodbye (Fugard) **5**:130; **9**:232-34; **14**:189; **40**:197, 201; **80**:62, 69, 74
"Hello Cheeverland, Goodbye" (Findley) **102**:100, 104, 108
"Hello, Dali" (Carroll) **143**:37
Hello, Darkness (Sissman) **18**:487, 489
"Hello, I Love You" (Morrison) **17**:290-91, 295
Hello, I'm Erica Jong (Acker) **111**:17
"Hello Mr. Soul" (Young) **17**:569, 577-78
"Hello, Mrs. Newman" (Levine) **54**:297
Hello, My Love, Goodbye (Weber) **12**:634
"Hello, Operator? I Don't Want a Policeman" (Perelman) **49**:258
Hello Out There (Saroyan) **10**:453; **56**:376
Hello...Wrong Number (Sachs) **35**:334
Hell's Angels: A Strange and Terrible Saga (Thompson) **9**:526; **17**:503-05, 510-11; **40**:426; **104**:337, 339, 343, 347-50
Hellstrom's Hive (Herbert) **12**:275-76; **35**:196; **44**:394
"The Helmet" (Levine) **118**:299
Helmet of Clay (Seifert) **34**:257; **93**:306, 319, 335, 343, 346
"Helmeted Boy" (Randall) **135**:386, 397
A Helmetful of Earth (Seifert)
See *Helmet of Clay*
Helmets (Dickey) **2**:117; **7**:80-1, 83-4; **109**:244
Helmets and Wasps (Mott) **15**:379
"The Helmsman" (Cunningham) **31**:97, 100, 102, 104
"The Helmsman" (H. D.) **73**:109
The Helmsman (Cunningham) **31**:96, 99
"The Helmsmen" (Merwin) **18**:334; **45**:277-78
Hèloïse (Hébert) **29**:239-41
"Help" (Lennon and McCartney) **35**:270, 274
"Help" (Tiptree) **48**:385
Help! (Lester) **20**:219-22
"Help, I'm a Rock" (Zappa) **17**:588
"Help Me, Rhonda" (Wilson) **12**:644, 647, 653
Help Stamp Out Marriage (Waterhouse)
See *Say Who You Are*
"Help Thou Mine Unbelief" (MacLennan) **92**:308, 330, 346
Help Wanted (Kroetz) **41**:241
"Help Your Child to Wonder" (Carson) **71**:104-05
"Helpful O'Malley" (Bainbridge) **62**:35-6, 38
"A Helping Hand" (Sansom) **6**:483
"Helpless" (Young) **17**:570, 574
Hemingway (Lynn) **50**:412-16, 418-20, 422-30
Hemingway: A Biography (Meyers) **39**:427-34
Hemingway at Midnight (Cowley) **39**:460
"Hemingway in Space" (Amis) **40**:43
Hemingway's First War (Reynolds) **44**:516-17
Hemligheter på vägen (Transtroemer) **52**:409-

10, 412; **65**:226, 229, 233-34, 236
"Hemlock" (Williams) **42**:442
Hemlock and After (Wilson) **2**:471, 473-74; **3**:535; **5**:513-14; **25**:459, 464; **34**:581
"Hemlocks" (Dorn) **10**:159
Hemmet och stjärnan (Lagerkvist) **54**:275
"The Hemorrhage" (Kunitz) **148**:87, 148
"The Hen" (Voigt) **54**:429
"The Hen Flower" (Kinnell) **3**:269; **29**:282; **129**:243, 252
"The Hen House" (Montague) **46**:267
"Hen Woman" (Kinsella) **138**:93, 101, 166
"Henceforth, from the Mind" (Bogan) **46**:84, 86-7, 89; **93**:61, 67, 69, 76, 81
Henceforward (Ayckbourn) **74**:19-20, 25, 31, 34-5
Henderson the Rain King (Bellow) **1**:28-31; **2**:49, 51, 53-4; **3**:48, 50, 53-9; **6**:53-5, 58, 60; **8**:69, 73-7, 79; **10**:44; **13**:71-3; **15**:47-9, 52, 54-5, 57; **25**:80-1, 85; **33**:66, 71; **34**:545; **63**:28, 32; **79**:76, 83
Hengest's Tale (Paton Walsh) **35**:429
Hennecke (Hein) **154**:176
Henri Christophe: A Chronicle in Seven Scenes (Walcott) **25**:453
Henri Matisse (Aragon) **22**:39
"Henrietta and Alexandra" (Barthelme) **46**:42
Henry Adams (Blackmur) **24**:66
Henry and Cato (Murdoch) **8**:405-06; **11**:384-85, 389-90; **31**:294
Henry and June (Nin) **127**:397, 399, 401-02
"Henry Bech Redux" (Updike) **5**:454
"Henry by Night" (Berryman) **13**:83; **25**:92
Henry Geldzahler (Warhol) **20**:415
"Henry James" (Nye) **42**:305
Henry James (West) **7**:525; **9**:560; **31**:450
"Henry James and His Cult" (Rahv) **24**:359
"Henry James as a Characteristic American" (Moore) **47**:268, 270
"Henry James by the Pacific" (Justice) **102**:277
Henry James: The Conquest of London, 1870-1881 (Edel) **29**:168-69
Henry James: The Master, 1901-1916 (Edel) **29**:171
Henry James: The Middle Years, 1882-1895 (Edel) **29**:168-69
Henry James: The Treacherous Years, 1895-1901 (Edel) **29**:169-70, 172
Henry James: The Untried Years, 1843-1870 (Edel) **29**:167
Henry Miller: Letters to Anaïs Nin (Miller) **84**:249
"Henry the Navigator" (McAuley) **45**:248
Henry Three (Krumgold) **12**:318-20
Henry V (Olivier) **20**:234-35, 237, 242-43
"Henry's Confession" (Berryman)
See "Dream Song 76"
"Henry's Fate" (Berryman) **8**:93
Henry's Fate and Other Poems, 1967-1972 (Berryman) **10**:46-8; **13**:83; **62**:43, 70, 74
"Henry's Understanding" (Berryman) **13**:83; **25**:92, 96
"A Hepcat May Look at a King" (Perelman) **49**:262
"Hephaestus" (Wilbur) **6**:570
"Heptonstall" (Hughes) **37**:178
"Heptonstall Graveyard, 22 October 1989" (Durcan) **70**:151-52
"Her" (Lessing) **94**:265
Her (Ferlinghetti) **2**:133; **10**:175, 177-78; **111**:59-66
Her (H. D.)
See *HERmione*
"Her and It" (Berryman) **25**:92
"Her Body, Mine, and His" (Allison) **153**:4
Her Brother (Ichikawa) **20**:182
"Her Dream House" (Bell) **8**:66
"Her Early Work" (Swenson) **106**:340-41
"Her Girls" (Ferber) **93**:162
"Her Hand" (Honig) **33**:213
"Her Hand Given Over" (Aleixandre) **36**:30
"Her Kind" (Sexton) **10**:468; **53**:314, 316, 318, 320, 324
"Her Long Illness" (Hall) **151**:223
"Her Longing" (Roethke) **101**:331
"Her Morning Dreams" (Fuller) **62**:187, 203
Her Mothers (Broner) **19**:71
Her Mother's Daughter (French) **60**:147-50
"Her Quaint Honor" (Gordon) **13**:248; **83**:231
"Her Report" (Ryan) **65**:215
"Her Reticence" (Roethke) **101**:331
"Her Second Career" (Rand) **79**:374
"Her Sense of Timing" (Elkin) **91**:217-19, 223
Her Side of It (Savage) **40**:376
"Her Smoke Rises Up Forever" (Tiptree) **48**:390, 392
"Her Strut" (Seger) **35**:384
"Her Sweet Jerome" (Walker) **58**:404; **103**:398, 406-07
"Her Table Spread" (Bowen) **3**:84; **22**:64-65; **118**:58-60, 97-98, 100
"Her Thighs" (Allison) **153**:25
"Her Three Days" (Ousmane) **66**:349
"Her Throat" (Wakoski) **2**:459
"Her Time" (Roethke) **101**:331
"Her Vertical Smile" (Kinsella) **138**:128
Her Victory (Sillitoe) **57**:396; **148**:159-60, 171-72, 175, 181, 184
"Her Voice Could Not Be Softer" (Clarke) **9**:168
"Her Whole Existence" (Himes) **108**:227
"Her Wisdom" (Merwin) **45**:269
"Her Words" (Roethke) **101**:331
"Her Wrath" (Roethke) **101**:266, 332-33
"Hera, Hung from the Sky" (Kizer) **80**:171, 184
"Heraclitus by the Lake" (Blaga) **75**:69
"Heraclitus on Rivers" (Mahon) **27**:292
"Herakleitos" (Davenport) **14**:140
Herakles (MacLeish) **3**:310; **8**:362; **14**:336-37
"Hera's Spring" (Thomas) **132**:381
"The Herb of Death" (Christie) **110**:144-45
L'herbe (Simon) **4**:495; **9**:482; **15**:485-86, 490-94; **39**:204-05, 207-10
Die Herberge (Hochwälder) **36**:238
"Herbert White" (Bidart) **33**:74, 76, 78
"Herbier de Bretagne" (Guillevic) **33**:193
Herbs and Apples (Santmyer) **33**:355-56
"Herbstmanöver" (Bachmann) **69**:38
"Herbsttag" (Hildesheimer) **49**:179
Hercule Poirot's Christmas (Christie) **48**:71, 73
"Hercules and Antaeus" (Heaney) **74**:158, 162
"Hercules, Deianira, Nessus" (Williams) **148**:362
Hercules, My Shipmate (Graves) **39**:322
A Herd of Deer (Dillon) **17**:98, 101
"The Herds" (Merwin) **88**:202
"Here" (Abse) **7**:2
"Here" (Creeley) **36**:121
"Here" (Larkin) **8**:332, 339; **9**:325; **18**:296-97, 301; **33**:260; **39**:341; **64**:266, 276, 279
"Here" (Monette) **82**:323
"Here and Elsewhere" (Walcott) **76**:275
"Here and Now" (Hospital) **145**:296, 316
"Here and Now" (Levine) **14**:321
Here and Now (Levertov) **28**:242; **66**:237-38
"Here and There" (Dunn) **36**:155
"Here and There" (Montale) **9**:387
"Here and There" (Wallace) **114**:347
"Here at Cubist College" (Grayson) **38**:210
Here at Eagle Pond (Hall) **151**:200, 213
"Here Be Dragons" (Baldwin) **42**:21
"Here Be Dragons" (Stevenson) **7**:463
"Here Be Monsters" (Baldwin) **127**:118
"Here, but Unable to Answer" (Hugo) **32**:250
"Here Come the Clowns—Didn't They?" (McGinley) **14**:367
"Here Come Those Tears Again" (Browne) **21**:38
Here Comes, and Other Poems (Jong) **6**:270; **83**:298
Here Comes Everybody: An Introduction to James Joyce for the Ordinary Reader (Burgess) **10**:86; **40**:122
Here Comes the Groom (Capra) **16**:160
"Here Comes the Maples" (Updike) **15**:546
"Here Comes the Night" (Wilson) **12**:653-54
"Here Comes the Weekend" (Weller) **26**:443-44
Here Comes There Goes (Saroyan) **56**:385
"Here Comes Yet Another Day" (Davies) **21**:94
"Here, Daphne!" (Masters) **48**:224
Here Endeth the Lesson (Bermant) **40**:92
"Here in the Night" (Jensen) **37**:186, 189
Here Is a Ghost (Abe)
See *Yurei wa koko ni iru*
"here is another bone to pick with you" (Clifton) **66**:83
Here Is Einbaum (Morris) **3**:344; **7**:247
"Here Is New York" (White) **39**:370, 377
"Here It Is" (Ignatow) **40**:260
"Here Lies a Lady" (Ransom) **4**:431
Here Lies Our Sovereign Lord (Hibbert) **7**:156
Here Lies: The Collected Stories of Dorothy Parker (Parker) **68**:327
Here, My Dear (Gaye) **26**:133-34
"Here Next the Chair I Was When Winter Went" (Graham) **29**:198
"Here on a Darkling Plain" (Derleth) **31**:133
"Here She Comes Now" (Reed) **21**:319
"Here the Legions Halted, Here the Ranks Were Broken" (Masefield) **47**:233
"Here There Be Tygers" (King) **37**:207; **61**:331
"Here to Learn" (Bowles) **53**:39-40, 44
Here to Stay: Studies in Human Tenacity (Hersey) **97**:305
"Here to Yonder" (Hughes) **108**:321
"Here Today" (Carruth) **84**:127
"Here Today" (McCartney) **35**:289-91, 293
"Here Today" (Wilson) **12**:646
"Here We Are a Point of Sanity" (Kogawa) **78**:167
"Here We Loved" (Amichai) **116**:95
"Heredity" (Harrison) **43**:179; **129**:171
Hérémakhonon: On doit attendre le bonheur (Condé) **52**:85; **52**:79-82, 85; **92**:99-100, 102, 104-05, 107-09, 111-12, 126, 130-31
"Here's Ronnie" (Amis) **62**:5
"Here's to the State of Mississippi" (Ochs) **17**:331
"Here's to the State of Richard Nixon" (Ochs) **17**:334
"The Heresy of Paraphrase" (Brooks) **110**:35
The Heresy of Self-Love: A Study of Subversive Individualism (Zweig) **34**:378
"Héréthique de l'amour" (Kristeva) **140**:156, 170, 186
"The Heretical Cricket" (Momaday) **85**:274
Los heréticos (Valenzuela) **31**:438; **104**:355-57, 376-77
The Heretics (Valenzuela)
See *Los heréticos*
Heretics of Dune (Herbert) **35**:206-08; **44**:393-94
"Herida en cuatro tiempos" (Rodriguez) **10**:440
"Heritage" (Barnes) **141**:58-9, 70
"Heritage" (Christie) **110**:127
"Heritage" (Still) **49**:363, 365
The Heritage (Lenz)
See *Heimatmuseum*
Heritage (West) **50**:359-60
A Heritage and Its History (Compton-Burnett) **1**:61
Heritage of Hastur (Bradley) **30**:27, 29-31
"A Heritage of Liberation" (Kunene) **85**:175
A Heritage of Stars (Simak) **55**:320
Herkules und der Stall des Augias (Duerrenmatt) **102**:61-2, 70, 76
Herkules und der Stall des Augias (Dürrenmatt) **15**:196
"Herlinda Leaves" (Castellanos) **66**:55-6
Hermaios (Rexroth) **11**:473; **22**:345
Herman and Alice (Mohr) **12**:446
Hermann Lauscher (Hesse)
See *Hinterlassene Schriften und Gedichte von Hermann Lauscher*
"El hermano mayor" (Castellanos) **66**:50
Hermes 3000 (Kotzwinkle) **35**:254

Hermes, Dog and Star (Herbert)
See *Hermes, pies i gwiazda*
"Hermes Hermeneutic" (Bernstein) **142**:39
"Hermes of The Ways" (H. D.) **73**:105, 115, 139
Hermes, pies i gwiazda (Herbert) **43**:183, 192
"Hermetic Definition" (H. D.) **8**:258; **14**:224; **31**:204-05, 208, 211; **73**:143-44
Hermetic Definition (H. D.) **73**:136, 139, 143
"Hermetic Poem" (Kunitz) **148**:76
"Hermetiques ouvriers" (Char) **11**:116
L'hermine (Anouilh) **13**:16, 19, 21; **40**:55; **50**:279
HERmione (H. D.) **14**:229, 231; **31**:209-12; **73**:135
"A Hermit" (Mahon) **27**:288
"The Hermit" (Smith) **64**:391
The Hermit (Ionesco)
See *Le solitaire*
The Hermit and Other Stories (Smith) **64**:391
"The Hermit at Outermost House" (Plath) **11**:446
"The Hermit Cackleberry Brown, on Human Vanity" (Williams) **13**:600
The Hermit of 69th Street: The Working Papers of Norbert Kosky (Kosinski) **53**:227-29; **70**:298, 302, 307-09
"The Hermit of Hudson Pond" (Van Duyn) **116**:410
"Hermonax" (H. D.) **31**:213
"Hernes" (Le Guin) **136**:346, 361
"Hero" (Creeley) **78**:140
"The Hero" (Friedman) **56**:97
"Hero" (Madhubuti) **73**:211
"The Hero" (Moore) **10**:350; **47**:270
"The Hero" (Neruda)
See "El héroe"
"The Hero" (Sassoon) **36**:385, 392; **130**:175, 178, 182, 184, 193, 215, 220
The Hero (Kopit) **33**:249-50
The Hero (Maugham) **15**:365, 370
A Hero Ain't Nothin but a Sandwich (Childress) **12**:106-08; **86**:306, 308, 312; **96**:91, 100, 108
The Hero and the Blues (Murray) **73**:230, 236, 238, 240, 243
"The Hero and the Hydra" (McAuley) **45**:246, 250-51, 254
A Hero in His Time (Cohen) **7**:51-2; **31**:93
"Hero Negative" (Coles) **67**:181
"The Hero of Currie Road" (Paton) **10**:388
"Hero of Our Time" (Megged) **9**:375
The Hero Rises Up (Arden) **6**:10; **15**:21-2, 25
The Hero with a Thousand Faces (Campbell) **69**:67-9, 72, 74, 76, 80-4, 88-91, 93, 95, 97, 99
The Hero with the Private Parts (Lytle) **22**:293
"Hero Worship" (Parker) **68**:336
Herod and Mariamne (Lagerkvist)
See *Mariamne*
"El héroe" (Neruda) **28**:315
"The Heroes" (Simpson) **32**:382
Heroes (Bowie) **17**:65-7
Heroes (McGinniss) **32**:301-02
Heroes (Poliakoff) **38**:377, 380, 385
Heroes (Shields) **97**:420, 423-24, 429, 432-33
Heroes and Saints (Moraga) **126**:287-88, 293, 301-02, 307, 309
"Heroes and Villains" (Wilson) **12**:645
Heroes and Villains (Carter) **5**:102; **41**:113; **76**:329
"Heroes Are Gang Leaders" (Baraka) **33**:55; **115**:15-6
Heroes Are Grazing in My Garden (Padilla)
See *En mi jardín pastan los héroes*
"Heroes are Made in Childhood" (Greene) **72**:151
"Heroes Die but Once" (Spinrad) **46**:384
"Heroes/Elders" (Creeley) **78**:160
"The Heroes in the Dark House" (Kiely) **23**:268; **43**:244
The Heroic Age (Haviaras) **33**:205-07
Heroic and Elegiac Song for the Lost Second Lieutenant of the Alb nian Campaign (Elytis)
See *Ázma iroikó ke pénthimo yia ton haméno anthipolohaghó tis Alvanías*
"Heroic and Elegiac Song for the Lost Second Lieutenant of the Albanian Campaign" (Elytis) **100**:155, 175, 190, 192
"Heroic Simile" (Hass) **18**:209, 211, 213
"The Heroics of Realism" (Hartman) **27**:179
"Heroin" (Reed) **21**:302, 307-08, 314, 316, 318-20, 322
"Heroine" (Dinesen) **10**:151; **29**:159; **95**:42
"The Heroine" (Highsmith) **102**:205, 220
"Heroines" (Rich) **36**:370
"The Heron" (Aksyonov) **101**:28, 41-2
"Heron" (Plumly) **33**:312
"The Heron" (Watkins) **43**:454
Heron (Aksyonov)
See *Caplja*
The Heron (Bassani) **9**:75-6
"The Heron and the Astronaut" (Lindbergh) **82**:166
"Heron at Port Talbot" (Clarke) **61**:82
Les Héros de mon enfance (Tremblay) **102**:372
"A Hero's Death" (Lagerkvist) **54**:276
"The Hero's Kitchen" (Johnston) **51**:243
"Hero's Return" (Hunter) **35**:226
Herovit's World (Malzberg) **7**:208
Herr F (Lem) **149**:116
Herr Nightingale and the Satin Woman (Kotzwinkle) **35**:255
The Herr Witch Doctor (Millin) **49**:250, 252
Hers (Alvarez) **5**:19-20
Herself (Calisher) **2**:96-7; **4**:87; **134**:7, 12-3, 15, 17, 20-4, 32-4, 41
Herself Defined: The Poet H.D. and Her World (Guest) **34**:441-45, 447
"Herself in Love" (Wiggins) **57**:433-34, 436
Herself in Love (Wiggins) **57**:433-36, 438-40
Herzog (Bellow) **1**:31-3; **2**:50-1, 53; **3**:48-51, 53-6, 58, 60-1; **6**:50, 52, 54-5, 58, 60-1; **8**:68-9, 73-7; **10**:42; **13**:66-7, 69, 73; **15**:46-7, 49-50, 54-6, 58; **25**:80-1, 84-6; **33**:65-6, 69-71; **34**:545; **63**:27, 30-2, 35, 38-9, 41; **79**:76, 79, 83
"He's a Real Gone Guy: A Short Requiem for Percival Angleman" (McGrath) **59**:175
"He's Misstra Know-It-All" (Wonder) **12**:657
He's My Boy (Gilbreth and Carey) **17**:156
"hesitate..." (Kinsella) **138**:89-90, 92-93, 101, 152
"An Hesitation on the Bank of the Delaware" (Barthelme) **5**:54
"Hesperides" (Prokosch) **48**:307
The Hessian (Fast) **23**:159; **131**:86
"The Hessian Prisoner" (Bates) **46**:51
Hester Street (Silver) **20**:341-44
"Heterosexism and Dancing" (Blount) **38**:45
Hets (Bergman) **16**:46; **72**:51, 61
Hetty Dorval (Wilson) **13**:607-09
"Hetty Sleeping" (Gardam) **43**:169
"He-Who-Came-Forth" (Levertov) **66**:237
"Hey Babe" (Young) **17**:576
Hey, Big Spender (Bonham) **12**:53-4
"Hey Cuba, Hecuba?" (Cabrera Infante) **120**:75
Hey, Dummy (Platt) **26**:350-51
"Hey, Have You Got a Cig, the Time, the News, My Face?" (Hannah) **90**:158, 160
"Hey Hey" (McCartney) **35**:291-92
"Hey Hey, My My" (Young) **17**:581, 583
Hey Jack! (Hannah) **90**:135-37, 145-46
"Hey Jude" (Lennon and McCartney) **35**:278, 294
Hey Little Walter (Alleyne) **65**:444-48
"Hey Nineteen" (Becker and Fagen) **26**:85
"Hey Sailor, What Ship?" (Olsen) **13**:433; **114**:192, 194, 198, 222-23, 232-35
"Hey, Taxi!" (Ferber) **93**:162
Hey, That's My Soul You're Stomping On (Corcoran) **17**:77
"Hey You" (Lightfoot) **26**:282
Heyday (Spackman) **46**:375-76, 378
"Heyfitz" (Cohen) **19**:113
H.G. Wells: Critic of Progress (Williamson) **29**:457
Hi Johnny (Hunter) **21**:161
Hi, Mom! (De Palma) **20**:74
"HIALOG (any number can play)" (Avison) **97**:114
"Hiatus" (Avison) **97**:69, 74
"Hibernaculum" (Ammons) **2**:13-14; **3**:11; **5**:29, 31; **8**:16, 18; **9**:27-30; **25**:47; **57**:58-9; **108**:33-4, 36, 42, 45, 53
Hibernaculum (Ammons) **108**:60
"Hibernation" (Blackburn) **9**:100
"Hiccups" (Damas)
See "Hoquet"
"Hickman Arrives" (Ellison) **86**:329; **114**:99, 102, 102
Hickory, Dickory, Dock (Christie) **110**:121
"Hid Life" (Avison) **97**:117
"The Hidden Bole" (FitzGerald) **19**:179, 181
The Hidden Canyon (Abbey) **59**:238
"Hidden Door" (Ferlinghetti) **2**:134; **111**:65
The Hidden Fortress (Kurosawa) **16**:397; **119**:338, 341
The Hidden God (Brooks) **24**:107, 109, 114; **86**:278, 287; **110**:10, 12, 28-9
The Hidden God (Goldmann)
See *Le Dieu caché*
The Hidden Ground of Love (Merton) **83**:404
"A Hidden History" (Okri) **87**:315
A Hidden Life (Dourado)
See *Uma vida em segredo*
Hidden Lives: A Family Memoir (Forster) **149**:97-100, 102-04
The Hidden Mountain (Roy)
See *La montagne secrète*
"Hidden Name, Complex Fate" (Ellison) **54**:141; **114**:116
The Hidden Target (MacInnes) **27**:283-84
The Hidden Waterfall (Zaturenska) **6**:585; **11**:579-80
The Hide (Unsworth) **127**:421
"Hide and Seek" (Gunn) **32**:213
"Hide and Seek" (Scannell) **49**:328
Hide and Seek (Potter) **58**:388-89, 391; **86**:346; **123**:230, 234
Hide and Seek (West) **17**:552
"Hideout" (Hugo) **32**:247-48
Hiding (Klein) **30**:240
"Hiding in Poems" (Nagy)
See "Versben bujdosó"
Hiding in Poems (Nagy)
See *Versben bujdosó*
"Hiding Man" (Barthelme) **115**:65-6, 71
Hiding Place (Wideman) **34**:298; **36**:454-55; **67**:374; **122**:287-90, 292, 297, 303, 305, 314, 321-23, 327, 331-32, 336, 340, 345-46, 348-51, 354-55, 363
"Hier ist Tibten" (Boell) **72**:72
Hier régnant désert (Bonnefoy) **58**:43-5, 47-54, 57-9
"The Hieroglyphic Monad" (Leiris) **61**:361
"Hieroglyphics" (Harjo) **83**:284
High (Hinde) **6**:240-41
"High and Dry" (Lightfoot) **26**:280
High and Low (Betjeman) **10**:52; **43**:42-3, 46
High and Low (Kurosawa) **16**:402-04; **119**:350-51, 379
The High and the Mighty (Gann) **23**:163-64
High Anxiety (Brooks) **12**:82-3
The High Cost of Living (Piercy) **14**:420-21; **18**:409; **62**:362, 365, 376; **128**:218, 241, 245
High Cotton (Pinckney) **76**:98-113
High Crimes and Misdemeanors (Greenberg) **30**:165-66
"High Dive" (Empson) **3**:147; **19**:154, 157
"High Gannet" (Parini) **54**:360-61
The High Green Hill (Bissett) **18**:61-2
"High Ground" (McGahern) **48**:272-73
High Ground (McGahern) **48**:272-73

High Hearts (Brown) **43**:85-6; **79**:169
High Heels (Almodovar)
See *Tacones lejanos*
The High House (Arundel) **17**:12-14, 16, 18
High in Vietnam Hot Damn (Pomerance) **13**:444
"High Island" (Murphy) **41**:318
High Island (Murphy) **41**:313-15, 317-20
"High John Is Risen Again" (Hamilton) **26**:152-53
The High King (Alexander) **35**:24
"The High Malady" (Pasternak)
See "Vysokaya bolesn"
"High Plains Rag" (Galvin) **38**:198
"The High Road" (Kinsella) **138**:101
The High Road (O'Brien) **116**:199-200
"The High Road of St. James" (Carpentier) **11**:101; **38**:95
"High School" (Beattie) **63**:18
High School (Wiseman) **20**:468-74, 476
"High Speed Car Wash" (Durcan) **43**:118
High Spirits (Davies) **42**:103; **75**:184
High Spirits (Jordan) **110**:275
High Stakes (Francis) **22**:152; **42**:149, 156
"A High Subjectivity" (Young) **82**:396, 412
"High Tension Lines across a Landscape" (Ciardi) **40**:154
High Tide in the Garden (Adcock) **41**:14-15, 17
"High Tide in Tucson" (Kingsolver) **130**:114, 120
High Tide in Tucson: Essays from Now or Never (Kingsolver) **130**:95, 99-100, 112-13, 119
High Time along the Wabash (Saroyan) **10**:454
"High to Low" (Hughes) **35**:222
High Towers (Costain) **30**:94-5
"High Water" (Mosher) **62**:312
High Water (Highsmith) **102**:205
The High White Wall (Sherburne) **30**:360-61
High, Wide, and Handsome (Mamoulian) **16**:423-24, 426
High Wind in Jamaica (Hughes) **1**:149
"High Windows" (Larkin) **5**:230-31; **8**:332, 339; **13**:339-40; **18**:301; **33**:261; **39**:346; **64**:265, 269, 272, 282, 284
High Windows (Larkin) **5**:225-31; **8**:332-33, 336-41; **9**:323; **13**:337-38, 340-41; **18**:297, 300-01; **33**:256, 259-62, 269; **39**:333-34, 338-39, 341, 344; **64**:259, 263-64, 270-72, 275, 277-78, 280, 285
Highcastle: A Remembrance (Lem)
See *Wysoki Zamek*
"Higher Arguments in Favor of Discipline..." (Milosz) **82**:297
"Higher Ground" (Wonder) **12**:657, 661
Higher Ground (Phillips) **96**:321-24, 326-33, 335, 337, 339, 341, 343, 350, 354
"The Higher Keys" (Merrill) **34**:229, 236
Highest Standard of Living (Reddin) **67**:268-69
Highgate Road (Ammons) **25**:45
Highland Fling (Mitford) **44**:489, 492
"Highland Games" (MacCaig) **36**:287
"A Highland Girl Studying Poetry" (Smith)
See "A Young Highland Girl Studying Poetry"
"Highland Portrait" (Smith) **64**:394
Highpockets (Tunis) **12**:596
High-Rise (Ballard) **14**:41; **36**:38; **137**:8-9, 12, 14, 23, 77-78
"High-Water Railers" (Hannah) **90**:158, 160
"The Highway" (Bradbury) **10**:71
"Highway" (Moure) **88**:230
"Highway 5" (Moure) **88**:230
"Highway 6" (Moure) **88**:230
Highway 61 Revisited (Dylan) **4**:149; **6**:155; **12**:181, 184, 199; **77**:162, 168, 170, 174, 179-80
"Highway 66" (Laughlin) **49**:222
"Highway in April" (Avison) **97**:112
"Highway: Michigan" (Roethke) **46**:356
"Hi-Ho the Ambulance-O" (Nash) **23**:322
La hija de Rappaccini (Paz) **10**:391-92
La hija del engaño (Bunuel) **80**:23
"El hijo de Andrés Aparicio" (Fuentes) **22**:171; **60**:165; **113**:257-58
Hijo de hombre (Roa Bastos) **45**:343-47
"El hijo de Karmaria" (Valenzuela) **104**:387
El hijo pródigo (Paz) **65**:176
Hijos de la ira (Alonso) **14**:16, 22
Hijos del aire (Paz) **19**:368
Los hijos del limo: Del romanticismo a la vanguardia (Paz) **4**:398; **6**:398; **10**:391, 393; **51**:336; **65**:176, 178, 180, 188; **119**:418
Los hijos muertos (Matute) **11**:362-65
Hikaya bi-la bidaya wa-la nihaya (Mahfouz) **153**:235, 273
Hikāya bilā bidāya walā nihāya (Mahfūz) **52**:292
Hikayat haratina (Mahfouz) **153**:235, 289, 308, 342
"Hiking on the Coast Range" (Rexroth) **49**:277; **112**:398
"Hikmat al-Hamawi" (Mahfouz) **153**:350
"Hilaire and the Marechal Petard" (Boyle) **121**:33
Hilaire Belloc (Wilson) **33**:457-58
"Hilda" (Ransom) **4**:431
Hilferufe (Handke) **8**:262; **15**:266-67; **134**:107-08, 161
"The Hill" (Creeley) **15**:149
"A Hill" (Hecht) **8**:268
"The Hill" (Ritsos) **31**:325
"The Hill" (Strand) **71**:285-86
"Hill Burial" (Winters) **32**:468-69
"Hill Field" (Montague) **46**:267
The Hill of Devi, and Other Writings (Forster) **45**:138; **77**:213, 217-18, 226, 228-29
"The Hill of Evening" (Merwin) **88**:212
The Hill of Evil Counsel (Oz) **54**:347, 352; **11**:428-29; **27**:359; **33**:302
The Hill of Summer (Drury) **37**:110-11
The Hill Road (Mayne) **12**:392
Hill Street Blues (Bochco and Kozoll) **35**:49-61
"Hill Walls" (Hughes) **119**:275
"The Hill Wife" (Frost) **10**:193, 198; **26**:113
"The Hillies" (Updike) **9**:537
"The Hills" (Brodsky) **13**:114
"Hills Like White Elephants" (Hemingway) **3**:234; **19**:211; **50**:413, 415
"Hills of Tuscany" (Lee) **90**:199
"Hilmar Enick" (Tolson) **36**:429
"Him" (Wright) **146**:336
Him (Cummings) **8**:160; **12**:144, 146, 153; **68**:35, 47
Him She Loves? (Kerr) **35**:250
"Him with His Foot in His Mouth" (Bellow) **33**:68; **63**:28, 39
Him with His Foot in His Mouth, and Other Stories (Bellow) **33**:67-71
Der Himbeerpflücker (Hochwälder) **36**:235, 237-39, 241
"El himen en México" (Arreola) **147**:26, 34
Himlens hemlighet (Lagerkvist) **54**:268, 271, 274, 277
Himmel auf Erden (Hein) **154**:182
Himmo (Kaniuk) **19**:239
"Himno entre ruinas" (Paz) **4**:396
Himnusz minden idöben (Nagy) **7**:252
Hind's Kidnap: A Pastoral on Familiar Airs (McElroy) **5**:279; **47**:237-39, 241-42, 244-45
Hindsight (Dickinson) **35**:136-38
The Hindsight Saga (Perelman) **23**:338; **44**:503
"A Hindu Sage at the Sorbonne" (Asturias) **8**:26
The Hindu View of Art (Anand) **93**:44
"Hindus" (Mukherjee) **53**:270
"The Hinge" (Gilliatt) **53**:146
Hinge Picture (Howe) **152**:150-51, 157-58, 195, 220-21, 235
"The Hint of an Explanation" (Greene) **72**:148
"Hinterland" (Shields) **113**:414
"Hinterlands" (Gibson) **63**:129-30
Hinterlassene Schriften und Gedichte von Hermann Lauscher (Hesse) **17**:198; **69**:198, 287
"Hints from Ariosto" (Porter) **33**:325
"Hiob" (Sachs) **98**:356
Hipogrifo violento (Sender) **8**:479
"Hipparchia" (H. D.) **73**:112
"A Hippocratic Oath for the Pluralist" (Booth) **24**:98
The Hippodrome (Colter) **58**:139-40, 143-44, 146
Hippolytus (Rexroth) **11**:472
Hippolytus Temporizes (H. D.) **31**:208; **73**:111, 117
"The Hippopotamus" (Eliot) **15**:216; **41**:151
"Der Hippopotamus" (Jünger) **125**:220
"Hips" (Cisneros) **69**:144; **118**:207
The Hired Man (Bragg) **10**:71-2
"Hiroshima" (Lowell) **15**:343
Hiroshima (Hersey) **1**:144; **7**:153; **40**:234, 239, 241; **81**:332-37; **97**:298-301, 303-07, 312, 315-22, 324
"Hiroshima Mon Amour" (Duras) **100**:124, 149
Hiroshima, mon amour (Duras) **34**:162; **40**:180-81, 185-86; **68**:74, 76-7, 81, 85, 87-9, 91, 94, 98; **100**:119, 130-31
Hiroshima, mon amour (Resnais) **16**:496-503, 505-07, 509-13, 517
Hiroshima Notes (Oe)
See *Hiroshima nōto*
Hiroshima nōto (Oe) **36**:347; **86**:213, 236, 238, 241
Hiroshima Poems (Purdy) **3**:408; **14**:432; **50**:246
"Hiroshima: The Aftermath" (Hersey) **81**:335; **97**:309-14
"Hiroshima, Watts, My Lai" (Hayden) **37**:153
"His Animal Is Finally a Kind of Ape" (Stern) **40**:408
"His Ashes" (Olds) **85**:306
His Band and the Street Choir (Morrison) **21**:232
His Butler's Story (Coles) **67**:180
"His Dog" (Prichard) **46**:345
His Enemy, His Friend (Tunis) **12**:598-99
"His Excellency" (Maugham) **67**:210
"His Excellency the Masquerader" (Clark Bekedermo) **38**:125
His Father's Hands (Kinsella) **19**:254; **138**:102-03, 106, 114
"His First Real Snow" (Shapcott) **38**:404
"His Foreboding" (Roethke) **101**:332
His Grace's Days (Johnson)
See *Hans nådes tid*
His Head (Ferlinghetti) **111**:64
His Human Majesty (Boyle) **19**:63; **58**:64; **121**:52-7
"His Last Day" (Himes) **108**:227, 258
"His Manner of Returning" (Williams) **45**:444
His Master's Voice (Lem) **40**:291, 297-98, 300; **149**:112-15, 123-24, 126-27, 132, 143-45, 147, 154, 159, 167-68, 202-4, 206-8, 217, 219, 243, 251, 261, 263, 275-76, 284
"His Middle-Class Blues" (Enzensberger) **43**:145
"His Mother Inside Him" (Updike) **139**:369
"His Night of Sadness" (Kunene) **85**:176
His Own Man (Gellhorn) **14**:195; **60**:186-87, 193
"His Plans for Old Age" (Meredith) **13**:373
His Present Discontents (Rosenthal) **28**:392, 394-95
"His Shining Helmet: Its Horsehair Crest" (Gallagher) **63**:125
"His Smell" (Olds) **85**:306-7
"His Son, in His Arms, in Light, Aloft" (Brodkey) **56**:60
"His Stillness" (Olds) **85**:308
His Toy, His Dream, His Rest: 308 Dream Songs (Berryman) **1**:34; **2**:56-7; **3**:67, 70; **8**:87; **13**:75, 80, 83; **25**:89-91, 93-4; **62**:43, 68
"His Wife Survived Him" (Brophy) **29**:91
"His-and-Hers Politics" (Kingsolver) **130**:94
The Hispanic Americans (Meltzer) **26**:308

"Hisperica Famina" (Spicer) **72**:357-58
"Hissen som gick ner i helvete" (Lagerkvist) **54**:287
The Hissing of Summer Lawns (Mitchell) **12**:438-40, 442-43
Hissing Tales (Gary) **25**:186
Histoire (Simon) **4**:495, 497; **9**:482, 484; **15**:488, 492-94; **39**:203, 205-07, 209-11
L'histoire d'Adele H. (Truffaut) **20**:397-98; **101**:396-97, 410-11
Histoire de la sexualité, Vol. 1: La volonté de savoir (Foucault) **31**:181-82, 185; **34**:339-42, 344; **69**:161-62, 165-69, 173-77, 179, 181, 183-84, 186, 189
Histoire de la sexualité, Vol. 2: L'usage des plaisirs (Foucault) **34**:342-43; **69**:166-68, 171-73, 176-77, 181, 187, 189, 191-92
Histoire de la sexualité, Vol. 3: Le souci de soi (Foucault) **34**:342-43; **69**:166-68, 171, 177, 181, 189
"Histoire de lipogramme" (Perec) **56**:256
Histoire de l'oeil (Bataille) **29**:39-42, 45, 48
"Histoire de lunes" (Carpentier) **11**:102-03; **110**:75-7
"Histoire de rats" (Bataille) **29**:38-9
Histoire d'une maison (Cayrol) **11**:110
Histoire et psychanalyse: Essai sur les possibilites et les limites de la psychohistoire (Friedlander) **90**:112
Histoire et utopie (Cioran) **64**:97-9
Histoire extraordinaire (Butor) **8**:117
Histoires d'amour (Kristeva) **77**:324; **140**:148-50, 167, 170, 180-81, 186, 195
"Historia" (Kadare) **52**:259
Historia de cronopios y de famas (Cortázar) **2**:103; **10**:118; **13**:164; **33**:135; **34**:329, 331-32; **92**:147-48
Historia de la eternidad (Borges) **44**:363, 368; **83**:163, 171
La historia de Mayta (Vargas Llosa) **42**:408-13; **85**:350, 352, 355, 362, 364, 366-68, 379, 383, 386-87, 389, 391, 395-96
Historia de una escalera (Buero Vallejo) **15**:97; **46**:93; **139**:10, 57
Historia del corazón (Aleixandre) **9**:18
"Historia del guerrero y de la cautiva" (Borges) **13**:104; **83**:161
"História do Carnaval" (Amado) **106**:74-5
História do Cerco de Lisboa (Saramago) **119**:154, 158, 170-72, 176
"Historia Minotaura" (Herbert) **43**:187
Historia personal del 'boom' (Donoso) **8**:179-80; **32**:154; **99**:216, 218, 220-21, 230
Historia secreta de una novella (Vargas Llosa) **10**:500
Historia universal de la infamia (Borges) **2**:77; **4**:74; **13**:106; **44**:362-63, 365, 368; **48**:35-6; **83**:163-66, 171
"Historial de un libro" (Cernuda) **54**:50
The Historian (Fuller) **28**:151
Historias de la Artámila (Matute) **11**:363
Historias desaforados (Bioy Casares) **88**:88
Historias fingidas y verdaderas (Otero) **11**:425-27
"Historical Afterword" (Berger) **19**:39, 41
"A Historical Approach to the Media" (McLuhan) **83**:367
The Historical Atlas of World Mythology (Campbell) **69**:82-3, 95
"Historical Criticism: Theory of Modes" (Frye) **24**:230
"Historical Emplotment and the Problem of Truth in Historical Representation" (White) **148**:298-99
Historical Evidence and the Reading of Seventeenth-Century Poetry (Brooks) **86**:288-89; **110**:16-17, 31, 38
"A Historical Footnote to Consider Only When All Else Fails" (Giovanni) **64**:191
"The Historical Interpretation of Literature" (Wilson) **24**:470
The Historical Novel (Lukacs) **24**:318-20, 334
"Historical Pluralism" (White) **148**:292
"Historical Process" (Enzensberger) **43**:146
"The Historical Text as Literary Artifact" (White) **148**:233, 286
"Histories" (Tomlinson) **45**:393
"History" (Berry) **27**:36
"History" (Hall) **59**:151, 155-56
"History" (Muldoon) **32**:320
"History" (Sherwood) **81**:102
"History" (Simic) **49**:342
"History" (Soto) **80**:280, 287
History (Lowell) **3**:302-05; **4**:301, 304; **5**:256-59; **8**:353-55, 357; **9**:334, 339; **11**:328-29, 331; **15**:344; **37**:235-38, 240; **124**:253, 255, 265, 270, 290-91, 303
"History: 13" (Olds) **85**:296, 298
History: A Novel (Morante) See *La storia*
"History: A Story Has Only a Few Good Years" (Wilson) **49**:416
History and Class-Consciousness (Lukacs) **24**:320, 324, 327, 338
History and Human Survival: Essays on the Young and Old, Survivors and the Dead, Peace and War, and on Contemporary Psychohistory (Lifton) **67**:142-43
History and Psychoanalysis: An Inquiry into the Possibilities and Limits of Psychohistory (Friedlander) See *Histoire et psychanalyse: Essai sur les possibilites et les limites de la psychohistoire*
"History and the New American Novel" (Alter) **34**:515
History and Tradition in Afro-American Culture (Lenz) **65**:379
History and Utopia (Cioran) See *Histoire et utopie*
"History as Apple Tree" (Harper) **7**:139
"History as Poetry" (Hill) **8**:295; **45**:185
"A History: for colored girls who have considered suicide/ when therainbow is enuf" (Shange) **74**:308-09
"History is Past and Present Life" (Barzun) **145**:80
History Is Your Own Heartbeat (Harper) **7**:138-39
"History Lesson" (Simic) **68**:378-79
"History Lessons" (Deane) **122**:74, 83
"History Lessons" (Komunyakaa) **94**:234
History Lessons (Deane) **122**:81-3
The History Man (Bradbury) **32**:52-3, 55-6; **61**:34-5, 37-40, 42, 44
"The History of a Contraoctave" (Pasternak) See "The Story of Counter-Octave"
"History of America" (Ostriker) **132**:302
"A History of Bitic Literature" (Lem) **40**:298
A History of Britain (Schama) **150**:202, 206, 208
A History of Britain with Simon Schama (Schama) **150**:203-04, 206
A History of Christian Thought (Tillich) **131**:353-54
A History of Christianity (Johnson) **147**:90-1, 102, 107-08, 134, 151, 158
"The History of Crome Manor" (Huxley) **79**:304
The History of Danish Dreams (Hoeg) See *Forestilling om det Tyvende Århundrede*
A History of Eternity (Borges) See *Historia de la eternidad*
"The History of Fire" (Hogan) **73**:158
"The History of Galadriel and Celeborn" (Tolkien) **38**:431
History of Humanism (Faludy) **42**:140
History of Infamy (Borges) See *Historia universal de la infamia*
A History of Modern Criticism, 1750-1950: Vol. 4, The Later Nineteenth Century (Wellek) **28**:443-44, 446-49, 451-52, 454, 447, 447, 450, 450
"History of My Heart" (Pinsky) **38**:355, 357-58, 362-63; **94**:298-99, 307, 309; **121**:446
History of My Heart (Pinsky) **38**:355-56, 358-59, 361-63; **94**:298-99, 305-6, 309, 322; **121**:435, 437, 446, 448
A History of Pan-African Revolt (James) **33**:219
The History of Polish Literature (Milosz) **31**:261-62
"The History of Rodney" (Bass) **143**:10-12
"The History of Sexuality" (Foucault) **69**:193
The History of Sexuality, Vol. l: An Introduction (Foucault) See *Histoire de la sexualité, Vol. 1: La volonté de savoir*
A History of the American Film (Durang) **27**:88-90
A History of the American People (Johnson) **147**:140, 143-46, 149-52, 157-58
A History of the English People (Johnson) **147**:90, 107, 114, 149
The History of the Growth of Heaven (Codrescu) **46**:102-03; **121**:157-8, 161-2, 175
The History of the Heart (Aleixandre) See *Historia del corazón*
A History of the Jews (Johnson) **147**:87, 90-2, 94, 96, 107, 114, 145, 149, 152, 157
"History of the Poet as a Whore" (Madhubuti) **73**:199
The History of the Siege of Lisbon (Saramago) See *História do Cerco de Lisboa*
"History of the Targo" (Borges) **48**:45
"History of the Warrior and the Captive" (Borges) See "Historia del guerrero y de la cautiva"
A History of the World in 10 1/2 Days Chapters (Barnes) **141**:32, 39, 48-9, 53, 56-8, 61-2, 65-7, 71, 77
The History Plays (Hare) **136**:259-60, 262
History: the Home Movie (Raine) **103**:205-07, 210-13
"A Hit Album" (Sorrentino) **40**:386
"The Hitch Hiker" (Williams) **42**:440
Hitchhike (Holland) **21**:151
The Hitchhiker (Simenon) **2**:399
"The Hitch-Hikers" (Welty) **33**:415; **105**:307
The Hitchhiker's Guide to the Galaxy (Adams) **27**:11-5; **60**:2-7
Hitchhiking (Havel) **123**:180
"The Hitchhiking Game" (Kundera) **9**:321; **32**:260; **115**:308, 346
"Hitherto Uncollected" (Moore) **47**:263
"Hitler, According to Speer" (Canetti) **86**:295
"The Hitler Diaries" (Hugo) **32**:249
Hitler er les États-Unis (1939-1941) (Friedlander) **90**:104, 112
The Hitleriad (Klein) **19**:263
"The Hitlerian Spring" (Montale) See "La primavera Hitleriana"
"Hitler's Daughter" (Federspiel) **42**:145
"Hitler's First Photograph" (Szymborska) **99**:198, 201
Hitsuji o megaru bōken (Murakami) **150**:38-49, 51-6, 58, 61, 63, 65, 67, 72-6, 78, 81, 85-6, 90, 92
Hitting Town (Poliakoff) **38**:375-78, 380, 383, 386
The Hive (Cela) See *La colmena*
Hiver Caraïbe (Morand) **41**:304
L'hiver de force (Ducharme) **74**:57, 68
"Hi-Way Songs" (Lightfoot) **26**:279
Hjarta høyrer sine heimlandstonar (Vesaas) **48**:405-06
Hjärtats sånger (Lagerkvist) **54**:275
H'm (Thomas) **6**:530, 532; **48**:380-82
H.M. Pulham, Esquire (Marquand) **10**:329-31
HMS Surprise (O'Brian) **152**:270-71, 281, 297-98
H.M.S. Ulysses (MacLean) **3**:309; **13**:359-61; **50**:347-50; **63**:259-64, 267-68
"Hoantteniate" (Kenny) **87**:258

"The Hoarder" (Sexton) **123**:418-19, 442
Hob taht al-Matar (Mahfūz) **52**:296-97
The Hobbit; or, There and Back Again (Tolkien) **1**:336, 338, 340; **2**:435; **3**:477, 480-81; **8**:515-16; **12**:563-64, 566-70, 577-80, 583-85; **38**:431-32, 435, 438-42
"The Hobbyist" (Pesetsky) **28**:357
"The Hobo" (Wild) **14**:581
The Hoboken Chicken Emergency (Pinkwater) **35**:317, 320
Die Hochzeit (Canetti) **14**:121; **75**:127; **86**:298, 301, 303
"The Hockey Hero" (Bowering) **47**:19
"The Hockey Poem" (Bly) **15**:63; **128**:32
The Hockey Sweater, and Other Stories (Carrier)
See *Les enfants du bonhomme dans la lune*
Hocus Pocus (Vonnegut) **111**:351-52, 354-58, 361-68
"Hoeing" (Soto) **80**:286, 288
"Hoffmeier's Antelope" (Swift) **41**:446
Hofmeyr (Paton) **25**:363
"Hofstedt and Jean—and Others" (Brodkey) **56**:60, 64
Hog Butcher (Fair) **18**:139, 141
"Hog Heaven" (Williams) **33**:446; **148**:344
"A Hog Loves Its Life: Something About My Grandfather" (Gurganus) **70**:191, 193, 195-96
Hogg (Delany) **141**:143
"Hoist High the Roof Beam, Carpenters" (Salinger)
See "Raise High the Roofbeam, Carpenters"
La hojarasca (García Márquez) **2**:148; **3**:180; **47**:145, 149-50, 153; **2**:149; **3**:180-81; **10**:216; **15**:254; **27**:147-48, 155; **47**:145; **55**:138; **68**:141, 145, 153, 156
Hojas de Parra (Parra) **102**:332-33
Hōjō no umi (Mishima) **2**:287; **4**:355-58; **6**:337-38; **9**:383-84; **27**:341-43
"Hojoki" (Rexroth) **112**:405
"Hokan" (Tanizaki) **28**:417
"Hokuro no tegami" (Kawabata) **107**:71, 104
"Hola Migvelin!" (Levine) **14**:317
"Holbein's Dead Christ" (Kristeva) **140**:182-83,
The Holcroft Covenant (Ludlum) **22**:289
Hold April (Stuart) **11**:510
"Hold Back the Tears" (Young) **17**:576-77
Hold Fast (Major) **26**:284-88
"Hold Me" (Levine) **118**:272-73
Hold Me! (Feiffer) **64**:151, 159, 164
"Hold Me Fast, Don't Let Me Pass" (Munro) **95**:310, 315
Hold On (Douglas) **73**:65-7, 81, 94
"Hold On, Hold Out" (Browne) **21**:41-2
"Hold On John" (Lennon) **35**:262
Hold Out (Browne) **21**:41-2
Hold Your Hour and Have Another (Behan) **79**:24-5, 27
Hold Zero! (George) **35**:176
The Holder of the World (Mukherjee) **115**:371-73
"Hölderlin" (Hamburger) **5**:159
Hölderlin (Weiss) **51**:386-87, 391, 393, 395, 397
"Hölderlin und das Wesen der Dichtung" (Heidegger) **24**:259
Hölderlin's Madness (Gascoyne) **45**:148, 152-54
"Holding Course" (Heaney) **74**:162
"Holding in the Sky" (Stafford) **29**:380
Holding On (Jones) **52**:246-48, 254
"Holding the Great Blind Man by the Hand" (Blaga) **75**:62, 77
"Holding the Great Blind Man's Hand" (Blaga)
See "Holding the Great Blind Man by the Hand"
Holding the Line: Women in the Great Arizona Mine Strike of 1983 (Kingsolver) **130**:74-78, 81-82, 84, 87, 91, 96, 101, 120
Holding the Pose (Thesen) **56**:414-16, 421
"Holding the Towel" (Swenson) **106**:337
"Holding Together" (Bell) **102**:5, 7
"Hold-Up" (MacNeice) **10**:325
The Hold-Up Man (Hart)
See *The Beloved Bandit*
"The Hole" (Dixon) **52**:99-100
"The Hole" (Hood) **28**:192
The Hole (Simpson) **29**:365-69
"The Hole/Birth Catalogue" (Ozick) **28**:352
"Hole in the Day" (Tilghman) **65**:106-07, 109-12
The Hole in the Flag (Codrescu) **121**:170, 172
"A Hole in the Floor" (Wilbur) **3**:530; **6**:570; **53**:399, 405; **110**:351
A Hole in the Head (Capra) **16**:156, 160
"The Hole in the Sea" (Bell) **8**:66; **31**:46
A Hole in the Sky (Konwicki)
See *Dziura w niebie*
"The Hole That Jack Dug" (Sargeson) **31**:362, 365, 370-71
"Holiday" (Ferber) **93**:153
"Holiday" (Grace) **56**:112
"Holiday" (Porter) **101**:256
"Holiday" (Rich) **125**:336
"Holiday" (Sitwell) **67**:319-20, 336
"The Holiday" (Smith) **44**:436, 440
Holiday (Middleton) **7**:219-21; **38**:333
The Holiday (Smith) **25**:416-17, 422-23; **44**:439
A Holiday for Murder (Christie) **48**:77
"A Holiday for Three" (Derleth) **31**:132
The Holiday Friend (Johnson) **27**:224
"A Holiday from Strict Reality" (Reid) **33**:351
"Holiday in Waikiki" (Davies) **21**:88-9
"Holiday Inn Blues" (Ferlinghetti) **111**:60
"Holidays" (Williams) **42**:443
Holland (Wilson) **12**:646, 654
"The Holland of the Mind" (Zoline) **62**:462-64
Holland's Glory (de Hartog) **19**:133
"Hollow" (L'Heureux) **52**:273
"Hollow" (Pancake) **29**:346-50
The Hollow (Christie) **6**:108; **12**:125; **48**:70-1, 73-6; **110**:135
"The Hollow Boy" (Calisher) **134**:11
"The Hollow Herring" (Aksyonov) **101**:42
The Hollow Hills (Stewart) **7**:468; **35**:393-96; **117**:369, 372, 376, 385
The Hollow Land (Gardam) **43**:170
The Hollow Lands (Moorcock) **5**:294; **58**:347-48
The Hollow Man (Carr) **3**:101
The Hollow Men (Eliot) **1**:90, 92; **2**:128-29; **6**:163; **9**:188; **10**:170; **13**:196-97; **15**:214, 216-17; **34**:525, 530; **41**:147, 151, 154, 161; **55**:346, 350-51, 373; **57**:187
"A Hollow Stone" (Oz) **27**:360
"A Hollow Tree" (Bly) **15**:63
"Holloway Jail" (Davies) **21**:92
"Holly" (Heaney) **37**:165; **74**:169
"The Holly and the Ivy" (Stevenson) **33**:383
Holly from the Bongs (Garner) **17**:135, 147
"Holly, Holly" (Diamond) **30**:112
"Hollywood" (Kaufman) **49**:202-03
Hollywood (Bukowski) **82**:23-6, 28; **108**:88-9, 91
Hollywood (Cendrars) **106**:190, 193-94
Hollywood (Kanin) **22**:231
Hollywood: A Novel of America in the 1920s (Vidal) **72**:400-04, 406; 273-75, 303, 321
"Hollywood and Vine" (Montague) **46**:265
"A Hollywood Diary" (Fuchs) **22**:159, 161
The Hollywood Kid (Wojciechowska) **26**:452-53
"Hollywood Nights" (Seger) **35**:383, 385
"Hollywood State of Mind" (Joel) **26**:214-15
Hollywood's Canada (Berton) **104**:46-7, 57
"The Holmes-Laski Correspondence" (Wilson) **24**:481
"Holocaust" (Ostriker) **132**:329
Holocaust (Reznikoff) **9**:449
"The Holy Bird" (Blaga) **75**:68
"The Holy Child's Song" (Merton) **83**:378, 392
"Holy Day" (Bissett) **18**:58
Holy Disorders (Crispin) **22**:110
"The Holy Earth" (Wheelock) **14**:571
Holy Europe (Adamov)
See *Sainte-Europe*
"Holy Face" (Huxley) **35**:241
The Holy Ghostly (Shepard) **17**:443
Holy Ghosts (Linney) **51**:259-60, 264
Holy Grail (Gilliam)
See *Monty Python and the Holy Grail*
The Holy Grail (Spicer) **18**:507, 512, 514; **72**:351
"Holy Grave" (Graham) **118**:227
"The Holy Land" (Updike) **43**:431
The Holy Land (Lagerkvist) **54**:281-85
"The Holy Man" (Hood) **28**:189
"Holy Moon" (MacCaig) **36**:283
"holy night" (Clifton) **66**:81
Holy Place (Fuentes)
See *Zona sagrada*
"Holy Saturday" (Oates) **15**:402
"Holy Satyr" (H. D.) **73**:109
"Holy Shit" (Kinnell) **129**:271
"The Holy Shroud" (Raine) **45**:334
Holy Smoke (Cabrera Infante) **45**:81-84; **120**:34-37, 68, 80
Holy Smoke (Howe) **47**:175-77
"Holy Sonnet" (Johnson) **7**:415
Holy Stones (Weldon) **36**:445; **122**:254
The Holy Terrors (Cocteau)
See *Les enfants terribles*
Holy the Firm (Dillard) **9**:178-79; **60**:70; **115**:168-75, 182-85, 187-88, 197, 199-207, 209
"Holy Thursday" (Hill) **45**:186
"Holy Thursday" (Muldoon) **72**:275
"Holy Thursday" (Wright) **146**:308
The Holy Tree (Jenkins) **52**:224, 226-27
"Holy Trinity" (Betjeman) **43**:41-2
"Holy Water" (Didion) **129**:78
"Holy Week" (Pasternak) **63**:313
Holy Week (Aragon)
See *La semaine sainte*
"The Holy Words of Tristan Tzara" (Rothenberg) **57**:381
Holzfällen: Eine Erregung (Bernhard) **61**:29-31
Holzwege (Heidegger) **24**:264, 277
"Homage" (Wright)
See "Homage to Cézanne"
Homage and Desecrations (Paz) **51**:336
"Homage to a Government" (Larkin) **5**:226; **8**:340; **33**:261; **64**:274
Homage to Adana (Kherdian) **6**:280-81; **9**:317
"Homage to Back to Methuselah" (Brophy) **105**:6
Homage to Blenholt (Fuchs) **8**:220-22; **22**:155, 158
"Homage to César Paladíon" (Borges) **19**:48; **48**:37
"Homage to Cézanne" (Wright) **28**:457-60; **146**:303, 305, 308, 312, 322, 330, 338, 343, 353, 360-64
"Homage to Clichés" (MacNeice) **10**:324; **53**:235
Homage to Clio (Auden) **3**:29
"Homage to Clotho: A Hospital Suite" (Sissman) **9**:492; **18**:488, 490
Homage to Creely (Spicer) **8**:499; **18**:510
Homage to Daniel Shays: Collected Essays, 1952-1972 (Vidal) **2**:450-51; **4**:553; **6**:550; **8**:528
"Homage to Dashiell Hammett" (Macdonald) **41**:270
"Homage to Duke Ellington on His Birthday" (Ellison) **86**:327
Homage to Edgar Allan Poe (Smith) **42**:346, 350, 353, 357
"Homage to Emerson, on Night Flight to New York" (Warren) **8**:539; **18**:536; **39**:267
"Homage to Ezra Pound" (Wright) **6**:579
"Homage to Horace" (MacNeice) **53**:242
Homage to John Dryden: Three Essays on Poetry of the Seventeenth Century (Eliot)

24:158, 167, 169, 171, 182
"Homage to Lorca" (Ciardi) **40**:156
"Homage to L.S. Lowry" (Longley) **29**:294
"Homage to Lucille, Dr. Lord-Heinstein" (Piercy) **62**:371; **128**:231
"Homage to Lucretius" (Whalen) **29**:446
"Homage to Marcus Aurelius" (Brodsky) **100**:61, 69, 74
"Homage to Matthew Arnold" (Rosenthal) **28**:391
"homage to mine" (Clifton) **66**:80
Homage to Mistress Bradstreet (Berryman) **2**:56, 58; **3**:65-8, 70; **4**:61-2; **6**:64-5; **8**:86-7, 91-3; **10**:47, 49-5; **13**:78-9, 81-2; **25**:89, 91, 94, 97-8; **62**:43-4, 46, 56, 72, 74, 76
"homage to my hair" (Clifton) **66**:69, 88
"homage to my hips" (Clifton) **66**:88
"Homage to Nadar" (Howard) **47**:169
"Homage to Paul Cézanne" (Wright)
See "Homage to Cézanne"
"Homage to Paul Robeson" (Hayden) **37**:158
"Homage to Pavese" (Levertov) **15**:338
"Homage to Postman Cheval" (Szirtes) **46**:393
Homage to QWERT YUIOP, and Other Writings (Burgess) **62**:124; **94**:76
"Homage to Sextus Propertius" (Pound) **2**:342, 344; **3**:396; **4**:408; **7**:335-36; **13**:459, 462; **48**:282, 284; **112**:309-12, 340
"Homage to Shakespeare" (Cheever) **64**:66
"Homage to Switzerland" (Hemingway) **30**:192
"Homage to the Chinese" (Haines) **58**:221
"Homage to the Empress of the Blues" (Hayden) **37**:155, 160
Homage to the Lame Wolf: Selected Poems (Simic) **130**:340
"Homage to the Memory of Wallace Stevens" (Justice) **102**:264, 283-84
"Homage to the Weather" (Hamburger) **14**:234
"Homage to Theodore Dreiser" (Warren) **6**:555; **8**:537; **39**:270
"Homage to William Cowper" (Davie) **5**:115
"Homage to Winter" (Rich) **73**:315
"Homage to Yalta" (Brodsky) **36**:80
"Hombre" (Purdy) **14**:435
"El hombre" (Rulfo) **80**:200, 213, 215
Un hombre (Gironella) **11**:234-35, 238
Hombre (Leonard) **71**:208, 211, 219-21, 225; **120**:266, 287-88, 296
"Un hombre anda bajo la luna" (Neruda) **62**:322
"El Hombre de la esquina rosada" (Borges) **13**:104; **48**:33, 35-6; **83**:166
Hombre de paso/Just Passing Through (Goldemberg) **52**:165, 168
El hombre junto al mar (Padilla) **38**:351
Hombre y Dios (Alonso) **14**:17, 23
El hombre y sus sueños (Marqués) **96**:224, 243
"El hombrecito" (Donoso) **8**:178; **11**:146
"Hombres de las orillas" (Borges)
See "El Hombre de la esquina rosada"
Hombres de maíz (Asturias) **8**:28; **13**:37, 39-40
"Los hombres XIX" (Neruda) **62**:334
Hombres y engranajes (Sabato) **10**:446; **23**:379
"Home" (Beer) **58**:32
"Home" (Creeley) **78**:141
"Home" (D'Aguiar) **145**:119
"Home" (Gordimer) **70**:178, 180
"Home" (Grau) **146**:132, 139, 153
"Home" (Hughes) **108**:315
"Home" (King) **53**:212
"Home" (Lorde) **71**:258
"Home" (Lowell) **37**:238
"Home" (O Hehir) **41**:324
"Home" (Phillips) **15**:419-21; **139**:208-11
"Home" (Shields) **113**:425
"Home" (Updike) **15**:540
Home (Olson) **28**:343
Home (Storey) **2**:424-25; **4**:528-29; **5**:415, 417; **8**:505
"Home Address" (Bronk) **10**:75
"Home after Three Months Away" (Lowell) **15**:347
"Home Again" (Johnston) **51**:240, 244
"Home Again" (Montague) **46**:270
Home Again (Montague) **46**:266
Home and Colonial (Coward) **29**:140
Home and Exile (Nkosi) **45**:294
The Home and the Star (Lagerkvist)
See *Hemmet och stjärnan*
The Home and the World (Ray)
See *Ghare Bahire*
"Home at Last" (Becker and Fagen) **26**:84
Home Before Dark (Bridgers) **26**:90-2
Home before Dark: A Biographical Memoir of John Cheever by His Daughter (Cheever) **48**:65-8
Home before Night (Leonard) **19**:282-83
The Home Book (Schuyler) **23**:388
"Home Burial" (Frost) **1**:110; **9**:227; **26**:111, 113, 119
"Home Burial" (Kennedy) **42**:256
Home Chat (Buck) **18**:80
Home Chat (Coward) **29**:131
Home Cooking: A Writer in the Kitchen (Colwin) **84**:142-43
Home Course in Religion (Soto) **80**:302
"Home Economics" (Castellanos)
See "Economía doméstica"
Home Fires (Guare) **29**:203
"Home for a Couple of Days" (Kelman) **58**:298
"Home for Thanksgiving" (Merwin) **88**:205
"Home for the Elderly" (Raine) **32**:349; **103**:186
A Home for the Heart (Bettelheim) **79**:111
"Home for Wayfarers" (Sayles) **14**:483
"Home Free" (Johnston) **51**:243, 245, 252
Home Free (Johnston) **51**:240-49, 251-52
"Home from Greece" (Stern) **40**:407
"Home from Hiroshima" (Clark Bekedermo) **38**:129
Home from the Hill (Humphrey) **45**:193-99, 201-02
Home from the War: Vietnam Veterans—Neither Victims nor Executioners (Lifton) **67**:143, 145, 150, 154
"The Home Front" (Stafford) **68**:422
Home Front Memo (Sandburg) **35**:354
Home Game (Quarrington) **65**:203
"Home Girl" (Ferber) **93**:145
"Home Ground" (Longley) **29**:295
"Home Home Home" (Ferlinghetti) **27**:139
"Home Is a Wounded Heart" (Diamond) **30**:112
"Home Is So Sad" (Larkin) **5**:227; **64**:266
"Home Is the Hangman" (Zelazny) **21**:474
Home Is the Sailor (Amado)
See *Os velhos marinheiros*
"Home Is Where You Hang Yourself" (Richler) **46**:352
"Home Movie" (Rule) **27**:423
"Home Movies" (Broumas) **73**:9
Home Movies (De Palma) **20**:80
"The Home of the Human Race" (Saroyan) **8**:468
"Home Paddock" (Shapcott) **38**:398
The Home Place (Morris) **1**:232; **37**:313, 316
"Home Revisited: Midnight and Thursday" (Ciardi) **40**:154
"Home Run" (Bukowski) **41**:73
Home: Social Essays (Baraka) **5**:45; **14**:48; **33**:53-4, 63; **115**:10, 45, 47-9
"Home Sweet Home" (Carroll) **10**:96-7
Home Sweet Home (Richler) **46**:351-53
"Home Thoughts" (Turco) **11**:552
Home Thoughts (Parks) **147**:198
"Home to Marie" (Beattie) **146**:59-60, 67, 69
"Home Town" (Snodgrass) **68**:388
"Home Town" (Waterhouse) **47**:417
Home Truths (Lodge) **141**:375
Home Truths: Selected Canadian Stories (Gallant) **38**:189-91, 193-94
Homeage to the American Indians (Cardenal)
See *Homenaje a los indios americanos*
Homeboy (Morgan) **65**:75-80
"Homecoming" (Alvarez) **93**:6
"Homecoming" (Lowell) **37**:238
"Homecoming" (Sanchez) **116**:276, 293
Homecoming (Alvarez) **93**:2, 6, 8-10
The Homecoming (Hamner) **12**:258
The Homecoming (Pinter) **3**:385-88; **6**:404, 410-14, 416-17, 420; **9**:420; **11**:442-45; **15**:422-23, 426; **27**:385, 392-95; **58**:369-71, 373, 375, 383-84; **73**:247-81
Homecoming (Sanchez) **116**:272, 274-76, 278, 282, 293-94, 301-02, 308-09, 313-14, 324
Homecoming (Snow) **4**:501; **13**:508-09, 511; **19**:425, 427
Homecoming (Voigt) **30**:417-19
The Homecoming (Wilson) **118**:398
Homecoming: Essays of African and Caribbean Literature, Culture, and Politics (Ngũgĩ wa Thiong'o) **36**:310-12, 318
"Homecoming in Late March" (Steele) **45**:363
"Homecoming of Emma Lazarus" (Kinnell) **29**:287
Homecoming: Reclaiming and Championing Your Inner Child (Bradshaw) **70**:425
"Homecomings" (Heaney) **25**:243, 247
Homecomings (Snow)
See *Homecoming*
Homefront (Walser)
See *Zimmerschlacht*
Home-girls (Moraga) **126**:289
Homegirls and Hand Grenades (Sanchez) **116**:287, 289, 299, 302-07, 309, 313, 317, 324
"Homegrown" (Young) **17**:576
"Homeland" (Kingsolver) **130**:73
Homeland, and Other Stories (Kingsolver) **81**:191; **130**:73, 75, 77-78, 80, 89, 96-97, 120
"The Homeless" (Merwin) **13**:386
"Homeless" (Seth) **43**:388
"Home-longing" (Atwood) **84**:105
"The Homely Heroine" (Ferber) **93**:140, 146
"Homemade" (McEwan) **66**:277-79
"Home-Made Beer" (Purdy) **14**:431; **50**:247
Homemade Love (Cooper) **56**:70-2
"Homenagem renovada a Marianne Moore" (Cabral de Melo Neto) **76**:160, 165
"Homenaje" (Cernuda) **54**:47
"Homenaje a Johann Jacobi Bachofen" (Arreola) **147**:10
Homenaje a los indios americanos (Cardenal) **31**:71-2
"Homenaje a Otto Weininger" (Arreola) **147**:31
"Homeplace" (Hooks) **94**:145
"Homer" (Katz) **47**:216
"Homer Nods" (Deane) **122**:82
Homer's Daughter (Graves) **45**:172
"Homes" (Montague) **46**:274
"Homesickness" (Bennett) **28**:27
"Home-Sickness...from the Town" (Huxley) **11**:282-83
"The Homesitter" (Binchy) **153**:75
Homespun of Oatmeal Gray (Goodman) **2**:169, 171
"Homestead, 1914" (Suknaski) **19**:432
"The Homestead Called Damascus" (Rexroth) **22**:344, 347; **49**:274-75, 279, 284-85; **112**:373-75, 379-80
"The Homestead Orchard" (Davis) **49**:91, 94, 97
"Hometown Piece for Messers Alston and Reese" (Moore) **47**:261, 263
"Homeward" (Alexander) **121**:8
"Homeward Bound" (Simon) **17**:465-66
The Homeward Bounders (Jones) **26**:231
Homeward to America (Ciardi) **40**:151, 153, 156-57; **44**:378; **129**:45
"Homeward, to Jayanta and Runu Mahapatra" (Alexander) **121**:5
"Homewards" (Transtroemer) **52**:418
"Homework" (Van Duyn) **7**:498; **63**:437, 440; **116**:402, 420, 428
"Homework Assignment on the Subject of Angels" (Rozewicz) **23**:363

Homeworld (Harrison) **42**:206-07
"Hommage à Bournonville" (Hoeg) **95**:116-17
"Hommage à Cezanne" (Durcan) **70**:151-52
"Hommage et famine" (Char) **9**:164
"Hommage to a Young Witch" (Cortázar) **10**:117
"Hommage to Malcolm Lowry" (Mahon) **27**:287
"Hommage to the British Museum" (Empson) **8**:202
L'homme assis dans le couloir (Duras) **68**:91
L'homme atlantique (Duras) **40**:181, 183-84; **68**:96
L'homme au petit chien (Simenon) **18**:483
L'homme aux valises (Ionesco) **9**:287-90; **11**:294; **41**:230; **86**:332, 341
Un homme comme un autre (Simenon) **8**:488
Un Homme de Broadway (Hart)
See *Act One: An Autobiography*
Un homme de Dieu (Marcel) **15**:363
"L'homme du parc Monceau" (Mandiargues) **41**:277
"L'homme et la bête" (Levine) **14**:317
"L'homme et la bête" (Senghor) **54**:410
"L'homme et les choses" (Sartre) **24**:418
L'homme foudroyé (Cendrars) **18**:93, 96, 98; **106**:167, 169, 172-73, 179, 182-83, 185, 187-88, 190, 192
"L'homme ligoté" (Sartre) **24**:417
L'homme nu (Lévi-Strauss) **38**:304, 306, 308
Un homme paisible (Michaux) **19**:311
Un homme qui dort (Perec) **56**:256-58; **116**:232-33, 235, 237-38, 246-48, 252-53, 261
L'homme qui ment (Robbe-Grillet) **4**:449; **8**:454; **14**:457; **43**:366; **128**:348, 362
L'homme révolté (Camus) **2**:97, 99; **4**:89, 91-2; **9**:143; **11**:95; **14**:107-09, 111-12, 115, 117; **32**:90, 97; **63**:62-3, 69, 71-3, 75, 82, 86, 117, 127, 133-36; **69**:117, 127, 133-36; **124**:7-9, 11-3, 23-4, 28-30, 33, 35, 38, 42-3
Les hommes abandonnés (Duhamel) **8**:187
Les hommes de bonne volonté (Romains) **7**:379-82
Les Hommes naissent tous le même jour (Gallo) **95**:98
"Hommunculus" (Bogan) **46**:86
Homo Faber: A Report (Frisch) **3**:167; **18**:163; **32**:188-90, 192, 194; **44**:183-85, 187-90, 199
Homo sexualis (Oe) **36**:347; **86**:225
Homo viator (Marcel) **15**:359
"The Homosexual Villain" (Mailer) **111**:104
Homosexuality and Literature, 1890-1930 (Meyers) **39**:433
"Homosexuality in Robert Duncan's Poetry" (Gunn) **32**:212
El hondero entusiasta, 1923-1924 (Neruda) **28**:312; **62**:323
Hondo (L'Amour) **25**:279; **55**:306-08
Honest Confession of a Literary Sin (Stuart) **34**:375
"Honest Confrontation" (Ritsos) **31**:325
"Honest Souls" (D'Aguiar) **145**:117
The Honest-to-God Schnozzola (Horovitz) **56**:149
"Honesty" (Joel) **26**:216-17
"Honey" (Beattie) **146**:58-61, 66
"Honey" (Johnston) **51**:243
"Honey" (Wright) **28**:469
Honey and Bread (Davies) **23**:141
Honey and Salt (Sandburg) **4**:463; **10**:449, 452; **15**:467; **35**:356
"Honey and Tobacco" (Silkin) **43**:401
"Honey at the Table" (Oliver) **34**:249; **98**:298
Honey for the Bears (Burgess) **13**:124; **22**:69, 78; **40**:115-16; **81**:301; **94**:25, 52, 64-5
"Honey, I'm Home!" (Bogosian) **141**:85
Honey in the Horn (Davis) **49**:80-5, 89-90, 94, 97-8
Honey out of the Rock (Deutsch) **18**:118
Honey Seems Bitter (Kiely) **23**:262; **43**:245
"The Honey Tree" (Oliver) **98**:299-300
The Honey Tree (Elliott) **47**:110-11
"Honey, We'll Be Brave" (Farrell) **66**:112, 131
Honeybath's Haven (Stewart) **14**:512
Honeybuzzard (Carter)
See *Shadow Dance*
Honeycomb (Saura) **20**:315
"The Honeyed Peace" (Gellhorn) **60**:183-84
The Honeyed Peace (Gellhorn) **60**:183-84
The Honeyman Festival (Engel) **36**:158-59, 162, 165
"Honeymoon" (O'Brien) **5**:311
"Honeymoon" (Seifert) **93**:333
"The Honeymoon" (Simmons) **43**:414
Honeymoon (Mahfouz)
See *Shahr al'asal*
Honeymoon (Seifert) **34**:256
"Honeymoon at Tramore" (Trevor) **71**:341; **116**:347, 363
The Honeymoon Voyage (Thomas) **13**:542; **31**:430; **132**:382
A Hong Kong House: Poems, 1951-1961 (Blunden) **56**:35-6, 40, 45, 47, 50
Honky Tonk Heroes (Jennings) **21**:202, 205
"Honky Tonk in Cleveland" (Sandburg) **35**:352
"Honkytonk" (Shapiro) **15**:476
"Honneurs funèbres" (Kiš) **57**:249
"Honolulu" (Dickey) **28**:119
"Honolulu" (Maugham) **67**:206
Honor Among Lovers (Arzner) **98**:69-70, 87
Honor, Power, Riches, Fame, and the Love of Women (Just) **27**:229
Honor Thy Father (Talese) **37**:393-94, 404
Honorable Men (Auchincloss) **45**:34-6
The Honorary Consul (Greene) **3**:212-15; **6**:219-20; **14**:219; **18**:197-98; **27**:173, 175-76; **37**:137; **70**:289, 292-93; **125**:175, 187
"The Honored Dead" (Pancake) **29**:347, 350
"Honoring Whitman" (Simpson) **149**:308, 313-16
"Honourable Estate" (Brittain) **23**:90
The Honourable Schoolboy (le Carré) **9**:326-27; **15**:324-26
"The Hon. Sec." (Betjeman) **2**:60; **43**:43
An Honoured Guest (Gordimer)
See *A Guest of Honour*
The Honours Board (Johnson) **27**:221, 223-24
"Hoodlums" (Sandburg) **35**:341
"Hoodoo Valley" (Roy) **14**:469
"The Hoofer" (Miller) **30**:264-65
"Hook" (Clark) **28**:78-9
"The Hook" (Weiss) **3**:517; **14**:556
Hook a Fish, Catch a Mountain: An Ecological Spy Story (George) **35**:177
"Hooks" (Williams) **56**:425
"Hooks and Feelers" (Hulme) **130**:44, 52
"Hoop Dancer" (Allen) **84**:39-40, 43
Hoops (Myers) **35**:298
Hooters (Tally) **42**:367
"Hop o' My Thumb" (Ashbery) **125**:15
Hop Signor! (Ghelderode) **11**:226
"Hope" (Avison) **97**:115
"Hope" (Hughes) **108**:336
"The Hope" (Ignatow) **4**:247
"Hope" (Lustig) **56**:182
"Hope" (Milosz) **31**:266
"Hope" (Mueller) **13**:399-400
"Hope" (Warren) **39**:270
Hope (Moravia)
See *La speranza*
Hope and Suffering: Sermons and Speeches (Tutu) **80**:357-59
"Hope Atherton's Wanderings" (Howe) **72**:204; **152**:165-66, 168, 170, 216
"The Hope Chest" (Stafford) **7**:457
A Hope for Poetry (Day Lewis) **10**:128, 133
Hope of Heaven (O'Hara) **42**:312, 320-21
"Hope Springs" (Loewinsohn) **52**:285
"Hope Stories" (Moure) **88**:232
Hopeful Monsters (Mosley) **70**:199-206
Hopelessness (Donoso)
See *La Desesperanza*
Hopes and Impediments: Selected Essays (Achebe) **127**:28, 33, 40
"Hopes Rise" (Boyle) **90**:62-3
"Hopi Overlay" (Rose) **85**:312
Hoping for a Hoopoe (Updike)
See *The Carpentered Hen and Other Tame Creatures*
"Hopkins to Whitman" (Dacey) **51**:83
"Hopper: The Loneliness Factor" (Strand) **71**:278
Hopscotch (Cortázar)
See *Rayuela*
Hopscotch (Horovitz) **56**:155
"Hoquet" (Damas) **84**:168, 177-78, 180
"La hora cero" (Cardenal)
See "La hora O"
A hora da estrela (Lispector) **43**:263-67, 271
La hora de todos (Arreola) **147**:4, 7-9, 11
"La hora O" (Cardenal) **31**:71, 75-7
"Horace and Margaret's Fifty-Second" (Baxter) **45**:51; **78**:17
"Horae Canonicae" (Auden) **14**:29; **123**:35, 39
"The Horatians" (Auden) **4**:33; **11**:17; **123**:16
"Horatio's Trick" (Beattie) **146**:59, 61, 67
Hore (Arghezi) **80**:6, 8
Horeb's Stone (Duhamel) **8**:187
"Horizon" (Soupault) **68**:405
Horizon (MacInnes) **27**:279-80
L'horizon (Marcel) **15**:363
"Horizon and Style" (Blaga)
See "Orizont şi stil"
"Horizons West" (Gregor) **9**:253
"The Horizontal Bop" (Seger) **35**:384-85
The Horn (Holmes) **56**:136-37, 140
Horn (Mano) **2**:270; **10**:328
"Horn Came" (Beckett) **29**:57
Horn of Africa (Caputo) **32**:104-06
Horn of My Love (p'Bitek) **96**:276-78, 291-92, 294, 299, 301-02, 306-07, 311
"Horn of Plenty" (Gordimer) **33**:179
Hornblower and the "Atropas" (Forester) **35**:170
Hornblower and the Crisis (Forester)
See *Hornblower during the Crisis*
The Hornblower Companion (Forester) **35**:172
Hornblower during the Crisis (Forester) **35**:171
"The Hornet's House" (Belitt) **22**:50-1
Hornet's Nest (Cornwell) **155**:69-72
Die Hornissen (Handke) **134**:128-30
"Horns" (Haines) **58**:215, 219
Horns Ende (Hein) **154**:59, 62, 72, 76, 96, 98-100, 103-05, 115, 133-36, 138-51, 160, 164-65, 167-68, 170, 182, 187-89, 191, 194
"Horoscope" (Clark Bekedermo) **38**:127
Les horreurs de la guerre (Perec) **56**:264
"Horror at Island Pond" (Harrison) **144**:112-13
"Horror Movie" (Dybek) **114**:64, 70
"Horror Movie" (Moss) **14**:375-76
"Horror Stories" (Jiles) **58**:271, 275, 277-78, 281
"Hors livre" (Derrida) **24**:156
"Horse" (Glück) **44**:217-18, 221-22
"The Horse" (Levine) **118**:274-75, 283
"The Horse" (Merwin) **8**:390; **18**:334
"The Horse" (Raine) **32**:349; **103**:186
"The Horse" (Wright) **28**:462
The Horse (Kurosawa)
See *Uma*
The Horse and His Boy (Lewis) **124**:236, 248
"Horse and Swan Feeding" (Swenson) **61**:398-99; **106**:313, 324-25, 340
"A Horse and Two Goats" (Narayan) **47**:304-06; **121**:369, 418, 420
A Horse and Two Goats, and Other Stories (Narayan) **28**:295; **121**:339
"The Horse Chestnut Tree" (Eberhart) **19**:144
"The Horse Fair" (Brown) **100**:81
Horse Feathers (Perelman) **44**:501-02, 504-05; **49**:270
The Horse Has Six Legs, (Simic) **130**:329, 334
"The Horse in the Cage" (Plumly) **33**:313
"Horse Latitudes" (Matthiessen) **64**:321, 324

"Horse Latitudes" (Morrison) **17**:291-92
The Horse Latitudes (Ferrigno) **65**:47-50
The Horse Show at Midnight (Taylor) **44**:301
The Horse Tamer (Farley) **17**:117-18
"The Horse That Died of Shame" (Momaday) **85**:247, 279
Horse under Water (Deighton) **7**:75; **22**:114-15
"Horseback" (Kizer) **80**:183
"Horseback in the Rain" (Still) **49**:363
The Horsehair Sofa (Hughes) **48**:181
"Horseman" (Zelazny) **21**:479
The Horseman (Haavikko) **34**:173, 175, 177-79
"The Horseman of Agawa" (Purdy) **50**:246-47
The Horseman on the Roof (Giono)
See *Le hussard sur le toit*
Horseman, Pass By (McMurtry) **2**:272; **7**:213-15; **11**:371; **27**:324-31; **44**:256; **127**:303, 311-12, 314-16, 319, 322, 328, 330, 333, 344-45, 349
"Horses" (Alexie) **154**:21
"Horses" (Hughes) **4**:235; **9**:281; **14**:270
"Horses" (Neruda) **7**:260
"Horses" (Smith) **12**:536
"Horses" (Smith) **73**:357
"Horses" (Walker)
See *Horses Make a Landscape Look More Beautiful*
Horses (Harjo)
See *She Had Some Horses*
Horses (Smith) **12**:535-40, 543
"Horses at Valley Store" (Silko) **74**:347
Horses Don't Bet on People and Neither Do I (Bukowski) **82**:13-14
"Horses Graze" (Brooks) **15**:93; **49**:36
A Horse's Head (Hunter) **31**:221
Horses Make a Landscape Look More Beautiful (Walker) **58**:407, 409
Horse's Neck (Townshend) **42**:378-81
Horses of Anger (Forman) **21**:116
"Horsie" (Parker) **68**:326, 334, 337
"Hortatory" (Dacey) **51**:80
Hosanna (Tremblay) **29**:418-19, 421; **102**:360-61, 364, 372, 374
"Hosanna Heysanna" (Rice and Webber) **21**:426
"Hose and Iron" (Kuzma) **7**:197
"The Hospice" (Aickman) **57**:3
"Hospital" (Bowering) **47**:19
"The Hospital" (Kavanagh) **22**:243
The Hospital (Chayefsky) **23**:116, 118
The Hospital (Fearing) **51**:107-08, 121-22
Hospital (Kieslowski) **120**:243
Hospital (Wiseman) **20**:469-70, 472
"A Hospital Christmas Eve" (McCullers) **4**:345
"Hospital Garden" (Jennings) **131**:233
"The Hospital in Winter" (Fisher) **25**:159
The Hospital of the Transfiguration (Lem)
See *Szpital Przemienienia*
The Hospital Play (Shawn) **41**:400
"Hospital / poem (for etheridge 9/26/69)" (Sanchez) **116**:295
Hospital Zone (Stolz) **12**:549-50
"A Host of Furious Fancies" (Ballard) **137**:63
"Hostage" (Oates) **108**:384
The Hostage (Behan)
See *An Giall*
Hostage (Household) **11**:277
The Hostage Towers (MacLean) **50**:348
"Hostages" (Banks) **72**:3, 5
"Hostages" (Wideman) **67**:379, 384
Hostages (Heym) **41**:210-11, 213, 215
Hostages to Fortune (Humphrey) **45**:201-02
Hosties noires (Senghor) **54**:390-91, 399-400, 407, 410; **130**:234-35, 238, 241-43, 247, 249, 258-59, 280, 284
Hostile Murmurs (Lezama Lima)
See *Enemigo rumor*
"Höstlig skärgård" (Transtroemer) **52**:418; **65**:233
Höstsonaten (Bergman) **16**:80-1; **72**:57, 59
"Hot" (Bukowski) **108**:113
Hot and Cold (Crommelynck)
See *Chaud et froid ou l'idée de Monsieur Dom*
"Hot as Sun Glasses" (McCartney) **35**:278-79
"Hot Ashes" (Arghezi) **80**:10
Hot August Night (Diamond) **30**:113
"Hot Broth" (Barnard) **48**:27
Hot Cars (Hunter) **31**:228
"Hot Coils" (McFadden) **48**:244
A Hot Country (Naipaul) **32**:327-28; **39**:355-57
Hot Day, Hot Night (Himes)
See *Blind Man with a Pistol*
"Hot Day on the Gold Coast" (Shacochis) **39**:199-200
"Hot Dog" (Stern) **100**:345
"Hot Flash" (Pollitt) **122**:207
The Hot Gates, and Other Occasional Pieces (Golding) **3**:199; **17**:169-70; **27**:164, 167, 169; **58**:190, 192-94; **81**:318
"Hot Ice" (Dybek) **114**:70-1, 74-7, 83
Hot Ice (Ludlam) **46**:240
The Hot Iron (Green) **25**:193
"Hot June" (Avison) **97**:77-8, 83
The Hot l Baltimore (Wilson) **7**:548; **14**:590, 592; **36**:465-66
Hot Money (Francis) **102**:128, 130-32, 148, 158
"Hot Night on Water Street" (Simpson) **7**:426; **149**:295, 306, 309
Hot Rats (Zappa) **17**:586, 590
The Hot Rock (Westlake) **7**:528; **33**:436, 438-40
Hot Rocks (Jagger and Richard) **17**:226
Hot Rod (Felsen) **17**:121-22
Hot Sleep: The Worthing Chronicle (Card) **47**:67-8
"Hot Spell" (Jensen) **37**:192
Hot Water Music (Bukowski) **41**:72-3
Hotcakes (Simon) **26**:408-09
"L'hôte" (Camus) **9**:144-45; **14**:114; **63**:71; **69**:135
"Hotel" (Creeley) **78**:154
"Hotel" (Dobyns) **37**:75
"Hotel" (Merwin) **45**:272
"The Hotel" (Singer) **69**:311-12
The Hotel (Bowen) **11**:62; **15**:78; **118**:107
Hotel (Hailey) **5**:157-58
"Hotel Behind the Lines" (Boyle) **58**:81
Hotel de Dream (Tennant) **13**:536-37; **52**:398
Hôtel du Commerce (Hochwälder) **36**:235
Hotel du Lac (Brookner) **34**:136-43; **51**:59, 61-3, 65; **136**:77-80, 88, 90, 92, 97-102, 104-05, 109, 112-15, 117, 119, 121, 127
The Hotel in Amsterdam (Osborne) **2**:328; **5**:333; **11**:421; **45**:313-16
A Hotel in the Hills (Havel) **123**:172
Hotel Insomnia (Simic) **130**:329, 332, 334, 336-38
Hotel Lautreamont (Ashbery) **77**:77; **125**:30-1, 35-8, 40
The Hotel New Hampshire (Irving) **23**:247-54; **38**:250-52; **112**:139-41, 154-58, 164-65
"The Hotel Normandie Pool" (Walcott) **25**:455-57; **76**:275
"The Hotel of Lost Light" (Kinnell) **129**:251
"The Hotel of the Idle Moon" (Trevor) **71**:326; **116**:371
"The Hotel of the Total Stranger" (White) **39**:375
Hotel Pastis: A Novel of Provence (Mayle) **89**:150-53
The Hotel Play (Shawn) **41**:399
Hotel "To the Lost Climber" (Strugatskii and Strugatskii) **27**:434
The Hotel Wentley Poems (Wieners) **7**:535-37
Hôtes de passage (Malraux) **9**:358; **57**:307, 320
Hothouse (Aldiss)
See *The Long Afternoon of Earth*
The Hothouse (Pinter) **27**:388, 392, 394; **58**:371, 385
Hothouse (Terry) **19**:441
The Hothouse by the East River (Spark) **3**:465-66; **5**:400; **8**:495; **13**:524-25; **94**:353
Hotline (Hyde) **21**:177
"Hots On for Nowhere" (Page and Plant) **12**:480
The Hottentot Room (Hope) **52**:214-17
"Houdini" (Weidman) **7**:517
"Houdini's Picnic" (Mitchell) **98**:180
"Hound" (Donnell) **34**:158
"The Hound" (Faulkner) **18**:149
The Hound of Earth (Bourjaily) **62**:84-9, 93
The Hound of Ulster (Sutcliff) **26**:433
Hounds on the Mountain (Still) **49**:362-63, 365
"The Hour" (Dunn) **40**:165
"An Hour" (Milosz) **22**:308; **82**:298
"The Hour and the Years" (Gordimer) **33**:177
An Hour Beyond Midnight (Hesse)
See *Eine Stunde hinter Mitternacht*
Hour of Gold, Hour of Lead: Diaries and Letters of Anne Morrow Lindbergh, 1929-1932 (Lindbergh) **82**:151
"The Hour of Letdown" (White) **10**:527
"The Hour of Not Quite Rain" (Young) **17**:569
The Hour of the Star (Lispector)
See *A hora da estrela*
The Hour of the Wolf (Bergman)
See *Vargtimmen*
The Hour We Knew Nothing of Each Other (Handke)
See *Die Stunde da wir nichts voneinander wußten*
Hourglass (Kiš)
See *Peščanik*
Hourra l'oural (Aragon) **3**:15
"The Hours" (Dubie) **36**:133
"An Hour's Restless Sleep" (McFadden) **48**:244
"The House" (Adcock) **41**:13
"The House" (Cisneros) **118**:176
"The House" (Coles) **46**:107
"The House" (Hogan) **73**:158
"The House" (Merwin) **45**:274
"House" (O Hehir) **41**:323-24
"The House" (Olson) **28**:343
"The House" (Sexton) **15**:472
"House" (Tomlinson) **45**:398, 400-01
"House" (Williams) **148**:367
"The House" (Zweig) **42**:470
House (Ferré)
See *The House on the Lagoon*
A House and Its Head (Compton-Burnett) **15**:135, 138, 141
"The House at Sagg" (Crase) **58**:161, 165
"House behind a House" (Seger) **35**:386
House, Bridge, Fountain, Gate (Kumin) **13**:326
"House by the Sea" (Montale)
See "Casa sul mare"
The House by the Sea: A Journal (Sarton) **14**:482; **49**:317-18, 322
A House by the Shore (Neruda) **28**:313-14
"House Dick" (Hammett) **47**:156
A House Divided (Buck) **7**:31-2; **11**:71, 73, 76-7; **18**:80
"House (fires)" (Alexie) **154**:
A House for Mr. Biswas (Naipaul) **4**:371-75; **7**:252-54; **9**:392-93; **13**:403-06; **18**:359-61, 363; **37**:323-25, 327, 329; **105**:140, 147, 149, 151-52, 154-56, 160, 170, 180-81
"The House Friend" (Singer) **69**:311-12
"The House Growing" (Updike) **23**:476
"House Guest" (Bishop) **32**:39
"House Hunting" (Chabon) **149**:22-4
"House Hunting" (Oates) **108**:381
The House in Blind Alley (Rice) **7**:364; **49**:305
The House in Clewe Street (Lavin) **18**:304; **99**:312
The House in Cornwall (Streatfeild)
See *The Secret of the Lodge*
The House in Darkness (Vesaas)
See *Huset i mørkret*
"A House in Festubert" (Blunden) **56**:30, 38, 44
"The House in French Village" (Strand) **41**:434
A House in Order (Dennis) **8**:173
The House in Paris (Bowen) **1**:39; **3**:82-83; **11**:59-60, 62-64; **15**:78-79; **118**:104, 109-10
"The House in the Acorn" (Redgrove) **41**:348

"House in the Country" (Davies) **21**:97
A House in the Country (Donoso)
See *Casa de campo*
The House in the Dark (Vesaas)
See *Huset i mørkret*
A House in the Middle of the Highway (Popa)
See *Kuća nasred druma*
A House in the Uplands (Caldwell) **14**:99; **60**:53
"House in the Wind" (Stuart) **34**:375
"The House in the Woods" (Ortese)
See "La casa del bosco"
"House in Toas" (Hughes) **108**:310
"The House in Turk Street" (Hammett) **47**:164
"House Is an Enigma" (Jensen) **37**:189-90
"House Lie, Believe the Lying Sea" (Hugo) **32**:247
House Made of Dawn (Momaday) **2**:289-90; **19**:318-21; **85**:226-30, 232-33, 238, 241, 245-48, 250-51, 255-57, 262, 270-73; **95**:214-81
"The House Martins" (Hamburger) **5**:159
House Mother Normal: A Geriatric Comedy (Johnson) **6**:262-63; **9**:300-02
"The House Next Door" (Dunn) **6**:149
A House Not Meant to Stand (Williams) **45**:455
"House o' Law" (Bennett) **28**:29
House of a Thousand Doors (Alexander) **121**:3-4, 6-8, 22
The House of a Thousand Lanterns (Hibbert) **7**:156
House of All Nations (Stead) **2**:420, 423; **5**:403-05; **8**:500; **32**:411-12, 415; **80**:307, 326, 329, 334, 336, 338, 341, 349
"The House of an Old Woman" (Kelman) **58**:295
The House of Assignation (Robbe-Grillet)
See *La maison de rendez-vous*
"The House of Asterión" (Borges)
See "La casa de Asterión"
The House of Blue Leaves (Guare) **8**:253; **14**:220; **29**:204-05, 208; **67**:78-9, 82-6, 88
The House of Brass (Queen) **11**:465
The House of Breath (Goyen) **5**:148-49; **8**:250; **14**:209-11, 214; **40**:215, 218
"House of Chirundo" (Mphahlele) **25**:340
The House of Connelly (Green) **25**:194, 196, 198-99
The House of Cornwall (Streatfeild)
See *The Secret of the Lodge*
House of Cowards (Abse) **29**:21-2
"House of Creation" (Akhmadulina)
See "Dom tvorchestva"
"The House of Darkstones" (Peake) **54**:372
The House of Dies Drear (Hamilton) **26**:147-48, 153-54
The House of Doctor Dee (Ackroyd) **140**:17, 36-7
The House of Dust: A Symphony (Aiken) **52**:22, 28
House of Earth (Buck) **11**:73, 75
The House of Fiction: An Anthology of the Short Story, with Commentary (Gordon) **6**:203; **13**:245; **83**:232, 235, 251
The House of Five Talents (Auchincloss) **4**:29; **45**:27-8
House of Flowers (Capote) **13**:134-35; **19**:81-2; **34**:322; **38**:82
"The House of God" (Hope) **51**:221
The House of Hanover: England in the Eighteenth Century (Garfield) **12**:232-34
"House of Haunts" (Queen) **11**:461
The House of Hospitalities (Tennant) **52**:405-06
House of Incest (Nin) **4**:378-79; **8**:425; **14**:381, 383-84; **60**:279, 281; **127**:361, 365, 370, 377-82, 397, 399-01, 403
The House of Intellect (Barzun) **51**:36-8; **145**:70, 72
"The House of Lamplight Alley" (Aksenov) **22**:27
House of Liars (Morante)
See *Menzogna e sortilegio*
House of Light (Oliver) **98**:276-80, 282-85, 290, 293-94, 302
The House of Mirth (Auchincloss) **9**:55
"The House of My Dreams" (O'Brien) **5**:311-12; **8**:429; **36**:341; **116**:194-95
"A House of My Own" (Cisneros) **69**:148; **118**:177, 180
"The House of Okumura VII" (Eshleman) **7**:99
"The House of Oliver Ames" (McGinley) **14**:366
"House of Rest" (Betjeman) **43**:50
The House of Roses (Endō) **99**:285-86
The House of Rothschild (Ferguson) **134**:64
The House of Rothschild: Money's Prophets: 1798-1848 (Ferguson)
See *The World's Banker: The History of the House of Rothschild*
The House of Rothschild: The World's Banker, 1849-1999 (Ferguson)
See *The World's Banker: The History of the House of Rothschild*
"House of Shade" (Kaye) **28**:198
The House of Sleep (Kavan) **13**:315; **82**:118-19, 126
House of Splendid Isolation (O'Brien) **116**:211, 213-15, 226
House of the Blue Horse (Kingman) **17**:244
"The House of the Heart" (Wakoski) **9**:554
"The House of the Injured" (Haines) **58**:215
The House of the Prophet (Auchincloss) **18**:25-7
"House of the Sleeping Beauties" (Kawabata)
See "Nemureru bijo"
House of the Sleeping Beauties, and Other Stories (Kawabata)
See *Nemureru bijo*
The House of the Solitary Maggot (Purdy) **10**:424; **52**:342-43, 347
The House of the Spirits (Allende)
See *La casa de los espiritus*
The House of Thunder (Koontz) **78**:200
The House of Women (Bermant) **40**:95
"House on a Cliff" (MacNeice) **53**:238
The House on Coliseum Street (Grau) **4**:207; **146**:128, 133, 138-42, 146-47, 149, 151, 156, 159-62, 165
"The House on Kings Road" (Monette) **82**:323
"The House on Lamplight Alley" (Aksyonov) **101**:19
"The House on Mango Street" (Cisneros) **118**:180
The House On Mango Street (Cisneros) **69**:144-45, 148-56; **118**:171, 173-46, 181, 187, 202, 207-09, 214, 217
The House on Marshland (Glück) **7**:118-19; **22**:174-76; **44**:215-16, 221, 224
The House on Quai Notre Dame (Simenon) **8**:486
"The House on Tenth" (Bowering) **47**:24
The House on the Bluff (Douglas) **73**:65-7, 74-5, 86, 94
House on the Corner (Dove)
See *The Yellow House on the Corner*
The House on the Embankment (Trifonov)
See *Dom na naberezhnoi*
"A House on the Heights" (Capote) **38**:84
The House on the Lagoon (Ferré) **139**:177, 184-87, 193-94
The House on the Mound (Derleth) **31**:138
The House on the Shore (Dillon) **17**:93
The House on the Strand (du Maurier) **6**:147; **59**:287
House Party: A Soulful Happening (Bullins) **5**:82; **7**:36
"House Party to Celebrate the Destruction of the Roman Catholic Church in Ireland" (Kavanagh) **22**:240
"The House Taken Over" (Cortázar)
See "Casa tomada"
"The House That Jack Built" (Davenport) **38**:143
"The House Through" (Motion) **47**:288-89, 293
"A House to Let" (Lavin) **99**:321-22
"The House Where I Was Born" (Day Lewis) **10**:131
The House without the Door (Daly) **52**:88
"Houseboat Days" (Ashbery) **25**:52
Houseboat Days (Ashbery) **13**:30, 35-6; **15**:29, 31-5; **25**:52-3, 58; **41**:35-6, 38, 40-1; **77**:44-5, 54-5; **125**:18, 30, 35
"The Housebreaker of Shady Hill" (Cheever) **64**:48
The Housebreaker of Shady Hill, and Other Stories (Cheever) **7**:49; **15**:127; **64**:54
"Housecleaning" (Giovanni) **117**:196
"Household" (Jensen) **37**:189
"Household Hints" (Longley) **29**:295
"Household recipe" (Arreola)
See "Receta casera"
Household Saints (Prose) **45**:325
Household Tales of Moon and Water (Willard) **37**:463-64
"The Householder" (Grau) **146**:153
The Householder (Jhabvala) **29**:254-56; **94**:167-68, 170, 176, 181, 184-85, 189-93, 205
"The Housekeeper" (Bishop) **32**:40
"Housekeeper" (Grau) **146**:132, 153
Housekeeping (Robinson) **25**:386-89
"Houseplants" (McFadden) **48**:250
"Houses" (Merwin) **88**:195
Houses and Travellers (Merwin) **8**:389-90; **18**:334; **88**:194
"Houses in North Oxford" (Raine) **103**:179, 186
The Houses of Children: Collected Stories (Dowell) **60**:107-109
"The Houses of Iszm" (Vance) **35**:420
"The Houses of the City" (Berriault) **109**:96
"Houses of the Holy" (Page and Plant) **12**:477, 482
Houses of the Holy (Page and Plant) **12**:476, 479-80, 482
Houses without Doors (Straub) **107**:284, 304
"The Housewarming" (Day Lewis) **10**:131
"Housewife" (Schaeffer) **11**:491
"Housewife" (Sexton) **8**:483; **53**:316
Housewives (Page) **40**:351
"Houston and History" (Steinem) **63**:381
"Houston, Houston, Do You Read?" (Tiptree) **48**:388-90, 395; **50**:358
"The Hovel" (Williams) **148**:360, 362
"How?" (Lennon) **35**:264-65, 267
"How" (Moore) **39**:84-5; **45**:279-80
"How about This?" (Carver) **36**:106
"How Beautiful Is Youth" (Hesse) **17**:218
"How 'Bigger' Was Born" (Wright) **21**:450; **48**:423, 428
"How Bozo the Button Buster Busted All His Buttons when a Mouse Came" (Sandburg) **15**:468
"How Claeys Died" (Sansom) **6**:484
"How Close" (Ortiz) **45**:303, 305
"How Crime Keeps America Healthy" (Puzo) **2**:352
"How Did I Get Away with Killing One of the Biggest Lawyers in the State? It Was Easy" (Walker) **103**:407, 410
"How Distant" (Larkin) **5**:223; **8**:333; **13**:335; **18**:300; **64**:282
"How Divine Is Forgiving?" (Piercy) **62**:379; **128**:273
"How Do I Feel" (Fearing) **51**:117
"How Do I Love You?" (Shapiro)
See "Sonnet VIII"
"How Do You Do, Dr. Berryman, Sir?" (Berryman) **3**:66
"How Do You Sleep?" (Lennon) **12**:367, 381; **35**:263-64, 268
"How Do You Think It Feels" (Reed) **21**:306
"How Does the State Imagine" (Updike) **139**:363
"How Duke Valentine Contrived" (Bunting) **47**:45, 49
"How Everything Happens (Based on a Study

of the Wave)" (Swenson) **61**:393; **106**:335, 339, 351
How Far Can You Go? (Lodge) **36**:273-74; **141**:344. 346-50, 359,371
How Far It Is From Here, How Near (Konwicki)
See *Jak daleko stad, jak blisko*
"How Gentle" (Oates) **6**:367; **33**:294
How German Is It (Abish) **22**:20-3
How Green Was My Valley (Ford) **16**:305, 316
How Green Was My Valley (Llewellyn) **7**:207; **80**:188-96
"How Hard It Is to Keep from Being King When It's in You and in the Situation" (Frost) **9**:229
How I Became a Holy Mother (Jhabvala) **8**:312-13; **29**:259; **94**:183-85, 187
How I Became a Writer (Gibbons) **145**:148-50
"How I Began" (Bainbridge) **130**:27
"How I Came to Be a Graduate Student" (Rose) **85**:311
"How I Came to Understand Irving Layton" (McFadden) **48**:248, 256
"How I Come to You" (Peacock) **60**:298
"How I Contemplated the World from the Detroit House of Correction and Began My Life Over Again" (Oates) **11**:400; **52**:338; **108**:367-68; **134**:248
"How I do What I Do If Not Why" (Vidal) **142**:284
"How I Escaped from the Labyrinth" (Dacey) **51**:79
How I Escaped from the Labyrinth, and Other Poems (Dacey) **51**:79-81
"How I Finally Lost My Heart" (Lessing) **10**:316; **22**:278
"How I Found America" (Yezierska) **46**:441
How I Got Him Back (Sayers) **122**:227-31, 233-34, 238, 240
"How I Got My Nickname" (Kinsella) **43**:256
How I Got That Story (Gray) **29**:200-01
How I Got to Be Perfect (Kerr) **22**:258
How I Grew (McCarthy) **59**:290-91
"How I Joined the Seal Herd" (Kroetsch) **23**:273
How I Met My Husband (Munro) **6**:341; **10**:357
"How I Missed the Million Dollar Round Table" (Kinsella) **43**:258
"How I Moved Anna Fierling to the Southwest Territories, or My Personal Victory over the Armies of Western Civilization" (Shange) **74**:308
"How I Painted Certain of My Pictures" (Bernstein) **142**:29
"How I Run Away and Make My Mother Toe the Line" (Mazer) **26**:295
"How I Saved Roosevelt" (Sondheim) **147**:244
"How I See Things" (Komunyakaa) **86**:192; **94**:224
How I Spent My Summer Holidays (Mitchell) **25**:327-28
"How I Started to Write" (Fuentes) **113**:256
How I Won the War (Lester) **20**:224-26
"How I Write" (Eberhart) **56**:89
"How I Write" (Welty) **105**:328, 333, 335
"How I Write My" (Foreman) **50**:167
"How I Wrote One of My Books" (Fuentes) **60**:162
"How I Wrote 'When Women Love Men'" (Ferré) **139**:150, 152
"How It Goes On" (Kumin) **13**:328; **28**:225
How It Is (Beckett)
See *Comment c'est*
"How It Was" (Milosz) **11**:380
How Late It Was, How Late (Kelman) **86**:180-89
How Life Began: Creation versus Evolution (Gallant) **17**:131
How Long Is Always (Weber) **12**:634
"How long, O Lord, how long?" (Sassoon) **130**:175
"How Long Will I Be Able To..." (Ashbery) **77**:42
"How Lousy Is Your Marriage: A 10-Minute Quiz That Could Help You Improve It" (Keillor) **115**:286
"How Many Friends" (Townshend) **17**:535-36
"How Many Goodly Creatures" (Fuller) **62**:199, 202
"How Many Heavens" (Sitwell) **67**:320
"How Many Midnights" (Bowles) **19**:60; **53**:37
How Many Miles to Babylon? (Fox) **2**:139; **121**:186, 198-99, 209, 211-12, 223, 225-26, 228
How Many Miles to Babylon? (Johnston) **7**:185-86; **150**:25, 32
"How Many More Times" (Page and Plant) **12**:473
"How Many Nights" (Kinnell) **29**:282
"How Mice Make Love" (Rosenblatt) **15**:446
"How Mickey Made It" (Phillips) **139**:206
"How Modern Christians Should Think about Man" (King) **83**:339
"How Morning Glories Could Bloom at Dusk" (Graham) **48**:145
"How Much" (Dybek) **114**:67
"How Much Earth" (Levine) **33**:271
How Much Is That in Dollars? (Buchwald) **33**:89-90
"How Not to Rate a Poet" (Carruth) **84**:127
"How Not to Write a Novel" (Grayson) **38**:211
"How Now We Talk" (Riding) **7**:374
"How Russian Is It: Lyn Hejinian's Oxota" (Perloff) **137**:303
"How Shall We Tell the Children" (Grass)
See "Wie sagen wir es den Kindern?"
How She Died (Yglesias) **7**:557-58; **22**:493
"How soon can I leave?" (Hill) **113**:293
How Stella Got Her Groove Back (McMillan) **112**:238, 240-46
"How Still the Hawk" (Tomlinson) **45**:392
"How 'Studs Lonigan' Was Written" (Farrell) **66**:134
"How Such a Lady" (Van Doren) **6**:541
"How Sweet and Proper It Is" (Dobyns) **37**:78
How Sweet It Is (Marshall) **17**:274-75
"How Sweet to Be an Idiot" (Monty Python) **21**:226
How the Dead Count (Johnson) **15**:480
How the Fishes Live (Lieber) **6**:311
How the Garcia Girls Lost Their Accents (Alvarez) **93**:2-5, 8-11, 13-8
"How the Last War Ended" (Garrett) **51**:140
"How the Mulatto Porciúncula Got the Corpse Off His Back" (Amado)
See "De como o Mulato Porciúncula Descarregou seu Defunto"
"How the Old Man Died" (Ferron) **94**:103, 119
How the Other Half Loves (Ayckbourn) **5**:35; **18**:29; **33**:42, 45, 47; **74**:3, 18-19, 29, 31, 33-5
"How the Piano Came to Be Prepared" (Cage) **41**:84
"How the Plains Indians Got Horses" (Plumly) **33**:312
"How the Story Ends" (Vanderhaeghe) **41**:450
How the West Was Won (L'Amour) **55**:308
"How the World Was Saved" (Lem) **149**:272
How to Be a Father (Gilbreth and Carey) **17**:155
"How to Be a TV Host" (Eco) **142**:101
"How to Be an Other Woman" (Moore) **39**:84; **45**:279-80; **68**:296
"How to Be Old" (Swenson) **106**:319
"How to Become a Writer" (Moore) **39**:84; **45**:279-80
"How to Build a Balcony" (Selzer) **74**:274
"How to Build a Slaughter-house" (Selzer) **74**:274
How to Cook a Wolf (Fisher) **76**:339, 341; **87**:118-20, 122
"How to Cover the Ground" (MacCaig) **36**:288
"How to Die" (Sassoon) **130**:182, 185, 215, 220
"How To Disembark from a Lark" (Benedikt) **14**:81
"How to Eat in Flight" (Eco) **142**:101
"How to Enter a Big City" (Merton) **83**:395
"How to Fill In a Crossword Puzzle" (Scannell) **49**:324
"How to Fry Chicken" (Colwin) **84**:142
"How to Get On in Society" (Betjeman) **6**:69; **43**:40
"How to Get There" (O'Hara) **78**:343
"How to Get to Green Springs" (Smith) **22**:386
"How to Grow a Wisteria" (O'Brien) **5**:313
"How to Hypnotize" (Gerstler) **70**:158
"How to Live on Long Island" (Simpson) **149**:352, 356, 360
"How to Make a Universe" (Barth) **89**:57-8
How to Make an American Quilt (Otto) **70**:91-5
"How to Make Stew in the Pinacate Desert" (Snyder) **5**:393
"How to Play Championship Tennis" (Muldoon) **32**:318-19; **72**:265
"How to Read" (Pound) **4**:411; **10**:402
"How to Read a Book" (Brodsky) **100**:70
How to Read a Novel (Gordon) **83**:251
How to Read a Page (Richards) **24**:395, 401
How to Read Donald Duck: Imperialist Ideology in the Disney Comic (Dorfman)
See *Para leer al Pato Donald*
How to Save Your Own Life (Jong) **8**:314-15; **83**:302, 304-05, 307, 310-11, 313, 318-19
How to See Deer (Booth) **23**:77
"How to Stuff a Pepper" (Willard) **7**:539; **37**:464
"How to Swing Those Obbligatos Around" (Fulton) **52**:158
"How to Take a Successful Nap" (Friedman) **56**:105
How to Talk Dirty and Influence People (Bruce) **21**:47
"How to Talk to Your Mother" (Moore) **39**:83-4; **45**:279-80
"How to Tell a True War Story" (O'Brien) **103**:137, 139-40, 161, 166, 174
How to Travel with a Salmon (Eco) **142**:101
"How to Win" (Brown) **32**:63-4
"How to Write a Long Autobiography" (Thurber) **125**:396, 398
"How to Write a Novel" (Lish) **45**:228, 230
How to Write a Play (Ludlam) **50**:342
"How to Write a Poem" (Lish) **45**:229-30
"How to Write a Poem about the Sky" (Silko) **23**:412; **74**:347
"How to Write a Short Story" (O'Faolain) **14**:406
"How to Write Like Someone Else" (Roethke) **46**:361
"How to Write the Great American Indian Novel" (Alexie) **154**:
"How Trurl's Perfection Led to No Good" (Lem) **149**:125, 272, 278
"How Truth—Leaps (Stumbles) Across Stage" (Foreman) **50**:164
"How Wang-Fo Was Saved" (Yourcenar) **38**:463; **87**:402-03
"How We Are Flowers" (Oates) **6**:367
"How Yesterday Looked" (Sandburg) **35**:352
"How You Get Born" (Jong) **83**:289
The Howard Fast Reader (Fast) **131**:95
Howard in Particular (Egoyan) **151**:136
Howards End (Forster) **1**:103, 106-07; **2**:134-36; **3**:160; **4**:165, 167-69; **9**:204-08; **10**:180-81; **13**:215-20; **15**:223-25, 231; **22**:131-32, 136-37; **45**:132-33, 135-38, 140, 142-43; 77;196, 216-17, 221, 223, 229-30, 234, 241
"Howard's Way" (Howard) **10**:275-76
Howbah Indians (Ortiz) **45**:301
"However Much I Booze" (Townshend) **17**:536
"Howl" (Ginsberg) **2**:162-63; **3**:194; **4**:181, 183; **6**:199; **13**:239-41; **36**:180-85, 192, 195-97; **69**:211-28; **109**:316-17, 323-28, 332-33,

335-37, 347-52, 355, 358, 369-72
Howl, and Other Poems (Ginsberg) **1**:118-19; **2**:162-64; **3**:193, 195; **6**:199, 201-02; **13**:239-41; **36**:183-84, 187-89, 191, 193-96, 198; **69**:211-12, 214, 219, 222; **109**:334, 337-42, 344, 350, 352-54, 356, 362, 363
"Howling for Love" (Scannell) **49**:332
Howrah Bridge, and Other Poems (Baxter) **14**:65
"How's the Night Life on Cissalda?" (Ellison) **42**:129-30
Hoy es fiesta (Buero Vallejo) **15**:98, 101; **139**:38
Hoyt's Child (Cassill) **23**:109
HPSCHD (Cage) **41**:83
"Hra na pravdu" (Klima) **56**:172-73
"Hřīšné město" (Seifert) **93**:339
Hrvatska rapsodija (Krleža) **114**:167, 170, 173
Hrvatski bog Mars (Krleža) **114**:167, 176-77
"Hub Fans Bid Kid Adieu" (Updike) **23**:463, 473
"The Hubbub" (Ammons) **57**:53
"Huckleberry Finn and the Hero" (Oe) **86**:226
"Huckleberry Woman" (Merwin) **13**:387
Hud (McMurtry) **2**:272; **7**:213-15; **127**:303, 319-27, 330
"Hudson Street" (Bronk) **10**:75
"The Hudsonian Curlew" (Snyder) **5**:395; **120**:313, 349-50
Hudsucker Proxy (The Coen Brothers) **108**:155-61, 166, 169
"Hue and Cry" (McPherson) **77**:358-59, 373, 375, 377
Hue and Cry (McPherson) **19**:309; **77**:350-52, 364-66, 374
Huelgistas (Valdez) **84**:395
Huey, the Engineer (Stuart) **14**:514
"The Hug" (Gunn) **81**:177, 180-81, 184, 187
"A Huge Cow Lying Down" (Cabral de Melo Neto)
See "Uma enorme rês deitada"
The Huge Season (Morris) **1**:231-33; **37**:310-12
Hugging the Shore: Essays and Criticism (Updike) **34**:284-87, 289-95; **139**:333, 352, 355, 362
The Hugh MacDiarmid Anthology (MacDiarmid) **4**:313; **19**:288
Hugh Selwyn Mauberley (Pound) **2**:340-42; **3**:395-96; **4**:412; **7**:332, 335; **10**:400, 404; **13**:456, 462; **18**:427-28; **34**:507; **48**:282-85, 287, 289, 290, 298-300; **50**:437; **112**:308-14
"Hughie" (O'Connor) **23**:331
"Hugo" (Mac Laverty) **31**:254
Hugo le terrible (Condé) **92**:132
Hugoliad; or, The Grotesque and Tragic Life of Victor Hugo (Ionesco)
See *Viata grotesca si tragica a lui Victor Jugo: Hugoliade*
"Huhediblu" (Celan) **82**:52
Huis clos (Sartre) **4**:476; **9**:470; **13**:501-02; **18**:470; **50**:370, 380, 382-84; **52**:376-77, 381, 383, 388
Hula (Shea) **86**:98-105
"Huleikat--the Third Poem about Dicky" (Amichai) **116**:130
"Hulk Couture" (Leyner) **92**:293
"The Hull Sit-In" (Dunn) **40**:166
Hullabaloo in the Guava Orchard (Desai) **119**:46-49
Hullabaloo over Georgie and Bonnie's Pictures (Jhabvala) **94**:171-72
Hulme's Investigations into the Bogart Script (Ghose) **42**:182-83
The Human Beast (Renoir)
See *La bête humaine*
"The Human Being and the Dinosaur" (Thurber) **5**:434
"The Human Bomb" (Lieberman) **36**:261
The Human Climate (Jacobsen) **48**:190
The Human Comedy (Saroyan) **8**:466; **56**:373-74
"A Human Condition" (Davies) **23**:145
"Human Condition" (Gunn) **18**:199
The Human Condition (Arendt) **66**:21-2, 24, 26, 36; **98**:3, 7-8, 14, 19-22, 27, 48, 52, 54
Human Desire (Lang) **20**:205, 216; **103**:88, 99
"The Human Element" (Maugham) **67**:211
The Human Factor (Greene) **9**:250-51; **14**:219-20; **18**:193-94, 197-98; **27**:175-77; **37**:138; **70**:289, 292-93; **72**:177; **125**:175, 177-78, 185, 187, 201
"The Human Fly" (Boyle) **90**:45
"Human Habitation" (Bowen) **118**:76
"Human Highway" (Young) **17**:580
"Human incense" (Randall) **135**:395
Human Landscapes (Hikmet)
See *Memleketimden ınsan manzaralari*
Human Landscapes from My Land (Hikmet)
See *Memleketimden ınsan manzaralari*
Human Nature and the Human Condition (Krutch) **24**:290
The Human Predicament (Hughes) **11**:278
The Human Province (Canetti)
See *Die Provinz des Menschen: Aufzeichnungen, 1942-1972*
"Human Relationships" (Ginzburg) **54**:201, 209
The Human Rights Book (Meltzer) **26**:306
Human Scale (Sale) **68**:350-53, 359
The Human Season (Wallant) **5**:477; **10**:511-13, 515-16
The Human Season: Selected Poems, 1926-1972 (MacLeish) **3**:311; **68**:293
"Human Sheep" (Oe) **86**:224, 227
"The Human Situation" (Spender) **10**:492
"Human Torso Gives Birth" (Sapphire) **99**:80
"The Human Universe" (Olson) **11**:417-19; **29**:327, 329, 334
The Human Voice (Cocteau) **43**:110
Human Voices (Fitzgerald) **19**:174-75; **51**:124; **61**:116-17; **143**:237-38, 246, 254, 258, 263-65, 267, 269-70
Human Wishes (Hass) **99**:139-43, 145-50, 154-55, 157
"Humane Letters" (Simpson) **149**:358
"Humanism and Naturalism" (Tate) **24**:439
"The Humanism of Irving Babbitt" (Eliot) **57**:183
"The Humanist" (Cunningham) **31**:104
"The Humanist" (Eberhart) **56**:77
"The Humanist" (Hill) **8**:295
"The Humanist's Tragedy" (Jeffers) **2**:212
Humanities in America: Report to the President, the Congress, and the American People (Cheney) **70**:362
"Humano ardor" (Aleixandre) **9**:15
The Humanoid Touch (Williamson) **29**:461
The Humanoids (Williamson) **29**:449, 452, 455-60
Humanscapes from My Land (Hikmet)
See *Memleketimden ınsan manzaralari*
"Humaweepi" (Silko) **74**:328
The Humble Administrator's Garden (Seth) **43**:387-88; **90**:337-8, 353, 361
The Humble Cemetery () **59**:363, 381
"The Humble Dollar" (Baker) **31**:29
"A Humble Protest" (Dos Passos) **82**:105
The Humbler Creation (Johnson) **1**:161; **27**:219-20, 223
Humboldt's Gift (Bellow) **6**:55-61; **8**:69-71, 80-1; **10**:44; **13**:73-5; **15**:54-5; **25**:82-6; **33**:71; **34**:545-46; **63**:27, 31, 33-5, 37, 39
"Hume" (Smith) **64**:398
"The Humiliation" (Friedman) **56**:97
"Humiliation with Honor" (Brittain) **23**:91
"Humility" (Chappell) **40**:149
"Humility" (Hoffman) **141**:296
"Humility, Concentration, and Gusto" (Moore) **10**:353; **47**:268, 270, 272
"The Hummingbird" (Paz) **51**:335
"The Hummingbird Comes Home" (Woolrich) **77**:389
"Hummingbirds" (Deane) **122**:82-3
"Hummingbirds" (Oliver) **98**:304
"Humor" (Yevtushenko) **126**:413
Humoresque (Odets) **98**:245
Humorous and/or Not So Humourous (Kenny) **87**:252
Humors of Blood and Skin: A John Hawkes Reader (Hawkes) **49**:155
"Hump" (Feldman) **7**:103
"Humpbacks" (Oliver) **98**:257, 271-72, 297-98
Humpty Dumpty (Hecht) **8**:270-73
Humulus le muet (Anouilh) **40**:57
"Hun" (Burgess) **62**:139
"The Hunch" (Dunn) **40**:165
"Hunchback Girl: She Thinks of Heaven" (Brooks) **49**:26
"The Hunchback of Dugbe" (Soyinka) **36**:409
"Hunchback on the Buga Road" (Musgrave) **54**:341
"Der Hund" (Dürrenmatt) **15**:194
Hundejahre (Grass) **1**:125-26; **2**:171-73; **4**:201-04, 206; **6**:207-08; **11**:247; **15**:261, 263; **22**:190; **32**:201; **88**:136, 139, 143-45, 159
Der Hundertjährige (Eliade)
See *Der Hundertjärige*
Der Hundertjärige (Eliade) **19**:148
A Hundred Camels in the Courtyard (Bowles) **53**:41
"A Hundred Collars" (Frost) **15**:240
The Hundred Days (O'Brian) **152**:292-94, 299
The Hundred Islands (Clark) **12**:132
The Hundred Secret Senses (Tan) **120**:413-15, 424
"A Hundred Years from Now" (Stern) **100**:340
Hundreds of Fireflies (Leithauser) **27**:240-43
"The Hungarian Insurrection" (Elytis) **49**:110
"The Hungarian Night" (Morand)
See "La nuit Hongroise"
"The Hungarian Professor" (Archer) **28**:14
"Hunger" (Haines) **58**:220
"Hunger" (Mahapatra) **33**:279, 283, 276
"Hunger" (Rhys) **6**:454-55; **51**:356
"Hunger" (Rich) **36**:374
"Hunger" (Shacochis) **39**:201
Hunger (Lessing) **22**:279; **94**:268
"Hunger and Cold" (Sandburg) **35**:356
Hunger and Thirst (Ionesco)
See *La soif et la faim*
The Hunger Artist Departs (Rozewicz)
See *Odejście Głodomora*
Hunger of Memory: The Education of Richard Rodriguez, An Autobiography (Rodriguez) **155**:234-40, 246-55, 261-70, 272, 274, 279-85, 288, 290, 295-97, 303-05, 308, 312-13, 315-20, 327, 330
The Hungered One: Early Writings (Bullins) **7**:37
"Hungerfield" (Jeffers) **54**:242, 245
Hungerfield and Other Poems (Jeffers) **54**:242; **11**:306-07
"Hungering" (Jong) **8**:314
Hungry as the Sea (Smith) **33**:376
"A Hungry Fighter" (Raine) **103**:186, 189
"Hungry for You" (Police, The) **26**:365
Hungry Fred (Fox) **121**:200
The Hungry Ghosts (Oates) **6**:371
Hungry Hearts (Prose) **45**:325-26
Hungry Hearts (Yezierska) **46**:441, 446
The Hungry Hill (du Maurier) **59**:286
Hungry Hills (Ryga) **14**:472-73
"Hunktown" (Mason) **82**:244
Hunky Dory (Bowie) **17**:58-9, 61-2, 64, 67
"Hunt" (Dumas) **6**:146
"The Hunt" (Jones) **7**:189, 191; **13**:311; **42**:241
"The Hunt" (Lem) **8**:345; **40**:295, 297
Hunt (Alvarez) **13**:8-10
The Hunt (Saura)
See *La caza*
The Hunt by Night (Mahon) **27**:293
The Hunt for Red October (Clancy) **45**:85-90; **112**:49-52, 54-66, 69, 72-4, 76-8, 81, 83-4, 88, 90
"Hunt the Thimble" (Abse) **7**:1; **29**:16, 18
The Hunted (Leonard) **28**:234; **71**:223
Hunted like a Wolf: The Study of the Seminole War (Meltzer) **26**:301-02

"The Hunter" (Doctorow) **37**:91, 93-4; **113**:152-52, 156
"Hunter" (Grau) **146**:131
"The Hunter" (Ignatow) **7**:177
"A Hunter" (Kelman) **58**:301
"The Hunter after Roots" (Neruda) **62**:327
Hunter of Worlds (Cherryh) **35**:103-05, 110
The Hunters (Salter) **52**:359, 363
Hunter's Green (Whitney) **42**:434
Hunter's Horn (Arnow) **7**:15-16; **18**:10, 12, 16
"Hunters in the Snow" (Wolff) **64**:449, 451
Hunters in the Snow (Wolff)
See *In the Garden of the North American Martyrs*
"A Hunter's Moon" (Thomas) **107**:337-38, 340
The Hunter's Year (Milosz)
See *Rok myśliwego*
"Hunting" (Head) **67**:98
"Hunting a Hare" (Voznesensky) **57**:414, 427
"A Hunting Accident" (Gordimer) **18**:190
"Hunting Civil War Relics at Nimblewill Creek" (Dickey) **4**:120
The Hunting Dark (Skelton) **13**:507
Hunting Flies (Wajda)
See *A Fly Hunt*
"Hunting Ivan Shark" (Dobyns) **37**:76
"The Hunting of Death: The Unicorn" (Lee) **46**:232
"Hunting on Sweetwater Creek" (Bottoms) **53**:31
The Hunting Party (Bernhard)
See *Die Jagdgesellschaft*
"Hunting Pheasants in a Cornfield" (Bly) **5**:61; **128**:13
"A Hunting Story" (Silko) **74**:347; **114**:316
Hunting Stuart (Davies) **7**:73
Hunting the Fairies (Mackenzie) **18**:316
"Hunting the Phoenix" (Levertov) **66**:251
Hunting the Wild Pineapple and Other Related Stories (Astley) **41**:47, 49
Hunting Tigers under Glass (Richler) **5**:376-77; **13**:481
"The Huntress" (Johnston) **51**:243
"The Huntress" (Stead)
See "The Dianas"
"The Huntsman's Apology" (Montague) **13**:391; **46**:269
Las Hurdes—Tierra sin pan (Bunuel) **80**:19, 21, 28, 30, 36, 38-9, 42, 49, 51
"Huria's Rock" (Grace) **56**:111
L'hurluberlu; ou, Le réactionnaire amoureux (Anouilh) **13**:17; **40**:57-8, 60-1
Hurlyburly (Rabe) **33**:344-47
Hurrah for Anything (Patchen) **18**:395
"Hurrah for Freedom" (Lind) **82**:129-30
"Hurrah for Thunder" (Okigbo) **25**:354, 356; **84**:316, 323
"A Hurricane at Sea" (Swenson) **61**:400; **106**:326
Hurricane Lamp (Cassity) **42**:99
"Hurricane Season" (Simic) **130**:306
Hurry Home (Wideman) **5**:489; **36**:451-54; **67**:371; **122**:286-87, 311, 314, 352-53, 356, 363
Hurry on Down (Wain)
See *Born in Captivity*
Hurry Sundown (Foote) **51**:131
"Hurry Up Please It's Time" (Sexton) **15**:472; **123**:441; **123**:441
"Hurrying Away from the Earth" (Bly) **10**:58; **128**:6
"The Hurrying Brook" (Blunden) **56**:29
Hurskas kurjuus (Sillanpaa) **19**:419-20
"Hurt" (Nowlan) **15**:398
"Hurt Hawks" (Jeffers) **54**:244
"The Hurt Trees" (Bell) **8**:67; **31**:48
"Husband and Wife with Newspaper" (Hall) **51**:172
"The Husband I Bought" (Rand) **79**:373-74
"Husband to Wife" (Simmons) **43**:407
Husbands (Cassavetes) **20**:46-7
"A Husband's Return" (Trevor) **71**:341, 343, 348
Huset i mørkret (Vesaas) **48**:404, 406-07, 413
Huskuld the Herald (Vesaas)
See *Sendemann Huskuld*
The Hussar (Rezzori) **25**:381
Le hussard sur le toit (Giono) **4**:184, 187-88; **11**:231
"The Hustler" (Lane) **25**:286
The Hustler (Tevis) **42**:369-70, 372, 374-75, 377
"Hut" (Pinsky) **94**:309
"Hut Five B" (Krleža)
See "Baraka pet be"
Huui, Huui (Burr) **6**:103-04
"Huxley Hall" (Betjeman) **6**:68; **43**:35-7
"Huzza!" (Stern) **40**:413
Hvězdy nad rajskou zahradou (Seifert) **44**:426
"Hyacinth" (Glück) **44**:217, 222
"Hyacinth" (H. D.) **73**:120
"The Hyacinth" (Raine) **45**:330
"A Hyacinth for Edith" (Smith) **15**:513
"The Hyacinth Symphony" (Elytis) **100**:172
"Hyacinths with Brevity" (Gustafson) **36**:218
"Hybrids of Plants and of Ghosts" (Graham) **48**:145
Hybrids of Plants and of Ghosts (Graham) **48**:144-47, 150-54; **118**:223-27, 230, 236, 239, 248, 250, 253-54, 258
The Hyde Park Headsman (Perry) **126**:334, 340
"Hydra" (Erdrich) **120**:144
The Hydra Head (Fuentes)
See *La cabeza de la hidra*
"Hydraulics" (Meredith) **4**:349
Hydrogen Box (Ginsberg) **109**:356
"Hyla Brook" (Frost) **26**:122
"The Hyland Family" (Farrell) **66**:129
"Hymen" (H. D.) **8**:258; **31**:201, 205, 208; **73**:119-20
Hymen (H. D.) **73**:105-07, 128
"The hymen in Mexico" (Arreola)
See "El himen en México"
"Hymeneal" (O'Faolain) **32**:343
"Hymie's Bull" (Ellison) **114**:131, 138
"Hymn" (Ammons) **5**:26-7; **8**:13; **25**:48; **57**:52; **108**:50-1, 54, 57-8
"Hymn" (Ginsberg) **3**:194; **36**:182, 187, 195
"Hymn" (Ian) **21**:186
"Hymn" (Milosz) **56**:240
"Hymn" (Randall) **135**:398
"Hymn" (Reading) **47**:350
"Hymn" (Smith) **12**:544
"Hymn" (Warner) **45**:429
"Hymn among the Ruins" (Paz)
See "Himno entre ruinas"
Hymn and Lament for Cyprus (Ritsos) **13**:487
"Hymn before Action" (Forster) **15**:228; **45**:132
Hymn for Anytime (Nagy)
See *Himnusz minden idöben*
"Hymn in Two Dimensions" (Elytis) **49**:109
"Hymn IV" (Ammons) **5**:27
"Hymn of Fire" (Wittlin) **25**:468
"Hymn of Not Much Praise for New York City" (Merton) **83**:395
"A Hymn of Restlessness, Madness, and Boredom" (Wittlin) **25**:468
Hymn of the Pearl (Milosz) **82**:310
"Hymn to a Spoonful of Soup" (Wittlin) **25**:467-68
"A Hymn to Chicago" (Brooks) **125**:108
"Hymn to Dispel Hatred at Midnight" (Winters) **32**:468
"Hymn to Ham" (Blount) **38**:47
"Hymn to Lanie Poo" (Baraka) **5**:45; **14**:45
Hymn to Life (Schuyler) **5**:383
"Hymn to Maria Neféli" (Elytis) **49**:110
"Hymn to Nessa" (Durcan) **43**:113
"Hymn to Ra" (Christie) **110**:128
"Hymn to the New Omagh Road" (Montague) **46**:270, 273
Hymn to the Rising Sun (Green) **25**:198
Hymne (Jouve) **47**:206, 212
Hymns (Wittlin) **25**:467-68
Hymns in Darkness (Ezekiel) **61**:107, 109
Hymns to St. Geryon (McClure) **6**:319
Hypnos Walking (Char) **55**:287
Hypnosis: The Wakeful Sleep (Kettelkamp) **12**:306-07
"Hypochondriac" (Swift) **41**:443
"Hypochondriac Logic" (Davie) **10**:121
"Hypocrite Swift" (Bogan) **39**:385; **46**:81; **93**:61
"Hypocrite Woman" (Levertov) **66**:238, 250
"Hyrdinden og Skorsteensfeieren" (Andersen)
See *Shepherdess of Sheep*
"Hysteria" (Eliot) **1**:90; **41**:150, 160
"I" (Lem) **149**:158
"I" (Merrill) **8**:386-87
I, a Man (Warhol) **20**:419
"I Accuse" (Neruda)
See "Yo acuso"
"I Ain't Got No Home in This World Anymore" (Guthrie) **35**:184, 191
I Ain't Marching Any More (Ochs) **17**:330-34
"I Always Wanted You to Admire My Fasting; or, Looking at Kafka" (Roth) **15**:449, 451
"I Am" (Riding) **7**:375
"I Am 21" (Robison) **42**:342-43
I Am a Camera (Isherwood) **44**:397
I Am a Cat (Ichikawa) **20**:187
"I Am a Child" (Young) **17**:572, 578, 583
"I Am a Child in These Hills" (Browne) **21**:35, 37
"I Am a Dangerous Woman" (Harjo) **83**:279
"I Am a Lonesome Hobo" (Dylan) **12**:185
"I Am a Rock" (Simon) **17**:459, 461, 463, 466
"I Am a Sioux Brave, He Said in Minneapolis" (Wright) **5**:520
"I Am a Victim of Telephone" (Ginsberg) **36**:188
"I Am a Woman" (Brown) **79**:154
"I Am Alive" (Momaday) **95**:243
"I Am an Animal" (Townshend) **17**:541
"I Am Bigfoot" (Carlson) **54**:39
I am Cuba (Yevtushenko) **126**:401, 409
"I Am Dreaming of a White Christmas: The Natural History of a Vision" (Warren) **6**:558; **8**:537; **10**:525; **13**:577
I Am Elijah Thrush (Purdy) **2**:350-51; **4**:423; **10**:424-25; **52**:343
"I Am Fourteen" (Voznesensky) **57**:426-27
I Am from Moscow (Krotkov) **19**:264
"I Am Goya" (Voznesensky) **57**:414-15, 423, 425-27
"I Am, I Said" (Diamond) **30**:112
"I Am in Danger—Sir—" (Rich) **76**:218
"I Am It and It Is I" (Campbell) **42**:90
I am Joaquin (Valdez) **84**:396
I Am Lazarus (Kavan) **13**:317
I Am Legend (Matheson) **37**:246-50
I Am Mary Dunne (Moore) **1**:225; **3**:341; **5**:296-97; **7**:237, 239; **8**:395; **19**:331; **32**:313; **90**:238, 240-2, 247, 249-51, 254-55, 265, 272, 304
"I Am No Son of the Fact" (Blaga) **75**:62, 78
"I Am Not a Son of Deed" (Blaga)
See "I Am No Son of the Fact"
"I Am Not Done Yet" (Clifton) **66**:72, 85
"I Am Not Myself" (Bates) **46**:55-6
"I Am Not Now, Nor Have I Ever Been, a Matrix of Lean Meat" (Perelman) **49**:265
I Am One of You Forever (Chappell) **40**:146-48; **78**:95, 98, 101, 114, 115
"I Am Peter" (Turco) **11**:549
"I Am Shaking to Death" (Hannah) **38**:234; **90**:137-38, 143
"I Am She" (Giovanni) **117**:199
"I Am That Face About Which Fire Fell" (Barker) **48**:9
I Am the Beautiful Stranger (Drexler) **2**:119-20; **6**:142
I Am the Bitter Name (Williams) **33**:443-45; **148**:311, 318-23, 328, 343
I Am the Cheese (Cormier) **12**:136-38; **30**:81-3, 85, 87-9, 91

I Am the Clay (Potok) **112**:293-94
"I Am the Daughter / Mother Who Has Learned" (Castillo) **151**:20
"I Am the Doorway" (King) **37**:205
I Am the Living (Cliff) **21**:65
"I Am the People, the Mob" (Sandburg) **35**:353
"I Am the Sun" (Hoffman) **6**:243
"I Am the Sun" (Kenny) **87**:240-41, 245
"I Am the Walrus" (Lennon and McCartney) **12**:360, 362; **35**:261-62, 268
I Am the World (Vansittart) **42**:399
"I Am Vertical" (Plath) **9**:433; **11**:447; **51**:340, 345
I Am Walking in the Garden of His Imaginary Palace (Urquhart) **90**:375, 377, 390, 398
"I am You" (Ferlinghetti) **111**:65
"I Am Your Singer" (McCartney) **35**:280
I and My True Love (MacInnes) **27**:280
"I and Your Eyes" (Knight) **40**:284-85, 287
"I Apologize" (Komunyakaa) **94**:235-36
I Apologize for the Eyes in My Head (Komunyakaa) **94**:218, 224, 230, 235, 240, 247
"I Ask Her" (Bowering) **15**:82
I Ask the Impossible (Castillo) **151**:104
"I Believe in Love" (Reed) **21**:312-13
"I Believe in You" (Dylan) **77**:176, 186-87
"I Believe in You" (Young) **17**:582
"I Blame It All on Mama" (Mitchell) **98**:187
"I Bought a Little City" (Barthelme) **46**:36
"I Bought a Palm-Tree" (Peake) **54**:372
I Brake for Delmore Schwartz (Grayson) **38**:211-13
"I Break the Sky" (Dodson) **79**:193
"I Build" (Rozewicz) **139**:236
"I Build an Orange Church" (Smith) **64**:394
"I Came from Yonder Mountain" (Connell) **45**:107
"I Came on a Slaveship" (Guillén) **79**:230
"I Came out of the Mother Naked" (Bly) **10**:57, 62; **38**:52; **128**:17, 22, 43
I Can Get It for You Wholesale (Polonsky) **92**:378, 405
I Can Get It for You Wholesale (Weidman) **7**:516-18
"I Can Hear Music" (Wilson) **12**:645
"I Can See for Miles" (Townshend) **17**:530, 538
"I Can Still Picture the Caribou" (Young Bear) **94**:364
I, Candidate for Governor and How I Got Licked (Sinclair) **11**:497; **15**:498
"I Cannot Forget the Woman in the Mirror" (Olds) **85**:295
I Cannot Get You Close Enough (Gilchrist) **143**:294, 299, 311, 313, 315-16, 329-30
"I Cannot Place the Face" (Deren) **102**:38
"I Cannot Stand Tears" (Bukowski) **41**:63, 66
"I Can't Explain" (Townshend) **17**:530, 539
I Can't Imagine Tomorrow (Williams) **45**:451
"I Can't Let My Heaven Walk Away" (Wonder) **12**:656
"I Can't Quit You Baby" (Page and Plant) **12**:479
"I Can't Reach You" (Townshend) **17**:529, 531
I Can't Remember Anything (Miller)
See *Danger: Memory!*
"I Can't See Your Face in My Mind" (Morrison) **17**:295
I Can't Stay Long (Lee) **90**:192, 198-99, 201
I Ching (Tillinghast) **29**:415
I, Claudius (Graves) **1**:128; **6**:211; **39**:321-24, 326-28; **45**:172-73
I Come as a Thief (Auchincloss) **4**:29-30; **6**:15
I Confess (Hitchcock) **16**:343, 351
"I Could Believe" (Levine) **118**:285, 314
"I Could Give All to Time" (Frost) **9**:225
"I Could Not Be Here at All" (Ammons) **57**:49-50
"I Could See the Smallest Things" (Carver) **22**:102
I Crossed the Minch (MacNeice) **10**:326; **53**:234-35
"I Cry, Love! Love!" (Roethke) **101**:274, 335, 339-41
"I Declare Myself an Impure Man" (Guillén) **48**:159
"I Declare, Under Penalty of Milkshake" (Perelman) **23**:336
I den tiden (Lagerkvist) **54**:286
"I Did It to Attract Women" (Musgrave) **54**:334
"I Did Not Learn Their Names" (Ellison) **114**:131
"I didn't want to" (Bukowski) **108**:106
"I Do/Dig Everything Swinging" (Williams) **13**:600
"I Do It for Your Love" (Simon) **17**:466
"I Do Not Know" (Musgrave) **54**:341
I Do Remember the Fall (Kelly) **55**:159
"I Do What I Can and I Am What I Am" (Weldon) **122**:269
I dol'she veka dlitsia den' (Aitmatov) **71**:7-9, 18-19, 21, 26-7, 30, 33
"I Don't Believe You" (Dylan) **77**:173
"I Don't Blame You At All" (Robinson) **21**:343, 345
I Don't Have to Show You No Stinking Badges! (Valdez) **84**:403-05, 407-08, 410, 413, 415, 417
"I Don't Know" (Carroll) **35**:77
"I Don't Know" (McFadden) **48**:252
I Don't Know (McFadden) **48**:251-52, 255
"I Don't Know How to Love Him" (Rice and Webber) **21**:424-25
"I Don't Know Why You Think" (Guillén)
See "No sé por qué piensas tú"
"I Don't Need a Bedsheet with Slits for Eyes to Kill You" (Bukowski) **82**:26
"I Don't Need You Any More" (Miller) **6**:333; **10**:345; **47**:249-50
I Don't Need You Any More (Miller) **47**:249
"I don't understand" (Yevtushenko) **126**:395
"I Don't Wanna Be a Soldier, I Don't Wanna Die" (Lennon) **35**:263-65, 267
"I Don't Wanna Face It" (Lennon) **35**:275
"I Don't Want to Be Alone" (Joel) **26**:220
"I Don't Want to Die" (Himes) **108**:227
"I Don't Want to Go to Chelsea" (Costello) **21**:68, 75
I Don't Want to Know Anyone Too Well, and Other Stories (Levine) **54**:293, 295, 299
"I Dream I'm the Death of Orpheus" (Rich) **7**:366; **11**:478
"I Dreamed I Saw St. Augustine" (Dylan) **12**:185
"I Dreamed that I Was Old" (Kunitz) **148**:81
"I Dreamed That in a City Dark As Paris" (Simpson) **7**:426; **9**:486; **149**:298
"I, Dreamer" (Miller) **30**:263
I Dreamt I Was a Nymphomaniac: Imagining (Acker) **45**:14; **111**:25, 32, 36
"I, Eliza Custis" (Grayson) **38**:210
"I Envy You Your Great Adventure" (Dowell) **60**:109
I, Etcetera (Sontag) **13**:516-19; **31**:411; **105**:197, 206
"I Expand My Horizons" (Trow) **52**:420
"I Expected to Spend My Time" (Alegria) **75**:34
"I Explain a Few Things" (Neruda)
See "Explico algunas cosas"
"I feel good in my trousers" (Amichai) **116**:98
"I Feel Pretty" (Sondheim) **30**:378, 387, 395; **147**:259
"I Feel, Therefore I Exist" (Voznesensky) **57**:425
"I Felt" (Ignatow) **7**:179
"I Find You" (Ignatow) **40**:261
"I fiumi" (Ungaretti) **11**:555
"I Fled Paris" (Butor) **11**:80
"I Fly in Dream" (Cocteau) **8**:146
I for One (Sargeson) **31**:364, 367
"I Found a Dead Fox" (Oliver) **98**:303
"I Found Out" (Lennon) **35**:262, 266
"I Gather the Limbs of Osiris" (Pound) **13**:454; **48**:288-89
I Gave at the Office (Westlake) **33**:436
"I Gave Up before Birth" (Beckett) **29**:57
"I Get Around" (Wilson) **12**:646, 649, 651, 653
"I Get By" (Robison) **98**:317
"I Get Wild/Wild Gravity" (Byrne) **26**:99
"I Give You Back" (Harjo) **83**:266
"I Go Back to May 1937" (Olds) **85**:292-93, 305
"I Got a Little Flat off Third and Yen" (Tate) **25**:430
"I Got By in Time" (Weller) **26**:443
"I Got Life" (Ragni and Rado) **17**:385
"I Got Plenty" (Carroll) **35**:77
"I Got the Blues" (Jagger and Richard) **17**:229, 242
"I Got the News" (Becker and Fagen) **26**:84
"I Had a King" (Mitchell) **12**:440
"I Had a Strange Dream" (Ratushinskaya) **54**:385
I Hardly Knew You (O'Brien)
See *Johnny, I Hardly Knew You*
"I Hate Paris" (Butor) **11**:80
"I Have" (Guillén)
See "Tengo"
I Have (Guillén)
See *Tengo*
"I Have a Dream" (King) **83**:343-46, 349
I Have Been Here Before (Priestley) **34**:361, 365
"I Have Been in You" (Zappa) **17**:592-93
"I Have Kept My Vigil" (Harrison) **42**:203
I Have Killed (Cendrars) **106**:191
"I Have No Mouth and I Must Scream" (Ellison) **13**:206; **42**:126; **139**:106-8, 112, 130-31, 133, 136, 140, 145
I Have No Mouth and I Must Scream (Ellison) **139**:129, 136-44
"I Have Nothing to Declare but My Genius" (Perelman) **5**:338
I Hear America Swinging (De Vries) **7**:78; **10**:136, 138; **28**:107
"I Hear the Oriole's Voice" (Akhmatova) **64**:16
"I Hear You, Doc" (Reed) **13**:480
"I Hear You Say So" (Bowen) **118**:67
"I Heard Her Call My Name" (Reed) **21**:314
I Heard My Sister Speak My Name (Savage) **40**:374-75
I Heard the Owl Call My Name (Craven) **17**:79-81
"I Heard Wild Geese" (Ekeloef) **27**:119
I, Judas (Caldwell) **28**:67; **39**:302
"I Just Love Carrie Lee" (Douglas) **73**:65-7, 82
"I Just Wasn't Made for These Times" (Wilson) **12**:646
"I Kill, Therefore I Am" (Ochs) **17**:332
I Knew a Phoenix: Sketches for an Autobiography (Sarton) **49**:316; **91**:245-48
"I Knew a Woman" (Roethke) **8**:460; **19**:401; **46**:363; **101**:328-29
I Knock at the Door: Swift Glances Back at Things That Made Me (O'Casey) **5**:320; **88**:237-38, 240
"I Know" (Berryman) **62**:58
"I Know a Man" (Creeley) **15**:153; **36**:121; **78**:120, 135, 137
"I Know I Remember, but How Can I Help You?" (Carruth) **7**:41
I Know What You Did Last Summer (Duncan) **26**:103-06, 108
"I Know What You Mean, Erdupps MacChurbbs: Autobiographical Myths and Metaphors" (Vizenor) **103**:281, 299
I Know Why the Caged Bird Sings (Angelou) **12**:9; **35**:30-3; **64**:24-5, 27-30, 34-9; **77**:2-13, 15-17, 19, 21-3, 31-3, 35; **155**:3-58
I, Laminarian (Césaire)
See *moi, Laminaire*
I Lay My Cards on the Table (Aragon)
See *J'abats mon jeu*

I Like It Here (Amis) **1**:5; **2**:4, 9; **129**:4-8, 16, 24
"I Like My Body" (Cummings) **3**:118
"I Live among the Shadows" (Salinas) **90**:332
I Live in Fear (Kurosawa)
See *Ikimono no kiroku*
"I Live in Music" (Shange) **126**:379
"I Live on Your Visits" (Parker) **68**:337
I Live under a Black Sun (Sitwell) **67**:314-15
I Lock My Door upon Myself (Oates) **108**:379-81, 385
"I Long for People through Whom the Past" (Coles) **46**:112
"I Look at My Hand" (Swenson) **106**:344
"I Look Out for Ed Wolfe" (Elkin) **51**:98
"I Love Every Little Thing about You" (Wonder) **12**:663
I Love Liberty (Brown) **79**:169
"I Love My Friend" (Hughes) **35**:214; **108**:331
"I Love My Rooster" (Still) **49**:366
I Love Myself When I Am Laughing...:A Zora Neale Hurston Reader (Walker) **103**:357, 372
"I Love Someone" (Stafford) **19**:431
"I Love Those Little Booths at Benvenuti's" (Brooks) **125**:90, 104
"I Love You" (Creeley) **78**:141
"I Love You Dear" (Robinson) **21**:343
I Married a Dead Man (Woolrich) **77**:389-91, 393-98, 400, 402-05
I Married a Witch (Clair) **20**:70
I Married You for the Fun of It (Ginzburg) **70**:282
I Marry You: A Sheaf of Love Poems (Ciardi) **40**:155-56, 163; **44**:380, 382; **129**:46
"I Maureen" (Spencer) **22**:406
I May Be Wrong, But I Doubt It (Royko) **109**:404
"I May Have Sung with Jerry Jeff" (Blount) **38**:46
"I May, I Might, I Must" (Moore) **8**:401; **47**:261
"I May Smoke Too Much" (Kristofferson) **26**:269
"I Meet Time" (Ali) **69**:32
"I, Mencius, Pupil of the Master ..." (Olson) **11**:416
I Met a Boy I Used to Know (Weber) **12**:634
"I Met a Little Girl" (Gaye) **26**:133-34
"I Must Have You" (Oates) **19**:352
I Myself Am a Woman (Ding Ling) **68**:66-7, 69
"I Need Help" (Hirsch) **50**:195, 198-99
"I Need Help from the Philosophers" (Stern) **40**:408; **100**:337
"I Need, I Need" (Roethke) **101**:279, 363, 381
"I Need You" (Weller) **26**:443
"I Need You Baby" (Berry) **17**:56
I Never Danced at the White House (Buchwald) **33**:93
I Never Loved Your Mind (Zindel) **6**:586; **26**:471-73, 475, 479-80
I Never Promised You a Rose Garden (Greenberg) **7**:135; **30**:161-66
I Never Said I Loved You (Bennett) **35**:46
I Never Sang for My Father (Anderson) **23**:32
"I Never Saw Morning" (Tyler) **103**:258
"I Nildeltat" (Transtroemer) **52**:409
"I No More Real than Evil in My Roof" (Graham) **29**:193
I, Olli, and Orvokki (Salama)
See *Minä, Olli ja Orvokki*
I On Feminine Culture (Castellanos)
See *Sobre cultura femenina*
"I Only Am Escaped Alone to Tell Thee" (Nemerov) **36**:305
I Ought to Be in Pictures (Simon) **31**:398-99, 403
"I, Ozymandias" (Ihimaera) **46**:200
I Passed This Way (Ashton-Warner) **19**:23-4
"I Peer Through Ugliness" (Nolan) **58**:366
"I, Pierre Rivière, Having Slaughtered My Mother, My Sister, and My Brother" (Foucault)
See "Moi, Pierre Rivière, ayant égurgé ma mer, ma soeur, et mon frère"
"I Pity the Poor Immigrant" (Dylan) **12**:185
"I Pity the Wind" (Stern) **40**:414
"I Plant Geraniums" (Giovanni) **117**:200
"I Play Chess with an Arab Professor" (Faludy) **42**:141
"I Pressed My Hands Together..." (Akhmatova) **64**:8
"I Put a Name in an Envelope..." (Barthelme) **46**:42
"I Put My Blue Genes On" (Card) **47**:67
"I, Quiyumucon" (Harris) **25**:217
I raconti accoppiamenti giudiziosi (Gadda) **11**:211
"I Remember" (Boland) **67**:39; **113**:82, 108
I Remember (Fellini)
See *Amarcord*
I Remember (Pasternak) **7**:295
I Remember (Perec)
See *Je me souviens*
"I Remember Babylon" (Clarke) **13**:148
"I Remember, I Remember" (Larkin) **5**:227; **8**:332; **18**:294, 301; **33**:256; **39**:336; **64**:266
"I Remember! I Remember!" (O'Faolain) **14**:406
I Remember! I Remember! (O'Faolain) **7**:275; **32**:340-41; **70**:319
I Remember Petersburg (Almedingen)
See *My Saint Petersburg*
"I Ride My High Bicycle" (Adcock) **41**:18
I, Robot (Asimov) **9**:50; **19**:27; **26**:35, 37, 46-7, 53; **76**:313-14, 318-20; **92**:1-23
I, Robot (Ellison) **139**:129-30
I Root My Name (Alexander) **121**:3
"I Said 'My Name Is "Ozzy" Manders, Dean of Kings'" (Frayn) **47**:135
"I Save Your Coat, but You Lose It Later" (Gallagher) **63**:117, 126
"I Saw Eternity" (Bogan) **46**:78, 81, 83; **93**:64-5
"I Saw Her Dancing" (Piercy) **62**:379
"I Saw Her Standing There" (Lennon and McCartney) **12**:374
I Saw in My Dream (Sargeson) **31**:364, 367-68, 371-73
"I Saw One Walking" (Avison) **97**:69, 75
"I Saw Three Ships" (Hospital) **145**:296, 304
"I Second That Emotion" (Robinson) **21**:342
"I See" (Redgrove) **6**:445; **41**:351
I See a Long Journey (Ingalls) **42**:232-35
I See By My Outfit (Beagle) **104**:4-5
"I See, Said the Blind Man, As He Put Down His Hammer and Saw" (Ashbery) **41**:39
"I see the sign and tremble" (Piercy) **128**:273
"I seek the word" (Szymborska) **99**:202
I Sent a Letter to My Love (Rubens) **19**:403-04
I Served the King of England (Hrabal)
See *Obsluhoval jsem anglického krále*
"I Set It My Task" (Ammons) **108**:19
"I Shall Laugh Purely" (Jeffers) **11**:306
"I Shall Marry the Miller's Son" (Sondheim) **30**:384, 392
I Shall Not Be Moved (Angelou) **64**:40
I Shall Not Hear the Nightingale (Singh) **11**:504, 506-07
"I Shot the Sheriff" (Marley) **17**:267-69
"I Should Tell You" (Larson) **99**:169
"I Shout Love" (Acorn) **15**:9
"I Sing of Olaf Glad and Big" (Cummings) **3**:118
"I Sing the Body Electric!" (Bradbury) **42**:37
I Sing the Body Electric! (Bradbury) **42**:34, 39
"I Sit by the Window" (Brodsky) **36**:78, 81; **100**:52
"I Sit in One of the Dives/On Fifty-Second Street" (Auden) **43**:22
i: Six Nonlectures (Cummings) **3**:117-18; **8**:155; **68**:46
"I Sleep a Lot" (Milosz) **82**:297
"I Smell Esther Williams" (Leyner) **92**:281
I Smell Esther Williams (Leyner) **92**:281, 285, 292-93
I sommersi e i salvati (Levi) **50**:330, 332, 336, 338-40
I Speak of Africa (Plomer) **4**:406
"I Speak of the City" (Paz) **51**:335; **65**:190
I Spy (Mortimer) **28**:283-84
"I Spy a Stranger" (Rhys) **51**:376; **124**:356
"I Spy Strangers" (Amis) **40**:43-5; **129**:6
"I Stand Here Ironing" (Olsen) **13**:432; **114**:192, 194, 197-98, 202, 207, 210, 212, 214, 221, 223, 231-35, 245
"I Stood with the Dead" (Sassoon) **36**:385
"I Substitute for the Dead Lecturer" (Baraka) **5**:45
"I Surrender in the March of My Bones" (Salinas) **90**:332
I Survive (Alegria)
See *Sobrevivo*
"I Swear" (Akhmadulina) **53**:14
"I Take Back Everything I've Said" (Parra) **102**:349-50, 352-53
"I Taste the Ashes of Your Death" (Bukowski) **41**:66
"I, Tekonwatonti" (Kenny) **87**:254
"I Tell Myself" (Sillitoe) **148**:155
"i thank You God for most this amazing" (Cummings) **15**:163
I That Was Born in Wales (Watkins) **43**:453-55
I, the Jury (Spillane) **3**:468-69; **13**:526-27
I, the Supreme (Roa Bastos)
See *Yo, el supremo*
"I Think: How Stupid I Have Been" (Akhmadulina)
See "La dumaiu: kak ia byla glupa"
"I Think It Rains" (Soyinka) **44**:277
"I Think of All Soft Limbs" (Gustafson) **36**:222
"I Thought I Was a Child" (Browne) **21**:35, 37
I Thought of Daisy (Wilson) **1**:373; **2**:474-75; **24**:468-69
I, Tituba, Sorceress, Black Woman of Salem (Condé)
See *Moi, Tituba, sorciére, noire de Salem*
"I Told You I Like Indians" (Ortiz) **45**:301
"I, Too, Sing America" (Hughes) **5**:191; **108**:283, 314, 324
"I Too Will End" (Barker) **48**:12
"I Tried to Be a Communist" (Wright) **21**:455-56
"I Understand the Sin That Weighs upon My House" (Blaga) **75**:62, 69, 78
"I Used to Live Here Once" (Rhys) **19**:390-91
"I Useta Live in the World (But Then I Moved to Harlem)" (Shange) **25**:402; **126**:349-50, 352
"I Visited the Poet..." (Akhmatova) **64**:20
I Waited on the King of England (Hrabal)
See *Obsluhoval jsem anglického krále*
"I Walked Out to the Graveyard" (Eberhart) **19**:143
"I Walked over the Grave of Henry James" (Eberhart) **56**:81
"I Walked the Boulevard" (Cummings) **68**:51
"I Wanna Be Black" (Reed) **21**:316
"I Wanna Be Your Lover" (Prince) **35**:323-24, 328
"I Wanna Pick You Up" (Wilson) **12**:652
"I Wanna Woman" (O'Casey) **11**:406
"I Want a Sunday Kind of Love" (Gold) **42**:192
"I Want a Twenty-Four-Hour Truce During Which There is No Rape" (Dworkin) **123**:75
"I Want, I Want" (Plath) **111**:164
I Want It Now (Amis) **2**:7, 9; **13**:12; **129**:16, 19, 22
"I Want to Ask a Terrifying Question" (Kaufman) **49**:207
"I Want to Be Honest" (Voinovich)
See "Khochubyt' chestnym"
I Want to Be Honest (Voinovich)
See *Kochu byt' chestnym*

"I Want to Be Your Love" (Robinson) **21**:348-49
"I Want to Boogie with You" (Reed) **21**:317, 321
"I Want to Dance" (Blaga) **75**:76
I Want to Go to Moscow (Duffy) **37**:116
"I Want to Live!" (Jones) **81**:63, 65, 69
"I Want to Play" (Blaga) **75**:69
"I Want to Sing" (Giovanni) **64**:191
"I Want You" (Dylan) **12**:182
I Want You (Gaye) **26**:132-33
"I Want You Women Up North to Know" (Olsen) **114**:221
"I Want You—She's So Heavy" (Lennon and McCartney) **12**:380
I Wanted a Year without Fall (Busch) **10**:91-2
"I Wanted to be There When My Father Died" (Olds) **85**:308
"I Wanted to Overthrow the Government but All I Brought Down Was Somebody's Wife" (Bukowski) **41**:67
I Wanted to Write a Poem: The Autobiography of the Works of a Poet (Williams) **22**:467-68; **42**:449
"I Wanted You to Know" (Levine) **33**:274
"I Was a Playboy Bunny" (Steinem) **63**:378, 380, 383
I Was Amelia Earhart (Mendelsohn) **99**:63-71
I Was Born But... (Ozu) **16**:447-48, 453
"I Was Born in Lucerne" (Levine) **33**:274-75; **118**:270, 302
"I Was Born in Náchod..." (Škvorecký) **69**:335-36
I Was Dancing (O'Connor) **14**:394
"I Was in Love" (Oates) **19**:348-49
"I Was Made to Love Her" (Wonder) **12**:655, 661
"I Was Taught Three" (Graham) **118**:248
"I Was Writing" (Rozewicz) **9**:463
"I Watched a Bird" (Souster) **14**:501
"I Watched a Snake" (Graham) **48**:148; **118**:228, 249
"I Went into the Maverick Bar" (Snyder) **120**:356
"I Went Out in the Sun" (Ammons) **108**:18
I Went to Russia (O'Flaherty) **34**:356-57
"I Went to See Irving Babbitt" (Eberhart) **56**:76
"I Will" (Spacks) **14**:511
I Will Call It Georgie's Blues (Newton) **35**:302
"I will die and go to my father" (Breytenbach) **126**:63
I Will Fear No Evil (Heinlein) **14**:252, 254-55; **26**:163, 165-66; **55**:303
"I Will Keep Her Company" (Davies) **23**:148
"I Will Lie Down" (Swenson) **106**:350
"I Will Live and Survive" (Ratushinskaya) **54**:385
I Will Marry When I Want (Ngũgĩ wa Thiong'o)
See *Ngaahika Ndeenda*
"I Will Not Crush the World's Corolla of Wonders" (Blaga) **75**:76
"I Will Pronounce Your Name" (Senghor) **130**:281
"I Will Sing You One-O" (Frost) **9**:220
"I Will Teach You about Murder" (Lerman) **9**:329
"I Wish" (Wonder) **12**:660, 662
I Wish This War Were Over (O Hehir) **41**:324-26
I Wonder As I Wander: An Autobiographical Journey (Hughes) **10**:279; **108**:284, 290-91, 298, 318, 324
"I Wore My New Canary Suit" (Christie) **110**:126
"I Would Die 4 U" (Prince) **35**:329, 331-32
"I Would Have Been a Trumpet Player If I Hadn't Gone to College" (Baraka) **115**:28
I Would Have Saved Them If I Could (Michaels) **6**:324-26; **25**:316
"I Would Like" (Yevtushenko) **51**:432; **126**:396
"I Would Like to Dance" (Ian) **21**:186
"I Would Like to Describe" (Herbert) **43**:188
I Would Steal Horses (Alexie) **96**:5, 8; **154**:17
"I Wouldn't Be in Your Shoes" (Woolrich) **77**:401, 403
I Write Your Name (Carroll) **35**:81; **143**:34
"I Wrote a Good Omelet" (Giovanni) **117**:177
"Iambic Feet Considered as Honorable Scars" (Meredith) **4**:348
"Ibadan" (Clark Bekedermo) **38**:117, 120, 126, 128
"Ibadan Dawn--After Pied Beauty" (Clark Bekedermo) **38**:128
Iberia: Spanish Travels and Reflections (Michener) **29**:311; **60**:256-57
"Ibn Gabirol" (Amichai) **116**:84
"Ibn Hakkan al-Bokhari, Dead in His Labryinth" (Borges)
See "Abencaján el Bojarí, muerto en su laberinto"
"Icarium Mare" (Wilbur) **110**:361
"Icarus" (Kaufman) **8**:317
"Icarus Descending" (Benford) **52**:64
Icarus's Mother (Shepard) **17**:436, 439, 445; **41**:407
"Ice" (Ai) **14**:8; **69**:6-7
"Ice" (Oliver) **98**:265
"Ice" (Tallent) **45**:387
"Ice" (Williams) **148**:365
Ice (Cristofer) **28**:97
Ice (Hunter) **31**:227
Ice (Kavan) **5**:205-06; **13**:316; **82**:122-26
"The Ice Age" (Gerstler) **70**:158
The Ice Age (Drabble) **10**:163-66; **53**:121-22, 124; **129**:111, 113-16, 118, 134, 145, 148
Ice Age (Livesay) **79**:344-45, 349
Ice and Fire (Dworkin) **43**:135; **123**:61, 89-90
"Ice at Last" (Johnston) **51**:251
"Ice Block" (Voznesensky) **57**:421
Ice Brothers (Wilson) **32**:449
Ice Cod Bell or Stone (Birney) **6**:72, 78
"Ice Cream" (Creeley) **78**:140
"The Ice Cream Man" (Raine) **103**:179, 186
Ice Crown (Norton) **12**:459-60, 467
"Ice Cube Culture: A Shared Passion for Speaking Truth: bell hooks and Ice Cube in Dialogue" (Hooks) **94**:158
"The Ice House Gang" (Rooke) **25**:390-91
The Ice in the Bedroom (Wodehouse) **2**:480
Ice Palace (Ferber) **18**:152; **93**:183-85, 188, 190
The Ice Palace (Vesaas) **48**:407-09
The Ice Saints (Tuohy) **37**:427-28, 431
Ice Station Zebra (MacLean) **13**:361-62; **50**:348-50; **63**:264-65, 269
"The Ice Storm" (Ashbery) **77**:65, 67
The Ice Storm (Moody) **147**:166-69, 170-74, 177-79, 181, 183, 185-92
"The Ice Wagon Going down the Street" (Gallant) **38**:194
Icebreaker (Gardner) **30**:158
An Ice-Cream War: A Tale of the Empire (Boyd) **28**:39-42; **53**:50-1, 53, 55-6; **70**:132, 138, 140, 142
"Icehouse" (Matthews) **40**:322
"The Icehouse, Pointe au Baril, Ontario" (Matthews) **40**:320
"Iceland" (MacNeice) **53**:231
The Ice-Shirt (Vollmann) **89**:279-86, 290-92, 294-301, 309-11, 313
"Ich bin ein Bewohner des Elfenbeinturms" (Handke) **134**:119, 128, 150
"Ich schreibe für Leser" (Frisch) **44**:189
"Ich schreibe kein Buch über Kafka" (Hildesheimer) **49**:174
Ichiban Utsukushiku (Kurosawa) **16**:399; **119**:339, 342, 345
Ici et ailleurs (Godard) **20**:153
Ici et maintenant (Adamov) **25**:19
The Icicle, and Other Stories (Sinyavsky) **8**:488
"Icicles" (Gass) **2**:154; **8**:244; **132**:162-63, 165
"Icicles" (Pinsky) **94**:308-9
Icoane de lemn (Arghezi) **80**:3, 6, 11
"icon" (Breytenbach) **126**:63
"Icon" (Piercy) **27**:373
L'iconoclaste (Marcel) **15**:361, 363
"The Iconoclasts" (Avison) **97**:68, 71, 80, 111
Iconographs (Swenson) **4**:534; **14**:519; **61**:392-94, 397, 400-01; **106**:320-21, 325, 327-28, 338, 342, 344, 349-50
"Icons" (Waddington) **28**:438
Icons on Wood (Arghezi)
See *Icoane de lemn*
I'd Rather Be Right (Hart and Kaufman) **38**:261, 265; **66**:175, 185
"Idaho" (Ashbery) **77**:42
"Idaho" (Hannah) **38**:233-35; **90**:138-39, 147
"Idaho Falls, 1961" (Hogan) **73**:148
"Idaho Out" (Dorn) **10**:159-61
"Idanre" (Soyinka) **36**:409; **44**:278
Idanre and Other Poems (Soyinka) **36**:409; **44**:277, 279
"The Idea" (Carver) **22**:97; **126**:142, 146
"The Idea" (Strand) **71**:287-88
"An Idea for Film" (Hannah)
See "Power and Light (An Idea for Film)"
The Idea of a Christian Society (Eliot) **6**:166; **9**:185
"The Idea of Ancestry" (Knight) **40**:279-81, 283-84, 286
"The Idea of Entropy at Maenporth Beach" (Redgrove) **41**:348, 352
"The Idea of Palestine in the West" (Said) **123**:344
"The Idea of Perfection" (Murdoch) **3**:346; **15**:388
"The Idea of the Good" (Wright) **28**:465
The Idea of the Humanities (Crane) **27**:72-4
"The Idea of the Modern" (Howe) **85**:149, 151
"The Idea of Trust" (Gunn) **18**:202
The Ideal Bakery (Hall) **151**:187
"Ideal Landscape" (Rich) **18**:446; **125**:336
"The Idealism of American Criticism" (Eagleton) **63**:106
"The Idealists" (Campbell) **32**:75
Ideals: A Book of Farce and Comedy (Scott) **43**:375-76
Ideas and the Novel (McCarthy) **24**:347-50; **59**:292
"Une idée fondamentale de phénoménologie de Husserl" (Sartre) **7**:391
Identification Marks: None (Skolimowski)
See *Rysopis*
The Identification of a Woman (Antonioni)
See *Identificazione di una donna*
Identificazione di una donna (Antonioni) **144**:2-3, 5-7, 37-6, 45, 49, 55, 57-8, 60, 62-3, 65, 67-8, 70, 81
Identität und Differenz (Heidegger) **24**:277
"Identities" (Muldoon) **72**:265
"Identity" (Ammons) **25**:43
"Identity" (Avison) **97**:76
"Identity and Argument for Prayer" (Warren) **13**:582
Identity and Difference (Heidegger)
See *Identität und Differenz*
"Identity Check" (Enzensberger) **43**:152
The Identity of Yeats (Ellmann) **50**:309
"Ideographs" (Olds) **39**:188
The Ideologies of Theory (Jameson) **142**:226-27, 230, 238-39
"The Ideology of Journeys in American Films" (Murakami) **150**:45
"The Ideology of Modernism" (Jameson) **142**:229-30
The Ideology of the Aesthetic (Eagleton) **132**:89, 91-2, 94, 98-100, 106, 110, 126, 130-33
The Ideology of the Aesthetic (Eagleton) **63**:110-14
"The Ideology of the Text" (Jameson) **142**:226, 230
"The Ides of March" (Fuller) **28**:149
The Ides of March (Wilder) **1**:364, 366; **5**:494, 496; **6**:572-73, 575-78; **15**:573; **82**:348, 353, 374, 376-77, 379
An Idiom of Night (Jouve) **47**:209

"The Idiom of the Argentines" (Borges)
See *El idioma de los Argentinos*
El idioma de los Argentinos (Borges) **44**:357, 363
"Idiosyncrasy and Technique" (Moore) **47**:268, 270
"The Idiot" (Randall) **135**:389
The Idiot (Kurosawa) **16**:401, 403-05; **119**:347-48
L'idiot de la famille: Gustave Flaubert de 1821 à 1857 (Sartre) **7**:397; **24**:421-22; **50**:382; **52**:373, 380, 385-87, 389
The Idiot Princess of the Last Dynasty (Klappert) **57**:261-66, 269-70
Idiotiki Odos (Elytis) **100**:187-88
"Idiots First" (Malamud) **18**:317-18; **27**:299, 306-07; **44**:412-13, 415; **85**:217
Idiots First (Malamud) **1**:198; **3**:321; **5**:269; **9**:346, 348; **18**:318; **27**:298, 301; **44**:413
The Idiots Karamazov (Durang) **27**:87-8
The Idiots Karamazov (Innaurato) **60**:201
"An Idiot's Love" (Tanizaki)
See "Chijin no ai"
The Idle Class (Chaplin) **16**:191
"Idle Speech" (Blanchot) **135**:133
"An Idle Visitation" (Dorn) **10**:158
"Idleness in South Africa" (Coetzee) **66**:99, 105; **117**:51
"The Idler" (Bitov) **57**:114-15
"Ido and Enam" (Agnon) **4**:12
"The Idol House of Astarte" (Christie) **110**:143
The Idol Hunter (Unsworth)
See *Pascali's Island*
"The Idol of the Cyclades" (Cortázar)
See "El ídolo de las cícladas"
"El ídolo de las cícladas" (Cortázar) **10**:114; **33**:129; **34**:332
The Idols of the Cave (Prokosch) **4**:420; **48**:312-14
"Idoto" (Okigbo) **25**:355
Idu (Nwapa) **133**:180-83, 190-93, 201, 216, 222-25, 230, 233, 235
Idut belye snegi (Yevtushenko) **26**:462
"An Idyll" (Castillo) **151**:5-7
"Idyll for a Fool" (Gustafson) **36**:214, 216
"L'Idylle" (Blanchot) **135**:81, 85, 113, 136-37
"Idylle" (Damas) **84**:179
"Idylls of Dugan and Strunk" (Stern) **39**:239
"If" (Hogan) **73**:149
"If" (Warren) **39**:258
If (Anderson) **20**:13-16, 18
"If All Men Were Brothers Would You Let One Marry Your Sister?" (Sturgeon) **39**:361-62
"If Anyone Had Told Me" (Aleixandre)
See "If Someone Could Have Told Me"
"If Anything Will Level with You Water Will" (Ammons) **108**:28
If Beale Street Could Talk (Baldwin) **4**:41-3; **5**:42-4; **15**:42; **17**:39, 45; **50**:297; **90**:31; **127**:124-25, 128-31
"If Beggars Were Horses" (Dowell) **60**:104-05, 109
If Birds Build with Your Hair (Snodgrass) **68**:387-88
"If Blood Were Not as Powerful as It Is" (Gallagher) **63**:126
"If Dogs Run Free" (Dylan) **77**:161
"If Ever You Go to Dublin Town" (Kavanagh) **22**:238
"If Everything Happens That Can't Be Done" (Cummings) **15**:163
If He Hollers Let Him Go (Himes) **2**:195; **4**:229; **7**:159; **58**:251, 254-55, 259, 261-63, 265-66; **108**:228, 231, 236, 253-55, 267, 271, 274
"If Hitler Had Invaded England" (Forester) **35**:173
"If I Could Only Live at the Pitch That Is Near Madness" (Eberhart) **19**:143; **56**:86
"If I Could Write This in Fire, I Would Write This in Fire" (Cliff) **120**:92, 94-96, 98, 113
If I Die in a Combat Zone, Box Me Up and Ship Me Home (O'Brien) **7**:271; **19**:357; **40**:348; **103**:132, 134, 136, 143, 149-50, 157, 169-76
"If I Fell" (Lennon and McCartney) **35**:268
"If I Forget Thee Jerusalem" (Amichai) **116**:128
"If I Had Children" (Swenson) **106**:342
"If I Had My Way" (Creeley) **15**:153
"if i have made, my lady, intricate" (Cummings) **3**:117; **15**:161
If I Love You, Am I Trapped Forever? (Kerr) **12**:297-98
"If I Only Had the Words" (Joel) **26**:218
"If I only knew" (Sachs)
See "Wenn ich nur wusste"
"If I Should Ever Travel!" (Ferber) **93**:146
"If I Should Open My Mouth" (Bowles) **53**:36-7
"If I Think of You Again It Will Be the Fifty-third Monday of Next Year" (Harjo) **83**:273, 275
"If I Were Sixteen Today" (Moore) **1**:227; **47**:267
"If Into Love The Image Burdens" (Baraka) **5**:45
If It Be Not I (Van Duyn) **116**:418-19, 423, 427
If It Must Be So (Buck)
See *Home Chat*
"If It Were Not for You" (Carruth) **7**:40
"If It Were You" (Page) **18**:379
"If It's Magic" (Wonder) **12**:659
"If Love Were All" (Coward) **29**:138
"If Men Could Menstruate" (Steinem) **63**:382, 384
"If Momma Was Married" (Sondheim) **30**:377, 387
"If Money" (Fearing) **51**:106
If Morning Ever Comes (Tyler) **18**:531; **28**:429-32; **44**:315; **59**:203; **103**:227, 235, 244, 258, 263-65, 269
If Mountains Die: A New Mexico Memoir (Nichols) **38**:342-44
"If Music Could Talk" (Clash) **30**:49
"If, My Darling" (Larkin) **33**:258; **64**:260, 262, 266
"If Never Again" (Gallagher) **18**:170
"If Not for the Blessing of a Son" (Castillo) **151**:48, 65
"If Not for You" (Dylan) **6**:156
If Not Now, When? (Levi)
See *Se non ora, quando?*
"If Not Poetry, Then What?" (Castellanos) **66**:56
"An 'If' of History" (Achebe) **26**:21, 24
If on a Winter's Night a Traveler (Calvino)
See *Se una notte d'inverno un viaggiatore*
"If Once in Silence" (Dunn) **36**:154
"If One Green Bottle. . ." (Thomas) **13**:539; **37**:420; **107**:318, 320, 334-36, 347-48
"If Poetry Were Not a Morality" (Gallagher) **63**:126
"If Someone Could Have Told Me" (Aleixandre) **36**:30
If Summer Should Return (Adamov) **25**:20
"If the Cap Fits" (Simmons) **43**:411
If the Earth Falls In (Clark) **12**:131
"If the Impressionists Were Dentists" (Allen) **52**:37
If the Old Could ... (Lessing) **40**:308-09, 315; **94**:258
"If the Owl Calls Again" (Haines) **58**:215
"If the Pope Doesn't Break with the U.S.A." (Parra) **102**:354
"If the River Was Whiskey" (Boyle) **90**:46-7, 50, 62
If the River Was Whiskey (Boyle) **90**:45-8
If the Stars Are Gods (Benford) **52**:59, 61
If the Sun Dies (Fallaci)
See *Se ïl sole muore*
"If There's a Reason" (Lightfoot) **26**:282
If They Come in the Morning: Voices of Resistance (Davis) **77**:108-10
"If They Knew Yvonne" (Dubus) **97**:197, 217, 228-29
If This Be a Man (Levi)
See *Se questo è un uomo*
"If This Goes On" (Heinlein) **55**:302, 304
If This Is a Man (Levi)
See *Se questo è un uomo*
"If We Had Bacon" (Roth) **6**:473
"If We Take All Gold" (Bogan) **39**:387; **93**:90
"If You" (Creeley) **36**:118
"If You Are About to Die Now" (Smith) **64**:393
If You Believe the Pythagoreans (Grossman) **41**:187-88
If You Call This Cry a Song (Carruth) **84**:128-31
"If You Could Read My Mind" (Lightfoot) **26**:281
If You Could Read My Mind (Lightfoot) **26**:278
If You Could See Me Now (Straub) **28**:409-10; **107**:266, 268, 274-78, 280-81, 302, 304-10
"If You Don't Like Hank Williams" (Kristofferson) **26**:269
"If You Forget the Germans" (Stern) **40**:406
"If You Know What I Mean" (Diamond) **30**:112
"If You Love the Body" (Tillinghast) **29**:415
"If You Only Knew..." (Guillén)
See "Ay negra, si tu supiera"
If You Please (Breton and Soupault)
See *S'il vous plaît*
"If You Saw a Negro Lady" (Jordan) **114**:145
"If You See Her, Say Hello" (Dylan) **77**:172-73
"If You Touched My Heart" (Allende) **97**:37
"If You Wanna Make Love" (Robinson) **21**:350-51
"If You're Dying, Choose a Mausoleum" (Miller) **14**:373
"If You're Glad I'll Be Frank" (Stoppard) **4**:524; **29**:394, 397
"The Igbo World and Its Art" (Achebe) **127**:33; **152**:77-9
The Ignoramus and the Madman (Bernhard)
See *Der Ignorant und der Wahnsinnige*
"Ignorance" (Middleton) **13**:389
Der Ignorant und der Wahnsinnige (Bernhard) **32**:24; **61**:12, 20
"Igor Stravinsky: The Selected Phone Calls" (Frazier) **46**:164-65
Igor-The Paris Years Chez Pleyel (The Brothers Quay) **95**:330-31, 336, 344, 353
Igre (Popa) **19**:373
The Iguana (Ortese)
See *L'iguana*
L'iguana (Ortese) **89**:191-97, 199
"Ihtidar M'taqadat wa Tawallud M'taqadat" (Mahfouz) **153**:336
"II" (Lem) **149**:158
"III" (Lem) **149**:158
Ikarian Dreamers (Nakos) **29**:323
"Ike" (Dove) **81**:137
"Ike and Nina" (Boyle) **36**:63
"Ikey" (Brown) **100**:82-3
Ikimono no kiroku (Kurosawa) **16**:399, 401, 403; **119**:379, 383, 385, 391, 397
Ikiru (Kurosawa) **16**:396, 400, 402; **119**:337, 340-41, 343, 347-49, 351, 353-56, 378-79, 382, 391, 403
"Ikons" (Mahapatra) **33**:279
The Ikons and Other Poems (Durrell) **4**:145
Ikuisen rauhau aika (Haavikko) **34**:180-81
Il cardillo addolorato (Ortese) **89**:199
Il castello dei destini incrociati (Calvino) **8**:126-28, 130-32; **22**:89; **33**:98, 100; **39**:306-07, 310, 313-14, 316-17; **73**:48, 51, 58; **48**:48-50, 59, 113, 127, 145, 150-51, 168
"Il cinema di poesia" (Pasolini) **106**:237
"Il continente sommerso" (Ortese) **89**:198-99
"Il diaul cu la mari" (Pasolini) **106**:230
Il Duetto (The Brothers Quay) **95**:329
"Il est des nuits" (Damas) **84**:173-74, 177
Il est par là, le soleil (Carrier) **13**:141-44;

78:39-40, 44, 46, 49, 51, 57, 61-2, 67-70, 79, 81, 83
Il était une fois dans l'est (Tremblay) **102**:361, 369
Il Fabulazzo Osceno (Fo) **109**:101, 109
Il Fanfani rapito (Fo) **109**:104
Il mare non bagna Napoli (Ortesè) **89**:191-92
"Il medioevo è già cominciato" (Eco) **28**:131
"Il neo-sperimentalismo" (Pasolini) **106**:212
"Il n'est pas de midi qui tienne" (Damas) **84**:158
"Il nini muart" (Pasolini) **106**:227-28, 233, 260-61
"Il n'y a pas d'amour heureux" (Aragon) **22**:38
Il n'y a pas de pays sans grand-père (Carrier) **13**:144; **78**:61, 63, 65-7, 70, 72, 80
Il pendolo di Foucault (Eco) **60**:114-15; **142**:66-9, 71-4, 81-7, 89-91, 93-5, 97-9, 102, 104, 106-07, 109, 114, 136-37
Il porto di Toledo (Ortese) **89**:195, 198
"Il sangue, il mare" (Calvino) **8**:127
"Il se pourrait bien que les arbres voyagent" (Carrier) **78**:63
"Il se sauve" (Davison) **28**:104
Il sesso inutile (Fallaci) **11**:190; **110**:189
"Il signor Lin" (Ortese) **89**:198
Il sogno di una cosa (Pasolini) **106**:231, 254
L'ile de la demoiselle (Hébert) **29**:240-41
L'île introuvable (Theriault) **79**:408
The Ilex Tree (Murray) **40**:333-34
Ílios o prótos (Elytis) **15**:220; **49**:106, 115; **100**:155, 175, 190
"I'll Be Home for Christmas" (Anderson) **23**:31
"I'll Be Waiting for You When the Swimming Pool Is Empty" (Tiptree) **48**:385-86
"I'll Be Your Baby Tonight" (Dylan) **12**:185
"I'll Bet He's Nice" (Wilson) **12**:651-52
"I'll Bring You Back Something Nice" (Levine) **54**:295
"I'll Cover You" (Larson) **99**:161, 164, 184
"I'll Do Anything" (Lightfoot) **26**:283
"I'll Fly Away" (Bottoms) **53**:32
"I'll Follow My Secret Heart" (Coward) **1**:65
I'll Get There; It Better Be Worth the Trip (Donovan) **35**:139-41, 143
I'll Leave It to You (Coward) **29**:139
I'll Love You When You're More Like Me (Kerr) **12**:300
I'll Never Be Young Again (du Maurier) **59**:284-86
"I'll Never See Johanna" (Sondheim) **30**:398
"I'll See You Again" (Coward) **1**:65; **29**:138
Ill Seen Ill Said (Beckett)
See *Mal vu mal dit*
"I'll Start Out by Talking" (Moure) **88**:220
"I'll Take My Stand" (Tate) **4**:535; **11**:527
"I'll Take My Stand" (Warren) **8**:538
Illa (Cixous) **92**:63
The Illearth War (Donaldson) **46**:140-43; **138**:4, 9, 11, 14, 19-20, 26, 38-40
The Ill-Fated Peregrinations of Fray Servando (Arenas)
See *El mundo alucinante: Una novela de aventuras*
Illiberal Education: The Politics of Race and Sex On Campus (D'Souza) **70**:400, 403-04
Illicit Interlude (Bergman)
See *Sommarlek*
"Illimitable Kingdom" (Parini) **54**:360
"The Illinois Enema Bandit" (Zappa) **17**:592
"The Illiterate" (Meredith) **13**:374; **55**:192
The Ill-Made Knight (White) **30**:440-41, 444-46
"Illness as Metaphor" (Muske) **90**:314
Illness as Metaphor (Sontag) **10**:487; **13**:519; **31**:411-13, 417; **105**:206, 214-15, 227
"The Illogic of Sumptuary Values" (Howe) **152**:158, 161-62
The Ill-Tempered Clavichord (Perelman) **49**:261, 272
"The Illuminated Man" (Ballard) **36**:34
"The Illumination" (Kunitz) **148**:79-80, 89, 101, 138, 145
Illumination Night (Hoffman) **51**:206-08
"Illuminations" (Glück) **22**:176
"Illuminatus!" (Wilson) **9**:576
"The Illumined Graves" (Lamming) **66**:220, 225
"Illusion" (Rhys) **51**:356
The Illusion (Caute) **29**:114-15, 118, 122
The Illusion (Kushner) **81**:197, 204
The Illusion of Technique (Barrett) **27**:20-1
"The Illusionist" (Kunitz) **148**:88
The Illusionist (Johnston) **150**:26, 32
"The Illusionists" (Friel) **42**:166
The Illusionists: A Tale (Fuller) **62**:198, 201, 203-05
"Illusions" (Blunden) **56**:38, 52
Illusions (Bach) **14**:36
The Illusions of Postmodernism (Eagleton) **132**:134, 136
"The (Illustrated) Body Politic" (Leyner) **92**:293-94
The Illustrated Man (Bradbury) **10**:70
"The Illustrated Woman" (Bradbury) **42**:33
"Illustration" (Ashbery) **77**:58
Illustrations (Butor) **15**:114, 119
The Illustrations (Dubie) **36**:131-33, 137-39
Illywhacker (Carey) **40**:130-35; **55**:112-18; **96**:26-9, 31-7, 43-7, 50, 53, 55, 58-9, 61, 63, 65, 70, 72, 74, 76, 81
"Ils ont" (Damas) **84**:167, 174
"Ils sont venus ce soir" (Damas) **84**:169, 171, 182, 185
Ilsa (L'Engle) **12**:344
"Ilu, the Talking Drum" (Knight) **40**:283-84, 287
La ilusion viaja en tranvia (Bunuel) **80**:24
Ilya Ehrenburg; Revolutionary, Novelist, Poet, War Correspondent, Propagandist: The Extraordinary Epic of a Russian Survivor (Goldberg)
See *Ilya Ehrenburg: Writing, Politics, and the Art of Survival*
Ilya Ehrenburg: Writing, Politics, and the Art of Survival (Goldberg) **34**:433-34, 436, 438
Ilyitch Slept Here (Carlisle) **33**:103
"I'm a Boy" (Townshend) **17**:529-31, 539
"I'm a Loser" (Lennon and McCartney) **35**:274
I'm a Lucky Guy (Gilbreth and Carey) **17**:153-54
I'm a Stranger Here Myself (Nash) **23**:318, 320
"I'm Carrying" (McCartney) **35**:285
"I'm Crazy" (Salinger) **56**:336; **138**:226
Im Dialog (Wolf) **150**:291, 294
"I'm Dreaming of Rocket Richard" (Blaise) **29**:70
I'm Dying Laughing (Stead) **80**:341
"Im Ei" (Grass) **32**:198, 201; **88**:179
I'm Everyone I Ever Loved (Mull) **17**:300
I'm Expecting to Live Quite Soon (West) **7**:523
"I'm Free" (Townshend) **17**:526
I'm Getting My Act Together and Taking It on the Road (Cryer) **21**:81-2
"I'm Going to Cut You into Little Pieces" (Pink Floyd)
See "One of These Days"
"I'm Herbert" (Anderson) **23**:31
"I'm Here" (Roethke) **19**:397
"I'm Here" (Sondheim) **30**:389
"Im Lande der Rujuks" (Boell) **27**:66; **72**:72
"I'm Losing You" (Lennon) **35**:272-73
"I'm Not Angry" (Costello) **21**:67
"I'm Not Down" (Clash) **30**:46-7
"I'm Not in Love" (Byrne) **25**:96
"I'm Not like Everybody Else" (Davies) **21**:95
I'm Not Rappaport (Gardner) **44**:208-12
I'm Not Stiller (Frisch)
See *Stiller*
"I'm Over Twenty-Nine" (Musgrave) **54**:341
I'm Really Dragged but Nothing Gets Me Down (Hentoff) **26**:182-84
"I'm Set Free" (Reed) **21**:303, 322
"I'm So Bored with the U.S.A." (Clash) **30**:43-5, 51-2
"I'm So Cute" (Zappa) **17**:592
"I'm Stepping Out" (Lennon) **35**:275-76
"I'm Still Here" (Sondheim) **30**:387, 396, 400; **147**:234, 264
"I'm Sure" (Ignatow) **40**:259
I'm Talking about Jerusalem (Wesker) **3**:517-19
"I'm the Face" (Townshend) **17**:534, 538
I'm the King of the Castle (Hill) **113**:281-82, 290, 293, 297, 300, 303, 305, 309-10, 312-14, 318, 321, 325, 330
"I'm Too Big but I Love to Play" (Tiptree) **48**:385
Im Wechsel der Zeit: Autobiographische Skizzen und Essays (Hochwälder) **36**:239
Im Westen nichts Neues (Remarque) **21**:324-27, 329-31, 334-37
"I'm Wide" (Lish) **45**:230
"Image" (Guillevic) **33**:193
"The Image" (Hass) **18**:212-13; **39**:147-48
"The Image" (Singer) **69**:306
"The Image" (Williams) **148**:352-53
Image and Idea (Rahv) **24**:351-52, 360
The Image, and Other Stories (Singer) **69**:305, 308-09
The Image and the Law (Nemerov) **6**:361; **36**:301, 304, 307
"The Image as Guide to Meaning in the Historical Novel" (Lytle) **22**:294
"An Image from Beckett" (Mahon) **27**:286, 288
"An Image from Propertius" (Longley) **29**:294
Image in the Snow (Deren) **16**:252
The Image Men (Priestley) **34**:361
"An Image of Leda" (O'Hara) **13**:427; **78**:354
"Image of Man as a Gardener after Two World Wars" (Ciardi) **44**:382
"Image of Man is Australian Poetry" (Buckley) **57**:129
The Image of Misfortune (Onetti)
See *La cara de la desgracia*
"An Image of Success" (Gordimer) **18**:185; **33**:180
The Image of the Beast (Farmer) **19**:164, 167
"The Image of the Shark Confronts the Image of the Little Match Girl" (Ashbery) **25**:54, 56
"The Image System of Grotesque Realism" (Oe) **86**:229, 242
"The Image-Maker" (Kunitz) **148**:110, 126
Image—Music—Text (Barthes) **83**:80-1
"Imagens em Castela" (Cabral de Melo Neto) **76**:167
"Images" (Aldington) **49**:2, 9, 12, 17
"Images" (Glück) **81**:170
"Images" (Hass) **99**:129-30, 135, 145, 148
"Images" (Munro) **19**:344; **95**:287, 292, 298
Images (Altman) **16**:23-4, 28, 35, 38, 41, 43; **116**:3-7, 21, 23, 67, 69, 73-4
Images (1910-1915) (Aldington)
See *Images Old and New*
"Images à Crusoe" (Perse) **46**:301
"Images and Images" (Simic) **68**:369
Images de Marque (Leiris) **61**:362
"Images for Godard" (Rich) **11**:476; **36**:373
"Images for Piano" (Corn) **33**:114
"Images in Castille" (Cabral de Melo Neto)
See "Imagens em Castela"
"Images of Angels" (Page) **7**:291
Images of Desire (Aldington) **49**:2-3, 7, 9-10, 17-18
"Images of Elspeth" (Berryman) **62**:64
Images of Kin (Harper) **22**:209
Images of Truth (Wescott) **13**:592
Images of War (Aldington) **49**:2-3, 5, 7-10, 17
Images Old and New (Aldington) **49**:2, 17
"A imaginação do pouco" (Cabral de Melo Neto) **76**:160, 165
Imaginación y violencia en América (Dorfman) **77**:155
L'imaginaire: Psychologie phénoénologique de l'imagination (Sartre) **24**:413; **44**:498
"Imaginary and Symbolic in Lacan" (Jameson) **142**:226

"The Imaginary Assassin" (Mukherjee) **53**:269
"Imaginary Countries" (Le Guin) **12**:211-13, 217-19, 248, **136**:395
"The Imaginary Dead Baby Sea Gull" (Shields) **97**:431, 433
Imaginary Friends (Lurie) **4**:306-07; **5**:260
The Imaginary Girlfriend (Irving) **112**:174-76
"Imaginary Homelands" (Rushdie) **55**:241
"The Imaginary Iceberg" (Bishop) **32**:43
"The Imaginary Jew" (Berryman) **3**:71; **10**:45
An Imaginary Life (Malouf) **28**:266, 268; **86**:196, 203, 208-09, 211
The Imaginary Lover (Ostriker) **132**:318-20
Imaginary Magnitude (Lem) **40**:292, 298-99; **149**:112-13, 116, 154, 156, 159, 173, 261-62, 277
Imaginary Paintings, and Other Poems (Baxter) **78**:24-25, 28
Imaginary Timber (Galvin) **38**:197-98
"The Imagination" (Richards) **24**:396-97
Imagination Dead Imagine (Beckett)
See *Imagination morte imaginez*
Imagination morte imaginez (Beckett) **2**:48; **3**:45; **6**:38, 42; **9**:83-4; **11**:40-1, 43; **14**:78; **16**:76-82, 85, 95-8, 102, 105, 107, 122, 123; **18**:50-1
"The Imagination of Disaster" (Gordon) **128**:109, 115
"Imagination on a Small Scale" (Cabral de Melo Neto)
See "A imaginação do pouco"
Imaginations (Williams) **2**:468-69; **5**:510
Imaginative Qualities of Actual Things (Sorrentino) **3**:461-62; **7**:449-52; **14**:499; **22**:391-93; **40**:385-86
"Imagine" (Lennon) **35**:263-65, 267, 270, 272-73, 275
Imagine (Lennon) **12**:366, 381; **35**:263-66, 269-70, 273
"Imagine a Day at the End of Your Life" (Beattie) **146**:53, 58, 60, 66, 85
"Imagine a Man" (Townshend) **17**:535-37
Imagine a Woman, and Other Tales (Selzer) **74**:285, 287
Imagine Kissing Pete (O'Hara) **3**:371; **42**:319, 326-27
"Imagined Scenes" (Beattie) **8**:56
Imaging American Women: Ideas and Ideals in Cultural History (Banta) **65**:327
"Imagining a Unicorn" (Spacks) **14**:511
Imagining a Unicorn (Spacks) **14**:511
"Imagining How It Would Be to Be Dead" (Eberhart) **56**:87
"Imagining Jews" (Roth) **9**:459
"Imagining the Reservation" (Alexie) **96**:4, 7; **154**:26
Imaginings of Sand (Brink) **106**:134-38
Imago (Butler) **121**:92-3, 96-7, 103, 105, 108, 118-20, 136, 139-40, 143, 145
Imago Bird (Mosley) **43**:318-20, 322; **70**:202, 205
Iman (Sender) **8**:479-80
"Imelda" (Colwin) **84**:146, 149, 151
"Imelda" (Selzer) **74**:274-76
Imerológhio enós athéatou Aprilíou (Elytis) **100**:175
Imitation of Christ (Warhol) **20**:420
"The Imitation of the Rose" (Lispector) **43**:268-70
Imitations (Lowell) **1**:180, 182; **2**:246, 249; **3**:300; **4**:297-28, 301; **5**:257; **8**:354; **124**:256, 270
Immaculate Man (Gordon) **128**:141-43
L'immaculée conception (Breton) **54**:32
Immanuel Kant (Bernhard) **32**:25; **61**:13, 26-7
"Immanuel Kant and the Hopi" (Stern) **40**:408
Immanuel Kant in England, 1793-1838 (Wellek) **28**:446, 452
The Immaterial Murder Case (Symons) **14**:523
"The Immigrant" (Rothenberg) **57**:374
The Immigrant Experience: The Long, Long Journey (Silver) **20**:341, 345
The Immigrant Jews of New York, 1881 to the Present (Howe)
See *World of Our Fathers: The Journey of the Eastern European Jews to America and the Life They Found and Made*
"Immigrant Song" (Page and Plant) **12**:474-75
"The Immigrant Story" (Paley) **140**:212, 219, 223, 227, 233-24, 262, 282
"Immigrant Voyage" (Murray) **40**:338, 340
The Immigrants (Fast) **23**:159-60; **131**:55, 59-61, 63, 70, 73, 86
The Immigrant's Daughter (Fast) **131**:86, 98, 100
"Immigration Blues" (Santos) **22**:365
The Immobile Wind (Winters) **32**:469
"Immobilism" (Graham) **118**:234
"An Immodest Proposal" (Brodsky) **100**:63, 72
"Immolatus" (Komunyakaa) **94**:241
"Immoral Allure" (Leyner) **92**:293
"The Immoral Proposition" (Creeley) **78**:124, 126
"The Immortal" (Borges)
See "El inmortal"
"An Immortal" (Murray) **40**:344
"The Immortal" (Simic) **68**:376; **130**:314
"Immortal" (Van Doren) **10**:496
"Immortal Autumn" (MacLeish) **68**:273-74, 285, 288
"Immortal Element" (Jacobsen) **48**:190
The Immortal One (Robbe-Grillet)
See *L'immortelle*
"The Immortal Story" (Dinesen) **10**:145; **95**:53-4
The Immortal Story (Welles) **20**:442, 445-47; **80**:391-93, 395-97
L'immortalité (Kundera) **68**:250-66; **115**:347-48, 357, 359; **135**:241, 252
Immortality (Kundera)
See *L'immortalité*
"Immortality over the Dakotas" (Warren) **39**:270
"The Immortals" (Amis) **62**:7, 10
"The Immortals" (Bioy Casares) **88**:78
"The Immortals" (Tate) **2**:432
L'immortelle (Robbe-Grillet) **1**:287; **2**:376; **6**:466; **128**:332, 336, 362
"Immortelles" (Merwin) **88**:210, 212
The Immovable Pilgrims (Lopez y Fuentes)
See *Los peregrinos inmóviles*
"Immram" (Muldoon) **32**:320-21; **72**:267-68, 270, 273-74, 278, 280
"Imogene Knode" (Broumas) **73**:3-4
"The Impalpabilities" (Tomlinson) **6**:534; **13**:549
"Impasse" (Stegner) **49**:351
Impatience (Trifonov)
See *Neterpenie*
"Impeccable Conception" (Angelou) **35**:32
"An Imperfect Copy of Antichrist" (Ayrton) **7**:18
"Imperfect Critics" (Eliot) **24**:169, 180
"The Imperfect Eye" (L'Heureux) **52**:272
Imperfect Thirst (Kinnell) **129**:265-66, 268, 271-72
"L'imperfection est la cime" (Bonnefoy) **58**:49, 59
"Imperial Adam" (Hope) **51**:210-12, 214, 216, 219-20
Imperial Caesar (Warner) **45**:436
Imperial City (Rice) **7**:359, 363
Imperial Earth (Clarke) **13**:150-51, 153, 155; **18**:106-07
The Imperial German Dinner Service (Hughes) **48**:184-85
The Imperial Presidency (Schlesinger) **84**:364-65, 367-68, 376, 381, 386
"The Imperial Theme" (Simmons) **43**:414
Imperial Woman (Buck) **7**:32; **127**:229-31
"Imperialism" (Graham) **48**:155; **118**:229, 251
"Impersonal Narration" (Booth) **24**:86
Implements in Their Places (Graham) **29**:196-98
"The Implements of Augury" (Simic) **49**:343
"Implosions" (Rich) **6**:457-58; **125**:321
"The Importance of Artists' Biographies" (Goldbarth) **38**:205-06
"The Importance of Being Earnest" (Ewart) **46**:153
"The Importance of Elsewhere" (Larkin) **13**:339; **64**:262
"The Importance of Green" (Galvin) **38**:199
"The Importance of Mozart's Operas" (Brophy) **105**:13
"The Important Thing" (Williams) **45**:447
Important to Me (Johnson) **7**:184; **27**:222
"Impossible" (Sondheim) **30**:378
Impossible Buildings (Johnson) **7**:414
"Impossible Iambics" (Sandburg) **35**:356
"The Impossible Indispensibility of the Ars Poetica" (Carruth) **84**:136
The Impossible Loves (Arrabal) **9**:39
Impossible Object (Mosley) **43**:314-16, 318-19, 321-22
The Impossible Proof (Nossack)
See *Un moegliche Bewiesaufrahme*
The Impossible Railway (Berton) **104**:39
"An Impossible Song" (Townshend) **42**:378, 380
"Impossible to Tell" (Pinsky) **121**:450
Impossible Vacation (Gray) **112**:114-17, 119, 126-27, 129-130
The Imposter (Brady) **86**:130, 133-34
"El impostor inverosímil Tom Castro" (Borges) **48**:36
"Impotence" (Williams) **42**:443
"Imprecated upon a Postal Clerk" (Nemerov) **36**:309
"Impresario on the Lam" (Perelman) **23**:336
"Impressions II" (Cummings) **68**:51
"The Imprisonment of Obatala" (Clark Bekedermo) **38**:126, 128
L'improbable (Bonnefoy) **58**:57
L'impromptu de l'alma; ou, Le cameleon du berger (Ionesco) **4**:251; **6**:248-49; **15**:298
L'impromptu du Palais-Royal (Cocteau) **8**:148-50; **43**:112
"Impromptu for Francis Webb" (Buckley) **57**:130
Impromptu in Moribundia (Hamilton) **51**:186, 195
The Impromptu of Outremont (Tremblay) **29**:424
"The Improved Binoculars" (Layton) **15**:322
"The Improvement" (Ashbery) **125**:31
"Improvisation" (Gunn) **81**:176, 187
"Improvisation" (L'Heureux) **52**:272
"An Improvisation for the Stately Dwelling" (Ammons) **108**:56
Improvisation; or, The Shepherd's Chameleon (Ionesco)
See *L'impromptu de l'alma; ou, Le cameleon du berger*
"Improvisations on Themes from Guillevic" (Justice) **102**:263
"The Improvisors" (Morgan) **2**:294
"Imprudent Lover" (Coles) **46**:113
"The Impstone" (Musgrave) **13**:401
The Impstone (Musgrave) **13**:401; **54**:341
Les impudents (Duras) **6**:149; **11**:165; **40**:179; **68**:92, 99; **100**:145-47, 149
"Impuissance" (Livesay) **79**:340
"Impulse" (Aiken) **10**:1-2
"The Impulse" (Smith) **64**:391
The Impuritans (Clarke) **6**:111
"In 1929" (Spender) **91**:266
"In 1940" (Akhmatova) **25**:29
"In a Bad Light" (Boland) **113**:100, 115, 126
"In a Blue Time" (Kureishi) **135**:284
"In a Boat" (Ashbery) **15**:34
"In a Buggy at Dusk" (Milosz) **82**:306
"In a Café" (Rhys) **19**:390-91
In a Café (Lavin) **18**:307
"In a Caledonian Forest" (MacDiarmid) **4**:309; **11**:333
"In a Churchyard" (Wilbur) **53**:402

"In a Cold Season" (Hamburger) **14**:234
"In a Country Church" (Thomas) **13**:543; **48**:381
"In a Country Churchyard" (Blunden) **56**:39
In a Dark Garden (Slaughter) **29**:373-75
"In a Dark Square" (Merwin) **2**:277
"In a Dark Time" (Roethke) **3**:433-34; **8**:456, 460; **11**:485; **46**:361, 364; **101**:267, 289, 309
In a Dark Wood (Warner) **59**:216
"In a Darkness" (Bowers) **9**:122
"In a Deserted Rest Home" (Akhmadulina)
See "V opustevshem dome otdykha"
In a Dusty Light (Haines) **58**:217, 219, 221
In a Farther Country (Goyen) **5**:148-49; **14**:210, 214; **40**:218
"In a Father's Place" (Tilghman) **65**:105, 108, 111-12
In a Father's Place (Tilghman) **65**:105-06, 108-09, 111-12
"In a Flemish Garden" (Fuentes) **22**:171
In a Free State (Naipaul) **4**:373-75; **7**:253-54; **9**:391-92; **13**:402, 404-05, 407; **18**:359; **37**:320, 329; **105**:142-43, 146, 157-58, 161, 164, 170, 176, 181
"In a Garden" (Clarke) **61**:73
"In a Great Man's House" (Jhabvala) **8**:312-13
"In a Green Night" (Walcott) **42**:421; **76**:273, 277-80, 282
In a Green Night: Poems, 1948-1960 (Walcott) **14**:549, 551; **25**:448-50; **42**:421; **67**:344
"In a Hand or a Face" (Townshend) **17**:535
In a Harbour Green (Kiely) **23**:259, 261-62; **43**:245
"In a Hard Intellectual Light" (Eberhart) **56**:75, 80
In a Hotel Garden (Josipovici) **153**:218, 224
"In a Jon-Boat during a Florida Dawn" (Bottoms) **53**:32-3
"In a Manner That Must Shame God Himself" (Vonnegut) **5**:469
In a Marine Light (Carver)
See *Ultramarine*
"In a Mental Hospital Sitting Room" (Jennings) **131**:240
"In a Mexican City" (Hughes) **108**:323
In a Mirror (Stolz) **12**:547-49
In a Moscow Street (Ehrenburg)
See *In Protochny Lane*
In a Narrow Grave: Essays on Texas (McMurtry) **7**:214-15; **27**:324, 328; **44**:260-62; **127**:304-06, 310
"In a Notebook" (Fenton) **32**:165-67, 169
"In a Polish Home for the Aged" (Hirsch) **50**:197
In a Province (van der Post) **5**:463
"In a Railway Compartment" (Fuller) **62**:200-02
"In a Right Angle: A Cycle of Quatrains" (Amichai) **57**:44
"In a Room and a Half" (Brodsky) **50**:132-33, 137
In a Shallow Grave (Purdy) **10**:424-25; **52**:348
"In a Simple Way I Love You" (Cryer) **21**:81
"In a Small Moment" (Simon) **26**:411-12
"In a Space" (Davies) **21**:105
"In a Station of the Metro" (Pound) **18**:428; **48**:283; **50**:436
"In a Strange Country" (Ellison) **114**:126
"In a Strange House" (Kunitz) **148**:102, 148
In a Strange Land (Middleton) **38**:332-33
In a Summer Season (Taylor) **29**:408, 411-12
In a Time of Violence (Boland) **113**:87, 90, 92-5, 99, 101, 108, 110, 112, 115, 119-21, 125-27
"In a Train" (Bly) **128**:20
"In a Troubled Key" (Hughes) **15**:291
"In a U-Haul North of Damascus" (Bottoms) **53**:32
In a U-Haul North of Damascus (Bottoms) **53**:31-3
"In a Vacant House" (Levine) **118**:290
In a Vast Dominion (Aleixandre)
See *En un vasto dominio*
"In a Warm Bath" (Rakosi) **47**:344
In a Year of Thirteen Moons (Fassbinder) **20**:119
In a Yellow Wood (Vidal) **4**:558; **22**:431-33
In Abraham's Bosom (Green) **25**:192-93, 195-96, 198-99
In Acht and Bann (Hein) **154**:180
In Adversity Be Ye Steadfast (Boyle) **19**:68
In Africa Even the Flies Are Happy (Breytenbach) **23**:84
In Agony (Krleža)
See *U agoniji*
"In Alien Flesh" (Benford) **52**:75-6
In Alien Flesh (Benford) **52**:75-6
"In Amalfi" (Beattie) **146**:58, 61, 66, 85
In America's Shoes (Codrescu) **46**:104-05; **121**:160, 162
"In Amicitia" (Ransom) **5**:365
In an Antique Land (Ghosh) **153**:86-91, 93-8, 103-07, 110, 113-14, 116, 126, 129
In and Out (Hine) **15**:282
"In Another Country" (Hemingway) **3**:241; **10**:269; **30**:182, 184-85, 196, 200; **61**:194, 203; **80**:136
"In Another Country" (Laughlin) **49**:221-23
In Another Country: Poems, 1935-1975 (Laughlin) **49**:220-22
In Any Case (Stern) **4**:523; **39**:236
"In April, In Princeton" (Kumin) **13**:327
"In Apulia" (Bachmann) **69**:61
"In Arden" (Tomlinson) **13**:549-50; **45**:394
"In Argos" (Davis) **49**:93
"In at the Birth" (Trevor) **71**:326
"In Athens Once" (Rodriguez) **155**:274, 276-77, 296, 301-02
"In Atrim" (Paulin) **37**:352
"In August" (Soto) **80**:289
In Aunt Mahaly's Cabin (Green) **25**:193
"In Baghdad" (Christie) **110**:125
"In Balthazar's Village" (Middleton) **13**:388
"In Barracks" (Sassoon) **130**:185, 222
In Battle for Peace (Du Bois) **96**:148
"In Bed" (Koch) **44**:248
"In Bed One Night" (Coover) **32**:127
In Bed One Night and Other Brief Encounters (Coover) **32**:126-27
"In between the Sheets" (McEwan) **66**:281
In between the Sheets (McEwan) **13**:371; **66**:275, 279-80, 282, 294
"In Blackwater Woods" (Oliver) **34**:249; **98**:273
In Bluebeard's Castle: Some Notes toward the Redefinition of Culture (Steiner) **24**:431-33
In Broken Country (Wagoner) **15**:559-60
"In Broken Images" (Graves) **45**:174
"In Buddy's Eyes" (Sondheim) **147**:230
"In California" (Simpson) **149**:310, 312
In Camera (Sartre) **44**:495
In Celebration (Anderson) **20**:17
In Celebration (Storey) **2**:424-25; **4**:529-30; **5**:414-15
"In Celebration of My Uterus" (Sexton) **53**:316; **123**:408, 441
"In Challenge, Not Defence" (MacLeish) **68**:288
In Character (Mortimer) **43**:304-05
"In Childhood" (Blunden) **56**:31
"In Church" (Thomas) **48**:383
"In City Hall Square" (Farrell) **66**:130
"In Clown Clothes" (Phillips) **28**:363
In Cold Blood: A True Account of a Multiple Murder and Its Consequences (Capote) **3**:99-100; **8**:132-33; **13**:133, 135-39; **19**:82-5, 87; **34**:320, 322-25, 327; **38**:78, 80, 82-5, 87; **58**:85-136
In Cold Hell, in Thicket (Olson) **5**:328; **29**:334
"In Cold Storm Light" (Silko) **74**:347
"In connection with a certain event" (Rozewicz) **139**:272-73
In Constant Flight (Tallent) **45**:386-90
"In Corner B" (Mphahlele) **25**:340, 342
In Corner B (Mphahlele) **25**:339, 341
In Country (Mason) **43**:286-90; **82**:236-39, 244, 251, 254, 256-58, 260; **154**:
In Cuba (Cardenal) **31**:71-2
In Custody (Desai) **37**:71-2
"In Cytherea" (Hoffman) **6**:243
"In Danger from the Outer World" (Bly) **10**:57
In Darkest America (Oates) **108**:376
"In Darkness" (Durban) **39**:44, 47
"In Darkness" (Williams) **148**:361-62
In Darkness and Confusion (Petry) **18**:403
"In Deep Waters" (Arghezi)
See "Apa mare"
In Defence of a Friend (Leonov) **92**:277
In Defence of Fantasy: A Study of the Genre in English and American Literature since 1945 (Swinfen) **34**:576-77
In Defence of Sensuality (Powys) **125**:302
"In Defense of a Passionate and Incorruptible Heart" (Lytle) **22**:294
"In Defense of Ellis Hollow Creek" (Crase) **58**:164
In Defense of Ignorance (Shapiro) **4**:484, 487; **53**:328, 330
"In Defense of Metaphysics" (Tomlinson) **45**:400
"In Defense of Milton" (Leavis) **24**:296
"In Defense of Purple Prose" (West) **96**:393
In Defense of Reason (Winters) **4**:589-90; **8**:552; **32**:459-60, 470
In Defense of Sensuality (Powys) **46**:319
In Defense of the Earth (Rexroth) **1**:283; **6**:450; **22**:346; **49**:277, 283; **112**:370
"In Defense of the Word" (Galeano) **72**:130
In den Wohnungen des Todes (Sachs) **14**:476; **98**:321-22, 324-25, 327-28, 332, 344-45, 348, 352-54, 356, 365
"In der Finsternis" (Boell) **72**:69
"In Distrust of Merits" (Moore) **8**:400; **10**:352
"In Dream: The Privacy of Sequence" (Young Bear) **94**:362, 366
"In Dreams Begin Responsibilities" (Schwartz) **4**:479; **10**:462-63, 466; **45**:353-55, 359; **87**:334-36, 339-43, 346-47
In Dreams Begin Responsibilities, and Other Stories (Schwartz) **45**:355; **87**:333
In Dubious Battle (Steinbeck) **1**:325; **5**:405; **9**:512, 514-18, 520; **13**:529-34; **21**:366, 371, 373, 381-83, 389-91; **34**:405, 412, 414; **45**:370, 374, 376; **59**:317, 333, 335-37, 344, 347, 354; **75**:341, 343-44, 348-49, 352-55, 357, 360; **124**:386, 393-94, 407, 410
"In Due Form" (Riding) **7**:374
"In Due Season" (Auden) **43**:15
"In Durance" (Pound) **7**:337; **13**:456; **48**:288
"In Ego with Us All" (Ciardi) **40**:155-56
In einer dunklen Nacht ging ich aus meinen stillen Haus (Handke) **134**:179
In England's Green And (Williams) **13**:600-01
"In Entropy's Jaws" (Silverberg) **140**:363-65, 367-70
"In Eporphyrial Harness" (Avison) **97**:77, 82
"In Evening Air" (Roethke) **101**:309
"In Evening Air" (Roethke) **3**:433
"In Every World" (Lane) **25**:288
In Evil Hour (García Márquez)
See *La mala hora*
"In Exchange for Haiku" (Niedecker) **10**:360
"In Exile" (Boland) **113**:93
In Fact (Ciardi) **10**:105; **40**:161
In Famine's Shadow (Jones) **52**:245
In Favor of the Sensitive Man (Nin) **14**:385-86
"In Fear of Harvests" (Wright) **3**:540; **10**:545
"In Festubert" (Blunden) **56**:41
In Fires of No Return (Baxter) **14**:62
"In Florida" (Swenson) **61**:402, 404
"In Fog, Taeit, Outside Cherbourg" (Hollander) **5**:186
"In Football Season" (Updike) **23**:473
In Form: Digressions on the Act of Fiction (Sukenick) **48**:368-69
"In France" (Dabrowska)
See "We Francji"
"In Gallarus Oratory" (Heaney) **5**:171; **7**:148; **91**:121

"In Genesis" (Lowell) **11**:329
"In Green Solariums" (Livesay) **79**:342, 352
"In Greenwich There Are Many Gravelled Walks" (Calisher) **8**:125; **38**:67; **134**:11
"In Guinea" (Cabral de Melo Neto)
See "Na Guiné"
"In Hardwood Groves" (Frost) **26**:118
"In Hefnerland" (Amis) **62**:5
In Her Day (Brown) **18**:73, 75; **79**:153, 155-56, 158-59, 169
"In Her Own Image" (Boland) **40**:99; **67**:44; **113**:58-60, 62
In Her Own Image (Boland) **40**:97-8, 100; **67**:41, 43-6; **113**:57-8, 60, 63, 74, 80-1, 87-8, 94, 96-7, 108-09, 117, 122-23
"In High Waters" (Graham) **48**:147
In His Country (Willard) **37**:462
In His Own Country (Callaghan) **41**:89
"In His Own Image" (Boland) **40**:100; **67**:44; **113**:58-60, 123
In His Own Write (Lennon) **12**:354-55; **35**:267
"In His Sixty-Fifth Year" (Fuller) **28**:157
"In Honor of David Anderson Brooks, My Father" (Brooks) **125**:53
"In Honour of Chris. Brennan" (McAuley) **45**:246
"In Horse Latitudes" (Pollitt) **122**:203
"In Hot Pursuit of Happiness" (Lem) **149**:289
"In Illo Tempore" (Heaney) **74**:169
"In India" (Ezekiel) **61**:102-03, 105
"In Isfahan" (Trevor) **7**:478; **71**:340; **116**:333, 374
"In It" (Johnston) **51**:239, 244, 249, 251
In Iwa's Country (Le Clézio) **31**:249
"In Jack-O'-Lantern's Weather" (Williams) **45**:443
"In January" (Clarke) **61**:83
In Joy Still Felt: The Autobiography of Isaac Asimov, 1954-1978 (Asimov) **19**:29; **26**:52
"In Just Spring" (Cummings) **12**:159
"In Khandesh" (Rao) **56**:291-92
"In Kildare Street" (Clarke) **9**:168
"In Lieu of the Lyre" (Moore) **13**:396
In Light of India (Paz)
See *Vislumbres de la India*
"In Lilliput" (O'Faolain) **70**:314
"In Limbo" (Wilbur) **9**:570; **53**:412; **110**:357
"In Llandough Hospital" (Abse) **29**:18
In London (Creeley) **36**:118; **78**:140, 159
"In Love" (Prince) **35**:323
In Love and Anger (Acorn) **15**:10
In Love and Trouble: Stories of Black Women (Walker) **5**:476-77; **6**:553-54; **27**:449; **46**:428; **103**:356-57, 363, 366, 372, 396, 398-99, 402, 406-13, 422
"In Love Made Visible" (Swenson) **106**:337, 347-48
"In Love with Ariadne" (Trevor) **71**:341, 348-49; **116**:363-64
"In Love's Place" (Padilla) **38**:351
"In Loving Memory of the Late Author of Dream Songs" (Meredith) **55**:193
"In Lower Town" (Levine) **54**:297, 300-01
"In Luss Churchyard" (Smith) **64**:388, 397
In Mad Love and War (Harjo) **83**:272, 274-77, 280-86
"In March" (Stevenson) **33**:380
În marea trecere (Blaga) **75**:62, 67, 69-70, 77
"In May, 1916: Near Richebourg St. Vaast" (Blunden) **56**:44
"In Me Two Worlds" (Day Lewis) **10**:128
"In Memoriam" (Arreola) **147**:16, 34
"In Memoriam" (Longley) **29**:292
"In Memoriam" (Schnackenberg) **40**:379
"In Memoriam" (Senghor) **54**:407; **130**:258, 266, 278, 280, 282
In Memoriam (Jennings) **131**:241
In Memoriam (Reznikoff) **9**:450
"In Memoriam: D.K." (Rich) **125**:325
"In Memoriam Francis Ledwidge" (Heaney) **25**:247
In Memoriam James Joyce (MacDiarmid) **4**:309, 312; **11**:333, 337-38; **19**:289-90; **63**:242, 250, 255
"In Memoriam Mae Noblitt" (Ammons) **108**:56
"In Memoriam Miss B." (Stevenson) **33**:379
"In Memoriam: Robert Fitzgerald" (Heaney) **74**:174
"In Memoriam Stratton Christensen" (Meredith) **13**:374
In Memoriam to Identity (Acker) **111**:34-6
"In Memoriam: Wallace Stevens" (Duncan) **41**:129
"In Memory" (Kinsella) **138**:137
"In Memory: After a Friend's Sudden Death" (Levertov) **66**:250
"In Memory of an Aristocrat" (Williams) **45**:453
"In Memory of Anton Webern" (Mueller) **51**:279
"In Memory of Anyone Unknown to Me" (Jennings) **131**:240
"In Memory of Arthur Winslow" (Lowell) **1**:182; **4**:297; **8**:358; **124**:285-86
"In Memory of Boris Pasternak" (Levertov) **15**:336
In Memory of David Archer (Barker) **8**:45; **48**:21, 24
"In Memory of Elena" (Forché)
See "The Memory of Elena"
"In Memory of Francis Webb" (Shapcott) **38**:402
"In Memory of H. F." (Klappert) **57**:256-57, 259-60
"In Memory of Leopardi" (Wright) **3**:543
"In Memory of Major Robert Gregory" (Kinsella) **138**:95
"In Memory of My Cat Domino" (Fuller) **28**:151
"In Memory of My Country" (Crase) **58**:163
"In Memory of My Feelings" (O'Hara) **78**:339, 350-51, 355-60, 365-66
In Memory of My Feelings (O'Hara) **2**:323; **13**:427, 430
"In Memory of Robert Macbryde" (Barker) **48**:19
"In Memory of Segun Awolowo" (Soyinka) **44**:277
"In Memory of Sigmund Freud" (Auden) **14**:31; **43**:27
"In Memory of the Horse David, Who Ate One of My Poems" (Wright) **3**:543; **5**:520
"In Memory of the Master Poet Robert Browning" (Nemerov) **36**:309
"In Memory of W. B. Yeats" (Auden) **43**:16, 27-8; **123**:12, 22, 25
"In Memory of W. H. Auden" (Matthews) **40**:320-21
"In Memory of W. H. Auden" (Stern) **100**:328
In Memory Yet Green (Asimov) **19**:27-9; **26**:51-2; **76**:312; **92**:5
"In Midas' Country" (Plath) **111**:200
"In Milan" (Milosz) **56**:248
"In Mind" (Levertov) **66**:238
"In Modern Dress" (Raine) **103**:186
"In Montgomery" (Brooks) **49**:28
"In My Country" (Castillo) **151**:20
"In My Day We Used to Call It Pussy-Whipped" (Bukowski) **82**:14
"In My Dream I Always Hear a Step on the Stairs" (Moravia) **46**:286-87
In My Father's Court (Singer)
See *Mayn Tatn's bes-din shtub*
"In My Father's House" (Baldwin) **127**:143
In My Father's House (Baldwin) **127**:109
In My Father's House (Gaines) **11**:217-18; **86**:173
"In My Father's House There Are a Few Mansions, More Hovels, and Probably Even More Ranch Houses" (Ciardi) **40**:161
"In My Life" (Dubus) **97**:195, 204-05, 208
"In My Mind" (MacCaig) **36**:284
"In My Room" (Wilson) **12**:644, 649, 651
"In My Time" (Blunden) **56**:44
"In My Time, In My Place" (Amichai) **57**:36
"In My Time of Dying" (Page and Plant) **12**:477, 479
"In Mysie's Bed" (MacDiarmid) **4**:310; **11**:334
"In Nature" (Haines) **58**:216
"In Nature There Is Neither Right Nor Left Nor Wrong" (Jarrell) **9**:298
In New England Winter (Bullins) **5**:83
"In Nine Sleep Valley" (Merrill) **34**:233
In Nueva York (Mohr) **12**:447
"In Ohnmacht gefallen" (Grass) **32**:199
In, on, or about the Premises: Being a Small Book of Poems (Blackburn) **43**:62
In Orbit (Morris) **1**:233; **3**:343; **7**:246; **37**:310-13
In Other Words (Katz)
See *Creamy and Delicious: Eat My Words*
In Other Words (Swenson) **61**:402-04; **106**:323, 333, 336, 340, 342-43, 346
"In Otto's Basement" (Simpson) **149**:316
In Our Lifetime (Gaye) **26**:134
In Our Terribleness (Some Elements and Meaning in Black Style) (Baraka) **2**:35; **5**:48; **33**:56
In Our Time (Hemingway) **1**:142; **3**:241-43; **6**:226, 233-34; **8**:285, 288-89, 292; **10**:263; **13**:273; **19**:210; **30**:178, 180-82, 184-86, 188-92, 195, 198-201; **34**:478; **39**:398, 401; **41**:197; **61**:191-92, 214; **80**:148, 150
In Our Time (Montale)
See *Nel nostro tempo*
"In Pain" (Simon) **26**:413
In Parenthesis (Jones) **2**:216-19; **4**:259-62; **7**:186-89, 191; **13**:307-12; **42**:238-43, 246-48
"In parte ove non e che" (Chappell) **40**:145
In Patagonia (Chatwin) **28**:70-5; **57**:141-43, 147-48, 150; **59**:274-78
In Peace as in War (Cabrera Infante)
See *Así en la paz como en la guerra*
In Place (Hollander) **14**:265
In Plain Russian (Voinovich)
See *Putëm vzaimnoj perepiski*
"In Plaster" (Plath) **17**:353; **51**:346; **111**:166, 180-81, 211
"In Plaster, with a Bronze Wash" (Meredith)
See "Thoughts on One's Head"
"In Praise of Ancestors" (Kunene) **85**:176-77
"In Praise of Cities" (Gunn) **32**:208
In Praise of Darkness (Borges)
See *Elogio de la sombra*
"In Praise of Diversity" (McGinley) **14**:367
"In Praise of Feeling Bad about Yourself" (Szymborska) **99**:205
"In Praise of Grief" (Bly) **15**:68
"In Praise of Limestone" (Auden) **3**:26; **6**:16, 20, 24; **9**:57; **14**:29; **123**:12, 16, 17, 19
In Praise of Love (Rattigan) **7**:355
"In Praise of Marriages" (Wright) **53**:428
"In Praise of Ms Navratilova" (Brophy) **105**:21
In Praise of Older Women: The Amorous Recollections of András Vajda (Vizinczey) **40**:432-34, 436-39
"In Praise of Shadows" (Tanizaki) **14**:526; **28**:416, 420
In Praise of Sleep (Blaga)
See *Lauda somnului*
In Praise of the Dangerous Life (Cendrars) **106**:191
"In Praise of the Earth" (Kunene) **85**:165
In Praise of the Stepmother (Vargas Llosa)
See "Elogio de la madrastra"
"In Praise of the Sword" (Wittlin) **25**:469
"In Praise of Unwashed Feet" (Willard) **7**:539
"In Praise of Vespasian" (Chester) **49**:54-6
"In Praise of Women's Bodies" (Steinem) **63**:383
"In Preparation" (Macdonald) **13**:356
"In Prison" (Bishop) **32**:40, 44
In Protochny Lane (Ehrenburg) **18**:131; **62**:175, 178-79

In Public, In Private (Denby) **48**:81, 83
"In Pursuit of the Angel" (Lieberman) **36**:261
In Pursuit of the English (Lessing) **22**:277-78
"In Quebec City" (Levine) **54**:296
In quel preciso momento (Buzzati) **36**:88, 96
In Radical Pursuit: Critical Essays and Lectures (Snodgrass) **10**:477-78
"In Railroad Yards" (Lane) **25**:288
In Re: Sherlock Holmes (Derleth) **31**:137
"In Re Solomon Warshawer" (Klein) **19**:261
"In Response to a Question" (Stafford) **29**:380
"In Retrospect" (Ezekiel) **61**:93, 103
"In Ruth's Country" (Bass) **79**:5
"In Salem" (Clifton) **19**:110
"In Santa Maria del Popolo" (Gunn) **18**:203; **81**:177
In Search (Levin) **7**:204-06
In Search of a Character (Greene) **9**:250
In Search of a Genre (Aksyonov) **101**:22
"In Search of a Language" (Boland) **113**:125
"In Search of a Majority" (Baldwin) **13**:53
In Search of Ancient Gods (von Daniken) **30**:425-26
In Search of Bisco (Caldwell) **50**:300
In Search of Columbus (Davies) **70**:339
In Search of Columbus: The Sources of the First Voyage (Henige) **70**:351, 353, 355
In Search of J. D. Salinger (Hamilton) **55**:334-37, 341
In Search of Love and Beauty (Jhabvala) **29**:261-63; **94**:171-72, 174, 183, 185-87, 194-96, 203-5; **138**:64, 72, 78
In Search of Melancholy Baby (Aksyonov) **101**:36-7, 39, 41-2, 52
"In Search of Our Mother's Gardens" (Walker) **103**:357
In Search of Our Mother's Gardens: Womanist Prose (Walker) **46**:428; **58**:408-09, 415; **103**:364, 367-70, 396-97, 400, 402, 414, 418
In Search of Owen Roblin (Purdy) **14**:432
In Search of Theatre (Bentley) **24**:47, 50
"In Season" (Davison) **28**:100
In Sepia (Anderson) **9**:31
In Sicily (Vittorini)
See *Conversazione in Sicilia*
"In Sickness and Health" (Humphrey) **45**:193
"In Sickness and in Health" (Auden) **2**:23; **123**:37
"In Sickness and in Health" (Gellhorn) **14**:195; **60**:184-85
"In Small Townlands" (Heaney) **14**:243
"In Snow, a Possible Life" (Smith) **42**:348
"In So Many Words" (Abish) **22**:19
"In So Sustained a Remarkable Amount of Motion" (Everson) **27**:134
"In Society" (Ginsberg) **36**:182
In soffitta (Buzzati) **36**:84
"In Some Doubt but Willingly" (Ciardi) **44**:382
In sonno e in veglia (Ortese) **89**:194-95, 197
In Spite Of (Powys) **125**:290, 293
"In Spring" (Squires) **51**:383
In Stahlgewittern (Jünger) **125**:220-21, 226, 248-52, 261
In Such a Night (Deutsch) **18**:118
In Suspect Terrain (McPhee) **36**:299
"In Sydney by the Bridge" (Cassity) **42**:98
"In Sylvia Plath Country" (Jong) **6**:267
"In Sympathy with Another Motherless Child (One View of the Profession of Writing)" (Giovanni) **117**:189
"In Terms of the Toenail" (Gass) **132**:165
"In Terror of Hospital Bills" (Wright) **5**:520
In That Dawn (Paustovsky)
See *The Beginning of an Unknown Century*
"In That Month of May" (Akhmadulina)
See "V tot mesiats Mai"
In That Time (Lagerkvist)
See *I den tiden*
In the Absence of Angels (Calisher) **38**:67-8; **134**:4-5, 10, 20, 40
"In the Absence of Horses" (Hearne) **56**:127
In the Absence of Horses (Hearne) **56**:126-27
"In the Alien Corn" (McNickle) **89**:184
"In the Alley" (Elkin) **51**:98
"In the American Grain" (Boyle) **121**:58
"In the American Grain" (Lowell) **124**:253
In the American Grain (Williams) **2**:467-68; **5**:508; **13**:602, 605; **22**:466; **42**:449, 451-53, 455; **67**:416, 427
"In the Aran Islands" (Mahon) **27**:287
"In the Attic" (Justice) **19**:233-34; **102**:256
"In the Attic" (Motion) **47**:286
"In the Back of My Car" (Zappa)
See "Cheap Thrills"
"In the Baggage Room at Greyhound" (Ginsberg) **36**:188
"In the Bahamas" (Hass) **99**:141
In the Bar of a Tokyo Hotel (Williams) **2**:465; **8**:549; **11**:571; **19**:472; **45**:449-52
"In the Basement" (Dybek) **114**:66
"In the Beach House" (Sexton) **10**:468
In the Beauty of the Lilies (Updike) **139**:369, 371-72, 375
"In the Beauty of the Lillies" (Auchincloss) **9**:54
"In the Beech" (Heaney) **74**:169
"In the Beginning" (Jennings) **131**:243
"In the Beginning" (Lamming) **66**:227
"in the beginning" (Rozewicz)
See "na początku"
"In the Beginning" (Sanchez) **116**:299, 300
"In the Beginning" (Simic) **130**:334, 336-37
In the Beginning (Potok) **7**:321-22; **26**:372-73; **112**:284
In the Beginning, Love: Dialogues on the Bible (Van Doren) **6**:541
"In the Beginning of the War" (Smith) **25**:421
"In the Beginning There Was Eva" (Castillo) **151**:110
In the Beginning Was Love: Psychoanalysis and Faith (Kristeva)
See *Au commencement était l'amour: Psychanalyse et foi*
"In the Beginning Was the Word: Logos or Mythos" (Fiedler) **4**:163; **13**:211
"In the Black Mill" (Chabon) **149**:22-3, 25
"In the Bleak Mid-Winter" (Thomas) **37**:419, 422; **107**:327
"In the Blue" (Kureishi) **135**:283
"In the Bodies of Words" (Swenson) **61**:402
In the Boom Boom Room (Rabe) **4**:425-27; **8**:450
"In the Bosom of the Country" (O'Faolain) **14**:405
"In the Briar Patch" (Garrett) **51**:144, 152
In the Briar Patch (Garrett) **51**:143-45
In the Burning Darkness (Buero Vallejo)
See *En la ardiente oscuridad*
In the Bus Shelter (Mahfouz)
See *Taht al-mizalla*
"In the Café" (Kadare)
See "Në kafe"
In the Cage (Abse) **29**:21
In the Castle of My Skin (Lamming) **2**:235; **4**:280; **66**:217, 219-21, 223-24, 227-30; **144**:126, 132, 136-37, 140, 142-44, 155-61, 163-66, 169-72, 174, 184, 187, 193-94, 196-97, 199-205
"In the Cell" (Olds) **85**:292, 298
"In the Cemetery Where Al Jolson Is Buried" (Hempel) **39**:68-70
"In the Children's Wing" (Johnson) **58**:291, 293
"In the City" (Weller) **26**:442-43, 448
In the City (Weller) **26**:442-43, 445
In the City of Fear (Just) **27**:229-30
"In the City of Red Dust" (Okri) **87**:319, 321
"In the Clear" (Transtroemer) **65**:223
"In the Clearing" (Butler) **81**:124
In the Clearing (Frost) **4**:176; **9**:220, 223; **13**:230
In the Cold Country (Howes) **15**:288-89
"In the Cold Kingdom" (Van Duyn) **116**:401
"In the Compartment" (Voinovich) **10**:505
"In the Corridor" (Fuller) **62**:196-97
In the Country of Last Things (Auster) **47**:16; **131**:5, 7, 24, 28-9
"In the Country of Modern Art" (Asturias) **8**:25
In the Country of Ourselves (Hentoff) **26**:183-84
"In the Country of the Black Pig" (Hope) **52**:209
In the Country of the Black Pig (Hope) **52**:208-09
In the Country of the Skin (Redgrove) **6**:445; **41**:349, 352, 355-56
In the Court of Yearning (Blaga)
See *La curţile dorului*
"In the Courtyard" (Montale) **9**:388
"In the Courtyard of the Isleta Mission" (Bly) **38**:59
In the Courtyard of Yearning (Blaga)
See *La curţile dorului*
"In the Crevice of Time" (Jacobsen) **48**:198
In the Crevice of Time (Jacobsen) **102**:242
"In the Crowd" (Weller) **26**:444
"In the Crypt at Bourges" (Grigson) **7**:136
"In the Dark" (Raine) **32**:352 ; **103**:184-85, 193
"In the Dark" (Smith) **64**:399
"In the Darkness" (Ding Ling)
See "Zai heianzhong"
"In the Darkness of Cities" (Purdy) **50**:246
"In the Days of Prismatic Color" (Moore) **47**:260, 262-63
In the Days of Simon Stern (Cohen) **7**:50-1; **31**:93
In the Dead of the Night (Dubie) **36**:129-30, 140
"In the Deep Museum" (Sexton) **53**:316
In the Deepest Part of Sleep (Fuller) **25**:180
"In the Department" (Sargeson) **31**:365
"In the Desert" (Coupland) **85**:35, 37, 41; **133**:8
"In the Desert War" (Simmons) **43**:407
In the Ditch (Emecheta) **14**:160; **48**:97-8, 101; **128**:54-6, 61, 68, 74, 76, 83
"In the Dream of My Grandmother's Tree" (Coles) **46**:113
"In the Dreaming" (Dickey) **28**:119
"In the Dry" (Pancake) **29**:346-48
In the Dwellings of Death (Sachs)
See *In den Wohnungen des Todes*
"In the Early Cretaceous" (Purdy) **50**:247
In the Early Morning Rain (Berrigan) **37**:44
"In the Egg" (Grass)
See "Im Ei"
"In the Egyptian Museum" (Lewis) **41**:254, 262
"In the Elegy Season" (Wilbur) **6**:570
"In the Evening" (Rich) **7**:365
"In the Eye of the Storm" (Spinrad) **46**:384
"In the Eyes of God" (Cheever) **15**:127
"In the Fair Field" (Thomas) **132**:382
"In the Fall" (MacLeod) **56**:193, 200
In the Fertile Land (Josipovici) **153**:208, 219, 221
In the Fictive Wish (Everson) **5**:122
"In the Field" (O'Brien) **103**:174
"In the Fifties" (Michaels) **6**:325
"In the Finland Woods" (Nowlan) **15**:398
"In the Flesh" (Barker) **52**:52, 55
In the Flesh (Barker) **52**:55-6
In the Flesh (Bowering) **15**:83; **47**:22
In the Flesh (Wolitzer) **17**:563-64
In the Fog of the Season's End (La Guma) **19**:272-76
"In the Foothills" (Purdy) **14**:432
In the Footsteps of the Prophet (Blaga)
See *Paşii profetului*
"In the Fourth Year of the War" (Ellison) **139**:132
In the Frame (Francis) **42**:150, 156-57; **102**:127, 131, 139
In the Freest State in the World (Traven) **11**:535
In the Future Perfect (Abish) **22**:17-18
"In the Gallery" (Abse) **29**:20
"In the Gallery" (Squires) **51**:382
"In the Garden" (Dylan) **77**:185-86, 190

"In the Garden" (Paley) **37**:333
"In the Garden of the North American Martyrs" (Wolff) **64**:448, 455
In the Garden of the North American Martyrs (Wolff) **64**:446-49, 450-51, 456-57
"In the Garret" (Van Vechten) **33**:385
"In the Giving Vein" (Porter) **5**:347; **33**:322
In the Great Passage (Blaga)
See *În marea trecere*
In the Great Passing (Blaga)
See *În marea trecere*
"In The Great War (II)" (Weldon) **122**:282
"In the Greyness of Isolated Time" (Brutus) **43**:92
"In the Groove" (Thomas) **107**:337-40
In the Habitation of Death (Sachs)
See *In den Wohnungen des Todes*
"In the Hands of the Senecas" (Edmonds) **35**:153, 155-56
"In the Heart of the Beast" (Williams) **33**:443-44; **148**:314, 319, 343
In the Heart of the Country (Coetzee) **23**:121-23, 125; **33**:106, 111; **117**:33, 44, 47-8, 65, 67-9, 72-3, 81, 83-4
"In the Heart of the Heart of the Country" (Gass) **8**:244-45; **15**:257-58; **132**:154, 164-65, 169-70, 172, 174, 181, 183, 192
In the Heart of the Heart of the Country, and Other Stories (Gass) **2**:154-55; **8**:244, 246-47; **11**:224-25; **39**:478, 482; **132**:142, 1490-53, 161, 190, 194
In the Heart of the Seas (Agnon)
See *Bilvav yamim*
In the Heart of the Valley of Love (Kadohata) **122**:193-94, 196-98
In the Heart or Our City (Rudnik) **7**:384
"In the Heat of the Summer" (Ochs) **17**:331
"In the Highlands" (Gellhorn) **60**:189, 192
"In the Hill at New Grange" (Jeffers) **54**:246
"In the Hills South of Capernaum, Port" (Olson) **29**:330
"In the Hills, the Cities" (Barker) **52**:53
"In the Hole" (Ciardi) **44**:383; **129**:47
In the Hollow of His Hand (Purdy) **52**:348-50
"In the Hospital" (Ding Ling) **68**:65
"In the Hospital" (Jensen) **37**:187-88
"In the Hospital for Tests" (Van Duyn) **63**:437
"In the Hotel" (Graham) **118**:223
"In the Hotel of Lost Light" (Kinnell) **13**:322; **129**:244
In the Hours Waiting for the Blood to Come (MacBeth) **9**:340
In the House of the Judge (Smith) **42**:349, 351, 353, 357
In the Houses of Death (Sachs)
See *In den Wohnungen des Todes*
"In the Icebound Hothouse" (Goyen) **40**:217
In the Illusion of the Threshhold (Bonnefoy)
See *Dans le leurre du seuil*
"in the inner city" (Clifton) **66**:68
"In the Islands" (Didion) **129**:76-78, 80, 82
"In the Jungle" (Dillard) **60**:74
"In the Kalahari Desert" (Raine) **32**:350; **103**:185, 188
"In the Kingdom of the Golden Dust" (Bissoondath) **120**:3, 5, 7
"In the King's Rooms" (Steele) **45**:365
In the Labyrinth (Robbe-Grillet)
See *Dans le labyrinthe*
In the Lake of the Woods (O'Brien) **103**:163-68, 176
"In the Land of Dreamy Dreams" (Gilchrist) **48**:114, 116; **143**:319, 322
In the Land of Dreamy Dreams (Gilchrist) **34**:165-66; **48**:114-18, 120; **143**:273, 276, 282, 294, 297-98, 309-10, 314-15, 319-32
In the Land of Israel (Oz) **54**:348-49, 351; **33**:300-04
In the Land of Morning (Petrakis) **3**:383
"In the Land of the Great Aunts" (Cassity) **42**:97
"In the Land of the Rujuks" (Boell)
See "Im Lande der Rujuks"
In the Last Analysis (Heilbrun) **25**:255
"In the Light" (Page and Plant) **12**:477, 479, 481
"In the Loyal Mountains" (Bass) **143**:10-11
In the Loyal Mountains (Bass) **143**:9-13, 17, 20-1
In the Lure of the Threshold (Bonnefoy)
See *Dans le leurre du seuil*
"In the Margin" (Blunden) **56**:40
"In the Matter of Miracles" (Feinstein) **36**:168
In the Meantime (Smart) **54**:425
"In the Meantime Darling" (Ashbery) **125**:31
"In the Mecca" (Brooks) **49**:28; **125**:69-70, 72, 94-9
In the Mecca (Brooks) **2**:82; **4**:78; **5**:75-6; **15**:92-3; **49**:22, 27-31, 34-7; **125**:45, 47-8, 50, 53-4, 61, 68, 70, 72-4, 85-6, 88, 94, 97, 103
"In the Memory of Andrée Rexroth" (Rexroth) **49**:279; **112**:375
"In the Men's Room" (Piercy) **27**:373
"In the Middle" (Smith) **64**:392, 400
In the Middle (Smith) **64**:394
In the Middle Distance (Delbanco) **6**:130
In the Middle Earth (Alexander) **121**:3
In the Middle of a Life (Wright) **6**:581-82
"In the Middle of America" (Haines) **58**:222
In the Middle of Nowhere (Howe) **47**:176-77
"In the Middle of the Fields" (Lavin) **99**:322
In the Middle of the Fields (Lavin) **4**:281; **18**:306-07; **99**:312, 322
"In the Middle of the Night" (Pearce) **21**:289
In the Middle of the Wood (Smith) **64**:401
"In the Middle of This Century" (Amichai) **116**:138
"In the Midst of Life" (Rozewicz) **9**:463, 465; **23**:363; **139**:226, 272, 288-89
"In the Midst of Life" (Sargeson) **31**:370, 373
In the Midst of My Fever (Layton) **15**:318
"In the Miro District" (Taylor) **18**:527-29; **37**:409; **50**:253; **71**:304, 306-07
In the Miro District, and Other Stories (Taylor) **18**:527-28
"In the Missouri Ozarks" (Van Duyn) **63**:442
"In the Mist" (MacCaig) **36**:285
"In the Mood" (Dowell) **60**:107
In the Mood (Waterhouse) **47**:422
"In the Morning" (Koch) **44**:246, 249
"In the Mortuary" (Raine) **32**:350, 352-53; **103**:200
"In the Mountains" (Blaga) **75**:77
"In the Mountains" (Strand) **18**:516
"In the Mountains" (Warren) **10**:521
"In the Mountains of Jerusalem" (Amichai) **116**:97
"In the Movies" (O'Hara) **78**:354
"In the Naked Bed, in Plato's Cave" (Schwartz) **10**:462; **45**:356; **87**:341, 347
In the Native State (Stoppard) **91**:192
"In the New Sun" (Levine) **14**:320
"In the Night" (Himes) **7**:159
"In the Night" (Kincaid) **43**:247-48; **137**:138, 163, 172
In the Night Café (Johnson) **58**:291-93
"In the Night the Night Sound Woke Us" (Rukeyser) **27**:411
"In the Nile Delta" (Transtroemer) **65**:226, 233
In the Ocean of Night (Benford) **52**:59-61, 63-5, 70-2, 76-7
"In the Old People's Home, 1914" (Ewart) **46**:148, 153
"In the Old Sun" (Hesse) **17**:218
"In the One Day" (Hall) **151**:182
In the Outer Dark: Poems (Plumly) **33**:310-13
In the Palace of the Movie King (Calisher) **134**:37-8, 41
In the Penal Colony (Berkoff) **56**:14
"In the Penile Colony" (Jong) **8**:314
"In the Penny Arcade" (Millhauser) **54**:325-26
In the Penny Arcade (Millhauser) **109**:157-58, 169-70, 174
"In the Pink" (Sassoon) **130**:178, 181, 217
In the Pink (Blackwood) **100**:16, 18
"In the Pond" (Johnston) **51**:239, 251
In the Presence of the Sun: Stories and Poems, 1961-1991 (Momaday) **85**:279-81
"In the Privacy of the Home" (Strand) **18**:516
"In the Protestant Cemetery, Rome" (Watkins) **43**:452
"In the Public Garden" (Moore) **47**:263
"In the Public Gardens" (Betjeman) **43**:41
"In the Reading Room of the British Museum" (Faludy) **42**:137
"In the Realm of the Herons" (Kaplan) **50**:55-7
In the Realm of the Senses (Oshima)
See *L'empire de sens*
"In the Red Light: A History of the Republican Convention in 1964" (Mailer) **111**:105-07
"In the Red Mountains" (Merwin) **45**:278
"In the Red Room" (Bowles) **53**:45
"In the Region of Ice" (Oates) **3**:360; **19**:348-49; **52**:338; **134**:247-48
"In the Reign of Peace" (Nissenson) **4**:381
In the Reign of Peace (Nissenson) **4**:380-81; **9**:399-400
"In the Ringwood" (Kinsella) **138**:87, 97-99
In the Room We Share (Simpson) **149**:353
"In the Ruins of New York City" (Merton) **83**:395
In the Scarlet Star (Williamson) **29**:454
In the Shade of the Old Apple Tree (Barker) **8**:44
"In the Shadow of War" (Okri) **87**:319
"In the Shetland Islands" (MacDiarmid) **4**:309; **11**:334
In the Skin of a Lion (Ondaatje) **51**:318-21; **76**:198, 202, 204, 206
In the Slammer With Carol Smith (Calisher) **134**:41
"In the Small Hotel" (Dunn) **6**:149
"In the Smoking Car" (Wilbur) **53**:405
In the Soop (Mull) **17**:300
In the Spirit of Crazy Horse (Matthiessen) **32**:292-95; **64**:315, 325
"In the Spring" (Fante) **60**:133
In the Stoneworks (Ciardi) **40**:158
"In the Stopping Train" (Davie) **8**:165-66; **31**:112, 118
In the Stopping Train, and Other Poems (Davie) **31**:111-12, 116-19
"In the Store" (Yevtushenko) **126**:413
"In the Street" (Tanizaki) **28**:414
"In the Street Today" (Weller) **26**:443
"In the Suburbs" (Simpson) **4**:498; **149**:323, 325, 360
"In the Suburbs" (Urdang) **47**:399
In the Summer House (Bowles) **68**:4-7, 9-15, 18, 21
"In the Tank" (Gunn) **32**:211
In the Terrified Radiance (Burnshaw) **3**:91
"In the Theatre: A True Incident" (Abse) **7**:2; **29**:18-19
"In the Thick of Darkness" (Salinas) **90**:332
"In the Thriving Season: In Memory of My Mother" (Mueller) **51**:279-80
"In the Time of the Blossoms" (Merwin) **45**:276-77
In the Time of the Butterflies (Alvarez) **93**:13-9
"In the Tradition" (Baraka) **33**:62
In the Tradition (Baraka) **115**:11, 18, 39
"In the Train" (O'Connor) **14**:398; **23**:326
"In the True Light of Morning" (Swan) **69**:361-64
"In the Tunnel" (Gallant) **38**:194
In the Twelfth Year of the War (Appleman) **51**:13
"In the Underworld" (Rukeyser) **27**:412
"In the Vacuum" (Williams) **42**:441
In the Valley of the Statues (Holdstock) **39**:152
"In the Village" (Bishop) **9**:90, 92; **13**:93; **32**:34, 40-1, 44
"In the Waiting Room" (Bishop) **9**:91, 97; **13**:89-90, 94; **15**:61; **32**:30-1, 33, 37, 39, 42-3

"In the Wake of Home" (Rich) **36**:378
"In the Wall" (Fisher) **25**:159
"In the Ward" (Lowell) **37**:238
"In the Ward: The Sacred Wood" (Jarrell) **13**:300
"In the Warehouse" (Oates) **134**:245
"In the Waxworks" (Shapiro) **53**:332
"In the Wee, Wee Hours" (Berry) **17**:51
"In the Wheatfield" (Blaga) **75**:69
"In the White Night" (Beattie) **63**:14, 16-17, 19; **146**:49, 52, 70, 72, 76, 85
"In the Wilderness" (Graves) **45**:169-70
"In the Wilderness" (Smith) **15**:515
"In the Wilderness" (Swan) **69**:363, 365
In the Wilderness, and Other Poems (Simmons) **43**:407, 411
"In the Wind My Rescue Is" (Ammons) **9**:28
In the Wine Time (Bullins) **1**:47; **5**:83
In the Winter of Cities (Williams) **45**:443
"In the Wood" (Pasternak) **63**:278
"In the Woods" (Rich) **3**:428; **11**:478; **125**:336
"In the Woods" (Robison) **98**:308, 317
In the World (Elliott) **2**:131
"In the X-Ray Room" (Moss) **50**:353
"In the Year of the Longest Cadillac" (Ciardi) **40**:155
"In the Zone" (Pynchon) **18**:440
"In the Zoo" (Stafford) **7**:459; **19**:431; **68**:422-23, 431-32
In Their Wisdom (Snow) **6**:517-18; **9**:498; **19**:427
"In This Age of Hard Trying, Nonchalance Is Good and ..." (Moore) **8**:400; **13**:397; **47**:261
"In This Country" (Brutus) **43**:89
"In This Country, But in Another Language, My Aunt Refuses to Marry the Men Everyone" (Paley) **140**:211
In This House of Brede (Godden) **53**:160-62
In This Our Life (Huston) **20**:158, 164
In This Quarter (Egoyan) **151**:124
In This Sign (Greenberg) **7**:135; **30**:162, 166
"In Thy Sleep/Little Sorrows Sit and Weep" (Rakosi) **47**:344
"In Time Like Air" (Sarton) **91**:253
In Time Like Air (Sarton) **4**:470
"In Time of Cloudburst" (Frost) **34**:475
"In Time of Plague" (Gunn) **81**:177, 181, 187-88
"In Time of the Hungarian Martyrdom" (Buckley) **57**:125
"In Time of War" (Auden) **123**:35, 48-9, 50-1
"In Time Which Made a Monkey of Us All" (Paley) **140**:267, 282
"In Times When My Head" (Simon) **26**:410-11, 413
"In Touch" (Fisher) **25**:160
In Tragic Life (Fisher) **7**:103
"In Transit" (Auden) **43**:27
In Transit: An Heroi-Cyclic Novel (Brophy) **6**:100; **29**:97; **105**:7, 10-11, 13-14, 22-30, 33
"In Trust" (Gilliatt) **53**:145
"In Tuscany" (Garrett) **3**:192
"In Two Degrees Cold" (Appleman) **51**:15
"In Umbria" (Moss) **45**:290
"In Verdi Square" (Tomlinson) **45**:403
"in viewpoint: poem for 14 catfish and the town of tama, iowa" (Young Bear) **94**:363, 366
"In Warsaw" (Milosz) **56**:248
In Watermelon Sugar (Brautigan) **1**:45; **3**:86-7, 90; **5**:67-8, 70-1; **9**:123; **12**:58-62, 66, 68, 70; **34**:314-15, 317-18; **42**:50, 57, 60, 62, 66
"In Weather" (Hass) **18**:209
"In West Flanders" (Blunden) **56**:44
"In Westminster Abbey" (Betjeman) **6**:68-9; **43**:33, 44
In What Hour (Rexroth) **1**:284; **22**:344-45; **49**:275, 277, 279-80, 284, 286; **112**:365, 374, 387, 390, 396-97, 400
"In What Manner the Body Is United with the Soule" (Graham) **118**:228, 239-40, 247
"In Which the Ancient History I Learn is Not My Own" (Boland) **113**:93
In Which We Serve (Coward) **29**:136, 140
"In White" (Frost) **10**:199
In White America (Duberman) **8**:185
"In Whose Garden I Am Sleeping / In Whose Garden I Am Sleeping Perfectly" (Moure) **88**:223
"In Willesden Churchyard" (Betjeman) **43**:45-6
"In Winter" (MacBeth) **5**:264
"In Winter" (Stevenson) **33**:379
In Winter (Ryan) **65**:211, 213
"In with the Doctor" (Kelman) **58**:298-99
In Words and the Poet (Thomas) **6**:530
"In Your Movements I See Drownings" (Lerman) **9**:329
"In Youth Is Pleasure" (Gallant) **38**:192
"In Zeno's World" (Nemerov) **36**:306
"The Inability" (Bronk) **10**:75
"Inaction" (Fuller) **28**:159
Inadmissible Evidence (Osborne) **1**:263; **2**:328; **5**:332-33; **11**:421-22; **45**:313-16, 319-21
The Inadvertent Epic (Fiedler) **24**:204-05
"Inaugural Lecture, Collège de France" (Barthes)
See *Leçon inaugurale faite le vendredi 7 janvier 1977*
"Inaugural Rose" (Jordan) **114**:146
"Inca" (Raine) **103**:186, 189
Incandescence (Nova) **31**:297-99
"Incantation" (Akhmadulina)
See "Zaklinanie"
"incantation" (Clifton) **66**:84
"Incantation" (Milosz) **56**:233, 251; **82**:303
"Incantation" (Swenson) **106**:351
The Incarnate (Campbell) **42**:90-1, 93
"Incarnation" (Rexroth) **49**:281; **112**:399
"The Incarnation of Sirius" (McAuley) **45**:248, 253
Incarnations of Immortality (Anthony) **35**:40
Incarnations: Poems, 1966-1968 (Warren) **4**:578; **6**:557-58; **8**:539; **10**:520; **13**:577; **18**:534, 536; **39**:265-66
"The Incendiary" (Scannell) **49**:326, 331
"L'incendio in via Keplero" (Gadda) **11**:209
"Incense to Idols" (Ashton-Warner) **19**:21
"The Inception of the Poem" (McAuley) **45**:248
"Incertus" (Heaney) **74**:193
"Incespicare" (Montale) **7**:225
"Incident" (Adcock) **41**:18
"Incident" (Fuller) **62**:206
"The Incident" (Smith) **64**:391
"Incident" (Stafford) **29**:387
Incident at Hawk's Hill (Eckert) **17**:107-08
"An Incident at Krechetovka Station" (Solzhenitsyn) **7**:435; **10**:479; **134**:284
"Incident at Twilight" (Dürrenmatt) **15**:195
Incident at Vichy (Miller) **1**:218; **2**:278-80; **6**:329-30; **10**:342-44; **15**:373-75; **47**:256
"Incident at Yalentay" (Castellanos) **66**:60
"An Incident at Yanagiyu" (Tanizaki) **28**:417
"Incident in a Saloon Bar" (Scannell) **49**:326
"Incident in Azania" (Waugh) **27**:477
"Incident in Hyde Park, 1803" (Blunden) **56**:33
"Incident in San Domingo" (Booth) **23**:75
"An Incident in the Early Life of Ebenezer Jones, Poet, 1928" (Betjeman) **43**:41
"An Incident in the 'Metropole': A True Story Resembling a Thriller" (Voinovich) **10**:507
"Incident on a Picnic" (Steele) **45**:362
"Incident on Fifty-Seventh Street" (Springsteen) **17**:477, 480, 488, 490
Incidental Music (Sagan) **36**:382-83
Incidents at the Shrine (Okri) **87**:314, 322, 325
Incidents in the Rue Laugier (Brookner) **136**:117-19
"Incipit" (Robbe-Grillet) **8**:454; **14**:462
Incitación al Nixonicidio y alabanza de la revolución Chilena (Neruda) **28**:314
The Incline (Mayne) **12**:399
"Including Myself" (Moure) **88**:219
Inclus (Guillevic) **33**:192, 194
"The Incognito Lounge" (Johnson) **52**:232-34
The Incognito Lounge, and Other Poems (Johnson) **52**:231-34
"The Incoherent Radio" (Ratushinskaya) **54**:385
The Incomparable Atuk (Richler) **5**:373, 376; **13**:481, 484, 486; **46**:347, 349; **70**:225, 230
"Incompatibilities" (Hughes) **9**:284
"The Incomprehensible Poets" (Yevtushenko) **126**:396
L'inconnu sur la terre (Le Clézio) **31**:250
The Increased Difficulty of Concentration (Havel) **25**:223, 225-26; **58**:240, 242; **123**:172, 181, 197-99, 204-05, 209
The Incredible Brazilian (Ghose)
See *The Native*
The Incredible Feeling Show (Swados) **12**:560
Incredible Floridas (Weir) **20**:424
The Incredible Planet (Campbell) **32**:74
"The Incredible Survival of Coyote" (Snyder) **120**:330
"Incunabula #3" (Daitch) **103**:78
"Ind Aff: Or Out of Love in Sarajevo" (Weldon) **122**:269-70
Indecent Dreams (Lustig) **56**:188-90
Indecent Exposure (Sharpe) **36**:399, 402
An Indecent Obsession (McCullough) **27**:321-22; **107**:135-36, 154
"Indecision" (Swados) **12**:557
"Indelible, Inedible" (Ashbery) **25**:54
Indemnity Only (Paretsky) **135**:308-09, 335-36, 343-44, 349, 356, 360, 363, 365
"Independence" (Bennett) **28**:27-8
Independence (Motion) **47**:287-94
"Independence Day" (Bukowski) **82**:14
"Independence Day" (Morrison) **21**:233
Independence Day (Ford) **99**:104, 107-15, 118-27
Independent People (Laxness)
See *Sjálfstaett fólk*
"The Independent Woman" (Govier) **51**:166-67
Les Indes (Glissant) **10**:231; **68**:171, 173, 179-80, 188
"A indesjada das gentes" (Cabral de Melo Neto) **76**:168
"Indeterminacy" (Cage) **41**:80
"India" (Mahapatra) **33**:277
"India" (Rodriguez) **155**:260, 296-97, 300
India: A Million Mutinies Now (Naipaul) **105**:174
India: A Wounded Civilization (Naipaul) **9**:393; **13**:407; **18**:363-64; **37**:321, 324, 328; **105**:155, 176
"India Again" (Forster) **77**:242
India Song (Duras) **100**:125, 127, 145, 148
India Song (Duras) **6**:150; **20**:100-04; **34**:162; **40**:178-80; **68**:77, 81, 89, 91, 95-6
"The Indian" (Updike) **139**:335
Indian (Ryga) **14**:472-73
The Indian Affair (Deloria) **21**:113
"Indian Boarding School: The Runaways" (Erdrich) **54**:165; **120**:134
"Indian Boy Love Song" (Alexie) **154**:27
"Indian Boy Love Songs" (Alexie) **154**:16, 27
"Indian Bread" (Kinnell) **5**:217; **13**:321
"Indian Camp" (Hemingway) **6**:231; **8**:289, 291; **10**:269; **13**:273; **19**:211; **30**:180, 186-87, 190, 192, 194, 196, 198-99; **50**:429; **80**:138
"Indian Country" (Alexie) **154**:47
"Indian Country" (Simpson) **7**:428-29; **149**:330
Indian Country (Matthiessen) **32**:295-97; **64**:315-16, 325
"Indian Dances" (Sarton) **49**:320
"Indian Education" (Alexie) **96**:7, 11; **154**:6, 26
Indian Foe, Indian Friend (Archer) **12**:17
"Indian Gift" (Hoffman) **141**:274, 280, 288
Indian Ink (Stoppard) **91**:192
Indian Journals, March 1962-May 1963 (Ginsberg) **2**:163; **3**:195; **6**:200; **36**:181, 186; **109**:351

Indian Killer (Alexie) **154**:16-20, 30-1, 37-9, 44, 47
Indian Man: A Life of Oliver La Farge (McNickle) **89**:181
"Indian Pipe" (Piercy) **27**:376
"The Indian Renaissance" (Waters) **88**:365
Indian Short Stories (Anand) **93**:42
"Indian Summer" (Barnes) **29**:27
"Indian Summer" (Hirsch) **50**:197
"Indian Summer" (Howes) **15**:290
"Indian Summer" (Moraga) **126**:297
"Indian Summer" (Pasternak) **63**:313
Indian Summer (Knowles) **1**:169; **4**:271-72; **26**:254-56, 258
"Indian Summer Poem" (Mahapatra) **33**:277, 282
Indian Tales and Others (Neihardt) **32**:331
the Indian Theatre (Anand) **93**:23
"The Indian Tribes of the United States: Ethnic and Cultural Survival" (McNickle) **89**:160-61
"The Indian Uprising" (Barthelme) **5**:53; **8**:50; **23**:44-5; **46**:36, 43; **115**:56-8, 65
The Indian Wants the Bronx (Horovitz) **56**:147-48, 150, 154
Indiana (Eshleman) **7**:97, 99
"Indianapolis/Summer/1969/Poem" (Sanchez) **116**:272, 278
"The Indians" (Wild) **14**:581
Indians (Coles) **108**:194
Indians (Kopit) **1**:170-71; **18**:290; **33**:247, 249-52
Indians and Other Americans: Two Ways of Life Meet (McNickle) **89**:168, 173, 175, 180-81
"Indians at the Guthrie" (Vizenor) **103**:281, 296
The Indians in the Woods, 1918-1928 (Lewis) **41**:252, 260-61
Indians of the Pacific Northwest (Deloria) **21**:114
"The Indians on Alcatraz" (Muldoon) **32**:315
Indicateur des chemins de coeur (Tzara) **47**:390
The Indifferent Children (Auchincloss) **45**:23-4
Gli indifferenti (Moravia) **2**:293; **7**:240-41, 244; **11**:382-83; **18**:343-49; **27**:354
"Indignities" (Gilchrist) **143**:319-20, 328
"The Indigo Engineers" (Vollmann) **89**:277
El indio (Lopez y Fuentes) **32**:278-80, 282-83
Indira Gandhi's Emergence and Style (Sahgal) **41**:372-73
"Indirect Method" (King) **53**:209, 212
Indirect Method, and Other Stories (King) **53**:209
Das indische Grabmal (Lang) **103**:86, 89
"Indischer Lebenslauf" (Hesse) **11**:272
Indiscretion (De Sica)
See *Stazione termini*
Indiscretions (Pound) **13**:461
"Indisposed" (Banks) **37**:24
The Individual and His Times (Fuller) **28**:157-59
"Individual and Mass Behavior in Extreme Situations" (Bettelheim) **79**:123, 125
"The Individualist" (Ritsos) **31**:324
"Individuals" (Simpson) **7**:428
"The Indivisible Incompatibles" (Swenson) **106**:348
"Indonesia" (Oliver) **98**:280, 290
"Indoor Games near Newbury" (Betjeman) **2**:60
"Indoor Perennials" (Hall) **51**:170
"Indosincrasia" (Ulibarrí) **83**:412
"Indulgences" (Godwin) **8**:248
"Industrija" (Bagryana) **10**:12
Inées Perée et Inat Tendu (Ducharme) **74**:61, 63-5
"The Ineffectual Marriage" (Loy) **28**:251
"The Ineluctabel Modality of the Vaginal" (Moody) **147**:190-91
Inessential Woman: Problems of Exclusion in Feminist Thought (Spelman) **65**:314
"The Inexhaustible Beginning" (Trifonov) **45**:411
"The Infallible Executors of Roman Law" (Haavikko) **34**:175
Infallible?--An Inquiry (Kung) **130**:131
Infamy (Borges)
See *Historia universal de la infamia*
"Infant" (Smith) **44**:442
Infante's Inferno (Cabrera Infante)
See *La Habana para un infante difunto*
"Infantiev" (Bitov) **57**:114-15
Les infants du sabat (Hébert) **13**:267-68; **29**:232, 238-41
Infants of the Spring: The Memoirs of Anthony Powell (Powell) **10**:417; **31**:313-16, 319-20, 322
"Infare" (Still) **49**:363
"The Infection" (King) **8**:321
The Infernal Desire Machines of Doctor Hoffman (Carter) **41**:114-15; **76**:323, 329
The Infernal Machine (Cocteau)
See *La machine infernale*
The Infernal World of Branwell Brontë (du Maurier) **59**:286
Inferno (Ciardi) **129**:28
"Inferno, I, 32" (Borges) **44**:354
The Inferno of Dante: A New Verse Translation (Pinsky) **121**:449
Inferno V (Arreola) **147**:33
Infidels (Dylan) **77**:179, 184
"El infierno tan temido" (Onetti) **10**:376
"Infiltration of the Universe" (MacLeish) **8**:362
L'infini turbulent (Michaux) **8**:392; **19**:312
The Infinite Atom (Campbell) **32**:74
The Infinite Conversation (Blanchot) **135**:91, 93-95, 109-10
Infinite Dreams (Haldeman) **61**:174-76, 178, 181
Infinite Jest (Wallace) **114**:366-68, 370, 372-76, 383-93, 395
"The Infinite Passion of Expectation" (Berriault) **109**:94
The Infinite Passion of Expectation (Berriault) **54**:4-5, 7; **109**:90, 92, 98
The Infinite Plan (Allende)
See *El plan infinito*
The Infinite Storm (Michaux)
See *L'infini turbulent*
"Infinitive" (Le Guin) **136**:395
"The Infinity Box" (Wilhelm) **7**:538
The Infinity Box (Wilhelm) **7**:538
An Infinity of Mirrors (Condon) **4**:107; **45**:93-6, 104; **100**:102, 111-12
"Infirmity" (Roethke) **3**:433; **46**:357
Inflation (Forman) **21**:121
"Influences" (Alexie) **96**:9; **154**:27
"Influences" (Carruth) **84**:127
The Influences (Watkins) **43**:455
"Influenza" (Adcock) **41**:18
"An Influx of Poets" (Stafford) **68**:443, 449
The Information (Amis) **101**:84-86, 88-99
"Information Density" (Ammons) **57**:53
El informe de Brodie (Borges) **2**:71-2, 77; **3**:81; **4**:75; **6**:88, 91; **10**:66-8; **13**:104; **44**:356-58, 364, 368; **48**:38, 40; **83**:182, 189
"Informe de Liberia" (Arreola) **147**:13, 34
"Informe sobre ciegos" (Sabato) **10**:444-46
The Informed Heart: Autonomy in a Mass Age (Bettelheim) **79**:110, 134-35
"Informer" (Randall) **135**:390
Informer (Ford) **16**:303, 315
The Informer (O'Flaherty) **5**:321; **34**:355-57
The Informers (Ellis) **117**:147-50
"The Ingoldsby Legends" (Wilson) **3**:540
Ingrid Babendererde: Reifeprüfung, 1953 (Johnson) **40**:270-71
The Inhabitant (Turco) **11**:550-51
"The Inhabitant of the Lake" (Campbell) **42**:92
The Inhabitant of the Lake and Less Welcome Tenants (Campbell) **42**:83, 89-91
The Inhabitants (Morris) **1**:232; **37**:313, 316
The Inhabited Island (Strugatskii and Strugatskii) **27**:434
Inhale and Exhale (Saroyan) **29**:363
"Inheritance" (Barnard) **48**:26
"Inheritance" (Ingalls) **42**:234
"Inheritance" (Louie) **70**:81
"Inheritance" (Merwin) **88**:213
"Inheritances" (Hacker) **72**:184
"Inheritor" (Wright)
See "Eroded Hills"
"The Inheritors" (Waters) **88**:333
The Inheritors (Golding) **1**:121-22; **2**:166, 168-69; **3**:197-98, 200; **8**:249; **10**:233-36, 239; **17**:158-62, 165-66, 171-72, 174, 177, 179; **27**:159-64, 167-68; **58**:185, 202; **81**:317-21, 323, 326
The Inheritors (Robbins) **5**:378
"The Inhuman Condition" (Barker) **52**:55
The Inhuman Condition (Barker) **52**:53-6
"The Inhumanist" (Jeffers) **54**:241; **3**:260; **11**:311
"Inicial" (Neruda) **28**:310-11
Inishfallen, Fare Thee Well (O'Casey) **88**:238-39, 262
"The Initiate" (Simic) **68**:375; **130**:314-15, 318
"Initiation" (McIlvanney) **42**:282
"Initiations" (Okigbo) **25**:349; **84**:299, 307-09, 313, 325, 327
"Initram" (Thomas) **13**:538, 540; **37**:416; **107**:319, 347
"Injun or Indian?" (Fiedler) **24**:198
Injury Time (Bainbridge) **10**:15-17; **14**:37; **62**:25, 30, 33, 36; **130**:9-10, 20
The Injustice Collectors (Auchincloss) **4**:31; **45**:24-5
"Ink Drawings" (Levertov) **28**:242
"The Ink Feather" (Swan) **69**:360-61
The Ink Truck (Kennedy) **6**:275; **28**:203-04; **53**:194, 197
The Inkling (Chappell) **40**:137-38, 140; **78**:97, 109
Inklings (Wolff) **41**:458-59
Inklings: Selected Stories (Jacobson) **14**:290
"Inland" (Motion) **47**:285-86, 289
"The Inlet" (Glück) **7**:119
"Inmarypraise" (Grass) **6**:209
The Inmates (Powys) **7**:349; **46**:321-22
"El inmortal" (Borges) **1**:39; **2**:69, 72, 76; **8**:98; **10**:66; **19**:47; **83**:156-57, 166
The Inmost Leaf (Kazin) **38**:272-74
Innansveitark-Skáldatími (Laxness) **25**:300
"Innard Life" (Macdonald) **13**:355
"Inner City" (D'Aguiar) **145**:117
"Inner City Blues" (Gaye) **26**:130, 132
The Inner Experience (Bataille)
See *L'expérience intérieure*
"The Inner Harbour" (Adcock) **41**:15-16
The Inner Harbour (Adcock) **41**:15-17
Inner Landscape (Sarton) **49**:308-09, 320; **91**:245, 254
The Inner Live of the Middle Class (Ehrenreich) **110**:180
"The Inner Part" (Simpson) **149**:310, 337
"The Inner Room" (Aickman) **57**:6
"Inner Voice" (Herbert) **9**:273
Inner Weather (Phillips) **28**:361, 363
The Inner Wheel (Roberts) **14**:463
The Inner World of the Outerworld of the Innerworld (Handke) **5**:165; **15**:266; **38**:219; **134**:159
Innervisions (Wonder) **12**:656-57
"Innings" (Williams) **148**:322
The Innkeeper's Song (Beagle) **104**:33-4
"Innocence" (Bates) **46**:52, 54
"Innocence" (Brodkey) **56**:58-60, 62, 65, 67
"Innocence" (Broumas) **10**:77; **73**:3, 16
"The Innocence" (Creeley) **8**:153
"Innocence" (Gunn) **18**:203; **32**:208
"Innocence" (Kavanagh) **22**:239
"Innocence" (Levine) **118**:305
Innocence (Fitzgerald) **51**:125-27; **61**:118-20, 122; **143**:
Innocence and Memory (Ungaretti) **7**:485
Innocence in Extremis (Hawkes) **49**:158-60

The Innocence of Age (Bissoondath) **120**:20-21, 26-27
The Innocent (McEwan) **66**:290-95
The Innocent (Visconti)
See *L'innocente*
"The Innocent and Infinite Windows of Childhood" (Schwartz) **45**:361
The Innocent and the Guilty (Warner) **7**:512
The Innocent Assassins (Eiseley) **7**:92
Innocent Blood (James) **18**:274-76; **46**:205-06; **122**:133-34, 136, 144, 146, 148-52, 155-56, 159, 169
Innocent Bystander (Sissman) **9**:492
An Innocent Millionaire (Vizinczey) **40**:436-39
The Innocent Party (Hawkes) **4**:213, 215; **7**:140
Innocent Sorcerers (Wajda) **16**:577-78
The Innocent Traveller (Wilson) **13**:607-09, 611
L'innocente (Visconti) **16**:573-74
The Innocents (Capote) **34**:322
Les innocents (Chabrol) **16**:182
The Innocents (Slaughter) **56**:412
"The Innocents Abroad" (Stafford) **4**:517
"Innoculated City" (Clash) **30**:52
L'innommable (Beckett) **2**:44-5; **3**:45; **4**:52; **6**:36-7, 42-3; **9**:78-9, 83-4, 87; **10**:28, 32; **11**:32-4, 37; **14**:71, 73, 76-7; **18**:41, 47, 50-1; **29**:53, 55-9, 61-2, 65-7; **59**:253, 257
"L'inoffensif" (Char) **14**:128
"Inquest" (Lem) **149**:276
"Inquest" (Snodgrass) **18**:491
The Inquest (Lem) **40**:295, 297
"L'inquilino" (Ortese)
See "Il signor Lin"
"The Inquisition" (Elytis) **49**:110
Inquisition (Arrabal) **58**:28-9
L'inquisitoire (Pinget) **7**:305-06; **37**:359-61, 363-64
The Inquisitory (Pinget)
See *L'inquisitoire*
"L'insaisissable Breyon!" (Theriault) **79**:407
"Insane Decisions" (Ashbery) **77**:66
"Inscribed in War-Books" (Blunden) **56**:30
"Inscription Facing Western Sea" (Merwin) **13**:386
"Inscription for the Tank" (Wright) **5**:520
"Inscriptions" (Rich) **125**:335
The Insect Colony (Larson) **31**:239
"The Insect World" (Rhys) **14**:447
"Insecurity" (Bissoondath) **120**:3-4, 18-19, 24
Ein Inselfrühling (Jünger) **125**:223
"Inselhin" (Celan) **19**:90
L'inserzione (Ginzburg) **54**:207; **70**:283
Inshallah (Fallaci) **110**:215-17
"Inside and Out" (Motion) **47**:293-94
"Inside Barbara Walters" (Grayson) **38**:211
Inside Big League Baseball (Kahn) **30**:230
"Inside from the Outside" (Jiles) **58**:280
Inside Mr. Enderby (Burgess) **4**:81, 84; **5**:88-9, 91; **8**:112; **10**:88; **22**:69; **40**:114, 122-23; **62**:130; **81**:301
"Inside Norman Mailer" (Apple) **9**:32; **33**:18, 21
The Inside of His Head (Miller)
See *Death of a Salesman*
"Inside Out" (Creeley) **78**:131
Inside, Outside (Wouk) **38**:452-53
"An Inside Outside Complex" (O'Faolain) **7**:274
"The Inside Rooms" (Giovanni) **4**:189
"Inside the Apple" (Amichai) **57**:47
Inside the Blood Factory (Wakoski) **4**:571; **7**:507; **9**:554
"Inside the Drop of Rain" (Plumly) **33**:311
Inside the Easter Egg (Engel) **36**:160-62
"Inside the Onion" (Nemerov) **36**:309
Inside the Onion (Nemerov) **36**:309
"Inside the Story" (Strand) **6**:521
"Inside the Tulip" (Bowering) **47**:28
"Inside-Out" (Knight) **40**:283-84, 286
"Insight" (Williams) **148**:357, 361
"Insight at Flame Lake" (Amis) **62**:7-10
"Insignificant Elephants" (Auden) **4**:33
"The Insoluble Problem: Supporting Art" (Barzun) **145**:77
"Insomnia" (Bishop) **32**:39
"Insomnia" (Bowers) **9**:122
Insomnia; or, The Devil at Large (Miller) **9**:380
"Insomniac" (Plath) **111**:171, 180, 214
L'insoumise (Blais) **6**:82; **13**:96
L'insourenable l'égrèté de l'être (Kundera) **32**:262-64, 267-68, 271; **68**:232-36, 238, 244-47, 249-50, 252-54, 256, 259-62, 264-66; **115**:309, 311, 315, 317, 321, 326, 329-30, 333, 344-45, 347-48, 351, 353-54, 359; **135**:205-58
"Inspeak: Your Streetwise Guide to Linguistics and Structuralism" (Bradbury) **61**:48
"The Inspector" (Reid) **33**:350
The Inspector (de Hartog) **19**:131
An Inspector Calls (Priestley) **5**:350; **34**:361-63, 365-66
The Inspector General (Rozewicz) **139**:279
Inspector Maigret and the Dead Girl (Simenon)
See *Maigret and the Young Girl*
Inspector Maigret and the Killers (Simenon) **47**:373, 377
Inspector Maigret and the Strangled Stripper (Simenon)
See *Maigret au "Picratt"*
Inspector Queen's Own Case (Queen) **11**:464
Inspector Saito's Small Satori (van de Wetering) **47**:411
"The Inspired Chicken Motel" (Bradbury) **42**:34
"Installation # 6" (Beattie) **146**:61, 70, 76
Instamatic Poems (Morgan) **31**:275-76
"L'instance de la lettre" (Lacan) **75**:286, 295
"Instances of Communication" (Jacobsen) **102**:241
"Instancing" (Ammons) **57**:50
"The Instant" (Levertov) **66**:241
L'instant de ma mort (Blanchot) **135**:136
The Instant Enemy (Macdonald) **1**:185; **2**:256; **14**:335
"L'instant II" (Chedid) **47**:87
An Instant in the Wind (Brink)
See *File on a Diplomat*
"Instant Karma!" (Lennon) **35**:265, 270-71, 273-74
"Instant of the Hour After" (McCullers) **12**:433
Instantanées (Robbe-Grillet) **128**:336, 376-77
"Instead of a Foreword" (Kunitz) **148**:142
"Instead of an Essay" (Tomlinson) **45**:397-98
"Instead of an Interview" (Adcock) **41**:16
"Instead of Camargue" (Swenson) **106**:320
"Instead of You" (Dunn) **36**:155
Instinct and Intelligence (Cousteau) **30**:107
The Institute (Cain) **11**:87; **28**:54
Institute Benjamenta, or This Dream Which People Call Human Life (The Brothers Quay) **95**:348, 351, 354, 356-58
"Instrucciones para John Howell" (Cortázar) **5**:109
"The Instruction Manual" (Ashbery) **9**:42; **41**:40; **77**:58, 70; **125**:14, 38
"Instructions for Bombing with Napalm" (Frame) **96**:200
"Instructions for Exiting the Building in Case of Fire" (Zoline) **62**:463
"Instructions for John Howell" (Cortázar) **5**:109
Instructions for Undressing the Human Race (Alegria) **57**:11
"Instructions from the Dean of Menopause" (Klappert) **57**:257-58
"Instructions to the Double" (Gallagher) **18**:170; **63**:122, 124
Instructions to the Double (Gallagher) **18**:168, 170; **63**:116, 118-20, 122
"Instructions to the Orphic Adept" (Graves) **45**:162, 166
"Instructions to the Player" (Rakosi) **47**:346
"Instructions to Vampires" (Adcock) **41**:13
"Instructions toward a Nude" (Dacey) **51**:79
The Instrument (O'Hara) **42**:319
"Instrument and Agent" (MacCaig) **36**:279
"Instrument of Destruction" (Spencer) **22**:406
Instrument of Thy Peace (Paton) **25**:364
"Instruments of Seduction" (Rush) **44**:91, 94-5
Insufficient Poppy (Enright) **31**:152
An Insular Possession (Mo) **46**:261-62; **134**:186, 188-92, 194-96, 203-06, 208-10
"The Insult" (Williams) **148**:348, 352
The Insurance Man (Bennett) **45**:59; **77**:91
"Una insurrección permanente" (Vargas Llosa) **85**:354
Insurrection (O'Flaherty) **5**:321; **34**:355-56
"Intacta" (Davison) **28**:100
"The Integers" (Leithauser) **27**:242
"Integraciones" (Neruda) **28**:309
"Integrity" (Rich) **36**:369, 377
"The Intellectual" (Ritsos) **31**:324
"The Intellectual Physiognomy of Literacy Characters" (Lukacs) **24**:316
Intellectual Things (Kunitz) **11**:319; **14**:313; **148**:67-69, 71, 86-88, 90-91, 94-97, 109, 111, 115-16, 123, 130, 137, 147-48
"The Intellectuals" (Randall) **135**:398
"The Intellectuals" (Shapiro) **53**:326
Intellectuals (Johnson) **147**:97, 99-100, 102, 104-13, 118-20, 145, 151
The Intellectuals on the Road to Class Power: A Sociological Study of the Role the Intelligentsia in Socialism (Konrád)
See *Az értlemiség utja az oszatályhatalomhoz*
Les intellectuels en question (Blanchot) **135**:130
Intelligent Life in the Universe (Sagan) **112**:416, 438
Intense Pleasure (McFadden) **48**:244-46, 250
"Intensive Care" (Smith) **73**:353, 356-57, 359
Intensive Care (Bennett) **77**:93
Intensive Care (Frame) **6**:190; **96**:173, 179-82, 191-92, 197, 199, 200, 217
"Intensive Care Unit" (Ballard) **137**:15-16
L'intention poétique (Glissant) **68**:173, 179, 181-82, 185, 189
Inter Ice Age 4 (Abe)
See *Daiyon kampyoki*
"Intercession" (Avison) **97**:115
"The Intercessors" (Derleth) **31**:133
The Intercom Conspiracy (Ambler) **9**:18, 20
Intercourse (Dworkin) **123**:62-4, 66-8, 83-5, 90, 92, 95, 102, 106
"An Interest in Life" (Paley) **6**:393; **37**:338; **140**:232-34, 247, 264, 267, 277, 281, 285
"Interference" (Ammons) **108**:21
"Interference" (Barnes) **141**:69-70
"Interferences" (Morgan) **31**:275-76
"Intérieur" (Bagryana) **10**:14
"L'intérieur" (Butor) **15**:117
"Interim" (Levertov) **5**:247-49
"Interim" (Wilson) **49**:416
"Interim in a Waiting Room" (Corn) **33**:114
Interim Report (Shapcott) **38**:401
"Interims" (Amichai) **116**:122
"The Interior Castle" (Stafford) **7**:457; **19**:431; **68**:422-23, 434, 449
"Interior Decorating" (Simmons) **43**:412
"Interior Decorator" (Betjeman) **43**:51
"The Interior Dialogue" (Mauriac) **9**:363
The Interior Landscape: The Literary Criticism of Marshall McLuhan, 1943-1962 (McLuhan) **83**:360
Interior Landscapes: Autobiographical Myths and Metaphors (Vizenor) **103**:311, 340
The Interior Life (Moravia)
See *La vita interiore*
"Interior Space" (Irving) **112**:172, 175
"Interiors" (Fisher) **25**:158
Interiors (Allen) **16**:9-11, 13-16; **52**:40, 46-8
"Interiors with Various Figures" (Fisher) **25**:161
"Interjection Number Four: Bad Year, Bad War: A New Year's Card, 1969" (Warren) **8**:538
"Interjection Number Three: I Know a Place Where All Is Real" (Warren) **8**:537

"Interjection Number Two: Caveat" (Warren) **8**:537
"Interlopers" (Wilding) **73**:399
"An Interlude of Winter Light" (Duncan) **41**:128-29
Interlunar (Atwood) **84**:68, 98, 102, 104
"An Intermediate Stop" (Godwin) **8**:249; **69**:232
"Intermission" (Coover) **46**:121
The Intermittent Quest (Ionesco)
See *La quête intermittent*
"Internal and External Forms" (Hall) **151**:196
Internal Colloquies: Poetries (Richards) **14**:453; **24**:401
Internal Foreigner (Klappert) **57**:266
"The International Crime of Genital Mutilation" (Steinem) **63**:384
"International Lover" (Prince) **35**:326, 328
The International Stud (Fierstein) **33**:152-53
"Interoffice Memorandum to James Seay" (Harmon) **38**:244
Interpersonal Perception: A Theory and a Method of Research (Laing) **95**:134, 141, 145, 174, 176
"Interplay" (Wright) **53**:424, 429
Interpretation and Overinterpretation (Eco) **142**:98-100, 105-06
Interpretation in Teaching (Richards) **24**:400-01
"The Interpretation of Dreams" (Koch) **44**:249
"The Interpretation of Dreams" (Matthews) **40**:323-24
"The Interpretation of Dreams" (Smith) **73**:353, 356-58
The Interpretation of Dreams (Breton) **15**:88, 90
"Interpretations" (Urdang) **47**:400
"The Interpreter" (Aldiss) **14**:11
The Interpreters (Soyinka) **3**:462; **5**:397; **14**:508, 509; **36**:410-11; **44**:291, 294-96
Interpreter's House (Dickey) **28**:118
"Interpreting the Past" (Lively) **32**:273
"Interpreting the Variorum" (Fish) **142**:156
The Interrogation (Le Clézio) **31**:242-43, 246, 249
"Interrogation II" (Williams) **148**:355-56, 358, 362
"The Interrogation of the Man of Many Hearts" (Sexton) **123**:407
"The Interrogation of the Prisoner Bung by Mister Hawkins and Sergeant Tree" (Huddle) **49**:181-82
The Interrupted Act (Rozewicz)
See *Akt przerywany*
"The Interrupted Class" (Hesse) **3**:248-49
"interrupted conversation" (Rozewicz)
See "przerwana rozmowa"
"An Interrupted Examination" (Rozewicz)
See "Przerwany egzamin"
Interrupted Praise: New and Selected Poems (Honig) **33**:216
"An Interruption" (Ciardi) **44**:383
"Interruptions From the West" (Paz) **119**:409
Intersect (Shields) **113**:412, 441
"I-80 Nebraska, m.490—m.205" (Sayles) **14**:483
"Interstellar Overdrive" (Pink Floyd) **35**:307
The Interstellar Search (Campbell) **32**:74
"Interstitial Office" (Berryman) **3**:69
Intertidal Life (Thomas) **37**:422-24; **107**:328, 330, 336-37, 340, 347, 349
"The Interval" (Motion) **47**:288, 291
"Interval in Sunlight" (Bradbury) **42**:35
Intervalle (Butor) **15**:119-20
"Interview" (Arreola) **147**:27
"The Interview" (Blackwood) **6**:80
"The Interview" (Bruce) **21**:44
"The Interview" (Creeley) **78**:136
"Interview" (Havel)
See *Audience*
"The Interview" (Ignatow) **40**:259
"The Interview" (Jhabvala) **94**:184
"Interview" (Randall) **135**:390, 398
"The Interview" (Singer) **69**:306
Interview (van Itallie) **3**:493
"An Interview Unlike Any Other" (Wiesel) **37**:451
"Interview with a Spirit Healer" (Abse) **29**:16
"Interview with Doctor Drink" (Cunningham) **31**:98
Interview with History (Fallaci)
See *Intervista con la storia*
"Interview with Myself" (Wolf) **150**:296, 317, 337, 339
Interview with the Vampire (Rice) **41**:361-67; **128**:278-79, 283, 286-92, 298-99, 303-04, 306-09, 311, 313-21
"An Interview with Tom Beckett" (Bernstein) **142**:8
"The Interviewer" (Hinde) **6**:239
Interviewing Matisse, or, The Woman Who Died Standing Up (Tuck) **70**:117-21
Interviewing the Audience (Gray) **112**:103, 111
Intervista (Fellini)
See *Federico Fellini's intervista*
Intervista con la storia (Fallaci) **110**:194-95, 207
"Intifada" (Jordan) **114**:147
"Intimacy" (Carver) **53**:62, 64-6; **55**:275, 277; **126**:183
"Intimacy" (Collins) **44**:37-8
"Intimacy" (Colwin) **84**:150
"Intimacy" (Montague) **46**:277
Intimacy (Kureishi) **135**:292-94
Intimacy, and Other Stories (Sartre)
See *Le mur*
Intimate Exchanges (Ayckbourn) **33**:47, 50; **74**:20
"Intimate Parnassus" (Kavanagh) **22**:238
Intimate Relations (Cocteau)
See *Les parents terribles*
Intimate Strangers (Prichard) **46**:337-38, 340-42
"Intimations" (Michaels) **25**:314
"Intimations of Mortality" (McGinley) **14**:366
"Intimidations of an Autobiography" (Tate) **6**:528
"Into Each Rain Some Life Must Fall" (Robinson) **21**:348-50
Into Eternity: The Life of James Jones, American Writer (MacShane) **39**:404-14
"Into Hades" (Young) **5**:523-25
"Into Mexico" (Van Duyn) **116**:400, 402
"Into My Own" (Frost) **26**:117-18
"Into My Own" (Levine) **33**:274
"Into the American Maw" (Frazier) **46**:164
"Into the Black" (Young)
See "Hey Hey, My My"
"Into the Dark Chamber" (Coetzee) **117**:74, 90, 98
"Into the Dusk-Charged Air" (Ashbery) **77**:57, 69
"Into the Green Night" (Faust) **8**:215
Into the Music (Morrison) **21**:238
"Into the Night" (Carroll)
See "When the City Drops"
Into the Night (Woolrich) **77**:405
"Into the Night Life" (Miller) **84**:250
"Into the Salient" (Blunden) **56**:30
Into the Slave Nebula (Brunner) **8**:111
Into the Stone (Dickey) **7**:79, 83; **109**:236, 244, 265
"Into the Tree" (Milosz) **82**:300
Into the Valley: A Skirmish of the Marines (Hersey) **40**:226; **81**:332, 334-35; **97**:297, 301, 303-04, 310
"Into the Wood" (Aickman) **57**:6-7
Into the Woods (Sondheim) **147**:227-29, 261
Into Their Labours (Berger) **19**:41
Into Your Tent I'll Creep (De Vries) **2**:114; **3**:125; **7**:76; **28**:107
"Intoxication" (Pasternak) **63**:313
"Intracom" (Le Guin) **45**:213, 216-17
"Intra-Political: An Exercise in Political Astronomy" (Avison) **97**:76, 79, 91, 109, 127
"Între două nopți" (Arghezi) **80**:6
"The Intrinsic Study of Literature" (Wellek) **28**:442
Introducción a la literatura inglesa (Borges) **9**:117
Introducción a los vasos órficos (Lezama Lima) **4**:288
Introducing David Jones: A Selection of His Writings (Jones) **42**:238, 241
Introducing Eavan Boland (Boland) **40**:97-9; **113**:69, 81
Introducing Shirley Braverman (Wolitzer) **17**:562
"Introduction (Queens of the Universe)" (Sanchez) **116**:299
Introduction to Dickens (Ackroyd) **140**:17
An Introduction to English Literature (Borges)
See *Introducción a la literatura inglesa*
"Introduction to History" (Galeano) **72**:130
Introduction to Metaphysics (Heidegger) **24**:270
"Introduction to Native American Literature" (Alexie) **154**:10
Introduction to Objectivist Epistemology (Rand) **30**:304
"Introduction to Poe and Performance" (Berkoff) **56**:15
"Introduction to the 'Collected Plays'" (Miller) **47**:250-51
An Introduction to the Metaphysical Poets (Beer) **58**:33
Introduction to the New Existentialism (Wilson) **14**:586
"Introduction to the Structural Analysis of Narrative" (Barthes) **83**:80
"Introduction to the Twentieth Century" (Dunn) **36**:155
"Introduzione" (Eco) **142**:89, 97
"The Intruder" (Borges)
See "La intrusa"
"The Intruder" (Dixon) **52**:98
"The Intruder" (Dubus) **97**:234, 237
"The Intruder" (Fisher) **25**:157
"The Intruder" (Kizer) **80**:172, 182
Intruder in the Dust (Faulkner) **3**:149, 156-57; **14**:179-80; **28**:143; **52**:139
"Intruders" (Abe) **81**:294, 296-97
The Intruders (Garner) **13**:236
"L'intrus" (Theriault) **79**:408
"La intrusa" (Borges) **1**:39; **2**:77; **6**:88; **44**:364; **48**:34; **83**:186, 188
Intrusion (Maugham) **93**:244
Intrusions (Aickman) **57**:3
"Intuition" (Lennon) **35**:266
The Intuitive Journey and Other Works (Edson) **13**:190
"The Inundation" (Dickey) **7**:79
"The Invaders" (Campbell) **32**:76, 78, 80
"The Invaders" (Winters) **32**:469
The Invaders (Plomer) **4**:406
Invaders from Earth (Silverberg) **140**:377
"Invaders from the Infinite" (Campbell) **32**:72-3
The Invaders Plan (Hubbard) **43**:206-07
The Invading Asteroid (Wellman) **49**:391
"The Invalid" (Merwin) **8**:390
"Invalid, Convalescing" (Raine) **103**:179
L'invasion (Adamov) **4**:5; **25**:12-15, 18-20
The Invasion (Adamov)
See *L'invasion*
The Invasion (Leonov)
See *Nashestvie*
The Invasion: A Narrative of Events concerning the Johnston Family of St. Mary's (Lewis) **41**:251-52, 259, 261-62
Invasion Earth (Harrison) **42**:207
"Invasion Exercise on the Poultry Farm" (Betjeman) **43**:34
"Invasion Footnote" (Ellison) **42**:131
Invasion from Aldebaran (Lem) **40**:290; **149**:282
The Invasion of Canada, 1812-1813 (Berton) **104**:41-4, 59
"The Invasion of the Airline Stewardesses" (Ritter) **52**:355

Invasion of the Space Invaders: An Addict's Guide (Amis) **38**:16
"Invasions" (Kunitz) **148**:87
"Invective against Denise, a Witch" (Hecht) **19**:208
La invención de Morel (Bioy Casares) **4**:63; **8**:94; **13**:84-5, 87; **88**:59-62, 64-5, 73, 75-7, 82, 84-7, 89, 91-3
"El inventario" (Poniatowska) **140**:295
Inventing the Flat Earth: Columbus and Modern Historians (Russell) **70**:341, 344
"L'invention" (Carrier) **78**:58
The Invention (Soyinka) **14**:505
"Invention for Shelagh" (Rule) **27**:420
"The Invention of Comics" (Baraka) **3**:35
The Invention of Morel, and Other Stories (from "La trama celeste") (Bioy Casares)
See *La invención de Morel*
The Invention of Poetry (Quarrington) **65**:203
"The Invention of Robert Herendeen" (Millhauser) **109**:158-59, 161
The Invention of Solitude (Auster) **47**:10-12; **131**:5, 7, 19, 24
"Invention of the Other" (Graham) **118**:222
"The Invention of the Telephone" (Klappert) **57**:258
The Invention of the World (Hodgins) **23**:228-36
The Inventor (Lind) **82**:143-44
"The Inventor of Franglais?" (Ewart) **46**:153
"Inventory" (Eich)
See "Inventur"
"The Inventory" (Poniatowska)
See "El inventario"
The Inventory (Josipovici) **43**:213-14, 218, 227-28
"The Inventory of Fontana Bella" (Williams) **5**:502
"Inventur" (Eich) **15**:204
"The Inverted Forest" (Salinger) **12**:498, 514
Investigating Psychics: Five Life Histories (Kettelkamp) **12**:307-08
Investigating UFO's (Kettelkamp) **12**:306
The Investigation (Lem) **8**:344; **15**:327; **40**:290; **149**:118, 132, 156, 159, 161, 165, 168, 172, 207-8, 251-52, 255, 260, 282, 284
The Investigation (Weiss)
See *Die Ermittlung: Oratorium in Elf Gesëngen*
Investigative Poetry (Sanders) **53**:309
"The Investigator" (Hinde) **6**:239
"Investigator" (Waddington) **28**:437
"The Investiture" (Sassoon) **130**:221
"The Investor" (Friedman) **56**:97
"Invictus" (Lattimore) **3**:277
"The Invincible" (Livesay) **79**:342
The Invincible (Lem)
See *Niezwyciezony*
An Invincible Memory (Ribeiro)
See *Vivo o povo brasileiro*
"The Invincible Slave-Owners" (Dinesen) **29**:159; **95**:35, 42
"Invischiato" (Moravia) **11**:382
"Invisibility in Academe" (Rich) **73**:322
"The Invisible Arch of Viñales" (Lezama Lima)
See "Arco invisible de Viñales"
Invisible Cities (Calvino)
See *Le città invisibili*
The Invisible Knight (Calvino)
See *Il cavaliere inesistente*
"The Invisible Man" (Phillips) **28**:362-63
Invisible Man (Ellison) **1**:93-5; **3**:141-46; **11**:179-81, 184; **54**:106-48; **86**:318-26, 328-29; **114**:85, 88-9, 91-3, 95, 98-9, 101-05, 107-08, 111-12, 114-15, 117, 124-27, 131-38
"Invisible Mending" (Morrissy) **99**:78
"Invisible Mending" (Williams) **148**:364
Invisible Mending (Busch) **47**:59-61
The Invisible Musician (Young Bear) **94**:371-73, 376
The Invisible One (Lagerkvist)
See *Den osynlige*
Invisible presencia (Alonso) **14**:23
The Invisible Pyramid (Eiseley) **7**:91
The Invisible River (Neruda)
See *El rio invisible*
"Invisible Sun" (Police, The) **26**:365
Invisible Threads (Yevtushenko) **26**:468
"The Invisible Woman" (Morgan) **2**:295
Invisible Woman: New and Selected Poems, 1970-1982 (Oates) **33**:292, 294; **108**:348; **134**:249
The Invisible Worm (Johnston) **150**:23-5, 31-2
The Invisible Writing (Koestler) **15**:312; **33**:235
"An Invitation" (Gunn) **81**:178, 182, 187
The Invitation (Castillo) **151**:3-5, 7, 30, 37, 45
Invitation à un concert officiel et autres récits (Kadare) **52**:261
L'invitation au château (Anouilh) **1**:7-8; **3**:11; **13**:17, 22; **40**:51, 54, 60; **50**:278-80
"L'invitation au voyage" (Wilbur) **14**:577
Invitation to a Beheading (Nabokov)
See *Priglashenie na kazn*
"Invitation to Juno" (Empson) **19**:155
"Invitation to the Dance" (Hughes) **9**:285
Invitation to the Waltz (Lehmann) **5**:235, 239
"Invitations" (Shields) **113**:425
"Invite" (O'Hara) **42**:320-21
L'invitée (Beauvoir) **1**:19; **2**:43; **8**:58; **31**:34, 40-2; **44**:343, 350; **71**:48-9, 51-6, 72, 85; **124**:137, 144, 146-47
Invocaciones (Cernuda) **54**:41-2, 47, 58, 60
"The Invocation" (Campbell) **42**:89
"The Invocation" (Hope) **51**:213, 215-16
"Invocation" (Jeffers) **54**:235
"Invocation" (Kinsella) **138**:101-03
"Invocation" (Kunitz) **148**:88
"Invocation" (Levertov) **66**:236
"Invocation" (McAuley) **45**:249-50
"Invocation" (Musgrave) **13**:401
"Invocation" (Raine) **45**:330, 341
"Invocation" (Sarton) **91**:244
"Invocation" (Sassoon) **130**:221-22
"Invocation" (Sitwell) **67**:320
"Invocation and Ritual Dance of the Young Pumpkin" (Zappa) **17**:585
"Invocation to Kali" (Sarton) **91**:254
"Invocation to the Guardian" (Montague) **46**:277
"Invocation to the Social Muse" (MacLeish) **8**:363; **68**:282, 290-92
Invocations (Cernuda)
See *Invocaciones*
"Invulnerable" (Ellison) **42**:131
"Inward Bound" (MacCaig) **36**:284-85
The Inward Eye (MacCaig) **36**:284
"The Inward Generation" (de Man) **55**:414
Inwards to the Sun (Shapcott) **38**:399
"Io" (Broumas) **73**:6
Io e lui (Moravia) **2**:293-94; **7**:242; **18**:347; **46**:284-85
"Ion Ion" (Arghezi) **80**:7
"Iona: The Graves of the Kings" (Jeffers) **54**:246
Ionesco the Great (Jacobsen) **102**:227
The Ionian Mission (O'Brian) **152**:278, 288, 300
"Iork" (Brodsky)
See "York: In Memoriam W. H. Auden"
"Iota" (Tolson) **105**:255
IOU's (Sebestyen) **30**:349-51
"Iowa" (Klappert) **57**:258
The Iowa Baseball Confederacy (Kinsella) **43**:257-60
The Ipcress File (Deighton) **4**:119; **7**:75-6; **22**:113-14; **46**:125, 128-29
"Iphigenia" (Dodson) **79**:194
Iphigenia at Aulis (Rexroth) **11**:472; **22**:345
"Ipomoea" (Glück) **81**:164
"Irani Restaurant Instructions" (Ezekiel) **61**:95
"Ireland" (Muldoon) **32**:320; **72**:266, 268
"Ireland, 1972" (Durcan) **43**:116
Ireland and the English Crisis (Paulin) **37**:355-56
Irene; o, El tesoro (Buero Vallejo) **15**:102; **139**:10, 16, 19, 57
Irene; or, The Treasure (Buero Vallejo)
See *Irene; o, El tesoro*
Irisches Tagebuch (Boell) **2**:68; **3**:75; **9**:109; **15**:70-2; **27**:60
The Irish (O'Faolain) **2**:275; **70**:317-18
"An Irish Childhood in England: 1951" (Boland) **67**:46; **113**:86, 92-93, 106, 108, 125
Irish Elegies (Colum) **28**:91
An Irish Faustus (Durrell) **4**:145; **13**:184
"The Irish Genius" (Allen) **52**:35
"Irish Hierarchy Bans Colour Photography" (Durcan) **43**:114-16
Irish Journal (Boell)
See *Irisches Tagebuch*
Irish Miles (O'Connor) **14**:397
The Irish Novelists, 1800-1850 (Flanagan) **25**:163
"Irish Revel" (O'Brien) **5**:313; **36**:338; **116**:207-11, 222
The Irish Signorina (O'Faolain) **47**:328-29, 331; **108**:407
Irish Sketch Book (Behan) **79**:30-1
"The Irish Unionist's Farewell to Greta Hellstrom in 1922" (Betjeman) **43**:34, 44, 52
The Irish Women (Boyle) **121**:36
"The Irish Writer" (Kinsella) **138**:139, 156
Irma La Douce (Wilder) **20**:460-61
"Iron" (Levi) **37**:226-27
"The Iron Age" (Blaga) **75**:79
Iron and Man (Lagerkvist)
See *Järn och människor*
The Iron Breadboard (Baxter) **14**:60
Iron Cage (Norton) **12**:465, 470
The Iron Cross (Rice) **7**:364
"The Iron Door" (Pratt) **19**:378, 385-86
The Iron Dream (Spinrad) **46**:386-87
The Iron Duke (Tunis) **12**:593
Iron Earth, Copper Sky (Kemal)
See *Yer demir gök bakir*
The Iron Giant (Hughes) **4**:236
The Iron Giant: A Story in Five Nights (Hughes) **119**:251
"Iron Horse" (Ginsberg) **36**:187, 193, 196
The Iron Horse (Ford) **16**:302
Iron John: A Book About Men (Bly) **70**:420-21, 424-26, 428-30, 435-61; **128**:32-41, 46-48
"The Iron Lady" (Ochs) **17**:331
"Iron Landscapes" (Gunn) **18**:199
"Iron Larks" (Gilliatt) **13**:237
"The Iron Lung" (Plumly) **33**:313
The Iron Man (Hughes) **119**:281
Iron Mountain (Clark) **12**:130
"Iron Palace" (Graves) **45**:166
"Iron Staircase" (Yevtushenko) **26**:467
"The Iron Thread" (Olsen) **114**:237
"The Iron Throat" (Olsen) **114**:221
"Iron Woman" (Rooke) **25**:391
Ironies of Fate (Mahfouz)
See *Abath al-aqdar*
Ironweed (Kennedy) **28**:205-06; **34**:206-11; **53**:191-97, 199-201
"Irony and Ironic Poetry" (Brooks) **24**:104
"Irony as Nursery" (Codrescu) **121**:162
"Irracionalismo y eficacia" (Cortázar) **92**:154
Irrational Man: A Study in Existential Philosophy (Barrett) **27**:16-17, 20
Irrefuhrung der Behörden (Becker) **7**:27
"The Irrelevant" (Campbell) **32**:74
"An Irrelevant Death" (Abe) **81**:297-98
"The Irresponsibles" (MacLeish) **68**:292
"An Irrevocable Diameter" (Paley) **140**:277
"Irtnog" (White) **10**:527
is 5 (Cummings) **12**:154, 158, 161; **15**:159-62; **68**:26-7, 34-6, 45-7
"Is Fiction the Art of Lying?" (Vargas Llosa) **42**:412

"Is Gender Necessary? Redux" (Le Guin) **136**:326, 328-29, 332-33, 347, 347, 356, 365
"Is It Far to Go?" (Day Lewis) **10**:131
"Is It in My Head?" (Townshend) **17**:532
"Is It Me?" (Townshend) **17**:532
"Is It Really Important to Think?" (Foucault) **69**:191-92
Is It Safe to Drink the Water? (Buchwald) **33**:90
Is It Something I Said? (Pryor) **26**:378
Is It the Sun, Philibert? (Carrier)
See *Il est par là, le soleil*
"Is It True?" (Sexton) **6**:494; **123**:418-19, 428
"Is Literary Criticism Possible?" (Tate) **24**:443
"Is/Not" (Atwood) **13**:44; **84**:65
"Is Paris Burning?" (Hooks) **94**:152
"Is Phoenix Jackson's Grandson Really Dead?" (Welty) **105**:333
"Is Poetry an American Art?" (Shapiro) **8**:486; **53**:328
Is Sex Necessary? or Why You Feel the Way You Do (Thurber) **125**:395, 402
Is Summer This Bear (Kenny) **87**:245-47
"Is That What You Are" (Merwin) **88**:192
Is That You, Miss Blue? (Kerr) **12**:298-99, 301; **35**:250-51
"Is the Pope Capitalized?" (Blount) **38**:46
Is There a Case for Foreign Missions? (Buck) **7**:32
"Is There a Text in This Class" (Fish) **142**:171
Is There a Text in This Class (Fish) **142**:150, 153-55, 158, 160, 162, 164, 169, 175-77, 183
"Is There No Love Can Link Us?" (Peake) **54**:373, 375
"Is There No Way Out?" (Paz)
See "¿No hay salida?"
"Is There Nowhere Else Where We Can Meet?" (Gordimer) **18**:185; **123**:130, 132
"Is This Love" (Marley) **17**:270, 272
"Is This Useful? Is This Boring?" (Grayson) **38**:211
"Is Verse a Dying Technique?" (Wilson) **24**:472
"Is Wisdom a Lot of Language?" (Sandburg) **35**:356
"Is You or Is You Ain't, Goober Man?" (Perelman) **23**:336
"Isaac" (Michaels) **25**:316
Isaac Asimov, The Complete Stories: Volume 2 (Asimov) **76**:319
Isaac Asimov's Book of Facts (Asimov) **26**:51
"Isaac Starbuck" (Sillitoe) **57**:388-89; **148**:163
"Isaak Babel" (Dubie) **36**:130
Isabel şi apele diavolului (Eliade) **19**:145
Isabella, tre caravelle e un cacciaballe (Fo) **109**:113, 115
"Isba Song" (McGuckian) **48**:278
"Ishmael, the Archer" (Colum) **28**:91
"Ishmael's Dream" (Stern) **100**:328
"Ishtar" (Wright) **53**:419
"Isidor" (Simpson) **7**:429; **149**:321
"Isis in Darkness" (Atwood) **84**:96-7
"Isis Wanderer" (Raine) **45**:332, 338
La isla (Goytisolo) **23**:183
"La isla a mediodía" (Cortázar) **5**:109; **34**:333
"Isla en Manhattan" (Marqués) **96**:240-41
"La Isla III" (Neruda) **62**:334
Isla Negra: A Notebook (Neruda)
See *Memorial de Isla Negra*
"Island" (Ezekiel) **61**:105, 107
"The Island" (Forché) **83**:211, 214
"The Island" (Honig) **33**:211-12
"The Island" (Jarrell) **9**:298
"The Island" (Jennings) **131**:240
"The Island" (Longley) **29**:296
"Island" (MacLeod) **56**:200
"The Island" (Rukeyser) **27**:408
"The Island" (Thomas) **6**:530
"The Island" (Williams) **148**:368
The Island (Creeley) **2**:105; **8**:151-52; **36**:122; **78**:125, 128, 144
The Island (Fugard) **9**:229-34; **14**:191; **25**:175; **40**:197-98; **80**:62-3, 65-6, 69, 70, 74-5, 80, 82
Island (Huxley) **1**:152; **3**:255; **4**:237-41, 243; **5**:193-94; **8**:303-04; **11**:282, 284-88; **18**:266-67; **35**:238-40, 242-44; **79**:309-10
"The Island at Noon" (Cortázar)
See "La isla a mediodía"
An Island Called Moreau (Aldiss) **40**:16
An Island Death (Yurick) **6**:583-84
"The Island Dream" (Hesse) **3**:248-49
Island Fling (Coward)
See *South Sea Bubble*
"Island Funeral" (MacDiarmid) **4**:309, 313; **11**:333
"The Island III" (Neruda)
See "La Isla III"
Island in the City: The World of Spanish Harlem (Wakefield) **7**:502-03
Island in the Sky (Gann) **23**:162
The Island of Crimea (Aksyonov)
See *Ostrov Krym*
The Island of Horses (Dillon) **17**:93, 95
"Island of Summer" (Warren) **10**:520
Island of the Blue Dolphins (O'Dell) **30**:267-71, 273-74, 276-77
The Island of the Day Before (Eco) **142**:114, 116
The Island of the Mighty (Arden) **6**:10
Island People (Dowell) **60**:96-101, 105-06, 109
The Island Stallion (Farley) **17**:116
"Island Storm" (Honig) **33**:211, 215
"The Island Ven" (Berriault) **109**:97
"The Islanders" (Booth) **23**:74
"The Islands" (Atwood) **4**:27
"The Islands" (H. D.) **73**:121
"The Islands" (Hayden) **37**:156
"Islands" (Merwin) **88**:203
"Islands" (Walcott) **67**:362
Islands (Brathwaite) **11**:67
Islands in the Net (Sterling) **72**:370-71, 373
Islands in the Sky (Clarke) **13**:153
Islands in the Stream (Hemingway) **1**:144; **3**:237, 243; **6**:229-30, 232; **8**:285, 288; **10**:269; **30**:199; **39**:430; **41**:204, 206; **50**:423; **80**:148, 151
Islands in the Stream (White) **7**:529
The Islands of Italy (Harrison) **144**:121
The Islands of Scotland (MacDiarmid) **4**:309; **11**:334
Islands of Space (Campbell) **32**:73
The Islands of Unwisdom (Graves) **45**:172
Íslandsklukkan (Laxness) **25**:297
"The Isle of Aves" (Hope) **51**:226
"Isle of Man Christmas 1967" (Kunene) **85**:165
Isle of the Dead (Zelazny) **21**:464, 470
Isle of the Sea Horse (Brinsmead) **21**:28
Islets/Irritations (Bernstein) **142**:55
Isma (Sarraute) **8**:471; **31**:381
"Ismael" (Chester) **49**:55-6
"Ismene" (Ritsos) **13**:488
Ismos (Gomez de la Serna) **9**:238
Isn't It Romantic (Wasserstein) **32**:440-43; **59**:219-21, 223-24; **90**:407-9, 412-15, 418-21, 425, 429-30, 431-33, 436
"Isn't She Lovely" (Wonder) **12**:659, 662
"Isobars" (Hospital) **145**:294-96, 305, 312
Isobars (Hospital) **145**:295, 297, 300, 302-05, 311-16
L'isola di Arturo (Morante) **47**:275, 280-81, 283
"Isolated Incidents" (Mukherjee) **53**:266, 268, 270
"Isolation" (Lennon) **35**:262
"Isolationist" (Page) **7**:291
"Isolda en el espejo" (Ferré) **139**:179
"Isolt of Brittany" (Christie) **110**:126
"Isomorphism" (L'Heureux) **52**:273
"Ispoved" (Voznesensky) **15**:554
"The Israeli Navy" (Bell) **8**:66
The Issa Valley (Konwicki)
See *Dolina Issy*
The Issa Valley (Milosz)
See *Dolina Issy*
Issei (Kogawa) **129**:284
"L'issue" (Char) **14**:128
"The Issue" (Grass) **49**:139
"The Issues" (Olds) **39**:187; **85**:290
"Iswaran" (Narayan) **28**:303
"It" (Olds) **85**:295
"It" (Sturgeon) **39**:361, 365-66
IT (King) **61**:318-25, 329-37; **113**:388-89, 391, 393
It (Mayne) **12**:405-06
It Ain't All for Nothin' (Myers) **35**:296-97
"It Ain't Me, Babe" (Dylan) **77**:167, 173
It Ain't Me Babe (Robbins) **21**:338
It All Adds Up (Amis) **101**:83
"It Always Breaks Out" (Ellison) **114**:100
It Catches My Heart in Its Hands: New and Selected Poems, 1955-1963 (Bukowski) **5**:80-1; **41**:64, 66-7; **108**:110, 114
It Changed My Life: Writings on the Women's Movement (Friedan) **74**:93-8
"It Fills You Up" (Morrison) **21**:237
"It Goes Without Saying" (Welsh) **144**:313-14
"It Had Wings" (Gurganus) **70**:192, 194, 196
"It Happened in Broad Daylight" (Duerrenmatt) **102**:60
It Happened One Night (Capra) **16**:153-54, 157-60, 163
It Happens Tomorrow (Fo) **32**:176
It Has No Choice (Bullins) **5**:83
"It Is 12.20 in New York a Friday" (O'Hara) **13**:423
"It Is a Living Coral" (Williams) **42**:462
"It Is a Spring Afternoon" (Sexton) **123**:407
"It Is Dangerous to Read Newspapers" (Atwood) **15**:38
"It is my own bones, Creeping" (Moure) **88**:229
"It Is Only Me" (Moure) **88**:217
"It Is Possible" (Rozewicz) **139**:226
It Is the Law (Rice) **7**:364; **49**:302
"It is the Responsibility" (Paley) **140**:274
"It Is the Season" (Jacobsen) **48**:193
"It Is This Way with Men" (Williams) **33**:442
It Is Time, Lord (Chappell) **40**:137; **78**:97
"It Is Very Distinct at the Ballpark" (Loewinsohn) **52**:284
"It Is Wonderful" (Ignatow) **40**:261
It Is Written (Duerrenmatt) **102**:56, 58, 60
It Is Written (Dürrenmatt)
See *Es steht geschrieben*
"It Isn't the Heat, It's the Cupidity" (Perelman) **49**:265
It Looked Like for Ever (Harris) **19**:205
"It May Not Always Be So: And I Say" (Cummings) **68**:30, 43-4
"It Must Be Sophisticated" (Ashbery) **77**:79; **125**:35
"It Spoke of Exactly the Things" (Hannah) **38**:233-34; **90**:138
"It Sure Is Cold Here at Night" (Freeman) **55**:57
"It Sure Was" (Kristofferson) **26**:268
It Takes a Long Time to Become Young (Kanin) **22**:232
"It Takes a Lot to Laugh, It Takes a Train to Cry" (Dylan) **77**:175
"It Takes a Thief" (Miller) **30**:262
"It Takes Two to Tango, but Only One to Squirm" (Perelman) **15**:418
"It Used to Be Green Once" (Grace) **56**:117
It Was (Zukofsky) **4**:599
"It Was a Funky Deal" (Knight) **40**:279, 287
"It Was Beginning Winter" (Roethke) **46**:362
"It Was Nothing—Really!" (Sturgeon) **22**:411
"It Was the Grape Autumn" (Neruda) **1**:247
"It Wasn't Me" (Berry) **46**:74
"It Will Be Darkness Soon" (Salinas) **90**:332
"It Won't Be Long" (Lennon and McCartney) **35**:274
Italian American Reconciliation (Shanley) **75**:323-25, 332
"Italian Days" (Wright) **146**:335, 339

Italian Days (Harrison) **144**:113-16, 121
An Italian Education: The Further Adventures of an Expatriate in Verona (Parks) **147**:208-10, 219
The Italian Element in Milton's Verse (Prince) **22**:339
"Italian Extravaganza" (Corso) **11**:123
Italian Fables (Calvino)
See *Fiabe italiene*
Italian Folktales (Calvino)
See *Fiabe italiene*
The Italian Girl (Murdoch) **1**:236; **3**:347; **6**:348-49; **8**:406; **31**:288-89
"Italian Hours" (Wright) **146**:314
The Italian Lesson (Elliott) **47**:115
Italian Light and Other Poems (Jennings) **131**:242
"Italian Morning" (Bogan) **46**:79-80, 85, 90
Italian Neighbors; or A Lapsed Anglo-Saxon in Verona (Parks) **147**:200-01, 206-09, 219
"Italian Postcards" (Urquhart) **90**:386
The Italian Straw Hat (Clair) **20**:59, 63, 70
An Italian Straw Hat (Cooney) **62**:145
An Italian Visit (Day Lewis) **6**:127; **10**:128
The Italian Wife (Humphreys) **47**:179-80, 188
Italianamerican (Scorsese) **20**:326, 329, 333-34; **89**:254
Italienische Reise (Rozewicz) **139**:253, 256
Itan no passporto (Abe) **81**:289
"Itansha no kanashimi" (Tanizaki) **28**:415
"The Itching Bear" (Edmonds) **35**:156
An Item from the Late News (Astley) **41**:48-9
"Items of a Night" (Grigson) **7**:136
"Ithaka" (Borges) **6**:93
"Ithaka" (Davenport) **14**:142
It's a Battlefield (Greene) **6**:219; **18**:194; **72**:148-49, 152-53, 158, 160-61
"It's a Dirty World" (Bukowski) **41**:73
"It's a Good Night" (Robinson) **21**:348
"It's a New Day" (Sanchez) **116**:301-02
It's a New Day: Poems for Young Brothas and Sistuhs (Sanchez) **116**:301, 309
"It's a Pity You Weren't With Us" (Aksyonov) **101**:18
It's a Slippery Slope (Gray) **112**:135-36
"It's a Woman's World" (Boland) **40**:100; **113**:79, 90, 109, 124
It's a Wonderful Life (Capra) **16**:156, 159-60, 162, 164-65
"It's All Over Now, Baby Blue" (Dylan) **77**:168, 173-74, 178
It's All True (Welles) **80**:413-16
"It's Always Tea-time in Chile" (Johnson) **147**:139
It's Beautiful (Sarraute)
See *C'est beau*
It's Called the Sugar Plum (Horovitz) **56**:147-48, 150
"Its Great Emptiness" (Pinsky) **38**:361
"It's Great to Be Back" (Heinlein) **26**:165
"It's Growing" (Robinson) **21**:346
"It's Half an Hour Later Before" (Ammons) **108**:12
"It's Hard to Be a Saint in the City" (Springsteen) **7**:487-88
"It's Hard to Dislike Ewart" (Ewart) **46**:147
Its Image on the Mirror (Gallant) **18**:172
"It's Just Another Day in Big Bear City, California" (Beattie) **63**:3, 9, 11-12
It's Like This, Cat (Neville) **12**:449-53
"Its Many Fragments" (Pinsky) **38**:361
It's Me, Eddie (Coles)
See *Eto ja—Edichka*
It's My Way! (Sainte-Marie) **17**:431
It's Never Over (Callaghan) **14**:100, 102; **41**:89
"It's Nice to Think of Tears" (Stern) **40**:413, 415
"It's Not for Me to Understand" (Nelson) **17**:305
It's Not the End of the World (Blume) **12**:44; **30**:20, 22
"It's Not True" (Townshend) **17**:530
It's Not What You Expect (Klein) **30**:237
"It's O.K." (Wilson) **12**:648
It's OK If You Don't Love Me (Klein) **30**:240
It's Only a Play (McNally) **41**:292-93; **91**:159
"It's Only Culture" (Epstein) **39**:468
"It's Only Rock 'n Roll" (Jagger and Richard) **17**:232-34, 236, 238
It's Over There, the Sun (Carrier)
See *Il est par là, le soleil*
"It's So Hard" (Lennon) **35**:263-64
"It's Still Rock 'n' Roll to Me" (Joel) **26**:220-21
It's Time, My Friend, It's Time (Aksyonov) **22**:26; **101**:3-4, 6, 10-11, 17, 29
"It's Too Dark in Here" (Berry) **17**:51
It's Too Late to Stop Now (Morrison) **21**:235
It's Trad Dad! (Lester) **20**:220
"It's Warm under Your Thumb" (Laughlin) **49**:222
"It's Worth Believin'" (Lightfoot) **26**:279
Itsuka (Kogawa) **78**:194-95; **129**:274-75, 280-81, 290, 298-301, 310, 312-17, 321
"Iva" (Akhmatova) **25**:24
"Ivan Meets G.I. Joe" (Clash) **30**:48
Ivan the Terrible and Ivan the Fool (Yevtushenko) **26**:468
Ivanca (Blaga) **75**:65-6
The Ivankiad; or, The Tale of the Writer Voinovich's Installation in His New Apartment (Voinovich)
See *Ivan'kiada: Ili rasskaz o vselenii pisatelia Voinovicha v novuiu kvartiru*
Ivan'kiada: Ili rasskaz o vselenii pisatelia Voinovicha v novuiu kvartiru (Voinovich) **10**:507-08; **49**:373-75, 377, 383-84; **147**:269-71, 289
Ivanov (Hare) **136**:299-300
"Ivanovo Calicoes" (Yevtushenko) **26**:468
Ivanovo Detstvo (Tarkovsky) **75**:369-72, 374, 382, 385, 388, 397-98, 402, 407
Ivan's Childhood (Tarkovsky)
See *Ivanovo Detstvo*
"Ivbie" (Clark Bekedermo) **38**:116, 125, 127-28
I've Always Been Crazy (Jennings) **21**:204-05
I've Been a Woman (Sanchez) **116**:272, 274-75, 281-82, 293, 298, 300, 302, 309-10, 315, 319
"I've Been Dead 400 Years" (Cliff) **21**:63
I've Got the Blues (Odets) **28**:332
"I've Got the Drimoleague Blues" (Durcan) **43**:114
"I've Got Time" (Seger) **35**:379-80
"I've Got to Tell You" (O'Hara)
See "Poem"
"I've Had Enough" (McCartney) **35**:285-86
"I've Had Her" (Ochs) **17**:331, 334
"I've Lost My Pal" (Sargeson) **31**:363-64
"I've Loved These Days" (Joel) **26**:215, 219-20
I've Tasted My Blood: Poems, 1956-1968 (Acorn) **15**:10
Ivona, Princess of Burgundia (Gombrowicz)
See *Iwona; Księżniczka Burgunda*
"Ivory, Apes, and People" (Thurber) **5**:434
The Ivory Grin (Macdonald) **14**:334; **41**:265, 269, 271
The Ivory Swing (Hospital) **42**:218-21; **145**:293, 297, 306, 308-09, 320
"The Ivory Tower" (Ashbery) **25**:54; **77**:61
"Ivy" (Sillitoe) **148**:199
"Ivy Gripped the Steps" (Bowen) **15**:77; **22**:64-5, 68
Ivy Gripped the Steps (Bowen)
See *The Demon Lover and Other Stories*
Ivy: The Life of I. Compton-Burnett (Spurling) **34**:494, 499, 501
The Ivy Tree (Stewart) **7**:467; **35**:390, 392
Iwona; Księżniczka Burgunda (Gombrowicz) **11**:239; **49**:121-26, 128
Ixion's Wheel (Gustafson) **36**:213, 216, 218
"Iya na yatsu" (Endō) **54**:157, 161
"Iz okna samoloyta" (Voznesensky) **15**:555
Iz shesti knig (Akhmatova) **25**:24
Izas, rabizas y colipoterras (Cela) **122**:21-2
Izlet u Rusiju (Krleža) **114**:168, 177
"The Izu Dancer" (Kawabata)
See "Izu no Odoriko"
"Izu no Odoriko" (Kawabata) **107**:100, 104, 106, 109
Izu no Odoriko (Kawabata) **107**:104-05, 108, 119
"J" (Merrill) **8**:384, 387
J. B. (Kazan) **63**:234
J. B. (MacLeish) **3**:310; **8**:362; **14**:336
"The J Car" (Gunn) **81**:179
"J. P. Donleavy's Dublin" (Mahon) **27**:286
J. P. Donleavy's Ireland: In All Her Sins and Some of Her Graces (Donleavy) **45**:127-29
J. P. Morgan Saves the Nation (Larson) **99**:160, 168, 171, 180, 186
J R (Gaddis) **6**:194-95; **8**:226-30; **10**:210-14; **19**:186-87; **43**:156-62; **86**:147-49, 151, 153, 155-58, 162-64, 166
J. S. Manifold: An Introduction to the Man and His Work (Hall) **51**:174
J'abats mon jeu (Aragon) **3**:14; **22**:38
Jabberwocky (Gilliam) **141**:247, 251, 260
Jablko z klína (Seifert) **34**:256; **44**:425; **93**:306, 318, 341
The Jacaranda Tree (Bates) **46**:64-5
J'accuse; the Dark Side of Nice (Greene) **27**:177; **70**:294
Jack (Sinclair) **14**:488
"Jack and Jill" (Thesen) **56**:414, 418-19
Jack and Jill (DeMarinis) **54**:98-9
Jack and the Beanstalk (Hunter) **31**:228
The Jack and the Joker (Ringwood) **48**:330, 333, 335-39
"Jack Frost" (Jacobsen) **102**:241
Jack Gelber's New Play: Rehearsal (Gelber) **14**:193-94
Jack Holborn (Garfield) **12**:215-17, 220, 224-28, 231, 235-36, 239
Jack in the Box (Kotzwinkle) **35**:255-56
Jack London, Hemingway, and the Constitution (Doctorow) **113**:174, 176
"The Jack of Diamonds" (Leonov) **92**:237
"The Jack of Hearts" (Ferlinghetti) **111**:65
Jack of Shadows (Zelazny) **21**:466, 473
Jack; or, The Submission (Ionesco)
See *Jacques; ou, La soumission*
"The Jack Randa Hotel" (Munro) **95**:319, 325
"Jack Schmidt, Arts Administrator" (Keillor) **40**:273
Jack Straw (Maugham) **11**:367-68; **15**:366
"Jack Stringer" (Nowlan) **15**:398
"Jack the Idiot Dunce" (Davies) **21**:101
Jack the Ripper (West)
See *The Women of Whitechapel and Jack the Ripper*
"Jack U Off" (Prince) **35**:324-26
Jack Winter's Dream (Baxter) **14**:64
"The Jackal-Headed Cowboy from Ra" (Reed) **13**:478
"The Jackdaw" (Hamburger) **5**:159
"The Jackdaw" (Hesse) **25**:259, 261-62
"A Jackeen Cries at the Loss of the Blaskets" (Behan) **79**:37, 51
"Jackhammer" (Dumas) **62**:155
Jackie Brown (Tarantino) **125**:373, 375-79, 383-84
"Jacklight" (Erdrich) **120**:184
Jacklight (Erdrich) **54**:164-65; **120**:132, 135, 137-38, 184
"Jacklighting" (Beattie) **146**:50
Jacklighting (Beattie) **146**:54, 85
Jacko the Great Intruder (Keneally) **117**:241-44
Jackpot: The Short Stories of Erskine Caldwell (Caldwell) **14**:96
"Jack's Girl" (Kadohata) **122**:195
"Jack's Straw Castle" (Gunn) **18**:201; **32**:209, 211
Jack's Straw Castle, and Other Poems (Gunn) **18**:199, 201-02; **32**:209, 211-12; **81**:178
Jackson Browne (Browne) **21**:34-5, 38

Jackson Pollock (Friedman) **7**:108
Jackson Pollock (O'Hara) **78**:375
"Jackstraws" (Ciardi) **129**:47
"The Jackstraws" (Fisher) **87**:131
"Jacob and the Angel" (Auden) **4**:35; **123**:7
Jacob Have I Loved (Paterson) **30**:283-85, 287-90
"Jacob: The Faith-Healing Priest" (Head) **67**:98
Jacob the Liar (Becker)
See *Jakob der Lügner*
Jacob Two-Two Meets the Hooded Fang (Richler) **5**:378
"Jacob y el otro" (Onetti) **10**:376
Jacobowsky and the Colonel (Behrman) **40**:88
The Jacob's Ladder (Levertov) **2**:242; **5**:246; **8**:345; **15**:336-37; **66**:235, 237-39, 253
"Jacob's Voice" (Celan)
See "Jakobs Stimme"
Jacob's Wake (Cook) **58**:154-55, 157-58
"Jacqueline Ess: Her Will and Testament" (Barker) **52**:51
"Jacquemard et Julia" (Char) **9**:165
Jacques and His Master (Kundera)
See *Jacques et son maitre: Hommage à Denis Diderot*
Jacques et son maitre: Hommage à Denis Diderot (Kundera) **68**:235, 264
Jacques; ou, La soumission (Ionesco) **4**:250-51; **6**:247-48, 253; **11**:290; **41**:222-23, 225, 230; **86**:332, 334, 340
"Jael" (Byatt) **136**:194
"Jael's Part" (Avison) **97**:91
Die Jagdgesellschaft (Bernhard) **32**:24-5; **61**:27-8
"Jäger des Spotts" (Lenz) **27**:245
"Jäger, mein Sternbild" (Sachs) **98**:330
The Jagged Orbit (Brunner) **8**:105-07, 110; **10**:78
Jagua Nana (Ekwensi) **4**:151-52
"The Jaguar" (Hughes) **14**:270
The Jaguar Smile (Rushdie) **59**:438
"Jah Live" (Marley) **17**:268
Jahrestage: Aus dem Leben von Gesine Cresspahl (Johnson) **40**:263
Jahrestage: Aus dem Leben von Gesine Cresspahl III (Johnson) **40**:269-70
Jahrestage: Aus dem Leben von Gesine Cresspahl IV (Johnson) **5**:201-02; **10**:284; **15**:307; **40**:263, 266-70
The Jail Diary of Albie Sachs (Edgar) **42**:114, 116, 120
"Jail Guitar Doors" (Clash) **30**:44-5
"Jail Poems" (Kaufman) **49**:204
Jailbird (Vonnegut) **22**:446-47, 449-51; **40**:441, 444-46; **111**:354-55, 358, 360-61
"The Jailer" (Plath) **9**:426; **14**:424; **51**:340, 345; **111**:166
"Jailer's Son" (Ferron) **94**:126
"Jailhouse Blues" (Guthrie) **35**:186
"Jailhouse Blues" (Randall) **135**:397
"The Jain Bird Hospital in Delhi" (Meredith) **55**:192
Jak daleko stad, jak blisko (Konwicki) **117**:257, 282-83
Jake and the Kid (Mitchell) **25**:322-23, 327-28
"Jake Bluffstein and Adolf Hitler" (Faust) **8**:215
Jake's Thing (Amis) **13**:14-15; **44**:135, 140, 144; **129**:5-6, 8, 16, 25
Jake's Women (Simon) **70**:238-40
Jakob der Lügner (Becker) **7**:27
Jakobowsky and the Colonel (Kazan) **63**:225
"Jakobs Stimme" (Celan) **53**:77
"À Jakobson" (Lacan) **75**:304
Jalamanta (Anaya) **148**:48-49
Jalna (de la Roche) **14**:148-49
La jalousie (Robbe-Grillet) **1**:286-90; **2**:374-75; **4**:446-50; **6**:464-66, 468; **10**:437; **14**:455-62; **43**:360, 364-66; **128**:326, 331-36, 341, 346-47, 349, 351, 353-54, 356, 359-60, 363, 364, 366 370, 376, 379, 382
Jalsaghar (Ray) **16**:476-77, 479-80, 482-83, 487, 491-93; **76**:360, 362, 367
Jamaica (Abrahams) **4**:2
"Jamaica Elevate" (Bennett) **28**:28
Jamaica Inn (du Maurier) **11**:162; **59**:280, 282-87
Jamaica Labrish (Bennett) **28**:27, 29-30
"Jamaica, Say You Will" (Browne) **21**:34-5
A Jamaican Airman Foresees His Death (D'Aguiar) **145**:124
"Jambalaya" (Berry) **17**:52
"James" (Joel) **26**:215
"James" (Simon) **26**:413
James and the Giant Peach (Dahl) **79**:177, 182
The James Bond Dossier (Amis) **2**:7, 10; **129**:18, 23
"James Dean" (Ai) **69**:18
"The James Dean Garage Band" (Moody) **147**:171, 183, 187
The James Dean Story (Altman) **16**:19, 41; **116**:11-12
James Joyce (Ellmann) **50**:305-06
"James Joyce, Marcel Duchamp, Erik Satie: An Alphabet" (Cage) **41**:85-6
The James Joyce Murder (Heilbrun) **25**:252
"James Pike, American" (Didion) **129**:78
"Jamesie" (Powers) **1**:282
Jamie Is My Heart's Desire (Chester) **49**:53-4, 56, 58
Jamie on a Flying Visit (Frayn) **7**:107
"Jamini Roy" (Ezekiel) **61**:91, 100
Jammin' the Greek Scene (Williams) **13**:600
"Jamming" (Marley) **17**:272
"Jamming with the Band at the VFW" (Bottoms) **53**:29-30
Jamming with the Band at the VFW (Bottoms) **53**:31
"Jamrag" (Lennon) **35**:265
"Jan. 6th" (Musgrave) **13**:400
Jan. 31 (Goldbarth) **5**:145; **38**:203
"Jan Godfrey" (Frame) **96**:185
Jana Aranya (Ray) **16**:495; **76**:358, 362, 367
Jane (Behrman) **40**:87-8
Jane and Prudence (Pym) **37**:368, 372-73, 379; **111**:229, 234, 243-48, 263-66, 269, 274, 279-81, 283-85
"Jane at Two" (Nowlan) **15**:399
Jane Eyre (Welles) **80**:379
Jane Franklin's Obsession (Berton) **104**:61
The Jane Poems (Spivack) **6**:520-21
"Jane, Steve, and Sarah" (Willingham) **51**:403
"Jane Witnesses the Destruction of the World" (Spivack) **6**:520
"Janek" (Dabrowska) **15**:165
"Janet Waking" (Ransom) **4**:431
A jangada de pedra (Saramago) **119**:153-54, 166-70
"Janice" (Cohen) **19**:113
"Janie Crawford" (Walker) **103**:371
"Janie Jones" (Clash) **30**:44-5
Janis Ian (Ian) **21**:184, 188
"Januaries" (Bishop) **13**:89
"January" (Barthelme) **59**:250
"January" (Chappell) **40**:142
"January" (Hass) **99**:140
"January 1918" (Pasternak) **63**:280
"January First" (Paz) **65**:187
"January Fugue" (Shapcott) **38**:404
The January Man (Shanley) **75**:325-27, 330
"January Oranges" (Brosman) **9**:135
"Janus" (Beattie) **63**:14, 16, 18; **146**:65, 85
Janus (Barker) **48**:10
Janus: A Summing Up (Koestler) **33**:242
"Japan" (Hecht) **8**:266-67; **19**:207
Japan and Her Ghosts (Gironella) **11**:237
"Japan First Time Around" (Snyder) **120**:346, 349-50
Japan, the Beautiful, and Myself (Kawabata) **107**:108
Japan, the Beautiful, and Myself (Kawabata) **107**:108
The Japanese Corpse (van de Wetering) **47**:406-07, 410
"Japanese in Warsaw" (Endō) **99**:301
"Japanese Jottings" (Aksyonov) **101**:17
"Japanese Movies" (Thesen) **56**:417
The Japanese of the Menam River (Endō) **99**:285
"Japanese Papers" (Sarton) **49**:307
"Japanese Print" (Clarke) **6**:112; **9**:168
"Japanese River Tales" (Hughes) **37**:179
"Japanese Tea Garden Golden Gate Park in Spring" (Whalen) **6**:566
"El jardín" (Borges)
See "El jardín de senderos que se bifurcan"
El jardín de al lado (Donoso) **32**:161; **99**:218, 220, 222-28, 233-38, 242-43, 245-49, 252-54, 274-77
"Jardin de France" (Senghor) **130**:266
"Jardín de invierno" (Neruda) **7**:261; **28**:310; **62**:333-35
"El jardín de senderos que se bifurcan" (Borges) **1**:39; **3**:80; **6**:93; **8**:102; **19**:54; **44**:362-63, 370; **48**:45-6; **83**:167
El jardín de senderos que se bifurcan (Borges) **48**:43; **83**:163-64
Le jardin des délices (Arrabal) **18**:21-2; **58**:17
Le jardin des délices (Carrier) **78**:65, 67-72, 79, 82
"Jardin du Palais Royal" (Gascoyne) **45**:159
Les jardins et les fleuves (Audiberti) **38**:33
The Jargoon Pard (Norton) **12**:469
Järn och människor (Lagerkvist) **54**:286
Jaro sbohem (Seifert) **93**:306, 332, 341
"Jasmine" (Mukherjee) **53**:270-71; **115**:364-65, 367-69
Jasmine (Mukherjee) **115**:365, 370, 373-75, 377-79, 386, 390-91
"Jason" (MacLeish) **8**:359
Jason and Medeia (Gardner) **3**:184-87; **5**:131, 133-35; **7**:115; **8**:236-238; **10**:219; **28**:167
Jason and the Money Tree (Levitin) **17**:265
Jason's Quest (Laurence) **3**:281; **50**:321
Jaune le soleil (Duras) **68**:94
"Jauregg" (Bernhard) **32**:27
"Javelina" (Harjo) **83**:274
"Javni" (Rao) **56**:312
Jawbreakers (Acorn) **15**:10
"Jaws" (Barthelme) **59**:251
Jaws (Benchley) **4**:53-4; **8**:82
Jaws (Spielberg) **20**:359-61, 363-66
Jazz (Morrison) **81**:241-48, 250, 252-62, 268, 270, 272
"A Jazz Age Clerk" (Farrell) **66**:131
Jazz Country (Hentoff) **26**:182, 184
"Jazz Fantazia" (Sandburg) **35**:358
Jazz Is (Hentoff) **26**:185
The Jazz Singer (Diamond) **30**:113-14
"Jazzonia" (Hughes) **108**:296
Jazz-set (Milner) **56**:225
Je l'entends encore (Cayrol) **11**:108
Je me souviens (Perec) **116**:241
"Je suis perdu" (Taylor) **18**:526
"Je Suis Une Table" (Hall) **151**:195
"Je t'adore" (Kinsella) **138**:90, 132
Je t'aime! (Simenon) **47**:374
Je t'aime, Je t'aime (Resnais) **16**:510-12
The Jealous God (Braine) **1**:43; **41**:57, 60
"Jealous Guy" (Lennon) **35**:263-65, 267, 274
"Jealous Twin" (Carroll) **35**:80-1
"Jealousy" (Williams) **148**:351
Jealousy (Robbe-Grillet)
See *La jalousie*
Jean Baudrillard: Selected Writings (Baudrillard) **60**:29, 33, 38-9
"Jean Beicke" (Williams) **42**:458
"Jean Harlow's Wedding Night" (Wasserstein) **90**:429
Jean le bleu (Giono) **4**:184; **11**:233
Jean Rhys: The Collected Short Stories (Rhys) **51**:375
Jean Rhys: The Complete Novels (Rhys) **51**:367
"Jeanne d'Arc" (Smith) **12**:535, 541
"La Jeannette" (Theriault) **79**:410
"Jean's TV" (Carver) **55**:276
Jeeves and the Tie That Binds (Wodehouse)

2:480-81; **5**:515
Los jefes (Vargas Llosa) **15**:550
Jefferson and/or Mussolini (Pound) **112**:315, 338
Jefferson in Paris (Jhabvala) **138**:73-4
The Jeffersons (Lear) **12**:331-32, 336
"Jeffrey, Believe Me" (Smiley) **53**:348
"Jeffty Is Five" (Ellison) **42**:129-30
"Jelängerjelieber Vergiβnichtmein" (Hein) **154**:166
J-E-L-L-O (Baraka) **5**:46
"A Jellyfish" (Moore) **8**:401
JEM: The Making of Utopia (Pohl) **18**:412-13
Jemima Shore's First Case (Fraser) **107**:50
"Jen jedno jsem spatřil..." (Seifert) **93**:343
Jennifer (Sherburne) **30**:361
"Jenny" (Davison) **28**:100
Jenny Kimura (Cavanna) **12**:100-02
Jenseits der Liebe (Walser) **27**:463, 466
"Jeopardy" (Dorris) **109**:308
"The Jerboa" (Moore) **2**:291; **4**:362; **8**:399; **10**:351; **47**:260, 265
Jeremiah (John Paul II) **128**:163-64, 168
Jeremy's Version (Purdy) **2**:350; **10**:421, 424; **28**:381; **52**:342-43, 347-48
"Jericho" (Ai) **69**:7
"Jericho" (Dickey) **7**:86
Jericho Road (Kogawa) **78**:181; **129**:300
Jericho Sleep Alone (Bermant) **40**:89-90
"Jericho's Brick Battlements" (Laurence) **62**:282
The Jerk (Martin) **30**:249, 251-52
The Jero Plays (Soyinka) **5**:398; **44**:286
"Jerome" (Fair) **18**:139, 141
"Jerome" (Jarrell) **13**:302-03
"Jeronimo" (Bishop) **9**:97
Jero's Metamorphosis (Soyinka) **44**:287-88
The Jersey Shore (Mayne) **12**:401-02
"Jerusalem" (Silkin) **43**:401
"Jerusalem 1967" (Amichai) **57**:39, 44
"Jerusalem Address" (Kundera) **115**:321, 324
Jerusalem Daybook (Baxter) **14**:66
"Jerusalem Prize Acceptance Speech" (Coetzee) **117**:89-90, 92
Jerusalem Sonnets (Baxter) **14**:66
Jerusalem Syndrome (Sobol) **60**:385-86
Jerusalem the Golden (Drabble) **2**:118; **3**:128; **5**:117; **10**:165; **22**:121; **53**:121; **129**:111, 117
"Jerusalem's Lot" (King) **26**:237
Jeruzalemski dijalog (Krleža) **114**:169
"Jesse" (Douglas) **73**:66-7, 73, 81
"Jesse" (Simon) **26**:413
"Jesse and Meribeth" (Munro) **50**:208-09, 211, 217-18, 221
The Jesse James Poems (Jiles) **58**:281-82
"Jesse Younger" (Kristofferson) **26**:268
Jessica (Campbell) **85**:4, 19-23, 26-7
Jessica Fayer (L'Heureux) **52**:278
"Jessica Kelley" (Hersey) **81**:329
A Jest of God (Laurence) **3**:278-81; **13**:341; **50**:311-17, 319, 321; **62**:269-71, 273, 279-81, 284-85, 289-91, 294-95, 306
Jestina's Calypso (Lovelace) **51**:271
Jesting Pilate (Huxley) **3**:255
"Jesuit Graves" (Wright) **119**:186, 188
"Jesus and Isolt" (Pinsky) **94**:306, 308, 310; **121**:446
"The Jesus Apparition" (Redgrove) **41**:352
Jesus, Break His Fall (Durcan) **43**:113
"Jesus Children of America" (Wonder) **12**:657
"Jesus Christ's Half-Brother Is Alive and Well on the Spokane Indian Reservation" (Alexie) **96**:5; **154**:6-7
Jesus Christ—Superstar (Rice and Webber) **21**:422-33
The Jesus Incident (Herbert) **23**:219; **35**:204-05, 209-10; **44**:393-94
"Jesus Is Easy" (Mull) **17**:299
The Jesus Myth (Greeley) **28**:170
Jesus on Mars (Farmer) **19**:168
"The Jesus Papers" (Sexton) **6**:491; **53**:321-23; **123**:420
"Jesus Suckles" (Sexton) **53**:322
Jesus Tales (Linney) **51**:260
Jesus Was a Capricorn (Kristofferson) **26**:268
"jesze próba" (Rozewicz) **139**:295
"Jet" (McCartney) **35**:282, 284, 289
"Jet Plane/Dhla-nuwa" (Allen) **84**:5
"Jet Stream: Betsy, 1980" (McNally) **82**:262
"Jets from Orange" (Ghose) **42**:178
Jets from Orange (Ghose) **42**:178-79
La Jeu avec Le feu (Robbe-Grillet) **128**:363
Le jeu du souterrain (Mallet-Joris) **11**:356
"La jeune fille" (Carrier) **78**:60
"La jeune fille et la mort" (Tournier) **23**:452
Le Jeune née (Cixous)
See *Newly Born Woman*
Les jeunes filles (Montherlant) **8**:393; **19**:322-23, 325, 328
Jeunesse (Green) **77**:273-74, 277-78, 281
Jeux de massacre (Ionesco) **86**:341
Les jeux incompris (Carrier) **78**:65
"Jew" (Abse) **29**:15
The Jew as Pariah (Arendt) **98**:27
"The Jew from Babylon" (Singer) **69**:310-11
A Jew in Love (Hecht) **8**:270
"A Jew of Persia" (Helprin) **7**:152; **10**:260
A Jew Today (Wiesel) **37**:450-51
"The Jewbird" (Malamud) **18**:317-19; **27**:298, 300; **44**:413, 417, 420; **85**:217
"The Jewel" (Moure) **88**:231
"A Jewel Box" (McFadden) **48**:251
The Jewel in the Crown (Scott)
See *The Raj Quartet*
The Jewel in the Skull (Moorcock) **58**:349
"Jewel Lotus Harp" (Broumas) **73**:9
"The Jewel of Amitaba" (Kotzwinkle) **35**:254
"The Jewel Stair's Grievance" (Pound) **10**:400
The Jeweler's Shop (John Paul II)
See *Sklep Jubüerski*
The Jewel-Hinged Jaw: Notes on the Language of Science Fiction (Delany) **14**:147; **38**:159; **141**:113, 145, 149-50
"The Jewels" (Clarke) **9**:168
The Jewels of Aptor (Delany) **141**:143, 149, 153, 155
"The Jewels of the Cabots" (Cheever) **7**:49; **11**:122
The Jewish Americans: A History in Their Own Words (Meltzer) **26**:308
"The Jewish Blues" (Roth) **66**:386, 389
"The Jewish Cemetery" (Kaufman) **8**:317
"A Jewish Cemetery by Leningrad" (Brodsky) **50**:120
"Jewish Graveyards, Italy" (Levine) **118**:285, 294
"The Jewish Hunter" (Moore) **68**:298, 300
"A Jewish Patient Begins His Analysis" (Roth) **66**:386, 407
"Jewish Princess" (Zappa) **17**:592-93
"The Jewish Refugee" (Malamud)
See "The German Refugee"
The Jews (Fast) **131**:86
"The Jews and Contemporary Literature" (de Man)
See "Les Juifs dans la littérature actuelle"
"Jews at Haifa" (Jarrell) **6**:261
"Jews in Contemporary Literature" (de Man)
See "Les Juifs dans la littérature actuelle"
"Jews in Present-Day Literature" (de Man)
See "Les Juifs dans la littérature actuelle"
"Jews in Today's Literature" (de Man)
See "Les Juifs dans la littérature actuelle"
The Jews of Silence: A Personal Report on Soviet Jewry (Wiesel)
See *Les Juifs du silence*
Jézabel (Anouilh) **13**:19; **40**:51, 55
JFK (Stone) **73**:384-86
JFK and LBJ (Wicker) **7**:533
A Jig for the Gypsy (Davies) **42**:104
The Jig of Forslin: A Symphony (Aiken) **52**:20-1, 27-8
Jiggery-Pokery (Hollander) **2**:197
Jig-Saw (Powell) **66**:368-69
"Jigsaw Puzzle" (Jagger and Richard) **17**:223, 241
Jihad vs. McWorld (Barber) **141**:14-15, 17, 19, 21-2, 25-6
Jill (Larkin) **5**:223-24, 229; **8**:333, 337-39; **9**:323-24; **13**:335, 337-38; **33**:262-66; **39**:334, 336, 340, 346-48; **64**:260, 280
Jill the Reckless (Wodehouse) **10**:538
"The Jilting of Granny Weatherall" (Porter) **7**:315; **101**:209, 212, 224, 244, 248, 253
"Jim Crow's Funeral" (Hughes) **108**:284
Jim Crow's Last Stand (Hughes) **108**:283
Jim Dandy: Fat Man in a Famine (Saroyan) **8**:467; **56**:376
"Jim Dean of Indiana" (Ochs) **17**:332
"Jim O'Neill" (Farrell) **66**:129-30
"Jimble" (Prichard) **46**:345
Jimmie Higgins (Sinclair) **15**:502; **63**:346, 349
"Jimmy Jazz" (Clash) **30**:46-7
Jimmy the Kid (Westlake) **33**:437, 440
"Jimmy's Chicky-Run" (Phillips) **28**:363
"Jingle" (Cohen) **38**:131
"Jinx" (Dickinson) **49**:102-03
Jitney (Wilson) **63**:454; **118**:372
Jitterbug Perfume (Robbins) **32**:373-74; **64**:377, 381-82, 384
"Jiving" (Dove) **81**:144
Jo Stern (Slavitt) **14**:491
"Joal" (Senghor) **54**:401, 409;
Joan Armatrading (Armatrading) **17**:7-8, 10
"Joan Didion: Only Disconnect" (Harrison) **144**:107
Joan Makes History (Grenville) **61**:156, 159-60, 167
Joan Miró (Cabral de Melo Neto) **76**:168
Joanna's Husband and David's Wife (Hailey) **40**:223-24
Joanna's Luck (Jones) **52**:254-55
"The Job" (Stafford) **7**:460
The Job (Burroughs) **75**:107-08, 111-13, 115
Job (John Paul II) **128**:163, 168
"Job 1957" (Rozewicz) **139**:236, 290
Job: A Comedy of Justice (Heinlein) **55**:303
Jobber Skald (Powys)
See *Weymouth Sands*
Job's Comforting (Richards) **14**:453
"Job's Discount" (Porter) **33**:319
Jobs in Fine Arts and Humanities (Berger) **12**:40
"Job's New Children" (Stanton) **9**:508
Job's Year (Hansen) **38**:239-40
"The Jockey" (McCullers) **12**:433; **100**:246
"Jody and the Kid" (Kristofferson) **26**:267, 270
"Jody Girl" (Seger) **35**:380-81, 383
Joe (Brown) **73**:24-8
"Joe and Pete" (Gellhorn) **60**:178
Joe Gould's Secret (Mitchell) **98**:168-70, 172-73, 175, 177, 180-81, 183, 187
Joe Hill: A Biographical Novel (Stegner)
See *The Preacher and the Slave*
Joe Louis Uncovers Dynamite (Wright) **14**:596
"Joe the Lion" (Bowie) **17**:66
"Joe the Painter and the Deer Island Massacre" (King) **89**:76-78
Joe Turner's Come and Gone (Wilson) **50**:268; **63**:447-48, 450-54, 456, 458; **118**:372-79, 384-85, 388, 390, 394, 401, 403-04, 406-07, 410, 412-15
Joe Versus the Volcano (Shanley) **75**:329-32
Joe's Ark (Potter) **86**:353; **123**:235
Joe's Bed-Stuy Barbershop: We Cut Heads (Lee) **105**:85, 102
Joe's Garage, Act I (Zappa) **17**:593-95
Joe's Garage, Act II (Zappa) **17**:594-95
Joe's Garage, Act III (Zappa) **17**:594-95
"Joey the Midget" (Soto) **32**:403
"Johann Joachim Quantz's Five Lessons" (Graham) **29**:196
"Johanna" (Sondheim) **30**:394, 398
John A.--Himself! (Findley) **102**:105
John and Mary (Jones) **52**:243, 245, 253

John Aubrey and His Friends (Powell) **7**:343; **31**:317
"John Aubrey's Antique Shop" (Szirtes) **46**:394
John Barry (Fearing) **51**:113
"John Billy" (Wallace) **114**:347, 349
"John Brown" (Hayden) **37**:158
John Brown (Du Bois) **64**:103
"John Cat" (Kinsella) **27**:236
"John Chapman" (Oliver) **98**:256, 258, 260
"John Chrysostom" (Wilbur) **110**:386
John Deth: A Metaphysical Legend and Other Poems (Aiken) **52**:20, 22, 26
John Dollar (Wiggins) **57**:436-41
"John Dos Passos and the Whole Truth" (Schwartz) **10**:462-63
"John Dryden" (Carruth) **84**:135
"John Duffy's Brother" (O'Brien) **7**:270
John Ford (Sinclair) **14**:489
"John John" (Arghezi) **80**:9
"John Keats, Surgeon" (Belitt) **22**:52
"John Knox" (Smith) **64**:397
John Lennon/Plastic Ono Band (Lennon) **12**:366, 380; **35**:261-62, 264-68, 271, 273-74
"John Marin" (Jones) **10**:285
"John Marston Advises Anger" (Porter) **33**:318, 322, 325
"John Maydew; or, The Allotment" (Tomlinson) **13**:549-50
"John Milton and My Father" (Beer) **58**:36
"John Napper Sailing through the Universe" (Gardner) **5**:133; **7**:111, 116
"The John O'Groats Theory" (Reading) **47**:350
John, Paul, George, Ringo, and Bert (Russell) **60**:319-20
"John Quixote" (MacCaig) **36**:282
"John Redding Goes to Sea" (Hurston) **7**:172; **30**:218
"John Sinclair" (Lennon) **35**:264
John Steinbeck (Parini) **133**:262-63, 265, 274, 283-85
"John the Baptist" (Simpson) **7**:427
"John Wayne's Teeth" (Alexie) **154**:40, 43
John Wesley Harding (Dylan) **4**:148; **6**:155, 158; **12**:185, 190, 199; **77**:169
"Johnnie Brewer" (Warner) **7**:512
Johnnie Cross (White) **49**:409-10
Johnno (Malouf) **28**:265, 267
"Johnny B. Goode" (Berry) **17**:54
"Johnny Bear" (Steinbeck)
See "The Ears of Johnny Bear"
"Johnny Carson" (Wilson) **12**:651-52
Johnny Crackle Sings (Cohen) **19**:111
Johnny Got His Gun (Trumbo) **19**:444-48
Johnny, I Hardly Knew You (O'Brien) **13**:415; **36**:337-38; **116**:185, 189, 191-92, 194
Johnny Johnson (Green) **25**:195, 198
Johnny Mangano and His Astonishing Dogs (Tremblay) **102**:365-66
"Johnny Mnemonic" (Gibson) **39**:139, 143; **63**:129, 134, 139
"Johnny on the Spot" (Woolrich) **77**:402
"Johnny Panic and the Bible of Dreams" (Plath) **11**:450-51; **17**:364; **111**:184, 212-13
Johnny Panic and the Bible of Dreams (Plath) **3**:390; **11**:450-51; **17**:364; **111**:179
"Johnny Spain's White Heifer" (Carruth) **84**:135
"Johnny Thomas" (Brown) **59**:262
Johnny Tremain (Forbes) **12**:207, 210-11
"Johnny Was" (Marley) **17**:269, 272
"John's Mysteries" (Stern) **100**:341-43
"Johnson as Critic and Poet" (Eliot) **24**:172, 178
"The Johnson Girls" (Bambara) **19**:33; **88**:21, 49
Johnson over Jordan (Priestley) **2**:347
"Johnson's Cabinet Watched by Ants" (Bly) **5**:64; **128**:29, 31
Joie de vivre (Rattigan) **7**:355
"Join Together with the Band" (Townshend) **17**:531
"Joke" (Dixon) **52**:100
"The Joke" (Singer) **3**:454
The Joke (Kundera)
See *Žert*
The Joker of Seville (Walcott) **25**:455; **67**:347, 350, 352; **76**:275
"Jokerman" (Dylan) **77**:179
"The Joker's Greatest Triumph" (Barthelme) **115**:65, 76
Jokes to Mislead the Police (Parra) **102**:347, 356
Joking Apart (Ayckbourn) **18**:30; **33**:44, 47-9
"Jokund ile Si-Ya-U" (Hikmet) **40**:245, 249-51
Jolis deuils, petites tragédies pour adultes (Carrier) **78**:46, 51, 59-60, 63, 65, 67
"Jonah" (Phillips) **28**:363
Jonah (Porter) **5**:347
Jonah: Christmas 1917 (Huxley) **11**:282-83
The Jonah Man (Carlisle) **33**:104-05
Jonah's Gourd Vine (Hurston) **7**:170-71; **30**:208-11, 215, 226-27; **61**:270
"Jonas ou l'artiste au travail" (Camus) **9**:144; **14**:114
Jonathan (Chedid) **47**:84-5
"Jonathan Edwards in Western Massachusettes" (Lowell) **8**:351
"Jonathan Livingston Seagull" (Diamond) **30**:113
Jonathan Livingston Seagull (Bach) **14**:35-6
Jonathan Livingston Seagull (Diamond) **30**:114
"Jonathan Sitting in Mud" (Giovanni) **117**:205
Jonathan Troy (Abbey) **36**:14
"Jonathan's Song" (Dodson) **79**:194
Jones (Humphreys) **47**:189
Jonica (Hart) **66**:176
"Jonna" (Haines) **58**:218
Jonoah and the Green Stone (Dumas) **62**:156-57, 159, 164
"Jools and Jim" (Townshend) **17**:541-42
Jordan County: A Landscape in Narrative (Foote) **75**:230-32, 239, 254, 257
The Jordans (Millin) **49**:239, 246
"Jorinda and Jorindel" (Gallant) **38**:190-91, 193-94
"La jornada" (Poniatowska) **140**:322
"Jornada de la soltera" (Castellanos) **66**:52
"José Ortega y Gasset" (Paz) **51**:332
"Josefina, Take Good Care of the Señores" (Cabrera Infante) **120**:73
"Joseph" (Forché) **25**:172; **83**:210
"Joseph" (Soyinka) **36**:415-17; **44**:285
Joseph (Jones) **52**:244-46
Joseph (Rathbone) **41**:340-42
"Joseph and His Brother" (Thomas) **37**:416; **107**:316, 318
Joseph and the Amazing Technicolor Dreamcoat (Rice and Webber) **21**:423, 427-28, 430
Joseph Banks: A Life (O'Brian) **152**:262, 264, 273
Joseph Conrad and the Fiction of Autobiography (Said) **123**:357
"Joseph Haydn and Captain Bligh" (MacLennan) **92**:342-43
Joseph Pasquier's Passion (Duhamel)
See *La passion de Joseph Pasquier*
"Joseph Pockets" (Stern) **40**:411
Josephine Herbst: The Story She Could Never Tell (Langer) **34**:448, 450-51, 453-54
"Jose's Country" (Winters) **32**:469
"Joshua" (Grau) **146**:126-27
Joshua Then and Now (Richler) **18**:452-56; **70**:219, 231
"Joshua Tree" (Ammons) **108**:21
"Josie" (Becker and Fagen) **26**:84
"Jottings of a Writer" (Olesha) **8**:430
Un joualonais, sa joualonie (Blais) **6**:80-2
"Un jour" (Michaux) **8**:390
Le jour (Wiesel) **3**:529; **5**:491
Le jour est noir (Blais) **6**:82; **13**:96; **22**:57-8
"Le jour où je devins un apostat" (Carrier) **78**:71
"Le jour qui fut" (Hébert) **29**:237
"Journal" (Pinget) **37**:364-65
"The Journal" (Shields) **113**:425
Journal (Green) **77**:273, 275, 283-84
Journal (Mauriac) **56**:210, 212
Journal, 1928-1958 (Green) **3**:204-05
Journal, 1936-1937 (Gascoyne) **45**:157-58
"Journal, August, 1968" (Blackburn) **9**:100
Journal du voleur (Genet) **5**:138; **14**:202; **44**:386-88, 390; **46**:175-76, 178, 182
Journal du voyageur (Green) **77**:284-85
Journal d'un contre-révolutionnaire (Kohout) **13**:323
Journal d'un curé de campagne (Bresson) **16**:103-04, 107-18
Le journal d'une femme de chambre (Bunuel) **16**:141, 148; **80**:47, 57
Journal en miettes (Ionesco) **41**:227-28; **86**:335, 340
"Journal for My Daughter" (Kunitz) **148**:84, 89, 100, 103, 149
Journal from Ellipsia (Calisher) **38**:71; **134**:13, 15, 18, 34, 36, 39, 41
"A Journal from France" (Clarke) **61**:78
Journal intime (Brossard) **115**:121
"Journal, June, 1971" (Blackburn) **9**:100
"Journal Night Thoughts" (Ginsberg) **36**:184; **109**:345
Journal/Nocturnal (Broner) **19**:70-1
Journal of a Living Experiment (Lopate) **29**:300
Journal of a Novel (Steinbeck) **124**:389
"Journal of a Poet" (Bogan) **93**:74
Journal of a Solitude (Sarton) **4**:471; **49**:317-18; **91**:247-48, 250-52
The Journal of Albion Moonlight (Patchen) **2**:332; **18**:391-94
"Journal of an Airman" (Auden) **11**:18; **14**:32
The Journal of Arthur Stirling (Sinclair) **63**:345, 347-48
"A Journal of English Days" (Wright) **146**:318-19, 329, 334-35, 364-65
The Journal of John Cardan (Cunningham) **31**:103
"A Journal of Southern Rivers" (Wright) **146**:338
Journal of the Fictive Life (Nemerov) **2**:307-08; **36**:304
"Journal of the Year of the Ox" (Wright) **146**:318-19, 328, 330, 334-35, 337-38, 340, 342, 358, 364
"A Journal of Three Questions" (Wright) **146**:338
"A Journal of True Confessions" (Wright) **146**:318-19, 321, 334, 336, 340
Journal sans date (Jouve) **47**:209
"The Journalist" (Ai) **69**:9-10, 17
The Journalists (Wesker) **3**:519-20; **42**:426-30
The Journals (Blackburn) **9**:99-100; **43**:65-6, 68
Journals (Wright) **146**:
Journals, 1939-1983 (Spender) **91**:264
Journals and Dreams (Waldman) **7**:509
Journals: Early Fifties, Early Sixties (Ginsberg) **13**:241; **36**:185-86; **69**:219; **109**:348, 351
Journals Mid-Fifties (1954-1958) (Ginsberg) **109**:350-51
The Journals of Susanna Moodie (Atwood) **3**:20; **8**:29-30, 32; **13**:42; **15**:37; **25**:63-4, 67-8; **84**:51, 62, 68, 97
The Journals of Sylvia Plath (Plath) **50**:448; **51**:347, 349-53; **111**:200
The Journals of Thornton Wilder, 1939-1961 (Wilder) **82**:377, 379, 380
"The Journey" (Abse) **29**:12
"The Journey" (Boland) **67**:36, 40, 42, 45-6; **113**:82, 84-5, 92, 94, 98, 110, 124
"Journey" (Clarke) **61**:73
"Journey" (Cook-Lynn) **93**:123
"A Journey" (Gordimer) **70**:177-78, 180
"Journey" (Grace) **56**:117, 119, 120, 123
"A Journey" (O'Brien) **5**:311; **8**:429
"The Journey" (Oliver) **98**:260

"The Journey" (Porter) **13**:451; **15**:429
"Journey" (Scott) **22**:373
"The Journey" (Thomas) **13**:544
"The Journey" (Thomas) **13**:542; **132**:381
"Journey" (Transtroemer) **65**:223
"The Journey" (Wright) **53**:428
Journey (Michener) **60**:261-62; **109**:376, 381
The Journey (Winters) **32**:469
The Journey, and Other Poems (Boland) **67**:36, 39, 45; **113**:69, 72-4, 77, 82, 84, 86-7, 94, 98, 108-09, 124
"Journey around My Room" (Bogan) **46**:88; **93**:103
Journey around My Room: The Autobiography of Louise Bogan, A Mosaic (Bogan) **39**:388-89, 391, 393-94; **46**:88; **93**:61, 73, 75-7, 88, 99
"Journey Back to the Source" (Carpentier) See "Viaje a la semilla"
"Journey beyond the Hills" (Still) **49**:363
"Journey by Air" (White) **49**:407
"A Journey by Night" (Warner) **19**:460
Journey Continued (Paton) **55**:311, 314; **106**:305-06
"The Journey East" (Livesay) **79**:338
The Journey Home (Abbey) **36**:14, 19; **59**:238, 241-42, 245
"A Journey in Love" (Shapcott) **38**:398, 400
Journey into Autumn (Bergman) See *Kvinnodröm*
Journey into Dustlessness (Sachs) **98**:326
Journey into Fear (Ambler) **6**:4; **9**:19, 21
Journey into Fear (Welles) **20**:444, 449
"A Journey into Speech" (Cliff) **120**:111, 119
Journey into the Beyond (Sachs) See *Fahrt ins Staublose*
"A Journey Into the Mind of Watts" (Pynchon) **123**:318, 325
"A Journey into the Mind of Watts" (Pynchon) **33**:334-35; **72**:332, 335
"Journey into the Night" (Lind) **82**:130
Journey into the Whirlwind (Ginzburg) **59**:384
Journey Inward (George) **35**:179
"The Journey of a Lifetime" (Carey) **96**:25, 38
"The Journey of a Poem Compared to All the Sad Variety of Travel" (Schwartz) **45**:355
The Journey of August King (Ehle) **27**:104-05
The Journey of Ibn Fattouma (Mahfouz) See *Rihlat Ibn Fattuma*
The Journey of Tai-me (Momaday) **85**:276
The Journey of the Fifth Horse (Ribman) **7**:357-58
"Journey of the Magi" (Eliot) **10**:168; **15**:217; **41**:151-52; **55**:374
Journey through Dark Night (Shiga) **33**:363-68
"Journey through the Past" (Young) **17**:582
Journey through the Past (Young) **17**:571, 574
Journey to a Known Place (Carruth) **4**:93
Journey to a War (Auden) **3**:25; **14**:26; **43**:18, 28; **123**:48
Journey to a War (Isherwood) **14**:278-79, 282; **44**:397-98
Journey to America (Levitin) **17**:263-64
Journey to Chaos: Samuel Beckett's Early Fiction (Federman) **47**:118-19, 129
Journey to Ithaca (Desai) **97**:189-90, 192
Journey to Ixtlan (Castaneda) **12**:88-9, 92, 95
"Journey to Love" (McFadden) **48**:256
Journey to Love (Williams) **22**:465; **42**:451, 463
"Journey to Nine Miles" (Walker) **58**:409
Journey to Nowhere: A New World Tragedy (Naipaul) See *Black and White*
"Journey to Nuremburg" (Hesse) **2**:191
Journey to Space (Nwapa) **133**:229
Journey to the Alcarria (Cela) See *Viaje a la Alcarria*
"The Journey to the Dead" (Updike) **139**:369
Journey to the East (Hesse) See *Die Morgenlandfahrt*
Journey to the End of the Night (Céline) See *Voyage au bout de la nuit*
"Journey to the Forks" (Still) **49**:364
"The Journey to the Interior" (Atwood) **8**:33
"Journey to the Interior" (Roethke) **8**:458; **19**:396; **101**:289, 306-07, 314-16, 319, 330
A Journey to the Interior (Newby) **2**:310; **13**:411
A Journey to the Rivers (Handke) See *Eine winterliche Reise*
"Journey to the Sacred Mountains" (Kunene) **85**:176-77
"Journey to the Sahel" (Cabral de Melo Neto) See "Viagem ao Sahel"
"A Journey to the Seven Streams" (Kiely) **23**:266; **43**:241
A Journey to the Seven Streams: Seventeen Stories (Kiely) **43**:239, 244
"Journey with Anita" (Fellini) **85**:64
The Journey with Jonah (L'Engle) **12**:347-48
Journey with My Selves: A Memoir, 1909-1963 (Livesay) **79**:354-55
Journey without Maps (Greene) **1**:134; **70**:293; **72**:149-50, 152, 161; **125**:198
Journeying and the Returns (Nichol) **18**:366, 368-69
Journeyman (Caldwell) **8**:122; **50**:299-300, 303; **60**:46-7, 49, 54, 64
"Journeys" (Prokosch) **48**:306
"Journeys" (Snyder) **120**:321
Journeys among the Dead (Ionesco) See *Voyages chez les morts: Thèmes et variations*
"Journeys and Faces" (Abse) **29**:14
Journeys between Wars (Dos Passos) **25**:137
Journey's End (Neruda) See *El fin del viaje*
Journey's End (O'Casey) **11**:407
Journeys to the Other Side (Le Clézio) **31**:249
Jours effeuillés: Poémes, essais, souvenirs, 1920-1965 (Arp) **5**:33
"Jóvenes" (Parra) **102**:343
"Joy" (Ashbery) **125**:30
"Joy" (Enzensberger) **43**:144-45
"Joy" (Gaye) **26**:135
"Joy" (Hughes) **108**:332
"Joy" (Moore) **68**:299-301
"Joy" (Rosenthal) **28**:395
"Joy" (Singer) **6**:508; **11**:502
"Joy" (Warren) **13**:577
Joy (Hunt) **70**:65-8
"Joy and Margaret" (Blunden) **56**:46-7
Joy in the Morning (Smith) **19**:424
"Joy inside My Tears" (Wonder) **12**:662
The Joy Luck Club (Tan) **59**:89-99; **120**:362-69, 371-73, 375-78, 380-85, 399-413, 415-18, 422; **151**:294-352
The Joy of Gay Sex (White) **27**:480; **110**:321, 323, 329
The Joy of Sex (Comfort) **7**:54
"The Joy of the Job" (Ferber) **93**:140, 142
"The Joy of the Just" (Gardner) **28**:162-63
Joy of the Worm (Sargeson) **31**:366-67, 374
"Joy Road and Livernois" (Piercy) **128**:273
"Joy-Bells" (Sassoon) **130**:183, 222
"Joyce" (Gilchrist) **143**:300, 329
"Joyce and Nationalism" (Deane) **122**:75-6
"Joyce and the Modern Novel" (Wilder) **82**:356, 359
"The Joycelin Schranger Story" (Disch) **7**:87
"Jóyenes alemanes" (Neruda) **62**:326
"The Joyful Black Demon of Sister Clara Flies through the Midnight Woods on Her Snowmobile" (Wakoski) **4**:573
"Joyful Mystery" (Castellanos) **66**:60
Joyful Noise: The New Testament Revisited (Moody) **147**:179, 184-85, 188
"Joyous Sound" (Morrison) **21**:237
Joyride (Cavanna) **12**:101
"The Joys of Being a Business Man" (Fearing) **51**:111
"The Joys of Gay Life" (White) **110**:335
The Joys of Motherhood (Emecheta) **14**:160; **48**:97, 99-101; **65**:329-33; **128**:54-5, 58-61, 64, 66-8, 74, 78, 83-6
Joysprick: An Introduction to the Language of James Joyce (Burgess) **4**:83
"József" (Murray) **40**:337
"J's Marriage" (Coover) **15**:145
"J's Wife" (Coover) **7**:58
"Juan" (Graves) **45**:166
Juan Bobo and the Lady of the Occident (Marqués) See *Juan Bobo y la dama de occidente*
Juan Bobo y la dama de occidente (Marqués) **96**:225
"Juan in Limbo" (Scannell) **49**:332
"Juan Muraña" (Borges) **2**:77; **10**:67
Juan sin tierra (Goytisolo) **10**:245; **23**:185, 187-88; **133**:25, 32, 44, 46-47, 57, 61-68, 72-73, 85, 95
Juan the Landless (Goytisolo) See *Juan sin tierra*
"Juanina Million" (Castillo) **151**:45
"Juan's Song" (Bogan) **4**:68; **46**:81
Jubal Sackett (L'Amour) **55**:306-08
Jubb (Waterhouse) **47**:418, 421
Jubiabá (Amado) **13**:11; **40**:25-7, 34, 36; **106**:57-8, 62-3, 71
"Jubilare" (Moure) **88**:227, 229
"Jubilate Matteo" (Ewart) **46**:151
Jubilee (Hart) **66**:176, 182
Jubilee Blues (Davies) **23**:145
"Jubilee Hymn" (Betjeman) **34**:308
Judah the Pious (Prose) **45**:322-24
"Judaism and Harold Bloom" (Ozick) **62**:349-51
Judaism: Between Yesterday and Tomorrow (Kung) **130**:147, 149, 151, 167, 169
"Judas" (Brunner) **8**:107
"Judas" (Chappell) **40**:141-42
"Judas" (O'Connor) **14**:399; **23**:332
The Judas Boy (Raven) **14**:441
The Judas Cloth (O'Faolain) **108**:423-24
Judas Eye (Breytenbach) **126**:94, 102
"The Judas Goat" (Musgrave) **54**:334
The Judas Goat (Parker) **27**:364, 366-67
"Judas Iscariot" (Spender) **10**:487
The Judas Kiss (Hare) **136**:300-02
Judas, My Brother (Yerby) **22**:489
The Judas Tree (Cronin) **32**:139
The Judas Window (Carr) **3**:101
The Judge (Mortimer) **28**:285-86
The Judge (West) **7**:525; **31**:451, 457; **50**:395, 398, 408
The Judge and His Hangman (Duerrenmatt) **102**:83
The Judge and His Hangman (Dürrenmatt) See *Der Richter und sein Henker*
"The Judge and Other Snakes" (Dubus) **97**:234
"The Judge Is Fury" (Cunningham) **31**:97, 100, 102
"Judge Not" (Roethke) **46**:356
"The Judgement" (Lind) **82**:128, 130
"Judgement Day" (O'Connor) **1**:257; **3**:366; **6**:382; **21**:268, 277, 279; **104**:103, 108, 115, 135, 160, 178, 187-88, 190, 198
Judgement Day (Lively) **32**:274-75
A Judgement in Stone (Rendell) **28**:385; **48**:320-21
The Judgement of Deke Hunter (Higgins) **10**:273-74
"The Judgement of Paris" (Merwin) **88**:205
"The Judge's Wife" (Allende) **97**:3, 33, 35
"The Judgment" (Akhmatova) **64**:12
"Judgment Day" (Hughes) **108**:297
Judgment Day (Farrell) **1**:98; **4**:157; **66**:112, 120, 127
Judgment Day (Rice) **7**:360-61; **49**:299-300, 302-03, 305
The Judgment of Paris (Vidal) **2**:448-49; **6**:549; **22**:434; **142**:322, 327
Judgment on Deltchev (Ambler) **6**:3; **9**:18
Judgment on Janus (Norton) **12**:457, 461, 469

"Judith" (Smith) **12**:535, 540
Judith (Abell) **15**:1, 5
Judith (Mosley) **43**:322; **70**:202-04
Judith, and Other Stories (Farrell) **4**:157-58; **8**:205
Judith Hearne (Moore)
See *The Lonely Passion of Judith Hearne*
"Judith Kane" (Spencer) **22**:402
Judith Madrier (Troyat) **23**:457
Judo Saga (Kurosawa) **119**:342, 350
Judy Garland and the Cold War (Simmons) **43**:409, 412
Jueces en la noche (Buero Vallejo) **139**:10, 12, 24-6, 39-43, 45, 48-52
Juegos de manos (Goytisolo) **10**:243; **23**:186; **133**:87-90, 93, 97
"El juez, mi rehén" (Ulibarrí) **83**:416
"Jug and Bottle" (Ross) **13**:496
"Jug Band Blues" (Pink Floyd) **35**:307
"Jug of Silver" (Capote) **1**:55
"Juggernaut" (Bass) **79**:3, 12; **143**:3
Juggernaut (Lester) **20**:229-30
"Juggernaut's Little Scrapbook" (Murray) **40**:335-36
"Juggler" (Wilbur) **53**:399, 407
Jugglers Three (Williamson) **56**:433-34
Juhannustanssit (Salama) **18**:460-61
Juhlat (Haavikko) **34**:170
Juicios sumarios (Castellanos) **66**:54
"Les Juifs dans la littérature actuelle" (de Man) **55**:383-84, 386, 398, 403-04, 408, 412, 419-20, 422
Les Juifs du silence (Wiesel) **3**:529; **37**:455
"Juilliard Lecture" (Cage) **41**:78, 80
"Juke Box Music" (Davies) **21**:102
The Jukebox (Handke)
See *Versuch über die Jukebox*
Jules and Jim (Truffaut)
See *Jules et Jim*
Jules et Jim (Truffaut) **20**:382, 387, 391-92, 394-97, 402-03; **101**:371, 373-75, 377-81, 383-85, 387-88, 391-94, 396, 406-408, 410, 412, 414-17
"Julia" (Hellman) **8**:282; **44**:530, 532; **52**:190-92, 194-95, 197-98, 200, 202-05
"Julia" (Lennon and McCartney) **35**:264, 266
Julia (Straub) **28**:409; **107**:264-66, 268, 274, 276-78, 281-83, 292, 304-10
Julia and the Bazooka, and Other Stories (Kavan) **5**:206; **82**:119-20, 122
Julia Paradise (Jones) **50**:51-4
Julian (Vidal) **2**:449; **4**:553-55, 557; **6**:549-50; **8**:528; **10**:502; **22**:433-35; **33**:407; **72**:386-87, 389, 399, 406; **142**:303, 320, 322, 326, 328, 334
Julian the Apostate (Vidal)
See *Julian*
Julian the Magician (MacEwen) **13**:357
"Julie: A Memory" (Brown) **73**:20
Julie of the Wolves (George) **35**:177-80
"Julie's on the Drug Squad" (Clash) **30**:43
Juliet of the Spirits (Fellini)
See *Giulietta degli spiriti*
"Julieta" (Guillén) **79**:241
Julio Jurenito (Ehrenburg)
See *The Extraordinary Adventures of Julio Jurenito and His Disciples*
"Julip" (Harrison) **143**:346-48, 353, 355, 359
Julip (Harrison) **143**:346-49, 359-60
Julius Caesar (Welles) **80**:379
"July" (Barnes) **127**:201
"July" (Lane) **25**:284
"July" (Swan) **69**:358-60, 363-64
July 7th (McCorkle) **51**:273-76, 278
"July Morning" (Bly) **128**:13-14,
July's People (Gordimer) **33**:181-85; **51**:156-59, 161-62; **70**:163, 165-67, 170-71, 182, 187; **123**:120, 158-60
"Jumbo's Wife" (O'Connor) **23**:329
La jument verte (Aymé) **11**:21-3
"Jump" (Gordimer) **123**:129
Jump, and Other Stories (Gordimer) **70**:166, 168, 176-77, 180; **123**:127, 129, 132-33, 135, 149
Jump Bad: A New Chicago Anthology (Brooks) **125**:109
Jump Ship to Freedom (Collier and Collier) **30**:73-5
Jumpers (Stoppard) **3**:470; **4**:525-27; **5**:411-14; **8**:501-04; **15**:518-20, 524; **29**:394, 397, 399-400, 402, 406; **34**:273-74, 280-81; **63**:404; **91**:184, 189-90
"Jumpin' Jack Flash" (Jagger and Richard) **17**:224, 229, 231
"Jumping Beans" (Lopate) **29**:302
Jumping Jupiter (Gilbreth and Carey) **17**:154
Jumping the Train Tracks with Angela (Durcan) **43**:116-17
"Jump-Up Day" (Kingsolver) **130**:73
"Junction" (Barnes) **141**:58, 70
"June" (Gunn) **32**:213
"June 30, 1974" (Schuyler) **23**:391
June 30th, June 30th (Brautigan) **12**:73-4
"A June Afternoon" (Wolf)
See "Juninachmittag"
"June Bug" (Gibbons) **145**:147
"June Cherries" (Asturias) **8**:25
"June: Dutch Harbor" (Meredith) **22**:302
"June Fugue" (Shapcott) **38**:402
"June Light" (Wilbur) **110**:351
June Moon (Kaufman) **38**:265
"June Rain" (Aldington) **49**:17
"June Rain" (Merwin) **18**:336-37
"June Recital" (Welty) **14**:564; **22**:456-58; **33**:420; **105**:299
The Juneberry Tree (Ferron)
See *L'amélanchier*
"Juneteenth" (Ellison) **114**:99, 102
Jung and Feminism: Liberating the Archetypes (Wehr) **65**:325
"Jung and the Theatre" (Davies) **13**:174
Jungfrukällen (Bergman) **16**:50, 61, 64-7, 74
"The Jungle" (Kavanagh) **22**:242
The Jungle (Samarakis)
See *I zoungla*
The Jungle (Sinclair) **1**:310; **11**:497-98; **15**:498-501; **63**:345-51, 354, 359-61, 366-70, 373-74, 376
"The Jungle and the Sea" (Aleixandre) **36**:29
"Jungle Fever" (Komunyakaa) **86**:192
Jungle Fever (Lee) **105**:95-97, 99-103, 111, 113, 127-30
"Jungle Knot" (Ammons) **25**:42
"The Jungle Line" (Mitchell) **12**:439
Jungle Lovers (Theroux) **5**:427; **8**:512; **28**:424-25
"The Jungle of Lord Lion" (Jacobsen) **102**:241
"Jungle Surrender" (Komunyakaa) **94**:230, 245
"Jungleland" (Springsteen) **17**:480-81, 489-90
"Jungletime" (Diamond) **30**:112
"The Juniata Diary: With Timely Repartees" (Codrescu) **46**:106; **121**:155
"Juninachmittag" (Wolf) **29**:464; **150**:237, 298, 315, 338
"Junior Addict" (Hughes) **15**:295
The Junior Bachelor Society (Williams) **13**:599
Junior Bonner (Peckinpah) **20**:276, 278
Junior Miss Series (Benson) **17**:48, 50
The Juniper Tree (Straub) **107**:304-05, 307-09
"Junk" (Wilbur) **6**:570; **53**:405; **110**:351
The Junkers (Read) **4**:444; **25**:375-76, 379
"Junkie Slip" (Clash) **30**:48
Junkie: The Confessions of an Unredeemed Drug Addict (Burroughs) **15**:111-12; **22**:83, 86; **42**:74-5, 77-8; **75**:97, 103-04
Junkies Are Full of Shhh. . . (Baraka) **115**:36
Junky (Burroughs)
See *Junkie: The Confessions of an Unredeemed Drug Addict*
Juno and Avos (Voznesensky) **57**:424
Juno and the Paycock (O'Casey) **5**:317-20; **9**:407-08; **11**:409-10; **15**:404-05; **88**:234-37, 242, 244, 247, 252, 254-58, 261-63, 265
Junta, the Body Snatcher (Onetti)
See *Juntacádaveres*
Juntacádaveres (Onetti) **7**:279-80; **10**:376
"Junto al Río de Cenizas de Rosa" (Sarduy) **97**:382, 384-86
"Jupiter Five" (Clarke) **136**:211
The Jupiter Legacy (Harrison) **42**:207
The Jupiter Plague (Harrison) **42**:207
Jupiter Project (Benford) **52**:63
Jupiter: The Largest Planet (Asimov) **26**:50
"El juramento" (Marqués) **96**:241, 245
Jurassic Park (Crichton) **90**:70, 72, 84-5, 87, 89, 91, 93, 96-7
Jürg Reinhart (Frisch) **3**:167; **9**:218; **44**:183, 185-86, 193, 204
The Jury (Klima) **56**:162-63, 165-67, 170
"Juryrigged" (Haldeman) **61**:174, 177
"Just a Little One" (Parker) **68**:335
Just a Little Simple (Childress) **86**:309, 311, 314
"Just a Smack at Auden" (Empson) **33**:142
"Just a Song at Twilight" (Aickman) **57**:4
"Just About Asleep Together" (Peacock) **60**:292
Just above My Head (Baldwin) **15**:41-4; **17**:41-5; **42**:17; **50**:297; **90**:31, 33; **127**:100, 105, 109, 121, 147, 151-53
Just Above My Head (Baldwin) **127**:100
Just Add Water and Stir (Berton) **104**:47
The Just and the Unjust (Cozzens) **1**:67; **4**:112-13, 115; **11**:124, 128, 131-32; **92**:178-81, 184-86, 189, 196, 211-12
"A Just Anger" (Piercy) **6**:404; **18**:406; **27**:375
Just Another Band from L.A. (Zappa) **17**:588, 593
Just As I Thought (Paley) **140**:277, 283, 285, 290-91
"Just as It Was" (Amichai) **57**:36
The Just Assassins (Camus)
See *Les justes*
Just Before Dark (Harrison) **143**:350, 355, 357-60
Just before Nightfall (Chabrol)
See *Juste avant la nuit*
"Just Before the War with the Eskimos" (Salinger) **138**:214
Just between Ourselves (Ayckbourn) **18**:30; **33**:41, 48-9; **74**:8, 18, 21, 23
"Just Boys" (Farrell) **66**:131
"Just Don't Never Give Up on Love" (Sanchez) **116**:287, 302, 310, 317
"Just Enough for the City" (McPherson) **77**:359, 378, 381-82
"Just for a Time" (Angelou) **77**:30
"Just For Starters" (Ashbery) **125**:40
"Just Friends" (Davies) **21**:92
Just Give me a Cool Drink of Water 'fore I Diiie (Angelou) **12**:13; **64**:32; **77**:15, 22, 28-9
Just, Human Time (Padilla)
See *El justo tiempo humano*
"Just Like a Man" (Shange) **126**:360
"Just like a Tree" (Gaines) **3**:179; **18**:167
"Just Like a Woman" (Dylan) **12**:182; **77**:177
"Just like Her Mother" (Callaghan) **41**:98
"(Just like) Starting Over" (Lennon) **35**:271-72, 274
Just Like the Resurrection (Beer) **58**:31, 36, 38
"Just like This Train" (Mitchell) **12**:443
"Just like Tom Thumb's Blues" (Dylan) **4**:149
"Just Living" (Lane) **25**:289
Just Looking (Updike) **139**:363
"Just Not True" (Simon) **26**:409
"Just Once" (Sexton) **123**:408-09
Just Relations (Hall) **51**:176-79
Just Representations: A James Gould Cozzens Reader (Cozzens) **92**:194, 203, 208
"Just Say Yes Calypso" (Ginsberg) **109**:318
"Just Tell Me Who It Was" (Cheever) **15**:131
"Just the Way You Are" (Joel) **26**:217, 221
Just to be Together (Antonioni) **144**:81
"Just to Keep You Satisfied" (Gaye) **26**:133
"Just Us" (Pryor) **26**:378

"Just Us Kids" (Crumb) **17**:83
"Just Walking Around" (Ashbery) **41**:35, 38
"Just Wednesday" (Ashbery) **125**:35
Juste avant la nuit (Chabrol) **16**:179, 183
"Juste présent" (Tzara) **47**:388
Les justes (Camus) **1**:54; **9**:146; **14**:108, 114-15; **32**:84-8, 90-2, 94, 96-101; **63**:63, 86; **124**:12, 24, 42
"A Justice" (Faulkner) **68**:128
"Justice" (Hughes) **15**:295
"Justice" (O'Hara) **42**:319
Justice and Her Brothers (Hamilton) **26**:152-53, 155-56
"Justice at Midnight" (Barker) **48**:15
"Justice Is Reason Enough" (Wakoski) **9**:554
"Justicia" (Kingsolver) **130**:84
Justification and Application: Remarks on Discourse Ethics (Habermas) **104**:91
Justine (Durrell) **1**:87; **4**:144, 146; **8**:190-92; **13**:185, 187-88; **27**:97-8; **41**:133, 136-37
El justo tiempo humano (Padilla) **38**:350, 352
Juvenile Court (Wiseman) **20**:474, 476
Juvenile Justice and Injustice (Hyde) **21**:178
"Juvenilia" (Smart) **54**:425
Juvenilia I (Nye) **42**:302, 304-05
Juvenilia II (Nye) **42**:302, 304-05
"Juventad" (Paz) **10**:392
Juxtaposition (Anthony) **35**:37
Jyotaro (Tanizaki) **28**:418
"K" (Merrill) **8**:385, 387
"The K" (Olson) **29**:330
"K, der Käfer" (Grass) **32**:201
"K filosofii postupka" (Bakhtin) **83**:36, 38
"The K. Leslie Steiner Interview" (Delany) **141**:115
"K Likomedu, na Skiros" (Brodsky) **50**:122-23
"K, the Beetle" (Grass)
See "K, der Käfer"
K Uranii (Brodsky)
See *To Urania: Selected Poems 1965-1985*
"The Kabbalah" (Borges) **48**:47-8
Kabbalah and Criticism (Bloom) **24**:79; **103**:2, 6-8, 12-13, 25, 27-8, 41, 48
"Kabnis" (Toomer) **4**:549; **13**:550-52, 554, 556; **22**:429
"Lo kabrosh" (Amichai) **116**:119-21, 124
"Kaddish" (Ginsberg) **2**:164; **3**:194-95; **4**:181; **6**:199; **13**:241; **36**:181, 183-85, 187-89, 192, 195, 197; **69**:217, 223, 225; **109**:324-26, 330, 332-33, 336, 338, 351, 358-62, 364, 371-72
"Kaddish" (Ignatow) **40**:259
Kaddish, and Other Poems (Ginsberg) **1**:119; **2**:162-64; **6**:198-99; **13**:239-40; **36**:183, 186, 193, 196, 199; **109**:328, 338-43, 348, 352, 359, 362-63
Kafatasi (Hikmet) **40**:245
Kaff auch Mare Crisium (Schmidt) **56**:391-92, 401, 405
Kafka (Soderbergh) **154**:332-33, 338-39, 341, 344, 347, 351, 353
"Kafka and His Executors" (Grass) **49**:138
"Kafka and His Precursors" (Borges)
See "Los precursores de Kafka"
"Kafka y sus precursores" (Borges)
See "Los precursores de Kafka"
"Kafkas" (Wiggins) **57**:434-36, 439
Kafka's Dick (Bennett) **45**:58-60; **77**:90-1
Kafka's Other Trial: The Letters to Felice (Canetti)
See *Der andere Prozeß: Kafkas Briefe an Felice*
Kagemusha (Kurosawa) **16**:406; **119**:338, 340, 342, 375-77, 380, 383-84, 396, 399
Kagi (Ichikawa) **20**:177, 181
Kagi (Tanizaki) **8**:510-11; **14**:525, 527; **28**:417
Kahawa (Westlake) **33**:439
"Kaiser and the War" (Ortiz) **45**:309, 311
Kak nam obustroit' Rossiiu?: Posil'nye soobrazheniia (Solzhenitsyn) **78**:427, 429-30, 432-33
Kakemono hôtel (Cayrol) **11**:110
"Kalaloch" (Forché) **25**:168-70; **83**:209, 211
Kalendarz i klepsydra (Konwicki) **117**:257-58, 272, 279, 284, 286
"Kali" (Clifton) **66**:80
"Kali's Galaxy" (Reed) **5**:368
Kalki (Vidal) **10**:501-04; **22**:435-36; **33**:407; **72**:386-87; **142**:301-02, 322, 326
Das Kalkwerk (Bernhard) **3**:64-5; **32**:17-21, 26; **61**:14-15, 19-21, 23-4, 28-9
Die Kälte: Eine Isolation (Bernhard) **32**:26; **61**:11
Kameliadamen (Abell) **15**:2, 7
Kamen no kokuhaku (Mishima) **2**:286-87, 289; **4**:355; **6**:338; **9**:381-82, 385; **27**:337-41, 345-46
Kamera Obskura (Nabokov) **1**:239; **2**:302; **3**:353-55; **6**:359; **8**:417; **15**:396; **44**:465; **46**:291, 294; **64**:348
Kammený most (Seifert) **44**:425; **93**:306, 328, 343
Kamouraska (Hébert) **4**:220; **29**:231-33, 235-38, 240-41
Kämpande ande (Lagerkvist) **54**:286
Der Kampf als inneres Erlebnis (Jünger) **125**:221, 236, 248, 259
Kanal (Wajda) **16**:577-79, 581-82
Kanchenjungha (Ray) **16**:481, 492, 494
"The Kandy-Kolored Tangerine-Flake Streamline Baby" (Wolfe) **51**:418, 420; **147**:322-23, 329, 374
The Kandy-Kolored Tangerine-Flake Streamline Baby (Wolfe) **35**:449-50, 452, 456, 458, 460, 465-66; **51**:418-20; **147**:310-11, 320-21, 328-30, 359
Kane and Abel (Archer) **28**:12-4
Kangaroo (Aleshkovsky) **44**:29-32
"The Kangaroo Communique" (Murakami) **150**:58
Kansakunnan linja (Haavikko) **34**:181
"Kansas City" (Harjo) **83**:271
Kansas City (Altman) **116**:71-4
Kanthapura (Rao) **25**:366-67, 369-72; **56**:284, 286-87, 289, 292-93, 295-96, 298-99, 301-04, 306-07, 315
Kaos (Lagerkvist) **54**:274, 277
"Kapetan Michalis" (Levi) **41**:245
"Das kapital" (Baraka) **33**:62
Kara-Bugaz (Paustovsky) **40**:363, 368
Karaoke (Potter) **86**:343-46, 348; **123**:275-80
"Karate" (Plumly) **33**:312
Karate Is a Thing of the Spirit (Crews) **6**:117-18; **23**:138; **49**:71-2, 76
"The Karate Kid" (Soto) **80**:298
"Karintha" (Toomer) **4**:549; **22**:425
The Karl Marx Play (Owens) **8**:434
"Kärleken och döden" (Lagerkvist) **54**:276, 286
"Karma" (Hughes) **37**:173
"Karma" (Raine) **103**:182
alKarnak (Mahfūz) **52**:297, 302-03
Karoton (Faludy) **42**:136
"Kartofel'nyy el'f" (Nabokov) **3**:354
Kartoteka (Rozewicz)
See *The Card File*
Die Kaschuben (Grass) **88**:144
"Kashmir" (Page and Plant) **12**:477-82
"A Kashmir Idyll" (Anand) **23**:18
"Kas-Kas" (Bennett) **28**:29
Kaspar (Handke) **5**:163, 165; **8**:262-63; **10**:254-56; **15**:267-68, 270; **38**:215, 217, 219; **134**:108, 110-11, 118, 130, 157-58, 161, 177
Kaspar and Other Plays (Handke) **38**:215, 219
Kassandra and the Wolf (Karapanou) **13**:314-15
Kassandra: Vier Vorlesungen; eine Erzählung (Wolf) **150**:215-16, 218-21, 223, 228-30, 235, 237-38, 241, 243, 245, 248-56, 271, 278-80, 286, 300, 306-10, 312, 318, 328-30, 336, 350-2, 354
"Kata Ucle" (Kawabata) **107**:73, 77, 86
Katar (Lem) **149**:118
Kate Vaiden (Price) **50**:229-33; **63**:323, 325-27, 329-30, 332-33, 335-36, 339, 341
"Kate Whiskey" (Muldoon) **32**:315
"Kategorier" (Ekelöf) **27**:111
"Käthe Kollwitz" (Rukeyser) **15**:457; **27**:413
"Katherine Anne Porter: The Eye of the Story" (Welty) **105**:322
Kathie and the Hippopotamus (Vargas Llosa)
See *Kathie y el hipopótamo*
Kathie y el hipopótamo (Vargas Llosa) **42**:407; **85**:380
Kathleen and Frank (Isherwood) **9**:292; **11**:298; **14**:281, 286; **44**:397-98
Kathleen Listens In (O'Casey) **88**:270
Kathleen, Please Come Home (O'Dell) **30**:275
"Kathleen's Field" (Trevor) **71**:332, 341, 348; **116**:363-64, 379-80, 395
Kathy and the Mysterious Statue (Kingman) **17**:244
Kathy Goes to Haiti (Acker) **45**:14; **111**:8-9, 11, 25
Katia (Almedingen)
See *Little Katia*
"Katia Reading" (Dobyns) **37**:79, 81
"Katmandu" (Seger) **35**:380-81, 383
"Kato slunce" (Bagryana) **10**:14
Katy Lied (Becker and Fagen) **26**:79-80, 83-4
Katz und Maus (Grass) **2**:171-72; **4**:202-03, 206; **32**:198; **49**:143; **88**:137, 143-45, 159
Katzelmacher (Fassbinder) **20**:106, 113
"Kava" (Marley) **17**:270
Kawa no Aru Shitamachi o Hanashi (Kawabata) **107**:121
Kaya (Marley) **17**:270-73
"Le Kaya-Magan" (Senghor) **130**:253, 255, 259
"Kayenta, Arizona, May, 1977" (Lewis) **41**:260-61
"Kazan University" (Yevtushenko) **126**:394
Kaze no uta o kike (Murakami) **150**:44, 70, 72, 82
Kean (Sartre) **7**:391; **13**:500
"Keats and the Embarrassments of Poetic Tradition" (Bloom) **24**:70
"Keats at Highgate" (Gunn) **32**:215
"Keel and Kool" (Frame)
See "Keel, Kool"
"Keel, Kool" (Frame) **96**:184-85
"Keel, Ram, Stauros" (Jones) **7**:190
"Keela, the Outcast Indian Maiden" (Welty) **33**:414; **105**:329, 349
"Keen" (Muldoon) **32**:318
Keep It Crisp (Perelman) **49**:259-60, 270
"Keep it Holy" (Ferber) **93**:162
"Keep Talking" (Levine) **33**:275
Keep the Change (McGuane) **127**:262, 267-69, 280, 298
"Keep the Customer Satisfied" (Simon) **17**:460, 465
Keep the Faith, Baby! (Powell) **89**:206-07, 209
Keep Tightly Closed in a Cool Dry Place (Terry) **19**:440
"Keep under Cover" (McCartney) **35**:292
Keep Your Eyes Down (Russell) **60**:319
"Keep Your Eyes on the Sparrow" (Cliff) **21**:64
"Keep Your Pity" (Boyle) **58**:66
"The Keeper of the Key" (Guthrie) **23**:199
The Keepers of the House (Grau) **4**:207-08; **146**:121, 128, 132-34, 136, 138-42, 144-45, 147-57, 159, 161-63
Keepers of the House (Teran) **36**:419-22
"Keeping Close to Home" (Hooks) **94**:144
Keeping Faith: Philosophy and Race in America (West) **134**:358, 362-63, 373-75, 377, 382, 388, 390
"Keeping Fit" (Gordimer) **70**:177-78; **123**:127, 144, 149
"Keeping Informed in D.C." (Nemerov) **6**:361
Keeping the Rabble in Line: Interviews with David Barsamian (Chomsky) **132**:68
"Keeping Things Whole" (Strand) **18**:518; **41**:436-38; **71**:278, 282, 284-85, 290
"Keeping Track" (Levertov) **66**:239
Keeping Watch (Pack) **13**:439
"Keeping Watch by Night" (O'Brien) **103**:145
"Keepsake" (Montale) **7**:232

Kehinde (Emecheta) **128**:80-1
Kein Ort. Nirgends (Wolf) **29**:463-64, 466-67; **58**:428, 431, 433-35, 437; **150**:214-15, 223-24, 227-30, 235-36, 250, 254-55, 271, 278, 280, 285, 287, 297, 301, 306, 325-27, 330, 350
"Kein Seeweg nach Indien" (Hein) **154**:179
"Keine Delikatessen" (Bachmann) **69**:57
Der Keller (Bernhard) **32**:25; **61**:11-13
The Kelpie's Pearls (Hunter) **21**:155
Kemet, Afrocentricity and Knowledge (Asante) **70**:389
"Ken Kesey at Stanford" (Cowley) **39**:461
Kennedy for the Defense (Higgins) **18**:234-35
Kennedy or Nixon: Does It Make Any Difference? (Schlesinger) **84**:375
Kennedy without Tears (Wicker) **7**:533
"Kennedy's Inauguration" (Bly) **38**:57; **128**:45
"Kennen" (Hein) **154**:158, 162
"The Kenneth James Interview" (Delany) **141**:116
Kennis van die Aand (Brink) **18**:66-7; **36**:68; **106**:95-7, 99, 101, 122-25, 137
"The Kensington Mass" (Jones) **42**:242
Kent Family Chronicles (Jakes) **29**:249-50
Kent State: What Happened and Why (Michener) **1**:214; **5**:290; **29**:311; **109**:375, 378-79, 382
"Kentucky Derby Day, Belfast, Maine" (Dobyns) **37**:82
Kentucky Fried Movie (Landis) **26**:271-73
Kentucky Is My Land (Stuart) **11**:509-10; **34**:373
"Kentucky Mountain Farm" (Warren) **6**:557
The Kentucky Trace: A Novel of the American Revolution (Arnow) **7**:15-16
"Kentucky Woman" (Diamond) **30**:110-11, 113
Kenyatta's Escape (Goines) **80**:94
Kenyatta's Last Hit (Goines) **80**:94
"Kenyon Review, After the Sandstorm" (Bukowski) **82**:14
"Keokuk" (Hugo) **32**:242
"Kepa" (Grace) **56**:116
Kepler (Banville) **46**:29, 31; **118**:10, 12, 15, 18, 23, 25, 27, 35, 38, 47
"Kept" (Bogan) **46**:80-1, 86, 89; **93**:65
"The Kerner Report on Camp Creek Road" (Allen) **84**:5, 38
Kerrisdale Elegies (Bowering) **47**:30-3
Kersti (Friis-Baastad) **12**:213
"Kerzen für Maria" (Boell) **72**:70
Kesey's Garage Sale (Kesey) **3**:267-68; **64**:231
Kesten and Cul-de-sac (Theriault)
See *Cul-de-sac*
The Kestrel (Alexander) **35**:27-8
"Kettle of Fire" (Davis) **49**:92, 94
Kettle of Fire (Davis) **49**:92-3
"Kew" (Sarton) **49**:307
"The Kew Stakes" (Hope) **51**:226
"The Key" (Asimov) **19**:25; **26**:45
"The Key" (Muldoon) **72**:282
"The Key" (Singer) **6**:509; **23**:419
The Key (Ichikawa)
See *Kagi*
The Key (Tanizaki)
See *Kagi*
Key Largo (Huston) **20**:159, 165
Key out of Time (Norton) **12**:468
"The Key to Everything" (Swenson) **106**:314, 345
A Key to Modern British Poetry (Durrell) **1**:84, 87
The Key to Rebecca (Follett) **18**:157
"Key to the Door" (Sillitoe) **148**:197
Key To the Door (Sillitoe) **1**:307; **3**:448; **6**:500; **57**:387, 392-93, 402-03; **148**:195, 197-98
A Key to the Suite (MacDonald) **3**:307; **44**:408
"The Keyboard" (Ellison) **139**:145
"Keys and Watercress" (Metcalf) **37**:306
"The Keys of Death" (Green)
See "Les clefs de la mort"
The Keys of the Kingdom (Cronin) **32**:135-36, 140
"The Keystone" (Powers) **57**:349
Keystone Kids (Tunis) **12**:594-95, 598
The K-Factor (Caute) **29**:124
"al- Khala" (Mahfūz) **55**:188
"Khalil'" (Leonov) **92**:237, 263-64
Khammārat al-qitt al-aswad (Mahfūz) **52**:297-98; **55**:174, 176, 188
Khan al-khalili (Mahfouz) **153**:249, 258, 271, 274, 276-77, 282-83, 336, 350, 352, 354-55, 366
Khan al-Khalīlī (Mahfūz) **52**:292-93, 300
"Khironomíes" (Ritsos) **6**:463
"Khochubyt' chestnym" (Voinovich) **147**:270, 272
"Khudozhnik" (Brodsky) **13**:115
"Kichli" (Seferis) **11**:493, 495
Kicking against the Pricks (Metcalf) **37**:307
"Kicking the Leaves" (Hall) **151**:192, 197
Kicking the Leaves (Hall) **13**:259-60; **37**:146-48; **59**:152, 154; **151**:181, 191, 193, 197-98, 204, 213
"Kicks" (Reed) **21**:311
"Kiczowaty" (Szymborska)
See "Kitschy"
"The Kid" (Ai) **69**:7, 13
"Kid" (Creeley) **11**:138
The Kid (Aiken) **10**:4; **52**:20, 24, 26, 32
Le kid (Beckett) **6**:39
The Kid (Chaplin) **16**:203, 207
The Kid (Coover) **32**:120; **46**:116; **87**:35
The Kid (Seelye) **7**:406
"Kid Charlemagne" (Becker and Fagen) **26**:81, 83
The Kid Comes Back (Tunis) **12**:595
"The Kid from Hell" (Strugatskii and Strugatskii) **27**:438
The Kid from Tomkinsville (Tunis) **12**:593, 598
"Kid MacArthur" (Vaughn) **62**:456, 459
"Kid Punch" (Beecher) **6**:48
Kid Stakes (Lawler) **58**:333, 336-37, 340-44
"Kidnap Poem" (Giovanni) **19**:192
The Kidnapped Saint (Traven) **11**:535
"Kidnapper" (Gallagher) **63**:123, 126
"The Kids Are All Right" (Townshend) **17**:525, 529
The Kids Are All Right (Townshend) **17**:539
"The Kids Downstairs" (Ihimaera) **46**:200
"The Kid's Guide to Divorce" (Moore) **39**:84; **45**:279-80
"Kierkegaard" (Smith) **64**:397
"Kierkegaard en la Zonz Rosa" (Fuentes) **113**:250-51
"Kierkegaard: The Singular Universal" (Sartre) **7**:472
"Kierkegaard Unfair to Schlegel" (Barthelme) **8**:50; **13**:56; **46**:40-1; **115**:60, 65, 70
Kieslowski on Kieslowski (Kieslowski) **120**:219, 221, 252
"Kiev" (Ehrenburg) **62**:170
Kifah Tiba (Mahfouz) **153**:249, 268, 270, 272, 274, 276-77, 309, 316-17, 319-20, 354, 372
Kifāh Tiba (Mahfūz) **52**:299
Kiiroi hito (Endō) **54**:154, 159; **99**:285-86
Kika (Almodovar) **114**:34-7
"Kiku on the Tenth" (Mishima) **27**:341
"Kilbinnen Men" (Dunn) **40**:171
"The Kilfenora Teaboy" (Durcan) **43**:114, 118
Kilgaren (Holland) **21**:149
"Kilka dni wojny o ktorej nie wiadomo, czy byla" (Konwicki) **117**:284
Kill Cure (Rathbone) **41**:338
"Kill Day on the Government Wharf" (Thomas) **13**:540; **37**:416; **107**:326
"Kill Your Sons" (Reed) **21**:309
Kill Zone (Estleman) **48**:105-06
The Killdeer (Reaney) **13**:472, 474-75
Killdeer Mountain (Brown) **47**:39-40
"Killdozer" (Sturgeon) **39**:361, 365, 368
"Killer" (Kesey) **46**:227
The Killer (Ionesco)
See *Tueur sans gages*
The Killer Angels (Shaara) **15**:474
Killer at Large (Thompson) **69**:378
"Killer Barracuda" (Kristofferson) **26**:270
Killer Dolphin (Marsh) **53**:248, 260
The Killer Elite (Peckinpah) **20**:281-83
The Killer Inside Me (Thompson) **69**:375-78, 380-81, 383-86, 388
"The Killer Poet" (Strand) **41**:439-41
"The Killers" (Bukowski) **41**:74; **108**:85
"The Killers" (Hemingway) **13**:273; **30**:179, 182, 184, 195-96; **41**:200; **80**:104
Killer's Head (Shepard) **6**:496-97
Killer's Kiss (Kubrick) **16**:376, 379-80, 385-86
"Killhope Wheel" (Silkin) **6**:498-99; **43**:403-04
The Killing (Kubrick) **16**:377, 379-80, 383-84, 386-87, 389
The Killing Doll (Rendell) **48**:323-24
Killing Everybody (Harris) **19**:204
"Killing Floor" (Ai) **69**:4
Killing Floor (Ai) **14**:8-9; **69**:3-8, 11-14, 16
A Killing for Christ (Hamill) **10**:251
The Killing Game (Ionesco)
See *Jeux de massacre*
"The Killing Ground" (Ballard) **137**:17
The Killing Ground (Settle) **61**:369-74, 376, 383-87
Killing in Verse and Prose, and Other Essays (Fussell) **74**:139
Killing Mr. Griffin (Duncan) **26**:104-06
Killing Mr. Watson (Matthiessen) **64**:325-29
The Killing of a Chinese Bookie (Cassavetes) **20**:51-2
"The Killing of Hastings Banda" (Theroux) **46**:401
Killing Orders (Paretsky) **135**:308-09, 313, 315-20, 322-24, 335-36, 344, 363-67
Killing Rage: Ending Racism (Hooks) **94**:159-61
The Killing Room (Bowering) **32**:47
"Killing the Calves" (Hayden) **37**:156
"Killing the Pig" (Montague) **46**:271
"Killing the Whale" (Plumly) **33**:310
Killing Time (Berger) **3**:63; **5**:60; **8**:83; **18**:57; **38**:41
Killing Time (Warner) **14**:553
The Killing Tree (Bennett) **35**:43
"Killings" (Dubus) **36**:145-46; **97**:201-02, 221, 223-24, 229-30
"The Killings in Atlanta" (Amis) **62**:2, 5
The Killings in Trinidad (Naipaul) **18**:363
The Kill-Off (Thompson) **69**:382, 386
Killshot (Leonard) **71**:218-19, 223; **120**:287, 304
"Kilmainham Jail" (Day Lewis) **10**:131
"Kilpeck" (Adcock) **41**:15
"Kilroy Was Here" (Farrell) **66**:129
"Kilroy's Carnival" (Schwartz) **45**:355, 360
The Kilterman Legacy (McCaffrey) **17**:281
"Kim" (Spivack) **6**:520
"Kimberley Solzhenitsyn's Calendar" (Frazier) **46**:164-65
"Kimberly" (Smith) **12**:539
Kimen (Vesaas) **48**:404-07, 409
"Kimono" (Graham) **118**:228, 240, 243
"Kimono" (Merrill) **13**:380
"Kimyōna shigoto" (Oe) **36**:349
"Kin" (Angelou) **77**:30
"Kin" (Szirtes) **46**:393
"Kin" (Welty) **105**:299, 323
"Kin" (Williams) **56**:426; **148**:364
"Kind" (Ammons) **108**:24
"Kind" (Miles) **14**:369
Ein Kind (Bernhard) **61**:11
Kind Are Her Answers (Renault) **17**:390
Kind Hearts and Gentle Monsters (Yep) **35**:472-73
A Kind of Anger (Ambler) **9**:18
"A Kind of Happiness" (Mahapatra) **33**:284
A Kind of Magic (Ferber) **18**:152; **93**:186
"A Kind of Nature" (Silkin) **43**:400
A Kind of Order, a Kind of Folly: Essays and Conversations (Kunitz) **6**:287; **11**:319;

148:81, 92, 96, 100, 102, 104-05, 118, 120, 123-24, 147
"A Kind of Parlance" (Peacock) **60**:297
"The Kind of Poetry I Want" (MacDiarmid) **4**:309, 312-13; **63**:244-46; 256
A Kind of Religion (MacInnes) **23**:286
"A Kind of Scar" (Boland) **113**:66, 90
A Kind of Scar (Boland) **113**:74
"A Kind of Survivor" (Steiner) **24**:428
A Kind of Testament (Gombrowicz) **49**:126-27, 134
"A Kind of Weakness" (Strand) **18**:516
"Kind Offices" (Johnston) **51**:250
Kinda Kinks (Davies) **21**:89
Kinder Brauchen Märchen (Bettelheim)
See *The Uses of Enchantment: The Meaning and Importance of Fairy Tales*
Kinder Capers (Snodgrass) **68**:388, 398-99
Kindergarten (Rushforth) **19**:405-07
Kindergeschichte (Handke) **134**:133, 151
"Kinderlied" (Grass) **2**:173; **32**:198
Ein Kinderspiel (Walser) **27**:462
"Kindertotenlieder" (Dubie) **36**:130
"Kindertotenlieder" (Longley) **29**:293
Kindheitsmuster (Wolf) **14**:594-95; **29**:464-68; **58**:422, 428, 430-36; **150**:214-17, 224-27, 230, 235, 237-38, 240-41, 243, 248, 254, 271, 280-81, 287-88, 296, 300, 318, 333, 341, 348-52
The Kindling (Elliott) **47**:106-07
Kindling (Shute) **30**:365
Kindly Light (Wilson) **33**:451
The Kindly Ones (Powell) **3**:400-02; **7**:340; **9**:435, 439
"Kindness" (Plath) **1**:271; **3**:392; **9**:426; **14**:424; **17**:360; **50**:446; **111**:203
Kindness (Ballard)
See *The Kindness of Women*
A Kindness Cup (Astley) **41**:46-8
"The Kindness of Mrs. Radcliffe" (Coward) **51**:74
The Kindness of Strangers: Poems, 1969-1974 (Whalen) **29**:445
The Kindness of Strangers: The Life of Tennessee Williams (Spoto) **39**:444-47, 449-53
The Kindness of Women (Ballard) **137**:20-21, 23, 35-42, 65, 76
Kindred (Butler) **38**:62, 65-6; **121**:77-8, 80-2, 85-9, 93-6, 102-05, 110, 116-17, 120-21, 125, 145-47, 149
Kindred (Carroll) **10**:96-7
Kinds of Affection (Miles) **2**:278; **14**:369; **39**:353
Kinds of Love (Sarton) **4**:471; **49**:313-14; **91**:241
Kindui nōgaku shū (Mishima) **4**:353; **27**:339
Kinflicks (Alther) **7**:11-4; **41**:19-24
Kinfolk (Buck) **11**:77
The King (Lagerkvist)
See *Konungen*
King and Joker (Dickinson) **12**:175-76; **35**:133-34, 138
The King and Me (Kureishi) **64**:246
"King and Shepard" (Brown) **48**:60
The King and the Queen (Sender)
See *El rey y la reina*
"King Bait" (Hulme) **130**:51
"King Bee" (Boyle) **90**:45, 48
King Blood (Thompson) **69**:384
"King Borborigmi" (Aiken) **52**:28
"King Caliban" (Wain) **46**:415
King Coal (Sinclair) **15**:498-99, 502; **63**:346, 348, 361-62, 371-73
"King Cobra" (Young Bear) **94**:370
"The King Cobra as Political Assassin" (Young Bear) **94**:370
King Coffin (Aiken) **52**:26
King Cole (Masefield) **11**:358; **47**:229
"King David Dances" (Berryman) **3**:66; **6**:64; **25**:92
The King David Report (Heym) **41**:215-16
"King Death" (Gallagher) **63**:122, 124
The King Dies (Ionesco)
See *Le roi se meurt*
King Fisher Lives (Rathbone) **41**:338-39, 341
"King Genius" (Lem) **149**:126
The King Goes Forth to France (Haavikko) **34**:175, 177-78
A King in New York (Chaplin) **16**:197-98, 203-04
"The King Is Dead" (Vanderhaeghe) **41**:450, 452
The King Is Dead (Queen) **11**:463
King James VI of Scotland, I of England (Fraser) **32**:183-84; **107**:32
King Jesus (Graves) **1**:128; **39**:322-23, 325; **45**:172-73
King John (Duerrenmatt)
See *König Johann*
King John (Dürrenmatt) **43**:126
"King John's Castle" (Kinsella) **138**:148
"King Kong" (Ondaatje) **51**:310
"King Kong Meets Wallace Stevens" (Ondaatje) **51**:310-12
King Lazarus (Beti)
See *Le roi miraculé*
"King Lear" (Simmons) **43**:410-12
King Leary (Quarrington) **65**:203-04
"A King Listens" (Calvino) **73**:50, 53, 60
King Log (Hill) **8**:293-96; **45**:178-79, 181-82, 184-87
"King Lord/Queen Freak" (Sanders) **53**:304
King Lord/Queen Freak (Sanders) **53**:304
King Midas: A Romance (Sinclair)
See *Springtime and Harvest: A Romance*
The King Must Die (Renault) **3**:426; **11**:472; **17**:393-97, 400-01
The King My Father's Wreck (Simpson) **149**:355, 357-59, 362
The King of a Rainy Country (Brophy) **11**:68; **29**:91; **105**:2, 7-10, 12, 30, 34-5
"The King of Asine" (Seferis) **5**:385
"King of Beasts" (MacCaig) **36**:283
The King of Comedy (Scorsese) **89**:237-42, 252, 261-68
"King of Death" (Honig) **33**:213
King of Egypt, King of Dreams (MacEwen) **13**:357
"The King of Harlem" (Kaufman) **49**:205
King of Hearts (Kerr) **22**:254
King of Hearts (Slavitt) **14**:491
King of Kazoo (Peck) **17**:341
"King of Pain" (Police, The) **26**:366
King of the Beggars (O'Faolain) **14**:402; **70**:317, 321
"King of the Bingo Game" (Ellison) **86**:324; **114**:113, 125, 131
King of the Castle (Russell) **60**:320
The King of the Fields (Singer) **69**:313-16
"King of the Gypsies" (Mitchell) **98**:153, 180
King of the Gypsies (Maas) **29**:305-07
"The King of the Hill" (Mailer) **74**:205
King of the Hill (Fleming) **37**:121-22
King of the Hill (SODERBERGH) **154**:338-39, 341, 344, 351
King of the Hill: On the Fight of the Century (Mailer) **2**:262; **3**:315; **8**:370
King of the Jews (Epstein) **27**:128-32
"King of the Mountain" (Garrett) **51**:140
King of the Mountain (Garrett) **51**:140, 142-43, 145
The King of the Rainy Country (Freeling) **38**:184
"King of the River" (Kunitz) **6**:286; **14**:313; **148**:71, 73, 76-77, 80, 93, 96, 100, 139, 142, 146
"King of the World" (Becker and Fagen) **26**:80
King Phoenix (Davies) **7**:73
King, Queen, Knave (Nabokov) **1**:243; **2**:299; **6**:352; **8**:417-18; **15**:396; **23**:312-13; **44**:465; **46**:294; **64**:348
King, Queen, Knave (Nabokov)
See *Korol, dama, valet*
King, Queen, Knave (Skolimowski) **20**:353-54
King Rat (Clavell) **25**:124-26, 128; **87**:2-3, 7, 9, 11-2, 17-9
"King Richard's Prison Song" (Blackmur) **24**:66
"King Saul and I" (Amichai) **9**:22; **116**:85, 87, 96
The King Snake (Eckert) **17**:106
"King Solomon's Ring" (Zelazny) **21**:466
"King Tut" (Martin) **30**:248
"King Userkaf's Forgiveness" (Mahfouz)
See "Afw al-malik Userkaf"
King Warrior Magician Lover: Rediscovering the Archetypes of the Mature Masculine (Gillette) **70**:426, 431, 458
"The King Who Lived on Air" (Bates) **46**:50
"King Yu" (Hesse) **25**:259
"The Kingdom" (MacNeice) **1**:186
A Kingdom (Hanley) **13**:261-62
"The Kingdom and the Glory" (McGinley) **14**:365
The Kingdom and the Power (Talese) **37**:391-93, 403-04
The Kingdom by the Sea: A Journey around Great Britain (Theroux) **28**:428; **46**:404
"Kingdom County Come" (Mosher) **62**:313
A Kingdom in a Horse (Wojciechowska) **26**:451
The Kingdom of Death (Allingham) **19**:14, 16
"The Kingdom of Earth" (Williams) **15**:580; **45**:452, 455
Kingdom of Earth: The Seven Descents of Myrtle (Williams) **1**:369; **2**:464-66; **5**:503; **11**:571, 573, 577; **45**:455
"Kingdom of Heaven" (Levertov) **66**:244
"The Kingdom of Poetry" (Schwartz) **10**:464
"The Kingdom of the Fathers" (Rich) **125**:332
The Kingdom of the Wicked (Burgess) **40**:124-26
The Kingdom of This World (Carpentier)
See *El reino de este mundo*
The Kingdoms of Elfin (Warner) **19**:459-60
Kingdoms of Gold, Kingdoms of Jade: The Americas Before Columbus (Fagan) **70**:331, 342
Kingdoms of the Wall (Silverberg) **140**:389, 397
"The Kingfisher" (Clampitt) **32**:115
"Kingfisher" (Oliver) **98**:292
The Kingfisher (Clampitt) **32**:115-18
"The Kingfishers" (Olson) **2**:326; **5**:328-29; **6**:388; **9**:412; **11**:417-20; **29**:329-30, 334
"Kingfishers at Condat" (Clarke) **61**:78, 82
"The Kingfisher's Boxing Gloves" (Fenton) **32**:165
Kingfishers Catch Fire (Godden) **53**:156-57
"Kinglidoma" (Ritsos) **6**:463
"The Kings" (Hope) **51**:215
The King's Fifth (O'Dell) **30**:268-70, 273
"The King's Indian" (Gardner) **5**:133-34; **7**:112-13, 115; **8**:238; **28**:167-68
The King's Indian (Gardner) **5**:132-35; **7**:111-14, 116; **8**:238; **18**:183; **28**:167
The King's Iron (Peck) **17**:341
The King's Persons (Greenberg) **7**:134; **30**:160-61
King's Ransom (Hunter) **31**:220
"Kingsbury Mill" (Fisher) **25**:161
"Kingsmeat" (Card) **47**:67
Kingstree Island (Ehle) **27**:102-03
"Kinjū" (Kawabata) **107**:73, 77, 86
Kink Kontroversy (Davies) **21**:88-9
The Kink Kronikles (Davies) **21**:93
Kinkakuji (Mishima) **2**:286; **4**:353-54, 357; **6**:338; **9**:383-84; **27**:335-36, 338-41
"Kinkies" (Trevor) **116**:371
The Kink's Greatest Celluloid Heroes (Davies) **21**:101
The Kinks Greatest Hits! (Davies) **21**:89
Kinks Kinkdom (Davies) **21**:89
Kinks Size (Davies) **21**:89
"Kinky Reggae" (Marley) **17**:267, 269
"The Kinnehorah" (Weidman) **7**:517
"Kinosaki nite" (Shiga) **33**:370

"Kinot al hametim bamilkhama" (Amichai) **116**:110-11
"The Kinsey Report" (Trilling) **24**:452
"Kinship" (Bottoms) **53**:31, 33
"Kinship" (Heaney) **14**:242, 244; **25**:243, 246, 251; **91**:117
Kinsman (Bova) **45**:71-3
Kiowa Trail (L'Amour) **25**:280
"Kip" (Grace) **56**:116-17, 120
Kipper's Game (Ehrenreich) **110**:175-79, 181-84
"Kira and Anya" (Bissoondath) **120**:13, 16, 19
"Kirchbachstrasse 121, 2800 Bremen" (Grayson) **38**:209
"Die Kirche im Dorf" (Boell) **72**:77
"The Kirk" (MacCaig) **36**:287
Kirlian Quest (Anthony) **35**:37
"Kirsten" (Shapcott) **38**:400
"Kiskatinaw Songs" (Musgrave) **13**:401
"The Kiss" (Blunden) **56**:39
"The Kiss" (Hall) **151**:195-96
"The Kiss" (Landolfi) **49**:216
"The Kiss" (Sassoon) **36**:385; **130**:181, 204, 213, 215
"The Kiss" (Sexton) **123**:407
Kiss (Warhol) **20**:421
The Kiss: A Memoir (Harrison) **151**:246-57
A Kiss before Dying (Levin) **3**:294
"A Kiss Errant" (Castillo) **151**:47, 65
"A Kiss in Galloway" (Fuller) **62**:197
Kiss, Kiss (Dahl) **79**:175-77, 183
Kiss Me Again, Stranger: A Collection of Eight Stories, Long and Short (du Maurier)
See *The Apple Tree: A Short Novel and Some Stories*
"Kiss Me Baby" (Wilson) **12**:644
Kiss Me, Deadly (Spillane) **13**:526-27
"Kiss Me, Hardy" (Bainbridge) **130**:28
Kiss Me Stupid (Wilder) **20**:461
The Kiss of Kin (Settle) **61**:374, 385
"The Kiss of Life" (Gardam) **43**:171
Kiss of the Spider Woman (McNally) **91**:159, 163
Kiss of the Spider Woman (Puig)
See *El beso de la mujer araña*
"Kiss on the Lips" (Prichard) **46**:332-33
Kiss on the Lips, and Other Stories (Prichard) **46**:332, 337, 343, 345
Kiss, Orchestra, Fish, Sausage (Aksyonov)
See *Potseluj, orkestr, ryba, kolbasa*
The Kiss to the Leper (Mauriac)
See *Le baiser au lépreux*
Kissing Cousins (Calisher) **134**:17, 31
"The Kissing Place" (Szirtes) **46**:394-95
"The Kissing Seat" (Muldoon) **32**:317
"Kissing Stieglitz Goodbye" (Stern) **100**:333
Kissing the Rod: An Anthology of Seventeenth-Century Women's Verse (Greer) **65**:316-17
"Kissing the Toad" (Kinnell) **29**:284
"Kitchen" (Jensen) **37**:191
"The Kitchen" (Lee) **90**:201
"The Kitchen" (O'Faolain) **32**:342
The Kitchen (Wesker) **3**:518; **5**:481-83; **42**:425-28, 430
Kitchen (Yoshimoto)
See *Kitchin*
"A Kitchen Allegory" (Fisher) **87**:128, 130
"The Kitchen Bitch" (D'Aguiar) **145**:115, 117, 121
The Kitchen God's Wife (Tan) **120**:365-69, 371, 386, 399-407, 409-413, 415-18, 422, 424; **151**:334
"The Kitchen Mandarins" (Erdrich) **120**:144
"The Kitchen Side of the Door" (Ferber) **93**:140-41
"The Kitchen Stairs" (Gombrowicz) **49**:127
"Kitchenette Building" (Brooks) **49**:31
Kitchin (Yoshimoto) **84**:421-30
"The Kite" (Eberhart) **11**:178; **56**:88
"The Kite" (Elytis) **100**:172
"Kite" (Jensen) **37**:191
"The Kite" (Strand) **71**:283
Kite (Minus) **39**:79-81
The Kite (Mitchell) **25**:322, 325-27
"Kite and Paint" (Robison) **42**:339
"Kite Flying at Doctor's Point" (Hulme) **130**:53
"A Kite for Michael and Christopher" (Heaney) **37**:165, 169
"Kite Man" (Wild) **14**:580
"Kites" (Merwin) **88**:210
"Kites" (Urdang) **47**:400
"Kitschy" (Szymborska) **99**:208
"Kitsilano Beach on a May Evening" (McFadden) **48**:258
"The Kitten" (Oliver) **34**:246, 249; **98**:256, 267
"Kittiwake" (Hall) **51**:170
"Kitty" (Appelfeld) **47**:5
Kitty Foyle (Trumbo) **19**:445
"Kitty Hawk" (Frost) **13**:230-31; **26**:120
"Kitty Partners" (Apple) **33**:22
Kitty Stobling (Kavanagh)
See *Come Dance with Kitty Stobling*
"Kitty's Back" (Springsteen) **17**:488
"The Kiwi Bird in the Kiwi Tree" (Bernstein) **142**:13, 16-17
Ki-Yu: A Story of Panthers (Haig-Brown) **21**:134, 139-40, 143-46
Kjeldene (Vesaas) **48**:404
"KKK" (Guillén) **48**:159
"Kladenec" (Bagryana) **10**:14
"Klagemauer Nacht" (Sachs) **98**:327
Klanger och spår (Transtroemer) **52**:410, 412; **65**:222-23, 229, 233
Klara and Two Men (Klima) **56**:166, 168
"Klare gerührt" (Jandl) **34**:196
"Klassik Komix #1" (Millhauser) **109**:160
"Klasyk" (Herbert) **43**:187
Klaxon, Trumpets, and Raspberries (Fo)
See *Clacson, trombette e penacchi*
"Kleckerburg" (Grass) **32**:198
"Klee Dead" (Coover) **15**:145
Klein und Wagner (Hesse) **69**:289, 297
"Kleine Aufforderung zum grossen Mundaufmachen" (Grass) **15**:263
"Eine Kleine mathmusik" (Perelman) **23**:336
"Kleiner Ausflug nach H" (Wolf) **150**:237, 320
Kleinzeit (Hoban) **7**:161; **25**:264, 266
Klingsohr (Hesse)
See *Klingsors letzter Sommer*
Klingsohrs letzter Sommer (Hesse)
See *Klingsors letzter Sommer*
Klingsor (Hesse)
See *Klingsors letzter Sommer*
Klingsor's Last Summer (Hesse)
See *Klingsors letzter Sommer*
Klingsors letzter Sommer (Hesse) **17**:206
The Klondike Stampede (Berton) **104**:61
Klondike: The Life and Death of the Last Great Gold Rush (Berton) **104**:39, 44-5, 47, 57
"Klounut govori" (Bagryana) **10**:14
"The Klupzy Girl" (Bernstein) **142**:55
The Knack (Jellicoe) **27**:206-10
The Knack (Lester) **20**:219, 223, 228-29
"The Knave of Diamonds" (Leonov)
See "Bubnovy valet"
Knave of Dreams (Norton) **12**:469-70
Kneading the Blood (Kenny) **87**:241
"Knee Song" (Sexton) **123**:408
"Kneel to the Rising Sun" (Caldwell) **1**:51; **14**:96; **60**:61
Kneel to the Rising Sun, and Other Stories (Caldwell) **60**:47, 50, 60-1
"Kneeling before You in a Gesture" (Brutus) **43**:91-2
"Kneeling Down to Look into a Culvert" (Bly) **38**:53; **128**:45
"Kneeshaw Goes to War" (Read) **4**:439
Der Knekht (Singer) **1**:313; **3**:453, 455, 457; **15**:504, 507; **23**:413-15, 418; **69**:316; **111**:294, 304-05, 307, 321-23, 328
"Knife" (Oates) **108**:382
"The Knife" (Samarakis) **5**:381
"The Knife" (Selzer) **74**:277-78
"Knife" (Simic) **9**:479; **22**:383; **49**:337, 339, 342; **68**:370, 379
"The Knife" (Tillinghast) **29**:416-17
A Knife All Blade (Cabral de Melo Neto)
See *Uma faca só lâmina*
The Knife and Other Poems (Tillinghast) **29**:415-17
"The Knife and the Bread" (Broumas) **73**:9
"The Knife and the Stone" (Hulme) **130**:52
"Knife Blows" (Mauriac)
See "Coups de couteaux"
Knife in the Water (Polanski) **16**:463-65, 467, 471-72
"The Knife Sharpener's Daughter" (Dybek) **114**:61
"The Knife Thrower" (Boell)
See "Der Mann mit den Messern"
"The Knight" (Hughes) **119**:270
"The Knight" (Rich) **6**:457; **11**:475-76; **36**:366
"The Knight, Death, and the Devil" (Jarrell) **13**:298
A Knight in Dried Plums (McFadden) **48**:245-46, 251
The Knight of the Swords (Moorcock) **27**:350
The Knightly Quest (Williams) **39**:449; **45**:447, 453
The Knightly Quest: A Novella and Four Short Stories (Williams) **1**:369; **45**:447
Knights and Dragons (Spencer) **22**:401, 405-06
Knight's Fee (Sutcliff) **26**:427-28, 431-36, 439, 441
Knight's Gambit (Faulkner) **3**:149, 156; **14**:179; **18**:148-49; **52**:128
The Knights of the Golden Table (Almedingen) **12**:1
"Knights of the Paper Spaceship" (Aldiss) **40**:17
The Knights of the Round Table (Cocteau)
See *Les chevaliers de la table ronde*
The Knights of the Round Table (Hein)
See *Die ritter der Tafelrunde*
"Knights of the White Camellia & Deacons of Defense" (Komunyakaa) **94**:249
"Knives" (Welch) **52**:428
"Knives of Pernambuco" (Cabral de Melo Neto)
See "As facas Pernambucanas"
Knjiga lirike (Krleža) **114**:166
"Knock, Knock" (Wilding) **73**:401, 403
Knock Knock (Feiffer) **8**:216; **64**:149-50, 159, 161
Knock on Any Door (Motley) **18**:355-57
"Knock on the Door" (Ochs) **17**:332
Knock upon Silence: Poems (Kizer) **15**:308; **39**:171; **80**:173-74, 177-79, 181
Knockdown (Francis) **22**:151-52; **42**:148-50, 155-58; **102**:140
"A Knocker" (Herbert) **9**:273
"Knockin' On Heaven's Door" (Dylan) **77**:187
"Knocking Around" (Ashbery) **15**:33
"Knocking Donkey Fleas off a Poet from the Southside of Chi" (Madhubuti) **73**:193, 214
Knocking on the Door (Paton) **10**:388; **25**:364
"Knocks Me off My Feet" (Wonder) **12**:660, 664
"Knole" (Fuller) **28**:152
"The Knot" (Kunitz) **148**:84-86, 93, 96, 99, 102-03, 142, 145
"A Knothole in Spent Time" (Ciardi) **129**:38
Knots (Laing) **95**:132, 137
"Knots in the Grain" (Snyder) **120**:331
The Knotting Sequence (Booth) **13**:103-04
Know about Alcohol (Hyde) **21**:179
Know about Drugs (Hyde) **21**:180
Know Nothing (Settle) **19**:409; **61**:372-73, 375-76, 381-87
Know Your Feelings (Hyde) **21**:177
"Know Your Rights" (Clash) **30**:51-2
"Knowing Bitches" (Ciardi) **129**:46
"Knowing He Was Not my Kind Yet I Followed" (Hannah) **90**:148-49

"Knowing the Human Condition" (Childress) **86**:314; **96**:104, 115
"Knowing Where to Stop" (Booth) **24**:91
"Knowledge" (Bogan) **46**:89; **93**:67
Knowledge and Experience in the Philosophy of F. H. Bradley (Eliot)
See "Experience and the Objects of Knowledge in the Philosophy of F. H. Bradley"
Knowledge and Human Interests (Habermas)
See *Erkenntnis und Interesse*
"Knowledge and the Image of Man" (Warren) **13**:576
Knowledge from the Abyss (Michaux)
See *Connaissance par les gouffres*
"Knowledge of Age" (Avison) **97**:76
Knowledge of Language: Its Nature, Origin, and Use (Chomsky) **132**:38-40, 67
"Knox" (Ellison) **13**:206
The Knox Brothers (Fitzgerald) **143**:266-68
"Knoxville, Tennessee" (Giovanni) **117**:194-96
Knuckle (Hare) **29**:213-14, 216-17; **58**:233; **136**:243, 259-61, 265, 286
Knulp (Hesse) **6**:237; **17**:218
Den knutna näven (Lagerkvist) **54**:274-75
Ko; or, A Season on Earth (Koch) **5**:219; **44**:248
"The Kobzar" (Gustafson) **36**:221
Kochu byt' chestnym (Voinovich) **10**:505, 507-08; **49**:373, 375-76; **147**:275-76
"Kodachrome" (Simon) **17**:466
Kodak (Cendrars) **18**:95; **106**:153, 158-59, 175, 185-86, 190-91, 198
Kodak Documentaires (Cendrars)
See *Kodak*
Kogda razglyaetsya (Pasternak) **18**:383
"Kogda v mrachneyshey iz stolits" (Akhmatova) **64**:9
"Koi" (Merrill) **91**:233
"Koisimi Buddhist of Altitudes" (Kinnell) **13**:320
Kojinteki na taiken (Oe) **10**:327, 374; **36**:343-48; **86**:215-16, 230, 236, 241, 244
"Koka Kola" (Clash) **30**:46
Kokkyō no minami, taiyō no nishi (Murakami) **150**:81, 90-2, 94
Koko (Straub) **107**:282-86, 288-91, 293-96, 298-302, 304, 306-07, 309-10
"Kolbel'naya treskovogo mysa" (Brodsky)
See "A Cape Cod Lullaby"
"Kolelo" (Bagryana)
See "Surce čoveško"
Kolkhida (Paustovsky) **40**:363, 368
Kollegi (Aksyonov)
See *Colleagues*
The Kolokol Papers (Bograd) **35**:62-3
Kolyma Tales (Shalamov) **18**:478-80
The Komagata Maru Incident (Pollock) **50**:224, 226
Kommentar till ett stjärnfall (Johnson)
See *Commentary on a Falling Star*
Die Komödie der Eitelkeit (Canetti) **14**:121; **75**:127-28, 143, 145-47; **86**:298, 301, 303
Komödie der Politik (Dürrenmatt) **15**:199
Kompleks polski (Konwicki) **28**:207-10; **54**:256-60, 262, 264; **117**:256-60, 262, 264, 271, 279-80, 284, 286, 290-91
"Kompromise Kompromisovich" (Yevtushenko) **26**:468
"Konarka" (Mahapatra) **33**:284
Koncert na ostrově (Seifert) **93**:336-37, 343
Konec prekrasnoj èpox (Brodsky)
See *Konets prekrasnoy epokhi*
Konek Landing (Figes) **31**:162
Konets melkogo cheloveka (Leonov) **92**:237-38, 242, 256, 265, 275, 278
Konets prekrasnoy epokhi (Brodsky) **13**:116-17
Konfessions of an Elizabethan Fan Dancer (Nichol) **18**:369
Kongi's Harvest (Soyinka) **5**:396; **36**:417-18; **44**:281-83, 286-88, 290
König Johann (Duerrenmatt) **102**:53, 55, 57, 62, 64
König Johann (Dürrenmatt) **15**:199
Kontakion for You Departed (Paton) **25**:363-64
Kon-Tiki: Across the Pacific by Raft (Heyerdahl) **26**:189-93
The Kon-Tiki Expedition (Heyerdahl) **26**:191, 193
"Kontrapunkti" (Bagryana) **10**:11, 13
Kontynenty (Milosz) **56**:236
Konungen (Lagerkvist) **54**:269-70, 275
"Kooks" (Bowie) **17**:58
Köp den blindes sång (Ekelöf) **27**:110
Kopfgeburten (Grass) **32**:201
Kora (Popa) **19**:373
Kora in Hell: Improvisations (Williams) **2**:468-70; **5**:507-09; **22**:466; **42**:449, 452, 460, 462-64; **67**:410
"Korab ot Ispanja" (Bagryana) **10**:12
"Kore" (Creeley) **8**:153; **36**:118
"Kore" (Merwin) **8**:389; **13**:384; **18**:335-36; **88**:203-04
"Korea" (McGahern) **48**:262
"Korea" (Selzer) **74**:269, 273, 285
Korol, dama, valet (Nabokov) **1**:243; **2**:299; **6**:352; **8**:417-18; **15**:396; **23**:312-13; **44**:465; **46**:294; **64**:348
Korrektur (Bernhard) **32**:21-3, 26; **61**:10, 14-15, 19, 21; **32**:21-2
Korsoniloff (Cohen) **19**:111
Koshikei (Oshima) **20**:246-49, 251-52
Kosmos (Gombrowicz) **7**:123, 127; **49**:121, 123, 127, 129, 133-34
Koto (Kawabata) **107**:98-9, 102, 104, 107-12
Koviakin's Notes (Leonov)
See *Zapisi nekotorykh epizodov, sdelannye v gorode Goguleve Andreem Petrovichem Koviakinym*
Kovyakin's Diary (Leonov)
See *Zapisi nekotorykh epizodov, sdelannye v gorode Goguleve Andreem Petrovichem Koviakinym*
Kovyakin's Journal (Leonov)
See *Zapisi nekotorykh epizodov, sdelannye v gorode Goguleve Andreem Petrovichem Koviakinym*
The Kozlotur Constellation (Iskander)
See *Sozvezdie Kozlotura*
Kōzui wa waga tamashii ni oyobi (Oe) **36**:350; **86**:215-17, 228, 230-32, 234, 238-39, 241
"Kral Majales" (Ginsberg) **36**:184; **109**:346-47, 355-56
"Kranich and Bach" (Hollander) **8**:299
"Krankheit und Liebesentzug" (Wolf) **58**:430; **150**:251
Krapp's Last Tape (Beckett) **1**:20; **2**:45-6; **6**:39, 45-7; **9**:77, 83-6; **10**:32; **11**:37-9; **14**:74; **18**:42-3, 47; **29**:58, 63; **57**:79, 89; **59**:252, 255, 257-58; **83**:114
Krasnoe koleso: Povestvovanie v otmerennykh srokakh. Uzel I, Avgust chetyrnadsatogo (Solzhenitsyn)
See *Avgust chetyrnadtsatogo*
Krazy Kat: The Unveiling and Other Stories (Dawson) **6**:125-26
"Kredowe koło" (Rozewicz) **139**:295, 297
The Kremlin Letter (Huston) **20**:171
"Kremlin of Smoke" (Schnackenberg) **40**:380-81
"Krestova Solitaire" (Lane) **25**:285
"Kretschmer's Types" (Durrell) **27**:97
Krik? Krak! (Danticat) **94**:93-100; **139**:85-9, 98-9
Krilon: A Novel about the Probable (Johnson) **14**:295
Krippendorf's Tribe (Parkin) **43**:336-39
Kris (Bergman) **72**:51
"Krishnamurti and His Hallucinating Devotees" (Asturias) **8**:25
Krisis: Ein Stuck Tagebuch (Hesse) **69**:275, 293, 297
"Kristallnacht" (Ai) **69**:9, 17
The Kristeva Reader (Kristeva) **140**:151, 181, 186, 201
Kristlein Trilogy (Walser) **27**:463
Kristnihald undir jökli (Laxness) **25**:300
Kristofferson (Kristofferson) **26**:266
Kristofor Kolombo (Krleža) **114**:166, 174-76
"Kristu Du" (Carey) **96**:25, 28, 36-7, 39
Kristy's Courage (Friis-Baastad) **12**:213
Kroliki i udavy (Iskander) **47**:195, 200-01
Kronika wypadków milosnych (Konwicki) **117**:257, 283, 285, 287
Kroniki (Milosz) **82**:297
Kroti film o milosci (Kieslowski) **120**:208, 210, 212-13, 215-16, 224, 227, 250
Kroti film o zabijaniu (Kieslowski) **120**:206, 208, 211-13, 215-16, 224-25, 236, 238-40, 242-43, 250-51
Kroxotnye rasskazy (Solzhenitsyn) **2**:412
"Die Krücke" (Hein) **154**:165, 167
Kruger's Alp (Hope) **52**:211-14, 217
Kruglie sutki non-stop (Aksyonov)
See *'Round the Clock Non-Stop*
Krumnagel (Ustinov) **1**:346
"Der Krüppel" (Hein) **154**:166
"Kto my,—fishki ili velikiye?" (Voznesensky) **57**:416
"Kto ty?" (Voznesensky) **15**:555
"Kublaikansky" (Raine) **32**:351
Kuća nasred druma (Popa) **19**:375
"Kudo" (Endō) **99**:293
"Kudzu" (Dickey) **15**:173
"The Kugelmass Episode" (Allen) **52**:41, 48
Kühe in Halbtrauer (Schmidt) **56**:391-92
Kujira no shimetsu suru hi (Oe) **86**:214
"Kukuvitsa" (Bagryana) **10**:12
Kullus (Pinter) **27**:388
"Die Kultur als Fehler" (Lem) **149**:278
"Kuma" (Shiga) **33**:368
Kumbha mela (Antonioni) **144**:70
Kumonoso-jo (Kurosawa)
See *Throne of Blood*
"Kumpel mit dem langen Haar" (Boell) **72**:69
Kumquat (Harrison) **129**:216, 219
"A Kumquat for John Keats" (Harrison) **129**:166
"A Kumquat for John Keats" (Harrison) **43**:179, 181; **129**:211
"Kuniko" (Shiga) **33**:367
"Kunst und Religion" (Boell) **27**:67
Der Künstliche Baum (Jandl) **34**:197
Kunstmakher fun Lublin (Singer) **1**:313; **3**:455, 457; **6**:508; **9**:488; **11**:500, 503; **15**:504-05, 508; **23**:414-15, 418, 422; **69**:307, 317; **111**:294, 300, 305, 307, 319, 321-22, 324-25, 328, 345
"Kurōdiasu no nikki" (Shiga) **33**:366-67, 371
Kuroi ame (Ibuse) **22**:224-27
Kuroi junin no ohna (Ichikawa) **20**:186
"Kurt and Natasha" (Janowitz) **145**:325
Kurt Gerstein ou l'ambiguité du bien (Friedlander) **90**:105-7, 112, 118
Kurt Gerstein: The Ambiguity of Good (Friedlander)
See *Kurt Gerstein ou l'ambiguité du bien*
"Kurt Vonnegut and His Critics: The Aesthetics of Accessibility" (Irving) **38**:250
Der kurze Brief (Handke)
See *Der kurze Brief zum langen Abschied*
Der kurze Brief zum langen Abschied (Handke) **5**:164-65, 167; **10**:255-56, 258; **38**:218-20, 222-23, 227; **134**:114-15, 118, 121, 130-31, 144-45, 148, 180
"Kurzgefasster Lebenslauf" (Hesse) **17**:204
"Kushta v poleto" (Bagryana) **10**:12
Kuşlar da gitti (Kemal) **14**:301
Kvaedakver (Laxness) **25**:295
"Kväll Morgon" (Transtroemer) **65**:235
Kvetch (Berkoff) **56**:17-19
Kvinnodröm (Bergman) **72**:41, 62
Kvinnor ropar heim (Vesaas) **48**:404, 406
Kvinnors väntan (Bergman) **16**:66; **72**:40, 62
"Kwa Mamu Zetu Waliotuzaa (for our mothers who gave us birth)" (Sanchez) **116**:273, 274, 281, 298, 301, 316

"Kyofu" (Tanizaki) **28**:417
Kyōko no ie (Mishima) **9**:383, 385; **27**:341
Kyōko's House (Mishima)
See *Kyōko no ie*
"Kyoto Born in Spring Song" (Snyder) **120**:317
"A Kyōto Garden" (Enright) **31**:149
"Kyoto: Her Nature, Food...and Women" (Tanizaki) **28**:416
"Kyrie" (Gascoyne) **45**:149
Kyrie (Jouve) **47**:212
"L" (Merrill) **8**:383-84, 387
"L" (Walcott) **67**:358
"La" (Tolson) **105**:262
"L.A." (Young) **17**:572
LA (Cixous) **92**:74, 93
L.A. (Wilson) **12**:653-54
"A la créole" (Audiberti) **38**:21
De la grammatologie (Derrida) **24**:137-40, 145, 147, 156; **87**:72-74, 77-80, 89-91, 100, 102, 104
"De la littérature considérée comme une tauromachie" (Leiris) **61**:341, 343, 352, 357-58
"A la mort" (Senghor) **130**:267
De la séduction (Baudrillard) **60**:24, 26, 33
De la vigilia estéril (Castellanos) **66**:45, 50
L.A. Woman (Morrison) **17**:290-91, 295-96
Labels: A Mediterranean Journal (Waugh) **19**:462; **107**:394
El laberinto (Arrabal)
See *La Labyrinthe*
El laberinto de la soledad (Paz) **3**:375-76; **6**:397; **10**:393; **19**:364, 366-67; **51**:331; **65**:176, 179, 181, 185-86, 188, 195; **119**:406-11, 413, 417, 419, 423
Laberinto de Pasiones (Almodovar) **114**:3, 14, 16-7, 30-2, 45, 46-9, 55
Labor in Vain (Garfield) **12**:234
Laboratories of the Spirit (Thomas) **13**:544-45; **48**:379-81
Laborem Exercens (John Paul II) **128**:179
Labors of Love (Cassill) **23**:109
"Labour Day Dinner" (Munro) **95**:302
The Labourers of Herakles (Harrison) **129**:220, 223-27
"The Labours of Hercules" (Fuller) **62**:186-87, 193-94, 201
LaBrava (Leonard) **28**:236-37; **34**:213-16; **71**:208-13, 216, 220, 222-23; **120**:270, 272, 274-77, 284, 287, 289, 295
"The Labrenas" (Landolfi)
See "La labrene"
"La labrene" (Landolfi) **49**:216-17
Laburnum Grove (Priestley) **2**:346; **34**:361
Labyrinth of Passions (Almodovar)
See *Laberinto de Pasiones*
The Labyrinth of Solitude (Paz)
See *El laberinto de la soledad*
La Labyrinthe (Arrabal) **58**:5-8, 12, 17-18
Le labyrinthe du monde (Yourcenar) **19**:484; **38**:461; **87**:382, 396, 432
Labyrinths (Borges)
See *Labyrinths: Selected Stories, and Other Writings*
Labyrinths of Voice (Kroetsch) **57**:287, 293; **132**:204-5, 212, 217-22, 230, 233, 250, 252-55, 286
Labyrinths: Selected Stories, and Other Writings (Borges) **2**:72; **3**:80; **8**:99; **44**:356; **48**:44, 46; **83**:171, 185, 188
Labyrinths, with Path of Thunder (Okigbo) **25**:349, 352, 355-56; **84**:305-06, 310, 312, 314, 316-19, 322-23, 328-34, 339-43
"Lac en coeur" (Dudek) **11**:161; **19**:137
"Laca" (Guillén) **79**:238
"Lace" (Boland) **67**:39; **113**:84
"The Lace Maker" (Watkins) **43**:446
"Der Lacher" (Boell) **2**:55; **15**:69; **27**:66
"Lachesis lapponica" (Enzensberger) **43**:145-46
"Lachrimae; or, Seven Tears Figured in Seven Passionate Pavans" (Hill) **8**:296; **18**:238, 242; **45**:178, 180-85, 187, 189
"Lackawanna" (Kinnell) **129**:271
"The Lackawanna at Dusk" (Parini) **54**:361
Laços de família (Lispector) **43**:267-72
"'Lacrimae rerum'" (Corn) **33**:116
"The Ladder" (Prince) **35**:331-32
"The Ladder" (Pritchett) **41**:334
"The Ladder and the Tree" (Golding) **58**:197
Ladder of Years (Tyler) **103**:274-77
Ladders to the Fire (Nin) **4**:376; **60**:279
Ladera este (Paz) **51**:324, 333; **65**:177, 181-83, 189, 198, 200; **119**:419
The Ladies (Grumbach) **64**:198-201
"Ladies Advice" (Thesen) **56**:421
Ladies Almanack (Barnes) **29**:27-9; **127**:161, 200-05
Ladies and Escorts (Thomas) **37**:416-17; **107**:316, 318, 326, 348
"Ladies and Gentleman" (Oates) **108**:385
"Ladies' and Gentlemen's Guide to Modern English Usage" (Thurber) **5**:435
"Ladies and Red Nights" (Vollmann) **89**:276, 304
"Ladies Auxiliary" (Guthrie) **35**:185
"Ladies by Their Windows" (Justice) **19**:232, 236; **102**:256
"Ladies from Lapland" (Chappell) **78**:114
"The Ladies in the Library" (Vidal) **33**:407; **142**:332
"Ladies, Listen to Me" (Wakoski) **7**:504
"Ladies Looking for Lice" (Kennedy) **42**:258
Ladies Love Outlaws (Jennings) **21**:201
Ladies' Man (Price) **12**:491-92
"Ladies Need Only Apply" (Astley) **41**:47
The Ladies of Missalonghi (McCullough) **107**:152, 154, 162
The Ladies of St. Hedwig's (Almedingen) **12**:1, 3
Ladies of the Canyon (Mitchell) **12**:436-37
Ladies of the Corridor (Parker) **68**:331, 333, 337
"Ladies Pay" (Reed) **21**:312-13
"The Ladies Who Lunch" (Sondheim) **30**:385-86, 391, 395, 400; **147**:240, 252-54
The Ladies-in-Waiting (Buero Vallejo)
See *Las meninas*
"El lado de la sombra" (Bioy Casares) **88**:94
El lado de la sombra (Bioy Casares) **88**:94
Ladri di biciclette (De Sica) **20**:85-9, 91-7
"Lady" (Carruth) **84**:135
"A Lady" (Donoso)
See "Una señora"
The Lady (Richter) **30**:316, 319, 324, 330
Lady (Tryon) **11**:548
"The Lady and the Pedlar" (Anand) **23**:18
"The Lady and the Unicorn" (Porter) **33**:322
"The Lady and the Unicorn and Other Tapestries" (Graham) **118**:240, 242, 246
"Lady Bates" (Jarrell) **2**:209; **6**:260
"Lady Cab Driver" (Prince) **35**:326-28
"Lady Day" (Reed) **21**:307
Lady Frederick (Coward) **29**:134
Lady Frederick (Maugham) **15**:366; **67**:215, 223, 228
The Lady from Dubuque (Albee) **25**:36-40; **53**:21-3, 25; **86**:120; **113**:28, 31-3, 40
"The Lady from Ferme-Neuve" (Ferron) **94**:120
"The Lady from Guatemala" (Pritchett) **5**:353-54; **41**:333
"The Lady from Lucknow" (Mukherjee) **53**:267
The Lady from Nowhere-At-All (Carroll) **10**:98
The Lady from Shanghai (Welles) **20**:434, 441, 443-44; **80**:382-84, 386, 388-91, 393, 395
"The Lady from the Land" (Thurber) **5**:433
"Lady Godiva" (Moravia) **7**:244
Lady Godiva and Other Stories (Moravia)
See *Un'altra vita*
"Lady Godiva's Horse" (Rooke) **25**:394
"Lady Godiva's Operation" (Reed) **21**:307
"Lady Immoraline" (Sitwell) **67**:325
"Lady in a Green Dress" (Callaghan) **41**:98
The Lady in Kicking Horse Reservoir (Hugo) **6**:244-45; **18**:260; **32**:239, 241-44, 246, 250
The Lady in the Car with Glasses and a Gun (Japrisot)
See *La dame dans l'auto avec des lunettes et un fusil*
Lady in the Dark (Hart) **66**:176, 178, 180, 182-83, 188-90
Lady into Fox (Garnett) **3**:188-89
The Lady Is Cold (White) **10**:528-29
Lady L (Gary) **25**:184
"Lady Lazarus" (Plath) **2**:335-36; **3**:390; **5**:342-44; **9**:427; **11**:445-48, 450; **14**:423, 425-26, 428; **17**:348, 354, 359, 361, 363, 365-66; **50**:440, 449; **51**:342-44, 346, 351, 353; **62**:390, 405; **111**:159, 173-74, 176-78, 180-81, 185, 199, 208-11, 216, 221
"Lady Lucifer" (O'Faolain) **70**:312
"Lady Luncheon Club" (Angelou) **35**:30
"A Lady of Fashion" (Phillips) **28**:362
The Lady of Larkspur Lotion (Williams) **45**:448
Lady of Luzon (Connelly) **7**:55
"A Lady of Quality" (Kinsella) **138**:159
The Lady of the Camelias (Abell)
See *Kameliadamen*
"The Lady of the House of Love" (Carter) **41**:117
"The Lady of the Lake" (Malamud) **9**:349; **11**:353; **27**:297; **44**:419; **85**:199
"Lady Olga" (Mitchell) **98**:168, 180
"The Lady on 142" (Thurber) **125**:401, 410-11
Lady Oracle (Atwood) **8**:30-31, 33-34; **13**:44-6; **15**:39; **25**:62-5, 67-8; **44**:147; **84**:70, 72, 77-9, 86 , 90-5, 105-07; **135**:7, 13, 18, 22, 67, 71
"Lady Stardust" (Bowie) **17**:65
The Lady Vanishes (Hitchcock) **16**:337-38, 340, 345, 347
The Lady Who Sold Furniture (Metcalf) **37**:299
"Lady with a Lamp" (Parker) **68**:326, 334, 339
Lady With a Laptop (Thomas) **132**:386
Lady with Chains (Carrier)
See *La dame qui avait des chaînes aux chevilles*
"The Lady with No One at All" (Williams) **45**:444
The Lady with the Compass (Haviaras) **33**:202
"The Lady with the Dog" (Baxter) **78**:28
"The Lady with the Pet Dog" (Oates) **52**:338; **108**:354, 368, 371
The Lady with the Unicorn (Watkins) **43**:441, 446, 451, 456
Lady Yesterday (Estleman) **48**:107
"Lady-Oh" (Diamond) **30**:112
"Lady's Boogie" (Hughes) **108**:299-304
Lady's Maid (Fisher) **149**:
Lady's Maid (Forster) **149**:78-9, 82
The Lady's Not for Burning (Fry) **2**:143, 145; **10**:200
"La'em" (Amichai) **116**:132
"El lago de los cisnes" (Neruda) **62**:332
"Lagoon" (Brodsky) **36**:78
"The Lagoon" (Frame) **96**:183-85, 188
The Lagoon and Other Stories (Frame) **66**:143-45; **96**:183-85, 188-89, 194, 209, 216
"Laguna Blues" (Wright) **146**:304, 343
"Laguna Ladies Luncheon" (Allen) **84**:8
Le lai de Barabbas (Arrabal) **18**:21
Laid Back in Washington (Buchwald) **33**:95
Laidlaw (McIlvanney) **42**:282-85
The Laird of Abbotsford: A View of Sir Walter Scott (Wilson) **33**:452-53
"The Laird's Son" (Brown) **100**:82
"Le lait de la mort" (Yourcenar) **38**:463; **87**:390
"Lajwanti" (Anand) **23**:21
Lak tar miyo kinyero wi lobo (p'Bitek) **96**:300
"The Lake" (Fuller) **28**:153
"The Lake" (Hall) **51**:171
"The Lake" (Jeffers) **54**:234
"The Lake" (Merwin) **13**:386
"The Lake" (Wright) **53**:424
The Lake (Kawabata) **5**:207-08; **9**:316; **107**:106, 108
"Lake Chelan" (Stafford) **4**:520

Lake Effect Country (Ammons) **57**:49-51, 59; **108**:16, 57
The Lake Goddess (Nwapa) **133**:219, 222, 224-27, 229, 233-36
"Lake in Spring" (Wright) **11**:578
"The Lake in the Sky" (Haines) **58**:218
"The Lake in Winter" (Shapcott) **38**:397
"Lake Michigan Morning" (Sandburg) **35**:356
The Lake of Darkness (Rendell) **28**:386-87; **48**:320-21
"The Lake of Loneliness" (Sagan) **17**:428
Lake of the Woods (Tesich) **40**:417, 422; **69**:373
"The Lake of Tuonela" (Roberts) **14**:464
"A Lake Scene" (Swenson) **61**:400; **106**:326
"Lake Stephen" (Baxter) **78**:26
"Lake Superior" (Niedecker) **42**:297, 300
Lake Wobegon Days (Keillor) **40**:275-77; **115**:261, 263-64, 269, 274-75, 277, 296
Lakeboat (Mamet) **46**:252
"Lakeshore" (Scott) **22**:372-74, 377-78
"Lakeside Incident" (Skelton) **13**:507
The Lakestown Rebellion (Hunter) **35**:229
Lakota Woman (Crow Dog) **93**:109-112
"Lamarck Elaborated" (Wilbur) **3**:533
"The Lamb" (Oliver) **19**:362
Lamb (Mac Laverty) **31**:253, 255-56
The Lamb (Mauriac) **56**:219
"Lamb to the Slaughter" (Dahl) **79**:180
"Lambda" (Tolson) **105**:284
The Lambert Mile (White) **49**:401-04
The Lambert Revels (White)
See *The Lambert Mile*
"Lambkin: A Fable" (Hope) **51**:217
The Lamb's War (de Hartog) **19**:133
"The Lame" (Bottoms) **53**:29
"Lame de fond" (Montague) **46**:269
"The Lame Duck" (Wright) **53**:425
"A Lame Idyll" (MacNeice) **53**:233
"The Lame Shall Enter First" (O'Connor) **3**:366; **13**:418; **15**:410; **21**:261, 263, 272, 276; **104**:103, 106, 108, 100, 113, 123, 135, 138, 141, 156, 173, 178-79, 184-85, 194, 196
"Lament" (Dodson) **79**:191
"Lament" (Gunn) **81**:179, 181, 184, 186-87
"Lament" (Livesay) **79**:345
"Lament" (Morrison) **17**:295-96
"Lament" (Plath) **17**:360
"Lament" (Sexton) **53**:318
Lament and Triumph (Barker) **48**:10-11, 16, 20
"Lament: Fishing with Richard Hugo" (Wright) **28**:469
"Lament for a Dead Policeman" (Simmons) **43**:414
"Lament for a Proprietor" (Porter) **33**:318
"Lament for Barney Flanagan" (Baxter) **14**:62
"Lament for Doormen" (Tomlinson) **45**:403
"The Lament for Galadriel" (Tolkien) **38**:440
Lament for Harmonica (Ringwood) **48**:330, 334-35, 339
"Lament for Moths" (Williams) **71**:360
"Lament for Pasiphaé" (Graves) **2**:175
"Lament for the Duke of Medina Sidonia" (Beer) **58**:38
"Lament for the Great Music" (MacDiarmid) **4**:309-10, 313; **11**:333
"Lament For The Lakes" (Frame) **96**:200
"Lament for the Makers" (Buckley) **57**:131
"Lament for the Makers" (Pinsky) **94**:308; **121**:437
"Lament for the O'Neills" (Montague) **46**:275-76
"Lament for the Poles of Buffalo" (Hass) **18**:209, 211
"The Lament of Edward Blastock" (Sitwell) **67**:325
"Lament of the Drums" (Okigbo) **84**:310-11, 315, 321, 326-27, 336, 341
"Lament of the Flutes" (Okigbo) **25**:351; **84**:328-30, 332
"Lament of the Frontier Guard" (Pound) **112**:344
"Lament of the Lavender Mist" (Okigbo) **25**:351, 354; **84**:310, 328-29, 331, 336
"The Lament of the Masks: For W. B. Yeats: 1865-1939" (Okigbo) **25**:353; **84**:311, 321
"Lament of the Normal Child" (McGinley) **14**:366
"Lament of the Sacred Python" (Achebe) **7**:6; **11**:4
"Lament of the Silent Sisters" (Okigbo)
See "Silences: Lament of the Silent Sisters"
"The Lament of the Tortured Lover" (Christie) **110**:126
"The Lament on the Death of a Master of Arts" (Anand) **23**:16; **93**:34
"Lament over Love" (Hughes) **35**:221
"The Lament upon the Waters" (Ashbery) **77**:45
"Lamentación de Dido" (Castellanos) **66**:45-6, 50-1, 53
"Lamentations" (Glück) **22**:175-77
"Lamentations" (Sassoon) **130**:182, 216, 220
"Lamentations on the War Dead" (Amichai)
See "Kinot al hametim bamilkhama"
"Lamento" (Transtroemer) **52**:410; **65**:235
Laments (Heaney) **91**:124
Laments for the Living (Parker) **15**:414; **68**:325
"A Lamia in the Cevennes" (Byatt) **136**:195
"Lamium" (Glück) **81**:173
De l'amour dans la ferraille (Carrier) **78**:79-82
"Lamp" (Rakosi) **47**:344
The Lamp and the Veil (Watkins) **43**:441-42
"The Lamp at Noon" (Ross) **13**:493
The Lamp at Noon, and Other Stories (Ross) **13**:492
A Lamp for Nightfall (Caldwell) **50**:302; **60**:64
"A Lamp in the Window" (Capote) **19**:85
"The Lamp of God" (Queen) **11**:461
A Lamp on the Plains (Horgan) **53**:172-75
"La lámpara en la tierra" (Neruda) **7**:259
Lampes à arc (Morand) **41**:303, 307
"Lampfall" (Walcott) **76**:279
"Lamplighter: 1914" (Kunitz) **148**:122
The Lamplighter's Funeral (Garfield) **12**:234-35, 237
The Lamplit Answer (Schnackenberg) **40**:380-81
"Lamp-Posts" (Dunn) **40**:169
"Lampshades" (Yevtushenko) **26**:467
Lamy of Santa Fe (Horgan) **9**:279
Lanark: A Life in Four Books (Gray) **41**:176-84
"Lancaster" (Sillitoe) **148**:
Lancelot (Percy) **8**:442-46; **14**:411, 414-15, 419; **18**:399, 402; **47**:341; **65**:257
Lancelot (Vansittart) **42**:396-98
Lancelot du Lac (Bresson) **16**:119
"Land" (Heaney) **5**:172
The Land (Colum) **28**:86-7, 90
Land (Lopez y Fuentes)
See *Tierra*
The Land and People of Ghana (Sale) **68**:349
The Land and the Promise (Slaughter) **29**:376
"The Land and the Water" (Grau) **146**:129
"The Land around Us" (Carson) **71**:104
"The Land Below" (Dorn) **10**:158-59
The Land beyond the River (Stuart) **11**:510; **34**:374
The Land Breakers (Ehle) **27**:103
The Land Is Bright (Kaufman) **38**:264, 266
"Land Israel" (Sachs) **98**:357
Land Israel (Sachs) **98**:357
"The Land Itself" (O'Brien) **8**:430
The Land Leviathan (Moorcock) **27**:348-49
Land of Carnival (Amado)
See *O país do carnaval*
"The Land of Cockaigne, 1568" (Dubie) **36**:135
"Land of Cotton" (Sorrentino) **7**:448
The Land of Look Behind: Prose and Poetry (Cliff) **120**:90, 92
"The Land of Loss" (Kinsella) **138**:132, 166
The Land of Lost Content (Hill) **113**:287
The Land of Lost Content (Phillips) **28**:362
Land of Muscovy (Almedingen)
See *Rus into Muscovy*
"Land of Promise" (Swan) **69**:363-64
The Land of Promise (Maugham) **11**:368; **93**:254
Land of Silence and of Darkness (Herzog) **16**:328
The Land of Silence and Other Poems (Sarton) **49**:312
The Land of the Blessed Virgin (Maugham) **93**:268
Land of the Free—U.S.A. (MacLeish) **8**:361; **14**:338; **68**:286, 292
"The Land of the Freeze" (Ekelöf) **27**:115
The Land of the Living (Connelly) **7**:57
The Land of Ulro (Milosz)
See *Ziemia Ulro*
Land of Unlikeness (Graham)
See *Region of Unlikeness*
Land of Unlikeness (Lowell) **1**:183; **4**:295, 297-98, 302; **5**:257; **8**:348, 356; **37**:235, 239, 241; **124**:253-54,263, 270, 281, 285-86
"The Land of Veils" (Peacock) **60**:293
The Land That Drank the Rain (Hoffman) **141**:267-68, 274-75, 277-78, 281, 296, 303-07
"The Land They Gave Us" (Rulfo)
See "Nos han dado la tierra"
The Land Unknown (Raine) **7**:353
"Land Where My Fathers Died" (Dubus) **97**:208, 213-16
Land Where My Fathers Died (Dubus) **97**:209
Land without Bread (Bunuel)
See *Las Hurdes—Tierra sin pan*
Land without Stars (Kiely) **23**:259, 261-62; **43**:239, 245
"Land Workers" (Masefield) **11**:358
"Landed Fish" (Piercy) **27**:374
Landed Gentry (Maugham) **11**:368
"Landfall" (Hoffman) **141**:270, 273, 280
"Landfall" (Mosley) **43**:317
Landfill Meditations (Vizenor) **103**:288
"Landing on the Moon" (Swenson) **61**:391
"Landing Zone Bravo" (O'Brien) **103**:145
"Landings" (Hoffman) **141**:294-95
"The Landlady" (Dahl) **79**:181
The Landlady (Behan) **79**:36, 53
Landlocked (Lessing) **3**:290, 292; **6**:291; **94**:281-82
"The Landlord" (Pritchett) **41**:334
The Landlord (Hunter) **35**:224-25, 227
Landlord (Vansittart) **42**:395
"The Landlord's Flower Beds" (Thesen) **56**:420
"The Landlord's Tiger Lilies" (Thesen) **56**:422
Lando (L'Amour) **25**:278
Landor's Poetry (Pinsky) **38**:360; **94**:302; **121**:448
Landru (Chabrol) **16**:169, 181
"Land's End" (MacLeish) **68**:273, 284, 287
Land's End (Stolz) **12**:555
"Landscape" (Ashbery) **41**:37
"Landscape" (Hooker) **43**:196-97
"Landscape" (Oliver) **98**:261, 267
Landscape (Pinter) **3**:386-87; **6**:416-17, 420; **9**:420; **11**:442-43; **15**:423-24; **27**:385, 394-96; **73**:268
Landscape after the Battle (Wajda) **16**:582
Landscape and Memory (Schama) **150**:152-62, 165-77, 179-80, 182-83, 188, 196, 202, 207
"Landscape as Poetic Focus" (Davie) **10**:125
"Landscape at Champrovent" (Dobyns) **37**:81
"Landscape, Figure, Cavern" (Le Guin) **45**:213
"Landscape for the Disappeared" (Komunyakaa) **94**:240
"Landscape, History and the Pueblo Imagination" (Silko) **114**:305-06
Landscape in Concrete (Lind)
See *Landschaft in Beton*
"Landscape in Spring" (Soto) **80**:290
"Landscape Near an Aerodrome" (Spender) **41**:427; **91**:260
Landscape of a Nightmare (Baumbach) **6**:32; **23**:52-3

"A Landscape of Cries" (Sachs)
See "Landschaft aus Schreien"
"Landscape of Fire" (Hooker) **43**:201
"Landscape of Love" (Page) **18**:376
"Landscape of My Young World" (Brutus) **43**:93
"The Landscape of Return" (Mahapatra) **33**:277
"Landscape of Screams" (Sachs)
See "Landschaft aus Schreien"
Landscape of the Body (Guare) **14**:221; **29**:204-06, 208; **67**:81-2, 85
Landscape of the Daylight Moon (Hooker) **43**:197, 199-200
"Landscape of the Star" (Rich) **7**:368
Landscape Painted with Tea (Pavic)
See *Predeo slikan cajem*
"Landscape Poetry Is a Dead Letter" (Bernard) **59**:45
Landscape West of Eden (Aiken) **52**:26
"Landscape with a Wish" (Levi) **41**:244
"Landscape with Door" (Alexander) **121**:22
Landscape with Figures (Hildesheimer)
See *Landschaft mit Figuren*
"Landscape with Little Figures" (Justice) **19**:234
"Landscape with Orphans" (Porter) **33**:320
"Landscape with Poet" (Levi) **41**:244
Landscape with Rain (Gustafson) **36**:220-22
"Landscape with Tractor" (Taylor) **44**:302-03
"Landscape without Figures" (McGinley) **14**:366
"Landscapeople" (Ashbery) **25**:53
"Landscapes" (Eliot) **13**:201; **15**:213
"Landscapes" (Oates) **3**:359; **6**:367
Landscapes After the Battle (Goytisolo)
See *Paisajes después de la batalla*
Landscapes of Living and Dying (Ferlinghetti) **27**:139; **111**:59
Landscapes of Watt (Beckett) **29**:59
Landscapes with Figures (Cabral de Melo Neto)
See *Paisagens com figuras*
"Landscapes with Termites" (Cabral de Melo Neto)
See "Paisagens com cupim"
The Landscapes Within (Okri) **87**:314, 316-19, 322, 325
"Landschaft aus Schreien" (Sachs) **98**:331, 335, 338-41, 343-44
Landschaft in Beton (Lind) **1**:177-78; **2**:245; **4**:292-93; **27**:271; **82**:128, 131-40, 142, 145
Landschaft mit Figuren (Hildesheimer) **49**:167
"Landslides" (Coles) **46**:112
Landslides: Selected Poems, 1975-1985 (Coles) **46**:113
"Lane" (Ali) **69**:31
Le langage et son double/The Language and Its Shadow (Green) **77**:285
"A l'ange avantgardien" (Scott) **22**:374, 377
"Der Lange Marsch" (Hofmann) **54**:225
"Der Längere Arm" (Lenz) **27**:245
The Langoliers (King) **113**:366-67, 385-87
Langsam im Schatten (Handke) **134**:161-62
Langsame Heimkehr (Handke) **134**:116, 123, 133, 143-46, 148, 154, 174
"Langston Blues" (Randall) **135**:398
Langston Hughes: A Biography (Meltzer) **26**:299
The Langston Hughes Reader (Hughes) **108**:285
"Langston, McKay, and Dubois: The Contradicitions of Art and Politics during the Harlem Renaissance" (Baraka) **115**:11
"Language" (Hooks) **94**:157
"Language" (Ciardi) **40**:156
"The Language" (Creeley) **78**:162
Language (Spicer) **8**:499; **72**:346, 348, 351
"Language and Gnosis" (Steiner) **24**:435
"Language and Literature from a Pueblo Perspective" (Silko) **114**:294-95, 303, 305-06, 311
Language and Mind (Chomsky) **132**:38
"Language (and Other) Problems" (Richler) **46**:352
"Language and Politics" (McCarthy) **39**:488-89
Language and Politics (Chomsky) **132**:68
Language and Problems of Knowledge: The Managua Lectures (Chomsky) **132**:40, 67-8,
Language and Responsibility (Chomsky) **132**:38
Language and Silence (Steiner) **24**:427-30, 432
"Language and the Destiny of Man" (Achebe) **152**:76-7
"Language as an Escape from the Discrete" (Jacobsen) **48**:192, 194-95
"Language as an Instrument of Domination" (Castellanos) **66**:56
Language as Gesture (Blackmur) **24**:57, 59-60, 63, 66
Language as Symbolic Action (Burke) **24**:132
"Language Barrier" (Warren) **39**:273
The L=A=N=G=U=A=G=E Book (Bernstein) **142**:4, 8
"The Language in the Present Day" (Brooks) **86**:282
"Language Is a Tool of Production" (Solzhenitsyn) **10**:480
"Language Journal" (Wright) **146**:339, 341
Language Lattice (Celan)
See *Sprachgitter*
Language Made Plain (Burgess) **81**:301
The Language of Clothes (Lurie) **39**:180
The Language of Fiction (Lodge) **36**:267-70; **141**:332-33
The Language of Goldfish (Oneal) **30**:279-80
"The Language of Love" (Hearne) **56**:127
"A Language of New York" (Oppen) **7**:281
"The Language of Religion" (Lewis) **124**:238
"The Language of Shadows" (Koch) **44**:246
The Language of the American South (Brooks) **86**:278, 283
"The Language of the Argentines" (Borges)
See *El idioma de los Argentinos*
"The Language of the Brag" (Olds) **32**:346; **39**:189
"The Language of the Gentry and the Folk" (Brooks) **86**:281
The Language of the Night: Essays on Fantasy and Science Fiction (Le Guin) **22**:269, 274; **136**:316, 318-19, 328, 362-63, 365, 379
"The Language of the Self" (Lacan)
See "Fonction et champ de la parole et du langage en psychanalyse"
"The Language of Weather" (Young Bear) **94**:369
"Language, Power, Force" (Eco) **60**:113
"(Language Struggle)" (Breytenbach) **126**:85
"Language-Mesh" (Celan)
See "Sprachgitter"
"Languages and Culture" (Brink) **106**:120
The Languages of Criticism and the Structure of Poetry (Crane) **27**:70-1
The Languages of Love (Brooke-Rose) **40**:102
The Languages of Love (Maitland)
See *Daughter of Jerusalem*
The Languages of Pao (Vance) **35**:422-23, 425
Langue (Jouve) **47**:206-08
"Langue de pierres" (Breton) **15**:91
"L'anguilla" (Montale) **9**:387
"Lantana" (Wakoski) **40**:456
The Lantern Bearers (Sutcliff) **26**:427, 429, 430, 432-37, 439
"Lantern Slides" (O'Brien) **65**:168, 171; **116**:210-11
Lantern Slides (O'Brien) **65**:167-71, 173; **116**:203-04, 222
Lanterna Magica (Bergman) **72**:60-2
"La lanterne magique de Picasso" (Prévert) **15**:439
"The Lanterns" (Koch) **44**:241
Lanterns across the Snow (Hill) **113**:309
Lanterns and Lances (Thurber) **5**:433; **11**:534; **125**:412
"Laocoon" (Piercy) **62**:367
The Laocoön Group (Rozewicz)
See *Grupa Laokoona*
"Lap Dissolves" (Coover) **46**:122
A Lap of Honour (MacDiarmid) **4**:310
"Lapis Lazuli" (Auden) **123**:48
"Lapis Lazuli" (Durcan) **70**:152
"L'Lapse" (Barthelme) **115**:65
"Lares" (Longley) **29**:293
"Large Bad Picture" (Bishop) **9**:94; **13**:95; **32**:29
"The Large Cool Store" (Larkin) **64**:269, 276
"A Large Number" (Szymborska) **99**:200
A Large Number (Szymborska) **99**:199
The Large Scale Structure of Space-Time (Hawking) **63**:149; **105**:44-5
"Largely an Oral History of My Mother" (Brodkey) **56**:60-1, 67
Larger than Life (Buzzati)
See *Il grande ritratto*
"The Largess" (Eberhart) **56**:86
"Largesse" (Muldoon) **32**:319; **72**:265
"The Largest Theme Park in the World" (Ballard) **137**:4
"Largo" (Celan) **53**:74
Largo Desolato (Havel) **58**:243, 245; **65**:420, 429, 435, 439, 441; **123**:177, 182, 188, 189-92, 196-99 206-07, 209
Largo Desolato (Havel) **123**:172
"Lark" (Blaga) **75**:77
"The Lark" (Merwin) **1**:213
The Lark (Anouilh)
See *L'alouette*
Lark Ascending (de la Roche) **14**:149
"Lark Descending" (Blunden) **56**:30
"The Lark in the Clear Air Still Sings" (O'Casey) **88**:261
The Lark. The Thrush. The Starling (Williams) **148**:311, 318-19
"The Larkin Automatic Car Wash" (Ewart) **46**:149
"Larkinesque" (Ryan) **65**:215
"Larmes de soleil" (Soupault) **68**:406-07
"Larry" (Gallant) **38**:195
Larry and the Undersea Raider (Farley) **17**:115
Larry's Party (Shields) **113**:444-46
"Las Vegas Tilt" (Ferlinghetti) **6**:183-84
"Lascelles Abercrombie" (Blunden) **56**:40
Lasher (Rice) **128**:295-96, 298, 306
Lasi Claudius Civiliksen salaliittolaisten pöydällä (Haavikko) **34**:170
"A Lass in Wonderland" (Scott) **22**:377
"The Lass of Aughrim" (Muldoon) **72**:277
Lassalle fragt Herrn Herbert nach Sonja (Hein) **154**:53
"Lasser" (Ammons) **5**:29
"Last Acts" (Olds) **85**:302
"The Last Adam" (Cozzens) **4**:112, 115; **11**:124, 128, 131-32
The Last Adam (Cozzens) **92**:179-81, 186, 192-93, 199
"The Last American Hero" (Wolfe) **147**:363-64
The Last Analysis (Bellow) **3**:49; **6**:49, 51; **8**:69, 76; **13**:70-1; **33**:71
Last and Lost Poems of Delmore Schwartz (Schwartz) **45**:354-57; **87**:344
The Last and the First (Compton-Burnett) **1**:63
"The Last Battle" (Parra) **102**:353-54
The Last Battle (Lewis) **6**:308; **27**:264; **124**:193-98, 236-37, 242, 248
The Last Battle (Ryan) **7**:385-86
The Last Beautiful Days of Autumn (Nichols) **38**:344-45
The Last Billionaire (Clair)
See *Le dernier milliardaire*
"The Last Bus" (Strand) **18**:516, 518
Last call, last call! Or we'll start without you (Arreola)
See *Tercera llamada; tercera! o Empezamos sin usted*
The Last Carousel (Algren) **4**:17-18; **33**:14-15
The Last Castle (Vance) **35**:417, 423, 426-27

The Last Catholic in America: A Fictionalized Memoir (Powers) **66**:379-80, 382-83
"The Last Charge" (Davidson) **13**:170
"Last Child" (Kennedy) **42**:255
"Last Class" (Roethke) **101**:266
"The Last Clock, a Fable for the Time, Such As It Is, of Man" (Thurber) **125**:403
The Last Command (Sternberg) **20**:377-78
"The Last Commander" (Yehoshua) **13**:617; **31**:468
The Last Cop Out (Spillane) **3**:469
"The Last Cottage" (Leavitt) **34**:77
Last Courtesies and Other Stories (Leffland) **19**:279-80
"The Last Covenant" (Riding) **7**:374
"The Last Crop" (Jolley) **46**:221
"Last Dance" (Young) **17**:572
"The Last Dance" (Zamora)
See "El último baile"
"The Last Dane" (Mahon) **27**:290
"The Last Day" (Dinesen) **10**:148
"Last Day" (Kogawa) **78**:167
"The Last Day" (Matheson) **37**:246
"The Last Day" (Stafford) **29**:379
The Last Day and the First (Weiss) **14**:557
"Last Day at the Job" (Cryer) **21**:81
"The Last Day in the Field" (Gordon) **29**:188; **83**:231, 247
The Last Day of Summer (Konwicki)
See *Ostatni dzien lata*
The Last Day the Dogbushes Bloomed (Smith) **25**:406, 408, 410; **73**:355
"Last Days" (Hall) **151**:223
"Last Days" (Oates) **33**:296
Last Days (Oates) **33**:296
"Last Days at Teddington" (Gunn) **18**:199
"Last Days of a Charming Lady" (Tate) **9**:523
"The Last Days of a Famous Mime" (Carey) **40**:129; **96**:53
"Last Days of a Squaw Man" (Cook-Lynn) **93**:127
"The Last Days of Alice" (Tate) **4**:535, 539; **6**:525; **9**:522
The Last Days of America (Erdman) **25**:155-56
The Last Days of British Honduras (Tavel) **6**:529
The Last Days of Louisiana Red (Reed) **5**:370-71; **6**:447-50; **13**:477, 480; **32**:357-59, 364; **60**:302, 305, 313
"Last Days of Prospero" (Justice) **19**:233; **102**:277
"The Last Deaths" (Williams) **148**:315, 323
"The Last Decision" (Bova) **45**:73
The Last Defender of Camelot: A Collection by Roger Zelazny (Zelazny) **21**:478-79
Last Delivery before Christmas (Buckler) **13**:120
"The Last Demon" (Singer) **38**:407; **111**:296, 329-32
The Last Detail (Towne) **87**:350-53, 360, 369, 374-77
"Last Diary" (Arguedas) **18**:8
"The Last Diet" (Gilchrist) **48**:120, 122; **143**:
The Last Ditch (MacNeice) **4**:315; **53**:237
Last Ditch (Marsh) **53**:247-51, 253
The Last Don (Puzo) **107**:210-14
"The Last Dream" (Young Bear) **94**:362
The Last Enchantment (Stewart) **35**:395-96; **117**:369, 372, 374-76, 379
The Last Epiphany (Aleixandre)
See *Nacimiento último*
"Last Evening" (Justice) **102**:267
"The Last Evolution" (Campbell) **32**:73-4, 77, 80
Last Exit to Brooklyn (Selby) **1**:306-07; **2**:390; **4**:481-82; **8**:474-77
"The Last Experiment of Dr. Brugge" (Gustafson) **36**:220
"The Last Fantasy" (Allen) **84**:5
"The Last Flight of Doctor Ain" (Tiptree) **48**:389, 394, 396; **50**:357
The Last Flower, a Parable of Pictures (Thurber) **5**:431-33, 435, 442; **25**:437; **125**:395, 403
Last Fragments (Pound) **48**:286
The Last Frontier (Fast) **23**:153-54; **131**:66, 73, 79, 81, 84-5, 93
The Last Frontier (MacLean) **50**:349-50
The Last Full Measure (Shaara) **119**:105-06
"The Last Galway Hooker" (Murphy) **41**:312, 314, 316
The Last Galway Hooker (Murphy) **41**:311
The Last Gamble (Graham) **23**:192
"Last Gang in Town" (Clash) **30**:44, 46
"The Last Gangster" (Corso) **11**:123
"The Last Gas Station" (Grau) **4**:210; **9**:240; **146**:128, 135
"The Last Generation" (Moraga) **126**:296
The Last Generation: Prose and Poetry (Moraga) **126**:288, 295-99
The Last Gentleman (Percy) **2**:332-34; **3**:379-81; **6**:399-400; **8**:440, 442, 444-45; **14**:413, 417; **18**:396-99, 401-02; **47**:338; **65**:254, 257-58, 260
"The Last Good Country" (Hemingway) **10**:269; **30**:194, 198-99
The Last Good Time (Bausch) **51**:54-5
The Last Guru (Pinkwater) **35**:317-18
"The Last Head" (Gascoyne) **45**:157
"The Last Hiding Places of Snow" (Kinnell) **129**:237-39, 249
"Last Hill in a Vista" (Bogan) **46**:89
Last Holiday (Priestley) **34**:362
The Last Hours of Sandra Lee (Sansom) **6**:484
The Last Houseparty (Dickinson) **35**:136, 138
The Last Human Being (Lagerkvist)
See *Sista mänskan*
The Last Hurrah (Ford) **16**:313, 315
The Last Hurrah (O'Connor) **14**:389-90, 392-94
"The Last Husband" (Humphrey) **45**:193, 203-04
The Last Husband, and Other Stories (Humphrey) **45**:193, 195
"The Last Incantation" (Smith) **43**:423, 425
The Last Jew in America (Fiedler) **4**:161; **13**:213
"Last Journal" (Wright) **146**:362
"Last Journey" (Montague) **46**:269
"The Last Kiss" (Gordimer) **33**:179-80
"The Last Laugh" (Betjeman) **43**:49
The Last Laugh (Perelman) **23**:338-40; **44**:502; **49**:269
"The Last Lawn of the Afternoon" (Murakami) **150**:58-9
"The Last Leaf" (Porter) **7**:310; **15**:429
"Last Letter" (Livesay) **79**:344
The Last Love (Costain) **30**:100
Last Loves (Sillitoe) **148**:
The Last Lunar Baedeker (Loy) **28**:251, 253
The Last Magi (Condé)
See *Les derniers rois mages*
The Last Magician (Hospital) **145**:296-302, 305-08, 310, 313
The Last Man (Lagerkvist)
See *Sista mänskan*
The Last Man and Other Verses (Daryush) **19**:118, 120
The Last Man's Head (Anderson) **37**:19
"Last May" (Dixon) **52**:94-5
"The Last Meeting" (Sassoon) **130**:185-86
The Last Metro (Truffaut) **20**:407-08; **101**:387, 396, 410
"The Last Mohican" (Malamud) **9**:346-48; **18**:317; **27**:297, 306; **44**:412
"The Last Moon" (Dubus) **97**:236-37
"The Last Morning" (Smith) **22**:385
Last Mornings in Brooklyn (Kenny) **87**:249
"The Last Mowing" (Frost) **4**:175; **10**:195
"The Last Mummer" (Heaney) **5**:170, 172
"Last Names and Empty Pockets" (Kinsella) **27**:237
"Last Night" (Hughes) **119**:271
Last Night at the Brain Thieves Ball (Spencer) **30**:404, 406
"Last Night I Drove a Car" (Corso) **11**:123
"Last Night in Darkness" (Lane) **25**:287
The Last Night of the Earth Poems (Bukowski) **82**:28
Last Nights of Paris (Soupault)
See *Les dernières nuits de Paris*
Last Notes from Home (Exley) **6**:172
"The Last of Autumn" (Blunden) **56**:28
The Last of England (Porter) **5**:346; **33**:319, 322
The Last of Mankind (Lagerkvist)
See *Sista mänskan*
The Last of Mr. Norris (Isherwood) **1**:156; **9**:293; **11**:298-300; **14**:283-84, 286; **44**:396-97, 399-400, 402
"The Last of Saturdays" (Elytis) **100**:190
Last of the Breed (L'Amour) **55**:306-07
"The Last of the Caddoes" (Humphrey) **45**:203
The Last of the Country House Murders (Tennant) **13**:536-37; **52**:397
The Last of the Crazy People (Findley) **27**:140-41; **102**:97, 105, 108, 111-16
The Last of the Duchess (Blackwood) **100**:18-21, 25, 27-8, 31
"The Last of the Fire Kings" (Mahon) **27**:288-90
"The Last of the Hapsburgs" (Hospital) **145**:295, 303, 305, 313, 315
The Last of the Just (Schwarz-Bart) **2**:388-89; **4**:479-80
The Last of the Lowries (Green) **25**:198
"The Last of the Masters" (Dick) **72**:113
The Last of the Pleasure Gardens (King) **53**:206-07; **145**:351
Last of the Red Hot Lovers (Simon) **11**:495; **31**:395-96, 403-04
The Last of the Savages (McInerney) **112**:211, 213, 215-19
"The Last of the Spanish Blood" (Garrett) **51**:152
The Last of the Wine (Renault) **3**:425-26; **17**:392-401
"The Last One" (Merwin) **13**:385; **88**:205-06
Last One Home Sleeps in the Yellow Bed (Rooke) **25**:390-91
Last Orders, and Other Stories (Aldiss) **40**:14-15, 20
The Last Outing (Leonov) **92**:278
The Last Pad (Inge)
See *Don't Go Gentle*
"The Last Painting or the Portrait of God" (Cixous) **92**:81, 94, 96
"The Last Pennant before Armageddon" (Kinsella) **43**:253, 255-57
"The Last People" (Merwin) **13**:383
"The Last Picasso" (Diamond) **30**:113
"The Last Picture Show" (Brown) **79**:154
The Last Picture Show (McMurtry) **2**:272; **3**:333; **7**:213-15; **11**:371; **27**:324-25, 328-31; **44**:254, 256-57; **127**:304, 314, 319-20, 322-23, 325-28, 330, 342, 354
The Last Plantagenets (Costain) **30**:100
"The Last Poem in the Series" (Jiles) **58**:277
Last Poems (Celan) **53**:82-3; **82**:34-6
Last Poems (Sexton) **53**:313
"The Last Post" (Graves) **39**:327
"Last Post" (O'Connor) **23**:331
"Last Puritan" (Bernstein) **142**:46
"Last Quarter" (Hollander) **5**:186
"The Last Quatrain of the Ballad of Emmett Till" (Brooks) **49**:36
"The Last Question" (Asimov) **9**:50, 52; **26**:55
"The Last Quixote" (Coover) **3**:114; **46**:115
"The Last Remarkable Man" (Cook-Lynn) **93**:115
The Last Resort (Johnson) **27**:217-18
Last Resort (Sommer) **25**:426
"The Last Resort on the Adriatic" (Welsh) **144**:316

A Last Resort—For These Times (Rathbone) **41**:342
"Last Respects" (Kiš) **57**:251, 253
"Last Respects" (Roth) **104**:284
Last Respects (Weidman) **7**:517
The Last Ride of Wild Bill (Brown) **59**:265, 266, 268
"Last Rites" (Scott) **22**:372, 376
"The Last River" (Kinnell) **5**:216; **29**:283; **129**:240, 255, 258, 260, 262-64, 268, 271
Last Round (Cortázar)
See *Ultimo round*
"Last Rung on the Ladder" (King) **113**:338
"Last Scene in the First Act" (Piercy) **18**:405; **27**:374
"Last Seen" (Ai) **69**:18
The Last September (Bowen) **11**:59-64; **15**:79; **118**:62, 68, 71, 73-74, 77-88, 92, 104-05
The Last Seven Wounds (Duhamel)
See *Les sept dernières plaies*
"Last Sheet" (Fuller) **28**:151
"The Last Song" (Harjo) **83**:270
The Last Song (Harjo) **83**:272, 278
The Last Song of Manuel Sendero (Dorfman)
See *La última canción de Manuel Sendero*
The Last Spike (Berton) **104**:44-5, 57
"Last Spring They Came Over" (Callaghan) **65**:250
Last Stand at Saber River (Leonard) **71**:224
Last Stands: Notes from Memory (Masters) **48**:220-24
The Last Station: A Story of Tolstoy's Last Year (Parini) **133**:253-56, 258, 261
"The Last Stop" (Seferis) **11**:492
"The Last Straw" (Brown) **79**:154
"The Last Struggle" (Davies) **23**:142
"The Last Summer" (Pasternak)
See "Provest'"
Last Summer (Hunter) **11**:279; **31**:222, 225
The Last Summer (Pasternak)
See *Povest*
Last Sunday (Peck) **17**:341-42
"Last Supper" (Endō) **99**:288, 296-97, 301, 307
"The Last Supper" (Nye) **42**:302
The Last Supper (Bermant) **40**:93
"The Last Supplement" (Kesey) **3**:267
The Last Sweet Days of Isaac (Cryer) **21**:78-9
Last Tales (Dinesen) **10**:145, 150; **29**:156; **95**:37, 47-50, 52, 55, 68
"Last Tango" (Steele) **45**:365
Last Tango in Paris (Bertolucci) **16**:89-94, 97-8, 100
"The Last Tea" (Parker) **68**:326, 339
The Last Temptation of Christ (Scorsese) **89**:249-54, 258, 260-63, 265, 267-68
The Last Testament of Oscar Wilde (Ackroyd) **52**:4-7, 10-12, 14-15; **140**:6, 10, 21, 24-5, 29-30, 33, 39, 50, 65
"The Last Thing He Wanted" (Didion) **129**:103-06
"Last Things" (Nemerov) **36**:309
"Last Things" (Plath) **5**:341
"Last Things" (Williams) **148**:363-64
Last Things (Snow) **4**:505; **6**:517; **9**:497-98; **19**:427
"The Last Thoughts of Sir Walter Raleigh in the Tower of London" (Padilla) **38**:352
"The Last Throw" (Pritchett) **41**:334
"The Last Time" (Jagger and Richard) **17**:231
"The Last Time" (Kristofferson) **26**:270
"The Last Time I Saw Her" (Lightfoot) **26**:278
"The Last Time I Saw Richard" (Mitchell) **12**:440
"The Last Time I Saw Trout Fishing in America" (Brautigan) **3**:88
"Last Time the Angels Came Up" (Kesey) **46**:228
"The Last to See Them Alive" (Capote) **13**:137
The Last Train Robbery (Theroux) **15**:533
"The Last Train to Malakhovka" (Voznesensky) **57**:415
"Last Trams" (Slessor) **14**:496-97
Last Treatments (Yehoshua) **13**:616; **31**:470
The Last Tresilians (Stewart) **7**:465
"Last Trip to Tulsa" (Young) **17**:572
The Last Trolley Ride (Calisher) **38**:72-3; **134**:13, 15, 19, 37, 42
The Last Trump (Gardner) **30**:156
The Last Tycoon (Kazan) **16**:373-74; **63**:225, 229
The Last Unicorn (Beagle) **7**:25-6; **104**:3-10, 15, 18-21, 23-34
The Last Valley (Guthrie) **23**:200-01
"The Last Veil" (L'Heureux) **52**:274
"The Last Virgin" (Howe) **47**:172
"The Last Voyage of the Ghost Ship" (García Márquez)
See "El último viaje del buque fantasma"
"Last Walk" (Lowell) **37**:238
The Last Waltz (Scorsese) **20**:332-34; **89**:260, 265
Last Waltz in Santiago, and Other Poems of Exile and Disappearance (Dorfman)
See *Pastel de choclo*
"The Last Wasp in the World" (Fiedler) **13**:213
The Last Wave (Weir) **20**:427-30
"The Last Will and Testament" (Auden) **43**:16
"Last Will and Testament" (Larkin) **64**:261
"The Last Will and Testament of Art Evergreen" (Pack) **13**:438
The Last Will of Dr. Mabuse (Lang) **20**:204
"Last Wishes" (Trevor) **9**:529
The Last Woman in His Life (Queen) **11**:464-65
The Last Word and Other Stories (Greene) **70**:289
"Last Words" (Abse) **29**:20
"Last Words" (Kunitz) **148**:77
"Last Words" (Plath) **3**:389; **14**:425; **51**:340, 346; **111**:214
"Last Words" (Roethke) **46**:356
The Last Words of Dutch Schultz (Burroughs) **5**:93
"Last Words to James Wright" (Hugo) **32**:250
"A Last World" (Ashbery) **41**:40; **77**:52
The Last Worthless Evening (Dubus) **97**:208-09, 213-16, 224
Last Year at Marienbad (Resnais)
See *L'annee derniére a Marienbad*
Last Year at Marienbad (Robbe-Grillet)
See *L'année dernière à Marienbad*
"Lastness" (Kinnell) **13**:322; **129**:247, 250-51, 253, 256
Latakia (Thomas) **37**:417-18, 423; **107**:330, 333-36, 340-41, 347-48
"Late" (Bogan) **93**:65, 92
"Late Afternoon of a Faun" (Brophy) **29**:91; **105**:9, 15, 30
"A Late Answer" (Levine) **14**:318
"Late at Night" (Rosenthal) **28**:395
"Late at Night" (Stafford) **29**:380
"A Late Aubade" (Wilbur) **53**:413; **110**:385
"Late August" (Atwood) **13**:44
"Late August" (Hacker) **72**:192
Late Autumn (Ozu) **16**:448-49, 451, 453-56
"Late Autumn in Venice" (Schwartz) **45**:355
The Late Bourgeois World (Gordimer) **5**:145, 147; **7**:132; **10**:239; **18**:186; **33**:182; **51**:161; **70**:162-65, 170, 172, 180; **123**:137, 141
The Late Breakfasters (Aickman) **57**:2
Late But in Earnest (Simmons) **43**:407, 411
Late Call (Wilson) **2**:472, 474; **3**:534-36; **5**:513-14; **25**:459, 461
A Late Divorce (Yehoshua) **31**:474-76
"Late Dusk" (Le Guin) **136**:395
"Late Echo" (Ashbery) **15**:33-4; **41**:38
"A Late Encounter with the Enemy" (O'Connor) **21**:256, 268-69; **104**:175
"Late Fall" (Jacobsen) **48**:192; **102**:242
Late for the Sky (Browne) **21**:35-6, 38
The Late George Apley (Kaufman) **38**:264
The Late George Apley (Marquand) **10**:329-31
"Late Ghazal" (Rich) **125**:335
"Late Gothic" (Gotlieb) **18**:191
The Late Great Human Road Show (Jiles) **58**:273-74, 278-79
The Late Great Me (Scoppettone) **26**:401-02
The Late Hour (Strand) **18**:517-18, 520-21; **41**:432, 434, 436; **71**:279, 287
"Late in the Evening" (Simon) **17**:467-68
"Late in the Season" (Matthiessen) **64**:321, 324
Late Innings (Angell) **26**:32-3
"Late, Late" (Starbuck) **53**:354
"Late Love" (Oz) **8**:436-37
Late Love (Oz)
See *Ad m'avet*
"Late Loving" (Van Duyn) **116**:411, 413, 415, 429
Late Marxism: Adorno, or, The Persistence of the Dialectic (Jameson) **142**:232, 236, 259
"Late Moon" (Bly) **38**:57; **128**:15
"The Late Mother" (Macdonald) **13**:356
"Late Naps" (Bell) **31**:51
"Late Night in Autumn" (Merwin) **88**:193
"Late Night, San Francisco" (Codrescu) **46**:103
"Late Night Telephone" (Jiles) **58**:271
Late Night Thoughts on Listening to Mahler's Ninth Symphony (Thomas) **35**:415-16
"Late Night with Fog and Horses" (Carver) **55**:273
A Late Picking: Poems, 1965-1974 (Hope) **51**:222
"Late Poem to My Father" (Olds) **85**:295, 299, 304
"The Late Public Figure" (Bates) **46**:55-6
"Late Requests" (Longley) **29**:295
"The Late Show" (Browne) **21**:36
"Late Sonnet" (Carruth) **84**:130
"Late Spring" (Hass) **99**:140-41
Late Spring (Ozu) **16**:448, 450-51, 453-56
"Late Summer" (Dunn) **36**:155
"A Late Sunday Afternoon by the Huron" (Baxter) **45**:52-3; **78**:17-18
"Late Train" (Simic) **130**:346
"Late Tutorial" (Buckley) **57**:130
"Late Victorians: San Francisco, AIDS, and the Homosexual Stereotype" (Rodriguez) **155**:254, 257, 268, 274-76, 303-08
"Late Winter" (Dudek) **11**:159
Latecomers (Brookner) **136**:85-91, 105, 111, 115-16
"Late-Flowering Lust" (Betjeman) **43**:34
"Lately" (Kureishi) **135**:276, 284
The Latent Heterosexual (Chayefsky) **23**:116
"Latent Rapists" (Shange) **25**:402
"Later" (Creeley) **78**:162
"Later" (Paley) **140**:291
"Later" (Sondheim) **30**:391, 402
Later (Creeley) **15**:153; **36**:121; **78**:141, 148, 150-52
"Later: Four Fragments" (Barnard) **48**:27
Later Poems (Thomas) **48**:381
"The Later Poetry of W. B. Yeats" (Blackmur) **24**:63
"Later Sonnets" (Denby) **48**:84
"Later Testament" (Belitt) **22**:49
Later than You Think (Kaye) **28**:198
Later the Same Day (Paley) **37**:333-35, 337, 339; **140**:207, 20911, 214, 221, 226, 228, 230-1, 234-36, 238, 247, 257, 260, 263, 265, 268, 272, 276-77, 281-83
"Later Today" (Stern) **100**:338-39
"Latest Face" (Larkin) **64**:262
"The Latest Injury" (Olds) **85**:293
Late-Winter Child (Buckley) **57**:133-36
The Lathe of Heaven (Le Guin) **13**:345, 350; **22**:273; **45**:213, 221
"The Latin American Novel" (Rodriguez) **155**:254
"The Latin Lesson" (Boland) **113**:92, 111
"Latitude" (Gotlieb) **18**:191
A látogáto (Konrád) **4**:273; **10**:304; **73**:174, 176-81, 184, 187
"Latorre, Prado, and My Own Shadow" (Neruda) **62**:325
"Latrine" (Eich) **15**:204
A Lattice for Momos (Everson) **27**:133-34

"Lauda" (Milosz) **56**:250; **82**:298, 303
Lauda somnului (Blaga) **75**:67, 70, 77-8
Laudatur (Faludy) **42**:139
"Das Läufer" (Lenz) **27**:245
"Laugh and Learn" (Royko) **109**:408
"Laugh? I Thought I'd Die" (Royko) **109**:408
"The Laugh of the Medusa" (Cixous)
See "Le Rire de la Méduse"
Laughable Loves (Kundera)
See *Směsné lásky*
"The Laughing Man" (Salinger) **12**:520; **56**:329
The Laughing Matter (Saroyan) **1**:301-02; **8**:467; **29**:361-62
The Laughing Policeman (Wahlöö)
See *Den skrattande polisen*
Laughing Stalks (Dudek) **11**:159; **19**:137-38
Laughing Stock (Linney) **51**:262
Laughing to Keep from Crying (Hughes) **10**:281; **108**:285
"Laughing with One Eye" (Schnackenberg) **40**:378-79
"Laughs in the Open Tombs" (Shapcott) **38**:403
"The Laughter" (Boell)
See "Der Lacher"
"Laughter" (Dybek) **114**:72, 81-2
"Laughter" (O'Connor) **23**:329
Laughter! (Barnes) **56**:4, 6, 8-9
"Laughter Beneath the Bridge" (Okri) **87**:314-15
Laughter in the Dark (Nabokov) **1**:239; **2**:302; **3**:353-55; **6**:359; **8**:417; **15**:396; **44**:465; **46**:291, 294; **64**:348
A Laughter in the Mind (Layton) **15**:319
"Laughter in the Peroration" (Klappert) **57**:268
"Laughter in the Slums" (Randall) **135**:376
The Laughter of Carthage (Moorcock) **58**:355-59
"The Laughter of Leen" (Richter) **30**:320
"The Laughter of the Wapishanas" (Harris) **25**:217
"The Laughters" (Howe) **152**:222
"Launcelot in Hell" (Ciardi) **40**:158
Laundrette (Kureishi)
See *My Beautiful Laundrette*
Laundromats (Altman) **116**:68
"Laura" (Aickman) **57**:4
"Laura" (Joel) **26**:223
"Laura's Funeral" (Johnston) **51**:249
"The Laureate" (Graves) **45**:173
"Laurel" (Walker) **27**:449; **103**:407, 409-10
"The Laurel Axe" (Hill) **45**:190
"Laurel Hole in the Day" (Vizenor) **103**:297
"Laurentian Shield" (Scott) **22**:372, 377
"Laurie" (Merwin) **45**:272
Laut und Luise (Jandl) **34**:196, 198
Lautaro (Alegria) **57**:9
Lautgedichte (Jandl) **34**:195
Lautréamont et Sade (Blanchot) **135**:112
"Lava" (Kinnell) **129**:256
Lava (Konwicki)
See *Lawa*
"Lava Cameo: A brooch carved on volcanic rock" (Boland) **113**:91-2, 94, 115, 125
Lavender-Green Magic (Norton) **12**:466
"Laventille" (Walcott) **25**:452; **67**:353-54; **76**:274
Laverne and Shirley (Marshall) **17**:276-78
"Lavin" (McGahern) **48**:262, 266, 268
"Lavinia: An Old Story" (Paley) **37**:339; **140**:208, 234, 238, 243-44, 249, 277
Law and Disorder (Forman) **21**:119
Law and Order (Wiseman) **20**:471-72
"The Law and the Grace" (Smith) **64**:398
The Law and the Grace (Smith) **64**:394, 398
The Law at Randado (Leonard) **71**:224
"Law Clerk, 1979" (Leithauser) **27**:240-41
A Law for the Lion (Auchincloss) **45**:25, 29
"Law like Love" (Auden) **43**:18
Law of Desire (Almodovar)
See *La Ley del Deseo*
The Law of Karma (Hall) **51**:170-72
"Law Song" (Sissman) **9**:491
"The Law Wishes to Have a Formal Existence" (Fish) **142**:199
Lawa (Konwicki) **117**:283, 290
Lawd Today (Wright) **1**:379; **4**:594-95; **14**:596; **21**:440, 448, 452, 460
The Lawless (Jakes) **29**:249
The Lawless Roads (Greene) **27**:173; **37**:137; **72**:150-51, 155, 160; **125**:184
Lawley Road, and Other Stories (Narayan) **28**:293, 296, 301, 303; **47**:306
"Lawn" (Ezekiel) **61**:109
"The Lawn Party" (Beattie) **13**:65; 146;64-5
"The Lawnmower" (Bowering) **47**:24
Lawrence and the Arabs (Graves) **39**:322
The Laws of Ice (Price) **63**:325, 333
The Laws of Practical Morality (Arghezi)
See *Pravila de morală practică*
Laws That Changed America (Archer) **12**:15-16
The Lawyers Know Too Much (Sandburg) **35**:341
"Lax though the Longing May Wear" (Barker) **48**:12
Lay By (Hare) **29**:216; **136**:286
"El lay de Aristotle" (Arreola) **147**:31
Lay Down Your Arms (Potter) **123**:229, 232
"Lay Down Your Weary Tune" (Dylan) **6**:154
"Lay, Lady, Lay" (Dylan) **77**:162, 186-87
The Lay of Barrabbas (Arrabal) **58**:15
"Lay of Errantry" (Césaire) **32**:112
"The Lay of Ike" (Berryman)
See "Dream Song 23"
"Lay of Maid Marion" (Hoffman) **6**:243
"The Lay of the Romance of the Associations" (O'Hara) **13**:424
"Lay Your Sleeping Head, My Love" (Auden) **11**:19; **43**:22
Layali alf layla (Mahfouz) **153**:306, 359-60
"Layaways" (Dixon) **52**:98, 100
"The Layers" (Kunitz) **148**:81, 86, 90-91, 93, 96, 101, 103, 109, 135-39, 142, 146-50
"A Layin on of hands" (Shange) **126**:352, 354
"Laying a Lawn" (Raine) **103**:195-96
"Laying on Our Backs Looking at the Stars" (Keillor) **115**:283
"Laying the Dust" (Levertov) **66**:237
A Layman Looks at Cancer (MacLean) **50**:349
"A Layman Looks at Medical Men" (MacLennan) **92**:342
Lazare (Malraux) **57**:307-08; **9**:358-59; **15**:354-55
Lazaretti; oder, Der Säbeltiger (Hochwälder) **36**:237, 239-40
Lazaretti; or, The Saber-Toothed Tiger (Hochwälder)
See *Lazaretti; oder, Der Säbeltiger*
"Lázaro" (Cernuda) **54**:48
Lázaro en el laberinto (Buero Vallejo) **139**:39-41, 43, 72-4
"Lazarus" (Achebe) **11**:4
"Lazarus" (Dybek) **114**:61, 63
"Lazarus" (Vanderhaeghe) **41**:452
"Lazarus and the Sea" (Redgrove) **41**:351
The Lazarus Effect (Herbert) **35**:204-06; **44**:393-94
A Lazy Eye (Morrissy) **99**:76-8
"Lazy Mornin'" (Lightfoot) **26**:279
"Lazy Sons" (Calvino) **33**:101
L.C. (Daitch) **103**:58-66, 70-8
"Lead" (Kinsella) **138**:98, 141
Leadbelly (Parks) **16**:460-61
"The Leader" (Clark Bekedermo) **38**:118, 125
"The Leader" (Clash) **30**:48
Leader (Horovitz) **56**:149
"Leader from a Quality Newspaper" (Kelman) **58**:300
Leader of the Band (Weldon) **122**:260-64
"The Leader of the People" (Steinbeck) **9**:515; **13**:530; **21**:376-78; **34**:409
"A Leader of the People (for Roy Wilkins)" (Randall) **135**:392
"The Leaders" (Vargas Llosa) **31**:444
"The Leading Lady" (Ferber) **93**:140
"Lead's the Best" (Auden) **9**:60
"The Leaf" (Warren) **8**:539; **18**:536; **39**:266-67
"Leaf by Niggle" (Tolkien) **12**:566, 570, 573-74, 586
"Leaf Eater" (Kinsella) **138**:118, 129
"A Leaf of Sage" (McAuley) **45**:250
Leaf Storm (García Márquez)
See *La hojarasca*
The Leafless American (Dahlberg) **7**:67
"Leaflets" (Rich) **6**:458
Leaflets: Poems, 1965-1968 (Rich) **3**:427; **6**:457-59; **7**:365-66, 371-72; **11**:476; **18**:445-46; **36**:372-73, 375; **73**:326, 328, 334; **76**:219; **125**:317, 336
Leafy Rivers (West) **7**:520; **17**:549-51
The League of Frightened Men (Stout) **3**:471
League of Frightened Philistines (Farrell) **66**:132
"Léah" (Migueis) **10**:341
Léah e outras histórias (Migueis) **10**:341
"Leah Goldberg Died" (Amichai)
See "Yehuda Halevi, Ibn Gabirol, Leah Goldberg meta"
"Lean Times in Lankhmar" (Leiber) **25**:310
"Leander of the Diving Board" (Cassity) **42**:97
Leaning Forward (Paley) **140**:210, 247
"The Leaning Tower" (Porter) **7**:309, 311, 314-17; **10**:398
The Leaning Tower, and Other Stories (Porter) **7**:309, 314; **101**:210, 215, 217, 224, 249, 255
"The Leap" (Barthelme) **13**:60-1; **46**:38, 41; **115**:66
Leap Before You Look (Oe) **86**:225, 227
Leap Before You Look (Stolz) **12**:554
Leap Year (Erickson) **64**:142-43, 145
"Leaping Falls" (Kinnell) **13**:322
"The Leaping Fire" (Montague) **46**:270
"Leaping Poetry" (Bly) **128**:43
Leaping Poetry: An Idea with Poems and Translations (Bly) **128**:42
Lear (Bond) **6**:87; **13**:99, 102; **23**:64, 68
Learn This Poem of Mine By Heart (Faludy) **42**:141-42
"The Learners" (Van Duyn) **63**:443
"Learning" (Scannell) **49**:332
"Learning a Dead Language" (Merwin) **5**:285; **45**:269; **88**:206
"Learning About the Indians" (Oliver) **98**:291
"Learning from the 60s" (Lorde) **71**:244
"Learning from the Tyrants" (Cioran) **64**:98
"Learning in War-Time" (Lewis) **124**:240
Learning Laughter (Spender) **91**:261
"Learning the Hero form Northrop Frye" (Kroetsch) **132**:282, 288
"Learning the Trees" (Nemerov) **9**:394
"Learning to Fall" (Beattie) **40**:64, 66; **63**:11-12, 17, 19; **146**:85
"Learning to Fly" (Hope) **52**:210
"Learning to Let Water Heal" (Bottoms) **53**:29-31
"Learning to See" (Welty) **105**:320-21, 378, 380-81
"Learning to Swim" (Swift) **41**:446
Learning to Swim, and Other Stories (Swift) **41**:443, 445-46; **88**:290, 318
"Learning to Write" (Lorde) **71**:256
The Learning Tree (Parks) **1**:265; **16**:457-59
"Learning Where to Stop" (Booth) **24**:91
"The Leather Man" (Doctorow) **37**:91, 93-4; **113**:135-36, 153-54
"Leave for Cape Wrath Tonight" (Auden) **3**:24; **11**:15
Leave It to Beany (Weber) **12**:632
Leave It to Me (Mukherjee) **115**:391-93
Leave It to Psmith (Wodehouse) **2**:479; **22**:482-83
"A Leave of Absence" (Simpson) **149**:361
"Leave Us Alone" (Rozewicz) **139**:235
Leave Well Enough Alone (Wells) **12**:638-39
Leaven of Malice (Davies) **13**:171, 173; **25**:130-

31; **42**:101-04, 106; **75**:184, 191, 213-14; **91**:203, 204
"Leaves" (Hughes) **119**:265
"Leaves" (Updike) **15**:543-44
Leaves and Flowers (Davenport) **6**:124
"Leaves Compared with Flowers" (Frost) **26**:117
Leaves from Satan's Book (Dreyer) **16**:259-60, 266
Leaves, News (Haavikko) **34**:169
Leaves of Hypnos (Char)
See *Feuillets d'Hypnos*
"Leaves that Talk" (Sexton) **15**:473; **123**:452
Leaves the Leaves (Haavikko)
See *Lehdet lehtiä*
"Leaves Without Trees" (Amichai) **116**:95
The Leavetaking (McGahern) **5**:280-81; **9**:369-70, 372-74; **48**:263-64, 269-73
The Leavetaking (Weiss)
See *Abschied von den Eltern: Erzählung*
"Leaving" (Harjo) **83**:271
"Leaving" (Suknaski) **19**:432
"Leaving" (Wilbur) **53**:409; **110**:361
"Leaving an Island" (Muldoon) **32**:316
"Leaving Barra" (MacNeice) **53**:231
"Leaving Belfast" (Motion) **47**:291
Leaving Cheyenne (McMurtry) **2**:272; **7**:213-15; **27**:325, 328-31, 333; **44**:255, 257; **127**:303-05, 307, 310, 312-14, 319, 327, 330
"Leaving Church Early" (Updike) **43**:430
"Leaving Early" (Plath) **3**:389; **5**:345; **51**:344
"Leaving Home" (Suknaski) **19**:432
Leaving Home (Keillor) **115**:267, 269, 274, 277, 288-92
"Leaving Inishmore" (Longley) **29**:292
"Leaving Ithaca" (Snodgrass) **68**:397
"Leaving My Bones Behind" (Hulme) **130**:44
"Leaving School" (Walcott) **67**:342
"Leaving the Atocha Station" (Ashbery) **9**:43
"Leaving the Cherries" (Smith) **64**:391
Leaving the Door Open (Ignatow) **40**:260-61
Leaving the Land (Unger) **34**:114-17
"Leaving the Yellow House" (Bellow) **25**:84
"Leaving This Island Place" (Clarke) **53**:89
"Leaving Town" (Brown) **73**:20
"Leaving Waterloo" (Wakoski) **40**:456
"Leavings" (Heaney) **91**:115
Lebensläufe (Hesse) **17**:197-98
Lebenszeichen (Herzog) **16**:321-23, 331
"Lección de cocina" (Castellanos) **66**:58-61
Lecherous Limericks (Asimov) **76**:315
"Lechery" (Phillips) **15**:420; **139**:201
La leçon (Ionesco) **1**:154; **4**:251-52; **6**:248, 253-54, 257; **9**:286; **11**:290; **15**:297-98; **41**:224-25, 230; **86**:332-33, 340
Leçon de choses (Simon) **9**:485; **15**:495-97; **39**:212, 214-15
Leçon inaugurale faite le vendredi 7 janvier 1977 (Barthes) **24**:37; **83**:96
Lector in Fabula (Eco) **142**:
"Lectura de domingo" (Guillén) **79**:229
"A Lecture by My Books" (Porter) **33**:320
"Lecture Noir" (Thesen) **56**:421
"Lecture on Nothing" (Cage) **41**:82
"Lecture Overheard" (Redgrove) **41**:358
Lectures and Essays (Heidegger)
See *Vorträge und Aufsätze*
Lectures on Literature (Nabokov) **23**:310-11, 314
"Led" (Voznesensky) **15**:554
Led Zeppelin (Page and Plant) **12**:473, 476-78
Led Zeppelin II (Page and Plant) **12**:473-74, 482
Led Zeppelin III (Page and Plant) **12**:474-75, 479
Led Zeppelin IV (Page and Plant) **12**:475-76, 478, 482
"Leda" (Huxley) **11**:284
"Leda" (Smith) **15**:517
"Leda" (Van Duyn) **63**:439; **116**:420
Leda (Chabrol) **16**:168
Leda (Krleža) **8**:329; **114**:168
"Leda and the Swan" (Van Duyn) **116**:401
"Leda Reconsidered" (Van Duyn) **63**:437, 440; **116**:400, 414, 419-20
"The Ledge" (Mathews) **52**:308
The Ledge between the Streams (Mehta) **37**:296-97
"The Ledger" (Kroetsch) **23**:273-75
The Ledger (Kroetsch) **132**:239, 282, 288
Lee in the Mountains and Other Poems (Davidson) **2**:111-12; **13**:166, 170; **19**:128
"Leela's Friend" (Narayan) **28**:302
"Left" (Ammons) **57**:58
The Left Bank (Rice) **7**:360-61, 363; **49**:295-96, 298, 300, 302
The Left Bank, and Other Stories (Rhys) **6**:452, 454-55; **14**:446; **19**:390; **51**:355-56, 359, 376; **124**:337, 344-45, 354
"The Left Eyelid" (Sagan) **17**:428
The Left Hand of Darkness (Le Guin) **8**:343; **13**:346-51; **22**:266-68, 272; **45**:214, 216-18, 221-23; **71**:187; **136**:318, 328-30, 332, 334, 337, 346-47, 349, 351, 353-56, 358, 363, 365, 383-84, 391
The Left in Europe since 1789 (Caute) **29**:110
Left of Centre (Johnson) **147**:101
"The Left, Right, Left, Right: Arrival of Tony Blair" (Barnes) **141**:68
"left with the day" (Bukowski) **108**:75
"The Left-Behind" (MacNeice) **53**:238
Left-Handed Liberty (Arden) **13**:26, 29; **15**:21
The Left-Handed Woman (Handke)
See *Die linkshändige Frau*
The Left-Hander's World (Silverstein and Silverstein) **17**:456
"The Leg" (Bitov) **57**:115
"The Leg" (Shapiro) **53**:331
A Leg to Stand On (Sacks) **67**:289-90, 292-96
"Legacies" (Giovanni) **64**:187
"Legacies" (Mahon) **27**:290-91
"Legacies" (Padilla) **38**:353
Legacies, after Villon (Mahon) **27**:286
Legacies: Selected Poems (Padilla) **38**:349-54
"Legacy" (Harjo) **83**:275, 281
"Legacy" (Kenny) **87**:241, 256
"The Legacy" (Motion) **47**:286, 293
"Legacy" (Ritsos) **13**:488
"Legacy" (Vinge) **30**:413-14
Legacy (Fast) **23**:161; **131**:86, 100
Legacy (Michener) **60**:258; **109**:382, 386
The Legacy (Shute) **30**:368-69
The Legacy of the Civil War (Warren) **59**:296
Legacy of the Desert: Understanding the Arabs (Archer) **12**:22
"Legal Fiction" (Empson) **19**:155; **34**:336
"The Legal System" (Hogan) **73**:158-59
"Legend" (Auden) **14**:33; **43**:17
"Legend" (Glück) **44**:218
"Legend" (Jones) **131**:269
"Legend for a Painting" (O'Faolain) **47**:327-28
"Legend in Bronze" (Davidson) **13**:169
"A Legend in Its Own Time" (Robinson) **21**:343
"Legend in Your Own Time" (Simon) **26**:407-08, 410
"Legend of Kalafaat" (Leonov) **92**:257
"The Legend of Success, the Salesman's Story" (Simpson) **7**:426
The Legend of Tarik (Myers) **35**:297-98
"Legend of the Last Jew on Earth" (Cohen) **7**:51
"The Legend of the Sleepers" (Kiš) **57**:251, 253
The Legend of the Thousand Bulls (Kemal) **29**:266
"A Legend of Viable Women" (Eberhart) **56**:91
Legenda (Krleža) **114**:166-67, 171-72, 174
Legenda emöke (Škvorecký) **15**:511-12l; **39**:221, 224, 229, 231-32; **69**:330-32, 334, 337, 341, 343-44, 346-48; **152**:304, 306, 315, 330, 332, 336
"Legende" (Celan) **82**:54
Legenden und Erzühlungen (Sachs) **98**:324
Légendes africanes (Tchicaya) **101**:355
"Legends" (Boland) **113**:94, 100, 126
Legends of Our Times (Wiesel) **3**:529
"Legends of the Fall" (Harrison) **66**:155-56, 159-60; **143**:335, 341, 345, 353
Legends of the Fall (Harrison) **14**:235-37; **33**:196-97, 199-200; **66**:154, 156, 158, 167-71; **143**:340-42, 344-45, 349
"Leggende" (Ungaretti) **7**:483
Legion: Civic Choruses (Harmon) **38**:242-43
The Legion of Space (Williamson) **29**:455-56, 461
The Legion of Time (Williamson) **29**:450-53, 456, 459-60
Legitimationsprobleme im Spätkapitalismus (Habermas) **104**:66, 69, 72
"The Legs" (Graves) **45**:169
Legs (Kennedy) **6**:274-75; **28**:204-06; **34**:206-10; **53**:192-94, 199
"The Legs of the Lame" (Garner) **13**:237
The Legs of the Lame (Garner) **13**:237
Lehdet lehtiä (Haavikko) **34**:170; **34**:170
Lehre der Sainte-Victoire (Handke) **134**:144, 146, 148
Die Lehre der Sainte-Victoire (Handke) **38**:224-25, 228; **134**:119, 123-27, 133, 158
"Leicestershire" (Davie) **31**:120
Leila (Donleavy) **45**:125-26
"Leila Lee" (Oates) **108**:384
Leiret og hjulet (Vesaas) **48**:406
Leisure Garden (Pa Chin)
See *Ch'i-yüan*
"Lejana" (Cortázar) **10**:114; **33**:128; **34**:332; **92**:155
"Leli" (Hrabal) **67**:121
"Lembrando Manolete" (Cabral de Melo Neto) **76**:161
"The Lemmings" (Masefield) **47**:233
"The Lemon" (Lustig) **56**:185
"Lemon Ode" (Galvin) **38**:198
Lemon Sky (Wilson) **7**:547
"The Lemon Song" (Page and Plant) **12**:474-76
"Lemonade" (Findley) **102**:108, 111-14
"Lemonade" (Lavin) **99**:322
Lemprière's Dictionary (Norfolk) **76**:86-92
"Lemuel's Blessing" (Merwin) **88**:194, 199, 201
"Léna ou le secret" (Yourcenar) **87**:385, 387
Lend Me a Tenor (Ludwig) **60**:251-53
"Lend Me Your Light" (Mistry) **71**:266
"The Lengthening Silence of a Poet" (Yehoshua) **31**:472-73
Lengua poética (Alonso) **14**:20
"Lenin" (Hughes) **108**:321
Lenin in Zurich (Solzhenitsyn) **7**:444-45; **18**:499; **34**:484, 489
"Lenin na tribune 18-ogo goda" (Voznesensky) **15**:555
"Lenny" (Asimov) **26**:47
Lenny (Fosse) **20**:123-25
"Lenny Bruce, American" (Bruce) **21**:44
Lenny Bruce at Carnegie Hall (Bruce) **21**:51
Lenny Bruce: I Am Not a Nut, Elect Me (Bruce) **21**:44
Lenny Bruce Live at the Curran Theater (Bruce) **21**:49, 51
"Lenny Bruce's Interviews of Our Times" (Bruce) **21**:44
"Lenore" (Moure) **88**:217, 229
"The Lens" (Williams) **56**:427
"Lenten Flowers" (Raine) **45**:340
"Lenten Thoughts of a High Anglican" (Betjeman) **10**:52; **43**:47
Lenuska (Leonov)
See *Lyonushka*
Leo and Theodore (Newlove) **6**:363-64
Léocadia (Anouilh) **8**:23-4; **13**:16, 20; **40**:51, 54; **50**:279
"Un león en el bosque de Palermo" (Bioy Casares) **88**:94
Leon Gaspard (Waters) **88**:363
Leon Trotsky (Howe) **85**:128

"Leonard Commits Redeeming Adulteries with All the Women in Town" (Erdrich) **54**:165
Leonardo's Last Supper (Barnes) **56**:5, 7-8
"Leontes, Solus" (Fuller) **62**:184
"The Leopard" (Nabokov) **3**:355
The Leopard (Bodker) **21**:11-12
The Leopard (Visconti) **16**:565-67, 574-75
The Leopard Hunts in Darkness (Smith) **33**:378
"Leopardi" (Strand) **41**:432-33
"The Leopard-Nurser" (Jacobsen) **48**:193
Leos Janacek: Intimate Excursions (The Brothers Quay) **95**:330, 332, 341-42, 344, 350, 353
The Leper Prince (Mishima) **2**:289
"The Leper's Helix" (Coover) **87**:52
"Lerici" (Gunn) **18**:199
"LeRoi Jones Talking" (Baraka) **115**:49
"Lesbia" (Aldington) **49**:6
The Lesbian Body (Wittig) **22**:476
Lesbian Images (Rule) **27**:417-20, 422
"Lesbos" (Plath) **14**:424; **17**:347-48; **51**:342; **62**:415; **111**:161, 169, 203
Lesen und Schreiben (Wolf) **150**:221
Leslie (Sherburne) **30**:363
"Leslie in California" (Dubus) **36**:147; **97**:228
De l'espirt: Heidegger et la question (Derrida) **87**:108
"The Less Deceived" (Larkin) **8**:339; **18**:294
The Less Deceived (Larkin) **3**:275; **5**:223, 225-28, 230-31; **8**:332-33, 336, 338, 340; **13**:335-38, 340; **18**:293-94, 297-99, 301; **33**:256, 261-63; **39**:334, 339, 341-42; **64**:259, 267-68, 270-71, 278-80
"Less Delicate than the Locust" (Bukowski) **41**:73
"Less Is Less: The Dwindling American Short Story" (Bell) **102**:16
Less than Angels (Pym) **37**:367-68, 373-74, 376-77; **111**:227, 234-36, 243-47, 249, 254-58, 263-67, 269, 271, 281-84
"Less Than One" (Brodsky) **50**:133; **100**:43
Less Than One (Brodsky) **50**:126, 130-33, 135-36; **100**:37, 49-50, 55, 58, 60-4
"Less than Zero" (Costello) **21**:66-7
Less than Zero (Ellis) **39**:55-9; **71**:147, 149-51, 157, 159, 162-64, 166, 168, 170, 172; **117**:105-09, 112-16, 118-24, 128-29, 131-32, 135, 138, 143, 146-48, 150
Lesser Evils: Ten Quartets (Soto) **80**:291, 300
Lesser Lives: The True History of the First Mrs. Meredith (Johnson) **48**:201-02
"Lesser Magellan" (Young) **82**:411
Lessico famigliare (Ginzburg) **11**:228-30; **54**:195-96, 200-07, 211, 214; **70**:280, 282-83
Lessness (Beckett)
See *Sans*
"The Lesson" (Bambara) **19**:33; **88**:12-3, 15, 21, 27
"The Lesson" (Lowell) **4**:303
"The Lesson" (Purdy) **28**:378
"The Lesson" (Simic) **49**:340; **130**:317
"The Lesson" (Tomlinson) **45**:396
The Lesson (Ionesco)
See *La leçon*
A Lesson before Dying (Gaines) **86**:170-79
"Lesson for the Day" (Stern) **39**:243-44
"A Lesson for This Sunday" (Walcott) **25**:451
"The Lesson for Today" (Frost) **10**:195
A Lesson from Aloes (Fugard) **25**:174-76; **40**:201, 203; **80**:62, 68, 70-2, 80-1
A Lesson from the Cyclops and Other Poems (Rudnik) **7**:384
A Lesson in Dead Language (Kennedy) **66**:214
"A Lesson in Geography" (Rexroth) **22**:346; **49**:285; **112**:397
"A Lesson in History" (Farrell) **66**:129
A Lesson in Love (Bergman)
See *En lektion i kärlek*
"A Lesson in Ourselves" (Brosman) **9**:135
"A Lesson in the Parts of Speech" (Thomas) **132**:381
"Lesson Number Eight" (Sondheim) **39**:174
"The Lesson of Poetry" (Cabral de Melo Neto)
See "A licão de poesia"
"The Lesson of Sainte-Victoire" (Handke)
See *Die Lehre der Sainte-Victoire*
"The Lesson of the Falling Leaves" (Clifton) **66**:81
"Lesson of the Master" (Dickey) **28**:117
"The Lesson of the Master" (Howard) **7**:169
"The Lesson of the Master" (Ozick) **28**:354; **155**:135
"Lesson One" (Johnston) **51**:255
Lesson Park and Belsize Square (Straub) **107**:304
"Lessons" (Amis) **40**:44
"Lessons: From Attica to Soledad" (Davis) **77**:108
"Lessons from the Art" (Selzer) **74**:264
The Lessons of Modernism (Josipovici) **153**:217, 219
The Lessons of Modernism, and Other Essays (Josipovici) **43**:220-21, 223, 226
"The Lessons of Stendhal" (Ehrenburg) **62**:178
"The Lessons of Theory" (Parini) **133**:288
"Lester Leaps In" (Kerouac) **14**:306
"Let America Be America Again" (Hughes) **108**:283
"Let Be" (Avison) **97**:117
Let Each Man Remember (Jacobsen) **48**:189, 196; **102**:235
"Let 'Em In" (McCartney) **35**:284-85
"Let Go" (Johnston) **51**:255
"Let Him Run Wild" (Wilson) **12**:644, 649
"Let History Be My Judge" (Auden) **6**:22
"Let It Be" (Lennon and McCartney) **12**:380; **35**:278-79, 292, 294
Let It Be (Lennon and McCartney) **12**:380
"Let It Begin" (Levine) **14**:318
Let It Bleed (Jagger and Richard) **17**:227, 229-32, 235, 236-37
Let It Come Down (Bowles) **1**:41; **2**:78; **19**:57; **53**:40-1, 43, 46
"Let It Go" (Empson) **8**:202
"Let It Go" (Nye) **13**:412
"Let It Last" (Armatrading) **17**:10
"Let It Loose" (Jagger and Richard) **17**:224
"Let It Rock" (Jagger and Richard) **17**:229
"Let It Rock" (Seger) **35**:381
"Let It Shine" (Young) **17**:576
"Let Koras and Balafong Accompany Me" (Senghor)
See "Que m'accompagnent Kôras et Balafong"
Let Live (Mphahlele) **25**:341
Let Love Come Last (Caldwell) **39**:302
Let Man Live (Lagerkvist) **54**:272
Let Me Alone (Kavan) **5**:205-06; **82**:121
"Let Me Be Your Clock" (Robinson) **21**:348-50
"Let Me Begin Again" (Levine) **33**:271; **118**:285, 301
Let Me Breathe Thunder (Attaway) **92**:25, 27-8, 32, 34-5, 37-8
Let Me Count the Ways (De Vries) **28**:106
"Let Me Die in My Footsteps" (Dylan) **77**:166
Let Me Fall before I Fly (Wersba) **30**:431-32
Let Me Hear You Whisper (Zindel) **26**:472
"Let Me Make This Perfectly Clear" (MacEwen) **55**:166-67
"Let Me Roll It" (McCartney) **35**:282
"Let My Love Open the Door" (Townshend) **17**:541-42
"Let My People Go" (Miller) **30**:264
Let No Man Write My Epitaph (Motley) **18**:357
Let Noon Be Fair (Motley) **18**:357
"Let Not This Plunder Be Misconstrued" (Brutus) **43**:92
Let the Buyer Beware (Bruce) **21**:54
"Let the Old Dead Make Room for the Young Dead" (Kundera) **32**:260; **115**:308
"Let the Rockets Roar" (Heinlein) **14**:249
"Let Them Call It Jazz" (Rhys) **14**:447; **51**:375; **124**:354
"Let Them Remember Samangan" (Bunting) **39**:299; **47**:45
Let There Be Light (Huston) **20**:165, 175
"Let Us Be Content with Three Little Newborn Elephants" (Miller) **43**:298
"let us begin again the / circle of Blackness" (Sanchez) **116**:300
"let us begin the real work" (Sanchez) **116**:327
Let Us Compare Mythologies (Cohen) **38**:130-32
"Let Us Go On This Way" (Wilson) **12**:652
"Let Us Now Praise Stupid Women" (Atwood) **84**:105
"Let Us Save the Universe" (Lem) **40**:295; **149**:149
Let X Be Excitement (Harris) **12**:263
"Let Your Hand Play First" (Livesay) **79**:347
Let Your Mind Alone! and Other More or Less Inspirational Pieces (Thurber) **5**:434, 437, 442; **25**:435; **125**:395
"Let Your Yeah Be Yeah" (Cliff) **21**:64
"Lethargy" (Justice) **6**:271
"Lethe" (Barnard) **48**:25, 27
"Lethe" (H. D.) **73**:109
"Letishta" (Bagryana) **10**:13
"Letizia" (Espriu) **9**:192
"Let's All Help the Cowboys Sing the Blues" (Jennings) **21**:203
Let's Do It Again (Poitier) **26**:360
"Let's Do the Time Warp Again" (O'Brien) **17**:322
Let's Get It On (Gaye) **26**:131-33, 135
Let's Get Small (Martin) **30**:246-47
"Let's Go Crazy" (Clash) **30**:49
"Let's Go Crazy" (Prince) **35**:329
"Let's Go, Daddy" (Bell) **31**:47
Let's Have Some Poetry (Jennings) **131**:238
"Let's Hear It for a Beautiful Guy" (Friedman) **56**:106-07
Let's Hear It for a Beautiful Guy (Friedman) **56**:107
Let's Hear It for the Queen (Childress) **86**:309
Let's Hear It from the Deaf Man (Hunter) **11**:279
Let's Kill Uncle Lionel (Creasey) **11**:135
"Let's Pretend We're Married" (Prince) **35**:326-27
"Let's Put Our Hearts Together" (Wilson) **12**:652
"Let's Say" (Dunn) **36**:154
"Let's See Action" (Townshend) **17**:531
"Let's See If I Have It Right" (Dunn) **36**:154-55
"Let's Seize the Time" (Cliff) **21**:62
"Let's Spend the Night Together" (Jagger and Richard) **17**:226, 238
Let's Talk about Men (Wertmueller) **16**:595-97
"Let's Work" (Prince) **35**:324-25
"The Letter" (Auden) **6**:24; **11**:15, 17; **123**:20-2, 24
"The Letter" (Blackburn) **43**:62
"A Letter" (Bogan) **93**:92-3
"Letter" (Cohen) **38**:131
"The Letter" (Creeley) **78**:135
"Letter" (Delany) **141**:152
"Letter" (Fuller) **62**:204
"A Letter" (Hecht) **13**:269
"Letter" (Hughes) **108**:291
"A Letter" (Justice) **6**:271; **102**:265
"The Letter" (MacEwen) **55**:168
"The Letter" (Malamud) **8**:375; **44**:416
"A Letter" (Mathias) **45**:238
"The Letter" (Maugham) **67**:206, 210
"The Letter" (Motion) **47**:288, 291, 293-94
"A Letter" (O'Faolain) **70**:314
"A Letter" (Simic) **68**:377
"Letter" (Strand) **18**:517; **71**:285-86
"Letter I" (Empson) **19**:157-58
"Letter II" (Empson) **8**:202; **19**:158
"Letter III" (Empson) **19**:157-58
"Letter IV" (Empson) **19**:159; **34**:335
"Letter V" (Empson) **19**:159

"A Letter about Unequivocal and Ambigious Meaning, Definiteness and Indefiniteness, about Ancient Conditions and New View Scopes, and about Objectivity" (Wolf) **58**:421
"Letter concerning the Yellow Fever" (Epstein) **7**:97
"Letter for Jan" (Lorde) **71**:240
"A Letter for Marian" (McGrath) **59**:181
"Letter for Those Who Grew Up Together" (Ciardi) **40**:153
"Letter from a City Dweller" (Davison) **28**:100
"Letter from a Distant Land" (Booth) **23**:73-4, 77
"Letter from a Far Country" (Clarke) **61**:74-6, 78-80
Letter from a Far Country (Clarke) **61**:74-7, 79, 82-3
"Letter from a Metaphysical Countryside" (Ciardi) **40**:157
"Letter from a Pander" (Ciardi) **40**:161
"Letter from a Region in My Mind" (Baldwin) See "The Fire Next Time"
"Letter from Assisi" (Jennings) **131**:238
Letter from Birmingham Jail (King) **83**:330, 332-34, 336-37, 346-48
"A Letter from Brooklyn" (Walcott) **25**:449; **67**:353
"Letter from Campus" (Turco) **63**:429
"Letter from Chicago" (Sarton) **91**:254
"A Letter from Copenhagen" (Keillor) **115**:267, 288
"Letter from Foreign Parts to Butcher" (Breytenbach) **126**:79
"A Letter from Gwyther Street" (Mathias) **45**:238
"Letter from Highgate Wood" (Adcock) **41**:16
"Letter from His Father" (Gordimer) **123**:118
"Letter From Home" (Wideman) **122**:315
"Letter from Johannesburg, 1976" (Gordimer) **70**:170
A Letter from Li Po, and Other Poems (Aiken) **52**:24, 26
"A Letter from Little Tobago" (Howes) **15**:289
"Letter from New Paltz" (Eshleman) **7**:99
"Letter from Our Man in Blossomtime" (Glück) **22**:173
"Letter from Paris" (Ciardi) **40**:155
Letter From Peking (Buck) **127**:231
"A Letter from Phillis Wheatley" (Hayden) **14**:240; **37**:153, 155, 158
"A Letter from Rome" (Hope) **51**:227
"Letter from the Alpes-Maritimes" (Hacker) **72**:189
"Letter from the House of Questions" (Atwood) **84**:98
"Letter from the North" (Bukowski) **41**:64
"A Letter from the Old Guard" (Walcott) **67**:360
"A Letter from the Pigmies" (Weiss) **14**:555
"A Letter Home" (Sassoon) **130**:184-85
"Letter I" (Eberhart) **56**:82
"Letter I" (Olson) **29**:334
"The Letter I" (Simpson) **7**:429
"A Letter in a Bottle" (Brodsky) **6**:96
"Letter in November" (Plath) **9**:427; **111**:204
"The Letter in the Cedarchest" (Goyen) **40**:217
"A Letter More Likely to Myself" (Graham) **29**:193
"Letter Number Forty-One" (Olson) **29**:329
The Letter of Marque (O'Brian) **152**:263, 282
"Letter of Recommendation" (Amichai) **9**:25
"A Letter of the Times, or Should This Sado-Masochism Be Saved?" (Walker) **103**:407-08, 412
"Letter on August 15" (Hacker) **72**:188, 190
"Letter on Humanism" (Heidegger) **24**:265
"A Letter That Never Reached Russia" (Nabokov) **8**:418; **15**:393
"Letter to a Bourgeois Friend Whom Once I Loved (and Maybe Still Do If Love Is Valid)" (Giovanni) **64**:194
Letter to a Child Never Born (Fallaci) See *Lettera a un bambino mai nato*
"Letter to a Conceivable Great-Grandson" (Birney) **6**:74
"Letter to a Faraway Friend" (Cioran) **64**:99
"Letter to a Friend About Girls" (Larkin) **64**:280
"Letter to a Poet" (Scannell) **49**:325
"Letter to a Poet" (Senghor) See "Lettre à un poète"
"Letter to a Prisoner" (Senghor) See "Lettre à un prisonnier"
"Letter to a Psychiatrist" (Sarton) **14**:481
"Letter to a Sailor" (Walcott) **76**:288
"Letter to a Sister Underground" (Morgan) **2**:294
"Letter to a Wrong Child" (Ciardi) **10**:105
"Letter to a Young Lady in Paris" (Cortázar) See "Carta a un senorita en París"
"Letter to a Young Poet" (Barker) **48**:17
"Letter to a Young Writer" (Price) **63**:326-27
"A Letter to Alex Comfort" (Abse) **29**:19
"Letter to Alexander Dubcek" (Havel) **123**:167
"Letter to all those who don't know what a Black is or who have forgotten what a White is" (Ouologuem) **146**:213
"Letter to all those who frequent Negroes" (Ouologuem) **146**:213
"Letter to an Exile" (Motion) **47**:292-93
"Letter to an Imaginary Friend" (McGrath) **59**:176, 183
Letter to an Imaginary Friend (McGrath) **59**:174-75, 177, 180-81
Letter to an Imaginary Friend: Parts One and Two (McGrath) **28**:276-79
"A Letter to Any Friend" (Riding) **7**:374
"A Letter to Basil" (Brutus) **43**:94
"Letter to Ben, 1972" (Durcan) **43**:113
"Letter to Bob Kaufman" (Komunyakaa) **94**:239
"Letter to California" (Mueller) **51**:284
"Letter to Dante" (Ciardi) **40**:152
"Letter to Dr. Gustáv Husák" (Havel) **65**:438
"Letter to Dr. Gustáv Husák General Secretary of the Czechoslovak Communist Party" (Havel) **123**:173, 191
"A Letter to Dr. Martin Luther King" (Sanchez) **116**:317
"Letter to Elaine Feinstein" (Olson) **11**:415
"A Letter to Elizabeth Mayer" (Auden) **3**:29
"Letter to Goldbarth from Big Fork" (Hugo) **32**:241, 250
"Letter to Hans Bender" (Celan) **53**:83
"Letter to Hanson" (Hugo) **32**:242
"Letter to Her" (Bly) **128**:29
"Letter to Hitler" (Laughlin) **49**:220-21
"Letter to Horace" (Brodsky) **100**:61
"A Letter to Ismael in the Grave" (Brown) **32**:64
"A Letter to J from Unwritten 'Greed, Part 10'" (Wakoski) **40**:456
"Letter to J. R. R., the Last Transcendentalist" (Ciardi) **40**:157
"A Letter to James Stephens" (Sarton) **49**:319
Letter to Jane (Godard) **20**:150
"Letter to Joe Brainard" (Waldman) **7**:509
"A Letter to John Dryden" (McAuley) **45**:246, 252
"Letter to John Fuller" (Fenton) **32**:166
"A Letter to John Steinbeck" (Yevtushenko) **26**:464
"Letter to Julie in a New Decade" (Hacker) **91**:110
"Letter to Levertov from Butte" (Hugo) **32**:247
Letter to Lord Byron (Auden) **14**:29; **43**:18-19, 27; **123**:48
"Letter to Man's Reasonable Soul" (Riding) **7**:374
"Letter to Marcel Proust" (Walker) **13**:566
"Letter to Mother" (Ciardi) **40**:152; **44**:379
"Letter to My Father" (McFadden) **48**:257-58
"A Letter to My Grandad on the Occasion of a Letter from Cousin Wanda Lee Saying Grandad is Too Infirm to Feed the Cows and Is Not Long for This World" (Jiles) **58**:281
"A Letter to My Grandsons" (Updike) **139**:326
Letter to My Judge (Simenon) See *Lettre à mon juge*
Letter to My Mother (Simenon) See *Lettre à ma mère*
"Letter to My Sisters at Home" (Ciardi) **40**:151
"Letter to N.Y." (Bishop) **32**:39
"A Letter to Pausanias" (Squires) **51**:377
A Letter to Queen Victoria (Wilson) **7**:550
"Letter to Reed" (Hugo) **32**:242
Letter to Sarah Blacher Cohen (Ozick) **155**:165, 169
"Letter to Seferis the Greek" (Durrell) **27**:97
Letter to Sister Benedicta (Tremain) **42**:383-84
Letter to Soviet Leaders (Solzhenitsyn) See *Pis' mo vozhdiam Sovetskogo Soiuza*
"Letter to the Academy" (Hughes) **108**:294
Letter to the Alumni (Hersey) **81**:335
"Letter to the Copy-Pissers, Negroes ghostwriters of Famous Writers" (Ouologuem) See "Lettre aux pisse-copie, Nères de "écrivains"
"Letter to the Finalists of the Walt Whitman First-Book Poetry Contest" (Wakoski) **40**:452-53
"Letter to the Fourth Congress of Soviet Writers" (Solzhenitsyn) **7**:445
Letter to Three Students (Solzhenitsyn) **78**:408
"Letter to Time" (Alegria) **75**:34, 37, 39, 42
"Letter to Tony: Suitable for Presentation as a Gift" (Goldbarth) **38**:201
"Letter to Virginia Johnson" (Ciardi) **40**:152
"A Letter to William Carlos Williams" (Rexroth) **112**:378, 394
"Letter to William Kinter of Muhlenberg" (Levertov) **66**:243
"Letter, Towards and Away" (Atwood) **4**:27
"The Letter Writer" (Singer) **38**:410
"Letter Written on a Ferry Crossing Long Island Sound" (Sexton) **6**:493; **53**:319
Lettera a un bambino mai nato (Fallaci) **11**:189-91; **110**:194-95, 207, 208
Lettera amorosa (Char) **9**:162
Lettere d'amore a Maria Cumani (Quasimodo) **10**:429
"The Letters" (Mott) **15**:380
"The Letters" (White) **69**:393
LETTERS (Barth) **14**:55-9; **27**:26-8; **51**:20-2, 26-8; **89**:47, 49
Letters (Castillo) See *The Mixquiahuala Letters*
Letters (Duncan) **15**:188
"The Letters II" (Mott) **15**:381
Letters: 1937-1954 (Powys) **125**:296
"Letters and Other Worlds" (Ondaatje) **51**:314, 316
"Letters and Poems to Nazim Hikmet" (Otero) **11**:425
Letters for Origin (Olson) **6**:387; **11**:417
"Letters for the Dead" (Levine) **4**:288; **14**:318; **118**:284, 292, 299-300
"Letters for the Next Time" (Ciardi) **40**:157
"Letters from a Father" (Van Duyn) **116**:408-10, 421, 425, 430
Letters from a Father (Van Duyn) **63**:441-44; **116**:408, 410, 412, 420, 426
Letters from a Lost Uncle from Polar Regions (Peake) **54**:369, 373
"Letters from a Man in Solitary" (Hikmet) **40**:248
Letters From a War Zone: Writings 1976-1989 (Dworkin) **123**:68, 70-1, 74, 77, 87
Letters from Africa, 1914-1931 (Dinesen) **29**:163-64; **95**:54-6, 58-60, 68-9, 77
"Letters from France" (Ousmane) **66**:350
Letters from Iceland (Auden) **3**:25; **43**:16, 18, 27
Letters from Iceland (MacNeice) **53**:234
"Letters from Jack" (Keillor) **115**:283
Letters from London (Barnes) **141**:61, 68

Letters from Maine (Sarton) **49**:321
"Letters from My Father" (Butler) **81**:129
"Letters from Rome" (Ciardi) **40**:155
Letters from the Earth to the Earth (McFadden) **48**:242-44, 246, 249, 251
Letters from the Field, 1925-1975 (Mead) **37**:281
"Letters from the Life-Watch" (Cixous) **92**:81
"Letters from the Ming Dynasty" (Brodsky) **36**:78
"Letters from the Poet Who Sleeps in a Chair" (Parra) **102**:351-53
"Letters from the Samantha" (Helprin) **22**:222
Letters from the Savage Mind (Lane) **25**:283, 285
"Letters from Tula" (Pasternak)
See "Pis'ma iz Tuly"
"Letters from Whetu" (Grace) **56**:116-17, 120
Letters Home (Nichol) **18**:366
Letters Home: Correspondence, 1950-1963 (Plath) **14**:427; **17**:367-68; **50**:441, 447-48; **51**:349; **62**:415; **111**:179
"Letters I Did or Did Not Get" (Ashbery) **77**:68
"Letters in a Time of Crisis" (Merton) **83**:383
"Letters in the Family" (Rich) **73**:332
Letters of Delmore Schwartz (Schwartz) **45**:357-59; **87**:344
Letters of E.B. White (White) **34**:431; **39**:377
The Letters of Evelyn Waugh (Waugh) **19**:465; **27**:474-76; **44**:520, 524; **107**:387, 392
Letters of Ezra Pound, 1907-1941 (Pound) **4**:410; **7**:335
The Letters of Great Ape (Orlovitz) **22**:337
The Letters of J. R. R. Tolkien (Tolkien) **38**:432-34
The Letters of Jean Rhys (Rhys) **51**:365-67; **124**:358, 362-63
Letters of Katherine Anne Porter (Porter) **101**:243, 250
Letters of Marshall McLuhan (McLuhan) **83**:372-74
The Letters of Robert Frost to Louis Untermeyer (Frost) **44**:459
The Letters of Sean O'Casey, Volume I, 1940-1941 (O'Casey) **9**:411; **88**:258
The Letters of T. S. Eliot: Volume One, 1898-1922 (Eliot) **55**:352-55, 359, 362, 369
The Letters of William S. Burroughs (Burroughs) **109**:227
Letters on Art and Literature (Mauriac) **56**:219
Letters on Literature and Politics (Wilson) **24**:486, 490
Letters to a German Friend (Camus)
See *Lettres à un ami allemand*
"Letters to a Roman Friend" (Brodsky) **36**:76
"Letters to a White Liberal" (Merton) **83**:382, 384
Letters to a Young Doctor (Selzer) **74**:272, 281
Letters to Alice on First Reading Jane Austen (Weldon) **36**:447-48
Letters to Allen Ginsberg, 1953-1957 (Burroughs) **42**:72
Letters to Christopher: Stephen Spender's Letters to Christopher Isherwood, 1929-1939 (Spender) **41**:424-25
Letters to Five Artists (Wain) **11**:561-63; **15**:561
Letters to Friends (Hugo) **6**:244
"Letters to Irish Poets" (Longley) **29**:293, 296
"Letters to Josef in Jerusalem" (MacEwen) **55**:163-65, 167-69
Letters to Louis Wilkinson (Powys) **125**:290
Letters to Malcolm: Chiefly on Prayers (Lewis) **3**:297; **6**:308; **124**:226, 228, 246
Letters to Martha and Other Poems from a South African Prison (Brutus) **43**:87-9, 92-4, 96
Letters to Mrs. Z (Brandys) **62**:119
Letters to Olga (Havel) **123**:173, 175-76, 185, 189-90, 196, 207, 211, 215
Letters to Olga: June 1979 to September 1982 (Havel) **65**:414-15, 419, 435, 438, 442
Letters to Olga: June 1979-September 1985 (Havel) **58**:240-44, 247
"Letters to Salonika" (Kroetsch) **57**:292
"Letters to Taranta-Babu" (Hikmet)
See "Taranta-Babuya mektuplar"
"Letters to the Princess" (Senghor)
See "Epîtres à la Princesse"
Letters to Tomasito (McGrath) **59**:176, 178
Letters to Yesenin (Harrison) **14**:235; **33**:197; **66**:158
"Letting Down the Side" (Garnett) **3**:189
"Letting Go" (Grau) **146**:130, 132, 138
"Letting Go" (McCartney) **35**:283
Letting Go (Roth) **31**:334-35, 343-44, 346; **66**:386, 401, 405, 415; **119**:120, 127
"Letting in Cold" (Bell) **31**:50
Letting in the Rumour (Clarke) **61**:83
"Un letto di passaggio" (Calvino) **33**:102
Lettre à la France nègre (Ouologuem) **146**:169-70, 174, 179, 183-85, 189, 213, 253
Lettre à ma mère (Simenon) **8**:487-88
"Lettre à Maurice Thorez" (Césaire) **112**:20, 25
Lettre à mon juge (Simenon) **2**:399; **18**:482; **47**:379
"Lettre à un poète" (Senghor) **130**:237, 258
"Lettre à un prisonnier" (Senghor) **130**:259
La lettre aérienne (Brossard) **115**:117, 127-28, 135, 137-39, 156
"Lettre aux pisse-copie, Nères de"e<´crivains" (Ouologuem) **146**:189, 213, 255
"Lettre d'amour" (Ferron) **94**:106-7, 126
"Lettre d'Angleterre" (Eliot) **24**:176
Lettres à un ami allemand (Camus) **11**:95; **69**:105
Lettres au Castor (Sartre) **52**:380
Lettres d'hivernage (Senghor) **130**:260
Letty Fox: Her Luck (Stead) **5**:404; **32**:412, 414-15; **80**:326-28, 331-33, 341-43, 345-46, 348-49
"Leuké" (H. D.) **31**:207
"leukemia as white rabbit" (Clifton) **66**:84
The Levant Trilogy (Manning) **19**:303-04
The Levanter (Ambler) **6**:2-3
"The Level at Which Sky Began" (Soto) **80**:287
"Levelling with Death" (Roberts) **48**:342
"Levels" (Mahapatra) **33**:277, 283
"Levels of Reality in Literature" (Calvino) **73**:39, 48
Levels of the Game (McPhee) **36**:294
"Leviathan" (Merwin) **13**:384; **45**:276
"Leviathan" (Wolff) **64**:451-52
Leviathan (Auster) **131**:22-3, 30, 42
Leviathan (Schmidt) **56**:392-93, 405
Leviathan (Wilson) **9**:576
"Lèviathan: La traversée inutile" (Green) **77**:265
Levine (Westlake) **33**:440
"Lévi-Strauss at the Lie-Detector" (Morgan) **31**:276
"Levitation" (Dacey) **51**:81
"Levitation" (Ozick) **62**:351, 353-54; **155**:167, 170, 178, 181, 184, 190
Levitation: Five Fictions (Ozick) **28**:349-50, 355; **62**:350; **155**:178, 180-82, 188-89, 216
Lew Archer, Private Investigator (Macdonald) **14**:336
Lewendood (Breytenbach) **126**:73, 83, 85, 89, 101
Lewis and Irene (Morand)
See *Lewis et Irène*
"Lewis Carroll au pays des petites Filles" (Tournier) **95**:378
Lewis et Irène (Morand) **41**:297, 303
Lewis Percy (Brookner) **136**:90-91, 107, 116
"Lexicon Rhetoricae" (Burke) **24**:118
"La ley" (Azorín) **11**:24
La Ley del Deseo (Almodovar) **114**:2-5, 7-16, 19-23, 30-32, 38, 53
"Leyenda" (Borges) **6**:90
La Lézarde (Glissant) **10**:231; **68**:170, 172-79, 181-82, 184, 187-89, 191
"Lezhat velosipedy" (Voznesensky) **57**:416
"Li letanis dal biel fi" (Pasolini) **106**:261
"Liaisons" (Sondheim) **30**:384-85
"Liaisons" (Tate) **25**:428
Liana (Gellhorn) **14**:194; **60**:182, 190, 194
"Liar!" (Asimov) **19**:27; **26**:55, 64; **92**:4, 6, 11
"The Liar" (Baraka) **5**:45; **115**:30-1
"The Liar" (Ihimaera) **46**:199
"The Liar" (Wolff) **64**:449-51, 454
The Liar (Savage) **40**:371-72
Liar, Liar (Yep) **35**:473-74
"The Liars" (Pritchett) **41**:334
Liars in Love (Yates) **23**:482-83
"Libbard's Last Case" (Turner) **48**:398-99
"Libby" (Simon) **26**:410
Le libera (Pinget) **13**:441-43; **37**:359-64
The Libera Me Domine (Pinget)
See *Le libera*
The Liberal Imagination (Trilling) **9**:530; **11**:539-42, 545-46; **24**:449, 450-54, 458-59, 461-62
"Liberalism Doesn't Exist" (Fish) **142**:199
"Liberality and Order: The Criticism of John Bayley" (Eagleton) **63**:106
Liberating Voices (Jones)
See *Liberating Voices: Oral Tradition in African American Literature*
Liberating Voices: Oral Tradition in African American Literature (Jones) **131**:257-8, 267
"Liberation" (Glück) **44**:218; **81**:173
"The Liberation" (Stafford) **68**:423, 431-32, 449
"La libertà stilistica" (Pasolini) **106**:246
"Libertad" (Aleixandre) **9**:14
Libertad bajo palabra (Paz) **65**:176, 189
Liberté d'action (Michaux) **8**:392
"La liberté des mers" (Reverdy) **53**:286
Liberté I: Négritude et humanisme (Senghor) **54**:399; **130**:251
"The Liberties" (Howe) **152**:196-97, 235-36, 239
The Liberties (Howe) **72**:208; **152**:151-52, 157, 162, 164
Le libertinage (Aragon) **22**:40
"The Libertine" (MacNeice) **4**:315
"Liberty" (Arreola)
See "Sinesio de Rodas"
Liberty Bar (Simenon) **47**:373, 376
Liberty behind the Words (Paz)
See *Libertad bajo palabra*
Liberty Tavern (Fleming) **37**:126
Liberty Tree (Paulin) **37**:354-55
Liberty Two (Lipsyte) **21**:210-11
Libra (DeLillo) **54**:86-94; **76**:171-72, 174-77, 179-83, 186; **143**:178, 182, 185, 189-91, 197, 199, 207-08, 224
"The Librarian" (Olson) **5**:328
"The Library" (Calisher) **38**:75
"The Library Horror" (Gardner) **28**:162-63
"The Library Is on Fire" (Char) **55**:289
"The Library of Babel" (Borges)
See "La biblioteca de Babel"
The Library Policeman (King) **113**:367
"The Library Revisited" (Weiss) **8**:546
"Libretto" (Thesen) **56**:414
Libretto for the Republic of Liberia (Tolson) **36**:425-27; **105**:231-35, 240, 254, 258, 261, 263, 271, 277, 281, 283-84, 286-88, 290-94
El libro de arena (Borges) **9**:117; **44**:364
Libro de las preguntas (Neruda) **7**:261; **28**:310; **62**:333, 336-37
The Libro de las profecias of Christopher Columbus: An en Face Edition (West) **70**:340-41, 355
El libro de levante (Azorín) **11**:27
El libro de los libros de Chilam Balam (Asturias) **13**:37
Libro de Manuel (Cortázar) **5**:109; **10**:115-16, 118; **13**:164; **15**:147-48; **33**:123, 125; **34**:329-30, 333-34
Libro que no muerde (Valenzuela) **31**:438; **104**:363, 377-78

"A licão de poesia" (Cabral de Melo Neto) **76**:152, 157
"Lice" (Merwin) **18**:334; **88**:187
Lice (Cendrars)
See *La Main Coupée*
The Lice (Merwin) **1**:212-13; **2**:277; **3**:339; **5**:286, 288; **8**:389; **13**:383-86; **18**:335; **45**:274, 278; **88**:187, 191, 195, 197, 199, 202, 204-06, 211
"A License" (Tuohy) **37**:430
License Renewed (Gardner) **30**:156-57
"the license to carry a gun" (Codrescu) **121**:159
License to Carry a Gun (Codrescu) **46**:101-03; **121**:155, 158-9
"License to Corrupt" (Barzun) **145**:71
"License to Kill" (Dylan) **77**:184
"Lichen" (Munro) **50**:209, 211-12, 216-17, 220
Lichtzwang (Celan) **53**:73, 82; **19**:91; **53**:73, 78, 82; **82**:34
Licking Hitler (Hare) **29**:215; **58**:225, 232; **136**:248, 262-63, 291, 306
"Licorice" (Theriault) **79**:408
"Liddy's Orange" (Olds) **85**:295, 300
"The Lie" (Angelou) **77**:31
"The Lie" (Banks) **37**:23
"The Lie" (Carver) **36**:106
The Lie (Moravia)
See *L'attenzione*
Lie Down in Darkness (Styron) **1**:329-30; **3**:472-74; **5**:418; **11**:515-16, 520-21; **15**:525; **60**:392
The Lie of the Land (Beer) **58**:37-8
A Lie of the Mind (Shepard) **44**:263-72
Eine Liebe in Deutschland (Hochhuth) **18**:255-56
Lieber Fritz (Kroetz) **41**:234
"Liebesgedicht" (Voigt) **54**:430-31
"(Liebeslied.)" (Celan) **82**.50-2
"Lieblingsspeise der Hyänen" (Lenz) **27**:245
Lieblose Legenden (Hildesheimer) **49**:173-74
"Ein Lied in der Wüste" (Celan) **53**:69
"Liedholz" (Read) **4**:439
"Liejyklos" (Brodsky) **36**:77
"Lies" (Canin) **55**:39
"Lies" (Endō) **99**:296
"Lies" (Shields) **97**:433
Lies (Newlove) **14**:377-78
Lies (Williams) **33**:441-42, 444-45; **148**:311, 320-22, 328, 343, 356
Lies and Secrets (Fuller) **62**:196-98, 201, 204
Lies of Silence (Moore) **90**:289-96, 298, 301
Lies of the Night (Bufalino)
See *Le menzogne della notte*
Lies of the Night (Bufalino)
See *Le menzogne della notte*
"Lieu de la salamandre" (Bonnefoy) **15**:76
The Lieutenant (Dubus) **13**:183; **97**:203, 209, 224, 230
"Lieutenant Bligh and Two Midshipmen" (Brown) **100**:82-3
Lieutenant Hornblower (Forester) **35**:169-70
Lieutenant Lookeast, and Other Stories (Ibuse) **22**:226-27
Lieutenant Schmidt (Pasternak) **18**:382; **63**:288, 292-93, 308, 313
"Life" (Aleixandre) **36**:29
"Life" (Head) **67**:96
"A Life" (Plath) **111**:181, 185
A Life (Leonard) **19**:282
A Life (Morris) **3**:343-44; **7**:246
A Life (Tesich) **40**:421
Life: A User's Manual (Perec)
See *La vie, mode d'emploi*
"The Life Adventurous" (Farrell) **66**:129
Life after God (Coupland) **85**:35-41; **133**:7-8, 10, 19
"Life After Jane" (Hall) **151**:217
"The Life Ahead" (Levine) **14**:321; **118**:285
Life among Others (Halpern) **14**:231-32
"Life among the Constipated" (Crumb) **17**:83
The Life and Adventures of Nicholas Nickleby (Edgar) **42**:117-21, 123
Life and Death (Breytenbach) **126**:73, 83
Life and Death (Dworkin) **123**:92-3, 95, 97, 100
Life and Death in a Coral Sea (Cousteau) **30**:104-05
Life and Death in the Charity Ward (Bukowski) **2**:84; **5**:80; **41**:68; **82**:3-4, 8; **108**:83
"Life and Death in the South Side Pavilion" (Carey) **96**:37, 67
Life and Death of an Oilman: The Career of E. W. Marland (Mathews) **84**:205, 211
"The Life and Death of God" (Ballard) **137**:13
The Life and Death of Nikolay Kurbov (Ehrenburg) **62**:174-75
The Life and Death of Yellow Bird (Forman) **21**:120
The Life and Extraordinary Adventures of Private Ivan Chonkin (Voinovich)
See *Zhizn i neobychainye prikliucheniia soldata Ivana Chonkina*
Life and Fate (Grossman)
See *Zhizn' i sud'ba*
Life and Limb (Reddin) **67**:265, 267, 270-71
The Life and Loves of a She-Devil (Weldon) **36**:448-49; **122**:259-60, 265, 268, 270-73, 278, 281-82
Life and Sun (Sillanpaa)
See *Elämä ja aurinko*
The Life and Times of an Involuntary Genius (Codrescu) **46**:103-04
The Life and Times of Chaucer (Gardner) **10**:220; **28**:164
The Life and Times of Joseph Stalin (Wilson) **7**:549-51; **9**:576
Life and Times of Michael K (Coetzee) **33**:106-12; **66**:91-2, 95-7, 99, 105-06; **117**:30-3, 39, 45-9, 59-60, 62-3, 66, 69, 71, 73, 75, 79, 81-7, 92, 102-03
"The Life and Times of Multivac" (Asimov) **26**:56; **92**:9
The Life and Times of Sigmund Freud (Wilson) **7**:549, 551
The Life and Work of Semmelweiss (Céline) **3**:104; **4**:99, 103; **7**:43; **9**:154; **124**:86
Life at the Top (Braine) **1**:43-4; **41**:57
"Life at War" (Levertov) **5**:248-49; **66**:239
Life before Man (Atwood) **15**:38-40; **25**:70; **84**:97; **135**:7, 9
"Life before Science" (Carlson) **54**:37-9
"Life Being the Best" (Boyle) **58**:77
Life Being the Best, and Other Stories (Boyle) **58**:77
"Life between Meals" (DeMarinis) **54**:99-100
"Life Class" (Montague) **13**:391; **46**:273
Life Class (Storey) **4**:530; **5**:415-17; **8**:505
Life Collection (Ivask) **14**:287
"Life Comparison" (Dugan) **6**:143
"Life Cycle of Common Man" (Nemerov) **6**:361
"Life Drawing" (Mac Laverty) **31**:255
"Life during Wartime" (Byrne) **26**:97
Life during Wartime (Reddin) **67**:270-72
"Life for a Life" (Paton) **25**:359
"Life for the Sake of Others" (Mahfouz)
See "Hayat l'l-ghayr"
A Life for the Stars (Blish) **14**:85
Life Force (Weldon) **122**:267-71, 274
"Life from a Goldfish Bowl" (Johnston) **51**:239, 243
"Life from a Window" (Weller) **26**:443-44
"Life Goes On" (Davies) **21**:102
Life Goes On (Sillitoe) **57**:399-400; **148**:
"The Life Guard" (Wain) **46**:417
The Life Guard (Wain) **46**:417
"The Life I Led" (Giovanni) **64**:191
The Life I Really Lived (West) **17**:554
Life in a Quiet House (Kohout) **13**:325
"Life in a Small Neighborhood" (Crase) **58**:165
"Life in an Explosive Forming Press" (Brunner) **8**:109
Life in an Explosive Forming Press (Brunner) **8**:109
Life in Folds (Michaux)
See *La vie dans les plis*
Life in Schools: An Introduction to Critical Pedagogy in the Foundations of Education (McClaren) **70**:366
"Life in the Earth" (Breytenbach) **126**:82
Life in the Forest (Levertov) **15**:338-39; **28**:242; **66**:236, 253
"Life in the Pre-Cambrian Era" (Janowitz) **145**:326
A Life in the Theatre (Mamet) **9**:360; **15**:355-56, 358; **46**:250-51
Life in the Universe (Silverstein and Silverstein) **17**:450
"Life in the Valley" (Strand) **71**:289
Life in the West (Aldiss) **40**:15, 19, 21
"Life in Windy Weather" (Bitov) **57**:114-15
Life in Windy Weather (Bitov) **57**:113-15, 117, 119
Life Is a Platform (Levi) **41**:245
Life Is Elsewhere (Kundera)
See *La vie est ailleurs*
"Life Is Happiness Indeed" (Sondheim) **147**:257
"Life Is No Abyss" (Stafford) **7**:457; **68**:423
"Life Is Trying to Be Life" (Hughes) **37**:172
Life, Law, and Letters (Auchincloss) **18**:25
Life Lessons (Scorsese) **89**:265, 267-68
Life/Lines: Theorizing Women's Autobiography (Brodzki) **65**:315
"A Life Membership" (Tuohy) **37**:430
Life Notes (Waldman) **7**:508
The Life of a Poet (Cocteau)
See *La vie d'un poète*
The Life of a Woman (Endō)
See *Onna no Issho*
"The life of Borodin" (Bukowski) **108**:111
"A Life of Goodbyes" (Bissoondath) **120**:14-15, 19
The Life of Henry James (Edel) **34**:537
"The Life of Imagination" (Gordimer) **123**:116
A Life of Jesus (Endō) **19**:161; **54**:160; **99**:285, 287, 301, 308
The Life of Jesus (Olson) **28**:342-44
The Life of John Milton (Wilson) **33**:455
"The Life of John Voe" (Brown) **48**:62
The Life of Juanita Castro (Warhol) **20**:415, 417
The Life of Langston Hughes, Volume I, 1902-1941: I, Too, Sing America (Rampersad) **44**:507-09, 511-13
"The Life of Lincoln West" (Brooks) **49**:23, 28, 36-7
The Life of Mahalia Jackson, Queen of the Gospel Singers (Jackson) **12**:291
"The Life of Poetry" (Tate) **25**:429
The Life of Poetry (Rukeyser) **15**:459-60; **27**:407, 412-13
A Life of Poetry: 1948-1994 (Amichai) **116**:137
The Life of Raymond Chandler (MacShane) **39**:411
The Life of Riot (Johnson) **15**:479
"The Life of Tadeo Isidoro Cruz" (Borges)
See "Biografía de Tadeo Isidoro Cruz (1829-1874)"
The Life of the Automobile (Ehrenburg) **18**:137-38
The Life of the Drama (Bentley) **24**:47-50
The Life of the Mind (Arendt) **98**:14-15, 38, 48, 52
The Life of the Self: Toward a New Psychology (Lifton) **67**:149, 151
The Life of Thomas More (Ackroyd) **140**:61
"A Life of Wonder" (Ignatow) **40**:259
"Life on Mars" (Bowie) **17**:58, 64
"Life on the Moon" (Smith) **73**:356, 358
"Life on the Road" (Davies) **21**:101
"Life on the Rocks: The Galápagos" (Dillard) **60**:75
"Life Portrait" (Steele) **45**:365
Life Quest (Aldington) **49**:17
Life Sentences (Hailey) **40**:222-23
Life/Situations (Sartre) **18**:472

Life Sketches (Hersey) **81**:329, 332
"Life Story" (Barth) **3**:41; **7**:24; **9**:68-9; **14**:53-4, 56; **51**:23; **89**:5-6, 9-10, 16, 19, 24, 28-30, 32, 34-6, 44-5, 47-8, 56, 61-2
Life Studies (Lowell) **1**:180-84; **2**:246-48; **3**:299-302, 304-06; **4**:295-96, 298-304; **5**:257-58; **8**:348, 350-51, 353, 355-58; **9**:333-35, 339; **11**:325-27, 331; **15**:342-48; **37**:232-33, 235-36, 238, 241-43; **124**:254-55, 257, 259, 261-63, 266-67, 269-76, 278-80, 285-86, 288-89, 291, 295, 299, 300-03
Life, the Universe, and Everything (Adams) **27**:13-15; **60**:2
"The Life to Come" (Forster) **3**:161; **13**:220; **22**:135; **45**:136
The Life to Come, and Other Stories (Forster) **2**:136; **3**:161-62; **15**:229, 231; **22**:135; **45**:131, 143
Life under Water (Greenberg) **57**:227-29
Life Vanquished (Lagerkvist)
See *Det besegrade livet*
"The Life with a Hole in It" (Larkin) **64**:272
"Life with Atlas" (West) **96**:363, 384
"Life with the Blob" (Macdonald) **41**:270
Life with the Lions: Unfinished Music Number Two (Lennon) **35**:267, 270
Life without Armour (Sillitoe) **148**:
Life Work (Hall) **151**:201-03, 207-09, 212
"The Life You Live (May Not Be Your Own)" (Cooper) **56**:71-2
"The Life You Save May Be Your Own" (O'Connor) **1**:257; **21**:256, 264, 276; **104**:104, 120, 123, 135
Lifeboat (Harrison) **42**:204
Lifeboat (Hitchcock) **16**:339, 345
"The Lifeguard" (Beattie) **146**:51
"The Lifeguard" (Dickey) **4**:120
"Lifeguard" (Updike) **7**:486; **13**:558; **139**:324
"Lifeline" (Heinlein) **14**:248; **55**:300, 302
Life's Long Days (Johnson)
See *Livsdagen läng*
"A Life's Unity" (Blunden) **56**:50
"Life's Work" (Kumin) **13**:327
The Lifestyle of Robie Tuckerman (Corcoran) **17**:71-2
Life-Terms (Canetti)
See *Die Befristeten*
"A Lifetime" (Castillo) **151**:47, 65
Lifetime (Sommer) **25**:424
A Lifetime Burning (Douglas) **73**:76-8, 84-8, 90, 97-9
A Lifetime Burning in Every Moment (Kazin) **119**:309, 311, 314-16, 320, 334
"The Lift Man" (Betjeman) **43**:51
"The Lift That Went Down into Hell" (Lagerkvist)
See "Hissen som gick ner i helvete"
"Lifting" (Heaney) **14**:243
"The Lifting" (Olds) **85**:308
"The Light" (Blaga) **75**:74
"light" (Clifton) **66**:87
"Light" (Jacobsen) **48**:190
"The Light" (Sarton) **91**:244
"Light" (Williams) **148**:347, 351
Light (Figes) **31**:168-70
Light a Penny Candle (Binchy) **153**:62-3, 67-8, 70, 78
Light Album (Wilson)
See *L.A.*
"Light and Dark" (Howes) **15**:289-90
Light and Dark (Bronk) **10**:75
Light and Darkness (Kawabata) **9**:314
"Light and Shade" (Rozewicz)
See "Światło i cień"
The Light and the Dark (Snow) **1**:317; **4**:501, 504; **6**:516; **13**:509-10; **19**:425
The Light and the Grief (Bufalino)
See *La luce e il lutto*
The Light around the Body (Bly) **1**:37; **2**:65-6; **5**:61-5; **10**:54-7; **15**:62, 65-8; **38**:55, 57; **128**:5-9, 11, 17, 19, 21-22, 29-30, 36
"The Light at Birth" (Berriault) **54**:7; **109**:98
The Light Beyond the Forest: The Quest for the Holy Grail (Sutcliff) **26**:440
"A Light Breather" (Roethke) **8**:455; **101**:304
Light Can Be Both Wave and Particle (Gilchrist) **65**:349; **143**:283, 294-95, 301, 311, 313-16, 325, 329
Light Compulsion (Celan)
See *Lichtzwang*
"Light Fiction" (Johnston) **51**:251
A Light for Fools (Ginzburg)
See *Tutti i nostri ieri*
"The Light from Beyond" (Smith) **43**:424
Light in August (Faulkner) **1**:100, 102; **3**:149-50, 152-53, 156-58; **6**:174, 176, 178, 180-81; **8**:207-09, 211; **9**:200-01; **11**:200, 202, 206; **14**:169, 172, 179-80; **18**:149; **28**:135-38, 140-45; **68**:116
The Light in the Forest (Richter) **30**:319-23
The Light in the Piazza (Spencer) **22**:399-400, 403
"The Light in the Window" (Woolrich) **77**:402
"A Light in Winter" (MacBeth) **2**:252
"A Light Left On" (Sarton) **91**:254
"Light Listened" (Roethke) **8**:456; **101**:332
"Light Music" (Mahon) **27**:292
"Light My Candle" (Larson) **99**:169
"Light My Fire" (Morrison) **17**:288, 290, 295
The Light of Day (Ambler) **4**:19; **6**:4; **9**:18
"The Light of Paradise" (Blaga) **75**:74
"The Light of the World" (Hemingway) **3**:241; **30**:185, 192
"The Light of the World" (Walcott) **67**:342, 359, 361-63; **76**:275
"Light on the Subject" (Komunyakaa) **94**:246
"The Light Put Out" (Moss) **45**:290
Light Shining in Buckinghamshire (Churchill) **31**:83-4
"The Light Symbolism in 'L'Allegro-Il Peneroso'" (Brooks) **110**:36-7
"the light that came to lucille clifton" (Clifton) **66**:85
Light Thickens (Marsh) **53**:260
"The Light Tree" (Elytis) **49**:111
The Light Tree and the Fourteenth Beauty (Elytis) **49**:108, 117; **100**:168, 170, 175, 180, 183, 185-86, 190
The Light under Islands (Squires) **51**:378
Light Up the Cave (Levertov) **28**:242-43; **66**:239
Light Up the Sky (Hart) **66**:176-79, 182-86, 188, 190
"Light Verse" (Asimov) **19**:28
Light Years (Gee) **57**:221-22
Light Years (Salter) **7**:387-38; **52**:360-61, 363, 365-67; **59**:195-98
"The Light-blue Sea Cannons" (Aksyonov) **101**:20
"Lightenings" (Heaney) **74**:188
Lightfall (Monette) **82**:316
"The Lighthouse" (Walcott) **67**:360; **76**:299
"Lighting Fires in Snow" (Richards) **14**:455
"Lightly Bound" (Smith) **25**:420
"Lightness" (Wilbur) **53**:397
"Lightnin' Blues" (Dove) **50**:157; **81**:144
"Lightning" (Barthelme) **46**:39-40, 43
"Lightning" (Oliver) **34**:247-48
"The Lightning" (Swenson) **106**:349
Lightning (Pa Chin)
See *Tien*
"The Lightning Rod Man" (Belitt) **22**:53, 52
"The Lightning Speed of the Past" (Carver) **55**:275
"Lightning Storm" (Schaeffer) **6**:489; **11**:491
"Lights" (Cardenal)
See "Luces"
"Lights among Redwood" (Gunn) **18**:200
"The Lights Are Always Near" (Kenny) **87**:256
"Lights I Have Seen Before" (Levine) **118**:298
"The Lights in the Sky are Stars" (Rexroth) **112**:377
The Lights of Earth (Berriault) **54**:5-7; **109**:90, 94
Lights On in the House of the Dead (Berrigan) **4**:58
"Lights Out" (Cassity) **42**:97
"The Lightship" (Lenz)
See "Das Feverschiff"
"The Light-Years" (Calvino) **8**:127
"Like a Banner" (Greenberg) **30**:166
Like a Bulwark (Moore) **8**:400; **47**:262
Like a Conquered Province (Goodman) **2**:171
"Like a Hurricane" (Young) **17**:577
"Like a Leaf" (McGuane) **45**:265-66; **127**:274
"Like a Message on Sunday" (Dorn) **10**:157
Like a Ripple in the Pond (Giovanni) **117**:185
"Like a Ripple on a Pond" (Giovanni) **117**:191
"Like a Rolling Stone" (Dylan) **6**:155; **12**:182, 193; **77**:165, 168, 171, 174-75, 179, 182, 186
"Like a Sentence" (Ashbery) **125**:30-1, 33-4, 40
"Like a Winding Sheet" (Petry) **1**:266
"Like All The Other Nations" (Paley) **140**:291
"Like an Old Proud King in a Parable" (Smith) **15**:516-17
Like Any Other Man (Boyle) **19**:67
Like Birds, Like Fishes (Jhabvala) **4**:257; **29**:256
"Like Dolmens round My Childhood, the Old People" (Montague) **13**:390; **46**:266, 275, 278
"Like Father, Like Sun" (Kaufman) **49**:207
Like Ghosts of Eagles (Francis) **15**:236
"Like Glass" (Beattie) **63**:18
Like I Say (Whalen) **29**:446
"Like Life" (Moore) **68**:297, 300-01
Like Life (Moore) **68**:297-302
Like Men Betrayed (Mortimer) **28**:282
"Like Mexicans" (Soto) **80**:284
"Like Morning Light" (Rosenthal) **28**:394
"Like Myself" (Ortiz) **45**:306
"Like O. M." (Cabral de Melo Neto)
See "A maneria de Olegário Mariano"
"Like Olegário Mariano" (Cabral de Melo Neto)
See "A maneria de Olegário Mariano"
Like One of the Family: Conversations from a Domestic's Life (Childress) **86**:309, 311; **96**:94-5
"Like Son" (Van Doren) **10**:495
"Like That" (McCullers) **12**:433
"Like the Inner Wall of a House" (Amichai) **116**:89, 93
Like the Lion's Tooth (Kellogg) **2**:224-25
"Like the Night" (Carpentier) **38**:94
"Like the Sad Heart of Ruth" (Taylor) **37**:407
"Like the Sun" (Narayan) **47**:304
"Like the Sunshine" (Bagryana)
See "Kato slunce"
"Like Things Made of Clay" (Kunze) **10**:310
"Like This One" (Moure) **88**:221
"Like This Together" (Rich) **6**:458; **7**:368; **125**:336
"Like This...So This" (Oates) **6**:367
"Like Three Fair Branches from One Root Deriv'd" (Hass) **18**:213
Like Water for Chocolate (Esquivel)
See *Como agua para chocolate*
"Like Whipporwills" (Simic) **22**:381, 383
A Likely Place (Fox) **121**:186, 198
A Likely story: The Writing Life (Kroetsch) **132**:281, 297
"Likenesses" (MacCaig) **36**:282
"Lila" (Brodkey) **56**:57, 59
Lila: An Inquiry into Morals (Pirsig) **73**:309-10
Lila the Werewolf (Beagle) **104**:5, 8, 19-23, 25
The Lilac Bus (Binchy) **153**:65-6, 70-1, 78
"Lilacs" (Lavin) **99**:322
"The Lilacs" (Wilbur) **6**:570
Lilacs out of the Dead Land (Billington) **43**:54
"Liliana llorando" (Cortázar) **33**:123-24
"Liliana Weeping" (Cortázar)
See "Liliana llorando"
"Liliane: Resurrection of the Daughter" (Shange) **126**:380-82

Liliane: Resurrection of the Daughter (Shange) **126**:380-82
Lilian's Story (Grenville) **61**:152-67
"Lilies" (Oliver) **98**:279, 281, 283
"The Lilies Break Open Over the Dark Water" (Oliver) **98**:283, 290
"The Lilies of the Field Know Which Side Their Bread Is Buttered On" (Harmon) **38**:243-44
Liliom (Lang) **20**:217; **103**:122
Lilít e altri racconti (Levi) **37**:224; **50**:323, 325, 334, 336
"Lilith" (Kennedy) **42**:255
Lilith (Salamanca) **4**:461-62; **15**:464-65
"Lilith, and Other Stories" (Levi)
See *Lilít e altri racconti*
"Det lilla fälttåget" (Lagerkvist) **54**:276, 287
Lillian Hellman: The Image, the Woman (Wright) **44**:526-32
"Lilly's Story" (Wilson) **13**:607
Lilo's Diary (Elman) **19**:149
"The Lily" (Bates) **46**:52, 54, 63
"Lily" (Smiley) **53**:348
Lily and the Lost Boy (Fox) **121**:231
"Lily Coe" (White) **49**:409
Lily Dale (Foote) **51**:135-37
"Lily Daw and the Three Ladies" (Welty) **2**:462; **22**:458; **105**:298, 385
"The Lily of the Valley Lay-By" (Tournier) **36**:439
"The Lily Pond" (Johnston) **51**:241, 243
Lily Tomlin on the Way to Broadway (Tomlin) **17**:517
"Lily's Party" (Purdy) **52**:350
The Lilywhite Boys (Poole) **17**:371
"Limbé" (Damas) **84**:168-69, 171-72, 176, 178, 182
"Limbo" (Carpenter) **41**:103
"Limbo" (Cernuda) **54**:58
"Limbo" (Heaney) **5**:170; **7**:148
"El Limbo" (Poniatowska) **140**:295, 323
Limbo (Huxley) **11**:284
"Limbo River" (Hillis) **66**:195
Limbo River (Hillis) **66**:194, 196-99
The Lime Twig (Hawkes) **1**:138; **2**:183, 185; **3**:221-23; **4**:214-18; **7**:141, 144, 146; **9**:263-64, 266, 268-69; **15**:271; **27**:191-92, 196, 199; **49**:161-62, 164
The Lime Works (Bernhard)
See *Das Kalkwerk*
Limelight (Chaplin) **16**:194-97, 201-02, 204
Limericks: Too Gross (Asimov) **76**:315
The Limey (SODERBERGH) **154**:344, 346-47, 349-51, 353-54
Limit of Darkness (Hunt) **3**:251
"Limited" (Sandburg) **10**:450
"Limites" (Borges) **6**:87; **10**:65
"Limits" (Ammons) **57**:50
"Limits" (Borges)
See "Limites"
"Limits" (Okigbo) **25**:349-50, 352, 355; **84**:317, 319
Limits (Okigbo) **25**:348-54; **84**:302, 306-10, 314-15, 319, 322, 325-28, 331, 336-37
The Limits of Interpretation (Eco) **60**:123; **142**:84-7, 89, 93, 96-7, 99, 105-06, 108-09, 126, 130-31
The Limits of Love (Raphael) **2**:366-67
"The Limits of Neopragmatism" (West) **134**:374, 383
"The Limits of the Novel" (Cowley) **39**:458
Lina (Arghezi) **80**:6
Lincoln: A Novel (Vidal) **33**:409-11; **72**:386-87, 389-93, 395-400, 402-04, 406; **142**:290, 296, 298, 320, 322-23, 328, 332-33
"The Lincoln Relics" (Kunitz) **148**:90, 108, 128, 150
"The Lincoln-Pruitt Anti-Rape Device: Memoirs of the Woman's Combat Army in Vietnam" (Prager) **56**:276-78
Lincoln's Doctor's Dog, and Other Stories (Grayson) **38**:210-11
"A Lincolnshire Church" (Betjeman) **43**:40, 42
"Linda" (Fuller) **62**:199
"Linda" (Nin) **127**:387
"Linda" (Smith) **12**:535
"Linda Paloma" (Browne) **21**:38
"The Linden Branch" (MacLeish) **8**:359
Linden Hills (Naylor) **52**:321-26
"The Linden Tree" (Leffland) **19**:280
The Linden Tree (Priestley) **2**:347
"Lindenbloom" (Clampitt) **32**:118
Lindmann (Raphael) **2**:366-67
"Lindow Man" (Selzer) **74**:287
"Lindsay and the Red City Blues" (Haldeman) **61**:181
"The Line" (Carruth) **84**:129
"The Line" (Hoffman) **6**:243
Line (Horovitz) **56**:149-50, 153
"Line and Form" (Dudek) **11**:160
"The Line of Apelles" (Pasternak)
See "Il tratto di Apelle"
The Line of Least Existence (Drexler) **2**:119
"The Lineman" (Miller) **30**:262, 264
"The Linen Industry" (Longley) **29**:296
"Linen Town" (Heaney) **7**:148
"The Linen Workers" (Longley) **29**:296
"Lines" (Dacey) **51**:82
"The Lines" (Motion) **47**:288
"Lines about the Recent Past" (Galvin) **38**:198
"Lines After Rereading T. S. Eliot" (Wright) **146**:345, 348, 353
Lines at Intersection (Miles) **39**:353
"Lines for a 21st Birthday" (Fuller) **62**:206
"Lines for a Bamboo Stick" (Dudek) **11**:159
"Lines for an Internment" (MacLeish) **68**:285
"Lines for Mr. Stevenson" (Turco) **63**:430
"Lines for My Grandmother's Grave" (Urdang) **47**:397
"Lines for Roy Fuller" (Spender) **91**:269
"Lines for the English" (Squires) **51**:383
"Lines for the Twice-Drowned" (Logan) **5**:255
"Lines for Translation into Any Language" (Fenton) **32**:169
"Lines for Winter" (Strand) **18**:517, 520
"Lines from My Grandfather's Journal" (Cohen) **38**:131
"Lines in Stasis in the Form of Sonnet That Didn't Get Written" (Montgomery) **7**:233
Lines of Life (Mauriac)
See *Destins*
"Lines on a Young Lady's Photograph Album" (Larkin) **5**:231; **18**:301; **33**:263; **64**:267, 279
Lines Scribbled on an Envelope and Other Poems (L'Engle) **12**:348
"Lines to Be Recited While Burning at the Stake" (L'Heureux) **52**:275
"Lines to Myself" (Heaney) **74**:152
"Lines to Robert Lowell" (Voznesensky) **57**:421
"Lines with a Gift of Herbs" (Lewis) **41**:262
"Lines Written for Allen Tate on His Sixtieth Anniversary" (Davidson) **2**:113
"Lines Written in a Guest Book" (Van Duyn) **116**:425
"Lines Written in the Euganean Hills" (Tomlinson) **45**:393-94
"Lines Written in the Library of Congress after the Cleanth Brooks Lecture" (Kumin) **28**:222
"Lines Written near San Francisco" (Simpson) **149**:307, 310, 312-13
"Lines Written on Dry Grape Leaves" (Blaga) **75**:76
"The Linesman" (Frame) **96**:182
"The Line-Up" (Randall) **135**:390, 397
Lingard (Wilson) **14**:589
"The Lingham and the Yoni" (Hope) **51**:214, 216
"La lingua seritta della realtà" (Pasolini) **106**:235
"Lining Up" (Howard) **47**:170-71
Lining Up (Howard) **47**:170
"Links on the Chain" (Ochs) **17**:330-31
Die linkshändige Frau (Handke) **15**:268; **38**:221-23, 227; **134**:118, 123, 130, 132-33, 137, 139
"Linoleum" (Gallagher) **63**:118
"Linoleum Roses" (Cisneros) **69**:146-47; **118**:173, 177, 184
Linotte: The Early Diary of Anaïs Nin, 1914-1920, Vol. I (Nin) **11**:398-99
"Lint" (Brautigan) **12**:65
"Liompa" (Olesha) **8**:432
"Lion" (Garrett) **51**:145
"The Lion" (Merton) **83**:388
"Lion" (Swenson) **61**:395, 400; **106**:326
The Lion and the Archer (Hayden) **37**:156, 160
The Lion and the Honeycomb: Essays in Solicitude and Critique (Blackmur) **24**:58-60, 65-6, 68
The Lion and the Jewel (Soyinka) **3**:463; **14**:506-07; **44**:280-83, 287, 290
The Lion and the Rose (Sarton) **49**:310, 320
Lion Country (Buechner) **2**:82-4; **4**:80; **6**:102-03; **9**:137
"Lion Dance" (Sondheim) **147**:258
"The Lion for Real" (Ginsberg) **36**:181, 199; **109**:356
"Lion Grove, Suzhou" (Seth) **90**:351
"Lion Hunt" (Beer) **58**:36
The Lion in Love (Delaney) **29**:144-47
The Lion in the Gateway (Renault) **17**:397
The Lion of Boaz-Jachin and Jachin-Boaz (Hoban) **7**:161; **25**:263
"The Lion of Comarre" (Clarke) **136**:209
The Lion of Comarre (Clarke) **35**:121; **136**:209, 211, 225
"A Lion on the Freeway" (Gordimer) **18**:189
Lion on the Hearth (Ehle) **27**:103
The Lion Skin (Baxter) **14**:63
The Lion, the Witch, and the Wardrobe (Lewis) **1**:177; **27**:262-63, 265; **124**:228, 232, 236, 246-47
"A Lion upon the Floor" (Olson) **29**:329
Lions and Shadows: An Education in the Twenties (Isherwood) **1**:157; **9**:290-93; **14**:279-80, 283; **44**:397-402
"Lions, Harts, Leaping Does" (Powers) **57**:356, 358
"Lions' Jaws" (Loy) **28**:251, 253
Lions Love (Varda) **16**:558
The Lion's Mouth: Concluding Chapters of Autobiography (Raine) **45**:340-41
Lionushka (Leonov)
See *Lyonushka*
"Lip Service" (Costello) **21**:68
"The Lippia Lawn" (Stafford) **4**:517; **19**:430
"Lips of My Love" (Prichard) **46**:337
Lips Together, Teeth Apart (McNally) **91**:159, 161, 164
"Lips Twisted with Thirst" (Ammons) **57**:49-50
Lipstick on Your Collar (Potter) **86**:347; **123**:250, 279
"Lipstick Vogue" (Costello) **21**:68
The Liquidator (Gardner) **30**:151-52
Lire "Le Capital" (Althusser) **106**:12, 17-19, 21, 29, 31, 38, 42-3
Lirika (Krleža) **114**:167
"Lisa" (Beauvoir) **31**:42
Lisa, Bright and Dark (Neufeld) **17**:308, 310
"Lisa Says" (Reed) **21**:304-05, 311
The Lisbon Traviata (McNally) **41**:291-92; **91**:159
al-Liss wa-al-kilāb (Mahfūz)
See *al-Liss wa'l-kilāb*
al-Liss wa'l-kilāb (Mahfūz) **52**:295-96, 300-01, 303-05; **55**:174, 181, 183
The List of Adrian Messenger (Huston) **20**:168
"A List of Assets" (Olesha)
See "Spisok blagodeyany"
"A List of Benefits" (Olesha)
See "Spisok blagodeyany"
"Listen Carefully" (Levine) **118**:314
"listen children" (Clifton) **66**:69
Listen for the Whisperer (Whitney) **42**:434

"Listen Put On Morning" (Graham) **29**:198
Listen! The Wind (Lindbergh) **82**:148, 150, 153, 158, 166-67
"Listen. This Is the Noise of Myth" (Boland) **67**:40, 46; **113**:86, 88, 98
Listen to the Mockingbird (Perelman) **49**:260, 272
Listen to the Warm (McKuen) **1**:211
Listen to the Wind (Brinsmead) **21**:29-30
Listen to the Wind (Reaney) **13**:475
"Listen to What the Man Said" (McCartney) **35**:282-83
"Listen with Mother" (Raine) **103**:186, 189
"Listenen to Big Black at S.F. State" (Sanchez) **116**:295
The Listener (Caldwell) **28**:62-3
"The Listener in the Corner" (Thomas) **13**:545
"Listening" (Paley) **37**:336-37, 339; **140**:222-23, 228-29, 232, 261, 263, 277, 283
"Listening" (Welty) **105**:320-21, 378-80, 382
Listening: A Chamber Play (Albee) **9**:10; **11**:13; **53**:21, 26; **113**:15, 17, 22, 24, 30-1, 33-5
The Listening Landscape (Zaturenska) **11**:579
Listening to America: A Traveler Rediscovers His Country (Moyers) **74**:249-51, 255
Listening to Billie (Adams) **13**:2; **46**:13-16, 21
"Listening to Distant Guns" (Levertov) **28**:242
"Listening to Marianne Moore on a Record" (Cabral de Melo Neto)
See "Ouvindo Marianne Moore em disco"
"Listening to Presiden Kennedy Lie about the Cuban Invasion" (Bly) **128**:6
"Listening to the Mourners" (Wright) **10**:544
"Listening to the Orchestra" (Hill) **113**:330
Listening to the Orchestra (Hill) **113**:330-31
"Listening Wind" (Byrne) **26**:98
The Listening Woman (Hillerman) **62**:251, 253, 256
"Liston Cows Patterson and Knocks Him Silly" (Rosenthal) **28**:394
Lisztomania (Russell) **16**:549
"The Litanies of the Beautiful Bay" (Pasolini) **106**:261
"Litany" (Ashbery) **15**:33-6; **25**:52-3, 58-9; **41**:33, 38; **77**:43
"A Litany for Mad Masters" (Zamora) **89**:387
"The Litany for Survival" (Lorde) **71**:241, 247, 257
"A Litany of Atlanta" (Du Bois) **64**:114, 116; **96**:130
"A Litany of Friends" (Randall) **135**:399
A Litany of Friends (Randall) **135**:392-93, 395, 397, 399
A Literary Affair (Blais) **22**:60
Literary Biography (Edel) **34**:534-35, 537
"The Literary Consequences of the Crash" (Wilson) **24**:481
Literary Criticism: A Short History (Brooks) **110**:9, 31
"Literary Criticism and Philosophy" (Leavis) **24**:298
"A Literary Discovery" (Betjeman) **43**:33
The Literary Essays of Ezra Pound (Pound) **4**:416
The Literary Essays of Thomas Merton (Merton) **83**:396
"Literary Gangsters" (Vidal) **142**:310
"The Literary Gathering" (Ewart)
See "Sestina: The Literary Gathering"
"A Literary History" (Brophy) **6**:100
"Literary History and Historical Writing" (White) **148**:301
"Literary History and Literary Modernity" (de Man) **55**:384, 386, 396
"A Literary History of Anton" (Cohen) **19**:113
"The Literary Life Today" (Epstein) **39**:467-68
Literary Lifelines (Durrell) **27**:96
"Literary Myths of the Revival" (Deane) **122**:103
"Literary Observations" (Fuller) **62**:196
"The Literary Process in Russia" (Sinyavsky) **8**:490
Literary Reflections (Michener) **109**:383
Literary Theory: An Introduction (Eagleton) **132**:84-7, 132, 135
Literary Theory: An Introduction (Eagleton) **63**:95-100, 104-05, 113
"Literary Theory and Historical Writing" (White) **148**:298-300
"Literary Theory and the Black Tradition" (Gates) **65**:386
"Literary Unions" (Ewart) **46**:150
"The Literate Farmer and the Planet Venus" (Frost) **26**:118
Literatur und Lustprinzip (Wellershoff) **46**:436-37
Literatur und Veränderung: Versuche zu einer Metakritik der Literatur (Wellershoff) **46**:434, 437
"A literatura como turismo" (Cabral de Melo Neto) **76**:169
"La literatura es fuego" (Vargas Llosa) **85**:354, 370-71
Literature and Existentialism (Sartre)
See *Qu'est-ce que la littérature?*
Literature and Morality (Farrell) **66**:132, 136
"Literature and Offence" (Brink) **36**:68
Literature and Reality (Fast) **131**:79, 83
"Literature and Revolution; or, The Idylist's Snorting Hobby-Horse" (Grass) **49**:140
Literature and Science (Huxley) **4**:241; **5**:192; **35**:242
"Literature and Society" (Leavis) **24**:298
"Literature and Technology" (MacLennan) **14**:343
Literature and the Press (Dudek) **19**:138
"Literature and the Right to Death" (Blanchot) **135**:88, 102-03, 108-10, 143
Literature and the Sixth Sense (Rahv) **24**:354-55
Literature and Western Man (Priestley) **34**:362-63
"Literature as Idol: Harold Bloom" (Ozick) **155**:168
"Literature as Knowledge" (Tate) **11**:522; **24**:444
"Literature as Tourism" (Cabral de Melo Neto)
See "A literatura como turismo"
"Literature as Utopia" (Bachmann) **69**:57
"Literature in the Reader: Affective Stylistics" (Fish) **142**:155-56
"Literature Is Fire" (Vargas Llosa)
See "La literatura es fuego"
The Literature Machine (Calvino)
See *Una pietra sopra: Discorsi di letteratura e societa*
"The Literature of Exhaustion" (Barth) **3**:41; **7**:22; **14**:55; **51**:20-2, 24-5; **89**:17, 21, 25, 35, 38-9, 44-7, 57
"The Literature of Replenishment" (Barth) **51**:20-2, 24-5; **89**:57
"The Literature of the Holocaust" (Alvarez) **5**:17
"Literature versus the Universities" (Hope) **51**:218
Literatuur in die strydperk (Brink) **106**:109
Lithium for Medea (Braverman) **67**:49, 53
"Lithuanian Divertissement" (Brodsky)
See "Litoviskij divertisment"
"Lithuanian Nocturne" (Brodsky) **100**:45, 53
"The Litigants" (Singer) **69**:306
"Litoviskij divertisment" (Brodsky) **36**:77; **50**:125, 131
"Litovskii noktyurn" (Brodsky)
See "Lithuanian Nocturne"
Litsom k litsu (Aitmatov) **71**:13-14, 16
La littérature et le mal (Bataille) **29**:46-7
"Littérature et metaphysique" (Beauvoir) **44**:345
"Littérature littérale" (Barthes) **24**:27
"Littérature objective" (Barthes) **24**:27
Little (Zukofsky) **2**:487
Little Badger and Fire Spirit (Campbell) **85**:15
"Little Ballad of Ploudiv" (Guillén) **79**:229
"A Little Beaded Bag" (Callaghan) **41**:98
Little Big Man (Berger) **3**:63-4; **5**:60; **8**:83-4; **11**:46; **18**:54-8; **38**:36-9, 41
Little, Big; Or the Fairies' Parliament (Crowley) **57**:158-60, 162-64
"Little Billy" (Townshend) **17**:534
"Little Bird" (Wilson) **12**:641
Little Birds (Nin) **127**:383-84, 386, 388-90
Little Birds: Erotica (Nin) **14**:387; **60**:269, 275; **127**:383-90
"Little Bit of Emotion" (Davies) **21**:105
"The Little Black Box" (Dick) **72**:113
"Little Black Heart of the Telephone" (Warren) **18**:537
"The Little Blond Fellow" (Farrell) **66**:113
"Little Bombadier" (Bowie) **17**:65
Little Book of Evening (Arghezi)
See *Cărticica de seară*
"Little Boy and Lost Shoe" (Warren) **8**:538
"Little Boy Impelling a Scooter" (Murray) **40**:343
A Little Boy in Search of God: Mysticism in a Personal Light (Singer) **11**:499; **23**:422; **38**:412; **69**:303
"Little Boy Sick" (Smith) **25**:418; **44**:442
"Little Boy Soldiers" (Weller) **26**:446
"The Little Boys" (Hughes) **4**:236
"Little Brother" (Wideman) **67**:379, 382-83, 385
"The Little Coat" (Spender) **41**:427
"The Little Cousins" (Taylor) **18**:523; **37**:411; **44**:305-06, 309
"Little Creatures" (Coupland) **85**:35-6, 39
"Little Curtis" (Parker) **68**:326-27, 334-36
The Little Dark Thorn (Arthur) **12**:26, 28
A Little Decorum, for Once (Spackman) **46**:380-81
"Little Deuce Coupe" (Wilson) **12**:651
Little Deuce Coupe (Wilson) **12**:642
"Little Did I Know" (Calisher) **134**:4, 7
The Little Disturbances of Man (Paley) **4**:391-92, 394; **6**:391-93; **37**:330-32, 334-35, 337; **140**:207,209, 226-27, 232-35, 237-38, 247, 251, 261-62, 265, 267, 276-77, 281, 283
"Little Dreams of Mr. Morgan" (Willingham) **51**:403
The Little Drummer Girl (le Carré) **28**:226-32
"The Little Duffer" (Stewart) **32**:421
Little Eden: A Child at War (Figes) **31**:166
"The Little Elderly Lady Visits" (Gustafson) **36**:212
"Little Elegy" (Kennedy) **42**:255, 257
"Little Elegy for Cello and Piano" (Justice) **102**:271
"Little Exercise" (Bishop) **9**:94-5
"Little Expressionless Animals" (Wallace) **114**:347-48, 350, 352, 359, 361
"Little Extras" (McGuane) **45**:265; **127**:274
"The Little Farm" (Bates) **46**:59
"Little Fishes" (Bates) **46**:63
"Little Flower" (Anand) **23**:18
The Little Flowers of Madame de Montespan (Urquhart) **90**:374-5, 381, 398
Little Footsteps (Tally) **42**:368
The Little Foxes (Hellman) **2**:187; **8**:281; **14**:256, 258-59; **18**:221; **34**:348-49, 351; **44**:527-28, 531-32; **52**:189, 191, 202
Little Friend, Little Friend (Jarrell) **2**:209-10; **6**:260; **13**:298, 300
"Little Fugue" (Plath) **5**:345; **111**:204, 214
A Little Geste (Hoffman) **6**:243; **13**:287; **23**:238
The Little Ghost (Preussler) **17**:375
"Little Gidding" (Eliot) **1**:89, 92; **2**:126; **3**:138; **6**:164-65; **9**:185, 187-88; **10**:171; **13**:196, 202; **15**:215-16; **34**:400, 524, 526, 530-32; **41**:147; **55**:346, 353, 360, 366, 374; **113**:183, 193, 219
"Little Gidding" (H. D.) **8**:257
"The Little Girl" (Paley) **6**:392; **37**:338; **140**:249, 252, 255, 262-63, 277, 282
"The Little Girl Continues" (Barnes)
See "The Grande Malade"
"Little Girl Lost" (Kristofferson) **26**:267

"Little Girl, My String Bean, My Lovely Woman" (Sexton) **53**:316, 324; **123**:441
"The Little Girl Sold with the Pears" (Calvino) **22**:94
"A Little Girl Tells a Story to a Lady" (Barnes)
See "Cassation"
The Little Girls (Bowen) **3**:82; **6**:94-5; **11**:63-4; **15**:79; **22**:62
"The Little Girl's Room" (Bowen) **22**:62
"The Little Gram Shop" (Rao) **56**:312
The Little Green Men (Le Guin) **136**:331
"The Little Green Monster" (Murakami) **150**:61
Little Ham (Hughes) **35**:217
"A Little Holiday" (O'Brien) **65**:173
The Little Horses of Tarquinia (Duras)
See *Les petits chevaux de Tarquinia*
The Little Hotel (Stead) **5**:403-05; **8**:499-500; **80**:336, 339
"The Little Hours" (Parker) **68**:326, 335
"Little Imber" (Forster) **22**:137; **45**:131, 133
"A Little Is Enough" (Townshend) **17**:541-42
"The Little John" (Dabrowska)
See "Janek"
Little Katia (Almedingen) **12**:2, 5-7
The Little Kingdom (Humphreys) **47**:184, 186-87
Little Kingdoms (Millhauser) **109**:165, 167, 170, 174
"The Little Knife" (Chabon) **149**:3-4, 7
"Little Lamb" (Sondheim) **30**:377
"Little Lamb Dragonfly" (McCartney) **35**:281
"Little League Try-Outs" (Soto) **80**:279
A Little Learning (Waugh) **27**:477; **44**:520, 522, 524; **107**:370, 392-93
"A Little Light" (Johnston) **51**:240, 245
"Little Lion Face" (Swenson) **106**:343
Little Little (Kerr) **35**:247-50
"Little Lobeila's Song" (Bogan) **4**:69; **39**:388; **93**:81
"Little Lost Robot" (Asimov) **9**:50; **92**:6, 11, 14
"The Little Man at Chehaw Station" (Ellison) **114**:108-12
"The Little Mariner" (Elytis) **100**:170-71, 175-76, 182, 184, 187, 189
The Little Mariner (Elytis) **100**:186-88
"Little Miracles, Kept Promises" (Cisneros) **69**:148; **118**:188, 196, 198, 201-02, 205
"Little Miss Queen of Darkness" (Davies) **21**:88
Little Murders (Feiffer) **2**:133; **8**:216; **64**:148-50, 159-64
"A Little Night Music" (Hospital) **145**:303
"A Little Night Music" (Seth) **43**:388
A Little Night Music (Sondheim) **30**:383-85, 387, 389, 391-92, 395-97, 399, 401-02; **147**:228, 230-31, 233, 237-38
The Little Nugget (Wodehouse) **5**:515
Little Ocean (Shepard) **6**:495; **17**:447
"A Little Old Funky Homeric Blues for Herm" (Carruth) **84**:129
"Little Old Lady Passing By" (King) **53**:209
"Little Old Miss Macbeth" (Leiber) **25**:304
"Little Old Spy" (Hughes) **108**:324
"The Little Old Woman" (Carroll) **10**:98
"The Little Ones" (Soto) **32**:402
A Little Order (Waugh) **27**:476
"Little Oscar" (Dybek) **114**:66
"A Little Outing to H." (Wolf)
See "Kleiner Ausflug nach H"
"Little Pad" (Wilson) **12**:645
Little People, Little Things (Pa Chin)
See *H siao-jen, h siao shih*
A Little Portable Cosmogony (Queneau)
See *Petite cosmogonie portative*
Little Portia (Gray) **36**:200
Little Prayers and Finite Experience (Goodman) **2**:170
"The Little Prince" (Lavin) **99**:320
"The Little Puppy That Could" (Amis) **62**:7-9, 10
A Little Raw on Monday Mornings (Cormier) **12**:133-34
"Little Red Corvette" (Prince) **35**:326-31
"Little Red Riding Hood" (Ferron) **94**:103, 123
"Little Red Rooster" (Jagger and Richard) **17**:227
"Little Red Twin" (Hughes) **119**:271
"Little Requiem" (Graham) **118**:263
"The Little Robber Girl Considers Some Options" (Hacker) **72**:190
"Little Rock" (Guillén) **48**:164; **79**:229-30
A Little Romance (Hill) **26**:207-08, 211-12
"The Little Room" (Carver) **53**:61
"The Little Sailor" (Elytis)
See "The Little Mariner"
The Little Sailor (Elytis)
See *The Little Mariner*
The Little Saint (Simenon)
See *Le petit saint*
"The Little Seafarer" (Elytis)
See "The Little Mariner"
The Little Seafarer (Elytis)
See *The Little Mariner*
"The Little Shoemakers" (Singer) **3**:453; **38**:407, 410; **69**:311; **111**:297
"Little Sister Pond" (Oliver) **98**:257
Little Sisters (Weldon) **11**:566; **19**:469; **122**:246, 268
"Little Sleep's-Head Sprouting Hair in the Moonlight" (Kinnell) **129**:240, 269
"The Little Soldier" (Aitmatov) **71**:16
"Little Songs for Gaia" (Snyder) **120**:325, 342
Little Songs of the Chief Officer of Hunar Louse, or This Unnameable Little Broom (The Brothers Quay) **95**:334, 337, 341-42, 344-45, 347, 351, 353-54
The Little Space: Poems Selected and New, 1968-1998 (Ostriker) **132**:327
The Little Swineherd and Other Tales (Fox) **121**:200, 230
Little Tales of Misogyny (Highsmith) **14**:261; **42**:214; **102**:173, 186, 190, 197
A Little Tea, a Little Chat (Stead) **32**:413-16; **80**:327, 329, 341
"Little Tembi" (Lessing) **22**:279
The Little That Is All (Ciardi) **40**:161; **44**:379, 381
The Little Theater of Jean Renoir (Renoir)
See *Le petit théâtre de Jean Renoir*
"Little Things" (Olds) **85**:296
"The Little Things You Do Together" (Sondheim) **30**:380, 391, 395, 402; **147**:251, 253-54
"The Little Time-Keeper" (Silkin) **43**:401
The Little Time-Keeper (Silkin) **43**:400, 404
"Little Triggers" (Costello) **21**:69
"Little Victories" (Seger) **35**:387
"The Little Virtues" (Ginzburg) **54**:209
The Little Virtues (Ginzburg) **70**:280
"The Little Ways that Encourage Good Fortune" (Stafford) **29**:384
"Little Whale, Varnisher of Reality" (Aksyonov) **101**:10, 18
Little Wheel, Spin and Spin (Sainte-Marie) **17**:431
"Little Willie" (Gordimer) **33**:179-80
Little Wilson and Big God (Burgess) **62**:126-28; **81**:300, 302, 305-06, 310; **94**:87
The Little Witch (Preussler) **17**:374
"The Little Wrens and Roses" (Kiely) **43**:239
"Littleblood" (Hughes) **119**:262
"The Littoral Zone" (Barrett) **150**:6-7, 17
"A Liturgy of Rofes" (Williams) **45**:444
Liubov'k elektrichestvu (Aksyonov)
See *Love of Electricity*
"Live" (Sexton) **10**:468; **53**:319; **123**:452
Live (Marley) **17**:269, 272
Live and Let Die (Fleming) **30**:132-33, 136, 138, 143, 148-49
Live Another Day (Ciardi) **40**:152-54, 156-57; **44**:375; **129**:42
Live at Leeds (Townshend) **17**:527-29
"Live Bait" (Tuohy) **37**:433
Live Bait, and Other Stories (Tuohy) **37**:430-32
Live Bullet: Bob Seger and the Silver Bullet Band (Seger) **35**:380-83, 385
Live Flesh (Rendell) **48**:326-27
Live Flesh (Vinc) **50**:263-64
Live from Golgotha: The Gospel According to Gore Vidal (Vidal) **142**:286-292, 296, 321, 326, 330, 333-35, 338
Live Like Pigs (Arden) **6**:4-5, 7-10; **13**:23-5, 28; **15**:18-19
Live Not by Lies! (Solzhenitsyn) **34**:482
Live or Die (Sexton) **2**:390-91; **4**:482; **6**:492-93; **8**:484; **10**:468; **15**:471-72; **53**:312, 316-17, 319-21, 324; **123**:406, 419, 430, 435, 440-42, 444, 447, 452
Live Peace in Toronto (Lennon) **35**:267, 271
Live Rust (Young) **17**:583
The Live Wire (Kanin) **22**:230
"Live with Me" (Jagger and Richard) **17**:226, 238
The Lively Dead (Dickinson) **35**:131, 133-34
"Lives" (Rukeyser) **15**:458; **27**:409, 413
Lives (Mahon) **27**:286-90
The Lives and Times of Bernardo Brown (Household) **11**:277
The Lives and Times of Jerry Cornelius (Moorcock) **27**:349
The Lives of a Cell: Notes of a Biology Watcher (Thomas) **35**:408-12, 414-15
"Lives of Girls and Women" (Munro) **95**:300
Lives of Girls and Women (Munro) **6**:341-42; **10**:357; **19**:345-46; **50**:210, 215; **95**:284-87, 289, 291, 293, 297, 299-303, 306, 311, 314-15, 317-18, 320, 323, 325
"The Lives of Gulls and Children" (Nemerov) **36**:304
"The Lives of Mrs. Gale" (Belitt) **22**:52
Lives of Short Duration (Richards) **59**:187, 189, 192
"Lives of the Artists" (Merwin) **88**:213
"Lives of the Artists" (Wright) **119**:181, 188
"The Lives of the Chosen" (Dobyns) **37**:76
"The Lives of the Dead" (O'Brien) **103**:136, 162, 175
"Lives of the Poest" (Van Duyn) **116**:410
"The Lives of the Poets" (Atwood) **13**:45-6
"Lives of the Poets" (Doctorow) **37**:93; **113**:135, 149-50, 152-55
Lives of the Poets: Six Stories and a Novella (Doctorow) **37**:91-4; **44**:166-68, 172, 175; **113**:135-36, 151-53, 155-56, 163, 171-72, 174, 176-77, 179
"Lives of the Saints" (Berriault) **109**:95
"Lives of the Saints" (Muldoon) **32**:315
"Lives of the Saints" (Wright) **119**:180-81, 185, 188; **146**:355
Lives of the Saints (Lemann) **39**:75-8
Lives of the Saints (Ricci) **70**:207-17
"The Lives of the Toll Takers" (Bernstein) **142**:24-5
Lives of the Twins (Oates) **52**:335, 339-40
Lives of X (Ciardi) **10**:106; **40**:163; **44**:375, 379, 381; **129**:42, 52
Livia; or, Buried Alive (Durrell) **13**:189; **27**:95, 98-100; **41**:134-35, 137-38
Livid Light (Castellanos)
See *Lívida luz*
Lívida luz (Castellanos) **66**:47, 52
"Livin' above My Station" (Mull) **17**:298
"Living" (Cooper) **56**:71
"Living" (Paley) **4**:392; **37**:332, 337; **140**:209, 211, 233
"The Living" (Pinsky) **38**:358; **94**:299
Living (Ayckbourn)
See *Living Together*
The Living (Dillard) **115**:194-96, 198, 201
Living (Green) **2**:178-79; **13**:251, 153-54; **97**:242, 245, 247-48, 254, 257-58, 267-68, 279-81, 284, 286-89, 292-93
Living (Kurosawa)
See *Ikiru*

"Living Alone in Iota" (Abbott) **48**:6
"Living among the Dead" (Matthews) **40**:320-21
"The Living and Dead" (Mphahlele) **25**:338, 342, 344
The Living and Dead, and Other Short Stories (Mphahlele) **25**:338, 341, 344; **133**:157
Living and Dying (Lifton) **67**:148
The Living and the Dead (White) **4**:586; **5**:486; **7**:531-32; **65**:275, 277, 279; **69**:394, 396, 401, 403, 407
Living at Home (Gordon) **128**:141-43
"Living at Random" (Landolfi) **49**:214
Living at the Movies (Carroll) **35**:78; **143**:27-9, 32, 34-5, 37, 42, 49
Living Authors (Kunitz) **148**:142
The Living Bread (Merton) **83**:403
The Living Buddha (Morand) See *Bouddha vivant*
Living by Fiction (Dillard) **60**:70-4; **115**:169-71, 175, 177, 179, 182-88, 198-201
Living by the Word: Selected Writings, 1973-1987 (Walker) **58**:408-10, 412
The Living End (Elkin) **14**:157-59; **27**:124-25; **51**:89, 91, 98, 100; **91**:213, 216, 224
"The Living Flag" (Keillor) **115**:272
"Living for Now" (Stevenson) **7**:464
"Living for the City" (Wonder) **12**:657
Living Free (Adamson) **17**:2-4
Living in a Calm Country (Porter) **13**:451-52; **33**:320, 325
Living in America (Stevenson) **33**:379-80
Living in Imperial Rome (Dillon) **17**:99
"Living in Paradise" (Costello) **21**:68
"Living in Sin" (Rich) **7**:370; **18**:446; **36**:372
"Living in the Cave" (Rich) **3**:428
"Living in the Country" (Kavanagh) **22**:237
"Living in the Interregnum" (Gordimer) **123**:136
Living in the Maniototo (Frame) **22**:148-49; **66**:145-46; **96**:186, 191, 193-94, 197-98, 202-05, 211, 217
"Living in the New Middle Ages" (Eco) **60**:113
Living in the Open (Piercy) **14**:420, 422; **27**:373; **128**:245-46
Living in the Present (Wain) **2**:457; **46**:408-10
Living in Time (Raine) **7**:352; **45**:330-32, 334
Living in Truth (Havel) **65**:442; **123**:172-73, 175, 185, 188, 191
Living Lights: The Mystery of Bioluminescence (Silverstein and Silverstein) **17**:451
"Living Like Weasels" (Dillard) **60**:74-5; **115**:202
"Living Loving Maid" (Page and Plant) **12**:473
"Living Memory" (Rich) **73**:328, 330, 332
The Living Novel and Later Appreications (Pritchett) **15**:440; **41**:328, 331
Living off the Country (Haines) **58**:221-22
"Living On: Border Lines" (Derrida) **87**:92
Living on the Dead (Megged) **9**:374-75
"A Living Pearl" (Rexroth) **49**:280; **112**:376, 399-400
The Living Principle (Leavis) **24**:307-08, 310, 314
Living Quarters (Canby) **13**:131
Living Quarters (Friel) **42**:173-74; **115**:224-25, 227-29, 233, 235, 237, 241-43
"The Living Reality of the Medicine World" (Allen) **84**:46
The Living Reed (Buck) **7**:32; **127**:238
"The Living Room" (Dobyns) **37**:81
"Living Room" (Jordan) **114**:147
The Living Room (Greene) **1**:135; **6**:212-13; **70**:292, 294
Living Room (Jordan) **114**:146-47
The Living Sea (Cousteau) **30**:102-03
The Living Temple: George Herbert and Catechizing (Fish) **142**:149-50, 173, 177
"Living Tissue/Dead Ideas" (Bernstein) **142**:9
"Living Together" (Bowers) **9**:121-22
"Living Together" (Merwin) **88**:195
Living Together (Ayckbourn) **5**:36-7; **74**:4-6
Living Together (Wilding) **73**:395, 397-98
"Living under a Threat" (Sachs) **98**:361
Living up the Street: Narrative Recollections (Soto) **80**:283-84, 298, 300
"Living with Beautiful Things" (McCarthy) **39**:485, 488, 490-91
"Living With Other Women" (Brown) **79**:154
Living with Your First Motorcycle (Felsen) **17**:124
Living-death (Breytenbach) **126**:83
Livingdying (Corman) **9**:169
"The Livingroom" (Turco) **11**:551
"Livings" (Larkin) **5**:230-31; **8**:337; **33**:259; **64**:261, 268
"Livings II" (Larkin) **5**:230; **33**:261
"Livings III" (Larkin) **18**:301; **33**:261
"Livingstone's Companions" (Gordimer) **123**:116, 144, 148-49
Livingstone's Companions (Gordimer) **3**:202; **5**:147; **10**:241; **18**:184; **33**:183; **123**:148
Un Livre (Brossard) **115**:106-07, 110-11, 117, 154-55
Le Livre à venir (Blanchot) **135**:78, 80, 96-98, 122
Le livre de mon bord: Notes, 1930-1936 (Reverdy) **53**:283-84, 286, 291-92
Le livre de mon pierrot (Nakos) **29**:322-23
Le livre du rire et de l'oubli (Kundera) **19**:268-71; **32**:260-71; **68**:232-36, 244-47, 252-54, 256-60; **115**:310-11, 317, 335-45, 347, 351, 354, 359; **135**:206, 211-12, 218, 241-42, 244-45, 247, 251-52
"Le livre est sur la table" (Ashbery) **77**:50-1
"Le livre, pour vieillir" (Bonnefoy) **15**:74
"Livres" (Butor) **15**:114
Livret de famille (Modiano) **18**:338
Livro de histórias (Ribeiro) **67**:276
Livsdagen läng (Johnson) **14**:296
"Livvie" (Welty) **105**:302-03, 385
Liza of Lambeth (Maugham) **15**:370; **67**:215, 227; **93**:227, 234, 244, 247, 271
The Lizard in the Cup (Dickinson) **12**:169-71; **35**:133-34
Lizard in the Grass (Hill) **113**:284-85, 295
Lizard Music (Pinkwater) **35**:319
The Lizard Woman (Waters) **88**:359
The Lizards (Wertmueller) **16**:586-87
The Lizard's Tail (Valenzuela) See *Cola de lagartija*
"Lizbeth: The Caterpillar Story" (Wideman) **36**:455; **122**:345, 355
Lizzie (Hunter) **31**:228-29
"Ljubov" (Bagryana) **10**:12
Ljubov (Brodsky) **13**:116
"Llama el océano" (Neruda) **62**:335
"El llano en llamas" (Rulfo) **80**:216, 224
El llano en llamas, y otros cuentos (Rulfo) **8**:462; **80**:199-200, 210, 213, 221, 223
"Llegada" (Guillén) **48**:166; **79**:240
Llegada de los dioses (Buero Vallejo) **46**:93-94, 96, 98; **139**:16, 19, 42
"Llyr" (Clarke) **61**:77
"De lo real-maravilloso americano" (Carpentier) **38**:98
"Lo, the Dear, Daft Dinosaur!" (Bradbury) **42**:42
Loaded (Reed) **21**:303, 308
"Loading Boxcars" (Lane) **25**:287
"The Load-Out" (Browne) **21**:39-40
"A Loaf of Bread" (McPherson) **19**:310; **77**:366
The Loafers (Fellini) See *I vitelloni*
"The Loan" (Malamud) **44**:418-19
Loaves and Fishes (Brown) **5**:78; **48**:51, 57; **100**:84
Loaves and Fishes (Maugham) **93**:249
Loblolly (Gilbreth and Carey) **17**:155
"Lobster" (Rakosi) **47**:343
"Lobsters in the Brain Coral" (Lieberman) **4**:292
"Loca Santa" (Castillo) **151**:34
Local Anaesthetic (Grass) **2**:172-73; **4**:202, 206; **6**:209; **11**:248; **15**:261; **32**:204; **49**:139, 143
Local Assays: On Contemporary American Poetry (Smith) **42**:355-56
Local Color (Capote) **3**:100; **8**:133; **19**:87; **34**:320; **38**:84; **58**:87
"Local Customs" (Thomas) **107**:333
"Local Family Keeps Son Happy" (Keillor) **40**:274
Local Lives (Brand) **7**:29-31
Local Measures (Miles) **1**:215; **39**:353
"Local Quarrels" (Bottoms) **53**:33
"Local Troublemaker Abramashvili" (Aksyonov) **101**:18
"Locale" (Crase) **58**:165
"Localizing" (Ammons) **57**:50, 52
Locations (Harrison) **6**:223; **143**:350
"Loch na Bearraig" (MacCaig) **36**:281
"The Loch Ness Monster's Song" (Morgan) **31**:276
The Lock at Charenton (Simenon) **47**:371
"Locked Doors" (Sexton) **123**:427
A Locked House (Snodgrass) **68**:388, 399
The Locked Room (Auster) **47**:14-16; **131**:4-5, 7, 9, 13-5, 24, 26, 33, 36-9
The Locked Room (Wahlöö) See *Det slutna rummet*
Locked Rooms and Open Doors: Diaries and Letters of Anne Morrow Lindbergh, 1933-1935 (Lindbergh) **82**:152-53
"Locker Room Conversation" (Ostriker) **132**:324
"The Locket" (Montague) **46**:277
"Locking Yourself Out, Then Trying to Get Back In" (Carver) **36**:107
"Lockout" (Ostriker) **132**:323, 325
"Locks" (Bukowski) **82**:14
"Locks" (Koch) **5**:219
"Locks without Doors" (Bernstein) **142**:26
The Lockwood Concern (O'Hara) **42**:316-17, 323-24
Locos: A Comedy of Gestures (Alfau) **66**:2-12
"Locus" (Allen) **84**:38
"Locus" (Hayden) **37**:157
"Locus Solus" (Bowering) **47**:19
"Locust Songs" (Hill) **8**:295
"The Locust Trees" (Klappert) **57**:257
The Locusts Have No King (Powell) **66**:359-60, 362, 364, 372, 374-76
The Lodge (Ringwood) **48**:335-39
Lodger (Bowie) **17**:66
The Lodger (Hitchcock) **16**:343-44, 352
Lodz--The Town (Kieslowski) **120**:209
"Lofty" (Beattie) **63**:18
"Lofty" (O'Connor) **23**:327
"Lofty in the Palais de Danse" (Gunn) **18**:200; **32**:207
"Log" (Merrill) **13**:380
The Log from the Sea of Cortez (Steinbeck) **34**:412; **124**:387, 392, 402
The Log of Christopher Columbus (Fuson) **70**:331, 351
Log Rhythms (Bernstein) **142**:56
"Logan Airport, Boston" (Lowell) **11**:331
Logan in Overtime (Quarrington) **65**:203
Logan Stone (Thomas) **13**:542
"Logarithms" (Singer) **69**:311
La logeuse (Audiberti) **38**:23, 26, 29
"Logging 15" (Snyder) **120**:341
"Logging and Pimping and 'Your Pal, Jim'" (Maclean) **78**:221-22, 231-32
"Logic" (Moore) **13**:396
"Logic of Empire" (Heinlein) **26**:163; **55**:302
The Logical Structure of Linguistic Theory (Chomsky) **132**:37
"Logopandocy" (Gray) **41**:179
"Logos" (Durrell) **27**:96
"Logos" (Hughes) **37**:173, 175; **119**:265
"Logos" (Warren) **10**:521
"Lohengrin's Tod" (Boell) **27**:59; **72**:70
Loin de rueil (Queneau) **5**:358; **42**:333
The Loiners (Harrison) **43**:174-78, 180; **129**:165, 174, 197, 203, 213, 217

Loitering with Intent (Spark) **40**:393-96, 398-400
Lola vs. Powerman and the Moneygoround, Part One (Davies) **21**:91, 97
"Lolita" (Parker) **68**:337
Lolita (Albee) **25**:38-9; **86**:120, 123; **113**:49
Lolita (Kubrick) **16**:377-80, 382, 384-87, 389, 392
Lolita (Nabokov) **1**:239-45; **2**:299-304; **3**:352-55; **6**:352, 355, 357-59; **8**:407-13, 417-18; **11**:391, 393, 395; **15**:390, 393, 395-96; **23**:304-05, 307; **44**:464-68; **46**:290-96; **64**:332-69
Lollingdon Downs, and Other Poems (Masefield) **11**:357; **47**:227, 229, 234
Lollipop (Southern)
See *Candy*
"Lollipops of the Pomeranian Baroque" (Fenton) **32**:165
"Lollocks" (Graves) **39**:323; **45**:170
Lolly Willowes (Warner) **19**:460
The Loman Family Picnic (Margulies) **76**:190, 193-94
A l'ombre des majorits silencieuses ou la fin du social (Baudrillard) **60**:14-15
Lona Hanson (Savage) **40**:370
"London" (Ezekiel) **61**:105
"London" (Morgan) **31**:275
"London" (Naipaul) **105**:160
London (Ackroyd)
See *Biography of London*
London (Morand)
See *Londres*
"London Ballads" (Plomer) **4**:406
"The London Boys" (Bowie) **17**:65
"London Bridge" (Ashbery) **77**:67
"London Calling" (Clash) **30**:48
London Calling (Clash) **30**:45-7, 49-51
The London Embassy (Theroux) **28**:428; **46**:398-99
"London Fantasy" (Peake) **54**:375
London Fields (Amis) **62**:12-20; **101**:63-67, 69-70, 77-79, 84-86, 88-90, 92, 95, 99
"London Girl" (Weller) **26**:443-44
"London Journal" (Wright) **146**:328
London Kills Me (Kureishi) **135**:265-67, 274, 285-86, 289, 291, 297-98
"London Letters" (Eliot) **9**:190
London Lickpenny (Ackroyd) **52**:2; **140**:9, 21
London Match (Deighton) **46**:131-32
The London Novels of Colin MacInnes (MacInnes) **23**:283
"London, Ontario" (Bowering) **47**:31
"London Rain" (MacNeice) **53**:237
"London, Rainy Day" (Ferlinghetti) **111**:65
"London Revisited" (Livesay) **79**:332
"London Songs" (Fuller) **62**:186
"London Town" (McCartney) **35**:285-87
London Town (McCartney) **35**:285
"London Traffic" (Weller) **26**:443
London Transports (Binchy) **153**:67, 70
"London Welshman" (Mathias) **45**:235
Londoners (Duffy) **37**:116-17
Londoners (Ewart) **46**:147-50
"London's Burning" (Clash) **30**:43-4
Londres (Morand) **41**:304, 306
"The Lone Pilgrim" (Colwin) **84**:140, 150-51
The Lone Pilgrim (Colwin) **23**:129-30; **84**:142, 146, 149-51
"The Lone Ranger" (Hall) **37**:142
The Lone Ranger (Baraka) **115**:29
The Lone Ranger and Tonto Fistfight in Heaven (Alexie) **96**:4-9, 11-13, 15-17; **154**:4, 6-9, 15-17, 19, 22-7, 29-30, 38, 40-2, 44, 47
"A Lone Striker" (Frost) **34**:475
The Lone Woman and Others (Urdang) **47**:399-400
"The Lone Woman of San Nicolas Island" (Urdang) **47**:399
Loneliest Girl in the World (Fearing) **51**:115-16, 121
"Loneliness" (Betjeman) **10**:52; **43**:48
"Loneliness" (Bukowski) **108**:86
"Loneliness" (Transtroemer) **52**:410; **65**:227
"The Loneliness" (Williams) **148**:345
Loneliness (Paz)
See *Soledad*
"Loneliness: An Outburst of Hexasyllables" (Carruth) **84**:129
The Loneliness of Mia (Beckman) **26**:88-9
"The Loneliness of the Long-Distance Runner" (Sillitoe) **1**:307-08; **6**:500; **19**:421; **57**:386, 391-92, 394-95
The Loneliness of the Long-Distance Runner (Sillitoe) **1**:308; **3**:448-49; **6**:501; **57**:388-89, 392, 396, 401; **148**:155-57, 159-62, 170-71, 173, 176-79, 181, 184, 186, 188, 190, 197-99
"Lonely Ache" (Ellison) **42**:126
Lonely Crusade (Himes) **2**:195; **4**:229; **7**:159; **58**:251, 255; **108**:220-21, 224, 228, 231-32, 236, 253-61, 271, 274
Lonely for the Future (Farrell) **66**:129, 132
The Lonely Girl (O'Brien) **3**:365; **5**:313; **116**:193
"The Lonely Guy's Apartment" (Friedman) **56**:105
The Lonely Guy's Book of Life (Friedman) **56**:105, 108
"The Lonely Guy's Cookbook" (Friedman) **56**:105-06
"Lonely Hearts Column" (Dorfman) **77**:141-43
"The Lonely Land" (Smith) **15**:515-17
"Lonely Looking Sky" (Diamond) **30**:111
"Lonely Love" (Blunden) **56**:40, 48, 52
"The Lonely Love of Middle Age" (Waddington) **28**:438
The Lonely Men (L'Amour) **25**:280
"The Lonely One" (Grau) **146**:125
The Lonely Passion of Judith Hearne (Moore) **1**:225; **3**:340-41; **5**:294-95; 297; **7**:235-37; **8**:394-95; **19**:330-31, 333-35; **32**:309, 312-13; **90**:238-40, 242, 249-52, 254, 256-7, 261-3, 267, 269, 273, 278, 288-90, 292, 301, 304
"The Lonely Psalmist" (Arghezi)
Scc "Psalmistul singuratic"
"Lonely School Days" (Berry) **17**:52
The Lonely Sea (MacLean) **50**:348; **63**:268-70
The Lonely Silver Rain (MacDonald) **44**:409
The Lonely Suppers of V.W. Balloon (Middleton) **13**:388-89
Lonely Vigils (Wellman) **49**:393-94
The Lonely Voice (O'Connor) **14**:397
"Lonely, White Fields" (Oliver) **98**:288
The Lonely Wife (Ray) **76**:357, 359
"Lonely Women" (Nyro) **17**:315
"A Loner" (Arghezi)
See "Un singuratic"
"The Loner" (Young) **17**:572, 582
The Loner: A Story of the Wolverine (Corcoran) **17**:77-8
Lonesome Cowboys (Warhol) **20**:420, 423
"The Lonesome Death of Hattie Carroll" (Dylan) **12**:180-81; **77**:166
"The Lonesome Death of Jordy Verrill" (King) **26**:243
Lonesome Dove (McMurtry) **44**:253-62; **127**:328, 330-34, 342-43, 350-52, 355
"The Lonesome Dream" (Mueller) **51**:280
The Lonesome Gods (L'Amour) **55**:308
Lonesome, On'ry, and Mean (Jennings) **21**:201
"Lonesome Pine Special" (Wright) **146**:313, 315, 342
"Lonesome Road" (Berriault) **54**:4
Lonesome Road (Green) **25**:193
"Lonesome Shorty" (Keillor) **115**:294
Lonesome Traveler (Kerouac) **14**:305
"LoneTree" (Simic) **130**:346
Long after Midnight (Bradbury) **42**:35
The Long Afternoon of Earth (Aldiss) **14**:10-12; **40**:18
"Long Ago" (Durrell)
See "Far Away"
The Long Ago (Lavin) **99**:312
Long Ago in France: The Years in Dijon (Fisher) **76**:333-36, 339
"The Long Alley" (Roethke) **11**:480; **46**:362; **101**:274, 280, 283, 335, 337-38
A Long and Happy Life (Price) **3**:404-06; **6**:425; **43**:342-44, 346-47, 349, 353; **50**:230-32; **63**:323-32, 334-36, 338, 341
"The Long and Winding Road" (Lennon and McCartney) **35**:281
Long before Forty (Forester) **35**:172
The Long Black Coat (Bennett) **33**:43-5
"Long Black Song" (Wright) **4**:595; **14**:596; **21**:445, 453-54
"The Long Boat" (Kunitz) **148**:110, 126, 128
The Long Christmas Dinner (Wilder) **82**:363-66, 386-87, 390
The Long Christmas Dinner, and Other Plays in One Act (Wilder) **5**:495; **10**:532-33; **15**:569, 574; **82**:345, 362, 386
"The Long Coyote Line" (Lane) **25**:289
The Long Dark Tea-Time of the Soul (Adams) **60**:4-7
"The Long Day" (Gordon) **13**:247; **29**:187; **83**:232
"The Long Day Called Thursday" (Neruda) **62**:326
A Long Day in November (Gaines) **11**:217; **86**:173
The Long Day Wanes: The Malayan Trilogy (Burgess)
See *The Malayan Trilogy*
A Long Day's Dying (Buechner) **2**:83; **4**:79-80
Un long demanche de fiancailles (Japrisot) **90**:170-73
A Long Desire (Connell) **45**:112-14
"Long Distance" (Ferber) **93**:139
"Long Distance" (O'Brien) **65**:168
"Long Distance" (Smiley) **53**:348-49
Long Distance (Mortimer) **5**:298-99
"Long Distance: An Octave" (Thesen) **56**:415
"Long Distance, II" (Harrison) **43**:180; **129**:197-98
"The Long Distance Runner" (Paley) **6**:392; **37**:336, 338; **140**:234, 238, 240, 242, 244, 255-59, 277, 279, 282, 284
"Long Division" (Rose) **85**:311
Long Division (Roiphe) **3**:435
Long Division: A Tribal History (Rose) **85**:311-12
The Long Divorce (Crispin) **22**:109
The Long Dream (Wright) **4**:595-96; **9**:584; **14**:598; **21**:436-37, 446, 449; **74**:380
Long Drums and Cannons (Laurence) **50**:314-15, 321; **62**:278
The Long Falling (Ridgway) **119**:93-4
The Long Farewell (Stewart) **14**:512
The Long Farewell (Trifonov)
See *Dolgoe proshchanie*
"The Long Flight" (Scannell) **49**:334
"A Long Fourth" (Taylor) **18**:524, 528; **37**:407, 409-11, 413; **44**:305; **50**:259-60; **71**:296-98, 308
A Long Fourth, and Other Stories (Taylor) **1**:334; **18**:523-24, 526
The Long Good-Bye (Altman) **16**:27-9, 31-2, 35-6, 43; **116**:3-7, 11, 13-14, 23, 44-6, 48, 59, 68
The Long Goodbye: Three Novellas (Trifonov) **45**:411-12, 417, 420
"Long Haired Lady" (McCartney) **12**:366, 372
"The Long Home" (Berryman) **13**:78
"Long House Valley Poem" (Ortiz) **45**:308
Long is the Cypress' Shadow (Delibes)
See *La sombra del ciprés es alrgada*
Long Island Light: Poems and a Memoir (Heyen) **18**:231-33
"The Long Island Night" (Moss) **45**:287
"Long Island Springs" (Moss) **45**:289
"Long Journey" (Fearing) **51**:114

The Long Journey (Corcoran) **17**:70
Long Lankin (Banville) **46**:24-27; **118**:2-4, 12, 28
The Long Lavender Look (MacDonald) **27**:274; **44**:408
"A Long Line of Doctors" (Kizer) **80**:180
"A long line of vendidas" (Moraga) **126**:274, 278-79, 282, 288, 298, 302-03, 305-06, 308-09
"Long Lines" (Goodman) **4**:196
Long Live Death (Arrabal)
See *Viva la muerte*
"Long Live Lord Kor!" (Norton) **12**:468
"Long Live the Bride" (Tchicaya) **101**:349
The Long Love (Buck) **11**:76
The Long March (Beauvoir)
See *La longue marche*
The Long March (Styron) **1**:329-30; **5**:418; **11**:514, 516-17; **15**:525; **60**:392
"The Long March from Hearth to Heart" (Breytenbach) **126**:94
"Long May You Run" (Young) **17**:576, 582
Long May You Run (Young) **17**:575-76
The Long Naked Descent into Boston (Eastlake) **8**:201
"The Long Naked Walk of the Dead" (Williams) **33**:442
"The Long Night" (Bambara) **88**:22, 28, 54, 55
The Long Night (Lytle) **22**:292, 296
The Long Night of Francisco Sanctis (Costantini) **49**:63-5
The Long Night of White Chickens (Goldman) **76**:46-55
"Long Nook" (Wieners) **7**:537
"Long Nose" (Stern) **40**:408
"Long Nose Tragedy, Short Nose Comedy" (Szirtes) **46**:394
"A Long Novel" (Ashbery) **77**:58
"The Long Piece" (Sillitoe) **148**:180
Long Remember (Kantor) **7**:194
"The Long River" (Hall) **37**:142-43; **59**:156; **151**:191, 196
The Long River (Smith) **64**:397
The Long Road to Paradise (Settle) **19**:410
"The Long Road to Ummera" (O'Connor) **14**:399; **23**:331-32
"The Long Shadow of Lincoln: A Litany" (Sandburg) **35**:354
The Long Shot (Monette) **82**:318
"Long Story Short" (Boyd) **28**:39
The Long Street (Davidson) **2**:112; **13**:167, 169; **19**:127
"Long Summer" (Lowell) **124**:255
"Long Summer 3" (Lowell) **124**:260-61
The Long Summer Still to Come (Simmons) **43**:408-09
Long Talking Bad Condition Blues (Sukenick) **48**:366, 369
"The Long Thoughts" (Dybek) **114**:64-5, 76
Long Time between Kisses (Scoppettone) **26**:404-05
Long Time Coming and a Long Time Gone (Farina) **9**:195
"Long Track Blues" (Brown) **59**:266
"Long Trip" (Hughes) **108**:333
"The Long Tunnel Ceiling" (Hughes) **119**:278
The Long Valley (Steinbeck) **9**:516; **13**:531, 534; **21**:381, 385; **34**:405; **45**:372, 374; **59**:348, 351; **124**:394
The Long View (Howard) **29**:242, 245
The Long Voyage Home (Ford) **16**:306-07
The Long Voyage: The Life Cycle of a Green Turtle (Silverstein and Silverstein) **17**:453
The Long Wait (Spillane) **13**:526-28
The Long Walk (King) **37**:201, 207; **61**:331, 333; **113**:388, 391
"The Long Walk at San Francisco State" (Boyle) **121**:60
"A Long Walk Before the Snows Began" (Bly) **128**:15
Long Walks and Intimate Talks (Paley) **140**:245 247, 255, 272, 274, 276
"The Long War" (Lee) **90**:177
"The Long Waters" (Roethke) **8**:456-57; **19**:399; **101**:285, 289, 299, 307, 316-19
"The Long Way Around" (Handke) **38**:228
A Long Way from Verona (Gardam) **43**:164-66
The Long Way Home (Benary-Isbert) **12**:33
The Long Way Home (Teran) **36**:419, 421
The Long Way 'Round (Handke) **134**:158, 176
"The Long Years" (Bradbury) **42**:38
"The Longe Nightes When Every Creature..." (Winters) **32**:468
"The Longer Better Forget-Me-Not" (Hein) **154**:
Longer Views (Delany) **141**:148-49, 159-60
The Longest Day (Ryan) **7**:385-86
"The Longest Day of the Year" (Beattie) **146**:59, 66, 72, 76
The Longest Journey (Forster) **1**:107; **2**:134; **3**:161; **9**:207; **10**:182; **13**:215-18, 220; **15**:222, 225; **22**:130-32, 136; **45**:131, 135-36, 138, 142; **77**:226, 236
The Longest Memory (D'Aguiar) **145**:117-19, 121, 123-24, 127
"The Longest Night" (Piercy) **27**:379
The Longest Weekend (Arundel) **17**:13-15, 17-18
"Longfellow Serenade" (Diamond) **30**:112
"Longfellow, Virgil, and Me" (Selzer) **74**:278, 283
"Longing" (Brutus) **43**:92
"Longing" (Oz) **11**:428-29
"The Longing" (Roethke) **8**:455; **19**:396, 398; **101**:305-06, 308, 312, 314, 316
"Longing for Lermontov" (Akhmadulina) **53**:9-10
"Longing for Mother" (Tanizaki)
See "Haha no kouru ki"
A Longing for the Light: Selected Poems of Vicente Aleixandre (Aleixandre) **36**:27, 29-30, 32
The Longings of Women (Piercy) **128**:253-56, 268
"Longjumeau" (Voznesensky) **57**:415
Longleaf (Hansen) **38**:237
"Long-Line Poems" (Laughlin) **49**:224
"The Longobards" (Herbert) **9**:274
The Longships in Harbour (McIlvanney) **42**:281, 285
Longshot (Francis) **102**:137-39, 141, 152, 158
Longshot O'Leary's Garland of Practical Poesie (McGrath) **59**:175-76
Longshot Poems for Broke Players (Bukowski) **41**:64
"The Longstop" (Bainbridge) **62**:37
Longtime Companion (Lucas) **64**:296
Longtime Passing (Brinsmead) **21**:32
La longue marche (Beauvoir) **8**:62; **44**:342-43
"Lonzhyumo" (Voznesensky) **57**:418
The Loo Sanction (Trevanian) **29**:430-32
"The Look" (Olds) **85**:306
"The Look" (Sartre) **13**:501
"Look" (Swenson) **61**:397
"Look" (Thomas) **48**:374
The Look (Marqués)
See *La Mirada*
"Look a Little on the Sunny Side" (Davies) **21**:94
Look after Lulu (Coward) **29**:140
"A Look at Alfred Metraux" (Leiris) **61**:362
"Look at All Those Roses" (Bowen) **118**:76
Look at All Those Roses (Bowen) **11**:66; **22**:67
"Look at Me" (Lennon) **35**:262
Look at Me (Brookner) **32**:60-1; **34**:137, 139, 142; **51**:62-3, 65; **136**:83-84, 89, 108-09, 112-14, 117
"Look at Me Go" (Robison) **42**:342
Look at the Harlequins! (Nabokov) **6**:354-56, 358-60; **8**:412-14; **15**:393; **44**:464, 466, 472-73; **46**:292
"Look at Us Play with Our Meat" (Stern) **40**:408
Look Back in Anger (Osborne) **1**:263; **2**:327-28; **5**:330-33; **11**:421, 423-24; **45**:313-21
Look Behind You, Neighbor (Ringwood) **48**:330, 334-36
"Look, Dick, Look. See Jane Blow It" (Dworkin) **123**:77
Look for Your Words, Look for Your Steps (Carrier)
See *Cherche tes mots, cherche tes pas*
"Look Homeward, Jack" (Ferlinghetti) **27**:139
"Look How the Fish Live" (Powers) **1**:282; **8**:447
Look How the Fish Live (Powers) **8**:447-48; **57**:349, 356-58
"Look it Up! Check it Out!" (Barzun) **145**:73
"Look Me in the Eyes" (Simon) **26**:409-10
"Look Out" (Redgrove) **6**:445
"Look Out for My Love" (Young) **17**:580
A Look round the Estate: Poems, 1957-1967 (Amis) **2**:6; **40**:41
"Look, Stranger, on This Island Now" (Auden) **3**:22, 24; **6**:20, 22-3; **11**:15; **14**:26-7, 32-4; **43**:15, 17-18; **123**:42
Look to the Lady (Allingham)
See *The Gyrth Chalice Mystery*
"Look to the Market" (Neruda) **62**:326
Look Who's Talking! (Perelman) **49**:257
"Lookalikes" (Beer) **58**:37
Looker (Crichton) **90**:69-71
"Lookin' Back" (Seger) **35**:380-82
"Lookin' for a Love" (Young) **17**:575
"Looking" (Snodgrass) **68**:397
"Looking Across Laguna Canyon at Dusk, West-by-Northwest" (Wright) **146**:357
"Looking Again at What I Looked At for Seventeen Years" (Wright) **119**:180; **146**:348
"Looking at a Dry Tumbleweed Brought in from the Snow" (Bly) **15**:63
"Looking at Each Other" (Rukeyser) **27**:411
"Looking at My Father" (Olds) **85**:292
"Looking at Native Prose" (Callaghan) **65**:246
"Looking at Pictures" (Wright) **146**:317
Looking at the Dance (Denby) **48**:81
"Looking at the Rain" (Lightfoot) **26**:278-79
"Looking at Them Asleep" (Olds) **85**:295-96
"Looking Back" (Beer) **58**:31
"Looking Back" (Heaney) **74**:167
Looking Back (Maugham)
See *Looking Backward*
Looking Back (Maynard) **23**:288-90
"Looking Back at the First Story" (Welty) **105**:306
"Looking Back at the Tin Drum" (Grass) **22**:195
"Looking Back from the Mud" (Rose) **85**:314
Looking Backward (Maugham) **11**:370; **67**:228
"Looking Down from Above" (Hood) **28**:193
"Looking 'Em Over" (Farrell) **66**:112
"Looking for a Rain God" (Head) **67**:98
"Looking for Buckhead Boys" (Dickey) **2**:117
"Looking for Chekov's House" (Simpson) **7**:428; **149**:315
"Looking for Climatic Asylum" (Aksyonov) **101**:41
"Looking for Dragon Smoke" (Bly) **128**:4, 36, 41
Looking for Holes in the Ceiling (Dunn) **36**:151-52, 155
"Looking for Love" (Reed) **21**:317
Looking for Mr. Goodbar (Rossner) **6**:469-70; **9**:457; **29**:352-56
"Looking for Mr. Green" (Bellow) **6**:52; **10**:44
"Looking for Mushrooms" (Oliver) **98**:265
"Looking for Mushrooms at Sunrise" (Merwin) **88**:203
"Looking for Poetry in America" (Vendler) **138**:264, 269
"Looking for Rilke" (Hass) **39**:150
"Looking for Snakes" (Oliver) **98**:282
"Looking for Something?" (Herbert) **35**:208; **44**:393
"Looking for Women" (Wieners) **7**:537
Looking for Work (Cheever) **18**:100-02; **48**:64-5
"Looking for Zora" (Walker) **58**:409

The Looking Glass War (le Carré) **3**:282; **5**:232-33; **9**:327
"Looking in a Mirror" (Atwood) **8**:32; **25**:67
"Looking in the Mirror" (Johnson) **15**:480
"Looking into a Tide Pool" (Bly) **15**:63
"Looking into Chaos" (Hesse) **69**:275
"Looking into You" (Browne) **21**:40
Looking on Darkness (Brink)
See *Kennis van die Aand*
"Looking Out for Number One" (Bogosian) **141**:86
"Looking Outside the Cabin Window, I Remember a Line by Li Po" (Wright) **146**:350, 353
Looking over Hills (Kherdian) **6**:281; **9**:317-18
"Looking over Jordan" (Gilchrist) **143**:282, 311, 315
"Looking Over the Acreage" (Ammons) **5**:27
"Looking Sideways" (Beer) **58**:38
"Looking Up" (Merwin) **88**:212
Looking Up at Leaves (Howes) **15**:289-90
"Looking Uptown" (Swenson) **14**:521
"Looking West from Laguna Beach at Night" (Wright) **146**:353, 357
"Looking-Glass" (Levertov) **66**:239
"The Look-Out" (H. D.) **73**:104, 108, 120
Lookout Cartridge (McElroy) **5**:279-80; **47**:238-44, 246
"Lookout Joe" (Young) **17**:574
"Lookout's Journal" (Snyder) **32**:389; **120**:345
"Looks" (Gunn) **81**:183
The Loom of Light (Brown) **48**:61
"Loon and Bebert" (Connell) **45**:109
Loon Lake (Doctorow) **18**:124-27; **37**:86-8, 90, 92-4; **44**:168, 170, 172, 175, 177, 179; **65**:137; **113**:144, 146-47, 150, 152, 156, 158, 160-61, 175-76, 180
"The Loon on Forrester's Pond" (Carruth) **84**:120, 132, 135
"The Loons" (Laurence) **50**:320; **62**:277
"The Loon's Cry" (Nemerov) **36**:304
The Loony-Bin Trip (Millett) **67**:258-62
"Loop" (Ondaatje) **51**:310
Der Loop Der Loop (The Brothers Quay) **95**:329
"Loophole" (Clarke) **136**:210, 212
"Loose" (Ortiz) **45**:310
"The Loose and Baggy Monsters of Henry James" (Blackmur) **24**:59, 64
Loose Change (Davidson) **9**:174-75
"Loose Ends" (Mukherjee) **53**:271; **115**:364
Loose Ends (Weller) **53**:386-93
"A Loose Mountain" (Frost) **26**:118
"Loose Reins" (Tilghman) **65**:106-08, 112
Loose Woman (Cisneros) **118**:209, 212
Loosely Tied Hands (Rosenblatt) **15**:448
"Loot" (Gunn) **6**:221
Loot (Orton) **4**:387-88; **13**:435-37; **43**:326-27, 329-30, 332-34
"Lopey" (Johnston) **51**:241, 243
"Loppy Phelan's Double Shoot" (Callaghan) **41**:98
Loquitur (Bunting) **39**:297; **47**:45-6, 49-50
"Lorca" (Thomas) **132**:382
The Lorca Story: Scenes from a Life (Albee) **113**:51-2
Lord Byron's Doctor (West) **96**:366, 373-74, 379-80, 387, 390, 392, 395
Lord Edgware Dies (Christie)
See *Thirteen at Dinner*
Lord Emsworth and Others (Wodehouse) **10**:537
Lord Foul's Bane (Donaldson) **46**:140-42; **138**:13-14, 16, 18-20, 35-9
"The Lord Giveth" (Yezierska) **46**:449
Lord Halewyn (Ghelderode)
See *Sire Halewyn*
Lord Hornblower (Forester) **35**:167-68, 170
Lord Malquist and Mr. Moon (Stoppard) **91**:184
Lord Malquist and Mr. Moon (Stoppard) **1**:328; **29**:394; **34**:278
"Lord Mountdrago" (Maugham) **67**:219
Lord Mullion's Secret (Stewart) **32**:421
"Lord Myth" (Dubie) **36**:137
Lord of Dark Places (Bennett) **5**:57-9
Lord of Darkness (Silverberg) **140**:397
Lord of Light (Zelazny) **21**:463-65, 467
"Lord of the Chalices" (Amis) **8**:11
Lord of the Dawn (Anaya) **148**:24
Lord of the Far Island (Hibbert) **7**:157
Lord of the Flies (Golding) **1**:119-22; **2**:165-68; **3**:196-98, 200; **10**:233-36, 239; **17**:157-58, 160-64, 166, 168-70, 172-77, 179; **27**:159-67, 169-70; **58**:169-212; **81**:315-19, 323, 325
The Lord of the Rings (Bakshi) **26**:72-4
The Lord of the Rings (Tolkien) **1**:335-41; **2**:433-36; **3**:477, 479-83; **8**:515-16; **12**:565-74, 576-84, 586; **38**:431-35, 437-43
Lord of the Shadow (Espriu) **9**:192
Lord of Thunder (Norton) **12**:457, 461
Lord Pengo (Behrman) **40**:85, 87-8
Lord Richard's Passion (Jones) **52**:248-49, 254
Lord Rochester's Monkey: Being the Life of John Wilmot, Second Earl of Rochester (Greene) **6**:220; **70**:293
"Lord Short Shoe Wants the Monkey" (Shacochis) **39**:199-201
Lord Valentine's Castle (Silverberg) **140**:357-59, 380
Lord Weary's Castle (Lowell) **1**:178-79, 182; **2**:246-47; **3**:302, 304-05; **4**:295, 298, 300, 302-03; **5**:257; **8**:348, 350-51, 353, 355-56; **9**:337-39; **11**:325-26, 328; **15**:343-44; **37**:235, 242; **124**:253-56, 261, 263, 270, 272-75, 283-85, 288, 303
"The Lordly and Isolate Satyrs" (Olson) **29**:335
The Lords and the New Creatures (Morrison) **17**:289
"The Lord's Chameleons" (Klappert) **57**:260
The Lords of Akchasaz: Murder in the Ironsmiths Market (Kemal) **29**:266, 268
The Lords of Discipline (Conroy) **30**:79-80; **74**:44-7, 49-52
The Lords of Limit: Essays on Literature and Ideas (Hill) **45**:186-89
The Lord's Pink Ocean (Walker) **14**:552
The Lord's Will (Green) **25**:193
"Lore" (Longley) **29**:295
"Lorelei" (Plath) **51**:343-44; **111**:178, 210
"Lorena's Army" (Pollitt) **122**:217
"Lorenzo de Medici, about 1480" (Faludy) **42**:137
"Lorgneau le grand" (Theriault) **79**:410
"Lorraine Goes to Livingston: A Rave and Regency Romance" (Welsh) **144**:320-21, 328, 334
Los Alamos Light (Bograd) **35**:63-4
"Los Angelenos" (Joel) **26**:214
"Los Angeles 1980" (Allen) **84**:8, 10
"The Loser" (Carroll) **10**:98
"The Loser" (Rich) **18**:445; **125**:337
The Loser (Konrád)
See *A cinkos*
Loser and Still Champion: Muhammad Ali (Schulberg) **48**:350
"Losers" (Friel)
See *Lovers*
"Losers" (Sandburg) **4**:463
Losers (Friel) **42**:166-67
"Losers, Finders: Strangers at the Door" (Findley) **102**:104, 106-08
"Losing Battles" (Welty) **2**:462-63; **5**:478, 479; **14**:564; **22**:462; **33**:415-16, 419, 421-24
Losing Battles (Welty) **105**:300, 303-06, 310, 312, 314, 329, 335, 349, 353-59, 363, 370-77, 390
"A Losing Game" (Powers) **1**:280; **57**:358
"Losing Game" (Swan) **69**:362
"Losing Merrygorounds" (Waddington) **28**:437
"Losing My Mind" (Sondheim) **30**:381; **147**:263
"The Losing Side" (Monette) **82**:332
"Loss" (King) **53**:212
"Loss" (Montague) **46**:270, 274
"Loss" (Williams) **33**:441
"The Loss" (Yevtushenko) **126**:407
The Loss of El Dorado (Naipaul) **7**:252-53; **9**:393; **18**:361; **105**:137, 139, 154, 156, 160
"The Loss of Faith" (Hospital) **145**:295-96, 303, 312
The Loss of India (Ghose) **42**:177, 179
"Loss, of Perhaps Love, in Our World of Contingency" (Warren) **59**:295
A Loss of Roses (Inge) **8**:307-08; **19**:226-29
"The Loss of Strength" (Clarke) **9**:168
"The Loss of the Creature" (Percy) **3**:378
"The Loss of the Magyar" (Beer) **58**:36
Loss of the Magyar (Beer) **58**:36, 38
"The Loss of The Nabara" (Day Lewis)
See "The Nabara"
"De L'Osservatore" (Arreola) **147**:13
Losses (Jarrell) **2**:207, 209-10; **6**:260; **13**:298, 300
"The Lost" (Boyle) **58**:81-2
"Lost" (Bukowski) **108**:113
"The Lost" (Campbell) **42**:84-5
"Lost" (Haines) **58**:220
"Lost" (Singer) **9**:486
The Lost (Nakos) **29**:322-23
"Lost and Found" (Levine) **118**:285, 300-01
Lost and Found (Gloag) **40**:211-12
The Lost and Found Man (Guild) **33**:186
The Lost and Found Stories of Morley Callaghan (Callaghan) **41**:98
The Lost and the Lurking (Wellman) **49**:390-91, 396
"The Lost Angel" (Levine) **4**:287
"The Lost Baby Poem" (Clifton) **19**:109; **66**:64, 73
"The Lost 'Beautifulness'" (Yezierska) **46**:441
"Lost Bodies" (Wright) **146**:338
"The Lost Camelia of the Bartrams" (Merwin) **88**:213
"Lost Child" (Anand) **23**:21
"The Lost Child" (Lavin) **99**:322
"The Lost Child" (Phillips) **28**:362
"The Lost Childhood" (Greene) **125**:175
The Lost Childhood, and Other Essays (Greene) **3**:211; **6**:217; **9**:250-51
"The Lost Children" (Jarrell) **2**:210
"The Lost Children" (Oliver) **34**:249; **98**:258
"Lost City of Mars" (Bradbury) **42**:34
The Lost Colony (Green) **25**:195-96, 199
"Lost Commagene" (Elytis) **100**:189
"The Lost Continent" (Spinrad) **46**:384
Lost Copper (Rose) **85**:312-13, 315, 317
"The Lost Cottage" (Leavitt) **34**:77-8
The Lost Country (Raine) **7**:353
The Lost Country (Salamanca) **4**:461-62; **15**:464
"Lost Cove and the Rose of San Antone" (Tillinghast) **29**:416
"The Lost Displays" (Wright) **6**:581
Lost Empires (Priestley) **5**:351; **34**:361
"The Lost Explorer" (McGrath) **55**:73
The Lost Father (Simpson) **146**:281-91, 293-94, 296
The Lost Father (Warner) **59**:211-17
"The Lost Federation" (Walcott) **14**:549; **76**:281
The Lost Flying Boat (Sillitoe) **57**:397-98; **148**:162, 184
"Lost Garden" (Lewis) **41**:254-55
"The Lost Girls" (Hogan) **73**:158-59
The Lost Grizzlies (Bass) **143**:12-15
"Lost Ground" (Trevor) **116**:383, 396
The Lost Honor of Katharina Blum: How Violence Develops and Where It Can Lead (Boell)
See *Die verlorene Ehre der Katharina Blum: oder, Wie Gewalt entstehen und wohin sie führen kann*
Lost Horizon (Capra) **16**:154-55, 160-62
"Lost in a Roman" (Morrison) **17**:286
Lost in America (Singer) **23**:422-23; **38**:408; **69**:303; **111**:320
"Lost in Calcutta" (Ginsberg) **36**:184

"Lost in Heaven" (Frost) **26**:118
"Lost in the Badlands" (Purdy) **50**:247
Lost in the Barrens (Mowat) **26**:336-37, 339, 341-43
Lost in the Bonewheel Factory (Komunyakaa) **94**:218-19, 246
Lost in the City (Jones) **76**:64-70
Lost in the Cosmos: The Last Self-Help Book (Percy) **47**:333-35, 339-40; **65**:257
"Lost in the Flood" (Springsteen) **17**:488
"Lost in the Funhouse" (Barth) **9**:66-7, 69; **14**:52-3; **51**:23; **89**:3-4, 6, 8-10, 13-17, 19-22, 33, 42-3, 45, 49-50, 54-5, 57, 59-60
Lost in the Funhouse: Fiction for Print, Tape, Live Voice (Barth) **1**:18; **2**:36-8; **3**:39, 41-2; **5**:51-2; **7**:22-5; **9**:65-6, 69, 71-2, 74; **10**:24; **14**:51, 53-4, 56; **51**:20-4, 26, 29; **89**:3-64
"Lost in the Supermarket" (Clash) **30**:46
"Lost in Translation" (Merrill) **8**:381; **13**:376; **18**:328; **34**:241
Lost in Yonkers (Simon) **70**:235-36, 239-45
The Lost Island (Dillon) **17**:93
Lost Island (Whitney) **42**:434
The Lost Lands (Vansittart) **42**:393
"The Lost Language" (Feldman) **7**:101
"The Lost Leader" (Blunden) **56**:47
"Lost Luggage" (Adams) **46**:17
"The Lost Man" (Wright) **53**:419
The Lost Ones (Beckett)
See *Le dépeupleur*
Lost Originals (Feldman) **7**:102-03
"Lost Paradise" (Seifert) **34**:362; **93**:331
The Lost Pilot (Tate) **2**:431; **25**:427-29
"Lost Possessions" (Hulme) **130**:53
Lost Profile (Sagan) **9**:468; **17**:427
"The Lost Romans" (Rukeyser) **15**:458
"The Lost Salt Gift of Blood" (MacLeod) **56**:196
A Lost Season (Fuller) **4**:177; **28**:152, 158
"The Lost Son" (Roethke) **11**:480-81; **19**:397; **46**:357, 362-64; **101**:263-64, 274, 277, 282-91, 301, 312, 325, 334-41
The Lost Son, and Other Poems (Roethke) **1**:291; **3**:433-34; **8**:455, 459-60; **11**:484-85; **19**:396-97; **46**:355-56, 358, 360-63; **101**:263, 265-66, 273, 285-89, 291-92, 298, 300-01, 303, 305, 312, 322-26, 334-35, 337-38
"Lost Sons" (Salter) **52**:369; **59**:196
"Lost Souls" (Wright) **146**:
"The Lost Speakers" (MacLeish) **68**:287-88
The Lost Steps (Carpentier)
See *Los pasos perdidos*
"A Lost Tradition" (Montague) **46**:276
"The Lost Tribe" (Muldoon) **32**:317
"Lost Unfound" (Gotlieb) **18**:191
The Lost Weekend (Wilder) **20**:456
"The Lost World" (Chabon) **149**:4, 6-7
"The Lost World" (Jarrell) **2**:210; **9**:296
The Lost World (Crichton) **90**:96-7
The Lost World (Jarrell) **2**:207-08, 210-11; **6**:260-62; **13**:301; **49**:200
Lost Worlds (Smith) **43**:419
"The Lost Young Intellectual" (Howe) **85**:147-48
"Lot and His Daughters" (Hope) **51**:216
"Lot Ninety-Six" (Day Lewis) **10**:131
"La lotería en Babilonia" (Borges) **1**:39; **2**:69, 77; **6**:90; **9**:116-17; **19**:51; **83**:156-57, 164
The Lothian Run (Hunter) **21**:157-58
Le lotissement du ciel (Cendrars) **18**:96; **106**:167, 172, 190
Lotna (Wajda) **16**:578, 582
"Lots" (Gunnars) **69**:260
"Lots of Ghastlies" (O'Faolain) **6**:383
"Lots of Lakes" (Loewinsohn) **52**:285
"Lot's Wife" (Akhmatova) **64**:16
"Lot's Wife" (Nemerov) **6**:361
"Lot's Wife" (Simmons) **43**:411
"Lot's Wife" (Szymborska) **99**:201
"Lotta Love" (Young) **17**:580
"The Lottery" (Jackson) **11**:302; **60**:211-16, 218, 221, 224-30, 232, 235-38; **87**:222-35
"The Lottery in Babylon" (Borges)
See "La lotería en Babilonia"
"The Lottery of Babylon" (Borges)
See "La lotería en Babilonia"
"The Lottery Ticket" (Greene) **125**:200
The Lotus Flowers (Voigt) **54**:432-34
Lou in the Limelight (Hunter) **35**:229-30
"Lou Marsh" (Ochs) **17**:330-32
Lou Reed (Reed) **21**:304
The Loud Boy's Life (Barker) **37**:37
The Loud, Resounding Sea (Bonham) **12**:51
"The Loudest Voice" (Paley) **37**:337; **140**:237, 252, 260, 266-67, 282
Lough derg (Kavanagh) **22**:244
"A Lough Neagh Sequence" (Heaney) **5**:170-71; **7**:147; **14**:243; **74**:157
Louie and Ophelia (Edwards) **43**:141-42
"Louie, His Cousin and His Other Cousin" (Cisneros) **118**:177
Louis 'David' Riel: Prophet of the New World (Flanagan) **25**:164
"Louisa, Please Come Home" (Jackson) **60**:235
Louise Bogan: A Portrait (Frank) **39**:383-84, 386-88, 390-91, 393
"Loulou; or, The Domestic Life of the Language" (Atwood) **84**:67
Le loup (Blais) **6**:81; **13**:97-8
"Loup Garoup Means Change Into" (Reed) **5**:368
"Lourdes: Syllables for a Friend" (Graham) **118**:225
"The Louse and the Mosquito" (Seth) **90**:353
"Lovborg's Women" (Allen) **52**:36
"Love" (Boland) **113**:92
"Love" (Butler) **81**:122, 129
"Love" (Char)
See "L'amour"
"Love" (Creeley) **36**:118
"Love" (Graham) **48**:149
"Love" (Kristofferson)
See "It Sure Was"
"Love" (Lennon) **35**:262
"Love" (Lispector) **43**:268-69
"Love" (MacDiarmid) **2**:253
"Love" (Milosz) **56**:233
"Love" (O'Hara) **13**:424
"Love" (Olesha) **8**:430, 432, 433-34
"Love" (Paley) **37**:333, 336
"Love" (Stevenson) **33**:379-80
"Love" (Wilson) **49**:413-16
Love (Brodsky)
See *Ljubov*
Love (Carter) **5**:103; **41**:113-14; **76**:328-30
Love (Dabrowska)
See *Miłość*
Love (Duras)
See *L'amour*
Love (Martin) **89**:116, 118
Love (Schaeffer) **22**:369
"Love, 20 the First Quarter Mile" (Fearing) **51**:117
"Love, 1944" (Rozewicz) **9**:463
Love: A Building on Fire (Byrne) **26**:98
Love: A Trilogy (Pa Chin)
See *Ai-ch'ing ti san-pu ch u*
A Love Affair (Buzzati)
See *Un amore*
Love Affair (Towne) **87**:378, 379
"Love after Love" (Walcott) **42**:422
"Love Again" (Larkin) **64**:263, 277, 281
Love Ain't Nothing but Sex Misspelled (Ellison) **13**:206; **42**:126-27
Love Alone: Eighteen Elegies for Rog (Monette) **82**:317, 321-23, 328, 331-34
Love Always (Beattie) **40**:66-9; **63**:15; **146**:47, 49, 52, 54, 69, 78
Love among the Cannibals (Morris) **1**:232; **37**:311-13
Love among the Ruins (Rice) **7**:363
"Love and Affection" (Armatrading) **17**:8-9
Love and Anarchy (Wertmueller) **16**:587-90, 595-96
"Love and Death" (Lagerkvist)
See "Kärleken och döden"
"Love and Death" (Oates) **134**:245
Love and Death (Allen) **16**:7, 10, 17; **52**:37, 39, 44, 48
Love and Death in a Hot Country (Naipaul)
See *A Hot Country*
Love and Death in the American Novel (Fiedler) **4**:159, 161; **13**:213; **24**:189-92, 197-99, 203-05
Love and Exile (Singer) **69**:304, 306
Love and Fame (Berryman) **2**:56-60; **3**:65-8, 70; **4**:60, 62-3; **6**:63-5; **8**:92-3; **10**:51; **13**:81-2; **25**:91-2, 95; **62**:43-4, 46, 54, 56-8, 66, 74-6
Love and Friendship (Lurie) **4**:305-06; **5**:259-60; **39**:180, 182
"Love and How to Cure It" (Wilder) **82**:362
"Love and Its Derangements" (Oates) **6**:367
Love and Its Derangements (Oates) **1**:251; **3**:359; **6**:367; **15**:401
"Love and Like" (Gold) **42**:195, 197-98; **152**:120
Love and Like (Gold) **42**:189, 197; **152**:120, 129, 144
"Love and Maple Syrup" (Lightfoot) **26**:280
"Love and Marilyn Monroe" (Schwartz) **45**:360
"Love and Marriage" (Johnston) **51**:249
Love and Napalm: Export USA (Ballard)
See *The Atrocity Exhibition*
Love and Other Deaths (Thomas) **13**:541-42; **132**:381
Love and Other Euphemisms (Klein) **30**:235-36
Love, and Other Stories (Olesha) **8**:432
Love and Responsibility (John Paul II)
See *Milose i odpowiedzialnosc: Studium etyczne*
Love and Salt Water (Wilson) **13**:608, 612
"Love and Separation" (Spender) **41**:427
Love and Separation (Spender) **41**:420
"The Love and the Hate" (Jeffers) **11**:311
Love and War, Art and God (Shapiro) **53**:330-31
Love and Work (Price) **3**:405-06; **43**:344-46, 353; **50**:229, 232; **63**:335, 341
"Love at First Sight" (Szymborska) **99**:202
"Love at Night" (Williams) **42**:443
"Love at Roblin Lake" (Purdy) **50**:239-41
Love at the Greek (Diamond) **30**:113
Love at Twenty (Truffaut) **101**:382, 386, 413
"Love Awake" (McCartney) **35**:286
"Love: Beginnings" (Williams) **148**:318, 320
"Love beyond Keeping" (Sandburg) **35**:356
Love Breeze (Robinson) **21**:347
"Love by Ambition" (Auden) **14**:32; **43**:15
"Love Calls Us to the Things of This World" (Wilbur) **6**:570; **53**:399, 401, 412; **110**:357, 359, 374, 385-87
Love Child (Duffy) **37**:115
Love Comes to Eunice K. O'Herlihy (Corcoran) **17**:76
Love, Dad (Hunter) **31**:224-26
"The Love Day" (Dunn) **40**:165
Love, Death, and the Changing of the Seasons (Hacker) **72**:185, 187-88, 191-92
"Love, Death, and the Ladies' Drill Team" (West) **7**:519; **17**:546, 548
Love, Death, and the Ladies' Drill Team (West) **7**:519, 521; **17**:546
The Love Department (Trevor) **7**:475; **71**:326, 345
The Love Eaters (Settle) **19**:408-09; **61**:374, 385
Love Feast (Buechner) **6**:102-03; **9**:136-37
"The Love for October" (Merwin) **88**:204
The Love for Three Oranges (The Brothers Quay) **95**:347, 350
"Love Fossil" (Olds) **32**:345-46; **39**:190
"The Love Gift" (Masefield) **11**:357
The Love Girl and the Innocent (Solzhenitsyn)
See *Olen'i shalashovka*

Love Goes to Press (Gellhorn) **60**:181-82
"Love Hard" (Alexie) **154**:4
"Love Has Its Own Action" (Dixon) **52**:95, 97-8
"Love Having You Around" (Wonder) **12**:656
"Love I Hear" (Sondheim) **30**:378
"Love in a Blue Time" (Kureishi) **135**:291
Love in a Blue Time (Kureishi) **135**:275-76, 284, 291, 293, 302
Love in a Burning Building (Purdy) **14**:430-31
"Love in a Bus" (McGrath) **59**:181
Love in a Cold Climate (Mitford) **44**:485, 491-92
"Love in a Colder Climate" (Ballard) **137**:4
Love in a Dry Season (Foote) **75**:231, 236, 238, 243, 252
"Love in a Song" (McCartney) **35**:282
"Love in a Valley" (Betjeman) **43**:35
"Love in a Valley" (Ewart) **46**:153
"Love in America?" (Moore) **47**:265
Love in Amsterdam (Freeling) **38**:185-86
"Love in Blood Time" (Olds) **85**:298
"Love in High Places" (Johnston) **51**:240-43, 247, 252
Love in Idleness (Rattigan) **7**:354
"Love in Moonlight" (Glück) **81**:167-69, 172
"Love in Reverse" (Amichai) **116**:107
Love in the Afternoon (Wilder) **20**:459
"Love in the Air" (Jin) **109**:54
Love in the Backrooms: The Sequel to City of Night (Rechy) **107**:259
Love in the Days of Rage (Ferlinghetti) **111**:59
"Love in the Depression" (McGinley) **14**:365
Love in the Environs of Voronezh (Sillitoe) **1**:308; **148**:155
"Love in the Luncheonette" (Rosenthal) **28**:391, 394
"Love in the Marble Foot" (O'Faolain) **47**:325
"Love in the Museum" (Rich) **7**:370
Love in the Ruins: The Adventures of a Bad Catholic at a Time Near the End of the World (Percy) **2**:334-35; **3**:378-79, 381; **6**:399-400; **8**:440, 442, 444-45; **14**:412-13, 418; **18**:397-98, 401-02; **47**:334, 336, 338-41; **65**:257-58
"Love in the Third World" (Cliff) **120**:92
Love in the Time of Cholera (García Márquez) **55**:134-40, 142-48
"Love Is" (Swenson) **106**:347
Love Is a Fervent Fire (Jenkins) **52**:221, 225, 227-28
"Love: Is a Human Condition" (Giovanni) **64**:192; **117**:203
Love Is a Missing Person (Kerr) **12**:298, 301; **35**:251
"Love Is a Piece of Paper Torn to Bits" (Bukowski) **41**:65-6
"Love Is a Rose" (Young) **17**:577
Love Is a Summer Word (Daly) **17**:90
"Love Is a Woman" (Wilson) **12**:652
"Love Is Always in Danger" (Yevtushenko) **126**:399
"Love is an Art of Time" (Rexroth) **112**:395
Love Is Colder than Death (Fassbinder) **20**:105
Love Is Eternal (Stone) **7**:469
"Love Is Not Concerned" (Walker) **58**:407
Love Is Not Enough: The Treatment of Emotionally Disturbed Children (Bettelheim) **79**:108, 111
"Love Is Not Relief" (Aleixandre) **36**:29
Love Is Not What You Think (West) **17**:547
Love Is One of the Choices (Klein) **30**:240-41
"Love Is So Short, Forgetting Is So Long" (Neruda)
See "Es tan corto el amor, y es tan largo el olvido"
Love Is the Crooked Thing (Abbott) **48**:4-7
"Love Is the Plan, the Plan Is Death" (Tiptree) **48**:386, 389, 392, 395-96; **50**:357-58
Love, Laurie (Cavanna) **12**:99
"Love Letta" (Bennett) **28**:29
"A Love Letter" (Ferron)
See "Lettre d'amour"
"Love Letter" (Plath) **111**:210
"Love Letter" (Schnackenberg) **40**:380-81
Love Letter from an Impossible Land (Meredith) **4**:348; **13**:373-74; **55**:193
Love Letters from Asia (Hochman) **3**:250; **8**:297
"Love Letters on Blue Paper" (Wesker) **5**:483-84
Love Letters on Blue Paper (Wesker) **5**:483-84; **42**:427
"Love Lies Sleeping" (Bishop) **1**:34; **32**:37
"Love Life" (Mason) **154**:303
Love Life (Mason) **82**:244 45, 251 52, 254 56, 258-59; **154**:237, 240, 294-95, 302-05
Love, Love at the End (Berrigan) **4**:56
The Love Machine (Susann) **3**:475
"Love Me, I'm a Liberal" (Ochs) **17**:334
"Love Me Now or Love Me Later" (Gaye) **26**:135
"Love Me till the Sun Shines" (Davies) **21**:90
Love Me Tonight (Mamoulian) **16**:419-20, 423-26, 428
"Love Me Two Times" (Morrison) **17**:292, 295
"Love Medicine" (Erdrich) **120**:137
Love Medicine (Erdrich) **54**:165-73; **39**:128-34; **120**:133-35, 138-45, 147-48, 150-53, 155-57, 162-68, 174, 181, 183-84, 186-87, 189-92, 195
"Love Minus Zero/No Limit" (Dylan) **6**:156; **77**:176-77
"Love, My Machine" (Simpson) **149**:312, 342
"Love Needs a Heart" (Browne) **21**:40
"The Love Object" (O'Brien) **8**:429; **36**:340; **116**:186, 208
The Love Object (O'Brien) **36**:337-38, 340; **116**:207-09, 222
The Love of a Good Man (Barker) **37**:34-7, 41
The Love of a Good Man. All Bleeding (Barker) **37**:37
Love of Electricity (Aksyonov) **101**:12, 22
A Love of Innocence (Jenkins) **52**:222-23, 225-27
The Love of Jenny Ney (Ehrenburg) **62**:174
The Love of Marcel Faber-Fabriczy for Miss Laura Warronigg (Krleža) **8**:330
"Love of My Life" (Gilchrist) **143**:300
"Love of Solitude" (Yevtushenko) **26**:467
"Love of the City" (Johnston) **51**:243-44, 247
"Love of the Scorching Wind" (Nagy) **7**:251
Love of the Scorching Wind (Nagy) **7**:251
A Love, on a Season (Stolz)
See *Two by Two*
"Love on My Mind" (Young) **17**:571
Love on Pyramid Hill (Mahfouz)
See *Al-Hubb fawq hadbat al-haram*
"Love on the Rocks" (Diamond) **30**:113
"Love on the Rocks" (Louie) **70**:79-80
Love on the Run (Truffaut) **20**:406; **101**:388, 396, 398, 400, 411-13
"Love on Toast" (Willingham) **51**:403
Love One Another (Dreyer) **16**:259-61
Love or Nothing (Dunn) **6**:148; **40**:167
"Love Out in the Street" (Simon) **26**:409
Love out of Season (Leffland) **19**:278-79
The Love Parlour (Rooke) **25**:391-92
"Love Passes" (Christie) **110**:126
"Love: Petulance" (Williams) **56**:429
"Love Philtre" (Prichard) **46**:337
"Love Poem" (Appleman) **51**:15
"Love Poem" (Ezekiel) **61**:101
"A Love Poem" (Knight) **40**:279, 283
"A Love Poem" (Kumin) **28**:224
"Love Poem" (Purdy) **14**:431
"Love Poem" (Raine) **7**:352; **45**:338
"Love Poem" (Rich) **73**:331
"Love Poem" (Steele) **45**:365
"Love Poem For Real" (Giovanni) **117**:186
"Love Poem on a Theme by Whitman" (Ginsberg) **6**:198; **109**:354, 358
"Love Poems" (Roethke) **8**:455; **101**:304
Love Poems (Amichai) **22**:33; **57**:36; **116**:96
Love Poems (Barker) **48**:14
Love Poems (Sanchez) **116**:272-73, 278, 289, 298, 302, 309, 323
Love Poems (Sexton) **2**:391; **4**:482-84, **6**:492, 494; **15**:471-72, 474; **53**:319, 321; **123**:406, 408-10, 427, 439-42, 450
Love Poems (Wild) **14**:580
Love Poems (Yevtushenko) **13**:620
Love Poems and Elegies (Smith) **64**:393, 399
"The Love Poems of Marichiko" (Rexroth) **112**:370, 383, 393, 398
The Love Poems of Marichiko (Rexroth) **49**:276, 286-88; **112**:387
The Love Poems of May Swenson (Swenson) **106**:336-37, 343-44, 347-48
The Love Poems of Myrrhine and Konallis (Aldington) **49**:2-3, 10
"Love Reign O'er Me" (Townshend) **17**:532
Love Respelt (Graves) **45**:166
Love, Roger (Webb) **7**:515
The Love Run (Parini) **54**:359
Love Scene (Coover) **15**:145; **32**:120
"Love Sickness" (Damas)
See "Limbé"
"Love So Fine" (Robinson) **21**:348
"Love Song" (Achebe) **11**:4; **26**:22
"Love Song" (Amichai) **116**:93
"Love Song" (Dabydeen) **34**:149
"A Love Song" (Dubus) **97**:235
"Love Song" (Eliot)
See "The Love Song of J. Alfred Prufrock"
"Love Song in Absence" (Wright) **53**:432
Love Song of a Puritan (Smith) **64**:388
"The Love Song of J. Alfred Prufrock" (Eliot) **1**:89, 91; **2**:127; **3**:136, 138-41; **6**:163, 167; **9**:183, 187; **10**:169-70; **13**:196-99, 201; **15**:210-211, 213; **24**:176; **34**:390, 397-98, 402, 525-26; **41**:146, 149-5; **55**:351-52, 371, 374; **57**:168, 175, 179, 181, 190, 207-08, 210; **113**:182-86, 188-97, 199-200, 202-11, 214-18, 220-23, 226
"Love Song to Idi Amin" (Knight) **40**:282
Love Songs (Loy) **28**:247, 251-52
Love Songs (Sanders) **41**:377
"Love Songs in Age" (Larkin) **3**:276; **33**:258
Love Songs to Joannes (Loy) **28**:247
"Love Sonnet" (Ezekiel) **61**:92, 100
"Love Story" (Abse) **29**:14
"A Love Story" (Bates) **46**:51
"A Love Story" (Bowen) **22**:62; **118**:75, 109
"A Love Story" (Graves) **2**:175; **45**:162, 173
Love Story (Segal) **3**:446-47; **10**:466-67
Love Story Black (Demby) **53**:114
"Love Street" (Morrison) **17**:288, 295
"Love Suffered" (Aleixandre) **36**:29
The Love Suicide at Schofield Barracks (Linney) **51**:259, 265
"Love Suicides" (Kawabata) **107**:113
"Love That I Bear" (H. D.) **73**:118
"Love the Butcher Bird Lurks Everywhere" (Stafford) **29**:381
"Love the Wild Swan" (Jeffers) **54**:249; **11**:306
"Love Thoughts" (Giovanni) **117**:177
"Love to Patsy" (Tuohy) **37**:431
"Love Too Long" (Hannah) **90**:141, 144-45
The Love Touch (Hoffman) **141**:264
Love! Valour! Compassion! (McNally) **91**:164-65
Love World (Arguedas)
See *Amor mundo y todos los cuentos*
"Love Wrapped Me in Darkness" (Rosenthal) **28**:394
Love You (Randall) **135**:377, 389, 392, 394, 396
"Love You by Heart" (Simon) **26**:413
Love You till Tuesday (Bowie)
See *David Bowie*
"Love, Your Only Mother" (Kaplan) **50**:55-7
"Love-Child" (O'Brien) **5**:311
The Loved and Envied (Bagnold) **25**:74-5
The Loved and the Lost (Callaghan) **14**:101-02; **41**:90, 92, 95; **65**:248-50
The Loved One (Isherwood) **44**:397

The Loved One: An Anglo-American Tragedy (Waugh) **1**:358-59; **3**:509; **19**:461; **27**:470, 477; **107**:360, 368-69, 374-76, 380, 382, 384, 400-02, 404-05
"Loved to Death" (Cooper) **56**:70
Love-Hate Relations: English and American Sensibilities (Spender) **5**:401-02; **91**:278, 280
"Loveland" (Sondheim) **30**:391
Loveland (Swarthout) **35**:401
The Loveliest Afternoon of the Year (Guare) **29**:204; **67**:79
Love-Life (Williams) **42**:443-45
"Lovelight" (Blunden) **56**:48
"The Loveliness of the Long Distance Runner" (Maitland) **49**:235
"Lovely" (Amis) **40**:40
"Lovely" (Sondheim) **30**:378
The Lovely Ambition (Chase) **2**:101
"The Lovely April" (Grau) **4**:210; **9**:240
"A Lovely Bit of Wood" (Gilliatt) **13**:237
The Lovely Ladies (Freeling) **38**:184
"The Lovely Leave" (Parker) **68**:328, 335, 339-40
"The Lovely Linda" (McCartney) **35**:278
"A Lovely Love" (Brooks) **49**:27
A Lovely Monster: The Adventures of Claude Rains and Dr. Tellenbeck (DeMarinis) **54**:96-8
A Lovely Morning (Yourcenar) **87**:405
A Lovely Summer for Crève Coeur (Williams) **19**:471
The Lovely Treachery of Words (Kroetsch) **132**:243, 286, 297
"Loveman's Comeback" (Campbell) **42**:88
"The Lover" (Aldington) **49**:5-6
"The Lover" (Creeley) **78**:134
"Lover" (Hoffman) **141**:270, 273, 280, 285, 309
"The Lover" (Walker) **103**:407-10, 412
"The Lover" (Williams) **148**:357
"The Lover" (Yehoshua)
See "Facing the Forests"
The Lover (Duras)
See *L'amant*
The Lover (Pinter) **1**:267; **3**:385-86; **6**:408; **15**:423-24; **27**:385-86, 394; **58**:373, 384; **73**:257
"Lover in a Mad World" (Salinas) **90**:332
"The Lover of Horses" (Gallagher) **63**:121, 124
The Lover of Horses (Gallagher) **63**:120-22, 124
"Loverboys" (Castillo) **151**:45
Loverboys (Castillo) **151**:45-48, 103
Loveroot (Jong) **6**:270; **8**:314-15; **18**:277; **83**:290, 299, 301
"The Lovers" (Berryman) **10**:45
"Lovers" (Cohen) **38**:131
"The Lovers" (Graham) **118**:249
"The Lovers" (Head) **67**:111
"Lovers" (MacBeth) **5**:265
"Lovers" (Oates) **9**:403
"The Lovers" (Souster) **14**:502
The Lovers (Farmer) **19**:165, 167
Lovers (Friel) **42**:166-67, 169; **59**:148; **115**:241
"Lovers Again" (MacBeth) **5**:265
"Lovers' Alley" (Mahfouz)
See "'Ushshaq al-hara"
A Lover's Almanac (Howard) **151**:281-85, 287, 289-90, 292
Lovers and Cohorts: Twenty-Seven Stories (Gold) **42**:197; **152**:120
Lovers and Tyrants (Gray) **22**:200; **153**:134, 138, 140, 143-45, 149-50
A Lover's Discourse: Fragments (Barthes)
See *Fragments d'un discours amoureux*
"The Lovers Go Fly a Kite" (Snodgrass) **68**:397
"Lovers in Middle Age" (Hall) **37**:142
"The Lovers Leave by Separate Planes" (Kumin) **28**:224
"Lovers of the Lake" (O'Faolain) **7**:274; **14**:405; **32**:341, 344; **70**:319
"Lovers of the Poor" (Brooks) **5**:75; **125**:90, 94
"Lovers of Their Time" (Trevor) **14**:537; **25**:443; **71**:349; **116**:377, 385
Lovers of Their Time, and Other Stories (Trevor) **14**:535-37; **25**:444-45; **71**:325, 346; **116**:374, 376
The Lovers of Viorne (Duras)
See *L'amante anglaise*
"Lovers on Aran" (Heaney) **25**:240; **74**:182
"Lovers' Quarter" (Mahfouz)
See "'Ushshaq al-hara"
"The Lover's Quarter" (Mahfūz) **52**:292
"Lover's Rock" (Clash) **30**:46-7
"A Lover's Woods" (Watkins) **43**:441
"Love's Heretical Ethics" (Kristeva)
See "Héréthique de l'amour"
"Love's in Need of Love Today" (Wonder) **12**:659-60, 664
Love's Labor: An Eclogue (O'Hara) **78**:364
Loves Lies Bleeding (Crispin) **22**:108-09
Love's Lovely Counterfeit (Cain) **3**:97; **28**:45, 47, 53
Love's Mansion (West) **96**:391-94, 396, 400
The Loves of Cass McGuire (Friel) **5**:128; **42**:164-65; **115**:216, 241-42, 244
The Loves of Harry Dancer (Sanders) **41**:382
The Loves of Ondine (Warhol) **20**:422
"Loves of the Puppets" (Wilbur) **53**:398, 405
Love's Old Sweet Song (Saroyan) **34**:458; **56**:376
Love's Pilgrimage (Sinclair) **63**:348-49
"Love's Progress" (Roethke) **3**:433; **8**:458; **101**:328
"Love's Young Dream" (O'Faolain) **70**:312, 319
Lovesick (Stern) **100**:327
"(Lovesong.)" (Celan)
See "(Liebeslied.)"
"Lovesong" (Hughes) **37**:177; **119**:259
"Lovestory" (Poniatowska) **140**:323-24, 332-33
Lovey Childs: A Philadelphian's Story (O'Hara) **2**:324; **42**:323-24
Lovhers (Brossard)
See *Amantes*
Loving (Green) **2**:178; **13**:253, 255; **97**:243, 245, 247-49, 251-57, 263, 269-70, 280-82, 288-91, 293
Loving a Woman in Two Worlds (Bly) **128**:16, 29, 32
"Loving Blackness as Political Resistance" (Hooks) **94**:153
A Loving Eye (Elliott) **47**:109-10
The Loving Game (Scannell) **49**:330
Loving Hands at Home (Johnson) **5**:198; **48**:201
Loving in the War Years: Lo que nunca paso por sus labios (Moraga) **126**:272-78, 280, 282, 285, 288, 291-94, 298, 302-06, 309
"Loving, Losing, Loving a Man" (Oates) **6**:370
"Loving Mad Tom" (Ashbery) **13**:30
Loving Memory (Harrison) **129**:183, 186, 210
Loving Roger (Parks) **147**:196-97, 200, 204
"The Loving Shepherdess" (Jeffers) **11**:305; **54**:237, 245, 249
The Loving Spirit (du Maurier) **59**:284-87
"Loving the Crone" (Piercy) **62**:378
"Loving the Killer" (Sexton) **123**:409
Low (Bowie) **17**:65-8
"Low Budget" (Davies) **21**:104
Low Budget (Davies) **21**:104-06
Low Company (Fuchs) **8**:220-21; **22**:158
Low Flying Aircraft (McNally) **82**:262-64, 267, 269-70
"Low Sunday" (Klappert) **57**:269
"Low Tide" (Szirtes) **46**:393
Low Tide (Eberstadt) **39**:48-51
"Low to High" (Hughes) **35**:222
"Low Water" (Hughes) **119**:295
The Lower Depths (Kurosawa) **16**:396, 401; **119**:338, 350, 378, 380
"Lower Field—Enniscorthy" (Olson) **29**:329
Lower Than The Angels (Perry) **126**:327
"The Lowering" (Swenson) **106**:320-21
The Lowest Trees Have Tops (Gellhorn) **60**:193
"Low-Flying Aircraft" (Ballard) **137**:20, 39
Low-Flying Aircraft, and Other Stories (Ballard) **14**:39, 41; **36**:37-38
"Lowland" (Gascoyne) **45**:153
"Low-Lands" (Pynchon) **33**:333-34, 338-40; **62**:432
"The Lowliest Bush a Purple Sage Would Be" (Keillor) **40**:274
"Loyal" (Matthews) **40**:323, 325
"LSD" (Ginsberg) **109**:325
The LSD Leacock (Rosenblatt) **15**:446-47
"The L-Shaped Room" (Banks) **23**:40-1
Lu Ann Hampton Laverty Oberlander (Jones) **10**:297
"Luau" (Wilson) **12**:647
"Luc and His Father" (Gallant) **38**:195
Luca (Moravia)
See *La disubbidienza*
Luca (Moravia) **27**:354
La lucarne ovale (Reverdy) **53**:285, 288
"Lucas, His Partisan Arguments" (Cortázar)
See "Lucas, sus discusiones partidarias"
"Lucas, sus discusiones partidarias" (Cortázar) **34**:334
La luce e il lutto (Bufalino) **74**:40
"Lucent and Inescapable Rhythms" (Perloff) **137**:302
"Luces" (Cardenal) **31**:77
"The Luceys" (O'Connor) **14**:399
Lucha (Urdang) **47**:401
Luci del varieta (Fellini) **16**:274, 298; **85**:55, 59, 67, 69, 71, 75, 78, 81
Lucid Stars (Barrett) **150**:2, 8, 13
"Lucifer" (Seger) **35**:378
Lucifer (Powys) **7**:347; **125**:278
Lucifer and the Lord (Sartre)
See *Le diable et le bon Dieu*
"Lucifer Ashore" (Davison) **28**:100
Lucifer Falling (White) **49**:400-01
"Lucifer in the Train" (Rich) **7**:368
"Lucifer Praying" (Klappert) **57**:259-60
Lucifer Wilkins (Garfield) **12**:235
"Lucinda" (Swan) **69**:359-61
"Luck" (Prichard) **46**:345
Luck and Pluck (Swarthout) **35**:403
The Luck of Ginger Coffey (Moore) **1**:225; **5**:295, 297; **19**:331; **32**:307, 309; **90**:238-9, 242-44, 251-2, 263, 277, 278, 280
"The Luck of Jad Peters" (Thurber) **125**:401
"The Luck of the Irish" (Lennon) **35**:264-65
"Luckenbach, Texas" (Jennings) **21**:204
"Luckily the Account Representative Knew CPR" (Wallace) **114**:347, 349
"Lucky" (Nyro) **17**:315
"Lucky Boy" (Pearce) **21**:289
"The Lucky Coin" (Clarke) **9**:168
Lucky Jim (Amis) **1**:5-6; **2**:4-10; **3**:9-10; **5**:20-3; **8**:11-12; **13**:12; **40**:41, 47-8; **44**:138, 140, 142; **129**:3, 5-6, 9, 11-12, 15-19, 22-25
"Lucky Jim Revisited" (Lodge) **141**:374
Lucky Life (Stern) **40**:405-08, 410-12; **100**:329
"The Lucky Pair" (Lavin) **99**:321
Lucky Poet (MacDiarmid) **4**:312-13; **19**:288
Lucky Starr and the Big Sun of Mercury (Asimov) **26**:36, 41, 64
Lucky Starr and the Moons of Jupiter (Asimov) **26**:41, 64
Lucky Starr and the Oceans of Venus (Asimov) **26**:35-6, 41, 64
Lucky Starr and the Pirates of the Asteroids (Asimov) **26**:41, 64
Lucky Starr and the Rings of Saturn (Asimov) **26**:36, 41, 64
"Lucky You" (Gerstler) **70**:156, 159
"Lucretius versus the Lake Poets" (Frost) **15**:243
"Luctus in Morte Infantis" (Barker) **48**:9, 12
Lucy (Kincaid) **68**:215-21; **137**:140, 146-52, 156, 161-62, 165-66, 174-75, 179, 188-89, 195, 197-203
"lucy and her girls" (Clifton) **66**:69
Lucy Crown (Shaw) **7**:411

"Lucy in the Sky with Diamonds" (Lennon and McCartney) **12**:357, 373; **35**:368
"Lucy's Daffodil" (Fuller) **62**:207
"Lud and Marie Meet Dracula's Daughter" (Tomlin) **17**:522-23
Lud Heat (Sinclair) **76**:227
Ludwig (Visconti) **16**:570, 575
"Ludwig Wittgenstein: Zu einem Kapital der jüngsten Philosophiegeschichte" (Bachmann) **69**:57
Ludzie stamtad (Dabrowska) **15**:166-68
"Lugar Ilamado Kindberg" (Cortázar) **33**:124, **34**:333
El lugar sin límites (Donoso) **4**:126-29; **8**:178-79; **11**:145-46; **32**:153-54, 159, 161; **99**:216, 218, 221, 223, 236, 240
Lugging Vegetables to Nantucket (Klappert) **57**:256-60, 263, 265-66
"Luigi's House" (Gellhorn) **60**:180-81
"Luis" (Selzer) **74**:287
Luisa en el páis de la realidad (Alegria) **75**:43-6, 48, 50-1
Luisa in Realityland (Alegria)
See *Luisa en el páis de la realidad*
Lukács and Heidegger: Towards a New Philosophy (Goldmann) **24**:251, 254
"Lukas, Sanftmütiger Knecht" (Lenz) **27**:245
"The Lull" (Green) **97**:276-77
"Lull" (Muldoon) **72**:266
"The Lull" (Peacock) **60**:294
"Lullabies" (Greenberg) **7**:134
Lullabies Twisters Gibbers Drags (Williams) **13**:600
"Lullaby" (Auden) **9**:56
"Lullaby" (Boland) **40**:100
"Lullaby" (Fearing) **51**:107
"Lullaby" (Glück) **81**:172-73
"Lullaby" (Poniatowska)
See "Canción de cuña"
"The Lullaby" (Riding) **7**:374
"Lullaby" (Sexton) **10**:468
"Lullaby" (Silko) **23**:409; **74**:344; **114**:314, 340
"Lullaby" (Sitwell) **67**:318-19, 325, 333, 336
"Lullaby" (Waddington) **28**:438
"Lullaby for Rachel" (Simmons) **43**:411
Lullaby for Sinners: Poems, 1970-1979 (Braverman) **67**:49
"Lullaby through the Side of the Mouth" (Wagoner) **3**:508
"Lullabye" (Broumas) **73**:9, 11
"Lulu" (Hesse) **25**:259
"Lumb Chimneys" (Hughes) **119**:288
"Lumber" (Barthelme) **36**:52; **117**:2
"The Lumens" (Olds) **85**:306
Lumeton aika (Haavikko) **34**:170
"La lumière, changée" (Bonnefoy) **15**:74
"Luminism" (Strand) **71**:288-89
"The Luminosity of Life" (Smith) **22**:386
"Lump" (Phillips) **28**:365
Lumpy Gravy (Zappa) **17**:588, 591
"Lumumba Lives" (Matthiessen) **64**:322, 325
Luna (Bertolucci) **16**:100
"Luna bark" (Mahfouz) **153**:359
Luna de enfrente (Borges) **19**:44-5; **44**:367
"Luna de miel" (Arreola) **147**:27
"Luna e G N A C" (Calvino) **33**:100; **73**:33
Luna silvestre (Paz) **65**:176, 196; **119**:412
"La luna sul muro" (Ortese) **89**:198
Lunar Attractions (Blaise) **29**:72
"Lunar Baedecker" (Loy) **28**:246, 248-49
"Lunar Changes" (Wright) **28**:470
"The Lunar Cycle" (Piercy) **27**:379
Lunar Landscapes (Hawkes) **4**:212
Lunatic Villas (Engel) **36**:164-65
Lunatics and Lovers (Kingsley) **44**:236, 238
"The Lunatic's Tale" (Allen) **52**:42
"The Lunch" (Cortázar)
See "El almuerzo"
"Lunch" (Koch) **5**:219; **44**:243, 248
"Lunch and Afterwards" (Abse) **29**:20
Lunch and Counter Lunch (Murray) **40**:336-38
"Lunch Hour" (O'Hara) **13**:431
Lunch Hour (Kerr) **22**:258-59
Lunch Hour (Mortimer) **28**:283-84
"Lunch in Winter" (Trevor) **71**:333
Lunch Poems (O'Hara) **2**:323; **13**:428; **78**:333
"Lunch with Pancho Villa" (Muldoon) **32**:318-19, 321; **72**:265-66, 268
"The Luncheon" (Archer) **28**:14
"Lunches of 1943" (Aksyonov) **101**:11, 15, 18, 20
Lunes en papier (Malraux) **4**:332; **15**:354-55
"Les lunettes" (Carrier) **78**:68
Lupercal (Hughes) **2**:197-98, 201-02; **4**:236; **9**:280-83; **14**:270, 273; **37**:171, 175, 180; **119**:265, 288, 291
"Lupercalia" (Hall) **51**:172
"The Lure of the Open Window" (Jong) **6**:268
"Lush Triumphant" (McGrath) **55**:75
Das Lusitania Songspiel (Durang) **27**:88
"Luss Village" (Smith) **64**:397
"Lust" (Urquhart) **90**:386
Lust for Life (Stone) **7**:468-71
"Lust in Action" (Glassco) **9**:237
"Lustig" (Jandl) **34**:195
"Lustra" (Okigbo) **25**:349, 355; **84**:299-300, 309, 313, 326
"Lustra" (Pound) **4**:408
Lustra (Pound) **1**:276; **10**:400; **13**:460; **48**:283-84
O lustre (Lispector) **43**:261, 265
Lusts (Blaise) **29**:76-7
O lutador (Andrade) **18**:3
"Luther" (Huddle) **49**:182
Luther (Osborne) **2**:328; **5**:331, 333; **11**:421-22; **45**:313-16
Lutheran Letters (Pasolini) **37**:351; **106**:259
Luv (Schisgal) **6**:489
"Luvina" (Rulfo) **80**:200, 213, 217
"Luxembourgh 1939" (Senghor) **130**:282
"Luxury" (Amichai) **116**:95
"Luzina Takes a Holiday" (Roy) **14**:467
Lvíce (Škvorecký) **15**:510; **69**:339, 341; **152**:315, 335-36
"Lychees for Tone" (Gardam) **43**:169
Den lyckliges väg (Lagerkvist) **54**:274
Lydia (Fast) **131**:100
Lydie Breeze (Guare) **29**:205-08; **67**:78-81
"Lyell's Hypothesis Again" (Rexroth) **49**:280, 285, 289; **112**:376, 383-84, 398, 400
"Lying" (Wilbur) **53**:405, 412; **110**:357, 360, 372
"The Lying Art" (Porter) **13**:452-53; **33**:320
"Lying Awake in a Desert" (Wagoner) **15**:560
The Lying Days (Gordimer) **10**:239; **18**:186; **33**:177-79; **70**:162-65, 170; **123**:137-39, 141
"The Lying Dear" (Graham) **29**:196
"Lying Doggo" (Mason) **82**:234, 236; **154**:254, 294, 320
Lying Figures (Warner) **14**:552
"Lying In" (Broumas) **73**:16
"Lying in a Hammock at William Duffy's Farm in Pine Island, Minnesota" (Wright) **3**:540, 543; **10**:546; **28**:468
"Lying in Politics: Reflections on the Pentagon Papers" (Arendt) **98**:11
Lying in State (Rathbone) **41**:345
Lying Low (Johnson) **13**:305-06; **48**:208
"Lying Together..." (Loewinsohn) **52**:285
Lying Together (Thomas) **132**:377-78
"Lymphater's Formula" (Lem) **149**:144
"Lynch" (Guillén) **48**:159
The Lynchers (Wideman) **5**:489-90; **36**:452-54; **122**:286, 289-90, 302, 311, 314, 352-53, 355, 363-64
"The Lynching" (Scannell) **49**:325, 331
"The Lynchings of Jesus" (Rukeyser) **27**:405
"Lyndon" (Wallace) **114**:348
"Lynn" (Dybek) **114**:62
"Lynz" (Orlovitz) **22**:337
Lyonesse (Vance) **35**:427-28
Lyonushka (Leonov) **92**:260, 270, 277
The Lyre of Orpheus (Davies) **75**:196-202, 206-08, 210-14, 216-17; **91**:203-4
"Lyric" (Raine) **7**:352
"The Lyric Physiognomy and Lyric Daring of Andreas Kalvos" (Elytis) **100**:177
"Lyric Sarcastic" (Gustafson) **36**:214
Lyrical and Critical Essays (Camus) **9**:146; **14**:108
Lyrical Ballads (Sandburg) **10**:448
The Lyrics of Noël Coward (Coward) **29**:134
Lyrics Unromantic (Gustafson) **36**:216
Lysistrata (Harrison) **129**:190
Lysistrata and NATO (Hochhuth) **18**:255
"M" (Merrill) **8**:383
M (Lang) **20**:202, 204, 213; **103**:90-5, 115
M. Butterfly (Cronenberg) **143**:57, 118, 125-32, 138
M. Butterfly (Hwang) **55**:150-55
"M. François Mauriac et la liberté" (Sartre) **24**:417
M. le modéré (Adamov) **25**:18, 21
"M. M. and the Rivers" (Cabral de Melo Neto)
See "Murilo Mendes e os rios"
"M., Singing" (Bogan) **93**:78
M/T (Oe) **86**:241
M: Writings, '67-'72 (Cage) **41**:81-3, 86
"Ma" (Muldoon) **32**:318
"Ma grand-mère toute-puissante" (Roy) **10**:440
"Ma lamadti bamilhamot" (Amichai) **116**:121
"Ma Lord" (Hughes) **108**:298
Ma mère (Bataille) **29**:44-5
Ma nuit chez Maud (Rohmer) **16**:529-31, 533, 536, 540
"Ma Provence" (Koch) **44**:243, 251
"Ma Rainey" (Brown) **59**:266, 270
Ma Rainey's Black Bottom (Wilson) **39**:276-82; **50**:267-68, 270-71; **63**:447-54, 457; **118**:372-73, 375-77, 379, 381-82, 388, 398, 403-05, 412
"Má vlast" (Klima) **56**:172-73
Mabel: A Story and Other Prose (Creeley) **78**:128
"Mabinog's Liturgy" (Jones) **42**:241
"Mabuti" (Highsmith) **102**:201
"Mac in Love" (Dixon) **52**:94, 96-7
A maçã no escuro (Lispector) **43**:261-66, 269-71
"Macabre" (Colter) **58**:146
"Macao" (Auden) **14**:26
"Macario" (Rulfo) **80**:200, 213, 216
Macario (Traven) **8**:520
Macaroon (Cunningham) **12**:164
"Macaw" (Bogan) **46**:77
"Macbech" (Updike) **43**:431
Macbeth (Polanski) **16**:469, 472
Macbeth (Welles) **20**:433-35, 438-39, 441-43, 447-49, 451, 453-54; **80**:382, 391, 397, 401, 410
Macbett (Ionesco) **6**:252-53; **11**:292; **86**:341
"Macchu Picchu" (Lane) **25**:284, 286
Macchu Picchu (Neruda)
See *Alturas de Macchu Picchu*
The MacGuffin (Elkin) **91**:213-14, 223
"La Macha" (Castillo) **151**:115
"Macherey and Marxist Literary Theory" (Eagleton) **63**:107
"The Machine" (Campbell) **32**:76, 78, 80
"La machine à detecter tout ce qui est américain" (Carrier) **78**:63
La machine àecrire (Cocteau) **43**:105-06, 108
Machine Dreams (Phillips) **33**:305-08; **139**:198-200, 203-4, 206-7, 214-15, 217-18, 220-22
La machine infernale (Cocteau) **8**:144, 147, 149; **15**:134; **16**:220; **43**:99-102, 105-06, 110-11
"The Machine Stops" (Forster) **77**:230
The Machine Stops (Forster) **10**:183; **22**:129-30
"The Machine-Gun Corps in Action" (O'Connor) **23**:329
The Machine-Gunners (Westall) **17**:555-58
The Machineries of Joy (Bradbury) **42**:33
"Machinery" (Kauffman) **65**:348
Machines and Men (Roberts) **14**:463
Macho Comacho's Beat (Sánchez) **23**:383-86

Die Macht der Gewohnheit (Bernhard) **32**:20, 23-4; **61**:12, 20, 26-8
"Macht und Überleben" (Canetti) **75**:129, 132
"Machu Picchu" (Birney) **6**:75
"Mackenzie River North" (Musgrave) **13**:400
"Mackerel" (Hoffman) **6**:244
The Mackerel Plaza (De Vries) **7**:76; **10**:136-38; **28**:106-07; **46**:135
"Mackinnon's Boat" (Tomlinson) **4**:548
"Mackintosh" (Maugham) **67**:206
The Mackintosh Man (Huston) **20**:173
Macquarie (Buzo) **61**:53-9, 64, 68
"Macquarie as Father" (Shapcott) **38**:398
Mad Dog Blues (Shepard) **4**:490-91; **17**:438, 443-44, 448; **41**:409, 412
Mad Dog Blues and Other Plays (Smith) **12**:534
"Mad Dogs and Englishmen" (Coward) **51**:76
Mad Ducks and Bears: Football Revisited (Plimpton) **36**:354-56
"The Mad Farmer in the City" (Berry) **27**:33
"The Mad Farmer Manifesto: The First Amendment" (Berry) **6**:61
"A Mad Fight Song for William S. Carpenter" (Wright) **5**:520; **28**:465
"Mad Housewife" (Nemerov) **36**:309
Mad in Pursuit (Leduc)
See *La folie en tête*
"The Mad Kitchen and Dong, the Cave Adolescent" (Jiles) **58**:273, 275
"The Mad Lomasneys" (O'Connor) **14**:399; **23**:332
Mad Love (Harjo)
See *In Mad Love and War*
The Mad Man (Delany) **141**:149
"Mad Marga" (O'Faolain) **47**:328
"A Mad Negro Soldier Confined at Munich" (Lowell) **124**:274-75
"A Mad One" (Gordimer) **18**:189
"The Mad One" (Mahfūz)
See "al- Majnūna"
The Mad Pomegranate and the Praying Mantis: An Andalusian Adventure (Luke) **38**:318
"The Mad Pomegranate Tree" (Elytis) **49**:106, 114
Mad Puppetstown (Keane) **31**:231-32
Mad Shadows (Blais)
See *La belle bête*
"The Mad Tea-Party" (Queen) **11**:462
The Mad Trapper (Wiebe) **138**:326, 337-39, 342, 372
"Mad Yak" (Corso) **11**:123
Madadayo (Kurosawa) **119**:338, 340, 402-03
"Madam" (Hughes) **108**:326
"Madam and Her Madam" (Hughes) **108**:326
"Madam and the Number Writer" (Hughes) **108**:297
Madam, Will You Talk? (Stewart) **7**:467; **35**:388-89, 391
Madame Bovary (Renoir) **20**:286, 293-94, 310
Madame de Pompadour (Mitford) **44**:485, 488-89
Madame de Sade (Mishima) **2**:286; **27**:337-38
"Madame Dodin" (Duras) **40**:184-85
Madame Edwarda (Bataille) **29**:45
Madame Maigret's Friend (Simenon) **18**:484-85
"Madame Moth" (Reaney) **13**:473
"Madame Rosette" (Dahl) **79**:174
Madame Sousatzka (Rubens) **31**:350-51
"Madame Zelena" (Carlson) **54**:38
"Madame Zilensky" (McCullers) **12**:433
"Madame Zilensky and the King of Finland" (McCullers) **100**:246
"Madam's Music" (Hall) **51**:170
Die Mädchen aus Viterbo (Eich) **15**:203
Madder Music (De Vries) **10**:137-38; **28**:107, 110, 112
Made in America (Maas) **29**:306-07
Made in Canada (Souster) **5**:395
"Made in Goatswood" (Campbell) **42**:85
Made in U.S.A. (Godard) **20**:137, 149
"Made to Last" (Durban) **39**:46
"Mademoiselle Claude" (Miller) **84**:262
Mademoiselle Colombe (Anouilh)
See *Colombe*
Mademoiselle Jaïre (Ghelderode) **11**:226
"Mademoiselle O" (Nabokov) **8**:414
"Mademoiselle Veronique" (Brodsky) **36**:81
The Maderati (Greenberg) **57**:227-30
Madigan (Polonsky) **92**:387-88, 405, 415
"Madimba: Gwendolyn Brooks" (Harper) **7**:139
"Madison at 69th, a Fable" (Gilchrist) **143**:300-01
"The Madison Experience" (Jordan) **114**:146
"The Madman" (Achebe) **26**:23; **75**:14
"The Madman" (Urdang) **47**:397
"The Madman and the Book" (Wiesel) **5**:490
The Madman and the Medusa (Tchicaya) **101**:356
"Madman of the Uncharmed Debris of the South Side" (Major) **19**:293
Madmen and Specialists (Soyinka) **3**:463; **5**:397; **14**:509; **36**:411, 417; **44**:286-88
"Madness" (Arghezi)
See "Streche"
"Madness" (Dickey) **2**:117; **109**:272
"Madness" (Jennings) **131**:240
"Madness" (Schaeffer) **6**:489
Madness (Blanchot)
See *La Folie du jour*
Madness and Civilization: A History of Insanity in the Age of Reason (Foucault)
See *Folie et déraison: Histoire de la folie à l'âge classique*
The Madness of George III (Bennett) **77**:103
"The Madness of Saul" (Sitwell) **67**:324
The Madness of the Day (Blanchot)
See *La Folie du jour*
"Madoc" (Mathias) **45**:236
"Madoc: A Mystery" (Muldoon) **72**:279-82
Madoc: A Mystery (Muldoon) **72**:279, 281-83
"The Madonna" (Barker) **52**:52, 55
"Madonna" (Kinsella) **138**:155
Madonna and Other Poems (Kinsella) **138**:153, 167
La madonna dei filosofi (Gadda) **11**:210
Madonna Red (Carroll) **38**:104, 107
"Madonnas Touched Up with a Goatee" (Simic) **49**:336; **68**:372
"The Madras Rumble" (Faust) **8**:215
"La madre" (Ginzburg) **54**:206
Una madre (Fo) **109**:109
"Madrid, 1974" (Van Duyn) **63**:442
"Madrid, May, 1977" (Van Duyn) **63**:442
"Madrigal" (Guillén) **48**:157; **79**:232, 238-40
Madrigal (Gardner) **30**:152
A Madrigal (H. D.)
See *Bid Me to Live (A Madrigal)*
"Madrigal trirrimo" (Guillén) **79**:238
"Madrigals" (Shapcott) **38**:400
Madrugada (Buero Vallejo) **15**:99, 101
"The Madwoman" (Nakos) **29**:321
The Madwoman in the Attic: The Woman Writer and the Nineteenth-Century Literary Imagination (Gubar) **145**:206-07, 209-22, 225-26, 232-33, 235-36, 239, 249-51, 254, 257-58, 266-72, 274-77, 279-83, 285, 287
The Madwoman's Underclothes (Greer) **131**:188-190
"Maelzel's Chess Player" (Hein) **154**:
"Maelzel's Chess Player Goes to Hollywood" (Hein) **154**:76, 146
"Maenad" (Plath) **11**:446, 448; **111**:159, 164-65
"Maestranzas de noche" (Neruda) **62**:322
"Maeterlinck in Ontario" (Cassity) **42**:99
Maeve's Diary (Binchy) **153**:67
Mafia Vendetta (Sciascia)
See *Il giorno della civetta*
"Magdalena" (Zappa) **17**:588
"Magdalene" (Kristofferson) **26**:270
Magdalene (Slaughter) **56**:408-09
The Magellan Nebula (Lem)
See *Oblok Magellana*
The Magellanic Clouds (Wakoski) **2**:459; **9**:555
"Maggid" (Piercy) **62**:379
Maggie Cassidy (Kerouac) **1**:167; **5**:215; **29**:270, 272; **61**:309
"Maggie Meriwether's Rich Experience" (Stafford) **68**:422, 449
Maggie Muggins (Waterhouse) **47**:421-22
"Maggie of the Green Bottles" (Bambara) **88**:16-17, 21, 23, 27, 47
Maggie-Now (Smith) **19**:424
"Maggie's Farm" (Dylan) **77**:176
"Maggie's Gift" (Paterson) **30**:283
A Maggot (Fowles) **87**:147, 149, 159, 161-62, 173-78, 181, 183
"Magi" (Brown) **48**:59
"The Magi" (Glück) **7**:118, 120
"Magi" (Plath) **5**:345; **51**:340; **111**:159
"Magias parciales del Quijote" (Borges) **13**:112; **83**:161
"Magic" (Kaplan) **50**:55, 57
"Magic" (Klein) **30**:236
"Magic" (Porter) **7**:320; **15**:432; **101**:209-210, 224
Magic (Elliott) **47**:114-15
Magic (Goldman) **48**:127-28
"Magic Affinities" (Moss) **7**:250
The Magic Animal (Wylie) **43**:472
Magic Animals: Selected Poems Old and New (MacEwen) **13**:358
The Magic Apple Tree (Feinstein) **36**:168
The Magic Apple Tree (Hill) **113**:326
"The Magic Apples" (O'Brien) **116**:187
"Magic at Ruth Lake" (Bass) **79**:17
"The Magic Barrel" (Malamud) **2**:266, 269; **3**:323; **8**:376; **18**:317; **27**:297, 306; **44**:412, 419-20; **78**:249, 264, 271; **85**:190-224
The Magic Barrel (Malamud) **1**:195-96, 200; **3**:320-24; **5**:269; **8**:376; **9**:346, 348; **11**:345-46; **18**:321; **27**:298, 301-02; **44**:411, 413, 415-16, 420; **78**:252, 281; **85**:191. 195, 200, 209
"The Magic Box" (Sillitoe) **57**:388
"The Magic Bus" (Townshend) **17**:527, 530, 536
The Magic Carpet, and Other Tales (Douglas) **73**:99
The Magic Carpets of Antonio Angelini (Ringwood) **48**:334
"Magic Castle" (Barthelme) **117**:5
The Magic Change: Metamorphosis (Silverstein and Silverstein) **17**:453-54
The Magic Christian (Southern) **7**:453
Magic City (Komunyakaa) **86**:191; **94**:218-220, 234, 237, 239, 240-41, 246, 248-49
"The Magic Curtain" (Kunitz) **148**:89-95, 105, 127
The Magic Finger (Dahl) **79**:177
"The Magic Flute" (Moore) **13**:396
The Magic Flute (Bergman)
See *Trollflöjten*
"Magic Fox" (Welch) **52**:428
"Magic, Inc." (Heinlein) **55**:302
The Magic Journey (Nichols) **38**:342, 344
The Magic Kingdom (Elkin) **91**:214, 220, 223-24
The Magic Lantern (Bergman)
See *Lanterna Magica*
The Magic Lantern of Marcel Proust (Moss) **50**:352
Magic Man, Magic Man (Wagman) **7**:500
"A Magic Mountain" (Milosz)
See "Dużo śpię"
"Magic Mountains" (Stafford) **4**:517
The Magic of Shirley Jackson (Jackson) **60**:211-13
The Magic of the Guts (Adler) **35**:13
Magic Papers (Feldman) **7**:101
"The Magic Poker" (Coover) **7**:58
"The Magic Strength of Need" (Cooper) **56**:70
"The Magic Striptease" (Garrett) **51**:149
The Magic Striptease (Garrett) **51**:149

"The Magic Study of Happiness" (Simic) **130**:326
The Magic Summer (Streatfeild) **21**:409-10
The Magic Toyshop (Carter) **5**:102; **41**:111-12, 114; **76**:323, 329
The Magic Will: Stories and Essays of a Decade (Gold) **42**:192-93; **152**:120, 138
"The Magical" (Eberhart) **56**:85
"Magical Lady" (Thurber) **11**:533
"Magical Mystery Pool" (McFadden) **48**:243
"The Magician" (Kotzwinkle) **35**:253
"Magician" (Rooke) **25**:391
"The Magician" (Tanizaki) **14**:527
The Magician (Abse) **29**:15, 17
The Magician (Bergman)
See *Ansiktet*
The Magician (Nabokov)
See *Volshebnik*
The Magician in Love (Rooke) **25**:393
The Magician of Lublin (Singer)
See *Kunstmakher fun Lublin*
The Magician's Feastletters (Wakoski) **40**:456-57
The Magician's Girl (Grumbach) **64**:201-05
The Magician's Nephew (Lewis) **27**:262-64; **124**:193, 221, 236, 241, 248
The Magicians of Caprona (Jones) **26**:230
"The Magician's Wife" (Gordon) **128**:118
The Magician's Wife (Cain) **28**:49, 52-3
Magie noire (Morand) **41**:300-01, 303-04, 306
Magie rouge (Ghelderode) **11**:226
"Magiel" (Herbert) **43**:186
"Der magische Tänzer" (Sachs) **98**:364, 367
Magister Ludi (Hesse)
See *Das Glasperlenspiel*
"Magna Mater" (Oates) **6**:373
"Magna Takes the Calls" (Dixon) **52**:100
"Magnanimity" (Kinsella) **138**:96, 148
The Magnanimous Cuckold (Crommelynck)
See *Le cocu magnifique*
"The Magnet" (Sarton) **49**:310
Magnet Fragments (Lezama Lima)
See *Fragmentos a su imán*
Magnetic Field (Loewinsohn) **52**:285-90
The Magnetic Fields (Breton and Soupault)
See *Les champs magnétiques*
The Magnetic Mountain (Day Lewis) **6**:128; **10**:132
"Magneto and Titanium Man" (McCartney) **35**:282-83
"Magnificat" (Guillevic) **33**:193
"Magnificat in Transit from the Toledo Airport" (Starbuck) **53**:354
Magnificence (Brenton) **31**:57, 60, 62, 64-7
The Magnificent Ambersons (Welles) **20**:435-36, 440, 444, 446-50, 452-54; **80**:368-69, 372-75, 377, 382, 386, 388-91, 393, 395-97, 409, 414-16
The Magnificent Century (Costain) **30**:96-7, 99
The Magnificent Cuckold (Crommelynck)
See *Le cocu magnifique*
The Magnificent Seven (Kurosawa)
See *The Seven Samurai*
The Magnificent Showboats of the Lower Vissel River, Lune XXIII South, Big Planet (Vance)
See *Showboat World*
The Magnificent Spinster (Sarton) **49**:321-23; **91**:240, 246-47, 249-50
"Magnolia Flower" (Hurston) **7**:172
"Magnum Opus" (Reid) **33**:350
Magnus (Brown) **48**:58-9, 61; **100**:78, 86
Magog (Sinclair) **2**:402; **14**:488
"Magpies" (King) **89**:97-8
"Magpies" (Wright) **53**:423
"Magpiety" (Milosz)
See "Śroczość"
"Magrette's Secret Agent" (Lee) **46**:234
"Magritte Dancing" (Stern) **100**:333, 343
"Mags" (Trevor) **116**:377
The Magus (Fowles) **1**:109; **2**:137-39; **3**:162-63; **4**:170-73; **6**:185, 187-89; **9**:210-17; **10**:184-87, 189; **15**:233-34; **33**:163, 166, 169, 171-75; **87**:136, 139-40, 147, 150-52, 154, 157-62, 176, 178-82
The Mahabharata: A Shortened Modern Prose Version of the Indian Epic (Narayan) **28**:301; **121**:353
Mahagony (Glissant) **68**:178-80, 182-84, 187
Mahanagar (Ray) **16**:480-84, 492; **76**:357
"The Maharajah" (White) **30**:451
The Maharajah, and Other Stories (White) **30**:451
Mahatma Gandhi and His Apostles (Mehta) **37**:292
"Mahatma Joe" (Bass) **143**:8-9
"Mahavaton Ki Ek Raat" (Ali) **69**:25
Mahler (Russell) **16**:548, 551
Mahler Grooves (Williams) **13**:600-01
"Mahoney the Bad Traveler" (Klappert) **57**:267
"Mahpiyato" (Cook-Lynn) **93**:124, 126, 130
"Mahr al-wazifa" (Mahfouz) **153**:350-51
Mai devi domandarmi (Ginzburg) **11**:228; **54**:196-97, 212
Mai Mai Peñi (Parra) **102**:356
The Maid (Audiberti)
See *La pucelle*
The Maid Silja (Sillanpaa)
See *Fallen Asleep While Young*
"The Maiden" (Stafford) **7**:457
Maiden Castle (Powys) **7**:348-50; **9**:441; **15**:433; **46**:320-21, 324; **125**:295, 299-301
"Maiden Name" (Larkin) **39**:339
"Maiden, Open" (Randall) **135**:392, 399
"Maiden Voyage" (Wolff) **64**:450
The Maids (Genet)
See *Les bonnes*
Maidstone: A Mystery (Mailer) **1**:193; **4**:323; **14**:351; **28**:256-57, 259; **74**:217-18
"Maighdean Mara" (Heaney) **7**:148; **74**:157
Maigret à New York (Simenon) **2**:399; **47**:381
Maigret Abroad (Simenon) **47**:370
Maigret Afraid (Simenon) **47**:382
Maigret and His Corpse (Simenon)
See *Maigret et son mort*
Maigret and M. Labbé (Simenon) **47**:372
Maigret and Monsieur Charles (Simenon) **47**:376
Maigret and the Apparition (Simenon) **8**:487; **18**:481
Maigret and the Black Sheep (Simenon) **8**:486
Maigret and the Bum (Simenon) **47**:377
Maigret and the Calame Report (Simenon)
See *Maigret and the Minister*
Maigret and the Coroner (Simenon)
See *Maigret chez le coroner*
Maigret and the Enigmatic Lett (Simenon)
See *Pietr-le-Letton*
Maigret and the Flea (Simenon) **47**:376
Maigret and the Gangsters (Simenon)
See *Inspector Maigret and the Killers*
Maigret and the Hotel Majestic (Simenon) **18**:486
Maigret and the Hundred Gibbets (Simenon)
See *Le pendu de Saint-Pholien*
Maigret and the Killer (Simenon) **47**:376
Maigret and the Loner (Simenon) **47**:377
Maigret and the Man on the Bench (Simenon)
See *Maigret et l'homme du banc*
Maigret and the Millionaires (Simenon) **47**:377
Maigret and the Minister (Simenon) **47**:375
Maigret and the Nahour Case (Simenon) **47**:378
Maigret and the Old Lady (Simenon)
See *Maigret et la vieille dame*
Maigret and the Wine Merchant (Simenon)
See *Maigret et le marchand de vin*
Maigret and the Young Girl (Simenon) **47**:373, 375
Maigret at the Coroner's (Simenon)
See *Maigret chez le coroner*
Maigret at the Crossroads (Simenon)
See *The Crossroad Murders*
Maigret au "Picratt" (Simenon) **47**:373
Maigret Bides His Time (Simenon) **47**:382
Maigret chez le coroner (Simenon) **47**:378; **47**:378, 381
Maigret cinq (Simenon) **47**:375
Maigret et la grande perche (Simenon) **3**:451
Maigret et la vieille dame (Simenon) **8**:487; **47**:375
Maigret et le client du samedi (Simenon) **47**:381
Maigret et le marchand de vin (Simenon) **47**:376, 381
Maigret et les vieillards (Simenon) **3**:450
Maigret et l'homme du banc (Simenon) **2**:398; **47**:377
Maigret et son mort (Simenon) **47**:380-81
Maigret Has Doubts (Simenon) **47**:378
Maigret Hesitates (Simenon) **2**:398
Maigret in Exile (Simenon) **18**:486; **47**:378
Maigret in New York's Underworld (Simenon)
See *Maigret à New York*
Maigret in Vichy (Simenon) **18**:481
Maigret Keeps a Rendez-Vous (Simenon) **47**:370
Maigret Loses His Temper (Simenon) **47**:375
Maigret Mystified (Simenon)
See *The Shadow in the Courtyard*
Maigret on the Defensive (Simenon) **47**:378
Maigret Rents a Room (Simenon)
See *Maigret Takes a Room*
Maigret Returns (Simenon) **47**:372
Maigret se trompe (Simenon) **47**:381
Maigret Sets a Trap (Simenon) **47**:376
Maigret Sits It Out (Simenon) **47**:371-72
Maigret Stonewalled (Simenon)
See *Monsieur Gallet, décédé*
Maigret Takes a Room (Simenon) **47**:374-75
Maigret to the Rescue (Simenon) **47**:371
Maigret Travels South (Simenon) **47**:369-70
A Maigret Trio (Simenon) **2**:399
Maigret's Boyhood Friend (Simenon) **47**:376
Maigret's Little Joke (Simenon) **47**:374-75
Maigret's Memoirs (Simenon) **8**:487; **47**:374, 383
Maigret's Pickpocket (Simenon) **47**:375
Maigret's Revolver (Simenon) **47**:382
Maigret's Rival (Simenon) **47**:378
Maigret's War of Nerves (Simenon)
See *A Battle of Nerves*
Maihime (Kawabata) **107**:121
"Mail at Your New Address" (Klappert) **57**:258
"Mail Call" (Jarrell) **9**:298
Mailer: His Life and Times (Manso) **39**:416-25
"The Mailman" (Strand) **18**:514, 516; **41**:437; **71**:283
"The Maimed Man" (Tate) **2**:429, 431; **11**:525, 527; **14**:529
"Maimuţoii judecători" (Arghezi) **80**:3
"La main" (Carrier) **78**:60, 68
La main (Simenon)
See *Maigret et l'homme du banc*
The Main (Trevanian) **29**:431-32
La Main Coupée (Cendrars) **106**:167, 183, 187-88, 190
"Main Currents of American Thought" (Shaw) **34**:369
"The Main Drag" (Boyle) **121**:53, 55-6
Main Line West (Horgan) **53**:172, 175
"The Main of Light" (Heaney) **74**:188
La main passe (Tzara) **47**:387
La main sèche (Tchicaya) **101**:354-55, 363, 366
"Main Theme" (Gaye) **26**:131
The Maine Massacre (van de Wetering) **47**:407-10
"Mainly By the Music" (Randall) **135**:391
"Les mains" (Hébert) **29**:238
Les mains négatives (Duras) **68**:92, 96
Les mains sales (Sartre) **4**:476; **9**:471; **13**:499-500; **18**:472; **50**:382; **52**:375, 381, 388
"Mainstreet" (Seger) **35**:381
"Maintaining a Home" (Dorris) **109**:311
Maíra (Ribeiro) **34**:102-04
Maisie (Taylor) **4**:543
Maison basse (Aymé) **11**:22
La maison de rendez-vous (Robbe-Grillet) **1**:287, 290; **2**:376; **4**:446, 448, 450; **6**:465-

66; **8**:452-54; **10**:437; **14**:457, 462; **43**:361; **128**:332-38, 346, 348-51, 353, 355, 357, 359-60, 363, 367, 370, 382
La maison du canal (Simenon) **47**:379
"Maison flake" (Tzara) **47**:393
La maison sans racines (Chedid) **47**:87-8
Le maître de la parole: Kouma lafôlô kouma (Laye) **38**:286-87, 290, 292
Le maître de Milan (Audiberti) **38**:33
Le maître de Santiago (Montherlant) **19**:326-27, 329-30
"La maîtresse servante" (Damas) **84**:179
Maitreya (Sarduy) **97**:390, 393-96, 399-400, 402-03, 405-07, 409-10
Maitreyi (Eliade) **19**:145
"The Maja" (Nin) **60**:276
"Majestic" (Johnston) **51**:249
"The Majesty of the Law" (O'Connor) **14**:398, 400; **23**:331-33
"al- Majnūna" (Mahfūz) **55**:176
The Major (Hughes) **48**:182, 184
The Major and the Minor (Wilder) **20**:455
Major André, Brave Enemy (Duncan) **26**:102
Major Dundee (Peckinpah) **20**:273, 279, 283-84
Major Elegies (Senghor) **130**:285
"Major Hoople" (Coles) **46**:112
"The Major of Hussars" (Bates) **46**:60
"Major Pugachov's Last Battle" (Shalamov) **18**:479-80
Makassar Reef (Buzo) **61**:63-7
Makbara (Goytisolo) **23**:188-89; **133**:24, 44-47
Make and Break (Frayn) **31**:191-93
"Make Believe Ballroom Time" (Strand) **71**:282
Make Death Love Me (Rendell) **28**:386
"Make It New" (Pound) **7**:327
"Make Me Wanna Holler" (Gaye)
See "Inner City Blues"
Make No Sounds (Corcoran) **17**:77
"Make Room for Me" (Sturgeon) **39**:363
Make Room! Make Room! (Harrison) **42**:205-06
"Make the Old Man Sing" (Shapcott) **38**:404
"Make Up" (Reed) **21**:305
"Make Way" (Lightfoot) **26**:282
"The Make-Believe Dance Hall" (Purdy) **10**:424
"The Maker" (Borges)
See "El hacedor"
"The Maker" (Wright) **53**:428
The Maker (Borges)
See *El hacedor*
"The Makers" (Nemerov) **36**:307-08
Makers and Finders (Brooks) **29**:85, 87-9
Makes Me Wanna Holler: A Young Black Man in America (McCall) **86**:73-81
"Makin' Thunderbirds" (Seger) **35**:386-87
"Making a Break" (Thesen) **56**:423
"Making a Movie" (Richler) **46**:351-52
"Making a Sacher Torte" (Wakoski) **40**:456
Making a TV Play (Taylor) **27**:441
"Making Amends" (Packer) **65**:350
"Making Arrangements" (Bowen) **118**:75
"Making Bricks Without Straw" (Rhys) **124**:370
Making Certain It Goes On (Hugo) **32**:250-51
"Making Change" (Busch) **47**:63
"Making Changes" (Michaels) **25**:317
Making Do (Goodman) **4**:197
"Making Good with Mother" (Ferber) **93**:136
Making History (Friel) **115**:237, 239, 243-46, 248-50
"Making, Knowing, and Judging" (Auden) **4**:34; **6**:16; **123**:21
"Making Much of Orioles" (Davison) **28**:103
The Making of a Martyr (Warren) **59**:296
"The Making of a New Zealander" (Sargeson) **31**:363-64, 370
The Making of Ashenden (Elkin) **6**:169; **27**:122, 125
"The Making of The Black Book" (Morrison) **87**:278
"The Making of the Book" (Fisher) **25**:160
The Making of the Popes, 1978 (Greeley) **28**:173-74
The Making of the Representative for Planet Eight (Lessing) **40**:302-06
"Making Peace" (Levertov) **66**:251
"Making Room" (Ammons) **57**:50
"Making Soda Pop" (Levine) **118**:287, 292
"Making Strange" (Heaney) **37**:169; **74**:168
"Making Tracks" (Grenville) **61**:152
Making Tracks (Ayckbourn) **33**:46, 50
"Making Tracks to Chittagong" (Theroux) **46**:402
"Making Up" (Boland) **67**:44; **113**:60, 63
"Making Up the Past" (Alvarez) **93**:17
"The Makings of a Music" (Heaney) **74**:178
The Makioka Sisters: A Tale of Disarrayed Chrysanthemums (Tanizaki)
See *Sasame yuki*
Makom aher (Oz) **8**:436
Mal aimées (Kavan)
See *Neige suivi de mal aimées*
Les mal aimés (Mauriac) **56**:215
Le mal court (Audiberti) **38**:22-4, 26, 28-31
Mal vu mal dit (Beckett) **29**:61-3, 65, 67; **59**:256
Mała apokalipsa (Konwicki) **28**:207-08, 211; **54**:254-63; **117**:264-65, 268, 271, 279-80, 283-84, 287-8, 292
La mala hora (García Márquez) **2**:148; **15**:253-54; **27**:147, 151, 155; **47**:153; **68**:153, 156
The Malacia Tapestry (Aldiss) **14**:14; **40**:14, 21
"Malacoda" (Beckett) **9**:80
Le maladie de la mort (Duras) **68**:73-4, 79-80, 87, 90-1, 99
Malady (Duras)
See *Le maladie de la mort*
The Malady of Death (Duras)
See *Le maladie de la mort*
The Malady of the Ideal (Brooks) **29**:86
Malafrena (Le Guin) **22**:270, 274-75; **45**:214, 216, 221
Malatesta (Montherlant) **19**:327, 329
"Malatesta Cantos" (Pound) **10**:402; **13**:461
The Malayan Trilogy (Burgess) **2**:85; **4**:81-2; **5**:89; **13**:124; **22**:69, 73-4, 77-8; **40**:113-14; **81**:301; **94**:56
Malcauchon; or, The Six in the Rain (Walcott) **9**:556; **25**:451
"Malcolm" (Sanchez) **116**:272, 274, 294
Malcolm (Albee) **5**:13; **9**:6; **13**:5; **25**:38; **113**:40
Malcolm (Purdy) **2**:347-50; **4**:422-24; **10**:422-24; **28**:376-78, 380-81; **52**:344, 347, 350-51
Malcolm Lowry's 'Volcano': Myth, Symbol, Meaning (Markson) **67**:190, 195
Malcolm Mooney's Land (Graham) **29**:196-98
"Malcolm Spoke/Who listened? (This Poem Is for My Consciousness Too)" (Madhubuti) **73**:199, 210
Malcolm X (Lee) **105**:104, 106, 109-10, 112-14, 127-29
Malcolm X Speaks: Selected Speeches and Statements (Malcolm X) **82**:173, 176, 188, 226; **117**:319
Malcolm X: The Last Speeches (Malcolm X) **82**:226-27
"Malcolm X: the Longed-for-Feminist-Manhood" (Hooks) **94**:158
The Malcontents (Snow) **4**:503
"Maldito amor" (Ferré) **139**:179-81, 183
Maldito amor (Ferré) **139**:153, 162, 179
"Maldrove" (Jeffers) **54**:235
Male and Female (Mead) **37**:273
The Male Animal (Thurber) **5**:432, 434-35, 442; **125**:388, 393, 414-15
Male Armor (Duberman) **8**:185
A Male Child (Scott) **60**:320
The Male Cross-Dresser Support Group (Janowitz) **145**:336, 346
"The Male Prison" (Baldwin) **42**:21
El male rahamim (Amichai) **116**:100-05, 118
"A Malebolge of Fourteen Hundred Books" (Shapiro) **53**:329-30
"Malediction" (Spacks) **14**:511
"The Malediction" (Williams) **15**:580; **45**:447
The Malefactors (Gordon) **6**:203-04, 206; **29**:190; **83**:236, 241-42, 244, 246, 251, 258-60
"Malefic Things" (Seth) **90**:350
Malemort (Glissant) **10**:231; **68**:174-82, 187, 189
Malempin (Simenon) **47**:371
"Malenkiī gigant bol'shogo seksa" (Iskander) **47**:201
Le malentendu (Camus) **1**:52; **9**:141-42, 146; **11**:93; **14**:108, 115; **32**:84-8, 92-6, 99-101; **69**:136; **124**:39; **124**:10, 39
"Malentendu à Moscou" (Beauvoir) **124**:183, 185-86
"Malest Cornifici Tuo Catullo" (Ginsberg) **109**:358
Malgudi Days (Narayan) **28**:301-03; **47**:302; **121**:354
Malhamat al-Harafish (Mahfouz) **153**:273, 299-301, 303, 306-8, 359-60, 367
"Malheur County" (Le Guin) **45**:216-17
"The Malice of Objects" (Gerstler) **70**:157
Malina (Bachmann) **69**:35-6, 51-2, 54, 59-62
"Malinche" (Castellanos) **66**:45, 53
"La Malnou" (Theriault) **79**:410
Malone Dies (Beckett)
See *Malone meurt*
Malone meurt (Beckett) **1**:23; **2**:44; **3**:45; **4**:52; **6**:37, 42-3; **9**:78, 80; **11**:33-4; **14**:71-3, 76; **18**:47, 50, 52; **29**:53, 55-7, 59, 65-7; **59**:253-54, 257
Malraux (Hartman) **27**:182
The Maltese Falcon (Hammett) **3**:219; **5**:162; **19**:193, 195-99; **47**:156-57, 161-64
The Maltese Falcon (Huston) **20**:157, 162, 165, 169, 172
Mama (McMillan) **50**:67-9; **61**:363-65; **112**:223, 226-27, 230, 234, 236-37, 239-40, 243, 247-49, 252
"Mama Come Home" (Tiptree) **48**:385
Mama Day (Naylor) **52**:324-27
Mama Dot (D'Aguiar) **145**:116-17, 121, 124, 127, 129
"Mama Dot's Treatise" (D'Aguiar) **145**:117
Mama Grande's Funeral (García Márquez)
See *Los funerales de la Mamá Grande*
"Mamá guantes" (Ulibarrí) **83**:416
"Mama Mercy" (Armatrading) **17**:8
The Mama Poems (Kenny) **87**:242, 245, 253-54, 258-59
"Mama Tuddi Done Over" (Rooke) **25**:394
Mama Turns 100 (Saura) **20**:322
Mamaji (Mehta) **37**:294
The Mambo Kings Play Songs of Love (Hijuelos) **65**:146-50
Maminka (Seifert) **44**:427; **93**:307, 317, 335, 343, 345
Mamma Roma (Pasolini) **20**:259-60, 265; **37**:347; **106**:206-08, 221-22, 226, 253, 273
Mammonart: A Study in Economic Interpretation (Sinclair) **63**:346
"Mammorial Stunzas for Aimee Simple McFarcin" (Birney) **6**:71, 75
The Mammoth Hunters (Auel) **107**:4-5, 8-10, 14-5, 19-20, 24-5
"A Mammy Encomium" (Nolan) **58**:366
MammyWater (Nwapa) **133**:201, 229-30
"The Man" (Bradbury) **10**:71; **42**:34
"A Man" (Bukowski) **108**:86
"The Man" (Clarke) **53**:91
"A Man. . ." (Le Guin) **136**:383, 85
"Man!" (MacLeish) **68**:270, 291
"The Man" (McCartney) **35**:291-92
"Man" (Roberts) **14**:463
"The Man" (Rulfo)
See "El hombre"
"The Man" (White) **30**:451
A Man (Fallaci)
See *Un uoma*
The Man (Wallace) **7**:509-10; **13**:567-69
"The Man Accursed" (Ali) **69**:31
"Man Alone" (Bogan) **46**:80, 83-4, 87; **93**:64
A Man and a Woman (Mull) **17**:299

"Man and Boy" (Heaney) **74**:188, 194
Man and Boy (Morris) **1**:232; **37**:310-11
Man and Boy (Rattigan) **7**:355
Man and God (Alonso)
See *Hombre y Dios*
"A Man and His Little Sister" (Wiesel) **37**:450
The Man and His Times (Malcolm X) **117**:317
"A Man and His Wife" (Sargeson) **31**:363-65
"Man and Socialism in Cuba" (Guevara) **87**:201, 216
Man and Time (Priestley) **34**:365
"A Man and Two Women" (Lessing) **2**:239; **10**:316; **22**:278
A Man and Two Women (Lessing) **94**:261
"Man and Wife" (Lowell) **4**:297; **15**:343; **124**:257-58
"Man and Wife" (Sexton) **123**:440
"Man and Wife" (Sorrentino) **7**:449
Man as an End: A Defense of Humanism; Literary, Social, and Political Essays (Moravia) **46**:283
"Man as Plaything, Life as Mockery" (Bissoondath) **120**:7
A Man Asleep (Perec)
See *Un homme qui dort*
"The Man beneath the Tree" (Wright) **53**:420
"The Man Born to Farming" (Berry) **46**:73
"Man Bring This Up Road" (Williams) **45**:446, 453, 455
"Man Can Face the Truth" (Bachmann) **69**:42
"Man Coming of Age" (Warren) **13**:573
"Man Descending" (Vanderhaeghe) **41**:448-49, 451-52
Man Descending (Vanderhaeghe) **41**:448-53
The Man Died: Prison Notes of Wole Soyinka (Soyinka) **3**:463; **5**:397; **44**:284-85
"Man Does, Woman Is" (Graves) **45**:172
Man Does, Woman Is (Graves) **11**:256
"The Man Doors Said Hello To" (Tiptree) **48**:385-86
"Man Dying on a Cross" (Scott) **43**:370
A Man Escaped (Bresson) **16**:115, 117
The Man Everybody Was Afraid Of (Hansen) **38**:237-38
A Man for All Seasons (Bolt) **14**:88-90
"Man Friday" (Hope) **51**:217, 221, 224, 226
"A Man from Benin" (Transtroemer) **52**:410; **65**:222, 227
The Man from Everywhere (Simenon) **47**:372
"The Man from Mars" (Atwood) **13**:46; **84**:70
Man from Mars (Lem)
See *Czlowiek z Marsa*
The Man from Monticello: An Intimate Life of Thomas Jefferson (Fleming) **37**:123
"The Man from P.I.G." (Harrison) **42**:203
"The Man from R.O.B.O.T." (Harrison) **42**:203
The Man from the Broken Hills (L'Amour) **25**:281
"Man from the South" (Dahl) **79**:189
"Man Gave Names to All the Animals" (Dylan) **77**:184, 186
"Man, God Ain't Like That" (Wright) **21**:438-39
Man Hunt (Lang) **20**:207; **103**:88
"The Man I Killed" (O'Brien) **103**:139, 142-43
"A Man I Knew" (Klappert) **57**:256, 259-60
A Man in a Mirror (Llewellyn) **80**:196
"A Man in Assynt" (MacCaig) **36**:284, 286
"Man in Black" (Plath) **9**:425; **14**:423
"The Man in Bogotá" (Hempel) **39**:68
A Man in Charge (Philipson) **53**:275
A Man in Full (Wolfe) **147**:372-73, 375-76, 378-79
"A Man in Louisiana" (McGuane) **45**:266
A Man in My Position (MacCaig) **36**:284, 286
Man in Space to the Moon (Branley) **21**:19
The Man in the Black Coat Turns (Bly) **38**:53-60; **128**:17, 23, 32, 43
"The Man in the Brooks Brothers Shirt" (McCarthy) **3**:329
The Man in the Brooks Brothers Shirt (McCarthy) **59**:290
The Man in the Brown Suit (Christie) **12**:113-14
The Man in the Cage (Vance) **35**:427
"Man in the Cellar" (O'Faolain) **108**:407, 413
Man in the Cellar (O'Faolain) **6**:382-83; **47**:330
A Man in the Divided Sea (Merton) **83**:390
"Man in the Drawer" (Malamud) **3**:323
The Man in the Glass Booth (Shaw) **5**:390-91
The Man in the Gray Flannel Suit (Wilson) **32**:444-49
The Man in the Gray Flannel Suit II (Wilson) **32**:449
The Man in the Gray Flannel Suit Twenty Years Before and After (Wilson) **32**:448
The Man in the High Castle (Dick) **30**:117, 121-22, 125, 127; **72**:105, 107, 117-22
Man in the Holocene (Frisch)
See *Der Mensch erscheint im Holozän*
"A Man in the House" (Colter) **58**:140, 146-47
"The Man in the Manmade Moon" (Kennedy) **42**:254
The Man in the Maze (Silverberg) **140**:343, 345, 359-62, 378
The Man in the Middle (Wagoner) **3**:507; **5**:473-74; **15**:558
"The Man in the Mirror" (Strand) **18**:516, 518; **41**:437; **71**:283-84
"A Man in the Moon" (MacDiarmid) **19**:286-87
"The Man in the Overstuffed Chair" (Williams) **45**:455-56
"The Man in the Toolhouse" (Swados) **5**:420
"The Man in the Tree" (Strand) **18**:515; **71**:284
"The Man in the Wind" (Stevenson) **33**:382
The Man in the Yellow Boots (Bowering) **15**:82
The Man in the Yellow Raft (Forester) **35**:172, 174
A Man in the Zoo (Garnett) **3**:188
Man Is an Onion (Enright) **4**:156
"Man Is—Nothing Is—No One" (Haavikko)
See "Mies ei—Mitaan, ei—Kukaan"
A Man Lay Dead (Marsh) **7**:210; **53**:247-48, 252
Man Lying on a Wall (Longley) **29**:294, 296
A Man Made of Smoke (Middleton) **38**:331
"The Man Made of Words" (Momaday) **85**:274; **95**:260, 262
"Man Must Live" (Mphahlele) **25**:336, 341
Man Must Live (Mphahlele) **25**:336, 338, 342; **133**:157
Man Must Speak: The Story of Language and How We Use It (Gallant) **17**:128
The Man Named East, and Other New Poems (Redgrove) **41**:358-59
"A Man Needs a Maid" (Young) **17**:570, 578
"Man of All Work" (Wright) **21**:438-39
"A Man of Destiny" (Castellanos) **66**:56
Man of England Now (Sargeson) **31**:366-67, 374
A Man of Honour (Maugham) **1**:204; **11**:368
"Man of Letters" (Dixon) **52**:97
A Man of Letters (Pritchett) **41**:335-36
"The Man of Letters in the Modern World" (Tate) **24**:443, 445
A Man of Little Evils (Dobyns) **37**:75
Man of Marble (Wajda) **16**:583-84
"Man of My Time" (Quasimodo) **10**:428
Man of Nazareth (Burgess) **13**:126; **22**:78; **40**:125
A Man of Power (Colegate) **36**:308, 113-14
"The Man of Sentiment" (Slessor) **14**:495
The Man of Slow Feeling: Selected Short Stories (Wilding) **73**:396
Man of Steel: Joseph Stalin (Archer) **12**:15
Man of the Moment (Ayckbourn) **74**:18-20, 27-9, 34-5
Man of the Monitor: The Story of John Ericsson (Latham) **12**:323
"A Man of the People" (Le Guin) **136**:383, 85
A Man of the People (Achebe) **1**:1-2; **3**:1-3; **5**:1, 3; **7**:3, 5-6; **11**:1, 3; **26**:13, 15-20, 25, 27; **51**:3, 6-7, 9; **75**:3-4, 6-8, 12, 14, 16, 18-26; **127**:27-8, 40, 42-3; **152**:17, 43
"A Man of the Thirties" (Grigson) **7**:135
Man of Two Worlds (Herbert) **44**:392
Man of Words/Man of Music (Bowie) **17**:58, 64, 67
Man Off Beat (Hughes) **48**:181
Man on a Tightrope (Kazan) **16**:361
The Man on All Fours (Derleth) **31**:127
"The Man on His Death Bed" (Aleixandre) **36**:28
The Man on the Balcony (Wahlöö)
See *Mannen på balkongen*
The Man on the Horse (Baxter) **14**:63
"Man on the Moon" (Ortiz) **45**:304, 309
"Man on the Pink Corner" (Borges)
See "El Hombre de la esquina rosada"
The Man on the Rock (King) **53**:205; **145**:365
"The Man on the Train: Three Existential Modes" (Percy) **14**:416; **65**:260
"The Man Outside" (Grau) **146**:141
Man Plus (Pohl) **18**:410, 412
"The Man Seeking Experience Enquires His Way of a Drop of Water" (Hughes) **14**:270
"The Man She Loved" (Simpson) **32**:377; **149**:332, 334
Man Should Rejoice (MacLennan) **92**:306, 308
Man Shy (Davison) **15**:170
The Man Sitting in the Corridor (Duras) **100**:130-31
"Man Smoking a Cigarette in the Barcelona Métro" (Durcan) **43**:118
"Man Splitting Wood in the Daybreak" (Kinnell) **129**:270-71
"Man Spricht Deutsch" (Enzensberger) **43**:145-46
"Man the Master" (Merton) **83**:397
Man the Measurer: Our Units of Measure and How They Grew (Gallant) **17**:129
"Man Thinks, God Laughs" (Kundera) **115**:350
A Man to Conjure With (Baumbach) **6**:32; **23**:53-4
A Man to Marry, A Man to Bury (Musgrave) **54**:333-34, 340
"A Man Told Me the Story of His Life" (Paley) **37**:339; **140**:222
"Man Track Here" (Derleth) **31**:131, 133
"The Man under the Bed" (Jong) **6**:268; **83**:291
"A Man Walks beneath the Moon" (Neruda)
See "Un hombre anda bajo la luna"
"Man We Was Lonely" (McCartney) **35**:278-79
"A Man Whistling" (Simmons) **43**:411
"The Man Who Became a Soprano" (Updike) **139**:368
"The Man Who Became Afraid" (Wesker) **3**:519; **5**:483-84
"The Man Who Blew Away" (Bainbridge) **62**:34, 37
"The Man Who Brought Happiness" (Federspiel) **42**:146
"The Man Who Came Back" (Singer) **111**:314
The Man Who Came to Dinner (Hart and Kaufman) **38**:262,265; **66**:174-76, 178, 182-87, 190-91
The Man Who Cried I Am (Williams) **5**:496-98; **13**:598-99
The Man Who Dared the Lightning: A New Look at Benjamin Franklin (Fleming) **37**:125
"The Man Who Didn't Eat Food" (Ulibarrí) **83**:418
The Man Who Died at Twelve O'Clock (Green) **25**:193
The Man Who Fell to Earth (Bowie) **17**:68
The Man Who Fell to Earth (Tevis) **42**:370-72, 374
"The Man Who Gave Up His Name" (Harrison) **14**:236-37; **66**:154-55, 159, 161; **143**:335, 344, 355
The Man Who Got Away (Elliott) **38**:179-80
"The Man Who Grew Younger" (Charyn) **5**:104
The Man Who Grew Younger, and Other Stories (Charyn) **5**:103
The Man Who Had All the Luck (Miller) **1**:216, 218
The Man Who Had No Idea (Disch) **36**:127

The Man Who Had Three Arms (Albee) **25**:40; **53**:18-21, 24-6; **86**:118, 120-21, 124-25; **113**:40-1
"The Man Who Invented Pain" (Raine) **32**:353; **103**:186, 189-90
"The Man Who Invented Sin" (O'Faolain) **1**:259; **32**:343-44; **70**:313, 318
The Man Who Invented Sin (O'Faolain)
See *Teresa, and Other Stories*
The Man Who Invented Tomorrow (Hughes) **48**:182, 184, 186
"The Man Who Killed a Shadow" (Wright) **9**:585; **21**:439
The Man Who Killed Himself (Symons) **2**:426; **14**:523; **32**:424
The Man Who Killed His Brother (Donaldson) **46**:140
The Man Who Killed the Deer (Waters) **88**:330, 334-37, 342-43, 345, 347, 349-52, 354-56, 358, 361-63
"The Man Who Knew Belle Starr" (Bausch) **51**:56-7
The Man Who Knew Kennedy (Bourjaily) **62**:96-9
The Man Who Knew Too Much (Hitchcock) **16**:342, 345
The Man Who Left His Will on Film (Oshima) **20**:249, 254
The Man Who Lived Alone (Hall) **37**:148-49;
The Man Who Lived His Life Over Again (Lagerkvist)
See *Han som fik leva om sitt liv*
"The Man Who Lived Underground" (Wright) **9**:585; **14**:597; **21**:438-40, 443, 445-46, 449; **74**:380
"The Man Who Lost His Memory Twice" (Mahfūz) **52**:292
The Man Who Lost His Wife (Symons) **14**:524
The Man Who Loved Children (Stead) **2**:420-23; **5**:403-05; **8**:499-500; **32**:408-09, 411-12, 414-18; **80**:305, 307, 309-10, 319, 322, 324-26, 331-34, 336, 339-42, 348-51, 353
"The Man Who Loved the Nereids" (Yourcenar) **38**:463
The Man Who Loved Women (Truffaut) **20**:404-05, 407; **101**:407, 411-13
"The Man Who Loves Hegel" (Dunn) **36**:154
"The Man Who Married Magdalene" (Hecht) **8**:268
"The Man Who Married Magdalene" (Simpson) **149**:355
The Man Who Mistook His Wife for a Hat, and Other Clinical Tales (Sacks) **67**:298-302, 304
"The Man Who Never Loses His Balance" (Dunn) **36**:153
The Man Who Risked His Partner (Donaldson) **46**:143
"The Man Who Saw the Flood" (Wright) **9**:585; **14**:598
The Man Who Shook Hands (Wakoski) **11**:564; **40**:455
The Man Who Shot Liberty Valance (Ford) **16**:308-11, 315, 319-20
The Man Who Shot the Albatross (Lawler) **58**:333
"The Man Who Sold the Moon" (Heinlein) **3**:224
The Man Who Sold the World (Bowie) **17**:57-9, 61-2, 64, 67
The Man Who Spat Silver (Calisher) **134**:42
"The Man Who Studied Yoga" (Mailer) **3**:315; **4**:319; **74**:224; **111**:135-36
"The Man Who Turned into a Statue" (Oates) **6**:370
The Man Who Turned into a Stick (Abe)
See *Bo ni natta otako*
"The Man Who Walked Home" (Tiptree) **48**:386; **50**:357
"The Man Who Was Almos' a Man" (Wright) **9**:585; **21**:438
The Man Who Was Given His Life to Live Again (Lagerkvist)
See *Han som fik leva om sitt liv*
"The Man Who Was Heavily into Revenge" (Ellison) **42**:129
"The Man Who Was Left Behind" (Ingalls) **42**:230
The Man Who Was Left Behind, and Other Stories (Ingalls) **42**:230-31
The Man Who Was Not with It (Gold) **4**:189, 191; **42**:191, 195; **152**:139
The Man Who Was There (Morris) **1**:232; **37**:311
The Man Who Wasn't There (Barker) **94**:3; **146**:41
The Man Who Watched the Trains Go By (Simenon) **1**:309
"The Man Who Went to Chicago" (Wright) **3**:545
The Man Who Went Up in Smoke (Wahlöö)
See *Mannen som gick upp i rök*
The Man Who Won the Pools (Stewart) **7**:464
The Man Who Would Be King (Huston) **20**:173
"The Man Who Would Never Write Like Balzac" (Wesker) **42**:426
The Man Who Would Not Come Back (Kabakov) **59**:395
"The Man Who Would Not Die" (Davidson) **13**:169
"The Man Who Wrote Books in His Head" (Highsmith) **14**:261; **102**:192
The Man Whose Dreams Come True (Symons) **2**:426; **14**:523
Man with a Bull-Tongue Plow (Stuart) **8**:507; **11**:509; **14**:513; **34**:373-74, 376
"Man with a Family" (Humphrey) **45**:193
"A Man with a Field" (Watkins) **43**:452
Man with a Sling (Neruda)
See *El hondero entusiasta, 1923-1924*
Man with Bags (Ionesco)
See *L'homme aux valises*
"The Man with Clam Eyes" (Thomas) **107**:333
"The Man with Night Sweats" (Gunn) **81**:178, 186
The Man with Night Sweats (Gunn) **81**:176-89
The Man with Nine Lives (Ellison) **139**:138
"Man with One Small Hand" (Page) **7**:291
The Man with Red Suspenders (Dacey) **51**:82-3
The Man with Seven Toes (Ondaatje) **14**:408; **29**:341; **51**:310-11, 316
The Man with the Coat (Callaghan) **65**:246-47
"The Man with the Dog" (Jhabvala) **4**:259; **94**:184
The Man with the Golden Arm (Algren) **4**:16; **10**:6; **33**:12-7
The Man with the Golden Gun (Fleming) **30**:137-39, 143-44, 148, 150
"The Man with the Knives" (Boell)
See "Der Mann mit den Messern"
"The Man with Three Violins" (MacEwen) **55**:164
The Man with Two Brains (Martin) **30**:251-52
The Man Within (Greene) **3**:211; **18**:193-94; **27**:175; **70**:291, 293; **72**:148-50, 177
The Man without a Face (Holland) **21**:148, 150-53
"Man without a Fig Leaf" (Garrett) **51**:147
Man without a Shadow (Wilson)
See *The Sex Diary of Gerard Sorme*
The Man without a Soul (Lagerkvist)
See *Mannen utan själ*
"A Man Writes to a Part of Himself" (Bly) **10**:57; **38**:58, 60
"The Management of Grief" (Mukherjee) **53**:272; **115**:366
El manana efímero (Goytisolo) **23**:186
Mañana los guerreros (Alegria) **57**:10-11
"Las Mañanitas" (Fuentes) **113**:257-58
Manassas: A Novel of the War (Sinclair) **63**:345-46, 348, 350, 366
Manchild in the Promised Land (Brown) **30**:33-41
"Manchouli" (Empson) **33**:142
The Manchurian Candidate (Condon) **4**:105-07; **6**:115; **8**:150; **45**:92, 96, 99, 101-02, 104; **100**:91, 94, 97-100, 102-07, 110-12
Mandabi (Ousmane) **66**:334-36, 338, 340-42
"Mandala" (Merrill) **2**:275
Mandala (Buck) **7**:33
The Mandarins (Beauvoir)
See *Les mandarins*
Les mandarins (Beauvoir) **2**:43; **4**:47-8; **8**:60-1; **14**:68; **31**:34, 38-9, 41-2; **44**:342-43, 345-46, 350; **50**:390; **71**:48-52, 54-6, 67-8, 70, 72, 74-5; **124**:127, 129-32, 140, 144, 183-86
Le Mandat (Ousmane)
See *Mandabi*
The Mandelbaum Gate (Spark) **2**:416-18; **3**:463-67; **5**:400; **8**:495; **18**:502-03, 505; **40**:393, 400; **94**:333, 339
"Mandolin" (Dove) **50**:153, 155
"Mandorla" (Celan) **53**:70
"Mandra" (Nin) **127**:385
"The Mandrill on the Turnpike" (Ashbery) **125**:32
The Man-Eater of Malgudi (Narayan) **28**:296-99; **47**:304, 308; **121**:333, 353, 356-57, 360, 384, 389, 407-08, 411, 413-14
Le manège espagnol (del Castillo) **38**:166-67
Man'en gan'nen no futtobōru (Oe) **10**:374; **36**:346; **86**:219, 225-26, 230, 232, 234, 241-42, 244
"A maneria de Olegário Mariano" (Cabral de Melo Neto) **76**:163
The Maneuver (Adamov)
See *La grande et la petite manoeuvre*
"Man-Fate" (Everson) **5**:123; **14**:166
Man-Fate: The Swan Song of Brother Antoninus (Everson) **5**:122
The Mangan Inheritance (Moore) **19**:332-35; **32**:310, 312-13; **90**:243, 247, 249-51, 254-5, 257, 260-61, 272-3, 277, 281, 289, 296, 305
"The Mangler" (King) **12**:311
"The Mango Community" (Jacobsen) **48**:196, 198; **102**:242
"Mango Says Goodbye Sometimes" (Cisneros) **69**:148; **118**:172, 180
"Mango Seedling" (Achebe) **11**:4; **26**:21; **127**:29
Mango Street (Cisneros)
See *The House On Mango Street*
"The Mango Tree" (Hospital) **145**:303
Manhattan (Allen) **16**:11-14, 18; **52**:39-41, 46-9
"Manhattan Island" (Stafford) **4**:517
Manhattan Made Me (Edwards) **43**:141
"Manhattan May Day Midnight" (Ginsberg) **109**:364
Manhattan Music (Alexander) **121**:20-2
Manhattan Pastures (Hochman) **3**:250
Manhattan Transfer (Dos Passos) **1**:77-9; **4**:131-32, 137-38; **11**:152, 154; **15**:183-85; **25**:137-38, 141-42, 145-47; **34**:419-24; **82**:61-2, 65-6, 68, 70, 73-4, 76, 86, 88, 102, 104-06
"Manhole Covers" (Shapiro) **15**:478
"Manhole Sixty-Nine" (Ballard) **36**:41
"Manhood" (Wain) **46**:415
Manhood: A Journey from Childhood into the Fierce Order of Virility (Leiris)
See *L'age d'homme*
Manhood in the Making: Cultural Concepts of Masculinity (Gilmore) **70**:425, 431
"Manhunt" (Carpentier) **11**:104
Manhunt (Carpentier)
See *El acoso*
A Mania for Sentences (Enright) **31**:155-56
"Manic and Depressive" (Matthews) **40**:325
"Manichean Geography" (Paulin) **37**:354
"Manifest Destiny" (Graham) **118**:237, 252
Manifest Manners (Vizenor) **103**:337-40
"The Manifestation" (Roethke) **3**:433
Manifeste dada (Tzara) **47**:393
Manifeste du surréalisme. Poisson soluble (Breton) **54**:16, 19-21, 33
"Manifesto" (Ewart) **13**:208

"Manifesto" (Monette) **82**:322-23, 332-33
"Manifesto" (Otero) **11**:427
"Manifesto" (Parra) **102**:348-49, 352-53
Manifesto of Surrealism (Breton)
See *Manifeste du surréalisme. Poisson soluble*
"Manifesto: The Mad Farmer Liberation Front" (Berry) **6**:61
Manifestoes of Surrealism (Breton) **54**:15-16
"The Manipulator" (Bell) **31**:46
La manivelle (Pinget) **13**:442
"Mankiewitz Won't Be Bowling Tuesday Nights Anymore" (Kinsella) **27**:237-38
"Mankind Journeys Through Forests of Symbols" (Chappell) **78**:117
The Mankind Thing (Shapcott) **38**:398, 400
"Manley Buckminster" (Avison) **97**:128
"The Man-Moth" (Bishop) **1**:34; **9**:98; **32**:33, 37-8, 43
"Der Mann mit den Messern" (Boell) **11**:58; **27**:66-7; **72**:69, 76
Mannen på balkongen (Wahlöö) **7**:501
Mannen som gick upp i rök (Wahlöö) **7**:501-02
Mannen utan själ (Lagerkvist) **54**:269-70, 272, 275, 278
"Le mannequin" (Robbe-Grillet) **4**:449
Männer Sache (Kroetz) **41**:234, 238, 240
"Manners" (Bishop) **32**:39
"Manners" (Peterkin) **31**:308
"Manners, Morals, and the Novel" (Trilling) **9**:531; **24**:450, 461
Människor (Lagerkvist) **54**:273, 286
Manny and Rose (Peters) **39**:91-3
"La mano" (Aleixandre) **36**:26
"Mano entregada" (Aleixandre) **9**:12
"Mano rubato" (Landolfi) **49**:214
The Manor (Singer) **1**:313; **3**:455-56; **9**:488; **11**:501; **15**:505; **23**:415-16
"The Manor Garden" (Plath) **14**:425; **111**:164, 179, 203
Las manos del día (Neruda) **7**:261; **7**:261; **28**:315
"Manos Karastefanís" (Merrill) **13**:376
A Man's Blessing (Sciascia)
See *A ciascuno il suo*
A Man's Blessing (Sciascia)
See *A ciascuno il suo*
A Man's Estate (Humphreys) **47**:179-80, 185-88
"Man's Fate" (Dubus) **97**:201
Man's Fate (Malraux)
See *La condition humaine*
"Man's Fulfillment in Order and Strife" (Duncan) **41**:130
Man's Hope (Malraux)
See *L'espoir*
Man's Life Is This Meat (Gascoyne) **45**:148, 153, 157
A Man's Place (Ernaux)
See *La place*
A Man's Place (Sender) **8**:481
"Man's Power over Things" (Kunene) **85**:165, 178
Man's Reach for the Stars (Gallant) **17**:128-29
Man's Reach into Space (Gallant) **17**:127-28
A Man's Road (Sillanpaa)
See *Miehen tie*
Man's Search for Meaning: An Introduction to Logotherapy (Frankl)
See *Ein psycholog erlebt das konzentrationslager*
"Manscape" (Tomlinson) **6**:534-35
Manseed (Williamson) **29**:461
Manservant and Maidservant (Compton-Burnett) **1**:60; **15**:137, 139, 141-42; **34**:496, 500, 502
"Mansion" (Ammons) **108**:21
The Mansion (Faulkner) **3**:151, 156; **14**:178-79; **18**:149; **28**:145; **68**:121
"The Mansion On The Hill" (Moody) **147**:191
"Le Manteau de Pascal" (Graham) **118**:263
The Manticore (Davies) **2**:113; **7**:72-4; **13**:173-74; **25**:129, 131, 133, 136; **42**:102, 105-07, 109; **75**:180, 184, 190, 192, 199, 215-16, 224; **91**:198, 201, 203, 204
Mantissa (Fowles) **33**:171-73, 175; **87**:149, 159, 162-67, 179-80
"The Mantle of Whistler" (Parker) **68**:336
Manual de morală practică (Arghezi) **80**:12
A Manual for Manuel (Cortázar)
See *Libro de Manuel*
"Manual for Sons" (Barthelme) **8**:51-52; **23**:47, 49; **115**:64
Manual Labor (Busch) **7**:38-9; **10**:91-3
A Manual of Instruction in Military Maps and Aerial Photographs (Maclean) **78**:244
"Manual System" (Sandburg) **35**:340
Manuale minimo dell'Attore (Fo) **109**:113, 119, 131, 135
Manuel de déification (Romains) **7**:381
"Manuela em dia de chuva" (Dourado) **23**:151
"Manuelzinho" (Bishop) **13**:89; **32**:37-8, 42
Manufacturing Consent: Noam Chomsky and the Media (Chomsky) **132**:55
Manufacturing Consent: The Political Economy of the Mass Media (Chomsky) **132**:40, 43-4, 55, 64, 67, 74
"Manuscript Found in a Pocket" (Cortázar)
See "Manuscrito hallado en un bolsillo"
"Manuscript Found under a Mattress in a Hotel Room" (Rudnik) **7**:384
The Manuscripts of Pauline Archange (Blais) **2**:63; **4**:67; **6**:80-2; **22**:58
"Manuscrito hallado en un bolsillo" (Cortázar) **33**:124
"Many Are Disappointed" (Pritchett) **41**:332
"Many as Two" (Avison) **4**:37; **97**:92
The Many Colored Coat (Callaghan) **14**:102-03; **41**:89-90; **65**:247-49, 252
"Many famous feet have trod" (Larkin) **64**:259
"Many Happy Returns" (Paterson) **30**:283
Many Happy Returns (Berrigan) **37**:43-4
Many Long Years Ago (Nash) **23**:320
"Many Loves" (Ginsberg) **36**:198; **109**:357
"Many Mansions" (Didion) **129**:76
"The Many Mansions" (Levertov) **66**:245
"Many Mansions" (Roth) **104**:284
"Many Mansions" (Silverberg) **140**:364
Many Moons (Thurber) **5**:430, 438, 442; **25**:437; **125**:406
"Many of Our Waters: Variations on a Poem by a Black Child" (Wright) **10**:544
"Many Problems" (Tate) **25**:428
"Many Rivers to Cross" (Cliff) **21**:61, 63-4
"Many Rivers to Cross" (Jordan) **114**:153
"Many Senses: Mexico City" (Moss) **45**:287
Many Smokes, Many Moons: A Chronology of American Indian History through Indian Art (Highwater) **12**:288
"Many Things of Death" (Salinas) **90**:326, 330, 331
Many Thousand Gone: An American Fable (Fair) **18**:140, 142
"Many Thousands Gone" (Baldwin) **42**:16; **67**:5; **127**:105, 126
"Many Wagons Ago" (Ashbery) **15**:36
"Many without Elegy" (Graham) **29**:193
The Many Worlds of Magnus Ridolph (Vance) **35**:422
"Manyone Flying" (Swenson) **106**:344, 346
A Many-Windowed House (Cowley) **39**:461
The Manzoni Family (Ginzburg)
See *La famiglia Manzoni*
Mao II (DeLillo) **76**:170-87; **143**:185, 188, 190, 197-98, 207, 209, 211, 223-26, 229
Mao Tse-Tung (Archer) **12**:18-21
Maori Girl (Hilliard) **15**:279
Maori Woman (Hilliard) **15**:279
"The Map" (Bishop) **9**:89, 93, 97; **32**:29, 32, 37, 43, 45
"Map" (Enright) **31**:150
"The Map" (Strand) **18**:516
"The Map of Harlem" (Dumas) **62**:159
A Map of Misreading (Bloom) **24**:74-5, 79, 81; **103**:2-4, 6, 12, 14, 20, 23-4, 26-7, 32-3, 41, 44, 46, 53-4
"A Map of Skye" (Hugo) **32**:244
"Map of the Antilles" (Walcott) **76**:279-80
"A Map of the City" (Gunn) **18**:203
A Map of the New Country: Women and Christianity (Maitland) **49**:231-32
"A Map of the Small Town" (Cassity) **42**:95
"A Map of the Western Part of the County of Essex in England" (Levertov) **5**:246
A Map of the World (Hare) **29**:219-22; **58**:230, 233
"Map to the Treasure" (Nyro) **17**:313, 316, 318
"El mapa de objetos perdidos" (Arreola) **147**:28-30
"Maple" (Frost) **9**:219
Mapmakers (Brink) **36**:68-9; **106**:109, 119-20
"Mappemonde" (Levertov) **66**:241
"Mappemounde" (Birney) **6**:72, 76, 78
"The Mapping of the Currents" (Olson) **28**:343
"Maps" (Reaney) **13**:473
Maps (Farah) **53**:140; **137**:80-81, 91, 93, 96-103, 110, 114-18, 130
Maps (Olson) **28**:342-43
Maps of Another Town: A Memoir of Provence (Fisher) **76**:335
Maquettes (Warner) **14**:552
"Mar del paraíso" (Aleixandre) **9**:16
"El mar del tiempo perdido" (García Márquez) **15**:254; **27**:148
"O mar e o canavial" (Cabral de Melo Neto) **76**:168
"Mar en la tierra" (Aleixandre) **9**:14
Mar morto (Amado) **13**:11; **40**:26-7, 36; **106**:58-60, 63
"Mar y aurora" (Aleixandre) **9**:12, 15
El mar y las campanas (Neruda) **7**:261; **28**:310-11; **62**:333,335-36
"Mar y noche" (Aleixandre) **9**:15
El mar y sus pescaditos (Castellanos) **66**:54
"Mara" (Jeffers) **11**:307
The Marabou Stork Nightmares (Welsh) **144**:317-18, 320-22, 324-27, 335, 337, 342-43, 345
"Marad tabib" (Mahfouz) **153**:349
"Marat Dead" (Tomlinson) **13**:550; **45**:401
Marat/Sade (Weiss) **3**:513-15; **15**:563, 565-69; **51**:386, 388, 391, 393-97
"Maratea Porto: The Dear Postmistress There" (Hugo) **32**:235
"Marathon" (Glück) **44**:216-17, 219-21, 223-24
Marathon Man (Goldman) **48**:126-28, 131
"The Marauder" (Johnston) **51**:254
al- Mārāyā (Mahfūz) **52**:299, 302
The Marble Faun (Faulkner) **9**:201; **68**:127
Marbles (Brodsky) **100**:58
Marbot: A Biography (Hildesheimer)
See *Marbot: Eine Biographie*
Marbot: Eine Biographie (Hildesheimer) **49**:173, 175-79
Marbre (Mandiargues) **41**:278-79
"Marburg" (Pasternak) **18**:382
"The Marburg Sisters" (Barrett) **150**:17
"Marcel" (Nin) **127**:385
Marcel Duchamp: Appearance Stripped Bare (Paz)
See *Marcel Duchamp o el castillo de la castillo de la pureza*
Marcel Duchamp o el castillo de la castillo de la pureza (Paz) **3**:375; **19**:365; **65**:176
Marcel Duchamp, or The Castle of Purity (Paz)
See *Marcel Duchamp o el castillo de la castillo de la pureza*
"Marcella" (Wilson) **12**:650
"The March" (Blaise) **29**:70-1
"The March" (Lowell) **3**:302
"March" (MacLeish) **68**:286
"March" (Pasternak) **63**:305, 313
"March 1, 1847. By the First Post" (Boland) **113**:110
"March 21" (Daryush) **19**:120

"A March Calf" (Hughes) **37**:180
"march eight/1979" (Young Bear) **94**:363
"March Evening" (Martinson) **14**:357
The March Hare (White) **49**:403
"March Journal" (Wright) **146**:328
"March Moon" (Hughes) **108**:330
"March Morning" (Ciardi) **40**:157
"March Morning Unlike Others" (Hughes) **37**:175
"A March on Washington" (Squires) **51**:381
"The March Past" (Larkin) **64**:262
"March Snow" (Berry) **4**:59
"March Song" (Ammons) **108**:20
March to the Monteria (Traven) **8**:522
Le marchand de regrets (Crommelynck) **75**:152, 168
Marchbanks' Almanack (Davies)
See *Samuel Marchbanks' Almanack*
"Marche" (Soupault) **68**:405
"Marche" (Tchicaya) **101**:350
"Marche Funèbre" (Seifert) **93**:337
Les marches de sable (Chedid) **47**:82
"Les marchés du temple" (Mandiargues) **41**:279
"Marching" (Simic) **22**:380; **130**:316
Marching Blacks: An Interpretive History of the Rise of the Black Common Man (Powell) **89**:202, 204-06
The Marchington Inheritance (Holland) **21**:153
The Marchioness of Loria (Donoso)
See *La misteriosa desaparición de la Marquesita de Loria*
"Marco Polo" (Slessor) **14**:492
Marco Polo, If You Can (Buckley) **37**:60-1
Marco Polo Sings a Solo (Guare) **8**:253; **29**:204-05; **67**:79
"Marcovaldo at the Supermarket" (Calvino) **33**:100; **73**:34
Marcovaldo: or, The Seasons in the City (Calvino)
See *Marcovaldo ouvero le stagioni in citta*
Marcovaldo ouvero le stagioni in citta (Calvino) **8**:127; **11**:91-2; **33**:99-100; **39**:306-07, 310-11; **73**:33-4, 42, 46
"The Mare" (Watkins) **43**:451-52, 454
Il mare colore del vino (Sciascia) **9**:475
La marea (Gironella) **11**:234, 238
La marée du soir (Montherlant) **8**:394
"Mares escarlatas" (Cernuda) **54**:52
"Margaret Are You Grieving" (Durcan) **70**:152
Margaret Mead: Some Personal Views (Mead) **37**:282-83
"Margaret Thatcher Joins the IRA" (Durcan) **43**:115
"Marge" (Carruth) **84**:135
La marge (Mandiargues) **41**:275-77, 279
Marges de la philosophie (Derrida) **87**:72, 84, 89
Margie (Fast) **131**:100
The Margin (Mandiargues)
See *La marge*
A Margin of Hope: An Intellectual Autobiography (Howe) **85**:132-35, 137, 139, 143-47, 155
The Marginal Farm (Buzo) **61**:70
"Marginal Notes in a Theology Text" (L'Heureux) **52**:273
"Marginalia" (Avison) **97**:93
"Marginalia" (Wilbur) **53**:412; **110**:357
"Margins" (Buckley) **57**:126
Margins (Booth) **23**:75-6
"Margrave" (Jeffers) **54**:248; **2**:212
"Marguerite" (Beauvoir) **31**:42
"Marguerite Landmine" (Kauffman) **65**:348
"Maria" (Sondheim) **30**:386
"María Concepción" (Porter) **7**:314; **13**:449; **101**:209-11
"Maria Giuseppa" (Landolfi) **49**:216
Maria Irene Fornes: Plays (The Conduct of Life; The Danube; Mud; Sarita) (Fornés) **39**:136-38; **61**:134-41
"Maria Minor" (Avison) **97**:71
Maria Neféli (Elytis) **49**:108-15, 117-18; **100**:170, 172-73, 175, 192
Maria Nephele (Elytis)
See *Maria Neféli*
"Maria Nephele's Song" (Elytis) **100**:173
"Maria Reiche: The Riddle of the Pampa" (Chatwin) **57**:153
"Maria Roberts" (Simpson) **149**:308, 319
María Sabina (Cela) **122**:66
Mariaagélas (Maillet) **54**:303-04, 307, 310-11, 314, 318; **118**:327, 329, 337-39, 341, 343, 345, 348-49
Mariaagelas: Maria, Daughter of Gelas (Maillet)
See *Mariaagélas*
Le mariage (Gombrowicz)
See *Slub*
Mariamne (Lagerkvist) **7**:200; **10**:312; **13**:333; **54**:288
Mariana o el alba (Marqués) **96**:241-43
Mariana, or the Dawn (Marqués)
See *Mariana o el alba*
"Marianne" (Celan) **10**:104
Marianne (Davies) **23**:146
A Marianne Moore Reader (Moore) **2**:291; **47**:267
Marianne Thornton, 1797-1887: A Domestic Biography (Forster) **4**:167; **77**:221
"Marie" (Jones) **76**:65
"Marie" (Kotzwinkle) **35**:253-54
"La Marie" (Theriault) **79**:410
Marie: A True Story (Maas) **29**:307-08
Marie and Bruce (Shawn) **41**:397-400, 402
"Marie at Tea" (Ostriker) **132**:324
Marie Blythe (Mosher) **62**:314-15
Marie Laveau (Prose) **45**:324, 326
"Marie, Marie, Hold On Tight" (Barthelme) **46**:40-1
La mariée etait en noir (Truffaut) **20**:383-84, 387, 390; **101**:375, 377-81, 383, 386, 390
Les mariés de la Tour Eiffel (Cocteau) **8**:146, 148; **15**:134; **43**:102, 105-06, 108-09
M'arifa (Mahfouz) **153**:294
Marigolds (Zindel)
See *The Effect of Gamma Rays on Man-in-the-Moon Marigolds*
Marigolds in August (Fugard) **25**:173
"Marihuana" (Woolrich) **77**:389-90, 396, 399
"Marijuana Notation" (Ginsberg) **109**:325
Marilyn (Steinem) **63**:385-88
Marilyn: A Biography (Mailer) **3**:315-20; **8**:372-73; **11**:344; **14**:351; **28**:259; **74**:205-06, 225, 227-28, 245; **111**:103, 114-15, 148
"Marilyn Miller" (Smith) **12**:535
Marilyn the Wild (Charyn) **8**:135-36
Marilyn's Daughter (Rechy) **107**:256, 258
"Marin" (Cisneros) **118**:184
"Marin" (Merwin) **88**:211
Le marin de Gibraltar (Duras) **6**:149-50; **11**:165; **40**:180-83; **68**:74, 79-80, 88, 98
"Marina" (Eliot) **9**:186-87, 189; **15**:210, 213, 217; **34**:529; **41**:148, 151; **55**:346, 374; **57**:206
"Marina and the Lion" (Ferré)
See "Marina y el leon"
"Marina y el leon" (Ferré) **139**:150, 152, 164
"Marin-an" (Snyder) **32**:387
Marine (Clancy) **112**:86-7
"Marine Surface, Law Overcast" (Clampitt) **32**:114
Mariner Dances (Newby) **2**:311
Marinero en tierra (Alberti) **7**:8-9
"Mariner's Carol" (Merwin) **5**:285
Mariners, Renegades, and Castaways (James) **33**:222
"Mariposa" (Guillén) **79**:238
"Mariposa de obsidiana" (Paz) **19**:366; **51**:327
"Marita" (Mason) **82**:255
"Marital Sonnets" (Simmons) **43**:408
Marjorie Morningstar (Wouk) **1**:376; **38**:444-47
"The Mark" (Bogan) **46**:77, 90; **93**:61, 90-1, 98
"The Mark" (Pancake) **29**:348, 350
Mark Coffin, U.S.S. (Drury) **37**:110
"Mark Ingestre: The Customer's Tale" (Aickman) **57**:4
Mark Lambert's Supper (Stewart) **7**:464
"The Mark of Apelles" (Pasternak)
See "Il tratto di Apelle"
"The Mark of Cain" (Yevtushenko) **26**:462
The Mark of Conte (Levitin) **17**:265
The Mark of the Horse Lord (Sutcliff) **26**:433-36, 439-40
Mark of the Vampire (Browning) **16**:125-26
The Mark of the Warrior (Scott) **60**:340
"The Mark of Vishnu" (Singh) **11**:505
The Mark of Zorro (Mamoulian) **16**:425, 428
Mark Twain and Southwestern Humor (Lynn) **50**:426
The Mark Twain Murders (Yep) **35**:472-73
"Mark Van Doren and the Brook" (MacLeish) **8**:363
Marked by Fire (Thomas) **35**:405-07
"The Market" (Snyder) **32**:387, 399
"Market Day" (Buckley) **57**:131
"Market Day" (Hacker) **72**:192
"The Market Where the Rivers Go" (Cabral de Melo Neto)
See "O mercado a que os rios"
"Markings" (Heaney) **74**:188
"Markiz w Grafie" (Lem) **149**:120
Marks of Identity (Goytisolo)
See *Señas de identidad*
Marksizm i filosofija jazyka (Bakhtin) **83**:3-7, 14, 16, 21, 25-6, 28-30, 33, 38, 45
Det märkvärdiga landet (Lagerkvist) **54**:287
"The Marl Pits" (Tomlinson) **13**:548
"The Marlboro Man" (Cisneros) **69**:155
Marle (Chambers) **35**:98
"Marlene American Horse" (Vizenor) **103**:281
Marlenes Schwester: Zwei Erzählungen (Strauss) **22**:407
"Marlin off the Moro" (Hemingway) **34**:478
"The Marlon Brando Memorial Swimming Pool" (Alexie) **96**:3, 12; **154**:29
"Marlon Brando, Pocahontas, and Me" (Young)
See "Pocahontas"
The Marlow Chronicles (Sanders) **41**:378
The Marmalade Bird (Sansom) **6**:483
"Marmilion" (McGrath) **55**:74, 76
The Marmot Drive (Hersey) **7**:153; **40**:227-28, 231, 239-40; **81**:334; **97**:302
Marnie (Graham) **23**:193
Marnie (Hitchcock) **16**:349-50, 353
"Maroon" (Dybek) **114**:61, 67
"Marooned" (Keillor) **115**:286
Marooned (Campbell) **32**:80
"Marooned off Vesta" (Asimov) **76**:313
"Marooned on Gilligan's Island: Are Women Morally Superior to Men?" (Pollitt) **122**:206, 218-19, 225
The Marquis de Sade (Beauvoir) **14**:66
Le marquis qui perdit (Ducharme) **74**:63, 65-6
The Marquise Goes Out at Five (Mauriac)
See *La Marquise sortit à cinq heures*
The Marquise of O (Rohmer)
See *Die Marquise von O*
La Marquise sortit à cinq heures (Mauriac) **9**:363-66
"Die Marquise von O" (Pasternak) **18**:385
Die Marquise von O (Rohmer) **16**:537-39
"Marrakesh" (Munro) **6**:342; **10**:357; **95**:302, 304
"Marriage" (Aickman) **57**:3
"Marriage" (Clarke) **9**:168
"Marriage" (Corso) **11**:124
"A Marriage" (Creeley) **36**:118
"Marriage" (Ezekiel) **61**:92, 94
"A Marriage" (Hoffman) **23**:237
"A Marriage" (Lavin) **99**:320
"Marriage" (Lowell) **11**:331
"Marriage" (Moore) **4**:362; **10**:351; **13**:393; **19**:336, 340, 342-43; **47**:260, 262
"Marriage" (Oates) **6**:367

"The Marriage" (Strand) **18**:518; **41**:438; **71**:283-84
"The Marriage" (Summers) **10**:494
"The Marriage" (Williams) **148**:325-26
"Marriage" (Wilson) **49**:413-15
Marriage (Feinstein) **36**:170
The Marriage (Gombrowicz)
See *Ślub*
The Marriage Ceremony (Gombrowicz)
See *Ślub*
"The Marriage Feast" (Lagerkvist) **54**:276-77
Marriage in Philippsburg (Walser)
See *Die Ehen in Philippsburg*
"Marriage Is a Private Affair" (Achebe) **26**:22; **75**:13
"Marriage Is Belonging" (Porter) **101**:241
Marriage Italian Style (De Sica) **20**:97
"Marriage No Field of Daisies" (Royko) **109**:407
"The Marriage Nocturne" (Ostriker) **132**:328
The Marriage of Bette and Boo (Durang) **38**:173-74
The Marriage of Cadmus and Harmony (Calasso)
See *Le nozze di Cadmo e Armonia*
"A Marriage of Convenience" (Morrissy) **99**:78
"The Marriage of John Keats and Emily Dickinson in Paradise" (Thomas) **132**:382
The Marriage of Maria Braun (Fassbinder) **20**:118-19
The Marriage of Mr. Mississippi (Dürrenmatt)
See *Die Ehe des Herrn Mississippi*
"The Marriage of Pocohantas" (Simpson) **7**:427
"The Marriage of Strongbow and Aoife" (Muldoon) **72**:279
"The Marriage of Theseus and Hippolyta" (Nemerov) **6**:360
"Marriage of Two" (Day Lewis) **10**:131
Marriage Play (Albee) **53**:26; **86**:119, 124
"A Marriage Poem" (Voigt) **54**:430-31
Marriage Poem (Ezekiel) **61**:105, 107
"A Marriage Poem for Peg and John" (Johnston) **51**:248
"A Marriage Portion" (Foote) **75**:230-31
"The Marriage Sculptor" (Van Duyn) **116**:422
"Marriage with Beasts" (Van Duyn) **3**:491; **63**:436, 439; **116**:401-01, 419, 429
"Marriages" (Larkin) **64**:262, 283
Marriages (Straub) **28**:408-09; **107**:266, 268, 274, 282-83, 291-92, 304-05
Marriages and Infidelities (Oates) **2**:315-16; **6**:370-71; **9**:402; **15**:400; **19**:351; **52**:338; **108**:354, 369, 370
The Marriages between Zones Three, Four, and Five (Lessing) **15**:334-36; **22**:285-86; **40**:303, 306; **94**:274-75
"Marriages, Births, Deaths" (Johnston) **51**:248-49, 254
"Married Dialogue" (Day Lewis) **10**:131
The Married Lovers (Horwitz) **14**:266
"The Married Man" (Phillips) **28**:362-63
A Married Man (Read) **25**:377-80
The Married Woman: Fragments of a Film Made in 1964 (Godard)
See *Une femme mariée*
"Married Woman's Complaint" (Bowering) **32**:47
"Le marronier" (Mandiargues) **41**:279
"The Marrow" (Le Guin) **45**:213
"The Marrow" (Roethke) **3**:433; **19**:396; **46**:364
"Marry Me a Little" (Sondheim) **30**:398; **147**:252, 254
Marry Me: A Romance (Updike) **9**:536-40; **13**:559, 563; **23**:472; **43**:431-32, 434; **139**:314-15, 336, 338, 347-53
"Marrying Damian" (Trevor) **116**:394-95
"Marrying the Hangman" (Atwood) **15**:36; **25**:69
Mars and Her Children (Piercy) **128**:274
La Marsellaise (Renoir) **20**:293, 295-98, 302, 311-12
"Marsh, Hawk" (Atwood) **84**:69
"Marshall Washer" (Carruth) **84**:135
"Marshallene at Work" (Engel) **36**:162
"Marshall's Dog" (Beattie) **63**:10-12
"Marshe O Pyus" (Voznesensky) **57**:416
Marshes (Konwicki)
See *Rojsty*
Le marteau sans maître (Char) **9**:164; **11**:114, 117; **55**:287-88
"Martello" (Paulin) **37**:354
Martello Towers (Buzo) **61**:58-67, 70
Martereau (Sarraute) **2**:384; **4**:464, 467, 469; **8**:471; **31**:377, 380; **80**:230, 236, 239-40, 252, 254
"Martha" (Lorde) **71**:235-36, 260
Martha (Fassbinder) **20**:108
"Martha Blake" (Clarke) **6**:113; **9**:168
"Martha Blake at Fifty-One" (Clarke) **6**:112-13; **9**:168
"Martha Graham" (Dodson) **79**:194
Martha Quest (Lessing) **3**:287, 290-91; **15**:334; **22**:283; **94**:255-57, 288
"Marthe" (Rexroth) **112**:388
"Marthe Away" (Rexroth) **49**:284
"The Martian" (Bradbury) **42**:38
The Martian Chronicles (Bradbury) **1**:42; **10**:68, 70; **15**:86; **42**:32, 35, 37-40, 43; **98**:111-12, 121, 141, 144
"A Martian Sends a Postcard Home" (Raine) **103**:191-94
A Martian Sends a Postcard Home (Raine) **32**:350-52, 354; **103**:181, 183, 186, 188, 190-91, 197-201, 211
Martian Time-Slip (Dick) **10**:138; **30**:116-17, 123, 125, 127; **72**:108, 114, 119, 121-22
The Martian Way, and Other Stories (Asimov) **3**:16
The Martians' Second Invasion (Strugatskii and Strugatskii) **27**:432, 434, 437
Martin and John (Peck) **81**:89-100
Martin Dressler: The Tale of an American Dreamer (Millhauser) **109**:165-69, 171-74
Martin Heidegger (Steiner) **24**:435-36
Martin Heidegger and the Question of Literature: Toward a Postmodern Literary Hermeneutics (Heidegger) **24**:277
Martin Mull (Mull) **17**:298-99
Martin Mull and His Fabulous Furniture (Mull) **17**:299
"Martin the Fisherman" (Knowles) **26**:258
"Martine" (Ferron) **94**:127-28
"Martinez" (Fish)
See "Dennis Martinez and the Uses of Theory"
"The Martinique" (Ondaatje) **51**:310
Martiríes (Ritsos) **13**:487
The Martlet's Tale (Delbanco) **6**:130
Marty (Chayefsky) **23**:111, 115
"The Martyr" (Ngũgĩ wa Thiong'o) **36**:317
"The Martyr" (Porter) **101**:235, 237, 239-40
The Martyr (O'Flaherty) **5**:321
"The Martyrdom of Bishop Farrar" (Hughes) **9**:284
"The Martyrdom of Saint Sebastian" (Durcan) **70**:153
"The Martyrdom of St. Magnus" (Brown) **100**:84, 86
The Martyrology, Books I-II (Nichol) **18**:368-70
"The Martyr's Corner" (Narayan) **28**:293
"The Martyr's Crown" (O'Brien) **10**:362
Maru (Head) **25**:233-38; **67**:92-7, 108-09
Marune (Vance) **35**:421
"The Marvelous Children" (Williams) **45**:443
"The Marvelous Girl" (Pritchett) **13**:468
The Marvelous Misadventures of Sebastian (Alexander) **35**:25
Marvelous Possessions: The Wonder of the New World (Greenblatt) **70**:356-57
"Marvelous Truth" (Levertov) **66**:236
"The Marvels of the City" (Simic) **49**:343
"Marvin McCabe" (Carruth) **84**:131, 135
The Marx Family Saga (Goytisolo) **133**:95-96
Marx: The Man and His Work (Prichard) **46**:337
Marxism and Form: Twentieth Century Dialectical Theories of Literature (Jameson) **142**:216-18, 224-27, 233, 251, 254-55, 261
"Marxism and Historicism" (Jameson) **142**:257
Marxism and Literary Criticism (Eagleton) **63**:94, 102-03
"Marxism and Literature" (Wilson) **24**:467, 470, 474
Marxism and the Philosophy of Language (Bakhtin)
See *Marksizm i filosofija jazyka*
Marxisme et le sciences humaines (Goldmann) **24**:242
"Marx's Three Voices" (Blanchot) **135**:134
Mary (Nabokov)
See *Mashen'ka*
"Mary and the Seasons" (Rexroth) **22**:346; **49**:283; **112**:377
Mary Anne (du Maurier) **59**:286
Mary Barnes (Edgar) **42**:113, 116
"The Mary Celeste Move" (Herbert) **44**:394
Mary Christmas (Chase) **2**:101
Mary Glenn (Millin) **49**:242-43, 246, 248
Mary Hartman, Mary Hartman (Lear) **12**:333-36, 338
Mary Hartman, Mary Hartman (Mull) **17**:300
"Mary in the Mountains" (Tilghman) **65**:106, 109, 111
"Mary Jane" (Smith) **12**:535
"Mary Jordan" (Kerrigan) **6**:276
"Mary Lou" (Seger) **35**:381
"Mary Magdalene at Easter" (Davison) **28**:100
Mary, Mary (Kerr) **22**:256
"Mary Moody Emerson, R.I.P." (Turco) **11**:549, 551
Mary of Scotland (Ford) **16**:312-13
Mary O'Grady (Lavin) **18**:304; **99**:312, 319
"Mary O'Reilley" (Farrell) **66**:129-30
"Mary, Queen of Arkansas" (Springsteen) **17**:487
Mary, Queen of Scots (Fraser) **32**:178-80, 183, 185; **107**:29,35,37,43,60-61,67
Mary Queen of Scots: The Fair Devil of Scotland (Hibbert) **7**:157
Mary Reilly (Martin) **89**:120-35, 137
"Mary Rowlandson" (Howe)
See "The Captivity and Restoration of Mrs. Mary Rowlandson"
"Mary Shelley" (Bowering) **32**:48
"Mary Stuart to James Bothwell" (Sitwell) **9**:493
"Mary Ure" (Murphy) **41**:319
"Mary Winosky" (Hughes) **108**:292
Marya: A Life (Oates) **52**:329-32, 334, 336-38; **108**:386, 390, 393
"Mary's Piece" (Dixon) **52**:97
"Mary's Song" (Plath) **111**:178, 199, 217, 219
"El más bello amor" (Aleixandre) **9**:14
"Masaccio's Expulsion" (Graham) **118**:244-45
Masante (Hildesheimer) **49**:170, 175, 179
Mascara (Dorfman) **77**:134-36, 139-42, 149-50, 152
Mascarets (Mandiargues) **41**:279
Die Maschine (Perec) **56**:256-57
Masculine Feminine (Godard) **20**:136, 139
*M*A*S*H* (Altman) **16**:20-1, 24-5, 28-9, 33, 40-1; **116**:3-6, 11, 14, 16-17, 21-3, 31, 36, 46, 48, 51, 54, 59, 66-7, 72
*M*A*S*H* (Gelbart) **21**:126-27, 129, 132; **61**:146-47
"Mash Flat" (Bennett) **28**:29
Mashen'ka (Nabokov) **1**:243, 245; **2**:300-01; **8**:418; **11**:395; **15**:396; **44**:469; **46**:295; **64**:348
"Mask" (Lem)
See *Maska*
"Mask" (Rozewicz) **139**:253
The Mask (Koontz) **78**:203
A Mask for Janus (Merwin) **1**:212; **2**:277; **5**:284, 287; **8**:388; **18**:335; **45**:268-70; **88**:194, 205, 207

The Mask of Apollo (Renault) **3**:425; **17**:398-99, 402
The Mask of Dimitrios (Ambler) **4**:18-19; **6**:3-4; **9**:19-20
"The Mask of the Bear" (Laurence) **62**:271
Maska (Lem) **149**:114, 152, 154, 181-82, 184-86
The Masked Days (Fuentes)
See *Los días enmascarados*
Masked Gods: Navaho and Pueblo Ceremonialism (Waters) **88**:341-43, 345-47, 352, 356, 362-64, 369
"The Masked Marvel's Last Toehold" (Selzer) **74**:279
"Masked Woman's Song" (Bogan) **4**:69; **39**:396
"The Mask-Maker" (Abse) **29**:14-15
"The Masks" (Prokosch) **48**:309
Masks (Brathwaite) **11**:67
Masks (Enchi) **31**:141
Masks: A Love Story (Bennett) **35**:43
The Masks of God (Campbell) **69**:72, 74, 76-7, 81-4, 88-9, 94-5, 99
The Masks of God: Creative Mythology (Campbell) **69**:74, 76
The Masks of God: Occidental Mythology (Campbell) **69**:73
The Masks of God: Oriental Mythology (Campbell) **69**:72-3
The Masks of God: Primitive Mythology (Campbell) **69**:70-1, 73
"The Masks of Love" (Scannell) **49**:325
The Masks of Love (Scannell) **49**:325, 331-32
"Masks of Satan" (Davies) **13**:174
The Masks of Time (Silverberg) **140**:343, 345, 364
Mason and Dixon (Pynchon) **123**:325-26, 328-32
"Mas'ot Binyamin ha'aharon mitudela" (Amichai) **22**:31, **57**:38, 40-2, 44, 46; **116**:119, 123, 138
A Masque for Janus (Merwin)
See *A Mask for Janus*
"Masque nègre" (Senghor) **130**:241, 253
"A Masque of Italy" (Christie) **110**:125, 128
A Masque of Mercy (Frost) **3**:170-71, 173; **9**:222; **10**:196-97; **13**:225-26; **15**:242-43
"The Masque of Princes" (Brown) **48**:57
A Masque of Reason (Frost) **3**:170, 173; **9**:222; **10**:193, 196; **13**:225-26; **15**:241-42
Masquerade (Berton) **104**:43-4, 47-8
The Masquerade (Clark Bekedermo) **38**:113, 115-16, 119, 122
The Masquerade of Souls (Lagerkvist)
See *Själarnas maskerad*
"Masquerades" (Okri) **87**:314
"Mass" (Jiles) **58**:271, 279
"Mass for the Day of St. Thomas Didymus" (Levertov) **28**:243; **66**:244
"Mass Man" (Walcott) **76**:274
Massachusetts Trust (Terry) **19**:440
"The Massacre" (Broumas) **73**:15
The Massacre at Fall Creek (West) **7**:522; **17**:553
Massacre in Mexico (Poniatowska)
See *La noche de Tlatelolco*
"Massacre of the Boys" (Rozewicz) **9**:465
Massacre of the Dreamers: Essays on Xicanisma (Castillo) **151**:30-1, 33, 36, 46, 48-9, 51, 70, 72, 83, 101-03, 107-08, 110
"The Massacre of the Innocents" (Davison) **28**:100
"Massacre of the Innocents" (Hope) **51**:212, 216
"The Massacre of the Innocents" (Simic) **130**:333
Masse und Macht (Canetti) **14**:119-21, 124; **25**:106-07, 109-14; **75**:124, 128-32, 134, 137, 139-42, 144-45; **86**:293-97, 299, 301-03
"Masses of Men" (Caldwell) **60**:60
"The Masses The Implosion of the Social in the Media" (Baudrillard) **60**:35
"The Masseuse" (Broumas) **73**:15-16
"Massive Retaliation" (Ciardi) **40**:155
"Mastectomy" (Boland) **40**:100; **67**:44, 46; **113**:58, 60, 90, 109, 117
"Mastectomy" (Ostriker) **132**:328
"The Mastectomy Poems" (Ostriker) **132**:328
"Master" (Carter) **5**:103
"The Master" (Merwin) **45**:268
The Master (Klima) **56**:164-65
The Master (White) **30**:444
Master and Commander (O'Brian) **152**:259, 261, 263, 266, 269, 273, 276-77, 281, 285-86, 289-91, 293, 295-97
"Master and Mistress" (Kunitz) **148**:98
The Master, and Other Stories (Kaufman) **8**:317
"The Master and the Victim" (Kunene) **85**:175
Master Georgie (Bainbridge) **130**:32-39
"Master Halcrow, Priest" (Brown) **48**:55
"Master Harold" ... and the Boys (Fugard) **25**:176-78; **40**:203; **80**:61, 63, 65, 68-70. 72, 77, 80-1
"Master Misery" (Capote) **3**:99; **13**:133-36, 138; **19**:79; **58**:86, 98
"Master of Days" (Kunene) **85**:165
"The Master of Doornvlei" (Mphahlele) **25**:344
The Master of Go (Kawabata) **5**:208; **18**:281; **107**:73-8, 81, 91, 101, 108
The Master of Petersburg (Coetzee) **117**:74-6, 79, 81, 87-93
"The Master of Secret Revenges" (Gass) **132**:195-96
"Master of the Asteroid" (Smith) **43**:420, 422
Master of the House (Dreyer) **16**:259-63
Master of the Moor (Rendell) **28**:388; **48**:321
The Master Puppeteer (Paterson) **12**:484; **30**:283-86, 288
"Master Richard" (Wain) **46**:411
"The Master Speech" (Frost) **34**:475
"Mastera" (Voznesensky) **15**:555-56; **57**:414-15, 417, 423
Master-Builder Manole (Blaga)
See *Meşterul Manole*
"Masterful" (Matthews) **40**:325
Mastergate: A Play on Words (Gelbart) **61**:145-50
"Mastering the Craft" (Scannell) **49**:332
"MAsterMANANiMAL" (Swenson) **61**:397
Masterpiece Theatre: An Academic Melodrama (Gubar) **145**:273-74
"Masters" (Amis) **40**:44
"The Masters" (Heaney) **74**:169
The Masters (Duhamel) **8**:189
The Masters (Snow) **1**:315-17; **4**:502-03; **6**:517; **9**:496; **13**:509-11; **19**:425, 427
Masters in Israel (Buckley) **57**:125-26, 129-31, 133
"Master's in the Garden Again" (Ransom) **2**:363; **11**:466
The Masters of Bow Street (Creasey) **11**:135
Masters of Life and Death (Silverberg) **140**:377
Masters of Modern Music (Berger) **12**:38-9
"The Master's Tools Will Never Dismantle the Master's House" (Lorde) **71**:244
"The Mastodon Palace of Westminster" (Aickman) **57**:2
"Masts" (Merwin) **88**:194
"Masts at Dawn" (Warren) **13**:577; **39**:267, 271
"A Mat to Weave" (Tchicaya) **101**:346
Matador (Almodovar) **114**:3-4, 6, 8-9, 11, 13-4, 19-20, 22-3, 29-34, 57-8
The Matador (Montherlant)
See *Le bestiaries*
"Matador: A Soliloquy" (Hall) **51**:170
The Matarese Circle (Ludlum) **22**:290-91
Matatabi (Ichikawa) **20**:183-84
"The Match" (Sillitoe) **6**:501; **148**:176
"Match Boxes" (Bowering) **47**:29
"Matchbox with a Fly in It" (Simic) **130**:339
The Matchmaker (Wilder) **82**:368, 376, 379
"Materia" (Aleixandre) **9**:12
Materia memorable (Castellanos) **66**:52-3
"Material" (Munro) **6**:341; **19**:344
Materialism (Graham) **118**:222-23, 254-55, 258, 260-62, 264
Matérialisme et révolution (Sartre) **24**:406
The Materials (Oppen) **7**:285; **34**:358-59
Materinskoe pole (Aitmatov) **71**:6, 13-14, 16, 22, 33
"The Maternal Feminine" (Ferber) **93**:139, 146
"Maternal Grief" (Raine) **45**:341
"Maternity Ward" (Selzer) **74**:272-73
"The Mathematicians of Grizzly Drive" (Škvorecký) **69**:339
"Mathematics of Love" (Hamburger) **5**:159
"Mathew VIII, 28ff" (Wilbur) **110**:385
"Mathilde" (Nin) **127**:387-88
Matière céleste (Jouve) **47**:208-09
Matière de Bretagne (Celan) **53**:71
Matière de rêves (Butor) **8**:120; **15**:115
Matière de rêves III (Butor) **15**:120
Matilda (Gallico) **2**:147
"Matilda's England" (Trevor) **116**:371, 374
Matilda's England (Trevor) **14**:536-37; **71**:325-27, 348; **116**:362, 367-68, 371, 374, 385
Les matinaux (Char) **11**:114; **55**:288
"Matinée" (Reverdy) **53**:289
"Matinees" (Merrill) **91**:229
Mating Birds (Nkosi) **45**:295-99
"Mating Calls" (Beer) **58**:38
"Matins" (Levertov) **66**:235, 243
"Matisse" (Hirsch) **31**:216
The Matisse Stories (Byatt) **136**:155, 163
"Matka powieszonych" (Rozewicz) **139**:305
The Matlock Paper (Ludlum) **22**:289; **43**:274
Matrena's House (Solzhenitsyn)
See "Matryonin Dvor"
The Matriarch (Ihimaera) **46**:202-03
"Matrix" (Fisher) **25**:160-61
Matrix (Fisher) **25**:159
"Matrix of Morning" (Watkins) **43**:454
The Matrix Trilogy (Johnson) **9**:301-03
The Matrons (Auchincloss) **18**:24
"Matryona's Home" (Solzhenitsyn)
See "Matryonin Dvor"
"Matryonin Dvor" (Solzhenitsyn) **2**:412; **4**:507; **7**:432, 436, 446; **10**:480; **18**:495; **26**:419, 423; **34**:489; **78**:408, 418; **134**:284, 298, 303, 305
Matsushima: Pine Islands (Vizenor) **103**:308
"Matter and Energy" (Oates) **3**:360
"A Matter of Chance" (Nabokov) **6**:358
A Matter of Conviction (Hunter) **31**:219-21
A Matter of Gravity (Bagnold) **25**:78-9
"A Matter of Origin" (Zamora)
See "Asunto de prinicpio"
"A Matter of Principle" (Archer) **28**:14
"A Matter of Taste" (La Guma) **19**:272
"A Matter of Teeth" (Sillitoe) **148**:199
The Matter of This World: New & Selected Poems (Olds) **85**:302
A Matter of Time (West) **7**:520; **17**:549, 551, 553
"A Matter of Vocabulary" (McPherson) **19**:309; **77**:358-61, 364, 366
Matters of Fact and Fiction: Essays, 1973-1976 (Vidal) **8**:528-29; **10**:501; **22**:436; **33**:404-405
Matthew Arnold (Trilling) **24**:458
"Matthew in the Marshes I" (Klappert) **57**:261
"Matthew in the Marshes II" (Klappert) **57**:261
"Matthew V. 29-30" (Mahon) **27**:290, 292
"The Mattress in the Tomato Patch" (Williams) **45**:447; **71**:364
"Mature Art" (MacDiarmid) **63**:242
"Maturity" (Parks) **147**:215
"Matzeln" (Hein) **154**:82, 166
Maud Martha (Brooks) **2**:82; **4**:79; **5**:75; **49**:23-5, 28; **125**:54-62, 64-6, 68, 72-3, 85-7, 97, 99, 104-07, 168-69
"Maude" (Auchincloss) **45**:24
Maude (Lear) **12**:331
"Maude Awake" (Piercy) **128**:218
Maudits soupirs pour une autre fois: Une version primitive de Féerie pour une

autre fois (Céline) **47**:76-7
Die Mauern von Jerichow (Hein) **154**:161, 175, 181
Maui the Demigod: An Epic Novel of Mythical Hawaii (Goldsberry) **34**:54-6
The Maul and The Pear Tree: The Ratcliffe Highway Murders 1811 (James) **122**:129, 131
Maule's Curse (Winters) **8**:552; **32**:454, 457, 463-65, 471
"Mau-Mauing the Flak Catchers" (Wolfe) **9**:578; **35**:454; **147**:333, 335-36
"Mau-Maus" (Guillén) **79**:229-30, 236-37
"Maumee Ruth" (Brown) **59**:262-63, 265
Maundy (Gloag) **40**:208-10
A Mauriac Reader (Mauriac) **56**:216
Maurice (Forster) **1**:109; **2**:135; **3**:161-62; **4**:165-66, 168; **9**:206-09; **10**:181-83; **13**:220-21; **15**:229-30; **22**:136; **45**:134, 137, 140-41, 143
Maurice's Room (Fox) **121**:186, 198
The Mauritius Command (O'Brian) **152**:261, 282, 288, 295
"Maurits Escher's Impossible/Buildings" (Johnson) **7**:415
Maus: A Survivor's Tale II: And Here My Troubles Began (Spiegelman) **76**:239-50
Maus: A Survivor's Tale: My Father Bleeds History (Spiegelman) **76**:240-42, 244-45, 247-48
Mausoleum (Enzensberger) **43**:149, 151
Le mauvais démiurge (Cioran) **64**:88-9, 93-4
Le mauvais lieu (Green) **77**:278, 280-82
Le Mauvais Sang (Tchicaya) **101**:348-49, 353, 357, 359
Mauve Desert (Brossard)
See *Le désert mauve*
Mauve Gloves and Madmen, Clutter and Vine (Wolfe) **9**:578-79; **15**:583, 585; **35**:457, 459
Mawrdew Czgowchwz (McCourt) **5**:277-79
"Mawu" (Lorde) **71**:262
Max (Fast) **131**:92-4, 100
Max: A Play (Grass)
See *Davor*
Max and the White Phagocytes (Miller) **1**:224; **2**:281; **9**:380; **84**:236
Max Jamison (Sheed) **2**:394-95; **4**:487-88; **10**:473
"Max Perkins in 1944" (Cowley) **39**:461
"Maxie Allen" (Brooks) **49**:31; **125**:74-5
"Maxims in Limbo" (Pack) **13**:439
Maximum Bob (Leonard) **71**:215, 227-28; **120**:285, 289, 291, 299
"Maximum Consumption" (Davies) **21**:94
Maximum Ned (Hannah) **90**:126
"Maximus, from Dogtown I" (Olson) **29**:334
The Maximus Letters (Olson) **5**:329
"Maximus of Gloucester" (Olson) **2**:326
The Maximus Poems (Olson) **1**:263; **2**:326-27; **5**:326, 328; **6**:386-88; **9**:412-13; **11**:417, 420; **29**:328-29, 335-36
"Maximus, to Himself" (Olson) **29**:334
Maximus, Vol. I (Olson) **29**:334
Maximus, Vol. III (Olson) **9**:413
Maximus, Vol. IV (Olson) **5**:327; **9**:413
Maximus, Vol. V (Olson) **5**:327
Maximus, Vol. VI (Olson) **5**:327
Max's Dream (Mayne) **12**:405
"Maxwell's Silver Hammer" (Lennon and McCartney) **12**:364, 380
"May" (Oliver) **34**:246; **98**:256-57
"May 15, 1982" (Kenny) **87**:242
"May 24, 1980" (Brodsky) **100**:55
"May, 1945" (Warner) **45**:433
"May and December: A Song" (Randall) **135**:399
"May and June" (Rendell) **48**:320
"May Be Left Untitled" (Szymborska) **99**:193
"The May Day Garland" (Blunden) **56**:47
"May Day Sermon" (Dickey) **7**:84; **10**:141; **109**:266-68, 273
"May Days" (Ginsberg) **109**:329
"May I Ask You a Question, Mr. Youngstown Sheet and Tube?" (Patchen) **18**:395
May I Cross Your Golden River? (Corcoran) **17**:74-5
"May I Feel Said He (I'll Squeal Said She)" (Cummings) **68**:29
"May It Be" (Pasternak) **63**:281
"May Night" (O'Connor) **23**:331, 331
May Out West (Swenson) **106**:351
"May the Ridge Rise" (Anand) **93**:57
May We Borrow Your Husband? and Other Comedies of the Sexual Life (Greene) **3**:211, 213, 215; **70**:293
"May We Entertain You?" (Sondheim) **30**:377
"May Wind" (Szirtes) **46**:393
"The Maya" (Nin) **127**:389
Mayan Letters (Olson) **29**:326
Maybe: A Story (Hellman) **18**:227-29; **34**:349, 352; **52**:190, 192-94, 198, 200, 204-05
"Maybe All This" (Szymborska) **99**:203
"Maybe I'm Amazed" (McCartney) **35**:278, 284, 289
Maybe the Moon (Maupin) **95**:204-10
"Maybe Your Baby" (Wonder) **12**:663
"Maybellene" (Berry) **17**:51, 53-5
Mayday (Faulkner) **28**:141-42
Maydays (Edgar) **42**:122-24
"Mayflower" (Aiken) **10**:3; **52**:24
"Maymeys from Cuba" (Ferber) **93**:141
Mayn Tatn's bes-din shtub (Singer) **3**:453; **11**:500; **15**:505; **23**:417, 419; **38**:412; **69**:310, 317; **111**:305
"The Mayo Accent" (Durcan) **70**:153
"Mayo Monologues" (Longley) **29**:295-96
"The Mayonnaise Chapter" (Brautigan) **12**:71
"Mayoo Sto Hoon" (Sainte-Marie) **17**:431
"Mayor Harold Washington and Chicago the "I Will" City" (Brooks) **125**:108
The Mayor of Castro Street: The Life and Times of Harvey Milk (Shilts) **85**:319, 321, 340-43
"The Mayors" (Asimov) **19**:26; **26**:63
"May-Ry" (Calisher) **38**:69; **134**:16
"May's Lion" (Le Guin) **136**:329
Mayta (Vargas Llosa)
See *La historia de Mayta*
"Mazatlán Sea" (Creeley) **78**:162
"Maze" (Eberhart) **56**:77
The Maze Maker (Ayrton) **7**:16-18, 20
A Maze of Death (Dick) **30**:124-25; **72**:121-22
"The Mazel Tov Revolution" (Haldeman) **61**:174, 176
Mazeppa (The Brothers Quay) **95**:347, 350
"Mazes" (Le Guin) **45**:213; **136**:329-30
"Mazie" (Mitchell)
See "Except That She Smokes, Drinks Booze and Talks Rough, Miss Mazie Is a Nun"
Mazurca para dos muertos (Cela) **122**:68-70
Mazurka for Two Dead Men (Cela)
See *Mazurca para dos muertos*
"M.B." (Brodsky) **36**:81
M.C. Higgins, the Great (Hamilton) **26**:149-52, 154, 157
McAuslan in the Rough (Fraser) **7**:106
The McBain Brief (Hunter) **31**:228
McCabe and Mrs. Miller (Altman) **16**:21-2, 25-6, 28-31, 35, 39, 41; **116**:3, 6-9, 11, 13-14, 17, 20, 22-3, 31, 37, 39-42, 44, 46, 48, 59, 65, 67, 72, 74
McCarthy and His Enemies: The Record and Its Meaning (Buckley) **37**:57
"McCarthy and the Intellectuals" (Fiedler) **4**:163
McCartney (McCartney) **12**:371; **35**:278-80, 285, 287
McCartney II (McCartney) **35**:287-89
"McCrimmon and the Blue Moonstones" (MacLean) **63**:269
"McDuff on the Mound" (Coover) **87**:25
"McKane's Falls" (Merrill) **13**:376
The McPhee Reader (McPhee) **36**:297
"McSorley's Wonderful Saloon" (Mitchell) **98**:165
McSorley's Wonderful Saloon (Mitchell) **98**:153-60, 164-65, 168-69, 171-73, 175, 177, 180-81, 183, 185
"M.D." (Fearing) **51**:114
"Me Again" (Rexroth) **112**:386, 400
Me Again: Uncollected Writings of Stevie Smith (Smith) **25**:420-22; **44**:435-36, 441, 444
"Me and Baby" (Castillo) **151**:20
"Me and Bobby McGee" (Kristofferson) **26**:267-70
"Me and Julio Down by the Schoolyard" (Simon) **17**:461, 465-66
"Me and Miss Mandible" (Barthelme) **46**:35, 40; **59**:247; **115**:65-7, 79
"Me and My Baby View the Eclipse" (Smith) **73**:357
Me and My Baby View the Eclipse (Smith) **73**:353, 356-59
Me and My Bones (Gallant) **17**:129-30
"Me and My Town" (Sondheim) **30**:387
"Me and Paul" (Nelson) **17**:303
"Me and the Girls" (Coward) **29**:141; **51**:74
"Me and the Runner" (MacEwen) **55**:164
"Me and the World" (Simmons) **43**:410
"Me and You and a Dog Named Blue" (Corcoran) **17**:78
"Me Bredda" (Bennett) **28**:29, 31
"Me Cago en la Leche (Robert Jordan in Nicaragua)" (Boyle) **90**:45
"Me, Hood!" (Spillane) **13**:528
Me, I'm Afraid of Virginia Woolf (Bennett) **77**:85-6, 88-9
Me Me Me Me Me: Not a Novel (Kerr) **35**:249-50, 252
Me, Myself, and I (Ayckbourn) **33**:50
Me Myself I (Armatrading) **17**:10-11
"Me Tarzan" (Harrison) **129**:166, 175
Mea Cuba (Cabrera Infante) **120**:71-72, 74-75, 77-82
"Mea culpa" (Sondheim) **30**:398
Mea culpa (Céline) **47**:79; **124**:57, 88
"The Meadow" (Carver) **55**:275
"Mead's Theory of Subjectivity" (Habermas) **104**:88
"A Meal" (Atwood) **4**:27
"The Meal" (Olds) **85**:294
"Mean Drunk Poem" (Thesen) **56**:418-19
"Mean Mother Mary" (Carroll) **35**:77
Mean Rufus (Smith) **22**:389
Mean Spirit (Hogan) **73**:160-64
Mean Streets (Scorsese) **20**:324-26, 337-38, 340; **89**:219-23, 231-32, 235-36, 239-40, 243-45, 247-49, 252-56, 260-61, 266-67
"The Meaning of a Literary Idea" (Trilling) **24**:456, 460-61
The Meaning of Contemporary Realism (Lukacs) **24**:320
The Meaning of Culture (Powys) **7**:349; **125**:297, 302
"The Meaning of Life" (Keillor) **115**:283
The Meaning of Meaning (Richards) **24**:370, 375, 385, 389, 400-01
"A Meaning of Robert Lowell" (Carruth) **84**:121, 124
"The Meaning of Simplicity" (Ritsos) **31**:331
Meaning of the Stars (Ivask)
See *Tähtede tähendus*
The Meaning of Treason (West) **9**:561, 563; **31**:455, 458; **50**:394-95, 398, 401, 404-06, 408, 410
"The Meaning of Western Defense" (Mailer) **111**:104
"Meaning the Meaning: Arakawa's Critique of Space" (Bernstein) **142**:9
"A Meaningless Institution" (Ginsberg) **36**:182
"Meaningless Midnight Musings" (McFadden) **48**:244, 250
"Meaningless Story" (Valenzuela) **31**:437-38

Meanings (Walcott) **25**:454; **76**:282
Means of Evil (Rendell) **28**:386-87
"Means of Protection" (Watkins) **43**:450
"Meant for You" (Wilson) **12**:641
"Measles" (Ashbery) **77**:42
"The Measure" (Lane) **25**:289
"The Measure" (Silkin) **6**:498
"Measure" (Williams) **13**:604
The Measure (Lane) **25**:288-89
The Measure of Man (Krutch) **24**:280
"The Measure of Poetry" (Nemerov) **9**:396
Measure of the Year (Haig-Brown) **21**:142
Measure with Metric (Branley) **21**:21
Measures (MacCaig) **36**:282, 288
"Measures for G.C." (Hoffman) **6**:243
"Measuring Death" (Mahapatra) **33**:281
"Meat" (Gunn) **81**:178
Meat (Wiseman) **20**:476-77
Meat Air: Poems, 1957-1969 (Loewinsohn) **52**:284-85
Meat Science Essays (McClure) **6**:318, 320; **10**:332
Mécanique jongleuse (Brossard) **115**:104-05
La meccanica (Gadda) **11**:215
The Mechanical Bride: Folklore of Industrial Man (McLuhan) **37**:252, 254, 256, 259-61, 263; **83**:354, 359, 361, 363, 366, 369, 373
"A Mechanic's Life" (Masters) **48**:224
"The Mechanics of Good Times" (Kauffman) **42**:252
"Mechanism" (Ammons) **108**:3, 4
"Les méchins" (Ferron) **94**:103
"Médaille d'or" (Soupault) **68**:406
"Les medailles flottent-elles sur la mer?" (Carrier) **78**:71
"Medal from Jerusalem" (Shaw) **7**:411; **23**:396; **34**:370
"Medallion" (Plath) **11**:446; **111**:199, 203
"Medallion" (Pound) **112**:313-14
"Medallions" (Davie) **8**:166
Meddle (Pink Floyd) **35**:311, 313
"Medea" (Raine) **45**:339
Medea (Anouilh)
See *Médée*
Medea (Fo) **32**:174-76
Medea (Jeffers) **54**:247; **11**:306, 310
Medea (Pasolini) **20**:265-68; **106**:226, 256
Medea:a Sex-War Opera (Harrison) **129**:169, 180, 182-83, 194, 203, 211, 225
Medea at Kolchis (Duncan) **55**:293
Medea: Stimmen (Wolf) **150**:333, 335, 337, 347, 350-52, 354-56
Médée (Anouilh) **8**:22; **13**:16-17, 20; **40**:51, 57; **50**:278
"Media Event" (Baxter) **45**:51, 53; **78**:17
"Media Man" (Vinge)
See "Mediaman"
"Media Vitae" (Duncan) **1**:82
"Mediaman" (Vinge) **30**:410
Le Médianoche amoureux (Tournier) **95**:377, 382, 390
"Mediation at Spring Hill" (Raine) **32**:349
Medical Center Lab (Berger) **12**:41
"A Medical Unit and a Half" (Aksyonov) **101**:9
"Medici Slot Machine" (Simic) **130**:328
A Medicine for Melancholy (Bradbury) **3**:86; **15**:85; **42**:32
Medicine in Action (Hyde) **21**:172
"The Medicine Man" (Caldwell) **14**:96
"Medicine Man" (DeMarinis) **54**:98, 102
Medicine River (King) **89**:79-82, 84, 86-91, 93-4, 97, 101
"Medicine Song" (Allen) **84**:39
"The Medieval" (Hall) **51**:175
Medieval Scenes (Duncan) **15**:187
"Medievalism" (Pound) **4**:410
Medina (McCarthy) **14**:358-59
El medio pollito (Ferré) **139**:153, 156
Una meditación (Benet) **28**:18-20, 22-3
"The Meditated Death" (Ungaretti) **7**:485
"Meditation" (Aldington) **49**:6
A Meditation (Benet)
See *Una meditación*
"Meditation Addressed to Hugh MacDiarmid" (Smith) **64**:397
"Meditation at Lagunitas" (Hass) **18**:210, 213; **39**:148; **99**:130, 144-46
"Meditation at Oyster River" (Roethke) **1**:291; **19**:399; **46**:364; **101**:289, 299, 306, 313-14, 319
"A Meditation in Seven Days" (Ostriker) **132**:318, 328
"Meditation in Summer and Sleeplessness" (Wright) **146**:360
"Meditation in Sunlight" (Sarton) **49**:310
"the Meditation of Simeon" (Auden) **123**:57
"Meditation on a Bone" (Hope) **51**:213
"Meditation on a Constable Picture" (Betjeman) **6**:67
"Meditation on Form and Measure" (Wright) **119**:186, 188
"A Meditation on John Constable" (Tomlinson) **13**:547; **45**:392
"Meditation on Play, Thoughts on Death" (Collins) **44**:36-7
"Meditation on Saviors" (Jeffers) **54**:237
"Meditation on Song and Structure" (Wright) **119**:186-87
Meditation on Statistical Method (Cunningham) **31**:97-9, 102
"Meditation on the BMT" (Blackburn) **43**:63
"Meditation on the Threshold" (Castellanos) **66**:60
Meditation on Violence (Deren) **16**:252-54; **102**:28, 31, 38, 40, 42-3, 48-9
"Meditation Two" (Eberhart) **11**:179
"Meditations" (Eberhart) **11**:178
"Meditations for a Savage Child" (Rich) **7**:373; **11**:477
"Meditations in an Emergency" (O'Hara) **5**:324; **78**:355
Meditations in an Emergency (O'Hara) **13**:424; **78**:347
Meditations in Green (Wright) **33**:467-70
"Meditations in Time of Divorce" (Simmons) **43**:412
"Meditations of an Old Woman" (Roethke) **3**:433; **8**:455, 459-60; **11**:486; **19**:398-99; **101**:288-89, 291, 304, 310, 312-13, 318-19, 327, 329-31, 333-34
"Meditations on History" (Williams) **89**:327, 343
"Meditations on Romans" (Garrett) **3**:192
"Meditations on the Problem of the Nation" (Herbert) **43**:189
"Meditations upon Survival" (Klein) **19**:262
"Mediterranean" (Senghor) **54**:392
"The Mediterranean" (Tate) **2**:429; **4**:535, 539; **6**:525; **9**:522; **11**:522, 525, 527
Mediterranean Cities (Denby) **48**:82-5
"Mediterraneo" (Montale) **7**:222, 227; **18**:339
"The Medium" (Voigt) **54**:431
The Medium (Weiss) **3**:516; **14**:557
The Medium Is the Massage: An Inventory of Effects (McLuhan) **37**:262-64; **83**:362, 366
"Medium Loser and Small Winner" (Brooke-Rose) **40**:106
"The Medium of Fiction" (Gass) **132**:165
"Medley" (Bambara) **88**:22-23, 28
"Medley" (McCartney) **35**:281
"Medusa" (Bogan) **46**:81-3, 86, 90; **93**:64, 67-9, 81, 85-7, 90, 93, 96
"Medusa" (Dove) **81**:152
"Medusa" (Plath) **5**:345; **9**:427; **11**:449; **17**:369; **51**:340; **111**:207
"Medusa" (Smith) **43**:422
The Medusa and the Snail: More Notes of a Biology Watcher (Thomas) **35**:410-12, 415
"Medusa's Ankles" (Byatt) **136**:163
Les Méduses, ou les orties de mer (Tchicaya) **101**:355
"Mee Too Buggi" (Cendrars) **106**:190
Meek Heritage (Sillanpaa) **19**:417
Meet John Doe (Capra) **16**:156, 160-62, 166
Meet Marlon Brando (Maysles and Maysles) **16**:443-44
Meet Me at Tamerlane's Tomb (Corcoran) **17**:74-5
Meet Me at the Morgue (Macdonald) **41**:271-72
Meet Me in St. Louis (Benson) **17**:48
Meet Me in the Green Glen (Warren) **1**:356; **4**:579, 581; **8**:540
Meet My Father (Ayckbourn) **33**:44
Meet the Austins (L'Engle) **12**:346-47, 350
Meet the Beatles (Lennon and McCartney) **12**:382
Meet the Maitlands (Streatfeild) **21**:417
Meet the Malones (Weber) **12**:631
Meet Whiplash Willie (Wilder)
See *The Fortune Cookie*
"The Meeting" (Abse) **29**:15
"The Meeting" (Bogan) **93**:81
"The Meeting" (Borges) **1**:39; **2**:77; **10**:67; **48**:33
"The Meeting" (Cortázar)
See "Reunión"
"The Meeting" (Dixon) **52**:97
"The Meeting" (Ewart) **46**:152-53
"Meeting" (Hughes) **9**:281
"Meeting" (Merwin) **88**:192
"A Meeting" (Montague) **13**:391
"A Meeting" (Nabokov) **1**:243
"A Meeting" (O'Faolain) **32**:341
"Meeting" (Pasternak) **63**:313
"Meeting" (Peterkin) **31**:308
"The Meeting" (Sillitoe) **57**:391, 396; **148**:159, 198
"Meeting, 1944" (Szirtes) **46**:395
"Meeting a Person" (Enright) **8**:204
The Meeting at Telgte (Grass) **22**:195-97; **32**:204
A Meeting by the River (Isherwood) **1**:157; **9**:294; **11**:300; **14**:280, 282, 285-86; **44**:397-98, 402
"Meeting Cheever" (Ryan) **65**:209, 214-15
Meeting Ends: A Play (Warner) **14**:553
"A meeting in Nowa Huta" (Rozewicz) **139**:273
"A Meeting in Rauch" (Bioy Casares) **88**:92, 94-5
"A Meeting in the Dark" (Ngũgĩ wa Thiong'o) **36**:311-12, 317
"The Meeting in the Kitchen, 1740" (Schnackenberg) **40**:379
"A Meeting in Valladolid" (Burgess) **62**:139
"Meeting Mrs. Milllar" (Aickman) **57**:5
"A Meeting of Eyes in Mexico" (Ferlinghetti) **111**:60
"A Meeting of Minds" (Lorde) **71**:256
"Meeting of Strangers" (Birney) **6**:74-5
"Meeting Place" (Ammons) **57**:50-1
Meeting Place (Mosley) **43**:312, 321
"Meeting Point" (MacNeice) **53**:231
The Meeting Point (Clarke) **8**:142; **53**:85, 87-9, 93-5
"Meeting the British" (Muldoon) **72**:276
Meeting the British (Muldoon) **72**:273-74, 277-79
"Meeting the Folks" (Grenville) **61**:152
"Meeting the Man Who Warns Me" (Bly) **10**:60
"Meeting the Mountains" (Snyder) **5**:393
"Meeting Together of Poles and Latitudes: in Prospect" (Avison) **97**:70, 76, 80, 90
"A Meeting with Medusa" (Clarke) **13**:148; **18**:107; **35**:123
Mefisto (Banville) **46**:31-33; **118**:7, 10-12, 15, 22, 24-25, 28, 33, 38, 47
Mefisto (Ellison) **139**:143
"Mefisto in Onyx" (Ellison) **139**:144
Meg (Gee) **29**:178-79
La meglio gioventù (Pasolini) **37**:348; **106**:227, 231, 243
Me-horei Kol Zeh Mistater Osher Gadol (Amichai) **9**:24; **22**:30; **116**:89-90, 92
Meier Helmbrecht (Hochwälder) **36**:235-38
Le meilleur de la vie (Gascar) **11**:222

Mein Jahr in der Niemandsbucht (Handke) **134**:174, 179, 180-81, 183
"Mein Judentum" (Hildesheimer) **49**:179
"Mein Karren knarrt nicht mehr" (Celan) **82**:52
Mein Name sei Gantenbein (Frisch) **3**:167; **9**:218; **18**:163; **32**:188-90, 192; **44**:183-85, 188-90, 193, 197, 199
"Mein Onkel Fred" (Boell) **72**:72
"Mein teures Bein" (Boell) **27**:65
"Mein trauriges Gesicht" (Boell) **27**:59; **72**:70-1
"Mein verdrossenes Gesicht" (Lenz) **27**:245
"Mein Vogel" (Bachmann) **69**:41
"Meiosis" (Auden) **43**:21, 27
"Mejdoub" (Bowles) **19**:59
"Los mejor calzados" (Valenzuela)
See "The Best Shod"
Los Mejores cuentos de Donoso (Donoso)
See *Cuentos*
"Meksikanskij romansero" (Brodsky) **50**:131; **100**:53
"Melancholia" (Bly) **10**:56
Melancholia (Sartre)
See *La nausée*
Melancholy Baby (O'Faolain) **47**:330
"Melancholy Breakfast" (O'Hara) **13**:424
Mélancolie nord (Rio) **43**:354-55
"Melancthon" (Moore) **47**:266
"Mélange adultère de tout" (Eliot) **3**:140
Meles Vulgaris (Boyle) **19**:68
"Mélie and the Bull" (Ferron) **94**:123
Melissa (Caldwell) **28**:59
"Melissa & Smith" (Shange) **126**:362
The Melodeon (Swarthout) **35**:403-04
"Melodic Trains" (Ashbery) **13**:30, 35-6; **15**:30
Melodien, der blev vaek (Abell) **15**:1
Melodrama Play (Shepard) **4**:489; **6**:497; **17**:436, 438, 441, 443; **41**:412
Mélodrame (Jouve) **47**:209-10
"Melografiadas" (Ferré) **139**:181-82
"Melon" (Barnes) **141**:58, 69
"The Melongene" (Wilbur) **110**:383
"The Melting Pot" (Randall) **135**:389
Melville Goodwin, U.S.A. (Marquand) **10**:329
"Melville's Marginalia" (Howe) **152**:183, 185, 193, 197, 199-200, 210-12, 221-25, 227-30
"Melville's Withdrawal" (Updike) **34**:290, 293
The Member for the Marsh (Mayne) **12**:386
"Member of the European Parliament" (Durcan) **70**:152
"A Member of the Family" (Spark) **40**:402
The Member of the Wedding (McCullers) **1**:208, 210; **4**:344-45; **10**:338; **12**:410-18, 420-24, 426, 430, 432; **48**:230-31, 234-36, 240; **100**:242-46, 249, 251-56, 260, 263, 270
"Membrane of Air" (Buckley) **57**:136
Memed, My Hawk (Kemal) **14**:299-300
"Memento" (Gotlieb) **18**:191
"Memento" (Spender) **41**:420
Memento mori (Spark) **2**:414-17; **3**:464-66; **5**:399; **13**:520-21, 525; **18**:501, 505-06; **40**:395-96, 400, 402; **94**:326-328, 332, 336, 353
Memleketimden ınsan manzaralari (Hikmet) **40**:244-45, 247, 251
Memnoch the Devil (Rice) **128**:306-07, 310-13
"Memo" (Fearing) **51**:106
"Memo" (Jordan) **114**:146, 152
"Memo from Purgatory" (Ellison) **139**:129
"Memo from Turner" (Jagger and Richard) **17**:226
"Memo: Preliminary Draft of a Prayer to God the Father" (Ciardi) **40**:161; **44**:382
"Memo to the 21st Century" (Appleman) **51**:15
"Memoir" (Ellison)
See "Memoir: I Have No Mouth, and I Must Scream"
"Memoir" (Pinsky) **94**:308
"Memoir" (Van Duyn) **63**:444-45; **116**:412
"Memoir: I Have No Mouth, and I Must Scream" (Ellison) **139**:129, 136-9
"Memoir of a One-Armed Harp Teacher" (Ciardi) **129**:40, 44, 49
Memoir of a Russian Punk (Coles)
See *Podrostak Savenko*
Mémoires d'Hadrien (Yourcenar) **19**:480-82; **38**:455-61, 463-64; **50**:361-65; **87**:383, 385-86, 390, 394-97, 401, 403-06, 409, 411-12, 417-19, 421, 423-24, 427-28, 431-32
Mémoires d'une jeune fille rangée (Beauvoir) **1**:19; **4**:48; **8**:58; **31**:42; **44**:343, 345, 349-50; **50**:389; **71**:59, 76, 80-1; **124**:144-46, 167
Mémoires intérieurs (Mauriac) **56**:218
Memoirs (Amis) **129**:12-13, 19, 25
Memoirs (Neruda)
See *Confieso que he vivido: memorias*
Memoirs (Sassoon)
See "Memoirs of an Infantry Officer"
Memoirs (Williams) **7**:545-46; **8**:547-48; **11**:573-75; **15**:581, 583; **19**:470, 472; **39**:445, 449-51, 453; **45**:443-44, 446, 452-53, 455; **111**:390-91
Memoirs, 1921-1941 (Ehrenburg) **18**:135, 137
Memoirs and Opinions (Tate) **9**:521; **11**:526
Memoirs Found in a Bathtub (Lem) **8**:344; **15**:327; **40**:291, 300; **149**:114, 159, 165, 243-48, 250-53, 255, 260, 264, 272-73, 275, 285
Memoirs from a Young Republic (Keneally) **117**:240-41
Memoirs from the Time of Immaturity (Gombrowicz)
See *Pamiętnik okresu dojrzewania*
"Memoirs in Oxford" (Prince) **22**:339-40
Memoirs of a Dutiful Daughter (Beauvoir)
See *Mémoires d'une jeune fille rangée*
Memoirs of a Fox-Hunting Man (Sassoon) **36**:387, 390, 394, 396-97; **130**:178, 194-95, 199-200, 202, 211-12, 223, 225-28
Memoirs of a Peon (Sargeson) **31**:365-67, 371, 373-74
"Memoirs of a Private Detective" (Hammett) **19**:195
The Memoirs of a Shy Pornographer (Patchen) **18**:392-93
Memoirs of a Space Traveler: Further Reminiscences of Ijon Tichy (Lem) **40**:294, 296; **149**:150-51, 165, 264, 273, 277-78
Memoirs of a Survivor (Lessing) **6**:299-305; **10**:315-16; **15**:333; **40**:312; **94**:253, 258, 261, 264, 282-83, 286
Memoirs of a Victorian Gentleman: William Makepeace Thackeray (Forster) **149**:66, 77
Memoirs of an Anti-Semite (Rezzori) **25**:382-85
Memoirs of an Ex-Prom Queen (Shulman) **2**:395
"Memoirs of an Infantry Officer" (Sassoon) **36**:387, 392, 394-97; **130**:178, 184, 194-97, 199-200, 202, 207, 211, 228-29
Memoirs of an Invisible Man (Saint) **50**:73-6
The Memoirs of Christopher Columbus (Marlowe) **70**:352
The Memoirs of George Sherston (Sassoon) **36**:388, 394, 396
The Memoirs of Hadrian (Yourcenar)
See *Mémoires d'Hadrien*
Memoirs of Hecate County (Wilson) **1**:373; **2**:474-75, 478; **8**:551
Memoirs of Many in One, by Alex Xenophon Demirjian Gray (White) **65**:275, 278, 282; **69**:410-13
Memoirs of Montparnasse (Glassco) **9**:236
The Memoirs of Solar Pons (Derleth) **31**:137-38
"The Memoirs of Stefan Czarniecki" (Gombrowicz) **49**:127
"Memoranda" (Dickey) **28**:117
The Memorandum (Havel) **25**:219-24, 226, 229; **58**:237, 239-40, 242, 244-45; **65**:419, 421, 429, 432, 435, 439-40; **123**:172-73, 177, 181, 186-87, 197-99, 204-05, 208
"Memorial" (Munro) **10**:357
"Memorial" (Sanchez) **116**:294, 325-26
"Memorial II" (Lorde) **71**:260
"The Memorial, 1914-1918" (Blunden) **56**:30, 39, 44-5
"Memorial Address" (Heidegger) **24**:266
"Memorial Day" (Berrigan) **37**:46
"Memorial Day" (Cameron) **44**:33, 35
"Memorial Day" (Lowell) **4**:304
"Memorial Day" (Simon) **26**:412-13
"Memorial Day" (Voigt) **54**:433
"Memorial Day, 1950" (O'Hara) **13**:423, 426-27; **78**:344, 348, 373-74
Memorial Day, 1950 (O'Hara) **13**:423
Memorial de Isla Negra (Neruda) **5**:303-04; **7**:261; **9**:399; **28**:312, 314-16; **62**:323, 325-26
"Memorial de Tlatelolco" (Castellanos) **66**:46, 53
Memorial do convento (Saramago) **119**:153-54, 164
"Memorial for the City" (Auden) **2**:23; **14**:27, 29; **123**:35, 38
"The Memorial Fountain" (Fisher) **25**:158, 160
The Memorial: Portrait of a Family (Isherwood) **1**:155-56; **9**:293; **11**:295, 297-300; **14**:280-82; **44**:396-97, 400-03
"Memorial Rain" (MacLeish) **68**:284-85, 293
"Memorial to Ed Bland" (Brooks) **49**:32
Memorial to Isla Negra (Neruda)
See *Memorial de Isla Negra*
"Memorial to Luthuli" (Paton) **10**:388
"Memorial Wreath" (Randall) **135**:387
Memorials of a Tour in Yorkshire (Simmons) **43**:408
Memorias de Ponce (Ferré) **139**:193
Memorias: Infancia, adolescencia y còmo sehace un escritor (Bioy Casares) **88**:95
Memorias inmemoriales (Azorín) **11**:27
Memories (Thomas)
See *Memories and Hallucinations*
Memories and Hallucinations (Thomas) **132**:357, 382
"memories for no one" (Young Bear) **94**:363
Memories of a Catholic Girlhood (McCarthy) **14**:363; **59**:290-93
"Memories of a Cross-Country Man" (Rooke) **25**:391
"Memories of a Lost War" (Simpson) **149**:345, 350
Memories of an Auctioneer (Auchincloss) **18**:24
Memories of Dying (Hughes) **48**:183-84
"Memories of Earth" (Morgan) **31**:274, 276
Memories of Happy Days (Green) **77**:276
"Memories of the Depression Years" (Justice) **102**:255
Memories of the Ford Administration (Updike) **139**:375
Memories of the Future (Horgan) **53**:181-82
"Memories of the Linen Room" (Raine) **103**:188
"Memories of West Street and Lepke" (Lowell) **11**:326-27; **15**:343; **124**:303
"Memories of Youghal" (Trevor) **116**:338
"Memory" (Bogan) **46**:83; **93**:64
"A Memory" (Hughes) **37**:176
"A Memory" (Lavin) **4**:282; **18**:305; **99**:312
"Memory" (Merwin) **18**:333-34
"Memory?" (Plath) **11**:449
"Memory" (Queneau) **42**:337
"Memory" (Raine) **32**:349
"Memory" (Roethke) **101**:329
"A Memory" (Welty) **14**:563; **33**:414; **105**:297, 334, 378-79
Memory (Jensen) **37**:191-92
"Memory, 1930" (Creeley) **36**:122; **78**:152
"Memory Albums" (Stuart) **8**:507
A Memory, and Other Stories (Lavin) **4**:282
Memory Box (Forster) **149**:106
Memory Gardens (Creeley) **78**:153-54, 158, 160, 162
"Memory Green" (MacLeish) **68**:273, 286
"Memory Hotel" (Jagger and Richard) **17**:236, 242
"Memory of a Porch" (Justice) **102**:252

"A Memory of Asia" (Ghose) **42**:185
A Memory of Asia: New and Selected Poems (Ghose) **42**:185
The Memory of Birds in Times of Revolution (Breytenbach) **126**:101
"The Memory of Elena" (Forché) **83**:211, 214, 216, 218-19
Memory of Fire (Galeano) **72**:131, 133-37, 139-41, 143-44
Memory of Fire: Century of the Wind (Galeano) **72**:135-38, 140
Memory of Fire: Faces and Masks (Galeano) **72**:132-37
Memory of Fire: Genesis (Galeano) **72**:131-38
A Memory of Murder (Bradbury) **42**:42
The Memory of Old Jack (Berry) **4**:59; **6**:62; **8**:85-6; **46**:73
"A Memory of Ottawa" (Levine) **54**:300
Memory of Snow and of Dust (Breytenbach) **126**:78-9, 90-1, 94
A Memory of Two Mondays (Miller) **1**:216, 219; **6**:329; **15**:373
A Memory of War (Fenton) **32**:166-67
"Memory of Wilmington" (Kinnell) **29**:285
"Memory pieces for Baby Jane" (Broumas) **73**:10-11
"Memory Unsettled" (Gunn) **81**:180, 188
Memos from Purgatory (Ellison) **13**:205
"Memphis" (Gilchrist) **48**:120-22
"Memphis" (Mason) **82**:251, 258; **154**:253
"Memphis Blues" (Brown) **23**:96; **59**:262,265
Me-mushiri Kouchi (Oe) **86**:226-27, 240-41
"Men" (Jong) **6**:267
"Men" (MacLeish) **68**:273, 283, 287-88, 293
Men and Angels (Gordon) **128**:96-99, 101-02, 111, 113-14, 116, 119-20, 122-23, 126-28, 140, 144, 149
"Men and Brethren" (Cozzens) **4**:113, 115; **11**:128, 131, 133
Men and Brethren (Cozzens) **92**:179-80, 182, 184, 198, 201
Men and Gods (Vittorini)
See *Uomini e no*
Men and Gods (Warner) **45**:439
Men and Wives (Compton-Burnett) **15**:138; **34**:500
"Men and Women" (Dabydeen) **34**:149
"Men and Women" (Seidel) **18**:475
Men at Arms (Waugh) **8**:543; **19**:461-62; **27**:471-72; **107**:371, 406
"Men at Forty" (Justice) **102**:261
Men at War (Waugh) **107**:406
Men Call It Dawn (Bunuel)
See *Cela s'appelle l'aurore*
"Men Fishing in the Arno" (Jennings) **131**:239
The Men from P.I.G. and R.O.B.O.T. (Harrison) **42**:202-03
"Men Have Forgotten God" (Solzhenitsyn) **78**:402
Men in Battle (Bessie) **23**:59-60
Men in Dark Times (Arendt) **98**:9, 11, 45, 52-3
The Men in the Jungle (Spinrad) **46**:383
Men in White (Kingsley) **44**:230-32, 234, 237-38
Men Inside (Bogosian) **45**:62; **141**:80-1, 84-5
"Men Loved Wholly beyond Wisdom" (Bogan) **39**:387; **46**:83, 86; **93**:64, 66, 69, 93
"Men Marry What They Need; I Marry You" (Ciardi) **44**:380; **129**:56
"Men Must Die" (Woolrich) **77**:403
Men of Distinction (Condon) **100**:93
"Men of Good Fortune" (Reed) **21**:306
"Men of Good Will" (MacNeice) **53**:231
Men of Good Will (Romains)
See *Les hommes de bonne volonté*
Men of Maize (Asturias)
See *Hombres de maíz*
"Men of Maize: Myth as Time and Language" (Dorfman) **77**:155
Men of Men (Smith) **33**:377-78
"Men of My Century Loved Mozart" (MacLeish) **68**:286
"Men of Our People" (Laurence) **50**:320, 322
Men of Stones (Warner) **45**:434-35, 437-40
"Men of the Great Man" (Cassity) **42**:98
Men of the Mountains (Stuart) **14**:513; **34**:373, 376
The Men of Tohoku (Ichikawa) **20**:181
Men on Bataan (Hersey) **40**:226; **81**:329, 332, 334-35; **97**:301, 303, 305, 310
"Men Running" (Cozzens) **92**:189
"Men Sign the Sea" (Graham) **29**:194, 198
"Men Suspected of Faggotry" (Donnell) **34**:159
"Men: The Man Who Ended His Story" (Wilson) **49**:413-16
The Men Who Treaded on the Tiger's Tail (Kurosawa) **119**:339, 342
"The Men with Long Faces" (Dobyns) **37**:78
Men Without Shadows (Sartre)
See *Morts sans sépulture*
Men without Women (Hemingway) **1**:143; **19**:211; **30**:180, 185, 192, 198-99; **39**:430; **44**:519
Men, Women, and Children (Sillitoe) **3**:449; **6**:500; **57**:392; **148**:158, 163-64, 167, 172
Men, Women, and Dogs (Thurber) **25**:436-37; **125**:412
"The Men XIX" (Neruda)
See "Los hombres XIX"
"Las ménades" (Cortázar) **33**:126-29
"Menage" (Luzi) **13**:353
"Ménage à trois" (Moss) **45**:292
"Menagerie" (Salinas) **90**:329
"Menagerie, a Child's Fable" (Johnson) **51**:234
Mencius on the Mind (Richards) **24**:390, 395
"A Mendicant Order" (Williams) **45**:444
"Mending Wall" (Frost) **3**:170, 174; **10**:197-98; **15**:240, 245-48; **26**:111-12, 116, 118, 123, 125-28
The Mendiola Trilogy (Goytisolo) **23**:185
"Mene, Mene, Tekel, Upharsin" (Cheever) **64**:65
"Menelaiad" (Barth) **2**:39; **3**:39, 41; **5**:50-1; **9**:70; **51**:23; **89**:6, 9-10, 15-17, 19, 21, 26-7, 45, 48, 54, 59, 61-3
Menéndez Pelayo, crítico literario (Alonso) **14**:20
"Meneseteung" (Munro) **95**:306, 311, 314, 320
"Los Menestrales" (Valenzuela) **104**:382, 387
Menfreya in the Morning (Hibbert) **7**:155
"Mengke" (Ding Ling) **68**:55, 64-5
Las meninas (Buero Vallejo) **15**:97-9, 101; **46**:95-6; **139**:7-10, 20, 33, 38, 43
"Menino de engenho" (Cabral de Melo Neto) **76**:160
"Meniscus" (Longley) **29**:295
Menneskebonn (Vesaas) **48**:404-05, 411
Men-of-War (O'Brian) **152**:277, 281
The Menorah (Škvorecký)
See *Sedmiramenný svícen*
Men's Business (Kroetz)
See *Männer Sache*
The Men's Club (Michaels) **25**:317-20
"Mens Creatrix" (Kunitz) **148**:67, 94, 98, 123
Men's Lives: The Surfmen and Baymen of the South Fork (Matthiessen) **64**:317-19, 325, 327
"The Men's Room in the College Chapel" (Snodgrass) **68**:397
"Men's Studies: 'Roman de la rose'" (Fulton) **52**:161
Der Mensch erscheint im Holozän (Frisch) **18**:162-63; **32**:192-94; **44**:192, 204, 206-07
Mensch Meier (Kroetz) **41**:240-41
Das Menschenbild der Seelenheilkunde (Frankl) **93**:194
"Menses" (Boland) **40**:98; **67**:44, 46; **113**:60-1, 109
Le mensonge (Sarraute) **10**:457; **31**:381-82; **80**:241
Mensonge: Structuralism's Hidden Hero (Bradbury) **61**:43-4, 47
Les mensonges (Mallet-Joris) **11**:355
"Menstruation at Forty" (Sexton) **4**:482; **123**:440
"Menthol Sweets" (Amichai) **116**:93
Mention My Name in Mombosa (Daly) **17**:89-90
"Menuchat kayits u-milam" (Amichai) **116**:133-35
"Menudo" (Carver) **53**:62; **55**:278
"Menus" (Cendrars) **106**:191
Menzogna e sortilegio (Morante) **47**:274-75, 279-80, 282-83
Le menzogne della notte (Bufalino) **74**:41
Mephisto (O'Hara) **78**:368-69
Le mépris (Godard) **20**:133, 143
"La mer" (Loewinsohn) **52**:283
Le meraviglie d'Italia (Gadda) **11**:215
Los mercaderes (Matute)
See *La trampa*
"O mercado a que os rios" (Cabral de Melo Neto) **76**:165
"The Mercedes" (Kavan) **82**:120
"A Mercedes Funeral" (Ngũgĩ wa Thiong'o) **7**:267; **36**:318
"Mercedes Hospital" (Bishop) **32**:44
"The Mercenaries" (Hemingway) **39**:399
"A Mercenary" (Ozick) **7**:288; **62**:353-54; **155**:178, 183-84, 191
Mercenary (Anthony) **35**:40-1
The Merchant (Wesker) **42**:425-26, 428-30
"The Merchant of Bristol" (Foote) **75**:230
"The Merchant of Heaven" (Laurence) **13**:341
The Merchant of Regrets (Crommelynck)
See *Le marchand de regrets*
The Merchant of the Four Seasons (Fassbinder) **20**:105-08, 119
The Merchant of Yonkers: A Farce in Four Acts (Wilder) **82**:359, 376, 379
"The Merchant Princes" (Asimov) **26**:63
Merchanter's Luck (Cherryh) **35**:109
Mercian Hymns (Hill) **5**:184; **8**:293-94, 296-97; **18**:238-43; **45**:178-83, 185-88, 191
Mercier and Camier (Beckett) **6**:42-5; **9**:84; **14**:70; **18**:52; **29**:55-6; **59**:254
Merciful Disguises: Published and Unpublished Poems (Van Duyn) **3**:491-92; **7**:499; **63**:438-39, 443; **116**:402, 406, 408
"Mercy" (Broumas) **73**:15-16
"Mercy" (Dickey) **47**:96; **109**:267-69, 272
"Mercy" (Kunene) **85**:175
Mercy (Dworkin) **123**:78-81, 83, 85-7, 98, 100
"Mercy, Mercy Me" (Gaye) **26**:130-31, 133
Mercy of a Rude Stream (Roth) **104**:284-86, 289, 317-21, 323-24, 326-29
Mercy Street (Sexton) **53**:321-22
"Mercy, the Cat's Got into the Budget" (Perelman) **49**:258
Mere Christianity (Lewis) **6**:311; **14**:323; **27**:263, 265-66; **124**:196, 224-25, 229, 232, 235, 237, 244, 246
"La Mère Noel" (Tournier) **95**:368
Meredithian Sonnets (Fuller) **28**:150-51
"Merging Traffic" (Greenberg) **30**:166
"Mericans" (Cisneros) **69**:155
"The Meridian" (Celan)
See "Der Meridian"
"Der Meridian" (Celan) **53**:74, 83; **82**:51, 57
Meridian (Walker) **9**:557-58; **19**:452; **27**:449-51; **46**:424, 428, 431; **58**:404, 406, 410; **103**:357, 366-67, 373, 383, 385-90, 392, 394-95, 405, 412
"La meridiana" (Piccolo) **13**:440
Merlin (Nye) **13**:414; **42**:305-06, 308
Merlin and the Snake's Egg (Norris) **14**:388
Merlin Trilogy (Stewart) **35**:397
"The Mermaid" (Mueller) **51**:279-80
Mermaids and Ikons (MacEwen) **13**:358
Mermaids in the Basement: Poems for Women (Kizer) **39**:170; **80**:181-83, 185
"Mermaids on the Golf Course" (Highsmith) **42**:216
Mermaids on the Golf Course (Highsmith) **42**:215

"The Merman" (Hesse) **25**:260
"The Merman" (Muldoon) **32**:318-19; **72**:264
The Merman's Children (Anderson) **15**:14
"Merriggi e ombre" (Montale) **7**:228
Merrily We Go to Hell (Arzner) **98**:69-70, 76, 78-9, 91
"Merrily We Pentagon" (Baker) **31**:31
Merrily We Roll Along (Hart and Kaufman) **33**:259-60, 263, 266; **66**:175, 182, 188-89
Merrily We Roll Along (Sondheim) **30**:399-403; **39**:174; **147**:227-28, 242-43, 263
The Merry Month of May (Jones) **3**:261-62; **10**:292; **39**:406-07, 412
The Merry Vineyard (Zuckmayer)
See *Der Fröliche Weinberg*
"Merry-Go-Round" (Crispin) **22**:112
"Merry-Go-Round" (Day Lewis) **10**:130-31
"Merry-Go-Round" (Hughes) **35**:218
The Merry-Go-Round (Maugham) **15**:365, 370; **93**:229-30
The Merry-Go-Round (Van Vechten) **33**:385
The Merry-Go-Round in the Sea (Stow) **23**:433; **48**:357-58, 360
"Merry-go-round with White Swan" (Seifert) **93**:330
Mert and Phil (Burr) **6**:104-05
Merton of the Movies (Connelly) **7**:56
Merton of the Movies (Kaufman) **38**:257
Mes débuts (Morand) **41**:304
Mes propriétés (Michaux) **8**:392; **19**:313
"A mesa" (Cabral de Melo Neto) **76**:151
"Mescaline" (Ginsberg) **109**:325
"Mesh Cast for Mackerel" (Bunting) **39**:299
Meshes of the Afternoon (Deren) **16**:251-53; **102**:28-31, 35-47
Meshugah (Singer) **111**:346-47
"Mesmerism" (Pound) **48**:288
"Mesopotamia" (Carver) **53**:61
"Mesquakie Love Song" (Young Bear) **94**:373
"Mess" (King) **53**:212
"A Mess of Clams" (Mitchell) **98**:174
"Message" (Berryman) **3**:66; **25**:95
"The Message" (Boell)
See "Die Botschaft"
"Message" (Forché) **25**:171; **83**:214
"Le Message" (Senghor) **130**:241, 266
"The Message" (Senghor)
See "Le Message"
"Message" (Whalen) **29**:445
"A Message All Blackpeople Can Dig (& A Few Negroes Too)" (Madhubuti) **6**:313; **73**:199, 210
"Message Clear" (Morgan) **31**:275
Message for Posterity (Potter) **123**:231, 233
"Message for the Sinecurist" (Gallagher) **63**:125
Message from Malaga (MacInnes) **39**:351
"Message from Mars" (McGinley) **14**:365
"Message from the Sleeper at Hell's Mouth" (Ostriker) **132**:328
"Message in a Bottle" (Gordimer) **33**:180; **123**:114
"Message in a Bottle" (Police, The) **26**:364
"The Message in the Bottle" (Percy) **65**:257, 260
The Message in the Bottle: How Queer Man Is, How Queer Language Is, and What One Has to Do with the Other (Percy) **6**:400-01; **8**:438-41; **14**:416; **18**:396, 402; **47**:333-35, 338-39
"the message of crazy horse" (Clifton) **66**:82
"Message to a Black Soldier" (Madhubuti) **73**:208
"Messages" (Dickey) **47**:96
"Messages" (Senghor) **54**:410;
"The Messenger" (Gunn) **18**:201
"The Messenger" (Kinsella) **138**:113-15, 127-30, 136, 148, 162
"The Messenger" (Merton) **83**:390
"Messenger" (Smith) **22**:389; **42**:353
"The Messenger" (Steele) **45**:362
The Messenger (Kinsella) **138**:166
The Messenger (Wright) **49**:425-27, 430-31, 434
Messenger Huskuld (Vesaas)
See *Sendemann Huskuld*
"Messengers" (Glück) **7**:120
"Messengers" (Martin) **89**:118
Messengers of Day: The Memoirs of Anthony Powell (Powell) **10**:417; **31**:316, 319, 322
Messengers of God: Biblical Portraits and Legends (Wiesel) **11**:570; **37**:459
The Messengers Will Come No More (Fiedler) **13**:212
Messiah (Vidal) **6**:549; **10**:502, 504; **22**:435; **33**:406-07; **72**:387; **142**:322, 334
The Messiah of Stockholm (Ozick) **62**:345-49, 353-54, 356-57; **155**:131-32, 138, 156-59, 161, 167, 170, 182, 184-85, 190, 196-97, 202, 208-09, 222
Meşterul Manole (Blaga) **75**:64, 66
Město v slzách (Seifert) **34**:256; **44**:424; **93**:305, 308, 316, 318, 331, 338-39
"A Meta Physic in Things" (Bowering) **47**:19
"Metacommentary" (Jameson) **142**:251
"Metafantasia: The Possibilities of Science Fiction" (Lem) **40**:300; **149**:121-24
Metahistory: The Historical Imagination in Nineteenth-Century Europe (White) **148**:217, 219-20, 223-25, 227-28, 231-34, 237, 241, 244, 246-48, 250, 255, 257-58, 264-66, 271-72, 282-83, 286-91, 297, 303
The Metal Horde (Campbell) **32**:73
The Metal Man (Williamson) **29**:454, 456
"Metamorfosis de la hechicera" (Castellanos) **66**:46, 53
"Metamorphic Journal" (Levertov) **15**:338
"Metamorphoses" (Cheever) **64**:65
"Metamorphoses" (Fisher) **25**:161
"Metamorphoses, I / Moon" (Walcott) **76**:270
"Metamorphosis" (Glück) **44**:215
"Metamorphosis" (Longley) **29**:295
"Metamorphosis" (Moravia) **46**:282
"The Metamorphosis" (Oates) **108**:354
"Metamorphosis" (Porter) **33**:322
"Metamorphosis" (Sachs) **98**:322
"Metamorphosis" (Sandburg) **35**:356
"Metamorphosis" (Sitwell) **9**:494, 496; **67**:324-25, 335
"The Metamorphosis" (Tomlinson) **45**:393
Metamorphosis (Berkoff) **56**:14, 16, 23
"Metamorphosis of a Witch" (Castellanos)
See "Metamorfosis de la hechicera"
"Metaphor & Memory" (Ozick) **155**:126
Metaphor and Memory (Ozick) **155**:124-26, 129, 135, 187-88, 190-91, 196-98, 203, 226, 228
"Metaphor and Reality" (Zamora) **89**:393
"Metaphor as Mistake" (Percy) **8**:439
"Metaphors" (Paz) **119**:422
"Metaphors" (Plath) **111**:167
"The Metaphysical Amorist" (Cunningham) **31**:102
"The Metaphysical Horse" (Hearne) **56**:125, 127
"Metaphysical Pictures of the Thistle" (MacDiarmid) **63**:244
"Metaphysical Poems" (Gascoyne) **45**:153
"The Metaphysical Poets" (Eliot) **10**:172; **24**:167, 171-72, 178; **55**:346; **113**:218, 220
Metapolitics (Viereck) **4**:560
"Meta-Rhetoric" (Jordan) **114**:146
"Métase mi prieta, entre el durmiente y el silbatazo" (Poniatowska) **140**:332, 334
Metel (Leonov) **92**:250, 252, 260, 268-70, 277
"Metempsychosis" (Slessor) **14**:492
Meteor (Behrman) **40**:73-4, 76, 78, 82, 87-8
The Meteor (Duerrenmatt)
See *Der Meteor*
Der Meteor (Duerrenmatt) **102**:54, 56, 62
The Meteor (Dürrenmatt)
See *Der Meteor*
Der Meteor (Dürrenmatt) **8**:194; **15**:199, 201
Les Météores (Tournier) **95**:361-63, 368-69, 373, 376-77, 381-82
"The Meterological Lighthouse at O" (Raine) **103**:182, 193-94
"Meters and Memory" (Justice) **102**:263, 284
"Metho Drinker" (Wright) **53**:418
"The Method" (Williams) **148**:346, 351
"Method for Calling up Ghosts" (Purdy) **50**:238
Méthode de méditation (Bataille) **29**:38-9
The Methods of Maigret (Simenon)
See *Mon ami Maigret*
Methods of the Novel (Oe)
See *Shosetsu no hoho*
Methuselah's Children (Heinlein) **3**:225; **8**:275; **14**:249; **26**:169; **55**:302, 304
"Métier: Why I Don't Write Like Franz Kafka" (Wilson) **49**:414, 416
"Metric Blues" (Scott) **22**:376
"Metrical Exercises" (Aldington) **49**:10
"Le métro" (Carrier) **78**:58-9, 68
Metro: A Novel of the Moscow Underground (Kaletski) **39**:72-4
"Metro-Goldwyn-Mayer" (Schwartz) **45**:356
Metroland (Barnes) **42**:24-7; **141**:31, 33-5, 53, 61-2, 65, 67-70
"Metropolis" (Shapcott) **38**:398
Metropolis (Lang) **20**:201-03, 210, 213, 215; **103**:82-5, 95, 108-10, 112, 114, 117-20, 122-28
The Metropolis (Sinclair) **63**:346, 348
Metropolitan Life (Lebowitz) **11**:322; **36**:248-49
"The Metropolitan Railway" (Betjeman) **43**:44
"Mews Flat Mona" (Plomer) **4**:407
"The Mexican Connection" (Joel) **26**:214
"Mexican Divertimento" (Brodsky) **36**:81; **50**:125
"Mexican Divertissement" (Brodsky)
See "Mexican Divertimento"
"Mexican Games" (Hughes) **108**:323
"Mexican Movies" (Cisneros) **69**:153
"Mexican Romancero" (Brodsky)
See "Meksikanskij romansero"
The Mexican Stove (Condon) **100**:91, 102, 110
"A Mexican Tale" (Kaplan) **50**:55, 57
"The Mexican Trinity" (Porter) **101**:241
"The Mexican Woman" (Simpson) **32**:379-80; **149**:331, 334
"Mexicans Begin Jogging" (Soto) **32**:403; **80**:278, 297
"Mexico" (Bass) **79**:5, 11; **143**:3
"Mexico" (Gilchrist) **65**:349; **143**:295, 311, 314, 325, 329-30
Mexico (Michener) **109**:383, 386
"Mexico Age Four" (Salinas) **90**:322, 329
Mexico and the United States (Archer) **12**:19
Mexico Bay: A Novel of the Mid-Century (Horgan) **53**:186-88
Mexico City Blues (Kerouac) **29**:270-71
"Mexico Is a Foreign Country: Five Studies in Naturalism" (Warren) **13**:574
Mexico Mystique: The Coming Sixth World of Consciousness (Waters) **88**:349-51, 361, 364-65
Mexico Set (Deighton) **46**:130-31
"Mexico's Children" (Rodriguez) **155**:268, 296, 298, 302
The Mezzanine (Baker) **61**:2-5
Mezzotints (Miller) **14**:372-74
MF (Burgess) **2**:86-7; **4**:80-1, 83; **5**:85; **10**:87-8; **22**:75; **40**:115-18, 120; **62**:125; **81**:303, 307; **94**:40, 51
MFM (Sassoon)
See *Memoirs of a Fox-Hunting Man*
"Mi" (Tolson) **105**:262
Mi abuela fumaba puros y otros cuentos de Tierra Amarilla/My Grandma Smoked Cigars, and Other Tales of Tierra Amarilla (Ulibarrí) **83**:409, 414, 418
"Mi caballo blanco" (Ulibarrí) **83**:413
"Mi chiquita" (Guillén) **79**:245
"Mi Comadre Me Aconseja" (Castillo) **151**:11
Mí general! (Lopez y Fuentes) **32**:279-81

Mi idolatrado hijo sisí (Delibes) **18**:110
"Mi vida entera" (Borges) **44**:367
Mia (Beckman) **26**:87-9
Mia Alone (Beckman)
See *Mia*
Miami (Wasserstein) **90**:417
"Miami 2017" (Joel) **26**:215, 220, 222
Miami and the Siege of Chicago: An Informal History of the Republican and Democratic Conventions of 1968 (Mailer) **1**:192; **2**:263; **3**:314; **4**:323; **8**:370-72; **11**:344; **14**:351; **28**:256-57; **74**:225; **111**:103, 107
"Miami Beach" (Moss) **45**:291
"MIA's (Missing in Action and Other Atlantas)" (Sanchez) **116**:302, 305, 317-18
Mica Mountain Poems (Wild) **14**:580
"Michael" (Brown) **5**:79
Michael (Dreyer) **16**:260-62
"Michael Angelo Looks Up Not Sleeping" (Gustafson) **36**:216
Michael Collins (Jordan) **110**:309-10
Michael Scarlett (Cozzens) **11**:124, 128, 131; **92**:196-97
"Michael X and the Black Power Killings in Trinidad" (Naipaul) **18**:363; **105**:155, 157, 163-64
"Michael's Wife" (O'Connor) **14**:398
"Micheaux's Films" (Hooks) **94**:153
Michelangelo (Krleža)
See *Michelangelo Buonarroti*
Michelangelo Buonarroti (Krleža) **114**:166, 174
Michelet (Barthes) **24**:25-6, 33; **83**:67
Michelet par lui-même (Barthes)
See *Michelet*
"Michelle" (Lennon and McCartney) **12**:358-59; **35**:278
Michigan: A Bicentennial History (Catton) **35**:94
Mick and Mick (Leonard) **19**:281
Mick Jagger (Highwater) **12**:285
Mickelsson's Ghosts (Gardner) **28**:163-66; **34**:548
The Microcosm (Duffy) **37**:113-14
"Microcosmic God" (Sturgeon) **22**:410, 412; **39**:361, 364-65
"The Microscopic Army Ants of Corsica" (Acorn) **15**:10
Microserfs (Coupland) **133**:8, 10-12, 20
Microworlds: Writings on Science Fiction and Fantasy (Lem) **40**:299-300; **149**:168, 170, 213, 230, 232, 236, 285-86
"MidAmerica" (Urdang) **47**:399
Midaq Alley (Mahfouz)
See *Zuqaq al-Midaqq*
Midaq Alley (Mahfūz)
See *Zuqāq al-Midaqq*
"Midas" (Winters) **4**:593
The Midas Consequence (Ayrton) **7**:19-20
Midas oder Die schwarze Leinwand (Duerrenmatt) **102**:91
Midas of the Rockies: The Story of Stratton and Cripple Creek (Waters) **88**:351, 360, 362
"Mid-August at Sourdough Mountain Lookout" (Snyder) **5**:393; **9**:501; **120**:315, 354
"Mid-Autumn" (Butler) **81**:124-26
Midcentury (Dos Passos) **1**:79; **4**:132, 137; **15**:187; **25**:141, 143, 145-46; **34**:420, 422-23
Mid-Century American Poets (Ciardi) **129**:37, 45
"Mid-Day" (H. D.) **73**:119
"The Middle against Both Ends" (Fiedler) **4**:160
"Middle Age" (Beer) **58**:33
"Middle Age" (Lowell) **8**:351
The Middle Age of Mrs. Eliot (Wilson) **2**:471-73; **3**:536; **5**:514-15; **25**:461, 463-64; **34**:584
"The Middle Ages" (Haines) **58**:216
The Middle Ages (Gurney) **54**:216-17; **32**:220-21; **50**:178-79, 183-84
Middle Class (Millin) **49**:239
Middle Class Radicalism: The Social Bases of the British Campaign for Nuclear Disarmament (Parkin) **43**:338
"The Middle Drawer" (Calisher) **134**:7-8, 33
The Middle Ground (Drabble) **22**:125-28; **53**:122, 124, 126, 128-29; **129**:115-19, 134, 145, 148-49
The Middle Kingdom (Barrett) **150**:3, 8, 17
The Middle Mist (Renault) **3**:425
The Middle of a War (Fuller) **28**:152-53, 158
The Middle of My Tether (Epstein) **39**:465
"The Middle of Nowhere" (Wagoner) **3**:508
The Middle of the Journey (Trilling) **9**:530-31; **11**:540-42, 544
Middle of the Night (Chayefsky) **23**:112
The Middle of the Night (Mahfūz)
See *Qalb al-layl*
"The Middle of the Night: The Hands" (Kallman) **2**:222
"Middle Passage" (Hayden) **5**:168-69; **14**:240-41; **37**:153, 155, 157-58, 160
Middle Passage (Johnson) **65**:152-59
The Middle Passage; Impressions of Five Societies: British, French, and Dutch—in the West Indies and South America (Naipaul) **4**:371-72, 374; **13**:406; **18**:363; **37**:323; **105**:138, 147-51, 154, 159, 180
The Middle Sister (Duncan) **26**:100
"The Middle-Aged" (Rich) **7**:368; **36**:372; **125**:336
"The Middle-Aged Man" (Simpson) **149**:304, 348
"The Middle-Aged Man and the Gulf" (Hannah) **90**:137
The Middle-Aged Man on the Flying Trapeze: A Collection of Short Pieces (Thurber) **5**:438, 442; **125**:395, 397, 401
"The Middle-American Prose Style" (Cowley) **39**:460
A Middle-Class Education (Sheed) **4**:487; **10**:473; **53**:339
"The Middle-Class Housewife" (Highsmith) **102**:197
"Middle-Class Pastoral" (Rodriguez) **155**:279, 312, 333
"Middle-Class Poem" (Dunn) **36**:156
The Middleman (Ray)
See *Jana Aranya*
The Middleman, and Other Stories (Mukherjee) **53**:269-72; **115**:363-64, 366-67, 386-87, 389
"Middle-Sea and Lear-Sea" (Jones) **42**:241
"Middlesex" (Davie) **8**:164
"The Midget" (Levine) **5**:251; **14**:317; **118**:302
Midis gagnés (Tzara) **47**:387, 390
Midland in Stilfs (Bernhard) **32**:17; **61**:9
"The Mid-Life Crisis of Dionysus" (Keillor) **115**:286
"Midnight" (Wright) **53**:428
Midnight (Green)
See *Minuit*
Midnight All Day (Kureishi) **135**:304
"Midnight and I'm Not Famous Yet" (Hannah) **38**:232; **90**:126, 148, 151, 163
The Midnight Bell: A Love Story (Hamilton) **51**:184-86, 190, 194-95, 197-98
"Midnight Chippie's Lament" (Hughes) **35**:221
A Midnight Clear (Wharton) **37**:439-43
"The Midnight Club" (Strand) **71**:288
"Midnight Cowboy" (Herlihy) **6**:234-35
Midnight Express (Stone) **73**:362-65, 367, 369-70, 382
The Midnight Folk (Masefield) **11**:356
The Midnight Fox (Byars) **35**:73
Midnight in the Desert (Priestley) **34**:365
Midnight in the Garden of Good and Evil: A Savannah Story (Berendt) **86**:33-40
"Midnight in the Mirror World" (Leiber) **25**:303
Midnight Is a Place (Aiken) **35**:18
"Midnight Lady" (Gaye) **26**:135
Midnight Line (Savage) **40**:374
"Midnight Log" (Clash) **30**:48
Midnight Love (Gaye) **26**:135
The Midnight Love Feast (Tournier)
See *Le Médianoche amoureux*
"Midnight Magic" (Mason) **82**:245, 256; **154**:234, 240, 302-05
Midnight Magic (Mason) **154**:302
The Midnight Man (Estleman) **48**:104, 107
Midnight Mass (Bowles) **53**:39-40, 45
"Midnight Meat Train" (Barker) **52**:51, 53
A Midnight Moon at the Greasy Spoon (Piñero) **55**:317-18
Midnight Movie (Potter) **123**:279
Midnight Oil (Pritchett) **5**:352-53; **13**:466; **41**:335
"Midnight on the Bay" (Young) **17**:576
"Midnight Rambler" (Jagger and Richard) **17**:224, 227, 230, 235-36
"The Midnight Reader" (Gardner) **5**:133
"The Midnight Skaters" (Blunden) **56**:30, 33, 45-7, 52
"Midnight Turning Gray" (Matthiessen) **64**:321, 324-25
Midnight Turning Gray (Matthiessen) **64**:321
"Midnight Verses" (Akhmatova) **64**:13
Midnight Was My Cry: New and Selected Poems (Kizer) **15**:309; **80**:179-80
Midnight's Children (Rushdie) **23**:364, 366-69; **31**:353-60; **55**:216-19, 223-25, 253-54, 263; **59**:406, 410, 412, 415, 417, 432, 434, 445, 447-48, 450; **100**:287-88, 290, 292, 295-96, 304, 310, 312, 315-18, 322-24
"Midnite Blue" (Nyro) **17**:318
"Midpoint" (Updike) **7**:486; **23**:465, 474-75; **43**:430
Midpoint, and Other Poems (Updike) **2**:441; **3**:485, 487; **13**:558; **23**:474-75; **43**:431
Midquest: A Poem (Chappell) **40**:143-48; **78**:91-7, 102, 111-12, 114-15
"Midrash on Happiness" (Paley) **140**:245, 272, 287
Midsommardalen (Martinson) **14**:355
"Midsummer" (Glück) **81**:167
"Midsummer" (Kinsella) **138**:121
Midsummer (Walcott) **42**:415-18, 421, 423; **67**:344, 348-49, 358-60; **76**:275, 300
Midsummer Century (Blish) **14**:83, 86
"Midsummer Christmas" (Avison) **97**:117
A Midsummer Dance (Salama)
See *Juhannustanssit*
"Midsummer, England" (Walcott) **14**:550
"Midsummer in Town" (Beer) **58**:37
"Midsummer Meditations" (McGinley) **14**:366
Midsummer Night and Other Tales in Verse (Masefield) **11**:358
"Midsummer Night Madness" (O'Faolain) **7**:273-74
Midsummer Night Madness, and Other Stories (O'Faolain) **1**:259; **7**:275; **14**:402; **32**:340, 343; **70**:313, 315-16, 321
Midsummer Night's Dream in the Workhouse (Lagerkvist) **54**:278
A Midsummer Night's Sex Comedy (Allen) **52**:48
A Midsummer-Night's Dream (Brenton) **31**:67
"The Midway Song" (Mitchell) **12**:435
The Midwich Cuckoos (Wyndham) **19**:474-76
The Midwife (Hochhuth) **18**:254-55
"Mid-winter Snowfall in the Piazza Dante" (Wright) **146**:350
"The Midwives" (Enzensberger) **43**:144, 146
"El miedo" (Marqués) **96**:244
Miehen tie (Sillanpaa) **19**:417-18, 420
"Mientras dura vida, sobra el tiempo" (Forché) **25**:169
Miernes (Breytenbach) **23**:86
"Mies ei—Mitään, ei—Kukaan" (Haavikko) **34**:175
"La migala" (Arreola) **147**:27
The Mightiest Machine (Campbell) **32**:72, 74, 76
"A Mighty Trauma Is Our Beginning" (Spielberg) **6**:519

Mignon (Cain) **28**:49, 52-3
"Mignotta" (Pasolini) **37**:347
Migraine: Evolution of a Common Disorder (Sacks) **67**:296-97
Migraine: Understanding a Common Disorder (Sacks)
See *Migraine: Evolution of a Common Disorder*
"Migrant Swift" (Wright) **53**:423
Migrants (Coles) **108**:194, 210-12
"Migration" (Boland) **40**:100; **113**:109
"Migration" (Carver) **55**:275
"A Migration" (Heaney) **74**:168
"Migration" (Neruda) **62**:332
Migrations (Josipovici) **43**:220-21; **153**:221
Migrations: An Arabesque in Histories (Scott) **43**:374, 385
Miguel Street (Naipaul) **4**:372, 375; **13**:403, 406; **37**:323-25, 327-28; **105**:142, 147-48, 150, 154-56, 165, 179
"Miisa" (Diamond) **30**:110
"Mike" (Acorn) **15**:8
Mikelandjelo (Krleža)
See *Michelangelo Buonarroti*
"Mike's View" (Royko) **109**:395
Mikey and Nicky (May) **16**:435-37
Mikkai (Abe) **22**:14-15; **53**:5-6; **81**:297
Mila Eighteen (Uris) **7**:491; **32**:433, 435
O milagre secundo Salomé (Migueis) **10**:340-41
The Milagro Beanfield War (Nichols) **38**:341-42, 344-47
"El milagro de Anaquillé" (Carpentier) **11**:102-03
"El milagro secreto" (Borges) **2**:76; **8**:98-9, 102; **44**:363; **83**:183
De milagros y de melancolías (Mujica Lainez) **31**:280, 282
Mildred Pierce (Cain) **3**:97; **11**:84; **28**:45, 47, 49-53
Mile High (Condon) **45**:97-8, 101-03
"The Mile Runner" (Waddington) **28**:438
"Mile Zero" (Kroetsch) **57**:292-93
"Miles City, Montana" (Munro) **50**:209-12, 216, 218-20; **95**:309-10, 314
"Miles Davis and Elizabeth Bishop Fake the Break" (Wright) **146**:359
Miles of Aisles (Mitchell) **12**:438
"Milford Junction, 1939: A Brief Encounter" (Coover) **46**:122
"Milgate" (Lowell) **11**:331
"Militant Black, Poet" (Randall) **135**:390
The Military Half: An Account of Destruction in Quang Ngai and Quang Tin (Schell) **35**:362-63
Military Men (Just) **4**:266; **27**:227
The Military Philosophers (Powell) **3**:400, 402; **7**:345; **9**:435; **10**:415; **31**:317
"Milk" (Carlson) **54**:37-8
Milk and Honey (Jolley) **46**:217-21
Milk and Honey (Lennon) **35**:275-76
"Milk Bread Beer Ice" (Shields) **113**:405
"Milk Is Very Good for You" (Dixon) **52**:95
"Milk of Death " (Yourcenar)
See "Le lait de la mort"
"The Milk of Paradise" (Tiptree) **48**:388, 392, 396
"Milk the Mouse" (Ryan) **65**:215
The Milk Train Doesn't Stop Here Anymore (Williams) **2**:465; **5**:499, 503; **11**:573; **19**:472; **45**:446, 450, 453, 455; **71**:387; **111**:379-80, 383, 391
Milkbottle H (Orlovitz) **22**:333-35
The Milk-Cheese (Pasolini)
See *La Ricotta*
"Milkman 2" (King)
See "Big Wheels: A Tale of the Laundry Game"
"Milkweed" (Levine) **14**:321
"Milkweed" (Wright) **3**:540; **5**:518
The Milky Way (Bunuel)
See *La voie lactée*
The Milky Way: Galaxy Number One (Branley) **21**:18
"Milky Way Vegetation I" (Gunnars) **69**:262
"Milky Way Vegetation II" (Gunnars) **69**:262
"The Mill" (Bates) **46**:66-7
"The Mill" (Morgan) **31**:275
"The Mill" (Wilbur) **53**:410; **110**:353
"Mill Cry" (Lane) **25**:288
"Mill Mountain" (Brown) **59**:265
"The Mill on the Po" (Bacchelli) **19**:31-2
"Mill Ruins" (Hughes) **119**:275, 288
Mille chemins ouverts (Green) **3**:204; **77**:276, 289
"Millenium" (McGinley) **14**:366
Millennium: A Novel about People and Politics in the Year 1999 (Bova) **45**:69-70, 72-3
"Millennium Also Ran" (Bates) **46**:52
"The Millennium, and What They Can Do With It" (Perelman) **9**:416
Millennium Approaches (Kushner) **81**:196-213
Miller's Crossing (The Coen Brothers) **108**:145-47, 149-51, 153, 156-58, 161-63, 166-67, 169
"The Miller's Tale" (Bates) **46**:66
Les Milles et une bibles du sexe (Ouologuem) **146**:169-70, 173-76, 218-21
Les Milles et une bibles du sexes (Ouologuem) **146**:
Millie's Boy (Peck) **17**:337-39
Le million (Clair) **20**:58-61, 67-8, 70
"Million Miles" (McCartney) **35**:286
"A Million Miles Away" (Alexie) **154**:43
"The Millionaire" (McGuane) **45**:265-66
"Millionaire" (Scannell) **49**:327
"Millionaires" (Chabon) **149**:4, 6
"Millions in His Firing Squad" (Royko) **109**:408
Millions of Strange Shadows (Hecht) **8**:269-70; **13**:269; **19**:207
"The Million-Year Picnic" (Bradbury) **42**:38
Un millón de muertos (Gironella) **11**:235, 238
"The Millpond" (Komunyakaa) **94**:238
"Millpond Lost" (Warren) **39**:265
"The Mills of the Kavanaughs" (Lowell) **1**:179, 182; **2**:246; **4**:295-96, 298, 300, 303; **8**:348, 351, 353, 356; **15**:344; **37**:232, 242; **124**:268, 272
The Mills of the Kavanaughs (Lowell) **1**:179, 182; **2**:246; **4**:295-96, 303; **8**:348, 351, 353, 356; **15**:344; **37**:232, 242; **124**:254
The Millstone (Drabble) **2**:118-19; **5**:118-19; **10**:162, 165; **22**:122-24; **53**:117-18, 121; **129**:112, 118, 145
"Millstream Memories" (Blunden) **56**:48
"Milne's Bar" (MacCaig) **36**:285
Miłość (Dabrowska) **15**:167
Milose i odpowiedzialnosc: Studium etyczne (John Paul II) **128**:166, 178, 193, 197
Milton in America (Ackroyd) **140**:50, 53-5, 75
"A Miltonic Sonnet for Mr. Johnson on His Refusal of Mr. Peter Hurd's Official Portrait" (Wilbur) **110**:371, 381
Milton's God (Empson) **8**:202; **33**:146, 148, 151; **34**:336-38
Milton's "Paradise Lost" (Wilding) **73**:390, 396
"Mimesis and Allegory" (Auden) **123**:6-8
"Mimesis and Diegesis in Modern Fiction" (Lodge) **141**:351
"Mimesis and the Motive for Fiction" (Alter) **34**:515
"Mimi the Fish" (Mazer) **26**:291
Mimic (SODERBERGH) **154**:356
The Mimic Men (Naipaul) **4**:373, 375; **7**:253; **9**:391-92; **13**:403-05; **18**:360-61; **37**:325; **105**:154, 156, 161, 170, 180-81
Mimi's Ghost (Parks) **147**:207-08, 219
Minä, Olli ja Orvokki (Salama) **18**:460-62
"Mind" (Wilbur) **9**:569-70; **110**:351
Mind Breaths: Poems, 1972-1977 (Ginsberg) **13**:241; **36**:185-86, 188, 191, 196; **109**:331
Mind Drugs (Hyde) **21**:174
Mind Fields (Ellison) **139**:142
The Mind Game (Spinrad) **46**:385
"Mind Games" (Lennon) **35**:265-66, 270-71
Mind Games (Lennon) **35**:265-67
The Mind Has Mountains (Hocking) **13**:285
The Mind Has Mountains (Jennings) **131**:232, 239-40
Mind in the Modern World (Trilling) **11**:539; **24**:458
"The Mind Is Still" (Le Guin) **45**:212
The Mind Murders (van de Wetering) **47**:408-09, 411-12
"A Mind of His Own" (Haldeman) **61**:174, 177
Mind of My Mind (Butler) **38**:61-2, 64, 66; **121**:73-76, 80, 89, 94, 97, 99, 103, 108-09, 113, 119, 120, 122, 144
"The Mind of Winter: Reflections on a Life in Exile" (Said) **123**:357
"Mind on My Man" (Simon) **26**:409
Mind over Murder (Kienzle) **25**:275
The Mind Parasites (Wilson) **3**:537
"Mind to Body" (Fuller) **4**:178
A Mind to Murder (James) **18**:273; **46**:205, 208; **122**:120, 122, 146, 148, 151, 153, 176, 185-87
Mindbridge (Haldeman) **61**:171-73, 176, 185
"The Mind-Reader" (Wilbur) **9**:568, 570; **53**:402-03
The Mind-Reader: New Poems (Wilbur) **9**:568-70; **14**:578-79; **53**:398-99, 401-02, 405, 409-11; **110**:352, 355, 361, 380
"The Mind's Games" (Williams) **42**:450
"Mind's Heart" (Creeley) **78**:156
Minds Meet (Abish) **22**:17, 22
The Minds of Billy Milligan (Keyes) **80**:166-67, 169
Mindwheel (Pinsky) **121**:429, 448
Mine Boy (Abrahams) **4**:1-2
"Mine Field" (Calvino) **33**:101
"The Mine Is Also of Nature" (Acorn) **15**:10
"Mined Country" (Wilbur) **53**:397
"Mineral" (Page) **7**:291
"Minerals of Cornwall, Stones of Cornwall" (Redgrove) **41**:351
"Miners" (Wright) **10**:543
The Miner's Pale Children (Merwin) **1**:214; **2**:277-78; **5**:288; **8**:390; **18**:332-33; **88**:198-200
"The Miner's Wake" (Parini) **54**:360
Minetoza (Paustovsky) **40**:362
Minetti (Bernhard) **32**:25; **61**:12-13
"The Mini Skirt" (Randall) **135**:399
Minick (Kaufman) **38**:258
"The Minimal" (Roethke) **8**:456; **19**:397; **101**:263
"Minimal Mahoney, in His Cups" (Klappert) **57**:265
The Minimal Self (Lasch) **102**:289-90, 295-96, 301-02
The Minimalist Program (Chomsky) **132**:67, 69
"Minims" (Leithauser) **27**:242
The Minister (Thomas) **13**:542; **48**:383
The Minister for Justice (White) **49**:404
"Minister of Defence" (Jhabvala) **138**:79
"Minister Opens New Home for Battered Husbands" (Durcan) **43**:115-16
The Ministry of Fear (Greene) **1**:130-31; **9**:250; **18**:194; **37**:140; **70**:289; **72**:148-50, 169-72
The Ministry of Fear (Lang) **20**:207, 213
"Mink" (Muldoon) **32**:321
The Min-Min (Clark) **12**:129-30
"The Minneapolis Poem" (Wright) **3**:541, 543; **5**:520; **28**:465
"Minneapolis Story" (Warren) **39**:259
Minnie and Moskowitz (Cassavetes) **20**:47-8, 55
"Minnie and Mrs. Hoyne" (Fearing) **51**:108
The Minnow Leads to Treasure (Pearce)
See *Minnow on the Say*
Minnow on the Say (Pearce) **21**:280-81, 283-89
"Minnows and a Monster" (Young) **82**:411
A Minor Apocalypse (Konwicki)
See *Mała apokalipsa*

Minor Characters (Johnson) **58**:286-92
"Minor Heroism: Something About My Father" (Gurganus) **70**:190, 193, 195-96
Minor Monuments: Selected Essays (Moss) **45**:292; **50**:353
"A Minor Mood" (Dybek) **114**:74-5
"The Minor Novelist" (Sheed) **53**:341
Minor Poems (Eliot) **15**:213
"A Minor Van Gogh" (Ostriker) **132**:303
"Minority Poem" (Ezekiel) **61**:97-9
"Minority Report" (Blunden) **56**:31
Minority Report (Rice) **7**:363
"Minotaur" (Dickey) **28**:117
"Minotaur" (Shapcott) **38**:399
"Le minotaure ou la halte d'oran" (Camus) **69**:112
Der Minotaurus (Wellershoff) **46**:435
"Minstrel" (Kinsella) **138**:95
The Minstrel (Kinsella) **138**:106
The Minstrel Boy (Cronin) **32**:140
"The Minstrels" (Valenzuela)
See "Los Menestrales"
"The Mint Quality" (Blackburn) **43**:63
Minty Alley (James) **33**:220
Minuit (Green) **11**:259; **77**:270, 276, 279-81
Minus Sign (Williamson) **29**:455
Minute by Glass Minute (Stevenson) **33**:381-82
"Minutes of the Last Meeting" (Updike) **15**:544, 546
Minutes to Go (Burroughs) **109**:183, 194-95
"La minutieuse" (Char) **9**:163
"Mio marito" (Ginzburg) **11**:229
Mirabell: Books of Numbers (Merrill) **13**:382; **18**:329-31; **34**:226-31, 235-38; **91**:228
"A Miracle" (Mahfūz) **52**:297
"The Miracle" (Pasternak) **63**:312
The Miracle (Jordan) **110**:304
Miracle (Škvorecký)
See *Mirákl*
Miracle at Indian River (Nowlan) **15**:398-99
Miracle de la rose (Genet) **1**:115-17; **5**:135, 137-39; **10**:225; **44**:386-90; **46**:173, 176-82
Miracle en Bohàme (Škvorecký)
See *Mirákl*
"A Miracle for Breakfast" (Bishop) **1**:36
The Miracle Game: A Political Whodunit (Škvorecký)
See *Mirákl*
Miracle in Saville (Michener) **109**:383
The Miracle Kittens (Nwapa) **133**:201, 229
"Miracle Man" (Costello) **21**:67
"The Miracle of the Birds" (Amado) **106**:73
Miracle of the Rose (Genet)
See *Miracle de la rose*
"Miracle on St. David's Day" (Clarke) **61**:79, 81-3
Miracle Play (Oates) **3**:364; **33**:289
Miracle Play (Shreve) **23**:404-05
Miracle Row (Ian) **21**:187
The Miracle Woman (Capra) **16**:153, 165-66
The Miracle Worker (Gibson) **23**:174-78
"Miracles" (Abse) **29**:18
Miracles (Lewis) **3**:296; **6**:311; **14**:323; **27**:262; **124**:194, 213, 232, 246
Miracles of the Gods (von Daniken) **30**:426
Miracolo a Milano (De Sica) **20**:85, 93
The Miraculous Day of Amalia Gómez (Rechy) **107**:254, 256, 257
"Miraculous Weapons" (Césaire)
See "Les armes miraculeuses"
La Mirada (Marqués) **96**:233, 235, 237-40, 244
Mirage (Ringwood) **48**:334-36, 338-39
"Mirages" (Boland) **113**:76
Mirages (Burnshaw) **13**:129
Mirákl (Škvorecký) **39**:229; **69**:330, 339, 341-43, 348-53; **152**:311-12, 314-15, 325, 330, 335-36
Miramar (Mahfouz) **153**:250, 262, 338, 354, 359, 369
Mīrāmār (Mahfūz) **52**:299, 301, 304-05; **55**:177-79, 181, 183, 185
"Miranda" (Barker) **8**:47
"Miranda Grows Up" (Van Duyn) **116**:427
"Miranda over the Valley" (Dubus) **13**:183; **97**:196, 201, 212
"Mirando aquellos desde los campos" (Zamora) **89**:368
"Miriam" (Capote) **3**:99; **13**:133; **19**:79; **34**:321
"Miriam" (Kerrigan) **6**:276
"Miriam" (Klima)
See "Myriam"
Miriam at Thirty-Four (Lelchuk) **5**:244-45
"Miriam Tazewell" (Ransom) **11**:470
"Miró in the Third Person: Eight Statements" (Cage) **41**:78
En miroir (Jouve) **47**:206
Le miroir de la production: ou, l'illusion critique du matérialism historique (Baudrillard) **60**:11-14
"Miroir de la tauromachie" (Leiris) **61**:341
Le miroir des limbes (Malraux) **9**:359; **15**:354; **57**:306-09, 319
Le miroir qui revient (Robbe-Grillet) **43**:366; **128**:366-68, 370, 376, 382
"The Mirror" (Bowers) **9**:122
"The Mirror" (Haines) **58**:222
"Mirror" (Plath) **5**:340; **111**:206-12
"Mirror" (Robison) **98**:306, 308
"The Mirror" (Singer) **15**:505; **38**:413-16; **111**:329-31
The Mirror (Singer) **38**:413-16
The Mirror and the Lamp (Abrams) **24**:11-12, 14, 18
"The Mirror and the Mask" (Borges) **13**:111; **48**:41
The Mirror Crack'd from Side to Side (Christie) **110**:121
A Mirror for Artists (Davidson) **19**:123-24
A Mirror for the Sky (West) **7**:520; **17**:544
A Mirror for Witches (Forbes) **12**:203
"Mirror Image" (Asimov) **26**:43-4
"Mirror in February" (Kinsella) **138**:118, 129, 136, 142, 150, 159, 161, 163, 165
Mirror in My House: The Autobiographies of Sean O'Casey (O'Casey) **5**:318
The Mirror in the Roadway (O'Connor) **14**:397
"The Mirror in Which Two Are Seen as One" (Rich) **18**:447
"Mirror, Mirror" (Tillinghast) **29**:414
Mirror, Mirror (Garfield) **12**:234-35
Mirror, Mirror (Waugh) **6**:559-60
The Mirror of Criticism: Selected Reviews, 1977-1982 (Josipovici) **43**:224-26
The Mirror of Her Dreams (Donaldson) **46**:143-45; **138**:41
Mirror of Her Own (Guy) **26**:145-46
The Mirror of Limbo (Malraux)
See *Le miroir des limbes*
The Mirror of Production (Baudrillard)
See *Le miroir de la production: ou, l'illusion critique du matérialism historique*
"The Mirror of the Enigmas" (Borges) **44**:355; **83**:162
The Mirror of the Mother: Selected Poems, 1975-1985 (Roberts) **48**:342-44
"The Mirror of the Unknown" (Kiš) **57**:251
Mirror on the Floor (Bowering) **47**:19-20
"Mirror Sermon" (Brutus) **43**:92
"The Mirror Stage as Formative of the Function of the I as Revealed in Psychoanalytic Experience" (Lacan)
See "Le stade du mirior"
"The Mirrored Man" (Avison) **97**:75, 80, 86, 90
"Mirrors" (Borges)
See "Los espejos"
"Mirrors" (Giovanni) **64**:192
"Mirrors" (Grace) **56**:116, 118-19
"Mirrors" (Graham) **48**:145
"Mirrors" (Jennings) **131**:230
Mirrors (Creeley) **36**:120-22; **78**:141-42, 151-53, 158
Mirrors (Mahfouz)
See *al-Maraya*
Mirrors (Mahfūz)
See *al- Mārāyā*
Mirrors and Windows (Nemerov) **2**:308; **36**:302-03, 305
Mirrorshades: The Cyberpunk Anthology (Sterling) **72**:370
A Misalliance (Brookner) **51**:61-4; **136**:88-90, 92, 103-04, 111, 115
The Misanthrope (Wilbur) **14**:576
"Misanthropos" (Gunn) **18**:203; **32**:208, 211
"Miscellaneous" (MacInnes) **23**:286
"A Miscellany of Characters That Will Not Appear" (Cheever) **7**:49
"The Mischief Done" (Crispin) **22**:112
The Mischief Makers (Truffaut) **20**:380, 397
"The Mischief of King Balerion" (Lem) **149**:125
"Misdeal" (Landolfi) **11**:321
"Misdemeanors" (Alexie) **154**:3
La mise à mort (Aragon) **22**:38
"Mise Eire" (Boland) **67**:40, 45-6; **113**:70, 82, 86, 98, 103, 105-08
Misérable miracle (Michaux) **8**:392; **19**:312-13
Miserable Miracle (Michaux)
See *Misérable miracle*
"Misère noire" (Damas) **84**:181
"Miserere" (Gascoyne) **45**:147, 153, 157
"Misericords" (Raine) **103**:186
"Misericords" (Szirtes) **46**:392
"Misery" (Ian) **21**:183
Misery (King) **61**:325-29, 337; **113**:350, 369-70, 388, 392
"Misery and Splendor" (Hass) **99**:140
"Misfit" (Heinlein) **3**:225; **14**:248; **55**:302
"Misfit" (Simon) **26**:408-09
Misfits (Davies) **21**:103-04
The Misfits (Huston) **20**:168
The Misfits (Miller) **1**:216, 218; **6**:332; **15**:374; **47**:249-50; **78**:311
"Misgiving" (Frost) **26**:117
Misgivings (Howard) **47**:169
Misgivings: My Mother, My Father, Myself (Williams) **148**:368-69
Mishima: A Vision of the Void (Yourcenar)
See *Mishima; ou, La vision du vide*
Mishima; ou, La vision du vide (Yourcenar) **50**:363; **87**:401
"Mismatched Shoes" (Komunyakaa) **94**:238
Misreadings (Eco) **142**:101
"Miss Amao" (Ding Ling)
See "Amao guniang"
"Miss Book World" (Abse) **29**:18
"Miss Briggs" (Sargeson) **31**:370
"'Miss Buttle' and 'Mr. Eliot'" (Wilson) **2**:477
"Miss Coynte of Green" (Williams) **5**:502-03; **45**:454
"Miss Crystal Confronts the Past" (Gilchrist) **143**:309
"Miss Drake Proceeds to Supper" (Plath) **111**:170-71
Miss Firecracker (Henley)
See *The Miss Firecracker Contest*
The Miss Firecracker Contest (Henley) **23**:217
"Miss Foote" (Thomas) **107**:333
"Miss Gada-Nigi" (Seifert) **93**:341
"Miss Gee" (Auden) **11**:16
"Miss God" (Ewart) **46**:153
Miss Gomez and the Brethren (Trevor) **7**:476; **9**:529; **71**:345; **116**:334-35
"Miss Gradenko" (Police, The) **26**:366
"Miss Hamilton in London" (Adcock) **41**:17
Miss Herbert (Stead) **8**:500-01; **32**:411-12, 414; **80**:326-27, 329, 342-44, 347-48
"Miss Holland" (Lavin) **18**:303
Miss Jairus (Ghelderode)
See *Mademoiselle Jaïre*
Miss Jane Pittman (Gaines)
See *The Autobiography of Miss Jane Pittman*
"Miss Jee" (Jin) **109**:52
"Miss Leonora When Last Seen" (Taylor) **37**:412

Miss MacIntosh, My Darling (Young) **82**:400-21
"Miss Marnell" (Clarke) **6**:112
Miss Morissa, Doctor of the Gold Trail (Sandoz) **28**:404
"Miss Muriel" (Petry) **1**:266; **7**:305
Miss Muriel, and Other Stories (Petry) **1**:266; **7**:305
"Miss Nora Kerrin Writes to Her Betrothed" (Shapcott) **38**:403
"Miss Nostradamus" (Simic) **130**:338
Miss Peabody's Inheritance (Jolley) **46**:215-19, 221
"Miss Peskova Regrets" (Škvorecký) **69**:345
"Miss Pulkinhorn" (Golding) **81**:319
"Miss Quirke" (Trevor) **116**:378
"La Miss Rose" (Castillo) **151**:47-8
"Miss Rosie" (Clifton) **66**:73, 86
"Miss Scarlett, Mr. Rhett and Other Latter Day Saints" (Angelou) **77**:28
Miss Silver's Past (Škvorecký)
See *Lvíce*
Miss Smilla's Feeling for Snow (Hoeg)
See *Smilla's Sense of Snow*
"Miss Smith" (Trevor) **71**:347; **116**:338
"Miss Twye" (Ewart) **46**:148
Miss Universal Happiness (Foreman) **50**:168, 171
Miss Vogel's Vacation (Binchy) **153**:75
"Miss Winczewska" (Dabrowska) **15**:169
"A Miss X" (Alberti) **7**:7
"Miss Yellow Eyes" (Grau) **146**:127, 161-62
"Miss You" (Jagger and Richard) **17**:239-40, 242
"Miss Zilphia Gant" (Faulkner) **18**:149
"Missile Base 612" (Yehoshua) **13**:617; **31**:471-72, 474
"The Missing" (Gunn) **81**:180
"Missing Child" (Simic) **130**:329
Missing Continents (Dorfman) **77**:150-52
"Missing Dates" (Empson) **19**:156
"The Missing Girl" (Jackson) **60**:230
"The Missing Line" (Singer) **69**:312
The Missing of the Somme (Dyer) **149**:46-7
"A Missing Person" (Mahapatra) **33**:282
"The Missing Person" (Wolff) **64**:450-51, 454
The Missing Person (Grumbach) **22**:205-06; **64**:198
Missing Persons, and Other Essays (Boell) **9**:112
The Missing Persons League (Bonham) **12**:55
"The Missing Piece" (Danticat) **94**:98; **139**:87
"Missing the Sea" (Kallman) **2**:221
"The Mission" (Friedman) **56**:97
"The Mission" (Warren) **18**:537
Mission Earth (Hubbard) **43**:206-08
Mission terminée (Beti) **27**:41-4, 46-9, 51-2
"Mission Tire Factory, 1969" (Soto) **80**:278, 293
Mission to Kala (Beti)
See *Mission terminée*
Mission to the Heart Stars (Blish) **14**:86
"The Missionaries" (Duncan) **41**:129
The Missionaries (Jenkins) **52**:221, 223, 227-28
"The Missionary" (Smith) **64**:392
"Missionary" (Thomas) **132**:381
"The Missionary Visits Our Church in Scranton" (Parini) **54**:362
"The Missions" (Rodriguez) **155**:260
"Mississippi" (Bass) **79**:4-5, 7; **143**:3
"Mississippi" (Dove) **81**:140, 150
"Mississippi" (Gilchrist) **143**:309
"Mississippi, Ham Rider" (Bambara) **88**:27
"Mississippi Levee" (Hughes) **15**:292
Mississippi Mermaid (Truffaut) **20**:386, 389-92; **101**:375, 379, 380-81, 383, 390, 407
"Missives to Max" (Hildesheimer) **49**:180
The Missolonghi Manuscript (Prokosch) **48**:316
"Missoula Softball Tournament" (Hugo) **32**:241
"Missouri" (Urdang) **47**:399-400
Missouri Bittersweet (Kantor) **7**:195-96
The Missouri Breaks (McGuane) **45**:261-62; **127**:258, 262-65, 267, 270, 280
"Missy" (Hill) **113**:281, 294, 297
"Missy's Twins" (Peterkin) **31**:306, 308
"Mist" (Graham) **118**:239-40
The Mist (King) **37**:207; **113**:341, 344-45, 359, 379-80
The Mist in the Mirror (Hill) **113**:315-16, 318
"The Mist Net" (Muldoon) **72**:277
"The Mistake" (Singer) **69**:306
Mistake (Havel) **123**:188-89
Mistaken Ambitions (Moravia)
See *Le ambizioni sbagliate*
"Mr. Andrews" (Forster) **77**:213
Mister Corbett's Ghost, and Other Stories (Garfield) **12**:217-18, 225, 237
Mister McGregor (Lytle) **22**:295, 298
Mister, Mister (Grass) **4**:201
Mr. (Calvino)
See *Palomar*
"Mr. Parker" (Colwin) **5**:108
"Mister Rock of Ages" (Lightfoot) **26**:282
"Mister Sparks:A Self-Portrait" (Tolson) **105**:249
"Mr. Tambourine Man" (Dylan) **6**:155; **12**:188-89; **77**:187
"Mister Toussan" (Ellison) **11**:183; **114**:93-4, 131
Mister White Eyes (Gold) **42**:196-97; **152**:120
Mr. Wilson's War (Dos Passos) **25**:145; **34**:424; **82**:96
El misterio del ramo de rosas (Puig) **65**:273; **133**:373
"Misterios gozosos" (Castellanos) **66**:45, 50
La misteriosa desaparición de la Marquesita de Loria (Donoso) **32**:160-61; **99**:242
Mistero Buffo (Fo) **109**:101, 104-06, 108-09, 113-18, 124-25, 127, 131, 142, 146
Il mistero di oberwald (Antonioni) **20**:42; **144**:15, 58, 65, 68-9, 81
Les mistons (Truffaut) **20**:380, 397; **101**:379, 382, 388, 405, 410
"Mistral" (Faulkner) **18**:147-48; **28**:136
"The Mistress" (Berriault) **54**:3; **109**:96
The Mistress and Other Stories (Berriault) **54**:3-4; **109**:90
"Mistress Mary" (Macdonald) **13**:356
Mistress Masham's Repose (White) **30**:441, 449
The Mists of Avalon (Bradley) **30**:31-2
"Misty Morning" (Marley) **17**:271
"Misty Mountain Hop" (Page and Plant) **12**:475
The Misunderstanding (Camus)
See *Le malentendu*
A Misunderstanding (Farrell) **66**:129
"Misunderstood" (Townshend) **17**:537
Misunderstood Games (Carrier)
See *Les jeux incompris*
"Mit Wechselndem Schlüssel" (Celan) **19**:90
"The Mitchells" (Murray) **40**:339, 341
"Der Mitmacher" (Duerrenmatt) **102**:61
Der Mitmacher (Duerrenmatt) **102**:61-2, 64, 69
Der Mitmacher: Ein Komplex (Duerrenmatt) **102**:61
Mito (Buero Vallejo) **15**:101-02; **139**:10, 19
"Mittags um zwei" (Eich) **15**:202
Mitteilungen an Max: Über der Stand der Dinge und anderes (Hildesheimer) **49**:179
"Mittelbergheim" (Milosz) **31**:265
Mixed Company (Shaw) **7**:411
"Mixed Doubles" (Shaw) **34**:370
"Mixed Feelings" (Ashbery) **15**:28, 32
"The Mixed Marriage" (Muldoon) **32**:319
"Mixed Sequence" (Roethke) **46**:364; **101**:304
"The Mixer" (MacNeice) **4**:318; **53**:243
The Mixquiahuala Letters (Castillo) **151**:3-9, 13-15, 17-25, 30-3, 37, 45-6, 48-9, 52-3, 57-8, 60-4, 83-4, 86-7, 100-02
A Mixture of Frailties (Davies) **13**:171; **25**:130-33; **42**:101-05; **75**:184, 192, 199, 204-05, 211-15; **91**:203-04
"Mizu kara waga namida o nuguitamo hi" (Oe) **36**:347-48; **86**:218, 225, 228, 239-40, 244
"M=L/T" (Goldbarth) **38**:205
"Mnemoka" (Smith) **43**:425
"A Mnemonic Wallpaper Pattern for Southern Two Seaters" (Williams) **13**:600
Mnemosyne Lay in Dust (Clarke) **6**:110, 112; **9**:168
Mo' Better Blues (Lee) **105**:89-91, 93, 95, 98, 102-03, 111, 127-28
"The Mob" (Brutus) **43**:92, 94
Mobile (Butor) **3**:93; **8**:117-18, 120; **15**:115, 118, 120
"The Mobile Bed-Object" (Highsmith) **102**:197
Mobius the Stripper (Josipovici) **6**:270; **153**:210
Moby Dick (Huston) **20**:163, 165-67
"Mocassin" (Kenny) **87**:240
"The Moccasin Telegraph" (Kinsella) **43**:254
The Moccasin Telegraph, and Other Stories (Kinsella) **43**:253, 257-58, 260
"The Mock Auction" (Lavin) **99**:319, 322
"Mock Orange" (Glück) **44**:216, 218, 221
Mocking the Fates (Mahfouz)
See *Abath al-aqdar*
Mockingbird (Tevis) **42**:371-73, 376-77
Mockingbird, Wish Me Luck (Bukowski) **5**:80; **82**:4
Mockinpott (Weiss) **51**:391, 395-96
"Mode of Existence of a Literary Work" (Wellek) **28**:452
"The Model" (Auden) **9**:59
"The Model" (Baxter) **78**:17
"The Model" (Malamud) **27**:307
"The Model" (Nin) **60**:277; **127**:385, 388-89
The Model (Aickman) **57**:4-5
Model (Wiseman) **20**:477-78
The Model Apartment (Margulies) **76**:188
A Model Childhood (Wolf)
See *Kindheitsmuster*
A Model for Death (Bioy Casares)
See *Un modelo para la muerte*
A Model World and Other Stories (Chabon) **149**:3-7, 10, 15, 23, 26, 32
Un modelo para la muerte (Bioy Casares) **88**:78
Moderate Fable (Young) **82**:396, 400, 405-06, 409, 411-12, 414
Moderato cantabile (Duras) **3**:129; **6**:149-50; **11**:165, 167-68; **34**:162; **40**:180-81, 184; **68**:74, 91; **100**:123-24, 130
The Modern American Novel (Bradbury) **32**:57
"Modern Dance Class" (Dunn) **36**:153
A Modern Day Yankee in a Connecticut Court, and Other Essays on Science (Lightman) **81**:76
Modern Dogma and the Rhetoric of Assent (Booth) **24**:92, 99
"The Modern Element in Modern Literature" (Trilling) **9**:532
The Modern Hebrew Poem Itself (Burnshaw) **3**:91
"Modern Literature and Sex" (Oe) **86**:229
"Modern Literature: Between the Whirlpool and the Rock" (Wilson) **24**:466
"Modern Love" (Boyle) **90**:47-8, 61
"Modern Love" (Morgan) **2**:295
Modern Poetry: A Personal Essay (MacNeice) **10**:324, 326; **53**:234-35, 244
"Modern Poetry and the Imagists" (Aldington) **49**:16
Modern Poetry and the Tradition (Brooks) **24**:101, 103-04; **86**:278-79, 286; **110**:3-4, 9, 11, 13-14, 26, 28-9, 32
"Modern Poetry Is Prose (But It Is Saying Plenty)" (Ferlinghetti) **27**:139
The Modern Poets (Rosenthal) **28**:389-90
The Modern Researcher (Barzun) **145**:73, 110
Modern Rhetoric (Brooks) **86**:278
"Modern Saint #271" (Janowitz) **43**:211; **145**:342
Modern Scream (Tomlin) **17**:516-17
The Modern Short Story: A Critical Survey (Bates) **46**:67
The Modern Temper (Krutch) **24**:281, 286-87, 289
"Modern Theatre" (Lagerkvist) **54**:271

"Modern Times" (Parra) **102**:355
Modern Times (Chaplin) **16**:190-92, 194-95, 197, 201-04, 207
Modern Times: The World From the Twenties to the Eighties (Johnson) **147**:90-1, 105, 107, 112-14, 117, 131, 143, 145, 149, 151
"The Modern Writer and His Community" (Brooks) **24**:111; **110**:8
"Moderne AE gteskab og andre Betragtninger" (Dinesen) **95**:61
"Modernism and Imperialism" (Jameson) **142**:230, 239
"Modernism and Its Repressed" (Jameson) **142**:230
"Modernism and Its Repressed" (Janis) **142**:
Modernism and the Harlem Renaissance (Baker) **65**:381
"Modernism" in Modern Drama: A Definition and Estima tion (Krutch) **24**:286
"The Modernist Event" (White) **148**:299
Modernities and Other Writings (Cendrars) **106**:190-91
"The Modernity of Keats" (Kunitz) **148**:
The Modes of Modern Writing: Metaphor, Metonymy, and the Typology of Modern Literature (Lodge) **36**:271-72, 274; **141**:330, 350. 369
"Modes of Pleasure" (Gunn) **18**:199
"A Modest Proposal" (Hughes) **14**:270
"A Modest Proposal" (Stafford) **7**:457; **68**:449
"A Modest Self-Tribute" (Wilson) **24**:480
"The Modesty of History" (Borges) **10**:65
La modification (Butor) **3**:92; **8**:113, 116-17, 119-21; **11**:78-9; **15**:112-13, 115-17, 119
"Modified Sonnets" (Moss) **14**:376
"Modulations for a Solo Voice" (Levertov) **15**:338-39
Modus Vivendi (Levinson) **49**:227-29
"Moe, Nat, and Yrd" (Pesetsky) **28**:358
Un moegliche Bewiesaufrahme (Nossack) **6**:365-66
A Moelna Elegy (Ekelöf)
See *En Mölna-elegi*
"Moeraki Conversations" (Hulme) **130**:53
Moetsukita chizu (Abe) **8**:1; **22**:12, 14; **53**:2-3, 5-6; **81**:285, 287, 289, 294, 297
"Moeurs contemporaines" (Pound) **10**:405
"Mogollon Morning" (Momaday) **85**:281
Mogu, the Wanderer (Colum) **28**:86
"Mohaq" (Shamlu) **10**:469
"The Mohawks in High Steel" (Mitchell) **98**:180, 184, 187
Mohn und Gedächtnes (Celan) **10**:101-02; **19**:89; **53**:69, 71, 74, 76-7, 80
M.O.I. American Pageant (Zappa) **17**:584-85
moi, Laminaire (Césaire) **32**:112-13; **112**:12, 22-3, 26, 30
Moi, Pierre Huneau (Theriault) **79**:414
"Moi, Pierre Rivière, ayant égurgé ma mer, ma soeur, et mon frère" (Foucault) **31**:185
Moi, Tituba, sorciére, noire de Salem (Condé) **52**:84-5; **92**:101-02, 108, 113-14, 124-31, 133-35
Moïra (Green) **77**:270-71, 274, 276-78, 290
Moires (Jouve) **47**:209
Moise and the World of Reason (Williams) **5**:505-06; **7**:544; **11**:574-75; **15**:581; **19**:472; **45**:453
Moj obracun s njima (Krleža) **114**:169, 175
"Moja ratna lirika" (Krleža) **114**:170
Moje první lásky (Klima) **56**:172-74
Mojo: A Black Love Story (Childress) **86**:309, 316; **96**:91, 103-04, 111
Mojo and the Russians (Myers) **35**:296
"The Mole" (Kawabata)
See "Hokuro no tegami"
Mole Notes (Benedikt) **4**:55
"The Mole-Catcher" (Blunden) **56**:37
"The Molecule as Mosaic" (Hall) **51**:175
Molecules Today and Tomorrow (Hyde) **21**:174
"Moles" (Oliver) **34**:247; **98**:274
"The Molesters" (Oates) **11**:402
"Molitva rezanova" (Voznesensky) **15**:554
Molloy (Beckett) **2**:44; **3**:45; **4**:52; **6**:34, 37, 42-3, 45; **9**:78-80, 84, 86; **11**:32-5; **14**:71-2, 76-7; **18**:47; **29**:53, 55-7, 59, 65-7; **57**:65, 92; **59**:253-54, 257, 260
"Molly" (Dubus) **97**:208, 213, 215-16, 218
Molly (Gray) **14**:214; **36**:203
"Molly Brant, Iroquois Matron, Speaks" (Allen) **84**:24
Molly Brant: Poems of War (Kenny)
See *Tekonwatoni/Molly Brant (1735-1795): Poems of War*
Molly Cottontail (Caldwell) **50**:302
"Molly: Passions" (Kenny) **87**:257
"Molly's Dog" (Adams) **46**:21
Molly's Dream (Fornés) **39**:138; **61**:129-31
En Mölna-elegi (Ekeloef) **27**:114-15
Molnen över Metapontion (Johnson) **14**:296
"Moly" (Gunn) **32**:208; **81**:179
Moly (Gunn) **3**:215-16; **6**:221-22; **18**:200, 203; **32**:208, 211
"Mom" (Smith) **73**:356, 358
"Mom in Your Boots" (Carroll) **38**:103
"Mom Luby and the Social Worker" (Hunter) **35**:226
Mom, the Wolf Man, and Me (Klein) **30**:236-37, 239, 241
Momatkom (Livesay) **79**:345
"Moment" (Kroetsch) **132**:275
"Moment" (Nemerov) **36**:303
"The Moment" (Raine) **45**:332, 338
"The Moment" (Roethke) **3**:433; **8**:456
"The Moment before the Gun Went Off" (Gordimer) **70**:177; **123**:128
The Moment Is All (Gustafson) **36**:222
"Moment of Eternity" (MacDiarmid) **4**:309; **11**:334
"The Moment of Green" (Merwin) **88**:213
"A Moment of Green Laurel" (Vidal) **33**:406-07
"The Moment of My Father's Death" (Olds) **85**:302
"The Moment of the Discovery of America Continues" (Kroetsch) **132**:239
A Moment of True Feeling (Handke)
See *Die Stunde der wahren Empfindung*
"The Moment of Truth" (Castellanos) **66**:56
"The Moment of Vision" (Eberhart) **56**:80
A Moment of War: A Memoir of the Spanish Civil War (Lee) **90**:200, 204-7, 209-10
"Moment of Wisdom" (Fisher) **87**:124
"The Moment the Two Worlds Meet" (Olds) **85**:293, 296
"Momentary Bafflement with Return Home at Dawn" (Codrescu) **46**:106
"Momentary Interrruption" (Wolf) **150**:298
A Momentary Taste of Being (Tiptree) **48**:388-89, 392
Moments (Hine) **15**:282
Moments of Grace (Jennings) **131**:241
"Moments of Light" (Chappell) **40**:141
Moments of Light (Chappell) **40**:141-43; **78**:95, 113
Moments of Reprieve (Levi)
See *Lilít e altri racconti*
Moments of the Italian Summer (Wright) **28**:469, 472
"Momma" (Barthelme) **46**:37
"Momma" (Seger) **35**:380
"Momma and the Neutron Bomb" (Yevtushenko) **51**:432; **126**:391, 396
"Momma Welfare Roll" (Angelou) **35**:30
Momo (Gary)
See *La vie devant soi*
"Mōmoku monogatari" (Tanizaki) **28**:414
Moms: A Praise Play for a Black Comedienne (Childress) **86**:309; **96**:110
Mon ami Maigret (Simenon) **8**:487; **47**:373
Mon oncle d'Amerique (Resnais) **16**:518
Mon temps n'est pas le vôtre (Marcel) **15**:361
"Mona" (Wilson) **12**:651-52
"Mona Lisa" (Herbert) **43**:189, 192
Mona Lisa (Jordan) **110**:274-76, 278, 282, 304, 306-09
Mona Lisa Overdrive (Gibson) **63**:134-38
Mona Minim and the Smell of the Sun (Frame) **96**:189
The Monarch (Vassilikos) **8**:524
The Monarch of the Glen (Mackenzie) **18**:316
"Monarchs" (Olds) **32**:345
"The Monastery at Vršac" (Wright) **146**:309
"The Monastery of Hosios Louikas" (Bowering) **32**:46
Moncrieff (Holland) **21**:149-50
Monday Begins on Saturday (Strugatskii and Strugatskii) **27**:434-35
"A Monday Dream at Alameda Park" (Thomas) **13**:538-39
Monday Morning (Hamilton) **51**:183, 194
Monday Night (Boyle) **5**:65; **58**:64, 66, 70, 73-4; **121**:53-4
Monday the Rabbi Took Off (Kemelman) **2**:225
The Monday Voices (Greenberg) **7**:134
Le monde cassé (Marcel) **15**:361, 364
Le Monde extérieur (Duras) **100**:134-35
"Le monde objet" (Barthes) **24**:27
Mondo et autres histoiries (Le Clézio) **31**:249-50; **155**:82-3
Il mondo salvato dai ragazzini (Morante) **47**:281, 283
"Monet" (Nemerov) **36**:307
"MONET: Les Nymphéas" (Snodgrass) **68**:393
"Monet's 'Waterlilies'" (Hayden) **37**:152
"Money" (Larkin) **8**:332; **9**:323; **64**:282
"Money" (Lennon) **35**:267
"Money" (Nemerov) **2**:308
"Money" (Nowlan) **15**:399
"Money" (Nyro) **17**:318-19
"Money" (Pink Floyd) **35**:306, 311, 313
"Money" (Williams) **148**:341
Money: A Jazz Opera (Baraka) **115**:10, 29
Money: A Suicide Note (Amis) **38**:16, 18-19; **62**:5-7, 9, 11, 13-17, 19; **101**:65-70, 77, 79-84, 86-91, 95
"Money and How It Gets That Way" (Miller) **43**:298
"Money Goes Upstream" (Snyder) **120**:326
Money Is Love (Condon) **6**:115; **8**:150; **100**:113
Money Is Love (Glanville) **6**:202
The Money Juggler (Auchincloss) **18**:24
Money, Money, Money (Wagoner) **3**:507; **5**:473
The Money Order (Ousmane)
See *Mandabi*
Money Pamphlets by £ (Pound) **7**:328
"Money Talks" (Davies) **21**:98
Money with Menaces (Hamilton) **51**:193
"Money Won't Save You" (Cliff) **21**:63
Money Writes! (Sinclair) **11**:498
The Moneychangers (Hailey) **5**:157-58
The Moneychangers (Sinclair) **63**:346, 348
"The Moneygoround" (Davies) **21**:91, 105
The Moneyman (Costain) **30**:93-5, 97
The Money-Order; with White Genesis (Ousmane)
See *Véhi-Ciosane; ou, Blanche-Genèse, suivi du Mandat*
"Mongolian Whiskey" (Katz) **47**:220, 222-23
The Mongrel (Rice) **7**:360
Mongrel (Seger) **35**:378, 381
Mongrel Mettel (Stuart) **34**:376
"Mónico" (Ulibarrí) **83**:411, 415
"Monique" (Gardam) **43**:167
"Monk" (Faulkner) **52**:128
Monk Dawson (Read) **4**:444-45; **10**:434, 436; **25**:376, 379
A Monk Swimming (McCourt) **119**:78-82
"Monkberry Moon Delight" (McCartney) **35**:279
"The Monkey" (Dinesen) **10**:152; **29**:154-55; **95**:59
"The Monkey" (King) **37**:207
Monkey Bridge (Cao) **109**:44-5
Monkey Business (Perelman) **9**:414-15; **44**:501-02, 504-05; **49**:270

"The Monkey Garden" (Cisneros) **118**:175, 186
The Monkey Grammarian (Paz)
See *El mono gramático*
Monkey Island (Fox) **121**:232
Monkey King (Chao) **119**:37-40
The Monkey King (Mo) **46**:257-59; **134**:189, 191, 194-96, 199, 204, 212
"Monkey Man" (Jagger and Richard) **17**:227, 228, 234
"The Monkey Puzzle" (Moore) **13**:394
The Monkey Wrench Gang (Abbey) **36**:13, 17, 19; **59**:238-39, 241-45
"Monkeybites" (Allison) **153**:25
"The Monkeys" (Moore) **8**:399; **47**:260
Monkeys (Minot) **44**:77-81
The Monkey's Wrench (Levi)
See *La chiave a stella*
Monkfish Moon (Gunesekera) **91**:33, 37, 41
"Monk's House, Rodmell" (Muske) **90**:316
"Monkshood" (Gunnars) **69**:260-61
El mono gramático (Paz) **10**:393; **51**:323-25
Monodromos (Engel) **36**:159, 162
"Monody on the Death of Aldersgate Street Station" (Betjeman) **34**:306; **43**:40
"The Monogram" (Elytis) **49**:109; **100**:173
The Monogram (Elytis) **100**:175, 188
"Monolog bitnika" (Voznesensky) **57**:417
"Monolog Merlin Monro" (Voznesensky) **57**:416
"Monolog rybaka" (Voznesensky) **57**:416
"Monólogo de la extranjera" (Castellanos) **66**:45-6
"Monologue" (Beauvoir) **124**:127, 130-31, 185
Monologue (Beauvoir) **14**:70
Monologue (Pinter) **15**:423; **27**:395-96; **58**:381
"Monologue of a Broadway Actress" (Yevtushenko) **26**:462; 388, 396
"Monologue of a Foreign Woman" (Castellanos)
See "Monólogo de la extranjera"
"Monologue of a Fox on an Alaskan Fur Farm" (Yevtushenko) **26**:464; **126**:399
"Monologue of a Loser" (Yevtushenko) **126**:388
"Monologue of a Polar Fox on an Alaskan Fur Farm" (Yevtushenko) **126**:399
"Monologue of a Shell" (Hooker) **43**:197
Monologue of a Whore in a Lunatic Asylum (Fo) **32**:176
"Monologue of an Actress" (Yevtushenko) **126**:388, 396
"Monologue of an American Poet" (Yevtushenko) **26**:462
"Monologue of Dr. Spock" (Yevtushenko) **26**:462
"Monologue of Isabel Watching It Rain in Macondo" (García Márquez) **3**:180
"Monologue of the Beatniks" (Yevtushenko) **26**:463
"Monologue on Life and Death" (Faludy) **42**:138
Monologues (Kundera) **19**:267
Monorail (Audiberti) **38**:32-3
"The Monosyllable" (Jacobsen) **48**:193; **102**:240
"Monotheism and Its Discontents" (Vidal) **142**:290
Monotones (Nichol) **18**:367
"Monotonies" (Boland) **113**:72
Monsieur (Durrell) **6**:151-54; **13**:187, 189; **27**:95, 98-100
"Monsieur Colin's Paint-Box Garden" (Grigson) **7**:136
Monsieur Gallet, décédé (Simenon) **47**:371, 374, 380
"Monsieur les deux chapeaux" (Munro) **50**:208-09, 211-12, 220
Monsieur Levert (Pinget)
See *Le fiston*
"Monsieur Maurice" (Pinget) **37**:364
Monsieur Monde Vanishes (Simenon) **8**:488
Monsieur; or, The Prince of Darkness (Durrell) **41**:134-35, 137-38
Monsieur Teste in America (Codrescu) **121**:163-64
Monsieur Toussaint (Glissant) **68**:173, 180-81
Monsieur Verdoux (Chaplin) **16**:193-97, 199-202, 204-06
Monsieur Vincent (Anouilh) **50**:279
"Monsieur X., Here Called Pierre Rabier" (Duras) **40**:188; **68**:75-6, 78, 83, 99
"Monsignor Missalwait's Interstate" (Vizenor) **103**:309
Monsignor Quixote (Greene) **27**:174, 176-77; **70**:287, 294; **72**:163-64
"The Monster" (Buzzati) **36**:94
Monster (Morgan) **2**:294-95
"The Monster and the Maiden" (Zelazny) **21**:466
"Monster Deal" (Barthelme) **36**:50; **117**:18
Monster in a Box (Gray) **112**:116-19, 126-27, 129-33, 135
Monster Lecture about Justice and Law (Duerrenmatt)
See *Monstervortrag über Gerechtigkeit und Recht*
The Monsters and the Critics, and Other Essays (Tolkien) **38**:439, 442
"The Monster's Belly" (Kingsolver) **130**:84
Monstervortrag über Gerechtigkeit und Recht (Duerrenmatt) **102**:58-9, 82
Les monstres sacrés (Cocteau) **43**:105, 112
Mont de piété (Breton) **9**:126; **54**:29-30
Montage of a Dream Deferred (Hughes) **10**:280; **35**:214, 218, 220-22; **108**:283, 291, 299, 328, 334-35
"La montagne du diev vivant" (Le Clézio) **31**:250
La montagne secrète (Roy) **10**:441; **14**:467
"Montana" (Zappa) **17**:589
"Montana Ecologue" (Stafford) **4**:521
"Montana Ranch Abandoned" (Hugo) **32**:237
Montauk (Frisch) **9**:217; **14**:183-85; **18**:163; **32**:193; **44**:190-93, 204-07
Mont-Cinère (Green) **3**:205; **77**:264, 266, 269, 271, 273, 288, 290
"Monte Niko" (Ulibarrí) **83**:416
"Monte Sant' Angelo" (Miller) **10**:345-46; **47**:249-50
"Montego Bay—Travelogue II" (Walcott) **25**:452
Montezuma's Revenge (Harrison) **42**:201
A Month and a Day (Saro-Wiwa) **114**:260, 262, 274-76
"A Month in Summer" (Kizer) **15**:308
A Month in the Country (Friel) **115**:250
A Month of Sundays (Updike) **5**:457-61; **7**:488-90; **9**:537-38; **13**:557, 559, 562; **43**:432; **139**:324, 336-38
"The Month Was April" (Auden) **43**:16-17
The Months (Brandys) **62**:117, 119
"Montjuich" (Levine) **14**:321
"Montmarte" (Hughes) **1**:149
"Montraldo" (Cheever) **7**:49; **15**:131
"La montre de Pâcome" (Theriault) **79**:408
Le montreur (Chedid) **47**:82, 87
Montserrat (Hellman) **2**:187; **18**:222
Monty Python and the Holy Grail (Gilliam) **141**:247, 260
Monty Python and the Holy Grail (Monty Python) **21**:224-25, 228
Monty Python: Live! At City Center (Monty Python) **21**:227
Monty Python's Big Red Book (Monty Python) **21**:223
Monty Python's Contractual Obligation Album (Monty Python) **21**:230
Monty Python's Flying Circus (Gilliam) **141**:253, 255
Monty Python's Flying Circus (Monty Python) **21**:224-25
Monty Python's Life of Brian (Monty Python) **21**:228-29
Monty Python's Matching Tie and Handkerchief (Monty Python) **21**:225-26
The Monty Python's Meaning of Life (Gilliam) **141**:240
Monty Python's Previous Album (Monty Python) **21**:224, 226
"Montypythonscrapbook" (Monty Python) **21**:229
"The Monument" (Bishop) **1**:34; **9**:92, 98; **32**:32-8, 41, 43
"A Monument" (Hughes) **37**:176; **119**:272, 290
"Monument" (Jeffers) **54**:248
"Monument" (Kunitz) **148**:124
The Monument (Johnson) **27**:213-14
The Monument (Strand) **18**:517, 520; **41**:434-35
The Monument Rose (Garrigue) **2**:153
Monuments and Maidens: The Allegory of Female Form (Warner) **59**:217
"Monuments not yet Erected" (Yevtushenko) **126**:386
Moo (Smiley) **144**:269-73, 295
Moo Pak (Josipovici) **153**:218-19, 225
"A Mood of Quiet Beauty" (Ashbery) **77**:63, 67
"Moods of Love" (Day Lewis) **10**:129
Moon across the Way (Borges)
See *Luna de enfrente*
"Moon and Flowering Plum" (Pollitt) **28**:366-68
"The Moon and GNAC" (Calvino)
See "Luna e G N A C"
The Moon and Sixpence (Maugham) **15**:368-70; **67**:219, 226; **93**:229-30, 233, 243-44, 250, 262-63, 267
"The Moon and the Yew Tree" (Plath) **1**:270; **5**:345; **9**:427, 433; **14**:425; **51**:353; **111**:203, 214
The Moon by Night (L'Engle) **12**:346
The Moon Children (Williamson) **29**:455
"The Moon Dance Skunk" (Guthrie) **23**:199
"Moon Deluxe" (Barthelme) **36**:52; **117**:17-18
Moon Deluxe (Barthelme) **36**:50-2, 54; **117**:2, 5, 9, 11, 13-18, 21
The Moon: Earth's Natural Satellite (Branley) **21**:17, 20
The Moon Era (Williamson) **29**:454
Moon Eyes (Poole) **17**:370-72
"The Moon, Falling" (Shields) **97**:429-30
"Moon Fishing" (Mueller) **51**:279
"The Moon in Its Flight" (Sorrentino) **22**:393
"Moon in My Window" (Sondheim) **30**:379
"The Moon in the Orange Street Skating Rink" (Munro) **50**:209, 211, 215-17, 219-20
"The Moon in Your Hands" (H. D.) **14**:223
The Moon Is a Gong (Dos Passos) **4**:133; **15**:84; **25**:144
The Moon Is a Harsh Mistress (Heinlein) **3**:226; **14**:254-55; **26**:174, 176; **55**:300, 303
"The Moon is Always Female" (Piercy) **128**:245
The Moon Is Always Female (Piercy) **27**:375-77, 379; **62**:373; **128**:243, 245-46
The Moon Is Down (Steinbeck) **1**:325; **9**:514; **13**:531-33; **21**:382; **34**:405, 411; **59**:335, 353
"The Moon Is Hell" (Campbell) **32**:75, 80
"The Moon Is the Number Eighteen" (Olson) **29**:334
"Moon Lady" (Hoffman) **141**:280, 283, 285
"Moon Lake" (Welty) **105**:339
"Moon Landing" (Auden) **6**:19; **9**:59; **14**:28
Moon Marigolds (Zindel)
See *The Effect of Gamma Rays on Man-in-the-Moon Marigolds*
"The Moon Momens" (Mahapatra) **33**:281, 284
"The Moon Moth" (Vance) **35**:419, 426
"Moon Object" (Abse) **7**:2
Moon of Desire (Prichard) **46**:337
Moon of Gomrath (Garner) **17**:135-43, 149
Moon of the Three Rings (Norton) **12**:458, 460, 462, 468
Moon on the Nile (Christie) **39**:437
"The Moon on the Water" (Derleth) **31**:138
"Moon on the Water" (Kawabata)
See "Suigetsu"
Moon Over Minneapolis (Weldon) **122**:268-70

"Moon over the Gasworks" (Seifert) **93**:333
Moon Palace (Auster) **131**:5-6, 8-9, 17, 22-7, 43
"The Moon Shines" (Rozewicz) **139**:236
The Moon Shines on Kylenamoe (O'Casey) **88**:269
"Moon Song, Woman Song" (Sexton) **123**:408
"The Moon, The Owl, My Sister" (Dowell) **60**:108-09
Moon Tiger (Lively) **50**:200-05
Moon-Bells and Other Poems (Hughes) **14**:271
Moonchildren (Weller)
See *Cancer*
Mooncranker's Gift (Unsworth) **76**:252; **127**:409-10, 412
Moondance (Morrison) **21**:232
Moonfleet (Lang) **20**:209, 216; **103**:89
"Moon-Freaks" (Hughes) **14**:271
"Moonlight" (Harjo) **83**:271
"Moonlight Alert" (Winters) **4**:591
"Moonlight Among the Pines" (MacDiarmid) **63**:252
"Moonlight Drive" (Morrison) **17**:290-91
The Moonlight Man (Fox) **121**:229-30
"Moonlight Mile" (Jagger and Richard) **17**:224, 228
Moonlight on the Highway (Potter) **123**:236, 266
"Moonlight on the Wall" (Ortese)
See "La luna sul muro"
"Moonlight Shadow" (Yoshimoto) **84**:421-24, 427-29
Moonlight Sonata (Ritsos) **13**:488; **31**:325, 328
"Moonlighters" (Lieberman) **36**:262
Moonraker (Fleming) **30**:139, 149
"Moonrise" (Plath) **111**:164, 178
Moonrise Moonset (Konwicki) **117**:266, 275, 279, 284, 288-89
"Moon's Farm" (Read) **4**:440
Moon's Farm (Read) **4**:439
The Moons of Jupiter (Munro) **95**:297, 301-02, 305-06, 308, 315-16, 320, 325
Moon's Ottery (Beer) **58**:34-5
"The Moon's Skull in the Lake" (Ivask) **14**:288
"Moonshine" (Marsh) **53**:255
Moonshine Light, Moonshine Bright (Fox) **22**:139-40
The Moonshine War (Leonard) **71**:224; **120**:283
"Moonshine Whiskey" (Morrison) **21**:232-33
"Moonshot" (Sainte-Marie) **17**:431
Moonshot (Sainte-Marie) **17**:431
"Moonshot: 1969" (Allen) **84**:4, 8
The Moon-Spinners (Stewart) **7**:467; **35**:390, 392
Moonstruck (Shanley) **75**:321-31
"Moontan" (Strand) **71**:284-85
"Moon-Watcher" (Clarke) **35**:122
Moon-Whales and Other Moon Poems (Hughes)
See *Moon-Bells and Other Poems*
"Moonwriter" (Bullins) **7**:37
"Moony-Art" (Hughes) **14**:271
Moorcock's Book of Martyrs (Moorcock) **58**:352
"Mooring" (Hoffman) **141**:270, 273, 283
"Moorings" (MacCaig) **36**:282
The Moor's Last Sigh (Rushdie) **100**:285-324
"Moortown" (Hughes) **37**:175, 177
Moortown (Hughes) **37**:172, 174-76, 178-80; **119**:249, 271-72, 279, 288
Moortown Elegies (Hughes) **37**:175; **119**:288-90
"The Moose" (Bishop) **9**:91-2, 96; **13**:89-91, 94-5; **32**:32, 37-8, 42
"Moose in the Morning, Northern Maine" (Van Duyn) **63**:442; **116**:410
"Moose Island" (H. D.) **31**:208
"Moot" (Colter) **58**:140, 147
"Moral Censorship" (Farrell) **66**:134
The Moral Circus (Honig) **33**:210
Moral Consciousness and Communicative Action (Habermas)
See *Moralbewusstsein und Kommunikatives Handeln*
"Moral Education" (Lustig) **56**:182
"Moral Fibre" (Amis) **40**:43, 45
The Moral Intelligence of Children (Coles) **108**:216
The Moral Life of Children (Coles) **108**:184, 186-88, 208, 211-12, 216
"Moral Problem" (Scannell) **49**:327, 331
Moralbewusstsein und Kommunikatives Handeln (Habermas) **104**:79-80, 82
"Moraldo in the City" (Fellini) **85**:64
Morale élémentaire (Queneau) **10**:430
"Morales élémentaires" (Perec) **56**:258
"The Moralists" (Winters) **4**:591
Moralities (Kinsella) **138**:84
"A Morality" (Forster)
See "What Does It Matter? A Morality"
"The Morality of Impersonal Narration" (Booth) **24**:88
"The Morality of Indian Hating" (Momaday) **85**:264-65; **95**:244, 275
Morality Play (Unsworth) **127**:416-20, 424-25
Moravagine (Cendrars) **18**:91, 95, 97; **106**:166, 183-85, 187-90, 192
Mord paas 31: A vaangin (Wahlöö) **7**:501
"Mordent for a Melody" (Avison) **97**:76, 90
Mordre en sa chair (Brossard) **115**:102
"More" (Ai) **69**:9
More (Pink Floyd) **35**:311
"The More a Man Has, the More a Man Wants" (Muldoon) **32**:321; **72**:270, 274, 279, 282
"More Benadryl, Whined the Journalist" (Vollmann) **89**:305, 307, 314
"More Catholic Than the Pope; Archbishop Lefebvre and a Romance of the One True Church" (Gordon) **128**:118
More Caviar (Buchwald) **33**:88-9
More Classics Revisited (Rexroth) **112**:387
"More Clues" (Rukeyser) **27**:410
More Collected Poems (MacDiarmid) **4**:313; **63**:246
More Collected Stories (Pritchett) **41**:334
"More de A.D." (Beckett) **14**:74
More Die of Heartbreak (Bellow) **63**:27-35, 40
"More Enterprise" (Merrill) **2**:274
"More Essex Poems" (Davie) **31**:117
More Experiments in Science (Branley) **21**:16
More Hardcore (Thompson) **69**:383
More Issues at Hand (Blish) **14**:83
More Joy (Comfort) **7**:54
More Joy in Heaven (Callaghan) **14**:100-01, 103; **41**:88, 90, 95; **65**:250, 252
"More Life" (Strand) **41**:439-41
"More Light! More Light!" (Hecht) **8**:268; **19**:207
"The More Little Mummy in the World" (Thomas) **37**:417; **107**:326,348
More Lives than One (Krutch) **24**:289
"More Love in the Western World" (Updike) **139**:360
"More of a Corpse than a Woman" (Rukeyser) **27**:404, 412
"More of the Insane" (Rosenblatt) **15**:448
"More Pleasant Adventures" (Ashbery) **41**:34, 39
More Poems, 1961 (Graves) **1**:127
More Poems for People (Acorn) **15**:10
More Poems to Solve (Swenson) **61**:402; **106**:340
More Pricks than Kicks (Beckett) **6**:38, 43; **10**:34; **11**:32, 36; **14**:79; **18**:41, 43; **29**:59, 62; **83**:135
More Shapes Than One (Chappell) **78**:116-17
More Songs about Buildings and Food (Byrne) **26**:95-8
"More Sonnets at Christmas" (Tate) **14**:531
More Tales of Pirx the Pilot (Lem) **40**:295, 297; **149**:262, 276
More Tales of the City (Maupin) **95**:191-94, 197, 199-201, 202
More Than a New Discovery (Nyro)
See *The First Songs*
More than Enough (Sargeson) **31**:369
"More Than Human" (Chabon) **149**:3, 5, 8
More than Human (Sturgeon) **22**:410-11; **39**:361-62, 364-68
"More Than the Sum of His Parts" (Haldeman) **61**:181
More Than You Deserve (Weller) **53**:390
The More the Merrier (Weber) **12**:633
More to Remember (Randall) **135**:376-77, 390, 392-94, 397-98
More under Saturn (Dickey) **3**:126-27
More Women than Men (Compton-Burnett) **15**:138, 140; **34**:494
More Words of Science (Asimov) **26**:38
More Work for the Undertaker (Allingham) **19**:13, 18
"Morgan Morgan" (Hospital) **145**:303
Morgan's Passing (Tyler) **18**:529-31; **28**:432; **44**:315; **59**:205; **103**:217, 222-24, 228, 235, 241-42, 244-45, 254, 259-60, 263
"Morgengabe" (Jeffers) **54**:234
Die Morgenlandfahrt (Hesse) **1**:146; **17**:204, 211; **25**:261, **69**:279
"Morgenlied" (Williams) **45**:443
"Moritat" (Jandl) **34**:197
Mork and Mindy (Marshall) **17**:277-78
Mörkerseende (Transtroemer) **52**:410; **65**:220, 222-23, 225, 229
Morley Callaghan's Stories (Callaghan) **65**:248
"Morn Advancing" (Keates) **34**:202-03
"Morning" (Arghezi) **80**:9
"A Morning" (Atwood) **84**:68
"Morning" (Barthelme) **13**:59-60, 62; **46**:37-8
"Morning" (Creeley) **78**:143
"Morning" (Davie) **31**:116, 118
"Morning" (Fuller) **62**:197
"Morning" (Glück) **44**:216, 218
"Morning" (MacCaig) **36**:279
"Morning" (Oliver) **98**:293
"A Morning" (Strand) **41**:432, 438
"Morning" (Williams) **42**:459
"The Morning" (Winters) **32**:469
Morning (Horovitz)
See *Chiaroscuro*
"Morning After" (Zamora) **89**:368
The Morning After (Sheed) **10**:473
The Morning after Optimism (Murphy) **51**:301-02, 304
"Morning and Evening" (Transtroemer) **65**:222
"Morning at Great Pond" (Oliver) **34**:246
Morning at Jalna (de la Roche) **14**:149
"Morning at the Window" (Eliot) **41**:151-52; **113**:187
"Morning Bedroom" (Dunn) **40**:165-66
"Morning Birds" (Transtroemer) **65**:227
"Morning Coffee" (Hope) **3**:250
"Morning Coffee" (Kinsella) **138**:167
"Morning Express" (Sassoon) **36**:386; **130**:191
Morning Face (Anand) **93**:29-30, 32-3, 36-7, 41, 55, 57
Morning Girl (Dorris) **109**:306-07, 309
"Morning Glory" (Moss) **45**:290
"Morning Glory" (Nemerov) **36**:308
The Morning Glory, Another Thing That Will Never Be My Friend (Bly) **15**:63, 65-6; **38**:50, 57-9; **128**:17, 22-23
"Morning Glory Blue" (Sandburg) **35**:356
"The Morning Half-Life Blues" (Piercy) **27**:373
"Morning in a New Land" (Oliver) **98**:294
Morning in Antibes (Knowles) **1**:169; **4**:272; **26**:247-48, 255-56, 258, 262
"Morning in Massachusetts" (Oliver) **19**:362
"Morning in Norfolk" (Barker) **48**:24
"A Morning in the Life of Intelligent People" (Mosley) **43**:314
"Morning in the Park" (Ciardi) **40**:157
Morning Is a Long Time Coming (Greene) **30**:170

"Morning Jitters" (Ashbery) **77**:66
"morning mirror" (Clifton) **66**:83
"The Morning Moon" (Walcott) **67**:351
Morning, Noon, and Night (Cozzens) **1**:67; **4**:116; **11**:132; **92**:189-94
"The Morning of the Day They Did It" (White) **10**:528
"The Morning of the Dead" (Wright) **53**:423-24
The Morning of the Poem (Schuyler) **23**:390-92
"Morning On This Street" (Soto) **80**:282
"Morning Poem" (Oliver) **98**:267
"Morning Prayer" (Berryman) **10**:46
"Morning Prayer" (Ezekiel) **61**:92
"The Morning Prayers of the Hasid, Rabbi Levi Yitzhak" (Gotlieb) **18**:193
"Morning Scene" (Huxley) **11**:284
"Morning Song" (Plath) **9**:428; **14**:422; **111**:207
The Morning Song of Lord Zero: Poems Old and New (Aiken) **52**:26
Morning Star (Dabrowska)
See *Gwiazda zaranna*
Morning Star (Williams) **15**:577
The Morning Star: Poems and Translations (Rexroth) **22**:349; **49**:275; **112**:370-71, 393
"Morning Sun" (MacNeice) **1**:186; **53**:234
"Morning Thinking of Empire" (Carver) **36**:100
"Morning Train" (Cliff) **21**:65
"The Morning Train" (Merwin) **88**:211
"A Morning Walk" (Ezekiel) **61**:92, 100, 104
"Morning with Broken Window" (Hogan) **73**:158
Morning Yet on Creation Day (Achebe) **75**:5; **127**:28; **152**:29-30, 65, 67, 89, 92
"Morning-Land" (Sassoon) **130**:176
"Mornings After" (Adcock) **41**:14, 17-18
"Mornings in a New House" (Merrill) **13**:381
"Mornings in Mexico" (West) **9**:562
Mornings Like This (Dillard) **115**:209
"morning-water train woman" (Young Bear) **94**:363
"Morocco" (Faludy) **42**:139
Morocco (Sternberg) **20**:369, 372
The Moronic Inferno and Other Visits to America (Amis) **62**:2-6; **101**:68, 77, 80, 82
Moros en la costa (Dorfman) **77**:145-46
Morový sloup (Seifert)
See *The Plague Column*
"Morpho Eugenia" (Byatt) **136**:151-52, 154, 180
"The Morphology of the Amorphous" (Perloff) **137**:302
Morreion: A Tale of the Dying Earth (Vance) **35**:422
"Morris Smith: The Man and the Myth" (Frazier) **46**:164-65
Morrison Hotel (Morrison) **17**:289, 291-92, 295-96
"Morse Moose and Grey Goose" (McCartney) **35**:286
Morskiye nabroski (Paustovsky) **40**:362
"Un Morso Doo Pang" (Ferber) **93**:139
"La mort" (Lee)
See "Elle est trois,"
Mort à crédit (Céline) **1**:56; **3**:102, 104-05; **4**:98, 100-02; **7**:43, 46-7; **9**:152, 158; **15**:125; **47**:71-5, 77, 79; **124**:52-3, 59-61, 72-4, 78-80, 87-9, 91-3, 95-6, 111-12, 115-16
La mort conduit l'attelage (Yourcenar) **50**:364; **87**:383
La mort dans l'âme (Sartre) **1**:305; **50**:383
Le mort de demain (Marcel) **15**:363
"La mort de l'auteur" (Barthes) **83**:81, 97
La Mort de Siegfried (Lang) **103**:88-9
Mort d'Oluwémi d'Ajumako (Condé) **52**:79, 81; **92**:99-100
La mort en ce jardin (Bunuel) **16**:147-48; **80**:25, 28, 30-1, 38-40
La mort heureuse (Camus) **2**:98-9; **9**:149-50; **124**:31
"La mort rose" (Breton) **54**:33
Mortal Acts, Mortal Words (Kinnell) **29**:284-86, 288-89; **129**:234, 238, 240, 249, 255-57, 264, 270
Mortal Coils (Huxley) **1**:151
Mortal Consequences: A History from the Detective Story to the Crime Novel (Symons) **14**:524; **32**:424-25
"The Mortal Danger" (Solzhenitsyn) **78**:403-06
"A Mortal Day of No Surprises" (Kumin) **13**:328; **28**:225
Mortal Engines (Lem) **8**:345; **40**:296; **149**:273
Mortal Friends (Carroll) **38**:104-08
Mortal Lessons: Notes on the Art of Surgery (Selzer) **74**:263-64, 268, 270, 276, 278-79, 281
"Mortal Limit" (Warren) **39**:265, 268, 270
"The Mortal Mountain" (Zelazny) **21**:465-66
A Mortal Pitch (Scannell) **49**:324, 330, 332
"Mortal Pride" (Clarke) **9**:168
Mortal Stakes (Parker) **27**:363-64, 366
"Mortality" (Betjeman) **6**:66
"Mortality and Mercy in Vienna" (Pynchon) **6**:430; **33**:333, 339
Morte accidentale di un anarchico (Fo) **32**:172-74, 176-77; **109**:104, 106, 117-18, 120-21, 136, 142, 144-45
La morte dell'inquisitore (Sciascia) **41**:388, 395
Morte d'urban (Powers) **1**:279-82; **4**:419; **57**:349-50, 352-54, 356-58
"A Morte e a morte de Quincas Berro Dágua" (Amado) **40**:30-1, 34; **106**:65-6, 70-1, 73, 77
Morte e vida severina e outraos poemas em voz alta (Cabral de Melo Neto) **76**:153, 155-56, 158, 160, 168-69
Une morte très douce (Beauvoir) **4**:47; **8**:62; **14**:67; **31**:35, 43; **44**:344-45, 349-51; **71**:58, 78-9
The Mortgaged Heart (McCullers) **1**:210; **4**:344-45; **12**:427, 432
"The Mortician's Twelve-Year-Old Son" (Ai) **69**:7
"Mortmain" (Warren) **13**:573; **39**:260, 266
"Morts pour la France" (Damas) **84**:176
Morts sans sépulture (Sartre) **9**:470-71; **13**:499; **52**:381
"Morvin" (Fuller) **62**:184-85
Morwyn; or, The Vengeance of God (Powys) **7**:350; **46**:322; **125**:291
"Mosaic" (Cage) **41**:78
"Mosaic Harlem" (Dumas) **62**:155
"The Mosaic Hunchback" (Macdonald) **19**:290
Mosby's Memoirs, and Other Stories (Bellow) **25**:85; **33**:67, 69, 71; **63**:43
"Moschus Moschiferus" (Hope) **51**:223
"Moscow" (Stern) **40**:414
Moscow 2042 (Voinovich) **49**:383-85; **147**:286, 293-94
Moscow Does Not Believe in Tears (Ehrenburg) **18**:131; **62**:176
"Moscow in the Wilderness, Segovia in the Snow" (Ferlinghetti) **27**:139; **111**:65
Moscow Novella (Wolf)
See *Moskauer Novelle*
Moscow Saga (Aksyonov) **101**:55-6
"The Moscow Symphony" (Hikmet) **40**:248
The Moscow Symphony and Other Poems (Hikmet) **40**:248
Mosén Milán (Sender) **8**:479, 481
Moses (Burgess) **8**:113; **22**:71, 78
"Moses at Darwin Station" (Purdy) **50**:247
"Moses' Death" (Hein)
See "Moses Tod"
Moses, Man of the Mountain (Hurston) **7**:171; **30**:212-13, 216, 219, 228
The Moses Of Beale Street (Tolson) **105**:281
Moses, Prince of Egypt (Fast) **23**:158; **131**:91
"Moses Tod" (Hein) **154**:167, 175, 181-82, 164-65
Moskauer Novelle (Wolf) **14**:593; **58**:432; **150**:227, 237, 260, 270-71, 278, 321-22, 329, 331
Moskaver Novelle (Wolf)
See *Moskauer Novelle*
Moskovskaia saga (Aksyonov)
See *Moscow Saga*
"Mosler Safe" (Lowell) **15**:343
The Mosquito Coast (Theroux) **28**:426-28; **46**:399-400, 403
"Mosquito Kingdom" (Cardenal)
See "Reino mosco"
"Mosquitoes" (Jones) **81**:63, 65, 67
Mosquitoes (Faulkner) **9**:199; **11**:200-01; **28**:140-41; **68**:127-28, 130-31
Moss and Blister (Garfield) **12**:234
"The Moss of His Skin" (Sexton) **53**:316-17
"Mossbawn: Sunlight" (Heaney) **25**:249; **74**:166, 193
"Moss-Gathering" (Roethke) **3**:432; **46**:362; **101**:294
Most (Bagryana) **10**:11
The Most Beautiful (Kurosawa)
See *Ichiban Utsukushiku*
"The Most Beautiful Legs in the World" (Kelley) **22**:247
"The Most Beautiful Protestant Girls in Muggalnagrow" (Durcan) **43**:118
The Most Beautiful World (Hall) **51**:176
"The Most Costly Passion of All" (Mayle) **89**:150
"The Most Difficult Position" (Fuller) **62**:196-97, 201, 203-04
"Most Exclusive Residence for Sale" (Davies) **21**:88
The Most High (Blanchot) **135**:112-13
"The Most Humble Poem" (Seifert)
See "Básežn nejpokornější"
"The Most Incredible Meal" (Kotzwinkle) **35**:253
"Most like an Arch This Marriage" (Ciardi) **40**:156-58
Most Likely to Succeed (Dos Passos) **4**:135; **15**:186; **25**:141, 146; **34**:422
"Most Lovely Shade" (Sitwell) **67**:324
"The Most of It" (Frost) **4**:175; **9**:219, 222, 228-29; **10**:194-95; **26**:128; **34**:471
"Most of My Life" (Stern) **100**:336
The Most of S. J. Perelman (Perelman) **15**:417-18; **44**:505
"A Most Peculiar Man" (Simon) **17**:458
"Mostly about Myself" (Yezierska) **46**:442
Mostly Baseball (Hall)
See *Fathers Playing Catch with Sons: Essays on Sport*
Mostly Canallers (Edmonds) **35**:146, 150-51
Il mostro (Buzzati) **36**:84
"Mostru o pavea" (Pasolini) **106**:229
"Mota Shel Assia G." (Amichai) **116**:118
The Mote in God's Eye (Niven) **8**:426
Motel (van Itallie) **3**:493
"A Motel in Troy, New York" (Jacobsen) **48**:193, 197
"A Motet for Tomas Luis de Victoria" (Shapcott) **38**:404
"The Moth" (Dobyns) **37**:81
"The Moth" (Scannell) **49**:328
"The Moth" (Wakoski) **40**:456
The Moth (Cain) **28**:48
"Moth Sonata" (Rosenblatt) **15**:448
"The Mother" (Brooks) **5**:75
"Mother" (Carruth) **84**:133
"Mother" (Hacker) **72**:182
"Mother" (Lennon) **35**:261-62, 266, 270
"The Mother" (Olds) **85**:286
"The Mother" (Ousmane) **66**:349
"Mother" (Paley) **140**:211
"Mother" (Police, The) **26**:366
"The Mother" (Snodgrass) **68**:381-82, 397
"The Mother" (Stevenson) **33**:382
The Mother (Buck) **11**:70, 74, 77; **18**:79
Mother (Seifert)
See *Maminka*

Mother and Child (Vinge) **30**:409-10, 413-14
"Mother and Child Reunion" (Simon) **17**:461, 465-66
"A Mother and Her Daughter" (Wiesel) **37**:450
"Mother and 'Miss E.'" (Fisher) **87**:131
"Mother and Son" (Lowell) **124**:261
"Mother and Son" (Tate) **9**:523; **14**:529, 531
Mother and Son (Compton-Burnett) **15**:140; **34**:495, 500
A Mother and Two Daughters (Godwin) **31**:194-96, 198; **69**:232, 234-35, 237-39, 241, 246, 252-53; **125**:126-27, 138-41, 144-45, 149, 151, 154-55, 157-58, 161-62, 168-70
"Mother/Child" (Ostriker) **132**:327
"Mother/Child: Codac" (Ostriker) **132**:318, 328
The Mother/ChildPapers (Ostriker) **132**:319
"Mother Coming" (Bly) **15**:62
Mother Courage and Her Children (Hare) **136**:278
Mother Courage & Her Children (Shange) **25**:399-400
"Mother Dressmaking" (Raine) **103**:182, 186, 189
"Mother Earth" (Asimov) **26**:42
"Mother Earth" (Gunn) **18**:200
Mother Earth (Aitmatov)
See *Materinskoe pole*
"Mother Earth: Her Whales" (Snyder) **120**:340
"Mother Earth, or the Folly of National Boundaries" (Kunene) **85**:178
Mother Field (Aitmatov)
See *Materinskoe pole*
Mother Figure (Ayckbourn) **18**:28; **33**:40
"Mother Gaia" (Snyder) **120**:343
"Mother Geese" (Niedecker) **42**:298-300
"Mother Goose" (Rexroth) **112**:400
"Mother in the Sky with Diamonds" (Tiptree) **48**:385
Mother Ireland (O'Brien) **8**:429-30; **116**:181-82, 185, 193-95, 197, 199
"Mother Knows Best" (Ferber) **93**:153, 162, 180
Mother Knows Best (Ferber) **93**:153
Mother Küsters Goes to Heaven (Fassbinder) **20**:112
Mother London (Moorcock) **58**:358-60
"Mother Marie Therese" (Lowell) **8**:353, 356; **15**:344
Mother Night (Vonnegut) **1**:348; **2**:453, 455; **3**:495-97, 499, 501-03, 505-06; **4**:561-65, 567; **5**:467-69; **8**:531, 533; **12**:601, 604, 606-07, 609-12, 614, 618-23; **40**:441, 443, 448-49; **60**:424, 431-32, 440; **111**:351, 354-55, 359, 361, 366
The Mother of Captain Shigemoto (Tanizaki)
See *Shōshō Shigemoto no haha*
"Mother of hanged men" (Rozewicz)
See "Matka powieszonych"
Mother of Pearl (Morrissy) **99**:73-8
"The Mother of the Child in Question" (Lessing) **94**:265
"The Mother of the Muses" (Harrison) **129**:216
"The Mother of Toads" (Smith) **43**:422
Mother Russia (Littell) **42**:276
"Mother to Son" (Hughes) **35**:216; **108**:296, 309
"Mother Tongue" (Simic) **9**:479
Mother World (Campbell) **32**:74
"Motherhood" (Swenson) **106**:335
"Motherhood according to Bellini" (Kristeva) **77**:312; **140**:175
Mothering Sunday (Streatfeild) **21**:400
"The Mother-in-Law" (Betts) **3**:73
Motherlode (Ferlinghetti) **111**:63
"Mothers" (Endō)
See "Haha naru mono"
"Mothers" (Giovanni) **117**:196
Mothers and Daughters (Hunter) **31**:220
"Mother's Boy" (Durcan) **70**:152
Mothers' Boys (Forster) **149**:96-7
"The Mother's Curses" (Schaeffer) **11**:491
"The Mother's Dance" (Kinsella) **43**:254
Mother's Field (Aitmatov)
See *Materinskoe pole*
Mother's Garden (Walker)
See *In Search of Our Mother's Gardens: Womanist Prose*
A Mother's Kisses (Friedman) **3**:165; **5**:127; **56**:95-6, 99, 102-3, 107-08
"Mother's Little Helper" (Jagger and Richard) **17**:226, 234-35
"The Mother's Tale" (Ai) **69**:9
"Mother's Voice" (Creeley) **36**:120; **78**:153
Mothersill and the Foxes (Williams) **13**:599
"Mothlady" (Rosenblatt) **15**:446
"Moths" (Boland) **113**:92
"The Motion" (Jacobsen) **48**:195
"The Motion" (Roethke) **3**:433; **19**:396
"Motion for Motion" (Ammons) **5**:28; **108**:23
The Motion of History and Other Plays (Baraka) **14**:48; **33**:57; **115**:10, 28-9
The Motion of Light on Water (Delany) **141**:99-100, 101, 116-17, 142, 145, 148, 150, 152, 155, 157, 160
"Motion of wish" (Kunitz) **148**:68, 87, 123
"Motion's Holdings" (Ammons) **57**:51, 56-7
Motives for Fiction (Alter) **34**:515-17
"Los motivos de son" (Guillén) **79**:238
Motivos de son (Guillén) **48**:157, 159, 161, 163, 165-69; **79**:228-29, 240-41, 244-46, 248
"Moto Shel Celan" (Amichai) **116**:118
La motocyclette (Mandiargues) **41**:275-77
"The Motor Car" (Clarke) **53**:89
Motor City (Morris) **76**:77-85
Motor City Blue (Estleman) **48**:103-04, 107
"A Motorbike" (Hughes) **37**:172
"Motorbike" (Williams) **42**:441
The Motorcycle (Mandiargues)
See *La motocyclette*
The Motorcycle Betrayal Poems (Wakoski) **2**:459; **4**:571-72; **7**:507; **9**:555
"Motorcycle Mama" (Young) **17**:580
"Motorcycle Stunts on the Vertical Wall" (Voznesensky) **57**:419
"O motorneiro de Caxangá" (Cabral de Melo Neto) **76**:168
"Les Mots" (Lowell) **124**:255
Les mots (Sartre) **1**:305; **4**:474, 476; **7**:389, 397; **13**:501; **18**:472-73; **24**:411; **44**:493, 496; **50**:370-72, 374, 376, 378, 381-82, 384; **52**:379, 385, 387
Les mots dans la peinture (Butor) **15**:114
Les mots et les choses: Une archéologie des sciences humaines (Foucault) **31**:174-78, 181, 185-86; **34**:339, 341; **69**:159, 168, 170
Mots sans memoire (Leiris) **61**:346
"Les mots sans rides" (Breton) **9**:125
"Motteti" (Montale) **7**:223-24; **18**:340
"The Motto on the Sundial" (Rexroth) **112**:396
Les mouches (Sartre) **4**:473; **7**:389; **9**:470-71; **13**:498-99; **18**:470; **44**:493; **50**:371, 373, 375, 381, 383; **52**:373, 388
Mouchette (Bresson) **16**:112-13, 115, 119
Mouchoir de nuages (Tzara) **47**:388, 390; **47**:388
"Mougins Provence, September, 1971" (Morgan) **31**:275
Le moulin de la sourdine (Aymé) **11**:22
Moulin premier (Char) **55**:288
Moulin Rouge (Huston) **20**:162
"The Mound Builders" (Kunitz) **148**:89, 128
The Mound Builders (Wilson) **7**:548-49; **14**:590; **36**:463
Mound Builders of Ancient America: The Archaeology of a Myth (Silverberg) **140**:396
"Mount Blank" (Hollander) **8**:299
"Mount Caribou at Night" (Wright) **146**:308, 310, 340
"Mount Eagle" (Montague) **46**:279
"The Mount of Olives" (Arghezi)
See "Muntele Măslinilor"
"Mount Royal" (Scott) **22**:374
"Mt. Zion" (Amichai) **116**:85, 88
"Mount Zion" (Hughes) **119**:275
Mount Zion; or, In Touch with the Infinite (Betjeman) **34**:306
"The Mountain" (Frost) **9**:219; **15**:247; **26**:112
"The Mountain" (Glück) **44**:216, 222
"The Mountain" (Mathias) **45**:238
"The Mountain" (Merwin) **1**:213; **88**:205
The Mountain (Troyat)
See *La neige en deuil*
"The Mountain and Maryann" (Lightfoot) **26**:278
"The Mountain and the Man Who Was Not God" (Jordan) **114**:151-52
The Mountain and the Valley (Buckler) **13**:118, 120
"Mountain and Tidewater Songs" (Epstein) **7**:97
"The Mountain Ash Tree" (Pack) **13**:438-39
Mountain City (Sinclair) **15**:498
"The Mountain Day" (Stafford) **68**:433
Mountain Dialogues (Waters) **88**:365
The Mountain in the Sea (Fuller) **62**:190-92, 195-97, 201-02, 204
Mountain Interval (Frost) **10**:193; **15**:248; **26**:117-19, 124, 128; **34**:468
Mountain Language (Pinter) **58**:385
"Mountain Liar" (Ammons) **108**:20
The Mountain Lion (Stafford) **4**:517; **7**:455, 456-59; **19**:430; **68**:421, 424-28, 430, 434-36, 439, 444, 447-49
"Mountain Meddler" (Guthrie) **23**:199
"Mountain Medicine" (Guthrie) **23**:203
"Mountain Mystery" (Warren) **39**:258
"Mountain Oysters" (Lane) **25**:285, 287
Mountain Paths (Arnow) **7**:15-16; **18**:10
"Mountain Pines" (Jeffers) **54**:234
"Mountain Plateau" (Warren) **18**:535
"Mountain Talk" (Ammons) **25**:44
Mountain Wolf Woman, Sister of Crashing Thunder: The Autobiographyof a Winnebago Indian (Mountain Wolf Woman) **92**:356-372
"The Mountaineers" (Abse) **29**:16
Mountaineers and Eskimos (Coles) **108**:194, 210
"Mountains" (Gascoyne) **45**:153
Mountains and Caverns (Sillitoe) **148**:176, 180-81
"Mountains and Rivers without End" (Snyder) **120**:318-19, 322
Mountains and Rivers without End (Snyder) **32**:387-89, 399; **120**:335, 358
"The Mountains of Dawn" (McIntyre) **18**:327
"The Mountains of Guatemala" (Connell) **45**:112
"The Mountains of Sunset" (McIntyre) **18**:327
"The Mountains of the Moon" (Powys) **7**:349; **125**:293
"Mountains, Polecats, Pheasants" (Norris) **14**:387
Mountains, Polecats, Pheasants and Other Elegies (Norris) **14**:387-88
Mounted Police Patrol (Haig-Brown) **21**:139
Mountolive (Durrell) **1**:87; **4**:144-45, 147; **8**:191; **13**:185-86
"The Mourner" (Friedman) **56**:107
"The Mourners" (Malamud) **9**:348; **27**:306; **85**:190
Mourners Below (Purdy) **28**:381-82; **52**:342-43, 346-48
The Mournful Demeanor of Lieutenant Boruvka (Škvorecký) **69**:333-34, 338, 346-47; **152**:315
"Mourning" (Strand) **6**:522
"A Mourning Forbidding Valediction" (Ashbery) **125**:35
"Mourning Letter" (Dorn) **10**:159
"Mourning Pablo Neruda" (Bly) **128**:44
"Mourning Poem for the Queen of Sunday" (Hayden) **37**:160
Mouroir (Breytenbach) **37**:47-50; **126**:70-2, 74-6, 87-9, 92-3
"The Mouse" (Ashbery) **77**:67

"The Mouse" (Nin) **60**:267
"The Mouse" (Snodgrass) **68**:382, 388
The Mouse and His Child (Hoban) **7**:161; **25**:263, 265
"Mouse Elegy" (Olds) **85**:295-96
Mouse on the Moon (Lester) **20**:220
Mouse Woman and the Mischief-Makers (Harris) **12**:268
Mouse Woman and the Vanished Princesses (Harris) **12**:266, 268
The Mousetrap (Christie) **6**:110; **12**:118, 125; **39**:437, 440-41; **48**:78; **110**:122-23, 146-48
La moustache (Carrere) **89**:67-71
Mouth (Ellison)
See *I Have No Mouth and I Must Scream*
"The Mouth of the Hudson" (Lowell) **5**:258
"Mouths" (Dudek) **11**:158
Le mouvement perpétual (Aragon) **22**:40
Mouvements (Michaux) **8**:392; **19**:316
"Movable Feast" (Weidman) **7**:517
"The Move" (Roy) **14**:467
Move! (Lieber) **6**:311
"Move On" (Sondheim) **30**:403; **147**:230
"Move On Up" (Bell) **102**:5-6, 8
Move Over, Mountain (Ehle) **27**:101-03
Move Over, Mrs. Markham (Cooney) **62**:144, 146
"Move Still, Still So" (Howard) **47**:171
"Move Un-noticed to be Noticed: A Nationhood Poem" (Madhubuti) **73**:215
A Moveable Feast (Hemingway) **3**:243; **6**:228; **8**:283; **13**:275; **19**:215, 224; **39**:402, 430, 432-33; **41**:198, 203-04, 207; **44**:519; **50**:427, 430; **80**:146
"The Move-In" (Bowen) **6**:96; **15**:78
"The Movement" (Bambara) **88**:54
Movement (Miner) **40**:327-31
"Movement of Autumn" (Watkins) **43**:450
"The Movement of Fish" (Dickey) **7**:83
"Movements" (Tomlinson) **4**:545; **13**:549
Movements (Michaux)
See *Mouvements*
"Movements IV" (Tomlinson) **13**:549
"The Movers" (Louie) **70**:79-80
The Movie at the End of the World (McGrath) **28**:277-78; **59**:175, 178, 181
"Movie House" (Updike) **23**:474
Movie Movie (Gelbart) **21**:130; **61**:149
"The Movie Run Backward" (Creeley) **78**:142
Movie Shoes (Streatfeild) **21**:399, 414-15
The Moviegoer (Percy) **2**:333-34; **3**:378-81; **6**:399-401; **8**:439-40, 442, 444-45; **14**:413, 416-18; **18**:396-400, 402; **47**:333, 336, 338, 340-41; **65**:255-60
"Moviegoing" (Hollander) **8**:299
Moviegoing and Other Poems (Hollander) **8**:298
"Movies" (Dixon) **52**:98
"Movies" (Hughes) **35**:222
Movies (Dixon) **52**:98-101
"Movin' Out" (Joel) **26**:215-17, 221
"Moving" (Jarrell) **2**:209
"The Moving" (Still) **49**:364, 366
"Moving Day" (Coles) **46**:107, 113
"The Moving Finger" (Masters) **48**:223
The Moving Finger (Christie) **39**:438; **48**:73
"The Moving Floor" (Szirtes) **46**:394
"Moving from Cheer to Joy, from Joy to All" (Jarrell) **9**:296
"Moving From Pain to Power: Black Self-Determination" (Hooks) **94**:159
"The Moving Image" (Wright) **11**:578; **53**:416, 418-19, 423-24, 426-27, 431
The Moving Image (Wright) **11**:578; **53**:416, 418-19, 423, 426-28, 430-31
Moving in Winter (Rich) **36**:378
"Moving Inward at Last" (Bly) **10**:57
"Moving: New York—New Haven Line" (Corn) **33**:117
Moving On (McMurtry) **2**:271-72; **3**:333; **7**:214-15; **27**:326, 328-30, 333; **44**:254; **127**:304, 315-17, 319
Moving Parts (Katz) **47**:217-19, 223
"Moving Pictures" (Johnson) **51**:234, 236
Moving Pictures: Memories of a Hollywood Prince (Schulberg) **48**:350-51
"A Moving Target" (Golding) **81**:321
A Moving Target (Golding) **27**:164-65, 168-69
The Moving Target (Macdonald) **1**:185; **14**:328, 334; **34**:417; **41**:265, 267-68, 270-71
The Moving Target (Merwin) **1**:212-13; **2**:276-77; **3**:340; **5**:285-86, 288; **88**:191-93, 197, 199, 201, 203-05
"Moving the Walls" (Simpson) **7**:428
"Moving through Spain" (Dobyns) **37**:77
"Moving to a New House" (Hesse) **17**:216
"The Moving to Griffin" (Ondaatje) **14**:407
Moving Towards Home (Jordan) **114**:152, 156
The Moving Toyshop (Crispin) **22**:108
Moviola (Kanin) **22**:232
"The Mower" (Bates) **46**:67
"The Mower" (Garrett) **51**:144
"Mowing" (Frost) **4**:177; **13**:227; **15**:246, 248; **26**:112, 115-16, 118
Mozaika (Voznesensky) **15**:555
Mozart (Hildesheimer) **49**:171, 175-76, 178-79
Mozart and the Wolf Gang (Burgess) **81**:304, 307-10
Mozart the Dramatist (Brophy) **29**:93-4, 98; **105**:3-4, 30, 37
"Mozart's Clarinet Concerto" (Dunn) **40**:171
Mr. Aa the Antiphilosopher (Tzara) **47**:390
Mr. Ames against Time (Child) **19**:101, 103
"Mr. and Mrs. Baby" (Strand) **41**:438-39, 441
Mr. and Mrs. Baby, and Other Stories (Strand) **41**:438-41; **71**:280
Mr. and Mrs. Bridge (Jhabvala) **138**:73
"Mr. and Mrs. Edgehill" (Coward) **29**:141
"Mr. and Mrs. Elliot" (Hemingway) **30**:191
"Mr. and Mrs. Jack Sprat in the Kitchen" (Van Duyn) **116**:421 22, 427
"Mr. & Mrs. Van Winkle" (Dybek) **114**:67
"Mr. Appollinax" (Eliot) **41**:160
"Mr. Arcularis" (Aiken) **5**:9; **52**:26
Mr. Arcularis (Aiken) **5**:9
Mr. Arkadin (Welles) **20**:434-35, 437, 440-41, 449; **80**:395, 413
Mr. Armitage Isn't Back Yet (Jones) **52**:246, 253
"Mr. Austin" (Farrell) **4**:158
"Mr. Bedford" (Godwin) **31**:197-99; **125**:144
Mr. Bedford and the Muses (Godwin) **31**:197-98; **69**:247; **125**:144, 146
Mr. Beluncle (Pritchett) **41**:332
"Mr. Big" (Allen) **52**:35
"Mr. Bleaney" (Larkin) **8**:339; **39**:341, 343; **64**:263, 272
"Mr. Blue" (Creeley) **4**:118; **8**:152; **36**:122; **78**:126, 132
Mr. Bone's Retreat (Forster) **149**:64
Mr. Bridge (Connell) **4**:108; **6**:116; **45**:111-12, 116
Mr. Campion's Lady (Allingham) **19**:17
"Mr. Churchill Says" (Davies) **21**:91
"Mr. Clean" (Weller) **26**:444
"Mr. Coffee and Mr. Fixit" (Carver) **126**:114, 133-35
Mr. Cogito (Herbert)
See *Pan Cogito*
"Mr. Cogito and Pure Thought" (Herbert) **9**:275
"Mr. Cogito and the Imagination" (Herbert) **43**:191, 193
"Mr. Cogito and the Soul" (Herbert) **43**:191
"Mr. Cogito Laments the Pettiness of Dreams" (Herbert) **9**:275
"Mr. Cogito on the Need for Precision" (Herbert) **43**:195
"Mr. Cogito on Virtue" (Herbert) **9**:276
"Mr. Cogito Reads the Newspaper" (Herbert) **9**:275
"Mr. Cogito Tells about the Temptation of Spinoza" (Herbert)
See "Pan Cogito opowiada o kuszeniu Spinozy"
"Mr. Costyve Duditch" (Toomer) **22**:429
"Mr. Crane and His Grandmother" (Boyle) **121**:58
Mr. Deeds Goes to Town (Capra) **16**:154-55, 158, 160-62, 164
"Mr. Durant" (Parker) **68**:326
"Mr. Eliot's Sunday Morning Service" (Eliot) **1**:92; **15**:210, 216
"Mr. Extinction, Meet Ms. Survival" (Appleman) **51**:17
Mr. Fairlie's Final Journey (Derleth) **31**:138
Mr. Gallet, Deceased (Simenon)
See *Monsieur Gallet, décédé*
Mr. Gourd (Endō)
See *Hechima kun*
"Mr. Green Genes" (Zappa) **17**:585
Mr. Happiness (Mamet) **15**:358; **46**:254
"Mr. Harrington's Washing" (Maugham) **67**:219
"Mr. Heine" (Smith) **64**:392
"Mr. Hoover or Mr. Coolidge" (Thurber) **125**:395
"Mr. Hunter's Grave" (Mitchell) **98**:161, 173, 182-84
"Mr. Jonas" (Green) **97**:274-77
"Mr. Jones" (Capote) **19**:85
"Mr. Krösing's Top Hat" (Seifert) **34**:261; **93**:310
"Mr. Levi" (Oz) **11**:429
"Mr. Lincoln and His Gloves" (Sandburg) **35**:358
Mr. Lincoln's Army (Catton) **35**:83-7
Mr. Love and Justice (MacInnes) **4**:314; **23**:282-87
"Mr. Loveday's Little Outing" (Waugh) **27**:477
Mr. MacKinley's Flight (Leonov)
See *Begstvo Mistera Mak-Kinli*
"Mr. Mahoney" (Jacobsen) **48**:195
Mr. Majestyk (Leonard) **71**:223; **120**:277, 283, 287
"Mr. McGregor's Garden" (McGuckian) **48**:276-77
Mr. McKinley Runs Away (Leonov)
See *Begstvo Mistera Mak-Kinli*
"Mr. McMirty" (Jacobsen) **102**:237
"Mr. McNamara" (Trevor) **71**:324, 335; **116**:361, 377
"Mr. Mendelsohn" (Mohr) **12**:446
Mr. Midshipman Hornblower (Forester) **35**:169
"Mr. Mine" (Sexton) **123**:408
"Mr. Monroe and the Moving Men" (Thurber) **125**:391
"Mr. Moore" (Dourado) **23**:151
"Mr. More and the Mithraic Bull" (Wilson) **2**:477
"Mr. Morgan" (Michener) **109**:378
Mr. Nicholas (Hinde) **6**:238, 241
Mr. Norris Changes Trains (Isherwood)
See *The Last of Mr. Norris*
Mr. Parker Pyne, Detective (Christie) **110**:112
Mr. Pope and Other Poems (Tate) **11**:527
"Mr. Powers" (Gordon) **13**:248; **83**:231
Mr. Pu (Ichikawa)
See *Poo-san*
Mr. Pye (Peake) **54**:366, 369-70, 375, 378
"Mr. Quintillian" (Hersey) **81**:330
"Mr. S. Karuma's Crime" (Abe)
See "S. Karuma-shi no hanzai"
Mr. Sammler's Planet (Bellow) **1**:33; **2**:52-3; **3**:51, 54-8; **6**:52-4, 56, 58-9, 61; **8**:71, 74-5, 78-80; **10**:39-42, 44; **13**:70-4; **15**:47, 49-50, 52, 54-5, 57; **25**:81-2; **33**:66-7, 69, 71; **34**:545; **63**:27, 33, 37-9
Mr. Sampath (Narayan) **28**:292, 298, 300; **121**:335, 356-58, 362, 371-72, 382, 389
Mr. Scobie's Riddle (Jolley) **46**:213-15, 217-18, 221
"Mr. Secrets" (Rodriguez) **155**:237, 239, 279, 312
"Mr. Seurat's Sunday Afternoon" (Schwartz)
See "Seurat's Sunday Afternoon along the Seine"
"Mr. Slaughterboard" (Peake) **54**:372

Mr. Smith Goes to Washington (Capra) **16**:155-58, 160-62
"Mr. Soul" (Young)
See "Hello Mr. Soul"
Mr. Stephen (White)
See *The Minister for Justice*
Mr. Stimpson and Mr. Gorse (Hamilton) **51**:192-95, 197
Mr. Stone and the Knights Companion (Naipaul) **4**:374-75; **7**:253; **13**:403-06; **105**:136, 147, 154, 156, 180
"Mr. Trill in Hades" (Smith) **64**:401
Mr. Vertigo (Auster) **131**:30-2, 43
"Mr. Vidal: Unpatriotic Gore" (Amis) **62**:3
"Mr. Waterman" (Redgrove) **41**:348, 359
Mr. Welk and Jersey Jim (Sackler) **14**:479
Mr. Whatnot (Ayckbourn) **33**:40, 42; **74**:29
"Mr. Whitney" (Kinsella) **27**:237
"Mr. Wilson, the World" (Jones) **10**:286
Mr. Witt among the Rebels (Sender) **8**:480
Mr. Wrong (Howard) **7**:164-65
"Mrs. Acland's Ghosts" (Trevor) **7**:477-78
Mrs. Beer's House (Beer) **58**:34-5
"Mrs. Benson" (Purdy) **28**:379
"Mrs. Bixby and the Colonel's Coat" (Dahl) **79**:176, 182
Mrs. Blood (Thomas) **7**:472; **37**:417, 423; **107**:316-21, 333-35, 340, 344-45, 348, 351
"Mrs. Box" (Chabon) **149**:22-3
Mrs. Bridge (Connell) **4**:108; **6**:116; **45**:107-09, 111-12, 116
Mrs. Caldwell habla con su hijo (Cela) **4**:96, 98; **122**:19, 43, 61, 65-6
Mrs. Caldwell Speaks to Her Son (Cela)
See *Mrs. Caldwell habla con su hijo*
Mrs. Caliban (Ingalls) **42**:230-31, 233-35
"Mrs. Cassidy's Last Year" (Gordon) **128**:114, 116
Mrs. Craddock (Maugham) **15**:370; **93**:244, 247, 257
"Mrs. Cross and Mrs. Kidd" (Munro) **95**:315
"Mrs. Darcy Meets the Blue-Eyed Stranger at the Beach" (Smith) **25**:409
Mrs. deWinter (Hill) **113**:316-19, 328-29
"Mrs. Digby's Picture Album" (Simic) **130**:314
Mrs. Doremi (Nakos) **29**:323
Mrs. Dot (Maugham) **15**:366
Mrs. Eckdorf in O'Neill's Hotel (Trevor) **7**:476; **71**:345; **116**:334-35, 338, 367, 374, 377, 382-83
"Mrs. Evan Nr. Six" (Davies) **23**:144
"Mrs. Fanchier at the Movies" (Fearing) **51**:114
"Mrs. Fay Dines on Zebra" (Calisher) **38**:69; **134**:7
Mrs. Fish, Ape, and Me, the Dump Queen (Mazer) **26**:293
"Mrs. Fornheim, Refugee" (Layton) **15**:322
"Mrs. Frankenstein" (Piercy) **62**:367
"Mrs. Franklin Ascends" (Chappell) **40**:141
"Mrs. Frost" (Clarke) **61**:78
Mrs. God (Straub) **107**:304-07
"Mrs. Golightly and the First Convention" (Wilson) **13**:609
"Mrs. Grobnik a Checker-Upper" (Royko) **109**:407
"Mrs. Hackett" (Dowell) **60**:107-08
Mrs. Harris: The Death of the Scarsdale Diet Doctor (Trilling) **129**:332-33, 336-37, 342, 356, 363
"Mrs. Hofstadter on Josephine Street" (Parker) **68**:336
"Mrs. Jinny's Shroud" (Prichard) **46**:333
"Mrs. Macintosh" (Hall) **51**:172
"Mrs. Mandford's Drawing Room" (Brophy) **29**:91
"Mrs. Mandrill" (Nemerov) **6**:361; **9**:394; **36**:300
"Mrs. Martino the Candy Store Lady" (Turco) **11**:552
Mrs. McGinty's Dead (Christie) **12**:117; **110**:133
"Mrs. McGonigle on Decorum" (Johnston) **51**:244
"Mrs. Mean" (Gass) **2**:154; **8**:244; **132**:165
Mrs. Munck (Leffland) **19**:277-79
Mrs. October was Here (Dowell) **60**:96, 99-100, 108
Mrs. Palfrey at the Claremont (Taylor) **29**:408-09, 412
"Mrs. Plum" (Mphahlele) **25**:339, 342; **133**:155
Mrs. Pooter's Diary (Waterhouse) **47**:423-24
"Mrs. Razor" (Still) **49**:366
"Mrs. Reinhardt" (O'Brien) **116**:186
"Mrs. Robinson" (Simon) **17**:460, 463, 465
"Mrs. Silly" (Trevor) **71**:336
Mrs. Silly (Bennett) **77**:97
"Mrs. Small" (Brooks) **15**:92; **125**:67
"Mrs. Snow" (Justice) **102**:285
Mrs. Stevens Hears the Mermaids Singing (Sarton) **4**:471-72; **14**:481; **49**:322-23; **91**:246-47, 249-50
Mrs. Ted Bliss (Elkin) **91**:114-15, 221-25
"Mrs. Todd's Shortcut" (King) **37**:206
"Mrs. Turner Cutting the Grass" (Shields) **113**:427, 429-30
"Mrs. Vandebilt" (McCartney) **35**:282
Mrs. Wallop (De Vries) **2**:113-14; **3**:126; **28**:107
"Mrs. Wentworth" (Reaney) **13**:473
"Mrs. Wienckus" (White) **10**:527
"Ms. Found in an Anthill" (Le Guin) **45**:217
"Mt. Vernon and Fairway" (Wilson) **12**:647
"MTX" (Moure) **88**:229
"Mu" (Tolson) **105**:250-51, 255
Much Obliged, Jeeves (Wodehouse)
See *Jeeves and the Tie That Binds*
"Mud Toe the Cannibal" (Purdy) **52**:350
"The Mud Vision" (Heaney) **74**:161
"Mudbone" (Pryor) **26**:378
"A Muddy Cup" (Montague) **46**:277
Muder Ahoy! (Christie) **110**:124
"The Mudtower" (Stevenson) **33**:381
Las muertas (Ibarguengoitia) **37**:182-84
"La muerte" (Aleixandre) **9**:14, 16
"La muerte" (Marqués) **96**:227
"Muerte constante más allá der amor" (García Márquez) **3**:182; **15**:254; **47**:146, 151
La muerte de Artemio Cruz (Fuentes) **8**:224; **13**:232; **22**:165; **41**:167, 171-72, 174; **60**:156-58, 160, 163, 172; **113**:230, 238, 253, 256-57, 262-63
"Muerte de Narcisco" (Lezama Lima) **101**:121, 125
La muerte no entrará en palacio (Marqués) **96**:224, 226-30, 232, 240-42, 250-52, 257-58, 260-61
"La muerte y la brújula" (Borges) **1**:39; **2**:72; **6**:87, 89, 91; **8**:97, 99; **10**:66; **19**:54; **44**:358, 362-63; **48**:33, 45; **83**:155, 177
"El muerto" (Borges) **19**:46; **48**:34, 38
"Les muets" (Camus) **9**:144; **14**:114; **124**:42-3
La muette (Chabrol) **16**:170, 174-75
"Mugging" (Ginsberg) **109**:365
A Mug's Game (Hamburger) **5**:159
"Mugumo" (Ngũgĩ wa Thiong'o) **36**:317
"Mugwump" (Silverberg)
See "Mugwump Four"
"Mugwump Four" (Silverberg) **140**:363-64
"Mujer" (Neruda) **62**:336
"Una mujer amaestrada" (Arreola) **147**:14
Mujer del río (Alegria) **75**:49
"Mujer imagen" (Ulibarrí) **83**:407
Mujer, levántate y anda (Gironella) **11**:234, 236
"Mujer nueva" (Guillén) **48**:157, 164, 166; **79**:233, 238-40
Mujer que sabe latín (Castellanos) **66**:43, 46-7, 54, 57, 61
"La mujer que se ahoga" (Cabrera Infante) **120**:83
Una mujer sin amor (Bunuel) **80**:23
"La mujer y su imagen" (Castellanos) **66**:46, 54
"Mujeres" (Parra) **102**:341
Mujeres al borde de un ataque de nervios (Almodovar) **114**:11-4, 19, 21-3, 37-45, 49, 52-5, 57
Mujeres No Son Rosas (Castillo) **151**:3, 5, 30-1, 37, 40, 45
"Mul Hayaarot" (Yehoshua) **31**:470
"Mulata" (Guillén) **48**:161; **79**:240, 245, 248
Mulata de tal (Asturias) **13**:37
"Mulatto" (Hughes) **10**:280; **35**:212, 217; **108**:327
Mulatto (Hughes) **108**:284, 291
"The Mulch" (Kunitz) **6**:286; **148**:102
"The Mule" (Asimov) **9**:52; **26**:46, 62-5
Mule Bone: A Comedy of Negro Life (Hurston) **61**:273
"Mule Song" (Ammons) **5**:29
"Mule Team and Poster" (Justice) **102**:255, 270
"Mules" (Muldoon) **32**:318-19
Mules (Muldoon) **32**:317-21; **72**:264-65, 273-74, 276
Mules and Men (Hurston) **7**:171; **30**:209-12, 215, 217, 220-21, 223-27; **61**:263, 267, 270, 275
Mulieris Dignitatem (John Paul II) **128**:169-70, 172-76, 178
"Mulleins Are My Arms" (Kenny) **87**:256
Mulligan Stew (Sorrentino) **14**:499-501; **22**:394-97; **40**:384-85, 389, 391
"Multiple Choice" (Brunner) **8**:109
The Multiple Man (Bova) **45**:69
"The Multiplicity of the Media'" (Eco) **142**:63
"Multitude" (Johnston) **51**:243
"Multiversity" (Duncan) **41**:128, 130
"Mulvihill's Memorial" (Trevor) **25**:445-46; **71**:348; **116**:377, 384
"Mum and Mr. Armitage" (Bainbridge) **62**:34, 37; **130**:28
Mum and Mr. Armitage: Selected Stories (Bainbridge) **62**:34-8; **130**:27
"Mumbo" (McCartney) **35**:280
Mumbo Jumbo (Reed) **2**:367-69; **3**:424; **5**:368-70; **6**:447-50; **13**:479-80; **32**:357, 359-60, 364; **60**:300, 302-05, 307-10, 312
The Mummy, or Ramses the Damned (Rice) **128**:281, 283
Mummy Slept Late and Daddy Fixed Breakfast (Ciardi) **44**:378
"The Mummy's Awakening" (Mahfouz)
See "Yaqzat al-mumya'"
Munchausen (Gilliam)
See *The Adventures of Baron Munchausen*
Münchhausen (Haavikko) **18**:208; **34**:169-70, 173
Munchmeyer (Thomas) **37**:415-16; **107**:314-15
Munchmeyer. Prospero on the Island (Thomas) **37**:415-16, 423; **107**:333, 348-49
Das Mündel will Vormund sein (Handke) **5**:166; **8**:262; **10**:256-57; **15**:267; **38**:217; **134**:109-10, 137, 161
Mundo a solas (Aleixandre) **9**:15; **36**:24, 28, 30
El mundo alucinante: Una novela de aventuras (Arenas) **41**:26-7
"El mundo está bien hecho" (Aleixandre) **9**:13
Mundo grande (Andrade) **18**:3
Mundome (Mojtabai) **5**:293; **9**:385-86; **15**:377-79
The Mundy Scheme (Friel) **42**:167; **115**:246
"La muñeca menor" (Ferré) **139**:155-57, 163-64, 167-68, 170-71, 178-81, 183
La muneca menor (Ferré) **139**:168
"La muñeca reina" (Fuentes) **113**:237
Una muñeca rusa (Bioy Casares) **88**:92-5
"Munich" (MacNeice) **4**:315
"The Munich Mannequins" (Plath) **5**:345; **9**:427; **111**:168, 182, 185-86, 206
"The Municipal Park" (L'Heureux) **52**:275
"Muntele Măslinilor" (Arghezi) **80**:2
Le mur (Sartre) **1**:305-06; **4**:473; **24**:406; **44**:495; **50**:371, 374, 382; **52**:379, 381
Murakami Haruki zensakuhin (Murakami) **150**:72-5, 78-9
"Mural" (Scott) **22**:375

"La muralla y los libros" (Borges) **13**:105; **83**:160, 162, 176
"The Murder" (Steinbeck) **21**:387-88
Murder à la mod (De Palma) **20**:72, 78
Murder After Hours (Christie)
See *The Hollow*
"Murder at Cobbler's Hulk" (O'Faolain) **7**:274
Murder at McQueen (Ritter) **52**:356-57
Murder at the ABA: A Puzzle in Four Days and Sixty Scenes (Asimov) **9**:49; **76**:313
Murder at the Gallop (Christie) **110**:124
Murder at the Savoy (Wahlöö)
See *Polis, polis potatismos*
The Murder at the Vicarage (Christie) **12**:122; **39**:438; **48**:74, 76; **110**:111-12, 116
Murder Being Once Done (Rendell) **28**:383, 385, 387
"Murder By Capitol" (Pound) **112**:315
Murder in Mesopotamia (Christie) **48**:74
Murder in Retrospect (Christie) **12**:123; **48**:72, 74; **110**:120
Murder in the Calais Coach (Christie) **1**:58; **6**:108; **8**:142; **12**:112-13, 117, 120, 122, 124; **48**:73, 77; **110**:112, 121-22, 132
Murder in the Cathedral (Eliot) **1**:89, 91; **2**:129; **6**:166-68; **13**:193, 195; **15**:206-08, 215; **34**:401; **41**:144, 152, 155; **55**:372; **57**:186, 208
Murder in the Dark (Atwood) **84**:70
Murder in the English Department (Miner) **40**:328, 330-31
"The Murder, Inc. Sutra" (Rothenberg) **57**:374
A Murder Is Announced (Christie) **12**:124; **39**:438; **48**:71-5; **110**:112, 116
Murder Most Foul (Christie) **110**:124
"Murder Mystery" (Reed) **21**:303, 307
"Murder Mystery" (Rooke) **25**:394
"Murder Mystery" (Wagoner) **3**:508
The Murder of Aziz Khan (Ghose) **42**:178-79
"A Murder of Crows" (Lane) **25**:287
"The Murder of Harry Keyes" (Durcan) **70**:147
The Murder of Otsuya (Tanizaki)
See *Otsuya Koroshi*
A Murder of Quality (le Carré) **3**:281; **5**:232-33
The Murder of Roger Ackroyd (Christie) **1**:58; **6**:108-09; **8**:140, 142; **12**:111-12, 114, 117-18, 120, 122-23; **39**:437, 440-41; **48**:71-73, 77; **110**:116, 122
"The Murder of the Frogs" (Carpenter) **41**:103
The Murder of the Frogs, and Other Stories (Carpenter) **41**:103, 105, 108
Murder on the Links (Christie) **12**:110, 122; **48**:74
Murder on the Orient Express (Christie)
See *Murder in the Calais Coach*
Murder on the Thirty-First Floor (Wahlöö)
See *Mord paas 31: A vaangin*
Murder, She Said (Christie) **110**:124
Murder Stalks the Wakely Family (Derleth) **31**:127
Murder with Mirrors (Christie) **48**:75
"The Murderer" (Smith) **44**:438
Murderer (Shaffer) **19**:415
The Murderer (Simenon) **1**:309
"The Murderer Guest" (Gordon) **128**:118
The Murderer Is a Fox (Queen) **11**:462
"The Murderers of Kings" (Herbert) **43**:191, 193
Murders in Volume 2 (Daly) **52**:87
Murdo and Other Stories (Smith) **64**:391
"Mureau" (Cage) **41**:82
Muriel (Elliott) **2**:131
Muriel (Resnais) **16**:501-02, 504, 506, 509-11, 515
"Murilo Mendes e os rios" (Cabral de Melo Neto) **76**:163
Murke's Collected Silences (Boell)
See *Doktor Murkes gesammeltes Schweigen, und andere Satiren*
"The Murmurers" (Jacobsen) **48**:190-91
Murmuring Judges (Hare) **136**:255-59, 261, 265, 267-75, 290, 306
Murmurs of Earth (Sagan) **30**:337; **112**:417
Murphy (Beckett) **2**:44, 48; **6**:34, 38-9, 43; **9**:78, 81; **10**:27-9, 34; **11**:34, 36-7; **14**:71, 75-6, 79-80; **18**:43, 50; **29**:53, 56, 65; **57**:92; **59**:253, 256, 258, 260
"Murphy in Manchester" (Montague) **46**:273
Murther & Walking Spirits (Davies) **75**:224-25; **91**:200-1, 204, 206, 209
The Muscular System: How Living Creatures Move (Silverstein and Silverstein) **17**:454
"The Muse" (Akhmatova) **64**:16
"The Muse" (Dunn) **36**:153
"The Muse" (Ewart) **46**:150
"The Muse" (Heaney) **37**:165
"The Muse" (Hope) **51**:215
"The Muse" (Kizer) **39**:169-70
"The Muse" (Sarton) **49**:314
"A Muse" (Simmons) **43**:410
"The Muse in Armor" (Benedikt) **14**:81
"The Muse Mother" (Boland) **67**:43, 45
"The Muse of History: An Essay" (Walcott) **67**:353
"A Muse of Water" (Kizer) **80**:172-73, 181, 185
"Muse, Poet, and Fountain" (Watkins) **43**:453
"Musée des Beaux Arts" (Auden) **3**:23-4; **9**:59; **11**:17; **43**:22; **123**:12
"Musée imaginaire" (Montague) **46**:266
Le musée imaginaire de la sculpture mondiale (Malraux) **15**:352
Le musée noir (Mandiargues) **41**:278
"Musées" (Butor) **15**:114
Museo d'ombre (Bufalino) **74**:39
The Muses Are Heard: An Account of the Porgy and Bess Tour to Leningrad (Capote) **3**:100; **8**:132-33; **34**:320, 322; **58**:87, 94
Museu de tudo (Cabral de Melo Neto) **76**:155-56, 160, 162, 169
"The Museum" (Duncan) **41**:129
"Museum" (Fearing) **51**:114
"Museum" (Hass) **99**:152
"Museum" (Niedecker) **10**:360
Museum (Dove) **50**:152; **81**:132-34, 136-38, 142-43, 145, 149
Museum (Friedman) **7**:108-09
Museum (Howe) **48**:171-75
The Museum of Cheats (Warner) **7**:511
"The Museum of Clear Ideas" (Hall) **151**:201
The Museum of Clear Ideas (Hall) **151**:200-02, 204, 208, 212-13, 219
Museum of Everything (Cabral de Melo Neto)
See *Museu de tudo*
"Museum of the Year 1937" (Panchenko) **59**:387
"Museum Piece" (Wilbur) **110**:385
"A Museum Piece" (Zelazny) **21**:465-66
Museum Pieces (Plomer) **4**:406
Museum Pieces (Tallent) **45**:388-90
"Museums and Women" (Updike) **9**:537; **23**:475; **139**:338
Museums and Women, and Other Stories (Updike) **2**:444-45; **3**:487-88; **7**:488; **13**:562; **23**:473, 475
Mushroom Book (Cage) **41**:82
"The Mushroom Gatherers" (Davie) **8**:162; **31**:109
"Mushroom Gathering" (Muldoon)
See "Gathering Mushrooms"
"Mushrooms" (Atwood) **84**:69
"Mushrooms" (Bradbury) **15**:85-6
"Mushrooms" (Derleth) **31**:138
"Mushrooms" (Fuller) **62**:195
"Mushrooms" (Oliver) **34**:246-47, 249; **98**:256
"Mushrooms" (Plath) **11**:447; **17**:350; **51**:344
"Mushrooms in the City" (Calvino)
See "Funghi in città"
"The Music" (Baraka) **115**:12
"Music" (Gilchrist) **143**:303, 314, 326-27
"Music" (Nabokov) **6**:357
"Music" (O'Hara) **13**:428-29
"Music" (Oliver) **34**:247; **98**:298
"Music" (Trevor) **71**:329, 333
Music (Slessor) **14**:497
The Music and Life of Carl Michael Bellman (Zuckmayer)
See *Ulla Winblad*
Music and Silence (Redmon) **22**:342
Music at Night (Huxley) **5**:192; **79**:310
A Music behind the Wall: Selected Stories, Volume One (Ortese) **89**:197-99
"The Music Box" (Montague) **46**:277
The Music Box Bird (Sarton) **91**:241
"The Music Critic's Tale" (Stead) **80**:326
Music for Chameleons: New Writing (Capote) **19**:84-5; **34**:320-21, 323, 326
"Music for Four Doors" (Graver) **70**:52
"Music from Spain" (Welty) **22**:461; **105**:339
Music from the Body (Pink Floyd) **35**:311
"Music in the Air" (Johnston) **51**:247
Music Late at Night (McAuley) **45**:253-54
"Music Lessons" (Oliver) **98**:267
Music Lessons (Akhmadulina) **53**:13
"The Music Lover" (Gardner) **28**:162-63
The Music Lovers (Russell) **16**:542, 544-46, 548
Music Maker (Cliff) **21**:62-3
"Music Must Change" (Townshend) **17**:538-39, 542
The Music of Chance (Auster) **131**:16-7, 30, 32, 42
"Music of Colonis" (Watkins) **43**:454
"Music of Colours" (Watkins) **43**:451, 453, 457
"Music of Colours—Dragonfoil and the Furnace of Colours" (Watkins) **43**:444
"Music of Colours—White Blossom" (Watkins) **43**:447, 451
Music of My Mind (Wonder) **12**:656, 661, 663
"The Music of Poetry" (Eliot) **15**:215; **113**:194
"The Music of Poetry" (Kinnell) **129**:265
"The Music of Prose" (Gass) **132**:188
The Music of This Sphere (Thomas) **35**:409
Music of Time (Newby) **2**:310
The Music of What Happens: Poems, Poets, Critics (Vendler) **138**:259, 262-64, 266-69
Music on Clinton Street (McCabe) **133**:113, 122
"Music on the Water" (Johnston) **51**:240, 242
The Music: Reflections on Jazz and Blues (Baraka) **115**:12, 37
The Music Room (McFarland) **65**:67-74
The Music Room (Ray)
See *Jalsaghar*
The Music School (Updike) **3**:488; **7**:487; **15**:543; **23**:473; **139**:335, 337-38
"Music Swims Back to Me" (Sexton) **53**:318
"The Music Teacher" (Cheever) **7**:49
"The Music That Hurts" (Komunyakaa) **94**:235
Music Walk (Cage) **41**:79
La musica (Duras) **20**:99
Música cercana (Buero Vallejo) **139**:40-43, 57, 72-3
La música en Cuba (Carpentier) **11**:103; **110**:59, 78
"Musical Chairs" (Fuller) **62**:196-97, 201
Musical Elaborations (Said) **123**:362, 370, 372, 377, 385
"Musical Moment in Assynt" (MacCaig) **36**:285
"Musical Offering" (Fuller) **28**:157
"Musician" (Bogan) **93**:78
"Musk" (Johnston) **51**:241, 243
Mussarniks (Grade) **10**:246, 248
"Mussel Hunter at Rock Harbour" (Plath) **11**:447
Mussolini's Italy (Gallo) **95**:93, 95-6
"Must the Novelist Crusade" (Welty) **14**:565
"Must We Burn Sade?" (Beauvoir) **124**:136, 140-41
The Mustache (Carrere)
See *La moustache*
Mustain (Price) **63**:330
Muswell Hillbillies (Davies) **21**:92-3, 95-7
"Mutability" (Snodgrass) **68**:388
"Mutable Hearts" (Avison) **97**:111
"Les mutations radieuses" (Tzara) **47**:387, 390

"The Mute" (Landolfi) **11**:321; **49**:211-12
Mute (Anthony) **35**:36
"Muted Music" (Warren) **39**:270
"Muteness" (Akhmadulina)
See "Nemota"
"The Mutes" (Levertov) **66**:238
The Mutilated (Williams)
See *The Gnädiges Fräulein*
"Mutilated Prayer" (Cocteau)
See "Prière mutilée"
Mutmassungen über Jakob (Johnson) **5**:200-02; **10**:283-84; **15**:302-04, 307; **40**:263, 267-68, 270
"Mutra" (Paz) **65**:182; **119**:419
Mutterschaft (Clayman) **65**:445-48
The Mutual Friend (Busch) **10**:93-4; **18**:84, 86; **47**:64
Mutuwhenua: The Moon Sleeps (Grace) **56**:114-17, 119-21, 123
Muzeeka (Guare) **8**:253; **14**:220; **29**:204-05
M.V. Sexton Speaking (Newton) **35**:301-02
"Mwilu/or Poem for the Living" (Madhubuti) **73**:215
"My '48 Pontiac" (Purdy) **50**:238
My Achilles Heart (Voznesensky)
See *Akillesovo serdtse*
"My Adolescent Days" (Tanizaki)
See "Sheishun monogatari"
My Aim Is True (Costello) **21**:66-70
My Amputations: A Novel (Major) **48**:215-18
"My Ancestors" (Cliff) **21**:65
My Animal Number Book (Nwapa) **133**:201, 229
"My Appearance" (Wallace) **114**:348, 350, 352
"My Aquatic Uncle" (Calvino)
See "Lo zio acquativo"
My Argument with the Gestapo: A Macaronic Journal (Merton) **11**:373-74
My Aunt Christina (Stewart) **32**:422
"My Baby Gives It Away" (Townshend) **17**:537
"My Back Pages" (Dylan) **6**:154; **77**:167
My Beautiful Laundrette (Kureishi) **64**:246-52, 254; **135**:261-62, 264-65, 267-68, 272, 274, 278-79, 284-85, 287-88, 293-94, 296-98, 300
"My Beginnings as a Writer" (Farrell) **66**:135
"My Belief" (Hesse) **17**:218
"My Belongings" (Endō)
See "Watakushi no mono"
"My Best Friend" (Reed) **21**:311
"My Best Soldier" (Jin) **109**:54
"My Big-Assed Mother" (Bukowski) **41**:68
My Body Was Eaten by Dogs: Selected Poems of David McFadden (McFadden) **48**:254-55
"My Bones Flew Apart" (Eberhart) **56**:76
My Brother (Kincaid) **137**:200-02
My Brother Fine with Me (Clifton) **66**:67
My Brother Michael (Stewart) **7**:467; **35**:389, 391-92; **117**:367
My Brother Sam Is Dead (Collier and Collier) **30**:71-5
"My Butterfly" (Frost) **10**:199
"My Cherie Amour" (Wonder) **12**:655, 661
"My Children at the Dump" (Updike) **3**:485
My Children! My Africa (Fugard) **80**:76-8
"My Children's Book" (Ewart) **46**:152
"My Company" (Read) **4**:437, 439
My Confession (Solzhenitsyn) **4**:508
"My Conversion" (Spark) **94**:344
"My Country" (Klima)
See "Má vlast"
"My Country" (Wright) **53**:423
"My Country Wrong" (Rule) **27**:419
My Cousin, My Gastroenterologist (Leyner) **92**:282, 284-85, 290-94
My Cousin Rachel (du Maurier) **11**:163; **59**:280, 284-85, 287
"My Cousins who could eat cooked turnips" (Frame) **96**:188
"'My Craft and Sullen Art':The Writers Speak--Is There a Feminine Voice in Literature?" (Thomas) **107**:348
"My Credo" (Fiedler) **4**:163; **13**:212
"My Crime Wave" (Lowell) **124**:278
"My Crow" (Carver) **53**:61
"My Crow, Pluto—A Fantasy" (Moore) **47**:266
My Crowd (Addams) **30**:16
"My Dad's Wallet" (Carver) **36**:107
"My Daily Horse" (Valenzuela) **104**:377
My Darling Clementine (Ford) **16**:305, 308, 310-11, 317
My Darling, My Hamburger (Zindel) **6**:586; **26**:471-73, 475, 479-80
"My Daughter" (Pack) **13**:438
My Daughter, My Son, The Eagle, The Dove (Castillo) **151**:46, 100, 103
My Daughter, Nicola (Arthur) **12**:24, 28-9
"My Daughter the Junkie on a Train" (Lorde)
See "To My Daughter the Junkie on a Train"
"My Day (With Apologies to Eleanor Roosevelt)" (Thurber) **125**:412
My Days: A Memoir (Narayan) **7**:254-55; **28**:296, 303; **121**:353, 357, 359, 403-04
My Days of Anger (Farrell) **66**:129
"My Dear Palestrina" (Mac Laverty) **31**:254
"My Death" (Smith) **15**:514
"My Death" (Strand) **18**:517; **41**:432
"My Ding-a-Ling" (Berry) **17**:54-5
My Dinner with André (Shawn) **41**:400-02
"My Dream" (Bennett) **28**:31
"My Dream" (Berry) **17**:52
"my dream about the cows" (Clifton) **66**:83
"My Dream by Henry James" (Ryan) **65**:209
"My Dream For Czechoslovakia" (Havel) **123**:194
"My Dream of Flying to Wake Island" (Ballard) **137**:65
"My Dungeon Shook" (Baldwin) **13**:53; **42**:19
"My Early Poems" (Justice) **19**:233
My Ears Are Bent (Mitchell) **98**:152-54, 163-64, 172, 177, 181, 183-84
My Education: A Book of Dreams (Burroughs) **109**:182, 230-31
My Emily Dickinson (Howe) **72**:195-201, 203, 209; **152**:153, 156-57, 159, 162, 164-65, 168-70, 174-77, 181, 192-93, 203-04, 207-10, 214-16, 218, 220, 229, 236, 239, 241-42, 244, 252-53
My Enemy, My Brother (Forman) **21**:117
"My Enemy's Enemy" (Amis) **40**:43-5
My Enemy's Enemy (Amis) **40**:45; **129**:6, 8
"My Entire Life" (Borges)
See "Mi vida entera"
"My Entry into the War" (Calvino)
See *L'entrada en guerra*
"My Erotic Double" (Ashbery) **15**:33
"My Evolving Program" (Du Bois) **96**:158
"My Expensive Leg" (Boell)
See "Mein teures Bein"
My Faith in Women's Suffrage (Masefield) **47**:233
"My Faithful Mother Tongue" (Milosz) **56**:246; **82**:290
"My Father" (Berrigan) **4**:58
"My Father" (Hillis) **66**:194
"My Father at 89" (Paley) **140**:210
"My Father Burns Washington" (Chappell) **78**:91
"My Father Died Imperfect as a Man" (Ciardi) **44**:379, 381
"My Father in the Dark" (Simpson) **7**:427
"My Father in the Night Commanding No" (Simpson) **7**:427-28; **149**:324, 342
"My Father Leaves Home" (Gordimer) **70**:177; **123**:127
"My Father Moved through Dooms of Feel" (Cummings)
See "My Father Moved through Dooms of Love"
"My Father Moved through Dooms of Love" (Cummings) **15**:162; **68**:50, 52
"My Father Paints the Summer" (Wilbur) **53**:397
My Father Photographed with Friends (Bronk) **10**:75
My Father Sits in the Dark (Weidman) **7**:516
"My Father Speaks to Me from the Dead" (Olds) **85**:306, 308
"My Father Was a River" (Dowell) **60**:104, 107-09
My Father Was a Toltec and Selected Poems, 1973-1988 (Castillo) **151**:11, 18-20, 30, 37, 45, 101-03
My Father Was a Toltec: New and Collected Poems (Castillo) **151**:30, 45
"My Father's Breasts" (Olds) **39**:187; **85**:302
"My Father's Country Is the Poor" (Walker) **103**:369
"My Father's Deaths" (Amichai)
See "The Times My Father Died"
"My Father's Fights" (Dybek) **114**:61
"My Father's God" (Fante) **60**:133
"My Father's House" (Rule) **27**:420
My Father's House (Troyat) **23**:458
My Father's House: A Memoir of Incest and Healing (Fraser) **64**:179-80
"My Father's Knee" (Scannell) **49**:326
"My Father's Life" (Richler) **46**:351-53
"My Father's Love Letters" (Komunyakaa) **94**:238, 241
"My Father's Red Indian" (Abse) **29**:21
My Father's Son (O'Connor) **23**:326
"My Father's Telescope" (Dove) **81**:135, 138
"My Father's Watch" (Ciardi) **40**:154
"My Father's Wedding" (Bly) **38**:58; **128**:46
My Fellow Devils (Hartley) **22**:214-15
"My Final Hour" (Laurence) **50**:316
"My First and Only House" (Adams) **46**:21
"My First Ball" (Ihimaera) **46**:199
My First Book (Binchy) **153**:67
"My First Hard Springtime" (Welch) **52**:429
My First Loves (Klima)
See *Moje první lásky*
"My First Marriage" (Jhabvala) **8**:312; **29**:256
My First Sorrow (Sarraute) **80**:243
"My First Two Women" (Gordimer) **33**:179
"My Flower Garden" (Christie) **110**:126
"My Fly" (Williams) **148**:358, 360
My Foot My Tutor (Handke)
See *Das Mündel will Vormund sein*
"My Forefathers" (Kunene) **85**:176
My Friend Hitler (Mishima)
See *Wagatomo Hitler*
My Friend Judas (Sinclair) **2**:401
My Friend Says It's Bullet-Proof (Mortimer) **5**:298-99
"My Friend the Instrument" (Simmons) **43**:414
My Friend Wants to Run Away (Hyde) **21**:180
My Garden Book (Kincaid) **137**:210-11
"My Genealogy" (Akhmadulina) **53**:14
"My Generation" (Townshend) **17**:525, 528-33, 536, 539-40
"My Generation Was Lost" (Milosz) **56**:233-34
"My Girl" (Robinson) **21**:347
My Glorious Brothers (Fast) **131**:75, 78, 91, 95, 97-8
"My God" (Amichai) **22**:33
"My Gold Chain" (Ashbery) **125**:30
"My Good Father" (Kizer) **80**:182-83
"My Goodbyes" (Alegria)
See "My Good-Byes"
"My Good-Byes" (Alegria) **75**:38-40
My Granddad the Monument (Aksyonov) **101**:22
"My Grandfather Gets Doused" (Chappell) **40**:145
"My Grandfather's Church Goes Up" (Chappell) **40**:145
"My Grandfather's Country" (Purdy) **50**:240-41
"My Grandfather's Wake" (Muldoon) **72**:273
My Grandma Smoked Cigars, and Other Tales of Tierra Amarilla (Ulibarrí)
See *Mi abuela fumaba puros y otros*

cuentos de Tierra Amarilla/My Grandma Smoked Cigars, and Other Tales of Tierra Amarilla
"My Grandmother" (Jennings) **131**:234
"My Grandmother's Dream of Plowing" (Chappell) **78**:92, 115
"My Grandmothersq1s Mirror" (Alexander) **121**:4, 8
"My Grave" (Levine) **118**:305
"My Handwriting" (Yevtushenko) **126**:388
My Happy Days in Hell (Faludy) **42**:135-36, 141
"My Hate" (Bell) **8**:65
"My Heart" (O'Hara) **78**:364
"My Heart Is Broken" (Gallant) **7**:110; **18**:171-72
My Heart's in the Highlands (Saroyan) **10**:452-53; **29**:362; **56**:367-71, 373, 375-80
"My Heavenly Shiner" (Lowell) **3**:306
"My Heroes Have Never Been Cowboys" (Alexie) **154**:9-11, 27
My Holy Satan (Fisher) **7**:103
My Home Is Far Away (Powell) **66**:358-59, 371
"My Homeland" (Klima)
See "Má vlast"
"My Honey" (Guillén)
See "Mi chiquita"
My Horse Gonzalez (Alegria)
See *Caballo de copas*
"My Hotel Year" (Coupland) **85**:35, 39
"My House" (Giovanni) **64**:187, 194; **117**:198-99
My House (Giovanni) **4**:189; **19**:192; **64**:186-87, 191, 194; **117**:181-86, 191-92, 196-97, 199
"My House in Umbria" (Trevor) **116**:372-73
My House in Umbria (Trevor)
See *Two Lives: Reading Turgenev; My House in Umbria*
My House Is on Fire (Dorfman)
See *Cría ojos*
"My Husband the Pig" (Sondheim) **147**:261
My Hustler (Warhol) **20**:420, 422
My Kinsman, Major Molineux (Lowell) **8**:350, 352; **11**:324-25
"My Lady the Lake" (Davison) **28**:104
"My Land Has a Voice" (Stuart) **11**:511; **34**:373, 376
"My Last Afternoon with Uncle Devereux Winslow" (Lowell) **11**:327; **15**:342; **37**:243; **124**:261-62, 272, 300
"My Last Name" (Guillén) **48**:158; **79**:229-30
My Last Two Thousand Years (Gold) **4**:193; **7**:121-22; **152**:122, 124-25, 128, 130, 137, 141
"My Lecture to the Writing Students" (Ostriker) **132**:302
My Left Foot (Brown) **63**:47-8, 55-6
"My Life" (Howe) **72**:198, 200
"My Life" (Joel) **26**:217
"My Life" (Ochs) **17**:332
My Life and Hard Times (Thurber) **5**:431-37, 439-40, 442; **11**:533; **25**:437, 439; **125**:386, 395, 397, 402-03, 405, 414-15
My Life and Times (Miller) **2**:283
My Life as a Man (Roth) **4**:454-59; **6**:475-76; **9**:459, 461; **15**:451-52, 455; **22**:353-54; **47**:357, 361-64, 366; **66**:416-17; **86**:250, 258
"My Life as a Writer" (Dworkin) **123**:93
"My Life as An Echo" (Miller) **84**:293
"My Life by Somebody Else" (Strand) **18**:517-19; **71**:279, 285
"My Life by Water: Collected Poems, 1936-1968" (Niedecker) **10**:360-61; **42**:297, 299
My Life in the Bush of Ghosts (Byrne) **26**:99
My Life in the Bush of Ghosts (Tutuola) **5**:443; **14**:538-39, 541; **29**:438, 440, 442
My Life, My Death by Pier Paolo Pasolini (Acker) **45**:17; **111**:8-10, 17, 21, 25-6, 32-3
My Life of Absurdity (Himes) **18**:250; **58**:263, 269-70; **108**:228-29, 234, 241, 256
"My Life on the Road with Bread and Water" (Willard) **37**:464
My Life, Starring Dara Falcon (Beattie) **146**:85
My Life to Live (Godard)
See *Vivre sa vie*
"My Life with R. H. Macy" (Jackson) **60**:211, 235
"My Life with the Wave" (Paz) **3**:375
My Little Poplar in the Red Kerchief (Aitmatov)
See *Topolek moi v krasnoi kosynke*
"My Little Town" (Simon) **17**:466
"My Little Utopia" (Simic) **22**:383
"My Little Woman" (Guillén) **79**:229
"My Livelihood" (Dickinson) **49**:103
"My Love" (McCartney) **35**:281, 283
"My Love Affair with James I" (Tremain) **42**:385
"My Love, My Umbrella" (McGahern) **48**:262, 268
"My Love Shooting the Buddha" (Lieberman) **36**:264
My Lovely Enemy (Wiebe) **138**:324, 326, 351, 379, 387-92, 394-95
"My Lover John" (Smart) **54**:425
"My Lucy Friend Who Smells Like Corn" (Cisneros) **69**:153
My Madness (Kavan) **82**:125-26
"My Man Bovanne" (Bambara) **88**:19-20, 27, 47
My Man-Coated Man (Lee) **90**:181-2, 185
"My Meadow" (Carruth) **84**:129, 132
"My Memory's Hyperbole" (Kristeva) **77**:320; **140**:183-84
My Merry Mornings: Stories from Prague (Klima) **56**:170-72, 174
My Michael (Oz) **54**:351-53, 355; **5**:334-35; **8**:436; **11**:427-28; **27**:359-60; **33**:302
"My Mind Reads ..." (Levi) **41**:243
"My Mistress" (Colwin) **84**:142
"My Moby Dick" (Humphrey) **45**:201, 205
"My Mother" (Brophy) **105**:8
"My Mother" (Kincaid) **43**:248; **68**:207-08; **137**:138, 140, 143, 172
My Mother (Bataille)
See *Ma mère*
"My Mother Breathing Light" (Vaughn) **62**:458
My Mother: Demonology (Acker) **111**:41
"My Mother Has Me Surrounded" (Kauffman) **42**:252-53
My Mother, My Father, and Me (Hellman) **18**:222, 224; **34**:348
"My Mother on an Evening in Late Summer" (Strand) **41**:432-33, 438
"My Mother Once Told Me" (Amichai) **116**:95
"My Mother Remembers She Was Beautiful" (Gallagher) **18**:170
"My Mother Remembers That She Was Beautiful" (Gallagher) **63**:118, 126
"My Mother Would Be a Falconress" (Duncan) **41**:128; **55**:298
My Mother's Body (Piercy) **62**:370-71, 373; **128**:231, 243, 246, 273
"My Mother's Hard Row to Hoe" (Chappell) **40**:143
"My Mother's Lips" (Williams) **33**:448; **148**:309-10, 344
My Mother's Music (West) **96**:399, 400
"My Mother's Nipples" (Hass) **99**:155
"My Mother's Novel" (Piercy) **27**:376
"My Mother's Pears" (Kunitz) **148**:127, 149
"My Mummy's Dead" (Lennon) **35**:262, 266
"My Muse" (Randall) **135**:392
"My Muse" (Smith) **25**:420
"My My, Hey Hey" (Young) **17**:581-82
"My nacional'nyj geroj" (Coles) **67**:173, 175, 179
"My Name" (Brautigan) **34**:318
"My Name" (Cisneros) **69**:146; **118**:177, 209
"My Name" (Levine) **33**:275; **118**:292
"My Name and I" (Graves) **45**:169
"My Name Blew Like a Horn Among The Payira" (p'Bitek) **96**:309
My Name is Aram (Saroyan) **1**:301; **8**:468
My Name Is Asher Lev (Potok) **2**:338-39; **7**:321; **26**:371-72; 263, 266, 269, 290-92, 295
My Name Is Ivan (Tarkovsky)
See *Ivanovo Detstvo*
My Name Is Legion (Zelazny) **21**:472
"My Name Is Red Hot. Yo Name Ain Doodley Squat" (Brooks)
See "Five Men against the Theme, 'My Name is Red Hot. Yo Name ain Doodley Squat'"
My Name Is Saroyan (Saroyan) **29**:362-63
"My Native Land" (Ignatow) **7**:177
"My Neighbor" (Ignatow) **7**:180
"My Neighborhood" (Dybek) **114**:62, 65, 67
"My Neighbour" (Williams) **148**:362
My Next Bride (Boyle) **58**:64, 66, 77-80; **121**:29, 46, 50, 62, 66, 68
My Night at Maud's (Rohmer)
See *Ma nuit chez Maud*
"My North Dakota Railroad Days" (Keillor) **40**:273-74
"My Nose Is Growing Old" (Brautigan) **3**:87
"My Oakland, There is a There There" (Reed) **60**:310
"My Oedipus Complex" (O'Connor) **14**:399; **23**:332
"My Old Man" (Hemingway) **6**:233; **8**:283; **19**:211; **30**:179, 191
"My Old Man" (Mitchell) **12**:436
"My Old Man" (Reed) **21**:320
"My Olson Elegy" (Feldman) **7**:102
My Organic Uncle (Pownall) **10**:419
My Own Ground (Nissenson) **9**:399-400
"My Own Native Land" (Singh) **11**:504
"My Own Sweet Good" (Brooks) **125**:74
"My Papa's Waltz" (Roethke) **101**:262, 264
"My Parents Village" (Rodriguez) **155**:275, 277
"My Perfect Soul Shall Manifest Me Rightly: An Essay on Blackfolks and the Constitution" (Jordan) **114**:151
My Petition for More Space (Hersey) **7**:154-55; **40**:240
"My Philosophy" (Allen) **52**:35
"My Poem" (Giovanni) **19**:191; **64**:182, 186
"My Poetry" (Rozewicz) **139**:289
"My Poets" (Levine) **118**:283
"My Pony Won't Go" (Lightfoot) **26**:279
My Present Age (Vanderhaeghe) **41**:450-53
My Properties (Michaux)
See *Mes propriétés*
"My Quarrel with Hersh Rasseyner" (Grade) **10**:247
"My Real Estate" (Apple) **9**:32
My Red Kerchiefed Young Poplar (Aitmatov)
See *Topolek moi v krasnoi kosynke*
"My Rival" (Becker and Fagen) **26**:85
"My Room" (Ali) **69**:31
"My Routine" (Matthews) **40**:319
"My Sad Captains" (Gunn) **18**:199; **32**:208, 211; **81**:180
My Sad Captains, and Other Poems (Gunn) **3**:215; **6**:221; **18**:200, 202; **32**:208, 211
My Saint Petersburg (Almedingen) **12**:1, 5-6
"My Second Marriage to My First Husband" (Fulton) **52**:162
"My Secret Identity Is" (Simic) **68**:378
My Several Worlds (Buck) **127**:227-29
"My Shoes" (Simic) **9**:479; **49**:337, 339, 341; **68**:370; **130**:330
"My Side of the Matter" (Capote) **1**:55; **19**:79-80
My Side of the Mountain (George) **35**:175-79
My Sister, Life (Pasternak)
See *Sestra moia zhizn*
"My Sisters" (Kunitz) **148**:84, 90-91, 118-19, 121
My Sister's Hand in Mine: An Expanded Edition of The Collected Works of Jane

Bowles (Bowles) **68**:10-11, 13
"My Sisters, O My Sisters" (Sarton) **4**:472; **14**:481; **49**:310; **91**:253
"My Son and I" (Levine) **14**:316, 318; **118**:277, 290
"My Son Austin" (O'Faolain) **14**:402
"My Son the Fanatic" (Kureishi) **135**:275, 284-86, 288, 298, 301, 303
My Son the Fanatic (Kureishi) **135**:287, 289, 292, 294-95
"My Son the Murderer" (Malamud) **8**:375; **27**:306; **44**:415
"My Son the Rastafarian" (Vargas Llosa) **42**:412
"My Songs Induce Prophetic Dreams" (Whalen) **6**:566
My Son's Story (Gordimer) **70**:167, 171-76, 180, 184, 187; **123**:128, 130-32, 138, 160
"My Soul and I" (Tolson) **105**:282
My Soul in China (Kavan) **5**:206
"My Speech to the Graduates" (Allen) **52**:42
My Squaring of Accounts with Them (Krleža) See *Moj obracun s njima*
"My Strange Quest for Mensonge" (Bradbury) **61**:48
"My Students" (Randall) **135**:399
"My Surgeons" (Kunitz) **148**:87-88, 105
"My Swazi Boy or Song of the Frog" (Kunene) **85**:176
"My Sweet Old Etcetera" (Cummings) **3**:119; **68**:46
"My Tears" (Oe) See "Mizu kara waga namida o nuguitamo hi"
"My Three Hoboes" (Scannell) **49**:327
My Times (Berton) **104**:62
"My Tocaya" (Cisneros) **118**:202
"My Trip Abroad" (Wilson) **24**:483
My True Love Waits (Weber) **12**:632-33
"My True Story" (Roth) **4**:454, 458-59; **9**:459
"My Uncle Daniel" (Cummings) **12**:159
My Uncle Dudley (Morris) **1**:232; **37**:310-12
My Uncle Oswald (Dahl) **18**:108-09; **79**:176, 179
My Uncle Silas (Bates) **46**:62-3, 66
"My Universities" (Yevtushenko) **51**:432
"My Vocation" (Ginzburg) **54**:201, 205
"My Voice Not Being Proud" (Bogan) **46**:83; **93**:64
"My War" (Fussell) **74**:125, 127, 134
"My War Poetry" (Krleža) See "Moja ratna lirika"
My War with the Twentieth Century (Berton) **104**:47
"My Warszawa:1980" (Oates) **33**:296
My Way (Bernstein) **142**:55-8
"My Weariness of Epic Proportions" (Simic) **68**:378
"My Whole Life" (Borges) See "Mi vida entera"
"My Wicked Uncle" (Mahon) **27**:290
My Wicked Wicked Ways (Cisneros) **69**:144, 150-51; **118**:210
"My Wife, My Car, My Color, and Myself" (Olson) **29**:328
My Wife's the Least of It (Gerhardie) **5**:139
My World (Stuart) **34**:375
My World—And Welcome to It (Thurber) **5**:438; **125**:412
My Year (Handke) See *Mein Jahr in der Niemandsbucht*
My Year in the No-Man's Bay (Handke) See *Mein Jahr in der Niemandsbucht*
My Younger Brother (Aksyonov) **101**:15
"My Youngest Child" (Shiga) **33**:368
My zdes' zhivem (Voinovich) **10**:504-05, 507; **147**:273
"Mycenae" (Denby) **48**:83
"Myeza and His Musical Instrument" (Kunene) **85**:176
Myko (Boyle) **19**:68
"Mymosh the Self-Begotten" (Lem) **8**:344
"My-ness" (Milosz) **56**:239
"Myopia: A Night" (Lowell) **11**:327-28; **124**:263-64
"Myra" (Berriault) **54**:3
Myra Breckinridge (Vidal) **2**:449; **4**:553-55, 557-58; **6**:548-50; **8**:525, 528; **10**:502, 504; **22**:438; **33**:408-09; **72**:386-87, 389; **142**:275-81, 292-96, 300, 302, 305, 307, 313, 319, 322, 329, 332, 334, 338
"Myremecology" (Rozewicz) See "Myrmekologia"
"Myriam" (Klima) **56**:172-73
"Myrisai to áriston" (Elytis) See "Smelling the Best"
"Myrmekologia" (Rozewicz) **139**:297
Myron (Vidal) **6**:548-50; **10**:502; **33**:409; **72**:387; **142**:275, 277-80, 293, 322, 334, 338
"Le myrte" (Bonnefoy) **15**:74
"Myself" (Ashton-Warner) **19**:22
"Myself" (Creeley) **78**:152
"Myself and India" (Jhabvala) **138**:74
"Myself in India" (Jhabvala) **138**:74, 77
Myself in India (Jhabvala) **4**:259; **94**:172, 177-79, 183, 185, 188
Myself When Young (du Maurier) **11**:164
Myself with Others: Selected Essays (Fuentes) **60**:162-64, 170; **113**:251, 256
Le mystère d'Alceste, Suivi de Qui n'a pas son minotaure? (Yourcenar) **87**:420
Mystère de la parole (Hébert) **29**:230, 236-38
"The Mysteries" (H. D.) **73**:121
Mysteries (Calisher) See *Mysteries of Motion*
The Mysteries (Harrison) **129**:167, 192-94, 203, 227
Mysteries (Wilson) **14**:584-85
"The Mysteries of Life in an Orderly Manner" (West) **7**:519
Mysteries of Motion (Calisher) **38**:73-5; **134**:9, 11, 19-20, 35-6, 39, 41
The Mysteries of Pittsburgh (Chabon) **55**:41-5; **149**:3-5, 7, 10, 14-17, 19-20, 23, 25-6, 28, 30-2
"The Mysteries of the Joy Rio" (Williams) **45**:453-54
Mysteries of the Mind (Hyde) **21**:176
Mysteries of Winterthurn (Oates) **33**:294-96; **52**:329, 331, 339; **108**:348-49, 351, 354, 385, 391
Les mystérieuses noces (Jouve) **47**:209
The Mysterious Affair at Styles (Christie) **1**:58; **6**:107-09; **12**:111, 114, 120, 122, 124, 127; **39**:438, 441; **48**:77; **110**:110, 116, 118, 122, 129
The Mysterious Disappearance of the Young Marchioness of Loria (Donoso) See *La misteriosa desaparición de la Marquesita de Loria*
"Mysterious Doings in the Metropolitan Museum" (Leiber) **25**:311
The Mysterious History of Columbus: An Exploration of the Man, the Myth, the Legacy (Wilford) **70**:331, 340, 342, 345, 354
"Mysterious Kôr" (Bowen) **22**:64-67; **118**:65, 67, 103
The Mysterious North (Berton) **104**:37-8, 47, 51-2
Mystery (Straub) **107**:283-86, 289-90, 302, 304, 306-07, 309-10
Mystery and Manners (O'Connor) **3**:365; **6**:380; **13**:417-18, 420-21
"Mystery at Euston" (Scannell) **49**:331
Mystery at Love's Creek (Cavanna) **12**:101
Mystery at the Edge of Two Worlds (Harris) **12**:269
"Mystery Dance" (Costello) **21**:67
Mystery in Little Tokyo (Bonham) **12**:50, 54
"Mystery in São Cristovão" (Lispector) **43**:267-68
"Mystery Mile" (Allingham) **19**:11, 14
The Mystery of Being (Marcel) **15**:359, 364
"The Mystery of Emily Dickinson" (Bell) **31**:49
"The Mystery of Hunter's Lodge" (Christie) **110**:111
The Mystery of Irma Vep: A Penny Dreadful (Ludlam) **46**:243-44; **50**:342-44
"The Mystery of Job's Suffering" (Spark) **40**:399
The Mystery of Kaspar Hauser (Herzog) See *Every Man for Himself and God against All*
The Mystery of Oberwald (Antonioni) See *Il mistero di oberwald*
"The Mystery of Personality in the Novel" (Gold) **42**:189
The Mystery of Phillis Wheatley (Bullins) **7**:37
The Mystery of Stonehenge (Branley) **21**:18
The Mystery of the Boquet of Roses (Puig) See *El misterio del ramo de rosas*
The Mystery of the Buddha (Cavanna) **12**:102
The Mystery of the Charity of Charles Péguy (Hill) **45**:182-87, 189-91
Mystery of the Fat Cat (Bonham) **12**:50-2
"The Mystery of the Initiate" (Blaga) **75**:62
Mystery of the Rose Bouquet (Puig) See *El misterio del ramo de rosas*
Mystery of the Verb (Hébert) **13**:268; **29**:232
Mystery of the Witch Who Wouldn't (Platt) **26**:350
"Mystic" (Plath) **5**:342; **11**:449; **14**:425; **17**:360; **51**:345; **111**:205
The Mystic Adventures of Roxie Stoner (Morgan) **6**:340
The Mystic Masseur (Naipaul) **4**:372, 375; **7**:252; **13**:402-04, 406; **18**:360; **37**:324-25; **105**:147-48, 155, 170, 179
"A Mystic of the Air Age" (Johnston) **51**:239, 251
"Mystic River" (Ciardi) **129**:39
"The Mystic River" (Kinnell) **129**:260, 263-64
Mysticism and Witchcraft (Waters) **88**:343
Mystics and Zen Masters (Merton) **1**:211
"Myten om människorna" (Lagerkvist) **54**:286-87
"The Myth" (Levine) **33**:274
"Myth" (Mahapatra) **33**:278, 282
"The Myth" (Oates) **108**:355, 357
"Myth" (Ritsos) **31**:325
Myth (Buero Vallejo) See *Mito*
Myth and Metaphor: Selected Essays, 1974-1980 (Frye) **70**:274
"Myth and Power" (Achebe) **152**:71
The Myth and the Powerhouse (Rahv) **24**:353, 361
"Myth, Dream, and Poem" (Read) **4**:444
"Myth in Education" (Hughes) **37**:171
Myth, Literature, and the African World (Soyinka) **14**:509; **36**:412
"The Myth Makers" (Lane) **25**:285
The Myth Makers (Pritchett) **15**:441-42; **41**:331
"The Myth of Arthur" (Jones) **7**:189-90; **13**:309
The Myth of Deliverance (Frye) **70**:277
"The Myth of Mankind" (Lagerkvist) See "Myten om människorna"
"Myth of Mountain Sunrise" (Warren) **39**:266
"The Myth of Quetzalcoatl" (Anaya) **148**:49
"The Myth of Sisyphus" (Blaga) **75**:69
The Myth of Sisyphus (Camus) See *Le mythe de Sisyphe*
"Myth on Mediterranean Beach: Aphrodite as Logos" (Warren) **10**:520
"Myth Today" (Barthes) **83**:93-4
Mythago Wood (Holdstock) **39**:151-54
Le mythe de Sisyphe (Camus) **1**:54; **2**:97; **4**:89, 91; **9**:141, 152; **11**:93, 95-6; **14**:104-05, 108-12, 117; **32**:88, 100; **63**:60-2, 83-4; **69**:105-06, 113-18, 121, 126, 128-29, 133-34, 136; **124**:9- 12, 21, 33, 35
"Mythic Fragment" (Glück) **44**:219, 222
The Mythic Image (Campbell) **69**:77-9, 81-2, 87
Mythistorema (Seferis) **5**:384; **11**:492-94

The Mythmakers (Barnard) **48**:27, 29
"The Mythmaker's Office" (Frame) **96**:192
"Mythological Beast" (Donaldson) **46**:143
"Mythological Introduction" (Larkin) **64**:262, 282
"The Mythological Poet" (Ashbery) **41**:40
Mythological Sonnets (Fuller) **28**:149, 151
"A Mythological Subject" (Colwin) **84**:149-50
Mythologies (Barthes) **24**:25-6, 30-1, 37; **83**:67, 69-71, 73-8, 80, 83, 85-7, 90, 93, 94-6, 98, 104
Mythologies: An Introduction to a Science of Mythology (Lévi-Strauss)
See *Mythologiques*
Mythologiques (Lévi-Strauss) **38**:303, 305, 308
"Mythos" (Gustafson) **36**:211
"Myths I" (Mott) **15**:381
"Myths VII" (Mott) **15**:381
Myths and Texts (Snyder) **5**:395; **9**:499, 503; **32**:387-89, 391, 396, 398-99; **120**:313, 316, 335, 340, 354
"The Myths of Bears" (Bass) **143**:17-18, 20-1
The Myths of Bears (Bass) **143**:20
Myths of Power: A Marxist Study of the Brontës (Eagleton) **63**:101-02, 104
"Myths of the Near Future" (Ballard) **137**:14
Myths of the Near Future (Ballard) **36**:44, 47; **137**:16, 37, 39
Myths to Live By (Campbell) **69**:77, 94
"Myths within Us" (Jennings) **131**:243
"Myxomatosis" (Larkin) **5**:225; **8**:340
"N" (Cummings) **15**:160
N or M? (Christie) **110**:111, 113
"--'n Spieelvars--" (Breytenbach) **126**:86
La nâ (Audiberti) **38**:22, 32-3
"Na audiart" (Pound) **48**:288
"Na cidade po porto" (Cabral de Melo Neto) **76**:161
Na czworakach (Rozewicz) **139**:229-30, 232, 249, 265, 281, 293
"Na Guiné" (Cabral de Melo Neto) **76**:167
"na początku" (Rozewicz) **139**:295
Na rannikh poezdakh (Pasternak) **18**:383; **63**:288, 290, 312
Na reke Baidamtal (Aitmatov) **71**:15
Na rubu pameti (Krleža) **8**:329, 331; **114**:168, 174, 176-77, 186
Na vlnách T. S. F. (Seifert) **34**:256; **44**:424; **93**:305, 318, 333, 340
"Na vystake Karla Veilinka" (Brodsky) **100**:55
Nabakov's Garden: A Guide to "Ada" (Mason) **82**:255
"The Nabara" (Day Lewis) **10**:131
"Nabo: The Black Man Who Made the Angels Wait" (García Márquez) **2**:150; **3**:181; **47**:148, 150
Nabokov: His Life in Art; A Critical Narrative (Field) **44**:465, 467-69
Nabokov: His Life in Part (Field) **44**:464-68, 470
"Nabonides" (Arreola) **147**:5
Nachdenken über Christa T. (Wolf) **14**:593-94; **29**:464-67; **58**:422-23, 431-36; **150**:217, 223-24, 227, 229-30, 235-37, 245, 248, 252-53, 258-60, 264, 271, 278, 280, 286, 288-93, 296, 300-02, 305-06, 317, 319, 322-23, 336-43, 345, 348, 351-52
Die nachholende Revolution (Habermas) **104**:87
Nachmetaphysisches Denken (Habermas) **104**:87, 89
Nachmittag eines Schriftsellers (Handke) **134**:136-40, 142, 151, 159, 166-68
"Nachtfahrt und früher Morgen" (Hein) **154**:194
Nachtfahrt und früher Morgen (Hein) **154**:135-38, 195
"Nachtflug" (Bachmann) **69**:38, 54
Nachtstück (Hildesheimer) **49**:169-71
Nacimiento último (Aleixandre) **9**:17
"Nackles" (Ellison) **139**:129
Nada (Chabrol) **16**:179, 183-84
Nada, nadie: La voces del temblor (Poniatowska) **140**:304, 309, 329-30, 338
"Nadie" (Aleixandre) **9**:15
"Nadir" (Le Guin) **45**:216
Nadja (Breton) **54**:22-6, 28, 32-4; **2**:80-1; **15**:87
Nafsika (Nakos) **29**:323
"Naga" (Narayan) **121**:414, 416
"La nageur" (Soupault) **68**:406-07
Några steg mot tystnaden (Johnson) **14**:296-97
"Nähe der gräber" (Celan) **19**:89
"Naiad" (Davidson) **13**:168; **19**:129
"A Nail" (Guillevic) **33**:191
"The Nail in the Middle of the Hand" (Brunner) **8**:108
Nail Polish (Layton) **2**:236
"The Nailhead" (Ignatow) **40**:258
"Nailing a Dock Together" (Bly) **128**:14
"The Nails" (Merwin) **88**:199
"Le nain rouge" (Tournier) **23**:452
"Nairobi" (Oates) **52**:331
Naissance de la clinique: Une archélologie du regard médical (Foucault) **31**:178-80; **34**:339; **69**:170
Naissance de l'Odyssée (Giono) **4**:188; **11**:232
The Naive and Sentimental Lover (le Carré) **3**:281; **5**:232-33; **15**:325
"A Naive Poem" (Milosz)
See "The World"
"The Naive Reader" (Reid) **33**:350
"Naked" (Oates) **108**:382
The Naked and the Dead (Mailer) **1**:187-93; **2**:258, 262-63, 265; **3**:311-15, 318; **4**:318-19, 321, 323; **5**:266; **8**:364, 368-73; **11**:339-40, 342-43; **14**:352; **28**:256-57; **39**:417-18, 420, 425; **74**:202-03, 205-06, 208-09, 211, 217, 219-21, 233, 238; **111**:94, 97, 108, 113, 126, 135-36, 139-42, 144-46, 148, 151
"The Naked and the Nude" (Graves) **45**:169
The Naked Beast at Heaven's Gate (Bataille)
See *Madame Edwarda*
"Naked Body" (Ritsos) **31**:332
"The Naked Eye" (Santos) **22**:363-64
"Naked Eye" (Townshend) **17**:534
"Naked Girl and Mirror" (Wright) **53**:425-26, 429
The Naked God (Fast) **23**:157-58; **131**:52-5, 57, 60, 66, 70-2, 74-7, 83, 87, 91, 98
"Naked in Arcadia" (Simic) **130**:328
Naked in Garden Hills (Crews) **6**:117; **23**:132, 138; **49**:68, 70, 72
"The Naked Lady" (Bell) **41**:54
Naked Lunch (Burroughs) **1**:48-9; **2**:90-3; **5**:91-2; **15**:108, 110-11; **22**:80-6; **42**:68-9, 71-7, 80; **75**:83-117; **109**:180-91, 194-95, 197, 207, 210-16, 220-22, 224, 226, 227-31
The Naked Lunch (Cronenberg) **143**:69-73, 76-77, 88, 93, 108-09, 116, 126, 134, 138, 152
"Naked Moon" (Rosenblatt) **15**:448
A Naked Needle (Farah) **53**:132, 134-35, 137-38; **137**:83-90, 105, 119-23, 131
The Naked Night (Bergman)
See *Gycklarnas afton*
Naked Poems (Webb) **18**:540-42
The Naked Sun (Asimov) **9**:50-1; **19**:28; **26**:40, 42, 46-8, 50, 53, 58; **76**:314; **92**:13
Naked Youth (Oshima) **20**:247
"Nakedness" (Ezekiel) **61**:105
The Nakedness of the Fathers: Biblical Visions and Revisions (Ostriker) **132**:321, 328
Nalini (Ezekiel) **61**:97-9
"Namaste" (Broumas) **73**:14
"Der Name" (Hein) **154**:166
"The Name" (Transtroemer) **52**:412; **65**:222-23
"Name and Address" (McCartney) **35**:286
"Name Changes" (Parra) **102**:348, 350
A Name for Evil (Lytle) **22**:293, 300
The Name of Action (Greene) **18**:194; **70**:291; **72**:158-59, 161
The Name of Annabel Lee (Symons) **32**:429
The Name of the Rose (Eco)
See *Il nome della rosa*
"The Name, the Nose" (Calvino)
See "Il nome il naso"
"Named for Victoria, Queen of England" (Achebe) **75**:13
"Name-Day Night" (Olson) **29**:330
The Nameless (Campbell) **42**:90, 93
"Nameless Flower" (Wright) **53**:424, 428, 431
"A Nameless One" (Avison) **97**:128
"The Nameless One" (Nakos) **29**:322
"The Nameless Stream" (Blunden) **56**:29
"Names" (Carruth) **84**:135
"Names" (Dixon) **52**:95
"Names" (Walcott) **76**:281-86
The Names (DeLillo) **27**:83-6; **39**:116-17, 119, 122, 125; **54**:79-83; **76**:171-72, 177, 179-80, 182, 185; **143**:176, 178-79, 208, 210, 215
The Names: A Memoir (Momaday) **19**:318, 320; **85**:235, 250, 256-57, 262, 267-68, 273, 279; **95**:267
"The Names and Faces of Heroes" (Price) **43**:341
The Names and Faces of Heroes (Price) **3**:404, 406; **43**:341-42, 344; **50**:229-30; **63**:325, 341
The Names of the Lost (Levine) **9**:332; **14**:315-16, 318-20; **33**:270-72, 274; **118**:267, 279, 284, 290, 296, 299, 301, 317
"The Name's the Same" (Findley) **102**:110-11
"Naming a Poem Called Tucker Drugs" (Moure) **88**:230
"Naming and Blaming: The Media Goes Wilding in Palm Beach" (Pollitt) **122**:206
"The Naming of Albert Johnson" (Wiebe) **138**:338, 379
"The Naming of Beasts and Other Poems" (Stern) **40**:414
"The Naming of Indian Boys" (Alexie) **154**:27
"The Naming of Names" (Bradbury)
See "Dark They Were, and Golden-Eyed"
Naming Our Destiny: New and Selected Poems (Jordan) **114**:143, 146, 149, 153, 157, 162
"Naming the Losses" (Parini) **54**:360
Nampally Road (Alexander) **121**:9-11, 14, 16, 18
Nana (Arzner) **98**:66, 69, 71, 75, 87, 90, 92-7, 99
Nana (Renoir) **20**:301
"The Nana-Hex" (Sexton) **53**:321
"Nancy and Sluggo" (Katz) **47**:216
"Nancy Culpepper" (Mason) **28**:274; **43**:288-89; **82**:235, 240; **154**:234, 236, 254, 205, 320
Nancy Mitford: A Biography (Hastings) **44**:483-84, 486-88, 491-92
"Nancy Reagan Wears a Hat: Feminism and Its Cultural Consensus" (Stimpson) **65**:339
"Nanji mo mata" (Endō) **99**:289, 290-95
Nanji mo mata (Endō) **54**:159; **99**:285-86
Nanna-ya (Condé) **52**:84
"Nanny" (Dick) **72**:118
"Naoise at Four" (Boland) **40**:96; **67**:43
Naomi's Road (Kogawa) **78**:183, 194
"The Nap" (Banks) **37**:23
"The Nap" (Hine) **15**:282
"Napier Court" (Campbell) **42**:84, 92
Napis (Herbert) **43**:186
The Napoleon Game (Hein)
See *Das Napoleon-Spiel*
Napoleon Symphony (Burgess) **4**:83-5; **5**:85-7, 90; **22**:78; **40**:118, 126; **62**:132; **81**:303, 307, 310; **94**:51, 61, 69, 75
Das Napoleon-Spiel (Hein) **154**:72, 80, 112-23, 125, 127, 179, 161, 163-64, 167-68, 172, 180-82, 188-89
Nappy Edges (Shange) **25**:397-99; **38**:393; **126**:364
"Naptha" (O'Hara) **78**:334
Nära livet (Bergman) **16**:47, 50, 80
"Narcissa" (Auchincloss) **45**:33
Narcissa, and Other Fables (Auchincloss) **45**:33
"Narcissus" (Disch) **36**:127
Narcissus (Scott) **43**:371-73

Narcissus and Goldmund (Hesse)
See *Narziss und Goldmund*
"Narcissus as Narcissus" (Tate) **6**:526; **14**:528
"Narcissus Explains" (Howard) **47**:171
"Narcissus Moving" (Berryman) **13**:78
"Narcissus Never Knew Her" (Alexander) **121**:5,6
Narracions (Espriu) **9**:192
The Narrative (Pasternak)
See *Povest*
"Narrative Art and Magic" (Borges)
See "El arte narrativo y la magia"
"Narrative Authority" (Sukenick) **48**:369
"Narrative, Description, and Tropology in Proust" (White) **148**:299, 304
"The Narrative of Jacobus Coetzee" (Coetzee) **23**:121, 124; **117**:34-6, 38, 44, 52, 79, 83
"Narrative Poetry" (Strand) **71**:288
"A Narrative with Scattered Nouns" (Dorn) **10**:160
"The Narrator" (Graham) **29**:193
The Narrow Corner (Maugham) **15**:367; **67**:206, 229-30
"A Narrow Heart: The Portrait of a Woman" (Gordon) **13**:244
The Narrow House (Scott) **43**:370-73, 380
The Narrow Land (Vance) **35**:427
Narrow Road to the Deep (Bond) **4**:69; **6**:85; **13**:98, 102
"The Narrow Road to the North" (Muldoon) **32**:318
Narrow Rooms (Purdy) **10**:425-26; **52**:343, 347-48
"The Narrow Way" (Pink Floyd) **35**:305
The Narrowing Circle (Symons) **14**:524
"Narrows" (Ammons) **8**:14
"The Narrows" (Jones) **42**:242-43
The Narrows (Petry) **7**:305; **18**:403-04
"Narsiga" (Rao) **56**:291, 306
"Narthex" (H. D.) **31**:208
Narziss und Goldmund (Hesse) **2**:189-92; **3**:243, 245-47; **11**:270-72; **17**:195, 204-06, 217-18; **69**:287, 289
Nascita d'aurora (Ungaretti) **15**:536
Nashestvie (Leonov) **92**:246, 260, 270-72, 277
Nashville (Altman) **16**:33-44; **116**:13-20, 22-6, 28-30, 36-7, 48, 50-1, 60-2, 64, 66, 68, 70, 72, 74
"Nashville Gone to Ashes" (Hempel) **39**:68-9
Nashville Skyline (Dylan) **3**:131; **4**:150; **6**:155; **12**:186-87, 189, 199; **77**:169
Nasty, Very: A Mock Epic in Six Parts (Rathbone) **41**:344
Nasz starszy brat (Rozewicz) **139**:291, 294
"Nat Bacon's Bones" (MacLeish) **68**:290
"Nat Koffman" (Ignatow) **40**:258
Natalie Mann (Toomer) **22**:425, 428, 430
Natalie Natalia (Mosley) **43**:316, 319, 321
"Natalya Nikolayevna Goncharov" (Coles) **46**:113
"Natasha" (Olesha) **8**:431
Nathalie Granger (Duras) **20**:99, 101
Nathan Coulter (Berry) **46**:73
"Nathan La Freneer" (Mitchell) **12**:436-37
Nathaniel (Saul) **46**:368-69
"Nathaniel Hawthorne" (Borges) **83**:164
Nathan's Run (Gilstrap) **99**:43-5
Natica Jackson (O'Hara) **42**:319, 327
"A Nation" (Milosz) **82**:297
Nation et voie africaine du socialisme (Senghor) **54**:399, 401; 130
"A Nation of Sheep" (Ferlinghetti) **111**:60
"A Nation of Wheels" (Barthelme) **46**:36
"National Day of Mourning for Twelve Protestants" (Durcan) **43**:114
"The National Debt" (Apple) **33**:21
National Dream (Berton) **104**:44-5
The National Dream (Findley) **102**:104, 106
The National Health (Nichols) **5**:305-07, 309; **36**:329, 331-32
National Health (Nichols) **65**:162
The National Interest (Edgar) **42**:116, 123
National Lampoon's Animal House (Landis) **26**:272-77
"National Liberation Movements" (Baraka) **14**:49
The National Line (Haavikko)
See *Kansakunnan linja*
"The National Pastime" (Cheever) **3**:107
"The National Pastime" (Spinrad) **46**:384
National Reality from the Bed (Valenzuela)
See *Realidad nacional desde la cama*
The National Theatre (Edgar) **42**:114-15
"National Thoughts" (Amichai) **57**:41
"National Trust" (Harrison) **43**:177; **129**:166
National Velvet (Bagnold) **25**:72-4
The National Weather Service (Berger) **12**:38
National Winner (Humphreys) **47**:181, 184
"La nationalisation de la littérature" (Sartre) **24**:419
Nationalism and the Jewish Problem (Jünger) **125**:256
Nationalism, Colonialism, and Literature (Jameson) **142**:235, 239
The Nations Within: The Past and Future of American Indian Sovereignty (Deloria) **122**:113-15
The Native (Ghose) **42**:180, 183-84
"The Native American Broadcasting System" (Alexie) **96**:12
Native American Tribalism: Indian Survivals and Renewals (McNickle) **89**:160-61, 181
Native Americans: 500 Years After, A Guide to Research in Native American Studies (Dorris) **109**:296
A Native Argosy (Callaghan) **41**:89
The Native Country (Haavikko)
See *Synnyinmaa*
"A Native Hill" (Berry) **27**:38, 40
The Native in Literature: Canadian and Comparative Perspectives (King) **89**:75
Native Intelligence (Sokolov) **7**:430-31
Native Land (Rich)
See *Your Native Land, Your Life*
"Native Land of My Return" (Ulibarrí)
See "Patria de retorno"
Native Realm: A Search for Self-Definition (Milosz)
See *Rodzinna Europa*
"Native Resistances" (Dickey) **3**:127
Native Son (Welles) **80**:382
Native Son (Wright) **1**:377-80; **3**:545-46; **4**:594-96; **9**:584-86; **14**:595-99; **21**:435, 441-42, 446-47, 458-59, 462; **48**:416, 418-21, 423-30; **74**:356, 359, 361, 363, 370, 378, 380-81, 383, 385, 390-91
Native Speaker (Lee) **91**:53-58
"Native Village" (Blaga) **75**:78
"Natives Don't Cry" (Boyle) **58**:66-7
Natives of My Person (Lamming) **2**:235; **4**:279; **66**:220, 223-25, 227-28, 230; **144**:126-27, 129, 131, 140, 143-46, 149-51, 174, 185-88, 191
"The Nativity" (Archer) **28**:14
"Nativity" (Livesay) **79**:334-36
"Nativity" (Raine) **45**:331, 335
The Nativity (Harrison) **129**:192
"Nativity, Caucasian" (Gurganus) **70**:191, 193, 195
"Nativity Poem" (Glück) **7**:118
"Nativity Scene" (Bottoms) **53**:32
"A Nativity Tale" (Brown) **100**:83
"Natrabach i na cytrze" (Milosz) **56**:235, 244, 249; **82**:295
Natsukashii toshi e no tegami (Oe) **86**:244
Natten är här (Johnson) **14**:295
Nattvardsgästerna (Bergman) **16**:52-5, 58, 61-2, 64, 74, 78, 80; **72**:33, 38-41, 46-7, 49, 52, 54-5, 59
Natty Dread (Marley) **17**:267-68, 270, 272-73
The Natural (Malamud) **1**:196-98, 201; **2**:266, 269; **3**:321, 324; **8**:375-76; **9**:341, 346, 348-50, 352; **11**:345-46, 349-53; **18**:321; **27**:295-96, 298-99, 301; **44**:411-17; **78**:248-49, 251-52, 264, 271-72, 282-83; **85**:200
Natural Affection (Inge) **8**:309; **19**:227-28
Natural Born Killers (Tarantino) **125**:350-51, 354-55, 357-59, 361-64, 366, 369, 372
Natural Child (Willingham) **5**:511; **51**:404-05, 411
A Natural Curiosity (Drabble) **129**:119-21, 123, 134-38, 141, 144-45, 148-50, 155-56, 160
Natural Enemies (Horwitz) **14**:267
"Natural Freaks" (Maitland) **49**:233
"A Natural Girl" (Yates) **23**:483
"Natural History" (Thomas) **37**:418-19, 421; **107**:325-26, 328, 349
"Natural History" (Warren) **8**:537
Natural History (Howard) **151**:264, 267-68, 270-77, 282-83, 285
Natural History (Urdang) **47**:397-98, 401
"Natural History II" (Walcott) **76**:285
"A Natural History of the Dead" (Hemingway) **30**:188
"A Natural Man" (Dumas) **62**:155
"Natural Mystic" (Marley) **17**:269-70
Natural Numbers: New and Selected Poems (Rexroth) **1**:284; **22**:346; **49**:274, 283, 285
A Natural Perspective: The Development of Shakespearean Comedy and Romance (Frye) **24**:213; **70**:271, 277
"Natural Resources" (Rich) **36**:374, 379; **125**:332
Natural Selection (Barthelme) **117**:9, 11, 13-14, 18, 21-3
Natural Shocks (Stern) **39**:241-43
Natural Stories (Levi)
See *Storie naturali*
Natural Supernaturalism (Abrams) **24**:12, 14, 16, 18
"Natural Theology" (Hass) **99**:142-43, 145-47
"Natural Tilts" (Vizenor) **103**:293
"Natural/Unnatural" (Avison) **97**:80-1
"Naturally" (Gallagher) **63**:116
"Naturally the Foundation Will Bear Your Expenses" (Larkin) **3**:275; **8**:340; **33**:258; **64**:272-74
"Nature" (McFadden) **48**:246
"Nature" (Oliver) **98**:292
"Nature and New Painting" (O'Hara) **78**:358
The Nature and Purpose of the Universe (Durang) **27**:88
"Nature Displayed" (Blunden) **56**:37
"Nature, Humanism, Tragedy" (Robbe-Grillet)
See "Nature, Humanisme, Tragédie"
"Nature, Humanisme, Tragédie" (Robbe-Grillet) **43**:360; **128**:345
"Nature in Literature" (Gerstler) **70**:158
"Nature morte" (Brodsky) **4**:78; **13**:116; **36**:81
"La nature morte de Samuel Beckett" (Johnson) **7**:415
"The Nature of a Mirror" (Warren) **8**:537
The Nature of Alexander (Renault) **11**:472; **17**:401
"The Nature of Almost Everything" (Robison) **42**:342-43
"The Nature of Beauty" (Ostriker) **132**:321
The Nature of Catastrophe (Moorcock) **58**:347-48
"The Nature of Cold Weather" (Redgrove) **41**:347, 351, 354
The Nature of Cold Weather and Other Poems (Redgrove) **41**:347, 349
"The Nature of Evidence" (Graham) **48**:144
"The Nature of Literature" (Wellek) **28**:442
The Nature of Love (Bates) **46**:65
The Nature of Love (Wright) **53**:425
The Nature of Passion (Jhabvala) **29**:253-54, 260; **94**:166-68, 170, 180; **138**:64
The Nature of Space and Time (Hawking) **105**:73-7
The Nature of the Universe (Gallant) **17**:126
"The Nature of Tragedy" (Miller) **10**:346
Nature: Poems Old and New (Swenson) **106**:346, 351
"Nature with Man" (Silkin) **6**:498; **43**:397, 400

Nature with Man (Silkin) **6**:498; **43**:397, 399, 404
Les naturels du Bordelais (Audiberti) **38**:22-4, 26
"Nature's Beauty" (Blunden) **56**:39
"Naufragi" (Ungaretti) **11**:559
"Naughty Boy" (Creeley) **36**:118
Nausea (Sartre)
See *La nausée*
La nausée (Sartre) **1**:305; **4**:473, 477; **7**:396, 398-99; **9**:472; **13**:503-06; **18**:463-66; **24**:406, 410, 421; **44**:493, 495; **50**:370-74, 377-80, 382-84; **52**:378-79, 384, 387-89
"A Navajo Blanket" (Swenson) **61**:398
Navegação de Cabotagem (Amado) **106**:91
"Navigator" (Sarton) **49**:310
The Navigator (Keaton) **20**:195
The Navigator (West) **3**:430-31
"The Navigator Returns to His Country" (Bioy Casares) **88**:92
Le navire night (Duras) **40**:178
Nayak (Ray) **16**:487, 494
Nayak—The Hero (Ray)
See *Nayak*
Näyelmät (Haavikko) **18**:208
The Nazarene Gospel Restored (Graves) **6**:211; **39**:325; **45**:173
Nazarin (Bunuel) **16**:130-31, 135, 148, 151; **80**:20, 25-6, 28, 30, 34, 38-41, 44, 47-50, 53
The Nazi Doctors: Medical Killing and the Psychology of Genocide (Lifton) **67**:155-61
Nazism (Forman) **21**:121
"Ndbele's People" (Hope) **52**:210
"Ndéssé on Blues" (Senghor) **130**:267, 275
"Ndéssé or Blues" (Senghor)
See "Ndéssé on Blucs"
"The ndioso Driver" (Cabral de Melo Neto)
See *O automobilista Infundioso*
"Në kafe" (Kadare) **52**:259
"Ne pisat' o groze" (Akhmadulina) **53**:13
Ne réveillez pas madame (Anouilh) **40**:59-60
Ne vahvimmat miehet ei ehjiksi jää (Haavikko) **34**:173, 178
"Neal vs. Jimmy the Fag" (Gelber) **79**:223
"Near Alexandria" (Brodsky) **100**:36
Near and Far (Blunden) **56**:49
"The Near and the Far" (Tomlinson) **45**:397
"Near Changes" (Van Duyn) **116**:414
Near Changes (Van Duyn) **63**:443-45; **116**:411-15, 418, 420, 423, 425, 427
The Near East (Asimov) **76**:312
Near False Creek Mouth (Birney) **6**:73-4
"Near Keokuk" (Sandburg) **35**:355
"Near of Kin" (Butler) **121**:141, 143
"Near Olympic" (Steele) **45**:364-66
"Near Pala" (Rush) **44**:91-2, 94-5
"Near Perigord" (Pound) **112**:352-53
"Near Périgord" (Stern) **40**:414
"Near the Haunted Castle" (Williams) **33**:445-46
"Near the Heart Place of Grue" (Abbott) **48**:3
"Near the Ocean" (Lowell) **8**:354; **9**:338; **11**:326; **15**:345; **37**:236
Near the Ocean (Lowell) **1**:181-82, 184; **2**:247, 249; **4**:302; **8**:351, 357; **11**:325, 331; **15**:342-43; **37**:234; **124**:301, 305-07
"Near the Unbalanced Aquarium" (Lowell) **124**:267
"Nearing La Guarira" (Walcott) **76**:279-80
"Nearing the Ancre Battlefield" (Blunden) **56**:30
"Nearing the Lights" (Moss) **14**:375
Nearing's Grace (Sommer) **25**:424-25
The Nearly Complete Collection of Woody Guthrie Folk Songs (Guthrie) **35**:184-85
"Nearly True Stories" (Riding) **7**:375
"Nearness of Graves" (Celan)
See "Nähe der gräber"
The Nearness of You (Kizer) **80**:182, 185-86
"Neato Keeno Time" (Crumb) **17**:83
Neb (Thomas) **48**:382-83
Nebanuitele trepte (Blaga) **75**:67, 71-2
Nebraska (Reddin) **67**:270
"Necessary Clarifications" (Aitmatov)
See "Neobkhodimye utochneniia"
Necessary Doubt (Wilson) **3**:537; **14**:589
Necessary Illusions (Chomsky) **132**:40, 67
Necessary Secrets: The Journals of Elizabeth Smart (Smart) **54**:425-26
"Necessities" (Mueller) **51**:283-84
"Necessities of Life" (Rich) **125**:336
Necessities of Life: Poems, 1962-1965 (Rich) **3**:427; **6**:457; **7**:365-66, 368, 371-72; **11**:476; **18**:446; **36**:366, 372, 375; **73**:325-26; **125**:336
"Necessity" (Eberhart) **56**:77
"Necessity" (Hughes) **35**:222
"The Necessity of Poetry" (Simic) **130**:334
"The Necklace" (Pritchett) **41**:334
The Necklace (Tomlinson) **2**:437; **4**:543-44, 546; **13**:545-46; **45**:393, 398-400, 402, 404
"Necrobes" (Lem) **40**:298
Necrocorrida (Codrescu) **121**:162
"Necrological" (Ransom) **2**:362; **4**:431, 435; **5**:365
"Necropsy of Love" (Purdy) **14**:432
Nectar in a Sieve (Markandaya) **8**:377; **38**:319-21, 323, 325
"The Nectarine Tree" (Sitwell) **9**:493
Ned Kelly (Buzo) **61**:58
"Ned Skinner" (Muldoon) **32**:317-18; **72**:276
"Need: A Chorale for Black Women's Voices" (Lorde) **71**:246
"The Need for Sleep" (Dybek) **114**:62
"A Need for Something Sweet" (Gordimer) **18**:190
"The Need of Being Versed in Country Things" (Frost) **3**:174; **15**:250
"The Need to Hold Still" (Mueller) **51**:280
The Need to Hold Still (Mueller) **51**:280, 282
"Need Ya" (Seger) **35**:380
Needful Things (King) **113**:388, 390, 392-93
"Needle" (Simic) **9**:480; **130**:305
The Needle (King) **8**:321-22
"The Needle and the Damage Done" (Young) **17**:570
"A Needle for the Devil" (Rendell) **48**:320
"The Needlecase" (Bowen) **22**:66
"Needles" (Cabral de Melo Neto)
See "Agulhas"
The Needle's Eye (Drabble) **2**:117-19; **3**:128; **5**:117-19; **10**:162-63; **53**:118-19, 121-23; **129**:112-13, 115, 124, 130-32, 143-44, 152
Needle's Eye (Oppen)
See *Seascape: Needle's Eye*
"Nefarious Times We Live In" (Allen) **52**:41-2
"Nefelegeretes" (Elytis) **100**:173
Nefertiti et le rêve d'Akhnaton (Chedid) **47**:86
"The Negative" (Williams) **39**:449
Negative Blue: Selected Later Poems (Wright) **146**:378
"Negative Capability and Its Children" (Simic) **49**:339; **130**:294-95, 321, 330
"Negative Pluses" (Ammons) **57**:50
"Negative Symbiosis" (Ammons) **57**:53
"Negative: The Little Engine That Could" (Smith) **42**:350
"Negatives" (Walcott) **14**:551
nege landskappe van ons tye bemaak aan 'n beminde (Breytenbach) **126**:100-01
"Neglect" (Williams) **148**:328, 354
"The Neglect of Ford Madox Ford's Fifth Queen" (Gass) **39**:482
"Negotations" (Rich) **73**:330
Les nègres: Clownerie (Genet) **2**:157-58; **5**:136-37; **10**:225; **14**:199, 207; **44**:385-89, 391; **46**:173, 178
"The Negress: Her Monologue of Dark Crepe with Edges of Light" (Dubie) **36**:132
Négritnde et Humanisme (Senghor) **130**:248, 250
"Negro" (Hughes) **108**:309
The Negro (Du Bois) **64**:116, 131; **96**:146
"The Negro Artist and the Racial Mountain" (Hughes) **35**:220; **108**:290, 294, 307, 320, 323, 325, 333
"Negro bembón" (Guillén) **48**:161, 168; **79**:245
The Negro Caravan (Brown) **59**:267
"The Negro Hero" (Brooks) **15**:93; **125**:58, 90
The Negro in American Fiction (Brown) **1**:47; **59**:271
"The Negro in Art" (Du Bois) **64**:124
The Negro in Virginia (Brown) **59**:272
"El negro mar" (Guillén) **79**:240
Negro Mask (Senghor)
See "Masque nègre"
"The Negro Mother" (Hughes) **108**:297
"A Negro Playwright Speaks Her Mind" (Childress) **86**:309
Negro Poetry and Drama (Brown) **1**:47; **59**:271
"A Negro Saw the Jewish Pageant, 'We Will Never Die'" (Dodson) **79**:194
"Negro Servant" (Hughes) **35**:214
"A Negro Speaks of Rivers" (Hughes) **5**:191; **10**:280; **44**:507, 511; **108**:296, 309, 311-12, 323, 334
"The Negro Writer and His World" (Lamming) **66**:226
"Negroes are anti-Semitic because they are anti-White" (Baldwin) **42**:22
"Nehotărîre" (Arghezi) **80**:2
"Neige" (Kavan) **13**:317
La neige en deuil (Troyat) **23**:458, 461
La neige était sale (Simenon) **1**:309; **2**:399; **18**:484, 486
Neige noir (Aquin) **15**:17
Neige suivi de mal aimées (Kavan) **13**:317
"Neige sur Paris" (Senghor) **54**:395-96; **130**:254, 259, 266
"Neiges" (Perse) **4**:399-400; **46**:303-05, 307, 309
"Neighbor" (Hugo) **32**:247-49
"Neighbor" (Silverberg) **7**:425
"Neighbor" (Simak) **55**:320
"The Neighborhood" (Gordon) **128**:110, 118
"Neighborhood Drunk" (Dybek) **114**:64, 74
"Neighborhood House" (Guillén) **79**:230
Neighboring Lives (Disch) **36**:125-26
"Neighbors" (Allison) **153**:4
"Neighbors" (Carver) **22**:97-8; **55**:277, 279-81; **126**:142, 164
"The Neighbors" (Friedman) **56**:97
"Neighbors" (Hogan) **73**:160
"Neighbors" (Singer) **111**:333
Neighbors (Berger) **18**:56-8; **38**:37-40
"Neighbours" (Clarke) **61**:83
Neil Young (Young) **17**:569, 572, 579
Neither Fish nor Fowl (Kroetz) **41**:240
"Neither in God nor in Marx" (Montale) **9**:387
"Neither Out Far nor in Deep" (Frost) **1**:110; **9**:219, 221; **13**:228; **15**:250; **26**:125
"Neither the Beginning ..." (Delany) **141**:101
"Neither the Most Terrifying nor the Least Memorable" (Valenzuela) **31**:437; **104**:378
"Neither Wanting More" (Swenson) **106**:347
Nejimaki-dori kuronikuru (Murakami) **150**:63-9, 82-3, 85-6, 88-90, 92-4
"Nekkid: Homage to Edgar Allan Poe" (Smith) **42**:353, 357
Nekrassov (Sartre) **13**:500-01
Nekrofánia (Haviaras) **33**:202
"Nel Bagno" (Jacobsen) **48**:192; **102**:241-42
Nel magma (Luzi) **13**:352-53
Nel nostro tempo (Montale) **18**:340
NELLIGAN (Tremblay) **102**:380
"Nelly Meyers" (Ammons) **5**:29; **108**:4
Nelly Sachs zu Ehren (Sachs) **98**:323
Nelly's Version (Figes) **31**:164-65
Nelson (Rattigan) **7**:355
Nemesis (Christie) **6**:108
"Nemota" (Akhmadulina) **53**:12
"Nemureru bijo" (Kawabata) **5**:208; **107**:77-8, 86, 114
Nemureru bijo (Kawabata) **9**:309; **18**:280, 286; **107**:77-78, 86, 106-09, 114

"Neobkhodimye utochneniia" (Aitmatov) **71**:14
Neobyknovennie rasskazy o muzhikakh (Leonov) **92**:258
"The Neo-Classic Drama" (Merwin) **45**:268-69
"The Neo-Classical Urn" (Lowell) **8**:351, 353; **11**:328
"Le néo-Français en déroute" (Queneau) **42**:333
"Neo-HooDoo Manifesto" (Reed) **3**:424; **13**:478; **60**:315
The Neon Bible (Toole) **64**:412, 415-17, 421-24
"Neon Sky" (Seger) **35**:379
Neon Vernacular: New and Selected Poems (Komunyakaa) **86**:190-94; **94**:239, 242, 246-49
The Neon Wilderness (Algren) **4**:16; **10**:5; **33**:13-5
"Neoplatonic Riff" (Ostriker) **132**:321
The Nephew (Purdy) **2**:348, 350; **10**:423-24; **28**:376-78, 380; **52**:343-44
The Nerd (Shue) **52**:392-93
"Nertheless" (Bernard) **59**:44
"Nerthus" (Heaney) **25**:245
Neruda and Vallejo: Selected Poems (Bly) **128**:22
Neruda and Vallejo: Selected Poems (Neruda) **1**:247
The Nerve (Bragg) **10**:72
Nerve (Francis) **2**:143; **22**:150; **42**:147, 149-50, 153, 155, 158; **102**:131-32, 144
Nerves (Wieners) **7**:536-37
"The Nervous Father" (Martin) **30**:248
Nervous Horses (Hearne) **56**:124-28
"Nervous Songs" (Berryman) **3**:67, 70; **8**:91; **13**:78; **62**:71
The Nervous System: The Inner Networks (Silverstein and Silverstein) **17**:452
"Nesselrode to Jeopardy" (Perelman) **49**:261, 272
"The Nest" (Nyro) **17**:320
The Nest (Kroetz) **41**:235-36, 239-40
"Nest Egg" (Stuart) **34**:374
"A Nest Egg for Paradise" (Singer) **69**:306-07
A Nest of Ninnies (Ashbery) **2**:17-18; **25**:50
A Nest of Ninnies (Schuyler) **23**:389
A Nest of Simple Folk (O'Faolain) **2**:275; **13**:402, 404-05; **70**:312-13, 315-16, 320-21
"Nest of Vampires" (Fenton) **32**:166
"Nested" (Nyro) **17**:320-21
The Nesting Ground (Wagoner) **3**:508; **5**:473
"The Nestling" (Williams) **42**:442
"Nestor's Bathtub" (Dove) **81**:137
"Nests" (Kinsella) **43**:253-54
"Nests in a Stone Image" (Goyen) **8**:251; **14**:212-13
Net of Jewels (Gilchrist) **143**:298-99, 301-07, 312-14, 323, 325, 327, 329, 332
"Net of Law" (Ding Ling) **68**:67
"The Net of Place" (Blackburn) **9**:100
Neterpenie (Trifonov) **45**:417, 422
Netherwood (White) **69**:410
The Nets (Blackburn) **43**:63
The Nets (Ghiselin) **23**:169
"Netting" (Graham) **48**:145
"Nettles" (Pollitt) **28**:366
"The Network" (Mathews) **52**:308
Network (Chayefsky) **23**:117-18
Netzahualcóyotl (Cardenal) **31**:73
"Neue Lebansansichten eines Katers" (Wolf) **29**:465
Neue Lebensansichten eines Katers (Wolf) **150**:237, 251, 286, 316, 323-24
"Der neuere (glücklichere) Kohlhaas" (Hein) **154**:165
"Neues Hörspiel" (Jandl) **34**:200
Neuromancer (Gibson) **39**:139-44; **63**:129-39
"Neurotics" (MacNeice) **53**:233
"The Neutral Love Object" (Kumin) **28**:223
"Nevada" (Cernuda) **54**:55
"Nevada" (Updike) **15**:545, 547
"Neve Forschungen über logik" (Heidegger) **24**:276
Never Again (King) **145**:351
Never Again (Nwapa) **133**:186, 188, 201, 222-27, 229-30, 233
"Never Again Would Birds' Song Be the Same" (Frost) **3**:174; **9**:228-29; **15**:250; **26**:114; **34**:471
"Never Any Dying" (Silkin) **6**:498
"Never Before" (Levine) **33**:274-75
Never Call Retreat (Catton) **35**:92-4
Never Come Morning (Algren) **4**:16; **10**:5; **33**:11, 13-14, 16
Never Cry Wolf (Mowat) **26**:335-36, 343, 346
Never Die (Hannah) **90**:140-41
Never Die Alone (Goines) **80**:96
"The Never Ending Wrong" (Porter) **15**:432
Never Enough! (Sargeson) **31**:371
"Never Give a Bum an Even Break" (Welch) **14**:559; **52**:429-30
"Never Had a Dream Come True" (Wonder) **12**:656
"Never Is Too Late" (Armatrading) **17**:8-9
"Never Marry a Mexican" (Cisneros) **69**:153-54; **118**:188-89, 193, 196, 198, 200, 202, 204-06
"Never More Will the Wind" (H. D.) **73**:119
Never Put Off to Gomorrah (Frayn) **31**:189
"Never Stronger" (Fuller) **62**:193
"Never to Dream of Spiders" (Lorde) **71**:262
Never to Forget: The Battle of the Warsaw Ghetto (Fast) **131**:83
Never to Forget: The Jews of the Holocaust (Meltzer) **26**:303-04
"Never Too Close" (Lightfoot) **26**:281
Never Victorious, Never Defeated (Caldwell) **28**:60-1; **39**:302-03
"Never Visit Venice" (Aickman) **57**:6-7
Never You Must Ask Me (Ginzburg) **70**:283
The Neverending Story (Ende) **31**:142-44
"Neverness; or The One Ship Beached on One Far Distant Shore" (Avison) **97**:70-2, 94, 111, 120
"Nevertheless" (Moore) **47**:264
Nevertheless (Moore) **8**:400
Neveryóna (Delany) **38**:159-60; **141**:130, 149, 153-54, 156-57
Nevesta z Texasu (Škvorecký) **152**:324-27, 329, 331-35
Névralgies (Damas) **84**:156, 158-60, 167, 170, 176, 179-80, 185
"New" (Matthews) **40**:322, 324
"The New Acquaintances" (Janowitz) **145**:325
The New Adventures of Ellery Queen (Queen) **3**:422; **11**:461
"The New Aestheticism" (Davie) **8**:163
"New Age" (Reed) **21**:303, 323
The New Age/Le nouveau siècle (Hood) **15**:287; **28**:191, 193, 195-96
The New Air Book (Berger) **12**:40
The New American Arts (Kostelanetz) **28**:213
New and Collected Poems (Paley) **140**:247,273,277
New and Collected Poems (Wilbur) **53**:409-10, 413; **110**:352, 357, 359-61, 372, 377, 380
New and Collected Poems, 1917-1976 (MacLeish) **8**:363; **14**:337
New and Collected Poems, 1950-1980 (Scannell) **49**:330-32
A New and Different Summer (Weber) **12**:633-34
New and Old Selected Writings (Clifton) **66**:78
New and Selected Poems (Davie) **31**:108-09
New and Selected Poems (Fearing) **51**:116-18
New and Selected Poems (Garrigue) **2**:154
New and Selected Poems (McGrath) **28**:276
New and Selected Poems (Meredith) **13**:374
New and Selected Poems (Nemerov) **2**:306; **9**:393
New and Selected Poems (Oliver) **98**:285-88, 290, 293-94, 302
New and Selected Poems (Richards) **14**:454-55
New and Selected Poems (Smith) **6**:512
New and Selected Poems (Wagoner) **3**:508
New and Selected Poems (Wild) **14**:580
New and Selected Poems (Williams) **148**:356
New and Selected Poems: 1923-1985 (Warren) **39**:264-70
New and Selected Poems, 1932-1967 (Viereck) **4**:559
New and Selected Poems, 1940-1986 (Shapiro) **53**:334
New and Selected Poetry (Warren) **59**:298
New and Selected Things Taking Place (Swenson) **14**:520-21; **61**:394-96, 398-99, 401; **106**:321-22, 324, 328-29, 331, 336, 338, 343-45
"New Approach Needed" (Amis) **2**:6
New Arrivals, Old Encounters (Aldiss) **14**:15
A New Athens (Hood) **28**:192-95
The New Atlantis (Le Guin) **45**:214, 216-17
New Axis (Newman) **2**:311
"New Babylons" (Abse) **29**:17
"The New Baseball" (Keillor) **40**:274
New Bats in Old Belfries (Betjeman) **34**:309; **43**:34
New Bearings in English Poetry (Leavis) **24**:292, 294, 298, 300, 306, 308
"New Best Friends" (Adams) **46**:22
"New Birds" (Davis) **49**:83
"A New Birth" (Hoffman) **6**:243; **23**:239
New Bodies for Old (Vance) **35**:419
The New Book of Forms: A Handbook of Poetics (Turco) **63**:431
"New Boots and Contracts" (Clash) See "All the Young Punks"
"The New Boy" (Dubus) **36**:147
The New British Poetry (D'Aguiar) **145**:117
"New Brunswick" (Nowlan) **15**:399
The New Cairo (Mahfouz) See *al-qahira al-jadida*
New Cairo (Mahfūz) See *al- Qāhira al-jadīda*
"The New Cathedral in Galway" (Clarke) **9**:168
The New Centurions (Wambaugh) **3**:509; **18**:532-33
The New City: A Prejudiced View of Toronto (Berton) **104**:47
New Collected Poems (Graves) **39**:325; **45**:168-69, 173-74
The New Confessions (Boyd) **53**:54-8; **70**:132-33, 135
The New Conservatism: Cultural Criticism and the Historians' Debate (Habermas) **104**:77-80
"The New Cosmogony" (Lem) **15**:329; **149**:113, 154
New Country (Spender) **10**:491
The New Criticism (Ransom) **2**:364; **4**:433-34, 436 37; **24**:363, 367
"The New Cultural Politics of Difference" (West) **134**:358, 374
"New Dawn" (Warren) **39**:264-65
"A New Day" (Levine) **118**:274-75, 299-300
"A New Day for Willa Mae" (Sapphire) **99**:80-1
New Days: Poems of Exile and Return (Jordan) **5**:203
A New Decade: Poems, 1958-1967 (Neruda) **5**:301
"A New Diary" (Abse) **7**:2
"The New Divan" (Morgan) **31**:276-77
The New Divan (Morgan) **31**:274, 276
A New Dominion (Jhabvala) **4**:256-59; **8**:311; **29**:256-61; **94**:171-74, 178-79, 181-86, 188, 192-94, 199, 201, 204
"New England" (Wright) **53**:430
"New England, 1868" (Dubie) **36**:130
"New England and Further" (Lowell) **124**:266
"A New England Bachelor" (Eberhart) **56**:91
"A New England Farm, August, 1914" (Murray) **40**:333
New England: Indian Summer (Brooks) **29**:81-2, 84-5, 88-9
"New England Theocritus" (MacCaig) **36**:283
"A New England View: My Report" (Eberhart) **11**:178
The New Equality (Hentoff) **26**:180-81

"The New Evangelical Right" (Amis) **62**:5
"New Every Morning" (Simmons) **43**:414
The New Ewart: Poems, 1980-1982 (Ewart) **46**:151-53
The New Food Book: Nutrition Diet, Consumer Tips, and Foods of theFuture (Berger) **12**:41-2
"New Forest Ponies" (Walker) **13**:566
New Found Land: Fourteen Poems (MacLeish) **8**:361; **14**:337; **68**:272-75, 292
"New Friends" (Rukeyser) **10**:443
"The New Frontier" (Gary) **25**:186
"The New Frontier" (Seidel) **18**:475
"The New Gardener" (Lavin) **99**:322
The New Genetics (Hyde) **21**:176
"The New Girl Friend" (Rendell) **48**:326
The New Girl Friend and Other Stories of Suspense (Rendell) **48**:326
"The New Gods" (Cioran) **64**:89, 94
The New Gods (Cioran)
See *Le mauvais démiurge*
New Green World (Herbst) **34**:452
"New Guinea Legend: The Finding of the Moon" (Wright) **53**:425
New Hampshire (Frost) **3**:170, 174; **9**:220, 228; **10**:195; **15**:240, 243-44, 249; **26**:110, 113, 119, 124; **34**:468, 471
"New Hampshire, February" (Eberhart) **11**:179; **56**:80, 85
"New Heaven and Earth" (Oates) **108**:356
A New Herball: Poems (Willard) **37**:462
A New History of Torments (Ghose) **42**:183-84
"New Home" (Richter) **30**:307
"The New Honesty" (Busch) **47**:63
"The New Hospital" (Raine) **103**:181
"The New House" (Bowen) **118**:75
The New India (Mehta) **37**:293-94
New Jersey: A Bicentennial History (Fleming) **37**:127
"New Jerusalem" (McAuley) **45**:251
"New Journalism" (Wolfe) **51**:417-18
"The New Journalism" (Wolfe) **147**:341, 353
The New Journalism (Wolfe) **147**:313, 340
The New Journalism, with an Anthology (Wolfe) **35**:457, 459, 463
"The New Kid" (Callaghan) **41**:98
"A New King for the Congo: Mobutu and the Nihilism of Africa" (Naipaul) **105**:155, 158
"New Lace Sleeves" (Costello) **21**:76
A New Leaf (May) **16**:431-37
A New Lease of Death (Vine) **50**:264
"The New Leda" (Howes) **15**:290
The New Left Church (Eagleton) **63**:101
"New Liberal Coalition" (Schlesinger) **84**:374
"New Liberty Hall" (Clarke) **9**:168
"A New Life" (Heaney) **5**:172
A New Life (Malamud) **1**:196-98; **2**:265-66, 268-69; **3**:321, 323-24; **9**:343, 346, 348-53; **11**:345-46, 349-53; **18**:321-22; **27**:295-96, 298, 302; **44**:413-14, 417; **85**:191
New Life (Pa Chin) **18**:373
A New Life (Rice) **7**:360; **49**:300, 304
"The New Life and Opinions of a Tomcat" (Wolf)
See "Neue Lebansansichten eines Katers"
"A New Look at the Language Question" (Paulin) **37**:355-57
"New Lots" (Simpson) **32**:378; **149**:308
New Maladies (Kristeva) **140**:201-02
"New Mama" (Young) **17**:574
"The New Man" (Jones) **76**:65
New Maps of Hell (Amis) **129**:18, 23
The New Meaning of Treason (West) **7**:525-26; **9**:562
The New Men (Snow) **1**:316; **4**:501-02; **6**:516; **9**:498; **13**:508-11; **19**:427
"New Mexican Confession" (Moraga) **126**:296
The New Military Humanism (Chomsky) **132**:74
The New Modern Poetry (Rosenthal) **28**:390-91
"The New Mood in Politics" (Schlesinger) **84**:355
"The New Moon Party" (Boyle) **36**:63
"The New Moreton Bay" (Murray) **40**:343
"New Morning" (Dylan) **77**:162
New Morning (Dylan) **3**:131; **4**:150; **6**:158; **12**:190; **77**:162
"The New Moses" (Stern) **100**:340
"New Mother" (Olds) **39**:187, 192; **85**:289
"The New Mothers" (Shields) **113**:441
"New Murders in the Rue Morgue" (Barker) **52**:51
"The New Music" (Barthelme) **13**:59-60
New Music (Price) **63**:325
"New Names" (Scott) **22**:373
The New Net Goes Fishing (Ihimaera) **46**:195, 198, 200
The New Nobility (Broner) **19**:70
"A New Notebook" (Hoffman) **13**:289
"New Novel, New Man," (Robbe-Grillet) **128**:340
"New Objectives, New Cadres" (Rexroth) **112**:397
The New Order (Prichard) **46**:337
"New Orleans Nuptials" (Shange) **74**:311
"The New Owner" (Barthelme) **59**:251
The New Oxford Book of Irish Verse (Kinsella) **138**:122, 124, 126, 128, 130, 143, 145, 158
"A New Pair" (Swenson) **61**:404
"The New Pastoral" (Boland) **40**:99; **113**:71
A New Path to the Waterfall (Carver) **55**:279-80; **126**:164
"A New Place" (McPherson) **77**:359
"The New Poem" (Wright) **146**:344
"New Poems" (Simpson) **7**:429
"New Poems" (Wright) **28**:471
New Poems (Fuller) **4**:178; **28**:151, 153, 157, 159
New Poems (Hope) **3**:251
New Poems (Montale) **7**:231; **9**:386-88
New Poems (Rexroth) **112**:386, 393
New Poems (Roethke)
See *Shorter Poems, 1951-53*
New Poems (Slavitt) **14**:490
New Poems (Transtroemer) **65**:223
New Poems, 1973 (Kinsella) **4**:271; **19**:252; **138**:105-06, 132, 166
"The New Poetries" (Kostelanetz) **28**:219
The New Poetry (Alvarez) **5**:16-18
"The New Poetry Handbook" (Strand) **71**:286, 290
The New Poets (Rosenthal) **28**:390-91
"A New Proletarian Art" (Seifert) **34**:263; **93**:340
New Provinces (Scott) **22**:371
The New Radicalism in America (Lasch) **102**:293, 297, 316-24
"The New Realism" (Ashbery) **2**:19
The New Realism (Spender) **10**:492
"A New Refutation of Time" (Borges)
See "Nueva refutación del tiempo"
"The New Ring" (Shapiro) **53**:332
"New Role for India's Holy Men" (Narayan) **121**:356
A New Romance (McFadden) **48**:248, 251-53, 255, 257
"New Rose Hotel" (Gibson) **39**:144; **63**:129-31, 134, 139
"The New Saddhus" (Pinsky) **38**:356; **121**:446
"A New School of Philosophy" (Rozewicz)
See "nowa szkoła filozoficzna"
"The New Sculpture" (Pound) **112**:315
"New Season" (Levine) **9**:332; **14**:316, 318-19; **118**:277, 300
"The New Season" (Merwin) **45**:276
"New Secondhand Clothes" (Raine) **103**:204
New Seeds of Contemplation (Merton) **83**:403
New Selected Poems (Hughes) **37**:177-78, 181; **119**:288, 295
New Selected Poems (Levine) **118**:296-300, 303, 305
New Selected Poems (Moss) **45**:290-91; **50**:352-53
New Selected Poems (Rothenberg) **57**:380, 382-83
New Shoes (Streatfeild)
See *New Town*
"A New Siege" (Montague) **13**:390; **46**:270-71, 275-76
"A New Song" (Heaney) **7**:148; **14**:242-43; **25**:249; **37**:162; **74**:157
"New Song" (Townshend) **17**:538
A New Song (Hughes) **10**:279; **108**:295, 297
New Songs (Arghezi)
See *Cîntece noi*
"The New Spirit" (Ashbery) **77**:49, 59; **125**:25
The New Spirit (Ashbery) **2**:19; **25**:50
"New Stanzas to Augusta" (Brodsky)
See "Novye stansy k Avguste"
"New Styles in Leftism" (Howe) **85**:156
"New Tables" (MacCaig) **36**:285
The New Tenant (Ionesco)
See *Le nouveau locataire*
"The New Tendency of the Avant-Garde Writers" (Kawabata) **9**:311
"New Territory" (Boland) **113**:96, 109
New Territory (Boland) **40**:100; **67**:46; **113**:69, 72, 74, 76, 81, 93, 96, 108-10, 114, 121-22
The New Testament (Asimov)
See *Asimov's Guide to the Bible, Volume II: The New Testament*
The New Theologian (Mehta) **37**:290
A New Time for Mexico (Fuentes) **113**:270-73
"The New Tourist" (Sarton) **49**:312
New Town (Streatfeild) **21**:402, 406
"The New Tradition" (Sukenick) **48**:369
"The New U" (Klappert) **57**:268
"New Views on Life by a Cat" (Wolf)
See "Neue Lebansansichten eines Katers"
New Wanderings and Misfortunes of Lazarillo de Tormes (Cela)
See *Nuevas andanzas y desventuras de Lazarillo de Tormes*
The New Water Book (Berger) **12**:40
New Weather (Muldoon) **32**:315-17, 319-21; **72**:264-65, 276, 279
New Wind in a Dry Land (Laurence)
See *The Prophet's Camel Bell*
"A New Window Display" (Mohr) **12**:446
The New Wolves (Bass) **143**:22
"The New Woman" (Guillén)
See "Mujer nueva"
"The New Woman" (Randall) **135**:399
"New World" (Momaday) **85**:268
"New World" (Walcott) **76**:285
The New World (Banks) **37**:24; **72**:4, 12, 14
The New World (Bogosian) **141**:89
The New World (Bronk) **10**:73, 76
The New World (Turner) **48**:399-402
New World Avenue and Vincinity (Konwicki)
See *Nowy swiat i okolice*
New World Writing (Roethke) **8**:456
New Writing (Lodge) **141**:
"New Year" (Clark Bekedermo) **38**:126
"A New Year Greeting" (Auden) **43**:27
"New Year Letter" (Auden) **123**:20-9, 32-5, 37, 39-40
New Year Letter (Auden) **1**:9-10; **2**:23; **3**:24; **4**:33, **14**:29; 35; **9**:55; **11**:19; **43**:16, 26-7; **123**:4, 6, 9-12, 20, 52-3
"New Year on Dartmoor" (Plath) **111**:202
"New Year Poem" (Larkin) **64**:282, 285
"New Year Verses" (Parshchikov) **59**:383
"New Year's at Lawrence's Grave" (Monette) **82**:332
"New Year's Day at Lepe" (Hooker) **43**:199
"New Year's Day at the End of a Decade" (Squires) **51**:379, 381-82
"New Year's Eve" (Ciardi) **40**:157
"New Year's Eve" (Eberhart) **56**:76
"New Year's Eve" (Prokosch) **48**:306-07
"New Year's Eve" (Schwartz) **4**:479; **45**:354; **87**:334
"New Year's Eve, 1979" (Wright) **146**:342

"A New Year's Garland for My Students" (Levertov) **3**:292
"New Year's Poem" (Avison) **97**:69, 74-5
"New Year's Resolution" (Appleman) **51**:15
"New Year's Song" (Seifert) **93**:334
"New York" (Gunn) **32**:213
"New York" (Hollander) **5**:187
"New York" (Moore) **8**:398; **19**:340
"New York" (Senghor) **54**:407; **130**:234, 281, 286
New York (Morand) **41**:301, 304, 306
New York: A Serendipiter's Journey (Talese) **37**:390-91
"New York Airport at Night" (Voznesensky) **57**:414, 419
"New York City" (Lennon) **35**:264
"New York City Serenade" (Springsteen) **17**:482-83
"New York Day Women" (Danticat) **94**:96-8
The New York Head Shop and Museum (Lorde) **71**:240, 248-49, 251
"The New York Intellectuals" (Howe) **85**:121-22, 149, 151, 153-54
New York Jew (Kazin) **34**:561; **38**:280-83; **119**:303, 305, 308, 311, 314, 318, 320, 331, 334
"New York Lady" (Parker)
See "From the Diary of a New York Lady"
New York, New York (Scorsese) **20**:330-32, 336, 339; **89**:231-32, 235-36, 241, 243, 245-46, 260, 263, 265, 267-68
"New York Power Crisis" (Matthias) **9**:361
"New York State of Mind" (Joel) **26**:219-20
New York Stories (Scorsese) **89**:265
"New York Taxis" (Yevtushenko) **126**:415
New York Tendaberry (Nyro) **17**:312-15, 317
"New York to Detroit" (Parker) **68**:325, 334, 339
The New York Trilogy (Auster) **47**:13-16; **131**:4-7, 9-10, 12-5, 17-8, 23-8, 30, 33-6, 39, 42, 45
"New York Variations" (Carroll) **143**:33
"The New York Woman" (Sissman) **9**:491
"The New Yorkers" (Giovanni) **117**:198
The New Yorkers (Calisher) **2**:96; **4**:87; **38**:74; **134**:7, 12, 15-19, 32, 34-6
The New Youth (Pasolini)
See *La nuova gioventù*
New Zealand (Marsh) **53**:255
"Newark, before Black Men Conquered" (Baraka) **14**:48
"Newborn Thrown in Trash and Dies" (Wideman) **122**:344
"Newcastle Is Peru" (Harrison) **43**:175; **129**:165, 220
Newcastle is Peru (Harrison) **129**:179, 219
"Newcomer" (Okigbo) **25**:347, 351; **84**:300, 306, 308-10, 314
"The Newest Bath Guide" (Betjeman) **43**:47
New-Found-Land (Stoppard) **8**:503-04
"Newhouse" (Major) **19**:297
Newly Born Woman (Cixous) **65**:328; **92**:51, 55, 64, 69-70, 72-3, 78-80, 83
The Newly Fallen (Dorn) **18**:128
"Newness" (Paulin) **37**:352
"Newport Jazz Festival" (Jordan) **114**:145
"The News" (Busch) **47**:63
"The News" (Cliff) **21**:63
News (Delbanco) **6**:130
"News Flash" (Cendrars) **106**:197
"News for the Mineshaft" (Price) **3**:406
"News from Avignon" (Weiss) **8**:546
News from Cold Point (Bowles) **2**:79
"The News from Ireland" (Trevor) **71**:329-33, 340, 346; **116**:367, 372, 382, 396
The News from Ireland, and Other Stories (Trevor) **71**:329, 332; **116**:367
News from Lake Wobegon (Keillor) **115**:296
"News from the Cabin" (Oliver) **98**:289
"News from the Cabin" (Swenson) **61**:399; **106**:325
News from the City of the Sun (Colegate) **36**:111
"News from the Glacier" (Haines) **58**:219
News from the Glacier: Selected Poems, 1960-1980 (Haines) **58**:220-22
"News from the Old Country" (Rakosi) **47**:343
"News from the Sun" (Ballard) **137**:14, 59-61
"News of the Death of the World's Biggest Man" (Macdonald) **13**:356
"News of the Human Universe" (Tillinghast) **29**:415
"News of the Phoenix" (Smith) **15**:516
News of the Phoenix (Smith) **15**:512-13
News of the Universe (Bly) **38**:51, 53-5; **128**:43
News of the World (Barker) **48**:17, 21, 23
The News of the World (Carlson) **54**:37-9
"News Photo" (Warren) **8**:537
"News Report at Ameliasburg" (Purdy) **50**:242
"News Wires of April 15, 1912" (Enzensberger) **43**:152
"New-Sense" (Baraka) **33**:56
"The Newspaper" (Gustafson) **36**:222
The Newspaper of Claremont Street (Jolley) **46**:213, 217
"Newspapers" (Lopate) **29**:302
"Newsreel" (Daryush) **19**:121
"Newsreel" (Day Lewis) **6**:127; **10**:133
"Newsreel: Man and Firing Squad" (Atwood) **25**:68
The Newton Letter (Banville) **46**:29-30, 32; **118**:7, 10-11, 15-16, 19, 20-23, 25, 27-28, 38, 47
Newton's Letter (Banville)
See *The Newton Letter*
"A New-Wave Format" (Mason) **28**:272-73; **82**:235; **154**:230, 253, 794, 304-05, 323
"Next" (Sondheim) **30**:388, 391; **147**:234, 258
Next (McNally) **4**:347; **7**:217; **41**:292
"Next Day" (Jarrell) **13**:302
"Next Door" (Harrison) **129**:198
"Next Door" (Wolff) **64**:446, 448
"The Next Glade" (Aickman) **57**:3, 7
"The Next Logical Step" (Bova) **45**:69
"Next My Spade's Going" (Graham) **29**:193
Next: New Poems (Clifton) **66**:81-5
Next of Kin (Egoyan) **151**:124, 127, 131-36, 138-41, 144-47, 150, 152, 154, 161, 166, 173
Next of Kin (Hopkins) **4**:234
"Next, Please" (Larkin) **5**:223; **8**:332; **13**:336; **18**:294-301; **33**:256
The Next Room of the Dream (Nemerov) **36**:302
"Next to Last Things" (Kunitz) **6**:288
Next to Nature, Art (Lively) **32**:275-76
"Next to the Cafe Chaos" (Broumas) **73**:15
"The Next to the Last Poem about God" (Williams) **148**:343
"Next to You" (Police, The) **26**:363
"Next Turn" (Slessor) **14**:492
"Next Year" (Carver) **36**:107
Next-to-Last Things: New Poems and Essays (Kunitz) **148**:106-08, 110-11, 120, 122-26, 136, 142, 147-49, 106-08
Nexus (Miller) **84**:251
Le nez qui voque (Ducharme) **74**:57, 59-61, 68
Ngaahika Ndeenda (Ngũgĩ wa Thiong'o) **36**:319, 322
"Ngiculela/Es una historia/I Am Singing" (Wonder) **12**:661
"Ngoma" (Dumas) **6**:146
N'Goola and Other Stories (Prichard) **46**:343, 345
"Niagara" (Jandl) **34**:195
"Niagara Daredevil, 37, Buried near the Falls" (MacEwen) **55**:168
"Niagara Falls" (Barth) **9**:67
Niaye (Ousmane) **66**:335
Die Nibelungen (Lang) **20**:200-01, 203; **103**:110, 121, 123-24
The Nibelungenlied (Almedingen) **12**:1
Nic albo nic (Konwicki) **8**:327; **117**:258, 277, 284-87
"Nic w plaszczu Prospera" (Rozewicz) **23**:359-60; **139**:291
"Nicaraguan canto" (Cardenal)
See "Canto nacional"
The Nice and the Good (Murdoch) **2**:297-98; **3**:347; **6**:344, 348; **11**:385
"A nice day" (Bukowski) **108**:112
"Nice Day at School" (Trevor) **71**:336
Nice Feeling Tonight (Ayckbourn) **33**:44
A Nice Pair (Pink Floyd) **35**:307
A Nice Place to Visit (Garner) **13**:235
"Nice to Be Nice" (Kelman) **58**:295
"A Nice Way to Go" (King) **8**:322
"Nice Weather, Aren't We?" (Grayson) **38**:211
Nice Work (Lodge) **141**:334-35, 341-47, 349, 352, 356, 367, 369, 371, 375
Nichijōseikatsu no boken (Oe) **86**:230, 241
The Nicholas Factor (Myers) **35**:299
Nicholson at Large (Just) **27**:227-28
"Nicht nur zur Weihnachtzeit" (Boell) **15**:70; **27**:56-7; **72**:72, 90-4
Nichts in den Windbruch getragen (Celan) **10**:101
The Nick Adams Stories (Hemingway) **3**:239, 241-42; **10**:269-70; **30**:193-94, 197-98
"Nick and the Candlestick" (Plath) **9**:426, 428; **111**:181-82, 199
"A Nickel Bet" (Knight) **40**:279
Nickel Mountain: A Pastoral Novel (Gardner) **3**:187-88; **5**:131-35; **7**:112, 114-15; **8**:237-38; **10**:218; **18**:177-78; **28**:167; **34**:550
"Ha nidah" (Agnon) **14**:3
The Niebelungs (Lang)
See *Die Nibelungen*
Die Niemandsrose (Celan) **10**:101; **19**:88, 90, 93; **53**:70, 72-7, 82; **82**:33, 37, 45
Niente e cosi (Fallaci) **110**:192, 197, 203, 210, 214-15
Niepokój (Rozewicz) **23**:358, 362-63; **139**:227, 260, 262, 299
"Nietzsche, Genealogy, History" (Foucault) **69**:194
Niezwyciezony (Lem) **8**:343-44; **15**:328; **40**:296; **149**:118, 156, 159, 161-62, 167-68, 173-74, 208-13, 216, 219, 243, 251, 260, 262-64, 283-84
Nigel Mole's Diary (Townsend) **61**:411
"Nigerian Unity/or Little Niggers Killing Little Niggers" (Madhubuti) **73**:199, 210-11
"A Nigger" (Himes) **108**:235
"Nigger" (Sanchez) **116**:276-77, 293
"Nigger" (Shapiro) **15**:475; **53**:330
"Nigger Can You Kill?" (Giovanni) **117**:177
Nigger Heaven (Van Vechten) **33**:390-400
"Nigger Song: An Odyssey" (Dove) **81**:134
The Niggerlovers (Tabori) **19**:437
"Nigger's Leap: New England" (Wright) **53**:418, 427, 432
"Night" (Akhmadulina)
See "Noch'"
"Night" (Bly) **5**:63; **10**:57
"Night" (Bogan) **4**:68; **39**:393; **93**:69, 78, 81-3
"The Night" (Bradbury) **42**:36-7
"Night" (Campbell) **32**:74-5
"Night" (Celan) **82**:37
"Night" (Giovanni) **117**:197
"Night" (Jeffers) **54**:236, 244
"The Night" (Kunene) **85**:165
"Night" (O'Brien) **116**:195
"Night" (Snyder) **120**:328
"Night" (Springsteen) **17**:489
Night (O'Brien) **3**:365; **5**:312-13; **36**:337; **116**:180, 184-85, 192, 194, 211, 227
Night (Pinter) **6**:417; **15**:423-24; **27**:394-95; **58**:373
Night (Wiesel)
See *La nuit*
"The Night / 1" (Galeano) **72**:139
"Night after Bushfire" (Wright) **53**:419
"A Night among the Horses" (Barnes) **3**:37; **29**:27
A Night among the Horses, and Other Stories (Barnes) **3**:36; **29**:26-7; **127**:161

Night and Day (Stoppard) **15**:521, 524; **29**:397, 401; **91**:187
Night and Fog (Resnais)
See *Nuit et brouilland*
Night and Hope (Lustig) **56**:182, 184
"Night and Morning" (Clarke) **9**:168
Night and Morning (Clarke) **6**:112; **9**:167-68
"The Night Apple" (Ginsberg) **36**:197
"Night Arrival at Seatrout" (Hughes) **37**:180
A Night at Green River (Hilliard) **15**:279
A Night at the Movies, or You Must Remember This (Coover) **46**:121-23
"A Night at the Opera" (Tomlinson) **13**:550
Night at the Vulcan (Marsh)
See *Opening Night*
Night Bathers (Walker) **13**:565
The Night before Christmas (Perelman) **49**:258
"The Night before Great Babylon" (Sitwell) **67**:318, 325
"The Night before Morning" (Bowering) **47**:19
"The Night before the Night before Christmas" (Jarrell) **2**:210
"Night Blooming Flowers" (Pollitt) **28**:367
"Night Call, Collect" (Bradbury) **42**:34
Night Chills (Koontz) **78**:203, 212, 216-17
"The Night City" (Graham) **29**:198
"The Night Club in the Woods" (Calisher) **38**:69
The Night Comers (Ambler)
See *A State of Siege*
Night Comes Softly: An Anthology of Black Female Voices (Giovanni) **117**:190
"Night Conference, Wood Quay: 6 Junte 1979" (Kinsella) **138**:155
The Night Country (Eiseley) **7**:91
Night Cries (Benedikt) **14**:81-2
Night Crossing (Mahon) **27**:286-87, 289-90
"Night Crow" (Roethke) **19**:397; **101**:263, 324
"The Night Dances" (Plath) **5**:345; **9**:427-28; **111**:167, 204
Night Desk (Ryga) **14**:472-73
"The Night Dream" (MacLeish) **68**:290
Night Dreams (Hoeg)
See *Fortællinger om Natten*
"The Night Driver" (Calvino) **73**:31-2
"Night Duty" (Transtroemer) **52**:415-16; **65**:220, 236
"The Night Express" (Moss) **45**:286, 289
"The Night Face Up" (Cortázar)
See "La noche boca arriba"
"Night Falls on Shiva's Hills" (Anand) **93**:57
"Night Feed" (Boland) **67**:42, 46; **113**:79, 92, 98, 124
Night Feed (Boland) **67**:41-4, 46; **40**:99-101; **113**:57, 72, 74, 79, 81, 87, 94, 97-99, 101, 108-09, 123-24
"Night Flight" (Bachmann)
See "Nachtflug"
"Night Flight" (Page and Plant) **12**:477
"Night Flight" (Updike) **23**:476
"Night Flight to Attiwapiskat" (Jiles) **58**:273
Night Flight to Hanoi (Berrigan) **4**:56
Night Flights (Cohen) **19**:112-13
"Night for Voyeurs" (Dybek) **114**:62
"The Night Game" (Pinsky) **94**:306-308; **121**:446
Night Has a Thousand Eyes (Woolrich) **77**:389-91, 393-97, 400, 402, 404-05
"The Night He Cried" (Leiber) **25**:304
"The Night He Was Left Alone" (Rulfo)
See "La noche que lo dejaron solo"
"Night Heron" (Snyder) **120**:349
"A Night in June" (Williams) **42**:458
The Night in Lisbon (Remarque) **21**:332-33
"Night in Martindale" (Raine) **45**:340
A Night in May (Yehoshua) **13**:616; **31**:470, 472
The Night in Motion (Michaux)
See *La nuit remue*
"Night in the City" (Mitchell) **12**:440
"Night in the Forest" (Kinnell) **29**:284
"A Night in the Garden" (Dickinson) **49**:102-03
"Night in the Province" (Krleža)
See *Noc u provinci*
Night in Tunisia (Jordan) **110**:275, 278
The Night Is Dark and I Am Far from Home (Kozol) **17**:252-54
The Night Is Here (Johnson)
See *Natten är här*
The Night Is Long: The Autobiography of a Person Who Can't Sleep (Millin) **49**:254
"Night Journal" (Wright) **146**:338, 351
"Night Journal II" (Wright) **146**:338
"Night Journey in the Cooking Pot" (Bly) **10**:60-1
"Night Letter" (Kunitz) **6**:286; **148**:69, 73, 87-88, 101, 148
"Night Letter" (Wright) **6**:580
"Night Letters" (Jordan) **114**:143
"The Night Lies" (Ciardi) **40**:157
"The Night Life" (Ignatow) **7**:177
Night Life (Kingsley) **44**:237-38
"Night Light" (Willard) **37**:463
Night Light (Justice) **19**:232-33; **102**:263-64, 270, 277, 283
"The Night Manny Mota Tied the Record" (Kinsella) **43**:255
Night Marc (Anthony) **35**:38-9
Night March (Lancaster) **36**:245
"Night Meeting" (Bradbury) **42**:38
The Night Mirror (Hollander) **2**:197; **5**:186-87; **8**:299; **14**:264
Night Monsters (Leiber) **25**:303
'night, Mother (Norman) **28**:319-21
"Night Movement" (Sandburg) **35**:341
"Night Moves" (Seger) **35**:383-86
Night Moves (Seger) **35**:381-86
"Night Muse & Mortar Round" (Komunyakaa) **94**:229
Night Music (Odets) **28**:328 29, 332-33, 341; **98**:198-200, 210, 229, 235, 237, 241, 244
"Night Must Fall" (Landolfi) **11**:321; **49**:212
Night Must Fall (Williams) **15**:577
"Night Notes" (Booth) **23**:78
The Night of a Thousand Nights (Mahfouz)
See *Layali alf layla*
Night of Camp David (Knebel) **14**:308
"Night of Endless Radiance" (McFadden) **48**:257-58
"The Night of Frost" (Harper) **7**:138
Night of January 16 (Rand) **44**:451; **79**:369-70, 373 77
Night of Light (Farmer) **19**:168
The Night of Long Knives (Gallo) **95**:87-90, 92-4
Night of Masks (Norton) **12**:468
The Night of One Hundred Heads (Sender)
See *La noche de las cien cabezas*
"Night of Sine" (Senghor)
See "Nuit de Sine"
"Night of Six Days" (Morand)
See "La nuit de seis jours"
"The Night of St. Bartholomew" (Akhmadulina) **53**:11
The Night of Stones (MacBeth) **2**:251
Night of the Aurochs (Trumbo) **19**:447-48
"Night of the Cabala and Passion" (Dourado)
See "Noite de cala e paixão"
"Night of the Chickens, North of Joplin" (Smith) **42**:346
"The Night of the Curlews" (García Márquez)
See "La noche de los alcaravanes"
"The Night of the Gifts" (Borges) **48**:47
"The Night of the Iguana" (Williams) **15**:579; **45**:446-47, 453, 455; **111**:380, 382-83, 388, 391-92
The Night of the Iguana (Huston) **20**:169
The Night of the Iguana (Williams) **1**:368; **2**:465; **5**:499-501; **7**:543; **8**:548-49; **11**:571, 573; **15**:580; **19**:472; **30**:466; **39**:444-46, 448, 451, 453; **45**:445-46, 449-50, 453-55; **71**:368-69, 371, 387
The Night of the Man on Stilts (Haviaras) **33**:202
"Night of the Meek" (Serling) **30**:358
Night of the Poor (Prokosch) **48**:307, 312
"Night of the Scorpion" (Ezekiel) **61**:102, 105-06
"Night of the Weeping Children" (Sachs) **98**:335
A Night of Their Own (Abrahams) **4**:1
Night on Bald Mountain (White) **7**:532
"Night on the Convoy" (Sassoon) **130**:186-87
"A Night Out" (Abse) **7**:1; **29**:18-19
A Night Out (Pinter) **11**:438-39; **15**:423; **27**:385-86, 394; **58**:372-74, 383
"Night Out, 1925" (Rhys) **14**:446; **124**:337
"A Night Outing" (Carroll) **143**:33
Night over Day over Night (Watkins) **55**:92-5
"The Night Parade" (Hirsch) **50**:196-97
"Night Passage" (Leiber) **25**:307
"Night Piece" (Belitt) **22**:49
"Night Pieces" (Strand) **18**:517, 520-21; **41**:432
"Night Pieces, II" (Strand) **18**:518
Night Play (Hildesheimer)
See *Nachtstück*
"The Night Raider" (Edmonds) **35**:155
"Night Rain" (Clark Bekedermo) **38**:117, 120-21, 125-29
"Night Rally" (Costello) **21**:68-9
"The Night Rhonda Ferguson Was Killed" (Jones) **76**:64
"Night Ride" (Saro-Wiwa) **114**:253
Night Rider (Warren) **1**:352-54; **4**:577-80, 582; **10**:518-19; **13**:570-71; **53**:359, 366, 376; **59**:298
Night Scene, the Garden (Alexander) **121**:12
"Night Scenes" (Duncan) **41**:128
"Night School" (Carver) **36**:106; **126**:166
Night School (Pinter) **11**:441; **27**:394; **58**:372, 383
Night Seasons (Foote) **91**:99
The Night Shapes (Blish) **14**:86
"Night Shift" (Marley) **17**:269
The Night Shift (Baxter) **14**:61
Night Shift (King) **12**:310; **26**:237; **37**:202, 207; **113**:335
"Night Song" (Clark Bekedermo) **38**:129
"Night Song" (Glück) **44**:217, 220
"Night Song for a Woman" (Purdy) **50**:238, 241
"Night Songs" (Kinsella) **138**:106, 132, 149, 161
"Night Sport" (Hoffman) **141**:282-83, 287-88, 310, 315
Night Studies (Colter) **58**:142-45
"Night Stuff" (Sandburg) **35**:341
"Night Sung Sailor's Prayer" (Kaufman) **49**:205
"Night Sweat" (Lowell) **11**:328; **15**:347; **124**:255
The Night Swimmers (Byars) **35**:73
"Night Taxi" (Gunn) **32**:212
"The Night the Bed Fell" (Thurber) **25**:440; **125**:414
"The Night the Ghost Got In" (Thurber) **11**:534; **125**:414
"The Night the Playoffs Were Rained Out" (Jacobsen) **102**:241
"The Night They Left Him Alone" (Rulfo)
See "La noche que lo dejaron solo"
"The Night They Murdered Boyle Somerville" (Durcan) **43**:114
"The Night They Put John Lennon Down" (Durcan) **43**:117
Night Thoughts (Gascoyne) **45**:148-53, 155, 157
"Night Thoughts in Greenwich Village" (O'Hara) **13**:426
"Night Thoughts of a Media Watcher" (Steinem) **63**:381
"Night Time" (Creeley) **78**:141
"Night Train" (Reaney) **13**:473
The Night Traveler (Oliver) **19**:362; **98**:259
Night unto Night (Wylie) **43**:463-64, 470
Night Vision (Transtroemer)
See *Mörkerseende*
"The Night Visitor" (Traven) **11**:536

"Night Visits with the Family" (Swenson) **106**:344
Night Voices: Strange Stories (Aickman) **57**:3-4
Night Walk (Daly) **52**:90
"The Night Was Young" (Wilson) **12**:651-52
"Night Watch" (Rich) **125**:336
"The Night Watchman" (Jacobsen) **48**:193; **102**:240
"The Night We Rode with Sarsfield" (Kiely) **23**:266; **43**:245
A Night with Cindy (Hugo) **18**:261
Night without End (MacLean) **13**:361-63; **50**:348-49; **63**:263
Night without Stars (Graham) **23**:192
"Night Women" (Danticat) **94**:94
"Night Words" (Steiner) **24**:429
"The Night Workers of Ragnarök" (Gunnars) **69**:263
The Night Workers of Ragnarök (Gunnars) **69**:262-63
Nightbirds on Nantucket (Aiken) **35**:20
The Night-Blooming Cereus (Hayden) **37**:151, 154, 160
Night-Blooming Cereus (Reaney) **13**:473, 475
Nightbook (Kotzwinkle) **5**:220; **35**:257
"Nightbreak" (Rich) **125**:318, 320
Nightclub Cantata (Swados) **12**:556-58, 560-61
"Nightfall" (Asimov) **19**:28; **26**:50; **76**:313-14; **92**:22
"Nightfall" (Mahapatra) **33**:283
"Nightfall" (Urdang) **47**:398
Nightfall (Silverberg) **140**:389
"The Nightfishing" (Graham) **29**:197, 199
The Nightfishing (Graham) **29**:195-98
"Nightgame" (Cherryh) **35**:107
"The Nightgown" (Dacey) **51**:83
"Nightgown" (Davies) **23**:145, 148
"Nightgown" (Merrill) **13**:380
"Nighthawks" (Dybek) **114**:68, 70-1, 81-2
"The Nightingale and the Frog" (Seth) **90**:354
The Nightingale of the Catholic Church (Pasolini)
See *L'usignuolo della Chiesa Cattolica*
The Nightingale Sings Badly (Seifert)
See *Slavík zpívášpatně*
The Nightingale Sings out of Tune (Seifert)
See *Slavík zpívášpatně*
The Nightingale Sings Poorly (Seifert)
See *Slavík zpívášpatně*
"Nightlight" (Kureishi) **135**:283
Nightlines (McGahern) **48**:262-63, 267-69, 271
"Nightmare" (Longley) **29**:293
The Nightmare (Forester) **35**:174
"Nightmare and Flight" (Arendt) **98**:51
Nightmare Begins Responsibility (Harper) **7**:138-39
"Nightmare Boogie" (Hughes) **108**:299, 301, 303-04
The Nightmare Factory (Kumin) **28**:221, 224-25
"Nightmare Island" (Sturgeon) **39**:361
"Nightmares" (Borges) **48**:47, 49
"Nightmusic" (Oates) **6**:370
"Night-Music" (Rukeyser) **27**:404, 410
"Night-Piece" (Sassoon) **130**:176
"A Night-Piece to Mrs. Treed" (Johnston) **51**:243
"Nightride" (Clarke) **61**:73
"The Night-Ride" (Slessor) **14**:492
"Nights and Days" (Salinas) **90**:323, 326, 328
Nights and Days (Dabrowska)
See *Noce i dnie*
Nights and Days (Merrill) **2**:273-75; **13**:376, 380; **91**:228, 230-31
Nights as Day, Days as Night (Leiris)
See *Nuits sans nuit et quelques jours sans jour*
Nights at Serampore (Eliade) **19**:146-47
Nights at the Alexandra (Trevor) **71**:348,350; **116**:367, 383
Nights at the Circus (Carter) **41**:119-21; **76**:329
"Nights before Battle" (Blunden) **56**:30
Nights below Station Street (Richards) **59**:186-92
Night's Black Agents (Leiber) **25**:307
"Night's Fall Unlocks the Dirge of the Sea" (Graham) **29**:194
"The Night's for Cryin'" (Himes) **58**:265
Nights in Aruba (Holleran) **38**:246-47
"Nights in Hackett's Cove" (Strand) **41**:432, 434
Nights in the Gardens of Brooklyn (Swados) **5**:420, 422
"Nights in the Gardens of Clare" (Durcan) **70**:149, 152
"Nights in the Gardens of Spain" (Berriault) **109**:97
Nights in the Underground: An Exploration of Love (Blais)
See *Les nuits de l'underground*
Night's Lies (Bufalino)
See *Le menzogne della notte*
Night's Lies (Bufalino)
See *Le menzogne della notte*
Night's Master (Lee) **46**:231, 234
"Night's Negation" (Read) **4**:439
"Night's Nothings Again" (Sandburg) **35**:341
"Nights of 1964-1966: The Old Reliable" (Hacker) **72**:191
The Nights of Cabiria (Fellini)
See *Le notti di Cabiria*
"The Nights of Goliadkin" (Bioy Casares)
See "Las noches de Goliadkin"
"The Nights of Goliadkin" (Borges) **48**:42
The Night's Orbit (FitzGerald) **19**:175
"Night-Sea Journey" (Barth) **2**:39; **9**:66; **14**:51; **27**:26; **51**:20, 23, 26; **89**:4, 6-10, 15-23, 27-8, 30, 32-3, 36, 39-45, 47-9, 52, 55, 59, 61, 64
"Nightshade" (Voigt) **54**:434
Night-Side (Oates) **9**:406; **11**:404; **52**:339; **134**:248
Nightsong (Williams) **5**:497
"Nightsong: City" (Brutus) **43**:91, 95-6
"Nightsong: Country" (Brutus) **43**:90
"A Nightsong for the Shining Cuckoo" (Hulme) **130**:52
Nightspawn (Banville) **46**:25-27; **118**:2-5, 11, 27-28
"The Night-Tender" (Govier) **51**:166-67
"Night-Time in the Cemetery" (Smith) **25**:419
Nighttime Talk with a Despised Man (Duerrenmatt) **102**:53
"Nightwalker" (Kinsella) **4**:271; **19**:251, 255; **138**:86, 89, 95, 99-100, 117, 133-34, 145, 149, 152, 159, 161-62, 166
Nightwalker and Other Poems (Kinsella) **4**:271; **19**:251, 253; **138**:89, 91, 94, 97-99, 105, 112, 119-20, 129, 131, 133, 136, 143, 146-48, 151, 158-59
Nightwatch (Sachs) **98**:322
Nightwatch (Soderbergh) **154**:356
Nightwatchmen (Hannah) **23**:208-09; **38**:232; 128, 152, 155, 156-59
Nightwebs (Woolrich) **77**:400
"Nightwind" (Banville) **46**:25; **118**:12
"Nightwind" (Swenson) **106**:318
Nightwing (Smith) **25**:412
"Nightwings" (Silverberg) **140**:378
Nightwings (Silverberg) **140**:343, 345, 358, 378
Nightwood (Barnes) **3**:36-8; **4**:43-4; **8**:47-8; **11**:29-31; **29**:23-32; **127**:160-64, 166-84, 186, 189, 194, 197-99, 203, 205-12
Nightwork (Hansen) **38**:240
Nightwork (Shaw) **7**:414
Night-World (Bloch) **33**:83-4
Der Nihilist (Duerrenmatt) **1**:81; **4**:140; **8**:195; **11**:170; **15**:195; **43**:120, 128
"The Nihilist as Hero" (Lowell) **8**:355
Niin katosi voitto maailmasta (Haavikko) **34**:170
"Nike Who Hesitates" (Herbert) **43**:184
"Nikki-Rosa" (Giovanni) **19**:191; **64**:191; **117**:167, 194, 201
Nilda (Mohr) **12**:445-46, 448
"The Nile" (Christie) **110**:127
"Nimram" (Gardner) **28**:161-63
"Nina" (Bates) **46**:49
"La niña que murió de amor" (Ulibarrí) **83**:416
"Nine" (Creeley) **78**:139
"IX" (Dunn) **40**:170
Nine (Kopit) **33**:251-52
"Nine Bean-Rows on the Moon" (Purdy) **14**:433
"Nine Beatitudes to Denver" (Barker) **48**:18
"Nine Below" (Harjo) **83**:272
Nine Coaches Waiting (Stewart) **7**:467; **35**:389, 392
Nine Days to Mukalla (Prokosch) **4**:421; **48**:312, 314-15
The Nine Guardians (Castellanos)
See *Balún-Canán*
"Nine Lives" (Le Guin) **8**:343
"Nine Lives" (Merrill) **91**:238
Nine Men Who Laughed (Clarke) **53**:96-7
The Nine Mile Walk (Kemelman) **2**:225
Nine Months in the Life of an Old Maid (Rossner) **9**:456
"Nine Months Making" (Mueller) **51**:280
"Nine Nectarines and Other Porcelain" (Moore) **2**:291; **13**:394, 397; **19**:340
The Nine O'Clock Mail (Sackler) **14**:479
The Nine Planets (Branley) **21**:16, 19, 23
Nine Poems (Goyen) **40**:218
"Nine Points of the Law" (Porter) **33**:318
"Nine Shaman Songs Resung" (Ferlinghetti) **6**:184
Nine Stories (Grau) **146**:159
Nine Stories (Salinger) **1**:298; **8**:463; **12**:519; **138**:182-83, 202, 215-17
Nine Tonight (Seger) **35**:385-86
Nine Women (Grau) **146**:131-32, 137-39, 142, 151, 153, 159-61, 163
Nine-Headed Dragon River: Zen Journals, 1969-1982 (Matthiessen) **64**:316-21, 326
The Ninemile Wolves (Bass) **79**:20; **143**:
"MCMXIV" (Larkin) **8**:340; **33**:261; **39**:336
"1989 cont./Gorilla in the Midst #6" (Sapphire) **99**:80
"1982" (Kenny) **87**:242
Nineteen Elastic Poems (Cendrars)
See *Dix-neuf poèmes élastiques*
"1911" (Kenny) **87**:242
"1915:The Queen's Own Oxfordshire Hussars" (Raine) **103**:211
"Nineteen Fifty-Five" (Walker) **103**:407, 412-13
"Nineteen Forty" (Dubie) **36**:131
"1948: Jews" (Rich) **76**:210
"1945-1985: Poem for the Anniversary" (Oliver) **98**:261
"1941" (Gilchrist) **143**:294-95
"Nineteen Hadley Street" (Schnackenberg) **40**:378-79
1900 (Bertolucci) **16**:100
1900 (Morand) **41**:304
1900 (West) **31**:459-60
"1901: In All Latin America" (Galeano) **72**:138
"1905" (Graves) **39**:323
Nineteen Masks for the Naked Poet (Willard) **7**:540; **37**:462
"1919: Back from the Front" (Raine) **103**:211
"1978 Reunion of Palmakh Veterans at Ma'ayan Harod" (Amichai) **57**:44
"1971" (Justice) **102**:277
"1977: Poem for Mrs. Fannie Lou Hamer" (Jordan) **114**:147
"1972" (Brodsky) **100**:54
"1906" (Raine) **103**:208
"1916 Seen from 1921" (Blunden) **56**:30, 38, 51
"1965 cont./Gorilla in the Midst #3" (Sapphire) **99**:80
Nineteen Stories (Greene) **37**:140
1939 (Boyle) **121**:53-4
"1937" (Danticat)
See "Nineteen Thirty-seven"

"Nineteen Thirty-seven" (Danticat) **94**:94, 96-7, 99
"1933" (MacLeish) **68**:281, 287
"1924: Lenin Takes a Long Bath" (Raine) **103**:212
1918 (Foote) **51**:132-36
1985 (Burgess) **13**:124-28; **22**:78; **40**:120; **62**:130-32; **94**:60-1
"1984" (Bowie) **17**:61
1984, Spring: A Choice of Futures (Clarke) **35**:128-29
1982 Janine (Gray) **41**:179-84
"1958" (MacEwen) **55**:167
"1959" (Tillinghast) **29**:415
"1959 Valentine" (Zukofsky) **18**:558
"1957, a Romance" (Gilchrist) **48**:115-16; **143**:274, 302, 306-07, 319, 322-28, 330
"1956—Ein Pilzjahr" (Hildesheimer) **49**:173-74
"1953" (MacNeice) **4**:316
"1940" (McFadden) **48**:251-52
"1944" (Gilchrist) **143**:320-21, 327
1941 (Spielberg) **20**:366
"1947 Blue Buick Convertible" (Sorrentino) **7**:448
"1942" (Brautigan) **12**:59, 61
1919 (Dos Passos) **1**:77; **11**:152-53; **15**:186; **34**:419, 424; **82**:62, 64-8, 71, 73, 80, 83-4, 86, 89, 91-2, 95, 98-103, 105, 108-10
1999 (Prince) **35**:326-28, 330-32
"1972" (Brodsky) **36**:76, 78
"1968" (Rakosi) **47**:345
1968 (Stern) **4**:523; **39**:239-40
1968, Year of Crisis (Archer) **12**:18
1969 Velvet Underground Live (Reed) **21**:308
"1966" (Achebe) **26**:21, 24
"1966 and All That" (Montague) **46**:271
"1963" (Dove) **81**:134
"Nineteenth Century as a Song" (Hass) **18**:213
"Nineteenth Nervous Breakdown" (Jagger and Richard) **17**:234-35
"The Nineteenth New York" (Doctorow) **113**:167
"The Nineteenth-Century Mexican Woman" (Castellanos) **66**:55
"The 1913 Massacre" (Guthrie) **35**:191, 193
"The Nineteen-Thirties Are Over" (Waddington) **28**:439
"1938" (Dacey)
See "A Surrealistic Photograph by Manuel Alvarez Bravo"
"1934" (Phillips) **15**:421; **33**:305
1934 (Moravia) **27**:355-57; **46**:285
"1939" (Taylor) **18**:526
1936... Peace? (Huxley) **35**:241
"1933" (Levine) **118**:277
1933 (Levine) **4**:288; **5**:250-52; **9**:332; **14**:319-20; **33**:271; **118**:272-73, 277, 284, 292, 299
1933 Was a Bad Year (Fante) **60**:133-34
"1928" (Sadoff) **9**:467
"1921" (Townshend) **17**:538
"Ninetieth Birthday" (Thomas) **6**:534
"Ninety Miles from Nowhere" (Phillips) **28**:364-65
"Ninety North" (Jarrell) **6**:260
"91 Revere Street" (Lowell) **124**:255, 263, 267, 272, 276, 279-80, 300
"91, Revere Street" (Raine) **103**:189
98 (Sukenick) **6**:523-24; **48**:365-70
95 Poems (Cummings) **1**:68; **8**:160; **12**:154; **15**:163; **68**:40-2, 48
Ninety-Nine Novels: The Best in English Since 1939 (Burgess) **81**:301
"91 Revere Street" (Kizer) **80**:183
"Ninety-One Revere Street: An Autobiographical Fragment" (Lowell) **4**:303; **5**:258; **8**:350; **9**:334-35
"A Ninety-Six-Year-Old Big Sister" (Gold) **42**:198; **152**:121
"92" (Brown) **73**:24
Ninety-Two Days (Waugh) **27**:477
Ninety-Two in the Shade (McGuane) **3**:330-31; **7**:212-13; **18**:323-26; **45**:258, 260, 262-63; **127**:245, 250-51, 155, 258-60, 262, 267, 269-70, 275-76, 279, 280, 283, 298
Un niño azul para esa sombra (Marqués) **96**:224, 226-28, 241-43, 245, 250-52
"El nino en el arbol" (Marqués) **96**:245
"Ninth Elegy: The Antagonists" (Rukeyser) **27**:407
"Ninth Fytte: La Donna" (Barnard) **48**:29
"The Ninth Part of Speech" (Davidson) **2**:113
"Ninth Psalm" (Sexton) **123**:404
"The Ninth Symphony of Beethoven Understood at Last as a Sexual Message" (Rich) **7**:367, 373
The Ninth Wave (Ehrenburg) **34**:440; **62**:177-78
"Niobe" (Watkins) **43**:446
Niobjeta ziemia (Milosz) **56**:238-40, 243, 246; **82**:290, 297
A Nip in the Air (Betjeman) **6**:66; **10**:53; **34**:306; **43**:46
"Nipples Rise to Spirit" (Dacey) **51**:80
"The Nipplewhip" (Benedikt) **14**:81
"Nippon, the Floating Kingdom" (Sondheim) **147**:234
The Nirvana Blues (Nichols) **38**:344, 346
"Nirvana Small by a Waterfall" (Perelman) **49**:261
"Nirvana Stair" (Broumas) **73**:17
"A Nite with Beau Willie Brown" (Shange) **25**:404; **126**:350, 352, 367
"Nitrate" (Levine) **118**:301
"Nitrous Oxide" (Ginsberg) **109**:325
The Nitty Gritty (Bonham) **12**:50-1, 53
"Nitya" (Narayan) **47**:304
Nixon: Ruin and Recovery 1973-1990 (Ambrose) **145**:31-5
Nixon: The Education of a Politician, 1913-1962 (Ambrose) **14**:11, 13-15, 19, 24, 26, 28
Nkrumah and the Ghana Revolution (James) **33**:221
"nNight Before the Journey" (Swenson) **106**:337
"No" (Berryman) **13**:83
"The No" (Dacey) **51**:83
"No" (Milosz) **82**:280
No (Ionesco)
See *Non*
NO (Major) **3**:320; **19**:293-94; **48**:212, 215
"No Answer" (Ignatow) **7**:175
"No Answer" (Thomas) **6**:530
"No Assistance" (Shange) **25**:402
"No Bells to Believe" (Hugo) **32**:247
"No Bird Does Call" (Warren) **39**:265
No Bugles Tonight (Lancaster) **36**:243-44
"No Bull Shit" (Smith) **12**:541
No Cause for Panic (Baker) **31**:26
No Chinese Stranger (Wong) **17**:567
"No Chocolates for Breakfast" (Jordan) **114**:152
No Clouds of Glory (Engel) **36**:157-58, 162
No Comebacks (Forsyth) **36**:176
"No Compassion" (Byrne) **26**:95
"No Connection" (Asimov) **26**:41
No Continuing City (Longley) **29**:291, 293-96
The No 'Count Boy (Green) **25**:193
No Country for Young Men (O'Faolain) **19**:360-61; **47**:326, 328, 330-31; **108**:406, 409-10, 414-15, 417-18, 422
No Country without a Grandfather (Carrier)
See *Il n'y a pas de pays sans grand-père*
No Country without Grandfathers (Carrier)
See *Il n'y a pas de pays sans grand-père*
"No Dancing" (Costello) **21**:67
No Deadly Drug (MacDonald) **44**:408
No Decency Left (Graves) **45**:171
"No Delicacies" (Bachmann)
See "Keine Delikatessen"
"No Direction Home" (Spinrad) **46**:384
No Direction Home (Spinrad) **46**:383-84
No Directions (Hanley) **13**:261
"No Dogs Bark" (Rulfo) **80**:200
"No Dove, No Covenant" (Vonnegut) **12**:607
No End (Kieslowski) **120**:206, 208-09, 22-, 224-25, 227, 232, 236, 238-40, 242, 244, 247, 250, 256-58, 260
No End of Blame (Barker) **37**:37-8
"No End of Fun" (Szymborska) **99**:201
No End of Fun (Szymborska) **99**:199
"No existe el hombre" (Aleixandre) **9**:15
No Exit (Sartre)
See *Huis clos*
No Fond Return of Love (Pym) **37**:373-74, 376-77, 379; **111**:227, 234, 238, 243-48, 263, 265-66, 269, 282-85
No Hassles (Waldman) **7**:508
"¿No hay salida?" (Paz) **19**:366; **65**:180-81
No Highway (Shute) **30**:367-68
"No I Don't" (Ashbery) **77**:64, 68
No, I'm Not Afraid (Ratushinskaya) **54**:380-82
No! in Thunder: Essays on Myth and Literature (Fiedler) **4**:163; **13**:211; **24**:189-91, 203
"No Joke" (Mac Laverty) **31**:255
"No Kaddish for Weinstein" (Allen) **52**:36-7
"No Land Is Waste" (Simmons) **43**:410, 412
No Land Is Waste, Dr. Eliot (Simmons) **43**:408
No Laughing Matter (Wilson) **2**:472-74; **3**:534-36; **5**:513-14; **25**:459, 463-64; **34**:581, 584
No Longer at Ease (Achebe) **1**:1; **3**:1-3; **5**:1, 3-4; **7**:3-6; **11**:1-3; **26**:12, 15-16, 18, 25-7; **51**:3-5; **75**:3, 6-7, 11, 13, 26; **127**:8-9, 28, 34-5, 40, 81-2; **152**:17
No Longer Two People (Lane) **25**:286, 288
"No Man Could Bind Him" (Vanderhaeghe) **41**:450, 452
No Man Is an Island (Merton) **83**:380, 382
"No Man, No Woman" (Rosa) **23**:353
"No Man's Land" (Heaney) **14**:244
"No Man's Land" (Seger) **35**:384-85
No Man's Land (Onetti)
See *Tierra de nadie*
No Man's Land (Pinter) **6**:418-19; **9**:418-21; **11**:444; **15**:423-25; **27**:387, 395-96; **58**:370, 374-76, 379, 383; **73**:277
No Man's Land (Shammas) **55**:86
No Man's Land: The Place of the Woman Writer in the Twentieth Century (Gilbert and Gubar) **65**:344-45, 347
No Man's Land: The Place of the Woman Writer in the Twentieth-Century, Volume 1: The War of the Words (Gubar) **145**:225, 233-36, 238-40, 245, 251-52, 254-55, 258, 260-61, 263-65, 267, 269-70, 285
No Man's Land: The Place of the Woman Writer in the Twentieth-Century, Volume 2: Sexchanges (Gubar) **145**:236, 239, 241, 258, 261-64, 267, 269-71, 273, 277
No Man's Land: The Place of the Woman Writer in the Twentieth-Century, Volume 3: Letters from the Front (Gubar) **145**:252-53, 258, 267-70, 274-77
No Man's Meat (Callaghan) **41**:89-92
No Man's Meat. The Enchanted Pimp (Callaghan) **41**:89, 91; **65**:248
No Man's Time (Yanovsky) **2**:485; **18**:550-51
"No Matter for History" (Brutus) **43**:89
No me agarran viva: La mujer salvadoreñna en lucha (Alegria) **75**:42-3
"No Money Down" (Berry) **17**:52-3
"No Moon Floods the Memory of That Night" (Knight) **40**:283
"No Moon for Me" (Miller) **30**:263
No More Dying Then (Rendell) **28**:383, 385; **48**:321
"No More Ghosts" (Graves) **45**:173
"No More Lonely Nights" (McCartney) **35**:293
"No More Looking Back" (Davies) **21**:101
"no more love poems" (Shange) **25**:402, 404
"No more love poems #3" (Shange) **126**:353
"No more love poems #4" (Shange) **126**:353-54, 375
No More Love Poems, Number Two (Shange) **25**:404
"No More Marching" (Madhubuti) **73**:209
"No more Parades" (Amis) **129**:24

"No More Sacrifices" (Ortiz) **45**:309
"No More Songs" (Ochs) **17**:332, 334
"No More Than Is" (Riding) **7**:374
"No Morning After" (Clarke) **136**:211
"No Name" (Atwood) **84**:102
"No Name for It" (Martinson) **14**:357
"No Name in the Street" (Baldwin) **13**:52; **42**:17, 19; **127**:140
"No Name in the Street" (Sillitoe) **19**:422; **57**:395
No Name in the Street (Baldwin) **2**:32-4; **4**:41; **13**:53; **15**:42; **17**:38; **42**:15, 17-19, 22; **127**:116-17, 124, 126-31, 145
"No Name is My Name" (Kroetsch) **132**:238, 290
No Nature: New and Selected Poems (Snyder) **120**:353-55
"No Neck and Bad as Hell" (Bukowski) **108**:86
"No News from the Old Country" (Motion) **47**:292
No Night without Stars (Norton) **12**:470
"No No No No" (Angelou) **77**:28
No, Not Bloomsbury (Bradbury) **61**:42
No Nudes Is Good Nudes (Wodehouse) **2**:479
"No Offense Intended But Fuck Christmas" (Ellison) **139**:134
"No One" (Merwin) **45**:270
"No One Remembers" (Levine) **14**:318-19; **118**:267, 300
"No One Talks about This" (Rakosi) **47**:344
"No One Will Laugh" (Kundera) **32**:260; **68**:241; **115**:332
No One Writes to the Colonel (García Márquez)
See *El colonel no tiene quien le escribe*
The No One's Rose (Celan)
See *Die Niemandsrose*
"No Orpheus, No Eurydice" (Spender) **41**:428; **91**:269
No Other Life (Moore) **90**:297-300, 302-3
"No oyes ladrar los perros" (Rulfo) **80**:224
No Parasan! (They Shall Not Pass): A Story of the Battle of Madrid (Sinclair) **15**:499; **63**:363
No Part in Your Death (Freeling) **38**:188
"No Particular Place to Go" (Morrison) **17**:291
No Particular Place to Go (Williams) **42**:444
"No Place" (O'Brien) **116**:210-11
No Place for an Angel (Spencer) **22**:401, 403, 405
No Place for Hiding (L'Heureux) **52**:275
"No Place for You, My Love" (Welty) **22**:459, 462; **105**:299
No Place on Earth (Wolf)
See *Kein Ort. Nirgends*
No Place to Be Somebody (Gordone) **1**:124-25; **4**:198-99
"No Pleasure" (Newlove) **14**:378
"No Quarter" (Page and Plant) **12**:476
No Quarter Given (Horgan) **53**:170-71, 175
No Regrets for Our Youth (Kurosawa)
See *Waga Seishun ni Kui Nashi*
No Relief (Dixon) **52**:93-7, 101
No Retreat (Hart) **66**:176, 182
"No Road" (Larkin) **13**:336, 340; **18**:294; **33**:258; **64**:258, 260, 262, 266
"No Room at the Inn" (Ferber) **93**:180
No saco nada de la escuela (Valdez) **84**:395
"No Sale" (Wagoner) **3**:508
"No Sanctuary" (Heaney) **14**:244
"No se culpa a nadie" (Cortázar) **10**:118
"No sé por qué piensas tú" (Guillén) **79**:251
No Secrets (Simon) **26**:408
"No Smiles" (Grekova) **59**:378
"No Solution" (Gascoyne) **45**:157
No Souvenirs: Journal, 1957-1969 (Eliade) **19**:148
"No Speak English" (Cisneros) **118**:177
No Star is Lost (Farrell) **66**:114, 116-17, 119-20
"No Starch in the Dhoti, s'il vous plaît" (Perelman) **49**:265
"No Succour!" (Stern) **100**:329
No Such Liberty (Comfort) **7**:52
"No Such Thing As a Free Lunch" (Grenville) **61**:152
"No Swan So Fine" (Moore) **10**:353
"No Swan so Fine" (Swenson) **106**:340
No Telephone to Heaven (Cliff) **120**:87-90, 92-97, 100-03, 108-10, 112-13, 115-16, 118-19, 121, 129
No Thanks (Cummings) **12**:145, 154; **15**:157, 161-62; **68**:35, 49
"No Theory" (Ignatow) **7**:179
No Third Path (Kosinski) **2**:232; **70**:300, 305
"No Ties" (Simmons) **43**:408
No Time (Avison) **97**:121-22
"No Time Ago" (Cummings) **8**:160
No Time for Comedy (Behrman) **40**:80-3
No Time for Sergeants (Levin) **6**:306
"No Time Is Passing" (Aickman) **57**:3
No Time like Tomorrow (Aldiss) **14**:11
No Time to Be Young (Jones) **52**:253
"No Title Required" (Szymborska) **99**:203
"No Turtles" (Klappert) **57**:258
"No Understand" (Sondheim) **30**:380
"No Use to Talk to Me" (Le Guin) **45**:213
No Vacancies in Hell (Epstein) **7**:97
No Vacation for Maigret (Simenon) **47**:373, 375
No Villain Need Be (Fisher) **7**:103, 105
"No Voyage" (Oliver) **19**:361; **98**:266
No Voyage (Oliver) **19**:361; **98**:256, 276-77, 288, 293
No Way (Ginzburg)
See *Caro Michele*
"No Way Out" (Johnston) **51**:241, 243, 252
"No Way Out but Through" (Maitland) **49**:235
No Way to Treat a Lady (Goldman) **48**:128
"No Whistle Slow" (Rooke) **25**:391
"No White Bird Sings" (Ciardi) **129**:47
"No Woman, No Cry" (Marley) **17**:271-72
"No Word" (Kunitz) **148**:74, 25, 117
Noah (Seger) **35**:378, 381
Noah and the Waters (Day Lewis) **10**:131, 133
"Noah's Ark" (Abe) **81**:298
"Noah's Ark" (Sillitoe) **148**:200
Noah's Ark (Blaga) **75**:65
Noaptea (Arghezi) **80**:6, 8
Nobel Lecture by Aleksandr Solzhenitsyn (Solzhenitsyn)
See *Nobelevskaia lektsii politerature 1970 goda*
The Nobel Prize (Krotkov) **19**:264-66
Nobelevskaia lektsii politerature 1970 goda (Solzhenitsyn) **4**:508, 512
Nobi (Ichikawa) **20**:177-78
Noble House: A Novel of Contemporary Hong Kong (Clavell) **25**:126-27; **87**:2, 8, 17-19
"Noble Savage Theme as Fetish" (White) **148**:286
The Noble Tale of Sir Lancelot of the Lake (Steinbeck) **21**:387
"Noblesse oblige" (O'Hara) **6**:385
Noblesse Oblige: An Enquiry into the Identifiable Characteristics of the English Aristocracy (Mitford) **44**:486, 491
Nobodaddy (MacLeish) **8**:360-61; **14**:336; **68**:271
Nobodaddy's Kinder: Trilogie (Schmidt) **56**:390, 393, 405
"Nobody" (Aleixandre)
See "Nadie"
Nobody Answered the Bell (Davies) **23**:147
"Nobody Answers the Door" (Tyler) **103**:258
"Nobody Better, Better than Nobody" (Frazier) **46**:166
Nobody Better, Better than Nobody (Frazier) **46**:165
"Nobody Gives" (Davies) **21**:98
Nobody Hears a Broken Drum (Miller) **2**:284
Nobody Knew They Were There (Hunter) **31**:222
"Nobody Knows" (McCartney) **35**:287-88
"Nobody Knows Anything about Art Anymore" (Donnell) **34**:158
"Nobody Knows My Name" (Baldwin) **42**:16
Nobody Knows My Name (Baldwin) **90**:28, 31, 34
Nobody Knows My Name: More Notes of a Native Son (Baldwin) **2**:31-2; **5**:42; **13**:52-3; **17**:21-3, 32, 38; **42**:14, 16, 18-19; **50**:282, 289, 292, 296; **127**:105, 114, 139, 144
Nobody Likes Me (Weldon) **122**:282
"Nobody Loses All the Time" (Cummings) **3**:119
"Nobody Loves Anybody Anymore" (Kristofferson) **26**:270
"Nobody Loves You" (Lennon) **35**:268-69
Nobody Owns th Earth (Bissett) **18**:58
"Nobody Said Anything" (Carver) **22**:96; **53**:65
Nobody to Blame (Greene) **37**:140
"Nobody Told Me" (Lennon) **35**:275-76
"Nobody Wanted to Sit behind a Desk" (Gray) **49**:152
"Nobody Will Laugh" (Kundera)
See "No One Will Laugh"
Nobody's Angel (McGuane) **45**:258-62, 265; **127**:245, 248, 250, 257, 262, 266, 269, 272, 293-98
"Nobody's Business" (Gilliatt) **10**:229
Nobody's Business (Gilliatt) **2**:160-61; **10**:229
Nobody's Fault (Jones) **52**:250
"Nobody's Fault but Mine" (Page and Plant) **12**:480
"Nobody's In Town" (Ferber) **93**:169
Nobody's In Town (Ferber) **93**:169
The Nobody's Rose (Celan)
See *Die Niemandsrose*
Noc u provinci (Krleža) **114**:167
Noce i dnie (Dabrowska) **15**:165-68
Noces (Camus) **1**:53; **14**:106-07, 111; **32**:86, 96; **63**:74, 84; **69**:112, 117, 127, 133; **124**:31
Les noces (Jouve) **47**:207-09, 212
Les noces rouges (Chabrol) **16**:178
"Noch'" (Akhmadulina) **53**:12
Noch feiert der Tod das Leben (Sachs) **98**:324
"La noche boca arriba" (Cortázar) **10**:113; **34**:332
"La noche cíclica" (Borges) **4**:71
La noche de las cien cabezas (Sender) **8**:480-81
"La noche de los alcaravanes" (García Márquez) **3**:181; **47**:148-49
"Noche de negros junto a la catedral" (Guillén) **48**:165
La noche de Tlatelolco (Poniatowska) **140**:294, 298, 304-06, 308-09, 327-28, 330-31, 337-38
"Noche del hombre y su demonio" (Cernuda) **54**:49
"Noche en claro" (Paz) **51**:337
"Noche final" (Aleixandre) **9**:12
"Noche incial" (Aleixandre) **9**:12
"La noche que lo dejaron solo" (Rulfo) **80**:200
"Noche sinfónica" (Aleixandre) **36**:29
De noche vienes (Poniatowska) **140**:295, 321-22, 325, 330, 332
"Nochebuena cincuenta y una" (Cernuda) **54**:46
"Las noches de Goliadkin" (Bioy Casares) **88**:68, 71, 77
"Noctamble" (Johnston) **51**:238, 240, 245
"Noctambule" (Smith) **15**:517
"Noctambules" (Gascoyne) **45**:152, 155, 159
Nocturna Artificialia: Those Who Desire Without End (The Brothers Quay) **95**:329-30, 333-34, 339, 347, 350-51, 353
"Nocturnal Games" (Hesse) **25**:260-61
"Nocturne" (Faulkner) **9**:201
"Nocturne" (Livesay) **79**:350
"Nocturne" (MacLeish) **68**:286
"Nocturne" (O'Hara) **78**:341
"Nocturne" (Prokosch) **48**:309
"Nocturne" (Transtroemer) **52**:410; **65**:222-23, 235
"Nocturne" (Voigt) **54**:434
"Nocturne" (Wright) **146**:378
Nocturne (Swinnerton) **31**:420-23, 425

"Nocturne among Grotesqueries" (Cernuda)
See "Nocturno entre las musarañas"
"Nocturne at Bethesda" (Bontemps) **1**:38; **18**:64
Nocturne of Remembered Spring and Other Poems (Aiken) **52**:22
"Nocturne with Neon Lights" (Tuohy) **37**:431
Nocturnes (Senghor) **54**:390, 402, 408-09; **130**:234-35, 238, 252, 259-60, 280
Nocturnes for the King of Naples (White) **27**:479-80, 482; **110**:316, 326-27, 330, 336-38
"Nocturno" (Castellanos) **66**:52-3
"Nocturno de San Ildefonso" (Paz) **51**:337; **65**:188, 190, 197, 200
"Nocturno entre las musarañas" (Cernuda) **54**:55, 58
Noé (Giono) **4**:188
The Noël Coward Diaries (Coward) **29**:139-41
Le noeud de vipères (Mauriac) **4**:339-40; **56**:206, 216, 219
Nog (Wurlitzer) **2**:482-84; **4**:597-98; **15**:587-89
No-Good Friday (Fugard) **14**:189; **80**:61, 63, 67-9, 80
"Noh Lickle Twang" (Bennett) **28**:29-30
Noh; or, Accomplishment (Pound) **48**:289
La noia (Moravia) **7**:240-42, 244; **11**:382-83; **18**:344, 349; **46**:283-85
La Noire de... (Ousmane) **66**:335
"noire et lippue, bien sûr" (Tchicaya) **101**:354
Noise in the Trees: A Memoir (Heyen) **13**:282, 284; **18**:230
"The Noise of a Match" (Char) **55**:288
"Noise of Strangers" (Garrett) **51**:149, 152
Noises Off (Frayn) **31**:192-93; **47**:137-40
"Noite de cala e paixão" (Dourado) **60**:85
"Noli Me Tangere" (Graham) **118**:259
Le Nom d'Oedipe (Cixous) **92**:88
"Nomad and Viper" (Oz) **27**:359-62
"Nomad Invasions" (Chatwin) **57**:153; **59**:277
"Nomad Songs" (Merwin) **88**:194
No-man's Rose (Celan)
See *Die Niemandsrose*
Les nombres (Chedid) **47**:82, 87
Il nome della rosa (Eco) **28**:130-33; **60**:111-14, 117-22, 124; **142**:62, 64-9, 71-8, 80-3, 85-7, 89, 91-5, 98, 105-07, 109, 114, 116, 136-38
"Il nome il naso" (Calvino) **73**:51, 53, 60
Non (Ionesco) **41**:225; **86**:334-35
"Non Linear" (Webb) **18**:541
"Non piangere, liù" (Porter) **13**:453
Non Sequitur O'Connor (Klappert) **57**:260-61
"Non serviam" (Lem) **15**:330; **149**:113-14, 125
Non Serviam (Ekeloef) **27**:114
"Nona" (King) **37**:207; **61**:333
"Nonaspettavano altro" (Buzzati) **36**:86
"Non-Commitment" (Achebe) **11**:4; **26**:22
"The Nonconformist's Memorial" (Howe) **152**:185
The Nonconformist's Memorial (Howe) **152**:182-83, 185-86, 192, 195-97, 203, 212
None but the Lonely Heart (Llewellyn) **80**:192, 194-96
None but the Lonely Heart (Odets) **98**:197, 199, 244-47
None Genuine without This Signature (Hood) **28**:194-95
None of Maigret's Business (Simenon)
See *Maigret's Little Joke*
None of the Above (Wells) **12**:637-38
"None of the Other Birds" (Smith) **25**:421
None Shall Look Back (Gordon) **6**:202-03, 207; **13**:242; **29**:186; **83**:227-29, 233, 240, 242, 247, 252-54, 258-59
None to Accompany Me (Gordimer) **123**:150-54, 156
Nones (Auden) **123**:16, 19
"A Non-Euclidean View of California as a cold Place to Be" (Le Guin) **136**:327-28, 334-35
The Nonexistent Knight (Calvino)
See *Il cavaliere inesistente*
Nongogo (Fugard) **14**:189, 191-92; **80**:61, 63, 67-8
"Non-Hymns" (Wittlin) **25**:468
The Nonny Poems (Kherdian) **6**:281; **9**:317-18
Nonsense and Happiness (Handke) **38**:218-19
Nonsequences: Selfpoems (Middleton) **13**:387
Non-Stop (Aldiss) **14**:10; **40**:20-1
"Non-Stop Dancing" (Weller) **26**:442
"Nonstop Jetflight to Halifax" (Johnston) **51**:245
"Non-Stop to Mars" (Williamson) **29**:455, 458
"Noon" (Apple) **9**:32
"Noon" (Dudek) **19**:136
"Noon" (Levine) **33**:271; **118**:299
"Noon" (Wright) **146**:
Noon (McNally) **4**:347; **7**:217; **41**:292
Noon: Twenty-Second Century (Strugatskii and Strugatskii) **27**:436
"Noon Wine" (Porter) **101**:224, 229, 242, 253
Noon Wine (Porter) **1**:273; **7**:311-14, 316-17, 319; **10**:394-96, 398-99; **13**:446, 448-50; **15**:429; **27**:398-99, 401; **101**:219
"Noon Wine: The Sources" (Porter) **101**:224
"Nooncoming" (Benford) **52**:75
"Noonday Axeman" (Murray) **40**:333-34, 340
Noonday Demons (Barnes) **56**:5-8
No-One Was Saved (Barker) **37**:32
Noontimes Gained (Tzara)
See *Midis gagnés*
Nopalgarth (Vance) **35**:427
Nor All Thy Tears (Swinnerton) **31**:428
Nor Shall My Sword (Leavis) **24**:306, 308, 310, 314
"Nora and Hilda" (Durcan) **43**:114
Nora Inu (Kurosawa)
See *Stray Dog*
Nora Jane and Company (Gilchrist) **143**:308-09
"Nora's Journal" (Klappert) **57**:259-60
Nord (Céline) **1**:57; **3**:104-05; **4**:98, 102; **7**:43, 45; **9**:152, 158; **47**:74-5, 79; **124**:64-6, 68, 70, 73, 78, 89, 93, 103-04, 107-08
Nordic Twilight (Forster) **1**:107
The No-Return Trail (Levitin) **17**:266
"Norfolk, 1969" (Tilghman) **65**:107-08, 110-11
The Norfolk Poems (Carruth) **4**:94
"Noria" (Césaire) **32**:113
Norm and Ahmed (Buzo) **61**:52-4, 56, 59-61, 64
"Norma" (Sanchez) **116**:302-03, 306
"Normal Circumstances and Other Special Cases" (Fish) **142**:157, 171
The Normal Heart (Kramer) **42**:270-73
The Norman Conquests (Ayckbourn) **5**:35, 37; **8**:34; **18**:27-9; **33**:42-3, 45, 49; **74**:6-7, 34
"Norman Mailer: The Avenger and the Bitch" (Amis) **62**:4-5
Normance (Céline) **124**:62, 66-8, 70-1
"North" (Heaney) **7**:151; **14**:244-45; **25**:245
"North" (Hoffman) **6**:244
"North" (Justice) **102**:258
"North" (Walcott) **76**:275
North (Céline)
See *Nord*
North (Heaney) **7**:148-52; **14**:242-45; **25**:243-51; **37**:163, 165, 168; **74**:156-60, 162-63, 165, 167, 171, 173-75, 180, 183, 190-91, 193; **91**:118, 121, 123, 128
"North America" (Newlove) **14**:377
North American Bear (Wright) **146**:378
A North American Education (Blaise) **29**:69-71, 73-5
"North American Sequence" (Roethke) **3**:433; **8**:457, 460; **11**:484-85; **19**:398-400; **46**:356, 361, 364; **101**:288-92, 299, 304-06, 308-13, 315-16, 318, 321, 327, 334
"North American Time" (Rich) **36**:378
The North American Turbine (Dorn) **10**:158; **18**:128
"North and South" (Walcott) **25**:457; **42**:422; **67**:348, 356
North & South (Bishop) **4**:65; **9**:89, 91, 93-4, 97; **13**:89, 91, 93, 95; **32**:28-9, 37-9, 41-2
North and South (Bishop)
See *North & South*
North and South (Jakes) **29**:250
"North Beach Birth" (Musgrave) **54**:335
North by Northwest (Hitchcock) **16**:346-47, 349, 353, 359
"North by the Creek" (Davison) **28**:102
North Central (Niedecker) **10**:360
"North Country" (Slessor) **14**:497
North Dallas Forty (Gent) **29**:180-83
"North Dublin" (Davie) **8**:167
North Face (Renault) **3**:425; **17**:392; **94**:353
"North in Winter" (Kenny) **87**:241
"North Light" (Helprin) **22**:221
North of Boston (Frost) **3**:172; **4**:176; **13**:222-23; **15**:239-40, 246-51; **26**:111, 118-19, 121, 124, 127; **34**:468, 470
North of Jamaica (Simpson) **4**:500; **7**:429; **149**:310, 326
"North of Sixty" (Richler) **46**:352
North of South: An African Journey (Naipaul) **32**:325-27; **39**:355-58
North of Summer (Purdy) **50**:246
North of the Danube (Caldwell) **50**:299
"The North Rim" (Swenson) **61**:401; **106**:329
"North Sea Off Carnoustie" (Stevenson) **33**:380-81
"North Sea Poem" (Musgrave) **13**:400
"The North Sea Undertaker's Complaint" (Lowell) **4**:299
"The North Ship" (Larkin) **13**:338
The North Ship (Larkin) **5**:223, 225-27, 230; **8**:338-40; **13**:335, 337; **18**:293, 298-300; **33**:261-62; **39**:334, 341-42, 344-45; **64**:257-61, 266-68, 270, 278
"North Shore" (Davison) **28**:100
North Shore Fish (Horovitz) **56**:157
The North Star (Hellman) **52**:191
"North Stream" (Scott) **22**:373
North to the Orient (Lindbergh) **82**:153, 158, 166-67
"North Winter" (Carruth) **4**:94; **84**:119
"Northeast Playground" (Paley) **140**:277
"Northern Elegies" (Akhmatova) **25**:26; **64**:5
"Northern Exposure" (Simic) **68**:373
"Northern Express" (Montague) **46**:277
"The Northern Gate" (Montague) **46**:269
"A Northern Hoard" (Heaney) **5**:170; **7**:148; **14**:243-44; **25**:241
"A Northern Legion" (Read) **4**:439
The Northern Light (Cronin) **32**:138-39
Northern Lights (O'Brien) **7**:272; **19**:357; **103**:134-35, 143, 166
"Northern Pass" (Rulfo)
See "El pasa del norte"
"Northern Philosopher" (Van Doren) **6**:541
"Northern Pike" (Wright) **5**:520
"Northern River" (Wright) **11**:578
The Northern Story (Paustovsky) **40**:367
"Northern Summer" (Faludy) **42**:141
Northfield Poems (Ammons) **2**:12; **5**:26; **57**:59; **108**:5
"Northhanger Ridge" (Wright) **6**:581
Northrop Frye on Shakespeare (Frye) **70**:271, 274-75
"Northumbrian Sequence" (Raine) **45**:332, 335, 337
"N.W.5 and N.6" (Betjeman) **43**:36, 40
Northwest Ecolog (Ferlinghetti) **27**:139
The Norton Anthology of Literature by Women: The Tradition in English (Gubar) **145**:222-24, 226, 228-30, 233, 236, 244, 250-51, 253, 258, 274, 283, 287
The Norton Book of Modern War (Fussell) **74**:133
Noruei no mori (Murakami) **150**:39-41, 51, 54-5, 72, 76-9, 83, 92
"Norwegian Wood" (Lennon and McCartney) **12**:360-61
Norwegian Wood (Murakami)
See *Noruei no mori*

"Nos han dado la tierra" (Rulfo) **80**:200, 210, 216, 221, 223
No's Knife (Beckett) **4**:51
"Nos mains au jardin" (Hébert) **29**:228, 232
De nos oiseaux (Tzara) **47**:392-93
"Nos vemos" (Allen) **84**:6
"The Nose" (Jong) **6**:269
The Nose of Sisyphus (Ferlinghetti) **111**:63
"Noses Run in My Family" (Mull) **17**:300
Nosferatu—The Vampyre (Herzog) **16**:330, 333-36
Nostalghia (Tarkovsky) **75**:385, 388-89, 392-94, 396, 398-99, 402, 411-13
"Nostalgia" (Mukherjee) **53**:267-68
"Nostalgia" (Strand) **71**:285
Nostalgia and Sexual Difference: Resistance to Contemporary Feminism (Doane and Hodges) **65**:324
Nostalgia for the Present (Voznesensky) **15**:557; **57**:420-22, 426
"Nostalgia of the Lakefronts" (Justice) **102**:272
"Nostalgic Suffering" (Voinovich) **49**:382
"Nostalgie de bonheur" (Coles) **46**:113
"Nostasia in Asia" (Perelman) **5**:338
The Nostradamus Traitor (Gardner) **30**:155
I nostri antenati (Calvino) **5**:97-8; **8**:127; **11**:88-9, 91; **22**:88, 90; **33**:97; **39**:307, 310, 314-15; **73**:34, 58
"A Nosty Fright" (Swenson) **61**:405; **106**:323
"Not" (Orlovitz) **22**:336
"Not a Day Goes By" (Sondheim) **30**:399-400; **147**:243
Not a Penny More, Not a Penny Less (Archer) **28**:11
Not a Word about Nightingales (Howard) **5**:188; **151**:275
Not after Midnight (du Maurier) **6**:146; **59**:285-87
"Not All There" (Frost) **13**:228
Not at These Hands (Wellman) **49**:388
"Not by Rain Alone" (Ross) **13**:492
"Not Charles" (Dixon) **52**:98, 100
"Not Correcting His Name Misspelled on the Mailing Label" (Dacey) **51**:82
Not Dancing (Dunn) **36**:156
"La not di maj" (Pasolini) **106**:229
"Not Dying" (Strand) **18**:515, 517; **71**:285-86
"Not Even a Blood Relation" (Weldon) **122**:282
"Not Fade Away" (Jagger and Richard) **17**:227
"Not for an Age" (Aldiss) **5**:15
Not for Children (Rice) **7**:363; **49**:301-03
"Not for Publication" (Gordimer) **33**:180, 182
Not for Publication, and Other Stories (Gordimer) **33**:180; **70**:162; **123**:113-15, 147
"Not for the Sabbath" (Singer) **23**:421
Not for the Sake of Remembering (Amichai) See *Ve-Lo al Menat Lizkor*
"Not Forgotten" (Davison) **28**:99-100, 102
Not George Washington (Wodehouse) **22**:485
"Not Going to New York: A Letter" (Hass) **18**:210
"Not Going to See a Movie about a Nuclear Holocaust's Aftermath" (Dacey) **51**:83
"Not Honey" (H. D.) **73**:105
Not I (Beckett) **3**:47; **4**:51; **6**:36-7, 39, 43; **9**:81-4, 86; **11**:37, 39; **14**:74; **18**:46-7; **29**:57, 65; **59**:253, 255
"Not in Baedeker" (Auden) **9**:60
Not in God's Image (O'Faolain) **108**:414
"Not in the Guide Books" (Jennings) **131**:238
"Not Just Bad Sex" (Pollitt) **122**:225
"Not just Because My Husband Said?" (Castillo) **151**:35
Not Just to Remember (Amichai) See *Ve-Lo al Menat Lizkor*
"Not Leaving the House" (Snyder) **32**:399
"Not Like a Cypress" (Amichai) See "Lo kabrosh"
"Not Looking at Pictures" (Forster) **4**:169
"Not Marble in the Gilded Monuments" (MacLeish) **68**:286
"Not Not While the Giro" (Kelman) **58**:295
Not Not While the Giro, and Other Stories (Kelman) **58**:295; **86**:181
Not Now But Now (Fisher) **76**:337, 342; **87**:119, 122, 126
Not Now, Darling (Cooney) **62**:141-44, 146, 148
"Not Now John" (Pink Floyd) **35**:315
Not of This Time, Not of This Place (Amichai) **9**:22-4; **57**:40, 46; **116**:78, 84, 128
"Not One of Us" (Highsmith) **42**:215; **102**:199
"Not Only Here" (Clash) See "Up in Heaven"
"Not Palaces" (Spender) **41**:428
"Not Planning a Trip Back" (Ashbery) **125**:40
"Not Quite Bernadette" (Bukowski) **41**:73
Not Responsible for Personal Articles (Gould) **10**:243
Not So Deep as a Well (Parker) **68**:326
"Not Somewhere Else, but Here" (Rich) **18**:449
Not That He Brought Flowers (Thomas) **48**:374, 380
"Not the End of the World" (Ryan) **65**:213
"Not the Sweet Cicely of Gerardes Herball" (Adams) **97**:89
"Not This Pig" (Levine) **118**:275
Not This Pig (Levine) **2**:244; **4**:285-87; **5**:251; **9**:332; **14**:317; **33**:271, 273-74; **118**:271, 275, 283, 285, 287-88, 299, 302
"Not to be Printed, Not to be Said, Not to be Thought" (Rukeyser) **10**:443
Not to Disturb (Spark) **2**:417-19; **3**:464; **5**:400; **8**:495; **13**:524; **40**:400
"Not Waiting for Godot" (O'Casey) **88**:260
"Not Waving but Drowning" (Smith) **25**:420, 422-23; **44**:438, 440, 443, 445
"Not While I'm Around" (Sondheim) **30**:394
Not With My Wife, You Don't! (Gelbart) **21**:125-26
Not without Laughter (Hughes) **1**:147, 149; **5**:190; **10**:280, 282; **35**:213; **108**:285, 293-94, 326
"Not Worth the Record" (Mathias) **45**:238
"Not Yet" (Alegria) **75**:45, 49
Notabilities (Bernhard) See *Die Berühmten*
The Notary from Le Havre (Duhamel) **8**:188
"Notas de viaje" (Parra) **102**:338-39
Notations (Cage) **41**:81
"The Notations of Love" (Livesay) **79**:337, 343
"Notations of Love" (Rosenthal) **28**:394-95
"The Note" (Arghezi) See "Biletul"
"A Note" (Turco) **63**:428
"Note eternelle du présent" (Reverdy) **53**:293
A Note in Music (Lehmann) **5**:235, 238
"A Note on a Poem by Thomas Hardy" (Hooker) **43**:199
"A Note on Balance at the Trot" (Hearne) **56**:126
"Note on Blues" (Hughes) **15**:291
"A Note on Eugenics" (Huxley) **79**:316
A Note on Literary Criticism (Farrell) **66**:111, 113, 131-32, 137
"Note on Local Flora" (Empson) **8**:202; **19**:155; **33**:142
"A Note on Metrics" (Dudek) **11**:160
"A Note on Poetry" (Barnard) **48**:27
"A Note on Puritans" (Smith) **64**:396
"A Note on Sherwood Anderson" (Farrell) **66**:138
"A Note on the Anti-Pornography of Samuel R. Delany" (Delany) **141**:130
"A Note on the Esthetic Significance of Photography" (Scott) **43**:385
"A Note on the Literary Life" (Schulberg) **48**:350
"A Note on the Truth of the Tales" (Vollmann) **89**:279
"Note on the Way" (Forster) **15**:227
"A Note on the Work of the Imagination" (Levertov) **66**:241
"A Note on This Poem" (Hall) **151**:187
"A Note on War Poetry" (Eliot) **41**:150
"A Note on Wittgenstein and Literary Criticism" (Abrams) **24**:13
"A Note on Wyatt" (Amis) **40**:44
"Note Slipped under a Door" (Simic) **22**:383
"Note sur la poésie" (Tzara) **47**:393
"A Note to Donald Davie in Tennessee" (Abse) **29**:20
"A Note to Olga" (Levertov) **66**:240, 246
"Note to the Reader" (Simpson) **149**:341
"Note to Wang Wei" (Berryman) **62**:76
"Notebook" (Durrell) **27**:96
"Notebook" (Levertov) See "From a Notebook, October '68—May '69"
Notebook (Lowell) **124**:265, 290, 300
Notebook, 1970 (Lowell) **1**:184; **3**:301-04; **4**:300, 302, 304; **5**:256-58; **8**:349, 356-58; **9**:334, 336, 338-39; **11**:328-31; **15**:342, 344, 347; **37**:232, 234, 236-37, 240
Notebook 1967-68 (Lowell) **1**:181-84; **2**:248; **3**:301-04; **4**:300, 302, 304; **5**:256-58; **8**:349, 356-58; **9**:334, 336, 338-39; **11**:328-31; **15**:342, 344, 347-48; **37**:232, 234, 236-37, 240; **124**:254-57, 260-61, 290
"Notebook of a Return to the Native Land" (Césaire) See *Cahier d'un retour au pays natal*
A Notebook on William Shakespeare (Sitwell) **67**:332
Notebooks (Camus) See *Carnets*
Notebooks, 1960-1977 (Fugard) **40**:198-201, 203
Notebooks from Lancarote (Saramago) **119**:175
The Notebooks of Captain Georges (Renoir) **20**:305
The Notebooks of David Ignatow (Ignatow) **4**:249; **7**:175, 177-79
The Notebooks of Lazarus Long (Heinlein) **55**:303
"The Notebooks of Robinson Crusoe" (Smith) **64**:389-90
The Notebooks of Robinson Crusoe (Smith) **64**:389-90, 400
The Notebooks of Susan Berry (Mott) **15**:379
"Notes" (Ciardi) **40**:161
"Notes" (Frost) **15**:243
"Notes" (Moore) See "How to Talk to Your Mother"
"Notes" (O'Brien) **103**:139, 174
"Notes" (Saroyan) **29**:362
Notes (Ackroyd) See *Notes for a New Culture: An Essay on Modernism*
Notes (Canetti) See *Aufzeichnungen, 1942-48*
Notes and Counter-notes (Ionesco) See *Notes et contre-notes*
"Notes d'un retour au pays natal" (Condé) **92**:130
Notes et contre-notes (Ionesco) **4**:251; **41**:222, 224; **86**:332
"Notes et variantes" (Camus) **63**:75
"Notes for a Book of Hours, A Confession" (Jennings) **131**:232
"Notes for a Case History" (Lessing) **22**:278
"Notes for a Hypothetical Novel" (Baldwin) **13**:53
Notes for a New Culture: An Essay on Modernism (Ackroyd) **52**:3, 13; **140**:20, 22-25, 28, 33, 49, 52, 65, 74
"Notes for a Novel about the End of the World" (Percy) **47**:338
"Notes for a Preface" (Merwin) **88**:191, 208
"Notes for a Proletarian Novel" (Thurber) **125**:396
"Notes for a Speech" (Baraka) **14**:42
"Notes for a Story" (Godwin) **8**:248-49
Notes for an African Orestes (Pasolini) **20**:270
"Notes for an Elegy" (Meredith) **13**:374; **22**:302

Notes for Another Life (Bridgers) **26**:92
"Notes for Oscar Wilde" (Wright) **6**:580
"Notes for the First Line of a Spanish Poem" (Galvin) **38**:198
"Notes for the Legend of Salad Woman" (Ondaatje) **51**:317
Notes from a Bottle Found on the Beach at Carmel (Connell) **4**:108-10; **6**:116; **45**:109-11
Notes from a Child of Paradise (Corn) **33**:119-21
"Notes from a Confession" (Birkerts) **116**:150
Notes from a Lady at a Dinner Party (Malamud) **8**:375
"Notes from a Nonexistent Himalayan Expedition" (Szymborska) **99**:199
"Notes From a Sububan Heart" (Van Duyn) **116**:424
"Notes from an Unfinished Novel" (Fowles) **87**:182
Notes from Isla Negra (Neruda)
See *Memorial de Isla Negra*
Notes from New York, and Other Poems (Tomlinson) **45**:403-04
"Notes From the Air" (Ashbery) **125**:37
"Notes from the Castle" (Moss) **45**:286, 289
Notes from the Castle (Moss) **45**:285-89, 292
Notes from the Century Before (Hoagland) **28**:180-81
"Notes from the Corner" (Bitov) **57**:114-15, 119
"Notes from the Delivery Room" (Pastan) **27**:368
"Notes from the Land of the Dead" (Kinsella) **4**:271; **19**:255-56; **138**:92-94, 114, 128, 136, 156
Notes from the Land of the Dead, and Other Poems (Kinsella) **4**:271; **19**:252-54, 257; **138**:88-90, 92, 94, 97, 99, 101-03, 105-06, 109, 112-13, 119-21, 131, 134, 142, 146, 148, 150-51, 158
"Notes Inspired by The Sleepwalkers" (Kundera) **115**:321
"Notes Made in the Piazzo San Marco" (Swenson) **61**:395
"Notes Mainly at the Clinic" (Abse) **29**:21
Notes of a Baden Patient (Hesse) **2**:190
Notes of a Dirty Old Man (Bukowski) **9**:138; **41**:74; **108**:80, 83
"Notes of a Native Son" (Baldwin) **1**:13, 15; **2**:31-3; **3**:32; **4**:41-2; **5**:41-2; **8**:41; **13**:52; **15**:43; **17**:21-4, 26, 28, 31, 38, 43; **42**:14, 15-6, 18; **50**:282, 291, 296
Notes of a Native Son (Baldwin) **90**:5, 10, 13; **127**:108, 114, 127, 140, 145
Notes of a Night Watchman (Zinoviev) **19**:488
"Notes of a Potential Suicide" (Bukowski) **41**:68
"Notes of a Submariner" (Szirtes) **46**:396
Notes of an Alchemist (Eiseley) **7**:91
Notes of the Author (Kosinski) **53**:221
Notes of Woe (Tate) **25**:427
"Notes on a Native Son" (Cleaver) **30**:54
Notes on a Poetry of Release (Graham) **29**:192
"Notes on a Possible Legend" (Wiebe) **138**:338
Notes on an Endangered Species and Others (Richler) **5**:378
"Notes on Camp" (Sontag) **105**:215-19, 226
"Notes on Class" (Fussell) **74**:125
"Notes on Dangerous Game" (Hemingway) **34**:478
"Notes on Poetics regarding Olson's 'Maximus'" (Duncan) **15**:189
"Notes on Poetry and History" (Simic) **130**:330
"Notes on Pornography" (Vidal) **142**:276, 278-80, 329, 334
"Notes on the Decline of Outrage" (Dickey) **7**:86; **109**:239
"Notes on the English" (Forster) **77**:227
"Notes on the Language of Aeschylus" (Warner) **45**:434, 439
"Notes on the Reality of the Self" (Graham) **118**:255-56, 261
"Notes on the Responsibility and the Teaching of Creative Writing" (Smith) **42**:356
"Notes on the Road: The SS. Formosa" (Cendrars) **106**:158
"Notes on the Wasteland" (Eliot) **113**:210-11
"Notes on the Writing of Horror: A Story" (Ligotti) **44**:54-5
"Notes on Thought and Vision" (H. D.) **73**:139
Notes on Translating Shakespearean Tragedies (Pasternak) **63**:291
"Notes on Writing a Novel" (Bowen) **15**:78
"Notes Toward a Dreampolitik" (Didion) **129**:80
"Notes toward a Nature Poem" (Ghose) **42**:185
"Notes toward a Poem That Can Never Be Written" (Atwood) **25**:65, 68; **84**:69; **135**:10
"Notes toward an Understanding of My Father's Novel" (Durban) **39**:44, 46
"Notes toward Finding the Right Question" (Ozick) **155**:180
"Notes Toward Home" (Jordan) **114**:146
Notes towards an Aesthetic (Baxter) **14**:62
Notes towards the Definition of Culture (Eliot) **2**:126, 128; **6**:165; **24**:177, 184; **41**:157-59, 162
Nothing (Green) **2**:178; **13**:252-54; **97**:245, 248, 250, 254, 257, 266, 276, 279, 283, 290-91, 293
"Nothing: A Preliminary Account" (Barthelme) **46**:36; **115**:71, 76, 98
Nothing, and So Be It (Fallaci)
See *Niente e cosi*
"Nothing Began as It Is" (Merwin) **18**:334
Nothing But Blue Skies (McGuane) **127**:245, 276-77, 279-85, 287-88, 290-91, 293
"Nothing but Color" (Ai) **14**:8; **69**:5-6, 11
Nothing but Light (Pack) **13**:438-39
Nothing but Love (Seifert)
See *Samá láska*
"Nothing but Poking" (Redgrove) **41**:348
Nothing Can Go Wrong (MacDonald) **44**:408
Nothing Can Rescue Me (Daly) **52**:88
"Nothing Down" (Dove) **50**:153, 157; **81**:139
"Nothing Ever Breaks Except the Heart" (Boyle) **58**:70-1
Nothing Ever Breaks Except the Heart (Boyle) **5**:67; **58**:70-1
"Nothing Ever Happens on the Moon" (Heinlein) **26**:175
Nothing for Anyone (Reading) **47**:350
Nothing Happens in Carmincross (Kiely) **43**:240-46
"Nothing in Heaven Functions As It Ought" (Kennedy) **42**:255-56
"Nothing in Prospero's Cloak" (Rozewicz)
See "Nic w plaszczu Prospera"
"Nothing Is Everything" (Townshend) **17**:528
"Nothing Is True" (Carroll) **143**:44
"Nothing Lasts a Hundred Years" (Rodriguez) **155**:299
Nothing Like It in the World: The Man Who Built the Transcontinental Railroad, 1863-1869 (Ambrose) **145**:57-9
Nothing Like the Sun: A Story of Shakespeare's Love-Life (Burgess) **2**:86; **4**:80, 84; **5**:86; **8**:112; **10**:89-90; **22**:70-1, 78; **40**:114, 116, 122, 126; **81**:313; **94**:41
"Nothing Makes Sense" (Giovanni) **117**:201
The Nothing Man (Thompson) **69**:379, 382, 385-86, 389
Nothing Missing but the Samovar (Lively) **32**:273
Nothing More than Murder (Thompson) **69**:379, 383, 387
Nothing More to Declare (Holmes) **56**:138-41
Nothing New under the Sun (Bacchelli) **19**:31-2
Nothing, Nobody (Poniatowska)
See *Nada, nadie: La voces del temblor*
"Nothing Now Astonishes" (Graves) **45**:173
Nothing or Nothing (Konwicki)
See *Nic albo nic*
Nothing Personal (Baldwin) **17**:28; **42**:18
Nothing Sacred (Carter) **41**:119; **76**:327, 329
Nothing Sacred (Walker) **61**:430-31, 433
Nothing to be Desired (McGuane) **127**:286
"Nothing to Be Said" (Larkin) **64**:271
"Nothing to Fear" (Amis) **2**:6
"Nothing to Say" (Davies) **21**:91
"Nothing Twice" (Szymborska) **99**:204, 207
"Notice" (Lowell) **11**:330
"Notice of Loss" (Enzensberger) **43**:151
"Notice the Convulsed Orange Inch of Moon" (Cummings) **68**:30
"Noţiunile" (Arghezi) **80**:11
Not-Knowing: The Essays and Interviews of Donald Barthelme (Barthelme) **115**:99
Notorious (Hitchcock) **16**:342, 345-46, 348, 359
"Notre Dame de Chartres" (Meredith) **4**:348
Notre dame des fleurs (Genet) **1**:115-17; **2**:157; **5**:137-38; **10**:225; **44**:386-90; **46**:168-76, 180, 182
"Notre hublot" (Chedid) **47**:87
Notre pain quotidien (Cendrars) **18**:96; **106**:173
"Notre petit continent" (Arp) **5**:34
La notte (Antonioni) **20**:19, 22, 26, 31; **144**:7-8, 11-16, 19, 27, 34, 36, 39, 41-42, 46, 48, 52, 54, 56-57, 59, 63, 67, 71, 73, 80-81, 84, 91-93, 95, 97
"La notte brava" (Pasolini) **37**:347
Le notti bianche (Visconti) **16**:563, 565
Le notti di Cabiria (Fellini) **16**:271, 273, 274, 292; **85**:59-60, 62, 74-6, 78-9
Le notti difficili (Buzzati) **36**:90
"Notting Hill" (D'Aguiar) **145**:119
Nottingham Lace (Forster) **22**:136-37; **45**:131
"Notwendiges Streitgespräch" (Wolf) **150**:248, 285
"Nouns" (Wright) **6**:580
Nourish the Beast (Tesich)
See *Baba Goya*
"Nourishments of Love" (Kunene) **85**:175
A nous la liberté (Clair) **20**:59-62, 70
Nous n'irons plus au bois (Crommelynck) **75**:152
"Nous tombons" (Char) **14**:128
Le nouveau locataire (Ionesco) **4**:251; **6**:248; **9**:286, 288; **41**:231; **86**:332, 340
Un Nouveau Patron pour l'Aviation (Cendrars) **106**:172
Nouveau recueil (Ponge) **18**:414
"nouvelle bonte" (Césaire) **112**:31
La nouvelle origine (Audiberti) **38**:21
La nouvelle somme de poèsie du monde noir (Damas) **84**:175, 180
Les nouvelles noces (Jouve) **47**:210
Nouvelles orientales (Yourcenar) **38**:462-64; **50**:363-64; **87**:401-02
Nouvelles pièces noires (Anouilh) **13**:19-20
"Nova" (Johnson) **7**:415
Nova (Delany) **8**:168; **14**:146-47; **38**:150-51, 153-57, 160-62; **141**:153
Nova Express (Burroughs) **2**:91-3; **5**:92; **15**:108, 110; **22**:83; **42**:71, 73, 77, 79; **75**:93, 96-8, 102, 106, 108, 111; **109**:183, 186, 195-96, 207, 209, 212, 229
"Nova Scotia Chronolog Number Three and Number Five" (Dunn) **36**:153
"The Novel" (Rich) **73**:332
The Novel (Michener) **109**:383
"The Novel and Communication" (Lodge) **141**:375
"The Novel and Europe" (Kundera)
See "The Depreciated Legacy of Cervantes"
The Novel and Our Time (Comfort) **7**:53
"The Novel and the Nation in South Africa" (Gordimer) **70**:163
"The Novel as Form" (Faulkner) **3**:156
"The Novel as History" (Mathews) **52**:312-13, 315
The Novel as Research (Butor) **8**:120

"The Novel as Spectacle" (Calvino) **73**:48
The Novel in the Third World (Larson) **31**:240-41
"The Novel Now" (Lodge) **141**:350
The Novel Now: A Guide to Contemporary Fiction (Burgess) **4**:82; **8**:112; **62**:131; **94**:33, 76
"The Novel of Manners Today" (Auchincloss) **45**:28
The Novel of the Future (Nin) **1**:248; **4**:379; **14**:384, 386; **60**:271; **127**:361, 363, 371, 397
Novel on Yellow Paper; or, Work It Out for Yourself (Smith) **25**:416, 422-23; **44**:432-35, 437-39, 443-45
"Novel, Screenplay, Stage Play" (Lodge) **141**:375
"Novel, Tale, and Romance" (McCarthy) **39**:485, 490
"The Novel Today" (Coetzee) **117**:65, 90, 93
Novela de entregas mensuales (Esquivel) **141**:176
Novela negra con arentinos (Valenzuela) **104**:379-82, 384-85, 389, 392-98
Novelario de donga novais (Dourado) **23**:151
A Novelette, and Other Prose (Williams) **2**:468-69
The Novelist (Fast) **131**:101-2
"The Novelist and His Characters" (Mauriac) **56**:211
The Novelist and the Narrator (Wilson) **34**:580
"Novelist as Teacher" (Achebe) **152**:43
The Novelist at the Crossroads (Lodge) **36**:270
Novelist before the World (Gironella)
See *El novelista ante del mundo*
"The Novelist, Diagnostician of the Contemporary Malaise" (Percy) **65**:261
"A Novelist to His Readers" (Green) **97**:293
"Novelist Today: Still at the Crossroads" (Lodge) **141**:373
El novelista ante del mundo (Gironella) **11**:234-35
"Novella" (Hass) **99**:143
The Novellas of Hortense Calisher (Calisher) **134**:41
Novelle del ducato in fiamme (Gadda) **11**:215
Novellen (Boell) **11**:55
"Novels and Children" (Barthes) **83**:95
The Novels of Dashiell Hammett (Hammett) **5**:161
"Novelty Booth" (Nowlan) **15**:399
"November" (Frost) **26**:128
"November" (Merwin) **18**:335
"November" (Smith) **25**:419
"November, 1889" (Howard) **7**:168
"November, 1961" (Smith) **64**:388
November and May (Szirtes) **46**:391-93, 395
"November Graveyard" (Plath) **111**:202
"November, l968" (Rich) **36**:366
"November: San Joaquin Valley" (Rose) **85**:314
"November through a Giant Copper Beech" (Honig) **33**:213
"November Walk near False Creek Mouth" (Birney) **6**:74, 76-7; **11**:51
"Novembers" (Peacock) **60**:293
Novembre (Simenon) **2**:398
"Novices" (Moore) **10**:350; **47**:260
"Noviembre" (Rodriguez) **10**:440
"Novilladas democráticas" (Murray) **40**:335
"Novotny's Pain" (Roth) **31**:335
"Novye stansy k Avguste" (Brodsky) **50**:125
"Now" (Barnard) **48**:26
"Now" (Jacobsen) **48**:198
"now" (Rozewicz)
See "teraz"
"Now" (Sondheim) **30**:391, 402
Now about These Women (Bergman)
See *For att ente tala om alla dessa kvinnor*
Now and Another Time (Hearon) **63**:159-60
Now and at the Hour (Cormier) **12**:133
Now and In Other Days (Amichai)
See *Akhshav Uveyamim*
Now and on Earth (Thompson) **69**:380, 383
"Now and Then" (Fuller) **62**:185
Now and Then: Poems, 1976-1978 (Warren) **13**:581; **18**:534-38; **39**:257-58, 260, 265, 270; **59**:296
Now Don't Try to Reason with Me (Booth) **23**:89, 99
Now Dowager (Bermant) **40**:92-3
"Now Full of Silences" (Pack) **13**:438
"Now I Am Married" (Gordon) **128**:110, 117-18
"Now I Become Myself" (Sarton) **91**:253
"Now I Come before You" (Cohen) **38**:137
"Now I Lay Me" (Hemingway) **8**:283; **10**:269; **13**:270; **30**:183, 187, 192, 196-97, 200
"now I love somebody more than" (Shange) **25**:402
"Now I'm a Farmer" (Townshend) **17**:534
Now Is Not Too Late (Holland) **21**:154
"Now Is the Air Made of Chiming Bells" (Eberhart) **19**:143; **56**:86
"Now Is the Time" (Himes) **7**:159
Now Is the Time for All Good Men (Cryer) **21**:77-9
Now Playing at Canterbury (Bourjaily) **8**:103-04; **62**:101-04
Now Sheba Sings the Song (Angelou) **64**:38; **77**:22, 32
"Now That April's Here" (Callaghan) **65**:250
Now That April's Here, and Other Stories (Callaghan) **14**:100
"Now That I Am Forever a Child" (Lorde) **71**:251
"Now That Men Can Cry..." (Sheed) **53**:336
"Now That My Father Lies Down beside Me" (Plumly) **33**:313
Now That the Buffalo's Gone (Sainte-Marie) **17**:431-32
"Now the Sidewise Easing into Night" (Plumly) **33**:310
"Now the Sky" (Van Doren) **10**:496
"Now the Sturdy Wind" (Graham) **48**:145
Now They Sing Again (Frisch)
See *Nun singen sie wieder*
Now They've Started Singing Again (Frisch)
See *Nun singen sie wieder*
"Now This Cold Man" (Page) **7**:291; **18**:378
"Now, Us" (Sexton) **123**:408
Now Wait for Last Year (Dick) **30**:115-16; **72**:121
"Now Wakes the Sea" (Ballard) **137**:12-13
Now We Are Enemies (Fleming) **37**:118, 120
"Now We Know How Many Holes It Takes to Fill the Albert Hall" (Kesey) **46**:228
"Now When We Think of Compromise" (Mahapatra) **33**:276, 282
"Now You Have to Push" (Hughes) **119**:289
"nowa szkoła filozoficzna" (Rozewicz) **139**:246
"Nowadays Clancy Can't Even Sing" (Young)
See "Clancy"
The Nowaks (Isherwood) **11**:300; **14**:278
Nowhere (Berger) **38**:41-2
"Nowhere but Here" (Fisher) **87**:128
Nowhere but Light (Belitt) **22**:50, 52-3
The Nowhere City (Lurie) **4**:305-07; **5**:259-60; **18**:310; **39**:182-83
The Nowhere Man (Markandaya) **8**:377; **38**:324
"No-Winter Country" (Lewis) **41**:255
Nowy swiat i okolice (Konwicki) **117**:276-77, 279, 281, 286, 289-90
Les noyers de l'Altenburg (Malraux) **1**:202; **4**:325-26, 328-29, 333, 336; **9**:355, 358-59; **13**:366-67, 369; **15**:352-54; **57**:302, 306, 308-09, 321
Le nozze di Cadmo e Armonia (Calasso) **81**:39-52
NP (Yoshimoto) **84**:430-31
N'Tsuk (Theriault) **79**:416
N.U.: Nettezza urbana (Antonioni) **20**:28; **144**:45, 68, 77
"Le nu parmi les cercueils" (Mandiargues) **41**:274
Le nu perdu, 1964-1970 (Char) **55**:288
"Le nu provençal" (Middleton) **13**:388
Le nuage rouge (Bonnefoy) **58**:56-7, 60
"Nube feliz" (Aleixandre) **9**:14
"Las nubes" (Azorín) **11**:25
Las nubes (Cernuda) **54**:42, 46, 53, 58, 60-1
"Nuchal (fragment)" (Kinsella) **138**:101-02
The Nuclear Age (O'Brien) **40**:345-48; **103**:132, 134-37, 143, 166
"Nuclear Umbrella" (Padilla) **38**:352
"Nude Descending" (Ostriker) **132**:326
Nude Descending a Staircase (Kennedy) **42**:254-55
"Nude Pictures" (Komunyakaa) **94**:231
The Nude Restaurant (Warhol) **20**:419, 422-23
"Nude Resting" (Dobyns) **37**:81
"The Nude Swim" (Sexton) **123**:409, 440, 450
Nude with Violin (Coward) **29**:136, 139
"Nude Women" (Asturias) **8**:25
Nuestra Natacha (Casona) **49**:40-5
"Nuestras imposibilidades" (Borges) **48**:45, 47; **83**:162
La nueva narrativa hispanoamericana (Fuentes)
See *La nueva novela hispanoamericana*
La nueva novela hispanoamericana (Fuentes) **10**:208
"Nueva refutación del tiempo" (Borges) **19**:55-6; **83**:160, 161-62, 178
Nuevas andanzas y desventuras de Lazarillo de Tormes (Cela) **4**:96; **59**:126, 135, 142; **122**:21-2, 53, 63
Nuevos sermones (Parra) **102**:356
La nuit (Ferron) **94**:106, 108, 110, 117-18, 124-26
La nuit (Wiesel) **3**:526-30; **5**:491; **11**:570; **37**:452
La nuit américaine (Truffaut) **20**:393, 396-97, 400, 406; **101**:379-80, 382-86, 396, 400, 407, 409-13
"Nuit blanche" (Damas) **84**:177-78, 183
"La nuit Catalane" (Morand) **41**:297, 308
Une nuit dans la fôret (Cendrars) **18**:96; **106**:166
La nuit de la Saint-Jean (Duhamel) **8**:189
"La nuit de seis jours" (Morand) **41**:297, 308
"Nuit de Sine" (Senghor) **54**:390; **130**:236, 275, 281
La nuit d'orage (Duhamel) **8**:187-88
La nuit du carrefour (Renoir) **20**:309-10
La nuit du décret (del Castillo) **38**:168-69
Nuit et brouilland (Resnais) **16**:502-03, 506, 512
"La nuit Hongroise" (Morand) **41**:296-97, 308
La nuit remue (Michaux) **8**:392; **19**:315
"La nuit Romaine" (Morand) **41**:297, 308
La nuit talismanique (Char) **14**:128; **55**:287-88
"La nuit Turque" (Morand) **41**:296-97, 307-08
"La nuit viennoise" (Lang) **103**:87
Les nuits de l'underground (Blais) **22**:59-60
Nuits sans nuit et quelques jours sans jour (Leiris) **61**:347, 360-61
Nuket (Haavikko) **34**:169-170, 173
"Nul ne se rappelle avoir vu" (Damas) **84**:180
"Null Class" (Young) **82**:396, 412
"Nullipara" (Olds) **85**:308
"Num bar da Calle Sierpes, Sevilha" (Cabral de Melo Neto) **76**:169
"Numa" (Benet) **28**:23
"# 5" (Alegria) **57**:10
"8. Normal" (Ostriker) **132**:326
"No. 80" (Amichai) **116**:98-9
"No. 52" (Amichai) **116**:97
"Number Four" (Major) **19**:297
"No. 14" (Amichai) **116**:95
"Number Man" (Sandburg) **15**:466
"Number Nine Dream" (Lennon) **35**:268, 270-71
The Number of the Beast (Heinlein) **26**:174-75; **55**:303
The Number of the Beast (Wilson) **33**:465
"No. 1" (Amichai) **116**:97

Number One (Dos Passos) **11**:156; **15**:183, 187; **34**:420
"Number One Rip-Off Man" (Cliff) **21**:63
"1. The Bridge" (Ostriker) **132**:326
"1. the supremes--cuz they dead" (Sanchez) **116**:294
"No. 74" (Amichai) **116**:97
"12. Epilogue: Nevertheless" (Ostriker) **132**:326
"No. 21" (Amichai) **116**:96
"No. 23" (Amichai) **116**:95
"No. 2" (Amichai) **116**:98
The Numbered (Canetti)
See *Die Befristeten*
"Numbered Apartment" (Merwin) **45**:274
"Numbers" (Creeley) **36**:121
"Numbers" (Hughes) **35**:222
"Numbers" (Sachs)
See "Zahlen"
"Numbers" (Weller) **26**:444
Numbers (Creeley) **2**:106; **78**:144
Numbers (Rechy) **7**:357; **18**:442; **107**:223-26, 228, 230, 238, 243, 254, 256, 258
"Numbers: 63" (Orlovitz) **22**:334-35
Numbers: A Further Autobiography (Lind) **2**:245; **4**:293
"Le numéro barbette" (Cocteau) **8**:148-49
Numero deux (Godard) **20**:153, 155
"The Nun at Court" (Blunden) **56**:48
"Nun, Geometry, Grief" (Lerman) **9**:330
"Nun, Ja! Das näschte Leben geht aber heute an. Ein Brief über die Bettine" (Wolf) **150**:328
"A Nun No More" (Fante) **60**:133
Nun singen sie wieder (Frisch) **9**:217; **14**:181-82; **32**:190; **44**:185, 194-96, 199, 204
"The Nun Who Returned to Ireland" (Carrier)
See "La religieuse qui retourna en Irlande"
"Nunc dimittis" (Brodsky) **4**:78; **36**:76, 79
"Nunc Dimittis" (Dahl) **79**:175, 178, 180
"Nunc Dimittis" (Lee) **46**:234
Nunca llegarás a nada (Benet) **28**:23-4
"Nuncle" (Wain) **46**:411
Nuncle and Other Stories (Wain) **46**:411
Nuni (Griffin) **68**:196-201
Nunquam (Durrell) **6**:153; **8**:193; **13**:185; **41**:136-37
Nuns and Soldiers (Murdoch) **22**:328-31; **31**:289, 291, 294
"A Nun's Mother" (Lavin) **99**:316
Nuorena nukkunit (Sillanpaa) **19**:420
La nuova gioventù (Pasolini) **106**:265, 267
Nuovi strani amici (Buzzati) **36**:84
Il nuovo questore (Buzzati) **36**:84
"Nuptial Hymn" (McAuley) **45**:254
"The Nuptial Torches" (Harrison) **129**:217
Nuptials (Camus)
See *Noces*
"Nur auf Sardinien" (Lenz) **27**:245
"Nuremburg" (Slessor) **14**:492
"Nurse Cora" (Cortázar) **3**:115
"Nurse Sharks" (Matthews) **40**:320
"The Nurselog" (Purdy) **50**:247
"Nursery Rhyme" (Simic) **130**:296
"A Nursery Tale" (Nabokov) **6**:357
"Nursie" (Kinsella) **43**:253, 255
The Nursing-Home Murder (Marsh) **53**:250
The Nutmeg of Consolation (O'Brian) **152**:259, 297, 300
La nuvola di smog (Calvino) **5**:98, 100; **11**:91, 92; **33**:100; **39**:315; **73**:42
"N.Y. Telephone Conversation" (Reed) **21**:305
"Nyassa" (Jeffers) **54**:234
Nyatt School (Gray) **49**:146-47; **112**:108
The Nylon Curtain (Joel) **26**:222-23
"N'yu-yorkskaya ptitsa" (Voznesensky) **57**:416
"O" (Merrill) **8**:386-87
"O" (Nowlan) **15**:398
"O" (Voznesensky) **57**:426-29
O Albany!: An Urban Tapestry (Kennedy) **53**:190-92, 194
O ano da morte de Ricardo Reis (Saramago) **119**:149, 154, 156-57, 162-64, 166, 168-70, 172
O Babylon (Walcott) **25**:454; **76**:275
O Beulah Land (Settle) **19**:408-09; **61**:372-74, 376, 381-87
"O Canada" (Richler) **46**:352
O Canada (Wilson) **2**:475
"O Cities, through Which the Armies Marched" (Haavikko) **34**:175
"O City of Broken Dreams" (Cheever) **64**:65
"The O. D. and Hepatitis Railroad or Bust" (Boyle) **90**:49
"O Daedalus, Fly Away Home" (Hayden) **5**:168
"O die Schornsteine" (Sachs) **98**:334, 348, 352, 355, 362
O Dreamland (Anderson) **20**:11, 17
"O Dreams, O Destinations" (Day Lewis) **10**:131
"O Earth, Turn!" (Johnston) **51**:251
O Evangelho segundo Jesus Cristo (Saramago) **119**:157-58, 165, 168-70, 175
"O Fat White Woman" (Trevor) **71**:337; **116**:363
O Gato Malhado e a Andorinha Sinhá (Amado) **106**:73
O Genteel Lady! (Forbes) **12**:202
"O Gentle Queen of the Afternoon" (Graham) **29**:193
"O Happy Melodist" (Hood) **15**:284; **28**:188
"The O in Jose" (Aldiss) **40**:21
"O întîlnire de necrezut" (Arghezi) **80**:13
"O leaves" (Hughes) **119**:263, 268
"O Love, Sweet Animal" (Schwartz) **45**:356
O Lucky Man! (Anderson) **20**:16-18
"O Lull Me, Lull Me" (Roethke) **101**:274, 282, 335, 340
"O Lung Flowering Like a Tree" (Frame) **96**:200
"O ma martelée" (Char) **9**:162
"O Marcel...Otherwise/I Also Have Been to Louise's" (Loy) **28**:253
O Master Caliban (Gotlieb) **18**:193
"O me donzel" (Pasolini) **106**:228
O Mikrós naftilos (Elytis) **100**:175, 187
O Mistress Mine (Rattigan)
See *Love in Idleness*
"O My God" (Police, The) **26**:366
O Pays, mon beau peuple (Ousmane) **66**:334
O risco do bordado (Dourado) **60**:85, 93-4
"O Rome" (Kinsella) **138**:161
O saisons, o chateaux (Varda) **16**:556
O Shepherd, Speak (Sinclair) **63**:365
O sorriso do lagarto (Ribeiro) **67**:282
"O Taste and See" (Levertov) **66**:250
O Taste and See (Levertov) **2**:242; **5**:246, 249; **15**:336; **66**:235-39
"O the Chimneys" (Sachs)
See "O die Schornsteine"
O the Chimneys (Sachs) **14**:475-76; **98**:362
"O, Thou Opening, O" (Roethke) **101**:273-74, 281, 284
O to Be a Dragon (Moore) **8**:400; **13**:396
"O Ugly Bird!" (Wellman) **49**:395
"O Waters" (Snyder) **120**:351
O Westport in the Light of Asia Minor (Durcan) **43**:113
"O Wha's the Bride" (MacDiarmid) **11**:334
"O What Is That Sound Which So Thrills the Ear" (Auden) **11**:15-16
"O Who Will Speak from a Womb or a Cloud" (Barker) **48**:10
"O Ye Tongues" (Sexton) **53**:320, 322-23
O Ye Tongues (Sexton) **123**:404, 420-23
"O Yes" (Olsen) **114**:192, 194, 213, 220-21, 223
"O Youth and Beauty!" (Cheever) **7**:49-50; **64**:46, 48
The Oak and the Calf (Solzhenitsyn)
See *Bodalsia telenok s dubom*
The Oak and the Ram (Moorcock) **5**:294
Oak Leaves and Lavender; or, A World on Wallpaper (O'Casey) **5**:318; **11**:408-09; **88**:239
"Oak Tree at the Entrance to Blackwater Pond" (Oliver) **98**:280
"Oasis" (p'Bitek) **96**:286
The Oasis (McCarthy) **3**:326-27; **14**:363; **39**:488; **59**:289, 291-92
Oasis in Space (Cousteau) **30**:105
The Oath (Wiesel)
See *Le serment de Kolvillàg*
"Oaxaca" (Shields) **97**:431
Obakasan (Endō) **7**:96; **54**:152, 156, 157, 159; **99**:284-85, 287, 302
"Obalaji as drummer, Ras as Poet" (Baraka) **115**:12
Obasan (Kogawa) **78**:165-69, 177, 179, 181, 183, 185-87, 192, 194-95; **129**:274-75, 277-280, 282-84, 286-88, 290-92, 295, 297-301, 304-06, 308-16, 318-21
"Obatala" (Clark Bekedermo) **38**:126
"Obeah Win de War" (Bennett) **28**:29
The Obedient Wife (O'Faolain) **47**:326-29, 331; **108**:413
"The Obelisk" (Forster) **45**:143
"Oberfeldwebel Beckstadt" (Raine) **32**:350, 352
Oberflächenübersetzungen (Jandl) **34**:195
"Obit Page" (Blackburn) **43**:68
"Obits" (Busch) **47**:65
Obituaries (Saroyan) **29**:360-61
"Obituary" (Asimov) **76**:320
"Obituary" (McGrath) **28**:277
"Obituary for a Living Lady" (Brooks) **49**:22
"Obituary of a Democracy" (Gellhorn) **60**:196
"Obituary of a Gin Mill" (Mitchell) **98**:165, 178, 180, 184
"Obituary of R. Fuller" (Fuller) **28**:151, 158
"Object into Subject" (Cliff) **120**:94
"Object Lessons" (Boland) **113**:94
Object Lessons: The Life of the Woman and the Poet in Our Time (Boland) **113**:108-09, 112-16, 120-21, 125-27
The Object of My Affection (McCauley) **50**:62-5
"Object Trouvé: Piazza San Marco" (Fuller) **62**:203
Objections to Sex and Violence (Churchill) **31**:82-3
"The Objectivist Ethics" (Rand) **79**:387
An "Objectivists" Anthology (Zukofsky) **1**:385
"Objectivity and Liberal Scholarship" (Chomsky) **132**:36
"Objects at Brampton Ash" (Middleton) **13**:387
Objects of Affection (Bennett) **77**:93
"Oblique Prayers" (Levertov) **66**:245
Oblique Prayers (Levertov) **66**:237, 239-41, 250
The Oblivion Ha-Ha (Tate) **2**:431; **25**:430
Oblok Magellana (Lem) **40**:289-90; **149**:152, 260, 282
Obmen (Trifonov) **45**:408-10, 413, 415-17, 419-21, 423
"La obra" (Bioy Casares) **88**:94
Obra Completa (Cela) **122**:21, 28
Obra gruesa (Parra) **102**:353
Obra poética (Guillén) **48**:162
Obras completas (Aleixandre) **9**:12, 17
Obras completas (Borges) **2**:73; **9**:117; **44**:361
Obras completas (Neruda) **2**:309; **28**:310
The Obscene Bird of Night (Donoso)
See *El obsceno pájaro de la noche*
The Obscene Fable (Fo)
See *Il Fabulazzo Osceno*
Obscene Gestures for Women (Kauffman) **65**:347
Obscenities (Casey) **2**:100
El obsceno pájaro de la noche (Donoso) **4**:126-30; **8**:178-80; **11**:146-47, 149-52; **32**:153-55, 159-61; **99**:216, 218-20, 222-23, 231-32, 240-41, 249-51, 254-56, 258, 267, 269, 274
"The Obscure" (Dubie) **36**:130
An Obscure Man (Yourcenar) **87**:404
Obscured by Clouds (Pink Floyd) **35**:311

"Obscurity and Clarity in Poetry" (Neruda) **5**:302
"The Obscurity of the Poet" (Jarrell) **9**:298
"Obsequies" (Longley) **29**:296-97
"Observance" (Berry) **46**:69
"Observation Car" (Hope) **51**:213, 216-17
Observations (Kissinger) **137**:219
Observations (Moore) **1**:228; **4**:363; **13**:393; **19**:337, 342
"Observations on the Uses of Autobiography in Fiction" (Stafford) **68**:441
"The Observer" (Rich) **36**:372
"Obsession" (Damas) **84**:173
"Obsession" (Montague) **46**:267-68
"Obsession" (Phillips) **28**:362
Obsession (Campbell) **42**:91-2
The Obsession (Levin) **7**:204-06
Obsession (De Palma) **20**:76-8
"Obsidian Butterfly" (Paz)
See "Mariposa de obsidiana"
Obsluhoval jsem anglického krále (Hrabal) **67**:114, 116, 120-26, 128-52
"Obsolescence" (Ciardi) **44**:383
"Obsolete Youth" (Bettelheim) **79**:126
"Obstacles" (Frame) **96**:189
Obstinate Cymric (Powys) **125**:293
"An Obstinate Exile" (Lee) **90**:203
"The Obvious" (Laing) **95**:141, 146
Obyknovenny chelovek (Leonov) **92**:246, 250-51, 260, 270, 277
Ocalenie (Milosz) **11**:377; **56**:236-37, 245; **82**:289
"Ocalony" (Rozewicz) **23**:363; **139**:235-36, 246, 272-73, 288
Occasion for Loving (Gordimer) **7**:132; **18**:186; **33**:183; **70**:161-62, 164; **123**:137, 139-40
Occasion of Sin (Billington) **43**:57-8
Occasional Prose (McCarthy) **39**:484-91
"The Occasional Room" (Loewinsohn) **52**:283
Le occasioni (Montale) **7**:222-24, 228, 230-32; **18**:340
"The Occasions" (Thesen) **56**:423
The Occasions (Montale)
See *Le occasioni*
The Occasions of Poetry (Gunn) **32**:210, 212-14
Occidental Mythology (Campbell)
See *The Masks of God: Occidental Mythology*
The Occult: A History (Wilson) **3**:538; **14**:583
"Occupant" (Summers) **10**:494
Occupant Please Forward (Summers) **10**:494
"The Occupation" (Abse) **29**:14
The Occupation (Caute) **29**:114-16, 122
Occupations (Griffiths) **13**:256; **52**:171-72, 174, 178, 180-82, 185
"The Ocean" (Cheever) **3**:107; **7**:49
"The Ocean" (Grace) **56**:112
"The Ocean" (Mason) **82**:240, 254; **154**:231, 272, 322
"Ocean 1212-W" (Plath) **62**:410; **111**:159, 209
"Ocean Avenue" (Chabon) **149**:3-6
"Ocean Girl" (Young) **17**:576
Ocean of Night (Ali) **69**:23
Ocean of Story (Stead) **80**:341-42
"Ocean of Words" (Jin) **109**:54
Ocean of Words (Jin) **109**:53-4
"Ocean Poem" (Moure) **88**:224
"Ocean Springs" (Gilchrist) **143**:309
The Ocean World of Jacques Cousteau (Cousteau) **30**:105-07, 109
Oceanography Lab (Berger) **12**:39
Ocean's Eleven (Soderbergh) **154**:356
"Ocean's Love to Ireland" (Heaney) **25**:245; **74**:157, 162
The Ocean's Musical March (Ritsos) **31**:324
L'océantume (Ducharme) **74**:57, 59-61, 68
Ocena mozliwooeci zbudowaniaetyki chrzeoecijańskiej przy zakozeniach systemu Maksa Schelera (John Paul II) **128**:192
Ochii Maicii Domnului (Arghezi) **80**:6
Ocnos (Cernuda) **54**:42, 53
Octaedro (Cortázar) **13**:164; **33**:124; **34**:333
Octagon Magic (Norton) **12**:458, 471
Octavian Shooting Targets (Gregor) **9**:253, 256
"October" (Johnston) **51**:248
"October" (Lane) **25**:284
"October" (Sassoon) **130**:176
"October" (Swenson) **61**:395, 397-98, 402; **106**:322
October 1916 (Solzhenitsyn)
See *Oktyabr' shestnadtsatogo*
"October, 1940" (Fuller) **28**:158
"October 1950" (Muldoon) **32**:319-20; **72**:265
"October Arriving" (Simic) **49**:343
"October at the Window" (Ashbery) **77**:66
October Blood (Gray) **153**:134-38, 140-41, 143-45, 149
The October Circle (Littell) **42**:275-76
"October Comes" (Blunden) **56**:30, 45
The October Country (Bradbury) **42**:46
"October Dawn" (Hughes) **9**:280-81
"October Frost" (Bly) **128**:15
"October Fugue" (Shapcott) **38**:402
"The October Game" (Bradbury) **42**:35
"October Ghosts" (Wright) **28**:466
"October in the Railroad Earth" (Kerouac) **61**:296, 309, 313
October Light (Gardner) **8**:233-38; **10**:220; **18**:183; **28**:162-63, 165, 167; **34**:550
"October Picnic Long Ago" (Warren) **39**:272
"October Prayer" (Pack) **13**:340
"An October Salmon" (Hughes) **37**:177, 179-81
"October Snow" (Johnston) **51**:253
"October Spring" (Appleman) **51**:14
October Wind: A Novel of Christopher Columbus (Wiggs) **70**:332, 349
"Octogenarians Die in Crash" (Leyner) **92**:281
"An Octopus" (Moore) **10**:348; **47**:260
The Octopus (Wurlitzer)
See *Nog*
"Oda a la pobreza" (Neruda) **9**:397
"Oda a las Américas" (Neruda) **9**:396-97
"Oda al átomo" (Neruda) **9**:397
"Oda al caldillo de congrio" (Neruda) **9**:397
"Odalisque" (Padilla) **38**:351
Odas elementales (Neruda) **5**:301, 303; **7**:259; **9**:396; **28**:307, 310-11, 313; **62**:333
"Odd" (Abse) **7**:1; **29**:16-17
The Odd Couple (Simon) **6**:503, 506; **31**:393, 396-98, 400, 403; **70**:235, 237-38, 240-41
Odd Girl Out (Howard) **7**:164
"An Odd Job" (Oe) **36**:346; **86**:226-27, 236
"Odd Jobs" (Cameron) **44**:33
Odd Jobs (Updike) **139**:362-63
Odd Number (Sorrentino) **40**:390-91
Odd Obsession (Ichikawa) **20**:177
The Odd Woman (Godwin) **5**:142-43; **8**:247-48; **22**:180-83; **31**:195-96, 198; **69**:232, 237-39, 243-46; **125**:117-18, 121-23, 128-29, 135, 137-38, 146-51, 158, 165, 167-70
"Oddball" (Aksyonov) **101**:11, 17
"Oddjob, a Bull Terrier" (Walcott) **14**:549
"The Odds" (Salinas) **90**:332
Odds Against (Francis) **2**:143; **22**:151; **42**:148-50, 153-54, 156; **102**:127, 146, 156-57, 162
Odds and Ends (Enzensberger)
See *Einzelheiten*
Odds and Sods (Townshend) **17**:534
"Odds: Roughs for Theatre and Radio" (Beckett) **9**:84; **14**:74
"Ode" (Kennedy) **42**:255
"Ode" (MacNeice) **10**:325
"Ode" (Prokosch) **48**:306, 309-10
"Ode" (Simic) **130**:296
Ode (Jouve) **47**:206
"Ode 32" (Bunting) **47**:45
"Ode 34" (Bunting) **47**:45
Ode à Charles Fourier (Breton) **9**:128
"Ode at the Spring Equinox" (Watkins) **43**:443
"Ode auf N" (Jandl) **34**:198
"Ode for James Downey" (Johnston) **51**:249
"Ode for the American Dead in Asia" (McGrath) **59**:181
"Ode on a Common Fountain" (Wieners) **7**:535
"Ode on Causality" (O'Hara) **13**:430
"Ode, on Contemplating Clapham Junction" (Middleton) **13**:387
"Ode on Human Destinies" (Jeffers) **54**:235
"An Ode on Nativity" (Olson) **29**:334
"Ode: On the Death of William Butler Yeats" (Smith) **15**:517
"Ode pour l'élection de son sépulchre" (Pound) **10**:405
"Ode: The Eumenides" (Smith) **15**:516
"The Ode to a Chinese Paper Snake" (Eberhart) **56**:82-3
"Ode to a Koala Bear" (McCartney) **35**:292
"Ode to a Model" (Nabokov) **8**:407
"Ode to a Paperclip" (Dunn) **40**:169
"Ode to Afternoon" (Porter) **33**:324
"Ode to an Absconding Bookie" (Algren) **33**:15
"Ode to Bill" (Ashbery) **15**:28
"Ode to Bread" (Neruda) **28**:307
"Ode to Curiosity" (Codrescu) **121**:161
"Ode to Duplicitous Men" (Holmes) **56**:145
"Ode to Ennui" (Dos Passos) **25**:143
"Ode to Failure" (Ginsberg) **36**:198
"Ode to Healing" (Updike) **43**:436
"Ode to Joy" (O'Hara) **13**:430
"Ode to Laryngitis" (Codrescu) **121**:161
"Ode to Lenin" (Neruda) **2**:309
"Ode to Man" (Arghezi)
See "Cînatre omului"
"Ode to Michael Goldberg's Birth and Other Births" (O'Hara) **5**:324
"Ode to Our Young Pro-Consuls of the Air" (Tate) **14**:533
"Ode to Picasso" (Elytis) **100**:173
"Ode to Rot" (Updike) **43**:436
"Ode to Stalin on His Seventieth Birthday" (Faludy) **42**:138
"Ode to Suburbia" (Boland) **67**:43; **113**:96, 122
"Ode to Terminus" (Auden) **43**:28
"Ode to the Bath" (McGinley) **14**:366
"Ode to the Brown Paper Bag" (Galvin) **38**:198
"Ode to the Confederate Dead" (Tate) **2**:427, 429-30; **4**:535, 539; **6**:527; **9**:523; **11**:522, 524, 527; **14**:528, 530
"Ode to the Runaway Caves" (Lieberman) **36**:262, 264-65
"Ode to the Spectral Thief, Alpha" (Dubie) **36**:139
"Ode to Willem de Kooning" (O'Hara) **5**:324
Odejście Głodomora (Rozewicz) **139**:231, 249, 265, 267, 293
"Odes" (Senghor) **54**:391
The Odes of John Keats (Vendler) **138**:251, 253, 265
Odes to Simple Things (Neruda)
See *Odas elementales*
The Odessa File (Forsyth) **2**:136-37; **36**:175
Odin den' Ivana Denisovicha (Solzhenitsyn) **1**:319-20; **2**:407-08, 410, 412; **4**:506-07, 511, 513-15; **7**:432, 436, 440, 444-45, 447; **10**:481; **18**:496; **24**:414-16, 418-23; **34**:481-82, 484-85, 489, 491; **78**:381, 389, 394, 408-09, 411, 416, 418; **134**:259-321
Odlévání zvonů (Seifert) **34**:257; **44**:422; **93**:310, 317, 324, 329, 332, 343
"Odnazhdy, pokanuvshis' na kraiu" (Akhmadulina) **53**:13
Ododo (Walker) **19**:454
"An Odor of Verbena" (Faulkner) **52**:132
"Odora Canum Vis" (Lewis) **124**:213
"Odour of Eucalyptus" (Wilding) **73**:398
An Odour of Sanctity (Yerby) **22**:488
ODTAA (Masefield) **11**:358
"Odysseus" (Merwin) **13**:384; **18**:333
"Odysseus at Rush Hour" (Dunn) **36**:155
Odysseus Elytis: Selected Poems (Elytis) **100**:192
"Odysseus on Hermes" (Gunn) **81**:182, 186
"Odysseus Speaking" (Barnard) **48**:27
"Odysseus to Telemachus" (Brodsky) **36**:76
"Odyssey" (Elytis) **100**:175, 187-88

"Odyssey" (Honig) **33**:211
The Odyssey (Walcott) **76**:297
"The Odyssey of a Manuscript" (Tolson) **105**:239
"The Odyssey of a Wop" (Fante) **60**:133
"Odyssey of Big Boy" (Brown) **23**:96; **59**:266
Odyssey of Courage: The Story of Alvar Nuñez Cabeza de Vaca (Wojciechowska) **26**:450-52
"Odyssey of Rancor" (Cioran) **64**:98
Ōe Kenzaburo dojidai ronshu (Oe) **86**:228-29
"Oeconomic divina" (Milosz) **11**:381
"Oedipus at Colonus" (Forster) **3**:162
"Oedipus Complex" (Durrell) **27**:97
Oedipus Rex (Cocteau) **8**:147; **43**:109, 111
Oedipus Rex (Pasolini)
See *Edipo Re*
Oedipus the King (Cocteau)
See *Oedipus Rex*
L'oeil du malin (Chabrol) **16**:169
L'oeuvre au noir (Yourcenar) **19**:482-84; **38**:454-60, 464-65; **50**:361, 363-65; **87**:386, 395-97, 399, 412, 433
Oeuvre de chair (Theriault) **79**:412-13
Oeuvres complètes (Bataille) **29**:41-2
Oeuvres complètes (Breton) **54**:32
Oeuvres complètes (Char) **55**:288
Oeuvres complètes (Genet) **44**:387
Oeuvres complètes (Green) **77**:279-81, 284-85
Oeuvres complètes, Volume I: 1912-1924 (Tzara) **47**:391, 393
Oeuvres complètes, Volume II: 1925-1933 (Tzara) **47**:391, 393
Of a Fire on the Moon (Mailer) **1**:192-93; **2**:262-63; **3**:318; **4**:323; **8**:369-71, 373; **11**:344; **14**:350; **74**:205, 225; **111**:103, 133
"Of a Jar You Are" (Nye) **13**:412
Of Age and Innocence (Lamming) **2**:235; **4**:279; **66**:218-19, 222-24, 227, 229-30; **144**:140, 143, 146, 152, 173-74, 184-86
"Of Alexander Crummell" (Du Bois) **64**:130
"Of an Etching" (Bowers) **9**:122
"Of Answers and Her Asleep" (Gustafson) **36**:217
Of Art and the Future (Miller) **84**:242
"Of Being Numerous" (Oppen) **7**:282-84, 286
Of Being Numerous (Oppen) **7**:282-84; **13**:434; **34**:358-59
"Of Birds and Beasts" (Kawabata)
See "Kinjū"
"Of Cabbages and Kings" (McPherson) **19**:309; **77**:359-61, 365-66
"Of Commerce and Society" (Hill) **8**:294
"Of Daumiers a Portfolio" (Klein) **19**:259
"Of Eastern Newfoundland, Its Inns and Outs" (Dorn) **10**:160
"Of Faith" (Clark Bekedermo) **38**:127
"Of Forced Sightes and Trusty Ferefulness" (Graham) **48**:152
"Of Friendship" (Steele) **45**:364
"Of Goats and Monkeys" (Walcott)
See "Goats and Monkeys"
"Of God and of the Gods" (Levertov) **66**:245
"Of Gods" (Levertov) **66**:241
Of Good and Evil (Gann) **23**:166
Of Grammatology (Derrida)
See *De la grammatologie*
"Of History Fiction" (Ciardi) **40**:156
"Of How the Lizards Live" (Brosman) **9**:135
Of Human Bondage (Maugham) **1**:204; **11**:370; **15**:366, 370; **67**:203-07, 211-14, 217-22, 228; **93**:225-73
Of Human Bondage, with a Digression on the Art of Fiction (Maugham) **93**:242
Of Human Freedom (Barzun) **51**:33-5
"Of Itzig and His Dog" (Abse) **29**:20
"Of John Davidson" (MacDiarmid) **63**:255
"Of Land and Love" (Ghose) **42**:177
"Of Languages" (Jennings) **131**:240
"Of Liberation" (Giovanni) **64**:182-83
Of Light and Sounding Brass (Yanovsky) **2**:485; **18**:551-52
"Of Love: A Testimony" (Cheever) **64**:65
Of Love and Death and Other Journeys (Holland) **21**:149
Of Love and Dust (Gaines) **11**:218; **18**:165-66; **86**:173
Of Love and Shadows (Allende)
See *De amor y de sombra*
"Of Memory and Desire" (Swan) **69**:358-360
Of Memory and Desire (Swan) **69**:359-60, 363
"Of Men and Cities" (Tolson) **105**:260
Of Mice and Men (Steinbeck) **1**:324-25; **5**:406, 408-09; **9**:512, 514, 517-18, 520; **13**:529, 531-32; **21**:366, 372, 378-86, 389-92; **34**:405, 410-11, 414; **45**:370-71, 382; **59**:322, 332-34, 351; **75**:335-65; **124**:382, 402
Of Miracles and Melancholies (Mujica Lainez)
See *De milagros y de melancolías*
"Of Missing Persons" (Browne) **21**:41-2
Of Mist and Grass and Sand (McIntyre) **18**:326
Of Mortal Love (Gerhardie) **5**:140-41
"Of Mourners" (Livesay) **79**:332
"Of Natural Reticence" (Garrett) **51**:141
"Of Necessity" (Levertov) **66**:241
Of Nightingales That Weep (Paterson) **12**:484-85; **30**:284-86, 288
"Of Poetry and Women and the World" (Paley) **140**:211-12
"Of Rabbi Yose" (Abse) **29**:20
Of Rats and Diplomats (Ali) **69**:31-2
"Of Rivers" (Levertov) **66**:241
"Of Robin Hood and Womanhood" (Dubus) **97**:233
"Of Rounds" (Swenson) **106**:339
"Of Sanctity and Whiskey" (O'Faolain) **14**:406
Of Smiling Peace (Heym) **41**:211-12
Of Snails and Skylarks (Brown) **63**:56
"Of Space/Time and the River" (Benford) **52**:76
Of Spirit: Heidegger and the Question (Derrida)
See *De l'espirt: Heidegger et la question*
"Of Suicide" (Berryman) **25**:95; **62**:74
Of Surrealism in Its Living Works (Breton)
See *Du surréalisme en ses oeuvres vives et d'ephemerides surréalistes*
"Of That Fire" (Ignatow) **40**:260
"Of the Coming of John" (Du Bois) **64**:117-18, 130, 133
"Of the Dead of a Forsaken Country" (Davis) **49**:93
"Of the Faith of the Fathers" (Du Bois) **64**:134
Of the Farm (Updike) **1**:344-45; **3**:487; **5**:451; **9**:538, 540; **15**:540, 543; **23**:469; **43**:430-31, 433; **70**:249; **139**:314, 368
Of the Festivity (Dickey) **28**:117-18
"Of the Passing of the First-Born" (Du Bois) **64**:130, 133
"Of the Quest of the Golden Fleece" (Du Bois) **64**:110
"Of the Scythians" (Pollitt) **28**:368; **122**:203
"Of the Sorrow Songs" (Du Bois) **64**:130
"Of the Training of Black Men" (Du Bois) **96**:129
Of the War: Passages (Duncan) **55**:293
Of the Well and Numa: An Essay and a Legend (Benet)
See *Del pozo y del Numa: Un ensayo y una leyenda*
"Of the Wings of Atlanta" (Du Bois) **64**:110, 130; **96**:129
Of Thee I Sing (Kaufman) **38**:258, 265
"Of This Time, of That Place" (Trilling) **9**:532; **11**:540
"Of Three or Four in a Room" (Amichai) **57**:41; **116**:89
"Of Tuor and His Coming to Gondolin" (Tolkien) **38**:431
"Of Tyranny, in One Breath: (translated from a Hungarian poem by Gyula Illyes, 1956)" (Avison) **97**:78
Of Whales and Women (Gilbreth and Carey) **17**:155
Of Women and Their Elegance (Mailer) **74**:225, 227
Of Women and Thomas Harrow (Marquand) **2**:271; **10**:328, 331
Of Women Born: Motherhood as Experience and Institution (Rich) **11**:474-76, 479; **18**:444; **36**:365, 375-76; **73**:323-24; **76**:219; **125**:321
Off Center (Harrison) **144**:107-12, 114, 116
Off into Space! Science for Young Travelers (Hyde) **21**:172
Off Keck Road (Simpson) **146**:293-97
Off Limits (Adamov) **25**:16, 20-2
"Off Point Lotus" (Kunitz) **148**:75
"Off Reservation Blues" (Allen) **84**:3
"Off The Campus: Wits" (Brutus) **43**:92
Off the Mainland (Shaw) **5**:390
"Off the Track" (Adcock) **41**:16
"Off to the Cemetery" (Ignatow) **7**:182
Offending the Audience (Handke)
See *Publikumsbeschimpfung*
"Öffentilich arbeiten" (Hein) **154**:97, 133-34, 178, 191
Der Öffentliche Ankläger (Hochwälder) **36**:235, 237-40
"Öffentlichkeit als Partner" (Frisch) **44**:191
"An Offering" (Apple) **33**:21-2
"An Offering" (Stafford) **29**:386
The Offering (Edwards) **43**:137-39, 141-42
"An Offering for Mr. Bluehart" (Wright) **3**:543
"Offerings" (Mason) **82**:235, 242; **154**:319
"The Office" (Munro) **10**:358; **95**:294, 297
The Office (Fornés) **39**:138
The Office (Kieslowski) **120**:243
"Office for the Dead" (Kinsella) **138**:86
Office Life (Waterhouse) **47**:421
Office Politics (Sheed) **2**:392 94; **4**:488; **10**:473; **53**:336
"Office Primitive" (Ewart) **46**:150
"Office Romances" (Trevor) **116**:333, 377
"Officers" (Miles) **34**:245
Officers and Gentlemen (Waugh) **8**:544; **19**:461; **27**:471-72; **107**:371, 406
"Officers' Mess" (Ewart) **46**:148, 150
The Officers' Wives (Fleming) **37**:128-29
"Offices" (Page) **18**:377
"Official Americans" (Rush) **44**:91-3, 95-6
Officina (Pasolini) **106**:232
Offret (Tarkovsky) **75**:385, 391-94, 396-99, 401, 411-13
Offshore (Fitzgerald) **19**:173-74; **51**:124-25; **61**:115-18, 120, 122; **143**:237-39, 246, 249, 251, 253-55, 258, 260, 262, 264-66
"Offshore Breeze" (Ashbery) **77**:67
"Offspring of the First Generation" (Pesetsky) **28**:357
Oficia de tinieblas cinquo (Cela) **13**:147
Oficio de tinieblas (Castellanos) **66**:60
"Oficio de tinieblas" (Carpentier) **110**:76-7
Un oficio del siglo XX (Cabrera Infante) **25**:105; **120**:34, 37, 65, 69-70
"La Ofrenda" (Moraga) **126**:299
"Oft in a Stilly Night" (O'Brien) **65**:167, 169-71, 173; **116**:203
"Often I Am Permitted to Return to a Meadow" (Duncan) **41**:124
Ogon no kuni (Endō) **7**:95
The Ogoni Nationality Today and Tomorrow (Saro-Wiwa) **114**:275
The Ogre (Tournier)
See *Le roi des Aulnes*
The Ogre Downstairs (Jones) **26**:224-26
Ogre, Ogre (Anthony) **35**:38
"Oh" (Sexton) **4**:483
Oh! (Robison) **42**:340-43; **98**:306, 308, 317-18
Oh, Boy! (Wodehouse) **22**:478
"Oh, Brother" (Leyner) **92**:293
Oh Dad, Poor Dad, Mamma's Hung You in the Closet and I'm Feelin' So Sad (Kopit) **18**:286-87; **33**:247-50, 252
"Oh! Darling" (Lennon and McCartney) **12**:364, 380

Oh, God! (Gelbart) **21**:128
"Oh Jamaica" (Cliff) **21**:60-1
"Oh, Joseph, I'm So Tired" (Yates) **23**:483
"Oh Khrushchev, My Khrushchev" (Grayson) **38**:212
Oh, Lady! Lady!! (Wodehouse) **22**:478
"Oh Louisiana" (Berry) **17**:52
"Oh Max" (Creeley) **36**:122
Oh Mercy (Dylan) **77**:181-85
"Oh, Moon of Mahagonny!" (Harrison) **43**:180
"Oh, My Love" (Lennon) **35**:263-64, 267
"Oh No" (Creeley) **36**:118
Oh Pray My Wings Are Gonna Fit Me Well (Angelou) **12**:13; **64**:32; **77**:15, 22, 29-30
"Oh, Sister" (Dylan) **77**:187
"Oh, the Big-Time, Game-Time, Show-Time Roll" (Wolfe) **147**:313
Oh, to Be a Swinger (Buchwald) **33**:93
Oh! What a Lovely War (Deighton) **46**:127
Oh What a Paradise It Seems (Cheever) **25**:119-22; **64**:49-52, 57, 59
"Oh What a Thrill" (Berry) **17**:56
"Oh, What Avails" (Munro) **95**:309, 314
"Oh Yoko!" (Lennon) **35**:263
"Oh! You Pretty Things" (Bowie) **17**:58
Ohayo (Ozu) **16**:447-48, 452-55
"Ohio" (Young) **17**:572
"Ohio Impromptu" (Beckett) **29**:59, 65-6
"Ohio River Blues" (Patchen) **18**:395
Ohio Town (Santmyer) **33**:357-58, 360
Ohitika Woman (Crow Dog) **93**:109. 111-12
Ohnmacht (Hein) **154**:
Der Ohrenzeuge: Fünfzig Charaktere (Canetti) **25**:108; **75**:145; **86**:294, 300-01
Oi for England (Griffiths) **52**:184
"Oil" (Hogan) **73**:154
Oil! (Sinclair) **11**:498; **15**:498-99; **63**:346, 349, 351, 361, 371, 373
"Oil at St. A. Barbara" (Eigner) **9**:181
Oil Notes (Bass) **79**:7-16, 18, 20; **143**:4-6
"L'oiseau des ruines" (Bonnefoy) **58**:53
"L'oiseau migrateur" (Breton) **9**:134
"L'oiseau spirituel" (Char) **14**:128
Oiseaux (Perse) **4**:398-400
"Les oiseaux du souci" (Prévert) **15**:437
Los ojos vendados (Saura) **20**:320, 322
"Okay, Mr. Pappendass, Okay" (Fuchs) **22**:157
"O'Keefe Retrospective" (Swenson) **61**:397
"Oklahoma" (Transtroemer) **52**:409
"Oklahoma Hills" (Guthrie) **35**:183
Oktyabr' shestnadtsatogo (Solzhenitsyn) **2**:411; **7**:444; **78**:413
Okurete kita seinen (Oe) **86**:228, 230
Ol' Waylon (Jennings) **21**:204
"Olber's Paradox" (Ferlinghetti) **111**:65-6
"Old" (Coles) **46**:108-09
Old Acquaintance (Guild) **33**:187
"Old Adam" (Avison) **97**:71
The Old Adam (Enright) **31**:147
"The Old Address" (Kavan) **82**:120
Old Age (Beauvoir)
See *La vieillesse*
Old Age from Antiquity to Post-Modernity (Johnson) **147**:161
"Old Age of an Eagle" (Ransom) **11**:466; **24**:366
"The Old Age of Michelangelo" (Prince) **22**:340
Old and New Poems (Hall) **151**:193-99, 209, 213, 216
"The Old and the New Masters" (Jarrell) **9**:296
"The Old Army Game" (Garrett) **51**:147
"The Old Artist: Notes on Mr. Sweet" (Walker) **58**:409
"The Old Asylum of the Narragansetts" (Dubie) **36**:133
"An Old Atheist Pauses by the Sea" (Kinsella) **138**:101
"Old Bapu" (Anand) **23**:21
"The Old Bird, a Love Story" (Powers) **1**:282
"Old Boards" (Bly) **128**:27-28,
"Old Bones" (Narayan) **28**:293
"The Old Books" (Scannell) **49**:327, 331
"Old Bottles" (Bowering) **47**:29
The Old Boys (Trevor) **7**:475-76; **25**:444-45; **71**:321, 333, 340, 342, 345; **116**:331, 334, 348, 366, 374-75, 381
"The Old Bucket" (Solzhenitsyn)
See "Staroe vedro"
"Old Bull" (Trevor) **116**:378
The Old Bunch (Levin) **7**:204, 206
The Old Capital (Kawabata)
See *Koto*
An Old Captivity (Shute) **30**:365-66
"The Old Century" (Sassoon) **36**:387
The Old Century and Seven More Years (Sassoon) **36**:394; **130**:178, 194, 202, 204, 207
"The Old Chevalier" (Dinesen) **29**:162; **95**:36, 42, 45
"The Old Chief Mshlanga" (Lessing) **22**:279
"Old Complaints Revisited" (Sontag) **13**:517-18
The Old Country (Bennett) **45**:58; **77**:83-5, 87, 100
"The Old Country Waltz" (Young) **17**:576
"Old Countryside" (Bogan) **46**:78, 83; **93**:64, 68-69, 78, 80-81, 96-97
"Old Couple" (Simic) **130**:318
"Old Coyote in the Adirondacks" (Kenny) **87**:253
"An Old Cracked Tune" (Kunitz) **6**:287; **148**:103, 127, 146, 148
The Old Crowd (Bennett) **45**:58; **77**:86, 88-9, 90-1,98
Old Dan's Records (Lightfoot) **26**:279, 282
The Old Dark House (Priestley)
See *Benighted*
"Old Desire" (Ammons) **57**:49
The Old Devils (Amis) **44**:134-44; **129**:3, 8, 10, 16, 18-21, 25
"Old Dirt Road" (Lennon) **35**:268
"Old Doc Rivers" (Williams) **9**:572; **42**:458
The Old Dog Barks Backwards (Nash) **23**:323
"Old Dominion" (Hass) **18**:213
"Old Dwarf Heart" (Sexton) **53**:318
The Old English "Exodus": Text, Translation, and Commentary (Tolkien) **38**:438, 440, 442
The Old English Peep-Show (Dickinson) **12**:168; **35**:133
"The Old Faith" (O'Connor) **23**:333
"The Old Fascist in Retirement" (Baxter) **78**:27, 30
Old Fashioned Pilgrimage (Clarke) **6**:112-13
"Old Fashioned Wedding" (Porter) **33**:325
"Old Favorites" (Santos) **22**:364
"An Old Field Mowed for Appearances' Sake" (Meredith) **4**:347
"Old Flame" (Lowell) **4**:303
"Old Flame" (Warren) **18**:535-36
"Old Florist" (Roethke) **101**:295
"Old Folks at Home" (Highsmith) **102**:199
"Old Folk's Home, Jerusalem" (Dove) **81**:152
The Old Foolishness (Carroll) **10**:98
"The Old Fools" (Larkin) **5**:230; **8**:332, 337; **9**:323; **18**:298-301; **33**:260, 262, 269; **39**:339, 341, 344; **64**:266, 270, 285
"The Old Forest" (Taylor) **37**:411-13; **44**:305-06, 309; **50**:251, 253, 255, 260; **71**:295-96, 298
The Old Forest, and Other Stories (Taylor) **37**:410-13; **44**:304-07, 309-10; **50**:251
"Old Francis" (Kelman) **58**:297, 300-01
"An Old Friend" (Abse) **29**:21
"Old Friends" (Bromell) **5**:74
"Old Friends" (Endō) **54**:161
"Old Friends" (Moure) **88**:218
"Old Friends" (Sondheim) **147**:243
"Old Gardener" (Simmons) **43**:410
The Old Glory (Lowell) **4**:299; **5**:256; **8**:350-53, 357; **11**:324-25; **124**:256, 303
"The Old Gods" (Kizer) **80**:172
The Old Gods Waken (Wellman) **49**:389, 396
"An Old Gourd" (Turco) **63**:429
"The Old Gray Couple" (MacLeish) **8**:363-64
The Old Gringo (Fuentes)
See *El gringo viejo*
"Old Harp" (Davidson) **13**:168; **19**:126
"Old Harry" (Kinsella) **138**:83, 99-100
"Old Homes" (Blunden) **56**:37
"The Old Horns" (Campbell) **42**:84-5
"The Old Hotel" (Swan) **69**:365
"Old House" (Redgrove) **6**:445
"The Old House at Home" (Mitchell) **98**:156, 184
"Old Houses" (Hall) **37**:142
"The Old Huntsman" (Sassoon) **36**:388-90; **130**:191-92
The Old Huntsman and Other Poems (Sassoon) **36**:385, 389-90, 392, 394; **130**:176, 178, 180-81, 184, 188, 202, 212, 218, 220
"The Old Icons" (Heaney) **74**:169
"The Old Italians Dying" (Ferlinghetti) **27**:139
The Old Jest (Johnston) **150**:22
"Old Jewelry" (Snodgrass) **68**:388, 399
"Old John's Place" (Lessing) **22**:279
Old Jules (Sandoz) **28**:400-02, 404-05, 407
"The Old Lady" (Jhabvala) **8**:312
"Old Lady Mandel" (Ferber) **93**:139, 142
"An Old Lady's Winter Words" (Roethke) **8**:455; **46**:363; **101**:304, 329
"An Old Lament Renewed" (Scannell) **49**:326, 329
"The Old Land Dog" (Betjeman) **43**:51
"Old Larkinian" (Ewart) **46**:151
"Old Leaves" (Squires) **51**:381
"Old Letters" (Schwartz) **45**:361
"Old Letters" (Steele) **45**:365
"The Old Liberals" (Betjeman) **43**:35, 37, 40
The Old Life (Hall) **151**:204, 212, 223
Old Lights for New Chancels: Verses Topographical and Amatory (Betjeman) **43**:34
"Old Lone Wolf" (Guthrie) **35**:185
"Old Love" (Archer) **28**:13-14
"Old Love" (Singer) **6**:511; **9**:487; **15**:507
Old Love (Singer) **15**:507-09; **23**:420-21; **111**:332-33
"The Old Lovers" (Aleixandre)
See "Los amantes viejos"
"Old Lovers at a Ballet" (Sarton) **91**:254
An Old Magic (Arthur) **12**:27-9
"The Old Man" (Coover) **32**:127
"Old Man" (Faulkner) **6**:174; **8**:211
"Old Man" (Hillis) **66**:194
"The Old Man" (Johnston) **51**:243
"Old Man" (MacCaig) **36**:288
"The Old Man" (Singer) **111**:294, 296-7
"Old Man" (Young) **17**:571
The Old Man (Trifonov)
See *Starik*
"The Old Man and the Child" (Roy)
See "Le veillard et l'enfant"
"The Old Man and the Child" (Wiesel) **5**:490
The Old Man and the Sea (Hemingway) **1**:143; **3**:231-34, 237, 241, 243; **6**:227-28, 230-32; **8**:283-85; **10**:264, 267; **13**:273, 275, 278-81; **19**:212, 224; **34**:478; **39**:428, 430; **41**:198, 202, 204; **50**:424, 427, 429; **61**:201, 225; **80**:146
"The Old Man and the Sun" (Aleixandre) **36**:28, 30
The Old Man and the Wolves (Kristeva)
See *Le Vieil Homme et les loups*
"Old Man at the Bridge" (Hemingway) **80**:135-36
The Old Man at the Railroad Crossing (Maxwell) **19**:307
"An Old Man Awake in His Own Death" (Strand) **41**:432
"Old Man Buzzard" (Brown) **59**:265, 268
"Old Man in the Crystal Morning" (Schwartz)
See "Poem"
"Old Man Isbell's Wife" (Davis) **49**:91
Old Man Joseph and His Family (Linney) **51**:260

"An Old Man, Light as a Feather" (Hein) **154**:
"Old Man Minick" (Ferber) **93**:145, 179-80
"Old Man of the Temple" (Narayan) **28**:293
"Old Man Playing with Children" (Ransom) **4**:435
Old Man Rubbing His Eyes (Bly) **15**:63
"Old Man's Fugue" (Shapcott) **38**:404
"An Old Man's Winter Night" (Frost) **1**:110; **9**:226; **15**:250; **26**:123-24
"Old Marrieds" (Brooks) **49**:21-2, 26; **125**:53
"The Old Master" (O'Faolain) **14**:402; **32**:342; **70**:317-18
"Old Master" (Shapcott) **38**:402
Old Masters (Bernhard)
See *Alte Meister*
Old Mazurka to the Rhythm of Rain (Ritsos) **31**:324
"The Old McGrath Place" (McGrath) **59**:175
"Old Meg" (Gunn) **81**:178
The Old Men at the Zoo (Wilson) **2**:471-474; **3**:535-36; **5**:513-14; **25**:463
"Old Men at Union Street Corner" (McIlvanney) **42**:282
"Old Men Go Mad at Night" (Williams) **45**:445
"Old Men Pitching Horseshoes" (Kennedy) **42**:256-57
"The Old Mill" (Tillinghast) **29**:415
"The Old Morality" (Fuentes)
See "Vieja moralidad"
"The Old Morality" (Fuentes) **22**:170-71
"Old Mortality" (Gilchrist) **143**:274
"Old Mortality" (Porter) **101**:224, 232, 251-52
Old Mortality (Porter) **1**:272; **3**:393; **7**:310, 312, 317, 319; **10**:396-99; **13**:448-51; **15**:428; **27**:401
Old Mother (Lane) **25**:289
"Old Mother Hubbard" (Guthrie) **23**:199
"Old Mountain Road" (Simic) **130**:306
"Old Mr. Busybody" (Capote) **34**:322
Old Mr. Flood (Mitchell) **98**:158-59, 165-66, 169, 172-73, 175, 177, 180-84
"Old Mr. Marblehall" (Welty) **14**:561; **33**:415; **105**:385-86
"Old Music for Quiet Hearts" (Sandburg) **35**:356
"Old Mythologies" (Montague) **46**:278
"Old Names Taste Like Ashes" (Haavikko) **34**:172
"Old New England" (Walcott) **25**:455, 457; **42**:421
"Old, Old Woodstock" (Morrison) **21**:232
The Old Ones (Wesker) **3**:518-20; **42**:426-28, 430
"The Old Order" (Porter) **3**:393; **7**:310; **13**:450
Old Order: Stories of the South (Porter) **10**:396; **13**:451
"Old Palaces" (Mahapatra) **33**:277-78
The Old Patagonian Express: By Train through the Americas (Theroux) **15**:533-35; **28**:425; **46**:402
"Old Peasant Woman Walks along the Beach" (Rozewicz) **9**:465
"Old People on the Nursing Home Porch" (Strand) **71**:282, 285
"Old People's Nursing Home" (Jennings) **131**:241
"Old Pewter" (Heaney) **37**:165; **91**:119
Old Phantoms (Edwards) **43**:139, 142
"An Old Photo in an Old Life" (Hoffman) **13**:287
"Old Photograph of the Future" (Warren) **39**:270
"The Old Play" (Slessor) **14**:496
"Old Pleasures Deserted" (Blunden) **56**:44
"Old poet" (Bukowski) **108**:111
The Old Poetries and the New (Kostelanetz) **28**:218
"The Old Poet's Tale" (Rakosi) **47**:348
Old Possum's Book of Practical Cats (Eliot) **55**:354
"The Old Prison" (Wright) **53**:418, 431
"Old Property" (Acorn) **15**:9
"An Old Pub near the Angel" (Kelman) **86**:185
"The Old Quarry, Part One" (Jones) **42**:242-43
"The Old Quarry, Part Two" (Jones) **42**:242
"Old Red" (Gordon) **29**:187-88; **83**:233, 239, 247-48
Old Red, and Other Stories (Gordon) **13**:245; **29**:189
"Old Rotting Treetrunk Down" (Snyder) **120**:326
"Old Sailor's Choice" (Davidson) **2**:112
"The Old Saybrook House" (Holmes) **56**:145
Old School Ties (Trevor) **71**:345
Old Shirts and New Skins (Alexie) **96**:2, 4, 8, 11; **154**:7-8, 10, 12-14, 26-7, 29
"Old Siam" (McCartney) **35**:286-87
Old Snow Just Melting (Bell) **31**:51
"Old Soldier" (Simpson) **7**:426
"Old Soldiers" (Brown) **73**:24
Old Soldiers (Bailey) **45**:45-7
"Old Song" (Livesay) **79**:340, 351
"Old Song" (Scott) **22**:373-74
"Old Song" (Voznesensky) **57**:427
"The Old Song and Dance" (Rexroth) **49**:289
"Old Souls" (Giles) **39**:64-6
"An Old Story" (Kelman) **58**:298-99
An Old Story about Travellers (Costantini)
See *Una vieja historia de caminantes*
"The Old System" (Bellow) **6**:53; **33**:71
"Old Tale" (Sorrentino) **40**:386
Old Tales of Old Castile (Delibes)
See *Viejas historias de castilla la vieja*
The Old Testament (Asimov)
See *Asimov's Guide to the Bible, Volume I: The Old Testament*
"Old Things" (Dunn) **40**:168
"Old Things" (Mason) **28**:273-74; **82**:242; **154**:317, 319
"An Old Time Indian Attack" (Silko) **74**:328
"Old Time Rock and Roll" (Seger) **35**:384
Old Times (Pinter) **3**:387-88; **6**:415-19; **9**:420-21; **11**:444; **15**:423-24; **27**:394-95; **58**:374, 376, 384; **73**:276
"Old Town" (Blaga) **75**:70
"Old Voices" (Norris) **14**:387
"Old Walt" (Hughes) **108**:333
The Old Ways (Snyder) **32**:394, 399; **120**:336
"The Old White Man" (Redgrove) **41**:348
"Old Whitey" (Van Doren) **10**:495
"An Old Whorehouse" (Oliver) **98**:256
"Old Wildwood" (Goyen) **40**:217
The Old Wives' Fairy Tale Book (Carter) **76**:329
"Old Woman" (Pinsky) **121**:433
"An Old Woman" (Sitwell) **67**:320, 335
"Old Woman" (Smith) **64**:388-89, 393-94, 398
"An Old Woman and Her Cat" (Lessing) **94**:261
The Old Woman and the Cow (Anand) **23**:13, 17
"The Old Woman and the Mayflowers" (Purdy) **50**:245
"An Old Woman Asked Me..." (Lopate) **29**:302
The Old Woman Broods (Rozewicz)
See *Stara kobieta wysiaduje*
"Old Woman Nature" (Snyder) **120**:326
"The Old Woman of Portrush" (Simmons) **43**:414
"An Old Woman of the Roads" (Colum) **28**:90
"Old Woman on Yonge Street" (Souster) **14**:504
"Old Woman with Flowers" (Smith) **64**:393
"The Old Women of Paris" (Randall) **135**:386
"Old Woodrat's Stinkiy House" (Snyder) **120**:358
"Old Words" (Sanchez) **116**:272, 279-80
The Olden Days Coat (Laurence) **50**:314
"Older Sister" (Simon) **26**:408-09
The Oldest Confession (Condon) **4**:105-07; **6**:115; **45**:95-6; **100**:91, 110-11, 113
The Oldest Killed Lake in North America (Carruth) **84**:136
Oldest Living Confederate Widow Tells All (Gurganus) **70**:190, 195-96
"The Oldest Man" (Fisher) **87**:124
The Oldest Man, and Other Timeless Stories (Kotzwinkle) **35**:254
"The Oldest Place" (Kinsella) **138**:106, 113, 121, 162
"Oldfashioned" (McGahern) **48**:273
"Old-Fashioned Chords" (Johnston) **51**:240
An Old-Fashioned Darling (Simmons) **57**:405
"An Old-Fashioned Story" (Colwin) **84**:146
"Old-Time Childhood in Kentucky" (Warren) **39**:265
"Olduvai and All That" (Connell) **45**:114
Ole Doc Methuselah (Hubbard) **43**:204
Oleanna (Mamet) **91**:147-50
Olen'i shalashovka (Solzhenitsyn) **10**:479
"Oleo: Demon Briefs and Dopey Ditties" (Kesey) **46**:227-28
Olinger Stories: A Selection (Updike) **15**:543; **23**:473; **139**:338
"The Olive Garden" (Gordon) **13**:246; **29**:188-90
The Olive of Minerva; or, The Comedy of a Cuckold (Dahlberg) **7**:71
The Olive Tree, and Other Essays (Huxley) **11**:286
"Oliver Plunkett" (Longley) **29**:296
"Oliver's Army" (Costello) **21**:71
Oliver's Story (Segal) **10**:466-67
"Olivia" (Rich) **76**:213
"Olivia" (Salinas)
See "Poem for Olivia"
Ölmez otu (Kemal) **14**:300-301
"Olson" (Howe) **152**:159
Los olvidados (Bunuel) **16**:131-33, 143, 146-47, 149; **80**:19-22, 27, 30-1, 38, 47, 51
Olympiad (Riefenstahl) **16**:521-22, 525-26
"The Olympian" (Dickey) **109**:246
The Olympian (Glanville) **6**:202
The Olympians (Priestley) **34**:362, 364
Olympic Games (Riefenstahl)
See *Olympiad*
"The Olympic Girl" (Betjeman) **43**:41
"Om pseudonumerog Gengaedelsens veje" (Dinesen) **95**:68
Omaenimo tsumi ga aru (Abe) **81**:294
"Omagh Hospital" (Montague) **46**:269
"Gli Ombra" (Ortese) **89**:198
"The Ombras" (Ortese)
See "Gli Ombra"
"Omega" (Tolson) **105**:247, 253, 274, 284-85
"Omegaman" (Police, The) **26**:365
"Omen" (Avison) **97**:111
"Omen" (Hirsch) **50**:195-96, 198-99
Omensetter's Luck (Gass) **1**:114; **2**:154-55; **8**:240-42, 245-46; **11**:224-25; **15**:255, 257; **39**:478, 482; **132**:164-65, 172-74, 181, 190, 194
Omeros (Walcott) **67**:361-68; **76**:288, 296-98
"Omicron" (Tolson) **105**:242, 274
Ommateum with Doxology (Ammons) **2**:12-13; **5**:25-6, 28; **8**:17; **25**:41; **57**:53-4; **108**:5, 12, 14, 26, 46, 60
The Omni-Americans: New Perspectives on Black Experience and American Culture (Murray) **73**:218-21, 230, 235-41
"Omnibus" (Cortázar) **34**:332
Omnivore (Anthony) **35**:40
"Omo" (Thomas) **107**:316-18
"On?" (Avison) **97**:112
"On a Beach in Southern Connecticut" (Klappert) **57**:257
"On a Bicycle" (Yevtushenko) **1**:382; **126**:396
"On a Book Entitled Lolita" (Nabokov) **64**:344, 365
"On a Bust of an Army Corporal Killed ... in the Boer War" (Coles) **46**:108
"On a Certain Engagement South of Seoul" (Carruth) **4**:93
"On a Child Who Lived One Minute" (Kennedy) **42**:257
On a Dark Night (West) **50**:360
On a Darkling Plain (Saro-Wiwa) **114**:258, 267, 275

On a Darkling Plain (Stegner) **49**:346-47; **81**:352
On a Deserted Shore (Raine) **7**:353; **45**:341
"On a Drawing by Flavio" (Levine) **118**:279, 293-94, 299
"On a Field Trip at Fredericksburg" (Smith) **42**:353
"On a Friend's Relapse and Return to a Mental Clinic" (Jennings) **131**:235, 240
"On a Gift in the Shape of a Heart" (Kinsella) **138**:90
"On a Line from Julian" (Kizer) **80**:179
"On a Line from Sophocles" (Kizer) **80**:179
On a mangé la dune (Maillet) **54**:305-06; **118**:327, 336, 344-46
"On a Morning Full of Sun" (Appleman) **51**:15
"On a Name for Black Americans" (Randall) **135**:390
"On a Painting by Patient B of the Independence State Hospital for the Insane" (Justice) **102**:261
On a Pale Horse (Anthony) **35**:39-41
"On a Photo of Sgt. Ciardi a Year Later" (Ciardi) **40**:157, 161; **44**:381
"On a Picture by Dürer" (Blunden) **56**:30
"On a Picture of Ezra Pound" (Carruth) **84**:127
"On a Pig's Head" (Tomlinson) **45**:401
"On a Portrait of a Scholar" (Winters) **32**:470
"On a Question Preliminary to Any Possible Treatment of Psychosis" (Lacan) **75**:288, 293
"On a Raised Beach" (MacDiarmid) **4**:312; **11**:338; **19**:287; **63**:242, 244-46, 249
"On a Small Steamboat" (Ding Ling)
See "Xiaohuolun shang"
"On a Son Returned to New Zealand" (Adcock) **41**:14
"On a Streetcar Named Success" (Williams) **45**:445
"On a Train to Rome" (Farrell) **8**:205; **66**:129
"On A Wagon" (Singer) **6**:509
"On a Winded Civilization" (Cioran) **64**:76, 78, 82, 96
On All Fours (Rozewicz)
See *Na czworakach*
"On an Old Photograph of My Son" (Carver) **126**:164, 169, 171
"On Angels" (Barthelme) **115**:71
"On Angels" (Milosz) **82**:296, 302
"On 'As for Poets'" (Snyder) **120**:329, 347
"On Balance" (Brunner) **8**:109
"On Ballistics" (Arreola)
See "De balística"
On Bear's Head (Whalen) **6**:565-66; **29**:445-46
"On Beauty" (Koch) **44**:249
On Becoming a Novelist (Gardner) **34**:548-49
"On Becoming a Writer" (Ellison) **86**:328; **114**:109-10
"On Being" (Kroetsch)
See "On Being An alberta Writer"
"On Being a Poet in America" (Simpson) **149**:312
"On Being a Self Forever" (Updike) **139**:326
"On Being An alberta Writer" (Kroetsch) **132**:210, 245, 282, 284, 286
"On Being an Intellectual" (McAuley) **45**:253
"On Being Asked to Write a Poem Against the War in Vietnam" (Carruth) **7**:41
"On Being Asked What It's Like to Be Black" (Giovanni) **64**:183
"On Being Blue" (Gass) **39**:477; **132**:186
On Being Blue: A Philosophical Inquiry (Gass) **8**:246-47; **11**:224; **15**:256, 258; **39**:478; **132**:166-67, 172, 174
"On Being Busted at Fifty" (Fiedler) **13**:212
On Being Christian (Kung)
See *Christ Sein (main title)*
"On Being Shot Again" (Hemingway) **34**:478
"On Being Twenty-Six" (Larkin) **64**:258, 260
"On Being Wrong: Convicted Minimalist Spills Beans" (Barthelme) **117**:9
On Boxing (Oates) **52**:333-35; **108**:362-63, 365-67, 374
"On Breaking the Forms" (Wain) **11**:563
On Call: New Political Essays (Jordan) **114**:152-53, 162
"On Charon's Warf" (Dubus) **97**:233
"On Chesterton" (Borges) **48**:46
"On Christ's Nature" (Amis) **129**:25
"On Circe's Island" (Simmons) **43**:410
"On Credo ut Intelligam" (Bronk) **10**:74
On Crime Writing (Macdonald) **41**:269
"On Criticism in General" (Pound) **10**:402
On Darkening Green (Charyn) **5**:104
"On Deck" (Plath) **111**:166
"On demande des dissidents" (Blanchot) **135**:131
"On Destiny, Language, and Translation; or, Ophelia Adrift in the C. & O. Canal" (Ferré) **139**:152, 177
On Difficulty, and Other Essays (Steiner) **24**:435, 437
"On Discovering Who We Are" (MacLennan) **92**:306, 341
On Distant Ground (Butler) **81**:121, 127
On Drink (Amis) **3**:9; **5**:22
"On Dry Land" (Motion) **47**:294
"On Each Journey" (Merwin) **88**:193
"On Each Other's Time" (Gilliatt) **53**:146
On Early Trains (Pasternak)
See *Na rannikh poezdakh*
"On Earth" (Broumas) **73**:17
"On Edge of Time Future" (Okri) **87**:324
On est toujours trop bon avec les femmes (Queneau) **42**:332-33, 335
On Extended Wings (Vendler) **138**:244-46, 253, 260, 264
"On Fairy Stories" (Tolkien) **3**:481; **12**:573, 581; **38**:440, 442-43
"On Falling Asleep by Firelight" (Meredith) **13**:375; **22**:301
"On Falling Asleep to Bird Song" (Meredith) **13**:375
"On Finding a Bird's Bones in the Woods" (Mueller) **51**:279
On First Looking Down from Lions Gate Bridge (Suknaski) **19**:432
"On Flower Wreath Hill" (Rexroth) **49**:276, 286; **112**:402-04
"On Flying" (Vidal) **142**:330, 333
"On Flying to a Political Convention" (Ciardi) **40**:157
"On for the Long Haul" (Boyle) **90**:46
"On F.R. Leavis and D.H. Lawrence" (Rahv) **24**:355
"On Freedom" (Ignatow) **40**:259
"On Freedom of Expression" (Warner) **45**:433
"On Freedom's Ground" (Wilbur) **53**:409, 411; **110**:356, 361, 384
"On Gay Wallpaper" (Williams) **42**:462
"On Getting a Natural (For Gwendolyn Brooks)" (Randall) **135**:390, 398
On Glory's Course (Purdy) **52**:345-48
On Going to Bed (Burgess) **40**:119
"On Goodbye" (Avison) **97**:116
On Grammatology (Derrida)
See *De la grammatologie*
On Grief and Reason (Brodsky) **100**:61-5, 68-70, 73
"On Guard" (Waugh) **27**:477
On Guerrilla Warfare (Guevara)
See *La guerra de guerrillas*
"On Handling Some Small Shells from the Windward Islands" (Swenson) **4**:532-34
"On Hearing a Recording of Marianne Moore" (Cabral de Melo Neto)
See "Ouvindo Marianne Moore em disco"
"On Hearing Russian Spoken" (Davie) **10**:125; **31**:109
"On Hearing the Airlines Will Use a Psychological Profile to Catch Potential Skyjackers" (Dunn) **36**:152
On Her Majesty's Secret Service (Fleming) **30**:143, 149
On Heroes and Tombs (Sabato)
See *Sobre héroes y tumbas*
"On Heroic Leadership and the Dilemma of Strong Men and Weak People" (Schlesinger) **84**:356
"On Highgate Hill" (Hope) **52**:209
"On His Back under the Night" (Cortázar)
See "La noche boca arriba"
"On His Own Face in a Glass" (Pound) **112**:330
"On His Sixty-Fifth Birthday" (Fuller) **28**:157
"On Hypotheses in 'Historical Criticism'" (Crane) **27**:74
"On Ibrahim Balaban's 'Spring Picture'" (Hikmet) **40**:249
On Ice (Gelber) **79**:217, 223-24
On Ice (Ingalls) **42**:233-35
"On 'Identity'" (Roethke) **101**:291, 328-29, 331
"On Inhabiting an Orange" (Miles) **14**:368
"On Initiation Rites and Power: Ralph Ellison Speaks at West Point" (Ellison) **114**:109
"On Its Way" (Swenson) **61**:396
"On John Donne" (Merwin) **45**:268
"On Keeping a Notebook" (Didion) **129**:77, 86, 99
On Keeping Women (Calisher) **38**:73; **134**:21, 35
"On Knowing Nothing" (Smith) **15**:514
"On Learning of a Friend's Illness" (Williams) **148**:344
On Learning to Read: The Child's Fascination with Meaning (Bettelheim) **79**:132-33
"On Leaving Norway, from a Mission, without a Penny" (Kunene) **85**:176
"On Leaving Wantage, 1972" (Betjeman) **10**:53; **43**:48
On Lies, Secrets, and Silence: Selected Prose, 1966-1978 (Rich) **18**:447-48; **73**:319, 321-22; **76**:215, 219; **125**:321
"On Listening: A Good Way to Hear" (Jordan) **23**:256
"On Living in Aztlán" (Zamora) **89**:361, 386
"On Looking Into Henry Moore" (Livesay) **79**:342, 346
"On Looking Up by Chance at the Constellations" (Frost) **3**:175; **26**:118
"On Love and Politics" (Ferré) **139**:173
"On Magical Thinking" (Blaga) **75**:63
"On Making Certain Anything Has Happened" (Frost) **26**:118
"On Medicine and Literature" (Coles) **108**:192
"On Minding One's Own Business" (Wright) **28**:463
On Modern Marriage, and Other Observations (Dinesen) **95**:60
On Moral Fiction (Gardner) **10**:222-23; **18**:176-77, 179, 180-81, 183-84; **28**:161-66; **34**:548-49
"On Moral Leadership as a Political Dilemma" (Jordan) **114**:146
"On Morality" (Didion) **129**:65, 76, 101
"On Mother's Day" (Paley) **140**:210
On Mozart: A Paean for Wolfgang (Burgess)
See *Mozart and the Wolf Gang*
"On My Birthday" (Amichai) **116**:95, 99
"On My Father" (Faludy) **42**:138
"On My Life" (Cliff) **21**:60
On My Master Döblin (Grass)
See *Über Mein Lehrer Döblin*
"On My Own" (Levine) **118**:303
"On My Own Work" (Wilbur) **14**:577
On My Way (Arp)
See *Jours effeuillés: Poémes, essais, souvenirs, 1920-1965*
"On My Way Out I Passed over You and the Verrazano Bridge" (Lorde) **71**:258-59
On Native Grounds (Kazin) **34**:556-57, 561; **38**:269-75, 279-80; **119**:303, 305-06, 308-11, 315-16, 319-21, 323, 331-34
"On Not Being a Dove" (Updike) **139**:326, 329, 363

"On Not Being a Jew" (Updike) **43**:431
"On Not Being Banned by the Nazis" (Acorn) **15**:10
"On Not Being Milton" (Harrison) **43**:177, 180; **129**:171, 174
"On Not Saying Everything" (Day Lewis) **10**:131
"On Open Form" (Merwin) **88**:193
"On Passing the New Menin Gate" (Sassoon) **130**:187
"On Passion as a Literary Tradition" (Ciardi) **129**:47
"On Pasternak Soberly" (Milosz) **82**:292
On Photography (Sontag) **10**:484-87; **13**:515, 518; **31**:411-13, 417-18; **105**:206, 208, 215, 226
"On Poetry" (Dudek) **11**:160
On Poetry and Poets (Eliot) **24**:171-72, 177-78; **113**:194
On Poets and Others (Paz) **51**:331-32
"On Poets and Poetry" (Olson) **11**:415
On Power and Ideology (Chomsky) **132**:32-3, 40
"On Prayer" (Milosz) **56**:248
"On Prettiness" (Vidal) **142**:304
On purge béé (Renoir) **20**:309
"On Quicksand Creek" (Still) **49**:366
"On Quitting a Little College" (Stafford) **29**:379
On Racine (Barthes)
See *Sur Racine*
On Radio Waves (Seifert)
See *Na vlnách T. S. F.*
"On Raglan Road" (Kavanagh) **22**:243
"On Reading Dickens" (Warner) **45**:434
"On Reading John Cage" (Paz) **51**:333
"On Reading That the Rebuilding of Ypres Approached Completion" (Blunden) **56**:43
"On Reading 'The Country of the Pointed Firs'" (Garrigue) **8**:239
"On Reading to Oneself" (Gass) **39**:478, 481
"On Realising He Has Written Some Bad Poems" (Purdy) **50**:246
"On Receiving a Postcard from Japan" (Van Duyn) **63**:445
"On Renoir's 'The Grape Pickers'" (Boland) **40**:100-01; **113**:108
"On Returning to Teach" (Bell) **8**:66
On Revolution (Arendt) **98**:11, 22-5, 39, 48, 51
"On San Gabriel Ridges" (Snyder) **120**:342
"On Saturday Afternoon" (Sillitoe) **57**:388
On Seduction (Baudrillard)
See *De la séduction*
"On Seeing Diana go Maddddddddd" (Madhubuti) **73**:213
"On Seeing England for the First Time" (Kincaid) **137**:188
"On Seeing Larry River's Washington Crossing the Delaware at the Museum of Modern Art" (O'Hara) **78**:352
"On Seeing the 100 percent Perfect Girl One Beautiful April Morning" (Murakami) **150**:51
"On Seeing 'The Day of the Dolphin'" (Livesay) **79**:332, 348
"On Self-Respect" (Didion) **8**:177; **14**:155
On sic Being Numersous (Oppen)
See *Of Being Numerous*
"On Sickness" (Cioran) **64**:88
On Site Inspection (Lem)
See *Wizja Lokalna*
"On Social Plays" (Miller) **47**:251
On Socialist Realism (Sinyavsky) **8**:488
"On Some Lines of Virgil" (Davenport) **38**:145, 148
"On Squaw Peak" (Hass) **99**:139, 142
On Stage (Tomlin) **17**:522-23
"On Stories" (Lewis) **124**:215
"On Style" (Sontag) **105**:201, 226
"On Sunday Walks" (Fuller) **62**:193
"On Talking to Oneself" (Gass) **39**:478, 481
"On Tearing up a Cynical Poem" (Blunden) **56**:51
"On That Century" (Milosz) **56**:232
"On the Air" (Jong) **6**:269
"On the Air" (Roth) **2**:379
"On the Appian Way" (Farrell) **8**:205
"On the Beach" (Abse) **7**:1
"On the Beach" (Young) **17**:576
On the Beach (Shute) **30**:369-74
On the Beach (Young) **17**:573-74, 576, 582
"On the Beach at Forte Dei Marmi" (Barker) **8**:47
On the Bearpaw Sea (Purdy) **14**:432
"On the Bestial Floor" (Merwin) **45**:269
"On the Birth of a Black/Baby/Boy" (Knight) **40**:286
"On the Birth of Bomani" (Clifton) **66**:77
"On the Birth of Good and Evil during the Long Winter of '28" (Levine) **14**:319
On the Black Hill (Chatwin) **28**:73-5; **57**:139, 141-42, 146, 148, 150; **59**:274-75, 278
"On the Blue Water" (Hemingway) **34**:478
"On the Body Politic" (Boyle) **58**:75
On the Brink of Reason (Krleža)
See *Na rubu pameti*
"On the Calculus" (Cunningham) **31**:97-8
"On the Cobb at Lyme Regis" (Beer) **58**:36
On the Contrary (Brink) **106**:130, 132-33, 137
On the Contrary (McCarthy) **14**:357; **24**:343; **39**:489; **59**:292
On the Contrary (McGinley) **14**:365
"On the Death of a Child" (Enright) **31**:155
"On the Death of a Murderer" (Wain) **11**:563
"On the Death of Friends in Childhood" (Justice) **102**:261, 268
"On the Death of Ghandi" (Scott) **22**:377
"On the Death of May Street" (MacBeth) **5**:265
"On the Death of My Father" (Kherdian) **6**:280
On the Death of My Father, and Other Poems (Kherdian) **6**:280; **9**:317
"On the Death of Senator James Walsh" (Winters) **32**:468
"On the Death of Shukskin" (Voznesensky) **57**:421
"On the Death of W. B. Yeats" (Hope) **51**:217
On the Decay of Humanism (Spackman) **46**:380
"On the Decipherment of Linear B" (Purdy) **6**:428
"On the Deck" (Barthelme) **59**:251
"On the Decline of Oracles" (Plath) **9**:422
"On the Demo, London, 1968" (McCarthy) **39**:485
"On the Disposal of My Body" (Disch) **36**:127
"On the Dressing Gown Lent Me by My Hostess the Brazilian Counsul in Milan, 1958" (Smith) **25**:422
"On the Edge" (Levine) **5**:251; **118**:274
"On the Edge" (Lorde) **71**:257
On the Edge (Koch) **44**:250
On the Edge (Levine) **4**:287; **5**:251; **14**:316; **33**:275; **118**:274, 283, 289-90, 302
"On the Edge of Darkness: What Is Political Poetry?" (Levertov) **66**:239
On the Edge of Reason (Krleža)
See *Na rubu pameti*
On the Edge of Reason (Krleža)
See *Na rubu pameti*
"On the Edge of the Cliff" (Pritchett) **15**:442, 444; **41**:334
On the Edge of the Cliff, and Other Stories (Pritchett) **15**:443-44; **41**:330
"On the Edge of the Desert" (Swan) **69**:355-56, 359, 362
On the Edge of the Desert (Swan) **69**:359, 363-64
"On the Edge of the Woods" (Gardner) **18**:178
"On the Eve of a Birthday" (Steele) **45**:365-66
"On the Eve of the Feast of the Immaculate Conception: 1942" (Lowell) **124**:281
"On the Eve of the Next Revolution" (Swan) **69**:358, 360-63
"On the Eve of Uncertain Tomorrows" (Bissoondath) **120**:14, 19
On the Eve of Uncertain Tomorrows (Bissoondath) **120**:14-15, 17-19
"On the Eyes of an SS Officer" (Wilbur) **110**:362, 381
"On the Far Edge of Kilmer" (Stern) **40**:413
"On the Ferry across Chesapeake Bay" (Bly) **5**:61
"On the Ferry from Suduroy to Torshavn" (Johnston) **51**:253
"On the Fragility of the Mind" (Eberhart) **56**:83
"On the Freedom of the Soul or the Praises of Métissage" (Senghor) **130**:250
On the Frontier (Auden) **1**:9; **11**:17
On the Frontier ... (Isherwood) **44**:396, 399
"On the Function of the Novel" (Farrell) **66**:137
"On the Ganges greenest isle" (Seth) **90**:353
"On the Geneology of Ethics: An Overview of Work in Progress" (Foucault) **34**:343-44
On the Golden Porch (Tolstaya) **59**:370-01, 385
On the Great Water Divide (Blaga)
See *La cumpana apelor*
"On the Hall at Stowey" (Tomlinson) **45**:393
"On the Heart's Beginning to Cloud the Mind" (Frost) **9**:228; **34**:475
On the High Wire (Arrabal)
See *En la cuerda floja*
On the Highest Hill (Haig-Brown) **21**:136, 141
"On the Home Front—1942" (Denby) **48**:85
"On the Human Condition" (Boyle) **58**:75
"On the Importance of Unimportant Poems" (Ciardi) **129**:46
On the Inside (Murphy) **51**:303, 305
"On the Island" (Jacobsen) **48**:192
On the Island (Jacobsen) **102**:241-42
"On the Killing of Pigs" (Rozewicz)
See "Świnobicie"
"On the Lake" (Douglas) **73**:94
"On the Last Afternoon" (Tiptree) **48**:389, 396; **50**:357
"On the Lawn at the Villa" (Simpson) **149**:295, 310-12, 321, 325, 329-30, 358
"On the Ledge" (Simpson) **149**:321
On the Ledge (Simpson) **32**:380
"On the Life That Waits" (Lieberman) **36**:262, 264
On the Limits of Poetry: Selected Essays, 1928-1948 (Tate) **24**:441
On the Line (Swados) **5**:420, 423
"On the Magellanic Clouds" (Wakoski)
See "George Washington Meets the King of Spain"
On the Marble Cliffs (Jünger) **125**:218, 251-52, 254-55, 257
"On the Margin" (Burgess) **4**:82
On the Margin (Huxley) **3**:256; **5**:192
"On the Materialist Dialectic" (Althusser) **106**:23
"On the Meeting of Garcia Lorca and Hart Crane" (Levine) **118**:322-23
"On the Morning After the Sixties" (Didion) **129**:77
On the Motion and Immobility of Douve (Bonnefoy)
See *Du mouvement et de l'immobilité de Douve*
"On the Mountain" (Gellhorn) **60**:188-89, 192
"On the Move" (Gunn) **32**:207; **81**:185
"On the Murder of Lieutenant José Del Castillo by the Falangist Bravo Martinez, July 12, 1936" (Levine) **9**:333; **14**:318; **118**:279, 294, 299, 302
"On the Nature and Use of This Book" (Davies) **75**:182
"On the Neglect of Poetry in the United States" (Simpson) **149**:362
On the Night of the Seventh Moon (Hibbert) **7**:155
On the Occasion of My Last Afternoon (Gibbons) **145**:186
"On the Occasion of the Open-Air Formation of the Olde Tymer's Walking and Nature Club" (Brooks) **125**:94

"On the Ocean Floor" (MacDiarmid) **63**:255
"On the Old Way" (Merwin) **88**:210-11
"On the Open Side" (Fisher) **25**:159
"On the Oregon Coast" (Kinnell) **129**:257-58
"On the Orthodoxy and Creed of My Power Mower" (Ciardi) **44**:383
"On the Other Side" (Milosz) **56**:237
On the Outside (Murphy) **51**:303, 305
On the Outskirts (Frayn) **31**:189; **47**:135
On the Perimeter (Blackwood) **100**:4-9, 11-12, 27
"On the Perpetuum Mobile" (Raine) **32**:351; **103**:180
"On the Persistence of Pastoral" (Fussell) **74**:129
"On the Philosophical Bases of the Humanities" (Bakhtin) **83**:13
"On the Photographs of Ansel Adams" (Salinas) **90**:332
"On the Platform" (Nemerov) **2**:308
"On the Pleasures of Formal Poetry" (Bogan) **93**:78
On the Poet and His Craft: Selected Prose (Roethke) **1**:292
"On the Poet as a Marionette" (Ciardi) **10**:107
"On the Porch" (Johnston) **51**:245
On the Prejudices, Predilections, and Firm Beliefs of William Faulkner (Brooks) **86**:278, 284-85, 287
"On the Quai at Smyrna" (Hemingway) **30**:189
On the Radio Waves (Seifert)
See *Na vlnách T. S. F.*
"On the Railway Platform" (Fuller) **4**:178
"On the Rainy River" (O'Brien) **103**:139
On the Razzle (Stoppard) **29**:398, 402
"On the Rebound" (Purdy) **52**:350
"On the Republic" (Elytis) **49**:108
On the Rim of the Curve (Cook) **58**:154
"On the River" (Levine) **118**:297, 305
On the River Baidamtal (Aitmatov)
See *Na reke Baidamtal*
"On the River Styx" (Matthiessen) **64**:322-23, 325
On the River Styx, and Other Stories (Matthiessen) **64**:321-22, 324-25, 327
"On the Rivershore" (Tilghman) **65**:107-08, 110-12
"On the Road" (Adams) **65**:348
"On the Road" (Didion) **14**:153
"On the Road" (Heaney) **74**:169, 197
"On the Road" (Richler) **46**:352
On the Road (Kerouac) **1**:165-67; **2**:226-29; **3**:265-66; **5**:212-15; **14**:303-07; **29**:271-74, 276-78; **61**:278-315
On the Road: A Search for American Character (Smith) **86**:266
On the Road Again (McFadden) **48**:247-48, 251, 255
"On the Run" (Boyle) **121**:40, 43-4
"On the Screaming of the Gulls" (Redgrove) **41**:353
"On the Self-Evident" (Grass) **49**:139
On the Shore of the Dead Sea (Endō) **99**:285, 287
"On the Skeleton of a Hound" (Wright) **28**:462
"On the Square and Across the River" (Aksyonov) **101**:11, 19-20
On the Staircase (Swinnerton) **31**:423
"On the Staten Island Ferry" (Kenny) **87**:259
"On the Steps of Low Library" (Trilling) **129**:329
"On the Steps of the Conservatory" (Barthelme) **13**:61
"On the Subway" (Olds) **85**:293, 298
"On the Teaching of Modern Literature" (Trilling) **11**:546; **24**:460
"On the Tennis Court at Night" (Kinnell) **29**:284-85
"On the Threshold of His Greatness, the Poet Comes Down with a Sore Throat" (Nemerov) **36**:301
"On the Time When the Surrealists Were Right" (Breton) **54**:16
"On the Trail of Big Bear" (Wiebe) **138**:361, 367
"On the Turmoil of Many Religions" (Milosz) **56**:232
"On the Via Margritta" (Connell) **45**:110
"On the Wagon" (Mitchell) **98**:157
On the Wasteland (Arthur) **12**:27-9
On the Waterfront (Kazan) **16**:362-74; **63**:222, 224, 226-29, 232-35
On the Waterfront (Schulberg) **7**:403; **48**:346-47, 351
"On the Waves" (Brodkey) **56**:64
On the Waves of Wireless Telegraphy (Seifert)
See *Na vlnách T. S. F.*
"On the Way" (McCartney) **35**:287-88
"On the Way" (Wiebe) **11**:568
"On the Way Back: A Work Not in Progress" (Greene)
See "An Appointment with the General"
"On the Way to Lycomedes of Scyrus" (Brodsky)
See "K Likomedu, na Skiros"
"On the Way to School" (Aleixandre) **36**:29
On the Way to the Sky (Diamond) **30**:114
"On the Wild Side" (Coles) **67**:177-78
On the Wire (Arrabal)
See *En la cuerda floja*
"On the Yankee Station" (Boyd) **28**:38
On the Yankee Station (Boyd) **28**:38-9; **53**:52
"On the Year of Many Conversions Etc." (Ciardi) **40**:157
"On the Zattere" (Trevor) **71**:329, 333
On This Island (Auden)
See "Look, Stranger, on This Island Now"
"On This Short Day of Frost and Sun" (Kumin) **28**:224
On This Side Nothing (Comfort) **7**:53
"On Those Islands (A Poem for Hector MacIver)" (MacNeice) **53**:231, 235
"On Top" (Snyder) **120**:326
On Tour (Streatfeild) **21**:408
"On Trains" (McPherson) **77**:361, 364, 366
"On Translating 'Eugene Onegin'" (Nabokov) **6**:359
On Trial (Rice) **7**:358, 363; **49**:291-92, 294, 300-02, 304
"On Triton" (Delany) **141**:153
On Troublesome Creek (Still) **49**:364, 366-67, 369
On Trust (Josipovici) **153**:225, 227
"On Tyranny" (Brodsky) **50**:132
"On Understanding" (Rao) **56**:306
"On Universalism" (Knight) **40**:279, 284
"On Utilitarianism" (Bell) **8**:66
"On Vacation" (Creeley) **78**:140
On Valentine's Day (Foote) **51**:134-36
On Violence (Arendt) **98**:12
"On Watching a World Series Game" (Sanchez) **116**:295
"On Which Side of the Curtain?" (Alegria)
See "A què lado de la cortina?"
"On Why I Would Betray You" (Graham) **118**:225
On Wings of Song (Disch) **36**:124-25
"On Writers and Writing" (Boyle) **58**:75
"On Writing" (Carver) **36**:99; **53**:66-7; **126**:145, 148, 153, 157
"On Writing" (Hemingway) **10**:269; **30**:194, 198
"On Writing" (Welty) **14**:565, 567
On Writing and Politics, 1967-1983 (Grass) **49**:136-38
"On Your Feet" (Tchicaya)
See "Debout"
"On Your Own" (Gallagher) **18**:170
"Once" (Celan) **82**:46
"Once" (Thomas) **6**:530
Once (Walker) **6**:553; **9**:558; **58**:405, 408-09; **103**:356, 364-65, 405
"Once a Great Love" (Amichai) **22**:33; **57**:37
Once a Greek... (Dürrenmatt)
See *Grieche sucht Griechin*
Once Again for Thucydides (Handke) **134**:181
Once and for All: Poems for William Bronk (Corman) **9**:170
The Once and Future King (White) **30**:445-52
Once Bitten, Twice Bitten: Poems (Porter) **33**:317-18, 322, 324
"Once by the Pacific" (Frost) **15**:241, 250; **26**:121, 124
"Once High upon a Hill" (Birney) **11**:51
"Once in a Lifetime" (Byrne) **26**:98-9
Once in a Lifetime (Hart and Kaufman) **38**:258, 265; **66**:175-78, 180-86, 188, 190-91
"Once in a Lifetime, Snow" (Murray) **40**:334
"Once in May" (Levine) **14**:318
Once Is Enough (Sargeson) **31**:368-69
Once Is Not Enough (Susann) **3**:476
"Once More" (Carruth) **84**:132
"Once More Out of Darkness" (Ostriker) **132**:318, 320
Once More Out of Darkness and Other Poems3 (Ostriker) **132**:318
Once More the Sea (Arenas)
See *Otra vez el mar*
"Once More to the Lake" (White) **10**:529; **34**:431; **39**:380
Once More upon a Totem (Harris) **12**:263, 266-67
"Once More with Feeling" (Kristofferson) **26**:270
"Once More with Feeling" (Williams) **42**:443-44
"Once on a Hill" (Blunden) **56**:47
"Once, Rocking on the Edge" (Akhmadulina)
See "Odnazhdy, pokanuvshis' na kraiu"
Once There Was a War (Steinbeck) **45**:382; **124**:391
Once upon a Droshky (Charyn) **5**:104
"Once upon a Picnic Ground" (Wagoner) **3**:508
"Once Upon a Time" (Gordimer) **70**:178
Once upon a Time (Dreyer) **16**:260-62
Once upon a Totem (Harris) **12**:261, 265, 267
"Den onda ängeln" (Lagerkvist) **54**:286
Onda sagor (Lagerkvist) **54**:274, 286
"Ondine" (Barnard) **48**:25-6
"1" (Cummings) **15**:161-62
"1" (Donnell)
See "Positions"
"One" (Kinsella) **138**:103, 113-15
"one" (Shange) **25**:402
One (Kinsella) **19**:253-54; **138**:88-89, 96-97, 99, 101-03, 106, 109, 142, 148, 150, 156
"The One About Coyote Going West" (King) **89**:101
One Across, Two Down (Rendell) **28**:383; **48**:322
"One Afternoon in 1939" (Brautigan) **12**:70
One against Another (Adamov)
See *Tous contre tous*
One against the Legion (Williamson) **29**:455, 460
"One against Thebes" (Gordon) **29**:188-90; **83**:258
One A.M. (Chaplin) **16**:204
"One A.M. with Voices" (Kennedy) **42**:257
One and Last Love (Braine) **41**:60-2
The One and Only (King) **145**:365
"The One and the Universe" (Sabato)
See *Uno y el universo*
"One Arab Flute" (MacEwen) **55**:163
"One Arm" (Kawabata)
See "Kata Ucle"
"One Arm" (Williams) **15**:579-80; **45**:447, 453, 456
One Arm (Wilson) **7**:547
One Arm, and Other Stories (Williams) **15**:579; **45**:447; **71**:366, 373
"One Art" (Bishop) **9**:98; **15**:60; **32**:36, 39, 44
"One Blink of the Moon" (Aldiss) **14**:15
"One Body: Some Notes on Form" (Hass) **39**:149; **99**:145

One by One (Gilliatt) **2**:160; **53**:142-43
"One Child of One's Own" (Walker) **103**:357
"One Chooses a Language" (Ghose) **42**:178
One Christmas (Capote) **38**:87
"One Christmas Knitting" (Jolley) **46**:220
One Clear Call (Sinclair) **63**:356-57
"One Crowded Hour of Glorious Strife" (McGinley) **14**:367
One Damn Thing after Another (Garner) **13**:235-36
"One Day" (Goldemberg) **52**:165
"One Day" (Lennon) **35**:266
"One Day" (Sapphire) **99**:82
One Day (Morris) **1**:233; **37**:311-12
The One Day: A Poem in Three Parts (Hall) **59**:151-57; **151**:181, 185, 187, 189-92, 197-99, 204-05, 208-13, 215
"One Day After Saturday" (García Márquez) **27**:147, 154; **47**:146, 150-51
One Day at a Time (Lear) **12**:334
"One Day in Spring" (Sitwell) **67**:319
One Day in the Afternoon of the World (Saroyan) **1**:301
One Day in the Life of Ivan Denisovich (Solzhenitsyn)
See *Odin den' Ivana Denisovicha*
"One Day in Wall Street" (Ferber) **93**:162
"One Day of Happiness" (Singer) **69**:309
One Day of the Life (Argueta)
See *Un dia en la vida*
One Day When I Was Lost (Baldwin) **3**:32; **17**:38-9
One Deadly Summer (Japrisot)
See *L'ete meurtrier*
"The One Desire" (Muldoon) **72**:267
One Dozen Roses (Robinson) **21**:343
One Earth, Four or Five Worlds: Reflections on Contemporary History (Paz) **51**:327-28, 330
"One Evening" (Lavin) **99**:322
One Eye and a Measuring Rod (L'Heureux) **52**:274
"One Fair Daughter and No More" (O'Faolain) **32**:341
One Fat Englishman (Amis) **1**:6; **2**:8-10; **3**:9; **5**:21-2; **129**:3-5, 7-8, 22
One Fat Summer (Lipsyte) **21**:212
One Fell Soup; or, I'm Just a Bug on the Windshield of Life (Blount) **38**:46-8
One Fine Day (Bennett) **77**:86-7
One Flew over the Cuckoo's Nest (Kesey) **1**:167; **3**:266-68; **6**:277-79; **11**:314, 316-18; **46**:224, 226, 228-29; **64**:206-44
"One Fond Embrace" (Kinsella) **138**:134, 137-38, 154-55, 163
One Fond Embrace (Kinsella) **138**:153-54
One Foot in the Grave (Dickinson) **35**:132
One for My Baby (Bessie) **23**:61-2
One for the Pot (Cooney) **62**:144
One for the Road (Davies) **21**:106
One for the Road (Russell) **60**:319, 322
One for the Rose (Levine) **33**:272-75; **118**:269-70, 272-73, 279-80, 285, 287, 292, 303, 318
"One Friday Morning" (Hughes) **35**:215; **108**:285
One from the heart (Coppola) **126**:260
One Generation After (Wiesel) **37**:450
"The One Girl at the Boys' Party" (Olds) **39**:189; **85**:289
"One Good Man" (Alexie) **154**:45, 48
"One Good Story, That One" (King) **89**:77-8, 98, 101
One Good Story, That One (King) **89**:98-9, 101
One Half of Robertson Davies: Provocative Pronouncements on a Wide Range of Topics (Davies) **13**:174; **25**:131-32; **75**:184; **91**:204
One Hand Clapping (Burgess) **4**:81; **22**:74; **40**:115-16; **81**:301; **94**:41
"One Hard Look" (Graves) **45**:166-67
One Hell of an Actor (Kanin) **22**:232
"One Holy Night" (Cisneros) **69**:153; **118**:201, 205
"One Human Minute" (Lem) **149**:112, 116
One Human Minute (Lem) **149**:263-64, 266
One Hundred and One Poems (Arghezi) **80**:10
One Hundred Best Books, With a Commentary and An Essay on Books and Reading (Powys) **125**:265-66
"100 Dollars and Nothing!" (Cooper) **56**:70
"The 184th Demonstration" (Piercy) **27**:374
The 158-Pound Marriage (Irving) **13**:293; **23**:244-45; **38**:250; **112**:155-57, 159, 165
One Hundred Love Sonnets (Neruda)
See *Cien sonetos de amor*
One Hundred More Poems from the Japanese (Rexroth) **112**:393
One Hundred More Poems from the Japanese (Rexroth) **11**:474
"One Hundred Per Cent" (Ferber) **93**:139
100
: The Story of a Patriot (Sinclair) **15**:502; **63**:346, 348
One Hundred Poems (Slessor) **14**:495
One Hundred Poems from the Chinese (Rexroth) **112**:370, 386, 392
One Hundred Poems from the Japanese (Rexroth) **11**:474; **112**:392
"107 Poems" (Fisher) **25**:159
"$106,000 Blood Money" (Hammett) **47**:161
110 Coca-Cola Bottles (Warhol) **20**:418
"110 West Sixty-First Street" (Barthelme) **46**:35
The 120 Days of Sodoma (Pasolini)
See *Salo: 120 Days of Sodom*
"125th Street and Abomey" (Lorde) **71**:232-33, 236
"One Hundred Years Ago" (Jagger and Richard) **17**:228, 232
"One Hundred Years of Proust" (Moss) **45**:287
One Hundred Years of Solitude (García Márquez)
See *Cien años de soledad*
One/ Interior/ Day (Harwood) **32**:225-26
"One is a Wanderer" (Thurber) **125**:403
One Is a Wanderer and Other Stories (King) **53**:212
One is Enough (Nwapa) **133**:170, 175-76, 190, 193, 201-02, 222-25, 227, 229-32, 234, 236-37
"One Is One and All Alone" (Thomas) **13**:539; **107**:316-18
"One Life" (Motion) **47**:293-94
"One Life" (Rich) **73**:330
One Life (Rukeyser) **15**:457-58; **27**:411
One Life at a Time Please (Abbey) **59**:238, 242
"One Life Furnished in Early Poverty" (Ellison) **13**:207
One Life to Live (Nixon) **21**:242-47
One Lonely Night (Spillane) **13**:526-28
One Long Poem (Harmon) **38**:243-44
"One Love" (Marley) **17**:269-70
"One Love/People Get Ready" (Marley) **17**:269
A One Man Protest (Ayckbourn) **74**:21
"One Man Works Silver, Another Works Red Gold" (Hein)
See "Der eine hauet Silber, der andere rotes Gold"
"One Man's Goose" (Starbuck) **53**:352
One Man's House (Ringwood) **48**:330, 335-36
"One Man's Hysteria—Real and Imagined—in the Twentieth Century" (Louie) **70**:80
One Man's Initiation—1917 (Dos Passos) **15**:184; **25**:137-38, 143-44, 146; **82**:78, 83, 86, 107
One Man's Meat (White) **10**:527-29; **34**:430; **39**:370, 372-73, 377, 379
"One: Many" (Ammons) **25**:42; **57**:59
One Million Dead (Gironella)
See *Un millón de muertos*
"One More Brevity" (Frost) **9**:228
"One More Day" (Milosz) **56**:250
One More July (Plimpton) **36**:355-56
"One More Kiss" (McCartney) **35**:281
One More Manhattan (McGinley) **14**:365
"One More Round" (Angelou) **35**:30
One More Sunday (MacDonald) **44**:407, 409
"One More Thing" (Carver) **22**:103
"One More Time" (Gordon) **29**:187-89; **83**:247
"One More Time" (Simon) **26**:407
"One More Way to Die" (Himes) **7**:159
"One Morning" (Steele) **45**:364
"One Morning in New Hampshire" (Swenson) **106**:321, 338
"One Must Have Willpower" (Guillén)
See "Hay que tené boluntá"
One Nation (Stegner) **81**:349
"One Night" (Merwin) **88**:194
"One Night in Turin" (O'Faolain) **1**:259
One Night Stand (Gardner) **44**:210
One Night Stand, and Other Poems (Spicer) **72**:352, 363
One Night Stood: A Minimal Fiction (Kostelanetz) **28**:218
"One Night's Standing" (Kogawa) **78**:167
"One of Many Epilogs" (Pasolini)
See "Uno dei tanti epiloghi"
"One of My Turns" (Pink Floyd) **35**:312
"One of Ours" (Boyle) **58**:66
"One of the Boys" (Dacey) **51**:80
One of the Children Is Crying (Dowell) **60**:96, 98-9, 109
One of the Founders (Newby) **13**:408
"One of the Muses" (Davison) **28**:100
"One of the Muses" (Williams) **33**:447-48; **148**:308, 314, 324, 344
"One of the Three Is Still Alive" (Calvino) **33**:99
"One of These Days" (García Márquez) **27**:147; **47**:146
"One of These Days" (McCartney) **35**:287
"One of These Days" (Pink Floyd) **35**:306, 311, 313
"One of Those Big-City Girls" (Carpenter) **41**:103
"One of Those Springs" (Seifert) **93**:337
"One of Us" (Fante) **60**:130
"One of Us Must Know (Sooner or Later)" (Dylan) **77**:174
"One Off the Short List" (Lessing) **22**:278
"1, 1/3, 1/3" (Brautigan) **12**:71
One or Another (Drexler) **2**:119-20
"One or Two" (Frost) **13**:230
"One or Two Things" (Oliver) **98**:259
"One Ordinary Day, with Peanuts" (Jackson) **60**:235
"One Out of Many" (Naipaul) **4**:373; **13**:407; **37**:320; **105**:157
"One Owner, Low Mileage" (Hood) **28**:189
One Plus One (Godard) **20**:140-41, 150
"One Pocket" (Carpenter) **41**:107-08
One Police Plaza (Caunitz) **34**:35-7
"A One Pound Stein" (Williams) **5**:510
"One Quiet Afternoon" (Buckler) **13**:120
"One Rainy Night of Winter" (Ali)
See "Mahavaton Ki Ek Raat"
"One Ran Before" (Winters) **32**:467
"1 September 1939" (Berryman) **62**:56, 71
"One Sided Shoot-Out" (Madhubuti) **73**:191, 214
One Sings, the Other Doesn't (Varda)
See *Une chant et l'autre pas*
"One Sister" (Jiles) **58**:278
"One XVI" (Cummings) **68**:26
One Size Fits All (Zappa) **17**:591
"One Slip-Slouch Twi" (Cummings) **15**:162
One Small Candle: The Pilgrims' First Year in America (Fleming) **37**:121
"The One Song" (Strand) **71**:285
"One Song Glory" (Larson) **99**:162, 169, 180, 187
"One Sort of Poet" (Smith) **15**:516
"One Spring Day" (Abse) **29**:15
One Step from Earth (Harrison) **42**:200
"One Step Towards Gomorrah" (Bachmann)
See "Ein Schritt nach Gomorrah"

"One Summer" (Grau) **146**:128, 139, 149
"One Summer" (Lavin) **4**:281; **99**:319, 322
"One Summer Morning" (Ihimaera) **46**:199
"One Sunday" (Mistry) **71**:270, 272
"One Sunday Afternoon" (Abse) **29**:20
One Thing and Another (Forbes) **12**:211
"One Thousand Cranes" (Purdy) **3**:408
"$1,000 a Week" (Farrell) **66**:129
$1,000 a Week, and Other Stories (Farrell) **66**:130
"One Thousand Fearful Words for Fidel Castro" (Ferlinghetti) **6**:182
1001 Afternoons in Chicago (Hecht) **8**:270
1003 (Hochwälder) **36**:236-38
"1,000 Years (Life after God)" (Coupland) **85**:36-7, 39; **133**:7-8, 10
The 1,000-Year Plan (Asimov) **92**:21
One Tiger to a Hill (Pollock) **50**:226
One Time, One Place (Welty) **14**:565; **22**:459; **105**:300, 324, 334
1x1 (Cummings) **8**:158; **12**:156; **15**:162-63, **68**:35, 48
"One Too Many Mornings" (Dylan) **77**:172-73
One Touch of Venus (Kazan) **63**:225
One Touch of Venus (Perelman) **44**:500-01, 503
The One Tree (Donaldson) **46**:141; **138**:41
One, Two, Buckle My Shoe (Christie) **12**:124; **48**:71-2
One, Two, Three (Endō) **99**:285
One, Two, Three (Wilder) **20**:459-60
"One Volume Missing" (Dove) **50**:157-58
"One Way Conversation" (Livesay) **79**:349
"One Way Journey" (MacCaig) **36**:285
One Way or Another (Cameron) **44**:33-5
One Way or Another (Sciascia) **9**:476
One Way Pendulum (Simpson) **29**:366-70
One Way Street (Engel)
See *Monodromos*
One Way Ticket (Hughes) **10**:279; **35**:214; **108**:291
One Way Ticket (Levine) **54**:292-93, 295, 297, 300
"One Way Ticket Home" (Ochs) **17**:333
"One Way to Spell Man" (Stegner) **49**:358-59
One Way to Spell Man (Stegner) **49**:358-59
"One Whale Singing" (Hulme) **130**:52
One Who Became Lost (Bowering) **32**:46-7
The One Who Has Escaped (Rozewicz) **139**:261
"The One Who Thinks Alone" (Arghezi)
See "Cel ce gîndeste singur"
The One Who Was Standing Apart from Me (Blanchot) **135**:144, 148
"One Winter Morning by the Footbridge" (L'Heureux) **52**:272
"The One with the Dog" (Kelman) **58**:298, 300
"One Woman Leads to Another" (Godwin) **125**:168
One Wonderful Sunday (Kurosawa)
See *Subarashiki nichiyobi*
"One World (Not Three)" (Police, The) **26**:365-66
One Writer's Beginnings (Welty) **33**:423-26; **105**:316, 319, 321-23, 326, 334, 349, 359-62, 367, 369, 377-80, 382-84, 387-88
"One Year" (Olds) **85**:306
"One Year Later" (Sagan) **36**:382
One-Act Plays for Stage and Study (Rice) **7**:358
"The One-Armed Crucifixion" (Durcan) **70**:153
"One-Eye" (Merwin) **1**:212
"One-Eye, Two-Eyes, Three-Eyes" (Sexton) **53**:314
One-Eyed Cat (Fox) **121**:215, 229
"The One-Eyed King" (Levine) **4**:287
One-Eyed Moon Maps (Gunnars) **69**:257-61
"The One-Horned Mountain Goat" (Harris) **12**:265
"One-Legged Man" (Sassoon) **36**:392; **130**:178, 182, 216
"The One-Legged Man" (Sexton) **4**:483
One-Man Masque (Reaney) **13**:475
"One-Night Homecoming" (Kennedy) **42**:256
"One-Play Oscar" (Fante) **60**:133
"One's a Heifer" (Ross) **13**:492
"Onesided Dialog" (Jordan) **114**:155
"One-Stringed" (Wiebe) **138**:388
One-Trick Pony (Simon) **17**:467-68
One-Woman Plays (Fo) **32**:174
Oni srazhalis' za rodinu (Sholokhov) **15**:482-83
The Onion Eaters (Donleavy) **4**:124-25; **6**:139, 141; **10**:154
The Onion Field (Wambaugh) **3**:509
Onion John (Krumgold) **12**:317-20
The Onion, Memory (Raine) **32**:348-52; **103**:179, 182, 186, 188-90, 197, 200
Onitsha (Le Clézio) **155**:84-6, 88-92, 99, 115-19
Onkel, Onkel (Grass) **15**:260
Onliness (Smith) **42**:346-47, 351
"Only a Few Left" (Madhubuti) **73**:209
"Only a Hobo" (Dylan) **77**:166
"Only among Walkers" (Padilla) **38**:349
Only as Far as Brooklyn (Kenny) **87**:241
"The Only Child" (Browne) **21**:39
"Only Child" (Page) **7**:291; **18**:377
"An Only Child" (Welty) **105**:363
An Only Child (O'Connor) **14**:395-96; **23**:326
Only Children (Lurie) **18**:310-11; **39**:180
"The only cool day of summer" (Broumas) **73**:12
The Only Daughter (Anderson) **37**:21
"The Only Death in the City" (Cherryh) **35**:107
Only Love (Seifert) **34**:256
Only Love (Seifert)
See *Samá láska*
"Only Love Can Break Your Heart" (Young) **17**:569-70
Only Make Believe (Potter) **58**:389, 391; **123**:230, 234
"The Only Man on Liberty Street" (Kelley) **22**:246
The Only Neat Thing to Do (Tiptree) **48**:394-95
"Only Once I Caught a Glimpse..." (Seifert)
See "Jen jedno jsem spatřil..."
The Only Ones Left (Char)
See *Seuls demeurants*
"Only People" (Lennon) **35**:266
"The Only Poem" (Warren) **39**:272
The Only Problem (Spark) **40**:396-400
"The Only Real Day" (Chin) **135**:156
The Only Sense Is Nonsense (Simpson) **29**:367
The Only Sun (Ozu) **16**:453
Only Ten Minutes to Buffalo (Grass) **4**:202; **15**:260; **88**:147
"Only the Dreamer Can Change the Dream" (Logan) **5**:255
"Only the Good Die Young" (Joel) **26**:216
Only the Heart (Foote) **51**:129
"Only the Little Bone" (Huddle) **49**:183-84
Only the Little Bone (Huddle) **49**:183-84
"Only the Presiden's Eggs Are Yellow" (D'Aguiar) **145**:115
"Only the Red Fox, Only the Crow" (Olson) **29**:329-30
"Only the World" (Urdang) **47**:401
Only the World (Urdang) **47**:400
"The Only Traffic Signal on the Reservation Doesn't Flash Red Anymore" (Alexie) **96**:4
"The Only Utopia Is in a Now" (Bernstein) **142**:23, 46
"The Only Way Around Is Through" (Ammons) **57**:49
"The Only Way to Make It in New York" (Brown) **32**:63
Only When I Larf (Deighton) **46**:126
Only When I Laugh (Simon) **70**:238
"Only Woman Blues" (Hughes) **15**:292
Onna no Issho (Endō) **99**:283, 285, 287
"Onnagata" (Mishima) **6**:339
Onnazaka (Enchi) **31**:140-41
"The Onset" (Frost) **13**:228; **26**:123
"Onset" (Johnston) **51**:248
De ontaarde slapers (Ruyslinck) **14**:472
"Ontario" (Muldoon) **72**:273
Ontological Proof of My Experience (Oates) **33**:289
"The Ontology of the Sentence; or, How to Make a World of Words" (Gass) **11**:224; **132**:166
"Oo You" (McCartney) **35**:278
"Oo-Ee Baby" (Reed) **21**:311
"Oona, The Jolly Cave Woman" (Highsmith) **102**:186
"Øowiany żønierzyk" (Rozewicz) **139**:263
O.P.: Orden público (Sender) **8**:477, 480-81
Open Air (Straub) **28**:408; **107**:304
Open All Night (Morand)
See *Ouvert la nuit*
"Open Arms" (Butler) **81**:125, 129
"The Open Boat" (Steinbeck) **9**:519
"Open Book" (Elytis) **100**:168
Open Book (Elytis)
See *Anihtá hártia*
The Open Cage: An Anzia Yezierska Collection (Yezierska) **46**:449
Open Couple (Fo) **109**:119
The Open Couple (Fo)
See *Coppia aperta*
"Open Court" (Kinsella) **138**:148, 154
Open Court (Kinsella) **138**:153-54
"The Open Door" (Sillitoe) **148**:197
The Open Door (Sillitoe) **57**:401-03; **148**:201-209
Open Door (Valenzuela) **104**:376, 380, 382, 388
Open Doorways (Appleman) **51**:14-15
"Open Eye, Open Heart" (Ferlinghetti) **27**:139
Open Eye, Open Heart (Ferlinghetti) **6**:183-84; **27**:139; **111**:65
Open Heart (Buechner) **2**:83-4; **4**:80; **6**:102-03; **9**:137
"Open House" (Gordimer) **18**:189
"Open House" (Roethke) **19**:396-97
Open House (Egoyan) **151**:131
Open House (Roethke) **1**:291; **8**:455, 459-60; **19**:396-97; **46**:356-57, 360-62; **101**:265-66, 287, 298, 301, 312
"Open It, Write" (Ekeloef) **27**:114
"Open Letter" (Dodson) **79**:194
"Open Letter" (Munro) **95**:291
"Open Letter" (Roethke) **19**:396-97; **101**:262-63, 334-36, 339, 341
"Open Letter from a Constant Reader" (Van Duyn) **116**:430
"Open Letter, Personal" (Van Duyn) **63**:440; **116**:408, 429
"An Open Letter to My Sister, Miss Angela Davis" (Baldwin) **50**:296
"Open Letter to President Husák" (Havel) **65**:419
"Open Letter to Richard Crossman" (Fenton) **32**:165
"Open Letter to the President of VAAP" (Voinovich) **147**:272
"An Open Letter to the South" (Hughes) **108**:294
Open Letters (Havel) **123**:166-67, 188, 200-01
"The Open Mind" (White) **49**:408
Open Papers (Elytis) **100**:190-91
The Open Poem (Rozewicz)
See *Poemat otwarty*
An Open Prison (Stewart) **32**:423
"The Open Road" (Farrell) **66**:129
Open Road (Dawson) **6**:126
The Open Sea (Meredith) **13**:374-75; **22**:301-02; **55**:193
Open Season: Sporting Adventures (Humphrey) **45**:205
"Open Secrets" (Motion) **47**:288, 290
Open Secrets (Munro) **95**:301, 319-25
Open Songs (McGrath) **59**:178
Open Songs: Sixty Short Poems (McGrath) **28**:278
"Open the Gates" (Kunitz) **6**:287; **148**:70, 77-79, 118, 125, 130, 136, 138

The Open Veins of Latin America: Five Centuries of the Pillage of a Continent (Galeano)
See *Las venas abiertas de América Latina*
"The Open Window" (Transtroemer) **65**:223
"Open Windows" (Hacker) **72**:182
"Open Winter" (Davis) **49**:91, 94, 97
The Open Work (Eco) **60**:118, 123
"Open-Air Museum" (Rich) **125**:336
The Opener of the Way (Bloch) **33**:82
"The Opening" (Olds) **32**:346
Opening Day (Gascoyne) **45**:152, 158
"Opening Her Jewel Box" (Matthews) **40**:320
Opening Night (Cassavetes) **20**:52-3
Opening Night (Marsh) **53**:253
The Opening of the Field (Duncan) **1**:82; **2**:122-23; **41**:126, 128-29; **55**:292-93, 295, 299
"The Opening of the Road" (Buzzati) **36**:92, 94
"Opening the Door of a Barn I Thought Was Empty on New Year's Eve" (Bly) **15**:63
Opening the Hand (Merwin) **45**:273-76; **88**:191, 194-95, 205-06
"Opening Up the Canon" (Fiedler) **24**:205
Openings (Berry) **4**:59; **27**:32, 34; **46**:70
Opéra (Cocteau) **8**:146; **15**:133
Opera aperta (Eco) **142**:73, 98, 129
"L'opéra des falaises" (Mandiargues) **41**:278
Ópera dos mortos (Dourado) **23**:149-52; **60**:83-4
L'opera mouffe (Varda) **16**:554, 556-57
Opera of the Dead (Dourado)
See *Ópera dos mortos*
Opéra parlé (Audiberti) **38**:23, 25-6, 29-30
Opera Wonyosi (Soyinka) **36**:412-13
"The Operation" (Livesay) **15**:341; **79**:338, 340, 343-44
"The Operation" (Sexton) **8**:483; **15**:472; **53**:312; **123**:408
"The Operation" (Snodgrass) **18**:491
Operation ARES (Wolfe) **25**:472
Operation Chaos (Anderson) **15**:11-12
Operation Harvest Moon (Harper) **22**:208
Operation Iskra (Edgar) **42**:115, 121
Operation Shylock: A Confession (Roth) **86**:247-64; **119**:129-30, 133, 135-36, 142
Operation Sidewinder (Shepard) **4**:489-90; **6**:497; **17**:436-37, 440, 447; **41**:409, 412
Operation Time Search (Norton) **12**:458, 468
Operation Wandering Souls (Powers) **93**:291 95, 299-301
Operetta (Gombrowicz) **4**:195; **49**:128-29
"Ophelia" (Hughes) **37**:179
"Ophelia" (Watkins) **43**:447
Ophelia (Chabrol) **16**:169-70, 177
"An Opinion on the Question of Pornography" (Szymborska) **99**:201
The Opinions of Oliver Allston (Brooks) **29**:82-4
"Opinions of the Press" (Reading) **47**:354
"Opium" (Ellison) **42**:130
The Opoponax (Wittig) **22**:471-74
Opowiadanie traumatyczne: Duszyczka (Rozewicz) **139**:227
Oppiano Licario (Lezama Lima) **101**:121, 129
"Opportunity" (Armatrading) **17**:8
The Opposing Self (Trilling) **9**:530; **11**:542-43, 546; **24**:452-53, 456, 458, 461-62
The Opposing Shore (Gracq)
See *Le rivage des Syrtes*
Opposite the Forests (Yehoshua)
See *Facing the Forests*
"Opposite the House of the Caryatids" (Pasternak) **7**:294
"Opposites" (Wilbur) **110**:364
Opposites (Wilbur) **6**:571; **110**:382, 387
Opposites—React (Williamson) **29**:455
"The Oppositional Gaze: Black Female Spectators" (Hooks) **94**:153
"Oppressed Hair Puts a Ceiling on the Brain" (Walker) **58**:409
"Oppression" (Hughes) **15**:295
Opticks: A Poem in Seven Sections (Goldbarth) **5**:143-44; **38**:203
"Optimism" (Hikmet) **40**:252
"Optimism and Critical Excess (Process)" (Bernstein) **142**:18
The Optimist (Gold) **4**:190-92; **42**:191; **152**:138
"Optimists" (Ford) **99**:115
"The Optimist's Daughter" (Welty) **105**:364
The Optimist's Daughter (Welty) **2**:463-64; **5**:479; **14**:564; **22**:462; **33**:415-16, 424; **105**:300, 308, 312, 322, 325, 335, 349-51, 353, 359-64, 367-70, 382-83, 390
"Optional" (Avison) **97**:71, 75
"Opulence" (Graham) **118**:256
Opus 21 (Wylie) **43**:465, 467, 470, 472
Opus 100 (Asimov) **26**:48
Opus 200 (Asimov) **19**:27-8
"Opus Dei" (Berryman) **3**:66, 68, 70; **13**:82; **25**:92
Opus Pistorum (Miller) **43**:301-02
"Op. posth. Nos. 1-14" (Berryman) **13**:80; **25**:93, 96, 98
L'or (Cendrars) **18**:95, 97; **106**:149, 153-54, 167, 182-83, 185, 190, 194
Or Else: Poem/Poems, 1968-1974 (Warren) **6**:555-59; **8**:536-37, 539, 542; **10**:520-22; **13**:577; **39**:260, 270-71
"Or, Solitude" (Davie) **5**:114
"...Or Traveller's Joy" (Tomlinson) **45**:394
"Or When Your Sister Sleeps Around for Money" (Knight)
See "The Violent Space (or when your sister sleeps around for money)"
"Una oracion" (Borges) **6**:90
Oración (Arrabal)
See *Oraison*
Oración (Arrabal) **9**:33, 38; **18**:18, 20; **58**:3, 7, 9, 11, 16, 18
"Oracle" (Cardenal)
See "Oraculoe"
"The Oracle" (Merton) **83**:391
"An Oracle" (White) **110**:340
The Oracle (O'Connor) **14**:392-93
The Oracle in the Heart, and Other Poems, 1975-1978 (Raine) **45**:339
"Oracle over Managua" (Cardenal)
See "Oráculo sobre Managua"
"Oracles" (Jiles) **58**:277-78
"Oráculo sobre Managua" (Cardenal) **31**:77
"Oraculoe" (Cardenal) **31**:77
"Orage" (Reverdy) **53**:289
Oraison (Arrabal) **58**:3, 7, 9, 11, 16, 18
Oraison (Arrabal)
See *Oración*
"Oral History" (Gordimer) **18**:190
Oral History (Smith) **73**:340-45, 347, 350, 352, 355, 357
"Oral Messages" (Ferlinghetti) **27**:138
"The Oral Tradition" (Boland) **67**:36; **113**:73, 82-3, 98, 119
"Orange County Plague" (Lieberman) **36**:263
"The Orange Fish" (Shields) **113**:408, 432
The Orange Fish (Shields) **113**:404-05, 407-08, 410-11, 413-14
"An Orange from Portugal" (MacLennan) **92**:340
"Orange Roses" (Stern) **40**:413
"The Orange Tree" (Belitt) **22**:53
The Orange Tree (Fuentes) **113**:262-65
The Orangery (Sorrentino) **14**:498-500; **40**:384, 386
"Oranges" (O'Hara) **78**:352, 355
Oranges (McPhee) **36**:293
Oranges (O'Hara) **2**:323; **13**:423, 426
"Oranges and Apples" (Munro) **95**:310
Oranges Are Not the Only Fruit (Winterson) **64**:426-27, 429-32, 434-35, 439-40, 442, 444
"Oranges from Morocco" (Aksyonov) **22**:27
Oranges from Morocco (Aksyonov) **101**:6-7, 10, 12, 16, 29-30
"Oranges on Her Windowsill" (Federspiel) **42**:145
"Orange-throats" (Zamora) **89**:392
"Orange-Tree" (Wright) **53**:419
"The Oranging of America" (Apple) **9**:32-3; **33**:19
The Oranging of America, and Other Stories (Apple) **9**:33; **33**:18-22
L'orare du discours (Foucault) **34**:341
"Oration at a Bonfire, Fourteen Years Late" (Dinesen) **95**:56
The Orators: An English Study (Auden) **2**:22; **6**:24; **9**:60; **11**:15, 18-19; **14**:31-2; **43**:15-16, 18, 21, 25
The Orb Weaver (Francis) **15**:235-36, 238
Orbita de Lezama Lima (Lezama Lima) **101**:109-10
"Orbital Radio Relays" (Clarke) **35**:128
"Orbiter 5 Shows How Earth Looks from the Moon" (Swenson) **61**:397
"Orbiting" (Mukherjee) **53**:271; **115**:385-87, 389
"Orchard" (Eberhart) **56**:77, 89
"Orchard" (H. D.)
See "Priapus"
The Orchard Keeper (Leonov)
See *Polovchanskie sady*
The Orchard Keeper (McCarthy) **4**:342-43; **57**:327-28, 330-32; **101**:133, 135, 147-48, 150, 154, 166-67, 175-78, 182, 185, 195, 197, 202-04
"Orchard Love" (Carlson) **54**:37
The Orchards of Polovchansk (Leonov)
See *Polovchanskie sady*
"Orchestra" (Purdy) **50**:247
"The Orchestra" (Turco) **11**:552
Orchestra and Beginners (Raphael) **14**:436
The Orchestra Rehearsal (Fellini)
See *Provo d'orchestra*
Orchéstration Théâtrale (Arrabal) **58**:4, 13-14
L'orchestre (Anouilh) **40**:58-9
"Orchids" (Roethke) **8**:461; **11**:484; **101**:294
Orchids in the Moonlight (Fuentes)
See *Orquídeas a la luz de la luna*
"L'ordalie" (Bonnefoy) **58**:53
Ordeal (Shute) **30**:364-65, 369
Ordeal by Ice (Mowat) **26**:334
Ordeal by Innocence (Christie) **12**:116, 124; **48**:75
The Ordeal of Gilbert Pinfold (Harwood) **32**:225
The Ordeal of Gilbert Pinfold: A Conversation Piece (Waugh) **1**:357; **3**:510, 513; **8**:544; **27**:474, 477; **44**:522-23; **107**:373, 385, 393, 398
The Ordeal of Mark Twain (Brooks) **29**:79-81, 86-7
The Order of Assassins (Wilson) **14**:589
"Order of Insects" (Gass) **8**:245; **15**:258
"The Order of Saying" (Tomlinson) **45**:398
"Order of the Black Cross" (p'Bitek) **96**:299
The Order of Things: An Archaeology of the Human Sciences (Foucault)
See *Les mots et les choses: Une archéologie des sciences humaines*
"Order to View" (MacNeice) **10**:323
"Orders" (Duncan) **55**:297
Orders of Chivalry (Vansittart) **42**:390-91
Orders of the Retina (Disch) **36**:127
Ordet (Dreyer) **16**:258, 260-61, 263-65, 267-69
L'Ordinaire (Brossard) **115**:106, 110
"An Ordinary Afternoon in Charlottesville" (Wright) **146**:353, 357
"An Ordinary Evening in Cleveland" (Turco) **63**:429
An Ordinary Evening in New Haven (Aiken) **3**:3
"Ordinary Homecoming" (MacCaig) **36**:282
Ordinary Love and Goodwill (Smiley) **76**:230, 233; **144**:251, 255
An Ordinary Lunacy (Anderson) **37**:18
"Ordinary Man" (Lightfoot) **26**:279
An Ordinary Man (Leonov)
See *Obyknovenny chelovek*
Ordinary Money (Jones) **65**:56-62

"An Ordinary Morning" (Levine) **118**:301
Ordinary, Moving (Gotlieb) **18**:192-93
"Ordinary Pain" (Wonder) **12**:660
"Ordinary People" (Davies) **21**:100
"Ordinary People" (Musgrave) **54**:341
Ordinary People (Guest) **8**:253-54; **30**:172-76
An Ordinary Person (Leonov)
See *Obyknovenny chelovek*
An Ordinary Woman (Clifton) **19**:109-10, **66**:66-7, 75-6, 80-1, 84-5
Ordinatio Sacerdotalis (John Paul II) **128**:193
Ordkonst och bildkonst (Lagerkvist) **54**:271, 273, 286, 289
"Ordo" (Westlake) **33**:438
The Ordways (Humphrey) **45**:195-200, 202
"Oread" (H. D.) **14**:223; **31**:205, 207; **73**:118, 121
Ore'ah natah lalun (Agnon) **4**:12; **8**:8-9; **14**:5
"Oregano" (Neruda) **28**:309
"Oregon" (Davis) **49**:92
L'oreille de l'autre (Derrida) **87**:92
Oreste (Anouilh) **40**:58; **50**:279
The Oresteia (Harrison) **129**:165, 168-71, 180-83, 192-93, 195, 203, 222, 226
The Oresteia of Aeschylus (Lowell) **15**:344, 348-49
"Orestes" (Davies) **23**:142, 145
"Orestes" (Ritsos) **31**:325
Orestes (Fugard) **14**:189; **40**:197; **80**:62, 64
Orestes (Ritsos) **13**:488
Orestes A. Brownson: A Pilgrim's Progress (Schlesinger) **84**:346
"Orestes at Tauris" (Jarrell) **2**:209; **13**:300
"Orf" (Hughes) **37**:174
The Organdy Cupcakes (Stolz) **12**:545-46, 549
"Organelle" (Swenson) **106**:314
"Organic Bloom" (Kunitz) **148**:87, 95, 123
Organic Trains (Carroll) **143**:39, 41
"Organized Guilt and Universal Responsibility" (Arendt) **98**:52
"The Organizer's Wife" (Bambara) **88**:7, 28, 37, 48, 52-54
"Organs" (Swenson) **106**:339
"The Orgasm: A Reappraisal" (Blount) **38**:46
Orgasmo Adulto Escapes from the Zoo (Fo) **32**:175-76; **109**:119
"Orghast" (Hughes) **119**:264-65, 272
La orgía perpetua: Flaubert y "Madame Bovary" (Vargas Llosa) **10**:500-01; **85**:355, 363, 385
Orgie (Brink) **106**:101
"The Orgy" (Amichai) **116**:107
The Orgy (Rukeyser) **27**:409
"O'Riada's Farewell" (Montague) **46**:272
"Orielton Empty" (Mathias) **45**:235-36
"Orient and Immortal Wheat" (Walcott) **67**:353
"The Orient Express" (Jarrell) **13**:298
Orient Express (Greene)
See *Stamboul Train*
"The Oriental Ballerina" (Dove) **50**:155, 158
Oriental Mythology (Campbell)
See *The Masks of God: Oriental Mythology*
Oriental Tales (Yourcenar)
See *Nouvelles orientales*
Orientale Lumen (John Paul II) **128**:207
Orientalism (Said) **123**:337, 341, 343-44, 346, 357-58, 369, 371, 374, 376, 379, 384, 390, 396-97
"Orientation Day in Hades" (Fulton) **52**:161
Orientations (Elytis)
See *Prosanatolizmí*
Orientations (Maugham) **67**:220
"Oriflamme" (Williams) **5**:502-03
An Origin Like Water: Collected Poems 1967-1987 (Boland) **113**:108, 112, 114, 120-21, 124, 127
"The Origin of Centaurs" (Hecht) **8**:268
The Origin of Evil (Queen) **11**:459, 463
"The Origin of Extermination in the Imagination" (Gass) **39**:481-82
"The Origin of Man" (Bowering) **32**:47
Origin of Satan (Pagels) **104**:222-28, 230, 233, 234
The Origin of the Brunists (Coover) **3**:114; **7**:57; **32**:124-26; **46**:116, 119, 121; **87**:23-6, 28-9, 32-3, 37-8, 43-6
"The Origin of the Scarecrow" (Farrell) **66**:131
"Original Child Bomb" (Merton) **83**:384
Original Child Bomb: Points for Meditation to Be Scratched on the Walls of a Cave (Merton) **11**:373
Original Light: New and Selected Poems, 1973-1983 (Goldbarth) **38**:204-07
"Original Memory" (Harjo) **83**:282
The Original Michael Frayn: Satirical Essays (Frayn) **47**:135
"Original Sin" (Jeffers) **15**:301
Original Sin (James) **122**:172-79, 186-87
Original Sin (Tabori) **19**:435-36
"Original Sin: A Short Story" (Warren) **8**:539; **13**:582; **39**:264
"Original Sin on the Sussex Coast" (Betjeman) **43**:38, 41
Original Sins (Alther) **41**:19-23
"The Original Sins of Edward Tripp" (Trevor) **71**:322, 335
"The Originators" (Merton) **83**:385, 397
"Origins" (Bowen) **6**:95
"Origins" (Walcott) **42**:418, 421
"Origins and History of Consciousness" (Rich) **36**:374, 376
"Origins of a Poem" (Levertov) **66**:241-43
Origins of Marvel Comics (Lee) **17**:258
"Origins of the Beat Generation" (Kerouac) **61**:310
Origins of the Sexual Impulse (Wilson) **14**:589
The Origins of Totalitarianism (Arendt) **66**:15-18, 22, 26, 31-2, 40; **98**:3, 9, 11, 17-18, 20-2, 31, 36, 45, 48, 50-2
Origins: The Lives and Worlds of Modern Cosmologists (Lightman) **81**:78
"O'Riley's Late-Bloomed Little Son" (Kennedy) **42**:256-57
"Orion" (Oliver) **98**:261
"Orion" (Rich) **18**:447; **36**:369
Orion (Bova) **45**:73-4
Orion aveugle (Simon) **39**:206
"Orion Iroquois" (Char) **55**:285
Orison (Arrabal)
See *Oración*
Orison (Arrabal)
See *Oraison*
"Orissa" (Mahapatra) **33**:283
"Orizont şi stil" (Blaga) **75**:72
Orkney: Pictures and Poems (Brown) **100**:84
An Orkney Tapestry (Brown) **48**:52; **100**:84
Orlando at the Brazen Threshold (Colegate) **36**:110, 113
Orlando King (Colegate) **36**:110, 113
Ormen's ägg (Bergman) **16**:80-2; **72**:55, 57, 59
Orn (Anthony) **35**:35, 40
"The Ornamental Water" (Blunden) **56**:45
Ornifle; ou, Le courant d'air (Anouilh) **13**:17, 20
El oro de los tigres (Borges) **6**:90; **13**:109-10; **48**:37; **83**:190
L'oro di Napoli (De Sica) **20**:90
"Orphan" (Jong) **6**:268
The Orphan (Rabe) **4**:425; **8**:450
The Orphan Genius (Dabrowska)
See *Geniusz sierocy*
"The Orphanage" (McCullers) **4**:345; **12**:432
"The Orphanage" (Reaney) **13**:473
"Orphanage Boy" (Warren) **18**:536
"The Orphaning" (Belitt) **22**:50, 52-3
"The Orphans" (Dubie) **36**:130
The Orphans (Murphy) **51**:300
Orphans and Other Children (Webb) **7**:515-16
The Orphan's Home (Foote) **51**:132-33, 136-37
Orphans of the Sky (Heinlein) **3**:225
Orphée (Cocteau) **8**:145, 147-49; **15**:134; **16**:223-29; **43**:102, 104-07, 109-10
"Orpheus" (Dybek) **114**:63
"Orpheus" (Rukeyser) **15**:457; **27**:407-08, 410-14
"Orpheus" (Smith) **64**:399-400
Orpheus (Blanchot)
See *The Gaze of Orpheus and Other Literary Essays*
Orpheus (Cocteau)
See *Orphée*
"Orpheus Alone" (Strand) **71**:287-88, 290
"Orpheus and Eurydice" (Graham) **48**:154
"Orpheus and His Lute" (O'Connor) **14**:398
Orpheus and Other Poems (Smith) **64**:399
"Orpheus Below" (Honig) **33**:214
"Orpheus' Brother" (Brunner) **8**:108
Orpheus Descending (Williams) **5**:499, 502; **11**:571-72, 577; **15**:578-79; **30**:466; **71**:369, 386, 405; **111**:393
"Orpheus in America" (Simpson) **149**:309
"Orpheus in the Underworld" (Gascoyne) **45**:148
"Orpheus in the Underworld" (Simpson) **7**:426
Orpheus in the Underworld of the Twentieth Century (Wittlin) **25**:467
"Orpheus to Eurydice" (Morgan) **23**:301-02
Orquídeas a la luz de la luna (Fuentes) **41**:168-72
Orsinian Tales (Le Guin) **8**:343; **45**:214, 216; **136**:343
Ortadirek (Kemal) **14**:299-300
"The Orthodoxy of Enlightenment" (Leavis) **24**:305
Örtlich betäubt (Grass) **15**:263
O'Ryan (Olson) **5**:328
The Osages: Children of the Middle Waters (Mathews) **84**:206, 209, 211, 221, 226
"Osai to minosuke" (Tanizaki) **8**:509
Oscar and Lucinda (Carey) **55**:112-19; **96**:36, 47, 49-50, 59, 61, 63, 70, 72, 76-82
Oscar Wilde (Ellmann) **50**:306, 309
"Oscar Wilde and San Miniato" (Wright) **6**:580
Osceola (Dinesen) **95**:67, 70
Oscura noticia (Alonso) **14**:16, 23, 26
"Osen'" (Voznesensky) **15**:555
"Osip Mandelstam" (Deane) **122**:83-4
Osm dnů (Seifert) **44**:425; **93**:306, 317, 334, 342
"Un oso y un amor" (Ulibarrí) **83**:415
Osoba i czyn (John Paul II) **128**:177, 193, 198
"Osobny zeszyt" (Milosz) **56**:231-32, 234, 239, 244, 251
"The Osprey" (Longley) **29**:292
The Osprey Suicides (Lieberman) **4**:291; **36**:261, 263
Ossessione (Visconti) **16**:563-64, 572, 575
Ossi di seppia (Montale) **7**:222, 224, 226-29, 231; **9**:387-88; **18**:339-40
"Ostanovka v pustyne" (Brodsky) **6**:96; **50**:123-24; **6**:96; **13**:114, 116; **50**:121-24, 131
Ostatni dzien lata (Konwicki) **117**:282
"Ostensibly" (Ashbery) **77**:63
Österjöar (Transtroemer) **52**:413-18; **65**:219, 226, 229, 233, 235
The Osterman Weekend (Ludlum) **22**:289; **43**:273
"Ostia Antica" (Hecht) **8**:268
"Ostinato and Drone" (Wright) **146**:372
Ostře sledované vlaky (Hrabal) **13**:290-91; **67**:121-22, 124-27, 129-31
Ostrov Krym (Aksyonov) **37**:12-13, 16; **101**:23-5, 29, 35, 47, 50
Den osynlige (Lagerkvist) **54**:268, 270-71, 274, 277
Otchaianie (Nabokov) **1**:242-43, **2**:302, **6**:359; **8**:412; **11**:394; **15**:396; **44**:465, 467; **46**:292, 294; **64**:351, 366
Othello (Welles) **20**:433-35, 438-41, 448-50; **80**:367, 410
"The Other" (Borges)
See "El otro, el mismo"
"The Other" (Dickey) **109**:235
"The Other" (Greene) **27**:174

"The Other" (Plath) **9**:426; **17**:361; **51**:340; **111**:203
"The Other" (Roethke) **101**:328
The Other (Tryon) **3**:483; **11**:548
"The Other Boat" (Forster) **2**:136; **4**:168; **15**:231; **22**:135-36; **45**:136, 140
"The Other Celia" (Sturgeon) **39**:366
Other Days (Haines) **58**:220
Other Dimensions (Smith) **43**:418-19
"The Other Eye of Polyphemus" (Ellison) **42**:130
"The Other Face" (Mahfūz)
See "al-Wahj al-ākhar"
"Other Factors" (Gaitskill) **69**:199-200
The Other Father (Hobson) **25**:271
The Other Glass Teat (Ellison) **139**:115, 129
Other Gods (Buck) **11**:75
"The Other Half" (Wright) **53**:425-26, 429
The Other Half (Wright) **53**:426, 429, 431
"The other, himself" (Borges)
See "El otro, el mismo"
Other Inquisitions, 1937-1952 (Borges)
See *Otras inquisiciónes, 1937-1952*
"The Other K" (Fuentes) **60**:162
"Other Kingdom" (Forster) **9**:207; **45**:140
"The Other Labrynth" (Bioy Casares)
See "El otro labertino"
"Other Manifestations of the American Scene" (Stafford) **4**:517
"The Other Margaret" (Trilling) **11**:544
"The Other Me" (McCartney) **35**:292
Other Men's Daughters (Stern) **4**:522-23; **39**:240-41
"Other Modes" (Updike) **2**:444; **3**:488
"Other Nations" (Kumin) **28**:223
"The Other Night at Columbia: A Report from the Academy" (Trilling) **129**:347, 365
"The Other One" (Borges)
See "El otro, el mismo"
The Other One (Green)
See *L'autre*
The Other Paris (Gallant) **18**:170
Other People: A Mystery Story (Amis) **38**:14-15; **62**:5, 17; **101**:65, 89
Other People's Children (Findley) **102**:106
"Other People's Legs" (Oe) **86**:226-27
Other People's Money (Weidman) **7**:517
"Other People's Stories" (Ozick)
See "Usurpation (Other People's Stories)"
Other People's Worlds (Trevor) **25**:442-44, 446; **71**:323, 326, 346, 348; **116**:338, 364, 377
Other Places (Pinter) **27**:392-93, 396-97; **58**:371, 375-78, 385
"The Other Rib of Death" (García Márquez)
See "La otra costilla de la muerte"
"The Other Ship" (Breytenbach) **126**:71
"The Other Shore" (Paz) **10**:392
"The Other Side" (Heaney) **25**:241
The Other Side (Alvarez)
See *El Otro Lado*
The Other Side (Gordon) **128**:127-28, 130-31, 140, 143-44, 149
The Other Side (Middleton) **38**:333
"The Other Side of Death" (García Márquez)
See "La otra costilla de la muerte"
The Other Side of Hugh MacLennan (MacLennan) **14**:343
"The Other Side of Lethe" (Howe) **47**:173-74
"The Other Side of the Border" (Greene) **72**:149
"The Other Side of the Fence" (Ihimaera) **46**:196, 199
The Other Side of the Fence (Tunis) **12**:596
The Other Side of the Fire (Ellis) **40**:192-93
The Other Side of the Hill (Luke) **38**:318
"The Other Side of the Lake" (Aldiss) **40**:21
"The Other Side of the River" (Wright) **146**:314, 338-39
The Other Side of the River (Wright) **146**:312-17, 321-22, 327, 330, 333, 336, 338, 341-42, 349, 363, 374-75, 380
The Other Side of the Sky (Clarke) **13**:148
"The Other Side of the Street" (Updike) **139**:368
The Other Side of the Sun (L'Engle) **12**:349
Other Skies (Ciardi) **40**:152-54; **44**:378
"The Other Tiger" (Borges)
See "El otro tigre"
"Other Times" (Nye) **13**:412
Other Times (Lawler) **58**:333, 336-37, 340-44
"The Other Tradition" (Ashbery) **77**:45, 54
The Other Trial (Canetti)
See *Der andere Prozeß: Kafkas Briefe an Felice*
"The Other Voice" (Paulin) **37**:353
The Other Voice (Paz) **119**:419
"The Other Voices" (Hogan) **73**:159
Other Voices, Other Rooms (Capote) **1**:55; **3**:99; **8**:132-33; **13**:132-35, 138-40; **19**:79-80, 85-7; **34**:320-25; **38**:78-9, 82-3, 85-7; **58**:86, 94, 102, 122, 133
"The Other Way" (Grau) **4**:210; **9**:240; **146**:128, 163
Other Weapons (Valenzuela)
See *Cambio de armas*
"The Other Whitman" (Borges)
See "El otro Whitman"
"The Other Woman" (Boland) **113**:78
"The Other Woman" (Dacey) **51**:83
"The Other Woman" (Gordon) **128**:110
"The Other Woman" (Lessing) **6**:292; **10**:316
"Other Women" (Vaughn) **62**:458-59
Other Women (Alther) **41**:22-4
Others (Shields) **113**:407, 412, 441
"Otherwise" (Ashbery) **15**:36
"Otherwise" (Niedecker) **42**:299
Otherwise Engaged (Gray) **9**:241-42; **36**:201-07, 210
Otherwise Known as Sheila the Great (Blume) **30**:22
"Otis and Marlena" (Mitchell) **12**:443
"Otkazom" (Brodsky) **13**:115
"Otoño" (Neruda) **62**:335
La otra casa de Mazón (Benet) **28**:20-1
"La otra costilla de la muerte" (García Márquez) **3**:181; **47**:147
"Otra no amo" (Aleixandre) **9**:12
Otra vez el diablo (Casona) **49**:40, 42-5, 47
Otra vez el mar (Arenas) **41**:29-30
"Otras aires" (Cernuda) **54**:60
Otras inquisiciónes, 1937-1952 (Borges) **2**:72; **3**:80; **8**:100; **10**:63; **44**:363, 366; **48**:39, 46-7; **83**:160-64, 166, 169, 171, 184
"El otro" (Borges)
See "El otro, el mismo"
Otro Canto (Castillo) **151**:3-5, 9, 30, 45
"El otro cielo" (Cortázar) **10**:113; **33**:126, 129
"Otro día nuestro" (Marqués) **96**:228, 243
"El otro, el mismo" (Borges) **13**:111; **44**:360, 365; **48**:38, 41
"El otro labertino" (Bioy Casares) **88**:59
El Otro Lado (Alvarez) **93**:17
"Otro rio: O Ebro" (Cabral de Melo Neto) **76**:168
El otro rostro del peronismo (Sabato) **23**:378
"El otro tigre" (Borges) **3**:81; **13**:107
"El otro Whitman" (Borges) **83**:163
Otros poemas (Parra) **102**:334, 341, 343, 356
"Otros tulipanes amarillos" (Cernuda) **54**:60
Ōtsu junkichi (Shiga) **33**:371
Otsuya Koroshi (Tanizaki) **8**:509
"The Ottawa Valley" (Munro) **19**:345; **95**:291
"The Otter" (Heaney) **14**:246; **25**:244; **37**:162
"An Otter" (Hughes) **2**:203; **4**:235
"Otto" (Roethke) **8**:457
"Otto and the Magi" (Connell) **45**:109
Otto e Mezzo (Fellini) **16**:274, 277, 282-84, 286-89, 291-92, 297-98; **85**:47-9, 55, 57-62, 64-6, 68-70, 73-6, 78-81
"Otto tis erate" (Elytis) **100**:178
Où boivent les loups (Tzara) **47**:387
Où: Le génie de lieu, Volume II (Butor) **11**:80; **15**:118, 120
L'oubli (Mauriac) **9**:366
Oublier Foucault (Baudrillard) **60**:13, 15
"Oughtiness Ousted" (Avison) **97**:121
"Oui" (Dorris) **109**:309
"Ouija" (Hughes) **119**:256
"Ouija" (Plath) **11**:447; **51**:344; **111**:178
"Ould Biddy—The Newsmonger" (Carroll) **10**:98
"Our Actors and the Critics" (McCarthy) **24**:344
"Our Afterlife I" (Lowell) **124**:301
"Our Afterlife II" (Lowell) **124**:298
"Our Aims Our Dreams Our Destinations" (Brutus) **43**:92-3
Our Ancestors (Calvino)
See *I nostri antenati*
Our Betters (Maugham) **1**:204; **11**:369; **15**:366; **67**:207, 223, 225; **93**:257
Our Blood: Prophecies and Discourses on Sexual Politics (Dworkin) **43**:132-33; **123**:89
"Our Bog Is Dood" (Smith) **25**:419
"Our Bourgeois Literature" (Sinclair) **63**:348
"Our Bovary" (Gordimer) **18**:186; **33**:180
Our Conquest (Hofmann) **54**:226, 229
Our Country and Our Children: Improving America's Schools and Affirming the Common Culture (Bennett) **70**:362
"Our Cousin, Mr. Poe" (Tate) **24**:445
Our Day Out (Russell) **60**:320
Our Dead Behind Us (Lorde) **71**:254-55, 257-59, 261-63
"Our Dead Poets" (Lowell) **11**:329
"Our Death" (Strand) **18**:516-17
Our England Is a Garden (Stewart) **14**:513
"Our Exagimation Round His Factification for Incamination of Work in Progress" (Beckett) **59**:254
"Our Father" (Durcan) **70**:153
Our Father (King) **8**:322
Our Father's Failing (Horovitz) **56**:155
"Our Fear" (Herbert) **43**:193
"Our Fearful Innocence" (O'Faolain) **32**:342
"Our First Day Together" (Simon) **26**:407
"Our Forward Shadows" (Swenson) **106**:339
Our Friends from Frolix-8 (Dick) **72**:121-22
Our Gang (Roth) **2**:378-80; **3**:437, 439; **4**:452-53, 456-57, 459; **6**:476; **15**:452; **22**:352; **47**:363; **119**:120
Our God's Brother (John Paul II) **128**:164-65, 168-69
Our Golden Ironburg (Aksyonov) **101**:25
"Our Grandmothers" (Angelou) **64**:41
Our Ground Time Here Will Be Brief (Kumin) **28**:222-25
"Our Hands in the Garden" (Hébert)
See "Nos mains au jardin"
Our Hospitality (Keaton) **20**:188
Our House in the Last World (Hijuelos) **65**:150
"Our Hunting Fathers" (Auden) **43**:17
"Our Hunting Fathers" (Simmons) **43**:411
"Our Inabilities" (Borges)
See "Nuestras imposibilidades"
"Our Inadequacies" (Borges)
See "Nuestras imposibilidades"
"Our King is Dead" (Dumas) **62**:160
"Our Lady of Ardboe" (Muldoon) **72**:266
Our Lady of Babylon (Rechy) **107**:259-60
Our Lady of Darkness (Leiber) **25**:306, 308
Our Lady of the Flowers (Genet)
See *Notre dame des fleurs*
Our Lady of the Snows (Callaghan) **41**:97-8
"Our Lady of the Well" (Browne) **21**:37
"Our Land" (Ritsos) **13**:488
"Our Lane" (Ali)
See "Hamari Gali"
Our Late Night (Shawn) **41**:396-97, 399-400
"Our Life Is War" (Chin) **135**:162
Our Little Trip (Ferlinghetti) **111**:63
"Our Love Is So Natural" (Wright) **53**:431
"Our Love Was" (Townshend) **17**:531
"Our Love Was Is" (Townshend) **17**:539
Our Man in Havana (Greene) **3**:212-13; **9**:250; **14**:219; **18**:197; **27**:176; **37**:140; **70**:289-90,

294; **72**:163-65, 169, 171-72; **125**:178, 185
"Our Many Different Businesses with Art" (Booth) **24**:98
Our Mother's House (Gloag) **40**:205-07, 210-11
Our Mrs. McChesney (Ferber) **93**:141
Our New Front Yard (Simak) **55**:320
Our Next President (Baker) **31**:27
"Our Northern Kind" (Carruth) **84**:129
"Our Old Aunt Who Is Now in a Retirement Home" (Shields) **113**:442
Our Older Brother (Rozewicz)
See *Nasz starszy brat*
"Our Own or Other Nations" (Brand) **7**:30
"Our Padre" (Betjeman) **43**:42
"Our Place in Winter" (Dobyns) **37**:77
Our Republic (Keneally) **117**:243
"Our Right-to-Lifer: The Mind of an Antiabortionist" (Pollitt) **122**:223
"Our Room" (Peacock) **60**:292
"Our Secret" (Allende) **97**:4, 10
"Our Story Begins" (Wolff) **64**:451-52, 454
"Our Strange and Loveable Weather" (Matthews) **40**:322
"Our Text for Today" (Pryor) **26**:378
"Our Time" (Sondheim) **147**:243
Our Town (Wilder) **1**:364, 366; **5**:494-96; **6**:572-78; **10**:532; **15**:569-73, 575; **35**:346-47; **82**:345-48, 352, 355, 357-66, 368, 373, 376, 379-80, 385-87, 389-90
"Our Trip (A Diary)" (Bioy Casares) **88**:92-3
"Our Turn" (Reed) **5**:368
"Our Vera Ivanovna" (Aksyonov) **101**:13
"Our Very Best People" (Ferber) **93**:153
"Our Visit to Niagara" (Goodman) **4**:196
"Our Western Furniture" (Fenton) **32**:164-65, 169
"Our Whole Life" (Rich) **7**:366
"Our Work and Why We Do It" (Barthelme) **23**:46
"Our Working Day May Be Menaced" (Avison) **97**:72, 91, 110
"L'Ouragan" (Senghor) **130**:253
"Ourselves or Nothing" (Forché) **83**:212, 219
Ourselves to Know (O'Hara) **2**:324; **42**:312, 318, 321-24
"Ousia and Grammé" (Derrida) **87**:85
"Out" (Hughes) **37**:180
Out (Brooke-Rose) **40**:104, 111
Out (Sukenick) **3**:475; **4**:531; **6**:523; **48**:363-70
"Out at Sea" (Martinson) **14**:356
Out Cry (Williams)
See *The Two-Character Play*
"Out Here" (Leavitt) **34**:77
"Out in the Midday Sun" (Thomas) **37**:419-21; **107**:316, 320, 328, 330
"Out in the Open" (Transtroemer) **65**:229
"Out in the Stream" (Hemingway) **34**:478
"Out Like a Lamb" (Dubus) **97**:233
Out of Africa (Dinesen) **10**:148-50, 152-53; **29**:153, 155-56, 158-60, 163-64; **95**:32-3, 37-8, 40-5, 47-9, 54, 56, 68, 72, 75, 77, 80-2
Out of Chaos (Ehrenburg) **18**:136; **62**:168
"Out of Darkness" (La Guma) **19**:274
"Out of Depth" (Waugh) **44**:520
"Out of His Window" (Van Doren) **6**:542
Out of India (Jhabvala) **94**:187-88; **138**:71, 77
"Out of Ireland" (Kinsella) **138**:128-29, 150
Out of Ireland (Kinsella) **138**:152
Out of Love (Wolitzer) **17**:563
"Out of Luck" (Tevis) **42**:372
"Out of Mind, Out of Sight" (Kristofferson) **26**:268
"Out of My Head" (Swenson) **106**:345
Out of My House (Foote) **51**:129
Out of My League (Plimpton) **36**:351-52, 356
"Out of My Mind" (Young) **17**:578
"Out of Night" (Campbell) **32**:75, 78, 80
"Out of Our Heads" (Jagger and Richard) **17**:232, 237
"Out of Season" (Aksyonov) **101**:22
"Out of Season" (Hemingway) **30**:181, 191; **61**:219
Out of Sheer Rage: Wrestling with D. H. Lawrence (Dyer) **149**:49-51, 53-4, 56-60
Out of Sight (Leonard) **120**:295, 297-300, 303-05
Out of Sight (Soderbergh) **154**:341-46, 348-51, 353-54, 356
"Out of Sleep Awakened" (MacLeish) **68**:290
"Out of Superstition" (Pasternak)
See "From Superstition"
"Out of the Blue" (Young)
See "My My, Hey Hey"
"Out of the Closet, onto the Bookself" (White) **110**:333, 342
"Out of the Dead City" (Delany) **14**:144
Out of the Everywhere and Other Extraordinary Visions (Tiptree) **48**:389-90
"Out of the Fray" (Gordon) **128**:110
"Out of the Garden" (Hall) **37**:148
Out of the Garden (MacInnes) **4**:314-15
"Out of the Hospital and Under the Bar" (Ellison) **54**:131-32; **114**:99
Out of the Picture (MacNeice) **10**:326; **53**:233, 237
"Out of the Pulver and the Polished Lens" (Klein) **19**:262
"Out of the Rubbish" (Piercy) **62**:371; **128**:230
"Out of the Sea, Early" (Swenson) **4**:533
Out of the Shelter (Lodge) **36**:270; **141**:343, 357-58
"Out of the Silence" (Findley) **102**:108
Out of the Silent Planet (Lewis) **1**:177; **3**:297-99; **6**:309-10; **14**:323-326; **27**:259-60; **124**:205, 207-09, 211, 225, 232, 246
"Out of the Snow" (Dubus) **97**:234, 237-38
"Out of the Sun" (Clarke) **13**:148
Out of the Sun (Bova) **45**:66
"Out of the Wardrobe" (Davies) **21**:103-04
Out of the Way: Later Essays (MacInnes) **23**:286
Out of the Whirlpool (Sillitoe) **57**:400-01; **148**:182
"Out of the Wood" (Fuller) **62**:185
Out of This World (Swift) **88**:284-90, 307, 310, 313, 315, 317-18, 322
"Out of Tune" (Davison) **28**:100
"Out of War" (Willard) **37**:464
"Out of Work Blues" (Hughes) **35**:221
"Out on the Week-End" (Young) **17**:571
"Out, Out—" (Frost) **9**:222
"Out Picking Up Corn" (Bly) **128**:15
"Out to the Hard Road" (Lorde) **71**:258
Out Went the Candle (Swados) **5**:420, 422
Outback (Keneally) **43**:232-33; **117**:240
"Outbound" (Sissman) **18**:488
Outcast (Sutcliff) **26**:426, 429-30, 439
The Outcasts of Heaven Belt (Vinge) **30**:414, 416
The Outcry (Antonioni)
See *Il grido*
"The Outdoor Amphitheatre" (Corn) **33**:117-19
"The Outdoor Concert" (Gunn) **18**:202
"Outdoors" (Johnston) **51**:248, 252-53
"The Outer Banks" (Rukeyser) **15**:459
Outer Dark (McCarthy) **4**:341-43; **57**:326-32, 334-36; **101**:135, 147-50, 154, 176-77, 183, 185, 195, 197, 201-04
"Outer Drive" (Honig) **33**:211
"The Outer Island" (Cassill) **4**:95
"The Outing" (Baldwin) **13**:52; **17**:33
"An Outing" (O'Brien) **5**:313
An Outland Piper (Davidson) **13**:166, 168; **19**:124, 126, 129
"Outlander" (Rule) **27**:423
Outlander (Rule) **27**:422-23
Outlanders (Weiss) **3**:515; **14**:555
"Outlandish Agon" (Van Duyn) **63**:440; **116**:402, 420
Outlandos d'amour (Police, The) **26**:363-64
"The Outlaw" (Heaney) **7**:148; **25**:244
"The Outlaw" (Ross) **13**:492
Outlaw Culture: Resisting Representations (Hooks) **94**:156-59, 161-62
"Outlaws" (Graves) **45**:166-67
"Outlaws of Callisto" (Wellman) **49**:391
Outline for the Study of the Poetry of American Negroes (Brown) **59**:267
Outline of a Jungian Aesthetics (Philipson) **53**:273
"Outlines" (Lorde) **71**:257
"The Outlook for American Culture, Some Reflections in a Machine Age" (Huxley) **18**:266
Outlyer and Ghazals (Harrison) **6**:224; **33**:197; **143**:345
Out-of-the-Body Travel (Plumly) **33**:312-16
The Out-of-Towners (Simon) **31**:395
"The Outpost" (Transtroemer) **65**:221, 226, 234, 236
Outrageous Acts and Everyday Rebellions (Steinem) **63**:378-79, 381-83
"The Outrider" (Livesay) **79**:342
Outrider (Stow) **23**:436
Outside (Duras) **68**:90
Outside (Norton) **12**:470-71
"Outside a Dirtroad Trailer" (Simic) **130**:313
An Outside Chance: Essays on Sport (McGuane) **45**:257-58; **127**:259, 271-72
"Outside History" (Boland) **113**:65-6, 73-4, 89, 92, 94, 104, 106, 125-26
Outside History 1980-1990 (Boland) **113**:68-9, 72-5, 80-1, 83, 87, 92-94, 99, 108, 111-12, 116, 118-19
"Outside of a Small Circle of Friends" (Ochs) **17**:333-34
"Outside the Diner" (Gunn) **81**:188
Outside the House of Baal (Humphreys) **47**:180-81, 184, 187-89
Outside the Law (Browning) **16**:124
"Outside the Machine" (Rhys) **6**:453, 456
"Outside the Ministry" (Lessing) **22**:278
"Outside the Operating Room of the Sex-Change Doctor" (Olds) **85**:294
"Outside the Wall" (Pink Floyd) **35**:313
"Outside-In" (Knight) **40**:283-84, 286
The Outsider (Camus)
See *L'étranger*
The Outsider (Fast) **131**:63, 86, 91
The Outsider (Sabato)
See *El túnel*
The Outsider (Wilson) **3**:537; **14**:583-85
The Outsider (Wright) **1**:379; **4**:596-97; **9**:584, 586; **14**:596-97; **21**:436, 443, 446, 448, 450-51, 462
Outsider in Amsterdam (van de Wetering) **47**:404-08
The Outsiders (Hinton) **30**:203-04, 206; **111**:75-83, 85-90
Outskirts (Kureishi) **64**:246; **135**:287
"The Outstation" (Maugham) **67**:206; **93**:257
The Outward Room (Brand) **7**:29-30
"Outwork, Prefacing" (Derrida) **87**:92
Ouvert la nuit (Morand) **41**:296-98, 303, 306-08
"Ouvindo Marianne Moore em disco" (Cabral de Melo Neto) **76**:160
"L'ouvrier modèle" (Carrier) **78**:58
The Oval Portrait, and Other Poems (Raine) **45**:339
"Ovando" (Kincaid) **137**:165
"La oveja negra" (Matute) **11**:364
"The Oven Bird" (Frost) **4**:174; **26**:123
"Ovenstone" (Guillén) **79**:229
"Over" (O'Brien) **5**:311; **8**:429; **36**:340-41
"Over 2,000 Illustrations" (Bishop)
See "Over 2,000 Illustrations and a Complete Concordance"
"Over 2,000 Illustrations and a Complete Concordance" (Bishop) **9**:97; **13**:94; **15**:59; **32**:37, 41
Over and Above (Hobson) **25**:272
"Over and Over Stitch" (Graham) **118**:226
"Over Back" (Frost) **13**:230
"Over Cities" (Milosz) **31**:262; **82**:294

Over on the Dry Side (L'Amour) **25**:281
"Over Russia's Wheatfields Once" (Ratushinskaya) **54**:386
Over the Border (Kesey) **3**:267-68; **46**:225
Over the Brazier (Graves) **1**:127; **39**:323; **45**:166
"Over the Edge" (Adcock) **41**:15
Over the Frontier (Smith) **25**:422; **44**:439
Over the High Side (Freeling) **38**:184
"Over the Hills and Far Away" (Page and Plant) **12**:476
Over the Hills and Far Away (Mayne) **12**:392, 398, 401
"Over the Hills in the Rain, My Dear" (Purdy) **50**:248
"Over the Moon" (Larson) **99**:167, 183-84
"Over the Ozarks, Because I Saw Them, Stars Came" (Smith) **22**:390
"Over the Red Line" (Wiebe) **14**:574
"Over the River" (Peterkin) **31**:306, 308
"Over the River and through the Wood" (O'Hara) **42**:326-27
"Over the Roof ..." (Levi) **41**:243
"Over the Valley" (Blunden) **56**:45
Over to You (Dahl) **79**:174, 177, 183
"The Overcoat" (Berriault) **109**:96
"The Overcoat II" (Boyle) **36**:63
"Overcome" (Gerstler) **70**:158
"Overcoming White Supremacy" (Hooks) **94**:159
The Overcrowded Barracoon (Naipaul) **7**:252-53; **13**:407; **105**:135-37, 155
An Overdose of Death (Christie) **110**:135
Overdrive (Buckley) **37**:61
"Overdue Pilgrimage to Nova Scotia" (Merrill) **91**:238
Overhead in a Balloon: Stories of Paris (Gallant) **38**:195
"Overheard" (Levertov) **66**:236
"Overheard in County Sligo" (Clarke) **61**:79, 82
Overlaid (Davies) **42**:104
Overland to the Islands (Levertov) **28**:242; **66**:235, 237, 241
"The Overload" (Byrne) **26**:98
"The Overloaded Packing Barrels" (Aksyonov) **101**:21
"Overlooking the Pile of Bodies at One's Feet" (Leet) **11**:323
Overnight (Inge) **8**:308
"The Over-Night Bag" (Greene) **3**:213
"Overnight to Many Distant Cities" (Barthelme) **46**:39, 43
Overnight to Many Distant Cities (Barthelme) **46**:38-9, 41-3; **59**:247, 249; **115**:80
Over-Nite Sensation (Zappa) **17**:589, 591
"Overpowered by Funk" (Clash) **30**:50-2
The Overreachers (Talese) **37**:391
"Overs" (Simon) **17**:459, 466
Overture (Scott) **22**:371
"Overture and Incidental Music for A Midsummer Night's Dream" (Carter) **41**:122
Overture to Death (Marsh) **53**:247, 250
Overtures to Death and Other Poems (Day Lewis) **10**:131, 133
"Ovid in the Third Reich" (Hill) **8**:293, 295; **45**:179-80, 183-84, 187, 189
"Ovid, Old Buddy, I Would Discourse with You a While" (Carruth) **84**:136
"O ovo da galinha" (Cabral de Melo Neto) **76**:167
"O ovo e a galinha" (Lispector) **43**:262
Owarishi michino shirubeni (Abe) **81**:292
Owen Glendower (Powys) **7**:348-50; **46**:320-22; **125**:274, 281, 294-96, 299, 301, 304
"Owen: Seven Days" (Williams) **148**:365
"Owl" (Plath) **111**:200
The Owl (Hawkes) **2**:183, 185; **3**:223; **4**:212-13; **7**:141, 145; **15**:270, 273; **27**:199; **49**:161, 164
The Owl Answers (Kennedy) **66**:202-07, 209
"The Owl Flower" (Hughes) **37**:173
The Owl in the Attic (Thurber) **5**:435-36; **125**:391, 395
"The Owl King" (Dickey) **47**:93
The Owl Service (Garner) **17**:136-49
"The Owls Are Leaving" (Ewart) **46**:152
Owls Do Cry (Frame) **6**:190; **22**:143, 145-47; **66**:144; **96**:166-67, 172-76, 178-83, 188-91, 195-96, 203, 206-09. 218
Owls in the Family (Mowat) **26**:335-36, 338-39, 343-44
The Owl's Insomnia (Alberti) **7**:10
The Owls of North America (Eckert) **17**:108
"The Owner of My Face" (Hall) **51**:175
Ownerless Earth (Hamburger) **5**:158-59
Owners (Churchill) **31**:81-3; **55**:126
"Owning a Wife" (Dacey) **51**:83
Owning Jolene (Hearon) **63**:168-70
"Owning Up" (Bowering) **47**:25
"The Ox" (Bates) **46**:55-6, 67
Ox (Anthony) **35**:35
Ox Bells and Fireflies (Buckler) **13**:122
The Ox-Bow Incident (Clark) **28**:76-83
Ox-Cart Man (Hall) **37**:145, 148;
"Oxen: Ploughing at Fiesole" (Tomlinson) **13**:547
"Oxenhope" (Warner) **7**:513
"Oxford" (Auden) **14**:26; **43**:16
"Oxford" (Dorn) **10**:159
Oxford Addresses on Poetry (Graves) **11**:254
Oxford Blood (Fraser) **107**:52
Oxford Book (Byatt) **136**:193
The Oxford Book of British Political Anecdotes (Johnson) **147**:128
Oxford Book of Canadian Verse (Smith) **15**:514
"Oxford Leave" (Ewart) **46**:150
"Oxford Town" (Dylan) **77**:166
"The Oxford Volunteers" (Huxley) **11**:283
Oxherding Tale (Johnson) **51**:229, 231-33, 235; **65**:156-57
Oye, patria, mi aflicción (Arrabal) **58**:27-8
Oyster (Hospital) **145**:317-20
"Oysters" (Heaney) **14**:244; **25**:247-48; **74**:159, 164-66; **91**:118
"Oysters" (McGahern) **48**:264
"Oysters" (Sexton) **53**:324
"Oysters" (Snyder) **32**:387
The Oysters of Locmariaquer (Clark) **19**:105
"Oza" (Voznesensky) **57**:413, 415, 426
Ozhog (Aksyonov) **22**:28; **37**:14-16; **101**:24-6, 28-38, 41-2, 44, 47-8, 50, 52
Ozidi (Clark Bekedermo) **38**:118, 124
"Oznob" (Akhmadulina) **53**:10, 13-14
"Ozone" (Dove) **81**:149, 151
O-Zone (Theroux) **46**:403-05
"P" (Merrill) **8**:385-88
"P. & O." (Maugham) **67**:206
P. D. Kimerakov (Epstein) **27**:127-28, 131
"P. S." (Reading) **47**:352
Pabellón de reposo (Cela) **4**:96, 98; **59**:126, 129, 142; **122**:54, 62
Pábitelé (Hrabal) **67**:121
"Pacelli and the Ethiop" (Cassity) **42**:97
"The Pacer" (Bogosian) **141**:85
"Pacific Door" (Birney) **11**:50
"Pacific Epitaphs" (Randall) **135**:386, 393, 397, 399
Pacific Highway (Wilding) **73**:394-96, 398-99
"Pacific Ideas—a Letter to Walt Whitman" (Simpson) **149**:310, 312
Pacific Interlude (Wilson) **32**:449
"Pacific Lament" (Olson) **29**:330
"Pacific Letter" (Ondaatje) **51**:314
Pacific Overtures (Sondheim) **30**:387-88, 390-82, 395-97, 399-402; **147**:228, 231, 234, 258, 260-61, 263
"Pacing..." (Creeley) **78**:141
Pack My Bag (Green) **13**:253-54; **97**:249-50, 257, 278, 280, 286-88, 291-92
Pack of Lies (Whitemore) **37**:445-48
"The Package Store" (Dixon) **52**:100
"Package Tour" (Binchy) **153**:75
"Packages" (Stern) **39**:243-44
Packages (Stern) **39**:243-44
"A Packet for Ezra Pound" (Pound) **48**:290
Paco's Story (Heinemann) **50**:186-93
"The Pact" (Musgrave) **54**:338
"The Paddiad" (Kavanagh) **22**:235, 240, 243
Paddy Clarke Ha Ha Ha (Doyle) **81**:156-61
"Paean to Place" (Niedecker) **10**:360; **42**:297-98, 300
Pagan Passport (Abe)
See *Itan no passporto*
A Pagan Place (O'Brien) **5**:313; **116**:179, 183-84, 192, 227
"The Pagan Rabbi" (Ozick) **7**:287, 288-89; **62**:341-44, 350-51, 353-54; **155**:126, 172-73, 177-79, 181, 183-84, 196-97, 208-09, 222, 226
The Pagan Rabbi, and Other Stories (Ozick) **3**:372; **7**:287-88; **28**:349-50, 355; **155**:126, 172, 177-78, 185, 216
Pagan Spain (Wright) **4**:596; **21**:443
"The Paganini Break" (West) **96**:375
The Pageant of England (Costain) **30**:95-6, 98-100
Pages from a Cold Island (Exley) **6**:170-72; **11**:186-87
"Pages from a Velvet Photograph Album" (Kiš) **57**:246
"Pages from a Voyage" (Corn) **33**:114
"Pages from a Western Journal" (Richler) **46**:352
"Pages from a Young Girl's Diary" (Aickman) **57**:3
"Pages from an Abandoned Journal" (Vidal) **33**:406-07
"Pages from Cold Point" (Bowles) **19**:61; **53**:46
Pages from Parra (Parra)
See *Hojas de Parra*
"Pages of a Wound Dresser's Diary" (Selzer) **74**:281-82
Pagoda of Long Life (Pa Chin) **18**:374
"Paho at Walpi" (Lewis) **41**:260
Paid on Both Sides (Auden) **2**:22; **6**:24; **11**:17; **14**:30-1, 33-4; **43**:17, 21, 24, 29
"The Pail" (Bly) **10**:62
"Pain" (Mahapatra) **33**:284
"Pain" (Simic) **9**:479
"Pain" (Webb) **18**:540
"The Pain Continuum" (Brodkey) **56**:61
"Pain for a Daughter" (Sexton) **10**:468
"A Pain I Dwell In" (Char) **9**:166
"The Pain Is Not Excessive" (Lenz)
See "Die Schmerzen sin zumutbar"
"Paingod" (Ellison) **13**:203, 206
Paingod and Other Delusions (Ellison) **13**:202; **42**:126
"Pains" (Enright) **31**:155
Paintbox Summer (Cavanna) **12**:98
The Painted Bird (Kosinski) **1**:171-72; **2**:231-32; **3**:272-73; **6**:282-85; **10**:306-09; **15**:313-17; **53**:218-22, 224-28; **70**:297-98, 300-09
"Painted Desert" (Barthelme) **117**:25-7
A Painted Devil (Billington) **43**:55
Painted Devils (Aickman) **57**:3
"The Painted Door" (Ross) **13**:492-93
Painted Dresses (Hearon) **63**:161-63
"Painted Finches" (Prichard) **46**:345
The Painted Garden (Streatfeild)
See *Movie Shoes*
"Painted Head" (Ransom) **4**:431; **5**:365
The Painted King (Davies) **23**:147
The Painted Lady (Sagan) **36**:380-82
Painted Rain (Allard) **59**:400-02
"Painted Steps" (Gallagher) **63**:118
The Painted Veil (Maugham) **15**:367, 370
"The Painted Window: Notes on Post-Realist Fiction" (Bowering) **47**:29
The Painted Word (Wolfe) **15**:585; **35**:455-56, 460, 464; **51**:416, 420
The Painted Word (Wolfe) **147**:310, 315-16, 321, 324, 329-31, 342-43
"The Painter" (Ashbery) **9**:42; **13**:35

"The Painter" (Hesse) **25**:261
"A Painter" (Matthias) **9**:361
"The Painter Dreaming in the Scholar's House" (Nemerov) **36**:301
The Painter Gabriel (Newlove) **6**:363
"Painter in Xyochtl" (Jacobsen) **48**:190
The Painter of Signs (Narayan) **7**:256; **28**:299, 302; **121**:354, 357, 363, 365, 367-68
The Painter Went Poor into the World (Seifert) See *Šel malíř chudě do světa*
"Painters" (Rukeyser) **10**:443
"Painting and Writing for Africa" (Breytenbach) **126**:94
Painting Churches (Howe) **48**:174-78
Painting the Roses Red (Malone) **43**:280
"Painwise" (Tiptree) **48**:385
"Le pair" (Carrier) **78**:58
A Pair of Baby Lambs (McFadden) **48**:257
"A Pair of Glasses" (Gallagher) **63**:122
"A Pair of Socks" (Sargeson) **31**:363
"Pairing" (Ammons) **57**:50
O país do carnaval (Amado) **40**:24-7; **106**:55, 57, 89-90
"Paisagens com cupim" (Cabral de Melo Neto) **76**:167
Paisagens com figuras (Cabral de Melo Neto) **76**:153, 158, 168
Paisajes (Goytisolo) See *Paisajes después de la batalla*
Paisajes después de la batalla (Goytisolo) **133**:23-29, 47, 56, 60, 86
"Paisley Park" (Prince) **35**:331-32
Paix dans les brisements (Michaux) **19**:312-14
A paixão segundo G. H. (Lispector) **43**:261-62, 266
"Pajaros sin descenso" (Aleixandre) **9**:16
Pal Joey (O'Hara) **1**:261; **6**:384; **11**:413; **42**:312
"La palabra" (Aleixandre) **9**:13
"Palabras antes de una lectura" (Cernuda) **54**:50
Palabras cruzadas (Poniatowska) **140**:130
"Palabras en el trópico" (Guillén) **48**:166
"The Palace" (Transtroemer) **65**:226
Le palace (Simon) **4**:495-96; **9**:484; **15**:487, 489-90, 492-93; **39**:203-05, 207, 209-11
The Palace (Simon) See *Le palace*
"The Palace at 4 A.M." (Barthelme) **46**:38-9, 43; **59**:251
"Palace Days" (White) **110**:340
Palace of Desire (Mahfouz) See *Qasr al-Shawq*
Palace of Ice (Vesaas) See *The Ice Palace*
Palace of Strangers (Masters) **48**:220
Palace of the Peacock (Harris) **25**:202-05, 210, 213, 218
Palace Walk (Mahfouz) See *Bayn al-Qasrayn*
Palace without Chairs (Brophy) **11**:68-9; **105**:16-18, 31, 33
"Paladin of the Lost Hour" (Ellison) **139**:125-29
"Palais de justice" (Helprin) **22**:220-21, 223
Le palais de sable (Marcel) **15**:360, 363
"Palais des Arts" (Glück) **22**:177; **81**:173
Palaver: Political Considerations (Enzensberger) See *Palaver: Politische Überlegungen*
Palaver: Politische Überlegungen (Enzensberger) **43**:154
The Palaverers (Hrabal) See *Pábitelé*
"A Pale and Perfectly Oval Moon" (Adams) **46**:16
Pale Blue Dot (Sagan) **112**:431, 433-34
"Pale Blue Eyes" (Reed) **21**:305, 308, 311, 318, 322
Pale Fire (Nabokov) **1**:240-41, 243-46; **2**:299-303; **3**:352-56; **6**:351-53, 355-59; **8**:407-15, 418; **11**:392-93, 396; **15**:392-93, 396-98; **23**:311; **44**:464-68; **46**:291-92; **64**:348, 366
"Pale Hands I Loathe" (Perelman) **49**:265
The Pale Horse (Christie) **12**:116; **110**:113, 122
"Pale Horse, Pale Rider" (Porter) **101**:228, 234, 252, 256
Pale Horse, Pale Rider (Porter) **3**:393; **7**:311, 315, 317; **10**:398; **13**:449-51; **15**:429; **27**:400-01
Pale Horse, Pale Rider: Three Short Novels (Porter) **7**:309, 312, 314, 317; **10**:398; **13**:446; **101**:212, 219, 229, 243, 249, 255
"Pale Light" (Montague) **46**:269
"The Pale Ones" (Spacks) **14**:511
"The Pale Panther" (MacNeice) **10**:324
"The Pale Pink Roast" (Paley) **37**:337; **140**:264, 277
"Pale Tepid Ode" (Justice) **102**:258
A Pale View of Hills (Ishiguro) **27**:202-04; **56**:158-61; **59**:159, 163, 166-67; **110**:220-25, 227-28, 231, 234, 236, 240, 246-47, 249-50, 257, 259, 261-62
The Paleface (Keaton) **20**:188
"Paleface and Redskin" (Rahv) **24**:352, 359
"A Paleolithic Fertility Fetish" (Szymborska) **99**:200
"Paleontology" (Cioran) **64**:89, 94
Palimpsest (H. D.) **31**:204, 208, 210; **73**:110-12, 123, 128-33, 135, 140
Palimpsest: A Memoir (Vidal) **142**:305-07, 309-12, 315-20, 322-23, 326, 331, 333
Palindroma (Arreola) **147**:26
"Palindrome" (Perec) **56**:254
Palindrome (Arrabal) See *Palindroma*
"Palinode" (Hamburger) **5**:159
"Palinodie" (Audiberti) **38**:21
Il palio dei buffi (Palazzeschi) **11**:432
Palladas: Poems (Harrison) **129**:165, 169
"A Palladian Bridge" (Tuohy) **37**:429
Palladium (Fulton) **52**:160-62
"Pallinode" (H. D.) **31**:207
"Palm Beach: Don't You Love It?" (Amis) **62**:5
Palm Latitudes (Braverman) **67**:50-3, 55
"Palm Sunday" (Bowers) **9**:121-22
"Palm Sunday" (Clampitt) **32**:114
"Palm Sunday" (Clifton) **19**:109
"Palm Sunday" (Muldoon) **72**:267-68
Palm Sunday (Marqués) **96**:224, 243
Palm Sunday: An Autobiographical Collage (Vonnegut) **22**:449-52; **40**:445-46; **111**:368
"A Palm Tree in the Desert" (Christie) **110**:125
Palmares (Jones) **131**:329
Palm-of-the-Hand Stories (Kawabata) See *Tanagokoro no Shōsetsu*
"The Palms" (Merwin) **88**:213
The Palm-Sized Stories (Kawabata) See *Tanagokoro no Shōsetsu*
The Palm-Wine Drinkard (Tutuola) **5**:443, 445; **14**:537-42; **29**:434-37, 439, 441-43
"A palo seco" (Cabral de Melo Neto) **76**:154, 161, 163
La paloma de vuelo popular: Elegiás (Guillén) **48**:158, 161, 164; **79**:229-30, 241
Paloma por dentro (Neruda) **62**:336
Palomar (Calvino) **39**:306, 311, 314-17; **73**:40-1, 43-7, 51, 57-9
"Palomas negras" (Ulibarrí) **83**:416
Palomino (Jolley) **46**:213, 217
A Palpable God (Price) **13**:464-65
Pals (Margulies) **76**:193
"Palymyra" (Plomer) **4**:407
Pamiętnik okresu dojrzewania (Gombrowicz) **49**:121, 127
"Pamjati T. B." (Brodsky) **50**:131
The Pamperers (Loy) **28**:251
A Pamphlet against Anthologies (Riding) **7**:373
"Pamphlet contre les catholiques de France" (Green) **77**:244, 278, 280-81, 289
"Pan" (Blaga) **75**:76
"Pan and Syrinx" (Rodgers) **7**:378
"Pan at Lane Cove" (Slessor) **14**:492
Pan Cogito (Herbert) **9**:274-76; **43**:188
"Pan Cogito opowiada o kuszeniu Spinozy" (Herbert) **9**:275; **43**:187
"Pan with Us" (Frost) **26**:117
Panama (McGuane) **18**:323-26; **45**:259-60, 262; **127**:245, 251, 253, 255, 258-59, 261-62, 267, 269, 275, 279, 283, 293-95, 298
"Panama, etc." (Cendrars) **106**:158
"Le Panama ou les aventures de mes sept oncles" (Cendrars) **18**:92, 94; **106**:152, 154, 158-59, 163, 167, 177, 181, 184, 186, 190-92, 196-97
"Pancakes for the Queen of Babylon" (Levi) **41**:246
Pancakes for the Queen of Babylon: Ten Poems for Nikos Gatsos (Levi) **41**:244-45, 248
Pandora (Fraser) **64**:166-68, 171, 175-77
"Pandora's Papers" (Ferré) **139**:161
Pandora's Papers (Ferré) See *Papeles de Pandora*
Pandor's Roles (Ferré) See *Papeles de Pandora*
"Panel Game" (Coover) **87**:40
Panels for the Walls of Heaven (Patchen) **18**:392
"The Pangolin" (Moore) **8**:401; **10**:353; **19**:340; **47**:265
"The Pangs of Love" (Gardam) **43**:171
"Pangs of Love" (Louie) **70**:78
Pangs of Love (Louie) **70**:78-81
The Pangs of Love, and Other Stories (Gardam) **43**:170-71
Panic: A Play in Verse (MacLeish) **68**:286, 293
Panic Encyclopedia: The Definitive Guide to the Postmodern Scene (Kroker) **77**:344
Panic in the Streets (Kazan) **16**:362, 367; **63**:225
Pankraz Awakens (Zuckmayer) **18**:554
Die Panne (Duerrenmatt) **102**:61-2, 64
"Panorama" (Guillén) **11**:262
"Pan's Fair Throng" (Moody) **147**:190
Pantagleize (Ghelderode) **6**:198; **11**:227
Pantaleón y las visitadoras (Vargas Llosa) **6**:543; **10**:498, 501; **15**:552; **31**:443-45, 449; **42**:404; **85**:352, 355, 362, 380, 389, 395
"Pantaloon in Black" (Faulkner) **3**:152; **8**:213-14
Panther (Haig-Brown) See *Ki-Yu: A Story of Panthers*
The Panther and the Lash: Poems of Our Times (Hughes) **10**:279; **15**:294; **35**:218-20; **108**:286, 290, 334
"The Panther Waits" (Ortiz) **45**:309, 311
"A Panting" (Enzensberger) **43**:145
"Pantomime" (Fearing) **51**:106
Pantomime (Walcott) **25**:454-55; **67**:342, 346, 351-52; **76**:275
"Pantoum" (Ashbery) **13**:34; **25**:50
"Panus Angelicus" (Muske) **90**:313
Paolo Paoli (Adamov) **4**:5; **25**:12, 15, 20-1
Les Paons (Tremblay) **29**:426
"Papa!" (Aksyonov) **101**:11
"The Papa and Mama Dance" (Sexton) **123**:409
Papa Boss (Ferron) **94**:106, 110, 113
"Papa Montero's Wake" (Guillén) See "Velorio de Papá Montero"
"Papa, What Does It Spell?" (Aksyonov) **101**:10, 15, 20
"Papa Who Wakes up Tired in the Dark" (Cisneros) **118**:184
Papeles de Pandora (Ferré) **139**:149-54, 160-62, 166-68, 177, 184, 186, 188, 193
Paper and Iron (Ferguson) **134**:46-8, 67-8
Paper Boy (Huddle) **49**:182-83
"Paper Children" (Jolley) **46**:213
"Paper Cities" (Schnackenberg) **40**:382
"Paper Cuts" (Jong) **6**:268
Paper Dragon (Hunter) **31**:221
The Paper Landscape (Aksyonov) See *Bumazhnyĭ peĭzazh*
Paper Lion (Plimpton) **36**:352-56
"Paper Matches" (Jiles) **58**:271, 279, 281
The Paper Men (Golding) **81**:315, 319-20, 322-23
"The Paper on the Floor" (Bukowski) **41**:63
The Paper People (Findley) **102**:98-9, 104

Paper Roses (Potter) **123**:237
Paper Trail (Dorris) **109**:298, 310
"Paperback Writer" (Lennon and McCartney) **35**:288
"Papers" (Popa) **19**:373
Papers from Lilliput (Priestley) **34**:361
"The Papers of Professor Bold" (Orlovitz) **22**:332
The Papers of Samuel Marchbanks (Davies) **42**:105; **75**:182-83, 187-89; **91**:204, 207
The Papers of Tony Veitch (McIlvanney) **42**:283-85
"The Paper-Spike" (Gustafson) **36**:220
"The Paperweight" (Schnackenberg) **40**:378
Papiers d'identité (Morand) **41**:304
"Paprika Plains" (Mitchell) **12**:443
"Papyrus" (Pound) **13**:460; **48**:292
Les pâques (Cendrars) **18**:93; **106**:159, 163, 177-78, 180, 184, 189-90, 195
Par derrière chez mon père (Maillet) **118**:327, 344-46, 363
"Par la fenêtre ouverte à demi" (Damas) **84**:180
"Para entrar al jardín" (Arreola) **147**:26
Para esta noche (Onetti) **7**:277
Para leer al Pato Donald (Dorfman) **48**:87-8, 94; **77**:134-36, 153
"Para llegar a Montego Bay" (Lezama Lima) **101**:121
"Para quién escribo" (Aleixandre) **36**:30
"Para una poética" (Cortázar) **92**:158
Para una tumba sin nombre (Onetti) **10**:376
"A Parable" (Glück) **44**:222
"Parable" (Wilbur) **110**:385
"Parable Island" (Heaney) **74**:161
Parable of a Drowning Man (Delibes)
See *Parábola del náufrago*
The Parable of the Blind (Hofmann)
See *Der Blindensturz*
"The Parable of the Palace" (Borges) **13**:112
The Parable of the Sower (Butler) **121**:121-22, 131-33, 142-43, 145-46, 148-49, 151
Parabola (Voznesensky) **15**:555
Parábola del náufrago (Delibes) **8**:169; **18**:114-15
"Parabolas" (Voznesensky) **57**:425
"Parabolicheskaya ballada" (Voznesensky) **57**:416
Paracelsus (Ryga) **14**:473
"Parachute" (Jagger and Richard) **17**:223
Parachutes & Kisses (Jong) **83**:310-2
"Parade" (Grace) **56**:111-13, 120
Parade (Cocteau) **8**:148; **15**:134; **43**:106, 108-09
The Parade Ends (Arenas)
See *Termina el desfile*
"A Parade in Town" (Sondheim) **30**:379, 387
The Parade is Over (Arenas)
See *Termina el desfile*
"Parade of Painters" (Swenson) **61**:390
"Parades Parades" (Walcott) **14**:549; **76**:274, 281
"Paradigm" (Allen) **84**:4
Le paradis perdu (Jouve) **47**:207
Paradísarheimt (Laxness) **25**:292, 299
"Paradise" (O'Brien) **36**:340-41; **116**:186, 189, 191
Paradise (Barthelme) **46**:43-5; **59**:247, 249; **115**:80-5
Paradise (Castedo) **65**:31-41
Paradise (Forbes) **12**:203-04
Paradise, and Other Stories (Moravia)
See *Il paradiso*
"Paradise Flycatcher" (Ezekiel) **61**:101-02, 105, 107
"Paradise Found" (White) **110**:333
Paradise Illustrated (Enright) **31**:152-53, 154-55
"Paradise Lost" (Kingsolver) **130**:112
Paradise Lost (Odets) **2**:318-19; **28**:324-25, 328, 332-33, 336, 340; **98**:198, 200, 204-05, 207, 212, 217-24, 229-31, 233, 236, 238, 241-42
"The Paradise Lounge" (Trevor) **25**:446; **116**:363
"Paradise Motel" (Simic) **130**:333, 334
Paradise News (Lodge) **141**:345-50, 352-53, 355-56, 367, 371
"Paradise of Children" (Mahfūz) **52**:298
"The Paradise of the Theologians" (Herbert) **9**:275
"Paradise Park" (Millhauser) **109**:170
Paradise Poems (Stern) **40**:411-14; **100**:333, 342
Paradise Postponed (Mortimer) **43**:305-09
Paradise Reclaimed (Laxness)
See *Paradísarheimt*
"Paradisets Have" (Andersen)
See *Sea Island Song*
Paradiso (Lezama Lima) **4**:288-91; **10**:317, 319-22; **101**:102-03, 106-15, 118-22, 124, 128
Il paradiso (Moravia) **2**:293; **7**:239, 242
"The Paradox of African-American Rebellions" (West) **134**:383
"Paradox of Time" (Warren) **39**:262
The Paradox Players (Duffy) **37**:114
"Paradoxes and Oxymorons" (Ashbery) **25**:54
"The Paradoxes of Creativity" (Barzun) **145**:72
"The Paraffin Lamp" (Brown) **100**:82-3
"Paráfrase de reverdy" (Cabral de Melo Neto) **76**:163
Parages (Derrida) **87**:92
The Paragon (Knowles) **1**:169; **4**:271-72; **10**:303; **26**:261-62
Paragon Walk (Perry) **126**:323, 328
"Paragraphs" (Carruth) **18**:88-9; **84**:119, 136
The Paraguayan Experiment (Wilding) **73**:396-97, 399, 405
"The Parallax Monograph for Rodin" (Dubie) **36**:135
"The Parallel World" (Martin) **89**:111-12, 118
"Parallel Worlds" (Martin)
See "The Parallel World"
"Paralytic" (Plath) **9**:427-28; **17**:360; **51**:341; **111**:160, 163
"Paraphrases" (Fisher) **25**:160
"Parapsyche" (Vance) **35**:425
Paras pathar (Ray) **16**:477, 482, 491-93
"Parashut" (Bagryana)
See "Vurni me"
The Parasite (Campbell) **42**:86-7, 90, 93
The Parasite Murders (Cronenberg)
See *They Came From Within*
"A Parasite of Rui Barbosa" (Cabral de Melo Neto)
See "Um piolho de Rui Barbosa"
"Parasites" (Jhabvala) **138**:78
Parasites of Heaven (Cohen) **38**:135-36
Les paravents (Genet) **1**:117; **2**:158; **14**:200; **44**:385-89, 391; **46**:173, 183
"Parce que la comédie" (Damas) **84**:159
"The Parcel" (Boland) **113**:93, 100, 127
A Parcel of Patterns (Paton Walsh) **35**:434
A Parcel of Trees (Mayne) **12**:389-90, 404, 407
"Pardon" (Shields) **113**:426
"The Pardon" (Wilbur) **6**:570
Pardon Me, You're Stepping on My Eyeball! (Zindel) **26**:474, 479-80
The Pardoner's Tale (Wain) **11**:564; **15**:561-62; **46**:418
"Pareille à la légende" (Damas) **84**:177
"Parentheses" (Ritsos) **31**:328, 330
Parentheses, 1946-47 (Ritsos) **31**:328-29
Parentheses, 1950-61 (Ritsos) **31**:328-29
"Parents" (Barthelme) **117**:5
"Parents" (Buckley) **57**:126, 131
"Parents" (Smith) **3**:460
Parents and Children (Compton-Burnett) **34**:500
"The parents left the child" (Amichai) **116**:98
"The Parents: People Like Our Marriage, Maxie and Andrew" (Brooks) **49**:26; **125**:74
Les parents terribles (Cocteau) **8**:148-49; **15**:132, 134; **16**:226, 228; **43**:104-06, 108-11
"Parergon" (Ashbery) **2**:19
"Parergon" (Derrida) **87**:92
"Paring the Apple" (Tomlinson) **13**:546; **45**:392, 399
"Paris" (Gilchrist) **143**:301, 314
"Paris" (Muldoon) **32**:319; **72**:266
"Paris" (Ondaatje) **29**:341
Paris (Green) **77**:288, 294
"Paris, 1968" (Rosenthal) **28**:394
"Paris and Cleveland Are Voyages" (Gold) **152**:120
"Paris and Helen" (Schwartz) **45**:355
Paris by Night (Hare) **136**:242, 263-64, 277
"Paris in the Snow" (Senghor) **130**:282
Paris Journal, 1937-1939 (Gascoyne) **45**:155, 157-58
Paris, New York: 1982-1984 (Brandys) **62**:116-17, 119-20
Paris! Paris! (Shaw) **34**:370
Paris qui dort (Clair) **20**:57, 66, 69
Paris, Texas (Shepard) **41**:413-14
"Paris: The May Revolution" (Fuentes) **60**:164
"Paris: This April Sunset Completely Utters; Post Impressions" (Cummings) **15**:155
Paris Trance (Dyer) **149**:52-3, 58-60
Paris Trout (Dexter) **55**:129-32
"Paris Without Rhyme" (Voznesensky) **57**:420
Parish Churches (Betjeman) **43**:49
Paris—Tombouctou (Morand) **41**:304
"The Park" (Fisher) **25**:157
"The Park" (Levertov) **1**:176
"The Park" (Williams) **56**:427
"Park City" (Beattie) **146**:85
Park City: New and Selected Stories (Beattie) **146**:84, 86
"Park-Bench Vacation" (Calvino) **33**:100
"Parker's Back" (O'Connor) **21**:268, 271, 276-77, 279; **104**:112, 115, 124, 138, 158-59, 166-67, 178, 187-88, 197
"Parker's Band" (Becker and Fagen) **26**:79
"Parker's Dog" (Vanderhaeghe) **41**:450, 452
"The Parking Lot" (Beattie) **63**:10
Parktilden Village (Elliott) **2**:130-31
Les parleuses (Duras) **6**:151; **68**:86-9; **100**:129
"Parliament Hill Fields" (Betjeman) **43**:32
"Parliament Hill Fields" (Plath) **51**:345; **111**:167, 201
Parlor, Bedlam, and Bath (Perelman) **23**:334; **44**:503
La parodie (Adamov) **4**:5; **25**:11-12, 17-20
The Parody (Adamov)
See *La parodie*
"Parody for the Poem 'Paterson'" (Williams) **42**:455
"Paroi" (Guillevic) **33**:194
"Parola" (Bagryana)
See "Kontrapunkti"
La parole des femmes (Condé) **92**:100-01, 112
La parole en archipel (Char) **14**:127; **55**:288
"Parole in agitazione" (Landolfi) **49**:215
Paroles (Prévert) **15**:437
"Parousia" (Glück) **81**:166
La parrocchie di Regalpetra (Sciascia) **8**:473; **9**:475; **41**:392-93
"The Parrot" (Bowen) **118**:62, 77
"The Parrot" (Ferron) **94**:126
"The Parrot" (Rozewicz) **139**:226
"The Parrot Who Met Papa" (Bradbury) **42**:35
"The Parrotfish" (Szirtes) **46**:393
Parrot's Perch (Rio)
See *Le perchoir du perroquet*
Parry of the Arctic (Berton) **104**:61
The Parsifal Mosaic (Ludlum) **43**:276
"Parsley" (Dove) **81**:134, 138
"The Parsley Garden" (Saroyan) **8**:468
Parsley, Sage, Rosemary, and Thyme (Simon) **17**:459-60, 464, 466
"Parsnips" (Tomlinson) **45**:397
Parson's Nine (Streatfeild) **21**:394-95
"Parson's Pleasure" (Dahl) **79**:176, 178, 183

The Parson's Progress (Mackenzie) **18**:314
Parson's Widow (Dreyer) **16**:259-61, 265
A Part (Berry) **27**:37; **46**:69-70
La Part du feu (Blanchot) **135**:78-79, 97-98, 102, 112, 122,
La part maudite (Bataille) **29**:42, 49-50
"Part of a Letter" (Wilbur) **53**:404, 407
"Part of a Novel, Part of a Poem, Part of a Play" (Moore) **13**:395
"Part of Mandevil's Travels" (Empson) **19**:154
Part of Nature, Part of Us (Vendler) **138**:249-50, 260, 262, 269
"A Part of Speech" (Brodsky)
See "Cast rěci"
A Part of Speech (Brodsky)
See *Cast rěci*
"Part of the Doctrine" (Baraka) **5**:48
"Part of What Might Have Been a Short Story, Almost Forgotten" (Warren) **39**:272
"Part One: Mr. and Mrs. Monroe" (Thurber) **125**:391
"Part Song, with Concert of Recorders" (Dickey) **28**:117
Partage formel (Char) **9**:161
"Parthenope" (West) **50**:405
Le parti pris de choses (Ponge) **18**:419
"Partial Accounts" (Meredith) **55**:191
Partial Accounts: New and Selected Poems (Meredith) **55**:190-93
"Partial Eclipse" (Snodgrass) **18**:491
"Partial Enchantments of the Quixote" (Borges)
See "Magias parciales del Quijote"
"Partial Magic in the Quixote" (Borges)
See "Magias parciales del Quijote"
"A Partial State" (Paulin) **37**:353
"A Partial View" (Scannell) **49**:331
"The PartialExplanation" (Simic) **130**:317
"La participación de la mujer mexicana en la educación formal" (Castellanos) **66**:46
Parti-Colored Blocks for a Quilt (Piercy) **62**:373; **128**:240, 243, 246
"Particular Lullaby" (Kunitz) **148**:86
The Particularity of the Aesthetic (Lukacs) **24**:330
Particularly Cats...and Rufus (Lessing) **94**:271-72
Une partie de campagne (Renoir) **20**:310-11
La Partie pour le tout (Brossard) **115**:103-05
Parties (Van Vechten) **33**:394-95, 397-99
"Parting" (Ammons) **25**:45; **108**:56
"Parting" (Bennett) **28**:26
"Parting" (Layton) **15**:319
"Parting" (Lorde) **71**:252
"Parting" (Pasternak) **63**:313
Parting from Phantoms (Wolf)
See *Auf dem Weg nach Taboo*
"Parting Is Such Sweet Sorrow" (Adcock) **41**:13
"Parti-pris" (Damas) **84**:179
Partir avant le jour (Green) **3**:204; **77**:271-73, 276-77, 289
Partisans (MacLean) **63**:266-67
Partisans (Matthiessen) **32**:285, 290; **64**:327
Partner (Bertolucci) **16**:87, 91, 94, 100
"Partners" (McGuane) **45**:265; **127**:274
The Partners (Auchincloss) **4**:30-1; **6**:15
Partners in Crime (Christie) **12**:112; **110**:111
A Partnership of Mind and Body (Kettelkamp) **12**:307
"The Partridge Festival" (O'Connor) **104**:178, 187-88
"Parts of Speech" (Thesen) **56**:415
"Parts of the Eagle" (Kinsella) **43**:254
"Part-Time" (p'Bitek) **96**:287
"Parturient montes" (Arreola) **147**:32
"Partway round the Course" (Sagan) **36**:382
"The Party" (Avison) **97**:68-9, 71
"The Party" (Barthelme) **115**:65
"The Party" (Creeley) **78**:126
"The Party" (Elkin) **51**:96
"Party" (Lively) **32**:273
"The Party" (Ochs) **17**:331-32
The Party (Griffiths) **13**:255-56; **52**:171-72, 174, 178, 185
"Party at Bannon Brook" (Nowlan) **15**:399
"A Party Down at the Square" (Ellison) **114**:125-26, 131, 138
A Party for Boris (Bernhard)
See *Eine Fest für Boris*
"A Party for the Girls" (Bates) **46**:67
Party Frock (Streatfeild) **21**:415
"Party Game" (Urquhart) **90**:375
"The Party Givers" (Deane) **122**:83
Party Going (Green) **2**:178; **13**:251, 253-55; **97**:242-43, 245-49, 254-55, 257, 268, 270-72, 277-82, 287-88, 290, 292
"Party Piece" (Muldoon) **72**:265
Party Shoes (Streatfeild) **21**:399
"Party Up" (Prince) **35**:324-25
"The Party-Givers" (Adams) **46**:16
The Party's Over (Goytisolo) **23**:189
"Parvardigar" (Townshend) **17**:528
"Les pas" (Carrier) **78**:60
Le pas au-delà (Blanchot) **135**:95, 99
"Le pas de Gamelin" (Ferron) **94**:129
Les pas perdus (Breton) **54**:32
"El pasa del norte" (Rulfo) **80**:200
"El pasado" (Borges) **6**:90
Pasado en claro (Paz) **10**:393; **19**:368; **51**:326-27, 333, 337; **65**:197, 200
Pasajes de la guerra revolucionaria (Guevara) **87**:199-200, 203-04, 206, 210
"Pasar" (Otero) **11**:427
"Pascal" (Huxley) **35**:241
"Pascal" (Muldoon) **72**:280
Pascal (Ringwood) **48**:330
Pascali's Island (Unsworth) **76**:252, 256, 259; **127**:409-10
"Pascal's Idea" (Simic) **130**:345
"Pascal's Sphere" (Borges) **8**:100; **83**:160, 163
Páscoa feliz (Migueis) **10**:341
"Pascoli e Montale" (Pasolini) **106**:232
Pascual Duarte's Family (Cela)
See *La familia de Pascual Duarte*
"Paseo" (Donoso) **11**:146-48; **32**:156-58
Paşii profetului (Blaga) **75**:65, 67-9, 74, 76-7
Pasión de la tierra (Aleixandre) **9**:10-11, 15; **36**:23, 25-6, 28-31
"Pasiphae" (Hope) **51**:220
Pasmore (Storey) **2**:425-26; **4**:529-30; **8**:505
"El Paso" (Phillips) **15**:420; **139**:220
El Paso de los Gansos (Alegria) **57**:12, 13-14
Los pasos perdidos (Carpentier) **8**:134; **11**:100, 102, 104-07; **38**:89-90, 92-6, 98-9; **110**:53, 56, 60, 64-7, 84, 90, 96-7, 103, 105
Pasqualino settebellezze (Wertmueller) **16**:590-93, 595-99
Pasque Flower (Ringwood) **48**:330, 334-39
The Pass (Savage) **40**:369-70
"Pass Away" (Berry) **17**:56
"Pass fe White" (Bennett) **28**:29
"Pass on by" (Guillén)
See "Sigue"
Pass th Food Release th Spirit Book (Bissett) **18**:60
"Pass to a Trail" (Yevtushenko) **126**:398
"Passacaglia on Getting Lost" (Harrison) **143**:355
Passacaille (Pinget) **7**:306; **13**:442-44; **37**:359-361
"Passage" (Levertov) **66**:245
"Passage" (Okigbo) **25**:347-48, 351, 355; **84**:300, 307-10, 312-13, 324, 326-27, 329, 331-32, 337, 342
"Passage" (Vliet) **22**:443
Passage (Hein) **154**:151
"Le passage de l'oiseau divin" (Breton) **9**:134
Passage de Milan (Butor) **3**:92; **8**:114-19, 121; **11**:79-80; **15**:115-17
Passage du malin (Mauriac) **56**:215
Passage of Arms (Ambler) **9**:19
"Passage of Land" (Wiebe) **138**:314
"Le passage Pommeraye" (Mandiargues) **41**:277-79
"Passage to Godhead" (Rukeyser) **27**:405
A Passage to India (Forster) **1**:103-04, 106-08; **2**:135; **3**:159-61; **4**:165, 167-69; **9**:206-09; **10**:179-81; **13**:215, 218-22; **15**:223, 227-28; **22**:130-35, 137; **45**:132-33, 135-39, 141-44; **77**:194-257
"Passage to More than India" (Snyder) **120**:309
"Passages" (Duncan) **41**:124, 128-30
Passages (Duncan) **2**:122; **4**:141; **15**:190-92
Passages (Michaux) **8**:392
Passages 24 (Duncan) **55**:297-98
Passages from the Revolutionary War (Guevara)
See *Pasajes de la guerra revolucionaria*
The Passages of Joy (Gunn) **32**:212-15; **81**:184
"Passages toward a Long Poem" (Aldington) **49**:11
"Passato prossimo" (Levi) **37**:224
"La passeggiata" (Landolfi) **49**:215
"The Passenger" (Calisher) **38**:76; **134**:10, 19
"The Passenger" (Nabokov) **15**:394
The Passenger (Antonioni) **20**:39-42; **144**:6, 25, 34-39, 41-43, 55-56, 58, 63, 70, 72, 76, 80-81, 97
Passenger (Keneally) **14**:301-03; **19**:248; **43**:236-37; **117**:224, 226-27
"Passenger Pigeons" (Jeffers) **54**:247
Passenger to Frankfurt (Christie) **12**:117-18; **39**:438
"Passengers" (Johnson) **52**:234
"Passengers" (Silverberg) **7**:425; **140**:378
"Passengers" (Wolff) **64**:446, 449
Passengers of Destiny (Aragon)
See *Les voyageurs de l'impériale*
"Passers-By on a Snowy Night" (Warren) **18**:539; **39**:265, 272
"A Passing" (Christie) **110**:127
Passing (Larsen) **37**:211-19
"The Passing Away of Old Beliefs and the Birth of New Beliefs" (Mahfouz) **153**:248
Passing Game (Tesich) **40**:420-21
"Passing It On" (Saner) **9**:469
The Passing of the Dragons (Roberts) **14**:464
The Passing of the Third-Floor Buck (Waterhouse) **47**:420
"Passing over Your Virtues" (Hearne) **56**:128
The Passing Scene (Ritter) **52**:354, 357
"Passing the Word" (Dobyns) **37**:75
Passing Through: The Later Poems New and Selected (Kunitz) **148**:127-28, 135-37, 141-43, 145, 147
"Passing Through—on my seventy-ninth birthday" (Kunitz) **148**:109, 134
"Passing Time" (Angelou) **77**:29
"Passing Time" (Ihimaera) **46**:200
Passing Time (Butor)
See *L'emploi du temps*
"Passion" (Elytis) **100**:156, 159, 161, 163, 165, 183
"Passion" (Oates) **108**:382
"Passion" (O'Faolain) **32**:341
A Passion (Bergman)
See *En Passion*
Passion (Bond) **23**:66
The Passion (Harrison) **129**:165, 192
Passion (Nichols)
See *Passion Play*
Passion (Sondheim) **147**:240, 242, 254, 260
The Passion (Winterson) **64**:428-30, 432-35, 440-42, 444
Passion and Affect (Colwin) **5**:107-08; **23**:128; **84**:146, 149-51
The Passion Artist (Hawkes) **15**:276-79; **27**:194-96, 198-99; **49**:163-65
La passion de Jeanne d'Arc (Dreyer) **16**:255-57, 259-66
La passion de Joseph Pasquier (Duhamel) **8**:189
La passion des femmes (Japrisot) **90**:169
"A Passion in Eden" (Greenberg) **7**:134
A Passion in Rome (Callaghan) **14**:102; **41**:90, 96; **65**:246, 248, 250

Passion: New Poems, 1977-1980 (Jordan) **23**:255-56, 258; **114**:142, 146, 155, 158, 161
The Passion of Anna (Bergman) See *En Passion*
The Passion of Ayn Rand (Branden) **44**:448, 450, 452-54
The Passion of Joan of Arc (Dreyer) See *La passion de Jeanne d'Arc*
The Passion of Joseph D (Chayefsky) **23**:114
The Passion of Molly T. (Sanders) **41**:382
The Passion of New Eve (Carter) **41**:115-16; **76**:324, 329
The Passion of Sacco and Vanzetti (Fast) **131**:83-4, 98
Passion of the Earth (Aleixandre) See *Pasión de la tierra*
The Passion of Women (Japrisot) See *La passion des femmes*
Passion Play (Kosinski) **15**:315-17; **53**:216, 220-22, 227; **70**:298, 306
Passion Play (Nichols) **36**:329-31
Passion simple (Ernaux) **88**:113-19
The Passionate Past of Gloria Gaye (Kops) **4**:274
"The Passionate Shopping Mall" (Baxter) **78**:29
"La passione" (Pasolini) **106**:268
Passione (Innaurato) **21**:197-99; **60**:200-01, 205-06
Passione e ideologia (Pasolini) **106**:245
Passionless Moments (Campion) **95**:2, 6
"Passions" (Singer) **9**:487, 489
Passions and Impressions (Neruda) **62**:324-27
Passions, and Other Stories (Singer) **6**:510-11; **9**:487, 489; **11**:499; **15**:509; **23**:420
Passions of the Mind (Byatt) **136**:150-51, 156-57, 161
The Passions of the Mind (Stone) **7**:470-71
The Passions of Uxport (Kumin) **28**:221-22
Passions Spin the Plot (Fisher) **7**:103
The Passport (Samarakis) See *To diav*
"The Passport Officer" (Bunting) **47**:53
Passport to Fame (Ford) **16**:307-08
Passport to the War (Kunitz) **14**:312; **148**:68-69, 71, 87-88, 91, 95, 111, 137, 148
"Past" (Sanchez) **116**:274, 280
The Past (Jordan) **110**:269-70, 272, 275
The Past (Kinnell) **129**:255-58, 264, 270
Past All Dishonor (Cain) **28**:51-3
"Past and Present" (Jones) **42**:245
The Past as Future (Habermas) **104**:98-99
The Past Is the Past (Wesley) **7**:518-19
"The Past Is the Present" (Moore) **8**:399
"Past Midnight" (Motion) **47**:293
The Past Now: New Poems (Gregor) **9**:255-56
"Past Paradise" (Wonder) See "Pastime Paradise"
"The Past, Present and Future" (Tolson) **105**:280
"The Past Reordered" (Ignatow) **7**:176
The Past through Tomorrow (Heinlein) **8**:275
Le Pastaga des loufs ou Ouverture orang-outan (Arrabal) **58**:18
Pastel de choclo (Dorfman) **77**:133
"Pastime Paradise" (Wonder) **12**:659, 662
Pastimes of a Red Summer (Vansittart) **42**:394
"Pastor Dowe at Tacaté" (Bowles) **19**:60; **53**:36-7
Pastor Prayers (Ezekiel) **61**:107
"Pastor Prayers—8" (Ezekiel) **61**:109
"Pastor Prayers—9" (Ezekiel) **61**:108
"A Pastoral" (Ashbery) **13**:35
"Pastoral" (Carver) **55**:279; **126**:157
"Pastoral" (Dove) **81**:150
"Pastoral" (Dubie) **36**:130
"Pastoral" (Hall) **59**:151, 154-56; **151**:188-89, 210
"Pastoral" (Landolfi) **49**:209
"Pastoral" (Mathias) **45**:235
"Pastoral" (Simic) **68**:368-69
Pastoral (Shute) **30**:372
"Pastoral Care" (Gardner) **5**:133-34; **7**:112-13, 116; **8**:238
Pastoral Jazz (Broumas) **73**:8-9, 13-14
Pastoral; or, Time for Cocoa (Hildesheimer) See *Pastorale; oder, Die Zeit für Kakao*
"Pastorale" (Cain) **28**:47
Pastorale; oder, Die Zeit für Kakao (Hildesheimer) **49**:167, 171
"A Pastorale of Sorts" (Turco) **63**:429
Pastorals: A Book of Verses (Blunden) **56**:40, 49
"Pastorela di Narcis" (Pasolini) **106**:230
Os pastores da noite (Amado) **40**:31-2; **106**:64, 73, 77
Pastors and Masters (Compton-Burnett) **1**:61; **3**:112; **10**:109-10; **15**:135, 138; **34**:495, 498, 500
"Pastrami Brothers" (Swados) **12**:558
"The Pasture" (Frost) **3**:170; **15**:247-48
"The Pasture Pond" (Blunden) **56**:29, 39, 51
The Pastures of Heaven (Steinbeck) **1**:325; **9**:513, 518; **13**:531; **21**:366, 380-81, 385; **34**:415; **45**:373-74, 382; **59**:317, 333-334; **75**:360; **124**:390, 393
"Pastures of Plenty" (Guthrie) **35**:187, 194
Pastures of the Blue Crane (Brinsmead) **21**:25-6, 30
"Pat Collins" (O'Hara) **42**:319
Pat Garrett and Billy the Kid (Peckinpah) **20**:278-79, 282, 284-85
Pat Hobby and Orson Welles (Welles) **80**:413
"Pat McGee" (Farrell) **66**:129
Pataphysical Poems (Queneau) See *Pounding the Pavements, Beating the Bushes, and Other Pataphysical Poems*
"Pataxanadu" (Middleton) **13**:389
Pataxanadu and Other Prose (Middleton) **13**:389
The Patch Boys (Parini) **54**:363; **133**:252
"Patchwork" (Boland) **113**:124
"Patchwork" (Longley) **29**:296
"Patent Leather" (Brooks) **49**:26; **125**:50
"Paterson" (Ginsberg) **4**:183; **36**:182; **109**:354
Paterson (Williams) **1**:369-72; **2**:466-70; **5**:506-10; **9**:571-73; **13**:602-05; **22**:465-69; **42**:449-52, 455-57, 459-61, 464; **67**:395-427
Paterson I (Williams) **9**:572-73; **13**:603; **22**:465, 467-68; **42**:455-56
Paterson II (Williams) **9**:572-73; **22**:465, 467; **42**:452-54, 456
Paterson III (Williams) **5**:508; **9**:572-73; **22**:465, 467
Paterson IV (Williams) **9**:571-73; **22**:465, 467
Paterson V (Williams) **5**:508; **9**:571-73; **13**:603; **22**:465-68; **42**:451, 460
"Path" (Hoffman) **6**:244
"Path" (Merwin) **8**:390
The Path (Delibes) See *El camino*
"The Path Among the Stones" (Kinnell) **129**:246, 251, 253-54
Path of Dalliance (Waugh) **7**:513-14
Path of Hunters: Animal Struggle in a Meadow (Peck) **17**:337-38
The Path of the Happy Man (Lagerkvist) See *Den lyckliges väg*
"The Path of the Moon's Dark Fortnight" (Gordimer) **33**:180
"Path of Thunder" (Okigbo) **84**:336, 342
The Path of Thunder (Abrahams) **4**:3
Path of Thunder (Okigbo) See *Labyrinths, with Path of Thunder*
The Path to the Nest of the Spiders (Calvino) See *Il sentiero dei nidi di ragno*
A Path Where No Man Thought (Sagan) **112**:429-30
Pather panchali (Ray) **16**:474-80, 482, 484-85, 489-91; **76**:356-58, 360-64, 366
"Pathology of Colours" (Abse) **29**:18
"Paths" (Miles) **14**:369
Paths (Transtroemer) See *Stigar*
Paths of Glory (Kubrick) **16**:377-80, 382-87
Pathways to the Gods (von Daniken) **30**:428
"Patience" (Graham) **118**:228
"Patience" (Reid) **33**:348
"Patience" (Reverdy) **53**:290
"Patience Is a Leveling Thing" (Jensen) **37**:189
The Patience of Maigret (Simenon) **47**:370
Les patients (Audiberti) **38**:31
"Patisserie" (Willard) **37**:463
"Patmos" (Elytis) **49**:110
Patooie (Peck) **17**:342
"Patria de retorno" (Ulibarrí) **83**:412
Patria mia (Pound) **13**:457; **112**:315-18, 320, 338
Patria o muerte! The Great Zoo, and Other Poems by Nicolás Guillén (Guillén) See *El gran zoo*
"The Patriarch" (Grau) **9**:240; **146**:128-30, 163
The Patriarch (Bermant) **40**:94-5
Patriarchal Attitudes (Figes) **31**:162-63, 167
"Patricia's Poem" (Jordan) **114**:145
Patrick Kentigern Keenan (Hunter) See *The Smartest Man in Ireland*
Patrimony: A True Story (Roth) **86**:249, 254, 257, 263; **119**:121, 127, 129-31, 134
"Patriot" (Hoffman) **141**:270
"The Patriot" (O'Faolain) **70**:314
The Patriot (Buck) **11**:75, 77
The Patriot (Connell) **45**:108-09
A Patriot For Me (Osborne) **5**:332; **11**:421; **45**:313-16, 321
Patriot Games (Clancy) **112**:50-1, 55-6, 63, 66-7, 72, 74-5, 77, 84, 90, 93
"Patriotic" (Kauffman) **42**:251-52
Patriotic Gore (Wilson) **1**:372-73; **2**:476; **3**:538; **8**:550; **24**:478, 481, 487-89
The Patriotic Murders (Christie) See *One, Two, Buckle My Shoe*
"Patriotic Poem" (Wain) **11**:562
Patriotic Suite (Montague) **46**:264, 270-71
"Patriotism" (Mishima) **6**:339; **27**:341-42
The Patriots (Kingsley) **44**:234
Patriots and Liberators: Revolution in the Netherlands, 1780-1813 (Schama) **150**:111, 136
"The Patriot's Dream" (Lightfoot) **26**:278
"The Patrol" (Lem) **40**:291
"A Pattern" (Jennings) **14**:292; **131**:233
The Pattern (Buckley) **57**:133-36
Pattern for a Tapestry (Dourado) See *O risco do bordado*
Pattern for a Tapestry (Dourado) See *Risco do bordado*
"Pattern for Death" (Still) **49**:363
"Pattern for Survival" (Matheson) **37**:246
The Pattern of the Future (Comfort) **7**:52
Patternmaster (Butler) **38**:61-2, 64, 66; **121**:73-76, 80, 88, 95, 97, 103, 105, 108, 119
"Patterns" (Janowitz) **43**:212; **145**:326
Patterns (Serling) **30**:353, 358
Patterns and Coincidences (Neihardt) **32**:336
Patterns in Comparative Religion (Eliade) **19**:147
Patterns of Childhood (Wolf) See *Kindheitsmuster*
"The Patterns of Dorne" (Sturgeon) **22**:411
"Patty Hearst" (Coupland) **85**:36
Paul Celan: Poems (Celan) **19**:95; **82**:34, 38-39, 41
"Paul Eluard" (Guillén) **79**:229
"Paul Klee" (Haines) **58**:220
"Paul Laurence Dunbar" (Hayden) **37**:153
"Paul Revere" (Jiles) **58**:273
Paul Revere and the World He Lived In (Forbes) **12**:205-07
"Paul Revere's Ride" (Whittemore) **4**:588
"Paul Robeson" (Brooks) **49**:30
Paul Robeson: The Life and Times of a Free Black Man (Hamilton) **26**:150
Paul Simon (Simon) **17**:461-66

Paula (Allende) **97**:56-64
Paulina, 1880 (Jouve) **47**:203, 210
"Paulo Freire" (Hooks) **94**:156
"Paul's Wife" (Frost) **9**:218; **26**:119
"The Pauper Witch of Grafton" (Frost) **1**:110; **9**:224-25; **15**:244
"Paura alla scala" (Buzzati) **36**:83-4, 86, 94, 96
Pauvre Bitos; ou, Le dîner de têtes (Anouilh) **1**:7; **13**:17, 20-2; **40**:56-8; **50**:279-81
Le pauvre Christ de Bomba (Beti) **27**:42-5, 49, 52
"Pavan for a Dead Prince" (Delaney) **29**:146
"Pavana dolorosa" (Hill) **45**:180
Pavane (Roberts) **14**:464
Pavannes (Pound) **7**:326
Pavarotti: My Own Story (Wright) **44**:527
"Paved Roads" (Aksyonov) **101**:13-14
Pavilion of Women (Buck) **11**:76-7
"Pawana" (Le Clézio)
See "Awaite Pawana"
Pawley's Peepholes (Wyndham) **19**:474
"Pawn to Bishop's Five" (Masefield) **47**:233
The Pawnbroker (Wallant) **5**:478; **10**:511-15
"The Pawnbroker's Wife" (Spark) **13**:519-20
"The Pawnshop" (Simpson) **149**:356
Pawnshop (Breton)
See *Mont de piété*
"Pax magna" (Blaga) **75**:68
Pay Day (Chaplin) **16**:191
"Pay It Back" (Costello) **21**:67
Payday (Carpenter) **41**:107
"The Paying Guests" (Mistry) **71**:272
Payment Deferred (Forester) **35**:165-66, 170
"Payne Whitney" (Schuyler) **23**:390
Les pays lointains (Green) **77**:283-90, 292-94
Pays mêlé (Condé) **52**:83-4; **92**:101
"Pays Natal" (Walcott) **76**:278
"Pays Perdu" (Garrigue) **8**:239
"Paysage de répons" (Butor) **3**:93
"Paysage de répons illustré par dialogues des règnes" (Butor) **3**:93
"Paysage Moralisé" (Auden) **11**:17; **14**:27
Le paysan de Paris (Aragon) **3**:14; **22**:36, 40
Le paysan de Paris (Breton) **15**:90
"Les paysans" (Malraux)
See "L'espoir"
Pe o palmă de ţărînă (Arghezi) **80**:13
"Pea Soup" (Reid) **33**:349
Pea Soup (Reid) **33**:349-51
"Peace" (Levine) **33**:271
"Peace" (Simon) **17**:461
Peace (Jünger)
See *Der Friede*
Peace (Kieslowski)
See *Spokoj*
Peace and Its Discontents (Said) **123**:397-98
Peace Breaks Out (Knowles) **26**:263-65
Peace Eye (Sanders) **53**:304
"Peace Frog" (Morrison) **17**:295-96
"Peace in Mind" (Armatrading) **17**:9
Peace in Our Time (Coward) **29**:136
Peace in the Middle East? (Chomsky) **132**:35-6
"Peace in the Welsh Hills" (Watkins) **43**:453-54
"Peace Is a Stratified Concept" (Allen) **84**:40
Peace like a River (Fisher) **7**:103
"The Peace of Cities" (Wilbur) **53**:397
"Peace of Mind" (Boyle) **90**:45, 48
"Peace of Mind" (Young) **17**:580
"The Peace of Utrecht" (Munro) **10**:358; **95**:305
Peace on Earth (Lem)
See *Pokój na Ziemi*
Peace Shall Destroy Many (Wiebe) **6**:567; **14**:572-74; **138**:308-10, 314, 326, 330, 336, 351-56, 372, 375-78
"The Peaceable Kingdom" (Piercy) **6**:401; **18**:406; **27**:374
The Peaceable Kingdom (de Hartog) **19**:132-33
The Peaceable Kingdom (Silkin) **6**:498; **43**:397-401
"The Peaceable Kingdom of Emerald Windows" (Chappell) **40**:144
"The Peacefulness of Vivyan" (Tiptree) **48**:385
"The Peacelike Mongoose" (Thurber) **5**:434
The Peacemaker (Forester) **35**:165-66
"The Peach Tree" (Sitwell) **67**:324
"The Peach Tree" (Swan) **69**:364
"Peaches" (McGahern) **48**:263, 266, 268
"The Peach-Tree" (Bates) **46**:50
"The Peacock" (Mosher) **62**:313
The Peacock Feather Murders (Carr) **3**:101
The Peacock Poems (Williams) **89**:320, 324-25, 332, 358
"Peacock's Superette" (Peacock) **60**:292
The Peacock's Tail (Hoagland) **28**:180
"Peak" (Ammons) **8**:16; **9**:30; **57**:59
Peake's Progress: Selected Writings and Drawings of Mervyn Peake (Peake) **54**:372, 378
"The Pealing" (Broumas) **73**:17
"Peals of Crying" (p'Bitek) **96**:287
"Peanuts" (Police, The) **26**:363
Peanuts (Schulz) **12**:522, 524-25, 527-31, 533
Peanuts Jubilee (Schulz) **12**:531-33
Peanuts Treasury (Schulz) **12**:525
"Pear Tree" (H. D.) **14**:223; **73**:118
"Pear Tree" (Livesay) **79**:338, 342, 350, 352
"Pear Tree Dance" (Jolley) **46**:220-21
"Pear-Brown Rome" (Denby) **48**:83
The Pearl (Steinbeck) **1**:325; **5**:407; **13**:533-34; **21**:368, 370-71, 382; **45**:374, 383; **75**:343
Pearl at the Bottom (Hrabal)
See *Perlička na dně*
"Pearl Harbor" (Howe) **152**:186-87
"Pearl May Lee" (Brooks) **125**:82-4
Pearl of the Deep (Hrabal)
See *Perlička na dně*
The Pearlkillers (Ingalls) **42**:234
"The Pearls" (Dinesen) **29**:159; **95**:35
"Pearls" (Graham) **118**:224
Pearls before Swine (Allingham)
See *Coroner's Pidgin*
Pearl's Progress (Kaplan) **59**:70-73
"Pears" (Kiš) **57**:246
"Peasant" (Merwin) **88**:206
"A Peasant" (Thomas) **6**:534
The Peasant from Paris (Aragon)
See *Le paysan de Paris*
The Peasant Mandarin (Murray) **40**:338-39
"Peasants" (O'Connor) **14**:398; **23**:332-33
"The Peat-Bog Man" (Simpson) **149**:328-29
La peau douce (Truffaut) **20**:383, 389, 405; **101**:375, 377, 379, 385
Peau noire, masques blancs (Fanon) **74**:71-2, 74-81, 83
"Pebble" (Herbert) **9**:272
Pebble in the Sky (Asimov) **26**:48, 64; **76**:315
"Peccatology" (Wright) **146**:365
Peckham's Marbles (De Vries) **46**:137-38
A Peculiar Treasure (Ferber) **93**:171, 177, 179, 186-87, 190
The Peddler and Other Domestic Matter (Summers) **10**:493
"A Peddler's Memories" (Goldemberg) **52**:165
"The Pedersen Kid" (Gass) **2**:154; **11**:224; **15**:255-56; **39**:478; **132**:154-158, 160, 162, 164-65, 181
"The Pedestrian" (Bradbury) **42**:32, 34
The Pedestrian (Bradbury) **42**:33
"A Pedestrian Accident" (Coover) **46**:116
"Pedestrian Crossin'" (Bennett) **28**:27, 29
The Pedestrian of the Air (Ionesco)
See *Le piéton de l'air*
"Pedestrian Pastoral" (Ryan) **65**:213
Pedestrian Subway (Kieslowski)
See *Przejscie podziemne*
Pedigree (Simenon) **1**:309
The Pedlar's Revenge, and Other Stories (O'Flaherty) **34**:356
Pedra do sono (Cabral de Melo Neto) **76**:150, 152, 156
"Pedro imaginário" (Dourado) **60**:85
Pedro Páramo (Rulfo) **8**:462; **80**:199-208, 210-14, 216-19, 221-24
"Pedro the Image Carver" (Dourado)
See "Pedro imaginário"
Peekskill, U.S.A.: A Personal Experience (Fast) **131**:83
Peel: An Exercise in Discipline (Campion) **95**:6, 11
Peel My Love Like an Onion (Castillo) **151**:46, 91-92, 101, 103
"Peeling" (Carey) **40**:128-29; **96**:24, 27, 35, 37, 67
"Peeling Fence Posts" (Kumin) **28**:223
"The Peeper" (Davison) **28**:100
"The Peeping Tom" (Knowles) **26**:258
"Peerless Jim Driscoll" (Scannell) **49**:331
"Peg" (Becker and Fagen) **26**:84
"Pegasus" (Kavanagh) **22**:235, 237
Pegasus and Other Poems (Day Lewis) **6**:126; **10**:128-29, 131
"Peggety's Parcel of Shortcomings" (Hersey) **81**:329
Peggy (Duncan) **26**:102
"Peggy Day" (Dylan) **12**:186
Pegil pes, begushchij kraem moria (Aitmatov) **71**:7-8, 11-12, 15, 21, 32-3
The Pegnitz Junction (Gallant) **7**:110-11; **38**:194
"Peirce and Communication" (Habermas) **104**:87
"Pel Tvardovsky v nochnoy Florentsii, B'yut zhenschinu" (Voznesensky) **57**:417
Pélagie: The Return to a Homeland (Maillet)
See *Pélagie-la-charrette*
Pélagie-la-charrette (Maillet) **118**:326-29, 335-38, 343-47, 349-50, 352, 354-58, 361-68
Die Pelerine (Eliade) **19**:147
"Pelican" (Wright) **53**:423
The Pelican Brief (Grisham) **84**:193-95, 198-99
A Pelican of Blondings (Wodehouse)
See *No Nudes Is Good Nudes*
"The Pen" (Carver) **55**:276
"The Pen" (Kinnell) **129**:271
"Pen in the Mouth" (Hope) **52**:209
The Pen Shop (Kinsella) **138**:160
Pen, Sword, Camisole: A Fable to Kindle a Hope (Amado) **40**:36-7
"Penal Rock/Altamuskin" (Montague) **46**:270
"Penalty of Godhead" (Achebe) **11**:4
"Penance" (Donaldson) **138**:41
"Penance" (Dybek) **114**:62
"Penance" (Kinsella) **27**:237
"Penance" (Williams) **33**:443
"The Pencil" (Crispin) **22**:111-12
Pencil Letter (Ratushinskaya) **54**:382
"Penda's Fen" (Rudkin) **14**:471
Le pendu de Saint-Pholien (Simenon) **3**:451; **8**:487; **47**:371, 374
"The Pendulum's Swing" (Brodsky) **100**:40
"Penelope" (Bitov) **57**:115
Penelope (Fast) **131**:100
Penelope (Maugham) **15**:366; **67**:223
Penelope (Vonnegut) **2**:452; **3**:500; **8**:530; **12**:605, 610, 619, 626; **40**:443
"Penelope at Her Loom" (Graham)
See "Self-Portrait as Hurry and Delay"
"Penelope Writes" (Pollitt) **122**:203
"Penelope's Despair" (Ritsos) **6**:464
"Penelope's Hall" (Bowering) **32**:48
Penetrations (Rozewicz)
See *Überblendungen*
"Penguin in Bondage" (Zappa) **17**:591
Penguin Touguet (Foreman) **50**:163
Penhally (Gordon) **6**:203-05, 207; **13**:242; **29**:185; **83**:226-27, 229, 232-33, 240-42, 247, 251, 253-54, 257, 259
"Penis Poem" (Phillips) **28**:363
The Penitent (Singer)
See *Der Bal-tshuve*
"Penitentes" (Zamora) **89**:363, 368, 382, 384, 387, 394
"Penitents" (Zamora)
See "Penitentes"
"The Pennacesse Leper Colony for Women, Cape Cod, 1922" (Dubie) **36**:130

"Pennants Must Have Breezes" (Weidman) **7**:517
Pennies from Heaven (Potter) **58**:389, 391-92, 395, 399-400; **86**:345-46, 348, 350-53; **123**:231-32, 236-37, 243, 245, 249-50, 265-66, 269, 273-74, 276-77, 279
Penniless Painter Goes Out into the World (Seifert)
See *Šel malíř chudě do světa*
"A Penniless Painter Went Out into the World" (Seifert)
See *Šel malíř chudě do světa*
The Penniless Redeemer (Ferron)
See *Le Ciel de Québec*
Penniless till Doomsday (Hall) **51**:170
"Pennstuwehniyaahtsi: Quuti's Story" (Ortiz) **45**:309
"Pennsylvania" (Sandburg) **10**:450
Pennsylvania Gothic (Sheed) **2**:392-94; **53**:339
"Penny Dreadful" (Coward) **51**:74
"Penny in the Dust" (Buckler) **13**:119-20
"Penny Parker's Mistake" (Ashbery) **25**:54
A Penny Saved Is Impossible (Nash) **23**:324
The Penny Wars (Baker) **8**:39
Penny Wheep (MacDiarmid) **11**:334, 338; **19**:286, 290; **63**:239
"El pensamiento en blanco" (Paz) **65**:182, 184
Pensamiento serpentino (Valdez) **84**:414
La Pensée (Brossard) **115**:106
La pensée sauvage (Lévi-Strauss) **38**:294, 296-97, 299, 304
Penser/Classer (Perec) **56**:264
"Penshurst Place" (Mahon) **27**:292
"Il pensiero fluttuante ddella felicità" (Luzi) **13**:353
"The Pension Grillparzer" (Irving) **112**:172, 175
"Pentagon: A Memory" (Carroll) **38**:103
"Pentecost" (Ai) **14**:8; **69**:4, 8
Pentecost Alley (Perry) **126**:337, 340, 343
"The Pentecost Castle" (Hill) **18**:238; **45**:178, 180, 182, 185, 190
Penthesilea (Riefenstahl) **16**:526
Penthesilia (Nye) **13**:413
"The Penthouse Apartment" (Trevor) **71**:322, 326, 339; **116**:371
Penthouse Legend (Rand)
See *Night of January 16*
Pentimento: A Book of Portraits (Hellman) **4**:220-22; **8**:280-82; **14**:259; **34**:348-50, 352-53; **44**:527-28, 530; **52**:190, 192-203
The Penultimate Truth (Dick) **30**:127; **72**:108, 123-24
"Peonies" (Oliver) **98**:287
"Peony Stalks" (Van Duyn) **116**:417, 424
"People" (Armatrading) **17**:10
"The People" (Silkin) **6**:499; **43**:404-05
People (Lagerkvist)
See *Människor*
People and Life, 1891-1921 (Ehrenburg) **18**:134
"People Are Fascinating" (Benson) **17**:46-7
People Are Living There (Fugard) **9**:232; **14**:189-90; **40**:197, 201; **80**:62, 69, 74
"People Are Strange" (Morrison) **17**:295
"The People at the Party" (Mueller) **51**:279
"The People behind This Peculiar Nation" (MacLennan) **14**:341
"People Don't Want Us" (Lewis) **41**:254
"People for Lunch" (Bainbridge) **62**:36-8
The People from Yonder (Dabrowska)
See *Ludzie stamtad*
"People Getting Divorced" (Ferlinghetti) **111**:65
People Have More Fun Than Anybody (Thurber) **125**:412
The People Immortal (Grossman) **41**:188
People in a Diary: A Memoir (Behrman) **40**:86-7
"People in Dreams" (O Hehir) **41**:322
People in Glass Houses (Hazzard) **18**:214-17
People in Summer Night (Sillanpaa) **19**:417-18
People Live Here: Selected Poems, 1949-1983 (Simpson) **32**:378, 380-84; **149**:309, 318-19, 321, 324, 327-32, 334, 336-38, 342, 351
The People Machines (Williamson) **29**:458
The People Named Chippewa: Narrative Histories (Vizenor) **103**:289, 291, 299, 311, 317, 348
People of Darkness (Hillerman) **62**:251-52, 256, 259
The People of Japan (Buck) **7**:33; **127**:239-40
The People of Kau (Riefenstahl) **16**:524-25
The People of Peoples and Their Gifts to Men (Du Bois) **96**:144-45
"A People of Solitaries" (Cioran)
See "Un peuple de solitaires"
People of the Buffalo (Campbell) **85**:4, 22
People of the City (Ekwensi) **4**:151
People of the Deer (Mowat) **26**:329-34, 341, 347
People of the Dream (Forman) **21**:119
"The People of the Night" (Duras) **100**:120
People of the Po Valley (Antonioni)
See *Gente del po*
"People of the Shell" (Piercy) **14**:420
People of the Valley (Waters) **88**:329, 334-37, 345, 351, 361, 366-70
People on a Bridge (Szymborska) **99**:192-93, 199, 203
"The People on the Bridge" (Szymborska) **99**:200
"People to People" (Ingalls) **42**:234
"The People v. Abe Lathan, Colored" (Caldwell) **1**:51
The People vs Ranchman (Terry) **19**:440
"People Who Died" (Carroll) **35**:79-81; **143**:29, 37, 53
People Who Knock on the Door (Highsmith) **42**:215-16; **102**:184, 209
People Who Led to My Plays (Kennedy) **66**:209-10
People Who Make Tomorrow (Kurosawa)
See *Asu o Tsukuru Hitobito*
People Will Always Be Kind (Sheed) **4**:488-89
The People with the Dogs (Stead) **32**:413, 416; **80**:341
People, Years, Life (Ehrenburg) **34**:434, 436; **62**:180-81
The People, Yes (Sandburg) **4**:463; **10**:448, 450-51; **15**:466, 468-70; **35**:347-48, 351-53, 357-58
A Peopled Landscape (Tomlinson) **2**:436-37; **4**:544, 546; **13**:545, 547; **45**:405
The Peoples of Kenya (Adamson) **17**:4
The People's Otherworld (Murray) **40**:342, 344
"People's Parties" (Mitchell) **12**:442
"People's Surroundings" (Moore) **13**:396
Pepi, Lucy, Bom and a Whole Lot of Other Girls (Almodovar)
See *Pepi, Lucy, Mom y Otros Chicas del Monton*
Pepi, Lucy, Mom y Otros Chicas del Monton (Almodovar) **114**:3, 16-17, 22, 25-6, 30-1, 35, 45
"The Pepper Plant" (Wakoski) **9**:555
Peppercanister Poems, 1972-1978 (Kinsella) **19**:254-56; **138**:85, 88, 94, 105-07, 110-13, 136
"Peppergrass" (Plumly) **33**:316
Peppermint frappé (Saura) **20**:320
Pequeña crónica de grandes días (Paz) **65**:190
"La Pequeña oda a un negro boxeador cubano" (Guillén) **48**:163; **79**:229-30
"Pequnea ode mineral" (Cabral de Melo Neto) **76**:159, 165
Perceval (Rohmer) **16**:538-40
Le perchoir du perroquet (Rio) **43**:355-57
"Percy" (Cheever) **11**:122
Percy (Davies) **21**:92
"Percy Lawson" (Purdy) **14**:434
"Percy's Song" (Dylan) **77**:166
Perdido (Robinson) **10**:438-39
"Perdón si por mis ojos..." (Neruda) **7**:261
"El peregrino" (Parra) **102**:338-39
Los peregrinos inmóviles (Lopez y Fuentes) **32**:282-83
"A Pereira da Costa" (Cabral de Melo Neto) **76**:163
Perelandra (Lewis) **1**:177; **3**:297-99; **6**:309, 311; **14**:323-26; **27**:260-61, 266; **124**:193, 213, 221, 223, 226, 228, 232, 236, 246
Perelman's Home Companion: A Collector's Item (The Collector Being S. J. Perelman) of Thirty-Six Otherwise Unavailable Pieces by Himself (Perelman) **49**:262
"The Perennial Answer" (Rich) **6**:459; **73**:330
The Perennial Philosophy (Huxley) **1**:152; **4**:239-41; **5**:193; **8**:303; **11**:286; **18**:269-70; **35**:241, 243-44; **79**:317
"The Perennial Poetry" (McAuley) **45**:249
"Perennials" (Levine) **118**:305
Perestroika (Kushner) **81**:197-98, 200-02, 207-08, 212
"The Perfect Body" (Kumin) **28**:223
A Perfect Circle of Sun (Pastan) **27**:368-69
A Perfect Couple (Altman) **16**:43-4; **116**:37
"The Perfect Critic" (Eliot) **24**:169, 180; **55**:356
"A Perfect Day for Bananafish" (Salinger) **3**:444; **12**:499, 503, 514, 520; **56**:324, 352; **138**:183, 198-99, 201, 204, 214, 216
The Perfect Fiction (Sorrentino) **7**:449, 451-52; **22**:391; **40**:384
A Perfect Ganesh (McNally) **91**:159
Perfect Happiness (Lively) **32**:275-77
"The Perfect Life" (Katz) **47**:222
"Perfect Morning" (MacCaig) **36**:282
"The Perfect Nazi Family Is Alive and Living in Modern Ireland" (Durcan) **43**:117
The Perfect Party (Fuller)
See *The Village: A Party*
The Perfect Party (Gurney) **54**:216-18, 220, 222; **50**:180-81, 183
A Perfect Peace (Oz) **54**:345-53, 355
"The Perfect Sky" (Gallagher) **63**:119
The Perfect Storm (Junger) **109**:56-62
"Perfect Things" (Barthelme) **117**:6
A Perfect Vacuum: Perfect Reviews of Non-Existent Books (Lem) **15**:329-30; **40**:292, 296, 298; **149**:112-13, 116, 125, 155-56, 159, 165, 168, 208, 261-62, 277-78
"The Perfect Warrior" (Bova) **45**:69, 75
"Perfect Weather" (Piercy) **62**:379
A Perfect Woman (Slaughter) **56**:411-12
"Perfect Women Who Are Bearable" (Wasserstein) **90**:430, 432
"Perfection" (Nabokov) **6**:357
"The Perfection of Dentistry" (Bell) **8**:65-6; **31**:47
"Perfection of Orchard View" (Edmonds) **35**:155
"Perfection Wasted" (Updike) **139**:346
The Perfectionist (Williamson) **56**:439-41
The Perfectionists (Godwin) **5**:142; **8**:248; **22**:179-80; **31**:198; **69**:246-47; **125**:128, 167-70
"Perfections" (Tomlinson) **45**:392-93
"A Perfectly, Clear View of Basketball" (Royko) **109**:408
"Perfectly Independent" (Ferber) **93**:153
"Perfectly Lovely Couple" (Sondheim) **30**:380
Perfil del aire (Cernuda) **54**:57-8
"The Performance" (Dickey) **15**:177; **109**:238, 287
"Performance" (Mahapatra) **33**:277, 283
"Performance as an extreme occasion" (Said) **123**:359
"The Performance of a Lifetime" (King) **53**:208
"The Perfume Sea" (Laurence) **62**:278
Perfume: The Story of a Murderer (Süskind) **44**:111-17
"Perhaps Hand" (Cummings) **68**:37
Perhaps Never (Derleth) **31**:131
"Perhaps No Poem But All I Can Say and I Cannot Be Silent" (Levertov) **66**:239
"Perhaps We Shall Meet Again" (Bates) **46**:55-6
"Perhaps You Should Talk to Someone" (Bainbridge) **62**:37

"Pericalypsis" (Lem) **15**:330; **149**:262
"Perichoresis and the Single Seminarian" (L'Heureux) **52**:274
"Peril" (Giles) **39**:64-5
Peril at End House (Christie) **6**:108; **12**:113, 122; **48**:71-2, 77; **110**:116, 137
"Perils of the Nile" (Gilchrist) **48**:115; **143**:320, 325, 327, 329
"Perils of Translation" (Parks) **147**:222
"Period" (Thomas) **6**:530
Period of Adjustment (Hill) **26**:196, 201
Period of Adjustment: High Point over a Cavern (Williams) **1**:368; **5**:500, 504; **11**:577; **15**:580; **19**:472; **71**:368-69
A Period of Transition (Morrison) **21**:237
"A Period of Youth" (Mahfouz)
See "Fatra min al-shabab"
The Periodic Table (Levi)
See *Il sistema periodico*
"Periodizing the Sixties" (Jameson) **142**:226, 230, 240
"Periodontics" (Simpson) **149**:349
"Periphery" (Ammons) **5**:27; **57**:59
The Perishable Quality (Davies) **23**:147
"El perjurio de la nieve" (Bioy Casares) **88**:60
"The Perjury of the Snow" (Bioy Casares)
See "El perjurio de la nieve"
Perlička na dně (Hrabal) **67**:121-22
"Perlmutter at the East Pole" (Elkin) **51**:99
Permanence and Change (Burke) **24**:119-21, 127-28
Permanent Errors (Price) **3**:406; **6**:423; **43**:344-45, 353; **63**:331, 341
"The Permanent Hell" (Ignatow) **7**:176
"A Permanent Insurrection" (Vargas Llosa)
See "Una insurrección permanente"
Permanently Bard (Harrison) **129**:211, 221
"Permission to Narrate" (Said) **123**:383
Permitted Fruit (Tzara)
See *Le fruit permis*
"Permutations" (Donnell) **34**:156
"The Pernambucan M. B." (Cabral de Melo Neto)
See "O pernambucano Manual Bandeira"
"O pernambucano Manual Bandeira" (Cabral de Melo Neto) **76**:163
"Perpetua" (Broumas) **73**:13-17
"The Perpetual Light" (Fulton) **52**:159
The Perpetual Orgy: Flaubert and "Madame Bovary" (Vargas Llosa)
See *La orgía perpetua: Flaubert y "Madame Bovary"*
"The Perpetual Present" (Paz) **4**:398
Perpétue (Beti) **27**:46-7, 53
"Perplex" (Bennett) **28**:29
"Perris Way" (Silverberg) **140**:378
Persécuté persécuteur (Aragon) **3**:14
"Persecution Smith" (Seger) **35**:378, 381
"El perseguidor" (Cortázar) **10**:113, 116; **13**:164; **33**:125-26, 128; **34**:332
"El Perseguidor" (Cortázar) **34**:332; **92**:149, 155-56
"Perseid" (Barth) **5**:52; **14**:54-5; **89**:38
"Persephone" (Barnard) **48**:26-7
"Persephone" (Ritsos) **13**:488
"Persephone" (Thomas) **132**:382
"Persephone Pauses" (Kizer) **80**:172-73
Persephone's Flowers (Grigson) **39**:332
"Pershore Station; or, A Liverish Journey First Class" (Betjeman) **43**:34, 36, 41
The Persian Boy (Renault) **3**:426; **17**:401
Persian Brides (Rabinyan) **119**:89-91
Persian Nights (Johnson) **48**:206-09
Persian Paintings (Anand) **93**:24
"Persistences" (Ammons) **25**:45
"Persistent Explorer" (Ransom) **4**:431
"The Person" (Laughlin) **49**:225
"...Person, or A Hymn on and to the Holy Ghost" (Avison) **97**:79, 93, 99, 104, 116
Person, Place, and Thing (Shapiro) **4**:485; **15**:475-76; **53**:331
"Person to Person" (Williams) **71**:368
Person to Person (Ciardi) **40**:159
"The Person Who Held the Job Before You" (Pesetsky) **28**:358
"Persona" (Banville) **46**:25
"Persona" (Jones) **131**:269
Persona (Bergman) **16**:56-9, 62, 67-9, 74, 78, 80; **72**:40, 46, 48-52, 55, 57, 59
Personae (Pound) **1**:276; **2**:343; **7**:323, 325; **13**:456; **48**:288, 299; **112**:340
"Personal and Sexual Freedom" (Major) **19**:293
A Personal Anthology (Borges)
See *Antologia personal*
Personal Anthology (Borges)
See *Antologia personal*
Personal Best (Towne) **87**:365-71, 373-78
"Personal Helicon" (Heaney) **25**:244
"A Personal History of Lesbian Porn" (Allison) **153**:4
A Personal History of the American Theater (Gray) **49**:148
A Personal History of the "Boom" (Donoso)
See *Historia personal del 'boom'*
"The Personal is Political" (White) **110**:336, 341, 343
"Personal Letter No. 2" (Sanchez) **116**:272, 278, 295
"Personal Letter No. 3" (Sanchez) **116**:274, 278, 295
A Personal Library (Borges)
See *Antologia personal*
A Personal Matter (Oe)
See *Kojinteki na taiken*
"Personal Place" (Kinsella) **138**:163
Personal Places (Kinsella) **138**:137, 153, 157, 167
"Personal Poem" (O'Hara) **78**:350-51, 376
"Personal Remarks" (McGinley) **14**:366
"A Personal Statement" (Longley) **29**:291, 293, 295-96
"Personal Tour" (Hall) **51**:172
Personality Plus (Ferber) **93**:136, 141, 147
Personality Quotient (Daly)
See *What's Your P.Q.*
"Personals" (Ginsberg) **109**:364
Personals (Bontemps) **18**:64
"Personism: A Manifesto" (O'Hara) **2**:322; **13**:423-24; **78**:350-51, 354, 362
Personnel (Kieslowski) **120**:246
"Persons" (MacNeice) **53**:234
"Persons from Porlock" (Hope) **51**:217, 221, 223, 225
Persons, Ideas, and Seas (Gironella) **11**:237
Persons of Consequence: Queen Victoria and Her Circle (Auchincloss) **18**:25
"Persons Unknown" (Capote) **13**:137
"Perspective" (Avison) **97**:67-71, 100, 102-04, 111
"Perspectives" (Ezekiel) **61**:93, 101
Perspectives (Tillich)
See *Perspectives on 19th and 20th Century Protestant Theology*
"The Perspectives and Limits of Snapshots" (Smith) **42**:353
Perspectives on 19th and 20th Century Protestant Theology (Tillich) **131**:353-54
"Persuasion" (Rozewicz)
See "Perswazja"
"Perswazja" (Rozewicz) **139**:249
Perto do coração selvagem (Lispector) **43**:261, 266
"Peru" (McNally) **82**:263
Peru (Lish) **45**:230-33
Pervigilium veneris (Tate) **4**:536
Pervyi uchitel' (Aitmatov) **71**:3, 6, 14, 16, 22
"A pesar de proponérselo" (Castellanos) **66**:56
Peščanik (Kiš) **57**:243-44, 246-50, 252
La peste (Camus) **1**:52-4; **2**:97-8; **4**:89-93; **9**:139-41, 144-46, 148, 150; **11**:93-4, 96-7; **14**:107, 110, 113, 115-17; **32**:86-8, 90; **63**:62, 64-8, 71, 73-7, 82-4, 86; **69**:109, 122, 128, 135-36; **124**:3, 7, 9-11, 13, 21-2, 25, 27, 29-31, 33-5, 46
"The Pet" (Gordimer) **123**:113-14
"Pet Milk" (Dybek) **114**:77
Pet Sematary (King) **37**:203-07; **61**:319, 321, 328, 331, 333, 335; **113**:335-36, 338, 346, 363-64, 367-68, 371-72, 374, 388-89, 391
Pet Sounds (Wilson) **12**:640-46, 649-52
Pet zvezdi (Bagryana) **10**:11
Petals of Blood (Ngũgĩ wa Thiong'o) **13**:583-84; **36**:313-17, 319, 322-24
"Peter" (Moore) **47**:261
"Peter" (Ondaatje) **14**:407; **29**:341
"Peter" (Simpson) **149**:307, 319-20, 336
"Peter and Rosa" (Dinesen) **29**:159
Peter Breaks Through (Membreno) **59**:399-402
Peter Camenzind (Hesse) **2**:190; **17**:195, 207-09, 216-17; **69**:287
"Peter in the Park" (Mazer) **26**:291
"Peter Kürten to the Witness" (Thomas) **31**:434
The Peter Pan Bag (Kingman) **17**:245-46
Peter Smart's Confessions (Bailey) **45**:42-4, 46-7
Peter Whiffle (Van Vechten) **33**:385, 388-89, 393-95, 398-99
"Peters" (Tolstaya) **59**:371
"The Peters Family" (Stafford) **29**:379
"Petersburg Tale" (Akhmatova) **11**:8
Petersen (Williamson) **56**:434
"Petey and Yotsee and Mario" (Roth) **104**:249
"Petit Cachou" (Bell) **102**:5, 7
"Petit désespoir" (Hébert) **29**:228
Le petit saint (Simenon) **2**:397; **18**:482-83
"Le petit salvié" (Williams) **2**:397; **56**:426, 428; **148**:318, 326-27, 341
Le petit soldat (Godard) **20**:130, 132
Le petit théâtre de Jean Renoir (Renoir) **20**:300, 302
Petite cosmogonie portative (Queneau) **5**:360-61
"La petite danceuse de quatorze ans" (Beattie) **146**:63
"A Petite Histoire of Red Fascism" (Codrescu) **121**:165
La petite marchande d'allumettes (Renoir) **20**:300, 309
La petite poule d'eau (Roy) **10**:442; **14**:465-66
"Petition" (Barth) **7**:24; **9**:67; **51**:23, 29; **89**:4-6, 8-10, 13, 15-16, 20, 26, 33, 43, 48, 53-5, 59-60
Les petits chevaux de Tarquinia (Duras) **6**:149; **11**:164; **40**:180; **68**:78, 80, 96; **100**:145
"Petit-Thouars" (Davie) **31**:124
"Pétres" (Ritsos) **6**:463
"The Petrified Man" (Welty) **5**:479; **14**:564; **33**:414-15; **105**:298, 310, 313, 323, 385-86
"The Petrified Woman" (Gordon) **29**:187; **83**:257
Pétrinos hrónos (Ritsos) **13**:487
Petrolio (Pasolini) **106**:272, 274
The Pets (Shaw) **5**:390
"Petting and Being a Pet" (Peacock) **60**:295, 297
Petulia (Lester) **20**:225, 227, 229
"Petunias" (Walker) **58**:405; **103**:412
Petushikha's Breakthrough (Leonov)
See *Petushikhinsky Prolom*
Petushikhin Notch (Leonov)
See *Petushikhinsky Prolom*
The Petushikhino Breakthrough (Leonov)
See *Petushikhinsky Prolom*
Petushikhinsky Prolom (Leonov) **92**:237, 242, 257, 264-65
"Un peuple de solitaires" (Cioran) **64**:74, 82, 84, 98
"Phaedo; or, The Dance" (Yourcenar) **38**:456
"Phaedra" (H. D.) **73**:105
Phaedra (Rexroth) **11**:472; **22**:345
Phaedra Britannica (Harrison) **129**:165, 168, 190, 193
"Phakeni's Farewell" (Kunene) **85**:176
Les phalènes (Tchicaya) **101**:357
"The Phallic Forest" (Wilding) **73**:395, 398
The Phallic Forest (Wilding) **73**:398

"Phallus in Wonderland" (Ewart) **46**:147, 150
"Phantasia for Elvira Shatayev" (Rich) **73**:332; **125**:309, 315-16
"Die Phantasie" (Lenz) **27**:251
"Phantasmagoria" (Gascoyne) **45**:152
Phantastik und Futurologie (Lem)
See *Fantastyka i futurologia*
"Phantom Africa" (Leiris) **61**:361
Phantom City: A Ghost Town Gallery (Beecher) **6**:49
Phantom Dwelling (Wright) **53**:432
"Phantom Eclipse" (Zamora) **89**:393
Phantom Fortress (Lancaster) **36**:244
Phantom Lady (Woolrich) **77**:389-97, 400, 403-04
Phantom of Liberty (Bunuel)
See *Le fantôme de la liberté*
"The Phantom of the Movie Palace" (Coover) **46**:121-22
"The Phantom of the Opera's Friend" (Barthelme) **115**:65, 70
Phantom of the Paradise (De Palma) **20**:75-6, 78
"Phantom Palace" (Allende) **97**:4
Phantoms (Koontz) **78**:197, 203, 206-12
Phantoms of My Brain (Gironella)
See *Los fantasmos de mi cerebo*
"Phar Lap in the Melbourne Museum" (Porter) **33**:318
La pharisienne (Mauriac) **9**:369; **56**:212, 219
Pharos and Pharillon (Forster) **13**:215, 221; **15**:228
"The Phase after History" (Graham) **118**:253, 260
Phases and Stages (Nelson) **17**:303-04, 306
The Phases of Love (Livesay) **79**:348
"The Pheasant" (Carver) **126**:142, 145
"Pheasant" (Plath) **51**:349; **111**:204, 214
"A Pheasant" (Szirtes) **46**:394
"Phenomena" (Carlson) **54**:38
"Phenomenal Woman" (Angelou) **35**:30; **77**:30
"The Phenomenology of Anger" (Rich) **6**:459; **7**:373; **11**:477; **125**:319
"The Phenomenon" (Shapiro) **53**:332
"A Phenomenon of Nature" (Howard) **10**:277
"Phi" (Tolson) **105**:271, 274
Phil Ochs' Greatest Hits (Ochs) **17**:332-34
Phil Ochs in Concert (Ochs) **17**:331
Philadelphia Fire (Wideman) **67**:380, 385-91; **122**:316, 337-42, 347-48, 356-57, 360, 363, 365, 367, 369-70
Philadelphia, Here I Come! (Friel) **5**:128-29; **42**:163-66, 169, 173-74; **59**:147, 149; **115**:213-14, 216, 224-25, 227-29, 231, 233-35, 237, 240-42, 251, 254-57
"Philadelphia Lawyer" (Guthrie) **35**:183, 191
The Philadelphia Negro (Du Bois) **64**:115, 128, 131; **96**:142, 146
The Philanthropist (Hampton) **4**:212
"Philemon and Baucis" (Gunn) **81**:178
Philip Larkin: A Writer's Life (Motion) **81**:417-64
Philip the King and Other Poems (Masefield) **47**:229
The Philippines' Fight for Freedom (Archer) **12**:18
"Phillida" (Fowles) **9**:214
"Phillips House Revisited" (Lowell) **124**:298
"Phillis Goldberg" (Durcan) **70**:151
"Philoclea in the Forest" (Huxley) **11**:282
"Philoctetes" (McAuley) **45**:250-51
"Philoctetes" (Ritsos) **31**:325
Philoctetes (Ritsos) **13**:488
Philoctetes: The Wound and the Bow (Wilson)
See *The Wound and the Bow*
"Philology Recapitulates Ontology, Poetry Is Ontology" (Schwartz) **45**:356
"The Philosopher" (Farrell) **66**:131
"The Philosopher and the Birds" (Murphy) **41**:317
"The Philosophers" (Merton) **83**:384
The Philosopher's Pupil (Murdoch) **31**:290-95; **51**:287
"Philosopher's Songs" (Huxley) **11**:284
The Philosopher's Stone (Lagerkvist) **54**:278
The Philosopher's Stone (Ray)
See *Paras pathar*
The Philosopher's Stone (Rowling)
See *Harry Potter and the Philosopher's Stone*
Philosophical Problems of Many Valued Logic (Zinoviev) **19**:485
"A Philosophico-Political Profile" (Habermas) **104**:87
"Philosophy" (Ezekiel) **61**:101
"Philosophy and Postwar American Criticism" (Wellek) **28**:446
"Philosophy as Stand-In and Interpreter" (Habermas) **104**:99
"The Philosophy Lesson" (Stafford) **68**:431, 433, 441-45
Philosophy of Chance (Lem)
See *Filozofia przypadku*
The Philosophy of Jean-Paul Sartre (Sartre) **1**:304
The Philosophy of Literary Form (Burke) **24**:121-22, 125-28
The Philosophy of Rhetoric (Richards) **24**:387-88, 394, 396, 399, 401
"Philosophy of Solitude" (Merton) **83**:403
A Philosophy of Solitude (Powys) **46**:319; **125**:302
"The Philosophy of Style" (Blaga) **75**:71
"The Philosophy of the Beat Generation" (Holmes) **56**:140
Phineas, and Other Stories (Knowles) **26**:257-58, 262
"Phobia and Composition" (Moody) **147**:189
"Phobias" (Appleman) **51**:17
"The Phoenix" (Cunningham) **31**:98-9, 102, 104
"Phoenix" (Ellison) **42**:127
"The Phoenix" (Le Guin) **45**:216
"Phoenix" (Nemerov) **36**:304
"The Phoenix" (Sarton) **91**:243
"The Phoenix and the Tortoise" (Rexroth) **49**:276-77; **112**:386, 394
The Phoenix and the Tortoise (Rexroth) **1**:284; **22**:345, 348; **49**:277; **112**:365-70, 373, 377, 387, 392, 400
"Phoenix in the Ashes" (Vinge) **30**:413
Phoenix Park (Kinsella) **138**:148
"Phoenix Park Vespers" (Durcan) **43**:114
A Phoenix Too Frequent (Fry) **2**:144; **10**:200; **14**:187-88
Phoenix under the Rain (Shamlu) **10**:470
Phogey! How to Have Class in a Classless Society (Bradbury) **32**:55
"Phone" (Creeley) **36**:118
"Phone for the Fishknives, Norman" (Betjeman) **43**:33
"A Phone of Her Own" (Wasserstein) **90**:429
"Phone-In" (Gilliatt) **13**:237
"Phonenix Park" (Kinsella) **19**:251-52, 255; **138**:86, 89-94, 99-102, 105-07, 109, 119, 127, 129, 133, 136, 140, 147-50, 152, 162, 165-66
"Phools" (Lem) **40**:294
"Phosphorus" (Levi) **37**:227
"Photini" (Nakos) **29**:322
"Photo of the Timbó Plantation" (Cabral de Melo Neto)
See "Fotografia do engenho Timbó"
Photo-Finish (Marsh) **53**:250, 255-56, 260
"Photograph" (Coles) **46**:107-08, 113
"Photograph" (Halpern) **14**:233
"The Photograph" (Oliver) **98**:256
"Photograph" (Page) **18**:376
A Photograph: A Still Life with Shadows/A Photograph: A Study of Cruelty (Shange)
See *A Photograph: Lovers in Motion*
Photograph: Cruelty (Shange)
See *A Photograph: Lovers in Motion*
A Photograph: Lovers in Motion (Shange) **25**:397-98; **74**:294, 307; **126**:365
"Photograph of the Girl" (Olds) **85**:291
"The Photograph of the Unmade Bed" (Rich) **6**:458
Photograph: Still Life (Shange)
See *A Photograph: Lovers in Motion*
"The Photographer" (Munro) **95**:291
"The Photographer in Winter" (Szirtes) **46**:395-96
The Photographer in Winter (Szirtes) **46**:395-96
"Photographer of Snow" (Hillis) **66**:194
"The Photographic Image" (Barthes) **83**:80, 85
"The Photographs" (Dobyns) **37**:78
"Photographs" (Van Duyn) **63**:441-42; **116**:408, 430
"Photographs" (Wright) **6**:581
The Photographs (Fuller) **28**:157
The Photographs (Vassilikos) **4**:551; **8**:524
"Photographs Courtesy of the Fall River Historical Society" (Olds) **85**:285
The Photographs of Chachaji (Mehta) **37**:294-95
"Photographs of Stanley's Grandfather" (Dunn) **40**:171
"photon scanner blue spruce" (Moure) **88**:232
"Photos of a Salt Mine" (Page) **7**:291-92
Phrases from Orpheus (Jones) **10**:285, 288
"Phrases in Common Use" (Jacobsen) **102**:240
"Phrenfy" (Reading) **47**:351
"The Phylactery" (Szirtes) **46**:391
"Phyladda, or the Mind/Body Problem" (Gilchrist) **143**:309
Phyllis (Fast) **23**:158; **131**:100
Physical Graffiti (Page and Plant) **12**:477-80, 482
"Physical Universe" (Simpson) **32**:381-82; **149**:316, 325, 349, 356
The Physicists (Duerrenmatt)
See *Die Physiker*
The Physicists (Dürrenmatt)
See *Die Physiker*
"Physics" (Janowitz) **43**:212
Die Physiker (Duerrenmatt) **102**:55-6, 59-60, 65, 69, 74, 77, 83
Die Physiker (Dürrenmatt) **8**:194, 197; **11**:171, 173; **15**:195-96, 198-99; **43**:128-30
The Physiology of Taste (Fisher) **87**:122, 129, 131
"Pi" (Tolson) **105**:242, 274
"Pi shnayim" (Agnon) **8**:9
"La pia" (Merwin) **45**:272; **88**:200
"Pian dei Giullari" (Ewart) **46**:152
"Piano" (Neruda) **7**:260
The Piano (Campion) **95**:9, 11-30
"Piano after War" (Brooks) **15**:95
The Piano Lesson (Wilson) **63**:452-58; **118**:375-79, 385, 388, 401, 404, 407-08, 410, 412
"Piano Man" (Joel) **26**:213, 218-19, 222
Piano Man (Joel) **26**:213-15, 217-18, 223
The Piano Man's Daughter (Findley) **102**:120-21
"A Piano Piece for the Left and Right Hand" (Jandl) **34**:196
"Piano Pieces" (Shapcott) **38**:404
"The Piano Player" (Barthelme) **46**:40
"Piano Practice" (Moss) **45**:290
"The Piano Tuner's Wives" (Trevor) **116**:394-95
The Pianoplayers (Burgess) **62**:124-26
"Piazza di Spagna, Early Morning" (Wilbur) **53**:413; **110**:348-49, 382
"Piazza Piece" (Ransom) **4**:431
Picasso (O'Brian) **152**:273
Picasso (Reverdy) **53**:280
Picasso and Poetry (Tzara) **47**:389
"The Picasso Poem" (Stern) **100**:333
"The Picasso Summer" (Bradbury) **42**:35
Picasso's Mask (Malraux)
See *La tête d'obsidienne*
Piccadilly (Seifert)
See *Deštník z Piccadilly*

The Piccadilly Bushman (Lawler) **58**:331-33, 337
"Piccola commedia" (Wilbur) **14**:578
"Pick and Poke" (Stern) **40**:409
The Pick of Paul Johnson (Johnson) **147**:87
Picked-Up Pieces (Updike) **9**:540; **34**:284-87, 290, 292; **43**:427-29; **139**:347, 351, 355, 357, 362
"Picking and Choosing" (Moore) **13**:393
"Picking Cloudberries by Moonlight" (Musgrave) **54**:334
"Picking Gooseberries" (Kenny) **87**:254
"Picking Pole Beans" (Piercy) **128**:231
"Picking the Roses" (Stern) **40**:412
"Picking Up the Beer Cans" (Carruth) **84**:129
"Pickle Belt" (Roethke) **19**:397
Pickpocket (Bresson) **16**:104-05, 114-15, 117
"The Picnic" (Creeley) **78**:134
"Picnic" (Graham) **118**:260
"Picnic" (Scott) **22**:372
Picnic (Inge) **1**:153; **8**:308; **19**:226-28, 230
"Picnic 1960" (Christie) **110**:125
Picnic at Hanging Rock (Weir) **20**:425-29
The Picnic at Sakkara (Newby) **2**:311; **13**:408
"A Picnic Contata" (Schuyler) **23**:388
Pic-nic en campaña (Arrabal) **9**:38; **18**:19; **53**:3, 8
Picnic in Babylon: A Jesuit Priest's Journal, 1963-1967 (L'Heureux) **52**:273, 275, 277, 279
The Picnic in the Cemetery (Urdang) **47**:398-99
Picnic on Paradise (Russ) **15**:461-62
Picnic on the Battlefield (Arrabal)
See *Pic-nic en campaña*
Picnic on the Grass (Renoir)
See *Le déjeuner sur l'herbe*
"Picnic on the Lawn" (Scannell) **49**:330
"Picnic with Moonlight and Mangoes" (Jhabvala) **8**:313
"Pico Blanco" (Zamora) **89**:392-93
"Pico Rico Mandorico" (Ferré) **139**:154, 158
Pictor (Hesse)
See *Piktors Verwandlungen*
A Pictorial History of English Architecture (Betjeman) **34**:308
"Pictor's Metamorphoses" (Hesse) **25**:259, 261
Pictor's Metamorphoses, and Other Fantasies (Hesse)
See *Piktors Verwandlungen*
Pictor's Transformations (Hesse)
See *Piktors Verwandlungen*
"The Picture" (Ionesco)
See *Le tableau*
"A Picture History of the War" (Barthelme) **115**:67
"Picture Layout in 'Life' Magazine" (Purdy) **50**:246
"Picture of a Black Child with a White Doll" (Merton) **83**:393, 397
"Picture of a Nativity" (Hill) **8**:294
"The Picture of J. T. in a Prospect of Stone" (Tomlinson) **13**:547, 549
"A Picture of Lee Ying" (Merton) **83**:393
"The Picture of Little J. A. in a Prospect of Flowers" (Ashbery)
See "The Portrait of Little J. A. in a Prospect of Flowers"
"A Picture of Soldiers" (Bell) **8**:66
"A Picture of the Virgin" (Kinsella) **27**:237-38
Picture Palace (Theroux) **11**:529-32; **15**:533; **28**:425; **46**:398, 400, 405
Picture Show (Sassoon) **36**:385; **130**:187
The Picture Story of Britain (Streatfeild) **21**:401
Picture Theory (Brossard) **115**:106, 108-09, 111, 121, 132, 134-36, 140-45
"The Picture: Wolves in the Tree" (Schaeffer) **11**:491
The Picturegoers (Lodge) **36**:266-67
"The Pictures" (Frame) **96**:188
"The Pictures" (Grace) **56**:116, 119
Pictures and Conversations (Bowen) **6**:94-6; **11**:64; **15**:78
Pictures at a Prosecution (Feiffer) **64**:153
Pictures at an Exhibition (Thomas) **132**:380-84
"Pictures for Crusoe" (Perse)
See "Images à Crusoe"
"Pictures from a Japanese Printmaker" (Redgrove) **41**:355
Pictures from an Institution (Jarrell) **2**:208; **6**:261; **9**:297; **13**:300; **49**:186-96, 201
"Pictures from Breughel" (Williams) **9**:575
Pictures from Brueghel, and Other Poems (Williams) **5**:507-08; **42**:455; **67**:407
Pictures in the Hallway (O'Casey) **5**:320; **88**:280
"Pictures of a Long-Lost World" (Souster) **14**:504
Pictures of Fidelman: An Exhibition (Malamud) **1**:200; **2**:266, 268; **3**:322, 324; **5**:269-70; **8**:375; **9**:346, 350; **11**:349, 351; **18**:321; **27**:296-97; **44**:413, 415, 417, 420; **85**:200
"Pictures of Lily" (Townshend) **17**:529-31, 535, 539
"Pictures of People in the War" (Glück) **22**:173
"Pictures of the Dead" (Price) **43**:351
Pictures of the Gone World (Ferlinghetti) **10**:174; **27**:137-38; **111**:50-4, 64, 71-2
"Pictures of the Ice" (Munro) **95**:315
"The Picturesque, the Sublime, and the South African Landscape" (Coetzee) **66**:99
Picturing Will (Beattie) **63**:20-3; **146**:46, 52-8, 69-70, 74-9, 83, 85
Pido la paz la palabra (Otero) **11**:425
"Pie Country" (Barthelme) **117**:17
"Pie Dance" (Giles) **39**:64
"Pie Song" (Sondheim) **30**:398
Pie XII et le IIIe Reich; documents (Friedlander) **90**:100-4, 106-7, 112, 118
Piebald Dog Running along the Shore (Aitmatov)
See *Pegil pes, begushchij kraem moria*
"A Piece" (Creeley) **78**:161
"A Piece of Advice" (Singer) **6**:508
A Piece of Mine (Cooper) **56**:69-72
"A Piece of Monologue" (Beckett) **29**:59, 65
A Piece of My Heart (Ford) **46**:156-59
A Piece of My Heart (Ford) **99**:105, 110, 116, 120-21
A Piece of My Mind (Greeley) **28**:178
A Piece of My Mind (Wilson) **8**:550; **24**:478
"A Piece of News" (Welty) **14**:561; **105**:325, 349, 368
A Piece of the Action (Poitier) **26**:361-62
A Piece of the Night (Roberts) **48**:340-42
"Pieces" (Rich) **7**:372
Pieces (Creeley) **1**:67; **2**:106-07; **4**:117; **8**:151, 153; **11**:138; **15**:151; **36**:117-21; **78**:124, 127-28, 130, 138-41, 147
Pieces and Pontifications (Mailer) **74**:207
Pièces brillantes (Anouilh) **1**:7; **13**:17, 19-20
Pièces costumées (Anouilh) **13**:19, 21
Pièces grinçantes (Anouilh) **13**:17, 19-20
Pièces noires (Anouilh) **1**:7; **8**:22; **13**:16, 19-21; **50**:278
Pieces of Another World: The Story of Moon Rocks (Branley) **21**:19
Pieces of Life (Schorer) **9**:473-74
Pieces of Soap (Elkin) **91**:213-14
"The Pieces of the Clock Lie Scattered" (Simic) **130**:314
Pieces of the Frame (McPhee) **36**:296
"Pieces of the One and a Half Legged Man" (Klappert) **57**:256, 258
Pièces roses (Anouilh) **1**:7; **13**:16, 19-21; **50**:278
"Pied à terre" (Johnston) **51**:240, 243, 247
Pied Piper (Shute) **30**:366-67
"Piedra" (Soto) **80**:287, 291-92
Piedra de sol (Paz) **6**:395; **10**:389, 391; **51**:333, 336-37; **65**:181, 185-87, 195, 199-200; **119**:406-07, 409, 413
Las piedras de Chile (Neruda) **28**:313-14
Piege pour Cendrillon (Japrisot) **90**:167-68
Pierce-Arrow (Howe) **152**:244
"Piere Vidal Old" (Pound) **10**:408; **48**:288
"The Pier-Glass" (Graves) **2**:176; **45**:167, 169
The Pier-Glass (Graves) **6**:210
"Pierre" (Nin) **127**:390
Pierre écrite (Bonnefoy) **9**:115; **58**:43-6, 49-54
"Pierre Menard, Author of the Quixote" (Borges)
See "Pierre Menard, autor del Quixote"
"Pierre Menard: Autor del Quijote" (Borges)
See "Pierre Menard, autor del Quixote"
"Pierre Menard, autor del Quijote" (Borges)
See "Pierre Menard, autor del Quixote"
"Pierre Menard, autor del Quixote" (Borges) **3**:77; **4**:74; **6**:87, 93; **8**:96; **9**:118; **13**:108; **19**:49; **44**:362, 369; **48**:37, 44-5; **83**:156-157, 161, 171-72, 181-82, 192
"La pierre qui pousse" (Camus) **9**:144, 150-51; **14**:114; **63**:71
"Pierre Ronsard and His Rose" (Lattimore) **3**:278
Pierrot le fou (Godard) **20**:139, 145, 149
Pierrot mon ami (Queneau) **5**:359-62; **42**:333
Pierrot ou les secrets de la nuit (Tournier) **95**:368, 372, 378-82
"Pieta" (Gascoyne) **45**:147
"Pietà" (Glück) **22**:178
"Pieta" (Krleža) **114**:170
"Pietà" (McAuley) **45**:252
"Pieta" (Thomas) **13**:543; **48**:374, 379
"La pietà" (Ungaretti) **7**:485; **11**:556; **15**:536
"The Pieta" (Van Duyn) **7**:498; **116**:425
Le piéton de l'air (Ionesco) **4**:252; **6**:252, 254-55; **9**:286-87; **11**:292; **41**:227, 229, 231; **86**:332, 340
La pietra lunare (Landolfi) **49**:216
Una pietra sopra: Discorsi di letteratura e societa (Calvino) **73**:39, 48
Pietr-le-Letton (Simenon) **18**:481; **47**:379
"Piety" (Simic) **49**:337
"Pig" (Hecht) **8**:269
"The Pig" (Lessing) **3**:288
"The Pig Boy" (Gardam) **43**:171
Pig Earth (Berger) **19**:39-41
"Pig Glass, 1973-1978" (Ondaatje) **51**:316-17
Pig in the Middle (Mayne) **12**:390, 392, 397
Pig in the Poke (Gray) **36**:201
Pig Island Letters (Baxter) **14**:62
The Pig Pen (Bullins) **5**:83
"Pig Pig" (Walker) **13**:566
Pig/s Book (Olson) **28**:343
"Pig Song" (Atwood) **13**:44
"Pig Sticking" (Rozewicz) **139**:297
"The Pigeon" (Oe) **86**:227
The Pigeon (Bennett) **35**:45
"Pigeon Eggs" (Van Duyn) **63**:445
Pigeon Feathers, and Other Stories (Updike) **3**:488; **5**:455; **13**:557, 562; **23**:473; **139**:327, 367-68
Pigeon Pie (Mitford) **44**:492
"Pigeons" (Larkin) **64**:271, 280
"The Pigeons" (Shapiro) **53**:334
"Pigeons at Daybreak" (Desai) **97**:152, 176
The Pigman (Zindel) **6**:586-87; **26**:470-76, 478-80
The Pigman's Legacy (Zindel) **26**:478, 480
Pigments (Damas) **84**:156-57, 159-61, 163-65, 169-71, 173-80, 182-83, 185-86
Pignight (Wilson) **33**:459, 464
Pigpen (Pasolini) **20**:264, 267
"Pigs" (Levi) **41**:246
Pigs (Fugard)
See *A Place with the Pigs*
Pigs in Heaven (Kingsolver) **81**:190-95; **130**:85-96, 103, 106, 110, 112-14, 120
Pigsty (Pasolini)
See *Pigpen*
"Pigtail" (Rozewicz) **139**:262
"The Pike" (Blunden) **56**:29, 32, 37, 45
"Pike" (Hughes) **4**:235-36; **9**:280-81; **37**:179; **119**:261, 271, 295

Pike's Peak: A Family Saga (Waters) **88**:349-51, 359, 364, 369
Piktors Verwandlungen (Hesse) **25**:259-61
"Pilatus" (Dürrenmatt) **15**:194
"Pile of Feathers" (Stern) **40**:408
A Pile of Stone (Nissenson) **4**:380; **9**:399
"A Pilgramage" (Ewart) **46**:154
The Pilgrim (Chaplin) **16**:188, 191, 201
Pilgrim at Sea (Lagerkvist) **54**:281-85
Pilgrim at Tinker Creek (Dillard) **9**:175, 177-78; **60**:70, 74, 76-7, 79, 80-1; **115**:160-61, 164-71, 175-82, 194, 197, 202-09
The Pilgrim Hawk: A Love Story (Wescott) **13**:591-92
Pilgrim of the Sea (Lagerkvist)
See *Pilgrim på havet*
The Pilgrim on the Earth (Green) **77**:264
Pilgrim på havet (Lagerkvist) **7**:200; **10**:312; **13**:332
"Pilgrimage" (Olds) **32**:346; **85**:286
"Pilgrimage" (Pinsky) **94**:308
Pilgrimage (Clarke) **9**:167
The Pilgrimage of Festus (Aiken) **52**:20, 22, 28
The Pilgrimage of Henry James (Brooks) **29**:81, 86-7
"Pilgrimage to Non-Violence" (King) **83**:347
"Pilgrimages" (Thomas) **48**:383
"The Pilgrim—Chapter Thirty-Three" (Kristofferson) **26**:267, 269
The Pilgrim's Regress (Lewis) **3**:299, **6**:310; **14**:322-24; **27**:265-66; **124**:205-07, 212-13, 216, 218, 220-22, 224, 241, 244
Piling Blood (Purdy) **50**:246, 248
Pili's Wall (Levine) **2**:244; **4**:286; **14**:317; **118**:283, 305
"The Pill Box" (Lively) **32**:277
The Pill versus the Springhill Mine Disaster (Brautigan) **3**:86-90; **12**:58-60, 69; **34**:315; **42**:61
"Pillar of Fire" (Bradbury) **42**:34; **98**:111
"Pillar of Fire" (Foote) **75**:230-31, 253, 257
A Pillar of Iron (Caldwell) **28**:65; **39**:303
"Pillar of Salt" (Jackson) **60**:211-12
Pillars of the Nation (Laurence) **50**:319
"Pillbox" (Blunden) **56**:43
"Pillow" (Hogan) **73**:158
"Pillow of Stone" (Grau) **146**:128
"The Pilot" (Turco) **11**:549, 551
"A Pilot from the Carrier" (Jarrell) **9**:298; **13**:300
"A Pilot Is Speaking" (Faludy) **42**:140
"Pilots, Man Your Planes" (Jarrell) **13**:300
Pimm's Cup for Everybody (Corcoran) **17**:76
Pinball (Kosinski) **53**:223-28; **70**:298, 307
Pinball, 1973 (Murakami)
See *1973-nen no pinbōru*
"Pinball Wizard" (Townshend) **17**:527, 535
The Pinballs (Byars) **35**:72, 75
Pincher Martin (Golding) **1**:121-22; **2**:166-69; **3**:196, 198-99; **8**:249; **10**:233, 237; **17**:159-66, 172, 174, 179; **27**:159, 162-64, 167-68; **81**:317-18, 320, 323
Pinchirannaa chōsho (Oe) **36**:350; **86**:215-18, 220-24, 228, 230-31, 238-40
The Pinchrunner Memorandum (Oe)
See *Pinchirannaa chōsho*
Pindare (Yourcenar) **87**:383
"Pine" (Dickey) **4**:120; **109**:266-67, 270-72
The Pine Barrens (McPhee) **36**:295
"Pine Tree Tops" (Snyder) **5**:395; **32**:389; **120**:312, 351, 354
The Pineapple Bay Hotel (Gardam)
See *Black Faces, White Faces*
"Pineapple Cake" (Desai) **97**:150
"The Pinewoods, Crows, and Owl" (Oliver) **34**:249
"Piney Wood Hills" (Sainte-Marie) **17**:432
"The Pineys" (Stern) **100**:329
Ping (Beckett)
See *Bing*
Ping-Pong (Adamov)
See *Le ping-pong*
Le ping-pong (Adamov) **4**:5-6; **25**:16, 20-1
"The Pink Corner Man" (Borges)
See "El Hombre de la esquina rosada"
"Pink Dog" (Bishop) **32**:37-8
Pink Floyd: The Wall (Pink Floyd) **35**:313-14
"Pink Hands" (Soto) **80**:302
"Pink Moon the Pond" (Oliver) **98**:266, 272
"Pink Tights and Ginghams" (Ferber) **93**:141
Pink Triangle and Yellow Star (Vidal)
See *The Second American Revolution and Other Essays, 1976-1982*
Pinktoes (Himes) **2**:195; **7**:159; **58**:253, 257, 261; **108**:228, 234
Pinky (Kazan) **16**:360-61; **63**:225, 229, 234
"Pinnacle Range" (Crase) **58**:163
"Pinnochio" (McFadden) **48**:258
Pinocchio in Venice (Coover) **87**:64-66, 68
"The Pinprick Speech" (Grass) **49**:139
Pin-Ups (Bowie) **17**:61-2, 64
"Um piolho de Rui Barbosa" (Cabral de Melo Neto) **76**:164
The Pioneers (Prichard) **46**:327, 332, 335-36, 338
The Pious Agent (Braine) **41**:59
"The Pious Brother" (Lind) **82**:128
Pipali Sahab: Story of a Childhood under the Rag (Anand) **93**:49
"Pipefish" (Oliver) **98**:283
The Piper at the Gates of Dawn (Pink Floyd) **35**:307
"Pipes of Peace" (McCartney) **35**:291
Pipes of Peace (McCartney) **35**:291-93
"Pipistrel" (Selzer) **74**:287
"A Pippa Lilted" (Stafford) **29**:382
Pippa's Challenge (Adamson) **17**:5
Pique-nique en Campagne (Arrabal)
See *Pic-nic en campaña*
Piracy Preferred (Campbell) **32**:73
Pirandello e la Sicilia (Sciascia) **41**:395
"The Piranha Brothers" (Monty Python) **21**:223
"Le pirate" (Soupault) **68**:406
The Pirate (Mamoulian) **16**:427
The Pirate (Robbins) **5**:380
"The Pirate of Penance" (Mitchell) **12**:437
"Pirates" (Škvorecký) **69**:333, 346
Pirates and Emperors: International Terrorism in the Real World (Chomsky) **132**:27, 67
Les pirates du Texas (Simenon) **47**:374
"The Pirate's Ghost" (Brown) **48**:55
"Pirx's Tale" (Lem) **149**:162
"Pis ma rimskomu drugu" (Brodsky) **50**:131
"Pis mo generalu Z." (Brodsky) **50**:131
Pis' mo vozhdiam Sovetskogo Soiuza (Solzhenitsyn) **4**:514; **7**:435, 439; **34**:488, 493; **78**:400, 403, 405, 424, 428-30
The Pisan Cantos (Pound) **3**:395, 399; **4**:417; **7**:326, 328-29; **13**:460-61, 463; **34**:505; **48**:282, 284-85, 287, 290, 293, 295, 299; **50**:434-38; **112**:301, 303-08, 332, 337, 339-40, 354-55, 357
Pisando la dudosa luz del día (Cela) **122**:20, 22
"Píseň o lásce" (Seifert) **93**:342
Píseň o Viktorce (Seifert)
See *The Song of Viktorka*
"Pis'ma iz Tuly" (Pasternak) **7**:293; **10**:387; **18**:385
"Piss Factory" (Smith) **12**:539
"Pissaro's Tomb" (Lane) **25**:287
"Pissing in a River" (Smith) **12**:539-40
The Pistachio Prescription (Danziger) **21**:84
The Pistol (Jones) **3**:261; **10**:290; **39**:406
A Pistol in Greenyards (Hunter) **21**:156-57, 161, 165
"The Pit" (Lessing) **94**:265
"The Pit" (Roethke) **11**:481
The Pit (Onetti)
See *El pozo*
"Pit Strike" (Sillitoe) **148**:172
"Pit Viper" (Momaday) **85**:262-63
Pitch Dark (Adler) **31**:14-18
"Pitch Memory" (Canin) **55**:37-8
"The Pitcher" (Dubus) **36**:146; **97**:210-11, 229
"Pitcher" (Francis) **15**:237, 239
"The Pitcher" (Hood) **28**:192
"The Pitchfork" (Heaney) **74**:194
"Pitching and Rolling" (Yevtushenko) **3**:547
"The Pitll Pawob Division" (Ellison) **42**:127
"The Pitt-Rivers Museum, Oxford" (Fenton) **32**:165-66
Pity in History (Barker) **37**:41
Pity Is Not Enough (Herbst) **34**:449, 451, 455
The Pity of War (Ferguson) **134**:51, 65-7, 69-71, 74-5, 79-81, 84-5, 88, 91, 93, 96
"A Pity. We Were Such a Good Invention" (Amichai) **57**:41; **116**:84, 90, 114-15
La più belle pagine di Tommaso Landolfi (Landolfi) **49**:216
Pius XII and the Third Reich: A Documentation (Friedlander)
See *Pie XII et le IIIe Reich; documents*
"The Pivot" (Kunitz) **148**:98
"A pizca" (Alonso) **14**:25
Pjesme u tmini (Krleža) **114**:167
Placard pour un chemin des écoliers (Char) **14**:127
"Placating the Gods" (Dacey) **51**:83
"Place" (Creeley) **78**:152
"The Place" (Simic) **130**:317
"The Place" (Warren) **39**:270
La place (Ernaux) **88**:98-99, 106-09, 111-13, 116-17, 120
Place (Forbes) **12**:211
A Place among People (Hall) **51**:173
"A Place and a Time to Die" (Ballard) **137**:17
A Place Apart (Fox) **121**:201-02, 232
"A Place as Good as Any" (Brodsky) **100**:69
The Place at Whitton (Keneally) **5**:210; **117**:209-11, 227, 245
Place Called Estherville (Caldwell) **60**:53
La Place de la Concorde Suisse (McPhee) **36**:299
A Place for Lovers (De Sica) **20**:95
A Place for my Head (Hoffman) **141**:264, 266, 276, 281, 296-97, 300-01
A Place for Us: How to Make Society Civil and Democracy Strong (Barber) **141**:24, 26
A Place in England (Bragg) **10**:72
"Place in Fiction" (Welty) **14**:565-67; **105**:321-22
The Place in Flowers Where Pollen Rests (West) **96**:363, 365-67, 371, 373, 375-76, 378, 381, 385-86
A Place in Space (Snyder) **120**:357
Place in the City (Fast) **131**:93
"A Place in the Country" (Simic) **49**:341
"A Place in the Sun" (Wonder) **12**:656
The Place of Dead Roads (Burroughs) **42**:73-6; **109**:197-99, 201
"The Place of Death" (Jarrell) **2**:207
"Place of Fire" (Purdy) **50**:246
A Place of Greater Safety (Mantel) **144**:215-20, 222, 224, 228, 232-33, 239-40
Place of Hawks (Derleth) **31**:128-31
"Place of Learning" (Sarton) **49**:310
"The Place of O" (Young Bear) **94**:362
"The Place of Pain in the Universe" (Hecht) **8**:266
"Place of Refuge" (Breytenbach) **126**:85, 87
"Place of the Salamander" (Bonnefoy)
See "Lieu de la salamandre"
The Place of the Skull (Aitmatov)
See *Plakha*
A Place on Earth (Berry) **8**:85; **46**:71, 73-4
"Place Pigalle" (Wilbur) **110**:381
"The Place the Musician Became a Bear on the Streets of a City Meant to Kill Him" (Harjo) **83**:286
A Place to Come To (Warren) **8**:540-42; **10**:523; **59**:302
A Place to Die (Bowering) **47**:29-30
A Place to Stand (Wagoner) **5**:473

"A Place to Stand On" (Laurence) **50**:320; **62**:280
The Place Whrere Souls are Born (Keneally) **117**:237
"The Place with No Name" (Ellison) **42**:127-29
A Place with the Pigs (Fugard) **80**:76, 78-80, 81, 83
A Place without Boundaries (Donoso)
See *El lugar sin límites*
Place Your Bets (Tzara)
See *Faites vos jeux*
"Placed by the Gideons" (Reading) **47**:350
Los placeres prohibidos (Cernuda) **54**:41, 43, 52-4, 58
"Place-Rituals" (Rukeyser) **15**:457
"Places" (Buckley) **57**:128, 131, 133
"Places in the World a Woman Could Walk" (Kauffman) **42**:250-51
Places in the World a Woman Could Walk (Kauffman) **42**:250-53
"Places I've Never Been" (Hood) **28**:189
"Places, Loved Ones" (Larkin) **64**:272
"Places, Names" (Le Guin) **136**:331
"Places to Look for Your Mind" (Moore) **68**:298-301
Places Where They Sing (Raven) **14**:442
"La Plage" (Robbe-Grillet) **128**:370-75
"Plague" (Hubbard) **43**:204
The Plague (Camus)
See *La peste*
"The Plague Children" (Hodgins) **23**:236
The Plague Column (Seifert) **34**:256-57, 259-61; **44**:422-23; **93**:304-05, 316-17, 320-22, 324, 329, 337-38, 341, 344, 346
The Plague Dogs (Adams) **18**:1
The Plague from Space (Harrison) **42**:207
The Plague Monument (Seifert)
See *The Plague Column*
Plague Ship (Norton) **12**:467
Plague Ship (Slaughter) **29**:378
Plagued by the Nightingale (Boyle) **5**:65; **19**:61; **58**:64-5, 70, 75; **121**:46, 52, 55, 62, 66
The Plague-Sower (Bufalino)
See *Diceria dell'untore*
The Plague-Sower (Bufalino)
See *Diceria dell'untore*
Plain (Rozewicz) **139**:260
A Plain Brown Rapper (Brown) **79**:153-54, 168
"Plain Fare" (Hine) **15**:282
"The Plain in Flames" (Rulfo)
See "El llano en llamas"
The Plain in Flames (Rulfo)
See *El llano en llamas, y otros cuentos*
The Plain Man (Symons) **14**:523
Plain Murder (Forester) **35**:165-66
Plain of Fire (Rulfo)
See *El llano en llamas, y otros cuentos*
"Plain Pleasures" (Bowles) **68**:3, 6, 11, 16
Plain Pleasures (Bowles) **68**:3, 9, 16
"Plain Song" (Raine) **103**:186
Plain Song (Harrison) **33**:197; **143**:344, 354
"A Plain Song for Comadre" (Wilbur) **53**:397, 405, 407, 410, 413; **110**:353
"A Plain Sonnet" (Mueller) **51**:280
"The Plain, the Endless Plain" (Aldiss) **40**:21
"Plain-chant" (Cocteau) **8**:145
The Plains of Cement (Hamilton) **51**:185-86, 190, 193-95, 197-98
The Plains of Passage (Auel) **107**:19-22, 24-5
Plains Song: For Female Voices (Morris) **18**:353-55; **37**:313
Plainsongs (Livesay) **15**:341; **79**:332, 337-38, 340
"Plaint" (Roethke) **3**:433
"Plainview: 1" (Momaday) **85**:256, 264-65
"Plainview: 2" (Momaday) **85**:247-48, 264-65, 269
"Plainview: 3" (Momaday) **85**:265
"Plainview: 4" (Momaday) **85**:265
Le plaisir du texte (Barthes) **24**:28-30, 37, 39; **83**:80, 96, 99-100, 102-04
Plakha (Aitmatov) **71**:21-33
Plameni vjetar (Krleža) **114**:167
"The Plan" (Cohen) **38**:137
"The Plan" (O'Brien) **36**:340
Plan B (Himes) **108**:234, 241-42, 251-53
Plan de evasión (Bioy Casares) **13**:84-7; **88**:62-3, 65-6, 73, 75-6, 79-81, 85-7, 91-2
Le plan de l'aiguille (Cendrars) **18**:97; **106**:169, 185-86
A Plan for Escape (Bioy Casares)
See *Plan de evasión*
"Plan for the Young English King" (Pound) **10**:407
El plan infinito (Allende) **97**:21-2, 24-6, 41-3, 57
"Plan Now to Attend" (Purdy) **28**:380
"Plan of Future Works" (Pasolini) **106**:241, 250
"The Planctus" (Hope) **3**:251
"Plane Landing in Tokyo" (Scott) **22**:373
"Planes of Language" (Gibbons) **145**:136
A Planet Called Treason (Card) **47**:67; **50**:143
Planet News: 1961-1967 (Ginsberg) **2**:163; **4**:181-82; **6**:198; **13**:240; **36**:183-85, 190-91, 194, 196
Planet of Adventure (Vance) **35**:423
Planet of Exile (Le Guin) **13**:345, 348; **22**:265, 273; **45**:213, 215, 218, 222;
The Planet of Junior Brown (Hamilton) **26**:148-49, 154, 156
The Planet of Lost Things (Strand) **41**:435-36
Planet of the Apes (Serling) **30**:357
"Planet of the Damned" (Vance) **35**:420
The Planet Savers (Bradley) **30**:26
Planet Waves (Dylan) **4**:150; **12**:199; **77**:190
"Planetarium" (Rich) **11**:478; **18**:447; **36**:372; **125**:317, 320, 321
The Planetarium (Sarraute)
See *Le planétarium*
Le planétarium (Sarraute) **1**:302; **2**:386; **4**:464, 466-67, 469; **8**:472; **31**:377-78, 380, 386; **80**:229-30, 236, 240, 252
"Planetesimal" (Hulme) **130**:52
Planets and Dimensions: Collected Essays of Clark Ashton Smith (Smith) **43**:420-21
"Planks" (Barnard) **48**:26
"The Planner's Dream Goes Wrong" (Weller) **26**:447
"Planning" (Ezekiel) **61**:104-05
"Planning the Perfect Evening" (Dove) **81**:134
Plans for Departure (Sahgal) **41**:374-75
"The Planster's Vision" (Betjeman) **6**:68; **43**:36-7, 40
Plant and Phantom (MacNeice) **4**:315; **53**:232
Plant Dreaming Deep (Sarton) **49**:316-17; **91**:251
The Plant, the Well, the Angel (Vassilikos) **4**:551
Plantain (Akhmatova) **25**:27; **64**:10
Plantain (Akhmatova)
See *Podorozhnik*
"Plantation Boy" (Cabral de Melo Neto)
See "Menino de engenho"
"Plantation Mistress or Soul Sister?" (Hooks) **94**:150, 152
"Planting a Magnolia" (Snodgrass) **68**:393
"Planting Bulbs" (Piercy) **128**:231
"Planting Strawberries" (Stern) **40**:408
"Planting Trees" (Updike) **43**:436
Plants Today and Tomorrow (Hyde) **21**:173
Planus (Cendrars)
See *Bourlinguer*
Płaskorzeźba (Rozewicz) **139**:291, 294-95, 297, 299, 308
"The Plaster Mask" (Oe) **86**:226-27
"The Plastic Abyss" (Wilhelm) **7**:537-38
"Plastic Man" (Katz) **47**:216
"Plastic People" (Zappa) **17**:585
Un plat de porc aux bananes vertes (Schwarz-Bart) **2**:389
"A Plate" (Popa) **19**:373
"The Platform Man" (Snodgrass) **68**:397
Platinum Blonde (Capra) **16**:159
Platitudes (Ellis) **55**:50-4
"Platko" (Alberti) **7**:7
The Plato Papers (Ackroyd)
See *The Plato Papers: A Prophecy*
The Plato Papers: A Prophecy (Ackroyd) **140**:63, 70-71, 73-75
"Platonic" (Ezekiel) **61**:93, 101, 105
"Platonic Drowse" (Warren) **39**:256
"Platonic Love" (Reaney) **13**:473
Platonic Scripts (Justice) **102**:268, 281, 283
Platoon (Stone) **73**:367-79, 381-83, 385
"Plato's Pharmacy" (Derrida) **24**:155; **87**:92
"Plato's Year" (Johnson) **7**:414
"Platsch" (Jandl) **34**:196
"Platte River" (Bass) **143**:8-9
Platte River (Bass) **143**:8-9, 21
"Platypus" (Murray) **40**:334
Plausible Prejudices: Essays on American Writing (Epstein) **39**:464-69
"A Play" (Alta) **19**:19
Play (Beckett) **6**:39, 43, 47; **9**:84, 86; **11**:37-9, 42-3; **18**:43, 46-8; **29**:54
The Play about the Baby (Albee) **113**:54
A Play by Aleksandr Solzhenitsyn (Solzhenitsyn) **1**:321
Play by Play (Goldemberg)
See *Tiempo al Tiempo*
"Play Ebony Play Ivory" (Dumas) **62**:155
Play Ebony Play Ivory (Dumas)
See *Poetry for My People*
"Play in Four Acts" (Dobyns) **37**:76
Play It Again, Sam (Allen) **16**:3-5; **52**:39, 44, 48
"Play It as It Lays" (Braverman) **67**:52
Play It as It Lays (Didion) **1**:74-5; **3**:127-28; **8**:173-77; **14**:151, 153; **32**:143, **129**:60, 69-70, 82-83, 85, 102- 03, 105
A Play of Giants (Soyinka) **36**:417-18
"A Play of Memory" (Updike) **23**:475
Play of Questions (Handke) **134**:158
The Play of the Eyes (Canetti)
See *Das Augenspiel: Lebensgeschichte 1931-1937*
Play Parade: Collected Plays of Noël Coward (Coward) **29**:134
Play Strindberg (Duerrenmatt) **102**:60-1
Play Strindberg (Dürrenmatt) **8**:195; **15**:195; **43**:126-27
Play with a Tiger (Lessing) **94**:272
La playa (Sarduy) **97**:370
"De playa a playa" (Otero) **11**:427
"Playa ignorante" (Aleixandre) **9**:15
"Playback" (Beattie) **63**:2, 9, 12, 19
"Playbox" (Reaney) **13**:473
"Playboy" (Wilbur) **110**:384
The Player (Altman) **116**:50-2, 55, 58-9, 62, 66-7, 71, 73
The Player King (Rovit) **7**:383
The Player on the Other Side (Queen) **3**:421; **11**:461, 464-65
"The Player Piano" (Jarrell) **13**:302
Player Piano (Vonnegut) **1**:348; **2**:453; **3**:495-96, 498, 500-01; **4**:562-63, 565-67; **5**:466-67, 469; **12**:600-03, 606, 609-12, 614, 616-18, 620-21, 623; **22**:445; **40**:441, 444; **60**:429, 431; **111**:351, 355, 363
Players (DeLillo) **8**:172; **10**:134-35; **13**:175, 178; **27**:80, 85-6; **39**:117, 123, 125; **54**:80, 82; **76**:171-72, 174, 182
Players (Williamson)
See *The Club*
The Players and the Game (Symons) **2**:426; **14**:523
Playground (Buell) **10**:81-2
The Playground (Levine) **54**:293, 299
"The Playhouse Called Remarkable" (Spark) **13**:523
"Playing an Obsolete Instrument" (Hollander) **5**:186
"Playing Cards" (Atwood) **4**:27
Playing Dead (Wiebe) **138**:374
Playing for Time (Miller) **26**:326-28
Playing House (Wagman) **7**:500

Playing in the Dark: Whiteness and the Literary Imagination (Morrison) **81**:239-40, 245-46, 248, 250-51, 255, 258, 260
"Playing in the Mines" (Parini) **54**:361
Playing Possum (Simon) **26**:409-10
"Playing with a Full Deck" (Bernstein) **142**:4
"Playing with Fire" (Simmons) **43**:414
"Playing with My Kinsman" (Kunene) **85**:176
Playland (Fugard) **80**:83
The Playmaker (Keneally) **117**:240, 243
"The Playroom" (Barnard) **48**:25-6
"The Playroom" (Turco) **11**:550
Plays for England (Osborne) **2**:328; **5**:332; **45**:314
Plays for the Poor Theatre (Brenton) **31**:69
Plays in Which Darkness Falls (Hildesheimer)
See *Spiele in denen es dunkel wird*
The Plays of J. P. Donleavy (Donleavy) **4**:125
"Plays: Self" (Foreman)
See "How I Write My"
The Playwright as Thinker (Bentley) **24**:45-7
"Plaza Real with Palm Trees" (Blackburn) **9**:100
"Plaza Real with Palm Trees: Second Take" (Blackburn) **9**:100
Plaza Suite (Simon) **6**:504; **31**:395-96, 403-04; **70**:240, 243
"Plea" (Kaufman) **49**:205
"A Plea to the Protestant Churches" (Brooks) **110**:28, 30
"Plea to Those Who Matter" (Welch) **52**:429-30
"A Pleasant Thought from Whitehead" (O'Hara) **13**:427
"A Pleasant Walk" (Enright) **31**:154
"Please" (Komunyakaa) **94**:242
Please Don't Eat the Daisies (Kerr) **22**:255
"Please Forward" (Summers) **10**:494
"Please Hello" (Sondheim) **30**:388; **147**:261
"Please Let Me Wonder" (Wilson) **12**:643
"Please, Master" (Ginsberg) **109**:333, 357, 364, 366
Please Pass the Guilt (Stout) **3**:472
"Please Please Me" (Lennon and McCartney) **35**:274
"Please Stay in the Family Clovis" (Durcan) **43**:114, 116
"Please Turn Off the Moonlight" (Wheelock) **14**:571
"Pleasure" (Schwartz) **10**:465
"Pleasure" (Wiggins) **57**:434-36
"Pleasure: A Political Issue" (Jameson) **142**:259
Pleasure City (Markandaya)
See *Shalimar*
The Pleasure Garden (Garfield) **12**:232-33, 236
"The Pleasure Ground" (Murphy) **41**:315-16
"The Pleasure of Her Company" (Smiley) **53**:348
The Pleasure of the Text (Barthes)
See *Le plaisir du texte*
The Pleasure Principle (Wilson) **33**:460-61, 464
Pleasure Seeker's Guide (Leet) **11**:323
"The Pleasure Steamers" (Motion) **47**:289, 291, 293-94
The Pleasure Steamers (Motion) **47**:285-86, 288-89, 292-94
Pleasure-Dome (Madden) **15**:350
The Pleasure-Dome: The Collected Film Criticism, 1935-40 (Greene) **70**:294
The Pleasures of Exile (Lamming) **2**:235; **66**:221-22, 224-27, 231; **144**:126, 140-42, 145, 186-87, 189-91, 193, 204
The Pleasures of Helen (Sanders) **41**:377
The Pleasures of Literature (Powys) **125**:300, 302
"The Pleasures of Peace" (Koch) **44**:243
The Pleasures of Peace and Other Poems (Koch) **44**:241, 243, 248-49
Pleasures of the Flesh (Ewart) **13**:208; **46**:148, 150
The Pleasures of the Harbour (Ochs) **17**:330-34
"Pleasuring Sunday" (Nagy) **7**:251
The Plebeians Rehearse the Uprising: A German Tragedy (Grass) **4**:201, 203; **6**:207; **15**:261; **49**:139
The Pledge (Duerrenmatt) **102**:59
The Pledge (Dürrenmatt)
See *Das Versprechen: Requiem auf den Kriminalroman*
The Pledge (Fast) **131**:63, 86, 90, 92, 95-6, 98
"The Pleiades" (Barnard) **48**:26
"The Plentitude" (Thesen) **56**:415
Plenty (Hare) **29**:213-20; **58**:225, 230, 233-35; **136**:243, 247-47, 248-49, 256-57, 259, 262-63, 265, 267, 274, 277, 284, 286, 290-93, 295, 306
"Plessy vs. Ferguson: Theme and Variations" (Merton) **83**:397
Plexus (Miller) **2**:281
"Plitsch" (Jandl) **34**:196
"Ploaie" (Arghezi) **80**:8
"Ploja fòur di dut" (Pasolini) **106**:267
"Ploja tai cunfins" (Pasolini) **106**:226-28, 267
"Pløjeren" (Dinesen) **95**:70-1
"Plot" (Oates) **6**:370-71
The Plot (Wallace) **13**:568
"The Plot against Proteus" (Smith) **15**:513, 516
The Plot Against Roger Rider (Symons) **32**:425
The Plot to Seize the White House (Archer) **12**:19-20
The plotters (Borges)
See *Los conjurados*
Plotting and Writing Suspense Fiction (Highsmith) **102**:185, 196, 209, 213
"Plotting with the Dead" (Szymborska) **99**:201
The Plough and the Stars (O'Casey) **5**:317-20; **11**:406-11; **15**:404-06; **88**:239, 242, 244-45, 247, 250, 254, 256-59, 262, 276-77
"The Plougher" (Colum) **28**:90
"Ploughman" (Kavanagh) **22**:238
Ploughman and Other Poems (Kavanagh) **22**:236
The Ploughman's Lunch (McEwan) **66**:286
Ploughmen of the Glacier (Ryga) **14**:474
"Plow Cemetery" (Updike) **43**:436
Plowman (Kavanagh)
See *Ploughman and Other Poems*
Plowshare in Heaven (Stuart) **34**:373, 376
Pluck the Flowers, Gun the Kids (Oe)
See *Me-mushiri Kouchi*
"Plug Body" (Howe) **47**:172-73
"Pluie" (Hébert) **29**:237
La Pluie d'Eté (Duras) **100**:120, 131
La pluie et le beau temps (Prévert) **15**:438
Pluie et vent sur Télumée Miracle (Schwarz-Bart) **7**:404-05
"Pluies" (Perse) **11**:433; **46**:303-05, 307, 309
"Plum Blossoms" (Peterkin) **31**:308
Plum Bun (Fauset) **19**:169, 171; **54**:176-77, 180-82, 187, 189-90
"The Plum Trees" (Oliver) **34**:247; **98**:257, 260, 296-97
"Plumb" (Zamora) **89**:369, 394
Plumb (Gee) **29**:177-79
The Plumber (Weir) **20**:429-30
"The Plumber as the Missing Letter" (Wheelock) **14**:571
"The Plumbing" (Merwin) **45**:277
Plume à Casablanca (Michaux) **19**:311
Plume au restaurant (Michaux) **19**:311
Plumelia (Piccolo) **13**:441
"The Plumet Basilisk" (Moore) **4**:362; **10**:353; **13**:396
"The Plum's Heart" (Soto) **80**:289
"Plunder" (Ammons) **25**:48
Plunder Squad (Westlake) **33**:437
"Plunge" (Gunn) **18**:199, 202
"A Plunge into Real Estate" (Calvino)
See "La speculazione edilizia"
"plunging into the improbable" (Broumas) **73**:5
"Plunking the Skagit" (Hugo) **32**:237
"Plurality" (MacNeice) **4**:317
Plus (McElroy) **47**:240-41, 243-44, 246
"Plutonian Ode" (Ginsberg) **36**:192, 196
Plutonian Ode: Poems, 1977-1980 (Ginsberg) **36**:188, 191-91, 194, 196
"Plutonium-186" (Asimov) **19**:26
PM/AM: New and Selected Poems (Pastan) **27**:371
Pnin (Nabokov) **1**:239, 243-45; **2**:299, 303; **3**:352-53, 355-56; **6**:351, 356; **8**:412, 418; **15**:393; **44**:467-68; **46**:291; **64**:351
The Pnume (Vance) **35**:422, 424
"Po' Boy Blues" (Hughes) **35**:221
"Po jagody" (Yevtushenko) **13**:620
"Po' Sammy" (Bennett) **28**:29
"Po' Ting" (Bennett) **28**:27
"The Poacher" (Le Guin) **136**:376
The Poacher (Bates) **46**:53-6
"Poachers Early Morning" (MacCaig) **36**:282
"Poaching" (Wolff) **64**:446, 449
Poarta neagră (Arghezi) **80**:6-7, 11
"Pobeda" (Aksyonov)
See "The Victory"
"Pocahontas" (Young) **17**:581
La poche parmentier (Perec) **56**:257-58
"Pochti elegiia" (Brodsky) **13**:116; **50**:121
"The Pocket Elephants" (Middleton) **13**:389
A Pocket Full of Miracles (Robinson) **21**:343
A Pocket Full of Rye (Christie) **12**:115-16, 124; **48**:75
The Pocket Mirror (Frame) **22**:145; **96**:189, 198, 201
"The Pocket Remembered" (Singer) **69**:306-07
"The Pocket Song" (Goldbarth) **38**:201
"The Pocket Wars of Peanuts Joe" (Harrison) **43**:175; **129**:176
Pocketful of Miracles (Capra) **16**:157, 160, 163
Pocketful of Rye (Cronin) **32**:140
Pocoangelini: A Fantography (Turco) **11**:552
Pocock and Pitt (Baker) **8**:39-40
"Pocock Passes" (Pritchett) **41**:334
"Pocomania" (Walcott) **42**:421; **76**:279
"Pocta Vladimíru Holanovi" (Seifert) **93**:343
"Pod of the Milkweed" (Frost) **9**:223; **10**:199
"Poderío de la noche" (Aleixandre) **9**:16
Podkayne of Mars (Heinlein) **55**:303
Podniataia tselina (Sholokhov) **7**:416-17, 420-21; **15**:481-84
Podorozhnik (Akhmatova) **25**:24; **126**:5, 24, 33
Podrostak Savenko (Coles) **67**:177, 182-83
Podstawy BHP w kopalni miedzi (Kieslowski)
See *Standards of Safety and Hygiene in a Copper Mine*
Podwojne zycie Weroniki (Kieslowski) **120**:216-18, 220-21, 223-28, 243-44, 249, 252, 254, 256
Poe Poe Poe Poe Poe Poe Poe (Hoffman) **6**:242; **13**:286-87; **23**:240-41
"Poem" (Alexie) **154**:27
"Poem" (Ashbery) **13**:35
"Poem" (Bernstein) **142**:47
"Poem" (Bishop) **9**:94-5, 97-8; **13**:95
"Poem" (Glück) **22**:174
"The Poem" (Hall) **37**:142
"The Poem" (Hoffman) **13**:289
"Poem" (Jensen) **37**:192
"Poem" (Justice) **6**:272; **19**:235; **102**:285
"The Poem" (Kinnell) **3**:269; **29**:284; **129**:234
"Poem" (Kunitz) **148**:86, 94-95
"Poem" (McGrath) **59**:183
"Poem" (O'Hara) **13**:423-25, 427, 430; **78**:333, 346
"Poem" (Oliver) **98**:260
"The Poem" (Paz) **4**:397
"Poem" (Purdy) **14**:431
"Poem" (Rukeyser) **27**:409
"Poem" (Schwartz) **45**:355; **45**:355
"Poem" (Simic) **9**:478, 481
"Poem" (Smith) **64**:395
"Poem" (Strand) **71**:281
"Poem" (Tomlinson) **13**:546
"Poem" (Turner) **48**:398-99
"The Poem" (Williams) **13**:605
"Poem" (Zweig) **34**:379
"Poem 1" (Ferlinghetti) **111**:50-1
"Poem I" (Larkin) **18**:293
"Poem II" (Larkin) **18**:298

"Poem 5" (Ferlinghetti) **111**:51
"Poem 6" (Ferlinghetti) **111**:53
"Poem 13" (Ferlinghetti) **111**:54
"Poem 14" (Ferlinghetti) **111**:54, 56
"Poem 15" (Ferlinghetti) **111**:57
"Poem 17" (Ferlinghetti) **111**:52
"Poem XX" (Larkin) **8**:340; **18**:293, 299
"Poem 22" (Ferlinghetti) **111**:55
"Poem 24" (Ferlinghetti) **111**:54, 58
"Poem 25" (Ferlinghetti) **111**:54
"Poem XXIX" (Larkin) **18**:298
"Poem XXXII" (Larkin) **8**:339-40
"Poem 177: The Law School Riots, Athens, 1973" (Levi) **41**:246
"Poem about a Ball in the Nineteenth Century" (Empson) **8**:201
"A Poem about George Doty in the Death House" (Wright) **5**:519
"A Poem about Intelligence for My Brothers and Sisters" (Jordan) **23**:255
"Poem about Morning" (Meredith) **13**:375
"Poem About My Rights" (Jordan) **114**:143-47, 158, 161, 163
"Poem about People" (Pinsky) **38**:359; **94**:305; **121**:435, 446
"A Poem about Poland" (Donnell) **34**:158
"Poem About Police Violence" (Jordan) **114**:142
"Poem about the Future" (Enzensberger) **43**:144
"Poem (All the Mirrors in the World)" (O'Hara) **78**:339
"Poem Almost Wholly in My Own Manner" (Wright) **146**:368
"The Poem and the Spear" (Laurence) **62**:280
"The Poem and the Water" (Cabral de Melo Neto)
See "O poema e a água"
"The Poem as a Field of Action" (Williams) **42**:450
"The Poem as Mask: Orpheus" (Rukeyser) **15**:459; **27**:413-14
"Poem at Thirty" (Sanchez) **116**:272, 275, 278, 280, 313
"Poem Beginning 'The'" (Zukofsky) **18**:558
"A Poem Beginning with a Line by Pindar" (Duncan) **2**:122; **15**:190, 192; **41**:124
"Poem by the Wellside" (Alexander) **121**:5
Poem Counterpoem (Randall) **135**:373, 377, 387, 390, 392, 394-96
"Poem Dedicatory" (MacLeish) **68**:273
"Poem Ended by a Death" (Adcock) **41**:16-17
"A Poem for 3rd World Brothers" (Knight) **40**:282, 285
"Poem for a Birthday" (Plath) **17**:368; **111**:164, 177-81, 203, 212
"A Poem for a Certain Lady on Her Thirty-Third Birthday" (Knight) **40**:283
"Poem for a Dead Neighbor" (Kingsolver) **130**:85
"Poem for a Fatherless Son" (Plath) **111**:167
"Poem for a Gone Woman" (Lane) **25**:287
"Poem for a Painter" (O'Hara) **13**:425
"Poem for a Poet" (Lorde) **71**:247
"A Poem for a Poet" (Madhubuti) **73**:213
"Poem for a Time of Change" (MacLeish) **68**:287
"Poem for a Tremendous Drunk" (Salinas) **90**:331
"Poem for Angela Elston" (Mahapatra) **33**:284
"Poem for Aretha" (Giovanni) **64**:186
"A Poem for Atheists" (Dunn) **36**:151
"Poem for Benn's Graduation from High School" (Ciardi) **40**:161
"A Poem for Black Hearts" (Baraka) **5**:48
"A Poem for Black Relocation Centers" (Knight) **40**:284
"Poem (For BMC No. 2)" (Giovanni) **117**:194
"Poem for Conrad" (Watkins) **43**:450, 453
"Poem for Etheridge" (Sanchez) **116**:295, 315
"Poem for Half-White College Students" (Baraka) **5**:48
"poem for jennifer, marla, tawana and me" (Sapphire) **99**:81
"Poem for Joy" (Jordan) **114**:154
"A Poem for Julia" (Hecht) **8**:266
"Poem for L. C." (Klappert) **57**:259
"Poem for Marie" (Heaney) **14**:243-44
"Poem for Mark" (Jordan) **114**:154
"A Poem for My Father" (Sanchez) **116**:281, 295, 313
"Poem for My Thirty-Second Birthday" (Ciardi) **40**:157
"A Poem for My Wife" (Sorrentino) **40**:386
"A Poem for Myself" (Knight) **40**:284
"Poem for Nana" (Jordan) **114**:143
"A Poem for Negro Intellectuals (If There Bes Such a Thing)" (Madhubuti) **73**:199
"Poem for Olivia" (Salinas) **90**:325
"Poem for One of the Annettes" (Purdy) **50**:245
"Poem for Personnel Managers" (Bukowski) **41**:64-5
"Poem for South African Women" (Jordan) **114**:158
"A Poem for Sterling Brown" (Sanchez) **116**:301
"A Poem for the Blue Heron" (Oliver) **98**:273
"A Poem for the Governments" (Williams) **148**:320, 343
"A Poem for the Students of Greece" (Boyle) **58**:76
"A Poem for the Teesto Diné of Arizona" (Boyle) **58**:76
"A Poem for Willie Best" (Baraka) **10**:20; **115**:33
"Poem XLII" (Cummings) **68**:47
"Poem From Taped Testimony in the Tradition of Bernhard Goetz" (Jordan) **114**:144
"Poem in April" (Gustafson) **36**:218
"Poem in March" (Levi) **41**:244
"Poem in Memory of an Earlier Poem" (Thesen) **56**:422-23
"Poem in Praise of the British" (Dunn) **40**:166
"Poem in Prose" (Bogan) **46**:90; **93**:65
"Poem in Three Parts" (Bly) **128**:5, 14-15, 17-21, 23-24, 26-29, 36, 43
A Poem in Time Frozen (Milosz) **22**:312; **82**:298
"A Poem in Translation" (Gallagher) **18**:170
"Poem Instead of a Columbus Day Parade" (Jordan) **114**:146
"A Poem Is a Walk" (Ammons) **5**:26
"Poem Issued by Me..." (Starbuck) **53**:353
"The Poem Itself" (Jacobsen) **48**:195
The Poem Itself (Burnshaw) **3**:91; **13**:129
"Poem (Khrushchev Is Coming on the Right Day!)" (O'Hara) **78**:360
"A Poem Looking for a Reader" (Madhubuti) **73**:193
"A Poem Nearly Anonymous" (Ransom) **24**:366
"Poem No. 4" (Sanchez) **116**:279
"Poem No. 7" (Sanchez) **116**:272, 274
"Poem No. 8" (Sanchez) **116**:315
"Poem (No Name No. 3)" (Giovanni) **64**:182
"Poem #5" (L'Heureux) **52**:273
"A Poem of Ecstasy" (Aksyonov) **101**:21
"The Poem of Flight" (Levine) **33**:274; **118**:301
"Poem of Lewis" (Smith) **64**:396-97
"Poem of Liberation" (Stern) **40**:410-11
"A Poem of Praise" (Sanchez) **116**:315
"Poem of the Gifts" (Borges)
See "Poema de los dones"
"Poem of the Wintry Fisherman" (Haines) **58**:215
"Poem of These States" (Ginsberg) **36**:191
"Poem on an Underground Wall" (Simon) **17**:459, 461
A Poem on Frozen Time (Milosz)
See *A Poem in Time Frozen*
"Poem on My Birthday" (Amichai) **9**:22
"A Poem on the First Battles" (Amichai)
See "Shir al hakravot harishonim"
"A Poem on the Nuclear War, from Pompeii" (Tillinghast) **29**:415
"Poem on the Road" (Jordan) **114**:146
"Poem, or Beauty Hurts Mr. Vinal" (Cummings) **8**:159; **68**:46
"Poem out of Childhood" (Rukeyser) **15**:457
"Poem Read at Joan Mitchell's" (O'Hara) **78**:372
"Poem LXVII" (Cummings) **68**:47
"Poem to a Foreign Lady" (Perse)
See "Poème à l'étrangère"
"Poem to Camus" (Kaufman) **49**:204
"A Poem to Complement Other Poems" (Madhubuti) **73**:199, 212
"Poem to My Daughter" (Stevenson) **33**:382
"Poem to My Husband from My Father's Daughter" (Olds) **32**:346; **85**:287
"Poem Two" (Snyder) **32**:387
"Poem V (F) W" (O'Hara) **78**:358
"A Poem with Children" (Guillén)
See "Poema con niños"
"A Poem with No Ending" (Levine) **118**:280, 301
"Poem with One Fact" (Hall) **37**:146
Poem without a Hero (Akhmatova)
See *Poema bez geroia*
Poem without a Hero: Triptych (Akhmatova)
See *Poema bez geroya: Triptykh*
"Poem without Theme" (Squires) **51**:377
"Poem Written After Reading Wright's 'American Hunger'" (Sanchez) **116**:303
Poema a fumetti (Buzzati) **36**:97
Poema bez geroia (Akhmatova) **11**:8-9; **25**:28-30; **64**:11, 13-15, 18-19; **126**:8, 11-3, 24, 35, 38, 44, 57
Poema bez geroya: Triptykh (Akhmatova) **126**:44
"Poema con niños" (Guillén) **79**:241
"Poema de los dones" (Borges) **6**:89
"O poema e a água" (Cabral de Melo Neto) **76**:150, 165
Poemas, 1923-1959 (Borges) **44**:363
Poemas (1953-1955) (Castellanos) **66**:50
"Poema(s) da cabra" (Cabral de Melo Neto) **76**:167
Poemas de amor (Guillén) **79**:241
Poemas de la consumación (Aleixandre) **9**:12, 17; **36**:25-7, 30-1
Poemas de un novelista (Donoso) **32**:161; **99**:270-72
Poemas para combatir la calvicie (Parra) **102**:356
Poemas puros (Alonso) **14**:16
Poemas y antipoemas (Parra) **2**:331; **102**:334, 337-38, 340, 342, 344-45, 348, 356
"Poemat autystyczny" (Rozewicz) **139**:290, 296, 299
Poemat otwarty (Rozewicz) **23**:362
"Pocmat równoczesny" (Rozewicz) **139**:295
"Poème" (Char) **14**:127
"Poème à l'étrangère" (Perse) **4**:399; **46**:305, 307, 309
Poeme noi (Arghezi) **80**:8
Le poême pulverisé (Char) **9**:161, 164
Poemele luminii (Blaga) **75**:67-70, 74-7
Poèmes (Genet) **44**:391
Poèmes (Senghor) **130**:236-37, 258
Poemes des deux années, 1953-1954 (Char) **9**:159
Poèmes en prose (Reverdy) **53**:286
Poèmes et poésies (1917-1973) (Soupault) **68**:408
Poèmes militants (Char) **14**:127
Poèmes nègres sur des airs africains (Damas) **84**:177, 179, 181, 184
Poèmes: Un champ d'îles, La terre inquiète, Les Indes (Glissant) **68**:182
Poem-Paintings (O'Hara) **13**:427
Poems (Amichai) **116**:84, 89-90, 95-6
Poems (Auden) **2**:22; **3**:24; **6**:19-24; **14**:26, 33; **43**:17; **123**:42
Poems (Barker) **48**:9, 11, 20
Poems (Beer) **58**:38
Poems (Berryman) **13**:77; **62**:71
Poems (Bishop) **4**:65
Poems (Celan) **53**:71, 74
Poems (Christie) **110**:125-26, 128

Poems (Clark Bekedermo) **38**:120, 125, 127
Poems (Eliot) **13**:193; **41**:151; **55**:350; **57**:167
Poems (Fearing) **51**:104-08, 110-11, 114-15
Poems (Finch) **18**:153
Poems (Fowles) **9**:216
Poems (Fuller) **28**:151-52
Poems (Golding) **27**:164; **81**:318
Poems (Hébert) **13**:268; **29**:231-32
Poems (Hope) **51**:213, 216-21
Poems (Ignatow) **7**:175, 177; **14**:274, 276; **40**:258
Poems (Jennings) **131**:237-38
Poems (Klein) **19**:260
Poems (Koch) **44**:240, 244
Poems (Laxness)
See *Kvaedakver*
Poems (MacNeice) **4**:315; **53**:233-34
Poems (Nabokov) **3**:351
Poems (Pasolini)
See *Poesi*
Poems (Ratushinskaya)
See *Stikhi/Poems/Poèmes*
Poems (Reaney) **13**:472
Poems (Slessor) **14**:492
Poems (Smith) **6**:512
Poems (Spender) **10**:488, 492; **41**:418, 424; **91**:263, 266, 269
Poems (Walcott) **25**:452; **76**:273
Poems (Warner) **45**:428-29
Poems, 1930 (Auden) **3**:25; **4**:34; **11**:15, 17; **14**:32; **43**:15-16, 18, 23-4, 26, 29
Poems, 1934 (Auden) **6**:19; **11**:18
Poems, 1934 (Empson) **34**:335
Poems, 1935 (Empson) **19**:152, 157, 159; **34**:335
Poems, 1950 (Bunting) **39**:297; **47**:44-5, 49
Poems, 1953 (Graves) **1**:127
Poems 1960 to 1967 (Levertov) **66**:251
"Poems 1946-56" (Spicer) **72**:362
Poems 1968-72 (Levertov) **66**:251-52
Poems, 1914-1926 (Graves) **1**:127; **45**:162-63
Poems, 1914-1930 (Blunden) **56**:30, 38, 40-1
Poems, 1918-1936 (Reznikoff) **9**:450
Poems, 1920-1945: A Selection (Tate) **14**:532
Poems, 1922-1947 (Tate) **4**:539; **14**:532
Poems, 1922-1961 (Davidson) **2**:112
Poems, 1923-1954 (Cummings) **15**:154; **68**:35, 40, 42
Poems, 1924-1933 (MacLeish) **8**:360; **68**:286
Poems, 1924-1944 (Lewis) **41**:255
Poems, 1925-1940 (MacNeice) **53**:231, 235
Poems, 1926-1930 (Graves) **45**:162
Poems, 1930-1940 (Blunden) **56**:30, 44
Poems, 1934-1969 (Ignatow) **4**:247-49; **7**:177, 180-82
Poems, 1937-1942 (Gascoyne) **45**:146-51, 153, 156, 158
Poems, 1938-1945 (Graves) **1**:126-27
Poems, 1938-1949 (Lowell) **9**:335
Poems, 1940-1953 (Shapiro) **8**:486; **15**:478
Poems, 1943-1947 (Day Lewis) **10**:130-31
Poems, 1943-1956 (Wilbur) **53**:396
Poems, 1955-1980 (Fisher) **25**:160-62
Poems, 1956-1973 (Kinsella) **19**:254-55; **138**:85, 94-95, 105, 107-09, 111-12, 117, 121, 141, 146, 149
Poems, 1957-1967 (Dickey) **1**:73; **2**:115; **4**:120; **7**:79; **15**:174; **47**:92; **109**:264
Poems, 1962-1978 (Mahon) **27**:291-92
Poems 1963-1983: Lies (Williams) **148**:318-22, 328, 356
Poems, 1964-1967 (Rothenberg) **6**:477
Poems, 1964-1980 (Rosenthal) **28**:398
Poems (1965-1973) (Van Duyn) **116**:426
Poems, 1965-1975 (Heaney) **25**:249-51; **37**:162
Poems, 1968-1970 (Graves) **2**:177; **6**:212
Poems, 1970-1972 (Graves) **1**:127; **2**:177; **6**:212; **45**:168-69
"Poems about Birch Trees" (Haines) **58**:218
Poems about God (Ransom) **2**:365; **4**:431, 436; **5**:366
"Poems about Paintings" (Snodgrass) **10**:477; **68**:393
"Poems about St. Petersburg, II" (Akhmatova) **64**:9
"Poems about War" (Achebe) **26**:21
Poems against Economics (Murray) **40**:335, 338
Poems All Over the Place, Mostly '70s (Ginsberg) **36**:196
Poems Ancient and Modern (Porter) **33**:318
Poems and Antipoems (Parra)
See *Poemas y antipoemas*
Poems and Epistles (Fuller) **62**:192, 194
Poems and Essays (Ransom) **2**:364; **5**:364
Poems and New Poems (Bogan) **39**:390; **46**:80-1, 83, 90
Poems and Poets (Grigson) **7**:135
Poems and Problems (Nabokov) **2**:304; **8**:407
Poems and Prose, 1949-1977 (Pinter) **27**:387
Poems and Satires (Graves) **1**:127
Poems and Songs (Ewart) **13**:208; **46**:147-49
"Poems Are a Complex" (Creeley) **78**:120
Poems by an Unknown (Abe)
See *Poems of an Unknown Poet*
"Poems by Women" (Levertov) **66**:244
"Poems for a Woman" (Amichai) **57**:43
Poems for All the Annettes (Purdy) **6**:428-29; **14**:433; **50**:236, 246
"Poems for Haruko" (Jordan) **114**:155
Poems for People Who Don't Read Poems (Enzensberger) **43**:144-46
Poems for the Game of Silence (Rothenberg) **6**:477
"Poems for the Living" (Olds) **85**:346
Poems Four (Dugan) **6**:144
"Poems from a Cycle Called 'Patriotic Songs'" (Amichai) **116**:91-2
"Poems from a Small Island" (Brown) **48**:57
Poems from a Voyage across the Sound (Haavikko) **34**:177
Poems from Centre City (Kinsella) **138**:153
"Poems from Issa" (Williams) **148**:316
Poems from Prison (Knight) **40**:278-80, 282-84
Poems from the House of Novgorod Merchant (Haavikko) **34**:177
"Poems from the Margins of Thom Gunn's 'Moly'" (Duncan) **41**:130; **55**:298
Poems from Three Decades (Lattimore) **3**:277-78
Poems, Golders Green (Abse) **29**:15-16
"The Poems I Have Lost" (Ortiz) **45**:307
Poems in Prose (Solzhenitsyn)
See *Kroxotnye rasskazy*
Poems in the Darkness (Krleža)
See *Pjesme u tmini*
Poems in the Porch (Betjeman) **43**:34, 49
Poems in the Shape of a Rose (Pasolini)
See *Poesia in forma di rosa*
"Poems in Transit" (Ferlinghetti) **6**:184; **27**:139
"Poems Looking In" (Ciardi) **40**:154
Poems New and Collected (Smith) **15**:517
Poems New and Selected (Brown) **48**:53, 57
Poems, New and Selected (Eberhart) **56**:79
Poems New and Selected (Lane) **25**:286-88
Poems New and Selected (Silkin) **43**:397-400
Poems New and Selected (Whittemore) **4**:588
"Poems Not about War" (Achebe) **26**:20, 22, 24
Poems of 9-10 P.M. (Hikmet)
See *Saat 21-22 siirleri*
Poems of a Jew (Shapiro) **4**:484; **53**:330-31, 333
"Poems of Air" (Strand) **18**:520
Poems of Akhmatova (Akhmatova) **25**:26; **64**:13-14
Poems of an Unknown Poet (Abe) **81**:292-93
Poems of André Breton: A Bilingual Anthology (Breton) **54**:30
Poems of Consummation (Aleixandre)
See *Poemas de la consumación*
Poems of Dedication (Spender) **91**:261, 263
"Poems of Exile" (Jordan) **5**:203
Poems of Jerusalem (Amichai) **116**:127-28
Poems of Light (Blaga)
See *Poemele luminii*
Poems of Love and Marriage (Ciardi) **129**:56
"Poems of Many Places" (Hall) **51**:171
Poems of Many Years (Blunden) **2**:65; **56**:29, 36, 40
Poems of Night (Kinnell) **29**:281
Poems of Paul Celan (Celan)
See *Paul Celan: Poems*
Poems of Places and People (Barker) **8**:46; **48**:19, 24
Poems of R. S. Thomas (Thomas) **48**:383
Poems of René Char (Char) **55**:287
The Poems of Richard Aldington (Aldington) **49**:11-13
The Poems of Richard Wilbur (Wilbur) **53**:405, 410; **110**:350, 352
The Poems of Stanley Kunitz, 1928-1978 (Kunitz) **14**:313; **148**:81, 83-84, 86, 91-92, 106, 111, 135, 141, 148-49
Poems of the Dispossessed (Kinsella) **138**:144
"Poems of the Forgotten" (Haines) **58**:220
"Poems of the Goat" (Cabral de Melo Neto)
See "Poema(s) da cabra"
Poems of the Negro Revolt (Randall) **135**:388
Poems of the War and After (Brittain) **23**:89
Poems of Thirty Years (Morgan) **31**:276
Poems of Two Worlds (Morgan) **23**:298, 301
Poems of Various Years (Yevtushenko)
See *Stikhi raznykh let*
Poems Old and New, 1918-1978 (Lewis) **41**:261-62
Poems Retrieved (O'Hara) **13**:423
Poems Selected and New (Page) **7**:292; **18**:379
Poems: Selected and New, 1950-1974 (Rich) **6**:459; **7**:369, 372-73; **36**:371, 375; **73**:323, 328
"Poems to a Brown Cricket" (Wright) **3**:541; **10**:544
Poems to Solve (Swenson) **61**:402; **106**:320, 339
Poems Unpleasant (Baxter) **14**:61
"Poems without Legs" (Hall) **37**:148
Poems Worth Knowing (McFadden) **48**:245
"Poems Written to Accompany Photographs by Rudy Burckhardt" (Denby) **48**:83
Poesi (Pasolini) **37**:348; **106**:250, 253
Poesí española: Ensayo de métodos y límites estilísticos (Alonso) **14**:20
Poesía, 1953-1966 (Rodriguez) **10**:439
"Poesía de comunión y poesía de soledad" (Paz) **65**:176, 180
La poesía de San Juan de la Cruz (Alonso) **14**:23
La poesia dialettale del Novecento (Pasolini) **37**:345; **106**:226, 231,
"Poesia e compoiçao—A inspiração e o trabalho de arte" (Cabral de Melo Neto) **76**:152, 157
Poesía en movimiento (Paz) **65**:177
Poesia in forma di rosa (Pasolini) **37**:346, 350; **106**:220, 253, 263
Poesía no eres tú: Obra poética, 1948-1971 (Castellanos) **66**:44, 53
"La poesia popolaine italiana" (Pasolini) **106**:231, 245
La poesia populace Italiana (Pasolini) **37**:343
Poesía y literatura (Cernuda) **54**:48
Poesías completas (Alberti) **7**:9
Poesias completas (Cabral de Melo Neto) **76**:156
Poesie a Casarsa (Pasolini) **37**:343, 348; **106**:228-29, 231, 234, 243, 271
La poésie antillaise (Condé) **92**:100
Poésie et connaissance (Césaire) **112**:13-14
Poesie IV (Jouve) **47**:208-09
Poésie pour pouvoir (Michaux) **8**:392
Poesie und Politik (Enzensberger) **43**:154
Poésies complètes: 1917-1937 (Soupault) **68**:404, 408
"The Poet" (Aleixandre)
See "El poeta"

"Poèt" (Bagryana) **10**:14
"The Poet" (Dinesen) **10**:145; **95**:42, 48, 53-4, 73
"A Poet" (Feldman) **7**:102
"The Poet" (Frost) **13**:227
"The Poet" (Kaufman) **49**:205
"The Poet" (Lowell) **37**:237
"The Poet" (Oates) **33**:294
"The Poet" (Randall) **135**:390
"Poet" (Shapiro) **53**:334
"The Poet" (Williams) **15**:579
"Poet" (Williams) **148**:366, 368
"Poet: A Lying Word" (Riding) **7**:374
"Poet and Critic" (Livesay) **79**:351
Poet and Dancer (Jhabvala) **94**:202-5; **138**:72-3
"Poet and Goldsmith" (Watkins) **43**:452
A Poet and His Camera (Parks) **1**:265
"The Poet and Revolution" (Day Lewis) **10**:132
"The Poet and the City" (Auden) **123**:21
"The Poet as a Creator of Social Values" (Sanchez) **116**:316
"The Poet as he writes" (Rozewicz)
See "Poeta w czasie pisania"
"The Poet as Hero: Keats in His Letters" (Trilling) **11**:543
"The Poet as Painter" (Tomlinson) **45**:404
"The Poet as Refugee" (Dobyns) **37**:76
"The Poet as Troublemaker" (Meredith) **4**:348
"Poet at Seventy" (Milosz) **56**:246; **82**:290
"Poet at the Market" (Yevtushenko) **26**:467
"The Poet Contemplates His Inaction" (Ezekiel) **61**:106
"The Poet Egan O'Rahilly, Homesick in Old Age" (Kinsella) **138**:149
"Poet for Time" (Lerman) **9**:331
"The Poet in New York in Detroit" (Levine) **118**:298
Poet in Our Time (Montale) **9**:390
"The Poet in Residence in Spite of Himself" (Montgomery) **7**:233
A Poet in the Family (Abse) **29**:20
The Poet in the Imaginary Museum: Essays of Two Decades (Davie) **10**:124-25; **31**:112
"The Poet in the World" (Levertov) **8**:346
The Poet in the World (Levertov) **3**:293; **5**:246-47, 250; **8**:346-47
"The Poet Is Dead" (Everson) **14**:163
"A Poet Is Not a Jukebox" (Randall) **135**:392, 399
"The Poet Is Not a Rolling Stone" (Neruda) **62**:324
"Poet, Lover, Birdwatcher" (Ezekiel) **61**:93-4, 101, 105, 110
"A Poet of the Thirteenth Century" (Borges)
See "Un poeta del siglo XIII"
"The Poet on the Island" (Murphy) **41**:311, 317
"The Poet Ridiculed by Hysterical Academics" (Snodgrass) **68**:388
"The Poet Says Good-Bye to the Birds" (Neruda) **62**:332
"Poet to Tiger" (Swenson) **61**:402; **61**:397; **106**:329, 343
"The Poet Turns on Himself" (Dickey) **47**:97
"Poet, When You Rhyme" (Jacobsen) **48**:190
The Poet Who Became a Worm (Alegria)
See *El poeta que se Volvío Gusano*
"El poeta" (Aleixandre) **9**:16
"Un poeta del siglo XIII" (Borges) **44**:367
El poeta que se Volvío Gusano (Alegria) **57**:11
"El poeta recuerda su via" (Aleixandre) **9**:12
"O poeta Thomas Hardy fala" (Cabral de Melo Neto) **76**:163
"Poeta w czasie pisania" (Rozewicz) **139**:307
Les poetès (Aragon) **22**:38
Poètes d'expression française (Damas) **84**:179
"Poet--For Irina Ratushinskaya" (Seth) **90**:351
The Poetic Art of Robert Lowell (Perloff) **137**:261, 273
Poetic Artifice (Perloff) **137**:290
"The Poetic Diction of John M. Synge" (Davie) **10**:124
A Poetic Equation: Conversations between Nikki Giovanni and Margaret Walker (Giovanni) **117**:192, 201, 204
"The Poetic Faculty" (MacDiarmid) **63**:248
The Poetic Image (Day Lewis) **10**:128
The Poetic Image in Six Genres (Madden) **5**:265
Poetic Justice (Heilbrun) **25**:255, 257
Poetic License: Essays on Modernist and Postmodernist Lyric (Perloff) **137**:278-80, 282, 288-89
Poetic Meter and Poetic Form (Fussell) **74**:117
"The Poetic Process" (Burke) **24**:118
"The Poetic Revelation" (Paz) **4**:397
The Poetic Self: Towards a Phenomenology of Romanticism (Alexander) **121**:3
"A Poetic State" (Milosz) **82**:307
"Poetic Structure in the Language of Aristotle" (Crane) **27**:71
Poetic Values (Neihardt) **32**:333
"Poetics" (Howe) **152**:161-62
"Poetics" (Nemerov) **36**:309
A Poetics (Bernstein) **142**:18-21, 42-44, 55-6
"A Poetics for Bullies" (Elkin) **4**:154
Poetics of Indeterminacy (Perloff) **137**:265, 267-70, 272-73, 287-91, 293-94
"Poetics of Miniature" (Simić) **130**:326
"The Poetics of Rita Kleinhart" (Kroetsch) **132**:281
"Poetics of the Americas" (Bernstein) **142**:57
"The Poetics of the Physical World" (Kinnell) **29**:282-83; **129**:235, 240, 267
Poetries and the Sciences (Richards) **24**:400
"Poetry" (Borges) **48**:47, 49
"Poetry" (Moore) **1**:227, **8**:397; **10**:349, **19**:342; **47**:271
"Poetry" (O'Hara) **78**:352, 364, 375-76
"Poetry" (Pasternak) **63**:281
"Poetry" (White) **10**:528
Poetry (Cocteau) **8**:145
"Poetry: A Note on Ontology" (Ransom) **5**:364-65, 367; **24**:365-68
"Poetry and Ambition" (Hall) **59**:153; **151**:185
"Poetry and Conflict in the Black World" (Mphahlele) **133**:134
"Poetry and Consciousness" (Williams) **148**:325, 329-30, 345
Poetry and Consciousness (Williams) **148**:363, 369
Poetry and Drama (Eliot) **6**:167; **24**:184
"Poetry and Experience" (Rich) **7**:371
Poetry and Fiction (Nemerov) **6**:360
"Poetry and History" (Paz) **4**:397
Poetry and Humanism (Mphahlele) **133**:151-52
"Poetry and Landscape" (Wilbur) **53**:400
"Poetry and Marriage" (Berry) **46**:75
Poetry and Metamorphosis (Tomlinson) **45**:405
Poetry and Morality (Buckley) **57**:132
"Poetry and Other Modern Arts" (Davie) **10**:125
"Poetry and Personality" (Carruth)
See "The Act of Love: Poetry and Personality"
"Poetry and Pleasure" (Pinsky) **94**:301, 303; **121**:438
"Poetry and Politics" (Enzensberger) **43**:148
Poetry and Repression (Bloom) **24**:80; **103**:2-4, 6, 8-9, 11-14, 24, 45, 47
"Poetry and Revolution" (Spender) **10**:489
"Poetry and Social Criticism" (Wain) **11**:563
"Poetry and the Absolute" (Tate) **24**:441, 445, 447
Poetry and the Age (Jarrell) **6**:261; **9**:296; **13**:299
Poetry and the Common Life (Rosenthal) **28**:392-94
"Poetry and the New Christians" (Buckley) **57**:130
"Poetry and the Primitive" (Snyder) **9**:499; **120**:327, 329, 331-32, 345
"Poetry and the Public World" (MacLeish) **68**:288
Poetry and the Sacred (Buckley) **57**:132
Poetry and the World (Pinsky) **94**:300-5, 311-12, 316; **121**:432, 446, 448
"Poetry as Imitation" (Schwartz) **4**:479
Poetry by Canadian Women (Sullivan) **65**:356
"Poetry, Community & Climax" (Snyder) **120**:331-32
Poetry for My People (Dumas) **6**:145-46; **62**:151, 155, 158, 160
Poetry for Supper (Thomas) **13**:542; **48**:374, 376, 380
"Poetry for the Advanced" (Baraka) **14**:49
Poetry, Gongorism, and a Thousand Years (Jeffers) **54**:244
A Poetry Handbook (Oliver) **98**:293, 302
"Poetry in English" (Dudek) **11**:160
Poetry in the Making (Hughes) **2**:203; **37**:171
"Poetry in Time of War" (Perloff) **137**:303
"Poetry is a great power" (Yevtushenko) **126**:395
"Poetry Is an Occupation" (Neruda) **9**:399
"Poetry is Not a Luxury" (Lorde) **71**:243, 263
"Poetry is the Smallest" (Ammons) **57**:58
"Poetry Manual" (Brooks) **110**:33
"Poetry Modern and Unmodern" (Tate) **11**:522
Poetry, Myth, Revolution (Paz) **119**:423
"Poetry needn't always" (Rozewicz)
See "poezja nie zawsze"
"The Poetry Notebook: Two" (Hall) **151**:193, 197
"Poetry of Departures" (Larkin) **33**:257, 268; **39**:345; **64**:272
The Poetry of George Herbert (Vendler) **138**:247-48, 265
The Poetry of Maya Angelou (Angelou) **77**:28
The Poetry of Place: Essays and Reviews, 1970-1980 (Hooker) **43**:200-02
"Poetry of Solitude and Poetry of Communion" (Paz)
See "Poesía de comunión y poesía de soledad"
The Poetry of Stephen Crane (Hoffman) **23**:240
"The Poetry of Tradition" (Pasolini) **106**:265
The Poetry of W. B. Yeats (MacNeice) **53**:244
The Poetry of Yevgeny Yevtushenko, 1953-1965 (Yevtushenko) **26**:461-62
Poetry On & Off the Page (Perloff) **137**:302
"Poetry, or Poems?" (Davie) **10**:124
"Poetry, Personality, and Death" (Kinnell) **29**:282; **129**:239-40, 269
"Poetry Reading" (Ezekiel) **61**:94, 97, 101, 103
"Poetry Reading" (Szymborska) **99**:206
"Poetry, Regeneration, and D.H. Lawrence" (Rexroth) **49**:278; **112**:371
"Poetry Review" (Jiles) **58**:279
"Poetry Shall Not Have Sung in Vain" (Neruda) **62**:324
"Poetry since Yeats" (Kinsella) **138**:151
"Poetry That Is Life" (Shamlu) **10**:470-71
Poetry to Enable (Michaux)
See *Poésie pour pouvoir*
The Poetry Wreck: Selected Essays, 1950-1970 (Shapiro) **8**:486
"The Poets" (Blaga) **75**:63, 79
"The Poets" (Boland) **113**:114
"Poets" (Boyle) **58**:76
"Poets" (Brown) **48**:59
"Poets" (Frame) **96**:200
"Poets" (Kennedy) **8**:320; **42**:257
Poets (Aragon)
See *Les poetès*
A Poet's Alphabet: Reflections on the Literary Art and Vocation (Bogan) **4**:68; **39**:388, 391; **46**:87; **93**:69-71, 105
Poets and Presidents (Doctorow) **113**:165
"Poets Are Still Writing Poems about Spring and Here Is Mine: Spring" (Waddington) **28**:440
"Poets, Children, Soldiers" (Hirsch) **31**:214
Poet's Circuits (Colum) **28**:91-2
"Poets in Canada" (Avison) **97**:105-11
"Poets in Late Winter" (Van Duyn) **116**:427
"A Poet's Lament: Concerning the Massacre of American Indians at Wounded Knee"

(Cook-Lynn) **93**:122
"A Poet's Life" (MacBeth) **9**:340
"The Poet's Mother" (Kroetsch) **57**:292-93
A Poet's Notebook (Sitwell) **67**:332
"The Poets Observe the Absence of God from the St. Louis Zoo" (Kumin) **28**:224
Poets of the 1950's (Enright) **31**:148
The Poet's Progress (McFadden) **48**:247, 251
"Poet's Pub" (MacDiarmid) **11**:334
"Poets Return" (Faludy) **42**:138
"Poets Survive in Fame" (Cunningham) **31**:102
The Poet's Town (Neihardt) **32**:331
"The Poet's Voice" (Moss) **45**:292
"Poets without Laurels" (Ransom) **5**:365; **24**:367
"The Poet's Words" (Ciardi) **10**:107
"Poet's Work" (Niedecker) **10**:360
A Poet's Year (MacBeth) **5**:264
Poezii: texte comentate (Blaga) **75**:76
"Poezijata" (Bagryana) **10**:14
Poezja (Rozewicz) **139**:263
"poezja nie zawsze" (Rozewicz) **139**:295
Poezja wybrane (Rozewicz) **139**:291, 299
Poezje zebrane (Rozewicz) **23**:363; **139**:263
"Poggio" (Durrell) **27**:97
Pogrzeb po polsku (Rozewicz) **139**:231, 265, 281, 293
"The Point" (Heaney) **74**:197
"The Point" (Montague) **46**:275
"The Point" (Soto) **32**:402
Point Counter Point (Huxley) **1**:150-51; **3**:252, 254-55; **4**:237-40, 243-44; **5**:192-94; **8**:304; **11**:281, 283-88; **18**:265, 268, 270-71; **35**:232, 235, 240-41, 243-44; **79**:304, 310, 312, 315, 326-27
"Point of Departure" (Calisher) **8**:125
"A Point of Identity" (Mphahlele) **25**:339, 342
Point of No Return (Marquand) **10**:329, 331
"Point Pelee in March" (Snodgrass) **68**:397
"Point Pinos and Point Lobos" (Jeffers) **11**:312
Point Reyes Poems (Bly) **15**:65
"Point Shirley" (Plath) **11**:446; **17**:367-68; **111**:177
La pointe courte (Varda) **16**:553, 556-57
Pointe-aux-coques (Maillet) **54**:303, 306; **118**:327, 329, 344-45, 364
"Points" (Hoffman) **141**:282, 313-14
Points for a Compass Rose (Connell) **4**:108-10; **6**:116
Points in Time (Bowles) **53**:38-40
The Points of My Compass (White) **10**:528, 530
Points of View (Maugham) **15**:368; **67**:219
Points on the Grid (Bowering) **15**:82; **47**:19
Point-to-Point (Keane)
See *Conversation Piece*
Poirot Investigates (Christie) **12**:110; **48**:71
Poison (Harrison) **151**:243-45, 257
"Poison Oak" (Huddle) **49**:183-84
"The Poison of Subjectivity" (Lewis) **124**:225
The Poison Oracle (Dickinson) **12**:171-72; **35**:131, 133-34
Poison Pen (Garrett) **51**:152-54
The Poison Tree (Ribman) **7**:358
The Poisoned Kiss and Other Stories from the Portuguese (Oates) **6**:373-74; **9**:402
"Poisoned Lands" (Montague) **46**:266, 275-76
Poisoned Lands and Other Poems (Montague) **13**:391; **46**:266, 273, 278-79
"The Poisoned Story" (Ferré) **139**:150-51, 155, 157
"The Poisonous Rabbit" (Calvino) **33**:100
The Poisonwood Bible (Kingsolver) **130**:103-07, 109-10, 112, 114-17, 119-23
Poisson d'or (Le Clézio) **155**:99, 110
Poisson soluble (Breton) **9**:132, 134; **54**:15, 17, 29, 33
Les poissons rouges; ou, Mon père, ce héros (Anouilh) **13**:21-2; **40**:57-60
"Poker Face" (Sturgeon) **22**:410
"The Poker Party" (Kelley) **22**:252
The Poker Session (Leonard) **19**:281
Pokój na Ziemi (Lem) **149**:116, 119, 152, 242-43, 263-64, 268, 276
Pokolenie zimy (Aksyonov)
See *Generations of Winter*
Poland (Michener) **29**:316-17; **60**:258; **109**:375, 377, 379, 382, 386, 388
"Poland/1931" (Rothenberg) **57**:380-81
Poland/1931 (Rothenberg) **6**:477-78; **57**:373-74, 382-83
"Poland: Legends" (Agnon)
See "Polin: Sipure agadot"
Polar Bear Hunt (Bissett) **18**:61
"Polar Bears and Others" (Boyle) **19**:62; **121**:25-6
Polaris and Other Stories (Weldon) **122**:260, 262
"Polaris, or Gulag Nightscapes" (MacEwen) **55**:164-65
"Polarities" (Atwood) **4**:26; **13**:46; **25**:62
Polaroids (Coupland)
See *Polaroids from the Dead*
Polaroids from the Dead (Coupland) **133**:17-19
"The Polatski Man" (Dybek) **114**:62, 64, 67, 71, 73, 75-6, 78
"Polder" (Heaney) **37**:162; **74**:162
"Poldi" (McCullers) **12**:433
"Pole Star" (MacLeish) **8**:361
"Pole Star for this Year" (MacLeish) **68**:286
"Poles Apart" (Bainbridge) **130**:28
Police (Baraka) **115**:36
Police at the Funeral (Allingham) **19**:14
"The Police Band" (Barthelme) **8**:50
"Police Dreams" (Bausch) **51**:55-7
Police Lab (Berger) **12**:40
"The Police: Seven Voices" (Murray) **40**:340
Police State: Could It Happen Here (Archer) **12**:23
"The Policeman and the Rose" (Rao) **56**:312-14
"Polin: Sipure agadot" (Agnon) **4**:11; **14**:3
Polis, polis potatismos (Wahlöö) **7**:502
"A Polish Anecdote" (Rothenberg) **57**:374
The Polish Complex (Konwicki)
See *Kompleks polski*
"Polish Displaced Persons" (Spender) **41**:421
"The Polish Question" (Weiss) **14**:554
Polismördaren (Wahlöö) **7**:502
"Polite Conversation" (Stafford) **7**:457; **68**:434, 450
"Politic" (Rose) **85**:314
"Political Code and Literary Code: The Testimonial Genre in Chile Today" (Dorfman) **77**:156
The Political Economy of Human Rights (Chomsky) **132**:34, 40
"Political Economy of the International Bond Market from the Age of Reason to the Present with Special Reference to the Period from 1850 to 1914" (Ferguson) **134**:67
A Political Fable (Coover) **32**:122
Political Fictions (Wilding) **73**:393, 399, 405
The Political Life of Children (Coles) **108**:184, 186-88, 210, 214
"Political Meeting" (Klein) **19**:262-63
Political Position of Art Today (Breton) **15**:90
"The Political Prisoner" (Kunene) **85**:166
"Political Relations" (Lorde) **71**:260
The Political Unconscious: Narrative as a Socially Symbolic Act (Jameson) **142**:222-23, 225-26, 243-44, 249-50, 253, 255, 259-60, 262-63
"Politician" (Garrett) **51**:144
"Politics" (Bukowski) **108**:87
"Politics" (Meredith) **13**:375
"Politics" (Paley) **4**:392; **37**:337
Politics (Acker) **111**:20
"Politics and Conscience" (Havel) **123**:174, 191, 214
Politics and Crime (Enzensberger)
See *Politik und Verbrechen*
"Politics and the Novel" (McCarthy) **39**:485
Politics and the Novel (Howe) **85**:117-19, 135, 147
"Politics and the World Itself" (Havel) **123**:215
"Politics Is Everyone's Privilege" (Yevtushenko) **126**:398
The Politics of Dispossession: The Struggle for Palestinian Self-Determination, 1989-1994 (Said) **123**:386-92
Politics of Experience (Castaneda) **12**:86
The Politics of Experience (Laing) **95**:124, 128, 131-34, 136, 138, 140-41, 144-47, 153, 167, 177-79, 182-83
"The Politics of Historical Interpretation: Discipline and De-Sublimation" (White) **148**:234, 236, 242, 245, 247, 249, 251, 267, 270, 272, 291-92
"The Politics of Hope" (Havel) **123**:217
The Politics of Hope (Schlesinger) **84**:355
"The Politics of Language" (Sukenick) **48**:370
"The Politics of Rich Painters" (Baraka) **5**:45
The Politics of the Family and Other Essays (Laing) **95**:132, 137, 149, 183-84
"The Politics of Theory: Idological Positions in the Postmodernism Debate" (Jameson) **142**:226, 230
The Politics of Upheaval (Schlesinger) **84**:382, 384
The Politics of Waste (Adamov)
See *La politique des restes*
The Politics of Women's Education: Perspectives from Asia, Africa, and Latin America (Conway) **152**:105
Politik und Verbrechen (Enzensberger) **43**:147-48, 150, 154
La politique des restes (Adamov) **25**:14-15, 17, 20-1
"Polka" (Sitwell) **67**:324
"Polling Day" (Scannell) **49**:330-31
"Pollock and Canvas" (Graham) **48**:150-51; **118**:250
Pollution Lab (Berger) **12**:39
Polonaise (Read) **10**:434-36; **25**:379
"Polonaise: A Variation" (Brodsky) **100**:41-2
Polovchansk Gardens (Leonov)
See *Polovchanskie sady*
Polovchanskie sady (Leonov) **92**:246, 260, 268-71, 277
"Polycarp" (Durcan) **43**:114, 116
The Polyglots (Gerhardie) **5**:140
Polylogue (Kristeva) **140**:196-98
"Polynesian" (Scott) **22**:373
"Pomade" (Dove) **81**:139
"The Pomegranate" (Boland) **113**:91, 120, 126
"Pomegranate" (Thomas) **132**:381
"Un pomeriggio Adamo" (Calvino) **33**:101
Pomes for Yoshi (Bissett) **18**:59, 61
Pomme, pomme, pomme (Audiberti) **38**:31
"Les pommes" (Carrier) **78**:59
"Pompeii" (Updike) **23**:475
Pompes funèbres (Genet) **1**:115; **2**:158; **5**:138-39; **44**:386-88, 390; **46**:173, 180-83
The Pomps of Hell (Ghelderode)
See *Fastes d'enfer*
"The Pond" (Nemerov) **36**:303, 305
"Pond" (Smith) **42**:353
The Ponder Heart (Welty) **1**:361; **2**:462-64; **5**:478; **14**:564; **33**:415-16, 419, 424; **105**:300, 318, 325, 335, 349
"Pondicherry Blues" (Jacobsen) **48**:195; **102**:240
"The Ponds" (Oliver) **98**:294
"Pondy Woods" (Warren) **18**:535
The Ponsonby Post (Rubens) **19**:403-04
Le pont aux trois arches (Kadare)
See *Ura me tri harqe*
Pont de Londres (Céline) **124**:62
Le Pont de Londres: Guignol's band II (Céline) **47**:71, 77; **124**:62, 91-2
"Pont Neuf at Nightfall" (Kinnell) **29**:284
"Pontifications" (Silverberg) **140**:396
Pony from Tarella (Clark) **12**:132
"Pony Rock" (MacLeish) **68**:286, 290

"Poodles. . .Great Eating!" (Martin) **30**:248
"The Pool" (Creeley) **78**:136-37
"The Pool" (H. D.) **73**:119
"The Pool" (Johnston) **51**:249-51
"The Pool" (Maugham) **15**:368; **67**:219
Pool and Rapid: The Story of a River (Haig-Brown) **21**:133, 141
"Pool Lights" (Barthelme) **117**:17
"Pool of Bethesda" (Sandburg) **35**:356
"The Pool Player" (Williams) **42**:440
"Pool Room in the Lion's Club" (Merwin) **45**:270
"The Pool Table Caper" (Hunter) **35**:226
"Pools" (Wesker) **5**:484
Pools of Mercury (Carroll) **143**:50-1
"The Poor" (Wild) **14**:581
Poor and Simple (Ortese)
See *Poveri e semplici*
"The Poor Are Always with Us" (Wolff) **64**:451-52
"Poor August von Goethe" (Rozewicz)
See "Biedny August von Goethe"
"Poor Baby" (Sondheim) **30**:401
Poor Bitos (Anouilh)
See *Pauvre Bitos; ou, Le dîner de têtes*
"Poor Charley's Dream" (Hope) **51**:222
The Poor Christ of Bomba (Beti)
See *Le pauvre Christ de Bomba*
"A Poor Christian Looks at the Ghetto" (Milosz) **56**:234
Poor Clare (Hartley) **2**:181-82
"Poor Dumb Butch" (Randall) **135**:399
"Poor Edward" (Johnston) **51**:239, 245
Poor Fool (Caldwell) **50**:300
Poor George (Fox) **2**:139-40; **121**:185-86, 218
"Poor Gum" (Bennett) **28**:29
"Poor Innocent" (Smith) **15**:515, 517
"A Poor Jew" (Bell) **8**:65
"Poor Koko" (Fowles) **6**:184, 187-88; **10**:188; **33**:174; **87**:154, 158
"The Poor Man's Pig" (Blunden) **56**:26-7
The Poor Mouth: A Bad Story about the Hard Life (O'Brien)
See *An Béal Bocht*
Poor Murderer (Kohout) **13**:323, 326
"Poor North" (Strand) **18**:520; **41**:432
"The Poor Poet" (Milosz) **56**:242
Poor Richard (Kerr) **22**:256-57
Poor Russell's Almanac (Baker) **31**:28
"A Poor Scholar of the 'Forties" (Colum) **28**:90
"Poor Slave" (Cliff) **21**:60
"Poor Superman" (Leiber) **25**:303-04
"The Poor Thing" (Powers) **1**:280, 282
The Poorhouse Fair (Updike) **1**:343-44; **2**:439, 442; **3**:485, 489; **5**:450, 453, 459-60; **9**:539; **13**:557-58, 562; **23**:463; **43**:431, 433; **70**:253; **139**:314, 331, 338
Poo-san (Ichikawa) **20**:181-82, 186
Pop. 1280 (Thompson) **69**:378-81, 383, 385-86, 389
"Pop Life" (Prince) **35**:332
The Pope and the Witch (Fo) **109**:142, 144
"The Pope's Penis" (Olds) **85**:294, 296, 303
The Pope's Wedding (Bond) **4**:69; **13**:99; **23**:64
Popeye (Altman) **116**:47, 59, 65
"Popham of the New Song" (Dubie) **36**:130
"Poplar Garden" (Bogan) **93**:93
"Poplar, Sycamore" (Wilbur) **6**:570
"The Poplars" (Fisher) **25**:159
Popo and Fifina (Hughes) **108**:294
Popol vuh (Asturias) **13**:37
"Popper's Disease" (Johnson) **51**:234-35
"Poppies" (Oliver) **98**:287, 291
"Poppies" (Smith) **12**:540
"Poppies" (Smith) **64**:388
"Poppies in July" (Plath) **5**:345; **17**:365-66; **51**:345; **111**:203-04
"Poppies in October" (Plath) **2**:336; **17**:359; **111**:203-04
Poppy (Nichols) **36**:329, 331-32; **65**:161
Poppy and Memory (Celan)
See *Mohn und Gedächtnes*
"Poppycock" (Francis) **15**:237
Pops (Linney) **51**:263
"Popular Songs" (Ashbery) **77**:58; **125**:36
"Populist Manifesto" (Ferlinghetti) **27**:137; **111**:66
Popytka k begstvu (Strugatskii and Strugatskii) **27**:433, 438
Pora, moi drug, pora (Aksyonov)
See *It's Time, My Friend, It's Time*
"The Porcelain Couple" (Hall) **151**:224
"The Porcelain Salamander" (Card) **47**:67
"Porcellina di terra" (Landolfi) **49**:214
"Porch" (Szirtes) **46**:393
"Porch Song" (Carroll) **35**:77
Porcilè (Pasolini) **106**:241, 256
"Porciúncula" (Amado)
See "De como o Mulato Porciúncula Descarregou seu Defunto"
"The Porcupine" (Kinnell) **2**:230; **3**:268-69; **29**:282, 284, 288; **129**:268
The Porcupine (Barnes) **141**:50-3, 55-7, 61-3, 67-8
"The Porcupine Puffer Fish" (Lieberman) **36**:263
"Porcupines at the University" (Barthelme) **23**:46; **115**:81
"Pore Perrie" (Goyen) **14**:211
Porgy (Mamoulian) **16**:424
Porius: A Romance of the Dark Ages (Powys) **7**:348; **15**:435; **46**:321-22; **125**:281, 291, 294-96, 299, 301, 304
The Pork Butcher (Hughes) **48**:185-88
"Pork Chop Paradise" (Himes) **58**:265
"Porn" (MacBeth) **5**:265
"Porn" (Walker) **27**:448, 450; **103**:407-08, 410-12
"Porno Flick" (Valenzuela) **31**:438
"Porno Love" (Dacey) **51**:79
Pornografia (Gombrowicz) **4**:194-95; **7**:122-25; **11**:242; **49**:123, 126-29, 133-34
The Pornographer (McGahern) **48**:264-67, 269, 271-73
"A Pornographer Woos" (Mac Laverty) **31**:253
"The Pornographic But Serious History" (Bell) **8**:67
"The Pornographic Imagination" (Sontag) **13**:516; **105**:225
"Pornography" (McEwan) **66**:279-80
"Pornography" (Raine) **103**:190
Pornography and Civil Rights (Dworkin) **123**:106, 109
"The Pornography Box" (Smith) **42**:346, 350, 353-54
"Pornography Happens to Women" (Dworkin) **123**:102
"Pornography Is a Civil Rights Issue" (Dworkin) **123**:76, 107
Pornography: Men Possessing Women (Dworkin) **43**:132-33, 135; **123**:68, 89-90, 92, 95, 102, 106
"Port" (Reverdy) **53**:281
Port Eternity (Cherryh) **35**:113-15
"Port of Call" (Abse) **29**:15
"Port of Call" (Codrescu) **121**:162
Port of Call (Bergman)
See *Hamnstad*
Port of Saints (Burroughs) **22**:83-5; **42**:80; **109**:195
The Portable Nabokov (Nabokov) **6**:357
Portable People (West) **96**:375, 392
"The Portable Phonograph" (Clark) **28**:78
Portable Steinbeck (Steinbeck) **59**:343, 345
"Porte cochère" (Taylor) **37**:409, 412-13; **44**:305-06; **50**:253, 258; **71**:299, 307
Porte des lilas (Clair) **20**:64-5
Porte dévergondée (Mandiargues) **41**:278
A Porter Folio: New Poems (Porter) **5**:346; **33**:318, 323
"The Porter Song Book" (Porter) **33**:318
Porterhouse Blue (Sharpe) **36**:399-400
"Porter's Metamorphoses" (Porter) **33**:318
Les portes de la forêt (Wiesel) **3**:529; **5**:492-93; **37**:452
"Porth Cwyfan" (Mathias) **45**:237
"Portland, 1968" (Glück) **22**:176
"The 'Portland' Going Out" (Merwin) **13**:383
Portnoy's Complaint (Roth) **1**:293; **2**:378-80; **3**:435-38, 440; **4**:451, 453-57, 459; **6**:475-76; **9**:459, 460-62; **15**:449, 451-52, 455; **22**:350-52; **47**:357-65; **66**:386-422; **86**:250-51, 255-57; **119**:120, 127, 130, 132, 135-37
"Il porto sepolto" (Ungaretti) **7**:484; **11**:559
"The Portobello Road" (Spark) **40**:403
"Portrait" (Ammons) **108**:24
"Portrait" (Bogan) **46**:77
"Portrait" (Boyle) **19**:62
"Portrait" (Fearing) **51**:106, 108
"Portrait" (Glück) **22**:177
"The Portrait" (Graves) **45**:169, 173
"Portrait" (Guillevic) **33**:191
"The Portrait" (Kunitz) **148**:98-100, 131, 138, 141
"Portrait" (Ostriker) **132**:310
"Portrait" (Senghor) **130**:266
"Portrait" (Thomas) **6**:534
"Portrait" (Urdang) **47**:399-400
The Portrait (Silkin) **43**:399
Portrait de l'artiste en jeune singe (Butor) **11**:81-2; **15**:114-15, 117-18
Portrait du soleil (Cixous) **92**:56
"Portrait d'un élu" (Camus) **14**:107
Portrait d'un inconnu (Sarraute) **1**:302; **2**:384-85; **4**:464, 466-67; **8**:469, 471-72; **10**:458-59; **31**:377, 380, 383; **80**:229, 236-37, 239, 241, 252, 254
"Portrait d'une femme" (Pound) **2**:343; **4**:408; **10**:401, 404
Portrait eines Planeten (Dürrenmatt) **15**:196
"The Portrait: Emmanuel Romano" (Williams) **22**:464
Portrait in Brownstone (Auchincloss) **4**:28, 30-1
"The Portrait of a Clown" (Turco) **11**:550
"Portrait of a Cog" (Fearing) **51**:108
"Portrait of a Deaf Man" (Betjeman) **43**:34
"Portrait of a Germanophile" (Borges) **48**:45
"Portrait of a Girl in Glass" (Williams) **5**:502; **15**:580; **45**:446-47, 452-54; **71**:365, 373
"Portrait of a Jew Old Country Style" (Rothenberg) **57**:374
"Portrait of a Lady" (Eliot) **1**:89-90; **3**:139; **9**:186-87, 189; **13**:201-02; **15**:213; **34**:397; **41**:146, 150; **55**:346, 362, 374; **57**:168, 207; **113**:183, 187, 190, 205, 209, 223
"Portrait of a Lady" (Gellhorn) **60**:179-181, 191
"Portrait of a Lady" (Ryan) **65**:215
"Portrait of a Lady" (Wakoski) **2**:459
"Portrait of a Lady" (White) **49**:409
Portrait of a Man Unknown (Sarraute)
See *Portrait d'un inconnu*
Portrait of a Planet (Duerrenmatt)
See *Porträt eines Planeten*
Portrait of a Romantic (Millhauser) **54**:324, 326-27; **21**:218-21; **109**:170, 174
"Portrait of a Short Story Writer" (Konwicki) **117**:281
"Portrait of an Artist" (Kavanagh) **22**:243
Portrait of an Artist with Twenty-Six Horses (Eastlake) **8**:199-200
"Portrait of Captain Logan" (Shapcott) **38**:399
Portrait of Delmore: Journals and Notes of Delmore Schwartz, 1939-1959 (Schwartz) **45**:360-61; **87**:344-46
"The Portrait of Diana Prochink" (Baker) **8**:40
"A Portrait of Elmer" (Faulkner) **18**:149
"Portrait of Georgia" (Toomer) **13**:551
Portrait of India (Mehta) **37**:290-92
Portrait of Ivan (Fox) **2**:139; **121**:199
Portrait of Jason (Clarke) **16**:218-19
Portrait of Joanna (McGuckian) **48**:274
"Portrait of Lady" (Smith) **42**:353
"The Portrait of Little J. A. in a Prospect of

Flowers" (Ashbery) **25**:57; **41**:40
"Portrait of Malcolm X" (Knight) **40**:279
Portrait of Margarita (Arthur) **12**:25, 28-9
"Portrait of Marina" (Page) **18**:377
Portrait of Max: An Intimate Memoir of Sir Max Beerbohm (Behrman) **40**:85
Portrait of Orkney (Brown) **48**:59; **100**:86
"A Portrait of Shunkin" (Tanizaki)
See "Shunkin shō"
"Portrait of the Artist" (Davie) **10**:121
"Portrait of the Artist" (Harrison) **42**:203
"A Portrait of the Artist" (Kinsella) **138**:135
"Portrait of the Artist as a Middle-aged Man" (Abse) **7**:2
"Portrait of the Artist as a New World Driver" (Murray) **40**:337
"Portrait of the Artist as a Young Woman" (Bogan) **39**:392
"Portrait of the Artist with Li Po" (Wright) **146**:338
Portrait of the Poet as Landscape (Klein) **19**:260
"Portrait with Flashlight" (Justice) **102**:265
"Portraits" (Cummings) **15**:160, 162
Portraits and Elegies (Schnackenberg) **40**:378-81
Porträt eines Planeten (Duerrenmatt) **102**:61, 81
"Portret epizodzisty" (Konwicki) **117**:281
The Poseidon Adventure (Gallico) **2**:147
"Poseshchenie muzeia" (Nabokov)
See "The Visit to the Museum"
"Posesión" (Aleixandre) **9**:13
"Position" (Damas) **84**:177
Position de l'inconscient (Lacan) **75**:295
"The Position of the Afrikaans Writer" (Brink) **36**:68
"Position Without Magnitude" (Simic) **130**:295
"Positional" (Johnson) **7**:415
"Positions" (Donnell) **34**:158
Positions (Derrida) **87**:72, 87, 105
Positions (Ernaux)
See *La place*
"Positive Edges" (Ammons) **57**:50
"Positive Obsession" (Butler) **121**:142, 147
"Positive Vibration" (Marley) **17**:268, 272
"Positively 4th Street" (Dylan) **77**:174-75
Positives (Gunn) **32**:211
"Positives: For Sterling Plumpp" (Madhubuti) **73**:215
"Posjaščaetsja Jalte" (Brodsky) **50**:131
"Poslanie k stikham" (Brodsky) **13**:116
Posle skazki (Belyj parokhod) (Aitmatov)
See *Belyj parokhod*
"Poslushnitsa" (Bagryana) **10**:12
Les possédés (Camus) **32**:88, 99-100; **63**:64
"The Possessed" (Barnes) **11**:31
"Possessed" (Olds) **39**:186
"The Possessed" (Sacks) **67**:299
The Possessed (Banville) **118**:3-5
The Possessed (Camus)
See *Les possédés*
Possessed (Gombrowicz) **49**:131-32
Possessing the Secret of Joy (Walker) **103**:419, 421, 424
Possession (Delbanco) **13**:174
Possession (de la Roche) **14**:150
Possession (Markandaya) **38**:322-23
Possession: A Romance (Byatt) **65**:122-29, 131-33; **136**:147, 150-51, 156-57, 159-63, 166-75, 180,81, 183, 186-91, 194
Possessions (Kristeva) **140**:200
"Possibilities" (Morrissy) **99**:78
Possibilities (Bradbury) **32**:51; **61**:40
"The Possibility of a Poetic Drama" (Eliot) **24**:175, 181
"The Possibility of Evil" (Jackson) **60**:215
"Possible" (Avison) **97**:79
"A Possible Fake" (Hollander) **5**:186
"Post aetatem nostram" (Brodsky) **50**:122-23, 131
Post Captain (O'Brian) **152**:266, 273, 281, 298-99
"The Post Card" (Boell)
See "Die Postkarte"
The Post Card: From Socrates to Freud and Beyond (Derrida)
See *La carte postale: De Socrate à Freud et au-delà*
"Post Modernism" (Apple) **33**:21
"Post modernism" (Jameson) **142**:230
"Post mortem" (Jeffers) **15**:300
Post Mortem (Coward) **1**:64; **29**:131-32, 135, 138
Post Office (Bukowski) **41**:68, 70; **82**:4, 10-13, 15-17, 24, 28; **108**:66, 70, 72, 81-3, 90, 96-7, 100, 106
"Post scriptum" (Bataille) **29**:38
"Postage Stamp with a Pyramid" (Simic) **130**:330
Postal Variations (Brandys) **62**:119
"Postcard" (Garrett) **3**:192
"Postcard" (McGrath) **59**:178
"The Postcard Collection" (Koch) **5**:219
"The Postcard from Chinatown" (Brautigan) **12**:59
"Postcard from Cornwall" (Abse) **29**:15
"Postcard from Florida" (Oliver) **34**:247
"A Postcard from Iceland" (Heaney) **74**:162
"A Postcard from John Ashbery" (O'Hara) **13**:427
"A Postcard from North Antrim" (Heaney) **74**:163
"Postcard to the Social Muse" (Winters) **32**:468
Postcards (Proulx) **81**:274-77, 279
"Postcards from Cape Split" (Van Duyn) **63**:442; **116**:400, 403, 406, 428
"Postcards from China" (Kroetsch) **57**:292
"Postcards to Columbus" (Alexie) **96**:11
Postcripts (Priestley) **34**:361, 364
"Poste restante" (Thomas) **48**:379
The Poster in History (Gallo) **95**:97
"Posterity" (Larkin) **5**:229; **9**:323; **33**:261; **39**:336
Postern of Fate (Christie) **12**:120; **110**:116, 125
"Posthumous Autobiography" (Scannell) **49**:332
"Posthumous Fiction" (Bowering) **47**:31
"A Posthumous Sketch" (Oates) **9**:403
The Posthumous Writings and Poems of Hermann Lauscher (Hesse)
See *Hinterlassene Schriften und Gedichte von Hermann Lauscher*
"Postigo" (Cabral de Melo Neto) **76**:161
Postille a Il Nome della rosa (Eco) **142**:76-7, 91, 93
A Postillion Struck by Lightning (Bogarde) **19**:41-2
"A Post-Impressionist Susurration for the First of November, 1983" (Carruth) **84**:136
"Post-Impressions" (Cummings) **15**:160-162
"Die Postkarte" (Boell) **11**:54; **72**:71
The Postman Always Rings Twice (Cain) **3**:96-7; **11**:85-6; **28**:43-5, 47-54
The Postman Always Rings Twice (Mamet) **46**:246
"Postman Cheval" (Breton)
See "Facteur Cheval"
"Postmark" (Abse) **29**:15
Postmarked the Stars (Norton) **12**:458-60, 467
Postmetaphysical Thinking (Habermas)
See *Nachmetaphysisches Denken*
"Postmodern Blackness" (Hooks) **94**:145
Postmodern Genres (Perloff) **137**:293
The Postmodern Scene: Excremental Culture and Hyper-Aesthetics (Kroker) **77**:343, 345
"Postmodernism and the impasse of lyric" (Perloff) **137**:273
"Postmodernism//Fin de Siecle" (Perloff) **137**:302
Postmodernism or, The Cultural Logic of Late Capitalism (Jameson) **142**:238-43, 245, 251, 253, 255, 259-60, 262, 265
Postmortem (Cornwell) **155**:60-1, 67-70
Poštovní holub (Seifert) **93**:306, 333-34, 340
Post-Prison Writings and Speeches (Cleaver) **30**:62-3, 65-6
Postřižiny (Hrabal) **67**:114-15, 120-21, 123
"Postscript" (Hooker) **43**:197
"Postscript" (Livesay) **79**:336
"Postscript" (Paley) **140**:291
"Postscript" (Thomas) **6**:530
"Postscript" (Wright) **6**:580
"Postscript: A Reply to the Angel at Blythburg" (Szirtes) **46**:394
"Postscript to an Autumn" (Wolf) **150**:315
"Postscript to an Erotic Novel" (Vizinczey) **40**:435
"Postscript to Duncan McNaughton" (Thesen) **56**:421
Postscript to me Name of the Rose (Eco)
See *Postille a Il Nome della rosa*
"A Postscript with Ntozake Shange" (Shange) **74**:307, 309
"Postulation" (Ammons) **57**:51
"The Postulation of Reality" (Borges) **83**:163, 165
Postures (Rhys) **2**:371-73; **6**:453-54, 457; **14**:446, 450; **51**:356-57, 359, 365, 368-70; **124**:322, 330-32, 334, 336-38, 341, 344-46, 348, 354, 365-66, 372, 374-75
"Postures of Unease" (Ashbery) **77**:68
"The Pot of Earth" (MacLeish) **8**:360-62; **68**:270-72, 275, 284, 286, 290, 293
"The Pot of Gold" (Cheever) **64**:65
"A Pot of Soothing Herbs" (O'Faolain) **47**:325; **108**:408-09
"Pot Pourri from a Surrey Garden" (Betjeman) **43**:41
"Pot Roast" (Strand) **18**:518, 520; **41**:435
"Potato" (Wilbur) **110**:383
"The Potato Dealer" (Trevor) **116**:395
"The Potato Elf" (Nabokov)
See "Kartofel'nyy el'f"
"Potato Flower" (Yevtushenko) **26**:467
Potch and Colour (Prichard) **46**:337, 343, 345
"Potential" (Campbell) **42**:92
The Pothunters (Wodehouse) **2**:478
Potiki (Grace) **56**:121-22
"The Potlatch of Esmerelda" (Tuohy) **37**:434
"Potomka" (Bagryana) **10**:12
"Pots and Pans" (Ammons) **57**:56
Potseluj, orkestr, ryba, kolbasa (Aksyonov) **37**:12
Potter on Potter (Potter) **123**:249-50
Potter's Field (Green) **25**:199
The Potting Shed (Greene) **6**:213; **70**:292, 294
Pounamu, Pounamu (Ihimaera) **46**:192, 195-96, 198-201
"The Pound Is Sinking" (McCartney) **35**:289-91
"Pound/Stevens: Whose Era?" (Perloff) **137**:273
"Pounding Fascism" (Bernstein) **142**:19
Pounding Nails in the Floor With My Forehead (Bogosian) **141**:90-3
Pounding the Pavements, Beating the Bushes, and Other Pataphysical Poems (Queneau) **42**:336-37
Pour Dante: Discours (Perse) **4**:399-400; **11**:433
"Pour faire le portrait d'un oiseaux" (Prévert) **15**:437
"Pour fêter une enfance" (Perse) **46**:300
Pour finir encour et Autres Foirades (Beckett)
See *Foirades*
"Pour Khalam" (Senghor) **54**:408
Pour la révolution africaine: Ecrits politiques (Fanon) **74**:72, 74
Pour l'amitié (Blanchot) **135**:130
"Pour le sport" (Sondheim) **30**:398
Pour Marx (Althusser) **106**:3, 17, 19, 29, 31, 39, 42
"Pour que tout soit en tout" (Damas) **84**:160
Pour saluer Melville (Giono) **4**:184
"Pour sûr" (Damas) **84**:175, 177
"Pour toi et moi" (Damas) **84**:167

Pour un malherbe (Ponge) **18**:413, 418
Pour un nouveau roman (Robbe-Grillet) **1**:287; **2**:375; **14**:462; **43**:360; **128**:326, 338, 344, 362, 367, 373
Pour un oui ou pour un non (Sarraute) **80**:241-42
"Pour un prométhée saxifrage" (Char) **9**:162
Pour une critique de l'économie politique du signe (Baudrillard) **60**:11-13, 15-16
Pour une morale de l'ambiguité (Beauvoir) **44**:344
"Pour une sémiologie des paragrammes" (Kristeva) **140**:184
Pour une sociologie du roman (Goldmann) **24**:235-36, 241, 243, 246
"Pouring the Milk Away" (Rukeyser) **27**:411
"Pourquoi la négritude? Négritude ou révolution?" (Condé) **52**:79, 82
'Pourquoi Pas?'—A Letter from Ottawa (Richler) **46**:352
Pouvoirs de l'horreur (Kristeva) **77**:306, 308-09, 324-25; **140**:147, 167, 170, 180-81
Povatek Filipa Latinovicza (Krleža) **8**:329-30; **114**:168, 176-81, 185
Poveri e semplici (Ortese) **89**:191
Poverkh barierov (Pasternak) **18**:381-82; **63**:289
"Poverty" (Ammons) **57**:49, 52
"Poverty" (Merwin) **8**:390
"Poverty in Athens, Ohio" (Bell) **8**:65
"The Poverty of Poverty" (Bernard) **59**:46
"Poverty Train" (Nyro) **17**:315, 318
Povest (Pasternak) **7**:298; **10**:384
Povest' o lesakh (Paustovsky) **40**:363
Povest' o zhizni (Paustovsky) **40**:358-61, 364-66
Povestri gor i stepei (Aitmatov) **71**:3, 21
Povestri i rasskazy (Aitmatov) **71**:7
"Pow Wow" (Alexie) **96**:4; **154**:3
"Powder Monkey" (Carver) **55**:275
"Powderday's Red Hen" (Stuart) **11**:511
Powdered Eggs (Simmons) **57**:404-05, 407-08
"Powder-White Faces" (Hughes) **108**:324
"Power" (Lorde) **71**:233, 236, 241, 246
"Power" (Redgrove) **41**:351
"Power" (Rich) **36**:376
Power (Fast) **131**:91-2, 103
Power (Konwicki)
See *Wladza*
"Power and Light" (Dickey) **2**:115; **15**:174
"Power and Light (An Idea for Film)" (Hannah) **38**:234-35; **90**:126, 138-39
"Power and Love" (MacLennan) **92**:342
"Power and Survival" (Canetti)
See "Macht und Überleben"
The Power and the Glory (Greene) **1**:130-33, 135; **3**:207-10, 213-14; **6**:215-19; **9**:251; **14**:216-18; **18**:195, 197; **27**:173, 175-76; **37**:136-37, 140; **70**:287, 289-91, 293, 295; **72**:148, 151-55, 157, 178-79; **125**:187, 189, 191, 194, 201, 208-14
The Power House (Comfort) **7**:54
Power/Knowledge: Selected Interviews and Other Writings (Foucault) **34**:343
"The Power of Creativity" (Kunene) **85**:166
"The Power of Darkness" (Anand) **23**:21
"The Power of Division" (Culler) **65**:339
The Power of History (DeLillo) **143**:215
The Power of Horses, and Other Stories (Cook-Lynn) **93**:124-27, 129-30
The Power of Light (Singer) **69**:306
"Power of Love" (Dorris) **109**:311
"The Power of Maples" (Stern) **40**:406
"The Power of Music to Disturb" (Mueller) **51**:279
The Power of Myth (Campbell and Moyers) **69**:87, 90-1, 93, 96, 98
The Power of Myth (Moyers) **74**:254
The Power of One (Courtenay) **59**:52-8
"Power of Reason" (Bissoondath) **120**:19
"The Power of Taste" (Herbert) **43**:193
The Power of the Dog (Barker) **37**:41
The Power of the Dog (Savage) **40**:371, 373, 376
"The Power of the Powerless" (Havel) **58**:243; **65**:420, 442; **123**:167, 173, 191-92
Power of Three (Jones) **26**:226-28
"Power Plays" (Ammons) **57**:51, 53
The Power Plays (Walker) **61**:424, 426-30, 432-33
Power Politics (Atwood) **2**:20; **3**:19-20; **4**:25; **8**:28-30; **13**:42-3; **15**:37; **25**:62-3, 67; **84**:68, 106; **135**:13
Power Shift: The Rise of the Southern Rim and Its Challenge to the Eastern Establishment (Sale) **68**:345-50, 353, 359
"A Power Struggle" (Head) **67**:98
The Power That Preserves (Donaldson) **46**:140; **138**:4, 6, 11-12, 14, 16, 18, 20-21, 36-37, 39
The Power to Change Geography (O Hehir) **41**:323-24
"Power to the People" (Lennon) **35**:264, 270-71
"Power to the Pussy" (Hooks) **94**:157
"Power-Cut" (McGuckian) **48**:276
"Powerfinger" (Young) **17**:581, 583
Powerful Long Ladder (Dodson) **79**:187-88, 190-91, 194, 198
"Powerhouse" (Welty) **14**:561; **33**:415, 424; **105**:314-15, 327, 329, 331, 336, 349
"Powerless, with a Guitar" (Grass)
See "In Ohnmacht gefallen"
"The Powerline Incarnation" (Murray) **40**:337
"Powers" (Milosz) **82**:303
Powers and Prospects (Chomsky) **132**:67
Powers of Attorney (Auchincloss) **4**:30; **9**:52; **45**:29
Powers of Darkness (Aickman) **57**:2
Powers of Horror (Kristeva)
See *Pouvoirs de l'horreur*
"Powrót prokonsula" (Herbert) **9**:274; **43**:184, 186, 189
"The POW's Suit" (Mahfouz)
See "Badlat al-asir"
"The Powwow at the End of the World" (Alexie) **154**:21
"Powwow Polaroid" (Alexie) **154**:13
"A Pox on You, Mine Goodly Host" (Perelman) **49**:259
El pozo (Onetti) **7**:276, 280; **10**:376-80
Practical Criticism (Richards) **24**:376, 386, 389, 392-93, 395-96, 398-400
"A Practical Joke" (Farrell) **66**:127
"Practical Recommendations in the Event of a Catastrophe" (Herbert) **43**:184
Practicalities (Duras)
See *La vie materielle*
The Practice Effect (Brin) **34**:135
"The Practice of the Craft" (Metcalf) **37**:299-300
The Practice of the Wild (Snyder) **120**:335-37, 339-40, 351-52
The Practice of Writing (Lodge) **141**:373-75
A Praed Street Dossier (Derleth) **31**:138
"Pragmatism and the Tragic" (West) **134**:375
Prague (Krizanc) **57**:274-76, 278-80
Prague (Seifert)
See *Praha*
"The Prague Orgy" (Roth) **47**:357-59, 362
Praha (Seifert) **93**:343
"Prairie" (Sandburg) **10**:448, 450; **35**:339-41, 343, 352
"Prairie" (Waddington) **28**:440
Prairie du chien (Mamet) **46**:254
"A Prairie Home Companion" (Keillor) **40**:272-75; **115**:261, 266, 268-69, 274, 276-77, 281, 284, 288, 293-94, 296
A Prairie Home Companion Anniversary Album (Keillor) **40**:274
The Prairie Home Companion Folk Song Book (Keillor) **115**:277
A Prairie Nightmare (Berton) **104**:61
"Prairie Poems" (Lane) **25**:289
Prairie-Town Boy (Sandburg) **35**:354, 357
"Praise" (Ciardi) **44**:381
"Praise" (Jensen) **37**:189
"Praise" (Oliver) **98**:283
Praise (Hass) **18**:209-13; **99**:139-42, 144, 148-50, 154, 157
"Praise/Complaint" (Goldbarth) **38**:205
"Praise for Death" (Hall) **151**:198
"Praise for Sick Women" (Snyder) **5**:394; **32**:387
"Praise in Summer" (Wilbur) **9**:569-70; **53**:399, 406
"Praise of Margins" (Gustafson) **36**:222
The Praise Singer (Renault) **11**:472; **17**:402
"Praise to the End!" (Roethke) **101**:274, 277-78, 281, 283, 334, 337-41
Praise to the End! (Roethke) **1**:291; **8**:455, 458; **11**:482; **19**:396-97; **46**:355, 360-61, 363; **101**:264, 266-67, 273, 286-88, 290-91, 303-05, 326-27, 334-35, 340-41
"Praised Be" (Elytis) **100**:155
"The Praises" (Olson) **5**:329; **11**:419
Praises (Jennings) **131**:243
"Praises IV" (McGrath) **59**:181
Praisesong for the Widow (Marshall) **27**:314-15; **72**:231-32, 236-37, 242-46, 248-50, 252-54
"Praising Dark Places" (Komunyakaa) **86**:192
"Praiso" (Hass) **18**:212
Prancing Novelist (Brophy) **6**:98; **29**:98; **105**:8, 14, 18, 29-30, 33
Der Präsident (Bernhard) **61**:27
Prater Violet (Isherwood) **1**:157; **9**:293; **11**:297, 299; **14**:278, 280, 282-85; **44**:397-98, 401-04
"Pratfalls" (Klein) **30**:235-36
Pratidwandi (Ray) **16**:487, 489, 492-93; **76**:358, 360
"Pravaya kist" (Solzhenitsyn) **4**:507; **7**:432; **18**:495
Pravda (Godard) **20**:141, 150
Pravda: A Fleet Street Comedy (Hare) **58**:225-30; **136**:247, 261, 267, 284, 286, 293
Pravila de morală practică (Arghezi) **80**:11
Praxis (Weldon) **11**:566; **19**:468-69; **36**:447
"Pray Eros" (Honig) **33**:211
Pray Love, Remember (Stolz) **12**:548-49
"Pray without Ceasing" (Ammons) **8**:14, 17; **9**:30; **57**:59
"Prayer" (Akhmatova) **64**:4
"Prayer" (Ezekiel) **61**:97
"Prayer" (Kinnell) **129**:248, 256
"Prayer" (Levertov) **15**:337
"A Prayer" (Mphahlele) **133**:135
"Prayer" (Olds) **85**:297, 305
"Prayer" (Sanders) **53**:304
"Prayer" (Simic) **130**:333
"Prayer Against Too Much" (Zweig) **34**:379
"Prayer before Birth" (MacNeice) **4**:315-16; **53**:239, 243
"Prayer for Aroniateka/Hendrick" (Kenny) **87**:254
A Prayer for Katerina Horovitzova (Lustig) **56**:183-84, 186-88
"Prayer for My Daughter" (Durcan) **70**:152
"A Prayer for My Daughter" (Van Duyn) **116**:426
A Prayer for Owen Meany (Irving) **112**:152-54, 156-58, 165, 173
"Prayer for Peace" (Lindbergh) **82**:155-56
"Prayer for Peace" (Senghor)
See "Prière de paix"
"A Prayer for Rain" (Mueller) **51**:280
"Prayer for Russia" (Ehrenburg) **62**:174
"Prayer in the Pacific" (Silko) **74**:347; **114**:316
"Prayer Meeting" (Hughes) **108**:297
The Prayer Meeting (Green) **25**:192
"Prayer of Mr. Cogito—Traveler" (Herbert) **43**:191
"Prayer of the Middle Class at Ease in Zion" (Nemerov) **36**:309
"The Prayer of the Middle-Aged Man" (Berryman) **13**:82

"Prayer Service in an English Church" (Bly) **38**:56
"A Prayer to Go to Paradise with the Donkeys" (Wilbur) **14**:577
"Prayer to Hermes" (Creeley) **78**:152
"Prayer to Masks" (Senghor)
See "Prière aux Masques"
"Prayer to the Good Poet" (Wright) **28**:466
"Prayer to the Lady, Queen Freak" (Sanders) **53**:304
"A Prayer to the Mountain" (Ciardi) **40**:161
"Prayers" (Ciardi) **40**:154
"Prayers" (Sondheim) **30**:388
Prayers (MacBeth) **5**:264
Prayers and Devotions (John Paul II) **128**:187
"Prayers and Sayings of the Mad Farmer" (Berry) **27**:33
Prayers of a Very Wise Child (Carrier)
See *Prières d'un enfant très très sage*
"Praying for Rain" (Bass) **79**:15
The Praying Man (Santos) **22**:365
Praying Mantis (Carroll) **143**:37, 47
"Prayrs for th One Habitation" (Bissett) **18**:58
"Praze" (Seifert) **93**:319
"Le pré" (Ponge) **18**:418-19
"Preach on Dusty Roads" (Shaw) **23**:396
"The Preacher" (Townshend) **17**:542
The Preacher and the Slave (Stegner) **49**:350-51
"The Preacher at the Corner" (Stafford) **29**:381
"Preaching to the Converted" (Porter) **5**:347; **13**:451; **33**:323
"Pre-Amphibian" (Atwood) **25**:66
"The Precedent" (Dodson) **79**:194
"Precession of the Equinoxes" (Rexroth) **112**:395
"The 'Precinct Station'—Structure and Idea" (Simpson) **149**:358
"Precious Angel" (Dylan) **77**:186-87
"Precious Five" (Auden) **14**:28
Precious Lives (Forster) **149**:103-04
"Preciousness" (Lispector) **43**:267-68
"The Precipice" (Wright) **53**:420
The Precipice (MacLennan) **2**:257; **14**:339-40, 342; **92**:306-07, 313-18, 322, 326, 328-31, 341, 344, 347
"Precipice—Encurled" (Byatt) **65**:125; **136**:138, 147-49
Precipitations (Scott) **43**:370, 384
"Precis" (Rozewicz) **139**:289
Précis de décomposition (Cioran) **64**:73, 91-2
"Precision" (Wakoski) **40**:455
A Precocious Autobiography (Yevtushenko) **26**:460; **51**:430; **126**:395, 398, 406
"Los precursores de Kafka" (Borges) **8**:100; **44**:359; **48**:44; **83**:193, 194
"The Predators" (Allen) **52**:35
Predatory Things of Our Age (Strugatskii and Strugatskii) **27**:433
Predeo slikan cajem (Pavic) **60**:288
"A Predicament" (Callaghan) **65**:250
"Prediction" (Himes) **7**:159; **58**:268; **108**:234, 251, 278
"The Prediction" (Strand) **18**:515, 518-20; **71**:284
Predilections (Moore) **47**:267
Predvaritel'nye itogi (Trifonov) **45**:408, 411, 413, 416-17, 420
Prefabrications (Miles) **39**:353
"A Preface" (Didion) **129**:98
"La préface" (Olson) **29**:330
"Préface" (Tchicaya) **101**:351-52
Préface à la Gita-Gavinda (Yourcenar) **38**:457
"Preface: Deciding to Live" (Allison) **78**:2
Preface: The screen test (Antonioni)
See *Prefazine: il provino*
"Preface to a Life" (Thurber) **125**:395
Preface to a Twenty Volume Suicide Note (Baraka) **2**:34; **5**:44-46; **10**:21; **14**:42; **115**:3, 10, 38, 40
"Preface to an Adaptation of Ibsen's An Enemy of the People" (Miller) **10**:346
"Preface to Blackness: Text and Pretext" (Gates) **65**:383
"Preface to My Poems—Frivolous Version" (Williams) **45**:443
A Preface to Paradise Lost (Lewis) **124**:193, 228
"Preface to 'The Galton Case'" (Macdonald) **14**:333
"Preface to the Reader" (Rukeyser) **15**:456
"Preface to The Unending Rose" (Borges) **13**:110
Prefazine: il provino (Antonioni) **144**:80
"Prefigurations: Prato" (Landolfi) **49**:217
"Pregão turístico do Recife" (Cabral de Melo Neto) **76**:153-54, 167-68
"The Pregnant Dream" (Swenson) **106**:337
The Pregnant Man (Phillips) **28**:362-64
"Preguntas" (Neruda) **28**:309
"Pre-History" (Akhmatova) **11**:8
"Preliminary Investigation of an Angel" (Herbert) **9**:272; **43**:188
"Preliminary Notes" (Moody) **147**:170-71, 187, 189
"Prelude" (Avison) **97**:74-7, 80-1, 106, 128
"The Prelude" (Frost) **9**:227
"Prelude" (Kavanagh) **22**:237
"Prelude" (Walcott) **25**:449; **67**:352; **76**:278, 280, 286
A Prelude (Wilson) **2**:475, 478; **24**:483
"Prelude for Spring" (Livesay) **79**:332, 334-36, 38
"Prelude: The Troops" (Sassoon) **130**:185, 219
"Prelude to a Fairy Tale" (Sitwell) **67**:313
Prelude to a Kiss (Lucas) **64**:294-99
"Prelude to a Parting" (Angelou) **77**:31
"Prelude to an Evening" (Ransom) **2**:363; **5**:365
"Prelude to Darkness" (Salinas) **90**:332
Prelude to Downfall: Hitler and the United States 1939-1941 (Friedlander)
See *Hitler er les États-Unis (1939-1941)*
Prelude to Foundation (Asimov) **76**:313
Prelude to Space: A Compellingly Realistic Novel of Interplanetary Flight (Clarke) **35**:118, 120-21, 124
Prelude to Terror (MacInnes) **27**:283-84
"Preludes" (Eliot) **13**:199, 201; **15**:213; **41**:152, 156; **57**:174; **113**:187
"Preludes" (Transtroemer) **52**:410; **65**:222-23
Preludes for Memnon; or, Preludes to Attitude (Aiken) **3**:3; **5**:9; **10**:3; **52**:22-4, 26, 29
Premier amour (Beckett) **6**:38; **10**:34-6
Le premier homme (Camus) **32**:99; **124**:7, 30-5, 36-9, 44, 47
Le Premier quartier de la lune (Tremblay) **102**:379
La première enquête de Maigret, 1913 (Simenon) **3**:451
Les premiers poèmes (Tzara) **47**:389
Los premios (Cortázar) **15**:146; **33**:135-36; **34**:329; **92**:138-39, 141, 155
"Premonition" (Montague) **13**:390; **46**:268
"The Premonition" (Roethke) **8**:460; **46**:361
"Pre-Mortem" (Purdy) **50**:247
Prenez Garde (White) **49**:399-400
Prenn Drifting (Lengyel) **7**:202
Prénom de Dieu (Cixous) **92**:56
Prénoms de personne (Cixous) **92**:52-3, 70, 90, 94
Preoccupations in Australian Poetry (Wright) **11**:578; **53**:432
Preoccupations: Selected Prose, 1968-1978 (Heaney) **25**:248-51; **74**:162, 165, 169, 173, 177-78, 181, 183, 193; **91**:115, 118, 121, 124, 128
"Preparation" (Butler) **81**:127
"Preparation" (Milosz) **56**:246, 251; **82**:290
"Preparation" (Silko) **74**:347
Preparation for the Ascent (Rogin) **18**:458-59
"Preparations for Victory" (Blunden) **56**:43
"Preparatory Exercise (Dyptych with Votive Tablet)" (Paz) **65**:198
Prepositions (Zukofsky) **4**:599
"The Pre-Presidential T.R." (Wilson) **24**:481
"A Pre-Raphaelite Ending, London" (Howard) **7**:168
"A Pre-Raphaelite Notebook" (Hill) **45**:180
"Pres Spoke in a Language" (Baraka) **115**:39
"Pre-School" (Purdy) **50**:246
"Prescience" (Angelou) **35**:32
"The Prescriptive Stalls As" (Ammons) **108**:13
Préséances (Mauriac) **4**:340; **56**:204, 206
"The Presence" (Elytis) **49**:109
"The Presence" (Gordon) **29**:188; **83**:247
"Presence" (Kunene) **85**:166
"Presence" (Levertov) **66**:241
Presence (Page and Plant) **12**:480
"The Presence of Grace" (Powers) **1**:280
The Presence of Grace (Powers) **4**:419; **8**:447; **57**:356
"The Presence of Presence" (Dacey) **51**:80-1
A Presence with Secrets (Spackman) **46**:377-78
"The Presences" (Jacobsen) **48**:198
"Presences" (Justice) **19**:233-34; **102**:263
Presences (Creeley) **78**:128, 130-33, 144, 147, 159
Présences (Jouve) **47**:203
Presences: Seven Dramatic Pieces (Taylor) **4**:542-43; **18**:524-27
"The Present" (Bell) **8**:67
"The Present" (Levine) **118**:315
"Present" (Sanchez) **116**:280
"The Present" (Stafford) **7**:457
The Present (Josipovici) **6**:270-71
The Present and the Past (Compton-Burnett) **34**:500
"Present Discontents" (Blunden) **56**:30
"A Present for Miss Merriam" (Buckler) **13**:120
Present Laughter (Coward) **29**:134-35, 138; **51**:68-70
Présent passé, passé présent (Ionesco) **41**:227-28; **86**:332, 335, 341
"The Present Past" (Nemerov) **36**:309
Present Past, Past Present (Ionesco)
See *Présent passé, passé présent*
The Present Takers (Chambers) **35**:101
"The Present Tense" (Oates) **33**:294
Present Tense (Gilroy) **2**:161
"Présentation des temps modernes" (Sartre) **24**:419-20
Presentation Piece (Hacker) **91**:94
"Presenting a Watch" (Howard) **47**:168
"Presents" (Wideman) **67**:379, 385
"Preservation" (Carver) **36**:100, 104; **126**:113-14, 122, 162-63, 179
Preservation, Act 1 (Davies) **21**:96-8
Preservation, Act 2 (Davies) **21**:98, 100
Preservation Hall (Spencer) **30**:404-07
Preserve and Protect (Drury) **37**:105, 107
"The President" (Barthelme) **8**:50; **23**:46
The President (Asturias)
See *El Señor presidente*
The President (Bernhard)
See *Der Präsident*
The President (Cassill) **23**:104-05
The President (Dreyer) **16**:259-61
The President (Hersey) **81**:332
"The President of the Louisiana Live Oak Society" (Gilchrist) **48**:116, 121; **143**:273-75, 283, 319-20, 322
Presidential Agent (Sinclair) **63**:355
Presidential Lottery (Michener) **109**:383, 386
Presidential Mission (Sinclair) **63**:355, 357
The Presidential Papers (Mailer) **1**:190, 192; **8**:370; **28**:256, 263; **74**:219; **111**:95-96, 100, 116
The President's Child (Weldon) **36**:445-47; **122**:255
The President's Man (Guild) **33**:188
"Presque Isle" (Glück) **81**:167
"La presqu'île" (Gracq) **48**:141
La presqu'île (Gracq) **48**:141
"Press Clippings" (Cortázar)
See "Recortes de prensa"
"Pressed Duck" (Seidel) **18**:475

"Pressing On" (Dylan) **77**:186, 190
"Pressure" (Davies) **21**:105-06
"Pressure" (Joel) **26**:223
"Pressure" (Waldman) **7**:508
Prêt-à-Porter (Altman) **116**:59, 61, 68, 70-1
"Pretend I'm Not Here" (Theroux) **11**:528
"Pretend We're French" (Freeman) **55**:57
"Pretended Homes" (Dunn) **40**:171
Pretendent Na prestol (Voinovich) **49**:376, 379-82; **147**:285
"The Pretender" (Browne) **21**:39-40
"The Pretender" (Gordimer)
See "My First Two Women"
The Pretender (Browne) **21**:38-41
Pretender to the Throne: The Further Adventures of Private Ivan Chonkin (Voinovich) **49**:376, 379-82
Pretending to Be Asleep (Davison) **28**:100-01
"Preternaturally Early Snowfall in Mating Season" (Warren) **39**:272
Prétexte: Roland Barthes (Barthes) **83**:89-90
"The Prettiest Star" (Bowie) **17**:60
Pretty Boy (Poliakoff) **38**:379-80, 385
"Pretty Boy Floyd" (Guthrie) **35**:183, 185, 190-91
Pretty Boy Floyd (McMurtry) **127**:350
"The Pretty Girl" (Dubus) **36**:147-48; **97**:199-202, 217, 221, 223, 228-30
"Pretty Ice" (Robison) **42**:339
"Pretty Lady" (Sondheim) **30**:397
Pretty Leslie (Cassill) **23**:104
"Pretty Little Picture" (Sondheim) **147**:255
"Pretty Maggie Moneyeyes" (Ellison) **13**:203, 206; **42**:126; **139**:130
Pretty Mournings, Small Tragedies (Carrier)
See *Jolis deuils, petites tragédies pour adultes*
The Pretty Pictures (Beauvoir)
See *Les belles images*
"Pretty Polly Barlow" (Coward) **51**:74
Pretty Poplar in a Red Kerchief (Aitmatov)
See *Topolek moi v krasnoi kosynke*
Pretty Tales for Tired People (Gellhorn) **60**:185, 187-88
"Pretty women" (Sondheim) **30**:393, 398; **147**:256
Pretzel Logic (Becker and Fagen) **26**:79, 83
"Preview of Death" (Woolrich) **77**:401
"The Previous Tenant" (Simpson) **32**:381; **149**:316, 322, 325, 335, 341, 351, 360
"Las previsiones de Sangiácomo" (Bioy Casares) **88**:67, 69
"Priapus" (H. D.) **14**:223; **31**:205
Priapus and the Pool and Other Poems (Aiken) **52**:20, 22
Příběh inženýra lidských duší (Škvorecký) **39**:221-22; **69**:327-30, 332, 335-37, 339, 342-44, 346-52; **152**:308, 315-17, 319-20, 325, 330-31, 335-37
The Price (Miller) **2**:279-80; **6**:330-33; **10**:342-43; **15**:373-74; **47**:251, 254-55
The Price of Diamonds (Jacobson) **4**:256; **14**:289
The Price of Gold (Waddington) **28**:439
"The Price of Office" (Mahfouz)
See "Mahr al-wazifa"
"The Price of Peace" (Cliff) **21**:60-1
The Price of Salt (Highsmith) **42**:211; **102**:210, 212, 219-21
"The Price of Stone" (Murphy) **41**:319
The Price of Stone: New and Selected Poems (Murphy) **41**:319-20
The Price of the Ticket: Collected Nonfiction, 1948-1985 (Baldwin) **42**:15-21; **127**:118, 141, 147-48
"The Price of Weakness" (Mahfouz)
See "Thaman al-d'f"
"Pricing" (Ignatow) **7**:177
The Prick of Noon (De Vries) **46**:134-36
Prick Up Your Ears (Bennett) **77**:85, 89-90, 98, 100, 102
"Prickli" (Tournier)
See "Prickly"
"Prickly" (Tournier) **36**:438; **95**:383-84, 387-89
Pricksongs and Descants (Coover) **3**:113-14; **7**:58; **32**:121-24, 126; **46**:119, 121-22; **87**:25, 32, 43
"The Pride" (Newlove) **14**:377
"Pride" (Urquhart) **90**:385
The Pride of Chanur (Cherryh) **35**:108-09
A Pride of Heroes (Dickinson)
See *The Old English Peep-Show*
Pride of the Bimbos (Sayles) **7**:399; **10**:460; **14**:484
"Pride of the Village" (Blunden) **56**:37
"Prière" (Damas) **84**:179
"Prière aux Masques" (Senghor) **130**:258, 282
"Prière de paix" (Senghor) **130**:234, 242, 249, 252, 254, 259
"Prière mutilée" (Cocteau) **8**:146
Prières d'un enfant très très sage (Carrier) **78**:83
"The Priest" (Thomas) **48**:375
"The Priest and the Matador" (Bukowski) **41**:64
"The Priest Says Goodbye" (Cohen) **38**:131-32
"A Priest to His People" (Thomas) **13**:542
"Priestly Fellowship" (Powers) **8**:447; **57**:349, 357-58
"The Priest's Confession" (Ai) **69**:9, 10
"The Priest's Wife" (L'Heureux) **52**:279
Priglashenie na kazn (Nabokov) **1**:239, 242-43; **2**:302; **3**:353; **8**:415, 418; **15**:393, 395-97; **46**:292; **64**:350-51
"Prikliuchenie v antikvarnom magazine" (Akhmadulina) **53**:12-13
Přilba hlíny (Seifert)
See *Helmet of Clay*
Prilli i thyer (Kadare) **52**:260
La prima Angélica (Saura) **20**:315-18, 321-22
"Prima Belladonna" (Ballard) **137**:66
The Primal Urge (Aldiss) **14**:10-11
Primary Colors (Klein) **154**:199-228
The Primary English Class (Horovitz) **56**:153-54
The Primary Language of Poetry in the 1640's (Miles) **39**:354
The Primary Language of Poetry in the 1740's and 1840's (Miles) **39**:354
The Primary Language of Poetry in the 1940's (Miles) **39**:354
"Primary Sources" (Moody) **147**:171
Primate (Wiseman) **20**:475, 477
"La primavera Hitleriana" (Montale) **9**:390
"Prime" (Ungaretti) **11**:559
"Prime Colours" (Watkins) **43**:451
"Prime Minister" (Enright) **31**:155
The Prime Minister (Clarke) **53**:89-90, 92, 95
"The Prime of Life" (Asimov) **26**:50
The Prime of Life (Beauvoir)
See *La force de l'âge*
The Prime of Miss Jean Brodie (Spark) **2**:415-17; **3**:465-67; **8**:493-94; **13**:520, 522-23; **18**:501-06; **40**:393-96, 399-400; **94**:327-28, 331-344, 350, 353-356, 358-359
Primeiras estorias (Rosa) **23**:352-54
"Primer" (Simic) **130**:317
"Primer for Blacks" (Brooks) **125**:107-08, 111
Primer for Blacks (Brooks) **49**:29; **125**:104, 107
Primer for Blacks--Three Preachments (Brooks) **125**:107
Primer for Combat (Boyle) **58**:70; **121**:31-2, 53
A Primer for Poets (Shapiro) **4**:487
A Primer of Ignorance (Blackmur) **2**:62
Primera història d'Esther (Espriu) **9**:192
Primera memoria (Matute) **11**:362-63, 365
"Primero sueño" (Guillén) **79**:246
Primeros encuentros/First Encounters (Ulibarrí) **83**:410-11, 415
"The Primitive" (Madhubuti) **73**:192
"The Primitive" (Swenson) **4**:533; **61**:391
The Primitive (Himes) **2**:195; **4**:229; **18**:248; **58**:252, 256-57, 263; **108**:229, 232, 254, 259
Primitive (Oppen) **13**:434; **34**:358
"Primitive Journal" (Wright) **146**:339
Primitive Mythology (Campbell)
See *The Masks of God: Primitive Mythology*
"Primitive Sources" (Atwood) **25**:66
"Primitives" (Randall) **135**:396
Primitivism and Decadence (Winters) **32**:451-52, 455, 460, 463, 466, 469
"Primo Levi's Suicide Note" (Ozick) **155**:125-26
The Primrose Path (Nash) **23**:317-18
"The Prince" (Winters) **32**:468
Prince (Prince) **35**:323-24
The Prince and Betty (Wodehouse) **10**:538
"The Prince and the Pauper" (Auchincloss) **45**:30
The Prince and the Showgirl (Olivier) **20**:238-39, 244
The Prince and the Wild Geese (Brophy) **29**:98-9
Prince Caspian: The Return to Narnia (Lewis) **124**:236, 248
Le Prince de Jaffar (Duhamel) **8**:187
"Prince Ferrix and Princess Crystal" (Lem) **15**:328; **149**:274
A Prince of a Fellow (Hearon) **63**:160-62
"Prince of Darkness" (Powers) **57**:355-56
Prince of Darkness (Mortimer) **43**:307
Prince of Darkness and Other Stories (Powers) **1**:279; **4**:419; **57**:356-7
The Prince of Jaffar (Duhamel)
See *Le Prince de Jaffar*
Prince of Naples (Walker) **61**:424, 428
Prince of Peace (Carroll) **38**:108-11
Prince of Players (Hart) **66**:182
"Prince of the Punks" (Davies) **21**:103
The Prince of Tides (Conroy) **74**:44-6, 50-3
"The Prince of Wales" (Pesetsky) **65**:349
The Prince of West End Avenue (Isler) **91**:45-52
"Princes and Powers" (Baldwin) **50**:292
"The Princes and the Feathers" (Harris) **12**:268
"The Prince's Land" (Murray) **40**:334
"Princess" (Mohr) **12**:446
"The Princess and the Bears" (Harris) **12**:268
"The Princess and the Pea" (Muldoon) **72**:278
The Princess Bride: S. Morgenstern's Classic Tale of True Love and Adventure; The "Good Parts" Version, Abridged (Goldman) **48**:126, 128
Princess in Denim (Sherburne) **30**:361
"The Princess with the Golden Hair" (Wilson) **8**:551
"Princesse, ton épître" (Senghor) **54**:396
"The Princessess" (Blaga) **75**:62
"Princeton Speech" (Weiss) **51**:386
"Principal in a Prairie Town" (Suknaski) **19**:432
Principal Products of Portugal (Hall) **151**:205-06
Principato (McHale) **3**:331; **5**:281-82
"Le principe d'utilité" (Cendrars) **18**:92
The Principle of Water (Silkin) **6**:499; **43**:400, 404
The Principles of Literary Criticism (Richards) **24**:370-76, 379-81, 384-85, 387-89, 393-400
Print of a Hare's Foot (Davies) **23**:146
"Printemps" (Le Clézio) **155**:84
Le printemps 71 (Adamov) **25**:13-21
Printemps et autres saisons (Le Clézio) **155**:83
The Printer of Malgudi (Narayan) **121**:332, 335-36, 338-39, 356
Printer's Devil (Moorcock) **58**:351
"Printer's Pie" (Hope) **51**:226
"The Prinzhorn Collection" (Coles) **46**:111-13
The Prinzhorn Collection (Coles) **46**:111-13
The Pripet Marshes (Feldman) **7**:103
"Priscilla" (Calvino) **11**:92
Prismatic Ground (Young) **82**:395-97, 405-06, 409, 411-12, 414

Prison (Bergman)
See *Fängelse*
The Prison (Simenon) **2**:398
Prison and Chocolate Cake (Sahgal) **41**:369
Prison and Peace (Aksyonov) **101**:55
The Prison Cell and Barrel Mystery (Reading) **47**:350
"The Prison House" (Ali) **69**:31
The Prison House (Ali) **69**:31
"Prison Island" (Fenton) **32**:165-66
"Prison Mass" (Himes) **108**:235
Prison Poems (Berrigan) **4**:57-8
The Prison Tree and the Women (Ritsos) **6**:463
"The Prisoner" (Ai) **69**:9, 15
"The Prisoner" (Jong) **6**:268
"The Prisoner" (Klappert) **57**:260
"The Prisoner" (Malamud) **3**:321
"The Prisoner" (Nkosi) **45**:295
"The Prisoner" (Paz)
See "El prisonero"
"The Prisoner" (Roa Bastos)
See "El prisonero"
"The Prisoner" (Simic) **22**:380; **130**:295, 311, 317-18
"Prisoner at a Desk" (Sarton) **91**:253
Prisoner of Azkaban (Rowling)
See *Harry Potter and the Prisoner of Azkaban*
"The Prisoner of Las Lomas" (Fuentes) **113**:242
The Prisoner of Second Avenue (Simon) **6**:504, 506; **31**:394-96; **70**:241
The Prisoner of Sex (Mailer) **2**:262; **3**:315; **4**:321-23; **8**:370, 373; **11**:341, 344; **39**:417, 420; **74**:205, 225-27; **111**:103
"The Prisoner of Zenda" (Wilbur) **110**:385
"Prisoner Who Wore Glasses" (Head) **67**:111
"El prisonero" (Paz) **19**:366; **119**:422
"El prisonero" (Roa Bastos) **45**:345
"Prisoners" (Boland) **40**:98; **67**:43
"Prisoners" (Komunyakaa) **94**:226
Prisoner's Dilemma (Powers) **93**:277, 279-86, 301
"A Prisoner's Ode to a Fine Lady from the Past" (Faludy) **42**:142
Prisoners of Jebs (Saro-Wiwa) **114**:254
Prisoners of Power (Strugatskii and Strugatskii) **27**:437
The Prisoners of September (Garfield) **12**:231-32, 236, 238-39
Prisoners of Silence: Breaking the Bonds of Adult Illiteracy in the United States (Kozol) **17**:255
The Prison-House of Language (Jameson) **142**:216-17, 225, 227, 260-61
Prisons (Settle) **61**:372-74, 379-86
"Privacy" (Rexroth) **112**:404
The Private Art (Grigson) **39**:332
"Private Audience" (Roa Bastos)
See "Audiencia privada"
Private Contentment (Price) **63**:325
"A Private Correspondence on Reality" (Graves) **45**:165
"Private Detentions" (Thomas) **132**:381
The Private Dining Room (Nash) **23**:322
"Private Domain" (McPherson) **19**:309; **77**:360, 366
"Private Drive" (Howard) **7**:165
The Private Ear (Shaffer) **5**:387
"Private Eye Lettuce" (Brautigan) **12**:59
Private Eyes: Adventures with the Saturday Gang (Kingman) **17**:245
A Private Function (Bennett) **77**:98, 101
"Private Ground" (Plath) **111**:203-04
Private Ground (Levi) **41**:247-48
"Private Hell" (Weller) **26**:445-46
"Private John Daniel Ramey" (Hersey) **81**:329
"Private Joy" (Prince) **35**:324-26
"Private Life" (Arreola)
See "La vida privada"
"The Private Life" (Mueller) **51**:281
Private Life (Elliott) **47**:108, 110
The Private Life (Mueller) **13**:399-400; **51**:281
A Private Life (Mueller)
See "The Private Life"
A Private Life (Seton) **27**:429-30
Private Life of an Indian Prince (Anand) **23**:13, 17; **93**:24-5, 29, 43, 50-2
"The Private Life of Mr. Bidwell" (Thurber) **5**:431
The Private Life of Sherlock Holmes (Wilder) **20**:463-64
Private Lives: An Intimate Comedy (Coward) **1**:64; **9**:173; **29**:133, 135-39; **51**:69-73, 75, 77
"A Private Lot" (Ghose) **42**:179
A Private Mythology (Sarton) **4**:471; **49**:314, 320
"Private Obsession" (Butler) **121**:143
"Private Parts" (Hope) **52**:211
Private Parts: A Memoir (Metcalf) **37**:301-03, 305-06
Private Parts, and Other Tales (Hope) **52**:210-11, 217
Private Potter (Harwood) **32**:222
"Private Sadness" (Kaufman) **49**:206
A Private Signal (Howes) **15**:289-90
A Private Treason (James) **122**:133
"Private Tuition by Mr. Bose" (Desai) **97**:150, 152-53, 171
"Private View" (Havel)
See "Vernisáz"
A Private View (Brookner) **136**:107-11, 132
A Private View (Havel) **58**:237-41, 243, 245; **123**:187-88, 196-97
"The Private War of Private Jacob" (Haldeman) **61**:177
"Private Worship" (Van Doren) **10**:495
The Private Wound (Day Lewis) **6**:128
Privateers (Bova) **45**:74
Privates on Parade (Nichols) **36**:327-28, 332; **65**:160-65
"Privilege" (Smith) **12**:543
The Privilege (Kumin) **28**:220
"Privilege of Being" (Hass) **99**:140, 142
"A Privileged Moment" (Day Lewis) **10**:131
Privileged Ones (Coles) **108**:194
"Privilegio del suicida" (Castellanos) **66**:53
The Prize (Wallace) **7**:509; **13**:567-68, 570
Prize Stock (Oe)
See *Shiiku*
"Prize-Winning Blank Verse" (Wilson) **24**:481
Prizzi's Family (Condon) **45**:104; **100**:92-5, 100, 109-11, 113
Prizzi's Glory (Condon) **100**:93-5, 100, 109-11, 113
Prizzi's Honor (Condon) **45**:99, 104-05; **100**:91-5, 97-8, 100, 102, 104-07, 109-13
Prizzi's Money (Condon) **100**:108-13
"The Pro" (Updike) **23**:473
"Pro femina" (Kizer) **39**:171; **80**:174-75, 178-79, 181-82, 184
Pro patria (Sender)
See *Iman*
"Próba rekonstrukcji" (Rozewicz) **139**:249
"Próba rozwiązania mitologii" (Herbert) **43**:187
A Probable Volume of Dreams (Bell) **8**:64-6; **31**:46-7, 49
Probing the Limits of Representation: Nazism and the Final Solution (Friedlander) **90**:120-1
"A Problem from Milton" (Wilbur) **3**:533
"A Problem in Spatial Composition" (Warren) **10**:522; **39**:270, 274
"The Problem of Anxiety" (Koch) **44**:246
"The Problem of Belief and the Problems of Cognition" (Brooks) **110**:15, 34-5
"The Problem of Change in Literary History" (White) **148**:286
"The Problem of Fornication in the Blarney Chronicle" (Durcan) **43**:116
The Problem of Pain (Lewis) **3**:296; **6**:308; **14**:322-23; **124**:232, 246
The Problem of the Green Capsule (Carr) **3**:101
"The Problem of the Text" (Bakhtin) **83**:9, 40
"The Problem Shop" (Rooke) **25**:394
"Problemas del subdesarrollo" (Guillén) **48**:159
"Problematica de la actual novela Latinoamericano" (Carpentier) **38**:94
"Problems" (Updike) **15**:544
Problems, and Other Stories (Updike) **15**:544-48; **139**:333, 336
"The Problems of a Catholic Writer" (Endō) **99**:285
"Problems of Adjustment in Survivors of Natural/Unnatural Disasters" (Oates) **6**:370
Problems of Dostoevsky's Poetics (Bakhtin)
See *Problemy tvorčestva Dostoevskogo*
"Problems of Knowledge" (Warren) **13**:573
Problems of Knowledge and Freedom (Chomsky) **132**:38
Problems of the Theatre (Dürrenmatt) **8**:194, 197; **11**:170, 173; **15**:199; **43**:123
"Problems of Underdevelopment" (Guillén)
See "Problemas del subdesarrollo"
"Problems Problems" (Bachmann) **69**:46-7
Problemy tvorčestva Dostoevskogo (Bakhtin) **83**:3-4, 6, 9, 13, 16, 18, 24-5, 30, 33, 40
"Procedures for Underground" (Atwood) **25**:67
Procedures for Underground (Atwood) **3**:20; **4**:24; **8**:30-1; **13**:44; **25**:63, 67; **84**:68
Proceed, Sergeant Lamb (Graves) **39**:322
Le procès (Welles) **20**:438-42, 444-45, 448, 450; **80**:389, 391, 396
Procès de Jeanne d'Arc (Bresson) **16**:105, 109, 113-15
Le procès de Shamgorod (Wiesel) **37**:452
"Process" (Livesay) **79**:338
"Processes" (Tomlinson) **13**:549
"The Procession" (Brodsky) **50**:120
"Procession" (Soyinka) **44**:285
"A Procession at Candlemas" (Clampitt) **32**:115-17
"The Procession of Life" (O'Connor) **23**:329
"Procession with the Madonna" (Yevtushenko) **3**:547
"Processional" (Enright) **31**:150
Le procès-verbal (Le Clézio) **31**:243-44, 251; **155**:80, 86-7, 115
Prochain Episode (Aquin) **15**:15, 17
"Prochorus Thompson" (Beer) **58**:36
"Prodigal" (Hoffman) **141**:295-96
"The Prodigal" (Simic) **130**:329
"The Prodigal" (Vanderhaeghe) **41**:452
The Prodigal Daughter (Archer) **28**:13-14
"The Prodigal Parent" (Gallant) **38**:190
"The Prodigal Son" (Bishop) **4**:66
"The Prodigal Son" (Bly) **38**:57-8; **128**:45
"Prodigal Son" (Montague) **46**:265
"The Prodigal Son" (Rozewicz) **139**:273
"The Prodigal Son" (White) **69**:403
The Prodigal Son (Hughes) **35**:218
"La prodigiosa tarde de Baltazar" (García Márquez) **27**:147-48; **47**:146, 151
"El prodigioso miligramo" (Arreola) **147**:31
"Prodigy" (Simic) **22**:382; **49**:337-38, 341; **130**:302, 317
"The Produce District" (Gunn) **32**:211
The Producers (Brooks) **12**:75-6, 78-82
"Proem" (McAuley) **45**:250
"Proem" (Paz) **65**:190
Proêmes (Ponge) **18**:417
The Profane Art (Oates) **33**:293
"La profesora" (Valenzuela) **104**:357
Le Professeur Taranne (Adamov) **25**:12, 14, 19-20
Professing Poetry (Wain) **11**:563-64
"Professing Stein/Stein Professing" (Bernstein) **142**:19
"Profession" (Asimov) **26**:53
"Profession" (Rodriguez) **155**:279, 312
Professional Correctness (Fish) **142**:201, 204-05, 207, 209
Professional Foul (Stoppard) **29**:395, 397, 404; **34**:272; **91**:190

"A Professional of Rememberances" (Cabral de Melo Neto)
See "O profissional da memória"
Professional Secrets (Cocteau) **8**:145-46
Professione: Reporter (Antonioni) **144**:36-37, 42
"The Professor" (Farrell) **66**:129
"Professor" (Hughes) **35**:215
"The Professor" (Valenzuela)
See "La profesora"
The Professor (Warner) **45**:429-32, 435, 437-41
"Professor A. Donda" (Lem) **149**:152
"Professor Cheeta" (Anand) **23**:18
"Professor Corcoran's Boxes" (Lem) **149**:150
"Professor Heller and the Boots" (Davie) **10**:124
"Professor Klaeber's Nasty Dream" (Raine) **32**:349
"Professor Nobody's Little Lectures on Supernatural Horror" (Ligotti) **44**:53-4
The Professor of Desire (Roth) **9**:460-62; **15**:449, 451-52, 455; **22**:354; **47**:359, 364; **66**:417, 420; **86**:255, 258; **119**:128, 138
"Professor Sea Gull" (Mitchell) **98**:168, 181, 187
Professor Taranne (Adamov)
See *Le Professeur Taranne*
Professors and Gods: Last Oxford Lectures on Poetry (Fuller) **4**:178
The Professor's Daughter (Read) **4**:444; **25**:376, 379
"The Professor's Houses" (Le Guin) **136**:376
"The Professor's Morning Ride" (Simmons) **43**:414
"Profile" (Auden) **14**:27; **43**:15
"The Profile on the Pillow" (Randall) **135**:386-87, 389, 396-97
Profiles of the Future: An Enquiry into the Limits of the Possible (Clarke) **35**:117, 128-29
"O profissional da memória" (Cabral de Melo Neto) **76**:169
Profit Over People (Chomsky) **132**:72-4
The Profits of Religion: An Essay in Economic Interpretation (Sinclair) **63**:346-47
Profound Today (Cendrars) **106**:191-92
"Profumo" (Muldoon) **72**:277
"De profundis" (Gascoyne) **45**:157
"Progenitor" (Zamora) **89**:384, 387
"Pro-Girl" (Ian) **21**:183
"Prognosis" (MacNeice) **53**:237
"Prognosis" (Roethke) **19**:397
"Prognostic" (Laughlin) **49**:220
"Program" (Burke) **24**:119
"The Program" (Fearing) **51**:106
A Program for Survival (Ruark) **3**:441
"Programme Note" (Tomlinson) **45**:397-98
"Progress" (MacCaig) **36**:285
The Progress of a Crime (Symons) **14**:522
"The Progress of Faust" (Shapiro) **53**:334
The Progress of Julius (du Maurier) **59**:284, 286
"The Progress of Love" (Munro) **50**:208-09, 211-12, 215, 217-18; **95**:306, 309
The Progress of Love (Munro) **50**:208-13, 215-19; **95**:318, 320
Progress of Stories (Riding) **7**:375
"Progression" (Christie) **110**:126
"Progulka" (Akhmadulina) **53**:15
Prohibido suicidarse en primavera (Casona) **49**:42-5, 48, 50
"Project" (Ammons) **25**:43
Project for a Revolution in New York (Robbe-Grillet)
See *Projet pour une révolution à New York*
"Project for a Trip to China" (Sontag) **13**:516, 518
Projective Verse (Olson) **6**:386; **11**:415-17; **29**:326, 335-37
Projet pour une révolution à New York (Robbe-Grillet) **2**:376-77; **4**:448, 450; **6**:464-65; **8**:454; **10**:437; **14**:462; **43**:366; **128**:350, 352-53, 360, 363
"Prolegomena to a Third Surrealist Manifesto or Not" (Breton) **54**:16
A Prolegomenon to a Theodicy (Rexroth) **22**:344; **49**:279, 285; **112**:375
"Proletarian Literature: A Political Autopsy" (Rahv) **24**:355
"The Proletariat Does Not Need Psychosis" (Yevtushenko) **126**:397
The Prolific and the Devourer (Auden) **14**:31; **43**:14-15, 26; **123**:6, 8
"Prolog" (Dixon) **52**:97
"Prolog" (Herbert) **43**:186
"Prólogo" (Guillén) **48**:160
Prólogos (Cela) **122**:22-27
"Prologue" (MacLeish) **8**:361
"Prologue" (Seifert) **93**:329-30
"Prologue" (Silkin) **43**:401
"Prologue" (Yevtushenko) **26**:461
Prologue (Brady)
See *The Unmaking of a Dancer*
"Prologue: An Interim" (Levertov)
See "Interim"
"Prologue at Sixty" (Auden) **14**:27; **43**:18; **123**:47
"Prologue for a Play" (Ciardi) **40**:157
"Prologue in Heaven" (Butor) **8**:118
"Prologue in the Theater" (Butor) **8**:118
"Prologue to an Autobiography" (Naipaul) **37**:325-29
A Prologue to Love (Caldwell) **28**:63
"Prologue to 'The Invention of Morel'" (Borges) **48**:47
"La prolongada busca de Tai An" (Bioy Casares) **88**:69
Proluky (Hrabal) **67**:122
"Promenade" (Ignatow) **40**:258
Promenade (Fornés) **39**:138; **61**:130-33, 140
"Promenade on Any Street" (Kunitz) **148**:87
"Proměny" (Seifert) **93**:342
La promesse de l'aube (Gary) **25**:185-86
"Prometheus" (Gray) **41**:179, 181
"Prometheus" (McAuley) **45**:246
"Prometheus" (Tomlinson) **4**:544; **13**:546, 548-49; **45**:392-93, 401
Prometheus Bound (Lowell) **3**:301; **8**:357; **11**:324; **15**:349; **124**:289
"Prometheus in Straits" (Ransom) **2**:363
"Prometheus Loved Us" (Barnard) **48**:25, 27
"Prometheus on His Crag" (Hughes) **37**:174-75, 177
Prometheus on His Crag (Hughes) **119**:272
Promieniowanie Ojcostwa (John Paul II) **128**:165, 168-69
Die Prominenten (Bernhard)
See *Die Berühmten*
"The Promise" (Steinbeck) **9**:515
The Promise (Buck) **11**:76-7
The Promise (Potok) **2**:338-39; **7**:321; **26**:369-70, 372-73, 376; **112**:260-61, 267, 276, 282, 290
Promise and Fulfillment: Palestine 1917-1949 (Koestler) **3**:271
Promise at Dawn (Gary)
See *La promesse de l'aube*
The Promise of Joy (Drury) **37**:107
Promise of Love (Renault) **17**:389-90
"Promise of Rain" (Taylor) **37**:411; **44**:305-06; **50**:260; **71**:299, 304
The Promise of Space (Clarke) **35**:117-18
The Promise: Requiem to the Detective Novel (Dürrenmatt) **8**:196
"The Promised Land" (Breytenbach) **126**:82
The Promised Land (Berton) **104**:44-6
Promised Land (Parker) **27**:363, 366-67
Promised Lands (Sontag) **31**:411
"The Promised One" (Wright) **53**:419
The Promisekeeper (Newman) **2**:311
Promises: Poems, 1954-1956 (Warren) **4**:578; **6**:557; **8**:539, 542; **10**:520, 522; **13**:572, 575, 577-78, 581; **39**:265-66, 270; **59**:297
"Promises, Promises" (Cassity) **42**:99
"Promises, Promises" (Muldoon) **32**:321; **72**:268
Promises, Promises (Simon) **31**:394, 403-04; **70**:235
Promises to Keep (Corcoran) **17**:73-4
Promises to Keep (Fleming) **37**:127-28
"A Promising Career" (Gellhorn) **60**:187-88
A Promising Career (Brown) **63**:56-7
Pronto (Leonard) **120**:291, 293-94, 304
"Proof" (Milosz) **22**:308
"The Proof" (Wilbur) **110**:386
"The Proof" (Winters) **32**:467-68
Proof (Francis) **42**:153, 159-60; **102**:131, 139, 148
"The Proofreader" (Huddle) **49**:182
"Propaganda Poem" (Ostriker) **132**:320
A Proper Gentleman (Scannell) **49**:332
"A Proper Halo" (Redgrove) **41**:359
A Proper Marriage (Lessing) **2**:238; **3**:291; **94**:256-57, 281, 286
"The Proper Respect" (Allende) **97**:29, 32
Proper Studies: The Proper Study of Mankind Is Man (Huxley) **18**:269; **35**:242; **79**:309
"Property" (Gilliatt) **10**:229
Property Of (Hoffman) **51**:199-202
"The Property of Colette Nervi" (Trevor) **71**:329; **116**:358
"Prophecy" (Hall) **151**:188, 191, 197
"The Prophecy" (Miller) **47**:249
Prophecy (Handke)
See *Weissagung*
"Prophecy on Lethe" (Kunitz) **148**:70, 78-80, 95
Prophesy Deliverance! (West) **134**:325-26, 328, 333, 346, 359
"The Prophet" (Blunden) **56**:29
"The Prophet of the New World" (Livesay) **79**:345
Prophetic Fragments (West) **134**:328, 353, 368, 376
Prophetic Thought in Postmodern Times (West) **134**:376
The Prophets (Mrozek) **3**:345
Prophets (Walker) **1**:351
The Prophet's Camel Bell (Laurence) **50**:314, 319; **62**:274, 278-81
The Prophet's Steps (Blaga)
See *Paşii profetului*
"Proposal for a Survey" (Adcock) **41**:16
"Propositions on the Death of Ana" (Guillén) **48**:159
The Proprietor (Schlee) **35**:374-76
"Propriety" (Moore) **2**:291
Proprioception (Olson) **5**:326
"Prosa aus der flüstergalerie" (Jandl) **34**:196
Prosanatolizmí (Elytis) **15**:220; **49**:106, 108, 115; **100**:155, 187, 189
"Prosas da maré na Jaqueira" (Cabral de Melo Neto) **76**:169
Proschai, Gul'sary! (Aitmatov) **71**:3, 7, 13-15, 17-19, 21-2
Prose and Poetry (Senghor) **130**:250
"Prose and Poetry of It All; Or, Dippy Verses" (Barth) **51**:26
"Prose and Verse" (Eliot) **113**:220
"Prose du transsibérien et de la petite Jeanne de France" (Cendrars) **18**:90, 92, 94, 97; **106**:151, 158-59, 163, 167, 177, 180-81, 184, 186, 189-90, 192, 196-97
"Prose of the Trans-Siberian" (Cendrars)
See "Prose du transsibérien et de la petite Jeanne de France"
"Prose Poem" (Tomlinson) **45**:393, 401
"The Prose Poem as an Evolving Form" (Bly) **128**:17, 24
"Prose Rhythms" (Voznesensky) **57**:425
"Proseball: Sports, Stories, and Style" (Hall) **37**:149
The Proselytizer (Mano) **2**:270
"Proserpina" (Lewis) **41**:253
Proserpina and the Devil (Wilder) **82**:384

"Prosody of the Transsiberian" (Cendrars)
See "Prose du transsibérien et de la petite Jeanne de France"
"Prospect" (Creeley) **78**:153
"Prospect" (Plath) **111**:201
The Prospect before Us (Dos Passos) **25**:145
The Prospect before Us (Gold) **4**:189; **42**:188; **152**:135, 144
"A Prospect of Swans" (Blunden) **56**:45
"Prospecting" (Ammons) **108**:20
"Prospective Immigrants Please Note" (Rich) **18**:446
"Prospects for an Expedition" (Federspiel) **42**:146
"Prospero and the Sycorax" (Hughes) **37**:177
Prospero on the Island (Thomas) **37**:416; **107**:315, 330, 349
Prospero's Cell: A Guide to the Landscape and Manners of the Island of Corcyra (Durrell) **8**:193; **13**:188
"Prospero's Soliloquy" (Zaturenska) **6**:586
Prostho Plus (Anthony) **35**:36
"Protean Man" (Lifton) **67**:142
"Protection" (Jacobsen) **48**:196, 198
"Protective Footwear" (Bowering) **47**:24-5
Protective Footwear: Stories and Fables (Bowering) **47**:24-5
"Protest" (Havel) **25**:227-28, 230; **58**:237-40, 243; **65**:413, 439
Protest (Havel) **123**:187-89, 191-92, 199
"A Protest against the Sun" (Millhauser) **54**:324-27
Protestant and Roman Catholic Ethics: Prospects for Rapprochement (Gustafson) **100**:197
"Protestant Drums, Tyrone, 1966" (Heaney) **74**:167
The Protestant Era (Tillich) **131**:354
"Protestant Old Folks' Coach Tour" (Durcan) **43**:114
"Proteus" (Borges) **13**:110
Proteus (West) **33**:431-32
"Prothalamium" (Smith) **15**:514
"Protivosloyaniye ochery" (Voznesensky) **15**:556
Protochny Lane (Ehrenburg)
See *In Protochny Lane*
"Protocol" (Lightfoot) **26**:281
The Proud and the Free (Fast) **131**:79
"Proud Are the Dead" (Oe) **86**:226-27
Proud Are the Dead (Oe) **86**:227
Proud Flesh (Humphrey) **45**:198-99
Proud Flesh (Warren) **8**:536; **53**:369
The Proud Highway: Saga of a Desperate Southern Gentleman (Thompson) **104**:348, 350
"The Proud Lady" (Dinesen) **10**:149
Proud Riders and Other Poems (Davis) **49**:83
"The Proud Walkers" (Still) **49**:364
"Proust" (Beckett) **1**:22; **10**:33, 35; **11**:36, 40; **18**:46; **57**:79, 95
The Proust Screenplay: À la recherche du temps perdu (Pinter) **15**:421-23; **73**:277
"Provazolezci" (Klima) **56**:172
"Prove It All Night" (Springsteen) **17**:483, 490
"Prove It to You One More Time" (Kristofferson) **26**:270
Provence (Mayle) **89**:152
The Proverb, and Other Stories (Aymé) **11**:21
"Proverbs" (Bennett) **28**:29
"Proverbs" (Gotlieb) **18**:193
"Provest'" (Pasternak) **18**:386
"Provide, Provide" (Frost) **1**:110; **9**:228; **15**:250; **44**:457
"Provided For" (Reznikoff) **9**:450
Providence (Brookner) **32**:59-61; **34**:139, 142; **51**:61-2, 65; **136**:83, 89-90, 97-101, 103-04, 111-13, 117
Providence (Resnais) **16**:515-18
Providence (Wolff) **41**:461-62
Providence Island (Willingham) **5**:511-12; **51**:408-09, 411
The Province of the Heart (McGinley) **14**:367
The Province of the Human (Canetti)
See *Die Provinz des Menschen: Aufzeichnungen, 1942-1972*
"Provincetown" (Dudek) **11**:159
Provincetown (Oliver) **98**:276
"Provincetown: Short-Suite" (Olson) **28**:343
"Provincial" (Barnard) **48**:25
"Provincial I" (Barnard) **48**:26
"Provincial II" (Barnard) **48**:26
"The Provincial Consciousness" (Stegner) **49**:359; **81**:339
"Provincial Narratives" (Paulin) **37**:352
"The Provincial Night" (Landolfi) **49**:217
A Provincial Story (Leonov)
See *Provintsialnaya istoriya*
"Provincialism the Enemy" (Pound) **7**:332; **112**:315
The Proving Trail (L'Amour) **25**:282
Provintsialnaya istoriya (Leonov) **92**:270
Die Provinz des Menschen: Aufzeichnungen, 1942-1972 (Canetti) **75**:144; **86**:295, 301
"Provisional Conclusions" (Montale) **7**:224
"Provisional Institutions" (Bernstein) **142**:57
Provo d'orchestra (Fellini) **16**:300; **85**:60, 69, 81
Provocation (Lem)
See *Prowokacja*
Provocations (Padilla) **38**:351
"The Prowler" (Malouf) **28**:269
The Prowler (Gunnars) **69**:264-66, 268
"The Prowler in the City at the End of the War" (Ellison) **139**:145
"Prowlers" (Baxter) **78**:27, 30
Prowokacja (Lem) **149**:113, 116, 263
Proxopera (Kiely) **23**:264-66; **43**:240, 242-43, 245
Der Proze um des Esels Schatten (Duerrenmatt) **102**:62
The Prudent Heart (Steele) **45**:364
Prufrock and Other Observations (Eliot) **41**:150, 161; **55**:350, 352, 354-55, 374
"Prufrock's Dilemma" (Berryman) **8**:91; **10**:45
"The Pruned Tree" (Moss) **50**:353
"Pruning Fruit Trees" (Pack) **13**:439
"Prurient" (Matthews) **40**:325
Prussian Nights: A Poem (Solzhenitsyn)
See *Prusskie nochi: pozma napisappaja vlagere v 1950*
Prusskie nochi: pozma napisappaja vlagere v 1950 (Solzhenitsyn) **9**:506-07; **10**:479, 483; **18**:499
Prywatne obowiazki (Milosz) **56**:237
Przejscie podziemne (Kieslowski) **120**:233
"Przekladaniec" (Lem) **149**:149
"przerwana rozmowa" (Rozewicz) **139**:298
"Przerwany egzamin" (Rozewicz) **139**:227, 249
"Przesłuchanie anioła" (Herbert) **43**:187
Przy budowie (Konwicki) **117**:284
Przypadek (Kieslowski) **120**:207-09, 232, 234 247, 256-57, 260
Przyrost naturalny: Biografia sztuki teatralnej (Rozewicz) **9**:464; **139**:229-30, 232-33, 235, 240-42, 276-78, 280-83, 293
"Ps. 19" (Avison) **4**:37; **97**:78, 81, 88, 93
P.S Wilkinson (Bryan) **29**:100-01
P.S. Your Cat Is Dead (Kirkwood) **9**:319
"Psalm" (Blaga) **75**:74, 77
"A Psalm" (Blunden) **56**:39
"Psalm" (Celan) **19**:94; **53**:70, 73, 75-6; **82**:42, 46, 48
"Psalm" (Rosenthal) **28**:394
"Psalm I" (Ginsberg) **36**:182, 195
"Psalm 72: Man Declared a Treasure" (Enright) **31**:149
"Psalm Concerning the Castle" (Levertov) **66**:236
"Psalm of Childhood" (Jennings) **131**:236
Psalmi (Arghezi) **80**:5-8
"Psalmistul singuratic" (Arghezi) **80**:2, 4-5
"Psalms" (Stern) **40**:408
Psalms (Arghezi)
See *Psalmi*
Psalms of Struggle (Cardenal) **31**:70, 80
The Psalms with Their Spoils (Silkin) **43**:401-03
"Psi" (Tolson) **105**:257, 277, 285
"Psi i knjige" (Kiš) **57**:240, 243
A psicologia da composicão com a fábula de Anfion e antiode (Cabral de Melo Neto) **76**:152-53, 157
Psion (Vinge) **30**:412
"P-s-s-t, Partner, Your Peristalsis Is Showing" (Perelman) **49**:259
Psuedo (Gary) **25**:188
"The Psyche of Riverside Drive" (Simpson) **149**:351
"The Psychedelic Children" (Koontz) **78**:201
"Psycho" (Ian) **21**:183
Psycho (Bloch) **33**:83-5
Psycho (Hitchcock) **16**:342-43, 347-49, 352, 356, 359
Psycho II (Bloch) **33**:84-6
"Psycho Killer" (Byrne) **26**:94-5
"Psychoanalysis" (Durrell) **27**:97
"Psychoanalysis: An Elegy" (Spicer) **18**:508
"Psychoanalysis and History" (Lifton) **67**:142
"The Psychohistorians" (Asimov) **26**:60
Ein psycholog erlebt das konzentrationslager (Frankl) **93**:193-95, 202, 206, 208-10, 216, 222-23
The Psychological Novel, 1900-1950 (Edel) **29**:168
La psychologie de l'art (Malraux) **4**:324-25; **9**:353, 358; **15**:351; **57**:301
"Psychology and Art" (Auden) **4**:34
"Psychology and Form" (Burke) **24**:118
"Psychology and the Troubadours" (Pound) **48**:285; **112**:310
Psychology in Action (Hyde) **21**:174
The Psychology of Art (Malraux)
See *La psychologie de l'art*
Psychology of Composition (Cabral de Melo Neto)
See *A psicologia da composicão com a fábula de Anfion e antiode*
Psychoneurotic Phantasies () **65**:444-48
"Psychopathologies of Black Envy" (Gubar) **145**:
"The Psychopathology of Everyday Life" (Matthews) **40**:323-24
"Psychopolis" (McEwan) **66**:278-82
Psychotherapy and Existentialism: Selected Papers on Logotherapy (Frankl) **93**:208, 218
"Ptitsata s motornoto surtse" (Bagryana) **10**:12
The Puberty Tree (Thomas) **132**:382
Pubis angelical (Puig) **28**:372; **65**:266, 269-70; **133**:300, 305, 324, 329, 338, 344-48, 350, 352-55, 372, 374-80
"Public and Political Poems" (Ferlinghetti) **6**:184; **27**:139
"Public Bar" (Enright) **31**:150
"Public Bart" (Hughes) **14**:271
The Public Burning (Coover) **15**:142-43, 145; **32**:122, 124-25; **46**:116-17, 119-22; **87**:24-5, 28-32, 35-9, 41-3, 46-7, 50, 56
"Public Execution in Pictures" (Achebe) **127**:31
"Public House Drunk" (Betjeman) **2**:61
The Public Image (Spark) **2**:416, 418; **3**:464; **5**:400; **13**:524; **40**:399-400
"Public Life" (Fearing) **51**:110
Public Order (Sender)
See *O.P.: Orden público*
"Public Outcry" (Oates) **15**:402
"A Public Pool" (Adams) **46**:21
The Public Prosecutor, and Other Plays (Hochwälder)
See *Der Öffentliche Ankläger*
"Public Silence, Private Terror" (Allison) **153**:4
"The Public Son of a Public Man" (Spender) **41**:428-29
"Public Speech and Private Speech in Poetry" (MacLeish) **68**:288, 290

Public Speech: Poems (MacLeish) **8**:361
"The Public vs. the Late Mr. William Butler Yeats" (Auden) **123**:6, 8, 21, 36
"The Public Ward" (Johnston) **51**:250
"The Public-House" (Davies) **23**:142
"Publicity Campaign" (Clarke) **136**:212
Publikumsbeschimpfung (Handke) **5**:166; **8**:262-63; **10**:256; **15**:265-68; **38**:215, 217, 228; **134**:106-07, 128, 137, 143, 157-58, 160, 175
"The Publisher to the Poet" (Laughlin) **49**:220
"La Pucelle" (Breytenbach) **126**:72
La pucelle (Audiberti) **38**:23
"Pueblerina" (Arreola) **147**:10, 17
"Pueblo, 1950" (Zamora) **89**:384, 386, 394
Pueblo en marcha (Goytisolo) **133**:45
Los pueblos (Azorín) **11**:24
Puella (Dickey) **47**:93-4; **109**:245, 264-65
"Puella Mea" (Cummings) **12**:146
The Puerile Lovers (Crommelynck)
See *Les amants puérils*
"La puerta cerrada" (Donoso) **4**:127; **32**:157
"Las puertas del cielo" (Cortázar) **33**:128
"Puerto Rican Song" (Guillén) **48**:158
"Puffball" (Weldon) **122**:255
Puffball (Weldon) **19**:468-70; **36**:446
"Puget Sound Country" (Davis) **49**:92
"The Pugilist at Rest" (Jones) **81**:63, 65, 67, 69
The Pugilist at Rest (Jones) **81**:61-70
I pugnalatori (Sciascia) **8**:474
Puhua, vastata, opettaa (Haavikko) **34**:179
"Pukeko" (Frame) **96**:201
Pułapka (Rozewicz) **139**:238-40, 265, 267, 292-93
"The Pull" (Olds) **85**:306, 308
Pull Down Vanity and Other Stories (Fiedler) **4**:160
"Pull My Daisy" (Ginsberg) **109**:365
"Pull of the Earth" (Plumly) **33**:312
"Pulled Up" (Byrne) **26**:94-5
"The Pulling" (Olds) **85**:307-08
"Pulling a Rowboat Up Among Lake Reeds" (Bly) **128**:13
Pullman Car Hiawatha (Wilder) **82**:345, 359, 364, 386-87, 390
Pulp (Bukowski) **108**:93-95, 115, 116
Pulp Fiction (Tarantino) **125**:349-65, 367-69, 371-83
"Pulse" (Dickey) **3**:127
"The Pulse" (Levertov) **5**:249
The Pump House Gang (Wolfe) **35**:451-54, 459,, 464; **147**:306, 310, 320, 357
"Pump It Up" (Costello) **21**:69
"Pumping" (Smith) **12**:539
The Pumpkin Eater (Mortimer) **5**:298-99
Pumpkin Seed Point (Waters) **88**:347, 356, 363-65
"The Pumpkins" (Pinget) **37**:364
"The Punch" (Friedman) **56**:97
Punch and Judy (The Brothers Quay) **95**:330-31
"Punch Minus Judy" (Simic) **130**:306
Punch: The Immortal Liar, Documents in His History (Aiken) **52**:20, 22, 24
Punch's Secret (Sarton) **4**:472
"Punctuation as Score" (Metcalf) **37**:307
"Puncture" (Ransom) **2**:363; **4**:431
The Puncture (Duerrenmatt) **102**:54
Punish the Sinners (Saul) **46**:366
"Punishable Innocence" (Breytenbach) **23**:87
"Punishment" (Heaney) **7**:149; **25**:243; **74**:158, 193
"Punishment" (Ritsos) **31**:325
Punishment Room (Ichikawa) **20**:181-82
Punishments (King) **145**:353-54
Punk et Punk et Colégram (Arrabal) **58**:18
"Punky Reggae Party" (Marley) **17**:271-72
"Punky's Dilemma" (Simon) **17**:459
Punta de Plata (Arreola) **147**:4
"The Pupils of the Eyes of Hungry People" (Hikmet) **40**:244
The Puppet Masters (Heinlein) **1**:139; **3**:225; **14**:247, 249, 254; **26**:178; **55**:303
Puppet on a Chain (MacLean) **50**:348; **63**:270
"The Puppet Show" (Rule) **27**:423
The Puppeteer (Kroetsch) **132**:262-63, 270-73, 275, 291-92, 294, 296
The Puppets (Haavikko)
See *Nuket*
The Puppy Sister (Hinton) **111**:90
Pupurupú (Ulibarrí) **83**:415-16
"Purdah" (Plath) **5**:345; **17**:363, 366; **51**:340-41, 343, 345; **111**:178, 210
"A Pure Accident" (Lavin) **4**:281; **99**:322
"Pure and Easy" (Townshend) **17**:528, 534
"Pure and Impure Poetry" (Warren) **8**:541
"The Pure and the Good" (Maclean) **78**:234-35
The Pure Clear Word: Essays on the Poetry of James Wright (Smith) **42**:346
"The Pure Food Act" (Murray) **40**:336
"The Pure Fury" (Roethke) **11**:486; **46**:363; **101**:265, 328, 331, 333
"Pure Memory" (Ondaatje) **51**:317
"Pure Sin" (Simon) **26**:413
Pure Smokey (Robinson) **21**:345-46, 349
"The Pure Suit of Happiness" (Swenson) **61**:395; **106**:322
"Purgation" (Dickey) **47**:93
"Purgatory" (Berryman) **62**:74
"Purgatory, Formerly Paradise" (Howard) **7**:170; **10**:276
"Purification" (Rozewicz) **139**:272
Purification (Williams) **71**:363, 369
"Purists Will Object" (Ashbery) **125**:4
"Puritan Poet Reel" (Buckley) **57**:126
Purity of Diction in English Verse (Davie) **5**:115; **8**:162, 167; **10**:123; **31**:113, 122
Purl and Plain, and Other Stories (Garnett) **3**:189
Purple America (Moody) **147**:171, 173-77, 179-88
"Purple Blooms" (Shields) **113**:426
The Purple Decades (Wolfe) **35**:464-66
Purple Dust (O'Casey) **5**:318, 320; **9**:407; **11**:408-10; **15**:405; **88**:270
Purple Gold Mountain (Ali) **69**:32
"The Purple Hat" (Welty) **1**:362; **14**:563
"Purple Loosestrife" (Ferron) **94**:120-21, 126
The Purple Plain (Bates) **46**:59-61, 64-5
Purple Rain (Prince) **35**:328-32
"The Purpose of the Moon" (Robbins) **32**:370
"The Purpose of This Creature Man" (Abbott) **48**:4-7
Purposes of Love (Renault)
See *Promise of Love*
"Les Pur-Sang" (Césaire) **19**:98
"Purse" (Gilliatt) **53**:145-46
A Purse of Coppers (O'Faolain) **1**:259; **14**:402; **32**:340, 343; **70**:317
"The Purse-Seine" (Blackburn) **9**:100; **43**:63
"The Pursuer" (Cortázar)
See "El Perseguidor"
"Pursuit" (Plath) **111**:165
"Pursuit" (Warren) **10**:525
Pursuit (Morgan) **6**:339-40
"The Pursuit of Gloom" (Willingham) **51**:403
Pursuit of Happiness (Jones) **52**:249
The Pursuit of Happiness (Rogers) **57**:360-64, 366-67
Pursuit of Honor (Sissman) **9**:491; **18**:488
The Pursuit of Love (Mitford) **44**:483, 485-87, 489-92
Pursuit of the Prodigal (Auchincloss) **9**:54; **45**:27
"A Pursuit Race" (Hemingway) **30**:179
"La Push" (Hugo) **32**:236
Push (Sapphire) **99**:82-8
A Pushcart at the Curb (Dos Passos) **15**:184; **25**:142-43
Pushkin (Troyat) **23**:457
Pushkin House (Bitov)
See *Pushkinskii dom*
"Pushkin's Photograph (1799-2099)" (Bitov) **59**:378
Pushkinskii dom (Bitov) **57**:114-24
The Pussy (McClure) **6**:317
"Pussywillows" (Lightfoot) **26**:278
Put On by Cunning (Rendell) **28**:387
Put Out More Flags (Waugh) **1**:359; **3**:513; **13**:585; **44**:522; **107**:359, 362, 370-71, 385, 393
Put Out the Lights (Seifert)
See *Zhasněte světla*
"Put the Money Down" (Townshend) **17**:534
"Put Your Head on My Shoulder" (Wilson)
See "Don't Talk"
"Put Your Muzzle Where Your Mouth Is (or shut up)" (Randall) **135**:390
"Put Yourself in My Shoes" (Carver) **55**:280; **126**:142-44, 164, 183
"Putamadre" (Dorfman) **77**:141-42, 144
Putëm vzaimnoj perepiski (Voinovich) **49**:375-77; **147**:270-71, 284
"Putney Garage" (Durcan) **70**:151-52
"Puttermesser and Xanthippe" (Ozick) **28**:349, 351; **62**:350-51; **155**:130-31, 170, 179, 181, 183, 189, 193, 208, 223
"Puttermesser: Her Work History, Her Ancestry, Her Afterlife" (Ozick) **28**:349; **155**:188
"Puttermesser Paired" (Ozick) **155**:167, 185
The Puttermesser Papers (Ozick) **155**:223
"Putting in the Person: Character and Abstraction in Current Writing and Painting" (Bradbury) **61**:34
"Putting in the Seed" (Frost) **26**:112
"Putting It All Away" (Dobyns) **37**:76
"Putting It Together" (Sondheim) **39**:174
Putting It Together (Sondheim) **147**:263-64
"Putting to Sea" (Bogan) **46**:84
"Putting Your Body to Sleep" (Dacey) **51**:81
Puut, kaikki heidän vihreytensä (Haavikko) **18**:205; **34**:170
"Puzzle" (Parra) **102**:350
"The Puzzle Factory" (Cassill) **4**:95
The Puzzle of Hind Foot (Strugatskii and Strugatskii) **27**:433
"The Puzzleheaded Girl" (Stead) **32**:408; **80**:305
The Puzzleheaded Girl (Stead) **2**:422-23; **5**:404; **32**:408-09; **80**:305, 323
"The Puzzling Nature of Blue" (Carey) **40**:133; **96**:25
"Pygmalion" (H. D.) **73**:104
"Pygmalion" (Hope)
See "The Invocation"
"Pygmy Twylyte" (Zappa) **17**:591
Pylon (Faulkner) **3**:153; **18**:143; **28**:140; **52**:112
"The Pylons" (Spender) **41**:418, 428
"pyramid" (Shange) **25**:402; **126**:352
The Pyramid (Golding) **1**:121-22; **2**:168; **3**:196, 198-200; **10**:237; **17**:172, 174, 176, 180; **27**:161, 163; **81**:315, 317-18, 322-23
"Pyramis; or, The House of Ascent" (Hope) **51**:213, 215, 217, 221
"Pyrography" (Ashbery) **13**:36; **15**:30; **25**:57; **77**:46
"Pyrography" (White) **110**:339, 343
"Pyrrhus et Cinéas" (Beauvoir) **31**:40-1
Pyrrhus et Cinéas (Beauvoir) **124**:134, 159-61
Pythagoras (Abse) **29**:17, 21-2
"Pythagoras and the Ladder" (Thurber) **125**:395
"Pythagoras in America" (Muldoon) **72**:281
"Pythagorean Silence" (Howe) **152**:193
Pythagorean Silence (Howe) **72**:195, 202, 207-08; **152**:152, 172, 186, 188-89, 192-93, 199, 201-02, 204-07, 232, 235
"The Pythoness" (Raine) **45**:333-34
The Pythoness and Other Poems (Raine) **45**:331-32, 334, 340
The Pyx (Buell) **10**:82
"Q" (Merrill) **8**:385-86; **13**:381
"Q & A" (Fearing) **51**:106
al- Qāhira al-jadīda (Mahfūz) **52**:292-93, 300; **55**:176
Qalb allayl (Mahfouz) **153**:235, 267
Qalb al-layl (Mahfūz) **55**:175

Qasr al-Shawq (Mahfouz) **153**:246-47, 249, 251-56, 282, 284-86, 293, 301, 304, 337, 372
Qasr al-Shawq (Mahfūz) **52**:293, 300; **55**:171, 174
QB VII (Uris) **32**:432-34
"Qiana" (Dorris) **109**:307
Quaderna (Cabral de Melo Neto) **76**:154, 158-59, 161, 168-69
Quaderno de quattro anni (Montale) **18**:340
Quadrille (Coward) **29**:136
Quadrille (Swinnerton) **31**:427
Quadrophenia (Townshend) **17**:532-40; **42**:379
Quaestio de fide apud s. Joannem a Cruce (John Paul II) **128**:192
Quag Keep (Norton) **12**:471
"The Quagga" (Enright) **31**:154
"Quai d'Orléans" (Bishop) **32**:42
The Quail and Autumn (Mahfouz)
See *al-Summan w'l-kharif*
Quail and Autumn (Mahfūz)
See *al-Summān wa-al-kharif*
"Quail for Mr. Forester" (Humphrey) **45**:193, 204
"A Quaint Disorder" (Scannell) **49**:328
Quake (Wurlitzer) **2**:484; **4**:597-98; **15**:588-89
"Quake Theory" (Olds) **32**:346; **85**:286
"The Quaker Graveyard at Nantucket (for Warren Winslow, Dead at Sea)" (Lowell) **1**:183; **2**:248; **4**:302; **8**:348, 350, 355, 358; **9**:335-37; **37**:234, 236; **124**:257, 261, 273, 288-89, 303
"Qualcosa era successo" (Buzzati) **36**:88, 92, 94, 96
The Quality of Hurt (Himes) **2**:195-96; **4**:229; **7**:159; **18**:248, 250; **58**:263-65; **108**:223, 228-29, 234, 241, 259-60
A Quality of Mercy (West) **96**:368
"Quality Time" (Kingsolver) **130**:73
Quand prime le spirituel (Beauvoir) **31**:38-9, 42; **44**:344-45; **71**:84
Quand vient le souvenir (Friedlander) **90**:111, 114-16,118, 121
Quantities (Howard) **7**:168; **10**:276; **47**:167-68
La Quarantaine (Le Clézio) **155**:87-8, 99-100, 103, 109
The Quarantine (Goytisolo)
See *La cuarentena*
"Il quarantotto" (Sciascia) **8**:474
The Quare Fellow (Behan) **1**:26; **8**:63-4; **11**:44; **15**:45; **79**:24-7, 34-6, 40-3, 47-9, 52-5, 58
"The Quarrel" (Brodkey) **56**:55-6, 63
"The Quarrel" (Buckler) **13**:119
"The Quarrel" (Kunitz) **148**:90-91
"Quarrel" (Voigt) **54**:430
"A Quarreling Pair" (Bowles) **68**:6-7
"The Quarry" (Clampitt) **32**:115
"Quarry" (Honig) **33**:212
"The Quarry" (Nemerov) **36**:305
The Quarry (Dürrenmatt)
See *Der Verdacht*
The Quarry (Eberhart) **11**:176
The Quarry Adventure (Kingman) **17**:243-44
Quartermaine's Terms (Gray) **36**:205-10
Quartet (Rhys)
See *Postures*
"A Quartet and Its Outcome" (Ferré)
See "Un cuarteto y su desenlace"
Quartet in Autumn (Pym) **13**:469-71; **19**:389; **37**:369, 372-73, 376-77; **111**:225-29, 231-32, 234-36, 242-44, 248-53, 258, 263, 266-71, 273, 275, 278, 280-85, 287
"Quartet: Uncollected Stories, 1979-1981" (O'Brien) **36**:340
"The Quartz-Stone" (Popa) **19**:373
Quasar (Butler) **121**:79
"Quasi una fantasia" (Montale) **18**:339
Quatorze juillet (Clair) **20**:61-2, 70
Quatrains (Hikmet) **40**:245
Les quatre cents coups (Truffaut) **20**:380, 382, 395, 399-400, 402-05, 407; **101**:370, 373, 375, 379, 381-82, 384-91, 396, 398-400, 403, 405-08, 410-11, 413
Les quatre vérités (Aymé) **11**:23
"89 et nous les noirs" (Damas) **84**:181
Le quatrième siècle (Glissant) **10**:231; **68**:172-78, 180-81, 183, 187-89
"Que así invade" (Aleixandre) **9**:12
"Que cante quetzal" (Allen) **84**:10
"Qué color" (Guillén) **48**:163-64
"Lo que el difunto dijo de sí mismo" (Parra) **102**:340
Qué He Hecho Yo para Merecer Ésto? (Almodovar) **114**:4, 6-7, 9, 11-13, 18-9, 23-8, 35, 39, 45-6, 49-53, 55
"A què lado de la cortina?" (Alegria) **57**:11-12
Que ma joie demeure (Giono) **4**:184; **11**:234
"Que m'accompagnent Kôras et Balafong" (Senghor) **54**:390, 395-98, 407, 409; **130**:246, 252, 255, 258, 267-68
"Lo que no se marchita" (Rodriguez) **10**:440
"Que siga el son" (Guillén) **79**:244
Que trate de España (Otero) **11**:425
"Quebec Night" (Gustafson) **36**:212
"The Queen" (Chappell) **40**:146
"Queen" (DeMarinis) **54**:101
"The Queen" (Nin) **127**:386
The Queen (Maysles and Maysles) **16**:440
Queen After Death (Montherlant)
See *Le reine morte*
The Queen against Defoe, and Other Stories (Heym) **41**:216-17
"Queen Bee" (Ihimaera) **46**:199-200
"Queen Bitch" (Bowie) **17**:58, 64
Queen Christina (Mamoulian) **16**:420-21, 423-24, 428
"The Queen Doll" (Fuentes)
See "La muñeca reina"
The Queen Elizabeth Story (Sutcliff) **26**:427-28, 432-33, 435, 439
"Queen for a Day" (Banks) **72**:5
"Queen Jane Approximately" (Dylan) **77**:174
The Queen of a Distant Country (Braine) **3**:86; **41**:58
"The Queen of Air and Darkness" (Anderson) **15**:12
The Queen of Air and Darkness (White) **30**:445-46
The Queen of Drum (Lewis) **27**:265
"The Queen of Egypt" (Schaeffer) **22**:369
The Queen of Egypt (Schaeffer) **22**:368-70
Queen of Greece (Tavel) **6**:529
"The Queen of Lop" (Johnston) **51**:239, 244
"Queen of Pentacles, Nine of Swords" (Hospital) **145**:304-05, 312
"Queen of Scots" (MacCaig) **36**:288
Queen of Stones (Tennant) **52**:399-401
Queen of Swords (Kotzwinkle) **35**:258
Queen of the Damned (Rice) **128**:279-80, 283, 293, 298-300, 302, 304, 311, 313, 318
The Queen of the Legion (Williamson) **29**:461
"Queen of the Night" (Oates) **33**:289
The Queen of What Ifs (Klein) **30**:242-43
The Queen on Tour (Abell) **15**:5
Queen Victoria (Streatfeild) **21**:402
Queen Victoria's Revenge (Harrison) **42**:202, 205
Queenie (Calisher) **2**:96; **134**:7, 20, 24, 26-8, 30-1, 35
"Queenie Fat and Thin" (Brooke-Rose) **40**:106
"Queenie White" (Bates) **46**:63
"Queens and Duchesses" (Johnston) **51**:244
The Queen's Gambit (Tevis) **42**:374-76
The Queens of France (Wilder) **15**:574; **82**:345, 362
The Queens of the Hive (Sitwell) **67**:325-28
"Queens of the Universe" (Sanchez) **116**:300
"The Queen's Red Race" (Asimov) **76**:320
Queer (Burroughs) **42**:77-8, 80-1; **109**:221, 229
"Queer Aztlan: The Re-formation of Chicano Tribe" (Moraga) **126**:295
"A Queer Heart" (Bowen) **22**:63
"A Queer Job" (Oe)
See "Kimyōna shigoto"
"A Queer Streak" (Munro) **50**:210, 214-16, 218-19
Quel bowling sul Tevere (Antonioni) **144**:38, 58, 62-62, 65-66, 70
"Quel histoire" (Grigson) **7**:137
Quel petit vélo à guidon chromé au fond de la cour? (Perec) **56**:257-58; **116**:232
Quelqu'un (Pinget) **13**:442
Quer pasticciacco brutto de via Merulana (Gadda) **11**:209, 216
Querelle de Brest (Genet) **5**:137-39; **44**:386, 388, 390; **46**:173, 176-77
Querelle of Brest (Genet)
See *Querelle de Brest*
Queremos tanto a Glenda (Cortázar) **33**:125-39; **34**:329, 334
"Queridinha da familia" (Dourado) **60**:85
Querido Diego, te abraza Quiela (Poniatowska) **140**:296, 300-02, 304, 330-31, 337
"The Query" (Allen) **52**:42
"Query, Not to Be Answered" (Oates) **33**:294
"The Quest" (Auden) **9**:59; **123**:5
"The Quest" (Olds) **85**:295-97
"The Quest" (Wright) **10**:544
Quest Crosstime (Norton) **12**:457, 471
Quest for an Island (Aksyonov) **101**:41-2
"The Quest for Blank Claveringi" (Highsmith) **102**:205
The Quest for Christa T. (Wolf)
See *Nachdenken über Christa T.*
Quest for Food (Cousteau) **30**:105-06
The Quest for God: A Personal Pilgrimage (Johnson) **147**:134-38, 145, 149
"The Quest for the South Land" (McAuley) **45**:251
"The Quest of Erebor" (Tolkien) **38**:431
The Quest of the Gole (Hollander) **5**:185
"The Quest of the Opal" (Cunningham) **31**:99-102, 106
The Quest of the Silver Fleece (Du Bois) **1**:80; **13**:182; **64**:110, 114, 117-18; **96**:133, 137
"Qu'est-ce que la critique?" (Barthes) **24**:26; **83**:88, 100
Qu'est-ce que la littérature? (Sartre) **13**:502; **18**:467; **24**:407, 410-12, 415, 417-21; **44**:494-96; **50**:380; **52**:373
"Question" (Creeley) **78**:142
"The Question" (Rukeyser) **27**:410
"Question" (Swenson) **106**:346, 350
"Question at Cliff-Thrust" (Warren) **39**:270
"A Question for the Frankfurt School" (Padilla) **38**:352
A Question of Attribution (Bennett) **77**:95, 97-8, 100, 103-04
"A Question of Class" (Allison) **153**:4, 41
"A Question of Climate" (Lorde) **71**:256
"A Question of Essence" (Lorde) **71**:260
The Question of Faith in St. John of the Cross (John Paul II)
See *Quaestio de fide apud s. Joannem a Cruce*
"A Question of Law" (Hein) **154**:
Question of Loyalty (Freeling)
See *Gun before Butter*
"A Question of Manners" (Hall) **51**:172
The Question of Max (Heilbrun) **25**:254, 257
"The Question of Narrative in Contemporary Historical Theory" (White) **148**:249, 251
The Question of Palestine (Said) **123**:347-48, 352, 358, 377, 390
"The Question of Poetic Form" (Carruth) **84**:117
"A Question of Power" (Hein)
See "Eine Frage der Macht"
A Question of Power (Head) **25**:233, 235-38; **67**:92-7, 99-100, 102-04, 109, 111
A Question of Proof (Day Lewis) **6**:129
"A Question of Rain" (Hoffman) **141**:
"The Question of Rain" (Hoffman) **141**:270, 273

A Question of Reality (Brandys) **62**:111-12, 119-20
"A Question of Re-Entry" (Ballard) **36**:37
A Question of Upbringing (Powell) **3**:400, 402-03; **7**:338, 340, 342; **9**:435; **10**:409, 412-14, 416, 418; **31**:317, 319-20
"The Question Party" (Barthelme) **115**:65
Questioned (Grass) **15**:259
The Questioning of Nick (Kopit) **33**:248-49
"The Questionnaire" (Snodgrass) **6**:514
"The Questions" (Pinsky) **38**:363; **94**:298
The Questions (Hawkes) **4**:213, 215
"Questions about a Spaniel of Eleven" (Dickey) **28**:117
Questions de méthode (Sartre) **18**:473; **24**:407; **52**:380-81, 386
"Questions for the Heart of Darkness" (Sapphire) **99**:81
Questions of Literature and Aesthetics (Bakhtin) **83**:2
"Questions of Method" (Foucault) **69**:190
"Questions of Travel" (Bishop) **13**:93-4; **15**:59; **32**:32, 36, 41
Questions of Travel (Bishop) **9**:90; **13**:89, 91-3; **32**:38-42
Questions Put to Myself (Szymborska) **99**:194, 199, 207, 211
"Questions to Tourists Stopped by a Pineapple Field" (Merwin) **45**:274
"Questions You Might Ask" (Oliver) **98**:294
La quête de l'ourse (Theriault) **79**:410-11, 414, 416
La quête intermittent (Ionesco) **86**:332, 337-38
"Quetzalcóatl" (Cernuda) **54**:48
Quetzalcoatl (Lopez Portillo) **46**:235-37
The Queue (Sorokin) **59**:369
"Quevedo" (Borges) **83**:162
Qui a ramené Doruntine? (Kadare) **52**:261
Qui je fus (Michaux) **19**:311-12, 315
Quia pawper amavi (Pound) **4**:408
Quick as Dandelions (L'Heureux) **52**:271-74
A Quick Graph: Collected Notes and Essays (Creeley) **78**:119-20, 145
"A Quick One While He's Away" (Townshend) **17**:524-25, 529-31
The Quick Red Fox (MacDonald) **27**:275; **44**:409
"The Quickening of St. John Baptist" (Merton) **83**:391
"Quicker with Arrows" (Santos) **22**:365
"The Quickest Way Out of Manchester" (Wain) **46**:411
"Quicksand" (Wiggins) **57**:435-36
Quicksand (Larsen) **37**:209-11, 213-16, 218
The Quicksilver Pool (Whitney) **42**:431
"Quicktime" (Ellison) **139**:127
Quién matú a Palomino Molero? (Vargas Llosa) **85**:362, 365-66, 368-69, 391, 395
"The Quiet" (Berry) **4**:59
Quiet Adventures (Lezama Lima)
See *Aventuras sigilosas*
"A Quiet Afternoon at Home" (Van Duyn) **63**:437
The Quiet American (Greene) **1**:131-33; **3**:208, 210, 212-14; **6**:219; **18**:194-95; **27**:173-74, 176; **37**:136-38; **70**:289-92, 294, 296; **72**:155-56, 173, 177; **125**:175, 177-78, 185, 187, 202
Quiet as a Nun (Fraser) **32**:184-85; **107**:34,51-52
"Quiet Days in Cliché" (Cabrera Infante) **120**:75
Quiet Days in Clichy (Miller) **9**:379; **84**:255
"Quiet Desperation" (Simpson) **32**:379; **149**:316, 333-34
The Quiet Don (Sholokhov)
See *Tikhii Don*
The Quiet Duel (Kurosawa) **16**:403
"Quiet Girl" (Hughes) **35**:214
Quiet in the Land (Chislett) **34**:144-46
"Quiet Lies the Locust Tells" (Ellison) **42**:131
A Quiet Life (Bainbridge) **8**:37-8; **10**:15-17; **62**:30, 36; **130**:8, 20
The Quiet Man (Ford) **16**:307, 315, 317
"A Quiet Place" (Jones)
See "A Quiet Place in the Country"
"A Quiet Place in the Country" (Jones) **131**:269
"Quiet Places" (Sainte-Marie) **17**:431
Quiet Places (Sainte-Marie) **17**:431
A Quiet Storm (Robinson) **21**:346
"Quiet Town" (Stafford) **29**:381
"The Quiet Woman of Chancery Lane" (Redgrove) **41**:359
"Quietness among Old Things" (Blaga) **75**:61
Quiller (Cook) **58**:151, 154, 157
"The Quince" (L'Heureux) **52**:273
"The Quince Bush" (Ammons) **25**:43
Quince Jam (Ferron)
See *La nuit*
"De Quincey's Status in the History of Ideas, 1944" (Wellek) **28**:446
"De Quincey's Three Opium Dream Sonnets on the Wordsworth Family" (Ewart) **46**:154
The Quincunx (Palliser) **65**:81-8
"Quinnapoxet" (Kunitz) **148**:90, 99, 132
Quinn's Book (Kennedy) **53**:197-201
"La quinque rue" (Blunden) **56**:43
Quintana and Friends (Dunne) **28**:128
Quintet (Altman) **16**:43; **116**:30, 59
Quintet (Vansittart) **42**:395-96
"Quintets for Robert Morley" (Murray) **40**:341
Quinx; or, The Ripper's Tale (Durrell) **41**:135-39
"Quisiera estar solo en el sur" (Cernuda) **54**:55
Quite Contrary: The Mary and Newt Story (Dixon) **52**:97-8, 101
"A Quite Incredible Dance" (Kinsella) **27**:238
"Quitting Time" (Lane) **25**:285, 288
A Quiver Full of Arrows (Archer) **28**:13-14
"Quixotic Expectation" (Salinas) **90**:328
A Quizaine for the Yule (Pound) **112**:331
Quo vadimus? or, The Case for the Bicycle (White) **10**:527, 529; **39**:377
Quoat-Quoat (Audiberti) **38**:22-5, 27-30
"Quod tegit omnia" (Winters) **32**:468
Quodlibet (Handke) **8**:262; **15**:267-68; **134**:161
Quoi? L'éternité (Yourcenar) **87**:382, 396, 405, 411-12, 417, 433
"Quoits" (Le Guin) **136**:346
Quoof (Muldoon) **32**:321-22; **72**:270, 272-74, 276, 282
"Quotations" (Sandburg) **35**:356
Quotations from Chairman Mao Tse-Tung (Albee) **113**:8-9, 15, 22-3
Quotations from Other Lives (Gilliatt) **53**:144-45
Qushtumur (Mahfouz) **153**:280, 289-90, 361
Qyteti i jugut (Kadare) **52**:258-59
"R" (Merrill) **8**:383, 385-86
R. Crumb and His Cheap Suit Serenaders (Crumb) **17**:85
R. Crumb's Big Yum Yum Book (Crumb) **17**:83, 86
The R Document (Wallace) **7**:510
R Is for Rocket (Bradbury) **42**:46
"R. S. I." (Lacan) **75**:287
The Ra Expeditions (Heyerdahl) **26**:192-93
"The Rabbi" (Hayden) **37**:160
The Rabbi of Lud (Elkin) **51**:96-8; **91**:213, 224
"La rabbia" (Pasolini) **106**:265
"The Rabbi's Daughter" (Calisher) **38**:71; **134**:7, 13
"The Rabbit" (Barnes) **3**:37; **29**:27
Rabbit at Rest (Updike) **70**:248-65; **139**:345-47, 354, 359-62, 364, 380
"The Rabbit Catcher" (Plath) **51**:340; **111**:204
"The Rabbit Fights for His Life the Leopard Eats Lunch" (Williams) **33**:443
"Rabbit in the Moon" (Swan) **69**:363-64
Rabbit Is Rich (Updike) **23**:467-72, 477; **43**:432-34; **70**:248-53, 255, 260; **139**:316, 332, 339-46, 354-55, 357-59
"Rabbit Man" (Sapphire) **99**:81
The Rabbit Race (Walser)
See *Eiche und Angora*
Rabbit Redux (Updike) **1**:345-46; **2**:442-45; **3**:486; **5**:451, 453-54, 456, 458, 460; **7**:485, 487-89; **9**:538-39, 541; **13**:558-59, 563; **15**:540-43; **23**:466-71, 477; **43**:430-31; **70**:248-53, 257, 259-60, 263; **139**:314, 332, 339, 341, 343, 345-46, 355-58
Rabbit, Run (Updike) **1**:344-46; **2**:439-44; **3**:485-86, 488; **5**:450-51, 453, 457-58; **7**:485-86, 488-89; **9**:537, 539, 541; **13**:562; **15**:540-42; **23**:463, 456-70, 473, 477; **34**:284, 291; **70**:248-49, 252-53, 257, 260-61; **139**:314, 332, 338-47, 354-55, 357-62
"The Rabbit-Hunter" (Frost) **26**:128
Rabbits and Boa Constrictors (Iskander)
See *Kroliki i udavy*
Rabbits and Redcoats (Peck) **17**:340
"The Rabbits Who Caused All the Trouble" (Thurber) **11**:533
Rabelais (Powys) **125**:291, 293
Rabelais and His World (Bakhtin)
See *Tvorčestva Fransua Rable i narodnaja kul'tura srednevekov'ja i Renessansa*
Rabelais et les traditions populaires en Acadie (Maillet) **118**:327, 344
Rabid (Cronenberg) **143**:81, 83, 85-87, 89, 92, 94-95, 104, 110, 112-14, 116, 134, 143, 152
Rabindranath Tagore (Ray) **16**:491
"Raby Head" (Everson) **27**:135
I racconti (Calvino) **5**:97; **11**:90; **39**:314
I racconti di Canterbury (Pasolini) **20**:266; **106**:226, 266
I racconti Romani (Moravia) **2**:293; **7**:240; **18**:343
Racconto d'autunno (Landolfi) **2**:293; **49**:216
"Raccoon" (Selzer) **74**:260
"Raccoon Journal" (Kunitz) **148**:107, 123, 126
"The Race" (Bates) **46**:62
"The Race" (Bukowski) **41**:66
"The Race" (Olds) **85**:306
"The Race" (Tomlinson) **45**:394
Race: A Study in Modern Superstition (Barzun) **51**:32-3
Race and Class (Joseph) **70**:370
"Race and Social Theory" (West) **134**:375, 383
"Race at Morning" (Faulkner) **18**:149
Race des hommes (Audiberti) **38**:21
Race et histoire (Lévi-Strauss) **38**:294
Race Matters (West) **134**:347-48, 352-63, 365, 372-74, 377, 380, 382, 384
"The Race of the Flood" (Williams) **33**:445; **148**:319
"Race Problems and Modern Society" (Toomer) **22**:424
Race Rock (Matthiessen) **7**:212; **32**:285; **64**:309, 327
'Race,' Writing and Difference (Gates) **65**:380
Racechanges: White Skin, Black Face in American Culture (Gubar) **145**:276, 278-80, 285
The Rachel Papers (Amis) **4**:19-21; **9**:25; **38**:11-12; **62**:5, 9, 11-12, 17; **101**:59, 61-63, 65-67, 69, 84, 86, 89, 92
"Racial Musings" (Christie) **110**:127
"Racine and the Tablecloth" (Byatt) **136**:137-38
Les racines du ciel (Gary) **25**:183-84, 186, 189
Racing Demon (Hare) **136**:245-46, 257-59, 261, 265, 267-71, 273-77, 267, 277, 283-84, 286, 290, 282-96
"Racing in the Street" (Springsteen) **17**:483-86, 490
"Racing with Utopias" (Grass) **49**:137
Racism 101 (Giovanni) **117**:200
"Racism: The Continuing Saga of the American Dream" (Giovanni) **117**:192
"Racists" (Williams) **148**:326, 329
The Rack (Serling) **30**:353
Racketeers in the Sky (Williamson) **29**:455
"Rada" (Arghezi) **80**:9
"Radar" (Bagryana) **10**:13
"Radar" (Spicer) **72**:361-63

Radcliffe (Storey) **2**:425; **4**:528; **8**:505
"The Radiance" (Rosenthal) **28**:394
The Radiant Future (Zinoviev) **19**:488-90
Radiant Mutations (Tzara)
See "Les mutations radieuses"
The Radiant Way (Drabble) **53**:123-29; **129**:119-23, 133-39, 141-42, 144-45, 148-51, 154-55, 160-62
"Radiare" (Moure) **88**:229
Radiation of Fatherhood (John Paul II)
See *Promieniowanie Ojcostwa*
Radical Artifice: Writing Poetry in the Age of Media (Perloff) **137**:283-93, 295-97
"Radical Chic" (Wolfe) **15**:584; **35**:454-57, 463-64; **147**:334-36
Radical Chic and Mau-Mauing the Flak Catchers (Wolfe) **2**:481; **15**:586; **35**:454, 465; **51**:422 **147**:312, 315, 317, 320
"A Radical Departure" (Tate) **25**:428
"Radical Departures" (Moss) **50**:353
Radical Poems, 1932-1938 (Klein) **19**:260
Radical Priorities (Chomsky) **132**:68
"Radio" (Bagryana) **10**:13
"The Radio" (Levine) **33**:275
"Radio I" (Beckett) **9**:84
"Radio II" (Beckett) **9**:84
Radio Days (Keillor) **115**:294
"Radio Ethiopia" (Smith) **12**:538, 540
Radio Ethiopia (Smith) **12**:538-39, 543
"The Radio in the Ivory Tower" (Pratt) **19**:385
"Radio Jazz" (Bowering) **15**:82
"Radio New France Radio" (Thesen) **56**:415, 421
"Radio, Radio" (Costello) **21**:71
"Radio Rick in Heaven and Radio Richard in Hell" (Foreman) **50**:165, 167
"Radio Waves" (Carver) **53**:61
"Radioactive Red Caps" (Hughes) **108**:284
The Radish Memoirs (White) **49**:406-07
Raditzer (Matthiessen) **32**:286, 290; **64**:309, 327
Radobis (Mahfouz)
See *Radubis*
Radubis (Mahfouz) **153**:260, 274, 309, 313, 316, 354, 372
Rādūbīs (Mahfūz) **52**:292, 299
"Radwick: A Child's Scrapbook" (Brown) **100**:81
"Rael" (Townshend) **17**:525, 530
"Rafaela Who Drinks Coconut and Papaya Juice on Tuesdays" (Cisneros) **118**:177, 216
"Rafferty" (Wain) **46**:411
The Raffle (De Sica) **20**:90
"The Raft" (King) **37**:206-07; **61**:331
The Raft (Clark Bekedermo) **38**:113-15, 119-20, 122-23
"The Raft of the Medusa" (Dickey) **28**:119
"Raftsman, Lumberjack" (Derleth) **31**:136
Rag and Bone Shop (Birney) **4**:64; **6**:77-8
The Ragazzi (Pasolini)
See *Ragazzi di vita*
Ragazzi di vita (Pasolini) **37**:341-43, 346-47; **106**:211, 216-18, 231, 242, 251, 253-54, 271
"Rage" (Oliver) **98**:259-60, 272, 293
Rage (King) **37**:207; **61**:331; **113**:375-77, 388, 391
Rage and Fire (Gray) **153**:166, 168, 171, 177-78, 180-81
"The Rage for the Lost Penny" (Jarrell) **2**:209-11; **6**:261
A Rage in Harlem (Himes)
See *For Love of Imabelle*
Rage in Heaven (Isherwood) **44**:397
The Rage of the Vulture (Unsworth) **76**:252, 259; **127**:409-11
A Rage to Live (O'Hara) **2**:324-25; **6**:386; **42**:313, 315, 317, 319
Raging Bull (Schrader) **26**:396-98
Raging Bull (Scorsese) **20**:334-36; **89**:233-36, 240-43, 247-49, 252, 254, 260-66, 268
"Raging Canal" (Edmonds) **35**:155
Ragioni d'una poesia (Ungaretti) **11**:555
"The Ragman's Daughter" (Sillitoe) **57**:393; **148**:198
The Ragman's Daughter, and Other Stories (Sillitoe) **57**:388-89, 392; **148**:156, 163, 167, 172
"Ragnarök" (Borges) **8**:101
"Ragtime" (Nin) **60**:267
Ragtime (Doctorow) **6**:131-38; **11**:140-45; **15**:178; **18**:120-27; **37**:83-9, 91-4; **44**:166-68, 170-72, 174-77, 179; **65**:137, 145; **113**:135-36, 144-48, 150, 152, 156, 158-60, 162, 166, 168-71, 176, 178, 180
Ragtime (Weller) **53**:393
Rahel Varnhagen: The Life of a Jewish Woman (Arendt) **98**:12, 53
"The Raid" (Steinbeck) **21**:381; **124**:394
Raiders of the Lost Ark (Spielberg) **20**:367
"The Rail" (Roth) **2**:378
"Railroad Bill, a Conjure Man" (Reed) **5**:368
"Railroad Bridge" (Ashbery) **77**:63, 67
Railroad Earth (Kerouac) **3**:265
"Railroad Sketches" (Dubus) **97**:233
"Railroad Standard Time" (Chin) **135**:156
The Railroad Track Triangle (Grass) **15**:259
"The Railway Children" (Heaney) **37**:165; **74**:190
The Railway Police (Calisher) **134**:13, 15, 17-18, 42
The Railway Police and The Last Trolley Ride (Calisher) **38**:71-2
The Railway Station Man (Johnston) **150**:28
"Rain" (Arghezi)
See "Ploaie"
"The Rain" (Creeley) **8**:151
"Rain" (Hogan) **73**:158
"Rain" (Hughes) **37**:175
"Rain" (Johnston) **51**:250
"Rain" (Kenny) **87**:246-47, 249
"Rain" (Lennon and McCartney) **35**:274
"A Rain" (Mahapatra) **33**:277
"Rain" (Maugham) **1**:204; **15**:369; **67**:206; **93**:249
"Rain" (Millhauser) **109**:160
"Rain" (Oliver) **98**:288
"Rain" (Soto) **80**:287
Rain (Brink)
See *Rumours of Rain*
Rain (Pa Chin)
See *Yü*
Rain, and Other Fictions (Kenny) **87**:247-49, 253
The Rain Ascends (Kogawa) **129**:290, 298, 303-04, 310-16
"Rain at Bellagio" (Clampitt) **32**:116
"Rain Charm for the Duchy, a Blessed, Devout Drench for the Christening of a Prince Harry" (Hughes) **119**:281
"Rain Check" (Barthelme) **117**:3, 18
"The Rain Child" (Laurence) **62**:278
"Rain Dance" (Carroll) **38**:103
"Rain Down Home" (Foote) **75**:230-31, 253-57
"Rain Downriver" (Levine) **118**:300-01
"Rain Eyes" (Berry) **17**:53
"The Rain Falling" (Mahapatra) **33**:284
The Rain Forest (Manning) **5**:273; **19**:301
Rain from Heaven (Behrman) **40**:77-80, 82, 88
"The Rain Glass" (Haines) **58**:222
"The Rain Guitar" (Dickey) **15**:177-78; **47**:91, 93, 98
"Rain in Ohio" (Oliver) **34**:247
"Rain in the Heart" (Taylor) **18**:526; **44**:305-06
The Rain in the Trees (Merwin) **88**:197, 205-06, 208, 212
"Rain Moving In" (Ashbery) **41**:35-6, 39
"A Rain of Rites" (Mahapatra) **33**:282
A Rain of Rites (Mahapatra) **33**:276-80, 282-83
"A Rain of Women" (Bukowski) **82**:8
"Rain on Tanyard Hollow" (Stuart) **14**:517
"Rain on the Battlefield" (Amichai)
See "Geshem bisdeh hakrav"
The Rain People (Coppola) **16**:232-33, 235, 239, 244-45, 249; **126**:262
"The Rain Song" (Page and Plant) **12**:476, 481
The Rain Stopped (Abell)
See *Regnen holdt op*
Rain upon Godshill (Priestley) **34**:365
"Rain Your Love on Me" (Cryer) **21**:79
The Rainbearers (Mosley) **43**:311
The Rainbirds (Frame) **2**:141; **6**:189; **22**:146; **96**:170-72, 179-80, 182, 189-91, 196, 200, 203, 216-17
"The Rainbow" (Kinnell) **29**:289
"Rainbow" (Plumly) **33**:313
Rainbow (Ragni and Rado) **17**:387-88
"Rainbow Body" (Snyder) **120**:329, 330
The Rainbow Grocery (Dickey) **28**:119
Rainbow Jordan (Childress) **86**:309; **96**:108, 114-18
Rainbow on the Road (Forbes) **12**:209-10
"The Rainbow Sign" (Kureishi) **64**:247-48; **135**:267, 279
The Rainbow Stories (Vollmann) **89**:276, 278-83, 285-86, 291, 296-304, 306-07, 311, 313
"Rainbow Trout" (Lightfoot) **26**:280-81
"Rainbow-Bird" (Wright) **53**:423
Rainbow's End (Cain) **28**:53-4
The Raining Tree War (Pownall) **10**:418-19
"The Rainmaker" (Humphrey) **45**:204
The Rainmaker (Ringwood)
See *Hatfield, the Rainmaker*
"Rains" (Perse)
See "Pluies"
"The Rainshore: Field, Rain, Heat" (Moure) **88**:230
Rainsong (Whitney) **42**:437
"The Raintree Street Bar and Washerteria" (Gilchrist) **143**:301, 315
"Rainy" (Ritsos) **31**:330
"Rainy Day in June" (Davies) **21**:88
"Rainy Day People" (Lightfoot) **26**:281
"Rainy Day Women #12 8 35" (Dylan) **77**:168
Rainy Mountain (Momaday)
See *The Way to Rainy Mountain*
"Rainy Mountain Cemetery" (Momaday) **85**:248, 266, 278
"Rainy Season: Sub-Tropics" (Bishop) **32**:31, 35-6, 42
"Raise High the Roofbeam, Carpenters" (Salinger) **1**:299; **3**:444, 446, **8**:463; **12**:499, 503, 513, 518, 521; **138**:184, 200-01, 204
Raise High the Roofbeam, Carpenters and Seymour: An Introduction (Salinger) **1**:299; **12**:518; **138**:216
Raise, Race, Rays, Raze: Essays since 1965 (Baraka) **14**:48; **33**:56
Raised by Puppets (Codrescu) **121**:175
"Raised on Robbery" (Mitchell) **12**:442
A Raisin in the Sun (Hansberry) **17**:182-85, 187-92; **62**:211-12, 214-21, 223-30, 232, 236-43, 247
Raising Arizona (The Coen Brothers) **108**:129-33, 135-44, 146-47, 149, 151, 156-57, 159-62, 165-66, 168-72, 175
Raising Demons (Jackson) **60**:211-12, 216, 228-29, 233-34
"The Raising of Elvira Tremlett" (Trevor) **71**:336, 350; **116**:377, 385
"Raising the Demon" (Kaplan)
See "Elisabetta, Carlotta, Catherine"
"Raising the Flag" (Vizenor) **103**:281
Raising the Moon Vines (Vizenor) **103**:296, 308
The Raj Quartet (Scott) **9**:477-78; **60**:329-51
"Raj teologów" (Herbert) **43**:186-87
The Rake's Progess (Auden) **43**:26
Rakovyi korpus (Solzhenitsyn) **1**:319-21; **2**:407-08; **4**:507-10, 512, 515; **7**:432, 434, 436, 442-45; **10**:480; **18**:495, 497-98; **26**:419; **34**:485, 492; **78**:381-83, 393-94, 396, 398, 409, 411, 420, 424; **134**:284, 296-97, 303
"Raleigh Was Right" (Williams) **67**:408
Ralentir travaux (Breton) **54**:32

Ralentir travaux (Char) **9**:165; **55**:286
Ralph and Tony (Forster) **22**:136-37; **45**:131-32
"Ram" (Clarke) **61**:79-80
Ram (McCartney) **12**:366, 371-72; **35**:279-80, 283, 289
"The Ram beneath the Barn" (Davison) **28**:104
"The Ram in the Thicket" (Morris) **37**:310
Ramayana (Narayan) **121**:353
"Ramblin' Gamblin' Man" (Seger) **35**:380, 384, 386
Ramblin' Gamblin' Man (Seger) **35**:378
Rambling Rose (Willingham) **5**:511-12; **51**:409-10
"Rambling Round" (Guthrie) **35**:190
"Ramifications" (Squires) **51**:379, 382
Ramona and the White Slaves (Walker) **61**:424, 426-27, 432
Ran (Kurosawa) **119**:338, 340--44, 380-81, 383-84, 386-95, 397-400, 402
Rancho Deluxe (McGuane) **45**:261-62; **127**:258, 262, 264, 267, 270, 280
Rancho Notorious (Lang) **20**:216; **103**:89
"Rancour" (Parks) **147**:215-16
"Randal" (Nye) **42**:309
Randall and the River of Time (Forester) **35**:172
"Randall Jarrell" (Lowell) **3**:302; **124**:255
Randall Jarrell's Letters: An Autobiographical and Literary Selection (Jarrell) **49**:197-201
"Randall, My Son" (Davidson) **13**:170
"Randevu" (Aksyonov)
See "Rendezvous"
Random Descent (Govier) **51**:163-64, 166
Randow (Hein) **154**:161-64
"R-and-R" (Enright) **8**:204
Raney (Edgerton) **39**:52-4
"Range" (Ammons) **25**:45
"The Range in the Desert" (Jarrell) **9**:299
Rangoon (Barthelme) **36**:49
Rani jadi (Kiš) **57**:245-47
Rannie zhuravli (Aitmatov) **71**:5, 7, 10-15, 32-3
Ransom (Duncan) **26**:101
Ransom (McInerney) **112**:180-82, 184, 203-04, 207-08, 212
"A Rant" (O'Hara) **78**:351
A Rap on Race (Baldwin) **90**:30
A Rap on Race (Mead) **37**:277-79
"Rape" (Andrade)
See "Rapta"
"The Rape" (Hein)
See "Die Vergewaltigung"
"Rape" (Rich) **3**:427, 429; **7**:367, 370, 373
Rape (Lennon) **35**:267
"Rape Fantasics" (Atwood) **25**:61
"Rape is Not a Poem" (Jordan) **114**:146, 148
The Rape of Clarissa (Eagleton) **132**:83
The Rape of Clarissa: Writing, Sexuality and Class Struggle in Samuel Richardson (Eagleton) **63**:97, 104
"The Rape of Persephone" (Dybek) **114**:61, 63, 66
"The Rape of Philomel" (Shapiro) **8**:486
The Rape of Shavi (Emecheta) **48**:99-100; **128**:68-9
The Rape of Tamar (Jacobson) **4**:254-56
"The Rape of the Drape" (Perelman) **49**:272
"Rape of the Leaf" (Kunitz) **148**:87
"Rape Poem" (Piercy) **62**:379
"Rape, Racism and the Myth of the Black Rapist" (Davis) **77**:124
"Rapids" (Ammons) **25**:45; **108**:56
"The Rapids" (Barnard) **48**:25
"Rappel" (Damas) **84**:173, 176
"Rapport" (Colter) **58**:147
"Rapta" (Andrade) **18**:4
"Rapture" (Johnston) **51**:239
"Rapunzel" (Sexton) **53**:321
"Rapunzel" (Thomas) **13**:540; **37**:417; **107**:316, 318, 320, 335
"Rapunzel, Rapunzel" (Chester) **49**:56
Rare Angel (McClure) **6**:319-21; **10**:333
"Rare Bird" (Barrett) **150**:5-6
"Rascacielos" (Guillén) **11**:262
The Rascals from Haskell's Gym (Bonham) **12**:55
"Rascasse" (Van Duyn) **116**:417, 422
Rashomon (Kurosawa) **16**:394-402, 404; **119**:337, 340-42, 345-50, 355-57, 360, 372-74, 399
"Raspberry Beret" (Prince) **35**:332
The Raspberry Picker (Hochwälder)
See *Der Himbeerpflücker*
Rasstoyanie v polkilometra (Voinovich) **147**:273
"Rassvet" (Pasternak) **18**:389
Rastaman Vibration (Marley) **17**:268-72
"the rat" (Bukowski) **108**:75
"The Rat" (McFadden) **48**:258
The Rat (Grass)
See *Die Rättin*
"A Rat and Some Renovations" (Mac Laverty) **31**:254
Rat Jelly (Ondaatje) **29**:341; **51**:310-12, 315-17
Rat Man of Paris (West) **96**:362, 365, 368-69, 377, 382, 385, 390, 393, 399-400
"Rat Race" (Marley) **17**:268-69, 272
Rat Race (Francis) **2**:142; **22**:151-52; **42**:148-50; **102**:131
Las ratas (Delibes) **18**:110
"Ratatouille" (Dunn) **40**:169
Rates of Exchange (Bradbury) **32**:56-8; **61**:39-41, 43, 45
"Rat-Faced Auntie" (Hannah) **90**:159
"A Rather Dull Introduction" (Pound) **48**:288
"Rather Like a Dream" (Warren) **18**:536
"Rational Man" (Rukeyser) **27**:411
Ratner's Star (DeLillo) **8**:171-72; **10**:134-35; **13**:175-76, 178; **27**:78-80, 82-3, 85; **39**:116-17, 119; **54**:81-2; **76**:171, 180, 182; **143**:180, 187
"Rats" (Hoffman) **6**:243-44
"The Rats" (Levine) **4**:287
"The Rats" (Sillitoe) **148**:195
The Rats (Sillitoe) **1**:307; **148**:195
"The Rats and Cats in the House of Culture" (Singh) **11**:504
Rats and Mice: Friends and Foes of Man (Silverstein and Silverstein) **17**:452
"Rat's Eye" (Hall) **51**:170
A Rat's Mass (Kennedy) **66**:208-09
"The Rats on the Waterfront" (Mitchell) **98**:161, 167, 182
Die Rättin (Grass) **49**:140-44
"Rattlesnake" (Wild) **14**:580
"Rattlesnake Country" (Warren) **8**:537; **10**:524; **39**:264-65
"Rattling Hail's Ceremonial" (Vizenor) **103**:281
Ravages (Leduc) **22**:262
"The Ravages of Spring" (Gardner) **5**:132; **7**:111, 113, 116
"Raven" (Hoffman) **6**:244
"The Raven" (Rich) **3**:428
"Raven II" (Bowering) **32**:47
"Ravenna" (Denby) **48**:82
"Ravens" (Hughes) **37**:175-76; **119**:271
"Ravens" (Jiles) **58**:279, 281
Raven's Cry (Harris) **12**:262, 264, 267
"Raven's Wing" (Oates) **52**:331-32
Raven's Wing (Oates) **52**:331-32
Ravensgill (Mayne) **12**:394-95, 397-98, 402-03
Ravenswood (McNally) **4**:347; **7**:218
"Le ravin" (Bonnefoy) **58**:53
"The Ravine" (Ai) **14**:8
"The Ravine" (Carruth) **84**:132, 135
"Raving and Drooling" (Pink Floyd) **35**:311
A Raving Monarchist (Rathbone) **41**:340
The Ravishing of Lol V. Stein (Duras)
See *Le ravissement de Lol V. Stein*
Le ravissement de Lol V. Stein (Duras) **40**:178, 180; **68**:73-4, 79, 81, 85, 87-9, 91, 93, 95, 99; **100**:122, 130, 143
The Raw and the Cooked (Lévi-Strauss)
See *Le cru et le cuit*
Raw Heaven (Peacock) **60**:292-94, 296-98
Raw Material (Sillitoe) **3**:448; **6**:500; **148**:174-75, 185-86
"Rawhead Rex" (Barker) **52**:53
The Rawhide Knot, and Other Stories (Richter) **30**:328-29
Ray (Hannah) **23**:210-13; **38**:232-35; **90**:127-30, 132, 134-37, 139-40, 144, 151, 160
"Rayme" (Phillips) **139**:205, 220
"Raymond Bamber and Mrs. Fitch" (Trevor) **7**:475; **71**:334; **116**:364
"Raymond of the Rooftops" (Durcan) **43**:118
"Raymond's Run" (Bambara) **88**:16, 18-19, 21, 39-40, 47, 49, 51
Rayuela (Cortázar) **2**:102-05; **3**:114-15; **5**:110; **10**:114, 118; **13**:157, 164; **15**:146-47; **33**:123, 125-26, 128, 130, 136; **34**:329-33; 136-74
"The Razor" (Shiga) **33**:367
"The Razor Shell" (Watkins) **43**:450
The Razor's Edge (Maugham) **1**:204; **11**:370; **15**:367; **67**:217, 219, 227, 229; **93**:245
"Re" (Duncan) **7**:88
"Re" (Tolson) **105**:262
"Re assessin the Critical Studies Movement" (West) **134**:383
Re: Colonised Planet 5 (Lessing) **94**:253
Re:Creation (Giovanni) **64**:186, 188, 195; **117**:183, 191-92, 195-97
Re Joyce (Burgess)
See *Here Comes Everybody: An Introduction to James Joyce for the Ordinary Reader*
"The Reach" (King) **37**:207; **61**:332-33
Reach for Tomorrow (Clarke) **18**:106
Reach to the Stars (Willingham) **5**:510; **51**:403-04
"Re-Act for Action" (Madhubuti) **73**:207
"The Reacting of Richard" (Updike) **9**:539
Reactionary Essays on Poetry and Ideas (Tate) **11**:527; **14**:530; **24**:439-40, 446
"Reactive Agent Tape Cut by Lee the Agent in Interzone" (Burroughs) **109**:195
"Read at the May Award Dinner, 1996" (Le Guin) **136**:395
"Reader" (Dorfman) **77**:141-43
Reader (Dorfman) **77**:136, 139, 152
"The Reader and the Writer" (Wolf) **150**:230, 260
The Reader and the Writer (Wolf) **150**:215, 323
"The Reader over My Shoulder" (Graves) **45**:167
Reader's nuestro que estás en la tierra: Ensayos sobre el imperialismo cultural (Dorfman) **48**:88-91, 93; **77**:134-35, 143, 150-51
"Readiness" (Monette) **82**:323
"Reading" (Blanchot) **135**:141
"Reading a View" (Malouf) **28**:268
"Reading Aloud" (Gallagher) **63**:124
"Reading and the Written Interview" (Delany) **141**:150
"The Reading and Writing of Short Stories" (Welty) **105**:327, 333
"Reading Apollinaire by the Rouge River" (Ferlinghetti) **111**:59
"Reading Books" (Rozewicz)
See "Czytanie książęk"
Reading Capital (Althusser)
See *Lire "Le Capital"*
"Reading Early Sorrow" (Williams) **56**:428
Reading for the Plot: Design and Intention in Narrative (Brooks) **34**:519-22
"A Reading Glass" (Johnson) **7**:415
Reading Henry James (Auchincloss) **9**:53
"Reading Her Old Letter about a Wedding" (Raine) **103**:179
"Reading History" (Simic) **130**:333
"Reading Holderlin on the Patio with the Aid of a Dictionary" (Dove) **81**:137
"Reading: I Dream My Schooling" (Acker) **111**:14

Reading in the Dark (Deane) **122**:87-96, 98-100, 102-03, 105
"A Reading in Trollope" (Stewart) **32**:421
"Reading Late at Night, Thermometer Falling" (Warren) **6**:556-58; **39**:260
"Reading Late in Winter" (Tillinghast) **29**:414
"The Reading Lesson" (Murphy) **41**:318
"Reading Miss Turgenev" (Trevor) **116**:372
"Reading Myself" (Lowell) **8**:355; **124**:256
Reading Myself and Others (Roth) **6**:476; **22**:357; **66**:417, 420-21; **86**:263
"Reading Nietzsche" (Moure) **88**:218
"A Reading of Rex Stout" (Van Duyn) **63**:442; **116**:411
"The Reading of the Will" (Knowles) **26**:258
"Reading Paradise Lost in Protestant Ulster, 1984" (Deane) **122**:82-3
"Reading Pascal in the Lowlands" (Dunn) **40**:171
"Reading 'Pericles' in New London" (Corn) **33**:117-18
"Reading Plato" (Graham) **48**:149; **118**:239-40, 250
"Reading Pornography in Old Age" (Nemerov) **36**:309
"A Reading Problem" (Stafford) **68**:423, 431
"Reading Robert Southey to My Daughter" (Nye) **42**:305
"Reading the Books Our Children Have Written" (Smith) **42**:346, 353
"Reading 'The Bostonians' in Algeciras Bay" (Fuller) **28**:153
"Reading the River" (McPhee) **36**:296
Reading the Signs (Wilding) **73**:396-97, 399, 401, 403
"Reading the South African Landscape" (Coetzee) **66**:99
Reading the Spirit (Eberhart) **11**:178; **19**:143; **56**:425, 429
"Reading: The Subway" (Williams) **56**:425, 429; **148**:318
"Reading the Tree" (Bernstein) **142**:12
"Reading to My Sick Daughter" (Buckley) **57**:126, 130
Reading to You (Hustvedt) **76**:58
"Reading Trip" (Kennedy) **8**:320; **42**:256
Reading Turgenev (Trevor)
See *Two Lives: Reading Turgenev; My House in Umbria*
"Reading Walt Whitman" (Vendler) **138**:265
"The Reading Wars" (Birkerts) **116**:166-67
"Reading, Writing, and the Rackets" (Fearing) **51**:117-18
"Reading Your Poems in Your House While You Are Away (for Richard Shelton)" (Kizer) **80**:183
"Readings" (Milosz) **56**:237
Readings (Cixous) **92**:95
"Readings, Forecasts, Personal Guidance" (Fearing) **51**:109
"Readings of History" (Rich) **18**:447
Reads (Brophy) **105**:31
Ready or Not (Stolz) **12**:546-47, 549
Ready to Wear (Altman)
See *Prêt-à-Porter*
"Reaffirmation" (Lindbergh) **82**:155-58
"Reagan, Begin, and God" (Blount) **38**:47
"Reaganism: The Spirit of the Times" (Howe) **85**:153
"Reah habenzin 'oleh be'api" (Amichai) **57**:44
The Real Cool Killers (Himes) **58**:265, 267, 269; **108**:237-38, 242, 244, 246-47, 250, 267, 275
The Real David Copperfield (Graves) **6**:211
Real Dreams (Griffiths) **52**:185
"Real Estate" (Muske) **90**:308
"Real Estate" (Waddington) **28**:440
Real Estate (Hamburger) **14**:234-35
Real Estate (Page) **40**:352-55
"A Real Fright" (Betjeman) **34**:309
"The Real Hero" (Amichai) **116**:130
"The Real Hero of the Agedah" (Amichai)
See "Hagibor ha'amiti shel ha'agedah"
"Real Impudence" (Calisher) **38**:75; **134**:10
"The Real Inspector Hound" (Stoppard) **1**:328; **3**:470; **4**:524-25, 527; **5**:412; **8**:504; **15**:518-19, 522-24; **29**:394, 397, 399-401; **34**:275; **63**:404, **91**:187, 190
"A Real Life" (Munro) **95**:320-21, 324
The Real Life of Alejandro Mayta (Vargas Llosa)
See *La historia de Mayta*
The Real Life of Sebastian Knight (Nabokov) **1**:240; **2**:302, 304; **3**:352; **6**:352, 354; **8**:412, 418; **11**:393; **15**:391; **46**:292; **64**:348, 366
"Real Life Writes Real Bad" (Findley) **102**:110-11
Real Losses, Imaginary Gains (Morris) **7**:247; **18**:351
"The Real Magic Opera Begins" (Ferlinghetti) **111**:65
"The Real Me" (Townshend) **17**:532-33
"Real Mothers" (Thomas) **37**:419-20, 422; **107**:328
Real Mothers (Thomas) **37**:418-20; **107**:316, 326-28, 330, 332, 349
"Real People" (Grayson) **38**:209
Real People (Lurie) **4**:306; **5**:259-60; **39**:179
"Real People in a Real Place" (Smith) **64**:400
"Real Places on How Sense Fragments--Thoughts on Ethnicity and the Making of Poetry" (Alexander) **121**:18
Real Presence (Bausch) **51**:51-4, 57
"The Real Revolution Is Love" (Harjo) **83**:273, 282
The Real Russia (Prichard) **46**:337
"Real Situation" (Marley) **17**:273
The Real Story of Alejandro Mayta (Vargas Llosa)
See *La historia de Mayta*
"The Real Thing" (Stewart) **32**:421
The Real Thing (Lessing) **94**:265, 272-73, 287
The Real Thing (Stoppard) **29**:402-06; **34**:273-82; **91**:187, 190
"The Real Work" (Snyder) **120**:329
The Real Work: Interview and Talks, 1964-1979 (Snyder) **32**:389-90, 393-94, 396, 399; **120**:325, 335
The Real World (Aragon) **3**:13
"The Real World of Manuel Córdova" (Merwin) **88**:211
Realidad nacional desde la cama (Valenzuela) **104**:389, 391
La realidad y el deseo (Cernuda) **54**:41-3, 46-52, 58-61
Realignment (Eshleman) **7**:99
Realism in Our Time (Lukacs) **24**:330
The Realists (Snow) **13**:514
"Réalité" (Damas) **84**:173, 176
"Realities" (MacLeish) **8**:359
"Realities" (Slessor) **14**:492
"Realities" (Williams) **42**:440
"Reality" (Damas)
See "Réalité"
"Reality" (Dudek) **19**:137
"A Reality" (Ekelöf) **27**:119
"Reality" (Pasolini) **106**:241, 250
"Reality Demands" (Szymborska) **99**:202
"Reality in America" (Trilling) **11**:541; **24**:460
Reality Sandwiches (Ginsberg) **6**:198; **13**:239; **36**:183, 185, 189, 195-96
"Realization" (Kunene) **85**:165
"Really, Doesn't Crime Pay?" (Walker) **58**:404; **103**:358-61, 372, 398-99, 406-07, 410
"Really Gone" (Redgrove) **41**:352
"The Really Practical People" (Snodgrass) **6**:514
The Really Short Poems of A.R. Ammons (Ammons) **108**:47, 61
"Realm" (Eberhart) **56**:77
The Realm of Prester John (Silverberg) **140**:396
The Realms of Gold (Drabble) **8**:183-85; **10**:162-65; **22**:127; **53**:118-20, 122; **129**:111, 113-15, 117-19, 124, 148
Realms of Strife (Goytisolo)
See *En los reinos de taifa*
"The Reaper and the Flowers" (Stuart) **11**:512
The Rear Column (Gray) **14**:215; **36**:205-06
"Rear Window" (Woolrich) **77**:400-01
Rear Window (Hitchcock) **16**:340-41, 346, 355, 358-59
"The Reardon Poems" (Blackburn) **43**:64
"The Rear-Guard" (Sassoon) **130**:214, 219
"Rearmament" (Jeffers) **3**:259
"Reason" (Asimov) **9**:51; **92**:4, 7, 9, 11, 21
"Reason" (McClure) **6**:318-19
"Reason" (Miles) **14**:369
Reason and Energy (Hamburger) **14**:233-34
Reason and Violence: A Decade of Sartre's Philosophy (Laing) **95**:123-25, 134, 140-42, 144, 171
"A Reason for Moving" (Strand) **18**:516
The Reason for the Pelican (Ciardi) **44**:378
Reason in Madness (Tate) **6**:527; **24**:440, 446
The Reason Why the Closet Man Is Never Sad (Edson) **13**:191
Reasonable Creatures: Essays on Women and Feminism (Pollitt) **122**:206-08, 216, 218-22, 224
"A Reasonable Man" (Beattie) **13**:65; **63**:3, 9; **146**:62-3, 81
"Reasonable People" (Fuentes) **113**:242-43
"Reasons for Attendance" (Larkin) **13**:336; **33**:256; **64**:258, 277
Reasons for Moving (Strand) **18**:514-16, 518; **41**:436; **71**:278, 282-86
Reasons of State (Carpentier)
See *El recurso del método*
Reasons of the Heart (Dahlberg) **7**:62
Reasons to Live (Hempel) **39**:67-70
"Reasons Why" (Hughes) **15**:295
"The Reassurance" (Gunn) **81**:179
"Reassurance" (Gurganus) **70**:190, 192, 195
Reave the Just an Other Tales (Donaldson) **138**:41
The Reawakening (Levi)
See *La tregua*
Rebecca (du Maurier) **6**:147; **11**:162-63; **59**:280-81, 283-87
Rebecca (Hitchcock) **16**:338, 343, 345, 357
The Rebecca Notebook and Other Memories (du Maurier) **59**:286
Rebecca West: A Celebration (West) **31**:458
Rebecca West: A Life (Glendinning) **50**:394-97, 399-401, 403, 405-10
The Rebel (Camus)
See *L'homme révolté*
The Rebel Angels (Davies) **25**:132-35; **42**:106-07, 109; **75**:184-85, 187, 190-202, 204, 206, 208, 211, 213, 215-16, 218, 223; **91**:201, 203-4
A Rebel in Time (Harrison) **42**:207
"Rebel Music" (Marley) **17**:267, 272
"Rebel, Rebel" (Bowie) **17**:62
"Rebel Waltz" (Clash) **30**:48
"Rebellion" (Campbell) **32**:74, 78, 80
"Rebellion" (Lowell) **8**:350; **11**:326; **124**:273, 285
The Rebellion of Young David, and Other Stories (Buckler) **13**:119
The Rebels (Jakes) **29**:248-49
Rebels of the Heavenly Kingdom (Paterson) **30**:287-88
"Rebirth" (Sanchez) **116**:280
Re-Birth (Wyndham) **19**:475
"Rebours" (Tchicaya) **101**:354
"Rebreaking Outlaw Horses in the Desert" (Hearne) **56**:127
Rebuilding Coventry (Townsend) **61**:417
Rebuilding Russia: Reflections and Tentative Proposals (Solzhenitsyn)
See *Kak nam obustroit' Rossiiu?: Posil'nye soobrazheniia*
Recalled to Life (Silverberg) **140**:377

"Recalling Manolete" (Cabral de Melo Neto)
See "Lembrando Manolete"
"Recalling War" (Graves) **39**:328; **45**:169
"Recapitulaciones" (Ferré) **139**:182-83
Recapitulation (Stegner) **49**:356-58, 361; **81**:350, 352
"Recapturing the Past in Fiction" (Settle) **61**:385-88
"Receipt" (Reading) **47**:352
A Recent Martyr (Martin) **89**:109, 111, 113, 116-19, 123, 125-27, 129
"Recent Negro Fiction" (Ellison) **114**:107
Recent Trends in New Zealand Poetry (Baxter) **14**:60
"The Reception" (Jordan) **114**:145, 154
"Reception" (McCartney) **35**:286
"The Reception Hall" (Mahfouz)
See "Al-Bahw"
Recessional (Michener) **109**:383, 386, 388-89
"Receta casera" (Arreola) **147**:26
Recherche de la base et du sommet (Char) **55**:289
Recherches dialectiques (Goldmann) **24**:239
Recherches pour une sémanalyse (Kristeva)
See *Semeiotke: Recherches pour une sémanalyse*
"Un récit?" (Blanchot) **135**:137
"The Recital" (Ashbery) **2**:19; **15**:28; **25**:50; **77**:54; **125**:17
"A Recital for the Pope" (Stern) **39**:244
"Recitatif" (Morrison) **81**:266
"Recitative of Palinurus" (Ungaretti) **7**:481, 485
Reckless (Lucas) **64**:290-96
Reckless Eyeballing (Reed) **60**:300-02, 304-06, 313
"The Reckoning" (Kunitz) **148**:97
The Reckoning (Elman) **19**:149-50
The Reckoning (Jellicoe) **27**:210-11
A Reckoning (Sarton) **14**:482; **49**:315, 322; **91**:245-46, 251
The Reckoning (Ward) **19**:457
"The Recluse" (L'Heureux) **52**:274
"Recluse" (O Hehir) **41**:324
"The Recluse" (Singer) **69**:312
"Recognition" (Blunden) **56**:43
"The Recognition" (Jennings) **131**:238
The Recognitions (Gaddis) **1**:113-14; **3**:177; **6**:193-95; **8**:227-30; **10**:209-14; **19**:185-90; **43**:156-63; **86**:147-49, 151-53, 156-57, 161-62, 164, 166, 168
Recoil (Thompson) **69**:386
Recollected Essays, 1965-1980 (Berry) **27**:37-9; **46**:75
"Recollection in Upper Ontario, from Long Before" (Warren) **39**:256, 272
"Recollection of Childhood" (Eberhart) **56**:86
Recollections of a Golden Triangle (Robbe-Grillet)
See *Souvenirs du triangle d'or*
Recollections of Gran Apachería (Dorn) **10**:159
"Recollections of Henry James" (Thurber) **125**:404
"Recollections of the Works Department" (Hood) **28**:187
"The Recompense" (Tomlinson) **45**:400, 403
"Reconaissance" (Bontemps) **1**:38
"Reconciliation" (Sassoon) **130**:187
Reconciliation (Shiga)
See *Wakai*
"Reconsidering the Madman" (Hugo) **32**:241
"Reconstruction and Its Benefits" (Du Bois) **64**:107
Record of a Living Being (Kurosawa)
See *Ikimono no kiroku*
"The Record of a Man" (Willingham) **51**:403
The Record of a Tenement Gentleman (Ozu) **16**:451
A Record of Certain Episodes Made in the Town of Gogulev by Andrey Petrovich Kovyakin (Leonov)
See *Zapisi nekotorykh epizodov, sdelannye v gorode Goguleve Andreem Petrovichem Koviakinym*
"A Record of Longing for Mother" (Tanizaki)
See "Haha no kouru ki"
"Records" (Giovanni) **19**:191; **64**:191
"Records" (Tate) **11**:525
"Recortes de prensa" (Cortázar) **33**:126
"Recourse" (Gallagher) **63**:121, 124
"Recoveries" (Ammons) **57**:53
The Recoveries (Adamov)
See *Les retrouvailles*
Recoveries (Jennings) **14**:291; **131**:239
Recovering: A Journal, 1978-1979 (Sarton) **49**:315, 317-18; **91**:251
"The Recovery" (Blunden) **56**:30
"The Recovery" (Dacey) **51**:79
"Recovery" (Milosz) **31**:268
"Recovery" (Scott) **22**:372
Recovery (Berryman) **3**:69, 71-2; **4**:63-4; **6**:63; **13**:83; **25**:95-7; **62**:45
"Recovery of Sexual Desire after a Bad Cold" (Chappell) **40**:147
"The Recruiting Officer" (McGahern) **48**:268
"Rectitude" (Ammons) **25**:42-3
The Rector of Justin (Auchincloss) **4**:29-31; **9**:52, 54; **18**:27; **45**:36-7
"Recuerdo" (Allen) **84**:6-8, 40
"Recuerdos de juventud" (Parra) **102**:338, 341
Recurrent Melody: Passcaglia (Pinget)
See *Passacaille*
El recurso del método (Carpentier) **8**:134-35; **11**:99-101, 107; **38**:101; **110**:57-9, 69, 91, 94-6
Recyclings (Kostelanetz) **28**:216
"Red" (Maugham) **1**:204; **15**:368
Red (Van Vechten) **33**:387
"The Red and Green Beads" (Hill) **113**:282, 312
The Red and the Green (Murdoch) **1**:236; **3**:346-47; **4**:368; **6**:348; **22**:326-27; **51**:291
The Red and the White (Troyat) **23**:459
"Red Angel Dragnet" (Clash) **30**:50-2
Red Anger (Household) **11**:277
Red Azalea (Min) **86**:82-97
The Red Badge of Courage (Huston) **20**:161, 163, 165
"The Red Balloon" (Abse) **29**:16
Red Beard (Kurosawa) **16**:402-03; **119**:338, 340, 352-54, 356, 362, 378-79, 382
"Red Blues" (Alexie) **154**:14
The Red Book and the Great Wall (Moravia) **7**:243
The Red Box (Stout) **3**:471
Red Burning Light; or, Mission XQ3 (Fornés) **61**:129, 131-32
"Red Buses" (Dunn) **40**:168
The Red Cabbage Café (Treitel) **70**:114-16
The Red Carnation (Vittorini) **6**:551
A Red Carpet for the Sun (Layton) **15**:320
"Red Chair" (DeMarinis) **54**:102
Red Chameleon (Kaminsky) **59**:171
"Red Clowns" (Cisneros) **118**:174, 177, 184, 186
"The Red Coal" (Stern) **40**:410
The Red Coal (Stern) **40**:409-12; **100**:329, 333
"The Red Cockatoos" (Kelman) **58**:298, 302
"The Red Cocoon" (Abe)
See "Akai mayu"
Red Cross (Shepard) **4**:489-90; **17**:434-36, 439, 448; **41**:409, 411
A Red Death (Mosley) **97**:331-39, 344-45, 348, 352-53, 355
The Red Desert (Antonioni)
See *Il deserto rosso*
The Red Devil Battery Sign (Williams) **11**:576; **45**:455
"The Red Dog" (Jensen) **37**:189
Red Dust (Levine) **4**:286-87; **14**:317; **33**:270-71; **118**:283, 299, 303
"The Red Dwarf" (Tournier) **36**:438-39
"The Red Flower Poems" (Zweig) **42**:465
The Red Fox (Hyde) **42**:225-28
"The Red Front" (Aragon) **22**:34
The Red Gang of Asakusa (Kawabata)
See *Asakusa Kurenaidan*
"The Red Girl" (Kincaid) **43**:249
The Red Glove (Rozewicz)
See *Czerwona rękawiczka*
Red Hart Magic (Norton) **12**:471
Red Harvest (Amado)
See *Seára vermelha*
Red Harvest (Hammett) **3**:218-19; **19**:193, 195-97; **47**:156-58, 160-63
The Red Heart (Reaney) **13**:473
"Red Hills" (Davies) **23**:144
Red Is for Murder (Whitney) **42**:431
The Red Kimono (Arzner) **98**:87
"Red Leaves" (Faulkner) **8**:212-13; **18**:147; **28**:143
Red Magic (Ghelderode)
See *Magie rouge*
"Red Maple Leaves" (Rexroth) **112**:404
The Red Monarch (Krotkov) **19**:264
"Red Money" (Bowie) **17**:66
"The Red Mullet" (Warren) **39**:267; **59**:295
"Red Music" (Škvorecký) **15**:511; **69**:343
"Red Neck Friend" (Browne) **21**:35
Red Noses (Barnes) **56**:6-10
Red Noses, Black Death (Barnes)
See *Red Noses*
The Red Notebook (Auster) **131**:42
"Red Pawn" (Rand) **79**:374-75, 377-78
Red Planet: A Colonial Boy on Mars (Heinlein) **3**:225; **14**:249; **26**:160, 163, 168, 171, 175-76; **55**:302
The Red Pony (Steinbeck) **1**:324-25; **9**:515-18; **13**:529, 533; **21**:378, 386, 389; **34**:405, 409, 415; **45**:374; **59**:317; **124**:386, 391, 394-95
"The Red Poppy" (Glück) **81**:165, 169-70
"Red Rabbit Running BAckwards (for A.W.)" (Carroll) **143**:40
Red Rebel: Tito of Yugloslavia (Archer) **12**:16
Red Ribbon on a White Horse (Yezierska) **46**:445, 447
Red River (Ford) **16**:318
"Red Rose and a Beggar" (H. D.) **14**:224
Red Rose Speedway (McCartney) **35**:280-83
"Red Roses" (Sexton) **123**:411
Red Roses for Bronze (H. D.) **31**:208; **73**:113, 121, 139
Red Roses for Me (O'Casey) **5**:318; **11**:407-10; **15**:404-05; **88**:257, 260, 262-70, 275-76, 280
"Red Runner" (Guthrie) **35**:185
"Red Sails" (Bowie) **17**:66
Red Sand (Stribling) **23**:445
"Red Shift" (Ammons) **57**:53
Red Shift (Garner) **17**:145-47, 149-50
"Red Shirt" (Atwood) **135**:70
"The Red Shoes" (Sexton) **4**:483
"Red Stamps with Lenin's Picture" (Kiš) **57**:251, 253-54
"Red Star, Winter Orbit" (Gibson) **63**:130
Red Storm Rising (Clancy) **45**:87-90; **112**:49-50, 52, 55-6, 62-3, 69, 74-7, 88, 90
"Red Termites" (Perelman) **49**:257
"Red Trousseau" (Muske) **90**:318
Red Trousseau (Muske) **90**:318
Red Wagon (Berrigan) **37**:44
The Red Wheel, Knot I: August 1914 (Solzhenitsyn)
See *Avgust chetyrnadtsatogo*
"The Red Wheelbarrow" (Williams) **42**:450, 457, 460
Red Wolves and Black Bears (Hoagland) **28**:182
"Rede und Nachrede" (Bachmann) **69**:56
"Rededication" (Cohen) **38**:130
"The Redeemer" (Sassoon) **130**:178, 181, 192, 194
The Redeemer of Man (John Paul II) **128**:201

"Redeeming the Time" (Hill) **45**:183, 186, 189
"Redemption" (Gardner) **28**:162
"Redemption Song" (Marley) **17**:273
"Redemption Songs" (Shacochis) **39**:199-200
Redemptor Hominis (John Paul II) **128**:160-61, 177, 179-80, 193
Redemptoris Missio (John Paul II) **128**:178
Reden im Herbst (Wolf) **150**:244, 294
"Redeployment" (Nemerov) **36**:304
Redevelopment (Havel) **123**:184
"Redfish" (Bass) **79**:5, 12; **143**:3
"The Red-Haired Miss Daintreys" (Lehmann) **5**:240
Red-Headed Stranger (Nelson) **17**:303-06
Redimiculum Matellarum (Bunting) **39**:297; **47**:43
"Rediscovering America" (Alexie) **154**:11
"Rediscovering Lost Values" (King) **83**:340
"Rediscovery" (McGrath) **59**:181
The Rediscovery of North America (Lopez) **70**:344
"Redondo Beach" (Smith) **12**:536, 539
"The Redress of Poetry" (Heaney) **74**:189
The Redress of Poetry (Heaney) **91**:124, 127-9
"Red-Tail Hawk and Pyre of Youth" (Warren) **13**:581-82; **18**:534-36; **39**:266
The Redundancy of Courage (Mo) **134**:202-04, 210
"Redundant! or the Wife's Revenge" (Weldon) **122**:273
"Redwing" (Gallagher) **63**:125
"Redwing Blackbirds" (Warren) **39**:262
"Red-Winged Blackbirds" (Cooper) **56**:72
"Redwood Hill" (Lightfoot) **26**:280
The Reed Cutter (Tanizaki) **8**:510; **28**:414, 416, 418
A Reed in the Tide (Clark Bekedermo) **38**:116-17, 125, 127-29
Reef (Gunesekera) **91**:33-39
"Reeling Back the Saffron" (Fulton) **52**:158
The Reeling Earth (Millin) **49**:251
"Reeling in the Years" (Becker and Fagen) **26**:79-80
"Reena" (Marshall) **27**:312; **72**:222
"Reencounter" (Kawabata)
See "Saikai"
"Reference Back" (Larkin) **39**:334; **64**:282
Refiner's Fire (Helprin) **10**:260-62; **22**:223; **32**:229, 233
"The Refinery" (Pinsky) **94**:305, 308-309; **121**:430, 447
"The Reflecting Trees of Being and Not Being" (Rexroth) **112**:373
"Reflection from Anita Loos" (Empson) **8**:201
"Reflection in an Ironworks" (MacDiarmid) **63**:255
"Reflections" (Carter) **5**:101-03
"Reflections" (Parini)
See "Reflections of a Nonpolitical Man"
"Reflections after a Poem" (McClure) **6**:319
Reflections and Refractions (Silverberg) **140**:376, 396-97
Reflections at Fifty (Farrell) **4**:157; **66**:132
"Reflections before a Glass Cage" (Enzensberger) **43**:149
"Reflections by a Mailbox" (Kunitz) **148**:88
Reflections from a Village (Swinnerton) **31**:427-28
"Reflections from Glass Breaking" (Sapphire) **99**:80
Reflections in a Golden Eye (Huston) **20**:170
Reflections in a Golden Eye (McCullers) **1**:208; **10**:338; **12**:409, 412-15, 417-18, 421-26; **48**:227-30, 240-41; **100**:246, 249, 251-52, 254, 256, 259, 261, 263
"Reflections in a Mirror" (Frye) **24**:225
"Reflections in a Spa" (Simpson) **149**:349
Reflections of a Jacobite (Auchincloss) **9**:52; **45**:33
"Reflections of a Kept Ape" (McEwan) **66**:280
"Reflections of a Middle-Aged Novelist" (Raven) **14**:440
"Reflections of a Nonpolitical Man" (Parini) **133**:288
"Reflections of India" (Forster) **77**:237, 239
Reflections of Nazism: An Essay of Kitsch and Death (Friedlander)
See *Reflets du nazisme*
"Reflections on a Lettuce Wedge" (Smiley) **144**:296-97, 300
Reflections on a Marine Venus (Durrell) **8**:193; **13**:188
"Reflections on Deafness" (Davie) **31**:108-09
Reflections on Espionage: The Question of Cupcake (Hollander) **8**:301-02; **14**:261, 264-65
"Reflections on Foreign Literature" (Enright) **8**:203
"Reflections on History in Missouri" (Urdang) **47**:400
Reflections on Language (Chomsky) **132**:18, 38
"Reflections on My Life" (Lem) **40**:300; **149**:161, 230, 232
"Reflections on My Own Name" (Porter) **33**:318
"Reflections on My Profession" (Giovanni) **64**:196
"Reflections on Narrative Poetry" (Simpson) **149**:316
"Reflections on the Black Woman's Role in the Community of Slaves" (Davis) **77**:122-23
Reflections on the Civil War (Catton) **35**:95
"Reflections on the Composition of Memoirs of Hadrian" (Yourcenar) **87**:394, 406-07, 411
Reflections on the Guillotine: An Essay on Capital Punishment (Camus)
See *Réflexions sur la peine capitale*
"Reflections on the Novel" (Anand) **93**:52
Reflections on the Psalms (Lewis) **3**:296; **124**:237, 246
"Reflections on Two Decades" (MacLennan) **92**:347
"Reflections outside a Gymnasium" (McGinley) **14**:366
Reflections upon a Sinking Ship (Vidal) **8**:528
"Reflective" (Ammons) **57**:59
Reflets du nazisme (Friedlander) **90**:118-19
Reflex (Francis) **22**:153-54; **42**:150, 154-58; **102**:144
Reflex and Bone Structure (Major) **19**:294-96; **48**:212-15
Réflexions sur la peine capitale (Camus) **4**:89; **14**:112, 117; **124**:29
"Reformers, Saints, and Preachers" (McGinley) **14**:368
"Refrain" (Dove) **81**:144
Refrain (Kieslowski) **120**:245
"The Refrigerator" (Moss) **14**:376
"Refuge" (Kingsolver) **130**:85
"The Refuge of the Roads" (Mitchell) **12**:442
Refugee (Anthony) **35**:39-41
"Refugee Blues" (Auden) **123**:29-31, 48
"Refugee in America" (Hughes) **1**:149
"Refugee Mother and Child" (Achebe) **11**:3; **26**:21, 24
"The Refugees" (Read) **4**:437, 439
"Refugees" (Tallent) **45**:387
"A Refusal to Mourn" (Mahon) **27**:290
"Refusal to Mourn the Death by Fire of a Child in London" (Ammons) **108**:21
"Refusing the Necessary" (Dobyns) **37**:77
"O regaço urbanizado" (Cabral de Melo Neto) **76**:167
Regain (Giono) **4**:186
Le Regard des femmes (Gallo) **95**:100
Le regard du roi (Laye) **4**:282-85; **38**:285-86, 288-91
"Regarding Chainsaws" (Carruth) **84**:132, 134-35
"Regarding Places" (Wilbur) **53**:406
"Regarding Wave" (Snyder) **32**:399; **120**:343
Regarding Wave (Snyder) **1**:318; **2**:406-07; **5**:393, 395; **32**:387-88, 391-92, 399; **120**:317, 325, 343, 354
"Regards d'outre-tombe" (Blanchot) **135**:98
"The Regatta" (Wilbur) **53**:400-01
"Regency Houses" (Day Lewis) **10**:131
Regeneration (Barker) **94**:4, 9-16, 18-19; **146**:2, 5-16, 18-19, 21-7, 30, 38, 41
The Regeneration Trilogy (Barker) **146**:38, 40
"Regent's Park Sonnets" (Hacker) **72**:182
"Regents' Professor Berryman's Crack on Race" (Berryman) **4**:62
Reggatta de blanc (Police, The) **26**:364
Un régicide (Robbe-Grillet) **43**:361, 364-67; **128**:364, 381
Regiment of Women (Berger) **3**:63-4; **5**:60; **18**:57; **38**:39
Regina (Epstein) **27**:131-32
Regina V. Rumpole (Mortimer) **28**:287
Regio (Rozewicz) **139**:227
"The Region Between" (Ellison) **139**:126-27, 140
La región más transparente (Fuentes) **8**:223-24; **13**:232; **22**:163-65; **41**:166-67, 171-72; **60**:153-54, 156-57, 163, 171-73; **113**:230, 235, 238, 244-45, 248-51, 253
Region of Unlikeness (Graham) **118**:222, 231, 233, 237-38, 248, 250-51, 253-54, 260-61
"Regionalism; or, Portrait of the Artist as a Model Farmer" (Montague) **46**:266
La règle du jeu (Leiris) **61**:341, 343-44, 347-60
La regle du jeu (Renoir) **20**:287, 294-95, 297, 299, 302-12
Regnen holdt op (Abell) **15**:5
"Regraduating the Lute" (Snodgrass) **68**:397
"Regreso" (Neruda) **62**:335
A Regular Guy (Simpson) **146**:288-92, 294, 296
"The Regulars" (Williams) **148**:354
"The Rehabilitation of Ginevra Leake" (Calisher) **38**:69; **134**:8
Rehabilitations and Other Essays (Lewis) **27**:265
The Rehearsal; or, The Punished Lover (Anouilh)
See *La répétition; ou, L'amoureux puni*
Rehearsals for Extinct Anatomies (The Brothers Quay) **95**:345-48, 351, 353, 355
Rehearsals for Retirement (Ochs) **17**:332
"Rehumanize Yourself" (Police, The) **26**:365-66
"Reichs-Kommissar, 1915-1944" (Hall) **51**:170
"Reification and Utopia in Mass Culture" (Jameson) **142**:247
The Reign of Sparrows (Fuller) **28**:156-57, 159
Reilly's Luck (L'Amour) **25**:282
"Reincarnation I" (Dickey) **109**:273
"Reincarnation II" (Dickey) **109**:247, 273
La Reine des Pommes (Himes) **108**:232, 241
Le reine morte (Montherlant) **8**:393; **19**:324, 327-28, 330
"Reinhabitation" (Snyder) **120**:328, 330-33, 345
Reinhart in Love (Berger) **3**:63; **5**:60; **8**:83; **18**:53-4, 57; **38**:36-8
Reinhart's Women (Berger) **38**:36-8
El reino de este mundo (Carpentier) **11**:100-05, 107; **38**:90-6, 98-9; **110**:61, 63, 69, 75-80, 82
"Reino mosco" (Cardenal) **31**:77
"Re-Interments: Recollections of a Grandfather" (Warren) **39**:265
Reinventing a Continent: Essays on South African Writing and Politics (Brink) **106**:138
"Reinventing America" (Urdang) **47**:399
Reinventing Womanhood (Heilbrun) **25**:254-55
"Die Reisebergegnung" (Seghers) **7**:409
"Reisekammeraten" (Andersen)
See "The Traveling Companion"
The Reivers (Faulkner) **14**:178; **28**:140
Reivindicación (Goytisolo)
See *La reivindicación del Conde Don Julián*
La reivindicación del Conde Don Julián (Goytisolo) **5**:150-51; **10**:245; **23**:184, 186-87; **133**:25, 32, 36-42, 44-47, 49-53,

55-58, 60, 65-67, 69-71, 74-81, 93, 95-97
"Rejoicing with Henry" (Kumin) **28**:223
Rejoicings: Selected Poems, 1966-1972 (Stern) **40**:408, 412-14; **100**:329, 333
"Rejoinder to a Critic" (Davie) **10**:125
Rekviem: Tsikl stikhotvorenii (Akhmatova) **126**:6, 34, 38, 42, 47, 53-4
"Relación del peregrino" (Castellanos) **66**:50
"Related Histories" (Adams) **46**:16-17
"The Relation of Environment & Anti-Environment" (McLuhan) **83**:370
The Relation Of My Imprisonment (Banks) **37**:27; **72**:8
The Relation of the Alabama-Georgia Dialect to the Provincial Dialects of Great Britain (Brooks) **86**:279
"Relations" (Allen) **84**:3
"Relations" (Robison) **42**:339
Relations (Slaughter)
See *The Story of the Weasel*
Relations and Contraries (Tomlinson) **4**:543, 546; **13**:546; **45**:396, 404
Relationship (Mahapatra) **33**:284
"Relationships" (Jennings) **131**:232
Relationships (Jennings) **14**:292; **131**:240
"A Relative and an Abosolute" (Van Duyn) **116**:406, 416
"A Relative Stranger" (Baxter) **78**:25, 27
A Relative Stranger, and Other Stories (Baxter) **78**:25-28, 30, 32
Relative Values (Coward) **29**:136
Relatively Speaking (Ayckbourn) **5**:35-6; **18**:27-8; **33**:40, 45, 47; **74**:19, 30-4
Relatives (Plante) **7**:307; **23**:344
"Relativistic Effects" (Benford) **52**:75-6
"Relativity" (Amichai) **57**:38
"Relato con un fondo de agua" (Cortázar) **10**:114
Relatos completos (Arguedas) **10**:10
"Relearning the Alphabet" (Levertov) **5**:249; **66**:242, 244-45
Relearning the Alphabet (Levertov) **3**:293; **5**:248-49; **28**:239, 241; **66**:235-37, 239, 245, 251
"The Release" (Gregor) **9**:254
"The Release" (MacLeish) **8**:361
Release (Schevill) **7**:400
"Release the Cranes" (Voznesensky) **57**:429
"Releases" (Fisher) **25**:161
Relentless as the Tarantula (Bukowski) **82**:22
"Relevance of African Cosmological Systems to African Literature Today" (Kunene) **85**:180
La relève du matin (Montherlant) **8**:394
"Relic" (Butler) **81**:122, 127, 129
"Relics" (Thomas) **107**:333
"Relief" (Blaise) **29**:70
"Relief" (Hughes) **35**:222
"Relief" (Padilla) **38**:349
"La religieuse qui retourna en Irlande" (Carrier) **78**:73, 78
"Religio Medici, 1643" (Borges) **6**:90
Religion and Career (Greeley) **28**:169
"Religion and Literature" (Brooks) **110**:9
Religion and Literature (Endō) **99**:285
"Religion and the Old South" (Tate) **4**:537; **11**:522; **24**:440
Religion and the Rebel (Wilson) **14**:587
"Religion and the Romantics" (Blunden) **56**:49
"Religion As Part of Culture" (Yevtushenko) **126**:398
Religion in the Year 2000 (Greeley) **28**:171
"The Religion of My Time" (Pasolini) **106**:239, 241, 253
La religione del mio tempo (Pasolini) **106**:220, 263, 265
La religione del nostro tempo (Pasolini) **37**:346
Religions East and West (Kettelkamp) **12**:306
"Religions, Inc." (Bruce) **21**:48, 53
"The Religious Button" (Brooke-Rose) **40**:106
"The Religious Poet" (Merwin) **88**:191
"The Reliquary" (Skelton) **13**:507
"Relocation" (Alexander) **121**:21
"Relocation" (Ortiz) **45**:303
Reluctant Guru (Narayan) **121**:353
"The Reluctant Poetess: Alicia Medina" (Kunene) **85**:166
"The Reluctant Voyage" (Bullins) **7**:37
Remain in Light (Byrne) **26**:98-9
The Remainderman (White) **49**:400
"The Remains" (Strand) **18**:515, 518; **41**:432; **71**:285
Remains (Snodgrass) **6**:514; **18**:491, 494; **68**:381-84, 388-90, 397
"Remains of Elmet" (Hughes) **119**:289
Remains of Elmet (Hughes) **14**:273; **37**:172-73, 175, 178; **119**:272-80, 288-90
The Remains of the Day (Ishiguro) **59**:158-64, 166-69; **110**:227, 229-34, 238-40, 243-46, 252-54, 256-65
The Remains of the Day (Jhabvala) **138**:73
"Remake the World" (Cliff) **21**:63
Re-Making Love (Ehrenreich) **110**:159-64, 178
"A Remark on Dedication" (Ekelöf) **27**:119
The Remarkable Andrew (Trumbo) **19**:445, 447
"The Remarkable Case of Mr. Bruhl" (Thurber) **5**:438; **125**:399-401
"Remarks of Soul to Body" (Warren) **6**:557; **10**:522
"Remarks of the Scholar Graduate" (Mathews) **52**:313-14
"Remarks on Discourse Ethics" (Habermas) **104**:91
"Rembrandt" (Lowell) **5**:256
Rembrandt's Eyes (Schama) **150**:188-202
"Rembrandt's Hat" (Malamud) **27**:306
Rembrandt's Hat (Malamud) **3**:323-25; **5**:269; **9**:349; **18**:318; **44**:411, 413, 415
"Remedies, Maladies, and Reasons" (Van Duyn) **63**:438, 441; **116**:408, 416, 424, 430
Remedy Is None (McIlvanney) **42**:279-81
"Remember" (Lennon) **35**:262
"Remember" (Rulfo)
See "Acuérdate"
"Remember" (Stafford) **29**:379
Remember Me (Tremblay)
See *Les anciennes odeurs*
Remember Me (Weldon) **9**:559-60; **11**:565; **19**:467, 469; **36**:446; **122**:247, 252-54
Remember Ruben (Beti) **27**:53
"Remember the Alamo" (Cisneros) **118**:201
"Remember the Moon Survives" (Kingsolver) **130**:85
"Remember Thy Creator" (Simmons) **43**:407
"Remember Young Cecil" (Kelman) **58**:295
"A Remembered Beat" (Kaufman) **49**:203
"Remembered Morning" (Lewis) **41**:254
Remembering Babylon (Malouf) **86**:195-211
"Remembering Christopher Smart" (Newlove) **14**:378
"Remembering Eliot" (Spender) **41**:421
"Remembering Esquimalt" (Skelton) **13**:507
"Remembering Hiroshima" (Purdy) **3**:408; **14**:432; **50**:246-47
Remembering Laughter (Stegner) **9**:510; **49**:345-47; **81**:344, 348-49
"Remembering Lunch" (Dunn) **40**:169
"Remembering Malibu" (Heaney) **74**:167
"Remembering Mykinai" (Corn) **33**:117
"Remembering Needleman" (Allen) **52**:40-2, 49
"Remembering Old Wars" (Kinsella) **138**:118, 165
"Remembering Poets" (Hall) **13**:260
Remembering Poets: Reminiscences and Opinions (Hall) **37**:143-45, 148; **59**:157; **151**:200
"Remembering the Children of Auschwitz" (McGrath) **59**:184
"Remembering the Movement" (Davie) **10**:124
"Remembering the Old Family Farmhouse" (Faludy) **42**:142
"Remembering the Thirties" (Davie) **8**:162; **10**:125; **31**:109
"Remembering Williams" (Tomlinson) **4**:548
"Remembrance" (Christie) **110**:126
"Remembrance" (Enzensberger) **43**:153
Remembrance (Walcott) **14**:550-51; **25**:454-55; **67**:352; **76**:275, 298
"Remembrance Day" (Achebe) **26**:21
"Remembrance Day" (Johnston) **51**:252
"Remembrance Day : 2010" (MacLennan) **92**:344
A Remembrance of Miracles (Ringwood) **48**:335, 338-39
"Remembrance of Things Past" (Ali) **69**:31
Remembrance Rock (Sandburg) **10**:448; **15**:467-68; **35**:351, 354
"Reminders of Bouselham" (Bowles) **19**:59
"Reminiscence" (Jennings) **131**:240
"Reminiscence of Carousels and Civil War" (Hirsch) **31**:216
"Reminiscence of My Beloved Mother" (Tanizaki)
See "Haha no kouru ki"
Reminiscences of the Cuban Revolutionary War (Guevara)
See *Pasajes de la guerra revolucionaria*
"Reminiscences: Places and People" (Allen) **52**:42
"The Remission" (Gallant) **18**:172
"Remittance Man" (Wright) **53**:427
"Remnant Water" (Dickey) **47**:92
"Remorse" (Betjeman) **43**:34
"Remorse" (Merwin) **8**:390
"Remorse" (Sassoon) **130**:182, 222
Remote (Shields) **97**:430, 433-36
"Remote Control" (Clash) **30**:44
Remote People (Waugh) **107**:381
"Remous" (Montague) **46**:269
"The Removal" (Merwin) **13**:386
The Removalists (Williamson) **56**:431-35, 439-40, 442
"The Remove" (Ghose) **42**:179
Remove Protective Coating a Little at a Time (Donovan) **35**:141
"Removing the Plate of the Pump on the Hydraulic System of the Backhoe" (Snyder) **120**:353
Le rempart des béguines (Mallet-Joris) **11**:355
"The Renaissance" (Pound) **112**:316-17
The Renaissance (Johnson) **147**:162
Renaldo and Clara (Dylan) **12**:197-98
"Renaming the Kings" (Levine) **118**:284
Renaud et Armide (Cocteau) **8**:149; **43**:112
"Rendevous-Vous with my Son" (Aitmatov) **71**:16
"Rendezvous" (Aksyonov) **101**:11, 22, 28, 30
"Rendezvous" (MacLean) **63**:270
The Rendezvous (O'Brian) **152**:273
Le rendez-vous (Robbe-Grillet)
See *Djinn*
The Rendez-Vous (Strugatskii and Strugatskii) **27**:433
The Rendezvous and Other Stories (du Maurier) **59**:286
Le rendez-vous de Senlis (Anouilh) **8**:24; **13**:16-17; **40**:51, 54-5
Rendezvous in a Landscape (Derleth) **31**:137
Rendezvous in Black (Woolrich) **77**:400, 403
"Rendezvous with America" (Tolson) **36**:424-25; **105**:259-60, 288, 291-92
Rendezvous with America (Tolson) **105**:231, 236, 239, 258-61, 263, 281-83, 285-86
Rendezvous with Rama (Clarke) **4**:105; **13**:150-51, 153-55; **18**:106-07; **35**:120, 123-24, 127; **136**:197-99, 201, 211, 237
"Renee" (Kelman) **58**:300-01
"The Renegade" (Camus)
See "Le renégat"
"Renegade" (Jackson) **60**:211-12
The Renegade (Graham) **23**:191
"Le renégat" (Camus) **4**:92; **9**:146; **14**:114

"The Renewal" (Roethke) **3**:433; **19**:396; **101**:265, 329
"Renewed Homage to Marianne Moore" (Cabral de Melo Neto)
See "Homenagem renovada a Marianne Moore"
Renga (Paz) **10**:390
Renga (Tomlinson) **4**:547; **45**:398
Renifleur's Daughter (Fraze) **50**:43-4
"Renner" (Powers) **1**:282
Renoir, My Father (Renoir) **20**:305
"Renouncing Sexual 'Equality'" (Dworkin) **43**:132
Rent (Larson) **99**:160-90
"Rent Control" (Tevis) **42**:372
Rent; or, Caught in the Act (Edgar) **42**:116, 123
"Rent-a-Womb" (Highsmith) **102**:201
"The Renunciatory Beauty" (Gascoyne) **45**:157
The Re-Ordering of the Stones (Silkin) **6**:498; **43**:396-98, 400, 404
Repair (Williams) **148**:363-69
"Repeat" (Kunene) **85**:178
"'Repent, Harlequin!' Said the Ticktockman" (Ellison) **42**:131-32; **139**:112, 131
"Repentance" (Behan) **79**:36-8
"Repentance" (Clarke) **9**:168
"Repentance" (Herbert) **24**:253, 268, 276
"Repentance and Self-Limitation in the Life of Nations" (Solzhenitsyn) **78**:385, 405-06; **134**:317
"Reperdiation of the Trilogy of Life" (Pasolini) **106**:268
Répertoire (Butor) **11**:78; **15**:119
Répertoire II (Butor) **11**:78; **15**:119
Répertoire III (Butor) **15**:114, 119
Répertoire IV (Butor) **15**:114, 119
Repetition (Handke)
See *Die Wiederholung*
La répétition; ou, L'amoureux puni (Anouilh) **1**:7; **13**:17; **40**:54-5; **50**:279
"The Replica" (Watkins) **43**:454
"The Reply" (Ginsberg) **36**:182
"The Reply" (L'Heureux) **52**:275
"The Reply" (Ignatow) **40**:259
"Reply" (Rozewicz) **139**:273
"Reply to a Reader" (Wolf) **150**:302
"A Reply to John Reichert" (Fish) **142**:157
"Reply to Mr. Wordsworth" (MacLeish) **8**:362
"Report" (Barthelme) **6**:29; **8**:50; **115**:59
"A Report" (Jin) **109**:54
"Report Cards" (Humphrey) **45**:193
"Report for Northrop Frye" (Everson) **27**:135
"Report from Normalia" (Hesse) **25**:261
"Report from Paradise" (Herbert) **9**:275; **43**:184
Report from Part One (Brooks) **2**:81-2; **4**:78-9; **125**:57, 65, 88, 110, 113
Report from the Aleutians (Huston) **20**:164
"Report from the Besieged City" (Herbert) **43**:191-93, 195
Report from the Besieged City and Other Poems (Herbert) **43**:191-92, 194-95
"Report from the Skull's Diorama" (Komunyakaa) **94**:245
Report of the Country Chairman (Michener) **109**:375, 378-79, 383, 386
"Report on an Unidentified Space Station" (Ballard) **137**:38
"Report on Experience" (Blunden) **56**:30, 33, 39, 49
Report on Planet Three and Other Speculations (Clarke) **35**:119, 122
Report on Probability A (Aldiss) **14**:10, 13; **40**:19-20
"Report on the Shadow Industry" (Carey) **40**:127; **96**:28, 37, 53
"Report on the Threatened City" (Lessing) **2**:242; **10**:316; **94**:261
"A Report to an Academy" (Oates) **33**:294
"Reportazh s otkrytiya GES" (Voznesensky) **57**:417
Reported Sightings (Ashbery) **125**:10, 13
"Reports from the Global Village" (Eco) **60**:112
Reports on the Ideological Situation of the Nation (Boell)
See *Berichte zur Gesinnungslage der Nation*
"Representation and the War for Reality" (Gass) **39**:477, 479-81; **132**:166
Representations of the Intellectual (Said) **123**:388-89, 391
The Representative (Hochhuth) **18**:252
Representing Super Doll (Peck) **21**:296
"Representing T. A. Buck" (Ferber) **93**:139
"Repression" (Williams) **56**:429
"Repression of War Experience" (Sassoon) **130**:184, 187, 217, 222
The Reprieve (Sartre)
See *Le sursis*
"The Reproach" (Glück) **44**:218, 221
"Reproach" (Graves) **45**:167
"Reproach to Dead Poets" (MacLeish) **68**:273, 287
The Reproductive System: How Living Creatures Multiply (Silverstein and Silverstein) **17**:453
"The Republic" (Ondaatje) **51**:310
A Republic of Insects and Grass (Schell) **35**:366-67
The Republic of Love (Shields) **91**:168, 171; **113**:433, 441, 445
The Republic of Whores (Škvorecký) **152**:323, 333-37
Repulsion (Polanski) **16**:463-65, 467, 471
"Una reputación" (Arreola) **147**:16, 18
"Requa" (Olsen) **114**:206-09, 223, 232
Request Concert (Kroetz)
See *Wunschkonzert*
"Request for Offering" (Eberhart) **56**:77
"Request to a Year" (Wright) **53**:420, 428
"Requiem" (Fearing) **51**:107
"Requiem" (Heinlein) **55**:302
"Requiem" (Ignatow) **40**:259
"Requiem" (Miller) **6**:334-35; **15**:372
Requiem (Akhmatova) **11**:8; **25**:25-8; **59**:384, 388, 391; **64**:6, 11-20; **126**:9-11, 13, 15, 17-8, 20, 24, 26-7, 40, 42-3, 45
Requiem (Bagryana)
See *Vechnata i svjatata*
Requiem (Guillevic) **33**:194
Requiem (Warner) **14**:553
Requiem: A Cycle of Poems (Akhmatova)
See *Rekviem: Tsikl stikhotvorenii*
"Requiem Before Renewal" (Brooks) **125**:107
Requiem for a Futurologist (Soyinka) **44**:298
Requiem for a Heavyweight (Serling) **30**:354-55, 358
Requiem for a Nun (Camus)
See *Requiem pour une nonne*
Requiem for a Nun (Faulkner) **3**:151, 156; **6**:175-76, 180; **28**:140
Requiem for a Princess (Arthur) **12**:25-6, 28-9
Requiem for a Spanish Peasant (Sender)
See *Mosén Milán*
"Requiem for Aberfam" (Thomas) **13**:541
"The Requiem for Christine Latrobe" (Epstein) **7**:97
Requiem for Fanny Goldmann (Bachmann)
See *Requiem für Fanny Goldmann*
"Requiem for the Champ" (Jordan) **114**:151
"Requiem for the Croppies" (Heaney) **74**:155; **91**:117
"Requiem for the Spanish Dead" (Rexroth) **49**:284-85
Requiem für Fanny Goldmann (Bachmann) **69**:36, 59
Requiem por un campesino espanol (Sender)
See *Mosén Milán*
Requiem pour une nonne (Camus) **9**:145; **14**:114; **32**:86, 88, 91, 96, 100
"Requiescat" (Hersey) **81**:329
"Requiescat" (Parker) **68**:325
Required Writing (Larkin) **33**:266-68; **39**:337, 341, 343; **64**:282, 284
"Reredos Showing the Assumption into Heaven of Frank O'Hara" (Feldman) **7**:102
"De rerum natura" (Blaga) **75**:62
"De rerum natura" (Boyle) **36**:58
"De rerum virtute" (Jeffers) **54**:244
Reruns (Baumbach) **6**:31-2
"Resaca" (Aleixandre) **9**:14
La resaca (Goytisolo) **23**:186; **133**:87, 90-93
El rescate del mundo (Castellanos) **66**:45, 50
"The Rescue" (Goyen) **14**:211
"A Rescue" (Green) **97**:274-76
"The Rescue" (McGuane) **45**:266
Rescue (Milosz)
See *Ocalenie*
"Rescue Mission" (Kristofferson) **26**:268-69
The Rescue of Miss Yaskell and Other Pipe Dreams (Baker) **31**:31-2
"Rescue Party" (Clarke) **35**:127; **136**:209-11, 213
"Rescue, Rescue" (Bell) **8**:66
"Rescue the Dead" (Ignatow) **4**:247; **7**:180; **14**:274; **40**:258
Rescue the Dead (Ignatow) **4**:247-48; **7**:175, 180-81; **14**:276; **40**:258
"Rescue with Yul Brynner" (Moore) **47**:261, 263
The Rescued Year (Stafford) **4**:519-20; **7**:461-62; **29**:385
"Research in Jiangsu Province" (Seth) **43**:388
"The Research of Dancers" (Moss) **45**:286-87
Réseau aérien (Butor) **8**:118, 120
"The Resemblance between a Violin Case and a Coffin" (Williams) **5**:502; **39**:450; **45**:447, 452-53; **111**:423
"Resentment" (Aldington) **49**:7
The Reservation (Ruyslinck) **14**:471
Reservation Blues (Alexie) **96**:13, 15-17; **154**:4-5, 7, 15-19, 22-5, 32, 38-9, 47
"The Reservation Cab Driver" (Alexie) **154**:27
"Reservation Drive-In" (Alexie) **96**:8; **154**:10
"Reservation Love Song" (Alexie) **154**:27
"Reservation Mathematics" (Alexie) **154**:12
"A Reservation Table of Elements" (Alexie) **154**:8, 27
"The Reservoir" (Frame) **96**:184-85, 191
Reservoir Dogs (Tarantino) **125**:342-47, 350-59, 362, 364-66, 368, 370-76, 383
Reservoir Ravine (Hood) **28**:195-96
The Reservoir: Stories and Sketches (Frame) **22**:143; **96**:188-89, 192, 216
Residence on Earth (Neruda)
See *Residencia en la tierra*
Residence on Earth and Other Poems (Neruda)
See *Residencia en la tierra*
Residencia en la tierra (Neruda) **1**:246; **2**:309; **5**:301, 303-05; **7**:257-60, 262; **9**:398; **28**:309, 311-13
Residencia en la tierra, Vol. 1, 1925-31 (Neruda)
See *Residencia en la tierra*
Residencia en la tierra, Vol. 2, 1931-35 (Neruda)
See *Residencia en la tierra*
Residencia I (Neruda)
See *Residencia en la tierra*
Residencia II (Neruda)
See *Residencia en la tierra*
Residencia III (Neruda)
See *Residencia en la tierra*
"Resident at the Club" (Motion) **47**:291, 294
Residential Quarter (Aragon)
See *Les beaux quartiers*
"Residents and Transients" (Mason) **82**:243; **154**:253-54, 256, 294, 315, 321
Residua (Beckett) **6**:36; **14**:80
The Residual Years: Poems, 1934-1948 (Everson) **1**:96; **14**:163
"Residue of Song" (Bell) **31**:48
Residue of Song (Bell) **8**:67; **31**:47-50
"Resign! Resign!" (Richards) **14**:455

Resignation; or, The Story of a Marriage (Hochhuth) **18**:253
"The Resistance" (Olson) **29**:329
"Resistance" (Simpson) **149**:350
Resistance (Archer) **12**:20
Resistance (Bernstein) **142**:4-5
"The Resistance Cabaret" (Simmons) **43**:409
Resistance, Rebellion, and Death (Camus) **2**:97
The Resistance to Theory (de Man) **55**:403-05, 409-10
"Resisting Amnesia" (Rich) **73**:322
"Resolution and Independence" (Bly) **128**:12
"Resolution of Dependence" (Barker) **48**:16, 20
"Resolve" (Jennings) **131**:240
Resonance and Foot-Tracks (Transtroemer)
See *Klanger och spår*
A Resounding Tinkle (Simpson) **29**:364-70
"Respectabilities" (Silkin) **43**:398, 400, 404
"A Respectable Woman" (Sillitoe) **148**:199
"Respected Graves" (Ignatow) **40**:259
Respected Sir (Mahfouz) **153**:250, 289
Respected Sir (Mahfūz) **52**:305
The Respiratory System: How Creatures Breathe (Silverstein and Silverstein) **17**:451
"El resplandor del ser" (Castellanos) **66**:45, 51, 60
"The Resplendent Quetzal" (Atwood) **13**:46; **25**:62
"Responding to Pain" (Govier) **51**:166
"Response" (Le Guin) **136**:317
"Response to Arthur Marwick" (White) **148**:277-78
"A Response to the Invitation to Respond" (Ballard) **137**:22, 24
Résponses (Sagan) **17**:428-29
Responses (Wilbur) **14**:578
"Responsibilities of the Poet" (Pinsky) **94**:300-304, 312; **121**:428, 432-33
"The Responsibility of Intellectuals" (Chomsky) **132**:36, 40, 55
"The Responsibility of Parentage" (Young) **82**:396
"Resposta a vinicius de moraes" (Cabral de Melo Neto) **76**:162
"The Rest" (Carver) **53**:61
Rest and Be Thankful (MacInnes) **27**:280
Rest beyond the Peaks (Bernhard)
See *Über allen Gipfeln ist Ruh: ein deutscher Dichtertag um 1980*
"Rest Cure" (Boyle) **121**:33, 56
Rest Home (Cela)
See *Pabellón de reposo*
"Rest Hour" (Johnston) **51**:250
"The Rest House" (MacNeice) **10**:323
Rest in Pieces (Brown) **79**:171
The Rest of Life (Gordon) **128**:141-43
The Rest of the Robots (Asimov) **26**:37, 42, 46-7, 53; **92**:5, 9, 13
Rest Pavillion (Cela)
See *Pabellón de reposo*
"Rest Stop" (Swan) **69**:362-64
Rest Ward (Cela)
See *Pabellón de reposo*
The Restaurant at the End of the Universe (Adams) **27**:12-15; **60**:2
"The Restaurant Window" (Moss) **45**:290
"Resting Places" (Watkins) **43**:450
"Restless" (Matthews) **40**:325
Restless Is the River (Derleth) **31**:131-33
Restless Nights: Selected Stories of Dino Buzzati (Buzzati) **36**:94-5
"Restless Serpents" (Zamora) **89**:380, 384, 386-87, 392
Restless Serpents (Zamora) **89**:361-63, 368-71, 373, 378, 381-82, 385, 388-91, 395
The Restless Years (Paustovsky) **40**:366-68
The Restless Youth (Paustovsky)
See *The Restless Years*
Restlessness (Rozewicz)
See *Niepokój*
"Restlessness and Experience" (Kunene) **85**:166
The Restoration of Arnold Middleton (Storey) **2**:425; **5**:415
Restoree (McCaffrey) **17**:280
"Restraint" (Barthelme) **117**:6
"The Resurection of Lazarus" (Fo) **109**:125
"Resurgam" (Tate) **14**:532
"The Resurgence of Miss Ankle-Strap Wedgie" (Ellison) **42**:126
"Resurrection" (Atwood) **15**:37
"Resurrection" (Davies) **23**:145
"Resurrection" (Graham) **118**:245
"Resurrection" (Harjo) **83**:273
"The Resurrection" (Jennings) **131**:232
"Resurrection" (Konwicki) **117**:281
"Resurrection" (Lind) **82**:129-30
"Resurrection" (Major) **19**:298
Resurrection (Blaga) **75**:64
Resurrection (Fitzgerald) **143**:315
The Resurrection (Gardner) **7**:112, 115; **8**:234, 237-38; **10**:218; **28**:167
Resurrection (Gerhardie) **5**:140
"La résurrection des morts" (Jouve) **47**:213
"Resurrection: Easter Sunday" (Allen) **84**:8
"Resurrection of Arp" (Smith) **15**:516
The Resurrection of Joseph Bourne (Hodgins) **23**:231-33, 235-36
"The Resurrection of the Dead" (Oates) **15**:402
Resurrection Row (Perry) **126**:323, 326
"The Retard" (Hein) **154**:
"The Retarded Children Find a World Built Just for Them" (O Hehir) **41**:324
Rethinking Camelot: JFK, the Vietnam War, and U.S. Political Culture (Chomsky) **132**:67
"Reticent" (Thomas) **13**:541
"The Retired Life of the Demons" (Enright) **31**:154
"The Retired Postal Clerk" (Betjeman) **43**:51
"Retirement" (Shapiro) **53**:334
"Retort" (Richards) **14**:453
Retour amont (Char) **55**:288
Retour au pays natal (Césaire)
See *Cahier d'un retour au pays natal*
Retour de Guyane (Damas) **84**:160, 164, 176, 179, 181
"Le retour de l'enfant prodigue" (Senghor) **54**:400, 406; **130**:259-60, 267
"Retratos anónimos" (Aleixandre) **9**:12
"The Retreat" (Mason) **82**:241, 246, 248-49; **154**:232, 285, 302-04, 322
"Retreat" (Shaw) **23**:396
The Retreat (Appelfeld) **47**:5-7
Retreat (Blunden) **56**:46
The Retreat (Newby) **2**:310; **13**:408, 410
"Retreat from Earth" (Clarke) **136**:209
The Retreat from Moscow (Almedingen) **12**:4
Retreat to Glory: The Story of Sam Houston (Latham) **12**:323-24
Retreat to Innocence (Lessing) **22**:280
"Retreating Wind" (Glück) **81**:164, 167, 169, 174
"Retribution" (Allen) **52**:40-1
"The Retrieval System" (Kumin) **28**:222
The Retrieval System (Kumin) **13**:327; **28**:222
"Retroduction to American History" (Tate) **11**:522; **14**:528, 532
"Retrospect" (Huxley) **11**:283
"Retrospective Forelook" (Eberhart) **56**:79
Les retrouvailles (Adamov) **25**:12
Retrouver la foi (Romains) **7**:381
"The Return" (Allen) **84**:3
"Return" (Blaga) **75**:78
"Return" (Bontemps) **18**:64
"The Return" (Bowen) **118**:74
"A Return" (Faulkner) **18**:148
"Return" (Forché) **25**:172; **83**:198-99, 211, 214, 216; **86**:144
"The Return" (Glück) **22**:177
"Return" (Heaney) **14**:243
"A Return" (Johnston) **51**:249
"The Return" (Jones)
See "The Return: A Fantasy"
"Return" (Lerman) **9**:331
"The Return" (Lustig) **56**:182, 184
"Return" (MacLeish) **68**:273
"The Return" (MacLeod) **56**:192, 194
"The Return" (McGrath) **28**:279-80
"Return" (Montague) **46**:267
"Return" (Neruda)
See "Regreso"
"The Return" (O'Brien) **36**:340
"Return" (Paz)
See "Vuelta"
"The Return" (Pound) **2**:343; **10**:405, 408; **18**:429; **48**:283
"The Return" (Roethke) **11**:481; **46**:362; **101**:263
"The Return" (Rozewicz) **139**:236
"The Return" (Silkin) **43**:400
"Return" (Tillinghast) **29**:416-17
"The Return" (Watkins) **43**:452
"Return" (Wright) **53**:424
Return (Paz)
See *Vuelta*
The Return (Turner) **48**:399-400
"The Return: A Fantasy" (Jones) **131**:250, 269
"Return from Ein Gedi" (Amichai) **116**:96
"The Return from the Freudian Islands" (Hope) **51**:211, 216, 221
Return from the Stars (Lem) **40**:289, 292-94, 296; **149**:117, 154, 162, 251, 263, 269-70
"The Return from Unlikeness" (Hine) **15**:280
"Return in Hinton" (Tomlinson) **13**:549
The Return Journey (Binchy) **153**:75-6
The Return of A. J. Raffles (Greene) **9**:250; **70**:292
"Return of a Popular Statesman" (Buckley) **57**:126
The Return of Ansel Gibbs (Buechner) **4**:79
"The Return of Chorb" (Nabokov) **15**:394
"The Return of Eva Perón" (Naipaul) **105**:155
The Return of Eva Perón (Naipaul) **18**:361-65; **37**:321, 323-24, 328-29; **105**:155, 171, 176
The Return of Frank James (Lang) **20**:206
"The Return of Inspiration" (Kunene) **85**:176
The Return of Iphigenia (Ritsos) **13**:488
The Return of Lanny Budd (Sinclair) **15**:500; **63**:357-59, 365
The Return of Lieutenant Boruvka (Škvorecký) **69**:346; **152**:315
"The Return of McCaughey" (Behan) **79**:36
The Return of Moriarty (Gardner) **30**:153-54
"Return of Peace" (Kunene) **85**:175
"The Return of Persephone" (Hope) **51**:216
The Return of Philip Latinovicz (Krleža)
See *Povatek Filipa Latinovicza*
"The Return of Robinson Jeffers" (Hass) **18**:211
The Return of Service (Baumbach) **23**:55
The Return of Solar Pons (Derleth) **31**:138
The Return of the Brute (O'Flaherty) **5**:321
"The Return of the Fisherman" (Clark Bekedermo) **38**:127
"The Return of the Goddess" (Graves) **2**:174
"Return of the Golden Age" (Kunene) **85**:175
"Return of the Hood" (Spillane) **13**:528
Return of the Jedi: The Storybook Based on the Movie (Vinge) **30**:415
"The Return of the Middle Ages" (Eco) **60**:112; **142**:
"Return of the Native" (Blunden) **56**:43
"The Return of the Native" (Cabral de Melo Neto) **76**:163
"Return of the Native" (Thurber) **125**:397
"The Return of the Prodigal Son" (Senghor)
See "Le retour de l'enfant prodigue"
"The Return of the Pronconsul" (Herbert)
See "Powrót prokonsula"
The Return of the Rivers (Brautigan) **34**:315
The Return of the Soldier (West) **7**:526-27; **9**:561; **31**:451, 454, 457, 459; **50**:395, 398, 401-02, 405-06
"The Return of the Son of Monster Magnet" (Zappa) **17**:589
"Return of the Sphinx" (MacLennan) **14**:342,

344; **92**:307, 344, 347
Return of the Sphinx (MacLennan) **92**:326, 343, 349-50
Return of the Traveller (Warner)
See *Why Was I Killed?*
The Return of the Vanishing American (Fiedler) **4**:161; **13**:211; **24**:197-99
"Return the Bridewealth" (p'Bitek) **96**:299
"The Return to a Cabin" (Leithauser) **27**:242
Return to a Place Lit by a Glass of Milk (Simic) **6**:502; **9**:478-79, 481; **49**:340; **130**:293, 298, 317, 319
"Return to Air" (Pearce) **21**:289
"Return to Cardiff" (Abse) **29**:15, 17
"Return to Chartres" (Sarton) **49**:310
"Return to D'Ennery, Rain" (Walcott) **67**:353; **76**:279
"Return to Frisco, 1946" (Snodgrass) **18**:490
Return to Goli (Abrahams) **4**:1
Return to Ithaca: The "Odyssey" Retold as a Modern Novel (Johnson)
See *Strändernas svall*
"Return to Kraków in 1880" (Milosz) **82**:305
"Return to Lewis" (Smith) **64**:396
Return to Lisca Bianca (Antonioni)
See *Ritorno a Lisca Bianca*
"A Return to Me" (Neruda)
See "Se vuelve a yo"
Return to My Native Land (Césaire)
See *Cahier d'un retour au pays natal*
"The Return to Mysticism" (Sadoff) **9**:467
Return to Nevèrÿon (Delany) **141**:154-55, 157
Return to Night (Renault) **17**:391
"Return to Oneself" (Neruda)
See "Se vuelve a yo"
Return to Paradise (Breytenbach) **126**:94, 96-9
Return to Paradise (Michener) **29**:310-11; **109**:378, 382
"Return to Pernambuco" (Cabral de Melo Neto)
See "Volta a Pernambuco"
"Return to Return" (Hannah) **38**:232
Return to Sender or, When the Fish in the Water Was Thirsty (Mungo) **72**:290
"Return to Solitude" (Bly) **5**:63; **10**:57; **38**:56; **128**:4
Return to the River (Haig-Brown) **21**:134-36, 141, 144-46
"The Return to the Trees" (Walcott) **76**:284
Return to Thebes (Drury) **37**:108-09
Return to Tomorrow (Hubbard) **43**:204
"Return to Varyinko" (Pasternak) **18**:388
"Return Trip Tango" (Cortázar) **33**:129-30
"Return Trips" (Adams) **46**:21
Return Trips (Adams) **46**:21-3
"Return Your Call" (Pinsky) **9**:417
"Returned to Say" (Stafford) **29**:381, 385
"Returning" (Lowell) **124**:255
"Returning" (Pastan) **27**:371
"Returning" (Rosenthal) **28**:394
Returning (O'Brien) **36**:336, 338, 341
"Returning a Lost Child" (Glück) **22**:173
"Returning North of Vortex" (Ginsberg) **36**:184
Returning to Earth (Harrison) **14**:235; **33**:197; **143**:344
"Returning to the Continent" (Brutus) **43**:89
Reubella and the Old Focus Home (Newton) **35**:301
Reuben (Wideman) **67**:374-78, 384; **122**:301-03, 319, 322-23, 331, 341, 348, 356, 360
"Reuben James" (Guthrie) **35**:193-94
Reuben, Reuben (De Vries) **2**:114; **3**:125; **10**:137; **28**:106, 112; **46**:137
"A Reunion" (Amis) **40**:40, 45
"ReUnion" (Bowering) **47**:24-5
"Reunion" (Cheever) **3**:106
"Reunión" (Cortázar) **5**:109; **92**:149
"The Reunion" (Dodson) **79**:193
"Reunion" (Swan) **69**:358, 361-64
"A Reunion" (Szirtes) **46**:392
"Reunion" (Vanderhaeghe) **41**:449
Reunion (Mamet) **15**:358; **46**:250-51
"Reunion in Brooklyn" (Miller) **1**:224; **84**:243
"Reunion in the Avenue" (Boell)
See "Wiedersehen in der Allee"
"Reunioning Dialogue" (Dickey) **15**:177
"Reunions" (Simon) **26**:406
The Reunions (Adamov)
See *Les retrouvailles*
"rev pinps" (Sanchez) **116**:294
Revaluation, Tradition, and Development in English Poetry (Leavis) **24**:293-94, 298, 300, 308
Un rêve fait à Mantoue (Bonnefoy) **58**:57
Le Réve Mexicain (Le Clézio) **155**:106, 108
"Revealed at Last! What Killed the Dinosaurs! And You Don't Look So Terrific Yourself" (Ellison) **13**:208; **139**:116
"Le réveille-matin" (Carrier) **78**:58
"The Revelation" (Bates) **46**:63
"The Revelation" (Elytis) **49**:110
"Revelation" (O'Connor) **3**:366; **13**:419; **15**:410; **21**:262-63, 271-72, 275-77, 279; **104**:103, 107, 110, 112, 115, 123-24, 138, 157, 159, 179-80, 185-89, 196-97
Revelation (Welty) **105**:359
"Revelations" (Barker) **52**:53, 55
"Revelations" (Dubie) **36**:142
"Revelations" (Macpherson) **14**:347
"Revenant" (McAuley) **45**:249
Les revenentes (Perec) **56**:256-57; **116**:233, 245, 267
"Revenge" (Allende)
See "Una venganza"
"Revenge" (Barth) **51**:26
"Revenge" (Gilchrist) **48**:115; **143**:274, 279, 297-98, 303, 310, 320-23, 327-28, 332
"Revenge" (Harrison) **14**:236-37; **66**:155-56, 159; **143**:335, 345
"Revenge" (Sillitoe) **57**:388-89; **148**:198
"Revenge" (Smith) **12**:544
Revenge (Brenton) **31**:56-7, 59-62, 65
"The Revenge of Hannah Kemhuff" (Walker) **58**:407; **103**:363, 365, 371, 406, 410, 412, 423
The Revenge of Moriarty (Gardner) **30**:154
Revenge of the Lawn: Stories, 1962-1970 (Brautigan) **1**:45; **3**:88-90; **12**:64-6, 70; **34**:315
"Revenge of the Poet-Critic" (Bernstein) **142**:57
Revenge of the Tribes (Berton) **104**:58-9
"Revenge of Truth" (Dinesen) **95**:49
The Revenge of Truth (Dinesen) **10**:145; **95**:41-2, 49, 61-2, 64, 67-8
The Revenger's Comedies (Ayckbourn) **74**:18, 28-9, 34-6
Reverberation Machines (Foreman) **50**:166
"Reverdure" (Berry) **27**:36
"Reverend Father Gilhooley" (Farrell) **66**:113, 131
The Reverend Ghost (Garrett) **3**:192; **51**:141, 145
Reverie (Aldington) **49**:2
"A Reverie of Bone" (Peake) **54**:369, 373
"Reveries on a pillow, Recife" (Cabral de Melo Neto)
See "Coisas de cabeceira, Recife"
"Reveries on a Pillow, Seville" (Cabral de Melo Neto)
See "Coisas de cabeceira, Sevilha"
"Reversal" (Ammons) **2**:14; **9**:28
"Reversal" (Dixon) **52**:100-01
Reversals (Stevenson) **7**:462
Reverse Psychology (Ludlam) **46**:242; **50**:342
"Reverse Pygmalion" (Avison) **97**:123
"Reverting Still Again" (Carruth) **7**:41
Les rêves et la jambe (Michaux) **19**:315
"Reviewers in Flat Heels: Being a Postface to Several Novels" (Markson) **67**:191
"Reviewing" (Wakoski) **9**:555
"Reviewing and Being Reviewed" (Epstein) **39**:467
Reviewing the Forties (Trilling) **129**:330, 337, 342
"The Revisionist" (Crase) **58**:159-61, 165
The Revisionist (Crase) **58**:159-66
Revisions (Bernhard)
See *Korrektur*
"Revisitation" (Sassoon) **130**:212
"Revisited Waters" (Watkins) **43**:447
"The Revival of Poetry" (Scott) **22**:371
"The Revival of Vaudeville" (Dickey) **28**:119
"Revolt against the Crepuscular Spirit in Modern Poetry" (Pound) **48**:288
Revolt in 2100: The Prophets and the Triumph of Reason over Superstition (Heinlein) **3**:225
Revolt in the South (Wakefield) **7**:503
The Revolt of the Fisherman of St. Barbara (Seghers) **7**:408-09
Révolte dans les Asturies (Camus) **32**:88, 100-01
"Revolucinations" (Morgan) **2**:295
"Revolution" (Fuller) **62**:185
"Revolution" (Lennon and McCartney) **12**:363; **35**:264, 266, 270
"Revolution" (Marley) **17**:267
"Revolution" (Montague) **46**:270
Revolution (Taylor) **27**:441
Revolution and Roses (Newby) **2**:311; **13**:408
"Revolution Blues" (Young) **17**:573
La révolution du langage poétique: L'avant-garde à la fin du XIXe siècle, Lautréamont et Mallarmé (Kristeva) **77**:299-302, 310, 313, 319-21, 323; **140**:147-50, 153-54, 157, 163, 168, 173, 179-80, 185, 193-97, 200
"Revolution I" (Lennon and McCartney) **12**:365
Revolution in Our Time (Archer) **12**:18
Revolution in Poetic Language (Kristeva)
See *La révolution du langage poétique: L'avant-garde à la fin du XIXe siècle, Lautréamont et Mallarmé*
A Revolution in Taste (Simpson) **32**:380; **149**:297, 327, 358
Revolution in Writing (Day Lewis) **10**:133
"Revolution Number Nine" (Lennon and McCartney) **35**:261, 270
"The Revolution of 1905" (Sadoff) **9**:467
"Revolution Rock" (Clash) **30**:47
The Revolution Script (Moore) **3**:341; **5**:296-97; **7**:236; **90**:255, 259, 269, 289
"Revolutionaries" (Ritsos) **31**:324
"The Revolutionary" (Bissoondath) **120**:3-4
"Revolutionary Dreams" (Giovanni) **64**:186; **117**:201
Revolutionary Immortality: Mao Tse-Tung and the Chinese Cultural Revolution (Lifton) **67**:140-41
"Revolutionary Music" (Giovanni) **19**:191; **64**:186
"Revolutionary Petunias" (Walker) **9**:558
Revolutionary Petunias (Walker) **103**:357, 364-66, 375, 395, 405
Revolutionary Road (Yates) **7**:553-56; **8**:556; **23**:482
"Revolutionary Situations" (Buckley) **57**:131
"A Revolutionary Tale" (Giovanni) **19**:192; **64**:183
"The Revolutionary Tradition in Afro-American Literature" (Baraka) **14**:49
A Revolutionary Woman (Fugard) **48**:110-12
"The Revolutionist" (Hemingway) **30**:189, 191; **80**:143
"Revolutions Revalued: The Attack on Credit Monopoly from a Cultural Viewpoint" (Williams) **22**:464
Revolver (Lennon and McCartney) **12**:357, 361, 376, 379, 384
Le revolver á cheveux blancs (Breton) **9**:127-28; **54**:18, 27, 30
"The Revolver in the Corner Cupboard" (Greene) **6**:216; **72**:151-52
The Revolving Door (Jones) **52**:247
"Revolving Meditation" (Kunitz) **148**:79, 92, 97, 101-02, 105

"Rewards of the Fountain" (Watkins) **43**:453
"El rey negro" (Arreola) **147**:27
El rey y la reina (Sender) **8**:478-79
Los reyes (Cortázar) **2**:101; **10**:113-14
Reynard the Fox; or, The Ghost Heath Run (Masefield) **11**:356-58; **47**:229-31, 233-34
"Reynolds & Chevrolet" (Kenny) **87**:241
The Rez Sisters (Highway) **92**:215-17, 219-21, 223-24, 227
Rhapsody in August (Kurosawa) **119**:338, 340, 378, 384-85, 397
"Rhapsody of Naked Light" (Ritsos) **31**:324
"Rhapsody on a Windy Night" (Eliot) **41**:156, 161; **55**:350, 374; **57**:169
"Rhenish Fourteenth C." (Van Duyn) **7**:498
"Rhetoric" (Fish) **142**:169-70, 185
"'Rhetoric' and Poetic Drama" (Eliot) **24**:185
"Rhetoric of a Journey" (Fuller) **28**:159
"The Rhetoric of Blindness" (de Man) **55**:401
The Rhetoric of Fiction (Booth) **24**:84-6, 89-92, 94-6
"The Rhetoric of Hitler's 'Battle'" (Burke) **24**:128
A Rhetoric of Irony (Booth) **23**:90-3
The Rhetoric of Romanticism (de Man) **55**:400, 404
"The Rhetoric of Temporality" (de Man) **55**:410
"The Rhetoric of the Image" (Barthes) **83**:85
A Rhetoric of the Unreal (Brooke-Rose) **40**:109, 111
"Rhetorical Meditations in Times of Peace" (Montague) **46**:265
The Rhetorical World of Augustan Humanism: Ethics and Imagery from Swift to Burke (Fussell) **74**:115, 137, 144
Rhine Journey (Schlee) **35**:372-76
The Rhinemann Exchange (Ludlum) **22**:288-89
"Rhinestone in the Rough" (Sorrentino) **40**:389
"The Rhino" (Soto) **80**:299
Rhinoceros (Ionesco)
  See *Rhinocéros*
Rhinocéros (Ionesco) **1**:154; **4**:250-52; **6**:250-53, 257; **9**:286, 289; **11**:289-90, 294; **15**:298-99; **41**:226, 229-31; **86**:331-34, 340
"Rho" (Tolson) **105**:255
"Rhobert" (Toomer) **13**:556
Rhoda, a Life n Stories (Gilchrist) **143**:313
Rhoda in Potatoland (Foreman) **50**:168, 172
"Rhode Island" (Meredith) **13**:373; **22**:303
"Rhododendron" (Stern) **40**:414
"Rhododendron Estranged in Twilight" (Middleton) **13**:387
"Rhododendrons" (Gallagher) **63**:124
"Rhody's Path" (Goyen) **14**:211
"Rhossili" (Watkins) **43**:454
"The Rhubarbarians" (Harrison) **43**:180; **129**:171
"The Rhyme of Reb Nachman" (Pinsky) **121**:446
"Rhyme of the Flying Bomb" (Peake) **54**:373
Rhymed Ruminations (Sassoon) **36**:389
"The Rhymer" (Blaga) **75**:63
"Rhymes" (Tomlinson) **13**:548
"Rhymes on Béthune, 1916" (Blunden) **56**:44
Rhymes without Reason (Peake) **54**:369
"Rhyming Max" (Updike) **23**:474
"The Rhythm" (Creeley) **8**:153; **78**:144, 156, 162
"Rhythm and Blues" (Baraka) **5**:45
The Rhythm of Violence (Nkosi) **45**:294-95
"Rhythms of Love" (Riding) **7**:374
"The Ribbon" (Williams) **42**:443
"Ribs, Roast, Chops, Bacon" (Johnston) **51**:254
"Ricardo and the Flower" (Bowering) **47**:22
"La ricchezza" (Pasolini) **37**:346
I ricci crescenti (Buzzati) **36**:84
"Rice" (Harris) **25**:212
"Rich" (Gilchrist) **48**:115-16, 120; **143**:273-74, 320, 322, 328, 332
"Rich" (Raine) **103**:186
"The Rich" (Tomlinson) **6**:535
Rich (Raine) **103**:185-90, 197-98, 206, 210
Rich and Famous (Guare) **8**:252-53; **14**:220; **29**:204-05
"Rich and Rare Were the Gems She Wore" (Kiely) **23**:261
Rich and Strange (Hitchcock) **16**:345
"Rich Boy's Birthday Through a Window" (Avison) **97**:69
"The Rich Brother" (Wolff) **64**:451-52, 454
Rich Desserts and Captain's Thin (Forster) **149**:102, 105
Rich in Love (Humphreys) **57**:233-38
Rich Like Us (Sahgal) **41**:373, 375
Rich Man, Poor Man (Shaw) **7**:413; **23**:398-400; **34**:368
The Rich Pay Late (Raven) **14**:441, 443
Rich Rewards (Adams) **46**:14-16, 21
"Richard Cory" (Simon) **17**:461
"Richard Greenow" (Huxley)
  See "The Farcical History of Richard Greenow"
Richard III (Olivier) **20**:237, 239-40, 243
Richard Pryor Live in Concert (Pryor) **26**:379, 381-84
Richard Pryor Live on Sunset Strip (Pryor) **26**:380-84
Richard Wright Reader (Wright) **14**:596
"Richard Wright's Blues" (Ellison) **11**:185
Richard's Cork Leg (Behan) **79**:27, 40, 47
Richard's Things (Raphael) **14**:437
Der Richter und sein Henker (Duerrenmatt) **102**:66, 69
Der Richter und sein Henker (Dürrenmatt) **4**:140-41; **11**:171, 174; **43**:122-23, 128
"The Rick of Green Wood" (Dorn) **10**:156, 159
"La ricotta" (Pasolini) **20**:271; **37**:347
La Ricotta (Pasolini) **106**:206-208, 221
"The Riddle" (Heaney) **74**:161
"A Riddle" (Hughes) **119**:277
"Riddle" (Snodgrass) **18**:491; **68**:388
"Riddle in the Garden" (Warren) **39**:266
"Riddle Me" (Ashbery) **77**:63, 65, 68-9
"The Riddle of the Ordinary" (Ozick) **62**:349, 352; 155167
"The Riddle of the Sphinx" (Du Bois) **64**:109, 112, 116
"Riddle: Post-Op" (Ostriker) **132**:326
"Riddles" (Guillén) **48**:157
"Riddles" (Parra)
  See "Rompecabezas"
Riddley Walker (Hoban) **25**:264-67
"Ride" (Miles) **14**:370
"The Ride" (Wilbur) **53**:412; **110**:357, 360, 372
Ride a Pale Horse (MacInnes) **39**:349-50
The Ride across Lake Constance (Handke)
  See *Der Ritt über den Bodensee*
"Ride, Fly, Penetrate, Loiter" (Hannah) **38**:233; **90**:138
"Ride My Llama" (Young) **17**:581
"Ride Natty Ride" (Marley) **17**:273
"Ride Off Any Horizon" (Newlove) **14**:377
"A Ride on the Short Dog" (Still) **49**:366-67
Ride Out (Foote) **75**:230-31, 236, 239
Ride Out the Wilderness: Geography and Identity in Afro-American Literature (Dixon) **65**:381
Ride Proud, Rebel! (Norton) **12**:457
Ride the Dark Trail (L'Amour) **25**:279
Ride the High Country (Peckinpah) **20**:272-75, 277, 279, 282-84
Ride with Me (Costain) **30**:93
"Rideau rideau" (Breton) **9**:127
"Riderless Horses" (Bly) **10**:57
"Riders" (Frost) **15**:241
"The Riders" (Voigt) **54**:433
"The Riders Held Back" (Simpson) **7**:427
Riders in the Chariot (White) **3**:521-22, 524; **4**:583-84; **5**:484-88; **7**:530, 532; **18**:545; **65**:275-79, 281-82; **69**:392-97, 400-01, 405-06, 408
Riders on the Earth: Essays and Recollections (MacLeish) **14**:338
"Riders on the Storm" (Morrison) **17**:294-95
"Riders to the Blood-Red Wrath" (Brooks) **5**:75; **15**:93; **49**:36; **125**:46, 48-9, 94
"The Ridge Farm" (Ammons) **57**:51-2, 54-6
Ridiculous Loves (Kundera)
  See *Směsné lásky*
Ridin' the Moon in Texas: Word Paintings (Shange) **74**:311, 313
"Ridin' up Front with Carl and Marl" (Wiggins) **57**:433-34, 439
"Riding a Jumper" (Hearne) **56**:124
"Riding a Nervous Horse" (Hearne) **56**:127
Riding High (Weber) **12**:632
Riding Lights (MacCaig) **36**:279-80, 284
"Riding the 'A'" (Swenson) **61**:401; **106**:328
Riding the Earthboy 40 (Welch) **14**:559; **52**:425-26, 428, 430, 433
Riding the Rap (Leonard) **120**:293-96, 299
Rien que la terre (Morand) **41**:304
Rien va (Landolfi) **49**:215-16
"RIF" (Barthelme) **59**:251
The Rifle and the Cross (Endō) **99**:287
Rifleman Dodd (Forester) **35**:165, 168, 170
The Rifles (Vollmann) **89**:286, 297, 304, 306, 309-13
Rigadoon (Céline)
  See *Rigodon*
"Right" (Matthews) **40**:324
"Right across the Great Plains" (Muldoon) **32**:317
"Right and Wrong Political Uses of Literature" (Calvino) **73**:48
"The Right Arm" (Muldoon) **72**:272
"Right Dress" (Scannell) **49**:330
Right from the Start (Hein) **154**:
"The Right Girl" (Sondheim) **147**:231
"The Right Hand" (Solzhenitsyn)
  See "Pravaya kist"
Right Hand Left Hand (Livesay) **15**:342; **79**:354
The Right Madness on Skye (Hugo) **32**:242-43, 250-51
The Right Moment for Humanity (Padilla)
  See *El justo tiempo humano*
"The Right of Eminent Domain versus the Rightful Domain of the Eminent" (Lebowitz) **36**:249
"Right of Sanctuary" (Carpentier) **38**:94
"Right On" (Ammons) **25**:43
"Right On" (Gaye) **26**:130
"The Right Profile" (Clash) **30**:47
"The Right Questions Is Theological" (Ozick) **155**:180
Right Royal (Masefield) **11**:357
The Right Stuff (Wolfe) **15**:584-87; **35**:458-60, 464-66; **51**:415, 418-21
The Right Stuff (Wolfe) **147**:303-04, 310, 313, 320, 323, 328-31, 334-37, 359-61, 363-65, 373, 375
The Right to an Answer (Burgess) **2**:85; **4**:81; **22**:70, 77; **40**:115-16; **62**:129; **94**:23-24, 26, 40-41
"The Right to Life" (Piercy) **27**:379
"Right to Loathsome Ideas" (Schlesinger) **84**:372
The Right to Remain Silent (Meltzer) **26**:300-01
"The Rightangled Creek: A Sort of Ghost Story" (Stead) **2**:423; **32**:408; **80**:306, 323
"The Rightful One" (Ignatow) **7**:175, 179
Rights of Passage (Brathwaite) **11**:66-7
Right-Wing Women (Dworkin) **43**:133-34; **123**:89-90, 106
Rigodon (Céline) **4**:101-04; **7**:45; **9**:153, 158; **47**:74-5, 79; **124**:64-6, 78, 89, 92-4, 103-04, 108, 112
"Rigor Viris" (Avison) **97**:69, 71, 106
"Rihaku" (Pound) **112**:343
Rihlat Ibn Fattuma (Mahfouz) **153**:264, 306, 359, 361
"Rikki Don't Lose That Number" (Becker and Fagen) **26**:79
Rima in the Weeds (McNamer) **70**:83-90
"Rimbaud and Verlaine" (Aiken) **52**:23
"Rimbaud and Verlaine" (O'Hara) **13**:424

"Rimbaud Fire Letter to Jim Applewhite" (Chappell) **78**:93, 96
"Rimbaud's Piano" (Merwin) **88**:213
"Rime of the Palmers" (Merwin) **45**:269
"Rimrock, Where It Is" (Carruth) **7**:41
"Rind of Earth" (Derleth) **31**:136
The Ring (Hitchcock) **16**:343
Ring around the Sun (Simak) **55**:320
Der Ring Gott Farblonjet (Ludlam) **50**:342, 344-45
"The Ring Of" (Olson) **5**:328
The Ring of Brightest Angels Around Heaven (Moody) **147**:170, 173, 183, 185-89
Ring of Truth (Scannell) **49**:333
Ring Roads (Modiano)
See *Le boulevards de ceinture*
Ring round the Moon: A Charade with Music (Anouilh)
See *L'invitation au château*
Ring the Judas Bell (Forman) **21**:116, 118
"Ringa Ringa Rosie" (Levine) **54**:293, 295
The Ringers on the Tower (Bloom) **24**:70, 73; **103**:3-4, 41
"Ringing the Bells" (Sexton) **53**:313
"Ringing the Changes" (Aickman) **57**:2, 5
Ringing the Changes: An Autobiography (de la Roche) **14**:150
"Ringling Brothers, Barnum and Bailey" (Van Duyn) **63**:443; **116**:410
Rings around Us (Gilbreth and Carey) **17**:155
Rings on a Tree (MacCaig) **36**:283, 286
The Rink (Chaplin) **16**:207
The Rink (McNally) **41**:290-91
"Río" (Aleixandre) **9**:12
El río (Matute) **11**:364
"Rio e/ou poço" (Cabral de Melo Neto) **76**:169
Rio Grande Fall (Anaya) **148**:32, 34
El rio invisible (Neruda) **62**:336
O rio ou relaçãode viagem que faz o Capibaribe sua nascente à cidade do Recife (Cabral de Melo Neto) **76**:153, 158, 162, 167-68
Un río, un amor (Cernuda) **54**:41, 51, 53-60
El rio y la muerta (Bunuel) **80**:24
"Riordan's Fiftieth" (Stern) **39**:244
Los ríos profundos (Arguedas) **10**:8; **18**:6-7, 9-10
"Riot" (Brooks) **49**:28
Riot (Brooks) **4**:78; **15**:92-3; **49**:23, 28, 31, 35, 37-8; **125**:45, 47, 88, 97, 106, 110
Riot: A History of Mob Action in the United States (Archer) **12**:20
Riot: A Poem in Three Parts (Brooks) **125**:106
Riotous Assembly (Sharpe) **36**:398-99, 402
"R.I.P." (Avison) **97**:76
Rip Awake (Coover) **32**:120
"Rip Off" (Cliff) **21**:60
Rip van Winkle (Frisch) **44**:194
The Ripening (Glissant)
See *La Lézarde*
Ripley Bogle (Wilson) **59**:105-08
Ripley under Ground (Highsmith) **4**:225; **42**:212; **102**:179, 193-95, 197, 207-09, 212
Ripley under Water (Highsmith) **102**:212
Ripley's End (Highsmith) **4**:226
Ripley's Game (Highsmith) **4**:226; **42**:214; **102**:174, 179-80, 183, 185, 193, 195, 208-09
The Rip-Off (Thompson) **69**:382-83, 387
"Riposte" (Hacker) **72**:191
Ripostes (Pound) **4**:408; **10**:405; **48**:288
A Ripple from the Storm (Lessing) **2**:238; **3**:290-92; **6**:298; **94**:256, 281-82
"Riprap" (Snyder) **120**:309
Riprap (Snyder) **5**:393-94; **9**:500-03; **32**:387-90, 396-98; **120**:313, 315-16, 338, 353
Riprap & Cold Mountain Poems (Snyder) **120**:315, 333
"Le Rire de la Méduse" (Cixous) **92**:54, 57, 69-70, 72, 75, 78-80, 87-9, 95-6
Risco do bordado (Dourado) **23**:150-51; **60**:85, 93-4
"The Rise" (Berry) **27**:38
"Rise and Fall" (Busch) **47**:62
"Rise and Fall" (Dacey) **51**:78
The Rise and Fall of Ziggy Stardust and the Spiders from Mars (Bowie) **17**:58-9, 61-3, 67-8
Rise of English Literary History (Wellek) **28**:443, 452
The Rise of Life on Earth (Oates) **108**:379, 381, 385
"The Rise of the Angry Generation" (Kunene) **85**:175
"The Rise of the Middle Class" (Banks) **37**:24
Risen from the Soil (Saramago) **119**:148
Risibles Amours (Kundera)
See *Směsné lásky*
"Risiko für Weihnachtsmänner" (Lenz) **27**:245
Rising and Falling (Matthews) **40**:320-22
The Rising Fire (MacEwen) **13**:357
The Rising Generation (Jellicoe) **27**:208-10
The Rising Gorge (Perelman) **5**:338; **9**:415; **23**:336
The Rising of the Moon (Ford) **16**:315
"The Rising of the Sun" (Milosz)
See "From Where the Sun Rises"
"The Rising Out" (McGuckian) **48**:278
Rising Sun (Crichton) **90**:76-83, 88, 90-1, 93, 96
"The Rising Tide" (Yehoshua) **31**:472
The Rising Tide (Keane) **31**:233
"Rising Up" (Gerstler) **70**:156
"Risk" (Asimov) **26**:55; **92**:13
"Risk" (Dickinson) **49**:102-03
Risk (Francis) **22**:151; **42**:150, 155, 157
"The Risk and the Clock" (Char)
See "Le risque et le pendule"
"Risky Bizness" (Kristofferson) **26**:269
"Le risque et le pendule" (Char) **11**:117
Risques et périls (Reverdy) **53**:286
"Risvegli" (Ungaretti) **11**:555
Rita Hayworth (Puig)
See *La traición de Rita Hayworth*
Rita Hayworth and Shawshank Redemption (King) **26**:240-42; **113**:351-52
"Rital and Raton" (Pasolini) **106**:270
"The Rite" (Randall) **135**:389
The Rite (Bergman)
See *Riten*
"Rite and Fore-Time" (Jones) **7**:190; **42**:241
Rite of Darkness (Castellanos)
See *Oficio de tinieblas*
"Rite of Passage" (Olds) **39**:187, 192; **85**:290
Rite of Passage (Fugard) **48**:110
Riten (Bergman) **16**:75; **72**:46-7, 56, 61
"Rites" (Cohen) **38**:130
"The Rites" (Creeley) **78**:133
"The Rites for Cousin Vit" (Brooks) **49**:27; **125**:67
"Rites for the Extrusion of a Leper" (Merton) **83**:397
"The Rites of Hysteria" (Gascoyne) **45**:148, 151
"Rites of Passage" (Gunn) **18**:200
"Rites of Passage" (Rexroth) **22**:345
Rites of Passage (Golding) **27**:160-63, 165-69; **81**:315, 317-25
Rites of Passage (Greenberg) **30**:162-63, 166
The Rites of Spring (Abbey) **36**:21
Ritmuri (Arghezi) **80**:6, 8
Ritorno a Lisca Bianca (Antonioni) **144**:38, 70
"Il ritorno di Lorenzo" (Levi) **37**:224
Ritsos in Parentheses (Ritsos) **31**:328-31
Der Ritt über den Bodensee (Handke) **5**:163; **8**:262; **10**:257; **15**:268-70; **134**:110, 114, 157, 161
Die ritter der Tafelrunde (Hein) **154**:55, 64-5, 158, 160, 172, 180-81
"Ritual" (Gregor) **9**:254
"Ritual" (Ignatow) **4**:248; **7**:180; **40**:258
"A Ritual" (Mahapatra) **33**:282
"Ritual" (Purdy) **50**:246
The Ritual (Bergman)
See *Riten*
"Ritual One" (Ignatow) **7**:180
"Ritual Two" (Ignatow) **7**:180
"Ritual Three" (Ignatow) **7**:180
"Ritual Drama as the Hub" (Burke) **24**:126
"Ritual for Eating the World" (Ammons) **108**:20
Ritual in the Dark (Wilson) **3**:537; **14**:588
Ritual in Transfigured Time (Deren) **16**:252; **102**:28, 31, 35, 38-9, 43-47
"Ritual of Departure" (Kinsella) **138**:85, 94, 99-100, 133, 156
"The Ritual of Memories" (Gallagher) **18**:170; **63**:123
Ritual of the Wind: North American Indian Ceremonies, Music, and Dances (Highwater) **12**:287
"Ritual XVII" (Blackburn) **9**:100
"Rituals" (Giovanni) **4**:189
"Rituals of Rejection" (Valenzuela)
See "Ceremonias de rechazo"
Rituals of Surgery (Selzer) **74**:263, 281, 285, 287
The Ritz (Lester) **20**:231
The Ritz (McNally) **7**:219; **41**:293; **91**:163
Le rivage des Syrtes (Gracq) **11**:245; **48**:136, 138-43
"A Rival" (Hughes) **37**:179
"The Rival" (Plath) **9**:427; **51**:344; **111**:214
"The Rivals" (Garrett) **51**:140
"The Rivals" (Scannell) **49**:331
The Rivals (Aitmatov)
See *Soperniki*
"Riven Doggeries" (Tate) **25**:429-30
Riven Doggeries (Tate) **25**:429
"River" (Aleixandre)
See "Río"
"River" (Ammons) **108**:22
"The River" (Carver) **55**:276
"The River" (Ciardi) **129**:39
"The River" (Dybek) **114**:72-3
"The River" (Kincaid)
See "At the Bottom of the River"
"The River" (Merwin) **88**:213
"The River" (O'Connor) **1**:257; **6**:381; **10**:368; **15**:412; **21**:256-57, 261, 271; **66**:309; **104**:120, 173
"The River" (Oliver) **98**:258
"The River" (Ostriker) **132**:324
"The River" (Salinas) **90**:322, 324
"The River" (Soto) **80**:301
The River (Cabral de Melo Neto)
See *O rio ou relaçãode viagem que faz o Capibaribe sua nascente à cidade do Recife*
The River (Godden) **53**:154-58, 161
The River (Hughes) **37**:178-81; **119**:281, 290, 295
The River (Renoir) **20**:287, 304
A River, A Love (Cernuda)
See *Un río, un amor*
River: A Poem (Chappell) **40**:143-45, 147; **78**:91
"River and Bridge" (Alexander) **121**:21
River and Bridge (Alexander) **121**:21
The River and I (Neihardt) **32**:335
"River and/or Well" (Cabral de Melo Neto)
See "Rio e/ou poço"
River at Her Feet (Sherburne) **30**:361
"The River Awakening to the Sea" (Chappell) **78**:111
"River Barrow" (Hughes) **37**:179
The River Between (Ngũgĩ wa Thiong'o) **3**:358; **7**:262, 264-66; **13**:583; **36**:312-13, 315-17, 319
"The River Bridged and Forgot" (Berry) **46**:72
"The River Flows Slowly along the Valley" (Akhmatova) **25**:27
River George (Lee) **52**:267-69
"River Going By" (Derleth) **31**:136
"The River House" (Blunden) **56**:29
"River Incident" (Roethke) **19**:397
River Lady (Waters) **88**:362

"The River Merchant's Wife: A Letter" (Pound) **1**:275; **112**:343, 346-47
A River Never Sleeps (Haig-Brown) **21**:135-36, 142
The River Niger (Walker) **19**:455
River of Death (MacLean) **63**:266
River of Earth (Still) **49**:363-69
"River of Names" (Allison) **78**:2; **153**:9, 18, 25
River of Stone (Wiebe) **138**:379-80
"River People" (Bass) **79**:17
River Rats, Inc. (George) **35**:178
"River Road" (Kunitz) **148**:81, 89, 128
"River Roads" (Sandburg) **10**:450
River Root: A Syzygy for the Bicentennial of These States (Everson) **14**:164, 167
"A River Running By" (Simpson) **149**:307
A River Runs Through It (Maclean) **78**:221-27, 229, 232, 235-37, 239-41
A River Runs Through It, and Other Stories (Maclean) **78**:221-22, 232, 235, 242, 244
"The River Song" (Pound) **112**:347
The River Sot' (Leonov)
See *Sot'*
The River Styx, Ohio (Oliver) **98**:276-77, 291
"The River That Is East" (Kinnell) **29**:281, 283-84, 287
The River to Pickle Beach (Betts) **3**:73; **28**:34
A River Town (Keneally) **117**:246-47, 249
Riverbed (Wagoner) **3**:508
"The Riverman" (Bishop) **9**:97; **13**:89; **32**:33-4, 42
"The Rivermen" (Mitchell) **98**:173, 182
"Riverroad" (Tilghman) **65**:107
"Rivers" (Milosz) **82**:298
Rivers among Rocks (Gustafson) **36**:212, 214, 216-18, 222
"Rivers and Mountains" (Ashbery) **77**:59-60
Rivers and Mountains (Ashbery) **2**:16, 19; **4**:22-3; **9**:43-4; **15**:26-7, 30; **25**:49, 58; **41**:40; **125**:4, 32
Rivers of Canada (MacLennan) **92**:306, 319, 343-44
The Rivers of Eros (Colter) **58**:138-41, 143-44, 146
"The Rivers of Roa Bastos" (Dorfman) **77**:156
"River's Story" (Tate) **25**:430
Rivers West (L'Amour) **25**:280-81
Riverside (Hamilton)
See *The Slaves of Solitude*
Riverside Drive (Simpson) **4**:499; **32**:379; **149**:332, 353, 359
The Riverside Villas Murder (Amis) **3**:7-10; **5**:22; **40**:41-3; **129**:8
La rivière sans repos (Roy) **10**:442; **14**:468
"Rivkala's Ring" (Gray) **112**:111
R.L.'s Dream (Mosley) **97**:348, 354-61
The Roaches (Tchicaya)
See *Les cancrelats*
"The Road" (Avison) **97**:111
"The Road" (Hillis) **66**:194
"The Road" (Sassoon) **130**:178
"The Road" (Sillitoe) **148**:198
"The Road" (Simpson) **7**:428
The Road (Anand) **23**:12, 17; **93**:48, 50, 55
The Road (Ehle) **27**:104
The Road (Fellini)
See *La strada*
The Road (Martinson)
See *Vägen till Klockrike*
The Road (Soyinka) **3**:463; **14**:508; **36**:410; **44**:277, 279-81, 283, 286-88, 290
The Road (Tesich) **40**:421
The Road Allowance People (Campbell) **85**:13-4
"The Road and the Sky" (Browne) **21**:36, 41
"The Road Atlas" (McGuane) **45**:265; **127**:274
The Road Back (Remarque) **21**:326-27, 330
"The Road Between Here and There" (Kinnell) **129**:248, 270
"Road Ends at Tahola" (Hugo) **32**:238
"The Road from Colonus" (Forster) **45**:136, 140-42
The Road from Coorain (Conway) **152**:102-4, 106-111
"Road from the Isles" (Laurence) **50**:320, 322; **62**:280-81
"A Road in Indiana" (Colwin) **84**:151
"The Road Not Taken" (Frost) **10**:193; **13**:230; **15**:248; **26**:116-17, 121, 123, 128; **34**:470, 474
"The Road of Dreams" (Christie) **110**:125
The Road of Dreams (Christie) **39**:437; **110**:125
"The Road of El Sueno by the Sea" (Salinas) **90**:332
The Road Past Altamont (Roy)
See *La route d'Altamont*
Road Scholar: Coast to Coast Late in the Century (Codrescu) **121**:173, 178-79
"Road Show" (Carpenter) **41**:103
The Road Sign at the End of the Street (Abe)
See *Owarishi michino shirubeni*
The Road through the Wall (Jackson) **60**:216-18, 232-34, 236
The Road to a Kingdom (Endō) **99**:287
The Road to Bithynia (Slaughter) **29**:374-75
The Road to Camlann: The Death of King Arthur (Sutcliff) **26**:440-41
"The Road to Emmaus" (Brown) **100**:82-3
The Road to Gandolfo (Ludlum) **43**:275
The Road to Joy (Merton) **83**:404
The Road to Klockrike (Martinson)
See *Vägen till Klockrike*
The Road to Lichfield (Lively) **32**:273
The Road to Los Angeles (Fante) **60**:133-35
Road to Mandalay (Browning) **16**:124
The Road to Many a Wonder (Wagoner) **5**:474-75
The Road to Mecca (Fugard) **40**:200-02; **80**:72, 74, 78-81, 84, 87
The Road to Miltown; or, Under the Spreading Atrophy (Perelman) **23**:335
"The Road to Platero" (Anaya) **148**:46-47
"The Road to Rankin's Point" (MacLeod) **56**:193, 196-97
The Road to Ruin (Sassoon) **36**:389
"The Road to Santiago" (Carpentier) **38**:94
The Road to Stratford (O'Connor) **14**:397
The Road to the City (Ginzburg)
See *La strada che va in città*
The Road to the Graveyard (Foote) **51**:133
Road to the Ocean (Leonov)
See *Doroga na okean*
"The Road to the Sea" (Clarke) **35**:122
Road to the Stilt House (Richards) **59**:187-89
Road to Volgograd (Sillitoe) **148**:185
The Road to Wellville (Boyle) **90**:56-9, 61, 64
"The Road to Yesterday" (Davison) **15**:170
"The Road You Didn't Take" (Sondheim) **30**:386, 391; **147**:234
Roadmarks (Zelazny) **21**:472, 474
"The Road's End" (Montague) **46**:267
"The Roads Must Roll" (Heinlein) **26**:171; **55**:302, 304
The Roads of Earth (Drury) **37**:111-12
The Roads of Freedom (Sartre)
See *Les chemins de la liberté*
"The Roads Round Pisa" (Dinesen) **10**:145, 152; **95**:35, 41, 49, 52, 64-5
The Roads That Lead Far Away (Haavikko)
See *Tiet eäisyyksiin*
Roadside Picnic (Strugatskii and Strugatskii) **27**:435-36
Roadside Valentine (Adler) **35**:14-15
"Roadwalkers" (Grau) **146**:158-61, 164-65
"Roadways" (Masefield) **11**:358
Roadwork (King) **37**:207-08
"Roan Stallion" (Jeffers) **54**:236, 238, 241, 243-44, 246; **3**:258
Roan Stallion, Tamar, and Other Poems (Jeffers) **11**:305; **54**:233, 235-37, 244
Roanoke: A Novel of the Lost Colony (Levitin) **17**:264
"Roar Lion Roar" (Faust) **8**:215
Roar Lion Roar (Faust) **8**:215
The Roar of Thunder (Smith)
See *The Sound of Thunder*
A Roaring in the Wind (Taylor) **14**:534-35
The Roaring Nineties: A Story of the Goldfields of Western Australia (Prichard) **46**:334, 337-38, 340, 342-43
"Roas Turkey" (Bennett) **28**:28
The Roast (Marshall) **17**:278
Roast Beef, Medium: The Business Adventures of Emma McChesney and Her Son, Jock (Ferber) **93**:135, 140-41, 147
"Roast Opossum" (Dove) **50**:153-54; **81**:139
Robbed in Light (Seifert) **44**:423
The Robber Bride (Atwood) **84**:108
The Robber Bridegroom (Uhry) **55**:265-66
The Robber Bridegroom (Welty) **1**:361; **2**:462-63; **14**:562; **22**:460; **33**:417-21; **105**:325, 341-46, 349, 384-85
The Robber Hotzenplotz (Preussler) **17**:374, 376
"The Robbery" (Mohr) **12**:447
"Robbie" (Asimov) **9**:50; **26**:54, 58; **92**:4, 10
"La robe de laine" (Theriault) **79**:407-08
"La robe déchirée" (Theriault) **79**:407
La robe mauve de Valentine (Sagan) **17**:424
La robe prétexte (Mauriac) **56**:206
"Robert" (Toomer)
See "Rhobert"
Robert Frost: A Life (Parini) **133**:289
"Robert Frost and the Poetry of Survival" (Parini) **133**:273
"Robert Frost at Bread Loaf His Hand against a Tree" (Swenson) **61**:394
Robert Frost Himself (Burnshaw) **44**:457-61
Robert Graves: The Assault Heroic, 1895-1926 (Graves) **44**:475-76, 479-80
Robert Hayden: Collected Poems (Hayden) **37**:159-60
"Robert Kennedy" (Seidel) **18**:475
Robert Kennedy and His Times (Schlesinger) **84**:368, 385
"Robert Kennedy Saved from Drowning" (Barthelme) **5**:53; **6**:30; **8**:50; **23**:46, 48; **46**:35, 43; **115**:57, 87, 92
"Robert Schumann" (Oliver) **98**:290
"Robert Schumann, Or: Musical Genius Begins with Affliction" (Dove) **81**:137
"Roberta" (Joel) **26**:214, 219
Robeson Street (Howe) **47**:177
Robespierre the Incorruptible: A Psychobiography (Gallo) **95**:87
"Robin" (Merwin) **18**:334
"The Robin" (Stolz) **12**:552
"The Robin" (Vidal) **33**:406-07
Robin and Marian (Lester) **20**:230-31
"Robin Redbreast" (Kunitz) **6**:287; **148**:87, 99, 128
"The Robin's House" (Barnes) **29**:27
Robinson (Spark) **2**:414-15, 417; **13**:520-21; **18**:505; **40**:393; **94**:326, 328, 331-333, 336, 353
Robinson Crusoe (Bunuel)
See *Las aventuras de Robinson Crusoe*
"Roblin's Mills" (Purdy) **50**:237
"Robot" (Davenport) **6**:124-25; **14**:140; **38**:144
Robot Fables (Lem)
See *Bajki Robotów*
"Robul"a (Arghezi) **80**:2
"Robust Meteors" (Char) **9**:167
Rocannon's World (Le Guin) **13**:345, 348, 351; **22**:265, 272; **45**:218, 222; **136**:330, 335, 384-85
Rocco and His Brothers (Visconti) **16**:570
"The Rock" (Jackson) **60**:214
Rock (Wagoner) **3**:507
The Rock: A Pageant Play (Eliot) **1**:91; **9**:190; **13**:194; **15**:206; **34**:525; **41**:159; **55**:348
"Rock and Fern" (Hooker) **43**:197
Rock and Other Four-Letter Words (Highwater) **12**:285
"Rock and Roll" (Page and Plant) **12**:475, 477-78
"Rock and Roll" (Reed) **21**:305, 307, 322-23

Rock and Roll Heart (Reed) **21**:312-13
"Rock and Roll Music" (Berry) **17**:53
"Rock and Roll Suicide" (Bowie) **17**:58, 61
"Rock and Roll Time" (Kristofferson) **26**:268-69
"Rock Bottom" (Ondaatje) **51**:313-14
"Rock Climbing" (Jiles) **58**:273
The Rock Cried Out (Douglas) **73**:70-6, 83, 85-6, 88, 90, 95-7, 99
The Rock Garden (Shepard) **17**:441; **41**:410
Rock It (Berry) **17**:55
"Rock Me on the Water" (Browne) **21**:35
Rock 'n' Roll (Lennon) **35**:269-71, 275
Rock 'n Roll Animal (Reed) **21**:307-09
"A Rock 'n' Roll Fantasy" (Davies) **21**:103-05
"Rock 'n' Roll Never Forgets" (Seger) **35**:385-86
"Rock 'n' Roll Nigger" (Smith) **12**:543
"Rock River" (Wideman) **67**:379, 385
"Rock Show" (McCartney) **35**:282-83
"Rock Springs" (Ford) **46**:161
Rock Springs (Ford) **99**:105-06, 110, 115-16, 120
"Rock Study with Wanderer" (Berryman) **62**:71
"Rock the Casbah" (Clash) **30**:50-2
"A Rock Thrown into the Water Does Not Fear the Cold" (Lorde) **71**:247
Rock Wagram (Saroyan) **29**:361-62
The Rock Woman (Baxter) **14**:63
"Rockaby" (Beckett) **29**:65
Rockaby, and Other Short Pieces (Beckett) **29**:59, 63-5; **59**:253, 255
"The Rocket and the Future of Warfare" (Clarke) **35**:128
"The Rocket Man" (Bradbury) **42**:44
"Rocket Man" (Jones) **81**:64-5, 67
Rocket Ship Galileo (Heinlein) **14**:247, 249; **26**:165, 171, 175; **55**:302
"Rocket Show" (Baxter) **14**:62
"Rocket Summer" (Bradbury) **42**:38
Rocket to the Moon (Odets) **2**:320; **28**:327-28, 332-33, 335; **98**:195, 198-200, 209, 215, 229-32, 237, 244, 252
"Rockin' after Midnight" (Gaye) **26**:135
Rocking Back and Forth (Grass) **15**:260
The Rocking Chair (Klein) **19**:259-62
"A Rocking Horse on Mars" (West) **96**:362
Rockinghorse (Kaniuk) **19**:239-40
"The Rockpile" (Baldwin) **17**:33
"The Rocks" (Creeley) **78**:144
"The Rocks" (Guillevic) **33**:191
"Rocks" (Mahon) **27**:288
"Rocks in Our Beds" (Holmes) **56**:143-44
"Rocks Off" (Jagger and Richard) **17**:224-25, 229, 236
Rockspring (Vliet) **22**:441-42
Rockway (Shanley) **75**:319
"Rocky Acres" (Graves) **45**:166-67, 169, 173
"Rocky Flats" (Levertov) **66**:239
The Rocky Horror Picture Show (O'Brien) **17**:322, 327
Rocky Mountain Foot (Bowering) **15**:82; **47**:20
Rocky Mountain Poems (Gustafson) **36**:212-13, 216-17
The Rocky Summer (Kingman) **17**:243
Rocky Time (Ritsos)
See *Pétrinos hrónos*
"The Rococo Seducer" (Brophy) **105**:8
Rod (Buzo) **61**:58
Rod Serling's Night Gallery (Serling) **30**:357
Roderick Hudson (Amis) **129**:8
Rodmoor (Powys) **7**:348, 350; **46**:313-14, 324; **125**:278-80, 294, 304
"Rodrigo Poems" (Cisneros) **69**:144
Rodzinna Europa (Milosz) **22**:309, 311-12; **31**:263-64, 267-68, 270; **56**:232, 242, 244, 250; **82**:277, 279, 281, 289, 291, 297
Roger's Version (Updike) **43**:437-39; **70**:249, 262-63; **139**:321, 323-24, 331, 375
RoGoPaG (Pasolini) **106**:226
Rogue Male (Household) **11**:277
"La roi Cophetua" (Gracq) **48**:141
Le roi des Aulnes (Tournier) **6**:536-38; **23**:452; **36**:433-44; **95**:361, 364, 366-67, 371-73, 375-78, 381, 390, 395
Le roi d'Yvetat (Renoir) **20**:300
Le roi miraculé (Beti) **27**:41-6, 49, 52
Le roi pêcheur (Gracq) **11**:246; **48**:134, 141
"Le roi s'amuse" (Urquhart) **90**:374
Un roi sans divertissement (Giono) **4**:184
Le roi se meurt (Ionesco) **4**:252; **6**:253; **9**:286; **11**:290-94; **15**:298; **41**:224, 227, 229, 231; **86**:332, 340
Rojo y negro (Arreola) **147**:6
Rojsty (Konwicki) **8**:325; **117**:256, 260, 274, 283-84
Rok myśliwego (Milosz) **82**:307-08
Roland Barthes by Roland Barthes (Barthes)
See *Roland Barthes par Roland Barthes*
Roland Barthes par lui-même (Barthes)
See *Roland Barthes par Roland Barthes*
Roland Barthes par Roland Barthes (Barthes) **24**:31, 36; **83**:79, 83-4, 88-9, 102-04
"Roland Hayes Beaten" (Hughes) **108**:319
The Role of the Reader (Eco) **142**:81, 94, 102, 106, 130
"The Role of the Writer in a New Nation" (Achebe) **51**:2; **127**:70
"Roll Another Number" (Young) **17**:574
"Roll Call" (Hoffman) **141**:294
"The Roll Call" (Johnston) **51**:238
Roll Call of Mirrors (Simic) **130**:340
Roll, Jordan, Roll (Peterkin) **31**:305, 307, 309, 311
"Roll Me Away" (Seger) **35**:386-87
Roll of Thunder, Hear My Cry (Taylor) **21**:419-21
"Roll On Bloomin' Death" (Luke) **38**:313
"Roll On, Columbia" (Guthrie) **35**:188, 194
"Roll Over, Beethoven" (Berry) **17**:51-5
Roll Shenandoah (Lancaster) **36**:245
Roll Sweet Chariot (Green) **25**:195, 198-200
"Roller Coaster" (Parra) **102**:348-49, 351
"Roller Skating Child" (Wilson) **12**:651-52
"Rolling Back" (Haines) **58**:222
"Rolling Dat Ole Debbil Electronic Stone" (Ellison) **139**:115
"The Rolling Machine" (Kelman) **58**:301
"rolling motion" (Moure) **88**:224
The Rolling Season (Mayne) **12**:392
The Rolling Stones (Heinlein) **26**:162, 165, 171-72, 176; **55**:302
Rolling Stones Now (Jagger and Richard) **17**:225, 232, 237
"Rolling Thunder" (Abbott) **48**:6
Rolling Thunder (Schrader) **26**:388-89, 399
Rolling Thunder Logbook (Shepard) **17**:445-46
"Rolling Up" (Simpson) **149**:316, 359
"Roly Poly" (Lem)
See "Przekladaniec"
Roma (Fellini) **16**:282-84, 298-300; **85**:53, 55, 59, 65-6, 69, 71, 74, 76, 78-9, 81
Roma (Palazzeschi) **11**:432
"Roma II" (Wright) **146**:335
"Romaiosyni" (Ritsos) **31**:325-26, 328
Le roman antillais (Condé) **92**:100, 112-13
Roman Balcony and Other Poems (Gascoyne) **45**:148, 150-51, 154
"Le roman comme recherche" (Butor) **3**:92
"Roman Diary, 1951" (Ciardi) **40**:162
The Roman Empire (Asimov) **76**:312
"Roman Fountain" (Bogan) **39**:387, 393; **46**:79-80, 86-7; **93**:76
Roman Hat (Queen) **11**:458
"A Roman Holiday" (Hecht) **8**:267
Roman Holiday (Sinclair) **15**:498
Le roman inachevé (Aragon) **22**:38
"Roman Incident" (Porter) **33**:322
"The Roman Night" (Morand)
See "La nuit Romaine"
"Roman Poem III" (Barker) **48**:18
"Roman Poem Number Five" (Jordan) **5**:203
"Roman Poems" (Garrett) **51**:144
"Roman Portrait Busts" (Updike) **23**:475
"The Roman Quarry" (Jones) **42**:242
The Roman Quarry and Other Sequences (Jones) **42**:242-43, 246-48
"Roman Reasons" (Enright) **31**:150
The Roman Republic (Asimov) **76**:312
"A Roman Sarcophagus" (Lowell) **1**:182
The Roman Spring of Mrs. Stone (Williams) **15**:580-81; **45**:453
Roman Tales (Moravia)
See *I racconti Romani*
La Romana (Moravia) **7**:240-41; **11**:382; **18**:344, 349; **46**:283, 285
"Romance" (Amis) **40**:40
"A Romance" (Dunn) **36**:153
"Romance" (Fuller) **28**:151
"Romance: A Prose Villanelle" (DeMarinis) **54**:101
"Romance I Think, Must Remain" (Lerman) **9**:330
"Romance in the Twilight" (Salinas) **90**:332
Romance of a Horse Thief (Polonsky) **92**:402, 415-17
The Romance of Atlantis (Caldwell) **39**:302-03
"A Romance of the Equator" (Aldiss) **40**:19
"Romance of the Thin Man and the Fat Lady" (Coover) **15**:145; **46**:115
Romancero (Pasolini) **106**:230-31
Le romancier et ses personnages (Mauriac) **56**:205
"Romania, Romania" (Stern) **40**:413
The Romanovs (Almedingen) **12**:2
"Romans Angry about the Inner World" (Bly) **128**:7, 12, 29
Romans, Countrymen, Lovers (Fleming) **37**:123-24
The Romans in Britain (Brenton) **31**:64, 66-9
"The Romantic" (Bogan) **46**:77-8, 83-4; **93**:64-5
"The Romantic Climacteric" (Pollitt) **122**:225
Romantic Comedy (Slade) **46**:371-72
The Romantic Egoists (Auchincloss) **45**:26
"The Romantic Entanglement" (Ashbery) **77**:69
The Romantic Manifesto (Rand) **79**:369
"The Romantic Movement" (Simic) **130**:327
"Romantic or Free?" (Auden) **123**:6-7
"Romantic Sonnet" (Simic) **130**:338
Romantic Times (Nabokov)
See *Glory*
"A Romantic Weekend" (Gaitskill) **69**:199-203
Romanticism and Consciousness (Bloom) **103**:47
Romanticism and the Modern Ego (Barzun) **51**:39-40; **145**:71, 94, 101
Romantics (Paustovsky) **40**:367
"Rome" (Antonioni) **144**:70
"Rome" (Williams) **13**:605
Rome 1630 (Bonnefoy) **58**:60
Rome and a Villa (Clark) **5**:106; **19**:105
"Rome, Anno Santo" (Montague) **46**:265-66
"The Rome Discourse" (Lacan)
See "Fonction et champ de la parole et du langage en psychanalyse"
Rome Haul (Edmonds) **35**:144-46, 148-49, 151, 153-54, 156-57
Rome n'est plus dans Rome (Marcel) **15**:360
"Rome: The Night Before" (Moss) **50**:353
Romeo and Jeannette (Anouilh)
See *Roméo et Jeannette*
Romeo and Juliet (Cocteau)
See *Roméo et Juliette*
Roméo et Jeannette (Anouilh) **13**:16-17, 20; **40**:51, 55-6
Roméo et Juliette (Cocteau) **8**:144; **43**:109
"Romiosini" (Ritsos)
See "Romaiosyni"
Rommel Drives On Deep into Egypt (Brautigan) **3**:87-8; **12**:59-60; **42**:61
"Rompecabezas" (Parra) **102**:346
Romulus (Vidal) **4**:553
"Romulus and Remus" (Hall) **51**:172
Romulus der Grosse (Duerrenmatt) **102**:53, 55, 58, 60, 74, 77, 79, 83
Romulus der Grosse (Dürrenmatt) **8**:194;

11:168-69, 171; **15**:194
Romulus the Great (Duerrenmatt)
See *Romulus der Grosse*
Romulus the Great: An Unhistorical Comedy (Dürrenmatt)
See *Romulus der Grosse*
"Ron Delph and His Fight with King Arthur" (Sillitoe) **148**:199
"La Ronde" (Le Clézio) **155**:83
La Ronde (Le Clézio) **155**:83
"Rondeau Redoublé" (Avison) **97**:76
Rondo (Brandys) **62**:118-21
Rond-Point des Champs Elysées (Morand) **41**:304
"Ronnie and Nancy: A Life in Pictures" (Vidal) **142**:303, 333
"Ronnie, Talk to Russia" (Prince) **35**:324-26
The Roof (De Sica)
See *Il tetto*
"Roof Beam" (Salinger)
See "Raise High the Roofbeam, Carpenters"
A Roof of Tiger Lilies (Hall) **151**:213
"The Roof Tableau of Kashikojima" (Lieberman) **36**:262
"The Roof, the Steeple and the People" (Ellison) **114**:99
"Roof Tree" (Murphy) **41**:320
"Roofs" (Levine) **33**:274
"Rooftop" (Moss) **45**:289
"The Roofwalker" (Rich) **7**:371; **11**:477-78; **18**:446; **36**:366; **125**:336
"Roog" (Dick) **72**:113
"The Rookers" (Mason) **28**:271; **154**:234, 238, 254, 317
Rookie of the Year (Tunis) **12**:595
"The Room" (Aiken) **52**:22
"The Room" (Ignatow) **7**:180; **40**:258
"A Room" (Lessing) **94**:261, 263-64
"The Room" (Sartre)
See "La chambre"
"The Room" (Strand) **6**:521; **18**:519
The Room (Altman) **116**:59
The Room (Day Lewis) **10**:128
The Room (Pinter) **1**:268; **6**:408, 410, 416-17; **9**:419; **11**:436-38, 440-41, 444; **15**:422; **27**:385, 388, 393-94; **58**:371-75, 377-78, 381, 384; **73**:252
The Room (Selby) **1**:307; **2**:390; **4**:481-82
"The Room and the Cloud" (Seidel) **18**:475
Room at the Top (Braine) **1**:43-4; **41**:55-60, 62
Room Enough to Caper (Brammer) **31**:53-4
"A Room Forever" (Pancake) **29**:346-47, 349
"Room Number Five" (Carey) **40**:129
"A Room of Frail Dancers" (Helprin) **22**:222
"Room of God and Door to Heaven" (Cook-Lynn) **93**:116
A Room of His Own (Beckman) **26**:87
Room Temperature (Baker) **61**:5-6
A Room with a View (Forster) **4**:169; **9**:207; **13**:215-16, 218-20; **22**:131; **45**:136, 138, 142; **77**:241
A Room with a View (Jhabvala) **94**:185, 187-88; **138**:64, 77
"The Room with the Tapestry Rug" (Giovanni) **117**:199
"A Roomful of Hovings and Other Profiles" (McPhee) **36**:294, 297
The Roominghouse Madrigals: Early Selected Poems, 1946-1966 (Bukowski) **82**:26-7
Rooms in the House of Stone (Dorris) **109**:310
"The Roosevelt and the Antinoe" (Pratt) **19**:379, 383
"The Rooster" (Orlovitz) **22**:333, 336
"The Roosters" (Bishop) **1**:34-5; **4**:66; **9**:92; **32**:29, 37-8, 42-3
"Root Cellar" (Roethke) **3**:432; **11**:484; **19**:397; **101**:293
"Root Hog or Die" (Guthrie) **35**:183
The Root of It (MacCaig) **36**:284
Rootabaga Stories (Sandburg) **5**:365-66; **10**:448; **15**:468; **35**:347, 357
Rooted (Buzo) **61**:51-6, 58-62, 64, 67-8
"Root-Light; or, The Lawyer's Daughter" (Dickey) **47**:91-2, 98
"Roots" (Clifton) **66**:70, 87
"Roots" (Haines) **58**:217
"Roots" (Heaney) **14**:244
"Roots" (Livesay) **79**:336, 350, 352
"Roots" (Meredith) **4**:349; **22**:302
"Roots" (Thomas) **107**:337, 340-41, 346
"Roots" (Walcott) **76**:277-78
Roots (Haley) **76**:343-45, 347-52
Roots (Wesker) **3**:517-19; **5**:481-82; **42**:425, 427
Roots and Branches (Duncan) **2**:122-23; **4**:141; **7**:87; **15**:192; **41**:129-30; **55**:293, 295
The Roots of Heaven (Gary)
See *Les racines du ciel*
The Roots of Heaven (Huston) **20**:163, 165
The Roots of Treason: Ezra Pound and the Secret of St. Elizabeths (Torrey) **34**:503-07, 509-12
"Roots, Rock, Reggae" (Marley) **17**:268
Roots: The Next Generations (Haley) **12**:253-55; **76**:344-45, 348
Roots: The Saga of an American Family (Haley) **8**:259-61; **12**:246-53; **76**:343-52, 346, 348
"Rope" (Porter) **15**:429; **101**:209-10
Rope (Hamilton) **51**:187, 189-90, 192, 194, 198
Rope (Hitchcock) **16**:340, 345, 355
Rope of Gold (Herbst) **34**:449, 451, 455
"Rope of Wind" (Dumas) **62**:162
Rope of Wind (Dumas) **62**:159, 164
"The Rope Trick" (Sillitoe) **57**:388; **148**:198
"The Rope-Makers" (Longley) **29**:293
"Ropes" (Townshend) **42**:379
Rope's End (Hamilton)
See *Rope*
"Roping, from A to B" (McGuane) **127**:271-72, 275
"Rosa" (Morrissy) **99**:78-9
"Rosa" (Ozick) **62**:353, 357-58; **155**:125-26, 129-30, 155, 170, 183-85, 192-93, 196-99, 202, 223
La rosa separada: obra póstuma (Neruda) **28**:310, 313; **62**:332-35
Rosaire (Ferron) **94**:126
"Rosalia" (Simic) **130**:306
"Rosalie" (Seger) **35**:379
"Rosalie's Folly" (Grenville) **61**:162
Rosalind Passes (Swinnerton) **31**:428
"Rosalinda's Eyes" (Joel) **26**:217
"Rosalita" (Springsteen) **17**:477, 482-85, 491
"Rosamund's Bower" (Aickman) **57**:4
A Rosario Castellanos Reader: An Anthology of Her Poetry, Short Fiction, Essays, and Journals (Castellanos) **66**:60-1
"Rosario de cuentos" (Ferré) **139**:182
The Rosary Murders (Kienzle) **25**:274-75
Rosas (Masefield) **11**:357
"The Rose" (Carey) **96**:25
"The Rose" (Cohen) **38**:137
"Rose" (Dixon) **52**:95
"Rose" (Dubus) **97**:203, 208, 214-16, 218, 222-24, 227-28, 230
"Rose" (Guillevic) **33**:193
"The Rose" (Roethke) **11**:485; **101**:289, 305, 308-09, 319-21
"The Rose and the Mignonette" (Aragon)
See "La rose et la reseda"
The Rose and the Puritan (Nowlan) **15**:398
The Rose and the Yew Tree (Christie) **12**:115
"The Rose Beetle" (Merwin) **88**:206
"The Rose Bush" (Giovanni) **64**:191
Rose Cottage (Stewart) **117**:394
La rose de sable (Montherlant) **8**:393; **19**:325
"La rose des vents" (Wilbur) **53**:405
Rose des vents (Soupault) **68**:404-05
"La rose et la reseda" (Aragon) **22**:37-8
"A Rose for Ecclesiastes" (Zelazny) **21**:466-68, 474
"A Rose for Emily" (Faulkner) **8**:213; **18**:149; **28**:143, 145; **52**:142;
A Rose for Winter: Travels in Andalusia (Lee) **90**:179-80, 184-5, 187
"Rose Harbours Whaling Station" (Bowering) **32**:47
A Rose in the Heart (O'Brien) **13**:415-16
"A Rose in the Heart of New York" (O'Brien) **13**:416; **36**:339-41; **116**:186, 189, 194
Rose Madder (King) **113**:383, 386-87
The Rose of Solitude (Everson) **5**:121; **14**:166
"Rose Petals" (Jhabvala) **138**:74-7
"Rose Street" (Lustig) **56**:182, 184
The Rose Tattoo (Williams) **1**:368; **2**:465; **5**:498, 500; **30**:470; **39**:446; **45**:446; **71**:382
"The Rose Warehouse" (Stern) **40**:410
Rose, Where Did You Get That Red? Teaching Great Poetry to Children (Koch) **44**:245
Roseanna (Wahlöö) **7**:501-02
"Rosedale Afternoon" (Phillips) **28**:361
"Rose-Johnny" (Kingsolver) **130**:73
Roseland (Jhabvala) **94**:184
"Roselily" (Walker) **58**:406; **103**:358-61, 363, 406, 410, 412
Rosemary (Stolz) **12**:548-49
Rosemary's Baby (Levin) **3**:294-95; **6**:305-07
Rosemary's Baby (Polanski) **16**:464-67, 471-73
A Rosen by Any Other Name (Horovitz) **56**:156
Rosencrantz and Guildenstern Are Dead (Stoppard) **1**:327-28; **3**:470; **4**:524-25, 527; **5**:412, 414; **8**:501-02, 504; **15**:518-19, 522-24; **29**:393-94, 397, 399-401, 406; **34**:273, 280-81; **63**:391-426; **91**:184, 187, 188-89
"Rosendo's Tale" (Borges) **10**:67; **13**:104; **48**:35
"Rosenschimmer" (Celan) **82**:49
"Roses" (Dove) **81**:138
"The Roses" (Oliver) **98**:256
"Roses and Revolutions" (Randall) **135**:389, 395
Roses Are Blooming in Picardy (Bermant) **40**:93
Roses Are Dead (Estleman) **48**:105-06
"Roses, Late Summer" (Oliver) **98**:281, 287
The Roses of Tretower (Mathias) **45**:235
"Roses, Rhododendron" (Adams) **46**:20
Les roses sauvages (Ferron) **94**:104-8, 112, 118, 124-27
"Rose's Turn" (Sondheim) **30**:389-90
The Rosewater Revolution: Notes on a Change of Attitude (Hughes) **48**:182
"Rosewood, Ohio" (Matthews) **40**:322
"Rosie" (Browne) **21**:39
Rosie and Sammy Get Laid (Kureishi)
See *Sammy and Rosie Get Laid: The Script and the Diary*
"Rosie Baby" (Huddle) **49**:182
"Rosie Won't You Please Come Home?" (Davies) **21**:88
Rosinante to the Road Again (Dos Passos) **1**:77; **25**:146; **82**:105
"Rosita, the Future Waits with Hands of Swans" (Salinas) **90**:332
Ross Macdonald (Bruccoli) **34**:416-17
Rosshalde (Hesse) **2**:190; **17**:195, 202, 217
"Rostered Duty" (Murray) **40**:337
"The rosy aureole of your affection" (Brutus) **43**:90
"Rosy Cheeks" (Howe) **47**:172
The Rosy Crucifixion (Miller) **2**:282; **9**:379; **14**:373; **43**:294, 297-98; **84**:277
Rosy Starling (Garfield) **12**:235
"Rotation of Crops" (Hollander) **8**:300
The Rotten Book (Rodgers) **12**:493
"Rotten Lake" (Rukeyser) **27**:406, 408
The Rotten Years (Wojciechowska) **26**:455-57
"Rouge High" (Hughes) **35**:215
"Rough Boys" (Townshend) **17**:541
The Rough Field (Montague) **13**:390-92; **46**:269-77, 279
Rough Mix (Townshend) **17**:537-38, 540
"Rough Outline" (Simic) **49**:336; **68**:373
"Rough Sketch" (Simmons) **43**:407

Rough Strife (Schwartz) **31**:387-90
Rough Trades (Bernstein) **142**:12-13, 41
"Rough Translations" (Giles) **39**:65-6
Rough Translations (Giles) **39**:64-6
Rough Treatment (Wajda) **16**:584-85
Roughneck (Thompson) **69**:383-84
Rougon-Macquart (Ehrenburg) **62**:179
"The Round" (Kunitz) **148**:125, 127, 143
Round about America (Caldwell) **50**:302
"Round and Round" (Seth) **90**:351
Round and Round the Garden (Ayckbourn) **5**:36-7; **74**:4-6
"The Round Dozen" (Maugham) **67**:209
"The Round House" (Jones) **131**:269
A Round of Applause (MacCaig) **36**:281-82
"Round Song" (McGrath) **28**:280
'Round the Clock Non-Stop (Aksyonov) **101**:22, 29
"The Roundhouse Voices" (Smith) **22**:389; **42**:346, 352-53
The Roundhouse Voices: Selected and New Poems (Smith) **42**:352, 354, 356-57
"Rounds" (Selzer) **74**:272
Rounds (Arghezi)
See *Hore*
Rounds (Busch) **18**:85-6; **47**:59, 64
"Rouse Him Not" (Wellman) **49**:396
"La route" (Gracq) **48**:141
"Route" (Oppen) **7**:283
La route d'Altamont (Roy) **10**:440; **14**:467
La route des Flandres (Simon) **4**:495-96; **9**:482, 484; **15**:487, 491-94; **39**:203-07, 209-11
"Route Six" (Kunitz) **148**:90
Route Two and Back (Dorris) **109**:298
Routines (Ferlinghetti) **111**:63
"The Rover" (Page and Plant) **12**:477-78
A Row of Tigers (Corcoran) **17**:70
Row with Your Hair (Tate) **6**:528
Rowan Farm (Benary-Isbert) **12**:31-2
"Rowayton at 4 P. M." (Klappert) **57**:256
"Rowing" (Sexton) **6**:492, 494; **53**:322; **123**:404, 424, 444
"The Rowing Endeth" (Sexton) **6**:492, 494; **53**:322; **123**:424, 444
"Równina" (Milosz) **56**:236
"Rows of Cold Trees" (Winters) **32**:468
"Roxanne" (Police, The) **26**:363-64
Roxy and Elsewhere (Zappa) **17**:590-91
"Roy Bradley, Boy Broadcaster" (Keillor) **115**:286, 295
The Roy Murphy Show (Buzo) **61**:52-3, 56, 60
"Royal Beatings" (Munro) **95**:290
"Royal Blue" (Loewinsohn) **52**:285
Royal Charles: Charles II and the Restoration (Fraser) **32**:184-85; **107**:35,42,67
Royal Chronicles (Mujica Lainez)
See *Crónicas reales*
"The Royal Commission" (Johnston) **51**:242, 252
"Royal Ebony" (Guillén)
See "Ebano real"
The Royal Family (Ferber) **93**:159, 165, 171
The Royal Family (Kaufman) **38**:258, 262
Royal Harry (Mayne) **12**:395, 399, 407
The Royal Hunt of the Sun (Shaffer) **5**:386-89; **14**:485-87; **18**:475-77; **37**:383-84; **60**:359, 361, 363, 373
"Royal Jelly" (Dahl) **79**:176, 180, 183
"Royal Orleans" (Page and Plant) **12**:480
"The Royal Palms" (Walcott) **76**:278
The Royal Pardon (Arden) **15**:21
"The Royal Scam" (Becker and Fagen) **26**:80
The Royal Scam (Becker and Fagen) **26**:80-1, 83, 85
"A Royal Visit" (Montague) **46**:266
The Royal Way (Malraux)
See *La voie royale*
Royaume farfelu (Malraux) **57**:301
"Rozmowa na Wielkanoc 1620 r." (Milosz) **56**:237
"rozmowa z Przyjacielem" (Rozewicz) **139**:295
"R.T.S.L." (Walcott) **42**:421
Le ru d'Ikoué (Theriault) **79**:418
Rubailer (Hikmet)
See *Quatrains*
"Rubaiyat" (Borges) **4**:75
Rubber Band (Bowie) **17**:65
Rubber Soul (Lennon and McCartney) **12**:357, 360, 366, 371-72, 375; **35**:274, 278
Rubbers (Reynolds) **38**:390
"Rubbing the Faces of Angels" (Bottoms) **53**:31
"Rubble" (Thomas) **13**:542; **132**:381
Rubble (Solzhenitsyn)
See *From under the Rubble*
"Rubens' Innocents" (Slessor) **14**:495
Rubicon Beach (Erickson) **64**:138-40, 142, 144
"Rublyovskoye shosse" (Voznesensky) **57**:416-17
Rubrics for a Revolution (L'Heureux) **52**:272-73
Ruby (Guy) **26**:142-43, 145
"Ruby and Amethyst" (Graves) **45**:166
"Ruby Brown" (Hughes) **108**:326
"Ruby on the 67" (Le Guin) **136**:376
Ruby Red (Fox) **22**:139-40
Rubyfruit Jungle (Brown) **18**:72-5; **43**:80-5; **79**:153, 155-57, 159-61, 163-69, 172
Ruce Venušiny (Seifert)
See *The Arms of Venus*
A Rude Awakening (Aldiss) **40**:15
Un rude hiver (Queneau) **5**:362
"Rudie Can't Fail" (Clash) **30**:46-7
Rudyard Kipling (Stewart) **7**:466
Rudyard Kipling and His World (Amis) **8**:11
Rue des boutiques obscures (Modiano) **18**:338
Rue deschambault (Roy) **14**:465-66, 468
Rue traversière (Bonnefoy) **9**:114; **58**:60
La rueda dentada (Guillén) **48**:159-60, 164; **79**:229
The Ruffian on the Stair (Orton) **4**:388; **43**:328-29, 331-34
Ruffles and Drums (Cavanna) **12**:101-02
Rufus (Fair) **18**:142
"The Rug" (O'Brien) **5**:313
"Rugaroo" (Erdrich) **54**:166; **120**:132
"Rugby Football Excursion" (MacNeice) **53**:231
"Rugby Road" (Garrett) **51**:147
"Ruidoso" (McPhee) **36**:296
"The Ruin" (Tomlinson) **13**:549
Ruin and Recovery (Ambrose)
See *Nixon: Ruin and Recovery 1973-1990*
Ruin the Sacred Truths (Bloom) **103**:36-9
"Las ruinas circulares" (Borges) **1**:38; **2**:76; **3**:80; **6**:87; **8**:97, 99, 102; **9**:121; **10**:65; **19**:46; **48**:33-5, 46; **83**:156-57, 175, 177, 181
Le ruine presque cocasse d'un polichinelle (Beti) **27**:53
The Ruined Boys (Fuller) **28**:149
The Ruined Map (Abe)
See *Moetsukita chizu*
Ruining the New Road: Poems (Matthews) **40**:318-19
"Ruins" (Thomas) **6**:530
Ruins and Visions: Poems, 1934-1942 (Spender) **41**:428; **91**:263
"Ruins of a Great House" (Walcott) **25**:450-51, 455; **42**:421; **76**:273, 278, 281
The Ruins of Isis (Bradley) **30**:32
Ruka a plamen (Seifert) **93**:343
"Rule 18" (Simak) **55**:321
Rule Britannia (du Maurier) **6**:147; **59**:284, 287
"The Rule of Names" (Le Guin) **71**:186
"Rule of Three" (Sturgeon) **39**:366
Rulers of the City (Fleming) **37**:127
Rules and Representations (Chomsky) **132**:17, 22, 38
The Rules of Attraction (Ellis) **71**:147, 149-51, 157, 162, 164, 166; **117**:105-07, 113, 123, 132-33, 135-38, 141, 143, 147, 150
The Rules of Chaos; or, Why Tomorrow Doesn't Work (Vizinczey) **40**:434-36
"Rules of Sleep" (Moss) **45**:290
Rules of Sleep (Moss) **45**:289-90; **50**:353
The Rules of the Game (Leiris)
See *La règle du jeu*
The Rules of the Game (Renoir)
See *La regle du jeu*
The Ruling Class (Barnes) **5**:49-50; **56**:2-5, 7-8
Rum and Coke (Reddin) **67**:265-68, 270-71
Rum Punch (Leonard) **120**:289-90, 299-300, 304-05
"Rumba" (Guillén) **48**:163; **79**:234, 239-40
Rumble Fish (Coppola) **126**:260
Rumble Fish (Hinton) **30**:205; **111**:77-83, 85, 90
"Rumble in Bavaria" (Royko) **109**:406
"Ruminant" (Scannell) **49**:327
"Rumination" (Eberhart) **56**:81, 87
"Ruminations of Luke Johnson" (Brown) **59**:263
Rumming Park (Mortimer) **28**:281
A Rumor of War (Caputo) **32**:102-06
"Rumor Verified" (Warren) **39**:258
Rumor Verified: Poems, 1979-1980 (Warren) **39**:257-61, 265
Rumors (Simon) **70**:240-41
Rumors of Peace (Leffland) **19**:278-80
Rumour at Nightfall (Greene) **18**:194; **72**:148, 158-59, 161
Rumours (Deane) **122**:74, 81-3
"Rumours of Foot" (Hillis) **66**:199
Rumours of Our Death (Walker) **61**:428
Rumours of Rain (Brink) **18**:68-9; **36**:65, 68; **106**:96-7, 99, 123-24, 130, 146
"Rumpelstiltskin" (Broumas) **73**:4, 7, 13
"Rumpelstiltskin" (Sexton) **53**:314
Rumplestiltskin (Hunter) **31**:226-27
"Rumpole for the Defence" (Mortimer) **28**:287
Rumpole of the Bailey (Mortimer) **43**:308
Rumpole's Return (Mortimer) **28**:287; **43**:305
Rumstick Road (Gray) **49**:146-47; **112**:97, 107, 114
"Run and Ask Daddy If He Has Any More Money" (Weldon) **122**:278
"The Run for the Elbertas" (Still) **49**:366-68
The Run for the Elbertas (Still) **49**:369-70
"Run for the Stars" (Ellison) **42**:127
Run for Your Wife! (Cooney) **62**:143-48
Run Man Run (Himes) **18**:245; **58**:254, 257, 263; **108**:234
A Run of Jacks (Hugo) **6**:244; **32**:234-38, 244, 247, 249
Run River (Didion) **3**:128; **8**:174, 177; **32**:143, 147, 150; **129**:82-83, 85, 89
Run Softly, Go East (Wersba) **30**:430-31
Run with the Hunted (Bukowski) **41**:64; **108**:94-5
"Runagate, Runagate" (Hayden) **5**:168; **37**:155, 157, 160
"Runaround" (Asimov) **26**:54; **76**:319; **92**:4, 11, 20
"The Runaway" (Frost) **26**:112
"The Runaway" (Ross) **13**:492
Runaway Horse (Walser) **27**:466-67
Runaway Horses (Mishima) **4**:355-58; **6**:337-38; **27**:341-42
Runaway Voyage (Cavanna) **12**:102-03
"Runaways" (Erdrich) **120**:135
Runaways (Swados) **12**:558-61
"Runaways Café I" (Hacker) **72**:187
"Runaways Café II" (Hacker) **72**:187
"Runes" (Brown) **5**:77
"Runes" (Nemerov) **6**:361-62; **9**:394; **36**:304-05
Runes (Baxter) **14**:60
"Runes from the Island of Horses" (Brown) **48**:57
"Rungstedlund: A Radio Address" (Dinesen) **95**:58
"The Runner" (Dacey) **51**:81
"The Runner" (Simpson) **4**:499; **7**:426-28; **149**:345, 350, 355
Runner in the Sun: A Story of Indian Maize (McNickle) **89**:160, 165, 168-69, 171-73, 175-79, 181
The Runner Stumbles (Stitt) **29**:389-91

"The Runners" (Purdy) **50**:242
"Runners" (Waddington) **28**:439
Runners (Poliakoff) **38**:385-86
"Running" (Dobyns) **37**:76-7
"Running" (Dubus) **97**:231
"Running" (Wilbur) **53**:413; **110**:384
"Running Away" (Marley) **17**:271
"Running Away from Home" (Kizer) **39**:169-71
"Running Child" (Coles) **46**:113
Running Dog (DeLillo) **13**:178-79; **27**:85-6; **39**:117, 123, 125-26; **54**:82, 90; **76**:177-78, 180, 182; **143**:185, 187, 189-90
"Running Dreams" (Beattie) **40**:64; **63**:12, 19
"Running Dry" (Young) **17**:569
"Running Gun Blues" (Bowie) **17**:57
Running in the Family (Ondaatje) **29**:342-43; **51**:313-14, 318, 320; **76**:202, 206
The Running, Jumping, and Standing Still Film (Lester) **20**:219, 228
The Running Man (King) **37**:201, 207; **113**:388
"Running of Streight" (Davidson) **13**:166
"The Running of the Grunion" (Rukeyser) **10**:442
The Running of the Tide (Forbes) **12**:208-09
"Running on Empty" (White) **110**:330, 340, 344
Running on Empty (Browne) **21**:39-41
Running on Empty (Phillips) **28**:364-65
"Running on the Spot" (Weller) **26**:447
"Running Stream" (Blunden) **56**:49
Running Wild (Ballard) **137**:14-15, 25-26, 28, 30, 33
"Rupee" (Willingham) **51**:403
"Rupert Beersley and the Beggar Master of Sivani-Hotta" (Boyle) **36**:63
"La ruptura" (Poniatowska) **140**:322-23, 330
"Ruptura" (Poniatowska) See "La ruptura"
"Rupture" (Pasternak) **63**:280, 291
La rupture (Chabrol) **16**:175, 182
"Rural Colloquy with a Painter" (Steele) **45**:363
"Rural Hazards" (Queneau) **42**:337
"Rural Objects" (Ashbery) **2**:17
Rus into Muscovy (Almedingen) **12**:6-7
Rush/What Fuckan Theory (Bissett) **18**:59
Rushes (Rechy) **18**:442-43; **107**:254-56, 258
"Rushing" (Young Bear) **94**:362
Ruski (Burroughs) **109**:182
"Russia and the Virus of Liberty" (Cioran) **64**:98
"The Russian Army Goes Into Baku" (Ostriker) **132**:321
"A Russian Beauty" (Nabokov) **6**:351-53
A Russian Beauty, and Other Stories (Nabokov) **3**:354-55; **6**:351-52
"The Russian Dancer" (Bates) **46**:51
Russian Dictionary of Linguistic Expression (Solzhenitsyn) **78**:434
"A Russian Doll" (Bioy Casares) **88**:92-3, 95
A Russian Doll, and Other Stories (Bioy Casares) See *Una muñeca rusa*
The Russian Forest (Leonov) See *Russkii les*
The Russian Girl (Amis) **129**:14-15
Russian Hide-and-Seek (Amis) **40**:42; **129**:12, 18
The Russian Interpreter (Frayn) **31**:189-90
Russian Journal (Lee) **36**:252-55, 257
The Russian People (Odets) **98**:196
"Russian Tanks in Prague" (Yevtushenko) **126**:394, 396-97
"Russian Winter Journal" (Ferlinghetti) **27**:139
The Russians and the Americans (Archer) **12**:21-2
"Die russischen Briefe des Jägers Johann Seifert" (Hein) **154**:136
Russkii les (Leonov) **92**:240, 247-48, 250-52, 254-55, 260, 266, 274, 277-78
Russkoe (Coles) **67**:175
Rust Never Sleeps (Young) **17**:580-81, 583
Rustic Elegies (Sitwell) **67**:312-13
"Rusticus" (Hall) **151**:180
"The Rustle of History's Wings, As They Said Then" (Amichai) **57**:37
The Rustle of Language (Barthes) See *Le bruissement de la langue*
"Rustling Taffetas" (Milosz) **56**:239
"Ruth" (Engel) **36**:162
"Ruth" (Oates) **19**:353; **134**:247
"Ruth" (Ozick) **155**:126
"Ruth" (Plumly) **33**:313
Ruth, a portrait (Cornwell) **155**:72
"Ruthanna Elder" (Purdy) **52**:350
"Ruth's Song (Because She Could Not Sing It)" (Steinem) **63**:379, 382-83
"Ruthy and Edie" (Paley) **37**:334, 336, 338; **140**:208, 211, 213-14, 229, 234, 277, 282
Rvach (Ehrenburg) **62**:175-76, 178
"Ryder" (Haines) **58**:220
"Ryder" (Rukeyser) **15**:457
Ryder (Barnes) **3**:36-7; **8**:47; **29**:27-9; **127**:161, 168, 173, 186, 189-91, 194, 201, 205, 212-14, 220-21
Rysopis (Skolimowski) **20**:348-50, 353
Ryugaku (Endō) **99**:285, 289-90, 293-96
Rzeka podziemna, podziemne ptaki (Konwicki) **117**:275, 279, 284, 288, 290-91
"s" (Piercy) See "In the Men's Room"
s (Loewinsohn) See *Magnetic Field*
S. (Updike) **70**:248-49; **139**:324-25
"S Angel" (Chabon) **149**:3-5, 10
"S. Dead" (Piercy) **27**:374
"S/He" (Paulin) **37**:354
S Is for Space (Bradbury) **42**:34, 39
S. J. Perelman: A Life (Herrmann) **44**:500-04
"S. Karuma-shi no hanzai" (Abe) **81**:293, 297
S. Karuma-shi no hanzai (Abe) **81**:285, 288
"S. L." (Brodkey) **56**:60, 68
S/Z (Barthes) **24**:28-31, 35-7; **83**:74, 77-8, 83, 85-7, 89-91, 95-6, 99, 103
S-1 (Baraka) **10**:19-20; **14**:48; **33**:57
Saat 21-22 siirleri (Hikmet) **40**:245, 247
"Sabás" (Guillén) **48**:157, 162
"Sabbath Park" (McGuckian) **48**:277-78
"Sabbatha and Solitude" (Williams) **5**:502; **15**:580
Sabbath's Theater (Roth) **119**:120, 123, 127, 129, 130-34, 137-38, 142
Sabbatical: A Romance (Barth) **27**:25-31; **51**:22, 24, 26-9
Sabella; or, The Blood Stone (Lee) **46**:231
"Sabélo" (Ulibarrí) **83**:414
"Sabeth" (Eich) **15**:202
"Sabina" (Nin) **127**:360
Sabine (Freeling) **38**:186
"The Sabine Farm" (Parini) **54**:360, 362
"Les sabines" (Aymé) **11**:23
Sabotage (Hitchcock) **16**:345, 358
The Sabre Squadron (Raven) **14**:441-42
"Sabrina" (Turco) **63**:429
Sabrina (Wilder) **20**:457
Sac Prairie People (Derleth) **31**:131
"Ein sächsischer Tartuffe" (Hein) **154**:165
Sackett's Land (L'Amour) **25**:280-81
"Sacks" (Carver) **126**:181
Sacktown Rag (Walker) **61**:425
"Le sacré dans la vie quotidienne" (Leiris) **61**:357
"Le Sacre du Printemps" (Piercy) **62**:377
Le sacre du printemps (Simon) **4**:495; **9**:485; **15**:487, 490-92; **39**:203-04, 209-11
"Sacred" (Silkin) **43**:398
The Sacred and Profane Love Machine (Murdoch) **4**:367-70; **6**:342-47; **8**:404; **15**:388-89; **31**:294
Sacred and Profane Memories (Van Vechten) **33**:395
Sacred and Secular Elegies (Barker) **48**:14, 17, 21
"The Sacred and the Suburban" (Phillips) **28**:363
"Sacred Chant for the Return of Black Spirit and Power" (Baraka) **5**:48
Sacred Cows and Other Edibles (Giovanni) **64**:195-96; **117**:189
"Sacred Elegies" (Barker) **8**:46
"The Sacred Factory" (Toomer) **22**:428, 430
Sacred Families (Donoso) **8**:179-80; **32**:154, 159-60; **99**:220
Sacred Families; Three Novellas (Donoso) See *Tres novelitas burguesas*
The Sacred Flame (Maugham) **67**:225
"The Sacred Hearth" (Gascoyne) **45**:147, 154, 157
"The Sacred Hoop: A Contemporary Indian Perspective on Native American Literature" (Allen) **84**:13, 29-30, 35
The Sacred Hoop: Recovering the Feminine in American Indian Traditions (Allen) **84**:14-15, 19-19, 22-4, 26-9, 31-3, 35-6, 39, 45
Sacred Hunger (Unsworth) **76**:252-60; **127**:413-18, 420-21, 424
"The Sacred Marriage" (Oates) **19**:351; **108**:354-58, 368-69
Sacred Monsters (Cocteau) See *Les monstres sacrés*
"The Sacred Mound" (Foote) **75**:230, 232, 257
"Sacred Objects" (Simpson) **149**:313-15, 319, 331
"The Sacred Rhino of Uganda" (Amis) **40**:43
The Sacred Wood: Essays on Poetry and Criticism (Eliot) **6**:166; **9**:190; **24**:158, 160-61, 163, 169, 171, 173, 178-84, 186; **34**:398 **55**:352; **57**:211-13
"The Sacred Wood Revisited" (McIlvanney) **42**:285
The Sacred Zone (Fuentes) See *Zona sagrada*
"The Sacrifice" (Auchincloss) **45**:30
"The Sacrifice" (Hamburger) **5**:159
"Sacrifice" (Kinsella) **138**:94, 101-02
The Sacrifice (Bidart) **33**:77, 79-81
The Sacrifice (Slavitt) **14**:491
Sacrifice (Vachss) **106**:362
The Sacrifice Consenting (Dickey) **28**:119
"A Sacrifice in the Orchard" (Bly) **38**:54-5, 57
"Sacrifice in the Temple" (Robbins) **21**:340
"Sacrifice of a Virgin in the Mayan Bull Court" (Dubie) **36**:134
"The Sacrificial Egg" (Achebe) **26**:22-3; **75**:13-14
Sacrificio en el Monte Moriah (Marqués) **96**:242-45, 250, 252
The Sacrilege of Alan Kent (Caldwell) **60**:46-8, 67
Sad as She Is (Onetti) See *Tan triste como ella*
"The Sad Ballad of the Fifteen Consecutive Rhymes" (Starbuck) **53**:354
"The Sad Boy" (Riding) **7**:374
Sad Cypress (Christie) **39**:438; **48**:72-3, 76
Sad Dust Glories: Poems during Work Summer in Woods (Ginsberg) **36**:188
A Sad Heart at the Supermarket (Jarrell) **2**:208; **6**:260; **9**:297
Sad Ires (Enright) **8**:203
"The Sad Phoenician" (Kroetsch) **23**:273-76; **132**:280
"Sad Song" (Kunitz) **148**:87
"Sad Steps" (Larkin) **5**:229; **8**:341; **13**:335; **33**:261; **39**:344; **64**:272, 276, 282
"Sadako" (Soto) **80**:294
"Sadastor" (Smith) **43**:424
The Saddest Summer of Samuel S (Donleavy) **1**:76; **4**:125; **6**:139, 141; **10**:154; **45**:126
"Saddle Up the Palomino" (Young) **17**:576
Sade, Fourier, Loyola (Barthes) **24**:31-2; **83**:83
The Sadeian Woman: An Exercise in Cultural History (Carter) **41**:117, 119; **76**:324, 327, 329
"Sad-Eyed Lady of the Lowlands" (Dylan) **12**:183; **77**:177-78
"Sadie" (Matthiessen) **64**:321-22, 324
"Sadie and Maude" (Brooks) **49**:22

Sadler's Birthday (Tremain) **42**:382-84
"Sadness" (Galvin) **38**:198
Sadness (Barthelme) **2**:41-2; **3**:43-4; **5**:53; **6**:30-1; **8**:50; **13**:55; **23**:44, 47; **46**:35-6, 41; **59**:247, 250; **115**:60, 68
"Sadness and Happiness" (Pinsky) **9**:416; **38**:355; **121**:445
Sadness and Happiness: Poems (Pinsky) **9**:416-17; **38**:359, 362; **94**:299, 308; **121**:432-35, 446
"Sadness and Joy" (Amichai)
See "Atsvut vesimha"
"The Sadness of Brothers" (Kinnell) **129**:236, 257
The Sadness of Days: New and Selected Poems (Salinas) **90**:332-33
"Sadness on a Deserted Evening" (Kunene) **85**:162
"Sado Machismo" (White) **110**:332
"Safe" (Gordon) **128**:115, 119
"Safe and Sound" (Simon) **26**:408
Safe Conduct (Pasternak) **7**:295-96; **10**:384; **18**:381; **63**:290-93
"Safe European Home" (Clash) **30**:43, 46
"Safe Houses" (Gordimer) **70**:177; **123**:129
"Safe Lives" (Beer) **58**:32
"Safe Places" (Urdang) **47**:399
"Safe Subjects" (Komunyakaa) **94**:239
The Safety Net (Boell)
See *Fürsorgliche Belagerung*
"The Safety-Valve" (Fuller) **62**:185
"Safeway" (Barthelme) **36**:50
"Saga" (Voznesensky) **57**:426
The Saga of a Seagull (Kemal)
See *Seagull*
The Saga of Anathan (Sternberg) **20**:373, 376
Saga of the Patient Footsoldier (Wittlin) **25**:466
Sagan om Fatumeh (Ekeloef) **27**:116-17
Sagarana (Rosa) **23**:348-51, 354-55
"Sagesse" (H. D.) **14**:223; **31**:208; **73**:143
"Sagg Beach" (Crase) **58**:162, 165
Sagittario (Ginzburg) **11**:228; **54**:209, 210, 213-14
La Sagouine (Maillet) **54**:303-06, 308, 310-11, 313-16, 318; **118**:326-36, 343-44, 346, 348, 362-63, 365
Said the Don (FitzGerald) **19**:178
"Said the Old Man to the Young Man" (Wesker) **42**:426
Said the Old Man to the Young Man (Wesker) **42**:426
Saigon Rose (Edgar) **42**:120-21
"Saikai" (Kawabata) **107**:104
"Sail Away" (Young) **17**:580
Sail Away (Coward) **1**:65
"Sail On, Sailor" (Wilson) **12**:646
"A Sailboat of Occasions" (Mahapatra) **33**:284
"Sailfish off Mombasa" (Hemingway) **34**:478
"Sailing" (Dacey) **51**:83
"Sailing Home from Rapallo" (Lowell) **8**:353; **37**:243; **124**:258, 276
Sailing into the Unknown: Yeats, Pound, and Eliot (Rosenthal) **28**:395-96
"Sailing Nights" (Seger) **35**:380
"Sailing the Back Water" (Smith) **22**:386
Sailing through China (Theroux) **46**:398
"Sailing to an Island" (Murphy) **41**:311, 314, 316, 318
Sailing to an Island (Murphy) **41**:311-12, 314-16, 318-19
"Sailor Ashore" (Merwin) **5**:288
"Sailor Boy of the Garden" (Elytis) **100**:175
"The Sailor Boy's Tale" (Dinesen) **29**:159; **95**:61
The Sailor from Gibraltar (Duras)
See *Le marin de Gibraltar*
The Sailor from Gibralter (Isherwood) **44**:397
"A Sailor in Africa" (Dove) **81**:138
"Sailor off the Bremen" (Shaw) **7**:411; **23**:395; **34**:370
Sailor off the Bremen (Shaw) **23**:395
The Sailor Who Fell from Grace with the Sea (Mishima)
See *Gogo no eiko*
"Sailors" (Nowlan) **15**:398
"Sailors" (Wild) **14**:581
The Sailor's Return (Garnett) **3**:188
"A Saint" (Johnston) **51**:239, 245
"Saint" (Rosenthal) **28**:395
The Saint and Mary Kate (O'Connor) **14**:395, 397, 400; **23**:328-30
"St. Anthony of the Desert" (Colwin) **84**:151
Saint Carmen de la main (Tremblay) **29**:419, 422, 424-25; **102**:362, 372, 374-75, 381
Saint Carmen of the Main (Tremblay)
See *Saint Carmen de la main*
"Saint Daniel the Paranoiac" (Klappert) **57**:269
The Saint Elias (Ferron)
See *Le Saint-Elias*
"Saint Francis and the Sow" (Kinnell) **129**:239, 270
Saint Genet, Actor and Martyr (Sartre)
See *Saint Genet, comédien et martyr*
Saint Genet, comédien et martyr (Sartre) **4**:475-76; **7**:393; **13**:498; **18**:473; **24**:404, 407-10; **44**:497; **50**:370; **52**:380
"Saint George and the Dragon: An Elizabethan Pageant" (Beer) **58**:38
Saint Glinglin (Queneau) **5**:361
Saint Jack (Theroux) **5**:427-28; **8**:512; **46**:405
"Saint Joey" (Demby) **53**:101
Saint John's Eve (Duhamel)
See *La nuit de la Saint-Jean*
"Saint Judas" (Wright) **10**:542
Saint Judas (Wright) **3**:540-43; **5**:520; **10**:542, 544-45; **28**:463, 468, 470-71
"Saint Junior" (Alexie) **154**:46-7
Saint Maybe (Tyler) **103**:247-48, 255-56, 261, 263, 267-70
Saint Oscar (Eagleton) **132**:125
"Saint Sex" (Williams) **148**:321
"Saint Valentine" (Moore) **10**:348
"Sainte Lucie" (Walcott) **9**:557; **14**:549-51; **42**:421-22
Sainte-Europe (Adamov) **25**:14-15, 17-18, 20-1
Le Saint-Elias (Ferron) **94**:106, 120, 124, 127
"The Saintly Men of Safed" (Michener) **5**:289
"Saints" (Gerstler) **70**:158
"Saints" (Mukherjee) **53**:266, 268, 270
"Saints" (Trevor) **116**:338-40, 345
Saints and Scholars (Eagleton) **132**:116-17, 126
Saints and Scholars (Eagleton) **63**:107-10
Saints and Strangers (Carter)
See *Black Venus*
"The Saints in Caesar's Household" (Tyler) **103**:258
"Saints Lose Back" (Willard) **7**:539
"The Saint's Path" (Blaga) **75**:77
Saint-Watching (McGinley) **14**:365, 368
"La Saison des pluies" (Le Clézio) **155**:84
Une saison à Rihata (Condé) **52**:81-2, 85; **92**:99-100, 109, 111, 130-31
Une saison au Congo (Césaire) **112**:3-4, 7, 21, 24, 28
Une saison dans la vie d'Emmanuel (Blais) **2**:63; **4**:66-7; **6**:80-1; **13**:96; **22**:60
"The Sake of Words for Their Own Sake" (Simpson) **32**:381
Sakhar-the-Pouch (Solzhenitsyn) **4**:507
Sakonnet Point (Gray) **49**:146; **112**:106-07
"Sakyamuni Coming Out from the Mountain" (Ginsberg) **3**:194; **4**:182
Sal Si Puedes: Cesar Chavez and the New American Revolution (Matthiessen) **7**:212; **32**:289-90, 292; **64**:303-04
"La sala" (Marqués) **96**:245
"Salad" (Nichol) **18**:369
"Salad Days" (Musgrave) **54**:335
Salad Days (Sagan)
See *Le chien couchant*
"The Saladmaker" (McFadden) **48**:246
The Saladmaker (McFadden) **48**:246-48
"Salamander" (McCartney) **35**:286
"Salamander" (Rukeyser) **27**:408
The Salamander (Paz)
See *Salamandra*
The Salamander (West) **6**:563-64
Salamandra (Paz) **51**:324; **65**:181
"Salami" (Levine) **4**:286; **9**:332; **118**:284
Salammbô (Ludlam) **50**:342
"Sale" (Desai) **97**:149, 171
"Sale Day" (Sargeson) **31**:370
"Salem" (Lowell) **8**:356
Salem's Lot (King) **12**:309; **26**:237, 239, 242; **37**:199, 201, 204-05; **61**:319, 323, 327, 331, 333; **113**:341, 344-47, 349, 354-55, 362, 365, 384, 387-91, 393
Salesman (Maysles and Maysles) **16**:438-39, 443
Salesman in Beijing (Miller) **47**:253-54
"A Salesman Is an It That Stinks, Excuse" (Cummings) **68**:41
"The Salesman's Son Grows Older" (Blaise) **29**:75
"Saliences" (Ammons) **5**:26-7; **8**:13, 16; **9**:26-8, 30; **57**:59; **108**:11, 23
"Salinas Sees Romance Coming His Way" (Salinas) **90**:332
The Saliva Milkshake (Brenton) **31**:65-7
Salka valka (Laxness) **25**:290, 295
"Sally" (Cisneros) **118**:177, 184
"Sally" (Durcan) **70**:152
Sally (Fast) **131**:100
Sally Bowles (Isherwood) **11**:300; **14**:284, 286; **44**:397, 399-400
Sally Can't Dance (Reed) **21**:308-09
"Salmon" (Graham) **118**:228
Salmos (Cardenal) **31**:75
Salo: 120 Days of Sodom (Pasolini) **20**:268-70; **106**:238-39, 241, 248-50, 257, 268, 273
Saloma (Krleža) **114**:172-73
"Salome" (Ai) **69**:9
"Salome" (Garrett) **51**:147-48
"Salome" (Komunyakaa) **94**:241
Salome (Egoyan) **151**:155, 175
Salome of the Tenements (Yezierska) **46**:441-42, 444-45
"Salomon's Story" (Anaya) **148**:47
"Salon des indépendents" (Szirtes) **46**:392
"Salon des refusés" (Thomas) **13**:539
Salonika (Page) **40**:351, 353-55
"Salsa" (Walcott) **67**:361
"Salt" (Levine) **33**:274; **118**:270
Salt (Gold) **4**:191-92; **42**:190-92, 198; **152**:135
Salt (Szymborska) **99**:199, 203
"Salt and Sawdust" (Narayan) **121**:419
The Salt Eaters (Bambara) **19**:33-35; **88**:9-11, 20-21, 23-24, 26-29, 31, 33-41, 43-44
"The Salt Garden" (Nemerov) **36**:304-05
The Salt Garden (Nemerov) **2**:305, 308; **6**:361; **36**:303, 305
Salt in the Wound (Sciascia)
See *La parrocchie di Regalpetra*
The Salt Lands (Shaffer) **14**:484
"Salt of the Earth" (Jagger and Richard) **17**:222, 238, 241
"The Salt of the Earth" (West) **31**:454; **50**:399
Salt of the Earth (Humphreys) **47**:190
Salt of the Earth (Wittlin) **25**:467-69, 471
"Salt Water" (Pinsky) **94**:302-3
"Salt Water Story" (Hugo) **32**:250
"Saltcod Red" (Lieberman) **36**:262
The Salterton Trilogy (Davies) **42**:102, 104; **75**:184, 191, 199; **91**:201, 204
Salto (Konwicki) **8**:326
Salto (Konwicki) **117**:282
"Salts and Oils" (Levine) **118**:292, 300
Salt-Water Ballads (Masefield) **11**:357; **47**:229, 233
Saltwater Summer (Haig-Brown) **21**:139-40
"Salud decimos cada día" (Neruda) **62**:335
"Salut à l'oiseau" (Prévert) **15**:437
Le salut de l'Irlande (Ferron) **94**:112, 115
"A Salute to My Friend Zo Nozizwe" (Kunene) **85**:176

"Salute to the Orient" (Forster) **15**:229
"Salute to the Passing" (Himes) **108**:235
Salvador (Didion) **32**:144-46; **129**:68-69, 78, 80-81, 83, 92-96
Salvador (Stone) **73**:365-67, 369-70, 375-77, 381-82
"El Salvador: An Aide Memoire" (Forché) **83**:197, 213-15
The Salvation Hunters (Sternberg) **20**:371
Salvation Now (Wilson) **33**:464
The Salvation of Ireland (Ferron)
See *Le salut de l'Irlande*
"The Salvation of Me" (Pancake) **29**:347, 350
Salwàre (Zuckmayer) **18**:556
The Salzburg Connection (MacInnes) **27**:282; **39**:349-50
The Salzburg Tales (Stead) **2**:422-23; **32**:407, 415; **80**:305, 307, 321-24, 326, 334, 340
Sam (Corcoran) **17**:69-70
Sam Ego's House (Saroyan) **8**:467
Sam O'Shanker (Russell) **60**:320
"Sam Palka and David Vishkover" (Singer) **6**:510
"Sam Sam the Candy Man" (Lane) **25**:284-85
"Sam Smiley" (Brown) **59**:262, 265-66
"Sam, Soren, and Ed" (Vanderhaeghe) **41**:448-49, 451-52
Sam the Sudden (Wodehouse) **5**:515
Sam Tucker (Green) **25**:192
Samá láska (Seifert) **34**:259; **44**:425-26; **93**:318, 339-41
Samantha (Fast) **131**:100
Samapti (Ray) **16**:494
"Samaritans" (Kelman) **58**:301
"Samba de los Agentes" (Codrescu) **121**:163
The Same Door (Updike) **1**:343; **3**:488
The Same Embrace (Lowenthal) **119**:76
"The Same Gesture" (Montague) **46**:278
"Same in Blues" (Hughes) **108**:328
"The Same Moon Above Us" (Stern) **100**:334
"Same Old Song" (Kristofferson) **26**:268
The Same Old Story (Fo) **32**:175
"The Same Poem Over and Over" (Rexroth) **112**:395
The Same River Twice (Walker) **103**:428
"Same Situation" (Mitchell) **12**:438, 440
Same Time, Next Year (Slade) **11**:507-08; **46**:370-73
"Same Time, Same Place" (Peake) **54**:372
Sammy and Rosie Get Laid: The Script and the Diary (Kureishi) **64**:248-51, 254-55; **135**:261-62, 264, 267, 272, 274, 277-80, 285-87, 289, 293, 296-98
"Sammy Chester" (Brooks) **15**:94
"Samos" (Merrill) **18**:331; **34**:235
Les samouraïs (Kristeva) **77**:325-26, 328, 334-37; **140**:161-62, 201
Samozerbuvh (Škvorecký) **152**:330
Sam's Cross (Durcan) **43**:113
Samson (Wajda) **16**:578, 582
"Samson and Delilah" (Abse) **29**:14
"Samson and Samsonella" (Aksyonov) **101**:9
"Samuel" (Paley) **37**:338; **140**:252
A Samuel Beckett Reader (Beckett) **29**:67
"Samuel Beckett's Dublin" (Davie) **31**:109
Samuel Johnson (Krutch) **24**:286
Samuel Johnson: A Biography (Wain) **15**:561
Samuel Johnson and the Life of Writing (Fussell) **74**:117, 119
Samuel Marchbanks' Almanack (Davies) **13**:173; **25**:129; **42**:103, 105; **75**:182-83
The Samurai (Endō) **54**:153-57, 160, 162; **99**:284-85, 287, 293
The Samurai (Kristeva)
See *Les samouraïs*
The Samurai (MacBeth) **9**:340
San Andreas (MacLean) **50**:348; **63**:267, 269
San Camilo, 1936 (Cela) **59**:141-43; **122**:27, 42-6, 61, 67, 70
"San Fernando Road" (Soto) **80**:286, 293-94
"San Francisco" (Olds) **85**:298
"San Francisco Dues" (Berry) **17**:52
"San Fruttuoso: The Divers" (Tomlinson) **45**:398
San Giorgio in casa Brocchi (Gadda) **11**:209
"San Ildefonso Nocturne" (Paz)
See "Nocturno de San Ildefonso"
San Martín Copybook (Borges)
See *Cuaderno San Martín*
San Martin Notebook (Borges)
See *Cuaderno San Martín*
"San Onofre, California" (Forché) **83**:214-16
The San Sebastian (Dillon) **17**:92-3
"San Sepolcro" (Graham) **118**:226-27, 230, 243-45
"Sanatorium" (Maugham) **67**:218
"The Sanatorium of Dr Vliperdius" (Lem) **149**:149
Sancho Panza en la ínsula Barataria (Casona) **49**:40
"The Sanctity" (Williams) **148**:322
The Sanctity of Marriage (Mamet) **15**:358
"The Sanctuaries" (Simpson) **149**:348
"Sanctuary" (Larsen) **37**:218
"Sanctuary" (Randall) **135**:397
"Sanctuary" (Wright) **53**:420
Sanctuary (Faulkner) **1**:100; **3**:149, 156; **6**:179-81; **8**:207-09, 211; **9**:201; **11**:198; **14**:179-80; **18**:143-44. 148-49; **28**:135-36, 140-42; **52**:107, 109, 112-13, 139
Sanctuary (Shange) **74**:314
Sanctuary V (Schulberg) **7**:403
"Sanctuary and the Southern Myth" (Tate) **4**:537
The Sanctuary Lamp (Murphy) **51**:303, 305, 307
"Sanctus" (Gascoyne) **45**:147
"Sanctus" (Moure) **88**:227
Sand (Mayne) **12**:390, 392-93, 397
Der Sand aus den Urnen (Celan) **10**:104; **19**:89; **53**:73, 81; **82**:48
"Sand Creek Survivors" (Vizenor) **103**:297
Sand from the Urns (Celan)
See *Der Sand aus den Urnen*
"Sand Pail" (Ashbery) **15**:28
Sand Rivers (Matthiessen) **32**:290-92; **64**:310-11, 326
The Sandalwood Tree (Vesaas)
See *Sandeltreet*
The Sandbox (Albee) **5**:10, 14; **9**:2-3, 9; **13**:7; **25**:33; **53**:22, 27; **86**:119-21; **113**:3, 17-8, 26, 47
The Sandbox Tree (Fleming) **37**:124
The Sandboy (Frayn) **31**:191
The Sandburg Range (Sandburg) **35**:354
The Sandburg Treasury: Prose and Poetry for Young People (Sandburg) **35**:357
"Sandcastle" (Coles) **46**:113
The Sandcastle (Murdoch) **1**:236; **2**:295; **3**:347; **6**:345, 349; **8**:406; **15**:384-85; **22**:327
Sandeltreet (Vesaas) **48**:405
"Sanders Theater" (Eberhart) **11**:179
Sandhedens Haevn (Dinesen)
See *The Revenge of Truth*
"Sandia Man" (Suknaski) **19**:432
Sandinista (Clash) **30**:47-51
"The Sandman" (Barthelme) **13**:57
"Sandpiper" (Bishop) **13**:93; **32**:42
"The Sandpit" (Heaney) **74**:167
"Sandra's Mobile" (Dunn) **40**:172
Sandro from Chegem (Iskander)
See *Sandro iz Chegema*
Sandro iz Chegema (Iskander) **47**:193-200; **59**:394
Sandro of Chegem (Iskander)
See *Sandro iz Chegema*
The Sands of Mars (Clarke) **13**:153; **35**:121; **136**:197, 210
"A Sandstone Farmhouse" (Updike) **139**:368
"Sandstone Keepsake" (Heaney) **37**:165, 169; **91**:117
"Sandstone Mountain" (MacCaig) **36**:283
"Sandwiched Between Proust and the Mummy: Seven Notes and an Epilogue on Carpentier's Reasons of State" (Dorfman) **77**:156
"Sandy" (Springsteen) **17**:488, 490-91
Sanford and Son (Lear) **12**:329, 330
"San-Fran-York on the Lake" (Royko) **109**:405
"Sång" (Transtroemer) **65**:235
Le sang des autres (Beauvoir) **1**:19-20; **8**:59; **31**:40-1; **44**:343, 345, 350; **50**:389; **71**:48-9, 55, 67-9, 72, 84; **124**:137, 140, 181; **124**:183-84
Le sang des gitanes (Simenon) **47**:374
Le sang d'un poète (Cocteau) **8**:145, 148; **15**:133-34; **16**:220-23, 225-30
Sång och strid (Lagerkvist) **54**:275
Le sang rive (Glissant) **68**:179, 181
"Sang satisfait du sens ancien du dit" (Damas) **84**:167
Sangre de amor correspondido (Puig) **65**:268, 271; **133**:318, 321, 355, 357-58, 378
Sangschaw (MacDiarmid) **11**:334, 338; **19**:285-86, 290; **63**:239
"A Sanguinary" (Goldbarth) **38**:205-06
Sanitized Sonnets (Porter) **33**:319, 324
"Sanity" (Leiber) **25**:304
Sanity, Madness and the Family (Laing) **95**:125, 127, 130, 135-36, 138, 141, 160, 168, 171, 174-76
Sanjuro (Kurosawa) **16**:399, 403-04; **119**:351, 361-66
Sanningbarriären (Transtroemer) **52**:410, 414-16, 418; **65**:226, 229-30
Sans (Beckett) **4**:52; **6**:36-8, 45; **11**:40; **14**:80; **18**:43; **29**:57, 59, 61
Sans coup férir (Tzara) **47**:395
"Sans remède" (Montherlant) **19**:325
Sanshiro sugata (Kurosawa) **16**:398-99; **119**:339, 345-55, 362, 375
Sanshiro Sugato, Part II (Kurosawa) **119**:339, 380
"Sanskrit" (Mahapatra) **33**:282
"Santa Ana a Oscuras" (Alegria) **75**:36, 38-9
"Santa Ana in the Dark" (Alegria)
See "Santa Ana a Oscuras"
"Santa Barbara Road" (Hass) **99**:140, 142
Santa Claus (Cummings) **15**:157-58
"Santa Claus's New Clothes" (Weldon) **122**:281
Santa Cruz (Frisch) **14**:181, 183; **18**:160; **44**:193-98, 200
"Santa Cruz Propositions" (Duncan) **41**:129-30
"Santa Fe" (Larson) **99**:167
"Santa Lucia" (Hass) **18**:211-13
"Santarém" (Bishop) **32**:37
Santaroga Barrier (Herbert) **12**:276, 279; **23**:226; **35**:196; **44**:393-94
"Santelices" (Donoso) **11**:147-48; **32**:158
Santorini (MacLean) **50**:347; **63**:270-71
"Santos: New Mexico" (Sarton) **49**:320
São Jorge dos Ilhéus (Amado) **40**:25, 27; **106**:60-1, 89
Sapetchatlionnoye vremya (Tarkovsky) **75**:389-91, 396, 401, 408-09, 412-13
Sapogonia: An Anti-Romance in 3/8 Meter (Castillo) **151**:18-20, 30, 33-5, 37-8, 40-3, 45, 84, 86-7, 92-3, 95, 101-02
"The Sapper" (Federspiel) **42**:145-46
"Sapphics against Anger" (Steele) **45**:366
Sapphics against Anger and Other Poems (Steele) **45**:365-66
A Sapphire for September (Brinsmead) **21**:27-8
Sappho (Delbanco) **6**:130
Sappho (Durrell) **13**:184
Sappho (Elytis) **100**:170
Sappho: A New Translation (Barnard) **48**:25, 27
"Sara" (Dylan) **77**:178
al- Sarāb (Mahfūz) **52**:292
Saracen Chronicles (Goytisolo) **133**:85-86
The Saracen Lamp (Arthur) **12**:26, 28
Sarafina! (Ngema) **57**:344-47
"Sarah" (Lavin) **99**:316-18
Sarah (Sackler) **14**:479
Sarah and Son (Arzner) **98**:69-71, 86-7, 90
Sarah Bastard's Notebooks (Engel) **36**:157, 163

Sarah Bishop (O'Dell) **30**:276-77
"Sarah Cole: A Type of Love Story" (Banks) **72**:3-5
Sarah Conley (Gilchrist) **143**:313
Sarah Phillips (Lee) **36**:255-58
"Sarandapikhou Street" (Vassilikos) **4**:552
"Saratoga" (Moss) **7**:249
Saratoga Headhunter (Dobyns) **37**:82
"Saratoga, Hot" (Calisher) **38**:75-6; **134**:10, 32
Saratoga, Hot (Calisher) **38**:75-6; **134**:10, 17, 19, 42
Saratoga Longshot (Dobyns) **37**:76, 78-9
Saratoga Swimmer (Dobyns) **37**:78-9
Saratoga Trunk (Ferber) **93**:173-75, 181, 186-87, 189-90
"Sarcophagi I" (Montale) **9**:388
"Sarcophagi II" (Montale) **9**:388
"Sarcophagus" (Selzer) **74**:262
"The Sarcophagus of the Esophagus" (Benedikt) **14**:81
Sard Harker (Masefield) **11**:357
Sardana Dancers (Jenkins) **52**:227-28
Sardines (Farah) **53**:132-40; **137**:84-85, 87, 89-90, 96-97, 105-07, 110, 114-16, 119-26, 128-29
Sargasso of Space (Norton) **12**:467
Sargento Getúlio (Ribeiro) **10**:436; **67**:273-79, 282
"Sarnesfield" (Mathias) **45**:238
Saroyan: A Biography (Gifford) **34**:457-59
Saroyan: A Biography (Lee) **34**:457-59
Sarton Selected (Sarton) **91**:240
"The Sartorial Revolution (I)" (Bioy Casares) **88**:78
Sartoris (Faulkner) **3**:153, 155, 158; **6**:180; **8**:210-11, 214; **9**:197, 199; **11**:197, 200, 202, 206; **14**:179-80; **28**:135, 140, 142-43; **52**:109, 112-13; **68**:127-30, 132
Sartre: A Life (Cohen-Solal) **50**:370-72, 374-76, 378, 381-82
Sartre on Theater (Sartre) **18**:473; **52**:372, 375
The Sartre: Origins of Style (Jameson) **142**:216, 257
Sartre: Romantic Rationalist (Murdoch) **3**:348; **15**:386; **51**:288
Sasame yuki (Tanizaki) **8**:510; **14**:525; **28**:414-15, 420-21
Sasayakadakeredo yakuni tatsu koto (Murakami) **150**:39
Sasha, My Friend (Corcoran) **17**.70
"Saskatchewan" (Lane) **25**:284
Såsom i en spegel (Bergman) **16**:50, 52, 54-5, 57, 59, 61-2, 64, 74, 79; **72**:33, 37-41, 47, 50, 52, 57, 59, 62
Sassafrass (Shange) **8**:485; **126**:360
Sassafrass, Cypress Indigo (Shange) **38**:392-94, 396; **74**:303, 307; **126**:360, 364, 380
Sassinak (McCaffrey) **17**:280-81
"Satan" (Tanizaki)
See "Akuma"
The Satan Bug (MacLean) **50**:348-49
"Satan Comes to Georgia" (Pritchett) **41**:331
Satan in Goray (Singer)
See *Shoten an Goray*
Satan Preaches (Mahfouz)
See *al-Shaytan y'iz*
Satan Says (Olds) **32**:345-46; **39**:190-93; **85**:285, 288-90, 292, 297, 305-06
"Satan Speaks" (Smith) **25**:420
"Satanic Form" (Swenson) **106**:337
The Satanic Mill (Preussler) **17**:376-77
The Satanic Verses (Rushdie) **55**:215-28, 230-51, 253-56, 258-59, 261-63; **59**:406-29, 431-55; **100**:287, 293-96, 299, 301-03, 305, 307-09, 311-12, 315-19, 321-23
Satan's Brew (Fassbinder) **20**:115
"Satellite" (Morgan) **2**:294
"Satellite of Love" (Reed) **21**:305, 314
"Sati Sapni" (Anand) **93**:57
"Satin Bower-Birds" (Wright) **53**:423
Satin-Legs Smith (Brooks)
See "The Sundays of Satin-Legs Smith"
"Satires" (Loy) **28**:253
"Satires and Occasions" (Garrett) **51**:144
The Satires of Persius (Merwin) **45**:269
Satirical Poems (Sassoon) **36**:387
"The Satirist" (MacNeice) **4**:318
"Satis Passio" (Murray) **40**:343
"Satisfaction" (Jagger and Richard) **17**:222, 225-27, 231, 234-35, 237, 239-40
"Satisfaction Guaranteed" (Asimov) **92**:13
"The Satisfactions of the Mad Farmer" (Berry) **8**:85
"The Satisfactory" (Pritchett) **41**:334
"Satisfied" (Morrison) **21**:239-40
"Satisfy My Soul" (Marley) **17**:270
Satori in Paris (Kerouac) **2**:227-28; **61**:296
Satura (Montale) **7**:224-25, 226, 230-01; **9**:386-87, 389; **18**:340
"Saturday" (Gallant) **38**:191, 194
"Saturday" (Salinas) **90**:324, 328
"Saturday Afternoon" (Caldwell) **8**:123
The Saturday Gang (Kingman) **17**:244-45
"Saturday Kids" (Weller) **26**:445-46
"Saturday Night" (Gunn) **81**:180
"Saturday Night" (Hughes) **108**:297
"Saturday Night" (Kenny) **87**:241
"Saturday Night" (Sondheim) **30**:398
"Saturday Night" (Wakoski) **40**:456
Saturday Night (Sondheim) **30**:387, 400; **147**:259
Saturday Night and Sunday Morning (Sillitoe) **1**:307-08; **3**:448-49; **6**:501; **19**:421; **57**:387, 389, 392, 396, 400-03; **148**:155-59, 163, 166, 169-71, 173, 176-78, 182, 184, 187, 190, 195-99, 201, 203, 205, 210
"A Saturday of Sun, Sand, and Sleep" (Calvino) **33**:100
"Saturday People" (Packer) **65**:350
"Saturday Sundae" (Scott) **22**:375
"Saturday Sweeping" (Levine) **4**:286; **118**:284, 292
Saturday the Rabbi Went Hungry (Kemelman) **2**:225
Saturday, the Twelfth of October (Mazer) **26**:290-91
"Saturday under the Sky" (Soto) **80**:283
"Saturdays" (Castillo) **151**:
"Saturn" (Grass) **32**:198, 200
"Saturn" (Olds) **85**:292, 294, 298, 304
"Saturn" (Wonder) **12**:660
Saturn and Beyond (Asimov) **26**:50-1
"Saturn, November 11th" (Ellison) **42**:131
"Saturn Rising" (Clarke) **13**:148
"Saturnalia" (Glück) **22**:173
Saturne (Malraux) **4**:335
"The Satyr" (Lewis) **27**:258
"The Satyr in the Periwig" (Sitwell) **67**:312
"The Satyr Shall Cry" (Garrett) **51**:149
Satyricon (Fellini) **16**:280-81, 283, 286-90, 292-93, 299; **85**:51, 53, 63-6, 68-70, 74, 76, 78, 82
Der Satz vom Grund (Heidegger) **24**:271
Sauce for the Goose (De Vries) **28**:108-10
"The Saucer Has Landed" (Buzzati) **36**:94
"The Saucer of Larks" (Friel) **115**:253
The Saucer of Larks (Friel) **42**:163; **115**:216
"Saucer of Loneliness" (Sturgeon) **39**:366
"A Saucerful of Secrets" (Pink Floyd) **35**:305
A Saucerful of Secrets (Pink Floyd) **35**:307, 310
Sauerkraut Soup (Dybek) **114**:64-4, 67-8, 76
"Saul Alone" (Gardam) **43**:167
"Saul and Patsy Are Getting Comfortable in Michigan" (Baxter) **45**:53; **78**:30
"Saul and Patsy Are Pregnant" (Baxter) **78**:26, 30
Saúl ante Samuel (Benet) **28**:21
Saul Bellow: Drumlin Woodchuck (Harris) **19**:206
"Saul Bellow in Chicago" (Amis) **62**:4
Saul Bellow: Vision and Revision (Fuchs) **34**:545-46
Das Sauspiel (Walser) **27**:463
La sauvage (Anouilh) **13**:17, 19, 21; **40**:50, 52, 55-6
Sauve qui peut (Durrell) **41**:139
Sauve qui peut (La vie) (Godard) **20**:153-55
The Savage (Anouilh)
See *La sauvage*
The Savage Gentleman (Wylie) **43**:461
The Savage God (Alvarez) **5**:18-19
Savage Holiday (Wright) **1**:379; **4**:596; **21**:443, 446
Savage in Limbo (Shanley) **75**:320
Savage Journey (Eckert) **17**:109
Savage/Love (Shepard) **41**:407
"Savage Memories" (Amichai) **116**:96
"Savage Menace" (Ashbery) **77**:62
Savage Messiah (Russell) **16**:543-44, 546, 548
Savage Night (Thompson) **69**:386, 389
Savage Sleep (Brand) **7**:29-30
"Savages" (O'Brien) **36**:339; **116**:186
Savages (Hampton) **4**:212
Savannah Bay (Duras) **34**:162
"Savata, My Fair Sister" (Goyen) **14**:211
"Save a Kitty from Extinction" (Royko) **109**:407
Save Every Lamb (Stuart) **34**:373, 376
Save Me, Joe Louis (Bell) **102**:17-9
"Save One for Mainz" (Huddle) **49**:183
"Save the Children" (Gaye) **26**:131
"Save the Country" (Nyro) **17**:316, 318
"Saved" (Dylan) **77**:186, 190-91
Saved (Bond) **4**:69; **6**:84, 86; **13**:98; **23**:63
Saved (Dylan) **77**:185, 188, 190
Saville (Storey) **8**:505-06
Saving and Spending: The Working-Class Economy in Britain, 1870-1939 (Johnson) **147**:89, 97
"Saving Grace" (Dylan) **77**:185-86, 189
Saving St. Germ (Muske) **90**:317
"Saving the Life That Is Your Own" (Walker) **103**:368, 414
Saving the Queen (Buckley) **7**:35-6; **37**:61
Saving the Text: Literature/Derrida/Philosophy (Hartman) **27**:187, 189
"Savings" (Hogan) **73**:158-59
Savings (Hogan) **73**:158-60
"Savior Machine" (Bowie) **17**:57
Savior, Savior, Hold My Hand (Thomas) **17**:498-501
"The Saviour" (Bullins) **7**:37
"Savitri" (Anand) **93**:57
Le savon (Ponge) **18**:413
Saw (Katz) **47**:216
"Sawdust" (Moss) **7**:250; **14**:376
Sawdust and Tinsel (Bergman)
See *Gycklarnas afton*
"Sawmill, Limekiln" (Montague) **46**:274
"Sawt min al'alam al-akhar" (Mahfouz) **153**:372-74
"A Saxon Tartuffe" (Hein)
See "Ein sächsischer Tartuffe"
Say Cheese! (Aksyonov)
See *Skazhi izjum!*
"Say Goodbye to Hollywood" (Joel) **26**:214
"Say Goodbye to the Wind" (Ballard) **137**:63-64
Say Hello to the Hit Man (Bennett) **35**:44
"Say It with Music" (Soupault) **68**:406
"Say Never" (Wallace) **114**:347
Say Nothing (Hanley) **5**:167
"Say Pardon" (Ignatow) **7**:177
Say Pardon (Ignatow) **7**:173-76, 179; **14**:275-76; **40**:258
"Say Say Say" (McCartney) **35**:291-93
Say Something Happened (Bennett) **77**:98
Say Who You Are (Waterhouse) **47**:418
"Say Yes" (Wolff) **64**:454
"Say You Love Me" (Peacock) **60**:297-98
"Saying Good-Bye to Hannah, 1907-1975" (McCarthy) **39**:487
"Saying Goodbye to Sally" (Yates) **23**:483
"Saying It to Keep It from Happening" (Ashbery) **77**:45-6
"A Saying of Anaximander" (Heidegger) **24**:270

Sayings and Doings (Berry) **27**:35
Sayonara (Michener) **11**:375; **29**:311; **109**:376, 378-79, 382
"The Scala Scare" (Buzzati)
See "Paura alla scala"
"A Scale in May" (Merwin) **88**:199-200
"The Scales" (Koch) **44**:242, 249
"The Scales of the Eyes" (Nemerov) **6**:361-62; **36**:302, 304-05
"Scaling Desire" (Ammons) **57**:53
Scandal (Endō) **54**:162-63; **99**:284-85, 289-91, 294, 299-300
Scandal (Kurosawa)
See *Shubun*
Scandal (Wilson) **33**:456-57
"Scandal d'Estime" (Hannah) **90**:162
"The Scandal on Via Sesotri" (Buzzati) **36**:93
The Scandalmonger (White) **30**:449
"A Scandalous Woman" (O'Brien) **36**:339-41; **116**:187, 194, 196, 198-99, 212, 216, 219-21
A Scandalous Woman, and Other Stories (O'Brien) **5**:311-12
"Scandinavian Skies" (Joel) **26**:223
A Scanner Darkly (Dick) **10**:138; **72**:110
Scanners (Cronenberg) **143**:57-58, 61, 65, 76, 87, 94-95, 116, 139, 143, 152-53
The Scapegoat (du Maurier) **59**:280-81, 284
The Scapegoat (Settle) **19**:410-12; **61**:371-76, 382-87
"Scape-Goats" (Barker) **52**:55
"The Scar" (Campbell) **42**:84
"Scar" (Lorde) **71**:259
"Scar" (McPherson)
See "The Story of a Scar"
"Scar" (Williams) **148**:348, 353
The Scar (Kieslowski) **120**:247, 252
"Scarborough Fair/Canticle" (Simon) **17**:462
A Scarcity of Love (Kavan) **5**:205; **82**:121
"The Scarecrow" (Farrell) **66**:131
"Scarecrow" (Pink Floyd) **35**:307
The Scarf (Bloch) **33**:83
"The Scarf of June" (Eberhart) **56**:77
Scarface (Hecht) **8**:274
Scarface (Norton) **12**:455
Scarface (Stone) **73**:364-65, 367, 369-70, 382
The Scarlatti Inheritance (Ludlum) **22**:288-89, 291
"The Scarlatti Tilt" (Brautigan) **12**:65
The Scarlet Cord (Slaughter) **29**:375
The Scarlet Empress (Sternberg) **20**:370, 372, 374
The Scarlet Goose (Almedingen) **12**:5-6
"Scarlet Ibis" (Atwood) **84**:67
The Scarlet Letters (Queen) **11**:464
"The Scarlet Moving Van" (Cheever) **7**:49
The Scarlet Patch (Lancaster) **36**:243
Scarlet Pilgrim (Robbins) **21**:338
The Scarlet Ruse (MacDonald) **3**:307; **27**:275
The Scarlet Sail (Cavanna) **12**:100
Scarlet Sister Mary (Peterkin) **31**:303-07, 309-10
Scarlet Street (Lang) **20**:207, 216; **103**:88, 102, 104-08
The Scarlet Sword (Bates) **46**:64-5
The Scarlet Thread (Betts) **28**:33-4
The Scarperer (Behan) **79**:25, 27
"Scars" (Williams) **42**:440
Scars (Kinsella) **27**:236-37; **43**:260
Scars on the Soul (Sagan)
See *Des bleus à l'âame*
Scattered Images of Childhood (Ionesco) **11**:290
Scattered Poems (Kerouac) **3**:264
Scattered Returns (Sissman) **9**:490; **18**:488
"Scattering As Behavior Toward Risk" (Howe) **152**:154, 157, 161, 176-78, 181
A Scattering of Salts (Merrill) **91**:227-28, 232, 237-38
"Scavengers at the Palm Beach County Landfill" (Bottoms) **53**:31
"Scenario" (Dunn) **36**:154
"Scenario" (Perelman) **44**:502; **49**:265
"Scenario for a Walk-On Part" (Fuller) **62**:186
"Scene" (Robbe-Grillet) **43**:361
Scène blanche (Brossard) **115**:110-11
La scène capitale (Jouve) **47**:203-06
"The Scene of the Crime" (Lem) **149**:112, 116-18, 152
The Scene of the Crime (Lem) **149**:112, 156
"A Scene of the Memorial Service for the War Dead" (Kawabata) **2**:222
"The Scene of War" (Read) **4**:439
"Scene Twelve: Take Seven" (Ciardi) **40**:162
"La sceneggiatura come 'struttura che vuol essene altia struttura'" (Pasolini) **106**:237
Scener ur ett äktenskap (Bergman) **16**:75, 77, 80-2; **72**:57, 59-61
Scenes from a Marriage (Bergman)
See *Scener ur ett äktenskap*
Scenes from American Life (Gurney) **54**:217; **32**:216-17, 219; **50**:175, 177-78
Scenes from American Life (Oates) **19**:350; **108**:389
Scenes from an Album (Trevor) **116**:338, 346
"Scenes from an Italian Restaurant" (Joel) **26**:215-16, 222
Scenes from Bourgeois Life (Jones) **52**:250
Scenes from the Life of a Faun (Schmidt)
See *Aus dem Leben eines Fauns: Kurzroman*
"Scenes from the Life of Behemoth" (Howard) **7**:168
"Scenes from the Life of Margaret" (Sillitoe) **148**:158
Scenes from the Life of the Future (Duhamel) **8**:188
"Scenes from the Lives of the Saints" (Nichol) **18**:368
"Scenes of J. C.'s Life" (Cabral de Melo Neto)
See "Cenas da vida de Joaquim Cardozo"
"Scenes of Passion and Desire" (Oates) **19**:352
Scenic Drive (Wilding) **73**:395, 398
The Scenic Route (Adcock) **41**:14-15, 17
Scent of Apples (Santos) **22**:365-66
"Scent of Camomile" (Derleth) **31**:138
Scented Gardens for the Blind (Frame) **2**:141; **6**:190; **96**:173-74, 176, 178-79, 182, 185-86, 189-91, 194, 196, 199, 203, 216-17
Die Schatten (Wellershoff) **46**:435
Der Schatten des Körpers des Kutschers (Weiss) **15**:563; **51**:389, 395
Der Schatten eines Traumes (Wolf) **58**:431, 433; **150**:288, 327
Die Schattengrenze (Wellershoff) **46**:433-34, 436
"Scheherazade" (Baxter) **78**:26
"Scheherazade in South Dakota" (Cassity) **42**:99
Der Schein trügt (Bernhard) **61**:11, 26
"Scherzo" (Berryman) **10**:51
Scherzo (Wheelock) **14**:571
Scherzo capriccioso (Škvorecký) **69**:327-32, 336, 344, 347; **152**:307-09, 315-16, 324, 330-37
"Schicksal einer henkellosen Tasse" (Boell) **15**:69
"Schiffman's Ape" (Sayles) **14**:483
Schinderhannes (Zuckmayer) **18**:555
Schindler's Ark (Keneally)
See *Schindler's List*
Schindler's List (Keneally) **27**:231-34; **43**:230-37; **117**:226-27, 229, 231, 233-35, 237, 239, 241, 243, 245, 250-51
"Schinz" (Frisch) **44**:194, 199
The Schirmer Inheritance (Ambler) **9**:19
Schismatrix (Sterling) **72**:368, 370
"Schizophrenic Girl" (Kennedy) **42**:256-57
Schizopolis (Soderbergh) **154**:341, 344, 347-48, 353-54, 356,
"Schläferung" (Hildesheimer) **49**:173
Schlaflose Tage (Becker) **19**:36
Schlötel, oder Was solls (Hein) **154**:53, 135, 165, 176
"Schmährede des alten B. auf seinen Sohn" (Hofmann) **54**:225
"Schmerz durch reibung" (Jandl) **34**:196
"Die Schmerzen sin zumutbar" (Lenz) **27**:252
Schmoedipus (Potter) **58**:400; **123**:235
"Schneebett" (Celan) **53**:72; **82**:39-40
Schneeglöckchenfeste (Hrabal)
See *Slavnosti sněženek*
Schneepart (Celan) **82**:34
"The Scholar" (Clarke) **6**:113
"Scholar and Gypsy" (Desai) **97**:150, 152
"Scholar I" (Deane) **122**:74, 91
"Scholar II" (Deane) **122**:74
"Scholars at the Orchid Pavillion" (Berryman) **25**:96
"Scholar's Wife" (Kennedy) **8**:320
Ein schöner Tag (Wellershoff) **46**:434-35
Die Schönheit des Schimpansen (Wellershoff) **46**:436-37
"Das Schönste Fest der welt" (Lenz) **27**:246
"The School Children" (Glück) **7**:119; **22**:174
"School Days" (Berry) **17**:53-5
School Daze (Lee) **105**:81-86, 95, 102, 109, 111, 128
"School Drawing" (Turco) **11**:550
"School Figures" (Matthews) **40**:323
A School for Fools (Sokolov) **59**:369, 388
"The School for Love" (Porter) **5**:347
"The School for Tenors" (Grass)
See "Die Schule der Tenöre"
"The School Friend" (Aickman) **57**:2
"The School Globe" (Reaney) **13**:473
The School of Darkness (Wellman) **49**:396-97
"The School of Desire" (Swenson) **106**:339, 347
The School of Donne (Alvarez) **5**:19
"The School of Eloquence" (Harrison) **43**:176-78, 181; **129**:172-76, 215
"The School of Eloquence"and Other Poems (Harrison) **129**:165-66, 197
"The School of Gordon Lish" (Birkerts) **116**:148, 151
"School of Knives" (Cabral de Melo Neto)
See "A escola das facas"
The School of Knives (Cabral de Melo Neto)
See *A escola das facas*
"A School Story" (Trevor) **71**:336; **116**:375
"School Teacher" (Smith) **64**:389
School Ties: Good and Bad at Games, and Dutch Girls (Boyd) **53**:53-4
Schoolboys in Disgrace (Davies) **21**:100-01
"Schoolcraft's Diary Written on the Missouri: 1830" (Bly) **128**:17, 24, 31
"Schooling" (Ammons) **2**:14
Schooling of Cyfran (Lem)
See *Edukacja Cyfrania*
"Schoolmaster" (Larkin) **64**:261
"Schoolmaster" (Yevtushenko) **1**:382
The Schoolmaster (Lovelace) **51**:267, 271
"The Schoolmaster in Spring" (Winters) **32**:470
"Schoolroom on a Wet Afternoon" (Scannell) **49**:324
"The Schooner Blue Goose" (Acorn) **15**:10
Schooner Cove (Jiles) **13**:304
"The Schooner Flight" (Walcott) **14**:551; **42**:420-22; **76**:272, 274-75, 296
"Schopenhauer und Marbot" (Hildesheimer) **49**:179
Das Schreien der Katze im Sack (Wellershoff) **46**:435
"The Schreuderspitze" (Helprin) **22**:221-22
"Ein Schritt nach Gomorrah" (Bachmann) **69**:35, 37
"Schrödinger's Cat" (Le Guin) **45**:213, 216; **136**:330
"Schtzngrmm" (Jandl) **34**:196, 198, 200
Schubertiana (Transtroemer) **52**:418
Die Schule der Atheisten: Novellen-Comödie in 6 Aufzügen (Schmidt) **56**:393-94
"Die Schule der Tenöre" (Grass) **32**:198
Schultz (Donleavy) **45**:123-26
The Schva (Broner) **19**:70
Das Schwanenhaus (Walser) **27**:466-67

"Schwartz between the Galaxies" (Silverberg)
See "Pontifications"
"Schwarze Flocken" (Celan) **19**:89; **19**:89
Der schwarze Schwan (Walser) **27**:462, 465
Schwarze Spiegel (Schmidt) **56**:390, 393, 405
"Die schwarzen schafe" (Boell) **2**:68
Schwarzenberg (Heym) **41**:219-20
"Schwierige Trauer" (Lenz) **27**:245-46
Die Schwierigen; oder, J'adore ce qui me brûle (Frisch) **9**:218; **44**:183-86, 188-89, 193, 203
Lo scialle andaluso (Morante) **47**:280
Lo sciecco bianco (Fellini) **16**:270, 272-74; **85**:52, 59, 66-7, 69, 71-2, 74, 76
"Science" (Jeffers) **11**:304
Science (Asimov)
See *Words of Science*
Science and Poetry (Richards) **24**:373, 378, 382, 387-89, 395, 400
"Science Fiction" (Bova) **45**:75
"Science Fiction" (Levi) **41**:244
"Science Fiction: A Hopeless Case—With Exceptions" (Lem) **40**:299; **149**:158
"The Science Fiction Hall of Fame" (Silverberg) **140**:343-46
"Science Fiction: Its Nature, Faults and Virtues" (Heinlein) **14**:252
The Science Fiction Source Book (Wingrove) **68**:456
The Science Fiction Stories of Walter M. Miller, Jr. (Miller) **30**:262
The Science: Glorious Entertainment (Barzun) **145**:72
"Science, Liberty and Peace" (Huxley) **4**:239; **18**:270
The Science of Hatred (Sholokhov) **15**:482
"The Science of the Night" (Kunitz) **148**:74
"Science-Fiction Cradlesong" (Lewis) **124**:213
"The Scientific Method" (Škvorecký) **69**:333
"Scilla" (Glück) **81**:164-65, 171
Scimitar (DeMarinis) **54**:97-9
"Scintillant Orange" (Vollmann) **89**:277-78, 304
Scion (Dickey) **109**:245
"Lo sciopero dei telefoni" (Buzzati) **36**:86
"Scissors" (Baxter) **78**:26
Sciuscia (De Sica) **20**:84, 92
La scomparsa di Majorana (Sciascia) **9**:476; **41**:389
Scoop (Waugh) **1**:359; **3**:512; **13**:585, 589; **27**:470; **44**:522; **107**:362, 370-71, 381, 383, 398, 400-01
The Scorched-Wood People (Wiebe) **11**:569; **14**:573; **138**:308, 312, 326, 330, 338, 343-44, 348-51, 357, 360, 372, 374
"The Score" (Bernard) **59**:46
"Score" (Rose) **85**:315
"A Score Settled" (Dourado)
See "Um ajuste de contas"
"The Scorpion" (Bowles) **19**:56-7; **53**:36
Scorpion and Other Poems (Smith) **25**:417
"The 'Scorpion' Departs but never Returns" (Ochs) **17**:332
The Scorpion God (Golding) **1**:122; **2**:168-69; **3**:200-01; **17**:177; **27**:163-64, 167; **81**:318, 323, 325-26
Scotchman's Return and Other Essays (MacLennan) **92**:298, 300, 306, 320
"Scotland's Fate: Canada's Lesson" (MacLennan) **14**:343
Scots Unbound (MacDiarmid) **63**:249, 255
Scotsman's Return and Other Essays (MacLennan)
See *Scotchman's Return and Other Essays*
Scott of the Antarctic (Brenton) **31**:59, 65
"Scottish Bards and an English Reviewer" (Barker) **48**:18
Scott-King (Waugh)
See *Scott-King's Modern Europe*
Scott-King's Modern Europe (Waugh) **27**:470; **107**:368-69
"Scottsboro" (Hughes) **108**:330
"Scoundrel" (Fante) **60**:133
The Scoundrel (Hecht) **8**:274
Scoundrel Time (Hellman) **8**:281-82; **14**:257, 260; **18**:225, 228-29; **34**:348, 350, 352; **44**:526, 528; **52**:189-90, 192-94, 198-205
"The Scour" (Ammons) **57**:49
"The Scourge" (Kunitz) **148**:77-78
"Scouting" (Levine) **118**:305, 310-11
"The Scoutmaster" (Taylor) **1**:334; **37**:412; **44**:305, 308; **50**:253; **71**:304-05
"Scram You Made the Pants Too Short" (Perelman) **23**:339-40
"The Scrap Merchant" (Mahfūz) **52**:292
"Scrapbook" (Appleman) **51**:15
"The Scrape" (Still) **49**:364
"Scrapeaway" (Weller) **26**:446
"The Scrapper" (Pancake) **29**:346-47, 350
"Scraps" (Graver) **70**:52
"Scratch" (Pesetsky) **28**:358
"Scratch Your Head" (Carroll) **35**:77
"Scratching the Surface: Some Notes on Barriers to Women and Loving" (Lorde) **71**:231, 244-46
"The Scream" (Hughes) **119**:270
"The Scream" (Smith) **64**:392
"The Scream" (Tomlinson) **45**:394
The Scream (Abell) **15**:3, 7
"A Scream of Toys" (Sillitoe) **19**:422; **57**:391, 396
"The Scream on Fifty-Seventh Street" (Calisher) **8**:125; **38**:69; **134**:41
"The Screamers" (Baraka) **33**:55-6, 62-3
"Screech Owl" (Davie) **31**:124
"A Screen Depicting the Fifty-Four Episodes of the Tale of Genji on a Background of Gold Leaf" (Pollitt) **28**:366
"The Screen Game" (Ballard) **137**:63, 65
Screen Test (Warhol) **20**:415
Screening History (Vidal) **142**:293-96
"SCREENO" (Schwartz) **87**:342
The Screenplays of Michelangelo Antonioni (Antonioni) **144**:15
The Screens and Other Poems (Richards) **14**:452, 455
"Screw: A Technical Love Poem" (Wakoski) **4**:573
"The Screwfly Solution" (Tiptree) **48**:389, 396; **50**:356, 358
The Screwtape Letters (Lewis) **1**:177; **3**:295, 297, 299; **6**:308; **14**:322-23; **27**:260, 263, 266; **124**:209-11, 225-26, 228-29, 232, 240, 244, 246
"Screwtop" (McIntyre) **18**:327
Scribble, Scribble (Ephron) **17**:113-14; **31**:159
"Scribbles" (Ammons) **57**:50
"Scribe" (H. D.) **73**:118
Scrieri (Arghezi) **80**:13
"Script" (Adcock) **41**:18
The Script (Anouilh) **50**:279
"Scripts for the Pageant" (Merrill) **18**:330-32; **34**:226, 228-31, 235-36; **91**:228
Scripture of the Blind (Ritsos) **31**:329, 331
Scritti corsair (Pasolini) **106**:245
"The Scriveners" (Buzzati) **36**:94
"Scroppo's Dog" (Swenson) **61**:398
Scuba Duba (Friedman) **5**:125, 127; **56**:98-9, 109
Le sculpteur de masques (Crommelynck) **75**:152, 155, 162-63, 166, 168
Sculpting in Time: Reflections on the Cinema (Tarkovsky)
See *Sapetchatlionnoye vremya*
"The Sculptor" (Christie) **110**:127
"The Sculptor" (Plath) **9**:423; **11**:447; **111**:201
The Sculptor of Masks (Crommelynck)
See *Le sculpteur de masques*
"Sculptors" (Purdy) **14**:433
Scum (Singer) **69**:316-21; **111**:341
"Scum Grief" (Bukowski) **41**:73
Scum of the Earth (Koestler) **15**:309; **33**:228-29
"Scumbag" (Lennon) **35**:265
Scumbler (Wharton) **37**:441-43
"Scyros" (Shapiro) **15**:478
"The Scythes" (Dubie) **36**:130
"Scything" (Clarke) **61**:80
SDS (Sale) **68**:343-44, 348, 353, 359
Se il sole muore (Fallaci) **110**:180, 191-92
"Se la vita e sventura...?" (Strand) **71**:288
"Se me ocurren ideas luminosas" (Parra) **102**:342
Se non ora, quando? (Levi) **37**:225, 228-30; **50**:327-28, 330, 332, 337, 339-40
"Se querían" (Aleixandre) **9**:12
Se questo è un uomo (Levi) **37**:220, 223, 225, 227; **50**:323-26, 332, 334, 336-37, 340
Se tavallinen tarina (Salama) **18**:461
Se una notte d'inverno un viaggiatore (Calvino) **22**:90-1; **73**:31, 34, 41, 48, 53-4, 56, 58, 60
"Se vuelve a yo" (Neruda) **62**:336
"The Sea" (Dudek) **11**:160
"Sea" (Ghiselin) **23**:170
"The Sea" (Oliver) **98**:271, 296-97, 299
The Sea (Bond) **4**:70; **13**:102; **23**:65
The Sea Anchor (Whitehead) **5**:488-89
"The Sea and Its Shore" (Bishop) **9**:90; **32**:40, 43
"Sea and Night" (Aleixandre)
See "Mar y noche"
The Sea and Poison (Endō)
See *Umi to dokuyaku*
"Sea and Sardinia" (West) **9**:562
The Sea and the Bells (Neruda)
See *El mar y las campanas*
"The Sea and the Canefield" (Cabral de Melo Neto)
See "O mar e o canavial"
"The Sea and the Mirror" (Auden) **123**:23-4, 26
"The Sea and the Mirror: A Commentary on Shakespeare's Tempest" (Auden) **1**:9-10; **2**:24; **3**:24, 27; **4**:33; **6**:20; **9**:59; **11**:17, 19; **14**:31; **43**:15; **123**:35, 40, 53
"The Sea and the Shore" (Amichai) **116**:122
"The Sea and the Shore" (Thurber) **5**:431
The Sea and the Wedding (Johnson) **27**:217
"The Sea and Tricks" (Aksyonov) **101**:22
"The Sea, around Us" (Loewinsohn) **52**:285
The Sea around Us (Carson) **71**:92-4, 99-111
The Sea at Dauphin (Walcott) **2**:460; **9**:556; **25**:451, 453-54; **67**:351
"Sea Bells" (Waddington) **28**:438
"The Sea Birds Are Still Alive" (Bambara) **88**:7-9, 20-23, 53-54
The Sea Birds Are Still Alive: Collected Stories (Bambara) **19**:33; 7, 27-28, 40, 42-3, 52, 54-5
"Sea Burial from the Cruiser 'Reve'" (Eberhart) **11**:178
"Sea Canes" (Walcott) **76**:285
"The Sea Caves of Dogashima" (Lieberman) **36**:261
"Sea Change" (Broumas) **73**:9
"The Sea Change" (Hemingway) **19**:219
"Sea Change" (Moss) **45**:291
The Sea Change (Howard) **29**:243
A Sea Change (Salamanca) **4**:462; **15**:463-65
The Sea Change of Angela Lewes (Seton) **27**:424, 426
"Sea Changes" (Bowering) **32**:48
"Sea Changes" (Montague) **46**:268-69
"Sea Charm" (Hughes) **35**:214
"The Sea Cliffs at Kailua in December" (Merwin) **45**:276
"The Sea Creature" (O Hehir) **41**:324
The Sea Does Not Wash Naples (Ortese)
See *Il mare non bagna Napoli*
"Sea Fever" (Masefield) **11**:358; **47**:233
Sea Garden (H. D.) **31**:205, 207-08, 211; **73**:106, 109
Sea Glass (Yep) **35**:470-71
"Sea Gods" (H. D.) **73**:121, 139
"Sea Graces" (Pollitt) **28**:367
"Sea Grapes" (Walcott) **42**:422; **76**:279, 285-86
Sea Grapes (Walcott) **9**:556-57; **14**:548-51;

25:452, 457; **42**:421-22 76;274
The Sea Gulls Woke Me (Stolz) **12**:546, 549
"Sea Heroes" (H. D.) **73**:105, 121
"The Sea Horse" (Graves) **39**:328
"Sea Horse" (Szirtes) **46**:393
The Sea in Being (Hemingway)
See *The Old Man and the Sea*
The Sea in Danger (Cousteau) **30**:107
"The Sea in Winter" (Mahon) **27**:292
"The Sea Is History" (Walcott) **42**:421
Sea Island Song (Childress) **86**:308-09, 314
Sea Lanes Out (Hugo) **32**:251-52
"Sea Lovers" (Martin) **89**:111-12, 118
"Sea Monster" (Merwin) **5**:288
"The Sea Mouse" (Oliver) **98**:303
Sea of Cortez: A Leisurely Journal of Travel and Research (Steinbeck) **9**:515-16; **21**:382-83, 389, 392; **34**:405, 412; **45**:383; **75**:344; **124**:424
Sea of Death (Amado)
See *Mar morto*
The Sea of Fertility: A Cycle of Novels (Mishima)
See *Hōjō no umi*
Sea of Grass (Kazan) **63**:225, 229
The Sea of Grass (Richter) **30**:307-09, 311-14, 316, 318-19, 324, 329
"The Sea of Hesitation" (Barthelme) **46**:38-9, 42-3
A Sea of Legends (Cousteau) **30**:107
Sea of Lentils (Benítez-Rojo) **70**:348, 359
"The Sea of Lost Time" (García Márquez)
See "El mar del tiempo perdido"
"The Sea of Sinbad" (Clarke) **35**:123
Sea of the Dead (Amado)
See *Mar morto*
"Sea of Tranquility" (Lightfoot) **26**:282
"Sea Poppies" (H. D.) **73**:119
Sea Routes to Polynesia (Heyerdahl) **26**:191-92
"Sea Sea Rider" (Brautigan) **12**:64
"The Sea Shell" (Bradbury) **98**:135
Sea Siege (Norton) **12**:467
The Sea, the Sea (Murdoch) **11**:388-89; **22**:328; **31**:287-89; **51**:287, 296
"The Sea to Hart Crane" (Moss) **45**:291
"Sea Treader" (Hoffman) **141**:288
Sea Trilogy (Golding) **81**:320, 325-26
"Sea Violet" (H. D.) **73**:119
"Sea Voyage" (Empson) **3**:147
The Sea Wall (Dillon) **17**:96
The Sea Wall (Duras)
See *Un barrage contre le Pacifique*
"The Sea When Absent" (Hemingway) **8**:285
"The Sea When Young" (Hemingway) **8**:285
"Sea Wolves" (Moorcock) **58**:347-48
"Sea Worms" (Ryan) **65**:215-16
"Sea-Beach" (Wright) **53**:428
A Sea-Change (Gould) **10**:241-42
"A Sea-Chantey" (Walcott) **76**:273, 279-80
"The Seacoast of Bohemia" (Garrett) **51**:140
Seademons (Yep) **35**:470
"The Seafarer" (Pound) **4**:408; **7**:336; **10**:408; **13**:454; **112**:305, 340, 343, 345-46
"The Sea-Gull" (Loewinsohn) **52**:283
Seagull (Kemal) **29**:267
The Seagull on the Step (Boyle) **58**:67; **121**:46
"The Seahorse and the Reef" (Ihimaera) **46**:200
"Seahorses" (Porter) **33**:323
"Seal" (Clarke) **61**:83
The Seal in the Bedroom (Thurber) **125**:395
"Seal Island Anthology" (Brown) **48**:60
"Seal Rock" (Pollitt) **122**:202
Seal Secret (Chambers) **35**:100
Sealed with a Loving Kiss (Hughes) **48**:181
The Seals (Dickinson)
See *The Sinful Stones*
The Seals (Dillon) **17**:97-8, 101
"Seals at High Island" (Murphy) **41**:313-14, 317
"Seals, Terns, Time" (Eberhart) **19**:144; **56**:86
Seamarks (Perse)
See *Amers*
"The Seamless Garment" (MacDiarmid) **11**:335; **63**:253
The Seamless Web (Burnshaw) **3**:90-1; **13**:128-30
The Seamless Web (Dickey) **10**:141
"Seamstress at St. Leon" (Clarke) **61**:83
"Seamus" (Pink Floyd) **35**:306
Seamus Heaney (Vendler) **138**:295, 301, 303
Seamus Heaney and Tom Paulin (Paulin) **37**:354
"Seamus Heaney's Fiftieth Birthday" (Durcan) **70**:151
"Sea-Music for My Sister Travelling" (Watkins) **43**:441
"The Sean Bhean Bhoct" (Montague) **46**:265-66, 275, 278
"Sean Flynn" (Clash) **30**:50-2
The Sean O'Casey Reader: Plays, Autobiographies, Opinions (O'Casey) **88**:253
"The Seance" (Creeley) **8**:152
The Séance, and Other Stories (Singer) **6**:508
"Seanchas" (Muldoon) **32**:315
Seára vermelha (Amado) **40**:27-8; **106**:57-59
"The Search" (Berryman) **25**:95
"The Search" (Blackburn) **43**:63
The Search (Dyer) **149**:44-5
The Search (Mahfouz)
See *al-Tariq*
The Search (Snow) **4**:500, 505
"Search by the Foundation" (Asimov) **26**:46, 60-3, 65
"Search by the Mule" (Asimov) **26**:63, 64
"A Search for a Future" (Miller) **47**:250
Search for a Method (Sartre) **52**:380-81, 386
Search for a Method (Sartre)
See *Questions de méthode*
The Search for Charlie (Corcoran) **17**:75
The Search for Harry Allway (Buzo) **61**:70-1
"The Search for J. Kruper" (Berriault) **54**:5; **109**:94
"The Search for Life—Is Anybody There?" (Branley) **21**:22
"The Search for Marvin Gardens" (McPhee) **36**:296
Search for Poetry (Andrade) **18**:4
Search for the Base and the Summit (Char)
See *Recherche de la base et du sommet*
A Search for the King (Vidal) **22**:433; **33**:406-07; **142**:322
The Search for the Perfect Language (Eco) **142**:112, 117, 121, 137
"The Search for Tom and Lucy" (Turner) **48**:398
Search for Tomorrow (Nixon) **21**:241, 245
"The Search for Wholes" (Livesay) **79**:348
"Search Party" (Merwin) **88**:210
"Search under Every Veil" (Bunting) **47**:54
The Searchers (Ford) **16**:310, 314, 316-17, 319
Searches and Seizures (Elkin) **4**:153-54; **6**:168-69; **9**:191; **14**:158; **27**:121-23; **91**:213
"Searching and Sounding" (Avison) **97**:80, 84-5
Searching for Caleb (Tyler) **7**:479; **11**:552; **28**:434; **44**:315, 320; **59**:202, 205; **103**:226, 235, 239-40, 243-44, 247-48, 259, 263, 265, 268-69, 273
Searching for Survivors (Banks) **37**:22-3; **72**:4-5, 12, 14
"Searching for Survivors II" (Banks) **37**:23
"Searching for the Ox" (Simpson) **149**:316, 354, 357
Searching for the Ox (Simpson) **7**:429-30; **9**:485-86; **149**:297, 299-300, 304-05, 316, 327, 338, 342, 346, 349-50
The Searching Image (Dudek) **19**:136
"Searching, Not Searching" (Rukeyser) **6**:480; **27**:413
The Searching Spirit (Adamson) **17**:5-6
The Searching Wind (Hellman) **2**:187; **8**:282; **18**:222; **52**:191
"Searchlight" (Heinlein) **26**:165
"Searchlight Practice" (Wright) **53**:428
Searoad (Le Guin) **136**:345-47, 361, 376
"Sea-Rose" (H. D.) **73**:105, 117, 121
Seascape (Albee) **5**:12-14; **9**:6; **11**:13; **25**:38; **53**:24; **86**:120, 124; **113**:15-6, 24, 28-31, 33, 40
Seascape: Needle's Eye (Oppen) **7**:284-85
"Seascape with Sun & Eagle" (Ferlinghetti) **111**:59
"A Seashell" (Snodgrass) **68**:388
"Seashells and Sandalwood" (Stow) **23**:436
"A Seaside Garden" (Gardam) **43**:171
"Seaside Resort" (Porter) **5**:347
"Season" (Soyinka) **44**:277
The Season at Sarsaparilla (White) **7**:531; **69**:407
A Season in England (Newby) **2**:311
A Season in Paradise (Breytenbach) **23**:85-6; **126**:60, 62, 66, 83, 94, 96, 98, 101
Season in Purgatory (Keneally) **8**:319; **10**:298; **14**:303; **19**:247; **117**:225, 235, 242
A Season in Rihata (Condé)
See *Une saison à Rihata*
"The Season in Scarborough, 1923" (Raine) **32**:353; **103**:186, 189-90
A Season in the Congo (Césaire)
See *Une saison au Congo*
A Season in the Life of Emmanuel (Blais)
See *Une saison dans la vie d'Emmanuel*
A Season in the Sun (Kahn) **30**:232
Season of Adventure (Lamming) **2**:235; **4**:279; **66**:219, 223-24, 227-32; **144**:132, 140, 143, 146, 152, 165, 173-75, 178, 183-86
Season of Anomy (Soyinka) **5**:398; **14**:509; **44**:294
The Season of Comfort (Vidal) **22**:432-33; **33**:405
A Season of Delight (Greenberg) **30**:167
A Season of Fear (Polonsky) **92**:378, 381, 402, 415, 417
"Season of Hard Wind" (Piercy) **27**:376
Season of Lights (Nyro) **17**:319
"Season of Lovers and Assassins" (Kizer) **80**:182
"The Season of Phantasmal Peace" (Walcott) **25**:456; **67**:355-56
Season of Ponies (Snyder) **17**:469
Season of the Briar (Brinsmead) **21**:26-7
"The Season of the Small, Small Spider" (Souster) **14**:505
Season of the Two-Heart (Duncan) **26**:100-01
"The Season of the Witch" (Herlihy) **6**:235-36
Season Songs (Hughes) **9**:282; **14**:271; **37**:175, 180; **119**:265-66, 268, 281
"Seasonal" (Ashbery) **125**:40
"Seasonal Greeting" (Simmons) **43**:412
"The Seasonless" (Wright) **28**:462
"The Seasons" (Fugard) **48**:109
"Seasons" (Haldeman) **61**:181
"Seasons" (Tomlinson) **13**:549; **45**:393
"Seasons and Meters" (Johnston) **51**:254
The Season's Difference (Buechner) **4**:79
Season's Greetings (Ayckbourn) **33**:43; **74**:7
Seasons in Flight (Aldiss) **40**:21
The Season's Lovers (Waddington) **28**:436
"Seasons of Love" (Larson) **99**:161, 173, 177, 180, 185, 187, 190
"The Seasons of the Soul" (Tate) **2**:428-30; **4**:540; **11**:522, 525, 527; **14**:529-31
Season's Reasons (Milner) **56**:225
The Sea-Thing Child (Hoban) **7**:161
"Seattle Art Society" (Acker) **111**:33
Seaview (Olson) **28**:344-45
Seawitch (MacLean) **13**:364
Sebastian; or, Ruling Passions (Durrell) **41**:133-35, 137-38
"La seca españa" (Azorín) **11**:24
"sechita" (Shange) **25**:402
"Der sechste Geburtstag" (Lenz) **27**:246
"Un secolo di studi sulla poesia popolare" (Pasolini) **106**:245
The Second American Revolution and Other Essays, 1976-1982 (Vidal) **33**:403-05, 409; **72**:386

"The Second Angel" (Levine) **4**:287
"Second Avenue" (O'Hara) **78**:344, 355, 359-60
Second Avenue (Mphahlele)
See *Down Second Avenue*
Second Avenue (O'Hara) **2**:323; **13**:423, 426-27
"The Second Bakery Attack" (Murakami) **150**:50, 58-9
"The Second Best Bed" (Nye) **42**:309
The Second Birth (Pasternak) **7**:292; **10**:383-84; **18**:382; **63**:289, 306
"The Second Birth of the Great Shaka of the Zulus" (Kunene) **85**:176
"Second Chance" (Auchincloss) **45**:30
"The Second Chance" (Sillitoe) **57**:391, 395
The Second Chance, and Other Stories (Sillitoe) **19**:422; **57**:391, 395; **148**:159
Second Chance: Tales of Two Generations (Auchincloss) **45**:30-1
"Second Chances" (Hugo) **32**:239
The Second Chronicles of Thomas Covenant, the Unbeliever (Donaldson) **46**:140-41; **138**:22, 27-8, 38, 40
"The Second Coming" (Abse) **7**:1
"Second Coming" (Livesay) **15**:340; **79**:339
The Second Coming (Percy) **18**:398-403; **47**:334, 337-38; **65**:257
"The Second Coming of Come-by-Chance" (Hospital) **145**:303, 305, 313
The Second Confession (Stout) **3**:472
"Second Cup of Coffee" (Lightfoot) **26**:278-79
The Second Curtain (Fuller) **4**:178; **28**:148
"Second Dawn" (Clarke) **136**:211-12
The Second Day (Ehrenburg) **34**:439; **62**:176, 178-79
The Second Deadly Sin (Sanders) **41**:379
The Second Death (Schell) **35**:366-67
The Second Dune (Hearon) **63**:160, 166
Second Ending (Hunter) **31**:218-20
"The Second Essay on Interest" (Murray) **40**:343
The Second Face (Aymé) **11**:21
Second Fall (O'Casey) **11**:406
A Second Flowering (Cowley) **39**:458-59
Second Foundation (Asimov) **3**:17; **26**:46, 58, 61, 64; **76**:313-14
Second Generation (Fast) **23**:160; **131**:86, 95-6, 100
Second Growth (Stegner) **49**:349-50
Second Heaven (Guest) **30**:174-76
"Second Hymn to Lenin" (MacDiarmid) **4**:311; **63**:253-55
Second Hymn to Lenin, and Other Poems (MacDiarmid) **63**:245, 250, 255
"The Second Interment" (Smith) **43**:420
"Second Language" (Gallagher) **63**:120
Second Language (Mueller) **51**:283-85
The Second Life (Morgan) **31**:272-73, 275-76
"A Second Look" (MacLennan) **92**:346
The Second Man (Behrman) **40**:72-3, 75-6, 78, 81, 87
Second Manifeste du surréalisme (Breton) **54**:20, 31
Second Manifesto of Surrealism (Breton)
See *Second Manifeste du surréalisme*
Second Marriage (Barthelme) **36**:52-5; **117**:4, 7, 11, 21, 26
"Second Meeting" (Dinesen) **10**:149, 152
"A Second Meeting with my Father" (Amichai) **116**:126
The Second Mrs. Whitberg (Bermant) **40**:94
Second Nature (Stolz) **12**:551
Second Poems (Graham) **29**:193
"Second Populist Manifesto" (Ferlinghetti)
See "Adieu á Charlot"
"Second Question" (Beattie) **146**:
The Second Ring of Power (Castaneda) **12**:95
"Second Sally" (Lem) **40**:296; **149**:155
The Second Scroll (Klein) **19**:258
"Second Sermon" (Brooks) **125**:73
"The Second Sermon on the Warpland" (Brooks) **15**:93; **125**:73, 96
The Second Sex (Beauvoir)
See *Le deuxième sexe*
The Second Shell (Williamson) **29**:454
"A Second Siege" (Montague) **13**:392
Second Skin (Hawkes) **1**:138; **2**:185-86; **3**:221-22; **4**:215, 218; **7**:141, 144-45; **9**:266-69; **15**:274-77; **27**:190-92, 199; **49**:161-64
"Second Son" (Pastan) **27**:368
"Second Son Day" (Honig) **33**:213, 215
"Second Song" (Bogan) **46**:81; **93**:67, 69
Second sous-sol (Butor) **15**:115
"Second Spring" (MacLeod) **56**:198-200
The Second Stage (Friedan) **74**:99-111
The Second Stone (Fiedler) **4**:160
"The Second Swimming" (Boyle) **36**:58
"Second Thoughts about Humanism" (Eliot) **6**:160
"Second Time Around" (Cortázar)
See "Segunda vez"
"The Second Time Around" (Fisher) **87**:124
The Second Tree from the Corner (White) **10**:527-28; **39**:370, 373, 375
The Second Trip (Silverberg) **140**:372, 379
"The Second War and Postmodern Memory" (Bernstein) **142**:20
"Second Wind" (Chappell) **78**:92
Second Words (Atwood) **135**:18
The Secondary Sky (Popa) **19**:373-74
Secondary Worlds (Auden) **6**:16; **43**:25; **123**:24-5
Second-Class Citizen (Emecheta) **14**:159; **48**:97-8, 101; **128**:54-6, 61-4, 66, 68, 73-4, 81-3
"Second-Class Matter" (Perelman) **49**:264
"The Second-Fated" (Graves) **45**:169
"Secrecy" (Watkins) **43**:454, 456
"The Secret" (Cohen) **19**:113
"The Secret" (Frame) **96**:184
"The Secret" (Mahapatra) **33**:284
"A Secret" (Plath) **51**:340
"The Secret" (Simic) **130**:335
A Secret (Akhmadulina) **53**:15
Secret (Andrade)
See *Segrafedo*
The Secret Adversary (Christie) **48**:73-4; **110**:111, 113, 123
Secret Agent (Hitchcock) **16**:345
The Secret beyond the Door (Lang) **20**:207, 216; **103**:87
"Le secret de Justine" (Theriault) **79**:408
Le Secret derrière la Porte (Lang)
See *The Secret beyond the Door*
The Secret Diary of Adrian Mole, Aged 13 3/4 (Townsend) **61**:407-16, 418-420
The Secret Diary of Margaret Hilda Roberts, Aged 14 1/2 (Townsend) **61**:420
Secret Friends (Potter) **86**:346, 353; **123**:248-49, 269
"The Secret Garden" (Hoffman) **141**:310-11
"The Secret Garden" (Kinsella) **138**:119
The Secret Glass (Bainbridge)
See *The Dressmaker*
The Secret Government: The Constitution in Crisis (Moyers) **74**:252
"A Secret Gratitude" (Wright) **10**:544
Secret Harmonies (Barrett) **150**:8
The Secret Heart of the Clock: Notes, Aphorisms, Fragments, 1973-1985 (Canetti)
See *Das Geheimherz der Uhr: Aufzeichnungen 1973-1985*
The Secret History (Tartt) **76**:119-37
Secret History of the Dividing Line (Howe) **152**:150, 169, 195, 220-31, 232, 235-36
The Secret History of the Lord of Musashi (Tanizaki)
See *Bushūkō hiwa*
Secret Honor (Altman) **116**:59, 68
"Le secret humain" (MacLeish) **68**:270, 285
"The Secret in the Cat" (Swenson) **14**:518
Secret in the Stlalakum Wild (Harris) **12**:263-67
"The Secret Integration" (Pynchon) **33**:334, 338-40; **62**:431, 434
Secret Isaac (Charyn) **18**:99
"Secret Journal" (Willingham) **51**:403
The Secret Journey of the Silver Reindeer (Kingman) **17**:245-46
The Secret Ladder (Harris) **25**:203, 205, 214
The Secret Life of Cartoons (Barker) **52**:54
"The Secret Life of Henry K" (Bova) **45**:75
"The Secret Life of James Thurber" (Thurber) **125**:395
The Secret Life of the Lord of Musashi (Tanizaki)
See *Bushūkō hiwa*
"The Secret Life of Walter Mitty" (Thurber) **5**:432, 440; **11**:533-34; **25**:440; **125**:388, 390, 399, 401-02, 407, 410-11
Secret Lives (King) **145**:358-59
Secret Lives, and Other Stories (Ngũgĩ wa Thiong'o) **36**:313, 317, 322
Secret Marriages (Longley) **29**:295
The Secret Meaning of Things (Ferlinghetti) **10**:174-75; **27**:139; **111**:65
"The Secret Miracle" (Borges)
See "El milagro secreto"
The Secret Muses: The Life of Frederick Ashton (Kavanagh) **119**:59-63, 69-70
"Secret Music" (Sassoon) **130**:181
Secret Narratives (Motion) **47**:288-94
The Secret of Chimneys (Christie) **110**:111, 113
The Secret of Dr. Honigberger (Eliade)
See *Secretul Doctorului Honigberger*
The Secret of Heaven (Lagerkvist)
See *Himlens hemlighet*
The Secret of J. Eddy Fink (Ian) **21**:183
The Secret of Luca (Silone) **4**:493
The Secret of the Lodge (Streatfeild) **21**:398, 406
Secret of the Lost Race (Norton) **12**:468
"The Secret of Their Voices" (Levine) **118**:267
Secret Passage (Cavanna) **12**:98
The Secret Passion (Huston)
See *Freud*
The Secret People (Wyndham) **19**:476
"Le secret perdu dans l'eau" (Carrier) **78**:63, 72, 77-8
Secret Places (Elliott) **47**:112-14
The Secret Rapture (Hare) **58**:231-35
Secret Rendezvous (Abe)
See *Mikkai*
The Secret Road (Lancaster) **36**:244
"The Secret Room" (Robbe-Grillet) **14**:462; **43**:361
"The Secret Sits" (Frost) **13**:228
Secret Stories of the Lord of Musashi (Tanizaki)
See *Bushūkō hiwa*
The Secret Tales of the Lord of Musashi (Tanizaki)
See *Bushūkō hiwa*
"The Secret Town" (Nash) **23**:317
Secret Training (Codrescu) **46**:104
Secret Understandings (Philipson) **53**:276
"A Secret Vice" (Tolkien) **38**:439-40, 442
Secret Villages (Dunn) **40**:170-71
The Secret Ways (MacLean) **13**:361; **63**:262-63
"Secret Weapons" (Cortázar)
See "Las armas secretas"
Secret Window, Secret Garden (King) **113**:367
"Secretary" (Gaitskill) **69**:199, 201
"Secretary" (Hughes) **2**:198; **9**:284
"The Secretary Chant" (Piercy) **6**:403
"Secrets" (Fuller) **62**:201
"Secrets" (Mac Laverty) **31**:253-54
"Secrets" (Williams) **148**:361
Secrets (Farah) **137**:113-16, 118
Secrets, and Other Stories (Mac Laverty) **31**:252-54
"Secrets and Surprises" (Beattie) **146**:66
Secrets and Surprises (Beattie) **13**:64-6; **18**:37; **40**:63, 66; **63**:3, 11, 15, 17/ **146**:47, 54, 66, 69, 78, 84

Secrets from the Center of the World (Harjo) **83**:272-73, 275-77, 279
Secrets of a Woman's Heart: The Later Life of I. Compton-Burnett, 1920-1969 (Spurling) **34**:495-98
"Secrets of Hans's Harem" (Sansom) **2**:383
"Secrets of Lord Bushu" (Tanizaki)
See *Bushūkō hiwa*
Secrets of the Shopping Mall (Peck) **21**:300
"Secrets of the Universe" (McFadden) **48**:257
Secrets of Women (Bergman)
See *Kvinnors väntan*
"Secrets of Wonder Women" (Hochman) **8**:297
Secrets on the Road (Transtroemer)
See *Hemligheter på vägen*
"Secrets on the Way" (Transtroemer) **65**:222-23
Secrets on the Way (Transtroemer)
See *Hemligheter på vägen*
Secretul Doctorului Honigberger (Eliade) **19**:145-47
"The Sect of the Phoenix" (Borges)
See "La secta del Fénix"
"The Sect of the Phoenix" (Borges)
See "La secta del Fénix"
"The Sect of Thirty" (Borges)
See "La secta de los treintas"
"La secta de los treintas" (Borges) **9**:117; **19**:51; **48**:38-9
"La secta del Fénix" (Borges) **83**:156-57
Section: Rock-Drill, 85-95 de los cantares (Pound) **4**:412, 414; **7**:331; **13**:463; **48**:282-83, 285-86, 293
"Secuestro de la mujer de Antonio" (Guillén) **48**:163
"Secular Conversions" (Burke) **24**:127
Secular Love (Ondaatje) **51**:313-15, 317, 320
The Secular Scripture (Frye) **24**:226, 229
"Security" (Bissoondath) **120**:13-16, 19, 24
"The Security Guard" (Dixon) **52**:95, 98
"Security Precedes Credibility" (Carr) **86**:47
"Sedan Chair" (Young) **17**:581
"Sediment" (Ignatow) **40**:258
Sedmiramenný svícen (Škvorecký) **39**:221; **69**:343
Seduced (Shepard) **17**:447-49; **41**:408-09
"Seduction" (Giovanni) **19**:190; **64**:186-87, 194-95
"Seduction and Betrayal" (Hooks) **94**:158
Seduction and Betrayal (Hardwick) **13**:264-66
The Seduction, and Other Stories (Oates) **6**:373; **9**:403
The Seduction of Mimi (Wertmueller) **16**:587-89, 595, 597-98
The Seduction of Mrs. Pendlebury (Forster) **149**:65, 76
The Seduction of Peter S. (Sanders) **41**:381-82
Seduction of the Minotaur (Nin) **4**:376, 378-79; **14**:385; **60**:275, 279-81; **127**:362, 379
"See Everything New" (Cryer) **21**:79
"See My Friends" (Davies) **21**:89
See Naples and Die (Rice) **7**:360; **49**:300
See No Evil: Prefaces, Essays, and Accounts, 1976-1983 (Shange) **38**:395
"See the Moon?" (Barthelme) **115**:62, 86
See the Old Lady Decently (Johnson) **6**:264-65; **9**:301
"See the Sky about to Rain" (Young) **17**:573
See Them Die (Hunter) **31**:220
See Under: Love (Grossman) **67**:65-72, 74
See You at Mao (Godard) **20**:141
See You Later Alligator (Buckley) **37**:62-3
See You Will Never Get Anywhere (Benet)
See *Nunca llegarás a nada*
The Seed (Vesaas)
See *Kimen*
The Seed beneath the Snow (Silone) **4**:493
"Seed Catalogue" (Kroetsch) **23**:273; **132**:239-242, 252
Seed Catalogue: Poems (Kroetsch) **23**:273; **132**:263-68, 280, 282-85, 287-88
"The Seed Cutters" (Heaney) **7**:152; **25**:245
"A Seed in the Sky" (Honig) **33**:216
"Seed Leaves" (Wilbur) **3**:533; **6**:568; **9**:568; **53**:404-05
"The Seed of My Father" (Swenson) **106**:351
"The Seed Picture" (McGuckian) **48**:275-77
"The Seed Thrower" (Scott) **22**:373
Seeds and Bran (Tzara)
See *Grains et issues*
"Seeds and Stones" (Kroetsch) **132**:283
Seeds for a Hymn (Paz)
See *Semillas para un himno*
Seeds of Change: A Quincentennial Commemoration (Viola) **70**:332, 344
Seeds of Contemplation (Merton) **1**:211; **83**:403
Seeds of Destruction (Merton) **1**:211; **83**:382-83
Seeds of Man (Guthrie) **35**:194
The Seeds of Time (Jameson) **142**:249-50, 252, 254, 256, 258, 262-63
The Seeds of Tomorrow (Sholokhov)
See *Podniataia tselina*
Seedtime on the Cumberland (Arnow) **7**:15-16; **18**:12
"Seeing Death in the Murderous Look of an Unknown Black Man Whom I Admire and Deducing from This Certain Proprietorial Privileges" (Hall) **51**:175
"Seeing Gender" (Acker) **111**:46
"Seeing Her Leave" (Davie) **31**:117
"Seeing in the Dark" (Komunyakaa) **94**:230
Seeing in the Dark (Transtroemer)
See *Mörkerseende*
Seeing Is Believing (Tomlinson) **2**:436-37; **4**:543-44, 546-47; **13**:545, 547; **45**:392-93, 396, 398-400, 402, 404
"Seeing Pablo Neruda" (Spacks) **14**:511
"Seeing Things" (Heaney) **74**:188, 194-95
"Seeing Things" (Peterkin) **31**:307
Seeing Things (Heaney) **74**:188-95, 197, **91**:124-25
Seeing through the Sun (Hogan) **73**:150-52, 154, 157, 159
Seeing Voices: A Journey into the World of the Deaf (Sacks) **67**:303-05
"Seeing You Have" (Snodgrass) **18**:491
Seek the House of Relatives (Cook-Lynn) **93**:121
"The Seeker" (Townshend) **17**:529, 531
"The Seekers" (McGrath) **59**:177, 181
The Seekers (Jakes) **29**:248
The Seekers and Other Poems (Sachs) **14**:476; **98**:362
"Seeking a Job" (Bennett) **28**:29
"The Seekonk Woods" (Kinnell) **129**:255, 270
Eine Seele aus Holz (Lind) **1**:178; **2**:245; **4**:292-93; **27**:271, 273; **82**:128-30, 132-38, 140, 142, 145
"Seele im Raum" (Jarrell) **6**:260; **13**:298
Die Seele und die Formen (Lukacs) **24**:324-25, 330
"Der seelische Ratgeber" (Lenz) **27**:245
Seembadha (Ray)
See *Simabaddha*
"Seen and Not Seen" (Byrne) **26**:98-9
"Seen the Lights Go Out on Broadway" (Joel)
See "Miami 2017"
"Seesaw" (Gerstler) **70**:156
"See-Saw" (Pink Floyd) **35**:307
The Seesaw Log (Gibson) **23**:175-76
Seetee Ship (Williamson) **29**:450
Seetee Shock (Williamson) **29**:450
Sefer ha-Maasim (Agnon) **8**:8; **14**:4
Seger i mörker (Lagerkvist) **54**:269-70, 272, 275, 278
"Un segno nello spazio" (Calvino) **8**:128
Ségou: La terre en miettes (Condé) **52**:83-5; **92**:108, 130
Ségou: Les murailles de terre (Condé) **52**:81-5; **92**:100, 102-03, 108-11, 113, 126, 130-31, 133-34
Segrafedo (Andrade) **18**:3
Segrêdo (Andrade) **18**:3
Segregation: The Inner Conflict in the South (Warren) **8**:538; **59**:298
La segretaria (Ginzburg) **54**:207
Il segreto del bosco vecchio (Buzzati) **36**:83, 97
Segu (Condé)
See *Ségou: Les murailles de terre*
Segues (Bell) **31**:51-2
"Seguir siguiendo" (Otero) **11**:427
"Segunda vez" (Cortázar) **33**:125
"Le sei della sera" (Ortese) **89**:198
Sein und Zeit (Heidegger) **24**:257, 260, 262, 264-65, 267, 269-71, 273, 275, 277, 279
"Las seis" (Aleixandre) **9**:12
Seis calas (Alonso) **14**:20
Seis problemas para Don Isidro Parodi (Bioy Casares) **13**:84, 106; **48**:36, 41-4; **88**:66, 69-73, 77-8, 85
"Seismograf" (Bagryana) **10**:13
"Seismograf na surtseto" (Bagryana) **10**:12, 14
Seize the Day (Bellow) **1**:27-8, 30-1; **2**:49, 51, 53; **3**:49-50, 52, 55-7, 60-1; **6**:56, 61; **8**:70, 72, 74, 77; **10**:37-9, 44; **13**:70, 72-3; **15**:47-8, 50, 52-3, 55, 57; **25**:80, 84-5; **33**:64, 67, 71; **63**:28, 36, 42-3; **79**:60-104
"Seize the Means of Projection" (Codrescu) **121**:172
"Seizing Control" (Robison) **98**:306-08, 317
"The Seizure" (Blaise) **29**:70-1
Seizure (Stone) **73**:364
A Seizure of Limericks (Aiken) **52**:26
The Seizure of Power (Milosz)
See *Zdobycie wladzy*
Sekai no owari to hādoboirudo wandārando (Murakami) **150**:39, 51, 53, 55, 62-3, 72, 74-6, 78, 81, 83, 86-7, 90, 92
Sekrya (Vaculik) **7**:494-97
Šel malíř chudě do světa (Seifert) **93**:306, 332, 335, 343
Le sel noir (Glissant) **68**:187
"Selahl" (Hughes) **108**:308
"Selbdritt, Selbviert" (Celan) **53**:77
Selbstbezichtigung (Handke) **5**:166; **8**:262-63; **15**:266-67; **38**:215; **134**:107-08, 161, 175
"Selbstversuch: Traktat zu einem Protokoll" (Wolf) **150**:228, 237, 253, 298, 320, 324-25
"The Select Party" (Ewart) **46**:150
Selected and New Poems (Dubie) **36**:139-41
Selected and New Poems, 1961-1981 (Harrison) **33**:197-98
Selected Cantos (Pound) **4**:416; **48**:295
Selected Criticism: Prose, Poetry (Bogan) **46**:84; **93**:65
Selected Declarations of Dependence (Mathews) **52**:307, 314, 316
Selected Essays (Eliot) **24**:173, 177, 183; **113**:218
Selected Essays (Farrell) **66**:132
Selected Essays (Montale) **18**:342-43
Selected Essays (Montherlant) **19**:324
Selected Essays (Williams) **5**:510; **67**:411
Selected Essays and Criticism (Dudek) **19**:139
Selected Essays of Delmore Schwartz (Schwartz) **45**:359
Selected Essays of Hugh MacDiarmid (MacDiarmid) **2**:254
Selected Failings (Neruda)
See *Defectos escogidos: 2000*
The Selected James Simmons (Simmons) **43**:411-12
Selected Letters (Frost) **44**:459, 462
Selected Letters, 1917-1961 (Hemingway)
See *Ernest Hemingway: Selected Letters, 1917-1961*
Selected Letters of Conrad Aiken (Aiken) **52**:30-2
Selected Letters of E. M. Forster, Volume I: 1879-1920 (Forster) **45**:137-38, 143
Selected Letters of E. M. Forster, Volume II: 1921-1970 (Forster) **45**:138-40, 143
Selected Letters of James Thurber (Thurber) **25**:438-40; **125**:393-94
Selected Letters of John O'Hara (O'Hara) **11**:414; **42**:318

The Selected Letters of Philip Larkin, 1940-1985 (Thwaite) **81**:417-64
Selected Letters of Theodore Roethke (Roethke) **46**:356
Selected Letters of William Faulkner (Faulkner) **9**:203
"A Selected Life" (Kinsella) **138**:88, 95, 105
A Selected Life (Kinsella) **19**:253
Selected Literary Criticism of Louis MacNeice (MacNeice) **53**:244
Selected Longer Poems (Ammons) **25**:44; **57**:59
Selected Notebooks: 1960-1967 (Cozzens) **92**:211
The Selected Paul Durcan (Durcan) **43**:115-18
Selected Plays (Friel) **115**:224
Selected Plays and Prose of Amiri Baraka/LeRoi Jones (Baraka) **14**:48
Selected Poems (Abse) **7**:1
Selected Poems (Adcock) **41**:17-18
Selected Poems (Aiken) **1**:4
Selected Poems (Akhmatova) **25**:25; **126**:31-2
Selected Poems (Ali) **69**:32
Selected Poems (Ammons) **2**:11-12; **5**:26; **9**:26; **25**:48; **57**:59; **108**:5, 17, 21-2, 24
Selected Poems (Ashbery) **41**:40-1; **77**:56, 60, 62; **125**:11, 33
Selected Poems (Auden) **123**:48
Selected Poems (Avison) **97**:120-22
Selected Poems (Baraka) **115**:38-9
Selected Poems (Barker) **48**:13-14
Selected Poems (Beer) **58**:36
Selected Poems (Betjeman) **6**:67
Selected Poems (Bly) **128**:17-19, 21, 23, 25, 27, 29-30
Selected Poems (Boland) **67**:45-6; **113**:108, 110
Selected Poems (Breton) **54**:17
Selected Poems (Brooks) **49**:23, 27, 32, 35; **125**:45, 48-9, 74, 88, 94
Selected Poems (Ciardi) **40**:162; **44**:375, 379-82; **129**:42, 44-45, 52-56
Selected Poems (Clarke) **9**:169
Selected Poems (Clarke) **61**:78-9, 82
Selected Poems (Creeley) **8**:153; **78**:161
Selected Poems (Daryush) **6**:122; **19**:119
Selected Poems (Day Lewis) **6**:127-28
Selected Poems (Deane) **122**:81
Selected Poems (Dorn) **18**:129
Selected Poems (Eberhart) **3**:135; **56**:80-4
Selected Poems (Eigner) **9**:181
Selected Poems (Ekelöf) **27**:113, 116
Selected Poems (Elytis) **49**:113-14
Selected Poems (Frost) **9**:219
Selected Poems (Glassco) **9**:236
Selected Poems (Graham) **29**:198-99
Selected Poems (Grass) **32**:197
Selected Poems (Gregor) **9**:253, 255
Selected Poems (Guillevic) **33**:191
Selected Poems (Gustafson) **36**:214, 216
Selected Poems (H. D.) **31**:203
Selected Poems (Hacker) **91**:110
Selected Poems (Hall) **51**:173-75
Selected Poems (Harrison) **43**:179-81; **129**:168, 171, 173-78, 204
Selected Poems (Hayden) **5**:168; **14**:240; **37**:160
Selected Poems (Hikmet) **40**:244, 247
Selected Poems (Hope) **51**:226-27
Selected Poems (Hugo) **18**:263-64; **32**:244-46
Selected Poems (Jarrell) **9**:297; **13**:300
Selected Poems (Jennings) **131**:237, 241
Selected Poems (Justice) **19**:232-34, 236-37; **102**:248-51, 253, 256, 261, 267-68, 270, 275, 277, 283
Selected Poems (Kinnell) **29**:288-89; **129**:260, 264, 266
Selected Poems (Laughlin) **49**:220
Selected Poems (Levertov) **66**:249-50
Selected Poems (Levine) **33**:275; **118**:274, 279-80, 296
Selected Poems (Lowell) **8**:353, 355-57
Selected Poems (MacCaig) **36**:284, 288
Selected Poems (Masefield) **47**:233
Selected Poems (Merrill) **91**:235
Selected Poems (Merton) **83**:393-94
Selected Poems (Merwin) **88**:204-06
Selected Poems (Milosz) **5**:292; **22**:308, 312; **31**:259, 262, 267; **56**:239-40, 244; **82**:297-98
Selected Poems (Montague) **46**:275-77, 279
Selected Poems (Moore) **1**:228-30; **2**:291; **13**:393; **19**:339; **47**:260
Selected Poems (Moss) **7**:247-49; **14**:375-76; **45**:289; **50**:352
Selected Poems (Murphy) **41**:319
Selected Poems (Neruda) **5**:301-02; **62**:333
Selected Poems (O'Hara) **13**:424
Selected Poems (Orlovitz) **22**:333, 336-37
Selected Poems (Pastan) **27**:370
Selected Poems (Patchen) **18**:394
Selected Poems (Paz) **51**:326-27, 334
Selected Poems (Pound) **4**:415
Selected Poems (Purdy) **3**:408
Selected Poems (Rakosi) **47**:342-43
Selected Poems (Ransom) **2**:365; **11**:467
Selected Poems (Rexroth) **49**:283-86
Selected Poems (Rich) **18**:446
Selected Poems (Riding) **7**:374-75
Selected Poems (Ritsos) **31**:325
Selected Poems (Rozewicz)
See *Poezja wybrane*
Selected Poems (Sachs)
See *Ausgewählte Gedichte*
Selected Poems (Sandburg) **35**:345
Selected Poems (Scannell) **49**:328-29
Selected Poems (Scott) **22**:373, 375, 377
Selected Poems (Senghor) **130**:233
Selected Poems (Shapcott) **38**:403-04
Selected Poems (Shapiro) **8**:486; **15**:478; **53**:331
Selected Poems (Silkin) **43**:403-04
Selected Poems (Simpson) **4**:497-99; **7**:428-29; **149**:313, 315, 341, 352
Selected Poems (Sitwell) **67**:324
Selected Poems (Skelton) **13**:506-07
Selected Poems (Smith) **43**:417, 422
Selected Poems (Strand) **41**:431-37; **71**:278, 286-88, 290
Selected Poems (Thomas) **31**:431, 434; **132**:362
Selected Poems (Transtroemer) **52**:415-16
Selected Poems (Voznesensky) **15**:552-53
Selected Poems (Walcott) **67**:353
Selected Poems (Warren) **59**:295-96
Selected Poems (Watkins) **43**:441
Selected Poems (Webb) **18**:542
Selected Poems (Wieners) **7**:536-37
Selected Poems (Williams) **148**:355-57, 362-63
Selected Poems, 1949 (Williams) **42**:462
Selected Poems, 1968 (Herbert) **43**:183, 188, 194
Selected Poems, 1977 (Herbert) **43**:188
Selected Poems, 1984 (Williams) **42**:461-62
Selected Poems 1954-82 (Fuller) **62**:203-04
Selected Poems: 1968-86 (Muldoon) **72**:275-76
Selected Poems, 1920-1970 (Everson) **27**:135
Selected Poems, 1923-1943 (Warren) **8**:539-40, 542; **10**:523, 525; **13**:578, 573-74; **18**:535
Selected Poems, 1923-1967 (Borges) **2**:71-2; **48**:46
Selected Poems, 1923-1975 (Warren) **8**:539-40, 542; **10**:523, 525; **13**:573, 578; **39**:265, 267
Selected Poems, 1928-1958 (Kunitz) **6**:285-86; **14**:312; **148**:69-74, 78-79, 84, 88-89, 91, 94-96, 105, 111, 137, 139, 145, 149
Selected Poems, 1930-1960 (Watkins) **43**:447, 455
Selected Poems, 1933-1980 (Faludy) **42**:142
Selected Poems, 1935-1985 (Laughlin) **49**:223-24
Selected Poems (1938-1958): Summer Knowledge (Schwartz)
See *Summer Knowledge: New and Selected Poems, 1938-1958*
Selected Poems: 1938-1988 (McGrath) **59**:180-84
Selected Poems, 1940-1966 (Birney) **6**:74-5, 78
Selected Poems, 1946-1968 (Thomas) **6**:531; **48**:380
Selected Poems 1947-1995 (Ginsberg) **109**:362-63, 365
Selected Poems, 1950-1975 (Gunn) **18**:202-04; **81**:184
Selected Poems, 1950-1982 (Koch) **44**:248, 250
Selected Poems, 1951-1974 (Tomlinson) **13**:546, 548-49; **45**:392, 394-96, 401
Selected Poems, 1951-1977 (Ammons) **25**:41-4
The Selected Poems, 1951-1986 (Ammons) **57**:51-2
Selected Poems, 1953-1976 (Alvarez) **13**:9
Selected Poems, 1954-1986 (Transtroemer) **52**:418
Selected Poems, 1954-1992 (Brown) **100**:88
Selected Poems, 1955-1976 (Honig) **33**:215
Selected Poems, 1955-1980 (Smith) **64**:393-96
Selected Poems 1956-1968 (Kinsella) **11**:252; **138**:89-92, 146-50, 161
Selected Poems, 1957-1967 (Hughes) **4**:235-36; **9**:281; **119**:295
Selected Poems, 1957-1987 (Snodgrass) **68**:387, 389, 395, 397-99
Selected Poems, 1958-1980 (Sorrentino) **40**:384, 386
Selected Poems, 1963-1980 (Longley) **29**:296
Selected Poems, 1963-1983 (Simic) **49**:337-43; **130**:311, 316, 340
Selected Poems 1965-1975 (Atwood) **8**:29-30; **15**:36-8; **25**:64, 67; **84**:68
Selected Poems 1966-1987 (Heaney) **74**:192-93, 195; **91**:124
Selected Poems, 1970-1980 (Codrescu) **46**:104-05; **121**:155, 158-62
The Selected Poems: Expanded Editions (Ammons) **108**:24
Selected Poems, Joseph Brodsky (Brodsky) **4**:77-8; **6**:97-8; **36**:74, 76-9, 81; **100**:49, 51-2, 58
Selected Poems: Loki Is Buried at Smoky Creek (Wah) **44**:328
Selected Poems: New and Old, 1923-1966 (Warren) **8**:539; **18**:534; **39**:266
The Selected Poems of Austin Clarke (Kinsella) **138**:107
The Selected Poems of David Ignatow (Ignatow) **7**:178-79, 181-82
Selected Poems of Dorothy Livesay 1926-1956 (Livesay) **15**:339
The Selected Poems of Langston Hughes (Hughes) **10**:279; **35**:216; **108**:292, 295, 315, 319, 334-35
Selected Poems of Luis Cernuda (Cernuda) **54**:58
Selected Poems of May Sarton (Sarton) **14**:482
The Selected Poems of Rosario Castellanos (Castellanos) **66**:60
Selected Poems: Poems Selected and New 1976-1986 (Atwood) **84**:68-9
Selected Poems: The Self-Completing Tree (Livesay) **79**:332-33, 336, 338, 353
Selected Poetry (Walcott) **14**:548; **25**:452; **42**:421
Selected Poetry of Amiri Baraka/LeRoi Jones (Baraka) **14**:48
The Selected Poetry of Hayden Carruth (Carruth) **84**:131, 133-34
The Selected Poetry of Jaroslav Seifert (Seifert) **44**:423; **93**:329, 331, 345
The Selected Poetry of Robinson Jeffers (Jeffers) **54**:238, 244, 246, 249; **11**:304
Selected Poetry of W. H. Auden (Auden) **2**:24
The Selected Poetry of Yehuda Amichai (Amichai) **57**:40-4; **116**:114, 130
Selected Prose (Celan) **82**:37
Selected Prose, 1909-1965 (Pound) **3**:397-99; **5**:349; **7**:333
Selected Short Stories of Mulk Raj Anand (Anand) **23**:21
Selected Shorter Poems (Reaney) **13**:476
Selected Stories (Gordimer) **7**:132-33; **10**:240;

33:182; **70**:163; **123**:116, 132, 144
Selected Stories (Hood) **28**:193
Selected Stories (Levine) **54**:295-97
Selected Stories (Pritchett) **13**:467; **15**:443; **41**:330
Selected Stories of Andre Dubus (Dubus) **97**:221-22, 227, 229-30, 235
Selected Stories of Roald Dahl (Dahl) **1**:71
Selected Stories of Seán O'Faoláin (O'Faolain) **14**:405-07
"Selected Strawberries" (Musgrave) **13**:400-01; **54**:340
Selected Tales of Jacques Ferron (Ferron) **94**:124
Selected Translations, 1968-1978 (Merwin) **45**:276
Selected Verse Translations (Watkins) **43**:455
Selected Works of Djuna Barnes (Barnes) **127**:162
Selected Writings (Barnes) **29**:25
Selected Writings (Capote) **3**:99; **13**:139; **58**:93
Selected Writings (Cendrars) **106**:177
Selected Writings (Olson) **5**:326
Selected Writings 1950-1990 (Howe) **85**:151-52
Selected Writings of William Goyen: Eight Favorites by a Master American Story-Teller (Goyen) **8**:250
Selected Poems of Tudor Arghezi (Arghezi) **80**:9
"Selene Afterwards" (MacLeish) **68**:271, 286
"Self" (Hacker) **72**:191
"Self" (de Man) **55**:410
The Self and Others: Further Studies in Sanity and Madness (Laing) **95**:124, 129, 131, 133-35, 138, 141, 156, 170-71, 173-74, 182
"The Self and the Mulberry" (Bell) **31**:49
"The Self and The Other" (Borges)
See "El otro, el mismo"
"Self as an Eye" (Squires) **51**:380
Self defence: Critique esthétique (Reverdy) **53**:280, 283, 285-86
"Self Defense" (Giles) **39**:65
"The Self in Fiction" (Barth) **51**:24
"Self Is a Very Iffy Word for Me" (Bell) **31**:51
"Self Portrait" (Castellanos)
See "Autorretrato"
"Self Portrait" (Wright)
See "Self-Portraits"
Self Portrait (Dylan) **4**:150; **6**:157; **12**:190, 199; **77**:164, 175, 178
Self Portrait (Kavanagh) **22**:236
"Self Portrait at Fourty-Four" (Pastan) **27**:369
Self Portrait/Deathwatch (Breytenbach) **126**:94
Self-Accusation (Handke)
See *Selbstbezichtigung*
The Self-Completing Tree (Livesay)
See *Selected Poems: The Self-Completing Tree*
Self-Consciousness (Updike) **70**:253, 263; **139**:327-28, 361, 363, 370-73
Self-Consuming Artifacts (Fish) **142**:144, 148-50, 160, 177-78, 183
"Self-Counsel in Old Age" (Wheelock) **14**:571
"The Self-Death" (Breytenbach) **126**:70
"Self-Experiment: Appendix to a Report" (Wolf)
See "Selbstversuch: Traktat zu einem Protokoll"
"The Self-Hatred of Don L. Lee" (Madhubuti) **73**:206
"Self-Help" (Beer) **58**:32
Self-Help (Moore) **39**:82-5; **45**:279-83; **68**:296-301
"Self-Interview" (Reed) **60**:313
Self-Interviews (Dickey) **1**:73; **2**:116; **109**:249-50
"The Selfish One" (Neruda)
See "El egoísta"
"Self-Portrait" (Blaga) **75**:61, 77
"Self-Portrait" (Creeley) **36**:120
"Self-Portrait" (Dixon) **52**:100
"Self-Portrait" (Graham) **48**:145; **118**:223
"Self-Portrait" (Stern) **40**:407
"Self-Portrait, 1969" (Bidart) **33**:74, 76
"Self-Portrait as a Bear" (Hall) **37**:142
"Self-Portrait as Apollo and Daphne" (Graham) **48**:154; **118**:249, 260
"Self-Portrait as Hurry and Delay" (Graham) **48**:155
"Self-Portrait as the Gesture between Them" (Graham) **48**:150; **118**:231
Self-Portrait: Ceaselessly into the Past (Macdonald) **34**:416; **41**:269-70
"Self-Portrait in a Convex Mirror" (Ashbery) **9**:44, 48; **13**:31, 33-4; **15**:28, 32, 35; **25**:52, 56; **41**:33, 37-8, 40-1; **77**:44, 46, 48-9, 55-6, 60, 62, 77-9; **125**:4-5, 7, 15, 33
Self-Portrait in a Convex Mirror (Ashbery) **6**:11-14; **9**:41-2, 44, 47-9; **13**:30-1, 33; **15**:28-9, 31, 35; **25**:58; **41**:38, 40; **125**:32, 24
"Self-Portrait, Nude with Steering Wheel" (Durcan) **70**:147
"Self-Portrait on a Summer Evening" (Boland) **113**:73, 82-3, 89, 94, 98
"Self-Portraits" (Wright) **28**:460; **146**:307, 343
"Self's the Man" (Larkin) **18**:299; **33**:258, 268; **39**:343; **64**:267-68, 282
"The Self-Seeker" (Frost) **15**:240
"Sell Me?" (Guillén) **79**:229
"Sell Me a Coat" (Bowie) **17**:65
"Sell Out" (Damas)
See "Solde"
"Selling Hot Pussy" (Hooks) **94**:150
Selling Illusions: The Cult of Multiculturalism in Canada (Bissoondath) **120**:21-22, 28
The Selling of the President, 1968 (McGinniss) **32**:299-302
The Sell-Outs (Valdez)
See *Los vendidos*
Selvä johdatus myöhempään historiaan (Haavikko) **34**:170; **34**:170
"La selva y el mar" (Aleixandre) **9**:14, 16
Sem' puteshestvii (Bitov) **57**:115
La semaine sainte (Aragon) **3**:14; **22**:35-6, 38
"The Semantic Waltz" (L'Heureux) **52**:273
"Semblance" (Bernstein) **142**:8
Semeiotke: Recherches pour une sémanalyse (Kristeva) **77**:299, 303; **140**:183-84
"Semejante a la noche" (Carpentier) **110**:48
"Semele Recycled" (Kizer) **39**:169-71
"Semicolon; for Philip Whalen" (Loewinsohn) **52**:284
"Semi-Fraudulent Direct from Hollywood Overture" (Zappa) **17**:587
Semillas para un himno (Paz) **19**:368
Semi-Monde (Coward) **51**:70
Séminaire XX (Lacan) **75**:304-05, 310
Séminaire, 1974-75 (Lacan) **75**:287
The Seminarian (del Castillo) **38**:167-68
"The Semiology of Silence: The Science Fiction Studies Interview" (Delany) **141**:114, 150
Semiotics and Structuralism (Bakhtin) **83**:24
Semiotics and the Philosophy of Language (Eco) **60**:116, 125; **142**:85, 93, 105-06, 130
"Semiprivate, Female" (Selzer) **74**:272
"The Semi-Sapphics" (Ewart) **46**:152-53
Semmel Weiss (Sackler) **14**:480
Semmelweiss (Céline) **124**:65
Il sempione strizza l'occhio al frejus (Vittorini) **9**:546; **14**:544
La señal que se espera (Buero Vallejo) **15**:101-02; **139**:72-4
Señas de identidad (Goytisolo) **5**:151; **10**:244-45; **23**:181, 186, 189; **133**:31-35, 44-47, 52, 56-57, 65-67, 71, 74, 87, 90, 93, 95-96
"Send in the Clowns" (Sondheim) **30**:384-85, 387, 396, 401; **147**:231, 263
"Send No Money" (Larkin) **5**:227; **18**:299; **33**:256
Send No More Roses (Ambler)
See *The Siege of the Villa Lipp*
Send Somebody Nice (Hilliard) **15**:280
"Send War in Our Time, O Lord" (Deane) **122**:83
Sendemann Huskuld (Vesaas) **48**:404-05, 410
"Send-Off" (Adcock) **41**:16
"The Send-Off" (Jong) **6**:268; **83**:300
"Séneca en las orillas" (Borges) **48**:47
A Seneca Journal (Rothenberg) **57**:374, 382
"Seneca Journal I" (Rothenberg) **57**:382
Senior Citizens (Jones) **52**:250
"Senior Service" (Costello) **21**:71
Seniority (Ziegenhagen) **55**:377-80
Senlin: A Biography (Aiken) **52**:20, 22, 24
Sennik współczesny (Konwicki) **8**:326; **117**:255, 257-58, 272, 282, 284-85, 287
"Señor Ong and Señor Ha" (Bowles) **53**:37
El Señor presidente (Asturias) **3**:17-8; **8**:28; **13**:37
"Señor (Tales of Yankee Power)" (Dylan) **77**:182
"Una señora" (Donoso) **11**:145; **32**:157
"La señora mayor" (Borges) **44**:365
Le Sens apparent (Brossard) **115**:107, 111, 114-15, 121, 136
Le sens de la marche (Adamov) **25**:12-13
Sens et non-sens de la révolte (Kristeva) **140**:193-97
"Sensation Time at the Home" (Merton)
See "A Song: Sensation Time at the Home"
"The Sense of an Ending" (Graham) **118**:249
A Sense of Danger (Scannell) **49**:326, 328, 331
A Sense of Detachment (Osborne) **45**:316, 320
"A Sense of Direction" (Gellhorn) **60**:180-81
The Sense of Glory (Read) **4**:441
A Sense of Honor (Webb) **22**:453-54
"Sense of Identity" (Herbert) **9**:275
"A Sense of Measure" (Creeley) **78**:147
A Sense of Measure (Creeley) **4**:118
The Sense of Movement (Gunn) **3**:215; **18**:200; **32**:207, 210; **81**:183-85
The Sense of Occasion (Kallman) **2**:221
"A Sense of Pilgrimage" (Levertov) **66**:242
"A Sense of Porpoise" (Grayson) **38**:211
"A Sense of Proportion" (Frame) **96**:189
A Sense of Reality (Greene) **3**:211; **70**:293
"A Sense of Shelter" (Updike) **23**:473
"A Sense of Story" (McPherson) **77**:365
"The Sense of the Past" (Trilling) **24**:450
A Sense of the World (Jennings) **131**:232, 238
A Sense of Values (Wilson) **32**:447
A Sense of Where You Are (McPhee) **36**:296
"The Sense of Wonder" (Carson) **71**:112
The Sense of Wonder (Carson) **71**:101, 103-08, 112-13
The Sense Organs: Our Link with the World (Silverstein and Silverstein) **17**:452
"Sensemayá" (Guillén) **79**:248
"Sensibility! O La!" (Roethke) **101**:274, 282, 335, 340
"The Sensitive Goldfish" (Stead) **80**:334
"The Sensitive Knife" (Stern) **40**:408
Senso (Visconti) **16**:564-66, 568-69, 572
"Il senso recondito" (Buzzati) **36**:96
"The Sensualists" (Roethke) **46**:363
"Sensuality" (Slessor) **14**:496
"The Sensuality of Truth" (Ezekiel) **61**:109
The Sensuous Dirty Old Man (Asimov) **76**:315
Sent for You Yesterday (Wideman) **34**:298-300; **67**:374, 378-79, 381-82, 384, 388; **122**:288, 290, 292, 297-98, 303, 307, 309, 314, 319-21, 323, 326-27, 332, 336, 340, 343, 345-46, 348, 350, 355-56, 363
Sent off the Field (Padilla)
See *Fuera del juego*
"The Sentence" (Barthelme) **23**:45; **115**:61
"The Sentence" (Graves) **45**:168
A Sentence of Life (Gloag) **40**:206-07
"Sentences" (Scannell) **49**:334
Sentences (Nemerov) **36**:305-08
"Sentences My Father Used" (Bernstein) **142**:32
"The Sententious Man" (Roethke) **101**:328
Il sentiero dei nidi di ragno (Calvino) **5**:97-8; **8**:127, 129; **11**:87-90, 92; **22**:89; **33**:97;

39:306-07, 309, 314, 317; **73**:52, 58
"Sentiment" (Parker) **68**:326, 334, 339
Sentiment of Time (Ungaretti)
See *Sentimento del tempo*
"Sentimental Education" (Brodkey) **56**:55-6
A Sentimental Education (Oates) **19**:356; **33**:289
"Sentimental Memory" (Colwin) **23**:129; **84**:149-50
"Sentimental Summer" (Huxley) **11**:282
Sentimento del tempo (Ungaretti) **7**:481-82, 485; **11**:555-57, 559-60; **15**:536-39
Sentimento do mundo (Andrade) **18**:5
"Sentiments fanés" (Reverdy) **53**:283
"Sentiments for a Dedication" (MacLeish) **68**:287
"The Sentinel" (Clarke) **35**:122; **136**:212, 225
"Sentry Duty" (Transtroemer) **65**:230
Separate but Unequal (Harlan) **34**:186
Separate Checks (Wiggins) **57**:431-33, 435, 439-40
A Separate Development (Hope) **52**:209-12, 217
"Separate Flights" (Dubus) **97**:197, 199, 201, 204, 206-07, 209, 215, 218
Separate Flights (Dubus) **13**:182-83; **36**:144, 146-48; **97**:195, 197, 199, 204, 209, 215, 218, 231, 235
"The Separate Notebooks" (Milosz)
See "Osobny zeszyt"
The Separate Notebooks (Milosz) **31**:267, 269; **56**:231-32, 234, 239, 244; **82**:283, 297-98, 301, 305, 310
The Separate Notebooks (Pinsky) **121**:448
A Separate Peace (Knowles) **1**:169; **4**:271-72; **10**:303; **26**:245-50, 252-53, 255-65
"Separate Planes" (Adams) **46**:21
A Separate Reality (Castaneda) **12**:86-90, 95
The Separate Rose (Neruda)
See *La rosa separada: obra póstuma*
Separate Tables (Rattigan) **7**:355-56
"Separating" (Coles) **46**:108
"Separating" (Updike) **7**:489; **15**:545-47
"The Separation" (Broumas) **73**:16
"A Separation" (Spender) **41**:427
La séparation (Simon) **39**:208
Separations (Hacker) **9**:257-58; **23**:205; **72**:188
"The Sepia Postcard" (Millhauser) **109**:157-58
Les sept dernières plaies (Duhamel) **8**:187-88
"September" (Hughes) **14**:270
September (Swinnerton) **31**:423
"September 1, 1939" (Auden) **4**:35; **6**:20; **9**:56-7; **43**:16; **123**:5-6, 34, 45-6, 48
"September 1, 1939" (Rexroth) **112**:396
"September 17" (Herbert) **43**:194
September, 1939 (Spender) **41**:427
September Blackberries (McClure) **6**:320
"September Dawn" (O'Connor) **23**:329
"September Eclogue" (Reaney) **13**:474
"September Elegy" (Moss) **45**:292; **50**:353
"September Fires" (Read) **4**:439
"September in Great Yarmouth" (Mahon) **27**:290
"September in the Park" (Snodgrass) **18**:491
"September Journal" (Spender) **41**:422-23
"September Moon" (Harjo) **83**:271
"September on Jessore Road" (Ginsberg) **36**:181
September September (Foote) **75**:262-63
"September Song" (Heaney) **74**:160, 165
"September Song" (Hill) **8**:293; **18**:236
"September Street" (Avison) **97**:76
"September Sun, 1947" (Gascoyne) **45**:147
"September, the First Day of School" (Nemerov) **6**:363
September Tide (du Maurier) **59**:286
"September Twilight" (Glück) **81**:167, 172
Septième (Audiberti) **38**:22
Septuagenarian Stew (Bukowski) **82**:25-8
"Septuagesima" (Betjeman) **34**:309-10
"Sepulture South: Gaslight" (Faulkner) **18**:149
"The Sequel" (Roethke) **3**:433; **8**:456
"Sequelae" (Lorde) **71**:241
"Sequence" (Ciardi) **40**:159
A Sequence for Francis Parkman (Davie) **5**:114-15; **10**:123
"Sequence, Sometimes Metaphysical" (Roethke) **11**:485; **46**:361, 364; **101**:288, 304, 326-27
"Sequences" (Sanchez) **116**:274, 279-80
Sequences (Sassoon) **36**:390, 392
Les séquestrés d'Altona (Sartre) **4**:476; **7**:392-93; **9**:470; **13**:502; **18**:471; **44**:493; **50**:381-82; **52**:381
Les séquestrés d'Altona (De Sica) **20**:90-1
"Ser de Sansueña" (Cernuda) **54**:61
Ser Visal's Tale (Donaldson) **46**:143
The Seraglio (Merrill) **13**:376-77, 381; **91**:228-29
"The Seraph and the Zambesi" (Spark) **13**:519; **40**:401, 403
Seraph on the Suwanee (Hurston) **30**:214, 216-17, 219, 228-29
The Seraphim (Barker) **48**:24
"Seraphion" (Baxter) **14**:62
"La serata a Colono" (Morante) **47**:281
"Serena" (Blunden) **56**:34
"Serena I" (Beckett) **9**:81
"Serena III" (Beckett) **9**:81
Serena Blandish (Bagnold) **25**:74, 76
Serena Blandish; or, The Difficulty of Getting Married (Behrman) **40**:73, 76, 78
Serena Cruz or True Justice (Ginzburg) **70**:282
"Sérénade" (Damas) **84**:179
Serenade (Cain) **3**:97; **11**:85-7; **28**:44-5, 47-8, 51-3
Serenade (Diamond) **30**:112-13
"Serenade: Any Man to Any Woman" (Sitwell) **67**:318-19, 322
"Serenade for Strings" (Livesay) **79**:354
Serenading Louie (Wilson) **7**:549; **36**:464-65
Serendipities (Eco) **142**:62, 136-38
"Serengeti" (Oliver) **98**:282
Serenissima: A Novel of Venice (Jong) **83**:321
"The Sergeant" (Barthelme) **8**:52
Sergeant Getúlio (Ribeiro)
See *Sargento Getúlio*
Sergeant Lamb of the Ninth (Graves) **39**:322, 325
Sergeant Pepper's Lonely Hearts Club Band (Lennon and McCartney) **12**:357-58, 361, 365, 373, 376, 379; **35**:267, 273, 275, 289-90
Sergeant Rutledge (Ford) **16**:308, 319
Sergio (Mujica Lainez) **31**:283
"The Serial" (Nemerov) **36**:308
Serial (Cabral de Melo Neto) **76**:154, 158-59
"Series and Nexus in the Family" (Laing) **95**:171-72
"A Series of Popes Had Been Devils" (Silko) **114**:333
"The Serious Artist" (Pound) **10**:405; **112**:318, 321
"A Serious Case" (Van Duyn) **63**:440-41
"Serious Comedy in Afro-American Literature" (Reed) **60**:310
Serious Money (Churchill) **55**:121-27
"A Serious Step Lightly Taken" (Frost) **10**:193
"A Serious Talk" (Carver) **22**:101; **36**:101
"Seriousness and the Inner Poem" (Carruth) **84**:117
Serjeant Musgrave's Dance (Arden) **6**:4-10; **13**:23-6, 28; **15**:18, 20, 23, 25
Le serment de Kolvillàg (Wiesel) **3**:528-30; **5**:490; **37**:453-54
"Sermon" (Purdy) **28**:378
"The Sermon" (Redgrove) **41**:348, 351
A Sermon (Mamet) **46**:246
"A Sermon Beginning with the Portrait of a Man" (Ciardi) **40**:157
"A Sermon by Doctor Pep" (Bellow) **33**:71
A Sermon on Swift (Clarke) **6**:112
"A Sermon on the Warpland" (Brooks) **125**:73, 96
Sermones y moradas (Alberti) **7**:10
Sermones y prédicas del Cristo de Elqui (Parra) **102**:347, 356
Sermons and Homilies of the Christ of Elqui (Parra)
See *Sermones y prédicas del Cristo de Elqui*
Sermons and Soda Water (O'Hara) **6**:384; **42**:319, 325-26
Serowe: Village of the Rain Wind (Head) **25**:238-39; **67**:97-8
"The Serpent" (Rothenberg) **57**:383
Serpent (Mosley) **43**:319-20; **70**:202
The Serpent (van Itallie) **3**:493
The Serpent and the Rope (Rao) **25**:365-68, 370-73; **56**:284-87, 289, 292-99, 301, 306-09, 312-15
Le serpent d'etoiles (Giono) **4**:184
"Serpent Knowledge" (Pinsky) **19**:372
"The Serpents" (Kunitz) **148**:137
The Serpent's Children (Yep) **35**:474
The Serpent's Egg (Bergman)
See *Ormen's ägg*
The Serpent's Gift (Lee) **86**:68-72
Serpent's Reach (Cherryh) **35**:106, 110-11
Serpico (Maas) **29**:304-05
The Serrated Wheel (Guillén)
See *La rueda dentada*
"O sertanejo falando" (Cabral de Melo Neto) **76**:164
"Servant" (Thomas) **48**:380
The Servant (Pinter) **11**:443; **27**:391
"Servant Boy" (Heaney) **25**:245
"Servant Boy" (Heaney) **74**:157
Servant of the Bones (Rice) **128**:307, 311-13
"The Servant Problem" (Kelley) **22**:246
"Servant Problem—Oriental Style" (Clarke) **35**:123
"A Servant to Servants" (Frost) **1**:110; **10**:198; **15**:240; **26**:119, 123
The Servants and the Snow (Murdoch) **4**:367-68
Servants of the Wankh (Vance) **35**:422, 424
A Servant's Tale (Fox) **121**:213-15, 217, 219, 221-22
Serve It Forth (Fisher) **76**:334, 336, 340-42; **87**:118, 120, 128-29, 132
"Service" (Thomas) **48**:374
Service inutile (Montherlant) **19**:326
Sesame, and Other Stories (Lem)
See *Sezam*
62: Modelo para armar (Cortázar) **2**:104-05; **3**:115; **10**:113, 116, 118; **15**:147; **33**:126-27; **34**:329, 333; **92**:149
"Seskilgreen" (Montague) **46**:271
"Sestina" (Bishop) **9**:90; **15**:60; **32**:38
"Sestina" (Eberhart) **56**:85
"Sestina: Altaforte" (Pound) **2**:343; **10**:408; **13**:461; **48**:288
"Sestina: Maria Maddalena" (Thomas) **132**:382
"Sestina of Sandbars and Shelters" (Lattimore) **3**:278
"Sestina on Six Words by Weldon Kees" (Justice) **102**:277, 283
"Sestina: The Literary Gathering" (Ewart) **46**:151-53
Sestra moia zhizn (Pasternak) **7**:293; **10**:382-83; **18**:383; **63**:275, 280, 289
Set in Motion (Martin) **89**:104-09, 116, 125, 129-30
A Set of Variations (O'Connor) **14**:396
A Set of Wives (Jones) **52**:242-43
Set on Edge (Rubens) **31**:350
Set the Bird Free! (Voznesensky) **15**:554
"Set the Controls for the Heart of the Sun" (Pink Floyd) **35**:305, 307
Set This House on Fire (Styron) **1**:329-30; **3**:472, 474; **5**:418; **11**:514-17; **15**:525, 527; **60**:397-98, 400-01
"Sette figli" (Moravia) **11**:383
I sette messaggeri (Buzzati) **36**:87, 93-4, 96-7
"Sette piani" (Buzzati) **36**:97
Setting Free the Bears (Irving) **13**:292; **23**:244-45; **38**:250-51; **112**:155-57, 159, 166
Setting Sons (Weller) **26**:444-46

The Setting Sun (Pa Chin) **18**:373
Setting the World on Fire (Wilson) **25**:461-64
"Settings" (Heaney) **14**:243; **74**:188-89
"The Settle Bed" (Heaney) **91**:125
Settle Down Simon Katz (Kops) **4**:275
"Settled Score" (Paretsky) **135**:370
"The Settlement of Mars" (Busch) **47**:62
Settlement Poems I (Gunnars) **69**:257-61
Settlement Poems II (Gunnars) **69**:257-61
Settlements (Donnell) **34**:155-59
"The Settlers" (Bradbury) **42**:38
The Settlers (Levin) **7**:204-06
"Settling Down" (Sadoff) **9**:466
Settling Down (Sadoff) **9**:466
Seuls demeurants (Char) **55**:287-88
"Seurat" (Dubie) **36**:130
"Seurat" (Sadoff) **9**:466
"Seurat's Sunday Afternoon along the Seine" (Schwartz) **45**:361; **87**:346-47
Seven (Seger) **35**:380
The Seven Ages of Man (Wilder) **82**:363
"Seven and the Stars" (Haldeman) **61**:181
Seven Arrows (Storm) **3**:470
"Seven Attempted Moves" (Fisher) **25**:158
Seven Beauties (Wertmueller)
See *Pasqualino settebellezze*
Seven Chances (Keaton) **20**:190, 193, 196
Seven Dada Manifestos and Lampisteries (Tzara) **47**:392
"The Seven Days" (Whittemore) **4**:588
Seven Days (Fast)
See *Seven Days in June*
Seven Days a Week (Kieslowski) **120**:243
Seven Days in June (Fast) **131**:79, 91, 102
Seven Days in May (Knebel) **14**:307-08
Seven Days in May (Serling) **30**:354-55
"The Seven Deadly Sins" (Smith) **73**:357
The Seven Deadly Sins (Nye) **13**:413
The Seven Deadly Sins (Shapcott) **38**:401
The Seven Descents of Myrtle (Williams)
See *Kingdom of Earth: The Seven Descents of Myrtle*
The Seven Dials Mystery (Christie) **12**:115; **110**:111, 113
"Seven Floors" (Buzzati) **36**:94
Seven Gothic Tales (Dinesen) **10**:147, 149-50, 152-53; **29**:154, 156-59, 161, 163-64; **95**:32, 35-7, 41, 43-7, 49-50, 53-4, 59, 61, 64, 68-9, 72-4
Seven Guitars (Wilson) **118**:411-13
The Seven Hells of Jigokv Zoshi (Rothenberg) **6**:477
"Seven Island Suite" (Lightfoot) **26**:280
Seven Japanese Tales (Tanizaki) **28**:421
Seven Journeys (Bitov)
See *Sem' puteshestvii*
The Seven Journeys (Graham) **29**:193-94
"Seven Laments for the Fallen in the War" (Amichai) **9**:25; **57**:41-2, 44; **116**:90, 115, 129, 137
"Seven Laments for the War-Dead" (Amichai)
See "Seven Laments for the Fallen in the War"
Seven Long Times (Thomas) **17**:500-02
"Seven Love Songs Which Include the Collective History of the United States of America" (Alexie) **96**:8, 10
The Seven Messengers (Buzzati)
See *I sette messaggeri*
"7, Middagh Street" (Muldoon) **72**:274, 277, 280, 282
The Seven Minutes (Wallace) **7**:510; **13**:568
"Seven Moments of Love" (Hughes) **15**:292
The Seven Mountains of Thomas Merton (Mott) **34**:460-67
Seven Nights (Borges) **44**:361; **48**:47-8
Seven Occasions (Summers) **10**:493
"Seven O'Clock News/Silent Night" (Simon) **17**:462, 466
"Seven O'Clock of a Strange Millennium" (Gilliatt) **53**:145
"Seven Odes to Seven Natural Processes" (Updike) **43**:436
"Seven Poems" (Strand) **18**:519; **71**:285
"Seven Points for an Imperilled Star" (Murray) **40**:335
Seven Poor Men of Sydney (Stead) **2**:422; **5**:403; **32**:406-09, 411-12, 414; **80**:307, 315, 319, 326, 331, 335-37
"Seven Rail Poems" (Moure) **88**:218
Seven Red Sundays (Sender)
See *Siete domingos rojos*
Seven Rivers of Canada (MacLennan)
See *Rivers of Canada*
"Seven Roses Later" (Celan)
See "Sieben Rosen später"
The Seven Samurai (Kurosawa) **16**:395-99, 403; **119**:337-38, 340-41, 348-49, 351, 355, 357, 364, 370-72, 381, 391, 403
"Seven Say You Can Hear Corn Grow" (Boyle) **58**:71
Seven Scenes from a Family Album (Gray) **49**:147
The Seven Sisters (Prokosch) **4**:421
"Seven Stanzas at Easter" (Updike) **23**:474
"Seven Steps to Love" (Day Lewis) **10**:131
The Seven Storey Mountain (Merton) **1**:211; **3**:337; **11**:372; **34**:461-65, 467; **83**:379, 382, 398-400, 403-04
Seven Summers (Anand) **23**:17; **93**:23-4, 29, 32, 37, 41-2, 55-6
Seven Suspects (Stewart) **14**:511; **32**:419
Seven Tales and Alexander (Bates) **46**:49-50
Seven Types of Ambiguity (Empson) **3**:147; **8**:201-02; **19**:153-55; **33**:137-38, 140-41, 145-50; **34**:336-38, 543
"Seven Ways of Going" (Smith) **12**:544
The Seven Who Fled (Prokosch) **4**:421; **48**:304-06, 309, 312-15
Seven Winters (Bowen) **11**:61; **118**:72
Seven Women (Ford) **16**:312, 317, 319-20
The Seven Year Itch (Wilder) **20**:457, 464
"Seven Years from Somewhere" (Levine) **33**:271
Seven Years from Somewhere (Levine) **14**:320-21; **33**:270-72, 274; **118**:279, 285, 297, 314, 317-18
The Seven-League Crutches (Jarrell) **2**:207-08, 210; **13**:298
"The Seven-Ounce Man" (Harrison) **143**:346-48, 350, 353
"Seventeen" (Farrell) **66**:128
Seventeen (Benson) **17**:49-50
Seventeen (Welles) **80**:380
Seventeen Chirps (Vizenor) **103**:296
17 Poems (Transtroemer)
See *17 dikter*
"The Seventeen Virgins" (Vance) **35**:428
"Seventeen Warnings in Search of a Feminist Poem" (Jong) **4**:263; **6**:267; **83**:289
1776, Year of Illusions (Fleming) **37**:126
"Seventeenth Century Landscape near Ballyferriter" (Kinsella) **138**:84
"A Seventeenth Century Suite" (Duncan) **55**:298
The Seventeenth Degree (McCarthy) **5**:276-77
Seventeenth Summer (Daly) **17**:87-9, 91
"A Seventeenth-Century Suite in Homage to the Metaphysical Genius in English Poetry, 1590-1690" (Duncan) **41**:128-30
The Seventeenth-Street Gang (Neville) **12**:450
Seventh Avenue Poems (Shapcott) **38**:402
The Seventh Babe (Charyn) **18**:99
The Seventh Book (Akhmatova) **11**:8; **64**:21
The Seventh Cross (Seghers) **7**:407-08
"Seventh Day" (Raine) **45**:333
The Seventh Game (Kahn) **30**:234
"Seventh Heaven" (Smith) **12**:535
Seventh Heaven (Smith) **12**:535, 540, 542
A Seventh Man (Berger) **19**:38-9
"Seventh Psalm" (Sexton) **123**:422-23
The Seventh Raven (Dickinson) **35**:135-36
"Seventh Seal" (Gotlieb) **18**:191
The Seventh Seal (Bergman)
See *Det sjunde inseglet*
"Seventh Street" (Toomer) **4**:549
"The Seventh Trunk" (Boell)
See "Warum ich kurze Prosa wie Jakob Maria Hermes and Heinrich Knecht schreibe"
"Seventh Voyage" (Lem) **40**:296
"Seventy Thousand Assyrians" (Saroyan) **29**:361
The 75th (Horovitz) **56**:155
"Seventy-five Dollars" (Hughes) **108**:292
Seventy-One Poems for People (Bowering) **47**:31, 33
Seventy-Seven Dream Songs (Berryman) **2**:56-7; **3**:65, 67-8, 70; **10**:48-9; **13**:75, 80; **25**:88-91, 93, 98; **62**:60, 71, 76
73 Poems (Cummings) **3**:118; **8**:160; **12**:154; **15**:163; **68**:40-2, 50
Several Observations (Grigson) **7**:135
Several Perceptions (Carter) **5**:102; **41**:112; **76**:323
"Several Species of Small Furry Animals Gathered Together in a Cave and Grooving with a Pict" (Pink Floyd) **35**:305, 311
"Several Voices Out of a Cloud" (Bogan) **39**:388; **46**:86, 90
"Several Voices out of a Cloud" (Gunn) **18**:202
Severance Pay (Whalen) **29**:447
"The Severed Head" (Lowell) **4**:299
"The Severed Head" (Montague) **46**:270
A Severed Head (Murdoch) **1**:234-37; **2**:296, 298; **3**:345, 347; **4**:367; **6**:343-45, 348; **15**:381-33, 385, 387; **31**:287-89, 295
"Severence Pay" (Macdonald) **13**:356
"Severnside" (Tomlinson) **45**:403
"Severo's Phases" (Cortázar)
See "Las fases de Severo"
Sevilha andando (Cabral de Melo Neto) **76**:161, 163
"A sevilhana que não se sabiae" (Cabral de Melo Neto) **76**:161
"The Seville Woman Unknown to Herself" (Cabral de Melo Neto)
See "A sevilhana que não se sabiae"
"The Sewing Harems" (Ozick) **62**:351; **155**:180-81
"Sex" (Carruth) **84**:136
Sex (Allen) **52**:43
Sex and Death (Purdy) **6**:428-29; **14**:432; **50**:246-47
"Sex and Death to the Age 14" (Gray) **49**:148-49, 152; **112**:97-8, 111, 114
Sex and Death to the Age 14 (Gray) **49**:148, 151
Sex and Destiny (Greer) **131**:179-90, 197, 199, 209, 218
"Sex and Love" (MacInnes) **23**:286
Sex and Power: The Rise of Women in America, Russia, Sweden, and Italy (Meyer) **65**:325
Sex and Subterfuge: Women Novelists to 1850 (Figes) **31**:168
Sex and Temperament in Three Primitive Societies (Mead) **37**:271-72
The Sex Diary of Gerard Sorme (Wilson) **3**:537; **14**:588
Sex, Drugs, Rock & Roll (Bogosian) **141**:86-90, 93
sex, lies, and videotape (Soderbergh) **154**:328-30, 332-33, 335, 337-39, 341, 344-45, 351, 353-54, 356
"The Sex of Poetry" (Smith) **22**:385
"The Sex Opposite" (Sturgeon) **39**:361
"Sex, Race, and Science Fiction" (Delany) **141**:114
The Sex War and Others: A Survey of Recent Murder Principally in France (Heppenstall) **10**:272
"Sex without Love" (Olds) **39**:188

"Le Sexe ou la tête?" (Cixous)
See "Castration or Decapitation?"
"The Sexes" (Parker) **68**:335-36
Sexing the Cherry (Winterson) **64**:434-44
"Sexism: An American Disease in Blackface" (Lorde) **71**:245
"Sex-'n'-Violence" (Brophy) **105**:9
"Sexplosion" (Lem) **15**:329
"Sext" (Berryman) **3**:69
Sextet in A Minor (Klein) **30**:242-43
El sexto (Arguedas) **10**:8; **18**:10
"Sexual Disaster Quartet" (Welsh) **144**:336
"Sexual Healing" (Gaye) **26**:135
The Sexual Liberals and the Attack on Feminism (Leidholdt and Raymond) **65**:317-19
The Sexual Outlaw (Rechy) **14**:445; **107**:236, 243-45, 247-51, 254, 256
Sexual Personae: Art and Decadence from Nefertiti to Emily Dickinson (Paglia) **65**:346; **68**:303-20
Sexual Perversity in Chicago (Mamet) **9**:360; **15**:356-57; **34**:223; **46**:247-48, 251-52, 255
Sexual Politics (Millett) **67**:234-43, 245, 247-48, 252-53, 256, 258, 260, 262
"The Sexual Revolution: Being a Rather Complete Survey of the Entire Sexual Scene" (Thurber) **125**:402
"Sexual Water" (Neruda)
See "Agua sexual"
"Sexuality" (Prince) **35**:325-26, 331
"Sexuality" (Vidal) **142**:334, 338
Sexuality Today—And Tomorrow: Contemporary Issues in Human Sexuality (Gordon) **26**:138
Sexus (Miller) **2**:282-83; **14**:371
"Sexy Dancer" (Prince) **35**:323
"A Sexy Little Giant" (Iskander)
See "Malenkiĭ gigant bol'shogo seksa"
"Seyh Bedreddin destani" (Hikmet) **40**:244-47, 249-51
"Seymour: An Introduction" (Salinger) **1**:295; **3**:444; **8**:463; **12**:503, 514, 518; **138**:179-80, 184, 198, 200-06, 209, 216
Seymour: An Introduction (Salinger)
See *Raise High the Roofbeam, Carpenters and Seymour: An Introduction*
Sezam (Lem) **40**:289; **149**:147-48, 282
"Sezoni dimëror i Kafe Rivierës" (Kadare) **52**:259
Shabbytown Calendar (Shapcott) **38**:402-03
"The Shack" (Laurence) **62**:280
Shackles (Césaire)
See *Ferrements*
"The Shad-Blow Tree" (Glück) **7**:120
Shade (Bernstein) **142**:47
A Shade of Difference (Drury) **37**:100-03, 105
"Shades of Caesar" (Weiss) **14**:556
"Shades of Scarlet Conquering" (Mitchell) **12**:439
"Shades of the Prison House" (O'Faolain) **32**:341
The Shade-Seller: New and Selected Poems (Jacobsen) **48**:191-92, 195; **102**:233
"Shadow" (Oliver) **98**:276
Shadow (Green) **77**:271
"Shadow: 1970" (Wright) **53**:426, 428-29, 432
Shadow and Act (Ellison) **54**:129; **86**:319, 323, 326; **114**:91-2, 104, 108-10, 112, 115-17, 123, 128
"Shadow and Ash" (Delany) **141**:159
Shadow and Substance (Carroll) **10**:95-100
Shadow Baby (Forster) **149**:100-01
The Shadow Box (Cristofer) **28**:94-6, 98
Shadow Box (Plimpton) **36**:356-57
The Shadow Cage and Other Tales of the Supernatural (Pearce) **21**:290, 292
"Shadow Country" (Allen) **84**:10
Shadow Country (Allen) **84**:2, 10-11, 28, 39-40
Shadow Dance (Carter) **5**:102; **41**:109-12; **76**:323, 328
Shadow Distance (Vizenor) **103**:340-41
"The Shadow Goes Away" (Bly) **10**:59; **128**:17
Shadow Hawk (Norton) **12**:460
The Shadow in the Courtyard (Simenon) **47**:369, 379
The Shadow Knows (Johnson) **5**:199-200; **13**:304-05; **48**:207-08
Shadow Land (Straub) **28**:411; **107**:265, 274-77, 279-82, 305-10
The Shadow Land (Vansittart) **42**:394
"The Shadow Life of Reading" (Birkerts) **116**:167
The Shadow Lines (Ghosh) **153**:83-6, 89, 93, 97-8, 100-02, 110, 114, 116-17, 121, 129
The Shadow Man (Gordon) **128**:146, 148-49, 151
The Shadow Master (Feinstein) **36**:170
Shadow of a Bull (Wojciechowska) **26**:449-53, 455-56, 458
"The Shadow of a Crib" (Singer) **111**:304-05
Shadow of a Doubt (Hitchcock) **16**:338, 340-41, 343, 345-46, 349-50, 355, 359
The Shadow of a Gunman (Carroll) **10**:97
The Shadow of a Gunman (O'Casey) **5**:317, 320; **11**:409-13; **15**:403, 405; **88**:234-37, 239, 242-43, 245-46, 254-55, 257-58, 262, 269
The Shadow of a Man (Moraga) **126**:275, 288, 292-94, 299-300, 302-04, 307
Shadow of a Man (Sarton) **49**:310-11
Shadow of a Sun (Byatt) **19**:75; **65**:127; **136**:157
The Shadow of Cain (Sitwell) **67**:336-37
The Shadow of Captain Bligh (MacLennan)
See "Joseph Haydn and Captain Bligh"
"The Shadow of Hiroshima" (Harrison) **129**:212
The Shadow of Hiroshima (Harrison) **129**:210-13
"Shadow of Night" (Derleth) **31**:136
Shadow of Paradise (Aleixandre)
See *Sombra del paraíso*
"The Shadow of Sound" (Voznesensky) **57**:425
The Shadow of the Coachman's Body (Weiss)
See *Der Schatten des Körpers des Kutschers*
"The Shadow of the Gods" (Miller) **10**:344
The Shadow of the Hawk (Forester) **35**:165-66
The Shadow of the Hawk (Scott) **43**:383
The Shadow of the Lynx (Hibbert) **7**:155
Shadow of the Moon (Kaye) **28**:197-201
The Shadow of the Torturer (Wolfe) **25**:473-79
The Shadow of Vesuvius (Dillon) **17**:100
A Shadow on Summer (Brown) **63**:51-3, 55-6
The Shadow on the Hills (Thiele) **17**:496
"Shadow Path (the encounter group)" (Allen) **84**:38
Shadow Play (Baxter) **78**:30-33
Shadow Play (Coward) **51**:70
"Shadow San" (Harrison) **129**:212
Shadow Train: Fifty Lyrics (Ashbery) **25**:54, 56-60; **41**:38; **77**:44
Shadowfires (Koontz) **78**:200, 203
The Shadow-Maker (MacEwen) **13**:358; **55**:163, 165
"Shadows" (Allen) **84**:37-8
"Shadows" (Delany) **141**:150
"Shadows" (Endō) **99**:296-97, 301, 307
"Shadows" (Norris) **14**:388
"Shadows" (Williams) **22**:465
"Shadows" (Williams) **148**:347
Shadows (Cassavetes) **20**:44, 55
Shadows (Clarke) **16**:216
Shadows (Lightfoot) **26**:283
"Shadows and Light" (Mitchell) **12**:439
Shadows in Paradise (Remarque) **21**:333-34
Shadows Offstage (Bennett) **35**:43-4
Shadows on Little Reef Bay (Adler) **35**:14-15
Shadows on Our Skin (Johnston) **150**:21, 32
Shadows on the Grass (Dinesen) **10**:146; **29**:156; **95**:35, 37, 43, 45-6, 48, 56, 81
"Shadows There Are" (Smith) **15**:516
"Shadow-Shamans" (Musgrave) **13**:401
"The Shadowy Land" (Grau) **146**:125
"The Shadowy Third" (Bowen) **118**:75
Shadrach in the Furnace (Silverberg) **140**:346, 300, 380
"Shad-Time" (Wilbur) **110**:361
"Shafei nüshi de riji" (Ding Ling) **68**:57, 59-60, 64-5, 67, 69
"The Shaft" (Tomlinson) **13**:548
Shaft (Parks) **16**:458-59
The Shaft (Tomlinson) **13**:548, 550; **45**:392-95, 401
Shaft's Big Score (Parks) **16**:459-61
Shagbark (Peck) **3**:377-78
Shaggy Dog (Potter) **123**:231
al- Shahhādh (Mahfūz) **52**:296, 300
Shahr al'asal (Mahfouz) **153**:359
Shake a Spear with Me, John Berryman (Honig) **33**:214
Shake Hands for Ever (Rendell) **28**:384, 387; **48**:320
Shake Hands with a Murderer (Rendell) **48**:324
"Shake Hands with the Devil" (Kristofferson) **26**:270
"Shakedown" (Waddington) **28**:437
"Shaker, Why Don't You Sing?" (Angelou) **77**:31
Shaker, Why Don't You Sing? (Angelou) **35**:32; **77**:22, 31
Shakespeare and Society (Eagleton) **63**:101, 112
Shakespeare and the Nature of Time (Turner) **48**:398
Shakespeare and the Students (Enright) **31**:150
"Shakespeare at Sonnets" (Ransom) **24**:362
"Shakespeare at Thirty" (Berryman) **10**:45-6
"Shakespeare in Harlem" (Hughes) **35**:220-21
"Shakespeare Say" (Dove) **81**:137
Shakespeare Wallah (Jhabvala) **29**:259; **94**:174, 185, 192; **138**:73
"A Shakespearean Sonnet: To a Woman Liberationist" (Knight) **40**:287
Shakespeare's Boy Actors (Davies) **13**:173; **25**:136
Shakespeare's Dog (Rooke) **34**:250-54
"Shakespeare's Grave" (Jeffers) **54**:246
"A Shakespearian Cycle" (Zaturenska) **11**:580
Shakha Proshakha (Ray) **76**:358-60, 364-65
Shaking the Pumpkin: Traditional Poetry of the Indian North Americans (Rothenberg) **57**:373, 375-77, 382
Shalako (L'Amour) **55**:308
Shalimar (Markandaya) **38**:326-27
"Shall Gaelic Die?" (Smith) **64**:395-96
"Shall I Compare Thee to a Summer's Day?" (Simmons) **43**:411
Shall We Gather at the River (Wright) **3**:540-43; **5**:518-20; **10**:543-45; **25**:463, 465-66, 469
Shall We Tell the President? (Archer) **28**:11-12
"Shallots" (Raine) **32**:350; **103**:184, 191
"The Shallowest Man" (Allen) **52**:40
"Shallowly Quicker" (Rozewicz) **9**:465
Shalvah gedolah: She'elot utshuvot (Amichai) **57**:37-8; **116**:97-8
"Shaman's Blues" (Morrison) **17**:288
"Shame" (Oates) **6**:370; **19**:348
"Shame" (Wilbur) **53**:405; **110**:384-85
Shame (Bergman)
See *Skammen*
Shame (Rushdie) **31**:353-60; **55**:216-19, 224, 253, 263; **59**:415-16, 431, 434, 444, 447, 450; **100**:287, 318-19, 322
Shame and Glory (Viereck) **4**:560
Shame the Devil (Appleman) **51**:15-16
Shame the Devil (O'Flaherty) **34**:357
"Shammu Khan" (Ali) **69**:31
"The Shampoo" (Bishop) **9**:93; **32**:37
Shampoo (Towne) **87**:354-55, 359-60, 366, 369, 372, 375-76
Shampoo Planet (Coupland) **85**:31-6, 39-41; **133**:3-8, 18, 20
"Shancoduff" (Kavanagh) **22**:238
"Shandy" (Kristofferson) **26**:269
Shanghai Express (Sternberg) **20**:370, 372, 379

The Shanghai Gesture (Sternberg) **20**:372, 378
"Shanghai, June 1989" (Durcan) **70**:147
"Shangri-La" (Davies) **21**:91, 93
"Shanley" (Farrell) **66**:129
Shannon's Way (Cronin) **32**:136
"The Shape of Death" (Swenson) **106**:328, 350
"The Shape of Flesh and Bone" (MacLeish) **8**:362
The Shape of Further Things: Speculations on Change (Aldiss) **14**:14
"A Shape of Light" (Goyen) **8**:251
"The Shape of the Fire" (Roethke) **11**:480, 482; **19**:397; **46**:363; **101**:262-63, 274, 281, 335, 337-40
"Shape of the Invisible" (Randall) **135**:376, 397
The Shape of the Journey: New and Collected Poems (Harrison) **143**:354
"The Shape of the Sword" (Borges) See "La forma de la espada"
"The Shape of Things" (Hogan) **73**:151
"The Shape of Things to Come" (Brown) **79**:153
Shapes and Sounds (Peake) **54**:366, 369, 373-74
"Shapes of Winter" (Sorrentino) **40**:386
A Shaping Joy: Studies in the Writer's Craft (Brooks) **24**:111, 113-14, 116; **86**:286-87; **110**:8, 15, 20
The Shaping of England (Asimov) **76**:312
The Shaping Spirit (Alvarez) **5**:16
"Shaping the World of My Art" (Marshall) **72**:249
Shardik (Adams) **5**:5-7
Shards of God: A Novel of the Yippies (Sanders) **53**:304
Shards of Memory (Jhabvala) **94**:212-13
Sharecroppers (Coles) **108**:194, 210
"The Shared Mystery" (Everson) **27**:134
"The Shark" (Pratt) **19**:380
"Shark Hunter" (Ciardi) **40**:155
"Shark in the Window" (Dickey) **109**:244
"The Shark: Parents and Children" (Wakoski) **40**:457
The Shark: Splendid Savage of the Sea (Cousteau) **30**:104
"Sharks" (Oliver) **98**:267
"The Shark's Parlor" (Dickey) **47**:97; **109**:266
"A Sharp Attack of Something or Other" (White) **30**:451
Sharra's Exile (Bradley) **30**:29
Shatranj Ke Khilari (Ray) **16**:495; **76**:357-59, 362-63, 365
"Shatterday" (Ellison) **42**:129-30
Shatterday (Ellison) **42**:129-30; **139**:129, 131-32
"Shattered" (Jagger and Richard) **17**:240
The Shattered Chain (Bradley) **30**:26, 30-2
"Shattered Image" (Betjeman) **10**:53-4
"Shattered Like a Glass Goblin" (Ellison) **42**:127
Shaved Fish (Lennon) **35**:270-71
Shaved Splits (Shepard) **17**:443; **41**:407
"The Shawl" (Ozick) **62**:357-58; **155**:129-30, 155, 104, 196-99, 201-02, 223
The Shawl (Mamet) **46**:254-55
The Shawl (Ozick) **62**:357-58; **155**:166-67, 169-70, 182, 184, 191, 196-97, 200-03
Shay Mouse (McCabe) **133**:113, 117
"She" (Konwicki) **117**:281
"She" (Nemerov) **36**:309
She (Rosenthal) **28**:394-95
"She and I" (Alexander) **121**:5
"She and the Muse" (Levertov) **66**:238, 250
"She Being Brand-New" (Cummings) **68**:43, 46, 51
"She Belongs to Me" (Dylan) **77**:176-77
She Came to Stay (Beauvoir) See *L'invitée*
"She Carries a 'Fat Gold Watch'" (Ondaatje) **14**:407
"She Contrasts with Herself Hippolyta" (H. D.) **73**:128
"She Didn't Even Wave" (Ai) **69**:7, 13
She Had Some Horses (Harjo) **83**:266, 268, 272, 276, 279, 285
She Had to Do Something (O'Faolain) **70**:315
"She Hid in the Trees from the Nurses" (Wright) **10**:545
She in Herland: Feminism as Fantasy (Gubar) **145**:261
"She in Summer" (Dickey) **28**:118
"She Knows Me Too Well" (Wilson) **12**:643, 651
"She Lays" (Peacock) **60**:292
"She Looked at the Sun" (Rozewicz) **139**:236
"She Loves" (Broumas) **73**:15-16
"She Loves You" (Lennon and McCartney) **12**:374
"She Rebukes Hippolyta" (H. D.) **73**:105
"She Seemed to Know" (Laughlin) **49**:224
"She Shall Be Called Woman" (Sarton) **14**:481; **49**:307
"She Shook Me Cold" (Bowie) **17**:57
"She Sings to Herself" (Alexander) **121**:4
"She, Though" (Williams) **148**:345-46, 348, 351
"She Touches Him" (Elliott) **2**:131
"She Unnames Them" (Le Guin) **136**:392
She Used to Wanna Be a Ballerina (Sainte-Marie) **17**:431
"She Waits for All Men Born" (Tiptree) **48**:388, 391, 397
She Walks in Beauty (Powell) **66**:366
"She Was Afraid of Upstairs" (Aiken) **35**:20
"She Went to Stay" (Creeley) **78**:144
"she won't ever forgive me" (Clifton) **66**:82
She Wore a Yellow Ribbon (Ford) **16**:305, 308
Shear (Parks) **147**:202, 204-06, 209, 219
"Shearing" (Clarke) **61**:78
"The Shearwaters" (Levi) **41**:247
"Sheds of Our Webs" (Bernstein) **142**:5-6
"Sheeba the Outcast Drag Queen" (Dickey) **28**:119
"Sheep" (Bates) **46**:51
"Sheep" (Oe) **10**:373
"Sheep" (Pink Floyd) **35**:311, 313
"Sheep" (Zoline) **62**:461-65
"The Sheep Child" (Dickey) **15**:173, 177; **47**:97; **109**:273
"Sheep Herding" (Davis) **49**:92
"Sheep in a Fog" (Plath) **51**:341; **111**:205, 215
The Sheep Look Up (Brunner) **8**:105-07, 110-11; **10**:78, 80-1
"Sheep Shearing at Ayot St. Lawrence" (Szirtes) **46**:391
"Sheep Trails Are Fateful to Strangers" (Spicer) **72**:349
"The Sheep Went On Being Dead" (Hughes) **14**:273
Sheepfold Hill: Fifteen Poems (Aiken) **52**:26
"Sheep-Fuck Poem" (Sanders) **53**:304
Sheepish Beauty, Civilian Love (Moure) **88**:231-32
Sheer Fiction (West) **96**:362, 394
Sheer Fiction II (West) **96**:394-95
Sheer Heaven (Bogosian) **141**:89
"The Sheer Joy of Amoral Creation" (Shields) **97**:429, 431
"Sheet Lightning" (Blunden) **56**:52
Sheik Yerbouti (Zappa) **17**:592-93
Sheiks and Adders (Stewart) **32**:421-22
"Sheishun monogatari" (Tanizaki) **28**:417
The Shelbourne Hotel (Bowen) **11**:61
"Shelf Life" (Heaney) **37**:165
"Shell" (Hoffman) **6**:244
"The Shell" (Humphrey) **45**:193
"Shell Game" (Dick) **72**:109
The Shell Lady's Daughter (Adler) **35**:13-14
"Shell Story" (Brown) **100**:83
Shella (Vachss) **106**:363-64
Shelley (Jellicoe) **27**:209
Shelley's Mythmaking (Bloom) **103**:11-12, 19, 22, 24
"Shells" (Redgrove) **41**:359
"Shells" (Williams) **148**:347, 358
"Shells by a Stream" (Blunden) **56**:29
"The Shells of the Ocean" (Wiebe) **138**:379
"Shelter" (Baxter) **78**:25-26, 29, 30
"Shelter" (Deane) **122**:74
"The Shelter" (Narayan) **47**:304
Shelter (Cryer) **21**:80
Shelter (Phillips) **139**:213, 215-19, 221-22, 224
The Shelter (Phillips) **96**:342, 354-55
"The Shelter of Your Arms" (Nelson) **17**:305
"Sheltered Garden" (H. D.) **31**:201; **73**:118
"A Sheltered Life" (Reed) **21**:312-13
"The Sheltered Sex: 'Lotus Eating' on Seven-and-Six a Week" (West) **31**:460
The Sheltering Sky (Bowles) **1**:41; **2**:78-9; **19**:56, 58-9; **53**:37-40, 42-4, 46
"Shemà" (Levi) **37**:223
Shema: Collected Poems of Primo Levi (Levi) **37**:223
Shenandoah, or the Naming of the Child (Schwartz) **4**:479; **87**:334-36, 339, 341-42
"The Shepards" (O'Connor) **23**:332
"The Shepherd" (Blunden) **56**:27, 32, 37
"The Shepherd" (Soto) **32**:401, 403; **80**:277, 282
"The Shepherd" (Williams) **31**:464
The Shepherd and Other Poems of Peace and War (Blunden) **56**:25, 28-9, 32, 36-8, 40-3, 51
"The Shepherd Corydon" (Howard) **10**:277
"The Shepherd Makhaz" (Iskander) **47**:196
Shepherd of the Streets (Ehle) **27**:102
Shepherdess of Sheep (Streatfeild) **21**:395-97
"Shepherds of the Nation" (Davies) **21**:98
Shepherds of the Night (Amado) See *Os pastores da noite*
"Shepherd's Song" (Milosz) **11**:380
Sheppey (Maugham) **1**:204; **15**:366-67; **67**:225-26
"Sheraton Gibson" (Townshend) **17**:528
Sherbrookes (Delbanco) **13**:174
"Sheridan" (Lowell) **11**:330
"Sheridan" (Merwin) **45**:274-76
"The Sheriff of McTooth County Kansas" (Dorn) **10**:161
Sherlock Holmes vs. Dracula; or, The Adventure of the Sanguinary Count by John H. Watson (Estleman) **48**:102
Sherlock Jr. (Keaton) **20**:195, 197-99
"Sherlock Spends a Day in the Country" (Fearing) **51**:119
"Sherston's Progress" (Sassoon) **36**:387, 395-97; **130**:178, 184, 193, 197-98, 200-02, 209, 211, 213
Sherwood Anderson (Howe) **85**:115
"She's a Woman" (Lennon and McCartney) **35**:285
"She's Always a Woman" (Joel) **26**:216-17
"She's Goin' Bald" (Wilson) **12**:643
"She's Gone" (Marley) **17**:271
"She's Got a Way" (Joel) **26**:217
"She's Got Medals" (Bowie) **17**:65
She's Gotta Have It (Lee) **105**:80-85, 95, 98, 100, 110, 119, 122-23, 128
"She's Leaving Home" (Lennon and McCartney) **12**:357; **35**:280
"She's My Baby" (McCartney) **35**:284-85
"She's Right on Time" (Joel) **26**:223
"She's the One" (Springsteen) **17**:489
Shibumi (Trevanian) **29**:431-32
"The Shield of Achilles" (Auden) **11**:20; **43**:26
The Shield of Achilles (Forman) **21**:116
The Shield of the Valiant (Derleth) **31**:136-37
"The Shield of Two Dreams" (Momaday) **85**:281
"The Shield of Which Less Said the Better" (Momaday) **85**:280
The Shield Ring (Sutcliff) **26**:426, 430-32, 434-35, 439
"The Shield That Died" (Momaday) **85**:280
"The Shield That Was Touched by Pretty Mouth" (Momaday) **85**:280
"Shift of Scene at Grandstand" (Swenson) **61**:405

"Shifting" (Beattie) **146**:81
"Shifting Colors" (Lowell) **37**:238; **124**:299
Shifting Landscape (Roth) **104**:282-85, 311, 317, 324
Shiiku (Oe) **10**:374; **36**:348; **86**:216, 226-27, 244
Shikasta (Lessing) **15**:331-36; **22**:285; **40**:303-04, 306, 309; **94**:253, 260-61
"Shiloh" (Mason) **28**:272, 274; **82**:235, 241, 246, 248, 250, 254-58, 260; **154**:231, 234, 236, 262, 263, 265-67, 280-81, 383, 290, 315, 317-18, 322
"Shiloh" (Mott) **15**:381
Shiloh (Foote) **75**:230, 238-40, 243, 251, 258
Shiloh, and Other Stories (Mason) **28**:271-74; **43**:286-88; **82**:233, 238-40, 244, 246, 249-50, 258-59; **154**:230, 236-40, 262, 264, 272, 284-85, 209, 294, 300, 302-05, 314
"Shine" (Damas) **84**:172, 176
"Shine a Light" (Jagger and Richard) **17**:225, 236
Shine On, Bright and Dangerous Object (Colwin) **23**:128-29; **84**:146, 150
"Shine on You Crazy Diamond" (Pink Floyd) **35**:308, 313
"Shine, Perishing Republic" (Jeffers) **54**:233, 245; **3**:259
"Shingles for the Lord" (Faulkner) **6**:179
"Shingling the New Roof" (Bottoms) **53**:33
The Shining (King) **12**:309-11; **26**:234, 237, 239-42; **37**:198-99, 201, 203, 205, 207-08; **61**:319, 321, 323, 328, 331, 335; **113**:335-36, 344, 347, 351, 353, 355, 362, 369, 378-79, 381-82, 388, 391-92
The Shining (Kubrick) **16**:393
"Shining Agate" (Dorris) **109**:309
"Shining Earth: A Summer Without Evil" (Buckley) **57**:126
"The Shining Houses" (Munro) **95**:285, 297
"The Shining One" (Bova) **45**:73
"The Shining Ones" (Brown) **5**:79
"The Shining Ones" (Clarke) **13**:148
"The Ship" (Bates) **46**:55-6
The Ship (Forester) **35**:164-68, 170, 174
"Ship Fever" (Barrett) **150**:6
Ship Fever and Other Stories (Barrett) **150**:5, 7-9, 11-13, 17
Ship Island, and Other Stories (Spencer) **22**:402
"Ship Master" (Graves) **45**:165
A Ship Named Hope (Klima) **56**:162-63, 174
Ship of Fools (Porter) **1**:271-74; **3**:393-94; **7**:311-21; **10**:398; **15**:426-27, 429-30, 432; **27**:401-02; **101**:215, 218-22, 224, 242-43, 249-50, 253, 255-56
The Ship of Men (Dourado)
See *A barca dos homens*
Ship of the Line (Forester) **35**:162-63, 166, 170
"The Ship Pounding" (Hall) **151**:224
"The Ship Sails at Midnight" (Leiber) **25**:304
The Ship Sails On (Fellini)
See *E la nave va*
"Shipapu iyetico" (Allen) **84**:38
"Shipbuilding Office" (O'Connor) **18**:377
"Shipbuilding Office" (Page) **18**:377
"A Ship-Load of Crabs" (Calvino) **39**:314
The Shipping News (Proulx) **81**:274-80
"Ships" (Masefield) **47**:233
"The Ships" (Redgrove) **41**:359
Ships and Other Figures (Meredith) **13**:374; **22**:302; **55**:193
"The Ship's Captain Looking Over the Rail" (Bly) **128**:45
Ships Going into the Blue (Simpson) **149**:353-54, 356, 358, 361
"Ships of Ashes" (Blaga) **75**:79
The Ship's Orchestra (Fisher) **25**:157-58, 160-61
"Shipwreck" (Barnes) **141**:77
Shipwrecked (Maugham) **15**:365
The Shipyard (Onetti) **7**:277, 280
The Shipyard (Onetti)
See *El astillero*
"Shir al hakravot harishonim" (Amichai) **116**:109
Shira (Agnon) **4**:14
"The Shires" (Betjeman) **43**:51
The Shires (Davie) **5**:115-16; **8**:163-67; **31**:112-13, 117-20, 123
Shirley (Fast) **131**:100
Shirley Valentine (Russell) **60**:321-25
Shiroi hito (Endō) **54**:154; **99**:283, 285, 307
"Shirt" (Pinsky) **94**:306, 308, 312; **121**:437-38, 446-47
"Shirt" (Simic) **49**:337; **130**:302
"The Shirt" (Soto) **80**:298
"The Shirt Poem" (Stern) **40**:410-11
"A Shirtsleeve Wedding" (Redgrove) **41**:358
"Shisei" (Tanizaki) **8**:509-10; **29**:415, 418
"Shisha no ogori" (Oe) **36**:349
"Shiva and Parvati Hiding in the Rain" (Pinsky) **94**:306, 308-9
Shiva Descending (Benford) **52**:66-7, 74
Shivers (Cronenberg)
See *They Came From Within*
Shizukanaru Ketto (Kurosawa) **119**:347, 379, 382
Shlemiel the First (Singer) **38**:415-16
"Shloimele" (Singer) **6**:509; **9**:488
"Shneynu beyahad vekhol ehad lehud" (Amichai) **116**:122
"The Shoals Returning" (Kinsella) **4**:271; **138**:136, 161
"The Shobies' Story" (Le Guin) **136**:385
"Shock" (Williams) **148**:369
Shock III (Matheson) **37**:245
"The Shock of Recognition" (Anderson) **23**:32
The Shock of Recognition (Wilson) **24**:472, 481, 488-89
The Shockwave Rider (Brunner) **10**:81
The Shoe Bird (Welty) **105**:335
Shoe Shine (De Sica) **20**:86-7, 94-5
"Shoe Soul" (Robinson) **21**:348
"Shoe Store" (Souster) **5**:396
"the shoelace" (Bukowski) **108**:75
Shoeless Joe (Kinsella) **27**:238-39; **43**:253, 255-60
"Shoeless Joe Jackson Comes to Iowa" (Kinsella) **27**:237-38
Shoeless Joe Jackson Comes to Iowa (Kinsella) **27**:237-38
"Shoes in the Rain Jungle" (Warren) **13**:573
The Shoes of the Fisherman (West) **6**:564; **33**:432-33
"The Shoes of Wandering" (Kinnell) **129**:243, 250-51
"Shoeshine Boys on the Avenida Juarez" (Purdy) **50**:241
Shōgun: A Novel of Japan (Clavell) **6**:113-14; **25**:126-28; **87**:2, 4-12, 16-19
Sholay (Ali) **69**:25
"Sholem Aleichem's Revolution" (Ozick) **155**:125
"Shōnen" (Tanizaki) **28**:415
Shoot the Piano Player (Truffaut)
See *Tirez sur le pianiste*
"The Shooter" (Welsh) **144**:317
"The Shooting" (Dubus) **36**:143; **97**:201
"Shooting Ducks in South Louisiana" (Tillinghast) **29**:417
Shooting in the Dark (Hougan) **34**:60-2
"The Shooting Party" (Bates) **46**:63
The Shooting Party (Colegate) **36**:112-14
"The Shooting Range" (Brodkey) **56**:60, 62, 64-5
"Shooting Rats at the Bibb County Dump" (Bottoms) **53**:29-30
Shooting Rats at the Bibb County Dump (Bottoms) **53**:28-33
"A Shooting Script" (Heaney) **74**:161
"Shooting Script" (Rich) **18**:446
"A Shooting Season" (Tremain) **42**:386
"Shooting Star" (Reed) **21**:314, 316
The Shooting Star (Benary-Isbert) **12**:31
A Shooting Star (Stegner) **9**:510; **49**:352-53
"Shooting Whales" (Strand) **41**:432-33
"Shootism versus Sport" (Hemingway) **34**:478
The Shootist (Swarthout) **35**:403
"Shoot-Out" (Moure) **88**:229
Shootout at Carnegie Hall (Ochs) **17**:333
"Shootout at Gentry's Junction" (Coover) **46**:121-22
"The Shop Ahoy" (Le Guin) **136**:361
"Shopgirls" (Barthelme) **36**:51-2; **117**:14, 17
"Shoppe Keeper" (Ellison) **42**:129
"Shopping" (Oates) **108**:381-82
"Shopping in Oxford" (Masefield) **47**:233
"The Shopping List" (Dacey) **51**:83
Shops and Houses (Swinnerton) **31**:421, 423
The Shopworn Tare of Barrels (Aksyonov)
See *The Tare of Barrels*
"The Shore" (Hearne) **56**:128
"Shore Leave" (Sturgeon) **39**:364
"Shore Life" (Brosman) **9**:135
"Shore Line" (Rakosi) **47**:346
"Shore Woman" (Heaney) **7**:148
The Shorebirds of North America (Matthiessen) **32**:288-89
"Shorelines" (Moss) **7**:249-50
"Shorelines" (Murray) **40**:335
The Shores of Light (Wilson) **3**:538; **8**:550; **24**:474-75, 479, 481
The Shores of Space (Matheson) **37**:246
"The Shorn Lamb" (Stafford) **7**:457
"The Short Biography of A. A. Darmolatov" (Kiš) **57**:252
The Short Cases of Inspector Maigret (Simenon) **47**:374
"A Short Course in Nietzschean Ethics" (Baxter) **45**:51; **78**:16
"Short Easterly Squall, With Low Visibility and Rising Gorge" (Perelman) **49**:265
"The Short End" (Hecht) **19**:207, 209-10
Short Eyes (Piñero) **4**:401-02; **55**:316-18
A Short Film About Killing (Kieslowski)
See *Kroti film o zabijaniu*
A Short Film About Love (Kieslowski)
See *Kroti film o milosci*
"Short Friday" (Singer) **38**:407, 409-10; **111**:295, 305, 311
Short Friday, and Other Stories (Singer) **3**:456; **15**:504; **23**:415-16, 418; **69**:313; **111**:299
"Short Glossary of Words Used by Poorer People" (Lebowitz) **36**:250
"Short Grotesque Litany on the Death of Senator McCarthy" (Guillén) **79**:229
"The Short Happy Life of Francis Macomber" (Hemingway) **3**:233-34; **8**:283; **10**:264; **13**:277-78; **19**:212; **30**:184; **39**:430-31; **41**:203, 205; **50**:424, 427, 429-31; **80**:141
"Short Histories of the Sea" (Muske) **90**:309
A Short History of a Small Place (Pearson) **39**:86-90
A Short History of Decay (Cioran)
See *Précis de décomposition*
A Short History of Irish Literature (Deane) **122**:79-81, 102
"A Short History of Judaic Thought in the Twentieth Century" (Pastan) **27**:369
"A Short History of Oregon" (Brautigan) **3**:88
"A Short History of Sex" (Soto) **80**:291
"Short History of the West" (Graham) **118**:237
Short Letter, Long Farewell (Handke)
See *Der kurze Brief zum langen Abschied*
A Short Life (Onetti)
See *La vida breve*
"The Short Life of Kazno Yamomoto" (Enright) **31**:155
"Short Mineral Ode" (Cabral de Melo Neto)
See "Pequnea ode mineral"
"Short Note on a Long Subject: Henry James" (Calisher) **134**:32
"Short Papa" (Purdy) **52**:350
"Short People Got No Reason to Live: Reading Irony" (Fish) **142**:169
"Short Poem" (Sanchez) **116**:277, 294
"Short Poem for Armistice Day" (Read) **4**:439

"A Short Poem in Color" (Boyle) **1**:42
Short Poems (Berryman) **6**:63; **8**:91; **25**:93
"A Short Recess" (Milosz) **31**:262
The Short Reign of Pippin IV: A Fabrication (Steinbeck) **21**:369, 382; **34**:405; **45**:382; **59**:353
"Short Riff for John Keats on his 188th Birthday" (Wright) **146**:318
A Short Sad Book (Bowering) **15**:81, 84; **47**:25
A Short Sharp Shock (Brenton) **31**:63-4
Short Sketches (Solzhenitsyn)
See *Kroxotnye rasskazy*
"Short Stories" (Moss) **14**:376
Short Stories from Berlin (Grass) **32**:200
"A Short Story" (Bowering) **47**:29
"Short Story" (Voigt) **54**:433
The Short Story Embassy: A Novel (Wilding) **73**:391, 393, 395-96, 398
"Short Story on a Painting of Gustav Klimt" (Ferlinghetti) **111**:65
"Short Summary" (Bogan) **46**:87
A Short Survey of Surrealism (Gascoyne) **45**:156-57
The Short Throat, the Tender Mouth (Grumbach) **22**:204
"Short Time" (Ewart) **13**:209
A Short Time to Live (Jones) **52**:251-52, 254
"Short Views in Africa" (Jacobsen) **48**:192, 197
"A Short Visit to a Failed Artist" (Bissoondath) **120**:3
A Short Walk (Childress) **15**:131-32; **86**:309, 312; **96**:91, 93, 108
"Short Wave" (Szirtes) **46**:393-94
Short Wave (Szirtes) **46**:393-95
Short Work of It: Selected Writing by Mark Harris (Harris) **19**:205-06
Shortcuts (Altman) **116**:51-3, 58-62, 64-9, 71, 73-4
Shorter Poems, 1951-53 (Roethke) **6**:451; **8**:455; **22**:346; **49**:274, 283, 286
"The Shorter View" (Kennedy) **42**:257
"The Shortest Way Home" (Kiely) **43**:244
"The Short-Story in England 1700-1753" (Jhabvala) **94**:207
"Shorty" (Gellhorn) **60**:183
"Shorty Leach" (Farrell) **66**:127
Shosetsu no hoho (Oe) **86**:227, 229, 240, 242
Shosetsu no Kenkyu (Kawabata) **107**:97
Shosha (Singer) **11**:499-503; **23**:416, 419-20; **69**:312; **111**:307, 310, 312, 321-24, 327-28, 333, 344-46
Shōshō Shigemoto no haha (Tanizaki) **28**:414, 419
The Shoshoneans (Dorn) **10**:159
The Shot (Buero Vallejo) **139**:44-5
"Shot Actress—Full Story" (Bates) **46**:55
"A Shot from Nowhere" (Highsmith) **42**:215
"Shot of Redeye" (Bukowski) **41**:67
Shoten an Goray (Singer) **1**:313; **3**:452, 455; **9**:488; **11**:500; **15**:503-04, 506, 508; **23**:413-20; **38**:408; **69**:306; **111**:293-94, 306, 311, 314-15, 318-22, 342-43
"Shotgun Days" (Lerman) **9**:329
"Shotgun Strategies" (Allison) **153**:19
Shotgun Willie (Nelson) **17**:302, 306
"Shots" (Ozick) **62**:350, 353-54
"Shottle Bop" (Sturgeon) **22**:410; **39**:361
"Should I Stay or Should I Go?" (Clash) **30**:51-2
"Should, Should Not" (Milosz) **82**:308
"Should Wizard Hit Mommy?" (Updike) **5**:455
The Shout (Graves) **45**:171, 173
The Shout (Skolimowski) **20**:354-56
Shout across the River (Poliakoff) **38**:382-83, 386
Shout at the Devil (Smith) **33**:377
"The Shovel Man" (Sandburg) **10**:448; **15**:468; **35**:355
Shovelling Trouble (Richler) **3**:431
The Show (Browning) **16**:123, 124, 126
"Show Biz" (Dickey) **28**:119
"Show Biz Connections" (Friedman) **56**:97
Show Boat (Ferber) **18**:151; **93**:149-52, 154, 156, 160, 164-65, 171-77, 179, 181, 185-87, 189-90
The Show Must Go On (Rice) **7**:363
"Show Saturday" (Larkin) **5**:230; **8**:332-33, 336, 339; **13**:340; **18**:301; **33**:259-60, 263; **64**:265, 282, 284-85
Show Some Emotion (Armatrading) **17**:8-9
Showboat World (Vance) **35**:427
Showdown (Amado)
See *Tocaia grande*
Showdown at Yellow Butte (L'Amour) **25**:279
"A Shower of Gold" (Barthelme) **46**:40; **115**:59, 65, 68, 69, 78, 79
"Shower of Gold" (Gustafson) **36**:220
"Shower of Gold" (Welty) **22**:459; **33**:419; **105**:338-39, 386-87
A Shower of Summer Days (Sarton) **49**:311
"The Showings; Lady Julian of Norwich, 1342-1416" (Levertov) **66**:251
Showman (Maysles and Maysles) **16**:442-43
Shrapnel (MacBeth) **5**:264
The Shrapnel Academy (Weldon) **122**:256
Shrapnel. Poet's Year (MacBeth) **5**:265
The Shrewsdale Exit (Buell) **10**:81-2
The Shrimp and the Anemone (Hartley) **22**:211, 214
"Shrine" (Gerstler) **70**:156-57
"The Shrine" (H. D.) **73**:109
The Shrine, and Other Stories (Lavin) **99**:312, 319
"Shrines" (Mahapatra) **33**:284
The Shrinking Man (Matheson) **37**:246-50
"The Shrink's Wife" (Olds) **85**:294
Shrivings (Shaffer)
See *The Battle of Shrivings*
Shroud for a Nightingale (James) **18**:272; **46**:205; **122**:120, 122, 125, 128, 135, 137, 146, 152-53
Shroud My Body Down (Green) **25**:197, 199
"The Shrouding" (Livesay) **79**:341
"Shrovetide" (Reed) **13**:480
Shrovetide in Old New Orleans (Reed) **13**:480; **32**:358-60; **60**:313
"Shrubs Burned Away" (Hall) **151**:197
"Shrubs Burnt Away" (Hall) **59**:152-56; **151**:181-82, 197
"The Shrunken Head of Pancho Villa" (Valdez) **84**:403, 405, 407, 413, 417
Shubun (Kurosawa) **16**:399; **119**:343, 347, 372, 378-79
"Shucking Corn" (Steele) **45**:365
"Shujia zhong" (Ding Ling) **68**:58
"Shunkin shō" (Tanizaki) **8**:510; **14**:527; **28**:414, 418
"Shut a Final Door" (Capote) **13**:133, 136, 140
Shut Down, Vol. 2 (Wilson) **12**:643-44
"Shutter Door" (Moure) **88**:231
A Shuttle in the Crypt (Soyinka) **36**:415; **44**:284-85
Shuttlecock (Swift) **41**:442-44; **88**:284-85, 287-90, 293-96, 307, 309, 311, 321-22
"Shuttles" (Swenson) **61**:403, 405; **106**:333
"The Shy Man" (Roethke) **101**:332-33
"Shy Rights: Why Not Pretty Soon?" (Keillor) **40**:273
"Si dorme come cani" (Calvino) **33**:102
Si j'étais vous (Green) **77**:275
Si l'été revenait (Adamov) **25**:16, 21-2
"Si souvent" (Damas) **84**:173, 176
"Si tú supiera" (Guillén)
See "Ay negra, si tu supiera"
Si usted no puedo, yo sí (Bunuel) **80**:22
The Siamese Twin Mystery (Queen) **11**:460
"The Siamese Twins Go Snorkeling" (Beattie) **146**:85
"Siamo spiacenti di..." (Buzzati) **36**:86
Siberian Lady Mac Beth (Wajda) **16**:579, 582
"The Siberian Olive Tree" (Johnston) **51**:243, 252
"Siberian Wooing" (Yevtushenko) **126**:391
"Sibirskiye bani" (Voznesensky) **57**:417
"Sibling Mysteries" (Rich) **36**:374
The Sibling Society (Bly) **128**:47-50
"Siblings" (Gordimer) **18**:189; **70**:183
"The Sibling's Woodcut" (Dubie) **36**:134
"A Sibyl" (Atwood) **25**:66
"Sibyl" (Heaney) **74**:159
"The Sibyl" (Watkins) **43**:450
The Sibyl (Lagerkvist) **54**:278-79, 281-83, 285; **13**:331
"Sicilia est insula" (Haavikko) **34**:175
The Sicilian (Puzo) **36**:361-63; **107**:196-99, 207, 213, 216
Sicilian Carousel (Durrell) **8**:193
Sicilian Uncles (Sciascia)
See *Gli zii di Sicilia*
"Sicilian Vespers" (White) **5**:487; **7**:532
"Sick Again" (Page and Plant) **12**:477
"A Sick Call" (Nowlan) **15**:398
"The Sick Child" (Glück) **22**:177
"The Sick Humor of Lenny Bruce" (Bruce) **21**:44
"Sick Leave" (Sassoon) **130**:184, 211
"Sick Love" (Graves) **39**:328; **45**:173
"Sick Visits" (Thomas) **48**:379
The Sickest Don't Always Die the Quickest (Jackson) **12**:290
"Sickness" (Akhmadulina)
See "Bolezn'"
"Sickness" (Sommer) **25**:425
"The Sickness unto Death" (Sexton) **6**:492; **123**:427
Siddharta (Hesse)
See *Siddhartha, eine indische Dichtung*
Siddhartha: An Indic Poem (Hesse)
See *Siddhartha, eine indische Dichtung*
Siddhartha, eine indische Dichtung (Hesse) **1**:145; **2**:191-92; **3**:245-48; **11**:271; **17**:195, 199, 206, 210-11, 214-17, 219; **69**:279, 289, 293
"Side by Side by Side" (Sondheim) **147**:240, 251-53
Side by Side by Sondheim (Sondheim) **30**:389; **147**:263
Side Effects (Allen) **52**:40-2
"Side Street" (Farrell) **66**:131
Side Street, and Other Stories (Farrell) **66**:129
"Sidere Mens Eadem Mutato" (Murray) **40**:337
"A Sidewalk Cafe: Budapest, Autumn" (Padilla) **38**:351
"The Sidmouth Letters" (Gardam) **43**:169-70
The Sidmouth Letters (Gardam) **43**:169, 171
"The Sidney Greenstreet Blues" (Brautigan) **12**:59
The Sidney Poet Heroical, in Twenty-Nine Scenes (Baraka) **10**:19; **115**:10, 20, 28
"Sieben Rosen später" (Celan) **19**:90
17 dikter (Transtroemer) **52**:408-10, 412, 415, 418; **65**:222, 226, 229, 231, 233-37
Siebzig verweht (Jünger) **125**:251
"Siefried's Journey" (Sassoon) **36**:387-88, 394, 396-97
Sieg des Glaubens (Riefenstahl) **16**:520
"The Siege" (Mueller) **51**:280
The Siege (Vansittart) **42**:391, 393
Le siége de l'air (Arp) **5**:33
The Siege of Krishnapur (Farrell) **6**:173-74
"The Siege of Mullingar" (Montague) **46**:268
The Siege of Pleasure (Hamilton) **51**:185-86, 190-91, 193-94, 197-98
The Siege of the Villa Lipp (Ambler) **9**:21-2
Der Sieger nimmt alles (Wellershoff) **46**:438-39
Siegfried (Lang) **20**:201, 204, 210; **103**:85
Siegfried Sassoon Diaries, 1915-1918 (Sassoon) **36**:396-97
Siegfried Sassoon Diaries, 1920-1922 (Sassoon) **36**:396-97
Siegfried's Journey (Sassoon) **130**:178, 182, 184, 186, 193, 202, 204-08, 211
Siegfried's Journey, 1916-1920 (Sassoon) **36**:388-89, 396
"Siegmund Freud" (Parra) **102**:343
"Siena" (Milosz) **56**:237

"Sierpes Street" (Cabral de Melo Neto)
See "Calle Sierpes"
"Sierra Leone" (McGahern) **48**:264
"Siesta" (Transtroemer) **65**:222
"Siesta in Xbalba and Return to the States" (Ginsberg) **36**:189-90
"Siesta: Mexico/Vermont" (Belitt) **22**:52
"Siestas" (Cortázar) **10**:113; **33**:129
Siete domingos rojos (Sender) **8**:477-78, 480
Sift in an Hourglass (Gustafson) **36**:212-13, 216-18
"The Sighing Time" (Blunden) **56**:37
"The Sight of the Horizon" (Brooks) **125**:88
Sight Unseen (Margulies) **76**:188-95
Sightings (Rothenberg) **6**:477; **57**:372
Sights and Spectacles, 1937-1956 (McCarthy) **24**:341-42
Sights Unseen (Gibbons) **145**:163-64, 186
The Sightseer (Wolff) **41**:456-57
El siglo de las luces (Carpentier) **11**:99-100, 102, 105-07; **38**:91-2, 94, 96-101; **110**:58, 60, 74, 78
"Sigma" (Tolson) **105**:255
"Sign" (Piercy) **128**:228-29
The Sign (Harrison) **6**:223
"Sign for My Father, Who Stressed the Bunt" (Bottoms) **53**:33
"A Sign in Space" (Calvino)
See "Un segno nello spazio"
"Sign In Stranger" (Becker and Fagen) **26**:81
The Sign in Sydney Brustein's Window (Hansberry) **17**:184-89, 191-92; **62**:216-18, 220
"The Sign of Apelles" (Pasternak)
See "Il tratto di Apelle"
Sign of Contradiction (John Paul II)
See *Znaki sprzecznosci*
The Sign of Jonas (Merton) **83**:379, 397-403
"Sign of Space" (Calvino)
See "Un segno nello spazio"
The Sign of the Chrysanthemum (Paterson) **12**:484; **30**:286
Sign of the Unicorn (Zelazny) **21**:468, 470, 473
The Sign of Three (Eco) **142**:85, 94
The Signal (Vesaas)
See *Signalet*
"The Signal from the House" (Kunitz) **148**:76-77, 94-95, 99
Signalet (Vesaas) **48**:407
"Signals" (Deane) **122**:74
Signature (Scott) **22**:373
"Signature Event Context" (Derrida) **87**:84
"Signature for Tempo II" (MacLeish) **68**:270
"The Signature of All Things" (Rexroth) **112**:385, 399
The Signature of All Things: Poems, Songs, Elegies, Translations, and Epigrams (Rexroth) **6**:450; **22**:345, 348-49; **49**:279; **112**:387, 405
"Signatures" (Dixon) **52**:99
Signatures of the Visible (Jameson) **142**:246, 258
"Signe ascendant" (Breton) **15**:91
Le signe de la croix (Marcel) **15**:364
Le signe de vie (Tzara) **47**:396
Le signe du lion (Rohmer) **16**:528, 530
"Le Signe du Mauvais Sang" (Tchicaya) **101**:349
"Signed, Sealed, Delivered" (Wonder) **12**:656, 663
Signed, Sealed, Delivered (Wonder) **12**:655-56
"Significant Moments in the Life of My Mother" (Atwood) **84**:67
Significant Others (Maupin) **95**:192-99, 201, 203-04, 208
Significant Sisters: The Grassroots of Active Feminism, 1839-1939 (Forster) **149**:66-71
"The Signifying Darkness" (Dodson) **79**:191
The Signifying Monkey: A Theory of Afro-American Literary Criticism (Gates) **65**:380, 387-91, 393-94, 404-05
Signifying Rappers (Wallace) **114**:360, 363
La Signora Senza Camelie (Antonioni) **20**:20-1; **144**:17, 67, 78-79
Signpost (Livesay) **15**:340; **79**:339
"Signs" (Blaga) **75**:70
"Signs" (Diamond) **30**:112
"Signs" (Merwin) **45**:273
"The Signs" (Olds) **85**:296
"Signs" (Redgrove) **41**:348
"Signs" (Wideman) **122**:344, 347
"Signs" (Williams) **148**:348, 351-53
"Signs and Portents" (Kunitz) **14**:313; **148**:81, 142
"Signs and Symbols" (Nabokov) **15**:393
Signs of Identity (Goytisolo)
See *Señas de identidad*
Signs of Life (Dabrowska)
See *Znaki zycia*
Signs of Life (Elliott) **38**:181-82
Signs of Life (Herzog)
See *Lebenszeichen*
Signs of the Gods (von Daniken) **30**:427
"Sigue" (Guillén) **79**:245-46
Siinä näkijä missä tekijä (Salama) **18**:460-62
S'il vous plaît (Breton and Soupault) **68**:408-13
Silabe (Arghezi) **80**:6-8
Silas and Ben-Godik (Bodker) **21**:13-14
"Silas and Goliath" (Bates) **46**:62
Silas and the Black Mare (Bodker) **21**:11-13
Silas and the Runaway Coach (Bodker) **21**:13-14
Silas Crockett (Chase) **2**:101
Silas Timberman (Fast) **131**:83-4, 98
"The Silence" (Berry) **46**:75
"Silence" (Bly) **5**:61
"Silence" (Ginzburg) **54**:201, 203-04; **70**:280
"Silence" (Moore) **47**:264
"The Silence" (Murakami) **150**:51-2
"Silence" (Simpson) **149**:353
"The Silence" (Williams) **148**:345
The Silence (Bergman)
See *Tystnaden*
Silence (Endō)
See *Chinmoku*
Silence (Pinter) **3**:386-87; **6**:416-17, 420; **9**:420; **11**:442-43; **15**:423; **27**:394-95; **58**:372, 374, 377; **73**:268
Le silence (Sarraute) **8**:470; **10**:457-58; **31**:381-82; **80**:241
The Silence (Sarraute)
See *Le silence*
"Silence and the Poet" (Steiner) **24**:429
Le silence des pierres (del Castillo) **38**:168
Le silence est d'or (Clair) **20**:64, 71
The Silence in the Garden (Trevor) **71**:339-42, 346, 349; **116**:348, 352, 354, 365, 376-77, 382-83, 396
Silence in the Snowy Fields (Bly) **2**:66; **5**:61, 63-5; **10**:54-7; **15**:62-3, 65-8; **38**:54-7; **128**:4-9, 11-17, 19-21, 23-24, 27-28, 30-31, 36
Silence: Lectures and Writings (Cage) **41**:76-83
"Silence Means Dissent" (Dworkin) **123**:102
The Silence Now (Sarton) **91**:244
A Silence of Desire (Markandaya) **38**:322-23
The Silence of History (Farrell) **11**:193; **66**:129, 139
"The Silence of Oswald" (Holmes) **56**:140
"The Silence of the Llano" (Anaya) **148**:45, 47
The Silence of the Llano (Anaya) **148**:27, 35, 44
"The Silence of the Night" (Kunitz) **148**:88
"The Silence of the Valley" (O'Faolain) **1**:259; **14**:402, 406; **32**:343-44; **70**:313, 318
Silence over Dunkerque (Tunis) **12**:598
"Silence Wager Stories" (Howe) **152**:184-85, 197, 212
"The Silences" (Dunn) **40**:169
Silences (Okigbo) **25**:349, 354
Silences (Olsen) **13**:432-33; **114**:199-202, 210, 215, 219, 221-24, 231, 237, 239
The Silences Between: Moeraki Conversations (Hulme) **39**:160; **130**:41, 43-4, 53
"Silences: Lament of the Silent Sisters" (Okigbo) **25**:354; **84**:302, 312, 315, 321-23, 325-26, 328, 332, 336
"Silences, When Writers Don't Write" (Olsen) **114**:193, 195-96
"El silencio de Dios" (Arreola) **147**:6
"The Silent Areas" (Feinstein) **36**:171
The Silent Areas (Feinstein) **36**:171
The Silent Cry (Oe)
See *Man'en gan'nen no futtobōru*
The Silent Cry (Perry) **126**:343
The Silent Duel (Kurosawa)
See *Shizukanaru Ketto*
"The Silent Generation" (Simpson) **4**:498; **149**:324
"Silent in America" (Levine) **5**:252; **9**:332; **118**:283, 287, 292, 298
"Silent in Gehenna" (Ellison) **13**:206
Silent Interviews (Delany) **141**:114-15, 118, 145, 149-52, 159
"Silent Journal" (Wright) **146**:352
"The Silent Man" (Phillips) **28**:364
"The Silent Marriage" (Simmons) **43**:410-11
"The Silent Men" (Camus)
See "Les muets"
"Silent Money" (Carroll) **143**:33
Silent Movie (Brooks) **12**:80-2
The Silent Mr. Palomar (Calvino)
See *Palomar*
"Silent Night, Lonely Night" (Anderson) **23**:30-2
"The Silent Piano" (Simpson) **149**:328
"The Silent Poet Sequence" (Kroetsch) **23**:273-75; **132**:284
The Silent Rooms (Hébert)
See *Les chambres de bois*
"Silent Service" (Sassoon) **36**:389; **130**:188
"Silent Sisters" (Okigbo)
See "Silences: Lament of the Silent Sisters"
The Silent Sky (Eckert) **17**:104-05
"The Silent Slain" (MacLeish) **68**:290
"Silent Snow, Secret Snow" (Aiken) **52**:26
The Silent Speaker (Stout) **3**:472
Silent Spring (Carson) **71**:97-9, 101-08, 110-13
"The Silent Towns" (Bradbury) **42**:38
The Silent World (Cousteau) **30**:101-04, 109
"Silhouette" (Ashbery) **15**:33
"Silhouette" (Hughes) **108**:328
Silhouette du scandale (Aymé) **11**:23
"Silhouettes" (Jones) **81**:65
"Sililoquy on the Rocks" (Bowering) **47**:19
"Silk of a Soul" (Herbert) **9**:271
Silk Stockings (Kaufman) **38**:268
Silk Stockings (Mamoulian) **16**:425, 428-30
Silkeborg (Abell) **15**:1, 5
Silken Eyes (Sagan) **9**:468; **17**:427-28
The Silken Net (Bragg) **10**:72
"The Silken Swift" (Sturgeon) **39**:361
"The Silken Tent" (Frost) **13**:228
"The Silken Tent" (Loewinsohn) **52**:285
Silkwood (Ephron) **31**:160
"The Silky Veils of Ardor" (Mitchell) **12**:443-44
"Sillat" (Haavikko) **34**:174
"Silly Boy Blue" (Bowie) **17**:65
"Silly Love Songs" (McCartney) **35**:284-85, 287-88, 290, 293-94
"Silly Talk about Suicide" (Valenzuela) **31**:437
The Silmarillion (Tolkien) **1**:338; **3**:481; **8**:515-16; **12**:585-87; **38**:431-32, 434-38, 441-43
"Siloam" (Davie) **31**:124
"Silvae" (Montale) **7**:222
"Silver" (Ammons) **5**:29; **108**:4
"The Silver Bangles" (Anand) **23**:21
The Silver Bears (Erdman) **25**:154
"The Silver Bird of Herndyke Mill" (Blunden) **56**:27, 31, 37
The Silver Branch (O'Faolain) **70**:315, 317
The Silver Branch (Sutcliff) **26**:426-28, 430, 433-35
"The Silver Bullet" (McPherson) **19**:310; **77**:365

The Silver Chair (Lewis) **27**:263; **124**:195, 236, 248
The Silver Chalice (Costain) **30**:97-8
"The Silver Crown" (Malamud) **3**:325; **8**:375; **18**:317-18; **27**:306
"A Silver Dish" (Bellow) **25**:84-5; **33**:68; **63**:29
The Silver Eggheads (Leiber) **25**:303
"Silver Gift Poem" (Elytis) **49**:114; **100**:175
"Silver Lamé" (Carpenter) **41**:103
"The Silver Lily" (Glück) **81**:172
"The Silver Locket" (McNickle) **89**:180
The Silver Metal Lover (Lee) **46**:232
"Silver Mirrors" (Carroll) **143**:27
Silver out of Shanghai: A Scenario for Josef von Sternberg, Featuring Wicked Nobles, a Depraved Religious Wayfoong, Princess Ida, the China Clipper, and Resurrection Lily (Cassity) **42**:96-7
"A Silver Plate" (Raine) **103**:210
"The Silver Porcupine" (Kinsella) **43**:258
"The Silver Stag" (Raine) **45**:332
The Silver Swan: Poems Written in Kyoto, 1974-1975 (Rexroth) **49**:283, 286; **112**:372, 404
"The Silver Swanne" (Dowell) **60**:108-09
The Silver Tassie (O'Casey) **5**:320; **11**:407-09; **15**:405-06, 408; **88**:242, 248, 251-54, 257, 259-61, 263-65, 267-70, 273, 275-77, 281
Silver: The Life of an Atlantic Salmon (Haig-Brown) **21**:139-40, 142-44
The Silver Tongued Devil and I (Kristofferson) **26**:267, 269-70
"Silver Wedding" (Scannell) **49**:329
Silver Wedding (Binchy) **153**:63, 67, 70, 78
Silver Wedding (Misharin) **59**:364
The Silver Wire (Bowering) **15**:82
Silverhill (Whitney) **42**:434
"Silvester-Unfall" (Lenz) **27**:245
"Silvia" (Cortázar) **10**:113
Sima kindynou (Samarakis) **5**:381
Simabaddha (Ray) **16**:487, 493, 495; **76**:357-58, 360, 362
"Simaetha" (H. D.) **73**:105
Simbi and the Satyr of the Dark Jungle (Tutuola) **5**:443; **14**:539; **29**:441-42
"Similar Triangles" (Raphael) **14**:438
"Simile" (Meredith) **55**:192
"Simile" (Momaday) **85**:247
"Similkameen Deer" (Lane) **25**:284
Simon (Sutcliff) **26**:425, 428-29, 432-35, 439
Simon and Garfunkel's Greatest Hits (Simon) **17**:463
"Simon Buckminster (SR)" (Avison) **97**:128
Simon del desierto (Bunuel) **16**:134-35, 139, 141, 151; **80**:41, 46
"Simon Frailman" (Scannell) **49**:331-32
"Simon le Mage" (Kiš) **57**:249, 251-52
"Simon Magus" (Kiš)
See "Simon le Mage"
Simon of the Desert (Bunuel)
See *Simon del desierto*
Simon Plunges Through Thousands of Years: A Dramatic Happening in Fourteen Scenes (Sachs) **98**:322
Simone de Beauvoir: A Life... a Love Story (Francis and Gontier) **50**:387-92
Simonetta Perkins (Hartley) **22**:211, 213
"Simple Autumnal" (Bogan) **46**:77-8, 89; **93**:92-3, 95-6
A Simple Honorable Man (Richter) **30**:317, 321-22, 326
"A Simple Language" (Clifton) **66**:86
"Simple Language, Simple People: Smith, Paton, Mikro" (Coetzee) **66**:99
"The Simple Life" (Bates) **46**:59-60
"The Simple Life" (Beer) **58**:38
"The Simple Life" (Richter) **30**:328
A Simple Lust: Selected Poems Including Sirens, Knuckles, Boots; Letters to Martha; Poems from Algiers, Thoughts Abroad (Brutus) **43**:88-9, 94, 96-7
"Simple Maria" (Allende) **97**:30, 32
Simple Passion (Ernaux)
See *Passion simple*
Simple People (Gray) **9**:241
"A Simple Sickness" (Jennings) **131**:233
Simple Speaks His Mind (Hughes) **10**:281
Simple Stakes a Claim (Hughes) **10**:281; **35**:215-16; **108**:284
Simple Takes a Wife (Hughes) **10**:281
"The Simple Truth" (Levine) **118**:324
The Simple Truth (Hardwick) **13**:264
The Simple Truth (Levine) **118**:308, 312, 322-24
"Simple Twist of Fate" (Dylan) **77**:178
Simple's Uncle Sam (Hughes) **35**:219; **108**:286
"The Simpleton" (Garfield) **12**:218
"Simplicity" (Rakosi) **47**:345
"The Simplification" (Piercy) **27**:374
"The Simply" (Bernstein) **142**:10-12
Simply Heavenly (Hughes) **35**:217-18
"Simply Passing Through" (Walcott) **25**:448
"Simply the Human Form" (Forster) **45**:131, 133
La simulación (Sarduy) **97**:404-06
The Simulacra (Dick) **30**:127; **72**:104, 121
Simulacra and Simulations (Baudrillard)
See *Simulacres et simulations*
"Le simulacre" (Pinget) **13**:443
Simulacres et simulations (Baudrillard) **60**:19
"Simultan" (Bachmann) **69**:47-8
Simultan (Bachmann) **69**:36, 46, 48, 59
Sin (Ai) **69**:8-10, 15-17
The Sin (Ichikawa)
See *Hakai*
The Sin Eater (Ellis) **40**:189-91
"The Sin Eaters" (Alexie) **154**:45, 48
"Sin título" (Zamora) **89**:387
"Sinaï, bis" (Tchicaya) **101**:353
The Sinai Sort (MacCaig) **36**:279-80
"Sinaloa" (Birney) **6**:75
"Sinbad" (Barthelme) **59**:251
"Since" (Auden) **4**:33; **6**:19-20
"Since 1939" (Lowell) **11**:330; **37**:238; **124**:301
"Since Donovan Died" (Scannell) **49**:327
"Since I Had You" (Gaye) **26**:132
"Since I've Been Loving You" (Page and Plant) **12**:480
"Since then" (Amichai) **116**:97
Sincerely, Willis Wayde (Marquand) **10**:329-30
"Sincerity and Art" (Huxley) **11**:283
Sincerity and Authenticity (Trilling) **9**:530; **11**:539, 543, 545; **24**:457-59
Sindbad and Me (Platt) **26**:348-50
"Sinesio de Rodas" (Arreola) **147**:3-5, 17, 34
"Sinesius of Rhodes" (Arreola)
See "Sincsio de Rodas"
"Sinew" (Carver) **55**:276
"Sinful City" (Seifert)
See "Hříšné město"
Sinful Davy (Huston) **20**:171
"The Sinful Life and Death of Tinkori" (Anand) **93**:57
Sinful Minds (Dourado)
See *As imaginações pecaminosas*
The Sinful Stones (Dickinson) **12**:169; **35**:133
Sinful Woman (Cain) **3**:97; **28**:53
"Sing a Song" (West) **134**:368
Sing Down the Moon (O'Dell) **30**:269-70
Sing for Your Supper (Weber) **12**:632
"Sing My Songs to Me" (Browne) **21**:35
"Sing Shaindele, Sing" (Charyn) **5**:104
"Sing This All Together" (Jagger and Richard) **17**:221
Sing to Me Through Open Windows (Kopit) **18**:287; **33**:249
"Singalong Junk" (McCartney) **35**:278-79
"Singapore" (Oliver) **98**:278, 280-81, 284
"The Singapore Hotel" (Hood) **28**:189
Singer of Sad Songs (Jennings) **21**:201
"The Singers" (Ai) **69**:5
"The Singers" (Boland) **113**:110, 119
"The Singer's House" (Heaney) **25**:247
"The Singer's Song" (Ekelöf) **27**:110
Singin' and Swingin' and Gettin' Merry Like Christmas (Angelou) **12**:13-14; **35**:31; **64**:24, 27, 29-31, 36, 39; **77**:3-4, 6-8, 10-13, 15, 22, 24-5
"Singing" (Shapcott) **38**:401
"Singing" (Stern) **40**:413-14
"Singing Aloud" (Kizer) **80**:174, 179, 181
"The Singing Bell" (Asimov) **26**:44-5
The Singing Cave (Dillon) **17**:94-5
The Singing Detective (Potter) **58**:393-401; **86**:345-53; **123**:240-50, 255-69, 271-74, 276-77, 279
Singing from the Well (Arenas)
See *Celestino antes del alba*
The Singing Head (Elliott) **47**:104
"Singing in the Clump" (Dowell) **60**:107-09
Singing in the Shrouds (Marsh) **53**:250
"The Singing Lesson" (West) **7**:519
"Singing Nigger" (Sandburg) **35**:352
"Singing School" (Heaney) **25**:245-46; **74**:163
"The Singing Statues" (Ballard) **137**:64, 66
Singing Strings (Kettelkamp) **12**:304
"Singing the Monthly Blues" (Jong) **83**:300
"Singing the Tree" (Goldbarth) **5**:144
Single Handed (Forester) **35**:159, 163
The Single Hound (Sarton) **49**:307-08; **91**:240, 245
A Single Lady, and Other Stories (Lavin) **99**:312
A Single Light (Wojciechowska) **26**:454, 458-59
A Single Man (Isherwood) **1**:156-57; **9**:294; **11**:300; **14**:280, 285; **44**:398-99, 402
A Single Pebble (Hersey) **1**:144; **7**:153; **40**:228-29, 231, 239-42; **81**:334-35; **97**:302
"Single Pigeon" (McCartney) **35**:281
"Single Sonnet" (Bogan) **46**:81, 90
Single Spies (Bennett) **77**:94-5, 97-8, 100-02
"Single Vision" (Kunitz) **148**:86
"Singleminded" (Brunner) **8**:107
"Singling & Doubling Together" (Ammons) **57**:49-51, 59-60; **108**:16, 38, 57, 58
A Singular Man (Donleavy) **1**:76; **4**:123, 125; **6**:139, 141-42; **10**:153-54
Singularities (Howe) **72**:209; **152**:154-55, 157, 192, 196, 203, 229, 248
"The Singularly Ugly Princess" (Brophy) **6**:99
"Un singuratic" (Arghezi) **80**:12
Sinister Street (Mackenzie) **18**:313-17
"Sink" (Celan) **53**:78
Sink the Belgrano! (Berkoff) **56**:17
"The Sinking House" (Boyle) **90**:48
"The Sinking of the Bismarck" (MacLean) **63**:270
The Sinking of the Odradek Stadium (Mathews) **6**:315-16; **52**:307, 309-10, 315-16, 318
The Sinking of the Odradek Stadium and Other Novels (Mathews) **52**:307
The Sinking of the Titanic (Enzensberger)
See "Der Untergand der Titanic"
Sinking Ship Blues (Breytenbach) **23**:84; **126**:61
"Sinn Fein: 1957" (Buckley) **57**:126
"Sinner" (Hughes) **10**:279; **108**:297
Sinning with Annie, and Other Stories (Theroux) **5**:427
Sins For Father Knox (Škvorecký) **69**:337-38, 344, 346-47; **152**:315
"Sins Leave Scars" (Cooper) **56**:70
The Sins of Philip Fleming (Wallace) **13**:567-68
"The Sins of the Fathers" (Porter) **33**:318
"Sins of the Third Age" (Gordimer) **33**:185; **70**:182
"Sintra" (Adams) **46**:21
"The Sipapu" (Loewinsohn) **52**:285
Sippi (Killens) **10**:300-02
Sippur pashut (Agnon) **4**:15
"Sipsy in the Rain" (Bass) **79**:17
"Sir" (McCartney) **35**:287
Sir Donald Wolfit (Harwood) **32**:224
"Sir Duke" (Wonder) **12**:660, 662
"Sir Francis Bacon" (Moore) **47**:268
"Sir Gawain and the Green Knight" (Winters) **4**:591; **32**:467

"Sir John Piers" (Betjeman) **43**:34
Sir Slob and the Princess: A Play for Children (Garrett) **51**:145
"Sir William Herschel's Long Year" (Hope) **51**:226
"Sir William Johnson: His Daily Journal" (Kenny) **87**:257
"Sire" (Cisneros) **118**:184
Sire Halewyn (Ghelderode) **11**:226
The Siren (Buzzati) **36**:95
"Siren Limits" (Okigbo) **25**:350, 352; **84**:301, 306-07, 314, 317-22, 326, 333
"The Siren of Sandy Gap" (Prichard) **46**:345
"Siren Song" (Atwood) **8**:29
La sirena varada (Casona) **49**:40, 42-6
Die Sirene (Wellershoff) **46**:437
"The Sirens" (Ferron) **94**:103, 125
"Sirens" (Gerstler) **70**:157-58
The Sirens (Wesley) **7**:519
"Sirens and Voices" (Swan) **69**:363-64
The Sirens of Titan (Vonnegut) **2**:453, 455; **3**:495-501, 503; **4**:561-63, 565-67, 569; **5**:466-67, 469; **8**:530-31; **12**:603-04, 606, 609, 612-14, 618, 620-21, 623, 628; **40**:448-49; **60**:424, 430-31, 438, 440; **111**:351, 358, 359, 366
"The Sirens' Welcome to Cronos" (Graves) **2**:174
The Sirian Experiments: The Report by Ambien II, of the Five (Lessing) **15**:336; **22**:285-87; **40**:303-06, 309
"Sirius: Midnight" (Derleth) **31**:138
"Sirmione Peninsula" (Spender) **41**:426
"Sirocco" (Piccolo) **13**:441
Sirocco (Coward) **29**:131
"Sirriamnis" (Lee) **46**:231-32
"Sirventes" (Blackburn) **43**:61
Sissie (Williams) **5**:498; **13**:598
Sista mänskan (Lagerkvist) **54**:268, 274, 277
Il sistema periodico (Levi) **37**:223, 226-27; **50**:323-24, 327-28, 332-34, 336, 338-40
"Sister" (Dunn) **36**:153
"Sister" (Farrell) **4**:158; **8**:205
"Sister" (Herbert) **9**:274
"Sister" (Hughes) **108**:328
"Sister" (Prince) **35**:324
"Sister" (Taylor) **5**:425
"Sister" (Voigt) **54**:429
"Sister" (Wolff) **64**:454
Sister Age (Fisher) **76**:341; **87**:124-25, 127-28, 130, 133
"Sister and Brother" (Welty) **105**:341
"Sister Ann of the Cornfields" (Kinsella) **27**:238
"Sister Imelda" (O'Brien) **36**:336, 339, 341; **116**:186, 195, 216-18
"Sister Lou" (Brown) **1**:47
"Sister Madeleine Pleads for Our Mary" (Fulton) **52**:161
Sister Mary Ignatius Explains It All for You (Durang) **27**:90-3; **38**:172-74
"Sister Morphine" (Jagger and Richard) **17**:223-24, 229, 234
"Sister Outsider" (Lorde) **71**:243
Sister Outsider: Essays and Speeches (Lorde) **71**:243-45, 260
"Sister Ray" (Reed) **21**:303, 314
Sister Son/ji (Sanchez) **116**:283, 301, 308, 316
"Sister Water" (Warren) **13**:582
"Sisterhood" (Steinem) **63**:379
Sisterhood Is Powerful (Morgan) **2**:294
Sisterly Feelings (Ayckbourn) **18**:29-30; **33**:42-3; **74**:31, 34
"The Sisters" (Jacobsen) **48**:198-99
"Sisters" (Kinsella) **138**:84
"The Sisters" (Wright) **53**:418
The Sisters (Angelou) **77**:21
The Sisters (Littell) **42**:277-78
Sisters (De Palma) **20**:74-8
"Sisters in Arms" (Lorde) **71**:260
The Sisters Materassi (Palazzeschi)
See *Sorelle Materassi*
The Sisters: New and Selected Poems (Jacobsen) **48**:197-99; **102**:240
Sisters of Darkness (Almodovar)
See *Entre Tinieblas*
"The Sisters of Mercy" (Cohen) **3**:109
"Sisters of the Princess" (Boyle) **58**:74
"Sisters of the Rain" (Cooper) **56**:71-2
Sisters of the Yam: Black Women and Self-Recovery (Hooks) **94**:154-55, 159
The Sisters Rosenweig (Wasserstein) **90**:435-40
"Sisters Under Their Skin" (Ferber) **93**:140
Sisyphus and Reilly: An Autobiography (Luke) **38**:317-18
"Sit Down Young Stranger" (Lightfoot) **26**:281
Sit Opposite Each Other (Summers) **10**:493
Sita (Millett) **67**:252-53, 258
"Sitalkas" (H. D.) **73**:104-05, 119
"Sitasq1s Story" (Alexander) **121**:9
"Sites" (Butor) **15**:114
Sitio a Eros (Ferré) **139**:149, 153, 162-63, 173-75
The Sittaford Mystery (Christie) **48**:72-3
"The Sitting" (McGuckian) **48**:278
"Sitting Around" (Harrison) **143**:350-51
"Sitting in Limbo" (Cliff) **21**:65
Sitting in Mexico (Bowering) **15**:83
"Sitting in My Hotel" (Davies) **21**:95
Sitting In: Selected Writings on Jazz, Blues, and Related Topics (Carruth) **84**:132
Sitting in the Club Car Drinking Rum and Karma Cola: A Manual for Ladies Crossing Canada by Train (Jiles) **58**:273-75
"Sitting in the Waters of Grasse River" (Kenny) **87**:255
Sitting Pretty (Young) **19**:479-80
"La situación insostenible" (Neruda) **28**:309
"The Situation at the End of the War" (Leavis) **24**:293
"Situation Comedy" (Jiles) **58**:272, 279
A Situation in New Delhi (Sahgal) **41**:372
"Situation in the West" (Ferlinghetti) **27**:139
Situation Normal (Miller) **1**:216
The Situation of Poetry: Contemporary Poetry and Its Traditions (Pinsky) **19**:369-70; **38**:355-56, 359-60; **94**:299-300, 302, 308; **121**:432, 434, 448
Situations (Sartre) **1**:304; **7**:397; **18**:473; **24**:416, 418, 421; **50**:370
Situations 2 (Sartre) **24**:419, 421
Situations 10 (Sartre) **9**:473
"VI" (Dunn) **40**:170
"The Six" (Randall) **135**:399
Six and One Remorses for the Sky (Elytis) **15**:220-21; **49**:107-09, 111, 117; **100**:175, 180, 192
"Six Beautiful in Paris" (McNickle) **89**:183-84
"Six Cemetery Poems" (Silkin) **43**:404
Six Darn Cows (Laurence) **50**:314
"Six Days before Christmas" (Kherdian) **6**:280
Six Days in Marapore (Scott) **60**:320
Six Degrees of Separation (Guare) **67**:86-90
"The Six Deliberate Acts" (Fisher) **25**:161
"6 della sera" (Ortese)
See "Le sei della sera"
Six Epistles to Eva Hesse (Davie) **5**:114-15; **8**:163, 165
"Six Feet of the Country" (Gordimer) **123**:144-49
Six Feet of the Country (Gordimer) **18**:185; **33**:178-79; **70**:162
"603 West Liberty Street" (Fulton) **52**:160
"Six Inches" (Bukowski) **41**:75; **108**:85
"Six Lectures in Verse" (Milosz) **56**:248; **82**:297-98, 301, 304
6 litres d'eau par seconde (Butor) **15**:115, 118
"Six Meditations after the Event" (Coles) **46**:108
Six Memos for the Next Millenium (Calvino) **73**:42, 49, 57, 59-60
"Six Nuns Die in Convent Inferno" (Durcan) **70**:151
Six of One (Brown) **18**:73-5; **43**:81; **79**:153, 155, 157-59, 169
"Six Places in New York State" (Crase) **58**:159-60
Six Plays of Clifford Odets (Odets) **98**:209, 211, 217
Six Problems for Don Isidro Parodi (Bioy Casares)
See *Seis problemas para Don Isidro Parodi*
"Six Sailors" (Feldman) **7**:103
Six San Francisco Poets (Kherdian) **6**:281
Six Sections from Mountains and Rivers without End (Snyder) **1**:318; **32**:388, 398
"Six Sentences" (Clarke) **9**:167
"Six Songs for Clöe" (Hope) **3**:251
"Six Songs for Tamar" (Amichai) **116**:96
"Six Songs of Khalidine" (Barnes) **127**:169
Six Stories (Bates) **46**:63
"Six Sundays in January" (Wesker) **3**:519; **5**:484
"The 6000" (Pratt) **19**:379-80
Six Troubadour Songs (Snodgrass) **18**:492
"Six Underrated Pleasures" (Piercy) **62**:370-71; **128**:231
"Six Varieties of Religious Experience" (L'Heureux) **52**:275
Six Walks in the Fictional Woods (Eco) **142**:99, 101, 103
"Six Winter Privacy Poems" (Bly) **10**:55, 61; **15**:63; **128**:22, 28, 31
The Six Wives of Henry VIII (Fraser) **107**:60-2, 64-5, 67
"Six Years" (Snyder) **32**:387, 391
"Six Years Later" (Brodsky) **36**:78
"The Six-Day Night" (Morand)
See "La nuit de seis jours"
Le sixième jour (Chedid) **47**:84-6
Sixpence in Her Shoe (McGinley) **14**:368
Sixteen, and Other Stories (Daly) **17**:90
"1614 Boren" (Hugo) **32**:244-47
"1692 Cotton Mather Newsreel" (Brautigan) **12**:69
"Sixteen-Year-Old Susan March Confesses to the Innocent Murder of All the Devious Strangers Who Would Drag Her Down" (Rooke) **25**:394
The Sixth (Arguedas)
See *El sexto*
Sixth Column (Heinlein) **14**:247
The Sixth Commandment (Sanders) **41**:380
"The Sixth Fleet Still Out There in the Mediterranean" (Starbuck) **53**:354
The Sixth Heaven (Hartley) **22**:211
Sixth Sense (Kettelkamp) **12**:305-06
"The Sixties" (Shields) **97**:430-31, 433
"Sixty Answers to Thirty-Three Questions from Daniel Charles" (Cage) **41**:83
Sixty Old (Le Guin) **136**:395
Sixty Poems (Ezekiel) **61**:96
Sixty Stories (Barthelme) **23**:47-9; **46**:42; **59**:246-47; **115**:78, 81
"A Sixty Year Old Man" (Endō) **99**:296, 301, 307
"65" (Reading) **47**:351
63: Dream Palace (Purdy) **2**:348-50; **4**:424; **10**:421-24; **28**:379; **52**:343-44
"Sixty-three Words" (Kundera) **115**:321
Sixty-Two: A Model Kit (Cortázar)
See *62: Modelo para armar*
"Sixty-Two Mesostics re Merce Cunningham" (Cage) **41**:82
"The Size of a Universe" (Ciardi) **40**:154
"The Size of Song" (Ciardi) **10**:107; **40**:159
"Sizwe Bansi Is Dead" (Purdy) **6**:429
Sizwe Bansi Is Dead (Fugard) **9**:229-34; **14**:191; **25**:175; **40**:197-98, 203; **80**:61-3, 65-6, 69-70, 74-5, 77, 79
Själarnas maskerad (Lagerkvist) **54**:276, 288-90
Sjálfstaett fólk (Laxness) **25**:291, 296
En Sjävbiografi: EfterKauamnade brev och anteckningar (Ekelöf) **27**:116
Det sjunde inseglet (Bergman) **16**:45-50, 52-5,

59-62, 64-7, 69, 71, 73-4, 77, 82; **72**:27-40, 52, 54-6, 59-60
Skammen (Bergman) **16**:60, 62, 74-5, 80-1; **72**:40, 49-50, 52, 54, 57, 59
Skapelsemorgon (Lagerkvist) **13**:331
"Skater in Blue" (Parini) **54**:360-61
"The Skaters" (Ashbery) **2**:19; **4**:23; **9**:43; **15**:27; **25**:50-1, 56; **41**:33, 40-1; **77**:52, 62; **125**:17
"The Skaters" (Jarrell) **13**:299
"Skating" (Motion) **47**:292
The Skating Party (Warner) **59**:212, 216
Skating Shoes (Streatfeild) **21**:400, 406-07, 410, 415
"Skaza harmonii" (Milosz) **56**:237
Skazhi izjum! (Aksyonov) **101**:29, 42-7, 50
"Skazka" (Pasternak) **18**:387-89; **63**:313, 318
"The Skein" (Kizer) **80**:174, 180
The Skeletal System (Silverstein and Silverstein) **17**:456
"The Skeleton" (Aldiss) **40**:19
"The Skeleton" (Pritchett) **13**:467
Skeleton Crew (King) **37**:207
"Skeleton Crow" (Szirtes) **46**:393
"Skeleton Key: Opening and Starting Key for a 1954 Dodge Junked Last Year" (Hollander) **2**:197
A Skeleton Key to "Finnegans Wake" (Campbell and Robinson) **69**:65-7, 90
"The Skeleton of Dreams" (Appleman) **51**:17
"The Skeleton of the Future" (MacDiarmid) **19**:287; **63**:253, 255
"The Skeletonizers" (Lieberman) **36**:261
"Skeletons" (Beattie) **63**:18; **146**:50
Skeletons (Swarthout) **35**:404
"Skepparhistoria" (Transtroemer) **65**:235
"Skeptic" (Frost) **13**:231; **26**:118
"Skeptic and Barbarian" (Cioran) **64**:88
"Skepticism and the Depth of Life" (Bellow) **10**:40
Skerrett (O'Flaherty) **5**:321; **34**:355-56
"SKETCH: CNR London to Toronto (II)" (Avison) **97**:113, 117
"SKETCH: End of a Day: OR, I as a blurry" (Avison) **97**:117
"Sketch for a Landscape" (Swenson) **106**:313
"Sketch from Life" (Sargeson) **31**:364
"Sketch in October" (Transtroemer) **65**:223
"Sketch of a Long Poem" (Voznesensky) **57**:418
"A Sketch of the Great Dejection" (Gunn) **81**:178, 182
"Sketch of the Old Graveyard at Col de Castillon" (Middleton) **13**:388
Sketchbook, 1946-1949 (Frisch)
See *Tagebuch, 1946-1949*
Sketchbook, 1966-1971 (Frisch)
See *Tagebuch, 1966-1971*
The Sketches (Turco) **11**:550, 552
Sketches and Studies of Present-Day Bohemian Paris (Rhys) **124**:337
Sketches from the Land of Kuty (Arghezi)
See *Tablete din ţara ke Kuty*
Sketches in Criticism (Brooks) **29**:83
The Skewbald Dog Running along the Seashore (Aitmatov)
See *Pegil pes, begushchij kraem moria*
The Skewbald Dog Running at the Edge of the Sea (Aitmatov)
See *Pegil pes, begushchij kraem moria*
"The Skewer" (McGrath) **55**:73, 75-6
"Skiddah and Kuziba" (Singer) **111**:305
The Skies of Crete (Forman) **21**:115
The Skies of Europe (Prokosch) **48**:311-12
"The Skills of Xanadu" (Sturgeon) **39**:364
"The Skimming Stone" (Steele) **45**:365
"Skin" (Selzer) **74**:278
The Skin (Silverstein and Silverstein) **17**:456
"Skin Boat" (Ondaatje) **51**:314
Skin Deep (Dickinson)
See *The Glass-Sided Ants' Nest*
"The Skin Game" (Phillips) **28**:362-63
The Skin of Dreams (Queneau)
See *Loin de rueil*
Skin of Grace (Willard) **37**:462-63
The Skin of Our Teeth (Kazan) **63**:225, 230, 234
The Skin of Our Teeth (Wilder) **1**:364-66; **5**:495-96; **6**:572-73, 575-78; **10**:531-32, 535; **15**:570-71, 573-75; **35**:442, 444; **82**:346-48, 352-53, 357-61, 363-64, 368, 376-77, 379-82, 384, 390-91
Skin Screen Utopia (Brossard) **115**:109-11
Skin: Talking about Sex, Class, and Literture (Allison) **153**:5, 10-12, 15, 17, 19, 25, 28, 30, 41, 44, 52
"Skin: Where She Touches Me" (Allison) **153**:3, 11
Skinflick (Hansen) **38**:238
"Skinned Alive" (White) **110**:340
Skinned Alive (White) **110**:339-40, 342-43
"Skinning a Deer" (Holmes) **56**:145
Skinny Legs and All (Robbins) **64**:380-84
"Skins" (Wright) **13**:612; **28**:457, 460; **146**:305, 326-27, 374
Skins and Bones (Allen) **84**:24
Skinwalkers (Hillerman) **62**:260
"The Skip" (Fenton) **32**:166
Skipper (Corcoran) **17**:78
Skippy (Sackler) **14**:479
Skipton (Johnson) **1**:161
"A Skirmish" (McGuane) **45**:265
Skirmish: The Great Short Fiction of Clifford D. Simak (Simak) **55**:319
Sklep Jubüerski (John Paul II) **128**:165, 168-69
"The Skokie Theatre" (Hirsch) **50**:198
"Skookumchuk" (Musgrave) **54**:336, 341
Den skrattande polisen (Wahlöö) **7**:501-02
Skryt (Breytenbach) **126**:79, 82, 102
The Skull (Hikmet)
See *Kafatasi*
"The Skull Ballad" (Voznesensky) **57**:414
The Skull Beneath the Skin (James) **46**:205-07; **122**:135, 145, 149-53, 165, 183, 186
A Skull in Salop and Other Poems (Grigson) **7**:135
"A Skull Picked Clean" (Day Lewis) **10**:131
"Skull Valley, Utah" (Squires) **51**:379
"The Skunk" (Heaney) **14**:245-46; **25**:242-44, 247; **74**:167
"Skunk Cabbage" (Oliver) **34**:246-47; **98**:257
"Skunk Hour" (Lowell) **3**:302; **4**:301; **5**:258; **8**:351, 354; **9**:336; **11**:326-27; **15**:344, 346-47; **37**:241, 243; **124**:254, 257, 264, 273
"Skurlatsky, Man of Letters" (Voinovich) **147**:285
Skutarevski (Leonov)
See *Skutarevsky*
Skutarevsky (Leonov) **92**:232, 240, 246, 250, 253, 259, 270, 274, 276-78
"The Sky" (Findley) **102**:111
"Sky" (Szymborska) **99**:198
Sky (Benedikt) **4**:54
"Sky and Earth" (Nagy) **7**:251
"The Sky and I" (McFadden) **48**:246
The Sky and the Forest (Forester) **35**:169
Sky Blue (Bataille)
See *Le bleu du ciel*
The Sky Changes (Sorrentino) **7**:451-52; **22**:392; **40**:387
"A Sky in Childhood" (Jennings) **131**:233
The Sky Is Free (Clark) **12**:131-32
"The Sky is Gray" (Gaines) **86**:178
"Sky Line" (Taylor) **37**:407
Sky Man on the Totem Pole? (Harris) **12**:263-67
"Sky of Grasses" (Young) **82**:411
Sky Stones (Neruda) **28**:313-14
"The Sky, the Stars, the Wilderness" (Bass) **143**:21
The Sky, the Stars, the Wilderness (Bass) **143**:17-19, 21
"Sky Valley Rider" (Wright) **6**:581
"Skybird" (Diamond) **30**:111
Skye Cameron (Whitney) **42**:432
Skyfall (Harrison) **42**:203-06
"Skylarks" (Hughes) **14**:271; **119**:271
"Skylight" (Mosley) **43**:317
"Skylight" (Muske) **90**:312
"Skylight" (Pastan) **27**:368
Skylight (Hare) **136**:276-77, 284-88
Skylight (Muske) **90**:309, 312-13
"Skylight One" (Aiken) **52**:26
Skylight One: Fifteen Poems (Aiken) **52**:26
"Skylights" (Gallagher) **63**:118
"Skyscape" (Oates) **33**:294
Skyscraper (Clarke) **16**:215
"The Skyscraper Loves Night" (Sandburg) **35**:341
"Skywriting" (Harrison) **43**:179
"Slabs of the Sunburnt West" (Sandburg) **35**:343
Slabs of the Sunburnt West (Sandburg) **15**:466; **35**:342-43, 352
"Slack" (Hooker) **43**:197
Slag (Hare) **29**:211, 213; **58**:233; **136**:248, 259-261, 263, 284, 286
"Slam, Dunk, & Hook" (Komunyakaa) **94**:237
The Slant Door (Szirtes) **46**:390-92, 394
Slap Shot (Hill) **26**:205-07
Slapstick; or, Lonesome No More! (Vonnegut) **8**:532-34; **12**:614, 618-20, 625-26, 628-29; **22**:446; **40**:441-42, 444-46; **111**:360, 368
Slapstick Tragedy (Williams)
See *The Gnädiges Fräulein*
"Slash Burning on Silver Star" (Lane) **25**:285
"Slate Mine" (Clarke) **61**:84
Slats Grobnik and Some Other Friends (Royko) **109**:404
"Slattery's Sago Saga; or, From Under the Ground to the Top of the Trees" (O'Brien) **7**:270; **10**:362
"The Slaughterer" (Singer) **3**:458
"The Slaughterer's Testimony" (Rothenberg) **57**:374
Slaughterhouse (Mrozek) **13**:399
Slaughterhouse-Five (Hill) **26**:198-201, 208, 211
Slaughterhouse-Five; or, The Children's Crusade: A Duty-Dance with Death (Vonnegut) **1**:347; **2**:451-53, 455-56; **3**:495-506; **4**:560, 562-64, 566-67, 569; **5**:465-70; **8**:529-32, 534-35; **12**:602-05, 607-11, 613-15, 617, 619, 623-24, 626-27, 629; **60**:416-41; **111**:351, 355, 358-59, 362-64, 366, 368-72
"Slave" (Phillips) **15**:419, 421
"Slave" (Simon) **26**:409-10
The Slave (Baraka) **1**:163; **2**:35; **3**:35-6; **5**:44-5; **14**:43-4; **33**:54, 57, 59-60; **115**:10-1, 33, 35
The Slave (Singer)
See *Der Knekht*
The Slave Dancer (Fox) **121**:198, 200-01, 206, 231-32, 234
The Slave Girl (Emecheta) **14**:159; **48**:97, 99, 10; **128**:54, 57-9, 61-2, 65, 67-8, 74-5, 79
The Slave of MS.H.6: (Ghosh) **153**:98, 103-04, 106
"Slave Quarters" (Dickey) **2**:115; **15**:174
Slave Ship: A Historical Pageant (Baraka) **14**:48-9; **33**:60; **115**:28, 34-5
Slave Song (Dabydeen) **34**:147-50
Slave Trade (Gold) **14**:208-09; **152**:138
Slavery: From the Rise of Western Civilization to the Renaissance (Meltzer) **26**:300-01
Slavery, Volume II: From the Renaissance to Today (Meltzer) **26**:301
"Slaves and Masters" (Brink) **36**:68
"The Slaves in New York" (Janowitz) **43**:211-12; **145**:332
Slaves of New York (Janowitz) **43**:210-12; **145**:323-27, 329, 332-35, 340-44, 346
Slaves of Sleep (Hubbard) **43**:207
The Slaves of Solitude (Hamilton) **51**:189-91, 193-95, 197-98
Slaves of Spiegel: A Magic Moscow Story (Pinkwater) **35**:319
"Slaves on the Block" (Hughes) **108**:328

"Slave-Woman's Song" (Dabydeen) **34**:149
Slavík zpívášpatně (Seifert) **34**:256, 260; **44**:424; **93**:305, 318, 333, 340-41
Slavnosti sněženek (Hrabal) **67**:121
"Slavnostní den" (Seifert) **44**:424
Slayground (Westlake) **33**:437
"Slaying the Dream: The Black Family and the Crisis of Capitalism" (Davis) **77**:128
Slayride (Francis) **42**:148, 154, 156-57
"The Sledding Party" (Millhauser) **54**:324-27
Śledztwo (Lem) **149**:207
Sleek for the Long Flight: New Poems (Matthews) **40**:319
"Sleep" (Murakami) **150**:38, 51, 55-7, 61-2
"Sleep" (Slessor) **14**:492-93
"The Sleep" (Strand) **71**:285
Sleep (Gelber) **14**:193
Sleep (Warhol) **20**:414-15, 417, 421
Sleep and Dreams (Silverstein and Silverstein) **17**:454
Sleep and His Brother (Dickinson) **12**:170-71; **35**:131, 133
Sleep Has His House (Kavan)
See *The House of Sleep*
"Sleep in the Majave Desert" (Plath) **111**:200-01
"Sleep Is the Silence Darkness Takes" (Lane) **25**:288
Sleep It Off, Lady (Rhys) **14**:446-47; **19**:390; **124**:342-44
"Sleep like a Hammer" (Ai) **14**:8; **69**:7
A Sleep of Prisoners (Fry) **2**:143-44; **10**:200, 202
The Sleep of Reason (Buero Vallejo)
See *El sueño de la razón*
The Sleep of Reason (Snow) **4**:501-02; **19**:427-28
The Sleep of the Great Hypnotist: The Life and Death and Life after Death of a Modern Magician (Redgrove) **41**:356
"Sleep of the Valiant" (Elytis) **49**:107; **100**:175
"Sleep Tight" (Purdy) **52**:350
Sleep Two, Three, Four! A Political Thriller (Neufeld) **17**:309
Sleep Watch (Tillinghast) **29**:414-15, 417
"The Sleeper" (Hope) **51**:214
"The Sleeper" (Moss) **45**:287
Sleeper (Allen) **16**:4-6, 9, 15; **52**:38-9
"The Sleeper Wakes" (Fauset) **54**:183-84, 186-87
"Sleepers" (Honig) **33**:211
The Sleepers (Tate) **25**:427
Sleepers Awake (Patchen) **18**:392
Sleepers in Moon-Crowned Valleys (Purdy) **2**:350; **10**:424
"Sleepers Joining Hands" (Bly) **38**:52, 57; **128**:30, 35
Sleepers Joining Hands (Bly) **2**:66; **10**:55-9, 61-2; **15**:63, 65-6; **128**:17, 21-22, 28, 30, 43
The Sleepers of Roraima (Harris) **25**:217
"Sleeping Beauty" (Broumas) **73**:3, 13
"Sleeping Beauty" (Ferré)
See "La bella durmiente"
"The Sleeping Beauty" (Sitwell) **9**:494-95
The Sleeping Beauty (Carruth) **84**:118-21, 123, 128-31, 136
Sleeping Beauty (Macdonald) **3**:308-09; **14**:328, 332, 335-36; **41**:270
The Sleeping Beauty (Sitwell) **67**:312, 317-18, 324, 334
The Sleeping Beauty (Taylor) **29**:407, 411-12
"The Sleeping Beauty Syndrome: The New Agony of Single Men" (Wasserstein) **90**:432
The Sleeping Car Murders (Japrisot)
See *Compartiment tueurs*
"Sleeping Compartment" (MacCaig) **36**:283
Sleeping Dog (Gray) **36**:200
Sleeping Dogs Lie (Gloag) **40**:210
"The Sleeping Fury" (Bogan) **39**:388, 390, 393, 395-96; **46**:80-1, 84; **93**:60-1, 67-8, 81, 85, 87-90
The Sleeping Fury (Bogan) **46**:79-81, 83, 89-90; **93**:105
The Sleeping Gypsy and Other Poems (Garrett) **3**:192; **51**:141-42, 145
"Sleeping in a Jar" (Zappa) **17**:586
"Sleeping in the Forest" (Oliver) **98**:267, 269, 271
"Sleeping in the Jon-Boat" (Bottoms) **53**:32
Sleeping in the Sun (Bioy Casares)
See *Dormir al sol*
Sleeping in the Woods (Wagoner) **5**:475; **15**:558
A Sleeping Life (Rendell) **28**:386-87; **48**:320
"Sleeping like Dogs" (Calvino)
See "Si dorme come cani"
"The Sleeping Lord" (Jones) **7**:191; **42**:240
The Sleeping Lord and Other Fragments (Jones) **4**:260, 262; **7**:187-89, 191; **13**:311; **42**:238, 242, 246-49
Sleeping Murder (Christie) **8**:142; **12**:121
"Sleeping on the Ceiling" (Bishop) **9**:97
"Sleeping on the Wing" (O'Hara) **78**:346
"Sleeping Out at Easter" (Dickey) **109**:265
"Sleeping Overnight on the Shore" (Swenson) **14**:518
The Sleeping Partner (Graham) **23**:192
"Sleeping Standing Up" (Bishop) **32**:34
"The Sleeping Trees" (Shapcott) **38**:400, 403
"Sleeping with Cats" (Piercy) **128**:231
"Sleeping with One Eye Open" (Strand) **71**:282-83
Sleeping With One Eye Open (Strand) **18**:514-16; **41**:436; **71**:278, 281-82, 284,
"Sleeping with the Television On" (Joel) **26**:220-22
"Sleeping with Women" (Koch) **44**:243, 251
"Sleeping with You" (Updike) **43**:435
"Sleepless at Crown Point" (Wilbur) **14**:580; **110**:383
"Sleepless Atlantic Boy" (Schwartz) **10**:465
Sleepless Days (Becker)
See *Schlaflose Tage*
"Sleepless Night" (Damas)
See "Nuit blanche"
"Sleepless Night" (Davies) **21**:102
Sleepless Nights (Hardwick) **13**:265-66
Sleepless Nights in the Procrustean Bed (Ellison) **139**:115, 129
"Sleep's Dark and Silent Gate" (Browne) **21**:39
"Sleeps Six" (Raphael) **14**:439
Sleeps Six, and Other Stories (Raphael) **14**:438
"A Sleepwalker" (Moravia) **7**:244
Sleepwalker (Davies) **21**:101, 104
"Sleepwalkers" (Le Guin) **136**:361
The Sleepwalkers (Ezekiel) **61**:97-9
The Sleepwalkers: A History of Man's Changing Vision of the Universe (Koestler) **33**:235
"Sleepwalking Solo" (Dybek) **114**:62
"Sleepy-Heads" (Sandburg) **35**:352
"Sleet" (MacCaig) **36**:283
Sleuth (Shaffer) **19**:413-15
"A Slice of Wedding Cake" (Graves) **45**:173
Slick But Not Streamlined: Poems and Short Pieces (Betjeman) **6**:68; **34**:305; **43**:32
"Slick Gonna Learn" (Ellison) **114**:93
Slide Rule (Shute) **30**:372
"The Slides" (Rich) **73**:330
Slides (Plante) **23**:342-44
"Slides from Our Recent European Trip" (Piercy) **62**:377
"Slides of Verona" (Wright) **6**:580
Sliding (Norris) **14**:388
Slight Abrasions (Vizenor) **103**:296
A Slight Ache (Pinter) **6**:408, 413, 420; **11**:437-38, 440-41; **15**:422; **27**:385-86, 393; **58**:373-74, 384; **73**:247, 251, 279
"A Slight Disorder" (Keates) **34**:201-03
"A slight relax of air where cold was" (Larkin) **64**:258
The Slightest Distance (Bromell) **5**:74
"Slightly Higher in Canada" (Grayson) **38**:212
The Slightly Irregular Fire Engine: Or; The Hithering Thithering Djinn (Barthelme) **59**:246
"Sligo and Mayo" (MacNeice) **53**:237
"Slim Greer" (Brown) **59**:262, 265-66
"Slim Hears 'The Call'" (Brown) **59**:262
"Slim in Atlanta" (Brown) **59**:266
"Slim in Hell" (Brown) **59**:266
"Slim Slow Slider" (Morrison) **21**:236
Slinger (Dorn) **10**:156-57, 161
"Slip Kid" (Townshend) **17**:536
"Slip, Slidin' Away" (Simon) **17**:467
"Slipfoot and How He Nearly Always Never Gets What He Goes After" (Sandburg) **15**:468
Slippage (Ellison) **139**:144
"Slippery Ice in New York" (Yevtushenko) **26**:464
A Slipping-Down Life (Tyler) **59**:202-04, 206; **103**:236-39, 241, 244, 259, 263-64, 267
"A Slip-Up" (McGahern) **48**:271
"Sliverlick" (Avison) **97**:114
"Sloe Gin" (Heaney) **37**:165
"Sloe Whisky" (Johnston) **51**:243
Slogum House (Sandoz) **28**:400-02, 405-07
"Sloop John B." (Wilson) **12**:643, 653
"The Slope" (Wright) **53**:429
"Sloth" (Dobyns) **37**:76
"Sloth" (Pynchon) **123**:328
"Sloth Moth" (Fuller) **28**:157
"Slouching Towards Bethlehem" (Didion) **129**:60, 76, 79, 82, 89, 96, 98-100
Slouching towards Bethlehem (Didion) **3**:127-28; **8**:174-77; **14**:151, 153; **32**:149; **129**:60, 86, 89,93, 95-96, 98-99, 101
Slouching towards Kalamazoo (De Vries) **28**:111-12; **46**:137
"Slough" (Betjeman) **6**:69; **43**:33, 37, 44-5, 50
"Slovenski vecheri" (Bagryana) **10**:12
"Slovo" (Akhmadulina) **53**:12
Slow Approach of Thunder (Paustovsky) **40**:360-61
"Slow Black Dog" (McFadden) **48**:248
"A Slow Boat to China" (Murakami) **150**:
"A Slow Burn" (Weiss) **8**:546
"The Slow Classroom" (Baxter) **78**:29
A Slow Dance (Montague) **13**:392; **46**:271-74, 279
"Slow Death" (Caldwell) **60**:60
"Slow Dissolve" (Grenville) **61**:155
Slow Homecoming (Handke)
See *Slow Journey Home*
Slow Journey Home (Handke) **38**:224-25, 228-29; **134**:158
Slow Learner: Early Stories (Pynchon) **33**:338-40; **62**:431, 433, 451; **123**:284-85, 294, 296-97
"Slow Music" (Tiptree) **48**:389; **50**:357
The Slow Natives (Astley) **41**:45-6, 48
"The Slow of Despond" (Thomas) **107**:338-42
"Slow Pace of the Future" (Char) **55**:288
"The Slow Pacific Swell" (Winters) **4**:593
"Slow Sculpture" (Sturgeon) **22**:412; **39**:361, 364, 366, 368
"Slow Tango for Six Horses" (Szirtes) **46**:394-95
"Slow Train" (Dylan) **77**:186-87, 189
Slow Train Coming (Dylan) **77**:176, 186-87, 189
The Slow Train to Milan (Teran) **36**:420-22
"Slow Walker" (Gunn) **32**:214
Slowly by Thy Hand Unfurled (Linney) **51**:257-58
Slowly, Slowly I Raise the Gun (Bennett) **35**:46
Slowly, Slowly in the Wind (Highsmith) **14**:261
"Slowly./Town" (Cummings) **68**:37
Slowness (Kundera) **115**:357, 359-60
Ślub (Gombrowicz) **11**:239; **49**:122-26, 128-29
Sluchai na stantsii Krechetovka i Matrenin dvor (Solzhenitsyn) **7**:435
"Slug in Woods" (Birney) **6**:78
"Sluggishness" (Akhmadulina) **53**:15

Slumber Party Massacre (Brown) **79**:169
Slumgullion Stew (Abbey) **36**:21
"The Slump" (Updike) **23**:473
Det slutna rummet (Wahlöö) **7**:502
Sly Fox (Gelbart) **21**:127-28
"The Small" (Roethke) **3**:433
"Small Action Poem" (Tomlinson) **13**:548
"Small Animals at Night" (Hogan) **73**:149
"The Small Assassin" (Bradbury) **42**:35, 42
"Small Avalanches" (Oates) **134**:246
"Small Bear" (Dixon) **52**:98
"The Small Blue Heron" (Wright) **3**:541
A Small Book of Poems (Laughlin) **49**:221
A Small Boy and Others (Baldwin) **13**:48
"Small Brother of the Sea Gulls" (Ritsos) **31**:324
Small Ceremonies (Shields) **91**:169, 176; **113**:395-401, 404-08, 410, 412-13, 424, 429, 437-38, 440, 442-45
Small Change (Truffaut)
See *L'argent de la poche*
Small Changes (Piercy) **3**:384-85; **6**:402-03; **27**:373, 378, 380; **62**:362-65, 373, 376, 381; **128**:222-27, 240, 244, 255-56, 268
Small Chronicle of Great Days (Paz)
See *Pequeña crónica de grandes días*
"Small Comment" (Sanchez) **116**:277
Small Craft Warnings (Williams) **2**:465-66; **5**:502, 504; **7**:544, 546; **8**:549; **11**:573, 575; **15**:581-82; **19**:472; **45**:450; **111**:392
A Small Desperation (Abse) **29**:16
"Small Dirge" (Redgrove) **41**:348
"Small Elegy" (Ciardi) **44**:382
Small Faces (Soto) **80**:284-85
"The Small Family" (Kelman) **58**:298
A Small Family Business (Ayckbourn) **74**:16-17, 19-20, 22, 24, 27-9, 31, 34-5
"Small Frogs Killed on a Highway" (Wright) **5**:520
Small g: A Summer Idyll (Highsmith) **102**:217-19, 221
"Small Game" (Levine) **14**:317
"Small Garden near a Field" (Gallagher) **63**:125-26
"A Small Girl Swinging" (Szirtes) **46**:395
"A Small, Good Thing" (Carver) **36**:101-04; **53**:63, 65; **126**:105, 107, 109-10, 112, 114, 125-26, 128, 130-33, 137-38, 141-42, 152-55, 157, 159-60, 163-64, 166-69, 171, 182-83
"Small Green Sea" (Elytis) **100**:173
Small Heroics (Richards) **59**:187
The Small Hours (Kaufman) **38**:266
Small Is Beautiful: Economics As If People Mattered (Schumacher) **80**:261-66, 268, 272-74
"Small Is My Cinema, Deep Is My Doze" (Perelman) **23**:336
"Small Island Republics" (Apple) **33**:21
"The Small Lady" (O'Faolain) **70**:315
"Small Memoriam for Myself" (Kaufman) **49**:205
"Small Ode to a Black Cuban Boxer" (Guillén)
See "La Pequeña oda a un negro boxeador cubano"
"A Small Personal Voice" (Lessing) **94**:252, 256, 287, 293
A Small Personal Voice: Essays, Reviews, Interviews (Lessing) **1**:175; **6**:296, 299; **22**:280
"Small Philosophical Poem" (Stevenson) **33**:382
"A Small Piece of Blue" (Levine) **54**:300
A Small Place (Kincaid) **68**:206-07, 209, 217; **137**:136-37, 140, 149-51, 153, 161-62, 164-65, 167-69, 173, 175, 188, 199-200, 202
"The Small Rain" (Pynchon) **33**:332-33, 338-40; **62**:431
Small Rain (Delbanco) **6**:130
The Small Rain (L'Engle) **12**:344
"The Small Room" (Fisher) **25**:158
The Small Room (Sarton) **4**:471; **49**:322; **91**:245
"A Small Room in Qingyün Lane" (Ding Ling) **68**:57
"Small Suite in Red Major" (Ritsos) **31**:332
"A Small Summit" (Ezekiel) **61**:107
"Small Tactics" (Atwood) **25**:67
A Small Town (Hearon) **63**:165-67
Small Town (Wilson) **32**:448-49
"Small Town Affair" (Arreola) **147**:5
A Small Town in Germany (le Carré) **5**:232-34
"A Small Variation" (Paz) **65**:201
The Small War of Sergeant Donkey (Daly) **17**:91
"Small White House" (Warren) **8**:538
"Small World" (Gotlieb) **18**:191
"Small World" (Sondheim) **30**:377
Small World (Lodge) **36**:277-78; **141**:329, 335-37, 339, 341, 343, 345, 348-49, 352, 354, 358-59, 361-62, 364-67, 369-71
The Smaller Sky (Wain) **46**:416-19
"The Smallest Part" (Gold) **42**:197; **152**:120
"The Smallest Woman in the World" (Lispector) **43**:269
"Smart" (Robison) **42**:342-43
"A Smart Cookie" (Cisneros) **118**:176-77, 186, 209, 216-17
A Smart Cunt (Welsh) **144**:316-17, 319, 324, 326, 336, 342, 344
Smarter and Smoother (Daly) **17**:88
The Smartest Man in Ireland (Hunter) **21**:155-56
"The Smartest Woman in America" (Colwin) **5**:108
Smash (Kanin) **22**:233
"The Smatterers" (Solzhenitsyn) **78**:403
"The Smell" (Clarke) **53**:96
"Smell" (Peacock) **60**:294
"The Smell of Death and Flowers" (Gordimer) **33**:178-79; **123**:116
"The Smell of Gasoline Ascends in My Nose" (Amichai)
See "Reah habenzin 'oleh be'api"
The Smell of Hay (Bassani) **9**:77
"Smelling the Best" (Elytis) **100**:171, 176
"Smerdyakov with a Guitar" (Belitt) **22**:52
Směsné lásky (Kundera) **4**:276-78; **9**:320; **19**:267, 269-70; **32**:259-60, 266; **68**:232, 234, 239-42, 244,250, 254, 266; **115**:307-08, 322, 346, 350; **135**:212
Śmieszny staruszek (Rozewicz) **139**:231, 240, 278
"The Smile" (Bradbury) **98**:109
"The Smile" (Finch) **18**:154
"The Smile" (Hughes) **2**:203
"The Smile" (Morgan) **23**:297
Smile (Nyro) **17**:317-19
"Smile a Beast-Smile" (Dacey) **51**:79
"Smile Away" (McCartney) **35**:279-80, 283
"The Smile beneath the Smile" (Colwin) **84**:146, 149-50
A Smile in His Lifetime (Hansen) **38**:238, 240
A Smile in the Mind's Eye (Durrell) **27**:94-5
"The Smile of a Turtle" (DeMarinis) **54**:99
The Smile of the Lamb (Grossman) **67**:73-6
"The Smile of Winter" (Carter) **5**:101-03
"Smile Please" (Abse) **29**:20
Smile Please: An Unfinished Autobiography (Rhys) **19**:391-95; **51**:366-67, 370-71; **124**:341-43, 346-47, 371-72
"The Smile Was" (Abse) **29**:18
"Smilers" (Johnston) **51**:240
Smiles of a Summer Night (Bergman)
See *Sommarnattens leende*
Smiles on Washington Square (Federman) **47**:130, 132
Smiley Smile (Wilson) **12**:641-43, 645, 649-50, 652
Smiley's People (le Carré) **15**:324-26; **28**:228-29, 231
Smilla's Sense of Snow (Hoeg) **95**:103-19
Smith (Garfield) **12**:217-18, 224-25, 227-32, 234-36, 239
Smith (Maugham) **15**:366
Smith of Wooton Major (Tolkien) **2**:434; **12**:570, 574
The Smithsonian Institution (Vidal) **142**:323, 325-27, 331, 333
"Smithy" (Duerrenmatt) **102**:61-2
"SMLE" (Murray) **40**:336
Smog (Calvino)
See *La nuvola di smog*
"Smoke" (Bissoondath) **120**:14, 19
"Smoke" (Chabon) **149**:3-4
"Smoke" (Faulkner) **3**:157
"Smoke" (Hoffman) **141**:270, 280, 288
"Smoke" (Robison) **42**:339
"Smoke" (Ryan) **65**:209
Smoke (Auster) **131**:32
Smoke, and Other Early Stories (Barnes) **29**:32
"Smoke and Steel" (Sandburg) **10**:450
Smoke Ghost (Leiber) **25**:303
Smoke on the Ground (Delibes) **8**:169
"Smoke over the Prairie" (Richter) **30**:307
"The Smoke Shop Owner's Daughter" (Garrigue) **8**:240
Smoke Signals (Alexie) **154**:30, 40-5
"Smokers" (Wolff) **64**:448-49
Smokescreen (Francis) **2**:142-43; **42**:148, 154, 156-57; **102**:156, 158
"Smokey" (Kristofferson) **26**:267
Smokey (Robinson) **21**:344
Smokey Robinson and the Miracles, 1957-1972 (Robinson) **21**:344
"Smokey the Bear Sutra" (Snyder) **120**:347-48
Smokey's Family Robinson (Robinson) **21**:347
Smokin' (Robinson) **21**:348
"Smokin' O.P.'s" (Seger) **35**:378-79
The Smoking Mountain: Stories of Postwar Germany (Boyle) **19**:64; **58**:64, 66, 74; **121**:38
"Smoky the Bear Bodhisattva" (Rexroth) **112**:364
"Smooth Gnarled Crape Myrtle" (Moore) **13**:396
"Smothered by the World" (Bly) **10**:57; **128**:5
"Smudging" (Wakoski) **7**:505
Smudging (Wakoski) **2**:459; **4**:572-73
Smug Minority (Berton) **104**:44, 47
"The Smuggler" (Singer) **69**:314
A Smuggler's Bible (McElroy) **47**:236-39, 241-42, 244
"The Smugglers of Lost Souls' Rock" (Gardner) **8**:234-36
Smultronstället (Bergman) **16**:47-50, 52-5, 59-62, 64-5, 69, 73-4, 79; **72**:31-7, 39-41, 52
"The Smurfette Principle" (Pollitt) **122**:217-18
"Smut-Hunting in Pretoria" (Fussell) **74**:124
"The Snail on the Slope" (Strugatskii and Strugatskii) **27**:432, 434, 437
"Snail Pie" (Still) **49**:366
"The Snail Watcher" (Highsmith) **102**:185, 205
"Snails" (Levine) **118**:305
"Snails" (Oliver) **98**:303
The Snail-Watcher, and Other Stories (Highsmith) **2**:194
"The Snake" (Abse) **29**:20
"The Snake" (Berry) **4**:59
"The Snake" (Steinbeck) **13**:529
"Snake Eyes" (Baraka) **5**:45
The Snake Has All the Lines (Kerr) **22**:256
The Snake Pit (Brand) **7**:29
"Snakecharmer" (Plath) **9**:432-33; **111**:201
"Snakes" (Mahapatra) **33**:281
"The Snakes" (Oliver) **34**:249
Snakes (Young) **19**:477-79
Snakes and Ladders (Bogarde) **19**:42
"Snakes in the Winter" (Oliver) **19**:362
"The Snakes of September" (Kunitz) **148**:124-25, 136-381
"Snake's Shoes" (Beattie) **8**:57
"The Snake-Song" (Narayan) **28**:303
"Snap Snap" (Barthelme) **6**:29
The Snapper (Doyle) **81**:156, 158-61
"Snapping the Fringe" (Alexie) **154**:13, 27
"Snapshot" (Fuller) **62**:185

"A Snapshot of the Auxiliary" (Hugo) **6**:245
"Snapshots" (Elytis) **100**:171, 179, 189
Snapshots (Robbe-Grillet)
See *Instantanées*
"Snapshots of a Daughter-in-Law" (Rich) **7**:366, 371; **11**:477-78; **18**:445, 447; **36**:366, 372-73, 375, 379; **76**:210; **125**:322, 331
Snapshots of a Daughter-in-Law: Poems, 1954-1962 (Rich) **6**:457-58; **7**:365, 368-69, 371-72; **11**:476-77; **18**:446; **36**:366, 371-73, 375; **73**:314, 324-25, 332; **76**:209; **125**:337
The Snare (Spencer) **22**:402-03, 405
The Snare of the Hunter (MacInnes) **27**:282; **39**:351
"A Snark in the Night" (Benford) **52**:61
The Snarkout Boys and the Avocado of Death (Pinkwater) **35**:318-20
The Snarkout Boys and the Baconburg Horror (Pinkwater) **35**:320-21
The Snarling Citizen (Ehrenreich) **110**:184-85
Sneaky People (Berger) **5**:60-1; **8**:83; **11**:47; **18**:58; **38**:39-41
"The Sneering" (Campbell) **42**:89
"The Sniper" (Sillitoe) **57**:391, 395
Snipe's Castle (Mathias) **45**:236-37
Snoopy and the Red Baron (Schulz) **12**:527
"Snoopy Come Home" Movie Book (Schulz) **12**:529
The Snoopy Festival (Schulz) **12**:531
"Snoring in New York—An Elegy" (Denby) **48**:84
"The Snow" (Amichai) **116**:105
"Snow" (Avison) **97**:99-100, 102-04, 116, 121-22, 124, 126, 128-36
"Snow" (Baxter) **78**:25
"Snow" (Beattie) **63**:14, 16-18; **146**:51, 73
"Snow" (Butler) **81**:127
"Snow" (Dobyns) **37**:78
"Snow" (Frost) **26**:112
"The Snow" (Hall) **37**:143
"Snow" (Kawabata) **107**:108
"Snow" (Levine) **118**:301
"Snow" (MacNeice) **4**:316
"Snow" (Mowat) **26**:347
"Snow" (Phillips) **15**:421
"The Snow" (Quasimodo) **10**:428
"Snow" (Wright) **146**:357, 374
Snow (Pa Chin) **18**:373
"Snow Angel" (Vaughn) **62**:456
"Snow at Roblin Lake" (Purdy) **14**:434
The Snow Ball (Brophy) **6**:99-100; **29**:92-4, 97-8; **105**:8, 10, 14, 29-30, 38
The Snow Ball (Gurney) **50**:180
"The Snow Child" (Carter) **41**:118
Snow Country (Kawabata)
See *Yukiguni*
"Snow Country Weavers" (Welch) **14**:558
"The Snow Curlew" (Watkins) **43**:450, 454
"Snow Door" (Moure) **88**:223-24
"Snow Drops" (Glück) **81**:173
Snow Falling on Cedars (Guterson) **91**:103-08
"Snow in New York" (Swenson) **14**:522
"Snow in San Anselmo" (Morrison) **21**:234-35
"Snow in Tokyo: A Japanese Poem" (Yevtushenko) **126**:397
"The Snow King" (Dove) **81**:137
"The Snow Lamp" (Hayden) **37**:157-59
The Snow Leopard (Matthiessen) **11**:358-61; **32**:290-91; **64**:308-11, 316-17, 320, 325-27
The Snow Leopard (West) **14**:568; **96**:383
"Snow Leopards at the Denver Zoo" (Matthews) **40**:320
"Snow Line" (Berryman) **25**:96
"Snow Log" (Ammons) **25**:42
"Snow Moon--Black Bear Gives Birth" (Oliver) **98**:265
Snow on Snow (Stanton) **9**:507-08
Snow on the Mountain (Clarke) **61**:73-4
"Snow out of Season" (Warren) **39**:262
"The Snow Party" (Mahon) **27**:288-89, 292
The Snow Party (Mahon) **27**:287-91
The Snow Pasture (Newby) **2**:311
"Snow People" (Blaise) **29**:73, 75
The Snow Poems (Ammons) **9**:30-1; **25**:41-3, 45; **57**:58-9; **108**:10-3, 24, 27-8, 35, 37, 55, 58
The Snow Queen (Vinge) **30**:410-16
"Snow Signs" (Tomlinson) **45**:400-01, 403
"Snow Smoking as the Fields Boil" (Hughes) **119**:271
"Snow Upon Paris" (Senghor)
See "Neige sur Paris"
The Snow Walker (Mowat) **26**:340-41, 344-45, 347
The Snow Was Black (Simenon)
See *La neige était sale*
"Snow White" (Broumas) **73**:5
"Snow White" (Sexton) **53**:314
Snow White (Barthelme) **1**:18; **2**:39-42; **5**:53-7; **6**:29-31; **8**:49-50; **13**:54-5, 58, 62; **23**:44-6, 48, 50; **46**:38-9, 43, 45; **59**:247-49; **115**:53, 55, 57-9, 64-5, 68-9, 71-4, 76-9, 81, 86, 94, 99
"Snowball" (Janowitz) **43**:212; **145**:325
"A Snowball in Hell" (Ashbery) **77**:65
"Snowbanks North of the House" (Bly) **128**:44-45
"Snowbed" (Celan)
See "Schneebett"
"Snowdrift" (Scott) **22**:373
Snowdrop Festivities (Hrabal)
See *Slavnosti sněženek*
"Snowfall" (Gunn) **32**:211
"The Snowfall" (Justice) **102**:269
"Snowfall" (Merwin) **18**:332
"Snowfall" (Oates) **33**:294
"Snowfall" (Strand) **41**:432
"Snowgoose" (Allen) **84**:4
"Snowing in Greenwich Village" (Updike) **13**:563
The Snowless Time (Haavikko)
See *Lumeton aika*
"The Snowman on the Moor" (Plath) **111**:165, 202
"Snowman, Snowman" (Frame) **66**:144; **96**:185-86, 192
Snowman, Snowman: Fables and Fantasies (Frame) **22**:143; **96**:188-89, 191
"Snowmen" (Millhauser) **54**:326-27
"Snows" (Perse)
See "Neiges"
"The Snows Are Melted, the Snows Are Gone" (Tiptree) **48**:385
"The Snows of Kilimanjaro" (Hemingway) **3**:234; **6**:226, 229-31; **8**:283; **10**:266; **13**:271, 277; **19**:212-13, 219; **30**:179, 183; **34**:478; **39**:430; **41**:197, 203, 206; **50**:427, 431; **61**:203; **80**:121, 150
"Snowshoeing Back to Camp in Gloaming" (Warren) **18**:539
The Snowstorm (Leonov)
See *Metel*
"A Snowy Day" (Shiga) **33**:367
"Snowy Heron" (Ciardi) **40**:157-58; **44**:382
"A Snowy Night on West Forty-Ninth Street" (Brennan) **5**:73
"Snuff" (Welsh) **144**:316
So All Their Praises (MacLennan) **92**:306, 308
"So Bad" (McCartney) **35**:292
So Big (Ferber) **18**:150; **93**:149, 156, 164, 171, 176-77, 179, 186-87
So Close to Life (Bergman)
See *Nära livet*
"So ein Rummel" (Boell) **72**:69
"So Far" (Merwin) **88**:209, 213
So Far and Yet So Near (Konwicki)
See *Jak daleko stad, jak blisko*
So Far From God (Castillo) **151**:22-4, 30, 33-5, 37, 44-6, 65-70, 72, 76-8, 83, 86-7, 91, 101-02, 104, 107-08, 110, 112, 114-17
So Far, So Good (Souster) **5**:395
"So, for the Moment, Sweet, Is Peace" (Brutus) **43**:91
"So Frost Astounds" (Warren) **13**:573
"So Glad to See You Here" (McCartney) **35**:286
So Going Around Cities: New and Selected Poems, 1958-1979 (Berrigan) **37**:45
"So I Said I Am Ezra" (Ammons) **57**:49; **108**:14
"So I Went Down to the Ancient Harbor" (Amichai) **57**:44
"So I Wrote You a Song" (Seger) **35**:379
"So Intricately Is This World Resolved" (Kunitz) **148**:74, 94
"So Little He Is" (Cummings) **15**:156
So Little Time (Marquand) **10**:329, 331
"So Lonely" (Police, The) **26**:364
So Long, and Thanks for All the Fish (Adams) **60**:2-4, 6-7
"So Long, Frank Lloyd Wright" (Simon) **17**:460-61, 465
So Long, It's Been Good to Know You (Guthrie) **35**:183-85, 189, 194
So Long on Lonely Street (Deer) **45**:119-21
So Long, See You Tomorrow (Maxwell) **19**:308-09
"So Long? Stevens" (Berryman)
See "Dream Song 219"
"'So Long' to the Moon from the Men of Apollo" (Swenson) **61**:400; **106**:327
"So Many Summers" (MacCaig) **36**:284
"So Many Things Terrify, So Many" (Cisneros)
See "Tantas Cosas Asustan, Tantas"
"So Many Worlds" (Grau) **146**:125
"So Much Things to Say" (Marley) **17**:270
"So Much Water So Close to Home" (Carver) **36**:100; **53**:64; **126**:131-35, 153
"So Not to be Mottled" (Zamora) **89**:369, 388, 390-91, 395
"So Often" (Damas)
See "Si souvent"
"So Old" (Snyder) **120**:324, 336
So Profit Disappeared from the World (Haavikko)
See *Niin katosi voitto maailmasta*
"So Speaks the Poet T. H." (Cabral de Melo Neto)
See "O poeta Thomas Hardy fala"
So the Wind Won't Blow It All Away (Brautigan) **34**:315; **42**:59-60
So This Is Depravity (Baker) **31**:28-9
"So This Is Male Sexuality" (Blount) **38**:46
"So Tired of Waiting for You" (Davies) **21**:89, 97
So ward Abend und Morgen (Boell) **27**:57; **72**:71, 74
"So Why Not a Visit..." (Thesen) **56**:419
"So You Say" (Strand) **41**:432
So, You're Getting Braces: A Guide to Orthodontics (Silverstein and Silverstein) **17**:456
"Soap" (Farrell) **66**:112, 129
"Soap" (Stern) **40**:413-14
Soap Opera (Davies) **21**:99-100
"The Soap-Pig" (Muldoon) **72**:273
Sobranie sochinenii (Yevtushenko) **126**:396
Sobranie sochnenii (Voznesensky) **57**:425
Sobre cultura femenina (Castellanos) **66**:54, 57
Sobre héroes y tumbas (Sabato) **10**:444-46; **23**:378-82
Sobre los ángeles (Alberti) **7**:7, 9
Sobrevivo (Alegria) **75**:33-4
"So-Called Sonnets" (Ewart) **46**:151
The Social Context of Modern English Literature (Bradbury) **32**:51
Social Organization of Manua (Mead) **37**:285
"Social Revolution in England" (Abse) **29**:16
"Social Science" (Louie) **70**:79-80
"Social Science Fiction" (Asimov) **92**:20
Social Studies (Lebowitz) **36**:248-50
"Social Work" (Kinsella) **138**:135
Socialism and America (Howe) **85**:138-39, 145, 150
La société de consommation (Baudrillard) **60**:14-15, 25, 33

"Society, Morality, and the Novel" (Ellison) **114**:112-13
"Society's Child" (Ian) **21**:184
Society's Child (Ian) **21**:182-84, 188
"Sociodowser" (Vizenor) **103**:293, 297-98
Sociologie d'une révolution (Fanon)
See *L'an V de la révolution algérienne*
"Sock It to Me Santa" (Seger) **35**:381
"Socks" (Hood) **28**:193
Les socles (Tremblay) **29**:426
"The Sod of Battlefields" (Davidson) **13**:169
"Sodomy" (Ragni and Rado) **17**:385
"Sofa Art" (Dickinson) **49**:102-04
"Soft and Hard" (Phillips) **28**:363
"Soft Come the Dragons" (Koontz) **78**:198
The Soft Machine (Burroughs) **2**:93; **5**:92; **15**:110-11; **22**:82-3; **42**:71, 73, 77, 79; **75**:93, 97, 102, 106; **109**:183, 185-86, 191, 194-96, 199, 207, 212, 229
"Soft Monkey" (Ellison) **139**:126
The Soft Parade (Morrison) **17**:288-89, 291-92, 295
"The Soft Psyche of Joshua Logan" (Talese) **37**:393, 403
The Soft Skin (Truffaut)
See *La peau douce*
"A Soft Spring Night in Shillington" (Updike) **139**:326, 361
Soft Targets (Poliakoff) **38**:386
"A Soft Touch" (Welsh) **144**:336
"Soft Toy" (Kinsella) **138**:111
"The Soft Voice of the Serpent" (Gordimer) **70**:178
The Soft Voice of the Serpent (Gordimer) **33**:176-79; **70**:162
"Soft Voices at Passenham" (White) **30**:451
"Soft Wood" (Lowell) **124**:298
Softcops (Churchill) **31**:90
"Softly My Soul" (Alexander) **121**:21
Sogliadatai (Nabokov) **1**:242; **2**:302; **15**:396; **64**:348
"Soho" (Morgan) **31**:273
"Soho Cinema" (Lorde) **71**:260
"The Soho Hospital for Women" (Adcock) **41**:16-17
"Soho: Saturday" (Abse) **29**:14
Soie sauvage (Broumas) **73**:8, 13-14
La soif et la faim (Ionesco) **6**:251, 253-54; **11**:292, 294; **41**:225, 227; **86**:340
"The Soil-Map" (McGuckian) **48**:277
"The Soirée of Velvel Kleinburger" (Klein) **19**:258
"Sojourn in X" (Boell)
See "Aufenthalt in X"
"Sojourner" (Dillard) **60**:75; **115**:205
"The Sojourner" (McCullers) **10**:335; **12**:413, 433
"Sol" (Tolson) **105**:262
"Sol de lluria" (Guillén) **79**:240
El sol y los MacDonald (Marqués) **96**:224-25, 228, 240
"Sola la muerte" (Neruda) **7**:257
"Solar" (Larkin) **5**:229-31; **8**:333; **18**:295-96; **33**:259-61; **64**:265, 268-69, 285
"The Solar Corona" (Swenson) **61**:397
Solar Lottery (Dick) **72**:120
"Solar System" (Wilson) **12**:652
"Solar Throat Slashed" (Césaire) **32**:113
Solaris (Lem) **8**:343-45; **15**:327-28; **40**:290, 293, 295-98, 300; **149**:112, 117-18, 132, 140, 144-45, 154, 156, 159, 161-62, 165-68, 172, 174-76, 178-79, 188-89, 191-93, 195-201, 217-19, 223-27, 230, 232, 234, 236-39, 242-43, 251, 255-56, 260, 272, 275-76, 281-85, 287-88
Solaris (Tarkovsky) **75**:370-72, 375-80, 382-85, 387, 389-90, 398, 402-03, 406-12
Soldado razo (Valdez) **84**:396, 406, 413, 415
"Soldados en Abisinia" (Guillén) **48**:158; **79**:235-37
Le soldat Dioclès (Audiberti) **38**:30
"Solde" (Damas) **84**:171-72, 176-77
"The Soldier" (Bitov) **57**:114
"Soldier" (Ellison) **139**:129
"A Soldier" (Frost) **13**:227
"Soldier" (Ignatow) **40**:258
The Soldier (Aiken) **52**:26
"Soldier Asleep" (McGinley) **14**:367
A Soldier Erect (Aldiss) **5**:14; **14**:14
"Soldier from the Wars Returning" (Brown) **48**:55
"Soldier in the Blanket" (Kotzwinkle) **35**:254
Soldier in the Rain (Goldman) **48**:124, 128
Soldier of Fortune (Gann) **23**:164
A Soldier of the Revolution (Just) **27**:226
Soldier, Soldier (Arden) **13**:28; **15**:19
"Soldiers" (Williams) **148**:314
The Soldiers (Hochhuth) **4**:231-32; **18**:251, 253
The Soldier's Art (Powell) **3**:400; **7**:345
"Soldiers Bathing" (Prince) **22**:338-39
"A Soldier's Declaration" (Sassoon) **36**:394; **130**:209, 212-13
"The Soldier's Dream" (Scannell) **49**:329-30, 332
"A Soldier's Embrace" (Gordimer) **123**:131
A Soldier's Embrace (Gordimer) **18**:188-91
"Soldier's Home" (Hemingway) **3**:242; **19**:211; **30**:181, 189-90, 192, 201-02; **50**:428
"Soldiers in Abyssinia" (Guillén)
See "Soldados en Abisinia"
Soldiers in Hiding (Wiley) **44**:118-20
"Soldier's Joy" (Wolff) **64**:450, 453-54
Soldier's Joy (Bell) **102**:4-5, 8, 11, 17, 22
The Soldiers of No Country (Ferlinghetti) **111**:63
"Soldiers of the Republic" (Parker) **68**:328, 336
Soldiers' Pay (Faulkner) **8**:214; **9**:199-201; **11**:201; **28**:140-41, 145; **52**:108, 112; **68**:127
A Soldier's Play (Fuller) **25**:181-82
"A Soldier's Son" (Boland) **40**:96, 98; **113**:122
"Soldiers Surround" (Ignatow) **40**:261
"The Soldier's Wish" (Smith) **64**:388
Sold-Out (Brossard) **115**:105-06, 110-11, 155
Sole Survivor (Gee) **29**:178-79
Soledad (Paz) **19**:367
"Soledad. =f. Solitude, Loneliness, Homesickness; Lonely Retreat" (Rich) **76**:219
"Soledades of the Sun and Moon" (Hope) **51**:215, 217-18, 226
"Soleil" (Reverdy) **53**:289
Soleil Cou-Coupé (Césaire) **112**:7, 15, 29
Soleil de la conscience (Glissant) **68**:180-81, 187
Le soleil des eaux (Char) **11**:115
Soleil des loups (Mandiargues) **41**:278
Soleil noir: Dépression et melancholie (Kristeva) **77**:314, 317-19, 324-25, 327, 333; **140**:148, 151, 182, 186, 200
"Le soleil placé en abîme" (Ponge) **18**:418
Soleils (Gascar) **11**:222
"Les soleils chanteurs" (Char) **14**:127
The Solemn Communion (Arrabal)
See *La communion solonelle*
Solemn Tightrope Walking (Oe)
See *Genshuku natsunawatari*
"A Solemne Musick" (L'Heureux) **52**:272, 274
Solemnly Walking the Tightrope (Oe)
See *Genshuku natsunawatari*
Solent Shore (Hooker) **43**:197-201
"Solent Winter" (Hooker) **43**:197
"Soles occidere et redire poussunt" (Huxley) **5**:192; **11**:284
Los soles truncos (Marqués) **96**:224, 226-28, 240-41, 249-50, 252
"Solfeggietto" (Rich) **73**:330
"Solid Geometry" (McEwan) **13**:370
The Solid Gold Cadillac (Kaufman) **38**:267
The Solid Gold Kid (Mazer) **26**:291-92
The Solid Mandala (White) **3**:521-23; **4**:583-86; **5**:485-88; **7**:529, 532; **65**:275-77, 279-82; **69**:401, 403-06, 408, 410, 412
"Solid Rock" (Dylan) **77**:185-89, 191
Solidão solitude (Dourado) **23**:150
"Soliloquies" (Williams) **148**:348
Soliloquies of a Chalk Giant (Hooker) **43**:197-99, 201
"Soliloquio del individuo" (Parra) **102**:344
"Soliloquy" (Jeffers) **54**:237, 242
"Soliloquy" (Prokosch) **48**:310
"Soliloquy of the Spanish Cloister" (Howard) **7**:168
"Soliloquy on a Southern Strand" (Montague) **46**:265-66
"Solipsism and Theology" (Warren) **6**:558
"The Solipsist" (Cunningham) **31**:100
"Solitaire" (Aleixandre)
See "El solitario"
"Solitaire" (Garrett) **3**:192; **51**:144
Solitaire (Anderson) **23**:33
Le solitaire (Ionesco) **6**:252, 256-57; **11**:290, 292-94; **86**:332
Solitaire/Double Solitaire (Anderson) **23**:33
The Solitaries (Walker) **13**:565
"El solitario" (Aleixandre) **9**:13
El Solitario (Cela) **122**:52, 54
"Solitary" (Boland) **113**:60-1
"Solitary" (Wideman) **36**:455; **122**:289, 320, 322, 349
A Solitary Blue (Voigt) **30**:420
"Solitary Confinement" (Kennedy) **42**:255
"The Solitary Daffodil" (Richards) **14**:455
"A Solitary Ewe" (Hood) **28**:189
"Solitary Man" (Diamond) **30**:111
"Solitary Swedish Houses" (Transtroemer)
See "Svenska hus ensligt belägna"
"Solitary Travel" (MacNeice) **4**:316
"A Solitude" (Levertov) **15**:338
"Solitude" (Transtroemer) **52**:412
"Solitude Late at Night in the Woods" (Bly) **10**:57; **128**:13
Solitudes (Vliet) **22**:441-43
Solitudes Crowded with Loneliness (Kaufman) **49**:202-03, 205
"Solja Work" (Bennett) **28**:29
Sollicitudo Rei Socialis (John Paul II) **128**:179
Solo: An American Dreamer in Europe, 1933-34 (Morris) **37**:314-16
"Solo Dance" (Phillips) **15**:419
Solo Faces (Salter) **52**:361-63, 366-68
Solo for Two Voices (Paz) **3**:377
"A Solo Song: For Doc" (McPherson) **19**:309; **77**:351-52, 364, 366-67, 369
Solomon Gursky Was Here (Richler) **70**:219-33
"Solomon's Mines" (Hill) **45**:182
Solomon's Temple (Hoffman) **5**:184-85
"Solstice" (Lorde) **71**:236
Solstice (Oates) **33**:297-98; **52**:329, 336; **108**:386, 389-90
Solstice and Other Poems (Jeffers) **54**:237
Solstices (MacNeice) **4**:318; **53**:241
Soltería (Castellanos) **66**:48
Soluble Fish (Breton)
See *Manifeste du surréalisme. Poisson soluble*
"Solus Rex" (Nabokov) **3**:354
"Solution Unsatisfactory" (Heinlein) **55**:302-03
"Solving the Riddle" (Simic) **9**:478
Solzhenitsyn: A Biography (Scammell) **34**:480-82, 484, 487, 489-92
"Somali Legend" (Jensen) **37**:192
"Somalia" (Ostriker) **132**:326
"Somber Prayer" (Berryman) **13**:82
La sombra de la sombra (Arreola) **147**:6
La sombra del ciprés es alrgada (Delibes) **18**:109, 111, 117
Sombra del paraíso (Aleixandre) **9**:11, 16; **36**:24, 26, 28, 30
Sombra e exílio (Dourado) **23**:150-51
"La sombra y su eco" (Ferré) **139**:182-83
"Sombre" (Reverdy) **53**:290
Sombrero Fallout: A Japanese Novel (Brautigan) **9**:124; **12**:73; **42**:49, 56
Some Achieve Greatness (Swinnerton) **31**:428
"Some Against Natural Selection" (Hirsch) **31**:214
Some American Feminists (Brossard) **115**:117

Some American People (Caldwell) **60**:53, 60-1, 66
Some Americans: A Personal Record (Tomlinson) **45**:395-96, 402-03, 405
Some Angry Angel: A Mid-Century Faeric Tale (Condon) **4**:107; **45**:92, 96; **100**:111-12
"Some Any" (Ammons) **57**:53
"Some Approaches to the Problem of the Shortage of Time" (Le Guin) **45**:216
"Some Are Born to Sweet Delight" (Gordimer) **70**:177, 180; **123**:129
"Some Autumn Characters" (Stafford) **29**:379
"Some Beasts" (Neruda) **1**:247
"Some Blind Alleys: A Letter" (Cioran) **64**:78, 99
"Some Blue Hills at Sundown" (Gilchrist) **143**:295
Some Business Recently Transacted in the White World (Dorn) **10**:160
Some Came Running (Jones) **1**:162; **3**:261; **10**:292; **39**:405-07, 412, 415
Some Can Whistle (McMurtry) **127**:329
some changes (Jordan) **5**:203
"Some Children of the Goddess" (Mailer) **8**:371
"Some collisions bring luck" (Piercy) **128**:229
Some Corner of an English Field (Abse) **29**:12
"Some Correspondence with Theodore Dreiser" (Farrell) **66**:138
"Some Dangers to American Writing" (Cowley) **39**:460
"Some Day I'll Find You" (Coward) **1**:65
"Some Day You'll Be Sorry" (Cozzens) **92**:201
Some Deaths in the Delta (Brown) **32**:62-3
"Some Different Meanings of the Concept of 'Difference'" (Barrett) **65**:339
Some Doves and Pythons (Elliott) **38**:178
"Some Dreamers of the Golden Dream" (Didion) **14**:153; **129**:77
"Some Dreams They Forgot" (Bishop) **32**:34
"Some Echo" (Creeley) **36**:121
"Some Elementary Comments on the Right of Freedom of Expression" (Chomsky) **132**:34
"Some Final Questions" (Webb) **18**:540
Some Follow the Sea (Felsen) **17**:120
"Some Foreign Letters" (Sexton) **15**:472; **53**:312, 321
"Some General Instructions" (Koch) **8**:323; **44**:244, 249, 251
"Some Get Wasted" (Marshall) **72**:248
Some Girls (Jagger and Richard) **17**:239-40, 242
"Some Good Things to be Said for the Iron Age" (Snyder) **120**:353
"Some Impediments to Christian Commitment" (Smith) **25**:421
Some Inner Fury (Markandaya) **38**:320-23
Some Kind of a Love Story (Miller) **47**:253
Some Kind of Grace (Jenkins) **52**:219, 225-26, 228
Some Kind of Hero (Kirkwood) **9**:320
"Some Kinda Love" (Reed) **21**:309, 311, 322
"Some Last Questions" (Merwin) **13**:385
Some Lie and Some Die (Rendell) **28**:384-85; **48**:320
Some Like It Hot (Wilder) **20**:459, 463, 465-66
"Some Like Poetry" (Szymborska)
See "Some People Like Poetry"
"Some Limitations of English" (Bunting) **47**:52
"Some Lines on the State of the Universe" (Faludy) **42**:141
"Some Love" (Ginsberg) **36**:197
"Some Marvelous Quarry" (Squires) **51**:383
"Some Memories of the Glorious Bird and an Earlier Self" (Vidal) **8**:527-28; **10**:501
Some Men Are Brothers (Enright) **31**:146, 148
Some Merry-Go-Round Music (Stolz) **12**:551
"Some Monday for Sure" (Gordimer) **10**:239; **33**:182-83
"Some Money" (Ashbery) **77**:68
"Some Mother" (Bukowski) **41**:73
"Some Mother's Son" (Davies) **21**:91
"Some Musicians Play Chamber Music for Us" (Bronk) **10**:75
"Some Natural Things" (Laughlin) **49**:224
Some Necessary Angels (Parini) **133**:288
"Some New Ruins" (Corn) **33**:116
"Some Notes on Montana" (McGuane) **127**:285
"Some Notes on Organic Form" (Levertov) **66**:242
"Some Notes on Recent American Fiction" (Bellow) **6**:58; **13**:73
"Some Notes on Silence" (Graham) **48**:151
"Some Notes on Time in Fiction" (Welty) **14**:567; **105**:378-80, 382
"Some Notions" (Arghezi)
See "Noţiunile"
"Some Novelists I Have Known" (Maugham) **67**:216
"Some Observations on Naturalism, So-Called, in Fiction" (Farrell) **66**:134-35, 137
"Some of the Forms of Jealousy" (Williams) **148**:345, 347-49, 351-52, 356, 361
"Some of These Days" (Purdy) **52**:350
"Some of Us Are Exiles from No Land" (O Hehir) **41**:322
Some of Your Blood (Sturgeon) **39**:361, 364-67
"Some Old Tires" (Ashbery) **25**:56
Some One Sweet Angel Chile (Williams) **89**:321, 324, 330, 332
Some Other Summer (Adler) **35**:13
"Some Passages of Isaiah" (Pinsky) **94**:303
"Some People" (Jordan) **114**:146, 149
"Some People Like Poetry" (Szymborska) **99**:208-10
"Some People Never Know" (McCartney) **35**:280
Some People, Places, and Things That Will Not Appear in My Next Novel (Cheever) **15**:127
"Some Poems for Max Ernst" (Bly) **15**:62
Some Prefer Nettles (Tanizaki)
See *Tade kū mushi*
"Some Quadrangles" (Swenson) **61**:403; **106**:335
"Some Real Mothers" (Delany) **141**:114
"Some Reasons Why I Tell the Stories I Tell the Way I Tell Them rather than Some Other Sort of Stories Some Other Way" (Barth) **51**:24-5
Some Recent Attacks: Essays Cultural and Political (Kelman) **86**:185
"Some Remarks on Humor" (White) **10**:531
"Some Secrets" (Stern) **40**:412
Some Soul to Keep (Cooper) **56**:71-2
"Some South American Poets" (Koch) **44**:243
"Some Sunny Day" (Beer) **58**:38
Some Sweet Day (Williams) **42**:442, 445
"Some Talk of Peace" (Blunden) **56**:30
Some Tame Gazelle (Pym) **37**:375-79; **111**:233-38, 240, 243-48, 254, 263-64, 267, 269-71, 273, 278, 283-87
"Some There Are Fearless" (Page) **18**:379
"Some Thoughts about the Line" (Simic) **68**:366; **130**:310
"Some Thoughts on Juvenile Delinquency" (Steinbeck) **21**:380
"Some Thoughts on Playwriting" (Wilder) **82**:356, 385
"Some Time with Stephen" (Kureishi) **135**:279
"Some Trees" (Ashbery) **41**:40
Some Trees (Ashbery) **2**:16-17; **4**:22-4; **9**:42-4; **13**:31, 34-5; **15**:26; **25**:49, 55, 57-8; **41**:40; **77**:42, 44, 50, 52, 58, 70; **125**:14, 31, 33, 36, 38
Some Unease and Angels (Feinstein) **36**:170
Some Versions of Pastoral (Empson) **8**:202; **19**:153-54; **33**:145, 147-48, 150; **34**:336-38, 340
"Some Wine Songs" (Hulme) **130**:66
"Some Women" (Garrett) **3**:192
"Some Words" (Ashbery) **4**:21
"Some Words" (Ballard) **137**:11, 21, 23
Some Write to the Future: Essays on Contemporary Latin American Fiction (Dorfman) **77**:153, 155
"Somebody Always Grabs the Purple" (Roth) **104**:249, 267
Somebody Else's Life (Philipson) **53**:276-77
Somebody in Boots (Algren) **4**:16; **10**:5; **33**:13
"Somebody Kept Saying Powwow" (Alexie) **154**:9
Somebody Owes Me Money (Westlake) **33**:436
"Somebody Who Cares" (McCartney) **35**:290-91
Somebody's Darling (McMurtry) **11**:371; **27**:331-33; **44**:254
"Somebody's Life" (Urdang) **47**:400
Someday (Seger) **35**:378
Someday, Maybe (Stafford) **4**:521; **7**:460-61
"Someday We're Gonna Tear Them Pillars Down" (Dodson) **79**:192
"Somehow we survive" (Brutus) **43**:90
Someone (Pinget) **37**:361
Someone Else (Tindall) **7**:473-74
Someone Else Is Still Someone (Pomerance) **13**:444
"Someone Has Disturbed the Roses" (García Márquez)
See "Alguien desordena estas rosas"
"Someone in a Tree" (Sondheim) **30**:388, 390, 397, 400, 402; **147**:258
"Someone in the Review Board" (Carroll) **38**:103
"Someone Is Beating a Woman" (Voznesensky) **57**:414
"Someone Is Probably Dead" (Bell) **31**:51
Someone Just Like You (Yurick) **6**:583-84
Someone Like You (Dahl) **79**:175, 177
Someone to Love (Mazer) **26**:296
"Someone Walking Around" (Cortázar)
See "Alguien que anda por ahí"
"Someone Writes to the Future: Meditations on Hope and Violence in García Márquez" (Dorfman) **77**:156
"Someone You Have Seen Before" (Ashbery) **77**:63-4
"Somersault" (MacDiarmid) **19**:286
Somersault (Konwicki)
See *Salto*
"Somerville" (Hill) **113**:281, 291, 312
"Something" (Oliver) **34**:247, 249; **98**:257
Something about a Death, Something about a Fire (Straub) **107**:305
Something about a Soldier (Harris) **19**:200, 203
"Something about a Viet Cong Flag" (Bukowski) **108**:87
"Something about England" (Clash) **30**:48
"Something about Him" (Williams) **45**:454
"Something about It" (Hollander) **8**:300
"Something Else" (Akhmadulina)
See "Drugoe"
Something Else (Davies) **21**:90, 105
"Something, Everything, Anything, Nothing" (O'Faolain) **14**:406
"Something for the Time Being" (Gordimer) **123**:114, 131
Something Going (Lipsyte) **21**:210
Something Happened (Heller) **5**:173-83; **8**:278-80; **11**:268; **36**:225-28, 230; **63**:203-04
"Something Happened to Me Yesterday" (Jagger and Richard) **17**:231, 238
Something I'll Tell You Tuesday (Guare) **29**:204
Something in Common, and Other Stories (Hughes) **10**:281
Something in Disguise (Howard) **29**:245-46
"Something in the Night" (Springsteen) **17**:483
"Something in the Water" (Prince) **35**:328
Something in the Wind (Smith) **25**:406-07, 410; **73**:342, 355
"Something Is in the Air" (Strand) **18**:516
"Something I've Been Meaning to Tell You" (Munro) **95**:286
Something I've Been Meaning to Tell You (Munro) **6**:341-42; **10**:356-57; **19**:344;

50:210; **95**:284, 293, 297, 301, 304, 313, 320, 322, 325
Something Left to Lose (Brancato) **35**:66, 68
"Something Like a Sonnet for Phillis Miracle Wheatley" (Jordan) **114**:145
Something Like an Autobiography (Kurosawa) **119**:339, 386, 402
"Something Missing" (L'Heureux) **52**:278
"Something Must Happen" (Boell) **39**:292
"Something Nice" (Gaitskill) **69**:199
"Something Other than Our Own" (Lane) **25**:289
"Something Out There" (Gordimer) **123**:118
Something Out There (Gordimer) **33**:183-85; **51**:157; **70**:163-66, 182; **123**:117
Something Said (Sorrentino) **40**:389-90
"Something So Right" (Simon) **17**:466
"Something Strange" (Amis) **40**:43
"Something the Cat Dragged In" (Highsmith) **42**:215
"Something There Is about You" (Dylan) **4**:150
Something to Answer For (Newby) **13**:409
Something to Be Desired (McGuane) **45**:263-65; **127**:245, 248-50, 254, 262, 269, 272-73, 280, 283, 287-88, 291, 298
"Something to Be Said for Silence" (Giovanni) **64**:191
"Something to Look Forward To" (Piercy) **62**:378
"Something to Nibble on in My Igloo" (Breytenbach) **23**:84
Something to Say: William Carlos Williams on Younger Poets (Williams) **42**:462
"Something to Tell Mother" (Orlovitz) **22**:333
"Something to Tell the Girls" (Gardam) **43**:167
"Something to Write Home About" (Ingalls) **42**:230
Something Unspoken (Williams) **11**:576
"Something Was Happening" (Hughes) **119**:270
Something Wicked This Way Comes (Bradbury) **3**:85; **10**:68-9; **42**:36, 42, 46; **98**:111, 144
"Something's Coming" (Sondheim) **30**:389, 395, 400
"Something's Going On" (Ortiz) **45**:301
Sometime in New York City/Live Jam (Lennon) **12**:372-73; **35**:264-66, 271, 273
"Sometime--Later--Not Now" (Findley) **102**:107-08
"Sometimes" (Nowlan) **15**:399
"Sometimes a Fantasy" (Joel) **26**:221
Sometimes a Great Notion (Kesey) **6**:277-78; **11**:318; **46**:224, 226; **64**:216
Sometimes a Stranger (Weber) **12**:635
"Sometimes All Over" (Coles) **46**:111
Sometimes All Over (Coles) **46**:107-11
"Sometimes, as a Child" (Broumas) **73**:2, 8
"Sometimes I Am Very Happy and Desperate" (Amichai) **116**:93
"Sometimes I Don't Mind" (Lightfoot) **26**:282
Sometimes I Live in the Country (Busch) **47**:63-5
"Sometimes . . . Injustice" (Kenny) **87**:259
"Sometimes They Come Back" (King) **113**:336
"Sometown" (Hoffman) **6**:243
"A Somewhat Static Barcarolle" (Cassity) **42**:98
Somewhere a Master: Further Hasidic Portraits and Legends (Wiesel) **37**:456-57
"Somewhere a Roscoe ..." (Perelman) **49**:258
"Somewhere above the Victim" (Yevtushenko) **26**:468
"Somewhere along the Line" (Joel) **26**:213
Somewhere among Us a Stone Is Taking Notes (Simic) **9**:480; **68**:376; **130**:311
"Somewhere Behind" (Kundera) **115**:321
"Somewhere, Belgium" (Kincaid) **43**:249
"The Somewhere Doors" (Chappell) **78**:116-17
"Somewhere Else" (Paley) **37**:339; **140**:262, 268, 277, 282
Somewhere Else (Kotlowitz) **4**:275
"Somewhere Far from This Comfort" (Coles) **46**:113
"Somewhere I Have Never Travelled, Gladly Beyond" (Cummings) **3**:117; **15**:154; **68**:44
"Somewhere in Africa" (Sexton) **123**:416-17
"Somewhere in Argentina" (Rosenblatt) **15**:447
Somewhere in the House (Daly) **52**:90
Somewhere in the Night (Moorcock) **58**:347-49, 351
"Somewhere Is Such a Kingdom" (Ransom) **2**:363; **4**:431
Somewhere Is Such a Kingdom: Poems, 1952-1971 (Hill) **8**:293-94, 296
"Somewhere, My Man" (Mahapatra) **33**:276
"Somewhere Near Phu Bai" (Komunyakaa) **94**:226, 228
"Somewhere U.S.A." (Lightfoot) **26**:280
Sommaren med Monika (Bergman) **16**:46, 60, 66
Sommarlek (Bergman) **16**:46-7, 51-2, 60, 66, 72; **72**:40-1, 62
Sommarnattens leende (Bergman) **16**:46-7, 49, 51-3, 61, 64, 66, 69, 73, 79, 82; **72**:30-1, 40, 52, 54-5, 60-2
Somme athéologique (Bataille) See *Summa Atheologica*
Le sommeil délivré (Chedid) **47**:83-5, 88
"Sommerbericht" (Celan) **53**:77
Sommerlicher Nachtrag zu einer winterlichen Reise (Handke) **134**:179
Sommerstück (Wolf) **150**:236, 248, 250, 290, 292-94, 301, 306, 329-30
The Somnambulists (Elliott) **47**:103
"Son" (Ian) **21**:183
"The Son" (Levertov) **66**:235, 237
"The Son" (MacBeth) **5**:263
"Son" (Olds) **39**:187
"The Son" (Swift) **41**:443, 446
The Son (Berriault) **54**:4; **109**:90, 92
"Son and Heir" (Cozzens) **92**:202
"Son and Heir" (Smith) **15**:517
"Son de cloche" (Reverdy) **53**:290
El son entero (Guillén) **48**:158, 162, 164, 168; **79**:229, 240, 250
"A son for Antillian Children" (Guillén) **79**:230
"The Son From America" (Singer) **6**:509; **111**:337
Son Motifs (Guillén) See *Motivos de son*
Son nom de Venise dans Calcutta désert (Duras) **40**:178; **68**:89, 96; **100**:145
Son number 6 (Guillén) See *Son número 6*
"Son numero 6" (Guillén) **48**:162; **79**:250
Son número 6 (Guillén) **79**:231
Son of a Hundred Kings (Costain) **30**:96
Son of a Smaller Hero (Richler) **5**:371-75; **13**:485-86; **18**:455; **46**:347
"The Son of Andrés Aparicio" (Fuentes) See "El hijo de Andrés Aparicio"
"Son of Celluloid" (Barker) **52**:53-4
"The Son of Karmaria" (Valenzuela) See "El hijo de Karmaria"
"The Son of Man" (Ginzburg) **70**:280
The Son of Man (Mauriac) **56**:219
Son of Man (Potter) **86**:346; **123**:232-34, 274, 278
Son of Man (Roa Bastos) See *Hijo de hombre*
Son of Man (Silverberg) **140**:372, 379
"Son of Msippi" (Dumas) **6**:145; **62**:155
"The Son of My Skin" (Redgrove) **41**:351-52
"Son of Orange County" (Zappa) **17**:591
"The Son of Perdition" (Cozzens) **11**:125, 131; **92**:196, 198-99, 201
"Son of Satan" (Bukowski) **82**:25
The Son of Someone Famous (Kerr) **12**:297-99
Son of the Black Stallion (Farley) **17**:115
A Son of the Circus (Irving) **112**:173-74
Son of the Great Society (Buchwald) **33**:91
Son of the Morning (Oates) **11**:404; **15**:401-02; **19**:350, 354; **33**:289
Son of the Morning Star: Custer and the Little Bighorn (Connell) **45**:117-18
"Son of the Tree" (Vance) **35**:420
Son of the Valley (Tunis) **12**:596, 598
"Son of the Wolfman" (Chabon) **149**:22-4
"Son the Beatiful Ones" (Kunene) **85**:175
"Son venezolano" (Guillén) **48**:161, 164
"A Son with a Future" (Reznikoff) **9**:450
"El soñado" (Arreola) **147**:10, 14, 17
Un soñador para un pueblo (Buero Vallejo) **15**:97, 99, 101; **46**:96; **139**:10, 63-5, 67-71
Sonar Kella (Ray) **76**:356
"Sonata" (Schnackenberg) **40**:380-81
"Sonatina in Blue" (Justice) **102**:253
"Sonatina in Green" (Justice) **102**:262-63, 265
"Sonatina in Yellow" (Justice) **102**:251-53, 255, 258, 264-65
Sonatinas (Ferré) **139**:158
Sonderbare Begegnungen (Seghers) **7**:409
Sondheim: A Musical Tribute (Sondheim) **30**:385, 387
"Sondra" (Van Duyn) **116**:422, 429
"Song" (Abse) **29**:16
"Song" (Bogan) **46**:81, 86, 89
"Song" (Boland) **40**:98, 100
"Song" (Creeley) **78**:152
"Song" (Durrell) **27**:97
"Song" (Fenton) **32**:165-66
"Song" (Glück) **81**:167, 173
"Song" (H. D.) **73**:118
"Song" (Heaney) **74**:159, 163
"The Song" (Johnson) **52**:232
"Song" (Justice) **102**:269
"The Song" (Milosz) **56**:233, 247
"The Song" (Roethke) **3**:433; **19**:399; **101**:263, 332
"Song" (Sitwell) **67**:320
"Song" (Snodgrass) **18**:491; **68**:395
"Song" (Thomas) **6**:530
"Song" (Winters) **32**:467
"Song III" (Bishop) **15**:59
"Song IV" (Bishop) **15**:59
A Song, a Twilight (Coward) **29**:139-40
Song about Death (Seifert) **34**:260
"Song About Love" (Seifert) See "Píseň o lásce"
"A Song about Major Eatherly" (Wain) **11**:562
"Song against Broccoli" (Blount) **38**:47
"Song and Dance" (Livesay) **79**:349, 351
Song and Idea (Eberhart) **11**:178; **19**:143; **56**:76-8
Song and Strife (Lagerkvist) See *Sång och strid*
Song at the Year's Turning: Poems, 1942-1954 (Thomas) **6**:532; **13**:542; **48**:377, 380
"Song But Oblique to '47" (Avison) **97**:68, 71
"Song by the Sea" (Lee) **90**:182
"Song for a Birth or a Death" (Jennings) **131**:231, 238-39
Song for a Birth or a Death (Jennings) **131**:235
"Song for a Dark Girl" (Hughes) **108**:299
Song for a Dark Queen (Sutcliff) **26**:437
"Song for a Lady" (Sexton) **123**:408, 439
"Song for a Lyre" (Bogan) **4**:68; **46**:81; **93**:78, 81-3
"Song for a Phallus" (Hughes) **119**:280
"Song for a Red Night Gown" (Sexton) **123**:407
"Song for a Slight Voice" (Bogan) **4**:68; **46**:81, 83; **93**:64, 96
"Song for Adam" (Browne) **21**:34
"Song for an Engraved Invitation" (McGinley) **14**:366
Song for an Equinox (Perse) **11**:436
Song for Anninho (Jones) **131**:246, 248, 253, 296-304
"Song for Bob Dylan" (Bowie) **17**:58
"Song for Disheartened Lute" (Dickey) **28**:118
"Song for Easter" (Wright) **53**:419
"Song for Marian" (Lamming) **66**:220
"Song for My Name" (Hogan) **73**:157
"Song for Myself" (Tolson) **105**:260, 282
"A Song for New-Ark" (Giovanni) **117**:198-99

"Song for Puerto Rico" (Guillén) **79**:230
"Song for Resurrection Day" (Buckley) **57**:125
"A Song for Rising" (Bowers) **9**:121
"Song for Sharon" (Mitchell) **12**:440
"A Song for Simeon" (Eliot) **15**:217; **41**:149, 151
"A Song for Soweto" (Jordan) **114**:161
"Song for Tamar" (Amichai) **57**:36
"A Song for the Asking" (Simon) **17**:460
"Song for the Death of Averroës" (Merton) **83**:394
"Song for the Deer and Myself to Return On" (Harjo) **83**:282
"A Song for the Degrees" (Pound) **13**:461
"Song for the Last Act" (Bogan) **39**:385; **46**:87; **93**:68-9, 76, 96
"Song for the Mothers of Dead Militiamen" (Neruda)
See "Canto a las madres de los milicianos muertos"
"Song for the Rainy Season" (Bishop) **13**:89
"Song for the Swifts" (Jennings) **131**:236, 241
"Song for Thomas Nashe" (Buckley) **57**:128
"Song for War" (Rodgers) **7**:378
"A Song from Armenia" (Hill) **8**:296
"Song (from Goodbye, Spring)" (Seifert) **93**:334
Song from the Earth: American Indian Painting (Highwater) **12**:285-86
"Song from the Multitude" (Livesay) **79**:353
Song: I Want a Witness (Harper) **7**:138-39
"A Song in Passing" (Winters) **32**:468
"Song in Praise of Willy" (Grass) **49**:139
"Song in Sligo" (Garrigue) **8**:240
"A Song in the Wilderness" (Celan)
See "Ein Lied in der Wüste"
"Song of a Child" (Morgan) **31**:275
"Song of a Citizen" (Milosz) **56**:238
Song of a Goat (Clark Bekedermo) **38**:113, 115-16, 118-22, 124
"Song of a Hebrew" (Abse) **29**:16
"The Song of a Shift" (O'Casey) **88**:239
Song of a Soldier (p'Bitek) **96**:299
"The Song of Abraham in the Fire" (Shamlu) **10**:472
"Song of Advent" (Winters) **32**:468
"A Song of Degrees" (Nemerov) **36**:304
Song of Deprivation (Ezekiel) **61**:97-9
"A Song of Experience" (Amis) **40**:40, 44
"The Song of Fire" (Blaga) **75**:79
The Song of Hendele (Seifert) **93**:328
"The Song of Hugh Glass" (Neihardt) **32**:329-31, 334, 338
"A Song of Innocence" (Ellison) **114**:108, 112
"The Song of Jed Smith" (Neihardt) **32**:334, 338
Song of Jubilee (Forman) **21**:119
Song of Kali (Simmons) **44**:273-75
Song of Lawino (p'Bitek) **96**:264-72, 277-79, 281-82, 290-91, 293-96, 299-312
The Song of Lazarus (Comfort) **7**:54
Song of Malaya (p'Bitek) **96**:274, 281-82, 286, 298-99, 301, 305
"The Song of Maria Neféli" (Elytis) **49**:109
The Song of My Sister (Ritsos) **31**:324
Song of Ocol (p'Bitek) **96**:268, 270, 280-81, 290-91, 294-99, 301, 305
"Song of Patience" (Cohen) **38**:131
"The Song of Peronelle" (Arreola) **147**:4
"A Song of Praise" (Sanchez) **116**:316
Song of Prisoner (p'Bitek) **96**:265-67, 270-73, 278, 280-81, 284-86, 288-89, 296-99, 301, 303-05
"Song of Reasons" (Pinsky) **38**:361
A Song of Sixpence (Cronin) **32**:139-40
"A Song of Sojourner Truth" (Jordan) **114**:145
Song of Solomon (Morrison) **10**:355-56; **22**:316-17, 319-20; **55**:195-96, 200, 205, 207-08, 210; **81**:217-18, 221, 223-25, 227-28, 230-38, 250, 256-57, 259-60, 262, 265, 268-69, 272; **87**:263-65, 292-94
"The Song of Songs" (Davies) **23**:144
Song of Songs (Mamoulian) **16**:421
"Song of the Blackbird" (Turco) **63**:429
"The Song of the Bongo" (Guillén)
See "La canción del bongo"
"Song of the Books" (Clarke) **6**:112
Song of the City (Abrahams) **4**:3
"The Song of the Cold" (Sitwell) **67**:336
The Song of the Cold (Sitwell) **2**:403
"Song of the Deportees" (Guthrie) **35**:193
"A Song of the Dust" (Sitwell) **67**:337
"The Song of the Final Meeting" (Akhmatova) **64**:8
"Song of the First and Last Beatnik" (Gold) **42**:192
"Song of the Flaming Sword" (Avison) **97**:111
"Song of the Forest" (Okigbo) **25**:350, 354; **84**:330, 332
"Song of the German Mercenaries" (Faludy) **42**:138-39
"Song of the GI's and MG's" (Laughlin) **49**:221
"The Song of the Honey Bee" (Hughes) **119**:292
The Song of the Horse (Kurosawa) **119**:399
"Song of the Immediacy of Death" (Bell) **8**:67
"The Song of the Indian Wars" (Neihardt) **32**:330-32, 334, 337-38
"Song of the Initiate" (Senghor) **130**:260
The Song of the Little Road (Ray)
See *Pather panchali*
"Song of the Lonely Bachelor" (Montague) **46**:265
Song of the Lusitanian Bogey (Weiss)
See *Gesang vom lusitanischen Popanz*
Song of the Lusitanian Bogeyman (Weiss)
See *Gesang vom lusitanischen Popanz*
"The Song of the Man of Light Who Passed into Gloom" (Shamlu) **10**:472
"The Song of the Messiah" (Neihardt) **32**:332 34, 338
"Song of the Native Land" (Seifert) **93**:335
"The Song of the Necromancer" (Smith) **43**:422-25
"Song of the Night" (Kinsella) **138**:97, 103
"Song of the Past" (Mahapatra) **33**:283
"The Song of the Poet" (Elytis) **49**:109
"Song of the River Sweep" (Lieberman) **36**:262
The Song of the Road (Ray)
See *Pather panchali*
"Song of the Shirt, 1941" (Parker) **68**:328, 334-35, 339-40
"The Song of the Shrouded Stranger of the Night" (Ginsberg) **36**:196
"Song of the Slip" (Snyder) **120**:327-28
"Song of the Smoke" (Du Bois) **64**:114; **96**:130
"Song of the Son" (Toomer) **13**:551; **22**:425-26
"A Song of the Soul of Central" (Hughes) **108**:309
"Song of the Spasskaya Tower" (Padilla) **38**:351
"Song of the Sweepings" (Seifert) **93**:331
"Song of the Tangle" (Snyder) **120**:328
"Song of the Taste" (Snyder) **32**:387
Song of the Trees (Taylor) **21**:418-20
"Song of the Whales" (Seifert) **34**:261-62
The Song of Three Friends (Neihardt) **32**:329-31, 334, 337
The Song of Viktorka (Seifert) **34**:262-63; **44**:422; **93**:307, 309, 323, 326-28, 332, 335-36, 343
"A Song of Wrinkles" (Whittemore) **4**:588
"Song Off-Key" (Wagoner) **3**:508
"Song on Porcelain" (Milosz) **82**:297-98
"A Song on the End of the World" (Milosz) **11**:381; **31**:259, 262; **56**:234
"The Song Remains the Same" (Page and Plant) **12**:481
The Song Remains the Same (Page and Plant) **12**:480, 482
"Song: 'Rough Winds Do Shake the Darling Buds of May'" (Simpson) **149**:344
"A Song: Sensation Time at the Home" (Merton) **83**:397
Song, Speech, and Ventriloquism (Kettelkamp) **12**:304
"The Song the Body Dreamed in the Spirit's Mad Behest" (Everson) **5**:122
"Song, the Brian Coral" (Rukeyser) **15**:457
"Song: The Organic Years" (Bell) **8**:66
"Song to Alfred Hitchcock and Wilkinson" (Ondaatje) **14**:407
Song to Grow On (Guthrie) **35**:187
"Song to Ishtar" (Levertov) **66**:235, 238
"A Song to No Music" (Brodsky) **36**:78, 81; **100**:52
"Song to Pie" (Blount) **38**:47
"A Song to Sing You" (Wright) **53**:419
"Song to Woody" (Dylan) **77**:166
"Song without Music" (Brodsky)
See "A Song to No Music"
"The Songbook of Sebastian Arrurruz" (Hill) **8**:293-95; **45**:178-79, 183, 190
Le songe (Montherlant) **8**:393; **19**:322-23
Le songe du critique (Anouilh) **40**:57
Les songes en equilibre (Hébert) **29**:227, 230, 236-37
The Songlines (Chatwin) **57**:139-48, 150, 153
Songlines (Chatwin) **59**:275-77
Songmaster (Card) **47**:67-9; **50**:143
Sóngoro cosongo: Poemas mulatos (Guillén) **48**:157, 159, 161-63, 166-68; **79**:229, 231, 238-40, 246-48, 250
"Songs" (Prokosch) **48**:309
Songs (Ostriker) **132**:318
Songs and Other Musical Pieces (Auden) **6**:17
"Songs and Recitations" (Simmons) **43**:414
"Songs for a Colored Singer" (Bishop) **1**:34; **9**:97; **15**:59; **32**:38
Songs for a Son (Peters) **7**:303
Songs for a Summer Day (MacLeish) **68**:285
"Songs for a Woman" (Amichai) **116**:96
Songs for an Autumn Rifle (Caute) **29**:109, 115
Songs for Eve (MacLeish) **8**:362
"Songs for Five Companionable Singers" (Corn) **33**:116, 118
"Songs for Masters" (Hope) **52**:209
"Songs for My Father" (Komunyakaa) **86**:192-93; **94**:239
Songs for Naëtt (Senghor)
See *Chants pour Naëtt*
"Songs/for Sanna" (Broumas) **73**:9
Songs for Soldiers and Tunes for Tourists (Guillén)
See *Cantos para soldados y sones para turistas*
"Songs for the Air" (Hecht) **8**:266
"Songs from Libretti" (Denby) **48**:83
Songs from the Stars (Spinrad) **46**:384-86
Songs in a Time of War (Saro-Wiwa) **114**:253
Songs in the Attic (Joel) **26**:222
Songs in the Key of Life (Wonder) **12**:659-62, 664
"Songs My Mother Taught Me" (Calisher) **134**:8
Songs My Mother Taught Me (Thomas) **7**:472; **13**:538; **37**:424; **107**:348
Songs of a Dead Dreamer (Ligotti) **44**:53-5
Songs of a Mountain Plowman (Stuart) **11**:509
"The Songs of Adrien Zielinsky" (Milosz) **11**:378
"The Songs of Distant Earth" (Clarke) **136**:225
The Songs of Distant Earth (Clarke) **136**:225
Songs of Enchantment (Okri) **87**:329-31
"Songs of Jerusalem and Myself" (Amichai) **116**:89, 114
"Songs of Life" (Diamond) **30**:113
"The Songs of Maximus" (Olson) **5**:329
"The Songs of Reba Love Jackson" (Wideman) **36**:455; **122**:289
Songs of Something Else (Ekeloef) **27**:119
"Songs of the Desert" (Baxter) **14**:61
Songs of the Doomed (Thompson) **104**:338-44, 347
Songs of the Heart (Lagerkvist)
See *Hjärtats sånger*
"Songs of the Land of Zion Jerusalem" (Amichai) **22**:30

"Songs of the Old Sod" (Simmons) **43**:412
"Songs of the Psyche" (Kinsella) **138**:128, 130, 162
Songs of the Psyche (Kinsella) **138**:148, 165
"Songs of the Sea-Witch" (Musgrave) **13**:400
Songs of the Sea-Witch (Musgrave) **13**:400; **54**:341;
"Songs of the Shade" (Senghor)
See *Chants d'ombre*
"Songs of the Transformed" (Atwood) **8**:29; **13**:44; **15**:37-8; **25**:67; **84**:65
Songs of Woody Guthrie (Guthrie) **35**:191
"Songs of Zion the Beautiful" (Amichai) **57**:41, 44
"Songs the Minstrel Sang" (Lightfoot) **26**:282
Songs to a Handsome Woman (Brown) **79**:153
"Songs to Survive the Summer" (Hass) **18**:212; **99**:140
Songs to the Seagull (Mitchell) **12**:435, 437, 440
"The Songs We Know Best" (Ashbery) **41**:34, 38
Sonim, di Geschichte fun a Liebe (Singer) **3**:456, 459; **11**:499, 501, 503; **23**:416, 419, 422; **111**:307, 309-12, 321-24, 327-28, 333, 341, 346
"Son-in-Law" (Gordimer) **123**:113
"Sonnet" (Bishop) **32**:37
"Sonnet" (Bogan) **46**:78; **93**:90, 96
"Sonnet" (Carruth) **84**:136
"Sonnet" (Hass) **99**:155
"Sonnet" (Justice) **102**:269, 278
"Sonnet" (Plumly) **33**:314
"Sonnet" (Reading) **47**:350
"Sonnet" (Watkins) **43**:450
"Sonnet" (Winters) **32**:468
"Sonnet" (Wright) **53**:427
"Sonnet VIII" (Shapiro) **4**:486
"Sonnet 14" (Berryman) **62**:51
"Sonnet 15" (Berryman) **62**:53
"Sonnet 16" (Berryman) **62**:51
"Sonnet 20" (Berryman) **62**:51
"Sonnet 23" (Berryman) **62**:52
"Sonnet 25" (Berryman) **62**:53
"Sonnet 40" (Berryman) **62**:50
"Sonnet 47" (Berryman) **62**:72
"Sonnet 52" (Berryman) **62**:51
"Sonnet 58" (Berryman) **62**:52
"Sonnet 75" (Berryman) **62**:51
"Sonnet 97" (Berryman) **62**:52
"Sonnet 100" (Berryman) **62**:50
"Sonnet 101" (Berryman) **62**:52
"Sonnet 103" (Berryman) **62**:52
"Sonnet 105" (Berryman) **62**:51
"Sonnet for Minimalists" (Van Duyn) **116**:412, 415
"Sonnet, Freely Adapted" (Zamora) **89**:361, 370, 372, 375, 394
"A Sonnet from the Stony Brook" (Jordan) **114**:145
"The Sonnet Hobby" (Pasolini) **106**:265-66
"Sonnet Number Eight" (Orlovitz) **22**:336
"Sonnet Number Ninety" (Orlovitz) **22**:336
"Sonnet on Rare Animals" (Meredith) **55**:192
"A Sonnet Sequence: Dishonor" (Denby) **48**:81, 84
"Sonnet: The Greedy Man Considers Nuclear War" (Ewart) **46**:151
"Sonnet III" (Cummings) **68**:44
"Sonnet to My Father" (Justice) **102**:268, 285
The Sonnets (Berrigan) **37**:42-5
Sonnets (Carruth) **84**:136
"Sonnets for Five Seasons" (Stevenson) **33**:383
"Sonnets for Roseblush" (Hollander) **5**:187
"Sonnets from China" (Auden) **123**:48
"Sonnets from the School of Eloquence"1 (Harrison) **129**:211
Sonnets of Love and Opposition (Brenton) **31**:63
"Sonnets of the Blood" (Tate) **11**:525, 527
Sonnets to Chris (Berryman)
See *Berryman's Sonnets*
"Sonnets—Actualities" (Cummings) **15**:159, 160
"Sonnets—Realities" (Cummings) **15**:159, 160, 162
"Sonnets—Unrealities" (Cummings) **15**:159
"Sonnet—To the Ocean" (Masefield) **11**:358
"Sonny Jim" (Williams) **42**:446
"Sonny's Blues" (Baldwin) **13**:53-4; **17**:33; **90**:2-41; **127**:106, 108
"Sono zenjitsu" (Endō) **54**:161
Sons (Buck) **7**:32; **11**:73, 77
Sons (Hunter) **31**:222
"Sons and Lovers" (Roth) **104**:283
Sons Come and Go, Mothers Hang in Forever (Saroyan) **8**:468
Sons of Cain (Williamson) **56**:439-42
"The Sons of Chan" (Chin) **135**:156-57
Sons of Darkness, Sons of Light (Williams) **5**:497
"The Sons of Medea" (Squires) **51**:381
The Sons of Mrs. Aab (Millin) **49**:247-48
Sons of My Skin: Selected Poems, 1954-1974 (Redgrove) **6**:447; **41**:350-54
Sons of the Conquistador (Fuentes) **113**:262
The Sons of the Falcon (Garnett) **3**:189
"Sons of the Silent Age" (Bowie) **17**:66
"Sons of Unless and Children of Almost" (Cummings) **68**:52
"Sons of Vulindlela" (Kunene) **85**:162
"Soolaimon" (Diamond) **30**:110
"Soon" (Sondheim) **30**:391, 402
"Soon I'll Be Loving You Again" (Gaye) **26**:132
Soon One Morning (Dodson) **79**:189
"Soonest Mended" (Ashbery) **13**:30, 33-4; **15**:33; **41**:40-1; **77**:51, 57-8
Soperniki (Aitmatov) **71**:5
Sophie's Choice (Styron) **15**:525, 528-31; **60**:392, 394-402
The Sophist (Bernstein) **142**:12, 22, 46, 55
Sor Juana Inés de la Cruz, o, Las trampas de la fe (Paz) **65**:176, 186, 189, 197; **119**:407, 410, 413, 416-17, 422
Sor Juana; Or, The Traps of Faith (Paz)
See *Sor Juana Inés de la Cruz, o, Las trampas de la fe*
"Sora no kaibutsu Aguwee" (Oe) **36**:348; **86**:215-16, 244
"The Sorcerer Postponed" (Borges)
See "El brujo postergado"
"The Sorcerer's Apprentice" (Johnson) **51**:234-36
The Sorcerer's Apprentice (Johnson) **51**:234, 236
"The Sorcerer's Daughter" (Bogan) **4**:69
The Sorcerer's Stone (Rowling)
See *Harry Potter and the Philosopher's Stone*
"Sorcery" (Livesay) **79**:338, 348, 353
"Sorcery or Foolishness" (Ulibarrí)
See "Brujerías o tonterías"
"A Sordid Tale, or, Traceleen Continues Talking" (Gilchrist) **143**:309
Sore Throats (Brenton) **31**:63, 67
Sorelle Materassi (Palazzeschi) **11**:431-32
"Soren Kierkegaard" (Auden) **123**:56
"Sorghum" (Mason) **154**:240
"La sorgue: Chanson pour Yvonne" (Char) **11**:117
"Soroche" (Barrett) **150**:6, 17
"Sorôco, His Mother, His Daughter" (Rosa) **23**:352-53
"Sorrel" (Fuller) **62**:199, 202
"Sorrow" (Alegria) **75**:34, 36-7, 39, 41, 53-5
The Sorrow and the Terror (Mukherjee) **115**:366, 386
A Sorrow beyond Dreams: A Life Story (Handke)
See *Wunscholses Unglück*
The Sorrow Dance (Levertov) **2**:242; **5**:248-49; **28**:238; **66**:236-39, 245-46
"Sorrow Is the Only Faithful One" (Dodson) **79**:191-92
"The Sorrow of the Pagan Outcast" (Tanizaki)
See "Itansha no kanashimi"
"Sorrow-Acre" (Dinesen) **10**:144, 146-47, 149-52; **29**:154; **95**:35, 38-42, 46, 48, 50, 52
"A Sorrowful Woman" (Godwin) **125**:168
"The Sorrows of Captain Carpenter" (Berryman) **10**:45
The Sorrows of Frederick (Linney) **51**:260, 262
"The Sorrows of Gin" (Cheever) **15**:131; **64**:47, 65
The Sorrows of Priapus (Dahlberg) **7**:64-5, 67, 71
Sorry... (Havel)
See *Audience*
"Sorry Fugu" (Boyle) **90**:45-7
"Sorry-Grateful" (Sondheim) **147**:251, 253
"A Sort of a Song" (Williams) **42**:457
"A Sort of Ecstasy" (Smith) **15**:516
A Sort of Forgetting (Vansittart) **42**:391
A Sort of Life (Greene) **3**:213; **6**:219-20; **27**:171-72, 174; **37**:138; **70**:289, 293; **72**:160, 179; **125**:187
"Sorties" (Cixous) **92**:52-3, 69, 78-9, 84-90, 92, 95
Sorties (Dickey) **2**:117; **7**:84; **10**:141; **47**:93
"Sorties: Out and Out: Attacks/Ways Out/Forays" (Cixous) **92**:77
"S.O.S" (Bagryana) **10**:14
"S.O.S." (Damas) **84**:169, 172, 177
Sos the Rope (Anthony) **35**:34-5
Sot' (Leonov) **92**:236-37, 245, 248, 256, 258-59, 276, 278
Sotto il sole giaguro (Calvino) **73**:50, 53, 59-60
"Sotto Voce" (Kunitz) **148**:88
The Sot-Weed Factor (Barth) **1**:17-8; **2**:35-9; **3**:38-9, 42; **5**:52; **7**:22-5; **9**:61, 68, 72-4; **10**:24; **14**:49-51, 56; **27**:28; **51**:20-1; **89**:8, 11, 14, 17
Le souci de soi (Foucault)
See *Histoire de la sexualité, Vol. 3: Le souci de soi*
Soudce z Milosti (Klima) **56**:173
"Souffrance" (Soupault) **68**:404
La soufriere (Herzog) **16**:328
"The Soul" (Amichai) **22**:33
"The Soul" (Amichai)
See "Hanefesh"
The Soul and Body of John Brown (Rukeyser) **27**:404
Soul and Form (Lukacs)
See *Die Seele und die Formen*
"Soul and Money" (Berriault) **109**:95
The Soul Brothers and Sister Lou (Hunter) **35**:225-29
Soul Catcher (Herbert) **12**:273; **35**:196; **44**:394
Soul Clap Hands and Sing (Marshall) **27**:309, 311-13, 315; **72**:212, 227, 231, 248, 254
A Soul for Sale (Kavanagh) **22**:234
Soul Gone Home (Hughes) **1**:148; **35**:217
"The Soul inside the Sentence" (Gass) **39**:479-80, 482; **132**:165
"Soul Kitchen" (Morrison) **17**:286, 290, 292
"The Soul Longs to Return Whence It Came" (Eberhart) **56**:77, 80, 87
Soul/Mate (Oates) **108**:386-88
The Soul of a Jew (Sobol) **60**:385
"The Soul of a Woman's College" (Rich) **73**:322
The Soul of Kindness (Taylor) **29**:408, 412
"The Soul of the Village" (Blaga) **75**:70, 78
Soul of the White Ant (Wilson) **33**:461, 464-65
Soul of Wood, and Other Stories (Lind)
See *Eine Seele aus Holz*
Soul on Fire (Cleaver) **30**:68-9
"Soul on Ice" (Cleaver) **30**:59
Soul on Ice (Cleaver) **30**:54-9, 61-2, 65, 67-9
"Soul Says" (Graham) **118**:234, 253
Soul Says (Vendler) **138**:273, 276, 290-94
"Soul Survivor" (Jagger and Richard) **17**:224, 236
"Soul under Water" (Aleixandre) **36**:29
Souls and Bodies (Lodge) **36**:274-76; **141**:352

The Souls of Black Folk (Du Bois) **1**:80; **2**:120-21; **13**:180, 182; **64**:103-05, 110, 116-17, 127-34; **96**:127-32, 137, 142, 146-48, 153-61
"The Souls of White Folk" (Du Bois) **64**:104
Souls on Fire: Portraits and Legends of Hasidic Masters (Wiesel)
See *Célébration hasidique: Portraits et legendes*
The Sound and the Fury (Faulkner) **1**:98, 100, 102; **3**:149-55, 157; **6**:176, 180; **8**:207-08, 211; **9**:197-203; **11**:197-202, 206; **14**:168-69, 171, 173, 175, 178-80; **18**:144, 148; **28**:140-42, 145; **68**:106-36
The Sound in Your Mind (Nelson) **17**:304
A Sound Investment (Sanchez) **116**:301
"The Sound Machine" (Dahl) **79**:181
Sound of a City (Farrell) **66**:127, 129
The Sound of a Scythe (Ellison) **139**:138
"Sound of a Wound" (Montague) **46**:276
The Sound of Bow Bells (Weidman) **7**:517
A Sound of Chariots (Hunter) **21**:159-60, 163, 165, 167-68
The Sound of Coaches (Garfield) **12**:230-31, 235, 237, 241
The Sound of Mountain Water: The Changing American West (Stegner) **49**:359
"The Sound of Pines" (Masters) **48**:224
"The Sound of Poets" (Sondheim) **30**:389
The Sound of the Mountain (Kawabata) **2**:223; **5**:207; **9**:309, 314-17; **18**:285; **107**:73, 87-89, 91, 101-02, 106, 111-12, 114, 117, 119-22
"Sound of the Sinners" (Clash) **30**:48
"The Sound of the Trees" (Frost) **10**:193; **26**:117
"A Sound of Thunder" (Bradbury) **42**:42
The Sound of Thunder (Caldwell) **28**:61
The Sound of Thunder (Smith) **33**:376
"The Sound of Waiting" (Calisher) **134**:5, 7
The Sound of Waves (Mishima) **2**:286; **4**:354; **6**:337; **9**:382, 385; **27**:340
"Sound Track" (Calisher) **38**:75-6; **134**:10
"Sounding Brass, Tinkling Cymbal" (Silverberg) **140**:376, 379
"Sounding Harvey Creek" (Bottoms) **53**:32
"Sounding My Name" (Kroetsch) **57**:292-93
"Soundings" (Baraka) **115**:12
"Soundings" (Muske) **90**:314
"Soundings: Block Island" (Belitt) **22**:52-4
"The sounds begin again" (Brutus) **43**:91, 96
Sounds, Feelings, Thoughts (Szymborska) **99**:192-93
"Sounds in the Night" (Lowell) **11**:329
"The Sounds of Silence" (Simon) **17**:459, 461, 463-64, 466
"Soup" (Creeley) **78**:141
"Soup" (Simic) **6**:502
Soup (Peck) **17**:338, 340
Soup and Me (Peck) **17**:339-40
"Soup du jour" (Shields) **113**:406-08
Soup for President (Peck) **17**:342
"Sour Milk" (Wakoski) **4**:573
Sour Sweet (Mo) **46**:259-61; **134**:189, 191, 194-96, 199, 204, 209-10, 212, 216-18, 220
"The Source" (Porter) **7**:310
"Source" (Walker) **103**:407, 410-13, 423
Source (Chappell) **40**:147, 149; **78**:97
The Source (Michener) **5**:288-90; **11**:375; **29**:311-14; **109**:375, 377, 379, 380, 382, 386
A Source of Embarrassment (McCarthy)
See *The Oasis*
"A Source of Innocent Merriment" (Tiptree) **48**:389
The Source of Light (Price) **43**:347-50, 353; **50**:229, 232
The Source of Magic (Anthony) **35**:35
"Sources" (Levine) **118**:301
"Sources" (Rich) **73**:316; **125**:316
Sources (Rich) **36**:371-72, 374, 377; **73**:327; **76**:210
Sources of Renewal (John Paul II) **128**:178, 180
Sources of Unrest (Vansittart) **42**:392
Le sourd dans la ville (Blais) **22**:60
"Sourdough Mountain Lookout" (Whalen) **29**:446
Sous bénéfice d'inventaire (Yourcenar) **19**:484; **87**:412
Sous les toits de Paris (Clair) **20**:57-62, 69-70
"Sousa" (Dorn) **10**:159
"The South" (Borges)
See "Le Sud"
"South" (Hoffman) **6**:244
"South" (Justice) **102**:258
"South" (Walcott) **76**:275
South (Green)
See *Sud*
"South Africa, 1986" (Levertov) **66**:251
The South African Quirt (Edmonds) **35**:157
The South Africans (Millin) **49**:246
"South America" (Dunn) **40**:170-71
South by Java Head (MacLean) **13**:361; **63**:262-64
"South by Southwest" (Alexie) **154**:46
"South Country" (Slessor) **14**:493
The South Goes North (Coles) **108**:210-11, 214
South of Heaven (Thompson) **69**:384
"South of My Days" (Wright) **53**:423, 427, 430
South of No North (Bukowski) **108**:77, 86-87
South of the Angels (West) **7**:519, 521; **17**:548, 551, 553
South of the Border, West of the Sun (Murakami)
See *Kokkyō no minami, taiyō no nishi*
"South Parade Pedler" (Bennett) **28**:26
"South Parks Road" (Fenton) **32**:165
South Pole Station (Berger) **12**:38
"South Sangamon" (Cisneros) **118**:174
South Sea Bubble (Coward) **29**:136, 139
South Street (Bradley) **23**:79-80; **118**:117, 120, 122
"South: The Name of Home" (Walker) **58**:405
South to a Very Old Place (Murray) **73**:222-24, 235-41
The South Wind of Love (Mackenzie) **18**:313
"Southbound on the Freeway" (Swenson) **106**:319
"Southeast Arkansia" (Angelou) **77**:29
"Southeast Corner" (Brooks) **49**:26
Southern Adventure (Paustovsky)
See *Brosok na yug*
"The Southern Belle" (Godwin) **125**:137-38, 155, 157
The Southern City (Kadare)
See *Qyteti i jugut*
"Southern Cop" (Brown) **59**:265-66
"The Southern Cross" (Konwicki) **117**:281
"The Southern Cross" (Wright) **28**:458; **146**:303, 308, 312, 327-28, 330-31, 336-37, 339, 341-43, 363-64
The Southern Cross (Wright) **28**:458-60; **119**:186; **146**:301-04, 306, 312-14, 321-22, 327-28, 330, 336-38, 341-43, 347, 353, 360-62, 374-75, 379
Southern Discomfort (Brown) **43**:81-3; **79**:153, 155, 158-59, 167-71
A Southern Family (Godwin) **69**:239, 241-49, 251-52; **125**:145-46, 149, 151, 167-70
Southern Fried (Fox) **22**:140
Southern Fried Plus Six (Fox) **22**:140
"Southern Gentlemen, White Prostitutes, Mill-Owners, and Negroes" (Hughes) **108**:318
"A Southern Landscape" (Spencer) **22**:406
"Southern Mammy Sings" (Hughes) **35**:221; **108**:325-26
"Southern Man" (Young) **17**:570, 572-73, 582
"Southern Mansion" (Bontemps) **1**:38; **18**:64
"A Southern Mode of Imagination" (Tate) **4**:537; **11**:522
"The Southern Quality" (McLuhan) **83**:360
"The Southern Road" (Randall) **135**:386-87, 395
Southern Road (Brown) **1**:47; **23**:95-8; **59**:262, 264-65, 267-68, 270-71, 273
"A Southern Sojourn" (Hoffman) **141**:283-84, 288
"The Southern Thruway" (Cortázar)
See "La autopista del sur"
"The Southerner" (Shapiro) **15**:476, 478
The Southerner (Renoir) **20**:287-88, 304
Southmost Twelve (FitzGerald) **19**:175
"Southpaw" (Mueller) **51**:284
The Southpaw (Harris) **19**:200, 203
Southways (Caldwell) **14**:96
"The Southwest Experimental Fast Oxide Reactor" (Gilchrist) **143**:309
"Southwestern Literature" (McMurtry) **127**:304, 333
"Souvenir" (Joel) **26**:214, 219
"Souvenir de temps perdu" (Smith) **15**:516
A Souvenir from Qam (Connelly) **7**:57
"A Souvenir of Japan" (Carter) **5**:102
"Souvenirs" (Randall) **135**:377
Souvenirs (Fuller) **28**:156-58
Souvenirs du triangle d'or (Robbe-Grillet) **43**:361-62, 365-68; **128**:359, 378, 382
Souvenirs pieux (Yourcenar) **19**:484; **87**:389, 396, 412, 417-18, 432-34
"Sovereign" (Voinovich)
See "Vladychitsa"
The Sovereign Sun: Selected Poems (Elytis) **15**:219-20; **49**:109; **100**:158, 174
The Sovereignty of Good over Other Concepts (Murdoch) **15**:387, 389; **51**:291
Soviet Poems (Gustafson) **36**:217-18, 221
Soviet River (Leonov)
See *Sot'*
Soviet Women: Walking The Tightrope (Gray) **153**:149-51, 156-59, 161-66
"Sow" (Plath) **5**:345; **9**:432; **17**:344, 348, 350; **51**:343; **111**:164
"The Sow and Silas" (Bates) **46**:63
"The Soy Cowboy" (Vollmann) **89**:314
"Soy Sauce" (Snyder) **120**:324
Sozaboy (Saro-Wiwa) **114**:258, 267, 275
Sozvezdie Kozlotura (Iskander) **47**:193, 196, 199-200
"The Space" (Soto) **80**:277
Space (Aleixandre)
See *Ambito*
Space (Michener) **29**:314-16; **60**:258; **109**:378-79, 381, 386
Space Ache (Wilson) **33**:463-66
The Space Beyond (Campbell) **32**:80
Space Cadet (Heinlein) **14**:250; **26**:161, 171, 175; **55**:302
"The Space Crone" (Le Guin) **136**:327-28, 387
Space Family Stone (Heinlein)
See *The Rolling Stones*
"A Space in the Air" (Silkin) **6**:498; **43**:397, 399-400
The Space Merchants (Pohl) **18**:412
"Space Monkey" (Smith) **12**:543
"Space Mowgli" (Strugatskii and Strugatskii) **27**:438
"Space Oddity" (Bowie) **17**:57, 59
The Space of Literature (Blanchot)
See *L'Espace littéraire*
The Space Pirate (Vance) **35**:420
"Space Rats of the C.C.C." (Harrison) **42**:203
"Space Sonnet and Pollyfilla" (Morgan) **31**:276
"The Space Spiders" (Hall) **37**:146
Space, Time, and Nathaniel (Aldiss) **14**:10
The Space Vampires (Wilson) **14**:589
"Spaced In" (Baker) **31**:29
The Spaces Between (Kingsolver) **130**:100
Spaces of the Dark (Mosley) **43**:321
"The space-ship" (Smith) **64**:393
"Spaceships Have Landed" (Munro) **95**:320, 325
Spacious Earth (Pasternak)
See *Zemnoy prostor*
"Spadanie czyli; o, Elementach wertykalnych i horyzontalnych w życiu czlowieka wspolczesnego" (Rozewicz) **23**:359; **139**:226

Spaghetti and the Sword (Rozewicz)
See *Spaghetti i miecz*
Spaghetti i miecz (Rozewicz) **139**:231, 293
"Spain" (Cocteau)
See "Espagne"
Spain (Auden) **3**:25; **14**:33; **43**:18, 21; **123**:22
"Spain, 1937" (Auden) **6**:20, 23; **11**:14, 19; **14**:27; **43**:16; **123**:48, 51
"Spain, 1934-1936" (Leiris) **61**:361
Spain: A Poem in Four Anguishes and a Hope (Guillén)
See *España: Poema en cuatro angustias y una esperanza*
Spain Again (Bessie) **23**:60
Spain at Heart (Neruda)
See *España en el corazón: himno a las glorias del pueblo en la guerra (1936-1937)*
Spain in My Heart (Neruda)
See *España en el corazón: himno a las glorias del pueblo en la guerra (1936-1937)*
Spain in the Heart (Neruda)
See *España en el corazón: himno a las glorias del pueblo en la guerra (1936-1937)*
Spain under Franco (Gallo) **95**:90, 92, 94, 96
"Span" (Avison) **97**:91
A Spaniard in the Works (Lennon) **12**:355; **35**:267
"The Spaniards Arrive in Shanghai" (Middleton) **13**:389
The Spanish Armadas (Graham) **23**:194
"Spanish Artifacts" (Dacey) **51**:80-1
"Spanish Balcony" (Beer) **58**:37
"The Spanish Bed" (Pritchett) **15**:442, 444
"Spanish Bombs" (Clash) **30**:46-7
The Spanish Cape Mystery (Queen) **11**:460
"The Spanish Civil War" (Carruth) **7**:41
"The Spanish Earl" (White) **30**:451
The Spanish Earth (Hemingway) **6**:226; **50**:412; **80**:107
The Spanish Gardener (Cronin) **32**:137
"The Spanish Lady" (Munro) **95**:293
The Spanish Letters (Hunter) **21**:155-56, 161, 166
"The Spanish Lie" (MacLeish) **68**:289
"Spanish Point" (Buckley) **57**:136
Spanish Roundabout (Daly) **17**:90
The Spanish Smile (O'Dell) **30**:277
The Spanish Temper (Pritchett) **41**:335
Spanish Testament (Koestler) **15**:309; **33**:243
The Spanish Virgin, and Other Stories (Pritchett) **41**:332
The Spanish World (Elliott) **70**:341
Spanking the Maid (Coover) **32**:125; **46**:117
Spare Ass Annie (Burroughs) **109**:185
"Spare Us from Loveliness" (H. D.) **73**:115
Spared (Horovitz) **56**:155
"A Spark in the Tinder of Knowing" (Rexroth) **112**:404
"A Spark of Laurel" (Kunitz) **148**:88, 95, 101-01, 105
Spark of Life (Remarque) **21**:330-31
Spark of Opal (Clark) **12**:130-32
Sparkling Cyanide (Christie) **12**:124
"Sparks Street Echo" (Creeley) **78**:161
"Sparrow" (Gaye) **26**:133-34
"Sparrow" (Gunn) **18**:202
"Sparrow Come in My Window" (Nowlan) **15**:398
A Sparrow Falls (Smith) **33**:376
"A Sparrow Hawk in the Suburbs" (Boland) **113**:111
"Sparrow Hills" (Pasternak) **63**:278
"Sparrows" (Lessing) **94**:265
"Sparrows in March" (Raine) **45**:330
Spartacus (Fast) **23**:156; **131**:55, 59-61, 63, 65-6, 70, 73, 75, 77, 81, 83-6, 94, 98
Spartacus (Kubrick) **16**:379-80, 382, 385-86, 389
Spartina (Casey) **59**:119-23
"Spasskoye" (Pasternak) **63**:279
"Spat" (Schaeffer) **11**:491
"Spät und tief" (Celan) **10**:102
"Spaţiul mioritic" (Blaga) **75**:72
"Spats" (Martin) **89**:111-12
The Spawning Run (Humphrey) **45**:198
"Speak" (Wright) **10**:544
Speak! (Buravsky) **59**:364
Speak, Answer, Teach (Haavikko)
See *Puhua, vastata, opettaa*
Speak for England (Bragg) **10**:72
"Speak, Memory" (Auden) **123**:43
Speak, Memory: An Autobiography Revisited (Nabokov) **1**:242, 245; **2**:299, 301, 304; **3**:354-55; **6**:357, 359; **8**:409, 412-15, 417-18; **11**:391-92, 395; **15**:390, 394; **46**:292
Speak Now (Yerby) **7**:557; **22**:491
Speak Out on Rape! (Hyde) **21**:177-78
"Speak to Me" (Pink Floyd) **35**:306
"Speak, You Also" (Celan) **19**:94; **53**:74-5; **82**:47
Speaker for the Dead (Card) **47**:69; **50**:143-51
Speaker of Mandarin (Rendell) **48**:323
Speaking and Language: Defense of Poetry (Goodman) **2**:169, 171; **4**:198
"Speaking in Tongues" (Moure) **88**:227
Speaking in Tongues (Byrne) **26**:99
"Speaking into Darkness" (Bottoms) **53**:29-31
"Speaking of Courage" (O'Brien) **103**:136, 139, 147, 163, 168, 174
"Speaking of LETTERS" (Barth) **51**:26
"Speaking of Which" (Moure) **88**:224
Speaking Parts (Egoyan) **151**:123-32, 134, 136, 139-40, 145, 147, 150-51, 153-54, 174
Spearpoint (Ashton-Warner) **19**:23
"Special Delivery" (Alexie) **154**:3
"Special Lovers" (Ransom) **4**:431
Special Occasions (Slade) **46**:372-73
A Special Providence (Yates) **7**:554; **23**:480
"A Special Sense of Place" (Momaday) **85**:237
"A Special Train" (Hoffman) **6**:243
The Special View of History (Olson) **11**:418-20
"Special-Constable" (Sassoon) **36**:385
"The Specialist" (Bogosian) **141**:86
Species of Spaces (Perec)
See *Espèces d'espaces*
"Speck's Idea" (Gallant) **38**:195
Spectacle (Prévert) **15**:438
The Spectacle at the Tower (Hofmann)
See *Auf dem Turm*
"The Spectacle of Youth" (Kunene) **85**:166
"Spectacles" (Butor) **15**:114
Spectacles (Beattie) **146**:47, 69
The Spectator Bird (Stegner) **9**:509; **49**:356; **81**:344, 348, 350
A Specter Is Haunting Texas (Leiber) **25**:304-05, 310
Spectral Emanations: New and Selected Poems (Hollander) **8**:302; **14**:263-64
"Spectral Lovers" (Ransom) **5**:365
"Spectre de la rose" (Davies) **23**:142
"The Spectrum Dream" (Shapcott) **38**:402
"The Speculation of the Building Constructors" (Calvino)
See "La speculazione edilizia"
Speculations about Jacob (Johnson)
See *Mutmassungen über Jakob*
"Speculations on the Present through the Prism of the Past" (Jordan) **114**:155
Speculative Instruments (Richards) **24**:390, 394-96
"La speculazione edilizia" (Calvino) **11**:89-91; **33**:100; **39**:315-16
"The Speech" (Pritchett) **41**:333
"Speech" (Sandburg) **35**:356
Speech and Phenomena, and Other Essays on Husserl's Theory of Signs (Derrida)
See *La voix et le phénomène: Introduction au problème su signe dans le phénoménologie de Husserl*
"Speech and Silence" (Ezekiel) **61**:105
"Speech for an Ideal Irish Election" (Montague) **46**:278
"Speech for the Repeal of the McCarran Act" (Wilbur) **14**:577; **53**:404; **110**:382
"Speech, Near Hope in Providence" (Honig) **33**:211
"Speech #38" (Baraka) **115**:39
"The Speech of a Man from the Backlands" (Cabral de Melo Neto)
See "O sertanejo falando"
"The Speech of Birds" (Raine) **7**:352
Speech on the Occasion of Receiving the Literature Prize of the Free Hanseatic City of Bremen (Celan) **53**:83; **82**:54
"Speech Rhythm" (Williams) **13**:604; **42**:460-61
"Speech Sounds" (Butler) **121**:110, 113-16, 142
"Speech to a Crowd" (MacLeish) **68**:287
"Speech to the Detractors" (MacLeish) **68**:287
"Speeches at the Barriers" (Howe) **72**:195; **152**:167
The Speeches of Malcolm X at Harvard (Malcolm X) **117**:317, 340
"Speech-Grille" (Celan)
See "Sprachgitter"
Speech-Grille, and Selected Poems (Celan)
See *Sprachgitter*
The Speed of Darkness (Rukeyser) **27**:409, 411
The Speed of Darkness (Tesich) **69**:368, 370-74
"Speed Queen among the Freudians" (Robbins) **21**:339-40
Speedboat (Adler) **8**:4-7; **31**:14, 16-17
Spektorsky (Pasternak) **10**:384; **18**:382-83; **63**:289, 311, 315
"Spel Against Demons" (Snyder) **120**:347
"Speleology" (Warren) **18**:539; **39**:265, 274
"The Spell" (Allen) **52**:35
"The Spell" (Kumin) **28**:220
"The Spell" (Lowell) **37**:238
"The Spell against Spelling" (Starbuck) **53**:354
A Spell before Winter (Nemerov) **36**:304
"Spell for a Traveller" (Mueller) **13**:400
A Spell for Chameleon (Anthony) **35**:35
A Spell for Green Corn (Brown) **48**:53-4
Spell #7: Geechee Jibara Quik Magic Trance Manual for Technologically Stressed Third World People (Shange) **25**:397-98; **74**:300-02, 307-10; **126**:357, 364-65, 367-68, 370
The Spell of Time (Levin) **7**:205
"The Spell of Wild Rivers" (McGuane) **127**:286
The Spell Sword (Bradley) **30**:27-8
Spella Ho (Bates) **46**:54-5
"Spellbound" (Zaturenska) **6**:586
Spellbound (Hitchcock) **16**:339, 345, 357
The Spellcoats (Jones) **26**:229-30
"Spelling" (Atwood) **25**:65
"Spelling" (Munro) **95**:293, 304
"Spells" (Raine) **45**:336
Spence + Lila (Mason) **82**:238-40, 245, 255, 257-58, 260; **154**:234, 236-37, 239-40, 272
Spencer's Mountain (Hamner) **12**:257-58
Spending (Gordon) **128**:149-53
"Spending the New Year with the Man from Receiving at Sears" (Wakoski) **40**:455-56
Spenser's Images of Life (Lewis) **124**:193
La speranza (Moravia) **46**:282
"Sphere" (Ammons) **57**:59; **108**:27
Sphere (Crichton) **54**:74-5
The Sphere (Sender)
See *La esfera*
"The Sphere of Pascal" (Borges)
See "Pascal's Sphere"
Sphere: The Form of a Motion (Ammons) **5**:30-1; **8**:13-16, 18; **9**:27-9; **25**:42; **57**:49, 57, 59; **108**:11, 13, 15, 24, 27-8, 35-8, 54-5, 60
Sphinx (Cook) **14**:131
Sphinx (Thomas) **132**:353-56, 377-78
The Spice-Box of Earth (Cohen) **38**:131-35, 137
"The Spider" (Cortázar)
See "La araña"
"The Spider" (Leiber) **25**:307

"Spider Blues" (Ondaatje) **51**:311-12
Spider Boy (Van Vechten) **33**:393-94, 397-98
"Spider Crystal Ascension" (Wright) **146**:306, 374
"The Spider Mathematician" (Ratushinskaya) **54**:385
"Spider on the Clothesline" (Hall) **51**:170
"The Spider Outside Our Window" (Souster) **5**:396
"Spider Rose" (Sterling) **72**:368
Spider Web (Dourado)
See *Teia*
Spider Woman (Puig)
See *El beso de la mujer araña*
Spider Woman's Granddaughters: Traditional Tales and Contemporary Writing by Native American Women (Allen) **84**:22, 24-7, 37, 45
"Spiders" (Schwartz) **45**:354
The Spiders (Lang)
See *Die Spinnen*
The Spider's House (Bowles) **1**:41; **19**:58; **53**:41-2, 46-9
The Spider's Strategy (Bertolucci) **16**:86-90, 92-5, 100
Spider's Web (Christie) **12**:125
Das Spiel vom Fragen (Handke)
See *Das Spiel vom Fragen oder Die Reise zum Sonoren Land*
Das Spiel vom Fragen oder Die Reise zum Sonoren Land (Handke) **134**:141, 150-54, 161, 177
Spiele in denen es dunkel wird (Hildesheimer) **49**:167, 171
"Spikes" (Chabon) **149**:23, 25
"Spillway" (Barnes) **3**:37; **29**:27, 31
Spillway, and Other Stories (Barnes) **29**:30, 32
Spin a Soft Black Song: Poems for Children (Giovanni) **117**:168, 191
"A Spin around the House" (Pack) **13**:340
"Spin It On" (McCartney) **35**:286
"Spindrift" (Kinnell) **29**:289
Die Spinnen (Lang) **20**:206, 209-10
"Spinnin' and Spinnin'" (Wonder) **12**:663
"Spinning" (Purdy) **50**:238
The Spinning Ladies (Wagoner) **3**:507
"The Spinning Wheel in the Attic" (Smith) **42**:356
"The Spinoza of Market Street" (Singer) **15**:505; **69**:306, 309
The Spinoza of Market Street, and Other Stories (Singer) **3**:456; **11**:502; **15**:504; **23**:413, 415, 418
"Spinster" (Ashton-Warner) **19**:20
"Spinster" (Plath) **111**:165
"The Spinsters and the Knitters in the Sun" (Beer) **58**:37
Spinsters in Jeopardy (Marsh) **53**:249-51, 254
"A Spinster's Tale" (Taylor) **18**:523; **37**:409
"Spinster's Wake" (Dunn) **40**:168
Spione (Lang) **20**:203, 209, 211; **103**:88
"The Spiral" (Calvino)
See "La spirale"
"Spiral" (Oates) **6**:370
Spiral (Leonov) **92**:274
"The Spiral of Perspectives" (Laing) **95**:145
"The Spiral Rag" (Ammons) **57**:49
The Spiral Road (de Hartog) **19**:130-31
"La spirale" (Calvino) **8**:127; **11**:91
"Spirals" (Fuller) **62**:196-97
"The Spire" (Voigt) **54**:430-31
The Spire (Golding) **1**:121-22; **2**:166-68; **3**:196-98, 200; **10**:237; **17**:166-68, 171-72, 174, 179; **27**:161, 163-64; **81**:315-18, 320-21, 323, 326
"The Spirit in Me" (Hoffman) **141**:283, 285-87, 308, 315
Spirit Lake (Kantor) **7**:196
The Spirit Level (Heaney) **91**:124, 129
"Spirit of America" (Wilson) **12**:643
"The Spirit of Place" (Rich) **36**:367, 370, 379; **73**:315
The Spirit of Romance (Pound) **7**:332, 335; **13**:457; **48**:288; **112**:331
The Spirit of St. Louis (Wilder) **20**:458
"Spirit of the House" (Weldon) **122**:254
"Spirit of Transgression" (Doctorow) **113**:162
Spirit Reach (Baraka) **115**:10
"The Spirit the Triumph" (Williams) **33**:443
"Spirits" (Bausch) **51**:55-7
Spirits, and Other Stories (Bausch) **51**:55-6
Spirits in Bondage: A Cycle of Lyrics (Lewis) **27**:265; **124**:213, 234
"Spirits in the Night" (Springsteen) **17**:487-88
Spirits of the Dead (Fellini) **16**:279
"Spirit's Song" (Bogan) **4**:68; **46**:81, 83; **93**:64-5, 81
"Spiritual" (Arghezi)
See "Sufletească"
"Spiritual" (Thesen) **56**:414
Spiritual (Pasolini) **106**:230
"The Spiritual Alchemy of Thomas Vaughn" (Rexroth) **112**:364
"A Spiritual Call" (Jhabvala) **94**:181, 184
The Spiritual Life of Children (Coles) **108**:203, 206-07, 209, 216
"The Spiritual Plan of Aztlán" (Zamora) **89**:378
"The Spiritual Roots of Democracy" (Havel) **123**:215
"Spiritual View of Lena Horne" (Giovanni) **64**:183
"Spiritus" (Beattie) **63**:14, 18; **146**:50
Spiritus, I (Rakosi) **47**:345
Spiritus Mundi (Frye) **70**:275
"The Spirokeet" (Ewart) **46**:150
"A Spism and a Spasm" (Mitchell) **98**:169
"Spisok blagodeyany" (Olesha) **8**:430-32
"Spit" (Williams) **33**:445; **148**:323, 328
Spit Delaney's Island (Hodgins) **23**:230, 232
Spite Marriage (Keaton) **20**:189
Splash! (Friedman) **56**:108
"Spleen" (O'Hara) **78**:351
Splender in the Grass (Inge) **8**:308
Splendid Lives (Gilliatt) **10**:229-30; **13**:237
The Splendid Wayfaring (Neihardt) **32**:331
Splendide-Hôtel (Sorrentino) **3**:462; **7**:448-50, 452; **14**:498; **22**:392-93; **40**:385-86, 389
Splendor and Death of Joaquin Murieta (Neruda)
See *Fulgor y muerte de Joaquín Murieta*
Splendor in the Grass (Kazan) **16**:367-71; **63**:226, 233, 235
"The Splendor of Being" (Castellanos)
See "El resplandor del ser"
The Splendor of Truth (John Paul II)
See *Veritatis Splendor*
Splendors of Hell (Ghelderode)
See *Fastes d'enfer*
"A Splinter" (Ryan) **65**:209
Split (Weller) **53**:387, 391-92
"Split, 1962" (Dunn) **36**:154
"Split at the Root" (Rich) **73**:321, 324
"Split Decisions" (Alexie) **154**:27-8
Split Images (Leonard) **28**:234-35; **120**:268, 270--72, 274-78, 301
Split Infinity (Anthony) **35**:36, 38
The Splits (Ritter) **52**:352, 357
Splitting (Weldon) **122**:276-77
"Splitting Wood at Six Above" (Kumin) **13**:327
"Splittings" (Rich) **18**:450
Spock Must Die! (Blish) **14**:86
The Spoil of the Flowers (Grumbach) **22**:204
Spoiled (Gray) **9**:241; **36**:201-03, 206-07
"The Spoiled Brat" (McFadden) **48**:250
"The Spoiler's Return" (Walcott) **42**:422; **67**:357; **76**:275
"The Spoiler's Revenge" (Walcott) **67**:356
"Spoils" (Gordimer) **70**:176, 178; **123**:129
The Spoils (Bunting) **10**:83-4; **47**:46, 48-50, 52-5
"Spoils of War" (Brodsky) **100**:61, 68
The Spoils of War (Fleming) **37**:129
Spoils of War (Weller) **53**:392-94
The Spoilt City (Manning) **19**:300-01
"Spokane Tribal Celebration, September, 1987" (Alexie) **96**:2; **154**:3
Spoken Opera (Audiberti)
See *Opéra parlé*
"The Spoken Word" (Davie) **10**:124
Spokoj (Kieslowski) **120**:203, 252
The Sponge Room (Waterhouse) **47**:417-18
"Sponono" (Paton) **25**:359-60
Sponono (Paton) **25**:361
Spookhouse (Fierstein) **33**:157
"Spooks" (Cooper) **56**:71
Spooky Lady's Sideshow (Kristofferson) **26**:268-69
Spooky Magic (Kettelkamp) **12**:304
"The Spool" (Belitt) **22**:49
"The Spoon" (Simic) **9**:479; **49**:337, 339, 342; **130**:330
"Spoons with Realistic Dead Flies on Them" (Simic) **49**:336
A Sport and a Pastime (Salter) **7**:387; **52**:359-60, 363-69; **59**:195-97
"Sport and Nationalism" (Sillitoe) **148**:181
The Sport of My Mad Mother (Jellicoe) **27**:205-08
A Sport of Nature (Gordimer) **51**:156-61; **70**:172, 175, 187; **123**:130-31, 137-38, 142, 155, 160
The Sport of Queens (Francis) **22**:150; **42**:148, 153-54; **102**:126, 140, 143-44, 153
The Sporting Club (McGuane) **3**:329-30; **7**:213; **18**:323, 325; **45**:258, 260, 262; **127**:245, 250, 254, 258, 262, 269, 279, 280, 283, 293
"A Sporting Life" (Moure) **88**:227
"A Sporting Man" (Mitchell) **98**:180
"Sports" (Guillén) **48**:164; **79**:230
$port$ (Tunis) **12**:592
"Sports Day in the Park" (Raine) **103**:186
Sports in America (Michener) **109**:382
"Sportsfield" (Hope) **51**:216
"The Sportsmen" (Dunn) **40**:167
"Sportsmen" (McGuane) **45**:265
Sportsworld (Lipsyte) **21**:211
The Sportswriter (Ford) **46**:159-62
The Sportswriter (Ford) **99**:105-08, 110-14, 116-25
"A Spot of Konfrontation" (Aldiss) **14**:15
"Spotlight" (Hulme) **130**:44
A Spotted Dog (Aitmatov)
See *Pegil pes, begushchij kraem moria*
The Spotted Sphinx (Adamson) **17**:5
Die Sprache (Heidegger) **24**:276
Sprache und Körperbau (Jünger) **125**:233
"Sprachgitter" (Celan) **53**:70; **82**:33, 37, 40, 57
Sprachgitter (Celan) **10**:101-02; **19**:90, 94-5; **53**:69-70, 72, 75-7
"Sprawozdanie z raju" (Herbert) **43**:186
"Spraying Sheep" (MacCaig) **36**:282
"Spread of Mrs. Mobey's Lawn" (Jacobsen) **48**:195
Spreading Fires (Knowles) **4**:272; **26**:262
Sprechblasen (Jandl) **34**:197-98
"The Spree" (Pritchett) **5**:353; **13**:467
"A Sprig of Dill" (Nemerov) **36**:309
Sprightly Running: Part of an Autobiography (Wain) **46**:411, 413, 420
"Spring" (Christie) **110**:127
"Spring" (Larkin) **64**:262, 266
"Spring" (Oliver) **98**:256, 280, 287
"The Spring" (Pound) **2**:343
"Spring" (Rexroth) **49**:283;
"Spring" (Sitwell) **67**:319
"Spring" (Squires) **51**:382
The Spring (Ehrenburg) **62**:178; **18**:132-34, 136; **34**:434, 440
The Spring (Ehrenburg)
See *The Thaw*
Spring (Pa Chin)
See *Ch'un*
Spring 71 (Adamov)
See *Le printemps 71*
"Spring, 1941" (Scott) **22**:372

"Spring, A Violin in the Void" (MacDiarmid) **63**:244
Spring and All (Williams) **2**:468-70; **5**:508-09; **9**:572-73; **22**:470; **42**:454-55, 457, 460, 462; **67**:407
"Spring and Summer" (Corn) **33**:116
"Spring Azures" (Oliver) **98**:294
"Spring Bulletin" (Allen) **52**:35
"Spring Chorus" (Johnston) **51**:248, 255
"Spring Cleaning" (MacNeice) **10**:325
"Spring, Coast Range" (Rexroth) **112**:390
Spring Comes Riding (Cavanna) **12**:98-9
"Spring Comes to Cambridge" (Updike) **139**:336
"Spring Day" (Ashbery) **2**:17-18
"Spring Drawing" (Hass) **99**:141, 143
"Spring Drawing 2" (Hass) **99**:141, 143
"Spring Evening" (Farrell) **66**:129, 131
"Spring Flood" (Pasternak) **63**:313
"Spring in the Academy" (Cassity) **42**:95
"Spring in the Classroom" (Oliver) **98**:288, 291
"Spring in the Igloo" (Atwood) **25**:66
"Spring in the New World" (Parini) **54**:360-61
"Spring Journal" (Honig) **33**:212
Spring Journal: Poems (Honig) **33**:212-13, 216
"Spring Light" (Ashbery) **15**:30
"Spring MCMXL" (Gascoyne) **45**:154
"Spring Moon" (Johnston) **51**:243, 248
Spring Moon: A Novel of China (Lord) **23**:278-80
Spring Morning (Boyle) **121**:25
"Spring Night" (Gustafson) **36**:215
Spring Night (Vesaas)
See *Vårnatt*
"Spring Northbound" (Honig) **33**:214, 216
"Spring Oak" (Kinnell) **5**:217
Spring of the Thief (Logan) **5**:252
"Spring on Troublesome Creek" (Still) **49**:363
"Spring planting in Korea" (Rozewicz) **139**:273
"Spring Poem" (Atwood) **13**:44
"The Spring Poem" (Smith) **42**:353
"Spring Pools" (Frost) **10**:195; **15**:241
"Spring Pools" (Nemerov) **9**:394
"A Spring Serpent" (Winters) **4**:593
Spring Shade (Fitzgerald) **39**:319, 473
"Spring Snow" (Matthews) **40**:321
Spring Snow (Mishima) **2**:287-88; **4**:355-56, 358; **6**:338; **9**:384; **27**:341-43
Spring Sonata (Rubens) **19**:405; **31**:350-51
"Spring Song" (Ciardi) **40**:151, 153, 157
"Spring Song" (Clifton) **66**:85
"A Spring Song" (Davie) **31**:116, 118
"Spring Song" (Purdy) **50**:244
Spring Sowing (O'Flaherty) **34**:356-57
"Spring Strains" (Williams) **42**:459
Spring Symphony (Ritsos) **31**:324
"Spring Thing" (Blackburn) **43**:63
"Spring Tide" (MacCaig) **36**:284
"Spring Victory" (Stuart) **34**:374
"Spring Voices" (MacNeice) **53**:234
Springboard (MacNeice) **4**:315
"Spring-Dance" (Rodgers) **7**:377
Springer's Progress (Markson) **67**:186-88, 191, 193, 195-97
The Springing of the Blade (Everson) **5**:122
The Springs (Vesaas)
See *Kjeldene*
"The Springs of Poetry" (Bogan) **93**:104
Springtime and Harvest: A Romance (Sinclair) **63**:345, 348
"Springtime in Touraine" (Senghor) **130**:275
"The Sprinter's Mother" (Dickey) **47**:92
"Sprocket Damage" (Bernstein) **142**:8
"Sprouts the Bitter Grain" (Webb) **18**:540
"Sprung Narratives" (Wright) **146**:347-48, 351, 354, 357
"Spunk" (Hurston) **7**:172; **30**:211, 215
Spurs: Nietzsche's Styles (Derrida)
See *Eperons: Les styles de Nietzsche*
"Spurwing Plover" (Murray) **40**:338
"Sputnik 57" (Guillén) **79**:229
"Spy" (Amichai) **116**:114
The Spy (Lang)
See *Spione*
Spy (Simon) **26**:412-13
A Spy in the House of Love (Nin) **4**:376; **8**:422; **14**:383
The Spy in the Ointment (Westlake) **7**:528; **33**:439
A Spy of the Old School (Rathbone) **41**:343
Spy Story (Deighton) **4**:119; **7**:74-6
The Spy Who Came in from the Cold (le Carré) **3**:281-82; **5**:233-34; **9**:327; **15**:324; **28**:227-28
The Spy Who Loved Me (Fleming) **30**:135-36, 139-40, 148
The Spyglass Tree (Murray) **73**:241-43
"SQ" (Le Guin) **45**:213
"Squandering the Blue" (Braverman) **67**:54
Squandering the Blue (Braverman) **67**:52-5
Le square (Duras) **3**:129; **6**:149; **11**:165; **40**:174, 180; **68**:76; **100**:129
The Square (Duras)
See *Le square*
The Square Cat (Ayckbourn) **74**:30-1
Square Dance (Boyle) **19**:68
Square in the Eye (Gelber) **79**:217, 222-24
Square One (Tesich) **69**:367-69
The Square Root of Wonderful (McCullers) **10**:334; **12**:425-26, 430
Square Rounds (Harrison) **129**:202, 221
The Squares of the City (Brunner) **8**:105; **10**:78-9
Square's Progress (Sheed) **2**:393; **4**:487
Squaring the Circle (Stoppard) **91**:190
"Squarings" (Heaney) **74**:188-91, 193-95, 197
Squat Betty (Waterhouse) **47**:417-18
"Squatter" (Mistry) **71**:266, 272
"Squatter's Children" (Bishop) **9**:93; **13**:89; **32**:31, 34
"Squeeze Box" (Townshend) **17**:535, 537
Squeeze Play (Auster) **131**:42-43
The Squire of Bor Shachor (Bermant) **40**:94
"Squirrel Disappears" (Peacock) **60**:292
The Squirrel Wife (Pearce) **21**:287-89
"The Squirrels of Summer" (Jacobsen) **48**:196
"S.R.O." (Ellison) **42**:127
"Śroczość" (Milosz) **56**:244
"An S.S. Officer" (Spicer) **18**:513
S.S. San Pedro (Cozzens) **4**:111; **11**:125, 128, 131; **92**:178, 186, 199-200
SS-GB: Nazi-Occupied Britain, 1941 (Deighton) **22**:116-17; **46**:128
"S.S.R., Lost at Sea" (Gustafson) **36**:214
"S-sss-ss-sh!" (Hughes) **108**:330
"St. Andrew's" (MacBeth) **2**:252; **5**:263
"St. Anne's Reel" (Ai) **69**:9
St. Augustine (West) **7**:525, 527; **31**:453
"St. Augustine and the Bullfight" (Porter) **101**:223
"St. Augustine's Pigeon" (Connell) **45**:109, 112, 115
St. Augustine's Pigeon: The Selected Stories of Evan S. Connell (Connell) **45**:114-15
"St. Barnabas, Oxford" (Betjeman) **34**:313
St. Burl's Obituary (Akst) **109**:39-42
"St. Catherine's Clock" (Kinsella) **138**:130, 136
"St Cecilia's Day" (Porter) **33**:323
"St. Christopher" (Brown) **100**:83
"St. Christopher" (Clarke) **9**:168
St. Dominic's Preview (Morrison) **21**:233-34
"St. Ebba of Coldingham" (Slavitt) **14**:491
"St. Francis and the Birds" (Heaney) **14**:243
"St. Francis of Assisi" (Elytis) **49**:110
St. Francis of Assisi (Almedingen) **12**:3
"St. George and the Dragon: Piecing It All Together" (Hearne) **56**:125-26
St. George and the Godfather (Mailer) **3**:315; **74**:225; **111**:103, 115
St. George of Ilhéus (Amado)
See *São Jorge dos Ilhéus*
"St. George's Basilica" (Seifert) **93**:345
"St. John" (Godwin) **31**:197
"St. Kilda's Parliament" (Dunn) **40**:170
St. Kilda's Parliament (Dunn) **40**:168-69, 171
St. Lawrence Blues (Blais)
See *Un joualonais, sa joualonie*
"St. Lawrence of the Cross" (McFadden) **48**:251
"St. Lawrence River" (Kenny) **87**:241
"St. Lemuel's Travels" (Amis) **8**:11
"St. Mark's" (Stern) **100**:344
St. Martin's (Creeley) **2**:108; **4**:117
"St. Paul Could Hit the Nail on the Head" (Mac Laverty) **31**:254
"St. Paul Outside the Walls" (Jennings) **131**:238
"St. Paul's Cathedral" (Hall) **51**:170
"St. Paul's Revisited" (Davie) **31**:112, 117
"St Paul's Rocks: 16 February, 1832" (Kinsella) **138**:120
"St. Roach" (Rukeyser) **10**:443
"St. Saviour's, Aberdeen Park" (Betjeman) **43**:35
"St. Thomas Aquinas" (Simic) **130**:318
"St. Thomas's Day" (Clarke) **61**:83
"St. Urbain Street Then and Now" (Richler) **46**:351-53
St. Urbain's Horseman (Richler) **3**:429-30; **5**:378; **18**:453, 455-56; **46**:347-51; **70**:220, 231-32
"St. Vincent's" (Merwin) **18**:334; **45**:274
Staalspanget (Wahlöö) **7**:501
"Stabat Mater" (Kristeva) **77**:317, 334; **140**:156-57, 170-71, 183, 186-88
"Stabat mater" (Wittlin) **25**:467
"The Stable" (Kinsella) **138**:135
Stad i ljus (Johnson) **14**:294
Stad i möerker (Johnson) **14**:294
"Le stade du miroir" (Lacan) **75**:282, 287, 292
Die Stadt (Dürrenmatt) **4**:140; **15**:193-96
Stadtgespräch (Lenz) **27**:244, 246, 249, 252-54
"The Staech Affair" (Boell)
See "Veränderungen in Staech"
"The Staff of Aesculapius" (Moore) **2**:291; **47**:263
"Staffordshire" (Davie) **8**:166
Stage Blood (Ludlam) **46**:241; **50**:343
Stage Door (Ferber) **93**:165
Stage Door (Kaufman) **38**:260
Stage Fright (Hitchcock) **16**:346
"The Stage Is Unlit" (Williams) **42**:440
"Stage Opens Case in New Delfer Trial" (Barnes) **127**:163
Stage Struck (Gray) **36**:205, 207
Stagecoach (Ford) **16**:304, 310, 314-15, 317
"Stages" (Gold) **42**:197; **152**:120
"Stages of a Journey Westward" (Wright) **3**:542
Stags and Hens (Russell) **60**:319-20
"Stained Glass" (Baxter) **45**:51, 53
Stained Glass (Buckley) **18**:81-3; **37**:60-1
Stained Glass Elegies (Endō) **54**:157, 160-61; **99**:301
"The Stained Glass Man" (Macdonald) **13**:356
"The Stained Glass Woman" (Macdonald) **19**:290
The Stainless Steel Rat (Harrison) **42**:200, 204-05
The Stainless Steel Rat for President (Harrison) **42**:207
The Stainless Steel Rat Saves the World (Harrison) **42**:204
The Stainless Steel Rat Wants You (Harrison) **42**:204
The Stainless Steel Rat's Revenge (Harrison) **42**:200-01, 204
"The Stains" (Aickman) **57**:4-5, 7
A Staircase in Surrey (Stewart) **14**:512
"The Stairs" (Moss) **14**:376
Stairs to the Roof (Williams) **71**:363, 367
"Stairway to Heaven" (Page and Plant) **12**:478-79, 481-82
"Staking Claim" (Ammons) **57**:58
"The Stalactite" (Blaga) **75**:61
Stalag 17 (Wilder) **20**:457, 460
"Stalin" (Elytis) **49**:110
The Stalingrad Elegies (Schevill) **7**:400

"Stalin's Heirs" (Yevtushenko) **3**:547; **26**:461, 464; **51**:431
Stalin's Heirs (Yevtushenko) **126**:390
"The Stalker" (Momaday) **85**:256
Stalker (Tarkovsky) **75**:382-85, 388-89, 394, 396-98, 401-02, 406-07, 412
"Stalking the Billion-Footed Beast: A Literary Manifesto for the New Social Novel" (Wolfe) **147**:321, 337, 340-46, 348-49, 366
Stalking the Nightmare (Ellison) **42**:131; **139**:115, 129, 133
"Stalkings" (Oates) **108**:371, 374
Stallerhof (Kroetz) **41**:234, 236-37
Stal'naja ptica (Aksyonov) **22**:26; **101**:19, 28-29
Stamboul Train (Greene) **3**:209, 213; **27**:173, 175; **37**:139; **70**:289-91, 293; **72**:159, 169, 171, 176
Stampe dell' ottocento (Palazzeschi) **11**:432
"The Stampede" (Williams) **42**:443
Stampede (Ringwood) **48**:329-30, 333, 335-38
"Stances" (Akhmatova) **126**:15, 20
The Stand (King) **12**:311; **26**:238, 240; **37**:200-01, 203, 205; **61**:327, 331-33, 335; **113**:343-47, 362, 364-66, 379, 388-93
"Stand, and Be Recognized" (Busch) **47**:61, 63
Stand Fast Beloved City (Almedingen) **12**:6
"Stand in a Row and Learn" (Abbott) **48**:4
A Stand in the Mountains (Taylor) **71**:295-96
Stand on Zanzibar (Brunner) **8**:105-07; **10**:78, 80
Stand Still like the Hummingbird (Miller) **43**:298
"Stand Up" (Marley) **17**:269
"Stand Up" (Salinas) **90**:324, 327
Stand Up, Nigel Barton (Potter) **86**:346, 349; **123**:229, 232, 265, 271, 273, 275
Stand We at Last (Fairbairns) **32**:163
Stand with Me Here (Francis) **15**:234-35, 239
"Stand with Your Lover on the Ending Earth" (Cummings) **68**:41
Standard Dreaming (Calisher) **2**:96-7; **4**:87; **134**:18, 35, 41
A Standard of Behavior (Trevor) **71**:339, 345; **116**:331, 334, 381
"The Standard of Living" (Parker) **68**:329, 335, 337
"Standardisation" (Hope) **51**:216
"Standards" (Doctorow) **113**:175
"Standards" (Moss) **45**:286
"Standards" (Weller) **26**:443
Standards of Safety and Hygiene in a Copper Mine (Kieslowski) **120**:209
Standing by Words (Berry) **46**:71, 75
Standing Fast (Swados) **5**:422-23
"Standing Fast: Fox into Hedgehog" (Davison) **28**:103
"Standing In for Nita" (Rooke) **25**:394
"Standing in My Ideas" (MacCaig) **36**:288
"Standing on the Streetcorner" (Denby) **48**:81
Standing Room Only (Ayckbourn) **74**:3
Standing Still and Walking in New York (O'Hara) **78**:358, 371, 375
"Standing Target" (Bernstein) **142**:22-4, 27-8, 34, 55
"Standing under a Cherry Tree at Night" (Bly) **15**:63
"The Stand-To" (Day Lewis) **10**:131
"Stand-to: Good Friday Morning" (Sassoon) **130**:181, 183, 214
"Stanislaw Lem" (Lem) **149**:268
"Stanley" (Grau) **146**:128-29, 161, 163
Stanley and the Women (Amis) **40**:45-8; **44**:135-36, 139, 141-42, 144; **129**:8-9, 12, 18-20, 23
Stanley Elkin's The Magic Kingdom (Elkin) **51**:92-6; **91**:213, 217
"Stanley Kunitz" (Oliver) **98**:290
"Stansy" (Akhmatova) **126**:15
"Stanza" (Bogan) **93**:92
"Stanzas" (Brodsky) **100**:51
"Stanzas Written at Night in Radio City" (Ginsberg) **6**:199
"The Star" (Clarke) **18**:107; **35**:122
"The Star" (Neruda)
See "La estrella"
Star (McClure)
See *The Surge*
The Star Beast (Heinlein) **26**:160-61, 172, 176-77; **55**:301, 303
Star Born (Norton) **12**:464
Star Bridge (Williamson) **29**:461
"Star Bright" (Williamson) **29**:455, 458
The Star Conquerors (Bova) **45**:65-6, 70
The Star Diaries (Lem) **8**:344-45; **15**:327; **40**:290, 296; **149**:112, 119, 145, 147-52, 156, 165, 255-56, 260, 264, 271, 273-75, 277, 284, 289
The Star Dwellers (Blish) **14**:86
"Star Food" (Canin) **55**:36-8
A Star for the Latecomer (Zindel) **27**:477-78
Star Gate (Norton) **12**:456, 461, 467
Star Guard (Norton) **12**:461, 463, 467
Star Hunter (Norton) **12**:467
"A Star in a Stone-Boat" (Frost) **13**:223
A Star in the Family (Faust) **8**:215
A Star in the Sea (Silverstein and Silverstein) **17**:450, 453
A Star Is Born (Hart) **66**:182
The Star King (Vance) **35**:421, 423
"Star Lummox" (Heinlein) **55**:303
Star Man's Son: 2250 A.D. (Norton) **12**:456, 461, 467
"Star of Bethlehem" (Young) **17**:577, 582
"Star of Day" (H. D.) **14**:224
The Star of Ethiopia (Du Bois) **64**:111, 121; **96**:145-46
"The Star of the Axletree" (Gray) **41**:183
Star Quality (Coward) **29**:140
Star Rangers (Norton) **12**:456, 461, 467
A Star Shines Over Mt. Morris Park (Roth) **104**:317, 319, 324-25, 327
Star Smashers of the Galaxy Rangers (Harrison) **42**:202-03, 205, 207
Star Songs of an Old Primate (Tiptree) **48**:388-89
"Star Spangled Banner" (Kristofferson) **26**:269
"Star Star" (Jagger and Richard) **17**:228, 234, 236, 238
A Star to the North (Corcoran) **17**:70, 72
"Star Trek" (Roddenberry) **17**:403-15
"Star Turn II" (Wright) **146**:380
The Star Turns Red (O'Casey) **5**:320; **11**:406-09; **15**:406; **88**:257-58, 270
Star Wars (Lucas) **16**:411-17
Star Watchman (Bova) **45**:66, 70
Stara kobieta wysiaduje (Rozewicz) **9**:463; **139**:230, 232, 265, 293
"The Star-Apple Kingdom" (Walcott) **42**:421-22; **67**:355
The Star-Apple Kingdom (Walcott) **14**:550-51; **25**:457; **42**:418, 421-22; **67**:358, 360; **76**:274
Starboard Wine (Delany) **141**:145, 149
Starbuck Valley Winter (Haig-Brown) **21**:138-41
Starcarbon, a Meditation on Love (Gilchrist) **143**:399, 312, 315-16
The Starched Blue Sky of Spain (Herbst) **34**:452
The Starcrossed (Bova) **45**:68-9
"Stardust" (Simon) **26**:413
Stardust Memories (Allen) **52**:46, 48-9
"Star-Fall" (Warren) **13**:582; **18**:535
"The Starfish" (Bly) **128**:17
"Starfucker" (Jagger and Richard)
See "Star Star"
"Stargazer" (Diamond) **30**:112-13
"Star-Gazer" (MacNeice) **53**:239
"Stargazing at Barten" (Steele) **45**:362
Starik (Trifonov) **45**:413-14, 417, 419-25
"Staring at the Sea on the Day of the Death of Another" (Swenson) **106**:328
Staring at the Sun (Barnes) **141**:32. 39, 48, 53, 61-2, 65, 77
"Stark Boughs on the Family Tree" (Oliver) **98**:266
"Stark County Holidays" (Oliver) **19**:362; **98**:265
"Starley" (Beattie) **146**:64
"Starlight" (Levine) **118**:277
"The Starlight Express" (Gilchrist) **65**:349
"Starlight Scope Myopia" (Komunyakaa) **94**:228, 240, 243-44, 247
"Starlight Scope Myopia" (Komunyakaa) **94**:228, 240, 243-244, 247
"Starman" (Bowie) **17**:59, 65
Starman Jones (Heinlein) **8**:275; **14**:250; **26**:162-63, 170-72, 176; **55**:301-02
"Staroe vedro" (Solzhenitsyn) **10**:479
"Starring: All People" (Arreola) **147**:14
Starring Sally J. Freedman as Herself (Blume) **12**:46
"Starry Night" (Sexton) **10**:468; **53**:316, 320
"The Starry Night" (Snodgrass) **68**:388
The Starry Rift (Tiptree) **48**:394-95
A Starry Ticket (Aksyonov) **22**:25, 27-8; **101**:3-4, 6, 9, 14-15, 28-9, 47
Starryveldt (Morgan) **31**:272
"Stars" (Hayden) **9**:270; **37**:153
"Stars" (Moss) **45**:287, 289
"Stars" (Slessor) **14**:494
"Stars" (Wright) **53**:418, 431
The Stars (Bernhard)
See *Die Berühmten*
Stars and Bars (Boyd) **53**:50-3, 55-6; **70**:132, 134-35
The Stars Are Ours! (Norton) **12**:456, 467
"The Stars are the Styx" (Sturgeon) **39**:366
The Stars at Noon (Johnson) **52**:239-41
"The Stars Below" (Saro-Wiwa) **114**:253
Stars in Her Eyes (Cavanna) **12**:100
Stars in My Pocket Like Grains of Sand (Delany) **38**:162; **141**:101-06, 119-26, 135-36, 138-39, 141, 148, 158
The Stars in Shroud (Benford) **52**:60, 65
"Stars in Your Name" (Broumas) **73**:15
The Stars, like Dust (Asimov) **26**:48
The Stars Look Down (Cronin) **32**:132-34
"Stars of the New Curfew" (Okri) **87**:319, 321
Stars of the New Curfew (Okri) **87**:315, 319-22
The Stars of the South (Green)
See *Les ètoiles du sud*
Stars over Paradise Garden (Seifert)
See *Hvězdy nad rajskou zahradou*
"Stars Over the Dordogne" (Plath) **111**:200, 214
"Stars Wheel in Purple" (H. D.) **73**:118
Stars Which See, Stars Which Do Not See (Bell) **31**:49-51
"Stars Won't You Hide Me" (Bova) **45**:73
Starship (Aldiss)
See *Non-Stop*
Starship Troopers (Heinlein) **14**:246-47, 250-254; **26**:162-63, 165-66, 170-71, 173, 177-78; **55**:303
The Star-Spangled Crunch (Condon) **100**:104
The Star-Spangled Future (Spinrad) **46**:384
The Star-Spangled Girl (Simon) **31**:393-94, 396
"The Star-Splitter" (Frost) **10**:195
Starswarm (Aldiss) **14**:11
"Start Again Somewhere" (Gallagher) **63**:118
Start from Home (Summers) **10**:493
A Start in Life (Brookner) **32**:59-61; **34**:139, 142; **136**:82, 87-88, 97-98, 100-01, 123
A Start in Life (Sillitoe) **1**:308; **57**:397, 399-400; **148**:156-57, 164, 168-69, 186-87
"Start of a Late Autumn Novel" (Transtroemer) **52**:416; **65**:230
Startide Rising (Brin) **34**:133-35
"Starting" (O'Brien) **13**:415
"Starting a New Life" (Morrison) **21**:232
"Starting Back" (Hugo) **32**:242
Starting: Early, Anew, Over, and Late (Yglesias) **22**:492
Starting from San Francisco (Ferlinghetti) **10**:175; **27**:139; **111**:64
Starting from Scratch (Castellanos)
See *Al pie de la letra*

Starting from Scratch: A Different Kind of Writer's Manual (Brown) **79**:166, 168, 171
Starting Out (Berton) **104**:62
Starting Out in the Thirties (Kazin) **38**:275-77, 280, 283; **119**:305, 311, 314, 318, 334
Starting Over (Wakefield) **7**:503
"Starving" (Faludy) **42**:141
"Starving Again" (Moore) **68**:300
"Starving Children" (Bogosian) **141**:86
Starworld (Harrison) **42**:206-07
"The State" (Pound) **112**:319-20
"State Champions" (Mason) **82**:244, 252
"State of Affairs" (Gustafson) **36**:222
"The State of Art" (Elkin) **14**:158
A State of Change (Gilliatt) **2**:160; **53**:143-44
"The State of Grace" (Brodkey) **56**:55-6, 63-4
State of Grace (Williams) **31**:461-63
A State of Independence (Phillips) **96**:317-18, 325, 333, 340, 343, 352, 354
The State of Ireland: A Novella and Seventeen Stories (Kiely) **23**:265-67; **43**:241-43, 245
A State of Justice (Paulin) **37**:352-53
A State of Peace (Elliott) **47**:107-08, 110
A State of Siege (Ambler) **4**:19; **9**:19
The State of Siege (Camus)
See *L'état de siège*
A State of Siege (Frame) **22**:144, 146; **96**:169, 179-80, 189-90, 192, 196, 203, 217, 219
"State of the Art" (Bernstein) **142**:19, 44
"State of the Art/1990" (Bernstein) **142**:9
State of the Nation (Dos Passos) **15**:183
State of the Union (Capra) **16**:159-61
"The State of the Union: 1975" (Vidal) **142**:298
"The Stately Roller Coaster" (Tremain) **42**:386
"Statement" (Francis) **15**:238
"Statement" (Kroetsch) **132**:239
"Statement By a Responsible Spinster" (Smith) **64**:394
"Statement for the New Poetics Colloquium, Vancouver, 1985" (Howe) **152**:163, 175-77
"Statement of Conservation" (Giovanni) **117**:203
Statements after an Arrest under the Immorality Act (Fugard) **9**:229, 232-35; **40**:197-98; **80**:65-6, 68, 70, 74
Statements: Two Workshop Productions (Fugard) **40**:197-98
States of Desire: Travels in Gay America (White) **27**:480-81; **110**:313-14, 316, 322-23, 327, 332
States of Emergency (Brink) **106**:107-08, 119-20, 123-25, 137
"Static" (Barnard) **48**:27
Station (Kieslowski) **120**:243, 245
"Station Island" (Heaney) **37**:164-66, 168-69; **74**:162-63, 165, 168, 175, 181, 184, 186-87, 193; **91**:115-17, 120, 122
Station Island (Heaney) **37**:164-69; **74**:162, 164-67, 169, 172, 174, 186, 189-90, 193, 197; **91**:119, 124
Station to Station (Bowie) **17**:63-4, 66, 68
Station Zima (Yevtushenko)
See "Zima Station"
"Stations" (Hughes) **119**:296
"Stations" (Lorde) **71**:260
"Stations" (Stow) **23**:436
Stations (Heaney) **74**:193; **91**:122
"The Statue" (Creeley) **78**:137
"The Statue" (Finch) **18**:155
"The Statue" (Fuller) **62**:184
"The Statue" (Gregor) **9**:254
"Statue and Birds" (Bogan) **46**:86; **93**:93
"Statue at Tsarskoye Selo" (Akhmatova) **64**:9
"The Statue in the Café" (Ritsos) **31**:331
"The Statue in the Hills" (Brown) **48**:57
"A Statue of Aphrodite" (Gilchrist) **143**:300-01, 325
"The Statue of Liberty" (Wideman) **67**:379, 382, 385
"The Statues" (Durcan) **70**:152
"The Statues" (Schwartz) **10**:462, 465
"Statues" (Wilbur) **53**:399
"Statues and Lovers" (Hall) **51**:170
Statues in a Garden (Colegate) **36**:109-11
Les statues meurent aussi (Resnais) **16**:505
"The Statues of Athens" (Squires) **51**:381
"The Status of Art" (Burke) **24**:119
"A Statute of Wine" (Neruda)
See "Estatura del vino"
Stavisky (Resnais) **16**:511, 513-15
"Stay" (Sondheim) **30**:379
"Stay Free" (Clash) **30**:43, 46
Stay with Me till Morning (Braine) **41**:58, 61
"Staying Alive" (Levertov) **8**:347; **66**:245-48
"Staying Alive" (Wagoner) **15**:558-59
Staying Alive (Wagoner) **5**:474
"Staying Alive by Going to Pieces" (Wagoner) **5**:474
"Staying at Ed's Place" (Swenson) **61**:397, 401
Staying On (Scott) **9**:478; **60**:336, 339, 341
"Staying Thin" (Dacey) **51**:82
Stazione termini (De Sica) **20**:94
"Steady, Steady, Six Already" (Cortázar) **34**:334
Steady Work: Essays in the Politics of Democratic Radicalism, 1953-1966 (Howe) **85**:150
The Steagle (Faust) **8**:215
"Steak Worship" (Priestley) **34**:362
The Stealer of Souls, and Other Stories (Moorcock) **58**:350
Stealing the Language: The Emergence of Women's Poetry in America (Ostriker) **132**:303-05, 308, 310, 312-18, 321, 327
"Stealing Tomorrow" (Ellison) **139**:116
"Stealing Trout on a May Morning" (Hughes) **37**:181
"Steam" (Wain) **46**:415
"The Steam Boiler Effect" (Grass)
See "Der Dampfkessel-Effekt"
"Steam Song" (Brooks) **49**:36, 38
Steambath (Friedman) **5**:127; **56**:98-100
Steamboat Bill Junior (Keaton) **20**:190, 193-96
"Steamed Carp's Cheeks" (Fuller) **62**:199
"The Steel" (Murray) **40**:343
Steel Across the Plains (Berton) **104**:61
"Steel and Glass" (Lennon) **35**:268, 271
The Steel Bird, and Other Stories (Aksyonov)
See *Stal'naja ptica*
"Steel Gang" (Davis) **49**:93
Steel Magic (Norton) **12**:457
Steel Magnolias (Harling) **53**:165-67
The Steel Spring (Wahlöö)
See *Staalspanget*
Steelwork (Sorrentino) **3**:462; **7**:447-48, 450-52; **22**:392-93; **40**:386-87
"Steely Silence" (Wakoski) **4**:573
The Steep Ascent (Lindbergh) **82**:166-67
Steeple Bush (Frost) **3**:169-70; **9**:220; **15**:241-42, 245; **26**:119
"A Steeple on the House" (Frost) **15**:242
"The Steeple-Jack" (Moore) **8**:397; **10**:348; **19**:338, 340; **47**:260-61, 264, 266, 270
Steeplejacks in Babel (Cassity) **6**:107; **42**:95, 97-8
"Steering Wheel" (Graham) **118**:223, 259
"Steersman, My Brother" (Walcott) **25**:450
"Stefano's Two Sons" (Landolfi) **11**:321; **49**:210, 212
Steffie Can't Come Out to Play (Arrick) **30**:17
"Steh auf, steh doch auf" (Boell) **72**:69
A Steinbook and More (Rothenberg) **6**:477
Das steinerne Herz: Historischer Roman aus dem Jahre 1954 (Schmidt) **56**:391-93, 405
The Steinway Quartet (Epstein) **27**:128
"Stele" (Aldington) **49**:3, 6
"Stèle aux mots" (Audiberti) **38**:21
"Stellar Manipulator" (Durcan) **70**:153
"Stellavista" (Ballard)
See "The Thousand Dreams of Stellavista"
Der Stellvertreter (Hochhuth) **4**:230; **11**:276
"The Stenographer" (Nowlan) **15**:399
"The Stenographers" (Page) **18**:379
The Step (Loewinsohn) **52**:285
"A Step Away from Them" (O'Hara) **13**:425; **78**:348-51, 353, 364, 376
"The Step Beyond" (Livesay) **79**:348
"Step on His Head" (Laughlin) **49**:220
A Step to Silence (Newby) **2**:310; **13**:408, 410-12
"Step-and-a-Half Waleski" (Erdrich) **54**:165
"Stepanida Ivanovna's Funeral" (Soloukhin) **59**:378
"The Stepchildren" (Elytis) **49**:111
The Stepdaughter (Blackwood) **9**:101; **100**:2-3, 9, 14-15, 19, 27, 31
Stepen' doveriia (Voinovich) **10**:506; **147**:279
The Stepford Wives (Levin) **3**:294; **6**:305-06
"Stephano Remembers" (Simmons) **43**:411
"Stephanotis" (Day Lewis) **10**:131
Stephen Crane: A Critical Biography (Berryman) **3**:71; **13**:76
Stephen D (Leonard) **19**:280
Stephen Hawking's A Brief History of Time: A Reader's Companion (Hawking) **105**:67-8
Stephen King's Danse Macabre (King) **26**:243; **37**:197-99, 202; **61**:326-27
A Stephen Sondheim Evening (Sondheim) **30**:400
Stephen Spender: Journals, 1939-1983 (Spender) **41**:426-27, 429
Stephen's Light (Almedingen) **12**:4-5
Steppenwolf (Hesse)
See *Der Steppenwolf*
Der Steppenwolf (Hesse) **1**:145-47; **2**:191; **3**:243-49; **6**:236; **11**:270-72; **17**:196-97, 201-02, 204, 206, 208, 211-16, 219; **25**:261, **69**:272, 274-79, 284, 286-87, 289, 292-98
"Steppin' Out" (Armatrading) **17**:10
"Stepping Outside" (Gallagher) **18**:168; **63**:120
"Stepping Westward" (Levertov) **66**:235
Stepping Westward (Bradbury) **32**:51, 53-6, 58; **61**:34, 39-40
"Steps" (O'Hara) **78**:334
Steps (Kosinski) **1**:171-72; **2**:231-33; **3**:272-73; **6**:282-85; **10**:306-08; **15**:313-14, 316-17; **53**:216-17, 219-20, 222, 226, 228; **70**:287-98, 300-01, 303, 306
The Steps of the Sun (Tevis) **42**:376-77
Steps: Selected Fiction and Drama (Josipovici) **153**:210
Stepsons of Terra (Silverberg) **140**:363
"Das Sterben der Pythia" (Duerrenmatt) **102**:61-2, 64, 69
Stereo (Cronenberg) **143**:87, 94, 152
The Sterile Cuckoo (Nichols) **38**:336-41, 343
"Sterling" (Hope) **52**:209
"The Sterling Letters" (Harper) **7**:140
Stern (Friedman) **3**:165; **5**:126-27; **56**:93-7, 99, 101-05, 107-09
Sternverdunkelung (Sachs) **98**:321-22, 324, 343-45, 352, 356-57, 364
Stet (Reading) **47**:354-55
"The Stethoscope" (Abse) **29**:18
"Steven Spielberg Plays Howard Beach" (Reed) **60**:310
"Stevens" (Harmon) **38**:243
"The Stevenson Poster" (Simpson) **149**:348
Stevie (Whitemore) **37**:444-45
Stevie: A Biography of Stevie Smith (Barbera and McBrien) **44**:432-35, 437, 440-41, 443-45
Stevie Smith: A Selection (Smith) **44**:433, 441
Stevie Wonder Presents Syreeta (Wonder) **12**:663
Stewards of Excellence (Alvarez) **5**:16
"Stick" (Abe) **81**:293
Stick (Leonard) **28**:235-36; **71**:207-08, 210-11, 213, 216-17, 219, 221-22, 224, 226; **120**:264-67, 274, 284, 287, 289, 295, 299, 305
"A Stick of Green Candy" (Bowles) **68**:4-6, 9
"A Stick-Nest in Ygdrasil" (MacDiarmid) **63**:244

Sticks and Bones (Rabe) **4**:425-27; **8**:449-51; **33**:341-44
"Sticks and Stones" (Michaels) **25**:315-16
Sticks and Stones (Bowering) **15**:81
Sticks and Stones (Reaney) **13**:475-76
Sticky Fingers (Jagger and Richard) **17**:224-26, 228-30, 232-33, 236, 238, 242
Stiff Upper Lip: Life among the Diplomats (Durrell) **41**:139
Stiffed: The Betrayal of the American Man (Faludi) **140**:106-11, 113-16, 118, 120, 122-26, 128-33
Stigar (Transtroemer) **65**:221, 233
"Stikhi pod epigrafom" (Brodsky) **13**:115
Stikhi/Poems/Poèmes (Ratushinskaya) **54**:379-80, 384, 386
Stikhi raznykh let (Yevtushenko) **13**:620
"Stikhii" (Bagryana) **10**:12
"Stiletto" (Joel) **26**:216-17, 220-21
"Still" (Ammons) **25**:48; **57**:58; **108**:23
"Still" (Beckett) **14**:74
"Still Afternoon Light" (Merwin) **1**:213
Still Another Day (Neruda) **62**:333
The Still Centre (Spender) **5**:401; **10**:492; **41**:424, 429
"Still, Citizen Sparrow" (Wilbur) **53**:410-11; **110**:354-55
"Still Crazy after All These Years" (Simon) **17**:465-66
"Still Do I Keep My Look, My Identity" (Brooks) **125**:52
"Still Hot from Filing" (Williams) **42**:439
"Still Hunting" (Lane) **25**:286
Still Is the Summer Night (Derleth) **31**:129
Still It Is the Day (Delibes)
See *Aún es de día*
"Still Jim and Silent Jim" (Pearce) **21**:288
"Still Just Writing" (Tyler) **103**:225, 257, 266
"Still Life" (Glück) **22**:174
"Still Life" (Graham) **118**:224
"Still Life" (Hughes) **14**:271
"Still Life" (MacCaig) **36**:282
"Still Life" (Olds) **85**:295
"Still Life" (Tchicaya) **101**:347
"Still Life" (Thomas) **31**:430
Still Life (Byatt) **65**:125, 131; **136**:135-36, 145, 149, 151, 156-59, 162, 164-65, 167, 177, 179, 181****
Still Life (Coward) **51**:69
Still Life (Daryush) **19**:119, 122
"Still Life: A Glassful of Zinnias on my Daughter's Kitchen Table" (Ostriker) **132**:324
"Still Life/Nature morte" (Byatt) **136**:151
"Still Life with Flowers" (Thomas) **13**:539
"Still Life with Fruit" (Betts) **6**:70
Still Life with Pipe (Donoso) **99**:222, 255, 273-75
"Still Life with Spring and Time to Burn" (Wright) **146**:345, 370
"Still Life with Stick and Word" (Wright) **146**:357
"Still Life with Watermelon" (Mason) **28**:274; **154**:322
"Still Life with Window and Fish" (Graham) **118**:241
Still Life with Woodpecker (Robbins) **32**:367-69, 371, 373-74; **64**:377, 381-83
"Still Lives" (Goldbarth) **38**:205
"A Still Moment" (Welty) **14**:563; **33**:424; **105**:299, 307, 385
"Still on Water" (Rexroth) **49**:281; **112**:398
Still Stands the House (Ringwood) **48**:329-39
"Still the Same" (Seger) **35**:383
"Still They Call It Marriage" (Musgrave) **54**:333
"The Still Time" (Kinnell) **29**:285
"Still Turning" (Swenson) **106**:351
Still Water (Nichol) **18**:369
Still Waters (Middleton) **38**:331
"Stillborn" (Plath) **5**:341; **14**:424; **111**:181, 212
Stille Nacht I (The Brothers Quay) **95**:351-52, 354
Stille Nacht II (The Brothers Quay) **95**:346-47, 351-52, 354
Stille Nacht III (The Brothers Quay) **95**:351-32, 355
Stille Nacht IIIA (The Brothers Quay) **95**:354
Stille Nacht IV (The Brothers Quay) **95**:354
Stiller (Frisch) **3**:167; **9**:217-18; **18**:163; **32**:188-94; **44**:183-90, 193-94, 200, 203
"Stillness" (Gardner) **28**:162
A Stillness at Appomattox (Catton) **35**:85-6, 88, 90
"The Stillness of the Poem" (Loewinsohn) **52**:282-83
"Stillpoint Hill at Midnight" (Chappell) **40**:145
"Stillpoint Hill That Other Shore" (Chappell) **40**:145; **78**:92
"Stills" (Montague) **46**:266
"Stimme des Heilegen Landes" (Sachs) **98**:349
"Stimmen" (Celan) **53**:69, 77
Stimmen (Eich) **15**:204
Stimmen (Wolf)
See *Medea: Stimmen*
Die Stimmen von Marrakesch: Aufzeichnungen nach einer Reise (Canetti) **14**:124; **25**:107-09, 111-12; **75**:130, 139; **86**:301, 303
Der Stimmenimitator (Bernhard) **61**:9
Stimmungen der See (Lenz) **27**:244-45
The Sting (Hill) **26**:201-05, 207-08, 211-12
"Stings" (Plath) **9**:424, 426, 431, 433; **17**:361, 366; **111**:169, 177
Stir Crazy (Friedman) **56**:108
Stir Crazy (Poitier) **26**:361-62
"Stir It Up" (Marley) **17**:268, 272
"The Stir-Off" (Still) **49**:364
Stirrings Still (Beckett) **59**:253, 255, 259
Stitch (Stern) **4**:523; **39**:237-39
"Stixi na smert T. S. Èliota" (Brodsky) **4**:77; **6**:97; **13**:114; **50**:131
"Stoat" (McGahern) **48**:264
"Stobhill" (Morgan) **31**:275-76
The Stochastic Man (Silverberg) **7**:425; **140**:343, 345, 380
"The Stocking" (Campbell) **42**:92
Stolen Apples (Yevtushenko) **1**:383; **3**:547; **126**:390
Stolen Hours (West) **17**:548
Stolen Kisses (Truffaut)
See *Baisers volés*
The Stolen Lake (Aiken) **35**:19-20
Stolen Life (Wiebe) **138**:396-97
The Stolen Melody (Nossack)
See *Die gestohlene Melodie*
"Stolen Pleasures" (Berriault) **109**:97
"Stolen Poems" (Laughlin) **49**:224
"The Stolen Stories" (Katz) **47**:222
Stolen Stories (Katz) **47**:220, 222-23
"Stolen Trees" (Hogan) **73**:156
Stomping the Blues (Murray) **73**:231-36, 242
"The Stone" (Ezekiel) **61**:104
"The Stone" (Herbert) **43**:193
"Stone" (Hoffman) **6**:244
"Stone" (Simic) **9**:479; **49**:338-40, 342; **68**:370, 378; **130**:316
"The Stone" (Soto)
See "Piedra"
"The Stone" (Thesen) **56**:420
"Stone" (Thomas) **13**:542
"Stone and Fern" (Norris) **14**:388
Stone and Flower Poems, 1935-1943 (Raine) **45**:330-32, 334, 341
The Stone Angel (Laurence) **3**:280; **13**:342-43; **50**:312-20; **62**:267, 269-71, 273, 278-84, 288-89, 306-07
"The Stone Bear" (Haines) **58**:218
The Stone Bird (Purdy) **50**:246, 248
The Stone Book (Garner) **17**:147-50
"The Stone Boy" (Berriault) **54**:3-4; **109**:95
The Stone Bridal Bed (Mulisch) **42**:287-88
The Stone Bridge (Seifert)
See *Kammený most*
The Stone Bull (Whitney) **42**:435
"Stone Canyon Nocturne" (Wright) **146**:374
"A Stone Church Damaged by a Bomb" (Larkin) **64**:261, 282
"Stone City" (Proulx) **81**:275
"The Stone Clasp" (Thomas) **132**:382
A Stone Country (La Guma) **19**:274-76
"The Stone Crab: A Love Poem" (Phillips) **28**:362-63
The Stone Diaries (Shields) **91**:167-80; **113**:437-41, 444-45
"Stone Dreams" (Kingsolver) **130**:73
A Stone for Danny Fisher (Robbins) **5**:379
The Stone from the Green Star (Williamson) **29**:454
"The Stone from the Sea" (Celan) **82**:36
"A Stone Garden" (Snyder) **120**:334-35
The Stone Hammer Poems (Kroetsch) **23**:272, 276; **132**:245, 275
The Stone Harp (Haines) **58**:215-17, 219, 221
"Stone Idols" (Silko) **114**:341
"The Stone in the Field" (Munro) **95**:305-06, 314
"Stone inside a Stone" (Simic) **9**:480
"Stone Keep" (Ammons) **57**:51
"The Stone Man" (Hill) **45**:179
"Stone Mania" (Murphy) **41**:319-20
Stone of Sleep (Cabral de Melo Neto)
See *Pedra do sono*
"The Stone on the Island" (Campbell) **42**:83
"Stone or Flame" (Swenson) **106**:337
Stone, Paper, Knife (Piercy) **27**:381; **62**:366-68, 373; **128**:246, 273-74
The Stone Raft (Saramago)
See *A jangada de pedra*
"Stone Reality Meditation" (Ferlinghetti) **111**:65
Stone Roots (Alexander) **121**:3
"Stone Serpents" (Zamora) **89**:386, 391, 393-94
Stone Telling (Le Guin) **45**:219
"Stone Trees" (Gardam) **43**:171
"The Stone Verdict" (Heaney) **74**:160
Stone Virgin (Unsworth) **76**:252-54; **127**:412-13
"The Stone without Edges" (Ciardi) **40**:156
"Stonebreaking" (Forster) **45**:134
"The Stonecarver's Poem" (Levertov) **66**:249
"Stoned Immaculate" (Morrison) **17**:293
"Stoned Soul Picnic" (Nyro) **17**:313
The Stone-Faced Boy (Fox) **121**:186, 199, 231
Stonehenge (Harrison) **42**:201
The Stonemason (McCarthy) **101**:168, 191-92, 194, 202-03
"Stones" (Hoffman) **141**:295
"The Stones" (Plath) **1**:270; **11**:446; **14**:425; **17**:365-68; **51**:340, 344, 346, 348-49; **111**:165, 178-79
"Stones" (Transtroemer) **65**:222
Stones (Findley) **102**:110, 117
The Stones (Hall) **1**:137
Stones (O'Hara) **13**:424, 427
"Stones and Angels" (MacEwen) **55**:165
Stones for Ibarra (Doerr) **34**:151-54
"Stones for My Temple" (Blaga) **75**:71
Stones from the Rubble (Montgomery) **7**:233
"Stones in My Passway, Hellhound on My Trail" (Boyle) **36**:64
The Stones of Chile (Neruda)
See *Las piedras de Chile*
The Stones of Florence (McCarthy) **14**:357; **59**:290
The Stones of the Field (Thomas) **6**:532; **13**:542; **48**:380
Stones Speak (Endō) **99**:285
The Stonewall Brigade (Slaughter) **29**:378
Stonewall Jackson: The Good Soldier (Tate) **11**:526-27
"Stonewall Jackson's Wife" (Wiggins) **57**:433-35
"Stoney End" (Nyro) **17**:315
"Stony Grey Soil" (Kavanagh) **22**:239
Stony Limits (MacDiarmid) **4**:309; **11**:333; **19**:290; **63**:249, 255
"Stop" (Dixon) **52**:99
"Stop" (Wilbur) **6**:570; **53**:413
A Stop in the Desert (Brodsky) **100**:59

Stop Press (Stewart) **14**:512
"Stop Staring at My Tits, Mister" (Bukowski) **41**:74; **108**:85
"Stopped Dead" (Plath) **5**:345; **17**:366; **51**:340, 345
"Stopped Frames and Set-Pieces" (Fisher) **25**:161
"Stopping by Woods on a Snowy Evening" (Frost) **3**:170, 174; **9**:220; **10**:198; **13**:223-24, 228, 230; **15**:240, 244, 246, 249; **26**:114-17, 119, 121-23; **34**:475
A Stopping Place (Mojtabai) **15**:378-79
"The Store" (Jones) **76**:65-6
The Store (Stribling) **23**:440, 442, 448-49
Det store spelet (Vesaas) **48**:404, 406, 409
"The Storeroom" (Weiss) **8**:546; **14**:554, 557
Störfall (Wolf) **150**:291-93, 330
La storia (Morante) **8**:402-03; **47**:276-77, 281-83
Storia della Tigre e altre storie (Fo) **109**:101, 108, 115
"La storia di Regalpetra" (Sciascia) **41**:392
Storie naturali (Levi) **50**:331
"Stories" (Anderson) **9**:31
"The Stories" (Dunn) **40**:171
"Stories" (Jarrell) **13**:301; **49**:196
"Stories" (Oliver) **98**:303
Stories (Lessing) **10**:316; **15**:331
Stories (Pasternak) **63**:290
Stories about Unusual Muzhiks (Leonov)
See *Neobyknovennie rasskazy o muzhikakh*
Stories and Plays (O'Brien) **4**:385; **7**:269-70; **10**:362
Stories and Prose Poems: by Aleksandr Solzhenitsyn (Solzhenitsyn) **4**:507; **78**:427
"Stories and Totalitarianism" (Havel) **123**:184, 188
Stories, Fables, and Other Diversions (Nemerov) **6**:360, 363
Stories for Children (Singer) **69**:306
"Stories from behind the Stove" (Singer) **3**:454
Stories from El Barrio (Thomas) **17**:502
Stories from Western Canada (Wiebe) **6**:567
"Stories I Tell Myself" (Cortázar) **33**:126, 130
Stories in an Almost Classical Mode (Brodkey) **56**:59-63, 65-7
The Stories of Bernard Malamud (Malamud) **27**:305-07; **44**:413
The Stories of Breece D'J Pancake (Pancake) **29**:346-51
The Stories of Elizabeth Spencer (Spencer) **22**:405
The Stories of Eva Luna (Allende) **97**:2-4, 9-11, 25-6, 28, 56, 63
Stories of Five Decades (Hesse) **2**:192; **3**:249
The Stories of Heinrich Böll (Boell) **72**:99
"Stories of Ideas" (Riding) **7**:375
The Stories of John Cheever (Cheever) **11**:120-21; **15**:129-31; **64**:66
The Stories of John Edgar Wideman (Wideman) **122**:343-44, 347
The Stories of Lilus Kikus (Poniatowska)
See *Los cuentos de Lilus Kikus*
"Stories of Lives" (Riding) **7**:375
Stories of Love (Agnon) **4**:11
"The Stories of Love and Sickness" (Calvino) **39**:314
The Stories of Mary Lavin (Lavin) **99**:322
Stories of Misbegotten Love (Gold) **42**:197
The Stories of Muriel Spark (Spark) **40**:400-03
"The Stories of Our Daughters" (Smith) **42**:350
The Stories of Ray Bradbury (Bradbury) **42**:35-7
The Stories of Raymond Carver (Carver) **36**:106; **53**:66
The Stories of Seán O'Faoláin (O'Faolain)
See *Finest Short Stories of Seán O'Faoláin*
"Stories of Snow" (Page) **7**:291-92; **18**:379
Stories of the Gods and Heroes (Benson) **17**:47
The Stories of William Trevor (Trevor) **71**:321, 324-5, 334; **116**:367
Stories that Could Be True: New and Collected Poems (Stafford) **29**:383, 385
Stories up to a Point (Pesetsky) **28**:357-59
Stories We Listened To (Haines) **58**:223
"The Storm" (Brown) **48**:57
"Storm" (H. D.) **73**:118
"The Storm" (L'Heureux) **52**:274
"Storm" (O'Brien) **65**:167-71
"Storm" (Oliver) **98**:266
The Storm (Ehrenburg) **18**:132; **62**:177-80
The Storm: A Poem in Five Parts (Alexander) **121**:8-9
Storm and Echo (Prokosch) **48**:312-15
The Storm and Other Poems (Brown) **100**:84
The Storm and Other Things (Montale)
See *La bufera e altro*
The Storm and the Silence (Walker) **14**:552
Storm at Castelfranco (Kallman) **2**:221
"Storm Awst" (Clarke) **61**:73
Storm Below (Garner) **13**:234
Storm Boy (Thiele) **17**:493, 496
"The Storm Cleared Rapidly" (Jacobsen) **48**:190
"Storm Coming in Wales" (Grigson) **7**:136
"Storm Ending" (Toomer) **1**:341
"Storm Fear" (Frost) **26**:113
"Storm Glass" (Urquhart) **90**:384-5
Storm Glass (Urquhart) **90**:383-5
Storm Haven (Slaughter) **29**:375
Storm in Chandigarh (Sahgal) **41**:371
"Storm in the Desert" (Squires) **51**:380, 382
Storm of Fortune (Clarke) **8**:142; **53**:93-4
The Storm of Steel (Jünger)
See *In Stahlgewittern*
"Storm on Fifth Avenue" (Sassoon) **36**:387
Storm over Warlock (Norton) **12**:467
"Storm Warnings" (Rich) **36**:365; **125**:310
"Storm Weather" (Shapcott) **38**:402
"Storm Windows" (Nemerov) **36**:305
The Storm Within (Cocteau) **16**:223
"The Storm-Cock's Song" (MacDiarmid) **63**:255
The Storming of Velikoshumsk (Leonov)
See *Vziatie Velikoshumska*
"Stormpetrel" (Murphy) **41**:314
Stormqueen (Bradley) **30**:27-8, 30
The Stormy Life of Lasik Roitschwantz (Ehrenburg) **18**:134; **34**:437, 439; **62**:173
"Stormy Night" (Blunden) **56**:49
The Stormy Night (Duhamel)
See *La nuit d'orage*
The Stormy Petrel (Stewart) **117**:384
"Stormy Sky" (Davies) **21**:102
"A Story" (Avison) **97**:115
"Story" (Cohen) **38**:131
"A Story" (Rich) **73**:330
"Story" (Sanchez) **116**:328
The Story (Pasternak)
See *Povest*
"A Story about Chicken Soup" (Simpson) **149**:324-25
"A Story about Greenery" (Valenzuela) **104**:388
"The Story Behind 'Foundation'" (Asimov) **92**:21
"Story Books on a Kitchen Table" (Lorde) **71**:247, 250
A Story for Teddy—And Others (Swados) **5**:422
"Story from Bear Country" (Silko) **114**:316
"The Story Hearer" (Paley) **37**:336; **140**:222, 226, 228, 230, 232, 234, 262
"A Story in an Almost Classical Mode" (Brodkey) **56**:60, 66-7
"Story in Harlem Slang" (Hurston) **30**:219
"Story into Film" (Oates) **134**:248-53
A Story like the Wind (van der Post) **5**:464
The Story of a Bad Horse (Kurosawa) **119**:399
"The Story of a Blind Man" (Tanizaki)
See "Mōmoku monogatari"
"The Story of a Citizen" (Gallagher) **63**:123, 125
"Story of a Coin" (Levi) **50**:335
The Story of a Country Boy (Powell) **66**:367
"The Story of a Dead Man" (McPherson) **77**:367-68, 373, 378-79, 382
The Story of a Humble Christian (Silone) **4**:494
The Story of a Life (Paustovsky)
See *Povest' o zhizni*
The Story of a Little Girl (Almedingen) **12**:1-2, 7
Story of a Love Affair That Never Existed (Antonioni)
See *Cronaca di un amore*
"Story of a Marriage" (Foote) **51**:137-38
"The Story of a Novel" (MacLennan) **92**:347
"The Story of a Panic" (Forster) **9**:207; **45**:140
The Story of a Round-House and Other Poems (Masefield) **47**:225
"The Story of a Scar" (McPherson) **77**:361, 365-69, 378, 380-82
The Story of a Shipwrecked Sailor (García Márquez) **47**:152-54
Story of a Staircase (Buero Vallejo)
See *Historia de una escalera*
Story of a Stairway (Buero Vallejo)
See *Historia de una escalera*
"The Story of a Story" (Smith) **25**:421
The Story of a Three-Day Pass (Van Peebles) **20**:409-10
A Story of a Town with a River (Kawabata)
See *Kawa no Aru Shitamachi o Hanashi*
"The Story of a Well-Made Shield" (Momaday) **85**:247
The Story of Adele H. (Truffaut)
See *L'histoire d'Adele H.*
"The Story of Africa" (Du Bois) **64**:112
The Story of an African Farm (Paton) **4**:395
"The Story of an Olson" (Olson) **29**:329
The Story of Aunt Shlomzion the Great (Kaniuk) **19**:240
"The Story of Counter-Octave" (Pasternak) **10**:387
A Story of Floating Weeds (Ozu) **16**:451
The Story of Folk Music (Berger) **12**:41
The Story of Gudrun (Almedingen) **12**:3
The Story of Henri Tod (Buckley) **37**:61-2
"A Story of How a Wall Stands" (Ortiz) **45**:303
The Story of Israel (Levin) **7**:206
The Story of Lola Gregg (Fast) **131**:83-4
"The Story of Lowry Maen" (Colum) **28**:91
The Story of Marie Powell: Wife to Mr. Milton (Graves) **39**:322, 325; **45**:173
The Story of Mist (Dybek) **114**:74
"The Story of My Experiment with a White Lie" (Anand) **93**:41-2
Story of My Life (McInerney) **112**:181-86, 190-91, 196, 202-04, 208-09, 212, 215, 218
"The Story of Our Lives" (Strand) **6**:521; **18**:519; **41**:433, 437; **71**:279, 289
The Story of Our Lives (Strand) **6**:521-23; **18**:519, 521; **41**:434, 436; **71**:279
The Story of Philosophy (Powys) **125**:302
"The Story of Richard Maxfield" (Wakoski) **7**:504
"The Story of Studs Lonigan" (Farrell) **66**:134
"Story of Sun House" (Silko) **74**:334-35, 338
"The Story of the Arrowmaker" (Momaday) **95**:238
Story of the Eye (Bataille)
See *Histoire de l'oeil*
The Story of the Heart (Aleixandre)
See *Historia del corazón*
"The Story of the Master and the Disciple" (Kiš) **57**:251
The Story of the Pencil (Handke) **134**:158
The Story of the Siren (Forster) **9**:207
"The Story of the State of Nature" (Gass) **132**:187
"Story of the Warrior and the Captive" (Borges)
See "Historia del guerrero y de la cautiva"
The Story of the Weasel (Slaughter) **56**:407-08, 410
"A Story of Tomoda and Matsunaga" (Tanizaki)
See "Tomoda to Matsunaga no hanashi"
"The Story of Tsoai" (Momaday) **85**:256
"The Story of Two Dogs" (Lessing) **22**:279

"Story of Two Gardens" (Paz)
See "Cuento de dos jardines"
The Story on Page One (Odets) **28**:336-37; **98**:211, 246
"The Story Teller" (Brown) **48**:52
"The Story Teller" (O'Connor) **23**:331
Story Teller (Kantor) **7**:195
The Story Teller (Vansittart) **42**:394, 400
"Story under Full Sail" (Voznesensky) **15**:557; **57**:422
"A Story Wet as Tears" (Piercy) **62**:366
"Story Which Should Have Happened" (Porter) **5**:347
"A Story with a Pattern" (Lavin) **18**:306
"The Storyteller" (Hillis) **66**:196, 199
"Storyteller" (Silko) **23**:411; **74**:322, 333, 338, 344; **114**:314
The Story-Teller (Highsmith)
See *A Suspension of Mercy*
Storyteller (Silko) **23**:411; **74**:326-27, 329, 331-32, 335-38, 341-44, 346-51; **114**:304, 310-12, 314-15, 317-19, 337-40, 343
The Storyteller (Sillitoe) **19**:420-21; **57**:403; **148**:163-64, 171, 184
The Storyteller (Vargas Llosa)
See *El hablador*
"Storyteller's Escape" (Silko) **74**:349
"Storytelling" (Silko) **74**:337; **114**:315
"Storytown" (Daitch) **103**:78
Storytown (Daitch) **103**:77-8
Stowaway to Mars (Wyndham) **19**:476
La strada (Fellini) **16**:270-73, 275-76, 278-79, 284, 286-87, 290, 292, 294, 297; **85**:46-8, 58-9, 66-7, 74, 76, 78, 80
La strada (Pasolini) **106**:230
La strada che va in città (Ginzburg) **11**:227; **54**:193, 196, 205; **70**:281-83
Strahlungen (Jünger) **125**:219-220, 222, 244, 251
Straight (Francis) **102**:135-37, 139, 158
Straight Cut (Bell) **102**:15-6
Straight from the Ghetto (Piñero) **55**:317
"Straight Talk from a Patriot" (Randall) **135**:399
Straight Through the Night (Allen) **59**:337
"Straight to Hell" (Clash) **30**:50-2
"Straight-Creek—Great Burn" (Snyder) **5**:395; **120**:313
The Straightening (Celan)
See *Sprachgitter*
Strains (Brutus) **43**:88-9
The Strait of Anian (Birney) **6**:74; **11**:51
"The Straitening" (Celan)
See "Engführung"
The Straitjacket (Parra) **102**:355
The Straits of Messina (Delany) **141**:145, 149, 159
"The Strand at Lough Beg" (Heaney) **25**:248; **37**:164; **74**:159-60, 163, 168, 171; **91**:115, 117
Strändernas svall (Johnson) **14**:295
"Strandhill, the Sea" (McGahern) **48**:268
Strands (Hulme) **130**:66
"The Strange Aberration of Mr. Ken Smythe" (Metcalf) **37**:300
The Strange Adventures of David Gray (Dreyer) **16**:258-61, 263-65, 269
The Strange Affair of Adelaide Harris (Garfield) **12**:223, 226, 230, 232, 235, 237
"A Strange and Sometimes Sadness" (Ishiguro) **27**:202
"The Strange and True Story of My Life with Billy the Kid" (Momaday) **85**:280
"Strange Archaeology" (Škvorecký) **69**:333, 346
The Strange Case of Mademoiselle P. (Norfolk) **76**:93-7
The Strange Children (Gordon) **6**:203, 207; **29**:190; **83**:232, 234-36, 244, 246-48, 258, 260-61
Strange Country (Deane) **122**:100-01
The Strange Country (Lagerkvist)
See *Det märkvärdiga landet*
Strange Days (Morrison) **17**:289, 291-92, 295
The Strange Death of Mistress Coffin (Begiebing) **70**:35-42
"Strange Encounters" (Chatwin) **57**:153
Strange Eons (Bloch) **33**:84
"Strange Fire" (Oz) **27**:359-60, 362
"Strange Fruit" (Harjo) **83**:272, 274
"Strange Fruit" (Heaney) **25**:243; **74**:158
Strange Fruit (Phillips) **96**:332, 334
Strange Fugitive (Callaghan) **14**:100, 102-03; **41**:89, 98; **65**:251-52
A Strange God (Savage) **40**:373-74
"Strange Hurt" (Hughes) **108**:330
The Strange Islands (Merton) **83**:394
"A Strange Job" (Oe)
See "An Odd Job"
"Strange Juice (or the murder of Latasha Harlins)" (Sapphire) **99**:81
"Strange Legacies" (Brown) **59**:265
"Strange Meeting" (Sassoon) **130**:186
Strange Meeting (Hill) **4**:226-28; **113**:280, 287, 291-92, 296-97, 300, 303-05, 312, 322-24, 330
Strange Moon (Stribling) **23**:445
"The Strange Museum" (Paulin) **37**:354
The Strange Museum (Paulin) **37**:353
The Strange Necessity (West) **7**:526; **31**:452, 459; **50**:394
Strange News from Another Star, and Other Tales (Hesse) **3**:249
"Strange People" (Erdrich) **54**:165
The Strange River (Green)
See *Epaves*
"Strange Things Happen Here" (Valenzuela) **104**:382
Strange Things Happen Here (Valenzuela) **31**:436-37; **104**:364, 376-78
"Strange Town" (Weller) **26**:446
Strange Wine (Ellison) **13**:208
Strange Yesterday (Fast) **131**:93
"The Stranger" (Brown) **48**:57
"The Stranger" (Joel) **26**:221
"The Stranger" (Kinsella) **138**:138
"The Stranger" (Rich) **125**:332
The Stranger (Camus)
See *L'étranger*
The Stranger (Joel) **26**:215-17, 221-22
The Stranger (Ray)
See *Agantuk*
The Stranger (Ringwood) **48**:330, 334-35, 338-39
The Stranger (Visconti) **16**:567-68, 575
The Stranger (Welles) **20**:433, 441; **80**:382, 387, 391, 393-96
"Stranger at Coney Island" (Fearing) **51**:114-15
Stranger at Coney Island and Other Poems (Fearing) **51**:113-14
The Stranger at the Gate (Neihardt) **32**:331
"Stranger at the Table" (Apple) **33**:21
"Stranger, Bear Words to the Spartans We..." (Boell)
See "Wanderer, kommst du nach Spa..."
A Stranger Came Ashore (Hunter) **21**:163-64
Stranger in a Strange Land (Heinlein) **3**:225-27; **8**:274-75; **14**:247, 250-252, 254-55; **26**:161-63, 166-70, 174; **55**:300-04
"Stranger in My Own Land" (Allen) **84**:18
"A Stranger in My Own Life: Alienation in American Indian Prose and Poetry" (Allen) **84**:3, 36
The Stranger in Shakespeare (Fiedler) **24**:200, 202
"Stranger in the House" (Costello) **21**:71
"Stranger in the House" (Wilhelm) **7**:537-38
Stranger in the House (Sherburne) **30**:363
A Stranger in the Kingdom (Mosher) **62**:315-18
"Stranger in the Village" (Baldwin) **2**:32; **42**:18; **50**:291; **90**:12
Stranger in Town (Hunt) **3**:252
Stranger in Town (Seger) **35**:382-86
"Stranger on a Train" (Theroux) **46**:402
Stranger on Horseback (L'Amour) **55**:308
"A Stranger with a Bag" (Warner) **7**:512
Stranger with My Face (Duncan) **26**:107-08
"Strangers" (Graham) **48**:144-45; **118**:225, 230
"Strangers" (Singer) **69**:309
Strangers (Jones) **52**:247-48, 253
Strangers (Koontz) **78**:197-98, 200, 203
The Strangers (Schlee) **35**:371-72
The Strangers All Are Gone (Powell) **31**:321-22
Strangers and Brothers (Snow) **1**:314-17; **4**:500-05; **6**:515-18; **9**:496-97; **13**:508-10, 511; **19**:425-28
Strangers in Paradise (Abbott) **48**:6-7
"The Stranger's Kingdom" (Carroll) **10**:98
Strangers on a Train (Highsmith) **2**:193; **4**:225-26; **42**:211; **102**:169-170, 172-73, 185-88, 190, 192-93, 199-201, 206, 210-13, 219-20
Strangers on a Train (Hitchcock) **16**:340, 344, 346, 349, 355, 358-59
Strangers on Earth (Troyat) **23**:459-60
Strangers to Ourselves (Kristeva)
See *Etrangers à nous-mêmes*
"Strangers When We Meet" (Kureishi) **135**:304
Strangers When We Meet (Hunter) **31**:219-21, 226
The Strangest Kind of Romance (Williams) **15**:580
"Strangled Thoughts" (Cioran) **64**:89, 94
Strapless (Hare) **58**:233; **136**:244-45, 248, 259, 264-65, 283
"Strata" (FitzGerald) **19**:180
Les stratégies fatales (Baudrillard) **60**:25-5, 33
"Strategy" (Gallagher) **63**:119
"Straus Park" (Stern) **40**:406, 408
Straw Dogs (Peckinpah) **20**:278, 282
"Straw Hat" (Dove) **50**:156; **81**:139
"Strawberries under the Snow" (Duncan) **15**:187
Strawberry Fields (Poliakoff) **38**:378-81, 386
"Strawberry Fields Forever" (Lennon and McCartney) **35**:268
"Strawberry Hill" (Ewart) **46**:150
"Strawberry Hill" (Hughes) **14**:270
"Strawberry Moon" (Oliver) **98**:265
"The Strawberry Window" (Bradbury) **42**:32
"Strawberrying" (Swenson) **61**:405; **106**:333
"Straw-Blond" (Hikmet) **40**:247, 251
Strawhead (Mailer) **74**:227
"Stray Cat Blues" (Jagger and Richard) **17**:222-23, 230, 235, 240
"Stray Children" (Oates) **52**:338
Stray Dog (Kurosawa) **16**:402-03; **119**:347, 362, 379, 382, 399-400
"The Stray Dog by the Summerhouse" (Justice) **19**:233
"Stray Dog Near Ecully" (Avison) **97**:70-1
"Stray Paragraphs in April, Year of the Rat" (Wright) **146**:372
"Strayed Crab" (Bishop) **32**:42
"The Straying Student" (Clarke) **9**:168
"Straż prozdkowa" (Rozewicz) **139**:276-78, 281-83
"The Stream" (Simic) **22**:381
"The Stream" (Van Duyn) **63**:441-42, 444; **116**:409-10, 421, 425, 430
Streamers (Altman) **116**:47
Streamers (Rabe) **8**:450-51; **33**:341-45
"Streams" (Auden) **14**:29; **43**:27
"Streamside Exchange" (Clark Bekedermo) **38**:120-21, 128-29
"Streche" (Arghezi) **80**:7
"The Street" (Dobyns) **37**:81
"The Street" (Pinsky) **38**:361-62; **94**:299
"The Street" (Soto) **80**:276-77, 281, 287, 292, 295-96
A Street (Brooks) **125**:89-90
The Street (Petry) **1**:266; **7**:304; **18**:403-04
The Street (Richler) **9**:450
"Street Boy" (Bennett) **28**:26, 29
"Street Crossing" (Transtroemer) **65**:229-30
"Street Fighting Man" (Jagger and Richard) **17**:222-24, 226, 229, 236-37, 241
Street Games (Brown) **32**:63-5

The Street Has Changed (Daly) **52**:88
Street Hassle (Reed) **21**:314-17, 319-21
"A Street in an Autumn Morning" (Krleža)
See "Ulica u jesenje jutro"
A Street in Bronzeville (Brooks) **1**:46; **2**:82; **5**:75-6; **15**:92-4; **49**:21-2, 25-6, 30-2, 35; **125**:45, 50, 53-4, 62, 68, 73-4, 80, 85, 88-9, 93, 105, 107
A Street in Moscow (Ehrenburg) **62**:168
"Street in the City" (Townshend) **17**:537
Street Legal (Dylan) **12**:197; **77**:189-90
"Street Life" (Diamond) **30**:112
Street of Crocodiles (The Brothers Quay) **95**:333-35, 338-45, 347-48, 350-57
"The Street of Furthest Memory" (Pinsky) **94**:307
Street of Riches (Roy)
See *Rue deschambault*
The Street of Today (Masefield) **11**:357
Street Players (Goines) **80**:91-2
Street Rod (Felsen) **17**:122
"Street Scene" (Simic) **130**:332
Street Scene (Rice) **7**:358-64; **49**:294-97, 299-302, 304-05
Street Scenes, 1970 (Scorsese) **20**:324
"Street Scenes II" (Hacker) **91**:110
Streetbird (van de Wetering) **47**:410, 412
"Streetcar" (Avison) **97**:106
A Streetcar Named Desire (Kazan) **16**:361, 367-69, 374; **63**:222, 225, 231, 234
A Streetcar Named Desire (Williams) **1**:367-69; **2**:465-66; **5**:498, 500-01, 503-06; **7**:541, 543, 545; **8**:547-48; **11**:572, 574-77; **15**:581; **19**:472; **30**:454-73; **39**:445-46, 449-50, 452-53; **45**:446-48; **71**:265-66, 382, 387, 399, 405; **111**:377, 380, 387-91, 398-404, 408-09, 411-19, 421-25
"Streetcorner Man" (Borges)
See "El Hombre de la esquina rosada"
Streetlife Serenade (Joel) **26**:214, 217, 219
"Streetlife Serenader" (Joel) **26**:214, 217
"The Streets" (Winters) **32**:468
Streets in the Moon (MacLeish) **8**:362; **68**:270-71, 273, 291
"The Streets of Ashkelon" (Harrison) **42**:203
"Streets of Fire" (Springsteen) **17**:483-85
Streets of Gold (Hunter) **11**:280; **31**:223
"The Streets of Laredo" (MacNeice) **1**:187
Streets of Laredo (McMurtry) **127**:343
Streets of Night (Dos Passos) **15**:184; **25**:137, 144
"Streets of Pearl and Gold" (Kizer) **80**:180, 182, 185
Strega (Vachss) **106**:355-59, 361, 365
"The Strength of Fields" (Dickey) **15**:177-78; **47**:92, 98; **109**:243
The Strength of Fields (Dickey) **15**:177-78; **47**:90-3, 95-6, 98; **109**:245
Strength of Steel (Serling) **30**:353
"Strength through Joy" (Rexroth) **112**:389
The Strength to Dream: Literature and the Imagination (Wilson) **14**:588
Strength to Love (King) **83**:328-30, 341
"Stretcher Case" (Sassoon) **130**:178
"The Stricken Child" (Dacey) **51**:79
A Stricken Field (Gellhorn) **60**:178-79, 190-91, 196
"Strictly Business" (Himes) **108**:235
Strictly from Hunger (Perelman) **49**:257
"Strictly Genteel" (Zappa) **17**:587
Strictly Personal (Maugham) **15**:367
Stride toward Freedom: The Montgomery Story (King) **83**:327, 331, 337-38, 347
"Striders" (Nemerov) **36**:309
"Strike" (Selby) **4**:481; **8**:475, 477, 475-76
"Strike and Fade" (Dumas) **6**:145; **62**:154-55
Strike the Father Dead (Wain) **46**:412, 418
Strike Three, You're Dead (Rosen) **39**:194-97
The Strikers (Valdez)
See *Huelgistas*
Strikes, Bombs, and Bullets: Big Bill Haywood and the IWW (Archer) **12**:19
"Striking at the Heart of the System" (Eco) **60**:113
Striking the Stones (Hoffman) **6**:243; **13**:287; **23**:237
Strindberg (Wilson) **14**:589
The String (Akhmadulina)
See *Struna*
String (Childress) **12**:104; **86**:309
String Horses (Holden) **18**:257, 259
String Too Short to Be Saved (Hall) **37**:146-47, 149; **59**:152; **151**:180, 216
Stringer (Just) **4**:266-67
"Strings" (Kinsella) **43**:253
The Strings Are False (MacNeice) **53**:244
The Strings, My Lord, Are False (Carroll) **10**:95-6, 98
"S-Trinity of Parnassus" (Tolson) **105**:256
Strip Jack Naked (Hill) **113**:296
"Strip/La Baleine" (Moure) **88**:219, 229
A Strip of Land (Arghezi)
See *Pe o palmă de ţărînă*
"Stripper" (Phillips) **15**:419
Striptease (Mrozek) **3**:345
Striptease of Jealousy (Arrabal) **9**:39
"Striptiz" (Voznesensky) **57**:417
Stripwell (Barker) **37**:32, 35-7
"Strivings of the Negro People" (Du Bois) **96**:154
"Strof och motstrof" (Transtroemer) **52**:410; **65**:235
"Strofy" (Brodsky)
See "Strophes"
"Stroke" (Buckley) **57**:126, 128, 131, 133
"The Stroke" (Dove) **50**:153; **81**:139
"The Stroke" (Smith) **25**:419
"The Stroke of Apelles" (Pasternak)
See "Il tratto di Apelle"
A Stroke of Genius (West) **96**:397
"A Stroke of Good Fortune" (O'Connor) **3**:366; **6**:381; **21**:268
"A Stroke of Luck" (Kotzwinkle) **35**:253-54
A Stroll in the Air (Ionesco)
See *Le piéton de l'air*
A Stroll with William James (Barzun) **51**:48, 50; **145**:63, 65-6, 71
The Stroller in the Air (Ionesco)
See *Le piéton de l'air*
The Strong Are Lonely (Hochwälder)
See *Das Heilige Experiment*
"The Strong Are Saying Nothing" (Frost) **10**:196
The Strong Breed (Soyinka) **14**:506-07; **36**:410-11; **44**:283, 287-90
The Strong City (Caldwell) **28**:57; **39**:302
Strong Democracy (Barber) **141**:2-3, 23
A Strong Dose of Myself (Abse) **29**:20
"Strong Horse Tea" (Walker) **5**:476; **103**:407, 412, 423
Strong Medicine (Foreman) **50**:168
"Strong Men" (Brown) **23**:96
"Strong Men, Riding Horses" (Brooks) **125**:53, 86
"Strong Men Riding Horses: Lester after the Western" (Brooks) **15**:92; **49**:32
"A Strong New Voice Pointing the Way" (Madhubuti) **73**:215
Strong Opinions (Nabokov) **3**:355; **8**:413-14; **23**:304
"A Strong Wind" (Clarke) **6**:112
Strong Wind (Asturias)
See *The Cyclone*
Stronger Climate (Jhabvala) **4**:257-58
The Strongest Men Don't Stay Unscathed; or, Mother Always Knows Best (Haavikko)
See *Ne vahvimmat miehet ei ehjiksi jää*
The Stronghold (Hunter) **21**:160, 165
The Stronghold (Levin) **7**:205
"Strophes" (Brodsky) **13**:115; **36**:77; **100**:55
"Strophes elegiaque: A la memoire d'Alban Berg" (Gascoyne) **45**:150, 158
Stroszek (Herzog) **16**:326-29, 331, 333
Strountes (Ekeloef) **27**:115
"The Structural Analysis of Science Fiction" (Lem) **149**:226
Structural Anthropology (Lévi-Strauss)
See *Anthropologie structurale*
"The Structural Study of Myth" (Rothenberg) **57**:383
The Structural Transformation of the Public Sphere (Habermas)
See *Strukturwandel der Offenlichkeit*
"La structure, le signe, et le jeu dans le discours des sciences humaines" (Derrida) **24**:153
"The Structure of Bad Taste" (Eco) **60**:118
"The Structure of Orlando Furioso" (Calvino) **73**:48
"The Structure of Rime" (Duncan) **41**:124, 128-29
The Structure of Rime (Duncan) **4**:141; **15**:190; **55**:297-98
"The Structure of the Plane" (Rukeyser) **15**:459; **27**:404
"Structures" (MacCaig) **36**:284
Les structures élémentaires de la parenté (Lévi-Strauss) **38**:294, 297, 300
Structures mentales (Goldmann) **24**:242
The Structures of Complex Words (Empson) **8**:201-02; **33**:145, 147-51; **34**:336-38
"The Struggle After Justice" (Neruda) **62**:328
The Struggle against Shadows (Duhamel) **8**:189
"The struggle for the Taal" (Breytenbach) **126**:63
Struggle Is Our Brother (Felsen) **17**:119-20
The Struggle of Thebes (Mahfouz)
See *Kifah Tiba*
"Struggle of Wings" (Williams) **42**:450
"The Struggle Staggers Us" (Walker) **6**:554
Struggling Man (Cliff) **21**:62
"The Struggling Masseur" (Naipaul) **13**:402
Struggling Spirit (Lagerkvist)
See *Kämpande ande*
Strukturwandel der Offenlichkeit (Habermas) **104**:85-6
Struna (Akhmadulina) **53**:9-11, 13, 15
Struna swiatła (Herbert) **43**:192
La Struttura Assente (Eco) **142**:127
Stuart Little (White) **34**:425-26, 430; **39**:369-70, 375-77, 380
The Stubborn Heart (Slaughter) **29**:374
"Stubborn Hope" (Brutus) **43**:89
Stubborn Hope: New Poems and Selections from "China Poems" and "Strains" (Brutus) **43**:89-90, 97
"The Stubborn Spearmen" (Davis) **49**:91, 97
The Stubborn Structure (Frye) **70**:275
"The Stucco House" (Gilchrist) **143**:300
"Stuck-Up" (Cryer) **21**:79
"The Student Aulach" (Spender) **41**:421
"The Students" (Bell) **8**:65
Students (Trifonov)
See *Studenty*
"The Students Take Over" (Rexroth) **49**:275
"The Student's Wife" (Carver) **126**:114
Studenty (Trifonov) **45**:407-11, 413, 417, 420-22
The Studhorse Man (Kroetsch) **5**:220-21; **23**:270-72; **57**:283-84, 288; **132**:200, 202, 205-9, 212, 244-47, 256
Studies (Fish) **142**:177
Studies (Ritsos) **13**:487
"Studies for an Actress" (Garrigue) **8**:239
Studies for an Actress and Other Poems (Garrigue) **8**:239
"Studies for an Andalusian Dancer" (Cabral de Melo Neto)
See "Estudos para uma bailadora andaluza"
Studies in a Dying Colonialism (Fanon)
See *L'an V de la révolution algérienne*
Studies in American Indian Literature: Critical Essays and Course Designs (Allen) **84**:13-14, 23, 28, 31, 34-6
Studies in Black American Literature: Black American Prose Theory, Volume I

(Fontenot) **65**:365
Studies in European Realism (Lukacs) **24**:315, 317, 321, 323
"Studies in Power" (Smith) **64**:398
"Studies in the Park" (Desai) **97**:149, 151-53, 171
"The Studies of Narcissus" (Schwartz) **45**:356
Studies of the Novel (Kawabata)
See *Shosetsu no Kenkyu*
Studies on the Life of Testaccio (Pasolini) **106**:270
The Studio (Dunne) **28**:121, 125
"Studio 5, The Stars" (Ballard) **137**:63, 66
"Studio Tan" (Zappa) **17**:592
Studium przedmiotu (Herbert) **9**:274; **43**:184, 192
Studs Lonigan: A Trilogy (Farrell) **1**:198; **4**:158; **8**:205; **11**:193, 195-96; **66**:112-14, 120-26, 128-29, 132, 134-36
"Study" (Harrison) **43**:180; **129**:170, 176
A Study in Choreography for Camera (Deren) **16**:252, 254
A Study in Choreography for Camera (Deren) **102**:28, 31, 37-8, 40-3
A Study in French Poets (Pound) **10**:400
"Study in Kore" (Plumly) **33**:311
A Study of Courage and Fear (Coles) **108**:193
"The Study of History" (Rich) **7**:368
"A Study of Reading Habits" (Larkin) **5**:223, 227; **39**:336, 343; **64**:266
"The Study of the Classics" (Warner) **45**:433
"Study of the Object" (Herbert) **43**:184-85, 188, 193
Study of the Object (Herbert)
See *Studium przedmiotu*
"Study War" (Styron) **11**:519
"The Stuff of Madness" (Highsmith) **42**:216
The Stuff of Sleep and Dreams: Experiments in Literary Psychology (Edel) **29**:174-75; **34**:534
"Stumbling" (Montale)
See "Incespicare"
"Stumbling" (Soupault) **68**:406
"The Stump" (Hall) **37**:142-43
"Stump" (Heaney) **14**:244
"Stumps" (Davison) **28**:101
Die Stunde da wir nichts voneinander wußten (Handke) **134**:157-62, 170, 177
Die Stunde der wahren Empfindung (Handke) **8**:264; **10**:255-56, 259-60; **38**:218-21, 223, 227; **134**:119-23, 126-27, 130, 133-34, 139, 145
Eine Stunde hinter Mitternacht (Hesse) **3**:248; **17**:198; **69**:287
"Stupid Girl" (Jagger and Richard) **17**:230, 233, 235
"Stupid Girl" (Young) **17**:579
"Stupid Man" (Reed) **21**:317
Sturgeon Is Alive and Well (Sturgeon) **22**:411, 413
Sturgeon's West (Sturgeon) **39**:366
Der Sturz (Dürrenmatt) **15**:196
Der Sturz (Walser) **27**:461
"Stuttgart: In a Nightclub" (Laughlin) **49**:221
"The Stygian Banks" (MacNeice) **10**:325
"Style" (Durrell) **27**:97
"Style" (Moore) **10**:349; **47**:263, 270
Le style Apollinaire (Zukofsky) **4**:600
"Style as Risk" (Cioran) **64**:75, 78-9
"The Style of Byron's 'Don Juan' in Relation to the Newspapers of His Day" (Avison) **97**:112
Styles of Radical Will (Sontag) **31**:407-10; **105**:225
"Stylistics, Poetics, and Criticism" (Wellek) **28**:452
"Styx" (Duncan) **55**:295-96
Su fondamenti invisibili (Luzi) **13**:352, 354
"The Sub" (Dixon) **52**:99
"Sub Contra" (Bogan) **93**:64, 67, 79-81
Sub Rosa (Benet) **28**:23, 25
"A Subaltern" (Sassoon) **130**:178, 180
"A Subaltern's Love Song" (Betjeman) **2**:60
Subarashiki nichiyobi (Kurosawa) **16**:398; **119**:342, 346, 349, 351, 378-79, 382
Subida al cielo (Bunuel) **80**:23, 29-30, 36
"Subiectul" (Arghezi) **80**:11
"The Subject and Power" (Foucault) **69**:190
"A Subject of Childhood" (Paley) **140**:227, 245-46, 277, 281
A Subject of Scandal and Concern (Osborne) **2**:328; **45**:313
The Subject Was Roses (Gilroy) **2**:161
The Subjection of Women (Mill) **65**:323
"Subjectivity" (Graham) **118**:222
"Subject-Matter of Poetry" (Huxley) **5**:192
"The Subjects of Discontent" (Klappert) **57**:268
"The Sublime and the Beautiful" (Murdoch) **8**:406
"The Sublime and the Beautiful Revisited" (Murdoch) **6**:347
"The Sublime and the Good" (Murdoch) **6**:346, 349
"The Sublime Art" (Hamburger) **14**:234
"The Sublime Child" (Berriault) **109**:96
"Subliminal Code" (Moure) **88**:218
"The Subliminal Man" (Ballard) **3**:32-3; **14**:41; **36**:33, 36
"Submarginalia" (Howe) **152**:192, 200, 213, 232, 237
Submarine (Clancy) **112**:77
Submarine Sailor (Felsen) **17**:120
"The Submerged Continent" (Ortese)
See "Il continente sommerso"
"Subpoena" (Barthelme) **5**:53
"Substitute" (Townshend) **17**:529-30, 532
"Subterranean Homesick Blues" (Dylan) **77**:161, 165, 188
The Subterraneans (Kerouac) **1**:165; **2**:226-27; **3**:265; **5**:214; **14**:303-04, 307; **29**:271-72; **61**:296, 298, 309
Os subterrâneos da liberdade (Amado) **106**:57, 59
Subtile Jagden (Jünger) **125**:226
"The Subtitle of This Book" (Barth) **51**:25
"Subtitles" (Castillo) **151**:47
"The Subtle Calm" (Blunden) **56**:46
Subtle Flame (Prichard) **46**:344-45
Subtraction (Robison) **98**:314-18
Suburb (Dos Passos) **25**:144
"Suburban" (Ciardi) **129**:46
Suburban Strains (Ayckbourn) **33**:42 4
The Suburban Wife (Stead)
See *Miss Herbert*
"Suburban Woman: A Detail" (Boland) **40**:98; **67**:39; **113**:89, 92, 96
"Suburbanite" (Moravia) **7**:244
"The Suburbans" (Kizer) **80**:172-73
"Suburbia" (Ciardi) **40**:162
The Suburbs of Hell (Stow) **48**:356-61
"Subversive Joy and Revolutionary Patience in Black Christianity" (West) **134**:353
"The Subverted Flower" (Frost) **9**:229; **34**:471
"Subverting the Standards" (Fiedler) **24**:205
"Subway" (Woolrich) **77**:401
The Subway (Rice) **7**:360, 362; **49**:300-02, 305
"Success" (Masters) **48**:223-24
Success (Amis) **38**:12-16; **62**:5, 11-12, 16-17; **101**:59, 61-63, 84, 86, 89-90
The Success and Failure of Picasso (Berger) **2**:54-5
Success Stories (Banks) **72**:2-5, 9, 11
"Success Story" (Townshend) **17**:535-36
The Successful Life of 3 (Fornés) **39**:138; **61**:129-33, 140
Successful Love, and Other Stories (Schwartz) **10**:462
The Succession: A Novel of Elizabeth and James (Garrett) **51**:149-51, 153
"Succotash" (Harmon) **38**:244
Such (Brooke-Rose) **40**:104-05, 111
Such a Gorgeous Kid Like Me (Truffaut)
See *A Gorgeous Bird like Me*
Such a Long Journey (Mistry) **71**:273-76
Such a Love (Kohout) **13**:323
"Such a Lovely Girl" (Jones) **52**:250
Such As (Breytenbach) **126**:89
"Such Counsels" (Plumly) **33**:313
"Such Counsels You Gave to Me" (Jeffers) **54**:238, 245-46
Such Counsels You Gave to Me and Other Poems (Jeffers) **11**:307; **54**:238
Such Darling Dodos (Wilson) **2**:470; **3**:534; **25**:464
Such Good Friends (Gould) **4**:199; **10**:241
Such Is My Beloved (Callaghan) **14**:101-03; **41**:90-1, 93, 95; **65**:246, 248-52
Such Nice People (Scoppettone) **26**:403-04
"Such Perfection" (Narayan) **121**:354
"Such Silences" (Livesay) **79**:333-34
Such Stuff as Screams Are Made Of (Bloch) **33**:84
"Such Things Only Happen in Books" (Wilder) **82**:362
Such Was the Season (Major) **48**:218
"Suchen wissen" (Jandl) **34**:199
"Sucker" (McCullers) **4**:345; **12**:432-33
"Le Sud" (Borges) **87**:97; **9**:116; **44**:362; **48**:36, 46
Sud (Green) **11**:258, 260; **77**:271, 276-77, 288-91, 294
Sudden Death (Brown) **43**:82-3, 85; **79**:153, 155, 169
A Sudden, Fearful Death (Perry) **126**:331
"Sudden Illness at the Bus-Stop" (Betjeman) **43**:32, 34
"The Sudden Sixties" (Ferber) **93**:145
"Sudden Things" (Hall) **37**:146
"A Sudden Trip Home in the Spring" (Walker) **103**:366, 407, 409-10, 412
"Suddenly" (Thomas) **48**:383
Suddenly Last Summer (Vidal) **142**:305, 325
Suddenly Last Summer (Williams) **1**:368; **2**:465-66; **5**:499, 501; **7**:543; **11**:571-72, 576; **39**:446; **45**:448; **71**:368, 386; **111**:380-83, 388, 391, 393, 424
"Suddenly, Walking along the Open Road" (Peake) **54**:375
Suder (Everett) **57**:214-17
"Sudor y látigo" (Guillén) **48**:158, 162, 164
"Sueño" (Soto) **80**:278
El sueño de la razón (Buero Vallejo) **15**:100-02; **46**:93-5; **139**:7-9, 15-16, 19, 33, 38, 42-3, 76, 79-80
"Sueño de las dos ciervas" (Alonso) **14**:25
El sueño de los héroes (Bioy Casares) **13**:85; **88**:88-93
"Sueño Real" (Ferlinghetti) **111**:65
Un sueño realizado y otros cuentos (Onetti) **7**:276
"Sueños" (Soto) **80**:278
Sueur de sang (Jouve) **47**:207-08, 212
"Suffer the Children" (Lorde) **71**:260
Suffer the Children (Saul) **46**:365, 369
Sufficient Carbohydrate (Potter) **58**:390-91
The Suffrage of Elvira (Naipaul) **4**:372, 375; **13**:402, 406; **37**:324-25; **105**:140, 147, 155, 179-80
"Suffragette City" (Bowie) **17**:61
"Sufletească" (Arghezi) **80**:8
"Sugar" (Byatt) **136**:146
Sugar (Byatt) **65**:125; **136**:135, 137-38, 146, 161
Sugar and Rum (Unsworth) **76**:254
"The Sugar Crock" (Gass) **8**:242
Sugar Daddy (Williams) **42**:441-42
"Sugar for the Horse" (Bates) **46**:62-3
Sugar for the Horse (Bates) **46**:62-3
"Sugar Loaf" (Hughes) **14**:271
"Sugar Mountain" (Young) **17**:572, 583
"Sugar Rises" (Goldbarth) **38**:201
Sugar Street (Mahfouz)
See *al-Sukkariyya*
"Sugarcane" (Guillén) **48**:157
The Sugarland Express (Spielberg) **20**:357-58, 365

Sugartown (Estleman) **48**:105, 107
"The Sugawn Chair" (O'Faolain) **32**:343; **70**:319
"The Suggestiveness of One Stray Hair in an Otherwise Perfect Coiffure" (Leyner) **92**:283
"The Suicide" (Davison) **28**:100
"Suicide" (Schaeffer) **6**:489
"Suicide" (Sturgeon) **22**:411
"Suicide: Anne" (Williams) **148**:318, 354
Suicide in B-Flat (Shepard) **41**:406, 412
"Suicide in the Trenches" (Sassoon) **36**:393; **130**:184, 202, 215, 221
"Suicide Notes" (Suknaski) **19**:432
"The Suicide of Hedda Gabler" (Dubie) **36**:130
"Suicide off Egg Rock" (Plath) **14**:424
"Suicide on Pentwyn Bridge" (Clarke) **61**:78
Suicide Prohibited in Springtime (Casona)
 See *Prohibido suicidarse en primavera*
Suicide: The Hidden Epidemic (Hyde) **21**:179
"Suicides" (Gilchrist) **48**:115-16, 121; **143**:273, 328
"The Suicides" (Justice) **102**:264
"Suicides" (Voigt) **54**:429
"Suicidio" (Aleixandre) **9**:14
"Suigetsu" (Kawabata) **107**:104
"Suishō Gensō" (Kawabata) **9**:311; **107**:114
"The Suit" (Levine) **118**:302
A Suit of Nettles (Reaney) **13**:474, 476
A Suitable Boy (Seth) **90**:351-60, 365-9
"The Suitcase" (Mphahlele) **25**:338, 342, 344
"The Suitcase" (Ozick) **28**:353; **62**:352; **155**:178, 209
Suitcase (Abe) **81**:291
"A Suite for Augustus" (Dove) **81**:134
"A Suite for Marriage" (Ignatow) **40**:258
Suite furlana (Pasolini) **106**:229, 233
"Suite in Prison" (Eberhart) **19**:143
Suite in Three Keys (Coward) **29**:135-36, 139
Suite logique (Brossard) **115**:106
"A Suite of Lies" (Webb) **18**:540
Suite to Appleness (Harrison) **6**:223
"Suites I and II" (Webb) **18**:540
The Suitors of Spring (Jordan) **37**:194
"Sujam o suicído" (Cabral de Melo Neto) **76**:164
"Le sujet en procès" (Kristeva) **77**:302; **140**:196, 198
al-Sukkariyya (Mahfūz) **52**:293, 300; **55**:171-72, 175-76
"Sul credere o non credere in Dio" (Ginzburg) **54**:207
Sula (Morrison) **4**:365-66; **10**:355; **22**:315-16, 318-19; **55**:196, 205, 207-08; **81**:217-19, 225-26, 228, 230, 232, 235-37, 254, 256, 260, 270; **87**:263-65, 291-94, 304, 306
Sulla poesia (Montale) **18**:341
Sullivan and Gilbert (Ludwig) **60**:251
"Sultry Rain" (Pasternak) **63**:277
"The Sum of All" (Blunden) **56**:34, 39
The Sum of All Fears (Clancy) **112**:56-9, 61-2, 77, 90
The Sum of Things (Manning) **19**:303-04
Suma y sigue (Alegria) **75**:38
Sumerian Vistas (Ammons) **57**:51-3, 55-6, 59; **108**:24
Summa Atheologica (Bataille) **29**:38, 44
Summa Technologiae (Lem) **149**:111, 116, 119, 145, 147, 149-50, 156, 164, 212-13, 255, 260-61, 264, 283
al-Summān wa-al-kharif (Mahfūz) **52**:295-96; 301
"Summary" (Sanchez) **116**:276, 280, 282, 294
"Summary" (Sarton) **49**:320
"Summer" (Ashbery) **2**:17
"Summer" (Blaga) **75**:69
"Summer" (Boyle) **121**:26
"Summer" (Cortázar)
 See "Verano"
"Summer" (Crase) **58**:162
"Summer" (Glück) **44**:216, 218, 221
"Summer" (Soto) **80**:287
Summer (Camus)
 See *L'été*
Summer (Grunwald) **44**:49-51
Summer (Leonard) **19**:282, 284
"Summer '68" (Pink Floyd) **35**:305
Summer: A European Play (Bond) **23**:72
A Summer Affair (Klima) **56**:173
The Summer after the Funeral (Gardam) **43**:165-66, 173
"Summer, an Elegy" (Gilchrist) **143**:320, 332
Summer and Smoke (Williams) **1**:367; **2**:465; **5**:498, 500; **7**:541, 543-44; **8**:548-49; **11**:572, 576; **30**:466; **39**:446, 448; **45**:446, 451, 453; **71**:405; **111**:380, 388, 392-93
"The Summer Anniversaries" (Justice) **102**:261, 270
The Summer Anniversaries (Justice) **19**:232-33; **102**:261, 263-64, 268, 270, 277, 283
The Summer before the Dark (Lessing) **3**:285-88, 291; **6**:300-01, 304; **15**:334; **22**:281; **40**:303; **94**:258, 261-62, 283-84, 286
"The Summer Belvedere" (Williams) **45**:443
A Summer Bird Cage (Drabble) **2**:118; **22**:120; **53**:121, 126; **129**:111, 141, 160
Summer Brave (Inge)
 See *Picnic*
"A Summer by the Sea" (Jhabvala) **94**:171-73; **138**:77-8
"Summer Camp" (Scott) **22**:376
"Summer Canyon" (Merwin) **45**:273
Summer Celestial (Plumly) **33**:315-16
Summer Crossing (Tesich) **40**:423-24
"The Summer Day" (Oliver) **98**:281, 294
"A Summer Day" (Stafford) **7**:457; **19**:430; **68**:422, 433
Summer Days (Wilson) **12**:649-50
"Summer Doorway" (Merwin) **18**:334
"Summer Dust" (Gordon) **29**:189; **83**:231-32, 241, 258
"The Summer Farmer" (Cheever) **15**:127
"The Summer Fire" (Dodson) **79**:199
The Summer Game (Angell) **26**:28-32
"Summer Garden" (Harrison) **43**:176
Summer Girls, Love Boys, and Other Short Stories (Mazer) **26**:295
"A Summer Gone" (Moss) **50**:353
"Summer Haiku" (Cohen) **38**:132
Summer Holiday (Mamoulian) **16**:427-28
"Summer Home" (Heaney) **25**:241; **74**:158
"Summer House" (Heaney) **7**:148
A Summer in Italy (O'Faolain) **70**:318
"A Summer in Maine" (Gilchrist) **143**:315, 330
"A Summer in Rouen" (Endō) **99**:289, 293-95
Summer in Salandar (Bates) **46**:65
Summer in the City (Stevens) **34**:111-13
Summer in the Spring: Ashinaabe Lyric Poems and Stories (Vizenor) **103**:341-47
Summer in the Spring: Ojibwe Lyric Poems and Tribal Songs (Vizenor) **103**:296, 298, 335-36, 342-48
A Summer in the Twenties (Dickinson) **35**:135
"Summer in Town" (Pasternak) **63**:313
Summer in Williamsburg (Fuchs) **8**:220-21
Summer Interlude (Bergman)
 See *Sommarlek*
Summer Knowledge: New and Selected Poems, 1938-1958 (Schwartz) **2**:387; **10**:465; **45**:354, 356
"Summer Landscape" (Eberhart) **56**:86
"Summer Landscape" (Sarton) **49**:309
"Summer Letter" (Deane) **122**:83
A Summer Life (Soto) **80**:298, 300-01
"Summer Lightning" (Clarke) **9**:168
"Summer Lightning" (Simmons) **43**:410-11
Summer Lightning (Cliff) **120**:87
Summer Love and Surf (Appleman) **51**:13
Summer Meditations (Havel) **123**:196, 200-02
"Summer Moon" (Winters) **32**:469
Summer Moonshine (Wodehouse) **22**:479
"Summer Morning" (Simic) **9**:480-81; **22**:380; **130**:291-92, 309
"Summer Morning" (Simpson) **149**:331
"A Summer Morning" (Wilbur) **53**:405, 413
"Summer near the River" (Kizer) **80**:174, 180
"A Summer Night" (Auden) **43**:17; **123**:34, 48, 51
"Summer Night" (Bowen) **22**:65-66; **118**:64-65, 67, 110
"The Summer Night" (Bradbury) **42**:38
"Summer Night" (Ekelöf) **27**:110
"Summer Night" (Harjo) **83**:276, 280
"A Summer Night" (Mahapatra) **33**:283-84
The Summer of 1925 (Ehrenburg) **18**:131; **62**:178
The Summer of Black Widows (Alexie) **154**:16, 20-2, 27, 35
"A Summer of Discovery" (Williams) **45**:445
Summer of Fear (Duncan) **26**:104
The Summer of My German Soldier (Greene) **30**:169-71
"The Summer of the Broad Jump Pit" (Gilchrist) **143**:279
The Summer of the Falcon (George) **35**:176
Summer of the Red Wolf (West) **6**:563
Summer of the Seventeenth Doll (Lawler) **58**:329-44
The Summer of the Swans (Byars) **35**:71-3, 75
Summer of the White Goat (Corcoran) **17**:76-7
The Summer Party (Poliakoff) **38**:383, 386
"Summer People" (Beattie) **63**:14, 18
"Summer People" (Hemingway) **10**:269; **30**:194; **39**:403
"Summer People" (Kaplan) **50**:55-7
"The Summer People" (Merrill) **6**:323
Summer People (Elliott) **47**:111-12
Summer People (Piercy) **62**:379-81; **128**:248, 256
"A Summer Pilgrim" (Tuohy) **37**:431
"A Summer Place" (Stevenson) **33**:381
A Summer Place (Wilson) **32**:445-46
"Summer Plain" (Transtroemer) **65**:223
"Summer Poem" (Enzensberger) **43**:144-45
"Summer Rain" (Read) **4**:439
Summer Rain (Duras)
 See *La Pluie d'Eté*
"The Summer Rebellion" (Calisher) **134**:21
"Summer Report" (Celan)
 See "Sommerbericht"
"Summer Resort" (Gellhorn) **60**:181
"Summer Rest and Words" (Amichai)
 See "Menuchat kayits u-milam"
"Summer School" (Davison) **28**:100
"Summer Session" (Ammons) **5**:29; **8**:15, 18; **25**:43-5
"Summer Session 1968" (Ammons) **57**:23, 59
"Summer Shore" (Grau) **146**:130
Summer Side of Life (Lightfoot) **26**:278, 282
"Summer Soft" (Wonder) **12**:659-60
The Summer Soldier (Guild) **33**:186-87
"Summer Solstice, New York City" (Olds) **85**:299
"Summer Song I" (Barker) **48**:24
"Summer Storm" (Montague) **46**:268
"Summer Storm" (Simpson) **149**:325
Summer Storm (Swinnerton) **31**:423
"Summer Storm in Japanese Hills" (Blunden) **56**:50
"The Summer Thunder" (Moss) **45**:290
"Summer time T. V. (is witer than ever)" (Sanchez) **116**:295
A Summer to Decide (Johnson) **1**:161; **7**:184
"A Summer Tragedy" (Bontemps) **1**:37
"Summer Tragedy Report" (Hillis) **66**:195-99
"Summer Vertigo" (Corn) **33**:116
"Summer Waterfall, Glendale" (MacCaig) **36**:283
"Summer Wish" (Bogan) **46**:78-9, 84, 90; **93**:65, 81, 90, 97
Summer with Monika (Bergman)
 See *Sommaren med Monika*
"Summer Words of a Sistuh Addict" (Sanchez) **116**:280
Summering (Greenberg) **7**:134

Summerplay (Bergman)
See *Sommarlek*
"A Summer's Day" (Collins) **44**:36, 38
"Summer's Day Song" (McCartney) **35**:287-89
"A Summer's Dream" (Bishop) **32**:34
"A Summer's Fancy" (Blunden) **56**:29
"Summer's Lease" (Haldeman) **61**:177-78
A Summer's Lease (Sachs) **35**:333
Summertime and Other Stories (Donoso)
See *Veraneo y otros cuentos*
"Summertime and the Living..." (Hayden) **37**:160
"Summertime Blues" (Townshend) **17**:525
Summertime Dream (Lightfoot) **26**:281
"Summertime in England" (Morrison) **21**:239
Summertime Island (Caldwell) **14**:95
The Summing Up (Maugham) **15**:367; **67**:211, 215-16, 219, 223, 226, 228; **93**:238-39, 246-47, 250, 253, 267, 270
"Summing Up by the Defendant" (Dodson) **79**:198
Summit (Thomas) **132**:356-57, 377-78
"Summit Beach, 1921" (Dove) **81**:147-48, 150
Summoned (O Hehir) **41**:322, 324
"Summoned By Bells" (Harrison) **129**:217
Summoned by Bells (Betjeman) **6**:69; **34**:306; **43**:37-9, 41-2
A Summoning of Stones (Hecht) **8**:266, 268-69; **13**:269; **19**:207
"Summons" (Dickey) **47**:94
A Summons to Memphis (Taylor) **50**:251-61; **71**:298
"The Sumo Revisions" (Hodgins) **23**:236
"Sumptuous Destitution" (Wilbur) **3**:532
"The Sun" (Ashbery) **15**:33-4; **41**:40
"The Sun" (Bottoms) **53**:30-1
"Sun" (Dickey) **7**:82
"Sun" (Kenny)
See "I Am the Sun"
"Sun" (Livesay) **79**:339
"Sun" (Moore) **4**:362; **10**:353
Sun: A Poem for Malcolm X Inspired by His Murder (Kennedy) **66**:205
The Sun Also Rises (Hemingway) **1**:141-44; **3**:231, 234-38, 240-41; **6**:226-27, 229-31, 233; **8**:283, 287, 289-90; **10**:263-64, 267; **13**:271-72, 274, 276, 278-79; **19**:211, 216-19, 221; **30**:179; **61**:190-232; **80**:111, 113, 117-18, 137, 141, 145 46, 151
The Sun Always Shines for the Cool (Piñero) **55**:316-18
"Sun and Fun" (Betjeman) **43**:35-6
Sun and Moon (Page) **18**:376-78
"Sun and Moon Flowers: Paul Klee, 1879-1940" (Dubie) **36**:131
Sun and Steel (Mishima) **2**:286-87, 289; **4**:354; **9**:381-83; **27**:342-43
The Sun and the Moon (Reaney) **13**:474
The Sun at Midnight: Notes on the Story of Civilization Seen as the History of the Great Experimental Work of the Supreme Scientist (Gascoyne) **45**:154
"The Sun between Their Feet" (Lessing) **94**:288-89, 295-96
"The Sun Came" (Knight) **40**:279
"The Sun Dance Shield" (Momaday) **85**:280
The Sun Dog (King) **113**:367
"Sun Dried" (Ferber) **93**:142
"The Sun Going Down upon Our Wrath" (Levertov) **66**:250
The Sun Has Begun to Eat the Mountain (Lane) **25**:284
Sun Horse, Moon Horse (Sutcliff) **26**:437
The Sun Is Axeman (Jones) **10**:285, 288
"Sun Is Shining" (Marley) **17**:270
"Sun King" (Lennon and McCartney) **12**:365, 380
The Sun King (Mitford) **44**:485, 488-89
The Sun My Monument (Lee) **90**:176-7, 181, 194
"Sun Poem" (Wakoski) **2**:459
"The Sun Rises Twice" (Bates) **46**:56
Sun Rock Man (Corman) **9**:170
"The Sun Room" (O'Hara) **6**:385
The Sun Shines Bright (Ford) **16**:316, 319
The Sun Shines on the Sanggan River (Ding Ling) **68**:62, 64, 66
The Sun: Star Number One (Branley) **21**:18
Sun Stone (Paz)
See *Piedra de sol*
"Sun the First" (Elytis) **100**:171-72
Sun the First (Elytis)
See *Ílios o prótos*
"Sun Threnody" (Komunyakaa) **94**:226-27
Sun Under Wood (Hass) **99**:155, 157-58
Suna no onna (Abe) **8**:1-2; **22**:11, 13; **53**:2-6; **81**:285, 287, 290-97
"Sunbathing on a Rooftop in Berkeley" (Kumin) **28**:225
The Sunbird (Smith) **33**:374-75
sunblue (Avison) **97**:111-18, 121
"Sunburst" (Mahapatra) **33**:280, 283
"Sunburst" (Seger) **35**:381
"Sundance" (Silverberg) **7**:425; **140**:346, 378
Sunday after the War (Miller) **43**:298; **84**:242-43
"Sunday Afternoon" (Munro) **95**:287, 297
"Sunday Afternoon" (Steele) **45**:362
"Sunday Afternoon at Home" (McFadden) **48**:256
"Sunday Afternoon at Two O'Clock" (Frame) **96**:201
"Sunday Afternoon in Buffalo, Texas" (Justice) **102**:259
"Sunday Afternoon near the Naval Air Base" (Ciardi) **40**:153
"Sunday Afternoon Service in St. Enodoc Church, Cornwall" (Betjeman) **43**:34
"Sunday at Home" (Smith) **25**:420-21
"Sunday at the Zoo" (Dybek) **114**:67
"Sunday before Noon" (Bukowski) **108**:113
Sunday Best (Rubens) **19**:403, 405; **31**:351
"Sunday Bloody Sunday" (Lennon) **35**:264
Sunday Bloody Sunday (Gilliatt) **2**:160-61; **53**:146
"Sunday Brunch in the Boston Restoration" (Starbuck) **53**:354
"Sunday by the Combination" (Hughes) **108**:297
"Sunday Chicken" (Brooks) **125**:74
"Sunday... Dig the Empty Sounds" (Salinas) **90**:324, 328
Sunday Dinner (Oates) **11**:400
"Sunday Drinks" (Trevor) **25**:445
"A Sunday Drive" (Atwood) **84**:69
"A Sunday Evening" (Kelman) **58**:298, 300
Sunday Father (Neufeld) **17**:310
"The Sunday Following Mother's Day" (Jones) **76**:65-6
"Sunday in Summer in Seatown" (Le Guin) **136**:376
Sunday in the Park with George (Sondheim) **30**:400, 402-03; **39**:172-74; **147**:227, 229-30, 260-62
"Sunday Lemons" (Walcott) **76**:285
Sunday, Monday and Always (Powell) **66**:372
"Sunday Mornin' Comin' Down" (Kristofferson) **26**:266, 270
"Sunday Morning" (Ammons) **5**:26
"Sunday Morning" (Avison) **97**:71
"Sunday Morning" (Ciardi) **40**:157
"Sunday Morning" (Dubus) **97**:237
"Sunday Morning" (Hass) **18**:212
"Sunday Morning" (Jacobsen) **48**:196
"Sunday Morning" (MacNeice) **1**:186; **53**:231, 238
"Sunday Morning, June 4, 1989" (Thomas) **107**:340, 346
"Sunday Morning Walk" (Smith) **64**:388, 394
The Sunday of Life (Queneau)
See *Le dimanche de la vie*
"The Sunday Poem" (Bowering) **15**:82
Sunday Punch (Newman) **14**:378-79
"Sunday Reading" (Guillén)
See "Lectura de domingo"
Sunday Runners in the Rain (Horovitz) **56**:154
"Sunday Siesta" (García Márquez) **47**:146
Sunday the Rabbi Stayed Home (Kemelman) **2**:225
"Sundays" (King) **53**:209, 212
"Sundays before noon" (Bukowski) **108**:112
"Sunday's Best" (Costello) **21**:71
"Sundays in Summer" (Oates) **108**:384
"Sundays Kill More Men than Bombs" (Bukowski) **41**:64
"The Sundays of Satin-Legs Smith" (Brooks) **5**:76; **15**:92; **49**:26, 32-3, 35; **125**:50, 89, 91
The Sundered Worlds (Moorcock) **58**:350
"The Sundial" (Clarke) **61**:73
"The Sundial" (Piccolo)
See "La meridiana"
The Sundial (Clarke) **61**:73-4, 79, 82
The Sundial (Jackson) **11**:303; **60**:211, 217, 219-20, 234
Sundiver (Brin) **34**:133-35
Sundog (Harrison) **33**:199-201; **66**:157, 160-61, 169; **143**:340-42, 344, 355, 357-59
"Sundown" (Lightfoot) **26**:280-81
Sundown (Lightfoot) **26**:280
Sundown (Mathews) **84**:203-04, 207, 209-11, 216, 225-26, 229-30
Sunfall (Cherryh) **35**:107
"Sunfast" (Livesay) **15**:340; **79**:337-38, 351
"Sunflower" (Breton)
See "Tournesol"
Sunflower (De Sica) **20**:95
Sunflower (West) **50**:394, 399
"Sunflower Sonnet Number Two" (Jordan) **11**:312
"Sunflower Sutra" (Ginsberg) **3**:194; **13**:239; **36**:181, 187; **109**:333, 365
"The Sunflowers" (Oliver) **98**:261
"Sunken Evening" (Lee) **90**:182
"Sunlight" (Gunn) **3**:216
"Sunlight" (Heaney) **7**:151; **25**:245
Sunlight (Van Peebles) **20**:410
The Sunlight Dialogues (Gardner) **2**:151-52; **3**:184-88; **5**:131-35; **7**:112, 114; **8**:234, 237-38; **10**:218-20; **28**:166-67; **34**:550
Sunlight on Cold Water (Sagan)
See *A Few Hours of Sunlight*
"The Sunlit Vale" (Blunden) **56**:44
"Sunny Afternoon" (Davies) **21**:88-90, 97
"A Sunny Place" (Kawabata) **107**:104, 107
"Sunny Prestatyn" (Larkin) **39**:340; **64**:262, 269-70
"Sunrise" (Hass) **18**:212-13
"Sunrise" (Seidel) **18**:475
"Sunrise" (Townshend) **17**:531
Sunrise (Seidel) **18**:474-75
Sunrise on Sarah (Ryga) **14**:473
"A Sunrise on the Veld" (Lessing) **22**:279
Sunrise with Seamonsters: Travels and Discoveries, 1964-1984 (Theroux) **46**:401-03
The Sun's Burial (Oshima) **20**:247, 251
The Sun's Net (Brown) **48**:55-6
"Sunset" (Ginsberg) **36**:182
"Sunset" (Glück) **81**:165, 172
Sunset at Blandings (Wodehouse) **22**:484
Sunset Boulevard (Wilder) **20**:456-57, 462
Sunset Gun (Parker) **68**:324
"Sunset Limited" (Harrison) **66**:167-71
"The Sunset Maker" (Justice) **102**:271
The Sunset Maker (Justice) **102**:269-72, 277, 283
The Sunset of a Clown (Bergman)
See *Gycklarnas afton*
"The Sunset Perspective" (Moorcock) **58**:348
"The Sunset Piece" (MacLeish) **68**:287-88
Sunset Village (Sargeson) **31**:369-70
"Sunset Walk in Thaw-Time in Vermont" (Warren) **8**:538; **18**:536
Sunshine (Klein) **30**:239

"Sunshine and Shadow" (Beattie) **40**:64, 66; **63**:19
The Sunshine Boys (Simon) **6**:506-07; **11**:496; **31**:399-401, 403; **39**:218; **70**:236, 238
The Sunshine Years (Klein) **30**:239
"Sunspot Baby" (Seger) **35**:381
Sunstone (Paz)
See *Piedra de sol*
"Sunstroke" (Landolfi) **11**:321
Suomalainen sarja (Haavikko) **34**:170
Suor (Amado) **40**:25-7
Superbia (Larson) **99**:160-61, 168, 171, 180, 186
Superboy—The Adventures of Superman When He Was a Boy (Siegel and Shuster) **21**:359
The Supercops (Parks) **16**:461
The Superhero Women (Lee) **17**:261-62
The Superintendent (Haavikko)
See *Ylilääkäri*
Superior Women (Adams) **46**:17-22
"Superiorities" (Wilbur) **110**:385
"Superman" (Davies) **21**:105
"Superman" (Updike) **23**:473
Superman (Puzo) **107**:213
Superman (Siegel and Shuster) **21**:354, 356, 359-60
"The Superman Comes to the Supermarket" (Mailer) **28**:257; **111**:96, 103-05, 107, 113
Superman II (Lester) **20**:232
Superman III (Kotzwinkle) **35**:257
"A Supermarket in California" (Ginsberg) **13**:239; **36**:192-93; **69**:211, 214; **109**:355
Supernation at Peace and War (Wakefield) **7**:502
The Supernatural: From ESP to UFOs (Berger) **12**:41-2
Superrealismo (Azorín)
See *El libro de levante*
"Supersonic Rocket Ship" (Davies) **21**:94
Superspies: The Secret Side of Government (Archer) **12**:23
"Superstition" (Wonder) **12**:657, 660, 663-64
Superstizione (Antonioni) **20**:28; **144**:77
"Superwoman" (Wonder) **12**:657
"Superwoman Drawn and Quartered, The Early Forms of She" (Atwood) **84**:89
"The Supper after the Last" (Kinnell) **29**:281; **129**:236
"The Supper at Elsinore" (Dinesen) **29**:157, 162
"Supper on the Blackbird's Field" (Popa) **19**:375
"Supplizio" (Ortese) **89**:198
"Suppose" (Mahapatra) **33**:284
A Supposedly Fun Thing I'll Never Do Again (Wallace) **114**:388-89
"Supposing You Have Nowhere to Go" (Musgrave) **54**:341
The Suppression of the African Slave-Trade to the United States of America, 1638-1870 (Du Bois) **64**:128; **96**:127, 146, 151, 160
"Supreme Fictions" (Squires) **51**:382
"Sur" (Le Guin) **45**:216
Sur la route de San Romano (Breton) **9**:128
"Sur le sein" (Damas) **84**:180
Sur les femmes (Montherlant) **19**:322
Sur Nietzsche (Bataille) **29**:38-9, 47
Sur Racine (Barthes) **24**:23, 25-6, 36, 41-2; **83**:67, 78, 98-9
"Sur une carte postale" (Damas) **84**:174
"Surce čoveško" (Bagryana) **10**:14
"Surcease" (Lane) **25**:287
"Sure ..." (Carroll) **143**:29
The Sure Hand of God (Caldwell) **60**:53
Sure of You (Maupin) **95**:197-204, 208
"'Sure,' Said Benny Goodman" (Carruth) **84**:136
"Surf" (Hansen) **38**:240
"The Surface" (Swenson) **106**:346
"Surface Calm" (Martin) **89**:116
The Surface of Earth (Price) **6**:423-26; **13**:463-64; **43**:348-50, 353; **50**:229, 232; **63**:332, 341
Surface of Meaning (Brossard)
See *Le Sens apparent*
Surface of Sense (Brossard)
See *Le Sens apparent*
Surface Tension (Blish) **14**:85
"Surface Textures" (Desai) **97**:149, 152-53, 171
Surfacing (Atwood) **2**:20; **3**:19-20; **4**:24-7, 28; **8**:28-31, 33-4; **13**:42-4; **15**:37, 39; **25**:61-4, 66, 68-9; **44**:146-48, 152-53, 160; **84**:49-53, 56, 59-60, 66, 69, 79, 90, 105, 107; **135**:7, 9, 18, 31, 62, 71
"Surfacing in Private Spaces" (Allen) **84**:5
Surfeit of Lampreys (Marsh)
See *Death of a Peer*
"Surfer Girl" (Wilson) **12**:642-44, 648-49
"Surfer in Winter" (Kessler) **4**:270
"Surfiction" (Wideman) **67**:379, 381-82, 384; **122**:348
Surfiction: Fiction Now and Tomorrow (Federman) **47**:121-23, 126
"Surfiction—Four Propositions in Form of an Introduction" (Federman) **47**:121, 126
"Surfin'" (Wilson) **12**:644, 647
"Surfin' Safari" (Wilson) **12**:647, 650
Surfin' Safari (Wilson) **12**:642, 644
"Surfin' U.S.A." (Wilson) **12**:647-48
Surfin' U.S.A. (Wilson) **12**:651
Surf's Up (Wilson) **12**:645, 648, 650
The Surge (McClure) **6**:317, 320
"The Surgeon as Priest" (Selzer) **74**:264, 276
"Surgeon at Two A.M." (Plath) **5**:345; **9**:433; **111**:203, 214
The Surgeon's Mate (O'Brian) **152**:259, 287, 299
"Surgery" (Thomas) **132**:382
"The Surname" (Guillén)
See "El apellido"
"Surplus Value Books: Catalogue Number 13" (Moody) **147**:190
Surplussed Barrelware (Aksyonov)
See *The Tare of Barrels*
"Surprise" (Hughes) **119**:271
"A Surprise in the Peninsula" (Adcock) **41**:14, 17
"Surprise, Surprise!" (Abse) **29**:15, 17
"Surprise Surprise" (Lennon) **35**:268
Surprise! Surprise! (Tremblay) **29**:419; **102**:367-68
"'Surprise, Surprise!' from Matron" (Jolley) **46**:214
"Surprised by Evening" (Bly) **38**:56
"Surprised by Joy" (Baxter) **45**:53; **78**:17-18
Surprised by Joy: The Shape of My Early Life (Lewis) **3**:296; **6**:310; **124**:213, 217, 226, 228, 232, 239-41, 248
Surprised by Sin (Fish) **142**:142, 144, 149, 160, 177, 183, 197, 210
"Surprises" (Aksyonov) **101**:9
Surprises of the Sun (McAuley) **45**:249, 252
Surreal Thing (Kristofferson) **26**:269
Surrealism (Read) **4**:443
Le surréalisme et l'après-guerre (Tzara) **47**:385
Surrealist Manifesto (Breton)
See *Manifeste du surréalisme. Poisson soluble*
"Surrealist Situation of the Object" (Breton) **54**:16
"A Surrealistic Photograph by Manuel Alvarez Bravo" (Dacey) **51**:79-80
"The Surrogate" (Blackburn) **43**:65
The Surrounded (McNickle) **89**:157-59, 161, 164-73, 175-88
"Surrounded by Children" (Smith) **25**:420
Surroundings (MacCaig) **36**:283
Le sursis (Sartre) **1**:305; **50**:383
"Surveillance" (Berryman) **62**:45
Surveiller et punir: Naissance de la prison (Foucault) **31**:180-81, 184-85; **34**:339-42; **69**:168-69, 174, 185, 190
A Survey of Modernist Poetry (Graves) **11**:254; **45**:173
A Survey of Modernist Poetry (Riding) **7**:375
"The Surveyor" (Roth) **104**:311
"A Survival" (Gold) **42**:193
"Survival" (Marley) **17**:272-73
Survival: A Thematic Guide to Canadian Literature (Atwood) **3**:20; **4**:25; **8**:31; **13**:42-3; **15**:37; **25**:62, 64; **84**:50-1, 55-6, 64, 68, 70, 89, 94; **135**:9, 62
"Survival Course" (Bowering) **47**:31
Survival in Auschwitz: The Nazi Assault on Humanity (Levi)
See *Se questo è un uomo*
"The Survival of the Bark Canoe" (McPhee) **36**:296
"The Survival of the Fittest" (Thomas) **107**:340-42
The Survival of the Fittest (Johnson) **27**:221, 224
"Survival Techniques" (Calisher) **134**:17
Survival Techniques (Calisher) **38**:76
Survival Zero (Spillane) **13**:527-28
Survivals (Honig) **33**:213, 216
Le survivant (Chedid) **47**:84-5
"Surviving" (Bettelheim) **79**:123, 136, 143
"Surviving" (Ostriker) **132**:328
Surviving (Green) **97**:291-93
Surviving, and Other Essays (Bettelheim) **79**:122, 124, 125-26
Surviving the Holocaust (Bettelheim)
See *Surviving, and Other Essays*
"Surviving the Life" (Diamond) **30**:112
"The Survivor" (Bambara) **88**:21, 27
"Survivor" (Cheever) **15**:127
"Survivor" (Kinsella) **138**:101-02
"The Survivor" (Levine) **118**:293
"Survivor" (MacLeish) **8**:363
"Survivor" (O Hehir) **41**:324
"The Survivor" (Rozewicz)
See "Ocalony"
Survivor (Butler) **38**:62-4; **121**:73-6, 80, 89-90, 94, 97, 100, 103, 105, 108, 113, 133
The Survivor (Forman) **21**:121
A Survivor (Jones) **52**:244-45, 254
The Survivor (Keneally) **5**:210-11; **10**:299; **117**:215-16, 224, 248
The Survivor (Lenz)
See *Stadtgespräch*
The Survivor (MacBeth) **9**:340
The Survivor and Other Poems (Rozewicz) **23**:361, 363; **139**:226-27, 288
"A Survivor in Salvador" (Tuohy) **37**:427
The Survivor: The Story of Eddy Hukov (Ehle) **27**:102
"Survivor Type" (King) **37**:206-07
"Survivors" (Sassoon) **130**:185, 216, 222
"The Survivors" (Snodgrass) **68**:382, 388
The Survivors (Beer) **58**:36, 38
The Survivors (Feinstein) **36**:171
The Survivors (Hunter) **35**:228-29
The Survivors (Raven) **14**:442-43
The Survivors (Shaw) **23**:397
The Survivors of the Crossing (Clarke) **8**:143; **53**:84-7, 91-2
"Susan and the Serpent—A Colonial Fiction" (Murray) **40**:334
A Susan Sontag Reader (Sontag) **31**:416-18; **105**:216-19
Susana, carne y demonio (Bunuel) **80**:29, 34
Susanna Moodie: Voice and Vision (Shields) **113**:396, 400, 413, 442
"Susanna on the Beach" (Gold) **152**:121
"Sushi" (Muldoon) **72**:273-74, 277
The Suspect (Wright) **44**:334-35
The Suspect in Poetry (Dickey) **109**:244
"The Suspended Life" (Ashbery) **2**:19
"A Suspense Story" (Macdonald) **13**:356
A Suspension of Mercy (Highsmith) **2**:192; **42**:212; **102**:170, 173-74, 177, 192
The Suspicion (Duerrenmatt) **102**:56, 59
Suspicion (Dürrenmatt) **4**:140

Suspicion (Hitchcock) **16**:338, 355
"Sussex" (Davie) **8**:165-66
"Suterareru made" (Tanizaki) **28**:418
"Suttee" (Auchincloss) **45**:30
Sutter's Gold (Cendrars)
See *L'or*
Suttree (McCarthy) **57**:329-31, 333-35; **101**:135-37, 147, 152-57, 167-69, 175-76, 178, 180-82, 186, 195, 198, 202-04
"Suvetski khora" (Bagryana) **10**:11
"Suzanne" (Cohen) **3**:109
Suzanne and the Young Men (Duhamel) **8**:189
"Suzerain" (Char) **9**:166
Den svåra stunden (Lagerkvist) **54**:268, 274
Svärmare och harkrank (Martinson) **14**:355
Svatby v domě (Hrabal) **67**:128
Svayamvara and Other Poems (Mahapatra) **33**:282
Svecha na vetru (Solzhenitsyn) **4**:510-11; **7**:432, 443; **10**:479
"Svengali" (Dybek) **114**:61
"Svenska hus ensligt belägna" (Transtroemer) **65**:233
Světlem oděná (Seifert) **44**:425; **93**:306, 309, 319, 328, 343
"Svijazhsk" (Aksyonov) **101**:29
Swag (Leonard) **28**:233; **71**:207, 213, 219, 224; **120**:264, 266, 277
Swallow (Thomas) **31**:434; **132**:353-56, 378
The Swallow and the Tom Cat: A Love Story (Amado)
See *O Gato Malhado e a Andorinha Sinhá*
Swallow the Lake (Major) **19**:292
The Swallower Swallowed (Ducharme)
See *L'avalée des avalés*
"Swallowing" (Barthelme) **115**:85
"Swallowing Darkness Is Swallowing Dead Elm Trees" (Waddington) **28**:437
"Swallows" (McGahern) **48**:264
Swami and Friends: A Novel of Malgudi (Narayan) **7**:255; **28**:299-300, 302; **47**:303, 307; **121**:333, 351, 356, 358, 417
"The Swamp" (Walcott) **42**:418
Swamp Angel (Wilson) **13**:607-08, 610-11
"Swamp Boy" (Bass) **143**:10
The Swamp Dwellers (Soyinka) **14**:506; **44**:281, 287
Swamp Man (Goines) **80**:91, 93, 97
"Swamp Pheasant" (Wright) **53**:423
Swamp Water (Renoir) **20**:304
"Swamps" (Oates) **6**:370; **108**:371
"The Swan" (Dacey) **51**:83
"Swan" (Hall) **37**:143
"The Swan" (L'Heureux) **52**:273
"The Swan" (Oliver) **98**:289
"The Swan" (Roethke) **19**:402
"Swan and Fox" (L'Heureux) **52**:278
"Swan and Shadow: The Last Shape" (Hollander) **2**:197; **5**:186
"The Swan Café" (Pinget) **37**:364
The Swan in the Evening (Lehmann) **5**:239
"Swan Lake" (Neruda)
See "El lago de los cisnes"
Swan Song (Binyon) **34**:32-4
The Swan Villa (Walser)
See *Das Schwanenhaus*
"Swanny Lake" (Aksyonov) **101**:22
"Swans" (Frame) **96**:184, 188
Swans on an Autumn River (Warner) **7**:512
"A Swan's Song Came from the Sky" (Blaga) **75**:69
"Swansong" (Muske) **90**:308, 311
The Swap (Klein) **30**:243
"The Swarm" (Murray) **40**:338
"The Swarm" (Plath) **9**:431; **14**:423
"Swarm" (Sterling) **72**:368, 372
A Swarm in May (Mayne) **12**:387-90, 397, 401-02
"The Swarming Bees" (Laughlin) **49**:220
The Swastika Poems (Heyen) **8**:231; **13**:282-84
"Sway" (Johnson) **52**:234
"Sway" (Simpson) **32**:377-78, 380; **149**:332
"Swaziland" (Giovanni) **117**:197
"Sweat" (Hurston) **7**:172
"Sweat" (Redgrove) **41**:352
"The Sweat" (Snyder) **120**:355
Sweat (Amado)
See *Suor*
"Sweat and the Lash" (Guillén)
See "Sudor y látigo"
"Sweat and the Whip" (Guillén)
See "Sudor y látigo"
"A Sweating Proust of the Pantry Shelves" (Van Duyn) **7**:498; **116**:402
Sweeney Agonistes: Fragments of an Aristophanic Melodrama (Eliot) **6**:166-68; **9**:190; **15**:206, 208; **41**:161; **55**:346-47, 350-51, 369, 371, **55**:346-47, 350-51, 369, 371
"Sweeney among the Nightingales" (Eliot) **1**:92; **10**:168; **34**:394; **55**:364-65
Sweeney Astray (Heaney) **37**:163-65, 167, 169; **74**:165-68, 193, 195, 197; **91**:122, 124
"Sweeney Erect" (Eliot) **1**:92; **57**:206
Sweeney in the Trees (Saroyan) **56**:376
"Sweeney Redivivus" (Heaney) **37**:169; **74**:162, 169, 174, 193, 197
Sweeney Todd: The Demon Barber of Fleet Street (Sondheim) **30**:392-402; **147**:228-31, 234-36, 239, 254, 256, 260, 263
"Sweeney's Return" (Heaney) **74**:169
Sweet Adelaide (Symons) **32**:428
Sweet and Sour Animal Book (Hughes) **108**:335-36
Sweet and Sour Milk (Farah) **53**:132, 134-40; **137**:83-87, 89-90, 96-97, 105-06, 108-09, 113-16, 118-27, 129-30
"Sweet Armageddon" (Hoffman) **141**:279, 283-84, 312
Sweet Bells Jangled out of Tune (Brancato) **35**:69
Sweet Bird of Youth (Williams) **1**:368; **2**:466; **5**:499; **7**:545; **11**:572; **15**:581; **19**:472; **30**:466-67; **39**:446; **45**:444-47; **71**:368; **111**:380, 391, 424
"Sweet Blindness" (Nyro) **17**:319
"Sweet Boy, Give me Yr Ass" (Ginsberg) **109**:358
"Sweet Burning" (Bogan) **93**:96
"Sweet Caroline" (Diamond) **30**:110-11, 113-14
Sweet Charity (Fosse) **20**:121
Sweet Charity (Simon) **70**:240
Sweet Danger (Allingham)
See *The Kingdom of Death*
Sweet Desserts (Ellmann) **61**:85-9
Sweet Diamond Dust and Other Stories (Ferré) **139**:153-54, 156-57, 184, 193
The Sweet Dove Died (Pym) **13**:470; **19**:386-87; **37**:377-78; **111**:227, 230, 232, 234-37, 242-48, 258, 262-63, 266, 269-71, 273, 281-82, 285
Sweet Dreams (Frayn) **3**:164-65
"Sweet Dreams, Son" (Tolstaya) **59**:372
"Sweet Everlasting" (Voigt) **54**:430
The Sweet Flypaper of Life (Hughes) **5**:190; **35**:215; **108**:289-90
Sweet Genevieve (Derleth) **31**:135
"Sweet Guinevere" (Lightfoot) **26**:282
"Sweet Harmony" (Robinson) **21**:344
The Sweet Hereafter (Banks) **72**:19-24
The Sweet Hereafter (Egoyan) **151**:147-51, 153-68, 170-74, 176
"Sweet Jane" (Reed) **21**:303, 306-07, 311, 315, 322
"Sweet Jesus" (Oliver) **98**:289
"Sweet like a Crow" (Ondaatje) **51**:317
"Sweet Little Girl" (Wonder) **12**:656
"Sweet Little Sixteen" (Berry) **17**:52, 54-5
Sweet Memories (Nelson) **17**:305
Sweet Reason (Littell) **42**:275
The Sweet Second Summer of Kitty Malone (Cohen) **19**:113-16
The Sweet Smell of Success (Odets) **98**:197, 245-48
Sweet Sue (Gurney) **54**:217-20, 223; **50**:180, 182-83
Sweet Sweetback's Baadasssss Song (Van Peebles) **2**:448; **20**:411-13
"Sweet Talk" (Vaughn) **62**:459
Sweet Talk (Vaughn) **62**:456-59
"Sweet Thing/Candidate" (Bowie) **17**:61
Sweet Thursday (Steinbeck) **1**:325; **5**:407; **9**:514, 517; **21**:382; **34**:405
"Sweet Time" (Peacock) **60**:292
"Sweet Town" (Bambara) **88**:12, 15, 27
"The Sweet Voice" (Kunene) **85**:166
Sweet Whispers, Brother Rush (Hamilton) **26**:157-59
"Sweet Will" (Levine) **118**:280, 287, 292
Sweet Will (Levine) **118**:274, 279-80, 283, 285, 287, 292, 294, 296, 301-02
Sweet William (Bainbridge) **8**:37; **10**:16; **18**:34; **62**:30; **130**:8-9, 20
"Sweetened Change" (Ammons) **25**:45; **108**:56
"Sweetest Little Show" (McCartney) **35**:291-92
"Sweetgrass" (Kenny) **87**:239
"The Sweetheart of the Song Tra Bong" (O'Brien) **103**:174
"Sweethearts" (Ford) **99**:115
Sweethearts (Phillips) **139**:200-1
"Sweethearts in a Mulberry Tree" (Knight) **40**:279
Sweetie (Campion) **95**:2-6, 8-9, 11-12, 18, 20, 23, 26
"Sweetly Sings the Donkey" (Delaney) **29**:146
Sweetly Sings the Donkey (Delaney) **29**:145-46
"The Sweetness of Bobby Hefka" (Levine) **118**:297
"The Sweetness of Life" (Stern) **40**:408
The Sweets of Pimlico (Wilson) **33**:450-51
The Sweet-Shop Owner (Swift) **41**:442-44, 446-47; **88**:288, 290-91, 294, 296, 307, 309, 311-12, 321
The Sweetshoppe Myriam (Klima)
See *Café Myriam*
Sweetsir (Yglesias) **22**:493-94
The Sweet-Vendor (Narayan) **121**:353-54, 356-57, 359, 361-62, 382, 385
Sweetwater (Yep) **35**:469, 471
The Swell Season: A Text on the Most Important Things in Life (Škvorecký) **39**:229; **69**:329, 332, 341, 343, 348, 352; **152**:315-16, 325, 334
A Swell-Looking Babe (Thompson) **69**:382, 386, 389
"Swells" (Ammons) **25**:45; **108**:56
Swept Away by an Unusual Destiny in the Blue Sea of August (Wertmueller) **16**:589-90, 592-96
"Swept for You Baby" (Robinson) **21**:343, 348
"Swept Sky" (Johnston) **51**:248
Świadkowie albo mała stabilizacja (Rozewicz) **139**:227, 229-30, 293
"Świadomość" (Milosz) **56**:243
Swiatlo dzienne (Milosz) **56**:238
"Światło i cień" (Rozewicz) **139**:307
"Swift Current" (Smith) **15**:515, 517
Swifter than a Dream (Rozewicz) **139**:261
Swiftie the Magician (Gold) **7**:120-22; **14**:208; **42**:195
A Swiftly Tilting Planet (L'Engle) **12**:352
"Swifts" (Stevenson) **33**:382
"The Swim" (Longley) **29**:296
A Swim Off the Rocks (Moss) **14**:375-76
"The Swimmer" (Cheever) **3**:107; **7**:49-50; **11**:120; **64**:46, 48, 53, 63, 66
"The Swimmer" (Ransom) **11**:469
"The Swimmer at Lake Edward" (Hugo) **32**:241
"The Swimmer in Hard Light" (DeMarinis) **54**:103
"A Swimmer in the Air" (Moss) **7**:248
Swimmer in the Secret Sea (Kotzwinkle) **35**:254-55
"Swimmers" (Swenson) **106**:339
"The Swimmers" (Szirtes) **46**:395-96

"The Swimmers" (Tate) **2**:429; **4**:541; **11**:525-26; **14**:529
The Swimmers and Other Selected Poems (Tate) **2**:430; **11**:526
"The Swimmer's Moment" (Avison) **97**:76, 80-1, 84, 121-22, 131, 135
Swimming Across the Hudson (Henkin) **119**:52-7
"Swimming Chenango Lake" (Tomlinson) **13**:548; **45**:401
Swimming Lessons, and Other Stories from Firozsha Baag (Mistry)
See *Tales from Firozsha Baag*
"The Swimming Pool" (Moss) **45**:291
The Swimming Pool Season (Tremain) **42**:387-88
"Swimming to Cambodia" (Gray) **49**:149
Swimming to Cambodia (Gray) **49**:148-52; **112**:97-8, 101-04, 111-20, 122-25, 127-31, 134
Swimming to Cambodia: The Collected Works of Spalding Gray (Gray) **49**:149, 152
The Swimming-Pool Library (Hollinghurst) **55**:55-63; **91**:132-34, 136-39, 141
The Swindle (Fellini)
See *Il bidone*
Swing, Brother, Swing (Marsh)
See *A Wreath for Rivera*
The Swing in the Garden (Hood) **15**:286; **28**:190-92, 195-96
"Swing Out, Sweet Chariot" (Perelman) **49**:259
Swinger (Ferlinghetti) **111**:64
"Swinging" (Clarke) **61**:73
"The Swinging Bridge" (Davidson) **13**:169; **19**:126
Swinging in the Rain (Bermant) **40**:92
Swinnerton (Swinnerton) **31**:425
"Świnobicie" (Rozewicz) **139**:297
The Swiss Family Perelman (Perelman) **49**:260-61, 266
The Switch (Leonard) **71**:221; **120**:287
Switch Bitch (Dahl) **6**:121-22; **79**:177, 181-82
"Switchblade" (Ryan) **65**:209, 211, 215
"The Switchman" (Arreola)
See "El guardagujas"
"Sword" (Hacker) **72**:184
"The Sword" (Landolfi) **11**:321; **49**:210-12
The Sword and the Circle: King Arthur and the Knights of the Round Table (Sutcliff) **26**:437, 440
The Sword and the Sickle (Anand) **23**:14, 20; **93**:24, 30-2, 41, 43, 48, 50
The Sword and the Stallion (Moorcock) **5**:294
Sword at Sunset (Sutcliff) **26**:432-33, 435, 438, 440
"Sword Eulogising Itself after a Massacre" (Kunene) **85**:175
The Sword in the Stone (White) **30**:436-41, 444-47, 449-50
The Sword of Aldones (Bradley) **30**:27, 29, 31
Sword of Honor (Waugh) **1**:358-59; **3**:510, 512; **19**:461; **27**:475; **107**:370, 372, 393, 401
The Sword of Parmegon (Ellison) **139**:132
Sword of the Lictor (Wolfe) **25**:476-77
"The Swords" (Aickman) **57**:3
Swords Like Lips (Aleixandre)
See *Espadas como labios*
"S.Y. Agnon and the First Religion" (Ozick) **155**:126
"The Sybarites" (Wilding) **73**:398
Sybil (Auchincloss) **45**:25
"Sycamore" (Watkins) **43**:450
The Sycamore Tree (Brooke-Rose) **40**:102-03
"The Sylko Bandit" (Raine) **103**:190
Syllogismes de l'amertume (Cioran) **64**:73
"Sylvester's Dying Bed" (Hughes) **108**:297
Sylvia (Fast) **131**:84, 100
Sylvia (Mackenzie)
See *The Early Life and Adventures of Sylvia Scarlett*
Sylvia (Sinclair) **63**:348
Sylvia Plath: A Biography (Wagner-Martin) **50**:439-41, 443-50
Sylvia Scarlett (Mackenzie)
See *The Early Life and Adventures of Sylvia Scarlett*
"Sylvia's Death" (Sexton) **123**:449-50
Sylvia's Marriage (Sinclair) **63**:348
The Symbol (Bessie) **23**:62
"Symbol as Hermeneutic in Existentialism" (Percy) **65**:260
"Symbol as Need" (Percy) **14**:415
"The Symbol of the Archaic" (Davenport) **38**:143
"Symbolic Action in an Ode by Keats" (Burke) **24**:125
The Symbolic City in Modern Literature (Ferlinghetti) **10**:174
Symbolic Exchange and Death (Baudrillard)
See *L'échange symbolique et la mort*
"The Symbolic Imagination: The Mirrors of Dante" (Tate) **2**:429; **6**:527; **14**:528
Symbolic Wounds: Puberty Rites and the Envious Male (Bettelheim) **79**:106-09
"Symbolism and Immortality" (Pasternak) **7**:296
"Symbols" (Williams) **148**:359-60
"Symmetrical Companion" (Swenson) **106**:336, 348
"A Symmetry of Thought" (Ammons) **9**:27
"A Sympathy, a Welcome" (Berryman) **62**:76
"Sympathy for the Devil" (Jagger and Richard) **17**:222-24, 226, 236, 241
Sympathy for the Devil (Godard)
See *One Plus One*
"Sympathy in White Major" (Larkin) **64**:283
"Symphonic Night" (Aleixandre)
See "Noche sinfónica"
"Symphony No. Three in D Minor, II" (Williams) **13**:600-01
"The Symposium" (Cunningham) **31**:102
"A Symposium" (Kundera) **9**:321; **32**:260
"The Symposium of the Gorgon" (Smith) **43**:422
Symposium of the Whole (Rothenberg) **57**:382
"Symptoms of Loss" (Williams) **42**:443
Symptoms of Loss (Williams) **42**:439-42
Synchronicity (Police, The) **26**:366
"Synchronicity I" (Police, The) **26**:366
"Synchronicity II" (Police, The) **26**:366
The Syncopated Cake Walk (Major) **19**:294, 299
"Syncrétisme et alternance" (Montherlant) **19**:325
"Syndrome" (Dunn) **40**:167
"The Syndrome" (Jones) **52**:250
"Synecdoche" (Corn) **33**:116
Synnyinmaa (Haavikko) **18**:205-07; **34**:168-69
"Synopsis" (Williams) **42**:442
Syntactics Structures (Chomsky) **132**:6-7, 14
"Syntax" (Graham) **118**:225
"Synthetic World" (Cliff) **21**:64
"Sypaichi" (Aitmatov) **71**:15
"The Syphilis Oozes" (Smith) **12**:541
"Syphoning the Spring" (Clarke) **61**:79
"Syracuse" (Denby) **48**:84
"Syracuse; or, The Panther Man" (Morand) **41**:300-01
"Syringa" (Ashbery) **13**:30, 36; **15**:30; **41**:41; **77**:42, 45, 55
"Syros" (Transtroemer) **52**:409; **65**:226
"Syrup of Figs Will Cast Our Fear" (Porter) **33**:322
"The System" (Ashbery) **2**:19; **15**:28; **25**:50; **77**:61; **125**:16
"The System" (Galeano) **72**:130
"The System and the Speaking Subject" (Kristeva) **140**:140, 168
The System of Dante's Hell (Baraka) **3**:35; **5**:44; **14**:46; **33**:52, 55, 57, 59, 63; **115**:3, 10, 15, 17, 49
The System of Dante's Inferno (Baraka)
See *The System of Dante's Hell*
The System of Objects (Baudrillard)
See *Le systéme des objets*
Systematic Theology (Tillich) **131**:352, 356
Systematics (Tillich)
See *Systematic Theology*
Système de la mode (Barthes) **24**:31, 36; **83**:94
Le systéme des objets (Baudrillard) **60**:9-11, 15, 25, 33
Szpital Przemienienia (Lem) **149**:163, 165-67, 251, 260, 267, 282
"Sztuka nienapisana" (Rozewicz) **139**:291, 294-95, 298
"Szyrk v. Village of Tantamount et al." (Gaddis) **86**:163
The T. E. Lawrence Poems (MacEwen) **55**:163
"T' Plays It Cool" (Gaye) **26**:131
"T. S. Eliot" (McFadden) **48**:244
T. S. Eliot (Spender) **91**:263
T. S. Eliot: A Life (Ackroyd) **34**:387-89, 392-96, 398-99, 402; **52**:7, 9-11, 14-15; **140**:21-22, 30
T. V. Baby Poems (Ginsberg) **109**:338
T. Zee (O'Brien) **17**:324
"t zero" (Calvino)
See "Ti con zero"
T Zero (Calvino)
See *Ti con zero*
t zero (Calvino)
See *Ti con zero*
"Ta" (Cummings) **15**:160
"Ta eleyía tis Oxó petras" (Elytis) **100**:189
"Ta zou hou" (Ding Ling) **68**:59
"Las tablas" (Parra) **102**:339-40
"The Table" (Cabral de Melo Neto)
See "A mesa"
"Table" (Simic) **22**:383
"The Table" (Trevor) **7**:475; **71**:339, 348
Table Manners (Ayckbourn) **5**:35, 37; **8**:35; **74**:4-6
Table Money (Breslin) **43**:76-8
"Table of Delectable Contents" (Simic) **22**:381
Table Talk (Ayckbourn) **33**:44
The Table Talk of Samuel Marchbanks (Davies) **13**:173; **25**:129; **42**:103, 105; **75**:182-83
Le tableau (Ionesco) **41**:229
"Tablet" (Shamlu) **10**:471
"Tableta de cronicar" (Arghezi) **80**:11
"Tablete. Despre cîteva lucruri ştiute" (Arghezi) **80**:13
Tablete din ţara ke Kuty (Arghezi) **80**:6, 11
Tablets from the Land of Kuty (Arghezi)
See *Tablete din ţara ke Kuty*
"Tabula rasa" (Carruth) **7**:41
Il taccuino del vecchio (Ungaretti) **11**:556
Tacey Cromwell (Richter) **30**:308, 310-11, 316, 319-20, 322, 324, 329
"Tacitus" (Trilling) **24**:450
Tacones lejanos (Almodovar) **114**:37, 55
"Tact and the Poet's Force" (Snodgrass) **10**:478
"The Tactful Saboteur" (Herbert) **44**:394
"The Tactics of Motivation" (Burke) **24**:127
Tade kū mushi (Tanizaki) **8**:509-10; **14**:525; **28**:417, 419, 421
"Tadeo Limardo's Victim" (Bioy Casares)
See "La vìctima de Tadeo Limardo"
"Tadeo Limardo's Victim" (Borges) **48**:42
Tadeusz Różewicz: Selected Poems (Rozewicz) **139**:288
"Tag och skriv" (Ekeloef) **27**:112
"Taga for Mbaye Dyôb" (Senghor) **130**:275
"Tage mit Hähern" (Eich) **15**:202
Tagebuch, 1946-1949 (Frisch) **14**:183-84; **44**:185-86, 190, 192, 194-96, 199-203, 207
Tagebuch, 1966-1971 (Frisch) **14**:184; **44**:192-93, 199, 204
Taht al-mizalla (Mahfouz) **153**:359, 371
Taht al-mizalla (Mahfūz) **55**:172
Tähtede tähendus (Ivask) **14**:287
"Tai An's Long Search" (Borges) **48**:41-2
"Taiko Dojo Messages from Haruko" (Jordan) **114**:154
"The Tailor's Wedding" (Simpson) **7**:428
"Tailpiece" (Barth) **9**:68

The Tain (Kinsella) **138**:96-97, 107, 121, 124, 160, 163
Tai-pan: A Novel of Hong Kong (Clavell) **6**:113; **25**:125-27; **87**:2-3, 8, 10, 17-19
"Tajinko Village" (Ibuse) **22**:227
"Tak durno zhit', kak ia vchera zhila" (Akhmadulina) **53**:12
Tak fordi du kom, Nick (Abell) **15**:5
Tak pobedim! (shest' p'es o Lenine) (Shatrov) **59**:359, 362
Take a Call, Topsy (Cavanna) **12**:98, 103
Take a Girl like You (Amis) **1**:6; **2**:4, 7-10; **5**:20; **8**:11; **13**:13; **44**:135, 143-44; **129**:4-8, 16, 18, 22, 25
"Take a Lesbian to Lunch" (Brown) **79**:153
"Take a Look at the Horizon" (Salinas) **90**:324
Take Heart (Peacock) **60**:296-98
"Take It Away" (McCartney) **35**:289-90
"Take It Easy" (Browne) **21**:35, 38
Take It or Leave It (Federman) **6**:181; **47**:122-24, 127, 129-30
Take Me Back (Bausch) **51**:53-4
"Take Me or Leave Me" (Larson) **99**:164, 169
"Take Me to the Mardi Gras" (Simon) **17**:466
"Take Me to the Water" (Baldwin) **127**:126
Take Me Where the Good Times Are (Cormier) **12**:134
"Take Me with You" (Prince) **35**:331
"Take My Saddle from the Wall: A Valediction" (McMurtry) **27**:328; **127**:311
"Take Off Your Socks!!" (Laughlin) **49**:224
"Take Pity" (Malamud) **27**:306; **44**:418
"Take the Moment" (Sondheim) **30**:379
Take the Money and Run (Allen) **16**:2-3, 5, 12, 15-16; **52**:39
"Take Them Out!" (Jordan) **114**:146
Take This Man (Busch) **47**:57-9
Take Three Tenses (Godden) **53**:153-56, 159, 161
"Take Your Clothes Off When You Dance" (Zappa) **17**:591
"Taken at the Flood" (Matthews) **40**:322
Taken at the Flood (Christie)
See *There Is a Tide*
"Takeoff" (Snodgrass) **68**:397
The Takeover (Spark) **8**:493-96; **40**:394-95, 398
The Taker/Tulsa (Jennings) **21**:201
"The Takers" (Olds) **39**:187
"takin a solo/ a poetic possibility/ a poetic imperative" (Shange) **126**:364
"Taking" (Ondaatje) **51**:311
Taking a Grip (Johnston) **51**:248, 253-54
"Taking a Hot Bath" (Piercy) **128**:231
"Taking a Visitor to See the Ruins" (Allen) **84**:24
"Taking a Walk with You" (Koch) **44**:243
"Taking a Walk with You" (Strand) **41**:436; **71**:281-82
"Taking Care" (Williams) **31**:464-65
Taking Care (Williams) **31**:464-65
Taking Care of Mrs. Carroll (Monette) **82**:315, 318, 328
Taking Chances (Keane) **31**:231
"Taking In Wash" (Dove) **50**:153; **81**:139
"Taking It All Off in the Balkans" (Fussell) **74**:139
Taking Liberties (Costello) **21**:75
"Taking My Baby Up Town" (Armatrading) **17**:9-10
Taking Notice (Hacker) **23**:204-05; **72**:182-83
The Taking of Miss Janie (Bullins) **5**:83-4; **7**:37
The Taking of Velikoshumsk (Leonov)
See *Vziatie Velikoshumska*
Taking Sides (Klein) **30**:238
Taking Steps (Ayckbourn) **33**:42-4, 50
Taking Stock (Trifonov)
See *Predvaritel'nye itogi*
Taking Terri Mueller (Mazer) **26**:294
"Taking the Forest" (Howe) **152**:153, 168, 172
"Taking the World in for Repairs" (Selzer) **74**:273, 275
Taking the World in for Repairs (Selzer) **74**:274-75, 281
Un tal Lucas (Cortázar) **33**:135-36; **34**:333-34
"Talbingo" (Slessor) **14**:492
"Talbot Road" (Gunn) **32**:213, 215
"A Tale" (Bogan) **46**:78; **93**:81, 85, 87, 92
A Tale (Pasternak)
See *Povest*
"A Tale about Rain in Several Episodes" (Akhmadulina)
See "A Fairytale about the Rain"
The Tale Bearers: Literary Essays (Pritchett) **41**:328-29, 331
A Tale for Midnight (Prokosch) **48**:315
Tale for the Mirror: A Novella and Other Stories (Calisher) **2**:96; **38**:69; **134**:4, 7, 41
"The Tale of a Turd" (Kureishi) **135**:283
"The Tale of Dragons and Dreamers" (Delany) **141**:155
The Tale of Fatumeh (Ekeloef)
See *Sagan om Fatumeh*
"The Tale of Fog and Granite" (Delany) **141**:156
"The Tale of Gorgik" (Delany) **141**:99, 154
The Tale of Life (Paustovsky)
See *Povest' o zhizni*
"The Tale of Macrocosmic Horror" (Smith) **43**:420
"Tale of Moons" (Carpentier)
See "Histoire de lunes"
"A Tale of Old Women" (Rozewicz) **139**:290
"The Tale of Plagues and Carnivals" (Delany) **141**:114, 154, 157
"The Tale of Rumor and Desire" (Delany) **141**:99, 154, 157
A Tale of Satisfied Desire (Bataille) **29**:45
The Tale of Sunlight (Soto) **32**:401-03; **80**:276-77, 281-83, 293, 295
"The Tale of the Beautiful Princess Kalito" (Maitland) **49**:233, 235
"The Tale of the Black Ring" (Akhmatova) **64**:16, 20
The Tale of the Body Thief (Rice) **128**:294, 299-300, 304-05, 313
"The Tale of the Children of Hurin" (Tolkien) **38**:431
"The Tale of the Furious Kalafat" (Leonov)
See "Legend of Kalafaat"
The Tale of the Triumvirate (Strugatskii and Strugatskii)
See *The Tale of the Troika*
The Tale of the Troika (Strugatskii and Strugatskii) **27**:434, 436
"Tale of the Wicker Chair" (Hesse) **25**:260-61
"The Tale of Three Story Telling Machines of King Genius" (Lem) **8**:344; **15**:327; **149**:170
"Tale of Time" (Warren) **13**:578; **39**:264
A Tale of Time: New Poems, 1960-1966 (Warren) **8**:539; **13**:573-74
"A Tale of Two Gardens" (Paz)
See "Cuento de dos jardines"
"A Tale of Two Liars" (Singer) **111**:297, 305
A Tale Told (Wilson) **36**:459-61, 463
"A Tale without Beginning or End" (Mahfūz) **52**:292
Talent and Work (Leonov) **92**:277
A Talent for Loving; or, The Great Cowboy Race (Condon) **4**:107; **45**:92, 96; **100**:94, 111, 113
Talent Is Not Enough (Hunter) **21**:164
The Talented Mr. Ripley (Highsmith) **2**:193; **4**:226; **42**:211; **102**:177, 179-80, 182-84, 193-94, 207-08, 211-12, 220
Tales (Baraka) **5**:45, 48; **14**:56; **33**:55, 57, 63; **115**:10, 15
Tales and Stories for Black Folks (Bambara) **88**:6
Tales and Texts for Nothing (Beckett) **2**:44
Tales for the Telling: Irish Folk and Fairy Stories (O'Brien) **116**:187
"Tales from a Family Album" (Justice) **102**:268
Tales from a Troubled Land (Paton) **4**:395; **25**:359
Tales from Bective Bridge (Lavin) **99**:312
Tales from Firozsha Baag (Mistry) **71**:266-67, 269-74, 276
Tales from Ovid (Hughes) **119**:250
Tales from the Plum Grove Hills (Stuart) **34**:374
Tales from the Uncertain Country (Ferron)
See *Contes du pays incertain*
Tales from the White Hart (Clarke) **13**:148-49; **18**:106; **136**:238
Tales I Told My Mother (Nye) **42**:304-05, 308
Tales of a Fourth Grade Nothing (Blume) **12**:47; **30**:20
"Tales of Afrikaners" (Coetzee) **117**:48
Tales of Beatnik Glory (Sanders) **53**:307
Tales of Burning Love (Erdrich) **120**:181-83, 190-94
Tales of Known Space (Niven) **8**:426
Tales of Love (Kristeva)
See *Histoires d'amour*
Tales of Love and Death (Aickman) **57**:3
Tales of Manhattan (Auchincloss) **4**:29; **18**:24; **45**:36
Tales of Mornings and Evenings (Mahfouz) **153**:289
Tales of Natural and Unnatural Catastrophes (Highsmith) **102**:201
Tales of Nevèryön (Delany) **14**:148; **38**:159; **141**:119, 130, 149, 153-57
Tales of Pirx the Pilot (Lem) **15**:330; **40**:291, 293, 295-96; **149**:262
Tales of Power (Castaneda) **12**:91-2, 95
"Tales of Queen Louisa" (Gardner) **5**:133; **8**:238
Tales of Tenderness and Power (Head) **67**:111
"Tales of the Art World" (Chatwin) **57**:153
Tales of the City (Maupin) **95**:192-97, 199, 201-07, 211
"Tales of the Islands" (Walcott) **25**:448; **42**:421; **67**:353-54; **76**:273, 275, 279
"Tales of the Marvellous and the Ridiculous" (Wilson) **24**:481
Tales of the Mountains and Steppes (Aitmatov)
See *Povestri gor i stepei*
Tales of the Quintana Roo (Tiptree) **48**:393-95; **50**:357
Tales of the South Pacific (Michener) **1**:214; **5**:289; **11**:375; **29**:309-12; **60**:258, 262; **109**:375-80, 382, 384, 385, 387, 388
"Tales of the Swedish Army" (Barthelme) **13**:59
Tales of the Unexpected (Dahl) **18**:108
"Tales of Two Old Gentlemen" (Dinesen) **95**:56
"Tales Told of the Fathers" (Hollander) **8**:301
Tales Told of the Fathers (Hollander) **8**:299-302
"Taliesin, 1952" (Thomas) **48**:377
"Taliesin and the Spring of Vision" (Watkins) **43**:447, 451, 453-54
"Taliesin in Gower" (Watkins) **43**:442, 451, 454
"A Taliessin Answer" (Redgrove) **41**:349
"A Talisman" (Moore) **13**:392; **19**:336
The Talisman (Alegria) **75**:51-2
The Talisman (King) **37**:205-06; **61**:328, 331; **113**:388-89, 391, 393
The Talisman (Straub) **107**:267-73, 275-77, 279-80, 282, 289, 291, 304-08, 310
"Talk I" (Cage) **41**:80
A Talk in the Park (Ayckbourn) **33**:41
Talk Radio (Bogosian) **141**:81-4, 89
Talk Radio (Stone) **73**:374-77, 382
"Talk Show" (Baxter) **45**:53; **78**:17, 21
"Talk to Me" (Mitchell) **12**:444
Talk to Me about Funes (Costantini)
See *Háblenme de Funes*
"A Talk with Doris Lessing" (Lessing) **94**:293
Talkative Man (Narayan) **47**:306-09
"Talkin 'Bout Sonny" (Bambara) **88**:21
"Talkin, John Birch Paranoid Blues" (Dylan) **77**:166, 168
Talkin' Moscow Blues: Essays about Literature, Politics, Movies, and Jazz (Škvorecký) **69**:334-36; **152**:314-15

"Talkin' World War III Blues" (Dylan) **77**:161
"Talking about Polylogue" (Kristeva) **140**:182
Talking All Morning (Bly) **38**:50-4
"The Talking Back of Miss Valentine Jones" (Jordan) **114**:145-46
Talking Back: Thinking Feminist, Thinking Black (Hooks) **94**:143-45, 159
"Talking Back (to W. H. Auden)" (Meredith) **55**:192
"Talking Birmingham Jam" (Ochs) **17**:331
Talking Book (Wonder) **12**:657, 659-60, 663
"Talking Cuba" (Ochs) **17**:330-31
"Talking Dust Bowl" (Kennedy) **42**:256
"Talking Dustbowl" (Guthrie) **35**:188
The Talking Earth (George) **35**:180
Talking God (Hillerman) **62**:262
Talking Heads (Bennett) **77**:92, 95, 98, 101-03
Talking Heads (Kieslowski) **120**:204, 243, 252
Talking Heads: Seventy-Seven (Byrne) **26**:94-5
"Talking Horse" (Malamud) **3**:323, 325; **27**:298, 300; **44**:417
"Talking in Bed" (Larkin) **33**:258
"Talking in the Train" (White) **49**:409
"Talking in the Woods with Karl Amorelli" (Knight) **40**:286
Talking It Over (Barnes) **141**:48, 50, 53, 61-3, 66-7, 77
"Talking Myself to Sleep at One More Hilton" (Ciardi) **40**:160
Talking Pictures (Foote) **91**:99
"Talking Shop Tanka" (Porter) **33**:323
"The Talking Stone" (Asimov) **26**:44
"Talking to a Stranger" (Grayson) **38**:209
"Talking to Little Birdies" (Simic) **130**:346
"Talking to My Grandmother Who Died Poor (While Hearing Richard Nixon Declare 'I Am Not a Crook')" (Walker) **58**:405
"Talking to Myself" (Auden) **2**:28; **6**:18-19
Talking to Myself: A Memoir of My Times (Terkel) **38**:424-25
"Talking to Sheep" (Sexton) **123**:405
Talking to Strange Men (Rendell) **48**:327
"Talking to the Moon" (Matthews) **40**:321
Talking to the Moon (Mathews) **84**:209-11, 216-18, 220-22, 224-26
"Talking to You Afterwards" (Porter) **33**:321
The Talking Trees (O'Faolain) **7**:273; **32**:342-43; **70**:319
"Talking United States" (Wilson) **24**:481
"Talking Vietnam Blues" (Ochs) **17**:330
"The Tall Grass" (Daly) **17**:90
Tall Houses in Winter (Betts) **28**:33
The Tall Hunter (Fast) **131**:93
Tall in the Saddle (Armatrading) **17**:9
"The Tall Men" (Davidson) **2**:111; **13**:166-67, 169; **19**:124-26
"The Tall Men" (Faulkner) **3**:149
"The Tall Sailing Ship" (Quasimodo)
See "L'alto veliero"
"Tall Windows" (Hass) **99**:143
"Taller Today" (Auden) **14**:32; **43**:15
The Talley Method (Behrman) **40**:80, 83, 87
Talley's Folly (Wilson) **14**:591-93; **36**:459-61, 465
"A Tally" (Creeley) **78**:137
"A Tally of the Souls of Sheep" (Hulme) **130**:53
"Talpa" (Rulfo) **80**:200-01, 216
Taltos (Rice) **128**:297-98, 306, 312
Talvipalatsi (Haavikko) **18**:205-06; **34**:170-71, 177
Tam o' the Wilds and the Many-Faced Mystery (MacDiarmid) **63**:249
"Tamar" (Helprin) **22**:221, 223; **32**:230-31
"Tamar" (Jeffers) **54**:233, 235-37, 244-46, 248-49; **2**:215; **3**:258; **11**:304-07; **15**:300
Tamar and Other Poems (Jeffers) **54**:235, 240, 250; **11**:304-05
Tamara (Krizanc) **57**:271-79
"The Tamarind Tree" (Anand) **23**:21
"Tambourine" (Prince) **35**:332
"The Tambourine Lady" (Wideman) **67**:379, 385
"Tambourine Life" (Berrigan) **37**:43, 46
"Tambourines" (Hughes) **108**:297
Tambourines to Glory (Hughes) **35**:216-18
Les tambours de la pluie (Kadare) **52**:261
"Tamer and Hawk" (Gunn) **18**:204; **32**:210
"The Taming" (Livesay) **15**:340-41; **79**:337, 339
The Taming of Badadoshkin (Leonov)
See *Usmirenie Badadoshkina*
"The Taming of the Shrew" (Peacock) **60**:295
Taming the Star Runner (Hinton) **111**:84-6
"Tamurlane" (Mukherjee) **53**:265-66, 268
An tan revolisyon (Condé) **92**:132
Tan triste como ella (Onetti) **10**:377-80
Tanagokoro no Shōsetsu (Kawabata) **107**:103, 108, 112
"Tancredi Continues" (Cixous) **92**:81-2, 93-4
Taneční hodiny pro starší a pokročilé (Hrabal) **67**:121
"Tang" (Himes) **108**:234-35
The Tangent Factor (Sanders) **41**:379-80
The Tangent Objective (Sanders) **41**:378-80
"Tangerine" (Page and Plant) **12**:475
"Tangi" (Ihimaera) **46**:196
Tangi (Ihimaera) **46**:193-97, 199, 202
Tangier Buzzless Flies (Hopkins) **4**:233
"Tangled Up in Blue" (Dylan) **6**:157; **12**:191; **77**:178
"A Tangled Web" (Haldeman) **61**:181
"Tango" (Glück) **22**:177
Tango (Mrozek) **3**:344-45; **13**:398
"The Tango Bear" (Hansen) **38**:240
"Tango: Maureen" (Larson) **99**:167, 169
Tango Palace (Fornés) **39**:138; **61**:129-30, 137, 139
The Tango Player (Hein)
See *Der Tangospieler*
Der Tangospieler (Hein) **154**:55-9, 61, 63-5, 71-2, 103-11, 119, 133-34, 136, 141, 144, 149-55, 158, 172, 177-78, 180-81, 184-87
"Tanhum" (Singer) **15**:507
Tanin no kao (Abe) **22**:12-13; **53**:2, 4, 6; **81**:285, 287-88, 293-94, 297
The Tank Corps (Škvorecký)
See *L'Escadron blindé*
"The Tank Trapeze" (Moorcock) **58**:347
"Tankas" (Borges) **13**:110
"Tanker Notes" (Snyder) **120**:330
Tankový prapor (Škvorecký)
See *L'Escadron blindé*
Tanner '88: The Dark Horse (Altman) **116**:50, 59
"Tantas Cosas Asustan, Tantas" (Cisneros) **69**:151
La tante (Simenon) **47**:379
"Tantric Ballad" (Ferlinghetti) **111**:65
"Tantrum" (Jensen) **37**:189
Tantrum (Feiffer) **64**:153
Tanya and the Two Gunmen (Škvorecký) **152**:336
"Die Tänzerin (D.H.)" (Sachs) **98**:354
"Tao and Unfitness at Inistiogue on the River Nore" (Kinsella) **138**:103, 116
"Tao in the Yankee Stadium Bleachers" (Updike) **23**:473
Tap Root Manuscript (Diamond) **30**:110-11
Tape for the Turn of the Year (Ammons) **2**:12-13; **5**:29, 31; **8**:14-15, 17-18; **9**:27; **25**:47; **57**:55, 58-9; **108**:5, 11-2, 48, 52-5, 58-9, 61
"Tape from California" (Ochs) **17**:332
Tape from California (Ochs) **17**:332
"Tapestries of Time" (Tolson) **105**:260, 282
"Tapestry" (Ashbery) **15**:33-4; **41**:40
"A Tapestry for Bayeaux" (Starbuck) **53**:353, 355
"Tapestry Makers" (Willard) **37**:463
"Tapiama" (Bowles) **2**:79
"Tapioca Surprise" (Goyen) **14**:211
Tapping the Source (Nunn) **34**:94-6
"The Taps" (Soto) **80**:298
Taps for Private Tussie (Stuart) **11**:511; **14**:517; **34**:373, 376
"Tapwater" (Jensen) **37**:191
Tar (Williams) **33**:447-49; **56**:426, 428-29; **148**:308-11, 313, 318, 320, 322, 324-25, 344, 359, 361
The Tar Baby (Charyn) **5**:104
Tar Baby (Morrison) **22**:320-23; **55**:195-96, 207-08; **81**:225, 228, 231-33, 236, 238, 256-57, 260; **87**:263, 288, 290-92, 294
"Tara" (Kinsella) **138**:133, 148
Tara (White) **49**:401
"Tara Diptych" (Hulme) **130**:61
Tara Road (Binchy) **153**:75-8
Taran Wanderer (Alexander) **35**:24-6
"Taranta-Babuya mektuplar" (Hikmet) **40**:245, 247
Tarantula (Dylan) **4**:148; **12**:184, 187; **77**:176
Taratuta (Donoso) **99**:222, 255, 273-75, 277
"Tardy" (Matthews) **40**:325
"Tardy Autumn" (Arghezi)
See "Tîrzui de toamnă"
The Tare of Barrels (Aksyonov) **101**:11-12, 28, 30
Tares (Thomas) **48**:374, 380
al-Tarīq (Mahfūz) **52**:295-96; **55**:174, 181-82
"The Tarn and the Rosary" (Brown) **48**:55, 60
Tårnet (Vesaas) **48**:407
The Tarot of Cornelius Agrippa (Morgan) **23**:299
"Tarquin" (O'Hara) **13**:426
"Tarry, Delight" (Belitt) **22**:48
"Tarsisius" (Buckley) **57**:129
"Tartan" (Brown) **48**:52
The Tartar Steppe (Buzzati)
See *Il deserto dei tartari*
Tarts and Muggers (Musgrave) **54**:338, 340
Tarzan and the City of Gold (Leiber) **25**:303
"Tarzan Is an Expatriate" (Theroux) **46**:402
"Tashlich" (Piercy) **62**:370
"A Task" (Milosz) **56**:238; **82**:307
Tasks and Masks: Themes and Styles of African Literature (Nkosi) **45**:295
The Tassie (O'Casey)
See *The Silver Tassie*
"The Taste" (Bitov) **57**:114-15
"Taste" (Dahl) **79**:180
"Taste" (Thomas) **13**:544
A Taste for Death (James) **46**:209-11; **122**:132, 134-35, 137-38, 145-46, 149-51, 153-55, 158, 164-66, 168, 180, 183
"A Taste for Perfection" (Vanderhaeghe) **41**:449-50
A Taste of Honey (Delaney) **29**:143-48
"The Taste of Metal" (Updike) **139**:327
A Taste of Salt Water (Shapcott) **38**:398, 400
"The Taste of the Age" (Jarrell) **6**:260
"Tasting the Wild Grapes" (Oliver) **98**:267, 297
"Tate Gallery" (Jennings) **131**:235
"Tatlin!" (Davenport) **6**:123
Tatlin! (Davenport) **6**:123-25; **14**:139-142; **38**:139-40, 144, 146, 148
"Tattered Banners" (Boyle) **121**:59
"Tattered Kaddish" (Rich) **76**:210, 212-14
"Tattoo" (Moss) **7**:249
"Tattoo" (Townshend) **17**:531, 533, 539
The Tattooed Countess (Van Vechten) **33**:387-88, 392, 398
"The Tattooed Man" (Hayden) **37**:155
"The Tattooed Man" (Raine) **103**:179
"Tattooer" (Tanizaki)
See "Shisei"
"Tattoos" (Wright) **13**:612; **28**:456, 460; **146**:326-27, 360, 366, 374
"Tattoos Twelve" (Wright) **13**:613
"Tau" (Tolson) **105**:255
Tau Zero (Anderson) **15**:11, 13
"Tauben" (Eich) **15**:202
Die tausend Augen des Dr. Mabuse (Lang)
See *The Thousand Eyes of Dr. Mabuse*
Tauw (Ousmane) **66**:336
Se tavallinen tarina (Salama) **18**:461
"The Tavern of Crossed Destinies" (Calvino) **8**:131

"The Tavern of the Black Cat" (Mahfūz) **52**:298
The Tavern of the Black Cat (Mahfouz) **153**:234
The Tavern of the Black Cat (Mahfūz)
See *Khammārat al-qitt al-aswad*
"Tavistock Square" (Williams) **42**:442
"Tawny Owl" (Clarke) **61**:82-3
The Tax Inspector (Carey) **96**:69 74, 76-8, 80-1, 83
The Taxi (Leduc) **22**:263
Taxi Driver (Schrader) **26**:385-89, 393-95
Taxi Driver (Scorsese) **20**:327-30, 334, 336-38, 340; **89**:223-26, 228-30, 232-33, 235-36, 239-41, 243-45, 248-49, 252, 254, 260-64, 266-67
"The Taxpayer" (Bradbury) **42**:38
Tayaout, fils d'Agaguk (Theriault) **79**:407, 418, 420
"Tayga" (Voznesensky) **57**:417
"Taylor Lake" (Ostriker) **132**:325
"T.B. Sheets" (Morrison) **21**:235
T.B. Sheets (Morrison) **21**:235
"TCB" (Sanchez) **116**:295
Te Kaihau (Hulme) **130**:48-9, 51-4
"Te lucis ante terminum" (Hill) **45**:180
"Tea and Sympathy" (Anderson) **23**:28-9, 31, 33
Tea and Sympathy (Kazan) **63**:234
"Tea for One" (Page and Plant) **12**:480
"Tea in the Rain" (Cryer) **21**:79
"Tea in the Sahara" (Police, The) **26**:366
Tea Party (Pinter) **15**:423; **27**:385, 394; **58**:373
"The Tea Time of Stouthearted Ladies" (Stafford) **68**:430
"Tea with an Artist" (Rhys) **51**:356
Tea with Dr. Borsig (Boell)
See *Zum Tee bei Dr. Borsig*
"Tea with Mrs. Bittell" (Pritchett) **15**:442; **41**:330
"Tea with the Devil" (Hope) **51**:226
"Teach the Gifted Children" (Reed) **21**:320-21
Teach Us to Outgrow Our Madness (Oe)
See *Warera no kyōki o ikinobiru michi o oshieyo*
"Teacher" (Ashton-Warner) **19**:21
"Teacher in 1980 America: What He Found" (Barzun) **145**:80
Teacher in America (Barzun) **145**:70, 73, 79, 94
"The Teacher's Mission" (Pound) **4**:416; **112**:322
"Teacher's Pet" (Thurber) **5**:432, **125**:413, 415
"Teaching a Dumb Calf" (Hughes) **119**:271
"Teaching a Stone to Talk" (Dillard) **60**:74
Teaching a Stone to Talk: Expeditions and Encounters (Dillard) **60**:74-5; **115**:170, 197-99, 202-03, 205-06, 208-09
"Teaching and Story Telling" (Maclean) **78**:239
"The Teaching of Literature" (O'Connor) **104**:167
"The Teaching Poet" (Roethke) **101**:266
"Teaching Poetry at Votech High, Santa Fe, the Week John Lennon Was Shot" (Allen) **84**:24
"Teaching the Ape to Write Poems" (Tate) **2**:432
Teaching the Penguins to Fly (Spacks) **14**:510
Teaching to Transgress: Educating as the Practice of Freedom (Hooks) **94**:155-59
"The Teachings of Don B.: A Yankee Way of Knowledge" (Barthelme) **115**:85-6
The Teachings of Don Juan (Castaneda) **12**:84-6, 88, 95
"Team Bells" (Davis) **49**:91
Team Bells Woke Me (Davis) **49**:90-1
"The Tear" (Kinsella) **19**:252, 254; **138**:101, 142
"A Tear" (Yevtushenko) **26**:467
"Tear Gas" (Rich) **6**:459
"Tears, Idle Tears" (Bowen) **22**:65; **118**:111-12, 114-15
"Tears in Sleep" (Bogan) **46**:78; **93**:90, 95-6
"The Tears of a Clown" (Robinson) **21**:342, 344, 347
"Tears of an Excavator" (Pasolini) **106**:241-249
"Tears of Rage" (Dylan) **6**:155
"Tears, Spray, and Steam" (Logan) **5**:255
"The Teasers" (Empson) **19**:156
Teater (Lagerkvist) **54**:273-74
Teatr (Rozewicz) **139**:276 82
"Teatr niekonsekwencji" (Rozewicz) **139**:282
El teatro en soledad (Gomez de la Serna) **9**:238
"Tecendo a manhã" (Cabral de Melo Neto) **76**:155
Technical Difficulties: African-American Notes on the State of the Union (Jordan) **114**:150-51, 153, 156
"Technical Notes" (Laughlin) **49**:220-21
"Technical Notes on My House-Arrest" (Havel) **65**:421
"A Technical Supplement" (Kinsella) **138**:113, 115, 130, 135-36, 162
Technical Supplement (Kinsella) **138**:88-89, 94, 106, 109, 120, 154, 156, 167
Technicians of the Sacred: A Range of Poetries from Africa, America, Asia, and Oceania (Rothenberg) **57**:373, 375, 379, 382
The Technicolor Time Machine (Harrison) **42**:200, 205
Technik und Wissenschaft als "Ideologie" (Habermas) **104**:68
"Technique as Discovery" (Schorer) **9**:473
Technique du roman (Queneau) **5**:360
The Technique of Fiction (Oe)
See *Shosetsu no hoho*
"Technologies" (Oppen) **7**:281
Technology and Culture (Dudek) **19**:139
Technology and the Canadian Mind: Innis/McLuhan/Grant (Kroker) **77**:341-42, 344
"Technology and the Soul" (Martinson)
See "Tekniken och själen"
"Tecumseh" (Oliver) **34**:246; **98**:257-58, 272, 278
Tecumseh (Eckert) **17**:108
Ted Hughes and Paul Muldoon (Hughes) **37**:179
Tedderella (Edgar) **42**:116
"Teddungal" (Senghor) **54**:410
"Teddy" (Salinger) **12**:520; **138**:183, 202
"Teddy Bears" (Swenson) **106**:333
"Teddy Boy" (McCartney) **35**:278
"The Teddy-Bears' Picnic" (Trevor) **116**:364
"Ted's Wife" (Thomas) **37**:421
Teeftallow (Stribling) **23**:439, 441, 445
Teen Kanya (Ray) **16**:479-80, 483-84, 490-491, 493; **76**:360
Teenage Survival Book (Gordon) **26**:139
A Teen-Ager's First Car (Felsen) **17**:124
Teendreams (Edgar) **42**:113
"Teeth" (Stern) **39**:237
Teeth, Dying, and Other Matters (Stern) **39**:237
The Teeth Mother Naked at Last (Bly) **128**:29
Teeth 'n' Smiles (Hare) **29**:211-14, 216; **58**:233; **136**:259, 261, 265, 286
"The Teeth of My Father" (Metcalf) **37**:301, 306
The Teeth of My Father (Metcalf) **37**:299-300
"The Teeth-Mother Naked at Last" (Bly) **2**:66; **5**:64; **10**:55, 58-9; **15**:62-3; **38**:55; **128**:6-9, 18, 21-22, 29-31
Tehanu: The Last Book of Earthsea (Le Guin) **71**:181-82, 184, 188-89, 191, 196, 198, 200-01; **136**:362, 365-69, 377, 381, 387-90
Teia (Dourado) **23**:149-51
"Teibele and Her Demon" (Singer) **15**:509; **38**:414-16
Teile dich Nacht (Sachs) **14**:477; **98**:347, 358-59
Teitlebaum's Window (Markfield) **8**:379-80
La tejedora de sueños (Buero Vallejo) **15**:99; **46**:96; **139**:10
"TeKaihau" (Hulme) **130**:53
"Tekniken och själen" (Martinson) **14**:355
Tekonwatoni/Molly Brant (1735-1795): Poems of War (Kenny) **87**:250-53, 258-59
"Telecommunication" (Reading) **47**:352
"Telegram" (Berrigan) **37**:44
"Telemachus" (Dickey) **28**:119
"Le téléphone" (Carrier) **78**:68
"Telephone Call" (Kenny) **87**:242
"A Telephone Call" (Parker) **68**:325, 329, 334, 339
"A Telephone Call on Yom Kippur" (Singer) **69**:305
"Telephone Conversation" (Soyinka) **14**:506; **44**:279
"The Telephone Number" (Scannell) **49**:326
"The Telephone Number of the Muse" (Justice) **19**:234, 236; **102**:265, 269
"Telephone Poles" (Updike) **23**:474
Telephone Poles, and Other Poems (Updike) **1**:344; **23**:474-75
Telepinus (Olson) **11**:420
"The Telescope" (Derleth) **31**:138
"Telescopic" (Frost)
See "A Loose Mountain"
"Television" (Beattie) **146**:67, 70
"Television" (Bennett) **28**:26
La télévision (Lacan) **75**:301
"Television Is a Baby Crawling Toward That Death Chamber" (Ginsberg) **36**:184; **109**:344
Television Plays (Chayefsky) **23**:111
"The Television Poems" (Dobyns) **37**:76-7
"Television's Junkyard Dog" (Crews) **49**:73
"Tell All the People" (Morrison) **17**:289
Tell Freedom (Abrahams) **4**:2
Tell It Me Again (Fuller) **62**:205
"Tell Me a Riddle" (Olsen) **114**:192-94, 197-99, 201-02, 207, 212-13, 215, 218-20, 222-24, 236-38, 240-42, 244
Tell Me a Riddle (Olsen) **4**:386-87; **13**:433; **114**:193, 195, 197-99, 201, 206, 232, 236, 239
"Tell Me a Story" (Warren) **13**:582
Tell Me Again How the White Heron Rises and Flies Across the Nacreous River at Twilight Toward the Distant Islands (Carruth) **84**:133, 136
"Tell Me, Doctor" (Redgrove) **41**:352
Tell Me How Long the Train's Been Gone (Baldwin) **1**:16; **2**:32; **4**:41-2; **5**:43; **13**:52; **15**:42-3; **17**:34-7, 45; **50**:283, 293, 296; **90**:31, 33; **127**:117-18, 121, 147, 151
Tell Me If the Lovers Are Losers (Voigt) **30**:418
Tell Me, Tell Me: Granite, Steel, and Other Topics (Moore) **8**:401; **47**:263
Tell Me that You Love Me, Junie Moon (Kellogg) **2**:223-24
Tell Me the Truth About Love (Auden) **123**:47
"Tell Me Who to Kill" (Naipaul) **13**:407; **105**:157
"Tell Me Why" (Young) **17**:570
"Tell Me Yes or No" (Munro) **6**:342; **10**:358; **19**:344
"Tell Miss Sweeny Good-Bye" (Tomlin) **17**:522-23
Tell My Horse (Hurston) **30**:212, 217
"Tell the Women We're Going" (Carver) **22**:102, 104
"Tell Them Good-by" (Foote) **75**:231
"Tell Them Not to Kill Me" (Rulfo)
See "Díles que no me maten!"
Tell Them Willie Boy Is Here (Polonsky) **92**:382-83, 387, 391-92, 396-97, 402-03, 405, 415-16
The Telling (Riding) **7**:375-77
"Telling about Coyote" (Ortiz) **45**:304, 306
"Telling Fortunes" (Brown) **59**:265
"Telling Moves" (Ammons) **57**:53
The Telling of Lies (Findley) **102**:112, 118
Telling Tales (Maitland) **49**:233-34
"Telling Them" (Beer) **58**:36
The Tell-Tale Heart (Symons) **32**:426-27
"El Tema del traidor y del héroe" (Borges) **6**:91; **19**:47; **48**:45; **83**:156
"Tema para San Jorge" (Cortázar) **10**:118
"Temenos" (Lane) **25**:288

Le témoignage de l'enfant de choeur (Simenon) **3**:450
Temol shilshom (Agnon) **14**:6
"Tempered Copper" (Richter) **30**:323
The Tempers (Williams) **42**:458
A Tempest: After "The Tempest" by Shakespeare, Adaptation for the Negro Theatre (Césaire)
See *Une tempête: d'après "La tempête" de Shakespeare, Adaptation pour un théâtre nègre*
Tempest-Tost (Davies) **13**:171, 173; **25**:129-31; **42**:101-02, 104; **75**:184, 191-93, 198, 213-14; **91**:201, 203-4
Une tempête: d'après "La tempête" de Shakespeare, Adaptation pour un théâtre nègre (Césaire) **19**:99; **112**:21, 26, 28, 39, 44
The Temple (Spender) **91**:264-68
The Temple (Weidman) **7**:518
The Temple of Dawn (Mishima) **4**:356, 358; **6**:338; **27**:341-42
The Temple of Gold (Goldman) **48**:123-24, 128
The Temple of My Familiar (Walker) **58**:410-17
The Temple of the Golden Pavillion (Mishima)
See *Kinkakuji*
"A Temple of the Holy Ghost" (O'Connor) **6**:376, 378; **13**:417; **15**:412; **21**:261, 263, 267-68
Tempo de amar (Dourado) **23**:150
The Temporary Kings (Powell) **3**:401-04; **7**:338-39, 343; **9**:436-37; **10**:415-16
A Temporary Life (Storey) **4**:529-30; **5**:416-17; **8**:505
"Temporary Secretary" (McCartney) **35**:287-89
"Temporary Shelter" (Gordon) **128**:110, 114-16
Temporary Shelter (Gordon) **128**:109, 111, 114-16, 122, 140
"Temporary Thing" (Reed) **21**:312
Le temps, ce grand sculpteur (Yourcenar) **50**:363-64; **87**:412, 433
Le temps d'Anaïs (Simenon) **18**:483
Le temps des assassins (Soupault) **68**:402-04
Le temps des morts (Gascar) **11**:220
Les temps du Carcajou (Theriault) **79**:417
Le temps du mépris (Malraux) **4**:324-26, 331, 336; **9**:354; **13**:366; **57**:301-02, 305-06, 312
Le temps immobile (Mauriac) **9**:367
"Le Temps ne passe pas" (Le Clézio) **155**:83
Le temps sauvage (Hébert) **29**:237-38
"Temptation" (Milosz) **82**:295, 298
"Temptation" (Prince) **35**:331-32
"The Temptation of Jack Orkney" (Lessing) **94**:261, 264
The Temptation of Jack Orkney, and Other Stories (Lessing) **2**:241-42; **3**:286; **6**:300; **94**:261
"The Temptation of Modernity" (Powell) **89**:206
"The Temptation of St. Anthony" (Barthelme) **13**:57; **46**:35
"The Temptation of St. Ivo" (Gardner) **8**:238
The Temptation to Exist (Cioran)
See *La tentation d'exister*
The Temptations of Big Bear (Wiebe) **6**:566-67; **14**:574; **138**:308-09, 311-12, 315, 318, 324, 326, 330-32, 334, 336, 338, 344, 351, 363-74, 386, 396
"The Temptations of Doctor Antonio" (Fellini)
See "Le tentazioni del Dottor Antonio"
The Temptations of Eileen Hughes (Moore) **32**:307-11, 313; **90**:260, 265, 268, 274, 304
The Temptations of Oedipus (Baxter) **14**:65
"The Temptress" (Jhabvala) **138**:78
"Tempul Firing" (Bissett) **18**:58
Temy i variatsi (Pasternak) **7**:293, 300; **18**:381-82; **63**:275, 280, 289
Temy i var'iatsii (Pasternak)
See *Temy i variatsi*
"10" (Reading) **47**:350
"Ten Accounts of a Monogamous Man" (Meredith) **4**:349
Ten Blocks on the Camino Real (Williams)
See *Camino Real*
"Ten Burnt Offerings" (MacNeice) **4**:317
"Ten Cents a Coup" (Ochs) **17**:333
The Ten Commandments (Kieslowski)
See *Dekalog*
Ten Dark Women (Ichikawa)
See *Kuroi junin no ohna*
"Ten Days Leave" (Snodgrass) **68**:387
Ten Days of Wonder (Queen) **11**:461-64
"Ten Degrees and Getting Colder" (Lightfoot) **26**:278
Ten Green Bottles (Thomas) **7**:472; **13**:539; **37**:417; **107**:314, 316-17, 326, 334, 347, 348, 350
Ten Horsepower (Ehrenburg) **62**:176
"Ten Indians" (Hemingway) **10**:269; **30**:181
"Ten Jack-Offs" (Bukowski) **41**:68
Ten Little Indians (Christie)
See *And Then There Were None*
Ten Little Niggers (Christie)
See *And Then There Were None*
Ten Million Ghosts (Kingsley) **44**:232
Ten North Frederick (O'Hara) **2**:324; **6**:385-86; **42**:313, 315, 319, 323-24
Ten Novelists and Their Novels (Maugham) **15**:368
10 Pastoral Poems (Alegria) **57**:10
"Ten Pecan Pies" (Major) **19**:298
"Ten Shots of Mr. Simpson" (Graham) **29**:198-99
The Ten Teacups (Carr)
See *The Peacock Feather Murders*
Ten Theatre Poems (Morgan) **31**:274
The 10:30 from Marseilles (Japrisot)
See *Compartiment tueurs*
Ten Thousand Light-Years from Home (Tiptree) **48**:385-86, 389, 393
"10,000 Men" (Dylan) **77**:182, 185
"Ten Thousand Words a Minute" (Mailer) **111**:106-07
Ten Times Table (Ayckbourn) **33**:41, 45
Ten Tiny Fingers, Nine Tiny Toes (Townsend) **61**:419
Ten Working Theses of the Writer in a Divided World (Weiss) **15**:567
"Ten Years Ago When I Played at Being Brave" (Ciardi) **44**:381
Ten Years Beyond Baker Street (Van Ash) **34**:118-19
"Ten Years Gone" (Page and Plant) **12**:479
"Ten Years' Sentences" (Laurence) **3**:280; **50**:321; **62**:269-70
Ten' zvuka (Voznesensky) **15**:554, 557
"Tenancies" (Thomas) **48**:375
"A Tenancy" (Merrill) **13**:379
"The Tenant" (Mukherjee) **53**:272; **115**:364, 366-67, 369
"The Tenant" (Ortese)
See "Il signor Lin"
"The Tenant" (Phillips) **28**:363
The Tenant (Polanski) **16**:472-73
The Tenants (Malamud) **1**:201; **2**:266-69; **3**:322, 325; **8**:375; **9**:343-46, 348-50; **11**:346-48, 351-54; **18**:319-21; **27**:295-96, 298, 300-04; **44**:413, 415, 419; **85**:200
The Tenants of Moonbloom (Wallant) **5**:478; **10**:512, 514-17
Tenants of the House (Abse) **29**:12-18
"Tenants of the Last Tree-House" (Gordimer) **33**:180
The Tenants of Time (Flanagan) **52**:153-56
"Tenato Suicidio" (Antonioni) **144**:79
Tenda dos milagres (Amado) **13**:11; **40**:33-4; **106**:56, 60, 62, 65
"Ten-Day Leave" (Meredith) **4**:348
Tender Is the Night (Potter) **123**:273
"A Tender Man" (Bambara) **88**:22, 28, 42
Tender Mercies (Brown) **32**:67-70
Tender Mercies (Foote) **51**:131-36, 138; **91**:101
"The Tender Offer" (Auchincloss) **45**:33
Tender Offer (Wasserstein) **32**:441
The Tender Skin (Truffaut)
See *La peau douce*
"The Tenderfoot and the Tramp" (Solzhenitsyn) **7**:432
"Tenderfoot in Space" (Heinlein) **26**:177
"Tenderloin" (Gunn) **81**:176, 178
Tenderness and Gristle: The Collected Poems (Niedecker) **42**:295
Tending to Virginia (McCorkle) **51**:275-78
Tendres stocks (Morand) **41**:295-98, 303, 306-08
"Tendril in the Mesh" (Everson) **5**:123; **14**:166
"Tenebrae" (Celan) **10**:104; **19**:88; **53**:75; **82**:45
"Tenebrae" (Clarke) **9**:168
"Tenebrae" (Gascoyne) **45**:148
"Tenebrae" (Hill) **45**:180
Tenebrae (Hill) **18**:238-40, 242-43; **45**:178-82, 185-87
Tenement of Clay (West) **96**:367-68, 384
"Tengo" (Guillén) **48**:161
Tengo (Guillén) **48**:158-59, 164, 167; **79**:229
Tennessee (Linney) **51**:260, 262
Tennessee Day in St. Louis (Taylor) **18**:522; **71**:293
"Tennessee June" (Graham) **48**:145
"Tennessee Line" (Wright) **146**:348
Tennessee Williams's Letters to Donald Windham, 1940-1965 (Williams) **19**:470; **45**:444-45
"Tennis" (Avison) **97**:69, 76, 81, 111, 129, 130-36
"Tennis" (Pinsky) **121**:435
"Tennis: A Portrait" (Moss) **14**:376
"The Tennis Court" (Dunn) **40**:171
"The Tennis Court" (Trevor) **9**:529
"The Tennis Court Oath" (Ashbery) **9**:43
The Tennis Court Oath (Ashbery) **2**:16, 18-19; **4**:22-3; **9**:42-43, 45; **15**:26-8, 34, 36; **25**:52, 55, 58; **41**:40-1; 42, 48, 52, 73; **125**:10, 37
The Tennis Handsome (Hannah) **38**:231-35; **90**:137, 148, 151
"Tennis Instructor, 1971" (Leithauser) **27**:240
Tennis Shoes (Streatfeild) **21**:397, 414
"Te-non-an-at-che" (Kenny) **87**:252
"Tenor" (Jensen) **37**:191
"Tense Night" (Faludy) **42**:140
"Tension in Poetry" (Tate) **4**:536; **6**:526; **11**:525
Tent of Miracles (Amado)
See *Tenda dos milagres*
The Tent of Orange Mist (West) **96**:397-99
"Tent on the Home Ground" (Ihimaera) **46**:200
"Tentation de la permanence" (de Man) **55**:404
La tentation d'exister (Cioran) **64**:73-5, 77-84, 87, 90, 92-3, 96-9
Tentativa del hombre infinito (Neruda) **28**:313
"Tentative Conclusion" (Frye) **24**:209
"Tentative Decisions" (Byrne) **26**:94
"Tentative Hour" (Avison) **97**:123
"A Tentative Welcome to Readers" (Stafford) **29**:387
Tentato suicidio (Antonioni) **144**:65
"Le tentazioni del Dottor Antonio" (Fellini) **16**:277; **85**:71
"Tenth Avenue Freeze-Out" (Springsteen) **17**:489
"The Tenth Child" (Calisher) **38**:76
"The Tenth Clew" (Hammett) **47**:164
The Tenth Commandment (Sanders) **41**:380-82
The Tenth Man (Chayefsky) **23**:113, 117
The Tenth Man (Greene) **37**:139-40; **70**:289
The Tenth Man (Maugham) **11**:368
The Tenth Month (Hobson) **7**:163
The Tenth Moon (Powell) **66**:367
"Tenth Symphony" (Ashbery) **15**:32
Ten-Thirty on a Summer Night (Duras)
See *Dix heures et demie du soir en été*
"Tents for the Gandy Dancers" (Engel) **36**:162
The Tents of Wickedness (De Vries) **2**:113; **3**:126; **28**:106, 110
"Tenzone" (Ciardi) **10**:105; **44**:381
"Los teólogos" (Borges) **13**:105; **44**:353; **83**:164
Teorema (Pasolini) **20**:261-65, 267; **37**:346-47,

349-51; **106**:226, 248, 256, 265, 273
"Teoría de Dulcinea" (Arreola) **147**:33
"Teoria delle giunte" (Pasolini) **106**:236
"Teo's Bakery" (Suknaski) **19**:434
"Tepeyac" (Cisneros) **118**:214
Tequila Sunrise (Towne) **87**:369-72, 374-78
"Ter le milicien" (Duras) **40**:188; **68**:75-6, 78, 83, 90, 94
"Ter of the Militia" (Duras)
See "Ter le milicien"
"Teraloyna" (Gordimer) **70**:177-78; **123**:128
"Teran" (Salinas) **90**:324
"teraz" (Rozewicz) **139**:296
"The Tercentenary Incident" (Asimov) **26**:50, 56; **76**:320
Tercera llamada; tercera! o Empezamos sin usted (Arreola) **147**:7, 9-11, 26
Tercera residencia, 1935-1945 (Neruda) **7**:258; **62**:328-29, 333, 336
"La tercera resignación" (García Márquez) **3**:181; **47**:147
"Teresa" (Adams) **46**:17
"Teresa" (Wilbur) **9**:570
Teresa, and Other Stories (O'Faolain) **14**:402; **32**:340, 343-44; **70**:318
"Teresa of Avila" (Jennings) **131**:231
Teresa of Jesus (Sender) **8**:480
"Teresa's Bar" (Durcan) **43**:113-14
Teresa's Bar (Durcan) **43**:113
"Teresa's Wedding" (Trevor) **71**:326; **116**:385, 395
"Tereseta-que-baixava-les-escales" (Espriu) **9**:192
Tereza Batista cansada de guerra (Amado) **13**:11; **40**:34-6; **106**:55, 59, 62, 73, 76, 86
Tereza Batista Home from the Wars (Amado)
See *Tereza Batista cansada de guerra*
"The Term" (Blackburn) **43**:61
Termina el desfile (Arenas) **41**:28
"The Terminal Beach" (Ballard) **3**:34; **14**:40; **36**:34, 46; **137**:37-38, 41
The Terminal Beach, and Other Stories (Ballard) **3**:33
"Terminal Day at Beverly Farms" (Lowell) **37**:243
Terminal Hip (Wellman) **65**:239, 242
The Terminal Man (Crichton) **2**:109; **6**:119; **54**:67-71, 76
Terminal Moraine (Fenton) **32**:164-66
"Terminal Note" (Forster) **3**:161; **9**:207; **15**:230
"Terminal Thoughts" (Brown) **63**:57
Terminal Visions (Ballard) **137**:11
Terminos del presagio (Sender) **8**:480-81
"Terminus" (Ammons) **25**:43
"Terminus" (Barthelme) **59**:251
"Terminus" (Mantel) **144**:240
"The Termitary" (Gordimer) **18**:189
"The Terms" (Simic) **130**:317
"The Terms in Which I Think of Reality" (Ginsberg) **4**:182
Terms of Endearment (McMurtry) **7**:214-15; **11**:371; **44**:255-57; **127**:320, 327, 330-32, 342
"The Terms of Life Itself: Writing 'Quiet Desperation'" (Simpson) **149**:360
Terms of Reference (Middleton) **38**:329-30
Terms of the Presage (Sender)
See *Terminos del presagio*
"The Terns" (Oliver) **98**:283
Terra amata (Le Clézio) **31**:245-47, 249
"Terra Australis" (McAuley) **45**:248
"Terra incognita" (Nabokov) **3**:354
Terra nostra (Fuentes) **8**:223-25; **10**:205-08; **41**:167-68, 171; **60**:152-53, 156, 162, 164-68, 171-72; **113**:243, 262-64
Terra nova (Tally) **42**:365-68
La terra promessa (Ungaretti) **7**:481-82; **11**:556, 558; **15**:537-39
La terra trema (Visconti) **16**:561-62, 564, 570
"Terrain" (Ammons) **108**:22
"The Terrapin" (Highsmith) **102**:172, 204, 220
Terraqué (Guillevic) **33**:192, 194
Terras do sem fim (Amado) **13**:11; **40**:24-5, 27, 29; **106**:58, 61-2
"La terre des hommes" (Durcan) **43**:113, 116
La terre inquiète (Glissant) **68**:171, 179
Terre lointaine (Green) **3**:204; **77**:276-80, 289
Terre sur terre (Tzara) **47**:388, 390, 396
"Les terres impossibles" (Theriault) **79**:408
"Terrestrial Magnetism" (Fulton) **52**:160
"Terribilis est locus iste: Gauguin and the Pont-Aven School" (Hill) **45**:181, 190
"Terrible" (Roethke) **11**:486
"Terrible Man, Barney" (Carroll) **10**:98
"The Terrible Redeemer Lazarus Morell" (Borges)
See "El espantoso redentor Lazarus Morell"
The Terrible Shears (Enright) **4**:155-56; **8**:203; **31**:154-56
Terrible Swift Sword (Catton) **35**:91-4
The Terrible Temptation (Arundel) **17**:15-18
The Terrible Threes (Reed) **60**:310-11, 313
The Terrible Threshold (Kunitz) **6**:287
The Terrible Twos (Reed) **32**:359-62; **60**:310-11, 313
Territorial Rights (Spark) **13**:525; **18**:505-06; **40**:395, 397, 400
"Territory" (Leavitt) **34**:77, 79
The Territory Ahead (Morris) **7**:245; **18**:353; **37**:311-13
"The Territory Is Not the Map" (Spicer) **72**:349
"Terror" (Aldington) **49**:7
Terror and Decorum (Viereck) **4**:559
"Terror and Erebus" (MacEwen) **55**:163-64, 166, 169
"The Terrorist, He Watches" (Szymborska) **99**:192, 196
"The Terrorist, He's Watching" (Szymborska)
See "The Terrorist, He Watches"
"Terrorist Trial and the Games" (Ostriker) **132**:302
"Le terroriste" (Theriault) **79**:408
Terrorists and Novelists (Johnson) **48**:202-03
Terrorizing the Neighbourhood: American Foreign Policy in the Post-Cold War Era (Chomsky) **132**:67
The Terrors of Dr. Treviles (Shuttle) **6**:446; **7**:423
The Terrors of Dr. Treviles: A Romance (Redgrove) **6**:446; **41**:355
Terrors of Pleasure (Gray) **49**:148; **112**:97-8, 119, 124, 130
"Terrors of Pleasure: The House" (Gray) **49**:152
"Terry Street" (Raine) **103**:189
Terry Street (Dunn) **6**:148; **40**:164-68, 172
"Tertiaries" (Ammons) **57**:57
Tertio Millenio Adveniente (John Paul II) **128**:207
Tess (Polanski) **16**:473
Tessie (Jackson) **12**:289-90
"The Test" (Lem) **40**:291, 296
"The Test" (Matheson) **37**:246
"Test" (Parra) **102**:350, 353
"The Test Is, If They Drown" (Grenville) **61**:156
"Test of Atlanta 1979" (Jordan) **114**:148
Test of Fire (Bova) **45**:72-3
"A Test of Poetry" (Zukofsky) **18**:561
"A Testament" (Creeley) **78**:140
"Testament" (Hoffman) **23**:238
The Testament (Wiesel) **37**:453-55
"Testament Coran" (Pasolini) **37**:348; **106**:243
Le testament d'Orphée (Cocteau) **16**:226-30
Le Testament du docteur Mabuse (Lang)
See *The Testament of Dr. Mabuse*
Le testament du Dr. Cordelies (Renoir) **20**:291, 298
"Testament for My Students" (Boyle) **58**:71-2
Testament for My Students (Boyle) **1**:42
Testament for My Students, 1968-1969, and Other Stories (Boyle) **1**:42; **58**:71-2
"The Testament of Athammaus" (Smith) **43**:420, 424
The Testament of Daedalus (Ayrton) **7**:20
The Testament of Dr. Cordelies (Renoir)
See *Le testament du Dr. Cordelies*
The Testament of Dr. Mabuse (Lang) **20**:206, 211; **103**:88, 121-22
Testament of Experience (Brittain) **23**:92-3
The Testament of Man (Fisher) **7**:103-04
The Testament of Orpheus (Cocteau)
See *Le testament d'Orphée*
"Testament of the Royal Nirvana" (Kallman) **2**:221
"Testament of the Thief" (Kinnell) **29**:283
"Testament of Youth" (Brittain) **23**:88-93
"Testamento de Hécuba" (Castellanos) **66**:53
Testaments Betrayed (Kundera)
See *Les testaments trahis*
Les testaments trahis (Kundera) **115**:355-56, 358, 360
Un testigo fugaz y disfrazado (Sarduy) **97**:404
Testimonies (O'Brian) **152**:267, 279-80
Testimonies (Ritsos) **31**:325, 327
"Testimonios" (Poniatowska) **140**:331
Testimony (Reznikoff) **9**:449
"The Testimony of J. Robert Oppenheimer" (Ai) **69**:9-10
"The Testimony of Light" (Forché) **86**:139, 141, 145
"Testimony of Pilot" (Hannah) **90**:132, 143, 164
Testimony of the Invisible Man: William Carlos Williams, Francis Ponge, Rainer Maria Rilke, Pablo Neruda (Willard) **37**:461-63
Testimony of Two Men (Caldwell) **2**:95; **39**:302-03
"The Testimony of Wine" (Smith) **22**:384-86
"Testimony on the War in France" (de Man) **55**:384
Testing the Current (McPherson) **34**:85 9
"The Testing Tree" (Kunitz) **148**:89, 97, 102, 111, 127, 138-39, 149
The Testing-Tree (Kunitz) **6**:285-87; **14**:313; **148**:69, 71-72, 76, 78-79, 83-84, 89-93, 95, 98, 109, 111, 117, 141-42, 149
"Tête" (Reverdy) **53**:290
Tête blanche (Blais) **4**:67; **6**:82; **13**:96
La tête d'obsidienne (Malraux) **9**:358; **57**:307
La tête du roi (Ferron) **94**:108, 112, 125
"Tetélestai" (Aiken) **52**:24, 27
Il tetto (De Sica) **20**:88, 94
Tex (Hinton) **30**:205-06; **111**:77-85
"Texarcana Was a Crazy Town" (Garrett) **51**:147, 152
Texas (Michener) **60**:255-57, 260-61; **109**:376-77, 379-81, 383, 386
Texas by the Tail (Thompson) **69**:386-87
Texas Celebrity Turkey Trot (Gent) **29**:181-82
"Texas Chainsaw Massacre" (Alexie) **154**:27
"The Texas Girls" (Lerman) **9**:331
"The Texas Principessa" (Goyen) **40**:217-18
Texas Town (Foote) **51**:129
A Texas Trilogy (Jones) **10**:296-97
Texasville (McMurtry) **127**:328, 331, 336, 342, 354-55
Text and Voice (Josipovici) **153**:217
"Text in a Notebook" (Cortázar) **33**:130, 132
"A Textbook of Poetry" (Spicer) **18**:511-12
La texte du roman: Approache semiologique d'une structure discursive transformationelle (Kristeva) **77**:299-300
Textes pour rien (Beckett) **4**:52-3; **6**:45; **9**:80; **10**:29; **11**:40; **29**:56, 59
Texts for Nothing (Beckett)
See *Textes pour rien*
Text-Sound Art in North America (Kostelanetz) **28**:219
The Texture of the Embroidery (Dourado)
See *Risco do bordado*
Textures of Life (Calisher) **38**:70; **134**:4, 6-7, 15, 21, 24-6, 30-1, 34
The Textures of Silence (Vorster) **34**:121-23
Thaddeus Stevens and the Fight for Negro Rights (Meltzer) **26**:298
"Thalassa" (MacNeice) **10**:325; **53**:238

"Thalidomide" (Plath) **5**:345; **51**:340; **111**:163
"Thaman al-d'f" (Mahfouz) **153**:350
"The Thames at Chelsea" (Brodsky) **36**:80
"Thames Forest" (Watkins) **43**:441
"Thammuz" (Mahon) **27**:288, 290
The Thanatos Syndrome (Percy) **47**:336-41; **65**:256-58
"Thank God for the Atom Bomb" (Fussell) **74**:129, 134, 140
Thank God for the Atom Bomb, and Other Essays (Fussell) **74**:129, 137
"Thank the Lord for the Nightime" (Diamond) **30**:111
Thank U Very Much for the Family Circle (Taylor) **27**:441
"Thank You" (Koch) **44**:243, 249
"Thank You" (Page and Plant) **12**:473
Thank You All Very Much (Drabble)
See *The Millstone*
Thank You and Other Poems (Koch) **44**:241, 248, 251
"Thank You, Christine" (Berryman) **2**:59
Thank You, Fog: Last Poems (Auden) **6**:18-20, 24-5; **9**:56; **43**:26, 29
"Thank You for the Lovely Tea" (Gallant) **38**:190, 194
Thank You, Masked Man (Bruce) **21**:58
Thank You, Miss Victoria (Hoffman) **40**:253
"Thank You Very Much" (Sondheim) **30**:379
"Thankfulness" (Milosz) **56**:239
"Thanking My Mother for Piano Lessons" (Wakoski) **4**:572
Thanks for Coming Home, Nick (Abell)
See *Tak fordi du kom, Nick*
"Thanks for the Ride" (Munro) **19**:344; **95**:285, 297
"Thanks to Joyce" (Behan) **79**:37-8
"Thanks to Miss Morrissey" (Ferber) **93**:141
Thanks to Murder (Krumgold) **12**:316
"A Thanksgiving" (Auden) **6**:25; **9**:55
"Thanksgiving" (Glück) **22**:173, 75
"Thanksgiving" (Nemerov) **36**:306
"Thanksgiving for a Habitat" (Auden) **11**:20; **43**:29; **123**:12, 39-40
"Thanksgiving Spirit" (Farrell) **66**:131
The Thanksgiving Visitor (Capote) **34**:322; **38**:84, 87
"A Thank-You Letter" (Swenson) **61**:405; **106**:323
Tharthara fawq al-Nil (Mahfouz) **153**:272, 305, 358, 371
Tharthara fawq al-Nīl (Mahfūz) **52**:296, 300-01; **55**:183
"Thasos" (Squires) **51**:381
"That" (Thomas) **48**:375
"That Abomination in the By-Now Twentieth Century Aesthetic Tradition: Meditation on a Wet Snowy Afternoon" (Wakoski) **4**:572
"That All Be in All" (Damas)
See "Pour que tout soit en tout"
"That Apple Was Mental" (Young) **82**:397, 412
That Bowling Alley on the Tiber: Tales of a Director (Antonioni)
See *Quel bowling sul Tevere*
That Championship Season (Miller) **2**:284-85
"That Chance" (Young) **82**:396-97, 412
"That Cloud" (Young) **82**:412
That Cold Day in the Park (Altman) **116**:47, 74
That Cold Day in the Park (Altman) **16**:20, 24-5, 31; **116**:11
"That Day" (Sexton) **123**:406-07
"That Dirty Old Man" (Sondheim) **30**:378
That Distant Afternoon (Fuller)
See *The Ruined Boys*
"That Distant Winter" (Levine) **5**:251
That Early Spring (Beckman)
See *The Loneliness of Mia*
"That Evening Sun" (Faulkner) **3**:156; **8**:213-14; **18**:147; **68**:128
"That Evening Sun" (Gilchrist) **143**:314
"That Falling We Fall" (Galvin) **38**:198
"That Girl Could Sing" (Browne) **21**:42
That Good between Us (Barker) **37**:33-5, 37
That Good between Us. Credentials of a Sympathiser (Barker) **37**:37
That Hideous Strength: A Modern Fairy Tale for Grown-Ups (Lewis) **1**:177; **3**:297-99; **6**:309-11; **14**:323-26; **27**:264, 266, 268; **124**:210-12, 222, 226, 232, 246-47
That Horse (Hogan) **73**:153-54
"That I Had the Wings" (Ellison) **11**:183; **114**:93-4, 126, 131
"That Kind of Thing" (Gallagher) **63**:124, 126
"That Lovely April" (Grau) **9**:240
That Mighty Sculptor, Time (Yourcenar)
See *Le temps, ce grand sculpteur*
"That Mortal Knot" (L'Heureux) **52**:273
That Most Distressful Nation: The Taming of the American Irish (Greeley) **28**:170-71
"That Mouth" (Rich) **76**:214
"That New Man, the American" (Stegner) **49**:359
That Night (McDonald)
See *A Bigamist's Daughter*
That None Should Die (Slaughter) **29**:372
That Obscure Object of Desire (Bunuel)
See *Cet obscure objet du désir*
That Old Gang O' Mine: The Early and Essential S. J. Perelman (Perelman) **49**:268-69
"That Old Picayune-Moon" (Keillor) **115**:294
"That Other World That Was the World" (Gordimer) **123**:157
"That Place Where Ghosts of Salmon Jump" (Alexie) **154**:21
"That Quick and Instant Flight" (Lane) **25**:285
That Red Wheelbarrow (Coles) **108**:195
"That Room" (Montague) **46**:267
"That Same Old Obession" (Lightfoot) **26**:279
"That Seed" (Wright) **53**:429
"That Star" (Dodson) **79**:193-94
"That Straightlaced Christian Thing between Your Legs" (Simic) **9**:479, 481
"That Summer" (Sargeson) **31**:363-64, 366, 368, 371-72
That Summer in Paris: Memories of Tangled Friendships with Hemingway, Fitzgerald, and Some Others (Callaghan) **3**:97; **14**:102-03; **41**:94; **65**:245-48, 250-53
"That Summer Shore" (Ciardi) **40**:156
That Summer—That Fall (Gilroy) **2**:161
That Tantalus (Bronk) **10**:74
"That the Science of Cartography Is Limited" (Boland) **113**:91, 100, 110, 113, 115
"That the Soul May Wax Plump" (Swenson) **61**:398, 402; **106**:329, 344
"That Thou Art Mindful of Him" (Asimov) **26**:50, 56; **92**:6-9
That Time (Beckett) **9**:84; **14**:74; **18**:46, 49; **29**:63-4; **59**:255
"That Time in Odessa" (Boell)
See "Damals in Odessa"
That Uncertain Feeling (Amis) **1**:5-6; **2**:4-5, 10; **5**:20-1, 23; **129**:8-9, 13
That Voice (Pinget) **37**:361, 363-66
"That Was Close, Ma" (Hannah) **90**:160
"That Was Me" (Chabon) **149**:22-3
"That Was the President" (Ochs) **17**:331
That Was The Week That Was (Potter) **123**:230
That Was Then, This Is Now (Hinton) **30**:204; **111**:77-78, 80-85
"That Which Cannot Be Spoken of Can Have a Song Sung about It by Art" (Hein) **154**:
"That Which Convinces" (Elytis) **49**:114
"That Would Be Something" (McCartney) **35**:278-79
"That Year" (McGuckian) **48**:275-76
"That Year" (Olds) **32**:346; **85**:285
"Thatch Retaliates" (Chappell) **40**:141
"The Thatcher" (Heaney) **25**:244
"That'll Show Him" (Sondheim) **30**:378
That's All (Duras) **100**:150
That's How We'll Win! (Six Plays about Lenin) ()
See *Tak pobedim! (shest' p'es o Lenine)*
"That's Marriage" (Ferber) **93**:138
"That's No Way to Spend Your Youth" (Clash) **30**:43-4
"That's Saul, Folks" (Grayson) **38**:211-12
"That's the Way" (Page and Plant) **12**:474-75
"That's the Way I've Always Heard It Should Be" (Simon) **26**:406-08, 410-11
That's What We Live For (Szymborska) **99**:194, 199, 203, 206, 211
That's Why We Are Alive (Szymborska)
See *That's What We Live For*
"ThatSurvey: Being Wedded is Not Always Bliss" (Pollitt) **122**:218
"Thaw" (Avison) **97**:77
"Thaw" (Longley) **29**:295
The Thaw (Ehrenburg) **18**:132-34, 136; **34**:434, 440; **62**:171-73, 178
"Thaw on a Building Site" (MacCaig) **36**:282
"Thawing Out" (Boyle) **90**:46-8, 50
"The" (Zukofsky)
See "Poem Beginning 'The'"
The The Birth-mark: Unsettling the Wilderness in American Literary History (Howe) **152**:182, 184, 192, 197, 199-200, 203, 208-16, 218-19, 221, 224, 228, 232, 237, 244, 250
"'The Black Swan' Revisted" (Selzer) **74**:273
"'The Monk' and Its Author" (Berryman) **10**:45
"Theater" (Toomer) **4**:549; **22**:425
Theater (Lagerkvist)
See *Teater*
"Theater Business" (Simpson) **149**:358, 361
The Theater Essays of Arthur Miller (Miller) **10**:346; **47**:250
Theater Piece (Cage) **41**:79
"Theater Problems" (Duerrenmatt) **102**:74
"Theaterprobleme" (Dürrenmatt) **15**:197
"Theatre" (Hellman) **52**:192
Theatre (Maugham) **67**:211
Théâtre (Sarraute) **31**:380-81
"Theatre I" (Beckett) **9**:84
Théâtre I (Arrabal) **58**:3, 11
"Theatre II" (Beckett) **9**:84
Théâtre III (Arrabal) **58**:10
Théâtre IV (Arrabal) **58**:9
Théâtre bouffe (Arrabal) **58**:16, 18
Théâtre cérémonie 'panique' (Arrabal) **58**:9, 19
Théâtre complet (Ionesco) **86**:340
Théâtre de Poche (Cocteau) **43**:107
Théâtre Eight (Arrabal) **9**:35
Théâtre et religion (Marcel) **15**:359
The Theatre of Commitment (Bentley) **24**:49, 51-2
"The Theatre of Hope and Despair" (Friel) **115**:251
"The Theatre of Inconsistency" (Rozewicz)
See "Teatr niekonsekwencji"
The Theatre of Mixed Means (Kostelanetz) **28**:213
Theatre of War (Bentley) **24**:52
"Theatre Party" (Coward) **51**:74
Theatre Shoes (Streatfeild) **21**:399
Theatre Works 1973-1985 (Harrison) **129**:204
"Thebais" (Howard) **47**:169-70
The Theban Mysteries (Heilbrun) **25**:252
Thebes' Struggle (Mahfūz)
See *Kifāh Tiba*
"Thee" (Aiken) **10**:4; **252**:27
"Theft" (Porter) **7**:314, 319-20; **10**:396; **27**:399; **101**:227, 253
Theft (Ingalls) **42**:229
"The Theft of Melko" (Tolkien) **38**:441
"The Theft Partial" (Simmons) **43**:407
Their Ancient Glittering Eyes: Remembering Poets and More Poets (Hall) **151**:200
"Their Behaviour" (Brutus) **43**:96
Their Blood is Strong (Steinbeck) **59**:340-41, 347

"Their Cities, Their Universities" (Murray) **40**:337, 340
Their Days Are Numbered (Canetti)
See *Die Befristeten*
Their Eyes Were Watching God (Hurston) **7**:171; **30**:210-12, 215-16, 218-19, 222-25, 227-28; **61**:237-75
"Their Frailty" (Sassoon) **130**:183, 186, 221
Their Heads Are Green and Their Hands Are Blue (Bowles) **19**:58; **53**:43
"Their Oxford" (Amis) **40**:45
"Their Quiet Lives" (Warner) **7**:512
Their Satanic Majesties Request (Jagger and Richard) **17**:220-21, 224, 229, 235, 237
"Their Son" (Green) **97**:292
"Their Thing" (Damas)
See "Ils ont"
"Their Very Memory" (Blunden) **56**:29, 43
Their Very Own and Golden City (Wesker) **3**:519; **5**:483; **42**:426, 428, 430
"Thelonious Monk and the Performance of Poetry" (Bernstein) **142**:57
"Them" (Simon) **26**:413
them (Oates) **1**:251-52; **2**:314; **3**:359, 361-62, 364; **6**:368-69, 371-72; **9**:403-06; **15**:400-01; **19**:349-50, 353; **33**:288-89, 293; **52**:329, 334-36, 338-39; **108**:374, 377-78, 391-92
"Them and Us" (Bukowski) **82**:28
"Them and uz" (Harrison) **129**:166, 173, 175, 211, 215
"Them Belly Full" (Marley) **17**:267, 269, 271-72
Them, Featuring Van Morrison (Morrison) **21**:234-35
Them That Glitter and Them That Don't (Greene) **30**:171
"Theme for Diverse Instruments" (Rule) **27**:420
Theme for Diverse Instruments (Rule) **27**:419-20
A Theme for Hyacinth (Symons) **32**:429
The Theme Is Freedom (Dos Passos) **25**:145
"Theme of the Traitor and the Hero" (Borges)
See "El Tema del traidor y del héroe"
"The Theme of the Traitor and the Hero" (Borges)
See "El Tema del traidor y del héroe"
Themes and Variations (Cage) **41**:84
Themes and Variations (Huxley) **4**:240
Themes and Variations (Pasternak)
See *Temy i variatsi*
Themes and Variations for Sounding Brass (Gustafson) **36**:213-14, 216-18, 221
Themes in My Poems (Jeffers) **54**:250
"Then" (Hacker) **72**:191
Then Again, Maybe I Won't (Blume) **30**:22
Then and Now (Maugham) **1**:204; **15**:368; **67**:207-09, 217
Then Badger Said This (Cook-Lynn) **93**:115, 118-120
"Then I Shall Be Able to Find Peace and Slumber" (Le Clézio) **31**:244
"Then Oblique Stroke Now" (Johnston) **51**:245
"Then or Now" (Rich) **125**:335, 336
Then Shall the Dust Return (Green) **77**:271
"Then We Were Three" (Shaw) **34**:370
Thendara House (Bradley) **30**:32
"Theodicy" (Milosz) **56**:239
"Theodore Dreiser: In Memoriam" (Farrell) **66**:139
Theodore Roethke: An American Romantic (Parini) **54**:358-59, 361
"Theodore Roosevelt: An American Sissy" (Vidal) **142**:303
"The Theologians" (Borges)
See "Los teólogos"
"Theological" (Ezekiel) **61**:108
A Theological Position (Coover) **3**:114; **15**:145; **32**:120, 124; **87**:24-5
Theology and Christian Ethics (Gustafson) **100**:196
Theophilus North (Wilder) **6**:577-78; **10**:536; **82**:367, 376, 378
Theorem (Pasolini)
See *Teorema*
Theorie des kommunikativen Handelns I-II (Habermas) **104**:85-6
Die Theorie des Romans (Lukacs) **24**:320, 323, 326-28
Theorie und Praxis (Habermas) **104**:66
"Theory" (Simic) **22**:381
"The Theory and Practice of Rivers" (Harrison) **66**:162; **143**:355, 358
The Theory and Practice of Rivers and New Poems (Harrison) **66**:162-63; **143**:344, 352, 354
The Theory and Practice of Rivers and Other Poems (Harrison) **66**:157, 161
"The Theory and Practice of the Strap-on Dildo" (Allison) **153**:11
"Theory as Liberatory Practice" (Hooks) **94**:157
The Theory of Communicative Action (Habermas)
See *Theorie des kommunikativen Handelns I-II*
A Theory of Fiction (Gass) **15**:257
Theory of Flight (Rukeyser) **10**:442; **15**:456, 458-59; **27**:403-05, 408, 410-11, 414
"A Theory of Language" (Percy) **6**:400; **8**:441
Theory of Literature (Wellek) **28**:441-44, 446, 452
"A Theory of Prosody" (Levine) **118**:286, 304
Theory of Prosody in Eighteenth-Century England (Fussell) **74**:144
A Theory of Semiotics (Eco) **142**:66-7, 92, 121-31
"The Theory of Sets" (Pesetsky) **28**:358
The Theory of the Novel (Lukacs)
See *Die Theorie des Romans*
"Theory of Truth" (Jeffers) **54**:250
Theory of War (Brady) **86**:130-36
"A Theory of Wind" (Goldbarth) **38**:205
"Theory, Pragmatism and Politics" (West) **134**:374
Therapy (Lodge) **141**:357-59, 367-68, 371-73
"Therapy 2000" (Roberts) **14**:463
"there" (Clifton) **66**:83
"There" (Creeley) **36**:121
"There" (Hooker) **43**:196
"There" (Taylor) **18**:526; **37**:412
"There Are a Lot of Ways to Die" (Bissoondath) **120**:3, 8
"There Are Delicacies" (Birney) **4**:64
There Are Facts (Blaga)
See *Ivanca*
"There Are More Things" (Borges) **48**:38, 40-1
"There Are Nights" (Damas)
See "Il est des nuits"
"There Are No Honest Poems About Dead Women" (Lorde) **71**:254
"There Are No Such Trees in Alpine, California" (Haines) **58**:218
"There Are No Thieves in This Town" (García Márquez) **27**:148, 154; **47**:146, 150-51
"There Are Not Leaves Enough to Crown to Cover to Crown to Cover" (Howe) **152**:208-9, 235, 237
"There Are Roughly Zones" (Frost) **10**:196; **26**:125
"There Are So Many Houses and Dark Streets without Help" (Bukowski) **82**:14
"There Are the Steps" (Ekeloef) **27**:119
"There Are Things I Tell to No One" (Kinnell) **29**:285; **129**:235, 270
"There But for Fortune" (Ochs) **17**:329, 331-32
"There But Where, How" (Cortázar) **33**:125
There Goes Rhymin' Simon (Simon) **17**:464-65
"There Has to Be a Jail for Ladies" (Merton) **83**:393
"There Is a Dream Dreaming Us" (Dubie) **36**:134, 136
"There Is a Happy Land" (Bowie) **17**:65
"There Is a Legend about a Piano That Somehow Got Flushed into the Sewers of Chicago" (Goldbarth) **38**:205
"There Is a Lone House" (O'Connor) **23**:331
"There Is a Right Way" (Welch) **52**:426
There Is a Tide (Christie) **12**:124; **48**:73
There Is a Tree More Ancient Than Eden (Forrest) **4**:163-64
There is Confusion (Fauset) **19**:169-71; **54**:175-76, 178, 180-81, 185, 187, 189
"There Is No Conversation" (West) **31**:453-54
"There Is No Such Thing as a Happy Love" (Aragon)
See "Il n'y a pas d'amour heureux"
"There Is Only One of Everything" (Atwood) **13**:44; **15**:37
There Is the Sun, Philibert (Carrier)
See *Il est par là, le soleil*
There Must Be More to Love Than Death (Newman) **8**:419
There Only Remains an Hour (Mahfouz) **153**:287-90
There Shall Be No Darkness (Blish) **14**:84
"There She Breaches" (Hemingway) **34**:478
"There Was a Child Went Forth" (Levine) **14**:317
There Was a Father (Ozu) **16**:451, 453, 456
There Was a Time (Caldwell) **28**:59
"There Was a Woman Bending" (Lane) **25**:284, 287
There Was an Ancient House (Kiely) **23**:263; **43**:245
There Was an Old Woman (Queen) **11**:462-63
"There Was an Old Woman She Had So Many Children She Didn't Know What to Do" (Cisneros) **118**:177
"There Was Earth inside Them" (Celan) **53**:75
"There Was Once" (Atwood) **84**:105
"There Was When Morning Fell" (Graham) **29**:193
"There Will Be Harvest" (Everson) **5**:122
"There Will Come Soft Rains" (Bradbury) **42**:38
There You Are (Simpson) **149**:361
There! You Died (Fornés)
See *Tango Palace*
Therefore (Grass)
See *Davor*
Therefore Be Bold (Gold) **4**:190-91; **42**:188-89; **152**:129, 141
"The Therefore Hag" (Guthrie) **23**:199
There'll Be No Teardrops Tonight (Nelson) **17**:305
There's a Bat in Bunk Five (Danziger) **21**:85-6
"There's a Better Shine" (Niedecker) **42**:298
"There's a Change in the Weather" (Davies) **21**:98
"There's a Garden of Eden" (Gilchrist) **48**:115, 120; **143**:274, 297, 319, 330
"There's a Grandfather's Clock in the Hall" (Warren) **8**:538
"There's a Maniac Loose Out There" (Vonnegut) **12**:610
"There's a Place" (Lennon and McCartney) **12**:375
There's a Trick with a Knife I'm Learning to Do: Poems, 1963-1978 (Ondaatje) **14**:410; **29**:341; **51**:316-17
"There's a Window" (Sapphire) **99**:80-1
"There's a World" (Young) **17**:570, 578
"There's No Difference" (Ashbery) **15**:36
"There's No Place like London" (Sondheim) **30**:398
"There's No Such Thing as Free Speech" (Fish) **142**:199, 207
There's No Such Thing as Free Speech and It's a Good Thing, Too (Fish) **142**:187, 191-93, 195-96, 198
"There's Not That Much to Say" (Neruda) **28**:311
"There's Nothing like a Good Foundation" (Asimov) **26**:63
There's Something in the Air (Bates) **46**:56-7
"There's the Sound of Rain" (Akhmadulina)
See "Vot zvuk dozhdia"

There's Wisdom in Women (Kesselring) **45**:206-07
Thérèse Desqueyrous (Mauriac) **4**:339, 341; **9**:368; **56**:204, 206
Thérèse et Pierrette à l'école des Saints-Agnes (Tremblay) **29**:424, 427; **102**:370-74, 376-77, 379
Thérèse's Creed (Cook) **58**:154
"The Thermal Stair" (Graham) **29**:196-97
"Theroux Metaphrastes" (Theroux) **25**:432
"Thesc" (Williams) **42**:452
"These Are My People" (Hayden) **37**:156
"These Are Poets Who Service Church Clocks" (Simic) **130**:326
"These Beautiful Girls" (Sondheim) **30**:382
"These Days" (Browne) **21**:41
These Golden Days (Braine) **41**:62
These Green-Going-to-Yellow (Bell) **31**:50-1
"These Lacustrine Cities" (Ashbery) **9**:44; **77**:56; **125**:4
These Our Mothers, or The Disintegrating Chapter (Brossard)
See *L'Amer*
"These Streets" (Levine) **118**:286, 301
"These Streets" (Milner) **56**:225
These the Companions (Davie) **31**:121-22, 124
These Thirteen (Faulkner) **3**:156; **8**:213; **28**:141
These Thousand Hills (Guthrie) **23**:197-98, 201
These Three (Hellman) **34**:348; **52**:191
"These Trees Stand" (Snodgrass) **18**:491
These Words: Weddings and After (McIlvanney) **42**:285
"These Yet to Be United States" (Angelou) **64**:40
"Theseus and Ariadne" (Graves) **2**:174; **45**:166, 173
"Thesis" (Dorn) **10**:159
"Theta" (Tolson) **105**:234
"Thetis" (Broumas) **73**:13
"They" (Creeley) **78**:140, 154, 157
"They" (Heinlein) **26**:165
"They" (Sassoon) **36**:385; **130**:177, 182-84, 191, 193, 216
"They" (Thomas) **48**:374, 381
"They Ain't the Men They Used to Be" (Farrell) **66**:131
"They All Go to the Mountains Now" (Brooke-Rose) **40**:106
"They All Made Peace—What Is Peace?" (Hemingway) **19**:218
"They Are All in Love" (Townshend) **17**:535-36
They Are Dying Out (Handke)
See *Die Unvernünftigen Sterben aus*
"They Are Not Ready" (Madhubuti) **73**:207
"They Arrive This Morning" (O Hehir) **41**:324
They Both Were Naked (Wylie) **43**:469
They Brought Their Women (Ferber) **93**:161-62
"They Called for More Structure..." (Barthelme) **46**:38, 42
They Came From Within (Cronenberg) **143**:57-59, 71, 81, 86-87, 92, 94, 104, 110-14, 116, 135-38, 140, 151-52, 157-58
They Came Here First: The Epic of the American Indian (McNickle) **89**:169, 172, 175, 181
They Came Like Swallows (Maxwell) **19**:305-06
"They Came That Night" (Damas)
See "Ils sont venus ce soir"
They Came to Baghdad (Christie) **12**:115; **39**:438; **48**:71, 74; **110**:113, 129
They Came to Cordura (Swarthout) **35**:399-400, 403
They Came to See a Poet (Rozewicz) **139**:290
They Caught the Ferry (Dreyer) **16**:268
"They Clapped" (Giovanni) **117**:197
"They Dirty the Suicide" (Cabral de Melo Neto)
See "Sujam o suicído"
They Do It with Mirrors (Christie) **110**:121
"They Dream Only of America" (Ashbery) **77**:42, 56
"They Feed They Lion" (Levine) **2**:244; **4**:286, 288; **9**:332; **14**:317-19; **118**:271-72, 276, 283, 303, 316, 318
They Feed They Lion (Levine) **2**:244; **4**:286-87; **5**:250-52; **9**:332; **14**:317, 320-21; **33**:271, 273; **118**:277, 283-85, 297, 290, 292-93, 297-99
"They Flee from Me" (Ewart) **46**:152
They Fought for Their Country (Sholokhov)
See *Oni srazhalis' za rodinu*
They Hanged My Saintly Billy: The Life and Death of Dr. William Palmer (Graves) **39**:322-23
"They Have Not Survived" (Mathias) **45**:237
"They Like" (Ashbery) **41**:37
They Never Came Home (Duncan) **26**:101-02
"They Never Were Found" (Jacobsen) **102**:237
"They Only Move" (Amis) **40**:44
"They Reach the Gulf of Mexico, 1493" (Neruda) **5**:302
"They Say Etna" (Bunting) **47**:45
They Shall Have Stars (Blish) **14**:85
They Shall Inherit the Earth (Callaghan) **14**:101-03; **41**:95; **65**:246, 248-50
"They Shall Not Grow Old" (Dahl) **79**:183
"They Shall Not Pass" (Ai) **69**:10
"They Shed the Load" (Rozewicz) **139**:290
"They Sleep without Dreaming" (Gilliatt) **53**:145-46
They Sleep without Dreaming (Gilliatt) **53**:145-46
They That Reap (Lopez y Fuentes)
See *El indio*
"They Warned Him Then They Threw Him Away" (Williams) **148**:321
They Went Thataway (Brown) **47**:36
They Were Expendable (Ford) **16**:306-07, 313, 315
"They Were Showing a Film of Bermuda in Hammond II" (Jacobsen) **48**:190
They Winter Abroad (White) **30**:449
They Won't Demolish Me! (Carrier)
See *Le deux-millième étage*
They Won't Take Me Alive (Alegria)
See *No me agarran viva: La mujer salvadorenña en lucha*
"They're Not Your Husband" (Carver) **36**:101
They're Playing Our Song (Simon) **31**:398, 400
They're Singing Again Now (Frisch)
See *Nun singen sie wieder*
"They've Given Us the Land" (Rulfo)
See "Nos han dado la tierra"
"Thick As Thieves" (Weller) **26**:446
"Thickening the Plot" (Delany) **38**:153
"Thicker than Liquor" (Berry) **46**:74
Thicker Than Water (Harrison) **70**:55-8; **151**:238-41, 245-46, 248-49, 251, 256-57
The Thicket of Spring (Bowles) **19**:60
"Thick-Lipped Nigger" (Guillén)
See "Negro bembón"
"The Thief" (Anand) **23**:21
"The Thief" (Govier) **51**:166
"The Thief" (Kunitz) **148**:77, 82, 88
"The Thief" (Tanizaki) **28**:414
"The Thief" (Tillinghast) **29**:416
The Thief (Leonov)
See *Vor*
The Thief and the Dogs (Mahfouz)
See *al-Liss w'l kilab*
The Thief and the Dogs (Mahfūz)
See *al-Liss wa'l-kilāb*
"The Thief Coyote" (Goyen) **14**:211
"The Thief of Poetry" (Ashbery) **77**:47
A Thief of Time (Hillerman) **62**:260-63
The Thief's Journal (Genet)
See *Journal du voleur*
"A Thief's Tale" (Klima) **56**:171
"The Thieves" (Grau) **146**:161, 163
Thieves (Gardner) **44**:210
Thieves' Carnival (Anouilh)
See *Le bal des voleurs*
Thieves in the Night: Chronicle of an Experiment (Koestler) **1**:170; **3**:270; **15**:310-11; **33**:231-33, 242
"Thieves' Kitchen" (Slessor) **14**:497
Thieves Like Us (Altman) **16**:28-31, 39; **116**:3-4, 7, 11-12, 14, 16, 21, 23, 31, 36-7
Thieves of the Kings and Queens of England (Fraser) **107**:33-34
"Thieving" (Rush) **44**:92-3, 95-6
"Thin Air" (Hass) **99**:139, 142
"The Thin Edge of Your Pride" (Rexroth) **49**:280; **112**:376
"Thin Ice" (Levine) **54**:298, 301
The Thin Man (Hammett) **3**:218-20; **5**:162; **19**:193-96; **47**:157, 163
The Thin Mountain Air (Horgan) **9**:279; **53**:185-86
"The Thin People" (Plath) **51**:340, 344; **111**:218
"The Thin Red Leash" (Thurber) **125**:413-14
The Thin Red Line (Jones) **1**:162; **3**:261; **10**:290-94; **39**:406-08, 414
The Thin Snow (Tanizaki) **8**:509
"The Thing" (Moravia) **46**:286-87
The Thing about Joe Sullivan (Fisher) **25**:159
"Thing from Inner Space" (Fuller) **62**:197
The Thing He Loves (Glanville) **6**:202
"The Thing Made Real" (Loewinsohn) **52**:283
A Thing of Beauty (Cronin) **32**:138
The Thing of It Is... (Goldman) **1**:123; **48**:125, 128
"A Thing of the Past" (Gordimer) **33**:180
"The Thing That Happened to Uncle Adolphe" (Callaghan) **41**:98
"A Thing They Wear" (Metcalf) **37**:299
"The Things" (Jacobsen) **48**:194
"The Things" (Kinnell) **129**:269
Things (Ponge) **18**:415
"Things as They Are" (Pritchett) **41**:332
Things as They Are (Horgan) **9**:278; **53**:180-82, 185
"Things Best Forgotten" (Bissoondath) **120**:15-16
Things Fall Apart (Achebe) **1**:1-2; **3**:1-2; **5**:1-3; **7**:3-7; **11**:1-4; **26**:11-16, 18-19, 21-2, 25-7; **51**:2-9; **75**:2-6, 8-13, 20, 23; **127**:9-10, 12, 28, 34-6, 39-42, 50, 52, 66, 68-72, 74-8, 81-2; **152**:2-98
Things Gone and Things Still Here (Bowles) **19**:59
"Things I Can Do in My Situation" (Swenson) **61**:394
"Things I Didn't Know I Loved" (Hikmet) **40**:251
Things I Didn't Know I Loved (Hikmet) **40**:246, 248
Things Invisible to See (Willard) **37**:464-66
"Things Not Solved Though Tomorrow Came" (Taylor) **44**:301
"Things of the World" (Waddington) **28**:440
"Things of This World" (Parini) **54**:363
Things of This World (Wilbur) **3**:530; **6**:568; **9**:569; **14**:576-77; **53**:396, 398-99, 404, 407-08, 410; **110**:348-49, 353
"Things Past" (Baker) **31**:31
"Things Past" (Skelton) **13**:508
Things Taking Place (Swenson)
See *New and Selected Things Taking Place*
Things That Are Caesar's (Carroll) **10**:95-9
"Things That Are Worse Than Death" (Olds) **39**:189; **85**:290
"Things That Fly" (Coupland) **85**:36, 39
Things that Happen Where There Aren't Any People (Stafford) **29**:386-87
"Things that have been lost" (Amichai) **116**:98
Things That I Do in the Dark: Selected Poetry (Jordan) **11**:312-13; **114**:146
The Things That I Know (Hemingway)
See *Across the River and into the Trees*
Things Themselves: Essays and Scenes (Price) **43**:346-47
"The Things They Carried" (O'Brien) **103**:143
The Things They Carried (O'Brien) **103**:133-34, 136-38, 140-43, 159-66, 168-69, 174-75
Things to Come (Norton) **12**:458

"Things to Do in Providence" (Berrigan) **37**:46
Things We Dreamt We Died For (Bell) **31**:46-7
The Things Which Are (Nowlan) **15**:398-99
"The Things You Keep" (Grau) **146**:125
Think Back on Us .?.?. (Cowley) **39**:461
"Think before You Shoot" (Adcock) **41**:13
Think Black! (Madhubuti) **2**:238; **6**:313; **73**:199-200, 202, 204-11, 214-15
"Think It Over" (Reed) **21**:320
"Think It Over America" (Beecher) **6**:49
"Think of It" (Celan) **53**:75
"Thinkability" (Amis) **62**:6-7, 9-10
Thinking about Christa T (Wolf)
See *Nachdenken über Christa T.*
"Thinking about Descartes" (Jennings) **131**:236
"Thinking about El Salvador" (Levertov) **66**:239, 250
"Thinking about Shelley" (Stern) **40**:410; **100**:333
"Thinking about the Past" (Justice) **102**:257, 285
"Thinking about the Poet Larry Levis One Afternoon in Late May" (Wright) **146**:372
"Thinking against Oneself" (Cioran) **64**:96-7, 99
"The Thinking Man's Wasteland" (Bellow) **8**:74
"Thinking of Death and Dogfood" (Kumin) **28**:228
"Thinking of Mr. D" (Kinsella) **138**:108-10, 161
"Thinking of That Contest" (Lane) **25**:287
"Thinking of the Goldfish" (Muldoon) **32**:315
"Thinking of the Lost World" (Jarrell) **2**:210; **9**:298
"Thinking of the World as Idea" (Pollitt) **28**:367
"Thinking Ourselves Into Trouble" (Thurber) **125**:405
The Thinking Reed (West) **31**:454, 457, 459; **50**:405-07
Thinks (Waterhouse) **47**:423
Thinner (King) **37**:206-08; **113**:369
The Third (Ezekiel) **61**:97
"The Third Autumn" (Dabrowska)
See "Trzecia jesién"
The Third Bank of the River, and Other Stories (Rosa)
See *Primeiras estorias*
The Third Book about Achim (Johnson)
See *Das Dritte Buch über Achim*
The Third Book of Criticism (Jarrell) **9**:296
The Third Deadly Sin (Sanders) **41**:381-82
"Third Degree" (Hughes) **35**:216
"The Third Dimension" (Levertov) **28**:242
"The Third Expedition" (Bradbury) **42**:37-8
The Third Eye (Hunter) **21**:169-70
The Third Face (Rozewicz)
See *Twarz trzecia*
"The Third Floor" (Rooke) **25**:391
The Third Generation (Fassbinder) **20**:118, 120
The Third Generation (Himes) **2**:195; **4**:229; **7**:159; **18**:247; **58**:250, 256, 263-65; **108**:224, 228-31, 259
Third Girl (Christie) **12**:117; **110**:121, 138
"Third Hymn to Lenin" (MacDiarmid) **63**:254-56
"Third Inning" (Hall) **151**:200
The Third Life of Grange Copeland (Walker) **5**:476-77; **6**:553; **9**:558; **19**:451-52; **27**:451, 453-54; **46**:423, 428, 431; **58**:404, 406, 408; **103**:356-57, 364-65, 368, 383, 385-89, 392, 395-96, 398, 405, 414, 418
"The Third Light" (Longley) **29**:296
The Third Lover (Chabrol)
See *L'oeil du malin*
The Third Man (Greene) **1**:134; **3**:207-210; **37**:139-40; **70**:288-89, 294; **72**:165-66, 168, 173-76
The Third Mind (Burroughs) **15**:112; **42**:71-2; **109**:182
"Third Monday" (Mason) **28**:271; **82**:245-46, 249-50; **154**:285, 322-23
"Third or Fourth Day of Spring" (Miller) **14**:375
"The Third Party" (Trevor) **71**:343, 348, 349; **116**:347, 375
The Third Policeman (O'Brien) **1**:252; **4**:383, 385; **5**:314, 317; **7**:270; **10**:362, 364; **47**:312-22
"A Third Presence" (Gordimer) **18**:185
"Third Psalm" (Sexton) **123**:420
Third Residence (Neruda)
See *Tercera residencia, 1935-1945*
The Third Residence (Neruda)
See *Tercera residencia, 1935-1945*
"The Third Resignation" (García Márquez)
See "La tercera resignación"
"The Third Sermon on the Warpland" (Brooks) **125**:106
"The Third Story" (Bitov) **57**:114-15
"Third Time Lucky" (Ingalls) **42**:234
"Third Voice: The Widower" (Davison) **28**:101
"Third Ypres" (Blunden) **56**:29-30, 38, 42-3, 51
"Third-World Literature in the Era of Multinational Capitalism" (Jameson) **142**:241-42
"Thirst" (Avison) **97**:117
"Thirst" (O'Brien) **7**:270; **10**:362
"Thirst" (Williams) **148**:356, 358, 361
Thirst (Bergman)
See *Törst*
Thirst (Trifonov) **45**:420
Thirst for Love (Mishima) **9**:382
Thirsting for Peace in a Raging Century: Selected Poems, 1961-1985 (Sanders) **53**:310
A Thirsty Evil (Vidal) **33**:406-07; **142**:305
"13" (Jones) **10**:287
"Thirteen" (Townshend) **42**:380-81
Thirteen (Morrison) **17**:290
Thirteen at Dinner (Christie) **6**:108; **12**:113-14
The Thirteen Clocks (Thurber) **5**:430, 432, 438, 440, 442; **25**:437-38; **125**:406
Thirteen Hands (Shields) **91**:178; **113**:440
"Thirteen O'Clock" (Fearing) **51**:116
"Thirteen Phantasms" (Smith) **43**:422
Thirteen Pipes (Ehrenburg) **62**:176, 179
The Thirteen Problems (Christie) **110**:139-46
Thirteen Stories and Thirteen Epitaphas (Vollmann) **89**:286, 291, 296-97, 302, 313
"Thirteen to Centaurus" (Ballard) **36**:37
"Thirteen Views of a Penis" (D'Aguiar) **145**:117
The Thirteen-Gun Salute (O'Brian) **152**:260, 265, 282, 285, 300
The Thirteenth Labor of Herucles (Iskander)
See *Trinadtsaty podvig Gerakla*
The Thirteenth Member (Hunter) **21**:158, 165
Thirteenth Night (Brenton) **31**:69
The Thirteenth Tribe: The Khazar Empire and Its Heritage (Koestler) **8**:324-25
The Thirteenth Valley (Del Vecchio) **29**:149-51
"The Thirteenth Voyage" (Lem) **149**:274, 277
"The Thirties" (Sadoff) **9**:467
The Thirties and After: Poetry, Politics, People, 1933-1970 (Spender) **41**:420-23, 427; **91**:242
Thirtieth Anniversary Report to the Class of '41 (Nemerov) **36**:302
"The Thirtieth Lie" (Deane) **122**:73
"The Thirtieth Year" (Bachmann)
See "Das dreissigste Jahr"
The Thirtieth Year (Bachmann)
See *Das dreissigste Jahr*
"Thirty Days" (Berry) **17**:53
"38 Phoenix Street" (Kinsella) **138**:95, 103, 106, 113, 140
"XXXI" (Auden) **14**:26
Thirty Pieces of Silver (Fast) **131**:96
Thirty Poems (Merton) **83**:389-91
Thirty Preliminary Poems (Barker) **48**:9, 11, 21
Thirty Seconds over Tokyo (Trumbo) **19**:445
Thirty Stories (Boyle) **5**:65; **19**:62; **58**:64, 70, 76; **121**:33
Thirty Things (Creeley) **11**:139
"Thirty Ways of Drowning in the Sea" (Levi) **41**:244
The Thirty-First of February (Symons) **14**:523
Thirty-Nine Poems (Ciardi) **40**:155, 158
The Thirty-Nine Steps (Hitchcock) **16**:337-38, 340, 345, 354, 357
Thirty-One Letters and Thirteen Dreams (Hugo) **18**:260, 262-63; **32**:241, 244, 250-51
Thirty-One Sonnets (Eberhart) **3**:134
Thirty-One Sonnets (Guillevic)
See *Trente et un sonnets*
"Thirty-Seven Haiku" (Ashbery) **41**:37
"XXXVI" (Walcott) **67**:358
Thirty-Six Poems (Warren) **1**:353; **13**:573, 575
Thirty-Two Votes before Breakfast (Stuart) **34**:376
"This" (Olds) **85**:295, 297
"This" (Rich) **73**:332
"This Age of Conformity" (Howe) **85**:134
"This Be the Verse" (Larkin) **9**:323; **33**:261, 268; **39**:336, 343; **64**:282
This Bed Thy Centre (Johnson) **1**:160; **27**:213
"This Black Rich Country" (Ammons) **57**:59
This Blessed Earth: New and Selected Poems, 1927-1977 (Wheelock) **14**:571
This Body Is Made of Camphor and Gopherwood (Bly) **10**:62; **15**:66-7; **38**:50; **128**:23
This Body the Earth (Green) **25**:195, 197
This Boy's Life (Wolff) **64**:456-61
This Bridge Called My Back: Writings by Radical Women of Color (Castillo) **151**:107
"This Bright Day" (Ammons) **2**:14; **57**:59
"This City!" (Stevenson) **33**:380
"This Cold Man" (Page)
See "Now This Cold Man"
This Crooked Way (Spencer) **22**:398-99, 403
This Crowded Planet (Hyde) **21**:173
"This Day" (Creeley) **15**:153
"This Day" (Fearing) **51**:114
"This Day" (Hoffman) **23**:238
"This Day" (Levertov) **66**:241
This Day's Death (Rechy) **1**:283; **107**:222-23, 225-26, 228, 230, 238, 254, 258
This Dear-Bought Land (Latham) **12**:323
"This Destination Not to Be Found in a Star" (Barker) **48**:9
"This Dreamer Cometh" (Ostriker) **132**:302
"This Farm for Sale" (Stuart) **11**:513
"This Fevers Me, This Sun on Green" (Eberhart) **19**:143; **56**:80
"This Form of Life Needs Sex" (Ginsberg) **36**:183; **109**:358
"This Golden Summer" (Lowell) **11**:331
"This Ground So Bare" (Van Doren) **10**:496
This Gun for Hire (Greene)
See *A Gun for Sale*
This Hallowed Ground: The Story of the Union Side in the Civil War (Catton) **35**:87-90
"This Hand, These Talons" (Cassill) **4**:94
This Happy Breed (Coward) **29**:135-36, 138; **51**:69
"This Heat" (Durban) **39**:44-6
This Hidden God (Goldmann)
See *Le Dieu caché*
"this house" (Young Bear) **94**:363
This Hunger... (Nin) **60**:267-68
"This I Believe" (Stegner) **49**:359
This Immortal (Zelazny) **21**:469
This in Which (Oppen) **7**:281; **34**:359
"This Is" (Ammons) **25**:42; **108**:28
"This Is..." (Chin) **135**:179
"This Is" (Steele) **45**:362-64
This Is (Williams) **11**:575
"This Is a Photograph of Me" (Atwood) **4**:27; **25**:66
"This Is a Poem I Wrote at Night, before the Dawn" (Schwartz) **45**:355
This Is a Recording (Corcoran) **17**:71
"This Is a Story about My Friend George, the Toy Inventor" (Paley) **37**:333; **140**:262
"This Is It" (Stern) **40**:406, 408

This is Lagos, and Other Stories (Nwapa) **133**:201, 229-30
This Is My Country Too (Williams) **5**:498
This Is My God (Wouk) **9**:580; **38**:444, 448, 452-53
"This Is Not..." (Chin) **135**:179
"This Is Not a Film, This Is a Precise Act of Disbelief" (Abish) **22**:17
This Is Not a Letter and Other Poems (Boyle) **58**:75-6
This is Not a Pipe (Foucault) **31**:186-87
"This Is Not For John Lennon (And This Is Not a Poem)" (Giovanni) **117**:198
This Is Not for You (Rule) **27**:417
"This Is the Beat Generation" (Holmes) **56**:139-40
This Is the Castle (Freeling) **38**:184
"This Is the Garden: Colors Come and Go" (Cummings) **68**:44
This Is the Modern World (Weller) **26**:443, 445
This Is the Rill Speaking (Wilson) **7**:547
"This Is the Road" (Silverberg) **140**:343
"this is the tale" (Clifton) **66**:82
"This Is Their Fault" (Forché) **83**:209
"This Is Tibet!" (Boell)
See "Hier ist Tibten"
"This Is What It Means to Say Phoenix, Arizona" (Alexie) **96**:5; **154**:30, 41
"This Is What Killed Dylan Thomas" (Bukowski) **108**:86
"This Island Formed You" (Smith) **64**:393
This Island Now (Abrahams) **4**:1-2
This Journey (Wright) **28**:467-69, 473
"This Land Is Your Land" (Guthrie) **35**:185, 188-91, 194
"This Last Pain" (Empson) **19**:155, 158; **33**:142; **34**:336
"This Life" (Dove) **81**:137
"This Life of Mine" (Van Doren) **6**:542
"This Loved One" (Fuller) **62**:193
This Man and Music (Burgess) **40**:119
This Man and This Woman (Farrell) **66**:128
"This Man for Fuck Sake" (Kelman) **58**:297
This Man Must Die (Chabrol) **16**:175-76
"This Man, My Father" (Callaghan) **41**:98
"This morning" (Simic) **130**:343
"This Morning Again It Was in the Dusty Pines" (Oliver) **98**:285
This Music Crept by Me on the Water (Eberhart) **11**:176
"This Must Be Wrong" (Ian) **21**:186
"This My Modest Art" (Nemerov) **36**:309
"This Neutral Realm" (Montague) **46**:277
"This Night Only" (Rexroth) **22**:346
This Noble Land (Michener) **109**:383
"This One's on Me" (Gotlieb) **18**:191
"This Page My Book" (Livesay) **79**:348
This Perfect Day (Levin) **6**:305-07
"This Poem" (Hall) **151**:192
"This Poem May Not Be Just What You Wrote to Santa for, But" (Johnson) **7**:415
"This Praying Fool" (Kumin) **28**:220
This Proud Heart (Buck) **11**:74-5
This Quiet Dust and Other Writings (Styron) **60**:392-94, 396
This Real Night (West) **9**:562
This Rock within the Sea (Mowat) **26**:338, 346-47
This Rough Magic (Stewart) **35**:390, 392; **117**:367
"This Sandwich Has No Mayonnaise" (Salinger) **12**:498
This School Is Driving Me Crazy (Hentoff) **26**:184-85, 187
"This Seems True" (Simmons) **43**:407
This Side Jordan (Laurence) **13**:342; **50**:314, 319, 322; **60**:278-79, 290, 306; **62**:278-79, 290, 306
This Side of Innocence (Caldwell) **28**:59; **39**:302-03
This Sporting Life (Anderson) **20**:12-13, 16-18
This Sporting Life (Storey) **2**:423-25; **4**:528; **5**:417; **8**:505
This Strange Passion (Bunuel)
See *El*
This Strangest Everything (Ciardi) **40**:160
"This Stupid Bitch" (p'Bitek) **96**:271-72
"This Summer" (Scannell) **49**:327
This Sunday (Donoso)
See *Este Domingo*
This Sweet Sickness (Highsmith) **2**:193; **42**:211; **102**:170, 173, 193
"This, That, and the Other" (Nemerov) **2**:307
This Thing Don't Lead to Heaven (Crews) **6**:117; **23**:132, 138; **49**:68
This Time (Jennings) **21**:202
"This Time Alone" (Wright) **53**:432
This Time of Morning (Sahgal) **41**:370
"This Time Tomorrow" (Davies) **21**:92
This Time Tomorrow (Ngũgĩ wa Thiong'o) **7**:266; **36**:320-21
"This Tokyo" (Snyder) **32**:399
"This Tournament" (MacNeice) **53**:233
This Tree Will Be Here for a Thousand Years (Bly) **15**:64, 68; **38**:50, 53, 56-7, 59; **128**:11-15, 17, 23, 30
"This Urn Contains Earth from German Concentration Camps" (Lorde) **71**:256
"This Was a Man" (Coward) **29**:131
This Was the Old Chief's Country (Lessing) **22**:279; **94**:261, 266
"This Way Down" (Johnston) **51**:244
"This Wilderness in My Blood: The Spiritual Foundations of the Poetry of Five American Indian Women" (Allen) **84**:11, 15, 36
"This World" (Creeley) **78**:148-49
This World and Nearer Ones: Essays Exploring the Familiar (Aldiss) **14**:15
This World, Then the Fireworks (Thompson) **69**:385, 387-88
"This Year's Girl" (Costello) **21**:68
This Year's Model (Costello) **21**:68, 70
"This You May Keep" (Zweig) **34**:379
The Thistle and the Grail (Jenkins) **52**:220, 225, 227-28
"The Thistle, The Nettle" (Milosz) **82**:311
"Thistles" (Hughes) **9**:284; **14**:271; **37**:179
"Thistles" (Levine) **4**:286
Thistles and Roses (Smith) **64**:393-94, 397-98
"Thix" (Thurber) **125**:410
Thomas and Beulah (Dove) **50**:152-58; **81**:132, 136, 138, 140-47, 151-52, 154
Thomas and the Warlock (Hunter) **21**:157
"Thomas at the Wheel" (Dove) **50**:153; **81**:139
"Thomas Bewick" (Gunn) **18**:199, 202
"Thomas Campey and The Coernican System" (Harrison) **129**:171
Thomas Hardy and British Poetry (Davie) **5**:114; **8**:162
"Thomas Jefferson" (Niedecker) **42**:296, 300
Thomas l'imposteur (Cocteau) **8**:146; **15**:132; **16**:220; **43**:103
Thomas l'obscur (Blanchot) **135**:76, 78-79, 83-84, 87-88, 94, 105, 109-10, 113-17, 119, 132, 142-43, 145-46
"Thomas Mann" (Szymborska) **99**:202
The Thomas Merton Reader (Merton) **83**:404
Thomas Muskerry (Colum) **28**:86-7, 90
"Thomas Nashe and 'The Unfortunate Traveler'" (Berryman) **10**:45
Thomas the Imposter (Cocteau)
See *Thomas l'imposteur*
Thomas the Obscure (Blanchot)
See *Thomas l'obscur*
"Thomas Traherne's Meditation for Love, 1672" (Dubie) **36**:130
"Thomasine" (Blunden) **56**:34, 38
Thor, with Angels (Fry) **10**:200
"Thoreau the Thorough Impressionist" (Barzun) **145**:73
"Thoreau Z" (Lowell) **37**:237
The Thorn Birds (McCullough) **27**:318-22; **107**:127-45, 147-63, 166-68, 170-71
Thorn in Our Flesh: Castro's Cuba (Archer) **12**:17-18
"Thornapple" (Rendell) **48**:320
"Thornbills" (Wright) **53**:423
Thorns (Silverberg) **140**:345, 377-78
Thornyhold (Stewart) **117**:384
The Thoroughbreds (Césaire) **112**:12
"Thoroughgo" (Char)
See "La minutieuse"
Thoroughly Modern Millie (Hill) **26**:196, 200-01, 204
"Thorow" (Howe) **72**:205, 209; **152**:154, 156-7, 162, 195, 197, 203, 229, 248-50, 252
"Those Awful Dawns" (Highsmith) **14**:261
Those Barren Leaves (Huxley) **1**:151; **4**:238-40, 244; **11**:281-82, 284-85; **18**:265, 267-69; **79**:304, 326
"Those before Us" (Lowell) **8**:351
"Those Being Eaten by America" (Bly) **15**:62; **128**:6
"Those Gods Are Children" (Achebe) **26**:24
Those Other People (Childress) **86**:309
"Those Paperweights with Snow Inside" (Peacock) **60**:295
"Those Times" (Sexton) **53**:322; **123**:435-36, 440
"Those Various Scalpels" (Moore) **13**:392; **19**:335
"Those Who Don't" (Cisneros) **118**:177, 184-85
"Those Who Have Burned" (Dickey) **28**:118
"Those Who Have No Turkey" (Hughes) **108**:292
Those Who Love (Stone) **7**:469-70
Those Who Perish (Dahlberg) **7**:66
Those Who Ride the Night Winds (Giovanni) **64**:192; **117**:170, 177, 187-88, 193, 198-99, 205
Those Who Walk Away (Highsmith) **2**:193; **4**:225; **102**:173, 185, 205-06
"Those Winter Sundays" (Hayden) **37**:153, 160
Those without Shadows (Sagan) **17**:419-20
"The Thou" (Montale)
See "Il tu"
"Thou Art Lovelier Than the Sky and Sea" (Cendrars) **106**:159
"Thou Didst Say Me" (Waddington) **28**:438
"Thou Good and Faithful" (Brunner) **8**:111
"Thou Shalt Not Kill" (Rexroth) **22**:346, 348; **49**:276-77, 280, 284; **112**:376, 400, 403
"Thou Unbelieving Heart" (Kunitz) **148**:87
"Thought" (Dumas) **62**:151-52
"Thought by Rembrandt's Wife and Model during the Painting of 'Flora'" (Rudnik) **7**:384
"The Thought Machine" (Stafford) **7**:460
"The Thought of Something Else" (Berry) **46**:70
"Thought of the Future" (Mahapatra) **33**:284
"Thought on June 26" (Kunene) **85**:166
Thought Reform and the Psychology of Totalism: A Study of 'Brainwashing' in China (Lifton) **67**:135-36, 140, 145, 154
"The Thought-Fox" (Hughes) **9**:281; **37**:172, 178-79; **119**:293-94
"Thoughts about a Doubtful Enterprise" (Simpson) **149**:358
"Thoughts about Lessing" (Arendt) **98**:50
"Thoughts about the Christian Doctrine of Eternal Hell" (Smith) **25**:417
"Thoughts about the Person from Porlock" (Smith) **25**:423
Thoughts after Lambeth (Eliot) **2**:126; **24**:177, 182-83
"Thoughts/Images" (Dumas) **62**:155
Thoughts in Solitude (Merton) **83**:389
"Thought's Measure" (Bernstein) **142**:31, 37, 56
"Thoughts on a Narrow Night" (Gustafson) **36**:222
"Thoughts on Being Bibliographed" (Wilson) **24**:474, 476

"Thoughts on Looking into a Thicket" (Ciardi) **44**:375, 382; **129**:42
"Thoughts on March 8" (Ding Ling) **68**:62, 68-9
"Thoughts on One's Head" (Meredith) **13**:375
"Thoughts on Politics and Revolution" (Arendt) **98**:11
"Thoughts on the Diary of a Nobody" (Betjeman) **43**:36
"Thoughts on the Poetic Discontent" (Ransom) **4**:436
"Thoughts on Turning Sixty-Five" (Johnson) **147**:139
"Thoughts on Women's Day" (Ding Ling) **68**:65
Thoughts, Words, and Creativity (Leavis) **24**:308-09, 314
A Thousand Acres (Smiley) **76**:229-38; **144**:252-67, 270-71, 273-75, 284, 286-90, 292, 295-97, 301-02, 304-06
"The Thousand and One Nights" (Borges) **48**:47
"The Thousand and One Nights" (Fuller) **62**:185
"The Thousand and Second Night" (Merrill) **2**:273-74; **13**:380-81
A Thousand Clowns (Gardner) **44**:209-10
Thousand Cranes (Kawabata) **2**:223; **5**:206-08; **9**:309, 316; **18**:285; **107**:73-4, 76, 98-101, 103-04, 106, 108-12, 114, 121
A Thousand Days: John F. Kennedy in the White House (Schlesinger) **84**:357, 359-60, 368, 375-76, 379-80, 384-85
"The Thousand Dreams of Stellavista" (Ballard) **137**:63-64, 66
The Thousand Eyes of Dr. Mabuse (Lang) **20**:208, 211; **103**:86
"The Thousand Islands" (Cendrars) **106**:190
A Thousand Orange Trees (Harrison) **151**:245, 249, 257
A Thousand Summers (Kanin) **22**:231
"The Thousand Things" (Middleton) **13**:387
"The Thousand Ways" (Chappell) **40**:142; **78**:95
Thousandstar (Anthony) **35**:36-7
"The Thrall" (Arghezi)
See "Robul"a
"Thrall" (Kizer) **80**:181-83, 185
"Thrasher" (Young) **17**:581
The Thread That Runs So True (Stuart) **14**:516; **34**:373, 375
Thread-Suns (Celan)
See *Fadensonnen*
"Threatened" (O Hehir) **41**:323-24
"The Threatened Man" (Borges)
See "The Threatened One"
"The Threatened One" (Borges) **83**:190
Threats Instead of Trees (Ryan) **65**:209, 211, 213
"Three" (Cummings) **15**:161
"Three" (Grau) **9**:240; **146**:128
"Three" (Gunn) **18**:199; **32**:208
"III" (Kinnell) **13**:322
"Three" (Lish) **45**:230
Three (Ashton-Warner) **19**:23
Three (Hellman)
See *Pentimento: A Book of Portraits*
Three (Quin) **6**:441-42
Three Act Tragedy (Christie) **48**:71-2
Three Actors and Their Drama (Ghelderode)
See *Trois acteurs: Un drame*
Three Actors, One Drama (Ghelderode)
See *Trois acteurs: Un drame*
Three Acts of Recognition (Strauss)
See *Trilogie des Wiedersehens*
Three Adventures: Galápagos, Titicaca, The Blue Holes (Cousteau) **30**:106
The Three Ages (Keaton) **20**:191
"3 AM" (Harjo) **83**:278-79
"3 A.M. Kitchen: My Father Talking" (Gallagher) **63**:126
The Three Arrows (Murdoch) **4**:367-68
"The Three Avilas" (Jeffers) **11**:306
"Three Awful Picnics" (L'Heureux) **52**:274
Three Bad Men (Ford) **16**:317
"Three Beyond" (Davie) **31**:124
"Three Blind Mice" (Christie) **48**:71
Three Blind Mice, and Other Stories (Christie) **12**:119
"The Three Boxes" (Chappell) **40**:141
Three by Ferlinghetti (Ferlinghetti) **2**:134
Three by Peter Handke (Handke) **38**:218
Three Cheers for the Paraclete (Keneally) **5**:210-11; **19**:245; **43**:236; **117**:215-17, 221, 224, 227
The Three Coffins (Carr) **3**:101
Three Colors (Kieslowski) **120**:217-33, 243-45, 247-56, 258
Three Colors: Blue (Kieslowski)
See *Three Colors*
Three Colors: Red (Kieslowski)
See *Three Colors*
Three Colours (Kieslowski)
See *Three Colors*
"Three Compositions on Philosophy and Literature" (Bernstein) **142**:37
Three Comrades (Remarque) **21**:327-28, 330-31
"Three Conservations" (Rosenthal) **28**:394
Three Continents (Jhabvala) **94**:186-87, 194-96, 204, 207-10, 213; **138**:64
"Three Conversations" (Rich) **125**:321
"Three Critics" (Silkin) **43**:400
"Three Darknesses" (Warren) **39**:265, 270
The Three Daughters of Madame Liang (Buck) **127**:240-41
"Three Days" (Simon) **26**:407
"Three Days and a Child" (Yehoshua) **31**:472
Three Days and a Child (Yehoshua) **13**:618; **31**:468-71
"Three Days and a Question" (Paley) **140**:272
"Three Deer One Coyote Running in the Snow" (Snyder) **120**:325
"Three Derivative Poems" (Sissman) **9**:490
Three Desks (Rcaney) **13**:474
Three Dialogues (Beckett) **6**:36
Three Dozen Poems (Everson) **27**:133
"Three Drawings" (Heaney) **74**:188
The Three Edwards (Costain) **30**:98-100
Three Essays on America (Brooks) **29**:83-4
Three Fantasies (Powys) **46**:324
"Three Fantasies in Minor Key" (Bioy Casares) **88**:92-3
Three Farmers on Their Way to a Dance (Powers) **93**:275-79, 281, 283-86, 289, 293, 296, 299, 301
The Three Fat Men (Olesha)
See *Tri tolstiaku*
"Three Fat Women of Antibes" (Maugham) **67**:211
"Three Fate Tales" (Creeley) **11**:135
"Three Floors" (Kunitz) **148**:89, 109, 112, 131, 141-42
"Three for Water-Music" (Davie) **31**:119
Three for Water-Music (Davie) **31**:119, 123
"Three Freuds" (Lowell) **37**:238
"Three from Tu Fu" (Kizer) **39**:171
The Three Generations of Superman (Siegel and Shuster) **21**:358
"3 Geniuses" (Wiggins) **57**:433, 435, 439
Three Godfathers (Ford) **16**:317
The Three Graces (Eliade)
See *Die drei Grazien*
"Three Halves of a House" (Hood) **28**:187, 193
Three Hundred and Sixty Degrees of Blackness Comin at You (Sanchez) **116**:293
"Three Hundred Men Made Redundant" (Durcan) **43**:116
365 Days (Glasser) **37**:131-34
334 (Disch) **36**:124
Three Hundred Years of Gravitation (Hawking) **105**:55
The Three Ill-Loved Ones (Cabral de Melo Neto)
See *Os três mal-amados*
"Three Illuminations in the Life of an American Author" (Updike) **43**:430
"Three Journeys" (Hirsch) **50**:196, 198
Three Journeys: An Automythology (Zweig) **34**:378-79; **42**:467
"Three Kills for One" (Woolrich) **77**:403
"Three Kinds of Pleasures" (Bly) **10**:56; **128**:19
"Three Knots in the Net" (Castellanos)
See "Tres nudos en la red"
"Three Laws of Robotics" (Asimov) **3**:17
Three Legions (Sutcliff) **26**:441
"Three Legs" (McCartney) **35**:279
"Three Lindens" (Hesse) **25**:259-60
"Three Little Birds" (Marley) **17**:269
"Three Little Men" (Boyle) **121**:55
"Three Long Songs" (Coles) **67**:171-72, 174
Three Lovers (O'Faolain) **19**:359; **108**:399, 424-25, 428
The Three Lovers (Swinnerton) **31**:423
Three Loves (Cronin) **32**:130-31
"Three Meditations" (Levertov) **15**:337
"Three Men" (Sargeson) **31**:365
Three Men Die (Millin) **49**:248
"Three Miles Up" (Howard) **7**:164
"Three Modes of History and Culture" (Baraka) **115**:38
"Three Moods of Princeton" (Clark Bekedermo) **38**:118, 128
"The Three Musicians" (Walcott) **67**:360
The Three Musketeers (Lester) **20**:227-28
"Three Notes toward Definitions" (Steele) **45**:363
Three Novels (Naipaul) **37**:324
Three Novels: The Blackmailer, A Man of Power, and The Geat Occasion (Colegate) **36**:113
"Three O'Clock" (Woolrich) **77**:403
Three of a Kind (Cain) **11**:85; **28**:45-7, 50
Three of a Kind (Ingalls)
See *I See a Long Journey*
"The Three of Us in the Dark" (Simon) **26**:413
"The Three of Us, the Four of Us" (Celan)
See "Selbdritt, Selbviert"
Three Old Brothers (O'Connor) **14**:401
Three on the Tower: The Lives and Works of Ezra Pound (Simpson) **9**:486; **149**:295-96, 300, 358
"Three or Four Things I Know about Him" (Bernstein) **142**:9
"Three Parabolic Tales" (Baxter) **78**:28
"Three Paths to the Lake" (Bachmann)
See "Simultan"
Three Paths to the Lake (Bachmann)
See *Simultan*
Three Pick-Up Men for Herrick (Van Peebles) **20**:410
"Three Pieces for Voices" (Redgrove) **41**:352
Three Places in Rhode Island (Gray) **49**:146; **112**:105, 118
Three Players of a Summer Game, and Other Stories (Williams) **5**:502; **45**:446-47, 452-53, 455
Three Plays (Brown) **48**:61
Three Plays (Buzo) **61**:67
Three Plays (Clark Bekedermo) **38**:113-15
Three Plays (Mrozek) **3**:345
Three Plays (Walker) **61**:424, 432
Three Plays (Wilder) **15**:572; **35**:442; **82**:361, 383, 385
Three Plus Three (Felsen) **17**:124
"Three Poems" (Elytis) **100**:175
"Three Poems" (Parra)
See "Tres Poesías"
Three Poems (Ashbery) **2**:18-19; **3**:15-16; **4**:22-4; **9**:43; **13**:33; **15**:26-8, 32, 35; **25**:58; **41**:35, 40-1; **77**:41-2, 52, 54, 60-1; **125**:11-2, 16-7, 26, 38
Three Poems (Wild) **14**:580
"Three Poems for James Wright" (Oliver) **98**:294
"Three Poems for Music" (Porter) **33**:318
"Three Poems for the New Year" (Wright) **146**:337-38
"Three Poems in Memory of My Mother, Miriam Murray nee Arnall" (Murray)

40:344
"Three Poems of Departure" (Wright) **146**:338
"Three Poems of Drowning" (Graham) **29**:194
"Three Poems of Sicily" (Davie) **31**:119
"Three Poems on Aaron Siskind's Photographs" (Logan) **5**:255
"Three Poems under a Flag of Convenience" (Elytis) **100**:179
"Three Poems with Yevtushenko" (Dickey) **47**:93
"III Poems Written in Surrey" (Barker) **48**:24
"Three Poets" (Rosenthal) **28**:394
Three Port Elizabeth Plays (Fugard) **9**:233
"Three Poses" (Johnson) **15**:480
Three Postcards (Lucas) **64**:289-90, 292
"Three Princes Carouse" (Iskander) **47**:200
"Three Prompters from the Wings" (Hecht) **8**:269
"Three Quatrains" (Sorrentino) **7**:449
"The Three Readings of the Law" (Handke) **5**:165
"three reasons for transgression" (Young Bear) **94**:363
"Three Rings" (Monette) **82**:323, 331-33
The Three Roads (Macdonald) **14**:332-33; **41**:268
Three Rooms in Manhattan (Simenon) **2**:399
"Three Seasons and a Gorilla" (Williams) **148**:321
Three Secret Poems (Seferis) **11**:493
"Three Sentences for a Dead Swan" (Wright) **3**:541
"Three Sermons to the Dead" (Riding) **7**:374
"Three Sheets in the Wind" (Chappell) **40**:145
Three Short Novels (Boyle) **5**:65; **58**:73
"Three Shots" (Hemingway) **10**:269; **30**:194
"Three Shrines" (Sandburg) **35**:356
The Three Sirens (Wallace) **7**:509; **13**:567-68
"Three Sisters" (Carroll) **35**:80
"The Three Sisters" (Cisneros) **69**:147; **118**:174, 177, 179
Three Sisters (Olivier) **20**:241, 244
Three Six Seven: Memoirs of a Very Important Man (Vansittart) **42**:397-98
"Three Sketches from House Made of Dawn" (Momaday) **85**:228
"Three Skies" (Stern) **100**:342
Three Soldiers (Dos Passos) **4**:137-38; **11**:154; **15**:184; **25**:140, 143, 147; **34**:419-20, 422-23; **82**:62-3, 78, 86
"Three Songs for a Cadaver" (Ciardi) **40**:154
"Three Sonnets" (Smith) **64**:398
The Three Stigmata of Palmer Eldritch (Dick) **30**:115-17, 121-22, 127; **72**:113, 117-19, 121-22
"Three Stories" (Sexton) **4**:482
Three Stories and Ten Poems (Hemingway) **6**:225
Three Stories and Ten Poems (McFadden) **48**:257
"Three Stratagems" (Vidal) **33**:406
"Three Subjects on the Study of Realism" (Herbert) **43**:188
"Three Swiss Inns" (Fisher) **87**:122
Three Tall Women (Albee) **86**:117-27; **113**:48-51, 53-4
"Three Tears" (Stern) **40**:408
"3:10 to Yuma" (Leonard) **120**:295
3001: The Final Odyssey (Clarke) **136**:235-38
Three Thousand Red Ants (Ferlinghetti) **2**:134; **111**:63
"Three Translations of Villon" (Gotlieb) **18**:193
"Three Transportations" (Porter) **33**:323
Three Trapped Tigers (Cabrera Infante)
See *Tres tristes tigres*
Three Travellers (Blais)
See *Les voyageurs sacrés*
"Three Travelogues" (Ammons) **8**:17; **9**:30
"Three Types of Poetry" (Tate) **11**:522; **24**:439
Three Uneasy Pieces (White) **69**:413-14
"Three Valentines to the Wide World" (Van Duyn) **63**:444; **116**:406, 421, 424
"Three Versions of Judas" (Borges)
See "Tres versiones de Judas"
"Three Views of a Mother" (Ciardi) **129**:48
"Three Views of Mount Rainier" (Deutsch) **18**:119
"Three Voices" (Abse) **29**:15
The Three Voices of Poetry (Eliot) **6**:167; **24**:184
"Three White Vases" (Swenson) **106**:333
Three Who Died (Derleth) **31**:128
Three Winters (Milosz) **11**:377; **22**:312
"Three Witches Go for Lunch in Elora" (Musgrave) **54**:341
Three Wogs (Theroux) **2**:433; **25**:431-34
"Three Women" (Ortiz) **45**:310
"Three Women" (Sargeson) **31**:364
Three Women (Altman) **16**:38-9, 41, 43; **116**:20-2, 28-30, 37-8, 59, 66-7, 69, 73-4
Three Women (Plath) **2**:338; **3**:391; **5**:342; **9**:428; **17**:361; **51**:342, 345, 349
"Three Women: A Poem for Three Voices" (Plath) **111**:159-60, 168, 177, 185, 203
"Three Women of the Country" (Hodgins) **23**:230
"Three Worlds" (Kunene) **85**:166
Three Years to Play (MacInnes) **23**:284
The Three-Arched Bridge (Kadare)
See *Ura me tri harqe*
"The Three-Cornered Pear" (Voznesensky)
See "The Triangular Pear"
"The Three-Day Blow" (Hemingway) **3**:242; **10**:267; **30**:180, 187, 189-90, 195-98
"The Three-Penny Opera" (O'Hara) **78**:349, 354-55
A Three-Pipe Problem (Symons) **14**:523
"The Thresher" (Ochs) **17**:331
Threshold (Fugard) **48**:109-10
Threshold (Le Guin)
See *The Beginning Place*
Threshold of Eternity (Brunner) **8**:105, 110
"The Thrice-Thrown Tranny Man; or, Orgy at Palo Alto High School" (Kesey) **46**:225
"Thrift" (Faulkner) **18**:149
"The Thrill of the Grass" (Kinsella) **43**:256
The Thrill of the Grass (Kinsella) **43**:253-57
"Thriller" (Havel) **123**:174, 200
Thrilling Cities (Fleming) **30**:135
The Throat (Straub) **107**:284-86, 288-92, 302, 304-10
Throne of Blood (Kurosawa) **16**:396, 401, 404; **119**:337, 341, 351, 357, 366-69, 380-81, 391-99
"The Throne of Good" (Nissenson) **4**:381
The Throne of Saturn: A Novel of Space and Politics (Drury) **37**:105-06
Thrones, 96-109 de los cantares (Pound) **4**:412, 414; **7**:331; **13**:463; **34**:505; **48**:282-83, 285-86, 293
Through a Brief Darkness (Peck) **21**:296, 298
"Through a Crack" (Ryan) **65**:211
"Through a Dustbin Darkly" (Weldon) **122**:281
"Through a Glass Brightly" (Bainbridge) **62**:35, 37
Through A Glass Darkly (Bergman)
See *Såsom i en spegel*
"Through Corralitos under Rolls of Cloud" (Rich) **73**:336; **76**:210
"Through Lifetime" (Young Bear) **94**:361
"Through My Sails" (Young) **17**:582
"Through Our Love" (McCartney) **35**:292
"Through Streets Where Smiling Children" (Rosenthal) **28**:395
Through the Broken Mirror with Alice (Wojciechowska) **26**:457
Through the Fields of Clover (De Vries) **1**:73
"Through the Hills of Spain" (Salinas) **90**:324-5, 329
Through the Hoop (del Castillo)
See *Le manège espagnol*
"Through the Inner City to the Suburbs" (Angelou) **35**:30
Through the Ivory Gate (Dove) **81**:140-41, 148, 152-55
Through the Leaves (Kroetz)
See *Männer Sache*
"Through the Long Night" (Joel) **26**:220
"Through the Mirror" (Elytis) **49**:110
Through the Night (Griffiths) **52**:173-74, 183
"Through the Night, 1" (Lowell) **124**:256
Through the Purple Cloud (Williamson) **29**:454
Through the Safety Net (Baxter) **45**:51-3; **78**:16-19, 21-22, 24-26, 32
"Through the Smoke Hole" (Snyder) **120**:333
Through the Vanishing Point: Space in Poetry and Painting (McLuhan) **83**:366, 368
Through the Villages (Handke) **38**:225-26
"Through Tristes Tropíques" (Leiris) **61**:361
"Through with Buzz" (Becker and Fagen) **26**:79
"Throughout Our Lands" (Milosz) **31**:259; **56**:240-41, 251
"Throw Back the Little Ones" (Becker and Fagen) **26**:80
A Throw to the South (Paustovsky)
See *Brosok na yug*
The Throwback (Sharpe) **36**:401
"The Thrower-Away" (Boell)
See "Der Wegwerfer"
Thru (Brooke-Rose) **40**:107-09, 111
Thrump-o-moto (Clavell) **87**:10, 13, 19
Thrush (Seferis)
See "Kichli"
"Thrush Song at Dawn" (Eberhart) **56**:87
"Thrushes" (Hughes) **9**:281; **37**:176, 179
"Thrushes" (Moure) **88**:226-28, 230
"Thrust and Riposte" (Montale)
See "Botta e riposta"
al-Thulatthiyya (Mahfūz) **55**:171, 174, 181-85, 187-88
"Thumb" (Dacey) **51**:80
"The Thumb Mark of Saint Peter" (Christie) **110**:142, 146
"Thumb-Nail Biography" (Kunitz) **148**:87
The Thumbstick (Mayne) **12**:388, 392
"Thunder among the Leaves" (Roa Bastos) **45**:346-47
Thunder among the Leaves (Roa Bastos)
See *El trueno entre las hojas*
"Thunder and Lightning" (Moravia) **11**:384
Thunder and Lightning (Klima) **56**:168
"Thunder and Roses" (Sturgeon) **39**:361
"Thunder Can Break" (Okigbo)
See "Come Thunder"
Thunder Heights (Whitney) **42**:433
Thunder on the Right (Stewart) **7**:467; **35**:389, 392
"Thunder Road" (Springsteen) **17**:479-81, 485, 489
"The Thunder Steers" (Elytis) **49**:110
Thunderball (Fleming) **30**:149-50
"Thunderbolt" (Tuohy) **37**:430
Thunderbolt (Sternberg) **20**:377
Thunderbolt and Lightfoot (Cimino) **16**:208
The Thurber Album (Thurber) **5**:430-31, 436, 442; **25**:437; **125**:414
Thurber and Company (Thurber) **125**:393
The Thurber Carnival (Thurber) **11**:534; **125**:401
Thurber Country (Thurber) **125**:395-97, 399-400
"Thurber: The Comic Prufrock" (De Vries) **7**:76
"Thursday Out" (Berryman) **10**:45
Thursday's Child (Streatfeild) **21**:410-11, 416
Thursday's Children (Anderson) **20**:15, 17
"Thurso's Landing" (Jeffers) **11**:306; **54**:237, 242-43, 248
Thurso's Landing, and Other Poems (Jeffers) **11**:306; **54**:237
"Thus" (Justice) **102**:250
"Thus" (Simic) **49**:336
"Thus Sings a Mockingbird in El Turquino" (Guillén) **79**:229-30
THX 1138 (Lucas) **16**:407-08, 411, 415-16
Thy Brother's Wife (Greeley) **28**:175-77
Thy Neighbor's Wife (O'Flaherty) **34**:355-57
Thy Neighbor's Wife (Talese) **37**:394-402

Thymus Vulgaris (Wilson) **36**:461
"Ti" (Tolson) **105**:262
"Ti con zero" (Calvino) **5**:99-101; **8**:127; **73**:31-2
Ti con zero (Calvino) **5**:99; **8**:127; **11**:89, 91-2; **22**:89; **73**:44, 47
"Ti ssu ping shih" (Pa Chin) **18**:374
La tiá Julia y el escribidor (Vargas Llosa) **10**:500; **85**:352, 355, 365, 368, 379, 383-84, 386, 389, 392, 394, 396
Tick, Tick . . . Boom! (Larson) **99**:160, 168, 180, 186
"Tick, Tock" (Sondheim) **147**:240, 251
A Ticket for a Seamstitch (Harris) **19**:200, 203
The Ticket That Exploded (Burroughs) **1**:48; **2**:90, 93; **5**:92; **15**:108, 110; **22**:82; **42**:71, 73-4, 79; **75**:93, 102, 106, 109-10; **109**:183, 186, 195, 207, 212, 229
Ticket to Ride (Potter) **58**:391-92, 401; **86**:346, 350, 352
A Ticket to the Stars (Aksyonov)
See *A Starry Ticket*
Tickets for a Prayer Wheel (Dillard) **115**:170, 201
The Tide (Gironella)
See *La marea*
"The Tide at Long Point" (Swenson) **106**:315
"Tide Pools" (Smith) **42**:354
"Tide Wash" (Clark Bekedermo) **38**:121, 126
"Tide-Reach" (Mathias) **45**:236
"Tides" (Hoffman) **141**:283-84, 288, 313
Tides (Montague) **13**:390-91; **46**:268-69, 271, 273-74, 278
Tides and Stone Walls (Sillitoe) **148**:195
The Tides of Lust (Delany) **14**:144; **38**:157-59; **141**:126-27, 129-32, 142
Tidewater Blood (Hoffman) **141**:288-92, 294, 296, 302-03, 316, 320, 322-23
The Tidewater Tales (Barth) **51**:27-9
"Tidings" (Milosz) **82**:291, 294-96
Tie Me Up, Tie Me Down (Almodovar)
See *Atame!*
The Tie That Binds (Haruf) **34**:57-9
Tied Up in Tinsel (Marsh) **7**:209
Tiefland (Riefenstahl) **16**:521, 523, 525-26
El tiempo (Matute) **11**:365
Tiempo al Tiempo (Goldemberg) **52**:167-69
Tiempo mexicano (Fuentes) **60**:152-53
Tien (Pa Chin) **18**:372-73
Tientos y diferencias (Carpentier) **11**:105; **38**:94; **110**:59
"Tieresias" (Harris) **25**:212
Tierra (Lopez y Fuentes) **32**:279-81
Tierra Amarilla: Cuentos du Nuevo México (Ulibarrí) **83**:408-09, 413
Tierra Amarilla: Stories of New Mexico/Cuentos de Nuevo México (Ulibarrí)
See *Tierra Amarilla: Cuentos du Nuevo México*
Tierra de nadie (Onetti) **7**:276
"La tierra que nos han dado" (Rulfo)
See "Nos han dado la tierra"
Tierra sin pan (Bunuel)
See *Las Hurdes—Tierra sin pan*
Tierras de Dios (Arreola) **147**:6
"The Ties That Bind" (Miller) **30**:263-64
Tiet eäisyyksiin (Haavikko) **34**:170
Tieta do Agreste, pastora de cabras; ou, A volta da filha pródiga (Amado) **13**:11-12; **40**:34-5; **106**:86
Tieta, the Goat Girl; or, The Return of the Prodigal Daughter (Amado)
See *Tieta do Agreste, pastora de cabras; ou, A volta da filha pródiga*
"Tiffany Alexander" (L'Heureux) **52**:275
Tiffany Street (Weidman) **7**:518
La tigańci (Eliade) **19**:146
"Tiger" (Hughes) **108**:307
The Tiger (Schisgal) **6**:489-90
The Tiger (Teran) **36**:422-23
The Tiger and the Horse (Bolt) **14**:90
The Tiger and the Rose (Scannell) **49**:328-29, 332-34
"Tiger Dream" (Raine) **45**:341
Tiger Eyes (Blume) **30**:22-4
A Tiger for Malgudi (Narayan) **47**:302-04; **121**:362, 374-77, 383
The Tiger in the Smoke (Allingham) **19**:13
The Tiger in the Tiger Pit (Hospital) **42**:220-21, 224; **145**:297, 308
The Tiger of Gold (Jenkins) **52**:222-23, 226
"Tiger Thoughts" (Hope) **51**:222
Der Tiger von Eschnapur (Lang)
See *Tigress of Bengal*
"Tigers" (Adcock) **41**:13
Tigers (Adcock) **41**:13
Tigers Are Better-Looking (Rhys) **6**:452-56; **14**:446; **19**:390
"The Tiger's Bride" (Carter) **41**:117
The Tiger's Daughter (Mukherjee) **53**:262-64, 268-70; **115**:386
The Tigers of Subutopia, and Other Stories (Symons) **32**:428-29
The Tiger's Revenge (Robbins) **21**:341
Tigers Wild (Rechy) **107**:256
Tight White Collar (L'Heureux) **52**:275-77, 279
"Tightrope Walker" (Scannell) **49**:327
The Tightrope Walker (Levine) **54**:292
"The Tightrope Walkers" (Klima)
See "Provazolezci"
"Tightrope Walking" (Atwood) **135**:36
Le Tigre du Bengale (Lang)
See *Tigress of Bengal*
A Tigress in Prothero (Swinnerton) **31**:427
Tigress of Bengal (Lang) **20**:209; **103**:86-9
The Tigris Expedition (Heyerdahl) **26**:194
Ti-Jean and His Brothers (Walcott) **2**:460; **4**:574; **9**:556; **25**:451, 454-55; **67**:351-52; **76**:273
Tikhii Don (Sholokhov) **7**:415-16, 418-21; **15**:480-85
Til Death (Hunter) **31**:219
"The Tilemaker's Hill Fresco" (Lieberman) **36**:262, 264
"Till Death Do Us Part" (Gellhorn) **14**:195; **60**:184
Till glädje (Bergman) **16**:72; **72**:62
"Till I Die" (Wilson) **12**:650
"Till It Shines" (Seger) **35**:384
"Till September Petronella" (Rhys) **19**:390-91; **51**:375
Till the Break of Day: Memories, 1939-1942 (Wojciechowska) **26**:457-58
"Till the Day I Die" (Odets) **28**:323-24, 332
Till the Day I Die (Odets) **98**:198, 201, 207, 213-15, 218, 224, 229, 231, 233-34, 241
"Till Victory" (Smith) **12**:543
Till We Have Faces: A Myth Retold (Lewis) **6**:310-11; **14**:324; **27**:266; **124**:197-200, 213, 222, 232, 241, 243, 246
"The Tillotson Banquet" (Huxley) **3**:256
Tillträde till festen (Beckman) **26**:86-7, 89
Tiln (Cook) **58**:157
"Tilth" (Graves) **45**:170, 175
Tim (McCullough) **27**:317; **107**:127-33, 137, 152, 154, 159
Tim, Tim: Anthologie de la littérature antillaise en néerlandais (Condé) **92**:100
Tim tim? Bois sec! (Condé) **92**:100
Timans and Justice (Johnson)
See *Timas och rä-ttfärdigheten*
Timas och rä-ttfärdigheten (Johnson) **14**:294
Timber (Haig-Brown) **21**:135, 141
"Timbuktu" (Thomas) **37**:421-22; **107**:316, 320-21, 327
Timbuktu (Auster) **131**:44-47
"Time" (Alegria)
See "Letter to Time"
"Time" (Creeley) **36**:121
"Time" (Merrill) **2**:273-74
"Time" (Pink Floyd) **35**:306-07
"Time" (Stafford) **29**:382
Time (Amichai)
See *Ha-Zeman*
Time (Burroughs) **109**:184
"Time: 1972" (Williams) **148**:363
"Time: 1975" (Williams) **148**:363
"Time: 1976" (Williams) **148**:355, 363
"Time: 1978" (Williams) **148**:355, 362
Time after Time (Keane) **31**:234-35
A Time and a Place (Humphrey) **45**:197-98
"Time and Again" (Bowering) **47**:22
"Time and Again" (Pancake) **29**:347-48
Time and Again (Simak) **55**:320
"Time and Description in Fiction Today" (Robbe-Grillet) **8**:453; **43**:360
"Time and Love" (Nyro) **17**:318
"Time and Music" (Lewis) **41**:261
"Time and Place" (Howe) **47**:174
Time and Place (Trifonov)
See *Vremia i mesto*
Time & Sense (Kristeva) **140**:192-93
"Time and the City" (Le Guin) **45**:220
Time and the Conways (Priestley) **2**:346; **5**:350; **34**:361, 365
"Time and the Garden" (Winters) **32**:469
Time and the Hunter (Calvino)
See *Ti con zero*
Time and the White Tigress (Barnard) **48**:28-9
Time and Tide (O'Brien) **116**:204-07, 212
Time and Time Again (Ayckbourn) **5**:35; **33**:40, 44; **74**:31, 33-6
"Time and Times" (Montale) **9**:387
"Time and Violence" (Boland) **113**:100
"The Time around Scars" (Ondaatje) **51**:310, 312
"Time as Hypnosis" (Warren) **6**:558; **10**:522; **39**:270
"Time as Now" (Scott) **22**:373
Time Bandits (Gilliam) **141**:240, 246-47, 249, 255-56, 259-60
"The Time Bomb" (Stewart) **32**:421
"The Time Capsule" (Gilchrist) **65**:349; **143**:294-95, 303
Time Cat (Alexander) **35**:22
"Time Considered as a Helix of Semi-Precious Stones" (Delany) **38**:149, 154
"Time Did" (Gordimer) **18**:190
"The Time Disease" (Amis) **62**:7-8
Time Enough for Love: The Lives of Lazarus Long (Heinlein) **3**:227; **14**:251-53, 255; **26**:169; **55**:303
"Time Fades Away" (Young) **17**:571
Time Fades Away (Young) **17**:571-75
Time for a Tiger (Burgess) **15**:103; **22**:73; **81**:301
A Time for Judas (Callaghan) **41**:92-8; **65**:252
"Time for Perjury" (Oe) **86**:226-27
"A Time for the Eating of Grasses" (Kumin) **13**:326
Time for the Stars (Heinlein) **26**:161, 171, 173, 177; **55**:302
"Time for Truth" (Weller) **26**:443
"Time Future" (White) **10**:527
"Time, Gentlemen!" (Calisher) **38**:69
Time Given (McAuley) **45**:253-54
"The Time Has Come" (Van Doren) **10**:496
The Time Hoppers (Silverberg) **140**:364
Time in a Red Coat (Brown) **48**:60-1
Time in Ezra Pound's Work (Harmon) **38**:243
Time in Its Flight (Schaeffer) **11**:491-92
Time in the Rock: Preludes to Definition (Aiken) **3**:3; **5**:8-9; **10**:3; **52**:21, 23-4, 26-7, 30
"Time Is Money" (Busch) **47**:62
The Time Is Noon (Buck) **7**:33
The Time Is Ripe (Odets) **98**:247
"Time Is the Artery of Space" (Ivask) **14**:287
"Time Is the Mercy of Eternity" (Rexroth) **49**:282-83; **112**:391, 399-400
Time Is the Simplest Thing (Simak) **55**:320
"Time Lapse with Tulips" (Gallagher) **63**:125
Time Must Have a Stop (Huxley) **1**:151-52; **4**:239-41, 243; **8**:303

Time No Longer (Caldwell) **39**:302-03
The Time Not Lost (Lem) **149**:165, 255, 263
"A Time of Bees" (Van Duyn) **63**:435, 440; **116**:401, 403, 420, 426
A Time of Bees (Van Duyn) **3**:491; **7**:498; **63**:435-36, 440
A Time of Changes (Silverberg) **140**:343, 365, 379
"The Time of Death" (Munro) **95**:296
A Time of Death (Cosic)
See *Vreme smrti*
Time of Desecration (Moravia)
See *La vita interiore*
"A Time of Difficulty" (Alexander) **121**:6
Time of Drums (Ehle) **27**:104-05
"A Time of Dying" (Wesker) **5**:483-84
"The Time of Friendship" (Bowles) **53**:44
The Time of Friendship (Bowles) **2**:79; **19**:60; **53**:40
The Time of Great Expectations (Paustovsky) **40**:364-65, 368
"The Time of Her Time" (Mailer) **3**:315; **28**:256, 261; **74**:207-08; **111**:135-37
The Time of History (Guillén)
See *Clamor*
Time of Hope (Snow) **13**:509-11; **19**:426-27
The Time of Illusion (Schell) **35**:363-64
The Time of Indifference (Moravia)
See *Gli indifferenti*
"A Time of Learning" (West) **7**:519
Time of Need: Forms of Imagination in the Twentieth Century (Barrett) **27**:18-20
"Time of Passage" (Ballard) **3**:33
A Time of Terror (Eckert) **17**:104
The Time of the Angels (Murdoch) **1**:236; **2**:296; **3**:347; **6**:348-49; **11**:386-87; **22**:327
The Time of the Assassins: A Study of Rimbaud (Miller) **9**:380; **84**:251
Time of the Butcherbird (La Guma) **19**:277
The Time of the Crack (Tennant) **13**:536-37; **52**:396, 398
The Time of the Ghost (Jones) **26**:231-32
The Time of the Hero (Vargas Llosa)
See *La ciudad y los perros*
"The Time of Their Lives" (O'Faolain) **32**:342
Time of Trial, Time of Hope: The Negro in America, 1919-1941 (Meltzer) **26**:297-98
"The Time of Year" (Trevor) **71**:348
The Time of Your Life (Saroyan) **8**:468; **10**:453, 455; **29**:359-60; **34**:459; **56**:367-85, 387-88
Time on Fire (Shapcott) **38**:397, 400
Time Out for Happiness (Gilbreth and Carey) **17**:156
Time Out of Joint (Dick) **30**:116, 125; **72**:110
"Time out of Mind" (Becker and Fagen) **26**:85
"Time Passing" (Townshend) **17**:528
"Time Passing, Beloved" (Davie) **5**:114; **31**:109, 118
"Time Past" (White) **10**:527
"Time Present" (White) **10**:527
Time Present (Osborne) **5**:333; **11**:421, 423; **45**:313-16, 320
"Time Quarry" (Simak) **55**:319
Time Remembered (Anouilh)
See *Léocadia*
"Time Shards" (Benford) **52**:76
"Time Sharing Angel" (Tiptree) **48**:389
"Time Spirals" (Rexroth) **112**:399-400
Time Thieves (Koontz) **78**:203
A Time to Be Born (Powell) **66**:357-59, 361, 363, 370-71
A Time to Be Happy (Sahgal) **41**:369
"A Time to Break Silence" (King) **83**:345-46, 349
A Time to Change (Ezekiel) **61**:104-05
"A Time to Dance" (Mac Laverty) **31**:255
A Time to Dance and Other Poems (Day Lewis) **6**:128; **10**:128, 131
A Time to Dance and Other Stories (Mac Laverty) **31**:254-55
A Time to Dance, No Time to Weep (Godden) **53**:163-64
A Time to Die (Wicker) **7**:534-35
"Time to Go" (Dixon) **52**:99-100
Time to Go (Dixon) **52**:99-101
Time to Go (O'Casey) **15**:405
"A Time to Keep" (Brown) **48**:52
"A Time to Keep" (Sillitoe) **57**:391, 396
A Time to Keep and Other Stories (Brown) **48**:52-5; **100**:83
A Time to Kill (Grisham) **84**:190, 195, 198-99
A Time to Laugh (Davies) **23**:141
Time to Love (Benary-Isbert) **12**:34
Time to Love (Dourado)
See *Tempo de amar*
A Time to Love and a Time to Die (Remarque) **21**:331-32
"A Time to Talk" (Frost) **15**:248
"The Time Tombs" (Ballard) **36**:37
The Time Traders (Norton) **12**:467
"Time Waits for No One" (Jagger and Richard) **17**:233, 236, 238
"Time Was Away" (MacNeice) **4**:315
"The Time We Climbed Snake Mountain" (Silko) **74**:335, 345
"Time We Took to Travel" (Bell) **8**:65
"Time Which Cannot Pass Away" (Hein) **154**:'
Time Will Darken It (Maxwell) **19**:306
"Time Will Tell" (Cliff) **21**:60
Time within Time: The Diaries of Andrey Tarkovsky (Tarkovsky) **75**:412
Time without Number (Berrigan) **4**:58
Time Zones (Cruz) **12**:185
Time-Jump (Brunner) **8**:108
Timeless Meeting (Graves) **6**:212
"Timeless, Twinned" (Warren) **39**:256
"The Timeless World of a Play" (Williams) **111**:394
"Timelight" (Skelton) **13**:507
Timelight (Skelton) **13**:507
Timequake (Vonnegut) **111**:371-73
"Timer" (Harrison) **43**:178
"Times" (Beattie) **63**:18
"Times" (Cummings) **15**:162
The Times Are Never So Bad: A Novella and Eight Short Stories (Dubus) **36**:146, 148; **97**:199, 201, 208-10, 224, 233
Time's Arrow (Amis) **101**:69-71, 77-78, 86-87, 89, 95
"The Times My Father Died" (Amichai) **116**:106-07
The Times of Melville and Whitman (Brooks) **29**:88-9
"Times of Sickness and Health" (Shields) **113**:405
Times of Surrender (Coles) **108**:192, 196
Time's Power: Poems, 1985-1988 (Rich) **73**:328, 330-32; **76**:211
"Time's Rub" (Benford) **52**:76
"Times Square" (Clark Bekedermo) **38**:118, 128
Times Square Red, Times Square Blue (Delany) **141**:160
"The Times They Are A-Changin'" (Dylan) **77**:164
The Times They Are A-Changin' (Dylan) **4**:149; **12**:182, 198-99
Times Three (McGinley) **14**:366, 368
Timescape (Benford) **52**:65-9, 72-4, 76-7
"Times-Square-Shoeshine Composition" (Angelou) **77**:28
"Timesweep" (Sandburg) **10**:449; **35**:356
Timmerlis (Bodker) **21**:12
"Timor dei" (Cunningham) **31**:102
"Timor Mortis" (Porter) **5**:347
Timothy Archer (Dick)
See *The Transmigration of Timothy Archer*
"Ti-Moune" (Gold) **42**:197-98; **152**:121
"The Tin Can" (Smith) **6**:513
The Tin Can and Other Poems (Smith) **6**:512
The Tin Can Tree (Tyler) **28**:430-31; **59**:203, 205, 207; **103**:236-37, 241, 244, 258, 264, 271, 273
The Tin Drum (Grass)
See *Die Blechtrommel*
The Tin Flute (Roy)
See *Bonheur d'occasion*
The Tin Lizzie Troop (Swarthout) **35**:402-03
The Tin Men (Frayn) **31**:189-90
"Tin Roof" (Ondaatje) **51**:313, 315
"Tin Roof Blues" (Brown) **23**:96
"Tin Soldier" (Rozewicz)
See "Øowiany żønierzyk"
"Tin Soldier" (Vinge) **30**:410
"Tin Tan Tann" (Cisneros) **118**:201, 205-06
"Tinder" (Heaney) **14**:244
"Tinieblas y consolación" (Castellanos) **66**:50
Tinisima (Poniatowska)
See *Tinísima*
Tinísima (Poniatowska) **140**:312-13, 320, 330, 336-38
Tinker, Tailor, Soldier, Spy (le Carré) **5**:232-35; **9**:327; **15**:324-26
"Tinkers" (Powers) **8**:447
Tinsel (Goldman) **48**:127-28
"Tintern Abbey" (Auden) **123**:35
Tiny Alice (Albee) **1**:5; **2**:1-4; **3**:7; **5**:10, 12-13; **9**:1, 5-7, 9; **11**:11; **13**:3-5; **25**:34, 37-8, 40; **53**:21, 23, 26; **86**:118, 123; **113**:15-17, 19-21, 25-6, 28, 30, 32, 34-6
"The Tiny Baby" (Strand) **41**:438-40
"Tiny Tears" (Fuller) **28**:157
"Tiny Treaties" (Alexie) **96**:8
"Tio e sobrinho" (Cabral de Melo Neto) **76**:163
"Tip on a Dead Jockey" (Shaw) **34**:370
Tip on a Dead Jockey (Shaw) **7**:412
Tips for Teens (Lebowitz) **36**:248
"Tirade for the Mimic Muse" (Boland) **67**:43; **113**:58-9, 87, 97-8, 122-23
"A Tirade Turning" (Roethke) **46**:361; **101**:266
"The Tire Hangs in the Woods" (Smith) **42**:346, 349
"Tired" (Hughes) **108**:320
"Tired and Unhappy, You Think of Houses" (Schwartz) **10**:462
"Tired Eyes" (Young) **17**:574
"Tires on Wet Asphalt at Night" (Warren) **39**:273
"Tiresias" (Clarke) **6**:112
"Tiresome Company" (Ferron) **94**:103
Tirez sur le pianiste (Truffaut) **20**:381-83, 397, 402-03; **101**:369, 373, 377, 380, 382-85, 387-91, 396, 406, 409-10
Les tiroirs de l'inconnu (Aymé) **11**:23
Tirra Lirra by the River (Anderson) **37**:20-1
"Tîrzui de toamnă" (Arghezi) **80**:7
Tis Pity She's a Whore (Ayckbourn) **74**:19
"Tis the Season to Be Jolly" (Matheson) **37**:245
Tissue (Page) **40**:355
"Titan" (Dorfman) **77**:141
Titania's Lodestone (Corcoran) **17**:75
"The Titanic" (Feldman) **7**:103
"The Titanic" (Milosz) **82**:299
Titanic (Durang) **27**:88
The Titanic (Pratt) **19**:378, 381-84
Titans (Pratt) **19**:378, 382
"Tithonus" (Brown) **48**:55
"Tithonus" (Thomas) **132**:381
Titicut Follies (Wiseman) **20**:467-69, 471-72, 476
"Title" (Barth) **3**:41; **9**:67, 69; **14**:53-4; **51**:23; **89**:5-6, 8-10, 12-16, 18-19, 23-24, 27, 30, 32, 34-5, 37, 44-6, 48, 50, 56, 59, 61-2
"The Title of This Book" (Barth) **51**:25
"Titre à Préciser" (Derrida) **87**:92
"Titties and Beer" (Zappa) **17**:592
"Titties Prayer" (Carrier) **78**:83
Titus Alone (Peake) **54**:367-68, 370-72, 376-78; **7**:302
Titus Andronicus (Duerrenmatt) **102**:54-6, 59, 61
Titus Groan (Peake) **54**:366-75, 377-78
Tiur'ma i mir (Aksyonov)
See *Prison and Peace*
"Tlactocatzine del jardin de Flandes" (Fuentes)
See "In a Flemish Garden"

"Tlactocatzine in the Garden of Flanders" (Fuentes)
See "In a Flemish Garden"
"Tlactocatzine, of the Flemish Garden" (Fuentes)
See "In a Flemish Garden"
"Tlön, Uqbar, Orbis Tertius" (Borges) **2**:69, 72; **3**:77; **6**:87, 92; **8**:94, 96, 98, 100; **9**:116-118; **10**:66; **44**:362, 369; **48**:33, 42-3, 45-6; **83**:155-57, 161, 164, 176, 183
Tlooth (Mathews) **6**:314-16; **52**:307, 309-10, 315-16, 318
"To a Beautiful Old Lady" (Christie) **110**:125
"To a Blackbird" (Kavanagh) **22**:236
To a Blossoming Pear Tree (Wright) **10**:546-47; **28**:466, 468, 472-73
"To A British Jar Containing Stephen's Ink" (Blunden) **56**:37
"To a Brother in the Mystery" (Davie) **31**:109
"To a Cedar Tree" (Christie) **110**:127
"To a Chameleon" (Moore) **8**:401
"To a Child" (Snodgrass) **68**:382
"To a Child" (Wright) **53**:419
"To a Communist" (MacNeice) **53**:234
"To a Conscript of 1940" (Read) **4**:439
"To a Contemporary Bunk-Shooter" (Sandburg) **35**:347
"To a Dead Lover" (Bogan) **93**:104
"To a Distant Statue of King George V" (Hall) **51**:170
"To a Fish Head Found on the Beach Near Malaga" (Levine) **118**:284
"To a Friend Going Blind" (Graham) **48**:154; **118**:240-42, 245
"To a Friend in Time of Trouble" (Gunn) **81**:184
"To a Friend in Trouble" (Wain) **11**:562
"To a Friend Parting" (Warren) **8**:539
"To a Friend Who Cannot Accept My Judgment of Him" (Wakoski) **4**:572
"To a Friend Who Has Moved to the East Side" (Ignatow) **14**:274
"To a Friend Who Threw Away Hair Dyes" (Van Duyn) **116**:415
"To a Friend Who Wished Always to Be Alone" (Wright) **13**:614
"To a Friend Whose Family Was Killed or Ngenimpi (A Late Recruit)" (Kunene) **85**:176
"To a Friend Whose Work Has Come to Triumph" (Sexton) **53**:316
"To a Friend with a Religious Vocation" (Jennings) **131**:235, 238
To a God Unknown (Steinbeck) **1**:325; **5**:406-07; **9**:512-13; **13**:530, 533; **21**:366, 381, 390; **34**:412; **59**:333; **75**:343; **124**:387, 393, 419
"To a Greek Marble" (Aldington) **49**:2-3, 6, 16
"To A. H., New Year, 1943" (Wright) **53**:427
"To a Happy Day" (Neruda) **7**:259
"To a Hostess Saying Goodnight" (Wright) **28**:462
"To a Husband" (Angelou) **77**:28
"To a Jealous Cat" (Sanchez) **116**:277, 294
"To a Lady in a Phone Booth" (McGinley) **14**:366
"To a Little Girl, One Year Old in a Ruined Fortress" (Warren) **39**:266
"To A. M., a Flamenco Singer" (Cabral de Melo Neto)
See *A Antonio Mairena, cantador*
"To a Mad Friend" (Davison) **28**:99-100
"To a Man" (Angelou) **64**:33-4
"To a Man on His Horse" (Prince) **22**:340
"To a Military Rifle" (Winters) **32**:468, 470
"To a Moth Seen in Winter" (Frost) **9**:226
"To a Muse" (Corn) **33**:116
"To a Navaho Boy Playing the Flute" (Kunene) **85**:176
"To a New Mother" (Levine) **33**:274
"To a Now-Type Poet" (Kennedy) **42**:257
"To a Painter in England" (Walcott) **76**:277
"To a Plum-Coloured Bra Displayed in Marks and Spencer" (Ewart) **46**:153
"To a Poet Who Has Had a Heart Attack" (Eberhart) **11**:177
"To a Red Hell" (Himes) **58**:264
"To a Sad Daughter" (Ondaatje) **51**:314, 317
"To a Snail" (Moore) **8**:400; **47**:272
"To a South African Policeman" (Kunene) **85**:175
"To a Steam Roller" (Moore) **47**:268
"To a Stranger" (Jensen) **37**:192
"To a Teacher of French" (Davie) **31**:116, 118
"To a Ten-Months' Child" (Justice) **102**:269
To a Tensed Serenity (Char)
See *À une sérénité crispée*
"To a Thinker" (Frost) **10**:193
"To a Wandering Albatross" (Neruda) **62**:331
"To a Waterfowl" (Hall) **37**:146
"To a Watertower" (Crase) **58**:160, 163
"To a Western Bard Still a Whoop and a Holler Away from English Poetry" (Meredith) **22**:302
"To a Winter Squirrel" (Brooks) **49**:28
"To a Woman on Her Defense of Her Brother" (Winters) **32**:468
"To a Young American the Day after the Fall of Barcelona" (Ciardi) **40**:157
"To a Young Girl Leaving the Hill Country" (Bontemps) **18**:64
"To a Young Writer" (Winters) **32**:470
"To Abolish Children" (Shapiro) **53**:329
To Abolish Children, and Other Essays (Shapiro) **53**:328-30
"To Acquire a Beautiful Body" (Dybek) **114**:62
"To Aegidius Cantor" (Howard) **10**:277
"To Alexander Graham" (Graham) **29**:199
To All Appearances: Poems New and Selected (Miles) **14**:369, 370
"To All Black Women, from All Black Men" (Cleaver) **30**:56, 59
"To All Sisters" (Sanchez) **116**:282
"To All Telephone Subscribers" (Enzensberger) **43**:145
"To an Adolescent Weeping Willow" (Bell) **31**:51
"To an American Poet Just Dead" (Wilbur) **110**:383
"To an Antarctic Traveller" (Pollitt) **122**:205
"To an Artist, to Take Heart" (Bogan) **46**:83; **93**:64
To an Early Grave (Markfield) **8**:378-79
"To an Honest Friend" (Sarton) **91**:254
"To an Old Lady" (Empson) **3**:147; **8**:202; **19**:155; **33**:142; **34**:540
"To an Old Man" (Randall) **135**:399
"To an Unknown American Friend" (Leonov) **92**:277
"To an Unknown Poet" (Kizer) **80**:183, 185
"To and Fro" (McEwan) **66**:275, 279, 281
"To Any Dead Officer" (Graves) **45**:166
"To Any Dead Officer Who Left School for the Army in 1914" (Sassoon) **36**:385; **130**:187, 193, 202, 215
"To Any Poet" (McAuley) **45**:249
"To Apollo" (Herbert) **43**:189
"To Artemis" (Carruth) **10**:100
"To Artina" (Hughes) **108**:333
"To Auden on His Fiftieth" (Eberhart) **11**:177
"To Aunt Rose" (Ginsberg) **2**:17
"To Autumn" (Glück) **7**:118
"To Autumn" (Logan) **5**:254
"To Autumn" (Smith) **64**:399
"To Autumn" (Wright) **146**:348
"To Be a Man" (Soto) **80**:284
"To Be a Poet" (Stevenson) **33**:381
To Be a Poet (Seifert)
See *Býti básníkem*
"To Be Collected" (Sillitoe) **57**:391
"To Be Discontinued" (Hospital) **145**:312
"To Be in Love" (Brooks) **49**:27-8; **125**:45
To Be of Use (Piercy) **6**:402-04; **18**:406; **27**:375; **62**:376; **128**:229, 244, 246
"To Be Quicker for Black Political Prisoners" (Madhubuti) **73**:215
"To Be Sung on the Water" (Bogan) **39**:387; **46**:81; **93**:77
"To Be Sung on the Water" (Bogan) **93**:65, 78
To Be Young, Gifted, and Black (Hansberry) **17**:187-88
To Bedlam and Part Way Back (Sexton) **2**:390-91; **4**:482-84; **6**:491; **8**:483; **15**:471-72; **53**:312, 316-18, 320-21; **123**:409, 412-16, 419, 423, 432-33, 435, 437, 439, 441, 451
"To Begin" (Strand) **6**:521
To Begin Again: Stories and Memoirs, 1908-1929 (Fisher) **87**:128, 130, 132-33
"To Belkis, When She Paints" (Padilla) **38**:349
"To Bev" (Behan) **79**:38
"To Bill Williams" (Eberhart) **11**:177
"To Bird-watching" (Neruda) **62**:331
To Bite the Flesh (Brossard)
See *Mordre en sa chair*
"'To Bodies Gone': Pygmalion Remembering" (Rosenthal) **28**:395
"To Build a House" (Hall) **59**:154-56; **151**:189-90
"To C. E. B." (Blunden) **56**:40
"To Canidia" (Jeffers) **54**:234
"To Carry the Child" (Smith) **44**:437
To Catch a Thief (Hitchcock) **16**:341, 346, 359
"To Cease" (Montague) **46**:269
"To Certain Friends" (Scott) **22**:377
"To Certain Negro Leaders" (Hughes) **108**:319
"To Change in a Good Way" (Ortiz) **45**:310-11
"To Christ" (Ritsos) **31**:324
"To Chuck" (Sanchez) **116**:278, 294
"To Cipriano, in the Wind" (Levine) **33**:273; **118**:273, 279-80, 285, 302, 318
To Circumjack Cencrastus (MacDiarmid) **11**:336; **19**:289-90; **63**:239
"To Cleave" (Bowering) **15**:82
"To Confirm a Thing" (Swenson) **106**:314, 341
"To Criticize the Critic" (Eliot) **24**:178
To Criticize the Critic (Eliot) **113**:193
"To Da-duh, In Memoriam" (Marshall) **27**:313-14
"To Death" (Senghor)
See "A la mort"
"To Delmore Schwartz" (Lowell) **3**:300
To Demosia ké ta Idiotika (Elytis) **100**:187
To diav (Samarakis) **5**:381 82
To diavatírio (Samarakis) **5**:381
"To Die for One's Country Is Glorious" (Kiš) **57**:251
To Die in Italbar (Zelazny) **21**:466, 468-69
"To Die in Milltown" (Hugo) **32**:240
"To Dinah Washington" (Knight) **40**:279
To Disembark (Brooks) **49**:23, 29
"To Don at Salaam" (Brooks) **49**:29
"To Dorothy" (Bell) **31**:50
"To Draw the Warmth of Flesh from Subtle Graphite" (Broumas) **73**:17
"To Dwell in Time" (Cabral de Melo Neto)
See "Habitar o tempo"
"To Earthward" (Frost) **9**:218; **26**:112
To Eat a Peach (Willingham) **51**:407
"To Elizabeth Ann Fraser" (McFadden) **48**:251
"To Elsie" (Williams) **67**:408
"To Eugene" (Brodsky) **50**:125
"To Eve in Bitterness" (Jones) **10**:286
"To Every Thing There Is a Season" (MacLeod) **56**:197-99
"To F." (Swenson) **106**:343
"To Fill" (Moore) **39**:82-3
To Fly (Breytenbach) **126**:81-3
"To Free Nelson Mandela" (Jordan) **114**:162
"To Gerhardt" (Olson) **11**:420
"To Giacomo Leopardi in the Sky" (Wright) **146**:315, 335, 338, 363-64
"To Girls at the Turn of Night Love Goes On Knocking" (Graham) **29**:193
"to gloria, who is she: on using a pseudonym" (Hooks) **94**:143
"To Happiness" (Neruda) **7**:259

To Have and Have Not (Hemingway) **1**:141; **3**:232, 235-36, 240; **6**:226-27, 229; **8**:283; **13**:271, 274, 278; **30**:179; **39**:430, 435; **41**:197-98; **80**:101, 103-04, 106, 108, 118, 135, 137, 143, 150-51
To Have and to Lose (Aitmatov)
See *Topolek moi v krasnoi kosynke*
"To Have Done Nothing" (Williams) **42**:460
To Heaven One Climbs on Foot (Ulibarrí)
See *Al cielo se sube a pie*
"To Helen" (Simic) **49**:341
"To Helen Whose Remembrance Leaves No Peace" (Jeffers) **54**:234
"To Hell with Dying" (Walker) **6**:553-54; **58**:409; **103**:399, 402, 409, 412, 423
To Hell with Picasso (Johnson) **147**:139
"To Here and the Easel" (Sturgeon) **22**:411; **39**:365
"To His Other Spirit" (Rosenthal) **28**:394-95
"To His Skeleton" (Wilbur) **110**:385
"To Hold a Poem" (Smith) **15**:515-16
"To Howard Hughes: A Modest Proposal" (Haldeman) **61**:174, 176-77
"To Hummingbirds" (Neruda) **62**:331
"To Incomprehensible Poets" (Yevtushenko) **126**:388
"To Isherwood Dying" (Gunn) **81**:186
To Jerusalem and Back: A Personal Account (Bellow) **8**:79-82; **15**:58; **25**:82, 86
"To Johnny Pole On The Forgotten Beach" (Sexton) **123**:409
"To Jorslem" (Silverberg) **140**:378
"To Jorslem" (Silverberg) **140**:
"To Joy" (Blunden) **56**:39
To Joy (Bergman)
See *Till glädje*
"To Juan at the Winter Solstice" (Graves) **1**:126; **2**:174; **39**:321; **45**:169, 173, 176
"To Judith Asleep" (Ciardi) **40**:153-54, 156-58; **44**:380
To Keep Moving: Essays, 1959-1969 (Hall) **37**:148
To Keep the Ball Rolling: The Memoirs of Anthony Powell (Powell) **31**:314, 317, 319-20, 322
"To Keorapetse Kgositsile (Willie)" (Brooks) **49**:29; **125**:85
"To Kill a Foreign Name" (Cabrera Infante) **120**:68
To Kill a Mockingbird (Foote) **51**:131, 133; **91**:101
To Kill a Mockingbird (Lee) **12**:340-42; **60**:240-50
To Leave before Dawn (Green)
See *Partir avant le jour*
"To Life" (Neruda) **7**:259
To Live and Die in Dixie (Beecher) **6**:48-9
"To Live as Foolishly as I Lived Yesterday" (Akhmadulina)
See "Tak durno zhit', kak ia vchera zhila"
To Live Forever (Vance) **35**:420, 423, 426
"To Lose the Earth" (Sexton) **6**:493; **123**:430
"To Love" (Neruda) **7**:259
"To Lucasta on Going to the Wars" (Graves) **45**:166
"To Lycomedes on Scyros" (Brodsky)
See "K Likomedu, na Skiros"
"To Maeve" (Peake) **54**:369, 372
"To Make a Play" (Swenson) **106**:339
"To Make a Poem in Prison" (Knight) **40**:279, 283
"To Marina" (Koch) **44**:246, 250
"To Marx" (Ritsos) **31**:324
"To Mary Gilmore" (Wright) **53**:429
To Meet the Sun (FitzGerald) **19**:176
"To M.E.L.M. in Absence" (Christie) **110**:126
"To Military Progress" (Moore) **8**:398
To Mix with Time: New and Selected Poems (Swenson) **4**:533; **61**:390-92, 395, 400; **106**:316, 319-20, 327, 336, 341, 345, 349
"To Ms. Ann" (Clifton) **66**:67
"To My Brother" (Bogan) **46**:80, 83, 87; **93**:64, 76
"To My Brother" (Sassoon) **130**:180, 213
"To My Brother Hanson" (Merwin) **88**:192, 201
"To My Brother on the Death of a Young Poet" (Levine) **33**:270
"To My Daughter the Junkie on a Train" (Lorde) **71**:232, 236
"To My Dog" (Aleixandre) **36**:30
"To My Elder Kinsman (Polycarp Dlamini)" (Kunene) **85**:176
"To My Father" (Bidart) **33**:76
"To My Father" (Olds) **85**:306
"To My First White Hairs" (Soyinka) **36**:409
"To My Friend, Behind Walls" (Kizer) **80**:12
"To My Friends" (Silkin) **43**:400
"To My God in His Sickness" (Levine) **14**:319; **118**:267, 279
"To My Godson, on His Christening" (Van Duyn) **63**:439; **116**:399, 425
"To My Mother" (Barker) **48**:22
"To My Mother" (Smith)
See "For My Mother"
"To My Mountain" (Raine) **45**:330
"To My Sister" (Roethke) **8**:455
To My Son in Uniform (Felsen) **17**:124
"To My Wife" (Cunningham) **3**:122; **31**:98
"To My Wife" (Larkin) **64**:262
"To My Wife at Midnight" (Graham) **29**:197-98
"To No End Ever" (Ciardi) **40**:159
"To Nomazwi—Reluctant Poetess" (Kunene) **85**:175-76
"To Old Asclepius—Lyric at Epidaurus" (Gustafson) **36**:218
"To One 'Investigated' by the Last Senate Committee, or the Next" (Ciardi) **40**:153, 157
"To One Who Was With Me in the War" (Sassoon) **130**:187
To Open the Sky (Silverberg) **140**:343, 345
To Our Father Creator Tupac (Arguedas)
See *Tupac amaru kampa Taytanchisman*
To Painting: A Poem of Color and Line (Alberti) **7**:10
"To Peter" (Rozewicz) **139**:297
"To Peter Taylor on the Feast of the Epiphany" (Lowell) **124**:254
"To P.L., 1916-1937: A Soldier of the Republic" (Levine) **118**:284, 294, 316
"To Please a Shadow" (Brodsky) **50**:132; **100**:61
"To Poets' Worksheets in the Air-Conditioned Vault of a Library" (Van Duyn) **116**:403
To Possess the Land: A Biography of Arthur Rochford Manby (Waters) **88**:364
To Praise the Music (Bronk) **10**:74
"To Professor X, Year Y" (Avison) **97**:133-34
"To Raja Rao" (Milosz) **56**:240; **82**:301
"To Ramona" (Dylan) **77**:174
"The To Read Dispossessed" (Delany) **141**:137, 146
"To Read or to Re-Read" (Goytisolo) **133**:86
"To Remember is a Kind of Hope" (Amichai) **116**:90
"To Revive Anarchism" (Shapiro) **53**:328
To Ride Pegasus (McCaffrey) **17**:281
"To Robby" (Wideman) **122**:328
"To Robinson Jeffers" (Milosz) **56**:241, 244; **82**:295-96, 300
"To Room Nineteen" (Lessing) **40**:310
To Room Nineteen (Lessing) **94**:261
To Sail beyond the Sunset (Heinlein) **55**:303
"To Saint George" (Le Guin) **136**:389
"To Say It" (Creeley) **78**:141
To See the Dream (West) **17**:546-47
"To See the Invisible Man" (Silverberg) **140**:377
"To See the Sun" (Amis) **40**:43, 45
To See, To Take (Van Duyn) **3**:491; **7**:498-99; **63**:436-38, 440, 442, 444; **116**:400-03, 406, 414, 419, 426
"To See You Again" (Adams) **46**:17
To See You Again (Adams) **46**:15-17, 21-2
"To September Wings" (Neruda) **62**:331
"To Sing a Song of Palestine" (Jordan) **114**:146
To Sir with Love (Clavell) **87**:18
To Skin a Cat (McGuane) **45**:265-66; **127**:262, 269, 274
"To Sleep, Perchance to Steam" (Perelman) **49**:265
To Smithereens (Drexler) **6**:142
"To Speak of My Influences" (Garrigue) **8**:240
"To Speak of Woe That Is in Marriage" (Lowell) **15**:343; **124**:259
"To Start, to Hesitate; to Stop" (Cummings) **8**:160
"To Statecraft Embalmed" (Moore) **8**:401; **47**:260
To Stay Alive (Levertov) **2**:243; **3**:293; **5**:248-250; **66**:245-46, 249, 251
"To Suzanne, from Prison" (Faludy) **42**:137-38
"To Take Objects Outs" (Herbert) **9**:275
To Teach, to Love (Stuart) **34**:375
To Tell Your Love (Stolz) **12**:545-46, 549, 552
"To the Adversary" (Wittlin) **25**:469
To the Air (Gunn) **18**:200
"To the American Negro Troops" (Senghor) **130**:234, 284
"To the August Fallen" (Wright) **5**:520
"To the Birds of Chile" (Neruda) **62**:331
"To the Blessed Virgin" (Buckley) **57**:125
To the Bone (Kristofferson) **26**:270
To the Boneyard (Rozewicz)
See *Do piachu*
"To the Botequim and Back" (Bishop) **32**:43
"To the Butterflies" (Dickey) **109**:246
"To the Chicago Abyss" (Bradbury) **98**:112
To the Chicago Abyss (Bradbury) **42**:33-4
"To the Dark Star" (Silverberg) **7**:425; **140**:351-53, 355-56
To the Dark Tower (King) **53**:204
"To the Days" (Rich) **125**:335
"To the Diaspora" (Brooks) **49**:23, 29
"To the End of the Pier" (Corn) **33**:115
To the End of the World (Cendrars)
See *Emmène-moi au bout du monde!*
To the Ends of the Earth (Golding) **81**:320
"To the Film Industry in Crisis" (O'Hara) **78**:354
To the Finland Station (Wilson) **1**:372-73; **2**:476; **3**:539-40; **24**:467, 473, 482-83, 486-87
"To the Foot from Its Child" (Neruda) **7**:260
"To the Governor and Legislature of Massachusetts" (Nemerov) **2**:308
"To the Gull" (Neruda) **62**:331
"To the Gulls of Antofagasta" (Neruda) **62**:331
"To the Hawk" (Justice) **19**:235
"To the Holy Spirit" (Winters) **4**:591; **32**:468-69
"To the Immaculate Virgin, on a Winter Night" (Merton) **83**:391
To the Indies (Forester) **35**:163-64
"To the Insects" (Merwin) **88**:206
To the Is-Land (Frame) **66**:143, 145, 150; **96**:187-88, 193-94, 201, 203, 206, 209-10, 217-18, 220
To the Islands (Stow) **23**:432-34; **48**:355-56, 358
"To the Lacedemonians" (Tate) **4**:539; **9**:522
To the Ladies! (Connelly) **7**:56
To the Ladies! (Kaufman) **38**:257, 264
To the Land of the Cattails (Appelfeld) **47**:7-9
To the Land of the Reeds (Appelfeld)
See *To the Land of the Cattails*
To the Limit (Armatrading) **17**:9-10
"To the Little Fort, San Lázaro, on the Ocean Front Havana" (Hughes) **108**:324
"To the Living" (Sarton) **49**:310
"To the Man Who Sidled Up to Me and Asked: 'How Long You In fer, Buddy?'" (Knight) **40**:279
"To the Members of the D.A.R." (Greenberg) **30**:163

"To the Mercy Killers" (Randall) **135**:386, 391, 398
"To the Migration of Birds" (Neruda) **62**:331
"To the Mother" (Amichai)
See "La'em"
"To the Mothers of the Dead Militia" (Neruda)
See "Canto a las madres de los milicianos muertos"
"To the Muse" (Levertov) **66**:238-39, 242
"To the Muse" (Wright) **3**:541, 543; **28**:466
"To the New Tenant" (Brodsky) **13**:114
"To the Nightingale" (McGuckian) **48**:278
To the North (Bowen) **3**:84; **11**:62, 65-66; **15**:79; **22**:61, 63; **118**:62, 89
"To the Oriole" (Neruda) **62**:331
"To the Painters: On the United States, Considered as a Landscape" (Howard) **47**:169
"To the Poet Who Happens to Be Black and the Black Poet Who Happens to Be a Woman" (Lorde) **71**:254, 256
"To the Poetry of Hugh McRae" (Slessor) **14**:496-97
"To the Poets in New York" (Wright) **3**:543
"To the Poets of Chile" (Levine) **14**:315, 318-19
To the Precipice (Rossner) **9**:456
To the Public Danger (Hamilton) **51**:190, 193
"To the Reader" (Cunningham) **31**:101-02
"To the Reader" (Jong) **6**:268
"To the Readers" (Blaga) **75**:62
"To the Sea" (Larkin) **5**:226, 230-31; **8**:332, 337, 339; **9**:323; **13**:340; **18**:301; **33**:259; **64**:277, 280, 282, 284
"To the Sea Serpent" (Fuentes)
See "A la Víbora de la mar"
"To the Secretariat of the Moscow Union of Writers" (Voinovich) **147**:272
"To the Senegalese tirailleurs Who died for France" (Senghor)
See "Aux Tirailleurs sénégalais morts pour la France"
"To the Sky" (Bell) **8**:67
"To the Snake" (Levertov) **66**:252
"To the Snake of the Sea" (Fuentes)
See "A la Víbora de la mar"
"To the Southdowns" (Blunden) **56**:45
"To the Soviet Union" (Ritsos) **31**:324
To the Stars (Hubbard)
See *Return to Tomorrow*
"To the Statues of the Gods" (Cernuda) **54**:58
"To the Stone-Cutters" (Jeffers) **54**:243, 248
"To the Storming Gulf" (Benford) **52**:71-2, 75-6
"To the Sun" (Bachmann)
See "An die Sonne"
"To the Unknown God" (Moravia) **46**:286
To the Unknown Hero (Nossack)
See *Dem unbekannten Sieger*
"To the Unknown Lady Who Wrote the Letters Found in the Hatbox" (Justice) **102**:279
To the Victors the Spoils (MacInnes) **23**:283
"To the Virgin as She Now Stands" (Codrescu) **46**:103
"To the Watcher of the Gates" (Kunene) **85**:166
"To the Western World" (Simpson) **7**:426; **9**:486; **149**:309, 325, 355
To the White Sea (Dickey) **109**:236, 257-60, 262-63, 273, 275, 287
"To the Wilderness" (Kinnell) **13**:320
"To the World Beyond I'm Posting" (Ratushinskaya) **54**:384, 386
"To Think Clearly" (Simic) **130**:332
"To Thom Gunn in Los Altos, California" (Davie) **31**:111
"To Those of My Sisters Who Kept Their Naturals" (Brooks) **125**:107
"To Thy Chamber Window, Sweet" (Gordon) **83**:247
To Transfigure, To Organize (Pasolini)
See *Trasumanar e organizzar*
"To Tu Fu, Beethoven, Va Dong, Magolwane and All the Great Poets of Humankind" (Kunene) **85**:176
"To Urania" (Brodsky) **100**:45-6
To Urania: Selected Poems 1965-1985 (Brodsky) **100**:41-2, 49-50, 53-5, 58, 61
"To Victor Hugo of My Crow Pluto" (Moore) **8**:401; **47**:263
"To Victory" (Sassoon) **130**:192
"To Violet Lang" (O'Hara) **13**:424
To Wake the Dead (Campbell)
See *The Parasite*
To Walk a Crooked Mile (McGrath) **28**:275-76; **59**:177-78
"To Westward" (Ciardi) **40**:151-52
To What End: Report from Vietnam (Just) **4**:266; **27**:227-28
"To What Red Hell" (Himes) **108**:227
To What Strangers, What Welcome (Cunningham) **3**:120-21; **79**:105
To Whom She Will (Jhabvala)
See *Amrita*
"To Wine" (Bogan) **93**:67
"To Wine" (Neruda) **7**:259
To X (Fuller) **28**:151
"To You" (Koch) **44**:251
To Your Scattered Bodies Go (Farmer) **19**:165
"To Yvor Winters, 1955" (Gunn) **18**:200
"Toad" (Oliver) **98**:304
"Toads" (Larkin) **3**:275; **13**:336; **33**:257, 263, 268; **39**:336, 342, 345; **64**:266, 272, 282
"Toad's Mouth" (Allende) **97**:9, 28-9, 32
"Toads Revisited" (Larkin) **5**:226; **33**:257, 268; **39**:341; **64**:282
"The Toad's Watch" (Castellanos)
See "La velada del sapo"
"A Toast" (MacNeice) **53**:231
A Toast to the Lord (Jenkins) **52**:225-26
Tobacco Road (Caldwell) **1**:51; **8**:123-24; **14**:94-5, 97-9; **50**:298-303; **60**:44-50, 53, 55-9, 61-7
Tobogán de hambrientos (Cela) **4**:97; **122**:19-20, 66
"Toby Dammit" (Fellini) **16**:279-81, 299; **85**:63-6, 81-2
Toby Lived Here (Wolitzer) **17**:564
Tocaia grande (Amado) **106**:84-5, 91
"Toccata and Fugue for the Foreigner" (Kristeva) **77**:336
"Der Tod der Elsa Baskoleit" (Boell) **72**:68, 71
"Der Tod ist ein Meister aus Deutschland" (Rozewicz) **139**:297
Todas las sangres (Arguedas) **10**:9; **18**:6-7
"Today" (Mahapatra) **33**:284
"Today" (O'Hara) **78**:345-46, 375-76
"Today a Leaf" (Stern) **40**:413
"Today I Was So Happy, So I Made This Poem" (Wright) **5**:518
"Today in the Cafe Trieste" (Tillinghast) **29**:416-17
"Today Is Friday" (Hemingway) **13**:280
"Today Is the Day" (Shields) **113**:408, 432
Today the Struggle (Jones) **10**:295; **52**:252-53
"Today Will Be a Quiet Day" (Hempel) **39**:68-70
Today's a Holiday (Buero Vallejo)
See *Hoy es fiesta*
"Today's Wish" (Kunene) **85**:175
Today's Young Barbarians (Arrabal) **58**:17
Todesarten (Bachmann) **69**:36, 59-60, 62
"Todesfuge" (Celan) **82**:33, 40, 44-5, 49
Todo empezó en domingo (Poniatowska) **140**:309, 312, 330-31
"Todo esto por amor" (Cernuda) **54**:54
Todo México (Poniatowska) **140**:330
Todo modo (Sciascia) **41**:387-88, 393-94
"Todorov's Fantastic Theory of Literature" (Lem) **149**:158
Todos los fuegos el fuego (Cortázar) **3**:115; **5**:109; **10**:115; **33**:123; **34**:329
Todos los gatos son pardos (Fuentes) **22**:168-70; **41**:168, 171; **113**:232
"Todos mis pecados" (Fuentes) **10**:206
Todos somos fugitivos (Gironella) **11**:236
"Todtnauberg" (Celan) **53**:74
"To-Em-Mei's 'The Unmoving Cloud'" (Pound) **112**:341, 348
"Toe'Osh: A Laguna Coyote Story" (Silko) **23**:412
"The Toe-Tag" (Muldoon) **72**:273
"Together" (Sassoon) **130**:222
A toi, pour toujours, ta Marie-Lou (Tremblay) **29**:419, 421-22, 425-26; **102**:360, 362, 370-71, 374-75, 381
The Toilet (Baraka) **5**:44; **14**:43, 46; **33**:54, 59; **115**:29, 47
"Toilet of a Dandy" (Slessor) **14**:492
Toinen taivas ja maa (Haavikko) **34**:170
"Token Drunk" (Bukowski) **82**:14
"Token Resistance" (Ashbery) **125**:30, 32-3
"Toki" (Grace) **56**:111, 118
Tokyo Boshoku (Ozu) **16**:449, 453
Tokyo Monogatari (Ozu) **16**:446-48, 450, 454, 456
Tokyo Olympiad (Ichikawa) **20**:179-80
The Tokyo Story (Ozu)
See *Tokyo Monogatari*
Tokyo Twilight (Ozu)
See *Tokyo Boshoku*
Tokyo Woes (Friedman) **56**:108-09
The Tokyo-Montana Express (Brautigan) **34**:315; **42**:49-50, 55-6, 60
"Told" (Levine) **118**:300
"Told in the Desert" (Smith) **43**:423, 425
"Tolerance and Taboo: Modernist Primitivism and Postmodernist Pieties" (Perloff) **137**:302
The Toll (Mewshaw) **9**:376
Tollow Waa Talee Ma (Farah) **137**:131
"The Tollund Man" (Heaney) **5**:170; **14**:243; **25**:243, 245, 248; **74**:155; **91**:116
Tolstoy (Troyat) **23**:460-61
Tolstoy and Dostoevsky (Steiner) **24**:423-24, 427
Tolstoy's Dictaphone: Technology and the Muse (Birkerts) **116**:174
"Tom" (Lavin) **99**:319
Tom (Buzo) **61**:53, 59-62, 64-5
Tom (Cummings) **12**:146; **68**:35
"Tom Carroll" (Farrell) **4**:158
"Tom Castro, the Implausible Imposter" (Borges)
See "El impostor inverosímil Tom Castro"
Tom Fobble's Day (Garner) **17**:147-50
Tom Horn (McGuane) **45**:261-62; **127**:258, 262, 265, 267, 270, 280
"Tom Joad" (Guthrie) **35**:183-84, 189-91
"Tom Mooney" (Hughes) **108**:294
Tom o'Bedlam's Beauties (Reading) **47**:351-52
"Tom Pringle" (Simpson) **7**:426
"Tom Riley" (Delaney) **29**:146
"Tom Rivers" (Gordon) **13**:247; **29**:187; **83**:231
"Tom Thumb Runs Away" (Tournier)
See "La Fugue du petit Poucet"
"Tom Whipple" (Edmonds) **35**:155
"Toma de conciencia" (Castellanos) **66**:52
"Tomás de Utrera's First Day of Spring" (Castillo) **151**:20
Tomas Tranströmer: Selected Poems, 1954-1986 (Transtroemer) **65**:224-27, 235
"Tomato" (Pollitt) **28**:367
"Tomatoes" (Merwin) **45**:272
A Tomb (Benet)
See *Una tumba*
"The Tomb at Akr Çaar" (Pound) **4**:408
"A Tomb for Boris Davidovich" (Kiš) **57**:241
A Tomb for Boris Davidovich (Kiš) **57**:240-44, 249-53
"The Tomb of Heracles" (McAuley) **45**:249
The Tomb of Ligeia (Towne) **87**:355-56
"The Tomb of Penthesilia" (Hope) **51**:220
"The Tomb of Pletone" (Forster) **45**:131-32
"The Tomb of Stéphane Mallarmé" (Simic) **130**:319-25
The Tomb of the Kings (Hébert)
See *Le tombeau des rois*
Tomb Tapper (Blish) **14**:86

Tombe (Cixous) **92**:90
"Le tombeau des rois" (Hébert) **4**:219; **29**:228-30, 236-38
Le tombeau des rois (Hébert) **13**:268; **29**:227-30, 232, 236-38
Le tombeau des secrets (Char) **11**:114
Le Tombeau hindou (Lang) **103**:86-9
"Les tombeaux de Ravenne" (Bonnefoy) **58**:58
The Tombs of Atuan (Le Guin) **13**:347; **22**:266, 271; **71**:180-82, 184, 188-89, 191, 196, 198, 200-01; **136**:314-15, 317, 330, 332, 362-64, 366, 377, 379-80, 387-88
"Tombstone Blues" (Dylan) **4**:149; **77**:161, 180
"The Tombstone-Maker" (Sassoon) **130**:178, 182
"Tombstones" (Ammons) **57**:53, 55-6
"Tom-Dobbin" (Gunn) **32**:208
"Tommy" (Wideman) **122**:289, 346
Tommy (Russell) **16**:547-59
Tommy (Townshend) **17**:525-27, 529-31, 533-38, 540; **42**:379
"The Tommy Crans" (Bowen) **22**:65, 67
Tommy Gallagher's Crusade (Farrell) **66**:130
The Tommyknockers (King) **61**:328-30; **113**:369, 388-93
"Tomoda to Matsunaga no hanashi" (Tanizaki) **14**:527
Tomodachi, enemoto takekai (Abe) **8**:1; **81**:295, 297
"Tomorrow" (Fearing) **51**:106
"Tomorrow" (McCartney) **35**:280
"Tomorrow" (Strand) **71**:286
Tomorrow (Foote) **51**:131
Tomorrow! (Wylie) **43**:467-68
"Tomorrow and Tomorrow" (Farrell) **4**:158
Tomorrow and Yesterday (Boell)
See *Haus ohne Hüter*
The Tomorrow Boy (Chislett) **34**:146
The Tomorrow File (Sanders) **41**:378
"Tomorrow Is a Long Time" (Dylan) **77**:172
Tomorrow Morning, Faustus! (Richards) **14**:453
Tomorrow the Warriors (Alegria)
See *Mañana los guerreros*
Tomorrow to Fresh Woods (Davies) **23**:143, 145
"Tomorrow, Tomorrow" (Walcott) **67**:361
Tomorrow Will Be Better (Smith) **19**:423
Tomorrow Will Come (Almedingen) **12**:1, 3-4
"Tomorrow You Shall Reap" (Mphahlele) **25**:336
"Tomorrow's Arrangement" (Gardam) **43**:170
The Tomorrow-Tamer, and Other Stories (Laurence) **13**:341; **50**:314-15, 319; **62**:278-79
Tomorrow-Today (Kureishi) **64**:246
Tom's Midnight Garden (Pearce) **21**:281, 283-87, 289
The Tom-Walker (Sandoz) **28**:407
"Ton père. Ta soeur" (Sarraute) **31**:383
Tone Clusters (Oates) **108**:376
"Tong Raa" (p'Bitek) **96**:307
"Tongue" (Herbert) **9**:271
Tongue of Flame: The Life of Lydia Maria Child (Meltzer) **26**:297
The Tongue Set Free: Remembrance of a European Childhood (Canetti)
See *Die gerettete Zunge: Geschichte einer Jugend*
"Tongues" (Govier) **51**:166
"Tongues" (Wright) **6**:580
Tongues (Shepard) **41**:407
The Tongues of Angels (Price) **63**:339-41
"Tongues of Fire" (Smith) **73**:353, 357-59
Tongues of Flame (Parks) **147**:201-02, 204, 221
"Tongues of Men" (Steiner) **24**:433
"Tongues of Men and of Angels" (Goyen) **40**:217
"Tongues of Stone" (Plath) **11**:451
Toni (Renoir) **20**:304, 309-10
To-Night at 8:30 (Coward) **51**:69
"Tonight at Noon" (Weller) **26**:443
"Tonight at Seven-Thirty" (Auden) **123**:12, 14-6
"Tonight I Hear the Water Flowing" (Mahapatra) **33**:281
"Tonight Is a Favor to Holly" (Hempel) **39**:68-9
"Tonight My Body" (Moure) **88**:218
"Tonight the Famous Psychiatrist" (Simpson) **7**:428
Tonight We Love (Linney) **51**:263
Tonight's the Night (Young) **17**:573-76, 580, 582-83
The Tontine (Costain) **30**:97-8
"Tonton-Macoute" (Guillén) **48**:159
"Tony's Story" (Silko) **23**:408; **74**:322, 346, 349; **114**:315-16
"Too Bad" (Parker) **68**:326, 335, 338
Too Bad about the Haines Girl (Sherburne) **30**:362
Too Bad Galahad (Cohen) **19**:115
"Too Dear" (Fuller) **62**:193
Too Dear for My Possessing (Johnson) **1**:161; **27**:214-15
Too Early Lilac (Almedingen) **12**:8
Too Far to Go: The Maples Stories (Updike) **13**:563; **43**:433
Too Far to Walk (Hersey) **40**:236-37, 240
Too Great a Vine (Clarke) **9**:167
"Too Happy, Happy Tree" (Ashbery) **77**:62, 69
"Too High" (Wonder) **12**:657
"Too Late" (Jin) **109**:54
"Too Late" (Thomas) **48**:376
Too Late (Dixon) **52**:96-7, 101
Too Late American Boyhood Blues (Busch) **47**:61-4
Too Late Blues (Cassavetes) **20**:45
"The Too Late Born" (MacLeish) **68**:272
"Too Late for Prayin'" (Lightfoot) **26**:280, 282-83
Too Late for the Mashed Potato (Mortimer) **28**:285
Too Late the Phalarope (Paton) **4**:395; **25**:357-63; **106**:288-89, 292-94, 296-97, 300, 304-06
Too Loud a Solitude (Hrabal)
See *Une trop bruyante solitude*
"Too Many Mornings" (Sondheim) **30**:387
"Too Many People" (McCartney) **12**:371
"Too Much" (Moore) **47**:265
Too Much Flesh and Jabez (Dowell) **60**:97-9, 101
"Too Much Information" (Police, The) **26**:365
Too Much Is Too Much (Cendrars) **106**:177-78
"Too Much Monkey Business" (Berry) **17**:53, 55
Too Much of Everything (Wylie) **43**:463
"Too Much of Nothing" (Dylan) **77**:178
"Too Much on My Mind" (Davies) **21**:88-9
"The Too Much Rain, or Assault of the Mold Spores" (Fitzgerald) **143**:
"Too Much Trouble" (Amis) **40**:43, 45
"Too Nice a Day to Die" (Woolrich) **77**:390, 392, 396
"Too Sensitive" (Bukowski) **41**:74; **108**:85
"Too Vague" (Fuller) **62**:193
Tool of the Trade (Haldeman) **61**:181-84
Tools of Modern Biology (Berger) **12**:38
"Toome" (Heaney) **7**:148; **14**:242-43; **25**:245
"The Toome Road" (Heaney) **74**:163; **91**:101, 117
"The Tooth" (Jackson) **60**:212, 235
"Tooth" (Swan) **69**:363
Tooth Imprints on a Corn Dog (Leyner) **92**:292-94
The Tooth of Crime (Shepard) **4**:490-91; **6**:496-97; **17**:441-44, 448; **41**:406, 410, 412; **44**:270
"Toothache" (Sargeson) **31**:365, 374
Tootsie (Gelbart) **61**:146-47
Top Girls (Churchill) **31**:87-9; **55**:122, 126-27
The Top of the Hill (Shaw) **23**:399
"Top of the Pops" (Davies) **21**:91
"Top Rock" (Stern) **40**:408
"Top Secret" (Voinovich) **147**:272
Top Soil (Rosenblatt) **15**:448
"The Top Ten Best Sellers" (Vidal) **8**:528
Topaz (Hitchcock) **16**:348, 353
Topaz (Uris) **7**:492; **32**:432-33
"The Topic" (Arghezi)
See "Subiectul"
Topoemas (Paz) **65**:199
"The Topography of History" (McGrath) **59**:180
Topolek moi v krasnoi kosynke (Aitmatov) **71**:3, 13-14, 16, 33
Topologie d'une cité fantôme (Robbe-Grillet) **8**:453-54; **10**:438; **14**:462; **43**:361-62, 367-68; **128**:359, 363, 370, 378, 382
Topology of a Phantom City (Robbe-Grillet)
See *Topologie d'une cité fantôme*
"Topos" (Arreola) **147**:14, 34
Tops and Bottoms (Streatfeild) **21**:395
"Topsy Turvy" (Powys) **46**:325
Tor Hapela'ot (Appelfeld) **23**:35, 38; **47**:2-5
"Torah as Feminism, Feminism as Torah" (Owens) **155**:
"Torahas Feminism, Feminism as Torah" (Ozick) **155**:180
The Torch in My Ear (Canetti)
See *Die Fackel im Ohr: Lebensgeschichte 1921-1931*
"Torch Procession" (Celan)
See "Fackelzug"
"Torch Song" (Cheever) **15**:127, 130; **64**:65
Torch Song (Roiphe) **9**:455-56
Torch Song Trilogy (Fierstein) **33**:152-57
Torches (Tate) **25**:427
"Torguyut arbuzami" (Voznesensky) **15**:555
Torment (Bergman)
See *Hets*
"Tormento del amor" (Aleixandre) **9**:12
"The Torments of Conscience" (Yevtushenko) **3**:547
"Tormer's Lay" (Le Guin) **22**:265
"The Torn Cloth" (Duncan) **41**:129
Torn Curtain (Hitchcock) **16**:347-48, 353
Torn Curtain (Moore) **90**:262
"The Torn Sky" (Jordan) **114**:146
"Torna Zeffiro" (Ekelöf) **27**:119
"Tornado" (Stafford) **29**:380
"Tornado Blues" (Brown) **23**:96; **59**:266
"Tornant al pais" (Pasolini) **106**:229
"Toronto Means the Meeting Place" (Crase) **58**:162
"Toronto the Ugly" (Lane) **25**:284
"Torpid Smoke" (Nabokov) **3**:354
"The Torque" (Forster) **3**:161
Torquemada (Fast) **23**:158
"La torre" (Olson) **29**:334
The Torrent (Hébert)
See *Le torrent*
Le torrent (Hébert) **4**:219-20; **13**:266-67; **29**:229-31, 237-38, 240
A Torrent of Faces (Blish) **14**:85
The Torrents of Spring: A Romantic Novel in Honor of the Passing of a Great Race (Hemingway) **6**:227; **8**:283; **30**:191; **39**:401, 403; **41**:200; **61**:192
"Torridge" (Trevor) **14**:536-37; **71**:323; **116**:374-75
Torse Three (Middleton) **13**:387
"Torso" (Brodsky) **36**:76
Törst (Bergman) **16**:51, 66, 72; **72**:40, 52
The Tortilla Curtain (Boyle) **90**:64-5
Tortilla Flat (Steinbeck) **1**:325; **5**:406-07; **9**:513-14, 517-18, 520; **13**:530-31; **21**:366, 368, 381-82, 386, 389-91; **34**:405, 409-10, 413-14; **45**:370, 373-74; **59**:317, 322, 334, 351; **75**:353, 357; **124**:393
Tortuga (Anaya) **23**:26; **148**:6-13, 15, 19, 27, 30, 35, 39, 47
"Tortuous Road" (Arghezi)
See "Cale frîntă"
"Torture" (Atwood) **25**:65
"Torture" (Ortese)
See "Supplizio"
"The Torturer" (Dürrenmatt)
See "Der Folterknecht"

"Tortures" (Szymborska) **99**:195, 206
"Tosca" (Allende) **97**:12
Tossing and Turning (Updike) **23**:475-76; **43**:429-30
"Total amor" (Aleixandre) **36**:29
Total Eclipse (Hampton) **4**:211
"The Total Library" (Borges) **48**:44
Total Loss Farm: A Year in the Life (Mungo) **72**:288-92
"Total Mobilisation" (Jünger)
See *Die totale Mobilmachung*
"Total Stranger" (Cozzens) **92**:202
Die totale Mobilmachung (Jünger) **125**:233, 245, 254, 259
Totalitarianism (Arendt)
See *The Origins of Totalitarianism*
"The Totally Rich" (Brunner) **8**:108; **10**:77
"Totem" (King) **89**:98
"Totem" (Plath) **9**:426-27, 433; **17**:365; **111**:182, 205
"Totem" (Senghor) **130**:266-67, 280
Le totémisme aujourd'hui (Lévi-Strauss) **38**:294, 305
Das Totenschiff (Traven) **8**:517-23; **11**:535-39
"Totentanz: The Coquette" (Hope) **3**:250; **51**:220
"Ein totes Kind spricht" (Sachs) **98**:364
"Toto, We're Back!" (Delany) **141**:151
"Tou Wan Speaks to Her Husband, Liu Sheng" (Dove) **81**:135, 137
"The Touch" (Blackburn) **9**:100
"The Touch" (Sexton) **123**:442
The Touch (Bergman)
See *Beröringen*
Touch (Gunn) **3**:215; **6**:221; **32**:208, 211; **81**:180
Touch (Josipovici) **153**:219-24
The Touch (Keyes) **80**:164
Touch (Leonard) **71**:217, 221; **120**:303-04
Touch and Go (Fisher) **76**:342
Touch and Go (Kerr) **22**:254
Touch and Go (Poole) **17**:373
"Touch Me" (Kunitz) **148**:128, 137, 141-42, 150
"Touch Me" (Morrison) **17**:289
Touch Not the Cat (Stewart) **7**:468; **35**:394
"A Touch of Autumn in the Air" (O'Faolain) **32**:343; **70**:312
A Touch of Chill (Aiken) **35**:18-19
A Touch of Danger (Jones) **3**:262
Touch of Evil (Welles) **20**:435, 442, 449, 452; **80**:386, 388-89, 391, 393, 395-96, 414
"A Touch of Gothic" (Gardam) **43**:169
A Touch of Infinity: Thirteen New Stories of Fantasy and Science Fiction (Fast) **23**:159
A Touch of Magic (Cavanna) **12**:100
"A Touch of Snow" (Davidson) **13**:168
Touch: Selected Poems, 1960-1970 (Bowering) **47**:21-2
Touch the Water, Touch the Wind (Oz) **5**:334-35; **8**:435
"Touched" (Broumas) **73**:15
"The Touching" (Livesay) **79**:337, 343, 350-51
"Touching" (Wolf) **150**:228
Touching (Neufeld) **17**:308-09
Touching Bottom (Tesich) **40**:421
"Touch-up Man" (Komunyakaa) **94**:240
"The Tough Guy" (Ferber) **93**:138
Tough Guys Don't Dance (Mailer) **39**:422, 424; **74**:207-10, 218-19, 224, 336
"The Toughest Indian in the World" (Alexie) **154**:45, 48
The Toughest Indian in the World (Alexie) **154**:45-8
Toujours (Audiberti) **38**:21
Toujours Provence (Mayle) **89**:145-47, 149-51, 153-54
"The Tour" (Plath) **14**:427; **51**:343; **111**:172-74
"La tour" (Theriault) **79**:407
"Tour 5" (Hayden) **37**:157-58
Tour of Duty (Dos Passos) **25**:145
"Touris" (Bennett) **28**:27
"The Tourist and the Geisha" (Enright) **4**:154
"The Tourist and the Town" (Rich) **7**:368; **73**:330; **125**:310, 330
"The Tourist from Syracuse" (Justice) **102**:279-80
"Tourist Pitch for Recife" (Cabral de Melo Neto)
See "Pregão turístico do Recife"
"Tourist Proclamation For Recife" (Cabral de Melo Neto)
See "Pregão turístico do Recife"
"Tourist Promotion" (Enright) **31**:150
"Tourists" (Alexie) **154**:22
"Tourists" (Amichai) **116**:127
"The Tourists" (McGrath) **59**:178
A Tourist's Guide to Ireland (O'Flaherty) **34**:356
"Tourists of the Revolution" (Enzensberger) **43**:148
"Tourists on Paros" (Ryan) **65**:209, 216
Tourmaline (Stow) **23**:433-35; **48**:356, 360
Tournament (Foote) **75**:230-31, 236-37, 240
The Tournament (Vansittart) **42**:392
"Tournesol" (Breton) **54**:27
Tours of the Black Clock (Erickson) **64**:139-42, 144-45
Tous contre tous (Adamov) **4**:5; **25**:12-13, 17-18, 20
Tous les hommes sont mortels (Beauvoir) **1**:19; **8**:60; **31**:40-1; **44**:343, 345, 350; **71**:48-9, 56, 67-8, 85
"toussaint" (Shange) **25**:402
Toussaint l'Ouveture: La Révolution Française et la problème colonial (Césaire) **19**:96
Tout compte fait (Beauvoir) **4**:47-9; **8**:58, 63; **44**:343, 349-50; **71**:79-80, 82-3; **124**:130, 144, 167
Tout l'or du monde (Clair) **20**:65-6
Tout va bien (Godard) **20**:146-47, 150
"Toute à ce besoin d'évasion" (Damas) **84**:180
Toute la mémoire du monde (Resnais) **16**:496, 503, 506, 510
"Toutes Directions" (Howard) **7**:164
Toutes les femmes sont fatales (Mauriac) **9**:363
"Toward" (Loewinsohn) **52**:284
"Toward a Definition of Marriage" (Van Duyn) **63**:435, 440; **116**:413, 426, 429
"Toward a Film on the River Po" (Antonioni) **144**:77
"Toward a More Feminist Criticism" (Rich) **73**:322
Toward a New Life (Nakos) **29**:322-23
"Toward a New Yiddish" (Ozick) **28**:352; **62**:349; **155**:128, 171
"Toward a Poetic Art" (Queneau) **42**:337
Toward a Radical Middle: Fourteen Pieces of Reporting and Criticism (Adler) **31**:12-13
Toward a Recognition of Androgyny (Heilbrun) **25**:253-54
"Toward a Socialist Theory of Racism" (West) **134**:379
"Toward a Successful Marriage" (Gordon) **26**:139
"Toward a Woman-Centered University" (Rich) **18**:448
"Toward an Organic Philosophy" (Rexroth) **22**:345; **49**:280, 284-85; **112**:376, 390, 397, 404
"Toward Certain Divorce" (Bell) **8**:65; **31**:47
"Toward Clairvoyance" (Fulton) **52**:158
"Toward Climax" (Snyder) **120**:332
"Toward Nightfall" (Simic) **49**:341
Toward the African Revolution: Political Essays (Fanon)
See *Pour la révolution africaine: Ecrits politiques*
Toward the End of Time (Updike) **139**:373-76, 380
"Toward the Imagination of Buffoonery and Regeneration" (Oe)
See "Dōke to saisei e no sōzōryku"
"Toward the Island" (Celan)
See "Inselhin"
"Toward the Jurassic Age" (Alegria) **75**:36, 38-9
"Toward the Piraeus" (H. D.) **73**:121
Toward Yoknapatawpha and Beyond (Brooks)
See *William Faulkner: Toward Yoknapatawpha and Beyond*
"Toward yYavnh" (Ozick) **155**:172
Towards a Better Life (Burke) **2**:87-8
Towards a Critique of a Political Economy of Signs (Baudrillard)
See *Pour une critique de l'économie politique du signe*
Towards a New Cold war: Essays on the Current Crisis and How We Got There (Chomsky) **132**:23, 40, 67
Towards a New Novel (Robbe-Grillet) **4**:449; **128**:340, 368
Towards a New Poetry (Wakoski) **40**:452-53, 458
"Towards a Philosophy of the Act" (Bakhtin)
See "K filosofii postupka"
"Towards a Semiological Guerrilla Warfare" (Eco) **142**:63
"Towards a Theory of Treason" (Enzensberger) **43**:149
"Towards an Essay: My Upstate New York Journals" (Kroetsch) **132**:202
"Towards Autumn" (Hacker) **72**:182
"Towards Dialectical Criticism" (Jameson) **142**:218
Towards the Human (Smith) **64**:400
"Towards the Imminent Days" (Murray) **40**:335-36, 340
Towards the Last Spike (Pratt) **19**:376, 380, 383-84
Towards the Mountain (Paton) **25**:361, 364; **55**:311, 313-14; **106**:299, 305
"Towards the Twenty-First Century" (Barzun) **145**:74, 77, 101
Towards Zero (Christie) **8**:142; **12**:114, 125; **48**:72; **110**:133
"The Tower" (Neruda) **7**:261
The Tower (Vesaas)
See *Tårnet*
The Tower (Weiss) **15**:563; **51**:387
"The Tower beyond Tragedy" (Jeffers) **54**:233, 235, 237-38, 246, 248; **11**:304-06, 310
The Tower Beyond Tragedy (Jeffers) **54**:251
The Tower of Babel (Arrabal) **58**:17
The Tower of Babel (Canetti)
See *Die Blendung*
The Tower of Babel (Merton) **83**:396
Tower of Glass (Silverberg) **140**:342, 378, 380
Tower of Ivory (MacLeish) **68**:285
The Tower Struck by Lightning (Arrabal) **58**:23-4
Towers of Healing (Oe)
See *Chiryō-tō*
The Towers of Silence (Scott)
See *The Raj Quartet*
"The Towers of Toron" (Delany) **14**:144
"Town" (Soto) **80**:287, 294
The Town (Faulkner) **6**:176; **14**:178-79
The Town (Richter) **30**:312-15, 318-19, 324-25, 328
"Town and Country Lovers" (Gordimer) **18**:190-91; **123**:130
Town and Country Matters (Hollander) **5**:187; **8**:302
The Town and the City (Kerouac) **2**:226; **3**:264; **5**:214-15; **14**:304; **29**:270, 272; **61**:310
The Town beyond the Wall (Wiesel)
See *La ville de la chance*
Town Burning (Williams) **14**:581, 583
"A Town Called Malice" (Weller) **26**:447
The Town Cats, and Other Tales (Alexander) **35**:28
"Town Center in December" (Corn) **33**:118
"The Town Clerk's Views" (Betjeman) **6**:68; **43**:37, 40, 42
"Town Crier Exclusive, Confessions of a Princess Manque: How Royals Found Me

Unsuitable to Marry Their Larry" (Elkin) **91**:218-19
"The Town Dump" (Nemerov) **2**:308
"Town Edge" (Shapcott) **38**:402
Town in Darkness (Johnson)
See *Stad i möerker*
"A Town in Eastern Oregon" (Davis) **49**:91
Town in Light (Johnson)
See *Stad i ljus*
Town in Tears (Seifert)
See *Město v slzách*
Town Life (Parini) **54**:363-64
A Town like Alice (Shute)
See *The Legacy*
"The Town of Hill" (Hall) **37**:147; **151**:196
The Town of Hill (Hall) **37**:146-47
"Town Report, 1942" (Cowley) **39**:460
The Town Scold (Johnson) **15**:480
"Townend, 1976" (Davie) **31**:112, 118
"Townies" (Dubus) **36**:145; **97**:201, 204, 206, 208, 223
The Townsman (Buck) **11**:76
Toxic Shock (Paretsky) **135**:361
Toxique (Sagan) **17**:424
A Toy Epic (Humphreys) **47**:180, 186-87
The Toy Fair (Moss) **7**:247; **45**:292
"The Toy Pilgrim" (Cohen) **19**:113
"Toyland" (Fisher) **25**:158-59
Toys in a Field (Komunyakaa) **94**:236
Toys in the Attic (Hellman) **2**:187; **4**:220; **18**:224; **34**:349, 351-52; **44**:529; **52**:191, 202
Toys in the Attic (Hill) **26**:204
"Toys of Tamison" (Norton) **12**:467
"Tra notte e giorno" (Luzi) **13**:353
"The Trace" (Fisher) **25**:159
"The Trace of Being" (Lane) **25**:286
"Traceleen at Dawn" (Gilchrist) **48**:120, 122
"Traceleen, She's Still Talking" (Gilchrist) **143**:329
"Traces of Living Things" (Niedecker) **42**:296-97
The Traces of Thomas Hariot (Rukeyser) **6**:479; **15**:459-60
Tracey and Hepburn (Kanin) **22**:231
Track 29 (Potter) **58**:400; **86**:346; **123**:243
"The Track Meet" (Schwartz) **45**:355-56; **87**:334
The Track of the Cat (Clark) **28**:77-84
Track of the Gloconda (Ellison) **139**:132
The Trackers of Oxyrhynchus (Harrison) **129**:194, 211, 221-24
"Tracking Level" (Ellison) **42**:131
"Tracks" (Montague) **13**:390
"Tracks" (Transtroemer) **65**:223, 226, 228
Tracks (Erdrich) **54**:170-73; **120**:139, 157-60, 162, 165-68, 174-78, 180-81, 184, 186-88, 190, 195
"The Tracks of My Tears" (Robinson) **21**:344, 347-48, 351
"Tractor" (Hughes) **37**:174; **119**:271
Tractor (Ritsos) **31**:324
"The Tractor in Spring" (Levi) **41**:244, 248
"The Trade" (Levine) **118**:323
Trade Wind (Kaye) **28**:199, 202
"Trade Winds" (Cortázar) **33**:124
"A Traded Car" (Updike) **15**:540-41
Trader to the Stars (Anderson) **15**:11
"The Traders" (Asimov) **26**:63
Il tradimento (Landolfi) **49**:216
Tradition and Poetic Structure (Cunningham) **31**:101, 103
"Tradition and the Individual Talent" (Eliot) **6**:160, 164; **13**:195-96; **15**:213; **24**:159, 163, 165, 170-72, 174-75, 178, 180-83, 187; **34**:528; **41**:155, 157; **55**:347, 356; **57**:206; **113**:218
"Tradition and the Individual Talent: The Bratislava Spiccato" (Mathews) **52**:308, 312-13
"Tradition and the West Indian Novel" (Harris) **25**:204-05
"Tradition and Value" (Auden) **123**:8
"Tradition, Society, and the Arts" (McAuley) **45**:251
Tradition, the Writer, and Society: Critical Essays (Harris) **25**:204
Traditional Hungarian Songs (Snodgrass) **18**:494
"Traditional Songs" (Shapcott) **38**:404
"Traditions" (Heaney) **7**:148; **14**:242; **74**:157
"Traducción do James Jogeo, la ultima hojo de Ulises" (Borges) **4**:71
Traduction et introduction à l'origine de la géométrie d'Edmund Husserl (Derrida) **87**:72
"Los traductores de las 1001 noches" (Borges) **83**:163
Traed mewn cyffion (Roberts) **15**:445
"Traffic" (Transtroemer) **65**:223
Traffic (SODERBERGH) **154**:350-56
"A Traffic Victim Sends a Sonnet of Confused Thanks to God as the Sovereign Host" (Ciardi) **129**:56
"Traficante, Too" (Castillo) **151**:11
El tragaluz (Buero Vallejo) **15**:98, 101-02; **46**:95-6; **139**:6, 10, 14-15, 19-20, 25, 32-3, 39, 43-4, 52-3, 57
"La tragedia" (Buero Vallejo) **139**:49-52
"The Tragedians" (Prokosch) **48**:309
"La tragédie du langage" (Ionesco) **41**:225
La tragédie du Roi Christophe (Césaire) **19**:96, 99; **32**:112; **112**:3-4, 7, 21, 28-9
"Tragedy" (Graham) **48**:149
"A Tragedy" (Lavin) **4**:281
Tragedy and Social Evolution (Figes) **31**:164-65
"Tragedy and the Common Man" (Miller) **6**:333; **10**:346; **15**:375; **26**:315-16; **47**:251
"Tragedy and the Whole Truth" (Huxley) **79**:310
"The Tragedy at Maradon Manor" (Christie) **110**:111
The Tragedy of King Christophe (Césaire)
See *La tragédie du Roi Christophe*
The Tragedy of Nan, and Other Plays (Masefield) **47**:225, 229
The Tragedy of Pompey the Great (Masefield) **11**:358
"The Tragedy of Taliped Decanus" (Barth) **9**:64, 69
"The Tragedy of the Leaves" (Bukowski) **41**:65; **108**:110
The Tragedy of X (Queen) **3**:421; **11**:459
The Tragedy of Y (Queen) **3**:421; **11**:459
The Tragedy of Z (Queen) **11**:459
"Tragic Architecture" (Simic) **130**:338
"The Tragic Fallacy" (Krutch) **24**:282
Tragic Ground (Caldwell) **14**:97; **50**:300; **60**:54-5, 66
"The Tragic Tryst" (MacDiarmid) **11**:334
Tragic Ways of Killing a Woman (Loreaux) **65**:327
La traición de Rita Hayworth (Puig) **3**:407; **5**:354-56; **10**:420; **28**:369-72; **65**:268, 271-73; **133**:296-300, 304, 306, 313, 315, 317-18, 320-21, 324, 332, 335, 339-41, 344, 347, 372-74
Trail Blazer of the Seas (Latham) **12**:322
"Trail Crew Camp at Bear Valley, 9000 Feet. Northern Sierra—White Bone and Threads of Snowmelt Water" (Snyder) **5**:394
Trail Driving Days (Brown) **47**:36-7
"The Trail into Kansas" (Merwin) **13**:386
Trailerpark (Banks) **37**:26-7; **72**:4, 9, 11, 14, 17
"The Train" (Carver) **126**:107, 110, 124, 173-74, 185
"Train" (Erdrich) **120**:132
"The Train" (Le Guin) **45**:219; **136**:361
"The Train" (Salinas) **90**:326
"The Train" (Walcott) **25**:452
"The Train" (Williams) **148**:366
The Train (Simenon)
See *Le train*
Le train (Simenon) **1**:397; **47**:379
Le train bleu (Cocteau) **15**:134
"Train for Dublin" (MacNeice) **53**:231, 234
"The Train from Bordeaux" (Duras) **100**:120
"Train from Rhodesia" (Gordimer) **18**:184
"Train in Vain" (Clash) **30**:46-7, 52
"Train Journey" (Wright) **53**:419, 431
A Train of Powder (West) **7**:525-26; **9**:561, 563; **50**:404
"Train Ride" (Berrigan) **37**:46
"Train Rising out of the Sea" (Ashbery) **15**:34; **41**:38
The Train Robbers (Read) **25**:376-77
"Train Song" (Bogan) **93**:77
"Train Time" (Bogan) **46**:90
Train to Pakistan (Singh) **11**:505-07
"Train Tune" (Bogan) **93**:65, 78
"The Train Was on Time" (Boell)
See "Der Zug war pünktlich"
Train Whistle Guitar (Murray) **73**:226-29, 231, 235-36, 238-42, 244
"The Trainee 1914" (Murray) **40**:333
"The Trains" (Aickman) **57**:4, 6-7
"The Trains" (Wright) **53**:427
Trainspotting (Welsh) **144**:312-31, 333-38, 342-43, 346
Traité du pianiste (Bonnefoy) **58**:57
Traité du style (Aragon) **22**:37, 41
"The Traitor" (Maugham) **67**:216
Traitor (Potter) **123**:232-33
The Traitor (Wouk) **38**:446-47
"Traitors" (Stern) **40**:408
The Traitors (Forman) **21**:117, 123
Traitors Gate (Perry) **126**:334, 336-38, 340
Traitor's Purse (Allingham) **19**:16, 17
"Traits and Stories" (Montague) **46**:270
"Trakat poetycki" (Milosz) **56**:235; **82**:297-300, 306
"Tralala" (Selby) **8**:475-76
The Tram (Kieslowski) **120**:243
"La trama" (Borges) **6**:90
La trama celeste (Bioy Casares) **88**:60
"Tramp" (Thomas) **48**:376
"The Tramp at Piraeus" (Naipaul) **105**:157
"A Tramp at the Door" (Roy) **14**:469
"La trampa" (Arreola) **147**:27
"La trampa" (Parra) **102**:337-38
La trampa (Matute) **11**:364-68
"Trampled under Foot" (Page and Plant) **12**:477, 480, 482
"The Tranced" (Roethke) **3**:433
"Tranquil River" (Milosz) **11**:378
"Transaction" (Updike) **15**:547
Trans-Atlantic (Gombrowicz)
See *Trans-Atlantyk*
Transatlantic Blues (Sheed) **10**:472-74; **53**:336, 339
A Transatlantic Tunnel, Hurrah! (Harrison)
See *Tunnel through the Deeps*
Trans-Atlantyk (Gombrowicz) **7**:124; **49**:122, 129-31
Transbluency (Baraka) **115**:38
"Transcedental Etude" (Rich) **18**:450; **36**:376; **125**:315
Transcendent Censorship (Blaga)
See *Cenzura transcendenta*
"Transcendental Experience in Relation to Religion and Psychosis" (Laing) **95**:178
"Transcendental Meditation" (Wilson) **12**:641
Transcendental Style in Film (Schrader) **26**:385, 387
"Transcendental View" (Blaga) **75**:78
"Transcending Destiny" (Ellison) **42**:131
"Transcontinental" (Derleth) **31**:136
Trans-Europ-Express (Robbe-Grillet) **6**:466; **14**:457; **128**:332, 346, 356, 362, 381
"Transfer of Title" (Phillips) **28**:363-64
The Transfiguration of Benno Blimpie (Innaurato) **21**:190, 192; **60**:199-202, 204, 206-07

The Transformation (MacBeth) **5**:265
Transformation: Understanding the Three Levels of Masculine Consciousness (Johnson) **70**:426
"Transformations" (Engel) **36**:160
"Transformations" (Harjo) **83**:269
"Transformations" (Oates) **108**:354
"Transformations" (Seifert)
See "Proměny"
"Transformations" (Waddington) **28**:438
Transformations (Sexton) **2**:392; **4**:482-83; **6**:494; **8**:483; **10**:468-69; **15**:470-72; **53**:314, 319, 321, 323; **123**:406, 420
"Transformed Nonconformist" (King) **83**:347
Transformer (Reed) **21**:304-06, 312
"Trans-Global Express" (Weller) **26**:447
The Transgressors (Thompson) **69**:384
"Transient Barracks" (Jarrell) **9**:299
"Transit" (Wilbur) **53**:413
Transit (Seghers) **7**:408
"Transit Bed" (Calvino)
See "Un letto di passaggio"
"Transit of the Gods" (Raine) **45**:337
The Transit of Venus (Hazzard) **18**:218-20
"Transit Passengers" (Gardam) **43**:169
A Transit to Narcissus (Mailer) **111**:135
"The Transition" (Grace) **56**:111
"Transition" (Okigbo) **84**:306-07, 309
Transitional Poem (Day Lewis) **6**:128; **10**:126-27, 131, 133
"The Translatability of Poetry" (Davie) **10**:124
"Translated from the American" (Alexie) **154**:12-13
"Translation" (Fuller) **28**:150, 159
"Translation" (Oates) **134**:246
"Translation" (Strand) **71**:280, 287-88
"Translation" (Wheelock) **14**:570
"Translation from Chopin" (Randall) **135**:399
"Translations" (Rich) **7**:372
Translations (Friel) **42**:171-74; **59**:146-49; **115**:221-24, 227-31, 233, 235, 237, 239-48, 250, 257
Translations (Tomlinson) **45**:405
"Translations from the English" (Starbuck) **53**:355
"The Translators of the 1001 Nights" (Borges)
See "Los traductores de las 1001 noches"
The Transmigration of Timothy Archer (Dick) **72**:114, 119-20
"The Transmutation into English" (Rakosi) **47**:347
"Transparencies" (L'Heureux) **52**:273
"Transparencies" (Stevenson) **33**:382-83
Transparencies (Johnson) **15**:480
"Transparent Garments" (Hass) **18**:213
The Transparent Sea (Dudek) **11**:159
Transparent Things (Nabokov) **2**:302-03, 305; **3**:353-54; **6**:351, 355; **8**:410, 412, 416, 418; **15**:393-95
"Transparently" (Ezekiel) **61**:105, 108
"Les transparents" (Char) **9**:161
"Transplanting" (Roethke) **101**:295
Transplants (Macdonald) **13**:355-56; **19**:290-91
"Transport" (Meredith) **55**:192
"Transport" (Simic) **130**:345
Transport from Paradise (Lustig) **56**:184
"The Transport of Slaves from Maryland to Mississippi" (Dove) **81**:137
"Transportation" (Oe) **86**:227
"Transsiberian" (Cendrars)
See "Prose du transsibérien et de la petite Jeanne de France"
"The Trap" (Tuohy) **37**:429
The Trap (Jacobson) **14**:289
The Trap (Rozewicz)
See *Pułapka*
Trap for Cinderella (Japrisot)
See *Piege pour Cendrillon*
"Trap Lines" (King) **89**:97
"Trapped Dingo" (Wright) **53**:418, 427
Trapped in the Arctic (Berton) **104**:61
"The Trapper" (Klappert) **57**:259
Trappers (Williams) **33**:442
"The Trappist Cemetery, Gethsemani" (Merton) **83**:393
Traps (Churchill) **31**:84
The Traps (Duerrenmatt)
See *Der Nihilist*
"Tras os montes" (Sissman) **18**:488, 490
"Trash" (Thomas) **107**:338, 340, 342
"Trash" (Williams) **33**:441; **148**:321
Trash (Allison) **78**:2-3, 5-7, 9, 11; **153**:5-7, 10, 12, 17-18, 20, 25, 28-30, 51
"Trashabet" (Redgrove) **41**:354
"Trasimeno" (Simpson) **149**:325, 328
"Trastevere" (Denby) **48**:82
Trasumanar e organizzar (Pasolini) **106**:253, 265-66
Tratados en la habana (Lezama Lima) **4**:288; **101**:121
"Il tratto di Apelle" (Pasternak) **7**:293; **10**:387; **18**:385
A Traumatic Tale (Rozewicz)
See *Opowiadanie traumatyczne: Duszyczka*
Träume (Eich) **15**:203-05
Travaux d'approche (Butor) **3**:93
"Travel" (Avison) **97**:123
"Travel" (Colwin) **23**:129
"Travel from Home" (Bullins) **7**:37
Travel Notes (Cendrars) **106**:190-91, 194, 198
"A Travel Piece" (Atwood) **25**:62
"Travel Report" (Wolf) **58**:421
"The Travel Sack" (Elytis)
See "Traveling Bag"
"The Traveler" (Stegner) **49**:351; **81**:346
The Traveler (Connelly) **7**:57
"Traveler, Conjuror, Journeyman" (Page) **18**:379
Traveler from a Small Kingdom (Neville) **12**:450-51
The Traveler in Black (Brunner) **8**:106
Travelers (Jhabvala)
See *A New Dominion*
"Traveler's Song" (White) **39**:376
Traveler's Tree (Tzara)
See *L'arbre des voyageurs*
"Travelin Man" (Matthiessen) **64**:321, 323-24
"Travelin' Man" (Seger) **35**:381, 383
"Traveling" (Alexie) **154**:4
"Traveling" (Paley) **140**:290
"Traveling Bag" (Elytis) **100**:171, 178, 187
"The Traveling Companion" (Padilla) **38**:349, 352
"Traveling Home: High School Reunion" (Theroux) **46**:401
"Traveling IV" (Hamburger) **5**:159
The Traveling Lady (Foote) **51**:130
"Traveling Light" (Fulton) **52**:160
Traveling on Credit (Halpern) **14**:231-32
"The Traveling Photographer: Circa 1880" (Smith) **42**:349
"Traveling Salesman" (Dybek) **114**:62-3, 67
"Traveling through the Dark" (Stafford) **29**:382
Traveling through the Dark (Stafford) **4**:520; **7**:460, 462; **29**:384
"Traveling with You" (Oates) **3**:359
Travelingue (Aymé) **11**:22-3
"The Traveller" (Berryman) **13**:76
"Traveller" (Gilchrist) **143**:274, 297, 320, 322, 331-32
"The Traveller" (Livesay) **79**:332
"A Traveller" (Paulin) **37**:352
"The Traveller" (Reid) **33**:350
"The Traveller" (Stevenson) **33**:379
The Traveller and His Child (Tindall) **7**:474
"Traveller, If You Come to the Spa" (Boell)
See "Wanderer, kommst du nach Spa..."
"Traveller, If You Go to Spa" (Boell)
See "Wanderer, kommst du nach Spa..."
"A Traveller in Time" (Young) **5**:524
Traveller without Luggage (Anouilh)
See *Le voyageur sans bagage*
"The Travellers" (Aldiss) **14**:13
"The Travellers" (Alexander) **121**:9
"Traveller's Curse after Misdirection" (Graves) **45**:169
Traveller's Litany (Baxter) **14**:61
"Travellin' Man" (McFadden) **48**:255
"Travelling" (Merwin) **88**:194
"Travelling" (Simic) **9**:481
Travelling (Hamburger) **5**:158; **14**:234
Travelling behind Glass (Stevenson) **7**:462-63; **33**:382
"The Travelling Companion" (Kinsella) **138**:133
The Travelling Entertainer (Jolley) **46**:213
"Travelling Even Farther North" (Astley) **41**:49
Travelling North (Williamson) **56**:435-36
Travelling People (Johnson) **6**:262; **9**:301
"Travelling Slaughterhouse" (Simic) **130**:317
"Travelling to My Second Marriage on the Day of the First Moonshot" (Nye) **42**:305
A Travelling Woman (Wain) **2**:457; **46**:409-10
"Travelogue" (Reading) **47**:350
"Travelogue in a Shooting Gallery" (Fearing) **51**:110
Travels (Amichai) **57**:41-2
Travels (Crichton) **54**:75-6
Travels (Merwin) **88**:209-13
"Travels in Georgia" (McPhee) **36**:296
"Travels in Hyperreality" (Eco) **60**:111; **142**:64
Travels in Hyperreality (Eco) **60**:111-13, 124; **142**:62, 65, 83, 93-4, 96
Travels in Nihilon (Sillitoe) **3**:448; **57**:397
"Travels of a Latter-Day Benjamin of Tudela" (Amichai)
See "Mas'ot Binyamin ha'aharon mitudela"
The Travels of Ibn Fattuma (Mahfouz)
See *Rihlat Ibn Fattuma*
The Travels of Jaimie McPheeters (Taylor) **14**:533-35
The Travels of Marrakesh (Canetti)
See *Die Stimmen von Marrakesch: Aufzeichnungen nach einer Reise*
"Travels of the Last Benjamin of Tudela" (Amichai)
See "Mas'ot Binyamin ha'aharon mitudela"
Travels through New England (Gray) **49**:147
Travels to the Enu: Stories of a Shipwreck (Lind) **27**:270-72; **82**:143-44
Travels with Charley in Search of America (Steinbeck) **5**:405; **21**:370, 392-93; **34**:409; **45**:382; **59**:353
Travels with My Aunt (Greene) **3**:208, 211, 214; **14**:219; **27**:173; **72**:164; **70**:292-93, 295; **125**:188
Travels with Myself and Another (Gellhorn) **14**:196; **60**:193, 195
Traversée de la mangrove (Condé) **92**:115-26, 132
Travesties (Stoppard) **4**:527; **5**:412-13; **8**:501-04; **15**:519-21, 524; **29**:394, 397, 399-401, 403, 406; **34**:280-81; **63**:404; **91**:187, 189
Travesty (Hawkes) **7**:143-45; **9**:269; **15**:278; **27**:190-91, 194-95; **49**:162-63
A Travesty (Westlake) **33**:438
Travnik Chronicle (Andrić) **8**:20
Trawl (Johnson) **6**:262-63; **9**:300-01, 303
Trayectoria del polvo (Castellanos) **66**:44, 50-1
Tread the Dark (Ignatow) **14**:275-77; **40**:259
Tread the Green Grass (Green) **25**:197, 199
Treason's Harbour (O'Brian) **152**:297-98
Treasure Hunt (Buechner) **9**:136-37
Treasure in Earthen Vessels (Gustafson) **100**:229
The Treasure Is the Rose (Cunningham) **12**:166
"The Treasure of Gold" (Carroll) **10**:98
The Treasure of Siegfried (Almedingen) **12**:1
The Treasure of the Sierra Madre (Huston) **20**:158, 162, 165
The Treasure of the Sierra Madre (Traven) **8**:518-20, 522
Treasures of Time (Lively) **32**:273-74
Treasury Holiday: Thirty-Four Fits for the Opening of Fiscal Year 1968 (Harmon) **38**:241-42
A Treasury of Yiddish Poetry (Howe) **85**:147

A Treasury of Yiddish Stories (Howe) **85**:126, 147
"Treat Her Gently—Lonely Old People" (McCartney) **35**:282
"Treatise on Poetry" (Milosz)
See "Trakat poetycki"
Treatise on Poetry (Milosz) **11**:377
Treatise on Style (Aragon)
See *Traité du style*
"Treatment" (Moody) **147**:189
"The Treble Recorder" (Seifert) **93**:336
Trece fábulas y media (Benet) **28**:21
"Tree" (Abse) **29**:14
"Tree" (Hoffman) **6**:244
"The Tree" (Pound) **48**:283
"A Tree" (Rozewicz) **139**:226
The Tree (Ehrenburg) **62**:170
"A Tree. A Rock. A Cloud." (McCullers) **12**:413, 416, 425, 433
Tree and Leaf (Tolkien) **12**:566, 581
"Tree and Sky" (Transtroemer) **65**:223
"Tree at My Window" (Frost) **13**:229; **15**:242; **26**:121
"Tree Change" (Fisher) **87**:130-31
"Tree Children" (Hall) **51**:173
"Tree Ferns" (Plumly) **33**:316
A Tree for Poverty: Somali Poetry and Prose (Laurence) **50**:312, 314; **62**:278, 280
"The Tree Fort" (Gilchrist) **65**:349
A Tree Grows in Brooklyn (Kazan) **16**:360, 362; **63**:225, 229, 231, 234
A Tree Grows in Brooklyn (Smith) **19**:422-23
"Tree in a Snowstorm" (Dudek) **11**:159
The Tree of Childhood (Iskander)
See *Dereva detstva*
The Tree of Hands (Rendell) **48**:323-24
Tree of Life (Condé)
See *La vie scélérate*
The Tree of Man (White) **3**:521-23; **4**:585-86; **5**:487; **7**:531; **18**:545, 548; **65**:275-77, 279, 282; **69**:392-97, 399-403, 405-06, 412
"A Tree of Night" (Capote) **1**:56; **3**:99; **13**:133; **19**:79; **58**:86
A Tree of Night, and Other Stories (Capote) **1**:55; **19**:79-80, 85-6; **34**:321; **38**:84, 87; **58**:94
"Tree of Rivers" (Rukeyser) **15**:457
The Tree of Swords and Jewels (Cherryh) **35**:113-14
The Tree of the Sun (Harris) **25**:211
A Tree on Fire (Sillitoe) **3**:448; **6**:500; **148**:154, 157, 164, 184-85, 189, 192-93, 208
"The Tree Seat" (Simpson) **149**:348
"Tree Surgeons" (Graham) **48**:154
"A Tree Telling of Orpheus" (Levertov) **66**:250
"The Tree that Became a House" (Haines) **58**:218
The Tree That Walked (Fuller) **62**:185-86, 201
"The Tree, the Bird" (Roethke) **3**:433; **19**:396
"Tree Trimming" (Ciardi) **129**:46
The Tree Where Man Was Born (Matthiessen) **5**:273; **7**:210; **11**:358, 360; **32**:290, 294; **64**:306-07, 309
"A Treeful of Cleavage Flared Branching" (Ammons) **108**:19
"Trees" (Hall) **151**:205
"The Trees" (Larkin) **5**:229; **8**:333, 339, 341; **13**:335; **39**:347; **64**:258, 266
"Trees" (Merwin) **13**:384
"Trees" (Nemerov) **36**:305
"The Trees" (Sarton) **49**:307
"Trees" (Williams) **42**:459
The Trees (Richter) **30**:308-15, 318-19, 324, 327
"Trees Abandon Something inside a Circle of Fog" (Ponge) **18**:419
The Trees, All Their Greenness (Haavikko)
See *Puut, kaikki heidän vihreytensä*
"Trees at the Arctic Circle" (Purdy) **50**:245
"Trees Die at the Top" (Ferber) **93**:170, 180
"Trees in the Open Country" (Simic) **49**:341, 343
Trees of Heaven (Stuart) **14**:514, 516; **34**:373, 376
Trees of Strings (MacCaig) **36**:286
"Treetops" (Bell) **8**:65; **31**:47, 49
"Der Treffpunkt" (Seghers) **7**:409
"Trefoil" (Ashbery) **41**:40
"Tregardock" (Betjeman) **10**:52; **43**:46
La tregua (Levi) **37**:222-23, 226-27, 229; **50**:323, 326-32, 334, 336-37
"Le 13 l'echelle a frôlé le firmament" (Breton) **9**:134
Le treizième César (Montherlant) **8**:394
Trelawny (Holland) **21**:149
"The Trellis" (Connell) **45**:107
"A Trellis for R." (Swenson) **4**:534; **106**:321, 344
"Tremayne" (Justice) **102**:270
"The Trembler" (Merwin) **88**:200
The Trembling Hills (Whitney) **42**:432
The Trembling of a Leaf (Maugham) **15**:369
A Trembling upon Rome (Condon) **45**:100-01; **100**:91, 110
The Tremor of Forgery (Highsmith) **2**:193-94; **102**:171, 173-78, 209
Tremor of Intent (Burgess) **10**:87, 90; **22**:70-1; **40**:114, 117; **62**:132; **94**:40, 51, 58-59
"Tren Fortynbrasa" (Herbert) **9**:274; **43**:183-84, 188, 193-94
"Trenchtown Rock" (Marley) **17**:267
The Trend is Up (West) **50**:360
"Trends" (Asimov) **26**:39
Trente et un sonnets (Guillevic) **33**:191, 194
Trepleff (Harris) **9**:258-59
Os três mal-amados (Cabral de Melo Neto) **76**:156, 165, 169
Tres novelitas burguesas (Donoso) **8**:179-80; **32**:154, 159-60; **99**:241-42
"Tres nudos en la red" (Castellanos) **66**:60-1
Las tres perfectas casadas (Casona) **49**:46
"Tres poemas" (Castellanos) **66**:52
"Tres Poesías" (Parra) **102**:344, 350
"Tres sorores" (Espriu) **9**:192
Tres tristes tigres (Cabrera Infante) **5**:95-97; **25**:100-04; **45**:78-81, 83; **120**:30-33, 36-38, 41-47, 49-59, 67, 69, 74-75, 78-83
"Tres versiones de Judas" (Borges) **19**:51; **48**:38; **83**:156, 164
Tres y un sueño (Matute) **11**:364
Le Très-Haut (Blanchot) **135**:136-37
"Trespass" (Matheson) **37**:246
Trespass (Knebel) **14**:308
The Trespassers (Hobson) **25**:268-69
Trespasses (Bailey) **45**:39-44
Treugol'naya grusa (Voznesensky) **15**:553-54, 556
Trevayne (Ludlum) **43**:274-75
"Trêve" (Damas) **84**:173-74, 177
"Trevenen" (Davie) **8**:167
Trevgol'naya grusa (Voznesensky)
See *Treugol'naya grusa*
Tri Simfonije (Krleža) **114**:173
Tri tolstiaku (Olesha) **8**:430, 432
Tría piímata me siméa efkerías (Elytis) **100**:175
"Triad" (Watkins) **43**:450
"The Trial" (Abse) **29**:16
"The Trial" (Havel) **123**:201
"The Trial" (Lem) **40**:291
The Trial (Berkoff) **56**:14
The Trial (Welles)
See *Le procès*
Trial Balances (Miles) **34**:244
"The Trial by Existence" (Frost) **10**:196; **13**:223; **15**:244; **26**:125-26
"Trial by Fury" (Bochco and Kozoll) **35**:60
Trial Impressions (Mathews) **52**:308, 314
Trial of a City (Birney) **6**:71-2, 78
Trial of a Judge (Spender) **10**:491; **41**:423-24; **91**:257, 261, 263
Trial of a Poet (Shapiro) **4**:485-86; **15**:476, 478
The Trial of Abigail Goodman (Fast) **131**:86
The Trial of Dedan Kimathi (Ngũgĩ wa Thiong'o) **36**:315, 321-22, 324
The Trial of Elizabeth Cree (Ackroyd) **140**:44-7, 57
The Trial of God (Wiesel) **37**:452, 455, 459
"The Trial of Jean Rhys" (Rhys) **19**:394
The Trial of Joan of Arc (Bresson)
See *Procès de Jeanne d'Arc*
"The Trial of Plucking Buds and Shooting Lambs" (Oe) **86**:241
The Trial of Sören Qvist (Lewis) **41**:254-58, 263
The Trial of the Catonsville Nine (Berrigan) **4**:57-8
"The Trial of the Old Watchdog" (Thurber) **5**:434
"The Trial of Thomas Builds-the-Fire" (Alexie) **96**:5
"Trial Run" (Jacobsen) **48**:194
Trial Run (Francis) **22**:152; **42**:156-57
"Trial Translation" (Burke) **24**:128
The Trials of Brother Jero (Soyinka) **3**:462; **14**:505, 507; **44**:281-82, 287-88
"Triangle" (Lightfoot) **26**:283
"Le triangle ambigu" (Mandiargues) **41**:279
"Triangle at Rhodes" (Christie) **48**:72
Triangle Junction (Grass)
See *Gleisdreieck*
Le triangle noir (Malraux) **4**:333
"The Triangular Pear" (Voznesensky) **57**:425-26
Triangular Pear (Voznesensky)
See *Treugol'naya grusa*
"Tribal Dance" (Montague) **46**:270
Tribal Justice (Blaise) **29**:70-1, 74-6
"Tribal Poems" (Ciardi) **40**:156
Tribal Scars (Ousmane)
See *Voltaïque*
Tribal Scenes and Ceremonies (Vizenor) **103**:296-97
"Tribal Stumps" (Vizenor) **103**:296
Tribunals Passages (Duncan) **41**:128-30
Tribunals: Passages 31-35 (Duncan) **2**:123; **4**:141
"Tribune or Bureaucrat" (Lukacs) **24**:339
The Tribune's Visitation (Jones) **4**:259; **7**:186-87; **13**:311
"The Tribute" (H. D.) **73**:104-05, 120
"Tribute" (Jennings) **131**:238
Tribute (Slade) **46**:370-72
"Tribute of a Legs Lover" (Dunn) **40**:167
"Tribute to a Reporter in Belfast, 1974" (Durcan) **43**:116
Tribute to Freud (H. D.) **8**:258; **14**:228; **31**:204, 208-10; **73**:122-27, 129-30, 137, 140
"Tribute to Mshongweni" (Kunene) **85**:176
Tribute to the Angels (H. D.) **8**:255, 257-58; **14**:223, 225-27; **31**:202-03, 208; **34**:445
"Tribute to Upanishads" (Ezekiel) **61**:109
"Tributes" (Jennings) **131**:235
Tributes (Jennings) **131**:235-36
"Tricentennial" (Haldeman) **61**:174, 176, 178
A Triche-coeur (Tchicaya) **101**:348, 350-51
Le tricheur (Simon) **4**:494-95; **9**:484; **15**:485-86, 489-92; **39**:203-04, 206, 209, 211
El triciclo (Arrabal)
See *Le tricycle*
"The Trick" (Campbell) **42**:88-9
"The Trick Is Consciousness" (Allen) **84**:3
A Trick of Light (Corcoran) **17**:71
The Trick of the Ga Bolga (McGinley) **41**:286-87
"Trick Scenery" (Barthelme) **117**:5-6
"Tricks" (Moure) **88**:217-19
Tricks of the Trade (Fo)
See *Manuale minimo dell'Attore*
"Tricks out of Time Long Gone" (Algren) **33**:15
"Tricks with Mirrors" (Atwood) **8**:29; **13**:44; **84**:50
The Trickster (Simon)
See *Le tricheur*
"Trickster 1977" (Rose) **85**:311
"Trickster Discourse" (Vizenor) **103**:325
The Trickster of Liberty (Vizenor) **103**:332-34

Tricolors (Kieslowski)
See *Three Colors*
The Tricycle (Arrabal)
See *Le tricycle*
Le tricycle (Arrabal) **9**:38; **18**:17, 21; **58**:4-5, 8, 17, 21
Trifles for a Massacre (Céline)
See *Bagatelles pour un massacre*
"The Triflin' Man" (Miller)
See "You Triflin' Skunk"
Trig (Peck) **17**:341
Trig Sees Red (Peck) **17**:342
The Triggering Town: Lectures and Essays on Poetry and Writing (Hugo) **18**:263; **32**:243, 245-47, 250
Trillion Year Spree: The History of Science Fiction (Wingrove) **68**:452, 456
"Trillium" (Glück) **81**:170
Trilobite, Dinosaur and Man (Simak) **55**:320
"Trilobites" (Pancake) **29**:346-50
Trilogia culturii (Blaga) **75**:58-61, 67
Trilogia cunoaşterii (Blaga) **75**:58, 67, 79-80
Trilogia della vita (Pasolini) **106**:248, 266, 268
Trilogia valorilor (Blaga) **75**:58, 67
Trilogie des Wiedersehens (Strauss) **22**:407
The Trilogy (Beckett) **6**:40; **29**:59
Trilogy (H. D.) **8**:255-57; **14**:225-28, 230; **31**:201, 206, 208-09, 211; **34**:442, 445; **73**:139-40, 142
The Trilogy (Mahfūz)
See *al-Thulatthiyya*
The Trilogy of Knowledge (Blaga)
See *Trilogia cunoaşterii*
Trilogy of Life (Pasolini)
See *Trilogia della vita*
The Trilogy of Values (Blaga)
See *Trilogia valorilor*
Trinadtsaty podvig Gerakla (Iskander) **47**:192-93, 198-99
"A Trinity" (Trevor) **71**:342-43, 348
Trinity (Uris) **7**:492; **32**:433, 437
"Trinity Peace" (Sandburg) **35**:340
"Trinity Place" (McGinley) **14**:365-66
"Trinket" (Bell) **31**:49-50
"The Trinket Box" (Lessing) **3**:288
"Trionfo della morte" (Ekeloef) **27**:111
Trios (White) **110**:331
"Trip" (Barthelme) **117**:15
"A Trip" (Hoffman) **6**:243
"The Trip" (Seidel) **18**:475
A Trip around Lake Erie (McFadden) **48**:253-56
A Trip around Lake Huron (McFadden) **48**:253-56
"The Trip Back" (Butler) **81**:128-29
The Trip Back Down (Bishop) **10**:54
The Trip to Bountiful (Foote) **51**:130-31, 134-36, 138; **91**:99
Trip to Hanoi (Sontag) **105**:197, 227
A Trip to Italy and France (Ferlinghetti) **27**:139
The Trip to Jerusalem (Lind) **4**:294
The Trip to London (Davies) **23**:142
"Trip to New York" (Cardenal)
See "Viaje a Nueva York"
A Trip to Russia (Krleža)
See *Izlet u Rusiju*
"A Trip to Southwell" (Sillitoe) **148**:158
A Trip to the North (Yevtushenko) **26**:466
Trip to the Village of Crime (Sender)
See *Viaje a la aldea del crimen*
"A Trip to Vigia" (Bishop) **32**:43
Trip Trap (Rathbone) **41**:338
Tripes d'or (Crommelynck) **75**:153, 156, 160, 162-63, 168-69
Triple (Follett) **18**:156
The Triple Echo (Bates) **46**:59, 61, 65-6
The Triple Thinkers (Wilson) **8**:550; **24**:470, 472-74, 481, 487
"Triple Time" (Larkin) **33**:256
"Triplicate" (Fuchs) **22**:156, 160
Tripmaster Monkey: His Fake Book (Kingston) **58**:318, 324-27
"Tripping" (Williams) **31**:462
Tripticks (Quin) **6**:442
"Triptych" (Eberhart) **56**:79
"Triptych" (Heaney) **25**:248
Triptych (Simon)
See *Triptyque*
"Triptych I, After a Killing" (Heaney) **74**:159
Triptych: Three Scenic Panels (Frisch)
See *Triptychon*
Triptychon (Frisch) **14**:184; **44**:192, 199, 204, 206-07
Triptyque (Simon) **4**:497; **15**:490, 493-96; **39**:208, 210-12, 214
"The Triskelion" (Stead) **80**:324
Tristan and Iseult (Sutcliff) **26**:435
"Tristan Vox" (Tournier) **36**:439; **95**:361
Tristana (Bunuel) **16**:135, 140, 147; **80**:40, 50, 57
"Tristan's Singing" (Masefield) **11**:357
"Triste conción para aburrir a cualquiera" (Neruda) **28**:309
Tristes tropiques (Lévi-Strauss) **38**:294, 296-99, 303, 311-12
Tristessa (Kerouac) **3**:265; **5**:214; **29**:271-72; **61**:296, 309
Triton (Delany) **8**:169; **14**:143-44, 146-47; **38**:151, 161-62; **141**:126-32, 135-36, 148, 152-53, 155, 159-60
"Triumf" (Arghezi) **80**:2
"Triumph" (James) **33**:221
"The Triumph" (Sassoon) **130**:222
Triumph (Wylie) **43**:468-69
"The Triumph of Achilles" (Glück) **44**:214, 217-18, 222
The Triumph of Achilles (Glück) **44**:214-24; **81**:164, 173
The Triumph of Inspector Maigret (Simenon) **47**:379
"The Triumph of Life: Mary Shelley" (Mueller) **51**:280-81
"Triumph of Man" (Kunene) **85**:165
"The Triumph of Poetry" (Frame) **96**:189
"The Triumph of Principles" (Boyle) **58**:74; **121**:60
"The Triumph of Reason" (Gilchrist) **143**:309
The Triumph of the Spider Monkey (Oates) **33**:289; **108**:386
Triumph of the Will (Riefenstahl) **16**:519-26
"Triumph of Thought" (Kunene) **85**:165
The Triumph of Time (Blish) **14**:85
Triumphal March (Eliot) **1**:89
Triumphs of Modern Science (Berger) **12**:37
"Triunfo del amor" (Aleixandre) **9**:14
Trivial, Vulgar, and Exalted (Cunningham) **31**:99
Troe (Coles) **67**:175
"The Troika" (Simpson) **149**:295
"The Troika Fairy Tale" (Strugatskii and Strugatskii) **27**:432
"Troilus" (Olson) **29**:329
Trois acteurs: Un drame (Ghelderode) **11**:227
Trois Couleurs: Bleu (Kieslowski)
See *Three Colors*
"Les trois frères" (Damas) **84**:179
Les trois Lumières (Lang) **103**:85, 88
Trois petits tours (Tremblay) **29**:419, 425
"Trois poèmes spontanés" (Ferlinghetti) **27**:139
"Les trois soeurs" (Char) **9**:164
Trois villes saintes (Le Clézio) **31**:251; **155**:106
Troisième bélvèdere (Mandiargues) **41**:277-79
The Trojan Brothers (Johnson) **27**:215-16
The Trojan Ditch (Sisson) **8**:490
The Trojan Horse: A Play (MacLeish) **68**:289-90
"The Trojan War" (Elytis) **49**:110
"The Troll" (White) **30**:452
Trolley Ride (Calisher)
See *The Last Trolley Ride*
Trollflöjten (Bergman) **16**:77; **72**:61
"Trolling for Blues" (Wilbur) **53**:412; **110**:357, 361
Trollope: His Life and Art (Snow) **9**:498
"Trompe l'oeil" (Perec) **56**:254
"Troop Train Returning" (Murray) **40**:335
Une trop bruyante solitude (Hrabal) **67**:128-33
"Tropes of the Text" (Gass) **39**:480-81
"The Trophy" (Hope) **51**:219
Tropic of Cancer (Miller) **1**:219-24; **2**:281-83; **4**:350; **9**:378-80; **14**:370, 372-75; **43**:293, 295-301; **84**:232-94
Tropic of Capricorn (Miller) **1**:220-22, 224; **9**:379-81; **14**:372-73; **43**:297-300; **84**:239, 241-42, 244-47, 250-51, 254, 258, 266, 269, 273, 287, 290
"Tropic Zone" (Walcott) **42**:416
Tropical Night Falling (Puig)
See *Cae la noche tropical*
The Tropical Night Falls (Puig)
See *Cae la noche tropical*
A Tropical Nightfall (Puig)
See *Cae la noche tropical*
"Tropics" (Voigt) **54**:429
Tropics of Discourse: Essays in Cultural Criticism (White) **148**:220-25, 233-34, 241, 244-48, 250, 255, 265-67, 270, 286-88, 290-91, 297, 299, 303
Tropismes (Sarraute) **2**:384; **4**:464, 466-67, 470; **8**:472; **10**:460; **31**:377, 380, 382-83, 386; **80**:233, 236, 238-40, 242, 250-52, 254-55, 257
Tropisms (Sarraute)
See *Tropismes*
"The Tropville Evening Express" (Yehoshua)
See "The Evening Journey of Yatir"
Trotsky (Howe)
See *Leon Trotsky*
Trotsky in Exile (Weiss)
See *Trotzki im Exil*
Trotsky: World Revolutionary (Archer) **12**:19-21
The Trotter-Nama (Sealy) **55**:78-83
Trotzki im Exil (Weiss) **15**:568; **51**:386-87, 391, 393-94
Trou de mémoire (Aquin) **15**:17
"The Trouble" (Powers) **1**:280, 282
Trouble (Weldon) **122**:272, 274
"Trouble Child" (Mitchell) **12**:438
"Trouble Coming Everyday" (Zappa) **17**:585, 588
Trouble Follows Me (Macdonald) **14**:332-33
Trouble in July (Caldwell) **1**:51; **50**:300; **60**:54-5
"Trouble in Mind" (Dylan) **77**:189
Trouble in Mind (Childress) **12**:104-05, 108; **86**:309-10, 314-15; **96**:88, 103-04, 109-10
The Trouble I've Seen (Gellhorn) **60**:177-79, 190-91, 195-96
"Trouble Man" (Gaye) **26**:131, 133
The Trouble with Being Born (Cioran) **64**:90, 98
"The Trouble with Being Food" (Busch) **10**:93
The Trouble with England (Raphael) **2**:367
The Trouble with Francis (Francis) **15**:236
Trouble with Girls (Amis) **129**:22
The Trouble with Harry (Hitchcock) **16**:341, 346
"The Trouble with Heroes" (Vanderhaeghe) **41**:450
The Trouble with Heroes, and Other Stories (Vanderhaeghe) **41**:450, 452
"The Trouble with Intellectuals" (Randall) **135**:391, 398
The Trouble with Lazy Ethel (Gann) **23**:165
Trouble with Lichen (Wyndham) **19**:475
The Trouble with Nigeria (Achebe) **75**:6, 17, 24; **127**:27-8
The Trouble with Principle (Fish) **142**:210-11
"Trouble with the Natives" (Clarke) **136**:211
Troubled Air (Shaw) **7**:411; **23**:397
"The Troubled Genius of Oliver Cromwell" (Carr) **86**:47
The Troubled Partnership (Kissinger) **137**:215, 229
Troubled Sleep (Sartre)
See *La mort dans l'âme*
Troublemaker (Hansen) **38**:237

"Troubles" (Stern) **39**:244
Troubles (Farrell) **6**:173
"The Troubles of a Book" (Riding) **7**:374
"The Troubles of Dr. Thoss" (Ligotti) **44**:53-5
The Troubling of the Waters (Blaga) **75**:64-6
Trouées (Guillevic) **33**:194-95
"Trout" (Heaney) **5**:173; **14**:243
"The Trout" (Montague) **46**:267, 275
"The Trout Farm" (Raine) **103**:201
Trout Fishing in America (Brautigan) **1**:44-5; **3**:86-90; **5**:68-71; **12**:57-66, 69-73; **34**:314-17; **42**:49-53, 56-8, 60, 62-6
"Troy Town" (Ondaatje) **14**:408
"The Truant" (Pratt) **19**:377, 379, 385
The Truants (Barrett) **27**:22-4
Truants (Carlson) **54**:36
Truants from Life: The Rehabilitation of Emotionally Disturbed Children (Bettelheim) **79**:111
"Truce" (Muldoon) **72**:266
The Truce: A Survivor's Journey Home from Auschwitz (Levi)
See *La tregua*
"The Truce and Peace" (Jeffers) **11**:305
Truck (Dunn) **71**:133-35
The Truck (Duras)
See *Le camion: Suivi de entretien avec Michelle Porte*
"A Trucker" (Gunn) **3**:215
"A Trucker Breaks Down" (Bottoms) **53**:29
"A Trucker Drives through His Lost Youth" (Bottoms) **53**:29
The True Adventures of Huckleberry Finn (Seelye) **7**:405-06
The True Adventures of John Steinbeck, Writer (Benson) **34**:404-08, 410, 412-15
The True and Only Heaven (Lasch) **102**:290-92, 295, 297-99, 301-03, 305, 311-12, 322, 324-25
"True Colors" (Adams) **46**:16
The True Confession of George Barker (Barker) **8**:46; **48**:16-18, 21-4
"True Confessional" (Ferlinghetti) **6**:184; **111**:65
True Confessions (Dunne) **28**:123-26
True Confessions of Adrian Albert Mole, Margaret Hilda Roberts and Susan Lilian Townsend (Townsend) **61**:419-21
The True Confessions of an Albino Terrorist (Breytenbach) **37**:50-2; **126**:67-8, 70-2, 74-9, 84, 87-9, 91-4, 96, 98-9, 101
"The True Discovery of Australia" (McAuley) **45**:248
The True History of Squire Jonathan and His Unfortunate Treasure (Arden) **15**:21
"The True Import of Present Dialogue, Black vs. Negro" (Giovanni) **64**:182, 185, 188, 191, 193
The True Life Story of Jody McKeegan (Carpenter) **41**:103-08
"True Love" (Le Guin) **136**:361
True Love (Gold) **42**:195-96; **152**:119-20
"True Love: Groping for the Holy Grail" (Ellison) **139**:115-16
"True Love Isn't Hard to Find" (Donnell) **34**:158
"True Loves" (Strand) **41**:438-41
"The True Nature of Time" (Warren) **6**:557; **13**:577
"True Night" (Snyder) **120**:324
True North: A Memoir (Conway) **152**:106-111
"The True Person" (Rexroth) **112**:372
"A True Picture Restored" (Watkins) **43**:452
True Repose (Oz) **33**:299
True Romance (Tarantino) **125**:347-48, 350-51, 354-55, 358, 362-66, 369, 371, 375
"The True Song" (Montague) **46**:268
True Stories (Atwood) **25**:65, 68-9; **84**:69; **135**:53
"True Stories of Bitches" (Mamet) **46**:255
The True Story of Ah Q (Hein)
See *Die wahre Geschichte des Ah Q*
"The True Story of Lavinia Todd" (Auchincloss) **9**:52
"True Tenderness" (Akhmatova) **64**:11
"True Thomas" (Nye) **42**:309
"True Trash" (Atwood) **84**:95, 97
"The True Tyrant" (Smith) **25**:419
True West (Shepard) **34**:266, 269-70; **41**:407-08, 411-12; **44**:264-65, 268-70
The Truelove (O'Brian) **152**:298
El trueno entre las hojas (Roa Bastos) **45**:344-47
Trullion (Vance) **35**:421
"The Truly Great" (Spender) **41**:428
"Truman Capote: Knowing Everybody" (Amis) **62**:5
Trumpet in Arms (Lancaster) **36**:243
The Trumpet of the Swan (White) **34**:426-27, 430; **39**:369, 375-78, 380
"The Trumpet Part" (Celan) **53**:75-6
Trumpet to the World (Harris) **19**:199, 203
The Trumpet Unblown (Hoffman) **141**:264-66, 271-72, 275-77, 281, 293, 296-97, 318-19
"Trumpeter" (Gardner) **28**:162-63
Trumpets and Rasperrries (Fo)
See *Clacson, trombette e penacchi*
"Trunk in Petöcki" (Boell) **72**:69
Trust (Costello) **21**:75
Trust (Fukuyama)
See *Trust: The Social Virtues and the Creation of Prosperity*
Trust (Ozick) **3**:372; **7**:287; **28**:349, 355; **62**:355; **155**:134-35, 168, 170, 177-78, 183-84, 216, 226
Trust in Chariots (Savage) **40**:370-71
"Trust Me" (Updike) **139**:336
Trust Me (Updike) **139**:327
Trust: The Social Virtues and the Creation of Prosperity (Fukuyama) **131**:147-49, 152, 158-59, 164, 169
The Truth about Stone Hollow (Snyder) **17**:472
"The Truth About the Floods" (Ezekiel) **61**:104, 107
The Truth about the Ku Klux Klan (Meltzer) **26**:309
Truth and Consequence (Stolz) **12**:547-48
"The Truth and Life of Myth" (Duncan) **2**:123; **4**:142; **7**:88; **41**:128; **55**:295, 298
"Truth and Power" (Foucault) **69**:194
"Truth and the Novelist" (Stafford) **68**:441
The Truth Barrier (Transtroemer)
See *Sanningbarriären*
Truth Barriers (Transtroemer)
See *Sanningbarriären*
"The Truth Game" (Klima)
See "Hra na pravdu"
"Truth in Fiction" (Stafford) **68**:441
"Truth in Melodrama" (Davies) **75**:197
The Truth in Painting (Derrida)
See *La verité en peinture*
"The Truth Is" (Hogan) **73**:151, 157
Truth Is More Sacred (Dahlberg) **7**:69; **14**:138
"Truth Is Never" (Miles) **14**:369
"Truth is on its Way" (Giovanni) **117**:191
"The Truth of Departure" (Merwin) **88**:195
"The Truth of Fiction" (Achebe) **152**:75-6
The Truth of Poetry (Hamburger) **5**:158
"The Truth of the Matter" (Ihimaera) **46**:200
"Truth or Consequences" (Adams) **46**:17
"The Truth the Dead Know" (Sexton) **10**:469; **53**:318; **123**:423, 446
"Try a Dull Knife" (Ellison) **42**:127
"Try a Little Priest" (Sondheim) **30**:398
"Try to Remember" (Herbert) **44**:394
"Try to See My Sister" (Walker) **58**:408
Try! Try! (O'Hara) **13**:431; **78**:332-33, 365-68
"Trying" (Robison) **98**:306-08
Trying Hard to Hear You (Scoppettone) **26**:400-03
The Trying Hour (Lagerkvist)
See *Den svåra stunden*
"Trying Out for the Race" (Yates) **23**:483
"Trying to Be" (Gaitskill) **69**:199, 201
Trying to Explain (Davie) **31**:115, 119
"Trying to Feel Something" (Ciardi) **129**:55
"Trying to Hold It All Together" (Eberhart) **19**:144
"Trying to Pray" (Wagoner) **15**:559
Trying to Save Piggy Sneed (Irving) **112**:174
"Trying to Talk with a Man" (Rich) **3**:428; **7**:369; **11**:478
"Trying to Write" (Smart) **54**:426
"Tryst" (Broumas) **73**:15
"Trzecia jesién" (Dabrowska) **15**:166
Trzy kolors: Bialy (Kieslowski)
See *Three Colors*
Trzy kolory: Czerwony (Kieslowski)
See *Three Colors*
Trzy kolory: Niebieski (Kieslowski)
See *Three Colors*
T.S. Eliot: A Study in Character and Style (Bush) **34**:524, 526-27, 530-32
"T.S. Eliot's Later Poetry" (Leavis) **24**:310
Tsar (Barnes)
See *Laughter!*
"Le tsar noir" (Morand) **41**:301
Tschai (Vance) **35**:422-24
Tsemakh Atlas (Grade) **10**:248
Tsing-Boum! (Freeling) **38**:184
Tsotsi (Fugard) **25**:173, 175-76; **40**:201; **80**:65, 67, 69
Tsuga's Children (Williams) **14**:582
"Tsvety" (Akhmadulina) **53**:11
"T.T. Jackson Sings" (Baraka) **5**:48
"Tú" (Borges) **13**:110
"Il tu" (Montale) **7**:224
"Tu Do Street" (Komunyakaa) **94**:236-37
"Tu entendras..." (Bonnefoy) **58**:53
Tu étais si gentil quand tu étais petit (Anouilh) **40**:57-8
Tu ne t'aimes pas (Sarraute) **80**:253, 256-57
"Tú no sabe inglé" (Guillén) **79**:245
"Tu ti spezzasti" (Ungaretti) **7**:485; **11**:556
"Tu y yo" (Arreola) **147**:10
"Tuatamur" (Leonov) **92**:237, 256, 263-64
"The Tub, 1934, Halifax, Mississippi" (Dubie) **36**:131-32
"Tubal-Cain Forges A Star" (García Márquez)
See "Tubal-Caín forja una estrella"
"Tubal-Caín forja una estrella" (García Márquez) **3**:181
"Tubes" (Hall) **151**:192
The Tubs (McNally) **4**:346; **7**:219
Tucker (Coppola) **126**:260, 267
"Tucker Drugs" (Moure) **88**:230
"Tucson: First Night" (Allen) **84**:2
El tuerto es rey (Fuentes) **113**:233
"Tuesday" (Ciardi) **129**:47
"The Tuesday Afternoon Siesta" (García Márquez)
See "Tuesday Siesta"
"Tuesday and Wednesday" (Wilson) **13**:606
"Tuesday Night" (Beattie) **146**:65
"The Tuesday Night Club" (Christie) **110**:141, 144
"Tuesday Night with Cody, Jimbo, and a Fish of Some Proportion" (Crews) **49**:73
"Tuesday, September 27" (Wolf)
See "Dienstag, den 27. September"
"Tuesday Siesta" (García Márquez) **27**:147-48; **47**:148, 150-51; **55**:148; **68**:151, 166
"Tuesday's As Good As Any" (O'Hara) **6**:385
Tueur sans gages (Ionesco) **4**:251-52; **6**:248-49, 253-54; **9**:286; **11**:290-92, 294; **15**:296; **41**:224, 229; **86**:332, 340
"The Tuft of Flowers" (Frost) **3**:174-75; **15**:246, 248; **26**:118, 121-22
Tug of War (McCartney) **35**:289-93
"Tugela River" (Plomer) **4**:407
The Tugman's Passage (Hoagland) **28**:186
"Tulane" (Berry) **17**:55
"Tulips" (Cummings) **15**:159
"Tulips" (McGuckian) **48**:274, 276
"Tulips" (Plath) **5**:341, 345; **9**:426, 428, 433; **11**:448-49; **14**:423, 425, 429; **17**:347, 355,

365, 368-69; **50**:446; **51**:340, 343-46; **111**:161-62, 168, 171-74, 210
"Tulips, Again" (Schaeffer) **11**:491
Tulips and Chimneys (Cummings) **3**:118-19; **8**:156, 158; **12**:139-40, 144-45, 160-61; **15**:159-60, 162, 164; **68**:27, 31, 35, 41, 44-6, 50
Tulku (Dickinson) **12**:177; **35**:131-32
"Tulpen" (Celan) **82**:49
"Tumannaya ulitsa" (Voznesensky) **15**:555
Tumatumari (Harris) **25**:207, 210, 213
Una tumba (Benet) **28**:19-20, 23
Una tumba sin nombre (Onetti)
See *Para una tumba sin nombre*
"La tumba viva" (Roa Bastos) **45**:345
Tumbleweed (van de Wetering) **47**:405-07, 410
"Tumbling Dice" (Jagger and Richard) **17**:229, 236
"Tumbling of Worms" (Kunitz) **148**:110
Tunc (Durrell) **1**:87; **6**:153; **8**:193; **13**:185; **41**:136-37
"A Tune for Festive Dances in the Nineteen Sixties" (Merton) **83**:397
"Tune, in American Type" (Updike) **23**:473
"Tuned In Late One Night" (Stafford) **29**:387
Tuned Out (Wojciechowska) **26**:454-55
"El túnel" (Parra) **102**:338
El túnel (Sabato) **23**:375-77, 379
Tunes for a Small Harmonica (Wersba) **30**:432-34
"Tuning of Perfection" (MacLeod) **56**:197-200
"Tunnel" (Barnes) **141**:58, 69
"Der Tunnel" (Dürrenmatt) **11**:172
"The Tunnel" (Rukeyser) **27**:404
"The Tunnel" (Strand) **18**:516, 518; **41**:437; **71**:281
"Tunnel" (Summers) **10**:494
The Tunnel (Gass) **15**:256-57; **39**:478; **132**:165, 171-78, 180-81, 185, 187-194
The Tunnel (Sabato)
See "Shooting Rats at the Bibb County Dump"
Tunnel in the Sky (Heinlein) **26**:161, 172, 176-77; **55**:302
The Tunnel of Love (De Vries) **1**:73; **3**:126; **28**:106, 112-13; **46**:137
Tunnel through the Deeps (Harrison) **42**:201-02, 205
Tunnel Vision (Arrick) **30**:18
Tunnel Vision (Paretsky) **135**:354-55
"Tunstall Forest" (Davie) **8**:164
"Tuolomne" (Starbuck) **53**:353
"Tupac amaru kampa Taytanchisman" (Arguedas) **18**:7
Tupac amaru kampa Taytanchisman (Arguedas) **18**:7-8
"Tupelo Honey" (Morrison) **21**:233
Tupelo Honey (Morrison) **21**:232-33
Tupelo Nights (Bradley) **55**:31-4
"Tupic" (Tournier) **95**:361
Turbott Wolfe (Plomer) **4**:406
Un turbulent silence (Brink) **36**:68
Turbulent Stream (Pa Chin)
See *Chi-liu*
"Turds" (Martin) **30**:248
La turista (Shepard) **4**:490; **17**:433-34; **41**:412
Turkey Hash (Nova) **7**:267; **31**:297, 299
"The Turkey Season" (Munro) **95**:302, 306
"Turkey Talk" (Janowitz) **145**:326
"Turkeyneck Morning" (Bukowski) **41**:73
"Turkish Delight" (O'Faolain) **108**:415
"The Turkish March" (Swan) **69**:363
"The Turkish Night" (Morand)
See "La nuit Turque"
"A Turkish Story" (Pollitt) **28**:366; **122**:202
"The Turmoil" (Pasternak) **10**:386
"Turn" (Saner) **9**:469
Turn, Magic Wheel (Powell) **66**:353-54, 356, 368
Turn of a Pang (Brossard)
See *Sold-Out*
"The Turn of the Moon" (Graves) **45**:166
"The Turn of the Screw" (Oates) **108**:354; **134**:246
The Turn of the Years (Pritchett) **41**:332
Turn Off the Lights (Seifert)
See *Zhasněte světla*
Turn Out the Lights (Seifert)
See *Zhasněte světla*
"Turn the Page" (Seger) **35**:379, 381, 384
"Turn, Turn Your Face Away" (Barker) **48**:14
"A Turn with the Sun" (Knowles) **26**:258
Turnaround (Carpenter) **41**:106-08
"The Turncoat" (Baraka) **5**:45; **14**:42
"turning" (Clifton) **66**:75
"Turning" (Howe) **152**:185, 211
"The Turning" (Levine) **14**:317; **118**:290
"Turning" (Rich) **73**:330
"Turning Away" (Dickey) **4**:120
"Turning Fifty" (Wright) **53**:431
"Turning Forty" (Jiles) **58**:272-73, 275, 278
"Turning Out the Bedside Lamp" (Williams) **45**:444
"The Turning Point" (Allen) **84**:5
"The Turning Point" (Stolz) **12**:552
Turning Point (Seferis) **5**:384
Turning the Tide: U.S. Intervention in Central America and the Struggle for Peace (Chomsky) **132**:26-7, 32, 65-7
"Turning Thirty" (Pollitt) **28**:367; **122**:203-04
"Turning to You" (Merwin) **45**:273
A Turning Wind (Rukeyser) **15**:456, 458; **27**:404, 406, 408, 410-11
Turns (Matthias) **9**:361-62
Turns and Movies and Other Tales in Verse (Aiken) **52**:20-2, 27
"Turns: Toward a Provisional Aesthetic and a Discipline" (Matthias) **9**:361
Turnstiles (Holden) **18**:257-59
Turnstiles (Joel) **26**:214-15, 219-20
"Turpentine" (Gallagher) **63**:121
"Turquoise Carnations" (Thesen) **56**:421
The Turquoise Lament (MacDonald) **3**:307
The Turquoise Mask (Whitney) **42**:435
"Turtle" (Hellman) **52**:193
"Turtle" (Lowell) **15**:238
"The Turtle" (Oliver) **98**:261, 274, 294
Turtle Diary (Hoban) **7**:160-62; **25**:266
Turtle Diary (Pinter) **58**:381
"The Turtle Dove" (Hill) **8**:294
Turtle Island (Snyder) **5**:395; **9**:498; **32**:387-88, 394, 396, 399-400; **120**:312-13, 322-23, 325, 339-40, 344-51, 354, 356
"Turtle Mountain Reservation" (Erdrich) **120**:136
"The Turtle Who Conquered Time" (Thurber) **5**:430
Turvey (Birney) **6**:70-1; **11**:49
"Tusten" (Vesaas) **48**:407
"The Tutelar of the Place" (Jones) **7**:188-89; **13**:311
"The Tutored Child" (Kunitz) **148**:88, 97
Tutti i nostri ieri (Ginzburg) **5**:142; **11**:228-29; **54**:193-94, 196, 201-05, 211; **70**:280, 283
Tutti uniti! tutti insieme! ma scusa quello non e'il padrone? (Fo) **109**:104, 112
TV (van Itallie) **3**:493
"TV in Black and White" (Soto) **80**:278
"TV Off" (Hughes) **37**:180
"TV People" (Murakami) **150**:51, 65
TV People (Murakami)
See *TV piipuru*
TV piipuru (Murakami) **150**:49
"TV Room at the Children's Hospice" (Ryan) **65**:212-14
"T.V. Talkin' Song" (Dylan) **77**:184
Två sagor om livit (Lagerkvist) **54**:286
"TVC One Five" (Bowie) **17**:67
"Tvoi dom" (Akhmadulina) **53**:11
Tvoj ubijca (Aksyonov)
See *Vash ubiytsa*
Tvorčestva Fransua Rable i narodnaja kul'tura srednevekov'ja i Renessansa (Bakhtin) **83**:13, 15, 17, 26, 28, 32, 57
Twarz trzecia (Rozewicz) **23**:362
"Twelfth Morning; or, What You Will" (Bishop) **9**:92; **32**:34, 43
"12 April 1974" (Breytenbach) **126**:90
Twelve around the World (Daly) **17**:89
"Twelve Bagatelles" (Shapcott) **38**:400
Twelve Chairs (Brooks) **12**:78-9, 82
The Twelve Dancers (Mayne) **12**:398, 406
"Twelve Études for Voice and Kazoo" (Sorrentino) **40**:386
"The Twelve Figures of the World" (Borges) **48**:41-2
"Twelve Flying Monkeys Who Won't Copulate Properly" (Bukowski) **41**:75; **108**:85
$1,200 a Year (Ferber) **93**:147
Twelve Million Black Voices: A Folk History of the Negro in the United States (Wright) **1**:377; **4**:595; **14**:598; **74**:390
12 Monkeys (Gilliam)
See *Twelve Monkeys*
Twelve Monkeys (Gilliam) **141**:250-51, 255-60
"Twelve Months After" (Sassoon) **130**:182, 220
Twelve Moons (Oliver) **19**:362-63; **98**:265, 269, 276-77, 290
"The Twelve Mortal Men" (McCullers) **12**:429; **48**:241
"Twelve O'Clock News" (Bishop) **9**:97-8; **13**:90; **32**:35, 39
"12 O'Clock News" (Bishop)
See "Twelve O'Clock News"
Twelve Poems (Warner)
See *Azrael*
Twelve Poems for Cavafy (Ritsos) **31**:328
"Twelve Propositions" (Burke) **24**:127
"Twelve Seasons" (Hall) **151**:197
The Twelve Seasons (Krutch) **24**:289
"12527th Birthday of the Buddha" (Komunyakaa) **94**:230, 232
"Twelve Versions of God" (Broumas) **10**:77
The Twelve-Spoked Wheel Flashing (Piercy) **14**:421-22; **128**:230, 245
"A Twelve-Step Treatment Program" (Alexie) **154**:27
The Twenties (Wilson) **24**:483
Twenties in the Sixties (Kostelanetz) **28**:218
Twentieth Century Authors (Kunitz) **148**:81, 115, 148
"Twentieth Century Fiction and the Black Mask of Humanity" (Ellison) **114**:108, 117
"Twentieth Century Fox" (Morrison) **17**:294
Twentieth Century Pleasures: Prose on Poetry (Hass) **39**:146-49; **99**:129-40, 144-50, 156-57
The Twentieth Century Revue (Arrabal) **58**:17
Twentieth Century Russian Poetry (Yevtushenko) **126**:401
"The Twentieth Voyage" (Lem) **149**:150-51, 275
"Twentieth-Century Blues" (Fearing) **51**:116
Twentieth-Century Britain (Johnson) **147**:137
Twentieth-Century Caesar: Benito Mussolini (Archer) **12**:15
Twentieth-Century Faith: Hope and Survival (Mead) **37**:280
A Twentieth-Century Job (Cabrera Infante)
See *Un oficio del siglo XX*
"Twentieth-Century Pharisee" (Thomas) **48**:379
"The Twentieth-First Voyage" (Lem) **149**:150-51, 267, 271, 275, 277
"The Twentieth-Fourth Voyage" (Lem) **149**:152, 273, 277
20 (Wilson) **12**:645
"Twenty and One" (Haavikko) **34**:178
Twenty Forty (Jong) **83**:319
Twenty Love Poems and a Despairing Song (Neruda)
See *Veinte poemas de amor y una canción desesperada*

Twenty Love Poems and a Desperate Song (Neruda)
See *Veinte poemas de amor y una canción desesperada*
Twenty Love Poems and a Song of Despair (Neruda)
See *Veinte poemas de amor y una canción desesperada*
Twenty Love Poems and One Song of Despair (Neruda)
See *Veinte poemas de amor y una canción desesperada*
"Twenty Minutes" (Salter) **52**:368-69; **59**:196-97
"Twenty or So" (Gregor) **9**:254
Twenty Poems (Aleixandre) **36**:25, 28, 32
Twenty Poems (Haines) **58**:217, 221
XX Poems (Larkin) **5**:230; **64**:257
Twenty Poems (Neruda)
See *Veinte poemas de amor y una canción desesperada*
Twenty Poems (Spender) **91**:260
Twenty Poems of Georg Trakl (Bly) **128**:19
Twenty Poems of Pablo Neruda (Bly) **128**:22
Twenty Poems of Tomas Tranströmer (Bly) **128**:22
Twenty Thousand Streets under the Sky: A London Trilogy (Hamilton)
See *The Siege of Pleasure*
Twenty Thousand Streets under the Sky: A London Trilogy (Hamilton)
See *The Plains of Cement*
Twenty Thousand Streets under the Sky: A London Trilogy (Hamilton)
See *The Midnight Bell: A Love Story*
"XXII" (Auden) **14**:26
"Twenty Years Gone, She Returns to the Nunnery" (Dickey) **28**:117
"28" (Levine) **118**:286, 301
The Twenty-Eighth Day of Elul (Elman) **19**:148
"The Twentyfifth Anniversary of a Republic, 1975" (Mahapatra) **33**:277, 281, 283
"Twenty-Fifth Floor" (Smith) **12**:543
Twenty-First Century Sub (Herbert) **12**:270, 273; **23**:224-26; **35**:196-98; **44**:392-95
"25 Norfolk Crescent" (Ewart) **46**:153
25 Poems (Walcott) **42**:421; **67**:344; **76**:273, 288
Twenty-Four Poems (Dudek) **19**:136
"Twenty-Nine Inventions" (Oates) **6**:369; **15**:400
Twenty-One Love Poems (Rich) **11**:478; **18**:450; **76**:209; **125**:309, 311, 312, 314-16, 322, 333
"Twenty-One Points about The Physicists" (Dürrenmatt)
See "Einundzwanzig Punkte du zen Physikern"
Twenty-One Stories (Greene) **3**:211
Twentyone Twice (Harris) **19**:201
"Twenty-Seven Wagons Full of Cotton" (Williams) **45**:454
The Twenty-Seventh Kingdom (Ellis) **40**:191-92
"Twenty-Six" (Ferlinghetti) **27**:138
"26 Days, On Earth" (Haldeman) **61**:176-77
Twenty-Six Starlings Will Fly through Your Mind (Wersba) **30**:433
20th Century Pleasures (Hass)
See *Twentieth Century Pleasures: Prose on Poetry*
"Twenty-Third Flight" (Birney) **6**:75
22 Stories (Gilliatt) **53**:146-47
"Twice as Much" (Agnon)
See "Pi shnayim"
"Twice Born" (Warren) **39**:259
Twice in Time (Wellman) **49**:387
"Twice More" (Williams) **148**:318
Twice Shy (Francis) **42**:150-57; **102**:162
Twice Shy (Neff) **59**:399-402
Twiddledum Twaddledum (Spielberg) **6**:519-20
"Twilight" (Campbell) **32**:74-5, 78-80
"Twilight" (Faludy) **42**:139-40
"Twilight" (Faulkner) **68**:128
The Twilight Book (Neruda)
See *Crepúsculario*
"Twilight Excursion" (Davidson) **19**:129
Twilight for the Gods (Gann) **23**:165
Twilight in Delhi (Ali) **69**:20, 23-7, 29-32
"Twilight in Southern California" (Fuchs) **22**:157, 161
Twilight: Los Angeles, 1992 (Smith) **86**:265-73
Twilight of the Day (Jones) **10**:295
The Twilight of the Elephants (Vittorini)
See *Il sempione strizza l'occhio al frejus*
"Twilight of the Gods" (MacNeice) **53**:233
The Twilight of the Gods of the Steppe (Kadare) **52**:259, 262
The Twilight of the Steppe Gods (Kadare)
See *The Twilight of the Gods of the Steppe*
The Twilight Zone (Serling) **30**:354, 358-59
The Twin In the Clouds (Pasternak)
See *Bliznets v tuchakh*
"Twin Peaks" (Whalen) **6**:566
Twin Peaks (Lynch) **66**:265-70
Twinkle, Twinkle, Little Spy (Deighton) **7**:76; **46**:127-29
"The Twins" (Bukowski) **41**:64; **108**:111
"Twins" (Kelley) **22**:247
"The Twins" (Livesay) **79**:348
"Twins" (Oates) **108**:384
"The Twins" (Spark) **13**:519; **40**:401
"The Twins" (Van Duyn) **116**:402
"Twin-Sets and Pickle Forks" (Dunn) **40**:170-72
"The Twist" (Olson) **29**:334
The Twisted Thing (Spillane) **13**:528
"The Twisted Trinity" (McCullers) **100**:260
"The Twitching Colonel" (White) **69**:406-07
"Two" (Allen) **84**:41
"Two" (Creeley) **78**:139
"Two" (Cummings) **15**:161
"2" (Seger) **35**:380
"Two" (Singer) **23**:421
The Two (Wallace) **13**:570
Two: A Phallic Novel (Moravia)
See *Io e lui*
Two Against One (Barthelme) **117**:7-8, 11, 14, 19, 21-2
"Two American Haikus" (Stern) **100**:329
The Two Americas (Fuentes) **113**:263
"Two and a Half Acres" (Shapcott) **38**:400
Two and the Town (Felsen) **17**:121-22
"Two Annas" (Greenberg) **7**:134
"Two Appearances" (Scannell) **49**:331
"Two Armies" (Spender) **41**:425
"Two Arts" (Rich) **76**:218
"The Two Audens" (Schwartz) **87**:346
"Two Bodies" (Paz) **51**:327
Two Books (Pasternak) **63**:289
"Two Boys" (Moore) **68**:297, 300
"Two Brothers" (Ai) **69**:9-10, 15, 17
"The Two Brothers" (Hesse) **25**:260
"The Two Brothers" (Pritchett) **41**:334
Two Brothers (Middleton) **38**:331-32
Two Bucks without Hair, and Other Stories (Millin) **49**:252
Two by Two (Gellhorn) **14**:195; **60**:184-85
Two by Two (Stolz) **12**:548, 553
"Two Campers in Cloud Country" (Plath) **11**:448; **111**:200-01, 210
"Two Castilians in Seville" (Cabral de Melo Neto)
See "Dois castelhanos em Sevilha"
"Two Centuries of Canadian Cities" (Avison) **97**:72
Two Cheers for Democracy (Forster) **1**:104; **2**:135; **45**:144; **77**:242
"Two Children" (Guillén)
See "Dos niños"
"Two Circuses Equal One Cricket Match" (Raine) **103**:180
Two Citizens (Wright) **3**:544; **5**:519-21; **10**:547; **28**:463, 465-66, 471-73
"Two Colonials" (Calisher) **38**:70
Two Comrades (Voinovich)
See *Dva tovarishcha*
"Two Conceits" (Tate) **14**:532
"Two Corpses Go Dancing" (Singer) **9**:487; **11**:499; **111**:314
Two Crimes (Ibarguengoitia)
See *Dos crímenes*
The Two Cultures and the Scientific Revolution (Snow) **1**:315-16; **13**:512-13
Two Daughters (Ray)
See *Teen Kanya*
"Two Deaths" (Ashbery) **13**:36
Two Deaths (Amado)
See "A Morte e a morte de Quincas Berro Dágua"
The Two Deaths of Christopher Martin (Golding)
See *Pincher Martin*
The Two Deaths of Quincas Wateryell (Amado)
See "A Morte e a morte de Quincas Berro Dágua"
Two Dedications (Brooks) **125**:107
"Two Died Together" (Cabrera Infante) **120**:78
"Two Dreamers" (Soto) **80**:298, 300
"Two Dreamtimes" (Wright) **53**:432
"Two Ears, Three Lucks" (Paley) **140**:266
"Two Egrets" (Ciardi) **40**:154; **44**:382
"The Two Elenas" (Fuentes)
See "Las dos Elenas"
Two English Girls (Truffaut)
See *Deux Anglaises et le continent*
"The Two Environments" (Trilling) **24**:460
"Two Eskimo Songs" (Hughes) **119**:261
The Two Executioners (Arrabal)
See *Les deux bourreaux*
The Two Faces of January (Highsmith) **2**:192; **4**:225; **42**:212; **102**:173, 189, 193, 196
The Two Faces of the Boss (Valdez)
See *Las dos caras del patroncito*
"Two Families" (Lish) **45**:230
"Two Fawns That Didn't See the Light this Spring" (Snyder) **120**:348-49
The Two Fiddlers: Tales from Orkney (Brown) **48**:55
Two Figures (Momaday) **85**:270
"The Two Fires" (Wright) **53**:420, 431
The Two Fires (Wright) **53**:419-20, 423, 428-29, 431
"Two Fish" (Pollitt) **122**:205
"Two for Heinrich Bleucher" (Weiss) **14**:557
Two for the Seesaw (Gibson) **23**:173-78
"Two Fragments: March 199-" (McEwan) **66**:280-81
"The Two Fraternities" (Peake) **54**:373
"The Two Freedoms" (Silkin) **43**:399-400
The Two Freedoms (Silkin) **6**:498; **43**:395-96
"Two Friends" (Voinovich)
See *Dva tovarishcha*
"Two from Ireland" (Davie) **31**:124
"Two Funerals" (Buckley) **57**:126
Two Gentlemen in Bonds (Ransom) **4**:436
"Two Ghosts" (Dubus) **97**:233
"Two Giants" (O'Brien) **116**:187
Two Girls, Fat and Thin (Gaitskill) **69**:203-08
"Two Hangovers" (Wright) **5**:519
"Two History Professors Found Guilty of Murder" (Durcan) **43**:114, 116
"Two Horses" (Merwin) **45**:276-77
"Two Horses" (Oliver) **98**:265
"Two Horses Playing in the Orchard" (Wright) **3**:540
"Two Hours in an Empty Tank" (Brodsky) **4**:77; **6**:97
"Two Hours to a Kill" (McGuane) **45**:266
"Two Houses" (Merwin) **45**:275
"252 or at the End of a Volume" (Kunene) **85**:176
"201 Upper Terrace, San Francisco" (Olds) **85**:297
200 Motels (Zappa) **17**:587-88
The 290 (O'Dell) **30**:274-75
"Two Hundred Years After" (Sassoon) **130**:186
"Two Images" (Ezekiel) **61**:93, 103

"Two Images of Continuing Trouble" (Silkin) **43**:404
Two in One (Smith) **3**:460
"Two in the Bush" (Thomas) **107**:316, 318, 320
"Two in the Bush, and Other Stories" (Thomas) **107**:316, 332
"Two Insomniacs" (Oates) **9**:403
Two Into One (Cooney) **62**:144
Two Is Lonely (Banks) **23**:42
The Two Jakes (Towne) **87**:369-70, 373, 377-78
Two Kinds of Angel (Edgar) **42**:123
"Two Kitchens in Provence" (Fisher) **87**:128
"Two Ladies in Retirement" (Taylor) **18**:522-23; **37**:409, 411; **44**:305
"Two Leading Lights" (Frost) **26**:118
Two Leaves and a Bud (Anand) **23**:15-16; **93**:33, 36, 42
"Two Letters" (Strand) **71**:288
"Two Little Hitlers" (Costello) **21**:71-2
Two Lives and a Dream (Yourcenar)
See *Comme l'eau qui coule*
Two Lives: Reading Turgenev; My House in Umbria (Trevor) **71**:350-52; **116**:365, 367, 372, 377
"Two Look at Two" (Frost) **26**:111
Two Lovely Beasts, and Other Stories (O'Flaherty) **34**:356-57
"Two Loves" (Eberhart) **56**:77
"Two Mayday Selves" (Avison) **4**:37; **97**:92
"Two Meditations" (Barth) **9**:67; **89**:5-6, 16, 21, 26, 44, 61-2
"Two Men" (Prichard) **46**:333
Two Men and a Wardrobe (Polanski) **16**:462, 464, 471
"Two Monsters" (Lem) **149**:155
Two Moons (Heppenstall) **10**:272-73
Two Moons (Johnston) **150**:28, 33
"Two More Gallants" (Trevor) **71**:333
"Two More under the Indian Sun" (Jhabvala) **8**:312
"Two Morning Monologues" (Bellow) **1**:31
"Two Motions" (Ammons) **8**:18
Two Much (Westlake) **7**:529
"Two Muses" (Jhabvala) **138**:78
"The Two Numantias" (Fuentes) **113**:262, 264
"Two of a Kind" (O'Faolain) **14**:405
"Two of Hearts" (Hogan) **73**:158
The Two of Them (Russ) **15**:462
The Two of Us (Braine) **41**:61-2
The Two of Us (Moravia)
See *Io e lui*
"Two of Us Staring into Another Dimension" (Oates) **3**:359
"The Two of Us Together and Each of Us Alone" (Amichai)
See "Shneynu beyahad vekhol ehad lehud"
"The Two Old Maids" (Landolfi) **49**:209-10
"Two on a Party" (Williams) **45**:452, 454
Two on an Island (Rice) **7**:361, 363; **49**:298, 300
"Two or Three Graces" (Huxley) **11**:281
Two or Three Things I Know about Her (Godard)
See *Deux ou trois choses que je sais d'elle*
Two or Three Things I Know for Sure (Allison) **153**:17-20, 28-9
"Two Organs" (Berryman) **62**:58
"Two Paintings by Gustav Klimt" (Graham) **118**:246-47, 261
"Two Pair" (Nemerov) **9**:395
"Two Peas in a Pod" (Škvorecký) **69**:337
Two People (Dreyer) **16**:263, 269
"II Peter, ii, 22" (Blunden) **56**:43
"Two Philosophers" (Welsh) **144**:319
"Two Pilgrims" (Taylor) **18**:524, 526
Two Plays (O'Casey) **88**:234, 236
Two Plays (Rice) **7**:361
"Two Poems" (Madhubuti) **73**:191
"Two Poems" (Plumly) **33**:313-14
Two Poems (Merrill) **3**:334
"Two Poems about President Harding" (Wright) **3**:541
"2 Poems from the Ohara Monogatari" (O'Hara) **78**:336
Two Poems in the Air (Dickey) **109**:244
"Two Poems of Flight-Sleep" (Dickey) **15**:178
"Two Poems of the Military" (Dickey) **15**:177
"Two Poems on the Catholic Bavarians" (Bowers) **9**:121
"Two Poems on the Passing of an Empire" (Walcott) **42**:421
"Two Portraits" (Abse) **29**:14
"Two Portraits of Sex" (Larkin) **64**:262, 282
"The Two Presences" (Bly) **15**:64; **128**:13-14
"Two Private Lives" (Tuohy) **37**:433
"Two Quatrains" (Amichai) **116**:95
"Two: Resurrections" (Williams) **148**:361
"Two Rides on a Bike" (Ryan) **65**:215
Two Rode Together (Ford) **16**:319
"The Two Roots of Judaism" (Wesker) **42**:430
Two Rothschilds and the Land of Israel (Schama) **150**:137
"Two Scenes" (Ashbery) **4**:23; **77**:57-8
"Two Seaside Yarns" (Katz) **47**:223
"Two Seedings" (Clark Bekedermo) **38**:126
"The Two Selves" (Avison) **4**:36; **97**:92
Two Serious Ladies (Bowles) **3**:84; **68**:2-13, 16, 18, 20-21
"Two Set Out On Their Journey" (Kinnell) **129**:237
"Two Ships" (Boyle) **90**:46
The Two Shorts (Fuentes) **113**:262
"The Two Sides of a Drum" (Smith) **15**:514
"Two Sides of a Story" (Wright) **53**:432
"Two Sisters" (Farrell) **66**:131
"The Two Sisters" (Fuller) **62**:186, 192, 203
"Two Sisters" (Nin) **127**:387
The Two Sisters (Arundel) **17**:12-13, 17
The Two Sisters (Bates) **46**:47-9, 54, 56
Two Sisters (Vidal) **2**:449; **4**:554; **6**:549-50; **8**:525; **33**:407; **72**:387; **142**:292
"Two Sisters of Persephone" (Plath) **17**:354
"Two Sketches from House Made of Dawn" (Momaday) **85**:228
"Two Soldiers" (Faulkner) **3**:149
Two Solitudes (MacLennan) **2**:257; **14**:339, 340, 342-43; **92**:298, 300-05, 307-10, 312-18, 321-23, 325-26, 341-43, 346, 350
"Two Songs" (Rich) **125**:336
"Two Songs for the Round of the Year" (Smith) **42**:350
"Two Songs from 'The Hunted Revolutionaries'" (McGrath) **59**:182
"Two Songs of Advent" (Winters) **32**:469
Two Sought Adventure (Leiber) **25**:302
Two Stars for Comfort (Mortimer) **28**:283-86
"Two Statements on Ives" (Cage) **41**:78
"Two Stories" (Gallagher) **18**:169
"Two Stories" (Wright) **146**:313, 349
"Two Summer Jobs" (Leithauser) **27**:240-42
"Two Suns in the Sunset" (Pink Floyd) **35**:315
Two Tales About Life (Lagerkvist)
See *Två sagor om livit*
Two Tales and Eight Tomorrows (Harrison) **42**:199
Two Tales of the Occult (Eliade) **19**:146-47
"Two Things, Dimly, Were Going At Each Other" (Hannah) **90**:160
2001: A Space Odyssey (Clarke) **1**:59; **4**:104-05; **13**:150-51, 153-55; **18**:105-06; **35**:118, 122-27
2001: A Space Odyssey (Kubrick) **16**:382-89, 391
Two Thousand Seasons (Armah) **1**:44-45; **33**:28-9, 32-6; **136**:2, 8-9, 14, 18-21, 23, 25-9, 33-4, 37-8, 42,52-4, 56-7, 59-65, 72-3
2061: Odyssey Three (Clarke) **136**:203-04, 235, 237
2010: Odyssey Two (Clarke) **35**:125-29; **136**:198, 204, 235, 237
"The 2003 Claret" (Amis) **40**:43
"2x2" (Dylan) **77**:183-84
Two to Conquer (Bradley) **30**:29-30
The Two Towers (Tolkien) **12**:565; **38**:434
Two Trains Running (Wilson) **63**:458; **118**:387-90, 402, 404, 408-10, 412
"Two Tramps in Mud Time" (Frost) **10**:195, 198; **26**:122; **34**:475
"221-1424 (San/francisco/suicide/number)" (Sanchez) **116**:295
Two Valleys (Fast) **23**:153; **131**:59, 81-2, 85, 93
"Two Variations" (Levertov) **5**:248
"Two Venetian Pieces" (Montale) **9**:388
"Two verdicts" (Rozewicz)
See "Dwa wyroki"
"Two versions of the imaginary" (Blanchot) **135**:104, 107, 123
Two Views (Johnson)
See *Zwei Ansichten*
"Two Views of a Cadaver Room" (Plath) **11**:446; **14**:426
"Two Views of Marilyn Monroe" (Clark Bekedermo) **38**:128
"Two Views of Nature: White and Indian" (Waters) **88**:343, 347
"Two Views of Withens" (Plath) **111**:202, 206
Two Virgins (Markandaya) **8**:376-77; **38**:325-26
Two Virgins: Unfinished Music Number One (Lennon) **35**:261, 267, 270
"Two Visits" (Barnard) **48**:27
"Two Voices" (Abse) **29**:17
"Two Voices" (Blunden) **56**:43
Two Voices (Cabral de Melo Neto)
See *Dois palamentos*
Two Voices (Thomas) **13**:541; **132**:381
"Two Voices in a Meadow" (Wilbur) **14**:577; **110**:374
Two Waters (Cabral de Melo Neto)
See *Duas aguas*
"Two Weddings and One Divorce" (Singer) **15**:509
Two Weeks in Another Town (Shaw) **7**:414; **23**:398, 400; **34**:368
"Two Went to Sleep" (Cohen) **38**:136
Two Wings the Butterfly (Vizenor) **103**:308
Two Wise Children (Graves) **39**:325
"Two Wise Generals" (Hughes) **9**:284
"Two Wise Men" (Kunene) **85**:166
Two Witches (Frost) **9**:224
Two Women (Lee) **90**:201
Two Women (Moravia)
See *La ciociara*
Two Women (Mulisch) **42**:288-89
Two Women (De Sica)
See *La ciociara*
Two Women and Their Man (Jones) **52**:252
"Two Working" (Clarke) **61**:73
"Two Worlds" (Maclean) **78**:239
Two Worlds and Their Ways (Compton-Burnett) **15**:140
"The Two Worlds of Ernst" (Wain) **46**:411
Two Years (O'Flaherty) **34**:357
Two-and-Twenty (Forester) **35**:165-66
The Two-Character Play (Williams) **5**:501-02, 504; **15**:582-83; **19**:472; **45**:444, 447-52, 455
The Twofold Vibration (Federman) **47**:127-29
"The Two-Headed Eagle" (Haavikko) **34**:175
Two-Headed Poems (Atwood) **15**:36-7; **18**:37; **25**:65, 69; **84**:66, 68
Two-Headed Woman (Clifton) **66**:68, 80-1, 84-6
Two-Lane Blacktop (Wurlitzer) **15**:589
Two-Part Inventions (Howard) **7**:167-68; **10**:274-76; **47**:168-69, 171
"Two-Part Pear Able" (Swenson) **61**:399; **106**:325
Twopence Coloured (Hamilton) **51**:183, 194
Two's Company (Middleton) **38**:329
"Two's Enough of a Crowd" (Hunter) **35**:226
2000 (Neruda) **28**:310
The Two-Thousand-Pound Goldfish (Byars) **35**:74-5
Two-Way Traffic (Lieber) **6**:312
The Twyborn Affair (White) **18**:546-49; **65**:275-76, 278, 281-82; **69**:410
"Tying One On in Vienna" (Kizer) **80**:172, 185

Tynset (Hildesheimer) **49**:167-68, 170, 175, 179
"Types Found in Odd Corners Round about Brooklyn" (Barnes) **127**:164, 166
Types of Shape (Hollander) **2**:197; **5**:186; **8**:302
The Typewriter (Cocteau) **43**:110, 112
Typewriter in the Sky (Hubbard) **43**:205, 207
The Typewriter Revolution and Other Poems (Enright) **4**:155
"Typhoid Epidemic" (Faludy) **42**:140
"Typhus" (Simpson) **32**:377-78, 380
Typical American (Jen) **70**:69-77
"A Typical Canadian Family Visits Disney World" (McFadden) **48**:250
"A Typical Day in Winnipeg" (Purdy) **50**:247
The Typists (Schisgal) **6**:489
"The Typographer's Ornate Symbol at the End of a Chapter or Story" (Avison) **97**:111
Tyrannus Nix? (Ferlinghetti) **111**:68
"The Tyranny of Trivia" (Thurber) **5**:433
"Tyrant of the Syracuse" (MacLeish) **8**:362
"Tyrants Destroyed" (Nabokov) **6**:357-60
Tyrants Destroyed, and Other Stories (Nabokov) **11**:391
Tystnaden (Bergman) **16**:56, 58, 62, 64, 67-8, 70-1, 74, 79-80; **72**:39-41, 52, 54-5, 59, 62
T-Zero (Calvino)
See *Ti con zero*
Tzili: The Story of a Life (Appelfeld) **47**:2-3, 5-6
"U" (Merrill) **8**:383-84, 387
U agoniji (Krleža) **8**:329; **114**:167, 177
U predvecerje (Krleža) **114**:173
The U.A.W. and Walter Reuther (Howe) **85**:115
Über allen Gipfeln ist Ruh: ein deutscher Dichtertag um 1980 (Bernhard) **61**:26
Über das selbstverständliche: Politische Schriften (Grass) **49**:139; **88**:168
Über den Schmerz (Jünger) **125**:259-60
"Über die Brücke" (Boell) **11**:53; **27**:56-7; **72**:69
Über die Dörfer (Handke) **134**:133, 161
Uber die Linie (Jünger) **125**:223, 231
"Über Lieblingswörter" (Handke) **134**:161
Über Mein Lehrer Döblin (Grass) **88**:147
Über mein Theater (Hochwälder) **36**:237
Überblendungen (Rozewicz) **139**:262
"Die Überflutung" (Hofmann) **54**:225
Die Überflutung: Vier Hörspiele (Hofmann) **54**:225
"Überlebende" (Sachs) **98**:328
Ubik (Dick) **30**:115-17, 119; **72**:104, 108, 110-12, 117, 119, 121-22
"Ubiquity" (Pinget) **37**:365
Uccellacci e uccellini (Pasolini) **20**:260, 271; **106**:220, 226, 273
"The UFO Menace" (Allen) **52**:42
"The Ugliest Woman" (Souster) **5**:396
"Ugly Corner" (MacCaig) **36**:285
"Ugly Honkies; or, The Election Game and How to Win It" (Giovanni) **19**:191; **64**:183
"The Ugly Little Boy" (Asimov) **76**:321
An Ugly Little Secret: Anti-Catholicism in North America (Greeley) **28**:173
"The Ugly Poem That Reluctantly Accepts 'Itself' As Its Only Title" (Dubie) **36**:132
Ugly Swans (Strugatskii and Strugatskii) **27**:434, 436
"Ugolino" (Heaney) **25**:248; **74**:190; **91**:115
Uh Huh; But How Do It Free Us? (Sanchez) **116**:284-85, 301
"Uh, Philosophy" (Ammons) **57**:52
"Uh-Oh, Love Comes to Town" (Byrne) **26**:94
Die Uhren (Hildesheimer) **49**:167
Ujawnienie (Rozewicz) **139**:228
"Ukhod Khama" (Leonov) **92**:237, 264
Ukulele Music (Reading) **47**:353-54
"Ulan Dhor Ends a Dream" (Vance) **35**:420
"Ulcer" (Pesetsky) **28**:358
"Ulica u jesenje jutro" (Krleža) **114**:166
"El Ulises de Joyce" (Borges) **4**:71
Ulla Winblad (Zuckmayer) **18**:556
"Ullswater" (Gunesekera) **91**:37
"Ulrich and the Doctor" (Vollmann) **89**:305
"Ulrike" (Borges) **13**:110; **48**:39-41; **83**:189
"Ulster Today" (Simmons) **43**:408
"An Ulster Twilight" (Heaney) **74**:167
La última canción de Manuel Sendero (Dorfman) **48**:92-5; **77**:133, 135, 137-43, 146-49, 152-53
"Ultima Thule" (Nabokov) **3**:354
The Ultimate Adventure (Hubbard) **43**:203
"The Ultimate City" (Ballard) **14**:39, 41-2; **36**:38
The Ultimate City (Ballard) **137**:45-46
The Ultimate Good Luck (Ford) **99**:105, 110, 116-17, 120-21
The Ultimate Good Luck (Ford) **46**:158-59, 161
"Ultimate Professor" (Redgrove) **41**:354
"The Ultimate Safari" (Gordimer) **70**:177-78, 180; **123**:127
Ultimate Values (Sassoon) **36**:392
"Ultimatum" (Gustafson) **36**:214
Ultimatum (Vesaas) **48**:406
"Ultime" (Ungaretti) **11**:559
"Ultimi cori" (Ungaretti) **7**:483
"El último amor" (Aleixandre) **9**:12
"El último baile" (Zamora) **89**:384, 386
El último guajolote (Poniatowska) **140**:330
Ultimo round (Cortázar) **5**:110; **92**:158
"El último viaje del buque fantasma" (García Márquez) **2**:149; **27**:147; **47**:151
Ultimo viene il corvo (Calvino) **39**:314
Ultramarine (Carver) **53**:60-1; **55**:275
"Uluru Wild Fig Song" (Snyder) **32**:396; **120**:323, 325
"Ulysses" (Ciardi) **40**:156
"Ulysses" (Ferron) **94**:103, 123, 125
"Ulysses" (Graves) **45**:161, 173
"Ulysses" (Kinsella) **138**:97
"Ulysses" (Soyinka) **36**:417; **44**:285
"Ulysses and Circe" (Lowell) **11**:325, 330; **37**:238
Ulysses in Traction (Innaurato) **21**:194-96; **60**:200-01, 205
"Ulysses, Order, and Myth" (Eliot) **10**:172
"De um avião" (Cabral de Melo Neto) **76**:167
Uma (Kurosawa) **119**:345, 350, 396, 399
Umberto D (De Sica) **20**:86-94, 96
Der umbewusste Gott: Psychotherapie und religion (Frankl) **93**:209-10, 216, 222
"The Umbilical Cord" (Gordimer) **18**:185
"The Umbrella" (Kureishi) **135**:304
"The Umbrella" (Plomer) **4**:407; **8**:446
An Umbrella from Piccadilly (Seifert) **34**:257, 261 62; **44**:423
Umbrella from Piccadilly (Seifert)
See *Deštník z Piccadilly*
The Umbrella from Piccadilly (Seifert)
See *Deštník z Piccadilly*
An Umbrella from Piccadilly (Seifert)
See *Deštník z Piccadilly*
"Umbrian Dreams" (Wright) **119**:180
"U.M.C." (Seger) **35**:380
Umi to dokuyaku (Endō) **19**:161; **54**:151-53, 159; **99**:283, 285, 299
"L'umile Itallia" (Pasolini) **106**:265
Ummagumma (Pink Floyd) **35**:305-08, 311
"Die Umsiedler" (Schmidt) **56**:391, 405
"Umykanie, ili Zagadka Endurtsev" (Iskander) **47**:196, 198
"U.N. Hymn" (Auden) **2**:28
U.N. Journal (Buckley) **7**:35
"Unaccompanied Sonata" (Card) **47**:68
Unaccompanied Sonata, and Other Stories (Card) **47**:67-8
"Unacknowledged Legislators and Art pour Art" (Rexroth) **49**:278; **112**:373
Un'altra vita (Moravia) **7**:242, 244
The Un-Americans (Bessie) **23**:60, 62
"The Un-Angry Young Men" (Fiedler) **24**:191
Unassigned Frequencies: American Poetry in Review, 1964-77 (Lieberman) **36**:259-60, 264
Unattainable Earth (Milosz)
See *Niobjeta ziemia*
"The Unattained" (Gascoyne) **45**:157
The Unavowable Community (Blanchot)
See *La Communauté inavouable*
The Unbearable Lightness of Being (Kundera)
See *L'insourenable l'égrèté de l'être*
"The Unbearable Ugliness of Volvos" (Fish) **142**:207
"Unbelievable Encounter" (Arghezi)
See "O întîlnire de necrezut"
"The Unbeliever" (Bishop) **9**:96; **32**:37
Unberechenbare Gäste (Boell) **72**:71
The Unblinding (Lieberman) **36**:261, 263
"Unborn" (Muldoon) **32**:316
"The Unborn" (Wright) **53**:419, 428
"Unborn Child" (Oates) **6**:367
"Unborn Song" (Rukeyser) **27**:411
"Unborn Things" (Lane) **25**:286
Unborn Things: South American Poems (Lane) **25**:284-85
"Unbroken Lineage" (Avison) **97**:76, 129-30, 133-34
"The Uncanny" (Hemingway) **8**:289
"Uncertain" (Kunitz) **148**:108
The Uncertain Certainty (Simic) **49**:339; **68**:370-71; **130**:313, 315, 330, 334, 340
Uncertain Friend (Heym) **41**:216
Uncertainties and Rest (Steele) **45**:362-65
"Unchain My Heart" (Jones) **81**:61, 63-5, 67
"The Unchangeable" (Blunden) **56**:41
Uncharted Stars (Norton) **12**:466-67
Uncivil Seasons (Malone) **43**:282
"Unclaimed" (Seth) **43**:388; **90**:338
"Uncle" (Levine) **118**:284, 292, 299
"Uncle" (Narayan) **121**:340
"Uncle" (Tate) **6**:528
"Uncle Albert/Admiral Halsey" (McCartney) **35**:279, 290-91
"Uncle and Nephew" (Cabral de Melo Neto)
See "Tio e sobrinho"
"Uncle Anne" (Boyle) **19**:62
"Uncle Arthur" (Bowie) **17**:65
"Uncle Ben's Choice" (Achebe) **26**:23; **75**:14
"Uncle Bernie's Farm" (Zappa) **17**:585
"Uncle Bullboy" (Jordan) **114**:146
"Uncle Casper" (Stuart) **14**:518
"Uncle Dockery and the Independent Bull" (Mitchell) **98**:187
"Uncle Fremmis" (Sturgeon) **22**:411
"Uncle Grant" (Price) **43**:341
"Uncle Jack" (Simmons) **43**:408, 410
"Uncle Jeff" (Stuart) **14**:514
Uncle Louis (Bowering) **47**:28-9
Uncle Meat (Zappa) **17**:585-87, 589, 591
"Uncle Meat Variations" (Zappa) **17**:585
"Uncle Roger" (Van Doren) **10**:495
Uncle Sandro and the End of the Goatibex (Iskander)
See *Diadia Sandro i konets kozlotura*
"Uncle Sandro and the Slave Khazarat" (Iskander) **47**:197
"Uncle Seaborn" (Hospital) **145**:295, 303, 305
"Uncle Spencer" (Huxley) **11**:281
"Uncle T" (Moore) **90**:277
"Uncle Theodore" (Dinesen) **10**:148-49; **95**:67
Uncle Tom's Children (Wright) **1**:379-80; **4**:594-95; **9**:585; **14**:596-98; **21**:435, 444, 452; **74**:363, 370, 378, 383, 385, 390, 393
"Uncle Tony's Goat" (Silko) **23**:412; **74**:347
"Uncle Wiggily in Connecticut" (Salinger) **12**:498; **138**:183, 214
"Uncles" (Atwood) **84**:96
"Uncles" (Taylor) **37**:409
"Uncle's Letters" (Narayan) **47**:305
Uncollected Poems (Betjeman) **34**:306; **43**:50-1
Uncollected Poems (Plath) **9**:425
The Uncollected Stories of William Faulkner (Faulkner) **18**:148-49
The Uncollected Wodehouse (Wodehouse) **22**:483-84
"Uncommon Visage" (Brodsky) **100**:69
Uncommon Women and Others: A Play about Five Women Graduates of a Seven Sisters

College Six Years Later (Wasserstein) **32**:439-40; **59**:219-21, 223; **90**:405, 407-8, 410-413, 416, 418-23, 429-31, 433
Unconditional Surrender (Waugh) **1**:358-59; **8**:543; **19**:461; **27**:472
The Unconquered (Ray)
See *Aparajito*
"Unconscious" (Breton) **54**:30
The Unconscious God: Psychotherapy and Theology (Frankl)
See *Der umbewusste Gott: Psychotherapie und religion*
Unconscious Motives of the Motion Picture Industry (Foreman) **50**:168
"The Unconsidered Life" (Musgrave) **54**:341
The Unconsoled (Ishiguro) **110**:257-58, 260-63, 265
"Uncontrollable Feeling of Ecstasy" (Kunene) **85**:176
The Uncorrected World (Hanson) **13**:263
"The Uncreating Chaos" (Spender) **41**:427, 429
"The Uncreation" (Pinsky) **94**:309; **121**:437
"Unctuous Platitudes" (Ashbery) **77**:59
Und diese verdammte Ohnmacht (Hein) **154**:121
Und Niemand weiss weiter (Sachs) **98**:321-22, 324
Und Sagte kein einziges Wort (Boell) **6**:83; **9**:102-04, 106-07, 109; **11**:57-9; **27**:54-9
"Und wir die Ziehlen" (Sachs) **98**:341
The Undanced Dance (Breytenbach) **126**:73, 84-5, 101-02
Undaunted Courage (Ambrose) **145**:43-4, 46, 49, 52-5, 57
"The Undead" (Graves) **11**:256
"The Undead" (Wilbur) **53**:405; **110**:384
"The Undecided" (Ritsos) **31**:324
"The Undefeated" (Hemingway) **13**:280; **19**:212; **30**:179, 182; **61**:190; **80**:137
"The Undefeated: An Acid House Romance" (Welsh) **144**:320, 322, 328-29, 334
"The Undelivered" (Cioran) **64**:89, 94
Under a Blanket of Stars (Puig) **133**:320-21
Under a Changing Moon (Benary-Isbert) **12**:34
"Under a Glass Bell" (Nin) **60**:267; **127**:373-74
Under a Glass Bell (Nin) **14**:381-82; **60**:267, 269
Under a Mantle of Stars (Puig) **133**:331, 366-68
Under a Soprano Sky (Sanchez) **116**:302, 307-08, 310-11, 318, 324-25
"Under a White Shawl of Pine" (Smith) **42**:350
Under Aldebaran (McAuley) **45**:245-47, 249, 252-54
"Under Arcturus" (Jones) **42**:242-43
"Under Black Leaves" (Merwin) **13**:383
"Under Capricorn" (Hollander) **2**:197
Under Capricorn (Hitchcock) **16**:345
"Under Carn Brea" (Thomas) **132**:381
"Under Cows" (Plumly) **33**:312
"Under Glass" (Atwood) **13**:46; **25**:62
"Under House Arrest" (Brutus) **43**:93
"Under Icebergs" (Hall) **51**:170
Under My Skin (Lessing) **94**:276-81, 283-84, 286-87
"Under My Thumb" (Jagger and Richard) **17**:226, 230, 234-35, 239
"Under One Small Star" (Szymborska) **99**:201
Under Plain Cover (Osborne) **45**:313-14, 316
"Under Pressure" (Transtroemer) **52**:411; **65**:223
Under Pressure (Herbert)
See *Twenty-First Century Sub*
"Under Sedation" (Hope) **51**:222
Under Sentence of Death (Genet) **44**:386
"Under St. Paul's" (Davie) **31**:109
"Under Stars" (Gallagher) **63**:122
Under Stars (Gallagher) **18**:169-70; **63**:119-20, 122
Under the Banyan Tree and Other Stories (Narayan) **47**:304-06; **121**:369
"Under the Bell Jar" (Nemerov) **6**:361
"Under the Boathouse" (Bottoms) **53**:32-3
"Under the Dog Star" (Ekelöf) **27**:110
Under the Eye of the Clock (Nolan) **58**:362-67
Under the Eye of the Storm (Hersey) **40**:237-39
"Under the Falling Sky" (Browne) **21**:38
"Under the Garden" (Greene) **3**:213, 215; **125**:175
Under the Ice (Nowlan) **15**:398
"Under the Influence" (Bowering) **32**:48
Under the Jaguar Sun (Calvino)
See *Sotto il sole giaguro*
"Under the Knife" (Singer) **15**:504
"Under the Lights" (Dubus) **97**:231-33
"Under the Maud Moon" (Kinnell) **5**:216-17; **129**:250
"Under the Moon's Reign" (Tomlinson) **45**:394
Under the Mountain Wall: A Chronicle of Two Seasons of the Stone Age (Matthiessen) **7**:210; **11**:360; **32**:287, 290; **64**:309
Under the Net (Murdoch) **1**:234, 236; **2**:295, 297; **4**:367-69; **6**:342, 345; **8**:404; **11**:386; **15**:384-86; **22**:328; **31**:293; **51**:289
Under the Red Flag (Jin) **109**:54
Under the Red Sky (Dylan) **77**:181-85
Under the Roofs of Paris (Clair)
See *Sous les toits de Paris*
"Under the Rose" (Pynchon) **33**:338, 340; **62**:433
Under the Rose (Davies) **23**:145
Under The Sea Wind: A Naturalist's Picture of Ocean Life (Carson) **71**:100, 102-09
Under the Shelter (Mahfouz)
See *Taht al-mizalla*
Under the Sign of Saturn (Sontag) **31**:411-13, 415-16
"Under the Skin of the Statue of Liberty" (Yevtushenko) **126**:394
Under the Skin of the Statue of Liberty (Yevtushenko) **13**:619
Under the Skin: The Death of White Rhodesia (Caute) **29**:122-24
"Under the Sky" (Bowles) **19**:60
Under the Sweetwater Rim (L'Amour) **25**:280
"Under the Tree" (Johnston) **51**:240-43, 245, 252
"Under the Tree" (Levertov) **28**:239
"Under the Trees" (Kaufman) **8**:317
"Under the Viaduct" (Dove) **50**:153; **81**:139
"Under the Vulture-Tree" (Bottoms) **53**:33
Under the Vulture-Tree (Bottoms) **53**:33-4
Under the Weather (Bellow) **6**:49-50
"Under the Wheat" (DeMarinis) **54**:99-101
Under the Wheel (Hesse)
See *Unterm Rad*
Under Venus (Straub) **107**:274, 283, 292, 304-05, 307, 310
"Under Water" (Strand) **41**:440
"Under Which Lyre" (Auden) **14**:28
Undercliff: Poems, 1940-1953 (Eberhart) **3**:133; **11**:178; **19**:144; **56**:81-3
"The Underdog" (Tolson) **105**:260
"The Underground" (Heaney) **74**:167, 190
Underground Alley (Mayne) **12**:389, 395, 405
The Underground Game (Mallet-Joris)
See *Le jeu du souterrain*
"The Underground Garage" (Beer) **58**:31
The Underground Man (Macdonald) **1**:185; **2**:255-56; **14**:332, 335-36; **41**:267, 269-70
Underground Man (Meltzer) **26**:301-02
The Underground River (Sarton) **91**:241
Underground River, Underground Birds (Konwicki)
See *Rzeka podziemna, podziemne ptaki*
"Underground the Darkness Is the Light" (Carruth) **84**:134, 136
The Underground Woman (Boyle) **5**:66-7; **121**:46
"Undergrowth" (p'Bitek) **96**:286
The Underneath (SODERBERGH) **154**:339-41, 343-44, 347, 354, 356
"The Undersea Farmer" (Howes) **15**:290
"Understanding Alvarado" (Apple) **33**:18-19
"Understanding and Politics" (Arendt) **98**:50, 52
"Understanding but not Forgetting" (Madhubuti) **73**:206-07, 209
Understanding Drama (Brooks) **110**:20, 29, 33
Understanding Fiction (Brooks) **110**:14, 20, 29, 33
Understanding Fiction (Warren) **59**:297, 299
Understanding Media: The Extensions of Man (McLuhan) **37**:255-63, 265-66; **83**:359-64, 367, 369, 373
Understanding Poetry (Brooks) **24**:111, 116; **86**:278-79; **110**:3, 14-15, 20, 29, 31, 33, 38, 40
Understanding Poetry (Warren) **39**:257; **59**:297, 299-300
Understrike (Gardner) **30**:151-52
The Understudy (Kazan) **6**:274; **63**:219
The Undertaker (Hawkes) **4**:213, 215
The Undertaker's Gone Bananas (Zindel) **26**:475-77, 479-80
"The Undertaking" (Glück) **22**:174
Undertones of War (Blunden) **2**:65; **56**:28, 31, 33, 38, 42-4, 51
"Underture" (Townshend) **17**:526
"Underwater" (Bioy Casares) **88**:92-3, 95
Underworld (DeLillo) **143**:196-200, 205-17, 219, 221
Underworld (Hecht) **8**:274
Underworld (Sternberg) **20**:368
"The Undesirables" (Huddle) **49**:184
Undesirables (Gunn) **81**:178
"The Undesireables" (Cabral de Melo Neto)
See "A indesjada das gentes"
"Undine" (Heaney) **37**:162; **74**:154
"Undine geht" (Bachmann) **69**:35, 37, 45
"Undine Goes" (Bachmann)
See "Undine geht"
The Undoing (Mastrosimone) **36**:291
"Undone Business" (Bernstein) **142**:9
"Undress the Bureaucrat" (Alegria) **57**:11
The Undying Grass (Kemal)
See *Ölmez otu*
"Uneasy Love" (Kunene) **85**:166
Unemí románu: Cesta Vladislava Vančuryza velkou epikou (Kundera) **68**:242-46, 248-50, 253-54, 263; **115**:320-21, 324-25, 355-56, 358, 360; **135**:223, 229-30, 233
The Unemployed Fortune-Teller (Simic) **130**:334-35
"Unemployment Monologue" (Jordan) **114**:145
Unending Blues (Simic) **49**:339, 341-43; **130**:312, 318
"The Unending Rose" (Borges) **13**:110
The Unending Rose (Borges) **13**:110
"Unes" (Bagryana) **10**:14
"The Unexceptional Drift of Things" (Alexander) **121**:21
"An Unexpected Adventure" (Gerstler) **70**:158
"Unexpected Freedom" (Peacock) **60**:298
The Unexpected Guest (Christie) **12**:125
Unexpected Night (Daly) **52**:86-7
The Unexpected Universe (Eiseley) **7**:90
"Unexpected Visit" (Adcock) **41**:18
Unexplained Laughter (Ellis) **40**:193-94
The Unexpurgated Code: A Complete Manual of Survival and Manners (Donleavy) **6**:142; **10**:153-55; **45**:125
Unfair Arguments with Existence (Ferlinghetti) **2**:134; **111**:63
"Unfinished After-Portrait (or: Stages of Mourning)" (Avison) **4**:36; **97**:76, 90
"Unfinished America" (Mott) **15**:380-81
"The Unfinished Business of Childhood" (Abbott) **48**:7
Unfinished Cathedral (Stribling) **23**:443-45, 447
"Unfinished Life" (Simpson) **149**:307-08
The Unfinished Man (Ezekiel) **61**:91-2, 95-7, 100-01
The Unfinished Novel (Aragon)
See *Le roman inachevé*
Unfinished Ode to Mud (Ponge) **6**:422
"Unfinished Poem" (Larkin) **64**:276-77
Unfinished Portrait (Christie) **48**:78

"Unfinished Short Story" (Forster) **45**:133
Unfinished Tales of Númenor and Middle-Earth (Tolkien) **38**:431-32, 442
An Unfinished Woman: A Memoir (Hellman) **4**:221-22; **8**:280-82; **14**:259; **18**:224, 226, 228; **34**:349, 352; **44**:527-28, 530; **52**:189-204
"Unflushed Urinals" (Justice) **102**:259, 261, 269
"Unfold! Unfold!" (Roethke) **101**:274, 281, 284, 335, 339-40
Unfolding in Fog (Shamlu) **10**:469-70
"The Unforeseen" (Gerstler) **70**:158
The Unforgiven (Huston) **20**:168
The Unfortunates (Johnson) **9**:300-03
"Unframed Originals" (Merwin) **88**:189
Unframed Originals: Recollections (Merwin) **45**:271-74, 276-77; **88**:198, 200, 202
"Unfriendly Witness" (Starbuck) **53**:353, 355
Ungenach (Bernhard) **32**:17-18; **61**:9
"El ungido" (Castellanos) **66**:50
"The Unglamorous but Worthwhile Duties of the Black Revolutionary Artist" (Walker) **103**:365
Unglück (Handke) **134**:164
The Ungrateful Garden (Kizer) **15**:308; **39**:171; **80**:171-75, 177, 179
The Ungrateful Land (Carrier) **78**:66
Unguarded Hours (Wilson) **33**:450-51
The Unguarded House (Boell)
See *Haus ohne Hüter*
"Unguided Tour" (Sontag) **13**:516, 518; **105**:206
"The Unhappy Composer" (Kunene) **85**:175
The Unheard Cry for Meaning: Psychotherapy and Humanism (Frankl) **93**:219-20
"Unhiding" (Kroetsch)
See "Unhiding the Hidden: Recent Canadian Fiction"
"Unhiding the Hidden: Recent Canadian Fiction" (Kroetsch) **132**:201, 208-9, 238-39, 276, 278
"Unholy Living and Half Dying" (O'Faolain) **32**:341
Unholy Loves (Oates) **15**:402-03; **33**:292; **52**:338; **108**:386, 390
The Unholy Three (Browning) **16**:122, 124
"Unhoped for Reunion" (Hein)
See "Unverhofftes Wiedersehen"
The Unicorn (Murdoch) **1**:236; **3**:345, 347; **6**:345; **8**:406; **11**:386-87; **15**:381-83; **22**:324-26
The Unicorn (Walser)
See *Das Einhorn*
The Unicorn and Other Poems, 1935-1955 (Lindbergh) **82**:158
"The Unicorn in the Garden" (Thurber) **5**:442; **11**:533; **125**:392, 408, 413
El unicornio (Mujica Lainez) **31**:282-83
"The Uninsured" (Gilchrist) **143**:300, 314
"Uninvited Guests" (Blaga) **75**:77
"The Union Dead" (Lowell) **124**:297
Union Dues (Sayles) **10**:460-62; **14**:483-84
L'union libre (Breton) **54**:17, 30; **9**:133
"Union Maid" (Guthrie) **35**:191, 194
Union Street (Barker) **32**:11; **94**:2-3, 9, 11, 14; **146**:5, 29, 31-4, 36, 40-1
"The Unique/Universal" (Oates) **108**:356
Unit of Five (Dudek) **19**:136
"The Unitas Oppositorium: Prose of Jorge Luis Borges" (Lem) **149**:158-62
"The United Church Observer" (McFadden) **48**:246, 248
"United Rapes Unlimited, Argentina" (Valenzuela) **31**:438
United States (Gelbart) **21**:131
"U.S. 1946 King's X" (Frost) **9**:223
United States: Essays 1952-1992 (Vidal) **142**:297, 299-301, 303, 310, 321, 331
U.S. Grant and the American Military Tradition (Catton) **35**:87-8
U.S.A. (Dos Passos) **1**:77-80; **4**:131-38; **8**:181-82; **11**:154-58; **15**:180-83, 185-87; **25**:137-38, 140-48; **34**:419-24; **82**:59-114
"U.S. One" (Rukeyser) **27**:406
U.S. One (Rukeyser) **15**:457-59; **27**:404-05, 408, 410
"The Unity" (Stern) **40**:414
The Unity of Marlowe's Doctor Faustus (Brooks) **24**:111
Unity of the Stream (Watkins) **43**:456-57
The Universal Baseball Association, Inc., J. Henry Waugh, Prop. (Coover) **3**:114; **7**:59-60; **15**:143; **32**:124-25; **46**:116-17, 119, 121; **87**:24-5, 27, 29, 35-8, 41, 43, 48, 50-1, 53, 58
A Universal History of Infamy (Borges)
See *Historia universal de la infamia*
"Universal Love" (Cliff) **21**:65
"Universe" (Heinlein) **26**:163; **55**:304
"The Universe" (Swenson) **61**:390; **106**:316, 345
The Universe, and Other Fictions (West) **96**:363, 373, 384
"The Universe as Seen Through a Keyhole" (Galeano) **72**:130
"Universe into Stone" (Smith) **15**:516
"The Universe Is Closed and Has REMs" (Starbuck) **53**:354
"The Universe Is Not Really Expanding" (Willingham) **51**:403
"The Universe of Death" (Miller) **84**:252
A Universe of Time (Farrell) **11**:192
"The Universe Responds" (Walker) **58**:410
"University" (Shapiro) **15**:476; **53**:331
"University Examinations in Egypt" (Enright) **4**:154
"University Hospital, Boston" (Oliver) **34**:247; **98**:257, 267
"The University Is Something Else You Do" (Bell) **31**:51
"The University Toilet" (Simmons) **43**:408
An Unkindness of Ravens (Rendell) **48**:325
The Unknown (Browning) **16**:121, 123-25
The Unknown (Maugham) **11**:368
Unknown Assailant (Hamilton) **51**:192-93, 195
"An Unknown Child" (Gardam) **43**:171
"Unknown Citizen" (Auden) **3**:23
"Unknown Girl in the Maternity Ward" (Sexton) **53**:317; **123**:412, 423
Unknown Man, No. 89 (Leonard) **28**:233; **71**:219; **120**:271, 275-79
The Unknown Men (Vesaas)
See *Dei ukjende mennene*
The Unknown Shor (O'Brian) **152**:280
"The Unknown Soldier" (Morrison) **17**:287, 291-92, 295-96
Unlawful Assembly (Enright) **31**:150, 154
Unlearning the Lie: Sexism in School (Harrison) **144**:100-01, 114
Unleaving (Paton Walsh) **35**:431-34
"Unless" (Warren) **18**:537
"The Unlikely" (MacCaig) **36**:284
Unlikely Stories, Mostly (Gray) **41**:178-79, 181-83
Unlimited (Cliff) **21**:60-1
The Unlimited Dream Company (Ballard) **14**:40; **137**:3, 8-9, 11-12, 14, 16, 37
"The Unlived Life" (Boland) **113**:77, 84
Unlocking the Air and Other Stories (Le Guin) **136**:375
The Unloved: From the Diary of Perla S. (Lustig) **56**:186-87
The Unlovely Child (Williams) **39**:100-01
The Unmade Bed (Sagan) **17**:428
"Unmailed Letter" (Harjo) **83**:273
"Unmailed, Unwritten Letters" (Oates) **19**:348, 351; **52**:338; **108**:369; **134**:246
The Unmaking of a Dancer (Brady) **86**:130, 133-34, 136
The Unmediated Vision (Hartman) **27**:179, 182
"The Unmentionable Subject" (Brophy) **105**:11
"The Unmirroring Peak" (Ammons) **8**:14
The Unnameable (Beckett)
See *L'innommable*
"Unnamed Islands in the Unknown Sea" (Hulme) **130**:51, 53
Unnatural Causes (James) **46**:205; **122**:120, 126-27, 134, 145, 150-53, 183
Unnatural Exposure (Cornwell) **155**:69, 72-3, 75
Unnatural Scenery (Canby) **13**:132
"Unnatural State of the Unicorn" (Komunyakaa) **86**:191; **94**:240
"Unnatural Writing" (Snyder) **120**:357
"Uno de dos" (Arreola) **147**:27
"Uno dei tanti epiloghi" (Pasolini) **106**:266
Uno y el universo (Sabato) **23**:378
An Unofficial Rose (Murdoch) **1**:236-37; **3**:347; **8**:406; **22**:327
The Unoriginal Sinner and the Ice-Cream God (Powers) **66**:381-83
Unpaniere di chiocciole (Landolfi) **49**:215
"The Unpeaceable Kingdom" (Mott) **15**:380
The Unpopular Ones (Archer) **12**:16
The Unquiet Bed (Livesay) **15**:340-41; **79**:332, 335-41, 349-52
"The Unquiet Ones" (Kunitz) **148**:90
"Unraveling" (Swan) **69**:355
"Unready to Wear" (Vonnegut) **12**:617
"Unreal City" (Eliot) **13**:198-99
Unreality (Brandys)
See *A Question of Reality*
"unrecovered losses/black theater traditions" (Shange) **126**:370
"The Unregenerate" (Belitt) **22**:49
"Unregierbarkeit" (Enzensberger) **43**:152
"Unreleased Movie" (Ashbery) **77**:65, 67
"Unrepresentative Verse" (Bernstein) **142**:57
Unrequited Loves (Baker) **8**:40
"Unrest" (Bly) **10**:56
"Unresting Death" (Larkin) **64**:258
"The Unreturning Footsteps" (Carroll) **10**:98
The Unrewarded Killer (Ionesco)
See *Tueur sans gages*
"Unrhymed Sonnet" (Ekelöf) **27**:117
"An Un-Romantic American" (Boland) **113**:103, 106, 108
"Unsaid" (Ammons) **25**:43; **108**:9
"An Unsaid Word" (Rich) **125**:310-11
"An Unscheduled Stop" (Adams) **46**:17
Der Unschuldige (Hochwälder) **36**:237
"Unscientific Postscript" (Nemerov) **6**:361
Unsecular Man: The Persistance of Religion (Greeley) **28**:171-72
"The Unseen" (Pinsky) **38**:359, 361-63; **94**:298-99; **121**:436
"The Unseen" (Singer) **38**:407; **111**:314
The Unseen Hand (Shepard) **4**:490; **6**:496-97; **17**:437-38, 442, 448; **41**:409
Unsent Letters: Irreverent Notes from a Literary Life (Bradbury) **61**:48
"Unsere Gier nach Geschdichten" (Frisch) **44**:188
"Unsere gute, alte Renée" (Boell) **72**:70
The Unshaven Cheek (Lawler) **58**:332
Unshorn Locks and Bogus Bagels (Perelman) **9**:415
Unsilent Night (Lee) **46**:231
"The Unspeakable" (Avison) **97**:81-4
The Unspeakable Gentleman (Marquand) **10**:330
Unspeakable Practices, Unnatural Acts (Barthelme) **2**:39; **6**:30; **8**:49, 50, 52; **13**:55; **23**:44; **46**:35-6, 39; **59**:247; **115**:57, 76
The Unspeakable Skipton (Johnson) **27**:217-18, 220, 224
"Unspoken" (Gascoyne) **45**:157
"An Unstamped Letter in Our Rural Letter Box" (Frost) **26**:118
"The Unsuccessful Husband" (Creeley) **4**:118
An Unsuitable Attachment (Pym) **37**:369-72; **111**:229-30, 232, 234, 236, 239, 242-44, 248, 258, 263, 265-66, 269-70, 279, 281-83, 285, 287
An Unsuitable Job for a Woman (James) **18**:272;

46:205-06; **122**:121, 133, 138, 144, 146-48, 151-52, 165, 183-84, 186-87
The Unsuspected Stair (Blaga)
See *Nebanuitele trepte*
The Unteleported Man (Dick) **72**:110, 121
"The Untelling" (Strand) **6**:521-22; **18**:520; **41**:433, 438; **71**:279, 289
"Unter den Linden" (Wolf) **150**:229, 237, 298, 319
Unter den Linden (Wolf) **29**:464, 467; **150**:237, 286
"Unter Mördern und Irren" (Bachmann) **69**:35-6, 45, 56
"Der Untergand der Titanic" (Enzensberger) **43**:150-53
Der Untergeher (Bernhard) **61**:22
Unterm Rad (Hesse) **2**:189; **3**:245; **17**:195-96, 201-02, 211, 215-17
"Das Unternehmen der Wega" (Dürrenmatt) **15**:196
Unterweggs zur Sprache (Heidegger) **24**:265, 277
"Until" (Tillinghast) **29**:415
"Until Forsaken" (Tanizaki)
See "Suterareru made"
Until I See You, Jesus (Poniatowska)
See *Hasta no verte, Jesús mío*
"Until It's Time for You to Go" (Sainte-Marie) **17**:432
Until the Celebration (Snyder) **17**:474
"Until the Night" (Joel) **26**:216-17, 220-21
"Until They Sail" (Michener) **109**:378
Until Your Heart Stops (McNally) **82**:264-70
Untilovsk (Leonov) **92**:255, 260, 270, 277
Untinears and Antennae for Maurice Ravel (Williams) **13**:601
"Untitled" (Ashbery) **25**:54
"Untitled" (Giovanni) **19**:192
"Untitled" (Swenson) **106**:336, 349
"Untitled" (Zamora)
See "Sin título"
"Untitled Piece" (McCullers) **12**:433
"Untitled Poem" (Silkin) **43**:400
Untitled Subjects (Howard) **7**:166-69; **10**:276; **47**:168-69
"Untitled Two" (Graham) **118**:263
Unto Deatht (Oz)
See *Ad m'avet*
Untold Millions (Hobson) **25**:272-73
"An Untold Story" (Colter) **58**:146-47
Untouchable (Anand) **23**:11, 13, 15, 17, 20-1; **93**:22, 24, 29-30, 36-8, 40-2, 45-6, 48-50
The Untouchable (Banville) **118**:37-38, 42, 44-45
The Untouchables (Mamet) **46**:255-56
The Untuning of the Sky (Hollander) **8**:298
The Unusual Adventures of Julio Jurenito and His Disciples (Ehrenburg)
See *The Extraordinary Adventures of Julio Jurenito and His Disciples*
The Unusual Life of Tristan Smith (Carey) **96**:75-80, 82, 84
Unusual Stories about the Peasants (Leonov)
See *Neobyknovennie rasskazy o muzhikakh*
Unutulan adam (Hikmet) **40**:245
The Unvanquished (Fast) **23**:154; **131**:55, 65, 73, 79, 81-2, 85, 93
The Unvanquished (Faulkner) **3**:149; **14**:179; **18**:148-49; **28**:138; **52**:137
"Unveiling" (Havel)
See "Vernisáz"
"The Unveiling" (Milosz) **31**:262-63
Unveiling Claudia: A True Story of a Serial Murder (Keyes) **80**:169
"Unverhofftes Wiedersehen" (Hein) **154**:166
Die Unvernünftigen Sterben aus (Handke) **8**:261; **10**:257; **15**:268-69; **134**:111, 114, 116-17, 158, 161
"The Unwanted" (Day Lewis) **10**:131
"Unwanted" (Lowell) **37**:238; **124**:254, 301
"The Unwithered Garland" (Kunitz) **148**:89
"The Unworldliness That He Creates" (Gregor) **9**:253
"The Unworthy Friend" (Borges) **10**:67; **13**:104
"Unworthy of the Angel" (Donaldson) **46**:143
"Unwritten Episodes" (Mphahlele) **25**:336
"The Unwritten Poem" (Simpson) **32**:380; **149**:336
"Unwritten Poem Review" (Szymborska) **99**:193, 202-03
"The Unwritten Work" (Rozewicz)
See "Sztuka nienapisana"
Un uoma (Fallaci) **110**:195-97
Uomini e no (Vittorini) **9**:546, 548
L'uomo che guarda (Moravia) **46**:287-88
Up (Sukenick) **3**:475; **4**:530-31; **48**:363, 366-67, 370
Up above the World (Bowles) **2**:78; **53**:38, 40-1, 43-5, 49
Up Against It (Royko) **109**:404
Up against It: A Screenplay for the Beatles (Orton) **43**:327-28, 331
"Up, Aloft in the Air" (Barthelme) **115**:65
"Up Among the Eagles" (Valenzuela) **104**:377, 388
Up Among the Eagles (Valenzuela)
See *Donde viven las águilas*
"Up and Down" (Fuller) **62**:191-92, 197
"Up and Down" (Merrill) **3**:335; **13**:378, 381; **18**:331
Up and Out (Powys) **46**:322; **125**:293
"Up at La Serra" (Tomlinson) **13**:547, 549
Up at the Villa (Maugham) **67**:217
"Up Country" (Kumin) **28**:224
Up Country: Poems of New England (Kumin) **5**:222
Up from Liberalism (Buckley) **37**:58, 60
"Up from the Earth" (Kumin) **13**:327
"Up From the Kitchen Floor" (Friedan) **74**:92
"Up in Heaven" (Clash) **30**:48
"Up in Michigan" (Hemingway) **30**:180, 198; **44**:518; **50**:415, 418-19, 426, 428
Up in Seth's Room (Mazer) **26**:292-93, 295
"Up in the Old Hotel" (Mitchell) **98**:161, 166, 173, 179, 182, 184
Up in the Old Hotel (Mitchell) **98**:169, 171-72, 174-78, 180, 183, 185, 187
"Up on Fong Mountain" (Mazer) **26**:291
Up the Agency: The Funny Business of Advertising (Mayle) **89**:150, 152
"Up the Bare Stairs" (O'Faolain) **1**:259
"Up the Dark Valley" (McGrath) **59**:183
Up the Line (Silverberg) **140**:364-65, 378
Up the Sandbox! (Roiphe) **3**:434-35; **9**:455
"Up the Shore" (Heaney) **14**:243
Up the Walls of the World (Tiptree) **48**:386-88, 391, 393, 397; **50**:355, 357-58
"Up to the Crater of an Old Volcano" (Hughes) **108**:323
Up to Thursday (Shepard) **17**:433; **41**:411
"Updraft" (Graham) **118**:227, 230
"An Upland Field" (Day Lewis) **10**:131
"Uplands" (Ammons) **5**:27; **57**:59
Uplands (Ammons) **2**:12; **5**:26-7; **9**:26-7; **25**:45; **57**:59; **108**:55
"Upon Apthorp House" (Hollander) **8**:299
"Upon Finding Dying: An Introduction, by L.E. Sissman, Remaindered at Is" (Sissman) **9**:490
"Upon Meeting Don L. Lee, in a Dream" (Dove) **81**:133, 137
"Upon the Sweeping Flood" (Oates) **134**:245, 248
Upon the Sweeping Flood, and Other Stories (Oates) **3**:360; **6**:370; **108**:341
"Upon This Evil Earth" (Oz) **27**:359, 361
Upon This Rock (Slaughter) **29**:377
Upper Austria (Kroetz) **41**:239-40
"Upper Berth" (Spielberg) **6**:519
"The Upper Class Twit of the Year Race" (Monty Python) **20**:223
"Upprätt" (Transtroemer) **52**:410
"Upprörd meditation" (Transtroemer) **65**:235
"Up-Rising" (Duncan) **7**:88; **41**:130
"Uprising" (Marley) **17**:273
"Upriver Incident" (Muldoon) **32**:315, 317
"Ups and Downs" (Kinsella) **27**:236
"The Upside Down Evolution" (Lem) **149**:264
"Upsilon" (Tolson) **105**:249-50, 252, 255-56
"Upstairs by a Chinese Lamp" (Nyro) **17**:313, 316, 318
"Upstairs, Downstairs" (Raphael) **14**:438
"Upstairs, Mona Bayed for Dong" (Hannah) **90**:160
The Upstart (Read) **4**:444-45; **10**:434-35; **25**:379
Upstate (Wilson) **2**:475-77; **8**:550
"Uptight" (Wonder) **12**:655, 661
Uptight (Grass)
See *Davor*
"Uptown" (Prince) **35**:324
Uptown Saturday Night (Poitier) **26**:359-60
"Ur en afrikansk dagbok" (Transtroemer) **52**:409-10
Ura me tri harqe (Kadare) **52**:259-60, 262
"L'uranium" (Theriault) **79**:408
Uranium Poems (Johnson) **7**:414; **15**:479
Uranus (Aymé) **11**:22-3
"Urban" (Ezekiel) **61**:91, 100
"An Urban Convalescence" (Merrill) **6**:323; **13**:379
Urban Scrawl (Ritter) **52**:355-56
"The Urbanization of a Shelter" (Cabral de Melo Neto)
See "O regaço urbanizado"
"Ur-Cantos" (Pound) **10**:401; **48**:285
Urfaust (Duerrenmatt) **102**:61
"The Urge to Self-Destruction" (Koestler) **6**:282
Urgent Copy (Burgess) **94**:56-7
"Uriah Preach" (Bennett) **28**:29
Urlicht (Innaurato) **60**:205, 207
"The Urn" (Olds) **85**:306
Die Ursache (Bernhard) **32**:25-6; **61**:11
"Der Ursprung des Kunstwerkes" (Heidegger) **24**:259
Urujac (Audiberti) **38**:32-3
"Úryvek z dopisu" (Seifert) **93**:344
"Us" (Codrescu) **121**:161
"US" (O'Hara) **13**:424
"Us" (Sexton) **53**:324
"Us and Them" (Pink Floyd) **35**:309, 313
Us Number One (Crumb) **17**:83
"Us Together" (Johnston) **51**:243
L'usage de la parole (Sarraute) **31**:381-83, 386
L'usage des plaisirs (Foucault)
See *Histoire de la sexualité, Vol. 2: L'usage des plaisirs*
The Use and Abuse of Art (Barzun) **51**:42-4
"The Use of Books" (McGrath) **59**:180
"The Use of Force" (Williams) **13**:606; **42**:458
"The Use of History" (Simmons) **43**:412
The Use of Pleasure: The History of Sexuality, Vol. 2 (Foucault)
See *Histoire de la sexualité, Vol. 2: L'usage des plaisirs*
The Use of Poetry and the Use of Criticism: Studies in the Relation of Criticism to Poetry in England (Eliot) **6**:167; **24**:161, 182-83; **41**:156; **113**:205
A Use of Riches (Stewart) **7**:464
The Use of Speech (Sarraute)
See *L'usage de la parole*
The Use of Words (Castellanos)
See *El uso de la palabra: Una mirada a la realidad*
"A Used Car Lot at Night" (Dacey) **51**:83
"The Used-Boy Raisers" (Paley) **140**:235, 245-46, 248-49
"Useful Fictions" (Roth) **4**:457; **9**:459
"Useless Knowledge" (Ciardi) **129**:51
The Useless Mouths (Beauvoir)
See *Les bouches inutiles*
The Useless Sex (Fallaci)
See *Il sesso inutile*
"The Uses of Anger" (Lorde) **71**:243

The Uses of Enchantment: The Meaning and Importance of Fairy Tales (Bettelheim) **79**:113-14, 123, 126, 135, 143-44, 146-47, 149-50,
"The Uses of Light" (Snyder) **120**:348
"The Uses of Literature" (Brooks) **24**:111; **110**:8
The Uses of Literature (Calvino)
See *Una pietra sopra: Discorsi di letteratura e societa*
"The Uses of the Erotic, The Erotic as Power" (Lorde) **71**:241, 243
"The Uses of Williamson Wood" (Carey) **96**:28, 38
USFS 1919: The Ranger, The Cook and a Hole in the Sky (Maclean) **78**:221, 231-33, 235-36
Ushant: An Essay (Aiken) **3**:3-5; **5**:8-9; **10**:3; **52**:19, 23-5, 31
"Usher II" (Bradbury) **98**:114
"'Ushshaq al-hara" (Mahfouz) **153**:235, 273
L'usignuolo della Chiesa Cattolica (Pasolini) **37**:347-48; **106**:228, 242, 250, 263, 265, 267-68
Using Biography (Empson) **34**:338, 538-43
Usmirenie Badadoshkina (Leonov) **92**:270, 277
El uso de la palabra: Una mirada a la realidad (Castellanos) **66**:49, 54, 56
Uspravna zemlja (Popa) **19**:374-75
"Ustica" (Paz) **4**:396
"A Usual Prayer" (Berryman) **13**:82
The Usual Story (Salama)
See *Se tavallinen tarina*
"Usufruct" (Clarke) **6**:112
"The Usurers" (Guillén) **48**:159
"Usurpation (Other People's Stories)" (Ozick) **7**:288-90; **28**:348; **62**:341, 343, 353-54; **155**:132, 167, 169-70, 178-79, 183-84, 190, 197, 210, 222
The Usurpers (Milosz)
See *Zdobycie wladzy*
Ut Unum Sint (John Paul II) **128**:207
Utah Blaine (L'Amour) **25**:279
"Utah Stars" (Matthews) **40**:322
Uterine Hunger (Miller) **84**:253
Utolenie zhazhdy (Trifonov) **45**:407-08, 410
"Utopia" (MacNeice) **10**:325
"Utopia" (Szymborska) **99**:192, 195
"Utopia de un hombre que está cansada" (Borges) **9**:117; **48**:39
Utopia Fourteen (Vonnegut)
See *Player Piano*
Utopia, Inc. (Ludlam) **46**:241
"Utopia, Modernism, and Death" (Jameson) **142**:253
"Utopia of a Tired Man" (Borges)
See "Utopia de un hombre que está cansada"
Utsikt från en grästuva (Martinson) **14**:355
Utsukushisa to kanashimi (Kawabata) **2**:222; **5**:208-09; **9**:316
Utwory poetyckie (Milosz) **11**:381; **22**:307
Utz (Chatwin) **57**:146-51; **59**:275-77
Las uvas y el viento (Neruda) **5**:301; **5**:301; **28**:312, 314
"V" (Merrill) **8**:383, 387
V. (Harrison) **43**:181; **129**:173, 176-78, 204-05, 207-08, 210-11, 219-20
V. (Pynchon) **2**:353-57; **3**:408-12, 414-15, 417, 419-20; **6**:430, 432-38; **9**:444-46; **11**:452-55; **18**:430, 433-35; **33**:327-30, 333-34, 338-40; **62**:431-33, 439, 443, 451, 453; **72**:296-99, 301-02, 308-09, 311, 325, 339; **123**:294-95, 300, 303, 306-07, 331
"V Amerika, propakhshey mrakom" (Voznesensky) **57**:416
"V, der Vogel" (Grass) **32**:201
"V dni neslykhanno bolevyye" (Voznesensky) **15**:556
"V gribnuiu osen" (Trifonov) **45**:408
V kruge pervom (Solzhenitsyn) **1**:319-21; **2**:407-10, 412; **4**:511, 515; **7**:432-36, 439, 440-42, 445; **9**:504; **10**:481; **18**:497-98; **26**:419; **34**:481, 485, 487, 491-92; **78**:382-85, 406-12, 418, 420, 424; **134**:296-97, 303, 305, 316-17
"V opustevshem dome otdykha" (Akhmadulina) **53**:12
V poiskakh grustnogo bebi: Kniga ob Amerike (Aksyonov)
See *In Search of Melancholy Baby*
"V, the Bird" (Grass)
See "V, der Vogel"
"V tot mesiats Mai" (Akhmadulina) **53**:11
"Vaarlem and Tripp" (Garfield) **12**:218
"The Vacant Lot" (Brooks) **125**:89
"The Vacant Lot" (O'Connor) **15**:409; **104**:123
"A Vacant Possession" (Fenton) **32**:165-66
A Vacant Possession (Fenton) **32**:165
Vacant Possession (Mantel) **144**:212, 220, 222, 228, 239
Vacant Sites (Hrabal)
See *Proluky*
"The Vacation" (Bradbury) **42**:33
Vacation Time: Poems for Children (Giovanni) **117**:178, 193
Václav Havel: Living in Truth (Havel) **123**:200
"The Vacuum" (Nemerov) **36**:305
"Vacuum Genesis" (MacEwen) **55**:163
Vaegen till Klockrike (Martinson)
See *Vägen till Klockrike*
"The Vagabond King" (Arzner) **98**:69
Vagabundos (Bonham) **12**:51
Vagadu (Jouve) **47**:203
"El vagamundo" (Otero) **11**:427
Vägen till Klockrike (Martinson) **14**:356
Vaghe stelle dell Orsa (Visconti) **16**:569
"A Vagrant" (Gascoyne) **45**:150, 157
A Vagrant and Other Poems (Gascoyne) **45**:147-51, 153
The Vagrant Mood (Maugham) **15**:368; **67**:219
"A Vague Word" (Mahfūz) **52**:297
Vägvisare till underjorden (Ekeloef) **27**:117
The Vaiden Trilogy (Stribling) **23**:446, 448
"Vain and Careless" (Graves) **45**:166-67
"The Vain Life of Voltaire" (Riding) **7**:373
Ein vakker dag (Vesaas) **48**:407
The Valachi Papers (Maas) **29**:303-05, 307
"Valaida" (Wideman) **67**:379, 382-84
"Valarie" (Zappa) **17**:586
Valdez Is Coming (Leonard) **71**:224
The Vale of Laughter (De Vries) **3**:125
"A Vale of Soulmaking" (Levertov) **66**:243
"Valediction" (Ciardi) **40**:151, 156
"Valediction" (Heaney) **25**:244
"Valediction" (MacNeice) **53**:231
"Valediction" (Thomas) **48**:380
"Valediction" (Weldon) **122**:281
"A Valediction Forbidding Mourning" (Rich) **36**:373; **125**:321
"Valentine" (Ashbery) **13**:36; **77**:45-7
"A Valentine" (Fuller) **62**:199, 204
"The Valentine" (Jones) **39**:410
The Valentine (Garfield) **12**:234
"Valentine Day" (McCartney) **35**:279
"Valentine for Ophelia" (L'Heureux) **52**:273
Valentines to the Wide World (Van Duyn) **3**:491; **63**:443; **116**:398, 406, 413, 426
Valentino (Ginzburg) **11**:228-29; **54**:210, 213-14
Valentino (Russell) **16**:551
"Valère et le grand canot" (Theriault) **79**:407
Valère et le grand canot (Theriault) **79**:407
"The Valiant Vacationist" (Avison) **97**:70-1, 76, 94, 100, 103-04, 131
"The Valiant Woman" (Powers) **1**:282
Validity in Interpretation (Hirsch) **79**:254-55, 257-58, 260-61
"Valina kukla" (Leonov) **92**:237, 262
VALIS (Dick) **72**:109, 116-20
El valle de las hamacas (Argueta) **31**:19
"La vallée" (Audiberti) **38**:21
"The Valley" (Bass) **143**:9-11
"Valley" (Grace) **56**:112-13, 118-19, 121
"The Valley Between" (Marshall) **72**:254
The Valley of Bones (Powell) **3**:400; **7**:340, 345; **10**:418; **31**:317
Valley of Decision (Middleton) **38**:335
The Valley of Horses (Auel) **31**:23-4; **107**:3-5, 8-11, 13-14, 24
The Valley of Issa (Milosz)
See *Dolina Issy*
"The Valley of Rest" (Kunene) **85**:165
Valley of the Dolls (Susann) **3**:475
"Valley of the Dragon" (Davidson) **13**:168; **19**:129
"Valo do Capibaribe" (Cabral de Melo Neto) **76**:168-69
Valparaiso (DeLillo) **143**:230-31
La valse aux adieux (Kundera) **9**:321-22; **19**:268, 270; **32**:261-62, 266; **68**:232, 239-43, 245, 260-61; **115**:351; **135**:206, 208, 212, 241, 243, 245-46, 249-50, 253
La valse des toréadors (Anouilh) **3**:11-12; **8**:24; **13**:17, 20-1; **40**:54-5, 59-60; **50**:278-80
La Valse mauve (Dinesen) **95**:69
"Valuable" (Smith) **3**:460
"The Value of Money" (Berger) **19**:39
"The Value of Narrativity in the Representation of Reality" (White) **148**:242, 247-48, 251, 291-92
"Values" (Blunden) **56**:33, 39
"Valya's Doll" (Leonov)
See "Valina kukla"
Vamp till Ready (Fuller) **28**:157-58
"Vampire" (Hughes) **2**:198; **9**:280
"Vampire" (Muldoon) **72**:265
Vampire (Wilson) **33**:460-64
"Vampire Blues" (Young) **17**:573
The Vampire Lestat (Rice) **41**:365-66; **128**:279, 283, 293, 298-302, 304, 307-08, 313
The Vampires (Rechy) **107**:223, 225-26, 228, 239, 256
Vampyr (Dreyer)
See *The Strange Adventures of David Gray*
The Van (Doyle) **81**:157-59, 161
"Van Gogh" (L'Heureux) **52**:272
"Van Gogh" (Jennings) **131**:240
Van Gogh (Resnais) **16**:502, 505, 508
"Van Gogh, Death and Summer" (Byatt) **136**:151, 159
Van Gogh's Room at Arles (Elkin) **91**:213-14, 217, 219-20
"Van Wyck Brooks on the Civil War Period" (Wilson) **24**:481
"Vanadium" (Levi) **37**:227
"Vancouver Lights" (Birney) **6**:74
The Vandal (Schlee) **35**:373
"Vandals" (Munro) **95**:320
Vandals of the Void (Vance) **35**:420
"Vandergast and the Girl" (Simpson) **7**:429; **149**:322
"The Vane Sisters" (Nabokov) **6**:360; **11**:391
The Vaněk Plays: Four Authors, One Character (Havel) **65**:440; **123**:191, 205
"Vanessa's Bower" (McGuckian) **48**:277
Il vangelo secondo Matteo (Pasolini) **20**:260, 263, 265-66, 271; **106**:202-05, 207-09, 221, 226, 248-49, 265, 272-73
Vanguard from Alpha (Aldiss) **14**:10
The Vanished Jet (Blish) **14**:86
"Vanished Mansard" (Hollander) **5**:186
Vanishing Act (Greenberg) **57**:227-28
Vanishing Cornwall (du Maurier) **59**:286
The Vanishing Hero (O'Faolain) **14**:404
Vanishing Point (Mitchell) **25**:323, 327
"Vanishing Point: Urban Indian" (Rose) **85**:311
"The Vanishing Red" (Frost) **26**:111
Vanities (Heifner) **11**:264
"Vanity" (Dobyns) **37**:76
"Vanity" (Merwin) **8**:390
"Vanity" (Oates) **6**:367
Vanity of Duluoz: An Adventurous Education, 1935-1946 (Kerouac) **2**:227, 229; **5**:214; **29**:270; **61**:296, 298, 309-10
"The Vanity of Human Wishes" (Ammons) **108**:22

"The Vanity of Human Wishes" (Gunn) **32**:213
"The Vanity of Human Wishes" (Lowell) **124**:305
The Vanquished (Antonioni)
See *I vinti*
"The Vantage Point" (Frost) **3**:174; **26**:117
"Vanvild Kava" (Singer) **38**:407
"Vanzetti—A Tribute and an Appeal" (Sinclair) **63**:371
"Vapor Trail Reflected in the Frog Pond" (Kinnell) **29**:290; **129**:255, 258, 268
"Vaquero" (Muldoon) **32**:318; **72**:264
Var the Stick (Anthony) **35**:35
Vargtimmen (Bergman) **16**:58-60, 68, 74, 81; **72**:40-1, 50, 52, 55, 62
Varia Invención (Arreola) **147**:4
"Variant" (Ashbery) **13**:35
"The Variant" (Simic) **130**:317
"Variation and Reflection on a Poem by Rilke" (Levertov) **66**:253
"Variation for Two Pianos" (Justice) **102**:258, 262
"Variation on a Noel" (Ashbery) **41**:36
Variation on a Theme (Rattigan) **7**:355
"Variation on a Theme of A. Huxley" (Ewart) **46**:150
"Variation on Gaining a Son" (Dove) **50**:156
"Variations" (Gregor) **9**:254
"Variations on a Text by Vallejo" (Justice) **19**:235; **102**:261, 263, 277, 283
"Variations on a Theme by William Carlos Williams" (Koch) **44**:250
"Variations on a Theme from James" (Justice) **102**:263, 283
"Variations on a Theme of the Seventeenth Century" (Hope)
See "The Elegy"
"Variations on Hopkins on the Theme of Child Wonder" (Clark Bekedermo) **38**:116, 127
Variations on the Theme of an African Dictatorship (Farah) **53**:134, 138-39; **137**:96, 104, 110, 113-14, 123
Varicose Moon (Leyner) **92**:285
"Varieties of Dramatic Criticism" (Crane) **27**:75
"Varieties of Exile" (Gallant) **38**:193
Varieties of Parable (MacNeice) **10**:323-24; **53**:240, 244
Variety Lights (Fellini)
See *Luci del varieta*
"Variety of Literary Utopias" (Frye) **24**:221
"A Variety of Religious Experience" (Brady) **86**:136
"Varioni Brothers" (Salinger) **12**:498
"The Various Arts of Poverty and Cruelty" (Bly) **15**:68
Various Inventions (Arreola)
See *Varia Invención*
The Various Light (Corn) **33**:116-20
"Various Miracles" (Shields) **113**:429
Various Miracles (Shields) **113**:403, 405-08, 410, 414, 419, 421, 424-25, 429
Various Persons Named Kevin O'Brien (Nowlan) **15**:399
Vårnatt (Vesaas) **48**:407-08, 412
The Varnishing Day (Havel)
See *Vernissage*
A városalapító (Konrád) **10**:304-05; **73**:173, 175-77, 179-82, 187
"Varsell Pleas" (Hersey) **81**:329
The Varsity Story (Callaghan) **65**:253
"The 'Varsity Students' Rag" (Betjeman) **43**:35
"The Vase and the Rose" (Major) **19**:298
"The Vase of Tears" (Spender) **41**:420
"The Vasectomy Bureau in Lisdoonvarna" (Durcan) **43**:117
Les vases communicants (Breton) **54**:21, 25-6; **9**:126-27; **15**:88
Vash ubiytsa (Aksyonov) **22**:26-7; **37**:12
"A Vast Common Room" (Price) **63**:333, 335
"A Vast Confusion" (Ferlinghetti) **111**:65
The Vast Earth (Pasternak) **63**:290
"Vaster than Empires and More Slow" (Le Guin) **45**:221; **136**:329, 375, 385
"The Vastness of the Dark" (MacLeod) **56**:193
"Vat 96" (Welsh) **144**:317
"Vatolandia" (Castillo) **151**:47
"Vaucanson" (Ashbery) **77**:64, 67
"Vaucanson's Duck" (Bernard) **59**:45
Vaudeville for a Princess, and Other Poems (Schwartz) **10**:462; **45**:359; **87**:348
The Vaudeville Marriage (Hochman) **3**:250
"Vault Centre" (Soyinka) **44**:285
"The Vaults of Yoh-Vombis" (Smith) **43**:418-19, 422
"Vaunting Oak" (Ransom) **5**:365
VD: The Silent Epidemic (Hyde) **21**:176
"V-Day" (McGinley) **14**:366
Vecher (Akhmatova) **25**:23-4; **64**:3, 8, 21; **126**:5, 11, 24, 27, 32, 47
"Vecher na stroyke" (Voznesensky) **15**:556
Vechnata i svjatata (Bagryana) **10**:11, 13
Den vedervaerdige mannen fraan saeffle (Wahlöö) **7**:502
Vedi (Mehta) **37**:295
Veedon Fleece (Morrison) **21**:236-37
Vefarinn mikli frá Kasmír (Laxness) **25**:291, 293
Vega and Other Poems (Durrell) **4**:147
Vegas (Dunne) **28**:121-23, 126
"Las Vegas (What?) Las Vegas (Can't Hear You! Too Noisy) Las Vegas!!!" (Wolfe) **51**:418
"The Vegetable King" (Dickey) **109**:272
The Vegetable Kingdom (Colum) **28**:91
"Vegetable Poems" (Pollitt) **122**:202
Vegetable Poems (Pollitt) **28**:367
"Vegetables" (Wilson) **12**:643
"Veglia" (Ungaretti) **7**:485; **11**:556
"Vegnerà el vero Cristo" (Pasolini) **106**:230
"Vehaya he'akov lemishor" (Agnon) **14**:3
Véhi-Ciosane; ou, Blanche-Genèse, suivi du Mandat (Ousmane) **66**:334-35, 338-44
"Vehicle" (Ammons) **57**:59
"Vehicles" (Honig) **33**:212
"Vehicles" (Williams) **56**:429
The Veil (Johnson) **52**:241
Veilchenfeld (Hofmann) **54**:228
"Le veillard et l'enfant" (Roy) **14**:469
Veillées noires (Damas) **84**:176, 178-81
"The Vein in the Pulse" (Cabral de Melo Neto) **76**:163
A Vein of Riches (Knowles) **10**:303-04; **26**:263
"Veins Visible" (Bissoondath) **120**:6-7
Veinte poemas de amor y una canción desesperada (Neruda) **2**:309; **7**:257, 259, 262; **9**:398; **28**:308, 311-13; **62**:333
Vejíř Boženy Němcové (Seifert) **93**:342
"La velada del sapo" (Castellanos) **66**:45, 47
The Veldt (Bradbury) **42**:33-4
Os velhos marinheiros (Amado) **13**:11; **40**:29-30, 32; **106**:57, 63-4
Velká povídka o Americe (Škvorecký) **152**:326
Ve-Lo al Menat Lizkor (Amichai) **22**:30
"Velocity Meadows" (Strand) **71**:288-89
"Velorio" (Cisneros) **118**:174
"Velorio de Papá Montero" (Guillén) **48**:161-63; **79**:248
"The Velvet Hand" (McGinley) **14**:367
The Velvet Horn (Lytle) **22**:293-97, 300
The Velvet Room (Snyder) **17**:469, 472
The Velvet Underground and Nico (Reed) **21**:303, 307, 314
"Ven al jardín" (Guillén) **79**:238
Las venas abiertas de América Latina (Galeano) **72**: 127-29, 131, 136, 143
Venceremos! The Speeches and Writings of Ernesto Che Guevara (Guevara) **87**:200-02
Le vendeur d'étoiles, et autres contes (Theriault) **79**:401, 408
Les vendeurs du temple (Theriault) **79**:400, 412, 416-17
Los vendidos (Valdez) **84**:395, 404, 416
The Vendor of Sweets (Narayan) **7**:254-55; **28**:295
Vendredi; ou, La vie sauvage (Tournier) **6**:536, 538; **23**:454; **36**:433, 435-37, 441; **95**:366-67, 369, 371-73, 375, 378, 380
Vendredi ou les limbes du Pacifique (Tournier) **95**:361, 377-78, 382, 390
The Venerable Bead (Condon) **100**:105-08
The Venetian Affair (MacInnes) **27**:281; **39**:349-51
"Venetian Interior, 1889" (Howard) **10**:275
"Venetian Stanzas" (Brodsky) **100**:38, 44-5
"Venetian Stanzas II" (Brodsky) **100**:38, 44, 50
"The Venetian Vespers" (Hecht) **19**:207-09
The Venetian Vespers (Hecht) **19**:208-10
"Venetsianskie strofy 2" (Brodsky)
See "Venetian Stanzas II"
"Venexia I" (Wright) **146**:346
"Una venganza" (Allende) **97**:33, 36
"Vengeance" (Iskander)
See "Vozmezdie"
"Vengeance" (Simon) **26**:412-13
La Vengeance de Krimhilde (Lang) **103**:88
"Vengeance for Nikolai" (Miller) **30**:265
Vengeance Is Mine (Spillane) **13**:526, 528
"Vengeance Is Mine, Inc." (Dahl) **79**:181
"The Vengeance of Nitocris" (Williams) **45**:452-55
"The Vengeful Creditor" (Achebe) **7**:6; **26**:23; **75**:15-16
"Veni creator" (Milosz) **56**:248
Veni, Vedi...Wendt (Stern) **4**:523; **39**:239
"Venice" (Denby) **48**:82
"Venice" (Moss) **7**:247; **50**:353
"Venice" (Tomlinson) **45**:399
"Venice 182-" (Berryman) **3**:70
"Venice Now and Then" (Lively) **32**:277
Venice Observed (McCarthy) **59**:292
"The Venice Poem" (Duncan) **15**:187; **55**:292
The Venom Business (Crichton) **54**:65-6
Le vent (Simon) **4**:494-96; **9**:484; **15**:485-87, 490-92, 494; **39**:203-04, 206-07, 209-11
Le Vent à Djémila (Camus) **124**:21
Le vent de la memoire (Cayrol) **11**:108
Le vent d'est (Godard) **20**:142, 144, 150
Le vent paraclet (Tournier) **23**:451-52; **36**:437; **95**:361-62, 364-65, 372, 376-80, 383-84, 387
"Vento a Tindare" (Quasimodo) **10**:428
Le Ventre (Tchicaya) **101**:348, 352, 358-59, 363
"le ventre reste" (Tchicaya) **101**:358
"Ventriloquist's Dummy" (Garrett) **51**:148
The Ventriloquist's Wife (Ludlam) **46**:241; **50**:342-44
Vents (Perse) **4**:399-400; **46**:303-05, 307-09
Venture of the Infinite Man (Neruda)
See *Tentativa del hombre infinito*
Venture Once More (Graham) **23**:192
"Venture to the Moon" (Clarke) **13**:148
"La Venue à l'écriture" (Cixous) **92**:90-1
La Venue à l'écriture (Cixous) **92**:52, 54-6, 69, 74-5, 82, 90-1
Venus and Mars Are Alright Tonight (McCartney) **12**:379; **35**:282-85
Venus and the Rain (McGuckian) **48**:277-79
"Venus and the Sun" (McGuckian) **48**:277-78
"Venus Androgyne" (Gascoyne) **45**:157
"Venus Ascendant" (Gellhorn) **60**:184
"Venus, Cupid, Folly, and Time" (Taylor) **18**:524; **37**:409, 413; **71**:299, 301, 303
Venus Envy (Brown) **79**:171
"The Venus Hunters" (Ballard) **36**:37; **137**:13
Venus in Sparta (Auchincloss) **4**:28, 30
"Venus in the Tropics" (Simpson) **149**:351
Venus, Near Neighbor of the Sun (Asimov) **26**:57-8
Venus Observed (Fry) **2**:143; **10**:200
"The Venus of Azombeii" (Smith) **43**:423
Venus on the Half-Shell (Farmer) **19**:166
Venus Plus X (Sturgeon) **22**:411; **39**:361, 363-64, 367
"Venus Rising" (Swan) **69**:365

"Venus Smiles" (Ballard) **137**:64, 66
"Venus Will Now Say a Few Words" (Auden) **14**:32; **43**:17
"Venusberg" (Barker) **8**:47
Venusberg (Powell) **10**:410-11
"Venus's-flytraps" (Komunyakaa) **94**:234, 241
"Venus—The Lark ..." (Blackburn) **43**:63
Vera Baxter (Duras) **68**:89-90
"Vera i Zoika" (Trifonov) **45**:408
"A Veranda on the Cane Field" (Cabral de Melo Neto)
See "O alpendre no canavial"
"Verandah" (Walcott) **76**:273, 281-82
"Veränderungen in Staech" (Boell) **72**:77, 101
"Veraneo" (Donoso) **8**:178; **32**:156
Veraneo y otros cuentos (Donoso) **11**:145; **99**:239
"Verano" (Cortázar) **13**:164; **33**:123
"The Verb to Kill" (Valenzuela) **31**:438; **104**:382
Verbal and Pictorial Art (Lagerkvist)
See *Ordkonst och bildkonst*
"The Verbalist of Summer" (Eberhart) **56**:82-3
Verbliuzhii glaz (Aitmatov) **71**:3-4, 16, 18
"Verbosity" (Yevtushenko) **126**:388, 396
Der Verdacht (Duerrenmatt) **102**:66-7, 69
Der Verdacht (Dürrenmatt) **4**:140-41; **11**:171, 174; **15**:195; **43**:122-23, 128
"Verdi and Postmodernism" (Bernstein) **142**:13
"The Verdict" (Dodson) **79**:193
Verdict (Christie) **12**:125
The Verdict (Mamet) **46**:253
"Vereda del cuco" (Cernuda) **54**:59
"Die Vergewaltigung" (Hein) **154**:75, 99, 166
"Vergüenza" (Zamora) **89**:363
Das Verhör von Habana (Enzensberger) **43**:146-47
Verikivi (Ivask) **14**:287
"The Veritable Years, 1949-1966" (Everson) **14**:167
Veritatis Splendor (John Paul II) **128**:183, 192, 194, 197, 202, 204
La verité en peinture (Derrida) **87**:90, 92-3, 96, 104, 106-08
Verklighet till döds (Martinson) **14**:355
"Verlie I Say unto You" (Adams) **13**:2
Die verlorene Ehre der Katharina Blum: oder, Wie Gewalt entstehen und wohin sie führen kann (Boell) **6**:84; **11**:58-9; **27**:67; **39**:292, 295-96; **72**:85-86, 88, 90
Der Verlust (Lenz) **27**:256
Vermilion Sands (Ballard) **3**:35; **6**:27-8; **36**:35; **137**:41, 63-67, 76, 78
"Vermont" (Beattie) **63**:22; **146**:84
"Vermont" (Carruth) **18**:88-9; **84**:123
"Vermont Ballad: Change of Season" (Warren) **39**:258
The Vermont Notebook (Ashbery) **6**:11-12; **25**:55
"A Vermont Tale" (Helprin) **22**:221
"Vermont Thaw" (Warren) **39**:265
Verna, U.S.O. Girl (Innaurato) **21**:195
The Vernacular Republic: Poems, 1961-1981 (Murray) **40**:340-41
"Vernisáz" (Havel) **65**:413, 439; **123**:191-92
Vernissage (Havel) **25**:224, 227, 230
Veronica's Room (Levin) **3**:294-95; **6**:306
"Vers de Société" (Larkin) **5**:227, 230; **8**:332, 337; **9**:323; **18**:299; **33**:256, 258, 268; **39**:345-46; **64**:258, 263, 270, 282
"Versben bujdosó" (Nagy) **7**:251
Versben bujdosó (Nagy) **7**:251
Das Verschwinden im Bild: Essays (Wellershoff) **46**:437
"Verse for Urania" (Merrill) **8**:384
"Verse Forms" (Randall) **135**:399
Verses and Poems (Brodsky) **100**:59
"Verses for a Centennial" (MacLeish) **68**:286
Verses: Fourth Book (Daryush) **19**:118, 120
"Verses in April" (Brodsky) **13**:114, 116
"Verses on the Death of T. S. Eliot" (Brodsky)
See "Stixi na smert T. S. Èliota"
"Verses versus Verses" (Bell) **8**:65
"Version Two" (Jones) **131**:269
Versos de salón (Parra) **102**:340-42, 356
Versos del capitán (Neruda) **5**:305; **28**:312
Los versos del capitán (Neruda)
See *Versos del capitán*
Die Verspätung (Hildesheimer) **49**:171
Das Versprechen: Requiem auf den Kriminalroman (Dürrenmatt) **4**:140-41; **11**:171; **15**:195-96; **43**:120, 122-23, 128; **102**:65, 68
Verstörung (Bernhard) **3**:65; **32**:16-22, 26-7; **61**:14, 18-19, 23-4, 29
Versuch über den geglückten Tag (Handke) **134**:156, 159, 171
Versuch über die Jukebox (Handke) **134**:156, 171
Versuch über die Müdigkeit (Handke) **134**:141, 150-54, 156, 171
Versus (Nash) **23**:321
Verteidigung der Wölfe (Enzensberger) **43**:146
"Vertical Man" (Kinsella) **138**:88, 102, 128
The Vertical Smile (Condon) **4**:106; **6**:115
"Vertigo" (Graham) **48**:153
"Vértigo" (Ulibarrí) **83**:407
Vertigo (Hitchcock) **16**:343, 350, 354, 356
"A Very Continental Weekend" (Stolz) **12**:552
A Very Easy Death (Beauvoir)
See *Une morte très douce*
The Very Eye of Night (Deren) **16**:254; **102**:28, 31, 36, 38, 40-1, 48-9
Very Far Away from Anywhere Else (Le Guin) **45**:212, 214
"A Very Good Second Man" (Heym) **41**:217
"A Very Indian Poem in Indian English" (Ezekiel) **61**:95
"Very Like a Whale" (White) **49**:408
A Very Long Engagement (Japrisot)
See *Un long demanche de fiancailles*
A Very Long Way from Anywhere Else (Le Guin)
See *Very Far Away from Anywhere Else*
A Very Private Eye (Pym) **37**:377-78; **111**:236-37, 263, 269, 272, 275
A Very Private Life (Frayn) **31**:190
A Very Proper Death (Hospital) **145**:297, 305
The Very Rich Hours of Count von Stauffenberg (West) **96**:362, 367, 370, 372-73, 377, 380, 382, 387, 392, 399
"The Very Sad Story of Salah Bourguine" (Chatwin) **57**:154; **59**:277
"The Very Same" (Monette) **82**:322, 332
A Very Scotch Affair (Jenkins) **52**:223-24, 227-28
"A Very Short Story" (Hemingway) **30**:181, 189-90, 192, 196
"A Very Stern Discipline" (Ellison) **114**:91
The Very Thing That Happens (Edson) **13**:190
"the very thought" (Rozewicz)
See "Coś takiego"
"Very Tree" (Kunitz) **148**:68, 87-8, 123
"Vesper Journal" (Wright) **146**:339
"Vespers" (Auden) **123**:39
"Vespers" (Berryman) **62**:46
"Vespers" (Johnson) **52**:234
"Vespers" (Muldoon) **32**:315-17
"Vespers" (Wright) **146**:
"Vessel" (Williams) **148**:352
"The Vessel of Wrath" (Maugham) **1**:204
Vessels (Bloom)
See *The Breaking of the Vessels*
Vestal Fire (Mackenzie) **18**:314
"La vestibule" (Butor) **15**:117
"Vestiges" (Brown) **23**:99
"Vestiges" (Bunting) **47**:45
"Vestigia" (Purdy) **6**:428
"Vesuvius" (Tolson) **105**:259
"Vesuvius at Home: The Power of Emily Dickinson" (Rich) **18**:447-48; **76**:218
"The Veteran" (Blunden) **56**:37, 42
"Veterans" (Coles) **46**:109
"Veterans" (Johnston) **51**:241, 243
"Veteran's Dream" (Heaney) **7**:148
"Vetiver" (Ashbery) **77**:63-5, 67-8
Vetsera blomstrer ikke for enhver (Abell) **15**:2
"La veuve Aphrodissia" (Yourcenar) **38**:463; **87**:390
La veuve couderc (Simenon) **2**:398
La veuve enragée (Maillet) **54**:304, 313-17; **118**:329-32
V.I. for Short (Paretsky) **135**:370
"Via Appia" (Denby) **48**:84
Via Dolorosa (Hare) **136**:302-03, 305-06
"Via negativa" (Salter) **52**:368; **59**:196
"Via negativa" (Thomas) **6**:530; **48**:382
"VIA: Tourism" (Moure) **88**:218
Les viaducs de la Seine-et-Oise (Duras) **11**:164-66; **40**:182
"Viagem ao Sahel" (Cabral de Melo Neto) **76**:169
I viaggi la morte (Gadda) **11**:211
"Viaggio agli inferni del secolo" (Buzzati) **36**:97
"Viaggio d'inverno" (Ortese) **89**:199
Viaggio in Sardegna (Vittorini) **9**:548
Viaje a la Alcarria (Cela) **13**:145, 147; **59**:128-30, 143; **122**:5-6, 22, 27, 50, 61, 64
Viaje a la aldea del crimen (Sender) **8**:481
"Viaje a la semilla" (Carpentier) **38**:94-5, 99; **110**:48, 52, 76, 88
"Viaje a Nueva York" (Cardenal) **31**:76-7, 79
Viaje a U.S.A. (Cela) **122**:22
Un viaje de invierno (Benet) **28**:20
Viata grotesca si tragica a lui Victor Hugo: Hugoliade (Ionesco) **86**: 336-7
"La víbora" (Parra) **102**:334, 337-39, 342
A Vicarage Family (Streatfeild) **21**:404, 416
The Vicar's Wife (Bennett) **77**:89
"Vice" (Baraka) **14**:46
"The Vice President of Insurance" (Kunitz) **6**:287
"The Vice-Consul" (Pritchett) **15**:443; **41**:334
Le vice-consul (Duras) **6**:149; **20**:101; **40**:178, 180; **68**:73, 89, 91; **100**:143, 148-49
The Vice-Consul (Duras)
See *Le vice-consul*
The Viceroy of Ouidah (Chatwin) **28**:72-3; **57**:141-42, 148, 150, 153; **59**:274-75, 279
"Los vicios del mundo moderno" (Parra) **102**:342-43
"Vicious Circle" (Reed) **21**:312-13
Vicious Circles (Blanchot) **135**:148
Vicissitude eforma (Luzi) **13**:354
"Vicissitudes of Presidential Reputations" (Schlesinger) **84**:380
"The Vicissitudes of te Avant-Garde" (Gass) **132**:186
"The Victim" (Garrett) **51**:143
"Victim" (O Hehir) **41**:323-24
The Victim (Bellow) **1**:27-31; **2**:49, 51, 53; **3**:48, 50-2, 56-7, 59, 61; **6**:50-3, 56, 61; **8**:74, 78; **13**:71-2; **15**:47-8, 50, 53-5; **25**:80-1, 85; **33**:66, 69, 71; **63**:31, 41; **79**:62, 76, 80, 83, 88
"The Victim of Aulis" (Abse) **7**:1; **29**:14
"La vìctima de Tadeo Limardo" (Bioy Casares) **88**:69
"La victime" (Jouve) **47**:203-05
Victimes du devoir (Ionesco) **4**:251; **6**:247-51, 253-54; **41**:225-27; **86**:332-33
"The Victims" (Olds) **39**:190; **85**:290
"The Victims" (Raine) **45**:334, 338
The Victims of Amnesia (Ferlinghetti) **2**:134; **111**:63
Victims of Duty (Ionesco)
See *Victimes du devoir*
"Victor" (Auden) **11**:16
"A Victor" (Hoffman) **6**:243
"Victor Blue" (Beattie) **63**:11
"Victoria" (Davies) **21**:91
"Victoria" (Haines) **58**:218
Victoria Line (Binchy) **153**:67
Victorian House, and Other Poems (Child) **19**:101
"The Victorians" (Blunden) **56**:51

The Victors (Ambrose) **145**:55-6
The Victors (Sartre)
See *Morts sans sépulture*
"The Victory" (Aksyonov) **101**:11-12, 18, 28, 30-1
"Victory" (Dickey) **2**:117; **47**:95; **109**:267, 273-75
"Victory" (Taylor) **5**:426
Victory: Choices in Revolution (Barker) **37**:38-41
Victory in the Dark (Lagerkvist)
See *Seger i mörker*
Victory of Faith (Riefenstahl)
See *Sieg des Glaubens*
Victory on Janus (Norton) **12**:461, 469
"Victory over Japan" (Gilchrist) **143**:302-03, 321
Victory over Japan (Gilchrist) **34**:164-66; **48**:119, 121; **143**:283, 296, 299, 309-11, 314-16, 321, 326-27, 329-30
"Vida" (Aleixandre)
See "Life"
Vida (Piercy) **18**:406-09; **27**:376, 378, 380; **62**:373, 376; **128**:218, 241, 245
La vida breve (Onetti) **7**:276-81; **10**:376, 380-81
"Vida de perros" (Parra) **102**:340-41
Uma vida em segredo (Dourado) **23**:149-51; **60**:83, 85
"La vida privada" (Arreola) **147**:4
"Vidal vs. Falwell" (Amis) **62**:5
Videodrome (Cronenberg) **143**:57, 65, 71, 76, 81, 83, 93-95, 97-98, 100-02, 104-05, 107-08, 116, 118, 126, 134-35, 138-39, 142-43, 152, 157
La vie (Godard)
See *Sauve qui peut (La vie)*
"La Vie Bohème" (Larson) **99**:162, 168-69, 178, 182, 185-86, 190
La vie dans les plis (Michaux) **19**:314, 316
Vie de l'art théatral, des origines a nos jours (Arreola) **147**:6
La vie devant soi (Gary) **25**:187-89
La vie d'un poète (Cocteau) **8**:147
"La vie écarlate" (Gascar) **11**:222
La vie est ailleurs (Kundera) **4**:276-78; **9**:320; **19**:270; **32**:260-61, 263; **68**:237-42, 244, 247, 257, 260-61, 264; **115**:307-08, 337-38, 342, 347, 350; **135**:245, 249
Vie et aventures de Salavin (Duhamel) **8**:186
La Vie et l'oeuvre de Philippe-Ignace Semmelweiss (Céline) **124**:86
Vie et mort dÉmile Ajar (Gary) **25**:191
La vie materielle (Duras) **68**:99-102; **100**:118-120, 124
La vie, mode d'emploi (Perec) **56**:255, 257-58, 260, 262-65, 267-74; **116**:232, 235-38, 242-43, 246, 248-53, 262, 264-65, 267, 270
"La vie parisienne" (Gallant) **38**:195
La vie passionée of Rodney Buckthorne (Cassill) **23**:107
La vie scélérate (Condé) **92**:102, 104, 107, 112-14, 125, 130-31, 133-34
La vie tranquille (Duras) **6**:149; **11**:165; **40**:179; **100**:145, 147
La vie unanime (Romains) **7**:379
Le Vieil Homme et les loups (Kristeva) **140**:161-66
"Le vieillard et l'enfant" (Roy) **10**:440
La vieillesse (Beauvoir) **2**:43-4; **4**:47, 49; **44**:343-44, 350; **71**:60-1, 75, 77-80, 82
Una vieja historia de caminantes (Costantini) **49**:61
"Vieja moralidad" (Fuentes) **22**:170-71; **113**:237
"La vieja rosa" (Arenas) **41**:28
Viejas historias de castilla la vieja (Delibes) **18**:113
"Vienna" (Spender) **10**:489-90
Vienna (Spender) **91**:260
"Vienna Blood" (Rothenberg) **57**:381
"Vienna. Zurich. Constance" (Thomas) **132**:334, 362-63, 382
"Vienne" (Rhys) **51**:356; **124**:354
"Vientos aliseos" (Cortázar) **34**:333
La vierge de Paris (Jouve) **47**:207-08, 212-13
Viet Journal (Jones) **39**:405, 410
Viet Nam Diskurs (Weiss) **15**:566, 568; **51**:387, 391-92, 395
Viet Rock (Terry) **19**:438-40
"Vietnam" (Cliff) **21**:60-1, 64
Vietnam (McCarthy) **14**:358-59
"The Vietnam Call of Samuel V. Reimer" (Wiebe) **14**:575
Vietnam Discourse (Weiss)
See *Viet Nam Diskurs*
"Vietnam Memorial" (Shapiro) **53**:334
"The Vietnam Project" (Coetzee) **23**:121, 124; **117**:34, 38, 44
"The Vietnam War" (Bly) **15**:68
A Vietnamese Wedding (Fornés) **61**:129, 131
The Vietnamization of New Jersey (Durang) **27**:88-9, 93
Vieux carré (Williams) **8**:549; **39**:452; **45**:443, 447-49, 455
"The View" (Milosz) **82**:299
"View" (Pastan) **27**:368
"A View" (Van Duyn) **63**:438, 440; **116**:404
The View from a Blind I (Barker) **48**:18
"View from a Height" (Vinge) **30**:410, 416
View from a Tussock (Martinson)
See *Utsikt från en grästuva*
"View from a Wheelchair" (Scannell) **49**:328
A View from Calvary (Boyle) **19**:68
"View from Charles Bridge" (Seifert) **93**:336
"The View from Here" (Stafford) **29**:380
"The View from Misfortune's Back" (Porter) **33**:323
The View from Serendip (Clarke) **35**:123
"The View from the Balcony" (Stegner) **49**:350
A View from the Bridge (Miller) **1**:216-17, 219; **2**:278, 280; **6**:326, 329-30; **15**:372-73; **26**.315, 318; **47**:252, 254; **78**:306, 318-19, 323
A View From the Diner's Club (Vidal) **142**:283, 285
The View from the Ground (Gellhorn) **60**:190-191, 193-96
The View from the Peacock's Tail (Rosenthal) **28**:392, 394
"View from the screen" (Bukowski) **108**:111
A View from the Source: Selected Poems (Hooker) **43**:200-01
"The View from the Stars" (Miller) **30**:260
The View from Tower Hill (Braine)
See *Stay with Me till Morning*
"The View Minus One" (Moss) **7**:247
A View of Dawn in the Tropics (Cabrera Infante)
See *Vista del amanecer en el trópico*
A View of the Harbour (Taylor) **2**:432; **29**:410
A View of the Promised Land (Duhamel) **8**:189
"A View of the Woods" (O'Connor) **10**:367; **21**:276; **104**:103, 108, 114, 135, 138, 154, 166-68, 173, 179, 183-84, 188, 192
"A View on Contemporary German Fiction" (de Man) **55**:420-21
"View with a Grain of Sand" (Szymborska) **99**:203
View with a Grain of Sand (Szymborska) **99**:194, 199, 203-04, 206
"Viewing a Leopard" (Honig) **33**:216
"Viewing the Body" (Snodgrass) **68**:382, 388, 397
"Viewpoint" (Hall) **51**:170
Views (Milosz) **56**:232
Views and Spectacles (Weiss) **14**:555
Views from a Window (Vidal) **22**:435
"Views of My Father Weeping" (Barthelme) **1**:18; **23**:46-8; **46**:36, 40, 43; **115**:67, 87, 89-93, 95
"Vigil" (Carver) **53**:61
"The Vigil" (Livesay) **79**:340
"The Vigil" (Winters) **32**:467
The Vigil (Williams) **148**:357, 359-63
"Vigilance" (Breton) **54**:30; **9**:127
"Vik" (Bagryana) **10**:14
"Viking Dublin: Trial Piece" (Heaney) **14**:244; **74**:193
The Viking Portable Library Dorothy Parker (Parker) **68**:328-30
Viktorka (Seifert)
See *The Song of Viktorka*
Det vilda torget (Transtroemer) **65**:226, 229, 233
Vile Bodies (Waugh) **1**:357-59; **3**:509-12; **8**:544; **13**:584, 586-89; **19**:461, 466; **44**:521-22, 524; **107**:356-57, 359-60, 362, 364, 366, 370-71, 376, 378-79, 383, 393, 394-97, 400-01
"Villa Adriana" (Rich) **7**:368
The Villa Golitsyn (Read) **25**:379-80
A Villa in France (Stewart) **32**:421-22
Villa Magdalena (Santos) **22**:362-63
Villa Stellar (Barker) **48**:19-20, 22, 24
"The Village" (Corn) **33**:117
"The Village" (Smith) **64**:402
"The Village" (Walcott) **76**:285-86
"The Village" (Wilhelm) **7**:538
The Village (Anand) **23**:12, 19; **93**:22, 24, 32, 43
The Village (Hinde) **6**:240
The Village (Smith) **64**:402
The Village: A Party (Fuller) **25**:179
The Village Band Mystery (Kingman) **17**:244
The Village by the Sea (Desai) **37**:68; **97**:175-76, 180, 190
Village Daybook (Derleth) **31**:137
"Village Ghetto Land" (Wonder) **12**:659, 662-63
The Village Green Preservation Society (Davies) **21**:90, 97
"The Village Idiot" (Hirsch) **50**:198
"The Village Inn" (Betjeman) **43**:37
"The Village Inside" (Hood) **28**:193
"A Village Life" (Walcott) **42**:419; **76**:286
The Village of Ben Sue (Schell) **35**:361-63
Village of God and the Devil (Alegria) **75**:51-2
"The Village of Miracles" (Blaga) **75**:78
The Village of Souls (Child) **19**:100, 103
"Village of the Sun" (Zappa) **17**:591
"Village of Winter Carols" (Lee) **90**:200
"A Village Priest" (Dubie) **36**:136
"The Village Priest" (Ngũgĩ wa Thiong'o) **36**:313
"The Village Saint" (Head) **67**:98
"Village Snow" (Levi) **41**:247-48
"Village Song" (Blunden) **56**:48
"The Village That Lost Its Children" (Lee) **90**:199
Village Year (Derleth) **31**:134
"Villages démolis" (Read) **4**:439
"Villa-Lobos" (Stern) **100**:333
"Villanelle of a Suicide's Mother" (Williams) **148**:355-56, 362
"Villanelle: The Psychological Hour" (Pound) **13**:460
"Ville" (Guillevic) **33**:194
Ville cruelle (Beti) **27**:45-6
La ville de la chance (Wiesel) **3**:529; **5**:490, 492
La ville dont le prince est un enfant (Montherlant) **19**:327, 329
"Villon" (Bunting) **10**:83; **39**:298; **47**:44-5, 49, 52-5
"Vilota" (Pasolini) **106**:228
Vimy (Berton) **104**:49
Vincent and Theo (Altman) **116**:46-8, 50, 65
Vindane (Vesaas) **48**:407
Vindication (Sherwood) **81**:101-10
Vindication of the Rights of Women (Wollstonecraft) **65**:323
"The Vindictives" (Frost) **10**:194-95
"The Vine" (Williams) **15**:580; **45**:447
"The Vinegar Mother" (Rendell) **28**:385
Vinegar Puss (Perelman) **5**:337-38
Vinegar Tom (Churchill) **31**:84

Vineland (Pynchon) **62**:439-54; **123**:293-98, 300, 302-12, 331
"The Vine—The Willow ..." (Blackburn) **43**:63
"The Vineyard Woman" (Wright) **53**:425
Vingt-cinq poèmes (Tzara) **47**:390-95
Vinland (Brown) **100**:77-81
Vinland the Good (Shute) **36**:367
"Vinland, Vinland" (Connell) **45**:113
"Víno a čas" (Seifert) **93**:341
"Vintage" (Hass) **99**:140
The Vintage (West)
See *On a Dark Night*
Vintage London (Betjeman) **6**:67
Vintage Murder (Marsh) **7**:210; **53**:247, 249-50, 255-60
"The Vintage of River Is Unending" (Hughes) **37**:181
Vintage Stuff (Sharpe) **36**:403
"A Vintage Thunderbird" (Beattie) **13**:64; **63**:17; **146**:47, 50, 52, 61-3, 71, 81
Vintage Thurber (Thurber) **5**:433
Vinter-Eventyr (Dinesen)
See *Winter's Tales*
"Vinterns formler" (Transtroemer) **52**:409, 411
Vinterns formler (Transtroemer) **65**:222
I vinti (Antonioni) **20**:19; **144**:34, 55, 67, 74, 79
Vinyl (Warhol) **20**:417, 422
Viola di morte (Landolfi) **49**:216
The Violated (Bourjaily) **62**:87-93, 101, 105-06
Violence and Glory: Poems, 1962-1968 (Schevill) **7**:401
The Violent Bear It Away (O'Connor) **1**:253-54, 257-58; **3**:365-67; **6**:375, 379; **10**:364, 367-70; **13**:418, 420, 422; **15**:408, 410-11, 413; **21**:257-63, 266, 271-73; **66**:309-10; **104**:103-06, 108, 120, 123, 135, 141, 178-79
The Violent Land (Amado)
See *Terras do sem fim*
"The Violent Noon" (Ballard) **14**:40
"The Violent Space (or when your sister sleeps around for money)" (Knight) **40**:279-81, 284, 286
"Violent Storm" (Strand) **41**:436; **71**:279, 282
The Violent West (Ghose) **42**:179
The Violent World of Hugh Greene (Wilson) **3**:537; **14**:588
Violet Clay (Godwin) **22**:180-83; **31**:195; **69**:232-33, 235, 238, 246; **125**:123-24, 128-29, 136, 139, 146, 149, 159, 165, 167
"Violet Hair" (Vollmann) **89**:278
"The Violet Rock" (Stafford) **7**:457
"Violets" (Glück) **81**:164, 170
"Violets" (O'Brien) **36**:340
Violette noziere (Chabrol) **16**:184
"A Violin" (Popa) **19**:373
The Violin Book (Berger) **12**:39-40
Violins and Shovels: The WPA Art Projects, a New Deal for America's Hungry Artists of the 1930's (Meltzer) **26**:304-05
Viollet (Cunningham) **12**:163-64
Viper Jazz (Tate) **25**:427-29
"Vipers" (Walker) **13**:567
La virgen del tepeyac (Valdez) **84**:397
"The Virgin and the Dynamo" (Auden) **123**:18
The Virgin and the Nightingale: Medieval Latin Poems (Adcock) **41**:18
"The Virgin and the Petri Dish" (Selzer) **74**:272-73
"Virgin Forest, Southern New South Wales" (Shapcott) **38**:400
The Virgin in the Garden (Byatt) **19**:76-7; **65**:125, 131
"The Virgin in the Rose-Bower; or, The Tragedy of Glen Mawr Manor" (Oates) **108**:349, 351, 353
Virgin Islands (Vidal) **142**:321
"The Virgin of Guadalupe" (Hughes) **108**:323
Virgin Planet (Anderson) **15**:15
Virgin Soil Upturned (Sholokhov)
See *Podniataia tselina*
The Virgin Spring (Bergman)
See *Jungfrukällen*
The Virgin Suicides (Eugenides) **81**:53-60
Virgin Territory (Maitland) **49**:233-35
"Virgin Violeta" (Porter) **101**:235, 237-38
"Virginal" (Ezekiel) **61**:96, 101
Virginia (O'Brien) **36**:335-36, 341-42
"Virginia Britannia" (Moore) **2**:291; **8**:399
"Virginia Reel" (Wright) **146**:308
Virginia Reels (Hoffman) **141**:283, 308-09
"Virginia Woolf: A Capsule Biography" (Borges) **48**:45
Virginie: Her Two Lives (Hawkes) **27**:196-98, 200-01; **49**:163-65
"Virgins" (Trevor) **71**:329, 332-33
Virgins and Vampires (Rosenblatt) **15**:447-48
"Virgo Descending" (Wright) **13**:614
"Virgo Hibernica" (Montague) **46**:267, 278
Viridiana (Bunuel) **16**:130-31, 134-35, 139; **80**:27-9, 31-2, 34-5, 37, 41, 45, 47, 49-51
"Virility" (Ozick) **7**:288; **28**:347; **62**:353-54; **155**:167, 170, 178, 183
"Virtu" (Ammons) **2**:14; **9**:28
Virtual History (Ferguson)
See *Virtual History: Alternatives and Counterfactuals*
Virtual History: Alternatives and Counterfactuals (Ferguson) **134**:48, 50, 53-4, 66, 85, 96
"Virtual History: Toward a 'Chaotic' Theory of the Past" (Ferguson) **134**:96
Las virtudes del pájaro solitario (Goytisolo) **133**:76, 85-86, 95
The Virtue of Selfishness: A New Concept of Egoism (Rand) **30**:304; **79**:369
The Virtues of the Solitary Bird (Goytisolo)
See *Las virtudes del pájaro solitario*
"Virtuoso" (Greenberg) **7**:134
Virtuoso Literature for Two and Four Hands (Wakoski) **7**:504-05, 507
"Virtuoso of the X" (Bell) **8**:66
A Virtuous Woman (Gibbons) **88**:123-28, 130-32; **145**:136, 138-45, 147, 149-51, 154, 164-65, 167
"Le visage nuptial" (Char) **9**:161-62; **11**:114; **55**:287
"Visakha" (Nye) **42**:309
Il visconte dimezzato (Calvino) **5**:97-8; **8**:129-30; **11**:88; **22**:87-8, 90; **33**:97; **39**:314, 317; **73**:58
Viscuous Circle (Anthony) **35**:37-8
Vishnevaya kostochka (Olesha) **8**:432
"The Visible Moments" (Squires) **51**:377
"Vision" (MacLeod) **56**:197-200
"Vision" (Scott) **22**:374
"The Vision" (Wright) **53**:432
The Vision (Koontz) **78**:203, 212, 214-17
"Vision (2)" (Alexie) **154**:8-9
"Vision and Late Supper" (Willard) **37**:464
Vision and Resonance (Hollander) **8**:298-99, 301-02; **14**:262
Vision and Verse in William Blake (Ostriker) **132**:301, 319
"A Vision beyond Time and Space" (Momaday) **95**:241
"Vision by Sweetwater" (Ransom) **4**:431
"La vision capitale" (Mandiargues) **41**:279
"Vision: Fire Underground" (O Hehir) **41**:324
"Vision: From the Drum's Interior" (Alexie) **154**:13
"Vision of a Woman Hit by a Bird" (Moure) **88**:229
A Vision of a World Language (MacDiarmid) **63**:255
"The Vision of Adam" (Ghiselin) **23**:169
A Vision of Battlements (Burgess) **4**:81; **5**:85; **10**:89-90; **13**:124; **22**:70, 72-4; **40**:113-14; **62**:132; 94;49, 51, 56, 75
A Vision of Beasts and Gods (Barker) **48**:15-16, 18
"Vision of Cathkin Braes" (Morgan) **31**:276
A Vision of Ceremony (McAuley) **45**:249, 252, 254
"A Vision of Democracy in the County of Meath" (Durcan) **70**:152
"Vision of England, '38" (Barker) **48**:10-11
"A Vision of the World" (Cheever) **15**:131; **64**:53, 58, 60-3
"A Vision of World Language" (MacDiarmid) **19**:289
"A Vision of Zosukuma" (Kunene) **85**:176
"Vision out of the Corner of the Eye" (Valenzuela) **31**:438; **104**:382
"The Vision Test" (Van Duyn) **63**:443
"Vision through Timothy" (Eberhart) **19**:144
"Vision under the October Mountain: A Love Poem" (Warren) **8**:537
"Visionary" (Ellison) **42**:131
The Visionary (Le Guin) **45**:219
The Visionary Company (Bloom) **24**:70, 75; **103**:11, 19, 30, 36-7, 41-3, 45, 47-8
The Visionary Farms (Eberhart) **11**:175, 178; **56**:81,88
"A Visionary Gleam" (Warner) **7**:513
"The Visionary Picnic" (Matthews) **40**:320
Le visionnaire (Green) **11**:259; **77**:267, 269, 276-77, 290
"Visions" (Heaney) **14**:243
"Visions" (Mukherjee) **53**:268
"Visions" (Wonder) **12**:657-58
Visions and Revisions of American Poetry (Turco) **63**:431-33
Visions from San Francisco Bay (Milosz)
See *Widzenia nad Zatoka San Francisco*
Visions from the Ramble (Hollander) **5**:186; **8**:299
Visions of America (Lynn) **50**:426
"Visions of Budhardin" (Dybek) **114**:62, 64-65, 71, 74, 76
Visions of Cody (Kerouac) **2**:228-29; **3**:264, 266; **5**:212-13; **29**:270, 272-74; **61**:297, 308-09
"Visions of Daniel" (Pinsky) **94**:309, 311-12
Visions of Eight (Ichikawa) **20**:185
Visions of Gerard (Kerouac) **1**:167; **14**:307; **29**:270; **61**:309
Visions of Glory: A History and Memoir of Jehovah's Witnesses (Harrison) **144**:101-06, 114, 116, 121
"Visions of Jesus" (Rothenberg) **57**:381, 383-84
Visions of Kerouac (Duberman) **8**:185-86
"Visit" (Ammons) **25**:45; **108**:28
"The Visit" (Ciardi) **40**:151
"A Visit" (Kavan) **82**:120
"A Visit" (Levertov) **15**:339
"A Visit" (Levine) **54**:297, 301
"Visit" (Senghor) **130**:280
"The Visit" (Smith) **64**:392
"The Visit" (Spencer) **22**:406
"The Visit" (Wesker) **42**:426
"The Visit" (Young) **82**:411
The Visit (Duerrenmatt) **102**:53-4, 83
A Visit (Fornés) **61**:129, 140
The Visit: A Tragi-Comedy (Dürrenmatt)
See *Der Besuch der alten Dame*
"A Visit at Tea-Time" (Wain) **46**:415
"A Visit from Johannesburg: Or Mr. Shaving's Wives" (Weldon) **122**:269
"A Visit from Mother" (Tevis) **42**:372, 377
"A Visit from Reverend Tileston" (Cook-Lynn) **93**:124, 127
"A Visit from the Footbinder" (Prager) **56**:276-77
A Visit from the Footbinder, and Other Stories (Prager) **56**:276-80
"A Visit in Bad Taste" (Wilson) **34**:581
"A Visit of Charity" (Welty) **105**:333
"The Visit of the Queen of Sheba" (Amichai) **9**:22; **57**:40, 44
Visit to a Small Planet (Vidal) **4**:558
"A Visit to Eggeswick Castle" (Davies) **23**:148
"A Visit to Grandmother" (Kelley) **22**:246
"The Visit to the Museum" (Nabokov) **3**:354

"A Visit to the Painter Vladimir Komarek" (Seifert) **34**:362
"A Visit to the Ruins" (Hope) **3**:251
"Visit with the Artist in Her Own Studio" (Robbins) **21**:341
"The Visitant" (Roethke) **11**:483; **101**:263
Visitants (Stow) **23**:437 38; **48**:358, 360-61
"Visitation" (Césaire) **32**:111
"Visitation" (Merwin) **88**:194
"A Visitation" (Snodgrass) **18**:491, 493; **68**:397
The Visitation (Roberts) **48**:341-42
Visitations (MacNeice) **4**:318; **53**:242
"Visite" (Reverdy) **53**:290
"Visiting a Dead Man on a Summer Day" (Piercy) **18**:405-06; **27**:374
A Visiting Card (Pound) **112**:356-57
Visiting Cards (King) **145**:354-55, 365
Visiting Mrs. Nabokov (Amis) **101**:77-78, 83
"Visiting the Farallones" (Bly) **128**:43
"Visiting the Tates" (Lowell) **124**:268, 270
"Visiting Thomas Hart Benton and His Wife in Kansas City" (Bly) **15**:63
"The Visitor" (Dahl) **6**:122; **79**:180-81, 183
"The Visitor" (Forché) **25**:172; **83**:216
"The Visitor" (Voigt) **54**:433
The Visitor (Poole)
See *Billy Buck*
The Visitor (Ray)
See *Agantuk*
"Visitor from Forest Hills" (Simon) **31**:396-97
"Visitor from Hollywood" (Simon) **31**:396
"Visitor: Jack Kerouac in Old Saybrook" (Holmes) **56**:143
"Visitors" (Barthelme) **46**:40, 43; **59**:249; **115**:80
"Visitors" (Lowell) **37**:238
"Visitors" (Mukherjee) **53**:267, 269
"Visitors" (Munro) **95**:305-06, 316, 318
Visitors (Brookner) **136**:123-24, 132
The Visitors (Kazan) **16**:369
The Visitors (Simak) **55**:319
"Visitors from Mlok" (Smith) **43**:422
The Visitors Have All Returned (Bowering) **32**:48
"Visitors to the Black Belt" (Hughes) **35**:214
"Visits to St. Elizabeths" (Bishop) **15**:60; **32**:37, 42
Viskningar och rop (Bergman) **16**:70-2, 75-6, 79, 82; **72**:52, 54-5, 57, 59, 62
Vislumbres de la India (Paz) **119**:419-23
La víspera del hombre (Marqués) **96**:233, 241, 244
"Vissi d'arte" (Moore) **68**:300
Vista del amanecer en el trópico (Cabrera Infante) **25**:100, 103-05; **45**:78; **120**:51, 59, 68-69, 73, 82
The Vistants (Waddington) **28**:440
Visual Language (Kostelanetz) **28**:218
"Vita amicae" (Le Guin) **45**:213
Vita d'un uoma (Ungaretti) **7**:483; **11**:556
Vita immaginaria (Ginzburg) **54**:197
La vita interiore (Moravia) **18**:346-49; **27**:356; **46**:284-85
"Vita Nuova" (Kunitz) **148**:95, 102
Una vita violenta (Pasolini) **37**:341-43, 347; **106**:209, 216, 218-19, 242, 253, 254, 269-70
The Vital Center: The Pollitics of Freedom (Schlesinger) **84**:348, 350, 355, 370-71, 374, 380-81
"Vital Message" (Phillips) **28**:363
Vital Parts (Berger) **3**:63; **5**:60; **38**:36-8
Vital Provisions (Price) **43**:350-51, 353; **63**:333
Vital Signs (Slavitt) **14**:490-91
"Vitamins" (Carver) **36**:104; **126**:107, 123, 155, 157-58, 165-66, 169, 183
I vitelloni (Fellini) **16**:271-77, 281, 283, 290-91, 293, 297, 299; **85**:55, 59, 64, 74-6, 78
"Vitrail" (Guillevic) **33**:195
Viudas (Dorfman) **48**:89-90, 92, 94; **77**:138, 141-42, 146, 148-49, 152-54
ViVa (Cummings) **15**:161-62, **68**:35, 47-8
Viva and Louis (Warhol)
See *Blue Movie*
Viva la muerte (Arrabal) **58**:14, 26, 28
"Viva Mi Fama" (Fuentes) **113**:242-43
"Viva Stalin" (Parra) **102**:354
Viva Zapata! (Kazan) **16**:368-69, 371-72; **63**:225, 235
Viva Zapata! (Steinbeck) **34**:415
"Vivaldi" (Dybek) **114**:66
"Vivaldi" (Schwartz) **45**:361
"Vivaldi, Bird and Angel" (Hope) **3**:251; **51**:227
"Vivaldi Years" (Stern) **40**:413
"Vivat! Vivat Regina!" (Bolt) **14**:91
Vive en poésie (Guillevic) **33**:194-95
Vive guitare (Audiberti) **38**:21
Vive Moi! (O'Faolain) **7**:272-73, 275; **70**:315, 319, 321
The Vivid Air (Gustafson) **36**:221-22
"Vivir para ver" (Otero) **11**:426
Vivir sin estar viviendo (Cernuda) **54**:60
The Vivisector (White) **3**:522-23; **4**:583-84; **5**:484-85, 487-88; **7**:529, 532; **65**:275-76, 278-79; **69**:400-02, 405
Vivo o povo brasileiro (Ribeiro) **67**:280-82
Vivre l'orange (Cixous) **92**:58, 62
Vivre sa vie (Godard) **20**:129, 148-49
Vivre! Vivre!: La suite des manuscrits de Pauline Archange (Blais) **4**:67
The Vixens (Yerby) **22**:487
Vizio di forma (Levi) **50**:331
Vladimir and Rosa (Godard) **20**:151
"Vladychitsa" (Voinovich) **10**:506
Vlaminck (Duhamel) **8**:188
"Vlemk the Box-Painter" (Gardner) **28**:161-63
"V-Letter" (Shapiro) **15**:475, 478; **53**:330, 334
V-Letter and Other Poems (Shapiro) **15**:475-76, 478; **53**:326, 331, 334
VN: The Life and Art of Vladimir Nabokov (Field) **44**:463-72
Vocabulaire (Cocteau) **15**:133
"The Vocabulary of Joy" (Ostriker) **132**:321, 325
"Vocation" (Stafford) **7**:462; **29**:388
"The Vocation of the Poet in the Modern World" (Schwartz) **87**:335
"Vocational Guidance" (Howard) **10**:276
"Vocations" (Williams) **148**:346-47
La voce della luna (Fellini) **85**:75, 77-8, 80
Le voci della sera (Ginzburg) **11**:228-29; **54**:194-96, 198, 200-01, 206, 211-12; **70**:279-80, 282-83
The Vodi (Braine) **41**:56
"Vodka" (Ciardi) **10**:105, 107
"Vodka and Small Pieces of Gold" (Delaney) **29**:146
"Voe Doe Dee Oh Doe" (Ellison) **139**:116
Voetskrif (Breytenbach) **23**:83; **126**:84, 101-02
"Vogel" (Cohen) **19**:113
Vogue la galère (Aymé) **11**:22
"The Vogue of the Marquis de Sade" (Wilson) **24**:481
"The Voice" (Levine) **33**:275; **118**:285, 301
"The Voice" (Nin) **14**:383-84; **60**:265-66
"The Voice" (Pritchett) **41**:333
The Voice at the Back Door (Spencer) **22**:399-400, 403
"A Voice Foretold" (Wideman) **122**:347
"A Voice from Croisset" (Rozewicz) **23**:360-61
Voice from the Attic (Davies)
See *A Voice in the Attic*
"Voice from the Cage" (Simic) **130**:343, 345
A Voice from the Chorus (Sinyavsky) **8**:488-90
"A Voice From the Other World" (Mahfouz)
See "Sawt min al'alam al-akhar"
"A Voice from under the Table" (Wilbur) **3**:533; **110**:349
A Voice in the Attic (Davies) **13**:172-74; **75**:184, 197, 205, 212; **91**:204
The Voice in the Closet/La voix dans la cabinet de débarras (Federman) **47**:123-25, 127-28, 132
A Voice in the Mountain (Davison) **28**:103-04
"Voice of a Dove" (p'Bitek) **96**:271, 286
The Voice of a Stranger (Humphreys) **47**:186
The Voice of Asia (Michener) **29**:310-11; **109**:376, 379, 382
The Voice of Experience (Laing) **95**:165
"The Voice of Night" (Arghezi)
See "Graiul noptii"
"The Voice of Rock" (Ginsberg) **6**:199
The Voice of Scotland (MacDiarmid) **63**:254
"The Voice of St. Lucia" (Walcott) **67**:344
"The Voice of the Beach" (Campbell) **42**:92
"The Voice of the Canefield" (Cabral de Melo Neto)
See "A voz do canavial"
"The Voice of the Holy Land" (Sachs)
See "Stimme des Heilegen Landes"
The Voice of the Moon (Fellini)
See *La voce della luna*
The Voice of the Mountain (Wellman) **49**:394-95
The Voice of the Sea, and Other Stories (Moravia) **11**:384
"The Voice of the Soul" (Pasternak) **7**:295
The Voice of the Victims (Boff) **70**:339
The Voice of the Void (Campbell) **32**:73
The Voice of Things (Ponge) **6**:422-23; **18**:415
The Voice That Is Great Within Us: American Poetry of the Twentieth Century (Carruth) **84**:118, 124
"A Voice through the Door" (Taylor) **18**:526
"Voices" (Celan)
See "Stimmen"
"Voices" (Josipovici) **6**:270
"Voices" (Plumly) **33**:310
"Voices" (Szymborska) **99**:198
Voices (Eich)
See *Stimmen*
Voices: A Memoir (Prokosch) **48**:317-18
Voices and Visions (Vendler) **138**:274
Voices at Play (Spark) **13**:519
"Voices by a River" (Blunden) **56**:29
Voices from the Forest (Mueller) **51**:280, 282
"Voices from the Moon" (Dubus) **36**:148-49; **97**:221, 223, 227, 229-30
Voices From the Moon (Dubus) **97**:203, 209-11, 213, 216, 224-25
"Voices from the Other World" (Merrill) **8**:387; **34**:235
Voices from the Sky: Previews of the Coming Space Age (Clarke) **35**:123
Voices from the Yiddish (Howe) **85**:147
Voices in an Empty Room (King) **53**:210-11; **145**:353
Voices in the City (Desai) **19**:133; **37**:64, 66, 69; **97**:142, 149, 152, 156, 161-62
Voices in the Evening (Ginzburg)
See *Le voci della sera*
"Voices in the Whirlwind" (Mphahlele) **133**:129, 134
Voices in the Whirlwind and Other Essays (Mphahlele) **25**:334-35, 341; **133**:129
Voices in Time (MacLennan) **92**:340, 343-45, 350
Voices of a Summer Day (Shaw) **7**:412
Voices of America (Bogosian) **45**:62; **141**:80-1, 84-5
"Voices of Expendable Superfluous? People" (Rozewicz) **139**:226
The Voices of Marrakesh: A Record of a Visit (Canetti)
See *Die Stimmen von Marrakesch: Aufzeichnungen nach einer Reise*
"Voices of Poor People" (Milosz) **11**:377-78; **56**:237-38
The Voices of Silence (Malraux)
See *Les voix du silence*
Voices of the Dead (Dourado)
See *Ópera dos mortos*
The Voices of the Heroic Dead (Mishima) **27**:341
Voices of the Moon (Fellini)
See *La voce della luna*
"The Voices of Time" (Ballard) **14**:40; **36**:37,

39-41, 44; **137**:54, 56, 58-59, 61
"Voices under the Ground" (Ekeloef) **27**:117
A Void (Perec)
See *La disparition*
The Void Captain's Tale (Spinrad) **46**:387-89
Void of Course (Carroll) **143**:46-7, 49
"Void Only" (Rexroth) **112**:404
La voie lactée (Bunuel) **16**:134 35, 139; **80**:41, 47, 51
La voie royale (Malraux) **4**:324-25, 330-31, 333, 336; **13**:367-68; **57**:300-01, 304, 308-09, 321
Voies de pères, voix de filles (Condé) **92**:104
Voina i tiur'ma (Aksyonov)
See *War and Prison*
"Voir la figure," de Jacques Chardonne (de Man) **55**:420
Les voisinages de Van Gogh (Char) **55**:288
Les voix du silence (Malraux) **4**:324; **13**:366; **57**:301, 307, 314, 324
La voix et le phénomène: Introduction au problème su signe dans le phénoménologie de Husserl (Derrida) **24**:136, 140; **87**:72, 103-04
Vol à voile (Cendrars) **18**:96
Le vol d'Icare (Queneau) **5**:362; **10**:430; **42**:331-32
Le Vol du Vampire (Tournier) **95**:370-71
"The Volcano" (Stegner) **81**:345
"Volcano" (Walcott) **76**:285-86
Volcano (Endō) **19**:161; **54**:152, 155; **99**:285
The Volcano (Santos) **22**:362-63
The Volcano Lover (Sontag) **105**:185-86, 188, 190-213, 224-25
Vole-moi un petit millard (Arrabal) **58**:18
"Les voleurs" (Burroughs) **42**:76
"Volhynia Province" (Simpson) **7**:428
Volk (Leonov) **92**:246, 260, 268, 270, 277
La volonté de savoir (Foucault)
See *Histoire de la sexualité, Vol. 1: La volonté de savoir*
Volshebnik (Nabokov) **44**:469; **46**:290-96; **64**:366
"Volta a Pernambuco" (Cabral de Melo Neto) **76**:167
"De volta ao Cabro de Santo Agostinho" (Cabral de Melo Neto) **76**:160
Voltaïque (Ousmane) **66**:334-35, 347
Voltaire in Love (Mitford) **44**:485, 488
The Voluntad (Azorín) **11**:26
"The Volunteer" (Stegner) **49**:351
Volunteers (Friel) **42**:169, 173-74; **115**:242-43, 246, 248
"Voluptuaries and Others" (Avison) **4**:36; **97**:72, 91, 94, 103-04, 107
Volverás a región (Benet) **28**:15-20
Volverás a región (Delibes) **8**:170
"Vom einem Land, einem Fluss und den Seen" (Bachmann) **69**:56
Vom hungrigen Hennecke (Hein) **154**:176
"Vom Sinn der Dichtung in Unserer Zeit" (Dürrenmatt) **15**:197
"Vom Steppenwolf" (Hesse) **6**:237
"Vomit" (Mahfouz)
See "al-Qay'"
Von allem Anfang an (Hein) **154**:164, 167-72, 182, 187-91, 195-6
The Von Bülow Affair (Wright) **44**:527
"Von diesen Stauden" (Celan) **82**:49
Von Schwelle zu Schwelle (Celan) **10**:101-02; **19**:90; **53**:69, 71, 74, 77
"Von Wesen der Wahrheit" (Heidegger) **24**:259
The Voodoo Gods (Deren)
See *Divine Horsemen: The Living Gods of Haiti*
Voodoo Gods: An Inquiry into Native Myths and Magic in Jamaica and Haiti (Hurston)
See *Tell My Horse*
"The Voodoo of Hell's Half-Acre" (Wright) **74**:387
Voprosy literatury i estetiki (Bakhtin) **83**:2, 14, 19, 32-4, 37, 44, 57, 59-60
Vor (Leonov) **92**:236-39, 243-50, 252, 254-55, 257-60, 266, 268, 274-79
Vor dem Ruhestand (Bernhard) **61**:11, 13, 26
Voraussetzungen einer Erzählung: Kassandra (Wolf) **58**:419-28, 431-34, 436-37; **150**:248, 297, 307-11, 321, 328-30, 334
Das Vorbild (Lenz) **27**:250-51
The Vortex (Coward) **29**:132-35, 137-39; **51**:69
"Vorticism" (Pound) **10**:400
Vorträge und Aufsätze (Heidegger) **24**:264, 277
Die Vorzüge der Windhühner (Grass) **6**:207; **32**:197-98, 200-01; **6**:207; **32**:197-98, 200-01
Voskhozhdenie na Fudzhiamu (Aitmatov) **71**:23
Voss (White) **3**:521-23; **4**:584-85; **5**:485-87; **9**:563, 565; **18**:545-46; **65**:275-76, 279-82; **69**:392-94, 396-97, 403, 405, 411
"Vot zvuk dozhdia" (Akhmadulina) **53**:11
Vote, Vote, Vote for Nigel Barton (Potter) **86**:346, 348-50; **123**:227, 231
"The Voter" (Achebe) **26**:20; **75**:14
"Votes and Boys" (Forster) **45**:133
"Votin' Ink" (Bennett) **28**:30
Votive Tablets: Studies Chiefly Appreciative of English Authors and Books (Blunden) **56**:46
"De votre bonheur etc." (MacLeish) **68**:286
Votre Faust: Fantaisie variable genre opéra (Butor) **3**:92; **8**:118-19
La vouivre (Aymé) **11**:22
Vous les entendez? (Sarraute) **2**:385-86; **4**:468-70; **31**:380; **80**:238, 241
Vous m'oublierez (Breton and Soupault) **68**:411-15
"A Vow" (Ginsberg) **36**:184, 191
"A Vow" (Hecht) **8**:269; **19**:207
The Vow of Conversation (Merton) **83**:403
"Voyage" (Levertov) **66**:243
"The Voyage" (Prokosch) **48**:309
"Voyage" (Rukeyser) **27**:406
Le voyage (Morand) **41**:304
The Voyage (De Sica) **20**:97
"Voyage à Rodrigues" (Le Clézio) **155**:115
Voyage au bout de la nuit (Céline) **1**:56-7; **3**:101, 103, 105; **4**:98, 100-03; **7**:42, 44-7; **9**:152-53, 155, 158; **15**:124; **47**:71-4, 77-9; **124**:52-5, 56-62, 66-70, 72-3, 75-7, 79-80, 85-91, 93, 95, 98, 102-03, 110, 112-17, 121-22
Le voyage de Patrice Périot (Duhamel) **8**:186
Voyage en Grande Garabagne (Michaux) **8**:392
Voyage en Italie (Giono) **4**:184
"A Voyage from Stockholm" (Tate) **25**:428
"The Voyage Home" (Appleman) **51**:17
Voyage Home (Hochman) **3**:250
Le voyage imaginaire (Clair) **20**:63, 69
"Voyage in the Blue" (Ashbery) **3**:16; **15**:28
Voyage in the Dark (Rhys) **2**:371-73; **6**:453-55; **14**:446-49, 451; **19**:393; **51**:359, 361, 364, 368-71; **124**:330, 332-33, 335, 338-39, 341, 346, 362, 372, 374
The Voyage of Saint Brandon (Brown) **48**:61
The Voyage of the Dawn Treader (Lewis) **124**:214, 221, 236, 248
The Voyage of the Destiny (Nye) **42**:307-08
The Voyage of the Narwhal (Barrett) **150**:6-18
"The Voyage of the Needle" (Dickey) **47**:92
A Voyage round My Father (Mortimer) **28**:286
Voyage to a Beginning: A Preliminary Autobiography (Wilson) **14**:584, 589
Voyage to Great Garabagne (Michaux)
See *Voyage en Grande Garabagne*
A Voyage to Pagany (Williams) **13**:602
Voyage to Somewhere (Wilson) **32**:444
"Voyage to Spring" (Aiken) **52**:24
Voyage to the First of December (Carlisle) **33**:103-04
"Voyage to the Moon" (Pinsky) **94**:309
Voyage to the Sonorous Land (Handke)
See *Das Spiel vom Fragen oder Die Reise zum Sonoren Land*
"Voyager" (Mueller) **51**:284
Voyager in Night (Cherryh) **35**:114
Voyagers (Bova) **45**:71-2, 75
Voyagers II: The Alien Within (Bova) **45**:75-6
"Les voyagerurs traques" (Montherlant) **19**:325
Voyages (Brown) **48**:60; **100**:80
Voyages and Homecomings (Neruda) **28**:314
Voyages chez les morts: Thèmes et variations (Ionesco) **41**:227-28; **86**:332, 341
Voyages de l'autre côte (Le Clézio) **31**:251
Le voyageur sans bagage (Anouilh) **8**:24; **13**:19, 21; **40**:52-3, 60; **50**:279
"Le voyageur sur la terre" (Green) **77**:266
Le voyageur sur la terre (Green) **11**:260; **77**:265, 274-76
Les voyageurs de l'impériale (Aragon) **22**:37
Les voyageurs sacrés (Blais) **2**:62; **4**:67; **6**:82; **13**:96; **22**:57
"The Voyeur" (Van Duyn) **63**:440; **116**:403, 426
The Voyeur (Moravia)
See *L'uomo che guarda*
Le voyeur (Robbe-Grillet) **1**:286-87, 289; **2**:373, 375; **4**:446, 449; **6**:464-66, 468; **8**:453; **10**:437; **14**:455-59, 461; **43**:361-62, 364, 366; **128**:325-26, 329-35, 339-40, 344-47, 353, 356, 359, 363, 365-66, 368, 379, 382
The Voyeur (Robbe-Grillet)
See *Le voyeur*
Voyou Paul. Brave Virginie. (Céline) **47**:72
"A voz do canavial" (Cabral de Melo Neto) **76**:155, 165
Una voz en la montana (Marqués) **96**:225
"Vozdushnye puti" (Pasternak)
See "Aerial Ways"
"Vozmezdie" (Iskander) **47**:201
Voznesensky: Selected Poems (Voznesensky) **57**:413-15
"Vozvrashcheniye v Siguldu" (Voznesensky) **57**:417
Vreme smrti (Cosic) **14**:132
Vremia i mesto (Trifonov) **45**:418, 420, 423
"V.R.T." (Wolfe) **25**:472
Všecky krásy světa (Seifert) **44**:426; **93**:322, 326
Vsegda v prodaže (Aksyonov) **22**:26-7; **37**:12
Vstrechniye korabli (Paustovsky) **40**:362
Vučja so (Popa) **19**:375
El vuelo de la celebración (Rodriguez) **10**:440
"Vuelta" (Paz) **51**:333, 335
Vuelta (Paz) **65**:198
La vuelta al día en ochenta mundos (Cortázar) **10**:118; **92**:155, 158
Vulcan's Hammer (Dick) **30**:127
"Vulthoon" (Smith) **43**:419
"The Vulture" (Beckett) **9**:81
"Vulture" (Wakoski) **2**:459
"Vulture Culture" (Breytenbach) **126**:78
"Vultures" (Achebe) **11**:4
"Vultures" (Oliver) **34**:246; **98**:274
Vuodet (Haavikko) **34**:170
"Vurni me" (Bagryana) **10**:12
Vurt (Noon) **91**:59-66
VV (Cummings)
See *ViVa*
"Vying" (Davie) **8**:164
"Vysokaya bolesn" (Pasternak) **7**:293-94; **18**:382
Vzgljad: Stix i poèmy (Voznesensky) **15**:553-54, 557
Vziatie Velikoshumska (Leonov) **92**:240, 242, 247, 260, 277
"W" (Merrill) **8**:387-88
"W. D. Assists in the Protection of Cock Robin's Roost" (Snodgrass) **68**:394
"W. D., Don't Fear That Animal" (Snodgrass) **68**:398
"W. D. Picks a Bouquet for Cock Robin but Cannot Separate the Thorns from the Flowers" (Snodgrass) **68**:394
"W. D. Tries to Warn Cock Robin" (Snodgrass) **68**:394, 398
"W drodze do Delf" (Herbert) **43**:187

W; or, The Memory of Childhood (Perec)
See *W; ou, Le souvenir d'enfance*
W; ou, Le souvenir d'enfance (Perec) **56**:258-62, 268, 271-73; **116**:233-35, 238, 246-47, 256-59, 267, 269
"W. S. Landor" (Moore) **47**:263
W. S. Merwin: The First Four Books of Poems (Merwin) **8**:388; **13**:384
"Wa ta se Na ka mo ni, Viet Nam Memorial" (Young Bear) **94**:373
"Die Waage der Baleks" (Boell) **11**:55; **27**:57; **72**:71, 74-6
"Wading at Wellfleet" (Bishop) **32**:37-8, 43
"Waga namida o nuguitamo, hi" (Oe)
See "Mizu kara waga namida o nuguitamo hi"
Waga Seishun ni Kui Nashi (Kurosawa) **16**:399-400; **119**:339, 346, 349, 379, 382
Wagatomo Hitler (Mishima) **2**:289
The Wager (Medoff) **6**:322-23
"The Wages of Fun" (Blount) **38**:47
Wages of Virtue (Middleton) **38**:330
"The Waggoner" (Blunden) **2**:65; **56**:37
The Waggoner and Other Poems (Blunden) **56**:25, 28-9, 32-3, 36-7, 40-2, 48
"Wagner/Artaud" (Delany) **141**:159
Wagner/Artaud (Delany) **141**:116, 148-49
"Wagon Wheel" (Reed) **21**:305
Wagonmaster (Ford) **16**:306-07, 311, 316
"al-Wahj al-ākhar" (Mahfūz) **55**:172-74
Wah'Kon-tah: The Osage and the White Man's Land (Mathews) **84**:203, 205, 207, 209, 211, 218-19, 226
Die wahre Geschichte des Ah Q (Hein) **154**:53, 90, 98-9, 136, 160
Die Wahrheit der Literatur: Sieben Gespräche (Wellershoff) **46**:437
"Waiariki" (Grace) **56**:112
"Waif" (Leiber) **25**:307
"The Wail" (Simic) **130**:336-37
Wailing Monkey Embracing a Tree (Shuttle) **7**:422
"The Wait" (Bass) **143**:11
"The Wait" (Clancy) **112**:63
"Wait" (Kinnell) **29**:285; **129**:270-71
"Wait" (Reed) **21**:315
"Wait" (Steele) **45**:362
"Wait for Me" (Creeley) **8**:153
Wait for Me, Michael (Stolz) **12**:552
"Wait till the Sun Shines" (Wain) **46**:417
Wait Until Spring, Bandini (Fante) **60**:128-29, 133-34
Wait until the Evening (Bennett) **5**:59
"Waiting" (Beattie) **40**:66; **63**:12, 18
"Waiting" (Creeley) **78**:151
"Waiting" (Dubus) **36**:145; **97**:202, 228
"Waiting" (Levine) **14**:316
"Waiting" (Mahapatra) **33**:279, 284
"Waiting" (Montague) **46**:267-68
"The Waiting" (Olds) **85**:308
"Waiting" (Thomas) **48**:382
"Waiting" (Warren) **13**:582
"Waiting" (Wright) **53**:427, 432
Waiting (Mahapatra) **33**:278-80, 282-83
"Waiting at Dachau" (Price) **3**:406; **6**:423
"Waiting for a Taxi" (Jordan) **114**:151
"Waiting for Ada" (Howard) **10**:277
Waiting for Cordelia (Gold) **14**:208; **42**:197; **152**:118, 137
"Waiting for Evening" (Sadoff) **9**:466
Waiting for Godot (Beckett)
See *En attendant Godot*
"Waiting for It" (Swenson) **61**:399; **106**:326
"Waiting for Lefty" (Odets) **2**:318-20; **28**:323-25, 329, 332, 338-40
Waiting for Lefty (Odets) **98**:194-95, 199-201, 205-07, 210, 212, 215, 218, 220-21, 224, 229, 231, 233-34, 236, 239, 243, 250, 252
"Waiting for Merna" (Sommer) **25**:425
Waiting for My Life (Pastan) **27**:370-71
"Waiting for Santy" (Perelman) **49**:259, 263
Waiting for Saskatchewan (Wah) **44**:323, 326-28
Waiting for Sheila (Braine) **41**:59
"Waiting for Stella" (Adams) **46**:22
Waiting for the Angel (McGrath) **28**:278-79
Waiting for the Barbarians (Coetzee) **23**:124-26; **33**:106-11; **66**:90-2, 95-7, 99, 102, 105-06; **117**:30-1, 33, 39-41, 43-5, 47, 59-60, 67, 74, 80-3, 86, 97-8, 100-03
Waiting for the Boat: Dennis Potter on Television (Potter) **86**:349; **123**:262
"Waiting for the Call" (Kinsella) **27**:237
Waiting for the End (Fiedler) **4**:161; **24**:193, 195-98
"Waiting for the End of the World" (Costello) **21**:70
Waiting for the End of the World (Bell) **41**:52-4; **102**:4, 6, 11, 16, 22
"Waiting for the Fire" (Appleman) **51**:15
"Waiting for the Girls Upstairs" (Sondheim) **30**:385, 397
Waiting for the King of Spain (Wakoski) **9**:554-55
Waiting for the Mahatma (Narayan) **7**:255; **28**:291, 300-01; **47**:307; **121**:354, 357, 363-68, 370-71, 381, 385, 400
Waiting for the Music (Fuller) **62**:204
"Waiting for the Poem to Come Through" (Souster) **14**:505
"Waiting for the Story to Start" (Martin) **89**:131
Waiting for the Sun (Morrison) **17**:289, 295
"Waiting for Tu Fu" (Wright) **146**:350, 355
"The Waiting Grounds" (Ballard) **36**:37; **137**:11, 13
"Waiting in the Bone" (Squires) **51**:378, 382-83
Waiting in the Bone and Other Poems (Squires) **51**:378, 380-81
Waiting in the Wings (Coward) **29**:139
Waiting in the Wings: Portrait of a Queer Motherhood (Moraga) **126**:311
"Waiting in Vain" (Marley) **17**:269-70
"Waiting Room" (Justice) **102**:258
The Waiting Room (Harris) **25**:208, 215
"Waiting to Be Fed" (Young Bear) **94**:362, 366
Waiting to Exhale (McMillan) **112**:226-34, 236-42, 244-45, 247, 249, 251-52
"Waiting Ward" (Wright) **53**:419
Waiting Women (Bergman)
See *Kvinnors väntan*
The Waiting Years (Enchi)
See *Onnazaka*
"Waiting—Afield at Dusk" (Frost) **26**:127
Waka Jawaka (Zappa) **17**:590
Wakai (Shiga) **33**:366-67, 371
"The Wake" (Dybek) **114**:64, 71, 73-4
"Wake for Papa Montero" (Guillén)
See "Velorio de Papá Montero"
A Wake for the Living (Lytle) **22**:298
Wake of the Great Sealers (Mowat) **26**:338
"Wake the World" (Wilson) **12**:641
Wake Up Britain!: A Latter-Day Pamphlet (Johnson) **147**:131, 133-34
Wake Up, Jonathan (Rice) **7**:360; **49**:301, 305
Wake Up, Stupid (Harris) **19**:200-01, 204
Wakefield Express (Anderson) **20**:17
"Wake-Pick" (Gunnars) **69**:260-61
Wake-Pick Poems (Gunnars) **69**:259-61
"Wake-Up Niggers" (Madhubuti) **6**:313; **73**:199, 207
"The Waking" (Roethke) **101**:271, 326
Waking (Figes) **31**:167-70
"Waking an Angel" (Levine) **4**:287
"Waking Early Sunday Morning" (Lowell) **8**:351; **15**:343; **37**:237; **124**:290, 299, 305-06
"Waking from Sleep" (Bly) **128**:10-11, 31
"Waking in a Newly-Built House" (Gunn) **6**:221
"Waking in March" (Levine) **118**:286
"Waking in the Blue" (Lowell) **11**:327; **15**:343
"Waking in the Dark" (Rich) **3**:428; **7**:369, 373
"Waking in the Endless Mountains" (Smith) **42**:357
"Waking Jed" (Williams) **33**:449; **148**:320
The Waking: Poems, 1933-1953 (Roethke) **1**:291; **8**:455; **19**:397; **46**:360, 363; **101**:266, 273, 287, 295, 302, 304
Waking Slow (Mewshaw) **9**:376-77
"Waking This Morning" (Swados) **12**:557
Waking Up (Fo) **32**:174, 176
"Waking Up in the Middle of Some American Dreams" (Jordan) **114**:152
"Wakulla: Chasing the Gator's Eye" (Bottoms) **53**:33
"Waldbruder Lenz" (Hein) **154**:128
Das Wäldchen 125 (Jünger) **125**:221-22
Der Waldgang (Jünger) **125**:223, 255
Waldo (Heinlein) **14**:250; **55**:302-03
Waldo (Theroux) **28**:422-23
"Wales and the Crown" (Jones) **7**:191
"Wales Visitation" (Ginsberg) **36**:184, 189-91; **109**:347
"Walimai" (Allende) **97**:9, 31
"The Walk" (Donoso)
See "Paseo"
"A Walk" (Snyder) **32**:391
"Walk" (Tchicaya)
See "Marche"
"A Walk After Dark" (Auden) **123**:54
"A Walk by the River" (Hoffman) **141**:283, 286
Walk Gently This Good Earth (Craven) **17**:80-1
"A Walk in Kyoto" (Birney) **6**:78
"A Walk in Late Summer" (Roethke) **3**:433
"A Walk in the Country" (Raine) **103**:184, 190
"A Walk in the Dark" (Clarke) **136**:210
A Walk in the Night, and Other Stories (La Guma) **19**:272-73, 275-76
"A Walk in the Woods" (Bowen) **118**:75
"A Walk in the Woods" (Davis) **49**:92
A Walk in the Woods (Blessing) **54**:8-13
A Walk in Wolf Wood (Stewart) **117**:369
Walk like a Dragon (Clavell) **87**:18
Walk Me to the Distance (Everett) **57**:216-17
Walk My Way (Corcoran) **17**:78
"A Walk on Moss" (Viereck) **4**:559
"A Walk on Snow" (Viereck) **4**:559
"A Walk on the Cliff" (Lavin) **99**:321-23
"Walk on the Moon" (Momaday) **85**:231
"Walk on the Water" (Broumas) **73**:15
A Walk on the Water (Leonard) **19**:280
A Walk on the Water (Stoppard) **15**:518; **29**:398
A Walk on the West Side: California on the Brink (Gold) **42**:194; **152**:120, 143
"Walk on the Wild Side" (Reed) **21**:304-05, 314
A Walk on the Wild Side (Algren) **4**:17; **10**:6-7; **33**:12, 15-16
Walk on the Wild Side: The Best of Lou Reed (Reed) **21**:314
A Walk to the River (Hoffman) **141**:266, 274, 276, 280, 296-97, 301, 307
"Walk with Eros" (O'Casey) **11**:406
A Walk with Love and Death (Huston) **20**:171-72
"A Walk with Raschid" (Jacobsen) **48**:192, 196 **102**:241
A Walk with Raschid, and Other Stories (Jacobsen) **48**:192, 196; **102**:225
"A Walk with the Accuser" (Gordon) **29**:188
"A Walk with Tom Jefferson" (Levine) **118**:286, 289, 302, 319, 321
A Walk with Tom Jefferson (Levine) **118**:281, 285, 296, 302, 304, 319
"Walked Two Days in Snow, Then It Cleared for Five" (Snyder) **120**:325
"The Walker" (Hope) **51**:213
"Walker Brothers Cowboy" (Munro) **50**:210; **95**:287, 298
"Walker in Darkness" (Wright) **53**:419
A Walker in the City (Kazin) **34**:561; **38**:272-73, 275, 280, 282; **119**:303, 305, 308-10, 318-19, 331-32
Walker Percy: An American Search (Coles) **108**:179

"Walkers Passing Each Other in the Park" (Rakosi) **47**:345
"Walkers with the Dawn" (Hughes) **35**:214
"Walking" (Creeley) **15**:151
"Walking at Whitsun" (Gascoyne) **45**:154, 158
Walking Dead (Dickinson) **12**:176-77; **35**:133-34
"Walking Down Park" (Giovanni) **117**:195-98
Walking Down the Stairs (Kinnell) **29**:281-82; **129**:239, 249, 252-54, 262, 268-69
The Walking Drum (L'Amour) **55**:308
"Walking Home at Night" (Ginsberg) **36**:182
Walking in Dead Diamond River (Hoagland) **28**:181
"Walking in the rain in Guyana" (Sanchez) **116**:318-19
"Walking in Your Footsteps" (Police, The) **26**:366
"Walking into Love" (Piercy) **18**:406; **27**:375
"Walking Lessons" (Price) **3**:406; **6**:423; **43**:345
"The Walking Man of Rodin" (Sandburg) **10**:448
"Walking on Sunday" (Murphy) **41**:317
"Walking on the Prayerstick" (Rose) **85**:312
"Walking on Water" (Munro) **10**:357; **19**:345; **95**:302, 304
"Walking Our Boundaries" (Lorde) **71**:232, 240, 247
"Walking Out" (Plumly) **33**:312
"Walking out Alone in Dead of Winter" (Kinnell) **13**:321
Walking Papers (Hochman) **8**:297-98
"Walking Parker Home" (Kaufman) **49**:203-04
The Walking Stones (Hunter)
See *The Bodach*
Walking the Black Cat (Simic) **130**:346
"Walking the Boundaries" (Davison) **28**:103
Walking the Boundaries: Poems, 1957-1974 (Davison) **28**:102-03
"Walking the Dog: a Diatribe" (Van Duyn) **63**:439
Walking the Indian Streets (Mehta) **37**:288-89
"Walking the New York Bedrock / Alive in the Sea of Information" (Snyder) **120**:358
"Walking the Trestle" (Parini) **54**:361
Walking Through Seville (Cabral de Melo Neto)
See *Sevilha andando*
"Walking to Sleep" (Wilbur) **14**:577; **53**:412; **110**:357, 360
Walking to Sleep: New Poems and Translations (Wilbur) **3**:532-33; **6**:568; **14**:577; **53**:396, 402, 406-07, 410-11; **110**:352, 355, 360, 372, 384-85
"Walking to the Cattle-Place" (Murray) **40**:335-36
Walking under Water (Abse) **29**:13-17
"Walking with Jackie, Sitting with Dog" (Soto) **32**:403
"Walking Wounded" (Scannell) **49**:327, 329, 332
"Walking Wounded" (Shaw) **7**:411; **23**:396
Walking Wounded: Poems, 1962-1965 (Scannell) **49**:327-29, 331-32
"The Walking-mort" (Barnes) **127**:163
"Walk-On" (Young) **17**:573
Walkover (Skolimowski) **20**:348, 350-51, 353
"The Wall" (Brooks) **49**:28, 38; **125**:112
"Wall" (Creeley) **2**:108; **78**:154
"The Wall" (Jones) **4**:259
"The Wall" (Sexton) **123**:427
"A Wall" (Simic) **49**:337; **130**:296
The Wall (Hersey) **1**:144; **7**:153; **40**:227, 230-31, 234, 241; **81**:332-34, 337; **97**:302-03, 305-06
The Wall (Pink Floyd) **35**:309-15
The Wall (Ringwood) **48**:330, 335-36, 338
The Wall, and Other Stories (Sartre)
See *Le mur*
"The Wall and the Books" (Borges)
See "La muralla y los libros"
Wall around a Star (Williamson) **29**:462
"The Wall of All Earth" (Akhmatova) **25**:28
"Wall of Death" (Voznesensky) **57**:428
"A Wall of Fire Rising" (Danticat) **94**:93, 98-9
The Wall of the Plague (Brink) **36**:70-2; **106**:119-22, 124
"Wall Songs" (Hogan) **73**:150-51, 153
Wall Street (Stone) **73**:367-68, 376-77, 381-82
The Wall: The Crime of Mr. S. Karuma (Abe) **22**:13
Wallace Stevens: Musing the Obscure (Sukenick) **3**:475
Wallace Stevens: The Poems of Our Climate (Bloom) **103**:12, 14, 16, 24
"A Walled Garden" (Taylor) **44**:305
Wallflower at the Orgy (Ephron) **17**:110-11, 113
"The Wallpaper Flower" (Snodgrass) **6**:514
The Wallpaper Fox (Philipson) **53**:274-75, 277
Walls and Bridges (Lennon) **12**:377; **35**:268-71, 274
The Walls Do Not Fall (H. D.) **8**:255, 257-58; **14**:223, 225-27; **31**:202-04, 208; **34**:445-46; **73**:117
"The Walls of Anagoor" (Buzzati) **36**:93-4
"The Walls of Shimpundu" (Pownall) **10**:419
"Walls That Hear You" (Woolrich) **77**:401
"Wally Whistles Dixie" (Beattie) **63**:12
The Walnut Door (Hersey) **9**:277
The Walnut Trees of Altenburg (Malraux)
See *Les noyers de l'Altenburg*
Walsh (Pollock) **50**:224, 226
"Walt and Will" (Apple) **33**:21
"Walt Whitman" (Dahlberg) **7**:63
"Walt Whitman" (Honig) **33**:211
"Walt Whitman at Bear Mountain" (Simpson) **4**:499; **7**:427, 429; **9**:486; **32**:380; **149**:310, 312, 321, 324, 330, 349
Walt Whitman: The Making of the Poet (Zweig) **34**:378-79; **42**:468-69
Walter (Taylor) **27**:443
Walter Benjamin (Eagleton) **132**:86-7
Walter Benjamin; or, Towards Revolutionary Criticism (Eagleton) **63**:97, 104, 110
"Walter Clark's Frontier" (Stegner) **81**:347
"Walter Llywarch" (Thomas) **6**:534
The Walter Mosley Omnibus (Mosley) **97**:360
"The Waltons" (Hamner) **12**:258-59
"The Waltz" (Parker) **15**:417; **68**:326, 335-36, 338
Waltz in Marathon (Dickinson) **49**:99-103
Waltz Into Darkness (Woolrich) **77**:389, 391, 393, 395-98
The Waltz of the Toreadors (Anouilh)
See *La valse des toréadors*
"The Waltzer in the House" (Kunitz) **148**:89
Wampeters, Foma, and Granfalloons: Opinions (Vonnegut) **4**:568-69; **5**:466, 469-70; **12**:610, 620, 626-27; **22**:449, 451; **60**:434
"The Wanderer" (Auden) **11**:15
"The Wanderer" (Christie) **110**:126
"The Wanderer" (Masefield) **47**:229
"The Wanderer" (Williams) **67**:405-06
The Wanderer (Leiber) **25**:302-03, 311
"The Wanderer Awaiting Preferment" (Stafford) **7**:462
A Wanderer in Japan (Blunden) **56**:50
"Wanderer, kommst du nach Spa..." (Boell) **6**:83; **27**:56, 58-9, 65-7; **39**:293-95; **72**:69, 70, 73, 76, 78, 79-84, 94, 98, 100
"Wanderers" (Stern) **39**:237
"The Wanderers" (Welty) **33**:420; **105**:340, 386
The Wanderers (Ichikawa)
See *Matatabi*
The Wanderers (Mphahlele) **25**:332-34, 340-42, 345; **133**:133, 138, 144, 147, 157
The Wanderers (Price) **6**:426-27; **12**:488-91
Wanderers and Travellers (Strugatskii and Strugatskii) **27**:433
"A Wanderer's Song" (Masefield) **11**:358
"The Wandering Islands" (Hope) **51**:216, 219-20, 224
"The Wandering Islands" (Walcott) **76**:279
The Wandering Islands (Hope) **51**:210, 213, 215-17, 219-20
The Wandering Jew (Heym) **41**:218-19
The Wandering of Desire (Montgomery) **7**:232
The Wandering Prince (Hibbert) **7**:156
"The Wandering Scholar's Prayer to St. Catherine of Egypt" (Cunningham) **31**:99, 101
The Wandering Unicorn (Mujica Lainez) **31**:283-85
Wanderings: Chaim Potok's History of the Jews (Potok) **14**:429-30; **26**:373-74; **112**:261-62, 269, 295
"Wanderlust" (McCartney) **35**:290-91
"Wanderung" (Jandl) **34**:195
"A Waning Moon" (Sansom) **6**:484
"The Want" (Olds) **85**:305
The Want Bone (Pinsky) **94**:305-12, 322; **121**:428, 431-32, 435-37, 448
"Want More" (Marley) **17**:268-69, 271
"Wantage Bells" (Betjeman) **43**:35
Wanted (Pryor) **26**:379
Wanted! A Horse! (Friis-Baastad) **12**:214
Wanted Alive (Moure) **88**:216-19, 227-29
"Wanted: An Ontological Critic" (Ransom) **4**:437; **5**:365; **24**:365
Wanted: Hope (Samarakis)
See *Zititai elpis*
"Wanted—An Enemy" (Leiber) **25**:304
"Wanting a Child" (Graham) **118**:249
"Wanting All" (Ostriker) **132**:327
The Wanting Seed (Burgess) **2**:85-6; **4**:84; **8**:112; **10**:87-8; **13**:123, 126; **22**:69-70, 74; **40**:116-17, 121; **62**:130-31; **94**:25-29, 31, 34, 39, 41, 43, 49, 51, 55, 57, 59, 65, 74, 77
"Wanting to Die" (Sexton) **6**:492; **53**:313, 316, 319-20; **123**:421
"Wanting to Experience All Things" (Bly) **38**:57; **128**:12
"Wanting to Help" (Bell) **8**:65
"Wanting to Live in Harlem" (Seidel) **18**:474
"The Wanton Song" (Page and Plant) **12**:477
"Wants" (Larkin) **5**:227; **18**:296, 301; **64**:260, 266
"Wants" (Paley) **37**:337; **140**:261, 263, 265, 276
The Wapshot Chronicle (Cheever) **3**:107, 109; **7**:50; **15**:127; **25**:118, 120; **64**:44, 48, 57, 65-7
The Wapshot Scandal (Cheever) **3**:106-07, 109; **7**:50; **25**:118; **64**:44, 48-9, 57-9, 66
"The War" (Duras)
See "La douleur"
"War" (Findley) **102**:108, 111-12, 116
"A War" (Jarrell) **49**:201
"War" (Scott) **22**:372
"War" (Simic) **130**:334
"War" (Williams) **56**:427
War (Le Clézio) **31**:247, 249
The War (Ehrenburg) **62**:177
The War: A Memoir (Duras)
See *La douleur*
"War All the Time" (Alexie) **154**:27
War All the Time: Poems, 1981-1984 (Bukowski) **41**:73; **82**:13
"War and Memory" (Jordan) **114**:146, 148, 157
War and Peace: Observations on Our Times (Fast) **131**:84, 102
War and Prison (Aksyonov) **101**:55
War and Remembrance (Wouk) **38**:449-52
"War and Silence" (Bly) **128**:21, 31
War and War (Barthelme) **36**:49
"War Autobiography" (Blunden) **56**:41
"The War between Desire and Dailiness" (Pastan) **27**:371
"The War between Men and Women" (Thurber) **11**:533; **25**:437
The War between the Tates (Lurie) **4**:305-07; **5**:259-61; **18**:310; **39**:178-80
"War Cemetary" (Blunden) **56**:30, 45
"War Cemetery, Ranville" (Scannell) **49**:330

War Comes to Willy Freeman (Collier and Collier) **30**:74-5
"The War Continues" (Moraga) **126**:297
"War Crimes" (Carey) **96**:28, 36, 38-9, 68, 71
"War Crimes" (Muske) **90**:309-10, 312
War Crimes (Carey) **96**:22, 24-5, 36, 38-9, 53, 55, 62-3, 68, 72
"War Cry" (Moraga) **126**:296
The War Diaries of Jean-Paul Sartre, November 1939-March 1940 (Sartre) **52**:377-80
War Fever (Ballard) **137**:4
"War Games" (Morgan) **2**:295
War Games (Morris) **7**:245
"The War Horse" (Boland) **40**:96, 98; **113**:96, 122
The War Horse (Boland) **40**:96-8, 100; **67**:43-6; **113**:74, 78, 81, 87, 94, 96, 99, 108-09, 114, 122
The War Hound and the World's Pain (Moorcock) **58**:354
"War: Impacts and Delayed Actions" (Blunden) **56**:38
"The War in the Bathroom" (Atwood) **13**:46; **25**:62
War Is Heaven! (Mano) **2**:270
"War Is Over" (Lennon)
See "Happy Xmas"
"The War Is Over" (Ochs) **17**:332, 335
The War Lords of Washington (Catton) **35**:82-3
The War Lover (Hersey) **40**:230-32, 234, 238-40; **81**:332, 334; **97**:302, 304
"War Memoir" (Kaufman) **49**:203
"War Movie Veteran" (Scannell) **49**:332
The War of Dreams (Carter) **5**:101
"The War of Men and Women" (Ostriker) **132**:328
The War of the End of the World (Vargas Llosa)
See *La guerra del fin del mundo*
The War of the Saints (Amado) **106**:86-91
"War of the Two Directions" (Wingrove) **68**:456
The War of the Worlds (Welles) **80**:378-81, 414-16
The War of Time (Carpentier)
See *Guerra del tiempo*
"The War of Vaslav Nijinsky" (Bidart) **33**:77-81
"The War on Poverty" (Shields) **97**:429-31
War on the Fourth Floor (Kohout) **13**:325
"War on the Periphery" (Johnston) **51**:240, 243, 250, 253
"The War Piece" (Bell) **8**:66
"War Poems" (Ciardi) **40**:154
"War Poems" (MacBeth) **5**:265
The War Poems of Siegfried Sassoon (Sassoon) **130**:181
"War Profit Litany" (Ginsberg) **36**:184
"A War Requiem" (Sissman) **9**:491
"War Sonnet" (Meredith) **13**:374
War Suite (Harrison) **6**:223
War Trilogy (H. D.)
See *Trilogy*
"War Winters" (Birney) **6**:74
War with the Newts (Kohout) **13**:324
War Within and Without: Diaries and Letters of Anne Morrow Lindbergh, 1939-1944 (Lindbergh) **82**:156-57, 159
"War Wounds" (Shields) **97**:430, 433
War Year (Haldeman) **61**:169
Ward 402 (Glasser) **37**:132-33
"Ward Number Four" (Pa Chin)
See "Ti ssu ping shih"
"The Warden" (Gardner) **7**:111, 116; **8**:238
"The Warden Said to Me the Other Day" (Knight) **40**:283
"The Warden's Wife" (Trevor) **116**:389
"Wardrobe Trunk" (Woolrich) **77**:399
"Warehouse Three" (Aldiss) **5**:15
Warera no jidai (Oe) **36**:350; **86**:214, 230, 239, 241
Warera no kyōki o ikinobiru michi o oshieyo (Oe) **86**:215-17, 225, 228, 243-44
Warlock (Harrison) **33**:196-201; **66**:155-56, 161, 169; **143**:336-37, 339, 341, 344, 355-56
Warlock of the Witch World (Norton) **12**:468
The Warlord of the Air (Moorcock) **27**:348; **58**:349
"Warm and Beautiful" (McCartney) **35**:284-85
A Warm December (Poitier) **26**:358-60
"Warm Flesh-Colored Ode" (Justice) **102**:258
"Warm Love" (Morrison) **21**:234
The Warm Nights of January (Tuohy) **37**:428, 431
"A Warm Room" (Tillinghast) **29**:414-15
"Warm Thoughts" (Robinson) **21**:348-50
Warm Worlds and Otherwise (Tiptree) **48**:386, 388-89, 393
"Warming Trends" (Louie) **70**:81
"The Warmth of the Sun" (Wilson) **12**:651
"Warning" (Cohen) **38**:131
"The Warning" (Creeley) **36**:120; **78**:134
"A Warning" (Ezekiel) **61**:96
"Warning" (Frost) **15**:246
"Warning" (Hughes) **35**:218
"Warning" (Rozewicz) **139**:236
Warning (Fassbinder) **20**:106
"Warning Sign" (Byrne) **26**:96
"Warning to Children" (Graves) **2**:176; **39**:328; **45**:170
"Warnings" (Parra) **102**:353
Warnings from the Grave (Plath) **9**:429
"Warnings to the Reader" (Parra) **102**:348-51
"A Warrant for Pablo Neruda" (McGrath) **28**:277
"Warren Pryor" (Nowlan) **15**:398
Warrendale (Maysles and Maysles) **16**:440
"Warrior" (Kenny) **87**:241
Warrior Marks (Walker) **103**:419-22
"The Warrior Princess Ozimbu" (Price) **43**:341
The Warrior Queens (Fraser)
See *Bodicea's Chariot: The Warrior Queens*
Warrior Scarlet (Sutcliff) **26**:426, 428, 430-36, 441
The Warriors (Jakes) **29**:248-49
The Warriors of Day (Blish) **14**:84
"The Wars" (Moss) **45**:291
The Wars (Findley) **27**:141-45; **102**:97, 99-101, 104-06, 109, 111-14, 116-17, 121
"The Wars in New Jersey" (Merwin) **88**:208
The Wars of the Jews (Sobol) **60**:385-86
A Warsaw Diary, 1978-1981 (Brandys) **62**:112-17, 119-20
"Warszawa" (Bowie) **17**:65
"A Wartime Dawn" (Gascoyne) **45**:154, 158-59
Wartime Journalism, 1939-1943 (de Man) **55**:411, 413
Wartime: Understanding and Behavior in the Second World War (Fussell) **74**:130-32, 135-39, 143
"The Wartons" (Blunden) **56**:37
"Warum ich kurze Prosa wie Jakob Maria Hermes and Heinrich Knecht schreibe" (Boell) **27**:67
"Was" (Faulkner) **6**:174-75
"Was" (Scott) **22**:374
Was bleibt (Wolf) **150**:244-45, 270, 272-75, 278-81, 292, 297-304, 306, 311, 314-16, 318-19, 329-30, 334-35, 347, 349-50, 352
Was Europe a Success? (Krutch) **24**:284, 289
Was Heisst Denken? (Heidegger) **24**:264, 267
"Was ich Rom sah und hörte" (Bachmann) **69**:42-3
Was soll aus dem Jungen bloss werden?: oder, Irgendwas mit Büchern (Boell) **27**:294; **72**:101
"Wash" (Faulkner) **52**:138-39
"Wash Far Away" (Berryman) **10**:45
"Wash of Cold River" (H. D.) **73**:108, 120
"The Washing Machine Tragedy" (Lem) **40**:294; **149**:149
"Washing Your Feet" (Ciardi) **129**:47
"Washington Bullets" (Clash) **30**:48-9
Washington, D.C. (Vidal) **2**:449; **4**:559; **6**:549-50; **8**:525; **22**:435; **33**:407, 409; **72**:377-79, 382-84, 389, 391-93, 395-97, 400-03; **142**:322, 334
"Washington in Love" (Berryman) **8**:93; **25**:96
Washington Is Leaking (Buchwald) **33**:94
Washington Jitters (Trumbo) **19**:446
Washington Square (Auchincloss) **9**:55
The Washington Square Ensemble (Bell) **41**:51-4; **102**:3-4, 16-7
Washington vs. Main Street: The Struggle between Federal and Local Power (Archer) **12**:21
"The Washroom Ballet" (Lieberman) **36**:261
"The Wasp" (Morrison) **17**:295
"Wasp" (Nowlan) **15**:399
The Wasp Factory (Banks) **34**:29-31
"Wasp Nest" (Fuller) **62**:199
"A WASP Woman Visits a Black Junkie in Prison" (Knight) **40**:285
"Wassermann Test" (Pasternak) **7**:297
"Die Wasserstrasse" (Schmidt) **56**:392
The Waste Land (Eliot) **1**:89-92; **2**:125-30; **3**:136-41; **6**:160-61, 164-66; **9**:182-88, 190; **10**:168-72; **13**:198, 201-02; **15**:210, 212, 214-17; **24**:163, 167, 172, 176, 185; **34**:388, 390,; **55**:346-48, 351-56, 358-60, 362, 366-70, 372, 374; **57**:167-213; **113**:182, 186, 189-91, 197, 209, 217, 219, 223
The Waste Land: A Facsimile and Transcript of the Original Drafts, Including the Annotations of Ezra Pound (Eliot) **57**:201-09
"Waste Sonata" (Olds) **85**:306
"Wasted Lives" (Weldon) **122**:278, 281
"Wasted on the Young" (Brunner) **8**:111
"Wasteland" (Weller) **26**:446
"Wasteland Berlin 1990" (Wolf) **150**:344
"Watakushi no mono" (Endō) **54**:158, 161
"The Watch" (Bass) **79**:4-6, 9
"The Watch" (Dixon) **52**:98
"The Watch" (Swenson) **14**:518; **61**:392
"The Watch" (Swift) **41**:443, 446; **88**:320
"Watch" (Ungaretti)
See "Veglia"
"The Watch" (Wagoner) **3**:508
The Watch (Bass) **79**:3-7, 10-11, 14-17, 19-20; **143**:3-4, 9, 12
"Watch Any Day His Nonchalant Pauses" (Auden) **14**:32; **43**:15
"Watch for Flag Man" (Loewinsohn) **52**:284
The Watch House (Westall) **17**:557-59
Watch It Come Down (Osborne) **45**:319-20
Watch on the Rhine (Hellman) **2**:187; **8**:281; **14**:258-59; **18**:222, 225, 227; **34**:348-49, 353; **44**:530; **52**:191, 202
"Watch Repair" (Simic) **49**:340
The Watch That Ends the Night (MacLennan) **2**:257; **14**:339-42, 344; **92**:305, 307-08, 321, 324-28, 331-40, 342-50
"Watch That Man" (Bowie) **17**:60
Watch the North Wind Rise (Graves) **11**:256; **45**:171-73
"Watch Your Step" (Costello) **21**:76
Watchboy, What of the Night? (Cassity) **42**:94-5
"The Watcher" (Cooper) **56**:71
"The Watcher" (Vanderhaeghe) **41**:449-50, 453
The Watcher (Calvino)
See *La giornato d'uno scruttatore*
The Watcher, and Other Stories (Calvino)
See *La giornato d'uno scruttatore*
Watcher in the Shadows (Household) **11**:277
"A Watcher of the Dead" (Gordimer) **33**:177
"The Watchers" (Blackburn) **43**:62
"The Watchers" (Bradbury) **42**:38
Watchers (Koontz) **78**:198, 200-01, 203, 219
"Watches of Grandfathers" (Dunn) **40**:168
Watchfires (Auchincloss) **45**:32
"The Watchful Gods" (Clark) **28**:79-80
The Watchful Gods, and Other Stories (Clark) **28**:78-9
"The Watching" (Dodson) **79**:194

"Watching" (O Hehir) **41**:324
"Watching 'Dark Circle'" (Levertov) **66**:239
"Watching Football on TV" (Nemerov) **36**:305
"Watching Him" (McFadden) **48**:243
"Watching. It Come" (Deane) **122**:74
Watching Me, Watching You (Weldon) **36**:443-45; **122**:254
"Watching Post" (Day Lewis) **10**:131
"Watching Running Water" (Blunden) **56**:29
"Watching the Detectives" (Costello) **21**:68, 74
Watching the Detectives (Rathbone) **41**:344
"Watching the Jets Lose to Buffalo at Shea" (Swenson) **61**:402; **106**:330
"Watching the River Flow" (Dylan) **6**:158
"Watching the Schoolyard" (Carroll) **143**:33
"Watching the Wheels" (Lennon) **35**:272-75
The Watchmaker of Everton (Simenon) **2**:396, 399
"Watchman, What of the Night?" (Barnes) **29**:24
"Water" (Creeley) **78**:137
"Water" (Larkin) **33**:259; **39**:344; **64**:268, 282-84
"Water" (Lowell) **4**:299
"Water" (Snyder) **32**:386; **120**:338
Water and Stone (Vliet) **22**:443
"Water and the Poem" (Cabral de Melo Neto) See "O poema e a água"
"Water and the Wine" (Armatrading) **17**:8
"The Water Bearer" (Williams) **42**:442
The Water Beetle (Mitford) **44**:489
"The Water Carrier" (Montague) **46**:275
"The Water Clock" (Boland) **113**:120
"The Water Diviner" (Abse) **29**:15
"The Water Drop" (Elytis) **49**:110-11
"Water Element Song for Sylvia" (Wakoski) **7**:504
The Water Engine: An American Fable (Mamet) **15**:355, 358; **46**:246, 249, 252-54
The Water Is Wide (Conroy) **30**:76-7; **74**:47-51
The Water Is Wide (Le Guin) **45**:213-14
"Water Island" (Moss) **45**:291-92
"Water Liars" (Hannah) **90**:143-45, 147, 160
"Water Maid" (Clark Bekedermo) **38**:121
Water Music (Boyle) **36**:58-60, 62-3; **90**:43, 49, 58-9, 61
"Water Music for the Progress of Love in a Life-Raft down the Sammamish Slough" (Wagoner) **5**:474
"The Water of Izli" (Bowles) **53**:36
"Water of Life" (MacDiarmid) **63**:244
"The Water of the Flowery Mill" (Rothenberg) **57**:374
Water on the Brain (Mackenzie) **18**:316
The Water Pourer (Coover) **87**:45
"The Water Rats" (Colwin) **5**:108; **84**:149
Water, Rock, and Sand (Levi) **41**:243-44
"Water Song" (Kogawa) **78**:167
Water Street (Merrill) **2**:273, 275; **13**:378-80; **91**:228, 230
Water under the Bridge (Elliott) **38**:181
"Water Widow" (Jensen) **37**:186
Water with Berries (Lamming) **2**:235; **4**:279; **66**:220, 225, 227-30; **144**:126-29, 131, 133-35, 140, 174, 176, 185, 187-91
Water with Berries (Lamming) **144**:126-29, 131, 133-35, 140, 174, 185, 187-91
Water with the Wines (Armatrading) **17**:9
"The Water Works" (Doctorow) **37**:91, 93; **113**:151-52
"Water Writes Always in Plural" (Paz) **19**:365
"Waterbird" (Swenson) **61**:402-03
"Waterclap" (Asimov) **19**:26
"Watercolor of Grantchester Meadows" (Plath) **51**:344; **111**:200, 203
"The Watercress Girl" (Bates) **46**:67
"The Water-Diviner" (Clarke) **61**:79-80, 83
"Waterfall" (Bass) **143**:15-16
"Waterfall" (Clarke) **61**:73
"The Waterfall" (Daryush) **19**:121
"Waterfall" (Heaney) **25**:242
"Waterfall" (O Hehir) **41**:323-24
"The Waterfall" (Oliver) **98**:288
"Waterfall" (Simon) **26**:409
The Waterfall (Drabble) **2**:117-19; **3**:128-29; **5**:118; **10**:165; **22**:122, 124-25; **53**:118-19, 121-22; **129**:112, 117-18, 124-25, 127, 145, 148
"Waterfalls" (McCartney) **35**:287
"Waterfalls" (Watkins) **43**:444, 453
Waterfront (Schulberg) **48**:346-47
Watergate: America in Crisis (Archer) **12**:21-2
"The Watergaw" (MacDiarmid) **11**:336; **19**:286-87; **63**:252
Watering (Brosman) **9**:135-36
Waterland (Swift) **41**:443-47; **88**:284-92, 294-303, 307-10, 313, 315-18, 320-22
"Waterlily Fire" (Rukeyser) **27**:408
Waterlily Fire: Poems, 1935-1962 (Rukeyser) **15**:456; **27**:408
"Waterloo Bridge" (Middleton) **13**:387
Waterloo Express (Jiles) **13**:304; **58**:271-73
"Waterloo Sunset" (Davies) **21**:90, 97
"Watermaid" (Okigbo) **25**:347-48, 351, 354; **84**:301, 305, 308-10, 313, 329-31
Watermark (Brodsky) **100**:38, 47, 56, 58
"Watermarked" (White) **110**:339-40
Watermelon Man (Van Peebles) **20**:410-12
Watermelons (Loewinsohn) **52**:283
"Water-Message" (Barth) **9**:66, 69; **89**:3, 6, 8-10, 14-16, 19, 22, 36, 41, 48-50, 54, 56, 59, 64
The Water-Method Man (Irving) **13**:292-93; **23**:244; **38**:250-51; 155-157, 159, 165
"A Waterpiece" (Blunden) **56**:29
"The Waters" (Matthews) **40**:322, 324
"The Waters" (Merwin) **45**:275
The Waters Are Come in unto My Soul (Oe) See *Kōzui wa waga tamashii ni oyobi*
"The Water's Edge" (Hooker) **43**:197
The Waters of Babylon (Arden) **6**:4, 9; **13**:26, 28; **15**:19
The Waters of Kronos (Richter) **30**:316-17, 321-22, 326
"Waters of Melis" (Kerrigan) **6**:276
The Waters of Siloe (Merton) **83**:398, 403
"The Watershed" (Auden) **6**:24
"Watershed" (Avison) **97**:128
Watership Down (Adams) **4**:6-10; **5**:4-7; **18**:2
The Waterworks (Doctorow) **113**:166-80
Watson's Apology (Bainbridge) **62**:32, 34; **130**:13, 20, 34
Watsonville: Some Place Not Here (Moraga) **126**:301-02
Watt (Beckett) **3**:45; **6**:34, 41-4; **9**:80, 84; **10**:27-8, 34-6; **11**:33-4, 36, 39, 40, 43; **14**:70-3, 75-6, 80; **18**:41, 50, 52; **29**:53, 56, 63, 65; **57**:65; **59**:253-54, 260; **83**:121
Watten: Ein Nachlass (Bernhard) **61**:9
Watusi (Clavell) **87**:18
"A Wave" (Ashbery) **41**:33-4, 36-41; **77**:62; **125**:3-7
"The Wave" (MacLeish) **8**:362
"Wave" (Smith) **12**:543
"Wave" (Snyder) **120**:310, 343
A Wave (Ashbery) **41**:33-40; **125**:40
The Wave (Scott) **43**:376-78, 383, 385
The Wave of the Future (Lindbergh) **82**:155-158, 164, 166-67
Wave the High Banner (Brown) **18**:70
Wave without a Shore (Cherryh) **35**:107-09, 112
Wavelength (Morrison) **21**:238
"The Waves" (Oliver) **98**:267
Waves (Pasternak) **63**:288
The Waves behind the Boat (King) **53**:207
"The Waves in Rio" (Ellison) **139**:140
The Waves of Night (Petrakis) **3**:382
"Waving" (Smith) **42**:348
The Wax Museum (Hawkes) **4**:213, 215
"The Way" (Creeley) **78**:127, 133
"The Way a Ghost Dissolves" (Hugo) **32**:247-48
"The Way a Sertanejo Speaks" (Cabral de Melo Neto) See "O sertanejo falando"
"The Way Back" (Grau) **9**:240
"The Way Down" (Kunitz) **148**:96, 99
The Way Home (Singer) **69**:306
"The Way I Feel" (Giovanni) **117**:192
"The Way In" (Tomlinson) **13**:549
The Way In and Other Poems (Tomlinson) **6**:534-36; **13**:548-49; **45**:396, 398, 401
A Way in the World (Naipaul) **105**:175-77, 179, 181-82
"The Way Is Not a Way" (Snyder) **32**:392
"The Way It Is" (Strand) **18**:516, 519; **41**:436; **71**:285
"The Way It Mostly Was" (O'Brien) **103**:144-45
"The Way It Sometimes Is" (Taylor) **44**:300
"the Way it Was" (Clifton) **66**:69
"The Way Love Used to Be" (Davies) **21**:92
"The Way of a Man" (Grau) **146**:127
The Way of a World (Tomlinson) **2**:437; **4**:544, 546-47; **13**:545-46, 548; **45**:393-94, 396, 398, 402
The Way of All Flesh (Compton-Burnett) **10**:109
Way of All the Earth (Akhmatova) **64**:13
The Way of It (Thomas) **13**:545; **48**:380-81
"The Way of Keys" (Dobyns) **37**:75
A Way of Life, like Any Other (O'Brien) **11**:405
A Way of Looking (Jennings) **131**:232, 237-38
A Way of Seeing (Mead) **37**:277-78
"A Way of Talking" (Grace) **56**:111-12
The Way of the Animal Powers (Campbell) See *The Historical Atlas of World Mythology*
The Way of the Seeded Earth (Campbell) See *The Historical Atlas of World Mythology*
"The Way of the Wind" (Oz) **27**:359
"The Way of the Wind" (Riding) **7**:374
"The Way of the World" (Martin) **89**:110, 112, 118
The Way of the World (Connelly) **7**:57
"A Way Out" (Adcock) **41**:16
"Way Out" (Rozewicz) **139**:289
A Way Out (Frost) **15**:249
Way Out in the Centre (Abse) **29**:20
The Way Some People Die (Macdonald) **14**:334; **41**:265, 267, 269, 271
The Way Some People Live (Cheever) **15**:127; **64**:66
"The Way the Bird Sat" (Young Bear) **94**:361, 366
The Way the Future Was (Pohl) **18**:412
"The Way Things Work" (Graham) **48**:145; **118**:248, 250, 258-59
The Way to Dusty Death (MacLean) **13**:359; **50**:348
"The Way to Eden" (Roddenberry) **17**:412
"The Way to Hump a Cow Is Not" (Cummings) **15**:162
"A Way to Love God" (Warren) **13**:578; **39**:267-69
The Way to Rainy Mountain (Momaday) **2**:290; **19**:317-20; **85**:227-28, 231-33, 235, 238, 246, 250-51, 253, 255-56, 258, 262, 266-67, 269, 273-79; **95**:218, 222, 234, 237-38, 274, 276-77
Way to the Ocean (Leonov) See *Doroga na okean*
"The Way up to Heaven" (Dahl) **79**:176
Way Upstream (Ayckbourn) **33**:45-6, 48; **74**:19-20, 24, 27, 29, 31
"The Way We Live" (Haines) **58**:216
"The Way We Live Now" (Bernard) **59**:46
"The Way We Live Now" (Sontag) **105**:197, 206
The Way West (Guthrie) **23**:197-98, 201
A Way with Words (Bowering) **47**:28
"The Way You Do the Things You Do" (Robinson) **21**:343, 346-47
"A Way You'll Never Be" (Hemingway) **10**:267; **30**:179, 183, 187-88, 196-97
"The Wayfarer" (Colum) **28**:85
"The Wayfarer" (Coover) **46**:116
"Wayne Foster" (Welsh) **144**:336

"Ways" (O'Brien) **13**:416; **36**:341; **116**:209-10
"Ways and Means" (Eberhart) **11**:178
Ways of a Sleeping Man, Ways of a Waking Man (Michaux)
See *Façons d'endormi, façons d'éveillé*
Ways of Death (Bachmann)
See *Todesarten*
Ways of Escape (Greene) **27**:171-74; **37**:138; **70**:289-90, 292; **72**:179; **125**:196
"Ways of Feeling" (Cassity) **42**:94
Ways of Telling (Dyer) **149**:38-9, 41
The Ways of White Folks (Hughes) **1**:149; **10**:281; **108**:313, 315
The Waystation (Simak) **55**:319-20, 322
The Wayward and the Seeking: A Collection of Writing by Jean Toomer (Toomer) **22**:428-29
The Wayward Bus (Steinbeck) **1**:325; **5**:406; **9**:517-18; **21**:366, 371, 382-83, 391; **34**:405; **45**:370, 372, 378; **75**:343, 350; **124**:402
"The Wayward Path" (Swan) **69**:362
The Wayward Saint (Carroll) **10**:97-100
"We" (McClure) **10**:333
We a BaddDDD People (Sanchez) **116**:272, 274-75, 278, 281, 295-96, 298, 301-02, 309, 313, 326
"We a BadddDDD People (for gwendolyn brooks/a fo real bad one)" (Sanchez) **116**:295, 309, 315
"We All Begin in a Little Magazine" (Levine) **54**:298, 301
We All Die Naked (Blish) **14**:86
We All Have the Same Story (Fo) **32**:176
"We All Wore a Green Carnation" (Coward) **29**:138
"We Also Walk Dogs" (Heinlein) **14**:249
We Always Treat Women Too Well (Queneau)
Scc *On est toujours trop bon avec les femmes*
"We and Europe" (Ehrenburg) **62**:177
"We and Them" (Marley) **17**:273
We Are All Fugitives (Gironella)
See *Todos somos fugitivos*
"We Are Always Too Late" (Boland) **113**:92
We Are Betrayed (Fisher) **7**:103
"We Are for the Dark" (Aickman) **57**:4
"We Are in Your Area" (Van Duyn) **116**:427
We Are Many (Neruda) **5**:303
"We Are Muslim Women" (Sanchez) **116**:299
"We Are Norsemen" (Boyle) **36**:57
We Are Still Married (Keillor) **115**:283, 286
"We Are the Dead" (Bowie) **17**:61
We Are the Living (Caldwell) **14**:96; **60**:48
"We Are the National Hero" (Coles)
See "My nacional'nyj geroj"
"We Are the Nighttime Travelers" (Canin) **55**:35-6, 38-9
"We Are the Only Animals Who Do This" (Boland) **113**:92
"We Are Very Poor" (Rulfo)
See "Es que somos muy pobres"
We Bombed in New Haven (Heller) **11**:265
We Can Build You (Dick) **30**:123, 127-28; **72**:104
"We Can Remember It for You Wholesale" (Dick) **72**:123-24
"We Can Work It Out" (Lennon and McCartney) **12**:361
We Can't Breathe (Fair) **18**:140-41
"We Come Back" (Rexroth) **112**:400
We Come to the River (Bond) **23**:66
"We Don't Know How . . . to think directly, to tell, we never learned in school" (Wolf) **150**:298
"We Don't Live Here Anymore" (Dubus) **36**:144, 146, 148-49; **97**:195-96, 199-200, 210, 218, 226
We Don't Live Here Anymore (Dubus) **97**:209, 218-20
"We Don't Want No Education" (Pink Floyd) **35**:313
"We Drink the Wine in France" (Walker) **103**:407
"We Encounter Nat King Cole as We Invent the Future" (Harjo) **83**:275, 282
"We Feed on Shadow" (Aleixandre) **36**:30
We Fished All Night (Motley) **18**:356-57
"We Francji" (Dabrowska) **15**:165
"We Free Singers Be" (Knight) **40**:285, 287
"We Get Smashed and Our Endings Are Swift" (Abbott) **48**:4-5
We Have Always Lived in the Castle (Jackson) **11**:301; **60**:211, 213-14, 217, 221-25, 234-35
"We Have Been Believers" (Walker) **6**:554
"We Have Known" (Bell) **31**:49
"We Have No Secrets" (Simon) **26**:408, 410, 413
We Have Ways of Making You Laugh (Gilliam) **141**:247
"We in Some Strange Power's Employ, Move on a Rigorous Line" (Delany) **38**:154; **141**:155
We Killed Christ (Bruce) **21**:54
"We Know You're Busy Writing, but We Thought You Wouldn't Mind If We Dropped In for a Minute" (Crispin) **22**:112
"We Laughed at Him" (Achebe) **11**:4
"We Learned" (Jong) **8**:314
We Live Again (Mamoulian) **16**:423
We Live Here (Voinovich)
See *My zdes' zhivem*
We Love Glenda So Much, and Other Tales (Cortázar)
See *Queremos tanto a Glenda*
"We Loved Here" (Amichai)
See "Ahavnu Kan"
We Might See Sights! and Other Stories (O'Faolain) **47**:325, 329
"We Must Call a Meeting" (Harjo) **83**:269, 280, 285
We Must March, My Darlings (Trilling) **129**:324-25, 327, 330-31, 337, 342, 347, 356
"We Never Know" (Komunyakaa) **94**:228, 243
We Never Make Mistakes (Solzhenitsyn)
See *Sluchai na stantsii Krechetovka i Matrenin dvor*
"We Real Cool" (Brooks) **15**:93; **125**:49, 81, 90, 94, 96, 109-11
"We Say 'Cheers' Every Day" (Neruda)
See "Salud decimos cada día"
We Talk, You Listen: New Tribes, New Turf (Deloria) **21**:109-10, 113; **122**:110
"We Teach" (Howard) **7**:168
We the Living (Rand) **30**:291-92, 296-98, 300; **44**:451; **79**:362, 371, 373-75, 377-81, 389
We, the People (Rice) **7**:360-61, 363; **49**:296-97, 300-05
"We Two" (H. D.) **73**:109
"We Walk the Way of the New World" (Madhubuti) **6**:313
We Walk the Way of the New World (Madhubuti) **2**:238; **73**:205, 212, 214-15
"We, We Ourselves" (Ammons) **57**:49-50
"We Went" (Montale) **9**:388
We Were Strangers (Huston) **20**:160-62
"We Were Three" (Alegria) **75**:36-7, 39
We Who Are About To (Russ) **15**:461-62
"We Who Stole the 'Dream'" (Tiptree) **48**:389
"We Will Never Retreat" (Fast) **131**:72
We Won't Pay! We Won't Pay! (Fo) **32**:173-76; **109**:100-01, 119-20, 122, 144, 146
"We Would Like You to Know" (Castillo) **151**:10, 20
"The Weaker Sex" (Kawabata)
See "Yowaki Utsuwa"
The Weaker Vessel (Fraser) **32**:186-87; **107**:35-36, 38, 40, 41-43, 45, 47, 51, 57, 59, 61, 67
The Weaker Vessel (Kawabata)
See "Yowaki Utsuwa"
"The Weald of Youth" (Sassoon) **36**:387, 394; **130**:178, 194, 202, 204, 206-7, 225
"The Wean and That" (Kelman) **58**:298
"Weapon Systems of the 21st Century" (Lem) **149**:116
Weapons of Happiness (Brenton) **31**:60-7
"The Weary Blues" (Hughes) **44**:507-09, 511
The Weary Blues (Hughes) **1**:147; **10**:279; **15**:292; **35**:212, 214; **108**:282, 290, 293-94, 296, 310, 312, 319, 323
"Weary Kingdom" (Irving) **112**:173, 175
"Weasels and Ermines" (Kinsella) **27**:239
Weasels Ripped My Flesh (Zappa) **17**:586, 590, 593
"The Weather" (Chappell) **40**:142; **78**:95
"The Weather" (Soto) **80**:299
Weather and Season (Hamburger) **14**:234
"The Weather as Cultural Determinator" (Giovanni) **19**:191
"Weather Bestiary" (Brown) **5**:76
The Weather for Poetry (Hall) **151**:206
Weather Forecast for Utopia and Vicinity: Poems, 1967-1982 (Simic) **49**:336-37, 339; **130**:318
"The Weather Gifts" (Szirtes) **46**:391
The Weather in Africa (Gellhorn) **14**:195; **60**:188-89, 192
The Weather in the Streets (Lehmann) **5**:235, 238
"The Weather Is Hot on the Back of My Watch" (Bukowski) **41**:67
The Weatherboard Cathedral (Murray) **40**:334, 336, 338
"Weathering by a Fire" (Brosman) **9**:135
"Weathering Out" (Dove) **50**:154; **81**:139
The Weathermakers (Bova) **45**:66-7
"Weatherman" (Dunn) **36**:153-54
The Weathermonger (Dickinson) **12**:167-68, 170, 172
Weathers and Edges (Booth) **23**:74-5
A Weave of Women (Broner) **19**:71-2
"The Weaver in the Vault" (Smith) **43**:420
Weaveworld (Barker) **52**:56-7
"Weaving the Morning" (Cabral de Melo Neto)
See "Tecendo a manhã"
"The Web" (Glassco) **9**:237
"Web" (Oliver) **34**:248
Web (Wyndham) **19**:476
"Web Central" (Weldon) **122**:282
"The Wedding" (Bates) **46**:52, 63
"The Wedding" (Carrier) **78**:38
"Wedding" (Dobyns) **37**:82
"Wedding" (Nagy) **7**:251
"The Wedding" (Pritchett) **15**:443; **41**:330, 334
"The Wedding" (Rothenberg) **57**:374
A Wedding (Altman) **16**:39-40, 42-44
The Wedding (Altman) **116**:30, 37-8, 51, 61, 66, 70
The Wedding (Canetti)
See *Die Hochzeit*
The Wedding (Kadare)
See *Dasma*
The Wedding (Wajda) **16**:580, 583
Wedding Album (Lennon) **35**:267
Wedding Band: A Love/Hate Story in Black and White (Childress) **12**:104-06; **86**:305-06, 309-10, 312, 314-16; **96**:88-93, 103-04, 109, 118-20, 123-24
"Wedding Bells Will Ring So Merrily" (Farrell) **66**:129
"Wedding Day" (Boyle) **58**:66-7, 71; **121**:26, 40, 42-4
"Wedding Day" (Hall) **51**:170
"Wedding Day" (Hemingway) **3**:240
Wedding Day, and Other Stories (Boyle) **5**:65; **19**:61
The Wedding Feast (Canetti)
See *Die Hochzeit*
The Wedding Feast (Wesker) **3**:519; **42**:426-27
The Wedding Group (Taylor) **2**:432-33; **29**:412
Wedding in Blood (Chabrol) **16**:179
"A Wedding in Hell" (Simic) **130**:346
A Wedding in Hell (Simic) **130**:333-34, 343, 345-46

"A Wedding in Jackson" (Gilchrist) **143**:300, 314, 327, 329
"The Wedding in the Garden" (Trevor) **71**:329, 348
"Wedding Night" (Landolfi) **11**:321; **49**:209
"The Wedding Night" (Sexton) **53**:316
"Wedding Night" (Tremain) **42**:386
"The Wedding of Galia" (Yehoshua) **31**:474
The Wedding on the Eiffel Tower (Cocteau)
See *Les mariés de la Tour Eiffel*
"The Wedding Party" (Dubie) **36**:132
The Wedding Party (De Palma) **20**:73, 78
"Wedding Pictures" (Phillips) **15**:420
"Wedding Song" (Dylan) **4**:150
"Wedding Song" (Robinson) **21**:346
"Wedding Song" (Smith) **42**:353
Wedding Song (Mahfouz) **153**:239, 242-43, 250
Wedding Song (Mahfūz) **52**:304-05
"A Wedding Toast" (Wilbur) **110**:385
"Wedding Wind" (Clarke) **61**:75
"Wedding Wind" (Larkin) **5**:227; **8**:332, 339; **18**:298; **33**:259; **39**:336, 345; **64**:259, 282
"The Wedding-Party" (Pasternak) **63**:313
Weddings (Yevtushenko) **26**:461
The Weddings at Nether Powers and Other New Poems (Redgrove) **41**:356
Weddings in the House (Hrabal)
See *Svatby v domě*
The Wedge (Williams) **42**:455
"The Wedge-Tailed Eagle" (Buckley) **57**:126
"Wednesday" (Fuller) **62**:206
"Wednesday" (Levine) **14**:318
"Wednesday at the Waldorf" (Swenson) **4**:534; **106**:339
Wednesday Morning Three A.M. (Simon) **17**:459
"Wednesday Night at Our House" (Grayson) **38**:210
"The Wee Boy Who Got Killed" (Kelman) **58**:300. 302
"Wee Horrors" (Kelman) **58**:295
"The Weed" (Bishop) **1**:34; **9**:92; **32**:34, 36-7, 42
"Weed" (Hass) **99**:140
The Weed Garden (Turco) **11**:551-52
"The Weed of Time" (Spinrad) **46**:383
"Weed Puller" (Roethke) **11**:484; **19**:397; **101**:293-94, 334
The Weedkiller's Daughter (Arnow) **7**:15-16; **18**:12, 16
"Weeds" (DeMarinis) **54**:100
"The Weeds" (Stern) **40**:408, 413
"Weeds and Peonies" (Hall) **151**:221
"Week of Sun" (Landolfi) **11**:321; **49**:212
"The Week of the Small Leaves" (Souster) **14**:505
"Weekend" (Beattie) **63**:17; **146**:63, 84
"Weekend" (Weldon) **36**:444
Weekend (Godard) **20**:137, 140, 151
"Weekend Glory" (Angelou) **35**:32
Weekend in Dinlock (Sigal) **7**:423-24
"Weekend in the Country" (Sondheim) **30**:397
"Weekend in the Neighborhood of Summer" (Ritsos) **31**:324
The Weekend Man (Wright) **6**:581-82
"Weekend Song" (Joel) **26**:214
A Weekend with Claude (Bainbridge) **4**:39, **22**:44; **62**:23-5, 30; **130**:20
"A Weekend with the Angels" (White) **10**:527
Weep before God (Wain) **11**:563
Weep Not, Child (Ngũgĩ wa Thiong'o) **3**:358; **7**:263-66; **13**:583; **36**:311, 313, 315-17, 319, 324
Weep Not for Me (Edwards) **43**:139-42
"Weeping and Wailing" (Stern) **40**:413
"The Weeping Headstones of the Isaac Becketts" (Durcan) **43**:114
"Weeping Willow" (Hikmet) **40**:244
"Weg zum Bahnhof" (Eich) **15**:204
"Weggebeizt" (Celan) **53**:79
"Der Wegwerfer" (Boell) **27**:66-7; **72**:67, 72-3, 107
Wei hu (Ding Ling) **68**:64-5
"Weiß sind die Tulpen" (Celan) **82**:50
Weighed in the Balance (Perry) **126**:339-40, 342
"The Weight" (Lane) **25**:289
The Weight of the Evidence (Stewart) **14**:512
The Weight of the World (Handke)
See *Das Gewicht der Welt*
"Weights" (Baxter) **45**:50-2; **78**:17
Weihnacht (Dürrenmatt) **8**:195; **15**:193-94
"The Weird of Avoosl Wuthoqquan" (Smith) **43**:420
Weird Scenes inside the Gold Mines (Morrison) **17**:290
"Weird Sister" (Phillips) **28**:361
"Weird Tales" (Chappell) **78**:116
Weird Tales (Hamilton) **1**:137
The Weirdstone of Brisingamen: A Tale of Alderly (Garner) **17**:134-38, 142-44, 149
Weissagung (Handke) **8**:262; **15**:266; **134**:108, 161
Weitere Aussichten (Kroetz) **41**:235
"The Welcome" (Blunden) **56**:43
Welcome! (Shapcott) **38**:404
"Welcome Back, Mr. Knight: Love of My Life" (Knight) **40**:287
Welcome Eumenides (Taylor) **5**:425-26
"Welcome Morning" (Sexton) **6**:493
"The Welcome Table" (Baldwin) **127**:118
"The Welcome Table" (Walker) **6**:554; **103**:361-63, 407
"Welcome the Wrath" (Kunitz) **148**:87-88
Welcome to Hard Times (Doctorow) **6**:136; **11**:143-45; **37**:84, 88-91, 93-4; **44**:168, 170, 176; **113**:131, 150-52, 156-58, 160-61, 166, 173, 176, 180
"Welcome to Kanagawa" (Sondheim) **147**:258
Welcome to Mars (Blish) **14**:86
"Welcome to the Machine" (Pink Floyd) **35**:308, 311
Welcome to the Monkey House: A Collection of Short Works (Vonnegut) **1**:348; **3**:495; **5**:467; **12**:602, 619; **40**:441
Welcome to the Moon (Shanley) **75**:319
Welcome to The Sibling Society (Bly) **128**:46
"Welcome to the Working Week" (Costello) **21**:67
Welcome to Thebes (Swarthout) **35**:400
Welcoming Disaster (Macpherson) **14**:346-47
Welfare (Wiseman) **20**:475-77
"Welfare Mothers" (Young) **17**:581
"Well" (Lennon) **35**:265
"The Well" (Levertov) **66**:238, 242-43, 253
"The Well" (Wiebe) **14**:575
The Well (Brown) **48**:61
The Well (Jolley) **46**:220-22
The Well (Onetti)
See *El pozo*
The Well (Ross) **13**:495-96
"Well Dennis O'Grady" (Gunn) **81**:176
"The Well Dreams" (Montague) **46**:277
"We'll Have Dinner at Eight" (Mphahlele) **25**:338, 342; **133**:155
"Well Moused, Lion" (Moore) **47**:272
"The Well of Baln" (Le Guin) **45**:213
"The Well of Bethlehem" (Goodman) **4**:197
"The Well of Lycopolis" (Bunting) **10**:83; **47**:45, 52, 54
Well of Shiuan (Cherryh) **35**:104-05, 112
"A Well Respected Man" (Davies) **21**:89, 95, 97
"We'll Run Away" (Wilson) **12**:651
"The Well Screened Lizette" (Škvorecký) **152**:338
We'll Shift Our Ground; Or, Two on a Tour (Blunden) **56**:47
We'll Take It from Here, Sarge (Trudeau) **12**:590
"Well Then" (Parra) **102**:355
"Well Water" (Jarrell) **2**:210; **13**:302
"Well Water" (Jensen) **37**:189
"Well We All Had Our Willie and Wade Records..." (Barthelme) **46**:42
"Well, Well, Well" (Lennon) **35**:262
"Well, What Are You Going to Do?" (Wright) **28**:466
The Well Wrought Urn (Brooks) **24**:102-08, 116; **86**:278-79, 286, 289; **110**:9, 14-17, 31-4, 36-7
The Well-Dressed Explorer (Astley) **41**:44, 46
Welle und Granit (Sachs) **98**:321
"Die Wellen des Balaton" (Lenz) **27**:252
"Wellesley Free" (Lowell) **11**:331; **37**:238; **124**:300
"The Wellfleet Whale" (Kunitz) **148**:107, 124-25, 127, 138-39, 141, 144
"Well-Found Poem" (Davie) **31**:123
"The Well-Intentioned Question" (Rose) **85**:313
The Well-Tempered Critic (Davies) **75**:191
The Well-Tempered Critic (Frye) **24**:214; **70**:275
"Welsh Blacks" (Clarke) **61**:80
"The Welsh Hill Country" (Thomas) **13**:543
"Welsh Incident" (Graves) **39**:328
The Welsh Sonata (Hanley) **13**:261-62
Welt im Kopf (Canetti) **75**:127
Weltanschauung (Ionesco) **9**:288
Der Weltverbesserer (Bernhard) **61**:13, 26
Wembly Arena (Zappa) **17**:595
Wenceslas Square (Shue) **52**:393-94
"Wendy" (Wilson) **12**:644, 650
"Wenishet-Jusmene" (Kunene) **85**:165
"Wenn ich nur wusste" (Sachs) **98**:348
Went South (Wiggins) **57**:431, 435, 438
Wer pa Lawino (p'Bitek)
See *Song of Lawino*
"We're at the Graveyard" (Ondaatje) **51**:310
We're Friends Again (O'Hara) **42**:319, 325
"We're Gonna Be All Right" (Sondheim) **30**:379
We're No Angels (Jordan) **110**:275-76, 278
"We're Not Gonna Take It" (Townshend) **17**:530
"We're Not Jews" (Kureishi) **135**:275
"We're Not Learnen to Be Paper Boys (for the young brothas who sell Muhammad Speaks)" (Sanchez) **116**:301
We're Not Pregnant: An Illustrated Guide to Birth Control (Mayle) **89**:142
"We're on TV in the Universe" (Vaughn) **62**:456-57
We're Only in It for the Money (Zappa) **17**:588-91
"We're Open Tonight" (McCartney) **35**:286-87
We're Right behind You, Charlie Brown (Schulz) **12**:532
"We're So Close" (Simon) **26**:412-13
"We're Very Poor" (Rulfo)
See "Es que somos muy pobres"
"The Wereman" (Atwood) **25**:67
"The Werewolf" (Carter) **41**:117
The Werewolf Trace (Gardner) **30**:154-55
"Werewolves in Their Youth" (Chabon) **149**:24
Werewolves in Their Youth (Chabon) **149**:22-4, 27
Werke: Essayistiche Schriften und Reden I, 1952-1956 (Boell) **72**:97
"Werner Herzog in Ghana" (Chatwin) **59**:277, 279
"The Werther Level" (Porter) **33**:321
Wesley (Brenton) **31**:59, 65
"West" (Hoffman) **6**:244
"The West" (Longley) **29**:293
"West" (Moure) **88**:219-20
West (Berkoff) **56**:21
"West Boulder Spring" (McGuane) **127**:290-91
"West Branch Ponds, Kokadjo, Maine" (Van Duyn) **63**:441
"West by the Road" (Davison) **28**:102
"West Central Pub" (Suknaski) **19**:432
"The West Coast" (Disch) **36**:127
"West Coast" (Livesay) **79**:346
West Country Churches (Betjeman) **34**:308
"West Indian Dutch Party" (Lamming) **66**:220
"The West Indian People" (Lamming) **66**:226
West Indies, Ltd.: Poemas (Guillén) **48**:157-59, 162-63, 166-69; **79**:229, 240, 244, 248-50

"West Marginal Way" (Hugo) **32**:236
"The West Midland Underground" (Wilding) **73**:398
The West Midland Underground (Wilding) **73**:397-98
West of Eden (Harrison) **42**:208-09
West of Suez (Osborne) **2**:328; **45**:316, 320
West of the Rockies (Fuchs) **8**:221; **22**:155-56, 159
West of Your City (Stafford) **7**:460, 462; **29**:385
West of Zanzibar (Browning) **16**:124
The West Pier (Hamilton) **51**:191-93, 195, 197
"West Point" (Vidal) **8**:529
West Side Story (Sondheim) **30**:376-78, 380, 385-87, 389-90, 395, 400, 402; **147**:259
West Strand Visions (Simmons) **43**:409
"West Twenty-Third" (Motion) **47**:291-92
"West Wind" (Wright) **53**:420
"West Window" (Jensen) **37**:192
West Window: The Selected Poetry of George Bowering (Bowering) **47**:28
West with the White Chiefs (Harris) **12**:262
"Westcottes Glanz und Ende" (Hildesheimer) **49**:174
"Westering" (Heaney) **74**:167
The Western Angler (Haig-Brown) **21**:136
The Western Approaches: Poems, 1973-1975 (Nemerov) **9**:394-96; **36**:301-02
"Western Australia" (Faludy) **42**:138
The Western Borders (Howe) **72**:202
The Western Canon (Bloom) **103**:50-6
The Western Coast (Fox) **2**:140-41; **8**:217-18; **121**:187-88, 214, 218
"Western Country" (Merwin) **13**:386
The Western Lands (Burroughs) **109**:197-99, 201, 230
"The Western Novel: A Symposium" (Waters) **88**:337, 364
"Western Star" (Wright) **53**:428
Western Union (Lang) **20**:206
"Western Wind" (Oppen) **7**:285
Western Wind (Fox) **121**:233-34
"Westland" (Baxter) **78**:25-27
Westmark (Alexander) **35**:27-8
Westmark Trilogy (Alexander) **35**:28
"West-Running Brook" (Frost) **13**:230; **15**:245, 250; **26**:125
West-Running Brook (Frost) **13**:223, 230; **15**:241, 249; **26**:117, 119, 124
Westviking (Mowat) **26**:342
Westward Ha!; or, Around the World in Eighty Clichés (Perelman) **5**:338; **9**:416; **23**:335; **44**:502; **49**:263, 266
"Westward the Course of Empire Takes Its Way" (Wallace) **114**:347, 349-50, 352, 354, 357-58, 361, 364
Westwego (Soupault) **68**:404-05
Westworld (Crichton) **54**:70-1, 76; **90**:69, 72-6
"Wet" (Colwin) **5**:108
"Wet" (Johnston) **51**:239
"Wet Are the Boards" (Ashbery) **77**:66, 69
"Wet Casements" (Ashbery) **13**:30; **15**:30, 33; **41**:40
"Wet Moccasins" (Kenny) **87**:249
"A Wet Night" (Beckett) **11**:32
The Wet Parade (Sinclair) **11**:497; **63**:349
"A Wet Sunday in Spring" (Fuller) **28**:159
Wetherby (Hare) **136**:244-45, 248, 263, 265, 274, 291-92,294
"Der Wetterfleck" (Bernhard) **32**:20
"We've Got Tonight" (Seger) **35**:383
Weymouth Sands (Powys) **9**:440; **46**:318-19, 324; **125**:287, 290-91, 294, 298-300, 304
"Wezwanie" (Milosz) **56**:238
"W.H. Auden as a Literary Critic" (Brooks) **24**:114
"Whacking Off" (Roth) **4**:451; **66**:386, 389
"Whakatu" (Hulme) **130**:44
"The Whale" (Ihimaera) **46**:196, 199
"Whale Constellations" (Gunnars) **69**:261
A Whale for the Killing (Mowat) **26**:337, 343, 346-47
"The Whale, His Bulwark" (Walcott) **76**:281
Whale Music (Quarrington) **65**:203-04
The Whale People (Haig-Brown) **21**:138-39
"The Whaleboat Struck" (Ammons) **108**:19
"The Whaler's Return" (Brown) **48**:52, 54
"Whales" (Olson) **28**:344
"The Whales" (Young) **82**:396
"The Whales' Graveyard" (Yevtushenko) **3**:547; **26**:462, 464; **126**:399
"Whales Off Sasketeewan" (Booth) **13**:103
Whanau (Ihimaera) **46**:194-95, 197, 202
"Wharf" (Merwin) **88**:192
"What" (Creeley) **78**:160
What? (Polanski) **16**:469-70
What a Kingdom It Was (Kinnell) **13**:321; **29**:279-80, 284; **129**:236, 266
What a Nighmare, Charlie Brown (Schulz) **12**:533
"What a Sky" (O'Brien) **65**:168
"What a View" (Montague) **46**:277
What a Way to Go (Morris) **1**:232-33; **37**:311-13
"What Ails Feminist Criticism?" (Gubar) **145**:280-81, 283, 288
What Am I Doing Here (Chatwin) **57**:152-54; **59**:276-79
"What America Would Be without Blacks" (Ellison) **114**:101
What Are Big Girls Made Of? (Piercy) **128**:270, 274
"What Are Poets For?" (Kroetsch) **132**:265
What Are the Bugles Blowing For? (Freeling) **38**:186-87
"What Are the Leftists Saying?" (Thurber) **25**:435; **125**:396, 398
"What Are the Odds?" (Acorn) **15**:10
"What Are Years" (Moore) **19**:339
What Are Years (Moore) **2**:292; **8**:399; **10**:346
What Are You Going to Do about It (Huxley) **35**:241
What Are You Up to, William Thomas (Newton) **35**:301
What Became of Jane Austen? And Other Questions (Amis) **3**:10; **5**:22; **129**:8, 17
"What Became of What-Was-His-Name?" (Enright) **31**:150
"What Became of Your Creature" (Gold) **152**:120
What Came Ashore at Lirios (Tiptree) **48**:395
"What Can I Do for You?" (Dylan) **77**:185-86, 189-90
"What Can You Do to Me Now?" (Nelson) **17**:306
What Century? (O'Hara) **78**:368-69
"What Comes Next" (Baumbach) **23**:54
"What Dante Means to Me" (Eliot) **113**:193
"What Destiny Wanted" (Fuentes)
See "Fortuna lo que ha querido"
"What Do the Scalds Tell Us?" (Johnston) **51**:248
What Do We Believe? (Greeley) **28**:172
"What Do You Call It When" (Ashbery) **125**:31
"What Do You Say?" (Giles) **39**:64-5
"What Does a Woman Need to Know?" (Rich) **73**:322
"What Does It Matter? A Morality" (Forster) **22**:135
"What Does Not Change" (Lane) **25**:284
"What Does Poetry Communicate" (Brooks) **110**:36
What Dreams May Come (Matheson) **37**:248
What Dreams May Come (Wellman) **49**:394, 396
"What Drives Saul Bellow?" (Ozick) **155**:170
What? Eternity (Yourcenar)
See *Quoi? L'éternité*
"What Feels like the World" (Bausch) **51**:55-6
"What Frightens Me..." (Ezekiel) **61**:105
"What Furies" (Hass) **39**:150; **99**:146
"What Gets In" (Hogan) **73**:160
"What Gives" (Eberhart) **56**:87
"What Goes On" (Reed) **21**:307
"What Happened Here Before" (Snyder) **120**:352
What Happened to the Corbetts? (Shute)
See *Ordeal*
What Happened When the Hopi Hit New York (Rose) **85**:315
What Happens Next? (Rogin) **18**:457-59
"What Has Happpened to These Working Hands?" (Hogan) **73**:158
"What Has Literature Got To Do With It?" (Achebe) **127**:6; **152**:78
What Hath a Man? (Millin) **49**:249-50
What Have I Done to Deserve This? (Almodovar)
See *Qué He Hecho Yo para Merecer Ésto?*
"What Have I Learned" (Snyder) **120**:325
What Have You Been Eating? (Hyde) **21**:177
"What Have You Done?" (Kunitz) **148**:97
"What He Saw" (Wideman) **122**:347
"What Holds Them Apart" (Galvin) **38**:199
"What I Believe" (Havel) **123**:214
What I Believe (Forster) **1**:108; **9**:204, 206; **15**:227, 229; **45**:132; **77**:218
What I Did Last Summer (Gurney) **54**:219; **32**:219; **50**:178
"What I Expected" (Spender) **41**:419
"What I Fear ..." (Oates) **6**:367
"What I Have Been Doing Lately" (Kincaid) **43**:248; **137**:143
"What I have Learned in the Wars" (Amichai)
See "Ma lamadti bamilhamot"
What I Know So Far (Lish) **45**:228-30
"What I Learned from Caesar" (Vanderhaeghe) **41**:449, 453
What I Lived For (Oates) **108**:394-95
What I Love (Elytis) **100**:172-74, 186-87
What I Might Have Become (Voinovich)
See *Kochu byt' chestnym*
"What I Might Have Been" (Voinovich) **49**:375-76; **147**:284
What I Really Think of You (Kerr) **35**:248-51
"What I Saw and Heard in Rome" (Bachmann)
See "Was ich Rom sah und hörte"
"What I Want to Say" (Van Duyn) **63**:437-38; **116**:403
What I Was (Michaux)
See *Qui je fus*
"What if God" (Olds) **85**:297, 299, 304
"What If I Said the Dinosaur's Not Dead" (Bradbury) **42**:42
What If You Died Tomorrow (Williamson) **56**:433-35, 442
What I'm Going to Do, I Think (Woiwode) **10**:542
"What Indians Do" (Ortiz) **45**:309-10
"What Is a Classic?" (Eliot) **24**:178; **41**:155
"What Is a Protestant, Daddy?" (Durcan) **43**:114, 116
What Is a Welshman? (Thomas) **48**:381
"What Is and Is Not" (Williams) **33**:441
"What Is Called Thinking" (Graham) **118**:238
What Is Called Thinking? (Heidegger)
See *Was Heisst Denken?*
What Is Contemplation? (Merton) **34**:465
"What Is Criticism?" (Barthes)
See "Qu'est-ce que la critique?"
What Is Existentialism? (Barrett) **27**:18
"What Is Fixed to Happen" (Paulin) **37**:354
What is Found There: Notebooks on Poetry and Politics (Rich) **125**:334
"What is it?" (Oliver) **98**:279, 292
"What Is Left to Link Us" (Lish) **45**:230
"What Is Left to Say" (Mueller) **51**:285
"What is Literature?" (p'Bitek) **96**:300
What Is Literature? (Sartre)
See *Qu'est-ce que la littérature?*
"What Is Minor Poetry?" (Eliot) **24**:178
What Is Money For (Pound) **7**:333
"What is Poetry" (Ashbery) **77**:47, 59
"What Is Possible" (Rich) **36**:367, 370
"What Is Poverty" (Salinas) **90**:331
"What Is Rape?" (Willingham) **51**:403

"What Is Seized" (Moore) **39**:82-3; **45**:280
"What Is the Basis of My Faith?" (Solzhenitsyn) **4**:508
"What Is the Connection between Men and Women" (Oates) **15**:401; **19**:348-49
"What Is the Language Using Us For?" (Graham) **29**:196, 198
"What Is the Voice That Speaks" (Warren) **39**:273
What Is Theatre? (Bentley) **24**:50-2
"What Is This Movie?" (Freeman) **55**:57
What Is to Be Done? (Gallant) **38**:190-93
What Is to Be Given? (Schwartz) **10**:463; **87**:346
"What is Winter?" (Blunden) **56**:46
"What It Cost" (Forché) **83**:208-09
"What It Costs" (Piercy) **27**:377
"What It Is I Think I'm Doing Anyhow" (Bambara) **88**:32-35
"What It Minns to Be a Minnow" (Perelman) **49**:264
"What Kind of Day Did You Have?" (Bellow) **33**:67-70
"What Kind of Formation Are B Specials?" (Paulin) **37**:354
"What Kind of Man" (Amichai)
See "Eyze min adam"
"What Lies Under" (Olson) **29**:327
What Love Has Joined Together (Robinson) **21**:342
"What Love Intended" (Boland) **113**:119
What Mad Pursuit (Gellhorn) **60**:177-78
What Makes Sammy Run? (Schulberg) **7**:401-03; **48**:346-47, 350, 352
"What Makes Us Human" (Donaldson) **138**:41
What Men Don't Tell Women (Blount) **38**:47-8
"What Men Have Instead of Skirts" (Donnell) **34**:159
What Moon Drove Me to This? (Harjo) **83**:268, 270, 272
"What Mrs. Felton Knew" (Findley) **102**:108
What Mrs. McGillicuddy Saw! (Christie) **48**:75; **110**:112
"What Must I Do To Be Lost" (Williams) **148**:321
"What My House Would Be Like If It Were a Person" (Levertov) **66**:236
"What Not to Say to Poorer People" (Lebowitz) **36**:248
"What of the Night?" (Kunitz) **148**:90
"What Really Happened" (Perloff) **137**:302
"What Remains" (Piercy) **62**:370-71; **128**:230-31, 243, 247
"What Remains" (Silone) **4**:493
"What Remains" (Wolf) **150**:300, 318, 320, 337
What Remains and Other Stories (Wolf)
See *Was bleibt*
"What Sally Said" (Cisneros) **118**:177, 184
"What Shall I Wear, Darling, to 'The Great Hunger'?" (Durcan) **70**:152
What Shall We Tell Caroline? (Mortimer) **28**:282-86
"What Shall We Tell Our Children?" (Grass) **49**:137
What Shall We Wear to This Party? (Wilson) **32**:447-48
"What Should Children Tell Parents?" (Thurber) **125**:402
"What Should I Have Done?" (Adams) **46**:19
"What Songs the Soldiers Sang" (Bell) **8**:65; **31**:46
"What Tempestuous Night" (Senghor) **130**:280
What the Birds Knew (Kurosawa) **119**:399
"What the Bones Know" (Kizer) **80**:172
What the Butler Saw (Orton) **4**:388; **13**:435-36; **43**:326-30, 334-35
What the Chairman Told Tom (Bunting) **39**:298
"What the Chroniclers Did Not Record" (Kenny) **87**:254
What the Crow Said in his Crow Journal (Kroetsch) **57**:283-84, 287; **132**:202, 230-34, 237, 247-48, 280, 288
"What the Deceased Had to Say About Himself" (Parra) **102**:350-51, 354
"What the Doctor Said" (Carver) **55**:282
"What the End Is For" (Graham) **48**:151, 153; **118**:250-51
"What the Fox Agreed to Do" (Bly) **38**:55, 57; **128**:23
"What the Frog's Eye Tells the Frog's Brain" (Fenton) **32**:166
What the Grass Says (Simic) **9**:480; **22**:379; **68**:376; **130**:311
"What the Heart Wants" (Moss) **45**:287
"what the mirror said" (Clifton) **66**:85, 88
"What the Motorcycle Said, A Small Excursion" (Van Duyn) **63**:439
What the Neighbors Did, and Other Stories (Pearce) **21**:288-90
"What the Pencil Writes" (Laughlin) **49**:220, 222
"What the Tapster Saw" (Okri) **87**:315, 320, 322
"What the Thunder Said" (Eliot) **10**:169; **41**:156
"What the White Had to Say" (Simic) **49**:340; **130**:298, 301-2, 304
What the Wine-Sellers Buy (Milner) **56**:222-28
What the Woman Lived: Selected Letters of Louise Bogan, 1920-1970 (Bogan) **4**:69; **39**:390, 394; **46**:87-8; **93**:71, 77, 84-5, 88
"What the Women Said" (Bogan) **93**:73
"What They Ate" (Le Guin) **45**:219
"What They Carried" (O'Brien) **103**:140
"What They Say about C. L." (Cabral de Melo Neto)
See "Contam de Clarice Lispector"
"What They Wore" (Le Guin) **45**:219
What Thou Lovest Well, Remains American (Hugo) **6**:245; **32**:241-42, 244, 250
"What to Do? A Problem Play" (Schuyler) **23**:388
"What to Do Next" (Barthelme) **115**:70-1
"What to Think Of" (Strand) **71**:284-86
What Use Are Flowers? (Hansberry) **17**:192-93
"What Use Have I Got for a Carnival" (Moravia) **46**:287
What Vedanta Means to Me (Isherwood) **14**:282
What Was Literature? Class Culture and Mass Society (Fiedler) **24**:205-06
"What Was Lost" (Ostriker) **132**:324, 326
"What Was Mine" (Beattie) **146**:59-61, 76, 78, 85
What Was Mine, and Other Stories (Beattie) **146**:58, 60, 66-7, 69-70, 84
What Was the Relationship of the Lone Ranger to the Means of Production?: A Play in One Act (Baraka) **115**:31
"What We Don't Talk About When We Talk About Poetry" (Perloff) **137**:302
"What We Lost" (Boland) **113**:73, 99
"What We Provide" (Bly) **128**:16
"What We Talk about When We Talk about Love" (Carver) **55**:276-77; **126**:148
What We Talk about When We Talk about Love (Carver) **22**:101-04; **36**:103-06; **53**:60; **126**:105-06, 108, 120, 125, 130-33, 135, 137, 141, 148-49, 152-54, 158, 163, 169, 179
What Where (Beckett) **29**:65-6
"What Whilwind Man Told Kochinanako, Yellow Woman" (Silko) **74**:333
"What Why When How Who" (Pinsky) **94**:308, 322; **121**:436
"What Will Happen to the Land?" (Momaday) **85**:229
"What Will Remain" (Mahon) **27**:288, 290
"What Work Is" (Levine) **118**:310, 321
What Work Is (Levine) **118**:296-97, 304-06, 310-11, 321
"What Would I Do White" (Jordan) **114**:146
"What You Hear from 'Em?" (Taylor) **18**:526, 528; **37**:409, 413
"What You Should Know to Be a Poet" (Snyder) **120**:353
"Whatever Gets You Through the Night" (Lennon) **35**:269-70
Whatever Is Moving (Moss) **45**:287-88; **50**:353
Whatever Love Declares (Kessler) **4**:270
"Whatever Time Is Past Was Worse" (Guillén) **79**:229
"Whatever You Say Say Nothing" (Heaney) **7**:149; **14**:245; **25**:246, 248
"Whatever's for Us" (Armatrading) **17**:7-8
What's Become of Waring (Powell) **10**:411-12; **31**:317, 319
What's Bred in the Bone (Davies) **42**:106-09; **75**:180-81, 184-87, 192, 196-202, 204-08, 211, 216-20, 222-24; **91**:201, 203-04
What's for Dinner? (Schuyler) **23**:389, 391
"What's Going On" (Gaye) **26**:130
What's Going On (Gaye) **26**:130-35
"What's Happening Brother" (Gaye) **26**:130
What's Happening! The Beatles in the U.S.A. (Maysles and Maysles) **16**:442-43
What's Happening to Me? (Mayle) **89**:141-42
"What's in Alaska?" (Carver) **22**:99; **53**:65; **126**:121
"What's in Your Life for Me" (Robinson) **21**:348-49, 351
"What's Meant by Here" (Snyder) **120**:324
"What's My Name" (Clash) **30**:44
What's So Big about Green? (Birney) **4**:64
"What's That Smell in the Kitchen?" (Piercy) **27**:382
"What's That You're Doing" (McCartney) **35**:290-91
"What's the Purpose of the Bayonet?" (Garrett) **51**:145, 152
"What's the Trouble: Social Crisis, Crisis of Civilization, or Both" (Howe) **85**:131
"What's the Use of Theorizing about the Arts?" (Abrams) **24**:13
What's to Become of the Boy? or, Something to Do with Books (Boell)
See *Was soll aus dem Jungen bloss werden?: oder, Irgendwas mit Büchern*
What's Up, Tiger Lily? (Allen) **16**:1, 3, 5, 15-16
"What's Wrong with Being a Slob?" (Naipaul) **105**:157
What's Wrong with This Picture? (Margulies) **76**:188, 193
What's Your P.Q. (Daly) **17**:89
Wheat that Springeth Green (Powers) **57**:349-54, 356-58
"The Wheel" (Ghiselin) **23**:170
The Wheel (Berry) **27**:40; **46**:71-2
The Wheel (Cendrars) **106**:185
The Wheel in Midsummer (Lewis) **41**:252
"The Wheel of Love" (Oates) **19**:348
The Wheel of Love, and Other Stories (Oates) **2**:313, 315; **6**:370; **19**:348, 351; **52**:338; **134**:227, 235, 242, 248
"The Wheelbarrow" (Pritchett) **13**:467; **41**:334
"Wheels" (Dixon) **52**:99-100
"Wheels" (McGahern) **48**:267-68
Wheels (Hailey) **5**:156
Wheels (Huxley) **11**:283-84
Wheels of Justice (Duerrenmatt) **102**:83
"Wheels Slowly Turning" (Montague) **46**:274
"Wheels within Wheels" (Heaney) **74**:188, 194
Wheelworld (Harrison) **42**:206
"Whelks" (Oliver) **98**:291
"When" (Lane) **25**:286
"When" (Olds) **39**:193; **85**:295
"When" (Williams) **148**:332, 344, 346, 349
"When a Man Needs a Woman" (Wilson) **12**:641, 643
"When Aliens Come" (Clarke) **35**:122
"When and Where and Whose Country is This, Anyway" (Jordan) **114**:152
When Angels Fall (Polanski) **16**:471
"When Are You Going Back?" (Gilliatt) **53**:145
"When Boyhood Dreams Come True" (Farrell) **66**:129
"When Death Came April Twelve 1945" (Sandburg) **10**:448

"When Death Comes" (Oliver) **98**:291, 294
"When Did You Stop Loving Me, When Did I Stop Loving You" (Gaye) **26**:133-34
When Dinah Shore Ruled the Earth (Durang) **27**:88
When Dinah Shore Ruled the Earth (Wasserstein) **90**:418
"When Doves Cry" (Prince) **35**:329-30
When Eight Bells Toll (MacLean) **13**:362; **50**:348
"When Everyone Was Pregnant" (Updike) **9**:537
"When first we faced" (Larkin) **64**:258
"when god decided to invent" (Cummings) **15**:162
"When Golden Flies upon My Carcass Come" (Eberhart) **56**:87
"When Half the Time They Don't Know Themselves" (Ashbery) **77**:65, 68
"When He Returns" (Dylan) **77**:185-87
When He Was Free and Young and He Used to Wear Silks (Clarke) **53**:89, 95-6
"When Heart Is Open" (Morrison) **21**:239-40
"When I Am Dead" (Dodson) **79**:193
"When I Am Dead" (MacBeth) **5**:263
"When I Banged My Head on the Door" (Amichai) **116**:136
"When I Die" (Giovanni) **19**:192; **64**:191
"When I Die" (Nyro) **17**:315, 319
"When I Grow Up to Be a Man" (Wilson) **12**:644, 649
"When I have a stomachache" (Amichai) **116**:97, 116
"When I Loved Her" (Kristofferson) **26**:267
"When I Nap" (Giovanni) **64**:187
"When I Sat Down to Play the Piano" (Purdy) **50**:247
"When I Set Fire to the Reed Patch" (Ammons) **108**:19
"When I Was a Freeport and You Were the Main Drag" (Nyro) **17**:313, 316, 319
"When I Was in Xia Village" (Ding Ling) **68**:67
"When I Was Young, the Whole Country Was Young" (Amichai) **57**:44
When I Whistle (Endō) **14**:161; **19**:160; **54**:152; **99**:285
"When I Wrote a Little" (Carruth) **84**:133
"When I'm among a Blaze of Lights" (Sassoon) **36**:388; **130**:184
"When I'm Gone" (Ochs) **17**:331
"When I'm Sixty-Four" (Lennon and McCartney) **12**:357, 360; **35**:279
When in Rome (Marsh) **7**:209; **53**:248
"When in Rome-Apologia" (Komunyakaa) **94**:235
"When in the Gloomiest of Capitals" (Akhmatova)
See "Kogda v mrachneyshey iz stolits"
"When It Comes" (Wain) **11**:562
"When It Happens" (Atwood) **13**:46; **44**:146
"When It's Human instead of When It's Dog" (Hempel) **39**:67-8
"When Its Shoesies That I Need" (Perelman)
See "Don't Bring Me Oscars"
"When It's Time to Go" (Wideman) **67**:379, 381, 385
"When Johnny ...." (Kelley) **22**:248
"When last I ranged and revelled" (Brutus) **43**:91
"When Life Begins" (Warren) **39**:272
"When Love Becomes Words" (Riding) **7**:374
"When Love Is Gone" (Hughes) **5**:191
"When Man Enters Woman" (Sexton) **6**:493
When Memory Comes (Friedlander)
See *Quand vient le souvenir*
When Memory Goes: Vichy France and the Jews (Gray) **153**:136
When Memory Speaks (Conway) **152**:111-12, 114
"When Men Got to the Summit" (Hughes) **119**:276
"When My Girl Comes Home" (Pritchett) **13**:468; **41**:332, 334
"When My Ship Comes Home" (Coward) **29**:139
"When My Sorrow Came Home" (Honig) **33**:211, 215
When One Has Lived a Long Time Alone (Kinnell) **129**:271
"When Our Dream World Finds Us, and These Hard Times Are Gone" (Abbott) **48**:5, 7
"When Poisoned Socrates" (Levi) **41**:242
When Queens Collide (Ludlam)
See *Conquest of the Universe*
When Rain Clouds Gather (Head) **25**:232-34, 236-38; **67**:92-3, 95, 110
"When Shall We Live?" (Hare) **136**:303
When She Was Good (Roth) **1**:292-93; **2**:378-79; **3**:436-38, 440; **4**:451, 457, 459; **6**:475-76; **9**:459, 461; **15**:449, 451-52; **22**:351-52; **31**:334-35, 343-44; **66**:386, 388, 391, 405; **119**:121
"When She Wears Red" (Hughes) **108**:293, 309
When the Atoms Failed (Campbell) **32**:72-3
When the Bough Breaks (Kellerman) **44**:225-28
When the Bridges Go Up (Aksyonov) **101**:17
"When the City Drops" (Carroll) **35**:79
"When the Clover Field Stirs" (Yevtushenko) **51**:432
"When the Dead Arise" (Kunitz) **148**:86
"When the Dumb Speak" (Bly) **15**:68; **128**:7, 12
"When the Fleet Was in in Mobile" (Highsmith) **102**:205-06
"When the Levee Breaks" (Page and Plant) **12**:475
"When the Light Falls" (Kunitz) **6**:287
"When the Lights Return" (Okri) **87**:315, 321-22
When the Lion Feeds (Smith) **33**:376
"When the Moment Is Over" (Pastan) **27**:371
"When the Music's Over" (Morrison) **17**:290-91
"When the Night" (McCartney) **35**:281
"When the Pipes Froze" (Collins) **44**:36-8
When the Rattlesnake Sounds (Childress) **12**:107; **86**:309, 316; **96**:103
When the Reds ... (Russell) **60**:319
"When the Saints Go Ma'chin Home" (Brown) **59**:263
"When the Shoe Is on the Other Foot for a Change" (Waddington) **28**:440
When the Siren Wailed (Streatfeild) **21**:412, 415
When the Skies Clear (Pasternak)
See *Kogda razglyaetsya*
When the Sky Burned (Bova) **45**:67, 73
"When the Stars Get Angry and Coo above Our Heads" (Salinas) **90**:332
"When the Statue Fell" (Blunden) **56**:34
When the Sun Tries to Go On (Koch) **44**:242-43
"When the Sun Went Down" (Ashbery) **41**:33
"When the Swimmers on the Beach Have All Gone Home" (Rooke) **25**:390-91
When the Time Comes (Blanchot) **135**:145, 148
When the Tree Flowered (Neihardt) **32**:335
When the Tree Sings (Haviaras) **33**:203-07
"When the Vacation Is Over for Good" (Strand) **18**:516; **71**:281-82, 285
When the War Began (Boell)
See "Als der Krieg ausbrach"
When the War Ended (Boell)
See *Als der Krieg zu Ende war*
When the War Started (Boell)
See "Als der Krieg ausbrach"
When the War Was Over (Boell)
See *Als der Krieg zu Ende war*
When the War Was Over (Frisch)
See *Als der Krieg zu Ende war*
"When the Whip Comes Down" (Jagger and Richard) **17**:240
When the Wind Blows (Sargeson) **31**:362-63
When the Wind Blows (Saul) **46**:366-67
"When the World Is Running Down, You Make the Best of What's Still Around" (Police, The) **26**:365
"When the World Stands Still" (Herbert) **9**:274
When Things of the Spirit Come First: Five Early Tales (Beauvoir)
See *Quand prime le spirituel*
"When Thou Hast Taken Thy Last Applause, and When" (Cummings) **68**:44
"When We are Able" (Zamora) **89**:384
When We Are Married (Priestley) **2**:347; **34**:361, 365-66
"When We Dead Awaken: Writing as Re-Vision" (Rich) **11**:477; **18**:445; **73**:321-23; **76**:215; **125**:311, 321, 332-33
When We First Met (Mazer) **26**:295-96
"When We Were Children" (MacNeice) **53**:237
"When We with Sappho" (Rexroth) **49**:289; **112**:383, 392, 398
"When Women Love Men" (Ferré)
See "Cuando las mujeres quieren a los hombres"
When Women Rule (Clarke) **53**:91, 95
"When You and I Were All" (Jarrell) **2**:209
"When You Are Silent, Shining Host by Guest" (Cummings) **8**:160
When You Comin' Back, Red Ryder? (Medoff) **6**:321-23
"When You Dance I Can Really Love" (Young) **17**:569, 582
"When You Gonna Wake Up?" (Dylan) **77**:186-87
"When You Kisses Me" (Armatrading) **17**:10
"When You Speak to Me" (Gallagher) **18**:169
"When You Were Mine" (Prince) **35**:324, 327
"When You're Down and Out" (Lennon)
See "Nobody Loves You"
"When You've Forgotten Sunday" (Brooks) **49**:38
"Where" (Berry) **27**:36
Where Adam Stood (Potter) **123**:237
Where All the Ladders Start (Loewinsohn) **52**:288-90
"Where Am I Kenneth?" (Koch) **44**:241
Where Angels Fear to Tread (Forster) **1**:103, 107; **2**:134; **4**:169; **9**:207; **13**:215-16, 219; **15**:222; **45**:136, 138, 142; **77**:241
"Where Are the Waters of Childhood?" (Strand) **18**:521; **41**:432, 434, 438; **71**:280
Where Are They Now? (Stoppard) **29**:394, 397
"Where Are Those People Who Did Hair" (Swados) **12**:558
"Where Are We Going? And What Are We Doing?" (Cage) **41**:77
"Where Are We Now" (Canin) **55**:38-9
"Where Are You Going, Where Have You Been?" (Oates) **3**:360; **9**:405; **11**:402-03; **19**:349-51; **52**:338; **108**:375, 386; **134**:224-54
Where Are You Going, Where Have You Been? (Oates) **134**:247
Where Are You Going, Where Have You Been? Stories of Young America (Oates) **134**:249
"Where but What" (Kelman) **58**:298
Where Did I Come From? The Facts of Life without Any Nonsense and with Illustrations (Mayle) **89**:141-42, 151
"Where Did the Spring Go?" (Davies) **21**:95
"Where Did They Go?" (Berry) **46**:74
"Where Do People Go?" (Swados) **12**:559
Where Do We Go from Here: Chaos or Community? (King) **83**:324, 328-31
"Where Do You Get Your Ideas From" (Le Guin) **136**:337
Where Eagles Dare (MacLean) **13**:362; **50**:348-49; **63**:265, 268, 270
Where East Is East (Browning) **16**:123-24
Where Elephants Go to Die (Donoso) **99**:223
Where Has Tommy Flowers Gone? (McNally) **4**:347; **7**:217-18
"Where Have All the Good Times Gone" (Davies) **21**:89
"Where Have You Gone, Charming Billy?" (O'Brien) **103**:144, 148-49
"Where I Come from God Is a Grandmother" (Allen) **84**:29, 31, 34

"Where I Live in This Honorable House of the Laurel Tree" (Sexton) **53**:317
Where I Live: Selected Essays (Williams) **19**:471; **45**:445-46
"Where I Lived, and What I Lived For" (Oates) **6**:370
"Where I Read What I Read" (Elkin) **51**:96
"Where I'd Quit" (Kauffman) **65**:348
"Where I'm Calling From" (Carver) **36**:101, 103-04; **53**:62-3, 65; **55**:275; **126**:126-28, 131, 133, 172-74, 179, 181-83
Where I'm Calling From (Carver) **53**:62-3, 65; **126**:129, 134-35, 137, 154-57, 159-60, 185
Where I'm Coming From (Wonder) **12**:656, 662
"Where Is Everybody?" (Serling) **30**:354
"Where Is Everyone?" (Carver) **36**:100; **126**:133-35
"Where Is Garland Steeples Now?" (Abbott) **48**:6
"Where is Home?" (Peacock) **60**:295
Where Is My Wandering Boy Tonight? (Wagoner) **5**:474
"Where Is the Love" (Hooks) **94**:159
"Where is the Voice Coming From" (Welty) **33**:425; **105**:298, 311, 314-15, 319
"Where Is the Voice Coming From" (Wiebe) **138**:321-24, 338, 379
Where Is the Voice Coming From? (Wiebe) **6**:567; **138**:326
"Where It Came From" (Brooks) **86**:280
"Where I've Been All My Life" (Kizer) **80**:181
"Where Knock Is Open Wide" (Roethke) **19**:396; **101**:273-74, 277-79, 290, 335, 339-40
Where Late the Sweet Birds Sang (Wilhelm) **7**:538
"Where Moth and Dust Doth Corrupt" (Wright) **13**:614
"Where Mountain Lion Lay Down with Deer" (Silko) **114**:316
Where Nests the Water Hen (Roy) See *La petite poule d'eau*
"Where Scars Come From" (Harmon) **38**:244
Where Shall We Go This Summer? (Desai) **37**:65, 67, 69-71; **97**:141, 144, 152, 158, 161-63, 172-73
"Where Solomon Was Wanting" (McAuley) **45**:251
Where Sparrows Work Hard (Soto) **32**:403; **80**:277, 282, 291, 293, 296
Where Speed Is King (Hyde) **21**:172
"Where, Tall Girl, Is Your Gypsy Babe" (Akhmatova) See "Gde, vysokaya, tvoy tsyganyonok"
"Where the Action Is" (Highsmith) **42**:216
Where the Air Is Clear (Fuentes) See *La región más transparente*
Where the Bluebird Sings to the Lemonade Springs: Living and Writing in the West (Stegner) **81**:341, 347-48, 353
Where the Boys Are (Swarthout) **35**:399-400
Where the Buffalo Roam (Potter) **123**:233
"Where the Car Turns at Eighteenth" (Ferber) **93**:140
Where the Compass Spins (Squires) **51**:381
"Where the Debris Meets the Sea" (Welsh) **144**:316
Where the Dreams Cross (Douglas) **73**:73-5, 83, 89
"Where the Eagles Dwell" (Valenzuela) See "Up Among the Eagles"
"Where the Girls Were Different" (Caldwell) **14**:96
Where the Going Was Good (Waugh) **107**:359-60
"Where the Hayfields Were" (MacLeish) **68**:289
"Where the Heart Is" (Shange) **74**:311
"Where the Hell Would Chopin Be?" (Bukowski) **41**:64
Where the Jackals Howl and Other Stories (Oz) See *Artsot hatan*
"Where the Kissing Never Stops" (Didion) **129**:77
Where the Long Grass Blows (L'Amour) **25**:278, 281
"Where the Rainbow Ends" (Lowell) **8**:348, 355; **11**:326
"Where the Rhododendrons Grow" (Aksyonov) **101**:10
Where the Rivers Flow North (Mosher) **62**:311-15
"Where the Sea Used to Be" (Bass) **143**:18, 20
Where the Sea Used to Be (Bass) **143**:18, 20, 22
"Where the Sidewalk Ends" (Dumas) **62**:155
"Where the Slow Fig's Purple Sloth" (Warren) **39**:266
Where the Soul Was Shallow (Gironella) See *Un hombre*
"Where the Tides Meet" (Mac Laverty) **31**:253
"Where the Track Vanishes" (Kinnell) **13**:320
"Where the World Began" (Laurence) **62**:280
"Where the World Begins" (Laurence) **50**:321
"Where There Is a Song" (Blaga) **75**:63
Where There's Smoke (Hunter) **11**:280
Where There's Smoke (Robinson) **21**:348
"Where They Disembarked" (Jiles) **58**:272
Where Water Comes Together with Other Water (Carver) **36**:107; **53**:60
"Where We Are Today, You Will Notice Is" (Smith) **22**:386
"Where We Must Look for Help" (Bly) **38**:60; **128**:17, 35
"Where We Were" (Dacey) **51**:81
"Where Will You Go, Sam Lee Wong" (Roy) **14**:469
"Where You'll Find Me" (Beattie) **63**:18, 22; **146**:49, 53
Where You'll Find Me, and Other Stories (Beattie) **63**:14-18; **146**:47, 53-4, 65, 69, 78, 84
Where's Daddy? (Inge) **8**:309
"Where's Esther?" (Goyen) **40**:217-18
"Wherever Home Is" (Wright) **28**:469
"Which New Era Would That Be?" (Gordimer) **7**:133; **33**:178-79
Which Ones Are the Enemy? (Garrett) **3**:190; **11**:220; **51**:143, 145
Which Tribe Do You Belong To? (Moravia) **7**:243
"Which Way to Inner Space" (Ballard) **137**:53
The Whicharts (Streatfeild) **21**:394
"While Driving North" (Ostriker) **132**:327
While Gods Are Falling (Lovelace) **51**:266-68, 271-72
"While Home" (Robison) **98**:306-07
"While Love Is Unfashionable" (Walker) **103**:364
"While My Guitar Gently Sings" (Hulme) **130**:48, 52
"While Reading Hamlet" (Akhmatova) **64**:15
While Reagan Slept (Buchwald) **33**:95
"While Seated on a Plane" (Swenson) **106**:335
"While Shepherds Watched" (Bunting) **47**:44
"While Sitting in the Tuileries and Facing the Slanting Sun" (Swenson) **106**:349
While Still We Live (MacInnes) **27**:279
While the City Sleeps (Lang) **20**:208; **103**:87, 89, 95-7
While the Sun Shines (Rattigan) **7**:354
"Whim" (Muldoon) **32**:320
"The Whimper of Whipped Dogs" (Ellison) **139**:112
The Whip (Creeley) **2**:106; **78**:130, 134
Whip Hand (Francis) **22**:152-53; **42**:150, 154, 156-57; **102**:128, 157, 162
"Whip Lady" (Davies) **21**:92
"A Whipbird Straps the Light Awake" (Shapcott) **38**:401
"Whiplash" (Matthews) **40**:325
Whipperginny (Graves) **45**:162-63
"The Whipping" (Hayden) **37**:160
Whipping Star (Herbert) **12**:279; **23**:221; **35**:196; **44**:393-94
Whipple's Castle (Williams) **14**:583
"The Whip-Poor-Will" (Thurber) **5**:432
The Whir of Gold (Ross) **13**:494, 496
The Whirlpool (Tanizaki) **28**:414-15
The Whirlpool (Urquhart) **90**:382-84, 386-93, 398, 401
Whirlwind (Clavell) **87**:10-5, 17-9
Whiskey (McNally) **4**:347
"Whiskey and Blood" (Blount) **38**:46
The Whiskey Vigil (Moure) **88**:229
"Whiskey, Whiskey" (Kristofferson) **26**:270
A Whisper in the Night: Stories of Horror, Suspense, and Fantasy (Aiken) **35**:20
"Whisper My Name" (Lightfoot) **26**:282
"The Whisper of Madness" (Mahfouz) See "Hams al-junun"
The Whisper of Madness (Mahfūz) See *Hams al-junūn*
The Whisper of the Axe (Condon) **6**:115; **8**:150; **45**:101, 103; **100**:91
Whisper to the Earth (Ignatow) **40**:259-60
"A Whispered Tale" (Sassoon) **130**:180
The Whispering Roots and Other Poems (Day Lewis) **6**:128-29; **10**:130-31
"Whispers" (Oliver) **98**:260, 267
Whispers (Koontz) **78**:197, 203-12, 215-17
Whispers in Bedlam (Shaw) **7**:413
"Whispers of Immortality" (Eliot) **1**:92
"Whistle" (Galvin) **38**:199
"The Whistle" (Komunyakaa) **94**:241
Whistle (Jones) **10**:290-94; **39**:406-09, 412, 415
A Whistle in the Dark (Murphy) **51**:300-01, 303-06, 308
"The Whistler" (Justice) **102**:254
The Whistling Boy (Arthur) **12**:25-6, 28
"Whit Monday" (MacNeice) **53**:239
"White" (Gilchrist) **143**:313
"White" (Johnston) **51**:249
"White" (Simic) **49**:338-40; **130**:297, 323
"White" (Strand) **18**:517
"White" (Wright) **6**:580
White (Simic) **9**:478, 481; **49**:339-40, 342; **130**:298-99, 301-6, 317, 319
"The White Album" (Didion) **129**:78-81, 104
The White Album (Didion) **14**:151-54; **129**:80, 85, 90, 105
The White Album (Lennon and McCartney) **12**:376, 379; **35**:266, 272
"White Apples" (Hall) **37**:146-47
"White as Snow" (Boyle) **58**:71
"The White Azalea" (Spencer) **22**:402
"The White Bird" (MacCaig) **36**:284-85
White Biting Dog (Thompson) **39**:250-53
"The White Boat" (Roberts) **14**:464
White Book (Kohout) **13**:325
White Boots (Streatfeild) See *Skating Shoes*
"White Boots Marching in a Yellow Land" (Ochs) **17**:332, 334
White Boy Running (Hope) **52**:216-17
"White Boys" (Ragni and Rado) **17**:385
The White Bus (Anderson) **20**:18
"The White Butterfly" (Longley) **29**:296
White Butterfly (Mosley) **97**:333-38, 344-46, 348, 352-53, 357
"The White Canoe" (Mowat) **26**:347
"White Center" (Hugo) **32**:243
White Center (Hugo) **32**:239, 250-51, 243
White Chappell, Scarlet Tracings (Sinclair) **76**:225, 227-28
White Coal or the Tears of Werther (Ehrenburg) **62**:176
White Coats (Dudintsev) See *White Robes*
"The White Coffin" (Bowering) **47**:24
The White Crow (Forman) **21**:121
The White Deer (Thurber) **5**:430, 433, 436, 442; **25**:437-38
"The White Devil" (Tate) **2**:428
White Dog (Gary) **25**:187

"The White Donkey" (Le Guin) **45**:216
The White Dragon (McCaffrey) **17**:283-84
White Dresses (Green) **25**:192
"White Dump" (Munro) **50**:209-12, 215-17, 220
"White Dwarfs" (Ondaatje) **29**:341-42; **51**:311-14
White Eagles over Serbia (Durrell) **1**:85
White Figure, White Ground (Hood) **15**:283, 285-86; **28**:188, 190
White Flock (Akhmatova)
See *Belaya staya*
"White Flowers" (Oliver) **98**:289
The White Gate (Chase) **2**:101
White Genesis (Ousmane)
See "Velorio de Papá Montero"
The White German Shepherd (Hearne) **56**:132-34
"White Girl, Fine Girl" (Grau) **146**:126
"White Goat, White Ram" (Merwin) **13**:384; **45**:270
The White Goddess: A Historical Grammar of Poetic Myth (Graves) **1**:128; **2**:177; **6**:210; **11**:255, 257; **39**:321-26, 328; **45**:165-66, 173
White Gold Wielder (Donaldson) **46**:141-44; **138**:6, 12, 16
"The White Holster" (Smith) **22**:390
"The White Horse" (Dumas) **62**:163
"The White Horse" (Jones) **81**:64-5
"The White Horse" (MacEwen) **55**:167
White Horses (Hoffman) **51**:203-04, 208
"The White Horses of Vienna" (Boyle) **58**:64, 66-7, 71, 75; **121**:33, 39, 46
The White Hotel (Thomas) **22**:418-22; **31**:430-35; **132**:333-36, 338-42, 344-45, 347-51, 353-54, 357, 359, 360-61, 363-66, 368-71, 373-81, 383-85, 389
"The White House" (Hughes) **108**:307
The White House (Murphy) **51**:302, 307-08
The White House Murder Case (Feiffer) **64**:150, 160
White House Years (Kissinger) **137**:216, 218, 241-42, 244, 250, 255-56
"The White Isle of Leuce" (Read) **4**:439
"White Key" (Muske) **90**:312
"White Kid Gloves" (Prichard) **46**:333
"The White Knights" (Vollmann) **89**:277-78
"The White Lantern" (Connell) **45**:113
The White Lantern (Connell) **45**:113-14
White Liars (Shaffer) **14**:487
"White Lies" (Theroux) **28**:425
White Light/White Heat (Reed) **21**:303-04, 307, 314, 319
"The White Lilies" (Glück) **81**:166, 172
White Lotus (Hersey) **40**:235, 239; **81**:332, 335; **97**:302-03
"White Magic" (Walcott) **67**:361
"White Man in Hammersmith Palais" (Clash) **30**:44-6
White Man, Listen! (Wright) **1**:377; **4**:596; **9**:585; **74**:383
White Man's Justice, Black Man's Grief (Goines) **80**:91-3
White Marriage (Rozewicz)
See *Białe małżeństwo*
"White Moon" (Swenson) **106**:351
White Mule (Williams) **2**:468; **5**:509-10
"White Mythology" (Derrida) **87**:85-6
"The White Negro" (Mailer) **1**:189; **3**:312; **8**:364, 366; **11**:341; **14**:349; **28**:256; **74**:211-12, 219, 223-24; **111**:94, 101, 104, 117, 121-22, 125, 133, 137, 148
"White Night" (Oliver) **98**:271, 296
"White Night" (Pasternak) **63**:313
"White Night" (Rich) **6**:459
"White Nocturne" (Aiken) **52**:22
White Noise (DeLillo) **39**:115-27; **54**:81-6; **76**:171-72, 174-75, 177, 179-82, 185-86; **143**:162-65, 169, 174, 176, 178, 180-81, 183, 186-94
"White Noises" (Hollander) **2**:197
The White Noon (Smith) **64**:397
"White Notes" (Justice) **102**:262
"White Oak" (Lewis) **41**:255
The White Oaks of Jalna (Findley) **102**:104, 106
White on Black on White (Dowell) **60**:99, 101-03, 106-07
"White on White" (Ferlinghetti) **27**:139
"White Owl Flies Into and Out of the Field" (Oliver) **98**:283, 289-90
White Palace (Savan) **50**:77-81
White Paper (Starbuck) **53**:353
White People (Gurganus) **70**:189-96
"White Petal Nanitch" (Davis) **49**:93
"White Pickney" (Bennett) **28**:29
White Pine (Oliver) **98**:302-04
The White Plague (Herbert) **35**:200-01, 205; **44**:394
"The White Pony" (Bates) **46**:56, 67
"The White Quail" (Steinbeck) **9**:516
"The White Queen" (Harrison) **129**:171, 219
"The White Rabbit" (Lustig) **56**:185
"The White Rabbit Caper" (Thurber) **5**:440; **11**:533
White Rain (Aitmatov)
See *Belyi dozhd*
"White Rat" (Jones) **131**:250, 269
White Rat (Jones) **131**:249-50, 253, 256, 267-68, 328
"White Riot" (Clash) **30**:44-5, 51
White Robes (Dudintsev) **59**:388-89
"The White Room" (Simic) **130**:313
"The White Rooster" (Goyen) **8**:250-51; **40**:217-18
The White Rose (Traven) **11**:535
White Sail (Sorrentino) **40**:386
The White Sheik (Fellini)
See *Lo sciecco bianco*
The White Ship (After the Fairy Tale) (Aitmatov)
See *Belyj parokhod*
"White Shroud" (Ginsberg) **36**:193
White Shroud (Ginsberg) **109**:324, 338, 356, 358
"White Shrouds" (Bottoms) **53**:34
White Stag of Exile (Shapcott) **38**:404-05
The White Steamer (Aitmatov)
See *Belyj parokhod*
The White Steamship (Aitmatov)
See *Belyj parokhod*
The White Steed (Carroll) **10**:95-100
"The White Stick" (Tuohy) **37**:431
White Sun, Black Sun (Rothenberg) **6**:477; **57**:371
"The White Sybil" (Smith) **43**:424
The White Thorntree (Davison) **15**:171
The White Threshold (Graham) **29**:194-95, 198
"The White Tiger" (Thomas) **48**:380
White Tiger (Browning) **16**:125
"The White Tower: A Novel in the Form of a Poem" (Leet) **11**:323
"White Trash" (Oates) **108**:383
"White, White Collars" (Johnson) **52**:234
"The White Wild Bronco" (Kiely) **43**:244
"White World" (H. D.)
See "The Whole White World"
White Writing: On the Culture of Letters in South Africa (Coetzee) **66**:98-101, 105; **117**:50-1, 70-5, 79=80
"Whitebait" (Grace) **56**:116
White-Haired Lover (Shapiro) **4**:486-87; **15**:479; **53**:333
The White-Haired Revolver (Breton)
See *Le revolver á cheveux blancs*
Whites (Rush) **44**:91-6
"Whites Only" (Hope) **52**:211
"Whitewash" (Damas)
See "Blanchi"
Whitewater (Horgan) **9**:278; **53**:183-84
Whither (Powell) **66**:366
"Whither Thou Goest" (Selzer) **74**:287
"Whitman: The Invisible World" (Hall) **37**:148
"Whitman's Line as a Public Form" (Bly) **128**:17
"Whitsun" (Plath) **5**:345
"The Whitsun Weddings" (Larkin) **3**:276; **5**:227, 230-31; **8**:332, 334-37, 339-40; **9**:325; **13**:335, 337, 340; **18**:297; **33**:259-60; **39**:342, 345; **64**:265-66, 269-71, 275, 282-84
The Whitsun Weddings (Larkin) **3**:275-76; **5**:223, 225-28, 230-31; **8**:332, 336-38, 340; **13**:337-38; **18**:293, 296-97, 299-301; **33**:256, 261-62; **39**:334, 338, 341-45; **64**:259-60, 269-72, 278-80, 283
"The Whittrick" (Morgan) **31**:275
Whity (Fassbinder) **20**:106
"Who" (Plath) **11**:448; **111**:159, 164
"Who?" (Weldon) **122**:261
"Who Actually Creates Gaps?" (Royko) **109**:405
"Who Are the Brain Police" (Zappa) **17**:588
Who Are the Violets Now (Waugh) **7**:514
Who Are We Now? (Ferlinghetti) **27**:139; 59, 65
Who Are You (Townshend) **17**:538-41
"Who Be Kind To" (Ginsberg) **6**:198; **36**:184, 188; **109**:347
"Who Began It and What For" (Gustafson) **36**:221
Who Brought Back Doruntine? (Kadare) **52**:261-62
Who Brought Doruntine Back? (Kadare)
See *Who Brought Back Doruntine?*
The Who by Numbers (Townshend) **17**:535-39, 542
Who Calls from Afar? (Brinsmead) **21**:30
Who Came First (Townshend) **17**:527, 531, 534
Who Can Replace a Man? (Aldiss) **14**:11
"Who Cares, Long as It's B-Flat" (Carruth) **84**:129
"Who Cares Who Killed Roger Ackroyd?" (Wilson) **24**:481
Who Do You Love (Sayers) **122**:229-31, 233, 235, 238, 240
Who Do You Think You Are? (Bradbury) **32**:53; **61**:39, 43
Who Do You Think You Are? (Munro) **19**:345-47; **50**:208, 210-12; **95**:283, 285-89, 291-95, 297, 301, 304-05, 310-11, 313, 321
Who Fears the Devil? (Wellman) **49**:389, 391, 393-94, 396
Who Gathered and Whispered behind Me (Goldbarth) **38**:203-04
"Who Goes There?" (Campbell) **32**:75-7, 80-2
"Who Has Lived from a Child with Chickens" (Kauffman) **42**:251
"Who Has Seen The Wind?" (Dodson) **79**:192
"Who Has Seen the Wind" (McCullers) **12**:432
Who Has Seen the Wind (Mitchell) **25**:321-22, 325-26
"Who Is Alienated from What?" (Rexroth) **49**:287
"Who is an SF Writer?" (Dick) **72**:106
Who Is Angelina? (Young) **19**:479
"Who Is Cherubino, What Is He?" (Brophy) **105**:37
Who Is Harry Kellerman and Why Is He Saying Those Terrible Things about Me? (Gardner) **44**:210
"Who Is It?" (Byrne) **26**:94-5
"Who Is It Can Tell Me Who I Am?" (Berriault) **109**:94-7
Who Is Teddy Villanova? (Berger) **8**:83-4; **11**:46; **18**:58; **38**:39, 41-2
"Who Is Your Mother? Red Roots of White Feminism" (Allen) **84**:29, 34
"Who Killed Feminist Criticism?" (Gubar) **145**:281, 288
Who Killed Palomino Molero (Vargas Llosa)
See *Quién matú a Palomino Molero?*
Who Killed Richard Cory? (Gurney) **32**:220
"Who Knows One?" (Gotlieb) **18**:191
Who Look at Me (Jordan) **114**:141, 153
Who Lost an American? (Algren) **33**:12

"Who Needs a Heart" (Shange) **74**:311
"Who Needs the Peace Corps" (Zappa) **17**:591
"Who Needs Theater Anymore" (Ionesco) **86**:332
"Who or What Was It" (Amis) **40**:43
Who Really Cares? (Ian) **21**:184
"Who Said It Was Simple" (Lorde) **71**:246
The Who Sell Out (Townshend) **17**:530-31, 533, 535, 537, 541
Who Shall Be the Sun? (Wagoner) **15**:559
Who Shall Die? (Beauvoir)
See *Les bouches inutiles*
The Who Sings My Generation (Townshend) **17**:524; **42**:379
Who Speaks for the Negro? (Warren) **8**:538; **59**:298
"Who Stands, the Crux Left of the Watershed" (Auden) **43**:17
"Who the Cap Fit" (Marley) **17**:268-69
"Who Then Is Crazy" (Spacks) **14**:511
Who Wants Music on Monday? (Stolz) **12**:552-53
Who Wants War? (Prichard) **46**:337
"Who Was Juana Gallo?" (Castillo) **151**:47-8, 65
"Who Was Leslie A. Fiedler?" (Fiedler) **24**:205
Who Was Oswald Fish? (Wilson) **33**:453-54, 457
"Who Watches from the Dark Porch" (Graham) **118**:252
"Who Will Know Us?" (Soto) **80**:302
Who Will Know Us?: New Poems (Soto) **80**:300-01, 303
"Whoever Was Using This Bed" (Carver) **53**:64-5; **55**:277
"Whoever You Are" (Purdy) **6**:428
The Whole Armour (Harris) **25**:203-05, 209, 214
Whole Days in the Trees (Duras)
See *Des journées entières dans les arbres*
"Whole Lotta Love" (Page and Plant) **12**:474-75, 478-79, 482
"Whole Love" (Graves) **45**:166
The Whole Man (Brunner) **8**:105; **10**:77
"A Whole School of Bourgeois Primitives" (Reid) **33**:348
"The Whole Soul" (Levine) **118**:282
"The Whole Story" (Nye) **42**:309
"The Whole Story" (Strand) **18**:515; **71**:281, 284
The Whole Voyald, and Other Stories (Saroyan) **1**:301
"The Whole White World" (H. D.) **73**:105, 118
The Whole Woman (Greer) **131**:209-11, 213-20, 223-7
"The Wholeness" (Silkin) **43**:399-400
(W)holes (Macdonald) **19**:290-91
"Who'll Be the Next in Line?" (Davies) **21**:89
Who'll Save the Plowboy? (Gilroy) **2**:161
"Wholly Numbers; or, The Meditations of St. Stitch" (Ciardi) **40**:159
"Whom I Write For" (Aleixandre)
See "Para quién escribo"
"Whooping Cranes" (Erdrich) **54**:165; **120**:136
Whoops-a-Daisy (Waterhouse) **47**:419
"The Whore of Mensa" (Allen) **52**:36-7, 40
"The Whorehouse in a Calcutta Street" (Mahapatra) **33**:279, 283
"Whores Die Hard" (Kristofferson)
See "Star Spangled Banner"
Whores for Gloria: Or, Everything Was Beautiful until the Girls Got Anxious (Vollmann) **89**:284-86, 290-91, 296, 304, 311, 313
Whoreson: The Story of a Ghetto Pimp (Goines) **80**:92, 95-6
"Whorl" (Young) **82**:411
"Whoroscope" (Beckett) **9**:82, 87; **14**:78
Who's Afraid of Virginia Woolf? (Albee) **1**:5; **2**:1-4; **3**:6-7; **5**:10-14; **9**:1-3, 5-7, 9-10; **11**:10-11, 13; **13**:3-7; **25**:34-8, 40; **53**:20-1, 24, 26; **86**:119-20, 122-25; **113**:5-7, 13, 15, 19-21, 26, 28, 30-3, 36, 40-1, 44, 49, 52, 54
Who's Got His Own (Milner) **56**:221-22
"Who's Most Afraid of Death? Thou Art of Him" (Cummings) **1**:68; **3**:117; **68**:44
Who's Next (Townshend) **17**:527-28, 535, 539-41
"Who's on First?" (Janowitz) **43**:212; **145**:327
Who's on First (Buckley) **18**:83; **37**:60-1
"Who's Paying for This Call?" (Hood) **28**:189
Who's Pinkus, Where's Chelm? (Taylor) **27**:440-41
"Who's Stronger in This Painting" (Yevtushenko) **126**:398
Who's That Knocking at My Door? (Scorsese) **20**:323, 325, 329-30; **89**:219-20, 249, 254-56, 260, 266-67
"Who's That Woman?" (Sondheim) **30**:382
"Who's to Bless and Who's to Blame" (Kristofferson) **26**:269
"Who's Who" (Auden) **9**:60
"Whose Deduction?" (Škvorecký) **69**:333
"Whose Dream Is This Anyway? Remythologizing and Self-Definition in Contemporary Indian Fiction" (Allen) **84**:36, 43
"Whose Goat?" (Stevenson) **33**:383
Whose Life Is It Anyway? (Clark) **29**:126-29
"Whose Side Are the Orixá On?" (Eco) **142**:94
"Whose Timeless Reach" (Ammons) **108**:19
"Whose Who" (Blount) **38**:46
"The Whosis Kid" (Hammett) **47**:164
"Why" (Oates) **134**:248
Why are Cross With Me, oh, Wind? (Arghezi)
See *Ce-ai cu mine, vîntule?*
Why Are We in Vietnam? (Mailer) **1**:191-92; **2**:262-63, 265; **3**:313-14; **4**:319, 323; **5**:267; **8**:370, 372-73; **11**:340, 342-43; **14**:352; **28**:256-57, 263; **74**:204, 206-07, 209, 224; **111**:95, 101-02, 108, 113, 117-18, 120-21, 141, 148
Why Are We So Blest? (Armah) **5**:32; **33**:27-32, 36-8
"Why Be a Poet?" (Heidegger) **24**:269
"Why Brownlee Left" (Muldoon) **72**:267, 272
Why Brownlee Left (Muldoon) **32**:319-21; **72**:365-66, 268-69, 273-74, 276-78
Why Call Them Back from Heaven (Simak) **55**:320
Why Can't They Be Like Us? America's White Ethnic Groups (Greeley) **28**:170
"Why Can't They Tell You Why?" (Purdy) **2**:349
Why Can't We Live Together Like Civilized Human Beings? (Kumin) **28**:222-25
"Why Clowns" (Fellini) **85**:82
"Why Crime is Good for America" (Puzo) **107**:189
"Why Did Benerjee Kill Himself?" (Hikmet)
See "Benerci kendini nicin öldürdü"
Why Didn't They Ask Evans? (Christie) **6**:108; **110**:113
"Why Do Human Beings Produce Literature?" (Oe) **86**:228, 241
Why Do You Live So Far Away? (Levine) **54**:299
"Why Do You Sing My Bird" (Ekeloef) **27**:119
"Why Do You Write about Russia?" (Simpson) **32**:377; **149**:316, 321, 337
Why Does Herr R. Run Amok? (Fassbinder) **20**:109, 115
"Why Does It Hurt When I Pee" (Zappa) **17**:593
"Why Dolphins Don't Bite" (Sturgeon) **39**:361
"Why Don't You Come Live with Me It's Time" (Oates) **108**:384
"Why Don't You Dance" (Carver) **22**:101; **36**:107; **55**:273, 277; **126**:153
"Why Don't You Look Where You're Going?" (Clark) **28**:78
"Why Don't You Write for Me?" (Ciardi) **10**:107
"Why Fortune Is Empress of the World" (Cassity) **42**:99
"Why Has Socialism Failed in America?" (Howe) **85**:151
"Why Have I Wandered the Asphalt of Midnight?" (Warren) **18**:539; **39**:273
Why Have the Birds Stopped Singing? (Sherburne) **30**:363
"Why Heisherik Was Born" (Singer) **69**:306
"Why Honey?" (Carver) **22**:96; **53**:65
"Why I Am Eight Years Younger Than Anthony Burgess" (Vidal) **142**:304
"Why I Am Not a Painter" (O'Hara) **78**:354
"Why I Died" (Jong) **83**:290
Why I Don't Write Like Franz Kafka (Wilson) **49**:414-16
"Why I Hate Family Values" (Pollitt) **122**:216, 221
"Why I like Country Music" (McPherson) **77**:366-67
"Why I Like England" (Townsend) **61**:420
"Why I Live at the P. O." (Welty) **14**:563; **22**:456; **33**:414-15; **105**:298, 309, 318, 385
"Why I Love Country Music" (Tallent) **45**:387
"Why I Love Sleep" (Lebowitz) **36**:249
"Why I Pray" (Moody) **147**:188
"Why I Quit the Gowanus Liberation Front" (Brown) **32**:63
"Why I Teach My Discipline" (Mphahlele) **133**:143
"Why I Went Up North, and What I Found When He Got There" (Kroetsch) **132**:275, 281
"Why I Write" (Didion) **129**:76, 79, 82, 93
"Why I Write" (Paton) **10**:388
"Why I'm Jewish" (Ginsberg) **109**:328
"Why Irish Heroines Don't Have to be Good Anymore" (O'Brien) **116**:188, 197
"Why Is Your Writing So Violent?" (Oates) **52**:337
"Why Literary Criticism Is Like Virtue" (Fish) **142**:193, 205
"Why Log Truck Drivers Rise Earlier Than Students of Zen" (Snyder) **120**:344
"Why Marry at All?" (Piercy) **62**:371; **128**:230
Why Me? (Westlake) **33**:440
Why Men Are The Way They Are (Farrell) **70**:422
"Why My Mother Made Me" (Olds) **85**:294
"Why Pornography Matters to Feminists" (Dworkin) **123**:76
"Why Rabbit Had to Go" (Updike) **139**:354-55, 361-62
Why Should I Have All the Grief? (Gotlieb) **18**:192
"Why So Many Shamuses?" (Škvorecký) **69**:339
"Why, Soldier, Does It Seem to You . . ." (Guillén) **48**:158
"why some people be mad at me sometimes" (Clifton) **66**:82
"Why Study Power: The Question of the Subject" (Foucault) **34**:343
"Why Suffering" (Paton) **25**:364
"Why the Castle" (Schaeffer) **22**:369
"Why the Classics" (Herbert) **9**:273; **43**:188
"Why There Will Never Be a Great Bowling Novel" (Blount) **38**:46
"Why Tribe" (Snyder) **120**:353
"Why Van Johnson Believes in ESP" (Grayson) **38**:211
Why Was I Killed? (Warner) **45**:430-31, 434, 438-40
Why We Act Like Canadians: A Personal Exploration of Our National Character (Berton) **104**:46-8, 60
Why We Can't Wait (King) **83**:328, 330, 347
"Why We Die" (Swenson) **106**:314
"Why We Do It" (Bass) **79**:2
Why We Fight (Capra) **16**:160
"Why We Read: Canon to the Right of Me" (Pollitt) **122**:206, 217, 222
"Why We Tell Stories" (Mueller) **51**:283
"Why We're Here" (McGahern) **48**:262

"Why, You Reckon?" (Hughes) **35**:215
"Whys/Wise" (Baraka) **115**:12
"Wichita Vortex Sutra" (Ginsberg) **2**:163; **4**:181, 183; **36**:183-84, 190, 192-93, 196-97; **109**:347, 372
Wichita Vortex Sutra (Ginsberg) **109**:338
The Wicked Cooks (Grass) **4**:202; **15**:260
The Wicked Day (Stewart) **35**:396-97
The Wicked Enchantment (Benary-Isbert) **12**:32, 34
"Wicked Girl" (Allende) **97**:9
"Wicked Gravity" (Carroll) **143**:30
The Wicked One (Hunter) **21**:167
The Wicked Pavilion (Powell) **66**:361, 372, 374-76
"A Wicked Story" (Shaw) **7**:412
Wicked Women (Weldon) **122**:278, 280-82
"The Wickedness of Peter Shannon" (Nowlan) **15**:398
"A Wicker Basket" (Creeley) **78**:161
"Wicket Maiden" (Scannell) **49**:330-31
Wickford Point (Marquand) **2**:271; **10**:329-31
"The Widder" (Bates) **46**:62
Wide Fields (Green) **25**:194
The Wide House (Caldwell) **28**:58; **39**:303
Wide Is the Gate (Sinclair) **15**:500; **63**:364
"The Wide Land" (Ammons) **25**:43-4; **108**:20
"The Wide Net" (Welty) **2**:462; **14**:562-63; **22**:459; **33**:419; **105**:307, 327-28, 368
The Wide Net, and Other Stories (Welty) **1**:362; **14**:562-63; **22**:460; **105**:384
"The Wide Prospect" (Jarrell) **13**:300
Wide Sargasso Sea (Rhys) **2**:371-73; **4**:445; **6**:452-55, 457; **14**:446-448, 451; **19**:392-93, 395; **51**:360-61, 364-72, 374-76; **124**:311-23, 326, 328-30, 334, 340, 342, 344-45, 348, 356, 358-59, 371-72, 374-75
The Wide Sleeve of Kwannon (Lancaster) **36**:241
"Widgeon" (Heaney) **37**:165
Widger's Way (Ringwood) **48**:329, 333, 335-36, 338
Die Widmung (Strauss) **22**:407-08
"The Widow" (Honig) **33**:211
"The Widow" (Jhabvala) **138**:71
"Widow" (Mueller) **51**:284
"The Widow" (O'Brien) **65**:169; **116**:203
"Widow" (Plath) **11**:448; **111**:214
"Widow" (Reading) **47**:350
"The Widow" (Smith) **64**:389, 394
The Widow (Fornés) **39**:138
The Widow (Freeling) **38**:187
The Widow Claire (Foote) **51**:136-37
The Widow in the Bye Street (Masefield) **47**:225-28, 230
"A Widow in Wintertime" (Kizer) **80**:172-73
"The Widow Interviewed" (Day Lewis) **6**:128
"The Widow Perez" (Soto) **32**:403
"Widower" (Raine) **103**:190
"The Widower" (Redgrove) **6**:445; **41**:351
"Widower" (Robison) **42**:339
"Widowers" (Davie) **31**:116
The Widower's Son (Sillitoe) **10**:477; **19**:421; **57**:395-96; **148**:158, 171, 174-75, 184, 194
"The Widows" (White) **49**:408
Widows (Dorfman)
See *Viudas*
Widows and Children First! (Fierstein) **33**:153, 155
"Widows and Orphans" (McPherson) **19**:310; **77**:359
The Widow's Children (Fox) **8**:218-19; **121**:188-89, 191-97, 214, 218
"Widow's Lament" (Brautigan) **12**:69
The Widows of Thornton (Taylor) **71**:293
"Widow's Walk" (Grau) **146**:132, 139
"The Width of a Circle" (Bowie) **17**:57, 59
Widzenia nad Zatoka San Francisco (Milosz) **31**:263-64; **56**:232, 242-44, 250
"Wie bei Gogol" (Lenz) **27**:252
"Wie das Gesetz es befahl" (Boell) **72**:98
"Wie sagen wir es den Kindern?" (Grass) **22**:195
"więc jednak żyje się pisząc wiersze sa długo" (Rozewicz) **139**:294-95
Wieczne zmartwiene (Dabrowska) **15**:167, 169
"Wieder Mitte geworden" (Sachs) **98**:359
"Wiederholen" (Breytenbach) **126**:70
Die Wiederholung (Handke) **134**:134-36, 139, 159, 164-66, 176
"Wiedersehen in der Allee" (Boell) **72**:69, 101
"Wiedersehen mit Drüng" (Boell) **72**:69
Die Wiedertäufer (Dürrenmatt) **4**:140; **15**:194, 197-98
Wier & Pouce (Katz) **47**:220-23
"Wife" (Faludy) **42**:139
"The Wife" (Highsmith) **102**:186, 197
Wife (Mukherjee) **53**:263-65, 268-69; **115**:386
The Wife of Martin Guerre (Lewis) **41**:253, 255-59, 262
"A Wife of Nashville" (Taylor) **18**:524; **50**:251
"The Wife of the Autumn Wind" (Kawabata) **107**:77
Wife to Mr. Milton: The Story of Marie Powell (Graves)
See *The Story of Marie Powell: Wife to Mr. Milton*
"The Wifebeater" (Sexton) **4**:483
"The Wife's Story" (Le Guin) **45**:216-17; **136**:330
"A Wife's Story" (Mukherjee) **115**:364, 367-69
"The Wife's Tale" (Bausch) **51**:55
"The Wife's Tale" (Heaney) **7**:148; **25**:244
"Wife-Wooing" (Updike) **9**:537; **13**:561
The Wig: A Mirror Image (Wright) **49**:426-31, 433-34
"Wiggle Wiggle" (Dylan) **77**:182, 184
Wigs on the Green (Mitford) **44**:483, 486, 492
"Wigtime" (Munro) **95**:307, 324
De wijn in drinkbaar dank zij het glas (Mulisch) **42**:288
"Wild" (Snyder) **120**:344
Wild 90 (Mailer) **74**:217
"A Wild and Crazy Guy" (Martin) **30**:248
A Wild and Crazy Guy (Martin) **30**:247-48
Wild Angels (Le Guin) **45**:214; **136**:389
Wild at Heart (Lynch) **66**:266-73
Wild Berries (Yevtushenko) **51**:425-30; **126**:398, 403
"Wild Billy's Circus Song" (Springsteen) **17**:481
"Wild Bird in a Living Room" (Walker) **13**:567
"The Wild Birds" (Berry) **46**:74
The Wild Birds: Six Stories of the Port William Membership (Berry) **46**:73-4
"The Wild Blue Yonder" (Thomas) **107**:342
The Wild Blue Yonder (Thomas) **107**:336-37, 339-41, 346
"Wild Boar Clough" (Davie) **31**:119, 124
The Wild Boys: A Book of the Dead (Burroughs) **2**:94; **5**:91-2; **15**:110-11; **22**:86; **42**:75, 78-80; **75**:102; **109**:184, 195
"Wild Boys of the Road" (Ashbery) **125**:37
The Wild Bunch (Peckinpah) **20**:273-76, 279, 281, 284
Wild Cat (Peck) **17**:339-40
"The Wild Cherry Tree" (Bates) **46**:60
"Wild Child" (Reed) **21**:304-05
The Wild Child (Truffaut)
See *L'enfant sauvage*
"Wild Children" (Morrison) **21**:234
The Wild Colonial Boy (Hynes) **65**:51-5
Wild Conquest (Abrahams) **4**:1, 3
"The Wild Dog Rose" (Montague) **13**:390; **46**:268-70, 276
Wild Dreams of a New Beginning (Ferlinghetti) **111**:59-60
"The Wild Duck" (Faludy) **42**:142
Wild Earth and Other Poems (Colum) **28**:85, 87
The Wild Earth's Nobility (Waters) **88**:327-28, 337, 339, 345, 349, 359
"Wild Escapes" (Pollitt) **28**:366
The Wild Flag: Editorials from The New Yorker on Federal World Government and Other Matters (White) **10**:529; **39**:377, 379
The Wild Frontier (Berton) **104**:47
Wild Frontier (Berton) **104**:47
The Wild Garden; or, Speaking of Writing (Wilson) **3**:534; **5**:512; **34**:581
"Wild Geese" (Oliver) **98**:260
The Wild Girl (Roberts) **48**:341-43
"The Wild Goose" (Buckler) **13**:123
The Wild Goose Chase (Warner) **45**:427-31, 433, 435, 437-38, 440-41
Wild Grape Wine (Purdy) **50**:246
"Wild Grapes" (Frost) **15**:244; **26**:111-12
"Wild Gratitude" (Hirsch) **50**:195-96, 198-99
Wild Gratitude (Hirsch) **50**:195-98
Wild Grow the Lilies: An Antic Novel (Brown) **63**:53-4
Wild Honey (Frayn) **47**:136-37, 139-41
Wild Honey (Wilson) **12**:641-43, 645, 649, 651-54
"Wild Horses" (Bass) **79**:5-7, 12
"Wild Horses" (Jagger and Richard) **17**:224, 229-30
"Wild Horses" (Lane) **25**:287
Wild Horses (Francis) **102**:158, 160-62
"The Wild Hunter in the Bush of the Ghosts" (Tutuola) **29**:439
Wild in the Country (Odets) **98**:247
Wild in the World (Donovan) **35**:140-42
"The Wild Iris" (Glück) **81**:165-66
The Wild Iris (Glück) **81**:163-74
The Wild Island (Fraser) **32**:185; **107**:37
Wild Justice (Smith) **33**:376
"Wild Life" (McCartney) **35**:280
Wild Life (McCartney) **12**:372; **35**:280, 293
"Wild Love" (Zappa) **17**:592
Wild Man Fragment (Olson) **11**:421
The Wild Man of Borneo (Connelly) **7**:56
The Wild Marketplace (Transtroemer)
See *Det vilda torget*
The Wild Market-Square (Transtroemer)
See *Det vilda torget*
"The Wild Mushroom" (Snyder) **120**:350
Wild Nights (Tennant) **52**:398-99, 406
"Wild Oats" (Larkin) **18**:299; **33**:258; **64**:272
Wild Oats (Epstein) **19**:162-63
Wild Oats (Le Guin) **136**:389
The Wild Oats of Han (Prichard) **46**:332, 335
A Wild Old Man on the Road (Callaghan) **65**:245-47, 250, 252
The Wild Old Wicked Man (MacLeish) **8**:362
The Wild One (Anouilh) **50**:279
"Wild Orchids" (Pollitt) **122**:205
The Wild Palms (Faulkner) **3**:152, 156; **8**:207, 211; **18**:149; **28**:138, 140, 145
"The Wild Parrots of Bloody Bay" (Jacobsen) **48**:191
The Wild Party (Arzner) **98**:63, 69, 74
A Wild Patience Has Taken Me This Far: Poems, 1978-1981 (Rich) **36**:366-68, 370, 376; **73**:315, 317, 326, 330; **125**:321, 323, 339
"Wild Raspberries" (Fuller) **62**:191, 202
Wild River (Kazan) **16**:367-69; **63**:226, 233, 235
"Wild Roses" (Christie) **110**:125
"Wild Roses" (Christie) **110**:126
Wild Roses (Ferron)
See *Les roses sauvages*
Wild Season (Eckert) **17**:105-06
Wild Seed (Butler) **38**:62, 66; **121**:73, 75, 81-2, 84-5, 88-9, 93-5, 97, 99, 103-05, 108-09, 119, 124, 144-45, 149
A Wild Sheep Chase (Murakami)
See *Hitsuji o megaru bōken*
The Wild Shore (Robinson) **34**:105-07
"The Wild Sky" (Rich) **7**:368
"Wild Sports of the West" (Montague) **46**:266
Wild Strawberries (Bergman)
See *Smultronstället*
"Wild Strawberry" (Kenny) **87**:239, 241, 248
A Wild Surmise (Raphael) **2**:366-67

Wild Swans: Three Daughters of China (Chang) **71**:114-29
The Wild, the Innocent, and the E Street Shuffle (Springsteen) **17**:477, 481, 484, 488, 490-91
"Wild Thing" (Sapphire) **99**:81-4
Wild to the Heart (Bass) **79**:3, 10, 15, 17-19; **143**:4, 9, 11
Wild Town (Thompson) **69**:382, 385
"Wild Water" (Swenson) **106**:337, 347
"Wild, Wild Night" (Morrison) **21**:232-33
"La Wild Woman" (Castillo) **151**:103
"Ein Wildermuth" (Bachmann) **69**:35, 37, 44
"A Wildermuth" (Bachmann)
See "Ein Wildermuth"
"Wildermuth's Passion" (Bachmann)
See "Ein Wildermuth"
"The Wilderness" (Fuller) **62**:197
"The Wilderness" (Mahfouz)
See "Al-Khala'"
"The Wilderness" (Mahfūz)
See "al- Khala"
"Wilderness" (Sandburg) **10**:449; **35**:339
"The Wilderness" (Snyder) **120**:346
Wilderness (Danvers) **70**:43-7
Wilderness (Parker) **27**:364
Wilderness: A Tale of the Civil War (Warren) **1**:356; **4**:578; **8**:540
Wilderness Empire (Eckert) **17**:106
"Wilderness Gothic" (Purdy) **14**:431; **50**:248
Wilderness of Ladies (Taylor) **5**:425-26
A Wilderness of Mirrors (Frisch)
See *Mein Name sei Gantenbein*
A Wilderness of Vines (Bennett) **5**:57-9
Wilderness Road (Green) **25**:198
Wilderness Stair: Poems, 1938-1954 (Belitt) **22**:49, 52
"A Wilderness Station" (Munro) **95**:319-22
"Wilderness Tips" (Atwood) **84**:97
Wilderness Tips (Atwood) **84**:95-7; **135**:62
The Wilderness War (Eckert) **17**:109
Wildest Dreams (Ayckbourn) **74**:30
Wildfire (Clark) **12**:131
Wildfire at Midnight (Stewart) **35**:388-90, 392
"Wildflowers" (Howard) **7**:169; **10**:274
Wildlife (Ford) **99**:104, 110, 116-17, 123
Wildlife in America (Matthiessen) **32**:285; **64**:309
"Wildness Makes a Form" (Silkin) **43**:402
Wild's Magical Book of Cranial Effusions (Wild) **14**:580
Wildtrack (Wain) **2**:458; **11**:562
"Wilf McKenzie" (Purdy) **50**:248
"Wilkie Fahnstock, The Boxed Set" (Moody) **147**:190
Wilkin's Tooth (Jones) **26**:224-25
"The Will" (Lavin) **99**:319
"The Will" (Merrill) **8**:386; **13**:377; **34**:235
"The Will" (Miller) **30**:262
The Will (Swados) **5**:420, 422
"Will I?" (Larson) **99**:184, 188
"Will I Go to Heaven?" (Mayle) **89**:141
"Will Not Come Back" (Lowell) **8**:354
"The Will of Stanley Brooke" (Campbell) **42**:83
"Will Scarlet" (Hoffman) **6**:243
Will Shakespeare: The Untold Story (Mortimer) **28**:286
"Will Someone Who Is Not Guilty" (Lerman) **9**:329
"Will the Circle Be Unbroken" (Dumas) **6**:145; **62**:154, 160-61, 163
The Will to Change: Poems, 1968-1970 (Rich) **3**:427-28; **6**:457-58; **7**:364, 366, 368, 371-72; **11**:476; **18**:446-47; **36**:366, 372-73, 375; **73**:323, 325-26, 334; **76**:217; **125**:317-18
"Will to Love" (Young) **17**:577, 579
The Will to Meaning: Foundations and Applications to Logotherapy (Frankl) **93**:210
The Will to Power (Foucault)
See *Histoire de la sexualité, Vol. 1: La volonté de savoir*
"Will to Win" (Scott) **22**:372
"Will You Please Be Quiet, Please?" (Carver) **22**:100; **55**:280; **126**:157, 180, 184
Will You Please Be Quiet, Please? (Carver) **22**:96-9, 101, 103; **36**:101, 103; **53**:60; **126**:105-06, 108, 114, 137, 142-44, 165, 179
"Will You Please Go Now" (O'Faolain) **47**:328
"Will You Tell Me" (Barthelme) **115**:56
"Will You Turn a Deaf Ear" (Auden) **14**:32; **43**:15
Willard and His Bowling Trophies: A Perverse Mystery (Brautigan) **9**:124; **12**:70-2; **42**:50, 56-7, 60
Willard Gibbs (Rukeyser) **6**:479; **15**:459-60
"The Willets" (Swenson) **61**:397-99; **106**:324-25, 337
"Willi" (Doctorow) **37**:91, 93; **113**:152, 163-65
"William" (Oliver) **98**:303
"William and Mareon Clark" (Brown) **48**:60
"William and Mary" (Dahl) **79**:181, 183
William Blake: The Complete Poems (Ostriker) **132**:318
"William Butler Yeats" (Hope) **51**:217
"William Butler Yeats Visits Lincoln Park and Escapes Unscathed" (Ochs) **17**:332
"William Carlos Williams: By Day and by Night" (Soupault) **68**:416
William Carlos Williams on Art and Artists (Williams) **22**:464
William Dean Howells: An American Life (Lynn) **50**:426
William Faulkner: A Critical Study (Howe) **85**:116
William Faulkner: First Encounters (Brooks) **86**:278, 285, 287
William Faulkner: The Yoknapatawpha Country (Brooks) **24**:107-08, 114, 116; **86**:278, 285, 287; **110**:5, 15, 24-5
William Faulkner: Toward Yoknapatawpha and Beyond (Brooks) **86**:285, 287; **110**:15, 24-5
"William Faulkner: Vision of Good and Evil" (Brooks) **86**:287
William Shakespeare (Eagleton) **132**:87-8
"William Street" (Slessor) **14**:497
"Williams Creek" (Oliver) **98**:303
"Willie" (Angelou) **35**:30; **77**:30
"Willie" (Brooks)
See "To Keorapetse Kgositsile (Willie)"
"Willie" (Tryon) **11**:549
Willie and Family Live (Nelson) **17**:305
Willie Masters' Lonesome Wife (Gass) **1**:114; **2**:155; **8**:242-43, 245-46; **15**:255; **39**:478; **132**:142-48, 167, 170, 172, 174, 181, 184, 190, 192
"Willie the Wandering Gypsy and Me" (Jennings) **21**:202
The Willie Way (Nelson) **17**:302
"The Willing" (Bell) **8**:67
"A Willing Slave" (Narayan) **28**:302
"Willingly" (Gallagher) **63**:123
Willingly (Gallagher) **63**:116-18, 120, 122, 124-25
Williwaw (Vidal) **2**:448; **4**:556-58; **22**:431, 433; **72**:387; **142**:274, 292, 303, 316
"The Willow" (Akhmatova)
See "Iva"
"Willow" (Armatrading) **17**:8
"Willow and Fig and Stone" (Buckley) **57**:131
"Willow He Walk" (Wellman) **49**:396
Willow Run (Swarthout) **35**:398
"Willow's Money" (Hansen) **38**:240
"Willowware Cup" (Merrill) **34**:235
Will's Boy: A Memoir (Morris) **37**:313-16
Willy Remembers (Faust) **8**:215
Wilt (Sharpe) **36**:400
The Wilt Alternative (Sharpe) **36**:401-02
Wilt on High (Sharpe) **36**:403-04
"The Wimp" (Gallagher) **63**:122, 124-25
"Winchester" (Squires) **51**:381, 383
"Wind" (Carver) **55**:275
"Wind" (Fenton) **32**:169
"Wind" (Hughes) **4**:235; **9**:281; **14**:270
"The Wind" (Pasternak) **63**:313
"The Wind" (Simic) **22**:382
"Wind" (Soto) **32**:405; **80**:286-87, 293
The Wind (Simon)
See *Le vent*
"The Wind and the Boy" (Head) **67**:98
"The Wind and the Snow of Winter" (Clark) **28**:78-9
"Wind and Trees" (Muldoon) **32**:317, 321
"Wind and Water and Stone" (Paz) **51**:336
The Wind at Djémila (Camus)
See *Le Vent à Djémila*
"The Wind at Your Door" (FitzGerald) **19**:176-77
The Wind Changes (Manning) **19**:299-300
"Wind Chimes" (Wilson) **12**:650
"Wind Chimes in a Temple Ruin" (Birney) **6**:75
"The Wind Coming Down From" (Ammons) **108**:21
The Wind Eye (Westall) **17**:556, 558-59
Wind from an Enemy Sky (McNickle) **89**:165-74, 181, 187
The Wind from Nowhere (Ballard) **3**:32; **14**:41; **36**:33; **137**:56
Wind from the East (Godard)
See *Le vent d'est*
The Wind from the Plain (Kemal)
See *Ortadirek*
"The Wind in the Cloisters" (Amis) **8**:11
A Wind in the Door (L'Engle) **12**:350
"The Wind in the Dooryard" (Walcott) **14**:550
Wind in the Eyes (Dabrowska) **15**:169
"Wind in the Street" (Gunn) **18**:203
The Wind in the Willows (Bennett) **77**:102
Wind Mountain: A Poem (Chappell) **40**:144-45; **78**:91
The Wind off the Small Isles (Stewart) **35**:391
Wind over All (Day Lewis) **1**:72
Wind over Wisconsin (Derleth) **31**:130, 133
"Wind Saves Woman in Leap from Building" (Jensen) **37**:192
"The Wind Shifting West" (Grau) **146**:129
The Wind Shifting West (Grau) **4**:210; **9**:240; **146**:128-29, 141, 160-61, 163
"The Wind Sleepers" (H. D.) **73**:118
Wind Song (Sandburg) **10**:450; **35**:357
"The Wind Took Your Answer Away" (Ellison) **139**:125
Wind, What Do You Want of Me? (Arghezi)
See *Ce-ai cu mine, vîntule?*
Windfalls (O'Casey) **11**:405
"Windigo" (Erdrich) **54**:165
"Winding Down the War" (Appleman) **51**:15
The Winding Stair: Francis Bacon, His Rise and Fall (du Maurier) **11**:163
"Winding Up" (Walcott) **42**:422
"Windingo" (Bowering) **15**:82
Windlestraws (Prichard) **46**:332, 335
"A Windmill in the West" (Carey) **40**:129, 133; **96**:27-8, 37
"Windmills of Dwinelle Hall" (Vizenor) **103**:288
"Windmühlen" (Schmidt) **56**:391
"The Window" (Carver) **53**:61
"The Window" (Creeley) **78**:137
"The Window" (Garrett) **51**:144
"Window" (Hoffman) **6**:244
"The Window" (Levine) **33**:275
"The Window" (Mahon) **27**:290
"A Window" (Merton)
See "The Blessed Virgin Mary Compared to a Window"
"A Window" (Murakami) **150**:58
"Window" (Pinsky) **94**:305; **121**:430
"The Window" (Ritsos) **13**:488
"The Window" (Samarakis) **5**:381
"The Window" (Sarton) **49**:310
"A Window" (Simpson) **149**:358
The Window (Dorris) **109**:298
"A Window Affair" (Dunn) **40**:166

"The Window Is an Almanach" (Goldbarth) **38**:203
"The window of a woman burning" (Piercy) **128**:230
"The Window of His Room" (Carroll) **38**:103
A Window on Russia (Wilson) **24**:482
"Window Seat" (Birney) **11**:51
"Windows" (Livesay) **79**:353
"The Windows" (Merwin) **8**:389
"Windows" (Tuohy) **37**:434
Windows (Creeley) **78**:160-62
Windows and Stones (Transtroemer) **65**:221-22
"Windröschen" (Celan) **82**:49
Windrose: Poems, 1929-1979 (Ghiselin) **23**:171-72
"Winds" (Auden) **43**:27
Winds (Perse)
See *Vents*
The Winds (Vesaas)
See *Vindane*
"Winds in the Western Suburbs" (Ritsos) **31**:324
The Winds of Altair (Bova) **45**:73
The Winds of Darkover (Bradley) **30**:27
The Winds of March (Weber) **12**:633
Winds of Morning (Davis) **49**:86-8, 90-1, 97-8
"The Winds of Orisha" (Lorde) **71**:231
"Winds of Passage" (Martinson) **14**:357
The Winds of Time (Corcoran) **17**:72
The Winds of War (Wouk) **1**:377; **9**:580-81; **38**:444, 449-52
The Wind's Twelve Quarters (Le Guin) **8**:342; **136**:325
"Windshield" (Ostriker) **132**:318
Windswept (Chase) **2**:101
"The Wind-Up Bird and Tuesday's Women" (Murakami) **150**:50, 56, 58-60
The Wind-Up Bird Chronicle (Murakami)
See *Nejimaki-dori kuronikuru*
"The Windy City" (Sandburg) **35**:342-43
"Windy Day at the Reservoir" (Beattie) **146**:60-1, 76, 81, 86
"Windy Evening" (Simic) **68**:377
"Windy Streets" (Johnston) **51**:243
"Wine" (Brooks) **125**:96
"Wine and Milk" (Barthes) **83**:94
"Wine and Time" (Seifert)
See "Víno a čas"
"The Wine Breath" (McGahern) **48**:263
Wine in the Wilderness: A Comedy Drama (Childress) **12**:106; **86**:310, 314, 316; **96**:91, 103-04, 107, 112-13
The Wine of Absurdity (West) **7**:522; **96**:383, 386
The Wine of Astonishment (Gellhorn) **60**:182, 192
The Wine of Astonishment (Lovelace) **51**:270-71
Wine of Choice (Behrman) **40**:79, 82
The Wine of the Puritans (Brooks) **29**:86
"Wine of Wyoming" (Hemingway) **30**:185
The Wine of Youth: Selected Stories (Fante) **60**:133
Wine, Writing (Haavikko) **18**:208; **34**:175
"The Wine-Dark Sea" (Aickman) **57**:6-7
The Wine-Dark Sea (Aickman) **57**:7
The Wine-Dark Sea (O'Brian) **152**:263-65, 267-69, 273, 276-78, 282, 298, 300
"The Winemaker's Beat-Étude" (Purdy) **50**:244
"Winesaps" (Smith) **42**:356-57
"Winged Flight" (Gustafson) **36**:221
Winged Seeds (Prichard) **46**:334, 338, 342-43
Winged Victory (Hart) **66**:178, 189
"Wingfoot Lake" (Dove) **50**:157
"Wingless" (Kincaid) **137**:138, 143
"Wings" (Goldbarth) **38**:207
"Wings" (Hughes) **2**:202
"The Wings" (Levertov) **66**:243
"Wings" (Voznesensky) **57**:419
Wings (Kopit) **18**:291; **33**:246-52
Wings of Desire (Handke) **134**:155
Wings of the Morning (Cunningham) **12**:165-66
"Wings over Africa" (Hemingway) **34**:478
Winkelberg (Hecht) **8**:271-72
The Winner (Rice) **49**:304
Winner Take All (Federman) **6**:182
Winner Take Nothing (Hemingway) **10**:271; **30**:180, 185, 192; **39**:430
"Winner Takes All" (Wasserstein) **90**:432
"Winner Takes All" (Waugh) **27**:477
Winner Takes All (Wellershoff)
See *Der Sieger nimmt alles*
"Winners" (Friel)
See *Lovers*
The Winners (Cortázar)
See *Los premios*
Winners (Friel) **42**:166-67
"winnie song" (Clifton) **66**:83
Winning (Brancato) **35**:66, 68-9
"The Winning of Etain" (Boland) **113**:96
A Winnipeg Childhood (Livesay) **4**:295; **79**:354
"The Winnower to the Winds" (Carruth) **84**:129
"The Winnowing" (Asimov) **26**:50
The Winslow Boy (Rattigan) **7**:354-56
"Winston" (Townshend) **42**:379-80
The Winston Affair (Fast) **131**:85
"Winter" (Celan) **82**:57
"Winter" (Dubus) **97**:223
"Winter" (Giovanni) **64**:194
Winter (Callaghan) **65**:249
Winter, 1671 (Ritter) **52**:354
"Winter: 1978" (Beattie) **40**:64, 66; **63**:12-13; **146**:50
The Winter Alone (Scott) **43**:377
"Winter at Roblin Lake" (Purdy) **14**:434
"Winter at the Track" (Voznesensky) **15**:557; **57**:420
"Winter Bouquet" (Snodgrass) **18**:491
"Winter Castle" (Jacobsen) **102**:235, 240
"A Winter Come" (Moss) **7**:248
"A Winter Convalescence" (Abse) **29**:18
"Winter Dog" (MacLeod) **56**:197-99
"Winter Drought" (Ryan) **65**:209, 212, 214
"A Winter Eden" (Frost) **15**:241
"Winter Evening" (Winters) **32**:469
"Winter Evening Poem" (Jensen) **37**:186
"A Winter Fable" (Boyle) **58**:69
"The Winter Father" (Dubus) **36**:146; **97**:209, 227
"Winter Fire" (Raine) **45**:331
"Winter Garden" (Neruda)
See "Jardín de invierno"
Winter Garden (Bainbridge) **22**:45-7; **62**:30-1; **130**:20
"Winter Harbour" (Bowering) **32**:47
The Winter Hero (Collier and Collier) **30**:72-3
"Winter Honey" (Jordan) **114**:148
"The Winter House" (Crase) **58**:161, 165
"Winter in Castile" (Dos Passos) **25**:143
"Winter in July" (Lessing) **6**:292; **22**:279
"Winter in the Abruzzi" (Ginzburg) **54**:201, 204, 208
Winter in the Blood (Welch) **6**:560-62; **14**:558-61; **52**:426, 428-36, 438
"Winter in the Country" (Oliver) **19**:362; **98**:266
A Winter in the Hills (Wain) **46**:416-18
"Winter Is Lovely, Isn't Summer Hell" (Rooke) **25**:394
"Winter Journey" (Baxter) **45**:53; **78**:17-18
Winter Journey (Broughton) **19**:73-4
Winter Journey (Figes) **31**:162-63
"Winter Kestrel" (Wright) **53**:417
Winter Kills (Condon) **4**:107; **6**:115; **8**:150; **45**:101-03; **100**:91, 94, 97, 100, 104, 110-11, 113
"Winter Landscape" (Berryman) **13**:77
"A Winter Landscape near Ely" (Davie) **5**:114
"Winter Landscape, with Rooks" (Plath) **111**:201-02, 205
"A Winter Legend" (Brown) **48**:59
"A Winter Light" (Haines) **58**:217
Winter Light (Bergman)
See *Nattvardsgästerna*
"Winter Lightning" (Nemerov) **36**:305
The Winter Lightning (Nemerov) **2**:306
"Winter Love" (H. D.) **73**:143
Winter Love (H. D.) **31**:208
"The Winter Man" (Scannell) **49**:329
The Winter Man (Scannell) **49**:329-30
"Winter Market" (Gibson) **39**:144
"The Winter Market" (Gibson) **63**:129
"Winter Mask" (Tate) **2**:429; **14**:529
Winter Morning in Charlottesville (Hass) **18**:213
The Winter Name of God (Carroll) **38**:103
"Winter Nelis" (Jolley) **46**:213
"Winter News" (Haines) **58**:214
Winter News (Haines) **58**:214-21
"A Winter Night" (Aldington) **49**:10
"Winter Night" (Boyle) **58**:80; **121**:33
"Winter Night" (Pasternak) **63**:313, 315, 317
Winter: Notes from Montana (Bass) **79**:12-20; **143**:5-6, 9, 15
Winter Numbers (Hacker) **91**:109-11
"Winter of '73" (Gold) **42**:197
"The Winter of Artifice" (Nin) **60**:265-66
The Winter of Artifice (Nin) **4**:379; **8**:421; **14**:381-83; **60**:265, 279; **127**:360, 374, 377
Winter of Madness (Walker) **14**:552
The Winter of Our Discontent (Steinbeck) **1**:326-27; **5**:405-06; **9**:520; **21**:371, 382, 391; **34**:405, 407, 410-11; **45**:382; **59**:350-51
Winter of the Luna Moth (Rosenblatt) **15**:446
Winter of the Salamander: The Keeper of Importance (Young Bear) **94**:363-64, 369-73, 376
The Winter of the World (Anderson) **15**:15
"Winter on Earth" (Toomer) **22**:429
"Winter on top of the Matterhorn" (Wright) **146**:311
The Winter Palace (Haavikko)
See *Talvipalatsi*
The Winter Palace (Haavikko) **18**:205-06; **34**:168-69, 177
The Winter People (Ehle) **27**:106-07
The Winter People (Whitney) **42**:434
"Winter Piece" (Tomlinson) **45**:393
"Winter Rain" (Adams) **13**:2
"The Winter Rain" (Berry) **4**:59
"Winter Remembered" (Ransom) **5**:365
"Winter Scene" (Ammons) **5**:30; **25**:43; **108**:24
"Winter Sleep" (Oliver) **98**:270
"Winter Sleepers" (Atwood) **25**:66
"Winter Solace" (Squires) **51**:379
Winter Soldiers (Santiago) **33**:354
"Winter Solstice" (Blackburn) **43**:69
"Winter Solstice" (Livesay) **79**:353
"Winter Song" (Kizer) **80**:180
"Winter Stars" (Blunden) **56**:47
Winter Station (Yevtushenko)
See "Zima Station"
Winter Sun (Avison) **4**:36; **97**:73-7, 79-86, 88-92, 105, 110-14, 117, 122, 128-30, 137
Winter Sun/The Dumbfounding: Poems 1940-1966 (Avison) **97**:110, 121, 128
"Winter Swan" (Bogan) **4**:68; **46**:90; **93**:65, 80, 90-1
A Winter Talent and Other Poems (Davie) **5**:114; **8**:162-63; **10**:125
Winter Tales (Brown) **100**:82-3
Winter Tales from Poland (Wojciechowska) **26**:457-58
Winter Thunder (Sandoz) **28**:407
"Winter Trees" (Oliver) **98**:271
Winter Trees (Plath) **2**:337-38; **3**:389-91; **5**:340-41, 343, 345; **9**:434; **14**:424-26; **17**:353, 355, 361-64, 366, 368; **51**:340, 353; **111**:158, 167-69, 181, 204
"Winter Tryst" (Van Doren) **6**:541
"Winter Verse for His Sister" (Meredith) **4**:349
"Winter Vineyard Workers" (Saroyan) **8**:468
"A Winter Visit" (Abse) **29**:20
"Winter Voyage" (Ortese)
See "Viaggio d'inverno"
"Winter Walk" (Blunden) **56**:46
"Winter Walking" (Purdy) **14**:433; **50**:238
"Winter Wheat" (Hoffman) **141**:294-96

"Winter Wind" (Munro) **95**:304
"Winterfold" (Brown) **48**:57
Winterfold (Brown) **48**:57-8; **100**:84
"Wintergreen Ridge" (Niedecker) **10**:360-62; **42**:297-98
"Wintering" (Plath) **9**:427, 431; **111**:177, 185
"Wintering in Victoria" (Rooke) **25**:391
Wintering Out (Heaney) **5**:170-72; **7**:147-48, 150-51; **14**:241-45; **25**:243, 245 46, 248; **37**:165; **74**:156-58, 167, 171, 193; **91**:121, 128
"Winterkill" (Ford) **46**:161
Eine winterliche Reise (Handke) **134**:175, 178
"Winterlong" (Young) **17**:577
Winterlude (Scannell) **49**:332
"A Winter-Piece" (Berryman) **13**:78
Winter's Edge (Miner) **40**:331
"Winter's Formulae" (Transtroemer)
See "Vinterns formler"
Winter's Formulae (Transtroemer)
See *Vinterns formler*
"Winter's King" (Le Guin) **136**:384
"Winter's Morning" (Deighton) **46**:127
"A Winter's Tale" (Brown) **48**:57
"A Winter's Tale" (Heaney) **7**:148
"The Winter's Tale" (Jarrell) **2**:209
"A Winter's Tale" (Plath) **51**:340
"A Winter's Tale" (Thomas) **13**:539; **107**:326, 343, 350
Winter's Tale (Helprin) **32**:229-33
"A Winter's Tale, by a Wife" (Van Duyn) **116**:410
Winter's Tales (Dinesen) **10**:146, 150; **29**:156, 158-59, 161; **95**:37-8, 46, 50-1, 68
The Winthrop Covenant (Auchincloss) **9**:54; **45**:32
"Winthrop Mackworth Redivivus" (Betjeman) **43**:37
"Winthrop Thorpe Tortuga" (Keillor) **115**:294
Wintle's Wonders (Streatfeild) **21**:402-03
"Wipeout" (Jones) **81**:63-5, 67
"The Wiper" (MacNeice) **53**:241-42
"Wir Besenbinder" (Boell) **11**:55; **72**:69
"Wir haben Angst zu verarmen" (Hein) **154**:66
"Wir werden lernen müssen" (Hein) **154**:134, 138-39, 141
"Wire" (Goldbarth) **38**:200
"Wired into Now" (Blount) **38**:46
"Wirers" (Sassoon) **130**:219
"Wires" (Larkin) **64**:262
"Wisconsin in Their Bones" (Derleth) **31**:138
Wisdom, Madness and Folly: The Making of a Psychiatrist (Laing) **95**:155, 184, 187
The Wisdom of the Heart (Miller) **43**:298; **84**:260
The Wisdom Tooth (Connelly) **7**:56
Wise Blood (Huston) **20**:174
Wise Blood (O'Connor) **1**:254-57; **3**:366; **6**:376, 379-81; **10**:364, 367-70; **13**:420-21; **15**:408-09, 411, 413; **21**:255-59, 261-62, 266, 271; **66**:299-330; **104**:104-06, 108, 119-20, 122, 124, 164, 179
Wise Child (Gray) **36**:201-04, 207
Wise Children (Carter) **76**:324-31
Wise Guys (Sondheim) **147**:264
The Wise Have Not Spoken (Carroll) **10**:95, 97
"The Wise Men" (Carpentier) **38**:94
"Wise Men at Their End" (Bausch) **51**:55-7
Wise Virgin (Wilson) **33**:454, 457
Wise, Why's, Y'z (Baraka) **115**:39
The Wise Wound (Carter) **76**:330
The Wise Wound: Everywoman and Eve's Curse (Redgrove) **41**:355-56, 359
"Wish" (Mason) **82**:258
"Wish" (Merwin) **5**:286
"Wish for a Young Wife" (Roethke) **46**:364; **101**:266, 333
"Wish Fulfilment" (Simmons) **43**:408
Wish in the Dark (Weber) **12**:631
"Wish to Be a Red Indian" (Plumly) **33**:312
"Wish You Were Here" (Aksyonov) **101**:28-9, 35
"Wish You Were Here" (Pink Floyd) **35**:313
Wish You Were Here (Brown) **79**:171
Wish You Were Here (Pink Floyd) **35**:307-13, 315
"The Wishbone" (Muldoon) **72**:277, 279
"Wishes" (Wright) **13**:614; **146**:310
Wishes, Lies, and Dreams: Teaching Children to Write Poetry (Koch) **8**:323; **44**:245
Wishful Thinking (Buechner) **4**:80
"The Wishing Box" (Plath) **3**:390
"Wishing More Dear" (Riding) **7**:374
"Wisteria" (Spencer) **22**:402
"A Wistful Poem Called 'Readers'" (Davie) **31**:112, 118
"Wit" (Hoffman) **141**:294
The Wit to Woo (Peake) **54**:366, 372-73, 375
"The Witch" (Beer) **58**:36
"The Witch" (Singer) **9**:487
"Witch Burning" (Plath) **17**:361; **111**:159, 163
The Witch Diggers (West) **7**:520; **17**:544-46, 552-53
"Witch Doctor" (Hayden) **37**:152, 158
The Witch from the Sea (Hibbert) **7**:156
The Witch in the Wood (White) **30**:438-41, 444-46
"The Witch of Coös" (Frost) **1**:110; **9**:218, 224-25; **15**:250
The Witch of Exmoor (Drabble) **129**:160-62
Witch Week (Jones) **26**:232-33
"Witchbird" (Bambara) **19**:33; **88**:28
"Witchcraft" (Head) **67**:93-5
The Witchcraft of Salem Village (Jackson) **60**:217, 223, 237
"The Witches' Brew" (Pratt) **19**:377-78, 383, 385
The Witches of Eastwick (Updike) **43**:432-35, 437; **70**:248-49, 253; **139**:319, 321, 324-25, 331-32, 336, 374
The Witches of Worm (Snyder) **17**:471-72
"Witch-Girl" (Dunn) **40**:168
"Witchgrass" (Glück) **81**:170
The Witch-Herbalist of the Remote Town (Tutuola) **29**:441-43
"Witching" (Boland) **40**:99-100; **67**:44; **113**:60, 62-3
The Witching Hour (Rice) **128**:283-86, 295-98, 306
"The Witchmark" (McGuckian) **48**:276-77
Witch's Business (Jones)
See *Wilkin's Tooth*
Witch's Cradle (Deren) **102**:37-9
"With a Gun" (Becker and Fagen) **26**:79-80
"With a Little Help from My Friends" (Lennon and McCartney) **12**:358
"With a Little Luck" (McCartney) **35**:285-86, 289
"With a Potpourri from Down Under" (Howard) **47**:169
"With All Deliberate Speed" (Madhubuti) **73**:215
"With All Due Respect" (Aleixandre) **36**:30
With All My Might (Caldwell) **50**:299
"With an Axe and an Auger" (Haines) **58**:220
With Bold Knife and Fork (Fisher) **76**:342; **87**:122
"With Burney and Dudek on Mount Royal" (Everson) **27**:133
"With Changing Key" (Celan)
See "Mit Wechselndem Schlüssel"
With Closed Eyes (Arenas)
See "Con los ojos cerrados"
"With Delicate Mad Hands" (Tiptree) **48**:389; **50**:357
With Eye and Ear (Rexroth) **112**:371
With Eyes at the Back of Our Heads (Levertov) **2**:242-43; **15**:336; **28**:242; **66**:238, 241, 252
"With Eyes Closed" (Paz) **65**:188
"With Eyes Veiled" (Simic) **130**:337
"With Folded Hands..." (Williamson) **29**:455-59
"With God on Our Side" (Dylan) **12**:183; **77**:161
"With Hands Like Leaves" (Still) **49**:363
With Hitler in New York, and Other Stories (Grayson) **38**:210
"With Hopes of Hemp" (Ammons) **108**:19
"With Horace" (Ignatow) **40**:259
"With Ignorance" (Williams) **33**:445; **148**:328
With Ignorance (Williams) **33**:444-48; **56**:426, 428-29; **148**:311, 314, 316, 318-20, 322-23, 325, 328-29, 344, 364
"With Janice" (Koch) **44**:248-49
"With Life and With Death" (Elytis) **100**:171, 177, 187
With Love to Lesbia: A Sheaf of Poems (Kenny) **87**:245
With Malice Toward All (Herrmann) **44**:503-04
"With Meaning" (Wieners) **7**:537
"With Mercy for the Greedy" (Sexton) **53**:319
With My Knives I Know I'm Good (Rathbone) **41**:338
With My Little Eye (Fuller) **4**:178
"With My Sons at Boarhills" (Stevenson) **33**:381
"With One Launched Look" (Stafford) **29**:381
With Open Eyes: Conversations with Matthieu Galey (Yourcenar)
See *Les yeux ouverts; entretiens avec Matthieu Galey*
"With or Without" (Dickinson) **49**:102-03
With or Without (Dickinson) **49**:102-03
With ou l'art de l'innocence (Cixous) **92**:62, 69, 94
"With Our Youth and with Our Aged" (Agnon)
See "Bin'arenu uvizkenenu"
"With Pale Women in Maryland" (Bly) **128**:8
"With Quevedo during Spring" (Neruda)
See "Con Quevedo en primavera"
With Shuddering Fall (Oates) **2**:314; **33**:293; **52**:335; **108**:341, 362, 386; **134**:247
"With So Little to Be Sure Of" (Sondheim) **30**:379, 400
With the Beatles (Lennon and McCartney) **12**:384
"With the Deep Voice of a Prophet" (Akhmadulina)
See "Glubokim golosom proroka"
"With the Grain" (Davie) **8**:165; **31**:109
"With the Old Ones" (Blaga) **75**:78
"With the Remover to Remove" (Howard) **47**:169
With the Victors (Gallo)
See *Le cortège des vainqueurs*
"With the World in My Bloodstream" (Merton) **83**:397
"With Trumpets and Zithers" (Milosz)
See "Natrabach i na cytrze"
"With Warm Regards to Miss Moore and Mr. Ransom" (Van Duyn) **63**:441
With Your Body upon My Hands (Grade) **10**:247
"With Your Tongue down My Throat" (Kureishi) **135**:276, 283-85, 292
"Withdrawal" (Carey) **40**:127-28
"The Withdrawal" (Lowell) **37**:238-39
"Withdrawal" (Williams) **42**:441
Withered Murder (Shaffer) **19**:413
The Withered Root (Davies) **23**:140, 143
"Withered Skin of Berries" (Toomer) **22**:428-29
"Within That Context, One Style: Eclectic, Reminiscent, Amused, Fickle, Perverse" (Trow)
See "Ahmet Ertegun"
"Within the Context of No Context" (Trow) **52**:420, 422
Within the Context of No Context (Trow) **52**:420, 422, 424
Within the Gates (O'Casey) **5**:320; **9**:407, 409-11; **11**:406-09; **15**:404, 406; **88**:239, 258, 270
Within the Zodiac (Gotlieb) **18**:191
"Without" (Hall) **151**:224
"Without" (Rozewicz)
See "Bez"
Without (Hall) **151**:212, 214, 221, 223-24

"Without a Counterpart" (Gunn) **18**:200
"Without a Hero" (Boyle) **90**:62-3
Without a Hero, and Other Stories (Boyle) **90**:62-3
"Without a Sough of Wind" (Simic) **49**:341; **130**:313
Without a Stitch in Time (De Vries) **2**:114
Without Anesthesia (Wajda) **16**:584
"Without Bark" (Zamora) **89**:393
"Without Benefit of Tape" (Livesay) **79**:336, 350
"Without Desolation" (Wakoski) **2**:459
Without End (Kieslowski)
See *No End*
Without Feathers (Allen) **52**:35-7, 40
"Without Love" (Cooper) **56**:70
Without Me You're Nothing (Herbert) **44**:393
Without Pausing for a Breath (Ehrenburg) **62**:176-78
Without Place (Alexander) **121**:3, 4
Without Remorse (Clancy) **112**:67, 77, 90
Without Sorcery (Sturgeon) **39**:361, 364, 366
Without Stopping (Bowles) **53**:43-5
"Without You" (Larson) **99**:164
"The Witness" (Garrett) **51**:140
"Witness" (L'Heureux) **52**:279
"The Witness" (Oates) **33**:296
"The Witness" (Porter) **7**:310; **15**:429
Witness (McNally) **7**:217
"Witness for the Prosecution" (Christie) **110**:112
Witness for the Prosecution (Christie) **12**:125; **48**:78; **110**:122-23
Witness for the Prosecution (Wilder) **20**:463
The Witness of Poetry (Milosz) **31**:264-66, 269; **56**:233, 250; **82**:284, 296, 299
"Witness, Secret and Not" (Alexie) **96**:5
"Witness to the Crucifixion" (Gilchrist) **143**:309
A Witness Tree (Frost) **9**:220; **10**:194; **13**:230; **15**:241-42; **26**:118; **34**:468, 470, 475
"The Witnesses" (Auden) **43**:16
"The Witnesses" (Hooker) **43**:197
The Witnesses (Simenon) **2**:397
The Witnesses, or Our Little Stabilization (Rozewicz)
See *Świadkowie albo mała stabilizacja*
"Wittenstein's Friends" (Eagleton) **132**:116
"Wittgenstein on Egdon Heath" (Morgan) **31**:276
Wittgenstein's Ladder (Perloff) **137**:298-301
Wittgenstein's Mistress (Markson) **67**:187-90, 193-94, 198-200
Wittgensteins Neffe: eine Freundschaft (Bernhard) **61**:22, 24
Wittgenstein's Nephew (Bernhard)
See *Wittgensteins Neffe: eine Freundschaft*
Wives and Other Women (Klein) **30**:242
"Wives at War" (Nwapa) **133**:187
Wives at War and Other Stories (Nwapa) **133**:186-87, 202, 229
The Wives of Henry VIII (Fraser)
See *The Six Wives of Henry VIII*
The Wizard Bird (Millin) **49**:251
A Wizard of Earthsea (Le Guin) **8**:343; **13**:347; **22**:266, 270, 273; **71**:178-84, 187-92, 194-98, 200-01, 203-04; **136**:314, 317-18, 320, 330, 362-64, 377-81, 387-89
The Wizard of Earthsea (Le Guin) **136**:332
The Wizard of Loneliness (Nichols) **38**:338-39, 341
Wizards (Bakshi) **26**:72, 74
"Wizard's World" (Norton) **12**:468
Wizja Lokalna (Lem) **149**:112, 152, 208, 263
Wladza (Konwicki) **8**:325; **54**:256; **117**:256, 284
"W.L.M.K." (Scott) **22**:371, 376
"WLT" (Keillor) **40**:274
WLT: A Radio Romance (Keillor) **115**:284-85
Wniebowstapienie (Konwicki) **8**:326; **117**:257-58, 284
Wo warst du, Adam? (Boell) **2**:68; **6**:83; **9**:102-03, 105, 107-08; **11**:53, 57-8; **27**:55-6, 58; **39**:293-94; **72**:78-80, 100
Der Wobbly (Traven) **11**:535
"Woden's Day" (Stafford) **68**:443
Wodwo (Hughes) **2**:197-98, 201-03; **4**:235-36; **9**:280, 283; **14**:271; **37**:172-75, 181; **119**:265, 281, 288, 291
"Woe or Wonder" (Cunningham) **31**:101, 103
Woe or Wonder (Cunningham) **31**:101-02
"Wohin" (Sachs) **98**:328
"The Wolf" (Davidson) **13**:168-69
The Wolf (Blais)
See *Le loup*
The Wolf (Leonov)
See *Volk*
Wolf: A False Memoir (Harrison) **6**:224-25; **33**:199; **66**:153, 155, 157-58, 160, 166; **143**:345, 349
"Wolf Alice" (Carter) **41**:117
"Wolf Dreams" (Beattie) **63**:3, 10; **146**:84
"Wolf Knife" (Hall) **13**:259
"Wolf Moon" (Oliver) **98**:288
"Wolf Net" (McClure) **6**:317
Wolf Solent (Powys) **7**:347-48; **9**:440-41; **15**:433-35; **46**:315-18, 320-21, 324; **125**:267-68, 272, 275-76, 278-82, 290, 294-98, 300, 302, 304
Wolf Willow: A History, a Story, and a Memory of the Last Plains Frontier (Stegner) **9**:510; **81**:339-40, 345, 349-50, 352
"Wolfbane" (Thomas) **13**:541
Wolfnight (Freeling) **38**:187
The Wolfpen Poems (Still) **49**:370-71
Wolf's Salt (Popa)
See *Vučja so*
"Wolfsberg" (O'Brian) **152**:273
Wolfwatching (Hughes) **119**:291
"The Wolves" (Kinnell) **13**:320
"The Wolves" (MacNeice) **53**:234
"Wolves Defended against the Lambs" (Enzensberger) **43**:145
"The Wolves of Aguila" (Matthiessen) **64**:321, 323-24
The Wolves of Willonghby Chase (Aiken) **35**:17, 19
"The Woman" (Creeley) **78**:134
"Woman" (Jarrell) **9**:297-98
"The Woman" (Jensen) **37**:192
"Woman" (Lennon) **35**:272, 274-75
"The Woman" (Levertov) **66**:238
"The Woman" (Livesay) **79**:343, 353
"Woman" (Lorde) **18**:309; **71**:252
"The Woman" (Mphahlele) **25**:337
"Woman" (Neruda)
See "Mujer"
"A Woman" (Pinsky) **121**:446
"Woman" (Salinas) **90**:328
The Woman (Bond) **23**:67
"The Woman Alone" (Day Lewis) **10**:131
A Woman Alone (Fo) **32**:175-76
A Woman Alone (Head) **67**:111
"A Woman and a Man" (Ding Ling)
See "Yige nüren he yige nanren"
"Woman and Her Image" (Castellanos)
See "La mujer y su imagen"
"Woman and the Sea" (Mott) **15**:381
"Woman and Tree" (Graves) **39**:325
Woman, Arise and Walk (Gironella)
See *Mujer, levántate y anda*
"The Woman as a Mummy's Head" (Boland) **40**:99-100
"Woman as Artist" (Taylor) **5**:425
"Woman as Knower" (Lifton) **67**:142
"Woman as Market" (Rukeyser) **15**:458
"Woman as Operator" (Williams) **22**:464
The Woman at Otowi Crossing (Waters) **88**:337, 342, 347-49, 358, 363-64
"The Woman at the Washington Zoo" (Jarrell) **2**:210; **9**:298
The Woman at the Washington Zoo (Jarrell) **2**:208, 210; **9**:296; **13**:302
Woman Beware Woman (Tennant) **52**:401-02
"The Woman Changes Her Skin" (Boland) **40**:99-100
"Woman Chopping Wood" (Hogan) **73**:157
"The Woman Destroyed" (Beauvoir) **124**:129-31
The Woman Destroyed (Beauvoir)
See *La femme rompue*
"The Woman Follows Me Home as I Walk" (Salinas) **90**:332
The Woman from Sicily (Swinnerton) **31**:427
"The Woman Hanging from the Thirteenth Floor" (Harjo) **83**:267
Woman Hating: A Radical Look at Sexuality (Dworkin) **43**:131-32; **123**:89, 95, 101, 106
"Woman Hollering Creek" (Cisneros) **118**:188-89, 193, 197-98, 204
Woman Hollering Creek and Other Stories (Cisneros) **69**:153-56; **118**:188-89, 198, 200, 202, 204, 214-17
The Woman I Abandoned (Endō)
See *The Girl I Left Behind*
"Woman in a Lampshade" (Jolley) **46**:221
Woman in a Lampshade (Jolley) **46**:213, 220-21
"The Woman in Black" (Moravia) **46**:286
The Woman in Black (Hill) **113**:316, 326-27
"A Woman in Heat Wiping Herself" (Olds) **85**:295
"Woman in Kitchen" (Boland) **113**:109, 124
Woman in Mind (Ayckbourn) **74**:9, 11, 13-15, 17-20, 23-4
A Woman in Sunshine (Swinnerton) **31**:426
"Woman in the Bar" (Shapcott) **38**:400
"the woman in the camp" (Clifton) **66**:81
The Woman in the Dunes (Abe)
See *Suna no onna*
"Woman in the House" (Stuart) **34**:376
The Woman in the Moon (Lang)
See *Die Frau im Mond*
"The Woman in the Ordinary" (Piercy) **27**:373
"Woman In the Rose Colored Dress" (Berriault) **109**:96
A Woman in the Sky (Hanley) **5**:167-68
Woman in the Window (Lang) **20**:207, 211, 216
"Woman Is the Death of the Soul" (Oates) **6**:367
"Woman Is the Nigger of the World" (Lennon) **12**:273; **35**:264, 270-71
A Woman like That (Shreve) **23**:402-03
"The Woman Lit by Fireflies" (Harrison) **66**:168-71; **143**:353, 355, 359-60
The Woman Lit by Fireflies (Harrison) **66**:167-71; **143**:344, 347, 351, 353, 359
A Woman Named Solitude (Schwarz-Bart) **2**:388-89; **4**:480
"A Woman Observed" (Ezekiel) **61**:96
The Woman of Andros (Wilder) **1**:364, 366; **5**:495; **6**:575, 577; **10**:536; **15**:572-74; **35**:442; **82**:339-40; 342-44, 364-65, 368, 372-73, 376, 379, 382
A Woman of Character (Gloag) **40**:209-10
A Woman of Destiny (Card) **47**:69
A Woman of Independent Means (Hailey) **40**:220-24
"Woman of Marrakech" (Castillo) **151**:11
A Woman of Means (Taylor) **37**:408; **44**:305; **50**:252-53, 258; **71**:297
A Woman of No Importance (Bennett) **77**:98
The Woman of Paris (Chaplin) **16**:187-88, 198, 201
The Woman of Rome (Moravia)
See *La Romana*
A Woman of Singular Occupation (Gilliatt) **53**:147
Woman of the Ganges (Duras)
See *La femme du Gange*
"The Woman of the House" (Murphy) **41**:311-12, 316, 320
Woman of the Inner Sea (Keneally) **117**:238-40, 243, 245
Woman of the River (Alegria)
See "A Temple of the Holy Ghost"
"The Woman of the Sumpul River" (Alegria) **75**:49
Woman on the Edge of Time (Piercy) **14**:419-

20; **18**:406; **27**:376; **62**:362-67, 371-74, 376; **128**:218, 224, 231-34, 241, 244-45, 250-52, 255-60, 263-68, 272
"The Woman on the Stair" (MacLeish) **8**:361; **68**:286-87
Woman on Trial (Rand)
See *Night of January 16*
"A Woman Pacing Her Room" (Levertov) **15**:339
"A Woman Painted on a Leaf" (Boland) **113**:92, 94-5, 111
"A Woman Playwright Speaks Her Mind" (Childress) **86**:316
"Woman Posing" (Boland) **40**:99, 101; **113**:108
A Woman Run Mad (L'Heureux) **52**:280-81
The Woman Said Yes: Encounters with Life and Death (West) **7**:522; **17**:553
"Woman Singing" (Ortiz) **45**:309
A Woman Speaks (Nin) **14**:385
"The Woman Takes Her Revenge on the Moon" (Boland) **113**:87
"The Woman, the Place, the Poet" (Boland) **113**:84, 105-06, 126
"The Woman Thing" (Lorde) **71**:232
"Woman to Child" (Wright) **53**:419, 427, 431
"Woman to Man" (Wright) **53**:418-19, 427, 431
Woman to Man (Wright) **53**:417, 419-20, 423-24, 427-28, 431
Woman to Woman (Duras)
See *Les parleuses*
"The Woman Turns Herself into a Fish" (Boland) **40**:99-100; **113**:124
"A Woman Unconscious" (Hughes) **9**:280, 285
A Woman under the Influence (Cassavetes) **20**:48-51, 55
A Woman Under the Surface (Ostriker) **132**:302, 318, 328
The Woman Warrior: Memoirs of a Girlhood among Ghosts (Kingston) **12**:312-14; **19**:249-50; **58**:308-18, 324, 327; **121**:244-47, 249, 252, 254-56, 261-62, 266-67, 269-72, 275, 279, 282, 284-302, 307-08, 310-16, 320-21
"The Woman Who Came at Six O'Clock" (García Márquez) **15**:254; **47**:148, 150
"The Woman Who Died Too Soon" (Steinem) **63**:380
"The Woman Who Fainted" (Dybek) **114**:74-6
"The Woman Who Had Imagination" (Bates) **46**:52, 54, 66
The Woman Who Had Imagination, and Other Stories (Bates) **46**:51-2
"The Woman Who Kept Her Poet" (Godwin) **8**:248
"The Woman Who Knew Too Much" (Ai) **69**:4
Woman Who Knows Latin (Castellanos)
See *Mujer que sabe latín*
"The Woman Who Loved Pigs" (Donaldson) **138**:41
"The Woman Who Loved to Cook" (Jong) **6**:267
The Woman Who Owned the Shadows (Allen) **84**:13, 17-20, 24, 28-33, 37-8, 41, 44
"A Woman Who Plays Trumpet Is Deported" (Cliff) **120**:89-90
"The Woman Who Raised Goats" (Gallagher) **18**:169; **63**:119
"The Woman Who Tried to Be Good" (Ferber) **93**:138, 180
"The Woman Who Was a Tree" (Huxley) **11**:282
The Woman Who Was Changed (Buck) **18**:80
The Woman Who Was God (King) **53**:213-14; **145**:351-53
"The Woman Who Was Never Satisfied" (Martin) **89**:111-12, 116, 118
"The Woman Who Was Not Allowed to Keep Cats" (White) **69**:398
A Woman Whose Heart Is Too Small (Crommelynck)
See *Une femme qu'a le coeur trop petit*
"Woman/Wilderness" (Le Guin) **136**:333
"Woman with Chrysanthemums" (Mueller) **51**:279
"Woman with Girdle" (Sexton) **8**:483
The Woman without a Face (Bergman) **72**:51
"Woman Work" (Angelou) **77**:30
"A Woman, Young and Old" (Paley) **37**:337; **140**:232, 234, 247, 277, 281
"Woman-Enough" (Gallagher) **18**:170; **63**:120
"The Womanhood" (Brooks) **5**:75; **49**:31
A Woman's Age (Billington) **43**:55-7
"A Woman's Breast" (Landolfi) **49**:214, 217
A Woman's Hand (White) **5**:486-87
"A Woman's Illness" (Ghose) **42**:179
"A Woman's Issue" (Atwood) **25**:65; **84**:68
"Woman's Song" (Wright) **53**:418-19, 427, 431
A Woman's Story (Ernaux)
See *Une femme*
"the woman's vision" (Young Bear) **94**:363
"Womanwork" (Allen) **84**:6
Womberang (Townsend) **61**:408-11
"Women" (Bogan) **39**:388, 390, 392; **46**:87
"The Women" (Boland) **113**:70, 92, 124
"Women" (Howe) **152**:159, 161-62
"The Women" (Jones) **131**:251, 269
"The Women" (Kenny) **87**:240
"Women" (Rich) **36**:372
"Women" (Scott) **43**:370
"Women" (Swenson) **61**:394, 397; **106**:342
"The Women" (Walker) **58**:405
Women (Bukowski) **41**:70-1, 73; **82**:10-11, 13, 28; **108**:96, 100-03, 105-09
Women and Angels (Brodkey) **56**:57-9
"Women and Blacks and Bensonhurst" (Harrison) **144**:112
Women and Children First (Benson) **17**:49
"Women and Honor: Some Notes on Lying" (Rich) **18**:448; **73**:324
Women and Men (McElroy) **47**:244-46
The Women and the Men (Giovanni) **19**:192; **64**:188-89, 191; **117**:184, 192, 197
Women and Wallace (Sherman) **55**:377-80
Women Are Different (Nwapa) **133**:222-27, 229, 233
"The Women Are Grieving" (Hogan) **73**:148
Women Are Not Roses (Casares) **151**:
"Women Artists and Contemporary Racechanges" (Gubar) **145**:283
The Women at Point Sur (Jeffers)
See *The Women of Point Sur*
Women Calling Home (Vesaas)
See *Kvinnor ropar heim*
Women, Class, and the Feminist Imagination: A Socialist-Feminist Reader (Hansen and Philipson) **65**:342
Women, Culture, & Politics (Davis) **77**:127-29
"Women in Egypt: A Personal View" (Davis) **77**:129
Women in Evidence (Japrisot)
See *La passion des femmes*
"Women in Love" (Mahapatra) **33**:284
Women in Love (Russell) **16**:541-42, 548
"Women in Marriage" (Stevenson) **7**:463
Women in Romanticism: Mary Wollstonecraft, Dorothy Wordsworth and Mary Shelley (Alexander) **121**:11
"Women in the Locker Room!" (Blount) **38**:47
Women in the Wall (O'Faolain) **6**:383; **19**:360; **47**:330-31; **108**:400-01
Women in Their Beds: New and Selected Stories (Berriault) **109**:95, 98
"Women Like Taverns I've Dreamt" (Salinas) **90**:332
"Women like You" (Ondaatje) **51**:313
"The Women Men Don't See" (Tiptree) **48**:389-90, 392; **50**:356-57
Women Men Don't Talk About (Calisher) **134**:42
"Women, Men, Theories, and Literature" (Heilbrun) **65**:344
The Women of Brewster Place (Naylor) **28**:304-05; **52**:320-24
Women of Crisis (Coles) **108**:188
"The Women of Dan Dance With Swords in Their Hands to Mark the Time When They Were Warriors" (Lorde) **71**:236
"Women of France" (Senghor)
See "Femmes de France"
Women of Messina (Vittorini)
See *Le donne di Messina*
The Women of Point Sur (Jeffers) **11**:305, 311; **54**:233, 236-37, 243, 245
The Women of Whitechapel and Jack the Ripper (West) **96**:369, 376, 386-90, 392-93, 396
The Women on the Porch (Gordon) **6**:203, 206; **29**:186, 190; **83**:234, 239, 243-44, 247-48, 250-51, 257, 260
Women on the Verge of a Nervous Breakdown (Almodovar)
See *Mujeres al borde de un ataque de nervios*
"The Women on the Wall" (Stegner) **49**:350; **81**:346
The Women on the Wall (Stegner) **49**:350; **81**:346
Women, Race, & Class (Davis) **77**:120-23, 128
"The Women Speaking" (Hogan) **73**:150
"Women We Never See Again" (Bly) **128**:13, 15
"Women Who Are Writers in Our Century: One Out of Twelve" (Olsen) **114**:197
The Women Who Hate Me (Allison) **78**:2-3, 7; **153**:5, 7, 17-18, 28
The Women Who Walk (Packer) **65**:350
Women Whose Lives Are Food, Men Whose Lives Are Money (Oates) **15**:402
"Women without Gardens" (Dunn) **40**:171
Women Writers of the Seventeenth Century (Wilson and Warnke) **65**:343
"Women-Identified" (Brown) **79**:159
"Women's House" (Muske) **90**:308
"Women's Liberation" (Vidal) **142**:333
"The Women's Movement" (Didion) **129**:64
"Women's Pentagon Action Unity Statement" (Paley) **140**:288
"A Women's Restaurant" (Boyle) **36**:56-8
The Women's Room (French) **10**:191; **18**:158-59; **60**:138, 141, 144, 147-50
"Women's Time" (Kristeva) **77**:306-09; **140**:142-151, 169, 181, 188, 202
"Woncha Come on Home" (Armatrading) **17**:8-9
Wonder Boys (Chabon) **149**:10-21, 23, 25-6, 30-2
"The Wonder Woman" (Giovanni) **64**:185-87
"Wonderful" (Wilson) **12**:645
The Wonderful Clouds (Sagan) **17**:422-23
Wonderful Fool (Endō)
See *Obakasan*
"Wonderful Future" (Nelson) **17**:302
"Wonderful Holidays" (Lehmann) **5**:240
The Wonderful O (Thurber) **5**:432, 438; **25**:437; **125**:406
"The Wonderful Old Gentleman" (Parker) **68**:326-27, 335, 337
"Wonderful Plant" (Goyen) **40**:218
The Wonderful Story of Henry Sugar and Six More (Dahl) **79**:177, 181
Wonderful Tennessee (Friel) **115**:237-38
Wonderful Words, Silent Truth (Simic) **68**:376; **130**:313, 334, 336, 340
"Wonderful World, Beautiful People" (Cliff) **21**:60
Wonderful World, Beautiful People (Cliff) **21**:60-1
"The Wonderful World of Winnebagos" (Crews) **49**:73
The Wonderful Years (Kunze) **10**:310
Wonderland (Oates) **1**:252; **2**:314-15; **3**:360-62; **6**:368-69; **9**:406; **15**:400-02; **19**:353; **52**:335, 338; **108**:374-75, 378, 385, 386, 391
"Wonderment" (Sassoon) **36**:385
"Wonders of Obligation" (Fisher) **25**:160-62
The Wonder-Worker (Jacobson) **4**:253-56

"Wonga Vine" (Wright) **53**:431
"Won't Get Fooled Again" (Townshend) **17**:527, 531, 535
Won't Know Till I Get There (Myers) **35**:298-99
Woo Havoc (Bell) **8**:67
"The Wood" (Green) **97**:292
"A Wood" (Merwin) **88**:192
"Wood" (Munro) **95**:311-12
"A Wood" (Wilbur) **53**:410-11; **110**:354-55
Wood and Stone (Powys) **7**:348; **46**:313; **125**:278-80, 304
"The Wood Dove at Sandy Spring" (MacLeish) **8**:362
"Wood Has No Mouth" (Lorde) **71**:255
Wood Mountain Poems (Suknaski) **19**:432-33
"Wood Scraps" (Hein)
See "Matzeln"
"The Woodcarver" (Brown) **100**:83
"Woodchucks" (Kumin) **28**:225
The Woodcock (Tournier)
See *Le coq de bruyère*
Woodcutters (Bernhard)
See *Holzfällen: Eine Erregung*
"Woodcutting on Lost Mountain" (Gallagher) **63**:124
"The Wooden Dove of Archytas" (Davenport) **14**:142
The Wooden Fish (Snyder) **120**:350
A Wooden Horse (Brandys) **62**:119
The Wooden Horse (Hine) **15**:282
Wooden Hunters (Cohen) **19**:115
Wooden Icons (Arghezi)
See *Icoane de lemn*
"The Wooden Madonna" (Coward) **51**:74
"Wooden Moscow" (Yevtushenko) **126**:398
"The Wooden Queen" (Leonov)
See "Dereviannaia koroleva"
The Wooden Shepherdess (Hughes) **11**:278
"The Wooden Umbrella" (Porter) **7**:310; **101**:223
"Wooding" (Motion) **47**:288-90
"The Woodlot" (Clampitt) **32**:114
"Woodpigeons at Rahenny" (Davie) **10**:122
"The Wood-Pile" (Frost) **9**:227; **15**:248; **26**:112, 122
"Woodrow Wilson (February, 1924)" (Jeffers) **54**:246
"The Woods" (Erdrich) **54**:165
The Woods (Mamet) **15**:356; **46**:251-52, 254
The Woods (Plante) **23**:347; **38**:365-67, 370-71
Woods and River Tales (Haig-Brown) **21**:146
"The Woods, New York" (Bronk) **10**:75
"Woodstock" (Mitchell) **12**:441
"The Wood-Weasel" (Moore) **8**:400
Woody Guthrie: Library of Congress Recordings (Guthrie) **35**:185
Woody Sez (Guthrie) **35**:193
Woody's Story (Guthrie) **35**:193
"Wool Tea" (Dowell) **60**:107-08
"The Wool Trade" (Heaney) **5**:170; **7**:151; **14**:242
The Woolgatherer (Mastrosimone) **36**:289-91
"Woolworth's" (Hall) **37**:142
The Worcester Account (Behrman) **40**:84
"Worcestershire" (Davie) **8**:165
"The Word" (Akhmadulina)
See "Slovo"
"The Word" (Smith) **25**:418
Word (Booth) **23**:77
The Word (Dreyer)
See *Ordet*
The Word (Wallace) **7**:510; **13**:567
A Word about Tolstoy (Leonov) **92**:277
Word Art and Picture Art (Lagerkvist)
See *Ordkonst och bildkonst*
The Word Became Sex (Sender) **8**:480
A Word Carved on a Sill (Wain) **11**:562
A Word Child (Murdoch) **6**:347-48; **8**:404-06; **11**:384, 389; **31**:288, 290, 294; **51**:288
"The Word Crys Out" (Ammons) **108**:12
"Word, Dialogue, and Novel" (Kristeva) **77**:310; **140**:146
"A Word for Me...Also" (Giovanni) **64**:192; **117**:177
"A Word for the Wind" (Ezekiel) **61**:104
"Word for Word" (Bachmann) **69**:46
The Word for World Is Forest (Le Guin) **8**:343; **13**:348, 350-51; **22**:266; **45**:222-23; **136**:322-23, 331-34, 383-85
"Word from the Right Wing" (Baraka) **5**:48
"A Word in Your Ear on Behalf of Indifference" (Davison) **28**:101
"The Word of Unbinding" (Le Guin) **71**:186, 199
A Word or Two Before You Go (Barzun) **145**:68
Word over All (Day Lewis) **6**:127; **10**:131
"A Word with You" (Bishop) **32**:38
Wordarrows (Vizenor) **103**:281, 284, 296-98
"Wordless Winter" (Davison) **28**:104
"Wordlists" (Harrison) **43**:176; **129**:198, 221
"Wordlists II" (Harrison) **43**:177
"Words" (Creeley) **15**:152
"Words" (Enright) **31**:154
"Words" (Levine) **33**:271; **118**:285
"Words" (Plath) **5**:346; **9**:428, 433; **14**:422, 424-25, 429; **17**:366; **62**:406
"Words" (Shields) **113**:426
Words (Creeley) **1**:67; **2**:106-07; **8**:151, 153; **11**:138; **15**:151-52; **36**:117-20; **78**:125, 127, 137, 143-44, 149
Words (Josipovici) **43**:214, 218-19, 227
Words (Kroetsch)
See *The Words of My Roaring*
The Words (Sartre)
See *Les mots*
Words and Experience (Hughes) **9**:282
Words and Music (Beckett) **6**:45, 47; **9**:83-4
Words and Music (Mayne) **12**:389-90, 403
"Words and Pictures" (Bernstein) **142**:9
Words and Things (Foucault) **34**:340
"Words Asleep" (Lee) **90**:194
Words by Heart (Sebestyen) **30**:345-51
Words Chosen Out of Desire (Vendler) **138**:253
"The Words Continue Their Journey" (Atwood) **84**:68
"Words for a Bike-Riding, Osprey-Chasing, Wine-Drunk Squaw Man" (Allen) **84**:10
Words for a Deaf Daughter (West) **7**:523; **14**:568-69; **96**:385, 393, 400
"Words for a Nursery" (Plath) **111**:167
"Words for a Song" (Lewis) **41**:261
Words for Dr. Y (Sexton) **53**:313
"Words for Hart Crane" (Lowell) **124**:275
"Words for Love" (Berrigan) **37**:43
"Words for Music" (Aldington) **49**:9-10, 17
"Words for the Dumb" (Van Duyn) **116**:427
"Words for the Unknown Makers" (Kunitz) **148**:84, 90, 127
"Words for the Wind" (Roethke) **46**:363; **101**:266, 328
Words for the Wind: The Collected Verse of Theodore Roethke (Roethke) **3**:432-33; **8**:455, 460; **46**:360, 363; **101**:265-67, 269, 285, 287, 290, 295, 302, 304, 311, 327-33
"Words for Winter" (Blaise) **29**:70
Words from History (Asimov) **76**:312
Words from the Exodus (Asimov) **76**:312
"The Words He Said" (Lessing) **22**:279
"Words heard, by accident, over the phone" (Plath) **111**:203
"Words in Commotion" (Landolfi) **49**:216-17
Words in Commotion, and Other Stories (Landolfi) **49**:215-17
Words in Genesis (Asimov) **76**:312
Words in Stone (Bonnefoy)
See *Pierre écrite*
Words in th Fire (Bissett) **18**:59
Words in the Mourning Time (Hayden) **5**:168; **37**:151-52, 160
The Words in the Sand (Buero Vallejo) **15**:100, 102
"Words in the Tropics" (Guillén) **79**:229-30
"Words into Fiction" (Welty) **105**:333
Words Made to Measure (Arghezi)
See *Cuvinte potrivite*
"Words of a Pilgrim" (Gregor) **9**:254
Words of Advice (Weldon) **11**:565
"Words of Comfort" (Ammons) **108**:12
The Words of My Roaring (Kroetsch) **5**:220-21; **23**:269-70; **57**:282-83, 288; **132**:202-9, 212, 244, 247-48, 250
Words of Science (Asimov) **26**:36, 38; **76**:312
"The Words of the Preacher" (Kunitz) **148**:74
"Words on a Page" (Raine) **103**:186
"The Words on Magnet" (Seifert) **93**:341
Words on the Map (Asimov) **76**:312
"Words Rising" (Bly) **38**:55, 59-60; **128**:32, 43
Words That Must Somehow Be Said: Selected Essays, 1927-1984 (Boyle) **58**:74-5; **121**:36-7
"Words to a Young Revolutionist" (Carruth) **84**:129
"Words to Frank O'Hara's Angel" (O'Hara) **78**:339
"Words with Marigold" (Tremain) **42**:386
Words with Power: Being a Second Study of 'The Bible and Literature' (Frye) **70**:272-73, 275, 278
"Words Words Words" (Randall) **135**:391
"Wordsharp" (Brunner) **8**:109
"Wordsworth and the Paradox of the Imagination" (Brooks) **110**:35
"A Wordsworthian Sonnet for Arnold Feinstein, Who Mended My Spectacles in Yugoslavia" (Ewart) **46**:154
Wordsworth's Poetry, 1787-1814 (Hartman) **27**:178, 182
"Work" (Arghezi) **80**:10
"Work" (Oliver) **98**:304
"Work" (Shields) **113**:442
Work (Dixon) **52**:94 7, 101
Work and Love (Dunn) **36**:155
"Work Diary" (Wolf) **58**:421
Work in Progress (Redgrove) **41**:348-49
"The Work of Art" (Oliver) **98**:302
"A Work of Artifice" (Piercy) **18**:405; **62**:379
The Work of Fire (Blanchot)
See *La Part du feu*
"Work Problem" (Hollander) **5**:186
"Work Song" (Berry) **27**:35-6
Work Suspended (Waugh) **13**:588-60; **19**:461
"Workday" (Hogan) **73**:159
"The Worker" (Blaga) **75**:70
The Worker (Jünger) **125**:238-39, 241-42, 244-45
"Worker in Mirror at his Bench" (Kinsella) **138**:89, 94, 105, 108, 111, 121, 129, 132, 149-50, 163
Workers '71 (Kieslowski) **120**:209, 245
The Workhouse Donkey (Arden) **6**:8; **13**:23-4, 29; **15**:20
"Working" (Harrison) **43**:176; **129**:166
Working Bullocks (Prichard) **46**:328, 330-32, 334, 336-38, 340-41, 343-44
"Working Class Hero" (Lennon) **35**:261-62, 267
Working Cotton (Williams) **89**:358
The Working Days: The Journals of 'The Grapes of Wrath,' 1938-1941 (Steinbeck) **59**:340-41, 346-49, 351, 353-54
"The Working Girl" (Beattie) **146**:59, 67, 70
Working Girls (Arzner) **98**:62, 71, 81, 87-90, 94
"Working Late" (Simpson) **32**:378; **149**:306, 325, 328, 357
Working Men (Dorris) **109**:298, 307-10
"The Working Novelist and the Myth-Making Process" (Lytle) **22**:293, 297
The Working of Water (Redgrove) **41**:359-60
"Working on the '58 Willys Pickup" (Snyder) **120**:325
"Working on Wall Street" (Swenson) **14**:521
"Working Out" (Ammons) **57**:53
Working Papers: Selected Essays and Reviews (Carruth) **84**:115, 118, 121, 123-24, 127

"A Working Party" (Sassoon) **130**:181, 187, 192, 214
Working: People Talk about What They Do All Day and How They Feel about What They Do (Terkel) **38**:422-25, 428
"Working the Face" (Parini) **54**:361
Working with Structuralism (Lodge) **36**:274, 276; **141**:330, 342, 369
"Workingman with Hand So Hairy-Sturdy" (Cummings) **68**:46
"The Workman" (Smith) **64**:390
"Works of Art" (Jennings) **131**:239
The Works of Love (Morris) **1**:230-33; **3**:343; **7**:246; **18**:354; **37**:310, 312-13
"The World" (Bowen) **11**:60
"The World" (Milosz) **11**:381; **31**:265-66, 268; **55**:232, 237, 245, 248, 251; **82**:285, 289, 298
"The World" (Simic) **130**:313, 318, 333, 341
The World about Us (Simon)
See *Leçon de choses*
The World Above (Polonsky) **92**:375-76, 402
The World according to Garp (Hill) **26**:208-10
The World according to Garp (Irving) **13**:293-97; **23**:244-47, 253; **38**:250, 252; **112**:139-40, 142-56, 158-60, 164-72, 174-75
"The World according to Hsü" (Mukherjee) **53**:265-67, 270
World Alone (Aleixandre)
See *Mundo a solas*
The World and Africa (Du Bois) **64**:118
The World and the Book: A Study of Modern Fiction (Josipovici) **43**:214-20, 223; **153**:217
"The World and the Jug" (Ellison) **86**:320
"The World as a Vision of the Unity in Flesh, Homage to Henry James" (Spacks) **14**:510
"The World as Holocaust" (Lem) **149**:112, 116
The World as I Found It (Duffy) **50**:33-6
"A World Awash with Fascism and Fear" (Ferlinghetti) **6**:183-84
The World before Us: Poems, 1950-70 (Weiss) **3**:517; **8**:545; **14**:557
"The World Began in Eden but Ended in Los Angeles" (Ochs) **17**:332
"The World behind Watergate" (Sale) **68**:346
A World Between (Spinrad) **46**:384
"The World Book, 1927" (Rich) **36**:366
"World Breaking Apart" (Glück) **22**:175
The World by Itself (Aleixandre) **36**:30
World Citizen: Woodrow Wilson (Archer) **12**:16
"The World Contracted to a Recognizable Image" (Williams) **9**:575
"The World Dance" (Le Guin) **45**:219
The World Doesn't End (Simic) **68**:370, 376, 378-79; **130**:318-19, 332
World Enough and Time (Warren) **1**:355; **4**:577-81; **8**:539, 541; **10**:518-19; **39**:266; **53**:376; **59**:298
World Enough: Rethinking the Future (Mead) **37**:280-81
"World Hymn 1914" (Christie) **110**:125, 127
A World I Never Made (Farrell) **66**:112, 114, 116, 120, 132, 136
A World in a Drop of Water (Silverstein and Silverstein) **17**:450
The World in the Attic (Morris) **1**:232; **7**:247
The World in the Evening (Isherwood) **1**:155, 157; **9**:293-94; **11**:294, 296-300; **14**:278, 280-81, 285; **44**:397-99, 402
The World Inside (Silverberg) **140**:342, 346-47, 350, 379-80, 382-87
"The World Is a Beautiful Place" (Ferlinghetti) **27**:137
The World Is a Room, and Other Stories (Amichai) **57**:38, 46; **116**:105, 107, 128
"The World Is a Wedding" (Schwartz) **45**:353-54
The World Is a Wedding (Schwartz) **4**:478; **10**:462-63; **45**:354; **87**:333-36
"The World Is Alive" (Le Clézio) **31**:243
"The World Is Almost Rotten" (Abbott) **48**:6
"The World Is Full of Poets" (Urdang) **47**:400
The World Is Made of Glass (West) **33**:433-34
The World Is My Home: A Memoir (Michener) **109**:375, 381, 385, 387-89
"The World Is Round Like an Orange" (Grenville) **61**:156
The World Jones Made (Dick) **30**:116
"The World Keeps Going Round" (Davies) **21**:89
World Light (Laxness)
See *Heimsljós*
A World More Attractive: A View of Modern Literature and Politics (Howe) **85**:121
"The World of 2001" (Clarke) **35**:123-24
World of Adventure (Vance) **35**:427
"The World of Apples" (Cheever) **3**:107; **7**:48, 50; **64**:50, 53
The World of Apples (Cheever) **3**:107-08; **7**:48-9; **25**:120
The World of Apu (Ray)
See *Apur sansar*
"The World of Charlie Brown" (Eco) **142**:103
The World of Dance (Berger) **12**:42
The World of Dew (Enright) **8**:203; **31**:148
A World of Difference (MacCaig) **36**:287-88
The World of Doonesbury (Trudeau) **12**:590
The World of Farley Mowat (Mowat) **26**:346-47
The World of Gwendolyn Brooks (Brooks) **1**:46; **4**:79; **49**:23; **125**:85
The World of Henry Orient (Hill) **26**:197, 204, 207-08
"World of Heroes" (Kavan) **82**:122
A World of Ideas: Conversations with Thoughful Men and Women about American Life Today and the Ideas Shaping Our Future (Moyers) **74**:253-54
"The World of J. Edgar Hoover" (MacBeth) **5**:264
The World of J.B. Priestley (Priestley) **34**:362
The World of Jesse Stuart (Stuart) **8**:507; **34**:373
The World of Lenny Bruce (Bruce) **21**:53
"A World of Light" (Jennings) **131**:239
A World of Love (Bowen) **3**:82, 84; **11**:63-64; **118**:77
The World of Mr. Mulliner (Wodehouse) **5**:517
"World of Nothing" (Fair) **18**:139, 141
World of Nothing (Fair) **18**:139
World of Og (Berton) **104**:47
World of Our Fathers: The Jews of Eastern Europe (Meltzer) **26**:302-03
World of Our Fathers: The Journey of the Eastern European Jews to America and the Life They Found and Made (Howe) **85**:123, 126-28, 133, 137, 147-49
The World of Paul Slickey (Osborne) **2**:328; **5**:331; **45**:313-14, 320
"World of Peace" (Cliff) **21**:61
A World of Profit (Auchincloss) **4**:29-30
World of Ptavv's (Niven) **8**:427
The World of Ray Bradbury (Bradbury) **42**:33
The World of Sex (Miller) **84**:242, 249-50, 252, 266, 287, 292
"The World of Simon Raven" (Porter) **33**:325
A World Of Strangers (Gordimer) **10**:239-40; **18**:186; **70**:162-63, 165-66, 169-70; **123**:137, 139-40
The World of the Lie (Loewinsohn) **52**:283-85
"World of the Myth" (Ellison) **42**:126
"World of the Red Sun" (Simak) **55**:320-21
The World of the Ten Thousand Things (Wright) **119**:180, 189; **146**:336, 339-42, 347, 349, 362, 365, 369, 373-75, 379
The World of Violence (Wilson)
See *The Violent World of Hugh Greene*
The World of Washington Irving (Brooks) **29**:88
"World of Women" (Durban) **39**:44-6
World of Wonders (Davies) **7**:73-4; **13**:173-74; **25**:133, 136; **42**:102, 105, 107, 109; **75**:180, 184, 192, 199, 204, 216; **91**:208
"World on a String" (Young) **17**:574
World Orders, Old and New (Chomsky) **132**:64-67, 71, 74
World Outside the Window: The Selected Essays of Kenneth Rexroth (Rexroth) **49**:286-87
The World Reformer (Bernhard)
See *Der Weltverbesserer*
A World Restored: Europe After Napeleon (Kissinger) **137**:241
A World Restored: Metternich, Castlereagh, and the Problems of Peace, 1812-1822 (Kissinger) **137**:214, 220, 227, 240
World Revolution, 1917-1936: The Rise and Fall of the Communist International (James) **33**:218
World Series (Tunis) **12**:593
"The World Still Needs" (Avison) **97**:89
"World Telegram" (Berryman) **62**:56, 71
"The World That Couldn't Be" (Simak) **55**:320
The World, the Text, and the Critic (Said) **123**:358, 380-81
The World, the Worldless (Bronk) **10**:73, 75
"The World (This One), the Flesh (Mrs. Oedipa Maas), and the Testament of Pierce Inverarity" (Pynchon) **72**:309, 323, 333
The World Upside Down (Mayne) **12**:386, 388-89
WWII (Jones) **39**:405
World War I (Smith) **64**:388
"The World War I Los Angeles Airplane" (Brautigan) **3**:89; **12**:65, 70
"World War III" (Bell) **8**:65
The World We Make (Kingsley) **44**:232-33
"The World Well Lost" (Sturgeon) **39**:361, 363, 366
"World Wisdom" (Kunene) **85**:175
"A World within a War" (Read) **4**:440
The World within the Word (Gass) **11**:224-25; **15**:258; **39**:477, 479-80, 482; **132**:142, 150, 153
World within Walls (Keene) **34**:567, 569
World within World (Spender) **5**:401; **41**:420-27; **91**:256-57, 261-65, 267-69
"A World Without a Name" (Deane) **122**:82
"World without End" (Gascoyne) **45**:153
World without End (Gray) **22**:201-02; **153**:134, 138, 140-41, 144-45
World without End, Amen (Breslin) **4**:76-7; **43**:72, 74, 76, 78
"A World without Objects Is a Sensible Emptiness" (Wilbur) **6**:570; **53**:399, 406; **110**:387
World without Stars (Anderson) **15**:13
"Worldliness" (Gregor) **9**:254
"Worldly Goods" (Wolff) **64**:448-49
Worldly Hopes (Ammons) **25**:46; **57**:49-50, 59
"Worlds" (Goldbarth) **38**:205
"Worlds" (Wilbur) **53**:413
The Worlds (Bond) **23**:71
Worlds: A Novel of the Near Future (Haldeman) **61**:178-80, 182-83
Worlds Apart: A Novel of the Near Future (Haldeman) **61**:179-80, 182, 186
The World's Banker: The History of the House of Rothschild (Ferguson) **134**:52, 60, 64, 67, 92
The World's Body (Ransom) **2**:362, 364; **4**:433, 436-37; **5**:364; **24**:362, 365-66
"World's End" (Ashbery) **125**:30, 40
World's End (Boyle) **55**:106-11; **90**:43-5, 47, 49, 51-2, 54, 57-60, 65
World's End (Johnson) **27**:212-14, 216
World's End (Neruda) **28**:315
World's End (Sinclair) **63**:354, 358
World's, End and Other Stories (Theroux) **28**:425; **46**:399
"World's Fair" (Berryman) **62**:71
World's Fair (Doctorow) **37**:94-6; **44**:166-79; **65**:137, 141; **113**:137, 150-51, 168, 170, 175-76, 178
"The World's Fastest Human" (Faust) **8**:215
The World's Flesh (Buckley) **57**:126, 129, 131, 133

"The World's Greatest Fisherman" (Erdrich) **120**:138
The Worlds of Fritz Leiber (Leiber) **25**:307
The Worlds of Robert A. Heinlein (Heinlein) **55**:303
The World's Room (MacCaig) **36**:285
"Worlds that Flourish" (Okri) **87**:315
"Worlds to Kill" (Ellison) **42**:127
"The World's Worst Boyfriends" (Wasserstein) **90**:432
The World-Thinker (Vance) **35**:419
The World-Wreckers (Bradley) **30**:31
"The Worm" (Ezekiel) **61**:104
The Worm and the Ring (Burgess) **2**:86; **5**:85; **40**:113-15, 117; **81**:301; **94**:49
"Worm Moon" (Oliver) **98**:265
"The Worms" (Kizer) **80**:172
Worms into Nails (Olson) **28**:343
The Worms of Kukumlima (Pinkwater) **35**:319-20
"Wormwood" (Kinsella) **19**:251, 254; **138**:89-90, 93, 128, 152, 159
Wormwood (Kinsella) **138**:98, 105, 109, 119, 133, 146, 165, 167
"The Wormwood Star" (Milosz) **82**:302, 305
"A Worn Path" (Welty) **33**:414, 419, 424; **105**:298, 301, 307, 319, 326, 349
"Worry" (Muske) **90**:309-10
Worse Things Waiting (Wellman) **49**:389, 392, 394, 396
"Worsewick" (Brautigan) **12**:64
"Worship" (Starbuck) **53**:353
"Worship of Art" (Wolfe) **147**:305
"The Worshippers" (Pritchett) **15**:442-43; **41**:330, 334
Worst Fears (Weldon) **122**:278-80
"The Worst of All Loves" (Dunn) **40**:167
"The Worst Pies in London" (Sondheim) **30**:398
"The Worst Policy" (Bainbridge) **62**:35, 37-8; **130**:28
"The Worst Thing in His Life" (Paton) **25**:360
"The Worst Thing of All" (Gordimer) **33**:181; **123**:113, 115
The Worst Years of Our Lives (Ehrenreich) **110**:178, 180, 187
Worstward Ho (Beckett) **29**:66-8; **59**:253
The Worthing Chronicle (Card) **47**:68; **50**:143
"Worthy It Is" (Elytis) **100**:155
Worthy It Is (Elytis)
See *The Axion Esti*
"Worüber man nicht reden kann" (Hein) **154**:134
"Worüber man nicht reden kann, davon kann die Kunst ein Lied singen" (Hein) **154**:97
Woton's Wake (De Palma) **20**:75
"Would You Do It for a Penny?" (Ellison) **42**:130
"Would You Like to Try for Infinity Years" (Montgomery) **7**:233
"Would You Suggest Writing as a Career?" (Bukowski) **41**:74-5; **108**:85
"The Would-Be Father" (Baxter) **45**:51-2
A Would-Be Saint (Jenkins) **52**:226, 229
"Wouldn't It Be Nice" (Wilson) **12**:647, 649
"The Wound" (Barthelme) **59**:251
"The Wound" (Glück) **22**:173
"The Wound" (Gunn) **18**:203
The Wound and the Bow (Wilson) **8**:550; **24**:468-70, 473, 476, 480-81, 487
The Wound and the Weather (Moss) **45**:290-91; **50**:352-53
"Wounded Knee" (Eiseley) **7**:92
The Wounded Land (Donaldson) **46**:140-41; **138**:4, 9, 11
"The Wounded Soldier" (Garrett) **51**:147, 152
The Wounded Stag (Santos) **22**:361
"Wounds" (Longley) **29**:292-93, 295-96
Wounds (Duffy) **37**:114-15, 117
"Wounds in the Rain" (McGrath) **28**:275
Woyzeck (Duerrenmatt) **102**:61
Woyzeck (Herzog) **16**:333-34
Woza Albert! (Mtwa) **47**:295-97
Woza Albert! (Ngema) **57**:340, 342, 344
"WPLJ" (Zappa) **17**:586
"Wrack" (Barthelme) **46**:43
"Das Wrack" (Lenz) **27**:245
Wraiths of Time (Norton) **12**:470-71
"Wrapped around Your Finger" (Police, The) **26**:366
"Wrapped in Black" (Bowering) **15**:82
"Wrapping the Wind" (Shange) **74**:311
"The Wrath of God" (Fante) **60**:131
"Wrath of the Purple" (Fast) **131**:93
"The Wreath" (Bates) **46**:56
"The Wreath" (Jacobsen) **102**:241
"Wreath for a Bridal" (Plath) **51**:344
"A Wreath for Alun Lewis" (Watkins) **43**:452
A Wreath for Rivera (Marsh) **53**:250, 254
"Wreath for the Dead" (Akhmatova) **64**:6
"A Wreath for the Gamekeeper" (Porter) **101**:223
A Wreath for Udomo (Abrahams) **4**:1
A Wreath of Christmas Legends (McGinley) **14**:368
A Wreath of Roses (Taylor) **29**:410
A Wreath of Sonnets (Seifert) **93**:346
A Wreath to Gorky (Leonov) **92**:277
"Wreaths" (Longley) **29**:296
"The Wreck" (Fuller) **62**:193
"The Wreck" (Haines) **58**:216
The Wreck of the 5:25 (Wilder) **6**:576
The Wreck of the Archangel (Brown) **100**:77, 80
The Wreck of the Cassandra (Prokosch) **4**:421
"The Wreck of the Edmund Fitzgerald" (Lightfoot) **26**:281
"The Wreck of the Thresher" (Meredith) **22**:303; **55**:191
The Wreck of the Thresher (Meredith) **4**:349; **13**:373, 375; **22**:302
"The Wreck of the Titanic" (Tolson) **105**:279
"Wreckage" (Momaday) **85**:281
The Wreckage of Agathon (Gardner) **2**:150-52; **3**:187; **5**:131, 135; **8**:237; **10**:218-19; **28**:167
Wrecked Eggs (Hare) **58**:230-31
Wreckers (Edgar) **42**:116
The Wrench (Levi)
See *La chiave a stella*
Wrestle with an Angel (Everson) **27**:133-34
The Wrestler (Andrade)
See *O lutador*
"Wretched" (Farah) **137**:94
The Wretched of the Earth (Fanon)
See *Les damnés de la terre*
Wright Morris: A Reader (Morris) **3**:343; **37**:310
"The Wrights' Biplane" (Frost) **13**:230
A Wrinkle in Time (L'Engle) **12**:346-52
"Wrinkled Linen" (Prager) **56**:276-77
"Wrinkles" (Jong) **6**:270
Wrinkles (Simmons) **57**:406-08
Write On (Lodge) **141**:329
"Write the Truth' My Son Said: 'Write About Me" (Harrison) **144**:107
"Write, Then" (Ekeloef) **27**:111
"The Writer" (Wilbur) **9**:569; **53**:413; **110**:361-63, 377, 385
"Writer and Critic" (Bradbury) **61**:42
"Writer and Critic" (Lukacs) **24**:316
"The Writer and His Community" (Achebe) **152**:74-5, 77, 79
"The Writer and the Concept of Adulthood" (Stegner) **49**:359
"The Writer as Detective Hero" (Macdonald) **41**:270
"The Writer as Exile" (Moore) **90**:277
"The Writer as Independent Witness" (Doctorow) **113**:162
"The Writer as Moralist" (Bellow) **8**:78
"Writer Devoured by Children" (Tournier) **95**:389
"The Writer in a State of Siege" (Brink) **106**:103
The Writer in America (Brooks) **29**:87-8
The Writer in Disguise (Bennett) **45**:58; **77**:93
"The Writer in the Family" (Doctorow) **37**:91-3; **44**:175, 177; **113**:136, 150-51, 153-55
"The Writer on, and at, Her Work" (Le Guin) **136**:361
A Writer's America: Landscape in Literature (Kazin) **119**:301
"Writers and Writing" (McCullers) **12**:427
Writers at Work (Didion) **129**:90
A Writer's Capital (Auchincloss) **18**:25
"The Writer's Commitment" (Alegria) **75**:53
The Writer's Dimension (Wolf) **150**:
Writers from the Other Europe (Roth) **15**:451
Writers in Politics (Ngũgĩ wa Thiong'o) **36**:318-19
A Writer's Ireland: Landscape in Literature (Trevor) **71**:327-29, 331; **116**:377
"The Writer's Kitchen" (Ferré)
See "La cocina de la escritura"
A Writer's Notebook (Maugham) **15**:368; **67**:218, 228-29
"The Writers of the American Revolution" (Williams) **13**:604
"Writers on Strike" (Lebowitz) **11**:322
The Writer's Point of View (Maugham) **15**:368
"The Writer's Situation" (Carruth) **84**:117
"A Writer's Story" (Levine) **54**:297-98, 300
Writes of Passage (Cabrera Infante) **120**:73
Writin' is Fightin': 37 Years of Boxing on Paper (Reed) **60**:310
"Writing" (Auden) **123**:23-4
"Writing" (Motion) **47**:288, 293
"Writing" (Nemerov) **36**:305
"Writing" (Paz)
See "Escritura"
"Writing a Book" (Hill) **113**:293, 326;
"Writing a First Novel" (Jong) **6**:270
Writing a Novel (Braine) **41**:59-61
"Writing a Résumé" (Szymborska) **99**:205
"Writing a Sketch of a Forgotten Poet" (Blunden) **56**:40
Writing a Woman's Life (Heilbrun) **65**:313
"Writing about Jews" (Roth) **15**:453
"Writing Again" (Bly) **38**:56
Writing Against: A Biography of Sartre (Hayman) **44**:493-94, 496-98
Writing against Time (Moss) **50**:353
"Writing American Fiction" (Roth) **4**:459
Writing and Being (Gordimer) **123**:157, 161-62
Writing and Difference (Derrida)
See *L'écriture et la différence*
Writing and the Body (Josipovici) **43**:223-26
"Writing and the Holocaust" (Howe) **85**:151-52
"writing autobiography" (Hooks) **94**:143
"Writing Autobiography" (Lee) **90**:199, 201
"The Writing Condition" (Sheed) **53**:341
Writing Degree Zero (Barthes)
See *Le degré zéro de l'écriture*
"Writing for Children Is No Child's Play" (Tournier) **95**:378-80
"Writing for Television" (Townsend) **61**:420
"Writing for the Fourth Time through 'Finnegans Wake'" (Cage) **41**:86
The Writing Game (Lodge) **141**:373-75
Writing Home (Williams) **42**:445
Writing in a State of Siege (Brink) **36**:68-70, 72; **106**:101, 103
"Writing in a Time of Violence" (Boland) **113**:93-4, 100, 111, 115-17, 127
"Writing in Latin America" (Allende) **57**:20
Writing in Restaurants (Mamet) **46**:255
"Writing in Wartime: The Uses of Innocence" (Fussell) **74**:140
"A Writing Lesson" (Gordon) **128**:110, 115
"The Writing Life" (Wright) **146**:372
The Writing Life (Dillard) **60**:79-81; **115**:193-94, 201
Writing Like a Woman (Ostriker) **132**:318, 327
"Writing Lives" (Merwin) **88**:209-10, 213
Writing Lives: Principia Biographica (Edel) **34**:534-37
The Writing of Disaster (Blanchot)
See *L'Ecriture du désastre*

"The Writing of God" (Borges)
See "La escritura del Dios"
The Writing of the Disaster (Blanchot)
See *L'Ecriture du désastre*
Writing on a Body (Sarduy)
See *Escrito sobre un cuerpo*
"Writing on Napkins at the Sunshine Club" (Bottoms) **53**:29-30
The Writing on the Wall and Other Literary Essays (McCarthy) **24**:344-46; **39**:487
"Writing Poetry in a Hotel Room" (Enright) **31**:150
Writing the Australian Crawl (Stafford) **29**:386
"Writing 'The Galton Case'" (Macdonald) **14**:333; **41**:270
"Writing through 'Finnegans Wake'" (Cage) **41**:84
Writing through 'Finnegans Wake' (Cage) **41**:84
"Writing through the Cantos" (Cage) **41**:85
"Writing to Aaron" (Levertov) **15**:339
Writing Was Everything (Kazin) **119**:303-04, 306-09, 313, 316, 334-35
Writing Well (Hall) **151**:184, 213
"Writing Your Love Down" (Jensen) **37**:188
Writings (Arghezi)
See *Scrieri*
Writings and Drawings (Dylan) **3**:130; **12**:189
"Writings on a Cave Wall" (Dowell) **60**:107-08
"Writings to an Unfinished Accompaniment" (Merwin) **88**:187
Writings to an Unfinished Accompaniment (Merwin) **3**:339-40; **5**:286-87; **8**:389; **13**:383; **45**:276; **88**:192-94, 200, 202, 205
Written by Herself: Authobiographies of American Women (Conway) **152**:103-4
"Written, Directed By, and Starring..." (Simmons) **43**:410
"Written in 1938" (Ewart) **46**:148
"Written in Dejection near Rome" (Bly) **10**:56
"Written in My Dream by W.C. Williams" (Ginsberg) **109**:324
"Written Off" (Enright) **31**:146
Written on Water (Tomlinson) **4**:544, 547-48; **13**:548-49; **45**:398
Written Stone (Bonnefoy)
See *Pierre écrite*
"Written Water" (Ammons) **57**:50
"Written While Riding the Long Island Rail Road" (Swenson) **61**:397
"Wrong" (Matthews) **40**:324
"The wrong anger" (Piercy) **128**:246
"Wrong Beauty" (Grass)
See "Falsche Schönheit"
The Wrong Box (Gelbart) **21**:125
"Wrong 'Em Boyo" (Clash) **30**:46-7
"The Wrong Folks" (Powers) **4**:419
"Wrong Formula" (McGinley) **14**:366
"The Wrong Lunch Line" (Mohr) **12**:446
The Wrong Man (Hitchcock) **16**:342-43, 346, 358
"Wrong Monday" (Piercy) **62**:378
"Wrong Number" (Bukowski) **41**:64
The Wrong Set, and Other Stories (Wilson) **2**:470; **3**:534
The Wrong Side of the Park (Mortimer) **28**:284-85
"The Wrong Stop" (Calvino) **33**:100; **73**:33
"The Wrong Sun" (Coupland) **85**:35, 39
"A Wrong Turning in American Poetry" (Bly) **38**:50; **128**:41
The Wrong Way Down (Daly) **52**:90
"Wrong Words" (Amis) **40**:44
WSW (West South West) (Moure) **88**:225-26, 230-31
Wu (Pa Chin)
See *Fog*
"The Wub" (Dick)
See "Beyond Lies the Wub"
"Wuden't Me" (Berry) **17**:56
"Wunderkind" (McCullers) **12**:433
Wünsche (Wellershoff) **46**:435
Wunschkonzert (Kroetz) **41**:234, 236-38
Wunscholses Unglück (Handke) **5**:163, 165-67; **8**:261, 263; **10**:255-56, 258; **38**:218-19, 221-24, 227; **134**:130-32, 139, 151, 154, 180
"Wunschzettel" (Weiss) **8**:545
"Wu-Sang-Kuei" (Guillén) **79**:229
"Wuthering Heights" (Plath) **51**:345; **111**:200, 202, 214
Wuthering Heights (Bunuel)
See *Abismos de pasion*
The Wycherly Woman (Macdonald) **2**:255; **14**:334
"Wygasnięcic Absolutu niszczy" (Rozewicz) **139**:295
"The Wykehamist" (Betjeman) **43**:35
"Wyncote: Pennsylvania" (Kinsella) **138**:126
Wyndmere (Muske) **90**:312-15
"Wyndmere, Wyndmere" (Muske) **90**:313
Wyrds (Allen) **84**:28
Wysoki Zamek (Lem) **149**:140-43, 145, 150, 255-58
Wyst: Alastor 1716 (Vance) **35**:421
Wyszedł z domu (Rozewicz) **139**:231, 240, 265, 293
"X" (Abbott) **48**:6
"X" (Merrill) **8**:382
"X" (Thesen) **56**:415
The X Factor (Norton) **12**:457, 468
X: Writings, '79-'82 (Cage) **41**:85-6
Xaipe: Seventy-One Poems (Cummings) **15**:163; **68**:31, 42, 48, 52
Xala (Ousmane) **66**:336, 341-42, 344-45
"Xanadu" (Thomas) **13**:539; **107**:315-19, 326
"Xavier Speaking" (Baxter) **45**:51; **78**:16
Xavier Villaurrutia en persona y obra (Paz) **119**:418
"Xeethra" (Smith) **43**:424
Xenia (Montale) **7**:224-25, 228, 231; **9**:386-88; **18**:340-41
"Xenia I" (Montale) **9**:387-89
"Xenia II" (Montale) **9**:387-8
Xenogenesis (Butler) **121**:97, 117, 134, 136-37, 144
Xénophiles (Breton) **54**:30; **9**:128
"Xerox" (Belitt) **22**:54
"Xi" (Tolson) **105**:242, 251
"Xiaohuolun shang" (Ding Ling) **68**:58
Xiccarph (Smith) **43**:418
Xionia (Wright) **146**:336, 338-39, 341-42, 375, 379
"Xmas Coming" (Rexroth) **112**:377
XPD (Deighton) **22**:118-19; **46**:129
"X-Ray" (Abse) **29**:20
"X-Ray Photograph" (Hope) **51**:227
Y and X (Olson) **29**:330
"Y/Me" (Grayson) **38**:211-12
Y pondrán esposas a las flores (Arrabal)
See *Et ils passèrent des menottes aux fleurs*
"Ya no es posible" (Aleixandre) **9**:12
"Yacht for Sale" (MacLeish) **68**:287, 290
"Yaddo" (Rakosi) **47**:347
"Yadkin Picnic" (Ammons) **57**:50
"Yadwigha, on a Red Couch, Among Lilies; A Sestina for the Douanier" (Plath) **111**:201
"Yage" (Ginsberg) **109**:325
The Yage Letters (Burroughs) **109**:184, 187
"Yaikini" (Kenny) **87**:241, 246
"Yajima Ryūdō" (Shiga) **33**:367
The Yakuza (Schrader) **26**:389
The Yakuza (Towne) **87**:360
Yan Tan Tethera (Harrison) **129**:169
Yancey's War (Hoffman) **141**:264, 266, 276, 281, 296, 298
"The Yang Self and the Old Writer" (Ozick) **155**:182
Yankee Doodle (Linney) **51**:263
Yankee Privateer (Norton) **12**:456
"The Yanks Are Coming, in Five Breathless Colors" (Perelman) **49**:265
Yanks Three Detroit Zero Top of the Seventh (Reynolds) **38**:387
"Yánnina" (Merrill) **13**:376, 381-82; **18**:328
"Yaqzat al mūmyā'" (Mahfūz) **55**:174
"Yaqzat al-mumya'" (Mahfouz) **153**:349, 351
"Yard Journal" (Wright) **146**:333, 338
A Yard of Sun: A Summer Comedy (Fry) **2**:143-44
"Yarrow" (Oates) **108**:384
"Yase: September" (Snyder) **32**:387
"The Yattering and Jack" (Barker) **52**:51
Yawar fiesta (Arguedas) **10**:8, 10; **18**:7, 9-10
Yawm qutila'l-z'im (Mahfouz) **153**:287-88, 324, 361, 364
The Yawning Heights (Aksyonov) **37**:13
The Yawning Heights (Zinoviev)
See *Ziyayuschiye vysoty*
"Ye Olde Ivory Tower" (Perelman) **49**:258
"Yea Tigers" (Souster) **5**:395
Yea! Wildcats (Tunis) **12**:598
"The Year" (Milosz) **82**:295
Year 501: The Conquest Continues (Chomsky) **132**:68
"The Year 1905" (Pasternak)
See "Devyatsat pyaty god"
A Year and a Day (Mayne) **12**:404-05
Year Before Last (Boyle) **58**:64-5; **121**:44, 46, 50, 55, 62, 66-8
Year Five of the Algerian Revolution (Fanon)
See *L'an V de la révolution algérienne*
A Year from Monday: New Lectures and Writings (Cage) **41**:77-83, 85-6
A Year in Provence (Mayle) **89**:143, 145-47, 149-54
A Year in the Dark: Journal of a Film Critic, 1968-1969 (Adler) **31**:11, 13
"The Year of Getting to Know Us" (Canin) **55**:36, 38-9
The Year of Living Dangerously (Koch) **42**:260-62, 264-65, 268
The Year of Living Dangerously (Williamson) **56**:437-38, 443
"The Year of Mourning" (Jeffers) **54**:235
The Year of My Rebirth (Stuart) **8**:507; **34**:375
The Year of Ricardo Reis's Death (Saramago)
See *O ano da morte de Ricardo Reis*
The Year of Silence (Bell) **102**:2-3, 8
"The Year of the Big Spring Clean" (Aldiss) **40**:17
The Year of the Century: 1876 (Brown) **47**:37-8
"The Year of the Child" (Hayden) **37**:156
"The Year of the Double Spring" (Swenson) **4**:534; **106**:338
The Year of the Dragon (Chin) **135**:162, 165, 167, 185, 191-93, 196-97, 202
Year of the Dragon (Stone) **73**:365, 370, 382
The Year of the French (Flanagan) **25**:163-67; **52**:148, 151-55
"The Year of the Green Pudding" (Weldon) **122**:268
"Year of the Indian" (Alexie) **154**:27
"The Year of the Jackpot" (Heinlein) **55**:304
"Year of the Ox" (Wright) **146**:
"Year of the Pigeons" (Still) **49**:365
The Year of the Raccoon (Kingman) **17**:245
"The Year of the Sloes, for Ishi" (Muldoon) **72**:279
The Year of the Unicorn (Norton) **12**:468
"The Year of the Whale" (Brown) **5**:77-8; **48**:57
The Year of the Whale (Brown) **100**:84
The Year of the Young Rebels (Spender) **41**:422; **91**:261
The Year One (Raine) **45**:331, 333-34, 341
A Year or So with Edgar (Higgins) **18**:233
"Yearning for My Mother" (Tanizaki)
See "Haha no kouru ki"
"Yearning for the Day" (Aleixandre) **36**:29
Yearning: Race, Gender, and Cultural Politics (Hooks) **94**:131, 145-50, 159
"Years" (Plath) **5**:339; **9**:426-27, 433; **111**:175, 204
The Years (Haavikko)
See *Vuodet*
The Years (Souster) **5**:396; **14**:504
The Years as Catches: First Poems, 1939-1946 (Duncan) **55**:293-94

The Years Between (du Maurier) **59**:286
"A Year's Changes" (Harrison) **33**:198
"Year's End" (Hacker) **91**:111
"Year's End" (Voigt) **54**:430-31
"Year's End" (Wilbur) **53**:401-02
"The Year's First Rain" (Clark Bekedermo) **38**:121, 128
"The Years from You to Me" (Celan) **82**:47
"The Years in Exile" (Metcalf) **37**:300, 306
Years of Hope (Paustovsky)
See *The Time of Great Expectations*
"Years of Indiscretion" (Ashbery) **13**:33
Years of Renewal (Kissinger) **137**:242, 245, 247-50, 252, 257-58
Years of Upheaval (Kissinger) **137**:241, 244, 249-50, 255
The Years with Ross (Thurber) **5**:436; **125**:394
"Yeats" (Plath) **5**:345
Yeats (Bloom) **24**:71; **103**:19, 36, 39
Yeats (Tuohy) **37**:430
"Yeats an Example?" (Heaney) **74**:178
"Yeats in Civil War" (Boland) **113**:93, 121
"Yeats in Dublin" (Watkins) **43**:453
Yeats: The Man and the Masks (Ellmann) **50**:308-09
Yeat's Vision and the Later Plays (Vendler) **138**:262
"Yeats's Tower" (Watkins) **43**:441
Yehuda (Levin) **7**:206
"Yehuda Ha-Levi" (Amichai) **57**:44
"Yehuda Halevi, Ibn Gabirol, Leah Goldberg meta" (Amichai) **116**:118
"Yeletov" (Shammas) **55**:86
"Yellow" (Jacobsen) **48**:195
The Yellow Admiral (O'Brian) **152**:284-90
Yellow Back Radio Broke-Down (Reed) **2**:368-69; **3**:424-25; **5**:368-70; **6**:448-50; **13**:479; **32**:359, 364; **60**:300, 302, 305, 307-08, 311-12
"The Yellow Bird" (Abse) **29**:13
"The Yellow Bird" (Williams) **15**:579; **45**:453, 456
"A Yellow Flower" (Cortázar)
See "Una flor amarilla"
Yellow Flowers in the Antipodean Room (Frame)
See *The Rainbirds*
Yellow for Peril, Black for Beautiful: Poems and a Play (Cassity) **42**:95, 98
The Yellow Heart (Neruda)
See *El corazón amarillo*
"The Yellow House" (MacEwen) **55**:169
The Yellow House on the Corner (Dove) **50**:152-53, 155; **81**:132-34, 136-37, 143, 145, 151
Yellow Leaf (Hoffman)
See *The Days In Yellow Leaf*
Yellow Man (Endō)
See *Kiiroi hito*
"Yellow Pages" (Raine) **103**:179, 188
"Yellow Pitcher Plant" (Gunn) **81**:178, 188
A Yellow Raft in Blue Water (Dorris) **109**:296-97, 299-301, 303, 306, 308-13
The Yellow Room (Hall) **1**:137; **37**:146
"The Yellow Rose" (Borges) **83**:159
Yellow Submarine (Lennon and McCartney) **12**:360, 365
"The Yellow Sugar" (Vollmann) **89**:278
"Yellow Tent" (Graver) **70**:51
"Yellow Trains" (Lively) **32**:277
The Yellow Wind (Grossman) **67**:57-64, 74
"Yellow Woman" (Silko) **23**:409-10, 412; **74**:321, 332-35, 338; **114**:314
"Yellowjackets" (Komunyakaa) **94**:241
"Yentl the Yeshiva Boy" (Singer) **6**:511; **15**:509; **38**:416-17; **69**:320
"Yer Blues" (Lennon and McCartney) **35**:266
Yer demir gök bakir (Kemal) **14**:299-301
"Yes and No" (Grigson) **7**:135
Yes from No-Man's-Land (Kops) **4**:274
"Yes: I Mean So OK—Love" (Bronk) **10**:74
"Yes, the Agency Can Handle That" (Fearing) **51**:117
Yes Yes No No (Kushner) **81**:204
"Yes Young Daddy" (Chin) **135**:152-53, 157
The Yeshira (Grade)
See *Tsemakh Atlas*
The Yeshiva (Grade) **10**:246, 248-49
"Yesterday" (Lennon and McCartney) **12**:359, 375; **35**:278, 289, 293
"Yesterday" (Merwin) **45**:274; **88**:205
Yesterday (Wideman)
See *Sent for You Yesterday*
Yesterday Came Suddenly (King) **145**:359-63
"Yesterday I Was Called Nigger" (Guillén)
See "Ayer me dijeron negro"
Yesterday, Today, Tomorrow (De Sica) **20**:91, 94
"Yesterday, Tomorrow, Always" (Derleth) **31**:136
Yesterday We Saw Mermaids (Friesner) **70**:332
"Yesterday's Light" (Blaga) **75**:61
"Yesterday's Love" (Farrell) **66**:129
Yesterday's Magic (Williams) **15**:577
Yesterday's Spy (Deighton) **7**:75-6
"Yesterday's Tomorrow" (Roberts) **14**:463
Yesterday's Wine (Nelson) **17**:304, 306
"Yester-Me, Yester-You, Yesterday" (Wonder) **12**:655
Les yeux bleux, cheveux noir (Duras) **68**:85, 87-8, 99-100; **100**:118, 127
Les yeux de la nuit (Woolrich) **77**:395
"Les yeux de la statue" (Laye) **38**:286
Les yeux et la memoire (Aragon) **22**:38
"Yeux Glauques" (Pound) **48**:287
Les yeux ouverts; entretiens avec Matthieu Galey (Yourcenar) **38**:457, 462, 464; **87**:402-04, 419, 424, 433-34
"The Yglesias of Ignatius Livingstone Island" (Schaeffer) **22**:370
"YgUDuh" (Cummings) **15**:162
"Yiddish in America" (Ozick)
See "Envy: or, Yiddish in America"
"Yiddishe Kopf" (Ginsberg) **109**:328
"Yige nüren he yige nanren" (Ding Ling) **68**:59, 66-7
Yikigunishu (Kawabata) **107**:107
Yin: New Poems (Kizer) **39**:169-71; **80**:186
"Yin Yang" (Mitchell) **12**:438
YK (Breytenbach) **126**:77, 89, 101
Yksityisiä asioita (Haavikko) **34**:170
Ylilääkäri (Haavikko) **34**:173
"Ylla" (Bradbury) **42**:38
Yo (Grade) **10**:246
"Yo acuso" (Neruda) **62**:327
Yo, el supremo (Roa Bastos) **45**:344, 347-51
Yo era un tonto (Alberti) **7**:9
Yobgorgle (Pinkwater) **35**:318-19
"A yoga class" (Muske) **90**:308
The Yogi and the Commissar and Other Essays (Koestler) **3**:270-71; **33**:230, 233
The Yogi of Cockroach Court (Waters) **88**:331, 333-34, 359-60
Yoidore Tenshi (Kurosawa)
See *Drunken Angel*
Yojimbo (Kurosawa) **16**:401, 403-06; **119**:337-38, 341, 351, 361, 364, 380, 382
Yokeham (Poole) **17**:372
The Yoknapatawpha Country (Brooks)
See *William Faulkner: The Yoknapatawpha Country*
"Yoko" (Gunn) **18**:204; **32**:209
"Yom Kippur 1984" (Rich) **73**:315
"Yonder Stands the Sinner" (Young) **17**:572
Yonnondio: From the Thirties (Olsen) **4**:385-87; **13**:432; **114**:194-96, 198, 201-03, 209, 211-12, 215, 220-29; 231-32, 235, 237
"York: In Memoriam W. H. Auden" (Brodsky) **36**:81; **100**:54
Yoru ni naruto sake wa (Murakami) **150**:42
"Yosaku the Settler" (Ibuse) **22**:227
"Yoshino: False Dawn of the Cherry Blossom" (Lieberman) **36**:261
Yoshinokuzu (Tanizaki) **28**:420-21
"You" (Borges)
See "Tú"
"You" (Dubie) **36**:133
"You" (Levine) **14**:318
"You All Know the Story of the Other Woman" (Sexton) **123**:408, 439
"You and I Are Disappearing" (Komunyakaa) **94**:225, 231, 233, 240
"You and I Saw Hawks Exchanging Prey" (Wright) **3**:544
You and Me (Lang) **20**:206; **103**:85
"You and the Boss" (Janowitz) **43**:211-12; **145**:343
"You, Andrew Marvell" (MacLeish) **14**:338; **68**:272-73, 284, 286, 290-91, 294
"You Angel You" (Dylan) **4**:150
"You Are" (Swenson) **106**:337, 347-48
"You Are as Brave as Vincent Van Gogh" (Barthelme) **8**:52
"You Are Forever" (Robinson) **21**:350-51
You Are Happy (Atwood) **8**:28-9; **13**:44; **15**:36; **25**:63-4, 66-7; **84**:64-5, 89; **135**:31
"You Are Not I" (Bowles) **53**:36-7
You Are Not Poetry (Castellanos)
See *Poesía no eres tú: Obra poética, 1948-1971*
You Are Now Entering the Human Heart (Frame) **66**:144
"You are the first generation raised without religion" (Coupland) **133**:8
"You Are the Sunshine of My Life" (Wonder) **12**:657, 663
"You Are Welcome!" (Forester) **35**:173
"You Are What You Own: A Notebook" (Adams) **46**:21
"You Belong to Me" (Costello) **21**:69
"You Belong to Me" (Simon) **26**:411-12
You Bright and Risen Angels: A Cartoon (Vollmann) **89**:275-76, 279-83, 286, 290-92, 298-304, 307, 310
"You Can Close the New York Stock Exchange" (Sondheim) **147**:247, 253-54
"You Can Cry" (Levine) **33**:274
"You Can Depend on Me" (Robinson) **21**:350
"You Can Get It If You Really Want" (Cliff) **21**:60, 63
"You Can Have It" (Levine) **33**:271; **118**:285, 287
"You Can Have It" (Oliver) **98**:263
"You Can Leave" (Gaye) **26**:134
"You Can Never Go Back" (Haldeman) **61**:181
"You Can Start the Poetry Now, Or; News from Crazy Horse" (McGrath) **59**:178, 181
"You Can Still Grow Flowers" (Greenberg) **7**:134
"You Can't Always Get What You Want" (Jagger and Richard) **17**:226, 236
"You Can't Be Any Poorer than Dead" (O'Connor) **15**:413
"You Can't Be Wrong and Get Right" (Cliff) **21**:63
You Can't Do Both (Amis) **129**:16, 20
"You Can't Do That" (Lennon) **35**:274
You Can't Get There from Here (Hamner) **12**:257-58
You Can't Get There from Here (Hood) **15**:286; **28**:189-91, 193-94
You Can't Get There from Here (Nash) **23**:322
You Can't Keep a Good Woman Down (Walker) **103**:357, 366-67, 369, 406-13, 422
"You Can't Rhumboogie in a Ball and Chain" (Fulton) **52**:158-59
"You Can't Step into the Same Street Twice" (Dybek) **114**:76
"You Can't Stop the Music" (Davies) **21**:99
You Can't Take It with You (Capra) **16**:155, 159-63
You Can't Take It with You (Hart and Kaufman) **38**:260, 262, 265-66; **66**:173-76, 178, 180, 182-86, 190-92

You Can't Take Twenty Dogs on a Date (Cavanna) **12**:102
You come at night (Poniatowska)
See *De noche vienes*
"You Could Drive a Person Crazy" (Sondheim) **30**:387, 391; **147**:240
You Could Live If They Let You (Markfield) **8**:380
"You Could Look It Up" (Thurber) **125**:389
You Didn't Even Try (Whalen) **29**:444-45
"You Didn't Fit" (Musgrave) **54**:341
You Don't Love Yourself (Sarraute)
See *Tu ne t'aimes pas*
"You Don't Pull No Punches but You Don't Push the River" (Morrison) **21**:236
"You, Dr. Martin" (Sexton) **53**:313
You, Emperors, and Others: Poems, 1957-1960 (Warren) **4**:578; **13**:573, 575, 577; **39**:265-66
"You Gave Me Hyacinths" (Hospital) **145**:313
"You Gave Me the Answer" (McCartney) **35**:282-83
"You, Genoese Mariner" (Merwin) **5**:285; **8**:389
"You Gotta Be Crazy" (Pink Floyd) **35**:311
"You Gotta Move" (Jagger and Richard) **17**:224
"You Had to Go to Funerals" (Walker) **58**:404
"You Hated Spain" (Hughes) **119**:295-96
"You Have Left Your Lotus Pods on the Bus" (Bowles) **53**:37
You Have Seen Their Faces (Caldwell) **8**:124; **50**:299, 301; **60**:53, 60-1, 66
You Have to Draw the Line Somewhere (Harris) **12**:261-62, 266
"You Haven't Done Nothin'" (Wonder) **12**:658, 661
"You, Heavenly" (Bell) **8**:66
"You Kissed Lilly" (Bukowski) **41**:72
"You Know Charles" (Robison) **42**:342
"You Know How to Turn On Those Lights" (Sainte-Marie) **17**:431
"You Know I Can't Hear You When the Water's Running" (Anderson) **23**:31
"You Know It Makes Sense" (Whalen) **29**:447
"You Know Me" (MacEwen) **55**:168
"You Know What" (Beattie) **146**:58-9, 61, 81
"You Lived in Glasgow" (Smith) **64**:393
"You Love the Thunder" (Browne) **21**:40
You Lovely People (Santos) **22**:361-62, 365
"You Make It All Worthwhile" (Davies) **21**:99
You Marry the Moon (Haavikko) **34**:169
"You May Be Right" (Joel) **26**:221
"You Must Meet My Wife" (Sondheim) **30**:400
"You Must Remember This" (Coover) **46**:121
You Must Remember This (Oates) **52**:334-37; **108**:374, 378, 390
"You mustn't show weakness" (Amichai) **116**:97
"You Never Can Tell" (Berry) **17**:54
You Only Live Once (Lang) **20**:206, 208, 213-14
You Only Live Twice (Fleming) **30**:138, 147-49
"You Pays Your Nickel" (Woolrich) **77**:401
"You Really Got a Hold on Me" (Robinson) **21**:347, 351
"You Really Got Me" (Davies) **21**:89, 102
"You Rope You Tie Me" (Armatrading) **17**:9-10
"You Shall above All Things Be Glad and Young" (Cummings) **68**:44
"You Shattered" (Ungaretti)
See "Tu ti spezzasti"
"You Shook Me" (Page and Plant) **12**:482
"You Should Have Seen the Mess" (Spark) **5**:400
"You Should Live So, Walden Pond" (Perelman) **49**:258, 264
"You Speak No English" (Guillén)
See "Tú no sabe inglé"
"You Still Believe in Me" (Wilson) **12**:646
"You Sure Love to Ball" (Gaye) **26**:133
You!: The Psychology of Surviving and Enhancing Your Social Life, Love Life, Sex Life, School Life, Home Life, Work Life, Emotional Life, Creative Life, Spiritual Life, Style of Life, Life (Gordon) **26**:137-39
You, Too Are Guilty (Abe)
See *Omaenimo tsumi ga aru*
"You, Too, Can Have a Body" (Scannell) **49**:328
You Touched Me! (Williams) **71**:360
"You Triflin' Skunk" (Miller) **30**:263
"You Wear It So Well" (Reed) **21**:312-13
You Were Marvellous (Fenton) **32**:167-68
"You Were Never Miss Brown to Me" (Williams) **89**:321
"You Were Perfectly Fine" (Parker) **68**:330, 335
"You Were Wearing" (Koch) **5**:219; **44**:243
"You Who Swim" (Updike) **23**:476
You Will Forget Me (Breton and Soupault)
See *Vous m'oublierez*
You Will Only Make Matters Worse (Cage)
See *Diary: How to Improve the World*
You Would If You Loved Me (Gordon) **26**:138-39
"You/Your" (Oates) **6**:367
"You'll Accomp'ny Me" (Seger) **35**:384-85
You'll Have Had Your Hole (Welsh) **144**:347
"You'll Never Be a Man" (Costello) **21**:76
"You'll Never Get Away from Me" (Sondheim) **30**:377
"You'll Never Know, Dear, How Much I Love You" (Updike) **5**:449
"You'll Never See Me Again" (Woolrich) **77**:389, 394
"You'll Take the High Road" (Brunner) **8**:111
"Young" (Sexton) **53**:318, 322, 324
Young Adolf (Bainbridge) **14**:36-9; **22**:45; **62**:30-1; **130**:10, 20, 22, 34
Young Adult Novel (Pinkwater) **35**:318-20
Young American Writers (Kostelanetz) **28**:212
Young Americans (Bowie) **17**:62-4, 66, 68
Young Ames (Edmonds) **35**:152, 156
The Young and Beautiful (Benson) **17**:49-50
Young and Innocent (Hitchcock) **16**:345
"Young and Innocent Days" (Davies) **21**:91
The Young and the Damned (Bunuel)
See *Los olvidados*
"The Young and the Old—Notes on a New History" (Lifton) **67**:142
The Young and the Passionate (Fellini)
See *I vitelloni*
"Young Archimedes" (Huxley) **3**:256; **5**:193; **11**:281
The Young Assassins (Goytisolo)
See *Juegos de manos*
"Young Bergdorf Goodman Brown" (Leyner) **92**:292, 294
The Young Caesar (Warner) **45**:435-36
"The Young Dancers" (Zaturenska) **6**:586
"Young David" (Amichai) **9**:22; **116**:85, 87
"Young Edgcumbe" (Causley) **7**:42
Young Entry (Keane) **31**:230
Young Felix (Swinnerton) **31**:422-23
"The Young Folks" (Salinger) **12**:521
Young Frankenstein (Brooks) **12**:77-80, 82
"The Young Girl" (Roethke) **101**:330
"The Young Girl at the Ball" (Hope) **3**:250
"Young Girls" (Souster) **14**:501
"Young Girls Growing Up (1911)" (Justice) **102**:277
"A Young Girl's Journal" (Aickman)
See "Pages from a Young Girl's Diary"
The Young Girls of Wilko (Wajda) **16**:584
"A Young Greek, Killed in the Wars" (Eberhart) **56**:88
The Young Grizzly (Corcoran) **17**:73
The Young Hemingway (Reynolds) **44**:515-18
"A Young Highland Girl Studying Poetry" (Smith) **64**:387, 396-97
The Young Idea (Coward) **29**:139
The Young in One Another's Arms (Rule) **27**:418, 420-21
The Young Lady from Paris (Aiken) **35**:20
The Young Landlords (Myers) **35**:296-97
"Young Lions" (Jones) **76**:65-6
The Young Lions (Shaw) **7**:409-11, 413-14; **23**:399-400; **34**:368-70
Young Lonigan (Farrell) **1**:98; **4**:157, 159; **11**:194; **66**:112-13, 121, 131-32
The Young Lovers (Garrett) **51**:145
Young Lust (Acker) **111**:11
"The Young Man" (Gilchrist) **48**:121
"Young Man Blues" (Townshend) **17**:525
The Young Man From Atlanta (Foote) **91**:113-18
"The Young Man from Kalgoorlie" (Bates) **46**:56
Young Man in a Hurry: The Story of Cyrus W. Field (Latham) **12**:323
Young Man in Chains (Mauriac)
See *L'enfant chargé de chaînes*
A Young Man in Search of Love (Singer) **11**:499, 503-04; **23**:422; **38**:412; **69**:303; **111**:310
The Young Man Who Arrived Late (Oe)
See *Okurete kita seinen*
"The Young Man with the Carnation" (Dinesen) **29**:159, 161; **95**:35, 51
The Young Manhood of Studs Lonigan (Farrell) **1**:98; **4**:157; **66**:120, 127
Young Mark: The Story of a Venture (Almedingen) **12**:3, 5-6
Young Martin Luther King (Childress)
See *The Freedom Drum*
The Young May Moon (Newby) **2**:311
"Young Men" (Scott) **43**:370
Young Men and Fire (Maclean) **78**:242, 243-44
"The Young Men Run" (Brooks) **49**:38
"Young Men Waking at Daybreak" (Williams) **45**:444
"Young Mothers I" (Olds) **85**:285
Young Mr. Lincoln (Ford) **16**:304, 310, 319
The Young One (Bunuel) **16**:133, 136, 148
"The Young Park" (Koch) **44**:249
Young Patullo (Stewart) **7**:466
A Young Person's Guide to Ballet (Streatfeild) **21**:412-13
The Young Pobble's Guide to His Toes (Ewart) **46**:153-54
Young Razzle (Tunis) **12**:596
The Young Rebecca: Writings of Rebecca West, 1911-17 (West) **31**:459-60
"The Young Rector" (Nowlan) **15**:398
Young Samurai (Mishima) **2**:286
The Young Scoundrel (Coles) **67**:180
Young Shoulders (Wain) **46**:418-19
The Young Unicorns (L'Engle) **12**:347-48
The Young Visitors (Wain) **46**:414, 416, 418
"The Young Wife" (Walcott) **67**:359, 361
A Young Wife's Tale (Sansom) **6**:483
"A Young Woman, A Tree" (Ostriker) **132**:318
"A Young Woman in Green Lace" (Parker) **68**:336
"Young Women" (Redgrove) **41**:348
"Young Women in Rollers" (Dunn) **40**:167
A Young World (De Sica) **20**:94
Youngblood (Killens) **10**:300
Youngblood Hawke (Wouk) **9**:580; **38**:448-49
Younger Brother (Ringwood) **48**:330
"The Younger Sister's Clothes" (Kawabata) **107**:107-08
The Youngest (Tindall) **7**:473
"The Youngest Doll" (Ferré)
See "La muñeca menor"
The Youngest Doll (Ferré)
See *Papeles de Pandora*
The Youngest Science: Notes of a Medicine Watcher (Thomas) **35**:412-14
"Younghusband" (Simmons) **43**:414
"Youngsters" (Parra)
See "Jóvenes"
"Your Attention Please" (Porter) **33**:319, 322, 326
"Your Birthday in the California Mountains" (Rexroth) **112**:386
"Your Body Is Stars Whose Million Glitter Here" (Spender) **41**:419, 427
"Your Bright Baby Blues" (Browne) **21**:39
"Your Errant Mom" (Robison) **98**:307-08
"Your Faces, O My Sisters! Your Faces Filled of Light!" (Tiptree) **48**:389